# ELLIOT'S GUIDE

## TO FILMS ON VIDEO

## SECOND EDITION

# John Elliot

**Boxtree**

*For Jack and Edith,*
*who made this possible*

First edition 1990
Second edition 1991

© John Elliot 1990, 1991

1 3 5 7 9 10 8 6 4 2

Designed by Penny Mills
Cover design by Paterson-Jones
Typeset by Bookworm Typesetting, Manchester
Printed and bound in Great Britain
by Richard Clay Limited, Bungay, Suffolk
for

Boxtree Limited
36 Tavistock Street
London WC2E 7PB

A catalogue record for this book is
available from the British Library.

ISBN 1–85283–142–1

# CONTENTS

# PREFACE TO THE SECOND EDITION

This edition of Elliot's Guide has undergone extensive revision in several important areas. Firstly, the need to ensure that the book accurately reflects video availability has led to the dropping (albeit reluctantly) of a large number of films. For unlike conventional film guides, one must not only keep abreast with new video releases but also monitor the market as a whole, ensuring that films that have become unavailable are not retained without good cause.

Accordingly, 588 such films have been dropped, where it was felt their inclusion could no longer be justified. However, this loss has been more than offset by the addition of 1,032 new video releases, bringing the book's content to just over 10,600 entries and making it a good deal more up-to-date.

It was not an easy decision to drop films, and I have been cautious where it was felt a film may merely be in the process of acquiring a new distributor or is likely to re-surface in the near future. The video market is in a constant state of flux, but I have done my best to meet the challenge inherent in covering such a volatile sector of the entertainment business. I need hardly add that the distributors list has been revised to reflect changes of address, the formation of new companies and the apparent cessation of old ones.

Additionally, the rapid growth of stereo and hi-fi sound-tracks has necessitated changes to a large number of films, and readers with these facilities are now amply served. At the same time, I have begun to indicate where films are available in a sub-titled form for the hearing impaired, as this was a neglected area.

Finally, I would like to thank the many readers who wrote in with suggestions, observations and most importantly, corrections of factual errors. Where possible, these have been incorporated into the book and I have spared no effort in revising and updating what has become a labour of love. I hope this shows.

**John Elliot, 1991**

# INTRODUCTION

This book comprises over 10,000 feature films that have been available on video. Though the bulk of them are English language films, many foreign works are included. For the purpose of this book, a feature film is defined as a work of fiction of at least 45 minutes. Compilations of TV series are included, but generally only when they have been formed into a full-length film of at least 45 minutes rather than being left as separate episodes. Additionally, in order to be included, episodes of a TV series that have not been made into a compilation must either have formed part of a complete story, or have each been a self-contained tale in its own right. Thus adaptations of novels or short stories are included but episodes of a soap opera are not.

The book excludes most documentaries, filmed artistic or sporting events, instructional tapes, shorts etc. In this respect it represents a departure from those guides available at present, which tend to include many such tapes.

Having listed a film, we cannot guarantee that it is still available; films change distributors frequently and sometimes become difficult to obtain. However, if a film is listed there is a good chance that it is still in circulation. Similarly, if any film is legally available on video in the UK, it is almost certainly listed here.

It is also important to remember that since the introduction of the Video Recordings Act 1984, it is illegal to sell or rent an uncertificated video unless its contents make it exempt (e.g. sporting or musical events or educational or documentary tapes). Where we have listed a film but provided no certification, this can mean one of two things:

a. To our knowledge the film is available on video but certification information was not available at the time of printing.

b. The film was available on video before the Act came into force and to our knowledge has been withdrawn. However, since it was available prior to the Act becoming law, we believe it to be likely that it will be submitted at some point for certification and have therefore included it.

We have tried not to lose sight of the purpose of the book, in that it is primarily a guide for those who see film as a form of entertainment, hence the general restriction to feature films. We have attempted to include films of every type, in order that the book will be used by all film lovers, whatever their taste or degree of interest. Our guiding principle in the inclusion of any feature film has been whether, to our knowledge, it has been available on video. We have tried not to sacrifice depth to scope in that the book is also aimed at the more serious film lover, who at present is obliged to make use of one of the more conventional film guides, which give scant details of video availability.

Particular regard has been paid to distributor and video recording format details, and an extensive and comprehensive list of distributors is provided, with every effort being made to keep up to date. Since there is no nationally agreed distributor code for films, it serves little purpose to include any of those used by individual distributors or wholesalers.

To sum up, our book attempts to break new ground in the degree of research we have carried out. For example, films for video are often cut, and in all cases the running times shown are for the video release. If we find that a film has been cut, we say so. In addition, we attempt to present a short synopsis for each film that is both informative and sometimes (we hope) amusing. Where relevant, films are related to similar works or placed in the historical context in which they were made. Outstanding music scores receive a mention as do other areas of interest.

The book takes the following form:

## 1. ABBREVIATIONS
This consists of a list of those used other than distributor codes.

## 2. FILMS LIST
This comprises the main section of the book. Note that although we try to provide full details for each entry, some gaps are unavoidable, particularly with regard to the more obscure films. For example, it sometimes is simply not possible to determine the year of production, country of origin or director of a given film, and rather than exclude it, we list it if we have most other details. However, we do not generally include films for which we had the barest details (e.g. the plot and year but no actors, running time or director). Information on all films included is as complete as it was possible to make it at the time of printing.

The film entries are arranged in alphabetical order with each entry taking the following form:

### Title:
Where the title starts with a numeral, this is treated as if spelt. Where titles begin with THE, A or AN, these are ignored and placed at the end. If an abbreviation formed part of the title and has not been expanded (e.g. Mr is sometimes altered to Mister) this will be because it is to be treated as it stands for the purpose of alphabetisation. However, titles that begin with a group of initials as in acronym based titles (e.g. C.A.T. Squad, C.H.O.M.P.S. etc.) are placed at the beginning of their letter group.

Note that American films have their titles spelt the American way (e.g. honor rather than honour). Foreign films are generally listed under an English title, unless the original title is widely known and used.

Films that were a vehicle for the star (e.g. Elvis Presley), or were part of a series (e.g. Marx Brothers films) are often grouped together for convenience. Check in the alternative titles section if a film cannot be located.

### Star Rating:
All films are given a star rating using the following scale:

| | |
|---|---|
| no stars | – abysmal: the film is so bad as to be unwatchable. |
| * | – poor to bad: the film is of poor quality or of minimal interest. |
| ** | – mediocre to fair: the film is watchable but unmemorable. (The vast majority of films in the book receive this rating.) |
| *** | – good to very good: the film is either well-made and worth watching or contains items or sequences that may be of interest. |
| **** | – excellent: the film has some remarkable and memorable qualities. |
| ***** | – outstanding: the film is felt to be a cinematic masterpiece. |

### British Board Of Film Censors Certification:
See abbreviations section for information on these.

### Director(s):
Attention is paid to the use of aliases. Where these are known to have been used, the real name follows in brackets.

### Country/Countries Of Origin:
This refers to the country (or countries) that had overall control and responsibility for production of the film, rather than the location or studio where the film was made (e.g. American films are often made in British studios).

### Year Of Production/Release:
Where the film was re-edited at a later date or not released until some time after production, the first year indicates the year of release, with further information being given where known.

### Principal Players:
Where an alias is used, the real name (if known) is given in brackets, if it is considered to be helpful in identifying the actor. In the case of animations or narrations, details of the voices used are given if known. Generally, an actor's name is given as it appeared in the credits; where

another more familiar name was also used (such as later on in an actor's career) this is given in brackets. As a rule, actors are listed in order of prominence in the film rather than in order of eminence.

## Plot Synopsis:

This includes any other details thought to be relevant and/or informative, such as outstanding scores, scriptwriters, historical context, sequels, alternative versions etc. Note that where other films are referred to, they are shown in capitals if they are included in the book, and in inverted commas if they are not. Additionally, if a sequel or remake is noted but its title is not given, this is because its title is similar to that of the earlier work. Where a film is a compilation, details are given. If the film received any Academy Awards (or in a few cases was nominated for them), details are provided, plus the full names of each recipient where space permits.

## Alternative Title(s):

These are given if known and where there are several they are listed alphabetically. Where a distributor has released the film under one of the alternative titles, that title is followed by the distributor code in brackets. Note that foreign titles that use the Roman alphabet are spelt just as they appear, but they are not accented. In addition, the convention by which German words taking the umlaut, have "e" inserted after the accented vowel (as in maedchen or ueber) is generally not adopted.

## Additional Information:

The name of the written work on which the film is based is given where known, but generally only when the film is truly derivative of it. Note that the title of the work is only given if it differs substantially from that of the film title.

Generally, for a written work to be noted in this section, it must have existed prior to the film being made (e.g. a novel rather than a screenplay), if performed, it must have been produced in a form other than as a film (e.g. a stage musical but not an earlier version of the film) and be the source of both characterisation and plot. In the case of made-for-TV films it is not always possible to determine whether on not the story existed prior to the film being made. This section is used for such references, unless we have information clearly showing that the work was not written as a story in its own right. Where the film has drawn some of its inspiration from works outside this group, such as songs, poems etc., mention of this is generally made in the Plot Synopsis section in preference to this one.

When the title film is included with others on the same cassette, this is indicated, with the names of the other films being given where known. If more than one distributor handles this film, it may be assumed that all the distributors carry it in this version unless a note indicates otherwise. In such cases the appropriate distributor codes would follow in brackets.

It is sometimes the case that either the title film or the other films included on the tape, are separately available from some of the distributors. When this is so it is clearly indicated, with the abbreviation asa (i.e. also separately available) following such additional titles.

## Film Category Code:

See abbreviations section for information on these.

## Running Time(s):

Alternative running times are given when they occur, each alternative being followed by the appropriate distributor code in brackets. Where the film is contained on several cassettes, this is indicated. In such cases each cassette may be assumed to be of approximately equal duration unless the contrary is indicated by a note of individual running times. All running times are rounded up or down to the nearest minute.

Films may be assumed to be in colour, to have the original soundtrack and to be in English, unless otherwise shown, e.g. silent, sub-titled or dubbed films. An exception to this rule is that where a film has been made in a non-English speaking country, it may be assumed to be in the language of that country and to have English sub-titles unless otherwise indicated, except in the case of Hong Kong made martial arts films, which are generally dubbed (though we do not mark them thus unless we are certain they have been).

Where the video running time of a feature film differs from its original cinema or TV running time (in the case of the former this often reflects differences between television scanning speeds and cinema speeds), the original running time is given if known. Original running times are also generally given in the case of TV mini-sagas and compilations of separate TV or feature film episodes. Where an original running time is provided, this is the longest one we have been able to determine for that film. In the case of silent films, original running times cannot be known with any certainty; times given are approximations only and unless otherwise indicated, assume a film speed of 24 frames per second.

Where the film is available together with others on the one cassette, the total running time of the cassette is given if known, it being clearly noted that this running time refers to this cassette rather than a single film. If an original running time is provided as well, it may be assumed to be for the given film only; original running times that refer to a cassette having several films are clearly indicated as such.

Different distributor video running times need not mean that a film has been censored. Sometimes films that are considered overlong (or compilations of TV series) are edited either before or after initial release; this may often be assumed to be so where the differences between the running times (and the original running time if given) are considerable. Smaller differences are often simply due to the mechanics of video production. This can generally be taken to be the case where the film is not marked as being cut, and the given discrepancy between tape and original running time is small.

Where no original running time is shown, it is because the video running time is not known to differ substantially. If several video running times are given, the longest one may generally be assumed to represent the closest approximation to the original running time.

Where a film is known to have been shortened for reasons of censorship rather than for a reason attached to the mechanics of video tape production, this is indicated. Note that a video film might, for example, be both marked as cut and be 20 minutes shorter than the original. This need not mean that it lost 20 minutes to the censor. Films can be both edited and cut, with the cuts made in a film often amounting to but a few minutes or even seconds. Note that a film can be cut twice, once at the film stage and once more on submission to the BBFC for certification prior to video release.

To the best of our knowledge, we mark a film as being cut where this was done at the video stage. This is a guide to video, and as such, our interest must primarily reflect what is available on video as compared to what may be publicly screened. However, if we have information that a film was cut prior to its screening, and that these cuts have been considered sufficient for video release, this is noted in brackets and it can be assumed that it is this version which is available. Wherever possible, we give the total duration of the cuts made. Note that if a film is available from more than one distributor, and the cuts made in each version differ in length, we generally simply give the longest duration unless the discrepancies are known to be considerable.

Of course, some films are never likely to be publicly shown in the UK. Where such films are marked as cut, this has almost certainly been done at the video stage. We do not mark as cut a film that a distributor voluntarily censored or shortened (this can occur when a distributor cuts a film before submission to the BBFC in order to gain a certification), but we certainly note it where to our knowledge it has been done. A film not marked as cut, but showing a large discrepancy between an original running time and the video time, may generally be assumed to have been edited by the distributor. Where this is definitely known to have occurred, the film is marked "abridged".

Films that were originally made for TV or compiled from several episodes of a TV series are indicated as being made for TV. If they are known to have been specifically made for cable/satellite TV or for video, this is shown.

### Video Format(s):
See abbreviations section for information on these.

### Distributor Code:
The abbreviation L/A (limited availability) follows any distributor if there are doubts as to the current availability of the film. This can be because we have reason to believe it to be no longer available from the distributor or because they appear to have ceased trading. It should be noted that a film may be unavailable from a distributor for the time being, simply because they were handling a version that had not been certificated. In all doubtful cases, reference should be made to the distributors list provided.

We can make no statement as to the legality or otherwise of any film listed as being available from a given distributor, nor does the code L/A imply that a given distributor was or is handling an illegal version of the film. At all times we have tried to ensure that our information is accurate. The inclusion of a given distributor is not an endorsement of them, nor is the use of the code L/A a criticism.

Note that when the film is available from several distributors, they are listed in chronological order, with the most recently known distributor given last.

## 3. ALTERNATIVE TITLES
Any film included in the book that has one or more alternative titles, is listed alphabetically in this section by its alternatives.

## 4. DISTRIBUTORS
This consists of a full and detailed list of all distributors referred to in the book, together with details of abbreviation codes and addresses. It is noted if, to the best of our knowledge, a distributor has ceased marketing videos or is a wholesale supplier only.

# JOHN ELLIOT'S TOP 10

## Cineastes' Choice

Although it's an impossible task, I have finally whittled down to ten my personal selection of the most outstanding films available on video.

Alexander Nevsky

All Quiet on the Western Front (1930)

The Battleship Potemkin

Bicycle Thieves

Cinema Paradiso

Ivan The Terrible: Parts 1 and 2

La Belle et la Bête

Les Enfants du Paradis

Monsieur Vincent

Orphée

## The Popular Choice

Of course, not every film can turn out to be a cinematic masterpiece. Here are ten of my favourites in terms of good, solid entertainment.

Crocodile Dundee

ET: The Extra-Terrestrial

The Godfather

Jaws

Midnight Cowboy

Moonstruck

Pretty Woman

Raiders of the Lost Ark

Star Wars

Superman

# ABBREVIATIONS

## 1. General Abbreviations

| | | | |
|---|---|---|---|
| /a: | suffix following format – active play | | distributor(s) |
| /h: | suffix following format – hi-fi soundtrack | LV: | Laservision optical videodisc format |
| /l: | suffix following format – long play | LVS: | Laservision format with stereo sound |
| /s: | suffix following format – stereo soundtrack | mCab: | made for cable TV |
| 12: | BBFC rating – only suitable for persons over the age of 12 | min: | minute(s) |
| 15: | BBFC rating – only suitable for persons over the age of 15 | MPAA: | Motion Picture Association of America |
| 18: | BBFC rating – only suitable for persons over the age of 18 | mPay: | made for Pay-TV |
| 8mm: | eight millimetre format | mSat: | made for Satellite-TV |
| AA: | Academy Award | mTV: | made for TV |
| AAN: | Academy Award nomination | mVid: | made for video |
| Aka: | also known as | NTSC: | TV standard – USA |
| asa: | also separately available | ort: | original running time |
| B: | Betamax format | Osca: | on the same cassette as |
| BBFC: | British Board of Film Classification | PAL: | TV standard – UK et al. |
| Boa: | based on a – (novel, play etc. if clearly derivative; the title being given if it differs from the film title) | PG: | BBFC rating – parental guidance |
| | | Quad: | 2 inch quadraplex open-reel videotape format |
| BTC: | 1 inch broadcast type "C" videotape format | R18: | BBFC rating – only available from licensed sex shops to those over the age of 18 |
| B/W: | black and white | | |
| CED: | capacitance-electronic-disc videodisc format | sec: | second(s) |
| comp: | compilation | SECAM: | TV standard – France et al. |
| CV: | ¼ inch compact videocassette format | SS: | surround sound |
| EIAJ: | ½ inch open reel "EIAJ" videotape format | subH: | subtitled version available for the hearing impaired |
| | | supV: | super VHS videocassette format |
| Ex: | Exempt from a BBFC certification because of its content | U: | BBFC rating – suitable for children |
| L/A: | limited availability – at time of writing video appears to be unavailable from | Uc: | BBFC rating – especially recommended for children |
| | | UMC: | ¾ inch U-matic cassette videotape format |
| | | V: | VHS format |
| | | V2: | Video 2000 format |
| | | WW: | World War (the appropriate number following, e.g. WW1) |

## 2. Film Category Codes

Where the categories are not self-explanatory a short note is given, but it must be understood that such explanations do not represent rigid definitions.

A — Adult films. (The main plot element in such films is sexual.)

A/AD — Action adventures. (These films are designed to

generate excitement by means of a series of action sequences.)

CAR Animations. (These are cartoons unless otherwise indicated in the write-up, e.g. puppet animations. The voices credited are generally those heard unless otherwise indicated, as in the case of non-English language animations that have not been dubbed into English.)

COM Comedies.

DOC Documentaries, artistic or historical films. (These are generally excluded.)

DRA Dramas. (The emphasis in these films is on human relationships and aspirations.)

EDU Educational films. (These are generally excluded.)

FAN Fantasy and science fiction films. (This category is generally not used to include fantasy films aimed solely at a juvenile audience.)

HOR Horror films. (In these films tension or excitement may arise out of human or non-human plot elements, but the main intention of the film is to shock, horrify or frighten.)

JUV Juvenile films. (This category also includes most animations except those clearly suited to another category.)

MAR Martial arts films. (This category does not generally include action adventures in which martial arts sequences occur, but are not central to the plot.)

MUS Musicals.

PER Performances, both artistic and/or sporting. (These are generally excluded.)

THR Thrillers. (In these films tension or suspense is deliberately maintained, and human activities are examined under these conditions.)

WAR War films.

WES Westerns.

## 3. Academy Awards

Because of the confusing range of Academy Awards presented each year, these abbreviations have been separately listed.

Over the years the names of the various awards have been altered, as new categories have been formed, or old ones replaced or expanded. The abbreviations listed below represent the generic names for awards in specific categories; where changes have occurred in the nature of these categories, an explanatory note is given.

Actor       Best Actor.
Actress     Best Actress.
Art         Best Art Direction. From the 1940 awards onwards, this category was split up so as to award B/W and colour films separately. The 1957/58 awards saw this become a single category, for both B/W and colour films, a period then followed, when B/W and colour films were awarded individually. But since the 1967 ceremony, both B/W and colour films have not merited separate awards. For the 1941/46 awards, recognition of Interior Decoration was made, but since the 1947 ceremony this has been modified to one of Set Decoration, and the two awards are now generally given together.
Assist Dir  Best Assistant Direction.

| | |
|---|---|
| Cin | Best Cinematography. This is sometimes referred to as Best Photography, and this award was split for B/W and colour films from the 1939 ceremony onwards. |
| Cost | Best Costume Design. Awarded separately for B/W and colour, this category was created for the 1948 awards onwards. |
| Dance Dir | Best Dance Direction. |
| Dir | Best Direction. |
| Doc | Best Documentary. Awarded separately for shorts and feature length films, from the 1941 awards onwards. |
| Edit | Best Film Editing. |
| Effects | Best Special Effects. Originally this category could include both visual and sound effects, but for the 1963/67 awards, sound effects were recognised in their own right. After the 1967 awards, only visual effects were awarded in their own category, but even these were not given each year, or were sometimes recognised by a Special Award only. Since the 1982 awards, both Special Visual Effects and Special Sound Effects Editing have been recognised, with the former awarded each year and the latter most years. If sound and visual effects are awarded separately, the abbreviations aud and vis are used. |
| Foreign | Best Foreign Language Film. Prior to the 1956 awards, these films were recognised by way of Special or Honorary Awards. |
| Hon Award | Honorary Award. This is noted when given for an outstanding contribution to a specific film and is sometimes referred to as a Special Award. |
| Int | Best Interior Decoration (See note on Best Art Direction.) |
| Make | Best Make-up. |
| Pic | Best Picture. |
| S. Actor | Best Supporting Actor. |
| S. Actress | Best Supporting Actress. |
| Score | Best Score. Over the years this category has generally been split so as to provide recognition for both musical and non-musical pictures. Up to the 1961 awards, recognition did not generally take account of the originality of the score, except in the case of non-musical pictures, and in some years only one award has been made. Generally, this category is now used to award Best Scores for musicals, regardless of whether they be original scores or adaptations from another medium. |
| Score (Orig) | Best Original Score. This category has generally been used for non-musical pictures. |
| Score (Adapt) | Best Score. This category is only used if the score has been clearly recognised as an adaptation. |
| Screen | Best Screenplay. Up to the 1939 ceremony, this was the only category for screenplay awards. For the 1940/47 awards, it occurred together with a Best Original Screenplay category. From the 1948 awards onwards, it occurred with a number of different categories, but was eventually dropped in 1974 in favour of awards recognising original and adapted screenplays. |

Screen (Orig)   Best Original Screenplay written directly for the screen, or based on material not previously published or produced. Screen (Adapt) Best Screenplay based on material adapted from another medium.

Set   Best Set Decoration. (See note on Best Art Direction.)

Short   Best Short Film. This is awarded separately for animations and live-action films.

Song   Best Original Song.

Sound   Best Sound Editing/ Recording.

Spec Award   Special Award. This category fell into disuse by the 1950 awards, and was replaced by one entitled Honorary Award. At the 1972 ceremony it was re-instituted to replace the Honorary Award category, but was known as a Special Achievement Award. It is given for outstanding technical achievement in a specific film.

Story   Best Story/Writing. This category was originally the only writing recognition awarded. By the 1930/31 awards, it was dropped in favour of categories covering original and adapted writing up to the 1934 awards. For the 1935/56 awards, only the Best Original Story category was retained, after which it was replaced by categories for Best Screenplay Adaptation, and Best Story/ Screenplay written directly for the screen.

Story (Orig)   Best Story written directly for the screen.

Story (Adapt)   Best Story based on material from another medium.

Story/Screen   Best Story/Screenplay with both story and screenplay written directly for the screen.

# A

## A-TEAM, THE: JUDGEMENT DAY ** PG
David Hemmings        USA          1985
*George Peppard, Mr T, Dwight Schultz, Dirk Benedict*
A dishonest lawyer arranges to have a judge's daughter kidnapped in order to ensure a favourable outcome for a client on trial. The A-Team are called in by the distraught judge and they obligingly help out with their own unique blend of organised mayhem. Based on the popular TV series.
A/AD                              90 min
V                                 CIC

## A-TEAM, THE: THE COURT MARTIAL ** PG
Tony Mordente/Les Sheldon/Michael O'Herlihy
                     USA          1986
*George Peppard, Mr T, Dwight Schultz, Dirk Benedict, Robert Vaughn, Eddie Velez*
Based on the popular TV series of the same name, this has the A-Team going to Barcelona in order to rescue a hijacked American plane. However, on board is a man, long believed dead, who can clear the A-Team of a number of serious charges.
Aka: A-TEAM, THE: TRIAL BY FIRE; LAST COURT MARTIAL, THE
A/AD                             140 min
B,V                               CIC

## A.W.O.L. ** 18
Herb Freed          SWEDEN/USA    1970
*Russ Thacker, Lenny Baker, Isabella Kaliff*
A little-known film following the strange adventures of US deserter.
DRA               89 min; 67 min (TAKE2)
B,V,V2                    VUL L/A; TAKE2

## A.W.O.L. ** 18
Sheldon Lettich     USA           1990
*Jean-Claude Van Damme, Harrison Page, Deborah Rennard, Lisa Pelikan, Ashley Johnson, Brian Thompson*
When his brother is badly injured in a dope deal that turned sour and later dies from his injuries, a tough Foreign Legionnaire deserts and takes up bareknuckle fighting to help the impoverished widow and her daughter. A brutal B-movie that's partly redeemed by the acting, especially Page in the role of Van Damme's manager and mentor. The screenplay is by Lettich and Van Damme.
Aka: A.W.O.L. ABSENT WITHOUT LEAVE
A/AD                             100 min
V                                 GHV

## ABBOTT AND COSTELLO MEET CAPTAIN KIDD ** U
Charles Lamont      USA           1952
*Bud Abbott, Lou Costello, Charles Laughton, Hillary Brooke, Fran Warren, Bill Shirley, Leif Erickson*
A lame pirate spoof with a generous helping of lousy songs which may be of slight interest if only for the presence of Laughton in a rare comic role. Our comic duo are stranded in Tortuga where they get hold of a treasure map. Captain Kidd in the guise of Laughton is however, in hot pursuit.
Aka: MEET CAPTAIN KIDD
Osca: THREE MUSKETEERS, THE
COM                               70 min
B,V                          KVD; VCC

## ABBOTT AND COSTELLO: AFRICA SCREAMS ***
Charles Barton      USA           1949
*Bud Abbott, Lou Costello, Max Baer, Hillary Brooke, Clyde Beatty, Frank Buck, Shemp Howard, Joe Besser*
Could just as well have been entitled Abbott and Costello on Safari, with our comic duo experiencing various crazy mishaps whilst on safari in Africa. One of their better efforts with a number of hilarious sequences.
Aka: AFRICA SCREAMS
COM                     79 min (ort 87 min)
B,V,V2                            EVP

## ABBOTT AND COSTELLO: JACK AND THE BEANSTALK *
Jean Yarbrough      USA           1952
*Bud Abbott, Lou Costello, Dorothy Ford, Barbara Brown, Buddy Baer*
Abbott and Costello version of this tale that begins and ends with black and white sequences. An anaemic A&C version of this famous fairytale with none of the funny routines common to their earlier films. Very poor.
Aka: JACK AND THE BEANSTALK
COM            73 min (ort 78 min) B/W and Colour
B,V                               KVD

## ABDUCTED ** 18
Boon Collins        CANADA        1985
*Dan Haggerty, Roberta Weiss, Lawrence King-Phillips, William Nunn, Steven Miller*
A female jogger out in the backwoods is kidnapped by a crazed mountainman and taken back to his cabin where she is obliged to stay until rescued by her ever-loving daddy. A violent and profane film that has little to recommend it except some rather good chase scenes. Set in Canada and said to to be based on a true story.
Aka: ABDUCTION
DRA                               90 min
B,V                          RCA; PARK

## ABDUCTION OF LORELEI, THE ** 18
Richard Rank        USA           1978
*Serena, John Galt, Charles Neal, Jenny Gillian, Monique Perrij*
A rich young woman is kidnapped whilst out shopping and raped in the back of a van. As the film progresses it gradually runs out of tension with our heroine enjoying a sexual encounter with the female member of her captors. When one of the male captors kills the other, Lorelei is able to affect her escape by seducing the other man and then killing him, thus enabling her to live happily ever after with her female friend.
A                                 90 min
V                                 RIP

## ABDUCTION, THE ***
Joseph Zito         USA           1975
*Gregory Rozakis, Judith-Marie Bergan, David Pendleton, Leif Erickson, Dorothy Malone, Lawrence Tierney*
This interesting story of a wealthy female student kidnapped by leftists might easily be thought to be based on the Patty Hearst kidnapping, but in fact arose from a novel written before that event took place. That being so, everything about it is strangely geared to the real-life kidnapping, so it may well have been influenced by that event.
Boa: novel Black Abductors by Harrison James.
DRA                               94 min
B,V,V2                        VCL/CBS

## ABIGAIL WANTED ** 15
Richard Taylor      USA           1978
*Sherry Jackson, Christopher Mitchum, Bill Watson, Les Lannom, Bert Hinchman, Sondra Theodore, Cliff Emmich*
An untidy blend of action and comedy that arises when two guys unwittingly purchase a car that's packed with drugs and stolen money. Filmed around St Louis, this has Jackson (disguised as a nun) setting out in murderous pursuit to regain said booty. A fast, violent and not particularly engaging comedy-drama.

Aka: STINGRAY
DRA                      90 min (ort 100 min) Cut (3 sec)
B,V                                                   ABC

## ABIGAIL'S PARTY **                                  PG
Mike Leigh            UK                              1977
*Alison Steadman, Tim Stern, John Salthouse*
One of Mike Leigh's sharp and barbed character
studies in which middle-class mores are put under the
microscope in the course of a single night. The first
full-length TV drama made in the UK to be partly
improvised.
COM                                         102 min mTV
V/h                                                   BBC

## ABILENE TOWN ***
Edwin L. Marin        USA                            1946
*Randolph Scott, Ann Dvorak, Edgar Buchanan,*
*Rhonda Fleming, Lloyd Bridges, Helen Boyce, Howard*
*Freeman, Richard Hale, Jack Lambert, Hank*
*Patterson, Eddy Waller, Dick Curtis*
The sheriff of a Kansas town tries to prevent conflict
between cattlemen and homesteaders out West after
the Civil War. An above-average Western that has a
good part for Dvorak as a dance-hall entertainer. This
has sometimes been shown in a colourised version.
WES                              86 min (ort 89 min) B/W
B,V,V2                                            VCL/CBS

## ABOMINABLE DOCTOR PHIBES, THE ***          15
Robert Fuest          UK                              1971
*Vincent Price, Joseph Cotten, Hugh Griffith, Terry-*
*Thomas, Virginia North, Aubrey Woods, Susan*
*TRavers, Alex Scott, Edward Burnham, Peter*
*Gilmore, Peter Jeffrey, Maurice Kaufman, Norman*
*Jones, John Cater, Sean Bury*
A man who was horribly disfigured in a car accident
that also took the life of his wife, seeks revenge on
those whom he considers were responsible. A horror
spoof that's a cut above many films of this genre.
Followed by the inferior DOCTOR PHIBES RISES
AGAIN.
HOR            90 min (ort 94 min) (Cut at film release)
V                                                     VIR

## ABOUT LAST NIGHT **                               18
Edward Zwick          USA                            1986
*Rob Lowe, James Belushi, Demi Moore, Elizabeth*
*Perkins, George DiCenzo, Michael Alldredge, Robin*
*Thomas*
A teenage love affair comes under threat from peer
pressure in this light romantic comedy aimed at the
under-twenties. An interesting if rather bland version
of a far more engaging one-act play. Let down by the
inconsistent direction and poor characterisation, this
gave Perkins her screen debut.
Boa: play Sexual Perversity In Chicago by David
Mamet.
COM                             102 min (ort 113 min)
V/h                                                   RCA

## ABOVE THE LAW **                                  18
Corey Yuen            HONG KONG                       1987
*Cynthia Rothrock, Yuen Biao, Peter Cunningham, Roy*
*Chiao, Karen Sheperd*
A tough female cop and martial arts expert finds
herself up against a group of hired killers when she
sets out to bring to book a man who has set himself up
as a self-appointed vigilante. A standard blend of
maximal action and minimal plotting, followed by a
sequel.
A/AD                                              87 min
V                                                     VPD

## ABOVE THE LAW 2: THE BLOND FURY **          18
Man Hoi               HONG KONG                       1987
*Cynthia Rothrock, Chin Siu Ho, Man Hoi, Ronnie Yu*
Another action vehicle for martial arts star Rothrock,
in this fast-paced tale of a reporter on the Hong Kong

Times, who is covering a fraud trial and finds that her
investigations lead to a couple of hitmen being sent to
silence her for good. Enjoyable if not all that original
in design or execution.
A/AD                                              85 min
V                                                     VPD

## ABOVE US THE WAVES ***                            U
Ralph Thomas          UK                             1956
*John Mills, John Gregson, Donald Sinden, James*
*Robertson Justice, Michael Medwin, James Kenney,*
*O.E. Hasse, Lee Patterson, Lyndon Brook, William*
*Russell, Thomas Heathcote, Theodore Bikel, Anthony*
*Newley, Harry Towb*
Realistic, documentary-style film that tells of the
relentless attempts on the part of the British to
destroy the German battleship Tirpitz during WW2. A
gripping submarine drama held together by an excel-
lent cast.
Boa: book by C.E.T. Warren and J. Benson.
WAR                              95 min (ort 99 min) B/W
B,V                                                   RNK

## ABRAHAM'S SACRIFICE **
John B. Hively        USA                            1979
*Gene Barry, Andrew Duggan, Beverly Garland*
Part of the "Greatest Heroes of the Bible" series, this
tells of Abraham and Isaac, and how the former's faith
was tested. Average.
DRA                                               49 min
B,V                                               VCL/CBS

## ABSENCE OF MALICE ***                             PG
Sydney Pollack        USA                            1980
*Paul Newman, Sally Field, Bob Balaban, Luther*
*Adler, Melinda Dillon, Barry Primus, Josef Sommer,*
*Don Hood, John Harkins, Wilford Brimley*
Absorbing drama telling of reporter Field who is
tricked by an unscrupulous government investigator
into printing a story that harms an innocent man, who
then tries to get even. Written by ex-reporter Kurt
Luedtke, this film raises some interesting points with
regard to press freedom versus the rights of the
individual. Filmed in Miami.
DRA                            111 min; 116 min (WHV)
B,V                             WHV; RCA (VHS only)

## ABSENT-MINDED PROFESSOR, THE ***               U
Robert Stevenson      USA                            1960
*Fred MacMurray, Nancy Olson, Keenan Wynn,*
*Tommy Kirk, Ed Wynn, Leon Ames, Elliott Reid,*
*Edward Andrews*
Lighthearted Disney story with MacMurray as the
title character discovering "flubber" or flying rubber;
a substance with most peculiar properties. The only
person who believes him is out to steal it. A bright and
breezy comedy with rather good special effects. Fol-
lowed by "Son Of Flubber".
Boa: short story A Situation Of Gravity by Samuel
Taylor.
COM             97 min B/W (colourised version available)
V                                                     WDV

## ABSOLUTE BEGINNERS **                             15
Julian Temple         UK                             1986
*Eddie O'Connell, Patsy Kensit, James Fox, Lionel*
*Blair, Ray Davies, David Bowie, Anita Morris, Steven*
*Berkoff, Mandy Rice-Davies, Sade Adu*
A lively and stylised musical set in 1950s London and
looking at the beginnings of teenage identity. Dis-
appointing in that the characters are rather flat, and
an examination of the rise of racism is a contrived
attempt to add substance to the film. Nonetheless, the
music of Bowie, Sade and jazz veteran Slim Gaillard
are compensations in an interesting if not entirely
satisfactory experiment.
Boa: novel by Colin MacInnes.
MUS                             100 min (ort 107 min
V/sh                                           PAL; VIR

## ABSOLUTION **
Anthony Page          UK          1978 (released 1981)
*Richard Burton, Dominic Guard, Dai Bradley,*
*Andrew Keir, Billy Connolly, Willoughby Gray, Hilda*
*Fenemore, Sharon Duce, Hilary Mason, Robert Addie,*
*Trevor Martin, Robin Soans, Preston Lockwood,*
*James Ottaway, Brook Williams*
In the cloistered atmosphere of a catholic boy's school
a humourless priest falls victim to a practical joke
played on him by his best student. Despite a strong
performance by Burton, the film's credibility degener-
ates as the story progresses. Written by Anthony
Shaffer and filmed in 1978 but not released in the
USA until 1988.
Aka: MURDER BY CONFESSION
DRA                              95 min (ort 105 min)
B,V,V2,LV                                ENT/HOM L/A

## ACAPULCO GOLD **                                      15
Burt Brinckerhoff        USA                        1978
*Marjoe Gortner, Robert Lansing, Ed Nelson, John*
*Harkins, Randi Oates*
Drug smuggling yarn shot on location on the
Hawaiian island of Kauai whose attractions slightly
compensate for the dullness of the plot.
DRA                              105 min Cut (49 sec)
B,V                              VTC L/A; VMA; STABL

## ACCIDENT ***
Joseph Losey          UK                            1967
*Dirk Bogarde, Stanley Baker, Jacqueline Sassard,*
*Delphine Seyrig, Alexander Knox, Michael York,*
*Vivien Merchant, Harold Pinter, Anne Firbank, Brian*
*Phelan, Freddie Jones, Nicholas Mosley*
The script by Harold Pinter sets the tone for a complex
story whose main elements – the love of an Oxford
professor for a student and the events surrounding a
fatal car crash provide a means of examination of the
inner thoughts and motives of the characters. A
thought-provoking and demanding film in which York
appears in his first major film role.
boa: novel by Nicholas Mosley.
DRA                              100 min (ort 105 min)
B,V                                            TEVP

## ACCIDENT AT MEMORIAL STATION **
Donald Brittain        CANADA                       1983
*Fiona Reid, Terence Kelly, Frank Perry, Kelly Anne*
*Anglin, Michael Hogan,*
A roof collapses at a hockey stadium and causes chaos
at the local hospital, with many of those trapped dying
before help can arrive. This film tends to concentrate
on the human interest stories of the victims rather
than on any big-budget special-effects but for all that,
it has very much the look of a made-for-TV film.
Average.
Aka: ACCIDENT, THE
DRA                              104 min (ort 166 min)
B,V                                            INT

## ACCIDENTAL TOURIST, THE ***                           PG
Lawrence Kasdan        USA                          1988
*William Hurt, Kathleen Turner, Geena Davis, David*
*Ogden Stiers, Amy Wright, Bill Pullman, Robert*
*Gorman, David Ogden Stiers, Ed Begley Jr*
A man who writes travel guides for a living has
become withdrawn following the accidental death of
his son in a shooting. This quirky and often wry story
follows him as he embarks on an affair with a bubbly
and zestful woman after his wife walks out on him,
only to find their affair threatened by her sudden
return. AA: S. Actress (Davis).
Boa: novel by Anne Tyler.
COM                              116 min (ort 121 min)
V/sh                                           WHV

## ACCUSED, THE ***                                       18
Jonathan Kaplan        USA                          1988
*Jodie Foster, Kelly McGillis, Bernie Coulson, Leo*
*Rossi, Ann Hearn, Carmen Argenziano, Steve Antin,*
*Tom O'Brien, Peter Van Norden*
After a young waitress is brutally gang raped in a bar,
a cool and efficient female D.A. bargains with the
accused men and the charge against them is reduced
to one of reckless endangerment. However, the victim
is outraged and in order to make amends, the D.A.
decides to press charges against those witnesses who
did nothing to prevent the rape. The violent rape
scene rather spoils this film's articulate and clear
stand. AA: Actress (Foster).
DRA                              106 min (ort 110 min)
V/sh                                           CIC

## ACE HIGH **                                            15
Guiseppe Colizzi        ITALY                       1968
*Bud Spencer (Carlo Pedersoli), Terence Hill (Mario*
*Girotti), Eli Wallach, Brock Peters, Kevin McCarthy,*
*Steffen Zacharias, Livio Lorenzon, Tiffany Hoyveld,*
*Remo Capitani, Armando Bandini, Isa Foster, Rick*
*Boyd*
Knockabout Western of the spaghetti variety with
little of the style of the Sergio Leone epics. One crook
steals a fortune from two others who in turn stole it
from another . . . and so on.
Aka: ASSO PIGLIA TUTTO; HAVE GUN, WILL
TRAVEL; I QUATTRO DELL'AVE MARIA;
REVENGE AT EL PASO; REVENGE IN EL PASSO
WES                            122 min Cut (2 sec) dubbed
B,V                                        CIC; FILV

## ACE UP MY SLEEVE *
Ivan Passer      UK/WEST GERMANY                   1975
*Omar Sharif, Karen Black, Joseph Bottoms*
Forgettable story of international high finance and
intrigue.
Aka: CRIME AND PASSION; FRANKENSTEIN'S
SPUKSCHLOSS
Boa: novel by James Hadley Chase.
THR                                          90 min
B,V                                          POLY

## ACES HIGH ***                                          PG
Jack Gold          UK                               1976
*Malcolm McDowell, Christopher Plummer, Simon*
*Ward, Peter Firth, Ray Milland, John Gielgud, Trevor*
*Howard, Richard Johnson, David Wood, David Daker,*
*Barry Jackson, Ron Pember, Tim Pigott-Smith,*
*Christopher Blake, Jane Anthony*
Competent remake of the early classic film Journey's
End", which in turn was based on the 1929 Sheriff
play. McDowell plays a cynical and embittered squad-
ron leader and Firth one of a fresh batch of WW1
pilots whose dislike of his superior turns to admira-
tion as he begins to understand him. Some exciting
aerial dogfight sequences highlight this remake.
Boa: play Journey's End by R.C. Sheriff/book
Sagittarius Rising by Cecil Lewis. WAR    109 min (ort
min)
B,V                                     TEVP; WHV

## ACROSS 110TH STREET ***                                18
Barry Shear        USA                              1972
*Anthony Quinn, Yaphet Kotto, Anthony Franciosa,*
*Richard Ward, Paul Benjamin, Ed Bernard, Antonio*
*Fargas, Norma Donaldson, Gilbert Lewis*
Three blacks disguised as police officers rob a Mafia-
controlled bank of $300,000 and are chased by both
the New York police and the Mob. Quinn was
co-executive producer in this exciting and often
violent film whose Harlem locations add considerable
atmosphere.
Boa: story by Wally Ferris.
THR                                          102 min
B,V                                          WHV

## ACROSS THE GREAT DIVIDE **    U
Steward Raffill          USA          1976
*Robert F. Logan, Heather Rattray, Mark Edward Hall, George "Buck" Flower*
Two orphans and a conman set out on a trek across the Rockies to start a new life in Oregon. A pleasant little film from the makers of those "Wilderness Family" films that concentrates on good scenic locations and wildlife shots rather than a strong plot.
JUV          98 min; 96 min (HER) (ort 102 min)
B,V,V2          VPD; HER

## ACT OF PASSION **          15
Simon Langton          USA          1984
*Kris Kristofferson, Marlo Thomas, George Dzundza, Jon De Vries, David Rasche, Linda Thorson, Edward Winter, Randy Rocca, Christine Estabrook, Steven Williams, Ron Parady, William Leach, Belinda Bremmer, Karen Cole*
A one-night stand with a suspected terrorist ruins a young woman's life; she is persecuted by the newspapers and receives sackfuls of poison-pen letters. The plot is derivative of the 1975 film "Dis Verlorene Ehre Von Katherine Blum" but the adaptation for an American audience (by Loring Mandel) is somewhat uneven.
Aka: LOST HONOR OF KATHRYN BECK, THE
Boa: novel The Lost Honor Of Katherina Blum by Heinrich Boll.
DRA          100 min mTV
B,V          CBS

## ACT OF PIRACY **          18
John (Bud) Cardos          USA          1988
*Gary Busey, Belinda Bauer, Ray Sharkey, Nancy Milford, Dennis Casey Park*
Action tale following a group of mercenaries who decide to capture a large motor yacht whose owner was in the process of delivering it to Sydney, Australia.
A/AD          100 min
V          CBS

## ACT OF VENGEANCE **          18
John Mackenzie          CANADA          1986
*Charles Bronson, Ellen Burstyn, Wilfred Brimley, Hoyt Axton, Ellen Barkin, Robert Schenkkan*
Film version of a book dealing with the murder of United Mineworkers Union official Jock Yablonski and his family, following his challenge to Tony Boyle – the incumbent president. The flat and matter-of-fact style does little to enhance this true-life drama.
Boa: book by Trevor Armbrister.
DRA          91 min mCab
B,V          GHV

## ACT OF VENGEANCE ***          18
Bob Kelljan          USA          1974
*Jo Ann Harris, Peter Brown, Jennifer Lee, Steve Kanaly, Lada Edmund Jr*
Rape victims band together to form a vigilante squad for revenge on a vicious sadist who forces his victims to sing while he rapes them. A vigilante tale that's a little more intelligent than is usual for films of this genre. See THE SISTERHOOD for a more brutal treatment of this theme.
Aka: RAPE SQUAD; VIOLATORS, THE
DRA          82 min (ort 90 min) Cut (4 min 48 sec)
B,V          RNK

## ACT OF VIOLENCE ***          15
Paul Wendkos          USA          1979
*Elizabeth Montgomery, James Sloyan, Sean Frye, Roy Poole, Biff McGuire, Michael Goodwin, Dolph Sweet, Linden Chiles, Ed Bernard, Tom Rosqui, Grand L. Bush, Victor Millan, Church Ortiz, Fredric Cook, Kate Zentall*
A sensitive story of the effects of a brutal gang mugging on the life of a liberal-minded, divorced newswriter and her young son.
DRA          92 min (ort 100 min) mTV
B,V          CIC

## ACT OF WILL: PARTS 1 AND 2 **          15
Don Sharp          USA          1989
*Victoria Tennant, Peter Coyote, Elizabeth Hurley, Kevin McNally, Jean Marsh*
Long weepie drama following the fortunes of three women, a grandmother, mother and daughter and their trials and tribulations through five decades of love and turmoil. Average.
Boa: novel by Barbara Taylor Bradford.
DRA          200 min (2 cassettes) mTV
V/sh          ODY

## ACT, THE **          15
Sig Shore          USA          1982
*Jill St John, Eddie Albert, Robert Ginty*
Political machinations about the re-election of a president are the subject of this satire. Average.
Aka: BLESS 'EM ALL
COM          92 min
B,V          EIV

## ACTION FORCE 3:          PG
## PYRAMIDS OF DARKNESS **
USA          198-
The wicked Cobra just never gives up. This time he has placed four cubes at four points on the Earth in order to create a field of darkness beneath which nothing can live. Will the mighty Action Force team save the world from destruction? Another lively tale in this series.
CAR          98 min Cut (12 sec)
V          MSD

## ACTION FORCE:          PG
## ARISE SERPENTOR, ARISE **
USA          198-
Another animated adventure following the changing fortunes of the Action Force team. In this tale their arch enemy the evil Cobra has created an invincible clone called Serpentor. Once more our team must battle to save the Earth from the forces of evil.
CAR          95 min
V          MSD

## ACTION FORCE: THE MOVIE ***          PG
USA          198-
Lively animation that follows the adventures of the Action Force team as they battle the forces of darkness, in particular the evil secret Cobra organisation that's out to dominate the world.
CAR          90 min
V          MSD

## ACTION HUNTERS, THE **          PG
Lee Bonner          USA          1986
*Ronald Hunter, Sean Murphy, Joe Cimino, Art Donovan*
An innocent couple suddenly find themselves thrust into an unbelievable adventure involving underwater treasure, gangsters, explosions and car chases.
Aka: ADVENTURES OF THE ACTION HUNTERS, THE
A/AD          79 min
V/h          PACE

## ACTION JACKSON **          18
Craig R. Baxley          USA          1987
*Carl Weathers, Craig T. Nelson, Vanity, Sharon Stone, Thomas F. Wilson, Bill Duke, Robert Davi, Jack Thibeau, Roger Aaron Brown, Stan Foster, Mary Ellen Trainor, Bob Minor, David Glen Eisley, Dennis Hayden, Brian Libby*
A Harvard law graduate turned cop and a nightclub singer, join forces in a desperate campaign to halt a

corrupt auto tycoon's political ambitions. Very much a routine good guys versus bad guys effort, with an abundance of car chases, killings and explosions.
A/AD     83 min (ort 95 min) Cut (9 sec including film cuts)
V/sh                                                      GHV

**ADAM ***                                              15**
Michael Turner          USA              1983
*JoBeth Williams, Daniel J. Travanti, Martha Scott, Richard Masur, Paul Regina, Mason Adams*
Powerful story of a couple who, after their child is kidnapped and murdered, lobby Congress so that parents of missing children may use the FBI national crime computer to help find them. Scripted by Allan Leicht and followed in 1986 by ADAM: HIS SONG CONTINUES.
DRA               92 min; 100 min (CH5) mTV
V/h                                          ODY; CH5

**ADAM AT 6 A.M. ***                                    15**
Robert Scheerer          USA              1970
*Michael Douglas, Lee Purcell, Joe Don Baker, Grayson Hall, Charles Aidman, Meg Foster*
A young college professor from California spends his summer working as a labourer in this unusual and rather absorbing character study.
DRA               96 min (ort 100 min)
V                                                 CBS

**ADAM: HIS SONG CONTINUES **                           15**
Robert Markowitz          USA              1986
*Daniel J. Travanti, JoBeth Williams, Richard Masur, Martha Scott, Paul Regina, Sam McMurray*
Sequel to the 1983 film that continues the tragic story of the parents of a small boy whose kidnapping and murder led to such public outcry that the government passed a special act in 1982 to deal with the problem of missing children. Adam's parents have moved to Washington to start again, but their lives are yet again filled with tragedy. Average.
DRA               90 min (ort 120 min) mTV
B,V                                              VIR

**ADDICTED TO HIS LOVE **                              PG**
Arthur Allan Seidelman USA              1988
*Barry Bostwick, Polly Bergen, Colleen Camp, Erin Gray, Dee Wallace Stone, Linda Purl, Hector Elizondo, Peggy Lipton, Rosemary Forsyth*
A totally unscrupulous man makes a good living out of the women he romances, exploiting their vulnerability and swindling them out of their money. When four of his most recent conquests meet, they discover they share a common misfortune and set about planning his downfall.
Aka: SISTERHOOD
DRA               94 min (ort 100 min) mTV
V                                                 EIV

**ADDICTION: A CRY FOR LOVE ***                        1980**
Paul Wendkos          USA
*Susan Blakely, Gene Barry, Powers Booth, Edie Dams, Lainie Kazan, Charles Siebert, Herb Edelman, Patricia Barry*
A female amphetamine addict and a divorced alcoholic meet, fall in love and try to help each other escape their addiction, in this above-average drama based on an autobiographical best-seller. The adaptation is by Renee Taylor and Joseph Bologna.
Aka: CRY FOR LOVE, A
Boa: book Bedtime Story by Jill Schary Robinson.
DRA               94 min (ort 100 min) mTV
B,V,V2                                         MED

**ADIOS AMIGO **                                       PG**
Fred Williamson          USA              1975
*Fred Williamson, Richard Pryor, Thalmus Rasulala,*

*James Brown, Mike Henry, Robert Phillips, Victoria Jee, Lynne Jackson, Suhaila Farhat, Liz Treadwell*
Unsuccessful off-beat Western with a mainly black cast. Pryor stars as a con-man with Williamson, playing his stooge. Written, directed and produced by Williamson and sorely in need of stronger direction to bring the comic elements together.
Aka: NO SWEAT (MOG)
WES                                          87 min
B,V                                  UFM L/A; MOG

**ADIOS GRINGOS **                                        **
George Finlay (Giorgio Stegani)
                         ITALY              1965
*Montgomery Wood (Giuliano Gemma), Evelyn Stewart (Ida Galli), Roberto Carmardiel, Peter Cross, Jesus Puente, Grant Laramy, Jean Martin, Dax Dean, Monique St Claire, Pierre Cressoy*
A rancher cheated out of his cattle and forced to kill a man in self-defence sets out to find the witness who can clear his name. Fair spaghetti Western.
WES                                         100 min
B,V,V2                                          VPD

**ADULT FAIRYTALES ***
Harry Tampa          USA              1979
*Don Sparks, Brenda Fogarty, Nai Bonet, Martha Reeves, Sy Richardson*
Adult sex comedy in which the Crown Prince seeks to lose his virginity to the voluptuous Snow White. Routine sex film.
Aka: FAIRY TALES
A                                            82 min
B,V,V2                                          VPD

**ADULTERESS, THE ***
Christian Lara          FRANCE              1973
*Patrice Pascal, Catherine Cozan, Laure Moutoussamy*
A look behind the scenes at a wedding, revealing the sexual dreams and fears of bride and groom.
Aka: LES INFIDELES
A                                            73 min
B,V                                             ACV

**ADULTERY ITALIAN STYLE ****
Pasquale Festa Campanile
                         ITALY              1966
*Catherine Spaak, Nino Manfredi, Vittorio Caprioli*
A wife avenges her husband's infidelity by tormenting him with an imaginary rival in this interesting Italian offering.
Aka: ADULTERIO ALL'ITALIANA
A                                            93 min
B,V                                             VIV

**ADVENTURE OF SHERLOCK HOLMES'          PG
SMARTER BROTHER, THE ****
Gene Wilder          USA              1975
*Gene Wilder, Madeline Kahn, Marty Feldman, Dom DeLuise, Leo McKern, Roy Kinnear, John Le Mesurier*
Spoof movie based on Conan Doyle's famous hero with "Sigerson Holmes" as the title character helping damsel in distress Kahn. Look out for DeLuise as a washed up opera star, he provides the liveliest moments in an otherwise weak story. Filmed in England and Wilder's first attempt at acting, writing and directing.
COM                                    87 min (91 min)
B,V,LV                                          CBS

**ADVENTURERS, THE ***                                  18**
Lewis Gilbert          USA              1970
*Bekim Fehimu, Candice Bergen, Ernest Borgnine, Olivia De Havilland, Leigh Taylor-Young, Thommy Bergren, Alan Badel, Rossano Brazzi*
Highly confusing adaptation of a Harold Robbins novel. The central theme is that of one man's quest for vengeance against a brutal security chief in an equally brutal Latin American dictatorship. The

strong cast are swamped by the disorganised and messy direction.
Boa: novel by Harold Robbins.
DRA    163 min (ort 171 min) (Abridged by distributor)
B,V                                            CIC

## ADVENTURERS, THE *                          U
David MacDonald         UK              1950
*Dennis Price, Jack Hawkins, Siobhan McKenna, Peter Hammond, Gregoire Aslan, Bernard Lee, Ronald Adam, Charles Paton*
Dreary South African Western involving the recovery of stolen diamonds that have been hidden in the African jungle.
Aka: FORTUNE IN DIAMONDS; GREAT ADVENTURE, THE
DRA                                     86 min B/W
B,V                                            CBS

## ADVENTURES IN BABYSITTING **            15
Chris Columbus          USA             1987
*Elizabeth Shue, Keith Coogan, Maia Brewton, Anthony Rapp, Calvin Levels, Vincent Philip D'Onofrio, Penelope Ann Miller, Albert Collins, John Fred Noonan, George Newborn, Bardaley Whitford, John Chandler, Ron Canada*
Stood up by her dream date, a girl settles down for a quiet evening babysitting some kids, but a call for help from a friend at the bus station in downtown Chicago plunges her and her charges into a series of breakneck adventures. Directorial debut for screenwriter Columbus and very much aimed at the teen-market.
Aka: NIGHT ON THE TOWN, A
COM                                        98 min
B,V                                          BUENA

## ADVENTURES OF A PLUMBER'S MATE *        18
Stanley Long            UK              1978
*Christopher Neil, Arthur Mullard, Stephen Lewis, Elaine Paige, Anna Quayle, Jonathan Adams, Graham Ashley, Neville Barber, Lindy Benson, Christopher Biggins, Richard Caldicott, Peter Cleall, Angela Daniels, Claire Davenport*
A plumber searches for a golden toilet seat in this dreary attempt at comedy. One in a series, and not a far cry from that "Confessions of a . . ." series.
COM                                        85 min
B,V,V2                           ALPHA/INT; STABL

## ADVENTURES OF A PRIVATE EYE *           18
Stanley Long            UK              1977
*Christopher Neil, Suzy Kendall, Harry H. Corbett, Fred Emney, Liz Fraser, Irene Handl, Ian Lavender, Julian Orchard, Jon Pertwee, Adrienne Posta, Anna Quayle, William Rushton, Robin Stewart, Diana Dors, Jonathan Adams*
Dull comedy about assistant private eye who investigates the case of a model who is being blackmailed with compromising photos. Very poor.
COM                                        96 min
B,V,V2                           ALPHA/INT; STABL

## ADVENTURES OF A TAXI DRIVER *           18
Stanley Long            UK              1976
*Barry Evans, Judy Geeson, Adrienne Posta, Diana Dors, Liz Fraser, Ian Lavender, Stephen Lewis, Robert Lindsay, Henry McGee, Angela Scoular, Brian Wilde, Rachel Dix, Natasha Staiteh-Masri, Jane Hayden, Gloria Walker*
Third in a series of tasteless and feeble comedies. This time round a young cab-driver gets involved with some jewel thieves and has a number of sexual adventures.
COM                                        89 min
B,V,V2                           ALPHA/INT; STABL

## ADVENTURES OF BARON MUNCHAUSEN, THE *** PG

Terry Gilliam  UK/WEST GERMANY          1988
*John Neville, Eric Idle, Sarah Polley, Oliver Reed, Uma Thurman, Jonathan Pryce*
Long, glossy and very expensively mounted story of this famous baron and his fantastic exploits, which though pure invention on his part, are shown in this lively and colourful production as if they really took place.
Boa: novel by Rudolph Erich Raspe.
FAN                                        121 min
V                                              RCA

## ADVENTURES OF BULLWHIP GRIFFIN, THE *** U
James Neilson           USA             1967
*Roddy McDowall, Suzanne Pleshette, Karl Malden, Harry Guardino, Richard Hadyn, Mike Mazurki, Hermione Baddeley, Bryan Russell*
Good fun film from Disney that's a spoof on those gold-rush Westerns with McDowall playing a Bostonian butler who together with two kids, embarks on a treasure hunt in the Wild West.
Boa: novel Bullwhip Griffin by Sid Fleischman.
COM                         106 min (ort 110 min)
B,V                                            WDV

## ADVENTURES OF CURLEY AND HIS            U
GANG, THE *
Bernard Carr            USA             1947
*Larry Olsen, Eileen Janssen, Frances Rafferty*
A boy and his gang get up to all kinds of mischief, such as playing pranks on their teacher, in this totally forgettable comedy. Originally shown with "The Fabulous Joe" as part of the "Hal Roach Comedy Carnival". See also CURLEY AND HIS GANG: IN THE HAUNTED MANSION.
Aka: CURLEY
COM                          51 min (ort 53 min)
B,V                         DFS; MAST (VHS only)

## ADVENTURES OF DON JUAN, THE ***        PG
Vincent Sherman         USA             1948
*Errol Flynn, Viveca Lindfors, Robert Douglas, Romney Brent, Alan Hale, Ann Rutherford, Robert Warwick, Jerry Austin, Douglas Kennedy, Una O'Connor, Aubrey Mather, Raymond Burr*
Flynn is in fine form in this boisterous and slightly tongue-in-cheek tale of the great lover who breaks the hearts of numerous maidens, even directing his blandishments at the Queen as he saves her from the plotting of her minister. Flynn's last big-budget film that contains some interesting attempts at parody.
AA: Cost (Leah Rhodes/Travilla/Marjorie Best).
A/AD                                  111 min B/W
V                                              WHV

## ADVENTURES OF ELIZA FRASER,
THE **
Tim Burstall           AUSTRALIA        1976
*Susannah York, Trevor Howard, John Waters, Rory McBride, Noel Ferrier*
A 19th century seafarer and his wife journey to Australia, the crew mutiny and they are captured by Aborigines. The husband is killed and the wife has many adventures before returning home in this likeable but inauspicious offering.
Aka: INTRIGUE
A/AD                        119 min (ort 130 min)
V                                             FILV

## ADVENTURES OF FRONTIER FREMONT, THE **
Richard Freidenborg     USA             1976
*Dan Haggerty, Denver Pyle, Tone Mirrati*
A tinsmith in the 1830s tires of life in St Louis and goes to live in the mountains. A pleasant outdoors adventure based on a true story.
A/AD                                       92 min
B,V                                            RNK

## ADVENTURES OF HAMBONE AND HILLIE, THE **                    15

Roy Watts            USA            1984
*Lillian Gish, Timothy Bottoms, Candy Clark, O.J.*
*Simpson, Robert Walker, Jack Carter, Alan Hale,*
*Anne Lockhart*
An old woman accidentally leaves her dog at an
airport over three thousand miles from home. Need-
less to say, the faithful mutt finds its way home.
Aka: HAMBONE AND HILLIE
COM                                            90 min
B,V                            VTC; MAST (VHS only)

## ADVENTURES OF HUCKLEBERRY            U
FINN, THE **

Jack B. Hively        USA            1981
*Kurt Ida, Dan Monahan, Brock Peters, Forrest Tucker,*
*Larry Storch, Lurene Tuttle, Mike Mazurki, Jack*
*Kruschen, Michele Marsh, Cliff Osmond*
Huck Finn and Tom Sawyer embark on a river
adventure as they float down the Mississippi on a raft
with a runaway slave. An engaging if uninspired
interpretation.
Aka: HUCKLEBERRY FINN
Boa: novel Huckleberry Finn by Mark Twain.
A/AD        97 min; 92 min (POR) (ort 100 min) mTV
V                            VSP; QUA; IPC; POR

## ADVENTURES OF MARCO POLO, THE ***        U

Archie Mayo          USA            1938
*Gary Cooper, Basil Rathbone, Sigrid Gurie, George*
*Barbier, Binnie Barnes, Ernest Truex, Alan Hale*
This somewhat comic treatment of the life and times
of one of the world's most famous explorers does not
always succeed but is nonetheless enjoyable, not least
for its exciting visual sequences. Look out for a brief
appearance of Lana Turner as a handmaiden.
DRA                                        100 min B/W
V                                              VGM

## ADVENTURES OF NELLIE BLY, THE **

Henning Schellerup    USA            1981
*Linda Purl, Gene Barry, John Randolph, Raymond*
*Buktenica, J.D. Cannon, Cliff Osmond, Elaine Heilveil*
A gutsy and determined journalist proceeds to put the
world to rights by way of exposing corruption, factory
abuses and brutality in an insane asylum. A glamou-
rised and highly fanciful look at the world of inves-
tigative journalism. Eminently forgettable.
Aka: LEGEND OF NELLIE BLY
Boa: story by Seeleg Lester.
DRA                                        100 min mTV
B,V                                            CBS

## ADVENTURES OF ROBIN HOOD, THE ****        U

Michael Curtiz/William Keighley
                    USA            1938
*Errol Flynn, Basil Rathbone, Claude Rains, Olivia De*
*Havilland, Alan Hale, Patric Knowles, Eugene*
*Pallette, Ian Hunter, Melville Cooper, Una O'Connor,*
*Herbert Mundin, Montagu Love, Howard Hill*
Splendid, classic version of the Robin Hood story, with
Flynn in fine form as Robin foiling the machinations
of the Sheriff of Nottingham and Sir Guy of Gisbourne
and thereby saving the throne for the absent King
Richard. A film that finely balances adventure and
comedy, its pace and verve are still unbeaten. Note
the early use of three-colour Technicolor. AA: Art
(Carl Jules Weyl), Score (Erich Wolfgang Korngold),
Edit (Ralph Dawson).
A/AD                                          102 min
B,V                                            WHV

## ADVENTURES OF SHERLOCK HOLMES, THE:   PG
A SCANDAL IN BOHEMIA ***

Paul Annett          UK            1984
*Jeremy Brett, David Burke, Gayle Hunnicutt, Wolf*
*Kahler, Michael Carter, Max Faulkner, Tim Pearce,*
*Rosalie Williams*
Holmes is engaged by the King of Bohemia to regain a
compromising photograph from a former mistress of
the King, in this first episode from the first series of
seven atmospheric stories. Written by Alexander
Baron.
Boa: short story by Arthur Conan Doyle. Osca:
ADVENTURES OF SHERLOCK HOLMES, THE:
THE SPECKLED BAND (HEND)
DRA    52 min; 105 min (HEND: 2 film cassette) mTV
V                                        VCC; HEND

## ADVENTURES OF SHERLOCK HOLMES, THE:   PG
THE BLUE CARBUNCLE ***

David Carson          UK            1984
*Jeremy Brett, David Burke, Rosalind Knight, Ros*
*Simmons, Ken Campbell*
Another story from this popular and well mounted
series. In this tale Holmes uses his remarkable powers
of deduction to return a priceless gem that was stolen
from the Countess of Morcar's hotel suite and later
turned up in the crop of a Christmas goose. The last
tale in the first season of seven stories. Written by
Paul Finney.
Boa: short story by Arthur Conan Doyle.
DRA                        47 min (ort 52 min) mTV
V                                              HEND

## ADVENTURES OF SHERLOCK HOLMES, THE:   PG
THE COPPER BEACHES ***

Paul Annett          UK            1985
*Jeremy Brett, David Burke, Joss Ackland, Natasha*
*Richardson, Lottie Ward, Patience Collier, Angela*
*Browne, Peter Jonfield*
Another tale in this well made TV series with Holmes
investigating strange occurrences at a large country
house when a woman who has misgivings about her
new post of governess comes to him for advice. This
episode was the first one in a second season of six
tales. Written by Bill Craig.
Boa: short story by Arthur Conan Doyle. Osca:
ADVENTURES OF SHERLOCK HOLMES, THE:
THE NORWOOD BUILDER
DRA                        103 min (2 film cassette) mTV
V                                              HEND

## ADVENTURES OF SHERLOCK HOLMES, THE:   PG
THE CROOKED MAN ***

Alan Grint            UK            1983
*Jeremy Brett, David Burke, Norman Jones, Lisa*
*Daniely, Denys Hawthorne, Flora Shaw, Paul*
*Chapman*
An episode from this excellent Granada TV series in
which Holmes is called on to investigate the mystery
surrounding a dead colonel that threatens the good
name of a regiment. Number five in the first series of
seven adventures. Written by Alfred Shaughnessy.
Boa: short story by Arthur Conan Doyle. Osca:
ADVENTURES OF SHERLOCK HOLMES, THE:
THE SOLITARY CYCLIST
DRA        52 min; 95 min (2 film cassette) mTV
V                                              HEND

## ADVENTURES OF SHERLOCK HOLMES, THE:   PG
THE DANCING MEN ***

John Bruce            UK            1984
*Jeremy Brett, David Burke, Terry Evans, Betsy*
*Palmer, David Ross, Eugene Lupinsky, Lorraine*
*Peters, Wendy Jane Walker*
Second episode from the first Granada series with
Holmes being called upon to solve the mystery of a
series of crudely drawn stick figures that appear to
represent a secret message and have terrified a man's
new wife. Written by Anthony Skene.
Boa: short story by Arthur Conan Doyle. Osca:
ADVENTURES OF SHERLOCK HOLMES, THE:
THE RESIDENT PATIENT
DRA        52 min; 95 min (2 film cassette) mTV
V                                              HEND

## ADVENTURES OF SHERLOCK HOLMES, THE: PG
THE FINAL PROBLEM ****
Alan Grint                UK                    1985
*Jeremy Brett, David Burke, Eric Porter, Rosalie
Williams, Olivier-Pierre, Claude Le Sache, Michael
Goldie, Robert Henderson*
In this tale Holmes confronts his old enemy Professor
Moriarty at the Reichenbach Falls in Switzerland.
One of the very best of an excellent series, with a
thrilling climax. This episode ended a series of
thirteen tales (shown in two seasons) and Holmes did
not appear on the TV screens again until 1986 with a
new set of tales, beginning with THE RETURN OF
SHERLOCK HOLMES: THE EMPTY HOUSE. Writ-
ten by John Hawkesworth.
Boa: short story by Arthur Conan Doyle. Osca:
ADVENTURES OF SHERLOCK HOLMES, THE:
THE RED-HEADED LEAGUE
DRA              52 min; 103 min (2 film cassette) mTV
V                                              HEND

## ADVENTURES OF SHERLOCK HOLMES, THE: PG
THE GREEK INTERPRETER ***
Derek Marlowe              UK                    1985
*Jeremy Brett, David Burke, Charles Gray, Alkis
Kritikos, George Costigan, Nick Field, Anton
Alexander, Victoria Harwood, Oliver Maguire, Rita
Howard, Peter Mackriel*
A further episode from the Granada TV series with
Holmes pitting his wits against kidnappers who have
abducted a Greek national and forced him to sign
important documents against his will. In this episode
our sleuth is helped by his brother Mycroft, played
with considerable panache by Charles Gray. Number
two from the second season of six episodes. Written by
Derek Marlowe.
Boa: short story by Arthur Conan Doyle. Osca:
ADVENTURES OF SHERLOCK HOLMES, THE:
THE NAVAL TREATY
DRA              52 min; 95 min (2 film cassette) mTV
V                                              HEND

## ADVENTURES OF SHERLOCK HOLMES, THE:
THE HOUND OF THE BASKERVILLES ****      PG
Brian Mills                UK                    1988
*Jeremy Brett, Edward Hardwicke, Raymond
Adamson, Neil Duncan, Ronald Pickup, Rosemary
McHale, Kristoffer Tabori, Edward Romfourt, James
Faulkner, Philip Dettmer, Stephen Tomlin, Fiona
Gillies, Bernard Horsfall, Donald McKillop*
An excellent adaptation of the famous tale, one in a
series of television productions that gave Brett an
opportunity to demonstrate his splendid interpreta-
tion of the part of Holmes, ably supported by Hard-
wicke as Watson.
Aka: HOUND OF THE BASKERVILLES, THE
Boa: novel by Arthur Conan Doyle. Osca:
ADVENTURES OF SHERLOCK HOLMES, THE:
THE SIGN OF FOUR (asa)
DRA              120 min; 210 min (boxed set) mTV
V                                              HEND

## ADVENTURES OF SHERLOCK HOLMES, THE: PG
THE NAVAL TREATY ***
Alan Grint                UK                    1984
*Jeremy Brett, David Burke, David Gwillim, Gareth
Thomas, Alison Skilbeck, Ronald Russell, Nicholas
Geake, Pamela Pitchford, John Malcolm*
In this episode Holmes has to locate a missing naval
document that deals with a secret treaty between
Great Britain and Italy, aware that it could spark off
an international crisis were it to fall into the wrong
hands. Number three in the first series of seven tales.
Written by Jeremy Paul.
Boa: short story by Arthur Conan Doyle. Osca:
ADVENTURES OF SHERLOCK HOLMES, THE:
THE GREEK INTERPRETER

DRA              52 min; 95 min (2 film cassette) mTV
V                                              HEND

## ADVENTURES OF SHERLOCK HOLMES, THE: PG
THE NORWOOD BUILDER ***
Ken Grieve                UK                    1985
*Jeremy Brett, David Burke, Rosalie Crutchley, Colin
Jeavons, Helen Ryan, Jonathan Adams, Matthew
Solon, Anthony Langdon*
Third tale in the second season of this excellent series,
with Holmes being called on to prove the innocence of
a man accused of the murder of one Joseph Oldacre.
Written by Richard Harris.
Boa: short story by Arthur Conan Doyle. Osca:
ADVENTURES OF SHERLOCK HOLMES, THE:
THE COPPER BEACHES
DRA              52 min; 103 min (2 film cassette) mTV
V                                              HEND

## ADVENTURES OF SHERLOCK HOLMES, THE: PG
THE RED-HEADED LEAGUE ***
John Bruce                UK                    1985
*Jeremy Brett, David Burke, Roger Hammond, Richard
Wilson, Tim McInnerty, Bruce Dukov, John Woodnutt,
John Labonowski, Eric Porter, Rog Stuart*
In this tale Holmes prevents a serious bank robbery
when he is called on to investigate a disbanded
organisation. Holmes' evil adversary, Professor
Moriarty is behind it all. Number five in the second
series of six tales. The script is by John Hawkesworth.
Boa: short story by Arthur Conan Doyle. Osca:
ADVENTURES OF SHERLOCK HOLMES, THE:
THE FINAL PROBLEM
DRA              52 min; 103 min (2 film cassette) mTV
V                                              HEND

## ADVENTURES OF SHERLOCK HOLMES, THE: PG
THE RESIDENT PATIENT ***
David Carson              UK                    1985
*Jeremy Brett, David Burke, Nicholas Clay, Patrick
Newell, Tim Barlow, Brett Forrest, Charles Cork, John
Ringham, David Squire*
In this tale Holmes tries is recruited by a young
medical man who wishes to help his benefactor, a
strange and secretive man who lives in a heavily
fortifies home. Having refused to confide in the
detective, the man is found hanged in mysterious
circumstances a short while later. Number four in the
second series of six stories. Written by Derek Mar-
lowe.
Boa: short story by Arthur Conan Doyle. Osca:
ADVENTURES OF SHERLOCK HOLMES, THE:
THE DANCING MEN
DRA              52 min; 95 min (2 film cassette) mTV
V                                              HEND

## ADVENTURES OF SHERLOCK HOLMES, THE:
THE SIGN OF FOUR ***                            PG
Peter Hammond              UK                    1987
*Jeremy Brett, Edward Hardwicke, Jenny Seagrove,
Ronald Lacey, John Thaw, Kiran Shah, Rosalie
Williams, Emrys James*
Following the strange disappearance of her father, a
young woman finds herself receiving a present each
year, and consults Holmes in an effort to solve the
mystery. Another fine TV adaptation of a Conan
Doyle mystery.
Aka: SIGN OF FOUR, THE
Boa: story by Arthur Conan Doyle. Osca:
ADVENTURES OF SHERLOCK HOLMES, THE:
THE HOUND OF THE BASKERVILLES (asa)
DRA              120 min; 210 min (boxed set) mTV
V                                              HEND

## ADVENTURES OF SHERLOCK HOLMES, THE: PG
THE SOLITARY CYCLIST ***
Paul Annett                UK                    1984
*Jeremy Brett, David Burke, Barbara Wilshire, John*

*Castle, Michael Siberry, Ellis Dale, Sarah Aitchinson,
Simone Bleackley*
Holmes finds himself working on a case in which a
man on a bicycle follows a music teacher for no
apparent reason each time she cycles off to give music
lessons to the daughter of a widower. Fourth tale in
the first series. The script is by Alan Plater.
Boa: short story by Arthur Conan Doyle. Osca:
ADVENTURES OF SHERLOCK HOLMES, THE:
THE CROOKED MAN
DRA          52 min; 95 min (2 film cassette) mTV
V                                           HEND

## ADVENTURES OF SHERLOCK HOLMES, THE:  PG
THE SPECKLED BAND ***
John Bruce          UK                      1984
*Jeremy Brett, David Burke, Jeremy Kemp, Rosalyn
Landor, Denise Armon, John Gill, Rosalie Williams*
Another adventure based on Conan Doyle's famous
sleuth in which he uncovers a vile murder plot that
makes use of a snake. Number six in the first set of
seven stories. Written by Jeremy Paul.
Boa: short story by Arthur Conan Doyle. Osca:
ADVENTURES OF SHERLOCK HOLMES, THE: A
SCANDAL IN BOHEMIA (HEND)
DRA    52 min; 105 min (HEND: 2 film cassette) mTV
V                                      VCC; HEND

## ADVENTURES OF SINBAD THE SAILOR,
THE **
Karel Zeman    CZECHOSLOVAKIA          1975
Cartoon version of the classic Sinbad tale in which our
hero finds a map giving the island location of a buried
cache of jewels. In his search for the treasure he falls
in love with a princess.
Aka: POHADY TISICE A JEDNE NOCI; TALES OF
1001 NIGHTS
CAR                                      87 min
B,V                                        HOM

## ADVENTURES OF SINBAD, THE **          Uc
UK                    1979
Cartoon animation introduced by Jon Pertwee telling
of how Sinbad sets off to regain Bagdad's magic
lantern that has been stolen by the wicked Old Man
Of The Sea. He does this in the hope of gaining the
riches and fame to seek the hand of the city's young
and beautiful princess.
CAR                                      47 min
V                                         STYL

## ADVENTURES OF SPORTS BILLY, THE **    U
USA                    1982
*Voices of: Lane Scheimer, Joyce Bulifant, Frank
Welker*
The evil Queen Vanda has a plan to spoil sport by
destroying fair play on Earth. Armed with his Omni-
Sac from which he can withdraw anything, Billy sets
out to do battle with the villainous Vanda and her evil
assistants. Compiled from a short-lived animated TV
series that lasted for one season.
Aka: SPORT BILLY
CAR                                      75 min
V                                         VGM

## ADVENTURES OF THE AMERICAN RABBIT,    U
THE ***
Fred Wolf/Stewart Moskowitz
USA                    1986
*Voices of: Bob Arbogast, Pat Freley, Barry Gordon,
Bob Holt, Lew Horn, Norm Lenzer, Ken Mars*
Feature-length cartoon about a super-rabbit which
uses its powers to fight against a biker gang holding
New York City in its evil grip. A cute and colourful
animation.
CAR                                      85 min
V                                          EIV

## ADVENTURES OF THE BENGAL
LANCERS ***
Humphrey Hubert (Umberto Lenzi)
ITALY/SPAIN                1965
*Richard Harrison, Wandisa Guida, Hugo Arden (Ugo
Sasso)*
Three sergeants in the Lancers foil the plans of a rebel
leader and rescue an English girl from captivity.
Average adventure from the Continent.
Aka: I TRE SERGENTI DEL BENGALA
A/AD                                     96 min
B,V                                        DER

## ADVENTURES OF THE WILDERNESS          U
FAMILY, THE: PART 1 ***
Stuart Raffill       USA                    1975
*Robert F. Logan, Susan Damante Shaw, Ham Larsen,
George "Buck" Flower, Hollye Holmes, William
Cornford, Heather Rattray*
The true story of a modern pioneer family who turn
their backs on civilisation and go off to live in a cabin
high in the Rockies, where they face their first winter
in the wilderness, the worst one in twenty years. A
sound human interest story that was followed by two
sequels.
Aka: WILDERNESS FAMILY, THE (CH5)
A/AD                    100 min; 95 min (IVS or CH5)
B,V,V2   VPD; IVS (Betamax and VHS only); CH5 (VHS
only)

## ADVENTURES OF THE WILDERNESS          U
FAMILY, THE: PART 2 ***
Frank Zuniga         USA                    1978
*Robert F. Logan, Susan Damante Shaw, William
Cornford, Ham Larsen, George "Buck" Flower, Brian
Cutler*
Continues the story of the Robinson family with the
same cast, the same magnificent Colorado scenery and
much the same kind of story. A lively and likeable
outdoors adventure, followed by MOUNTAIN FAMI-
LY ROBINSON.
Aka: FURTHER ADVENTURES OF THE
WILDERNESS FAMILY; WILDERNESS FAMILY
PART 2, THE
A/AD                    104 min; 101 min (IVS)
B,V V2          VPD; IVS (Betamax and VHS only)

## ADVENTURES OF TOM SAWYER, THE ***     U
Norman Taurog        USA                    1938
*Tommy Kelly, Ann Gillis, Jackie Moran, May Robson,
Walter Brennan, Victor Jory, Spring Byington,
Margaret Hamilton*
Excellent David O. Selznick colour adaptation of
Twain's classic work which is a little more light-
hearted than the original tale but contains a number
of entertaining sequences for all that. Originally
made with a running time of 93 min but shortened for
general release.
Boa: novel Tom Sawyer by Mark Twain.
COM                         76 min (ort 93 min)
B,V                     GHV; VCC; STRAND

## AENIGMA **                            18
Lucio Fulci          ITALY                  1987
*Jared Martin, Caitlin O'Heaney, Susan Kendall*
A shy and awkward college girl is the victim of a cruel
prank played on her at college. As she runs away she
is knocked down by a car and fatally injured. Lying in
hospital in a coma, her spirit animates a devilish
double in order to have revenge in this stilted,
incomprehensible and utterly overblown shocker.
Screenplay is by Fulci and Giorgio Mariuzzo
HOR                                      86 min
B,V                                        VPD

## AEROBICIDE **                         18
David A. Prior       USA                    1986
*Fritz Matthews, David Campbell, Ted Prior, Marcia*

*Kerr*
Thriller set in an exercise clinic whose patrons seem
to be at risk from more than just shortness of breath.
Average.
THR                90 min; 82 min (APX) Cut (18 sec)
B,V                                    VIP/IVS L/A; APX

**AFFAIR, THE \*\*\***                              PG
Gilbert Cates          USA                 1973
*Natalie Wood, Robert Wagner, Bruce Davison, Jamie
Smith-Jackson, Kent Smith, Pat Harrington, Paul
Ryan, Frances Reid, Mark Roberts, Anna Aries, Steve
Riskas, Brett Ericson, Robert Stull, Anna Karen, Paul
Pepper, Sue Taylor*
Above-average TV movie telling the story of a female
songwriter with polio who falls in love with a lawyer.
An excellent cast do justice to Barbara Turner's
sensitive script.
DRA                          74 min; 71 min (CH5) mTV
B,V                              PRV L/A; CH5 (VHS only)

**AFFAIRS OF JANICE \*\*\***
Zebedy Colt            USA                 1976
*C.J. Laing, Crystal Harris, Annie Sprinkles, Bobby
Astyr, Ras Keen, Zebedy Colt*
George, an alcoholic artist, discovers that his wife has
a female lover. Finding that there is also a man in love
with her, he tricks both into posing in a sexually
provocative manner, murders them and calls the
police. He has so arranged things that it is his wife
who is accused of murder. In between all of this occur
various sexual interludes with a sadistic tone. This
film may be disagreeable, but it certainly isn't
forgettable.
A                                            90 min
V                                               RIP

**AFRICA EXPRESS \*\***                             PG
Michele Lupo           ITALY               1967
*Ursula Andress, Jack Palance, Guiliano Gemma*
Tale of a young American running a haulage service
in Africa, who meets a nun in disguise on the trail of a
war criminal. Average.
Aka: TROPICAL EXPRESS (VDEL or KRP)
A/AD                73 min (VDEL); 93 min (KRP)
B,V,V2                  IFS/CBS L/A; VDEL L/A; KRP

**AFRICA: TEXAS STYLE! \*\***
Andrew Marton          USA                 1967
*Hugh O'Brian, John Mills, Nigel Green, Tom Nardini,
Adrienne Corri, Ronald Howard, Charles Hayes,
Hayley Mills*
This dull pilot for the TV series "Cowboy In Africa"
has O'Brian working with Mills senior to preserve
wildlife from predatory poachers and other hazards.
A/AD                              109 min mTV
B,V                                         GHV

**AFRICAN DREAM, AN \*\*\***                        PG
John Smallcombe SOUTH AFRICA               1988
*Kitty Aldridge, John Kani, Dominic Jephcott*
Story of a friendship between a white woman and a
black man in South Africa, that attempts to examine
some of the implications that flow from the doctrine of
apartheid.
DRA                                          90 min
B,V                                             CHV

**AFRICAN QUEEN, THE \*\*\*\***                       U
John Huston            USA                 1951
*Humphrey Bogart, Katharine Hepburn, Robert
Morley, Peter Bull, Theodore Bikel, Walter Gotell,
Peter Swanwick, Richard Marner*
Wonderfully successful combination of Bogart and
Hepburn in the tale of an untidy skipper being
persuaded by a prim spinster to take his boat up the
Congo during WW1. Together they face both the
elements and hostile Germans and in the process
learn to respect and, ultimately, love each other. A

classic film. AA: Actor (Bogart).
Boa: novel by C.S. Forester.
DRA                                         105 min
B,V                                             CBS

**AFTER DARKNESS \*\*\***                           15
Dominique Othenin-Giraud/Sergio Guerrez
                        SWITZERLAND/UK     1985
*John Hurt, Julian Sands, Victoria Abril, Pamela
Salem, William Jacques, Michael Herzog, Philippe
Herzog*
A study in schizophrenia in which a man attempts to
cure his young brother himself, after years spent in a
mental home have failed to produce any improvement.
This turns out to be a dangerous undertaking.
Aka: AFTER DARK; NACH DER FINSTERNIS
DRA                                         109 min
B,V                                             AVA

**AFTER HOURS \*\*\***                              15
Martin Scorsese        USA                 1985
*Griffin Dunne, Rosanna Arquette, Verna Bloom,
Thomas Chong, John Heard, Teri Garr, Linda
Fiorentino, Cheech Marin, Catherine O'Hara, Dick
Miller, Bronson Pinchot*
Strange, surrealistic account of a word processor
operator who, after a date with a strange girl in New
York's Soho district, finds himself effectively
marooned there, unable to get away as he experiences
a night of weird and crazy encounters.
COM                          93 min (ort 97 min)
V/h                                             WHV

**AFTER MIDNIGHT \***                               18
Ken Wheat/Jim Wheat   USA                  1989
*Jillian McWhirter, Pamela Segall, Ramy Zade, Marc
McClure, Nadine Van Der Velde, Marg Helgenberger,
Billy Ray Sharkey*
A group discussion by members of a college psycholo-
gy class concerning what they find scary, forms the
linking device for four tedious tales, which tend to rely
rather heavily on violence for effect. A poor effort that
received limited theatrical exposure – deservedly so.
HOR                                          90 min
V                                               MGM

**AFTER PILKINGTON \*\*\***                         15
Christopher Morahan    UK                  1988
*Bob Peck, Miranda Richardson, Gary Waldhorn,
Barry Foster, Reina James, Richard Brenner, Mary
Miller*
The quiet life of an Oxfod don is shattered when his
childhood girlfriend involves him in a hunt for a
missing archaeologist. Interesting made-for-TV mys-
tery.
DRA                                       99 min mTV
V/h                                             BBC

**AFTER THE FALL OF NEW YORK \*\***                 18
Martin Dolman (Sergio Martino)
                        FRANCE/ITALY       1983
*Michael Sopkiw, George Eastman (Luigi Montefiore),
Roman Geer, Edmund Purdom, Anna Kanakis,
Valentine Monnier*
Another post-nuclear holocaust film. Here one side
infiltrates the other's city to discover the secret of an
anti-missile shield, and at the same time atttempts to
smuggle out the last fertile woman on Earth to start a
new civilisation on another planet.
Aka: 2019 (MGM or VIR); 2019: AFTER THE FALL
OF NEW YORK (XTASY); 2019: DOPO LA CAPUTA
DI NEW YORK
FAN        90 min Cut (7 sec); 81 min Cut (VIR: 54 sec)
B,V                    VTC L/A; MGM; VIR; XTASY

**AFTER THE PROMISE \*\*\***                        PG
David Greene           USA                 1987
*Mark Harmon, Diana Scarwid, Rosemary Dunsmore,*

*Donnelly Rhodes, Trey Ames, Mark Hildreth, Richard Billingsley*
Powerful drama based on actual events that tells of the long struggle of an itinerant carpenter to regain custody of his four sons, who were taken from him and institutionalised following the death of their mother. Set during the Depression period, this presents an uneasy look at bureaucracy, bungling and abuse.
Boa: book by Sebastion Milito.
DRA                     89 min (ort 100 min) mTV
V/h                                             NWV

## AFTERMATH, THE **                              18
Steve Barkett          USA                    1979
*Dayle Kerry, Steve Barkett, Larry Latham, Lynne Margulies, Christopher Barkett, Sid Haig*
Three astronauts return to Earth from a three month mission into deep space, only to find the planet devastated by nuclear war. They are forced to fight for survival against horribly maimed mutants, who are roaming the planet in search of the now scarce resources, whilst attempting to destroy the remnants of civilisation.
Aka: ZOMBIE AFTERMATH
HOR              100 min; 87 min (TGP)
B,V                             WOV; TGP

## AFTERNOON DELIGHTS **                         R18
Warren Evans           USA                    1981
*Eric Edwards, Merle Michaels, Veronica Hart, Vanessa Del Rio, Larry O'Brien, Serena, Bobby Astyr, Vanessa Del Rio, Samantha Fox*
Five guys usually meet every Tuesday night to have a game of poker. However, on this particular night they decide to write down the sex lives of their former wives and read them to each other. This beginning is no more than a device for five flashback sequences intended to show how each wife spent her time while her husband was out working. Despite some amusing sequences this one is rather too contrived to work all that well.
Aka: AFTERNOON DELIGHT
A                                          80 min
B,V                                           EVI

## AFTERSHOCK *                                   15
Frank Harris           USA                    1989
*Jay Roberts Jr, Elizabeth Kaitan, Christopher Mitchum, John Saxon, Richard Lynch, James Lew, Michael Berryman, Russ Tamblyn*
A friendly alien emissary sent to Earth to find out how to avoid nuclear war arrives just at the conclusion of WW3. This flabby premise is soon drowned in a welter of generalised mayhem that's occasionally interrupted by dollops of moralistic philosophising.
HOR                      87 min (ort 91 min)
V                                             MED

## AGAINST A CROOKED SKY **                        U
Earl Bellamy           USA                    1979
*Richard Boone, Stewart Peterson, Geoffrey Land, Jewel Blanch, Clint Ritchie, Henry Wilcoxon, Shannon Farnon, Vincent St Cyr*
Simple old-fashioned Western tale of a boy's search for his sister who has been kidnapped by the Indians. An engaging family film that leaves no permanent impression but offers an hour and a half of light entertainment.
WES                                         89 min
B,V                                       VCL; APOL

## AGAINST ALL ODDS **                             18
Taylor Hackford        USA                    1983
*Jeff Bridges, James Woods, Rachel Ward, Jane Greer, Alex Karras, Richard Widmark, Dorian Harewood*
An unemployed American football player in need of cash accepts a job from a former team-mate who is now the owner of a shady nightclub. The job involves finding his girlfriend who has run off to Mexico. He

not only finds her but falls in love with her, getting enmeshed in a complex web of corruption and intrigue. This loose remake of OUT OF THE PAST (Greer plays the mother of her character in the original) suffers badly from an over-complex plot.
DRA                     116 min (ort 128 min)
V                                             RCA

## AGATHA **                                      PG
Michael Apted          USA                    1979
*Dustin Hoffman, Vanessa Redgrave, Timothy Dalton, Helen Morse, Tony Britton, Celia Gregory, Paul Brooke, Timothy West, Alan Badel*
A speculative film examining what happened to mystery writer Agatha Christie when she disappeared for 11 days in 1926. Redgrave is convincing as Christie, with Hoffman somewhat less so as the reporter who tracks her down.
DRA                                        100 min
V                                             WHV

## AGATHA CHRISTIE COLLECTION, THE:               PG
## IN A GLASS DARKLY **
Desmond Davies         UK                     1982
*Emma Piper, Nicholas Clay, Shaun Scott, Elspet Gray*
A man has a premonition about a murder and ends up marrying the victim. One of the episodes from an adequate rather than inspired series of Agatha Christie tales, originally shown on Thames Television.
Aka: AGATHA CHRISTIE HOUR, THE: IN A GLASS DARKLY; IN A GLASS DARKLY
Boa: story by Agatha Christie.
DRA                               52 min mTV
V                                             VCC

## AGATHA CHRISTIE COLLECTION, THE:                U
## THE CASE OF THE MIDDLE-AGED WIFE **
Michael Simpson        UK                     1982
*Maurice Denham, Peter Jones, Gwen Watford*
A woman seeks advice on her husband's unfaithfulness with unexpected results. Another episode from a forgettable series of adaptations of Christie stories – mild, muddled and forgettable.
Aka: AGATHA CHRISTIE HOUR, THE: THE CASE OF THE MIDDLE-AGED WIFE; CASE OF THE MIDDLE-AGED WIFE, THE
Boa: story by Agatha Christie.
DRA                               52 min mTV
V                                             VCC

## AGE OF CONSENT **                               15
Michael Powell         AUSTRALIA              1969
*James Mason, Helen Mirren, Jack MacGowran, Neva Carr-Glyn, Frank Thring*
A jaded painter seeks fresh inspiration in the Great Barrier Reef and meets a young girl only too willing to pose for him. Limp and predictable with the clumsy attempts at comedy an added annoyance. The pretty Australian scenery is, however, a slight compensation.
Boa: story by Norman Lindsay.
DRA                      95 min (ort 103 min)
B,V                                           RCA

## AGE OF INNOCENCE, THE **
Alan Bridges           CANADA/UK             1977
*David Warner, Honor Blackman, Trudy Young, Cec Linder, Tim Henry, Robert Hawkins, Joey Davidson, Jon Granik, Lois Maxwell, Michael Tait, John Swindells, John Bayliss, John Frieson, Vincent Dale, Spencer Harrison*
Silly story of a teacher with pacifist views who flees to Canada after WW1. There he once again faces persecution for his views.
Aka: RAGTIME SUMMER
DRA                      96 min (ort 101 min)
B,V                                           RNK

## AGENCY **
George Kaczender    CANADA             1981
*Lee Majors, Robert Mitchum, Valerie Perrine, Saul*
*Rubinek, Anthony Parr, Alexandra Stewart*
Mitchum plots to gain political influence through the
subliminal use of TV ads. An interesting idea that
falls prey to a flat and tedious treatment.
Boa: story by P. Gottlieb.
DRA                                   110 min
B,V,V2                                    GHV

## AGENT ON ICE ***                        15
Claude Worswick       USA              1985
*Tom Ormeny, Clifford David, Matt Craven, Louis*
*Pastore*
A tough former CIA agent now works as a private
detective and finds that an old enemy he thought was
dead is plotting to kill him – and the CIA want to help.
A fast-paced and complex espionage tale with some
sharp dialogue and a good performance from David as
a sinister CIA man.
THR                                    95 min
B,V                                       MED

## AGENT ORANGE **                         15
Robert Davies              1989 (released 1990)
*Michelle Bestbier, Phillip Brown*
Lumbering thriller set in Africa where the land of a
woman farmer is slowly being poisoned by the illegal
manufacture of the title compound – a powerful
defoliant first used by the US in Vietnam. A CIA
agent posing as a reporter turns up and together they
set about putting the matter to rights.
THR                                    85 min
V                                         CIC

## AGNES OF GOD ***                        15
Norman Jewison        USA              1985
*Jane Fonda, Anne Bancroft, Meg Tilly, Anne Pitoniak,*
*Winston Reckert, Gratien Gelinas*
A nun is accused of murdering the child she is alleged
to have given birth to in the convent. A court
psychiatrist appointed to find out the truth finds that
her task is not an easy one. The three leads do their
very best in an intense but ultimately unsatisfying
film. Screenplay was by Pielmeyer with photography
by Sven Nykvist.
Boa: play by John Pielmeyer.
DRA                                   113 min
B,V                                       RCA

## AGONY AND THE ECSTASY, THE **            U
Carol Reed            USA              1965
*Charlton Heston, Rex Harrison, Diane Cilento, Harry*
*Andrews, Adolfo Celi*
Epic account of the life of Michelangelo that examines
his conflicts with Pope Julius II and concentrates on
his painting of the Sistine Chapel ceiling. A lavish
and detailed production that entirely over-shadows
the actors, it is preceded by a short documentary on
the work of the artist.
Boa: novel by Irwin Stone.
DRA                                   134 min
B,V,V2                                    CBS

## AGUIRRE, WRATH OF GOD ***
Werner Herzog   WEST GERMANY           1974
*Klaus Kinski, Ruy Guerra, Del Negro, Helena Rojo,*
*Cecilia Rivera, Peter Berling, Danny Ades*
Beautifully made but empty account of a doomed
expedition of Spanish conquistadors in search of seven
legendary cities of gold. Led by Aguirre, their deluded
and slightly insane leader, they leave Pizarro's ex-
pedition and strike out on their own, meeting with
death in the remote jungles of the Amazon. A
dreamlike, hypnotic and ultimately pointless film.
Written by Herzog.
DRA                             90 min (ort 95 min)
B,V                                       PAL

## AI NO BOREI **
Nagisa Oshima       JAPAN              1978
*Kazuko Yoshiyuki, Tatsuya Fuji, Takahiro Tamura,*
*Takuzo Kawatani*
A peasant woman has an affair with good-for-nothing
and together they plot to murder her husband.
However, his ghost returns to haunt them. A follow-
up to AI NO CORRIDA that does little with the
interesting subject matter, but offers tedium in large
measure.
Aka: EMPIRE OF PASSION
DRA                                   108 min
B,V                                       PVG

## AI NO CORRIDA **
Nagisa Oshima   FRANCE/JAPAN           1976
*Tatsuya Fuji, Eiko Matsuda, Aio Nakajima, Meika*
*Seri*
Erotic drama about the sexual relationship between a
young couple, with the insatiable appetite of young
wife Matsuda leading to a series of experiments in
sensual experience that end in tragedy. A well-acted
and often explicit film that offers little of real
substance beneath its glossy and sensual surface.
Followed by AI NO BOREI.
Aka: IN THE REALM OF THE SENSES
DRA                           97 min (ort 105 min)
B,V                                       PVG

## AIR FORCE **                            PG
Howard Hawks          USA              1943
*John Garfield, John Ridgely, Gig Young, George*
*Tobias, Arthur Kennedy, James Brown, Charles*
*Drake, Harry Carey*
Fairly typical look at a WW2 bomber crew, the
exciting action sequences compensating for the banal-
ity of the dialogue.
WAR                     120 min (ort 124 min) B/W
V                                         WHV

## AIR HAWK **
David Baker         AUSTRALIA          1983
*Eric Oldfield, Louise Howill, Ellie Maclure*
A pilot and his brother become marked men through
swamping the gem market with too many stones, in
this standard and rather cliched action tale.
A/AD                                   92 min
B,V,V2                                    INT

## AIRPLANE 2: THE SEQUEL **                15
Ken Finkleman         USA              1982
*Robert Hays, Julie Hagerty, William Shatner, Peter*
*Graves, Chad Everett, Lloyd Bridges*
A poor sequel to AIRPLANE! with the fun centring
around the first passenger space shuttle to the moon.
Despite the many cameo appearances and the hard
work of all concerned, this one just can't match the
pace of the original. The laughs when they do come
are few and far between. Look out for Raymond Burr,
Chuck Connors, Sonny Bono, Rip Torn and many
others. Written by Finkleman.
COM                                    82 min
B,V,V2                                    CIC

## AIRPLANE! ***                           PG
Jim Abrahams/David Zucker/Jerry Zucker
                      USA              1980
*Robert Hays, Julie Hagerty, Robert Stack, Lloyd*
*Bridges, Peter Graves, Kareem Abdul-Jabbar, Leslie*
*Nielsen, Lorna Patterson, Stephen Stucker*
Wildly anarchic spoof on AIRPORT and all those
other disaster-in-the-air type movies. A fast-paced
series of mainly visual gags revolving around the
plight of the passengers and crew aboard a troubled
flight, as ground-control battle to bring it safely down.
Inventive, witty and very, very funny. The infinitely
inferior AIRPLANE 2: THE SEQUEL followed.
COM                                    87 min
B, V/h, V2, LV                            CIC

**AIRPORT ✶✶** PG
George Seaton USA 1970
*Burt Lancaster, Dean Martin, George Kennedy, Helen
Hayes, Jean Seberg, Van Heflin, Jacqueline Bisset,
Maureen Stapleton, Barry Nelson, Dana Wynter, Lloyd
Nolan, Barbara Hale*
Top-heavy with a star cast, this boring long film looks
at the comings and goings of a busy airport. The
inevitable crisis-in-flight goes some way towards
enlivening a dull film that spawned three equally
boring sequels. AA: S. Actress (Hayes).
Boa: novel by Arthur Hailey.
DRA 130 min (ort 137 min)
V/h CIC

**AIRPORT '75 ✶✶** PG
Jack Smight USA 1974
*Charlton Heston, Karen Black, George Kennedy,
Gloria Swanson, Helen Reddy, Efrem Zimbalist Jr,
Susan Clark, Sid Caesar, Linda Blair, Dana Andrews,
Roy Thinnes, Nancy Olson, Ed Nelson, Myrna Loy*
Yet another one of these interminable jetliner disaster
movies. Once more a very full cast has been assem-
bled, including Helen Reddy as a singing nun, yet the
banality of the script proves to be the film's most
enduring if not endearing feature. Swanson plays
herself in her final film. Look out for Sharon Gless
who pops up briefly.
Aka: AIRPORT 1975
A/AD 101 min (ort 106 min)
V/h CIC

**AIRPORT '77 ✶✶** PG
Jerry Jameson USA 1977
*Jack Lemmon, Lee Grant, Brenda Vaccaro, Joseph
Cotten, Olivia de Havilland, James Stewart, Darren
McGavin, Robert Foxworth, Kathleen Quinlan, Monte
Markham, Christopher Lee, James Booth*
Third in the series of "Airport" dramas. Here a private
Boeing 747 crashes in the ocean and sinks, necessitat-
ing a daring rescue bid. Lemmon is good as the pilot in
an otherwise glossy and fairly vacuous disaster movie.
Entertaining if you like that sort of thing.
DRA 116 min
V/h CIC

**AIRPORT '80: THE CONCORDE ✶** PG
David Lowell Rich USA 1979
*Alain Delon, Susan Blakely, Sylvia Kristel, Robert
Wagner, Bibi Andersson, John Davidson, Andrea
Marcovicci, Martha Raye, Cicely Tyson, Jimmie
Walker, David Warner, Mercedes McCambridge*
Last in the series of "Airport" films with the usual
collection of stars doing little for a disaster movie
that's one big yawn from start to finish. The Concorde
does however, act beautifully.
Aka: AIRPORT '79; CONCORDE, THE: AIRPORT '79
DRA 108 min (ort 123 min)
B,V CIC

**AIRPORT S.O.S. HIJACK ✶✶**
Barry Pollack USA 1973
*Adam Roarke, Lynn Borden, Neville Brand, Jay
Robinson, Dub Taylor*
A reckless gambler owes money to the Mafia and
decides that the only way he can pay off his debt is to
kidnap a millionaire. This scheme leads to the hijack-
ing of an aircraft which is then held to ransom,
causing terror for all concerned.
Aka: HIJACK (VDEL)
A/AD 90 min (VUL); 85 min (VDEL)
B,V,V2 VUL L/A; VDEL

**AIRWOLF ✶✶** 18
David Bellisario USA 1984
*Jan-Michael Vincent, Ernest Borgnine, Alex Cord,
Belinda Bauer, David Hemmings*
Super-helicopter with massive firepower has to be
recovered from Colonel Gaddaffi and a plot to deliver

it into the hands of the Russians must be thwarted.
The services of a super-agent are enlisted with this
end in mind in this ludicrous and unbelievable yarn.
Pilot for a TV series.
A/AD 85 min (ort 98 min) mTV
B,V,V2 CIC

**AIRWOLF 2 ✶✶** PG
Nicholas Cora/Harvey Laidman
USA 1984
*Jan-Michael Vincent, Ernest Borgnine, Alex Cord*
Compiled from two episodes of a popular TV series
about a highly sophisticated helicopter which is used
for dangerous assignments. Average piece of high-
flying nonsense.
Aka: AIRWOLF 2: DEADLY MISSION; AIRWOLF 2:
THE SEARCH
A/AD 91 min mTV
B,V CIC

**AIRWOLF 3: FLIGHT INTO DANGER ✶✶** PG
Steve Dollinger USA 1984
*Jan-Michael Vincent, Ernest Borgnine, Alex Cord*
Another full-length adventure compiled from two
episodes of a TV series of the same name featuring a
powerful helicopter. The unbelievable plots are as
before, little more than an excuse for the fast-paced
action sequences.
A/AD 88 min mTV
B,V CIC

**AIRWOLF: THE STAVOGRAD INCIDENT ✶** PG
Ken Jubenvill USA 1986
*Barry Van Dyke, Michelle Scarabelli, Anthony
Sherwood, Geraint Wyn-Davies*
After the demise of the original "Airwolf" series, a
Canadian company bought the rights to the show and
released these cheaper and even more banal clones. In
this one a serious nuclear accident in the USSR
releases a deadly cloud of radioactive dust and the
Russians ask the USA for help in dealing with it.
Together with his team, pilot St John Hawke races to
the rescue in this badly made and wretchedly acted
story.
A/AD 83 min mTV
B,V CIC

**ALADDIN ✶✶**
Jean Image FRANCE 1979
A competent but unmemorable cartoon version of the
classic fairytale.
Aka: ALADDIN AND HIS MAGIC LAMP; ALADDIN
ET LA LAMPE MERVEILLEUSE
CAR 70 min
B,V VDM/GHV

**ALADDIN ✶✶✶** PG
Bruno Corbucci ITALY 1986
*Bud Spencer (Carlo Pedersoli), Luca Venantini, Janet
Agren*
Updated version of the famous tale with Al Addin a
14-year-old Miami boy with no father, but a chorus
girl mother and a gambling drunk of a grandfather.
When he comes across an old oil lamp and starts
cleaning it, he releases the genie, who can grant his
wishes but only operates by day. In the course of his
many adventures he decides to take on his mother's
protection racket boss in this amusing Disney-style
story.
JUV 92 min (Cut at film release by 1 sec)
B,V RNK

**ALAMO BAY ✶✶** 15
Louis Malle USA 1985
*Ed Harris, Amy Madigan, Ho Nguyen, Donald Moffat,
Truyer V. Tran, Rudy Young, Cynthia Carle*
Story of ethnic conflict in a Texan fishing village
between local fishermen and newly arrived Viet-
namese refugees. One of those annoyingly tiresome

"we-are-all-racists" films in which the director makes no attempt to give a balanced view of the American characters. It is, however, said to be based on a real incident in which the new arrivals were threatened by the Ku Klux Klan. Well made but surprisingly unmoving.

DRA                          95 min (ort 98 min)
B,V                          CBS; RCA (VHS only)

## ALAMO, THE ***                          PG
John Wayne              USA              1960
*John Wayne, Richard Widmark, Laurence Harvey,*
*Richard Boone, Frankie Avalon, Carlos Arruza,*
*Patrick Wayne, Linda Cristal, Chill Wills, Joseph*
*Calleia, Joan O'Brien, Ken Curtis, Hank Worden,*
*Denver Pyle, Alissa Wayne*
Wayne directed this over-long account of the heroic stand by 185 Americans who held off 7,000 Mexican troops. A long, rambling and verbose offering that is redeemed by the truly memorable final attack. The excellent score is by Dimitri Tiomkin. AA: Sound (Gordon E. Sawyer/Fred Hynes).

WES                          154 min (ort 199 min)
V                            WHV

## ALAMO, THE: THIRTEEN DAYS              PG
## TO GLORY **
Burt Kennedy            USA              1987
*James Arness, Brian Keith, Lorne Greene, Alec*
*Baldwin, Jim Metzler, Isela Vega, Raul Julia,*
*Kathleen York, David Ogden Stiers, Gene Evans,*
*Ethan Wayne, Fernando Allende*
A less than enthralling account of this famous battle, a milestone in Texas' struggle for independence from Mexico. Raul Julia as Santa Anna and the well-handled battle scenes are good points in an otherwise unimaginative and cliche-ridden offering.
Aka: ALAMO, THE; ALAMO, THE: PARTS 1 AND 2
Boa: book Thirteen Days To Glory by J. Lon Tinkle.

WES                          178 min (2 cassettes) mTV
V                            VIR

## ALAMUT AMBUSH, THE ***                 15
Ken Grier               UK               1983
*Terence Stamp, Robin Sachs, Carmen du Sautoy,*
*Michael Culver, John Horsley, John Rowe, John*
*Grillo, Oscar Quitak, Rosalie Crutchley, Richard*
*Wilson*
Complex thriller involving a British intelligence operative who is an expert on the Middle East, being sent to thwart the activities of a group of terrorists.
Aka: CHESSGAME: ENTER HASSAN
Boa: novel The Alamut Ambush by Anthony Page.

THR                          94 min (ort 100 min) mTV
B,V                          GRN

## AL CAPONE ***                          15
Richard Wilson          USA              1959
*Rod Steiger, Fay Spain, James Gregory, Martin*
*Balsam, Nehemiah Persoff, Murvyn Vye, Joe de Santis*
A reasonably straightforward account of Capone's years of power, taking us up to his fall when convicted on a charge of tax evasion. A solid film, done in semi-documentary style, and only slightly marred by Steiger's over-acting.

DRA                          104 min B/W
V                            CBS

## ALCATRAZ 1: THE WHOLE SHOCKING
## STORY **
Paul Krasny             USA              1980
*Michael Beck, Art Carney, Telly Savalas, Alex Karras,*
*Ronny Cox, John Amos, Will Sampson, Richard*
*Lynch, Robert Davi, Charles Aidman, James*
*MacArthur, Peter Coyote*
The story of Clarence Carnes, said to be the youngest person ever to be sent to Alcatraz, and the decades he spent planning his escape. A simple prison tale whose

dramatic moments must be measured against the periodic descents into cliche. Look out for Carney as Robert Stroud, the legendary Birdman of Alcatraz. The first part of a 240 minute TV film.
Boa: story by Clarence Carnes and Don DeVevi.

DRA                          108 min (ort 120 min) mTV
B,V,V2                       VUL

## ALCATRAZ 2: THE FINAL ESCAPE **
Paul Krasny             USA              1980
*Michael Beck, Art Carney, Telly Savalas, Alex Karras,*
*Ronny Cox, John Amos, Will Sampson, Richard*
*Lynch, Robert Davi, Charles Aidman, James*
*MacArthur, Peter Coyote*
The second part of ALCATRAZ 1: THE WHOLE SHOCKING STORY, telling of Clarence Carnes, and the years he spent planning his escape from this island prison. Originally both parts were shown as a 240 min TV movie.

DRA                          98 min (ort 120 min) mTV
B,V,V2                       VUL

## ALCHEMIST, THE **
James Amante (Charles Band)
                        USA              1981
*Robert Ginty, Lucinda Dooling, John Sanderford,*
*Viola Kate Stimpson, Robert Glaudini*
Minor horror tale of demonic possession set in the Fifties, with Ginty being cursed a century ago to live like an animal by Glaudini, his rival in love. He is eventually saved by a modern-day double of the woman who originally came between the two men. Some prints may be cut to about 85 minutes.

HOR                          106 min
B,V                          VFP

## ALEX: THE LIFE OF A CHILD ***          PG
Robert Markowitz        USA              1986
*Bonnie Bedelia, Craig T. Nelson, Jennie James,*
*Danny Corkill, Mark Withers, Melonie Mazman,*
*Brenda Bazinet, Cherry Jones, Elva Mae Hoover, Dann*
*Florek, Sean McCann, Ted Simonette, Jane Schoetle,*
*Lindsay Amelio, Harley Cross*
The sad story of a young girl and her losing battle with cystic fibrosis, based on the book by sportswriter Frank Deford. The sensitive script is by Carol Evan McKeand and Nigel McKeand. Good but depressing.
Boa: book by Frank Deford.

DRA                          90 min (ort 100 min) mTV
B,V                          NOVA

## ALEXANDER NEVSKY *****                 PG
Sergei Eisenstein       USSR             1938
*Nikolai Cherkassov, Dmitri Orlov, Nikolai Okhlopkov,*
*Alexander Abrikossov, Vassily Novikov*
Powerful epic tale of Nesky and the Russian army repelling an attack by the Teutonic knights in the 13th century. Replete with the required propaganda of the time, this presents a remarkable vision of art in the service of the state. Yet for all that (and the strangely unconvincing battle on the ice), this is a masterwork that rises, together with the brilliant Prokofiev score, far above the stultifying constraints of socialist-realism.

DRA                          106 min B/W
V                            HEND

## ALEXANDRA: QUEEN OF SEX **
Robert Freeman          USA              1983
*Eva Sternberg, Reg Wilson, Lauren Wilde, Joanna*
*Storm, Ashley Summer (Rachel Ashley), Red Wilson,*
*R. Bolla, Michael Gaunt, Steve Douglas*
Slight tale of a woman who has learnt through her sexual conquests of the infidelities of three other married women. Having invited each couple to a party she telephones the wives to warn them that she intends to reveal their extramarital affairs, but to the relief of each woman the film ends with her getting

caught in her own trap.
Aka: ALEXANDRA
A                                                99 min
B,V                                       LOTUS/CBS

**ALF ** **                                        U
Tom Patchett            USA               1987
*Max Wright, Ann Schedeen, Andrea Elson, Benji
Gregory, Liz Sheridan, John LaMotta, Anne Meara*
Inspired by E.T. THE EXTRA-TERRESTRIAL, this
tale follows the adventures of an ugly but lovable
alien, who travels across galaxies from his own planet
and takes up residence at the home of an unsuspecting
family. See also MAC AND ME.
JUV                                        48 min mTV
V                                                VCC

**ALFIE ** ** **                                    15
Lewis Gilbert           UK                1966
*Michael Caine, Julia Foster, Vivien Merchant, Shelley
Winters, Alfie Bass, Millicent Martin, Jane Asher,
Shirley Ann Field, Eleanor Bron, Denholm Elliott,
Graham Stark, Murray Melvin, Sydney Tafler, Peter
Graves*
Caine is perfect in this brilliant story of a working-
class Romeo who casually enters into relationships
with women until a tragedy finally produces in him a
sense of responsibilty. Fine performances from Win-
ters and the rest of the cast are coupled to a witty and
perceptive script. One of the best films of the 1960s.
Followed by ALFIE DARLING.
Boa: play by Bill Naughton.
DRA                             109 min (ort 114 min)
V                                                CIC

**ALFIE DARLING ***                                18
Ken Hughes              UK                1975
*Alan Price, Joan Collins, Jill Townsend, Paul Copley,
Annie Ross, Sheila White, Rula Lenska, Hannah
Gordon, Roger Lumont, Minah Bird, Derek Smith,
Vicki Michelle, Brian Wilde, Robin Parkinson, Jenny
Hanley, Sally Bulloch*
An attempt to produce a sequel to the smash hit
ALFIE from 1966. This time Alfie is a lorry driver
pulling the birds along the motorways of Europe. A
film having none of the insight or bittersweet humour
of the original, with Price an utterly inadequate
replacement for Caine. Quite missable.
Aka: OH, ALFIE
COM          98 min (ort 102 min) (Cut at film release)
B,V                                             TEVP

**ALFREDO, ALFREDO ***                             U
Pietro Germi            ITALY             1972
*Dustin Hoffman, Stefania Sandrelli, Carla Gravina,
Clara Colosimo, Danielle Patella, Duilio Del Prete*
Feeble comedy about a wimp who marries a sexy
woman, and lives to regret it. A typical Italian comedy
full of the usual cliches and sexual innuendo that is of
curiosity value in observing Hoffman playing with a
dubbed voice.
COM                             98 min (ort 110 min)
B,V                                              FFV

**ALIAS THE JESTER ** **                           U
                        UK                1985
*Voices of: Richard Briers, Brian Wilde, Jimmy
Hibbert, Myfanury Talog, Brian Trueman*
A spaceman lands on Earth during the Middle Ages,
when his machine goes crazy owing to faulty spark
plugs. Compiled from five 30 minute TV episodes.
CAR                             52 min (ort 150 min) mTV
V                                       THAMES/VCC

**ALICE ** **
Jerry Gruza/Jacek Bromski
              BELGIUM/POLAND/UK          1981
*Jean-Pierre Cassel, Sophie Barjac, Susannah York,
Paul Nicholas*
A competent but hardly memorable musical, based on

Lewis Carroll's books.
Boa: novel Alice's Adventures In Wonderland/
Through The Looking Glass by Lewis Carroll.
MUS                                        92 min
B,V,V2                                          AVP

**ALICE DOESN'T LIVE HERE ANYMORE ** * **           15
Martin Scorsese         USA               1975
*Ellen Burstyn, Billy Green Bush, Kris Kristofferson,
Alfred Lutter, Diane Ladd, Jodie Foster, Harvey
Keitel, Vic Tayback, Valerie Curtin*
Excellent and enjoyable account of a young widow
coming to terms with her own life after the death of
her husband leaves her penniless. Kristofferson is
memorable as the gentle man who tries to win her
love, as is the fine Robert Getchell screenplay. AA:
Actress (Burstyn).
DRA                             108 min (ort 112 min)
V                                               WHV

**ALICE GOODBODY ***                               18
Tom Scheuer             USA               1976
*Sharon Kelly, Daniel Kauffman, Keith McConnell*
Dullish sex spoof on a lonely girl's misadventures in
Hollywood.
Aka: GOSH
A                             83 min; 77 min (XTASY)
B,V               XTASY; WOV/FREN; STABL

**ALICE IN THE CITIES ***                          
Wim Wenders        WEST GERMANY           1974
*Rudiger Vogeler, Yella Rottlander, Elizabeth Kreuzer*
Another slab of pretentious and heavy Teutonic
symbolism. A cynical and world-weary photographer
gets saddled with a lovable little girl and gradually
loses his negative attitudes in this beautifully photo-
graphed but ponderous tale.
DRA                                        110 min B/W
B,V                                              PVG

**ALICE IN WONDERLAND ***                          U
Harry Harris            USA               1985
*Beau Bridges, Lloyd Bridges, Patrick Duffy, Ringo
Starr, Shelley Winters, Telly Savalas, Sammy Davis
Jr, Robert Morley, Scott Baio, Red Buttons*
Star-packed version of Lewis Carroll's classic fantasy
produced by Irwin Allen – of TOWERING INFERNO
and POSEIDON ADVENTURE fame. A colourless
and dreary production not helped by some remarkably
banal songs.
Boa: novels Alice's Adventures In Wonderland/
Through The Looking Glass by Lewis Carroll.
JUV                             176 min (2 cassettes)
V/h                                             WHV

**ALICE IN WONDERLAND ** **                        18
Bud Townsend            USA               1976
*Kristine De Bell, Terri Hall, Juliet Graham, Bradford
Alexander*
Alice is a librarian who loses her inhibitions by
indulging in a series of wildly erotic encounters in this
adult sex comedy.
A                     70 min (ort 88 min) Cut (2 min 30 sec)
B,V                                    INT L/A; IVS

**ALICE IN WONDERLAND ** * **                      U
Clyde Geronimi/Hamilton Luske/Wilfred Jackson
                        USA               1951
*Voices of: Kathryn Beaumont, Ed Wynn, Richard
Hadyn, Sterling Holloway, Pat O'Malley, Jerry
Colonna, Verna Felton, Bill Thompson, Heather
Angel, Joseph Kearns, Larry Grey, Queenie Leonard,
Dink Trout, Doris Lloyd*
Cartoon version containing elements from both "Alice
in Wonderland" and "Alice through the Looking
Glass". Walt Disney animation at its best, with
several entertaining songs and some good character-
isations compensating for the uneven script.
Boa: novels Alice's Adventures In Wonderland/

Through The Looking Glass by Lewis Carroll.
CAR                                    72 min (ort 75 min)
V                                                    WDV

## ALICE'S RESTAURANT **                              15
Arthur Penn              USA                        1969
*Arlo Guthrie, Pat Quinn, James Broderick, Michael
McClanathan, Geoff Outlaw, Tina Chen*
This attempt to capture the anti-Vietnam sentiments
of the song on which the film is based doesn't really
work. An overlong film that sags badly at times
though the odd mixture of social commentary, drama,
comedy and whimsy is intermittently engaging. The
song that inspired the film was written by Guthrie.
DRA                                   106 min (ort 111 min)
V                                                    WHV

## ALIEN **                                           18
Ridley Scott             USA                        1979
*Sigourney Weaver, Yaphet Kotto, Tom Skerritt, Ian
Holm, Harry Dean Stanton, John Hurt, Veronica
Cartwright*
Incredible special effects are wasted on a routine
horror story of a terrifying alien creature that slaugh-
ters the crew of a commercial spaceship one by one.
Made with infinite care in terms of effects, but poor
dialogue and plot development let it down badly. From
the opening, it's downhill all the way. Followed by
ALIENS which is even more gory. AA: Effects (Vis)
(H.R. Giger/Carlo Rambaldi/Brian Johnson/Nick
Allder/Denys Ayling).
HOR                                   111 min (ort 117 min)
B, V/sh, V2, LV                                      CBS

## ALIEN ENCOUNTERS *                                 15
Ed Hunt                  CANADA                      1977
*Robert Vaughn, Christopher Lee, Daniel Pilon, Tiiu
Leek, Helen Shaver, Henry Ramer, Victoria Johnson,
Doreen Lipson, Kate Parr, Sherri Ross, Linda
Rennhofer, Richard Fitzpatrick, Ted Turner, Sean
McCann, Bob Warner*
Good aliens help Earth resist a take-over by bad
aliens. Low-budget film with extremely poor special
effects.
Aka: PROJECT GENOCIDE (VDEL); STARSHIP
INVASIONS
FAN                             90 min; 84 min (VDEL)
B,V                                          VCL; CROS

## ALIEN FROM L.A. *                                  PG
Albert Pyun              USA                        1988
*Kathy Ireland, Thom Mathews, Linda Kerridge*
A lonely young woman, while looking for her missing
archaeologist father in Africa, falls into a bottomless
pit where she meets a strange character who takes her
to the lost city of Atlantis. A silly adventure tale of
rubbishy effects and stupid dialogue, not helped by a
dismal and squeaky-voiced performance from Ireland
in the role of the heroine.
FAN                                   84 min Cut (21 sec)
B,V                                                  CAN

## ALIEN NATION ***                                   18
Graham Baker             USA                        1988
*James Caan, Mandy Patinkin, Terence Stamp, Kevin
Major Howard, Leslie Bevins*
Offbeat SF police thriller set at some future period
when alien immigrants live and work on Earth. A
police detective has his partner killed by some of the
aliens in the course of a robbery and is none to pleased
to find his new partner is an alien too. Early promise
and many clever touches are hampered by a disappointing script. A TV series followed.
FAN                                    86 min (ort 94 min)
V                                                    CBS

## ALIEN PRIVATE EYE **                               15
Vik Rubenfeld            USA                        1987
*Nikki Fastinetti, Cliff Aduddel, John Alexander,*

*Robert Axelrod*
A blend of detective and SF genres that sees the title
character visiting Earth for a short break, and
discovering the presence of other alien visitors when
gang warfare breaks out over the possession of a
strange artifact. A not altogether successful melding
of two disparate threads, but undeniably ambitious in
conception.
FAN                                                95 min
V                                                    GHV

## ALIEN TERROR *                                     18
Jack Hill/Juan Ibanez                               1971
            MEXICO/USA  (re-released 1986)
*Boris Karloff, Enrique Guzman, Christa Linder,
Maura Monti, Yerye Beirute, Tere Valez, Sergio
Kleiner, Mariela Flores, Griseld Mejia, Rosangela
Balbo, Tito Novarro*
A deranged scientist discovers a powerful new form of
energy that's capable of destroying the entire planet.
However, it can only operate within a human body, in
this low-grade and forgettable nonsense. One of four
horror/SF films shot in Mexico with footage of the
ailing Karloff just prior to his death. This one was
re-written using a story Karloff had approved, but it's
still an embarrassing mess.
Aka: INCREDIBLE INVASION, THE; LA
INVASION SINIESTRA; SINISTER INVASION,
THE
FAN                                    73 min (ort 90 min)
B,V                                                 CINE

## ALIEN TERROR **                                    18
Chuck McNeil             USA                        1977
*Jackie Earl Haley, Alfred W. Lutter, Chris Barnes,
Kathi Carey, John Woods*
A returning space capsule brings to Earth a danger-
ous alien. Average.
Osca: NIGHMARE CITY
FAN                                                100 min
B,V                                             VTC L/A

## ALIEN TERROR, THE **                               18
Donald M. Dohler        USA                        1978
*John Leifert, Tom Griffiths, Mary Martens*
A spaceship crashes near a small town and a host of
grotesque monsters wreak havoc on the surrounding
countryside.
FAN                                                82 min
B,V                                              AVI L/A

## ALIENATOR, THE *                                   15
Fred Olen Ray            USA                        1989
*Jan-Michael Vincent, John Phillip Law, Ross Hagen,
Teagan, Dyann Ortelli, Jesse Dabson, Dawn
Wildsmith, P.J. Soles, Robert Clarke, Richard Wiley,
Leo V. Gordon, Robert Quarry*
A kind of distant cousin to THE TERMINATOR in
which an alien escapes from a prison spaceship and
crash-lands on Earth, but is pursued by a murderous
android. Forest ranger Law and his companions come
across the injured fugitive and set about offering
assistance. A film of weak plotting and dialogue; its
passable effects and mediocre acting do little to
sustain one's interest.
FAN                                    87 min (ort 89 min)
V                                                  PRISM

## ALIENS **                                          18
James Cameron            USA                        1986
*Sigourney Weaver, Carrie Helm, Michael Biehn, Paul
Reiser, Lance Henriksen, Bill Paxton, Jeanette
Goldstein*
A sequel to ALIEN with our heroine arriving at a
planet, where she has to do battle with a host of
monsters, this time round. The effects are more
gruesome, though the film is as empty as ever. A kind
of horror film in space rather than a true science
fiction film, the speculative element of this genre

completely overwhelmed by gory special effects. AA:
Effects (Aud) (Don Sharpe), Effects (Vis) (R. Skotak/S.
Winston/J. Richardson/S. Benson).
Aka: ALIENS: THIS TIME IT'S WAR
FAN                              131 min (ort 137 min)
V/sh                                             CBS

## ALIENS ARE COMING, THE ***                    PG
Harvey Hart           USA                        1980
Tom Mason, Melinda Fee, Eric Braeden, Fawne
Harriman, Caroline McWilliams, Matthew
Laborteaux, Ron Masak, John Milford, Max Gail, Ed
Harris, Hank Brandt, Laurence Haddon, Gerald
McRaney, Curtis Credel, Peter Schuck
SF thriller in which an advance mission of aliens
leave their dying planet and land in rural America,
taking over the minds and bodies of the locals as part
of their plan to gain control of Earth's resources. A
slick reworking of the theme handled in THE INVA-
SION OF THE BODY SNATCHERS.
FAN                                       97 min mTV
B,V                                             ACAD

## ALIENS FROM SPACESHIP EARTH *
Don Como              USA                        1977
Donovan, Lynda Day George
Was Earth inhabited millions of years ago by alien
beings? Has the course of history been influenced by
extra-terrestrials? A rubbishy and incompetent
pseudo-documentary that attempts to answer these
and other burning questions of our time.
Aka: ALIENS FROM SPACESHIP EARTH
WANTED
FAN                               87 min (ort 107 min)
B,V,V2                                           INT

## ALISON'S BIRTHDAY **                           15
Ian Coughlan          AUSTRALIA                   1979
Lou Brown, Joanne Samuel, Bunny Brooke, Vincent
Ball, Marion Johns, Belinda Giblin, Lisa Peers,
Margie McCrae, Martin Vaughan, Rosalind Speirs,
Robyn Gibbes, Lou Brown, Ian Coughlan, Ralph
Cotterill
Horror tale about a girl warned by her dead father,
during a seance, to leave her uncle's house before her
19th birthday. She doesn't and discovers that her
birthday party is to take the form of a black magic
ritual, designed to transfer her personality into the
wizened remains of a dead witch in order to make her
the cult's new leader. Standard yarn of poor direction
and plotting.
HOR                                94 min (ort 99 min)
B,V,V2                                   INTMED; APX

## ALL ABOUT EVE ****                              U
Joseph L. Mankiewicz   USA                       1950
Bette Davis, George Sanders, Anne Baxter, Celeste
Holm, Gary Merrill, Thelma Ritter, Marilyn Monroe,
Hugh Marlowe, Gregory Ratoff
Brilliantly acted and scripted story of a young aspir-
ing actress and her ruthless rise to stardom. Davis is
superb as the ageing star with Merrill playing her
young lover. The witty characterisations are too
numerous to mention, though Sanders as a critic and
Marlowe as a playwright stand out. Basis for the
Broadway musical "Applause". AA: Pic, Dir, S. Actor
(Sanders), Screen (Mankiewicz), Cost (Edith Head/
Charles LeMaire), Sound (Fox Studios).
DRA                               133 min (ort 138 min)
V/h                                              CBS

## ALL ABOUT GLORIA LEONARD **
Gloria Leonard        USA                        1978
Gloria Leonard, Jamie Gillis, Gloria Todd, Ming Toy,
Marc Stevens
Hardcore pseudo-documentary on High Society maga-
zine publisher Gloria Leonard, in which a tediously
detailed account of her sexual experiences is intercut
with film sequences illustrating them. Almost certain

to be cut for the UK.
A                                             108 min
B,V                                        XTACY/KRP

## ALL COPPERS ARE . . . *
Sidney Hayers         UK                         1972
Julia Foster, Ian Hendry, Nicky Henson, Wendy
Allnut, Sandra Dorne, Glynn Edwards, Carmel
McSharry, Queenie Watts, Eddie Byrne, David Baxter,
Norman Jones, Ellis Dale, Robin Askwith, David
Essex, Nicola Davies, Stephen Leigh
Pointless story of a married constable who has an
affair with a robber's girlfriend.
DRA                                84 min (ort 87 min)
B,V                                              RNK

## ALL CREATURES GREAT AND SMALL:            U
THE HOMECOMING **
Terence Dudley        UK                         1983
Christopher Timothy, Robert Hardy, Peter Davidson,
Carol Drinkwater
Special Christmas feature based on the popular TV
series which in turn was based on the books of James
Herriot, telling of his life as a Yorkshire country vet
in the 1930s. A fairly pleasant and undemanding TV
film.
Aka: HOMECOMING, THE
DRA                                       90 min mTV
B,V                                              BBC

## ALL DOGS GO TO HEAVEN **                        U
Don Bluth             USA                         1989
Voices of: Loni Anderson, Judith Barsi, Dom DeLuise,
Melba Moore, Charles Nelson Reilly, Burt Reynolds,
Vic Tayback
An orphan is adopted by an ex-con mutt who has
returned from heaven to perform a good deed. The
vivid animation work of Bluth is one of the few strong
points in this silly and disorganised romp of weak
plotting and cliched characterisations.
CAR                               81 min (ort 85 min) subH
V/sh                                             WHV

## ALL GOD'S CHILDREN **
Jerry Thorpe          USA                         1980
Richard Widmark, Ned Beatty, Ossie Davis, Ruby Dee,
Mariclare Costello, Ken Swofford, John Harkins,
Fredric Lehne, George Spell, Trish Van Devere,
Harvey Vernon, Vincent Duke Milana, Kenneth
Kimmins, Brad English
Feeble attempt to deal with the issues raised by forced
bussing and racial equality. Widmark is good as the
judge who must decide the issue though the William
Blinn script could be better.
DRA                               97 min (ort 100 min) mTV
B,V                                              ATA

## ALL IN A NIGHT'S WORK **
Joseph Anthony        USA                         1961
Shirley MacLaine, Dean Martin, Charlie Ruggles,
Cliff Robertson, Jerome Cowan, Jack Weston, Gale
Gordon
When an innocent office girl is caught in a compromising position with an important business executive,
various complications arise. Not least the fact that the
nephew of said executive, who just happens to be the
heir of the company, suspects that his uncle's "mistress" will reveal the affair unless he pays her to keep
silent. A scatty and lightweight comedy that is sorely
in need of a more spirited script.
COM                                           94 min
B,V                                              CBS

## ALL NIGHT LONG ***                              15
Jean-Claude Tramont   USA                         1981
Gene Hackman, Barbra Streisand, Diane Ladd,
Dennis Quaid, Kevin Dobson, Ann Doran, William
Daniels

When a middle-aged executive is demoted by his company, becoming manager of a downtown all-night drugstore, the favoured hangout of assorted weirdos; he finds solace by embarking on an affair with his neighbour's wife. Streisand replaced Lisa Eichhorn at short notice in this one and she's not well-cast, yet Hackman performs well in a comedy of considerable charm.

COM                                    84 min (ort 96 min)
B,V,V2                                                    CIC

## ALL NIGHT LONG ***                                      15
Basil Dearden             UK                            1961
*Patrick McGoohan, Marti Stevens, Betsy Blair,*
*Richard Attenborough, Keith Michell, Paul Harris,*
*Bernard Braden, Maria Velasco, Harry Towb, Dave*
*Brubeck, Johnny Dankworth, Charles Mingus, Tubby*
*Hayes, Keith Christie*
A retelling of "Othello" in a modern setting involving rivalry between jazz musicians. In this updated setting "Desdemona" becomes a white singer and "Othello" a black bandleader. Patrick McGoohan is memorable as a drummer playing "Iago" to this couple. Look out for guest appearances of Charlie Mingus, Johnny Dankworth and Dave Brubeck. Not entirely successful but a brave and spirited attempt nonetheless.

DRA                                                 95 min
B,V                                          RNK; STRAND

## ALL OF ME ***                                           15
Carl Reiner               USA                          1984
*Steve Martin, Lily Tomlin, Victoria Tennant, Madolyn*
*Smith, Dana Elcar, Richard Libertini, Jason Bernard,*
*Selma Diamond*
A lawyer finds that the left side of his body has been taken over by the soul of an extremely wealthy and eccentric woman. Martin is superb as the idealistic lawyer driven to distraction by an often hilarious chain of events, though the script suffers from unevenness. An ambitious mixture of fantasy and comedy that actually improves as the story progresses.

COM                                    88 min (ort 93 min)
V/h                                TEVP; WHV (VHS only)

## ALL QUIET ON THE WESTERN FRONT ***              PG
Delbert Mann              USA                          1979
*Richard Thomas, Ernest Borgnine, Ian Holm, Donald*
*Pleasence, Patricia Neal, Mark Drewry, Mark Elliott,*
*Dai Bradley, Mathew Evans, George Winter, Dominic*
*Dephcott, Colin Mayes, Ewan Stewart, Simon*
*Haywood, Kevin Stoney*
A remarkably good remake of the 1930 classic anti-war film telling of the experiences of a group of raw recruits in the German trenches of WW1. Borgnine gives one of his best performances as a world-weary and cynical sergeant whose job is to mould these recruits into a competent force. The adaptation from Remarque's novel is by Paul Monash.
Boa: novel by Erich Maria Remarque.

WAR                           103 min (ort 180 min) mTV
V/h                                        PRV L/A; CH5

## ALL QUIET ON THE WESTERN FRONT ****             PG
Lewis Milestone           USA                          1930
*Lew Ayres, Louis Wohlheim, John Wray, Slim*
*Summerville, Russell Gleason, Ben Alexander, Beryl*
*Mercer*
A moving and powerful adaptation of Remarque's great anti-war novel tracing the fortunes of a group of German teenagers who volunteer for service on the Western Front in 1914. Their passage from naive patriotism to cynical disillusionment is vividly portrayed with the final sequence being one of the most haunting on film. Considerably shortened on release, it was followed in 1937 by "The Road Back", a poor sequel. Remade in 1979. AA: Pic.
Boa: novel by Erich Maria Remarque.

WAR                               103 min (ort 140 min) B/W
B,V                                                      CIC

## ALL SHOOK UP! **                                        15
Miklos Lente          CANADA                           1984
*Foster Brooks, Mike McDonald, Konnie Krome, Terrea*
*Foster, Milan Cheylov, Jason Sorokin, Wally Wodchis,*
*Donnie Bowes, Ruddy Hall, Andrew Perkins, Kim*
*Cayer, Darlene Burlie, Kimberly Brooks*
Young people at a summer camp enjoy high-spirited frolics in a good, clean harmless lightweight film. See LITTLE DARLINGS for a similar treatment of this perennial juvenile theme.
Aka: ODDBALLS (AVP)

COM                                92 min; 88 min (AVP)
B,V                                       AVP L/A; VDEL

## ALL THAT JAZZ ***                                       15
Bob Fosse                 USA                          1979
*Roy Scheider, Jessica Lange, Ann Reinking, Leland*
*Palmer, Cliff Gorman, Ben Vereen, Erzsebet Foldi,*
*Sandahl Bergman, John Lithgow*
Surrealistic musical fantasy based on the director/choreographer Fosse's own life, that offers one a strange combination of self-indulgence and gloom. The great opening and splendid dance numbers are enjoyable interludes that compensate to some extent for the film's overall lack of direction or purpose. AA: Art/Set (Philip Rosenberg and Tony Walton/Edward Stewart and Gary Brink), Score (Ralph Burns), Cost (Albert Wolsky), Edit (Alan Heim).

MUS                               118 min (ort 123 min)
V                                                        CBS

## ALL THE KIND STRANGERS **
Burt Kennedy              USA                          1974
*Stacy Keach, Samantha Eggar, John Savage, Robby*
*Benson, Arlene Farber, Tim Parkison*
Grisly film about seven backwoods orphans who lure prospective adoptive parents to a remote farmhouse they have turned into a prison. Those who fail to make the grade are killed and their bodies disposed of. An unsuspecting Keach and Eggar are the latest couple to be "assessed".

HOR                            74 min (ort 78 min) mTV
B,V,V2                                                   VUL

## ALL THE PRESIDENT'S MEN ***                            15
Alan J. Pakula            USA                          1976
*Robert Redford, Dustin Hoffman, Martin Balsam,*
*Jason Robards, Hal Holbrook, Jack Warden, Jane*
*Alexander, Stephen Collins, Meredith Baxter, Ned*
*Beatty, Robert Walden, Polly Holliday, F. Murray*
*Abraham, Lindsay Ann Crouse*
The film of the book about the Washington Post reporters Bob Woodward and Carl Bernstein, whose investigation into the Watergate break-in ultimately led to the resignation of President Nixon and his political disgrace. A film that skilfully tells a true story without any unnecessary embellishment. AA: S. Actor (Robards), Screen (Adapt) (William Goldman), Art/Set (George Jenkins/G. Gaines), Sound (A. Plantadosi/L. Fresholtz/D. Alexander/J. Webb).
Boa: book by Carl Bernstein and Bob Woodward.

DRA                               130 min (ort 138 min)
B,V                                                     WHV

## ALL THE RIGHT MOVES **                                  15
Michael Chapman           USA                          1983
*Tom Cruise, Lea Thompson, Craig T. Nelson, Charles*
*Cioffi, Paul Carafotes, Christopher Penn*
A young boy living in a Pennsylvania steel town sees a football scholarship to university as his only hope of a better life. However, in the process he comes into conflict with his equally ambitious coach. A light-hearted and engaging film very much aimed at the youth audience.

DRA                               86 min (ort 91 min)
B,V                                                     CBS

**ALL THE SENATOR'S GIRLS ✶✶**
En Cognito        USA              1977
*Valerie Parker, Connie Burnett, Lois Parsons, Glen*
*Swallow, Alan Sterling, Beverly Hutton, Rod Harris*
A man is so busy running for senator that he has no
time to satisfy his wife. He decides to pep up his
campaign with an anti-porn crusade. From here the
story moves on to a wild campaign party thrown by
one of his millionaire supporters on his yacht. If this
sounds like an incoherent plot, it's probably because it
is. Amusing in parts, this chaotic film soon degenerates into a mere sequence of sundry couplings on
board the yacht.
A                                    90 min
V                                    DFS

**ALL THE WAY BOYS ✶✶**                 PG
Giuseppe Colizzi      ITALY          1973
*Terence Hill (Mario Girotti), Bud Spencer (Carlo*
*Pedersoli), Cyril Cusack, Michele Antoine, Rene*
*Koldehoff*
Modern outlaws fly a beat-up old plane over the Andes
in this sorry sequel to the "Trinity" films of Spencer
and Hill. Comic opportunities quickly get bogged
down in excessive contributions from the pathos
department.
COM                    88 min (ort 105 min)
B,V,V2            EHE/CBS; CH5 (VHS only)

**ALL THIS AND HEAVEN TOO ✶✶✶**          U
Anatole Litvak        USA            1940
*Bette Davis, Charles Boyer, Jeffrey Lynn, Barbara*
*O'Neil, Virginia Weidler, Walter Hampden, Helen*
*Westley, George Couloris, Montagu Love, June*
*Lockhart, Anne Todd, Fritz Leiber*
In 19th century France, an aristocrat falls in love with
a governess and the pair embark on a doomed love
affair that ends in scandal and death. A full-blooded
adaptation of the Field novel with a script that
provides many opportunities for the assorted stars to
give of their best.
Boa: novel by Rachel Field.
DRA              135 min (ort 143 min) B/W
V                                    WHV

**ALLAN QUATERMAIN AND THE**             PG
**LOST CITY OF GOLD ✶✶**
Gary Nelson/Newt Arnold (additional scenes only)
                      USA            1986
*Richard Chamberlain, Sharon Stone, James Earl*
*Jones, Henry Silva, Robert Donner, Doghmi Larbi,*
*Aileen Marson, Cassandra Peterson, Martin Rabbett*
A sequel to KING SOLOMON'S MINES with Quater-
main and his fiancee going off in search of his missing
brother. He soon finds himself and his companions
menaced by spears, serpents, savages and lions as
they trek through uncharted regions in this derivative
and lacklustre adventure tale.
A/AD                  96 min (ort 110 min)
B,V                                  RNK

**ALLEY CAT ✶**                          18
Edward Victor (Eduardo Palmos/Victor Ordonex/Al
Valleta)              USA            1984
*Karin Mani, Robert Torti, Brit Helfer, Michael Wayne,*
*Jon Greene, Timothy J. Cutt*
Routine and exploitative urban violence tale with a
young girl coming into conflict with a nasty street
gang and using her martial arts skills to good effect
following an attack on her grandparents.
DRA              78 min (ort 82 min) Cut (40 sec)
B,V                                  EIV

**ALLEY CATS, THE ✶**
Radley Metzger        USA            1966
*Uta Leuka, Karin Field, Sabrina Koch*
American sex film of minimal plot, almost certain to
be cut for the UK.

A                                    76 min
B,V,V2                               DER

**ALLIGATOR ✶✶✶**
Lewis Teague          USA            1980
*Robert Foster, Michael Gazzo, Robin Riker, Perry*
*Lang, Henry Silva, Jack Carter, Bart Braverman,*
*Dean Jagger*
When a pet alligator gets flushed down the toilet it
returns as a 20 foot monster to terrorise and kill the
inhabitants of Chicago. Strange as it may sound, the
script (by John Sayles) provides a number of comic
moments that nicely balance the expected horror; not
least is a wonderful performance by Silva as an
egocentric and obsessive Great White Hunter.
HOR                    90 min (ort 94 min)
B,V,V2                               INT

**ALLNIGHTER, THE ✶**                    PG
Tamar Simon Hoffs     USA            1987
*Susanna Hoffs, Dedee Pfeiffer, Joan Cusack, Michael*
*Ontkean, John Terlesky, James Anthony Shanta, Pam*
*Grier*
A pretty co-ed, searching for her "Mr Right", makes a
last ditch attempt to find romance on the last night
before graduation day whilst her silly, scatter-brained
colleagues embark on a series of sexual encounters.
Tedious, empty and not terribly funny.
COM                    92 min (ort 108 min)
V/sh                                 CIC

**ALL'S FAIR ✶✶**                        15
Rocky Lang            USA            1989
*George Segal, Sally Kellerman, Jennifer Edwards,*
*Lou Ferrigno, Robert Carradine, John Kapelos, Jane*
*Kaczmarek*
Mediocre American comedy that examines the battle
of the sexes within the context of some weekend
war-games. When the blonde go-ahead marketing
chief of a confectionary company decides to teach her
chauvinist boss a lesson, she gathers together an army
of disgruntled wives to take on him and his macho
pals at a weekend war-games exercise. A tired script
and limp direction waste comic opportunities in this
one.
COM                                  90 min
B,V                                  BRAVE

**ALMOST ANGELS ✶✶✶**                    U
Steve Previn          USA            1962
*Peter Weck, Hans Hott, Fritz Eckhardt, Bruni Lobel,*
*Vincent Winter, Sean Scully*
Two boys in the famous Vienna Boys choir become
firm friends in this engaging Disney feature. A little
on the sentimental side, especially when one of the
boys saves the day at an important performance; yet
the fine singing and convincing acting are compensa-
tions.
JUV                    89 min (ort 93 min)
B,V                                  WDV

**ALMOST PERFECT AFFAIR, AN ✶✶**         15
Michael Ritchie       USA            1979
*Keith Carradine, Monica Vitti, Raf Vallone, Christian*
*De Sica, Dick Anthony Williams, Henri Garcia*
A novice cinema verite film-maker attending the
Cannes Film Festival, has an affair with a producer's
wife in order to promote his work. Very much set
against the background of this famous film festival,
its appeal will mainly be restricted to determined
film-buffs, despite one or two satirical touches.
DRA                    87 min (ort 93 min)
V/h                                  CIC

**ALMOST YOU ✶**                         15
Adam Brooks           USA            1984
*Brooke Adams, Griffin Dunne, Karen Young, Marty*

*Watt, Christine Estabrook, Josh Mostel, Laura Dean,*
*Miguel Pinero, Joe Silver, Joe Leon*
A couple living in New York are obliged to hire a
live-in nurse when the wife dislocates her hip. One of
those tedious romantic comedies that tries to present
some kind of "message" about love, marriage and
commitment.
COM                     92 min (ort 110 min)
V/h                                          CBS

## ALOHA SUMMER **                          PG
Tommy Lee Wallace     USA              1988
*Chris Makepeace, Yuji Okumoto, Don Michael Paul,*
*Lorie Griffin, Tia Carrere, Andy Bumatai, Sho Kosugi,*
*Blaine Kia, Warren Fabro, Scott Nakagawa*
A nostalgic, coming-of-age drama set on the Hawaiian
island of Waikiki with six American, Japanese and
Hawaiian boys coming of age during the summer of
1959. Remarkably earnest and well-meaning but the
utter banality of the script is a serious drawback.
Disengage mind and enjoy scenery.
COM         92 min (ort 98 min) Cut (1 min 13 sec)
B,V                                          MGM

## ALOHA, BOBBY AND ROSE **
Floyd Mutrux          USA              1975
*Paul Le Mat, Dianne Hull, Tim McIntire, Leigh*
*French, Martine Bartlett, Robert Carradine, Eddie*
*(Edward James) Olmos*
A car mechanic and his girl friend are inevitably
drawn into crime when a hold-up meant as a joke,
misfires and a liquor store clerk is killed. With the
police in pursuit, the couple are forced to flee in this
well made but somewhat predictable crime-drama.
DRA                                   90 min
B,V                                          VCL

## ALONE IN THE DARK **                      18
Jack Sholder          USA              1982
*Jack Palance, Donald Pleasance, Martin Landau,*
*Dwight Schultz, Erland van Lidth de Jeude, Deborah*
*Hedwell*
During a power-cut, three inmates of a mental
hospital escape and invade the home of a psychiatrist,
forcing him into violence in this uneven and muddled
horror yarn.
HOR                          93 min Cut (15 sec)
B,V,LV                                       RNK

## ALPHA BETA ****
Anthony Page          UK               1973
*Albert Finney, Rachel Roberts*
The break-up of a marriage in all its misery, with
Finney and Roberts in splendid form tormenting each
other prior to their split-up. An engrossing but
depressing work. See also Bergman's SCENES FROM
A MARRIAGE.
Boa: play by E.A. Whitehead.
DRA                                   65 min mTV
B,V,V2                                       INT

## ALPHA CITY ***                            18
             WEST GERMANY               1985
*Claude-Olivier Rudolph, Isabelle Gutzwiler, Al Corley,*
*J. Draeger, Peter Von Strombeck, Sybille Rauch*
Fast-paced but rather cliched tough urban thriller.
Aka: ABGERECHNET WIRD NACHTS
THR                                   96 min
V                                            CFD

## ALPHA INCIDENT, THE **
Bill Rebane           USA              1977
*Ralph Meeker, John Goff, Stafford Morgan, Carole*
*Irene Newell*
A Mars probe returns to Earth, contaminated by a
deadly organism that can destroy civilisation as we

know it. A familiar theme with the government
desperately attempting to cover up this hazard; but a
leak of radiation foils their plans.
FAN                          81 min (ort 84 min)
B,V,V2                                       REP/VPD

## ALPHABET CITY *                           18
Amos Poe              USA              1984
*Vincent Spano, Kate Vernon, Michael Winslow, Zohra*
*Lampert, Raymond Serra*
A picture of the life of an unpleasant gangster on New
York City's Lower East Side that is practically devoid
of a storyline, relying almost solely on arty direction
and surface imagery. A shallow and unsatisfying
offering that could easily have been very much better,
but not much worse.
DRA                          85 min (ort 98 min)
B,V                                          CBS

## ALPHAVILLE **
Jean-Luc GoddardFRANCE/ITALY           1965
*Eddie Constantine, Anna Karina, Akim Tamiroff,*
*Howard Vernon*
Confused account of Saris, a computer controlled city
of the future where a private detective is sent to
rescue a scientist. A tedious and erratic film that
suffers badly from the director's failure to impose
clarity of vision. Good ideas swim about in there but
remain undeveloped. Pity.
FAN                     98 min (ort 100 min) B/W
B,V                                          PVG

## ALTERED STATES **                         18
Ken Russell           USA              1980
*William Hurt, Blair Brown, Bob Balaban, Charles*
*Haid, Thaao Penghilis, Dori Brenner, Miguel*
*Godreau, Drew Barrymore*
A scientist involved in primal brain research subjects
himself to a series of mind-affecting experiments with
dire results. Employing some memorable special
effects, this excessively talky film had Chayefsky
disowning it as an adaptation of his novel (the novel is
now credited to Sidney Aaron – his pen-name). This
was Hurt's film debut.
Boa: novel by Paddy Chayefsky.
FAN                                   102 min
V/sh                                         WHV

## ALTERNATIVE WAR ***
Clyde Ware            USA              1971
*Martin Sheen, Davey Davidson, Rod McCary, Denine*
*Terry*
A conscientious objector in West Virginia opts out of
the Civil War, spending three years living as a recluse
in a cave in this well handled drama. Based on a
legendary tale with a nice performance from Sheen,
who's the only one on the screen for most of the time.
Aka: NO DRUMS, NO BUGLES (SVC)
WES                     85 min; 90 min (SVC)
B,V                          SVC L/A; MARKET/GOV

## ALVAREZ KELLY ***                         PG
Edward Dmytryk        USA              1966
*William Holden, Richard Widmark, Janice Rule,*
*Patrick O'Neal, Victoria Shaw, Roger C. Carmel,*
*Richard Rust, Arthur Franz, Donald (Don "Red")*
*Barry, Harry Carey Jr, Mauritz Hugo, Robert Morgan,*
*Stephanie Hill, Paul Lukather*
A cattle-owner is caught between both sides, in this
slow-moving Civil War tale, as Holden who sells to the
Yankees, is kidnapped by the Confederates who want
him to steal cattle for them. Very much a standard
Civil War yarn, complete with some incongruous love
scenes. The screenplay is by Franklin Coen/Elliott
Arnold.

WES                                          116 min
B,V                                            RCA

## ALWAYS ***                                  PG
Steven Spielberg        USA                    1989
*Richard Dreyfuss, Holly Hunter, John Goodman, Brad
Johnson, Audrey Hepburn, Roberts Blossom, Keith
David, Marg Helgenberger*
In this flashy remake of "A Guy Named Joe", a
daredevil pilot firefighter is tragically killed at work
but returns in spirit form to oversee the welfare of his
former girlfriend, who has another chance of happi-
ness with a young pilot. An optimistic and entertain-
ing film of little depth but much sentimentality.
COM                                117 min (ort 121 min)
V                                              CIC

## AMADEUS ****                                PG
Milos Forman            USA                    1984
*F. Murray Abraham, Tom Hulce, Elizabeth Berridge,
Simon Callow, Roy Dotrice, Christine Ebersole, Jeffrey
Jones*
A brilliant film version of a play on the life and death
of Mozart, filmed in Prague (by Miroslav Ondricek)
and boasting one of the most literate film scripts of the
1980s. The story revolves around the unpleasant
rivalry between Salieri and Mozart – musical
mediocrity and genius respectively. AA: Pic, Dir,
Actor (Abraham), Screen (Adapt) (Schaffer), Sound
(Berger et al), Art/Set (Von Brandenstein/Cerny),
Cost (Pistek), Make (LeBlanc/Smith).
Boa: play by Peter Schaffer.
DRA                                153 min (ort 158 min)
V/sh                                   TEVP L/A; WHV

## AMATEUR, THE *                              15
Charles Jarrott         CANADA                 1981
*John Savage, Christopher Plummer, Ed Lauter,
Marthe Keller, Arthur Hill, Nicholas Campbell,
Graham Jarvis, John Marley*
A CIA computer wizard uses his skills to hunt down
the terrorists who seized the American Consulate in
Munich and murdered his girlfriend. This foolish and
over-complex spy thriller has Savage totally miscast
as the computer buff (Plummer would have been a
better choice) and suffers badly from the want of a
more intelligent script.
Boa: novel by R. Littell.
THR                                109 min (ort 111 min)
B,V,V2,LV                                      CBS

## AMAZING ADVENTURES OF
## BARON MUNCHAUSEN, THE ***
Joseph Von Baky         GERMANY                1943
*Hans Albens*
A high spirited and entertaining version of this tale of
arch exaggerator Baron Munchausen.
COM                                            101 min
B,V                                            TEVP

## AMAZING ADVENTURES OF JOE 90, THE **  PG
Gerry Anderson/Alan Perry/Leo Easton/Desmond
Saunders                UK                     1981
*Voices of: Len Jones, Rupert Davies, David Healey,
Keith Alexander*
Compilation of a popular TV puppet series about a boy
with strange mental powers. So-so.
JUV                                        90 min mTV
B,V                               PRV L/A; CH5 (VHS only)

## AMAZING CAPTAIN NEMO, THE ***            U
Alex March              USA                    1978
*Jose Ferrer, Burgess Meredith, Lynda Day George*
Captain Nemo and his submarine, Nautilus, are
shaken free from their resting place, where they have
been trapped for decades by a blast in the course of
some US Navy war-games. He sets out to defeat an
evil professor who, together with his robot crew, is

threatening Washington with a nuclear device, in this
entertaining piece of nonsense.
A/AD                                98 min (ort 102 min)
V/h                                            WHV

## AMAZING DOBERMANS, THE ***
David Chudnow/Byron Chudnow
                        USA                    1976
*James Franciscus, Barbara Eden, Fred Astaire, Jack
Carter, Billy Barty*
Action-comedy with a bible-quoting Astaire as a
former con-man, using his five remarkable dogs to
help a treasury agent foil the criminal plans of a
racketeer. An enjoyable high-budget sequel to THE
DOBERMAN GANG and THE DARING DOBER-
MANS that has a lot going for it; not least owing to
the wise casting of Astaire.
A/AD                                90 min (ort 99 min)
B,V,V2                                         VUL

## AMAZING HOWARD HUGHES, THE **           PG
William A. Graham       USA                    1977
*Tommy Lee Jones, Ed Flanders, James Hampton,
Tovah Feldshuh, Lee Purcell, Jim Antonio, Sorrell
Brooke, Arthur Franz, Howard Hesseman, Ed Harris*
TV movie covering the career of Howard Hughes, from
eccentric millionaire to psychotic recluse, that belies
the title by managing to make the weird and faintly
sinister career of Hughes seem surprisingly unin-
teresting. Flanders as Hughes' associate Noah Diet-
rich, easily steals the scenes from Jones as the
millionaire recluse. Feldshuh is interesting too, as the
actress Katherine Hepburn. Below average. First
shown in two parts.
Boa: book Howard The Amazing Mr Hughes by Noah
Dietrich.
DRA                                119 min (ort 240 min) mTV
B,V                                            TEVP

## AMAZING MISTER BLUNDEN, THE ***
Lionel Jeffries         UK                     1972
*Laurence Naismith, Lynne Frederick, Garry Miller,
Rosalyn Landor, Marc Granger, Diana Dors, James
Villiers, Madeleine Smith, David Lodge, Dorothy
Alison, Stuart Lock, Deddie Davis*
Whimsical tale of two children befriended by a ghost
after the death of their father in WW1 and taken back
in time on a series of adventures. Despite a somewhat
muddled plot it remains a gentle work of some charm.
Boa: novel The Ghosts by Antonia Barber.
JUV                                            98 min
B,V,V2                                     VCL/CBS

## AMAZING STORIES **                        15
                        USA                    1985
*Kevin Costner, Kiefer Sutherland, Bronson Pinchot,
Christopher Lloyd, Scott Coffey, Mary Stuart
Masterson*
A compilation of three short stories, written and
presented by Steven Spielberg – "The Mission",
"Mummy, Daddy" and "Go To The Head Of The Class".
An uneven mixture of horror, comedy and adventure
that was followed by several sequels.
FAN                                            120 min
B,V                                            CIC

## AMAZING STORIES: 2 **                      15
Steven Spielberg        USA                    1985
*Robert Blossom, Lukas Haas, Gregory Hines, Danny
DeVito, Rhea Perlman*
Three more short stories combining elements of
fantasy, adventure and comedy, and once more presented by Steven Spielberg. The stories are entitled:
"Ghost Train", "The Amazing Falsworth" and "The
Wedding Ring". The first story has an old man
dismayed to find his son has built his home over the
spot where a train nearly killed him years ago. The
other tales are similar fantasy mixtures – all are let
down by an excess of sentimentality.

FAN                                    74 min
B,V                                       CIC

## AMAZING STORIES: 3 **                 PG
Joe Dante/Robert Stephens/Tom Holland
          USA                          1986
*Hayley Mills, Stephen Geoffreys, Jon Cryer, Dennis
Lipscomb*
Director Steven Spielberg once more presents three
fantasy tales: "The Greibble", "Moving Day" and
"Miscalculation". The first tells of a woman's attempts
to get rid of an uninvited guest – her son's lovable
monster, the second story examines a boy's plight
when he discovers that both he and his parents are
extra-terrestrials, and the last tale tells of a photographer with a recipe that can bring photographs to
life. Average.
FAN                                    68 min
B,V                                       CIC

## AMAZING STORIES: 4 ***               PG
Brad Bird/Thomas Carter/Matthew Robbins
          USA                          1986
*Joe Seneca, Natalie Gregory, Lane Smith*
Three more short fantasy tales in this series – "Family
Dog", "Dorothy And Ben" and "The Main Attraction".
The first tale examines the exploits of a hound after
his return from a bizarre obedience school, in the
second a man awoken from a forty year coma has in
fact been on another world, and in the last tale a
meteor shower enhances the attractiveness of a high
school romeo. More entertaining fantasy shorts let
down by sentimentality.
FAN                                    71 min
B,V                                       CIC

## AMAZING STORIES: 5 ***               PG
Philip Joanou/Mick Garris/Todd Holland
          USA                          1986
*John Lithgow, Patrick Swayze, David Carradine*
Fifth in the series with another three tales of the
supernatural. "The Doll" tells of two shy people
brought together by the magic of a supernatural
toymaker, "Life On Death Row" has Patrick Swayze in
the role of a condemned prisoner, and "Thanksgiving"
is a humorous episode in which a greedy prospector
finds some unearthly carnivores living at the bottom
of a well beneath his property. A much better
collection with well handled effects.
FAN                                    98 min
V/sh                                      CIC

## AMAZING STORIES: 6 ***               U
Martin Scorsese/Paul Michael Glaser/Donald Petrie
          USA                          1986
*Sam Waterstone, Max Gail, Kate McNeil, Sid Caesar*
Three more strange stories: "Mirror, Mirror" which
has the author of horror tales being chased by a nasty
ghoul, "Blue Man Down" in which a cop whose partner
was shot dead loses his confidence, and "Mr Magic"
which examines the changing fortunes of a washed-up
magician who finds a rather special pack of playing
cards.
FAN                                    72 min
B,V                                       CIC

## AMAZING STORIES: 7 **                U
          USA                          1987
*Robert Townsend, Charles Durning, M. Emmet Walsh*
Four magic stories: "The 12 Inch Sun", "Magic Sunday", "You Gotta Believe It", and "One Amazing
Night". An uneven blend of fantasy, comedy and the
sentimental. The first tale follows the changing
fortunes of a struggling scriptwriter, the second is a
cliched story of an old man and grandson who swap
bodies, the third episode is the predictable story of a
man dreaming of a plane crash and the last episode
has Santa Claus getting himself arrested.

FAN                                    91 min
B,V                                       CIC

## AMAZING STORIES: 8 **                PG
Norman Reynolds/Leslie Limka Glatter/Bob Balaban
          USA                     1985/1986
*June Lockhart, Milton Berle*
Another set of supernaturasl tales from this variable
series: "The Pumpkin Tale", "Without Diana" and
"Fine Tuning". This time round the stories are by
Steven Spielberg. Average.
FAN                                    69 min
B,V                                       CIC

## AMAZON WOMEN ON THE MOON **          15
John Landis/Joe Dante/Carl Gottlieb/Peter Horton/
Robert Weiss    USA                    1987
*Rosanna Arquette, Ralph Bellamy, Carrie Fisher,
Griffin Dunne, Ed Begley Jr, Steve Guttenberg, Sybil
Danning, Steve Forrest, Paul Bartel, B.B. King, Lou
Jacobi, Howard Hesseman, Steve Allen, Russ Meyer,
Arsenio Hall*
A parody of those tacky SF films of the 1950s
(especially "Cat Women On The Moon") that tells of
three American space voyagers who, with their pet
monkey, fall into the clutches of a group of love-
starved space maidens. One joke is that the movie is
being shown on TV and constant breakdowns in
transmission provide the excuse for a series of essentially unrelated skits and parodies, most of which are
remarkably unfunny.
COM             82 min (ort 87 min) Colour and B/W
V/h                                       CIC

## AMAZONIA *                           18
Roy Garrett (Maurio Gariazzo)
          ITALY                        1984
*Elvire Audrey, Alvaro Gonzales, Dick Marshall,
Andrew Louis Coppola, Dick Campbell*
During a boat trip down the river Amazon, Cather-
ine's parents are murdered and she is taken captive by
a tribe of cannibals. Later she escapes with the help of
a native, who informs her that her parents were
murdered by a jealous uncle and aunt. She sets out to
have her revenge in this utterly dull, cliched and
gratuitously gory effort.
Aka: AMAZONIA: THE CATHERINE MILES
STORY; AMAZONIA INFERNO VERDE;
L'AMAZZONE BIANCA; WHITE AMAZON; WHITE
SLAVE
A/AD                          90 min Cut (52 sec)
B,V                                       AVA

## AMAZONS **                           18
Alex Sessa       USA                   1986
*Windsor Taylor Randolph, Penelope Reed, Joseph
Whipp, Danitza Kingsley, Wolfram Hoechst, Jacques
Arnot, Charles Finch, Frank Cocza, Santiago Mallo,
Annie Larronde, Armand Capo, Mary Fournery,
Noelle Balfour, Esther Velazquez*
Two female warriors go on a quest for the legendary
Sword of Adzundati, the only means by which they
can overcome the evil wizard who threatens their
tribe. Another sword-and-sorcery romp of pretty
female warriors and their dastardly enemies.
FAN               84 min Cut (1 min 13 sec)
B,V                                       MED

## AMBASSADOR, THE ***                  18
J. Lee Thompson   USA                  1984
*Robert Mitchum, Ellen Burstyn, Rock Hudson, Fabio
Testi, Donald Pleasence, Michal Bat-Adam*
An American ambassador in the Middle East gets
caught up in the Arab-Israeli conflict as he attempts
to mediate between the warring groups. Burstyn as
the ambassador's adulterous wife is especially good in
an intelligent and exciting adaptation of the Leonard
novel, which was in fact remade in 1986 as FIFTY-
TWO PICK-UP.

Boa: novel 52 Pick-up by Elmore Leonard.
THR                                    93 min (ort 95 min)
B,V                                    GHV

## AMBER WAVES ***
Joseph Sargent          USA               1980
Dennis Weaver, Kurt Russell, Mare Winningham,
Fran Brill, Wilford Brimley, Ross Harris, Grainger
Hines, Penny Fuller, Eloy Phil Casados, Bill Morey,
Michael Talbott, Robby Weaver
A tough wheat farmer and an arrogant male model
clash over their opposing views of life whilst stranded
in a small Mid-West town. Essentially a study of
personality and character, with excellent perform-
ances all round, not least that of Winningham, who
won an Emmy for her portrayal of Weaver's daughter.
The literate script is by Ken Trevey with the music
composed by John Rubinstein.
DRA                                    92 min (ort 105 min) mTV;
B,V                                    VTC

## AMBUSH MURDERS, THE **                PG
Steven Hilliard Stern   USA               1982
James Brolin, Dorian Harewood, Alfre Woodard,
Louis Giambalvo, John McLiam, Teddy Wilson,
Antonio Fargas, Amy Madigan
The true story of a compassionate lawyer defending a
black activist, at his third trial for the murder of two
white cops gunned down in a Californian black
neighbourhood. Suffers badly from an excess of dia-
logue if not of good intentions.
Boa: book by Beb Bradlee Jr.
DRA                    110 min; 90 min (IVS) mTV;
B,V                    DIPLO/VFP; HER; IVS

## AMBUSHERS, THE *                       PG
Harry Levin             USA               1967
Dean Martin, Senta Berger, Janice Rule, Kurt
Kasznar, James Gregory, Albert Salmi
The third (and silliest) film in the "Matt Helm" series,
with our secret agent out to save the world from an
experimental flying disc, that has gone astray in the
jungles of Mexico. Neither the jokes nor the gadgets
are up to much, and this tired spy spoof rapidly
becomes very irritating. See also THE SILENCERS
and THE WRECKING CREW. The script is by
Herbert Baker.
A/AD                                   97 min (ort 102 min)
V                                      RCA

## AMERICA 3000 *                         15
David Engelbach         USA               1985
Chuck Wagner, Laurene Landon
A futuristic comedy set 900 years after a nuclear war,
with a primitive female dominated society existing, in
which men are little better than slaves. However,
when a rebel stumbles across an underground cache of
21st century weaponry, he obtains the means to take
on the wicked Queen Vada and her Amazon followers.
An utterly silly "Max Max" style spoof in which stupid
ideas vie with dopey dialogue.
COM                                    89 min Cut (3 sec)
B,V                                    MGM

## AMERICAN ANGELS **                     18
Beverly C. Sebastian/Ferd Sebastian
                        USA               1989
Jan Mackenzie
A decidedly offbeat but quite absorbing film that deals
with the world of female wrestling and the hardships
they endure to reach the top of their chosen profession.
Aka: BAPTISM OF FIRE
A/AD                                   95 min
V                                      CIC

## AMERICAN ANTHEM **                     PG
Albert Magnoli          USA               1986
Mitch Gaylord, Janet Jones, Michelle Phillips, R.J.

Williams, Michael Pataki, Patrice Donnelly, Stacy
Maloney, Maria Anz, Andrew White
Born on the wrong side of the tracks, a bright and
talented youth is forced to make adult decisions for
the first time. Should he desert his family to pursue
gymnastics, or follow his father's wishes and continue
his work as a mechanic? This corny and rather
poorly-written tale gave Olympic gymnast Gaylord,
his film debut, but the incessant music-video approach
of the director (of PURPLE RAIN) does little to make
use of his acting talents.
DRA 97 min (ort 100 min) (Cut at film release by 3 sec)
B,V                                    GHV

## AMERICAN BLUE NOTE ***                 15
Ralph Toporoff          USA               1989
Peter MacNichol, Carl Caportorto, Tim Guinee,
Jonathan Walker, Charlotte D'Amboise, Bill
Christopher-Myers, Trini Alvarado, Zohra Lampert
A comedy-drama that focuses on a month in the life of
a 1960s jazz band. An enjoyable film that provides
solid entertainment, uncomplicated by any great
insights or messages.
Aka: FAKEBOOK
COM                                    93 min (ort 97 min)
V                                      ODY

## AMERICAN BOYFRIENDS **                 15
Sandy Wilson            CANADA            1989
Margaret Langrick, John Wildman, Jason Blicker,
Delia Brett
This sequel to MY AMERICAN COUSIN moves the
action onto the 1960s and largely concentrates on the
career of Sandy (Langrick) who has matured some-
what since her appearance in the earlier film. A
bittersweet coming-of-age story, enjoyable but largely
unremarkable.
DRA                                    90 min (ort 100 min)
V                                      VES

## AMERICAN CHRISTMAS CAROL, AN **
Eric Till               USA               1979
Henry Winkler, David Wayne, Dorian Harewood,
Chris Wiggins, R.H. Thompson, Susan Hogan
An adaptation of Charles Dickens' much filmed
classic, in a New England town during the era of the
Depression. An abundance of makeup turns Winkler
into our aged miser, but to little avail in this plodding
tale.
Boa: short story by Charles Dickens.
DRA                                    100 min mTV;
B,V                                    PVG

## AMERICAN COMMANDO NINJA **            18
                                          1988
Patrick L'Argent, Daniel Garfield, Kelvin Wong,
Laura Yang
A scientist who has developed a bacteriological
weapon that could be used to dominate the world, is
kidnapped and a Ninja warrior must do battle with
hordes of warriors in order to prevent a cataclysm.
Routine martial arts adventure.
Aka: COMMANDO THE NINJA
MAR                                    86 min Cut (22 sec)
B,V                                    CINE

## AMERICAN COMMANDOS *                   18
Bobby A. Suarez         USA               1985
Christopher Mitchum, John Phillip Law, Franco
Guerrero, Willie Williams, Ken Metcalfe
Formula "Vietnam veteran sent back to kill 'em" film;
after killing the drug dealer who raped his wife, a man
is forced to go on a mission to tackle heroin dealers in
the Golden Triangle. A violent and innaccurate
portrayal of a very real problem; the opening scenes
supposedly set in California but using ridiculous
Filipino locations, are an apt comment on the level of
direction for the entire film.

Aka: HITMAN; MISTER SAVAGE
A/AD                    85 min (ort 88 min) Cut (13 sec)
B,V                                                        GHV

## AMERICAN DREAMER **        PG
Rick Rosenthal          USA                         1984
*JoBeth Williams, Tom Conti, Giancarlo Giannini,*
*Coral Browne, James Staley, Huckleberry Fox, C.B.*
*Barnes*
An American housewife writes a novel and wins a trip
to Paris where events drive her to the belief that she is
in fact the daring heroine of a series of adventure
thrillers. A muddled and miscast comedy-adventure
that puts one in mind of ROMANCING THE STONE,
only don't expect any suprises with this one.
COM                                             105 min
B,V                                                      CBS

## AMERICAN EAGLE **        18
Robert J. Smawley       USA                         1988
*Asher Brauner, Robert F. Lyons, Vernon Wells*
A former commando who worked for the CIA, is forced
out of retirement when his girlfriend is kidnapped by
white slavers. Together with an old war buddy, the
pair roam the streets of Casablanca in search of her, in
this formula action yarn.
DRA                                              90 min
V                                                     FUTUR

## AMERICAN FLYERS **        PG
John Badham             USA                         1985
*Kevin Costner, David Grant, Rae Dawn Chong,*
*Alexandra Paul, Janice Rule, Luca Bercovici, Robert*
*Townsend, John Amos, Jennifer Grey*
Two brothers, one terminally ill, take part in a tough
professional cycling marathon, in a good-natured if
rather glossy look at this gruelling sport. Written by
Steve Tesich who also wrote the story for BREAKING
AWAY.
DRA                           108 min (ort 114 min)
V/sh                                                    WHV

## AMERICAN FRIEND, THE ***        PG
Wim Wenders
          USA/FRANCE/WEST GERMANY        1977
*Dennis Hopper, Bruno Ganz, Lisa Kreuzer, Gerald*
*Blain, Jean Eustache, Sam Fuller, Nicholas Ray*
Vague and ponderous film about the planned assas-
sination of a gangster, that makes a statement of sorts
on the Americanisation of European life. The tale has
Ganz, as a German picture-framer being hired to
carry out the assassination, with film directors Fuller
and Ray appearing as thugs.
Boa: novel Ripley's Game by Patricia Highsmith.
DRA                          123 min (ort 127 min) Subtitled
B,V                                                      PVG

## AMERICAN GIGOLO *        18
Paul Schrader           USA                         1980
*Richard Gere, Lauren Hutton, Nina Van Pallandt,*
*Hector Elizondo, Frances Bergen*
A male prostitute is falsely accused of murder and a
client of his who can clear him, not unnaturally is
reluctant to do so. A poor excuse for a thriller, this
look at the seamy side of life in L.A. has little to
commend it, not least some remarkably poor acting
and dialogue.
THR                           112 min (ort 117 min)
V/h                                              CIC (VHS only)

## AMERICAN IN PARIS, AN ****        U
Vincente Minnelli       USA                         1951
*Gene Kelly, Leslie Caron, Oscar Levant, Nina Foch,*
*Georges Guetary*
An ex-GI stays in Paris after WW2, and tries to make
it as an artist whilst finding himself torn between
Caron and Foch. The story has few surprises but this
dazzling musical (built around a Gershwin score)
hosts an array of fine songs and dances. AA: Pic, Cin

(A. Cilks/J. Alton), Story/Screen (Alan Jay Lerner),
Score (J. Green/S. Chaplin), Art/Set (C. Gibbons and
P. Ames/Edwin B. Willis and K. Gleason), Cost (W.
Plunkett/I. Sharaff).
MUS                           108 min (ort 113 min)
V                                                        MGM

## AMERICAN MURDER, AN **        18
Doug Campbell           USA                         1988
*Michael Bowen, Ray Wise, Clancy Brown, Clare Wren,*
*Michael J. Pollard*
A man deserted by his father years ago, is invited to
meet him and embarks on a passionate affair with the
woman he discovers is now his stepmother. This
situation leads him into an intrigue of violence in this
routine melodrama.
DRA                                              90 min
B,V                                                    CASVIS

## AMERICAN NIGHTMARE **       
Don McBrearty           CANADA                      1982
*Lawrence S. Day, Lora Stanley, Lenore Zann, Paul*
*Bradley, Claudia Udy, Charles Page Fletcher, Larry*
*Aubrey, Michael Copeman, Bunty Webb, Tom Harvey,*
*Peter Lavender, Martin Doyle, Nancy Oliver*
A brutal tale of urban squalor involving a vengeful
psychotic and a young man, whose search for his
missing sister uncovers a nasty truth about his own
father. Average.
HOR                                              85 min
B,V                                                      VPD

## AMERICAN NINJA **        18
Sam Firstenberg         USA                         1985
*Michael Dudikoff, Steve James, Judie Aronson,*
*Tadashi Yamashita, Phil Brock, Guich Koock, John*
*Fujioka, John LaMotta, Tony Carreon, Roi Vinzov,*
*Willie Williams, Jerry Bailey, Christopher Hoss, Joey*
*Galvez, Nick Nicholson*
Routine martial-arts tale set at a US Army base in the
Phillipines, where Dudikoff, as an American soldier,
uses his fighting skills to wipe out drugs dealers, with
not a little help from his army pal James. An
uninspired stab at the martial arts genre with AMER-
ICAN NINJA 2: THE CONFRONTATION following
soon after.
Aka: AMERICAN WARRIOR
MAR                    91 min (ort 95 min) Cut (24 sec)
V/s                                                      MGM

## AMERICAN NINJA 2:        18
## THE CONFRONTATION ***
Sam Firstenberg         USA                         1987
*Michael Dudikoff, Steve James, Larry Poindexter,*
*Gary Conway, Jeff Weston, Michelle Botes, Michael*
*Stone*
Tough GIs Dudikoff and James team up once more as
they pit their Ninjitsu skills against a psychotic
Caribbean drugs baron and his band of warriors, in
order to rescue a group of captured US Marines; they
are to be trained by the drugs baron for his own evil
purposes. A superior sequel to AMERICAN NINJA
that benefits from the better script; the work of actors
Gary Conway and James Booth. AMERICAN NINJA
3 followed.
A/AD         86 min (ort 105 min) (Cut at film release by 28
sec)
B,V                                                      RNK

## AMERICAN NINJA 3: BLOODHUNT *        18
Cedric Sundstrom        USA                         1989
*David Bradley, Marjoe Gortner, Yehuda Effroni, Steve*
*James, Evan J. Klisser, Michele Chan, Calvin Jung*
Following his father's murder by gangsters in the
course of a martial arts contest, a young boy is
brought up and trained in the martial arts. Now a
young man, he sees his mentor kidnapped by a group
of Ninja during a tournament and traces them to a

secret research plant. Later, he breaks in only to discover that he has in fact been deliberately enticed there to gauge the effectiveness of a deadly experimental virus. Very disappointing.
Aka: AMERICAN NINJA 3

| MAR | 86 min |
| V | PATHE |

### AMERICAN NINJA THE MAGNIFICENT **    18
Charles Lee          USA          1988
*Pierre Kirby, Danny Raisebeck*
A master of modern weaponry and a master of the martial arts are rivals, but they join forces to combat an evil Ninja group responsible for the deaths of their families. Average.
Aka: NINJA OF THE MANIFICENCE

| A/AD | 90 min |
| B,V | CINE |

### AMERICAN PIE **
Jeffrey Fairbanks          USA          1981
*Arcadia Lake, Lysa Thatcher, Eric Edwards, Kitty Shane*
Two losers kidnap two debutantes but their rich father refuses to pay the ransom as he thinks they are playing a trick on him. He jokingly tells the kidnappers they can keep the girls and so they do exactly that in this routine offering; the first to be produced with Dolby sound.

| A | 88 min Cut |
| B,V | EVI |

### AMERICAN RASPBERRY **    18
Brael Swirnoff          USA          1977
*Art Fleming, Connie Fox, Fred Franklin, Warren Oates, David Spielberg*
A satire on the power of American TV. The president is forced to take drastic steps to stop a series of programmes making fun of sacred American values. Average.
Aka: PRIME TIME

| COM | 72 min |
| B,V | RNK |

### AMERICAN ROULETTE *    15
Maurice Hatton    AUSTRALIA/UK          1988
*Andy Garcia, Kitty Aldridge, Robert Stephens, Al Matthews, Susannah York*
Political thriller in which the deposed president of a South American country lives in exile in London, where he is constantly threatened by death squads sent from home. Overburdened with dialogue and meaningless chase sequences, this loosely plotted and dreary tale wastes the talents of all concerned.

| A/AD | 98 min (ort 102 min) |
| V | VIR |

### AMERICAN STUD IN PARIS, AN ***    18
USA
*John C. Holmes, Gloria Leonard, Betsy Ward*
An American expatriate writer down on his luck, is commissioned by a lusty female philanthropist to write a novel detailing life on the famous left bank of Paris. An amusing French farce that was mutilated in order to obtain a BBFC certification. The 75 minute running time shown on the tape is made up of trailers.

| A | 37 min (ort 75 min) Cut (4 min 31 sec) |
| B,V | CASS/IVS; GLOB |

### AMERICAN TAIL, AN **    U
Don Bluth          USA          1986
*Voices of: Dom DeLuise, Christopher Plummer, Madeline Kahn, Phillip Glasser, Nehemiah Persoff, John Finnegan, Cathianne Blore, Will Ryan*
During the late 19th century, a young Russian mouse gets separated from his family as they are about to arrive in America. A glossy and occasionally poignant cartoon feature, the charm of which is seriously hampered by the poorly plotted script. Produced by

Steven Spielberg, this was his first attempt at producing a cartoon.

| CAR | 78 min (ort 80 min) |
| V/sh | CIC |

### AMERICAN WAY, THE **    15
Maurice Phillips          UK          1986
*Dennis Hopper, Michael J. Pollard, Eugene Lipinski, James Aubrey, Nigel Pegram*
A group of Vietnam veterans runs a pirate TV station which they use to jam right-wing broadcasts, as well as doing their best to scupper the chances of a female presidential candidate who they oppose. The idea is sound, the acting is fine but the end result is tired and unconvincing.
Aka: RIDERS OF THE STORM

| A/AD | 101 min (ort 105 min) |
| V | RCA |

### AMERICAN WEREWOLF IN LONDON, AN ***    18
John Landis          USA          1981
*David Naughton, Griffin Dunne, Jenny Agutter, Brian Glover, John Woodvine*
Two young American lads are attacked by a werewolf whilst out walking on the moors. One dies whilst the other finds himself drawn into an increasingly nightmarish world where dreams and reality intermingle and eventually become indistinguishable. At its very best when horror is mixed with a measure of grisly humour, the ending is a sad anti-climax. Landis scripted this one. AA: Make (Rick Baker).

| HOR | 98 min |
| B,V,LV | POLY; CH5 (VHS only) |

### AMERICANA ***    15
David Carradine          USA          1973 (released 1981)
*David Carradine, Barbara Hershey, Michael Greene, Bruce Carradine, John Barrymore III, Fran Ryan*
An interesting and offbeat look at the problems facing Vietnam veteran Carradine in adjusting to civilian life, as he attempts to rebuild a merry-go-round in a small town in Kansas. A quirky little drama that takes a more refreshing look at the very real problems these veterans faced on their return.

| DRA | 91 min |
| B,V | CBS |

### AMERICANO, THE **    PG
William Castle          USA          1955
*Glenn Ford, Cesar Romero, Frank Lovejoy, Abbe Lane, Ursula Theiss, Rodolfo Hoyos, Tom Powers, Dan White, Frank Marlowe*
A Texan cowboy runs into trouble delivering Brahma bulls to Brazil, in this routine Western whose inadequacies of script are somewhat mitigated by the refreshing change of scenery.
Osca: HIGH NOON (VCC)

| WES | 85 min; 81 min (VCC) Cut (3 sec) |
| B,V | BBC; VCC (VHS only) |

### AMERICATHON *    PG
Neil Israel          USA          1979
*Harvey Korman, John Ritter, Nancy Morgan, Fred Willand, Zane Buzby, Peter Riegart, Richard Schaal, Elvis Costello, Chief Dan George, Tommy Lasorda, Jay Leno, Peter Marshall, Meat Loaf, Howard Hesseman,*
The year is 1998 and a bankrupt USA must raise money to save itself by holding a telethon. Buzby as a Vietnamese punk-rocker is one small high-spot in a tedious and sterile waste of an idea of great comic potential. The narration is by George Carlin.

| COM | 80 min (ort 86 min) |
| B,V,V2 | GHV |

### AMERIKA: PARTS 1, 2 AND 3 ***    15
Donald Wyre          USA          1987
*Kris Kristofferson, Sam Neill, Robert Urich, Mariel Hemingway, Christine Lahti, Cindy Pickett, Wendy Hughes, Dorian Harewood, Richard Bradford, Ford*

Rainey, Armin Mueller-Stahl, Ivan Dixon, Don Reiley,
Lara Flynn Boyle
Set in the year 1997, 10 years after the USA has been
taken over by the Soviet Union, this paints a grim
picture of a country with its economy in ruins, and
with Soviet-controlled troops patrolling the streets.
The US President is now a mere puppet, but American
pride is rekindled on the release from prison of the last
true Presidential candidate. A gloriously overblown
and hysterical flag-waver that now looks very dated
indeed.
DRA          545 min (3 cassettes – ort 840 min) mTV
B,V                                                SHEER

## AMITYVILLE 2: THE POSSESSION *          18
Damiano Damiani          USA               1982
James Olson, Burt Young, Moses Gunn, Andrew
Prine, Rutanya Alda, Jack Magner
More of a prequel to THE AMITYVILLE HORROR
than a sequel, this purports to be the story of the
previous owners of the house, with the older son being
eventually compelled by evil forces to murder the rest
of the family. A dismal spin-off that's both dull and
unpleasant.
Boa: novel Murder In Amityville by H. Holzer.
HOR                     100 min (ort 104 min)
B,V                     TEVP; WHV (VHS only)

## AMITYVILLE 3-D **
Richard Fleischer        USA               1983
Tony Roberts, Tess Harper, Robert Joy, Candy Clark,
John Beal, Leona Dana, John Harkins, Lori Loughlin,
Meg Ryan
3-D version which ends with the destruction of the
house-of-horror after a large number of people have
met grisly deaths, following purchase of the house by
Roberts and his family. Good production values hold
up this utterly predictable and gory journey.
Aka: AMITYVILLE: THE DEMON
HOR                                        93 min
B,V,V2                                     TEVP

## AMITYVILLE 4: THE EVIL ESCAPES **          18
Sandor Stern             USA               1989
Patty Duke, Jane Wyatt, Frederic Lehne, Norman
Lloyd, Brandy Gold, Aron Eisenberg, Geri Betzler
Fourth outing in the series for another set of unfortun-
ates and this notorious house, where the latest
occupants find their daughter falling victim to evil
forces. Strong on performances, but no new insights
are on offer here.
Aka: AMITYVILLE: THE EVIL ESCAPES;
AMITYVILLE HORROR, THE: THE EVIL ESCAPES
PART 4
HOR                     95 min (ort 100 min) mTV
V                                          MED

## AMITYVILLE HORROR, THE *          15
Stuart Rosenberg         USA               1979
James Brolin, Rod Steiger, Margot Kidder, Don
Stroud, Murray Hamilton, Michael Sacks, Helen
Shaver, Natasha Ryan, Meeno Peluce, K.C. Martel,
Val Avery, John Larch
Story of a family who move into a haunted Long
Island house and endure numerous grisly happenings.
A re-run of just about every haunted house cliche
going, with Steiger wonderfully hammy as a local
priest. Based on a rubbishy pulp fiction novel that was
presented as a factual account of real events. A
prequel and some sequels followed. Very poor.
Boa: novel by Jay Anson.
HOR          116 min; 114 min (VIR) (ort 118 min)
B,V,V2                  GHV; VCC; VIR (VHS only)

## AMONG WOLVES *          18
Jose Giovanni
          FRANCE/MALTA/SWITZERLAND          1985
Claude Brasseur, Bernard-Pierre Donnadieu, Niels

Arestrup, Jean-Hugues Anglade, Daniel Duval, Jean-
Roger Milo
A band of mercenaries is recruited to rescue a NATO
general held captive by terrorists. Dull co-production
Eurofilm recalling many a dud from the 1960s.
A/AD                    108 min Cut (51 sec)
B,V                                        RCA

## AMOROUS ADVENTURES OF A YOUNG          15
POSTMAN, THE *
Anthony Baker            USA
Eva Renzi, Richard Jordan, Amadeus August
The title says it all. Forget the film and put the kettle
on.
A                                          79 min
B,V                     INT L/A; MPV

## AMOROUS MILKMAN, THE *
Derren Nesbitt           UK                 1976
Julie Ege, Diana Dors, Brendan Price, Donna
Reading, Nancie Wait, Alan Lake, Bill Fraser, Fred
Emney, Patrick Holt, Roy Kinnear, Ray Barrett,
Anthony Sharp, Megs Jenkins, Arnold Ridley, Sam
Kydd, Janet Webb
Women find a milkman just irresistible. Dull. Very
dull.
Aka: AMOROUS ADVENTURES OF A MILKMAN,
THE
Boa: novel by Derren Nesbitt.
COM                                        93 min
B,V                     WAL L/A; EIV

## AMOS **                                 PG
Michael Tuchner          USA               1985
Kirk Douglas, Elizabeth Montgomery, Dorothy
McGuire, Pat Morita, James Sloyan, Ray Walston
An old man who was once a baseball coach but now in
his late seventies, goes into an old people's home very
much against his will. A number of the home's
residents have met untimely ends and in investigat-
ing this he finds himself crossing swords with the
head nurse. Despite some superficial similarities to
ONE FLEW OVER THE CUCKOO'S NEST (in which
Douglas starred on Broadway), this one never rises
above a pedestrian level.
Boa: novel by Stanley West.
DRA                     91 min (ort 100 min) mTV
B,V                                        PRV

## AMSTERDAM AFFAIR, THE ***
Gerry O'Hara             UK                 1968
Wolfgang Kieling, William Marlow, Catherine Von
Schell, Pamela Ann Davy, Josef Dubin-Behrman, Will
Van Selst, Lo Van Hensbergen, Guido de Moor
Thriller set in Amsterdam and involving the murder
of a young woman. Despite the fact that all the clues
appear to point to her lover as the culprit, an inspector
Van der Valk decides to investigate further. Pretty
fair thriller set in a pleasing location that later gave
rise to the British TV series "Van der Valk".
Boa: novel Love In Amsterdam by Nicolas Freeling.
THR                                        91 min
B,V,V2                                     INT

## AMSTERDAM KILL, THE **          15
Robert Clouse           HONG KONG          1977
Robert Mitchum, Bradford Dillman, Richard Egan,
Leslie Nielsen, Keye Luke
A drug-bust film with Mitchum as a retired narcotics
investigator, who comes back to help a friend who's
under suspicion of being part of an international
drugs ring. A world-weary and cynical Mitchum does
his best with a plot that has little in the way of
surprises or fresh ideas. The script is by Robert Clouse
and Gregory Tiefer.
THR                     86 min (ort 93 min)
B,V,V2                  RNK; VCC (VHS only)

## AMSTERDAMNED ** 18
Dick Maas     NETHERLANDS     1988
*Huub Stapel, Monique Van De Ven, Serge-Henri Valcke, Hidde Maas, Wim Zomer*
Thriller set in Amsterdam with a police inspector on the trail of a nasty serial killer, unaware that his girlfriend can help him bring the killer to justice. Average urban slasher movie. Written and directed by Maas.
THR     113 min
V     VES

## AMY *** 15
John Llewellyn Moxey     USA     1989
*Kathleen Beller, Mariette Hartley, Gary Graham, Keir Dullea, Sandy McPeak*
A tense thriller in which a woman is pursued by a sinister figure in dark glasses but can get no-one to believe her. However, when she takes a trip to her mother's lakeside house the series of events that follows prove her fears to be real enough.
THR     91 min
V     INTMED

## AMY *** U
Vincent McEveety     USA     1981
*Jenny Agutter, Barry Newman, Kathleen Nolan, Chris Robinson, Lou Fant, Lance LeGault, Margaret O'Brien, Nanette Fabray, Lucille Benson*
At the turn of the century, a woman leaves her husband to go and teach deaf children at a school for the handicapped, when her husband puts their own son, who happens to be deaf, into an institution. A good-hearted and most enjoyable Disney yarn that was originally made for TV but came to be released at cinemas instead.
JUV     90 min (ort 100 min) mTV
B,V     WDV

## AMY JOHNSON STORY, THE ** PG
Nat Crosby     UK     1984
*Harriet Walter, Clive Francis, Patrick Troughton*
The story of this famous female aviator, who on May 5th 1930 became the first woman in aviation history to make a solo flight, going on to make many more until her dramatic disappearance. At its best during the airborne sequences, but considerably less successful when it attempts an examination of her personal life.
DRA     90 min mTV
V     START

## ANASTASIA ** PG
Marvin J. Chomsky     USA     1986
*Amy Irving, Olivia De Havilland, Jan Niklas, Nicolas Surovy, Susan Lucci, Elke Sommer, Edward Fox, Claire Bloom, Omar Sharif, Rex Harrison, Jennifer Dundas, Christian Bale, Andrea Bretterbauer, Sydney Bromley, Arnold Diamond*
Mini-series about Anna Anderson who was dragged from a Berlin river in 1919 after a failed suicide attempt. After months of amnesia she gradually begins to regain her memory, claiming to be the youngest daughter of Czar Nicholas. However, her failure to offer anything as proof results in her being branded an imposter. This opulent exercise in tedium has a red-eyed Irving hovering on the verge of tears throughout. Watch this and you'll do the same.
Aka: ANASTSIA: THE MYSTERY OF ANNA
Boa: book Anastasia: The Riddle Of Anna Anderson by Peter Kurth.
DRA     194 min (2 cassettes – ort 200 min) mTV
B,V     CAN

## ANATOMY OF A SEDUCTION **
Steven Hilliard Stern     USA     1979
*Susan Flannery, Jameson Parker, Rita Moreno, Ed Nelson, Michael LeClair, Allan Miller, Roger C.*

*Carmel, Sandy Baron, Bryan O'Byrne, Ron Prince, Rod Colbin, Barry Michlin, Ernest Halada, Peter Turgeon, Eldon Quick*
Glossy soap opera about the romance of a beautiful but aloof 40-year-old divorcee with her best friend's son, who just happens to be the friend of her own son. Watchable but very much a made-for-TV drama.
DRA     96 min (ort 100 min) mTV
B,V     VFP

## ANCHORS AWEIGH *** U
George Sidney     USA     1945
*Frank Sinatra, Gene Kelly, Kathryn Grayson, Dean Stockwell, Jose Iturbi, Pamela Britton, Billy Gilbert, Henry O'Neill*
Popular musical about a couple of sailors who go on shore leave with 4-day passes and are out for a good time. Meeting up with a Hollywood extra who yearns to be a star, the two buddies decide to help. Features Kelly's memorable dance routine where live action blends with animation as he partners Jerry Mouse. If the story is a little weak the musical numbers do more than compensate. AA: Score (Georgie Stoll).
MUS     144 min
V     MGM

## AND A NIGHTINGALE SANG ** PG
Robert Knights     UK     1988
*Tom Watt, Phyllis Logan, Joan Plowright, John Woodvine, Pippa Hinchley, Stephen Tomkinson*
Typical British comedy-drama following the affairs of a Geordie family during WW2. Moderately amusing in places but fairly forgettable.
DRA     97 min
V/h     ODY

## AND BABY MAKES SIX ** PG
Waris Hussein     USA     1979
*Colleen Dewhurst, Warren Oates, Maggie Cooper, Al Corley, Timothy Hutton, Allyn Ann McLerie, Mildred Dunnock, Mason Adams, Maria Melendez, Bill Smillie, Lee Wallace, Christopher Allport, Tamu, Joshua Greenrock*
Pregnancy poses a dilemma for a middle-aged couple who already have three grown-up children. Dewhurst does well with a weak story (the script is by Shelley List), but it's not half as good as it might have been. Followed by BABY COMES HOME.
DRA     93 min (ort 100 min) mTV
B,V,V2     GHV

## AND GIVE US OUR DAILY SEX *
Jose Ramon Larraz ITALY/SPAIN     1980
*Laura Gemser, Nils Stanic, Barbara Ray*
Feeble and typically Continental sex comedy all about a pubescent youth and his awakening interest in the opposite sex.
Aka: GIVE US OUR DAILY SEX; MALIZIA EROTICA
A     94 min
B,V,V2     FFV

## AND GOD CREATED WOMAN * 18
Roger Vadim     FRANCE     1957
*Brigitte Bardot, Curt Jurgens, Jean-Louis Trintignant, Christian Marquand, Georges Poujouly, Jean Tissier, Jane Marken, Paul Faivre*
A dated and dreary vehicle for a display of Bardot's charms in which she plays a young woman with a healthy appetite for men. Filmed on location in St Tropez and remade after a fashion in 1987.
Aka: AND WOMAN WAS CREATED; ET DIEU CREA LA FEMME
DRA     95 min
V     CASPIC

## AND GOD CREATED WOMAN ** 18
Roger Vadim     USA     1987

Rebecca DeMornay, Vincent Spano, Frank Langella,
Donovan Leitch, Judith Chapman, Jaime McEnnan,
Benjamin Mouton, David Shelley
A woman marries merely to avoid a prison term, but
neglects her husband in favour of a rock career and a
flirtation with a politician. This watery variation of
Vadim's former success has more in common with
Goldie Hawn's OVERBOARD than his earlier film. A
dull and dreary remake in name alone.
COM                              94 min (ort 100 min)
B,V                                              VES

### AND JUSTICE FOR ALL ***                       15
Norman Jewison        USA                        1979
Al Pacino, Jack Warden, John Forsythe, Lee
Strasberg, Jeffrey Tambor, Sam Levene, Christine
Lahti, Craig T. Nelson, Joe Morton
Unfunny attempt at a satire on the American system
of justice, with a lawyer getting into all kinds of
trouble on account of his clients, as he mounts a
one-man crusade against the inadequacies of Mary-
land's legal system. Firing off its shots in all directions (and scoring a few hits along the way), this
sometimes sad, sometimes funny movie has the stars
performing well despite a basically weak story. Written by Valerie Curtin and Barry Levinson.
DRA                             116 min (ort 119 min)
V                                                RCA

### AND NOW FOR SOMETHING              PG
### COMPLETELY DIFFERENT ***
Ian McNaughton        UK                         1972
John Cleese, Eric Idle, Graham Chapman, Terry
Gilliam, Terry Jones, Michael Palin, Connie Booth,
Carol Cleveland
Repetition of well known Monty Python sketches from
the popular TV show and featuring many examples of
their anarchic sense of humour such as "The Dead
Parrot", "The Lumberjack Song", "The Upper-Class
Twit Of The Year" and "The World's Deadliest Joke".
The first entry into films for the Monty Python team
and not unnaturally a somewhat uneven collection.
Followed by MONTY PYTHON AND THE HOLY
GRAIL, the first of several more consistent efforts.
COM                      88 min; 85 min (PREST)
B,V                                  RCA; PREST

### AND NOW THE SCREAMING STARTS ***
Roy Ward Baker        UK                         1973
Peter Cushing, Herbert Lom, Stephanie Beacham,
Patrick Magee, Ian Ogilvy, Geoffrey Whitehead, Guy
Rolfe, Rosalie Crutchley, Janet Key, Gilliam Lind,
Sally Harrison, Lloyd Lamble, Norman Mitchell
Bizarre story of horror in a country house, with a
newly-wed Beacham finding that she is living in a
house that has been under a curse for many years.
Better than the usual run of British horror films, this
one is helped along by a strong cast.
Boa: novel Fengriffen by David Case.
HOR                              87 min (ort 91 min)
B,V,V2                                           GHV

### AND SOON THE DARKNESS **
Robert Fuest          UK                         1970
Pamela Franklin, Michele Dotrice, Sandor Eles, John
Nettleton, Clare Kelly, Hana-Maria Pravda, John
Franklyn
Two nurses go on a cycling holiday in France. One is
murdered by the local sex maniac, and the other is
gripped by panic as she tries to avoid the same fate. A
brooding and ponderous thriller with sexual over-
tones; it may be cut for the UK.
THR                              94 min (ort 98 min)
B,V                                             TEVP

### AND THE WALL CAME TUMBLING DOWN **
Paul Annett          UK                          1984
Peter Wyngarde, Gareth Hunt, Brian Deacon, Barbi
Benton, Richard Hampton, Pat Hayes, Carol Royle,

Ralph Michael, Gary Waldhorn, Robert James
Strange horror tale revolving around the demolition
of a church and the reincarnation of a Satanist, out for
revenge against a coven member who betrayed others
in return for a blessing.
HOR                                            72 min
B,V                                          BWV/VSP

### AND THEN YOU DIE ***                          18
Francis Mankiewicz   CANADA                      1987
Kenneth Welsh, Wayne Robson, R.H. Thomson, Tom
Harvey, George Bloomfield, Graeme Campbell
Based on a true story, this tells of the last nine days of
an Irish drugs baron operating in Montreal. Using
Hell's Angels as his muscle, he becomes locked in a
power struggle with the Mafia for control of the
lucrative cocaine market. Fair action tale.
A/AD                         96 min (ort 115 min) mTV
B,V                                             CINE

### AND YOUR NAME IS JONAH **                      U
Richard Michaels      USA                        1979
Sally Struthers, James Woods, Randee Heller, Penny
Santon, Titos Vandis, Ruth Manning, Jeff Bravlin,
Robert Davi, Erica Yohn, Lee Kessler, Antony Ponzini,
Robin Pearson Rose, Bernard Bragg, Rose Barbato,
Paula Shaw
A couple find that their son has been wrongly
diagnosed as retarded and placed in an institution.
They now have to cope with the fact that he is merely
profoundly deaf. An interesting human-interest dra-
ma in which the patent earnestness of the script
outweighs any real strengths of the plot.
DRA            96 min; 90 min (PARA) (ort 100 min) mTV
B,V                               HER; PARA (VHS only)

### ANDERSON TAPES, THE ****                       15
Sidney Lumet          USA                        1971
Sean Connery, Martin Balsam, Dyan Cannon, Ralph
Meeker, Alan King, Margaret Hamilton, Christopher
Walken, Garrett Morris
An ex-con plans to rob a building, not knowing that
his every action is being recorded by surveillance
equipment that has been in operation since he left
prison. A fast and exciting thriller that has a particu-
larly good climax. The catchy score is by Quincy
Jones. This was Walken's film debut.
Boa: novel by Lawrence Sanders.
A/AD                             95 min (ort 98 min)
B,V                                              RCA

### ANDREA THE NYMPHO *
Hans Schott-Schobinger
                      WEST GERMANY               1968
Dagmar Lassander, Joachim Hansen
Andrea leaves her home in the country for life in the
city. See title for plot.
Aka: NYMPHO, THE
A                                              84 min
B,V,V2                                           DER

### ANDROID ***
Aaron Lipstadt        USA                        1982
Klaus Kinski, Don Opper, Brie Howard, Norbert
Weisser, Crofton Hardester, Kendra Kirchner
Stylish and thoroughly enjoyable film about the
controller of a strange space station and his android
helper Max, who he soon plans to replace with a more
up-to-date creation. When three escaped criminals
arrive at the space station their quiet routine is
interrupted, but the scientist has plans for using one
of them. A slightly wacky and offbeat film using sets
left over from BATTLE BEYOND THE STARS.
Low-budget but good fun. Co-written by Opper.
FAN                              80 min (ort 82 min)
B,V,V2                                        IFS/CBS

### ANDROMEDA STRAIN, THE **                       PG
Robert Wise           USA                        197⁷

*Arthur Hill, David Wayne, James Olson, Kate Reid, Paula Kelly*
A team of scientists race against time to isolate a deadly organism brought to Earth by a satellite that has crashed in New Mexico. Seriously overlong, this one was in need of severe editing.
Boa: novel by Michael Crichton.
FAN                              124 min (ort 130 min)
B,V                                                CIC

## ANDY COLBY'S INCREDIBLE ADVENTURE ** PG
Deborah Brock           USA            1988
*Randy Josselyn, Jessica Puscas, Dianne Kay, John Franklin, Vince Edwards, Bo Svenson, Richard Thomas, Erik Estrada*
Fantasy adventure with a 12-year-old boy agreeing to babysit for his sister on condition that he can hire a video to watch. However, he gets more than he bargained for when he brings home one entitled "The Incredible Video Adventure".
Aka: ANDY AND THE AIRWAVE RANGERS
A/AD                                          87 min
V                                              MGM

## ANDY WARHOL'S BAD ***
Jed Johnson/Andy Warhol
                USA                     1971
*Carroll Baker, Penny King, Susan Tyrell, Stefania Cassini, Cyrinda Foxe*
An expensive, almost mainstream drama (it cost $1,500,000 to make), about a woman who runs a facial-hair removal business but supplements her income by running a contract killer service; she specialises in children and animals. Sometimes funny, more often sick, this was Warhol's most conventionally plotted film. A lot better than one would expect.
Aka: BAD
DRA                                          100 min
B,V                                            PVG

## ANDY WARHOL'S DRACULA **
Paul Morrissey/Anthony M. Dawson (Antonio Margheriti)
                ITALY/FRANCE            1973
*Joe Dallesandro, Udo Kier, Arno Juerging, Vittorio De Sica, Maxime McKendry, Roman Polanski*
Mildly pornographic spoof on the Dracula story with our vampire discovering that he must have the blood of virgins in order to survive. A lot less gory than his production of Frankenstein, this has some funny moments but the plot remains in serious need of a blood transfusion.
Aka: ANDY WARHOL'S YOUNG DRACULA; BLOOD FOR DRACULA; DRACULA CERCA SANGUE DI VERGINE E MORI DI SETE; DRACULA VUOLE VIVERE: CERCA SANGUE DI VERGINA; YOUNG DRACULA
HOR                                          106 min
B,V,V2                                        VIPCO

## ANDY WARHOL'S FRANKENSTEIN *
Paul Morrissey/Anthony M. Dawson (Antonio Margheriti)
           FRANCE/ITALY/WEST GERMANY    1973
*Joe Dallesandro, Monique Van Voorien, Udo Kier, Srdjan Zelenovic, Dalia di Lazzaro*
Shot in 3-D, this companion piece to ANDY WARHOL'S DRACULA is a real camp version, with plenty of blood and severed limbs, as our demented Baron embarks on the creation of a series of beautiful creatures from the assorted pieces of human anatomy. Definitely not one for the squeamish. Unlikely to be available in an uncut form in the UK.
Aka: CARNE PER FRANKENSTEIN; DEVIL AND DR FRANKENSTEIN, THE; FLESH FOR FRANKENSTEIN; FRANKENSTEIN; FRANKENSTEIN EXPERIMENT; IL MOSTRO E IN TAUOLA . . . BARONE FRANKENSTEIN; UP

FRANKENSTEIN; WARHOL'S FRANKENSTEIN
HOR                                          95 min
B,V,V2                                        VIPCO

## ANGEL **                                    18
Robert Vincent O'Neil   USA            1983
*Cliff Gorman, Susan Tyrell, Dick Shawn, Rory Calhoun, John Diehl, Donna Wilkes, Elaine Giftos*
A young high school student is a devoted scholar by day and a Hollywood hooker by night. Having said that, little remains in terms of plot as this one goes nowhere. However, do look out for Shawn as a drag queen. AVENGING ANGEL followed.
DRA                                          92 min
B,V                                          TEVP

## ANGEL **                                    15
Neil Jordan             EIRE            1982
*Stephen Rea, Veronica Quilligan, Alan Devlin, Honor Hefferman, Marie Kean, Peter Caffrey*
After a saxophonist witnesses the brutal murder of the band's leader and a deaf-and-dumb girl, he sets out to have his revenge on the culprits, in this formula thriller.
Aka: DANNY BOY
THR                                90 min (ort 92 min)
B,V                                            PVG

## ANGEL 3: THE FINAL CHAPTER **              18
Tom De Simone           USA            1988
*Mitzi Kapture, Maud Adams, Richard Roundtree, Mark Blankfield, Kim Shriner*
This time round, our heroine's quest is to rescue her sister from a white slavery ring before she is sold into a fate worse than death. Average.
Aka: ANGEL 3
A/AD            95 min (ort 100 min) Cut (37 sec)
B,V                                            NWV

## ANGEL AND THE BADMAN ***                    U
James Edward Grant      USA            1947
*John Wayne, Gail Russell, Bruce Cabot, Harry Carey, Irene Rich, Lee Dixon, Stephen Grant, Tom Powers, Paul Hurst, Olin Howlin, John Halloran, Joan Barton, Craig Woods, Marshall Reed, Hank Worden, Pat Flaherty*
A gunfighter is won over to an honest life through the love of a young Quaker girl. Despite the simplicity of the plot this fine Western is warm, human and engaging.
WES          100 min B/W (colourised version available – VCC)
B,V,V2      WOV; EVC L/A; MOV L/A; VCC (VHS only)

## ANGEL CITY ***
Philip Leacock          USA            1980
*Ralph Waite, Paul Winfield, Jennifer Warren, Mitchell Ryan, Jennifer Jason Leigh, Roman Macnaughton, Red West, Bob Minor, Ken Renard, Paulene Meyers, John David Allen, Joe Dorsey, Wallace Wilkinson, Sandra Dorsey, Bob Hannah*
Moving drama about a West Virginia family who find themselves prisoners in a camp for migrant labourers. Harsh and uncompromising, this draws on the main strengths of the originating book via the James Lee Barrett script. A good cast adds conviction.
Boa: book by Patricia Smith.
DRA                                        100 min mTV
B,V,V2                                        VUL

## ANGEL CLOUD **                              U
                USA                     1975
A flower spirit called "Angel" is sent on a mission by the king of a distant planet to find the magical "Flower of Seven Colours". This plant has the power of generating love and kindness and is needed to save the life of her ruler. First in a series telling of the adventures Angel encounters in her search for the magical flower.

Aka: ANGEL; FLOWER ANGEL, THE (HVM)
CAR                60 min; 46 min (HVM) (ort 94 min)
B,V                          HVM; MAST (VHS only)

## ANGEL DUST **                                    15
Edouard Niermans    FRANCE                    1987
*Leon Senza, Vincent-Marie Bourot, Bernard*
*Giraudeau, Fanny Bastien, Fanny Cottencon, Jean-*
*Pierre Sentier, Michel Aumont, Gerard Blain*
Routine crime drama with a police inspector trying to
get a lead on a murder and a bank robbery whilst
enduring marital difficulties. Average.
Aka: POUSSIERE D'ANGE
DRA                             91 min (ort 94 min)
V/h                                            PAL

## ANGEL HEART ***                                 18
Alan Parker            USA                     1987
*Robert De Niro, Mickey Rourke, Lisa Bonet, Charlotte*
*Rampling, Stocker Fountelieu, Brownie McGhee,*
*Michael Higgins, Charles Gordone, Kathleen Wilhoite*
A tough New York detective pits his wits against a
fearsome adversary in a story blending action and the
occult and set in the backwoods of New Orleans. The
striking visual images are the film's greatest asset,
though after a while even they begin to pale in the
face of the serpentine plot. Parker scripted and
directed. A torrid sex scene was cut just prior to
release and has not yet been restored.
Boa: novel Falling Angel by William Hjortsberg.
THR     109 min (ort 113 min) (Cut at film release by 4
sec)
V/sh                                     GHV/PARK

## ANGEL IN EXILE ***                               PG
Allan Dwan/Philip Ford USA                    1948
*John Carroll, Adele Mara, Thomas Gomez, Barton*
*MacLane, Alfonso Bedoya*
After his release from jail a man heads for the gold
mines of Arizona, but has a change of heart and plan,
when circumstances cause Mexican villagers to re-
gard him as a kind of religious saviour. Produced by
Republic, this unusual Western has quite a lot going
for it.
WES                       89 min; 86 min (STABL)
V                                VMA L/A; STABL

## ANGEL IN GREEN, THE **                           15
Marvin J. Chomsky      USA                    1987
*Susan Dey, Bruce Boxleitner, Milo O'Shea, Peter*
*Smith, Dan Lauria*
A poor and dismal remake of "Heaven Knows Mr
Allison" with a nun and an army captain marooned on
a remote island in the Pacific. As ever, the scenery is a
partial compensation.
DRA               93 min (ort 100 min) mTV
V                                              TGP

## ANGEL OF HEAT **                                 18
Meryl A. Schreibman    USA                    1981
*Marilyn Chambers, Stephen Johnson, Mary Woronov,*
*Remy O'Neill, Dan Jesse*
Daft adult adventure movie with a female super-agent
sent on a mission to prevent the world being des-
troyed.
Aka: ANGEL FROM H.E.A.T.; ANGEL OF H.E.A.T.;
PROTECTORS, THE: BOOK 1
A                                          90 min
B,V              VTC L/A; XTACY/KRP; PICPAL

## ANGEL OF VENGEANCE **                            18
Abel Ferrara          USA                     1980
*Zoe Tamerlis, Steve Singer, Jack Thibeau, Peter*
*Yellen, Darlene Stuto, Editta Sherman, Albert Sinkys,*
*Jimmy Laine*
After being raped twice in the course of one evening, a
young mute woman arms herself and turns vigilante,
gunning down lecherous men, in this nasty and
exploitative clone of films like DEATHWISH and

THE VIGILANTE.
Aka: MS. 45
THR                       80 min Cut (1 min 42 sec)
B,V                                            WHV

## ANGEL OF VENGEANCE **                            18
Ted V. Mikels         USA                     1988
*Jannina Poynter, David O'Hara, Macka Foley, Carl*
*Irwin*
After having researched her father's military diaries,
the journalist daughter of a former Green Beret goes
into the woods to practice survival techniques. Once
there, she's accosted by the psychopathic member of a
survival group who murder a gang of bikers in an
ambush and then turn their attentions to her, forcing
her to make use of some of her new survival skills.
Violent and predictable exploiter.
Aka: WAR CAT
A/AD                                       90 min
B,V                                            IVS

## ANGEL ON MY SHOULDER **
John Berry            USA                     1980
*Peter Strauss, Richard Kiley, Barbara Hershey, Janis*
*Paige, Seymour Cassel, Scott Colomby, Peter MacLean,*
*Billy Jacoby, Douglas Kirkson, Anne Newman*
*Mantee, Murray Matheson, Terry Alexander, Frank*
*Campanella, Anne Seymour*
Remake of classic 1947 comedy, with a wrongfully
executed gangster being sent back to Earth by the
Devil in the body of a lookalike D.A. In the course of
working as a D.A. he learns the value of truth, justice
and decency; thus gaining a reprieve from hell. Corny
in a very 1980s way and not a patch on the Paul Muni
original.
COM                                  96 min mTV
B,V                             VFP L/A; HER

## ANGELA **
Boris Sagal           CANADA                  1977
*Sophia Loren, John Vernon, Steve Railsback, John*
*Huston, Luce Guilbeault, Michelle Rossignol, Jean*
*Lapointe, Andree Cousineau, Ji Tu Cumbuka, Yvon*
*Dufour, Denis Payne*
Wonderfully weepie tale of a woman who falls for a
23-year-old young enough to be her son, the insur-
mountable problem being that (unknown to her), he is
exactly that.
DRA                           91 min (ort 100 min)
V                                              EHE

## ANGELO, MY LOVE ***                              15
Robert Duvall         USA                     1983
*Angelo Evans, Michael Evans, Ruthie Evans, Tony*
*Evans, Steve "Patalay" Tsigonoff, Debbie Evans, Millie*
*Tsigonoff, Cathy Kitchen*
Absorbing story of some modern-day gypsies, with a
loose plot built around the exploits of streetwise New
York kid Angelo Evans. Written by Duvall, this is his
second directorial offering and offers a fascinating
glimpse of a side of the city few ever see.
DRA                                       115 min
B,V                                          POLY

## ANGELS **                                        18
Joe Williams          USA                     1986
*Ginger Lynn, Annette Haven, Kelly Nichols, Jamie*
*Gillis, Paul Thomas, Colleen Brennan, Jill Ferrar,*
*Eric Edwards, Herschel Savage*
A second hardcore spoof on American TV series
"Charlie's Angels" with our heroines using their
charms to rescue the kidnapped daughter of a US
senator. However, the kidnapping is no more than a
plot for mother and daughter to revenge themselves
on their callous husband and father.
Aka: COMING OF ANGELS, A: THE SEQUEL
A               53 min (ort 80 min) Cut (8 min 23 sec)
B,V                                            ELV

## ANGELS' BRIGADE **
Greydon Clark          USA                1979
*Jack Palance, Neville Brand, Jim Backus, Pat
Buttram, Alan Hale Jr, Peter Lawford, Jacqueline
Cole, Susan Kiger, Sylvia Anderson*
A sort of clone of the TV series "Charlie's Angels" with
seven women teaming up and fitting out a super-van
to combat drug dealers. Mindless high-action saga.
A/AD                                     87 min
B,V                                      HOK

## ANGELS DIE HARD **                    18
Richard Compton        USA                1970
*Tom Baker, William Smith, Connie Nelson, R.G.
Armstrong, Beach Dickerson, Rita Murray, Dan
Haggerty, Bambi Allen, Alan De Witt, Gary Littlejohn,
Michael Stringer*
Gang warfare between a group of Hell's Angels and
the locals, leads to some unpleasantness but in this
one our Angels are the goodies and save some folk
trapped in a mine disaster. Average two-wheeled
action story.
Aka: ROUGH BOYS (KRP)
A/AD                    84 min; 82 min (FOX)
B,V                     HOK; FOX; KRP

## ANGELS IN HELL **                     15
Larry Buchanan         USA                1977
*Victor Holchak, Lindsay Bloom, David McLean, Royal
Dano, Adam Roarke, Linda Cristal*
A story based on Howard Hughes' experiences during
the making of "Hell's Angels" in 1930, its subsequent
gala premiere and his discovery of Jean Harlow.
Average.
Aka: HUGHES AND HARLOW: ANGELS IN HELL
(ODY)
DRA                                      91 min
B,V                     VUL L/A; ODY

## ANGELS OF THE CITY ***                18
Lawrence-Hilton Jacobs USA               1989
*Kelly Galindo, Cynthia Cheston, Michael Ferrare,
Lawrence-Hilton Jacobs, Renny Stroud*
Two college co-eds take a trip to some of the less
salubrious parts of L.A. for a sorority prank, but when
they witness a shooting they find themselves on the
killer's hit-list. A fairly straightforward and enjoyable
action thriller, that gave Jacobs his directorial debut.
A/AD                                     90 min
V                       INT; CINE

## ANGELS OF THE STREETS **
Jurgen Roland    WEST GERMANY             1969
*Horst Frank, Herbert Fux, Werner Pochath, Karl
Lieffen, Rainer Baselow, Gernot Endemann, Irmgard
Riessen, Margot Mahler, Uwe Carstens, Horst
Hesslein, Esther Daniels, Reinhold W. Timm, Jochen
Serndt*
Formula German murder melodrama set in the
red-light district of Hamburg.
Aka: DIE ANGEL VON ST PAULI
DRA                                      100 min
V                                        INT

## ANGELS WITH DIRTY FACES ****          PG
Michael Curtiz         USA                1938
*James Cagney, Pat O'Brien, Humphrey Bogart, Ann
Sheridan, George Bancroft, Billy Halop, Leo Gorcey,
Huntz Hall, Gabe Dell, Bobby Jordan, Bernard
Punsley*
Excellent gangster movie telling of the uneasy
friendship between two boyhood friends who go their
separate ways, one becoming a priest and the other a
gangster who's idolised by some street punks our
priest hopes to reform (played by the "Dead End Kids"
of the 1937 film DEAD END). Fine entertainment and
beautifully acted – the closing electric chair sequence
is an all-time great. Scripted by John Wexley and
Warren Duff.

Boa: story by Rowland Brown.
DRA                     94 min (ort 97 min) B/W
B,V                                      WHV

## ANGIE BABY *                          18
Argen Ciel             USA
*Linda Neal, David Douglas, Barney Bossick*
Pretty forgettable sex film enlivened to some extent
by a Mafia plot. Cut before video submission by 6 min
23 sec.
A                       76 min Cut (7 sec)
B,V                     PPL L/A; CRAW

## ANGRY BREED, THE *                    15
David Commons          USA                1969
*Jan Sterling, James MacArthur, William Windom,
Jan Murray, Murray McLeod, Lori Martin, Melody
Patterson*
A Vietnam veteran comes to Hollywood following his
discharge, in the hope of becoming an actor but gets
mixed up with a bunch of bikers, in this confusing and
unbelievable dud.
DRA                                      89 min
B,V                                      VFP

## ANGRY DRAGON, THE **
Chiang Hung      HONG KONG                1974
*Cheong Lik, Christine Hui Shan, Lee Wan Chung*
Kung Fu all the way – the plot hardly matters. For
devotees.
MAR                                      80 min
B,V,V2                                   GOV

## ANGRY FIST, THE **                    18
Tien Han         HONG KONG
*Wong Kwan Hsung, Chin Hum, Tzu Lang, Wong Fei
Lung*
Standard martial arts mayhem: honour must be
avenged, the guilty must be punished and so forth.
Very much an average affair.
MAR                                      90 min
V                                        MART

## ANGRY GUN, THE ***                    15
Duccio Tessari         ITALY              1966
*Montgomery Wood (Giuliano Gemma), Fernando
Sancho, Hally Hammond, George Martin, Lorella de
Luca, Nieves Navarro, Antonio Casas, Jose Manuel
Martin, Paco Sanz*
When his fiancee and her father are held hostage in
their ranch house by a wounded Mexican bandit and
his gang, a sheriff is forced to turn elsewhere for help
and joins forces with a gunman to stage a rescue.
Aka: BALLAD OF DEATH VALLEY; PISTOL FOR
RINGO, A; UNA PISTOLA PER RINGO
WES                     91 min (ort 97 min)
B,V                                      WARAD

## ANGRY JOE BASS **
Thomas G. Reeves       USA                1976
*Henry Bal, Molly Mershon*
Tale of racial prejudice and greed, with a struggle over
fishing rights between Indians and a wealthy
businessman leading to conflict and violence.
Average.
Aka: WILD JOE BASS
DRA                                      82 min
B,V,V2                  IFS L/A; IVS/CBS

## ANGRY RED PLANET, THE **              15
Ib Melchior            USA                1959
*Gerald Mohr, Nora Hayden, Les Tremayne, Jack
Kruschen, Paul Hahn*
An expedition to Mars comes up against a variety of
perils, not least being a collection of tentacled mons-
ters sent to destroy them by the planet's inhabitants.
A slow-moving film that takes forever to get going,
but endearing in its way and making use of several

unusual ideas. Filmed using "Cinemagic", an unusual process of dubious value.

FAN                                                          80 min (ort 83 min)
V                                                                          RCA

## ANGUISH ***                                                          18
Bigas Luna              SPAIN                                          1988
*Zelda Rubinstein, Talia Paul, Michael Lerner, Clara Pastor*
A mad killer is on the loose in a cinema whose audience are watching another mad killer film – both unspool together. This imaginative and well handled story loses its way in a welter of violence; the overblown effects dissipate the strength of the compelling ideas.

HOR                                                          81 min (ort 89 min)
B,V                                                                       CBS

## ANIMAL BEHAVIOUR **                                                  PG
H. Anne Riley            USA                                           1989
*Karen Allen, Armand Assante, Holly Hunter, Josh Mostel, Richard Libertini*
Pleasant comedy-drama set on a university campus, where a music teacher and a researcher on inter-species communication meet but fail to realise how attracted they are to each other, until a neighbour and mother of an autistic child inadvertently brings them together.

COM                                                                   88 min
V                                                                          RCA

## ANIMAL FARM **                                                        U
John Halas/Joy Bachelor UK                                            1955
*Voices of: Maurice Denham, Gordon Heath*
Cartoon version of Orwell's cautionary tale, with an ending changed from that of the book to give it a more optimistic flavour. This straightforward adaptation offers a largely diluted set of critical observations on the nature of power and corruption. Not a kiddie film, but only just.
Boa: novel by George Orwell.

CAR                                                                   75 min
B,V                                                                   RNK; BBC

## ANIMALYMPICS **                                                       U
Steven Lisberger         USA                                          1979
*Voices of: Gilda Radner, Billy Crystal, Harry Shearer, Michael Fremer*
Animated send-up of the Olympics with the human participants replaced by various animals. OK for kids not yet out of nappies, its surfeit of cuteness will turn others off.

CAR                                                          78 min (ort 80 min)
B,V,LV                                                       BAR/PRV L/A; VGM

## ANITA *                                                               18
                        SWEDEN                                        197-
*Christa Lindberg*
A traumatic sexual encounter as a child leads a girl into a fantasy world of self-gratification. Made in the 1970s and truly looking its age.

A                                                           88 min (Cut at film release)
V                                                                   PHV; SHEP

## ANNA ****                                                            15
Yurek Bogayevicz         USA                                          1987
*Sally Kirkland, Paulina Porizkova, Robert Fields, Ruth Maleczech, Stefan Schnabel, Larry Pine*
Kirkland plays an ageing Czech actress living in impoverished exile in New York. When a young and struggling actress faints at her feet she takes her home and later teaches her the basics, only to see her succeed where she failed. A touching and original film with a remarkable performance from Kirkland and a fair one from ex-model Porizkova in her screen debut.

DRA                                                          96 min (ort 100 min)
V                                                                          VES

## ANNA KARENINA ****                                                    U
Clarence Brown           USA                                          1935
*Greta Garbo, Fredric March, Freddie Bartholomew, Maureen O'Sullivan, May Robson, Basil Rathbone, Reginald Owen, Reginald Denny*
An opulent and carefully made romantic tragedy, telling of the wife of a Russian aristocrat who falls hopelessly in love with a handsome cavalry officer. Garbo is excellent in the title role, and March gives fine support as her lover. Filmed once before as "Love" (also with Garbo) and made several more times since.
Boa: novel by Leo Tolstoy.

DRA                                                                   96 min B/W
V                                                                          MGM

## ANNA KARENINA **
Julien Duvivier          UK                                           1947
*Vivien Leigh, Ralph Richardson, Kieron Moore, Marie Lohr, Sally Ann Howes, Niall MacGinnis, Michael Gough, Martita Hunt, Hugh Dempster, Mary Kerridge, Heather Thatcher, Helen Haye, Austin Trevor, John Longden, Ruby Miller*
Second attempt to film Tolstoy's classic novel of a married woman in love with a handsome Russian officer. The good cast can do little with this dismally stilted and overlong production.
Boa: novel by Leo Nikolai Tolstoy.

DRA                                                  110 min (ort 139 min) B/W
B,V                                          SPEC/POLY; WHV (VHS only)

## ANNA KARENINA: PARTS 1 AND 2 **                                      PG
Basil Coleman            UK
*Nicola Pagett, Eric Porter, Stuart Wilson*
Tolstoy's classic tale of an aristocratic lady and her tragic love for a count gets the standard TV treatment in this competent but far from inspired production.
Boa: novel by Leo Tolstoy.

DRA                                                                  365 min mTV
V/h                                                                        BBC

## ANNA KARENINA **                                                      PG
Simon Langton            USA                                          1985
*Jacqueline Bisset, Paul Scofield, Christopher Reeve, Ian Ogilvy, Anna Massey, Joanna David, Judi Bowker, Valerie Lush, Judy Campbell*
Later remake of Tolstoy's classic, with Bisset playing the title character who, although already married, falls in love with a dashing Russian count and becomes pregnant by him. Set during the reign of Czar Nicholas I of Russia, this is a glossy and visually pleasing production of little passion or force. Worth seeing for one of Scofield's rare screen appearances.
Boa: novel by Leo Nikolai Tolstoy.

DRA                                                                  130 min mTV
V                                                                          RCA

## ANNA TO THE INFINITE POWER **                                        PG
Robert Wiemer            USA                                          1983
*Dina Merril, Marsha Byrne, Mark Patton, Donna Mitchell, Loretta Divine, Jack Ryland, Jack Gilford*
A young girl discovers that her mental abilities are the result of a cloning experiment and sets out to find her sisters to whom she is linked by telepathy. Pleasant and fairly undemanding fantasy-thriller largely aimed at youngsters. Written by Robert Wiemer.
Aka: GENETIC CONTACT (GLOB)
Boa: novel by Mildred Ames.

THR                                                                   101 min
B,V                                                     VTC; VIZ; GLOB

## ANNE OF GREEN GABLES ***
Kevin Sullivan           CANADA                                      1985
*Megan Follows, Colleen Dewhurst, Richard Farnsworth, Patricia Hamilton, Marilyn Lightstone, Schuyler Grant, Rosemary Radcliffe, Jonathan Crombie, Charmion King, Jackie Burroughs, Joachim Hansen, Christiane Krueger*

Remake of the 1934 classic film, following the adoption of the title character by a bachelor farmer and his sister through to her blossoming growth into a young woman. Originally shown in two parts, this handsome adaptation of the famous children's classic is always good to look at. Followed by "Anne Of Avonlea".
Boa: novel by Lucy Maud Montgomery.
DRA                          202 min (2 cassettes) mTV
V                                                    BUENA

## ANNE OF THE THOUSAND DAYS **          PG
Charles Jarrott          UK                      1969
*Richard Burton, Genevieve Bujold, Anthony Quayle,*
*John Colicos, Irene Papas, Michael Hordern,*
*Katherine Blake, Valerie Gearson, Michael Johnson,*
*Peter Jeffrey, Joseph O'Conor, William Squire,*
*Esmond Knight, Brook Williams*
Wooden film version of a boring play about Anne Boleyn, her courtship by Henry VIII, marriage and subsequent execution. Good scenery and costumes plus a nice performance from Bujold are compensations. AA: Cost (Margaret Furse).
Boa: play by Maxwell Anderson.
DRA                           140 min (ort 145 min)
V/h                                                  CIC

## ANNIE *                                   U
John Huston              USA                      1982
*Albert Finney, Carol Burnett, Aileen Quinn, Ann*
*Reinking, Bernadette Peters, Tim Curry, Geoffrey*
*Holder, Edward Herrmann*
Film adaptation of the smash Broadway musical about Little Orphan Annie, a famous comic strip character created during the Depression by Harold Gray. Nice performances from Quinn as Annie and Finney as Daddy Warbucks are wasted in a large, ponderous and glitzy effort. Uninspired, unimaginative and unmoving. Written by Carol Sobieski from his play, with music by Charles Strouse and lyrics by Martin Charnin.
Boa: play by Carol Sobieski/book by Thomas Meecham.
MUS                        128 min; 122 min (PREST)
B,V                              RCA; PREST (VHS only)

## ANNIE HALL ****                          15
Woody Allen              USA                      1977
*Woody Allen, Diane Keaton, Tony Roberts, Carol*
*Kane, Paul Simon, Shelley Duvall, Janet Margolin,*
*Colleen Dewhurst, Christopher Walken*
Romantic comedy looking at the relationship between a Jewish comedian and a girl from the mid-West. Full of Allen observations on life, love and fame with a warm script and appealing performances and not let down by the unevenness that afflicts so many of Allen's films. One of his best efforts. AA: Pic, Dir, Actress (Keaton), Screen (Orig) (Woody Allen/ Marshall Brickman).
COM                           89 min (ort 94 min)
V                                                    WHV

## ANNIE OAKLEY ***                         U
George Stevens           USA        -            1935
*Barbara Stanwyck, Preston Foster, Melvyn Douglas,*
*Pert Kelton, Moroni Olsen, Andy Clyde, Chief*
*Thundercloud, Delmar Watson*
Western tale of the famed female sharp-shooter and her love for Toby Walker, who claimed to be the world's greatest marksman. A lively and episodic jaunt through the Wild West. Look out for Olsen in his role as Buffalo Bill.
WES                                           87 min B/W
V                                                    PARK

## ANNIE'S COMING OUT ***                   PG
Gil Brealey              AUSTRALIA               1983
*Angela Punch MacGregor, Tina Arhondis, Drew*
*Forsythe, Liddy Clark, Wallas Eaton, Simon Chilvers,*
*Monica Maugham, Mark Butler*
A disabled teenager is incarcerated in a hospital for the handicapped, and is believed to be mentally retarded. A new teacher-therapist fights a heroic court battle to prove that she is in fact of high intelligence.
Aka: TEST OF LOVE, A
Boa: novel by Rosemary Crossley and A. McDonald.
DRA                                           92 min
B,V                                       IPC/VSP; APX

## ANNIHILATOR, THE **                      15
Michael Chapman          USA                      1986
*Mark Lindsay Chapman, Susan Blakely, Lisa Blount,*
*Brion James, Earl Boen, Geoffrey Lewis, Catherine*
*Mary Stewart, Nicole Eggert, Barry Pearl, Paul*
*Brinegar, Channing Chase, Barbara Townsend,*
*Christopher Johnston*
A man must destroy the woman he loves after she and a group of people have returned from a trip transformed into murderous robots. Stylish pilot for a TV series let down by poor pacing and dialogue. Make-up artists Michael Westmore and Zoltan Elek were Emmy nominated.
HOR                        90 min (ort 100 min) mTV
B,V                                                  CIC

## ANNIHILATORS, THE *                      18
Charles E. Seiller Jr    USA                      1985
*Christopher Stone, Andy Wood, Lawrence Hilton-*
*Jacobs, Gerrit Graham, Dennis Redfield, Paul Koslo*
Vietnam veterans are hired by the inhabitants of a small southern town in order to break the grip of local youth gangs. A dull and trashy vigilante film with minimal plot and maximal violence.
DRA                                           87 min
B,V                                                  NWV

## ANOTHER CHANCE **                        15
Jesse Vint               USA                      198-
*Bruce Greenwood, Anne Ramsey, Vanessa Angle, Jeff*
*East, Bernard Behrens*
A successful fellow has everything he wants in life until he falls in love, in this lighthearted and fairly innocuous effort.
COM                                           80 min
V                                                    WATER

## ANOTHER COUNTRY ***                      15
Marek Kaniewska          UK                       1984
*Rupert Everett, Colin Firth, Michael Jenn, Robert*
*Addie, Anna Massey, Betsy Brantley, Rupert*
*Wainwright, Tristan Oliver, Cary Elwes, Geoffrey*
*Bateman, Frederick Alexander, Adrian Ross-Magenty,*
*Philip Dupuy, Jeffrey Wickham*
Set in a boys' public school in the 1930s, this film focuses on the oppressive and cloistered atmosphere of corruption and betrayed ideals that influences the lives of some of the pupils there. Based on Mitchell's successful London play, that attempted an examination of the public school system that produced traitors such as Guy Burgess and Donald MacLean. A Cannes Festival Award Winner.
Boa: play by Julian Mitchell.
DRA                         90 min; 86 min (VIR)
B,V                              PVG; STABL; VIR (VHS only)

## ANOTHER TIME, ANOTHER PLACE ***
Michael Radford          UK                       1983
*Phyllis Logan, Giovanni Mauriello, Denise Coffey,*
*Tom Watson, Gian Luca Favilla, Gregor Fisher, Paul*
*Young, Claudio Rosini, Jennifer Piercey, Yvonne*
*Gilan, Carol Ann Crawford, Ray Jeffries, Scott*
*Johnston, Nadio Fortune*
A farmer's wife in the Scottish Highlands gradually falls in love with one of a group of Italian POWs billetted on the tiny farming community. A nice WW2 drama, originally made for TV but released to cinemas instead.
Boa: novel by J. Kesson.

DRA                                    102 min mTV
B,V,V2                                         VCL

## ANOTHER WAY ***
Karoly Makk        HUNGARY              1982
*Jadwiga Jankowska-Cieslak, Grazyna Szapolowska,*
*Jozef Kroner*
Two female journalists on a Budapest newspaper fall
in love, but a tragedy is the result. An interesting
European melodrama.
Aka: EGYMASRA NEZRE
DRA                                       109 min
B,V                                       CAP/PVG

## ANOTHER WOMAN ***                           PG
Woody Allen        USA                 1988
*Gena Rowlands, Mia Farrow, Ian Holm, Blythe*
*Danner, Gene Hackman, Betty Buckley, Martha*
*Plimpton, John Houseman, Sandy Dennis, David*
*Ogden Stiers, Philip Bosco, Harris Yulin, Frances*
*Conroy*
Another Allen stab at a Bergmanesque study of
misery, complete with Sven Nykvist as cameraman.
This story focuses on the usual collection of angst-
ridden New Yorkers, particularly a woman whose
cosy and sheltered lifestyle is shattered by unforeseen
events. A mature adult drama of powerful if decidedly
narrow appeal.
DRA                            77 min (ort 84 min)
V                                             VIR

## ANTAGONISTS, THE **                          15
Boris Sagal        USA                 1981
*Peter O'Toole, Peter Strauss, Barbara Carrera, Nigel*
*Davenport, Paul Smith, Alan Feinstein, Giulia*
*Pagano, Anthony Quayle, Denis Quilley, Timothy*
*West, Anthony Valentine, David Warner, Clive*
*Francis, George Innes, David Opatoshu*
Cut-down version of the TV film "Masada", telling of
the Jewish fortress that defied the might of Rome.
There are a few good things in this glossy and
overlong TV production, but O'Toole's dreadful over-
acting is not one of them.
Aka: MASADA
Boa: novel by Ernest K. Gann.
DRA                      128 min (ort 448 min) mTV
V/h                                           CIC

## ANTHROPHAGUS 2 *
Joe D'Amato (Aristide Massaccesi)
                   ITALY               1980
*George Eastman (Luigi Montefiore), Annie Belle, Ian*
*Danby, Charles Borromel, Katja Berger, Edmond*
*Purdom, Ted Rusoff, Anja Kochansky*
Sequel to the first film with a lab experiment creating
an unstoppable monster whose body keeps regenerat-
ing at the expense of his (and the director's) brain
cells. Another messy and cliched horror yarn that
stumbles along from one ponderously scored shock to
another without ever building up to anything of note.
Aka: ABSURD
HOR                                        90 min
B,V                                           MED

## ANTONY AND CLEOPATRA **                       U
Charlton Heston    USA                 1972
*Charlton Heston, Hildegard Neil, Eric Porter, John*
*Castle, Fernando Rey, Freddie Jones, Peter Arne,*
*Roger Delgado*
Uninspired and sluggish attempt to bring
Shakespeare's tragedy alive on film that was severely
hampered by a limited budget.
Boa: play by William Shakespeare.
DRA                          159 min (ort 170 min)
B,V,V2                                    VUL; PRV

## ANTONY AND CLEOPATRA ***                      U
Jonathan Miller    UK

*Colin Blakely, Jane Lapotaire*
Competent BBC made-for-TV production of this
famous play.
Boa: play by William Shakespeare.
DRA                                    172 min mTV
V/h                                            BBC

## ANTS: PANIC AT LAKEWOOD MANOR **
Robert Sheerer     USA                 1977
*Lynda Day George, Myrna Loy, Suzanne Somers,*
*Robert Foxworth, Gerald Gordon, Bernie Casey,*
*Moosie Drier, Steve Franken, Brian Dennehy, Stacy*
*Keach Sr*
Poisonous ants go on the rampage at a family
residence that has been turned into a hotel. Predict-
able horror-thriller of little note.
Aka: ANTS; IT HAPPENED AT LAKEWOOD
MANOR; PANIC AT LAKEWOOD MANOR
THR                                    100 min mTV
B,V                                           TEVP

## ANY GUN CAN PLAY ***
Enzo G. Castellari ITALY               1967
*Edd Byrnes, Gilbert Roland, George Hilton, Kareen*
*O'Hara, Pedro Sanchez, Gerard Herter*
Routine spaghetti Western in which a bandit, a
stranger and a banker join forces in order to divide a
fortune in stolen gold. A good deal better than is usual
for this genre, but more for the strong presence of
Roland than for any novel aspects of plot.
Aka: FOR A FEW BULLETS MORE (INT); GO KILL
AND COME BACK; I'LL GO . . . I'LL KILL HIM AND
COME BACK; VADO . . . L'AMMAZO E TORNO
WES              96 min; 100 min (INT) (ort 105 min)
B,V,V2      GOV (Betamax and VHS only) L/A; VPD

## ANY WHICH WAY YOU CAN **                      15
Buddy Van Horn     USA                 1980
*Clint Eastwood, Ruth Gordon, Sondra Locke, William*
*Smith, Harry Guardino, Ruth Gordon, Glen Campbell,*
*Anne Ramsey, Logan Ramsey*
Offbeat and mindless follow-up to the successful
EVERY WHICH WAY YOU CAN in which bare-fist
boxer Eastwood is still slugging it out. Despite a few
funny moments the best actor is still our orangutan –
Clyde.
COM                  110 min (ort 116 min) Cut (45 sec)
B,V                                           WHV

## ANYONE FOR DENIS? *                           PG
Dick Clement       UK                  1982
*Angela Thorne, John Wells*
Tiresome adaptation of a tedious stage farce based on
the lives of Denis and Margaret Thatcher. The story
revolves around a weekend of fun and mischief when
Denis invites two of his drinking cronies down to
Chequers while his wife is away at a Euro-Conference.
Boa: play by John Wells.
COM                                        76 min mTV
V                                      THAMES; VCC

## ANZIO **                                      PG
Edward Dmytryk
                   FRANCE/ITALY/SPAIN  1968
*Robert Mitchum, Peter Falk, Robert Ryan, Earl*
*Holliman, Mark Damon, Arthur Kennedy, Reni*
*Santoni, Anthony Steel, Patrick Magee*
Uninspired account of WW2 Allied Anzio landings
with plenty of large-scale action and a star-studded
cast, but still short on interest.
Aka: BATTLE FOR ANZIO, THE
WAR                                       117 min
B,V                                           RCA

## APACHE MASSACRE **                            18
William A. Graham  USA                 1972
*Harry Dean Stanton, Xochitl, Cliff Potts, Don*
*Wilbanks, Woodrow Chambliss, James Gammon, Roy*
*Jenson, William Carstens, Richard Breeding*

An impulsive gunman befriends an Indian woman who has escaped the massacre of her people by the US Cavalry. But even for them, tragedy strikes. An obscure and rather violent Western of little merit.
Aka: BILLY; COUNT YOUR BLESSINGS; CRY FOR ME; CRY FOR ME, BILLY; FACE TO THE WIND; LONG TOMORROW, THE
WES                                   93 min, 88 min (CINE)
B,V                                   CBS; CINE; DIAV

## APACHE WOMAN *
Roger Corman            USA                    1955
*Lloyd Bridges, Joan Taylor, Lance Fuller, Morgan Jones, Paul Birch, Dick Miller, Paul Dubov, Jonathan Hale, Chester Conkliln*
A government expert tries to mediate between whites and Apaches but gets tangled up with fiery halfbreed Taylor. A low-budget and low-grade Corman effort that is so bad it's often quite funny, but not often enough to make it worth watching.
WES                                          83 min
B,V                                     MMA; PORVI

## APARTMENT, THE ****                         PG
Billy Wilder           USA                     1960
*Jack Lemmon, Shirley MacLaine, Fred MacMurray, Ray Walston, Jack Kruschen, Edie Adams, David Lewis, Joan Shawlee*
Sharp and witty story of an ambitious executive who lends his apartment to his superiors to curry favour with them, with unforeseen results when he falls in love with his boss's latest girlfriend. Later made into the Broadway musical "Promises, Promises". AA: Pic, Dir, Story/Screen (Wilder/ A.L. Diamond), Art/Set (Alexander Trauner/Edward G. Boyle), Edit (Daniel Mandell).
COM                          119 min (ort 125 min) B/W
V                                             WHV

## APARTMENT ZERO ***                          15
Martin Donovan         UK                      1988
*Colin Firth, Hart Bochner, Dora Bryan, Liz Smith, Fabrizio Bentivoglio*
Arty drama set in Buenos Aires where the central character is the owner of a flea-pit cinema who is forced to take in a tenant, a former American mercenary who may or may not be a serial killer. A plethora of movie references and a good suspenseful atmosphere cannot entirely mask the lack of substance. Screenplay is by Donovan and David Koepp.
DRA                                          120 min
V                                            20VIS

## APHRODITE **                                18
                       USA                     1983
*Valerie Kaprisky*
Kaprisky plays a nymphomaniac mistress who embarks on a wild career of debauchery in this censored sex film.
A                    77 min (ort 90 min) Cut (6 min 50 sec)
V                                             VES

## APOCALYPSE MERCENARIES ***                  15
John R. Dawson         USA
*Karl Landgren, Vassili Karris, Peter Hiats, Thomas Rauser, Maurice Poli, Brigitte Christensen*
Four tough commandos and their leader, embark on a hazardous mission to Bosnia in Yugoslavia in order to attack a German command post. Once there they are confronted by tanks, fighter planes and an assortment of heavy artillery in this routine high-action adventure.
A/AD                                         85 min
B,V                                          VPD

## APOCALYPSE NOW ***                          18
Francis Ford Coppola    USA                    1979
*Marlon Brando, Martin Sheen, Robert Duvall, Frederic Forrest, Sam Bottoms, Dennis Hopper, Albert*

*Hall, Harrison Ford, Larry Fishburne, G.D. Spradlin*
Hollywood finally discovered the Vietnam War with an epic story of a secret agent sent into the jungle with orders to kill an officer who has set up his own little kingdom in the heart of the Cambodian jungle. A strange rather surreal journey up river for Sheen, is followed by a muddled climax. A film of unforgettable images and opaque ideas. AA: Cin (Vittorio Storaro), Sound (Walter Murch/Mark Berger/Richard Beggs/Nat Boxer).
Boa: short story Heart Of Darkness by Joseph Conrad.
WAR                              148 min (ort 153 min)
B, V/sh, LV                                   CIC

## APOLOGY ***                                 15
Robert Bierman         USA                     1986
*Lesley Anne Warren, Peter Weller, John Glover, George Loros, Jimmie Ray Weeks, Harvey Fierstein, Charles S. Dutton, Skye Bassett, Garrett M. Brown, Christopher Noth, Ellen Barber, Reathel Bean, Diana Reis, Joe Zaloom*
Thriller involving a female sculptor in Manhattan who becomes drawn into a strange web of murder and intrigue, since her latest art form makes use of confessions she hears on her telephone hot line. She eventually finds herself being pursued by a psychotic killer whilst a tough detective is not far behind. A film of implausible ideas and flashes of occasional intensity. The script is by playwright Mark Medoff.
Aka: APOLOGY: FOR MURDER
THR                                          98 min mCab
B,V                                          MED

## APPLE DUMPLING GANG RIDES                   U
## AGAIN, THE **
Vincent McEveety       USA                     1979
*Tim Conway, Don Knotts, Tim Matheson, Kenneth Mars, Elyssa Davalos, Cliff Osmond, Jack Elam, Robert Pine, Harry Morgan, Ruth Buzzi, Audrey Totter, Richard X. Slattery, John Crawford, Ted Gehring*
Slapstick sequel to THE APPLE DUMPLING GANG with Knotts and Conway bumbling outlaws out in the Old West. Tiresomely predictable Disney kiddie comedy that adds nothing whatsoever to the earlier film.
WES                                          88 min
B,V                                          WDV

## APPLE DUMPLING GANG, THE **                 U
Norman Tokar           USA                     1975
*Bill Bixby, Susan Clark, Don Knotts, Stacy Manning, Tim Conway, David Wayne, Slim Pickens, Harry Morgan, Clay O'Brien, Brad Savage, Irish Adrian*
A gambler becomes the guardian of three homeless children and later tries to pull off a daring bank robbery in this kid's comedy-Western. The usual slapstick capers one expects from Disney, with Knotts and Conway doing their worst as a pair of bumbling villains. Followed by THE APPLE DUMPLING GANG RIDES AGAIN which just shows that you can't keep a good dumpling down.
Boa: novel by Jack M. Bickham.
WES                                          100 min
B,V                                          WDV

## APPLE, THE *
Menahem Golan          USA                     1980
*Catherine Mary Stewart, Allan Love, George Gilmour, Vladek Sheybal, Grace Kennedy, Joss Ackland*
Futuristic musical set in 1994, when a couple's entry in a song contest is sabotaged by an evil rock promoter. Nonsensical and tedious dross of the highest order.
MUS                                          84 min
B,V                                          RNK

## APPOINTMENT WITH DEATH *                    PG
Michael Winner         USA                     1988
*Peter Ustinov, Lauren Bacall, Carrie Fisher, John*

*Gielgud, Piper Laurie, Hayley Mills, Jenny Seagrove, David Soul, Nicholas Guest, Valerie Richards, John Terlesky, Amber Bezer, Douglas Sheldon, Mike Sarne, Michael Craig*
Oh dear, it's another one of those depressingly lack-lustre detective yarns that collapses under its surfeit of stars. In this one a posh 1937 tour of the Holy Land turns nasty when a malicious and wealthy dowager is poisoned. Each of her fellow tourists could have done it but luckily Hercule Poirot is on hand to uncover the culprit. The script is by Winner, Anthony Shaffer and Peter Buckman.
Boa: novel by Agatha Christie.
DRA                    102 min (ort 108 min)
B,V                    CAN

## APPOINTMENT WITH FEAR ** 15
Alan Smithee (Ramzi Thomas)
                    USA          1986
*Michele Little, Michael Wyle, Kerry Remsen, Douglas Rowe, Garrick Dowhen, Mike Gomez, Deborah Sue Voorhees, Pamela Bach, Vincent Barbour, Danny Dayton, James Avery, Sergia Simone, Stephen B. Gregory, Charlotte Speer*
An asylum patient becomes the reincarnation of the Egyptian god Attis, the King of the Woods. In order to retain his powers he is obliged to kill, and kidnaps a baby for this purpose, but is relentlessly pursued by a police detective.
HOR                    90 min (ort 96 min)
B,V                    MED

## APPOINTMENT, THE ** 
Lindsey C. Vickey      UK           1981
*Edward Woodward, Samantha Weyson, John Judd, Ken Julian, Lindsey C. Vickey*
Horror story about a young girl with strange powers which she uses to get things her own way. Average.
HOR                    90 min
B,V,V2                 3MVID

## APPRENTICE TO MURDER ** 15
R.L. Thomas            USA          1987
*Chad Lowe, Mia Sara, Donald Sutherland, Rutanya Alda, Eddie Jones, Mark Burton, Knut Husebo*
Murder story set in the Pennsylvania Dutch community, and revolving around the personality of a charismatic small-town doctor with supernatural powers who takes on the local demon. Odd and quirky mixture of drama and horror with little of value. Filmed in Norway.
DRA                    90 min (ort 97 min)
V                      NWV

## APPRENTICESHIP OF DUDDY KRAVITZ, THE ***
Ted Kotcheff           CANADA       1974
*Richard Dreyfuss, Micheline Lanctot, Jack Warden, Randy Quaid, Joseph Wiseman, Denholm Elliott, Joe Silver*
Well acted and lively comedy-drama following the rise of an ambitious Jewish boy from Montreal's Jewish quarter who is determined to make good, no matter what it takes. Set in the 1940s and containing many vivid and comical highlights.
Boa: novel What Makes Duddy Run? by Mordecai Richler.
DRA                    121 min
B,V,V2                 GHV

## APRIL FOOL'S DAY ** 18
Fred Walton            USA          1986
*Deborah Foreman, Deborah Goodrich, Griffin O'Neal, Clayton Rohner, Jay Baker, Amy Steel, Ken Olandt, Leah King Pinsent*
An attempt to bring some humour to the FRIDAY THE 13TH genre with a young girl inviting some college chums over to her parents' secluded island home for the weekend; one by one they meet a grisly

end. An uneasy film that can never quite decide which way it's going.
HOR                    86 min (ort 88 min)
B,V                    CIC

## APRIL IN PARIS * U
David Butler           USA          1952
*Doris Day, Ray Bolger, Claude Dauphin, Eve Miller, George Givot*
Dismal star vehicle for Day, with her playing a chorus girl who is invited by mistake to an American arts festival in Paris. Once there she captivates the chief diplomat. The sprinkling of humour (such as various onboard problems for Bolger and Day en route to France) simply cannot hide the sheer lack of ideas in this drab and dull musical.
MUS                    100 min
V                      WHV

## AQUANASTA JOE ** 
Mario Gariazzo         ITALY        1971
*Richard Harrison, Ty Hardin, Lee Banner, Lincoln Tate*
Western tale of a bounty hunter's revenge on the gang that robbed him. Average.
WES                    90 min
B,V,V2                 VPD

## ARABIAN ADVENTURE *** U
Kevin Corner           UK           1979
*Christopher Lee, Milo O'Shea, Oliver Tobias, Emma Samms, Peter Cushing, Mickey Rooney, Capucine, Puneet Sira, John Wyman, John Ratzenberger, Shane Rimmer, Elizabeth Welch, Suzanne Danielle, Milton Reid*
Colourful reworking of some of the fantasy elements from THE THIEF OF BAGDAD that's largely aimed at kids but with enough effects to appeal to adults as well.
A/AD                   94 min (ort 98 min)
B,V                    TEVP

## ARCH OF TRIUMPH *** 
Lewis Milestone        USA          1948
*Ingrid Bergman, Charles Boyer, Charles Laughton, Louis Calhern*
Classic story of a romance between prostitute and refugee in WW2 France, with both being pursued by a Gestapo chief. Slow pacing is a drawback. Remade for TV in 1985.
Boa: novel by Erich Maria Remarque.
DRA                    81 min (ort 120 min)
B,V                    INT

## ARCHER AND THE SORCERESS, THE ** PG
Nick Corea             USA          1981
*Lane Caudell, Belinda Bauer, Victor Campos, George Innes, Kabir Bedi, Marc Alaimo, Allan Rich, John Hancock, Priscilla Pointer, George Kennedy, Robert Feero, Richard Dix, Ivan J. Rado, Sharon Barr, Tony Swartz, Richard Moll*
Action fantasy set in prehistoric times telling of a young wanderer who seeks a sorcerer who can help him regain his rightful title. Pilot for a short-lived TV series, "Archer – Fugitive From The Empire". A lightweight comic-strip yarn that never develops into anything substantial.
Aka: ARCHER, THE: FUGITIVE FROM THE EMPIRE; FUGITIVE OF THE EMPIRE
FAN                    95 min (ort 100 min) mTV
B,V                    ARENA/CIC

## ARCHER'S ADVENTURE ** PG
Denny Lawrence         AUSTRALIA    1985
*Brett Climo, Robert Coleby, Ned Lander, Doreen Warburton, Claire Corbett, John Spicer*
The tale of the first winner of the Melbourne Cup in 1862. His handler volunteers to trek with the horse across 600 miles of bush and the pair endure many

hardships before arriving at their destination. Pleasant little adventure yarn that will appeal mostly to kids.
Aka: ARCHER

| | |
|---|---|
| A/AD | 99 min |
| B,V | NWV |

### ARCTIC HEAT *** 18
Renny Harlin  FINLAND/USA  1985
*Mike Norris, David Coburn, Steve Durham, Thalmus Rasulala, Albert Salmi, Pitta Vuosalmi, Laura Meimo, Vesa Vierikko*
Three young American seamen on leave in Finland go reindeer hunting, and then foolishly cross the Soviet border as a dare. Getting back, however, proves to be much harder for they are caught and sent to a prison camp with little hope of release. Action film let down by a shallow script.
Aka: BORN AMERICAN

| | |
|---|---|
| A/AD | 92 min Cut (14 sec) |
| B,V | GHV |

### ARE YOU BEING SERVED? * PG
Bob Kellett  UK  1977
*Mollie Sugden, John Inman, Frank Thornton, Trevor Bannister, Wendy Richard, Arthur Brough, Nicholas Smith, Arthur English, Harold Bennett, Andrew Sachs, Karan David, Glyn Houston, Penny Irving, Derek Griffiths, Sheila Staefel*
One of those feeble TV spin-offs from a popular British sit-com. This one has the staff of Grace Brothers, the department store, going on holiday and enduring a series of catastrophes – the making of this film being one of them.

| | |
|---|---|
| COM | 91 min (ort 95 min) |
| B,V | TEVP; WHV (VHS only) |

### ARENA ** 15
Peter Manoogian  USA  1988
*Paul Satterfield, Claudia Christian, Hamilton Camp*
In the year 4038 the universe is ruled by one government and has a single common language. "Arena" is the name for a popular sport whose contestants compete for cash prizes, but can find themselves up against any kind of creature. This disappointing fantasy tells of a drifter badly in need of some money to return to Earth who decides to try his luck.

| | |
|---|---|
| FAN | 93 min |
| V | EIV |

### ARENA, THE ** 
Steve Carver  USA  1974
*Pam Grier, Margaret Markov, Lucretia Love, Paul Muller*
Quite well mounted gladiator spectacle set in acient Rome with all the participants being women and the film having a rather pro-female stance. Women's lib with swords – the display of attractive combatants is the best thing in this nonsense.
Aka: NAKED WARRIORS

| | |
|---|---|
| A/AD | 79 min |
| B,V | TEVP |

### ARIZONA HEAT ** 18
John G. Thomas  USA  1988
*Michael Parks, Denise Crosby, Hugh Farrington, Ron Briskman, Renata Lee, Dennis O'Sullivan*
A cop who refuses to obey the rules is given a tough woman partner and together they investigate a series of strange slayings. Average.

| | |
|---|---|
| A/AD | 88 min |
| B,V | VPD |

### ARK OF THE SUN GOD, THE **
Anthony M. Dawson (Antonio Margheriti)
ITALY  1984
*Donald Warbeck, John Steiner, Alan Collins, Susie Sudlow, Riccardo Palacios, Aytekin Akkaya, Suleyman Turhan*
A professional safe-cracker is recruited for the purpose of stealing the Ark of Gilgamest the Sun God. Filmed in Turkey.
Aka: ARK OF THE SUN GOD . . . TEMPLE OF HELL, THE

| | |
|---|---|
| A/AD | 92 min |
| B,V | VTC |

### ARM OF FIRE ** 
Richard McNamara  ITALY  1964
*Gordon Scott, Gabriella Pallota, Massimo Serato*
Historical epic about a man who saved Rome from surrendering to Tarquin the Proud in 55 BC. A standard Italian costumer.
Aka: IL COLOSSO DI ROMA

| | |
|---|---|
| DRA | 87 min |
| B,V,V2 | VPD; WAT |

### ARMED AND DANGEROUS ** 15
Mark L. Lester  USA  1986
*John Candy, Eugene Levy, Robert Loggia, Kenneth McMillan, Meg Ryan, Brion James, Jonathan Banks, Don Stroud, Steve Railsback*
A lawyer and a cop, both unjustly dismissed from their jobs, are forced to earn a living as private security guards. However, this does not stop them from waging a private war against corruption in the police and unions. Lame comedy with an episodic script made up of bits and pieces.

| | |
|---|---|
| COM | 88 min |
| B,V | RCA |

### ARMED RESPONSE ** 18
Fred Olen Ray  USA  1986
*Lee Van Cleef, David Carradine, Michael Berryman, Mako, Lois Hamilton, Ross Hagen, Brent Huff, Laurene Langdon, Dick Miller*
Action story set in the Chinatown area of Los Angeles with a retired cop and his eldest Vietnam veteran son hitting the vengeance trail, when the two youngest sons are murdered in a double-cross after they get involved in retrieving a jade statuette for a local Chinese gangster. A fast and brainless story for those who like their action undiluted by a plot.
Aka: JADE JUNGLE, THE

| | |
|---|---|
| A/AD | 83 min Cut (1 sec) |
| B,V | EIV |

### ARMOUR OF GOD, THE *** 15
Jackie Chan  HONG KONG  1986
*Jackie Chan, Alan Tam, Lola Forner, Rosamund Kwan*
Kung fu actioner with Chan obliged to borrow back some religious artefacts (the "Armour of God") from an antiques dealer to whom he sold them, in order to use the pieces as bait to retrieve his girlfriend from an evil cult. As ever, Chan does his own stunts in this fast and furious action tale.

| | |
|---|---|
| MAR | 88 min |
| B,V | VPD |

### AROUND THE WORLD IN 80 DAYS *** U
Michael Anderson  USA  1956
*David Niven, Cantinflas, Robert Newton, Shirley MacLaine, Marlene Dietrich, Charles Boyer, Joe E. Brown, Martine Carol, John Carradine, Charles Coburn, Ronald Colman, Melville Cooper, Noel Coward, Finlay Currie, Fernandel*
Lavish version of Jules Verne's famous story of a Victorian gentleman and his valet who together win a bet that they can go round the world in eighty days. No less than 44 star cameos come together in this long, expensively mounted and extremely tiring jaunt. Remade in 1988. AA: Pic, Dir, Cin (Lionel Lindon), Screen (Adapt) (S.J. Perelman/James Poe/John Farrow), Score (Victor Young), Edit (Gene Ruggiero/Paul Weatherwax).
Boa: novel by Jules Verne.

COM 178 min
B, V/sh FFV; WHV

## AROUND THE WORLD IN EIGHTY DAYS: PG
## PARTS 1 AND 2 **
Buzz Kulik USA 1988
*Pierce Brosnan, Eric Idle, Peter Ustinov, Jill St John,*
*Jack Klugman, John Mills, Robert Wagner, Robert*
*Morley, Julia Nickson, Henry Gibson, Lee Remick,*
*John Hillerman, Christopher Lee, Roddy McDowall*
Overlong and glossy adventure tale loosely based on
the Verne classic, with Victorian gentleman Phileas
Fogg embarking on his epic journey. By way of a
foolish sub-plot, he is pursued by a bumbling detective
who suspects him of robbing the Bank of England of
£55,000.
Boa: novel by Jules Verne.
A/AD 275 min (2 cassettes) mTV
B,V GHV

## AROUND THE WORLD WITH FANNY HILL **
Mac Ahlberg SWEDEN 1973
*Shirley Corrigan, Gaby Fuchs, Peter Bonke*
A woman leaves her husband in Stockholm and
becomes a sex-film star in Hollywood. No apparent
connection with the famous erotic novel for this dull
offering.
Aka: JÖRDEN RUNT MED FANNY HILL
A 80 min
B,V PMA

## ARRANGEMENT, THE **
Elia Kazan USA 1969
*Kirk Douglas, Fay Dunaway, Richard Boone, Deborah*
*Kerr, Hume Cronyn*
The director's own novel forms the basis for this film
about an advertising executive who suddenly decides
to chuck it all in and re-evaluate his life but has to put
up with opposition from those closest to him. A good
cast are largely wasted in this flawed and incoherent
treatment of a potentially interesting tale.
Boa: novel by Elia Kazan.
DRA 120 min (ort 127 min)
V WHV

## ARSENIC AND OLD LACE ****
Frank Capra USA 1941 (released 1944)
*Cary Grant, Priscilla Lane, Raymond Massey, Peter*
*Lorre, Jack Carson, Jean Adair, Josephine Hull,*
*James Gleason, Grant Mitchell, John Alexander,*
*Edward Everett Horton*
Extremely funny film version of the famous stage
comedy about two old ladies who murder their guests
(for the very best of motives). Lorre and Massey are
especially good as a couple of unsuspecting murderers
who are hiding out in the house. Unfortunately, with
the demise of the CED disc system this film is not yet
widely available.
Boa: play by Joseph O. Kesselring.
COM 118 min B/W
CED WHV L/A

## ARTHUR ***
Steve Gordon USA 1981
*Dudley Moore, Liza Minnelli, John Gielgud, Geraldine*
*Fitzgerald, Stephen Elliott, Ted Ross, Barney Martin*
Some good moments in an uneven comedy about a
young spoiled millionaire who must choose between
money and a planned marriage or true love and
possible penury. Often quite witty with Moore rather
endearing as an amiable drunken brat, but Gielgud
steals the show as his caustic butler. Written by
Gordon and followed by a sequel. AA: S.Actor (Giel-
gud), Song ("Best Thing You Can Do" – Burt Bachar-
ach/Carole Bayer Sager/Christopher Cross/Peter
Allen).
COM 93 min (ort 97 min)
V/h WHV

## ARTHUR 2 ** PG
Bud Yorkin USA 1988
*Dudley Moore, Liza Minelli, John Gielgud, Cynthia*
*Sikes, Stephen Elliot, Paul Benedict, Geraldine*
*Fitzgerald, Barney Martin, Kathy Bates, Jack Gilford,*
*Ted Ross, Daniel Greene, Brogan Lane*
A disappointing sequel in which Arthur loses all his
money and his wife decides that they ought to adopt a
baby. All the charm and freshness of the original has
long since evaporated. Gielgud pops up briefly – as a
ghost.
Aka: ARTHUR 2: ON THE ROCKS
COM 108 min (ort 110 min)
V/sh WHV

## AS SUMMERS DIE ** 15
Jean-Claude Tramont USA 1986
*Scott Glenn, Jamie Lee Curtis, Bette Davis, John*
*Randolph, Ron O'Neal, Beah Richards, Richard*
*Venture, Paul Roebling, Penny Fuller, Bruce McGill,*
*C.C.H. Pounder, John McIntire, Tammy Baldwin,*
*Nadia Gay Brown, Bill Coates*
Steamy, Southern melodrama about a scheming rich
family out to deprive an elderly black woman of her
rightful claim to part of their land. Glenn plays a
smalltown Louisiana lawyer who sets out to help her
and picks up a couple of unlikely allies in the process.
The few scenes with Davis make this otherwise
forgettable film worth seeing.
Boa: novel by Winston Groom.
DRA 84 min (ort 87 min) mCab
B,V CHV; BRAVE (VHS only)

## AS YOU LIKE IT *** U
Basil Coleman UK 198-
*Helen Mirren, Brian Stirner, Richard Pasco, James*
*Bolam, Clive Francis*
A well made BBC TV production slightly hampered by
the constraints that apply to filmed TV plays but still
worth seeing. This comic tale of love and intrigue that
takes place in a mythical forest was made on location
at Glamis Castle.
Boa: play by William Shakespeare.
DRA 152 min mTV
V BBC

## ASCENDANCY **
Edward Bennett UK 1982
*Julie Covington, Ian Charleson, John Phillips, Susan*
*Engel, Philip Locke, Kieran Montague, Rynagh*
*O'Grady, Philomena McDonagh, Michael McKnight,*
*Jeremy Sinden, Walter McMonagle, Shay Gorman,*
*Liam O'Callaghan, Sean Caffrey*
Belfast in 1920 is the setting for this psychological
drama about a woman obsessed by her brother's death
in WW1 and unable to come to terms with the
sectarian killing all around her. Despite a strong
performance from Covington this one fails to make
any clear statements.
DRA 90 min
B,V LNG

## ASH WEDNESDAY * 15
Larry Peerce USA 1973
*Elizabeth Taylor, Henry Fonda, Helmut Berger, Keith*
*Baxter, Margaret Blye*
An ageing woman undergoes massive plastic surgery
in an attempt to regain her youth and hold onto her
husband, but discovers that beauty is not enough.
Tiresome and plodding dud with a story that needed
major surgery too.
DRA 99 min
B,V,V2 VUL; MIA (VHS only); PARK

## ASHANTI ** 15
Richard Fleischer SWITZERLAND 1979
*Michael Caine, Peter Ustinov, Beverly Johnson, Kabir*
*Bedi, Omar Sharif, Rex Harrison, William Holden*
The wife of a World Health Organisation doctor is

kidnapped by slave traders, in this absurd attempt at an adventure yarn. A flabby script competes with insipid dialogue – the result is one long yawn.
Aka: ASHANTI: LAND OF NO MERCY
Boa: novel Ebano by A. Vasquez-Figueroa.
A/AD                                                    117 min
B,V                                                      RCA

## ASHES AND DIAMONDS ****
Andrzej Wajda          POLAND              1958
Zbigniew Cybulski, Ewa Krzyzanowska, Adam Pawlikowski, Bogumil Kobiela, Waclaw Zastrzezynski
The last part of Wajda's trilogy about the Polish resistance (following A GENERATION and KANAL) traces the conflict between the Communists and the Nationalists at the end of WW2. Cybulski gives a remarkable performance as a young Resistance fighter in this harsh and articulate study.
DRA                              100 min (ort 104 min) B/W
B,V                                                     TEVP

## ASPHALT WARRIORS *                              18
Patrick Millet          FRANCE               1985
Daniel Auteuil, Marisa Berenson, Marcel Bozzufi
Two ruthless detectives, who hate each other, are assigned the task of clearing the tough drug-pushers from the streets of Paris. A badly acted and violent French clone of all those mindless urban actioners from the States, dubbed into hip American for good measure.
Aka: L'ARBALETE
A/AD          86 min (ort 91 min) Cut (59 sec) dubbed
B,V                                                      RCA

## ASPHYX, THE ***
Peter Newbrook          UK                   1972
Robert Stevens, Robert Powell, Jane Lapotaire, Fiona Walker, John Lawrence, Alex Scott, Ralph Arliss, Terry Sculler, David Gray, Tony Caunter, Paul Bacon
A 19th century scientist discovers the key to immortality when he finds a way to isolate the spirit of death that hovers over each individual creature at the moment of its death. However, his experiments go horribly wrong and although he gains immortality, he is left to brood for all time on the tragic death of his daughter. Highly unusual and worthy fantasy tale somewhat hampered by a wordy script.
Aka: HORROR OF DEATH; SPIRIT OF THE DEAD
HOR                                76 min (ort 99 min)
B,V,V2                             INT; MARKET/GOV L/A

## ASSASSIN **                                      PG
Sandor Stern            USA                  1986
Robert Conrad, Karen Austin, Richard Young, Jonathan Banks, Robert Webber, Ben Frank, Jessica Nelson, Nancy Lenehan, Len Birman, Robert F. Hoy, Nick Angotti, Grace Simmons, Allan Graf, Richard Newton, Scott Lincoln
An ex-CIA agent is recalled in order to track down a humanoid assassin on the loose who has been programmed to kill leading US government officials. Somewhat inspired by the success of THE TERMINATOR but of no great value.
FAN                              96 min (ort 100 min) mTV
B,V                                                      IVS

## ASSASSIN OF YOUTH
Elmer Clifton            USA                  1935
Luanna Walters, Arthur Gardner, Dorothy Short, Earl Dwire, Fern Emmett
A film that purports to describe the hazards and horrors of smoking marihuana, with a bunch of those crazy kids smoking just one too many joints at a wild dope party. Meanwhile, an intrepid reporter investigates. A laughable piece of nonsense that's hugely enjoyable after a few beers, especially for the short film within it – "The Marihuana Menace". See also REEFER MADNESS and MARIHUANA: THE DEVIL'S WEED.

DRA                                                71 min B/W
B,V,V2                                                   VCL

## ASSASSIN, THE *                                  18
Chan Tong Man    HONG KONG
Li Sin Kun, Yang Tze Kiang
Standard kung fu mayhem – and all in the defence of honour.
MAR                                                     72 min
V                                        XTACY/KRP; XTASY

## ASSASSINATION *                                  15
Peter Hunt              USA                  1986
Charles Bronson, Jill Ireland, Stephen Elliott, Jan Gan Boyd, Randy Brooks, Michael Ansara, William Prince, James Staley, Kathryn Leigh Scott
An agent is hired to protect the President's wife from a vicious assassin whose orders are coming from inside the White House. A wildly ridiculous and over-the-top exercise in explosions and bad directing.
THR                               85 min (ort 88 min)
B,V                                                     RNK

## ASSASSINATION OF TROTSKY, THE **            15
Joseph Losey    FRANCE/ITALY/UK        1972
Richard Burton, Alain Delon, Romy Schneider, Valentina Cortese, Giorgio Albertazzi, Luigi Vannucchi, Duilio Del Prete, Jean Desailly, Carlos Miranda, Peter Chatel, Hunt Powers, Gianni Lofredo, Claudio Brook
Unconvincing melodrama dealing with the last days of Trotsky. Delon is the murderer hired to kill Trotsky, who lives in a fortress in self-imposed exile. A strange film of symbolism and quirky psychological insights that, despite strong performances, remains completely unmoving.
DRA                               103 min Cut (23 sec)
B,V                              POLY; CH5 (VHS only)

## ASSASSINATION RUN, THE **                     15
Ken Hannam              UK                   1984
Malcolm Stoddard, Mary Tamm, Sandor Eles
The wife of a retired British Intelligence man is held captive by German terrorists. She will be killed unless he assassinates a newspaper publisher. A compilation of three 50 minute episodes. Average.
Aka: TREACHERY GAME, THE
THR                                              108 min mTV
B,V,V2                                                   BBC

## ASSASSINATION, THE **
Reza S. Badiyi
                    ISRAEL/WEST GERMANY        1972
Hardy Kruger, Gila Amagor, Jason Roberts
The Israeli secret service create the legend of a mythical agent, leading to the death of an innocent tourist at the hands of Arab terrorists. Rather cliched thriller.
Aka: DEATH MERCHANTS, THE; DEATH OF A STRANGER; DER TOD EINES FREMDEN; EXECUTION, THE
THR                                                     87 min
B,V                                                     VCL

## ASSAULT *                                         18
Vincent Dawn                                 1989
Brent Huff, Mary Stavin
A man attempts to rescue a group of forgotten American POWs still being held in a Vietnamese prison camp that's under the control of terrorists. When the CIA send a man to infiltrate them he turns out to be a double agent.
A/AD                                                    91 min
V                                                   TGP L/A

## ASSAULT **
Sidney Hayers           UK                   1971
Frank Finlay, Lesley-Anne Down, Suzy Kendall, James Laurenson, Freddie Jones, Tony Beckley, Dilys

*Hamlett, Anthony Ainley, James Cosmo, Patrick Jordan, Allan Cuthbertson, Anabel Littledale, Tom Chatto, David Essex*
Mystery surrounds the identity of a rapist/killer at loose in a girl's school. A victim struck dumb as a result of an attack is unable to help. Eventually, the art mistress catches him in this predictable thriller best described as run-of-the-mill. The script is by John Kruse.
Aka: IN THE DEVIL'S GARDEN; TOWER OF TERROR
Boa: novel The Ravine by Kendal Young.
THR                                    87 min (ort 91 min)
B,V                                              RNK

## ASSAULT AND MATRIMONY **                     15
James Frawley        USA              1987
*Jill Eikenberry, Michael Tucker, John Hillerman, Michelle Phillips, Joseph Cortese*
This slapstick comedy has battling couple Eikenberry and Frawley spending their time devising ever more weird ways to bump each other off. OK as a broad and brash comedy but the sheer lack of genuine wit is a handicap.
COM                            90 min (ort 100 min) mTV
B,V                                            BRAVE

## ASSAULT OF FINAL RIVAL **                     PG
                     HONG KONG              1989
Like Samson, a martial arts fighter owes his incredible strength to his long, flowing locks. A jealous rival sends a girl to seduce him and cut his hair when he is asleep, thus rendering him powerless. A slightly more original theme enlivens this otherwise fairly conventional offering.
MAR                                           87 min
V                                              VPD

## ASSAULT OF THE PARTY NERDS *                  15
Richard Gabai        USA              1989
*Linnea Quigley, Troy Donahue, Richard Gabai, C. Paul Demsey, Michelle McClellan, Marc Silverberg, Robert Mann, Richard Rifkin*
The "nerds" decide to change their image by throwing the frat house party of all time. More mindless comedy capers.
COM                                           90 min
B,V                                             COM

## ASSAULT ON PRECINCT 13 ****                   18
John Carpenter       USA              1976
*Austin Stoker, Darwin Joston, Laurie Zimmer, Martin West, Tony Burton, Nancy Loomis, Kim Richards, Henry Brandon*
A nasty gang of psychopaths decide to embark on a series of murders. When one of their members is killed they follow the killer to a nearly totally deserted police station and stage a siege, intending to kill everyone in it. A well made and extremely tense film with minimal dialogue. Written by Carpenter, who also did the score.
THR                                           91 min
B,V                                         RNK; PAL

## ASSAULT ON THE WAYNE **                       PG
Marvin J. Chomsky    USA              1970
*Joseph Cotten, Lloyd Haynes, Dewey Martin, Leonard Nimoy, William Windom, Keenan Wynn, Malachi Throne, Sam Elliott, Ivor Barry, Ron Masak, Gordon Hoban, Lee Stanley, David Thorpe, Dale Tarter, John Winston, Henry Olek*
A nuclear submarine puts out to sea with a new commander who is unaware of the presence onboard of foreign agents, intent on getting hold of a top secret device. A good cast do their best with a pretty average script.
THR                            71 min (ort 90 min) mTV
B,V                                              CIC

## ASSAULT, THE ****                             PG
Fons Rademakers NETHERLANDS           1986
*Derek de Lint, Marc van Uchelen, Monique van de Ven, John Kraaykamp, Huub van de Lubbe, Eilly Weller*
A young boy witnesses the brutal murder of his family in the final days of WW2. Haunted by this memory, he finally comes to terms with the truth as he grows to manhood. A long and often harrowing story, suspenseful, intense and without a cliche in sight. The superb performances are matched by Gerard Soeteman's fine screenplay. AA: Foreign.
Aka: DER AANSLAG
Boa: novel by Harry Mulisch.
DRA                                  120 min (ort 146 min)
B,V                                             MGM

## ASSIGNMENT MUNICH **                          PG
David Lowell Rich    USA              1972
*Roy Scheider, Richard Basehart, Lesley Warren, Werner Klemperer, Robert Reed, Pernell Roberts, Keenan Wynn*
A pilot for a short-lived TV series called "Assignment Vienna" that ran for eight episodes. After WW2 an American bar-owner in Germany becomes an undercover agent for the US Government, being given the job of recovering $5,000,000 dollars in gold that was stolen during the war. Average.
THR                            96 min (ort 100 min) mTV
V                                              MGM

## ASSIGNMENT, THE **                            15
George Bisset       SWEDEN            1977
*Christopher Plummer, Thomas Hellberg, Carolyn Seymour, Fernando Rey, Per Oscarsson, Walter Gotell*
A Swedish diplomat is sent to mediate in the turbulent political situation of a Latin American country. A slow moving and unconvincing drama that fails to come to life.
Boa: novel by Per Wahloo.
DRA                                           95 min
B,V,V2                             IFS/CBS L/A; ODY

## ASSISI UNDERGROUND, THE **                    PG
Alexander Ramati     USA              1985
*Ben Cross, Maximilian Schell, James Mason, Irene Papas*
A group of Italian monks help Jews to escape from the Nazis towards the end of WW2 in this disappointing story. What might have been gripping remains largely unrealised.
Boa: book While The Pope Kept Silent by A. Ramati.
DRA                                  109 min (ort 178 min)
B,V                                             GHV

## ASTERIX AND CLEOPATRA ***                     U
Rene Goscinny/Albert Uderzo
                BELGIUM/FRANCE        1968
An enjoyable cartoon animation following the adventures of the celebrated comic book character. In this adventure Asterix, Obelix and Getafix go to Egypt with their dog Dogmatic. Here their intention is to help an architect friend build a palace for Queen Cleopatra.
CAR                                           70 min
B,V               MOV L/A; SEL; PARK (VHS only)

## ASTERIX IN BRITAIN ***                        U
Pino Van Lamsweerde
                DENMARK/FRANCE        1986
*Voices of: Robert Barr, Peter Hudson, Patrick Floersheim, Steve Gadler, Judy Rosen-Martinez, Ken Starcevic, Gordon Heath, Jack Beaber, Bill Kearns, Sean O'Neil, Graham Bushnell, Ed Marcus, Herbert Baskind, Jimmy Schuman*
Just across the English channel an invasion force of Romans are gathering to invade Britain. Only Asterix, Obelix and friends can save the day in this adventure of Britons in 50 BC. A lively and enjoyable

animation, based on this popular comic-book character.
Aka: ASTERIX CHEZ LES BRETONS; ASTERIX IN BRITAIN: THE MOVIE
CAR                                75 min (ort 89 min)
V                                                    PAL

**ASTERIX THE GAUL 2:**                          U
**THE TWELVE TASKS OF ASTERIX ***
Rene Goscinny/Albert Uderzo/Matt McCarthy
(English version)        FRANCE            1975
*Voices of: Paul Bacon, George Baker, Sean Barett,*
*Christina Greatex, Ysanne Churchman, Alexander*
*John, Michael Kilgarriff, Barbara Mitchell, Geoffrey*
*Russell, Genni Nevinson, Paddy Turner*
Asterix comes to the rescue of his village when it is set
twelve impossibly difficult tasks by the Emperor
Julius Caesar who wants to take it over.
Aka: LES DOUZE TRAVAUX D'ASTERIX;
TWELVE TASKS OF ASTERIX, THE
CAR                                            84 min
B,V                 SEL L/A; FUTVI; VCC (VHS only)

**ASTERIX THE GAUL: 1 ***                        U
Rene Goscinny/Albert Uderzo
                    BELGIUM/FRANCE            1967
*Voices of: Paul Bacon, George Baker, Sean Barett,*
*Christina Greatex, Ysanne Churchman, Alexander*
*John, Michael Kilgarriff*
Cartoon featuring this popular comic strip character –
a little warrior with super-human strength, who in
the company of his trusty companions, gets into a
variety of scrapes in the course of his battles with the
might of Rome.
Aka: ASTERIX LE GAULOIS
CAR                                            67 min
B,V                 MOV; VFP; SEL; VCC (VHS only)

**ASTERIX THE GAUL:**                            U
**ASTERIX AND THE BIG FIGHT ***
Philippe Grimond        FRANCE
*Voices of: Bill Odie, Ron Moody, Brian Blessed, Sheila*
*Hancock*
A pleasant cartoon version of two Goscinny-Uderzo
tales, one of several adaptations of the popular series
of comic book stories, following the affairs of the
ancient Gauls and Romans. This story revolves
around a custom that requires a would-be chief to
defeat another in order to become leader. Getafix has
promised Vitalstatistix a magic potion to help him do
this, but the former has an accident and forgets how to
make it.
Aka: ASTERIX AND THE BIG FIGHT
CAR                                            75 min
V/h                                                PAL

**ASTONISHED ***                                 18
Travis Preston/Jeff Kahn
                        USA                    1988
*Liliana Komorowska, Tommy Hollis, Charles S.*
*Dutton, William Foeller*
When an actress is propositioned by her pimp landlord
who offers her an alternative way of paying her rent,
she kills him in a fury, but is seen doing so by a hooker
and has to silence her as well.
DRA                                            93 min
V                                              BIGPIC

**ASTRO ZOMBIES**
Ted V. Mikels          USA                    1967
*John Carradine, Wendell Corey, Tom Pace, Tura*
*Satana, Vince Barbi, Victor Izay, Joe Hoover, Wally*
*Moon, Egon Sirany, John Hopkins, Lynette Lantz,*
*Janis Saul, Vic Lance, Rod Wilmoth*
Human transplants go on the rampage in one of the
worst films of all time. One that Edward D. Wood Jr
could have been proud of; this wonderfully inept film

delights in a script by Mikels and Wayne Rogers.
Aka: SPACE VAMPIRES
HOR                                78 min (ort 83 min)
B,V                                                MOV

**ASYLUM ***
Roy Ward Baker          UK                    1972
*Robert Powell, Herbert Lom, Patrick Magee, Geoffrey*
*Bayldon, Barbara Parkins, Richard Todd, Sylvia*
*Sims, Peter Cushing, Barry Morse, Ann Firbank, John*
*Franklyn-Robbins, Britt Ekland, Charlotte Rampling,*
*James Villiers*
Quartet of stories recounted by the inmates of an
asylum, interwoven with the mystery that surrounds
the former director, now an inmate himself. A few
chilling moments with segments of Prokofiev's "Pictures at an Exhibition" used to good effect. The shorter
running time refers to the film as marketed under its
alternative title. Scripted by Robert Bloch. Stories
are: "Frozen Fear", "The Weird Tailor", "Lucy Comes
To Stay" and "Mannikins Of Horror".
Aka: HOUSE OF CRAZIES
HOR                                       95 min; 86 min
B,V                                                GHV

**AT CLOSE RANGE ***                             15
James Foley            USA                    1985
*Sean Penn, Christopher Penn, Christopher Walken,*
*Mary Stuart Masterson, Millie Perkins, Eileen Ryan,*
*Alan Autry, Candy Clark, Tracey Walter, Crispin*
*Glover, Kiefer Sutherland*
A teenager and his half-brother meet their father
whom they have not seen for many years, only to find
that he is a dangerous and violent small-time crook.
Based on a true incident, but despite good performances, this brooding and moody story remains rather
aloof and uninvolved.
DRA    111 min (ort 115 min) (Cut at film release by 14
sec)
B,V                                                RCA

**AT MOTHER'S REQUEST: PARTS 1 AND 2 ***    15
Michael Tuchner        USA                    1987
*Stefanie Powers, E.G. Marshall, Doug McKeon,*
*Frances Sternhagen, Corey Parker, Penny Fuller, John*
*Wood, E.G. Marshall*
A psychological drama based on a true story, with
Stefanie Powers as a divorced mother who is constantly pleading for cash from her wealthy father. When he
is shot to death there are several suspects. A sluggish
and uneven drama of little impact. Based on the
notorious Frances Schreuder murder case and originally shown in two parts.
Boa: book by Jonathan Coleman.
DRA                        198 min (2 cassettes) mTV
B,V                                                CBS

**AT THE EARTH'S CORE ***                        PG
Kevin Connor          UK                      1976
*Doug McClure, Peter Cushing, Caroline Munro, Cy*
*Grant, Godfrey James, Keith Barron, Sean Lynch*
A Victorian scientist burrows down to the Earth's core
and discovers a land inhabited by subhumans and
prehistoric monsters of assorted varieties. A follow-up
to THE LAND THAT TIME FORGOT. Occasionally
entertaining but generally just rather dull.
Boa: novel by Edgar Rice Burroughs.
FAN                                            86 min
B,V                                        TEVP; WHV

**AT WAR WITH THE ARMY ***                       U
Mal Walker            USA                      1950
*Jerry Lewis, Dean Martin, Polly Bergen, Angela*
*Greene, Mike Kellin*
Dated comedy about a private helping his sergeant
who has girl trouble. A high-spot is a soda machine
gag in this strained comedy – the first starring feature

for Lewis and Martin.
Boa: play by James Allardice.
COM                          90 min (ort 93 min) B/W
B,V,V2                            EVC; PORVI/MOV

## ATLANTA CHILD MURDERS, THE *** 15
John Erman            USA              1985
*Jason Robards, James Earl Jones, Martin Sheen, Rip
Torn, Morgan Freeman, Calvin Levels, Lynne Moody,
Ruby Dee, Gloria Foster, Paul Benjamin, Andrew
Robinson, Percy Rodrigues*
Three-part account of a shocking series of child
murders that took place in Atlanta's black community
in the 1970s. Originally a made-for-TV mini-series
that follows events leading up to the conviction of
Wayne Williams in 1982 for these crimes. Robards
and Torn are good as lawyers on opposite sides. The
excellent script by Abby Mann caused controversy due
to its suggestions that Williams may not have been
guilty.
DRA                      300 min (3 cassettes) mTV
B,V                                      HER

## ATLANTIC CITY **** 15
Louis Malle      CANADA/FRANCE             1980
*Burt Lancaster, Susan Sarandon, Kate Reid, Al
Waxman, Robert Goulet, Wallace Shawn, Micel
Piccoli, Hollis McLaren, Robert Joy*
Strange offbeat character study with Lancaster as an
ageing small-time crook whose life becomes intert-
wined with that of some other losers. The film focuses
on a series of people who pursue their dreams in a
town whose best times have long since gone. Excellent
screenplay is by John Guare with Lancaster giving
one of his strongest performances.
Aka: ATLANTIC CITY, USA
THR                      105 min; 100 min (VGM)
B,V,LV              ENT/HVP; VGM (VHS only)

## ATLANTIS INTERCEPTORS, THE * 18
Roger Franklin (Ruggero Deodato)
                    ITALY                  1983
*Christopher Connelly, Mike Miller, Ivan Rassimov,
Marie Fields, Tony King*
Radioactive waste raises Atlantis from the depths.
With it come the Interceptors, marauding invaders on
motorcycles. Two Vietnam vets dare to discover the
source of their power. Plenty of action in this non-
sense.
Aka: RAIDERS OF ATLANTIS
A/AD                89 min (ort 100 min) Cut (8 sec)
B,V,V2                                    MED

## ATOR THE INVINCIBLE ** PG
David Hills        ITALY/USA              1983
*Miles O'Keeffe, Lisa Foster (Lisa Raines), David Cain
Houghton, Charles Borromel, Chen Wong*
More sword-and-sorcery adventures on the theme of
Good versus Evil. Sequel to ATOR, THE FIGHTING
EAGLE with O'Keeffe a prehistoric warrior out to
save Earth from the "Geometric Nucleus" - a primi-
tive atomic bomb. Utterly silly effort of far-fetched
and unbelievable encounters, but enjoyable in an
undemanding way. See also IRON WARRIOR.
Aka: BLADE MASTER, THE; ATOR L'INVINCIBLE
FAN                          88 min Cut (27 sec)
B,V                                      VTC

## ATOR, THE FIGHTING EAGLE * PG
David Hills        USA                    1982
*Miles O'Keeffe, Sabrina Siani, Ritza Brown, Edmund
Purdom, Brooke Hart, Laura Gemser, Warren Hillman,*
A sword-and-sorcery fantasy in which our young hero
battles the Forces of Evil. A ridiculous Italian effort,
inspired by those "Conan" films but lackining pace or
acting ability from muscle-bound hero O'Keeffe. Fol-
lowed by ATOR THE INVINCIBLE.
Aka: ATOR

FAN                          98 min (ort 100 min)
B,V                                TEVP; STABL

## ATTACK FORCE NORMANDY ** 
Henry Mankiewirk       USA                1976
*Jack Palance, John Douglas, Carlos Estrada*
The story of a commando raid in France made in
preparation for the D-Day landings. Standard war
film – no more than competent.
Aka: HELL'S BRIGADE; HELL'S BRIGADE: THE
FINAL ASSAULT
WAR                                      83 min
B,V,V2                           VHS L/A; MED

## ATTACK FORCE Z *** 15
Tim Burstall    AUSTRALIA/TAIWAN         1981
*John Phillip Law, Mel Gibson, Sam Neill, Chris
Haywood, John Waters*
Commando group sets out to rescue survivors of a
plane that's crashed on a Japanese-held island in the
Pacific during WW2. A taut and well made little war
drama.
WAR                                      92 min
B,V,V2                      GHV; ELE (VHS only)

## ATTACK OF THE KILLER TOMATOES * PG
John De Bello          USA                1980
*David Miller, Sharon Taylor, George Wilson, John
DeBello, Jack Riley*
The title is the best thing in this low-budget spoof on
SF films, dealing with vicious vegetables. Some say it
should have been called The Ketchup Killers. Others
say it should never have been made. See also SOUR
GRAPES, another masterpiece from this director.
RETURN OF THE KILLER TOMATOES! followed.
COM                                      87 min
B,V                        VPD; CH5 (VHS only)

## ATTACK OF THE NORMANS ** 
Mario Bava          ITALY                 1961
*Cameron Mitchell, Genevieve Grad, Joe Robinson*
Mediocre historical costume drama dubbed (or should
we say drubbed?) into English.
Aka: BLADESTORM; CONQUEST OF THE
NORMANS; INVADERS, THE
A/AD                                 90 min dubbed
B,V,V2                                    VPD

## ATTIC, THE *** 
George Edwards         USA                1979
*Carrie Snodgress, Ray Milland, Ruth Cox, Rosemary
Murphy, Francis Bay, Marjorie Eaton*
Psychological thriller about a spinster revolting
against her domineering and crippled father. A touch
above average, mostly thanks to fine performances
from Snodgress and Milland.
THR                                      97 min
B,V,V2                                    INT

## ATTIC, THE *** 18
Doug Adams           USA                 1988
*Carol Lynley, Gail O'Grady, Michael Hall Keys,
Joseph Gian, Joanna Miles*
A PSYCHO style tale of a young woman who returns
to her home town and to the house where her father
was murdered. Every night she hears strange sounds
that seem to come from the attic where the murder
took place. A complex and quite gripping chiller.
Aka: BLACKOUT
HOR                                      90 min
B,V                                      CHV

## ATTICA **** PG
Marvin J. Chomsky      USA                1980
*Henry Darrow, Charles Durning, Joe Fabiani, Morgan
Freeman, George Grizzard, David Harris, Roger E.
Mosley, Arlen Dean Snyder, Glynn Turman, Anthony*

*Zerbe, Andrew Duncan, Ron Foster, William Flatley, Noble Lee Lester*
Gripping and moving account of the Attica prison riot of 1971 which left 39 dead after Governor Nelson Rockerfeller sent in the New York state troopers. Despite some network-instigated changes to the script to tone down the criticism of Rockerfeller, this powerful film remains a searing and bitter condemnation of needless slaughter. Adapted from Wicker's best-seller by James Henerson.
Boa: book A Time To Die by Tom Wicker.
DRA                                  104 min mTV
B,V                                    VFP; HER

**ATTILA THE HUN ***                           PG
Pietro Francisci   FRANCE/ITALY              1955
*Anthony Quinn, Sophia Loren, Henri Vidal, Irene Papas*
Ludicrous film about Attila, who marches off to capture Rome but when met by Pope Leo I becomes as gentle as a lamb. Some lamb.
Aka: ATTILA (STABL)
DRA                            76 min (ort 88 min)
B,V                      VDM L/A; VMA L/A; STABL

**AU PAIR GIRL ***                             18
                                             ITALY
*Gloria Guida, Oreste Lionello, Rosello Como*
A buxom girl becomes involved with various members of a strange Roman family in this so-so softcore sex film.
A                                           80 min
B,V                                   VFP L/A; HER

**AU PAIR GIRLS ***                            18
Val Guest          UK                        1972
*Gabrielle Drake, Astrid Frank, Nancie Wait, Me Me Lay, Richard O'Sullivan, John Le Mesurier, Geoffrey Bayldon, Rosalie Crutchley, Julian Barnes, Lyn Yeldham, Ferdy Mayne, Steve Patterson, John Standing, Norman Chappell*
Four au pairs have a series of amorous adventures in London in this feeble and dated attempt at a sex comedy.
COM                                         86 min
B,V                                      VDM; HER

**AUDREY ROSE ***                              15
Robert Wise        USA                       1977
*Marsha Mason, John Beck, Anthony Hopkins, Susan Swift, John Hillerman, Norman Lloyd, Robert Walden*
Supernatural thriller in which Mason and Beck are a happily married couple who are told by a stranger that their 12-year-old girl is the reincarnation of the man's dead daughter. Overlong and under-developed, with a script by DeFelitta.
Boa: novel by Frank DeFelitta.
HOR                          109 min (ort 113 min)
V                                             WHV

**AUNT MARTHA ***                              18
Thomas Casey       USA
*Abe Zwick, Scott Lawrence, Don Craig, Robert Hughes, Sandra Laurie*
A male transvestite finally cracks up under the pressure of drug taking and living a double life in this earnest but somewhat overwrought drama.
DRA                                         95 min
V                                           FIFTH

**AUNT PEG ***
Wes Brown          USA                       1980
*Juliet Anderson, John C. Holmes, Jamie Gillis, Mike Ranger, Seka, Serena, Michael Morrison, Shirley Woods*
First of several "Aunt Peg" movies with our heroine the producer/director of porno films. With an insati-

able sexual appetite she demonstrates that she's better than any of her stars in a series of encounters that comprise the bulk of this easygoing, uncomplicated tale. See also AUNT PEG'S FULFILLMENT.
A                                           80 min
B,V                                           CAL

**AUNT PEG'S FULFILLMENT ***
Wes Brown          USA                       1982
*Juliet Anderson, John Leslie, Suzy Reynolds, Jonny Keyes, Richard Pacheco, Sharon Mahlberg, John C. Holmes, Aaron Stunt*
Routine hardcore sequel to AUNT PEG with Anderson once more giving her all as the porno film producer with the insatiable appetite. This film has even less of a story than the original and is largely a simple look at Aunt Peg in action, as she works her way through five guys and three women.
A                                           77 min
B,V                                           CAL

**AURORA ***                                   PG
Maurizio Ponzi     ITALY/USA                 1984
*Sophia Loren, Daniel J. Travanti, Edoardo Ponti, Angela Goodwin, Ricky Tognazzi, Marisa Merlini, Anna Strasberg, Franco Fabrizi, Philippe Noiret, Antonio Alloca, Gianfranco Amoroso, David Caneron, Vittorio Duce*
A mother and son track down her former lovers to persuade each of them that they are the boy's father so that they will pay for an operation to restore his sight. Ponti as the boy in question is good in his acting debut, but this tedious and far-fetched tale boasted four writers and even more production companies. A family affair for Loren; Edoardo Ponti is her son and the film was produced by Alex Ponti – her stepson.
Aka: AURORA BY NIGHT; QUALCOSA DI BLONDA; SOMETHING BLONDE
DRA                          91 min (ort 100 min) mTV
B,V                          IPC/VSP L/A; AVG; CBS

**AURORA ENCOUNTER, THE ***                    U
Jim McCullough Sr  USA                       1985
*Jack Elam, Peter Brown, Dottie West, Mindy Smith, Spanky McFarland, Carol Bagdasarian*
A small Western town at the turn of the century is visited by a pint-sized alien with strange and terrifying powers, but fortunately a benevolent disposition. Average.
FAN                                         86 min
V/h                                           NWV

**AUTHOR! AUTHOR! ****                         PG
Arthur Hiller      USA                       1982
*Al Pacino, Dyan Cannon, Tuesday Weld, Eric Gurry, Bob Dishy, Alan King, Bob Elliott, Ray Goulding, Andre Gregory*
Comedy about the marital troubles of a playwright whose wife leaves him with the kids just as his new play is about to open on Broadway. A slight but enjoyable and undemanding tale with some nice performances. The script is by by playwright Israel Horovitz.
COM                          105 min (ort 110 min)
B,V,V2,LV                                     CBS

**AUTOBIOGRAPHY OF A FLEA, THE ****
Jim Mitchell/Artie Mitchell
                   USA                       1976
*Jean Jennings, John C. Holmes, Annette Haven, Paul Thomas*
Hardcore porno based on an anonymous Victorian novel about a young virgin's sexual initiation. The flea in question tells his story from the body of a girl who is led by priests into a life of sin. A strange, humorous and explicit sex film, with a strong connecting thread linking each tale.
A                            76 min (ort 86 min) Cut
B,V                                           TCX

## AUTOBIOGRAPHY OF A PRINCESS ***   15
James Ivory          UK          1975
*James Mason, Madhur Jaffrey, Keith Varnier, Diane*
*Fletcher, Timothy Bateson, Johnny Stuart, Nazrul*
*Rahman*
Skilfully made comment on the British Raj, struc-
tured around an Indian princess showing home
movies to a former retainer who has come to tea.
Osca: DELHI WAY, THE
DRA          59 min; 100 min (VIR – 2 film cassette)
B,V                                    PVG; VIR

## AUTUMN SONATA ****   15
Ingmar Bergman       SWEDEN       1979
*Ingrid Bergman, Liv Ullmann, Lena Nyman, Halvar*
*Bjork, Gunnar Bjornstrand*
Painful exploration of the relationship between a
self-absorbed mother, who enjoys success as a famous
concert pianist, and her dowdy resentful daughter,
who pays her a visit for the first time in seven years.
The last theatrical film for Bergman. As ever, the
photography of Sven Nykvist is outstanding.
DRA                          89 min (ort 97 min)
B,V                        PRV L/A; CH5 (VHS only)

## AVALANCHE *   15
Corey Allen          USA          1978
*Rock Hudson, Mia Farrow, Robert Foster, Jeanette*
*Nolan, Steve Franken, Rick Moses, Barry Primus*
Disaster at a newly opened ski resort where the
holidaymakers are at the mercy of a giant avalanche.
When it does arrive, the disaster provides a welcome
break from a boring script and lacklustre perform-
ances.
A/AD                                     91 min
B,V                                    EHE; VGM

## AVALANCHE EXPRESS *   PG
Mark Robson          EIRE/USA      1979
*Lee Marvin, Robert Shaw, Linda Evans, Maximilian*
*Schell, Joe Namath, Mike Connors, Horst Buchholz*
Confused story about a defecting KGB head trapped
on a snowed-in Dutch train, whilst CIA agents are out
to get information on biological warfare from him. The
last film for both the director and Shaw, most of whose
dialogue had to be dubbed in by an impressionist. A
sad and dismal effort.
THR                                      88 min
B,V,V2,LV                                  CBS

## AVANTI! *   15
Billy Wilder         USA          1972
*Jack Lemmon, Juliet Mills, Clive Revill, Edward*
*Andrews, Gianfranco Barra, Franco Angrisano*
An American millionaire goes to Italy to collect the
body of his father who died whilst on holiday there. He
discovers that he had a mistress who was killed in the
same accident. He then finds that the woman's
daughter is also at the hotel. From this unpromising
beginnning develops ... nothing; just an endless
series of contrived catastrophes and car chases as
events pile on top of events in a desperate search for
laughs.
COM                          139 min (ort 144 min)
B,V                                        WHV

## AVENGER, THE **   18
David Blyth          USA          1987
*Scott Feraco, Rosanna Davon, Robert Sedgwick, Carlo*
*Palomino, Mike Starr, Raymond Serra, Teresa Blake*
A violent action thriller in which a man who makes
his living delivering expensive cars all over the
country, is set up by a bunch of rich kids on a false
charge of transporting stolen vehicles and serves a
term in jail. On being released he returns to Miami
determined to have his revenge.
Aka: NASTY HABITS
THR                                      76 min
B,V                                        EHE

## AVENGING ANGEL *   18
Robert Vincent O'Neill  USA       1985
*Betsy Russell, Rory Calhoun, Susan Tyrrell, Robert F.*
*Lyons, Osie Davis*
Sequel to ANGEL, in which our heroine graduates
from college only to find that the cop who got her off
the streets has been murdered. She sets out to avenge
his death in this dreadful rubbish.
DRA                                      93 min
B,V                                        RCA

## AVENGING BOXER ***   18
                     HONG KONG
*Peter Chen, Casanova Wong*
A man learns kung fu to avenge his father's murder
and the theft of a treasured golden plate. A better
than average martial arts tale with an exciting finale
in a booby-trapped warehouse.
Aka: FEARLESS YOUNG BOXER, THE (VTM)
MAR                                      94 min
B,V                                    VTM; KFM

## AVENGING EAGLE **   15
Sun Chang            HONG KONG
*Ti Lung, Fu Shong, Ku Feng, Tu Lung*
After being rejected by his childhood sweetheart a
man takes to crime and becomes a notorious criminal,
in this simple martial arts tale.
MAR                                      81 min
B,V                                    HOT L/A; VPD

## AVENGING FORCE ***   18
Sam Firstenberg      USA          1986
*Michael Dudikoff, Steve James, John P. Ryan, James*
*Booth, Bill Wallace, Karl Johnson*
An ex-secret service agent is forced into action to help
his best friend, a black man who is running for office.
When a right-wing terrorist group kidnaps the man's
sister he is forced to go on a manhunt through the
remote swamplands of Louisiana. A better than
average action yarn with an exciting climax. Scripted
by Booth, who also plays Dudikoff's former boss.
A/AD                                     103 min
B,V                                        MGM

## AVIATOR, THE **   PG
George Miller        USA          1985
*Christopher Reeve, Rosanna Arquette, Tyne Daly,*
*Scott Wilson, Jack Warden, Sam Wanamaker, Marcia*
*Strassman*
An embittered pilot and his passenger, a spoilt rich
teenage girl, have to pull together to survive when
their plane crashes in the wilderness in a tale set in
1928. A dull and plodding effort.
Boa: story by Ernest Gann.
DRA                          96 min (ort 98 min)
V/sh                                       WHV

## AWAKENING, THE **   15
Mike Newell          UK          1980
*Charlton Heston, Susannah York, Jill Townsend,*
*Stephanie Zimbalist, Patrick Drury, Bruce Meyers,*
*Nadim Sawalha, Ian McDiarmid, Ahmed Osman,*
*Miriam Margolyes, Michael Mellinger, Ishia*
*Bennison, Leonard Maguire*
Remake of BLOOD FROM THE MUMMY'S TOMB,
with an Egyptian Queen reincarnated after 3,800
years, in the body of the daughter of the archaeologist
who opens her tomb. Tedious and slow-moving. See
also THE TOMB.
Boa: novel Jewel Of The Seven Stars by Bram Stoker.
HOR          100 min; 96 min (WHV) (ort 105 min)
B,V                          TEVP; WHV (VHS only)

## AWKWARD CUSTOMER, THE *   18
                     USA
The adventures of five pretty ladies who are attending
a course to learn how to sell erotic underwear.

Determined to get the job, they all set about seducing the sales manager who readily gives in to their charms. A slightly plotted sex film of no great value.

A | 53 min Cut (57 sec)
V | SFI

# B

## B.L. STRYKER: BLUES FOR BUDER ** 15
Burt Reynolds USA 1989
*Burt Reynolds, Ossie Davis*
A further outing for Reynolds as our unconventional detective, who this time is hired to ensure that a rich, spoiled brat finds a school that doesn't expel him. The usual blend of action and humour prevails. Average.
Aka: BLUES FOR BUDER
THR | 91 min mTV
V | CIC

## B.O.R.N. ** 18
Ross Hagen USA 1988
*Ross Hagen, P.J. Soles, Hoke Howell, Russ Tamblyn, William Smith, Amanda Blake, Rance Howard, Clint Howard, Claire Hagen, Kristine Gillespie, Dawn Wildsmith*
Title refers to "Body Organ Replacement Network", whose nefarious activities involve the kidnapping of youngsters for use as involuntary organ donors. A film that uses the same premise as COMA, though plot development involves a good deal more action, as Hagen and Howell set out to destroy the organisation in question.
THR | 87 min (ort 92 min)
V | CINE

## B.R.A.T. PATROL, THE ** U
Mollie Miller USA 1986
*Sean Astin, Tim Thomerson, Nia Long, Jason Presson, Joe Wright, Dustin Berkovitz, Dylan Kussman, Brian Keith, Stephen Lee, John Quade, Billy Jacoby, Dean Anthony, Lisa Dinkins, Greg Finley, John Hafrancis, Ira Heiden*
A group of mischievous kids discover that weapons are being stolen from a military base. When army officials refuse to believe their story they are forced to take matters into their own hands. Average.
Aka: BRAT PATROL, THE
JUV | 88 min mTV
B,V | WDV

## BABAR: THE MOVIE ** U
Alan Bunce CANADA/FRANCE 1990
Enjoyable but rather bland animation based on the writings of Brunhoff, and following the adventures that befall a baby elephant as he grows to maturity. Compiled from a series of about 24 episodes.
Boa: short stories by Jean de Brunhoff.
CAR | 73 min
V/sh | ABBEY

## BABE ** R18
John Christopher USA 1981
*Bobbi Jackson, Samantha Fox, Tiffany Clark, Roderic Pierce, Ron Jeremy, George Payne*
A woman working in a top New York modelling agency is left a fortune by her grandfather, but will only inherit if she marries in 30 days. Her employer doesn't want to lose her and conspires for Babe to marry an out of work actor with grandiose dreams for mounting expensive plays, hoping this will use up her inheritance and thus keep her working. Her scheme backfires when his play is a success but luckily Babe decides to keep her career. Average.
A | 74 min (ort 80 min) Cut (8 sec)
B,V | SHEP; TCX

## BABES IN TOYLAND * U
Clive Donner USA 1986
*Drew Barrymore, Richard Mulligan, Eileen Brennan, Keanu Reeves, Jill Schoelen, Pat Morita, Googy Gress, Walter Buschoff, Rolf Knie, Gaston Haeni, Pipo Sosman, Shari Weiser, Chad Carlson, Elizabeth Schot, Mona Lee Goss*
Sluggish and uninspired remake of the Victor Herbert operetta with only "Toyland" and "March of the Wooden Soldiers" remaining, plus a new and totally forgettable score by Leslie Bricusse. Barrymore is transported to a fantasy village and has to break the domination of the evil Barnaby in this insipid kid's adventure. Written by playwright Paul Zindel.
JUV | 91 min (ort 150 min) mTV
V/sh | RCA

## BABES IN TOYLAND ** U
Jack Donohue USA 1961
*Ray Bolger, Annette Funicello, Tommy Kirk, Gene Sheldon, Henry Calvin, Ed Wynn, Kevin Corcoran, Tommy Sands*
A remake of the 1932 Laurel & Hardy original, with Mary and Tom travelling through the Forest Of No Return to Toyland, where they assist in making toys for Christmas. But the villainous Mr Barnaby has other ideas. A miscast remake of the earlier film that doesn't lack for special effects but could do with a more talented cast.
MUS | 101 min
B,V | WDV

## BABETTE'S FEAST **** U
Gabriel Axel DENMARK 1987
*Stephane Audran, Jean-Philippe Lafont, Jarl Kulle, Bibi Andersson, Hanne Steensgard, Gudmar Wivesson, Bodil Kjer, BIrgitte Federspiel*
Critically acclaimed story set in an austere community in the 1870s, with two spinster sisters living quietly in their small Danish village using religion as a substitute for life. They take in a mysterious Parisian refugee as a cook who later wins a lottery, using the money to prepare a banquet for the community. A fresh, evocative and exquisite film. The screenplay is by Axel. AA: Foreign.
Aka: BABETTES GAESTEBUD
Boa: short story by Isak Dinesen (Karen Blixen).
DRA | 103 min (ort 105 min) (English language and subtitles)
B,V | SHEER; BRAVE

## BABY AND THE BATTLESHIP, THE ** 
Jay Lewis UK 1956
*John Mills, Richard Attenborough, Bryan Forbes, Lionel Jeffries, Andre Morell, Michael Howard, Lisa Gastoni, Ernest Clark, Harry Locke, Michael Hordern, Clifford Mollison, Thorley Walters, Duncan Lamont, Cyril Richard*
Two sailors sneak an Italian baby on board a battleship and have quite some time hiding it from their superiors. Dated and unfunny.
Boa: novel by Anthony Thorne.
COM | 96 min
B,V | STJ

## BABY BOOM *** PG
Charles Shyer USA 1987
*Diane Keaton, Harold Ramis, Sam Wanamaker, Sam Shepard, James Spader, Pat Hingle, Britt Leach, Kristina Kennedy, Michelle Kennedy, Kim Sebastian, Mary Gross, Patricia Estrin, Elizabeth Bennett, Peter Elbling, Shera Danese*
A female workaholic yuppie "inherits" a 13-month-old baby girl from a relative and finds it impossible to reconcile the demands of motherhood with her career. An amiable comedy that makes a few sharp points in between comic lulls. The script is by Shyer and Nancy Meyers. A TV series followed.

COM                                   107 min
V/sh                                     WHV

## BABY CAT **                           18
Pierre Unia         FRANCE             1984
*Julie Margo, Felix Marten, Corinne Carson*
A wealthy Parisian model hatches a plan to rob her
employer and lover by arranging her own "kidnap".
However, her plan backfires when she really is
kidnapped and she is forced to use all her female wiles
to make her escape.
A                         80 min; 77 min (ATLAN)
B,V                                ELV; ATLAN

## BABY COMES HOME **                     PG
Waris Hussein       USA               1980
*Colleen Dewhurst, Warren Oates, Devon Ericson,
Fredric Lehne, Christopher Marcantel, Mildred
Dunnock, Paul McCrane, David Huffman, Dena
Dietrich, James Noble, Lee Wallace, Floyd Levine,
Toni Gellman, Maria Melendez*
Sequel to AND BABY MAKES SIX with our middle-
aged couple finding themselves parents once more
after having raised three kids. Average.
Aka: AND BABY COMES HOME
DRA                    91 min (ort 100 min) mTV
B,V,V2                                  GHV

## BABY FACE ***
Alex de Renzy       USA               1977
*Amber Hunt, Linda Wong, Otis Sistrunk, Cuddles
Malone*
Amusing story of a man who seduces a 15-year-old girl
and then has to go on the run to escape the girl's
vengeful mother. Most of the film is taken up with his
stay at his chosen place of sanctuary, a male brothel
patronised by some very demanding ladies.
A                                    85 min
B,V                                     TCX

## BABY FACE 2 **                         18
Alex De Renzy       USA               1987
*Lois Ayres, Stacey Donovan, Candie Evens, Kevin
Gibson, Melissa Melendez, Tom Byron, Marc Wallace,
Taija Rae, Careena Collins, Kristara Barrington,
Jerry Butler, Jamie Gillis*
This in-name-only sequel to the earlier film tells of an
all-girl party that turns into an interminable orgy
with the arrival of a male stripper (Gillis). A few
funny lines and a good performance from Gillis
enliven this formula sex romp.
A                                    44 min
V                                      FAST

## BABY IT'S YOU ***                      15
John Sayles         USA               1982
*Rosanna Arquette, Vincent Spano, Joanna Merlin,
Nick Ferrari, Jack Davidson, Dolores Messina, Leora
Dana, Sam McMurray, Tracy Pollan, Matthew
Modine, Robert Downey Jr, Caroline Aaron, Fisher
Stevens*
An amusing look at life in 1960s New Jersey, with a
middle-class high school girl being wooed by a deter-
mined working-class Italian boy. Good attention to
detail and engaging dialogue help prolong interest,
despite the basic emptiness of the plot.
Boa: short story by Amy Robinson.
COM                      101 min (ort 105 min)
V                                       CIC

## BABY LOVE *                            18
Dan Wolman  ISRAEL/WEST GERMANY       1983
*Zachi Noy, Yftach Katzor, Jonathan Segal*
Israeli story of three teenage nerds who have their
revenge on the freshmen of a frat house. One more in
the interminable LEMON POPSICLE series. Fol-
lowed by PRIVATE MANOEUVRES.
Aka: LEMON POPSICLE 5

COM                              90 min dubbed
B,V                                GHV; VCC

## BABY LOVE **                           18
Alastair Reid       UK                1968
*Ann Lynn, Keith Barron, Linda Hayden, Diana Dors,
Derek Lamden, Patience Collier, Dick Emery, Sheila
Staefel, Bernard Miles, Timothy Carlton, Troy Dante,
Christopher Witty*
Lolita-type teenager causes trouble when she goes to
live in the house of the former lover of her dead
mother and sets out to seduce her mother's ex-lover,
his son and his wife. A sleazy and unsatisfying tale.
Boa: novel by Tina Chad Christian.
DRA                                  96 min
B,V,V2                                  EHE

## BABY MAKER, THE **                     18
James Bridge        USA               1970
*Barbara Hershey, Collin Wilcox-Horne, Sam Groom,
Scott Glenn, Jeannie Berlin*
A film that attempts to tackle the issue of surrogate-
motherhood, with a childless couple hiring a young
semi-hippie girl to have a kid for them as the wife is
sterile. Not much of a story and not much of a film.
DRA                                  109 min
B,V,V2                      VDM/GHV; STABL

## BABY ROSEMARY *
Harold Perkins      USA               1976
*Sharon Thorpe, John Leslie, Leslie Bovee, Ken Cotton*
The story of Rosemary, a frigid woman who leaves her
husband and takes up with a strange religious cult.
Later, the action moves to a funeral parlour where
Rosemary has arrived to bury her stepfather. Rosem-
ary's friends turn up and her stepfather is heard in a
voice-over, begging not to be buried as he is still alive.
Whether he is buried or not we cannot say, as a
general orgy finally brings this dreary and inconsis-
tent mess to its conclusion.
A                                    80 min
B,V                             IPC/VSP L/A

## BABY, THE **
Ted Post            USA               1972
*Anjannette Comer, Ruth Roman, Marianna Hill*
A social worker becomes a murderess in order to keep
a mentally retarded youth for herself. A sad and
dreary tale.
HOR                      93 min (ort 102 min)
B,V,V2                                   VCL

## BABY: SECRET OF THE LOST LEGEND **     PG
B.W.L. Norton       USA               1985
*William Katt, Sean Young, Patrick McGoohan, Julian
Fellowes, Hugh Quarshie, Kyalo Mativo*
Two people attempt to save a couple of prehistoric
brontosauri from the attentions of a game hunter. A
good start is soon spoilt by some remarkably predict-
able developments.
Aka: BABY
DRA                        89 min (ort 93 min)
B,V                                     WDV

## BABYLON *
Franco Rosso        UK                1981
*Brinsley Forde, Karl Howman, Trevor Laird, Brian
Bovell, Victor Romero Evans, David N. Haynes, Archie
Pool, T. Bone Wilson, Mel Smith, Beverly Michaels,
Stephen Kalipha, Beverly Dublin, Mark Monero,
David Cunningham*
Noisy and unpleasant drama about the lives of black
youths in South London. The plot (such as it is) has a
black youth turning criminal when racists smash up
his reggae sound system. All the expected stereotypes
are here; bigoted and hateful whites and alienated
and equally disagreeable blacks. A film that presumably was intended to explore black culture winds up as
yet another mass of formula characterisations.

DRA                          90 min
B,V                         CHRY/PVG

**BABYSITTER, THE ***                15
Peter Medak        CANADA            1980
*Patty Duke Astin, William Shatner, Quinn Cummings,*
*David Wallace, Kenny Tigar, Stephanie Zimbalist,*
*Virginia Kiser, John Houseman, Hildy Brooks, Frank*
*Birney, Richard Ty Haller*
Psychological thriller about a family who fall under
the domination of an attractive babysitter who rapidly
begins to exploit their needs and vulnerabilities. It
starts off well enough but ultimately is a let-down.
DRA                          96 min mTV
B,V                        VFP L/A; HER

**BACHELOR GIRL ***                  15
Rivka Hartman     AUSTRALIA          1987
*Lyn Pierse, Kim Gyngell, Jan Friedl, Bruce Spence*
Engaging comedy from Down Under that chronicles
the experience of a 32-year-old single girl and would-
be writer whose meddlesome aunt and uncle are
determined to play matchmaker. When an old university friend comes back into her life, he creates
complications that are mirrored in the lives of characters of the TV soap opera she is writing. A lighthearted and entertaining comedy.
COM                          79 min
V                            GHV

**BACHELOR MOTHER ***                U
Garson Kanin       USA               1939
*Ginger Rogers, David Niven, Charles Coburn, Frank*
*Albertson, Ernest Truex, E.E. Clive, Elbert Caplen Jr*
A woman accidentally gets left in charge of an
abandoned baby in this happy and lively Norman
Krasna comedy. Remade in 1956 as BUNDLE OF
JOY.
COM                          81 min B/W
V                            VCC

**BACHELOR PARTY ***                 18
Neil Israel        USA               1984
*Tom Hanks, Tawny Kitaen, Adrian Zmed, Bibi Besch,*
*George Grizzard, Robert Prescott*
Preparations for a bachelor party get a little out of
hand in a comedy that starts off well but rapidly
descends into tastelessness in a desperate search for
laughs.
COM                          106 min
V/h                          CBS

**BACK FROM ETERNITY ***
John Farrow        USA               1956
*Robert Ryan, Anita Ekberg, Rod Steiger, Phyllis Kirk*
Plane crash drama set in the jungles of South America
where only five of the eight survivors can be carried
on the repaired plane. A fair remake of the 1939 film
"Five Came Back".
Osca: FIRST REBEL, THE
DRA                          93 min B/W
B,V                          KVD

**BACK ROADS ***                     15
Martin Ritt        USA               1981
*Sally Field, Tommy Lee Jones, David Keith, Miriam*
*Colon, Dan Shor, Michael V. Gazzo, M. Emmett*
*Walsh, Nell Carter*
Humdrum tale of a prostitute and a tramp who fall in
love on a journey from Mobile in California. The
attractive leads can do little with the flat and
uninventive script.
COM                          95 min
B,V,LV                       CBS

**BACK TO BATAAN ***                 PG
Edward Dmytryk     USA               1945
*John Wayne, Anthony Quinn, Beulah Bondi, Fely*

*Franquelli, Lawrence Tierney, Richard Loo, Philip*
*Ahn*
Routine story of a colonel in the US marines who
organises resistance against the Japanese on Bataan
in the Philippines. A solid action tale whose good
action sequences help mask the dullness of the script.
Osca: ROADBLOCK (KVD)
WAR                     91 min; 88 min (VCC) B/W
B,V                     KVD; VCC (VHS only)

**BACK TO SCHOOL ***                 15
Alan Metter        USA               1986
*Rodney Dangerfield, Burt Young, Sally Kellerman,*
*Keith Gordon, Robert Downey Jr, Paxton Whitehead,*
*Terry Farrell, M. Emmett Walsh, Adrienne Barbeau,*
*Ned Beatty, Severn Darden, Kurt Vonnegut Jr*
A self-made millionaire decides to join his son who is
having difficulties fitting in as a college freshman and
so his uneducated dad buys his way into the Ivy
League college. A simple story that gives ample scope
for a winning and hilarious performance from Danger-
field and a funny sequence of sight gags and one-
liners.
COM                          93 min
V/sh                         RCA

**BACK TO THE BEACH ***               PG
Lyndall Hobbs      USA               1987
*Frankie Avalon, Annette Funicello, Connie Stevens,*
*Pee-Wee Herman (Paul Reubens), Don Adams, Lori*
*Loughlin, Bob Denver, Tommy Hickley, Demian Slade*
A couple take a break and visit their daughter at her
Southern California beach apartment. At first bewil-
dered by the swinging lifestyle, they soon adapt,
becoming the "beach couple" of the 1980s. The efforts
of over six writers achieve little in this thin and
uninspired comedy. Contains a host of guest stars
from 1950s and 1960s TV sit-coms, but they add little
to this one.
COM                          88 min
B,V                          CIC

**BACK TO THE FUTURE ***              PG
Robert Zemeckis    USA               1985
*Michael J. Fox, Crispin Glover, Lea Thompson,*
*Christopher Lloyd, Wendie Jo Sperber, Marc McClure,*
*Claudia Wells, Thomas F. Wilson, James Tolkan*
A clever and lighthearted look at the adventures that
befall a teenager who, as a victim of an eccentric
scientist, is whisked back into the 1950s where he
meets his parents as teenagers, and has the task of
persuading them to fall for each other so that he can
be born. Features one of John De Lorean's ill-fated
gull-winged cars that doubles as the time machine.
Followed by a sequel. AA: Effects (Aud) (Charles L.
Campbell/Robert Rutledge).
COM                     113 min (ort 116 min)
B,V                          CIC

**BACK TO THE FUTURE: PART 2 ***      PG
Robert Zemeckis    USA               1989
*Michael J. Fox, Christopher Lloyd, Lea Thompson,*
*Thomas F. Wilson, Harry Waters Jr, Charles*
*Fleischer, Joe Flaherty, Elisabeth Shue, James*
*Tolkan, Casey Siemaszko*
A frantic, production-line sequel to the first film, with
Fox and Lloyd venturing into both the future and the
past, as Marty McFly tries to save the future from the
effects of his first trip into the past. Incredible plot
complications and superb effects mask a film of little
warmth, whose ideas inexorably lead to Part 3 for
their resolution.
Aka: PARADOX: BACK TO THE FUTURE 2
FAN                     104 min (ort 107 min)
V                            CIC

**BACK TO THE FUTURE: PART 3 ****     PG
Robert Zemeckis    USA               1989

*Michael J. Fox, Christopher Lloyd, Mary Steenburgen, Thomas F. Wilson, Lea Thompson, Elisabeth Shue, Matt Clark, Richard Dysart, Pat Buttram, Harry Carey Jr, Dub Taylor, James Tolkan, ZZ Top*
This excellent follow-up to Part 2 makes up for the failings of the earlier film, with Fox now back in the Old West of 1885, where he attempts to change the course of history and thereby save the life of his inventor buddy. A noisy comic-book fantasy, imaginative, fast-paced and fun.

FAN 113 min (ort 118 min) (wide-screen version available)
V CIC

## BACKFIRE **
Gilbert Cates     USA     18
    1987
*Karen Allen, Keith Carradine, Bernie Casey, Dean Paul Martin, Jeff Fahey, Dinah Manhoff*
A married woman meets a mysterious stranger and is drawn into an exciting and intensely erotic relationship, unaware that his intentions and his past are equally obscure.
THR 89 min
B,V VIR

## BACKSTAGE **
Jonathan Hardy     USA     15
    1987
*Laura Brannigan, Michael Aitkens*
Story of a superstar who attempts to prove herself as a serious dramatic actress but faces great opposition, especially from one critic who indulges in savage and scathing reviews. Average.
DRA 94 min
B,V FUTUR

## BAD BLOOD **
Chuck Vincent     USA     18
    1988
*Linda Blair, Ruth Raymond, Gregory Patrick, Troy Donahue*
Low-budget horror story with a demented middle-aged woman regaining the son who was taken from her at birth by her womanising husband, and then embarking on an orgy of revenge. A gory, screaming and frenzied offering.
HOR 100 min
V CFD

## BAD BLOOD ***
Mike Newell     NEW ZEALAND/UK     18
    1981
*Jack Thompson, Carol Burns, Dennis Lill, Donna Akersten, Martyn Sanderson, Marshall Napier*
True story of a New Zealand farmer who went berserk and killed seven people in 1941, instigating a massive manhunt. A competent action drama that gave Thompson an early starring role.
Aka: GRAHAM MURDERS, THE; SHOOTING, THE
Boa: book Manhunt: The Story Of Stanley Graham by Howard Willis.
DRA 114 min mTV
B,V RNK

## BAD BOYS ***
Richard Rosenthal     USA     18
    1983
*Sean Penn, Reni Santoni, Esai Morales, Eric Gurry, Jim Moody, Ally Sheedy, Clancy Brown*
Tough film that examines the treatment of juvenile delinquents at a detention centre and follows the story of a personal vendetta that reaches its climax within the prison walls. Violent and not always believable, but never less than fully absorbing. Sheedy's film debut.
DRA 99 min
B,V TEVP; WHV

## BAD BUNCH, THE **
Greydon Clark     USA     1976
*Greydon Clark, Aldo Ray, Tom Johnigarn, Jacquline*

*Cole, Jock Mahoney, Pamela Corbett*
Story set in the L.A. district of Watts, where a white liberal tries in vain to make friends with a black gang, but finds out to his cost that prejudice cuts both ways. Average urban thriller.
THR 82 min
B,V MOG

## BAD COMPANY **
Wesley Emerson     USA     15
    1972
*Mandy Lane, Traci Butler, Dorothy LeMay*
The story of a female police officer who uses her body to seduce young men and women in order to blackmail them.
Osca: STORMY
A 93 min; 89 min (CIC)
B,V CAL L/A; CIC

## BAD DREAMS *
Andrew Fleming     USA     18
    1988
*Jennifer Rubin, Bruce Abbott, Richard Lynch, Harris Yulin, Sy Richardson, Dean Cameron, Susan Barnes, E.G. Daily, Susan Ruttan, Charles Fleischer*
The sole survivor of a Jim Jones-style mass suicide by members of a cult awakens after 13 years spent in a coma. However, she is haunted by visions of the cult's evil leader and when members of her therapy group start being found murdered, she becomes convinced that the cult leader's spirit is responsible. A visually unpleasant horror tale whose inadequate script is a major failing.
HOR 81 min (ort 84 min)
V CBS

## BAD GIRLS' DORMITORY **
Tim Kincaid     USA     18
    1985
*Carey Zuris, Teresa Farley, Rick Gianasi, Marita Jennifer DeLora, Natalie O'Connell*
The endless saga of exploitative studies of women in prison rolls inexorably on. This one's set in a juvenile detention centre that is privately run. Cut before video submission by 33 sec.
DRA 92 min
B,V ODY

## BAD GUYS, THE **
Joel Silberg     USA     PG
    1986
*Adam Baldwin, Mike Jolly, Michelle Nicastro, Ruth Buzzi, James Booth, Gene LeBell, Norman Burton*
Two ex-cops turn to wrestling to make a living after they are kicked out of the force. Moronic and dim-witted comedy with a bunch of real-life wrestlers adding little to this one except in terms of bulk.
COM 86 min
B,V RCA; PARK

## BAD JIM **
Clyde Ware     USA     1989
*James Brolin, Richard Roundtree, John Clark Gable, Harry Carey Jr, Rory Calhoun, Ty Hardin, Pepe Serna*
Posing as Billy the Kid and his gang, three bank robbers carry out a series of raids. A simple-minded story, mildly entertaining and well supported by a good cast of Western veterans.
WES 86 min (ort 90 min)
V CASPIC

## BAD MANNERS *
Bobby Houston     USA     15
    1984
*Edy Williams, Karen Black, Martin Mull, Anne DeSalvo*
Five orphans make a pact that they will never be separated; when one of them is adopted by a wealthy couple the others decide to mount a "rescue". Poorly conceived comedy of few ideas.

COM 85 min
B,V CBS

## BAD MAN'S RIVER **
Gene (Eugenio) Martin
FRANCE/ITALY/SPAIN 1972
*Gina Lollobrigida, Lee Van Cleef, James Mason,*
*Eduardo Fajarado, Simon Andreu, Diana Lorys*
Slightly tongue-in-cheek Western with plenty of action, robberies etc. In 1905 Mexico, a revolutionary hires an outlaw gang to blow a safe, but the gang leader is continually outsmarted and double-crossed by a female mastermind. The touches of comedy add very little to the film, which is too patchy to work effectively.
Aka: E CONTINUANO A FREGARSI IL MILIONE DI DOLLARI; EL HOMBRE DEL RIO MALO; EL RIO DE LOS MALDITOS
WES 90 min (ort 100 min)
B,V PREM/VFP

## BAD MEDICINE **
Harvey Miller USA 15
1985
*Steve Guttenberg, Alan Arkin, Julie Hagerty, Bill*
*Macy, Robert Romanus, Curtis Armstrong, Julie*
*Kavner, Joe Grifasi, Taylor Negron*
Unfunny medi-comedy about an American student who is forced, by the lack of a place at any US college, to attend a shady medical school somewhere in Central America that's run by Arkin.
COM 96 min
B,V CBS

## BAD PENNY *
Mark Ubell (Chuck Vincent)
USA 1978
*Samantha Fox, Molly Malone, Don Peterson, Kurt*
*Mann, Roger Caine*
A woman has to solve a riddle before she can inherit a vast fortune left by her uncle, and in the course of her investigations is obliged to sleep with about five men, in this trite and ridiculous effort.
Osca: BODY LUST/HARD UP (asa)
A 80 min
B,V HVS L/A; HAR

## BAD TASTE **
Peter Jackson NEW ZEALAND 18
1988
*Peter O'Herne, Mike Minett, Terry Potter, Peter*
*Jackson, Craig Smith, Doug Wren, Dean Lawrie*
An insane and overdone celebration of gore, with a bunch of uncontrollable thugs sent on a mission to stop the planet being taken over by a group of aliens, who intend to use the human race as raw material for a string of intergalactic fast-food restaurants. Funny in places, but definitely not one to see having just eaten.
COM 90 min
B,V CFD

## BAD TIMING ***
Nicolas Roeg UK 18
1980
*Art Garfunkel, Theresa Russell, Harvey Keitel,*
*Denholm Elliott, Daniel Massey, Dana Gillespie,*
*William Hootkins, Eugene Lipinski, George Roubicek,*
*Stefan Gryff, Sevilla Delofski, Robert Walker, Gertan*
*Klauber, Ania Marson*
An American divorcee has an affair with a strange Viennese psychiatrist which eventually leads to tragedy. Despite serious miscasting of Garfunkel, this one has many good things in it, not least being a fine performance from Russell as a woman of self-destructive urges and a good backing score with music from The Who, Keith Jarrett and Billie Holiday. One of the few Roeg films in which his flashy direction adds to the movie.
Aka: BAD TIMING: A SENSUAL OBSESSION
DRA 118 min (ort 123 min)
B,V,V2 RNK; VCC (VHS only)

## BADGE 373 *
Howard W. Koch USA 15
1973
*Robert Duvall, Verna Bloom, Henry Darrow, Eddie*
*Egan, Felipe Luciano, Tina Christiana*
After his partner is killed a New York police launches a one man war against a crime syndicate. A dull FRENCH CONNECTION-style movie lacking pace or interest.
THR 116 min
B,V CIC

## BADGE OF THE ASSASSIN ***
Mel Damski USA 15
1985
*James Woods, Yaphet Kotto, Alex Rocco, David*
*Harris, Steven Keats, Larry Riley, Pam Grier, Rae*
*Dawn Chong, Richard Bradford, Kene Holliday,*
*Tamu Blackwell, Richard Brooks, Akosua Busia,*
*Lewis Arquette, Alan Blumenfeld*
Dramatisation of the real-life manhunt for the murderers of two New York cops in the early 1970s, which involved a nationwide search masterminded by an assistant Manhattan D.A. Woods gives a performance of some intensity in this harsh and gritty police thriller.
Boa: book by Robert K. Tannebaum and Philip Rosenberg.
THR 96 min mTV
B,V EIV

## BADLANDS **
Terence Malick USA 18
1973
*Martin Sheen, Sissy Spacek, Warren Oates, Ramon*
*Bieri, Alan Vint*
Two young lovers go on a killing spree in this grim thriller based on an infamous killing spree of the 1950s by Starkweather and Fugate. Now a film with a devoted if minor cult following.
THR 95 min
B,V WHV

## BAGDAD CAFE ***
Percy Adlon WEST GERMANY PG
1988
*Mariane Sagebrecht, C.C.H. Pounder, Jack Palance,*
*Monica Calhoun, Darron Flagg, Christine Kaufmann,*
A buxom West German woman on holiday in the USA becomes involved with a very strange set of characters who patronise the title establishment, a roadside greasy spoon in the California desert. A largely plotless but endearing comedy from the director of "Sugarbaby", with a nice performance from Palance as a former Hollywood set decorator who decides to paint her portrait.
Aka: OUT OF ROSENHEIM
COM 88 min
B,V VES

## BAGTHORPE SAGA, THE **
Paul Stone UK U
1983
*Dandy Nichols, Angela Thorpe, Richard Orme*
Compiled effort from a TV series about an eccentric English family. Average.
DRA 96 min mTV
B,V BBC

## BAIT **
Hugo Haas USA 1954
*Hugo Haas, Cleo Moore, John Agar, Emmett Lynn,*
*Cedric Hardwicke*
Goldminers fight amongst themselves over women, in this clumsy menage-a-trois story. Hardwicke appears as the Devil in an intriguing pre-credit opening.
A/AD 79 min
B,V RAIN/MOV

## BAIT, THE **
Leonard Horn USA 1973
*Donna Mills, Michael Constantine, William Devane,*
*June Lockhart, Arlene Golonka, Noam Pitlik,*
*Thalmus Rasulala, Gianni Russo, Xenia Gratsos,*

*Brad Savage, Timothy Agoglia Carey, Don Keefer,*
*Mitzi Hoag, Wendy Wagner*
A widowed policewoman agrees to act as a decoy in
order to trap a rapist and murderer in this unpleasant
and unconvincing thriller.
Boa: novel by Dorothy Uhnak.

| | |
|---|---|
| THR | 72 min mTV |
| B,V | RNK |

### BAJA OKLAHOMA ***     PG
Bobby Roth   USA   1988
*Lesley Ann Warren, Peter Coyote, Swoosie Kurtz, Billy*
*Vera, Anthony Zerbe, Willie Nelson, Emmylou Harris,*
*Alice Krige, Bob Wills Jr*
A lively and lighthearted tale of a cocktail waitress
living in a small Texas town who dreams of fame as a
singer/songwriter, whilst juggling her aspirations
with her romantic interests. This engaging comedy-
drama hosts a number of singing stars plus Krige as
singer Patsy Cline.
Boa: novel by Dan Jenkins.

| | |
|---|---|
| COM | 100 min (ort 105 min) mCab |
| V | WHV |

### BAKER STREET BOYS, THE **     U
Marilyn Fox   UK   1984
*Jay Simpson, Damion Napier, Adam Woodyat*
Adaptation from a TV series about a gang of Victorian
street urchins who help Sherlock Holmes. Fairly
forgettable TV drama.

| | |
|---|---|
| DRA | 99 min mTV |
| B,V | BBC |

### BALBOA **     15
James Polakof   USA   1982 (released 1983)
*Tony Curtis, Chuck Connors, Lupita Ferrer, Carol*
*Lynley, Steve Kanaly, Sonny Bono, Catherine*
*Campbell, Cassandra Peterson, Jennifer Chase,*
*Martine Beswicke, Henry Jones*
Steamy drama of power and passions among Califor-
nia's idle rich, with Curtis a nasty tycoon in Balboa
who's about to pull off a real estate deal whilst
everyone else is too busy sleeping around to notice. An
episodic and uneven soap opera, edited down from a
longer and unsold mini-series.
Aka: BALBOA: MILLIONAIRE'S PARADISE

| | |
|---|---|
| DRA | 100 min |
| B,V | QUA/VSP; SQUIR |

### BALL GAME **
Anne Perry   USA   1980
*Lisa De Leeuw, Mike Ranger, Connie Peters, Candida*
*Royalle, Laurence Rothschild*
A baseball game has been arranged between the
inmates of the Women's County Jail and their male
guards. To improve their chances, the girls capture
the guards the night before the match and wear them
to a frazzle, in this rather banal sex comedy.

| | |
|---|---|
| A | 84 min |
| B,V,V2 | ELV |

### BALLAD OF A GUNFIGHTER **
Bill Ward   USA   1963
*Marty Robbins, Joyce Redd, Bob Barron, Nestor Paiva,*
*Michele Davis, Laurette Luez, Gene Davis*
Two outlaws fall for the same girl. One of them robs a
stagecoach but the other takes both the loot and the
girl. Robbins' first starring feature is a low-budget
and unmemorable affair, but he does get to sing "El
Paso" and "San Angelo".

| | |
|---|---|
| WES | 84 min B/W |
| B,V | MMA |

### BALLAD OF CABLE HOGUE ***     PG
Sam Peckinpah   USA   1970
*Jason Robards, Stella Stevens, L.Q. Jones, Strother*
*Martin, R.G. Armstrong, David Warner, Slim Pickens,*
*Peter Whitney, Gene Evans, William Mims, Kathleen*
*Freeman, Vaughn Taylor, James Anderson*

Comedy Western telling of a tough prospector who,
after being left to die in the desert by his unscrupulous
greedy partners, plots a complex revenge. Stevens is
good as a whore who joins him in his quest for the
better things in life, in this entertaining feature.

| | |
|---|---|
| WES | 117 min (ort 121 min) |
| B,V | WHV |

### BALLAD OF DEATH VALLEY **
Duccio Tessari   ITALY
*Montgomery Wood, Giuliano Gemma, Fernando*
*Sancho, Holly Hammond*
A gang of Mexican bandits on the run seek refuge at a
remote farmhouse where they hold the farmer and his
daughter hostage. Standard Italian Western.

| | |
|---|---|
| WES | 90 min |
| B,V,V2 | VPD |

### BALLAD OF GREGORIO CORTEZ, THE ***     15
Robert M. Young   USA   1982
*Edward James Olmos, James Gammon, Tom Bower,*
*Bruce McGill, Brion James, Alan Vint, Rosana*
*DeSoto, Pepe Serna, William Sanderson, Barry*
*Corbin, Tim Scott, Michael McGuire, Jack Kehoe,*
*Victoria Plata*
True story of a Mexican who, after killing a sheriff in
1901, evaded capture by a 600-strong posse for almost
a fortnight. An harshly realistic story, told from
several viewpoints and with a nice restrained per-
formance from Olmos.

| | |
|---|---|
| WES | 100 min mTV |
| B,V | EHE |

### BALLAD OF JOE HILL, THE **
Bo Widerberg   SWEDEN   1971
*Thommy Berggren, Ania Schmidt, Kelvin Malave,*
*Everl Anderson, Cathy Smith*
Romanticised account of Joe Hill – a legendary
American labour organiser at the turn of the century.
A glossy and unrealistic study with a few good
moments and a nice title song, sung by Joan Baez.
Aka: JOE HILL

| | |
|---|---|
| DRA | 100 min |
| B,V | TEVP |

### BALLERINA **     U
Noramn CampbelIDENMARK/USA   1965
*Kirsten Simone, Mette Honnigen, Henning*
*Kronstantam*
A crippled girl is determined to become a ballerina in
this weepie Disney effort.

| | |
|---|---|
| DRA | 92 min |
| B,V | WDV |

### BALTIMORE BULLET, THE **     15
Robert Ellis Miller   USA   1980
*James Coburn, Omar Sharif, Bruce Boxleitner, Ronee*
*Blakeley, Calvin Lockhart*
A smooth-talking con-man and his young apprentice
set out to hustle a suave gambler (Sharif miscast once
again) in a high-stakes game of pool. Skip this one and
see an infinitely better film – THE HUSTLER.

| | |
|---|---|
| DRA | 98 min |
| B,V,LV | RNK; VCC (VHS only) |

### BAMBOO BROTHERHOOD, THE **
   HONG KONG
*Yuo Tien Lung, Tang Mei Fung, Lei Ming*
Typical kung fu fisticuffs with some nice action but
little plot.

| | |
|---|---|
| MAR | 92 min |
| B,V,V2 | EVC |

### BANANAS ***     15
Woody Allen   USA   1971
*Woody Allen, Louise Lasser, Carlos Montalban,*
*Howard Cosell*
Very uneven Woody Allen comedy set against a
guerilla revolution in a backward Latin American

dictatorship and winding up as their new president. The funny moments are very funny but there are too few of them, though the courtroom scene is a joy. Look out for Sylvester Stallone, he pops up briefly as a hoodlum. Score is by Marvin Hamlisch.

COM                                78 min (ort 82 min)
B,V                                                WHV

## BAND OF THE HAND **                              18
Paul Michael Glaser      USA                        1986
*Stephen Lang, Michael Carmine, Lauren Holly, John Cameron Mitchell*
A court order sends five young Miami tearaways to a detention project in the Florida Everglades, where they meet a tough Vietnam veteran who straightens them out and sends them back to the city to fight corruption, in this formula nonsense.

A/AD                                              116 min
V/sh                                                 RCA

## BAND WAGON, THE ****                               U
Vincente Minnelli      USA                          1953
*Fred Astaire, Cyd Charisse, Jack Buchanan, Oscar Levant, Nanette Fabray*
Astaire plays a washed-up movie star who goes to Broadway to try his luck in this classic Hollywood musical. If the story is not up to much the numbers are and include highlights such as: "Dancing In The Dark", "Shine On Your Shoes" and "That's Entertainment", all of which are by Howard Dietz and Arthur Schwartz. One of the best numbers is a Mickey Spillane spoof – "The Girl Hunt".

MUS                                108 min (ort 112 min)
V                                                    MGM

## BANDIDA ***                                       PG
Louis Malle      FRANCE/ITALY                       1965
*Jeanne Moreau, Brigitte Bardot, George Hamilton, Paulette Dubost, Claudio Brook, Gregor Von Rezzori*
An Irish anarchist girl comes to Mexico, where she and another girl become involved with strolling players and revolutionaries. A flashy, bouncy show of a film, whose superficial first half gives way to a more substantial and entertaining second half.
Aka: VIVA MARIA!

COM                                107 min (ort 119 min)
V                                                    KRP

## BANDIDOS **
Max Dillman (Massimo Dallamme)
              ITALY/SPAIN                           1967
*Terry Jenkins, Enrico Maria Salermo, Venantino Vernatini*
Story of one man's revenge against a gang leader in this routine spaghetti Western.
Aka: BANDIDOS O CREPA TU . . . CHE VIVO IO

WES                                                95 min
B,V,V2                                              FFV

## BANDITS **
Sergio Corbucci
   ITALY/MONACO/SPAIN/WEST GERMANY  1972
*Tomas Milian, Susan George, Telly Savalas, Rosanna Janni, Eduardo Fajardo, Franco Giacobini, Herbert Fux, Laura Betti, Alvaro De Luna*
An escaped convict teams up with a wild and spirited girl as he robs his way across Mexico, all the time tracked by a persistent lawman. A lighthearted and tongue-in-cheek spaghetti Western.
Aka: J+S, A CRIMINAL STORY OF THE FAR WEST; LA BANDA; LA BANDA J+S: CRONICA CRIMINALE DEL WEST; SONNY + JED; LOS HIJOS DEL DIA Y DE LA NOCHE

WES                                                91 min
B,V                                              PPL; GOV

## BANDITS FROM SHANTUNG **
              HONG KONG                             1971
*Chang Yi*

Kung fu Western in which a town is held to ransom after a silver robbery.

MAR                                                79 min
B,V                                                  RNK

## BANDITS, THE **
Robert Conrad/Alfredo Zacharias
              MEXICO                                1967
*Robert Conrad, Roy Jenson, Jan-Michael Vincent, Pedro Armendariz Jr, Manuel Lopez Ochoa, Antonio Aguilar, Maria Duval, Pilar Pellicar*
Three cowboys are saved from a hanging and escape with their rescuer to Mexico, where they set out to find a hidden treasure. A mediocre offering, not released in the States until 1979.
Aka: LOS BANDIDOS

WES                                                89 min
B,V,V2                                          INT; PPL

## BANDOLERO! **                                     15
Andrew V. McLaglen      USA                         1968
*James Stewart, Dean Martin, Raquel Welch, George Kennedy, Andrew Prine, Will Geer, Denver Pyle, Tom Heaton, Rudy Diaz, Sean McClory, Harry Carey Jr, Donald (Don "Red") Barry, Guy Raymond, Perry Lopez, Jock Mahoney, Dub Taylor*
A couple of outlaw brothers flee across the border with Welch as a hostage, and experience some difficulties from their Mexican colleagues. A tired saga in which the pleasant outdoors scenery only slightly compensates for the formula plot.

WES    102 min (ort 106 min) (Cut at film release by 16 sec)
B,V,LV                                              CBS

## BANG BANG **
Chuck Vincent      USA                              1975
*C.J. Laing, Jeffrey Hurst, Lynn Bishop, Misty Grey, Jennifer Jordan, Jaime Blume, David Savage, Wade Nichols, Mariene Willoughby, Annie Sprinkles, John Christopher*
Fast and furious sex comedy inspired by "Rowan And Martin's Laugh In" – a popular comedy show of the 1970s. An interminable series of sexual skits are presented with very little to link them except their explicitness. Some are very funny but many, with the demise of the type of TV shows that inspired them, appear very dated.
Aka: BANG, BANG, YOU'VE GOT IT!; PORN FLAKES
OSCA: SIZZLE/SLIPPERY WHEN WET (asa)

A                                   56 min (ort 81 min)
B,V                                                  HAR

## BANG BANG GANG, THE *                             18
Jan Guylder      USA                                1970
*Jae Miller, Marland Proctor, Mark Griffin*
A kind of BONNIE AND CLYDE times two. Two female robbers team up with two male robbers. The rest is violence and sex in this unpleasant offering.

THR                                                76 min
B,V                                              PRV L/A

## BANG BANG KID, THE ***                             U
Stanley Prager  ITALY/SPAIN/USA                     1967
*Guy Madison, Tom Bosley, Sandra Milo, Riccardo Garrone, Jose Maria Caffarel, Dianik Zurakowska, Giustino Durano*
A gunfighting robot helps the townsfolk regain control of their town from a wealthy mine-owner, in this offbeat comedy-Western set at the turn of the century.
Aka: BANG BANG

WES                                 84 min (ort 90 min)
B,V                                          PRV L/A; CH5

## BANG THE DRUM SLOWLY ****
John Hancock      USA                               1973
*Robert De Niro, Michael Moriarty, Vincent Gardenia, Tom Ligon, Heather MacRae, Barbara Babcock, Phil*

*Foster, Ann Wedgeworth, Selma Diamond, Patrick McVey, Danny Aiello*
Story of two baseball buddies who play for a New York team. When one of them finds that he is dying from cancer he conspires with the other to keep this from the rest of the team. Episodic and a little overlong, but superb performances from the two leads carry it through. Screenplay is by Harris from his novel. First done with Paul Newman for TV, but this is the better adaptation.
Boa: novel by Mark Harris.
DRA                                                    98 min
B,V                                                       GHV

**BANK SHOT ***                                          PG
Gower Champion          USA                  1974
*George C. Scott, Joanna Cassidy, Sorrell Brooke, G. Wood, Clifton James, Bob Balaban, Bibi Osterwald*
A criminal plans to rob a bank – by moving the entire building! A crazy and entertaining comedy that's a sequel of sorts to THE HOT ROCK.
Boa: novel by Donald E. Westlake.
COM                                                    83 min
B,V                                                       WHV

**BANKER, THE ***                                         18
William Webb            USA                  1989
*Robert Forster, Jeff Conaway, Richard Roundtree, Shanna Reed, Leif Garrett, Duncan Regehr, Deborah Richter*
A demented banker is in reality also a crossbow-wielding serial killer, whose penchant is to murder and mutilate prostitutes. The usual tough cop is out to nail him in this standard slasher offering. The script is by Webb.
HOR                                       92 min (ort 95 min)
V                                                          RCA

**BANZAI RUNNER ***                                       15
John G. Thomas          USA                  1986
*Dean Stockwell, John Shephard, Charles Dierkop, Dawn Schneider, Ann Cooper, Barry Sattles*
A Highway Patrol officer turns the enforcement of speed limits into a lone crusade, when a bunch of rich young brats start using the roads as a racing track for their sports cars. Average.
A/AD                                                   85 min
B,V                                                       MED

**BARABBAS ***                                            PG
Richard Fleischer    ITALY/USA              1962
*Anthony Quinn, Jack Palance, Silvana Mangano, Vittorio Gassman, Valentina Cortese, Katy Jurado, Harry Andrews, Arthur Kennedy, Michael Gwynn*
Interminable biblical epic that attempts to tell of what happened to Barabbas who was set free instead of Jesus. Sent to the silver mines he becomes a Christian and then a gladiator. Well acted but this one just goes on and on.
Boa: novel by P. Lagerkvist.
DRA                                                  127 min
B,V                                                       RCA

**BARBARELLA ***                                          15
Roger Vadim        FRANCE/ITALY            1967
*Jane Fonda, John Phillip Law, David Hemmings, Milo O'Shea, Ugo Tognazzi, Anita Pallenberg, Marcel Marceau, Claude Dauphin*
In the 41st century Barbarella is sent on a mission to investigate the disappearance of a famous scientist. A highly imaginative attempt to bring to life a French comic strip character, let down by a flawed script and poor direction. It now looks very dated, not least because of its musical score.
Aka: BARBARELLA, QUEEN OF THE GALAXY
FAN                                                    97 min
B,V                                                       CIC

**BARBARIAN MASTER ***                                    18
Michael E. Lemick (Franco Prosperi)
                        ITALY              1983
*Peter MacCoy, Margareta Range, Yvonne Fraschetti, Anthony Freeman, Sabrina Siani*
Sword-and-sandal epic like hundreds before it.
A/AD                                                   90 min
B,V                                              OREG/BUDGE

**BARBARIAN QUEEN ***                                     18
Hector Oliviera         USA                  1985
*Lana Clarkson, Dawn Dunlap, Katt Shea, Frank Zagarino*
Standard sword-and-sandal epic of female warriors on the warpath.
Aka: LA REINA BARBARA; QUEEN OF THE NAKED STEEL; REINA SALVAJE
A/AD            76 min (ort 85 min) Cut (2 min 21 sec)
B,V                                                       MED

**BARBARIAN REVENGE ***                                   15
Al Bradley (Alfonso Brescia)
                     HONG KONG/ITALY
*Nick Jordan, Mark Hannibal, Yueh Hua, Malissa Longo*
Fantasy adventure, in which a beautiful young woman, Valleria, enlists the help of an ex-prisoner of the Amazons to fight back against their evil domination of the men of her village.
FAN                                       94 min Cut (22 sec)
B,V                                              AVR; BARBAR

**BARBARIAN, THE ***                                      18
Rudolph Mate        ITALY/USA              1961
*Jack Palance, Milly Vitale, Richard Wyler*
One of those endearingly typical Italian costumers of the 1960s. This one is set at the time of the Second Punic War.
Aka: BARBARIANS, THE; FREEDOM FOR REBEL; REVAK, LO SCHIAVO DI CARTHAGINE; REVAK, SLAVE OF CARTHAGE; REVAK THE REBEL
DRA                                                    84 min
B,V,V2                                            VPD; WHV

**BARBARIANS, THE ***                                     U
Ruggero Deodato         USA                  1987
*David Paul, Peter Paul, Richard Lynch, Eva La Rue, Virginia Bryant, Sheeba Alahani, Michael Berryman*
Twin brothers battle evil in a primitive world of long ago when they embark on a quest to rescue the queen of their native tribe. This wonderfully silly sword and sorcery tale is only memorable for the muscular presence of the Pauls – twin wrestlers billed as the Barbarian Brothers in real life.
A/AD                                                   84 min
V/sh                                                      WHV

**BARBARIAN AND THE GEISHA, THE ***                       U
John Huston             USA                  1958
*John Wayne, Eiko Ando, Sam Jaffe, So Yamamura*
The story of the first US diplomat to visit Japan in 1856, who encounters a good deal of local opposition, but finds solace in the charms of a beautiful geisha. A flabby and disjointed costume epic, not helped by a ludicrous piece of miscasting of Wayne as the ambassador.
DRA                                      101 min (ort 105 min) B/W
V                                                          CBS

**BARBAROSA ***                                           PG
Fred Schepisi            USA                  1982
*Willie Nelson, Gary Busey, Isela Vega, Gilbert Roland, Danny De La Paz, George Voskovec, Alma Martinez, Howland Chamberlain, Wolf Muser, Kai Wulf, Harry Caesar, Sharon Compton, Roberto Contreros, Luis Contreros*
A legendary outlaw befriends a young cowhand, who's

on the run for the accidental killing of his brother-in-law. Our outlaw takes him on as a protege and teaches him how to survive, in this spirited and offbeat Western.
WES                                    90 min; 86 min (CH5)
B,V,V2,LV                              PRV L/A; CH5 (VHS only)

### BARBARY COAST ★★★★
Howard Hawks            USA                    1935
*Joel McCrea, Walter Brennan, Edward G. Robinson, Brian Donlevy, Frank Craven, Miriam Hopkins*
Richly melodramatic account of San Francisco in the days of the Gold Rush, with plenty of excellent acting and a lively plot, as a dance-hall queen comes into conflict with a local big-shot. David Niven appears very briefly as an extra.
DRA                                           90 min B/W
B,V                                               VGM

### BARBIE'S FANTASIES ★★
Claude Goddard          USA                    1974
*Jenny Lane, Jamie Gillis, Jeffrey Hurst, Jennifer Hurst, Sue Kelly*
A loosely structured sex film that is virtually a compilation of separate sequences intended to illustrate some very private fantasies.
A                                                90 min
B,V                                                 RIP

### BARCELONA KILL, THE ★★★
Jose Antonio de la Fuente
                        SPAIN                  1972
*Linda Hayden, John Justin, Simon Andrew*
An enjoyable crime thriller set in Barcelona's gypsy quarter.
THR                                              86 min
B,V,V2                                             VCL

### BARE KNUCKLES ★
Don Edmonds             USA                    1976
*Robert Viharo, Sherry Jackson, Michael Heit, John Daniels, Gloria Hendry, Richard Kennedy*
A modern bounty hunter goes after a mad slasher whose victims are, as is usual in these films, all women. Turgid nonsense
THR                                              90 min
B,V,V2                                             VPD

### BARE NECESSITIES ★                              18
Keith Jon               USA
*Robert Egan, Hilary Scott, Paul Wheeler, Bonnie Paine*
A Beverly Hills business big-shot engages the services of an escort agency to help him entertain some lonely clients.
A                                                85 min
B,V                                              VEXCEL

### BAREFOOT CONTESSA, THE ★★★               PG
Joseph Mankiewicz       USA                    1954
*Humphrey Bogart, Ava Gardner, Edmond O'Brien, Marius Goring, Rossano Brazzi, Elizabeth Sellars, Valentina Cortesa*
A mentor-director propels a beautiful Spanish dancer to Hollywood stardom but she eventually marries a Count. However, he is unable to father children so she embarks on an extramarital affair but is eventually shot by him. An absorbing and well produced melodrama slightly spoilt by an over-wordy and often obscure script. AA: S. Actor (O'Brien).
DRA                                         122 min B/W
V                                                 WHV

### BAREFOOT EXECUTIVE, THE ★★                   U
Robert Butler           USA                    1971
*Kurt Russell, Joe Flynn, Harry Morgan, Wally Cox, Heather North, Heydon Rorke, Alan Hewitt, John Ritter*
Thanks to some help from his pet chimp, an employee

of a TV station is able to climb to the top of the executive ladder. Formula Disney film with a few good moments that float about in the slapstick script.
COM                                              96 min
B,V                                                WDV

### BAREFOOT IN THE PARK ★★                      PG
Gene Saks               USA                    1967
*Jane Fonda, Robert Redford, Charles Boyer, Mildred Natwick, Herb Edelman, Mabel Albertson, Fritz Feld,*
Plotless and pointless comedy about a couple who live five storeys up in an apartment block that has no lift. The Neil Simon script delivers a few laughs but the running-joke about climbing the stairs begins to grow thin after a while.
Boa: play by Neil Simon.
COM                                             102 min
B,V                                             ARENA/CIC

### BARFLY ★★★                                     18
Barbet Schroeder        USA                    1987
*Mickey Rourke, Faye Dunaway, Alice Krige, Frank Stallone, Jack Nance, J.C. Quinn, Sandy Martin, Roberta Bassin, Gloria Leroy, Leonard Termo, Fritz Feld*
Screenwriter Charles Bukowski's autobiographical account follows the adventures of Skid Row writer Henry, an independent spirit who begins a turbulent romance with fellow barfly Wanda. Their rocky relationship is threatened when a female literary editor "discovers" his talent. A boozy and semi-comic look at assorted Los Angeles derelicts and low-lifes.
DRA                                              96 min
B,V                                                WHV

### BARKLEYS OF BROADWAY, THE ★★★               U
Charles Walters         USA                    1949
*Fred Astaire, Ginger Rogers, Oscar Levant, Billie Burke, Gale Robbins*
After a ten year break Astaire and Rogers teamed up again for this witty Comden-Green story of a showbiz couple who split up but eventually get back together again. Songs include: "You'd Be Hard To Replace" and "They Can't Take That Away From Me".
MUS                                             105 min
B,V                                                MGM

### BARNABY AND ME ★★
Norman Panama    AUSTRALIA                     1977
*Sid Caesar, Juliet Mills, Sally Boyden, John Newcombe*
An American con-man gets involved with a girl and her pet koala bear in this enjoyable little family comedy. Pretty innocuous stuff but good pleasant fun.
COM                                              90 min
B,V                                             CYC/VUL

### BARON AND THE KID, THE ★★                    PG
Gary Nelson             USA                    1984
*Johnny Cash, Darren McGavin, Greg Webb, Tracy Pollan, June Carter Cash, Claude Akins, Richard Roundtree, Dan Albright, Harvey Andrews, Bill Ash, Earl Poole Ball, Ron Baskin, Jere Beery, Tracey Bise, Ned Bridges*
Film based on a song by Johnny Cash. A pool player comes up against a young challenger who turns out to be the son he never knew. Inevitably reminds one of the Kenny Rogers film THE GAMBLER, with a similar shortage of material for a full-length film.
Aka: BARON, THE
DRA                              91 min (ort 100 min) mTV
B,V                                               CBS

### BARON BLOOD ★★★
Mario Bava
                ITALY/WEST GERMANY             1972
*Joseph Cotten, Elke Sommer, Alan Collins (Luciano Pigozzi), Massimo Girotti, Antonio Canatafora, Humi*

*(Umberto) Raho, Nicoletta Elmi, Dieter Tressler, Rada Rassimov*
Gruesome vampire story telling of the attempts made by the descendants of a vampire nobleman to rejuvenate him. The usual plot is helped by some interesting settings and intelligent use of lighting.
Aka: BLOOD BARON, THE; CHAMBER OF TORTURES; GLI ORRORI DEL CASTELLO DI NORIMBERGA; THIRST OF BARON BLOOD, THE; TORTURE CHAMBER OF BARON BLOOD, THE
HOR                                        90 min
B,V                                        GHV

## BARRACUDA **
Harry Kerwin            USA              1978
*Wayne-David Crawford, Jason Evers, Bert Freed, Roberta Leighton, Cliff Emmich*
River pollution affects the fish and then the people in a small Florida town, leading to the expected mayhem.
Aka: LUCIFER PROJECT, THE
HOR                                        90 min
B,V                                        AVP

## BARREL FULL OF DOLLARS, A **            15
Miles Deem              USA              1970
*Klaus Kinski, Hunt Powers, Gordon Mitchell, Simone Blondell, Rai Saunders*
Story of feuding and revenge set against the background of the American Civil War. A typical action Western of little merit.
Aka: PER UNA BARA PIENA DI DOLLARI
WES                          98 min; 83 min (STABL)
B,V,V2                              VDM/GHV L/A; STABL

## BARRY LYNDON **                         PG
Stanley Kubrick          UK              1975
*Ryan O'Neal, Marisa Berenson, Patrick Magee, Hardy Kruger, Steven Berkoff, Gay Hamilton, Marie Kean, Diana Koerner, Murray Melvin, Frank Middlemass, Andre Morell, Arthur Sullivan, Godfrey Quigley, Leonard Rossiter*
Based on a story of a young Irish boy who desires success but is spoilt by it, this is little more than an exquisitely detailed look at 18th century England. An overlong, languid and beautiful film, but a terribly empty one. Written by Kubrick and with narration by Michael Hordern. AA: Cin (John Alcott), Art/Set (Ken Adam and Roy Walker/Vernon Dixon), Cost (Ulla-Britt Sonderlund/Milena Canonero), Score (Leonard Rosenman).
Boa: novel The Memoirs Of Barry Lyndon by William Makepeace Thackeray.
DRA                                        185 min
B,V                                        WHV

## BARRY McKENZIE HOLDS HIS OWN *          18
Bruce Beresford     AUSTRALIA           1974
*Barry Humphries, Barry Crocker, Donald Pleasence, Dick Bentley, Tommy Trinder, Ed Devereaux, Frank Windsor, Deryck Guyler, Arthur English, Roy Kinnear, John Le Mesurier, Desmond Tester, Louis Negin, Paul Humpoletz*
A stupid sequel to "The Adventures Of Barry McKenzie" with both him and his brother plus Dame Edna (who is mistaken for Queen Elizabeth II) being kidnapped and taken to Transylvania. Crocker plays the bill-swilling twit first encountered in the Private Eye comic-strip as well as his twin brother. As tiresome as it is witless and a waste of the considerable talents of both Humphries and Crocker.
COM                          95 min; 93 min (MIA)
B,V                              INT; VGM; MIA

## BASKET CASE ***                         18
Frank Henenlotter        USA            1981
*Kevin Van Hentenryck, Terri Susan Smith, Beverly Bonner, Lloyd Pace, Robert Vogel, Diana Browne*
Low-budget horror film about a man who arrives in

New York, together with a mysterious padlocked wicker basket that contains his deformed telepathic mutant brother. Very tongue-in-cheek and often quite effective, with a few intriguing animated sequences.
HOR       85 min (ort 91 min) Cut (35 sec in addition to film cuts)
B,V                                        PAL

## BASKET CASE 2 ***                       18
Frank Henenlotter        USA            1990
*Kevin Van Hentenryck, Annie Ross, Heather Rattray, Jason Evers, Kathryn Meisle, Ted Sorel*
A potent sequel to the earlier film with Duane and his mutant brother Belial arriving at a community of freaks, where they experience a large number of monstrous encounters and the unwelcome attentions of an investigative journalist. A gruesome, gory, entertaining shocker.
HOR                          84 min (ort 89 min)
V                                          MED

## BASTARD, THE **                         15
Lee H. Katzin            USA            1978
*Andrew Stevens, Noah Beery, Peter Bonerz, Tom Bosley, Kim Cattrall, John Colicos, William Daniels, Buddy Ebsen, Lorne Greene, James Gregory, Olivia Hussey, Cameron Mitchell, Harry Morgan, Patricia Neal, Eleanor Parker*
Flat and unconvincing story of the illegitimate son of a French aristocrat who searches through England and France for his birthright and later goes off to America where he takes part in the War of Independence. The first of three adaptations of the historical novels of John Jakes. THE REBELS and THE SEEKERS were his other two works in the series. Raymond Burr narrates.
Aka: KENT CHRONICLES, THE
Boa: novel by John Jakes.
DRA                                        210 min mTV
B,V                                        CIC

## BAT 21 ***                              15
Peter Markle             USA            1987
*Gene Hackman, Danny Glover, Jerry Reed, Clayton Rohner, David Marshall Grant, Erich Anderson, Joe Dorsey, Michael Ng, Theodore Chan Woei-Shyong, Don Ruffin, Scott Howell, Michael Raden, Timothy Fitzgerald, Stuart Hagen*
A lieutenant colonel is shot down behind enemy lines in Vietnam and a rescue mission is mounted, using a pilot to guide him from the air. Having spent his entire career away from ground combat, the officer is shocked at the devastation wrought by American bombing and for the first time in his life sees the horrors of war. A mature film, echewing "Rambo" style cliches in favour of a look at how both sides have become de-humanised by the conflict.
Aka: BAT. 21
Boa: book by William C. Anderson.
WAR                          101 min (ort 105 min)
B,V                                        GHV

## BAT PEOPLE, THE *
Jerry Jameson            USA            1974
*Stewart Moss, Paul Carr, Marianne McAndrew, Michael Pataki, Arthur Space*
Doctor on honeymoon is bitten by bat with expected results. Would have been more interesting if it were the other way round.
Aka: IT LIVES BY NIGHT
HOR                          91 min (ort 95 min)
B,V,V2                                     INT

## BAT, THE ***
Crane Wilbur             USA            1958
*Vincent Price, Agnes Moorehead, Gavin Gordon, John Sutton, Lenita Lane, Darla Hood*

A woman writer sets a trap for the prowler who breaks into the spooky house she has rented. A good adaptation of Rinehart's much-filmed novel with some spooky moments.
Boa: play by Mary Roberts Rinehart.
HOR                                          78 min
B,V                                          RNK

**BATES MOTEL ***                            15
Richard Rothstein      USA                   1987
Bud Cort, Jason Bateman, Lori Petty, Greggy Henry, Khrystyne Haje, Moses Gunn
Film inspired by PSYCHO and a ill-conceived pilot for a TV series. After 27 years together in an asylum Norman bequeathes the Bates Motel, scene of countless happy times, to his young friend Alex who is about to be released. A misguided and rubbishy spin-off.
HOR                    91 min (ort 104 min) mTV
B,V                                          CIC

**BATMAN ****                                U
Leslie Martinson       USA                   1966
Adam West, Burt Ward, Cesar Romero, Frank Gorshin, Burgess Meredith, Lee Meriweather, Alan Napier, Neil Hamilton, Madge Blake, Reginald Denny
The only feature film spin-off from the 1960s TV series, in which Batman and his sidekick Robin thwart a united attempt by the four greatest criminal masterminds to hold the entire world to ransom. Kids may enjoy watching the Joker, the Riddler, the Penguin and the Catwoman go about their nefarious business but this one has little appeal for adults.
Aka: BATMAN: THE MOVIE
JUV                                          105 min
V                                            CBS

**BATMAN *****                               15
Tim Burton             USA                   1989
Michael Keaton, Jack Nicholson, Kim Basinger, Jack Palance, Billy Dee Williams, Jerry Hall, Pat Hingle, Michael Gough, Robert Wuhl, Tracey Walter, Lee Wallace
The film whose release in the UK prompted a new cinema certification to keep out the tots, this is a dark and moody rendition, bringing the famous D.C. Comics character to the screen, where he is all but swamped by the spectacular sets and Nicholson's wildly overblown portrayal of arch-criminal The Joker. A sombre tale, flawed by weak plotting. Screenplay is by Sam Hamm.
AA: Art (Anton Furst and Peter Young).
A/AD                   121 min (ort 126 min)
V/sh                                         WHV

**BATTERIES NOT INCLUDED ****                PG
Matthew Robbins        USA                   1987
Hume Cronyn, Jessica Tandy, Frank McRae, Elizabeth Pena, Michael Carmine, Dennis Boutsikaris
Tenants faced with the demolition of their building get help from an unexpected quarter when small friendly aliens pay them a visit. Another cloyingly sweet sugar-coated Steven Spielberg production.
COM                                          102 min
B,V                                          CIC

**BATTLE BEYOND THE STARS ***               PG
Jimmy T. Murakami      USA                   1980
Richard Thomas, Robert Vaughn, Sybil Danning, John Saxon, George Peppard, Sam Jaffe, Morgan Woodward, Darlanne Fluegel
SEVEN SAMURAI in space. A real cheapo attempt to cash in on the success of STAR WARS. But for the fact that it's lousy it might have been watchable.
FAN                                          98 min
V                                            WHV

**BATTLE FOR THE PLANET OF THE APES ****    PG
J. Lee Thompson        USA                   1973
Roddy McDowall, Claude Akins, John Huston, Natalie Trundy, Severn Darden, Paul Williams, Lew Ayres
This is the fifth and last sequel to PLANET OF THE APES (we hope!) and has a society in which man and ape live in harmony facing a threat from two opposing factions, one ape and the other mutant-human. A generally sub-standard sequel with footage from earlier films. A TV series followed.
FAN                                          83 min
V                                            CBS

**BATTLE OF ALGIERS, THE ******
Gillo Pontecorvo   ALGERIA/ITALY            1965
Yacef Saadi, Jean Martin, Brahim Haggiag, Tommaso Neri, Samie Kerbash
In Algeria of 1954, an ex-convict joins in the fight for independence in this politically oriented, excellent semi-documentary examination of the origins of this struggle.
Aka: LA BATTAGLIA DI ALGERI
WAR                                      135 min B/W
B,V                                        CAPS/PVG

**BATTLE OF AUSTERLITZ, THE ****
Abel Gance                                   1959
FRANCE/ITALY/LIECHTENSTEIN/YUGOSLAVIA
Claudia Cardinale, Martine Carol, Leslie Caron, Vittorio De Sica, Rossano Brazi, Jean Marais, Ettore Manni, Jack Palance, Orson Welles
This somewhat over-elaborate costume drama tells the story of Napoleon's battle with the Austro-Russian army at Austerlitz. A star-studded cast acts as though wading through concrete in this stilted and stultifying effort.
Aka: AUSTERLITZ
WAR                                          166 min
B.V                                          INT

**BATTLE OF BILL'S POND, THE ****
Harley Coklis          UK                    1978
Ben Buckton, Andrew Ashby, Talfryn Thomas, Ann Beach, Keith James, Geoff Hinsliff, Derek Ware, Geoffrey Palmer, Miriam Margoyles, Inda Robson
The authorities are reluctant to act, when two boys discover that the pond they fish in has become polluted by industrial waste from a local detergent factory. A fair little drama.
DRA                                          56 min
B,V                                          RNK

**BATTLE OF BRITAIN, THE ****               PG
Guy Hamilton           UK                    1969
Laurence Olivier, Robert Shaw, Michael Caine, Susannah York, Christopher Plummer, Kenneth More, Trevor Howard, Ralph Richardson, Patrick Wymark, Curt Jurgens, Michael Redgrave, Nigel Patrick, Robert Flemyng, Edward Fox
Overlong attempt to tell the story of the Battle of Britain that focuses so closely on the details of the conflict that it becomes tedious rather than exciting. Weighed down almost to the point of collapse with star cameos (as is so often the case with British films), the superb flying sequences offer some compensation in the cinema, but will be largely wasted on TV.
Boa: book The Narrow Margin by D. Wood and D. Dempster.
WAR                    110 min (ort 132 min)
V                                            WHV

**BATTLE OF EL ALAMEIN *****                PG
Calvin Jackson Paget (Giorgio Ferroni)
                       ITALY/FRANCE          1968
Frederick Stafford, Ettore Manni, Robert Hossein, Michael Rennie, George Hilton, Ira Furstenberg
Uneasy WW2 partners Italy and Germany use their soldiers to fight the British in the North African

desert of 1942. A fairly strong action tale following the events leading up to Rommel's defeat (a good performance from Hossein), with the British shown in a rather poor light this time round.
Aka: DESERT TANKS
WAR          105 min; 85 min (QUICK); 102 min (SID)
B,V,V2                                  IFS/CBS; QUICK; SID

## BATTLE OF MIDWAY, THE **                    PG
John Smight              USA                 1976
Toshiro Mifune, Charlton Heston, Henry Fonda, Robert Mitchum, Glenn Ford, Edward Albert, James Coburn, Hal Holbrook, Robert Wagner, Robert Webber, Ed Nelson, James Shigeta, Monte Markham, Chris George, Glenn Corbett
Account of the 1942 battle when the Japanese attacked the island of Midway during WW2 but found the tide of the war in the Pacific turning against them. A noisy and confused story that concentrates on too many stars and too little action.
Aka: MIDWAY
WAR                                     126 min
V/h                                        CIC

## BATTLE OF OKINAWA **
Kihachi Okamoto         JAPAN               1971
Keiju Kobayashi, Tetsuro Tanba
An account of the fanatical opposition the Americans encountered, in their attempt to take the island of Okinawa from the Japanese defenders during WW2. Average.
WAR                                     150 min
B,V,V2                                  CRYS/DFS

## BATTLE OF THE ACES **                        PG
Roger Corman            USA                 1971
John Phillip Law, Barry Primus, Peter Masterson, Karen Huston, Robert La Tourneaux, Hurd Hatfield, Corin Redgrave
Set during WW1, this tells of a Canadian pilot who joins the Royal Flying Corps and takes on a German air ace. The flying sequences are excellent but the film fails dismally on the ground, where all pace and sense of action is lost in the stilted dialogue.
Aka: RED BARON, THE; VON RICHTHOFEN AND BROWN
WAR                           97 min; 90 min (KRP)
B,V                                  FILV L/A; KRP

## BATTLE OF THE ANTILLES ***                    PG
Gillo Pontecorvo   FRANCE/ITALY            1969
Marlon Brando, Evaristo Marquez, Renato Salvatori, Tom Lyons, Norman Hill
Hard-hitting account of how the British send one of their diplomats to a Portuguese Caribbean island to instigate a slave revolt and thus bring the island (and its sugar industry) under British control.
Aka: BURN!; QUEIMADA
DRA                           90 min (ort 132 min)
B,V                                         FILV

## BATTLE OF THE BULGE **                        PG
Ken Annakin             USA                 1965
Henry Fonda, Robert Shaw, Robert Ryan, Charles Bronson, James MacArthur, Dana Andrews, George Montgomery, Ty Hardin, Pier Angeli, Telly Savalas
Account of the last major German offensive of WW2; it took place in the Ardennes in the middle of the winter of 1944. Apart from some good performances such as Shaw's, this overlong and dull effort never allows the action to distract one from the banality of the script.
Boa: book by R.E. Merriam.
WAR                                     135 min
B,V                                         WHV

## BATTLE OF THE COMMANDOS **
Umberto Lenzi           ITALY               1969
Jack Palance, Curt Jurgens, Tomas Hunter, Diana Lorys, Wolfgang Preiss, Robert Hundar

To assist the D-day invasion, a group of commandos led by Palance are sent to destroy a powerful German cannon. Average.
Aka: LEGION OF THE DAMNED
WAR                                      94 min
B,V                                  VFP L/A; HER

## BATTLE OF THE CORAL SEA **                    PG
Paul Wendkos            USA                 1959
Cliff Robertson, Gia Scala, Patricia Cutts, Teru Shimada, Gene Blakely, Gordon Jones
During WW2, a tough submarine captain is given the task of photographing the Japanese Pacific fleet, is captured but eventually escapes. A watchable but unenthralling war story, with adequate action sequences but little else.
WAR                          83 min (ort 85 min) B/W
V                                           RCA

## BATTLE OF THE DAMNED **                       PG
Robert Montero          ITALY               1969
Dale Cummings, Monty Greenwood, Herbert Andrews
A group of American demolition experts are sent on a suicide mission to Tunisia to blow up an underground fuel dump behind German lines. Another in a long line of forgettable Italian war epics.
WAR                                      83 min
V                                           VPD

## BATTLE OF THE JAPAN SEA **
Seiji Maruyama          JAPAN               1969
Toshiro Mifune, Toshio Kurosawa, Tatsuyo Nakadai
Account of a decisive battle that took place between Russia and Japan in their war of 1905. Average war film of no great merit.
Aka: NIHONKAI DAIKAISEN
WAR                                     120 min
B,V,V2                                      DFS

## BATTLE OF THE RIVER PLATE, THE **
Michael Powell/Emeric Pressburger
                        UK                  1956
Peter Finch, John Gregson, Bernard Lee, Anthony Quayle, Michael Goodliffe, William Squire, Andrew Cruickshank, Christopher Lee, Ian Hunter, Jack Gwillim, Lionel Murton, Anthony Bushell, Peter Illing
Rather talky and stilted tale of the British Navy's pursuit and trapping of the German pocket battleship the Graf Spee, in Montevideo harbour in 1939. Done in semi-documentary style with a few good moments, but too many characters vie for attention in this undisciplined effort.
Aka: PURSUIT OF THE GRAF SPEE
Boa: book Graf Spee by Michael Powell.
WAR                                     106 min
B,V                                         RNK

## BATTLE OF THE SEXES **                         U
Charles Crichton        UK                  1959
Peter Sellers, Robert Morley, Constance Cummings, Jameson Clark, Moultrie Kelsall, Alex Mackenzie, Roddy McMillan, Donald Pleasence, Ernest Thesiger
The uneventful and staid lives of the employees of a stuffy Edinburgh company are upset by the arrival of a pushy female efficiency expert, and one of their number contemplates murder. An interesting attempt at a black comedy that is only intermittently effective.
Boa: short story The Catbird Seat by James Thurber.
COM                          81 min (ort 84 min) B/W
V                                           CH5

## BATTLE OF THE STARS **                         15
Al Bradley (Alfonso Brescia)
                        ITALY               1979
John Richardson, Jason Palance, Gisella Hatin, Yanti Somer, West Buchanan, Kathy Christine, Max Karis, Percy Hogan, Pamela Mason, Mamie Van Doren, Anthony Eisley, Nicolas Barte, Gaetano Balestrieri

An alien spaceship penetrates Earth's defences and lands, whereupon friendly aliens arrive to offer their help in the search for the invaders in this endearing nonsense.

FAN 86 min (ort 96 min)
B,V PRV L/A; CH5

## BATTLE ON THE RIVER NERETVA, THE *** PG
Veljko Bulajic
    YUGOSLAVIA/ITALY/WEST GERMANY 1970
*Yul Brynner, Sergei Bondarchuk, Curt Jurgens, Orson Welles, Hardy Kruger, Sylva Koscina, Franco Nero*
This tells of one of the bloodiest battles of WW2; the one that took place in Yugoslavia between the Partisans and the Germans. A solid and expensive account of this famous battle that might well have won an Academy Award as Best Foreign Film (it was nominated), had it not been mutilated in a clumsy attempt to shorten its running time.
Aka: BATTLE OF NERETVA; BITKA NA NERETVI
WAR 127 min (ort 175 min) Cut (7 sec)
B,V,V2 VDM; STABL

## BATTLE RATS ** 18
Benjamin Briggs Sr USA
*Jack Gilbert, Corwyn Sperry*
War drama set in Vietnam where the title group of brave American fighting men fearlessly attacks an underground Vietcong hideout. Yet one more celluloid victory to make up for the less-than-glorious shortcomings of reality. Average.
A/AD 93 min
V RCA

## BATTLE SQUADRON *** 15
Tom Raymonth (Enzo G. Castellari) 1969
    FRANCE/ITALY/SPAIN (re-released 1983)
*Van Johnson, Francisco Rabal, Evelyn Stewart, Bekim Fehmiu, George Taylor, Gloria Samara, Peter Roland, Frank Phillips, Frederick Stafford*
WW2 story of the formation of the Partisan Air Force after the debacle of Dunkirk and following the exploits of a group of German agents who penetrate the British High Command on the eve of the Battle of Britain. A strong and enjoyable war story.
Aka: BATTLE COMMAND; BATTLE OF THE EAGLES; EAGLES OVER BRITAIN; EAGLES OVER LONDON; LA BATTAGLIA D'INGHILTERRA; LA BATTALLA SOBRE BRETANA
WAR 122 min
B,V VDM L/A; MERL/VCL; ACAD

## BATTLESHIP POTEMKIN, THE ***** PG
Sergei Eisenstein USSR 1925
*Alexander Antonov, Grigory Alexandrov, Vladimir Barsky, Mikhail Gomorov, Levshin*
A partly fictitious account of the mutiny in 1905, aboard a battleship in Czarist Russia at the port of Odessa, brought vividly to life in a series of powerful images and the brilliant use of montage. Rightfully considered a masterpiece, the scene at the Odessa Steps when innocent civilians are mown down by troops is one of the most famous sequences ever filmed.
Aka: BRONENOSETS POTEMKIN; POTEMKIN
DRA 65 min B/W silent
V HEND

## BATTLESTAR GALACTICA * PG
Richard A. Colla USA 1978 (re-released 1979)
*Lorne Greene, Richard Hatch, Dirk Benedict, Ray Milland, Ed Begley Jr, John Colicos, Patrick MacNee, Lew Ayres, Jane Seymour, Laurette Spang, Terry Carter*
Feature film clipped together from the first and fifth episodes of a TV series, and it looks it too. Plenty of special effects in this rather poor story of how the survivors of an attack by evil robots, the Cyclons,

escape from their doomed planet in search of a haven on planet Earth, led by a huge spaceship commanded by Greene. The special effects are by John Dykstra. See also MISSION GALACTICA: THE CYCLON ATTACK and CONQUEST OF THE EARTH.
FAN 119 min (ort 125 min) mTV
V/h CIC

## BATTLETRUCK ** 15
Harley Cokliss USA 1982
*Michael Beck, Annie McEnroe, James Wainwright, John Ratzenberger, Randolph Powell, Diana Rowan, John Bach, Bruno Lawrence*
Yet another post-nuclear holocaust film in which a brutal ruler dominates a devastated and radioactive world by means of a monster battletruck. This one is set in 1994. Filmed in New Zealand.
Aka: WARRIORS OF THE 21ST CENTURY
FAN 89 min
B,V,V2 GHV; VCC (VHS only)

## BAWDY ADVENTURES OF TOM JONES, THE * 15
Cliff Owen UK 1976
*Nicky Henson, Trevor Howard, Terry-Thomas, Arthur Lowe, Georgia Brown, Joan Collins, William Mervyn, Murray Melvin, Madeleine Smith, Geraldine MacEwan, Jeremy Lloyd, Janie Greenspun, Michael Bats, Hilda Fenemore, Isabel Dean*
A failed attempt at a bawdy version of the London stage musical that is generally acknowledged to be inferior to the 1963 film TOM JONES. Set in 18th century Somerset, this follows the amorous adventure of our country squire's son, with various women of the time, including Joan Collins as a highwaywoman.
Boa: novel Tom Jones by Henry Fielding/play by Paul MacPherson and Paul Holden.
COM 94 min
B,V CIC

## BAY BOY, THE ** 15
Danie Petrie CANADA/FRANCE 1984
*Kiefer Sutherland, Liv Ullmann, Peter Donat, Isabelle Mejias, Mathieu Carriere, Joe MacPherson, Iris Currie, Kevin McKenzie, Alan Scarfe, Chris Wiggins, Francis MacNeil, Michael Egges, Leah Pinsent, Robert Taylor*
A boy in a small Canadian town in the 1930s is torn between his mother's wish for him to become a priest and his normal sexual desires. An earnest but limp coming-of-age tale with one-dimensional characterisations and a predictable and cliched script.
Aka: LE PRINTEMPS SOUS LA NEIGE
DRA 97 min
B,B RNK; ORION

## BAY COVE ** 15
Carl Schenkel USA 1987
*Pamela Sue Martin, Tim Matheson, Barbara Billingsley, James Sikking, Jeff Conaway, Woody Harrelson, Susan Ruttan, Inga Swenson, John Dee, Nigel Bennett, Michael Caruana, Patrick Brymer, Cree Summer Francks, David Harvey*
Tired and tedious supernatural drama of modern witchcraft with a couple moving into a quaint village and finding that their neighbours belong to a witches' coven.
Aka: BAY COVEN
HOR 95 min (ort 100 min) mTV
B,V SONY

## BAYWATCH: PANIC AT MALIBU PIER * PG
Richard Compton USA 1989
*David Hasselhoff, Parker Stevenson, Shawn Weatherly, Billy Warlock, Erika Eleniak, Gina Hecht, Monte Markham, Richard Jaeckel*
A dullish pilot for a TV series following the exploits of a bunch of Californian lifeguards, whose stretch of Malibu beach appears to be remarkably over-burdened with accident-prone beauties.

DRA                    97 min (ort 100 min) mTV
V                                            VCC

## BEACH BALLS *                               18
Joe Ritter            USA                    1988
*Phillip Paley, Heidi Helmer, Amanda Goodwin*
A youngster finally plucks up the courage to introduce
himself to a beautiful girl he has been admiring on the
beach, but finds that she merely wants to use him to
gain an introduction to one of his friends – a local rock
star. A silly teen comedy-drama that mixes in the
usual blend of humour, action and inanity; the heavy
metal soundtrack and occasional doses of tension that
never amount to anything are considerable
annoyances.
COM                                       75 min
V                                            CINE

## BEACH GIRLS, THE *                          18
Pat Townsend          USA                    1982
*Debra Blee, Val Kline, Jeana Tomasina, Judson
Vaughn, James Daughton, Adam Rourke, Herb Braha*
A feeble and predictable sex comedy, about three
schoolgirls given the run of a beach house that belongs
to the uncle of a friend.
COM                                       89 min
B,V                                          TEVP

## BEACH HOUSE, THE **                         15
John Gallagher        USA                    1982
*Kathy McNeil, Richard Duggan, John Cosola, Ileana
Seidel, Spence Waugh, Paul Anderson*
Kids share a beach house for a week of sun, sea, sand
and sex in this mild and vacuous film.
Aka: DOWN THE SHORE
COM                                       76 min
B,V                                           CBS

## BEACH OF THE WAR GODS **
Wang Yu               CHINA                  1974
*Wang Yu, Lung Fei, Tien Yeh*
Some good scenes in this story of Chinese villagers
fighting off Japanese pirates.
Aka: ZHAN SHEN TAN
MAR                       78 min (ort 100 min)
B,V                                           RNK

## BEACHES ***                                 15
Gary Marshall         USA                    1988
*Bette Midler, Barbara Hershey, John Heard, Spalding
Gray, Lainie Kazan, James Read, Grace Johnston,
Mayim Bialik, Marcie Leeds*
An aspiring singer and a poor little rich girl meet
under the boardwalk in Atlantic City and keep alive
their friendship over the course of several years by
writing letters. Later they become flatmates and the
film follows their changing fortunes, with our singer
enjoying success but her friend succumbing to a fatal
virus. An absorbing comedy-drama.
DRA                      118 min (ort 123 min)
V                                           BUENA

## BEAR, THE ***                               PG
Jean-Jacques AnnaudFRANCE                    1989
*Jack Wallace, Tcheky Karyo, Andre Lacombe*
An orphaned bear cub has to fend for itself until its
"adoption" by a huge Kodiak. However, the two now
face danger from a couple of hunters. An absorbing
nature story, made over several years and about a
million miles removed from the Disney Studios
output.
Aka: L'OURS
Boa: novel The Grizzly King by James Oliver
Curwood.
A/AD                      90 min (ort 93 min)
V                                            RCA

## BEAR ISLAND                                 PG
Don Sharp         CANADA/UK                  1979
*Donald Sutherland, Vanessa Redgrave, Richard
Widmark, Christopher Lee, Barbara Parkins, Lloyd
Bridges, Lawrence Dane*
One of the most boring films ever made. Boredom on a
grand scale. Although it is supposedly based on an
Alistair MacLean novel, it fails to bring to life his
story of a hunt for Nazi gold at an Arctic base.
Redgrave totally miscast as a Norwegian is its most
memorable feature.
Boa: novel by Alistair McLean.
THR                      102 min (ort 118 min)
B,V                                           RCA

## BEARHEART OF THE GREAT NORTHWEST ***
Rand Brooks           USA                    1964
*Marshall Reed, Fritz Feld, Joey Young, Dub Taylor,
Sugar, Buck Taylor, Denver Pyle*
An old man and his dog live alone in the mountains.
The dog was suspected of being savage but was found
to have saved a little girl from a bear. When the dog's
master is killed, it sets out to find the culprits. A
pleasant little family film, enlivened by the nice
outdoor locations.
Aka: BEARTOOTH; LEGEND OF THE
NORTHWEST
A/AD                                      75 min
B,V     AJAX/VAL L/A; PMA L/A; CHM/PPL L/A; IFS

## BEARS AND I, THE **
Bernard McEveety      USA                    1974
*Patrick Wayne, Chief Dan George, Andrew Duggan,
Michael Ansara*
A Vietnam veteran tries to mediate between Indians
and white bigots and also becomes a foster father to
three bear cubs in this mildly diverting Disney yarn.
DRA                                       89 min
B,V                                          WDV

## BEAST IN THE CELLAR, THE **
James Kelly           UK                     1970
*Flora Robson, Beryl Reid, John Hamill, T.P.
McKenna, Tessa Wyatt, David Dodimead, Christopher
Chittell, Peter Craze, John Kelland, Vernon Dobtcheff,
Dafydd Harvard*
Two unmarried sisters hide their demented brother in
a cellar. Pretty soon he escapes and goes on the
traditional murderous rampage. An average film,
sustained (but only just) by a couple of nice perform-
ances from Reid and Robson.
HOR                       90 min (ort 101 min)
B,V                                           GHV

## BEAST OF WAR, THE **                        18
Kevin Reynolds        USA                    1988
*Jason Patric, Steven Bauer, George Dzundza, Stephen
Baldwin, Don Harvey, Kabir Bedi, Erick Avari, Haim
Gerafi*
Finding themselves trapped in the desert, a Soviet
tank crew tries to reach their battalion while fighting
off Afghan tribesmen. When a soldier from the tank is
deserted by his comrades, he joins the rebels. A cliched
and slow-moving story, of poor characterisation and
dialogue, and with the standard violent action sequ-
ences. Only the nationality of the protagonists is
unusual. Filmed in Israel.
Aka: BEAST, THE
WAR                      105 min (ort 109 min)
V                                            RCA

## BEAST WITH FIVE FINGERS, THE **            15
Robert Florey         USA                    1946
*Robert Alda, Andrea King, Peter Lorre, Victor
Francen, J. Carrol Naish*
A disembodied hand gets up to the usual naughtiness.
Lorre as an ageing servant is of course excellent, in
this otherwise fairly unremarkable film. Said to have
had some of the effects worked on by Luis Bunuel but
hardly any better for that. See THE HAND for an
update of this tale.

Boa: book by W.F. Harvey.
HOR 85 min B/W
B,V WHV

**BEAST WITHIN, THE *** 18
Phillipe Mora USA 1982
*Ronny Cox, Bibi Besch, Paul Clemens, Don Gordon,*
*R.G. Armstrong, Kitty Moffat, L.Q. Jones*
Poor Besch is raped by "something" whilst on holiday
and later gives birth to a son. He grows into a
teenager/monster and goes on a killing spree, in this
pointless and bloody exercise in nastiness.
HOR 90 min (ort 98 min) Cut (1 min 7 sec)
B,V WHV

**BEAST, THE *** 15
Hilmar Oddson ICELAND 1986
*Edda Heidrunn Backmann, Trostur Gunarsson,*
*Johann Sigudarson*
After many years, a young author returns with his
girlfriend to his childhood home, a place which only
holds disturbing memories for him. An intense and
absorbing melodrama.
Aka: AS THE BEAST DIES; EINS OG SKEPNAN
DEYR
DRA 96 min
V/sh ATA L/A; RCA

**BEAST, THE *** 18
Walerian Borowczyk FRANCE 1972
*Sirpa Lane, Lisbeth Humel, Pierre Benedetti,*
*Elisabeth Kaza, Guy Trejan, Dalio, Roland Amontel,*
*Jean Martinelli, Pascale Rivault*
An elegantly erotic version of the "Beauty and the
Beast" tale, made with a good deal more care than is
usually shown for films of this genre. Unlikely to be
available in an uncut form in the UK.
Aka: DEATH'S ECSTACY
A 102 min; 93 min (VIZ)
B,V VTC L/A; JVI L/A; VIZ

**BEASTMASTER, THE *** 15
Don Coscarelli USA 1982
*Marc Singer, Tanya Roberts, Rip Torn, John Amos,*
*Rod Loomis*
More sword and sorcery as our hero, who can communicate with animals, falls in love with a slave girl
and does battle with the forces of evil, in the shape of a
wicked priest who had his father killed. Good ideas
and cinematography (by John Alcott) are largely
wasted on a film that never rises above the level of a
comic-book.
FAN 111 min (ort 118 min) (Cut at film release)
B,V,V2 TEVP; WHV

**BEASTS *** 15
Don Hawks USA 1983
*Tom Babson, Kathy Christopher, Vern Porter, Dutch*
*Schindler*
A perfect weekend reunion for two high school lovers
at a remote cabin retreat in the Rockies turns into a
nightmare as they are threatened by a prowling
grizzly and a pair of ruthless convicts. Enjoyable but
predictable thriller.
THR 92 min
B,V IDS L/A; PAN

**BEAT STREET *** 15
Stan Lathan USA 1984
*Rae Dawn Chong, Guy Davis, John Chardiet, Leon W.*
*Grant, Robert Taylor, Saundra Santiago*
Lively and noisy film, telling of the efforts of a group
of youngsters to escape the poverty of their surround-
ings through dance and music. Shot entirely on
location in New York City. A slick and flashy version
of WILD STYLE aimed clearly at the breakdancing
set and produced by Harry Belafonte.
MUS 104 min
B,V RNK; ORION

**BEAT THE DEVIL *** U
John Huston USA 1954
*Humphrey Bogart, Jennifer Jones, Peter Lorre, Ivor*
*Bernard, Marco Tulli, Gina Lollabrigida, Robert*
*Morley, Edward Underdown*
Confused satire about con-men in Africa who are
intent on double-crossing each other in the search for
a uranium mine. Scripted by Huston and Truman
Capote but for all that, one of Bogart's less well known
films, and rightly so.
Boa: book by J. Helvick.
COM 89 min; 96 min (VCC) B/W
B,V CBS; VCC (VHS only)

**BEAT, THE *** 18
Paul Mones USA 1987
*John Savage, David Jacobson, Kara Glover, William*
*McNamara, Jeffrey Horowitz*
A strange misfit joins the toughest class in a New
York high school and is at first pushed around by the
street gangs but eventually wins them over with his
love of poetry and mystical fantasy. A confused and
earnest film that says nothing original; and takes a
long time doing it.
DRA 98 min
V VES

**BEATLES: A HARD DAY'S NIGHT *** U
Richard Lester UK 1964
*George Harrison, Paul McCartney, John Lennon,*
*Ringo Starr, Wilfrid Brambell, Norman Rossington,*
*Victor Spinetti, Anna Quayle, John Junkin, Deryck*
*Guyler, Kenneth Haigh, Richard Vernon, Lionel Blair*
Wonderfully fresh at the time, this is a zany musical
comedy vehicle for The Beatles, that follows them on a
train journey from Liverpool to London to take part in
a TV show. The first venture for the group into film
and containing some of their best songs from that
period.
Aka: HARD DAY'S NIGHT, A
MUS 89 min (ort 98 min) B/W
B,V VES/PVG

**BEATLES: HELP! *** U
Dick Lester UK 1965
*John Lennon, Paul McCartney, George Harrison,*
*Ringo Starr, Leo McKern, Eleanor Bron, Victor*
*Spinetti, Roy Kinnear, Patrick Cargill*
Very much a vehicle film for the Fab Four, this
episodic and anarchic attempt to build on the success
of A HARD DAY'S NIGHT has The Beatles being
chased by a religious sect from the Far East, who wish
to regain a sacred ring. Frenetic and tiring, but worth
seeing if only for songs such as "Ticket To Ride" and
"You've Got To Hide Your Love Away."
Aka: HELP!
MUS 90 min (ort 92 min)
V/sh VCC

**BEATLES: THE MAGICAL MYSTERY TOUR *** PG
John Lennon/Ringo Starr/Paul McCartney/George
Harrison UK 1967
*John Lennon, Ringo Starr, Paul McCartney, George*
*Harrison, Jessie Robins, Victor Spinetti*
A silly, plotless and self-indulgent vanity vehicle for
The Beatles, that follows the fortunes of a coachload of
travellers who, having had their day out hijacked by
some magicians, stagger from one inconsequential
adventure to another. Well worth hearing, but too
dated and turgid to be worth watching. Songs include
"The Fool On The Hill", "Blue Jay Way" and "Your
Mother Should Know".
Aka: MAGICAL MYSTERY TOUR, THE
MUS 50 min (ort 60 min) mTV
V/sh VCC

**BEATLES: YELLOW SUBMARINE **** U
George Dunning UK 1968

*Voices of: Paul Angelis, John Clive, Dick Emery, Geoff Hughes, Lance Percival*
A charming musical fantasy that offers brilliant animated sequences and Beatles tunes – an unbeatable combination. The story takes The Beatles on a journey to Pepperland, where they have to free its music-loving folk from the wicked Blue Meanies. A film of rich inventiveness that marked a highpoint for British animation; it has yet to be equalled.
Aka: YELLOW SUBMARINE
CAR                                              82 min
V                                                 WHV

### BEAUTY AND DENISE **                          15
Neal Israel            USA                       1988
*David Carradine, Julia Duffy, Dinah Manoff*
A woman witnesses the murder of a top politician at the White House and finds herself in danger, so a tough cop is assigned to protect her. However, they discover that the murder was carried out by a sinister secret organisation and soon find themselves embroiled in a political intrigue.
A/AD                                             92 min
V                                                 MED

### BEAUTY AND THE BEAST ***
Fielder Cook           USA                       1976
*George C. Scott, Trish Van Devere, Virginia McKenna, Bernard Lee, Patricia Quinn, Michael N. Harbour, William Relton*
A newer version of the classic fairy tale of the father who is forced to give his youngest daughter to the Beast. Though it cannot compare to Cocteau's masterpiece LA BELLE ET LA BETE, good acting and some striking make-up (by Del Acevedo, John Chambers and Dan Striepke) make it worthwhile.
JUV                                         86 min mTV
B,V                                            VCL/CBS

### BEAUTY AND THE BEAST ***                       U
Eugene Marner          USA                       1987
*Rebecca DeMornay, John Savage, Yossi Graber, Michael Schneider, Carmela Marner, Ruth Harlpa, Joseph Bee, Jack Messenger, Tzipi Mor, Fira Kanter, Rafi Godlvasser, Eduardo Hobshar, Nitzan Zytzer, Eran Lavy, Deborah Sherph*
Another reworking of this classic fairy tale, intended to show that the value of individuals should not be based on their physical appearance. An enjoyable and competent rendition.
JUV                                              90 min
V/sh                                              WHV

### BEAUTY OF THE BARBARIAN **                     18
Al Bradley (Alfonso Brescia)
                       ITALY/SPAIN
*Lincoln Tate, Lucretia Love, Paola Tedesco, Mirta Miller, Genia Woods, Benito Stefanelli, Solly Stubbing, Robert Vidmark*
Fantasy adventure story, in which the Queen of the Barbarians seeks out the secret of the sacred fire, in an effort to conquer The Kingdom, protected by Darma, a supposed god, made immortal by the flames of the sacred fire. Another costumed romp, OK in its way but hardly memorable.
FAN                                90 min Cut (31 sec)
B,V                                               AVR

### BECAUSE HE'S MY FRIEND ***
Ralph Nelson           AUSTRALIA                 1978
*Karen Black, Keir Dullea, Jack Thompson, Tom Oliver, Don Reid, Barbara Stephens, Warwick Poulsen*
Touching story of a couple with a mentally retarded son, and the problems they face in trying to cope with this.
DRA                                         91 min mTV
B,V,V2                                            GOV

### BECKET ****                                    PG
Peter Glenville        UK                        1964
*Richard Burton, Peter O'Toole, Donald Wolfit, Martita Hunt, Pamela Brown, John Gielgud, Sian Phillips, Paolo Stoppa, Gino Cervi, David Weston, Percy Herbert, Nial McGinnis, Felix Aylmer, John Phillips, Frank Pettingell*
A film version of Anouilh's play telling of Becket's career and eventual martyrdom, that moves at a leisurely pace from his early days and friendship with King Henry II to his eventual death at the instigation of the monarch. A powerful and absorbing study, filmed on location in England and strikingly photographed by Geoffrey Unsworth. AA: Screen (Adapt) (Edward Anhalt).
Boa: play by Jean Anouilh.
DRA                             142 min (ort 149 min)
B,V                          ODY/CBS; CH5 (VHS only)

### BED OF A THOUSAND PLEASURES ***
Anthony M. Dawson (Antonio Margheriti)
                       ITALY                     1972
*Barbara Bouchet, Femi Benussi, Barbara Marzano*
Film version of several of these classic Arabic tales. A colourful and fairly well made romp.
Aka: 1001 NIGHTS; FINALMENTE . . . LE MILLE E UNA NOTTE
A/AD                                             92 min
B,V                                          DER; VPD

### BEDAZZLED **                                   PG
Stanley Donen          UK                        1967
*Peter Cook, Dudley Moore, Eleanor Bron, Raquel Welch, Alba, Michael Bates, Bernard Spear, Parnell McGarry, Howard Goorney, Barry Humphries, Daniele Noel, Robert Russell, Michael Trubshawe*
Limp, unfunny and terribly dated attempt to update the Faust legend, with a short-order chef selling his soul to the Devil in return for the girl of his dreams. One of the few redeeming features is Peter Cook's portrayal of the Devil.
COM                                             103 min
B, V/h, V2, LV                                    CBS

### BEDFORD INCIDENT, THE ***                      PG
James B. Harris        USA                       1965
*Richard Widmark, Sidney Poitier, James MacArthur, Martin Balsam, Wally Cox, Donald Sutherland, Eric Portman*
Cold War story of a US naval destroyer on a routine NATO patrol near the coast of Greenland, that encounters an unidentified submarine. A battle of wits now takes place, driving all concerned to near breaking point. A strong cast and tightly directed story hold one's attention right to the end.
Boa: book by M. Rascovich.
WAR                                        98 min B/W
V                                                 RCA

### BEDKNOBS AND BROOMSTICKS ***                    U
Robert Stevenson       USA                       1971
*Angela Lansbury, David Tomlinson, Sam Jaffe, Roddy McDowall, John Ericson, Roy Snart, Cindy O'Callaghan, Ian Weighill, Bruce Forsyth, Tessie O'Shea*
Set in 1940, this film tells the story of three evacuee children who defeat an invasion attempt against Britain. They are helped by a kind witch who owns a magic bedstead. Not brilliant but it has a certain charm. The animated sequences are directed by Ward Kimball. AA: Effects (Vis) (Alan Maley/Eustace Lycett/Danny Lee).
Boa: novel Bedknob And Broomstick by Mary Norton.
COM                             97 min; 112 min (WDV)
B,V                                     RNK L/A; WDV

### BEDMANIA **
Jacques LemoineCANADA/FRANCE                     1974
*Alice Sapritch, Michel Balabra, Jean Leferre*

A bed provides the link in a number of stories in this uneven sex farce.
Aka: LE LIT; LE PLUMARD EN FOLIE
A                                                    80 min
B,V                                                     INT

## BEDROOM EYES ***                          18
William Fruet          USA                  1984
*Kenneth David Gilman, Dayle Haddon, Barbara Law, Christine Cattle*
A man out jogging becomes fascinated when he glimpses a beautiful woman, and finds himself driven to spy on her constantly. When she is murdered, he becomes the prime suspect and is forced to search for the culprit in order to clear his name. An offbeat and sometimes comical murder mystery, fairly entertaining but often illogical. Followed by a sequel.
DRA                                                 89 min
B,V                                        PRV L/A; CBS

## BEDROOM EYES 2 **                         18
Chuck Vincent (Mark Ubell)                  1988
*Wings Hauser, Kathy Shower, Linda Blair, Jane Hamilton, Joe Giardina, Kevin Thomsen, Jennifer Delora, Harvey Siegel, Stan Schwartz*
A sequel to the earlier film, telling of a man who embarks on an affair in order to make his wife jealous. However, when his partner is found murdered all the evidence would appear to point to his wife being the suspect. Average.
THR                                                 90 min
V                                                   CINE

## BEDROOM WINDOW, THE ***                   15
Curtis Hanson          USA                  1987
*Steve Guttenberg, Terry Lambert, Elizabeth McGovern, Isabelle Huppert, Paul Shenar, Frederick Coffin, Carl Lumbly, Wallace Shawn, Brad Greenquist*
A man having an affair with his boss' wife, finds himself the main suspect in a series of brutal killings after reporting an attack on a girl, seen from his bedroom window by his lover, who is not prepared to report it herself. A suspenseful and complex homage to Hitchcock that may be unbelievable but is always engrossing.
THR                                                108 min
B,V                                                  CBS

## BEDTIME WITH ROSIE *
Wolf Rilla             UK                   1974
*Una Stubbs, Diana Dors, Ivor Burgoyne, Johnny Briggs, Margaret Lewis, Ned Lynch, Tony Doohan, Nicky Henson*
A young pregnant girl stays overnight at her aunt's on her way to a new life in Holland, but tries to seduce auntie's lodger during her stay. Another feeble celebration of smutty humour masquerading as an honest sex comedy; the Italians do this sort of thing so much better.
COM                                   70 min (ort 76 min)
B,V,V2                                          IVER/CBS

## BEER **                                   15
Patrick Kelly          USA                  1985
*Loretta Swit, Rip Torn, Kenneth Mars, David Alan Grier, William Russ, Saul Stein, Dick Shawn*
A woman advertising executive mounts a campaign for a brand of beer which is claimed to turn ordinary wimps into real macho men. Failed spoof on Madison Avenue marketing techniques that goes flat very quickly.
Aka: SELLING OF AMERICA, THE
COM                                                 80 min
B,V                                                  RNK

## BEES, THE *
Alfredo Zacharias      USA                  1978
*John Saxon, Angel Tompkins, John Carradine, Claudio Brook, Alicia Encinias*

Low-budget horror yarn, about killer bees threatening the very existence of mankind. Uninspired and nonsensical dross. See also THE SWARM.
HOR                                                 93 min
B,V,V2                                               INT

## BEETHOVEN'S NEPHEW *                      15
Paul Morrissey
AUSTRIA/FRANCE/WEST GERMANY  1985
*Wolfgang Reichmann, Jane Birkin, Nathalie Baye*
A glossy and rather irritating drama, following the relationship between this great composer and his nephew, who was brought up by Beethoven and lived with him for many years. Undeniably beautiful to look at, but a superficial study at best. However, at least the music is worthwhile.
Aka: LE NEUVEU DE BEETHOVEN
DRA                                  99 min (ort 102 min)
V                                                    NWV

## BEETLEJUICE ****                         15
Tim Burton             USA                  1988
*Michael Keaton, Geena Davis, Alec Baldwin, Jeffrey Jones, Sylvia Sidney, Susan Kellerman, Catherine O'Hara, Winona Ryder, Robert Goulet, Glenn Shadix, Dick Cavett, Annie McEnroe*
A newly deceased couple have a hard time coping with the obnoxious family who've moved into their home, so they call on the services of the title spirit. A celebration of incredible special effects and some very funny moments, most of which take place in the hereafter. The story is by Michael McDowell and Larry Wilson, with cinematography by Thomas Ackerman and a score by Danny Elfman. AA: Make (Steve Laporte/Robert Short).
COM                                                 89 min
V/sh                                                 WHV

## BEFORE AND AFTER **                       PG
Kim Friedman           USA                  1979
*Patty Duke Astin, Bradford Dillman, Barabara Feldon, Art Hindle, Conchata Ferrell, Rosemary Murphy, Kenneth Mars, Randolph Powell, Betty White, Vern Taylor, Eve Roberts, Jennifer Kramer, Tara Lynn Bottorf, Rick Johnson*
After her husband turns forty and walks out on her, a woman sets out to lose weight in order to regain her self esteem. Attractive once more, she has to decide whether she should wait for her husband to return or make a new life for herself in this mild comedy-drama.
DRA                                 92 min (ort 100 min) mTV
V                                                    VCC

## BEGGAR'S OPERA, THE ***
Peter Brook            UK                   1953
*Laurence Olivier, Stanley Holloway, Dorothy Tutin, Daphne Anderson, Mary Clare, George Devine, Hugh Griffith, Yvonne Furneaux, Sandra Dorne, Athene Seyler, George Rose, Margot Grahame, Kenneth Williams, Dennis Cannan*
A captured highwayman puts on an opera in Newgate jail based on his own exploits, in this potted version of a work from 1728 by John Gay. A rousing and spirited adaptation, from stage director Brook in his film directing debut. Co-produced by Olivier.
Boa: opera by John Gay.
DRA                                  90 min (ort 94 min)
B,V                                                 TEVP

## BEGINNER'S LUCK **                        18
Frank Mouris/Caroline Ahlfors Mouris
USA                  1984
*Sam Rush, Riley Steiner, Charles Homet, Kate Talbot, Mickey Coburn*
Story of a strange menage-a-trois involving a lusty couple and their lonely and shy law student neighbour. A bright and cheerful little comedy which, if a little silly is nonetheless redeemed by its endearing and zany humour.

COM                                     85 min
B,V                                     NWV

## BEGINNING OF THE END, THE *
Bert I. Gordon          USA             1957
*Peter Graves, Peggie Castle, Morris Ankrum, Richard
Benedict*
Giant grasshoppers threaten the world, in this en-
dearingly silly B-picture of the 1950s.
FAN                                 74 min B/W
B,V                                     VIV

## BEGUILED, THE ***                    15
Don Siegel              USA             1971
*Clint Eastwood, Geraldine Page, Elizabeth Hartman,
Jo Ann Harris, Darleen Carr, Pamelyn Ferdin, Mae
Mercer*
Brooding atmospheric film about a wounded Yankee
soldier who hides out at a Confederate school for
young ladies. His presence there leads to jealousy and
eventual death. An extremely well made and unusual
Eastwood film.
Boa: novel by T. Cullinan.
DRA                         100 min (ort 109 min)
B,V                                     CIC

## BEHIND CONVENT WALLS ***             18
Walerian Borowczyk      ITALY           1977
*Ligia Branice, Marina Pierro, Howard Ross, Gabriella
Goaccobe, Loredana Martinez*
A classic interpretation of the sexual feelings and
fantasies of the women who spend their lives in the
cloistered atmosphere of a 19th century convent. A
confusing narrative detracts, but this film does not
lack for atmosphere.
Aka: BEHIND THE CONVENT WALLS; INTERIOR
OF A CONVENT; L'INTERNO DI UN CONVENTO
Boa: story Roman Walks by Stendhal (Marie Henri
Beyle).
DRA        90 min Cut (9 sec in addition to film cuts)
V                                   VPD; ROGUE

## BEHIND THE GREEN DOOR *
Jim Mitchell/Artie Mitchell
                        USA             1972
*Marilyn Chambers, John Keyes, George S. McDonald*
A woman is kidnapped by a strange sex club and
forced to participate in every form of sex imaginable,
in this ugly hardcore film, that now has a certain cult
status in the USA.
A                                       72 min
B,V                                     TCX

## BEHIND THE SCENES OF AN ADULT MOVIE **
                                        R18
Joe Sherman             USA             1981
*Samantha Fox, Veronica Hart, John Leslie, Danielle,
Herschel Savage, Jesie St James, Ron Jeremy,
Georgina Spelvin, Joey Civera*
Most of this film consists of cuts from other Cal Vista
movies together with conversation and comments
from the various stars interspersed throughout. They
discuss how they got into the business and their
feelings about it and the film has a behind-the-scenes
look at the making of EXPOSE ME NOW.
Aka: BEHIND THE SCENES OF AN X-RATED
MOVIE
A              68 min (ort 84 min) Cut (4 min 25 sec)
B,V,V2                              TCX; SHEP

## BEING THERE **                        15
Hal Ashby               USA             1980
*Peter Sellers, Shirley MacLaine, Jack Warden, Melvyn
Douglas, David Clennon, Richard Dysart*
A childlike gardener whose only knowledge of the
world comes from TV is, on the death of his employer,
thrust out into the real world where he is taken into
the homes of the powerful, following a chance acci-

dent. His simple words charm all, who read into them
great wisdom. A witty but overlong attack on Amer-
ican politics reminding one of Hans Andersen's tale
"The Emperor's New Clothes" but minus the ending.
AA: S. Actor (Douglas).
Boa: novel by Jerzy Kosinski.
COM                 121 min; 124 min (PARK)
B,V,V2,LV               CBS; PARK (VHS only)

## BEING, THE *                          15
Jackie Kong             USA             1980
*Martin Landau, Jose Ferrer, Dorothy Malone, Ruth
Buzzi, Rexx Coltrane (Johnny Commander), Kent
Perkins, Marianne Gordon Rogers, Murray Langston,
Kinky Friedman, Johnny Dark*
A number of people go missing in a small town and it
would seem that they have fallen victim to a mutant
monster spawned by nuclear waste. A trashy grade-Z
horror film with a touch of humour here and there, but
still a dismal experience. Producer William Oscoe was
Kong's husband at the time and appears under the
name Rexx Coltrane but was also known as Johnny
Commander.
Aka: EASTER SUNDAY
HOR                                     82 min
B,V                                     ARF

## BELIEVERS, THE ***                    18
John Schlesinger        USA             1987
*Martin Sheen, Helen Shaver, Harley Cross, Robert
Loggia, Elizabeth Wilson, Harris Yulin, Lee
Richardson, Richard Masur, Carla Pinza, Jimmy
Smits*
A widowed police psychologist moves with his son to
New York City and finds himself threatened by a
demonic cult whose followers believe in child sacrifice
when he's called upon to investigate a series of
ritualistic child murders. A well crafted and gripping
story.
Boa: novel The Religion by Nicholas Conde.
HOR                                    110 min
V/sh                                    RCA

## BELL JAR, THE ***                     1979
Larry Peerce            USA             1979
*Marilyn Hassett, Julie Harris, Anne Jackson, Mary
Louise Weller, Barbara Barrie, Robert Klein, Donna
Mitchell, Jameson Parker, Thaao Penghlis*
Strong but uneven version of Sylvia Plath's incredibly
depressing and partly autobiographical novel, telling
of the mental breakdown of an intellectual girl in the
1950s. Joyful it is not.
Boa: novel by Sylvia Plath.
DRA                                    107 min
B,V                                     VTC

## BELL OF HELL, THE **
Claudio Guerin Hill    FRANCE/SPAIN     1973
*Viveca Lindfors, Renaud Verley, Alfredo Mayo,
Maribel Martin, Nuria Gimeno, Christine Betzner,
Saturno Cerra, Nicole Vesperini, Erasmo Pascual,
Susana Latour*
A young man plans his revenge on the relatives whom
he holds responsible for placing him in an asylum.
Average.
Aka: BELL FROM HELL, A; LA CAMPANA DEL
INFIERNO
THR                                     97 min
B,V                             DVP L/A; VCL/CBS

## BELLA **
Alexander Kubelka       USA             1974
*Eric Edwards, Dana Stone, Jake Teague, Tracy
Adams, Arcadia Lake*
Arriving home from school, Tracy discovers her
mother making passionate love in the basement
garage of Tom, their neighbour. Later Tracy visits
Tom and he makes love to her too. However, she

becomes jealous and threatens to expose her mother's affair to her father. Finally, a truce is called and mother and daughter agree to share Tom. And what of Tracy's father? Well he never finds out anything.
Osca: SUMMER HEAT (asa)

| A | 52 min |
| B,V | HAR |

### BELLBOY, THE **   U
Jerry Lewis   USA   1960
*Jerry Lewis, Alex Corry, Bob Clayton, Sonny Sands, Milton Berle, Walter Winchell*
Lewis' directorial debut is the comic tale of a blundering bellboy working at the Fountainbleau Hotel in Miami Beach. No plot, just a series of madcap slapstick adventures as Lewis clumsily staggers from one mishap to another. A dated comedy.

| COM | 72 min B/W |
| V | COL |

### BELLE STARR STORY, THE **
Nathan Wich (Lina Wertmuller)
ITALY   1967
*Elsa Martinelli, Robert Woods, George Eastman (Luigi Montefiore), Francesca Righini, Dan Harrison*
A romantic Western with Martinelli as the notorious female outlaw being spurned by her outlaw lover and taking revenge in a way he is certain to appreciate.
Aka: BELLE STARR; IL MIO CORPO PER UN POKER; QUEEN OF DIAMONDS

| WES | 95 min |
| B,V,V2 | ALPHA/INT (Betamax and VHS only); FFV |

### BELLES OF ST TRINIANS, THE **   U
Frank Lauder   UK   1954
*Alastair Sim, Joyce Grenfell, George Cole, Hermione Baddeley, Beryl Reid, Betty Ann Davies, Irene Handl, Mary Merrall, Renee Houston, Joan Sims, Balbina, Guy Middleton, Sidney James, Arthur Howard, Richard Wattis*
First in a series of slapstick films centred on an unruly school for girls where more time is spent reading up racing form than on the study of the "three Rs". Based on Ronald Searle's cartoons of a dotty school and its uncontrollable pupils. Occasional sparks of humour are never enough to get this patchy comedy going, though Sim does his best in two roles. BLUE MURDER AT ST TRINIANS followed.

| COM | 92 min B/W |
| V | WHV |

### BELLMAN AND TRUE ***   15
Richard Loncraine   UK   1987
*Bernard Hill, Kieran O'Brien, Richard Hope, Frances Tomelty, Derek Newark, John Kavanagh, Ken Bones*
Hill stars as a timid computer programmer who is drawn into an association with criminals without realising the consequences. When they kidnap his stepson he is forced to use his expertise in a bank robbery. A low-key and understated film whose elements serve as a framework for an interesting character study rather than simply as part of a straight crime film.

| A/AD | 117 min |
| B,V | CAN |

### BELLS **   15
Michael Anderson   CANADA   1980
*Richard Chamberlain, John Houseman, Sara Botsford, Robin Gammell, Gary Reineke, Barry Morse, Alan Scarfe, James B. Douglas, Kenneth Pogue, Neil Munro, Jefferson Mappin, Tom Butler, Colin Fox, Luba Goy, Lenore Zann*
Telephones are turned into deadly devices by an ingenious long-distance killer. When a girl is killed, her former tutor sets out to find out who is behind the killings. A cliched and unexciting thriller, cut to 80 minutes in a TV version.
Aka: MURDER BY PHONE

| THR | 119 min |
| B,V,V2 | GHV |

### BELLS OF ST MARY'S, THE **   U
Leo McCarey   USA   1945
*Ingrid Bergman, Bing Crosby, Henry Travers, William Gargan, Ruth Donnelly, Joan Carroll, Martha Sleeper, Rhys Williams*
A Catholic priest is sent to a poor community where he becomes involved in running a parish school where Bergman is the Sister Superior. Meandering and over-sentimental sequel to "Going My Way", with Bing introducing the song "Aren't You Glad You're You?". AA: Sound (Stephen Dunn).

| DRA | 121 min B/W |
| V | VCC |

### BELLY OF AN ARCHITECT, THE ***   15
Peter Greenaway   ITALY/UK   1987
*Brian Dennehy, Chloe Webb, Lambert Wilson, Sergio Fantoni, Stephania Casini, Vanni Corbellini*
A hard-drinking American architect and his beautiful wife travel to Rome to set up an exhibition. As he becomes increasingly obsessed with his failing health and his wife's unfaithfulness the beauty of Rome becomes no more than a backdrop for some symbolic and fascinating observations on art, life and mortality. The striking cinematography is by Sacha Vierny.

| DRA | 113 min |
| V/h | PAL |

### BELOW THE BELT ***
Robert Fowler   USA   1974
*Regina Baff, Mildred Burke, John C. Becher, Annie McGreevey, Ric Mancini, Jane O'Brien, Shirley Stoler, Dolph Sweet*
A strange off-beat and low-budget film about a waitress who becomes a lady wrestler in a search for fame and fortune. An inconsistent but often fascinating series of character studies.
Boa: novel To Smithereens by Rosalyn Drexler.

| DRA | 91 min |
| B,V,V2 | VPD; TCX |

### BELSTONE FOX, THE **   PG
James Hill   UK   1973
*Eric Porter, Rachel Roberts, Jeremy Kemp, Dennis Waterman, Heather Wright, Bill Travers*
Story of an orphaned fox cub reared with the hounds. This leads to tragic consequences in a somewhat mediocre film. Disappointing.
Aka: FREE SPIRIT
Boa: novel The Ballad Of The Belstone Fox by David Rook.

| DRA | 99 min (ort 103 min) |
| B,V | RNK; MIA (VHS only) |

### BEN HUR **
1987
Competent animation based on Wallace's classic novel and following some of the hero's most memorable adventures.
Boa: novel by Lew Wallace.

| CAR | 60 min |
| V | STYL |

### BEN HUR ****   PG
William Wyler   USA   1959
*Charlton Heston, Jack Hawkins, Martha Scott, Stephen Boyd, Hugh Griffith, Sam Jaffe, Finlay Currie, Terence Longdon, Andre Morrell, Haya Harareet, Cathy O'Donnell, John Le Mesurier*
A lavish remake of the 1926 silent classic, telling of the conflict between the Jews and Romans at the time of Christ, and of the bitter rivalry that develops between two ex-friends, culminating in a spectacular chariot race. AA: Pic, Dir, Actor (Heston), S. Actor (Griffith), Cin (R. Surtees), Art/Set (Horning and Carfagno/Hunt), Edit (Winters/Dunning), Cost (Haf-

fenden), Score (M. Rozsa), Sound (F. Milton), Effects (R. MacDonald – vis/M. Lory – aud).
Boa: novel by Lew Wallace.
DRA                                                209 min
V                                                      MGM

## BENEATH THE PLANET OF THE APES **        15
Ted Post              USA              1969
*Charlton Heston, James Franciscus, Kim Hunter,
James Gregory, Maurice Evans, Linda Harrison,
Victor Buono, Paul Richards, Thomas Gomez, Natalie
Trundy*
This first sequel to PLANET OF THE APES has our astronauts caught up in a battle between the apes and human mutants, who have survived the nuclear holocaust and now live underground. Good ideas are let down by tired and often pompous script. Followed by ESCAPE FROM THE PLANET OF THE APES.
FAN                                                95 min
B,V,LV                                               CBS

## BENGAZI **
John Brahm            USA              1954
*Richard Conte, Victor McLaglen, Richard Carlson,
Mala Powers*
Routine adventure yarn is set in the African desert, with an assortment of unsavoury characters who find themselves trapped in a desert shrine by marauding natives.
THR                                            77 min B/W
B,V                                                  KVD

## BENJI ***                                      U
Joe Camp              USA              1974
*Peter Breck, Christopher Connelly, Deborah Walley,
Edgar Buchanan, Frances Bavier, Patsy Garrett, Allen
Fiuzat, Cynthia Smith, Terry Carter, Tom Lester,
Mark Slade, Herb Vigran, Larry Swortz, J.D. Young,
Erwin Hearne*
Lovable mutt saves three children from being kidnapped. An ideal family oriented film; followed by FOR THE LOVE OF BENJI and BENJI THE HUNTED.
COM                                                85 min
B,V,V2      VES/PVG; WDV (Betamax and VHS only)

## BENJI THE HUNTED **                            U
Joe Camp              USA              1987
*Red Steagall, Frank Inn, Nancy Francis, Mike Francis*
Benji gets lumbered with the task of finding a home for some orphaned cougar cubs in this combination of canine and wilderness adventure films. A mediocre sequel to FOR THE LOVE OF BENJI.
Aka: HUNTED, THE
JUV                                                86 min
B,V                                          WDV; BUENA

## BERENSTAIN BEARS MEET BIG PAW, THE ***    U
                      USA              1980
One in a series of likeable animated adventures involving a family of bears. In this one they hear of the legend of "Big Paw" – a voracious giant bear who, should a bear ever become too greedy, will descend on the town with the intention of gobbling it up. When the bears are confronted by Big Paw they discover that their ideas were mistaken.
CAR                                                47 min
V                                                    EHE

## BERK, THE ***                                 PG
Robert Moore          USA              1971
*Gene Wilder, Ellen Burstyn, Bob Newhart, Cloris
Leachman, Nancy Walker, Valerie Harper, Norman
Fell, Martha Scott, Rob Reiner, Richard Schaal, Gino
Conforti, Robert Sampson, Dick Gautier, Gerald
Michenaud, John Archer*
The story of two poker-playing buddies and their domestic troubles; one has an unhappy marriage whilst the other has just lost his job. Together they decide to paint the town red in this witty and

engaging comedy, scripted by James L. Brooks.
Aka: NIGHT CAPER (MANHAT or KRP);
THURSDAY'S GAME (CBS)
COM                       93 min; 98 min (IVS) mTV
B,V                        CBS; MANHAT; IVS; KRP

## BERLIN AFFAIR, THE ***                        18
Liliana Cavini  ITALY/WEST GERMANY     1985
*Gudrun Landgrebe, Kevin McNally, Mio Takaki, Hans
Zischler, Massimo Girotti, Philippe Leroy, William
Berger, Andrea Prodan, Tomoko Tanaka, John
Steiner, Enrica Mario Scrivano*
The daughter of the Japanese ambassador to Nazi Germany, seduces both a woman and her husband, drawing them both into a self-destructive if passionate affair. Captures well the claustrophobic atmosphere of Berlin in 1937 and the creeping totalitarian takeover of all aspects of German life.
Aka: AFFAIRE BERLINESE; BERLIN INTERIOR;
INTERNO BERLINELE; LEIDENSCHAFTEN
Boa: novel The Buddhist Cross by Junichiro Tanizaki.
DRA                                  93 min (ort 121 min)
B,V                                                  RNK

## BERLIN BLUES **                               15
Ricardo Franco                         1989
*Julia Migenes-Johnson, Keith Baxter*
The story of a romance between a Berlin nightclub singer and an East German musician. A pleasant soap opera of no great depth.
DRA                                               101 min
V                                                  PATHE

## BERLIN EXPRESS ***
Jacques Tourneur      USA              1948
*Merle Oberon, Robert Ryan, Charles Korvin, Paul
Lukas, Robert Coote, Reinhold Schunzel, Roman
Toporow, Peter Von Zerneck, Otto Waldis*
Taut spy thriller set in post-WW2 Berlin, with the members of several nations working together to prevent a German statesman being kidnapped by an underground Nazi movement.
Osca: ISLE OF THE DEAD
THR                                            83 min B/W
B,V                                                  KVD

## BERSERKER *                                   18
Jeff Richard          USA              1988
*Josef Alan Johnson, Valerie Sheldon, Greg Dawson,
George Flower*
An ancient Viking warrior with a taste for human flesh, comes back to life and threatens six college students on vacation. A new variation on the well-played theme of kids in mortal danger, atrociously made, badly acted, ludicrously plotted.
Aka: BERSERKER: THE NORDIC CURSE (PENG)
HOR              80 min (ort 85 min) Cut (1 min 4 sec)
B,V                                   VIDMO L/A; PENG

## BERT RIGBY, YOU'RE A FOOL **                 15
Carl Reiner           USA              1989
*Robert Lindsay, Robbie Coltrane, Bruno Kirby, Corbin
Bensen, Anne Bancroft, Cathryn Bradshaw, Jackie
Gayle*
A coal miner who dreams of a singing career is spotted by a director of TV commercials when he enters a talent contest. He soon finds himself on his way to Hollywood. Written by Reiner, this flabby musical comedy is nothing more than a vehicle for Lindsay, who achieved great success in the stage musical "Me And My Girl". Passable, but hardly exhilarating.
MUS                                  90 min (ort 95 min)
V                                                    WHV

## BEST BIT OF CRUMPET IN DENMARK, THE *
Ole Ege              DENMARK           1972
*Lonny Feddersen, Leni Kjellander, Ingerlije Gaarde,
Gotha Andersen, Sune Pilgaard, Ulla Bjergskov, Palle
Arrestrup, Soren Hansen, Ole Ege, Connie Nielsen*

Tedious sex film about a young girl's progress from country wench to luxury whore.
Aka: BORDELLET: EN GLAEDESPIGES ERINDRINGER; BORDELLO

| | |
|---|---|
| A | 90 min |
| B,V | XTACY/KRP |

## BEST DEFENSE *
Willard Huyck        USA                     18
                                            1984
*Eddie Murphy, Dudley Moore, Kate Capshaw, George Dzundza, Helen Shaver, David Rasche*
An industrial engineer accidentally obtains plans for a super-tank that are being sought by the KGB. Almost totally unfunny and often quite unpleasant.
Boa: novel Easy And Hard Ways Out by R. Grossbach.

| | |
|---|---|
| COM | 90 min |
| V/h | CIC |

## BEST FRIENDS **                         PG
Norman Jewison        USA
*Burt Reynolds, Goldie Hawn, Jessica Tandy, Barnard Hughes, Audra Lindley, Keenan Wynn, Richard Libertini, Ron Silver, Carol Locatell*
Unexpected complications arise when two screenwriters who have lived together as lovers for 5 years get married. Some funny moments, and a few good cameos from supporting stars, are not enough in this lacklustre comedy. The script is by screenwriting team Barry Levinson and Valerie Curtin.

| | |
|---|---|
| COM | 105 min |
| B,V | WHV |

## BEST LITTLE WHOREHOUSE IN TEXAS, THE **15
Collin Higgins        USA                   1982
*Burt Reynolds, Dolly Parton, Dom DeLuise, Charles Durning, Jim Nabors, Robert Mandan, Lois Nettleton, Theresa Merritt, Noah Beery, Barry Corbin*
Musical about the predicament a local sheriff faces when he comes under pressure to close down a rural bordello whose madam happens to be his lady friend. A flashy and ambitious venture that is at its best when it doesn't try to take itself seriously, which is not often enough. Based on a hit Broadway show.

| | |
|---|---|
| MUS | 110 min |
| B, V/h, LV | CIC |

## BEST OF BOTH WORLDS ***
Douglas Williams    CANADA                   1983
*Gaye Burgess, Sugith Varughese, Malika Mendez*
Asian parents living in Canada arrange a marriage for their son, even though he already has a girlfriend, in this likeable comedy.

| | |
|---|---|
| COM | 87 min |
| B,V,V2 | INT |

## BEST OF ENEMIES ***                      PG
Guy Hamilton        ITALY/USA               1961
*David Niven, Alberto Sordi, Michael Wilding, Amedeo Nazzari, Harry Andrews, David Opatoshu, Kenneth Fortescue, Noel Harrison, Dino De Laurentis, Duncan Macrae*
A gently satirical study of the futility of war, with an Italian and a British officer learning respect for each other during the Abyssinian campaign of WW2. The film makes a few useful points, but its impact is hardly major.

| | |
|---|---|
| WAR | 100 min (ort 104 min) |
| V | RCA |

## BEST OF FRIENDS, THE **
Michael Robertson  AUSTRALIA                1982
*Angela Punch McGregor, Graeme Blundell*
A man and woman who are friends find that their friendship is threatened when they become lovers. Average melodrama.

| | |
|---|---|
| DRA | 97 min |
| B,V | PRV L/A |

## BEST OF THE BADMEN **
William D. Russell    USA                    1952
*Robert Ryan, Claire Trevor, Robert Preston, Jack Buetel, Walter Brennan, Bruce Cabot, John Archer, Lawrence Tierney, Barton MacLane, Tom Tyler, Robert Wilke, John Cliff, Lee MacGregor, Emmett Lynn, Carleton Young*
A wrongly accused former Union cavalry officer obtains help from assorted outlaws (including the James and Younger brothers) in a bid to clear his name in this verbose and stilted Western.
Osca: SEALED CARGO

| | |
|---|---|
| WES | 81 min (ort 84 min) |
| B,V | KVD |

## BEST OF THE BEST **                       15
Bob Radler          USA                      1989
*Eric Roberts, James Earl Jones, Sally Kirkland, Phillip Rhee, John P. Ryan, John Dye, David Agresta, Tom Everett, Louise Fletcher, Simon Rhee, Christopher Penn*
Having sworn to have his revenge for the murder of his brother by a Korean karate master, a young man joins the American karate team in order to take part in an international competition. A cliched exercise in fisticuffs that blends together elements of ROCKY and THE KARATE KID.

| | |
|---|---|
| MAR | 93 min (ort 97 min) |
| V | EIV |

## BEST OF TIMES, THE **                     15
Roger Spottiswoode    USA                    1986
*Robin Williams, Kurt Russell, Pamela Reed, Holly Palance, Donald Moffat, Margaret Whitton, M. Emmet Walsh, Donovan Scott, R.G. Armstrong*
Williams plays a guy who has never been able to forget the time he muffed a winning pass in a football game at his high school, and decides to arrange a rematch for all concerned twenty years later. A patchy and almost plotless comedy, whose winning performances are chained to a losing script. Written by Ron Shelton.

| | |
|---|---|
| COM | 99 min (ort 104 min) |
| V | WHV |

## BEST REVENGE **                           18
John Trent          CANADA                   1983
*John Meard, Levon Helm, John Rhys-Davies, Alberta Watson, Moses Znaimer, Benjamin Gordon, Hrant Alianak, Tim McCauley, Lorenzo Campos, David Caldersi, Michael Ironside, Angus MacInnes, Rob Garrison, Sean Sullivan*
A small-time drug dealer is blackmailed into taking an enormous shipment of cannabis from Morocco to the USA and finds himself running into a lot of unsavoury characters and situations. Average.

| | |
|---|---|
| A/AD | 91 min |
| B,V | POLY |

## BEST SELLER **                            18
John Flynn          USA                      1987
*Brian Dennehy, James Woods, Victoria Tennant, Allison Balson, Paul Shenar, George Coe, Anne Pitoniak*
A policeman/author survives a violent robbery but remembers something of the appearance of one of his masked attackers. Several years later his life is saved by a man of this appearance, who then approaches him to write the story of his life as a hitman for a crooked businessman whom he wants to expose. Two great performances from the leads cannot mask the flaws in the Larry Cohen script.

| | |
|---|---|
| THR | 92 min (ort 110 min) |
| V/sh | RCA |

## BEST SHOT ***                             PG
David Anspaugh      USA                      1986
*Gene Hackman, Barbara Hershey, Dennis Hopper,*

*Sheb Wooley, Fern Parsons, Brad Boyle, Steve Hollar,*
*Brad Long, David Neidorf*
A former top college coach arrives at a small farming
community in the 1950s with plans to make a winning
basketball team out of the local school players as a
way of redeeming himself. Hackman gives a great
performance in this contrived but often entertaining
story. The script is by Angelo Pizzo.
Aka: HOOSIERS
DRA                                              111 min
B/h, V/h                                             RCA

## BEST YEARS OF OUR LIVES, THE ****        U
William Wyler          USA                       1946
*Dana Andrews, Teresa Wright, Virginia Mayo, Cathy*
*O'Donnell, Fredric March, Myrna Loy, Harold Russell,*
*Hoagy Carmichael, Gladys George, Steve Cochran,*
*Ray Collins*
Fine and highly moving drama about three American
soldiers returning home to civilian life at the end of
WW2 and finding it difficult to adjust. Harold Russell
is memorable in this outstanding drama. The script is
by Robert Sherwood. AA: Pic, Dir, Actor (March), S.
Actor (Russell), Edit (Daniel Mandell), Screen (Robert
E. Sherwood), Score (Hugo Friedhofer), Spec Award
(Harold Russell for bringing hope and courage to his
fellow veterans).
Boa: novel Glory For Me by MacKinlay Kantor.
DRA                    159 min (ort 172 min) B/W
V                                                 VGM

## BETRAYAL **                              15
David Jones            UK                         1983
*Jeremy Irons, Ben Kingsley, Patricia Hodge, Avril*
*Edgar, Ray Marioni, Caspar Norman, Chloe*
*Billington, Hannah Davies, Michael Konig, Alexander*
*McIntosh*
This film version of a Pinter play about the rela-
tionship between a husband, his wife and her lover,
makes use of an unusual device in that the story is
told backwards in time. A slack and dull effort despite
strong performances from all concerned.
Boa: play by Harold Pinter.
DRA                                               95 min
B,V                                                 PVG

## BETRAYAL AND REVENGE ***                 15
Zheng Kangyu           CHINA                      1986
*An Yaping, Chen Kang, Fang Jian, Pang Lin Tai,*
*Shao Xiao Kui, He Fu Sheng*
The son of an executed revolutionary who led an
abortive uprising in 1864, takes revenge for his
father's death after a period of ten years.
MAR                    104 min (ort 113 min) Cut (11 sec)
V                                                 TRAX

## BETRAYED *                               18
Constantin Costa-Gavras USA                      1988
*Tom Berenger, Debra Winger, John Heard, Betsy*
*Blair, John Mahoney, Ted Levine, Jeffrey DeMunn,*
*Albert Hall, David Clennon, Richard Libertini*
A foolish and muddled tale following the exploits of a
female FBI agent who is sent to investigate a white
supremacist group, but winds up falling in love with
her quarry instead.
DRA                    122 min (ort 127 min)
V/sh                                               WHV

## BETRAYED BY INNOCENCE **                 15
Elliot Silverstein     USA                       1986
*Barry Bostwick, Cristen Kauffman, Lee Purcell, Craig*
*Richard Nelson, Joel Colodner, Thom Christopher,*
*Paul Sorvino, Susan Marie Snyder, Philip Bruns,*
*Dendrie Allyn Taylor, Jim Townsend, Vincent*
*Pandoliano, Joe D'Angerio*
A respected documentary film-maker is seduced by a
precocious but under-age girl, and then finds himself
charged with statutory rape by her father, an over-
protective cop. A controversial issue is treated in an

entirely predictable way, in this exploitative and
formula account.
DRA                                              90 min mTV
B,V                                                 CIC

## BETSY, THE **                            18
Daniel Petrie          USA                       1978
*Laurence Olivier, Robert Duvall, Katherine Ross,*
*Tommy Lee Jones, Jane Alexander, Lesley-Anne*
*Down, Kathleen Beller, Edward Herrmann*
Film version of a novel about the wheelings and
dealings behind the scenes at a giant car company run
by the company patriarch and his family. Hammy but
enjoyable trash.
Boa: novel by Harold Robbins.
DRA                                              122 min
B,V                                                 WHV

## BETTER LATE THAN NEVER **
Richard Crenna         USA                       1979
*Harold Gould, Strother Martin, Tyne Daly, Harry*
*Morgan, Marjorie Bennett, Victor Buono, George*
*Gobel, Jeanette Nolan, Donald Pleasence, Larry*
*Storch, Lou Jacobi, Paula Trueman, Bill Fiore, Joyce*
*Bulifant, William Bogert*
A rather contrived comedy in which the old people in a
home, revolt against the petty rules and restrictions
imposed by a disagreeable matron, helped in this by
the arrival of a free-spirited newcomer.
COM                    90 min (ort 104 min) mTV
B,V,V2                                             VUL

## BETTER LATE THAN NEVER **                PG
Bryan Forbes           USA                       1982
*David Niven, Art Carney, Maggie Smith, Kimberly*
*Partridge, Catherine Hicks, Melissa Prophet*
Two older men compete for the affections of a 10-year-
old girl who just happens to stand to inherit a vast
fortune and is the granddaughter of one of them. The
pleasant South of France location is a plus but the
rubbishy script is a definite minus.
COM                    92 min (ort 95 min)
B,V,V2                                             GHV

## BETTER OFF DEAD **                       15
Savage Steve Holland   USA                       1985
*John Cusack, David Ogden Stiers, Kim Darby,*
*Demian Slade, Curtis Armstrong, Scooter Stevens,*
*Diane Franklin*
A teen comedy about a young guy who loses his
girlfriend to the butch captain of a ski team. To regain
his self-respect and win her back, he challenges him to
a downhill race. A lightheaded comedy that starts off
with lots of funny gags and then slides rapidly
downhill into cliche. A highlight is the early clay-
animation sequence by Jimmy Picker. The feature
debut for writer/director Holland.
COM                                               93 min
B,V                                                 CBS

## BETTER TOMORROW, A **                    18
John Woo               HONG KONG                  1990
A suspense-thriller set in Hong Kong's dangerous
underworld, that involves two brothers, one of whom
has become a policeman and the other a criminal.
Despite their different pathways, a series of violent
episodes and double crosses teach them both the value
of family ties.
THR                                               92 min
V                                                  RCA

## BETTY BLUE ****                          18
Jean-Jacques Beineix FRANCE                      1986
*Jean-Hugues Anglade, Beatrice Dalle, Consuelo De*
*Haviland, Gerard Darmon, Clementine Celarie,*
*Jacques Mathou, Claude Confortes, Philippe*
*Laudenbach, Vincent Lindon, Raoul Billeray, Claude*
*Aufaure, Andre Julien, Nataly Dalyan*
A disgruntled, tempestuous waitress, embarks on a

wild and stormy love affair with a 35-year-old handyman after she discovers that he has written an
unpublished novel. Putting his job and emotional
stability in jeopardy, they head for Paris and then a
provincial town, where finally, tired, drugged and
disillusioned, she goes mad. A tragi-comedy of impressive power that won the Grand Prize at the 10th
Montreaux Film Festival.
Aka: 37.2 LE MATIN; 37.2 DEGRES LE MATIN; 37.2
DEGREES IN THE MORNING
Boa: novel 37.2 Le Matin by Philippe Dijan.
DRA                              117 min (ort 121 min)
B,V                                             CBS

### BETWEEN FRIENDS ***                          15
Lou Antonio            USA                      1983
*Elizabeth Taylor, Carol Burnett, Barbara Bush,*
*Stephen Young, Henry Ramer, Bruce Grey, Charles*
*Shamata, Lally Cadeau, Vera Cudjoe, Stephen Young,*
*Michael J. Reynolds, Patricia Idlette, Jim Morris, Jeri*
*Craden, Nancy Kerr*
Taylor is a recently divorced woman who wants a man
in her life as someone to keep her in furs and
diamonds. Burnett is a recently divorced estate agent
who just wants male companionship. When a snow-
storm strands the latter at the mansion of the former,
who is putting her home on the market, the pair strike
up a friendship which brings about change in both
their lives. A tour-de-force for the two stars and well
above average.
Boa: novel Nobody Makes Me Cry by Shelley List.
DRA                              100 min mCab
B,V                                             VES

### BETWEEN THE LINES ***                        15
Joan Micklin Silver    USA                     1977
*John Heard, Lindsay Crouse, Jeff Goldblum, Jill*
*Eikenberry, Bruno Kirby, Gwen Welles, Stephen*
*Collins, Michael J. Pollard, Marilu Henner*
A Boston underground newspaper is threatened with
being bought up by a press baron. An extremely
enjoyable and little known film, with first-rate per-
formances from the cast, who at that time were
largely unknowns.
DRA                              100 min
B,V                                             HER

### BETWEEN THE SHEETS **                        R18
Anthony Spinelli       USA                     1984
*John Leslie, R.J. Reynolds, Randy West, Richard*
*Pacheco, Eric Edwards, Joey Silvera, Seka, Annette*
*Haven, Chelsea Manchester, Arcadia Lake, Veronica*
*Hart, Vanessa Del Rio*
A six-part account of the various lovers who have used
an ancient brass bed, with the female mattress and
male bed talking about their long experience of lovers.
The stories vary across time, with the best tales being
the last ones. An interesting, if contrived idea for a
film that, not all that good to begin with, will hardly
be worth seeing in the mutilated 29 minute version.
Aka: DIARY OF A BED (VTEL)
A                                29 min (ort 90 min) Cut
V                                       BLUES; VTEL

### BETWEEN TWO WOMEN ***                        PG
John Avnet             USA                     1986
*Michael Nouri, Farrah Fawcett, Colleen Dewhurst,*
*Bridgette Anderson, Danny Corkhill, Steven Hill,*
*Terry O'Quinn, Kenneth Danziger, Carmen*
*Argenziano, Bronson Pinchot*
Psychological study of a man torn between the
emotional demands of his wife and his strong-willed
mother, who is living in the same house. Powerful
performances from the two leads (especially De-
whurst's Emmy-winning role) enliven this one. The
script is by Larry Grusin and Avnet.
Boa: novel Living Arrows by Gillian Martin.
DRA                              91 min (ort 100 min) mTV
B/s, V/s                                         WHV

### BEVERLY HILLS BODY SNATCHERS **              15
Jon Moston/Titus R. Soles
                       USA                     1988
*Vic Tayback, Frank Gorshin*
A greedy mortician and a mad scientist hatch a crazy
scheme to make money by bringing dead rich people
back to life.
COM                              90 min
V                                               CHV

### BEVERLY HILLS BRATS *                        15
Dimitri Sotirakis      USA                     1988
*George Kirby, Peter Billingsley, Terry Moore, Martin*
*Sheen, Burt Young, Ramon Sheen, Fernando Allende,*
*Cathy Podewell*
A satirical look at the Beverly Hills lifestyle and
values that has the teenage son of a wealthy cosmetic
surgeon staging his own kidnapping (with the assistance of a kindly but incompetent burglar) in order to
remind the family of his existence. Matters get out of
hand, however, when a pair of vicious crooks decide to
get in on the act. A good premise is wasted in this
vacuous comedy.
COM                              91 min
V                                               VIR

### BEVERLY HILLS CONNECTION **                  15
Corey Allen            USA                     1985
*Lisa Hartman, James Brolin, David Hemmings, Irina*
*Ferris, Michael C. Gwynne, Alexa Hamilton, Lane*
*Smith, Drake Hogestyn, Aharon Ipale, Stuart*
*Whitman, John McCook, Eric Server, Robin Bach,*
*Brenda Bolte, Wally Dalton*
A tough Laramie lady cop investigates her close
friend's murder in Beverly Hills, and is mismatched
with a casual Beverly Hills cop who is assigned to help
her catch a killer from Wyoming. A flat and dullish
thriller, lacking both bite and pace.
Aka: BEVERLY HILLS COWGIRL BLUES
THR                              92 min (ort 100 min) mTV
B,V                                             CIC

### BEVERLY HILLS COP ***                        15
Martin Brest           USA                     1984
*Eddie Murphy, Judge Reinhold, Lisa Eilbacher,*
*Bronson Pinchot, John Ashton, Ronny Cox, Steven*
*Berkoff, James Russo, Jonathan Banks, Stephen*
*Elliott*
After the death of his friend, a Detroit cop takes to the
streets of L.A. in search of those responsible. Comedy
and drama are blended cleverly with Murphy perfect-
ly cast as a streetwise and unconventional cop. The
script is by Daniel Petrie Jr. Followed by a sequel.
DRA                              101 min
V/sh                                            CIC

### BEVERLY HILLS COP 2 **                       15
Tony Scott             USA                     1987
*Eddie Murphy, Ronny Cox, Judge Reihold, John*
*Ashton, Brigitte Nielsen, Paul Reiser, Jurgen*
*Prochnow, Allen Garfield, Dean Stockwell, Paul*
*Reiser, Paul Guilfoyle, Gilbert Hill, Robert Ridgley,*
*Brian O'Connor, Alice Adair*
Sound-and-fury sequel that has everything except
good acting and a credible, coherent plot. Trite,
tiresome and directed with all the sensitivity of a cosh.
A/AD                             99 min
V/sh                                            CIC

### BEVERLY HILLS MADAM **                       15
Harvey Hart            USA                     1986
*Faye Dunaway, Melody Anderson, Louis Jourdan,*
*Marshall Colt, Donna Dixon, Terry Farrell, Robin*
*Givens, William Jordan, Nicolas Coster, William*
*Taler, Gary Hershberger, Rod McAru, Beulah Quo,*
*Seymour Cassel, Aki Aleong*
The story of an exclusive brothel keeper and her
clientele. Little more than a parade of beautiful girls
and a wonderfully hammy performance from Dun-

away in a glossy and trashy piece of nonsense.
DRA                                    93 min mTV
B,V                                        RNK

## BEVERLY HILLS VAMP **                    18
Fred Olen Ray           USA              1989
*Eddie Deezen, Britt Ekland, Jay Richardson, Tim
Conway Jr, Michelle Bauer, Robert Quarry, Dawn
Wildsmith, Pat McCormick*
A young man out to make it in the film world comes up
against a vampire madam and her coterie of hookers.
This silly spoof on vampire movies is alternately
amusing and annoying, the inclusion of numerous
Hollywood in-jokes and Deezen's Jerry Lewis-style
slapstick don't make it any more palatable.
COM                          86 min (ort 89 min)
V                                          NWV

## BEYOND A REASONABLE DOUBT **
Fritz Lang              USA              1956
*Dana Andrews, Joan Fontaine, Sidney Blackmer,
Philip Bourneuf, Barbara Nichols*
A novelist is persuaded to fake evidence that gets him
convicted for murder and is then unable to prove his
innocence. And why does he do this? To get a
first-hand look at the legal system of course. An
intriguing but utterly unbelievable idea, that just
doesn't hold up in this poor effort.
Osca: FLYING LEATHERNECKS
DRA                                   77 min B/W
B,V                                        KVD

## BEYOND ATLANTIS *
Eddie Romero    USA/PHILIPPINES          1973
*Patrick Wayne, John Ashley, Leigh Christian, Lenore
Stevens, George Nader, Sid Haig, Eddie Garcia, Vic
Diaz*
Fantasy about a lost civilisation, perhaps of slight
interest for its feminist sub-plot. Low-budget non-
sense that mixes up amphibious humanoids with
various philosophical ramblings.
FAN                                        89 min
B,V                                         INT

## BEYOND EVIL **
Herb Freed              USA              1980
*John Saxon, Lynda Day George, Michael Dante, Mario
Milano, Janice Lynde, David Opatoshu*
A couple move into a house that's inhabited by the
hostile spirit of a 100-year-old woman who doesn't
take kindly to this intrusion. So-so horror yarn of no
great consequence.
HOR                                        90 min
B,V,V2                                    VIPCO

## BEYOND REASON *
Telly Savalas           USA              1977
*Telly Savalas, Laura Johnson, Diana Muldaur,
Douglas Dirkson, Marvin Laird, Bob Basso, Biff Elliot,
Barney Phillips, Walter Brooke*
A psychiatrist struggling for the right to treat the
mentally ill with respect, begins to crack under the
strain of his work. This writing and directing debut
for Savalas is a dull, carelessly-made effort that was
never released theatrically; Priscilla Barnes was
replaced as leading lady but she still appears in a few
sequences.
Aka: MATI
THR                                        94 min
B,V,V2                                      VCL

## BEYOND REASONABLE DOUBT ***              PG
John Laing      NEW ZEALAND              1980
*David Hemmings, John Hargreaves, Martyn
Sanderson, Grant Tilly, Diana Rowan, Ian Watkin*
A man wrongly accused of a double murder fights to
prove his innocence, in this fairly competent docu-
drama loosely based on the real case of innocent
farmer Arthur Thomas, who was wrongfully convicted

on trumped-up charges. Hemmings is the cop who
instigates the whole nasty business.
Boa: book by David Yallop.
DRA                                       127 min
B,V                                    SPEC/POLY

## BEYOND THE DARKNESS *                    18
Joe D'Amato (Aristide Massaccesi)
                        ITALY            1979
*Kieran Canter, Cinzia Monreale, Franca Stoppa*
Another one of those psychotic-killer-on-the-loose
films. In this one our murderer is a crazed young man
who is so upset by the death of his girlfriend that he
decides to dig her body up and preserve her. When a
hitchhiker drops in whilst this is in progress he
decides to dismember her rather then engage in any
long-winded explanations. A brutal and messy film,
but one with most of the gratuitous gore removed.
Aka: BLUE HOLOCAUST; BUIO OMEGA
HOR                          85 min (ort 94 min)
B,V                                        VPD

## BEYOND THE POSEIDON ADVENTURE *          15
Irwin Allen             USA              1979
*Michael Caine, Sally Field, Telly Savalas, Karl
Malden, Peter Boyle, Jack Warden, Slim Pickens,
Shirley Knight, Shirley Jones, Mark Harmon,
Veronica Hamel*
A weak sequel to THE POSEIDON ADVENTURE,
telling of attempts by two crews to loot the capsized
liner of its valuables before it sinks. The plot in this
one is the first thing to go down.
Boa: novel by Paul Gallico.
THR                                       110 min
B,V                                        WHV

## BEYOND THE VALLEY OF THE DOLLS ***
Russ Meyer             USA              1970
*Dolly Read, Cynthia Myers, Marcia McBroom, David
Gurian, John LaZar, Michael Blodgett, Edy Williams,
Erica Gavin*
A sequel in name only, that parodies all those trashy
soap operas of the time. In this one a female rock band
tries to make the big time in L.A. This Hollywood
debut for Meyer has many good things in it, not least
the utterly over-the-top script by film critic Roger
Ebert.
DRA                     102 min (ort 109 min) Cut
V                                          CBS

## BEYOND THE WALLS **                      18
Uri Barbash             ISRAEL           1984
*Arnon Zadok, Muhammed Bakri, Assi Dayan, Rami
Danon, Adib Jahashan, Boaz Sharambi*
Story of life in a maximum security Israeli prison that
largely focuses on the tensions between the Arab and
Israeli inmates. What could have been a powerful
study is just one more noisy prison saga.
Aka: MEIACHOREI HASORALIM
DRA                          99 min (ort 103 min)
B/h, V/h                                   WHV

## BEYOND THERAPY *                         15
Robert Altman           USA              1986
*Jeff Goldblum, Julie Hagerty, Glenda Jackson, Tom
Conti, Christopher Guest, Genevieve Page, Cris
Campion, Sandrine Dumas*
A manic and utterly superficial story of nutty New
Yorkers and their equally peculiar therapists. A
strong cast is wasted in a story that needed the talents
of a more gifted writer to make it work. Filmed in
Paris.
Boa: play by Christopher Durang.
COM                                        98 min
B,V                                        NWV

## BEYOND, THE **                           18
Lucio Fulci             ITALY            1981
*Katherine McColl, David Warbeck, Sarah Keller,*

*Antoine St John, Veronica Lazar, Anthony Flees,*
*Giovanni de Nava, Michelle Mirabella, Al Cliver (Pier*
*Luigi Conti)*
Story of a young woman who inherits a rundown
Louisiana hotel that just happens to be built over one
of the gateways to Hell. A series of violent deaths take
place. Average shocker. See also THE SENTINEL for
another treatment of this theme.
Aka: AND YOU'LL LIVE IN TERROR! THE
BEYOND; E TU VIVRAI NEL TERRORE!
L'ALDILA; L'ALDILA; SEVEN DOORS OF DEATH
HOR                     89 min (Cut at film release)
B,V                             VDM/GHV; ELE

**BEZHIN MEADOW **                          PG
Sergei Eisenstein        USSR              1937
*Vitya Kartashov, Boris Zakhava, Igor Pavlenko,*
*Telesheva*
Some fragments of an incomplete Eisenstein film were
reconstructed in 1966. Now seen as a series of freeze
frames, these few sections show the loss his failure to
complete this film represents.
Aka: BEZHIN LUG
Boa: story by Ivan Turgenev. Osca: TIME IN THE
SUN
DRA             91 min (2 film cassette) B/W
V                                         HEND

**BIBLE, THE ***                              U
John Huston        ITALY/USA              1966
*George C. Scott, Peter O'Toole, Ava Gardner, Richard*
*Harris, Ulla Bergryd, Michael Parks, Stephen Boyd,*
*Franco Nero, John Huston*
A dreadful and stilted attempt to film the first 22
chapters of Genesis, following the exploits of Adam
and Eve, Cain and Abel, Noah and the Flood and
Abraham and his sacrifice. Heavy-handed, ponderous
and pompous; the book is a lot better.
Aka: BIBLE . . . IN THE BEGINNING, THE; LA
BIBLIA
DRA                     155 min (ort 174 min)
V/h                                       CBS

**BICYCLE THIEVES *****
Vittoria De Sica        ITALY             1948
*Lamberto Maggiorani, Lianella Carell, Enzo Staiola,*
*Elena Altieri*
Wonderfully moving film telling of an Italian work-
man who, after a long period of unemployment finally
gets a job. When the bicycle he needs for the job is
stolen he embarks on a long and painful search. A
cinema landmark. AA: Spec Award (most outstanding
foreign language film released in the USA during
1949).
Aka: BICYCLE THIEF, THE; LADRI DI
BICICLETTE
Boa: novel by L. Bartolini.
DRA                              90 min B/W
B,V                               LNG/PVG

**BIDDY ***
Christine Edzard         UK               1983
*Celia Bannerman, Sam Ghazoros, Luke Duckett, Miles*
*Parsey, David Napier, Kate Elphick, Sabine Goodwin,*
*Emily Hone, Patricia Napier, Sally Ashby, John*
*Dalby, Amelda Brown, Jason Morell*
This skilful reconstruction of a mid-Victorian house-
hold looks at the life of a nursemaid.
DRA                                   86 min
B,V                                   NARROW

**BIG ****                                   PG
Penny Marshall          USA               1988
*Tom Hanks, Elizabeth Perkins, Robert Loggia, John*
*Heard, Jared Rushton, David Moscow, Jon Lovitz,*
*Mercedes Ruehl, Josh Clark, Tracy Reiner*
With the aid of a wishing machine at a carnival
fairground, a youngster gets his chance to become an
adult, waking up the next day as a 30-year-old. What

might so easily have been mawkish and cloying is
sharp and pleasing, mainly thanks to a wonderfully
fresh performance from Hanks as the child in a man's
body.
COM                     100 min (ort 102 min)
V/sh                                      CBS

**BIG BAD MAMA ***
Steve Carver            USA               1974
*Angie Dickinson, Tom Skerritt, William Shatner,*
*Susan Sennett, Robbie Lee, Dick Miller, Joan Prather,*
*Royal Dano, Sally Kirkland*
A mother turns to robbery in order to escape from
grinding poverty and goes off on a crime jaunt with
her two teenage daughters. A sexy answer to BON-
NIE AND CLYDE with a good performance from
Dickinson. The catchy score is by David Grisman. A
poor sequel followed thirteen years later.
DRA                                   82 min
B,V                                      TEVP

**BIG BAD MAMA 2 ***                          18
Jim Wynorski            USA               1987
*Angie Dickinson, Robert Culp, Danielle Brisebois,*
*Julie McCullough, Bruce Glover*
A pointless and largely witless sequel to the earlier
film, with Mama McClatchie and her two daughters
robbing banks, and stealing the son of a crooked
politician as a way of avenging her husband's death.
Incorporates excerpts from the original film and it's
not hard to see which is the better of the two.
A/AD                                  85 min
B,V                                      MGM

**BIG BANG, THE ***                           18
Jean-Marc Picha  BELGIUM/FRANCE           1987
*Voices of: David Lander, Carol Androfsky, Marshall*
*Efron, Alice Playten*
Adult futuristic cartoon comedy set on the eve of
WW4, with the shattered USA and USSR forming a
single country, the USSSR, but finding that they are
in conflict with the nation of Vagina, formed by the
remaining women who survived WW3. A film that
tries hard to be satirical but ends up being merely
crude.
CAR             73 min (ort 90 min) Cut (10 sec)
B,V                                       EIV

**BIG BET, THE ***                            18
Bert I. Gordon           USA              1986
*Sylvia Kristel, Kimberley Evenson, Lance Sloan, Ron*
*Thomas, John Smith, Deanna Claire, Kenneth Ian*
*Davies, Stephanie Blake, Elizabeth Blake, Elizabeth*
*Cochrell, Robert Marucci*
Trivial teenage fare from a renowned director (of
rubbishy SF movies), telling of a nerd who wagers his
car against the school bully, that he can bed one of the
girls in his class before the week is out. He turns to his
beautiful and sophisticated new neighbour for advice.
COM                     90 min; 87 min (VPD)
B,V                      CINGRO; VPD (VHS only)

**BIG BIRD CAGE, THE ***                      18
Jack Hill               USA               1972
*Pam Grier, Anitra Ford, Sid Haig, Candice Roman,*
*Vic Diaz, Carol Speed*
Amusing spoof on Filipino prison movies with a gang
of thieving mercenaries engineering an escape from
the outside. A sequel to "The Big Doll House".
A/AD            87 min (ort 90 min) Cut (2 min 24 sec)
B,V                                       WHV

**BIG BLUE, THE ***                           15
Luc Besson             FRANCE             1988
*Rosanna Arquette, Jean-Marc Barr, Jean Reno, Paul*
*Shenar, Sergio Castellito, Marc Buret, Griffin Dunne*
A colourful action story that traces the changing
relationship between a young woman and a man who
decides to take up the hazardous sport of free diving.

The shallow plot and characterisation are handicaps but the pretty locations will compensate slightly. Filmed in Sicily, Corsica, Paris, New York, the Virgin Islands and the Riviera.

A/AD                                        114 min (ort 119 min)
V                                                                CBS

## BIG BOSS 2 ***
Cheng Kay Ying    HONG KONG
*Bruce Cheung, Yeung Wai, Li Ying Ying, Nam Chi I, Casanova Wong, Mu King, David Cheung, Stella Ma, Wong Yen Tong*
A fast-paced high-kicking kung fu tale of revenge bearing no relation to Bruce Lee's film THE BIG BOSS. As ever, the plot is strictly of secondary importance to the well-choreographed fighting sequences.
Aka: BRUCE AGAINST THE ODDS
MAR                                                    83 min
B,V,V2                                              VIPCO

## BIG BRAWL, THE ***                          15
Robert Clouse        USA                          1980
*Jackie Chan, Jose Ferrer, Mako, Rosalind Chao, Kristine DeBell, Ron Max, Lenny Montana, H.B. Haggerty*
Set in the USA in the 1930s, this tells of a fight contest which offers a huge cash prize to the winner. An interesting melding of martial arts and gangster genres with a good deal of humour and a strong cast. Clouse also directed ENTER THE DRAGON.
Aka: BATTLE CREEK BRAWL
MAR                        95 min; 91 min (VCC) Cut (2 sec)
B,V,V2                                 GHV; VCC (VHS only)

## BIG BUS, THE **                                PG
James Frawley        USA                          1976
*Joseph Bologna, Lynn Redgrave, John Beck, Sally Kellerman, Rene Auberjonois, Stockard Channing, Bob Dishy, Stuart Margolin, Howard Hesseman, Jose Ferrer, Ned Beatty, Harold Gould, Larry Hagman, Richard Mulligan, Ruth Gordon*
Feeble spoof on all those disaster-movies. Here an atomic-powered bus is involved in a number of misadventures on its first cross-country run.
COM                                                    86 min
B,V                                                        CIC

## BIG BUSINESS **                                PG
Jim Abrahams        USA                          1988
*Bette Midler, Lily Tomlin, Fred Ward, Edward Herrmann, Michele Placido, Daniel Gerroll, Barry Primus, Michael Gross, Joe Grifasi, Mary Gross, Deborah Rush, Nicolas Coster*
Two sets of identical twins, accidentally separated and switched at birth, meet up years later in New York when one set arrives for a showdown with the corporation that's going to erase their little home town, only to find that the other set of girls is in charge of the company. A nice idea for a comedy, but it never really takes off, despite winning performances from Midler and Tomlin. After a while the special effects tend to irritate too.
COM                                                    94 min
B,V                                                   BUENA

## BIG CAT, THE **                                U
Tom Leetch          USA                          1988
*Jeremy Slate*
Pleasant Disney outdoors adventure that centres on a family who live in a remote log cabin high up in the mountains and find their peaceful lifestyle threatened, by a big cat which struck the young daughter dumb in an earlier frightening encounter.
Aka: RETURN OF THE BIG CAT
A/AD                                                    90 min
B,V                                                        WDV

## BIG CHILL, THE ***                             15
Lawrence Kasdan     USA                          1983
*Tom Berenger, Glenn Close, William Hurt, Kevin Kline, Mary Kay Place, Jeff Goldblum, JoBeth Williams, Meg Tilly, Don Galloway*
A look at a group of former college hippies who have now dropped back into society and meet at the funeral of a friend who has just committed suicide. This excellent piece of ensemble acting has the group examining their lives and careers as they come to terms with the suicide. The fine cast and a nice 1960s soundtrack compensate for any deficiencies in the plot. Written by Kasdan and Barbara Benedek.
DRA                                                   101 min
V                                                          RCA

## BIG CIRCUS, THE ***                            U
Joseph Newman       USA                          1959
*Victor Mature, Rhonda Fleming, Red Buttons, Kathryn Grant, Peter Lorre, Vincent Price, Gilbert Roland, David Nelson, Howard McNear, Steve Allen, Adele Mara*
A lively story that sees the near-bankrupt owner of a circus making an attempt to keep on the road whilst keeping his business rivals at bay at the same time. Despite a loose plot, the film delivers enough thrills to keep it going. Lorre as a clown is one of several highlights.
DRA                                                   109 min
V/h                                                        CBS

## BIG COMBO, THE ***
Joseph H. Lewis     USA                          1955
*Cornel Wilde, Jean Wallace, Brian Donlevy, Earl Holliman, Richard Conte, Lee Van Cleef, Robert Middleton, Helen Walker*
Violent film about the struggle between a crime syndicate and the forces of law and order, in the shape of a persistent cop who is out to nail a cunning racketeer. A slick and well directed story.
THR                                                89 min B/W
B,V,V2                                                   VUL

## BIG COUNTRY, THE ***                           PG
William Wyler       USA                          1958
*Gregory Peck, Charlton Heston, Burl Ives, Jean Simmons, Carroll Baker, Chuck Connors, Charles Bickford, Alfonso Bedoya, Chuck Hayward, Buff Brady, Jim Burk, Dorothy Adams, Cuck Roberson, Bob Morgan, John McKee, Jay Slim Talbot*
A sea captain goes west to claim his intended, a rancher's daughter, and finds himself involved in a feud over water rights between his prospective father-in-law and a hillbilly clan. Overlong, overblown, overrated Western where even the excellent acting is overshadowed by the title player, the spectacularly rugged landscape of the Southwest. The fine musical score is by Jerome Moross. AA: S. Actor (Ives).
Boa: novel by Donald Hamilton.
WES                                                   161 min
V                                                          WHV

## BIG EASY, THE ***                              15
Jim McBride         USA                          1987
*Dennis Quaid, Ellen Barkin, Ned Beatty, John Goodman, Ebbe Roe Smith, Lisa Jane Persky, Charles Ludlam, Tom O'Brien, Marc Lawrence, Solomon Burke, Jim Garrison*
A smart homicide detective finds himself at odds with the new female D.A. whilst investigating a local Mob murder, but the two become romantically involved even though they remain at odds professionally. A vigorous and highly unusual crime drama with a great Cajun music score and some nice New Orleans locations. Written by Daniel Petrie Jr.
DRA                                                    98 min
V/sh                                                      RCA

## BIG FIX, THE ***
Jeremy Paul Kagan     USA     15     1978
*Richard Dreyfuss, Susan Anspach, Bonnie Bedelia,*
*John Lithgow, F. Murray Abraham, Ofelia Medina,*
*Fritz Weaver, Mandy Patinkin*
A twist to the poacher-turned-gamekeeper theme in
which a hippie turned private eye investigates a
conspiracy involving many former hippie figures. The
screenplay is by Simon from his novel.
Boa: novel by Roger L. Simon.
THR                     104 min (ort 108 min)
B,V                                      CIC

## BIG FOOT AND THE MUSCLE MACHINES ***  U
USA     1987
A lively cartoon telling of a girl who discovers a map
giving directions to the Fountain Of Youth, but a
certain Mr Big is out to get it. However, help arrives
in the shape of Yank Justice and his muscle machines
who, together with the girl, foil the plans of the evil
Mr Big.
CAR                                    52 min
V                                        MSD

## BIG HURT, THE ***
Barry Peak     18     1987
*David Bradshaw, Lian Lunson, Simon Chilvers, Nick*
*Waters*
A Melbourne journalist newly released from prison
investigates an exclusive club run by a mysterious
woman, and uncovers strange experiments in which
hormones are used to transform pain into pleasure. A
suspenseful blend of thriller and fantasy genres.
THR                                    94 min
V                                        RCA

## BIG JAKE **
George Sherman     USA     15     1971
*John Wayne, Richard Boone, Maureen O'Hara,*
*Patrick Wayne, Chris Mitchum, Bobby Vinton, Bruce*
*Cabot, Glenn Corbett, Harry Carey Jr, John Agar*
With the kidnapping of his grandson, an elderly
Texan decides to take the law into his own hands and
goes after the boy's abductors. A violent and over-
blown blend of fisticuffs and action, with good produc-
tion values but an unfortunate element of self-parody.
WES                                   109 min
V                                        CBS

## BIG JOB, THE **
Gerald Thomas     UK     U     1965
*Sidney James, Sylvia Syms, Dick Emery, Joan Sims,*
*Jim Dale, Lance Percival*
After fifteen years in jail, a bunch of inept crooks are
released and return to retrieve their buried loot, but
find that a new police station has been built over the
field they buried it in.
COM                                84 min B/W
V                                        WHV

## BIG LAND, THE ***
Gordon Douglas     USA     1957
*Alan Ladd, Virginia Mayo, Edmond O'Brien, Anthony*
*Caruso, Julie Bishop, John Qualen, Don Castle, David*
*Ladd, Jack Wrather Jr, George J. Lewis, James*
*Anderson, Don Kelly, Charles Watts*
Amiable post-Civil War story of wheat farmers and
cattlemen who join forces against cheating business-
men, and bring a rail link to Texas in order to reach
better markets.
Aka: STAMPEDED
Osca: PIONEER BUILDERS
WES                                    88 min
B,V                                      KVD

## BIG MAN, THE **
David Leland     UK     18     1990
*Liam Neeson, Joanne Whalley-Kilmer, Ian Bannen,*
*Billy Connolly*
A Scottish miner unemployed since the 1985 strike
(during which he was imprisoned) enters the brutal
world of bare-knuckle fighting that's controlled by a
cynical and world-weary criminal. A dour, harsh and
uncompromisingly gritty tale, whose plot elements
never quite hold together, consequently blurring the
impact and message of the original novel. The music is
by Ennio Morricone.
Boa: book by William McIlvanney.
A/AD                                  111 min
V/sh                                     PAL

## BIG MEAT EATER *
Chris Windsor     CANADA     18     1984
*George Dawson, Andrew Gillies, Big Miller*
Horror spoof about the strange things that keep
happening to a small town butcher whose freezer is
used to stow the corpse of the town's mayor, after a
psycho has made fillets of his fingers. A low-budget
effort, endearing in a trashy way.
COM                                    78 min
B,V                                      PVG

## BIG MOUTH, THE *
Jerry Lewis     USA     U     1967
*Jerry Lewis, Harold J. Stone, Buddy Lester, Susan*
*Bay, Del Moore, Paul Lambert*
A timid bank employee discovers that he is the double
of a dying gangster and becomes embroiled in murder
and a search for stolen loot. A dull and enervating
comedy vehicle for Lewis – one of his poorer efforts.
COM                       103 min (ort 107 min)
V                                        RCA

## BIG RASCAL, THE **
Chi Kuan-Chun     HONG KONG     18     1980
*Chi Kuan-Chun, Wang Cheng, Chi Kang, Peng Kang,*
*King Kung*
A man seeks revenge for the murder of his brother by
a gang boss. Standard "honour must be avenged" plot
is a vehicle for some nice punch-ups.
MAR                                    90 min
B,V                     CHM/PPL L/A; NORM; STABL

## BIG RED **
Norman Tokar     USA     Uc     1962
*Walter Pidgeon, Gilles Payant, Emile Genest, Janette*
*Bertrand, Doris Lussier*
A young boy gets a job working for a wealthy dog
fancier and makes friends with a champion Irish
setter. Typical family fare from Disney, in which the
usual series of adventures are followed by the compul-
sory happy ending. Filmed in Canada.
Boa: novel by J.A. Kjelgaard.
JUV                                    85 min
B,V                                      WDV

## BIG RED ONE, THE ***
Samuel Fuller     USA     15     1980
*Lee Marvin, Mark Hamill, Robert Carradine, Bobby Di*
*Cicco, Kelly Ward, Siegfried Rauch, Stephane Audran*
Gritty and realistic WW2 film about a tough infantry
sergeant who, together with his seasoned section,
survive while the fresh recruits die all around them.
The title refers to their infantry badge.
WAR                                   111 min
B,V,V2,LV                CBS; PARK (VHS only)

## BIG RISK, THE **
HONG KONG
*Cheung Nick, Cheung Long, Tong Tin Sze, Queenie*
*Kong*
Set during the Japanese occupation of China, this
kung fu adventure has a secret agent getting involved
in a furious struggle with a rival gang when he is sent
to retrieve some secret documents.
MAR                                    90 min
B,V                                      VPD

**BIG SCORE, THE ** **                    15
Fred Williamson          USA          1983
*John Saxon, Fred Williamson, Richard Roundtree,
Nancy Wilson, Bruce Glover, Ed Lauter, D'Urville
Martin, Michael Dante, Joe Spinell*
A narcotics cop takes the law into his own hands when
he decides to take on the local crooks. Typical
black-oriented thriller that uses a script originally
commissioned for a Clint Eastwood film that never got
made. Disappointing.
THR                         82 min Cut (6 sec)
B,V                                   MED

**BIG SHOT ***
Charles S. Dubin          USA          1983
*Telly Savalas, Keith Gordon, Dora Volonaki, Michael
Constantine, Yula Gavala*
Effective drama telling of a Greek-American who
returns with his teenage American-born son to the
village of his birth after 35 years in New York, but
receives a less than warm welcome from the locals.
Savalas gives one of his better performances. Scripted
by George Kirgo.
Aka: MY PALIKARI; SILENT REBELLION
Boa: story by Leon Capetanos.
DRA                            88 min mTV
B,V                                   POLY

**BIG SHOTS ** **                         15
Robert Mandel          USA          1987
*Ricky Busker, Darius McCrary, Robert Joy, Robert
Prosky, Jerzy Skolimowski, Paul Winfield*
A naive white kid teams up with a streetwise black
kid and together they get involved in murders,
mysteries and mayhem in this production-line effort.
COM                          87 min Cut (47 sec)
B,V                                   GHV

**BIG SKY, THE ***
Howard Hawks          USA          1952
*Kirk Douglas, Dewey Martin, Arthur Hunnicutt,
Buddy Baer, Jim Davis, Steven Geray, Hank Worden,
Elizabeth Threatt, Henri Letonal, Robert Hunter,
Booth Coleman, Frank De Kova, Guy Wilkerson, Cliff
Clark, Fred Graham, Sam Ash*
A classic Western that tells the story of an expedition
to set up a trading post in 1830, with fur-trapper
Douglas leading a bunch of adventurers up the
Missouri River. Its original running time proved to be
too long and it was edited down. The script is by
Dudley Nichols.
Boa: novel by A.B. Guthrie Jr. Osca: CODE OF THE
WEST
WES                    117 min (ort 141 min) B/W
B,V                                   KVD

**BIG SLEEP, THE ***                      15
Michael Winner          UK          1978
*Robert Mitchum, Sarah Miles, Richard Boone, Candy
Clark, Edward Fox, John Mills, James Stewart, Joan
Collins, Oliver Reed, Harry Andrews, Richard Todd,
Colin Blakely, Diana Quick, James Donald, John
Justin, Simon Turner*
Follow-up to FAREWELL, MY LOVELY that's a
fairly faithful adaptation of Chandler's book, albeit
one that's updated and set in London, thus largely
destroying the flavour if not the plot elements of the
novel. As before, private eye Marlowe finds himself
embroiled in murder, blackmail and violence when he
is hired to protect the daughter of a general. Competent rather than powerful and best not compared to
the Howard Hawks classic.
Boa: novel by Raymond Chandler.
THR                         95 min (ort 99 min)
B,V,V2                  PRV L/A; CH5 (VHS only)

**BIG SLEEP, THE ****                     PG
Howard Hawks          USA      1944 (released 1946)

*Humphrey Bogart, Lauren Bacall, John Ridgely,
Charles Waldron, Martha Vickers, Louis Jean Heydt,
Regis Toomey, Peggy Knudsen, Dorothy Malone, Bob
Steele, Elisha Cook Jr*
Classic film noir adapted from Chandler's first book,
with private detective Philip Marlowe being hired by
a rich society lady and getting drawn into a complex
web of intrigue and murder, mostly brought about by
the woman's uncontrollable younger sister. The con-
voluted plot is wellnigh impossible to follow (even
Chandler couldn't explain one murder), but the power-
ful script, by Faulkner, Jules Furthman and Leigh
Brackman, carries it through.
Boa: novel by Raymond Chandler.
THR                            110 min B/W
V                                     WHV

**BIG STEAL, THE ***                      PG
Don Siegel          USA          1949
*Robert Mitchum, Jane Greer, William Bendix, Ramon
Novarro, Patric Knowles, Don Alvarado, John Qualen,
Pascual Garcia Pena*
An army officer framed for a payroll robbery sets out
to pursue the real culprits and gets involved with
Greer along the way. Well made and complex story
with some surprising plot twists.
Boa: novel by Richard Wormser. Osca:
UNDERWATER!
THR                             68 min B/W
B,V                    KVD L/A; VCC

**BIG SWEAT, THE ** **                    18
Ulli Lommel          USA          1989
*Robert Z'dar, Ken Letner*
Having just been released from prison, a petty crook is
all too ready to slip back into his old ways, but has a
chance to make a fresh start when the FBI ask for his
help in breaking up a criminal gang.
A/AD                              90 min
V                                     BCB

**BIG SWITCH, THE **
Pete Walker          UK          1968
*Sebastian Breaks, Virginia Weatherall, Erika Raffael,
Jack Allen, Derek Aylward, Douglas Blackwell, Julie
Shaw, Jane Howard, Roy Stone, Brian Weske, Tracey
Yorke, Lena Ellis*
After being implicated in a murder, a playboy is
blackmailed into posing for obscene photos, in this
unmemorable and lacklustre effort.
Aka: STRIP POKER
A/AD          68 min; 75 min (HVS) (ort 81 min)
B,V                           WEC; HVS

**BIG TIME **                             PG
Andrew Georgias          USA          1977
*Christopher Joy, Leon Isaac, Andrew Georgias*
A man down on his luck, resorts to fraud and finds
himself in big trouble. Average.
COM                               88 min
B,V                           AVA/CBS

**BIG TOP PEE-WEE ***                     U
Randal Kleiser          USA          1988
*Pee-Wee Herman (Paul Reubens), Kris Kristofferson,
Penelope Ann Miller, Susan Tyrell, Valeria Golino.
Voices of: Wayne White, Susan Tyrell, Albert
Henderson, Kevin Peter Hall, Kenneth Toby*
A farmer gets a chance to join the circus when a freak
storm dumps a big top on his doorstep. Offbeat and
moderately amusing Pee-Wee comedy vehicle, with a
few good moments but no great laughs. Clever but
somewhat insipid. The film was co-written and pro-
duced by Reubens.
COM                               82 min
B,V                                   CIC

**BIG TOWN, THE ** **                      15
Ben Bolt              USA                  1987
*Matt Dillon, Diane Lane, Tommy Lee Jones, Tom
Skerritt, Lee Grant, Bruce Dern, Suzy Amis, David
Grant*
A small-time gambler comes to Chicago in the 1950s
to try his luck. A flashy and cliched story with Dillon
finding the going tougher than he expected and
getting involved with two girls along the way.
DRA                                    106 min
B,V                                        RNK

**BIG TRAIL, THE *** **                     U
Raoul Walsh            USA                1930
*John Wayne, Marguerite Churchill, El Brendel, Tully
Marshall, David Rollins, Tyrone Power Sr, Ward
Bond, Helen Parrish, Ian Keith*
The story of a wagon train and the hazards faced by its
members as they travel along the Oregon trail. Wayne
got his first starring role in this enjoyable early talkie
and though he took several more years to reach
stardom, shows considerable promise. The film was
made using an early 70 mm process known as
Grandeur, and is best enjoyed on the wide-screen. A
dated but impressive early Western epic.
WES            116 min (ort 121 min) B/W
V                                          CBS

**BIG TROUBLE ** **                         15
John Cassavetes        USA                1986
*Peter Falk, Alan Arkin, Beverly D'Angelo, Charles
Durning, Robert Stack, Paul Dooley, Valerie Curtin,
Richard Libertini*
An insurance salesman gets drawn into a crazy plot to
kill a woman's husband when he finds he's short of
funds to put his kids through college. Messy and
contrived nonsense with a few humorous moments,
but not too many of them.
COM                                     90 min
B,V                                        RCA

**BIG TROUBLE IN LITTLE CHINA *** **        15
John Carpenter         USA                1986
*Kurt Russell, Kim Catrall, Dennis Dun, James Hong,
Kate Burton, Victor Wong, Suzee Pai*
Russell plays a trucker who finds himself involved in
a strange Chinatown adventure when his friend's
fiancee is kidnapped and he sets out to rescue her,
venturing into the underground domain of a 2,000-
year-old wizard in the process. Amusing and tongue-
in-cheek action story of spectacular effects and im-
aginative fantasy elements. The electronic score is by
Carpenter.
A/AD                         96 min Cut (9 sec)
B,V                                        CBS

**BIG WEDNESDAY *** **                      PG
John Milius            USA                1978
*Jan-Michael Vincent, William Katt, Gary Busey, Lee
Purcell, Barbara Hale, Patti D'Arbanville*
Following their stint in Vietnam, three surfing bud-
dies get together to face the challenge of the waves
once more. Starts as an amusing surfing comedy set in
the 1960s, but as it moves into the 1970s the comic
elements give way to drama. Later re-cut to 104 min
by Milius and re-titled "Summer Of Innocence" for
pay-TV release.
Aka: SUMMER OF INNOCENCE
DRA                                    119 min
B,V                                        WHV

**BIG WHEEL, THE *** **
Edward Ludwig          USA                1949
*Mickey Rooney, Thomas Mitchell, Mary Hatcher,
Spring Byington, Allen Jenkins, Michael O'Shea*
Despite the fact that his racing car father was killed
on the track, his son still decides to follow in his
footsteps. Standard plot but quite nicely handled.
DRA                                     92 min

B,V                                    PORVI/MOV

**BIG ZAPPER ** **
Lindsay Shonteff       UK                 1973
*Linda Marlowe, Richard Monette, Gary Hope, Sean
Hewitt, Michael O'Malley, Jack May, Penny Irving,
Stuart Lock, Bobby Anne, Kristopher Kum, William
Ridoutt, Graham Ashley, Gavin Douglas, Nora
Llewellyn, Jeanette Marsden*
Low-grade thriller about a violent and unorthodox
private eye and her trusty and masochistic sidekick,
who get involved in bringing a murderous pimp to
justice.
THR                                     90 min
B,V                                        VFO

**BIGAMIST, THE *** **                      PG
Ida Lupino             USA                1953
*Edmond O'Brien, Joan Fontaine, Ida Lupino,
Edmund Gwenn, Jane Darwell, Kenneth Tobey*
A man married to two women finds himself torn apart
by his love for both of them. A well acted and often
quite touching character study with good directing
work from Lupino – her only stint directing herself.
DRA                                 80 min B/W
V                                  VMA; STABL

**BIGFOOT ** **                              U
Danny Huston           USA                1987
*Colleen Dewhurst, James Sloyan, Gracie Harrison,
Joseph Maher, Adam Karl, Candace Cameron*
Familiar family-style adventure about a big furry
creature and its mate who get involved with various
humans. Quite similar in theme to BIGFOOT AND
THE HENDERSONS. Pretty routine stuff though the
make-up work of Robert Schiffer stands out.
A/AD                     90 min (ort 100 min) mTV
B,V                                        WDV

**BIGFOOT AND THE HENDERSONS *** **         PG
William Dear           USA                1987
*John Lithgow, Melinda Dillon, Don Ameche, David
Suchet, Kevin Peter Hall*
Story of a family who run over a huge beast on their
return from a camping outing. Thinking he might sell
the carcass, the father straps it to his car roof but later
finds that it wasn't killed after all. Whereupon the
family decide to adopt the creature. A pleasant,
undemanding comedy outing.
COM                                    106 min
V/sh                                       CIC

**BIGGEST BATTLE, THE ** **
Humphrey Longan (Umberto Lenzi)
             ITALY/WEST GERMANY/YUGOSLAVIA 1977
*Helmut Berger, Samantha Eggar, Giuliano Gemma,
John Huston, Stacy Keach, Henry Fonda, Edwige
Fenech*
Overlong and mediocre account of WW2 tank battles
in North Africa during the campaign to chase Rom-
mel's Africa Corps out of the continent.
Aka: BATTLE FORCE; BATTLE OF THE
MARETHLINE; GREAT BATTLE, THE; IL
GRANDE ATTACCO
WAR                                     97 min
B,V,V2                             HOK/VIDMOV

**BIGGLES GETS OFF THE GROUND * **          PG
John Hough             UK                 1986
*Neil Dickson, Alex Hyde-White, Peter Cushing, James
Saxon, Michael Siberry, Marcus Gilbert, Fiona
Hutchinson, William Hootkins*
But the film stays put. A disjointed account of a young
businessman thrown back in time to 1917 where he
teams up with our fictional flying ace. The characters
are drawn from the "Biggles" WW1 novels of Captain
W.E. Johns but the film is firmly rooted in the
teen-fantasy adventure genre. Very poor indeed.
Aka: BIGGLES; BIGGLES: ADVENTURES IN TIME
A/AD                       89 min (ort 92 min)

B,V                                    CBS

## BIKINI SHOP, THE **                   15
David Wechter          USA               1985
*Bruce Greenwood, Michael David Wright, Debra Blee,*
*Barbara Horan, Ami Julius, Calyn Gorg, Jay*
*Robinson*
Two men run a bikini shop and have a little difficulty
making ends meet, in this pleasant sun, sand and surf
Californian comedy.
Aka: MALIBU BIKINI SHOP, THE
COM                                    90 min
B,V                              POLY; CH5

## BIKO INQUEST, THE **                  PG
Albert Finney          UK                1987
*Albert Finney, Nigel Davenport, Michael Gough, John*
*Standing, Richard Johnson, Michael Aldridge*
Dramatisation, based on the acclaimed theatre pro-
duction, of the events surrounding the death in police
custody of South African civil rights activist Steve
Biko. Long, wordy, earnest and dull, in roughly that
order. See also CRY FREEDOM.
DRA                                   102 min mTV
V                                        VCC

## BILITIS *                             18
David Hamilton         FRANCE            1977
*Patti d'Arbanville, Bernard Giraudeau, Mona*
*Kristensen, Mathieu Carriere, Gilles Kohler*
Soft-focus pretentious portrayal of a girl's coming of
age and sexual initiation. An incredible, implausible
and utterly French film, full of silly visual imagery
and little else, made by a director better known for his
glossy coffee-table books of nude models. See also A
SUMMER IN SAINT TROPEZ, a similar film that
works in a way this one fails to.
A                              91 min Cut (25 sec)
B,V                                  INT/CBS

## BILL ***                              PG
Anthony Page           USA               1981
*Mickey Rooney, Dennis Quaid, Largo Woodruff, Harry*
*Goz, Anna Maria Horsford, Kathleen Maguire, Jenny*
*Dweir, Tony Turco, Ray Serra, John Towey, Breon*
*Gorman, George Hamlin, Phil Oxnam, Harriet Rogers,*
*Lotta Palfi, Bill Winkler*
Sensitive and moving drama about a mentally re-
tarded adult who is struggling to adapt to life outside
the institution he has spent 46 years in. Rooney gives
one of the finest performance of his career (for which
he won an Emmy), in a film which, but for some
contrived padding, would have been quite outstand-
ing. Based on the true story of William Sackter. An
Emmy also went to Corey Blechman for the script.
Followed by BILL: ON HIS OWN.
Boa: story by Barry Morrow.
DRA                     93 min (ort 100 min) mTV
B,V                  GHV; VCC; ODY (VHS only)

## BILL AND TED'S EXCELLENT ADVENTURE ** PG
Stephen Herek          USA               1989
*Keanu Reeves, Alex Winter, George Carlin, Bernie*
*Casey, Amy Stock-Poynton, Tony Camilieri, Dan Shor,*
*Ted Steedman, Rod Loomis, Al Leong, Robert V.*
*Barron*
Two brainless teenagers must avoid flunking their
history exam and their discovery of a time-travelling
telephone booth gives them the chance to do so when
they meet various characters from the past. An
empty-headed jaunt through time that provides a
trifle of amusement.
COM                       86 min (ort 90 min)
V                                      CASPIC

## BILL OF DIVORCEMENT, A **
George Cukor           USA               1932
*John Barrymore, Katharine Hepburn, Billie Burke,*
*David Manners, Henry Stephenson*

Drama of a man who returns home after years in a
mental home and gets to know his daughter for the
first time, despite the fact that his wife is preparing to
divorce him. Interesting but rather stilted and now
chiefly remembered as Hepburn's screen debut.
Aka: NEVER TO LOVE
Boa: play by C. Dane.
DRA                     75 min; 96 min (INT) B/W
B,V                                 GHV; INT

## BILL: ON HIS OWN ***                  PG
Anthony Page           USA               1983
*Mickey Rooney, Helen Hunt, Edie McClurg, Tracey*
*Walter, Teresa Wright, Paul Lieber, Dennis Quaid,*
*Harry Goz, Largo Woodruff, Terry Evans, Marianna*
*Clore Blase, Jerry Michael Hayes, Marina Astudillo,*
*Sharon Menzel, Mona Fultz*
This sequel to BILL tells the story of an ex-patient of a
mental home and the problems he faces in readjusting
to the outside world. Not quite as good as the earlier
film, but Rooney's fine performance carries it along.
DRA                                   92 min mTV
B,V                  CBS; ODY; CH5 (VHS only)

## BILLION DOLLAR BRAIN ***              PG
Ken Russell            UK                1967
*Michael Caine, Karl Malden, Ed Begley, Oscar*
*Homolka, Francoise Dorleac, Guy Doleman, Vladek*
*Sheybal, Milo Sperber, Mark Elwes, Donald*
*Sutherland, Susan George*
This flawed attempt to film Deighton's novel suffers
from both stilted dialogue and over-indulgence.
However, it's enjoyable for Ed Begley's superb por-
trayal of a rabid commie-hating billionaire, who plans
an attack on the USSR but is foiled by Homolka as a
wily KGB colonel. Caine, as agent Harry Palmer is as
lifeless as ever, though some see this as his chief
strength. Preceded by THE IPCRESS FILE and
FUNERAL IN BERLIN.
Boa: novel by Len Deighton.
THR                                    111 min
B,V                                      WHV

## BILLION FOR BORIS, A **               PG
Alex Grasshoff         USA               1984
*Seth Green, Lee Grant, Scott Tiler*
A man finds a way to make money, after his friend
builds a TV set that can predict the future. An
unusual idea for a comedy that doesn't really come
together – pity.
Boa: novel by Mary Rodgers.
COM                                    90 min
B,V                                      HER

## BILLIONAIRE BOY'S CLUB **             15
Marvin J. Chomsky      USA               1987
*Judd Nelson, Ron Silver, Fredric Lehne, Brian*
*McNamara, Raphael Sbarge, John Stockwell, Barry*
*Tubb, Stan Shaw, Jill Schoelen, James Sloyan, Ron*
*Silver, James Karen*
Based on the true story of convicted killer Joe Hunt,
this tells of how a criminal embroiled a group of L.A.
youthful millionaires into a dubious money-making
scheme, whose eventual outcome was murder. An
interesting saga spoilt by stilted dialogue and lack of
pace.
Aka: BILLION DOLLAR BOY'S CLUB
DRA    175 min; 180 min (VIR) (ort 200 min) (2 cassettes)
mTV
B,V                     IVS; VIR; VCC (VHS only)

## BILLY GALVIN ***                      PG
John Gray              USA               1985
*Karl Malden, Lenny Von Dohlen, Toni Kalem, Joyce*
*Van Patten, Keith Szarabajka, Alan North, Paul*
*Guilfoyle, Barton Heyman*
Story of the title character who wants to be a
construction worker just like dad, despite the serious

reservations of his father, who wants his son to have a better life. Nice performances hold the interest when the cliched and formula script has long since ceased to.
DRA 91 min
V RCA

**BILLY JACK ** **                                    18
T.C Frank (Tom Laughlin)
                                    USA                1971
Tom Laughlin, Delores Taylor, Clark Howat, Bert Freed, Julie Webb
Our hero is a mixed race Vietnam vet who uses his karate expertise to save a school, protect wild mustangs and help a runaway teenager. Followed by two sequels: "The Trial Of Billy Jack" and "Billy Jack Goes To Washington". None of them are particularly good, all have a simplistic "peace and love" message that is ill-served by the violence of the plots.
DRA 111 min
B,V WHV

**BILLY LIAR ** ** **                                 PG
John Schlesinger        UK                1963
Tom Courtenay, Julie Christie, Wilfred Pickles, Mona Washbourne, Finlay Currie, Ethel Griffies, Gwendolyn Watts, Helen Fraser, Leslie Randall, Rodney Bewes, George Innes, Patrick Barr, Godfrey Winn, Leonard Rossiter
An excellent adaptation of a novel, of a bored undertaker's clerk whose only escape from the dullness of his drab North Country existence is via his own imagination. Imaginative, touching and rather poignant.
Boa: novel by Keith Waterhouse/play by Keith Waterhouse and W. Hall.
COM 96 min; 89 min (WHV) (ort 98 min) B/W
B,V TEVP; WHV (VHS only)

**BILLY THE KID ** **                                 15
William A. Graham        USA                1988
Val Kilmer, Duncan Regehr, Ned Vaughan, Patrick Massett, Julia Carmen, Nate Esformes, Rene Auberjonois, Albert Salmi, Gore Vidal
Screenplay is by Gore Vidal, in this sanitised tale of a poor misunderstood lad who just happened to become a killer through events outside his control. An entertaining film that does little to increase our knowledge of the true nature of this legendary Wild West character. An earlier teleplay by Vidal in the 1950s formed the basis for the Paul Newman film, THE LEFT-HANDED GUN. Vidal has a cameo as a graveside minister.
Aka: GORE VIDAL'S BILLY THE KID
WES 93 min (ort 100 min) mCab
V TURNER

**BILLY THE KID VERSUS DRACULA ** *                   PG
William Beaudine        USA                1965
Chuck Courtney, John Carradine, Melinda Plowman, Virginia Christine, Walter Janovitz, Bing Russell, Harry Carey Jr
Ridiculously inept spoof in which Billy the Kid unwittingly marries a girl whose uncle just happens to be Dracula.
HOR 80 min
B,V EHE

**BILOXI BLUES ** ** **                               15
Mike Nichols        USA                1988
Matthew Broderick, Christopher Walken, Matt Mulhern, Corey Parker, Markus Flanagan, Casey Siemaszko, Michael Dolan, Penelope Ann Miller
Semi-autobiographical account of Neil Simon's wartime experiences, set in 1943 at an army base in Missouri. This continues the tale of Eugene Jerome that began with BRIGHTON BEACH MEMOIRS and follows him through his ten tough weeks of army basic training. A witty and perceptive look at a young man's

journey to manhood. The stage play "Broadway Bound" followed up its success.
COM 103 min
V/sh CIC

**BIM ** ** **                                        
Hugh A. Robertson   TRINIDAD        1974
Ralph Maharaj, Hamilton Parris, Wilbert Holden
Strong and thoughtful drama that examines the tensions between the black and Indian communities of Trinidad before 1962.
DRA 98 min
B,V WOV

**BINGO BONGO ** **                                   15
Pasquale Festa Campanile
                                    ITALY                1982
Adriano Celentano, Carole Bruquet, Walter D'Amore
A boy reared by apes is brought back to civilisation and falls in love with the scientist who teaches him to speak, in this foolish comedy.
COM 102 min
B,V RCA

**BIOHAZARD ** *                                      18
Fred Olen Ray        USA                1983
Aldo Ray, Angelique Pettyjohn, Arthur Peyton, William Fair, Frank McDonald, Christopher Ray, David Pearson, Richard Hench, Carroll Borland
A psychic experiment releases a being from a parallel universe that immediately sets out to hunt for its favourite food – humans. A lacklustre offering from a renowned B-film director.
FAN 75 min
B,V VIR

**BIONIC NINJA ** **                                  18
Tim Ashby        HONG KONG        1986
Kelly Steve, Alan Hemmings, Rick Wilson, Peter Chan, Andy Man, Jack Young, Pauline Chao, Alex Baker
The CIA send their best agent to recover a top secret microfilm, after it has been stolen for the KGB by a criminal Ninja organisation. The mission seems hopeless, our agent is blocked at every turn, but he discovers the power of Ninjitsu, a power so great that our mighty hero is able to smash his way into the heart of this evil empire. High-action nonsense with a low-grade plot.
MAR 86 min Cut (14 sec)
B,V VPD

**BIONIC SHOWDOWN, THE ** *                           PG
Alan Levi        USA                1989
Lee Majors, Lindsay Wagner, Richard Anderson, Sandra Bullock, Jeff Yagher, Geraint Wyn Davies, Martin E. Brooks, Robert Lansing, Josef Sommer, Lee Majors II
More bionic shenanigans in this spin-off from "The Six Million Dollar Man", with the pair from the TV series and a couple of similarly equipped youngsters out to foil the work of a bionic spy whose intention is to blight East-West relations. Poorly plotted production-line nonsense.
Aka: BIONIC SHOWDOWN: THE SIX MILLION DOLLAR MAN AND THE BIONIC WOMAN
A/AD 92 min (ort 100 min) mTV
V CIC

**BIRD ** ** **                                       15
Clint Eastwood        USA                1988
Forest Whitaker, Diane Venora, Michael Zelniker, Samuel E. Wright, Keith David, Michael McGuire, James Handy
The story of legendary jazz saxophonist Charlie Parker, whose playing dominated jazz in the 1940s. When it's good it's very good, but this film spends too long looking at Parker's self-destructive urges, most especially his drug addiction. Whitaker's bravura

performance and Parker's music (most of the sound-track features his playing) are considerable compensations. AA: Sound (Les Frescholtz/Dick Alexander/Vern Poore/William D. Burton).

DRA 154 min (ort 161 min)
V WHV

## BIRD WITH THE CRYSTAL PLUMAGE, THE ** 18
Dario Argento
             ITALY/WEST GERMANY    1969
*Tony Musante, Suzy Kendall, Eva Renzi, Enrico Maria Salerno, Mario Adorf, Renato Romano, Umberto Rano, Werner Peters*
An American writer living in Rome witnesses a murder and draws himself and his mistress into a tangled web of intrigue as he embarks on an amateur sleuthing exercise. Disjointed and uneven thriller that would have been far more gripping with a tighter script.
Aka: BIRD WITH THE GLASS FEATHERS, THE; DAS GEHEIMNIS DER SCHWARZEN HANDSCHUHE; GALLERY MURDERS, THE; L'UCCELLO D'ALLE PIUME DI CRISTALLO; PHANTOM OF TERROR, THE
THR 92 min (ort 98 min) (Cut at film release)
B,V,V2 VDM L/A; STABL

## BIRDS OF PREY ** 18
Jorge Montesi    CANADA    1984
*Jorges Montesi, Linda Elder, Joseph Patrick Finn, Maurice Brand, Jennifer Keene, Sam Motrich, Mike Douglas, Peter Haynes, Toby M. Lawrence, Deryck Hazel, Suzanne Tessier, Rolanda Lee, Paul Wood, Mark Olafson, Mike Gazely*
When the body of a brutally murdered pimp is discovered, the evidence appears to point to a small-time criminal. However, his detective friend suspects that he has been framed and the two men try to discover the real culprits. Average.
Aka: TRAPPED
THR 90 min
B,V RCA

## BIRDS, THE ** 15
Alfred Hitchcock    USA    1963
*Rod Taylor, Tippi Hedren, Suzanne Pleshette, Jessica Tandy, Veronica Cartwright, Ethel Griffies, Charles McGraw*
One of Hitchcock's less successful films in that it fails to develop in any substantial way. In it, groups of birds join for some unknown reason and begin to make murderous attacks on the people living in a small and isolated California community. The plodding and opaque script is by Evan Hunter. Loved by the critics, but on careful viewing it's really hard to see why.
Boa: story by Daphne Du Maurier.
DRA 113 min
V CIC

## BIRDY *** 15
Alan Parker    USA    1984
*Matthew Modine, Nicolas Cage, John Harkins, Sandy Baron, Karen Young*
Two friends are reunited after having fought in Vietnam. One of them is confined to an asylum where his obsession with birds has led to his complete isolation from the outside world. Wharton's powerful WW2 novel is updated to the Vietnam War and works surprisingly well, despite a disappointing ending. Modine is quite outstanding. Scripted by Sandy Kroopf and Jack Behr.
Boa: novel by William Wharton.
DRA 115 min
V/sh RCA

## BIRTH OF A NATION, THE **** 
D.W. Griffith    USA    1915
*Lillian Gish, Mae Marsh, Miriam Cooper, Robert Harron, Josephine Cromwell, Henry B. Walthall,*

Wallace Reid, Donald Crisp, Joseph Henabery, Raoul Walsh, Eugene Pallette, Spottiswood Aiken, J.A. Beringer, John French
First and most famous cinema epic depicting the story of the American Civil War and the post-war period, seen through the eyes of two families. A classic and often moving film that is as successful in its depiction of the battle scenes as it is in portraying more intimate moments. The film, originally shown as "The Clansman", is slightly marred by its expression of questionable sentiments. Written by Griffith and Frank E. Woods.
Boa: novel The Klansman by Thomas Dixon Jr.
DRA 158 min B/W silent
B,V SPEC/POLY

## BIRTHDAY PARTY, THE *** 15
William Friedkin    UK    1968
*Robert Shaw, Patrick Magee, Dandy Nichols, Sydney Tafler, Moultrie Kelsall, Helen Fraser*
Film version of a Harold Pinter play about a lodger in a seaside boarding house who is menaced by two strangers. An overlong display of Pinter's talent for the obscure that works quite well, despite the absence of a meaningful plot.
Boa: play by Harold Pinter.
THR 122 min (ort 124 min)
B,V RNK; VGM

## BISCUIT EATER, THE ** U
Vincent McEveety    USA    1972
*Earl Holliman, Lew Ayres, Godfrey Cambridge, Patricia Crowley, Johnny Whitaker, Beah Richards, George Spell*
Typical Disney kiddie-fare in which a discarded mongrel is rescued by our juvenile heroes and as per formula, goes on to win a championship. OK if you like your films sugar-coated. A remake of a 1940 film of the same name.
JUV 87 min Cut (4 sec)
B,V WDV

## BISEXUAL ** 18
Eric Lipman    FRANCE    1975
*Yves-Marie Mauvin, Florence Caybrol, Marion Game, Jenny Arasse, Bernadette Robert, Guy Bertil, Sylvain Levignac*
The erotic fantasies of a young computer operator involving himself and his girlfriend (but alas, not his computer).
Aka: LES ONZE MILLE VIERGES; 11,000 SEXES, THE
Boa: novel Les Onze Milles Vierges by Guillaume Apollinaire.
DRA 80 min Cut (19 sec in addition to film cuts)
B,V DER; XTASY

## BITCH WANTS BLOOD, THE ** 
             FRANCE
*Monica Vitti, Maurice Ronet, Robert Hussein*
Unedifying exploiter about a rape victim who seeks revenge.
DRA 83 min
B,V PAE L/A; MRV

## BITCH, THE * 18
Gerry O'Hara    UK    1979
*Joan Collins, Michael Coby, Kenneth Haigh, Ian Hendry, Carolyn Seymour, Sue Lloyd, Mark Burns, John Ratzenberger, Pamela Salem, Anthony Heaton, Maurice O'Connell, Peter Wight, Doug Fisher, George Sweeney, Chris Jagger*
In this sequel to THE STUD our heroine, facing divorce from her wealthy husband, will stop at nothing to save her failing disco, and engages in a temporary liaison with a gangster on the run from the Mafia. A weak, noisy disco-style follow-up that unashamedly seeks to cash in on the success of the earlier film.

Boa: novel by Jackie Collins. Osca: STUD, THE
(PARK)
DRA   90 min; 99 min (VGM); 189 min (PARK – 2 film
cassette)
B,V   BWV/VSP; VGM (VHS only); PARK (VHS only)

**BITE THE BULLET ***                               PG
Richard Brooks          USA            1975
*Gene Hackman, Candice Bergen, James Coburn, Jan-
Michael Vincent, Ian Bannen, Ben Johnson, John
McLiam, Jerry Gatlin, Robert Donner, Robert Hoy,
Dabney Coleman, Paul Stewart, Jean Willes, Sally
Kirkland, Buddy Van Horn*
This story of an epic 600-mile endurance horse race in
the old West suffers badly from a thin plot and an
episodic treatment. The beautiful photography of
Harry Stradling Jr is however, a considerable com-
pensation. Written by Brooks.
WES                       125 min (ort 131 min)
V                                       RCA

**BITE, THE ***                                    18
Fred Goodwin        ITALY/JAPAN        1989
*Jill Schoelen, J. Eddie Peck, Jamie Farr, Savina
Gersak, Bo Svenson, Sydney Lassick*
A young couple travelling through the desert inadver-
tently come across an abandoned nuclear test site.
Unfortunately the man is bitten by one of the mutated
snakes that infest the area and eventually becomes a
rampaging snake-like creature that must be des-
troyed. A conventional but rather well made horror
film that harks back to the 1950s. Apart from having
the same producer, the film bears no relation to THE
CURSE.
Aka: CURSE 2: THE BITE
HOR                        94 min (ort 98 min)
V                                       EIV

**BITTER HARVEST ***                               PG
Roger Young            USA             1981
*Ron Howard, Art Carney, Tarah Nutter, David Knell,
Barry Corbin, Richard Dysart, Michael Bond, Jim
Haynie, Robert Hirschfeld, G.W. Bailey, Robert
Behling, Ken Hixon, Dwight Schultz, Joe Miksak,
Charlotte Stewart*
Based on a true incident, this tells of a young dairy
farmer's race against time to identify a deadly chemic-
al that is killing his cattle and has poisoned his child.
An effective drama with an intelligent script by
Richard Friedenberg.
DRA                       90 min (ort 100 min) mTV
V                                       VPD

**BITTER TEARS OF PETRA VON KANT, THE ***
Rainer Werner Fassbinder
              WEST GERMANY            1972
*Margit Carstensen, Irm Hermann, Hanna Schygulla,
Eva Mattes, Katrin Schaake, Gisela Fackelday*
Ponderous and pretentious film about a lesbian
love-triangle, with wealthy fashion designer Carsten-
sen fretting over her unreliable lover Schygulla. Slow,
tedious and vastly over-rated. Written by Fassbinder.
DRA                                     124 min
B,V                                     PVG

**BITTERSWEET LOVE ***                             
David Miller           USA             1975
*Lana Turner, Robert Lansing, Celeste Holm, Robert
Alda, Scott Hylands, Meredith Baxter Binney*
A couple marry and after the wife conceives, they
discover that they are in fact half-brother and sister.
To this unlikely plot is added the additional tedium of
endless discussion regarding abortion and the ter-
mination of their marriage.
DRA                                     95 min
B,V                                     CBS

**BLACK ARROW ***                                  U
John Hough             USA             1983

*Oliver Reed, Fernando Taylor, Benedict Taylor,
Stephan Chase, Georgia Slowe, Donald Pleasence, Roy
Boyd, Aldo Sanbrell, Carol Gotell, Frank Brana,
Robert Russell, Ralph Brown*
In 15th century England an outlaw battles a corrupt
lord. Entertaining but rather bland remake of the
superior 1948 film.
Boa: novel by Robert Louis Stevenson.
A/AD                                    90 min mCab
B,V                                     WDV

**BLACK ARROW, THE ***                             Uc
              AUSTRALIA              1973
Fairly well made animation set against the background of the English Civil War, and following the
exploits of a young squire who teams up with a band of
forest outlaws and attempts to capture a traitor to his
cause.
CAR                                     60 min
V                                       STYL

**BLACK BEAUTY ***                                 U
James Hill              UK             1971
*Mark Lester, Walter Slezak, Peter Lee Lawrence, Uschi
Glas, Patrick Mower, John Nettleton, Maria Rohm,
Eddie Golden, Clive Geraghty, Johnny Hoey, Patrick
Gardiner, Margaret Lacey, Fernando Bilbao, Vincente
Rola, Jose Niero*
Film based on the classic story by Anna Sewell about
an unhappy horse that is mistreated by a series of
cruel owners before finally returning to its original
young master. No more than adequate. Screenplay is
by Hill and Wolf Mankowicz and the music is by
Lionel Bart.
Boa: novel by Anna Sewell.
DRA                                     105 min
B,V,V2                     HOK; VGM (VHS only)

**BLACK BEAUTY ***                                 U
              USA                    1978
A cartoon version of the famous children's classic by
Anna Sewell that tells of a horse that is separated
from its kiowner and suffers great hardship before
being reunited with him. Somewhat sugary, but a
likeable enough tale.
Boa: novel by Anna Sewell.
CAR                        60 min; 44 min (CH5)
B,V                       SKY/VFP; CH5 (VHS only)

**BLACK BEAUTY ***          Uc            1988
Pleasant but unmemorable animation based on
Sewell's classic story of a young horse that endures
many hardships following its separation from its
master.
Boa: novel by Anna Sewell.
CAR                                     49 min
V                                       VCC; PICK

**BLACK BELT JONES ***                             18
Robert Clouse          USA             1973
*Jim Kelly, Gloria Hendry, Scatman Crothers, Alan
Weeks, Eric Laneuville, Nate Esformes*
Black kung fu in this story of a school of self-defence,
battling with the Mafia in the Watts district of L.A. A
fairly enjoyable action film from the same team that
brought us ENTER THE DRAGON. Followed by a
sequel.
MAR         82 min (Cut at film release by 1 min 27 sec)
B,V                                     WHV

**BLACK BOUNTY KILLER, THE ***                     15
Jack Arnold            USA             1974
*Fred Williamson, D'Urville Martin, R.G. Armstrong,
William Smith, Carmen Hayworth, Barbara Leigh,
Don Barry, Ben Zeller*
A black bounty hunter becomes a sheriff and cleans up
the town. Reminiscent of BLAZING SADDLES but
more of a true Western.
Aka: BOSS; BOSS NIGGER

WES           87 min; 89 min (SHEP)
B,V                  VPD; SHEP

## BLACK CAESAR **          18
Larry Cohen       USA           1973
*Fred Williamson, Art Lund, Julius W. Harris, Gloria Hendry, D'Urville Martin, Val Avery, William Wellman*
Black version of THE GODFATHER, tracing the rise of a petty criminal, with the usual gore and violence. Followed by a sequel the same year – "Hell Up In Harlem".
DRA                    92 min
B,V                STARB L/A

## BLACK CARRION **
John Hough       UK            1984
*Season Hubley, Leigh Lawson, Norman Bird, Alan Love, Diana King, William Hootkins*
A journalist and a photographer on the trail of two missing pop stars are led to a strange village that is not marked on any map. Average horror yarn.
HOR                  72 min
B,V                   BWV

## BLACK CAT, THE **
Lucio Fulci      ITALY        1981
*Patrick Magee, Mimsy Farmer, David Warbeck, Dagmar Lassander, Daniela Doro, Al Cliver (Pier Luigi Conti), Bruno Corazzari, Geoffrey Copleston*
Slightly Poe-inspired tale that opens with a strange man who wanders through cemeteries recording messages from the dead. A detective is sent to investigate a series of nasty murders, but it is a female photographer who connects them to the man's sinister cat. A stodgy low-budget affair.
Aka: IL GATTO NERO
HOR                  88 min
B,V                   VTC

## BLACK COBRA, THE **      18
Stelvio Massi    USA          1987
*Fred Williamson, Karl Lundgren, Eva Grimaldi, Riccardo Moni, Vassili Karis*
A woman photographer sees a murder being committed and takes a photo of the killer, a vicious gang leader, thereby putting herself at the top of his personal hit list. Average.
THR      87 min (ort 95 min) Cut (1 min 14 sec)
B,V                  VPD

## BLACK DEEP THROAT **     18
Albert Moore (Guido Zurli)
             ITALY        1976
*Ajita Wilson, Ivano Staccioli, Agnes Kalpagos, Ronald Mardanbo, Patricia Webley*
A black female journalist becomes involved in sexual scandals in high places.
Aka: GOLA PROFUNDA NERA; QUEEN OF SEX (XTASY)
A    79 min (ort 90 min) Cut (XTASY: 4 min 5 sec)
B,V,V2     INT/CBS L/A; VPD L/A; XTASY

## BLACK DRAGON AVENGES THE    18
## DEATH OF BRUCE LEE, THE **
Tommy Loo Chung HONG KONG      1975
*Ron Van Clief, Charles (La Pantera) Bonet, Thomson Kao Kan*
A wealthy businessman hires a martial arts champion to find out the truth about the death of Bruce Lee. Yet one more tedious martial arts caper trading on the reputation of Lee.
MAR          90 min; 83 min (SHEP)
B,V,V2            VPD L/A; SHEP

## BLACK DRAGON, THE **
Tommy Loo Chung (Lu Chun)

---

         HONG KONG         1974
*Ron Van Clief, Jason Pai Piao, Jorge Estraga, Nancy Veronica*
A young farm boy teams up with a narcotics agent to penetrate a drugs syndicate. Average.
MAR          60 min (ort 93 min)
V                    HVS

## BLACK EAGLE, THE ***      15
Eric Karson      USA          1986
*Jean Claude Van Damme, Sho Kosugi, Doran Clark, Bruce Doran, Vladimir Skomarovsky, William H. Bassett, Jan Triska, Kane Kosugi, Shane Kosugi*
Under the cover of a Japanese marine biologist, a CIA agent undertakes a hazardous mission to recover top-secret laser navigation equipment from a crashed USA fighter. Fast-paced formula actioner with a liberal dose of martial arts combat.
A/AD         89 min (ort 93 min)
B,V                  VPD

## BLACK EMMANUELLE *      18
Albert Thomas (Adalberto Albertini)
             ITALY        1975
*Laura Gemser, Karin Schubert, Angelo Infanti, Don Powell*
First in an interminable series. Here our heroine is a photographer sent to Nairobi on an assignment. Various sexual adventures follow in this glossy but utterly tedious softcore effort.
Aka: EMMANUELLE NERA
A         98 min Cut (1 min 28 sec)
B,V                  WHV

## BLACK EMMANUELLE 2 **
Albert Thomas (Adalberto Albertini)
             ITALY        1976
*Shulamith Lasri, Angelo Infanti, Dagmar Lassander, Don Powell, Percy Hogan, Sharon Leslie, Pietro Torrisi, Franco Daddi, Attilio Pottesio, Danielle Ellison, Franco Cremonini*
Our voluptuous heroine is wounded in Beirut in the course of the Lebanese Civil War and loses her memory. She travels to New York for treatment and is slowly nursed back to health. A flimsy story that provides the excuse for much petting in this formula softcore tale.
Aka: BLACK EMMANUELLE NO. 2;
EMMANUELLE NERA NO. 2; NEW BLACK EMMANUELLE, THE (VPD)
A          90 min; 85 min (VPD)
B,V              PFS; VPD

## BLACK EMMANUELLE GOES EAST **  18
Joe D'Amato (Aristide Massaccesi)
             ITALY        1976
*Laura Gemser, Gabriele Tinti, Ely Galleani, Ivan Rassimov, Kioke Mahoco*
This time our heroine is in the Far East. Various sexual adventures follow. Another dreary softcore session enlivened by the exotic locations.
Aka: BLACK EMMANUELLE IN BANGKOK;
EMMANUELLE NERA: ORIENT REPORTAGE
A       86 min Cut (3 min 25 sec)
B,V          CANON/VPD; ROGUE

## BLACK EMMANUELLE,         18
## WHITE EMMANUELLE **
Brunello Rondi   ITALY        1976
*Laura Gemser, Annie Belle, Al Cliver (Pier Luigi Conti), Gabriele Tinti, Susan Scott, Theodore Challapin*
Set in a magnificent villa on the banks of the Nile, this is the story of the strange effect a young female student has on an extravagant group of expatriates. Various sexual adventures follow.
Aka: EMMANUELLE IN EGYPT; VELLUTO NERO
A 77 min (ort 83 min) Cut (1 min 52 sec in addition to

film cuts)
B,V                                    DFS; XTACY/KRP

## BLACK FIST ***
Timothy Galfas          USA              1976
*Richard Kaye, Richard Lawson, Annazette Chase,*
*Dabney Colman, Robert Burr*
A tough martial arts fighter is hired by a crime boss as
a streetfighter, and comes into conflict with a crooked
cop in this black kung fu actioner. More or less a
formula offering, but Colman's performance as the
corrupt cop makes it worthwhile.
Aka: BLACK STREETFIGHTER, THE; FIST
THR                       90 min (ort 105 min)
B,V                                    VIPCO; CIC

## BLACK GESTAPO, THE **
Lee Frost               USA              1975
*Rod Perry, Charles P. Robinson, Lee Frost, Ed Gross,*
*Angela Brent, Phil Hoover*
When a black nurse is raped and then murdered, a
black vigilante group is formed in the ghetto under
the leadership of a Vietnam vet, but this people's
army soon becomes embroiled in a violent internal
power struggle.
DRA                       81 min (ort 89 min)
B,V,V2                                 IFS/CBS

## BLACK GOLD **
                    FRANCE/ITALY         1961
*Richard Harrison, Florence Cayrol, Jean Marie*
*Lemaire, Fay Spain, William Phipps, Dub Taylor, Ken*
*Mayer, Vincent Barbi, Rusty Westcoatt*
Four men and a woman are sent to the Middle East by
an oil company, to sabotage the wells of an Arab
Emirate that does not wish to abide by a contract.
Much murder, intrigue and espionage takes place.
A/AD                                    102 min
B,V,V2                                 VPD

## BLACK GUNN **
Robert Hartford-Davis   USA              1972
*James Brown, Martin Landau, Brenda Sykes, Luciana*
*Paluzzi, Stephen McNally*
After his brother is killed, a black nightclub owner
goes on a revenge-hungry rampage in this formula
black action film.
THR                                     100 min
B,V                                    CIC

## BLACK HAND, THE **
Antonio Racioppi    ITALY/SPAIN          1973
*Lionel Stander, Philippe Leroy, Rosanna Fratella*
A young immigrant arrives in New York and is
gradually drawn into criminal activities. Average.
THR                                     104 min
B,V,V2                                 VPD

## BLACK HOLE, THE ***                        PG
Gary Nelson             USA              1979
*Anthony Perkins, Maximilian Schell, Ernest Borgnine,*
*Yvette Mimieux, Robert Forster, Joseph Bottoms*
A film that could have been much better. Poor
dialogue and characterisation let down this story of
the arrival of an expedition to an almost deserted
spaceship, perched precariously on the edge of a black
hole, the only inhabitants of which are a crazed
scientist and a sinister army of robots. The best
features are the effects, and the strange "Heaven or
Hell" ending that follows the passage of the ship
through the hole.
FAN                                     92 min
B,V,V2                                 RNK; WDV

## BLACK JACK **
William T. Naud         USA              1972
*Georg Stanford Brown, Brandon De Wilde, Keenan*
*Wynn, Tim O'Connor, James Daly, Dick Gautier,*
*Robert Lansing*

A failed attempt at a screwball comedy with three
convicts hijacking a B-52 bomber. Too patchy to really
work, but there are a few nice comic touches. Written
by Naud and Gautier.
Aka: BLACKJACK; WILD IN THE SKY
COM                                     87 min
B,V                                    VCL

## BLACK MAMA, WHITE MAMA **                   18
Eddie Romero            USA              1972
*Pam Grier, Margaret Markov, Sid Haig, Lynn Borden,*
*Zaldy Zshornack, Laurie Burton, Eddie Garcia*
This virtual remake of "The Defiant Ones" has two
female convicts escaping from a Filipino prison camp,
but chained together. Hammy actioner in which any
superficial resemblance to the outstanding earlier
film is no more than accidental.
Aka: CHAINED WOMEN; CHAINS OF HATE; HOT,
HARD AND MEAN
THR             81 min (ort 90 min) Cut (23 sec)
B,V                                    RNK

## BLACK MARBLE, THE **                        15
Harold Becker           USA              1980
*Robert Foxworth, Paula Prentiss, Harry Dean Stanton,*
*Barbara Babcock, John Hancock, Raleigh Bond, Judy*
*Landers, James Woods*
Forgettable police romance with a beautiful female
cop being assigned a new partner who's an alcoholic.
Stiff and unmoving with none of the wit or punch of
the novel.
Boa: novel by Joseph Wambaugh.
DRA                                     106 min
B,V,V2,LV                              EHE

## BLACK MARKET BABY **                        PG
Robert F. Day           USA              1977
*Bill Bixby, Linda Purl, Desi Arnez Jr, Tom Bosley,*
*David Doyle, Jessica Walter, Lucille Benson, Annie*
*Potts, Tracy Brooks Swope, Allan Joseph, Mark*
*Thomas, Argentina Brunetti, Tom Pedi, Beulah Quo,*
*Robert Resnick*
A college student gets pregnant and she and her
boyfriend have a hard time fending off a black market
adoption ring that's out to take away the child. An
unpleasant and exploitative tale that never really
tries to examine the complexities of this social issue.
Aka: DANGEROUS LOVE, A; DON'T STEAL MY
BABY
Boa: novel A Nice Italian Girl by Elizabeth
Christman.
DRA                                     96 min mTV
B,V                                    CINE

## BLACK MOON RISING *                          18
Harley Cokliss          USA              1985
*Tommy Lee Jones, Robert Vaughn, Linda Hamilton,*
*Bubba Smith, Keenan Wynn, Richard Jaeckel, Lee*
*Ving, William Sanderson*
A thief steals a computer tape and hides it in the boot
of a high-tech hydrogen-powered supercar. When the
car is stolen a chase ensues. Plot minimal, action
maximal.
A/AD 90 min; 95 min (WHV) (ort 100 min) (Cut at
film release by 40 sec)
B, V/s                       CAN; WHV (VHS only)

## BLACK NARCISSUS ****                         U
Michael Powell/Emeric Pressburger
                    UK                   1946
*Deborah Kerr, David Farrar, Jean Simmons, Sabu,*
*Shaun Noble, Nancy Roberts, Flora Robson, Ley On,*
*Eddie Whaley Jr, Kathleen Byron, Esmond Knight,*
*Jenny Laird, May Hallatt, Judith Furse*
Well filmed story of the problems, emotional and
otherwise, that face a group of nuns trying to start a
mission in the Himalayas. Dramatic and often mov-
ing, with absolutely sumptuous photography that
earned it a well-deserved Oscar. A highpoint is the

flashback sequence (originally excised from the US prints) in which Kerr recalls her former life. AA: Cin (Jack Cardiff), Art/Set (Alfred Junge).
Boa: novel by Rumer Godden.

| | |
|---|---|
| DRA | 98 min (ort 100 min) |
| B,V | RNK; VCC (VHS only) |

**BLACK PANTHER, THE \***      18
Ian Merrick     UK     1977
*Donald Sumpter, Debbie Farrington, Marjorie Yates, Sylvia O'Donnell, Andrew Burt, Alison Key, Ruth Dunning, David Swift, Michael Barrington, Lila Kaye, Delia Paton, Edwin Apps, Gerry Sundquist, Ruth Kettlewell, Graham Ashley*
Film based on the true story of the notorious British psychopath, Donald Neilson, who kidnapped and murdered the heiress Leslie Whittle in Bradford, Yorkshire in 1972. A tasteless and exploitative re-enactment.

| | |
|---|---|
| THR | 99 min |
| B,V,V2 | ALPHA/INT; AVR |

**BLACK PIRATE, THE \***      PG
Mario Costa     ITALY     1962
*Ricardo Montalban, Giulia Rubini, Liana Orfei, Mario Feliciano, Vincent Price, Giustino Durano, Gisella Sofio, Jose Jaspe, Edoardo Toniolo*
A pirate stops the slave trade and marries the governor's daughter, in this rather laughable pirate adventure.
Aka: GORDON IL NERO PIRATA; GORDON THE BLACK PIRATE (ELE)

| | |
|---|---|
| A/AD | 88 min; 83 min (ELE) |
| B,V | APX; ELE (VHS only) |

**BLACK PIRATE, THE \*\***      PG
Vincent Thomas     ITALY     1976
*Terence Hill (Mario Girotti), Bud Spencer (Carlo Pedersoli), Silvia Monti*
Passabake of the 1926 pirate classic.
Aka: IL CORSAREO NERO

| | |
|---|---|
| A/AD | 103 min |
| B,V | VDM/GHV; PHE |

**BLACK PIRATE, THE \*\***      PG
Mario Costa     ITALY     1962
*Ricardo Montalban, Giulia Rubini, Liana Orfei, Mario Feliciano, Giustino Durano, Gisella Sofio, Jose Jaspe, Edoardo Toniolo*
A pirate stops the slave trade and marries the governor's daughter, in this rather laughable pirate adventure.
Aka: GORDON IL NERO PIRATA

| | |
|---|---|
| A/AD | 88 min |
| B,V | APX |

**BLACK PIRATE, THE \*\*\***
Albert S. Parker     USA     1926
*Douglas Fairbanks Sr, Billie Dove, Anders Randolph, Donald Crisp, Fred Becker, Tempe Piggott, Sam De Grasse*
Fairbanks plays a shipwrecked mariner who turns pirate, to have his revenge on the gang of cutthroats who blew up his father's ship. A thoroughly enjoyable silent classic, replete with athletic feats and sword-play and with the star in top form. It was filmed using an early Technicolor process but most available prints are B/W.

| | |
|---|---|
| A/AD | 83 min B/W silent |
| B,V | POLY |

**BLACK RAIN \*\*\***      18
Ridley Scott     USA     1989
*Michael Douglas, Andy Garcia, Ken Takakura, Kate Capshaw, Yusaki Matsuda, Shigeru Koyama, John Spencer*
A hardbitten New York cop (is there any other kind?) is given the job of delivering a Japanese mobster to the police in Osaka. When the crook escapes, the cop

insists on staying in Japan and helping to recapture him, but he now finds himself on unfamiliar terrain. A visually exciting rollercoaster of a film with simple plotting and violent action. AA: Sound (Donald O. Mitchell/Kevin O'Connell/Greg P. Russell/Keith A. Webster).

| | |
|---|---|
| THR | 121 min (ort 126 min) |
| V | CIC |

**BLACK RAINBOW \*\*\***      15
Mike Hodges     USA     1989
*Rosanna Arquette, Jason Robards, Tom Hulce, Mark Joy*
A well crafted thriller about a father-and-daughter team who perform clairvoyance tricks at small-town carnivals. When the daughter begins receiving messages apparently warning her about forthcoming murders the two find their lives in danger. Scripted by Hodges.

| | |
|---|---|
| THR | 103 min (ort 113 min) |
| V/h | PAL |

**BLACK ROOM, THE \*\***
Elly Kenner/Norman Thaddeas Vane
    USA     1981
*Stephen Knight, Cassandra Gaviola, Jim Stathis*
Visitors to a sinister mansion fall prey to modern day vampires. Average.

| | |
|---|---|
| HOR | 90 min |
| B,V,V2 | INT/CBS |

**BLACK ROSES \***      18
John Fasano     USA     1988
*John Martin, Ken Swofford, Julie Adams, Carla Gerrigno, Sal Viviano, Carmen Appice*
Small-town kids turn into monsters after a sleazy hard rock band arrives, and set about murdering their troublesome parents. A gloriously bad teen monster feast, whose promising tongue-in-cheek beginning soon gives way to a disjointed series of over-the-top encounters.

| | |
|---|---|
| HOR | 83 min (ort 90 min) Cut (31 sec) |
| B,V | VPD |

**BLACK SABBATH \*\*\***
Mario Bava     ITALY     1963
*Boris Karloff, Mark Damon, Michele Mercier, Jacqueline Pierreux (Jacqueline Soussard), Gustavo de Nardo, Glauco Onorato, Rika Dialina, Milly Monti, Harriet White*
Three tales of horror involving various forms of supernatural happening are hosted by Karloff, who appears in the final episode in which a vampire controls an entire family. Episodes are: "The Wurdalak", "A Drop Of Water" and "The Telephone". Above average and often quite atmospheric.
Aka: BLACK CHRISTMAS; I TRE VOLTI DELLA PAURA; THREE FACES OF FEAR, THE; THREE FACES OF TERROR, THE

| | |
|---|---|
| HOR | 99 min |
| B,V | VPD |

**BLACK SISTER'S REVENGE \*\***      15
Jamaa Fanaka     USA     1979
*Jerri Hayes, Ernest Williams II, Charles D. Brooks III*
A girl takes revenge for her boyfriend's betrayal, and takes to crime to keep her carwash going in the face of white hostility. Set in L.A. and another fine example of racism-exploitation, with white people portrayed as hateful bigots.

| | |
|---|---|
| DRA | 100 min |
| B,V,V2 | VDM; STABL |

**BLACK SIX, THE \***
Matt Cimber (Matteo Ottaviano)
    USA     1974
*Gene Washington, Carl Eller, Lem Barney, Willie Lanier, Rosalind Miles*
A real racism-exploitation movie – six black Vietnam

vets come up against racism, when the brother of one of them is murdered for dating a white girl by a group of Hell's Angels. Our vets soon sort them out in this tiresome and exploitative rubbish.

DRA                                    85 min
B,V                                  INT/CBS

**BLACK STALLION RETURNS, THE ***        U
Robert Dalva          USA              1983
*Kelly Reno, Vincent Spano, Woody Strode, Allen Goorwitz, Ferdinand Mayne, Jodi Thelan, Teri Garr*
Sequel to THE BLACK STALLION with our boy, now a teenager, searching the Sahara for his Arabian steed. Tired and disappointing sequel with none of the sparkle of the earlier film. The directorial debut for Dalva, who worked on the earlier film as editor.
Boa: novel by Walter Farley.
JUV                                    99 min
V/sh                                     WHV

**BLACK STALLION, THE ***                U
Carroll Ballard       USA              1979
*Kelly Reno, Mickey Rooney, Teri Garr, Clarence Muse, Hoyt Axton, Michael Higgins*
Adventures of a boy and a magnificent black stallion. They are shipwrecked on an island, and after being rescued go on to win a major horse race. A trifle overlong, but the beautiful photography and a great performance from Rooney as a veteran horse trainer help it along. A rather poor sequel, THE BLACK STALLION RETURNS followed in 1983. AA: Spec Award (Alan Splet for sound editing).
Boa: novel by Walter Farley.
JUV                                   110 min
V/s                                      WHV

**BLACK SUNDAY ***                       15
John Frankenheimer    USA              1977
*Robert Shaw, Bruce Dern, Marthe Keller, Fritz Weaver, Steven Keats, Bekim Fehimu, Michael V. Gazzo, William Daniels*
With the help of the pilot of a television blimp, a group of international terrorists plans to blow up an American Super Bowl sports stadium. Dern gives his usual psychotic performance as the slightly unbalanced pilot, a former Vietnam POW. Some great aerial photography and a strong script by Ernest Lehman, Kenneth Ross and Ivan Moffat, make us forget the implausibility of the plot.
Boa: novel by Thomas Harris.
THR                                   140 min
B,V                                  ARENA/CIC

**BLACK SUNDAY ***                       15
Mario Bava           ITALY             1960
*Barbara Steele, John Richardson, Ivo Garrani, Andrea Checchi, Arturo Dominici, Enrico Olivieri, Clara Bindi, Antonio Pierfederici, Tino Bianchi, Germana Dominici*
A beautiful witch was put to a cruel death hundreds of years ago. For one day each century she rises from the dead to have her revenge on the descendants of her original tormentors. An atmospheric and intriguing tale, well acted and directed.
Aka: LA MASCHERA DEL DEMONIO; DEMON'S MASK, THE; HOUSE OF FRIGHT; REVENGE OF THE VAMPIRE
Boa: short story The Vij by Nikolai Gogol.
HOR                                83 min B/W
B,V,V2                             VDM L/A; SCV

**BLACK TORMENT, THE ***                 15
Robert Hartford-Davis  UK             1964
*John Turner, Heather Sears, Ann Lynn, Peter Arne, Francis De Wolff, Edina Ronay, Raymond Huntley, Patrick Troughton, Annette Whitely, Joseph Tomelty, Norman Bird*
Spooky goings-on take place in 18th century England when a baronet whose first wife apparently committed

suicide returns to his estate with his new bride. The baronet begins to fear for his sanity following a series of nasty incidents that appear to be his own handiwork. There is however, a rational and rather neat explanation that can be traced to the jealousy of his dead wife's sister. Ponderously directed but replete with atmosphere.
Aka: ESTATE OF INSANITY
HOR                                    85 min
B,V,V2                        VAMP/VDM L/A; STABL

**BLACK TULIP, THE ***
Christian Jaque      ITALY             1963
*Alain Delon, Virna Lisi, Dawn Addams*
Adventure film based on a Dumas novel that tells of the exploits of the title character. Average costumer.
Boa: novel by Alexandre Dumas.
A/AD                                  109 min
B,V,V2                               VCL/CBS

**BLACK VEIL FOR LISA, A ***
Massimo Dallamano
                ITALY/WEST GERMANY      1969
*John Mills, Luciana Paluzzi, Robert Hoffman, Renate Kasche, Enzo Fiermonte, Carlo Hinterman, Louis Bazzocchi, Giuseppe Terranova, Rodolfo Licari, Bernandino Solitari, Vanno Polverosi, Robert Van Daalen*
The head of Hamburg's drugs squad spends more time tailing his wife than dealing with a drugs ring, as potential informers are killed one after the other. Fair thriller.
Aka: DAS GEHEIMIS DER JUNGEN WITSE; LA MORTE NON HA SESSO; VICOLO CIECO
THR                                    88 min
B,V                                  DIPLO/CBS

**BLACK VENUS ***                        18
Claude Mulot         USA               1983
*Mandy Rice Davies, Josephine Jacqueline Jones, Jose Antonio Ceinos, Emiliano Rodando, Florence Guerin, Karin Schubert*
A young woman rises from the brothel to better things. Made for America's Playboy cable channel and pretty much what one would expect.
Boa: short story by Honore de Balzac.
A    95 min (ort 110 min) (Cut at film release by 31 sec)
mCab
B,V                                      MGM

**BLACK WIDOW ***                        15
Bob Rafelson         USA               1986
*Debra Winger, Theresa Russell, Dennis Hopper, Nicol Williamson, Sami Frey, Terry O'Quinn, D.W. Moffett, Lois Smith, Mary Woronov, Rutanya Alda, James Hong, Diane Ladd*
A female investigator at the Justice Department, begins to follow the exploits of a young woman who seduces wealthy men, marrying and then killing them. However, her interest develops into an unhealthy obsession, in this slick and absorbing thriller, full of sexual intensity and often making intriguing comparisons between the two women and their motivations. The photography is by Conrad Hall and the score is by Michael Small.
THR                                    97 min
V/sh                                     CBS

**BLACK WINDMILL, THE ***                PG
Don Siegel           USA               1974
*Michael Caine, Donald Pleasence, Delphine Seyrig, Clive Revill, Janet Suzman, Joseph O'Connor, John Vernon, Joss Ackland*
Disappointing espionage thriller from a director who has done much better work. An espionage agent (played by Caine) faces a lone, uphill task, as he sets about trying to rescue his kidnapped son. Adequate,

but no more than that.
Boa: novel Seven Days To A Killing by Clive Egleton.
THR                                                   102 min
B,V                                                       MCA

## BLACKBEARD THE PIRATE **                            U
Raoul Walsh             USA                    1953
*Robert Newton, Linda Darnell, Keith Andes, William*
*Bendix, Irene Ryan, Richard Egan*
Classic story of pirates in the Caribbean, with re-
formed pirate Sir Henry Morgan being charged to rid
the seas of the dastardly Blackbeard. A rambling and
tedious yarn, with Newton having great fun hamming
up his pirate role. Partially redeemed by exceptional
Technicolor photography. Music is by Victor Young.
A/AD                                                   95 min
B,V                                                       KVD

## BLACKBEARD'S GHOST **
Robert Stevenson        USA                    1968
*Peter Ustinov, Dean Jones, Suzanne Pleshette*
The ghost of a famous pirate, returns to help prevent
gangsters taking over a hotel owned by his descen-
dants and turning it into a casino. Dreary and
uninspired comedy-fantasy despite a vigorous per-
formance from Ustinov.
Boa: story by B. Stahl.
COM                                                   102 min
B,V                                                       RNK

## BLACKENSTEIN
William A. Levey        USA                    1973
*John Hart, Ivory Stone, Andrea King, Liz Renay,*
*Roosevelt Jackson, Joe Disue, Nick Bolin, Cardella di*
*Milo, James Cougar, Marva Farmer*
A man wounded in Vietnam undergoes experimental
surgery to regain the use of his limbs, but is deliber-
ately given the wrong injection by a medical assistant
who lusts after his girlfriend. This produces "Blacken-
stein" – an unstoppable monster who has the honour
of appearing in one of the trashiest variants on the
Frankenstein legend ever made.
Aka: BLACK FRANKENSTEIN
HOR                                                    87 min
B,V                                                       VPD

## BLACKMAIL ***
Alfred Hitchcock        UK                     1929
*Anny Ondra, John Longden, Donald Calthrop, Cyril*
*Ritchard, Sara Allgood, Charles Paton, Harvey*
*Braban, Phyllis Monkman, Hannah Jones, Percy*
*Parsons, Johnny Butt, Sam Livesey (in the silent*
*version only)*
A woman kills a man who tried to rape her. She then
finds herself caught between the demands of a black-
mailer and her boyfriend, a Scotland Yard detective
assigned to the case. Some exciting moments in
Hitchcock's (and Britain's) first talkie, which was
originally shot as a silent. (Ondra's voice was dubbed
over by Joan Barry in the sound version, because of
her heavy accent.)
Boa: play by Charles Bennett.
THR                                  92 min (ort 96 min) B/W
B,V                                          TEVP L/A; WHV

## BLACKOUT **
Eddy Matalon    CANADA/FRANCE                  1978
*Robert Carradine, Belinda Montgomery, June Allyson,*
*Don Granbery, Terry Haig, Victor B. Tyler, Camille*
*Ange, Maurice Attias, David Bairstow, Thor*
*Bishopric, David Bloom*
During the 1977 New York power blackout, the
inhabitants of an apartment block are terrorised by
criminals. A mediocre and violent thriller with a few
inappropriate moments of black comedy.
THR                                                    90 min
B,V,V2                                        MERL/VCL/CBS

## BLACKOUT **                                         18
Douglas Hickox          CANADA                 1985
*Richard Widmark, Keith Carradine, Michael Beck,*
*Kathleen Quinlan, Gerald Hiken, Paul Drake, Don*
*Hood, Martina Deignan, Lawrence Lott, Kenneth*
*Kimmins, Murray Ord, Sheila Moore, Jason Michas,*
*Shana Lane-Block, Dan Shea*
A madman kills his family and then disappears
without trace. Seven years later the detective who led
the investigation learns of an amnesiac road accident
victim who may be the wanted man. He sets out to
investigate in this average crime thriller.
THR                                               95 min mTV
B,V                                         POLY L/A; CH5

## BLACKSTAR **                                        U
                        USA                    1981
Animated sword-and-sorcery feature with the highly
original theme of good versus evil. Enjoyable enough
in its way, but hardly a memorable animation.
JUV                                   63 min; 41 min (PARK)
B,V                          SEL L/A; PARK (VHS only)

## BLADE ***
Ernest Pintoff          USA                    1973
*John Marley, Jon Cypher, Kathryn Walker, William*
*Prince, John Schuck, Rue McClanahan, Joe Santos,*
*Steve Landsburg*
A tough New York cop hunts down a psychotic
woman-hating killer, in this over-complex but well
made thriller.
THR                                                    91 min
B,V                                                       SHV

## BLADE IN HONG KONG **                              PG
Reza Badiyi             USA                    1985
*Terry Lester, Keye Luke, Mike Preston, Jean-Marie*
*Hon, Ken Fagan, Leslie Nielsen, Nancy Kwan, Ellen*
*Regan, James Hong, Anthony Newley, Alice Lau,*
*Patricia Duff, Melanie Vincz, Diana Haye, Alex Ng,*
*David Ho*
A private eye in Hong Kong battles its underworld,
searching for the criminals who tried to kill his father.
Nothing new in this prospective pilot.
A/AD                     91 min (96 min) Cut (10 sec) mTV
B,V                                                       VIR

## BLADE IN THE DARK, A **                            18
Lamberto Bava           ITALY                  1983
*Andrea Occhipinti, Lara Nassinski, Anny Papa,*
*Fabiola Toledo, Michele Soavi, Valeria Cavalli,*
*Stanko Molnar*
A young composer rents a quiet villa to work undis-
turbed on his latest work, but is disturbed by a series
of mysterious and frightening events.
Aka: HOUSE OF THE DARK STAIRWAY; LA CASA
CON LA SCALA NEL BUIO; QUELLA CASA CON
LA AL BUIO
HOR              90 min (ort 110 min) Cut (1 min 50 sec)
B,V                                                       VES

## BLADE RIDER: ATTACK OF THE                         PG
## INDIAN NATION ***
Harris/Bernard M. Eveety/Reisner
                        USA                    1965
*Chuck Connors, Robert Lansing, David Brian, Kathie*
*Brown, Noah Beery Jr, H.M. Wynant, Michael Pate,*
*Lee Van Cleef, William Bryant*
A former army officer has to refute charges of
cowardice, and at the same time, work to prevent a
new Indian uprising following the death of Custer at
the Battle of Little Big Horn. Compiled from three
episodes of the NBC TV series "Branded" and released
as a feature film outside the USA. A lively little
Western.
Aka: CALL TO GLORY; RIDE TO GLORY (MEV)
WES                                 90 min; 97 min (MEV) mTV
B,V                                      MEV L/A; WARAD

**BLADE RUNNER \*\*\***                                15
Ridley Scott            USA            1983
*Harrison Ford, Rutger Hauer, Sean Young, Edward*
*James Olmos, Daryl Hannah, William Sanderson, Joe*
*Turkel, Joanna Cassidy, Brion James*
In the 21st century, an ex-cop is forced out of
retirement and given the job of hunting down a group
of dangerous androids who are hiding out on Earth.
Poor dialogue and characterisation are major flaws,
but for sheer visual impact this film takes some
beating. Voice-over is an annoyance, try to ignore it.
Boa: novel Do Androids Dream Of Electric Sheep? by
Philip K. Dick.
FAN                          112 min (ort 118 min)
V/sh                                      WHV

**BLADES OF STEEL \*\***                              15
Randy Bradshaw        CANADA            1987
*Christianne Hurt, Colm Fedre, Stuart Hughes, Tom*
*Butler, Rosemary Dunsmore, Patricia Hamilton*
A fairly entertaining look at the world of professional
ice skating, with the story of a talented young skater,
who encounters many difficulties on the way to the
top.
Aka: BLADES OF COURAGE; SKATE
DRA                                100 min mTV
B,V                                      CINE

**BLAKE'S SEVEN: AFTERMATH \***                  PG
Vere Lorrimer          UK              1980
*Josette Simon, Cy Grant, Alan Lake, Sally Harrison,*
*Steven Pacey, Richard Franklin, Michael Melia*
Episode 1 from the third season of the dreary BBC
space opera. In this tale Earth has beaten off an
invasion from Andromeda, but the crew of the "Liber-
ator" have to leave their damaged vessel, and several
of them land on a primitive planet.
FAN                                119 min mTV
V                                        BBC

**BLAKE'S SEVEN: ORAC \***                         PG
Michael E. Briant/Vere Lorrimer
              UK              1978
*Gareth Thomas, Sally Kygrette, Robert Beatty*
Compiled from a lousy TV series about a band of
ex-convicts who fight to overthrow a totalitarian
society. A typical BBC attempt at SF.
FAN                                118 min mTV
B,V                                      BBC

**BLAKE'S SEVEN: THE BEGINNING \***               PG
Terry Nation           UK              1978
*Gareth Thomas, Paul Darrow, Jan Chappell, Michael*
*Keating, Sally Knyvette*
Condensed from one of the BBC's cheap attempts at a
space saga, this tells of a group of prisoners who
escape and seize a superpowerful starship, thus
starting a rebellion against a tyrannical galactic
empire. STAR WARS on a flea's budget, with acting to
match.
FAN                                120 min mTV
B,V                                      BBC

**BLAKE'S SEVEN: THE DUEL \***                    PG
Michael E. Briant      UK              1978
*Gareth Thomas, Paul Darrow, Jacqueline Pearce*
Continues the story of a band of rebels and their
struggle against the Federation. A mediocre and
dreary made-for-TV attempt to do SF on the cheap.
FAN                                119 min mTV
B,V                                      BBC

**BLAME IT ON RIO \*\***                            15
Stanley Donen          USA              1984
*Michael Caine, Joseph Bologna, Valerie Harper,*
*Michelle Johnson, Demi Moore, Jose Lewgoy*
While on holiday in Rio de Janeiro, Caine has an
affair with his best friend's teenage daughter. Even
Michael Caine can do little with a lousy script that is

based on the French film "One Wild Moment". Written
by Charlie Peters and Larry Gelbart.
COM                          110 min; 96 min
V/h                        RNK; WHV (VHS only)

**BLAME IT ON THE NIGHT \***                      PG
Gene Taft              USA              1985
*Nick Mancuso, Byron Thomas, Leslie Ackermann,*
*Billy Preston, Merry Clayton, Richard Bakalyan,*
*Merry Clayton, Billy Preston, Ollie E. Brown*
A pop star's young son comes to live with him when
his mother dies. Brought up in strict private schools,
he finds it hard to appreciate his father's way of life. A
dull plodder with a script by Taft and Mick Jagger.
DRA                          86 min Cut (15 sec)
B,V                                      CBS

**BLASTFIGHTER \*\***                               18
Lamberto Bava
              FRANCE/ITALY/SPAIN        1983
*Michael Sopkiw, George Eastman (Luigi Montefiore),*
*Mike Miller, Valerie Blake, Raymond Richard*
An ex-cop comes out of prison determined to avenge
the murder of his daughter and his friend and employs
a sophisticated gun for the purpose. A typical story of
bloody revenge, highly reminiscent of STRAW DOGS.
Aka: BLASTFIGHTER: L'EXECUTEUR;
BLASTFIGHTER: THE FORCE OF VENGEANCE
A/AD                          86 min Cut (12 sec)
B,V                                      MED

**BLAZE \*\*\***                                    18
Ron Shelton            USA              1989
*Paul Newman, Lolita Davidovitch, Jerry Hardin,*
*Gailard Sartain, Jeffrey De Munn, Garland Bunting,*
*Richard Jenkins, Robert Wuhl*
A fictionalised account of Earl K. Long, the larger-
than-life governor of Louisiana, whose political career
took a nosedive in the 1950s following his affair with
Blaze Starr, a stripper of the time. Newman gives a
flamboyant performance as the Governor, and Davido-
vitch is appealing as his girlfriend, but the film
remains too distanced from its characters and never
really develops. The real-life Starr appears in a cameo
as the stripper Lily.
Boa: book Blaze Starr: My Life As Told To Huey Perry
by Blaze Starr and Huey Perry.
DRA                          113 min (ort 119 min)
V                                        TOUCH

**BLAZING FLOWERS \*\***
Griseppe Zappulla      ITALY            1978
*George Hilton, Marc Porel, Anna Maria Rizzol, Al*
*Cliver (Pier Luigi Conti), Anthony Freeman, Barbara*
*Magnolfi*
Formula crime story involving the Mafia.
THR                                      90 min
B,V,V2                                  INT/CBS

**BLAZING MAGNUMS \***                            18
Martin Herbert (Alberto de Martino)
              CANADA/ITALY              1977
*Stuart Whitman, John Saxon, Martin Landau, Tisa*
*Farrow, Carole Laure, Gayle Hunnicutt, Jean Leclerc,*
*Jean Marchand, Anthony Forest, Andree St Laurent,*
*Peter MacNeil, Julie Wildman, James Tapp, Jerome*
*Thibergien, Terence Ross*
A detective has to crack the toughest case of his
career; the murder of his sister, who turns out to be far
from the innocent college student she has always
seemed. His investigations lead him on a tangled trail
through the seamier side of Montreal, in this fast and
furious nonsense.
Aka: BLAZING MAGNUM; SHADOWS IN A ROOM;
STRANGE SHADOWS IN A ROOM; UNA
MAGNUM SPECIAL PER TONY SAITTA
DRA          94 min Cut (52 sec in addition to film cuts)
B,V,V2                        VNET/VFO L/A; MED

## BLAZING NINJA, THE *
Godfrey Ho    HONG KONG    18
1985
*Philip Cheung, Sony Tanaka, Ronny Lee, Alex Lim,
Tim Chen, Sandy Peng*
Kung fu tale set against the background of the
Japanese occupation before and during WW2. A
virulently anti-Japanese exercise in fisticuffs, with
absolutely nothing to do with Ninjas (the title was
intended to exploit the Ninja craze) that's neither well
made nor interesting.
MAR    90 min
B,V    NET; PACE; AMBER

## BLAZING SADDLES ***
Mel Brooks    USA    15
1970
*Cleavon Little, Gene Wilder, Harvey Korman,
Madeline Kahn, Slim Pickens, David Huddleston,
Alex Karras, John Hillerman, Liam Dunn, Carol
Arthur, Dom DeLuise, George Furth, Don Megowan,
Burton Gilliam, Count Basie, Tom Steele*
Western spoof that was a big hit at the time but now
seems very dated. The plot loosely revolves around the
arrival in town of the new sheriff, who happens to be
black. Crazy events rapidly pile up until they climax
in the breakdown of the entire film – the cast simply
rushes off the set and out into the street. Ambitious
and high-spirited, but little more than a series of
one-liners and visual gags – though some are very
funny indeed.
COM    89 min (ort 94 min)
V    WHV

## BLAZING SAND **
Raphael Nussbaum
ISRAEL/WEST GERMANY    1960
*Daliah Lavi, Gert Guenter Hoffman*
A girl persuades four men to undertake a risky
mission in order to save her lover.
THR    85 min
B,V    EVI

## BLAZING STEWARDESSES ***
Al Adamson    USA    1976
*Yvonne De Carlo, Bob Livingston, Geoffrey Land, Don
"Red" Barry, The Ritz Brothers, Connie Hoffman,
Regina Carrol, T.A. King, Lon Bradshaw, John
Shank, David Sharpe*
The tale of some crazy air stewardesses. The title is
the best part of the film, the inspiration for which is
BLAZING SADDLES. Three stewardesses come to the
rescue of a rancher friend being robbed by his crooked
foreman, together with the local madam who is
pursuing the rancher. Apart from some brief initial
sex scenes, this is no more than a mildly amusing
Western spoof.
A    82 min
B,V,V2    IFS/CBS

## BLEAK HOUSE: PARTS 1, 2 AND 3 ***    PG
Ross Devenish    UK    1985
*Diana Rigg, Denholm Elliot, Fiona Walker, Graham
Crowden, Bernard Hepton, Peter Vaughn, Robin
Bailey, Frank Windsor, T.P. McKenna*
Dickens' classic tale of tragedy, intrigue and love, and
a stinging satire on the English legal system that
follows the course of a ruinous lawsuit. A meticulous
and highly realistic work. First shown as eight 50
minute episodes.
Boa: novel by Charles Dickens.
DRA    390 min mTV
B,V    BBC

## BLEAK MOMENTS ***    PG
Mike Leigh    UK    1971
*Anne Raitt, Sarah Stephenson, Eric Allen, Liz Smith*
In a south London suburb a typist and her retarded
sister live out their drab and pointless existence.
Scripted by Leigh, this long and difficult film makes a

few sharp and witty comments on life in general.
DRA    111 min
V    CONNO

## BLESS THIS HOUSE *    U
Gerald Thomas    UK    1971
*Sid James, Diana Coupland, Terry Scott, June
Whitfield, Peter Butterworth, Sally Geeson, Robin
Askwith, Carol Hawkins, Janet Brown, George A.
Cooper, Patsy Rowlands, Bill Maynard, Wendy
Richard, Marianne Stone, Julian Orchard*
Another limp British TV spin-off based on a series of
the same name. As ever, the material is insufficient to
make a full-length film. Stories in the TV series
focused on the trials and tribulations of a couple and
their two teenage kids – this film offers us more of the
same.
COM    87 min; 85 min (VCC)
B,V    RNK; VCC (VHS only)

## BLIND ALLEY **    18
Larry Cohen    USA    1983
*Anne Carlisle, Brad Rijn, John Woehrle, Matthew
Stockley, Stephen Lack, Otto Von Wernherr*
A contract killer murders a drug dealer but is seen by
a two-year-old. Later he strikes up a relationship with
the boy's mother and finds himself growing fond of the
kid, even though he would be wiser to kill him. A
suspense-free and rather clumsy thriller, in which our
kid seems to be more at risk from his divorced parents
than from the killer.
Aka: PERFECT STRANGERS
A/AD    90 min
B,V    EHE

## BLIND CHESS **
USA    1988
*Burt Reynolds*
A standard detective thriller, with Reynolds once
again playing private detective B.L. Stryker, who this
time finds himself working on a case that involves the
boyfriend of his assistant. See also CAROLANN, THE
DANCER'S TOUCH and DIRTY DIAMONDS.
THR    90 min mTV
V    CIC

## BLIND DATE *    15
Blake Edwards    USA    1987
*Bruce Willis, Kim Basinger, William Daniels, John
Larroquette, Phil Hartman, Alice Hirson, George Coe,
Mark Blum, Graham Stark*
A yuppie gets fixed up with a blind date but is warned
that the girl cannot tolerate alcohol. He takes her
along to impress his friends but after giving her
champagne she reduces a restaurant and his career to
a shambles. Boring and predictable farce with little
going for it. Willis' screen debut.
COM    91 min
V    RCA

## BLIND DATE ***
Nico Mastorakis    USA    1984
*Joseph Bottoms, Kirstie Alley, James Daughton, Lana
Clarkson, Keir Dullea, Charles Nicklin, Michael
Howe, Gerald Kelly, Jerry Sundquist, Marina Sirtis,
Kathy Hill, Louis Sheldon, Danos Lygizos, Spyros
Pafafranzis, Ankie Grelson*
Thriller about a blind executive who can "see" thanks
to computer techniques and a brilliant surgeon, who
also happens to be responsible for some nasty mur-
ders. The plot, which has Bottoms becoming obsessed
with catching the killer, is a contrived one if ever
there was one, but the good cast gives it a semblance
of credibilty. Filmed in Greece.
THR    99 min
V/sh    VDM L/A; VMA

## BLIND FEAR **    15
Tom Berry    USA    1988

*Shelly Hack, Jack Langedijk, Kim Coates, Heidi Von Palleske, Ron Lea, Jan Rubes*
A blind girl "witnesses" a serious crime and the crooks set out to silence her. A fairly taut thriller.
THR                                              87 min
V                                                   VIR

## BLIND FURY ***                                   18
Phillip Noyce            USA                      1989
*Rutger Hauer, Terrance O'Quinn, Lisa Blount, Brandon Call, Meg Foster, Nick Cassavetes, Randall "Tex" Cob, Noble Willingham, Rick Overton, Sho Kosugi*
In this violent parody of a martial arts movie, a blind swordsman who has been trained in the fighting arts comes to the aid of an ex-army buddy; a chemist whose son has been kidnapped in order to force the father to work for crooks synthesising designer drugs. A kind of westernised adaptation of a popular Japanese character ("Zatoichi") that's played for laughs much of the time.
A/AD                          82 min (ort 85 min) subH
V                                                   RCA

## BLIND JUSTICE ***                                15
Rod Holcomb              USA                      1986
*Tim Matheson, Mimi Kuzyk, Tom Atkins, Lisa Eichhorn, Philip Charles MacKenzie, John Kellogg, Marilyn Lightstone, Anne Haney, David Froman, John M. Jackson, Linda Thorson, Jack Blessing, Ann Ryerson, Sam Dalton*
A series of unfortunate circumstances lead to the arrest of an innocent man who is accused of a number of armed robberies. He then spends the next 18 months fighting to establish his innocence. Based on a true incident, this is an interesting examination of the forces that operate against a person who is wrongly convicted. Matheson is excellent as the man whose life is blighted by these events.
DRA                                      90 min mTV
B,V                                                 CBS

## BLIND TERROR ***                                 15
Richard Fleischer        UK                       1971
*Mia Farrow, Robin Bailey, Dorothy Alison, Diane Grayson, Norman Eshley, Brian Rawlinson, Christopher Matthews, Paul Nicholas, Michael Elphick, Barrie Houghton, Lila Kaye, Donald Bissett*
A blind girl is the only survivor after a maniac's attack on an isolated estate. A cliched but often highly effective thriller.
Aka: SEE NO EVIL
THR                           84 min (ort 89 min)
B,V                                                 RCA

## BLINDED BY THE LIGHT **
John A. Alonzo           USA                      1980
*Kristy McNichol, James Vincent McNichol, Anne Jackson, Michael McGuire, Jenny O'Hara, Phillip R. Allen, Keith Andes, Sandy McPeak, Gail Edwards, Sean Thomas Roche, Benjamin Bottoms, Stephan Burns, Michael LeClair*
A girl tries to rescue her brother from a sect that has brainwashed him. A disappointing film that never gets to grips with this fascinating subject. The two McNichols are real-life brother and sister.
Boa: novel by Robin F. Brancato.
DRA                                      100 min mTV
B,V,V2                                              VTC

## BLINDSIDE *                                      18
Paul Lynch           CANADA/USA                   1987
*Harvey Keitel, Lori Hallier, Allan Fawcett, Lolita David*
An ex-surveillance expert owns a block of flats where he has installed security cameras on every window. When he is approached by a couple of thugs who want to use his expertise in order to spy on one of the tenants, he finds himself drawn into a tangled conflict

between rival gangs. A confused, boring and disjointed mess of a film.
A/AD                                             98 min
B,V                                               SHEER

## BLISS **                                         18
Ray Lawrence        AUSTRALIA                     1985
*Barry Otto, Lynette Curran, Helen Jones, Miles Buchanan, Gia Carides, Tim Robertson*
A high-powered businessman has a major heart attack and sees himself dying, but returns to life with a major change in his outlook. A good opening to this satire never really develops into anything of consequence. Written by Lawrence and Carey from his novel.
Boa: novel by Peter Carey
COM                               106 min (ort 111 min)
V/h                                                 NWV

## BLOB, THE *                                      15
Irvin S. Yeaworth Jr     USA                      1958
*Steve McQueen, Aneta Corseaut, Earl Rowe, Olin Howlin*
Some remarkably cheap effects in this story of a meteorite that brings a monster to Earth. It takes the form of a lump of jelly that grows by absorbing whatever gets in its way. A good idea is spoilt by cheap sets and poor direction but somehow the film is endearing for its very ineptness. A comedy sequel – SON OF BLOB followed. Remade in 1988. The title song was composed by Burt Bacharach. This was McQueen's first starring role.
FAN                          76 min; 81 min (BRAVE)
B,V                              MOV; BRAVE (VHS only)

## BLOB, THE **                                     18
Chuck Russell            USA                      1988
*Kevin Dillon, Shawnee Smith, Donoven Leitch, Jeffrey DeMunn, Ricky Paull Goldin, Kevin Dillon, Billy Beck, Candy Clark, Joe Seneca*
Remake of a 1958 dud, with little improvement except in the special effects department (courtesy of Lyle Conway). This $30,000,000 film (the budget was 120 times as much as the original) follows our Blob as he lands at the small ski resort of Arborville and begins tucking into the residents. He proves to be a lot harder to tackle than his earlier namesake, and in one repulsive sequence sucks a restaurant worker down a sink plughole.
FAN                               91 min (ort 95 min)
V/sh                                     CHV L/A; RCA

## BLONDE AMBITION ***                             R18
John Amero/Lem Amero     USA                      1980
*Suzy Mandell, Dory Devon, Eric Edwards, Molly Malone, Jamie Gillis, Richard Bolla, Wade Parker*
A sex film with a comedy plot that opens with two sisters performing their hammy musical act at a saloon in Wyoming. Lured to New York by their agent with the promise of a job if they'll send him a $100 retainer, they arrive to find that he has absconded. They enjoy various adventures and even appear in a porno version of GONE WITH THE WIND, in this insane, confusing and often very funny story.
Aka: CAN I COME AGAIN?; CAN I COME TOO?
A       85 min Cut (2 min 29 sec in addition to film cuts)
B,V                                                 TCX

## BLONDE FIRE **                                   18
Bob C. Chinn             USA                      1979
*John C. Holmes, Seka (Dorothy Hundley Patton), Jesie St James*
Unlikely as it sounds, this is a porno film about a private eye who is hired to bring the Blonde Fire diamond from South Africa to New York, after a client has purchased it for $1,000,000. In the course of this task he beds several women, loses the diamond, but regains it from a woman who hid it in an unusual place. Cut before video submission by 17 min 1 sec.

A                    71 min; 40 min (CRAW) (ort 96 min)
B,V,V2                            CAL L/A; CRAW

## BLONDE GODDESS, THE ***
Bill Eagle              USA              1982
*Susanna Britton, Jacqueline Lorians, Jonathan Ford,*
*Loni Sanders, Ron Jeremy, Jane Kelton, Tamara West*
A comic book artist is so enmeshed in his characters
that he lives his life through them. First he is seen
rescuing his heroine in a RAIDERS OF THE LOST
ARK spoof; later the action moves on to a role as a
WW1 flying ace, during which he shoots down the
Black Baron and lands his plane on a French country
estate for a little dalliance with two contessas.
Further adventures follow in this crazy and amusing
sex film.
A                                       82 min
B,V                            XTACY/TCX; KRP

## BLONDE HEAT *
Timothy McDonald        USA                  18
*John Leslie, Gina Carrera, Richard Pacheco, Angel,*
*Seka, Renee Lovin, Jill Jason, Laurie Smith, David*
*Friedman, Billy Dee, Jon Martin*
A silly sex spoof on THE MALTESE FALCON (it's
sub-titled "The Case Of The Maltese Dildo") in which
a private eye is hired by an art collector to find the
dildo Julius Caesar gave to Cleopatra. However, he
spends most of the time making love to his secretary
and the various women he meets on his travels.
Enlivened by some slightly amusing dialogue but too
thinly plotted to entertain. Cut before video submission by 16 min 14 sec.
A                              61 min (ort 77 min)
V                                      SCRN L/A

## BLONDE NEXT DOOR, THE **
Joe Sherman             USA              1981
*Danielle Martin, Ron Jeremy, Lisa De Leeuw, Mai Lin*
A woman's secretions act as a powerful aphrodisiac. A
con-man discovers this and begins to market the fluid
with great success. His only problem is how to keep
the woman in a state of constant arousal. Tepid
nonsense.
A                                       82 min
B,V                                        CAL

## BLONDE VENUS ***
Joseph Von Sternberg   USA               PG
                                         1932
*Marlene Dietrich, Cary Grant, Herbert Marshall,*
*Dickie Moore, Sidney Toler*
An aspiring young actress who gives up the stage to
marry a hopeful scientist, is forced to return to cabaret
life after her husband is afflicted with radium poison-
ing. Episodic and superficial, but it's hard to resist a
film with Dietrich at her most engaging.
DRA                                 95 min B/W
V                                          CIC

## BLONDES HAVE MORE FUN ***
John Seeman             USA              R18
                                         1981
*Seka (Dorothy Hundley Patton), Jesie St James, John*
*Leslie, Jack Wright, Joan Seeman, Dorothy Le May*
A near bankrupt businessman comes across a mad
scientist who has perfected a genuine aphrodisiac. It
can grow hair on bald heads, turn old ladies into
nymphomaniacs and make men into indefatigable
lovers. John Leslie has a lot of fun with it, enjoying
himself at a whorehouse, as do other characters. A
crude burlesque-style romp that, despite the silliness
of the plot, is often quite funny.
A              58 min (ort 76 min) Cut (1 min 41 sec)
B,V                                  SHEP; TCX

## BLONDES LIKE IT HOT **
                WEST GERMANY             18
                                         1986
*Olinka (Olinka Hardimann), Dominique St Clair,*
*Ester Allen, Jeff Moore, Paul French, Kathy Kay,*
*Sadrina, Lisa Anderson*

A country girl comes to the big city to work as an
assistant to a doctor and is easily, and not too
unwillingly corrupted. With the arrival of her boyfriend matters become complicated, but she eventually
returns home with him where her mama catches them
in bed together and starts making wedding plans. An
innocuous little tale, not over-burdened in the plot
department.
A                                       80 min
B,V                                   CASS/IVS

## BLOOD AND BLACK LACE **
Mario Bava                               18
        FRANCE/ITALY/WEST GERMANY        1965
*Cameron Mitchell, Eva Bartok, Mary Arden, Thomas*
*Reiner, Arianna Gonni*
Thriller about a series of nasty murders of fashion
models. A lifeless script and unconvincing perform-
ances spoil this one. Not for the squeamish.
Aka: SEI DONNE PER L'ASSASSINO
THR                    80 min (Cut at film release)
B,V,V2                            IFS/CBS; VPM

## BLOOD AND BULLETS **
Fernando Di Leo        ITALY             1977
*Jack Palance, Edmund Purdom, Al Cliver (Pier Luigi*
*Conti), Harry Baer, Gisela Hahn, Enzo Pulcrano*
A formula Italian Mafia crime drama.
Aka: MISTER SCARFACE
DRA                                     90 min
B,V                                        APX

## BLOOD AND GUNS **
Guilio Petroni         ITALY             1968
*Tomas Milian, Orson Welles, John Steiner, Jose*
*Torres, Luciano Casamonica, Anna Maria*
*Lanciaprima, Giancarlo Badessi*
Even the presence of Orson Welles does little to
enliven this routine spaghetti Western set during the
Mexican revolution (1910-1920). Both an English
doctor and government troops seek revenge on the
illiterate peasant leader of a small rebel group.
Generally violent and often incomprehensible.
Aka: TEPEPA; VIVA LA REVOLUCION
WES                     90 min (ort 103 min)
B,V                              ABA L/A; INT

## BLOOD AND GUTS **
Paul Lynch              CANADA           18
                                         1978
*William Smith, Micheline Lanctot, Brian Clark, Henry*
*Beckman*
Predictable film about a wrestling troupe and the
youngster who joins it.
Aka: HEAVY THUNDER
DRA                        95 min; 90 min (MKR)
B,V                              QUA/VSP; MKR

## BLOOD AND HONOUR **
Bernd Fischerauer
                WEST GERMANY             1982
*Rolf Becker, Marlies Engel, Steven Higgs*
A nicely sanitised story of the rise to power of Hitler,
and of the way an ordinary German family is affected
by this. A glossy and utterly unrealistic melodrama,
that inevitably reminds one of HOLOCAUST, a film
of similar merits.
DRA                                    220 min
B,V                                        HER

## BLOOD AND ORCHIDS ***
Jerry Thorpe            USA              15
                                         1986
*Kris Kristofferson, Sean Young, Jose Ferrer, Jane*
*Alexander, Susan Blakely, George Coe, David*
*Clennon, Richard Dysart, Elizabeth Lindsey, Haunani*
*Minn, William Russ, James Saito, Matt Salinger,*
*Madeline Stowe*
Story of four native Hawaiians accused in 1937 of
having raped the wife of a US Navy officer. A strong
examination of racial prejudice and the caste system

of the islands, which would have been considerably improved with better casting; Kristofferson as a laid-back detective just does not convince. Based on a script by Katkov, which is in turn based on his book about a real-life case. First shown in two parts.
Boa: book by Norman Katkov.

DRA 175 min (2 cassettes – ort 240 min) mTV
B,V NWV; PVG

### BLOOD AND SAND ***
Fred Niblo USA 1922 PG
*Rudolph Valentino, Nita Naldi, Lila Lee, George Field, Rose Rosanova, Walter Long, Leo White*
A silent classic about the tragic rise and fall of a matador and the women in his life. The dated seduction scenes have not aged well but as a whole the film packs a punch, not least thanks to the star's undeniable charisma. Remade in 1941.
Boa: novel by Vicente Blasco Ibanez.

DRA 80 min B/W silent
B,V CBS

### BLOOD AND SAND **
Rouben Mamoulian USA 1941 PG
*Tyrone Power, Linda Darnell, Rita Hayworth, Nazimova, Anthony Quinn, J. Carroll Naish, John Carradine, Laird Cregar, Lynn Bari, George Reeves, Monty Banks*
A sluggish remake of the 1921 Valentino silent, with a dashing matador finding himself torn between two women. Undeniably handsome to look at, but stilted and lacking in impact. The story was filmed once more in 1989. AA: Cin (Ernest Palmer/Ray Rennahan).
Boa: novel by Vicente Blasco Ibanez.

DRA 120 min (ort 123 min)
V/h CBS

### BLOOD AT SUNDOWN **
Albert Cardiff (Alberto Cardone) 18
ITALY 1972
*Anthony Steffen, Carol Brown, Jerry Wilson, John Garko, Frank Varrell*
A man gets out of prison only to find that in his absence his brother has taken charge of both his girlfriend and the town.

WES 100 min Cut (10 sec)
B,V VPD

### BLOOD BATH **
Joel M. Reed USA 1975
*Harve Presnell, Curt Dawson, Doris Roberts, Jack Somack, Richard Niles, Jerry Lacy, Stefan Schnable, Norman Bush, Tom Yammi, William C.C. Chen, Sharon Shayne, Deborah Loomis, P.J. Soles*
Plenty of blood and unexplained killings in this standard shocker.

HOR 82 min
B,V RNK

### BLOOD BEACH **
Jeffrey Bloom USA 1981
*John Saxon, David Huffman, Mariana Hill, Otis Young, Burt Young, Stefan Gierasch*
There's something nasty lurking beneath the sand of a local beach. A number of people have disappeared into it. A good idea is spoilt by the painfully slow progress of the story and lack of focus on any specific character.

HOR 92 min
B,V,V2 VPD

### BLOOD BEAST TERROR, THE *
Vernon Sewell UK 1967
*Peter Cushing, Robert Flemyng, Wanda Ventham, Vanessa Howard, David Griffin, John Paul, Kevin Stoney, Roy Hudd, Glynn Edwards, Russell Napier*
A turgid and totally unconvincing film about the daughter of a Victorian entomologist who is able to change into a giant death's head moth. Should be put into mothballs (and left there).

Aka: VAMPIRE-BEAST CRAVES BLOOD, THE
HOR 88 min
B,V VAMP/VDM L/A; GHV

### BLOOD BEAT **
Fabrice A. Zaphiratos USA 18
1985
*Helen Benton, Terry Brown, Claudia Peyton, James Fitz Gibbons, Dana Day, Peter Spelson, Frank Miley, Carol Wagner, Andrea Cauchon, Charlie White, Bill Madlener, Duane Albrecht, Clinton Gouldman, Mark Johnson, David End*
Evil forces descend upon an American family as they gather to celebrate a traditional Christmas. Average.

HOR 83 min
B,V REP/VPD

### BLOOD BRIDE **
Robert J. Avrech USA 1980
*Ellen Barber, Philip English*
A woman marries a man at a low point in her life only to discover that he is a crazed killer, in this formula effort.

HOR 89 min
B,V VIPCO

### BLOOD BROTHERS ***
Pasquale Squitieri ITALY 18
1974
*Claudia Cardinale, Franco Nero, Lina Polito, Fabio Testi, Antonio Orlando*
Mafia drama set in Naples at the end of the century. A young man who aspires to become a lawyer finds his ambitions complicated by his close ties with the criminal family in which he grew up. A competent crime melodrama.
Aka: I GUAPPI

DRA 122 min (ort 149 min)
B,V ELE

### BLOOD DINER *
Jackie Kong USA 18
1987
*Rick Burks, Carl Crew, Roger Dauer, Sheba Jackson, Lisa Geuggenheim, Lanette La France, Max Morris*
Two demented brothers run a popular restaurant which serves as a front for their worship of an evil dark goddess whom they plan to revive with body parts taken from their patrons. Amateurish and way over-the-top shocker that tries very hard to be bad and succeeds.

HOR 80 min Cut (3 min 53 sec)
V VES

### BLOODFIST **
Terence H. Winkless USA 18
1989
*Don Wilson, Joe Mari Avellana, Michael Shaner, Riley Bowman, Vic Diaz*
The usual revenge plot (this time over a dead brother) is incidental to this enjoyable display of flying fists and feet as various martial arts champs from the World Kickboxing Association go through their paces.

A/AD 83 min (ort 86 min)
V MGM

### BLOOD FROM THE MUMMY'S TOMB **
Seth Holt/Michael Carreras
UK 1971
*Andrew Keir, Valerie Leon, James Villiers, Hugh Burden, George Coulouris, Mark Edwards, Rosalie Crutchley, Aubrey Morris, David Markham, Joan Young, James Cossins, David Jackson, Jonathan Burne, Tamara Ustinov, Penelope Holt*
Based on a novel by Bram Stoker, this film tells of the revenge that a long dead Egyptian princess takes, on the members of the team of archaeologists who have disturbed her tomb. Carreras completed the film following the death of Holt. Disjointed and muddled, with Leon being taken over by the spirit of the princess in a silly and contrived reincarnation sub-plot. Made by Hammer Films and very much a typical example. Remade as THE AWAKENING and THE

TOMB.
Boa: novel Jewel Of The Seven Stars by Bram Stoker.
HOR 90 min
B,V TEVP

## BLOOD HARVEST ** 18
Bill Rebane USA 1987
*Tiny Tim, Itonia, Dean West, Ed Bevin, Cari Saloch*
The daughter of a bank official is placed in danger when her father's bank decides to foreclose on all the outstanding debts of a local farming community. Another gory, low-budget offering from a veteran B-movie director. Cut before video submission by 2 min 10 sec.
HOR 83 min (ort 90 min) Cut (2 min 51 sec)
B,V SCRN

## BLOOD HOOK ** 18
James Mallon USA 1986
*Dan Winters, Paul Drake, Mark Jacobs, Lisa Todd, Patrick Danz, Sara Hauser, Christopher Whiting*
Five college kids on holiday in a remote area find themselves being stalked by a sadistic demented killer, with the local fishing competition gradually degenerating into a murderous bloodbath.
HOR 90 min (ort 106 min) Cut (16 sec)
B,V AVA

## BLOOD MONEY ** 15
Jerry Schatzberg USA 1987
*Andy Garcia, Ellen Barkin, Morgan Freeman*
A small-time smuggler and a hooker find themselves threatened with death by a group supplying weapons to the Contras, in this competent action tale.
Aka: BLOOD MONEY: THE STORY OF CLINTON AND NADINE
A/AD 91 min
B,V VIR

## BLOOD OF A POET, THE ** 
Jean Cocteau FRANCE 1930
*Lee Miller, Enrico Rivero, Jean Desbordes, Feral Benga, Odette Talazac*
A young poet muses on life and then passes through a mirror and witnesses a series of strange fantasies, which he sees through the keyholes of the doors in a hotel corridor. A Mexican revolutionary shot and then restored to life, and a boy killed by a snowball, are but two examples of the images seen. Raved over by the critics on release, this is an intriguing experiment in surrealistic imagery – a film of little meaning but much opacity.
Aka: LE SANG D'UN POETE
DRA 58 min B/W
B,V PVG

## BLOOD OF DRAGON PERIL ** 18
Rocky Mann HONG KONG
Martial arts film set against the Japanese invasion of Manchuria in the 1930s. The master of one of the top kung fu schools is killed by the Japanese and his eldest son is beaten so badly that he suffers permanent brain damage. The second son joins the army, but the third disappears. When a masked fighter appears and begins to attack Japanese bases, the second son is instructed to kill him and the inevitable conflict occurs. Average.
MAR 83 min
V VPD

## BLOOD OF OTHERS, THE * 15
Claude Chabrol CANADA/FRANCE 1983
*Jodie Foster, Sam Neill, Michael Ontkean, Stephane Audran, Lambert Wilson, Alexandra Stewart, Monique Mercure, Roger Mirmont, Jean Francois Balmer, Marie Bunel, John Vernon, Christine Laurent, Michel Robin, Kate Reid*
Mini-series about a woman who joins the French Resistance to get her lover out of the hands of the Gestapo. A well below average TV saga, spoilt by bad casting and hammy dialogue.
Aka: LE SANG DES AUTRES
Boa: novel by Simone de Beauvoir.
DRA 273 min (2 cassettes) mCab
B,V MGM

## BLOOD OF THE DRAGON ** 18
Kao Pao Shu HONG KONG 1974
*Jimmy Wang Yu, Chiao Chiao, Nu Lang, Yang Yang*
Kung fu tale of an uprising against an evil warlord, led by a Master of the Steel Spear. Standard martial arts plot, but lots of good swordplay enlivens this one.
Aka: DESPERATE CHASE
MAR 93 min; 97 min (GLOB) Cut (13 sec)
V FIFTH; GLOB

## BLOOD ON SATAN'S CLAW *** 
Piers Haggard UK 1970
*Patrick Wymark, Linda Hayden, Barry Andrews, Simon Williams, Tamara Ustinov, Michele Dotrice, Wendy Padbury, Anthony Ainley, James Hayter, Avice Landone, Charlotte Mitchell, Robin Davies, Howard Goorney*
The discovery of a devil's claw, sparks off a spate of devil worship among a group of farm children in a 17th century English village. A competent horror tale with a gruesome and evocative atmosphere.
Aka: SATAN'S CLAW; SATAN'S SKIN
HOR 95 min
B,V GHV

## BLOOD ON THE SUN *** PG
Frank Lloyd USA 1945
*James Cagney, Sylvia Sydney, Robert Armstrong, Wallace Ford, Rosemary De Camp*
An American newspaperman in Japan before WW2 discovers plans for world domination. He attempts to smuggle them out whilst being pursued by the agents of a warlord. A fast-paced and suspenseful story. AA: Art/Int (Wiard Ihnen/A. Boland Fields)
DRA 94 min; 88 min (VIR) B/W
B,V PORVI/MOV; GLOB; VIR (VHS only)

## BLOOD ORGY OF THE SHE-DEVILS * 
Ted V. Mikels USA 1972
*Linda Zaborin, Tom Pace, William Bagdad, Leslie McRae, Ray Myles*
Not as exciting as it sounds. A horror film purporting to deal with all aspects of demonology.
HOR 73 min
B,V VCL/CBS

## BLOOD QUEEN ** 
Radley Metzger
WEST GERMANY/YUGOSLAVIA 1972
*Christine Kruger, Siegfried Rauch, Mark Damon*
Dull biopic on the life and death of Evita (Eva) Peron.
Aka: DON'T CRY FOR ME LITTLE MOTHER, LITTLE MOTHER
DRA 100 min
B,V,V2 VUL

## BLOOD RANSOM * 18
Cedric Sundstrom 1988
*Oliver Reed, Peter Vaughan, Claudia Udy, Sharon Schaffer*
A ruthless drugs baron captures the daughter of the CIA agent who arrested his son, hoping to use her as a hostage, but she and her companions escape and find some weapons with which to attack their tormentors. A low-budget violent action thriller that's virtually devoid of redeeming features.
Aka: FAIR TRADE
A/AD 88 min
V MGM

**BLOOD RELATIONS *** 18
Graeme Campbell   CANADA   1988
*Jan Rubes, Kevin Hicks, Lydie Denier, Lynne Adams,*
*Sam Malkin, Stephen Saylor*
A son plans to kill his father whom he blames for the
death of his mother in a car crash and this develops
into a nasty rivalry when dad brings home his new
fiancee. Ponderous and lacking in humour.
COM                          81 min (ort 90 min)
B,V                                SONY

**BLOOD RELATIVES *** 18
Claude Chabrol  FRANCE/CANADA   1978
*Donald Sutherland, Aude Landry, Lisa Langlois,*
*Laurent Malet, Micheline Lanctot, Stephane Audran,*
*Donald Pleasence, David Hemmings*
A detective, investigating a brutal sex murder, sus-
pects her employer, who was her cousin and is a
known sexual offender. Careful and suspenseful mur-
der mystery, unreleased in the States until 1981.
Boa: novel by E. McBain.
THR                                90 min
B,V,V2              VCL/CBS L/A; VCL/VIR

**BLOOD SABBATH ** 18
Brianna Murphy        USA        1972
*Susan Damante, Tony Geary, Dyanne Thorne*
A GI seeks the sea nymph who saved his life and
becomes caught up in a strange world of voodoo.
HOR                                82 min
B,V                            AVA/CBS

**BLOOD SIMPLE *** 18
Joel Cohen/Ethan Cohen
                      USA        1984
*John Getz, Frances McDormand, Dan Heyada, Samm-*
*Art Williams, M. Emmett Walsh*
A Texan bar-owner hires a private eye to kill his wife
and her lover. However, the murders are faked. This
leads to complications. A convoluted and flamboyant
homage to film noir with good touches of black
humour.
THR                                98 min
B,V                                 PVG

**BLOOD SISTERS ** 18
Roberta Findlay        USA        1986
*Amy Bretano, Shannon McMahon, Brigette Cossu,*
*Dan Erikson, Marla Machant, Elizabeth Rose, Cjerste*
*Thor, Patricia Finneran, Gretchen Kingsley*
Seven girls are forced to stay in a haunted brothel as
part of the initiation rites of a sorority and face a night
of terror in the company of the undead. Formula
sorority-sisters-in-peril offering. Average.
Aka: SLASH
HOR                       83 min Cut (28 sec)
B,V                         CAN L/A; CAREY

**BLOOD TIDE *** 
Richard Jeffries   GREECE/UK   1980
*Jose Ferrer, James Earl Jones, Lila Kedrova, Deborah*
*Shelton, Martin Kove, Mary Louise Weller, Lydia*
*Cornell*
An American artist living on a remote Greek island,
becomes fascinated by the legend of a sinister sea
creature, to which virgin girls were said to have been
sacrificed. Her brother and sister-in-law visit her, and
at the same time a string of brutal murders occurs.
Eventually they are traced to our monster, which
appears but briefly; just as well as it is a remarkably
unconvincing one.
Aka: BLOODTIDE; RED TIDE, THE
HOR                                97 min
B,V                                 VFP

**BLOOD TIES *** 18
Giacomo Battiato       ITALY        1986
*Brad Davis, Vincent Spano, Tony LoBianco, Barbara*
*DeFossi; Arnoldo Foa, Angelo Infanti, Delia Boccardo,*

*Ricky Tognazzi, Michael V. Gazzo, Maria Conchita*
*Alonso, Joe Spinell, James Andronica, Anita*
*Bartolucci*
The Mafia blackmail a young American into agreeing
to kill his cousin, a courageous anti-drugs examining
magistrate, by the simple expedient of holding his
father as hostage. A well-made but often brutal
gangster movie.
Aka: AMERICAN COUSIN, THE; IL CUGINO
AMERICANO
DRA                    98 min (ort 240 min) mTV
B,V                                 PAL

**BLOOD TRACKS** 18
Mike Jackson (Mats Olsson)
                      SWEDEN        1986
*Brad Powell, Tina Shaw, Michel Fitzpatrick, Frances*
*Kelly, Karina Lee, Jeff Harding, Naomi Kaneda*
A rock band shooting a video discover a nasty secret in
a deserted factory. A worthy addition to any collection
of all-time worst movies.
HOR                        81 min Cut (23 sec)
B,V                                 AVA

**BLOOD VENGEANCE ** 
                      ITALY
*George Eastman (Luigi Montefiore), Mary Kristal,*
*Rose Marie Lind*
A slight little tale of love, jealousy, intrigue and
revenge.
DRA                                99 min
B,V                EIV L/A; MMA; PORVI

**BLOOD VOWS ** PG
Paul Wendkos        USA        1987
*Melissa Gilbert, Joe Penny, Eileen Brennan, Talia*
*Shire, Tony Franciosa, Carmine Caridi*
A young girl is mugged soon after arriving in New
York and the only help she receives is from a
handsome and sophisticated lawyer. Having fallen in
love with him she marries, only to find that she has in
fact married into a Mafia family. Average.
Aka: BLOOD VOWS: THE STORY OF A MAFIA
WIFE
THR                    90 min (ort 100 min) mTV
B,V                                 VIR

**BLOOD-SPATTERED BRIDE, THE *** 18
Vincent Aranda        SPAIN        1972
*Maribel Martin, Simon Andreu, Alexandra Bastedo,*
*Dean Selmier, Montserrat Julio*
A poor and unimaginative adaptation of a Sheridan
Le Fanu story, with the ghost of a murderess, dead for
200 years, terrorising a newlywed couple who are
staying at a secluded mansion.
Aka: BLOOD SPLATTERED BRIDE, THE; BLOODY
FIANCEE; LA NOVIA ENSANGRETADA; 'TIL
DEATH DO US PART; TILL DEATH DO US PART
Boa: novel Carmilla by Sheridan Le Fanu.
HOR        96 min Cut (26 sec in addition to film cuts)
B,V                             MOV; SHEP

**BLOODBATH AT THE HOUSE OF DEATH ** 18
Ray Cameron        UK        1984
*Kenny Everett, Pamela Stephenson, Vincent Price,*
*Gareth Hunt, Don Warrington, John Fortune, Sheila*
*Staefel, John Stephen Hill, Cleo Rocos, Graham Stark,*
*Pat Ashton, David Lodge, Davilia David, Oscar Quitak*
An over-ambitious send-up of the whole horror film
genre which uses every horror cliche in the book (and
a few more besides). The story has scientists investi-
gating a series of deaths that are possibly linked to a
local ritual. A most uneven work, best suited to those
who are fans of Everett's zany brand of humour.
COM                        88 min (ort 92 min)
B,V                                TEVP

**BLOODBROTHERS ** 18
Robert Mulligan        USA        1978

Richard Gere, Tony LoBianco, Paul Sorvino, Lelia Goldoni, Yvonne Wilder, Kenneth McMillan, Marilu Henny, Danny Aiello
A young man is caught between two demands, that he become a construction worker like his father or that he break away to live his own life. Gere stands out in this otherwise overblown big-city melodrama.
Aka: FATHER'S LOVE, A
DRA     93 min (ort 118 min) (Abridged by distributor)
B,V                                                         WHV

## BLOODFIGHT *                                              18
Shuji Goto          HONG KONG              1989
Yusuaki Kurata, Bolo Yeung, Yam Tat Wah
The inevitable revenge theme crops up once more, as a former champion trains his latest protege, only to see him callously murdered in the course of a bout with the reigning champion. A poorly plotted and unconvincingly acted mess, with a silly sub-plot involving a thuggish former student and lush, scenic-style photography that makes the film resemble a Hong Kong tourist brochure.
MAR                                                     93 min
V                                                          VPD

## BLOODHOUNDS OF BROADWAY ***              PG
Howard Brookner        USA                 1989
Madonna (Madonna Ciccone), Matt Dillon, Jennifer Grey, Julie Hagerty, Rutger Hauer, Esai Morales, Anita Morris, Randy Quaid, Madeleine Potter, Ethan Phillips
A loose adaptation of a Runyon story revolving around the exploits of a set of gangsters, gamblers and general hangers-on, all of whom are out to celebrate New Year's Eve 1928. A lightweight but engaging period comedy that captures a good deal of the flavour if not the verve of Runyon's writing. This was documentary-maker Brookner's first work of fiction, unfortunately he died just prior to its release. First filmed in 1952.
Boa: short story by Damon Runyon.
COM                                       88 min (ort 93 min)
V                                                         20VIS

## BLOODLINE *                                               18
Terence Young       USA                   1979
Audrey Hepburn, Ben Gazzara, James Mason, Michelle Phillips, Omar Sharif, Romy Schneider, Irene Papas, Gert Frobe, Beatrice Straight, Maurice Ronet
A dull adaptation of a Sidney Sheldon bestseller. A woman finds herself in charge of a business empire following the death of her father, but someone is planning to murder her. This turgid and cliche-ridden effort is even worse than the novel that inspired it.
Aka: SIDNEY SHELDON'S BLOODLINE
Boa: novel by Sidney Sheldon.
DRA                                               117 min mTV
B,V                                                       CIC

## BLOODLUST **
Marijan Vajda     SWITZERLAND             1976
Werner Pochath, Ellen Umlauf, Birgit Zamula, Gerhard Ruhnke, Fred Berhoff, Peter Hamm, Marion Messner, Roswitha Guether, Charley Hiltl
Some terrifying childhood experiences have left a young man both deaf and dumb and obsessed with death. When events at work trigger a descent into madness, he takes to mutilating cemetery corpses and eventually commits murder. A macabre and gruesome tale, said to be based on an actual case history.
Aka: MOSQUITO; MOSQUITO DER SCHÄNDER
HOR                                        86 min (ort 88 min)
B,V,V2                                                    DFS

## BLOODSPORT **                                             18
Newt Arnold        USA                    1987
Jean Claude Van Damme, Leah Ayres, Donald Gibb, Norman Burton, Forest Whitaker, Bolo Yeung

Kung Fu adventure set at a secret martial arts competition held in Hong Kong. Based on the true story of American Frank Dux – the first Westerner ever to win the ultra-tough kumite contest. A violent, low-budget affair that has a few good moments, but not too many of them.
MAR                                                     89 min
V/sh                                                     WHV

## BLOODSTAINED SHADOW **
Antonio Bido          ITALY
Craig Hill, Stefania Casini, Lino Capolicchio
A series of nasty murders have taken place in a small Italian village. A young professor from Venice comes to the village to visit his brother who is the local priest. Having witnessed a murder himself, the priest is now in danger.
HOR                                                    133 min
B,V                                                 DIPLO/VFP

## BLOODSTONE **                                             15
Dwight Little        USA                  1988
Christopher Neame, Jack Kehler, Charles Brill, Brett Stimely, Rajni Kanth, Anna Nicolas
A thief steals a priceless ruby but is forced to hide it in the luggage of a couple on honeymoon who are on their way to India. Said couple are soon being pursued by a motley collection of rogues. Average.
A/AD                                       83 min (ort 90 min)
V/sh                                                      GHV

## BLOODSUCKERS *
Michael Burrows (Robert Hartford-Davis)
                      UK                   1970
Peter Cushing, Patrick Macnee, Alex Davion, Johnny Sekka, Madeline Hinde, Patrick Mower, Imogen Hassall, Edward Woodward, William Mervyn, David Lodge
Vampire movie with a Mediterranean setting that explores the ancient vampire cult of the Greek island of Hydra and its link with sinister Oxford dons. A disjointed hotchpotch that includes some narrated silent sequences and shows evidence of clumsy post-production alteration.
Aka: BLOODSUCKER; DOCTORS WEAR SCARLET; INCENSE FOR THE DAMNED
Boa: novel Doctors Wear Scarlet by Simon Raven.
HOR                                        76 min (ort 87 min)
B,V,V2                                                 INT/CBS

## BLOODY BIRTHDAY **
Ed Hunt              USA                   1980
Susan Strasberg, Jose Ferrer, Lori Lethin, Melinda Cordell, Julie Brown, Joe Penny, Billy Jacoby, Michael Dudikoff
Three women are killed during a solar eclipse. Ten years later a small town is shaken by a series of gruesome murders as three kids born on the day of the eclipse go on a rampage. Despite the unusual basis for the plot this one just serves up the usual gore.
Aka: BLOODY SUNDAY
HOR                                                     83 min
B,V,V2                                                 IFS/CBS

## BLOODY FISTS, THE **                                      18
Ng Sze Yuen         HONG KONG             1969
Cheng Hsing, Chen Kuan-Tai, Lui Ta Chuan, Lindy Lim, Yue Mi, San Lau, Fong Yeh, Henry Yue Young
A group of Japanese invade a Chinese village to obtain a miraculous herb. After a series of bloody encounters, they are defeated by the villagers, who are aided by a mysterious stranger. A low-grade martial arts film with a fair plot but poor action sequences.
Aka: BLOODY FIST, THE; DANG KOU-TAN
MAR 86 min; 75 min (SHEP or GLOB) Cut (57 sec in addition to film cuts)
B,V OCEAN/CVC L/A; REV L/A; SHEP; GLOB

**BLOODY FRIDAY \*\***
Rolf Olsen ITALY/WEST GERMANY 1972
*Raimund Harmstorf, Gila von Weiterschausen,*
*Amadeus August*
Terrorists make a mess of a bank robbery and take
refuge in a deserted house in this unmemorable
melodrama.
Aka: BLUETIGER FREITAG
DRA 97 min
B,V MERC/VPD

**BLOODY KIDS \*\***
Stephen Frears UK 1979 (released 1983)
*Derrick O'Connor, Gary Holton, Richard Thomas,*
*Peter Clark, Gwynneth Strong, Caroline Embling,*
*Jack Douglas, Billy Colvill, Neil Cunningham,*
*Stewart Harwood, Mel Smith, Roger Lloyd Pack,*
*Julian Hough*
Two 11-year-old boys at a British seaside town find
that a childish prank goes terribly wrong, and results
in violence and a police hunt. Average.
DRA 87 min (ort 91 min)
B,V PRV L/A; CH5 (VHS only)

**BLOODY MAMA \*\*\***
Roger Corman USA 1970
*Shelley Winters, Pat Hingle, Don Stroud, Diane Varsi,*
*Robert Walden, Robert De Niro, Pamela Dunlap,*
*Bruce Dern, Clint Kimbrough*
Tense and gripping tale of a psychotic mother and her
degenerate offspring who together wage war on
society. Though violent and sordid it remains one of
Corman's better films.
Boa: novel by Robert Thom.
DRA 89 min (VIR); 82 min; Cut (11 sec)
B,V RNK; VIR (VHS only)

**BLOODY MISSION \*\***
HONG KONG
*Liu Yung, Cheng Le, Tsui Siu Keung, Chi Chen,*
*Raymond Liu*
Kicking and punching kung fu tale like a thousand
similar efforts.
MAR 88 min
B,V VTEL

**BLOODY NEW YEAR \*\***
Norman J. Warren UK 1987
*Suzy Aitchinson, Nikki Brooks, Colin Heywood, Mark*
*Powley, Catherine Roman, Julian Ronnie*
After a brawl at a funfair, three lads decide to leave
town and set off on a sailing boat together with three
girls. They are soon shipwrecked on an island which
they discover is locked in a time warp owing to a
nuclear accident there in 1959. The gory special
effects are the best thing in this nonsense.
Aka: TIME WARP TERROR
HOR 85 min
B,V IVS

**BLOODY WEDNESDAY \***
Mark G. Gillhuis USA 1985
*Raymond Elmendorf, Pamela Baker, Navarre Perry,*
*Terese Mae Allen*
The true story of a psychotic who shot 35 people in a
MacDonald's restaurant in 1985, as seen from the
killer's point of view. A violent, exploitative and
disagreeable film.
HOR 86 min; 88 min (PALAN) Cut (3 min 52 sec)
B,V PVG; PALAN

**BLOOMFIELD \*\*\***
Richard Harris ISRAEL/UK 1969
*Richard Harris, Romy Schneider, Kim Burfield,*
*Maurice Kaufmann, Yossi Yadin, Shraga Friedman,*
*Aviva Marks, Yossi Grabber, David Heyman*
A 10-year-old boy hitch-hikes to Jaffa to see his
'ootball idol play in his last game. A simple, old-
'ashioned and enjoyable story, filmed partly in Israel.

Written by Wolf Mankowitz and Richard Harris.
Aka: HERO, THE
DRA 95 min
B,V RNK

**BLOW OUT \*\*\*** 18
Brian De Palma USA 1981
*John Travolta, Nancy Allen, John Lithgow, Dennis*
*Franz, Peter Boyden*
Interesting variation on the BLOW UP theme. A
sound technician accidentally records an accident in
which a politician plunges his car into a river, with a
girl in the passenger seat; probably suggested by the
Chappaquiddick incident that involved US senator
Edward Kennedy in controversy. The intriguing story
reveals a politically motivated murder, but flaws in
the plot and irritating camerawork let it down.
THR 108 min
B,V,V2,LV ORION/RNK; VIR (VHS only)

**BLOW UP \*\*** 15
Michelangelo Antonioni UK 1966
*David Hemmings, Sarah Miles, Vanessa Redgrave,*
*Peter Bowles, John Castle, Jane Birkin, Gillian Hills,*
*Verushka, Jill Kennington, Harry Hutchinson, Julian*
*Chagrin, The Yardbirds*
How a good idea can be ruined by a lack of plot or
characters. A fashion designer taking photos in the
park seems to have been an unwitting witness to a
murder. After a moment of genuine tension as he
develops the film, it's downhill all the way. Written by
Antonioni with a score by Herbie Hancock. See also
BLOW OUT, which tried a similar idea – but with
sound.
Boa: short story by Julio Cortazar.
THR 104 min (ort 111 min)
B,V MGM

**BLUE ANGEL, THE \*\*** 18
Joe D'Amato (Aristide Massaccesi)
ITALY 1988
*Tara Buckingham, Richard Brown, Rick Anthony*
*Monroe, Jayne Gray, Moses Gibson, Ken Werbinski*
A reworking of the Dietrich classic but updated and
set in the USA, where a senator falls for a sultry
nightclub singer. Over-complex and often contrived,
but quite watchable.
DRA 90 min
V CFD

**BLUE BELLE \***
Massimo Dellamano ITALY/UK 1975
*Annie Belle, Felicity Devonshire, Ciro Ippolito, Charles*
*Fawcett, Maria Rohm, Tim Street, Linda Ho, Ted*
*Thomas, Linda Slade, Al Cliver (Pier Luigi Conti),*
*Chan Yiu Lin, Ines Pellegrini, Rik Battaglia*
A high-class whore makes a bet on the loss of virginity
of a financier's mistress, in this dreary sex melod-
rama.
Aka: END OF INNOCENCE, THE; LA FINE
DELL'INNOCENZA
DRA 86 min
B,V DFS L/A; MARKET

**BLUE BLOOD \*\*** 18
Andrew Sinclair UK 1973
*Oliver Reed, Fiona Lewis, Anna Gael, Derek Jacobi,*
*Meg Wynn Owen, John Rainer, Richard Davies,*
*Gwyneth Owen, Patrick Carter, Elaine Ives-Cameron,*
*Tim Wylton, Hubert Rees, Dilys Price, Sally Anne*
*Newton*
A German governess arrives at an English stately
home where she finds the butler engaged in a scheme
to undermine the authority of his master and usurp
him. A disagreeable version of THE SERVANT,
lacking the style of that earlier film.
Boa: novel The Carry-Cot by Alexander Thynne.
DRA 86 min; 78 (TURBO)
B,V,V2 INT/CBS; TURBO

## BLUE CITY ** 18
Michelle Manning USA 1986
*Judd Nelson, Ally Sheedy, Anita Morris, Scott Wilson,*
*David Caruso, Julie Carmen, Luis Cantreras*
Returning after a five year absence to his hometown
in Florida in order to seek a reconciliation with his
father, a young man discovers that he has been
murdered and that the case remains unsolved.
Moreover, his stepmother has inherited the bulk of his
father's estate and moved in with his father's former
business partner. He decides to carry out his own
investigation in this over-complex melodrama. The
music soundtrack is by Ry Cooder.
Boa: novel by Ross MacDonald.
DRA 80 min
B,V CIC

## BLUE COLLAR *** 18
Paul Schrader USA 1978
*Richard Pryor, Harvey Keitel, Yaphet Kotto, Lane*
*Smith, Ed Begley Jr*
Three workers in a car plant find that they are being
exploited by their own union and decide to do
something about it. A harsh and uncompromising
study of exploitation, helped by a literate script and
good performances.
DRA 109 min (ort 114 min)
B,V CIC

## BLUE DE VILLE ** PG
Jim Johnston USA 1986
*Jennifer Runyon, Kimberly Pistone, Mark Thomas*
*Miller, Robert T. Prescott, Toni Sawyer, Noel Conlen,*
*Micole Mercurio, William Frankfather, Toni Sawyer,*
*Laurel Adams, John LaFayette, Paul Scheurr, Hal*
*Havins, Joe Lynn Turner*
A free-spirit anxious to locate her missing father,
convinces her friend to set off with her in a 1959
Cadillac De Ville that she won in a bar. Along the way
they pick up a college drop-out/musician who has a
mysterious past. An offbeat and slightly wacky com-
edy-drama that was made as a pilot for a TV series.
DRA 97 min mTV
B,V RCA

## BLUE EYES OF THE BROKEN DOLL, THE **
Carlos Aured SPAIN 1973
*Paul Naschy (Jacinto Molina), Diana Lorys, Maria*
*Perschy, Eva Leon, Eduardo Calvo, Ines Morales,*
*Antonia Pica, Luis Ciges*
An ex-convict is given a job by a girl who lives in a
large house, together with her sister. A series of
brutal murders begins with her arrival. Average.
Aka: HOUSE OF PSYCHOTIC WOMEN, THE;
HOUSE OF DOOM; LOS OSOS AZULES DE LA
MUNECA ROTA
HOR 85 min (ort 91 min)
B,V,V2 CAN/VPD

## BLUE FANTASIES * 18
Walter Boos WEST GERMANY 1978
*Karin Kernke, Elizabeth Welz, Helene Rosenkranz,*
*Nicole Avril*
The sex fantasies of a group of college students who
are aroused whilst reading a batch of letters. One in a
long line of tired and dated German sex films.
Aka: SCHOOLGIRL REPORT NO. 1 (DER);
SCHULMADCHEN: REPORT 12 TEIL
A 72 min
B,V VIDMOV/HOK L/A; DER L/A; ELV; HOK

## BLUE FIRE LADY **
Ross Dimsey AUSTRALIA 1978
*Cathryn Harrison, Mark Holden, Peter Cummins,*
*Marion Edward, John Wood*
The story of a young girl and her obsession with
horses. Standard outdoors tale for the horse-loving
set.
Aka: BLUE FYRE LADY

DRA 90 min
B,V,V2 VCL/CBS

## BLUE GRASS: PARTS 1 AND 2 ** 15
Simon Wincer USA 1987
*Cheryl Ladd, Anthony Andrews, Mickey Rooney,*
*Wayne Rogers, Kieran Mulrony, Brian Kerwin, Diane*
*Ladd, Shawnee Smith*
A girl who has grown up with horses on the Kentucky
Blue Grass is determined to gain recognition as an
equal among the horse breeders of Kentucky but her
plans are opposed by a group of breeders who aim to
keep their circle exclusive. A pleasant little soap
opera tale that will appeal to horse lovers, though the
foaling sequence may be a little strong for some.
DRA 177 min (available as a 1 or 2 tape package) mTV
B,V CBS

## BLUE HEAVEN ** 15
Kathleen Dowdey USA 1984
*Leslie Denniston, James Eckhouse, Lisa Sloan,*
*Marsha Jackson*
Dreary and sordid tale of an unhappy marriage and of
a wife who suffers violence at the hands of her
husband, and yet cannot bring herself to leave him.
DRA 112 min
V VPD

## BLUE HOTEL ** 15
Rob Cohen USA 1987
*Michael Woods, Josh Brolin, Bill Sadler, Lisa Jane*
*Persky*
Two men set out to track down the murderers of their
rock idol, but when one of them falls in love with the
rock star's former girlfriend, h soon finds himself
being framed for murder.
Aka: BLUE HOTEL: PRIVATE EYE; PRIVATE
EYE: BLUE HOTEL
DRA 90 min mTV
B,V CIC

## BLUE IGUANA, THE ** 15
John Lafia USA 1988
*Dylan McDermott, Jessica Harper, James Russo,*
*Pamela Gidley, Dean Stockwell, Tovah Feldshuh*
A none-too-successful bounty hunter tries to enrich
himself by helping the IRS recover $20 million from a
small Latin American bank. A spoof on all those
"private eye goes south of the border" films, that
suffers badly from messy script and tries too hard for
laughs.
COM 86 min (ort 88 min)
B,V VES

## BLUE JEAN COP ** 18
James Glickenhaus USA 1988
*Peter Weller, Patricia Charbonneau, Sam Elliott,*
*Antonio Fargas, Blanche Baker*
A tough cop teams up with a defence attorney to fight
corruption within the force. A solid action film with
good dialogue and an unusual car chase.
A/AD 96 min
B,V BRAVE

## BLUE KNIGHT, THE **
J. Lee Thompson USA 1975
*George Kennedy, Alex Rocco, Glynn Turman, Verna*
*Bloom, Michael Margotta, Seth Allen, John Steadman,*
*Richard Hurst, Bart Burns, Ji-Tu Cumbuka, Walter*
*Barnes, Marc Alaimo, Eric Christmas, Joseph*
*Wambaugh, Britt Leach*
A cop looks for the killer of an ageing fellow officer. A
nice performance from Kennedy in the role of Wam-
baugh's Bumper Morgan is let down by the formula
script. Both a remake of the superior 1973 TV film and
a pilot for a TV series of thirteen 60 min episodes.
Look out for Wambaugh, who appears as the desk
sergeant.
Boa: novel by Joseph Wambaugh.

A/AD                          70 min (ort 78 min) mTV
B,V                                        SPEC/POLY

## BLUE LAGOON, THE *                         15
Randal Kleiser          USA                1980
*Brooke Shields, Christopher Atkins, Leo McKern,*
*William Daniels*
Remake of the 1949 film, telling the story of the
growing sexual awareness of a young boy and girl,
both shipwrecked on an island. Much nudity and
adolescent frankness about sex but little else in a
thoroughly insipid film. Written by Douglas Day
Stewart. The excellent photography is by Nestor
Almendros.
Boa: novel by Henry de Vere Stacpoole.
DRA                                     104 min
V/sh                                        RCA

## BLUE LAMP, THE ***                         PG
Basil Dearden           UK                 1949
*Jack Warner, Jimmy Hanley, Dirk Bogarde, Robert*
*Flemyng, Bernard Lee, Peggy Evans, Gladys Henson,*
*Tessie O'Shea, Patric Doonan, Bruce Seton, Clive*
*Morton, Frederick Piper, Dora Bryan, Norman*
*Shelley, Campbell Singer*
A police sergeant on the eve of retirement is shot and
killed by a gang robbing a cinema. However, the
murderer is brought to justice in a manhunt where
even members of the criminal fraternity lend a
helping hand as they despise the use of firearms. A
very British film in style and attitudes. The dead
sergeant later starred in a very long-running TV
police series – "Dixon Of Dock Green". A solid and
low-key film.
DRA                          81 min (ort 84 min) B/W
V                                           WHV

## BLUE LIGHTNING, THE **                     15
Lee Philips           AUSTRALIA            1986
*Sam Elliott, Rebecca Gilling, Robert Culp, John*
*Meillon, Robert Coleby, Max Phipps, Ralph Cotterill,*
*Jack Davis, Ray Meaghr, Michael Carman, Norm*
*Erskine, Gary Waddell, Jeff Truman, Gary Who, Bob*
*Barrett, Chris Pang*
An American private eye goes to Australia and finds
himself in the outback where he has to recover a
valuable gem from a wily villain, ably assisted by a
pretty female associate. Plenty of violent and unbe-
lievable action, but nothing new in the plot depart-
ment.
THR                          93 min (ort 100 min) mTV
B,V                                         VIR

## BLUE MAGIC **                              R18
Larry Revene            USA                1981
*Samantha Fox, Veronica Hart, Jack Wrangler,*
*Candida Royalle, Ron Hudd, George Payne, Josh*
*Andrews, Merle Michaels*
Gothic sex film set at Woodhurst Castle which is
owned by Natalie Woodhurst, a woman who has lived
for several centuries. Her longevity is related to her
insatiable sexual appetite and the story has her
inviting three couples to her castle for the weekend, in
order to satisfy her needs. Eventually they all fall
under her spell and a most enjoyable time is had by
all. A pleasant costumed fantasy let down by a rather
static and unconvincing plot.
A                                   68 min (ort 82 min)
B,V                                    TCX; SHEP

## BLUE MAX, THE **                           PG
John Guillermin         USA                1966
*George Peppard, James Mason, Ursula Andress,*
*Jeremy Kemp, Karl Michael Vogler, Anton Diffring,*
*Harry Towb, Peter Woodthorpe, Derek Newark, Derren*
*Nesbitt, Loni Von Friedl, Friedrich Ledebur, Carl*
*Schell*
Overlong saga of German WW1 combat pilot and his
struggle to achieve fame, in his eyes represented by

the Blue Max award, even if it means risking the lives
of his comrades and seducing the wife of a superior
officer. Good photography and aerial sequences compensate for the dullness of the plot.
Boa: novel by Jack D. Hunter.
DRA           146 min (ort 156 min) (Cut at film release)
B, V/sh, LV                                 CBS

## BLUE MONEY ***                             PG
Colin Bucksey           UK                 1982
*Billy Connolly, Tim Curry, Debbie Bishop, Dermot*
*Crowley, Frances Tomelty, George Irving, John Bird*
A cab driver discovers a huge amount of money left by
mistake in his cab, and soon finds various villains are
after both it and him, in this likeable and enjoyable
romp.
COM                                  85 min mTV
B,V                                        TEVP

## BLUE MOVIES **                             18
Ed Fitzgerald/Paul Kova  USA              1987
*Larry Linville, Steve Levitt, Lucinda Crosby, Darien*
*Mathias, Larry Poindexter, Christopher Stone, Don*
*Calfa*
Comedy set in the world of moviemaking where an
incompetent director with big dreams and small
talents attempts to recoup his losses by making a sex
film. Average story in a slightly unusual setting.
COM                                      90 min
B,V                                         IVS

## BLUE MURDER AT ST TRINIANS *               U
Frank Launder           UK                 1958
*Joyce Grenfell, Terry-Thomas, George Cole, Alistair*
*Sim, Lionel Jeffries, Sabbrina, Thorley Walters, Eric*
*Barker, Richard Wattis, Lloyd Lamble, Michael*
*Ripper, Judith Furse, Lisa Gastoni, Dilys Laye,*
*Kenneth Griffith*
Dreadfully dated and unfunny film, the second in the
series, with our anarchic schoolgirls off to Rome,
having won a UNESCO prize trip. There they become
involved with a jewel thief, who hides out at their
school. A film that skilfully epitomises all that was
and still is wrong with the British film industry. Do
miss it. Followed by THE PURE HELL OF ST
TRINIANS.
COM                        86 min; 83 min (WHV) B/W
B,V                            STJ; WHV (VHS only)

## BLUE SKIES AGAIN **                        PG
Richard Michaels        USA                1983
*Harry Hamlin, Robyn Barton, Mimi Rogers, Dana*
*Elcar, Kenneth McMillan, Marcos Gonzales*
Story of a young woman and her attempts to enter the
world of professional baseball. An amiable film let
down by poor direction and acting – strictly minor-
league stuff.
COM                                      87 min
V                                           GHV

## BLUE STEEL ***                             U
Robert N. Bradbury      USA                1934
*John Wayne, George "Gabby" Hayes, Yakima Canutt,*
*Eleanor Hunt, Ed Peil Sr, George Cleaveland, George*
*Nash, Lafe McKee, Hank Bell, Earl Dwire*
Outlaws discover gold deposits beneath the town and
resort to murder and extortion until the Duke comes
onto the scene. A good, old-fashioned Western with an
excellent opening sequence that takes place during a
thunderstorm whilst a robbery is in progress.
WES                                      54 min B/W
V                                           CH5

## BLUE SUNSHINE ***                          18
Jeff Lieberman          USA                1976
*Zalman King, Deborah Winters, Mark Goddard,*
*Robert Walden, Charles Siebert*
A young man accused of a series of murders discovers
that they were really committed by former college

mates who were all users of a certain brand of LSD some ten years previously. A violent psychological thriller.

| | |
|---|---|
| THR | 95 min |
| B,V | VIDMO |

## BLUE THUNDER *** 15
John Badham          USA          1983
*Roy Scheider, Warren Oates, Daniel Stern, Malcolm McDowell, Candy Clark, Joe Santos*
Action film that centres around the L.A. police department's use of a super-helicopter, one that is equipped with a formidable arsenal of surveillance devices as well as devastating weaponry. Scheider plays a Vietnam-veteran-turned-cop who steals the title craft. A slick and well-made film that starts off well but gets bogged down in the ludicrous aspects of the plot. Written by Dan O'Bannon and Don Jakoby.

| | |
|---|---|
| A/AD | 108 min |
| B,V | RCA |

## BLUE THUNDER: REVENGE IN THE SKY ** PG
USA          1984
*James Farentino, Dana Carvey, Sandy McPeak, Bubba Smith, Dick Butkus, Ann Cooper, Katherine Justice, David Spielberg, Kal Wulff*
An episode from the "Blue Thunder" TV series, all about a high-tech police helicopter. In this tale they embark on a race against time to prevent the KGB from stealing a restored jet plane. Average mindless action.
Aka: REVENGE IN THE SKY

| | |
|---|---|
| A/AD | 47 min mTV |
| V | RCA |

## BLUE THUNDER: SECOND THUNDER ** PG
USA          1984
*James Farentino, Dana Carvey, Sandy McPeak, Bubba Smith, Dick Butkus, Ann Cooper, Richard Lynch, David Wiley*
An episode from the TV series "Blue Thunder". This action tale has our helicopter team becoming the target of a mysterious fighter plane, that has already attacked a couple of police helicopters. Standard noise and action.
Aka: SECOND THUNDER

| | |
|---|---|
| A/AD | 47 min mTV |
| V | RCA |

## BLUE THUNDER: SKYDIVER ** PG
USA          1984
*James Farentino, Dana Carvey, Sandy McPeak, Bubba Smith, Dick Butkus, Ann Cooper*
Yet another adventure drawn from the "Blue Thunder" TV series, with a special task force and their sophisticated helicopter now being given the job of protecting a visiting foreign head of state. Average.
Aka: SKYDIVER

| | |
|---|---|
| A/AD | 47 min mTV |
| V | RCA |

## BLUE THUNDER: TROJAN HORSE **
USA          1984
*James Farentino, Dana Carvey, Sandy McPeak, Bubba Smith, Dick Butkus, Ann Cooper, Dennis Holahan, Elizabeth Hoffman, Ralph Manza, Brian Kale, Ralph M. Clint, Leigh Lombardi, Vincent Howard, Dean Wein, Nick Konakas*
An episode from the "Blue Thunder" TV series, with our intrepid helicopter team on a secret undercover mission to foil a jail breakout on the part of a crooked financier. So-so offering in a routine action series.
Aka: TROJAN HORSE

| | |
|---|---|
| A/AD | 47 min mTV |
| V/sh | RCA |

## BLUE VELVET *** 18
David Lynch          USA          1986
*Isabella Rosselini, Dennis Hopper, Kyle MacLachlan, Laura Dern, Hope Lange, Dean Stockwell*
A weird but original film, telling of a young man and his involvement with a nightclub singer and a sadistic kidnapper, in a seemingly innocent small American town. Hopper gives an outstanding performance as the town's resident psycho, in this bizarre and disturbing study of the seamy side of life, written by Lynch; the use of widescreen will suffer on TV. A minor cult film. Rosselini is the daughter of Ingrid Bergman.

| | |
|---|---|
| DRA | 115 min |
| B,V | CBS |

## BLUE YONDER, THE *** U
Mark Rosman          USA          1985
*Peter Coyote, Huckleberry Fox, Art Carney, Dennis Lipscomb, Joe Flood, Frank Simons, Mitty Smith, Stuart Klitsner, Morgan Upton, Bennett Cale, Cyril Clayton, Charles Adams, Gretchen Grant, Doug Morrison, Jerry Landis*
A youngster, obsessed with his grandfather's pioneering aviation exploits, travels back in time to the 1920s to meet him, the old man having died before he was born. The two hit it off so well they get involved in a series of adventures and change the course of history. Sentimental but enjoyable family entertainment.
Aka: TIME FLYER

| | |
|---|---|
| COM | 86 min (ort 105 min) mCab |
| B,V | WDV |

## BLUEBEARD **
Edward Dmytryck
          FRANCE/ITALY/WEST GERMANY          1972
*Richard Burton, Raquel Welch, Virna Lisi, Joey Heatherton, Sybil Danning (Sybelle Danninger), Nathalie Delon, Karin Schubert*
Story of an Austrian aristocrat who keeps the bodies of his murdered mistresses frozen in the vaults of his castle. An utterly wooden performance from Burton doesn't make for much of a film, despite some moments of black humour and a parade of beautiful girls.

| | |
|---|---|
| HOR | 123 min |
| B,V | TEVP |

## BLUES BROTHERS, THE *** 15
John Landis          USA          1980
*John Belushi, Dan Aykroyd, Cab Calloway, Kathleen Freeman, Chaka Khan, The Blues Brothers Band, Carrie Fisher, James Brown, Henry Gibson, Aretha Franklin, Ben Piazza, Ray Charles*
Comedy about two brothers, both musical performers, who become involved in a race against time to save their old orphanage – nearly destroying Chicago in the process. A zany and quite enjoyable story that skilfully intercuts some great music, with scenes of wholesale destruction whenever the pace appears to be in danger of slackening. Numerous cameo appearances include Steven Spielberg, Frank Oz, Steve Lawrence, John Lee Hooker and Paul Reubens.

| | |
|---|---|
| COM | 127 min (ort 133 min) |
| V/sh | CIC |

## BLUME IN LOVE ** 15
Paul Mazursky          USA          1973
*George Segal, Susan Anspach, Kris Kristofferson, Marsha Mason, Donald F. Muhich, Shelley Winters, Paul Mazursky*
A divorced lawyer refuses to accept that his ex-wife no longer loves him and sets out to win her back. Some nice touches but overlong and rambling. Kristofferson gives a nice performance as the man who moves in with Anspach.

| | |
|---|---|
| COM | 117 min |
| B,V | WHV |

## BMX BANDITS ** PG
Brian Trenchard-Smith
          AUSTRALIA          1984
*David Argue, John Ley, Bryan Marshall*

Three kids on BMX bikes foil the plans of a gang of crooks in this formula kid's adventure.

A/AD                             87 min
B,V                               RNK

## BOARDWALK ***
Stephen Verona          USA           1979
*Ruth Gordon, Lee Strasberg, Janet Leigh, Joe Silver, Eli Mintz, Eddie Bart*
An elderly Jewish couple struggle to survive in a decaying neighbourhood, and face harassment from a street gang. A film that starts off as a poignant study of urban decay is spoilt by an implausibly violent DEATH WISH-style climax. Leigh gives a nice performance as the couple's devoted daughter.

DRA                              95 min
B,V,V2                    VIDMOV/HOK

## BOAT HOUSE **                    15
Aiken Scherberger    CANADA        1985
*Wendy Crewson, David Ferry, Keith Knight, Robby Benson*
An aspiring young reporter is intrigued by the doings of a mysterious woman and her involvement with a boat house on a remote island. He eventually stumbles across a 25-year-old murder mystery. Average.

HOR                              90 min
B,V                               MOG

## BOAT, THE ***                   15
Wolfgang Peterson
         WEST GERMANY        1981
*Jurgen Prochnow, Herbert Gronemeyer, Klaus Wennemann, Hubertus Bengsch, Martin Semmelrogge, Bernd Tauber, Erwin Leder, Martin May*
This account of a German U-boat on a mission during WW2, provides a stark and realistic picture of submarine warfare, spoilt by a terribly contrived ending. A longer version with a running time of 300 minutes was made for TV. Not a film for the claustrophobic as most of the action centres on the behaviour and stresses among the crew, with little respite from the confined space. Written by Peterson.
Aka: DAS BOOT
Boa: novel by Lothar-Guenther Buchheim.

WAR                  128 min (ort 145 min)
V/sh                               RCA

## BOATNIKS, THE **              U
Norman Tokar        USA           1970
*Phil Silvers, Norman Fell, Robert Morse, Stefanie Powers, Mickey Shaughnessy*
An accident-prone coastguard trying to live up to the reputation of his war hero father, becomes a hero himself when he finally catches three jewel thieves. Likeable but formula Disney comedy.

COM                             100 min
B,V                               WDV

## BOB AND CAROL AND TED AND ALICE **    15
Paul Mazursky        USA           1969
*Natalie Wood, Robert Culp, Elliot Gould, Dyan Cannon, Horst Ebersberg, Lee Bergiere*
A sophisticated and sexually liberated Californian couple try to persuade their less trendy friends to join them in a menage a quatre. Some sharp observations on the morality of a vanished era are marred by a stupid ending. Written by Mazursky and Larry Tucker and the directorial debut for the former. Later a short-lived TV series.
Boa: novel by P. Welles.

COM                             101 min
B,V                               RCA

## BOBBIE JO AND THE OUTLAW *        18
Mark L. Lester        USA           1976
*Marjoe Gortner, Lynda Carter, Jesse Vint, Merrie Lynn Ross, Belinda Belaski, Gerrit Graham*

A bored girl joins a criminal gang on their violent robbing and killing spree. A few in-jokes for film-buffs are the only relief in a nasty and often brutish film. The script is by Vernon Zimmerman.
Aka: BOBBIE JOE AND THE OUTLAW; BOBBY JOE AND THE OUTLAW

THR                  84 min (ort 89 min)
B,V                       VFO L/A; WISE

## BOBBY DEERFIELD *            PG
Sydney Pollack        USA           1977
*Al Pacino, Marthe Kelly, Anny Duperey, Walter McGinn, Romolo Valli, Stephen Meldegg*
A real weepie in which our hero, a Grand Prix racer, only learns the meaning of life when he falls for a Florentine aristocrat who is dying from some unnamed disease. Get in a good supply of paper hankies for this one.
Boa: novel Heaven Has No Favourites by Erich Maria Remarque.

DRA                             123 min
B,V                               WHV

## BODY AND SOUL *              18
George Bowers        USA           1981
*Leon Isaac Kennedy, George Bowers, Jayne Kennedy, Peter Lawford, Michael V. Gazzo, Muhammad Ali, Perry Lang, Kim Hamilton*
A dreary remake of the 1947 classic in which a welterweight resists the corruption of the fight world (this time round) and goes on to become the champion. Kennedy does his best, but the thin storyline is his toughest opponent.

DRA                              95 min
B,V                               RNK

## BODY AND SOUL ****
Robert Rossen        USA           1947
*John Garfield, Lilli Palmer, Hazel Brooks, Ann Revere, William Conrad, Canada Lee, Joseph Pevney*
Classic boxing film that follows the career of a young man who sets out to reach the top of his profession but is corrupted in the process. He finally regains his self respect when, at the end of his career, he beats a young contender for his title after having previously agreed to take a dive. This tough, final match is one of the best ever put on screen. Written by Abraham Polonsky and remade in 1981. AA: Edit (Francis Lyon/Robert Parrish).

DRA                        104 min B/W
B,V,V2                          INT/CBS

## BODY CHEMISTRY **           18
Kristine Peterson      USA           1990
*Marc Singer, Mary Crosby, Lisa Pescia, David Kagen, H. Bradley Barneson, Doreen Alderman, Laureen Tuerk, Joseph Campanella*
The married director of a research lab investigating sexual behaviour is seduced by a psychopathic female colleague and embarks on a relationship from which he is unable to break free. A blatant clone of FATAL ATTRACTION, well handled but all too familiar.

DRA                       84 min (ort 87 min)
V                               20VIS

## BODY COUNT *                18
Ruggero Deodato     ITALY         1986
*Bruce Penhall, Mimsy Farmer, David Hess, John Steiner, Charles Napier, Luisi Maneri, Andrew J. Lederer, Cynthia Thompson, Stefano Madia, Nancy Brilli*
College kids go off in search of an old Indian legend of a mythical creature that's half-beast and half-man, and are horror struck when they find it. So will you be if you watch this nonsense.

HOR            83 min (ort 90 min) Cut (14 sec)
B,V                        IVS; BRAVE

## BODY DOUBLE ** 18
Brian De Palma        USA        1984
*Craig Wasson, Deborah Shelton, Melanie Griffith,*
*Gregg Henry, Guy Boyd, Dennis Franz*
An unemployed actor spies on a woman who performs
a striptease in front of her bedroom window every
night. Her sudden murder with a drill is witnessed by
him and he soon finds himself drawn into a complex
and tangled web of murder. A sleazy film of fetishes
and porno movies that has a few good moments even if
it does copy Hitchcock's REAR WINDOW. Co-
produced and co-written by De Palma. The music is by
Frankie Goes To Hollywood.
THR                      109 min (ort 114 min) Cut (5 sec)
V/sh                                              RCA

## BODY FEVER *** 15
Ray Dennis Steckler    USA        1969
*Caroline Brandt, Bernard Reion, Gary Kent, Brett*
*Pearson, Herb Robins, Ray Dennis Steckler, Dina*
*Bryan, Julie Connors*
Plenty of action in this story of a private eye and his
search for a girl who has ripped off the leader of a
drugs ring.
Aka: LAST ORIGINAL B-MOVIE, THE: SUPER
COOL
A                                              80 min
B,V                          MARKET/GOV L/A; MPV

## BODY HEAT *** 18
Lawrence Kasdan        USA        1981
*William Hurt, Kathleen Turner, Richard Crenna, Ted*
*Danson, J.A. Preston, Mickey Rourke*
Somewhat reminiscent of DOUBLE INDEMNITY and
THE POSTMAN ALWAYS RINGS TWICE, with a
rich married socialite inveigling a Florida lawyer into
a plot to kill her husband. Though somewhat over-
derivative, it improves as it develops. The directorial
debut for Kasdan and the screen debut for Turner.
DRA                                            113 min
B,V                                             WHV

## BODY LOVE * 
Lusse Braun (Alberto Hunderte)
                    WEST GERMANY        1977
*Lolita Da Nova, Jack Gatteau, Glenda Farrel, Gene*
*Sorlin, Tony Morena, Gilda Jacobs, Roberta Jones,*
*Carmen Royale*
A strange, surrealistic sexual fantasy that follows
Martine, the daughter of a baron, who owns a chateau
in an unidentified country. Leaving her father's
castle, she arrives at another chateau and enjoys a
sexual encounter with three men. Martine returns
home and some lesbian encounters follow. This rather
pointless story then ends with her initiating an orgy
among some entranced people who have been waiting
at the chateau for her arrival.
A                                              82 min
B,V                                             CAL

## BODY LUST * R18
Henry Paris (Radley Metzger)/Gerard Kikoine
                    USA        1981
*Arlene Manhattan, Desiree Cousteau, Veronica Hart,*
*George Payne, Ron Jeremy, Misty, Samantha Fox,*
*Vanessa Del Rio, Merle Michaels*
A woman leaves a note for her husband telling him
that she wants to have her freedom, and sets off in
search of adventure. First she enjoys a lesbian encoun-
ter and then moves on to a bar and then a health club.
Intercut with this action are shots of Del Rio and her
radio chat show, in which members of a studio
audience discuss sex. This tiresome and contrived
mess ends with our woman returning home to destroy
the note before her husband gets back.
Aka: TALE OF TIFFANY LUST, THE (HVS)
Osca: BAD PENNY/HARD UP (asa)
A     79 min; 74 min (HVS); 72 min (TAR) (Cut at film
release)
B,V                            HVS L/A; HAR; TAR

## BODY MAGIC *** R18
Sven Conrad        USA        1982
*Rick Ardonne, Kathleen Kristal, Joey Silvera, Sarah*
*Fenton, Terri Starr, Victoria Slick, Bill Dee, Kelly*
*Cole, Penny Arcade, Linda Templeton*
This film opens with Mark, a renowned erotic photographer, explaining his craft to Laura, who is new to
the business. Fifteen minutes of erotic stills are
followed by several explicit sex scenes, whilst the
dialogue consists of a voice-over commenting on or
appraising the photographer, who is never seen
taking part in the events he films. Mark finally makes
love to Laura, concluding an unusual and fairly
sophisticated adult movie.
A                      73 min (Cut at film release)
B,V                              EVI; SEL; SHEP

## BODY OF EVIDENCE ** 18
Roy Campanella II      USA        1987
*Margot Kidder, Barry Bostwick, Tony LoBianco,*
*Caroline Kava, Jennifer Barbour, David Hayward*
A pathologist involved in the hunt for a serial killer
comes under suspicion from his wife who gradually
begins to suspect that he and the murderer could very
well be one and the same. Something of a revamp of
SUSPICION with a few good moments in a generally
poor script. Written by Cynthia Whitcomb and Cam-
panella.
THR                      90 min (ort 100 min) mTV
B,V                                             CBS

## BODY ROCK * 15
Marcelo Epstein        USA        1984
*Lorenzo Lamas, Vicki Frederick, Cameron Dye, Ray*
*Sharkey, Michelle Nacastro*
Another one for the breakdance set, with Lamas
dumping all his friends when he's hired to run a smart
uptown club. A noisy music video with burly Lamas
totally miscast, in the role of our ghetto kid bound for
glory. The good cinematography of Robby Muller is
largely wasted on a tenth-rate script.
MUS                                            91 min
B,V                                             TEVP

## BODY SLAM *** 15
Hal Needham        USA        1987
*Dirk Benedict, Tanya Roberts, Roddy Piper, Lou*
*Albano, Barry Gordon, Charles Nelson Reilly, Billy*
*Barty, John Astin*
A seedy music producer down on his luck, gets
accidentally involved with the world of professional
wrestling. An engaging comedy featuring a number of
cameos from grapplers of the ring such as the Wild
Samoans, Ric Flair and Bruno Sammartino. The
screen debut for Piper.
COM                                            90 min
B,V                                             CHV

## BODY SNATCHER, THE *** PG
Robert Wise        USA        1945
*Boris Karloff, Henry Daniell, Bela Lugosi, Edith*
*Atwater, Russell Wade, Rita Corday*
Set in Scotland in the 19th century, this tells of a
doctor who is forced to employ a bodysnatcher in order
to obtain the corpses he requires for his experiments.
He eventually finds himself being blackmailed by a
villainous coachman, in this atmospheric adaptation
of Stevenson's chiller.
Boa: story by Robert Louis Stevenson.
HOR                                       77 min B/W
V                                               VCC

## BODY SNATCHERS, THE * 18
Norman Thaddeus Vane USA        1981
*Luca Bercovici, Nita Talbot, Jennifer Starrett, Leon*
*Askin, Barbara Pilavin, Alan Stock*
A group of kids steal the body of a famous horror
movie star, who comes back from beyond, to take

bloody revenge on those who disturbed his rest. Enjoy your rest by giving this one a miss.
Aka: FRIGHTMARE
HOR                                        90 min
B,V                                          AVR

## BODY STEALERS, THE *
Gerry Levy          UK/USA              1969
*George Sanders, Maurice Evans, Patrick Allen, Neil Connery, Lorna Wilde, Hilary Dwyer, Robert Flemyng, Allan Cuthbertson, Michael Culver, Sally Faulkner, Shelagh Fraser*
Silly attempt at SF in which parachutists keep on disappearing, being taken to another planet to revitalise a dying civilisation.
Aka: INVASION OF THE BODY STEALERS; THIN AIR
FAN                                        91 min
B,V                                          GHV

## BODY TALK: THE LANGUAGE OF LOVE ***
Pedie Sweet          USA              1982
*Angelique Pettijohn, Randy West, Kay Parker, Steven Tyler*
This story has Mark, a young sculptor, being introduced to Cassie, an older woman. They fall in love and Cassie ends a relationship with a man who has been supporting her for years. She buys Mark a studio but later discovers she has bone cancer and under pressure from Mark's father, ends their relationship. Knowing none of this, Mark goes off on a year-long seminar but later returns to be with her as she dies in this well made adult soap opera.
A                                          79 min
B,V                                          ELV

## BODYGUARD, THE **
Simon Nuchtern          USA              1977
*Sonny (Shinichi) Chiba, Aaron Banks, Bill Louie, Judy Lee*
A martial arts expert seeks revenge for a friend's death at the hands of an international drugs smuggler. Average.
MAR                                        89 min
B,V                                      CIC L/A; RCA

## BOGEY MAN, THE ***
Ulli Lommel          USA              1980
*Suzanna Love, Ron James, John Carradine, Nicholas Love, Raymond Boyden, Felicite Morgan, Bill Rayburn, Llewelyn Thomas, Jay Wright*
A woman is haunted by the spirit of her mother's lover, who was murdered years ago by her now mute brother. Returning to her childhood home in an attempt to purge herself of this trauma, she comes across a mirror which reflects an image of the long-dead lover. She smashes it, but a fragment is imbued with evil power and causes much bloodshed. An intriguing and imaginative fantasy-horror, followed in 1983 by a sequel (banned so far).
Aka: BOOGEY MAN, THE
HOR                                        91 min
B,V                                        VIPCO

## BOGIE *
Vincent Sherman          USA              1979
*Kevin O'Connor, Kathryn Harrold, Anne Wedgeworth, Patricia Barry, Alfred Ryder, Donald May, Richard Dysart, Carol Vogel, Tobias Anderson, Anne Bellamy, Michael Bond, Herb Braham, Normann Burton, Michael Currie*
Below-average biopic that attempts to reconstruct the Hollywood years of Bogart, using actors and actresses hired for their resemblance to Bogart, Bacall and Mayo Methot rather than for their acting ability. A flat and dismal effort; years before, Sherman directed several Bogart movies. The script is by Daniel Taradash.
Aka: BOGIE: THE LAST HERO

Boa: book by Joe Hyams.
DRA                                      110 min mTV
B,V                                          VFP

## BOILING POINT *
Paul Levis          USA          R18
                                          1983
*Seka (Dorothy Hundley Patton), Kay Parker, Lisa De Leeuw, John Leslie, Paula Brown, Phaedra Grant, Sylvia Rogers, Jon Martin, John Seeman, Constance Penny, Desiree Cousteau*
This disjointed and incoherent account of some individuals and their sex lives, opens with a prostitute getting caught up in a raid that's foiled by a plainclothes cop. Later she winds up at the cop's apartment, but so does the raider, and he goes to bed with the cop's wife. The film then moves on to an encounter between a babysitter and the woman she has come to sit for, and finally a disco orgy sequence brings the whole mess to its conclusion.
A                                    62 min (ort 71 min)
B,V                              SEL L/A; EVI; SHEP

## BOLDEST JOB IN THE WEST, THE *
Anthony Loma (Jose Antonio de la Loma)
                    FRANCE/ITALY/SPAIN          1971
*Mark Edwards, Carmen Sevilla, Charlie Bravo, Piero Lulli, Yvan Verella*
After having carried out a big safecracking job, a gang falls out when it comes to dividing up the spoils. A trite and forgettable Italian effort.
Aka: EL MAS FABULOSO GOLPE DEL FAR-WEST; NEVADA
WES                                        100 min
B,V                                      INT/CBS

## BOLERO          18
John Derek          USA              1984
*Bo Derek, George Kennedy, Andrea Occhipinti, Ana Obregon, Olivia d'Abo, Greg Bensen*
A film of mind-numbing stupidity, bad dialogue and worse acting, made by the director as a vehicle with which to show off his wife. Set in the 1920s, it follows a spoiled, rich graduate of an English girls school who, with the help of her chauffeur, is determined to lose her virginity to a handsome Arab sheikh. But he fails her by falling asleep, so she hurries to Spain where a bullfighter eventually helps her out in this laughable effort.
A                                          100 min
B,V                                          GHV

## BOMB AT 10-10 *
Casey Diamond (Charles Damic)
                    YUGOSLAVIA              1966
*George Montgomery, Rada Popovic, Peter Banicevic, Branko Plesa*
An American pilot escapes from a POW camp and makes his way to occupied Belgrade. Here he becomes involved in an underground plot to assassinate a sadistic SS colonel. A messy and disjointed effort, haphazardly made and directed.
WAR                                        87 min
B,V                                          DFS

## BOMBAY TALKIE **
James Ivory          INDIA              1970
*Jennifer Kendal, Shashi Kapoor, Zia Mohyeddin*
Story of a sophisticated American woman who comes to Bombay and gets involved with two men in the film industry there. A so-so romantic drama whose backdrop of film studios adds surprisingly little to the film. The script is by Ruth Prawer Jhabvala.
DRA                                        105 min
B,V                                        HOME

## BOMBS AWAY **
Bruce Wilson          USA          PG
                                          1985
*Michael Santo, Pat McCormack, Michael Huddleston, Ben Tone, Lori Larsen*

The story of a missing atom bomb and the complications its loss causes, especially when it turns up in a surplus store in Seattle. Average.

COM 90 min
B,V AVR

## BON APPETIT ** R18
Chuck Vincent USA 1980
*Kelly Nichols, Randy West, Gloria Leonard*
A wealthy jetsetting woman bets a waitress $250,000 that she cannot seduce the world's ten best lovers within 50 days. A frantic sex tour of the world follows, with Nichols hopping in and out of bed in San Francisco, then New York, Paris, Munich, Amsterdam and Rome, with a few extra stops on the way. A film of nice locations and breathless activity, with our waitress winning both the money and a husband as well.

A 59 min (ort 83 min) Cut (7 min 11 sec)
B,V SHEP; TCX

## BON VOYAGE ** PG
Mike Vardy UK 1985
*Nigel Havers, Judy Parfitt, Ursula Howells*
A simple tale following the changes in relationships between a group of people in the course of a voyage from San Francisco to Hong Kong. Nicely photographed but fairly unremarkable.
Boa: story by Noel Coward.

DRA 58 min mTV
V PICK

## BON VOYAGE! * U
James Neilson USA 1962
*Fred McMurray, Jane Wyman, Deborah Whalley, Michael Callan, Tommy Kirk, Kevin Corcoran*
Tedious Disney comedy about an American family and their disastrous first trip abroad, when they holiday in Paris. A simple-minded and forgettable effort that goes nowhere.
Boa: book by M. Hayes and J.A. Hayes.

COM 126 min
B,V WDV

## BONANZA: THE NEXT GENERATION ** PG
William F. Claxton USA 1988
*John Ireland, Barbara Anderson, Michael Landon Jr, John Amos, Robert Fuller, Brian A. Smith, Peter Mark Richman, Gillian Green*
The original TV series "Bonanza" ran from 1959 to 1973 – this is a pilot for an entirely new series with a fresh cast. In this tale the late Ben Cartwright's brother is now running the Ponderosa but has turned drilling rights over to some unscrupulous landgrabbers. Cartwright's nephews come to the rescue. Produced and written by David Dortort, who created the original series, which Claxton worked on too. Average.

WES 92 min; 90 (MSD) (ort 100 min) mTV
B,V COL; MSD

## BONDITIS *
Karl Suter WEST GERMANY 1966
*Gerd Baltus, Marion Jacob, Herbert Weicker*
A man is diagnosed as suffering from "Bonditis" – that is, he is obsessed with all the James Bond paraphernalia of spies, guns, women etc. A daft and forgettable comedy.

COM 100 min
B,V,V2 INT/CBS

## BONDS OF LOVE ** PG
Michael Anderson USA 1988
*Burt Lancaster, Ben Cross, Olivia Hussey*
Romantic drama based on Wojtyla's novel of two couples who are separated by WW2 and the German invasion of Poland, and do not meet until many years later, when in New York they find that their respec-

tive children have embarked on a love affair of their own. Average.
Boa: novel The Jeweller's Shop by Karol Wojtyla (Pope John Paul II).

DRA 88 min
V FUTUR

## BONNIE AND CLYDE **** 18
Arthur Penn USA 1967
*Warren Beatty, Faye Dunaway, Michael J. Pollard, Denver Pyle, Gene Hackman, Estelle Parsons, Gene Wilder, Dub Taylor*
A slick, stylish but heavily glamorised story of Bonnie Parker and Clyde Barrow – two of the most notorious gangsters to operate in the 1930s, when they specialised in robbing banks. Perceptive, funny and violent – this potent mixture is directed with enormous flair and has great performances from the leads. The climax is almost unbelievably ferocious. Wilder's screen debut. AA: S. Actress (Parsons), Cin (Burnett Guffrey).

DRA 106 min
V WHV

## BONNIE'S KIDS **
Arthur Marks USA 1975
*Tiffany Bolling, Robin Matson, Steve Sandor, Alex Rocco, Scott Brady*
Two sisters, victims of a brutal upbringing by their stepfather, turn to murder and robbery. Average.

DRA 90 min
B,V ARF

## BOOB TUBE, THE **
Christopher Odin USA 1974
*John Alderman, Sharon Kelly, Lois Lanne*
The story of KSEX, a television station with a difference and the effect its unique programmes have on the viewers.

A 74 min
B,V MMA

## BOOBY TRAP ** 18
Franky Schaeffer USA 1986
*Emily Longstreth, Devin Hoelscher, Merritt Buttrick, Frank Collinson, Garth Gardner, Tom Lister Jr, Kim Milford, Michael Wollet, Kristina David, Don Blakely, Dorothy Patterson, June C. Ellis, Elliot Berk, Phillip Clark*
Now it's an incurable disease rather than nuclear war that's led to the end of civilisation as we know it. Set in 1998, a plague has killed off most of the population and among the ruins, a boy, a girl and a robot battle crazed mutants for survival.
Aka: WIRED TO KILL

FAN 90 min (ort 96 min)
B,V MED

## BOOK OF NUMBERS **
Raymond St Jacques USA 1973
*Raymond St Jacques, Phillip Thomas, Freda Payne, Hope Clarke, D'Urville Martin, Gilbert Green*
Action film that follows the rivalry between two numbers operations that run in a small Arkansas town; one being operated by blacks and the other by whites. Eventually the two opposing groups make ready for a violent battle in this so-so story.

A/AD 81 min
B,V CINE

## BOOT HILL ** PG
Giuseppe Colizzi ITALY 1969
*Terence Hill (Mario Girotti), Bud Spencer (Carlo Pedersoli), Woody Strode, Victor Buono, Lionel Stander, Eduardo Ciannelli*
Confused tale of an escaped prisoner who joins a circus as cover, whilst waiting to be joined by his two

companions, so that they can get their revenge on an outlaw gang. A variable mishmash of comedy and action.
Aka: LA COLLINA DEGLI STIVALI
WES                                                87 min
V                                                  ACTEL

**BOOTLEG **                                          15
John Prescott      AUSTRALIA              1989
*Ray Meagher, Carmen Duncan, John Gregg, Max Meldrum, Ian Nimmo, Shelley Friend, John Flaus*
A private eye hired to find a missing woman is mistaken for a talented saxophonist, but eventually unravels the complex threads of the case he is working on, in this competent thriller.
THR                                                90 min
V                                                  GHV

**BOOTLEGGERS **
Charles B. Pierce      USA                1974
*Paul Koslo, Dennis Fimple, Slim Pickens, Jaclyn Smith, Chuck Pierce Jr*
Action comedy set in 1930s Arkansas and dealing with the attempts of rival moonshining families to outwit each other as they run their produce to Memphis. Fair.
Aka: BOOTLEGGER'S ANGEL
COM                              84 min (ort 101 min)
B,V                                                VFO

**BORDER, THE **                                      18
Tony Richardson      USA                  1982
*Jack Nicholson, Harvey Keitel, Valerie Perrine, Warren Oates, Elpidia Carrillo*
A lukewarm drama about the corruption of an honest border guard who begins accepting bribes to allow in Mexican illegal immigrants. When the child of a poor Mexican girl is kidnapped to be sold on the black market, his sense of decency is put to the test. A film that needed stronger direction and a tighter script to really work.
DRA                                               107 min
B,V,LV                                             CIC

**BORDER, USA, THE **
Christopher Leitch      USA               1980
*Telly Savalas, Eddie Albert, Danny La Paz*
An honest cop discovers that his colleagues are being bribed by dishonest businessmen so as to turn a blind eye to the import of cheap Mexican labour. Average.
Aka: BLOOD BARRIER; BORDER, THE
DRA                                                97 min
B,V,V2                                         VCL/CBS

**BORDERLINE **                                       15
Jerrold Freedman      USA                 1980
*Charles Bronson, Wilford Brimley, Bruno Kirby, Ed Harris*
Bronson plays a US Border Guard who is trying to protect the country, from a flood of illegal Mexican immigrants who attempt to cross the border annually. He becomes involved in a murder hunt when his partner and a poor youth are murdered. Uninspired melodrama.
DRA                              106 min; 99 min (CH5)
B,V                          PRV L/A; CH5 (VHS only)

**BORN A NINJA **                                     15
                          1988
*Patrick L'Argent, Daniel Garfield, Laura Wong, Kelvin Wong*
Action tale in which a Japanese war criminal with a secret formula for germ warfare, is pursued by Ninjas who steal his formula, forcing him to embark on a battle in order to retrieve it. Average action, below-average plot.
A/AD                        83 min Cut (2 min 42 sec)
B,V                                                CINE

**BORN AGAIN **                                       PG
Irving Rapper      USA                    1978
*Dean Jones, Anne Francis, Jay Robinson, Dana Andrews, Raymond St Jacques, George Brent*
Little of interest in this film account of the religious rebirth of an adviser to President Nixon following the Watergate affair. A flat and pretentious account.
Boa: book by C. Colson.
DRA                                               106 min
B,V,V2                                             EHE

**BORN BEAUTIFUL **                                   PG
Harvey Hart      USA                      1982
*Erin Gray, Ed Marinaro, Polly Bergen, Lori Singer, Ellen Barber, Judith Barcroft, Michael Higgins, P.J. Benjamin, Barbara Blackburn, Paul Dumont, Andrea Kessler, Nancy Everhard, Albert Stratton, Kevin Conroy*
A TV movie about models trying to hit the big time in New York's fashion world and experiencing the usual frustrations and jealousies. A kind of dull soap opera set in the world of fashion models. Filmed on location in New York.
DRA                                          100 min mTV
B,V                                                MGM

**BORN FREE **                                         U
James Hill      UK                        1966
*Virginia McKenna, Bill Travers, Geoffrey Keen, Peter Lukoye, Omar Chambati, Bill Godden, Bryan Epsom, Robert Cheetham, Robert Young*
Fair adaptation of Adamson's book based on her experiences working together with her husband, as game wardens in Kenya. Having raised a lion cub in captivity, they are obliged to teach it to fend for itself before releasing it into the wild. A syrupy outdoors adventure saved by the colourful locations and good animal shots. LIVING FREE followed. AA: Score (Orig) (John Barry), Song ("Born Free" – John Barry – music/Don Blake – lyrics).
Boa: book by Joy Adamson.
DRA                                                96 min
B,V                                                RCA

**BORN IN EAST L.A. **                                15
Cheech Marin      USA                     1987
*Cheech Marin, Daniel Stern, Paul Rodriguez, Jan-Michael Vincent, Tony Plana, Kamala Lopez, Alma Martinez*
A third-generation American Hispanic who gets caught in an immigration raid without any identification, is taken to be an illegal immigrant and deported to Tijuana. Based on Marin's successful Bruce Springsteen parody record, this follows his crazy antics to get back into the States. A pleasant comedy vehicle whose humour begins to wear thin after the first 30 minutes.
COM                                                81 min
V/h                                                CIC

**BORN INNOCENT ***
Donald Wyre      USA                      1974
*Linda Blair, Joanna Miles, Kim Hunter, Richard Jaeckel, Mary Murphy, Allyn Ann McLerie, Janit Baldwin, Nora Heflin, Tina Andrews, Mitch Vogel, Sandra Ego*
Harrowing if somewhat overdone account of the experiences of a runaway teenager in a tough juvenile detention home. A graphic rape scene of Blair by her fellow inmates was subsequently cut from the film, following a lawsuit against the network in 1978. This was Blair's TV movie debut.
DRA                                          100 min mTV
B,V                                            ODY/CBS

**BORN LOSERS **                                      18
T.C. Frank (Tom Laughlin)
                          USA             1967
*Tom Laughlin, Elizabeth James, Jeremy Slate, William Wellman Jr, Jane Russell, Robert Tessier*

Violent biker film in which a young female dropout is rescued from the clutches of a nasty bike gang by a tough half-breed, who eventually routs the entire gang. An unpleasant and brutal tale that features the debut of Billy Jack – a Laughlin creation who is not averse to using violence in the pursuit of peace. Followed by BILLY JACK.
DRA                              112 min Cut (52 sec)
B,V,V2                                            GHV

## BORN ON THE FOURTH OF JULY ****        18
Oliver Stone          USA                    1989
*Tom Cruise, Willem Dafoe, Raymond J. Barry, Caroline Kava, Kyra Sedgewick, Bryan Larkin, Jerry Levine, Josh Evans, Frank Whaley, Stephen Baldwin, John Getz, Tom Berenger, Abbie Hoffman*
The story of anti-war activist Ron Kovic, who joined the Marines as a raw recruit in the 1960s, saw action in Vietnam and returned home a cripple, paralysed from the chest down. Based on his memoirs, the film charts his early patriotism, later disillusionment and final ordeal of mental and physical rehabilitation. Cruise is superb in this powerful film. The score is by John Williams. AA: Dir, Edit (David Brenner/Joe Hutshing).
DRA                          138 min (ort 144 min)
V                                                CIC

## BORN TO BE BAD **                        PG
Nicholas Ray          USA                    1950
*Joan Fontaine, Robert Ryan, Zachary Scott, John Leslie, Mel Ferrer*
A ruthless woman uses her charms to get want she wants, completely oblivious to the suffering she causes. A good cast helps maintain the interest in this overblown melodrama.
Boa: novel All Kneeling by A. Parrish.
DRA                                        90 min
V                                             VCC

## BORN TO BE SOLD **
Burt Brinckerhoff      USA                   1981
*Lynda Carter, Harold Gould, Dean Stockwell, Philip Sterling, Sharon Farrell, Lloyd Haynes, Ed Nelson, Joy Garrett, Claire Malis, Donna Wilkes, Rita Taggart, Bernard Behrens, Gordon Haight, Joyce Temple-Harris, Ken Hill*
A mediocre film loosely based on a book telling of the attempts of a social worker to expose an illegal baby-selling racket. A muddled and exploitative tale.
Boa: novel The Baby Brokers by Lynn McTaggart.
DRA                          94 min (ort 100 min) mTV
B,V,V2                                          VUL

## BORN TO KILL ***
Robert Wise           USA                    1947
*Claire Trevor, Lawrence Tierney, Walter Slezak, Audrey Long, Elisha Cook Jr, Philip Terry*
Absorbing film about a murderer who marries one woman but becomes involved with her divorced sister. This cold and cynical study, a good example of the genre of film noir, has now achieminor cult status.
Aka: LADY OF DECEIT
Boa: novel Deadlier Than The Male by J.E. Gunn.
DRA                                  92 min B/W
B,V                                           GOV

## BORN TO RUN ***                           U
Don Chaffey           USA                    1977
*Tom Farley, Robert Bettles, Andrew McFarlane, Mary Ward, Julieanne Newbould*
A boy trains his pony to win a race and uses the prize money to help his grandfather. An amiable kid's adventure, set in New South Wales of 1911.
JUV                                        89 min
B,V                                           WDV

## BORN WILD **                              18
Maury Dexter          USA                    1968

*Tom Nardini, Patty McCormack, David Macklin*
Rival Mexican and white gangs fight over their turf with predictable results in this formula urban melodrama.
Aka: YOUNG ANIMALS, THE
DRA                                        98 min
B,V,V2                                    ORION/RNK

## BORROWED HERO **
Lewis D. Collins       USA                   1941
*Alan Baxter, Florence Rice, John Hamilton, Stanley Andrews, Constance Worth, Wilma Francis, Mary Gordon, Richard Terry, Jerry Marlowe, Paul Everton, John Maxwell, Guy Usher, George Dobbs, Dorothy Gulliver, Eba Larson*
A district attorney attempts to clean up big-city corruption in this competent but unmemorable drama.
DRA                                      65 min B/W
V                                            WOOD

## BORSALINO ***                             15
Jacques Deray      FRANCE/ITALY             1970
*Jean-Paul Belmondo, Alain Delon, Michael Bouquet, Catherine Rouvel, Francoise Christophe*
A stylish and witty film about the growing friendship between two 1930s Marseilles gangsters who decide to join forces. A semi-comic film with the leads giving great performances as two rather likeable hoodlums. The catchy score is by Claude Bolling. A kind of French tribute to American gangster films of the period. The inferior BORSALINO AND CO. followed.
DRA                                       126 min
B,V                                            CIC

## BORSALINO AND CO. *
Jacques Deray
          FRANCE/ITALY/WEST GERMANY         1974
*Alain Delon, Catherine Rouvel, Riccardo Cuccialla*
A forgettable sequel to the 1970 film BORSALINO that continues the saga of 1930s Marseilles gangsters, but minus Belmondo, who was shot in the first film. A flat and disappointing follow-up lacking the style and verve of the original.
DRA                                       107 min
B,V,V2                                         VTC

## BOSS'S WIFE, THE*                         15
Ziggy Steinberg       USA                    1986
*Daniel Stern, Arielle Dombasle, Fisher Stevens, Melanie Mayron, Lou Jacobi, Martin Mull, Christopher Plummer, Thalmus Rasulala, Robert Costanzo*
An ambitious young stockbroker, trying to advance his career, has to deal with a demanding boss, a sleazy fellow employee and the oversexed wife of his boss. Disappointing comedy that never really catches fire, despite the best efforts of a strong cast.
COM                                        80 min
B,V                                            CBS

## BOSS, THE ***
Fernando di Leo        ITALY                  1973
*Henry Silva, Richard Conte, Antonia Santili*
When the daughter of a criminal boss is abducted, a dangerous game ensues, involving police, politicians and gangsters. A fair thriller.
Aka: IL BOSS; MURDER INFERNO
THR                            87 min (ort 109 min)
B,V,V2                                         VPD

## BOSTON STRANGLER, THE ****               18
Richard Fleischer      USA                   1968
*Tony Curtis, Henry Fonda, George Kennedy, Mike Kelin, Hurd Hatfield, Murray Hamilton, Jeff Corey, Sally Kellerman, William Marshall, George Voskovec, William Hickey, James Brolin*

Tony Curtis is superb in this low-key, almost documentary account of the mass murderer who terrorised Boston in the 1960s. A totally absorbing drama, documenting his appearance, career and eventual capture, with a look at his motivations. A chilling film, but the use of complex multi-images will tend to be lost on TV.
Boa: book by Gerold Frank.
DRA        110 min (ort 120 min) Cut (1 min 5 sec)
V/h        CBS

**BOSTON WARRIORS ** **                        PG
Maury Dexter        USA        1969
Tom Stern, Jeremy Slate, Jocelyn Lane, Angelique Pettyjohn
One of those low-grade biker films that are seen once, and never remembered.
Aka: HELL'S BELLES
DRA        91 min
B,V        KSV; KRP

**BOSTONIANS, THE ***                          PG
James Ivory        UK        1984
Christopher Reeve, Vanessa Redgrave, Madeleine Potter, Jessica Tandy, Nancy Marchand, Barbara Bryne, Wesley Addy, Linda Hunt, Maura Moynihan, Wallace Shawn, Nancy New, Charles McCaughan, John Van Ness Philip, Martha Farrar
Adaptation of Henry James' story of Boston society in the 19th century, with Redgrave well cast as the feminist heroine who tries to interest naive Potter in the women's movement, whilst Southern gent Reeve, vies for her attentions. A slow, literate and somewhat aloof study. The script is by Ruth Prawer Jhabvala.
Boa: novel by Henry James.
DRA        117 min (ort 122 min)
B,V        EHE

**BOULEVARD NIGHTS **                          18
Michael Pressman        USA        1979
Richard Yniguez, Marta Du Bois, Danny De La Paz, Betty Carvalho, Carmen Zapata, James Victor, Victor Millan
Dull story of a Chicano youth who makes an unsuccessful attempt to break away from the influence of his street gang, but is drawn back in, on account of his excitable young brother. Well meaning, but the story unfolds in an all too predictable way. Filmed in Los Angeles.
DRA        100 min
B,V        WHV

**BOUND FOR GLORY ****                         PG
Hal Ashby        USA        1976
David Carradine, Ronny Cox, Melinda Dillon, Randy Quaid, Gail Strickland, John Lehne, Ji-Tu Cumbuka
Biography of Woody Guthrie, the folk balladeer and poet – the eloquent voice of America's downtrodden during the dark years of the Depression and beyond. Carradine is perfectly cast as Guthrie, who travels the country, fighting and singing for the underdog, against the background of Leonard Rosenman's great score adaptation. AA: Cin (Haskell Wexler), Score (Leonard Rosenman).
Boa: book by Woody Guthrie.
DRA        142 min
V        WHV

**BOUNTY KILLER, THE ***                       PG
Spencer G. Bennet        USA        1965
Dan Duryea, Rod Cameron, Audrey Dalton, Richard Arlen, Buster Crabbe, Fuzzy Knight, Johnny Mack Brown, Bob Steele, G.M. "Bronco Billy" Anderson, Peter Duryea, Eddie Quillan, Norman Willis, Edmund Cobb, I. Stanford Jolley
Intelligent Western in which a mild-mannered Easterner gets involved in a life of violence and bounty-hunting. A cast of former Western stars from old movies is well used in this literate and low-key story.
Aka: BOUNTY KILLERS

Osca: MACAO
WES        90 min (ort 92 min)
B,V        KVD

**BOUNTY MAN, THE ***
John Llewellyn Moxey        USA        1972
Clint Walker, Richard Baseheart, John Ericson, Margot Kidder, Arthur Hunnicutt, Gene Evans, Rex Holman, Wayne Sutherlin, Paul Harper, Dennis Cross, Vincent St Cyr, Glenn Wilder, Robert Townsend, Hal Needham
A man sets out to have his revenge on the criminal responsible for his wife's death, and chases him to an isolated valley where he comes up against an entire gang. A routine story is improved by Jim Byrnes' intelligent but sombre script.
WES        74 min mTV
B,V        GHV

**BOUNTY, THE ***                              15
Roger Donaldson        UK        1984
Anthony Hopkins, Mel Gibson, Edward Fox, Laurence Olivier, Daniel Day Lewis, Bernard Hill, Philip Davis, Liam Neeson, Wi Kuki Kaa, Tevaite Vernette, Philip Martin Brown, Simon Chandler, Malcolm Terriss, Simon Adams
Third version of the story of the Bounty Mutiny. A well made and lavish study that attempts to paint a truer picture of Captain Bligh and Fletcher Christian, and the events that led up to the famous mutiny. Always good to look at, but directed in a rather clinical and uninvolved way. The use of wide screen will tend to be largely lost on TV.
Boa: book Captain Bligh And Mr Christian by R. Hough.
DRA        128 min (ort 133 min)
B,V        TEVP

**BOUQUET OF BARBED WIRE, A ***
Tom Wharmby        UK        1976
Frank Finlay, James Aubrey, Susan Penhaligon, Sheila Allen
A dreary saga of a wealthy publisher's obsessive love for his daughter, and how it leads to a tragic breakup of his family. Well made and acted, but never really convincing. Originally a six-part TV serial. Followed by the TV sequel ANOTHER BOUQUET.
Boa: novel by Andrea Newman.
DRA        343 min mTV
B,V        SONY

**BOURNE IDENTITY, THE ***                     15
Roger Young        USA        1988
Richard Chamberlain, Jaclyn Smith, Yorgo Voyagis, Donald Moffat, Anthony Quayle, Denholm Elliott
Having been washed up on a beach with amnesia and bullet wounds, a man sets about trying to piece together his true identity, but finds that he may in fact have been a professional terrorist and killer. A tense and intriguing thriller.
Boa: novel by Robert Ludlum.
THR        176 min (ort 192 min) mTV
V/sh        WHV

**BOX OF DELIGHTS, THE **                      U
Renny Rye        UK        1984
Patrick Troughton, Devin Stanfield, Robert Stephens, Geoffrey Lander, Jonathan Stephens, Carol Frazer
Film adaptation of a six part serial based on a classic John Masefield novel. The story tells of a magic box and the adventures it leads a young boy into. A well made and fairly entertaining kid's fantasy.
Boa: novel by John Masefield.
JUV        166 min mTV
B,V        BBC

**BOXCAR BERTHA **                             18
Martin Scorsese        USA        1972
Barbara Hershey, David Carradine, Barry Primus,

*John Carradine, Bernie Casey*
Set against the background of the Depression, this is an account of a small-town Arkansas girl who falls in with a bunch of train robbers. A kind of BONNIE AND CLYDE without the glamour, with David Carradine taking on the railroad establishment, aided by the real-life title character. Scorsese's first film shows some of the flair of his later works, but is at heart superficial and unsatisfying.

| DRA | 92 min; 88 min (VIR) (ort 97 min) |
| B,V | RNK; VIR (VHS only) |

**BOXER BLOW \***                                    18
Joseph Lai          HONG KONG          1989
*Jonathan James, Kenneth Woods*
Two US agents are dispatched to the Middle East to de-fuse a delicate situation that could trigger off WW3. They find themselves caught up in a clash between a band of fanatics and a criminal gang. This thin framework provides the minimal plot for the usual blend of action and martial arts mayhem.

| MAR | 86 min |
| V | VPD |

**BOXER'S ADVENTURE, THE \*\***
                       HONG KONG
*Pai Ying, Ling Yun, Yen Han-Hhsi*
Standard kung fu fare with a boxer fighting criminals at the time of the Tang Dynasty. Average.
Aka: BOXER ADVENTURE

| MAR | 80 min |
| V | ACE L/A; OCEAN |

**BOY AND HIS DOG, A \*\***
L.Q. Jones          USA          1975
*Don Johnson, Susanne Benton, Alvy Moore, Helene Winston, Charles McGraw, Tim McIntire (voice only)*
A black comedy set in a post-WW4 world of 2024, with a boy and his highly intelligent and telepathic dog foraging for food, eventually being lured by a woman into a bizarre underground society, where the boy's services are required for procreation purposes. A faithful adaptation of Ellison's novella, but severely hampered by a low-budget.
Boa: novella by Harlan Ellison.

| FAN | 90 min |
| B,V | VPD; MED |

**BOY FROM HELL, THE \*\***                          18
Deryn Warren          USA          1987
*Anthony Jenkins, Aaron Teich, Alexandra Kennedy, Theodora Louise, John Reno*
A nasty little horror film that has a mother placing her son in a boarding school, to keep him out of the hands of his father whose intention is to cast a demonic bloodspell over him. Having murdered the boy's mother, the father comes to get his son, who has in the meantime begun to kill his classmates.
Aka: BLOODSPELL

| HOR | 88 min |
| B,V | RCA |

**BOY IN BLUE, THE \*\***                             15
Charles Jarrot          CANADA          1986
*Nicolas Cage, Christopher Plummer, Cynthia Dale, David Naughton, Sean Sullivan, Melody Anderson*
Dreary romantic biopic devoted to Ned Hanlan; a Canadian who was a famed international rowing champion for some ten years at the start of the century. Filmed in Montreal, with Cage miscast as this brutish and unpleasant rower, who comes to Philadelphia at around 1900 to show up the snobs at the first of many regattas.

| DRA | 93 min |
| B,V | CBS |

**BOY ON A DOLPHIN \*\***                            U
Jean Negulesco          USA          1957
*Allan Ladd, Clifton Webb, Sophia Loren, Laurence*

*Naismith, Alexis Minotis, Jorge Mistral*
When a Greek girl diver discovers a valuable sunken treasure, the news attracts a ruthless collector and an American archaeologist. An Aegean adventure yarn, in which the beautiful scenery out-acts the sadly miscast male lead; expect no surprises. This was Loren's US film debut.
Boa: novel by David Divine.

| A/AD | 110 min |
| V/h | CBS |

**BOY TAKES GIRL \*\***                              PG
Michal Bat-Adam     ISRAEL          1983
*Gabi Eldor, Hillel Neeman, Dina Limon*
A girl is sent to a farming co-operative for the summer holidays and finds it hard to adjust to new and unfamiliar surroundings. Forgettable drama.

| DRA | 84 min (ort 93 min) Cut (32 sec) |
| V | GHV |

**BOY WHO COULD FLY, THE \*\*\***                    PG
Nick Castle          USA          1986
*Lucy Deakins, Bonnie Bedelia, Colleen Dewhurst, Jay Underwood, Fred Savage, Louise Fletcher, Fred Gwynne, Mindy Cohen, Janet MacLachlan, Michelle Bardeaux, Aura Pithart*
A young girl moves to a small town after her father dies and discovers a strange autistic boy there, whose only method of coping with reality is to believe he can fly. She gradually gets to know him and in doing so, overcomes her own problems. Though the film's change from drama to fantasy tends to undermine its impact, this sensitive and warm story treats serious ideas with a light touch.

| DRA | 103 min |
| V/h | CBS |

**BOY WHO HAD EVERYTHING, THE \***                   18
Stephen Wallace     AUSTRALIA          1984
*Jason Connery, Laura Williams, Lewis Fitz-Gerald, Ian Gilmour, Diane Cilento*
Set in Sydney in 1965, this rather superficial account of a boy's first year at university, examines his emotional problems with his mother and girlfriend. An inconsequential and trite study of adolescence and growing pains. Cilento plays Connery's mom – as she is in real life.

| DRA | 90 min |
| B,V | SONY |

**BOY WHO TURNED YELLOW, THE \*\*\***
Michael Powell          UK          1972
*Mark Dignam, Robert Eddison, Helen Weir, Brian Worth, Esmond Knight, Laurence Carter, Patrick McAlinney, Lem Kitaj*
A boy sent home for sleeping in class, turns yellow on the way home. So does everyone else on the same underground train. A series of slight but enjoyable adventures follow in this charming little work. Scripted by Emeric Pressburger, who worked with Powell on "A Matter Of Life And Death" – a somewhat better known fantasy.

| JUV | 55 min |
| B,V | RNK |

**BOYFRIEND, THE \*\***                              U
Ken Russell          UK          1971
*Twiggy (Lesley Hornby), Christopher Gable, Max Adrian, Barbara Windsor, Bryan Pringle, Murray Melvin, Moyra Fraser, Georgina Hale, Sally Brant, Vladek Sheybal, Tommy Tune, Brian Murphy, Graham Armitage*
Ostensibly an attempt to create a screen version of the Sandy Wilson stage pastiche. The plot (such as it is) follows the attempts of a provincial company to put on a musical. Russell's homage to the genre of the Hollywood musical has a number of good fantasy sequences that mirror the work of Busby Berkley, but the lack of a strong storyline is a drawback.

Boa: musical by Sandy Dennis.
MUS                          104 min (ort 125 min)
V/sh                                        MGM

## BOYS AND GIRLS TOGETHER *                 18
Ralph Lawrence Marsden  UK            1979
*Roger Furse, Christine Maskelle, Cherry Patel, Paul
Ong, Helen Fitzgerald, Anthony Thomas*
Four men and four women live out their sexual
fantasies among a group of tenants in a multi-racial
house in Hampstead. Dull and trite.
A      53 min (ort 57 min) Cut (15 sec in addition to film
cuts)
B,V                                        CLOCK

## BOYS FROM BRAZIL, THE **                  18
Franklin J. Schaffner   USA           1979
*Gregory Peck, Laurence Olivier, James Mason, Lilli
Palmer, Rosemary Harris, John Dehner, John
Rubinstein, Uta Hagen, Steven Guttenberg, Denholm
Elliott, Anne Meara, Bruno Ganz, Michael Gough,
Prunella Scales*
Based on a bestseller, this tells of a post-war Nazi plan
to use genetic implantation to breed a group of Hitler
clones. Sometimes tense, more often nasty, with
Olivier totally miscast as a Simon Wiesenthal-type
Nazi hunter coming up against Peck's sinister Nazi
scientist.
Boa: novel by Ira Levin.
THR                                       120 min
B,V                        PRV L/A; CH5 (VHS only)

## BOYS IN BLUE, THE *                       PG
Val Guest           UK                1983
*Bobby Ball, Tommy Cannon, Suzanne Danielle, Roy
Kinnear, Eric Sykes, Jack Douglas, Edward Judd, Jon
Pertwee, Arthur English, Billy Burden, Nigel
Lambert, Eric Francis, Ken Barker, Richard
Borthwick, Su Douglas*
A throw-back to those silly British comedies of years
gone by (we hoped). Based on a 1939 Will Hay film
"Ask A Policeman", the plot follows village policemen
and their attempts to catch some art thieves. Written
and directed by Guest. An inept cast flounders about
in an inept comedy – we deserve better.
COM                                        91 min
B,V,V2,LV                                  RNK

## BOYS IN COMPANY C, THE ***
Sydney J. Furie  USA/HONG KONG        1978
*Stan Shaw, Andrew Stevens, James Canning, Michael
Lembeck, Craig Wasson, Scott Hylands, James
Whitmore Jr, Noble Willingham, Santos Morales,
Drew Michaels, Lee Ermey*
The fortunes of five recruits to the US Marines are
followed as they are whipped into shape for action in
Vietnam. Tough, sometimes brutal film, with a great
performance from Shaw. Written by Furie and Rick
Natkin.
WAR                          121 min (ort 127 min)
B,V                                        RNK

## BOYS IN THE BAND, THE ****                15
William Friedkin    USA               1970
*Kenneth Nelson, Leonard Frey, Cliff Gorman, Frederik
Combs, Laurence Luckinbill, Keith Prentice, Robert
LaTourneaux, Reuben Greene*
Film version of a Broadway play dealing with the
lives and loves of a group of men who meet at a
birthday party – eight are homosexual, but the ninth
insists he isn't. Despite the limitations of a single set,
this superbly acted drama is sometimes funny, often
sad, but never less than totally absorbing. A badly cut
108 minute version was produced for TV.
Boa: play by Mart Crowley.
DRA                                       114 min
B, V/sh                        MGM; CBS (VHS only)

## BOYS NEXT DOOR, THE **                    18
Penelope Spheeris     USA             1985
*Maxwell Caulfield, Charlie Sheen, Patti D'Arbanville,
Christopher McDonald, Hank Garrett, Moon Zappa*
Violent tale of two high school graduates who embark
on an orgy of killing on a weekend trip to L.A., as a
form of protest at their bleak futures. A senseless and
despairing character study.
Aka: BLIND RAGE; KILLERS
A/AD                           87 min Cut (19 sec)
B,V                                        CBS

## BRAIN DAMAGE ***                          18
Frank Henenlotter     USA             1988
*Rick Herbst, Gordon MacDonald, Jennifer Lowry,
Theo Barnes, Vicki Darnell, Lucille Saint-Peter, Kevin
Van Hentryck*
An offbeat and fairly outrageous horror yarn concern-
ing a young man who acquires a monster parasite
named Elmer, who requires fresh human brains in
order to live. His host agrees to help him in his quest,
in return for a euphoria-inducing fluid Elmer pumps
into his brain. Look out for an amusing cameo by Van
Hentryck, the star of BASKET CASE – Henenlotter's
first film. Cut before video submission by 22 sec.
HOR                                        86 min
V                                          PAL

## BRAIN, THE **                             PG
Gerard Oury         FRANCE            1969
*David Niven, Jean-Paul Belmondo, Bourvil, Eli
Wallach, Silvia Monti, Fernand Valois*
The story of a master crook who poses as a NATO
colonel in order to carry out the theft of 14 million
dollars in assorted currencies from a Paris-Brussels
train. Meanwhile a pair of small-time crooks are
planning the same heist. Niven does his best in this
slight and rather laboured crime caper.
COM                                        97 min
B,V                                        CIC

## BRAIN, THE ***                            18
Edward Hunt         USA               1988
*Tom Breznahan, Cyndy Preston, David Gale*
The rapid rise in the ratings of a popular new TV show
called Independent Thinking is followed by a spate of
murders and suicides among its viewers. It transpires
that an alien with plans for domination of the planet
is behind the show, in this interesting and unusual
horror yarn.
HOR                                        99 min
V                                          RCA

## BRAIN DEAD **                             15
Adam Simon          USA               1989
*Bill Pullman, Bill Paxton, Bud Cort, Patricia
Charbonneau, Nicholas Pryor, George Kennedy*
A neurologist is called in to examine the mind of a
brilliant but insanely murderous physicist, whose
disturbed brain holds the key to a piece of vital
research. However, the neurologist soon finds himself
plunged into a nightmarish fantasy world where
nothing is as it seems. A few unusual ideas are all
that's on offer in this incoherent shocker.
HOR                                        85 min
V                                          MGM

## BRAIN MACHINE, THE ***                    U
Ken Hughes          UK                1954
*Patrick Barr, Elizabeth Allan, Maxwell Reed, Russell
Napier, Vanda Godsell, Gibb McLaughlin*
With the use of an electro-encephalograph, a female
psychiatrist at a hospital discovers that a drug
smuggler is a dangerous psychopath, but is kidnapped
by him. The unusual opening premise helps add some
zest to a solid but basically conventional crime story.
THR                         80 min (ort 83 min) B/W
V                                          WHV

## BRAINSTORM *** 15
Douglas Trumball     USA     1983
*Natalie Wood, Christopher Walken, Louise Fletcher,*
*Cliff Robertson, Joe Dorsey, Jordan Christopher, Alan*
*Fudge, Donald Hotton, Stacy Kuhne-Adams,*
*Georgianne Walken, Jason Lively, Lou Walker, John*
*Hugh, David Wood*
Two scientists have perfected a sensory device in the
form of a headset that can relay images directly into
one's consciousness. With potential for both good and
evil, the device is sought by some unscrupulous
parties. The incredible visual effects (designed for 70
mm stereophonic projection) do not translate well to
TV, but hold up an otherwise routine "mad-scientist"
type tale. Natalie Wood's last film; she died during
production in 1981.
FAN     101 min
V     MGM

## BRAINWASH *** 
Bobby Roth     USA     1982
*Yvette Mimieux, Cindy Pickett, Christopher Allport,*
*John Considine, Julius Harris, Scott Marlowe, Fran*
*Ryan, Walter Olkewicz, Danny Dayton, Denny Miller*
A company requires its top executives and their wives
to undergo "Executive Development Training" which
consists of a humiliating series of exercises undergone
at encounter group workshops, the purpose of this
being to control the behaviour of its employees. A
disturbing tale, made more so by the fact that it is
loosely based on true events.
Aka: CIRCLE OF POWER; MYSTIQUE; NAKED
WEEKEND, THE
HOR     98 min (ort 103 min)
B,V,V2     VCL/CBS

## BRAINWASHED **
Eric Le Mung     FRANCE/ITALY     1972
*Omar Sharif, Florinda Bolkan*
A girlfriend has waited years to visit a former leader
now imprisoned on an island, but her visit ends in
tragedy. Average.
Aka: LE DROIT D'AIMER; IL DIRITTO D'AMARE;
RIGHT TO LOVE, THE
DRA     98 min
B,V,V2     VCL

## BRAINWAVES ** 18
Ulli Lommell     USA     1982
*Tony Curtis, Keir Dullea, Suzanna Love, Vera Miles,*
*Percy Rodrigues, Paul Wilson, Ryan Seitz, Nicholas*
*Love, Corinne Alphen, Eve Brent Ashe, Philipe Carr,*
*Roger Burgraff, Michael DeFrancisco, Jason Fong*
A young girl is injured in a hit-and-run accident, but
is saved from a coma by being given the brain of a
murdered girl. She then experiences strange night-
mares and hallucinations and finds herself being
stalked by the murdered girl's killer. A new twist on
the Frankenstein legend fails to develop, in this
unimaginative and stolid thriller.
Aka: SHADOW OF DEATH
THR     100 min; 77 min (MAST)
B,V,V2     VTC L/A; VMA L/A; MAST (VHS only)

## BRANNIGAN ** 15
Douglas Hickox     UK     1975
*John Wayne, Richard Attenborough, Judy Geeson,*
*Mel Ferrer, John Vernon, Daniel Pilon, John Stride,*
*James Booth, Del Hanney, Lesley-Ann Down, Barry*
*Dennen, Anthony Booth, Brian Glover, Ralph Meeker,*
*Jack Watson*
An Irish-American cop is sent to England to catch a
fugitive gangster who has fled to London to avoid
extradition. Routine cop thriller with Wayne in an
unusual setting.
THR     107 min (ort 111 min)
V     WHV

## BRASS TARGET ** 15
John Hough     USA     1978
*Sophia Loren, John Cassavetes, Robert Vaughn,*
*George Kennedy, Max Von Sydow, Patrick McGoohan*
Complex but rambling thriller in which Patton does
not die in an accident at the end of the war, but is
murdered because he knows about a robbery by his
subordinates, of 250 million dollars worth of Nazi
gold. A rambling and muddled story of little merit,
though Von Sydow is good as the killer.
Boa: novel The Algonquin Project by Frederick Nolan.
THR     111 min
B,V     MGM

## BRAT, THE * R18
    USA
*Jamie Summers, Sioban Hunter, Rebecca Lynn, Jerry*
*Butler*
A spoilt brat of a woman is in danger of losing her
husband to one of his sexy secretaries. No great
shakes when it comes to fidelity herself, she decides to
use her prowess to keep her husband happy. A tedious
little sex film.
A     53 min
V     VEXCEL

## BRAVADOS, THE *** PG
Henry King     USA     1958
*Gregory Peck, Joan Collins, Stephen Boyd, Albert*
*Salmi, Henry Silva, Barry Coe, Kathleen Gallant,*
*George Voskovec, Herbert Rudley, Lee Van Cleef, Ken*
*Scott, Andrew Duggan, Gene Evans, Joe Da Rita,*
*Robert Adler, Robert Griffin*
An overlong, rambling Western, in which Peck is bent
on pursuit of the man who raped and murdered his
wife, but realises after a while that he is little better
than his quarry. Peck gives a nice, restrained per-
formance and Da Rita an intense one as the "hang-
man" in this rather austere above-average Western.
WES     93 min (ort 98 min)
V/h     CBS

## BRAVE FROG, THE: A VERY FROGGY AFFAIR **U
Michael Reynolds     1985
Cartoon animation following the exploits of a little
frog who escapes with his parents from the monsters
of a pond, and heads off in search of a new home.
Settling in Rainbow Pond he meets a little girl frog
and together they set out in pursuit of adventure.
Average.
CAR     91 min
V     MAST

## BRAVE FROG, THE: GREATEST ADVENTURE **U
Michael Reynolds
Another story in the "Brave Frog" series, with all the
little frogs of the pond community fighting a nasty
villain in the shape of a leopard frog.
Aka: BRAVE FROG'S GREATEST ADVENTURES,
THE
CAR     91 min Cut (2 min 16 sec)
V     MAST; XTASY

## BRAVE LITTLE TOASTER, THE *** U
Jerry Rees     USA     1987
*Voices of: Jon Lovitz, Tim Stack, Timothy Day*
Animated feature that follows the adventures of five
household items left alone in a holiday home who have
faithfully carried out their daily duties despite the
fact that no-one lives there anymore. Eventually they
tire of this pointless existence and set off in search of a
little boy they once knew as "Master". An offbeat but
pleasing and well executed effort.
CAR     90 min
V     BRAVE

## BRAVESTARR: THE LEGEND ** U
Tom Tatarnowicz     USA     1986

*Voices of: Charlie Adler, Susan Blu, Pat Fraley*
Animated space Western about an Indian marshal sent to tame "New Texas", a rough planet whose citizens have pleaded for help in fighting the forces of evil. Fair.
Aka: BRAVESTARR; MARSHAL BRAVESTARR
CAR             88 min; 48 min (VCC) (ort 101 min)
B,V             CHV; VCC (VHS only)

## BRAZIL ***        15
Terry Gilliam             UK             1985
*Jonathan Pryce, Katherine Helmond, Robert De Niro, Ian Holm, Bob Hoskins, Ian Richardson, Michael Palin, Peter Vaughan, Kim Griest, Jim Broadbent, Barbara Hicks, Charles McKeown, Derrick O'Connor, Kathryn Pogson*
A chilling and imaginative portrayal of an inefficient but brutal Britain of the not-too-distant future, where a clerk clings to his ideals in the face of opposition from the police state. A visually impressive film full of great moments of black comedy, but also a film that goes on far too long. The screenplay is by Gilliam, Tom Stoppard and Charles McKeown.
COM             137 min (ort 142 min)
V/sh             TEVP; WHV

## BREAKAWAY ***        U
Warren Skaaren             USA
*Walter Yates*
Autobiographical account of one man's longing to leave the city for a more natural life in the wilderness. Yates plays himself in this enjoyable outdoors drama.
DRA             90 min
V             FIFTH

## BREAKDANCE 2: ELECTRIC BOOGALOO **   PG
Sam Firstenberg             USA             1984
*Lucinda Dickey, Adolfo (Shabba-Doo) Quinones, Michael (Boogaloo-Shrimp) Chambers, Susie Bono*
Happy but empty sequel to the first film, with a rich college-bound kid and some underprivileged youths uniting to save a community centre. A noisy, cheerful stomper for the breakdancing set. Numbers include "Do Your Thang" and "Oye Mamacita".
Aka: BREAKIN' 2 ELECTRIC BOOGALOO
MUS             89 min (ort 94 min) (Cut at film release)
B, V/s             GHV; VCC

## BREAKDANCE: THE MOVIE **      PG
Joel Silberg             USA             1984
*Lucinda Dickey, Adolfo (Shabba Doo) Quinones, Michael (Boogaloo Shrimp) Chambers, Ben Lokey, Christopher McDonald, Phineas Newborn*
The plot is minimal in this story of three breakdancers who try to make it big on Broadway. A breakdancer's answer to FLASHDANCE, with loud music and plenty of breakin'. A sequel followed in 1984.
Aka: BREAKIN'
MUS             88 min
B,V             GHV; MSD

## BREAKER MORANT **** 
Bruce Beresford             AUSTRALIA             1979
*Edward Woodward, Jack Thompson, John Waters, Charles Tingwell, Bryan Brown, Vincent Ball, Lewis Fitz-Gerald*
An excellent film that's set in the Boer War and tells the story of three Australian soldiers who were court-martialled ostensibly for murdering prisoners, but in reality for political reasons. A powerful drama based on true events and a winner of several Australian Academy Awards.
Boa: play by Kenneth G. Ross.
WAR             106 min
B,V,V2             GHV

## BREAKER! BREAKER! *       15
Don Hulette             USA             1977
*Chuck Norris, George Murdock, Terry O'Connor, Don Gentry*

A trucker searches for his brother in a town that's run by a corrupt judge, in this stupid comedy-actioner that trades on the CB craze but does little with it.
A/AD             85 min
B,V             VIPCO; THV/RHIHOM

## BREAKFAST AT TIFFANY'S ***    PG
Blake Edwards             USA             1961
*Audrey Hepburn, George Peppard, Patricia Neal, Buddy Ebsen, Mickey Rooney, Martin Balsam, John McGiver*
The bittersweet story of a relationship between a struggling young writer and a zany New York playgirl who comes from a small town. Based on a Truman Capote story, this film has some good moments and a memorable Mancini score. AA: Score (Henry Mancini), Song ("Moon River" – Henry Mancini – music/ Johnny Mercer – lyrics).
Boa: novel by Truman Capote.
COM             109 min (115 min)
B,V             CIC

## BREAKFAST CLUB, THE ***     15
John Hughes             USA             1984
*Emilio Estevez, Judd Nelson, Molly Rinwald, Anthony Michael Hall, Ally Sheedy, Paul Gleason*
Five students who have to spend a Saturday morning in detention, sit talking about themselves in a perceptive, honest and poignant study that's rather constrained by a predictable script.
DRA             93 min
V/h             CIC

## BREAKFAST IN PARIS * 
John Lamond             AUSTRALIA             1981
*Barbara Parkins, Rod Mullinar, Jack Lenoir, Elspeth Ballantyne, Jeremy Higgins, Graham Stanley*
A fashion designer packs her bags and flies off to Paris after she discovers her boyfriend in bed with another woman. There she has a romance with a photographer. A weak and dreary attempt at comedy.
COM             96 min
B,V,V2             3MVID

## BREAKHEART PASS *       PG
Tom Gries             USA             1976
*Charles Bronson, Charles Durning, Ben Johnson, Richard Crenna, Ed Lauter, Jill Ireland, David Huddleston, Roy Jenson, Casey Tibbs, Archie Moore, Joe Kapp, Read Morgan, Robert Rothwell, Rayford Barnes, Scott Newman*
Even the story, based on an Alistair Maclean novel, cannot help in a film that is dull, dull, dull. The confusing plot has Bronson starring as a government undercover agent on the trail of gun-runners. Most of the action or lack of it takes place on an interminable train journey.
Boa: novel by Alistair MacLean.
WES             95 min (Cut at film release)
B,V             WHV

## BREAKING ALL THE RULES **    15
James Orr             CANADA             1984
*Carl Marotte, Carolyn Dunn, Rachel Hayward, Thor Bishopric*
A fairly run-of-the-mill teen-appeal movie that is quite watchable if modest in scope. Here, the action, backed up by a loud musical accompaniment, is set in an amusement park where four teenagers get caught up in the theft of a valuable diamond.
Aka: BREAKING THE RULES; FUN PARK
COM             90 min
V/h             NWV

## BREAKING AWAY **       PG
Peter Yates             USA             1979
*Dennis Christopher, Dennis Quaid, Daniel Stern, Jackie Earle Haley, Robyn Douglass, Barbara Barrie, Paul Dooley*

A film which, despite critical acclaim, never really comes to life. All about four friends who, having left school, don't know what to do with their lives. This sincere and well-meaning effort suffers from a distinct lack of direction. Later a brief TV series. AA: Screen (Orig) (Steve Tesich).

COM                                        100 min
B,V,LV                                        CBS

**BREAKING GLASS **                             15
Brian Gibson            UK                    1980
*Hazel O'Connor, Phil Daniels, Jon Finch, Jonathan Pryce, Peter Hugo Daly, Mark Wingett, Gary Tibbs, Charles Wegner, Mark Wing-Davey, Hugh Thomas, Derek Thompson, Nigel Humphreys, Ken Campbell, Lowri-Anne Richards*
A girl singer forms her own band but cannot cope with the fame that success brings her. Powerful performance from O'Connor as the singer, is largely wasted on a predictable script.

DRA                                        104 min
B,V,V2               VCL; VIR; ODY (VHS only)

**BREAKING LOOSE ***                            18
Rod Hay             AUSTRALIA                 1988
*Peter Phelps, Vince Martin, Abigail*
A brash young man gets involved in some unexpected adventures when he leaves the city and heads for the beach, in this forgettable little action tale. The script is by Hay.

A/AD                                        83 min
V                                            MED

**BREAKING POINT **
Peter Markle            USA                   1989
*Corbin Bernsen, Joanna Pacula, John Glover*
The story of a US Army major who is abducted by the Nazis and undergoes brainwashing, eventually coming to believe that WW2 is over and that he has been in a military hospital for the past two years. Fair.

DRA                                        91 min
V                                          TURNER

**BREAKING UP ***
Delbert Mann            USA                   1978
*Lee Remick, Granville Van Dusen, Vicki Dawson, David Stambaugh, Fred J. Scollay, Stephen Joyce, Cynthia Harris, Michael Lombard, Meg Mundy, Ed Crowley, Linda Sorenson, Kenneth McMillan, James Noble, Bruce Gray*
Drama about a sophisticated suburban couple who split up after fifteen years of marriage. When her husband walks out, Remick is left to cope with the house and kids. An effective drama with a convincing performance from Remick. Scripted by Loring Mandel.

DRA                                  100 min mTV
B,V                                           VTC

**BREAKOUT ***
Tom Gries               USA                   1975
*Charles Bronson, Robert Duvall, John Huston, Alejandro Rey, Jill Ireland, Sheree North, Randy Quaid*
Tough action film in which Bronson plays a lush pilot, who rescues a man from a seedy Mexican jail after he has been framed for a murder. Fast paced and often quite funny, but spoilt by excessive dependence on violence. Written by Howard B. Krietsek, Marc Norman and Elliott Baker.
Boa: novel Ten Second Jailbreak by C. Asinof.

A/AD                                        96 min
B,V                                           RCA

**BREAKTHROUGH **
Andrew V. McLaglen
            WEST GERMANY/UK                  1979
*Richard Burton, Robert Mitchum, Rod Steiger, Curt Jurgens, Klaus Loewitsch, Helmut Griem, Michael*

*Parks*
A disappointing sequel to CROSS OF IRON. Burton plays a German sergeant who becomes emmeshed in a plot to assassinate Hitler in the summer of 1944.
Aka: SERGEANT STEINER

WAR                                        111 min
B,V,V2                                        GHV

**BREATHLESS **                                 18
Jim McBride             USA                   1983
*Richard Gere, Valerie Kaprisky, Art Metrano, William Tepper, John P. Ryan, Gary Goodrow, Robert Dunn*
Lukewarm remake of Godard's 1959 film "A Bout De Souffle" that lacks any of the punch of the original. Gere is effective as the young amoral punk on the run from the police, who embarks on a whirlwind affair with a beautiful foreign student, but after a while the pointlessness of the whole exercise begins to tell.

DRA   96 min (RNK); 98 min (VIR) (ort 100 min) Cut (24 sec)
B,V,V2               RNK; VIR (VHS only)

**BREED APART, A **                             15
Philippe Mora          USA                    1984
*Powers Boothe, Rutger Hauer, Kathleen Turner, Donald Pleasence, Jayne Bentzen, John Dennis Johnston, Brion James*
A collector of bird's eggs becomes obsessed with the idea of obtaining those of a rare breed of eagle, and hires a mountain climber to steal two rare eggs from a conservationist-recluse, even though this theft will lead to the extinction of the species. A picturesque but empty and strangely uninteresting account.

DRA                           101 min; 90 min (VCC)
B,V                       GHV; VCC (VHS only)

**BREEDERS **                                   18
Tim Kincaid             USA                   1986
*Theresa Farley, Lance Lewman, Francis Raines, Natalie O'Connell*
Nasty mutant spores arrive on Earth and, having assumed human form, indulge in a rape orgy – the intention being to reproduce in the form of human duplicates. A chilling idea that's let down by cliched development.

FAN                                        75 min
B,V                                           EIV

**BREWSTER McCLOUD ***                          15
Robert Altman           USA                   1970
*Bud Cort, Sally Kellerman, Michael Murphy, Shelley Duvall, Jennifer Salt, Stacy Keach, William Windom, Margaret Hamilton, Rene Auberjonois, John Shuck*
Bizarre and offbeat film about a boy who yearns to fly like a bird, a weird "birdwoman" who has the power to help him, and a series of inexplicable murders. Almost impossible to describe and harder to sit through – though it does have a few extremely funny moments.

COM                                        105 min
B,V                                           MGM

**BREWSTER'S MILLIONS ***                       PG
Walter Hill             USA                   1985
*Richard Pryor, John Candy, Lonette McKee, Stephen Collins, Jerry Orbach, Pat Hingle, Tovah Feldshuh, Joe Grifasi, Hume Cronyn*
A man is left a vast fortune by a long-lost uncle, with the stipulation that he spend 30 million dollars in 30 days. Remake of a 1945 film of the same name which it cannot compare to, mainly due to the poor script and lousy direction. A waste of Pryor and Candy – good comedians both. The seventh outing for McCutcheon's novel.
Boa: novel by G.B. McCutcheon.

COM                                        98 min
V/sh                                         CIC

**BRIAN'S SONG ****                             PG
Buzz Kulik              USA                   1970

*James Caan, Billy Dee Williams, Jack Warden,
Shelley Fabares, Judy Pace, Bud Furillo, Bernie
Casey, David Huddleston, Ron Feinberg, Jack
Concannon, Abe Gibron, Ed O'Bradoviich, Dick
Butkus, Mario Machado, Stu Nahan*
A true story of the real life friendship between two
famous baseball stars, one white and the other black,
who played for the Chicago Bears. This film attempts
to examine how the team as a whole was affected
when one of them developed cancer and died at the age
of 26. A fine and moving story, scripted by Edward
Blinn and with an outstanding score by Michel
Legrand.
Boa: story I Am Third by Gale Sayers.
DRA                      74 min (ort 76 min) mTV
V                                          PREST

### BRIDE CAME C.O.D., THE ** U
William Keighley      USA                    1941
*James Cagney, Bette Davis, Stuart Erwin, Eugene
Palette, William Frawley, Jack Carson, George Tobias*
A charter pilot agrees to kidnap an heiress but gets
stuck with her when they crash in the desert. A limp
and empty-headed comedy that's worth a look, if only
to see the stars squeeze a few laughs out of such
unpromising material.
DRA                            88 min B/W
V                                          WHV

### BRIDE OF BOOGEDY ** PG
Oz Scott              USA                    1987
*Richard Masur, Mimi Kennedy, Tammy Lauren,
David Faustino, Joshua Rudoy, Leonard Frey,
Howard Witt, Eugene Levy*
A 300-year-old ghost has decided to get himself a wife,
so he attends a local carnival where he casts a spell on
the entire town, with a pretty girl the object of his
attentions. Typical Disney haunted-house comedy
that followed a pilot for a prospective TV series.
COM                       89 min (ort 100 min) mTV
B,V                                        WDV

### BRIDE OF FRANKENSTEIN, THE **** PG
James Whale          USA                    1935
*Boris Karloff, Colin Clive, Valerie Hobson, Dwight
Frye, Elsa Lanchester, Ernest Thesiger, Una
O'Connor, E.E. Clive, Gavin Gordon, Douglas Walton,
O.P. Heggie, John Carradine*
Classic sequel to FRANKENSTEIN with Franken-
stein being forced by mad doctor Thesiger to make a
mate for his monster. Contains a number of highlights
such as the blind hermit scene and an excellent
creation sequence. This shortened version omits part
of the Mary Shelley prologue plus the murder of the
mayor. Scripted by John L. Balterton and William
Hurlbut and scored by Franz Waxman. Followed by
"Son Of Frankenstein" and the remake, THE BRIDE.
Osca: FRANKENSTEIN
HOR 75 min (ort 90 min) 134 min (2 film cassette) B/W
V                                          CIC

### BRIDE TO BE ** 15
Moreno Alba        SPAIN/USA                 1975
*Stanley Baker, Sarah Miles, Peter Day, Jose Martin
Caffarell, Maria Vico, Eduardo Bea, Vicente Soler*
A woman, betrothed to a wealthy landowner, falls in
love with a young priest. Fair melodrama, based on a
19th century Spanish novel.
Aka: PEPITA JIMENEZ
Boa: novel by Juan Valera.
DRA                           108 min
B,V                                        PRV L/A

### BRIDE, THE ** 15
Frank Roddam         UK                      1985
*Sting (Gordon Sumner), Jennifer Beals, Clancy
Brown, David Rappaport, Anthony Higgins, Geraldine
Page, Alexei Sayle, Veruschka, Quentin Crisp, Phil
Daniels, Andrew De La Tour, Tony Haygarth,*

*Matthew Guinness, John Sharp*
A flawed attempt both to remake THE BRIDE OF
FRANKENSTEIN and rethink the legend. Here our
Baron falls madly in love with the female he supposedly created for his monster. A film that succeeds
in terms of the look of a gothic horror film, but fails at
any deeper level – mainly due to the poor performances of Sting and Beals. Rappaport is however,
outstanding as the midget who befriends our Baron's
male monster.
HOR                          114 min (ort 119 min)
V/sh                                       RCA

### BRIDESHEAD REVISITED *** 15
Charles Sturridge/Michael Lindsay-Hogg
                     UK                      1981
*Jeremy Irons, Anthony Andrews, Diana Quick,
Laurence Olivier, Claire Bloom, Simon Jones,
Stephane Audran, Mona Washbourne, John Le
Mesurier, John Gielgud*
This massive, fanatically faithful adaptation of
Waugh's novel is a slow, ponderous account of how an
Oxford student becomes deeply involved with a wea-
lthy upper-class family. Beautifully made and acted,
this TV drama hosts an array of unpleasant charac-
ters but lacks both pace and impact.
Boa: novel by Evelyn Waugh.
DRA                     664 min (6 cassettes) mTV
V                                     GRN L/A; VES

### BRIDGE AT REMAGEN, THE ** PG
John Guillermin      USA                     1968
*George Segal, Ben Gazzara, Robert Vaughn, Bradford
Dillman, E.G. Marshall, Peter Van Eyck*
Account of a true incident in WW2 when Allied troops
had to hold a vital bridge over the Rhine prior to the
final onslaught on Nazi Germany. Well made but
hampered by the utter predictability of the material –
a standard war film.
Boa: book by K. Hechler.
WAR                           113 min
B,V                                        WHV

### BRIDGE ON THE RIVER KWAI **** PG
David Lean           UK                      1957
*Alec Guinness, Jack Hawkins, Sessue Hayakawa,
William Holden, James Donald, Andre Morell,
Geoffrey Horne, Ann Sears, Peter Williams, John
Boxer, Percy Herbert, Harold Goodwin, Henry Okawa*
During WW2, British soldiers in a Japanese POW
camp build a bridge under the orders of their comman-
der whilst Holden plots to blow it up. A vigorous but
utterly glamorised picture of war that whitewashes
the cruelties of the Japanese, yet for all that, contains
sequences of great power. AA: Pic, Dir, Actor (Guin-
ness), Cin (Jack Hildyard), Edit (Peter Taylor), Score
(Malcolm Arnold), Screen (Adapt) (Pierre Boulle/Carl
Foreman/Michael Wilson).
Boa: novel by Pierre Boulle.
WAR                          155 min (ort 161 min)
B,V                                        RCA

### BRIDGE TO HELL ** PG
Luis Ciccarese/Umberto Lenzi
                     ITALY                   1986
*Jeff Connors, Francis Ferre, Paky Valente, Andy
Forrest*
Three escaped POW's, not content with winning just
their freedom, go on to try to steal a golden treasure
from the Germans, in this run-of-the-mill war film.
WAR                          88 min (ort 96 min)
B,V                                        AVA

### BRIDGE TO NOWHERE ** 18
Ian Mune           NEW ZEALAND               1985
*Bruno Lawrence, Philip Gordon, Alison Routledge,
Margaret Umbers, Stephen Judd, Matthew Hunter,
Shelley Luxford*
A group of teenagers have to survive various hazards

in a trek across country and are forced into a war of survival when they arouse the wrath of a hermit. A well made but rather uninteresting tale.

HOR                                              82 min
B,V                                        EHE; NELS

### BRIDGE TO SILENCE **                          15
Karen Arthur          USA              1988
*Maree Matlin, Lee Remick, Michael O'Keefe, Josef*
*Sommer, Phyllis Frelich*
In her TV acting debut, Matlin plays a woman with a hearing disability who tries to rebuild her life, shattered in a car crash that killed her husband. Remick is her cold and heartless mother, with whom she comes into conflict over the fate of her daughter. A soap opera style tearjerker which never rises above the trite script, despite excellent performances all round.
Boa: story by Louisa Burns Bisogno.
DRA                     88 min (ort 100 min) mTV
V                                             PARK

### BRIDGE TOO FAR, A *                            15
Richard Attenborough   UK              1977
*Dirk Bogarde, James Caan, Edward Fox, Michael*
*Caine, Sean Connery, Hardy Kruger, Ryan O'Neal,*
*Robert Redford, Maximilian Schell, Laurence Olivier,*
*Liv Ullman, Elliott Gould, Gene Hackman, Anthony*
*Hopkins, Arthur Hill*
An unsuccessful attempt to tell the tragic story of the failed 1944 Arnhem operation, when Allied commandos dropped behind the German lines in occupied Holland. A star-studded cast plus thousands of extras, succeed in producing a film that collapses under its own weight.
Boa: book by Cornelius Ryan.
WAR                     169 min (ort 175 min)
V                                             WHV

### BRIDGES AT TOKO-RI, THE ***                    U
Mark Robson           USA              1954
*William Holden, Grace Kelly, Mickey Rooney, Fredric*
*March, Earl Holliman, Robert Strauss*
This drama, based on a bestseller by James Michener, tells the story of a lawyer recalled to fly jets during the Korean War. A powerful yet sensitive film showing the ultimate futility of war. AA: Effects (Paramount Studios).
Boa: novel by James Michener.
WAR                                          99 min
V                                             CIC

### BRIEF AFFAIR, A ***                          R18/18
Louie Lewis           USA              1981
*Annette Haven, Loni Sanders, Lisa De Leeuw, Brigette*
*Monet, Paul Thomas, Mike Horner, Joey Civera,*
*Sharon Mitchell, Nicole Noir*
Story set at the Lewis Academy of Performing Arts, that's essentially a series of separate episodes focusing on some of the girls studying there and the things they do to achieve sexual satisfaction. A kind of hardcore version of FAME with a few good moments, but just as episodic a storyline. The Harmony version was cut before video submission by 34 min 44 sec.
Osca: NIGHTLIFE (INTMED)
A 76 min (SEX); 40 min (HAR: Cut – 2 min 22 sec); 73 min (INTMED) (ort 90 min)
B,V
XTACY/KRP L/A; INTMED (VHS only); SEX (R18 version); HAR (18 version)

### BRIEF ENCOUNTER *                              PG
Alan Bridges          USA              1974
*Sophia Loren, Richard Burton, Jack Hedley,*
*Rosemary Leach, Ann Firbank, Gwen Cherrell,*
*Benjamin Edney, John Le Mesurier, Jumoke Debayo,*
*Madeline Hinde, Marco Orlandini, Patricia Franklin,*
*Ernest C. Jennings, Jack Harding*
A poor remake of the 1945 film, lacking any of its

predecessor's qualities and as before telling of the stolen meetings between two married people. A woefully inadequate and unappealing effort.
Boa: play Still Life by Noel Coward.
DRA                                          99 min mTV
B,V,V2   PRV L/A; CH5 (VHS only); POLY (VHS only)

### BRIEF ENCOUNTER ***                            PG
David Lean            UK               1945
*Celia Johnson, Trevor Howard, Stanley Holloway,*
*Cyril Raymond, Joyce Carey, Everley Gregg, Margaret*
*Barton, Dennis Harkin, Valentine Dyall, Irene Handl,*
*Marjorie Mars, Nuna Davey, Edward Hodge, Sydney*
*Bromley, Avis Scott*
A suburban housewife and a local doctor, both less than content with their own marriages, meet and enjoy a brief romance. Their stolen meetings take place at a dismal railway station between trains. Fine acting and a good score (Rachmaninov's Second Piano Concerto) serve to point out the serious deficiencies in a stilted film, complete with the obligatory stereotyped working-class characters. Enjoyable but very, very dated. Remade in 1974.
Boa: play Still Life by Noel Coward.
DRA                                          86 min B/W
V                                             RNK

### BRIGADOON ***                                  U
Vincente Minnelli     USA              1954
*Gene Kelly, Cyd Charisse, Van Johnson, Elaine*
*Stewart, Jimmy Thompson, Barry Jones, Hugh Laing*
This adaptation of a Broadway musical, tells the story of a ghost village in the Scottish Highlands that comes to life once in every hundred years. Two Americans on holiday in Scotland discover it. Not all that inventive, but the enjoyable Alan Jay Lerner score makes it worthwhile.
Boa: musical by Alan Jay Lerner and Frederick Loewe
MUS                                          103 min
B,V                                           MGM

### BRIGHT LIGHTS, BIG CITY ***                    18
James Bridges         USA              1988
*Michael J. Fox, Phoebe Cates, Kiefer Sutherland,*
*Jason Robards, Swoosie Kurtz, Frances Sternhagen,*
*Tracy Pollan, John Houseman, Dianne Wiest, William*
*Hickey, Charlie Schlatter, David Warrilow, Alex Mapa*
A young man comes to New York from the Midwest and takes on a job as a fact-checker at a Manhattan magazine, but is soon caught up in a lifestyle that revolves around an endless cycle of drugs and alcohol. Fox is good as a fellow whose frenzied lifestyle threatens to cost him his sanity, but the more complex aspects of the novel are not brought out.
Boa: novel by Jay McInerney.
DRA                     104 min (ort 110 min)
V/sh                                          WHV

### BRIGHTON BEACH MEMOIRS **                      15
Gene Saks             USA              1986
*Blythe Danner, Jonathan Silverman, Bob Dishy, Brian*
*Drillinger, Judith Ivey, Stacey Glick, Lisa Waltz*
Neil Simon's semi-autobiographical story, that follows the affairs of two families sharing the same house in Brooklyn of 1937. Story is seen through the eyes of the young Simon, whose interests in life are largely confined to baseball and girls. A pleasant but cloying outing, with none of the sharpness of the successful Broadway play.
Boa: play by Neil Simon.
COM                                          105 min
B,V                                           CIC

### BRIGHTON ROCK ***                              
John Boulting         UK               1947
*Richard Attenborough, Hermione Baddeley, William*
*Hartnell, Carol Marsh, Nigel Stock, Wylie Watson,*
*Harcourt Williams, Alan Wheatley, George Carney,*
*Charles Goldner, Reginald Purdell, Constance Smith*

Film version of Graham Greene's novel about 1930s Brighton gangland life. A teenage hoodlum kills a rival but meets his Nemesis in the shape of a music hall artiste. Attenborough is superb as the gangster who finally meets a fitting end. The script is by Terence Rattigan and Greene.
Aka: YOUNG SCARFACE
Boa: novel by Graham Greene.
DRA                                    89 min (ort 91 min) B/W
B,V                                                      TEVP

## BRIMSTONE AND TREACLE ***                    18
Richard Loncraine        UK                    1983
Sting (Gordon Sumner), Denholm Elliott, Joan Plowright, Suzanna Hamilton
A handsome young man charms his way into the home of a middle-class couple on the pretext of being a friend of their daughter, now in a coma following an accident. A compelling but often unpleasant film with a fine performance from Sting, as the amoral stranger who eventually takes over the household, ultimately raping the daughter. The script is by Potter from his play. Originally made as a TV play in 1976, but the BBC banned it.
Boa: play by Dennis Potter.
DRA                                            87 min mTV
B,V                                            BWV/VSP

## BRINDAMORE ISLAND CONSPIRACY, THE **  15
Waris Hussein            USA                   1988
Ted Danson, Richard Masur, Rachel Ticotin, Marcie Leeds, James Noble, Kim Miyori, David Huddleston, Merritt Buttrick
A fair drama telling of a group of businessmen whose secret intrigues were threatened by one of their number, who was going to expose their activities but committed suicide instead. However, this is only the beginning of their problems.
Boa: novel by Jonathan Kellerman.
DRA                                            96 min
V                                              TGP

## BRING ME THE HEAD OF ALFREDO GARCIA *  18
Sam Peckinpah            USA                   1974
Warren Oates, Isela Vega, Gig Young, Robert Webber, Helmut Dantine, Emilio Fernandez, Kris Kristofferson
A sleazy story set in Mexico, with a small-time American piano player getting mixed up with some nasty characters, such as the wealthy Mexican who offers a million dollars for the head of his daughter's seducer. A gruesome and sickly melodrama, well directed but of little purpose or logic.
DRA                                            108 min
B,V                                            WHV

## BRING ME THE HEAD OF DOBIE GILLIS **    U
Stanley Z. Cherry        USA                   1988
Dwayne Hickman, Bob Denver, Connie Stevens, Sheila James, Scott Grimes, William Schallert, Tricia Leigh Fisher, Steve Franken
Stars of the American sitcom "The Many Loves Of Dobie Gillis" are reunited after 25 years, in this trivial little comedy which has wealthy Thalia Menninger returning to town with the intention of persuading old flame Dobie to dump his wife for her. Many stars from the original series pop up, though Stevens takes over the role originally played by Tuesday Weld.
COM                                    93 min (ort 100 min) mTV
V/h                                            CBS

## BRINGING UP BABY ****                           U
Howard Hawks             USA                   1938
Cary Grant, Katharine Hepburn, Charles Ruggles, May Robson, Walter Catlett, Fritz Feld, Jonathan Hale, Barry Fitzgerald, Ward Bond, Leona Roberts, George Irving, Tala Birell, Virginia Walker, John Kelly
Screwball comedy in which a zany heiress with a pet leopard sets her sights on a paleontology professor and

pursues him relentlessly, bringing chaos and havoc into his life. A well-paced comedy that cracks along at breakneck speed, moving from one crazy situation to the next. WHAT'S UP DOC? was an attempt at a remake, but this earlier film is by far the better of the two.
Osca: MY FAVOURITE WIFE (VCC)
COM          98 min; 183 min (VCC – 2 film cassette) B/W
B,V                                    TEVP; VCC (VHS only)

## BRITANNIA HOSPITAL *                           15
Lindsay Anderson         UK                    1982
Leonard Rossiter, Brian Pettifer, John Moffatt, Fulton Mackay, Jill Bennett, Vivian Pickles, Barbara Hicks, Graham Crowden, Peter Jeffrey, Marsha Hunt, Catherine Wilmer, Mary McLeod, Joan Plowright, Robin Askwith, Mark Hamill
An old crumbling hospital, threatened by a strike, demonstrations and an impending royal visit, is used as a metaphor for the state of the UK. A ponderous satire of occasional wit and considerable repulsiveness.
COM                                    111 min (ort 116 min)
B,V,V2                                         TEVP

## BROADCAST NEWS ***                             15
James L. Brooks          USA                   1987
William Hurt, Holly Hunter, Albert Brooks, Robert Prosky, Lois Chiles, Joan Cusack, Jack Nicholson, Peter Hackes, Christian Clemenson, Robert Katims, Ed Wheeler
A behind-the-scenes look at the world of TV news broadcasting with a highly strung and neurotic woman producer finding herself attracted to the handsome anchorman who has joined the network, despite the fact that he represents everything she loathes in broadcasting. Meanwhile, her best friend, who is a first-class reporter, is in love with her. An intelligent and witty comedy by writer/director/producer Brooks. Set and filmed in Washington D.C.
COM                                    127 min (ort 132 min)
V/sh                                           CBS

## BROADWAY DANNY ROSE **                         PG
Woody Allen              USA                   1984
Woody Allen, Mia Farrow, Nick Apollo Forte, Howard Storm, Jackie Gayle, Sandy Baron, Corbett Monica, Monty Gunty, Will Jordan, Milton Berle, Joe Franklin
A Broadway theatrical agent remains ridiculously loyal to his no-talent acts. He complicates his life even further by falling for the wife of a Mafia hoodlum. Despite good performances. the humour becomes a bit strained. Highpoints are some of the over-the-hill untalented performers our agent is trying to push. Written and directed by Allen.
COM                        86 min; 81 min (VIR) Cut B/W
B,V                                    RNK; VIR (VHS only)

## BROKEN ANGEL **                                15
Richard T. Heffron       USA                   1988
William Shatner, Susan Blakely, Roxann Biggs, Jason Horst, Brock Peters, Millie Perkins, Erika Eleniak, Collin Davis
This unmemorable thriller has Shatner searching for his daughter in Southern California following her disappearance after a gang shoot-out. He encounters the kind of treatment these thrillers reserve for folk who ask the wrong people the wrong questions. Bears some similarities to Dennehy's quest in A FATHER'S REVENGE.
DRA                                            96 min mTV
B,V                                            MGM

## BROKEN DREAMS **
Peter Levin              USA                   1981
Lucie Arnaz, Richard Jordan, Tony Bill, Tarah Nutter, Charles Levin, Peter Hobbs, Pat Hingle, Bridgette Anderson, Mimi Maynard, Michael Prince, Eda Zahl, Dorothy Fielding

Passions and intrigues in the American seat of government, with a bright and ambitious congressional aide falling for a lobbyist. A slight romantic drama of little warmth or interest.
Aka: WASHINGTON MISTRESS
DRA                              90 min mTV
B,V                             POLY; HER

### BROKEN MIRRORS *                    18
Marleen Goris    NETHERLANDS           1985
Lineke Rijxman, Henriette Tol, Elda Barrends
A view of life in an Amsterdam brothel with a sub-plot that revolves around a sadistic sex murderer. One of those all-men-are-rapists films; man-hatred on a grand scale.
Aka: GERBOKEN SPIEGELS
DRA                              112 min
B,V                             TEVP; CAN

### BROKEN PROMISE **                   15
Sandy Tung        USA                  1983
Ric Gitlin, Isabel Glasser, Jane Darby, Lela Higgins, Donna Jo Ford, Tom Archen, Jack Rose
The story of an unsuccessful marriage between two teenagers. Good enough in its way but unmemorable.
Aka: MARRIAGE, A
DRA                     84 min (ort 94 min)
B,V                             ODY/CBS

### BROKEN SABRE, THE **
Bernard McEveety   USA            1965/1966
Chuck Connors, Kamala Devi, Peter Breck, MacDonald Carey, John Carradine, Wendell Corey, Rochelle Hudson, Robert Q. Lewis, Cesar Romero, Patrick Wayne, William Bryant, Steve Malo, H.M. Wynant, John Lormer, Jay Jostyn
A man convicted of cowardice at the Battle of Bitter Creek is dismissed from the army. He tries to redeem himself in Arizona, by posing as a traitor in order to join a band of Mexican outlaws and lure them into a trap. However, his plans don't quite work out. This film is made up from some segments of the TV series "Branded" and was released theatrically in the UK. Average.
WES                              79 min mTV
B,V                             MEV

### BROKEN VOWS **                      15
Jud Taylor          USA                1986
M. Emmet Walsh, Tommy Lee Jones, Annette O'Toole, Milo O'Shea, David Groh, Madeleine Sherwood
A parish priest is called to administer the last rites to a dying man, who has been stabbed. Though the murder victim makes no confession nor shows any interest in the desire of the priest to help him, the latter becomes obsessed with finding out more about him. He becomes involved with the man's former girlfriend, getting drawn into a sinister mystery in the process. A competent but depressing TV drama, scripted by James Costigan.
Boa: novel Where The Dark Streets Go by Dorothy Salisbury Davis.
DRA                              95 min mTV
B,V                             CAREY L/A; CHEV

### BRONCO BILLY **                     PG
Clint Eastwood     USA                 1980
Clint Eastwood, Sondra Locke, Geoffrey Lewis, Scatman Crothers, Bill McKinney, Sam Bottoms, Dan Vadis, Sierra Pecheur
A self-styled cowboy runs a small-time Wild West show which is joined by a spoiled heiress. A screwball comedy that digs deep for laughs but has a modicum of charm if not wit.
Aka: BILLY BRONCO
DRA                     111 min (ort 119 min)
B,V                             WHV

### BRONSON LEE, CHAMPION **            15
Yukio Noda          USA                1978
Tadashi Yamashita, Dale Ferguson, Steve Fisher, Shingo Yamashiro, Yoko Horikoshi, Masafumi Suzuki
A martial arts expert has to fight those trying to stop him taking part in the karate world championships. Routine high-kicking martial arts tae.
MAR          73 min (ort 81 min) Cut (2 min 5 sec)
B,V                    VTC L/A; VMA; STABL

### BRONX WARRIORS *                    18
Enzo G. Castellari    ITALY            1983
Vic Morrow, Christopher Connolly, Fred Williamson, Mark Gregory, Stefania Girolami
Set in the Bronx of 1990, this film tells the story of the warfare between Bronx gang leaders and the unsavoury head of a corporation. Violent, trashy nonsense, filmed in the Bronx and Rome. Followed in 1983 by BRONX WARRIORS 2: THE BATTLE OF MANHATTAN.
Aka: 1990: THE BRONX WARRIORS
DRA                              84 min
B,V                             EIV

### BRONX WARRIORS 2:
### THE BATTLE OF MANHATTAN *
Enzo G. Castellari    ITALY            1983
Henry Silva, Mark Gregory, Valeria d'Obici, Timothy Brent (Giancarlo Prete) Thomas Moore, Andrea Coppola, Paolo Malco
The continuation of the story of THE BRONX WARRIORS. Here the entire Bronxdistrict has been bought up by a multi-national for development, in the face of furious opposition from the local gangs. A blundering, thudding sequel.
Aka: ESCAPE FROM THE BRONX
DRA                              89 min
B,V                             EIV

### BROOD, THE ***                      18
David Cronenberg    CANADA             1979
Samantha Eggar, Oliver Reed, Art Hindle, Cindy Hinds, Nuala Fitzgerald, Susan Hogan, Robert Silverman, Gary McKeehan, Henry Beckman, Michael Magee, Joseph Shaw, Larry Solway, Reiner Schwartz, Felix Silla
Mental derangement, murderous midgets and buckets of blood – a psychiatrist tries to help his patients by getting them to give birth to physical manifestations of their disturbances. One especially disturbed patient produces a brood of ghastly midget children who attack her perceived enemies, beating them to death with mallets. A sickening but compelling shocker in Cronenberg's inimitable style. Grade 10 on the yuck scale.
HOR              90 min; 88 min (PLACE)
B,V,V2       ALPHA/INT/CBS L/A; EMP; PLACE

### BROTHER FROM ANOTHER PLANET, THE **   15
John Sayles         USA                1984
Joe Morton, Darryl Edwards, Steve James, Leonard Jackson, Maggie Renzi, Tom Wright, Caroline Aaron, Rossette Le Noire, Dee Bridgewater, Ren Woods, John Sayles
A black mute alien appears in Harlem where he feels at home, and just like Sellers in BEING THERE, impresses everyone he meets, just by letting them do all the talking. He is, however, on the run from his own planet. Made on a miniscule budget, but good dialogue helps it along. A worthy but flawed effort; a foolish drug dealing subplot could have been excised to the film's advantage.
FAN                              108 min
B,V                             PVG

### BROTHER SUN, SISTER MOON **         PG
Franco Zeffirelli    ITALY/UK          1973
Graham Faulkner, Judi Bowker, Leigh Lawson,

*Kenneth Cranham, Lee Montague, Valentina Cortese,*
*Alec Guinness, Michael Feast, Nicholas Willatt, John*
*Sharp, Adolfo Celi, Francesco Guerrieri*
A flower-power view of the life of St Francis of Assisi,
complete with the songs of Donovan. Gentle and
well-meaning with excellent photography, but the
performances lack dramatic impact, resulting in a
lifeless endeavour.

DRA                        116 min (ort 122 min)
V                                          CIC

## BROTHERHOOD OF DEATH **
Bill Berry              USA              1976
*Roy Jefferson, Le Tari, Haskell V. Anderson, Mike*
*Thomas, Larry Jones, Mike Bass*
Three black Vietnam veterans form a secret society to
avenge themselves on the Ku Klux Klan, who control
the area where they live. Exploitative melodrama
starring some former members of the Washington
Redskins.

DRA                                    86 min
B,V                                       HER

## BROTHERHOOD OF JUSTICE **                 15
Charles Braverman      USA              1986
*Kiefer Sutherland, Kenau Reeves, Lori Loughlin, Joe*
*Spano, Darren Dalton, Evan Mirand, Don Michael*
*Paul, Gary Riley, Billy Zane, Danny Nucci, Danny De*
*La Paz, Jim Haynie, Sean Sullivan, Perla Walter,*
*Walter Brown, Kent Minault*
School friends band together in a heroic attempt to
free a town from the ruthless grip of nasty criminals,
doing this largely at the instigation of the school
principal. Below average action story with the cliched
and disagreeable "fight fire with fire" type message.
Pilot for a TV series.
Boa: story by Noah Jubelirer.

A/AD                   93 min (ort 100 min) mTV
B,V                                CASTLE/IVS

## BROTHERHOOD OF SATAN ***                  18
Bernard McEveety       USA              1971
*Strother Martin, L.Q. Jones, Charles Bateman, Ahna*
*Capri, Charles Robinson, Geri Reischl, Alvy Moore,*
*Helene Winston, Debi Storm, Jeff Williams, Judy*
*McConnell, Joyce Easton, Robert Ward, John Barclay,*
*Phyllis Coughlan*
A witches' coven takes over an entire town in this
compelling little chiller.

HOR                                    92 min
B,V                                       RCA

## BROTHERS IN ARMS **                       18
George Jay Bloom III   USA              1988
*Todd Allen, Jack Starrett, Charles Grant, Dedee*
*Pfeiffer, Mitch Pileggi, Dan Bell, Shannon Norfleet*
A strange band of isolated mountain dwellers practice
a religion that involves human sacrifice and they go
hunting for suitable victims. Eventually a tracker and
his brother, out on a search for a long-lost friend, come
up against them.

HOR                           88 min (ort 95 min)
V                                         GHV

## BROTHERS OF THE WILDERNESSS **
David Michael Hillman  USA              1984
*George Randall, Stephen Mara, Chs Kivette, Mark*
*Sawicki, Stephen Fleet, Alina Szpak*
The story of the struggle of a boy and his dog against
the elements. An OK outdoors adventure.

A/AD                                   77 min
B,V                                PRIME/CBS

## BROTHERS O'TOOLE, THE **
Richard Erdman         USA              1972
*John Astin, Pat Carroll, Steve Carlson, Hans Conreid,*
*Allyn Joslyn, Jesse White, Richard Jury, Richard*
*Erdman, Miranda Barry, Jacques Hampton*

Western comedy in which a man was sentenced to
hang for crimes he did not commit because of his
resemblance to a notorious outlaw. He escapes and
sets off with his brother to track down the real outlaw.
A bland but amiable tale, best enjoyed by kids – at
whom it is probably aimed.
Aka: DOUBLE TROUBLE

COM                        91 min (ort 94 min)
B,V,V2                               VCL/CBS

## BROTHERS-IN-LAW **                        PG
E.W. Swackhamer        USA              1985
*Mac Davis, Joe Cortese, Robert Culp, John Saxon,*
*Daphne Ashbrook, Gerald O'Loughlin, John S. Regan,*
*Candi Brough, Randi Brough, Dennis Burkley, Frank*
*McCarthy, Randolph Powell, Bill Morey, Jack Riley,*
*Geno Silva, Lukas Haas*
The title characters are a highway patrolman and a
trucker and though linked by marriage they loathe
each other. However, they forget their differences for
a while in order to oppose the machinations of a
corrupt businessman. Pilot for a TV series. Average.

A/AD                                73 min mTV
V                                         CIC

## BROWNING VERSION, THE ****                 U
Anthony Asquith        UK                1951
*Michael Redgrave, Jean Kent, Nigel Patrick, Bill*
*Travers, Ronald Howard, Wilfrid Hyde-White, Brian*
*Smith, Paul Medland, Ivan Sampson, Peter Jones,*
*Josephine Middleton, Sarah Lawson, Scott Harold,*
*Judith Furse*
A classic tale, with Redgrave starring as a once
brilliant scholar who's now a middle-aged classics
teacher at a boarding school. On the eve of his
retirement because of ill health, a single act of
kindness gives him courage to face the future, despite
the realisation that he is held in contempt by his
adulterous wife, his pupils and fellow teachers. A
moving and sensitive adaptation of a fine play.
Boa: play by Terence Rattigan.

DRA                                90 min B/W
V                                         CH5

## BRUBAKER **                               15
Stuart Rosenberg       USA              1980
*Robert Redford, Yaphet Kotto, Jane Alexander,*
*Murray Hamilton, David Keith, Morgan Freeman,*
*Matt Clark, Tim McIntire, Linda Haynes, M. Emmet*
*Walsh, John McMartin, Richard Ward, Albert Salmi,*
*Wilford Brimley*
An idealistic prison chief faces opposition in his
attempts to introduce humane conditions and retain
his principles. After a harrowing introduction that
effectively depicts the horror and brutality of prison
life, the film reverts to a predictable black-and-white
tale of how reaction triumphs over reform. Redford
plays the title character as an enigmatic loner whose
inner feelings and motivations are never brought to
the surface. Disappointing.

DRA                                   130 min
B,V,V2,LV                                 CBS

## BRUCE AGAINST IRON HAND **
To Lo-Po               HONG KONG
*Bruce Li (Ho Tsung-Tao), Shao Lung, Bruce Liang*
Inspector Li investigates the mysterious deaths of two
masters of the martial arts. Another run-of-the-mill
kung fu adventure with a Bruce Lee clone.

MAR                                    89 min
B,V,V2                                    VPD

## BRUCE AND SHAOLIN KUNG FU 1 **
James Nam              HONG KONG        1982
*Bruce Le (Huang Kin Lung), Chan Xing, Chang Lee,*
*Kong Tau, Yeung See, James Nam*
Standard fisticuffs with a martial arts fighter going to
Korea on a mission of revenge following the murder of
his master by Japanese assailants.

MAR                                          86 min
V                                               ICL

## BRUCE AND SHAOLIN KUNG FU 2 **
James Nam          HONG KONG
*Bruce Le (Huang Kin Lung), Chan Xing, Chang Lee,*
*Kong Tau, Yeung See, James Nam*
The story continues . . .
MAR                                          83 min
V                                               ICL

## BRUCE AND THE SHAOLIN BRONZEMEN **
Joseph Kong         HONG KONG
*Bruce Le (Huang Kin Lung), Chang Lee, Lita Vasquez*
Our kung fu hero searches for a buried treasure but
pauses along the way to rescue a man arrested and
tortured for a crime he did not commit.
Aka: BRUCE AND THE SHAOLIN BRONZEMEN
MASTER
MAR                                          90 min
B,V                                            MIN

## BRUCE LEE AGAINST SUPERMEN **
                    HONG KONG
*Bruce Li (Ho Tsung-Tao)*
A doctor discovers a secret formula that would help
solve the world's food crisis. He is kidnapped by an
international syndicate. Kung fu to the rescue!
MAR                                          80 min
B,V,V2                                         VPD

## BRUCE LEE IN NEW GUINEA **
C.Y. Yang           HONG KONG          1980
*Bruce Li (Ho Tsung-Tao), Chen Sing, Ho Chung Dao,*
*Chan Wai Man, Danna, Yang Sze*
Two kung fu masters visit an island where a tribe
worships the legendary Snake Pearl. They find them-
selves having to defend the daughter of the murdered
chief against a cruel wizard. New Guinea locations are
an asset in a routine saga from Hong Kong's kung fu
factory.
Aka: BRUCE LI IN NEW GUINEA
MAR                                          90 min
B,V                                       OCEAN/GVC

## BRUCE LEE STORY, THE **
Shih Ti             TAIWAN/USA          1974
*Li Hsiao-Lung, Tang Pei, Yamada*
Another biopic about the late Bruce Lee. Average
Bruce-ploitation offering.
Aka: DRAGON STORY, A; SUPERDRAGON
MAR                                          80 min
B,V,V2                                          WOV

## BRUCE LEE THE INVINCIBLE *
                    HONG KONG          1980
*Bruce Li (Ho Tsung-Tao), Chen Sing, Ho Chung Dao,*
*Chen Wai Man*
A young kung fu expert battles it out with evil martial
arts students, bandits, et cetera, et cetera. Very dull.
Aka: BRUCE LI: THE INVINCIBLE; INVINCIBLE,
THE
MAR                                          90 min
B,V                                       OCEAN/GVC

## BRUCE LEE: THE MAN – THE MYTH **          18
Ng See Yuen         HONG KONG          1976
*Bruce Li (Ho Tsung-Tao), Donnie Williams, Liang*
*Shao-Sung, Hsiao Ch'i Lin*
Biopic about the life and times of Bruce Lee, from his
student days to his involvement in films. Formula
martial arts outing trading on the old Bruce magic.
Aka: BRUCE LEE: THE TRUE STORY; LI HSIAO-
LUNG CH'UAN-CH'I
MAR                                 90 min (ort 104 min)
B,V                               DFS; MIA (VHS only)

## BRUCE LEE'S GREATEST REVENGE **
Tu Lu-Po            HONG KONG          1978
*Bruce Li (Ho Tsung-Tao), Ku Feung, Mi Hsuen, Han*
*Vo Tsai, Li I Min, Tang Yen Tsan, Yang Sze, Michelle*
Anti-Chinese prejudice forms the background to this
story of the conflict and rivalry between a European
and a Chinese martial arts club, with our Bruce
coming home to find that his master has been killed
by the Japanese. Largely a remake of an earlier Lee
film – "The Chinese Connection". Average.
Aka: BRUCE LI'S GREATEST REVENGE;
DRAGON'S GREATEST REVENGE
MAR                                          94 min
B,V                                        ACE; VGM

## BRUCE THE KING OF KUNG FU **              18
Bruce Le (Huang Kin Lung)
                    HONG KONG          1984
*Bruce Le (Huang Kin Lung), Shih King*
OK biopic about the famous kung fu actor whose
career was so abruptly cut short. This one traces his
life from birth in America to his introduction in Hong
Kong to the martial arts.
MAR                                          87 min
V                                               VPD

## BRUCE THE SUPERHERO **                    18
Bruce Le (Huang Kin Lung)
                    HONG KONG          1984
*Bruce Le (Huang Kin Lung), Lito Lapid*
Bruce avenges his father's murder by the Black
Dragon Society. If only he would avenge himself on
the writers of these interminable Bruce-films.
MAR                              84 min Cut (1 min 38 sec)
V                                               VPD

## BRUCE'S FINGERS **
Joseph Kong         HONG KONG          198-
*Bruce Le (Huang Kin Lung), Chan Wai Man, Nora*
*Miao, Rose, Yuen Man Chi, Chang Leih, Young Zee,*
*Wuk Ma No Hans*
A disciple of the late Bruce Lee goes to the USA to
claim a Kung Fu manual that describes the fighter's
secret finger techniques. However, the book is also
sought by an evil kung fu gang led by a vicious
criminal. To achieve their ends they kidnap the
Master's ex-girlfriend who now has to be rescued by
one of his followers.
Aka: BRUCE'S DEADLY FINGERS
MAR                                          91 min
B,V,V2                                       INT L/A

## BRUTAL GLORY **                           15
Loos Roets          SOUTH AFRICA       1987
*Timothy Brantley, Robert Vaughn, James Ryan*
Set in New York circa 1918, this tale follows the
career of boxer Kid McCoy from his early beginnings
to his success as a top prize-fighter. Fair.
DRA                                         107 min
V                                               RCA

## BRUTE, THE **
Gerry O'Hara        UK                 1977
*Sarah Douglas, Julian Glover, Suzanne Stone, Bruce*
*Robinson, Jenny Twigge, Peter Bull, Charlotte*
*Cornwell, James Farrar, Roberta Gibbs, Clive*
*Graham, Sylvester Morand, Kenneth Nelson, Nicholas*
*Barnes, Carol Cleveland*
Drama about the problems of marital violence in
which a young wife decides to leave her brutal
husband. Average.
DRA                                          90 min
B,V                                        BWV/VSP

## BUCK AND THE PREACHER ***               PG
Sidney Poitier      USA                1972
*Sidney Poitier, Harry Belafonte, Ruby Dee, Cameron*
*Mitchell, Denny Miller, Nita Talbot, John Kelly, Tony*
*Brubaker, James McEachin, Clarence Muse, Ken*

*Menard, Julie Robinson*
Poitier's directorial debut tells of a scout and con-man preacher helping a band of escaped slaves on the run. Good characterisations and the music of Benny Carter help make up for the serious lack of action.
WES                             99 min (ort 102 min)
B,V                                              RCA

## BUCK ROGERS IN THE 25TH CENTURY *          15
Daniel Haller          USA                      1979
*Gil Gerard, Pamela Hensley, Erin Gray, Tim O'Connor, Henry Silva, Joseph Wiseman, Felix Silla, Mel Blanc (voice only)*
Pilot for a TV series with Buck Rogers, the legendary space hero, returning in this modern version of the 1930s serial. In this adventure he has to prove that he is not in league with space pirates. A glossy and superficial effort, using much of the hardware and sets left over from shooting another made-for-TV SF outing, BATTLESTAR GALACTICA, which had the same producers. This pilot was released to cinemas first. Mediocre.
Aka: BUCK ROGERS
FAN                             89 min mTV
B,V,LV                                          CIC

## BUCKAROO BANZAI **                          15
W.D. Richter          USA                        1984
*Peter Weller, John Lithgow, Ellen Barkin, Clancy Brown, Jeff Goldblum, Christopher Lloyd*
A multi-talented pulp-fiction hero does battle with aliens from another dimension, who threaten to unleash a nuclear war by taking over the body of a mad scientist. A confused attempt at a credible SF adventure that could have worked well, but was badly let down by the incoherent script. Despite this (or perhaps because of it), the film now has something of a cult following.
Aka: ADVENTURES OF BUCKAROO BANZAI ACROSS THE EIGHTH DIMENSION
FAN                             94 min (ort 103 min)
B,V                                              CAN

## BUCKEYE AND BLUE **                          PG
J.C. Compton          USA                        1988
*Robyn Lively, Jeffrey Osterhage, Rick Gibbs, Michael Horse*
The story of an American Civil War hero who becomes involved with a gang of crooks together with his young companion, whilst trying to avoid capture by the US Cavalry.
WES                             90 min
V                                               BOX

## BUCKSTONE COUNTY PRISON **                   18
Jimmy Huston          USA                        1978
*Earl Owensby, Don (Red) Barry, Sunset Carson*
Prison drama involving an Indian half-breed who helps track down runaways and is in turn sentenced to a term in jail. Another run-of-the-mill prison story.
DRA                             89 min Cut (1 min 5 sec)
B,V,V2                                          INT; AVR

## BUD AND LOU **
Robert C. Thompson          USA                 1978
*Harry Korman, Buddy Hackett, Michele Lee, Arte Johnson, Robert Reed, William Tregoe, Danny Dayton, Art Ergner, Tracy Morgan, Judith Hanson, Henry Brandon, Edmund Penney, Betty Hartford, Ronn Wright, George Barday*
Unsuccessful attempt to chart the career of Abbott and Costello and portray some of the sadness behind the laughter, following their careers from early burlesque and vaudeville days to the later successes in movies. Interesting rather than funny, with stilted and unconvincing performances from Korman and Hackett as the title characters.
COM                             100 min mTV
B,V                                              VFP

## BUDDY BUDDY ***                              15
Billy Wilder          USA                        1981
*Jack Lemmon, Walter Matthau, Paula Prentiss, Klaus Kinski, Ed Begley Jr, Dana Elcar, Miles Chapin, Joan Shawlee*
An adaptation of the French film farce, "A Pain In The A---", this black comedy revolves around a hitman and the complications he is caused by a would-be suicide, who's unhappy over the break-up of his marriage. A funny and uncomplicated farce, with the two leads playing their parts to perfection.
COM                             92 min
V                                               MGM

## BUDDY HOLLY STORY, THE ****                  PG
Steve Rash          USA                          1978
*Gary Busey, Don Stroud, Charles Martin Smith, Maria Richwine, Amy Johnston, Conrad Janis, Dick O'Neill, William Jordan, Will Jordan (different actors), Fred Travalena, "Stymie" Beard*
Musical drama about the life and death of this great rock 'n roll star, with Busey quite outstanding as the singer, in a film that steers well clear of the usual Hollywood glossy excesses and goes for a straight biopic instead. Busey, Smith and Stroud sing and play "live" in this memorable musical docu-drama; Busey is in real-life a part-time rock musician. AA: Score (Joe Benzetti).
DRA                             110 min
B,V,V2                                          CBS; EIV

## BUDDY SYSTEM, THE **                         PG
Glenn Jordan          USA                        1984
*Richard Dreyfuss, Susan Sarandon, Nancy Allen, Jean Stapleton, Wil Wheaton, Edward Winter, Keene Curtis*
A kid plays matchmaker between his single mother and a would-be novelist and inventor, but there are complications. A pleasant romantic comedy whose familiar storyline provides little scope for comedy.
COM                             110 min
B,V                                              CBS

## BUFFALO BILL AND THE INDIANS, OR
## SITTING BULL'S HISTORY LESSON **            PG
Robert Altman          USA                       1976
*Paul Newman, Burt Lancaster, Joel Grey, Kevin McCarthy, Harvey Keitel, Allan Nicholls, Geraldine Chaplin, John Considine, Robert Doqui, Mike Kaplan, Bert Remsen, Bonnie Leaders, Denver Pyle, Will Sampson, Pat McCormick*
Buffalo Bill's Wild West Show serves as a vehicle to show how history has been re-written and glamorised. A dull effort that makes a few interesting points regarding the glamorisation of the past, and then has little more to offer.
Aka: BUFFALO BILL
Boa: play Indians by Arthur Kopit.
WES                             118 min (ort 135 min)
B,V                                              TEVP

## BUG **                                       15
Jeannot Szwarc          USA                      1975
*Bradford Dillman, Joanna Miles, Richard Gilliland, Jamie Smith Jackson, Alan Fudge, Patricia McCormack, Jesse Vint*
An earthquake releases strange beetles that set fire to everything they come into contact with. An unpleasant and messy shocker.
Boa: novel The Haphaestus Plague by Thomas Page.
HOR                             95 min (ort 101 min)
B,V                                              CIC

## BUGSY MALONE ***                            U
Alan Parker          UK                          1976
*Scott Baio, Jodie Foster, Florrie Dugger, John Cassisi, Martin Lev, Paul Murphy, Humpty Jenkins, Davidson Knight, Sheridan Earl Russell, Paul Christelson,*

*Dexter Fletcher, Vivienne McKonne, Helen Corran, Andrew Paul*
A 1920s gangster musical spoof with all the parts played by kids. The machine-guns fire custard pies and the sedans are driven with pedals. Only the lack of a decent story lets it down. A unique "homage" of sorts, as sweet and messy as the custard pies the kids fire at each other.

| MUS | 93 min; 90 min (VCC) |
| B,V,LV | RNK; VCC (VHS only) |

### BULL DURHAM *** 18
Ron Shelton          USA          1989
*Kevin Costner, Susan Sarandon, Tim Robbins, Trey Wilson, Robert Wuhl, Jenny Robertson, Max Patkin*
Story set against the world of major league baseball, where an attractive groupie feels it is her mission in life to pick a new promising youngster each season and teach him some maturity. Costner plays a tough older veteran of the game who has been assigned to one particular player to teach him some discipline. When she chooses this very player a clash of personalities becomes inevitable. A leisurely but charming romantic comedy.

| COM | 103 min (ort 108 min) |
| V | VIR |

### BULLDANCE, THE ** 15
Zelda Barron          USA          1989
*Lauren Hutton, Cliff De Young, Robert Beltran, Viveka Duns, Renee Estevez*
A group of young American schoolgirls staying on a Greek island become obsessed with the mythology of ancient Greece, and place their lives in danger when their re-enactment of an ancient pagan festival disturbs the local villagers.
Aka: FORBIDDEN SUN

| THR | 90 min |
| B,V | CHV |

### BULLDOG BREED, THE ** 
Robert Asher          UK          1960
*Norman Wisdom, Ian Hunter, David Lodge, Robert Urquhart, Edward Chapman, Eddie Byrne, Peter Jones, Liz Fraser, John Le Mesurier, Terence Alexander, Sydney Tafler, Brian Oulton, Johnny Briggs, Penny Morell, Claire Gordon*
Slapstick comedy with a grocer bungling his way through life from the Navy to Outer Space. An adequate vehicle for a star whose talents always outshone his material.
Aka: NORMAN WISDOM: THE BULLDOG BREED
Osca: SQUARE PEG, THE

| COM | 97 min |
| B,V | RNK |

### BULLDOG DRUMMOND COMES BACK ** U
Louis King          USA          1937
*John Barrymore, John Howard, Louise Campbell, Reginald Denny, E.E. Clive, J. Carrol Naish, John Sutton, Helen Freeman*
A spin-off from the earlier Ronald Colman adventure, with Howard a poor replacement in the role of the super-sleuth. In this tale Drummond comes up against a villainous criminal in the form of Naish. One of about ten in the series.

| A/AD | 58 min B/W |
| V | CH5 |

### BULLDOG DRUMMOND ESCAPES ** U
James Hogan          USA          1937
*Ray Milland, Guy Standing, Heather Angel, Porter Hall, Reginald Denny, E.E. Clive, Fay Holden, Clyde Cook, Walter Kingsford*
Our dashing hero helps unmask a fiendish gang of counterfeiters. The start of a minor series in which Milland took over the role as this amateur sleuth. Later he handed over to John Howard. Average.

| THR | 65 min; 67 min (CH5) B/W |
| B,V,V2 | VCL/CBS L/A; CH5 (VHS only) |

### BULLDOG DRUMMOND IN AFRICA *** U
Louis King          USA          1938
*John Howard, Heather Angel, H.B. Warner, J. Carrol Naish, Reginald Denny, Anthony Quinn, Michael Brooke*
Howard as Drummond shows Scotland Yard how to solve one of their crimes, but gets involved in a mystery of his own when his girlfriend decides to do some sleuthing. Fair.

| A/AD | 58 min B/W |
| V | CH5 |

### BULLDOG DRUMMOND'S BRIDE ** PG
James Hogan          USA          1939
*John Howard, Heather Angel, H.B. Warner, Reginald Denny, Elizabeth Patterson, Eduardo Ciannelli*
One of the last in this particular series has our super-sleuth finally marrying his long-suffering girlfriend. However, he decides to take on one last case before getting wed in this fast-paced, above average story. After 1939 Bulldog Drummond remained dormant until his resurrection with the 1967 film "Deadlier Than The Male".

| A/AD | 57 min B/W |
| V | CH5 |

### BULLDOG DRUMMOND'S PERIL ** U
James Hogan          USA          1938
*John Barrymore, John Howard, Louise Campbell, Reginald Denny, E.E. Clive, Porter Hall, Elizabeth Patterson, Nydia Westman*
Drummond follows a diamond thief on a wild chase that takes him from London to Switzerland. Average.

| A/AD | 66 min B/W |
| V | CH5 |

### BULLDOG DRUMMOND'S REVENGE ** U
Louis King          USA          1937
*John Barrymore, John Howard, Louise Campbell, Reginald Denny, E.E. Clive, Nydia Westman, Lucien Littlefield, John Sutton*
One of the many vehicles for this war-hero and adventurer, inspired by the play "Bulldog Drummond" by Sapper (H.C. McNeile). In this tale Drummond goes after a man who has stolen some powerful explosives.
Osca: WOMAN ALONE, A (WOOD)

| A/AD | 55 min (ort 60 min) B/W |
| B,V | WOOD L/A; CH5 (VHS only) |

### BULLDOG DRUMMOND'S SECRET POLICE ** U
James Hogan          USA          1939
*John Howard, Heather Angel, H.B. Warner, Reginald Denny, Leo G. Carroll, Elizabeth Patterson*
In this adventure our super-sleuth searches for a treasure that's been hidden beneath a medieval castle.

| A/AD | 54 min B/W |
| V | CH5 |

### BULLET FOR PRETTY BOY, A ** 15
Henry Rosenbaum          USA          1970
*Fabian Forte, Jocelyn Lane, Astrid Warner, Michael Haynes, Adam Roarke, Anne MacAdams, Robert Glenn, Camilla Carr, Jeff Alexander, Desmond Dhooge, Bill Thurman, Hugh Feagin, Jessie Lee Fulton, James Harrell, Gene Ross*
Mediocre biopic on the career of notorious gangster "Pretty Boy" Floyd that follows his unpleasant and bloody career.
Aka: BULLET FOR A GANGSTER

| A/AD | 85 min |
| V | VIR/PVG |

### BULLET FOR THE GENERAL, A ** 18
Damiano Damiani          ITALY          1967
*Klaus Kinski, Gian Maria Volante, Lou Castel, Martine Beswick, Bianca Manini, Jaimie Fernandez, Andrea Checci, Jose Manuel Martin, Spartaco Conversi, Joaquin Parra, Aldo Sambrell*

During the Mexican revolution, a government agent is hired to kill a revolutionary general, and has to win the loyalty of the guerilla leader in order to accomplish this task. Average Italian outing to Mexico.
Aka: QUIEN SABE
A/AD                                    118 min; 112 min (PHE)
B,V,V2                       VDM/GHV; PHE (VHS only)

## BULLETS OR BALLOTS ***                       PG
William Keighley         USA                    1936
*Edward G. Robinson, Joan Blondell, Barton MacLane,*
*Humphrey Bogart, Frank McHugh, Dick Purcell,*
*George E. Stone*
A city cop pretends to quit the force, but this is only a ploy in his attempt to infiltrate a mobster's gang. A taut and energetic crime story, one or two rungs short of classic status.
DRA                            79 min (ort 81 min) B/W
V                                               WHV

## BULLETPROOF *                                 15
Steve Carver            USA                     1987
*Gary Busey, Darlanne Fluegel, Henry Silva, Thalmus*
*Rasulala, L.Q. Jones, Rene Enriquez, Mills Watson,*
*James Andronicu, R.G. Armstrong, William Smith,*
*Luke Askew, Lincoln Kilpatrick, Lydie Denier,*
*Ramon Franco, Juan Fernandez*
A former CIA agent turned Los Angeles cop, is given the task of rescuing some army personnel and retrieving a top-secret 28-ton super-tank, which has fallen into the hands of terrorists. To do this he has to go across the Mexican border and locate the terrorist base. An old familiar tale, done in an old familiar way.
A/AD                                          90 min
B,V                                             VIR

## BULLFIGHTER AND THE LADY, THE ***            PG
Budd Boetticher         USA                     1951
*Robert Stack, Joy Page, Gilbert Roland, Katy Jurado,*
*Virginia Grey, John Hubbard*
A young American skeetshooting champ on holiday in Mexico, becomes fascinated with bullfighting and tries his hand, with tragic results. An engrossing drama and certainly one of the best examinations of the subject on film. Produced by John Wayne and unfortunately cut down from 124 minutes, but this original version has now been restored.
DRA                          87 min (ort 124 min) B/W
V                                        VMA; STABL

## BULLIES **                                    18
Paul Lynch              USA                     1986
*Janet Laine Green, Dehl Berti, Stephen B. Hunter,*
*Jonathan Crombie, Olivia D'Abo, Bill Croft*
A peaceful family move to a quiet mountain community, only to discover that the town is terrorised by the Cullen family who hold a grip of fear over all. A brutal and predictable revenger in which our clean-cut new arrivals are pushed too far and finally come out fighting. Edifying it is not.
DRA                                           92 min
B,V                                           SHEER

## BULLITT ****                                  15
Peter Yates             USA                     1969
*Steve McQueen, Robert Vaughn, Jacqueline Bisset,*
*Simon Oakland, Robert Duvall, Don Gordon, Norman*
*Fell*
Now best remembered for a classic car chase, this film stars McQueen as an anti-hero cop who's suspicions are aroused when he's put on an assignment guarding a Mafia squealer. A taut action film with some great San Francisco locations. AA: Edit (Frank P. Keller).
Boa: play Mute Witness by Robert L. Pike.
THR                                          109 min
B,V                                             WHV

## BULLSHOT *                                    PG
Dick Clement            UK                      1984
*Alan Shearman, Diz White, Ron House, Frances*
*Tomelty, Michael Aldridge, Ron Pember, Christopher*
*Good, Mel Smith, Billy Connolly, Geoffrey Bayldon,*
*Christopher Godwin, Bryan Pringle, Angela Thorne,*
*Peter Bayliss, John Wells*
A 1930s comedy spoof with fiendish Huns, a stolen formula, a mad professor and a steely aristocratic and dashing hero. And how dated it all seems! A celebration of slapstick and one-liners; uneven, incoherent and far too laboured to be funny. The script is by Shearman, White and House from their play.
Boa: play by Alan Shearman, Diz White and Ron House.
COM                            84 min (ort 88 min)
B,V                                             TEVP

## BUNDLE OF JOY **
Norman Taurog           USA                     1956
*Debbie Reynolds, Eddie Fisher, Adolphe Menjou, Nita*
*Talbot, Tommy Noonan, Melville Cooper, Una Merkel,*
*Robert H. Harris*
Musical comedy in a department store setting. A remake of Ginger Rogers' BACHELOR MOTHER with a salesgirl causing complications by taking care of an abandoned baby. Occasionally funny, but generally heavy-going.
Osca: MONTANA BELLE
COM                            95 min (ort 98 min)
B,V                                             KVD

## BUNKER, THE ***
George Schaefer         USA                     1980
*Anthony Hopkins, Richard Jordan, Cliff Gorman,*
*James Naughton, Michael Lonsdale, Piper Laurie,*
*Susan Blakely, Martin Jarvis, Michael Kitchen,*
*Andrew Ray, Robert Austin, Yves Brainville, Michael*
*Culver, Julian Fellowes*
Above-average version of Hitler's last days, with a chilling performance from Hopkins, for which he won a well-deserved Emmy. The script is adapted from O'Donnell's book by John Gay. See also HITLER: THE LAST TEN DAYS.
Aka: ADOLF HITLER: THE BUNKER
Boa: book by James P. O'Donnell.
DRA                                       154 min mTV
B,V                                             VFP

## BURBS, THE **                                 PG
Joe Dante               USA                     1989
*Tom Hanks, Corey Feldman, Rick Ducommon, Carrie*
*Fisher, Bruce Dern*
The tale of a fairly ordinary guy, whose nosey neighbours get more than they bargained for when their snooping gets out of hand, especially regarding the eerie Klopeks, whose house looks as though it's haunted. A mildly amusing comedy outing from the director of GREMLINS.
COM                                           97 min
                                                CIC

## BURGLAR *                                     15
Hugh Wilson             USA                     1987
*Whoopi Goldberg, Bobcat Goldthwait, G.W. Bailey,*
*Lesley Ann Warren, James Handy, Anne DeSalvo,*
*John Goodman, Barbara Simpson, Elizabeth Ruscio,*
*Vyto Ruginis, Larry Mintz, Raye Birk, Eric Poppick,*
*Scott Lincoln, Thorn Bray*
A cool cat burglar witnesses a murder and then finds that she has been framed as the culprit. With the aid of a crazy friend, she causes general chaos in San Francisco, trying to solve the crime in order to clear herself, whilst both avoiding the police and the killer, who wants to make her his next victim. This clumsy mixture of comedy and suspense is neither funny not taut, but is well and truly a waste of Goldberg's considerable talents.
COM                    98 min (Cut at film release by 11 sec)
V/sh                                            WHV

## BURGLARS, THE **
Henri Verneuil  FRANCE/ITALY  1971
*Jean-Paul Belmondo, Omar Sharif, Dyan Cannon, Robert Hossein*
A policeman chases three burglars, one of whom is an ace safe-cracker who has stolen some priceless emeralds. A remake of "The Burglar" (1956), but incorporating elements from many other heist films. This routine crime thriller has some nice Greek locations and one good chase sequence, but little more.
Aka: LA CASSE
THR                                                            120 min
B,V                                                                RCA

## BURIED ALIVE *
Gerard Kikoine  USA  1989
*Donald Pleasence, John Carradine, Robert Vaughn*
A highly strung female teacher takes a post at a reform school for girls that's run by a charismatic principal. Difficult girls tend to meet nasty ends (such as being buried in concrete) and when our teacher's suspicions are aroused by several disappearances she decides to investigate. A dreary little shocker of little force or originality. The alternative title is misleading as there is little similarity between this any any Poe story.
Aka: EDGAR ALLAN POE'S BURIED ALIVE
HOR                                                             90 min
V                                                                  EIV

## BURIED ALIVE ***
Frank Darabont  USA  1990
*Tim Matheson, Jennifer Jason Leigh, William Atherton, Hoyt Axton, Jay Gerber*
A scheming wife persuades her lover to assist in the murder of her husband, but the victim apparently has other ideas and escapes from his grave, no doubt to have his revenge. A weird but rather clever black comedy, nicely put together and delivering a few neat twists.
HOR                                        89 min (ort 96 min) mTV
V                                                                  CIC

## BURNING BED, THE ***
Robert Greenwald  USA  1984
*Farrah Fawcett, Paul LeMat, Grace Zabriskie, Richard Masur, Christa Denton, Penelope Milford, James Callahan, Gary Grubbs, David Friedman, David Andrews, James Hampton, Virgil Frye, Dixie Wade, Heather Rich, Justin Gocke*
A battered working-class wife suffers years of beatings and humiliation at the hands of her violent husband until she snaps and sets him on fire, whilst he's in bed. A harrowing and compelling drama with Fawcett giving a fine portrayal of a woman driven to take an appalling revenge. The script is by Rose Leiman Goldenberg.
Boa: novel by Faith McNulty.
DRA                                        91 min (ort 100 min) mTV
B,V                                                                CBS

## BURNDOWN *
James Allen  USA  1989
*Peter Firth, Cathy Moriarty, Michael McCabe, Hal Orlandini, Hugh Rouse*
A bizarre series of murders takes place at a ghost town that was once the centre of a thriving nuclear industry. The deaths take a more sinister turn when the body of the latest victim is found to be highly radioactive. When a sheriff and a reporter begin their investigations, they find the murders are linked to a now-closed nuclear reactor. A dull thriller with anti-nuclear sentiments, plodding in its development and incoherent in its resolution.
THR                                          83 min (ort 87 min)
V                                                                  MED

## BURNING SECRET ***
Andrew Birkin                                                    PG

UK/USA/WEST GERMANY  1988
*Faye Dunaway, Klaus Maria Brandauer, Ian Richardson, David Eberts*
A charming but amoral baron, is recovering from a WW1 bayonet wound at a sanitarium, and embarks on an affair with a woman who has brought her asthmatic son there, initiating a friendship with the son in order to reach the mother. An absorbing drama slightly spoilt by miscasting of Dunaway, though Brandauer as the baron is excellent. Filmed in Prague and Marienbad and made once before in 1933 by Robert Siodmak as "Brennendes Geheimnis".
Boa: short story by Stefan Zweig.
DRA                                                            103 min
B,V                                                                VES

## BURNING, THE *
Tony Maylam  USA  1980
*Brian Matthews, Leah Ayres, Brian Backer, Larry Joshua, Shelley Bruce, Lou David, Holly Hunter*
Five teenagers at summer camp play a nasty trick on a caretaker which goes horribly wrong. Years later, he comes back to claim his revenge. A gory rip-off of an idea that's generally been cultivated by all those FRIDAY THE 13TH films – the gruesome make-up is by Tom Savini. Hunter's screen debut. Unlikely to be available in an uncut form in the UK.
HOR                                                             90 min
B,V                                                               TEVP

## BURY ME AN ANGEL ***
Barbara Peeters  USA  1975
*Dixie Peabody, Terry Mace, Joanne Jordan, Clyde Ventura, Dan Haggerty, Stephen Whittaker, Gary Littlejohn, Beach Dickerson*
Well made biker film in which our heroine sets out with a shotgun intent on avenging her brother's murder. An effective melodrama, the more so for being shown from the woman's point of view.
DRA                                                             86 min
B,V                                                           VCL/CBS

## BURY THEM DEEP **
John Bird  ITALY  1973
*Craig Hill, Ken Wood, Jose Greci*
Standard spaghetti Western about a gang robbing a bullion train. You've seen the story a hundred times before.
WES                                          93 min (ort 100 min)
B,V                                                                VPD

## BUS STOP ****
Joshua Logan  USA  1956
*Marilyn Monroe, Arthur O'Connell, Don Murray, Hope Lange, Betty Field, Robert Bray, Eileen Heckart, Hans Conried, Casey Adams*
Marvellously entertaining comedy about a hick co-whand who falls for a nightclub singer, and sets out to pursue her in the only way he knows how, his intention being to make her his wife. Monroe's first film on her return to Hollywood from the Actors' Studio. A highlight is Monroe singing "That Old Black Magic". Scripted by George Axelrod. Gave rise to a brief TV series.
Aka: WRONG KIND OF GIRL, THE
Boa: play by William Inge.
COM                                                             96 min
V                                                                  CBS

## BUSHIDO BLADE, THE ***
Tom Kotani  JAPAN/USA  1980
*James Earl Jones, Richard Boone, Toshiro Mifune, Sonny Chiba, Frank Converse, Laura Gemser*
A 19th century martial arts tale, with Captain Perry in Japan helping to recover a sacred ceremonial sword, that was intended to be a gift to the USA, but has been stolen by three samurai opposed to this.
Aka: BLOODY BUSHIDO BLADE, THE

DRA 103 min
B,V TEVP

## BUSINESS AS USUAL ** 15
Lezli-An Barrett UK 1987
*Glenda Jackson, Cathy Tyson, John Thaw, Mark McGann, Eamon Boland, James Hazeldine, Buki Armstrong, Stephen McGann, Philip Foster, Natalie Duffy, Jack Carr, Mel Martin, Michelle Byatt, Robert Keegan, Angela Elliott*
A woman is sacked from her job as a boutique manageress, when she rejects the advances of an executive. She fights to win a claim for unfair dismissal in a campaign that galvanises both her union and the country.
DRA 86 min (ort 89 min)
B/sh, V/sh WHV

## BUSTED UP ** 18
Conrad E. Palmisano CANADA 1986
*Irene Cara, Tony Rosato, Frank Pellegrino, Paul Coufos, Stan Shaw*
A small-time boxer and the owner of a gym take a stand against mobsters, who are trying to force them out in order to build a health club on their premises.
DRA 92 min
B,V MED

## BUSTER *** 15
David Green UK 1988
*Phil Collins, Julie Walters, Larry Lamb, Martin Jarvis, Sheila Hancock, Stephanie Lawrence, Ellen Beaven, Michael Attwell, Ralph Brown, Anthony Quayle*
It's homage to train-robbers time as we salute one of the gang who took part in the Great Train Robbery of August 1963. This tells of how Buster Edwards fled to Mexico after the raid. A well made and enjoyable drama that tends to overlook some of the nastier aspects of this famous raid. (In the course of the actual robbery, the train driver was viciously beaten – he died not long afterwards.)
DRA 98 min (ort 102 min)
B,V VES

## BUSTER AND BILLIE ** 18
Daniel Petrie USA 1974
*Jan-Michael Vincent, Joan Goodfellow, Pamela Sue Martin, Clifton James, Robert Englund*
Soppy story of teenage high school romance set in Georgia in 1948 with a handsome boy falling for a homely but loving girl. Initially a gentle tale, but about halfway through it abruptly changes tone and becomes a nasty and cliched story of revenge.
DRA 97 min (ort 100 min)
V RCA

## BUSTER KEATON: COLLEGE **
James W. Horne USA 1927
*Buster Keaton, Ann Cornwall, Harold Goodwin, Snitz Edwards, Florence Turner*
Silent film about a brainy but inept college student, who still manages to make everyone else look foolish, and eventually becomes a college football star. An episodic effort from Keaton, with a few good gags but badly in need of stronger plotting.
Aka: COLLEGE
COM 65 min B/W silent
B,V SPEC/POLY

## BUSTER KEATON: OUR HOSPITALITY *** U
Buster Keaton/Jack Blystone
USA 1923
*Buster Keaton, Natalie Talmadge, Joe Keaton, Buster Keaton Jr, Kitty Bradbury, Joe Roberts*
A satirical look at the legendary Hatfield-McCoy feud, with Keaton as the last surviving McCoy, who goes South to claim his inheritance and falls in love with the daughter of the rival clan. An inventive silent comedy with a great finale. Keaton married Talmadge in real life too.
Aka: OUR HOSPITALITY
COM 66 min B/W silent
V VIR

## BUSTER KEATON: SHERLOCK JR **** U
Buster Keaton/Donald Crisp
USA 1924
*Buster Keaton, Kathryn McGuire, Ward Crane, Joseph Keaton*
In one of his most inventive films, Keaton plays a movie projectionist who is falsely accused of stealing a watch. With his head filled with fantasies of being a great detective, he dreams himself into the movies he is showing and merges with the figures and background on the screen. A joyful, funny romp that ranks as one of Keaton's best films.
Aka: SHERLOCK JR
COM 46 min B/W silent
V VIR

## BUSTER KEATON: THE GENERAL **** U
Buster Keaton/Clyde Bruckman
USA 1926
*Buster Keaton, Marion Mack, Glen Cavender, Jim Farley, Joseph Keaton*
In one of the best of his slapstick silents, Keaton plays a Confederate whose train is stolen by spies from the North. He infiltrates the Union lines with the intention of retrieving his locomotive, but finds that things go far from smoothly. Not as fanciful as some of his other films but made with great care and beautifully photographed by Matthew Brady. The same tale was done in a more serious vein by Disney as THE GREAT LOCOMOTIVE CHASE.
Aka: GENERAL, THE
COM 76 min; 74 min (CH5) B/W silent
B,V SPEC/POLY; CH5 (VHS only)

## BUSTER KEATON: THE NAVIGATOR **** U
Buster Keaton/Donald Crisp
USA 1924
*Buster Keaton, Kathryn McGuire*
One of Keaton's best comedies, with the star and his girlfriend finding themselves adrift on a deserted liner that's marooned in the middle of the ocean. A highlight is a crazy chase sequence when they run aground on an island inhabited by cannibals.
Aka: NAVIGATOR, THE
COM 62 min B/W silent
B,V VIR

## BUSTIN' LOOSE *** 15
Oz Scott USA 1981
*Richard Pryor, Cicely Tyson, Angel Ramirez, George Coe, Bill Quinn, Roy Jenson, Robert Christian, Alphonso Alexander, Janet Wong, Fred Carney*
Rather touching film about an ex-con on probation who drives a busload of handicapped kids and their teacher to a new life in Seattle. Mainly filmed in 1979 but following an accident to Pryor, completion was delayed until 1981. The film debut for Broadway director Scott. Co-written and co-produced by Pryor. Gave rise to a TV series.
COM 90 min
B,V,V2 CIC

## BUSTING ** 18
Peter Hyams USA 1973
*Elliot Gould, Robert Blake, Allen Garfield, Antonio Fargas, Michael Lerner, Sid Haig, Cornelia Sharpe*
Two unorthodox L.A. vice cops fight corruption both inside and outside the police force, in this fast-paced but rather brainless action-comedy. Fargas went on to play "Huggy Bear" in the TV series "Starsky and Hutch". Scripted by Hyams.

COM                          88 min Cut (27 sec)
B,V                                          WHV

## BUTCH AND SUNDANCE:          PG
## THE EARLY YEARS **
Richard Lester        USA            1979
*William Katt, Tom Berenger, Jeff Corey, Peter Weller,*
*Christopher Lloyd, John Schuck, Michael C. Gwynne,*
*Brian Dennehy, Jill Eikenberry, Arthur Hill, Vincent*
*Schiavelli*
A good-looking and nicely photographed prequel to
BUTCH CASSIDY AND THE SUNDANCE KID,
that's badly let down by a trite and empty plot. This
amiable film meanders along quite pleasantly, but
ultimately the lack of a decent script weighs heavily
against it.
WES                              107 min mTV
B,V,V2                                       CBS

## BUTCH CASSIDY AND THE        PG
## SUNDANCE KID ****
George Roy Hill       USA            1969
*Paul Newman, Robert Redford, Katherine Ross,*
*Strother Martin, Sam Elliott, Henry Jones, Jeff Corey,*
*George Furth, Cloris Leachman, Ted Cassidy, Kenneth*
*Mars, Donnelly Rhodes, Jody Gilbert, Timothy Scott,*
*Don Keefer*
A glamorised film about the celebrated outlaws and
train robbers, that's a pure delight to watch and has
many memorable moments – the dynamite episode is
a highspot. A semi-comic tale that follows their
exploits and deaths in Bolivia, where they had fled to
avoid capture. AA: Story/Screen (William Goldman),
Cin (Conrad Hall), Score (Orig) (Burt Bacharach),
Song ("Raindrops Keep Falling On My Head" – Burt
Bacharach – music/Hal David – lyrics).
WES                          105 min (ort 112 min)
V                                            CBS

## BUTCHER, THE ***                          15
Claude Chabrol    FRANCE/ITALY        1970
*Stephane Audran, Jean Yanne, Antonio Passallia,*
*Mario Beccaria, Pasquale Ferone*
A series of brutal murders of young girls shocks a
small French town. They are eventually traced to a
seemingly inoffensive local butcher. A chilling thriller
that explores the psychology of the murderer and his
relationship with a local schoolteacher.
Aka: LE BOUCHER
THR                          98 min; 88 min (VIR)
B,V,V2    VCL/CBS L/A; VIR (Betamax and VHS only)

## BUTTERFLIES *                            PG
Gareth Gwenlan        UK             1978
*Wendy Craig, Andrew Hall, Bruce Montague*
Yet another of those British TV compilations; this
one's culled from six 30 minute episodes of a soppy and
simpering series, all about an affair between a
divorced man and a housewife. As light as candyfloss
but considerably sweeter.
COM                              60 min mTV
B,V                                          BBC

## BUTTERFLIES ARE FREE ***                  PG
Milton Katselas       USA            1972
*Goldie Hawn, Edward Albert Jr, Eileen Heckert, Mike*
*Warren, Michael Glasser*
A blind boy falls for the unconventional girl-next-door
and comes into conflict with his over-possessive
mother. Good performances from Hawn as the daffy
aspiring actress, who comes into Albert's life, and
Heckert as his mother, for which she won a well-
deserved Oscar. Based on the successful Broadway
play. AA: S. Actress (Heckert).
Boa: play by Leonard Gershe.
COM                              105 min
V                                            RCA

## BUTTERFLY *                               18
Matt Cimber (Matteo Ottaviano)
                      USA            1981
*Stacy Keach, Orson Welles, Pia Zadora, James*
*Franciscus, Lois Nettleton, Stuart Whitman, Edward*
*Albert Jr, Ed McMahon, June Lockhart, Paul*
*Hampton*
A dull and rubbishy film telling of an amoral and
selfish young woman who uses her beauty to get what
she wants. She ends up seducing Keach, who is
supposed to be her father. Welles, as a judge, is the
only good thing in an otherwise worthless film, set in
Nevada's silver-mining regions during the late 1930s.
Boa: novel The Butterfly by James M. Cain.
DRA                              103 min
B,V    TEVP L/A; VIP L/A; CAN; VGM; PARK (VHS
only)

## BUTTERFLY REVOLUTION, THE **             15
Bert L. Dragin        USA            1986
*Chuck Connors, Charles Stratton, Adam Carl, Harold*
*P. Pruett, Tom Fridley, Melissa Brennan, Stuart*
*Rogers, Shawn McLemore, Samantha Neward, Rick*
*Fitts, Nancy Calabrese, Michael Cramer, Doug Toby,*
*Shirley Mitchell, Chris Hubbell*
Connors stars as the new director of a summer camp,
hopelessly out of touch with the youngsters and their
teenage counsellors. Stratton stars as one of the
counsellors, who challenges his domination, resulting
in a coup and the imprisonment of the adults. A
contrived and downright peculiar tale, which sees the
kids sliding rapidly into barbarism in true "Lord Of
The Flies" style.
Aka: SUMMER CAMP NIGHTMARE; SUMMER
CAMP MASSACRE
Boa: novel by William Butler.
DRA                              85 min
B,V                                          CBS

## BUY AND CELL **                          15
Robert Boris          USA            1987
*Robert Carradine, Ben Vereen, Michael Winslow,*
*Malcolm McDowell, Randall "Tex" Cobb, Imogene*
*Coca, Fred Travalena, Roddy Piper, Lise Cutter, Tony*
*Plana, Michael Goodwin*
A stockbroker is framed by his boss and sent to jail,
but takes his entrepreneurial talents with him,
setting up a business with the help of the inmates. A
mediocre comedy, filmed in Italy but set in the USA.
COM                          92 min (ort 95 min)
B,V                                          EIV

## BUYING TIME **                           18
Mitchell Gabourie     CANADA         1988
*Jeff Schultz, Page Fletcher, Laura Cruikshank, Dean*
*Stockwell, Leslie Toth, Michael Rudder*
A man is arrested while helping his ne'er-do-well of a
friend steal some money back from the bookies to
whom he is heavily in debt. A detective offers them
the chance to have all charges dropped in return for
help in an undercover operation against a drugs
dealer. Their agreement soon plunges them into
danger and excitement, and the cast do what they can
in this low-budget and rather unoriginal thriller.
THR                              90 min
V                                            PATHE

## BY DAWN'S EARLY LIGHT ***                15
Jack Sholder          USA            1990
*Powers Boothe, Rebecca DeMornay, Martin Landau,*
*Rip Torn, Darren McGavin, James Earl Jones, Peter*
*MacNichol, Jeffrey DeMunn*
A nuclear missile is launched from an unknown
source in the Middle East and it strikes the Soviet
Union. When the Russian leaders become convinced
that it represents an American first strike they
respond in kind. An effective nuclear thriller that
carefully balances tension against plausibility.
Boa: novel Trinity's Child by William Prochnau.

DRA            97 min (ort 100 min) mCab
V/sh                              WHV

**BY DESIGN ***                     18
Claude Jutra      CANADA          1981
*Patty Duke Astin, Saul Rubinek, Sara Botsford, Sonia
Zimmer*
A love triangle with a difference; a lesbian fashion
designer decides to become a mother, despite the
knowledge that her decision will shock those around
her. An interesting idea is let down by a muddled and
uneven script.
COM                            88 min
B,V              ALPHA/INT/CBS; VEXEL

**BYE BYE BABY ***            18
Enrico Oldini      ITALY            1989
*Brigitte Nielsen, Carol Alt, Luca Barbareschi, Jason
Connery*
A love triangle set in a tropical paradise where a
female billiards player falls for the husband of her
doctor girlfriend. Though able to satisfy him sexually,
she finds him unwilling to give up his wife.
DRA                             82 min
B,V                             CINE

# C

**C.A.T. SQUAD, THE ***         PG
William Friedkin      USA          1986
*Joseph Cortese, Stephen W. James, Jack Youngblood,
Bradley Whitford, Barry Corbin, Patricia
Charbonneau, Eddie Valez, Sam Grey, Al Shannon,
Anna Maria Horsford, Frank Military, Anne Curry,
Hans Bogild*
A special anti-espionage tactical assault team – the
Counter Assault Tactical Squad, is brought in by the
US government after three of its best scientists
working on a top-secret project are killed in a series of
violent attacks. A fast-paced but fairly routine action
tale, the pilot for a TV series that was pulled.
Followed by C.A.T. SQUAD 2: OPERATION
PYTHON WOLF.
THR           97 min (ort 100 min) mTV
B,V                             IVS

**C.A.T. SQUAD 2:**            15
**OPERATION PYTHON WOLF ****
William Friedkin      USA          1988
*Steve James, Jack Youngblood, Deborah Van
Valkenburgh, Joseph Cortese, Miguel Ferrer, Ted
Dillon, Alan Scarf*
Sequel to the 1986 film, with our Counter Assault
Tactical Squad swinging into action once more. Apart
from some exciting sequences and a good plot twist,
it's more of the same cliched nonsense.
Aka: CAT SQUAD: PYTHON WOLF
A/AD                        94 min mTV
B,V                      CHV; MED

**C.C. AND COMPANY ***        18
Seymour Robbie      USA          1970
*Joe Namath, Ann-Margret, William Smith, Jennifer
Billingsley, Teda Bracci, Greg Mullavey, Sid Haig,
Bruce Glover, Wayne Cochran and the C.C. Riders*
A mindless biker film with Namath in his first
starring role, playing a motorcyclist who comes into
conflict with a biker gang whilst enjoying some
romantic interludes with Ann-Margret. A badly acted
and juvenile effort, with a few unintentionally funny
moments along the way.
DRA         94 min (Cut at film release)
B,V                        CBS; EHE

**C.H.O.M.P.S. ****           PG
Don Chaffey        USA          1979

*Wesley Eure, Valerie Bertinelli, Conrad Bain, Chuck
McCann, Red Buttons, Larry Bishop, Hermione
Baddeley, Jim Backus*
A spate of burglaries inspires a young inventor to
develop a mechanical canine to protect homes. His
robot doggy has a fault however, and this causes the
inevitable complications for all concerned. A banal
Disney-style comedy that was, believe it or not,
originally made with a few profanities spoken by
another dog, but was re-dubbed to make it more
suitable for the kiddies. Title is an acronym for
Canine HOMe Protection System.
COM                            89 min
B,V,V2                            GHV

**C.H.U.D. ****               18
Douglas Cheek      USA          1984
*John Heard, Daniel Stern, Kim Greist, Brenda Currin,
Justin Hall, Michael O'Hare, Christopher Curry*
A strange colony of sub-humans live in the sewers of
New York but come up to the surface at night to enjoy
some human flesh. Title is an acronym for Cannibalis-
tic Humanoid Underground Dwellers. A nasty little
film that was followed by a slightly better sequel.
HOR           83 min (ort 90 min)
B,V                             MED

**C.H.U.D. 2 ****             15
David Irving        USA          1988
*Brian Robbins, Tricia Leigh Fisher, Bill Calvert,
Gerrit Graham, Robert Vaughn, Jack Riley, Norman
Fell, Larry Linville, Bianca Jagger*
A group of students steal the body of one of the
creatures from the first movie as a prank. It's soon
thawed out and walking the streets, turning the
townsfolk into similar zombie-like creatures. A crack-
pot colonel tries to keep the lid on things as our
flesh-eating monster starts to get out of control, in this
enjoyable but production-line piece of nonsense.
Aka: C.H.U.D. 2: BUD THE CHUD
HOR                            81 min
V                                VES

**CABARET *****            15
Bob Fosse          USA          1972
*Liza Minnelli, Joel Gray, Michael York, Helmut
Griem, Fritz Wepper, Marisa Berenson*
Excellent account of the growing Nazi take-over, seen
against and through the setting of a sleazy Berlin
cabaret, with the story a loose adaptation of the career
of nightclub performer Sally Bowles. The great dance
numbers are highspots in a fine musical. AA: Dir,
Actress (Minnelli), S. Actor (Grey), Edit (D. Brether-
ton), Cin (G. Unsworth), Score (Adapt) (R. Burns),
Art/Set (R. Zehetbauer and J. Kiebach/H. Strabel),
Sound (R. Knudson/D. Hildyard).
Boa: book Goodbye To Berlin by Christopher
Isherwood.
MUS            120 min (ort 128 min)
B,V                        RNK; VGM

**CABINET OF DOCTOR CALIGARI, THE ****
Robert Wiene      GERMANY      1919
*Werner Krauss, Conrad Veidt, Lil Dagover, Friedrich
Feher, Hans Von Twardowski, Rudolf Lettinger*
A landmark Expressionist film in which it would
appear that a fairground hypnotist has complete
control of a victim he uses for the purpose of murder.
Ultimately the sinister acts the victim is forced to
carry out are found to be nothing more than the
dreams of a disturbed lunatic being treated in a
sanatorium. An immensely powerful film of stylised
sets and grotesque angles; faded but still potent.
Remade in 1962.
Aka: DAS CABINET DES DR CALIGARI
HOR         44 min (ort 73 min) B/W silent
B,V                             TEVP

**CABOBLANCO \***
J. Lee Thompson          USA          1980
*Charles Bronson, Jason Robards, Dominique Sanda,*
*Camilla Sparv, Gilbert Roland, Fernando Rey, Simon*
*MacCorkindale, Denny Miller*
Rip-off of CASABLANCA with Bronson as a saloon-
owner in a Peruvian village just after WW2. Robards
is a Nazi, whilst Rey is a police captain and Sanda is a
Frenchwoman who's looking for her lover. Derivative
and hammy, a dud on all counts.
THR                                 90 min
B,V,V2                              GHV

**CACTUS \*\*\***                        PG
Paul Cox          AUSTRALIA          1986
*Isabelle Huppert, Norman Kaye, Robert Menzies,*
*Monica Maughan, Sheila Florence, Peter Aanensen,*
*Banduk Marika*
A French woman in Australia is injured in a car
accident and her sight is damaged. Whilst convalesc-
ing, she meets an attractive blind man. This slow tale
of her growing relationship with him and of the
difficulties they face, is not without its moments, but
it does tend to wander off the story from time to time.
DRA                                 95 min
B,V                                 POLY

**CACTUS FLOWER \*\*\***                    PG
Gene Saks          USA          1969
*Walter Matthau, Ingrid Bergman, Goldie Hawn, Jack*
*Weston, Rick Lenz, Vito Scotti, Irene Hervey*
Wonderfully enjoyable comedy about a dentist who
persuades his nurse to pretend to be his wife so that he
will not have to marry his girlfriend. The plot is pretty
thin, but the fresh and winning performances carry it
off. Hawn's first major role, for which she won a
well-deserved Oscar. The script is by I.A.L. Diamond
from the Broadway play. AA: S. Actress (Hawn).
Boa: play by Abe Burrows.
COM                                 99 min
V                                   RCA

**CACTUS JACK \*\***                        PG
Hal Needham          USA          1979
*Kirk Douglas, Ann-Margret, Arnold Schwarzenegger,*
*Paul Lynde, Foster Brooks, Ruth Buzzi, Jack Elam,*
*Strother Martin, Robert Tessier*
Wildly over-the-top spoof Western that sends up both
whites and Indians, telling of an outlaw who pursues a
girl and her tough protector.
Aka: VILLAIN, THE
COM                        85 min (ort 105 min)
B,V                                 RCA

**CADDIE \*\***
Donald Crombie          AUSTRALIA          1976
*Helen Morse, Takis Emmanuel, Jack Thompson, Ron*
*Blanchard, Drew Forsythe, Kirrili Nolan, Lynette*
*Currin, Philip Hinton, Simon Hinton, Sean Hinton,*
*Deborah Kounnas, Mariane Howard, Mary Mackay*
Autobiographical account of an independent-minded
woman, who is left by her husband with their two
children to bring up. Set in the late 1920s and early
1930s, this bland and cliched tale has a few perceptive
moments in charting the heroine's road to independ-
ence, but there are too few of them.
Boa: book Caddie Woodlawn by C.R. Brink.
DRA                                 107 min
B,V                                 ENT/HVP

**CADDYSHACK \*\***                        15
Harold Ramis          USA          1980
*Chevy Chase, Rodney Dangerfield, Ted Knight,*
*Michael O'Keefe, Bill Murray, Sarah Holcomb, Scott*
*Colomby, Brian Doyle Murray, Cindy Morgan*
Slapstick and zany comedy set in a country club that
runs an exclusive golfing establishment. The first

opening sequences are very funny, but this effort soon
runs out of ideas. Followed by CADDYSHACK 2.
COM                                 94 min
V                                   WHV

**CADDYSHACK 2 \*\***                        15
Alan Arkush          USA          1988
*Jackie Mason, Robert Stack, Dan Aykroyd, Chevy*
*Chase, Dyan Cannon, Jonathan Silverman, Dina*
*Merrill, Randy Quaid, Jessica Lundy, Chynna*
*Phillips, Brian McNamara*
This borrows the title of the 1980 film but little else.
Mason is good as a self-made construction millionaire,
who takes a fitting revenge when his daughter is
snubbed by the snooty members of a local country
club. This one idea does not suffice to sustain the film
throughout its entire length and after the first half it
soon runs down.
COM                                 94 min
V                                   WHV

**CAESAR AND CLEOPATRA \*\***                 U
Gabriel Pascal          UK          1945
*Vivien Leigh, Claude Rains, Stewart Granger, Flora*
*Robson, Francis L. Sullivan, Cecil Parker, Basil*
*Sydney, Ernest Thesiger, Michael Rennie, Anthony*
*Eustrel, Renee Asherson, Raymond Lovell, Olga*
*Edwardes, Esme Percy*
Film version of Shaw's play about the teenage Egyp-
tian queen and her relationship with Caesar. A stilted
and utterly tiresome effort with a surprise ending –
just when you think it's never going to end it does.
Boa: play by George Bernard Shaw.
DRA                        121 min (ort 138 min)
B,V                                 RNK

**CAGE, THE \*\***                        18
Lang Elliott          USA          1989
*Lou Ferrigno, Reb Brown*
Standard formula mayhem with Ferrigno a brain-
damaged Vietnam veteran who runs a bar with his
buddy and is not averse to using his physical prowess
to eject troublemakers, usually through the nearest
window. Some gangsters witness this and persuade
him and his buddy to go in for "cage fighting", a tough
and brutal form of combat. People who like Chuck
Norris movies will like this one.
A/AD                                97 min
B,V                                 BRAVE

**CAGED FURY \*\***
Cirio H. Santiago          ITALY          1983
*Bernie Williams, Taffy O'Connell, Jennifer Lane,*
*Catherine March*
Ten women POWs are held in a prison camp and are to
be trained to assassinate heads of state, but they
escape and endure many ordeals in the jungle before
reaching civilisation.
WAR                                 90 min
B,V                        VFP L/A; TCE L/A; INT

**CAGED HEAT \*\***                        18
Jonathan Demme          USA          1974
*Juanita Brown, Erica Gavin, Roberta Collins,*
*Rainbeaux Smith, Barbara Steele, Toby Carr-*
*Refelson, Desiree Cousteau*
Tiresome women-in-prison movie set for once in the
US and not in the jungle hell, so beloved of this genre.
Inevitably, a group of inmates go on the rampage and
take their violent revenge. Now has a sizeable cult
following. Demme's first feature has a few semi-comic
moments, but apart from these, it's business as usual.
Aka: RENEGADE GIRLS
DRA                        92 min; 83 min (ODY)
B,V,V2                  IFS/CBS; ODY (VHS only)

**CAGED WOMEN \*\***
Vincent Dawn (Bruno Mattei)
                        FRANCE/ITALY          1982

*Laura Gemser, Gabriele Tuti, Lorraine de Selle, Jack Stany*
An undercover journalist infiltrates a women's prison. Standard exploiter that offers a few titillating moments but little in the way of a plot.
Aka: EMMANUELLE REPORTAGE DA UN CARCERE FEMMINILE; EMMANUELLE REPORTS FROM A WOMEN'S PRISON
DRA 96 min
B,V VIP

## CAGNEY AND LACEY ***  15
Ted Post USA 1980
*Loretta Swit, Tyne Daly, Joan Copeland, Al Waxman, Ronald Hunter, Yvette Hawkins, Carl Lumbly, Gerard Parkes, Ben Hammer, Harvey Atkin, Anna Berger, Patrick Brymer, Neil Dainard, Lili Francks, Richard Yearwood, Nicky Fylan*
Two female detectives solve a tough murder case involving a diamond broker. Fair pilot for a TV series that got progressively more earnest and preachy as it ran. This pilot shows how good it was when it started.
DRA 100 min; 91 min (CH5) mTV
B,V VFP L/A; HER; CH5 (VHS only)

## CAGNEY AND LACEY: A FAIR SHAKE **  15
Reaza Badiyi USA 1988
*Sharon Gless, Tyne Daly, Martin Kove, Sidney Clute, Harvey Atkin, Robert Hegyes, John Karlen*
A simple case of bank fraud proves to be more complex than at first sight, when links with the Mafia are revealed. Feature-length spin-off from the popular TV series.
DRA 120 min mTV
V VIR

## CAGNEY AND LACEY: TURN, TURN, TURN **  15
Sharon Miller USA 1987
*Sharon Gless, Tyne Daly, Martin Kove, Sidney Clute, Harvey Atkin, Robert Hegyes, John Karlin, Al Waxman, Carl Lumbly*
Another feature-length spin-off from the popular TV series, with Detective Cagney hitting the bottle when her father dies, whilst Beth rescues a baby from a burning car and tries to locate the mother. Average.
DRA 89 min mTV
V VIR

## CAHILL: U.S. MARSHAL **  15
Andrew V. MacLaglen USA 1972
*John Wayne, George Kennedy, Gary Grimes, Neville Brand, Clay O'Brien, Marie Windsor, Morgan Paull, Dan Vadis, Royal Dano, Scott Walker, Denver Pyle, Jackie Coogan, Rayford Barnes, Dan Kemp, Harry Carey Jr, Walter Barnes*
A US Marshal finds that his own sons are involved in a robbery that he is investigating. A preachy and earnest Western that follows a well-trodden path – one of Wayne's poorer efforts.
Aka: CAHILL
WES 97 min (ort 103 min)
V WHV

## CAINE MUTINY COURT MARTIAL, THE ***  PG
Robert Altman USA 1987
*Eric Bogosian, Brad Davis, Jeff Daniels, Michael Murphy, Peter Gallagher, Kevin O'Connor, Daniel Jenkins*
A sort of unofficial sequel to THE CAINE MUTINY, that concentrates on the subsequent court-martial of the officers involved in the mutiny, a highlight being the sequence where Captain Queeg effectively convicts himself. An absorbing and literate study.
DRA 96 min mTV
B,V EIV

## CAINE MUTINY, THE ****  U
Edward Dmytryk USA 1954
*Humphrey Bogart, Fred MacMurray, Van Johnson,*
*Robert Francis, Jose Ferrer, May Wynn, E.G. Marshall, Lee Marvin, Tom Tully, Claude Akins*
Based on the Pulitzer Prize-winning novel, this tells of a ship's captain who hovers on the threshold of breakdown, and receives scant pity from his sullen and contemptuous crew. Bogart as the captain was never better, his courtroom monologue is harrowing. Johnson, Francis and MacMurray play his mutinous chief officers.
Boa: novel by Herman Wouk.
DRA 119 min B/W
V RCA

## CAIRO ROAD **  U
David McDonald UK 1950
*Eric Portman, Laurence Harvey, Maria Mauban, Karel Stepanek, Harold Lang, Camelia, Gregoire Aslan, Oscar Quitak*
In his determination to catch drug smugglers, an Egyptian police colonel devises a series of traps. A standard cops and robbers tale, given a touch more sparkle thanks to the unusual setting.
A/AD 86 min (ort 95 min) B/W
V WHV

## CAIN'S CUT-THROATS **
Kent Osborne/Bud Dell USA 1970
*Scott Brady, Bruce Kimball, Robert Dix, John Carradine, Don Epperson, Adair Jamison, Darwin Jaston, Teresa Thaw, Willis Martin*
A blend of SF and Western genres, with seven bikers in a small town going back in time to the Wild West of the 1870s. There they team up with a former Confederate army captain and a bounty hunting preacher, to get even with the renegade soldiers who raped the latter's wife and killed his son.
Aka: CAIN'S WAY
WES 89 min (ort 95 min)
B,V,V2 VTC

## CAL ***  15
Pat O'Connor UK 1984
*Helen Mirren, John Lynch, Donal McCann, John Kavanagh, Steven Rimkus, Ray McAnally, Catherine Gibson, Louis Rolston, Tom Hickey, Gerald Mannix Flynn, Seamus Ford, Edward Byrne, Audrey Johnson, Brian Munn*
A young unemployed man in Northern Ireland is reluctantly drawn into the murder of a policeman and then becomes romantically involved with the dead man's wife. A literate and engrossing study, with a strong performance from Mirren for which she won the Best Actress award at Cannes. Produced by David Puttnam and scripted by MacLaverty.
Boa: novel by Bernard MacLaverty.
DRA 102 min
B/h, V/h WHV

## CALAMITY JANE ***  U
David Butler USA 1953
*Doris Day, Howard Keel, Allyn Ann McLerie, Philip Carey, Gale Robbins, Dick Wesson, Paul Harvey, Chubby Johnson*
Bright and bouncy musical Western, with Day in fine form as the tomboyish female gunslinger who changes her ways when she falls in love with Keel. AA: Song ("Secret Love" – Sammy Fain – music/Paul Francis Webster – lyrics).
MUS 97 min
V WHV

## CALENDAR GIRL MURDERS, THE **  15
Willaim A. Graham USA 1985
*Tom Skerritt, Sharon Stone, Barbara Bosson, Robert Beltran, Pat Corley, Robert Morse, Alan Thicke, Silvana Gallardo, Michael C. Gwynne, Robert Culp, Barbara Parkins, Wendy Kilbourne, Victoria Tucker, Pamela West*
Month by month the pretty girls who grace the centre

pages of a men's magazine are being murdered. Having murdered Miss January and Miss February, it would appear that Miss March is next in line. Presumably Miss December is glad she's on the back page. A minor murder mystery.
Boa: story by Gregory S. Dinallo.
THR                                    95 min (ort 104 min) mTV
B,V                                                        CBS

**CALIBRE .357 ** **                                    18
Eddie Nicart          PHILIPPINES                     1982
*Nelson Anderson, Jean Seaburt, Marilon Bendingo, Carole O'Nei, Azenitu Briones*
A martial arts expert and secret agent, avenges the death of his friend at the hands of drug dealers.
A/AD                                             98 min
B,V                                                        GHV

**CALIBRE 9 ** **
Fernando Di Leo          ITALY                         1971
*Barbara Bouchet, Philippe Leroy, Gastone Moschin*
An ex-con is released but is then pursued by a gang of currency smugglers who accuse him of stealing $300,000 from them. Average European thriller.
Aka: MILANO CALIBRO NOVE
THR                                             100 min
B,V,V2                                                     VPD

**CALIFORNIA BULLS ** **                               15
                       USA                            1987
*Delta Burke, Geoffrey Scott, Clayton Landey, Marshall Teague, Reid Shelton, Jeff East, Ruta Lee, Sam Scarber*
A beautiful woman acquires a football team as part of a divorce settlement, and faces tough opposition from its members, a bunch of sex-crazed beer-swilling slobs, in order to turn it into a winning team.
COM                                              90 min
B,V                                                        MOG

**CALIFORNIA DOLLS, THE *** **                         18
Robert Aldrich          USA                            1981
*Peter Falk, Vicki Frederick, Laurene Landon, Burt Young, Tracy Reed, Richard Jaeckel, Ursaline Bryant-King, Claudette Nevins*
Entertaining film about two female wrestlers and their manager, who dream of the big time. Messy, disjointed and uneven, but the great performances are considerable compensations. Aldrich's last film.
Aka: ALL THE MARBLES
DRA                                             113 min
B,V                                                        MGM

**CALIFORNIA GIRLS ** **
William Webb          USA                              1982
*Al Music, Mary McKinley, Alicia Allen*
A disc jockey dreams up a beauty competition to save an ailing radio station, and three of California's prettiest girls set out to win the cash prize.
COM                                              90 min
B,V,V2                                                     VCL/CBS

**CALIFORNIA GOLD RUSH ** **
John B. Hively          USA                            1979
*John Dehner, Ken Curtis, Henry Jones, Gene Evans, Victor Mohica, Robert Hays, Cliff Osmond, Don Haggerty, Coleman Creel, Henry Max Kendrick, Bill Zuckert, Bert Santos, John Aspiras, Tim Bailey, John G. Bishop, Don Casto*
A newly built town is besieged by gold prospectors and a young writer heads West to follow the gold rush. A glossy and lightweight Western.
Boa: short stories The Luck Of Roaring Camp and The Outcasts Of Poker Flat by Bret Harte.
WES                                    96 min (ort 100 min) mTV
B,V                                                        RNK

**CALIFORNIA KID, THE *** **                           PG
Richard T. Heffron          USA                        1974

Martin Sheen, Nick Nolte, Vic Morrow, Michelle Philips, Stuart Margolin, Jait Baldwin, Gary Morgan, Joe Estevez, Donald Mantooth, Frederic Downs, Michael Richardson, Norman Bartold, Britt Leach, Barbara Collentine
A demented small-town sheriff likes nothing better than punishing speeding motorists by forcing them off hairpin mountain curves. The hot-rodding brother of one of his latest victims (played by Estevez – Sheen's brother in real life) forces the sheriff into a deadly duel, in this well-made and taut thriller. The script is by Richard Compton.
A/AD                                    71 min (ort 78 min) mTV
B,V                                                        CIC

**CALIFORNIA SUITE *** **                              15
Herbert Ross          USA                             1978
*Jane Fonda, Alan Alda, Richard Pryor, Bill Cosby, Maggie Smith, Michael Caine, Walter Matthau, Elaine May, Gloria Gifford, Sheila Frazier, Herb Edelman, Denise Galik*
Adaptation of a Neil Simon play about four couples who occupy the same suite in a Beverly Hills Hotel. An uneven series of episodes. Smith and Caine as a British couple in town for the Academy Awards are a delight, as are Jewish couple Matthau and May. The divorce drama of Alda and Fonda and the bitchy Pryor and Cosby effort are both duds. AA: S. Actress (Smith).
Boa: play by Neil Simon.
COM                                             99 min
V                                                          RCA

**CALIGULA ** **
Tinto Brass          USA                              1980
*Malcolm McDowell, Teresa Ann Savoy, Helen Mirren, Peter O'Toole, Guido Mannari, John Gielgud*
An attempt to relate the story of this particularly repulsive Roman Emperor that is merely an excuse for sex (six minutes of hardcore in the uncensored version) and explicit violence as we follow this lovable Roman through a seemingly endless series of depravities and decapitations. Written by Gore Vidal and produced by Penthouse, this was the first $15,000,000 porno film. We can't say it was money well spent. Re-issued at 105 min.
A                                               156 min
B,V,V2                                                     ELV

**CALIGULA AND MESSALINA ** **                         18
Anthony Pass (Antonio Passalia)
                       FRANCE/ITALY                   1982
*John Turner, Betty Roland, Kathy Sadik, Francoise Blanchard*
An erotic version of Roman history that attempts to cash in on the success of the US film CALIGULA. A colourful and thoroughly over-the-top romp.
Aka: CALIGULA E MESSALINA; CALIGULA ET MESSALINA; FALL AND RISE OF THE ROMAN EMPIRE, THE (ROXY or GLOB)
A                                               98 min Cut
B,V                          INT L/A; VIDMID; ROXY; GLOB

**CALIGULA EROTICA ** **                               18
Roberto Montero          ITALY                         1977
*Carla Colombo, Cinzia Romanazzi, Roberto Montero, Gastone Dascucci*
We are now in Roman times and poor old Caligula is impotent. Naturally he goes to a sex clinic for help but once there, he is no longer under the protection of the Praetorian Guard. From such small beginnings . . .
Aka: CALIGULA'S HOT NIGHTS
A                                      68 min (ort 75 min)
B,V                                           VPD; NET; TCX

**CALL HARRY CROWN ** **                               15
John Frankenheimer          USA                        1974
*Richard Harris, Edmond O'Brien, Bradford Dillman,*

*Chuck Connors, Ann Turkel, Constance Ford,*
*Katherine Baumann*
Ridiculous attempt at a spoof on gangster films which
is both confused and unfunny.
Aka: 99 AND 44/100% DEAD
COM                                              98 min
B,V                                              CBS

**CALL HIM MISTER SHATTER \*\***
Michael Carreras  HONG KONG/UK         1976
*Stuart Whitman, Peter Cushing, Anton Diffring, Ti*
*Lung, Lily Lee, Yemi Ajibade, Liu Ka Yong, Liu Ya*
*Ying, Lo Wei, James Ma*
Kung fu movie with a burnt-out hitman being given
an assignment in Hong Kong and getting involved in
the obligatory web of double-crosses and political
assassination. A stab at the kung fu market on the
part of Hammer Films, with plenty of action but no
discernible plot.
Aka: MISTER SHATTER; SHATTER
MAR                          86 min; 90 min (VFO)
B,V                                    VFO L/A; EHE

**CALL IT MURDER \*\***
Chester Erskine        USA              1934
*Sidney Fox, O.P. Heggie, Henry Hull, Margaret*
*Wycherly, Lynne Overman, Helen Flint, Humphrey*
*Bogart, Richard Whorf, Cora Witherspoon*
The foreman of a jury in a murder trial, sends a
woman to the electric chair but is hounded by the
press when his own daughter kills her lover. Stilted
melodrama that takes quite a while to get going.
Aka: MIDNIGHT
Boa: play by Paul Sifton and Claire Sifton.
DRA                                      70 min B/W
B,V,V2                                     VCL/CBS

**CALL ME \*\***                                18
Sollace Mitchell       USA              1987
*Patricia Charbonneau, Sam Freed, Patti D'Arbanville,*
*Boyd Gaines, Stephen McHattie, Steve Buscemi, John*
*Seitz*
A woman recipient of obscene phone calls which she
thinks come from her boyfriend, becomes drawn into a
game of cat and mouse when she witnesses a murder.
A psychological thriller hampered by clumsy develop-
ment, and poor characterisation of the supporting
cast.
THR        98 min (Cut at film release by 3 min 56 sec)
B,V                                           VES

**CALL OF THE WILD \*\***                       PG
Ken Annakin
FRANCE/ITALY/SPAIN/UK/WEST GERMANY
                                            1972
*Charlton Heston, Maria Rohm, Michele Mercier,*
*Raimund Harmstorf, George Eastman (Luigi*
*Montefiore), Friedhelm Lehmann, Horst Heuck,*
*Sancho Garcia, Juan Luis Galiardo, Rik Battaglia, Alf*
*Malland, Alfredo Mayo, Sverre Wilberg*
Film version of a classic Jack London story with the
beautiful countryside of Finland standing in for the
Yukon, as two men and a dog trek across 200 miles of
frozen wasteland during the 1896 Klondike Gold
Rush. A flat and insipid effort that wastes the talents
of a good cast, though the beautiful scenery is a
compensation.
Boa: novel by Jack London.
DRA                            100 min (ort 105 min)
B,V                            GHV; MIA (VHS only)

**CALL TO GLORY \*\***                           PG
Thomas Carter        USA                1984
*Craig T. Nelson, Cindy Pickett, Joseph Hacker,*
*Gabriel Damon, Keenan Wynn, Elisabeth Shue, G.D.*
*Spradlin, David Hollander*
Pilot for a cancelled TV series following the lives of a
family, the father of which is an Air Force pilot, flying
reconnaissance missions at the time of the Cuban

missile crisis. Average.
Aka: CALL TO GLORY: JFK
DRA                        92 min (ort 104 min) mTV
V/h                                           CIC

**CALLAN \*\*\***                               15
Piers Haggard/Reginald Collin
                     UK                 1970
*Edward Woodward, William Squire, Patrick Mower,*
*Russell Hunter*
Two episodes from the popular television series about
a solitary and ruthless secret agent, who operates
according to his own unconventional rules. Episodes
are "Suddenly – At Home" and "Breakout". Fair. See
also THIS IS CALLAN.
A/AD                             104 min mTV
V                                           VCC

**CALLER, THE \*\***                            18
Arthur Allan Seidelman USA              1987
*Malcolm McDowell, Madolyn Smith*
A woman in a lonely cottage is expecting the arrival of
her boyfriend, but is surprised by a knock on the door,
the caller being a man who claims that his car has
broken down. Inviting himself in to use a telephone,
he stays, and a deadly battle of wits takes place. An
interesting psychological thriller, badly spoilt by a
foolish ending.
THR                            92 min (ort 104 min)
B,V                                           VES

**CALLIE AND SON \*\***
Waris Hussein         USA               1981
*Lindsay Wagner, Jameson Parker, Dabney Coleman,*
*Joy Garrett, Michelle Pfeiffer, John Harkins, James*
*Sloyan, Andrew Prine, Richard McKenzie, Macon*
*McCalman, Ed Call, Jim Calvert, Dawn Jeffory,*
*Katherine DeHetre, Hugh Gillin*
A woman who has an obsessive love for her son, rises
from poverty to power and wealth in Texas. Overlong
and overblown melodrama, scripted by author Tho-
mas Thompson.
DRA                              150 min mTV
B,V                                           VDB

**CAME A HOT FRIDAY \*\*\***                    PG
Ian Mune          NEW ZEALAND           1985
*Peter Bland, Philip Gordon, Billy T. James, Michael*
*Lawrence, Marshall Napier, Erna Larsen, Patricia*
*Philips, Don Selwyn*
A man plans to get even with a casino owner who has
cheated him. To do this he enlists the aid of a local
criminal. An old-fashioned caper film that's set in
1949 and delivers the laughs in an open and uncompli-
cated way.
COM                                     101 min
B,V                                     EHE; NELS

**CAMEL BOY, THE \*\***                          U
Yoram Gross        AUSTRALIA            1984
*Voices of: Barbara Frawley, Ron Haddrick, John*
*Meillon, Robyn Moore, Michael Pate*
Feature length animated adventure about a young
boy and his camel friend, who journey across the dry
and dusty deserts of the Middle East. Fair.
CAR                                      78 min
V                                            VES

**CAMELOT \***                                   U
Joshua Logan          USA               1967
*Richard Harris, Vanessa Redgrave, David Hemmings,*
*Franco Nero, Lionel Jeffries*
Film version of the Lerner and Loewe musical that
still has the same good songs but is ruined by actors
with lousy voices. Excessive use of close-ups is an
added annoyance, though on TV this will be less so. A
dreary effort. AA: Art/Set (John Truscott and Edward
Carrer/John W. Brown), Cost (John Truscott), Score
(Adapt) (Alfred Newman/Ken Darby).

Boa: musical by Lerner and Loewe.
MUS 175 min (ort 181 min)
V/h WHV

## CAMERON'S CLOSET ** 18
Armand Mastroianni USA 1987
*Cotter Smith, Mel Harris, Chuck McCann, Scott
Curtis, Leigh McCloskey, Kim Lankford, Tab Hunter*
A 10-year-old boy has had his psychic powers tampered with by his father and a scientist partner. In the course of their experiments the boy has brought to life an evil demon that lives in his bedroom cupboard. He loses control of it and a series of grisly murders takes place. A detective assigned to the case forms a close bond with the boy, and now has the task of rescuing him. A mediocre horror yarn, not all that far removed from POLTERGEIST.
Boa: novel by Gary Bradner
HOR 83 min (ort 86 min)
B,V MED

## CAMILLE ** PG
Desmond Davies UK 1984
*Greta Scacchi, Colin Firth, John Gielgud, Billie
Whitelaw, Ben Kingsley, Patrick Ryecart, Denholm
Elliott, Lila Kaye, Rachel Kempson, Ronald Pickup,
Julie Dawn Cole, Shelagh MacLeod, Natalie Ogle,
Nicholas Hawtrey*
Film version of the Dumas story telling of a 19th century courtesan who dies for love. A lavish but somewhat bland production – best to stick to the 1936 Garbo one.
Boa: novel The Lady Of The Camelias (La Dame Aux Camelias) by Alexandre Dumas.
DRA 90 min (ort 100 min) mTV
B,V VES/PVG

## CAMILLE 2000 ** 18
Radley Metzger USA 1969
*Danielle Gaubert, Nino Castelnuovo, Philippe Forquet,
Eleanora Rossi-Drago*
Modern version of a Dumas tale of an expensively kept woman who falls for a young boy. Cut before video submission.
Aka: CAMILLE
Boa: novel La Dame Aux Camelias by Alexandre Dumas.
DRA 94 min (ort 119 min)
B,V ALPHA/INT L/A; TOW

## CAMORRA *** 18
Lina Wertmuller ITALY 1985
*Angela Molina, Harvey Keitel, Francisco Rabal, Isa
Danieli, Daniel Ezralow, Paolo Bonicelli*
A passionate drama set in Naples against the backdrop of drug abuse, with the lives of a Mafia family, a boy, some female vigilantes and a businessman drawn together through their involvement with an ex-prostitute. Winner of four Italian Oscars.
Aka: COMPLICATED INTRIGUE OF BACK ALLEYS AND CRIMES; INTRIGO COMPLICATO DI VICOLI E DELITTI; MAMA SANTISSIMA; NAPLES CONNECTION, THE (WAL); UN COMPLICATO INTRIGO DI DONNE, VICOLI E DELITTI
DRA 89 min (ort 106 min)
B,V WAL L/A; RNK

## CAMP 708 ** 18
Dan Cohen ISRAEL 1983
*Michael Beck, Sigourney Weaver, F. Murray Abraham,
Alan Feinstein*
Fair biopic of Jewish activist Boris Abramovitch and his struggles with the Soviet authorities. Caught attempting to escape from the USSR, he was imprisoned and then transferred to a mental hospital, where he was tortured.
Aka: MADMAN

DRA 95 min mTV
B,V EXC/CBS

## CAMPAIGN BURMA ** PG
John Sturges USA 1959
*Frank Sinatra, Gina Lollobrigida, Peter Lawford,
Steve McQueen, Richard Johnson, Paul Henreid,
Brian Donlevy, Dean Jones, Charles Bronson*
This WW2 action movie has all the standard cliches in its far-fetched tale of combat and romance, but the performances of the stars generally hold it up.
Aka: NEVER SO FEW
WAR 124 min
V FILV

## CAMPBELL'S KINGDOM *** U
Ralph Thomas UK 1957 (re-issued 1960)
*Dirk Bogarde, Stanley Baker, Michael Craig, Barbara
Murray, James Robertson Justice, Athene Seyler,
Robert Brown, John Laurie, Sidney James, Mary
Merrall, George Murcell, Finlay Currie, Peter Illing*
Big-budget adventure film set in the Canadian Rockies and following the conflict between a sick man who inherits an oil valley and a crooked contractor who intends to build a dam that will flood his property.
Boa: novel by Hammond Innes.
A/AD 97 min (ort 119 min)
B,V RNK; VCC

## CAMPUS KILLINGS * 18
Richard Haines USA 1984
*Francine Forbes, Ric Randing, Cathy Lacommare*
Standard psychopath-on-the-loose story with the usual nutter roaming the campus bumping off the students. Made on a flea's budget.
Aka: SPLATTER UNIVERSITY
HOR 75 min Cut (1 sec)
V BRAVE

## CAMPUS MAN ** PG
Ron Casden USA 1987
*John Dye, Kim Delaney, Steve Lyon, Morgan
Fairchild, Kathleen Wilhoite, Miles O'Keeffe*
A college student convinces his hunky amateur diver buddy to pose for an all-male calendar. He finds that sales soar, but his friend arouses the interest of a female magazine editor, theatening his amateur status, and dreams of a gold medal at the Olympics. Vacuous teen comedy inspired by a real calendar produced by the Arizona State University. The script is by Todd Headlee, a former student there.
COM 96 min
V VES

## CAN BE DONE AMIGO ** 
Maurizio Lucidi
FRANCE/ITALY/SPAIN 1971
*Jack Palance, Bud Spencer (Carlo Pedersoli),
Francisco Rabal, Dany Saral, Renato Cestie, Luciano
Catenacci, Roberto Camardiel, Franco Giacobini, Sal
Borgese, Serena Michelotti, Manuel Guitan, Marcello
Verziera, Cleri Dante*
The comic misadventures of a man unwise enough to seduce the sister of a ruthless gunfighter. Average.
Aka: BIG AND THE BAD, THE; SI PUO FARE, AMIGO
WES 88 min (ort 105 min)
V INT

## CAN I DO IT TILL I NEED GLASSES? * 18
T. Robert Levy USA 1980
*Roger Behr, Robin Williams, Debra Klose, Jeff
Doucette, Victor Dunlop, Moose Carlson, Patrick
Wright, Walter Olkewicz*
The title is the most risque thing in this tired and limp sex comedy. From the same team who produced IF YOU DON'T STOP IT YOU'LL GO BLIND.
COM 73 min; 80 min (CHV)
B,V VPD L/A; CHV

## CAN SHE BAKE A CHERRY PIE? *
Henry Jaglom            USA                    15
                                              1983
*Karen Black, Michael Emil, Frances Fisher, Michael
Margotta, Martin Harvey Friedberg*
Believe it or not this was the official US entry at the
1983 Cannes Film Festival, and is about a neurotic
woman who takes up with a man who never seems to
stop talking, after her husband walks out on her. By
the way, it didn't win.
COM                         90 min (ort 118 min)
B,V                                        PVG

## CAN YOU FEEL ME DANCING? ***        PG
Michael Miller          USA                  1987
*Justine Bateman, Max Gail, Jason Bateman, Roger
Wilson, Frances Lee McCain, Vicki Eaton, Cheryl
McMannis, Santos Morales, Phil Rubinstein, Joe
Nasser, Kurek Ashley, Harold Diamond, Francis
Florio, Marty Schiff, Jason Stuart*
A sensitive and perceptive drama of a young blind
woman trying to maintain her independence in the
face of an over-protective family. She is dismayed to
discover that her boyfriend tends to treat her in the
same way. Inspired by the lives of Cheryl McMannis
and Joe Nasser, both of whom have small roles in this
film. Written by husband and wife team J. Miyoko
Hensley and Steven Hensley.
DRA                      95 min (ort 100 min) mTV
V                                        PACEV; APOL

## CAN YOU KEEP IT UP FOR A WEEK? *
Jim Atkinson            UK                    1974
*Jeremy Bulloch, Jill Damas, Neil Hallett, Richard
O'Sullivan, Sue Longhurst, Jenny Cox, Joy
Harrington, Valerie Leon, Olivia Munday, Mark
Singleton, Venica Day, Jules Walters, Catherine Howe,
Wendy Wax, Mandy Morris*
A girl promises to marry her boyfriend if he can keep
his hands off other women (and thus keep his job) for a
whole week. An utterly dated and dismal sex farce.
COM                                       94 min
B,V                                     INT/CBS

## CAN-CAN **                              U
Walter Lang             USA                  1960
*Frank Sinatra, Shirley MacLaine, Maurice Chevalier,
Juliet Prowse, Louis Jourdan*
A Paris nightclub owner faces constant police harass-
ment because of an exciting new dance being per-
formed on his premises. Film version of a dull but
tuneful musical set in Paris of the 1890s. Songs
include: "C'est Magnifique", "I Love Paris", "Let's Do
It" and "Just One Of Those Things".
Aka: CAN CAN
Boa: play by Abe Burrows.
MUS                                      131 min
B,V                                          CBS

## CANADIAN PACIFIC **
Edwin L. Marin          USA                  1949
*Randolph Scott, Jane Wyatt, J. Carrol Naish, Victor
Jory, Nancy Olson, Robert Barrat, Walter Sande, Don
Haggerty, Brandon Rhodes, Mary Kent, John Parrish,
John Hamilton, Richard Wessel, Howard Negley*
Adventure story of railway construction, in wild
country full of hostile Indians and other hazards. A
fair Randolph Scott epic.
A/AD                        81 min (ort 95 min) B/W
B,V                                     INT/CBS

## CANDI GIRL **                            18
John Christopher        USA                  1977
*L'Orielle, Brenda Lockwood, Samantha Fox, John C.
Holmes, Serena, Bobby Astyr, Ron Hudd, Steven
Mitchell, Herschel Savage*
A simple-minded story following the exploits of two
guys who own a used car lot. Their day starts with a

series of interviews of girls for the job of saleswoman –
most of the interviews taking place in the back of a
pick-up truck. Back at home, their wives are enjoying
each other's company more than their husbands'.
They get home and the local gangster arrives demanding a share of their profits; he winds up with a share
of their wives instead.
Aka: JET SEX
A                                         83 min
V                                    VTEL; GLOB

## CANDIDATE FOR A KILLING **
Jose Maria Elorrieta
                        ITALY/SPAIN         1969
*Anita Ekberg, Fernando Rey, Margaret Lee*
Routine crime thriller
Aka: CANDIDATO PER UN ASSASSINO; UN
SUDARIO A LA MEDIA
THR                                      95 min
B,V                                    VCL/CBS

## CANDIDATE, THE ***                      PG
Michael Ritchie         USA                  1972
*Robert Redford, Peter Boyle, Don Porter, Allen
Garfield, Karen Carlson, Melvyn Douglas*
Political satire about a young Californian lawyer who
decides to run for the Senate on a platform of total
honesty. A sharp and witty drama that combines a
great feel for political campaigning, with a winning
performance from Redford. Ritchie and screenwriter
Larner were actually involved in some of the cam-
paigns of the 1960s. AA: Story/Screen (Jeremy
Larner).
DRA                                      106 min
B,V                                          WHV

## CANDIDO EROTICO **                       18
Claudio de Molinis      ITALY                1978
*Lilli Carati, Mircha Garven, Maria Baxa, Ajita Wilson*
A porno performer in a Copenhagen live-sex club,
meets the daughter of a couple who hire him to
improve the husband's sluggish performance in bed.
Aka: CANDIDO EROTICA; COPENHAGEN
NIGHTS
A                            95 min; 90 min (NET)
B,V                                VPD; NET; TCX

## CANDLE FOR THE DEVIL, A **
Eugenio Martin          SPAIN               1973
*Judy Geeson, Aurora Bautista, Esperanza Roy*
Two sisters run a little hotel in a quiet village in
Spain, but beneath the deceptive calm, strange forces
are at work.
Aka: UNA VELA PARA EL DIABLO
HOR                                      84 min
B,V                                          VDM

## CANDLESHOE ***                           U
Norman Tokar            UK                   1977
*David Niven, Helen Hayes, Jodie Foster, Leo McKern,
Veronica Quilligan, Ian Sharrock, Sarah Tamakuni,
David Samuels, John Alderson, Mildred Shay,
Michael Balfour, Sydney Bromley, Vivian Pickles*
A smart butler foils the plans of a con-man who
intends passing off a phoney heiress in an English
stately home, in order to locate a hidden family
treasure. Entertaining Disney tale with Niven, a man
of limited dramatic range, rather well-cast as the
butler. Filmed in England.
Boa: novel Christmas At Candleshoe by Michael
Innes.
COM                                      101 min
B,V                                          WDV

## CANDY CANDY **                           U
                        USA                  1981
Animated feature best described as a cartoon soap
opera. Two girls living in an orphanage are always at

odds with one of the boys and only realise how much
they really like him when he is adopted.
CAR                              48 min (ort 60 min)
V                                INT L/A; XTASY

## CANDY GOES TO HOLLYWOOD **
Gail Palmer          USA                   1979
Carol Connors, John Leslie, Richard Pacheco, Howie
Gordon, Wendy Williams
A dumb blonde comes o Hollywood and enjoys various
adventures. A kind of sequel to THE EROTIC
ADVENTURES OF CANDY with some crude satires
on popular TV shows of the period. Average.
Osca: EIGHT TO FOUR (asa)
A                                          88 min
B,V                                        HAR

## CANDY MAN, THE **
Herbert J. Leder        USA                1969
George Sanders, Leslie Parrish, Gina Roman, Manolo
Fabregas, Carlos Cortez
A film star's young child is kidnapped in Mexico City,
and a tired British drug-pusher living there, hatches a
plot to exploit the situation and make some easy
money. A flat and dull thriller with nothing going for
it except some nice locations.
THR                                    98 min B/W
B,V                                    IPC L/A; QUA

## CANDY STRIPE NURSES *                    18
Allan Holleb            USA                1974
Candice Rialson, Robin Mattson, Maria Rojo,
Kimberly Hyde, Dick Miller, Stanley Ralph Ross,
Monte Landis, Tom Baker
Dull sex comedy revolving around the antics of
volunteer nurses at a local hospital. The last of Roger
Corman's "nurse" picture. For this, much thanks.
COM                              76 min (ort 80 min)
B,V                                        TEVP

## CANDY TANGERINE MAN, THE **              18
Matt Cimber (Matteo Ottaviano)
                        USA                1975
John Daniels, Tom Hankerson, Eli Haines, Marva
Farmer, Buck Flower
Story of a respectable L.A. businessman, married and
with a family, who leads an incredible double life,
becoming at night one of the most powerful pimps in
town.
Aka: TANGERINE MAN, THE
DRA            84 min (ort 95 min) Cut (4 min 18 sec)
B,V                                        SAT

## CANNERY ROW **                           15
David S. Ward           USA                1982
Debra Winger, Nick Nolte, Audra Lindley, Frank
McRae, M. Emmet Walsh, Sunshine Parker, Santos
Morales, John Huston (narration)
Romance between basketball player turned marine
biologist and female drifter, is set against the seedy
background of a once thriving fishing town in Califor-
nia. Attractive sets by Richard MacDonald and a
couple of great performances, are lost in a welter of
sloppy direction. Ward's directorial debut.
Boa: novellas Cannery Row and Sweet Thursday by
John Steinbeck.
DRA                                       120 min
B,V,V2                                      MGM

## CANNIBAL **
Reggero Deodati      ITALY                 1977
Massimo Foschi, Me Mehay
An oil exploration expedition in the Philippines falls
into the hands of cannibals.
DRA                                        88 min
B,V,V2                                      DFS

## CANNIBAL APOCALYPSE **                    PG
Anthony M. Dawson (Antonio Margheriti)
                        ITALY              1980
John Saxon, Elisabeth Turner, John Morghen, Cindy
Hamilton, May Heatherley, Cinzia Carolis, Tony King,
Giovanni Lombardo Radice, Wallace Wilkinson,
Ramiro Oliveiros, Venantino Venantini
Two POWs returning from Vietnam discover that
they have acquired a taste for human flesh. Pretty
much what you would expect from a film with this
basis for a plot. Unlikely to be available in an uncut
form in the UK.
Aka: APOCALISSE DOMANI; APOCALIPSE
CANNIBAL; APOCALYPSE DOMANI; CANNIBAL
APOCALIPSIS; CANNIBALS ARE IN THE
STREETS, THE; CANNIBALS IN THE CITY;
INVASION OF THE FLESH HUNTERS;
SLAUGHTERERS, THE; LAST HUNTER; VIRUS
HOR                      90 min; 103 min (INT)
B,V                              VPD L/A; INT

## CANNIBAL MAN, THE **
Eloy de la Iglesias     SPAIN              1974
Vincente Parva, Emma Cohen, Vicki Lagos
A man who works in the canning plant of a slaughter-
house kills a taxi driver in self defence. This sparks off
a wave of horrific crimes, in this cliched but violent
melodrama. Unlikely to be available in an uncut form
in the UK.
Aka: APARTMENT ON THE 13TH FLOOR; LA
SEMANA DEL ASESINO
DRA                                        98 min
B,V,V2                                     INT/CBS

## CANNON OPERATION *                        18
                        USA                1984
David Ilveria, William Byrum
The outcome of the Korean War is in jeopardy, when a
high-ranking spy who might reveal damaging secrets
falls into the hands of the North Koreans. To some
extent based on a true incident but no more interest-
ing for that.
Aka: CANON OPERATION, THE
A/AD                                       90 min
V                                          FALCON

## CANNONBALL FEVER *                        PG
James R. Drake          USA                1989
Melody Anderson, Peter Boyle, Donna Dixon, John
Candy, Joe Flaherty, Eugene Levy, Tim Matheson,
Brooke Shields, Shari Belafonte, Matt Frewer, Mimi
Kuzyk, Lee Van Cleef, Smothers Brothers
Yet one more comedy built around the idea of a
coast-to-coast autorace, where a bunch of wealthy folk
with nothing better to do decide to hold an illegal
cross-country race with no-holds-barred. Despite the
new director and cast (Candy replaces Burt Reynolds
as the central character), this follow-up to the earlier
"Cannonball" films is virtually devoid of new ideas.
COM                                        92 min
V                                          VES

## CANNONBALL RUN, THE *                     PG
Hal Needham            USA                 1980
Burt Reynolds, Roger Moore, Farrah Fawcett, Dom
DeLuise, Sammy Davis Jr, Edward Asner, Dean
Martin, Adrienne Barbeau, Terry Bradshaw, Jack
Elam, Bert Convy, Jackie Chan, Molly Picon, Jamie
Farr, Bianca Jagger, Mel Tillis
It's no holds barred time when it comes to winning in
an illegal car race from New York to California. A
noisy and almost unbearable rip-off of THE GUM-
BALL RALLY. Followed in 1984 by CANNONBALL
RUN 2
COM                                        96 min
V                                          CBS

## CANNONBALL RUN 2 *                        PG
Hal Needham            USA                 1984

Burt Reynolds, Dom DeLuise, Dean Martin, Sammy Davis Jr, Shirley MacLaine, Jamie Farr, Marilu Henner, Telly Savalas, Susan Anton, Joe Theismann, Frank Sinatra, Sid Caesar
Sequel to the 1980 film and once more, about a cross-country car race. A sloppy and carelessly thrown together mess, featuring a host of stars in cameo roles.
Aka: CANNONBALL 2
COM                              108 min; 103 min (POLY)
B,V          CH5 (VHS only); HER; POLY (VHS only)

## CAN'T BUY ME LOVE **                                    15
Steve Rash              USA              1987
Patrick Dempsey, Amanda Peterson, Dennis Dugan, Cortney Gains, Seth Green, Tina Caspary, Sharon Farrell, Ami Dolenz, Steve Franken
A despised nerd (i.e. he wears glasses) achieves overnight popularity when he bribes the most attractive girl in the school to pose as his girlfriend. Peterson gives a great performance in a film that would have been a certain winner if the makers could have dispensed with the obligatory sentimentality.
COM                                                90 min
B,V                                    BUENA; TOUCH

## CAN'T STOP THE MUSIC *                                  PG
Nancy Walker            USA              1980
The Village People, Valerie Perrine, Bruce Jenner, Steve Guttenberg, Paul Sand, Tommy Grimes, June Havoc, Barbara Rush, Leigh Taylor-Young, Jack Weston
A Greenwich Village pop group become overnight stars in this wooden comedy on the music business. A couple of good numbers can't save it.
COM                                               120 min
B, V/sh                                            TEVP

## CANTERVILLE GHOST, THE ***                              U
Paul Bogart             USA              1986
John Gielgud, Ted Wass, Andrea Marcovicci, Alyssa Milano, Jeff Harding, Lila Kaye, Harold Innocent, George Baker, Dorothea Phillips, Bill Wallis, Spencer Chandler, Brian Oulton, Deddie Davies, Celia Breckon
A likeable romp through this famous Oscar Wilde tale of a restless 17th century ghost, who will only be released when he can persuade one of his descendants to perform a deed of bravery. Gielgud does justice to the role taken by Laughton in the fondly remembered 1940 version, and the rest of the cast gives good support. Filmed in England.
Boa: short story by Oscar Wilde.
JUV                                                96 min mTV
V                                                   VGM

## CANTON IRON KUNG FU **                                  15
Li Chao           HONG KONG              197-
Liang Jia Ren, Wang Chung
A kung fu movie featuring Canton-style fighting, with one of the ten "tigers" of Quon Tung perfecting his fighting techniques, as a prelude to revenge for a previous defeat.
Aka: CANTONEN IRON KUNG FU; CANTONESE IRON KUNG FU; IRON FIST OF KWANGTUNG
MAR                                                90 min
B,V                                                 VPD

## CAPERS **                                               
Richard Michaels        USA              1973
Adam Roarke, Larry Bishop, Alexandra Hay
Two stuntmen and a girl plan to smuggle mariujuana across the Mexican border, in this somewhat pedictable comedy.
Aka: HOW COME NOBODY'S ON OUR SIDE?
COM                                                90 min
B,V,V2                                              GOV

## CAPONE *                                                
Steve Carver            USA              1975
Ben Gazzara, Susan Blakely, Harry Guardino, John

Cassavetes, Sylvester Stallone, Peter Maloney, Frank Campanella, John D. Chandler, John Orchard, Mario Gallo, Russ Marin, George Chandler, Royal Dano
A tedious attempt to chart the rise and fall of one of America's most notorious gangsters. Gazzara's dialogue is muffled and incomprehensible for most of the time but this is no great loss; the best thing in this movie is the stock footage from THE SAINT VALENTINE'S DAY MASSACRE.
A/AD                                               101 min
V/sh                                                CBS

## CAPONE'S ENFORCER ***                                   15
Michael Switzer         USA              1988
Anthony LaPaglia, Trini Alvarado, Vincent Guastaferro, Michael Moriarty, Michael Russo, Louis Guss, Bruno Kirby
Gangster tale focusing on the career of one Frank Nitti, who was one of Capone's most trusted henchmen. Atmospheric and often bloody, with a strong performance from LaPaglia and a largely unknown cast.
Aka: NITTI; NITTI: THE ENFORCER
A/AD                                                95 min
V                                                   SONY

## CAPRICORN ONE ***                                       PG
Peter Hyams             USA              1978
Elliot Gould, James Brolin, Hal Holbrook, Sam Waterston, Karen Black, O.J. Simpson, Telly Savalas, Brenda Vaccaro, Denise Nicholas, David Huddleston, Robert Walden, David Doyle
Complications arise when a reporter discovers that the first manned flight to Mars was a fake. The capsule has been reported as burning up on re-entry and the pilots killed, but they are understandably not too willing to help in this hoax. An implausible but entertaining film of intrigues and chases.
A/AD                                               118 min
B,V,V2,LV       PRV L/A; CH5 (VHS only); POLY (VHS only)

## CAPTAIN AMERICA **                                      U
Rod Holcomb             USA              1979
Reb Brown, Len Birman, Heather Menzies, Steve Forrest, Robin Mattson, Joseph Ruskin, Lance LeGault, Frank Marth, Chip Johnson, Dan Barton, Nocana Aranda, Michael McManus, James Ingersoll, Jim B. Smith, Ken Chandler, Jason Wingreen
One of Marvel's comic-strip heroes is brought to the screen in this routine tale, which has his ex-Marine son carrying on the crime-busting family tradition, by fighting a master criminal who has planted a neutron bomb in Phoenix. Well below average and followed by a sequel of similar quality.
A/AD                                               100 min mTV
B,V,V2                                              CIC

## CAPTAIN BLOOD ****                                      PG
Michael Curtiz          USA              1935
Errol Flynn, Olivia de Havilland, Basil Rathbone, Lionel Atwill, Ross Alexander, Guy Kibbee
An unjustly punished surgeon is deported from England and turns to piracy in this first Flynn swashbuckler. Brilliant high adventure, with Flynn at his very best, ably supported by a fine cast. Has also become available in a computer coloured version for those who like icing on their caviar.
Boa: novel by Rafael Sabatini.
A/AD                                   94 min (ort 119 min) B/W
V                                                   WHV

## CAPTAIN FUTURE: SPECIAL AGENTS AND ALIEN CUT-THROATS ***                                    U
Robert Barron           USA              1985
A dying spaceman returns to Earth with the dreaded "apeman" disease, and tells a tale of destruction and disaster in a far-off galaxy, before he dies. In this

lively cartoon adventure, Captain Future is assigned the dangerous task of finding a missing Special Agent and tracking down the cause of the deadly disease.

| CAR | 94 min |
| V | MAST |

## CAPTAIN HARLOCK VOL. 1 **
JAPAN                    1977

A space pirate is the only one who can save Earth from being taken over by evil aliens, in this so-so compilation of several episodes of the TV series.

| CAR | 60 min mTV |
| V | JVC L/A; ART |

## CAPTAIN COSMOS **                         PG
Roy Thomas        HONG KONG        1989

Animated space opera set in the not-too-distant future when an emergency signal from Earth reaches the headquarters of a group of galactic warriors. Their help is required to defeat the female head of an evil empire that has been abducting and enslaving space travellers. A fierce battle now ensues as they fight to defeat this empire and free its captives. A watchable film of adequate animation. See also THE COSMOS CONQUEROR and FALCON 7.

| CAR | 77 min |
| V | VPD |

## CAPTAIN LUST ***                          18
Beau Buchanan        USA        1977

*Jake Teague, Beau Buchanan, Sharon Mitchell, Nancy Dare, Jamie Gillis, Wade Nichols, Veri Knotty, Ming Toy*

This adult pirate spoof is set in the 18th century, with the son and daughter of the Count of Monte Christo being cheated out of their inheritance – a hidden fortune in gold and jewels. They smuggle themselves onto a ship heading for an island where the treasure is buried, but soon discover that a pirate captain and his crew of women are after the loot as well. A bawdy romp of high-spirits and colourful locations.
Aka: CAPTAIN LUST AND THE PIRATE WOMEN
Osca: INSPIRATIONS/TEENAGE BRIDE (ROXY)

| A | 52 min (ort 82 min) Cut (3 min 47 sec) |
| B,V | ILV L/A; TOW; GLOB; ROXY |

## CAPTAIN SCARLETT **                       U
Thomas Carr        USA        1953

*Richard Greene, Leonora Amar, Nedrick Young, Eduardo Norriega*

Adventure story set just after the Napoleonic War, with Greene riding into action in best Robin Hood tradition, as a people's protector against the villainous Duke of Corlaine, who rules over a vast swathe of southern France. A flimsy costumed romp of no great note.

| A/AD | 72 min |
| V | VCC |

## CAPTAIN SCARLET: REVENGE OF THE
MYSTERONS FROM MARS *                        Uc
Bryan Burgess/Robert Lyon/Ken Turner
UK
1961 (re-edited/re-released USA 1981)

*Voices of: Francis Matthews, Donald Gray, Paul Maxwell, Ed Bishop, Jeremy Wilkin, Gary Files, Cy Grant, Charles Tingwell, Sylvia Anderson, Janna Hill, Lian-Shin, Liz Morgan*

Feature clipped together from a TV puppet series in which Earth is menaced by mysterious aliens.

| JUV | 91 min mTV |
| B,V | PRV L/A; CH5 (VHS only) |

## CAPTAIN SINBAD **                          PG
Byron Haskin
WEST GERMANY/USA        1963

*Guy Williams, Pedro Armendariz, Heidi Bruhl, Abraham Sofaer, Bernie Hamilton*

Predictable but colourful Sinbad adventure, with our dashing adventurer setting off to save a princess, and battling an assortment of monsters along the way.

| A/AD | 82 min |
| B,V | MGM |

## CAPTAIN YANKEE AND THE JUNGLE        PG
RAIDERS **
Anthony M. Dawson (Antonio Margheriti)
ITALY        1984

*Christopher Connelly, Lee Van Cleef, Alan Collins*

A successful but dubious explorer has to face pirates and crooks in the wilds of Borneo just prior to WW2, as he leads an expedition in search of a legendary and priceless ruby. Fair adventure yarn with some good special effects.
Aka: JUNGLE RAIDERS

| A/AD | 95 min |
| B,V | MED |

## CAPTAINS COURAGEOUS ****              U
Victor Fleming        USA        1937

*Spencer Tracy, Freddie Bartholemew, Lionel Barrymore, Melvyn Douglas, Mickey Rooney, John Carradine, Walter Kingsford, Charley Grapewin, Christian Rub*

Bartholemew plays a spoilt rich brat who falls off a cruiser and is picked up by a fishing vessel. Tracy gives a remarkable portrayal of the Portuguese fisherman who takes the boy in hand and wins his affection. A splendid film with some great scenes both on land and sea. Tracy won an Oscar in this one, and no wonder. The script is by John Lee Mahin, Marc Connelly and Dale Van Every. Remade as a TV film in 1977. AA: Actor (Tracy).
Boa: novel by Rudyard Kipling.

| DRA | 112 min B/W |
| V | MGM |

## CAPTAIN'S TABLE, THE ***                 U
Jack Lee        UK        1958

*John Gregson, Peggy Cummins, Donald Sinden, Nadia Gray, Maurice Denham, Richard Wattis, Reginald Beckwith, Bill Kerr, Nicholas Phipps, John Le Mesurier, Lionel Murton, Joan Sims, Miles Malleson, James Hayter*

The captain of a freighter is given trial command of a luxury liner and has to make a number of compromises to get things running smoothly. A lively and spirited adaptation of Gordon's book, written by John Whiting, Bryan Forbes and Nicholas Phipps.
Boa: novel by Richard Gordon.

| COM | 86 min |
| B,V | RNK; STRAND; VCC (VHS only) |

## CAPTIVE *                                   18
Paul Mayersberg        FRANCE/UK        1985

*Oliver Reed, Irina Brook, Corinne Dacla, Xavier Deluc, Hiro Arai, Nick Reding*

A young heiress is kidnapped by a bunch of rich kids playing at being terrorists. Arty and irritating film with nothing of interest to say.
Aka: HEROINE

| DRA | 97 min |
| B,V | VIR |

## CAPTIVE **                                 18
Robert Emenegger/Allan Sandler
USA        1980

*David Ladd, Cameron Mitchell, Lori Sanders, Dan Sturkie, Donald Bishop, Ashley Emenegger, Dan Sandler, Michael Gregory, Augie Tribach, Helen Price Marshall, Jerry Prell, Michael Catlin, Robert Emenegger*

Earth is at war with the planet of Styrolia and two aliens crash-land after being shot down by fighters, and take a farming family captive. Average.

FAN                                        91 min
V                                   EXC/CBS; VIR

**CAR CRASH ★★**
Anthony M. Dawson (Antonio Margheriti)
            ITALY/MEXICO/SPAIN              1981
*Joey Travolta, Vittorio Mezzogiorno, John Steiner,*
*Ana Obregon, Ricardo Palacios*
Two American stuntmen have a series of adventures
in Mexico, in this obscure and forgettable action story.
A/AD                                       90 min
B,V,V2                                 3MVID/PVG

**CAR NAPPING ★★**                           PG
Wigbert Wicker   WEST GERMANY              1979
*Eddie Constantine, Adolfo Celi, Anny Duperey, Ivan*
*Desny, Michael Gelabru, Hans Beerhenke, Bernd*
*Stephan*
A young motor car designer plans to steal forty
Porsches in one go. Fair.
Aka: ESCAPADE (VDEL); FORTUNE IS
STANDING AROUND IN THE STREETS, A
THR                                        85 min
B,V,V2                               VUL L/A; VDEL

**CAR TROUBLE ★★★**                           18
David Green            UK                   1985
*Julie Walters, Ian Charleson, Stratford Johns,*
*Vincenzo Ricota, Hazel O'Connor, Dave Hill, Anthony*
*O'Donnell, Vanessa Knox-Mayer, Roger Hume, John*
*Blundell, Veronica Clifford, Laurence Harrington, Jeff*
*Hall, Roy Barraclough*
A young wife is forbidden to drive the family car but
does so, and in the process becomes somewhat entang-
led with a young mechanic. A humorous and percep-
tive farce with Walters and Charleson hilarious as the
ill-fated couple.
COM                                        90 min
B,V                                          TEVP

**CAR WASH ★★**                              PG
Michael Schultz        USA                 1976
*Richard Pryor, Irwin Corey, George Carlin, Franklin*
*Ajaye, Ivan Dixon, Melanie Mayron, The Pointer*
*Sisters, Garrett Morris, Antonio Fargas*
A boisterous, offbeat comedy set in a Los Angeles car
wash to the music of Rose Royce and The Pointer
Sisters. More a collection of vignettes than a coherent
story, and all done to music too. Often funny, but its
unevenness is a drawback. Written by Joel Schu-
macher.
COM                                        92 min
V/h                                           CIC

**CARAVAN OF COURAGE:**                        U
**AN EWOK ADVENTURE ★★★**
John Korty             USA                  1984
*Eric Walker, Warwick Davis, Fionnuala Flanagan,*
*Guy Boyd, Daniel Frishman, Debbie Carrington, Tony*
*Cox, Kevin Thompson, Maragarita Fernandez, Pam*
*Grizz, Bobby Bell, Aubree Miller, Burl Ives (narration)*
A spin-off from the STAR WARS films, with two
children who are searching for their parents crash-
landing on a strange planet and being rescued by the
Ewoks – the benevolent creatures that inhabit it. A
wholesome kid's adventure packed with visual mar-
vels. Producer George Lucas' first TV movie, and
followed by EWOKS: THE BATTLE FOR ENDOR.
Aka: CARAVAN OF COURAGE; EWOK
ADVENTURE, THE
Boa: story by George Lucas.
FAN                     95 min (ort 100 min) mTV
B,V                                           CBS

**CARAVAN TO VACCARES ★★**                   15
Geoffrey Reeve    FRANCE/UK                1974
*Charlotte Rampling, David Birney, Michel Lonsdale,*
*Michael Bryant, Marcel Bozzuffi, Manitas De Plata,*
*Serge Marquand, Marianne Eggerickx, Francois*

*Brion, Graham Hill, Jean-Pierre Cargol, Jean-Pierre*
*Castaldi, Gordon Tanner*
A plot to smuggle a Hungarian scientist to the US,
involves an American drifter and his girlfriend.
Others, however, are after him and will stop at
nothing to get him. An uneven and flat thriller that
could have worked with tighter direction and editing.
Boa: novel by Alistair MacLean.
A/AD                          81 min (ort 98 min)
B,V DFS L/A; RNK L/A; VGM (VHS only); PARK
(VHS only); XTACY/KRP

**CARAVANS ★★**
James Fargo          IRAN/USA              1978
*Anthony Quinn, Jennifer O'Neill, Michael Sarrazin,*
*Christopher Lee, Joseph Cotten, Barry Sullivan*
A James Michener novel forms the basis for this story,
of a diplomat who is sent back to the Middle East, for
the daughter of a US senator who has married an
Arab and joined a Bedouin caravan. A glossy 1940s
style adventure yarn, lacking pace and focus.
Boa: novel by James Michener.
A/AD                                      129 min
B,V,V2                                        GHV

**CARBON COPY ★★**                           15
Michael Schultz        USA                 1981
*George Segal, Susan St James, Denzel Washington,*
*Jack Warden, Dick Martin, Paul Winfield, Tom Poston*
A successful corporate executive who has hidden the
fact that he is Jewish from his colleagues, gets a
sudden shock when his black 17-year-old illegitimate
son turns up. A blend of social drama and comedy that
scatters a few laughs in several directions, but
ultimately runs out of steam. The script is by Stanley
Shapiro.
COM                           87 min (ort 92 min)
B,V                                           GHV

**CARD, THE ★★★**
Ronald Neame           UK                  1952
*Alec Guinness, Glynis Johns, Valerie Hobson, Petula*
*Clark, Edward Chapman, Veronica Turleigh, George*
*Devine, Joan Hickson, Frank Pettingell, Gibb*
*McLaughlin, Michael Hordern, Alison Leggatt,*
*Wilfrid Hyde-White*
A bright young clerk finds that there are many ways
in which he can improve his social status (and his
bank balance). A lively and endearing comedy,
scripted by Eric Ambler.
Aka: PROMOTER, THE
Boa: novel by Arnold Bennett.
DRA                                    90 min B/W
B,V                                           RNK

**CARDIAC ARREST ★★**
Murray Mintz      USA     1975 (released 1980)
*Garry Goodrow, Mike Chan, Maxwell Gail, Susan*
*O'Connell, Ray Reinhardt*
The San Francisco police are baffled by a bizarre
series of murders in which the victim's hearts have
been removed with surgical precision. Average mur-
der mystery of no great merit.
THR                                        90 min
B,V                          POLVID/CEN L/A; HOK

**CARE BEARS' ADVENTURE IN WONDERLAND,**
**THE ★★**                                    U
Raymond Jafelice     CANADA                1987
*Voices of: Bob Dermer, Eva Almos, Dan Hennessy, Jim*
*Henshaw, Colin Fox*
This insipid and dull cartoon animation has the Care
Bears following Alice through the looking glass and
embarking on a series of adventures. The music is by
John Sebastion.
CAR                           72 min (ort 75 min)
B,V                                           VIR

**CARE BEARS MOVIE 2:**      U
**A NEW GENERATION ***
Dale Schott      USA      1986
*Voices of: Hadley Kay, Chris Wiggins, Cree Summer
Francks, Alyson Court, Dan Hennessey, Michael
Fantini, Sunny Besen Thrasher, Maxine Miller, Pam
Hyatt, Brillie Mae Richards, Eva Almos, Bob Dormer,
Patrice Black, Nonnie Griffin*
Sugary and shallow animation telling of the Care
Bears and their adventures in the Kingdom of Caring.
Made with neither imagination, care nor wit, this is a
fine example of a cartoon that ties in with marketing
concepts but has no merits in its own right. A dismal
conveyer-belt type production.
CAR      77 min
V      RCA

**CARE BEARS MOVIE, THE *****      U
Arna Selznick      USA      1985
*Voices of: Harry Dean Stanton, Georgia Engel, Mickey
Rooney, Jackie Burroughs, Sunny Besen Thrasher*
Full-length cartoon about a group of lovable bears
who perform good deeds by helping lonely and unhap-
py children. Based on heavily merchandised charac-
ters, this soppy and sentimental animation will
appeal to toddlers; older kids will find it tiresome.
Music is by Carole King with narration by Mickey
Rooney.
Boa: story by Frank M. Bickham.
CAR      75 min (ort 90 min)
B,V      VES

**CAREFREE *****      U
Mark Sandrich      USA      1938
*Fred Astaire, Ginger Rogers, Ralph Bellamy, Luella
Gear, Clarence Kolb, Jack Carson, Franklin
Pangborn, Walter Kingsford, Hattie McDaniel*
Typical Astaire and Rogers vehicle with the story of a
psychologist falling for one of his wacky female
patients sent to him by his best friend. The plot is
paper-thin but this happy and enjoyable musical has
some outstanding Irving Berlin numbers such as
"Change Partners" and "I Used To Be Color Blind".
Osca: EASY LIVING (KVD)
MUS      79 min (ort 81 min) B/W
B,V      VCC; KVD

**CAREFUL, HE MIGHT HEAR YOU *****      PG
Carl Schultz      AUSTRALIA      1983
*Wendy Hughes, Nicholas Gledhill, Robyn Nevin, John
Hargreaves, Geraldine Turner*
Depression-era tale with twins, one poor and the other
wealthy, fighting a legal battle over custody of their
nephew, following the death of his mother and the
abandonment of his father. A sensitive and absorbing
drama, well acted and made with considerable care.
Boa: novel Signs Of Life by Summer Locke Elliott.
DRA      116 min
B,V      IPC/PVG

**CAREY TREATMENT, THE *****      15
Blake Edwards      USA      1972
*James Coburn, Pat Hingle, Jennifer O'Neill, Skye
Aubrey, Elizabeth Allen, Alex Dreier*
Medical whodunnit set in a Boston hospital, and
revolving round the efforts of a pathologist, to clear a
colleague who has been charged with performing an
abortion on the chief surgeon's fifteen-year-old daugh-
ter. A competent and involved thriller, filmed in
Boston.
Boa: novel The Case Of Need by J. Hudson.
THR      101 min
B,V,V2      MGM

**CARHOPS, THE *****      18
Peter Locke      USA      1980
*Kitty Carl, Fay De Witt, Lisa Ferringer, Pamela Miller,
Marcie Barkin. Jack DeLeon*

Three girlecome waitresses at a busy drive-in res-
taurant and have many sexual adventures.
Aka: CALIFORNIA DRIVE-IN GIRLS (PANA or
DIAM); KITTY CAN'T HELP IT
A      81 min; 84 min (DIAM) Cut (49 sec)
B,V      DER/MOV L/A; PORVI; PHE; PANA; DIAM

**CARIBE *****      18
Michael Kennedy      CANADA      1987
*John Savage, Kera Glover, Stephen McHattie, Sam
Malkin, Zack Neiss*
Action tale in which a beautiful munitions sales-
woman travels with her partner to Central America,
where they hope to sell dynamite to the local revolu-
tionaries and make their fortune from the deal. When
her partner is killed and the arms they were to deliver
are stolen, she is forced to run for her life.
A/AD      85 min
B,V      VES

**CARMEN *****      PG
Francesco Rosi      FRANCE/ITALY      1984
*Julia Migenes-Johnson, Placido Domingo, Ruggero
Raimnodi, Faith Esham, Jean-Philippe Lafont,
Gerard Gardino*
This poor film production of the famous opera is stilted
and awkward in just about every way except for the
singing. On TV the deficiencies are even more appa-
rent, in a film that's best appreciated with one's eyes
closed.
Boa: opera by Bizet.
PER      148 min (ort 152 min)
V/sh      RCA

**CARMEN *****      15
Carlos Saura      SPAIN      1983
*Antonio Gades, Laura Del Sol, Paco de Lucia, Cristina
Hayos, Juan Antonio Jimenez, Sebastian Moreno*
Flamenco interpretation of Bizet's famous opera with
the action set among the members of a dance company
and following the exploits of a choreographer, who is
captivated by the women he is to cast in the title role.
Considerably more spirited than many a more conven-
tional interpretation, with superb performances from
Gades and Del Sol.
Boa: opera by Bizet.
MUS      103 min; 97 min (VIR)
B,V      FOD; VIR (VHS only)

**CARMEN BABY *****      18
Radley Metzger      NETHERLANDS      1967
*Barbara Valentine, Claude Ringer, Uta Levka, Walter
Wiltz, Carl Mohner*
Fairly unmemorable softcore version of Carmen.
A      82 min
B,V      ABC; NET

**CARNAL GAMES *****
Ralph Lander      USA
*John Leslie, C.J. Laing, Sharon Mitchell, Jake
Teague,*
The tale of a middle-aged wealthy man who marries a
woman because she looks exactly like his sister, who
was killed in a car crash. He used to enjoy watching
his sister make love to her various suitors prior to
making love to him and aims to employ his new wife
in the same way. A rather kinky tale, not badly acted,
but the extended orgy scene and incestuous elements,
will be certain to lose sections to the UK censor.
A      90 min
V      RIP

**CARNAL KNOWLEDGE *****      18
Mike Nichols      USA      1971
*Jack Nicholson, Candice Bergen, Art Garfunkel, Ann-
Margret, Rita Moreno, Carol Kane*
This perceptive and thoughtful look at the changing
sexual attitudes of two men, from college youthfulness
through to middle age, is undeniably absorbing but

ultimately a depressing experience. Scripted by Jules
Feiffer with an excellent performance from Ann-
Margret as Nicholson's sexy mistress.
DRA                                    96 min
B,V,LV                    CBS; EHE; CH5 (VHS only)

**CARNAL REVENGE ***                    18
Alfredo Rizzo          ITALY            1974
*Erna Schurer, Femi Benussi, Mario Pisu, Pupo De
Luca, Carlo Rizzo, Jacques Stangslave, Fiorella
Galgano, Michelina Cavalierre*
Sex film that tells the erotic tale of two randy girls
who use their wiles to win the favours of a wealthy
count.
Aka CARNALITA; EROTIC REVENGE; HOT
PLAYMATES (ELV)
A              85 min; 80 min (ELV); 95 min (ATLAN)
B,V                       ACV; ELV; ATLAN

**CARNIVAL OF BLOOD ***                 18
Leonard Kirtman        USA             1971
*Burt Young, Earle Egerton, Judith Resnick*
A maniac is on the loose in a carnival park, in this
gruesome but unmemorable effort.
HOR                        78 min; 85 min (WIZ)
B,V                             VPD; WIZ

**CARNY ****                            18
Robert Kaylor          USA             1980
*Gary Busey, Jodie Foster, Meg Foster, R Robertson,
Bert Remsen, Kenneth McMillan, John Lehne, Elisha
Cook, Craig Wasson*
Two carnival hustlers fall in love with a young
runaway who joins them on the road. An intimate and
atmospheric look at life on the road, with a great score
by Alex North. The abrupt ending is, however, a
letdown. Co-written by Robertson.
DRA                       107 min; 102 min (CINE)
B,V,V2          CBS; CINE (Betamax and VHS only)

**CAROLANN ***                          15
Tony Wharmby           USA             1989
*Burt Reynolds, Ossie Davis, Deborah Raffin*
A Miami private eye becomes involved in a case in
which an Arab arms dealer was blown up on his
private yacht, and discovers that the man's wife is an
old school friend. He is given the task of protecting
her. Another film in the "Stryker" series. See also
THE DANCER'S TOUCH, BLIND CHESS and DIR-
TY DIAMONDS.
THR                            90 min mTV
V                                  CIC

**CAROUSEL ****                          U
Henry King             USA             1956
*Gordon MacRae, Shirley Jones, Cameron Mitchell,
Barbara Ruick, Claramae Turner, Robert Rounseville,
Gene Lockhart*
A rough carnival barker tries to improve when he
marries, but is killed while committing a robbery to
provide for his child. However, he has another chance
to put his affairs in order. A colourful but stilted film
version of the famous musical, based in its turn on a
fantasy play. Songs include "If I Love You", "Solilo-
quy" and "You'll Never Walk Alone". Filmed before as
"Liliom" in 1930 and 1934. The use of super-wide-
screen will be lost on TV.
Boa: play Liliom by Ferenc Molnar/musical by
Richard Rodgers and Oscar Hammerstein.
MUS                            128 min
V                                  CBS

**CARPENTER, THE ****                    18
David Wellington       USA             1987
*Wings Hauser, Lynn Adams, Pierre Lenoir, Barbara-
Ann Jones, Beverly Murray*
A young couple move into their new home and proceed
to renovate it, but soon discover that it's haunted by
the spirit of the former occupant, a demented mass

murderer. Quite an effective little chiller.
HOR                            90 min
V                                  PARK

**CARQUAKE ***
Paul Bartel      HONG KONG/USA         1976
*David Carradine, Bill McKinney, Veronica Hamel,
Robert Carradine, Judy Canova, Carl Gotleib, Roger
Corman, Sylvester Stallone, Martin Scorsese,
Jonathan Kaplan, Joe Dante*
There are no holds barred in an illegal cross-country
car race with a grand prize of $100,000 for the winner.
A low-grade rip-off of THE GUMBALL RALLY with a
few attempts at humour and a clutch of cameo roles.
Aka: CANNONBALL
Osca: SPEEDTRAP (double cassette)
A/AD                           91 min
B,V                                VCL

**CARRIE ***                            18
Brian De Palma         USA             1976
*Sissy Spacek, Amy Irving, Nancy Allen, William Katt,
John Travolta, Piper Laurie, Betty Buckley, P.J. Soles,
Priscilla Pointer*
A girl with terrifying psychic powers finally turns on
the classmates who have tormented her, when they
play a spiteful trick on her at a school dance. A nasty,
depressing film with some gory moments. Screenplay
is by Lawrence D. Cohen. The film debut for Irving,
Buckley and Soles. Believe it or not, this one formed
the basis for a stage musical.
Boa: novel by Stephen King.
HOR                        98 min; 94 min (WHV)
B,V,V2            INT/CBS; WHV (VHS only)

**CARRIER, THE ***                      18
Nathan J. White        USA             1987
*Gregory Fortescue, Steve Lee, Steve Dixon*
When a small American town is cut off from the world
by the effects of a violent storm, the townsfolk
struggle to escape from death. Average.
HOR                            94 min
V/h                                MED

**CARRINGTON V.C. ****
Anthony Asquith        UK              1954
*David Niven, Margaret Leighton, Noelle Middleton,
Maurice Denham, Geoffrey Keen, Laurence Naismith,
Clive Morton, Mark Dignam, Allan Cuthbertson, John
Glyn-Jones, Victor Maddern, Newton Blick, Raymond
Francis, John Chandos*
Courtroom drama about an army major who has
embezzled regimental funds and is subsequently
court-martialled. As the story unfolds, the reasons
behind this become clear, in this solid and absorbing
tale.
Aka: COURT MARTIAL
Boa: play by Dorothy Campbell Christie.
DRA              102 min (ort 106 min) B/W
B,V                                CBS

**CARRY ON ABROAD ***                    PG
Gerald Thomas          UK              1972
*Sidney James, Kenneth Williams, Charles Hawtrey,
Joan Sims, Kenneth Connor, Peter Butterworth,
Jimmy Logan, Barbara Windsor, June Whitfield,
Hattie Jacques, Bernard Besslaw, Derek Francis, Sally
Geeson, Carol Hawkins*
This time round, a holiday abroad is not quite what
the brochures promised, when a bunch of English
tourists find themselves spending their holiday at an
unfinished hotel in the Mediterranean.
COM        89 min; 85 min (VCC) (Cut at film release)
B,V                 RNK; FUTVI; VCC (VHS only)

**CARRY ON AGAIN, DOCTOR ***              PG
Gerald Thomas          UK              1969
*Sidney James, Kenneth Williams, Charles Hawtrey,
Jim Dale, Joan Sims, Hattie Jacques, Barbara*

*Windsor, Patsy Rowlands, Peter Butterworth, Patricia Hayes, William Mervyn, Harry Locke, Valerie Leon, Elspeth Baxter, Wilfrid Brambell*
More medical antics from the same team who brought you CARRY ON DOCTOR etc. In this one a surgeon sets up a slimming clinic using a potion supplied by an island orderly.
COM   88 min; 85 min (VCC or FUTVI) (Cut at film release)
B,V   RNK; FUTVI; VCC (VHS only)

## CARRY ON AT YOUR CONVENIENCE **   PG
Gerald Thomas   UK   1971
*Sidney James, Kenneth Williams, Charles Hawtrey, Joan Sims, Hattie Jacques, Bernard Bresslaw, Kenneth Cope, Jacki Piper, Richard O'Callaghan, Patsy Rowlands, Bill Maynard, Davy Kaye, Margaret Nolan, Renee Houston, Harry Towb*
This farce is set on the premises of Messrs W.C. Boggs and Sons, manufacturers of fine toiletware, and follows the exploits of the factory foreman, whose pet budgie is able to predict race winners. A tired and dated effort.
COM   86 min (ort 90 min) (Cut at film release)
B,V   RNK; FUTVI; VCC (VHS only)

## CARRY ON BEHIND **   PG
Gerald Thomas   UK   1975
*Elke Sommer, Kenneth Williams, Joan Sims, Bernard Bresslaw, Jack Douglas, Windsor Davies, Kenneth Connor, Liz Fraser, Peter Butterworth, Patsy Rowlands, Adrienne Posta, Ian Lavender, Carol Hawkins, Patricia Franklin*
A professor of archaeology and his attractive assistant find that they are sharing a caravan site with a lot of buxom beauties. Average.
COM   87 min (ort 90 min) (Cut at film release)
B,V   RNK; FUTVI; VCC (VHS only)

## CARRY ON CABBY **   PG
Gerald Thomas   UK   1963
*Sidney James, Hattie Jacques, Kenneth Connor, Charles Hawtrey, Esma Cannon, Liz Fraser, Bill Owen, Milo O'Shea, Judith Furse, Ambrosine Philpotts, Renee Houston, Jim Dale, Cyril Chamberlain*
The neglected wife of a taxi firm owner decides to get her own back by setting up a rival business staffed by buxom girls. Originally entitled "Call Me A Cab" but later retitled to form part of the "Carry On" series.
Aka: CALL ME A CAB
COM   88 min (ort 91 min) B/W
V/h   WHV

## CARRY ON CAMPING *   PG
Gerald Thomas   UK   1968
*Sidney James, Kenneth Williams, Charles Hawtrey, Terry Scott, Joan Sims, Barbara Windsor, Hattie Jacques, Dilys Laye, Bernard Bresslaw, Peter Butterworth, Julian Holloway, Betty Marsden, Trisha Noble*
Two men hit on the idea of going on a camping site holiday in Devon as a way of stimulating their unresponsive girlfriends. Later various other groups arrive, including a bunch of hippies intent on holding a pop festival. One of the weakest of the "Carry On" films.
COM   85 min (ort 88 min)
B,V   RNK

## CARRY ON CLEO **   PG
Gerald Thomas   UK   1965
*Sidney James, Kenneth Williams, Kenneth Connor, Amanda Barrie, Joan Sims, Charles Hawtrey, Jim Dale, Julie Stevens, Victor Maddern, Sheila Hancock, David Davenport, Jon Pertwee, Tanya Billing, Francis de Wolff, Tom Clegg*
Now it's the turn of Cleopatra to get the treatment – in Rome in 50 B.C., British slaves save Caesar from

assassination at the hands of an ambitious soldier and the Egyptian Queen.
COM   92 min; 88 min (WHV) (Cut at film release)
B, V/h   TEVP; WHV (VHS only)

## CARRY ON CONSTABLE **   U
Gerald Thomas   UK   1959
*Sid James, Eric Barker, Kenneth Connor, Charles Hawtrey, Leslie Phillips, Joan Sims, Hattie Jacques, Shirley Eaton, Cyril Chamberlain, Joan Hickson, Irene Handl, Terence Longdon, Jill Adams, Freddie Mills*
This early entry to this long-running series is set in a police training college, and looks at the various mishaps that occur when a new bunch of students arrive. Slightly amusing in a rather episodic way.
COM   83 min (ort 86 min) (Cut at film release) B/W
V/h   WHV

## CARRY ON COWBOY **   PG
Gerald Thomas   UK   1965
*Sid James, Kenneth Williams, Jim Dale, Percy Herbert, Joan Sims, Davy Kaye, Bernard Bresslaw, Charles Hawtrey, Peter Butterworth, Angela Douglas, Sydney Bromley, Sally Douglas, Joan Pertwee, Edina Ronay, Peter Gilmore*
A former sanitary engineer takes over a town in the Wild West as their new sheriff, and a girl helps him thwart an outlaw who shot her father. An inept period comedy that now looks very dated.
Aka: RUMPO KID, THE
COM   91 min (ort 95 min) (Cut at film release)
B, V/h   TEVP; JVC L/A; WHV (VHS only)

## CARRY ON CRUISING **   U
Gerald Thomas   UK   1962
*Sidney James, Kenneth Williams, Liz Fraser, Kenneth Connor, Dilys Laye, Lance Percival, Jimmy Thompson, Cyril Chamberlain, Esma Cannon, Vincent Ball*
The captain of the "Happy Wanderer" has to contend with the fact that, just prior to setting sail on a Mediterranean cruise, the crew of his luxury liner has been replaced with a bunch of inexperienced incompetents. This was the first colour "Carry On" film but the episodic plot of mishaps and risque jokes remains unchanged.
COM   86 min (ort 89 min)
V/h   WHV

## CARRY ON DICK **   PG
Gerald Thomas   UK   1974
*Sidney James, Barbara Windsor, Kenneth Williams, Hattie Jacques, Bernard Bresslaw, Joan Sims, Kenneth Connor, Peter Butterworth, Jack Douglas, Patsy Rowlands, Bill Maynard, Margaret Nolan, John Clive, David Lodge, George Moon*
More broad comedy of the nudge-nudge wink-wink variety based on the legend of Dick Turpin, with our highwayman posing as a village vicar in order to outwit the Bow Street Runners. A pleasant costumed outing.
COM   89 min; 86 min (FUTVI or VCC) (ort 91 min)
B,V   RNK; FUTVI; VCC (VHS only)

## CARRY ON DOCTOR *   PG
Gerald Thomas   UK   1968
*Frankie Howerd, Sidney James, Kenneth Williams, Charles Hawtrey, Jim Dale, Barbara Windsor, Joan Sims, Hattie Jacques, Anita Harris, Bernard Bresslaw, Peter Butterworth, Dilys Laye, Derek Francis, Peter Jones, Dandy Nichols*
None of these medical spoofs are much good; this one is no exception. It follows the exploits of a group of patients who revolt against the medical staff, plus the misadventures of a charlatan who thinks he's only got a week to live – but don't pity him, pity us. Very poor.

COM               91 min (ort 94 min)
B,V          RNK; FUTVI; VCC (VHS only)

### CARRY ON DON'T LOSE YOUR HEAD ***  PG
Gerald Thomas       UK           1966
*Sidney James, Kenneth Williams, Joan Sims, Jim Dale, Charles Hawtrey, Dany Robin, Peter Butterworth, Peter Gilmore, Michael Ward, Leon Greene, Diana Macnamara*
One of the best of the "Carry On" films, this is a fairly amusing send-up of the Scarlet Pimpernel story. Here our hero is called The Black Fingernail, and easily outwits the leaders of the French Revolution in his fight to save members of the French nobility from the guillotine.
Aka: DON'T LOSE YOUR HEAD
COM      87 min (ort 90 min) (Cut at film release)
B,V             RNK; VCC (VHS only)

### CARRY ON EMMANUELLE **
Gerald Thomas       UK           1978
*Suzanne Danielle, Kenneth Williams, Kenneth Connor, Jack Douglas, Joan Sims, Peter Butterworth, Larry Dann, Beryl Reid, Henry McGee, Howard Nelson, Claire Davenport, Norman Mitchell, Tricia Newby, Robert Dorning, Bruce Boa*
Spoof on the well-known sex film with the sexually unsatisfied wife of the French ambassador causing various mishaps.
COM              78 min (ort 88 min)
B,V,V2                  VCL

### CARRY ON ENGLAND **  PG
Gerald Thomas       UK           1976
*Kenneth Connor, Windsor Davies, Patrick Mower, Judy Geeson, Joan Sims, Jack Douglas, Diane Langton, Melvyn Hayes, Peter Joans, David Lodge, Peter Butterworth, Julian Holloway, Johnny Briggs, Brian Osborne, Jeremy Connor*
A mixed sex anti-aircraft battery of 1940 is the setting for this wartime Carry On comedy. The plot revolves around the attempts of their C.O. to thwart their sexual shenanigans. A weak and foolish story whose risque jokes dealing with sexual and bodily functions, now look remarkably stale.
COM    86 min; 84 min (VCC or FUTVI) (ort 89 min) (Cut at film release)
B,V          RNK; FUTVI; VCC (VHS only)

### CARRY ON FOLLOW THAT CAMEL **  PG
Gerald Thomas       UK           1967
*Phil Silvers, Kenneth Williams, Jim Dale, Charles Hawtrey, Joan Sims, Angela Douglas, Peter Butterworth, Bernard Bresslaw, Anita Harris, John Bluthal, William Mervyn, Peter Gilmore, Vincent Ball*
This time the Foreign Legion gets the "Carry On" treatment, with an English gentleman who has been accused of fraud, joining up and saving the fort from Arab attackers.
Aka: FOLLOW THAT CAMEL
COM            94 min; 91 min (VCC)
B,V           RNK; VCC (VHS only)

### CARRY ON GIRLS **  PG
Gerald Thomas       UK           1973
*Sidney James, Joan Sims, Kenneth Connor, Barbara Windsor, Bernard Bresslaw, June Whitfield, Peter Butterworth, Jack Douglas, Patsy Rowlands, Joan Hickson, David Lodge, Valerie Leon, Margaret Nolan, Sally Geeson*
When Sid Fidler bulldozes Fircombe Council into holding a beauty contest, the local Women's Lib Action Group opposes the plan. Average "Carry On" capers.
COM     88 min; 84 min (VCC or FUTVI) (Cut at film release)
B,V          RNK; FUTVI; VCC (VHS only)

### CARRY ON HENRY ***  PG
Gerald Thomas       UK           1971
*Sidney James, Kenneth Williams, Joan Sims, Charles Hawtrey, Terry Scott, Barbara Windsor, Kenneth Connor, Julian Holloway, Peter Gilmore, Julian Orchard, Gertan Klauber, David Davenport, William Mervyn, Bill Maynard*
Period farce in this comedy series which takes a look at Henry VII and two of his wives, one of whom is a garlic-loving woman who gets pregnant by her lover. One of the better "Carry On" films, with James at his lecherous, leering best.
COM              87 min (ort 89 min)
B,V          RNK; FUTVI; VCC (VHS only)

### CARRY ON JACK **  PG
Gerald Thomas       UK           1963
*Bernard Cribbins, Kenneth Williams, Juliet Mills, Charles Hawtrey, Jim Dale, Peter Gilmore, Donald Huston, Percy Herbert, Ed Devereaux, Ian Wilson, Barry Gosney, George Woodbridge, Cecil Parker, Frank Forsyth, Jimmy Thompson*
The mixture as before. This time, the Carry On team direct their efforts towards spoofing the British Navy in 1805. This was the first film in the series to use period costumes.
Aka: CARRY ON SAILOR; CARRY ON VENUS
COM        87 min (Cut at film release)
V/h                  WHV

### CARRY ON LOVING *  PG
Gerald Thomas       UK           1970
*Sidney James, Kenneth Williams, Charles Hawtrey, Joan Sims, Hattie Jacques, Terry Scott, Richard O'Callaghan, Bernard Bresslaw, Jacki Piper, Imogen Hassall, Julian Holloway, Joan Hickson, Janet Mahoney, Bill Maynard*
Action is set in a phoney marriage agency run by Sid James and Hattie Jacques. Nineteenth in the "Carry On" series and one of the poorer efforts.
COM    90 min; 86 min (VCC or FUTVI) (Cut at film release)
B,V          RNK; FUTVI; VCC (VHS only)

### CARRY ON MATRON *  PG
Gerald Thomas       UK           1972
*Sidney James, Kenneth Williams, Hattie Jacques, Charles Hawtrey, Barbara Windsor, Terry Scott, Joan Sims, Kenneth Cope, Bernard Bresslaw, Kenneth Connor, Bill Maynard, Jacki Piper, Marianne Stone, Derek Francis*
Another of the hospital comedies in the "Carry On" series and little better than the 1959 film. This one is set in a maternity hospital with James and a team of crooks intent on stealing a supply of birth control pills. The period farces are generally better.
COM    89 min; 86 min (VCC or FUTVI) (Cut at film release)
B,V          RNK; FUTVI; VCC (VHS only)

### CARRY ON NURSE *  PG
Gerald Thomas       UK           1960
*Shirley Eaton, Kenneth Connor, Charles Hawtrey, Hattie Jacques, Wilfrid Hyde-White, Terence Longdon, Bill Owen, Leslie Phillips, Joan Sims, Susan Stephen, Kenneth Williams, Michael Medwin, Susan Beaumont, Ann Firbank*
One of the earliest and feeblest of the "Carry On" films. We are subjected to a display of juvenile antics by patients and staff in a men's hospital ward. A banal plot combines with a paucity of jokes to make this a trial rather than a pleasure. As the series progressed the leading stars developed their personalities – this one is of interest in that it shows a few flashes of undeveloped potential, but little more than that.
COM       83 min (Cut at film release) B/W
B, V/h             TEVP; WHV (VHS only)

**CARRY ON REGARDLESS \*\***                      PG
Gerald Thomas          UK              1961
*Sid James, Charles Hawtrey, Kenneth Williams,*
*Kenneth Connor, Joan Sims, Bill Owen, Liz Fraser,*
*Terence Longdon, Hattie Jacques, Esme Cannon,*
*Sydney Tafler, Julia Arnall, Terence Alexander,*
*Stanley Unwin, Joan Hickson*
The owner of an agency set up to provide temporary
staff for any occasion, endures one comic mishap after
another, from his well-meaning but clumsy staff. As
always, a series of blundering episodes are presented
for our amusement, culminating in the demolition of a
house that the employees merely intended to spruce
up.
COM                    87 min (ort 93 min) B/W
V/h                                   WHV

**CARRY ON SCREAMING \*\***                      PG
Gerald Thomas          UK              1966
*Harry H. Corbett, Kenneth Williams, Fenella Fielding,*
*Charles Hawtrey, Jim Dale, Angela Douglas, Peter*
*Butterworth, Bernard Bresslaw, Jon Pertwee, Tom*
*Clegg, Billy Cornelius, Frank Thornton, Denis Blake*
Lightweight spoof on the horror genre, set in a
potential Dracula Development Area, with a detective
investigating a revived corpse and his vampiric sister,
who vitrifies girls for use as shop-window dummies.
Aka: CARRY ON VAMPIRE
COM                         93 min (ort 97 min)
V/h                                   WHV

**CARRY ON SERGEANT \*\***                       U
Gerald Thomas          UK              1959
*William Hartnell, Bob Monkhouse, Shirley Eaton,*
*Kenneth Connor, Charles Hawtrey, Kenneth Williams,*
*Terence Longdon, Hattie Jacques, Gerald Campion,*
*Cyril Chamberlain, Gorden Tanner, Frank Forsyth,*
*Basil Dignam, John Gatrell*
The very first of the "Carry On" films, this feeble
comedy centres on the experiences of a bunch of raw
recruits at an army training unit. Hartnell plays a
sergeant who accepts a bet that the last squad he is to
train before retiring, will win the "Star Squad" award.
A creaky farce that is slightly redeemed by energetic
performances.
Boa: novel The Bull Boys by R.F. Delderfield.
COM                           80 min B/W
V/h                                   WHV

**CARRY ON SPYING \*\***                         U
Gerald Thomas          UK              1964
*Barbara Windsor, Kenneth Williams, Bernard*
*Cribbins, Charles Hawtrey, Eric Barker, Dilys Laye,*
*Jim Dale, Richard Wattis, Eric Pohlman, Victor*
*Maddern, Judith Furse, John Bluthal, Renee Houston*
Windsor plays a trainee spy who joins the rather inept
British Secret Service, hoping to put her talents (such
as a photographic memory) to good use. In the
company of three other trainee spies, she is sent to
Vienna and Algiers to prevent a secret formula falling
into the hands of a bisexual mastermind.
COM                          84 min (ort 87 min)
V/h                                   WHV

**CARRY ON TEACHER \*\***                        U
Gerald Thomas          UK              1959
*Ted Ray, Charles Hawtrey, Leslie Phillips, Joan Sims,*
*Kenneth Wulliams, Hattie Jacques, Rosalind Knight,*
*Cyril Chamberlain, Richard O'Sullivan, Carol White*
The humour centres on a secondary school with
headmaster Ted Ray, whose pupils get up to an
assortment of pranks when school inspectors visit,
their intention being to block their master's transfer
to another school. Look out for O'Sullivan in an early
appearance as one of the pupils.
COM      83 min (ort 86 min) (Cut at film release) B/W
V/h                                   WHV

**CARRY ON UP THE JUNGLE \*\***                  PG
Gerald Thomas          UK              1970
*Sid James, Kenneth Connor, Joan Sims, Frankie*
*Howerd, Charles Hawtrey, Terry Scott, Kenneth*
*Connor, Bernard Bresslaw, Jacki Piper, Reuben*
*Martin, Valerie Leon*
An explorer recalls his amazing adventures in darkest
Africa when, whilst searching for a rare bird, he was
captured by a tribe of girls. A slight and lacklustre
spoof on jungle adventure films, with Scott doing his
Tarzan bit as Jungle Boy.
COM                         87 min (ort 89 min)
B,V                      RNK L/A; VCC (VHS only)

**CARRY ON UP THE KHYBER \*\*\***                PG
Gerald Thomas          UK              1968
*Sidney James, Kenneth Williams, Charles Hawtrey,*
*Joan Sims, Roy Castle, Terry Scott, Bernard Bresslaw,*
*Peter Butterworth, Angela Douglas, Cardew Robinson,*
*Julian Holloway, Leon Thau, Alexandra Dane, Jeremy*
*Spenser*
This is one of the best "Carry On" films and is set in
the North West Frontier during the British Raj, when
fearless British soldiers faced hostile Afghan tribes-
men undaunted. Full of the usual double entendres
and with a stronger plot than was usual for this series.
COM                         86 min (Cut at film release)
B,V                    RNK; FUTVI; VCC (VHS only)

**CARTEL \*\***                                  18
John Stewart          USA              1989
*Miles O'Keefe, Don Stroud, Crystal Carson, Suzanne*
*Slater*
A pilot is set up by the leader of a drug-smuggling ring
that had his sister murdered, but escapes from prison
and joins his girlfriend in a vengeance crusade. A
fast-paced action thriller, competently made and
acted.
A/AD                                  95 min
V/h                                   NWV

**CARTHAGE IN FLAMES \*\***                      PG
Carmine Gallone FRANCE/ITALY           1960
*Terence Hill (Mario Girotti), Anne Heywood, Jose*
*Suarez, Pierre Brasseur, Daniel Gelin, Illaria Occhini,*
*Paolo Stoppa, Aldo Silvani, Edith Peters, Erno Crisaa,*
*Ivo Garrani, Cesare Fantoni, Gianric Tadeschi,*
*Fernand Ledoux*
Story of a young slave girl who avenges the death of
the warrior who rescued her, set against the back-
ground of the destruction of Carthage during the
Third Punic War. Good action scenes prop up this
formula tale of love and intrigue.
DRA                                   110 min
B,V,V2                   VDM L/A; VMA; STABL

**CARTIER AFFAIR, THE \*\***                     PG
Rod Holcomb           USA              1984
*Joan Collins, Telly Savalas, David Hasselhoff, Ed*
*Lauter, Stephen Apostle Pec, Jordan Charney, Joe*
*LaDue, Charles Napier, Randi Brooks, Rita Taggart,*
*Jay Gerber, Hilly Hicks, Louisa Moritz, Liz Sheridan,*
*Donald Torres*
The private secretary of a businesswoman is more
interested in getting his hands on her diamonds than
on her, in order to pay off a debt to a former prison
cellmate. Glossy and only moderately amusing,
though Collins does a nice send-up of her public
image.
Boa: story by Eugenie Ross-Leming, Brad Buckner
and Michael Devereaux.
COM                         100 min mTV
B,V                      ODY; CH5 (VHS only)

**CARTOUCHE \*\*\*\***                           PG
Philippe De Broca FRANCE/ITALY         1962
*Jean-Paul Belmondo, Claudia Cardinale, Odile*
*Versois, Philippe Lemaire, Marcel Dalio, Noel*
*Roquevert*

In 18th century France, a group of thieves takes over a Paris crime syndicate, eventually avenging the death of one of their leaders. Based to some extent on a French legend, this vivid blend of action, comedy and drama gave Belmondo and Cardinale roles they clearly relished; they have rarely been better.
Aka: SWORDS OF BLOOD
A/AD                                          114 min
V                                            CASPIC

**CARVE HER NAME WITH PRIDE ***        PG
Lewis Gilbert           UK                   1958
*Virginia McKenna, Paul Scofield, Jack Warner, Denise Grey, Maurice Ronet, Avice Landone, Anne Leon, Nicole Stephane, Billie Whitelaw, William Mervyn, Michael Goodliffe, Bill Owen, Sydney Tafler, Noel Willman*
A low-key account of a young and courageous girl – Violette Szabo, who parachuted into Nazi-occupied Europe as a secret agent, only to be betrayed and executed at Ravensbruck. A restrained and well-acted account that is all the more effective for its semi-documentary style.
Boa: book by R.J. Minney.
WAR                114 min (ort 119 min) B/W
V                                            VCC

**CASABLANCA ****                            U
Michael Curtiz          USA                  1943
*Humphrey Bogart, Ingrid Bergman, Paul Henreid, Claude Rains, Peter Lorre, Conrad Veidt, Sydney Greenstreet, Dooley Wilson, Marcel Dalio, S.K. Sakall, Madeleine LeBeau, Joy Page, John Qualen, Ludwig Stossel, Leonid Kinskey*
By no means a perfect film, but nevertheless one of Hollywood's finest, and used by others as a touchstone for excellence. It tells of the lonely owner of a nightclub in Vichy-controlled Casablanca, and of the brief return of his former lover who now works for the Resistance. A highly enjoyable film that enjoys a classic reputation. AA: Pic, Dir, Screen (Julius Epstein/Phillip G. Epstein/Howard Koch).
Boa: play (unstaged) Everybody Comes To Rick's by Murray Burnett and Joan Alison. DRA   102 min B/W
B,V,V2                              INT/CBS; WHV

**CASANOVA **                               18
Frederico Fellini       ITALY                1976
*Donald Sutherland, Cicely Brown, Tina Aumont, John Karlsen, Daniel Emilfork Berenstein*
Good-looking but essentially flat account of the many adventures of the famous 18th century lover. The music of Nino Rota is a slight compensation in this absurdly stylised and pretentious effort. AA: Cost (Danilo Donati).
Aka: FELLINI'S CASANOVA
A                          147 min (ort 163 min)
V                                            CBS

**CASANOVA: PART 2 ***
Troy Benny              USA                  1982
*John C. Holmes, Jesie St James, Rhonda Jo Petty, Danielle, Bjorn Beck, Sheila Parks, Anne Perry, Carlos Tobalina William Margold, Bill Kershner, Dorian Kupl*
An erotic version of Casanova, that opens in Paris in 1751 with the arrival of Casanova. He wounds a woman who was disguised as a man in the course of a duel, but she recovers sufficiently to get pregnant by him. From here he moves on to greater things, screwing half the women of Europe with the aid of a secret aphrodisiac perfume. Costumes and acting are good in a rather lighthearted tale that has its conclusion in the 20th century.
A                                            93 min
B,V,V2                                       ELV

**CASANOVA: PARTS 1 AND 2 ***              15
Simon Langton/Ken Russell

USA                                          1987
*Richard Chamberlain, Faye Dunaway, Sylvia Kristel, Ornella Muti, Hanna Schygulla, Sophie Ward, Frank Finlay*
Another attempt to bring the story of the famous lover of the 17th century to the screen. This lighthearted romp is helped along by the witty script of George MacDonald Fraser and is directed with considerable verve. It's only drawback is its excessive running time.
DRA                 168 min (2 cassettes) mTV
B,V                                          WHV

**CASE CLOSED **                            15
Dick Lowry              USA                  1988
*Byron Allen, Charles Durning, Marc Alaimo, James Greene, Eddie Jones, Erica Gimpel, Christopher Neame, Charles Weldan*
A misfire cops versus robbers comedy, with a young police detective teaming up with a retired cop to solve three murders and a jewel theft. A senseless and unfunny attempt to cash in on the success of BEVERLY HILLS COP and those similar 1980s cop comedies. This one's written and co-produced by former stand-up comic Allen.
COM                  92 min (ort 100 min) mTV
B,V                                          CBS

**CASE OF DEADLY FORCE, A ***              PG
Michael Miller          USA                  1986
*Richard Crenna, John Shea, Lorraine Toussaint, Frank McCarthy, Tom Isbell, Tate Donovan, Michael O'Hare, Dylan Baker, Anna Maria Horsford, Elizabeth J. Fowler, Tracy Fitzpatrick, Kristin Rhone, Paul O'Brien, Ken Cheeseman*
A black widow hires a lawyer to clear her husband's name after he was shot by two cops in Boston, and the police force carry out an unsatisfactory investigation. A strong and engrossing drama based on a true case, adapted from O'Donnell's book by Dennis Nemec.
Boa: novel Deadly Force: The Story Of How A Badge Can Become A License To Kill by Lawrence O'Donnell Jr.
DRA               120 min; 91 min (CAREY) mTV
B,V                            WHV L/A; CAREY

**CASE OF HONOUR, A *                       15
Eddie Romero            USA                  1988
*Timothy Bottoms, John Phillip Law*
After having been held for ten years by their Vietnamese captors, five American POWs escape and head for an old helicopter one of them ditched in the jungle years ago. A strictly second-rate adventure yarn.
A/AD                                         88 min
V                                            BRAVE

**CASE OF LIBEL, A **                       PG
Eric Till            CANADA/USA              1983
*Edward Asner, Daniel J. Travanti, Lawrence Dane, Gordon Pinsent, Robin Gammell*
Fair courtroom drama based on Nizer's book about a 1954 libel case, in which a prize-winning war correspondent and a conservative newspaper columnist crossed swords in a legal battle.
Boa: book by Louis Nizer.
DRA                                          92 min mTV
B,V                                          VPD

**CASE OF THE HILLSIDE STRANGLERS, THE ** 18
Steven Gethers          USA                  1988
*Richard Crenna, Dennis Farina, Billy Zane, Tony Plana, Tazia Valenza, James Tolkan, Karen Austin, Roert Harper*
Crenna is one of the investigators trying to track down a nasty serial killer, in this talky and ponderous tale, based on a true series of killings that took place around the L.A. area in the late 1970s.
Aka: HILLSIDE STRANGLERS, THE
DRA                        90 min (ort 96 min)
V                                            CHV

## CASEY'S SHADOW ** PG
Martin Ritt　　　　USA　　　　1978
*Walter Matthau, Alexis Smith, Robert Webber, Murray Hamilton, Andrew A. Rubin, Stephen Burns*
A horse trainer is left to raise his three sons alone when his wife walks out on him, in this amiable but aimless romp.
Boa: short story Ruidoso by John McPhee.
COM　　　　　　　93 min (ort 117 min)
B,V　　　　　　　　　　　　　　RCA

## CASINO ROYALE ** PG
V. Guest/J. Huston/K. Hughes/R. Parrish/J. McGrath/
R. Talmadge
　　　　　　　UK　　　　　1967
*Peter Sellers, David Niven, Ursula Andress, Joanna Pettet, William Holden, Woody Allen, Daliah Lavi, John Huston, Jacqueline Bissett, Peter O'Toole, Derek Nimmo, Charles Boyer, Deborah Kerr, Orson Welles, George Raft*
A perfect illustration of the old adage about too many cooks. This unlucky, unhappy spy spoof – nominally about the retired Sir James Bond being asked to resume active service and join the fight against the evil SMERSH – is such a welter of cliches, overblown effects and poor dialogue that it defies description. Never before has so much talent and money been thrown away in the achievement of so little.
Boa: novel by Ian Fleming.
COM　　　　　　126 min (ort 131 min)
V　　　　　　　　　　　　　　RCA

## CASSANDRA *** 18
Colin Eggleston　　AUSTRALIA　　1987
*Shane Briant, Briony Behets, Kit Taylor, Lee James, Tim Burns, Tessa Humphries, Susan Barling*
A girl begins to investigate the causes of her ghastly nightmares and finds those around her beginning to die in nasty circumstances. A compelling tale that unfortunately has a disappointing resolution, though there are a few nasty jolts along the way.
HOR　　　　　　　89 min (ort 93 min)
B,V　　　　　　　　　　AVS L/A; VIR

## CASSANDRA CROSSING, THE ** PG
George Pan Cosmatos
　　　ITALY/WEST GERMANY/UK　　1976
*Sophia Loren, Richard Harris, Burt Lancaster, Martin Sheen, Ava Gardner, John Phillip Law, Ingrid Thulin, Lee Strasberg, Lionel Stander, Ann Turkel, O.J. Simpson, Ray Lovelock, Alida Valli, Tom Hunter*
Tedious disaster film in which mankind must be saved somehow from a deadly virus, which a terrorist on board a transcontinental train is infected with. Filmed in France and Italy.
DRA　　　　　　123 min (ort 129 min)
B,V　　　　　　　　　　PRV L/A; CH5

## CASTAWAY *** 15
Nicolas Roeg　　　UK　　　　1986
*Oliver Reed, Amanda Donohoe, Tony Rickards, Todd Rippon, Georgina Hale, Frances Barber*
Based on the real-life experiences of Lucy Irving, who responded to an advert from a man seeking a woman to join him for a year on an isolated desert island, far removed from the complexities of civilisation. Visually satisfying, but this tale of conflict and disagreement between two basically rather selfish people eventually loses its impact.
Boa: book by Lucy Irving.
DRA　　　　　　112 min (ort 117 min)
B/sh, V/sh　　　　　　　　　　WHV

## CASTAWAY COWBOY, THE ** U
Vincent McEveety　　USA　　　1974
*James Garner, Vera Miles, Robert Culp, Eric Shea, Elizabeth Smith, Gregory Sierra, Shug Fisher, Manu Tupou*
A Texan is shanghaied to Hawaii in the 1850s, where he helps a widow turn her land into a ranch and fight off the local villain who is after her property. Standard Western plot slightly helped by the Hawaiian locations.
WES　　　　　　　87 min (ort 90 min)
B,V　　　　　　　　　　　　　　WDV

## CASTAWAYS: A LOVE STORY ** 15
John Wilder
*Sabrina Siani, Fabio Meyer*
A man and a woman are castaway on a desert island in this softcore adult adventure. Average.
A　　　　　　　　　　　　　80 min
V　　　　　　　　　TROPIC/CENCOM

## CASTLE KEEP ** 15
Sydney Pollack　　　USA　　　1969
*Burt Lancaster, Peter Falk, Patrick O'Neal, Jean-Pierre Aumont, James Patterson, Scott Wilson, Al Freeman Jr, Tony Bill, Bruce Dern, Astrid Hereen, Michael Conrad*
Classic war story about a group of US soldiers who take over a 10th century castle as a stronghold. It is owned by an aristocrat whose only concern is for his priceless collection of art treasures. Expensive looking but rather uneven adaptation of Eastlake's book, with the strong cast slightly compensating for the deficiencies of the plot.
Boa: novel by William Eastlake.
DRA　　　　　　　　　　　103 min
V/sh　　　　　　　　　　　　　RCA

## CASTLE OF EVIL * 15
Frances D. Lyon　　USA　　　1966
*Scott Brady, Virginia Mayo, David Brian, Lisa Gaye, Hugh Marlowe*
A frightened group of prospective heirs gather on an isolated island in the Caribbean for the reading of a will. They fear that something terrible is going to happen – and sure enough it does; for the deceased was an inventor who created a robot man who now runs amok, killing off the survivors in this laughably ludicrous display of ineptitude.
HOR　　　　　　　　　　　85 min
B,V　　　　　　　　　　　　　VFP

## CASUAL SEX? ** 18
Genevieve Robert　　USA　　　1988
*Lea Thompson, Victoria Jackson, Andrew Dice Clay, Mary Gross, Stephen Stellan, Jerry Levine, Peter Dvorsky*
Two young women on vacation at a health resort cautiously look for that elusive meaningful relationship. A slight romantic comedy for the AIDS age, largely told from the female point of view.
Boa: play by Wendy Goldman and Judy Toll.
COM　　　　　　　　　　　84 min
B,V　　　　　　　　　　　　　CIC

## CASUALTIES OF WAR ** 18
Brian De Palma　　　USA　　　1989
*Michael J. Fox, Sean Penn, Don Harvey, John C. Reilly, John Leguizamo, Thuy Thu Le, Erik King, Sam Robards*
War drama based on a true incident, when an American patrol kidnapped, raped and finally murdered a Vietnamese girl. Fox is the solitary voice of reason in this thought provoking work, but the jumbled script and interminable moralising dilute the strong anti-war sentiments.
Boa: article in the New Yorker by Daniel Lang.
DRA　　　　　　　　　120 min subH
V　　　　　　　　　　　　　　RCA

## CAT AND MOUSE *** 1974
Daniel Petrie　　　USA　　　1974
*Kirk Douglas, Jean Seberg, John Vernon, Bessie Love, Beth Porter, Sam Wanamaker, James Bradford, Suzanne Lloyd, Stuart Chandler, Valerie Colgan,*

*Mavis Villiers, Elliott Sullivan, Robert Sherman, James Berwick*
A mild mannered biology teacher will stop at nothing to have his revenge on his ex-wife, after learning during their divorce proceedings that he is not the father of their son. A taut thriller with a wonderfully sinister performance from Douglas. Douglas' TV movie debut.
Aka: MOUSEY
THR                                   87 min mTV
B,V                                   TEVP

### CAT AND THE CANARY, THE ***                15
Radley Metzger          UK              1978
*Honor Blackman, Edward Fox, Michael Callan, Wendy Hiller, Olivia Hussey, Beatrix Lehmann, Daniel Massey, Carol Lynley, Peter McEnery, Wilfrid Hyde-White*
A comedy suspense tale that has been remade several times. Seven distant relatives gather in a strange house on a stormy night to hear the reading of a will. A nice remake with a few good touches and a strong cast.
Boa: play by John Willard.
THR                       98 min; 94 min (PARK)
B,V,V2        VUL; MIA (VHS only); PARK (VHS only)

### CAT BALLOU **                                PG
Elliott Silverstein     USA             1965
*Jane Fonda, Lee Marvin, Michael Callan, Dwayne Hickman, Tom Nardini, John Marley, Reginald Denny, Jay C. Flippen, Nat King Cole, Stubby Kaye, Arthur Hunnicutt, Bruce Cabot, Burt Mustin, Paul Gilbert, Harvey Clark, Oscar Blank*
Western spoof about a girl who hires a drunken gunfighter to protect her father and turns outlaw when her dad is killed. Very uneven and only funny in a few places. The best thing in this movie is Lee Marvin's two roles – as the drunken gunman and his twin desperado brother (complete with false tin nose). A disappointing effort. The script is by Walter Newman and Frank R. Pierson. AA: Actor (Marvin).
Boa: novel The Ballad Of Cat Ballou by R. Chansler.
COM                          92 min (ort 96 min)
B,V                                    RCA

### CAT CHASER ***                              18
Abel Ferrara            USA             1989
*Peter Weller, Kelly McGillis, Charles Durning, Frederic Forrest, Tomas Milian, Juan Fernandez*
A kind of modern stab at film noir, this follows the exploits of an ex-soldier who now runs a hotel in Santa Domingo. His affair with the wife of the country's head of the secret police plunges him into a world of intrigue, treachery and murder.
Boa: novel by Elmore Leonard.
THR                                   93 min
V                                     EIV

### CAT CITY *                                  PG
                        USA             1987
Set in the year 80 A.M.M. (anno Mickey Mouse), this story tells of a cat organisation out to rid the world of mice. However, the rodents engage a scientist to help them fight back.
CAR                                   96 min
B,V                        APOL; VGM (VHS only)

### CAT FROM OUTER SPACE, THE **               U
Norman Tokar           USA             1978
*Ken Berry, Sandy Duncan, Roddy McDowall, Harry Morgan, MacLean Stevenson, Ronnie Schell*
Silly kid's comedy in which an extra-terrestrial cat seeks the help of US scientists in order to repair its spaceship. A few complications but little in the way of surprises, in this very typical Disney effort.
COM                                   99 min
B,V                                    WDV

### CAT IN A CAGE **
Tony Zarindast          USA             1983
*Behvooz Vossoughi, Sybil Danning, Colleen Camp, Frank DeKova, Tony Bova, Mel Novak*
Members of a wealthy family plan to kill each other, in their attempts to gain an inheritance. Average. Written by Richard Vasques.
Aka: CAT IN THE CAGE
THR                                   100 min
B,V                                    DFS

### CAT ON A HOT TIN ROOF ***                  15
Jack Y. Hofsiss         USA             1984
*Jessica Lange, Tommy Lee Jones, Rip Torn, Kim Stanley, David Dukes, Penny Fuller*
Williams' powerful story of a rich plantation owner who, dying of cancer, is beset with problems caused by his two sons, one being a schemer and the other a neurotic who no longer sleeps with his wife. A more faithful version than the 1958 adaptation, retaining the portions skipped in the earlier work, especially with regard to "Maggie the Cat" and her efforts to get her husband back into her bed.
Boa: play by Tennessee Williams.
DRA                                   148 min mTV
B,V                                    VES/PVG

### CAT ON A HOT TIN ROOF ****                 15
Richard Brooks          USA             1958
*Elizabeth Taylor, Paul Newman, Burl Ives, Jack Carson, Judith Anderson, Madeleine Sherwood, Larry Gates*
Powerful adaptation of a play by Tennessee Williams about a Southern family; an autocratic plantation owner is dying of cancer but still dominates his greedy family who are all, with the exception of one son, competing to win his favour. Adapted by Brooks and James Poe and remade for TV in 1984.
Boa: play by Tennessee Williams.
DRA                          103 min (ort 108 min)
V                                     MGM

### CAT O'NINE TAILS *                          18
Dario Argento
          FRANCE/ITALY/WEST GERMANY      1971
*James Franciscus, Karl Malden, Catherine Spaak, Cinzia De Carolis, Carlo Alighiero*
A former reporter is now blind and spends much of his time doing crossword puzzles. He teams up with an active reporter in order to track down a nasty psycho who has left a gruesome trail of corpses. A brutish murder mystery, loaded with sex and gore and badly dubbed for good measure.
Aka: DIE NEUNSCHWANZIGE KATZE; IL GATTO A NOVE CODE
HOR                                   108 min dubbed
V                                     WHV

### CAT PEOPLE **                               18
Paul Schrader           USA             1982
*Nastassia Kinski, Malcolm McDowell, John Heard, Annette O'Toole, Ruby Dee, Ed Begley Jr, Scott Paulin, John Larroquette*
A not terribly good attempt at a remake of a 1942 film, with a brother and sister having a strange feline ancestry and the power to turn into panthers. This film concentrates more on the sexual aspects of the tale, with Kinski falling in love with a zoo curator whilst a black panther leaves a trail of bloodshed in the community. A good-looking but incoherent story.
HOR                                   112 min
V/h                                    CIC

### CATACLYSM **
Tom McGowan/Greg Tallas/Phillip Marshak
                        USA             1972
*Cameron Mitchell, Faith Cliff, Mark Lawrence, Charles (Richard) Moll, Robert Bristol*
Demonic horror epic that builds up to a blood chilling

climax. It involves a hunt for an SS officer who seems not to have aged at all. Footage from this tale was used in one of the stories in the anthology film NIGHT TRAIN TO TERROR.
Aka: NIGHTMARE NEVER ENDS, THE; SATAN'S SUPPER
HOR                                              94 min
B,V,V2                                    VUL L/A

**CATACOMBS ****                                    18
David Schmoeller        USA              1988
*Timothy Van Patten, Laura Schatta, Jeremy West, Vernon Dobtcheff, John Petter, Mapi Golan, Ian Abercrombie, Donald Pleasence, Katrine Michelson, Feodor Chapliani, Brett Porter*
For hundreds of years an Italian monastery has been haunted by the legend of a demon that once attacked the previous occupiers and is now imprisoned deep within the catacombs of the ancient building. The arrival of a woman at this formerly male-only community, sparks off a series of events that lead to the release of this creature. Formula creature-released-from-hell horror yarn with some nice settings.
HOR                          84 min Cut (12 sec)
V                                               EIV

**CATCH 22 ****                                     15
Mike Nichols            USA              1970
*Alan Arkin, Martin Balsam, Richard Benjamin, Jon Voight, Art Garfunkel, Bob Newhart, Anthony Perkins, Paula Prentiss, Martin Sheen, Orson Welles*
Joseph Heller's brilliant anti-war novel contains so much that no film could ever do it justice. This is a worthy but only partially successful attempt to do so and follows the adventures of Yossarian, a bomber pilot who will do anything so as not to have to go on flying.
Boa: novel by Joseph Heller.
DRA                                             122 min
B,V                                             CIC

**CATCH ME A SPY ***
Dick Clement          FRANCE/UK          1971
*Kirk Douglas, Marlene Jobert, Trevor Howard, Tom Courtenay, Patrick Mower, Bernadette Lafont, Bernard Blier, Sacha Pitoeff, Richard Pearson, Garfield Morgan, Angharad Rees, Isabel Dean, Jonathan Cecil, Robert Raglan*
Pathetic comedy about a British agent who smuggles Russian manuscripts into the UK and falls for the wife of a Russian spy. An uneven mixture of comedy and mystery, filmed in Scotland and Bucharest. The script is by Dick Clement and Ian La Frenais.
Aka: TO CATCH A SPY
Boa: novel by George Marton and Tibor Meray.
COM                          91 min (ort 94 min)
B,V,V2                                          VCL

**CATCH ME IF YOU CAN ****                          PG
Stephen Sommers         USA              1989
*Matt Lattanzi, Loryn Locklin, M. Emmet Walsh, Geoffrey Lewis*
When a high school is threatened with closure, the class president enlists the services of a drag racer and arranges a series of illegal races in order to raise enough money to keep the school open. A pleasant but remarkably bland high school frolic, clearly aimed at the teen set.
A/AD                         101 min (ort 105 min)
V                                               MED

**CATCH US IF YOU CAN ****                          PG
John Boorman            UK               1965
*Dave Clark, Barbara Ferris, Lenny Davidson, Rick Huxley, Mike Smith, Denis Payton, David Lodge, Yootha Joyce, Robin Bailey*
In the company of a model, a group of happy-go-lucky stuntmen have various adventures in the west of England. Boorman's first film is a glossy but empty attempt to capture some of the verve of A HARD DAY'S NIGHT, and do for the Dave Clark Five what the earlier film did for The Beatles. Songs include "I Can't Stand It", "Having A Wild Weekend" and the title song.
Aka: HAVING A WILD WEEKEND
MUS                       87 min (ort 91 min) B/W
V                                               WHV

**CATHERINE CHERIE ****                             18
Hubert Frank
           SPAIN/WEST GERMANY           1982
*Berta Cabre, Micha Kapteijn, Ajita Wilson, Peter Steiner, Dagmar Altman, Racquel Evans, Miguel Avedis*
Predictable sex film with a young girl yearning to become a pop star but finding that her manager only wants to exploit her sexually.
Aka: CATHERINE
A                93 min (ort 97 min) Cut (1 min 17 sec)
B,V                           BLUMO/GOLD; CAN

**CATHIE'S CHILD *****
Donald Crombie         AUSTRALIA         1977
*Michelle Fawdon, Alan Cassell, Harry Michael, Bob Hughes, Sophia Haskas, Sarah McKenzie, Judy Stevenson, Bobbie Ward, Gerry Gallagher, Annibale Migliucci, Arthur Dignam, Willie Fennell*
Moving story of a young mother and her fight to get her 3-year-old daughter back from Greece, where her estranged husband has taken her. She turns to the media for help. Based on a true story.
Aka: CATHY'S CHILD
Boa: book by Dick Wordley.
DRA                                             89 min
B,V                                         ENT/HVP

**CATHOLIC BOYS *****                               15
Michael Dinner          USA              1985
*Donald Sutherland, John Heard, Andrew McCarthy, Mary Stuart Masterson, Kevin Dillon, Malcolm Danare, Jennie Dundas, Kate Reid, Wallace Shawn, Philip Bosco*
A look at the lives of a group of boys studying at a Catholic seminary in Brooklyn in 1965. Often very funny, with a good cameo from Shawn as a priest obsessed with preventing lustfulness. Writing debut for Dinner and Charles Purpura.
Aka: HEAVEN HELP US
DRA                                             99 min
B,V                      TEVP; WHV (VHS only)

**CATLOW *****                                      PG
Sam Wanamaker          UK               1971
*Yul Brynner, Leonard Nimoy, Richard Crenna, Daliah Lavi, Julian Mateos, David Ladd, Bessie Love, Bob Logan, John Clark, Dan Van Husen, Cass Martin, Jeff Corey, Jo Ann Pflug, Jose Nieto, Angel Del Pozo, Victor Israel*
Following the Civil War, an outlaw and drifter is intent on recovering a fortune in gold, but he finds that he is being chased by a former friend who is now a marshal. A lighthearted comedy Western with an unusual role for Brynner.
Boa: novel by Louis L'Amour.
WES                          98 min (ort 101 min) Cut
B,V                                             MGM

**CAT'S EYE ****                                    15
Lewis Teague            USA              1985
*Drew Barrymore, James Woods, Alan King, Kenneth McMillan, Robert Hays, Candy Clark, James Naughton, Tony Munafo, Mary D'Arcy*
Three Stephen King stories form the basis for this compilation film, in all of them a cat provides a linking theme. A trio of nasty tales, all of which are lacking in inventiveness if not in unpleasantness.
Boa: short stories by Stephen King.

HOR 93 min
B,V TEVP

## CATTLE ANNIE AND LITTLE BRITCHES ***
Lamont Johnson  USA  1977
*Burt Lancaster, Rod Steiger, Amanda Plummer,*
*Diane Lane, John Savage, Scott Glenn, Michael*
*Conrad*
The year is 1893, and two girls from the East go West,
join up with the remnants of a gang of robbers and
persuade them to pull off a few more jobs. A likeable
little tongue-in-cheek tale that, strangely, sank with-
out a trace on release, possibly due to poor promotion.
Filmed in Mexico. This was Plummer's film debut.
Boa: novel by Robert Ward.
WES 88 min (ort 95 min)
B,V,V2 VCL/CBS

## CATWALK KILLER **
Gus Trikonis  USA  PG  1982
*Connie Sellecca, Eleanor Parker, Jessica Walter*
Story of murder and intrigue in the fashion industry,
with a former fashion designer planning to make a
comeback at her mountain retreat. When there is a
power failure, horror strikes in the form of a killer
who begins to murder the models one by one. Average.
Aka: SHE'S DRESSED TO KILL
HOR 94 min
V VPD

## CAUGHT ***
Max Ophuls  USA  1949
*James Mason, Robert Ryan, Barbara Bel Geddes,*
*Frank Ferguson, Curt Bois, Natalie Schafer*
A woman marries a vicious millionaire who makes
her unhappy so she leaves for a doctor, even though
she is expecting his child. A moving and absorbing
melodrama, well acted and directed.
Boa: novel Wild Calendar by Libbie Block.
DRA 88 min B/W
B,V INT/CBS

## CAULDRON OF BLOOD *
Edward Mann (Santos Alocer)
SPAIN/USA  1967
*Boris Karloff, Viveca Lindfors, Jean-Pierre Aumont,*
*Jacqui Speed, Rosenda Monteros*
A blind sculptor is supplied with skeletal remains for
use in modelling but they are actually the remains of
victims that have been murdered by his sadistic wife.
A gruesome exercise in boredom, that wastes a fine
cast on a dull story.
Aka: BLIND MAN'S BLUFF; CHILDREN OF
BLOOD; CORPSE COLLECTORS, THE; DEATH
COMES FROM THE DARK; EL COLECCIONISTA
DE CADAVERES
HOR 87 min (ort 97 min)
B,V,V2 VAMP/VDM/GHV

## CAVE GIRL *
David Oliver  USA  15  1986
*Daniel Roebuck, Cindy Ann Thompson, Bill Adams,*
*Larry Gabriel, Jeff Chayette, Valerie Greybe*
An anthropology student is thrown back in time
whilst exploring a cave, and gets to experience Stone
Age living at first hand, in this clumsy and unfunny
effort.
COM 84 min
B,V CBS

## CAVE OF DIAMONDS *
Frank Kramer  15
FRANCE/ITALY/WEST GERMANY  1964
*Paul Hubschmid, Marianne Hold, Brad Harris, Horst*
*Frank, Chris Howland, Dorothee Parker, Philip*
*Lemaire*
A woman doctor and a reporter join forces to fight
diamond smugglers in South East Asia, in this dull

Euro-adventure.
Aka: DIE DIAMANTENHOHLE AM MEKONG
A/AD 88 min
B,V STR L/A; DAV L/A; VTEL

## CAVEMAN **
Carl Gottlieb  USA  PG  1970
*Ringo Starr, Barbara Bach, John Matuszak, Shelley*
*Long, Dennis Quaid, Avery Schreiber, Jack Gilford*
Feeble comedy set in prehistoric times, with Ringo
Starr playing a misfit who forms his own tribe
consisting of outcasts from other caves. A dumb
comedy that's slightly helped by some good special
effects (dinosaurs were created by David Allen), and
one or two funny moments. A brave effort, that
probably looked a lot funnier on paper than when it
came to the screen.
COM 90 min
B,V EHE; WHV

## CAVERN DEEP **
Ian Dalgleish  Uc
*Colin Forsythe, Mark Fidelo, Michele Quinn*
This story involves a Canadian journalist investigat-
ing the Loch Ness Monster and in the process meeting
up with three kids and an old hermit. Pleasant but
unmemorable little adventure.
A/AD 52 min
B,V GHV

## CEASEFIRE **
David Nutter  USA  15  1984
*Don Johnson, Lisa Blount, Robert F. Lyons, Richard*
*Chaves, Rick Richards, Chris Noel*
A Vietnam veteran is haunted by his wartime experi-
ences but cannot face up to the fact that he is
psychologically disturbed. An honest and well-meant
attempt to focus on the problems faced by these
veterans, but a little too earnest and predictable for its
own good. Scripted by Fernandez.
Boa: play Vietnam Trilogy by George Fernandez.
DRA 93 min (ort 97 min)
V VCC

## CELEBRITY **
Paul Wendkos  USA  15  1984
*Michael Beck, Joseph Bottoms, Ben Masters, James*
*Whitmore, Tess Harper, Karen Austin, Ned Beatty,*
*Claude Akins, Dinah Manoff, Debbie Allen, Jennifer*
*Warren, Hal Holbrook, Bonnie Bartlett, Rhonda*
*Dotson, Jerry Hardin*
Sprawling TV mini-series about three Fort Worth
buddies from a high school class of 1950, whose lives
are linked together 25 years later by a crime they
committed in the past.
Boa: novel by Thomas Thompson.
DRA 300 min (2 cassettes) mTV
B,V MGM

## CELESTINE **
Clifford Brown (Jesus Franco)
FRANCE  1974
*Linda Romay, Jean-Pierre Granet, Howard Vernon*
Adult movie in which a prostitute takes work as a
maid in a stately home and has the usual encounters
with all and sundry.
Aka: CELESTINE, MAID AT YOUR SERVICE;
CELLESTINE, BONNE A TOUT FAIRE
A 79 min
B,V,V2 GOV

## CELIA ***
Ann Turner  AUSTRALIA  15  1988
*Rebecca Smart, Nicholas Eadie, Maryanne Fahey,*
*Victoria Langley*
In a dully oppressive 1950s Melbourne suburb, a
9-year-old girl experiences a series of minor dis-
appointments, the effect of which is cumulative. Her
growing sense of isolation and mental disturbance

leads to an unexpected resolution. A highly unusual study of paranoia, fantasy and childhood fears, it makes several interesting observations despite a slackening of pace towards the climax. Turner's feature debut.

| DRA | 90 min (ort 102 min) |
|-----|-----|
| V | CFD |

### CELLAR DWELLER ** 18
John Carl Buechler    USA    1987
*Debrah Mullawney, Brian Robbins, Vince Edwards, Jeffrey Combs, Pamela Bellwood, Yvonne De Carlo, Cheryl-Ann Wilson*
Back in 1951 an imaginative comic book artist was working on his latest creation, when it rose from the page and destroyed him. Thirty years pass and his house is converted to an artist's institute. However, one of the students unwittingly resurrects the title creature and the expected series of gruesome deaths occur. Worth seeing perhaps for the repulsive effects, but certainly not for the plot, which is largely absent.

| HOR | 80 min |
|-----|-----|
| B,V | EIV |

### CELLAR, THE *** 18
Kevin S. Tenney    USA    1988
*Patrick Kilpatrick, Chris Miller, Suzanne Savoy, Ford Rainey*
A man is forced to sell his house despite the fact that he knows an evil creature lurks in his cellar. The son of the new owners is convinced of the existence of the creature, despite the refusal of his father to believe him, and eventually the expected confrontation takes place. A gripping chiller with a refreshing lack of gore.

| HOR | 90 min |
|-----|-----|
| B,V | CHV |

### CEMETERY OF THE LIVING DEAD ** 18
Ralph Zucker (Massimo Pupillo)
ITALY    1965
*Barbara Steele, Walter Brandt, Marilyn Mitchell, Alfred Rice, Richard Garret, Alan Collins, Tide Till*
This charming film tells of a man who reaches out from beyond the grave to take revenge on those responsible for his death. Bloody and unpleasant, with little to redeem it.
Aka: CINQUE TOMBE PER UN MEDIUM; FIVE GRAVES FOR THE MEDIUM; TERROR: CREATURES FROM THE GRAVE

| HOR | 92 min B/W |
|-----|-----|
| B,V,V2 | VDM L/A; SCV; STABL |

### CENTRE SPREAD ** 18
Tony Paterson    USA
*Paul S. Trahair, Kylie Foster*
Futuristic sexual fantasy, set in a society in which sex is freely available and telling of a top photographer whose assignment is to find a girl with a "new century" image.
CENTRESPREAD

| A | 70 min Cut |
|-----|-----|
| B,V | ELV |

### CENTREFOLD FEVER ** 
Richard Milner    USA    1981
*Samantha Fox, Kandi Barbour, Tiffany Clark, Ron Jeremy, Marc Stevens, Annie Sprinkles, Richard Bolla, Lisa Be, Veri Knotty*
Totally over-the-top hardcore comedy consisting of numerous sex sequences and a largely minimal plot; this one has the editor of a sleazy porno magazine searching for the perfect Centrefold Girl.

| A | 80 min |
|-----|-----|
| B,V | XTACY/KRP |

### CENTREFOLD GIRLS ** 
John Peyser    USA    1974
*Andrew Prine, Tiffany Bolling, Aldo Ray, Ray*

*Danton, Francine York, Jeremy Slate, Mike Mazurki, Dan Seymour*
A deranged man is determined to kill girls who have posed naked for the centre pages of a men's magazine. Formula murder-thriller.

| THR | 92 min |
|-----|-----|
| B,V,V2 | INT/CBS L/A; VPD |

### CENTURION ** PG
*Carl Mohner, Jim Dolen, Laura Rocca*
Standard costume drama, telling of a centurion who is trained to fight in the arena, but begins to question his actions and eventually joins up with the Barbarians, thus incurring the wrath of Rome.

| A/AD | 84 min Cut (3 sec) |
|-----|-----|
| B,V | VPD |

### CERTAIN FURY * 18
Steven Gyllenhaal    USA    1985
*Tatum O'Neal, Irene Cara, Nicholas Campbell, Peter Fonda, Moses Gunn*
During a courtroom gun battle in which some convicts escape, two juvenile delinquent girls also seize the opportunity to get free, but find that they are in far worse trouble as they are now thought to be accomplices. An inept and rubbishy effort, badly acted and sloppily directed. Made in Canada.

| DRA | 83 min |
|-----|-----|
| B,V | MED |

### CERTAIN SACRIFICE, A * 18
Stephen Lewicki    USA    1980
*Madonna Ciccone, Jeremy Patosh, Charles Kurtz*
A poorly made and filmed student effort devoted to the seamy side of life among New York's outcasts and misfits. It was probably only released to cash in on Madonna's subsequent fame, this being her first film. Of curiosity interest only.

| A | 62 min |
|-----|-----|
| B,V | ABC; MIA |

### CHAIN GANG *** 18
Worth Keeter    USA    1984
*Earl Owensby, Robert Bloodsworth, Carol Bransford, James Eric, Leon Rippy, Terry Loughlin, Paul Holman, Steve Boles, Gene Kusterer, Mark Ferri, Lash LaRue*
A drifter sentenced to hard labour on a chain gang, plots revenge against his tormentors in this harsh and brutal drama.

| DRA | 90 min |
|-----|-----|
| B,V | MED |

### CHAIN REACTION, THE *** 15
Ian Barry    AUSTRALIA    1980
*Steve Bisley, Anna-Maria Winchester, Ross Thompson, Ralph Cotterill, Patrick Ward*
A tense drama about the ruthless attempts made to cover up an accidental spillage of radioactive material. A security team searches for a contaminated scientist who has escaped to warn the public.

| FAN | 92 min |
|-----|-----|
| B,V | WHV |

### CHAIN, THE * PG
Jack Gold    UK    1985
*Herbert Norville, Denis Lawson, Rita Wolf, Maurice Denham, Nigel Hawthorne, Billie Whitelaw, Judy Parfitt, Leo McKern, Tony Westrope, Bernard Hill, Warren Mitchell, Gary Waldhorn, Ron Pember, Carmen Munroe, David Troughton*
Story of the trials of house-moving, revolving around the difficulties faced by seven interlinked households. An utterly predictable and tedious comedy, consisting of a series of dreary and trite vignettes. Screenplay is by Jack Rosenthal.

| COM | 92 min (ort 100 min) |
|-----|-----|
| B,V | RNK |

**CHAINED HEAT ***  18
Paul Nicolas  USA/WEST GERMANY  1983
*Linda Blair, John Vernon, Tamara Dobson, Stella*
*Stevens, Sybil Danning, Nita Talbot, Michael Callan,*
*Henry Silva*
Innocent girl in prison finds herself at the mercy of the
warden. One of those women-in-prison movies, with
plenty of violence and titillation, but nothing of
substance.
DRA  92 min Cut (1 min 37 sec)
B, V/sh  TEVP

**CHAINS ***  18
Roger J. Barski  USA  1989
*Jim Jordan, Michael Dixon, John L. Eves*
Two couples out on a double-date find themselves
caught up in a gangland war in South Chicago and
soon learn just how ruthless they'll need to be in order
to stay alive. A violent and exploitative action tale,
quite well-mounted for all its lack of originality.
A/AD  94 min
V  VPD

**CHAINS OF GOLD ***  18
Rod Holcomb  USA  1990
*John Travolta, Marilu Henner, Bernie Casey, Hector*
*Elizondo, Joey Lawrence*
Violent action tale set among the drug dealers and
street gangs of downtown Miami, where an idealistic
social worker battles against brutality and indiffer-
ence in his efforts to rescue kids from a life of crime
and exploitation. Average urban action tale with a
social conscience.
A/AD  91 min
V  MED/RCA

**CHAIR, THE ***  18
Waldemar Korzeniowsky
USA  1987
*James Coco, Paul Benedict, Gary McCleery, Trini*
*Alvarado*
Coco makes his last screen appearance in this tale of a
haunted electric chair, that claimed the life of the
prison governor in a riot years ago. With the reopen-
ing of the prison, a series of inexplicable events take
place in this rather disappointing horror yarn.
HOR  89 min
V  MED

**CHALLENGE OF DEATH ***
HONG KONG
*Delung Tam, Wang Tao, Chang Yi*
Two fighters called Golden Snake and Dragon Fists
join forces to combat an evil arms smuggler.
MAR  90 min
V  OCEAN/GVC

**CHALLENGE OF THE GOBOTS:**  U
**INVASION FROM THE 21ST LEVEL ***
William Hanna/Joseph Barbera
USA  1985
On the planet Gobotron a fierce battle is being fought
between the wicked Gobots and the good Guardian
Gobots. The evil Gobots hatch a plan to take over the
Earth by unleashing a plague of insects.
CAR  50 min; 44 min (PREST)
B,V  CBS; PREST (VHS only)

**CHALLENGE OF THE GOBOTS:**
**THE GOBOTRON SAGA ***  U
William Hanna/Joseph Barbera
USA  1985
Continues the story of good versus bad in the form of
the robots or Gobots of Gobotron, who are divided into
evil Renegade Gobots and good Guardian Gobots. In
this tale our good Gobots get a little help from some
Earth robots, who change themselves into vehicles
and travel to Gobotron to do battle. Compiled from
five episodes of a TV series, the idea for which was

taken from actual toy robots.
CAR  101 min mTV
B,V  PREST/VES

**CHALLENGE OF THE MACKENNAS, THE ***  15
Leon Klimovsky  ITALY  1969
*John Ireland, Robert Woods, Annabella Incontrera,*
*Robert Carmardiel, Daniela Giordano*
The story of Don Diego de Castro, a rancher who rules
his family and lands as a tyrant, but begins to
encounter opposition from his own family as well as
from a gunman, and is prevented from lynching a man
who has been after his daughter. Standard gory
Italian Western.
WES  90 min (ort 101 min)
B,V  PRV L/A

**CHALLENGE OF THE MASTERS ***  15
Chang Hsin-Yi  HONG KONG  1981
*John Lui, Chin Lung*
Two rival martial arts schools battle it out after a
student is killed in a fight. OK if you know what to
expect, just don't look for anything new in the plot
department.
MAR  88 min
B,V  VPD

**CHALLENGE OF THE NINJA ***  18
Godfrey Ho  HONG KONG  1989
*Bruce Baron, Pierre Tremblay, Eric Redner, Alison*
*Ellis, Silvia Rod, Richard Berman, Gerry Broad, Billy*
*Lee, Mike Powell, Alex Yang, Michael Wong*
A corrupt Ninja gang has spread a reign of terror and
murder and a police officer and secret master of
Ninjitsu sets out to defeat them. However, a youngster
he has befriended is also determined to fight them,
and sets out to learn the fighting arts for himself.
MAR  82 min
V  VPD

**CHALLENGE OF YOUNG BRUCE LEE ***
HONG KONG
Romanticised account of the early years of Bruce Lee.
He is adopted by monks and taught the secrets of kung
fu whereupon he leaves for life in the city and settles
down, using his talents to fight crime.
MAR  88 min
B,V,V2  VPD

**CHALLENGE THE NINJA ***  18
Godfrey Ho  HONG KONG  1986
*Bruce Baron, Pierre Tremblay, Eric Redner, Alison*
*Ellis, Silvia Rod, Janet Hansen*
A man who lost his family in the struggle with an evil
Ninja boss is helped by a policeman who is secretly
also a Ninja warrior.
MAR  82 min Cut (3 min 54 sec)
B,V  NINJ; VPD

**CHALLENGE TO BE FREE ***  U
Tay Garnett/Ford Beebe
USA  1972 (released 1975)
*Mike Mazurki, Jimmy Kane, Fritz Ford, Vic Christy,*
*Tay Garnett, John McIntire (narration)*
A fur-trapper and a golf champion are chased across
1,000 miles of frozen territory in the Arctic, by a posse
of lawmen and dogs. They have to survive blizzards
and avalanches in their struggle to escape. A simple-
minded action tale, the last film from Garnett, who
appears briefly as Marshall McGee.
Aka: MAD TRAPPER OF THE YUKON
A/AD  90 min
B,V  VPD; IVS

**CHALLENGE, THE ***  18
John Frankenheimer  USA  1982
*Scott Glenn, Toshiro Mifune, Atsuo Nakamura, Donna*
*Kei Benz, Calvin Young, Clyde Kusatsu, Sab*
*Shimada, Yoshio Inaba, Seiji Miyaguchi, Miko Taka,*
*Kenta Fukasaku, Kiyoako Nagai*

An American boxer becomes involved in a conflict between two Japanese brothers over their rights to family swords. Entertaining but rather contrived action tale, scripted by John Sayles and Richard Maxwell. Outdoors sequences were filmed in Kyoto.

DRA 112 min
B,V,V2,LV CBS

**CHALLENGE, THE **** U
Milton Rosmer/Luis Trenker
UK 1938
*Luis Trenker, Robert Douglas, Joan Gardner, Mary Clare, Ralph Truman, Fred Groves, Frank Birch, Geoffrey Wardwell, Norman Caplat, Lyonel Watts, Ralph Truman, Lawrence Baskcomb, Reginald Jarman, Tony Sympson, Cyril Smith*
Standard man-against-the-Matterhorn saga set in 1865, when a guide proves an English climber was not responsible for the deaths of his friends. Fair.

THR 77 min B/W
V PICK

**CHAMP, THE *** PG
Franco Zeffirelli USA 1979
*Jon Voight, Faye Dunaway, Ricky Schroder, Strother Martin, Jack Warden, Arthur Hill, Joan Blondell, Elisha Cook*
Remake of a 1931 film that deals with a washed-up prize fighter and his son. The boy's mother, having remarried and become a rich and successful fashion writer, turns up and wants to take the boy away. A tiresome and utterly unbelievable tale, made more so by young Schroder as the boy, who just cries and cries and cries.

DRA 118 min (ort 121 min)
V/sh MGM

**CHAMPAGNE CHARLIE **** 15
Allan Eastman CANADA/FRANCE 1988
*Hugh Grant, Megan Gallagher, Megan Follows, Jean-Claude Descrieres, Stephane Audran, R.H. Thomson,*
The romanticised story of Charles Heidsieck, who introduced champagne to America at the time of the Civil War. Arriving in America with his wife, he becomes involved with a Southern girl, is arrested as a spy and experiences various other vicissitudes. An opulent and handsome drama, fatally flawed by excessive length (it was originally broadcast in two parts).

DRA 200 min mTV
V CINE

**CHAMPAGNE FOR TWO **** PG
Lewis Furey CANADA 1987
*Nicholas Campbell, Kirsten Bishop*
A female architect thinks only of her career until the arrival of an unexpected room-mate. However, their budding romance is threatened by her boss and his former lover.
Boa: story by Serita Deborah Stevens.

DRA 74 min
V VCC

**CHAMPION ***** 
Mark Robson USA 1949
*Kirk Douglas, Marilyn Maxwell, Arthur Kennedy, Ruth Roman, Lola Albright, Paul Stewart*
A ruthless boxer will stop at nothing to get to the top in the fight game. Douglas gives a nice performance as our unlovable pugilist in this somewhat loose adaptation of Lardner's story. AA: Edit (Harry Gerstad).
Boa: short story by Ring Lardner.

DRA 98 min B/W
B,V SPEC/POLY

**CHAMPIONS **** PG
John Irvin UK 1983
*John Hurt, Edward Woodward, Jan Francis, Ben Johnson, Peter Barkworth, Ann Bell, Judy Parfitt, Alison Steadman, Kirstie Alley, Michael Byrne,*

*Carolyn Pickles, Fiona Victory, Mark Burns, Richard Leech, Frank Mills*
Based on the story of Bob Champion, the jockey who overcame cancer and went on to win the Grand National, this film is at its best when it focuses on the treatment he has to undergo, otherwise a somewhat dull film that fails to do justice to the man who was its inspiration.
Boa: book Champion's Story by Bob Champion and J. Powell.

DRA 115 min
B,V EHE; RACE

**CHAMPIONSHIP SEASON, THE *****
Jason Miller USA 1982
*Stacy Keach, Robert Mitchum, Bruce Dern, Martin Sheen, Paul Sorvino, Arthur Franz*
At the 24th annual reunion of a high school basketball squad and their paternalistic coach, a group of five former players re-live their moment of triumph when they won a basketball match over twenty years ago. A success on stage, this Pulitzer prize-winning play does not translate well to film and the characters appear as little more than caricatures. Written by Miller.
Aka: THAT CHAMPIONSHIP SEASON
Boa: play by Jason Miller.

DRA 106 min
B,V GHV

**CHANCES ARE ****** PG
Emile Ardolino USA 1989
*Cybill Sheperd, Ryan O'Neal, Robert Downey Jr, Mary Stuart Masterson, Josef Sommer, Christopher McDonald, Joe Grifasi, Susan Ruttan, Fran Ryan, James Noble*
A college student recalls a previous life as a lawyer who was murdered, and for good measure discovers that the mother of his current girlfriend was in fact his wife in that past incarnation. A rather silly but endearing comedy, its derivative fantasy elements are effective if not all that original.

COM 104 min (ort 108 min) subH
V/sh 20VIS

**CHANEL SOLITAIRE **** 15
George Kaczender FRANCE/USA 1981
*Marie-France Pisier, Timothy Dalton, Rutger Hauer, Karen Black, Brigitte Fossey*
Highly romanticised account of the life of Coco Chanel, one of the most famous fashion designers in the world. This one follows her first 38 years and is largely devoted to her love life. Average.
Boa: novel by Claude Dulay.

DRA 107 min (ort 124 min)
B,V TEVP

**CHANGE OF SEASONS, A **** 15
Richard Lang USA 1980
*Shirley MacLaine, Anthony Hopkins, Bo Derek, Michael Brandon, Mary Beth Hurt, Ed Winter*
When a college professor has an affair with one of his students, his wife decides to embark on an affair of her own. Typical mid-life crisis film that is very mildly entertaining but says nothing new. Co-written by Erich Segal.

COM 97 min (ort 102 min)
B,V WHV

**CHANGELING, THE *****
Peter Medak CANADA 1979
*George C. Scott, Melvyn Douglas, Trish Van Devere, John Colicos, Jean Marsh, Madeleine Thornton-Sherwood*
A recently widowed musician moves into an old house, which is inhabited by the ghost of a crippled child who was murdered by his father about 70 years ago. A patchy and slightly disjointed tale that has a few genuinely scary moments, but ultimately disappoints. A shorter film would have been far more effective.

HOR                                          113 min
B,V,V2                                          VTC

## CHANGELING 2: THE REVENGE **          18
Lamberto Bava                                 1988
*Gina Scola, David Brandon*
A woman helped her lover dispose of the body of her
murdered husband, but was unknowingly carrying his
child. The couple decide to bring up the child, but are
unprepared for some sinister events that unfold ten
years later, with the arrival of a mysterious stranger
at their house.
HOR                                           91 min
V                                               TGP

## CHANT OF JIMMY BLACKSMITH, THE ***     18
Fred Schepisi         AUSTRALIA               1978
*Tommy Lewis, Freddy Reynolds, Ray Barrett, Jack
Thompson, Peter Carroll, Elizabeth Alexander*
A half-caste Aborigine who was brought up by a
Methodist minister, exacts a bloody revenge on those
who humiliated him. Strong if predictable indictment
of racism, set in 1900 and based on some true events.
See also UTU.
Boa: novel by Thomas Keneally.
DRA                                          124 min
B,V                                          ODY/CBS

## CHAPTER TWO **                          PG
Robert Moore          USA                     1979
*James Caan, Marsha Mason, Valerie Harper, Joseph
Bologna*
Screen version of a Neil Simon semi-autobiographical
play, about a writer who embarks on a romance before
he has really got over the death of his wife. An
overlong story whose downbeat tone tends to dissipate
what little humour there is.
Boa: play by Neil Simon.
COM                                          121 min
B,V                                             RCA

## CHARGE OF THE LIGHT BRIGADE, THE ****   PG
Michael Curtiz        USA                     1936
*Errol Flynn, Olivia De Havilland, Patric Knowles,
Henry Stephenson, Nigel Bruce, Donald Crisp, David
Niven*
A lavish and stirring action epic, that distorts history
to make the fateful charge of the 27th Lancers at
Balaclava little more than the work of one over-
ambitious officer. That said, its production values are
such that, taken as entertainment, it is very good
indeed. Allegedly based on the famous poem of Alfred
Lord Tennyson and remade in 1968. AA: Assist Dir
(Jack Sullivan).
A/AD                        111 min (ort 116 min) B/W
V                                               WHV

## CHARIOTS OF FIRE ***                    U
Hugh Hudson           UK                      1981
*Ben Cross, Ian Charleson, Nigel Havers, Nicholas
Farrell, Daniel Gerroll, Cheryl Campbell, Alice Krige,
John Gielgud, Lindsay Anderson, Nigel Davenport,
Struan Rogers, Ian Holm, Patrick Magee, Dennis
Christopher*
True story of two Cambridge students who competed
in the 1924 Olympics. Much acclaimed by the critics,
it nicely illustrates the British nostalgic yearning for
the glories of the past. Nevertheless, a well made and
enjoyable if ponderous effort. The feature debut for the
director. AA: Pic, Screen (Orig) (Colin Welland), Score
(Orig) (Vangelis), Cost (Milena Canonero).
Boa: book Dollar Bottom And Taylor's Finest Hour by
J. Kennaway.
DRA                               118 min (ort 124 min)
V                                               CBS

## CHARLES AND DIANA: A ROYAL LOVE STORY **
James Goldstone       USA                     1982
*David Robb, Caroline Bliss, Christopher Lee, Rod*

Taylor, Margaret Tyzack, Mona Washbourne, Charles
Gray, David Langton*
This British-acted and American-financed version of
the most important event of this century will be
certain to appeal to the masses. Enjoyable candyfloss
with a Royal flavour. One of two films made on this
subject, the other one being "The Royal Romance Of
Charles And Diana".
DRA                                           95 min
B,V                                          IFS/CBS

## CHARLESTON **
Marcello Fondato      ITALY                   1976
*Bud Spencer (Carlo Pedersoli), James Coco, Herbert
Lom*
Crime farce in which an art-faking con-man steals
from Scotland Yard and is pursued by a determined
police officer. Coco gives a nice performance as a rich
American gangster who also crosses the path of
Spencer.
COM                                           91 min
B,V                                             FFV

## CHARLEY AND THE ANGEL **               U
Vincent McEveety      USA                     1973
*Fred McMurray, Cloris Leachman, Harry Morgan,
Kurt Russell, Vincent Van Patten, Kathleen Cody*
A shopkeeper whose days are numbered, changes his
mean ways after a visit from an angel. Fluffy Disney
comedy with the usual production-line warmth and
obligatory sincerity.
Boa: novel The Golden Evenings Of Summer by W.
Stanton.
COM                                           91 min
B,V                                             WDV

## CHARLEY HANNAH'S WAR **               15
Peter H. Hunt         USA                     1986
*Robert Conrad, Shane Conrad, Christian Conrad, Red
West, Joan Leslie, Stephen J. Cannell*
When a police captain accidentally shoots a young boy
whilst chasing a gang, he takes a teenage member of
the gang under his wing. He subsequently mounts his
own private war against international drug smug-
glers. Pilot for a series, with Conrad starring with his
two sons. The acting debut for TV producer Cannell.
Aka: CHARLEY HANNAH
DRA                          91 min (ort 142 min) mTV
V/sh                                            GHV

## CHARLEY ONE-EYE **                    18
Don Chaffey           USA                     1973
*Richard Roundtree, Roy Thinnes, Nigel Davenport,
Jill Pearson*
A black deserter from the Union Army and an Indian
outcast are thrown together in a desert wilderness,
but find that outside forces cause their relationship to
take a tragic turn. An interesting tale.
THR              96 min; 85 min (XTASY) (ort 107 min)
B,V                               INT/CBS L/A; XTASY

## CHARLEY'S AUNT *
Graeme Muir           UK                      1977
*Eric Sykes, Jimmy Edwards, Barbara Murray, Gerald
Flood, Alvin Lewis, Osmond Bullock*
Dreadfully inept comedy about the attempts of two
men to be alone with their girlfriends, with one
obliged to pose as his maiden aunt in a scheme that
gets somewhat out of hand. Thomas' play has been
filmed about six or seven times, but the 1941 version
by Archie Mayo is probably the best one. And as for
this one – well the less said the better.
Boa: play by Brandon Thomas. Osca: MISTER
AXELFORD'S ANGEL
COM                                           75 min mTV
B,V                                             GHV

## CHARLIE AND THE TALKING BUZZARD **    Uc
                      USA                     1979

*Christopher Penn, Duncan McLeon, Bruce Kemp*
Charlie and his friends give an evil mayor his
come-uppance in this lighthearted kid's adventure.
JUV                                          81 min
B,V                                           MED

## CHARLIE BROWN: A BOY NAMED        U
## CHARLIE BROWN **
Bill Melendez          USA              1969
The first full-length animated feature based on the
characters created in the famous Schulz comic strip
"Peanuts". A pleasant but slight series of vignettes
following the adventures of the Peanuts gang, as
Charlie Brown and friends prepare for the baseball
season. See also SNOOPY, COME HOME!
Aka: BOY NAMED CHARLIE BROWN, A
CAR                                          80 min
B,V,V2,LV                                     CBS

## CHARLIE BROWN: BON VOYAGE **       U
Bill Melendez          USA              1980
*Voices of: Daniel Anderson, Scott Beach, Casey
Carlson, Debbe Muller, Patricia Patts, Arrin Skelley*
Celebrating the 30th anniversary of Schulz's
"Peanuts" comic strip, this tale takes the Peanuts
gang to France for a fortnight as exchange students. A
flimsy effort that may appeal to fans of the comic strip.
Aka: BON VOYAGE, CHARLIE BROWN; BON
VOYAGE, CHARLIE BROWN (AND DON'T COME
BACK!)
CAR                                          73 min
B,V                                           CIC

## CHARLIE BROWN: RACE FOR YOUR LIFE **    U
Bill Melendez          USA              1977
*Voices of: Duncan Watson, Greg Felton, Stuart
Brotman, Gail Davis, Liam Martin*
Third animated "Peanuts" adventure based on the
famous strip cartoon by Schulz with this one set in a
summer camp just prior to a treacherous raft race.
Pleasant but insipid animation.
Aka: RACE FOR YOUR LIFE, CHARLIE BROWN
CAR                               72 min (ort 75 min)
B,V                                           CIC

## CHARLIE CHAN AND THE              PG
## CURSE OF THE DRAGON QUEEN *
Clive Donner           USA              1981
*Peter Ustinov, Lee Grant, Angie Dickinson, Richard
Hatch, Brian Keith, Roddy McDowall, Rachel Roberts,
Paul Ryan, Johnny Sekka*
Attempt to present a slapstick update of the famous
detective that quickly degenerates to the level of a bad
farce. The story has a curse put on Chan and his
descendants by the evil Dragon Queen, but the
greatest curse was to be a member of a good cast
appearing in rubbish like this.
COM                                          92 min
B,V                                           WHV

## CHARLIE CHAPLIN: A DAY'S PLEASURE **    U
Charles Chaplin        USA              1919
*Charles Chaplin, Edna Purviance, Henry Bergman,
Babe Lincoln*
The story of a family picnic and the mishaps that
befall it. Mild Chaplin comedy short, consisting of a
series of vignettes rather than a complete story.
Osca: CHARLIE CHAPLIN: THE CIRCUS
COM         20 min; 72 min (2 film cassette) B/W silent
V                               PGV L/A; CH5

## CHARLIE CHAPLIN: CITY LIGHTS ****   U
Charles Chaplin        USA              1931
*Charles Chaplin, Virginia Cherrill, Florence Lee,
Harry Myers, Hank Mann*
Chaplin at his most inventive in this fine if rather
sentimental story of a blind flower girl and a penniless
tramp, who somehow finds the money to pay for an

operation to restore her sight. Highlights are the
sequences dealing with his friendship with a drunken
millionaire, who doesn't know him when he's sober,
and the finale, when the girl meets up with her
benefactor.
Aka: CITY LIGHTS
COM                              87 min B/W silent
B,V            SPEC/POLY; CH5 (VHS only)

## CHARLIE CHAPLIN: LIMELIGHT ***     U
Charles Chaplin        USA              1952
*Charles Chaplin, Claire Bloom, Sydney Chaplin, Nigel
Bruce, Norman Lloyd, Buster Keaton*
Rather sentimental story of a washed-up comic from
the days of the music-hall who befriends a beautiful
young ballerina. Though it suffers badly from stilted
dialogue, some flashes of brilliance light it up. It won
an Oscar for the music in 1972 when it became eligible
for entry; it had not been shown in a Los Angeles
theatre until then. AA: Score (Orig) (Charles Chaplin/
Raymond Rasch/Larry Russell).
Aka: LIMELIGHT
DRA               145 min; 135 min (CH5) B/W
B,V                                   POLY; CH5

## CHARLIE CHAPLIN: MODERN TIMES ****  U
Charles Chaplin        USA              1936
*Charles Chaplin, Pauette Goddard, Henry Bergman,
Chester Conklin, Stanley "Tiny" Sandford, Hank
Mann, Louis Natheaux, Allan Garcia*
Chaplin's last silent (apart from some contrived sound
sequences) is a savagely witty attack on the dehuma-
nising effects of modern industry. Our hero's struggles
against the might of big business, his "marriage", a
fine ending and Chaplin's own score (including
"Smile") make this a classic work.
Aka: MODERN TIMES
COM                              89 min B/W silent
B,V                     POLY; CH5 (VHS only)

## CHARLIE CHAPLIN:                   PG
## MONSIEUR VERDOUX ****
Charles Chaplin        USA              1947
*Charles Chaplin, Martha Raye, Marilyn Nash, Isobel
Elsom, Irving Bacon, William Frawley, Mady Correll,
Allison Roddan, Robert Lewis, Fritz Leiber*
A sacked bank clerk becomes a murderer, bumping off
rich women after marrying them in order to support
his family. Overtones of Landru the Bluebeard are
treated in a savage and witty attack on the morality of
the arms trade. The dialogue is less stilted than most
other Chaplin talkies and, as ever, he provides the
music.
Aka: MONSIEUR VERDOUX
DRA                                  118 min B/W
B,V                                   POLY; CH5

## CHARLIE CHAPLIN: THE CIRCUS ***    U
Charles Chaplin        USA              1928
*Charles Chaplin, Merna Kennedy, Allan Garcia, Betty
Morrissey, Harry Crocker*
A tramp joins a circus in order to escape the attentions
of the law, but finds his attention being drawn to the
attractive horse-riding stepdaughter of the circus
owner. Though not one of his great films, this comic
tale has many hilarious sequences and culminates in
a memorable finale. AA: Spec Award (Chaplin).
Aka: CIRCUS, THE
Osca: DAY'S PLEASURE, A (PGV – short) or ONE
(CH5)
COM               72 min (ort 82 min) B/W silent
B,V                     PVG L/A; POLY L/A; CH5

## CHARLIE CHAPLIN: THE GOLD RUSH ****  U
Charles Chaplin        USA              1925
*Charles Chaplin, Georgia Hale, Mack Swain, Tom
Murray*
Brilliant Chaplin comedy about a lone Yukon prospec-
tor who makes the big time. Still wonderfully funny

with some marvellous visual gags, as our hero battles privation and the elements. A highlight is the brilliant sequence when Chaplin and his partner are trapped in their hut as it's about to tumble over a precipice.
Aka: GOLDRUSH, THE
COM      72 min B/W silent
B,V      SPEC/POLY; VIDCLB; CH5

### CHARLIE CHAPLIN: THE GREAT DICTATOR *** U
Charles Chaplin    USA    1940
*Charles Chaplin, Paulette Goddard, Jack Oakie, Reginald Gardiner, Maurice Moscovitch, Billy Gilbert, Henry Daniell*
Chaplin said that he would never have been able to make a lighthearted spoof on Hitler had he known the true horrors that would emerge from WW2. Even so, after 45 years that stilted satire on the Nazi dictatorship still retains some interest, even if most of the humour seems a little strained. The story is one of mistaken identity, with a Jewish barber being mistaken for the dictator of Tomania – Adenoid Hynkel.
Aka: GREAT DICTATOR, THE
COM    128 min; 120 min (CH5) B/W
B,V      POLY; CH5

### CHARLIE CHAPLIN: THE IDLE CLASS ** U
Charles Chaplin    USA    1922
*Charles Chaplin, Edna Purviance, Mack Swain*
A tramp who desires the good things in life finds that he has been mistaken for a wealthy woman's husband. A modest little comedy that lacks much of the liveliness of his better works.
Osca: CHARLIE CHAPLIN: THE KID
COM      31 min B/W silent
V      POLY; CH5

### CHARLIE CHAPLIN: THE IMMIGRANT *** U
Charles Chaplin    USA    1917
*Charles Chaplin, Edna Purviance, Albert Austin, Henry Bergman, Stanley Sanford, Eric Campbell*
A penniless immigrant makes friends with a girl on a boat, later helping her in a cafe, in this charming early Chaplin work, that skilfully mixes comedy and social comment.
COM      20 min B/W silent
V      EMI

### CHARLIE CHAPLIN: THE KID *** U
Charles Chaplin    USA    1921
*Charles Chaplin, Jackie Coogan, Edna Purviance, Lita Grey, Chuck Reisner*
Chaplin's first feature is a touching comedy about a tramp who brings up an abandoned baby and has a tough time preventing welfare agencies from taking him into care. A wonderful blend of comedy, tragedy and slapstick. This film launched Coogan as a child star.
Aka: KID, THE (POLY)
Osca: CHARLIE CHAPLIN: THE IDLE CLASS
COM    60 min; 50 min (CH5) B/W silent
B,V      POLY; CH5

### CHARLIE CHAPLIN: VOLUME 1 *** U
Charles Chaplin    USA    1915/1917
*Charles Chaplin, Edna Purviance, Bud Jamison, Leo White, Paddy McGuire, Lloyd Bacon, Albert Austin, Eric Campbell*
A compilation of three classic Chaplin shorts – "The Tramp", "The Pawnshop" and "Easy Street". In the first tale a tramp saves a girl from crooks but is wounded in the process. However, she takes care of him. The second story is an amusing farce that revolves around the activities of a pawnbroker, and the final tale sees Chaplin as a tramp who's reformed by an attractive missionary, becomes a policeman and takes on the local bully.
COM    114 min (3 film cassette) B/W silent
V      EMI L/A; PAL L/A; CH5

### CHARLIE GRANT'S WAR ** 15
Martin Larut    CANADA    1985
*R.H. Thomson, Joan Orensten, Jan Rubes, Douglas Campbell*
A young Canadian living in Vienna becomes involved in a plot to save Jews from the Nazis in this formula adventure yarn.
A/AD      125 min
B,V      CAREY/PVG; PARK

### CHARLIE MUFFIN ** 15
Jack Gold    UK    1979
*David Hemmings, Sam Wanamaker, Jennie Linden, Ralph Richardson*
A defecting KGB agent will only surrender to the black sheep of MI6, shabby and scruffy Charlie Muffin. But there is more to this than meets the eye.
Boa: novel Charlie M by Brian Freemantle.
THR      104 min
B,V    THAMES/TEVP; VCC (VHS only)

### CHARLIE, THE LONESOME COUGAR *** U
Winston Hibler    USA    1967
*Ron Brown, Brian Russell, Linda Wallace, Jim Wilson, Clifford Peterson, Lewis Sample, Edward C. Moller, Rex Allen (narration)*
A small cougar makes friends with the people working at a logging camp in the Pacific Northwest. A pleasant Disney comedy-adventure with excellent outdoor photography.
A/AD      75 min
B,V      WDV

### CHARLIE'S BALLOON *** Uc
Larry Elikann    USA    1981
*Jack Albertson, Adrienne Barbeau, John Reilly, Slim PIckens, William Bogert, Pat Cooper, Bert Freed, Anne Seymour, William Sadler, Moosie Drier, Laurence Haddon, Jack Knight, Morgan Farley, Robert Lussier, Edward Ansara*
A youngster fulfils his ambition of crossing America in a hot-air balloon with his grandfather. Complications arise due to a large amount of Mafia money hidden in their luggage. A pleasant and visually pleasing romp.
Aka: CHARLIE AND THE GREAT BALLOON CHASE
COM      98 min mTV
B,V      ODY

### CHARLOTTE *** 18
Roger Vadim    FRANCE    1974
*Sirpa Lane, Roger Vadim, Mathieu Carriere, Michel Duchaussoy*
A man writes a book about a girl's murder and discovers the identity of the killer in this rather offbeat sex film.
Aka: CHARLLOTTE: A GIRL MURDERED; LA JEUNE FILLE ASSASSINEE
A    86 min (ort 100 min) (Abridged at film release)
B,V      WOV; STABL; XTASY

### CHARLOTTE'S WEB ** U
Charles A. Nichols/Iwao Takamoto
     USA    1973
*Voices of: Debbie Reynolds, Agnes Moorehead, Paul Lynde, Henry Gibson, Charles Nelson Reilly*
Cartoon feature based on a children's story about a spider who befriends a piglet and saves his bacon. A fair animation let down by some totally forgettable songs by Richard and Robert Sherman. A Hanna-Barbera production.
Boa: novel by E.B. White.
CAR      94 min
B,V    HVM L/A; WEC L/A; VGM; MIA; KRP

### CHARLY *** PG
Ralph Nelson    USA    1968
*Cliff Robertson, Lilia Skala, Dick Van Patten, Claire*

Bloom, Leon Janney
Based on a Hugo winning short SF story, this is a look at what happens when a mentally retarded adult undergoes experimental neuro-surgery and becomes a genius, but only temporarily. An interesting film that would have been far more convincing minus the touches of sentimentality that tend to spoil it. AA: Actor (Robertson).
Boa: novel Flowers for Algernon by Daniel Keys.

DRA                                              103 min
B,V                                          RNK; VGM

**CHASE ***                                      15
Rod Holcomb              USA              1985
Jennifer O'Neill, Robert S. Woods, Michael Parks, Terence Knox, John Philbin, Kathleen York, J.E. Freeman, Cooper Huckabee, Richard Farnsworth, Michol Sullivan, John Walter Davis, Douglas Newell, Richard Arnold
A female lawyer returns to her small home town and finds herself defending a man accused of murdering an old friend. The case takes on more sinister aspects when she discovers that a group of assassins are out to silence the suspect.

DRA                                        90 min mTV
B,V                                               CBS

**CHATO'S LAND ***                               18
Michael Winner           USA              1972
Charles Bronson, Jack Palance, Richard Basehart, James Whitmore, Simon Oakland, Ralph Waite, Richard Jordan, Victor French, William Watson, Roddy McMillan, Paul Young, Lee Paterson, Rudy Ugland, Sonia Rangan, Verna Harvey
An Indian half-breed kills a white man in self defence and finds that he is pursued by a posse. A competently made film in which the Indian finds that once the posse has entered his land he has the advantage. A violent and often bloody Winner offering, best described as a pointless exercise in nastiness.

WES                   95 min (ort 100 min) Cut (41 sec)
B,V                                               WHV

**CHATTANOOGA CHOO CHOO ***                      PG
Bruce Bilson             USA              1984
George Kennedy, Barbara Eden, Joe Namath, Melissa Sue Anderson, Bridget Hanley, Clu Gulager, Christopher McDonald, Davis Roberts, Tony Azito, Parley Baer
A man must restore the famous train and make a final run before he can collect an enormous inheritance. Enjoyable comedy with a strong cast doing their best with the rather limited story.

COM                                              102 min
B,V                                               MED

**CHATTERBOX ***                                 18
Tom De Simone            USA              1977
Candice Rialson, Larry Gelman, Jane Kean
Sex comedy about a woman's strange way of expressing herself; through her sexual organ. Despite an amusing beginning this one soon degenerates into tiresome nonsense.

A                                                73 min
B,V                                       VTC L/A; STABL

**CHATTERBOX ***
Joseph Santley           USA              1943
Joe E. Brown, Judy Canova, Rosemary Lane, John Hubbard, Gus Schilling, Anne Jeffreys, Chester Clute
A timid radio-cowboy visits a dude ranch for publicity purposes and becomes a hero, with a little help from a girl who works there.

COM                                           76 min B/W
B,V                                               VTC

**CHE! ***                                       15
Richard Fleischer        USA              1969
Omar Sharif, Jack Palance, Cesare Danova, Robert

Loggia, Woody Strode
Flat biopic about the life and death of a famous revolutionary who helped Castro come to power and then went off to instigate revolution elsewhere. A dismal, plodding effort that fails in just about every way, though perhaps worth seeing if only to catch Palance playing Castro.

DRA                               92 min (ort 113 min)
B,V                                               CBS

**CHECKING OUT ***                               15
David Leland             USA              1988
Jeff Daniels, Melanie Mayron, Michael Tucker, Ann Magnuson, Kathleen York, Allan Harvey, Jo Harvey Allen, Felton Perry, Alan Wolfe
Following the sudden death of his best friend from a heart attack, an executive experiences an acute attack of hypochondria, and spends the rest of the movie wondering if he will experience the same fate. A botched attempt at a black comedy whose amusing moments are few and far between.

COM                                              90 min
V/sh                                              CBS

**CHEECH AND CHONG: STILL SMOKIN' ***            18
Thomas Chong             USA              1983
Cheech Marin, Thomas Chong, Hansman In't Veld, Carol Van Herwijnen, Shirleen Stroker, Susan Hahn
Silly pothead comedy with our dope crazy duo, all about a film festival in Amsterdam. As thin as all those Cheech and Chong films and a good deal harder to watch, not least owing to the inclusion of about twenty minutes of concert footage.
Aka: STILL SMOKIN'

COM                               87 min (ort 92 min)
V/h                                               CIC

**CHEECH AND CHONG:**                            15
**THINGS ARE TOUGH ALL OVER ***
Tom Avildsen             USA              1982
Cheech Marin, Thomas Chong, Shelby Fiddis, Rikki Marin, Evelyn Guerero, Rip Taylor, Shelby Chong
Cheech and Chong comedy with two brothers driving a car to California, unaware that it contains $5,000,000. One of their better efforts, with the stars also playing a couple of Arab brothers who cross the path of the first pair. Written by Marin and Chong.
Aka: THINGS ARE TOUGH ALL OVER

COM                                              92 min
B,V                                               RCA

**CHEECH AND CHONG'S NEXT MOVIE ***             18
Thomas Chong             USA              1980
Cheech Marin, Thomas Chong, Evelyn Guerrero, Betty Kennedy, Sy Kramer, Rikki Marin
Unfunny collection of dope-jokes by two of the most famous potheads in the world. Incoherent, uneven and only sporadically amusing.
Aka: HIGH ENCOUNTERS OF THE ULTIMATE KIND

COM                                              99 min
V/h                                               CIC

**CHEECH AND CHONG'S NICE DREAMS ***            18
Thomas Chong             USA              1981
Cheech Marin, Thomas Chong, Stacy Keach, Evelyn Guerrero, Timothy Leary
Cheech and Chong decide to use an ice-cream van as a front for selling dope, which naturally leads to complications but not much in the way of real humour.
Aka: NICE DREAMS

COM                               83 min (ort 97 min)
V                                                 RCA

**CHEECH AND CHONG'S**                           15
**THE CORSICAN BROTHERS ***
Thomas Chong/Cheech Marin
                         USA              1984

*Cheech Marin, Thomas Chong, Roy Dotrice, Shelby Fiddis, Rikki Marin, Edie McClurg, Rae Dawn Chong, Robbi Chong*
Spoof remake of the 1941 film of Dumas' story of the twins who, though separated at birth, still maintain a psychic link. Their first non-pothead parody that falls flat on its face, despite our boys playing three roles each. Watch it for the nice French locations, but don't expect to laugh.
Aka: CORSICAN BROTHERS, THE
COM 86 min (ort 90 min)
B,V RNK; VIR (VHS only)

### CHEECH AND CHONG'S UP IN SMOKE *** 18
Lou Adler USA 1978
*Cheech Marin, Thomas Chong, Stacy Keach, Tom Skerritt, Edie Adams, Strother Martin, Zane Busby*
The first in a seemingly endless number of "Cheech and Chong" pothead comedies, based on two dope-smoking, beer-swilling slobs they created in a series of record albums. This one features a vehicle made entirely of pressed dope, and tells of how our two dope-crazy potheads go in search of some good grass. Episodic and largely disjointed, but undeniably funny in parts.
Aka: UP IN SMOKE
COM 82 min
B,V CIC

### CHEERLEADERS' BEACH PARTY ** 
Alex E. Goiten USA 1978
*Stefanie Hastings, Linda Jenson, Mary Lou Lovedan*
Sexy cheerleaders come to the rescue of a university that is in danger of losing its best football players. Happy, brainless, forgettable – in roughly that order.
COM 83 min
B,V RNK

### CHEERLEADERS' WILD WEEKEND ** 18
Jeff Werner USA 1979
*Jason Williams, Kristine De Bell, Anthony Lewis, Ann Wharton, Janet Blythe*
When 15 cheerleaders are kidnapped, their captors find that they are too much to handle in this pretty average comedy.
COM 87 min
B,V TEVP

### CHEERLEADERS, THE **
Paul Glickler USA 1973
*Stephanie Fondue, Denise Dillaway*
Locker-room hi-jinks form the basis for this comedy about American football teams and a squad of uninhibited cheerleaders. Another flimsy effort in this rather limited comedy genre.
COM 81 min
B,V VDM

### CHEETAH ** U
Jeff Blyth USA 1989
*Keith Coogan, Lucy Deakins, Collin Mothupi, Timothy Landfield, Breon Gorman, Ka Vindia, Kuldeep Bhakoo, Paul Onsongo*
Two teenagers join their scientist parents in Kenya for several months, where they befriend a young Masai tribesman and adopt an orphaned cheetah cub. A predictable and simplistic Disney adventure which, despite its lack of depth, makes some useful points about respect for the wild.
A/AD 80 min (ort 84 min)
V WDV

### CHEQUE IS IN THE POST, THE ** 15
Joan Darling USA 1985
*Brian Dennehy, Anne Archer, Nita Talbot, Dick Shawn, Hallie Todd, Chris Herbert, Michael Bowen*
The story of one man's revolt against the American way of life in its more crass and materialistic form, with credit cards, status symbols etc. He decides to make his home self-sufficient, but complications arise.

A patchy and uneven comedy that takes a nice idea and fails to build on it.
Aka: CHECK IS IN THE MAIL, THE
COM 90 min
B,V AVR

### CHERRY 2000 ** 15
Steve De Jarnatt USA 1988
*Melanie Griffith, David Andrews, Ben Johnson, Tim Thomerson, Pamela Gidley*
In the world of 2017, sexual partners have been replaced by robot playmates, and one man is forced to embark on a long and arduous search for spare parts when his girlfriend breaks down. An implausible action fantasy let down by poor casting and the lack of a decent plot, though one or two spectacular effects slightly compensate.
FAN 98 min
B,V RCA

### CHERRY HILL HIGH **
Alex E. Goitein USA 1976
*Carrie Olsen, Nina Carson, Lynn Hastings, Gloria Upson, Stephanie Lawlor, Linda McInerney*
Five American teenage girls hold a contest to see who will be the first to lose her virginity. Formula teen-comedy.
Aka: VIRGIN CONFESSIONS
COM 86 min
B,V RNK

### CHERRY PICKER, THE *
Peter Curran UK 1972
*Lulu, Bob Sherman, Spike Milligan, Wilfrid Hyde-White, Patrick Cargill, Robert Hutton, Priscilla Morgan, Arthur Blake, Barry Wilsher, Bruce Boa, Henry McGee, Jack Hulbert, Fiona Curzon, Terry-Thomas*
A feeble comedy in which an American VIP hires a girl and her father in an attempt to reform his hippy son. Worth about two minutes of anyone's time, unfortunately it lasts for seventy-nine.
Boa: novel Pick Up Sticks by Mickey Phillips.
COM 79 min (ort 92 min)
B,V,V2 IFS/CBS

### CHESTY ANDERSON, U.S. NAVY **
Ed Forsyth USA 1976
*Shari Eubank, Scatman Crothers, Fred Willard, Rosanne Katon, Dorri Thomson, Frank Campanella, Marcie Barkin*
Timid sexploitation movie about a squad of female naval recruits with buxom Eubank bouncing into action. Written by Paul Pompian and H.F. Green.
Aka: ANDERSON'S ANGELS
COM 88 min
B,V CHM/PPL

### CHEYENNE AUTUMN *** U
John Ford USA 1964
*Richard Widmark, Carroll Baker, Karl Malden, Ricardo Montalban, Sal Mineo, Edward G. Robinson, James Stewart, Gilbert Roland, Patrick Wayne, Elizabeth Allen, Victor Jory, John Carradine, Mike Mazurki, John Qualen, Denver Pyle*
A dramatic story chronicling the US Government's horrendous treatment of a group of Cheyenne Indians who attempted, in 1878, to migrate north from their squalid reservation in Oklahoma, where they lived almost as prisoners. A good-looking if overlong and disorganised tale; Ford's last Western.
Boa: novel by Mari Sandoz.
WES 126 min (ort 154 min)
V WHV

### CHICAGO JOE AND THE SHOWGIRL ** 18
Bernard Rose UK 1990
*Kiefer Sutherland, Emily Lloyd, Patsy Kensit, Alexandra Pigg*

BONNIE AND CLYDE is transferred to WW2 Britain in this dark tale (based on a real case) of a GI with delusions of grandeur and a liking for the good life, who falls for a British dancer. Together, they embark on a killing spree until finally captured. The sparse and realistic portrayal of wartime Britain is an asset, but the film lacks depth and provides no insight into the motivations of the duo.

DRA                                    103 min
V                                        PAL

## CHICAGO STORY ***                     PG
Jerry London          USA              1981
*Vincent Baggetta, Dennis Franz, Kene Holliday, Jack Kehoe, Craig T. Nelson, Kristoffer Tabori, Gail Youngs, Michael Horton, Charles Hallahan, Allan Rich, Richard Venture, Brooke Alderson, Luca Bercovici, Kelly Hayden*
This good pilot for a TV series that was intended to mix legal, medical and police elements, follows the ordeal of an innocent man who is held for the sniper shooting of a young girl in a park. A solid and intelligent drama, written by Eric Bercovici.
DRA                    92 min (ort 104 min) mTV
B,V                                      MGM

## CHICKEN CHRONICLES, THE **             18
Francis Simon         USA              1977
*Steven Guttenberg, Ed Lauter, Lisa Reeves, Meridith Baer, Branscombe Richmond, Gino Baffa, Phil Silvers*
One of those innumerable comedies set in an American high school. This time a teenage boy has problems with his employer, his school-work and of course, with his girlfriend. Guttenberg's screen debut. A highlight is Silvers in a semi-serious role, running the fast-food shop where some of the kids work after school.
Boa: novel by P. Diamond.
COM                                     95 min
B,V,V2,                                 EHE

## CHICKIE TETTRAZZINI **
Charles Dodgson       USA              1975
*Blaise Pascal, Emmeline Parkhurst, William Booth, Cotton Mather, I.M. Zoroaster, Thomas Paine, Jamie Gillis*
A good-natured female cop moonlights at a massage parlour and is generous with her favours. Everyone falls in love with Chickie and when she wins the New York lottery she is overwhelmed with offers of friendship in this trite and plot-empty sex film.
Aka: CHICKIE
A                                       90 min
V                                        RIP

## CHIEFS ***                             15
Jerry London          USA              1980
*Charlton Heston, Keith Carradine, Stephen Collins, Brad Davis, Tess Harper, Paula Kelly, Wayne Rogers, Paul Sorvino, Victoria Tennant, Billy Dee Williams, Lane Smith, Kaiulani Lee, Novella Nelson, Danny Glover*
Study of a small-town and the tensions that are generated by the murder of a young boy, which has remained unsolved for over 40 years. A compilation of an atmospheric mini-series, originally shown in three 96 minute episodes.
Aka: ONCE UPON A MURDER
Boa: novel by Stuart Woods.
DRA                                    206 min mTV
B,V                              VFP L/A; HER

## CHILD BRIDE OF SHORT CREEK, THE **
Robert Michael Lewis  USA              1981
*Christopher Atkins, Diane Lane, Conrad Bain, Kiel Martin, Helen Hunt, Warren Vanders, Dee Wallace, Joan Shawlee, Babetta Dick, Melinda Almquist, Julianne Slocum, C. Duane Tuft, Robert E. Hartenberger, Alan Nash, Jay Bernard*

A returning Korean War veteran comes into conflict with his fundamentalist father who plans to add a teenage bride to his many wives, in their isolated Arizona community where polygamy is practiced. An offbeat story, based on true events, with a raid made on just such a community in the 1950s.
Boa: story Jessica's Story by Michael Fessier Jr.
DRA                                    120 min mTV
B,V,V2                                IFS/CBS

## CHILD OF GLASS ***                      U
John Erman            USA              1978
*Barbara Barrie, Biff McGuire, Anthony Zerbe, Nina Foch, Katy Kurtzmann, Steve Shaw, Olivia Barash, Katy Kurzman, Denise Nickerson, Jack Rader, Irene Tedrow, Lilyan Chauvin, David Hurst, Sue Ann Gilfillan*
An enjoyable family tale in which a young boy moves with his parents into an old Southern mansion. Once there they find that strange forces are at work and young Alexander is drawn into an adventure involving witchcraft, a lost fortune in diamonds and an encounter with a crazy caretaker.
Boa: novel The Ghost Belonged To Me by Richard Park.
A/AD                                    93 min mTV
B,V                                      WDV

## CHILD, THE **
Robert Voskanien      USA              1977
*Rosalie Cole, Laurel Barnett, Frank Janson*
An old isolated farmhouse set in the middle of a dark wood, is the setting for a story of a little girl with strange mental powers who communicates with ghoul-like creatures that roam the woods.
Aka: KILL AND GO HIDE; ZOMBIE CHILD
HOR                                     95 min
B,V                                      VFO

## CHILDHOOD OF MAXIM GORKY, THE ****     PG
Mark Donskoi          USSR             1938
*Alexei Lyarsky, Y. Valbert, M. Troyanovski, Valeria Massalitinova*
The first part of the Maxim Gorky trilogy, with the orphaned writer being brought up by his grandparents, and learning about life and the tribulations of the Russian people. A rich and detailed film, full of humour and strong characterisations. Followed by MY APPRENTICESHIP and MY UNIVERSITIES.
Aka: DETSTVO GORKOVO
DRA                    95 min (ort 110 min) B/W
V                                       HEND

## CHILDREN IN THE CROSSFIRE **            PG
George Schaefer       USA              1984
*Charles Haid, David Huffman, Julia Duffy, Karen Valentine, Niall Tobin, James Norris, Peter Gilroy, Grainne Clark, Geraldine Hughes, Kirk Cameron, Penelope Windust, David Held, Henry G. Sanders, Garn Stephens*
Tells of children from both Catholic and Protestant communities of Northern Ireland who were taken to the USA for a summer holiday. What begins as a sincere examination of this troubled province very quickly develops into a series of simplistic observations. This is a great pity, because it is actually very well made. Filmed partly in Dublin.
Aka: SUMMERTIME YANKS
DRA                                     96 min mTV
B,V                                      VES

## CHILDREN OF A LESSER GOD ***            15
Randa Haines          USA              1986
*William Hurt, Marlee Matlin, Piper Laurie, Philip Bosco, Alison Gompf, John F. Cleary, John Basinger, Philip Holmes, Georgia Ann Cline, William D. Byrd, Frank Carter Jr, John Limnidis, Bob Hiltermann, E. Katherine Kerr*
An idealistic teacher of the deaf is intrigued by his

discovery of an intelligent deaf woman who works there as a janitor and is isolated owing to her refusal to learn lip-reading. Though less powerful than Medoff's Tony award-winning play, this unusual love story owes much to the convincing and moving performances of its leads. The film debut for both Matlin and Haines. AA: Actress (Matlin).
Boa: play by Mark Medoff.
DRA                                           115 min
V/h                                           CIC

## CHILDREN OF AN LAC, THE **                    U
John Llewellyn Moxey   USA                    1980
*Shirley Jones, Alan Fudge, Ina Balin, Beulah Quo, Ben Piazza, Lee Paul, Kieu Chinh, Vic Diaz, Vic Silayan, Robert Padua, Bongchi Miraflor, Anita Linda, Manila Gumila, Nguyet Balin, Andy Del Mundo, Tony Malanca, Dexter Doria*
Story of three women who try to evacuate hundreds of orphans from Saigon just before it falls, largely based on the experiences of Balin, who plays herself. A competent drama, scripted by Blanche Hanalis from Balin's story.
Boa: story by Ina Balin.
DRA                                       92 min mTV
V                                             VPD

## CHILDREN OF DIVORCE **                        PG
Joanne Lee            USA                     1980
*Barbara Feldon, Lance Kerwin, Stacey Nelkin, Billy Dee Williams, Olivia Cole, Zohra Lampert, Christopher Ciampa, Stella Stevens, Fritz Weaver, Greg Mullavey, Carmine Caridi, Mary-Robin Redd, Carmen Zapata, Pamela McMyler*
A look at the effects of divorce on the children of three socially different families, with most of the film consisting of discussions between the kids involved, who commiserate with each other and try to understand what has happened. Average social drama, scripted by Lee.
DRA                                       97 min mTV
B,V                                        PRV L/A

## CHILDREN OF RAGE **                            15
Arthur Allan Seidelman
                      ISRAEL/UK               1974
*Simon Ward, Cyril Cusack, Simon Andrew, Helmut Griem, Olga Georges-Picot, Richard Alfieri*
An attempt to explain both sides of the Arab-Israeli conflict in which a young Palestinian joins the struggle after his brother is killed, is wounded and then treated by the same idealistic Israeli doctor who operated on his brother. Average.
DRA                                          106 min
B,V,LV                                     ODY/CBS

## CHILDREN OF THE CORN *                         18
Fritz Kiersch         USA                     1984
*Peter Horton, Linda Hamilton, R.G. Armstrong, John Franklin, Courtney Gains, Robby Kiger*
Adaptation of a Stephen King short story about a young couple who get involved with a strange cult, in a small Iowa town in the American corn belt. Laughable but gory nonsense.
Boa: short story by Stephen King.
HOR                                           88 min
B,V                                TEVP; WHV (VHS)

## CHILDREN OF THE FULL MOON **                   15
Tom Clegg             UK                      1973
*Christopher Cazenove, Diana Dors, Robert Urquhart, Celia Gregory, Adrian Mann, Victoria Wood, Sophie Kind*
A couple are lent a weekend cottage but find that the journey there is full of perils when they meet up with a family of werewolves. A standard Hammer House of Horror offering.
Osca: VISITOR FROM THE GRAVE (CH5)
HOR          90 min; 105 min (2 film cassette) mTV

B,V,V2                        PRV L/A; CH5 (VHS only)

## CHILDREN OF THE NIGHT **                       15
Robert Markowitz      USA                     1985
*Kathleen Quinlan, Nicholas Campbell, Lar Park-Lincoln, Mario Van Peebles, Wally Ward, Eddie Velez, David Crowley, Donald Hotton, Marta Kober, Laura Esterman, Sherri Stone, Michael Shaner, Vincent J. Isaac, Monica Calhoun*
A young student opens a refuge for the rehabilitation of child prostitutes, in this flimsy and exploitative attempt at social drama. Based on the real-life experiences of Lois Lee, who attempted to research into the roots of female crime, as part of her doctoral thesis.
Boa: book by Dr Lois Lee/story by William Wood.
DRA                           89 min (ort 100 min) mTV
B,V                                           MGM

## CHILDREN SHOULDN'T PLAY WITH               18
DEAD THINGS *
Benjamin (Bob) Clark   USA                    1973
*Alan Ormsby, Anya Ormsby, Valerie Mauches, Jane Daly, Jeffrey Gillen*
A film company goes to an island to make a film and takes over a rural graveyard, unwittingly resurrecting the dead when witchcraft is dabbled in. Unusual but totally unfrightening – the stupid script sees to that.
HOR                             90 min; 78 min (SID)
B,V,V2                           INT/CBS L/A; SID

## CHILDREN, THE *                                18
Max Kalmanowicz      USA                      1980
*Martin Shakar, Gil Rogers, Gale Garnett*
Mysterious gas from a nuclear plant contaminates a school bus full of kids, they become radioactive and burn anyone who touches them. And if this plot sounds like something from a 1950s B-movie, that's just what it resembles.
Aka: CHILDREN OF RAVENSBACK
HOR                                           89 min
B,V          INT/CBS; VCL L/A; ALPHA/INT; APX

## CHILD'S PLAY *
Val Guest             UK                      1984
*Mary Crosby, Nicholas Clay, Debbie Chasan, Suzanne Church, Joanna Joseph*
A couple wake up one day to find that their home is encased in a solid wall. If that wasn't sufficient to spoil their day, they find that the TV screen displays a strange symbol and green slime begins to pour down the chimney.
HOR                                           72 min
B,V                                           BWV

## CHILD'S PLAY ***                               15
Tom Holland           USA                     1988
*Catherine Hicks, Brad Dourif, Chris Sarandon, Alex Vincent, Dinah Manoff, Tommy Swerdlow, Jack Colvin*
Horror yarn in which a child is the only one aware of the fact that his new doll is possessed by the spirit of a dead murderer. Eventually he gets the grown-ups to believe him, but not before several murders have taken place. A highlight of this well-made chiller is the excellent special effects in which the doll comes to life.
HOR                             81 min (ort 87 min)
V/sh                                          WHV

## CHILLER **                                     15
Wes Craven            USA                      1985
*Michael Beck, Beatrice Straight, Paul Sorvino, Laura Jackson, Dick O'Neill, Alan Fudge*
A man deep frozen for 10 years is revived but starts to behave rather strangely, eventually conducting a reign of terror. Variable quality horror yarn that fails to make the best of its plot.

HOR                    94 min (ort 100 min) mTV
B,V                                         CBS

## CHINA CAT, THE **
Robert C. Chinn        USA              1977
*John C. Holmes, Desiree Clearbranch, Eileen Welles,*
*Jennifer Richards, Kyoto, John Seeman, Monte*
*Stevens*
Five girls go to bed with private detective Johnny
Wadd, as each one attempts to get hold of a stolen jade
figurine of a cat he has obtained. A happy, harmless
and plotless film; a futher instalment to THE SILKEN
PUSSYCAT.
Osca: LITTLE ANGEL PUSS
A                       70 min (ort 80 min)
B,V                                         CAL

## CHINA GIRL **
                                            R18
Paolo Uccelo           USA              1974
*Annette Haven, James Young, Pamela Yen, Tom*
*Douglas, Barry Fry*
A secret formula that can affect memory is eagerly
sought by a foreign country, whose agent will pay any
price to get it. It was created by a male and female
scientist team, and to obtain it they are both kidnap-
ped to be tortured with pleasure by a sinister Madame
Wu and her associates. The female scientist exhausts
every man Madame can find and this mildly amusing
spoof ends with their rescue by a US agent.
Aka: EMBODIMENT OF FORBIDDEN PLEASURE,
THE
Osca: EXPOSE ME NOW (asa)
A                                       87 min
B,V                          EVI; WEC; HAR

## CHINA GIRL ***
                                            18
Abel Ferrara           USA              1987
*James Russo, Richard Panebianco, Sari Chang, David*
*Caruso, Russell Wong, Joey Chin, James Hong*
An ethnic romance story with the relationship be-
tween an Italian boy and his Chinese girlfriend
leading to gang warfare between the respective
communities who disapprove of this liaison. An
energetic and violent updating of WEST SIDE
STORY, set as before among the street gangs of New
York City.
A/AD                        89 min Cut (7 sec)
B,V                                         VES

## CHINA LAKE MURDERS, THE **
                                            15
Alan Metzger           USA              1989
*Tom Skerritt, Michael Parks, Nancy Everhard, Lara*
*Parker, Lauren Tewes, Bill McKinney, Lonny*
*Chapman*
A big-city cop has a breakdown and goes off on
vacation, where he embarks on a series of murders at
a small desert town. A fairly well made thriller
over-burdened with excessive dialogue.
THR                    85 min (ort 100 min) mCab
V                                           CIC

## CHINA O'BRIEN **
                                            18
Robert Clouse          USA              1989
*Cynthia Rothrock, Richard Norton, Patrick Adamson,*
*David Blackwell*
A tough female cop and martial arts expert kills in
self defence, promptly resigning from the force and
returning to her home town. Once there, she finds that
she is once more called upon to use her prowess, even
though she has sworn never again to use violence.
A/AD                                    86 min
V                                           EIV

## CHINA O'BRIEN 2 **
                                            18
Robert Clouse          USA              1989
*Cynthia Rothrock, Richard Norton, Keith Cooke,*
*Frank Magner, Harlow Marks, Tiffany Soter, Tricia*
*Quai, Don Re Sampson*
This sequel to the first martial arts action thriller has

better production values but essentially provides more
of the same. As sheriff of a small town our intrepid
heroine is involved with investigations into some
gangland killings and soon meets the baddies headon.
A/AD                                    82 min
V                                           EIV

## CHINA ROSE **
Robert Day             USA              1983
*George C. Scott, Ali McGraw, Michael Biehn, Denis*
*Lill, David Snell, James Hong, Carolyn Ellis Levine,*
*John Nisbet, Tong Lan Hwa, Harry Ip, Alice Lau,*
*Lillian Lee, Ray Burrus, Kan Tien Chi, Eric Chan, Yu*
*Fu, Charles Woo*
An American businessman searches for his son who
disappeared during the Chinese Cultural revolution.
He engages the services of an interpreter with whom
he becomes emotionally involved, and the pair soon
find themselves involved with drug traffickers.
Absorbing but rather spoilt by slow development and
poor casting.
DRA                              100 min mTV
B,V                                         VFP

## CHINA SYNDROME, THE ***
                                            PG
James Bridges          USA              1979
*Jane Fonda, Jack Lemmon, Michael Douglas, Scott*
*Brady, James Hampton, Peter Donat, Wilford Brimley,*
*James Karen*
Exciting drama about an attempted cover-up of an
accident at a nuclear power station in California. The
title is the nickname that has been used to describe
what could happen in the event of a reactor core
meltdown taking place. Tense and quite chilling, with
fine performances from Fonda as a TV reporter and
Lemmon as a dedicated executive working for the
company that runs the plant. Written by Mike Gray,
T.S. Cook and James Bridges.
THR                                    120 min
B,V                                         RCA

## CHINATOWN ***
                                            15
Roman Polanski         USA              1974
*Jack Nicholson, Faye Dunaway, John Huston, Perry*
*Lopez, John Hillerman, Darrell Zwerling, Diane Ladd,*
*Burt Young, Bruce Glover, Roman Polanski*
Film set in Los Angeles in 1937, where a private
detective hired by a woman to investigate her hus-
band's love-affairs, stumbles onto a complex web of
corruption and intrigue. A broodingly atmospheric
film rather spoilt by an excessively convoluted plot,
though Nicholson as the detective conveys just the
right tone of world-weary cynicism. Look out for
Polanski who pops up briefly as a knife-happy midget.
AA: Screen (Orig) (Robert Towne).
THR                                    131 min
B,V,LV                                      CIC

## CHINATOWN KID **
                                            18
Chang Cheh             HONG KONG        1978
*Shirley Yu, Alexander Fu Sheng, Shaw Yin-yin, Kuo*
*Che, Sun Chien, Lo Meng, Tsai Hung*
A martial arts expert is forced to leave Hong Kong in
a hurry, and finds he can make a good living in San
Francisco's Chinatown.
MAR                    108 min Cut (1 min 30 sec)
B,V                                         WHV

## CHINESE BOXER, THE **
                                            18
Jimmy Wang Yu          HONG KONG        1968
*Jimmy Wang-Yu, Wu Szu-Yuan, Yang Chin-Chen, Lo*
*Lieh, Wang Ping, Chen Hsing*
One of the first of the kung fu films to reach the West,
this one has the highly original plot of a disciple who
has to avenge to death of his master.
Aka: LUNG HU TOU
MAR              90 min (ort 94 min) Cut (1 min 3 sec)
B,V                                  VPD; TEVP

**CHINESE BOXES ★★**  15
Chris Petit  UK  1984
*Will Patton, Gottfried John, Adelheid Arndt, Robbie*
*Coltrane, Beate Jensen, Susanne Meierhofer, Jonathan*
*Kinsler, Kit Carson, Chris Sievernich, Martin Muller,*
*Christopher Petit*
A young heroin smuggler in Berlin, finds himself
drawn into a complex intrigue that involves a girl's
murder.
THR  87 min
B,V  VES/PVG

**CHINESE DRAGON ★★**
Chang I  HONG KONG
*Chang I, Yueh Yong, Chang Feng*
Standard kung fu punch-up; honour must be avenged
etc. Average.
MAR  80 min
B,V  IFS/CBS

**CHINESE DRAGON, THE ★★**
  HONG KONG
*Man Ting, Chan Shun Yet, Wei Tze Han, Lee Quan, Le*
*Yuen*
More kung fu action in this routine martial arts tale.
MAR  80 min
B,V  NORM; VIDTAP

**CHINESE HERCULES ★★**
Choy Tak  HONG KONG  1974
*Yang Sze, Chaing Fan*
A young girl prevents a villain from attacking poor
labourers in this slightly unusual martial arts tale.
Aka: FROM CHINA WITH DEATH
MAR  92 min
B,V,V2  IFS/CBS

**CHINESE STUNTMEN ★★**
  HONG KONG
*Bruce Li (Ho Tsung-Tao), Jimmy Coban*
A famous actor has his life insured for 2 million
dollars by his producer who is planning to kill him.
Fair if ludicrously plotted martial arts action, with a
Bruce Lee clone.
MAR  90 min
B,V  VPD

**CHINESE TYPEWRITER, THE ★★★**  PG
Lou Antonio  USA  1979
*Tom Selleck, James Whitmore Jr, Don Ameche, Jamie*
*Lyn Bauer, Marlena Amey, William Daniels, Lane*
*Bradbury, Kathryn Leigh Scott, David Palmer, George*
*Fisher, Walt Davis, Elizabeth Halliday, Michael Brick,*
*June Whitley Taylor*
Pilot for a TV series called "Boston And Kilbride"
about a pair of rather happy-go-lucky private eyes.
Here, they are given the task of recovering a stolen jet
plane and getting it back safely to its owner. When
they fail in their efforts they decide to appeal to the
crook's greed, by offering him what they claim is the
blueprint for a workable Chinese-script typewriter.
Quite enjoyable in a bland and easy-going way.
Aka: BOSTON AND KILBRIDE: THE CHINESE
TYPEWRITER
COM  78 min mTV
B,V  CIC

**CHISHOLMS, THE ★★★**
Mel Stuart  USA  1978
*Robert Preston, Rosemary Harris, Ben Murphy, Brian*
*Kerwin, Jimmy Van Patten, Stacey Nelkin, Susan*
*Swift, Charles Frank, Glynnis O'Connor, Sandra*
*Griego, David Hayward, Anthony Zerbe, Brian Keith,*
*Doug Kershaw, Tom Taylor*
Epic dealing with a large family who go from Virginia
to California and on the way have a number of
adventures. Typical family Western with splendid
location work and production detail, but a few inci-
dents too many. Music is by Elmer Bernstein with

extracts from Aaron Copeland's "Appalachian
Spring", "Billy the Kid" and "Rodeo". Compiled from a
TV series that consisted of six 96 min episodes.
WES  300 min (2 cassettes) mTV
B,V,V2  GHV

**CHISUM ★★**  PG
Andrew V. McLaglen  USA  1970
*John Wayne, Forrest Tucker, Christopher George,*
*Pamela McMyler, Geoffrey Deuel, Ben Johnson, Glenn*
*Corbett, Bruce Cabot, Andrew Prine, Patric Knowles,*
*Richard Jaeckel, Lynda Day (George), John Agar,*
*Lloyd Battista*
Unbelievable Western in which a cattle baron teams
up with Billy the Kid (!) to fight corrupt officials.
Forgettable all the way through until the climax,
which is a laughable, utterly overdone saloon fight.
WES  107 min (ort 110 min)
V  WHV

**CHITTY CHITTY BANG BANG ★**  U
Ken Hughes  UK  1968
*Dick Van Dyke, Sally Ann Howes, Lionel Jeffries, Gert*
*Frobe, Anna Quayle, Benny Hill, James Robertson*
*Justice, Robert Helpmann, Heather Ripley, Adrian*
*Hall, Barbara Windsor, Davy Kaye, Stanley Unwin,*
*Peter Arne, Victor Maddern*
An inventor rescues a derelict car which he then
imbues with fantastic properties, enabling it to fly.
Sloppy special effects and a lousy score make this kid's
musical adventure a most forgettable experience.
Scripted by Roald Dahl and Hughes.
Boa: novel by Ian Fleming.
JUV  145 min
V/sh  WHV

**CHOCKY ★★**  U
Vic Hughes/Christopher Hodson
  UK  1984
*Andrew Ellams, James Hazeldine, Carol Drinkwater*
A young boy becomes the host for a strange disembo-
died visitor from another planet. Compiled from four
30-minute episodes of a TV serial. Average.
Boa: novel by John Wyndham.
FAN  112 min mTV
B,V  THAMES/TEVP

**CHOCOLATE KILLER, THE ★**  15
Michael Adrien  USA  1986
*Rod Browning, Robert Chapel, Tabi Cooper, Michael*
*D. Roberts*
A man has to catch a crazed sex killer in order to
restore his reputation as a folk hero, in this tasteless
and unfunny comedy.
Aka: LIFE AND TIMES OF THE CHOCOLATE
KILLER, THE
COM  80 min
B,V  MOG

**CHOCOLATE WAR, THE ★★**  15
Keith Gordon  USA  1988
*Ilan Mitchell-Smith, Wally Ward, Jenny Wright, Doug*
*Hutchinson, John Glover, Bud Cort, Adam Baldwin*
A Catholic boys school is largely controlled by a secret
society of student fascists. An idealistic student
clashes with both them and his sadistic teacher when
he starts bucking the system, most notably by refusing to take part in a fund-raising chocolate sale, hence
the title. Gordon's directorial debut is fairly assured,
but this strange blend of comedy and drama is both
oppressive and heavy-handed.
Boa: novel by Robert Cormier.
DRA  99 min (ort 103 min)
V  MED

**CHOICE, THE ★★**  15
David Greene  USA  1981
*Susan Clark, Mitchell Ryan, Largo Woodruff, Paul*
*Regina, Kathleen Lloyd, Lisa Jane Persky, Joanne*

Naile, Justin Lord, Jennifer Warren, Karen Machon, John Chappell, Jack Rader, Vernon Weddle, Cynthia Grover, Mary Ellen O'Neill
A young pregnant girl contemplating abortion discovers that her mother faced the same dilemma years before. Run-of-the-mill melodrama that's inevitably hampered by the contrived script. Not to be confused with another mTV film made in 1986 called CHOICES, that also dealt with this issue.
DRA                                              96 min mTV
B,V                                         VFP L/A; HER

## CHOICES **
David Lowell Rich        USA                    1986
George C. Scott, Jacqueline Bisset, Melissa Gilbert, Laurie Kennedy, Steven Flynn, Nancy Allison, Kirsten Bishopric, Daliah Bache, Nicholas A. Bourdon, Catherine Colney, Richard Dumont, Lorena Gale, Barbara Ann Jones
A self-righteous judge who opposes abortion is placed in a dilemma when his second wife and unmarried teenage daughter both become pregnant and want to have abortions. A glossy soap opera style movie that attempts to present the pros and cons of this issue, but is hampered by the superficial nature of the script, written by Judith Parker. See THE CHOICE, that also dealt with the issue of unwanted pregnancies.
DRA                                          104 min mTV
B,V                                                CAN

## CHOICES **                                        18
Silvio Narizzano        USA                     1981
Paul Carafotes, Demi Moore, Val Avery, Victor French, Dennis Patrick, Leila Goldoni, Pat Buttram
A partially deaf player is dropped from the school football team and soon becomes alienated and in danger of becoming a drug-taking drop-out. Good performances help this sincere but mawkish effort.
Aka: DILEMMA (MOG); TOUCHDOWN (FOX)
DRA                                              87 min
B,V,V2        HOK; FOX; MOG (Betamax and VHS only)

## CHOIRBOYS, THE *                                  18
Robert Aldrich           USA                    1977
Charles Durning, Louis Gossett Jr, Perry King, Clyde Kusatsu, Stephen Macht, Tim McIntire, Randy Quaid, Chuck Sacci, Don Stroud, James Woods, Burt Young, Robert Webber, Jeanie Bell, Blair Brown, Michele Carey
Black comedy that looks at the lives of the officers in a police department in Los Angeles, who relieve the pressure of their job with some riotous forms of entertainment. A ponderous and vulgar effort, about as witty as a cosh, and only slightly more articulate. From the novel by Wambaugh, who is said to have disowned this adaptation – and no wonder.
Boa: novel by Joseph Wambaugh.
COM                                             119 min
V/h                                                CBS

## CHOOSE ME ****                                    15
Alan Rudolph             USA                    1984
Lesley Ann Warren, Keith Carradine, Genevieve Bujold, Rae Dawn Chong, Patrick Bauchau, John Larroquette, John Considine
Story of lonely people in a big city. A radio counsellor ends up sharing a flat with one of her confidantes and becomes involved with her emotional problems. An inventive, witty and perceptive look at the roles people play in life, with fine performances and a great script. Filmed in Los Angeles.
DRA                                    106 min (ort 114 min)
B,V                                    ODY; CH5 (VHS only)

## CHOPPING MALL **                                  18
Jim Wynorski             USA                    1986
Paul Bartel, Mary Woronov, Barbara Crampton, John Terlesky, Kelli Maroney, Tony O'Dell, Russell Todd, Dick Miller, Karrie Emerson, Suzee Slater, Nick Segal,

Mel Welles, Gerrit Graham, Angela Aames, Paul Coufos, Arthur Roberts
Teenagers holding an impromptu party in a store's bed department after closing, come under threat from three high-tech security robots that a thunderstorm has caused to malfunction. The plot is reminiscent of WESTWORLD as well as countless teenagers-in-peril movies, and despite a few in-jokes and cameo roles, quickly lapses into cliche.
Aka: KILLBOTS; R.O.B.O.T.
HOR                                              73 min
B,V                                                VES

## CHOPPY AND THE PRINCESS **                        U
                         USA                    1984
Pilot for a series of cartoons about the adventures of a princess and a leprechaun in Silverland. In this first story, the queen bears a princess, but she cannot inherit due to an ancient law. Choppy is sent down from heaven to put things right.
Aka: ADVENTURES OF CHOPPY AND THE PRINCESS, THE (WISE); SECRET OF THE PHANTOM KNIGHT
CAR                                    75 min (ort 80 min)
V                                          AST L/A; WISE

## CHORUS CALL **                                    18
Antonio Sheppard        USA                     1978
Kay Parker, Susan London, Richard Bolla, Bob Hollander, Beth Anne, Darby Lloyd Raines, Joe Nassivera (Joey Civera), Bobby Astyr
Carefully made sex film very loosely tied to the story of a Broadway superstar, who can hire or fire members of the cast of the shows she appears in. Most of the action in this one takes place in a Broadway theatre and the story is soon forgotten amid a welter of sexual couplings. In between, there are a few well-mounted numbers and these help compensate for the weaknesses of the plot.
Osca: FEMALE FANTASIES/MARY! MARY! (asa)
A                          67 min (ort 78 min) Cut (5 min 21 sec)
B,V                                                HAR

## CHORUS LINE, A **                                 PG
Richard Attenborough   USA                      1985
Michael Douglas, Alyson Reed, Terrence Mann, Audrey Landers, Blane Savage, Pam Klinger, Charles McGowan, Justin Ross, Gregg Burge, Nicole Fosse, Janet Jones, Cameron English, Vicki Frederick, Michael Belvins, Yamil Borges
This failed attempt to recreate the feeling of the Broadway hit musical, has performers auditioning for a place on a chorus line and revealing their hopes and fears as they perform before cynical director Douglas. A dismal filming of an excellent musical.
Boa: musical by Nicholas Dante and James Kirkwood.
MUS                                    112 min (ort 118 min)
B, V/sh                                      EHE; CH5

## CHORUS OF DISAPPROVAL, A **                       PG
Michael Winner          UK                      1988
Jeremy Irons, Anthony Hopkins, Prunella Scales, Sylvia Syms, Gareth Hunt, Lionel Jeffries, Jenny Seagrove, Richard Briers, Patsy Kensit, Alexandra Pigg
Having moved to a small seaside town, a shy widower joins an amateur theatrical troupe that's dominated as much by its romantic intrigues as it is by the overbearing director. Ayckbourn's stage play is clumsily translated to the screen, where the solid performances of the players can mask neither the uninspired direction nor the shallowness of the material.
Boa: play by Alan Ayckbourn.
COM                                    95 min (ort 100 min)
V                                                  MGM

## CHOSEN, THE ***
Jeremy Paul Kagan    USA    1982
PG

*Robby Benson, Maximilian Schell, Rod Steiger, Barry Miller, Hildy Brooks, Ron Rifkin, Val Avery*
Adapted from Potok's novel, this is a wonderfully evocative recreation of post-war Brooklyn, in which a young Jewish boy forms a friendship with an orthodox Chasidic boy. Steiger as a Chasidic rabbi was never more convincing. The film contains some death camp sequences that some may find distressing.
Boa: novel by Chaim Potok.
DRA                              112 min
B,V,V2                        EHE; CH5

## CHRISTIANE F. **
Ulrich Edel    WEST GERMANY    1981
18

*Nadja Brunkhorst, Thomas Haustein, Jens Kuphal, Reiner Wolk*
Realistic drama about teenage junkies and one girl who turns to prostitution in order to support her habit. A sincere, uneven and rather forgettable effort, based on a real story. David Bowie appears briefly in a short concert sequence.
Boa: book by Christiane F.
DRA                    120 min Cut (5 min 2 sec)
B,V,V2          SPEC/POLY; CH5 (VHS only)

## CHRISTINA **
Paco Lara    USA/SPAIN    1984
18

*Jewel Shepard, Ian Serra, Enrique Johnson*
Story of one of the richest women in the world and her quest for new sexual experiences.
Aka: CHRISTINA AND SEXUAL RETRAINING; CHRISTINA Y LA RECONVERSION SEXUAL
A                              85 min Cut (3 min)
B,V                                 MGM

## CHRISTINE **
John Carpenter    USA    1982
18

*Keith Gordon, John Stockwell, Alexandra Paul, Robert Prosky, Harry Dean Stanton, Christine Belford, Roberts Blossom*
A 1958 Plymouth is a demonic automobile that kills and maims all who come between it and its owner. A gruesome but flimsy horror yarn that starts off with promise but rapidly rolls downhill. Written by Bill Phillips.
Boa: novel by Stephen King.
HOR                              106 min
V/sh                                  RCA

## CHRISTMAS CAROL, A ***
Edwin L. Marin    USA    1938
U

*Reginald Owen, Gene Lockhart, Kathleen Lockhart, Terry Kilburn, Leo G. Carroll, Barry MacKay, Lynne Carver, Ann Rutherford, June Lockhart*
With the arrival of several ghosts, the life of Scrooge the miser is transformed on the eve of Christmas. An early and carefully made adaptation of the famous Dickens classic, with good period detail. Owen replaced Lionel Barrymore, the latter's lameness preventing him from starring as Scrooge, to which role he gave substance in a number of Christmas radio broadcasts. June Lockhart appears in her screen debut.
Boa: short story by Charles Dickens.
FAN                              69 min B/W
V                                     MGM

## CHRISTMAS CAROL, A **
AUSTRALIA    1979
U

Cartoon animation of the famous Dickens classic, with miserly old Scrooge having a change of heart after a visit from the ghosts of Christmas. Fair.
Boa: short story by Charles Dickens.
CAR              45 min; 72 min (RPTA or MSD)
B,V   RPTA; MSD (VHS only); VCL; CHILD; STYLUS
(VHS only)

## CHRISTMAS CAROL, A ****
Clive Donner    USA    1984
U

*George C. Scott, Nigel Davenport, Frank Finley, Edward Woodward, Lucy Gutteridge, Angela Pleasence, Roger Rees, David Warner, Susannah York, Anthony Walters, Timothy Bateson, Michael Carter, Michael Gough*
An excellent version of this famous tale, with Scott in fine form as a memorable Scrooge. A beautifully made film offering much to delight, not least being the film location – Shrewsbury in England. The excellent script is by Roger O. Hirson.
Boa: short story by Charles Dickens.
DRA                              100 min mTV
V/sh                                  MED

## CHRISTMAS EVIL ***
Lewis Jackson    USA    1980

*Brandon Maggart, Jeffrey de Munn, Ray Barry, Dianne Hull, Andy Fenwick, Joe Jamrog, Brian Neville, Scott McKay, Peter Friedman, Bobby Lesser, Sam Gray*
Three children wait for Santa Claus on Christmas Eve, but it turns out to be not their father, but a deranged toy-factory worker who dresses up as Santa to go on a killing spree. A gruesome little chiller that deserved more success than it achieved on release.
Aka: TERROR IN TOYLAND; YOU BETTER WATCH OUT
HOR                    89 min (ort 100 min)
B,V,V2                            IFS/CBS

## CHRISTMAS MOUNTAIN **
Pierro Moro    USA    1980

*Slim Pickens, Mark Miller, Barbara Stanger, Fran Ryan, Tina Minard, John Hart*
An old cowboy discovers the true meaning of Christmas when he helps a pregnant woman who has recently been widowed, during a blizzard in 1888. Pleasant little family drama.
DRA                              90 min
B,V                                  VUL

## CHRISTMAS STAR, THE ***
Alan Shapiro    USA    1986
U

*Edward Asner, Fred Gwynne, Jim Metzler, Rene Auberjonois, Susan Tyrell, Karen Landry, Alan North, Philip Bruns, Nicholas Van Burek, Vicki Wauchope, Zachary Ansley, Peter Bibby, Lillian Carlos, David Glyn-Jones, Clair Brown*
A con man breaks out of jail dressed as Santa in order to recover some hidden loot, but is taken for the genuine article by a couple of kids. An amiable Disney fantasy.
Boa: story by Alan Shapiro, Jeffrey White and Carol Dysinger.
JUV                    90 min (ort 100 min) mTV
B,V                                  WDV

## CHRISTMAS STORY, A ***
Bob Clark    USA    1983
PG

*Peter Billingsley, Melinda Dillon, Darren McGavin, Ian Petrella, Scott Schwartz, Tedde Moore, Jean Shepherd (narration)*
An account of a young boy growing up in the 1950s and of the many devious schemes he invents in order to be given an air rifle for Christmas. A charming and warm-hearted tale, partly based on Shepherd's novel, and narrated by her in the first person. Directed, believe it or not, by the man who gave us PORKY'S.
Boa: novel In God We Trust, All Others Pay Cash by Jean Shepherd.
COM                    89 min (ort 98 min)
B,V                                  MGM

## CHRISTMAS TO REMEMBER, A ***
George Englund    USA    1978

*Jason Robards, Eva Marie Saint, Joanne Woodward, George Perry, Bryan Englund, Mary Beth Manning,*

*Nora Martin, Arvid Carlson, Mildred Carlson, Alex Mayer, Pamela Danser, Guy Paul, Allen Hamilton, Sally Chamberlin*
A city boy goes to stay for Christmas with his grandparents in the country, in a tale set in the years of the Depression. A sentimental but enjoyable drama, helped along by a strong cast.
Boa: novel The Melodeon by Glendon Swarthout.
DRA                           95 min (ort 104 min) mTV
B,V                                                    VTC

## CHRISTMAS WITHOUT SNOW, A ***            PG
John Korty            USA                          1979
*Michael Lerned, John Houseman, Valerie Curtin, Ramon Bieri, James Cromwell, David Knell, Calvin Levels, Ruth Nelson, Beah Richards, William Swetland, Ed Bogas, Daisietta Kim, Joy Carlin, Anne Lawder, Barbara Tarbuck*
Sentimental story with a seasonal flavour, telling of a new divorcee who joins an amateur choir struggling to mount a performance of Handel's Messiah, under the autocratic hand of a perfectionist music director.
Boa: story by John Korty.
DRA                                            96 min mTV
V                                                      VCC

## CHRISTOPHER COLUMBUS **                   PG
Alberto Lattunda    ITALY/USA                     1984
*Gabriel Byrne, Oliver Reed, Faye Dunaway, Rossano Brazzi, Virna Lisi, Raf Vallone, Max Von Sydow, Eli Wallach, Nicol Williamson, Michel Auclair, Massimo Girotti, Murray Melvin, Jack Watson, Larry Lamb, Massimo Girotti*
Compiled from a TV mini-series about the life of the famous voyager. A good-looking but essentially flat account, not helped by the wooden and unconvincing acting of the lead. Originally shown in six 50 minute episodes.
Aka: CRISTOFORO COLOMBO
DRA                           178 min (ort 360 min) mTV
B,V                                          HER L/A; CH5

## CHRISTY **
Steve Harris            USA                        1975
*Andrea True, Cindy West, Anne Christian, Harry Reems, Mark Stevens, Eric Edwards, Peter Smith*
A couple who live by their wits have a 15-year-old daughter who pretends to be older. Much to the disgust of her boyfriend, she gets a job as a stripper at a local pub and later cons a wealthy guy out of money, by getting him to make love to her. Meanwhile, mom and dad engage in various pursuits of their own.
A                                              60 min
V                                                      RIP

## CHROME AND HOT LEATHER **                 15
Lee Frost            USA                          1971
*William Smith, Tony Young, Michael Haynes, Peter Brown*
A bunch of Green Berets have a run-in with a gang of tough bikers and the conflict soon escalates. Unfortunately, the bikers do not realise that their adversaries are trained to kill, in this violent action film.
A/AD                                           91 min
B,V                                                    RNK

## CHRONICLE OF A DEATH FORETOLD ***         15
Francesco Rosi        ITALY                        1987
*Rupert Everett, Gian Maria Volonte, Ornella Muti, Anthony Delon, Irene Papas, Lucia Bose*
A steamy tale of sexual passion, intrigue, jealousy and death, set in a small Columbian town where a man rejects his bride when he discovers that she is not a virgin.
Aka: CRONACA DI UNA MORTE ANNUNCIATA
Boa: novel by Gabriel Garcia Marquez.
DRA                           105 min (ort 110 min)
B,V                                                    RCA

## CHRONICLES OF NARNIA, THE: PRINCE CASPIAN **                                     U
Marilyn Fox            UK                          1989
*Sophie Wilcox, Sophie Cook, Jonathan Scott, Richard Dempsey, Barbara Kellerman, Michael Aldridge*
The second part of a competent BBC adaptation of the "Narnia" books of C.S. Lewis that began with "The Lion, The Witch And The Wardrobe". In this adventure the four children arrive in the magical land of Narnia and find that King Miraz is plotting to take over the kingdom and that Prince Caspian has fled for his safety.
Boa: novel by C.S. Lewis.
JUV                                            57 min mTV
V/h                                                    BBC

## CHRONICLES OF NARNIA, THE: THE VOYAGE OF THE DAWN TREADER **                     U
Marilyn Fox            UK                          1989
*Sophie Wilcox, Sophie Cook, Jonathan Scott, Richard Dempsey, Barbara Kellerman, Michael Aldridge*
The third part of this enjoyable BBC adaptation. In this adventure three of the children journey to Narnia and sail with Prince Caspian in search of seven missing lords of Narnia.
Boa: novel by C.S. Lewis.
JUV                                           109 min mTV
V/h                                                    BBC

## CHUCK MOOL **                             PG
E.B. Clucher (Enzo Barboni)
                       ITALY                      1969
*Leonard Mann, Woody Strode, Peter Martell*
A young man suffering from amnesia, escapes from a mental asylum in order to search for his past.
Aka: CIAK MULL, L'UNO DELLA VENDETTA
WES                                            90 min
B,V                                           VFP L/A; HER

## CHURCHILL'S LEOPARDS **
Maurizio Pradeaux
                       ITALY/SPAIN               1970
*Richard Harrison, Klaus Kinski, Pilar Velasquel*
British saboteurs and resistance fighters join forces in order to blow up a vital dam.
Aka: I LEOPARDI DI CHURCHILL; LOS LEOPARDOS DE CHURCHILL
WAR                                            84 min
B,V,V2                                                 FFV

## CIAO! MANHATTAN **                        18
John Palmer/David Weisman
                       USA                         1972
*Edie Sedgwick, Wesley Hayes, Isabel Jewell, Jane Holzer, Viva, Roger Vadim*
A clumsy attempt to splice two films together, with the first one (in B/W) a kind of mystery thriller set in the 1960s, and the second (in colour) a study of Sedgwick living out her last days at the home of her parents. Not an appealing effort, but this comment on the pathetic life of the star (who died at 28 just after the second film) is as disturbing as it is disjointed.
DRA                           95 min B/W and Colour
V                                                      PAL

## CINCINNATI KID, THE ***                   15
Norman Jewison        USA                          1965
*Steve McQueen, Edward·G. Robinson, Karl Malden, Ann-Margret, Tuesday Weld, Cab Calloway, Rip Torn, Joan Blondell, Jack Weston*
In New Orleans in the 1930s a bunch of roving card-sharks get together for a big game, with a young challenger taking on an older champion. Inevitably reminding one of THE HUSTLER, though as with that film, some contrived romantic interest detracts from the story. Scripted by Ring Lardner Jr and Terry Southern, with Jewison replacing Sam Peckinpah as director.

Boa: novel by Richard Jessup.
DRA 101 min
B,V MGM

**CINDERELLA \*\*** U
Charles S. Dubin USA 1964
*Ginger Rogers, Jo Van Fleet, Lesley Ann Warren,*
*Stuart Damon, Celeste Holm, Walter Pidgeon*
Amiable musical version of the fairytale.
MUS 77 min
V CASPIC

**CINDERELLA \*\*** Uc
1989
A competent animated version of this much-filmed
classic tale, part of the Pickwick series of "Animated
Classics".
CAR 40 min
V PICK

**CINDERELLA 2000 \*\*\*** 18
Al Adamson USA 1977
*Catherine Erhardt, Vaughn Armstrong, Jay B. Larson*
In the year 2047 the Earth is run by computers and
robots. Sex is strictly controlled and only allowed for a
fortunate few. This forms the background to a space-
age revamping of the Cinderella story.
A 89 min
V VPD

**CINDERELLA LIBERTY \*\*\*** 15
Mark Rydell USA 1973
*James Caan, Marsha Mason, Eli Wallach, Kirk*
*Calloway, Burt Young, Bruce Kirby Jr, Allyn Ann*
*McLerie, Dabney Coleman, Sally Kirkland*
Whilst on shore leave, a good-natured but rather
simple sailor meets a streetwise prostitute with a
black son and falls in love with her. An awkward
blend of romance and squalor, held together by
sensitive performances from the leads.
Boa: novel by Darryl Ponicsan.
DRA 112 min (ort 117 min)
V CBS

**CINDERELLA'S WONDERWORLD \*\*** U
USA 1980
A young girl and her widowed father live happily
together until the arrival of a crafty fortune teller and
her scheming daughter.
Aka: CINDERELLA'S
WONDERLAND
CAR 77 min
B,V ALPHA/INT; VGM (VHS only)

**CINDERFELLA \*** U
Frank Tashlin USA 1960
*Jerry Lewis, Ed Wynne, Judith Anderson, Anna*
*Maria Alberghetti, Henry Silva, Robert Hutton, Count*
*Basie*
A garish and overblown adaptation of the famous
fairytale suitably adjusted to serve as a vehicle for the
comic talents (such as they are) of Lewis. Talky and
ineffectual, this exercise in pretentiousness works
neither as a comedy nor as a fantasy. A dull and
dismal dud.
COM 91 min
V COL

**CINDY'S LOVE GAMES \*\*** 18
Aldo Grimaldi ITALY 1979
*Cindy Leadbetter, Anna Maria Clementi, Maurice*
*Poli, Vassili Karis*
Story of an insatiable woman who uses her sexuality
to take advantage of all the men who lust after her.
Aka: AMANTI MIEI; TIGHT FIT (DRUM or HTM)
A 84 min Cut (CAN: 3 min 40 sec); 89 min Cut
(DRUM: 1 min 3 sec) (ort 100 min)
B,V VSP L/A; HTM L/A; BLUMO; CAN; DRUM

**CINEMA PARADISO \*\*\*\*** PG
Giuseppe Tornatore
FRANCE/ITALY 1989
*Philippe Noiret, Jacques Perrin, Antonella Attili, Enzo*
*Cannavale, Isa Danieli, Leo Gullota, Mario Leonardi,*
*Pupella Maggio, Leopoldo Trieste, Salvatore Cascio,*
*Agnese Nano*
Set in Sicily just after WW2, this loving tribute to the
cinema explores the fascination a local cinema exerts
on a youngster, where he enjoys a friendship with the
kindly projectionist. A warm, poignant and moving
film that recaptures the magic of the picture palaces of
old. First released at 155 minutes but prudently
shortened, it won the Special Jury Prize at Cannes
1989. Written by Tornatore with music by Ennio
Morricone. AA: Foreign.
DRA 124 min
V PAL

**CIRCLE OF CHILDREN, A \*\*\*\*** 
Don Taylor USA 1977
*Jane Alexander, Rachel Roberts, David Ogden Stiers,*
*Nan Martin, Matthew Laborteaux, Peter Brandon,*
*Jason Tyler, Kyle Richards, Susan Pratt, Judy Lewis,*
*Ray Buktenica, Pearl Shear, Christopher West, Niki*
*Dantine*
Moving story of a school for emotionally disturbed
children, and the rich suburban woman who finds
some meaning in her life by working there as a
volunteer. MacCracken's autobiographical novel is
translated to screen with superb performances from
both Alexander and Roberts, as the demanding
teacher who at first regards Alexander as little more
than a wealthy woman killing time. Followed by a
sequel.
Boa: novel by Mary MacCracken.
DRA 100 min mTV
B,V WDV L/A

**CIRCLE OF TWO \*\*** 15
Jules Dassin CANADA 1980
*Richard Burton, Tatum O'Neal, Nuala Fitzgerald,*
*Robin Gammell, Patricia Collins, Kate Reid*
A 60-year-old artist falls for a 16-year-old student and
has a romantic but platonic relationship with her, in
this superficial and rather empty effort.
Boa: story A Lesson In Love by Marie Terese Baird.
DRA 102 min
B,V VIPCO

**CIRCLEMAN \*\*\*** 18
Damien Lee CANADA 1987
*Vernon Wells, William Sanderson, Franco Columbo,*
*Sonja Bellivue*
A washed-up fighter takes a job as a caretaker at a
local gym, and is forced back into the fight game in
order to help out his girlfriend's dad, who has got
mixed up with gangsters. Despite some similarities to
all those ROCKY films, this tale is held up by strong
performances and good characterisation.
DRA 87 min
B,V MED

**CIRCLES IN A FOREST \*\*** U
Regardt Van Den Bergh 1988
*Ian Bannen, Judi Trott, Arnold Vosloo*
An eco-tale for our age that's set in South Africa in the
19th century, where hardship forces a woodcutter to
turn to hunting elephants for their ivory. However,
his son refuses to join him and takes a job at the local
woodyard. There, he attempts to prove his worth to his
boss (and prospective father-in-law) by prospecting for
gold, setting off a chain of events that could destroy
his beloved forest. An earnest but rather dull drama.
Boa: novel by Darlene Matthee.
DRA 96 min
V AVALON

## CIRCUS OF HORRORS **
Sidney Hayers          UK               1959
*Anton Diffring, Erika Remberg, Yvonne Monlaur,*
*Donald Pleasence, Jane Hylton, Kenneth Griffith,*
*Conrad Phillips, Jack Gwillim, Vanda Hudson,*
*Yvonne Romain*
A plastic surgeon hides out in a circus after making a
series of botched operations. Here he recruits perfor-
mers from the ranks of criminals whose faces he
alters. Rather predictable and flat, and with a totally
contrived ending.
HOR                    87 min (ort 91 min)
B,V                                    TEVP

## CITIZEN KANE ****                    U
Orson Welles           USA               1941
*Orson Welles, Joseph Cotten, Agnes Moorehead,*
*Everett Sloane, Dorothy Comingore, Ray Collins,*
*George Coulouris, Ruth Warwick, William Alland,*
*Paul Stewart, Erskine Sanford*
Ambitious account of the career of a megalomaniac
newspaper tycoon, seen as a series of flashbacks, with
a reporter investigating the circumstances of his
death. A powerfully atmospheric film, its thin story is
partially hidden beneath erratic flashes of brilliance.
The newspaper tycoon William Hearst saw the film as
a veiled personal attack and ensured that none of his
papers gave it publicity. AA: Screen (Orig) (Herman J.
Mankiewicz/Orson Welles).
DRA                    120 min B/W
B,V                    HER; CH5 (VHS only)

## CITY BENEATH THE SEA ***             U
Irwin Allen            USA               1970
*Stuart Whitman, Rosemary Forsyth, Richard*
*Basehart, Robert Wagner, Joseph Cotten, James*
*Darren, Robert Colbert, Paul Stewart*
Futuristic tale of an underwater city, which is under
threat from a stray planetoid and other perils, in its
first year of existence. Fair fantasy adventure,
scripted by John Meredyth Lucas.
Aka: ONE HOUR TO DOOMSDAY
FAN                    90 min (ort 98 min) mTV
V                                      WHV

## CITY FOR CONQUEST ***                PG
Anatole Litvak         USA               1940
*James Cagney, Ann Sheridan, Frank Craven, Donald*
*Crisp, Arthur Kennedy, Frank McHugh, George*
*Tobias, Elia Kazan, Anthony Quinn, Jerome Cowan,*
*Lee Patrick, Blanche Yurka, Thurston Hall*
A New York truck driver takes up boxing, in the hope
of making a better life for himself and his composer
brother, but is injured in the course of a fight and loses
his sight. Corny and superficial it may be, but both in
terms of acting and production it's hard to fault.
Kennedy's first adult role and a rare appearance
before the cameras for Kazan as a small-time gangster. See also PARADISE ALLEY, a kind of 1978
update.
Boa: novel by Aben Kandel.
DRA                    94 min (ort 105 min) B/W
V                                      WHV

## CITY GIRL ***                        18
Martha Coolidge        USA               1984
*Laura Harrington, Joe Mastroianni, Carole McGill,*
*Peter Riegert, Jim Carrington, Geraldine Baron,*
*Colleen Camp*
A woman photographer trying to advance her career,
becomes drawn into a series of tragic events. A sound
and entertaining story, well acted and directed.
DRA                    81 min
B,V                                    CBS

## CITY HEAT *                          15
Richard Benjamin       USA               1984
*Clint Eastwood, Burt Reynolds, Jane Alexander,*
*Madeline Kahn, Irene Cara, Richard Roundtree, Rip*

*Torn, Tony LoBianco, William Sanderson*
A mean cop teams up with a slick private eye to solve
a murder case in Kansas City in the 1930s. Occasionally funny, but most of the time this brutish and
simple-minded gangster-versus-cop spoof is just plain
nasty. Written by Sam O. Brown (Blake Edwards).
COM                    93 min
V                                      WHV

## CITY KILLER *                        PG
Robert Lewis           USA               1984
*Heather Locklear, Gerald McRaney, Terence Knox,*
*Peter Mark Richman, John Harkins, Jeff Pomerantz,*
*Jason Bernard, Todd Susman, Audrey Totter,*
*Jeanetta Arnette, Adam Gregor, John Nesnow, Tom*
*Kindle, John Gamble, Sharon Madden*
A rejected lover takes to demolishing buildings as a
bizarre form of revenge, in this ponderous and unin-
spired thriller.
THR                    120 min mTV
B,V                                    EHE

## CITY LIMITS *                        15
Aaron Lipstadt         USA               1984
*Darrell Larson, John Stockwell, Kim Cattrall, Rae*
*Dawn Chong, John Diehl, Don Opper, Robby Benson,*
*James Earl Jones, Danny De La Paz, Norbert Weisser*
Futuristic urban adventure movie, in which a plague
wipes out the world's adult population, and gangs of
young thugs are left to battle it out. A messy and
incoherent disaster of a movie, set 15 years into the
future and best left there. Narration is by Jones. See
also GAS.
FAN                    85 min
B,V                                    POLY

## CITY OF BLOOD **                     15
Daryl Roodt      SOUTH AFRICA           1987
*Ian Yule, Ken Gampu, Joe Stewardson*
A series of murders of prostitutes sends a coroner in
search of the killers, strange supernatural beings that
can materialise at will. A flawed attempt to add
supernatural elements to a standard murder mystery,
and at the same time take a few swipes at the South
African political system.
HOR                    92 min
B,V                                    NWV

## CITY OF THE DEAD **
John Moxey             UK               1960
*Christopher Lee, Dennis Lotis, Betta St John, Patricia*
*Jessel, Venetia Stevenson, Valentine Dyall, Norman*
*MacOwen, Tom Naylor, Fred Johnson*
A woman burnt at the stake as a witch 250 years ago
still "lives", in a small town where she runs a hotel
and lures unwary strangers into becoming human
sacrifices. And as ever, it's set in Massachusetts. Slow
to start, but it eventually develops a good atmosphere.
Aka: HORROR HOTEL
HOR                    78 min B/W
B,V                                    INT

## CITY OF THE LIVING DEAD **           18
Lucio Fulci            ITALY            1980
*Christopher George, Janet Agren, Katriona MacColl,*
*Carlo de Mejo, Antonella Interlenghi, Giovanni*
*Lombardo Radice, Daniela Doria, Luca Paismer,*
*Fabrizio Jovine*
A priest commits suicide in a churchyard, and in New
York a young girl goes into a trance, heralding a
somewhat serious turn of events, in which the dead
rise up in a small Massachusetts town and terrorise
the living. A gory and carelessly made shocker,
ostensibly set in H.P. Lovecraft's town of Dunwich,
but actually shot in Italy.
Aka: FEAR; GATES OF HELL, THE; PAURA
NELLA CITTA DEI MORTI VIVENTI
HOR        87 min (ort 94 min) Cut (ELE: 2 min 21 sec;
NET: 1 min 29 sec)
B,V        INT L/A; ITL L/A; PACE L/A; ELE; NET

## CITY ON FIRE **
Alvin Rakoff          CANADA          1979
*Barry Newman, Henry Fonda, Shelley Winters, Ava*
*Gardner, Susan Clark, Leslie Nielsen, James*
*Franciscus, Jonathan Welsh*
A cigarette falls onto some dry grass just as petrol is
leaking into the sewers. This forms the basis for a
disaster movie, which is in turn the background for a
story of revenge, by a former employee of an oil
refinery.
DRA                                      103 min
B,V,V2,LV                                   RNK

## CITY RATS **                               18
Valentin Trujillo     MEXICO
*Rodolfo de Anda, Angelica Chain, Enrique (Flaco)*
*Guzman*
The story of gangs of abandoned children who have
taken to a life of crime.
Aka: RATAS DE LA CIUDAD
A/AD                  92 min Cut (1 min 14 sec)
B,V                                         VPD

## CITY UNDER THE SEA **
Jacques Tourneur       UK               1965
*Vincent Price, David Tomlinson, Susan Hart, Tab*
*Hunter, Henry Oscar, John Le Mesurier, Derek*
*Newark, Roy Patrick, Anthony Selby*
Tells of a strange community of Victorian smugglers
who do not age, and live in the ruins of a sunken city.
Dull and unimaginative plot development spoils a
good idea which has Price sending his gill-men to
kidnap a woman who reminds him of a long-lost love.
Tourneur's last film.
Aka: WAR GODS OF THE DEEP
DRA                         80 min (ort 84 min)
B,V                                        TEVP

## CITY, THE **                               15
Harvey Hart            USA              1977
*Robert Forster, Don Johnson, Ward Costello, Jimmy*
*Dean, Mark Hamill, Susan Sullivan, Felton Perry,*
*Leslie Ackerman, Paul Cavonis, Paul Fix, Joby Baker,*
*William Conrad, Jay Varela, George Clifton, Vivi*
*Janis, Joaquin Martinez*
A disappointing attempt to create a suspenseful
account of a country singer menaced by a psychotic
killer. Two cops are assigned to track down the killer
before it's too late.
DRA                                   75 min mTV
B,V                                       TURBO

## CITY'S EDGE, THE *                          15
Ken Quinnell          AUSTRALIA         1983
*Tommy Lewis, Katrina Forster, Hugo Weaving, Mark*
*Lee, Ralph Cotterill*
A youngster comes to the big city and rents a room in
a sleazy apartment block, getting mixed up with the
local gangsters and no-hopers.
Aka: EDGE OF THE CITY; RUNNING MAN, THE
Boa: novel by W.A. Harbison.
DRA                                       86 min
B,V                                         MGM

## CLAIRE'S KNEE ***
Eric Rohmer            FRANCE           1970
*Jean-Claude Brialy, Aurora Cornu, Beatrice Romand,*
*Laurence De Monaghan, Michele Montel, Gerard*
*Falconetti, Fabrice Luchini*
The delicate tale of a man who spends the summer
enjoying the company of three lovely ladies on the
shores of Lake Geneva. Though about to get married,
he finds himself becoming obsessed with the knee of a
girl towards whom he is otherwise completely indifferent. The fifth in Rohmer's series of "Six Moral Tales",
this is a talky but minutely observed drama of
manners.
Aka: LE GENOU DE CLAIRE

DRA                        100 min (ort 106 min)
V                                           INT

## CLAIRVOYANT, THE ***                        U
Maurice Elvey          UK               1934
*Claude Rains, Fay Wray, Ben Field, Jane Baxter,*
*Mary Clare, Athole Stewart, C. Denier Warren, Frank*
*Cellier, Donald Calthrop, Felix Aylmer, Jack Raine,*
*Graham Moffat, George Merritt, Eliot Makeham, Percy*
*Parsons*
A phoney mind-reader finds that some of his predic-
tions come true, in this effective and atmospheric
minor tale. The good photography is by Glen MacWil-
liams.
Aka: EVIL MIND, THE
Boa: story by Ernst Lothar.
DRA                                    80 min B/W
B,V                                 RNK; STRAND

## CLAN OF THE CAVE BEAR, THE *                 15
Michael Chapman        USA              1986
*Daryl Hannah, Pamela Reed, James Remar, Thomas*
*G. Waites, Curtis Armstrong, John Doolittle*
Film version of a bestseller about a young cave-girl
who is adopted by a tribe of Neanderthals and
becomes their first female warrior. Insipid and ex-
tremely silly, with subtitles being used to translate
the primitive language of the cave folk. Screenplay is
by John Sayles.
Boa: novel by Jean M. Auel.
FAN           92 min (ort 99 min) (Cut at film release)
B,V                                   EHE; CH5

## CLARA'S HEART **                            15
Robert Mulligan        USA              1988
*Whoopi Goldberg, Michael Ontkean, Kathleen*
*Quinlan, Spalding Gray, Beverly Todd, Neil Patrick*
*Harris, Hattie Winston*
A Jamaican housekeeper takes a post with an obno-
xious couple hovering on the brink of divorce, and
befriends the youngster placed in her care. A mawkish
confection of sentimentality and homespun wisdom,
that's both badly edited and singularly unmoving.
Goldberg's strong screen presence does little for this
film.
DRA                        104 min (ort 108 min)
V/sh                                        WHV

## CLARISSA **                                 18
                       FRANCE
*Brigitte Lahaye*
A man gets his kicks by sending his wife off to make
love to his friends. With his demands becoming more
and more depraved, she is obliged to consent or risk
losing him. A slight and pretentious film.
Aka: CLARISSE
A                     62 min Cut (5 min 18 sec)
B,V                                    ELV; TAR

## CLASH BY NIGHT **
Fritz Lang             USA              1952
*Barbara Stanwyck, Paul Douglas, Robert Ryan,*
*Marilyn Monroe, Keith Andes, J. Carrol Naish*
Drama of personal relationships in a small fishing
village, involving the skipper of a fishing boat, his
wife and his friend. An atmospheric but overblown
tale, with Monroe and Andes providing a little
distraction in a love-interest sub-plot.
Boa: play by Clifford Odets.
DRA                                    90 min B/W
B,V,V2                                  VCL L/A

## CLASH OF THE TITANS **                       15
Desmond Davis          UK               1981
*Harry Hamlin, Judi Bowker, Ursula Andress, Maggie*
*Smith, Laurence Olivier, Burgess Meredith, Claire*
*Bloom, Sian Phillips, Flora Robson, Tim Pigott-*
*Smith, Neil McCarthy, Susan Fleetwood, Anna*
*Manahan, Jack Gwillim*

Fantasy adventure based on Greek and Nordic myths. The Gods high up on Olympus, watch Perseus as he battles against various monsters in his march towards everlasting glory. The enjoyable special effects are by Ray Harryhausen. If only the dialogue was better.
FAN                              113 min (ort 118 min)
V/sh                                                MGM

## CLASH OF THE WARLORDS **                    15
                    ITALY
*Will Williams, Gabby Farro, Robert Marios, Tom Romano, Teresa Hunt*
Inconsequential post-WW4 survival epic of the MAD MAX type.
FAN                                           73 min
B,V                                               AMB

## CLASS **                                      15
Lewis John Carlino        USA             1983
*Rob Lowe, Jacqueline Bisset, Andrew McCarthy, Cliff Robertson, Stuart Margolin, John Cusack*
A film with some wonderfully choreographed humorous moments which very quickly runs out of steam. Rich kids go to college where one rather naive young boy has an affair with the mother of his room-mate. The film largely consists of a series of high spirited episodes, with little attempt at an over-riding plot and an abrupt and jarring ending.
COM                              97 min; 94 min (VIR)
B,V,V2            ORION/RNK; VIR (VHS only)

## CLASS OF '44 **                               15
Paul Bogart               USA             1973
*Gary Grimes, Jerry Houser, Oliver Conant, Deborah Winters, William Atherton, Sam Bottoms*
Sequel to SUMMER OF '42 with our hero going to college, growing up and falling in love. Nice period detail but this one has very little to say.
DRA                                           95 min
B,V                                               WHV

## CLASS OF '63 ***
John Korty                USA             1973
*James Brolin, Joan Hackett, Cliff Gorman, Woodrow Chambliss, Ed Lauter, Colby Chester, Graham Beckel, Tom Peters, Ann Noland, Jessica Rains, Lou Picetti, Burke Byrnes, Don McGovern, Tom McFadden, Andrew Scott*
A college reunion forms the background to this tale of unhappy love and marital breakdown, with a remarkable performance from Hackett as the unhappy wife who meets an old college flame. A nostalgic and often quite touching study, with the fine performances raising the film above its soap opera material.
DRA                                       74 min mTV
B,V                                           IFS/CBS

## CLASS OF '84 **
Mark L. Lester            CANADA          1982
*Perry King, Timothy Van Patten, Merrie Lynn Ross, Roddy McDowall, Stefan Amgrom, Al Waxman, Michael J. Fox*
Obnoxious film about the harassment of a high school teacher by a psychotic student and his gang of bullies. A thoroughly nasty work from start to finish, though teachers may well relate to the sequence where McDowall uses the threat of death to make his students do some work.
Aka: CLASS OF 1984
DRA                                           90 min
B,V,V2                                           TEVP

## CLASS OF 1999 **                              18
Mark L. Lester            USA             1990
*Bradley Gregg, Traci Lin, John P. Ryan, Pam Grier, Joshua Miller, Stacy Keach, Malcolm McDowell, Patrick Kilpatrick, Darren E. Burrows*
THE TERMINATOR meets "Blackboard Jungle" in this gruesome sequel to CLASS OF '84, that has a

gang of high school thugs meeting their match when they come up against some experimental android teachers. An overblown celebration of violence masquerading as a film with a message.
FAN                               90 min (ort 98 min)
V                                                  VES

## CLASS OF MISS MacMICHAEL, THE *               15
Silvio Narizzano          UK              1978
*Glenda Jackson, Oliver Reed, Michael Murphy, Rosalind Cash, John Standing, Riba Akabusi, Phil Daniels, Patrick Murray, Sylvia O'Donnel, Sharon Fussey, Herbert Norville, Perry Benson, Tony London*
A clumsy and shrill comedy-drama that has Jackson as a dedicated teacher, devoting her life to her pupils in her attempts to get them to make a success of their studies, even to the extent of refusing an offer of marriage. Hers is a meaningless sacrifice however, for they are shown to be utterly unable to rise above their slum background. TO SIR, WITH LOVE minus the charm.
Boa: novel 'Eff Off by Sandy Houston.
DRA                               94 min (ort 99 min)
V                                         PARK; HOLLY

## CLASS OF NUKE 'EM HIGH *                      18
Richard W. Haines/Samuel Weill
                          USA             1986
*Janelle Brady, Gilbert Brenton, Robert Pritchard, R.L. Ryan, James Nugent Vernon*
Nuclear waste turns high school kids into little horrors, in this fairly mindless exercise in low-brow humour, replete with sadistic gags and various overblown episodes.
Aka: NUKE 'EM HIGH
COM                               85 min (ort 92 min)
V                                                  VIR

## CLAUDIA **                                    18
Anwar Kawadri             UK              1985
*Deborah Raffin, Nicholas Ball, John Moulder-Brown, Barbara Jefford, Mark Eden, Elizabeth Counsel, Ed Devereaux, Belinda Mayne, Sam Douglas, Josephine Buchan, Paul Herzberg, Bruce Boa, Nuala Barrie, Shirley Dixon, Ros Simmons*
After three years of marriage, a woman leaves her rich property developer husband only to find that her happiness with a lover is short-lived, when he is murdered on her husband's orders. Naturally, she takes her revenge and one that enriches her to boot. Filmed and acted in true soap opera style with well-scrubbed faces in the leading roles, chocolate-box photography and slushy music. Best suited to lovers of romantic fiction.
Aka: CLAUDIA'S STORY; DINNER DATE
DRA                                           85 min
B,V                                               SONY

## CLAWS **
Richard Bansbach/Robert Pierson
                          USA             1977
*Jason Evers, Leon Ames, Dick Robinson, Myron Healey, Anthony Caruso, Carla Layton, Glenn Sipes*
No, this is not a tale of a barbaric budgie, but of a gigantic grizzly bear that goes on a murderous rampage. (Is there any other kind?)
Aka: DEVIL BEAR
DRA                                           90 min
B,V                       WAL L/A; MMA; PORVI

## CLEAN AND SOBER ***                           18
Glenn Gordon Caron        USA             1988
*Michael Keaton, Kathy Baker, Morgan Freeman, M. Emmet Walsh, Tate Donovan*
A real-estate salesman who has borrowed a client's money to finance his drug addiction, goes into a treatment centre to stay out of trouble and avoid the police. Once there, he gradually comes to realise that he has a problem and emerges a changed man, if not

an entirely reformed character. A gripping drama, despite its length and somewhat deliberate pacing.
DRA 119 min (ort 121 min)
V/sh WHV

**CLEAN SLATE ***
Bertrand Tavernier FRANCE 1981
*Philippe Noiret, Isabelle Huppert, Jean-Pierre Marielle, Stephane Audran, Irene Skobline, Eddy Mitchell, Guy Marchand, Michel Beaune, Jean Champion, Victor Garriver, Gerard Hernandez, Abdoulaye Dico, Daniel Langlet*
Deals with the effects of colonialism in French West Africa in the late 1930s. A meek government constable pushed too far by some crooks, resorts to murder as a way of resolving his problems, but finds himself unable to stop. An interesting, if heavy-handed study of mania, with touches of black humour.
Aka: COUP DE TORCHON
Boa: novel Pop. 1280 by Jim Thompson.
DRA 128 min
B,V PVG

**CLEOPATRA *** PG
Joseph L. Mankiewicz USA 1963
*Elizabeth Taylor, Richard Burton, Rex Harrison, Pamela Brown, George Cole, Hume Cronyn, Cesare Danova, Kenneth Haigh, Andrew Keir, Martin Landau, Roddy McDowall, Robert Stephens, Francesca Annis, Martin Benson, Herbert Berghof*
Overlong and overblown retelling of the saga of Cleopatra. Remarkable for its stilted dialogue and cardboard characterisations. An expensive flop that could have been produced far more cheaply without such an emphasis on the overwhelming sets. AA: Cin (Leon Shamroy), Art/Set (DeCuir, Smith, Brown, Blumenthal, Webb, Pelling and Juraga/Scott, Fox and Moyer), Cost (Sharaff, Novarese and Renie), Effects (Vis) (Emil Kosa Jr).
Boa: novel The Life And Times Of Cleopatra by C.M. Franzero.
DRA 176 min (ort 243 min)
V/h CBS

**CLEOPATRA JONES *** 15
Jack Starett USA 1973
*Tamara Dobson, Bernie Casey, Shelley Winters, Brenda Sykes, Antonio Fargas, Bill McKinney, Esther Rolle*
A black female karate-chopping government agent goes after drug runners. Plenty of action in this violent nonsense. Followed by CLEOPATRA JONES AND THE CASINO OF GOLD.
THR 89 min
B,V WHV

**CLEOPATRA JONES AND THE** 15
**CASINO OF GOLD ***
Chuck Bail HONG KONG/USA 1974
*Tamara Dobson, Stella Stevens, Tanny, Norman Kell, Albert Popwell, Caro Kenyatta, Christopher Hunt*
Sequel to CLEOPATRA JONES, in which our athletic amazon takes on a Hong Kong drugs ring. A slick, violent and overwrought effort.
A/AD 92 min
B,V WHV

**CLIFF RICHARD: SUMMER HOLIDAY *** U
Peter Yates UK 1963
*Cliff Richard, Lauri Peters, David Kossoff, Ron Moody, Melvyn Hayes, The Shadows, Lionel Murton, Madge Ryan, Una Stubbs, Teddy Green, Pamela Hart, Nicholas Phipps*
Young people have a holiday on the Continent in a borrowed double decker bus. A cute vehicle for Cliff with its appeal largely confined to his large and faithful fan-club. Yates' directorial debut with a script by Peter Myers and Ronnie Cass. Musical direction is by Stanley Black.
Aka: SUMMER HOLIDAY
MUS 109 min
B,V/h TEVP; WHV

**CLIFF RICHARD: TAKE ME HIGH *** U
David Askey UK 1973
*Cliff Richard, Hugh Griffith, Debbie Watling, George Cole, Richard Wattis, Anthony Andrews, Madeline Smith, Moyra Fraser, Ronald Hines, Jimmy Gardner, Noel Trevarthen, Graham Armitage, John Franklyn-Robbins, Elisabeth Scott*
Cliff Richard vehicle in which he plays a bank employee who is sent to Birmingham to set up a major hamburger restaurant. During his stay there he meets a young girl and falls in love. A tired and empty youth musical, with little of the bounce of Richard's earlier films.
Aka: TAKE ME HIGH
MUS 86 min (ort 90 min)
V/h WHV

**CLIFF RICHARD: THE YOUNG ONES *** U
Sidney J. Furie UK 1961
*Cliff Richard, Robert Morley, Carole Gray, Teddy Green, Richard O'Sullivan, Melvyn Hayes, Annette Robertson, Robertson Hare, Sonya Cordeau, Gerald Harper, The Shadows*
Syrupy vehicle for Cliff Richard, who plays a young man fighting to stop his youth club being demolished by his father's company. A badly dated youth musical, made slightly more bearable by a few good songs. The music is by Stanley Black.
Aka: WONDERFUL TO BE YOUNG; YOUNG ONES, THE
MUS 104 min (ort 108 min)
B,V/h TEVP; WHV (VHS only)

**CLIFF RICHARD: WONDERFUL LIFE *** U
Sidney J. Furie UK 1964
*Cliff Richard, Susan Hampshire, Walter Slezak, Melvyn Hayes, The Shadows, Richard O'Sullivan, Una Stubbs, Derek Bond, Gerald Harper*
Routine Cliff vehicle, with our star getting pressed into service as a stuntman for a film being made on the Canary Islands. So sweet and syrupy it should carry a dental warning; as usual our Cliff combines maximum goodness with minimum personality. He gets to sing too. Written by Peter Myers and Ronald Cass.
Aka: WONDERFUL LIFE
MUS 104 min (ort 113 min)
B,V/h TEVP; WHV (VHS only)

**CLIFTON HOUSE MYSTERY, THE ***
Hugh David UK 1978
*Ingrid Hafner, Sebastian Breaks, Peter Sallis*
Compiled from a TV series of six 30 min episodes, this is the story of a family who move into a house which they find is home also to some spectral lodgers.
JUV 150 min mTV
B,V GHV

**CLINIC, THE *** 18
David Stephens AUSTRALIA 1982
*Chris Haywood, Simon Burke, Gerda Nicholson, Rona McLeod, Suzanne Roylance, Veronica Lang, Pat Evison*
Pre-AIDS comedy-drama set in a clinic for sexually transmitted diseases, that focuses on various funny occurrences but has little of interest to say. A slight little work.
COM 92 min Cut
B,V MED

**CLOAK AND DAGGER *** PG
Fritz Lang USA 1946
*Gary Cooper, Lilli Palmer, Robert Alda, Vladimir Sokoloff, Ludwig Stossel, J. Edward Bromberg, Helene Thimig, Marc Lawrence*

A university professor is sent on a secret mission to Germany by the OSS and attempts to locate a kidnapped scientist. A slackly directed and rather cold espionage tale, that might so easily have been far better. A few flashes of inspiration occasionally appear.
DRA                                   106 min B/W
V                                           VIR

## CLOAK AND DAGGER ** PG
Richard Franklin        USA              1984
*Henry Thomas, Dabney Coleman, Michael Murphy,*
*John McIntire, Jeanette Nolan, Christine Nigra*
A young boy who tells tall stories, actually witnesses a murder which leads to his life being in danger, but of course nobody will believe him. A patchy reworking of "The Window", chiefly remembered for a nice peformance from Coleman as the boy's father and his imaginary hero "Jack Flash".
DRA                99 min (ort 101 min) Cut (14 sec)
B,V                                        CIC

## CLOCKWISE * PG
Christopher Morahan      UK              1985
*John Cleese, Penelope Wilton, Alison Steadman,*
*Stephen Moore, Sharon Maiden*
Contrived comedy about a headmaster, whose obsessive need for punctuality is severely tested as he makes his way to an important meeting of head-teachers. An unutterably tedious film, scripted by Michael Frayn, it tries hard to make much of little, but finally collapses for sheer lack of ideas.
COM                                       92 min
B, V/h                        CAN; WHV (VHS only)

## CLOCKWORK TERROR ** 18
USA
*Chris Mitchum, Sue Lyon, David Carpenter*
A bike gang terrorises a small town but comes up against a strange and powerful force.
DRA                    97 min Cut (2 min 6 sec)
B,V                            EMPIR L/A; PLACE

## CLONE MASTER, THE ** PG
Don Medford             USA              1978
*Ralph Bellamy, Art Hindle, Robyn Douglass, Ed*
*Lauter, John Van Dreelen, Stacy Keach Sr, Lew*
*Brown, Bill Sorrells, Ken Sansom, Robert Karnes,*
*Betty Lou Robinson, Vernon Weddle, Steve Austin,*
*Phillip Pine, Kirk Duncan*
When a biochemist working on the production of clones is kidnapped, his fellow worker goes to Washington only to discover that no-one has heard of their research. He decides to create thirteen replicas of himself and embarks on a mission to take on the government and its corrupt officials. This mystery adventure was the pilot for a TV series that never cloned.
A/AD              93 min (ort 104 min) mTV
B,V                                        CIC

## CLONES OF BRUCE LEE, THE ** 
Joseph Kong        HONG KONG            1980
*Dragon Lee, Bruce Le (Huang Kin Lung), Bruce Lai,*
*Bruce Thai, John Benn, Yan Tze*
Kung fu movie with an absolutely ludicrous plot, in which three new clones of Bruce Lee are created from a syringeful of the original's blood. Switch the brain off and enjoy the action.
MAR                                       85 min
B,V,V2                             VIDMOV/HOK

## CLONES, THE ** 
Lamar Card/Paul Hunt  USA              1973
*Michael Greene, Otis Young, Susan Hunt, Gregory*
*Sierra, Stanley Adams, Barbara Burgdorph, John*
*Barrymore Jr, Alex Nicol, Bruce Bennett, Angelo*
*Rossito*
After he has fled from a secret laboratory, a research

scientist discovers that he has been cloned as part of a plot to take over the world. Despite a promising start and a good sequence in which original and clone come face to face, ponderous direction and attempts at self-parody let it down badly.
FAN                                       90 min
B,V                            AVP L/A; INT

## CLONUS ** 18
Robert S. Fiveson       USA              1978
*Timothy Donnelly, Dick Sargent, Peter Graves, David*
*Hooks, Keenan Wynn*
An insidious government plan to start cloning the population must be kept secret at all costs. Confused and uneven attempt at a horror-thriller, watchable, but no more than that.
Aka: ALTER EGO (MANHAT or KRP); CLONUS HORROR, THE; PARTS: THE CLONUS HORROR
THR              90 min; 85 min (MANHAT or KRP)
B,V,V2              AVP L/A; MANHAT; KRP

## CLOSE ENCOUNTERS OF THE THIRD KIND: PG
## SPECIAL EDITION ***
Steven Spielberg     USA   1977 (re-released 1980)
*Richard Dreyfuss, Teri Garr, Melinda Dillon, Cary*
*Guffey, Bob Balaban, Francois Truffaut*
Several people are obsessed with strange images linked to imminent alien landings. The government tries at all cost to keep this event secret, but fails to stop a determined few from reaching the contact zone. A film of enormous visual impact, but overlong and rather disjointed. This version was re-edited and has footage not included in the earlier work. AA: Cin (Vilmos Zsigmond), Spec Award (Frank Warner for sound effects editing).
FAN                          127 min (ort 135 min)
V/sh                                       RCA

## CLOSE KUNG FU ENCOUNTER, THE ** 18
Raymond Chin        HONG KONG
*Jackie Chang, Roger Mao, Jurang In-Shik, Kim*
*Jung-Sung, Choi Min Kyu, Lee Ye-Min, Hong Sung-*
*Jung, Kim Kee Joo, King Sung-Nam, Han Myung-*
*Han*
A kung fu expert working for the army, attempts to recover some of China's gold from the Japanese. He is captured and forced to fight for his life.
MAR                                       88 min
B,V                                        VPD

## CLOSE YOUR EYES AND PRAY * 18
Skip Schoolnik        USA              1987
*Brittain Frye, Donna Baltron, George Thomas,*
*Annette Sinclair*
A bunch of kids set out to spend the night at the furniture store owned by the father of one them, but fall victim to a psychopathic murderer who kills several of them, forcing the others to hunt him down. A standard slasher movie of little merit that's not helped by its daft ending.
Aka: HIDE AND GO SHRIEK
HOR              86 min (ort 90 min) Cut (50 sec)
B,V                                        TGP

## CLOUD DANCER ** 
Barry Brown          USA   1978 (released 1980)
*David Carradine, Jennifer O'Neill, Joseph Bottoms,*
*Colleen Camp, Albert Salmi, Salome Jens, Nina Van*
*Pallandt*
Love story set against the background of aerobatics and telling of a man who is obsessed with this sport. A loosely made and episodic drama with a few nice aerial sequences, but little happening on the ground. Written by William Goodhart, Barry Brown and Daniel Tamkus.
DRA                                      107 min
B,V,V2                                     GHV

**CLOUD WALTZER ** **
Gordon Flemyng UK/USA
PG
1986
*Kathleen Beller, Francois Eric Gendron, Paul*
*Maxwell, Therese Liotard, Claude Gensac, David Baxt,*
*Dora Doll*
A woman journalist ends up falling in love with a
millionaire recluse she has been sent to interview. A
lush chocolate-box romance, based on a novel in the
Harlequin series of romantic fiction. Beautiful photo-
graphy and competent acting, but the plot is as thin as
tissue paper.
Aka: CLOUD WALTZING
Boa: novel by Tony Cates.
DRA 90 min (ort 103 min) mTV
V CIC

**CLOWNHOUSE ** **
Victor Silva USA
15
1989
*Nathan Forest Winters, Brian McHugh, Sam Rockwell*
The youngest of three brothers has a pathological fear
of clowns, but is forced to accompany his eldest
brother and girlfriend to the circus, where three
escaped lunatics now disguised as clowns, provide the
requisite entertainment. A predictable and rather
bloodless horror yarn that has a few moments of terror
despite the unimaginative direction.
HOR 78 min
V EIV

**CLOWN MURDERS, THE ** **
Martyn Burke CANADA
15
1975
*Stephen Young, Susan Keller, Lawrence Dane, John*
*Candy, Al Waxman, Gary Reineke, Cec Linder*
At a Halloween party, a bunch of bored, rich friends
decide to add a little excitement to their lives by
staging a crime for fun, so they kidnap the former
girlfriend of one of them. However, their crime has
tragic repercussions, with two of them getting killed,
as tension mounts at their hideout. Reineke adds a
nice air of menace to a film that's otherwise undistinguished. The screenplay is by Martyn Burke.
DRA 95 min
B,V VPD

**CLUB LIFE ** **
Norman Thaddeus Vane USA
18
1986
*Tony Curtis, Dee Wallace Stone, Michael Parks, Tom*
*Parsekian, Jamie Barrett, Pat Ast, Yana Nirvana*
A young motorcross champion leaves home for Hollywood, and winds up working as a bouncer at a disco
owned by Curtis. Shocked by the immorality he sees
all around him, he resolves to fight against moral
decay and decadence. A bright and gaudy action film
of little interest.
Aka: KING OF THE CITY
A/AD 86 min (ort 90 min) (Cut at film release)
B,V PACEV; SCRN

**CLUB MED ***
Bob Giraldi USA
PG
1986
*Jack Scalia, Patrick Macnee, Linda Hamilton, Janis*
*Lee Burns, Traci Lin-Tavi, Jeff Kaake, Bill Maher,*
*Adam Mills, SinBad, Timothy Williams, Allison Argo,*
*Lorraine Chanel, Jason Cook, William Coss, John P.*
*Nadeu*
Romantic comedy following the fortunes of five holi-
daymakers in a tropical paradise resort. A glossy and
insubstantial effort, set against some colourful back-
grounds. The TV movie debut for Giraldi, whose
directing experience before this film, was largely
confined to commercials and music videos.
COM 88 min (ort 104 min) mTV
B,V STABL; CAPIT

**CLUB PARADISE ** **
Harold Ramis USA
15
1986
*Robin Williams, Rick Moranis, Peter O'Toole, Twiggy*
*(Lesley Hornby), Adolph Caesar, Eugene Levy, Jimmy*
*Cliff, Joanna Cassidy, Andrea Martin, Brian Doyle*

*Murray Robin Duke, Mary Gross, Simon Jones*
An ex-Chicago fireman teams up with a musician/
nightclub owner to transform a seedy Caribbean
cottage resort into a swinging singles hotspot. Likeable but aimless comedy, worth seeing more for Cliff's
almost non-stop music than for any virtues inherent
in the vapid plot. Screenplay is by Ramis and Brian
Doyle-Murray.
COM 92 min
V/sh WHV

**CLUB, THE ***
Bruce Beresford AUSTRALIA
1981
*Jack Thompson, Graham Kennedy, Frank Wilson,*
*Harold Hopkins, John Howard, Alan Cassell, Maggie*
*Doyle*
The story of an Australian football club and the
pressures and problems which the game imposes on
those who devote their lives to it. An excellent drama
largely concentrating on the political intrigues that
take place off field – Thompson is excellent as the
coach. Screenplay is by Williamson.
Aka: PLAYERS
Boa: play by David Williamson.
DRA 102 min
B,V VDB

**CLUE ** **
Jonathan Lynn USA
PG
1985
*Eileen Brennan, Tim Curry, Madeline Kahn,*
*Christopher Lloyd, Martin Hull, Michael McKean,*
*Martin Hull, Lesley Anne Warren, Colleen Camp, Lee*
*Ving, Bill Henderson, Howard Hesseman*
Inspired by the board game "Cluedo", this is a murder
mystery set in one of those Gothic mansions so beloved
by murder mystery writers. Reminiscent of, but far
inferior to "Ten Little Indians". Released in three
versions, each with a different ending, but now all
three versions are cobbled together into a single film.
A brave attempt, but heavy-going for all concerned.
The directorial debut for Lynn.
THR 97 min
B,V CIC

**CLUE ACCORDING TO SHERLOCK HOLMES, THE
** **
Murray Golden UK
U
1980
*Keith Michell, Dody Goodman, Keith McConnell,*
*Laurie Main*
A Sherlock Holmes-style adventure, in which the
mystery of a hidden fortune, reputed to have been left
behind by an eccentric millionaire when he died, is
eventually solved by our sleuth, with a little help and
a good deal of patient endeavour.
JUV 45 min (ort 50 min) mTV
V PICK

**COACH OF THE YEAR ***
Don Medford/Andy Sidaris
PG
USA 1980
*Robert Conrad, Erin Gray, Daphne Maxwell, Red*
*West, David Hubbard, Ricky Paul, Lou Carello, Alex*
*Paez, Radames Torres, Joneal Joplin, Dean Hill, Kelly*
*Keefe, Ed O'Bradovich*
A former football player crippled in the Vietnam War,
builds a new life for himself coaching young offenders
from his wheelchair. A warm and enjoyable film with
a strong performance from Conrad. Pilot for an
unmade TV series.
DRA 93 min mTV
B,V CIC

**COACH, THE ** **
Bud Townsend USA
1978
*Cathy Lee Crosby, Michael Biehn, Keenan Wynn, Steve*
*Nevil, Channing Clarkson, Sydney Wicks, Jack David*
*Walker, Meredith Baer, Myron McGill, Robyn Pohle,*
*Kristine Greco, Brent Huff*

A female Olympic gold medallist is accidentally hired to be coach to a boy's high school basketball team. A tame and tedious dud.

DRA 100 min
B,V VPD; MED

## COAL MINER'S DAUGHTER **** PG
Michael Apted USA 1980
*Sissy Spacek, Tommy Lee Jones, Levon Helm, Phyllis Boyens, Beverly D'Angelo, Bill Anderson Jr, Foister Dickerson, Malla McCown, Pamela McCown, William Sanderson, Kevin Salvilla, Sissy Lucas, Pat Paterson, Brian Warf*
Rags-to-riches film biography of country singer Loretta Lynn, that's not always all that accurate, but is never less than totally engrossing. Spacek did her own singing, for which she received a well-deserved Oscar. The screenplay was by Tom Rickman. AA: Actress (Spacek).

DRA 125 min
V MCA; RCA

## COBRA * 18
George P. Cosmatos USA 1986
*Sylvester Stallone, Brigitte Nielsen, Reni Santoni, Andrew Robinson, Lee Garlington, John Herzfeld, Art Le Fleur, Brian Thompson, David Rasche, Val Avery*
Repellent vigilante drama with Stallone as a cop whose solution to crime is to shoot anything that moves. A DIRTY HARRY clone with our tough cop given the assignment of tracking down serial killers. Some good action sequences, but little more.
Boa: novel Fair Game by Paula Gosling.

A/AD 83 min Cut (4 sec)
V WHV

## COBRA AGAINST NINJA ** 15
Joseph Lai HONG KONG
*Richard Harrison, Stuart Smith, Alan Friss, Paul Branney, Gary Carter, Alfred Pears, Jimmy Busco*
Standard adventure fare with the head of the Ninja Empire battling to uphold its honour and integrity.

MAR 87 min Cut (7 sec)
B,V NINJ; VPD

## COBRA MISSION * 18
Larry Ludman (Fabrizio De Angelis) ITALY 1986
*John Ethan Wayne, Donald Pleasence, Oliver Tobias, Christopher Connelly, John Steiner, Manfred Lehmann*
Another Vietnam POW rescue saga with all the stock characters – sadistic Vietnamese captors, heroic POWs etc. I dare say you've seen it all before.
Aka: OPERATION NAM; RAINBOW PROFESSIONALS

A/AD 79 min
B,V EIV

## COBRA VERDE *** PG
Werner Herzog WEST GERMANY 1987
*Klaus Kinski, King Ampaw, Jose Lewgoy, Salvatire Basile, Nana Agyfei Kwame of Nsein*
As a punishment for seducing his employer's young daughters, Kinski is sent to Africa to work as a slave trader. In hostile Dahomey he escapes the clutches of a tyrant ruler and sets out to form an army of female warriors with the intention of overthrowing the monarch and seizing power.

A/AD 95 min
B, V/h PAL

## COCA-COLA KID, THE ** 15
Dusan Makavejev AUSTRALIA 1985
*Eric Roberts, Bill Kerr, Greta Scacchi, Chris Haywood, Kris McQuade, Max Gilles, Rebecca Smart*
A Coca-Cola salesman in Australia discovers a small valley where the local bigshot is making his own soft drink and refusing to allow any other to be sold. An offbeat and quirky little film of few laughs.

COM 90 min
B,V PVG; WHV

## COCAINE COWBOYS 18
Ulli Lommel USA 1979
*Jack Palance, Tom Sullivan, Andy Warhol, Suzanna Love, Pete Huckabee*
A rock band supports itself in between gigs by smuggling cocaine. A rubbishy and flat effort, filmed at Warhol's Montauk home.

DRA 87 min
B,V VUL L/A; HEND/PVG

## COCAINE FIENDS, THE
William A. O'Connor USA 1939
*Noel Madison, Lois January, Sheila Manners, Dean Benton, Lois Lindsay, Eddie Phillips*
Classic melodramatic warning about the horrors of drug addiction, with a young girl introduced to the pleasures of cocaine (she believes she's taking "headache powder") by a mobster on the run from the law. A tacky and exploitative effort, so bad it's quite funny in places, but not funny enough to rank as a full-blooded comedy. See also REEFER MADNESS and COCAINE: ONE MAN'S POISON.
Aka: PACE THAT KILLS, THE
Osca: MULTIPLE MADNESS

DRA 74 min
B,V PVG

## COCAINE WARS ** 18
Hector Olivera ARGENTINA/USA 1986
*John Schneider, Kathryn Witt, Royal Dano, Frederico Luppi, Rodolfo Ranni, John Vitaly, Heidi Paddle, Ricardo Jordan, Nan Grey, Edgar Moore*
John Schneider stars as a US drug enforcement agent, in this fast-moving but simple-minded tale in which he is sent to combat an evil South American cocaine baron. Heavy-going and confusing.
Aka: COCAINA; FINE WHITE LINE, THE; MUERTA BLANCA

A/AD 79 min Cut (22 sec)
B,V MED

## COCAINE: ONE MAN'S POISON *** 15
Paul Wendkos USA 1983
*Dennis Weaver, Karen Grassle, David Ackroyd, Pamela Bellwood, James Spader, Jeffrey Tambor, Richard Venture*
Story of a successful businessman who develops an addiction to cocaine during a slump in his business. Weaver gives a remarkable performance as a man whose drug habit threatens to ruin his life. A little melodramatic at times, but always absorbing. The script is by Barry Schneider and David Goldsmith.
Aka: COCAINE: ONE MAN'S SEDUCTION

DRA 100 min mTV
B,V VFP L/A; HER

## COCKTAIL ** 15
Roger Donaldson USA 1988
*Tom Cruise, Bryan Brown, Elisabeth Shue, Lisa Banes, Laurence Luckinbill, Kelly Lynch, Gina Gershon, Ron Dean, Paul Benedict*
A young arrival in New York dreams of making his fortune with a chain of bars, after he become a bartender and falls under the influence of an older barman. A cute, empty and strangely pointless effort.

DRA 103 min
V TOUCH

## COCOON *** PG
Ron Howard USA 1985
*Don Ameche, A. Wilford Brimley, Hume Cronyn, Steve Guttenberg, Tahnee Welch, Brian Dennehy, Jessica Tandy, Maureen Stapleton*
A tale of contact between three feisty senior citizens and some benevolent aliens on a mission to Earth,

who have hidden a power source with remarkable properties in an unattended swimming pool. It just happens to be the one our trio are in the habit of using. Excessive sentimentality and a slow start are handicaps. A sequel followed. AA: S. Actor (Ameche), Effects (Vis) (Ken Ralston/Ralph McQuarrie/Scott Farrar/David Berry).
Boa: novel by David Saperstein.
FAN 112 min
V CBS

## COCOON: THE RETURN **
Daniel Petrie USA PG 1988
Don Ameche, Jack Gilford, Gwen Verdon, Maureen Stapleton, Hume Cronyn, Jessica Tandy, Wilford Brimley, Elaine Stritch, Tahnee Welch, Courteney Cox
The elderly folk who were taken to distant stars in the first film, now return to Earth for a visit in this thoroughly disappointing and predictable sequel. None of the sparkle of the first film is here, although Ameche and company do their best with the tired script. An unnecessary sequel if ever there was one.
Aka: COCOON 2
FAN 111 min
V/sh CBS

## CODE OF SILENCE **
Andy Davis USA 18 1985
Chuck Norris, Henry Silva, Bert Remsen, Molly Hagan, Nathan Davis, Joseph Guzaldo, Mike Genovese, Dennis Farina
A tough Chicago cop has to fight both an underworld boss and his own colleagues. Standard action movie of little depth but much mayhem.
A/AD 101 min
B,V ORION/RNK

## CODE OF THE WEST **
William Berke USA 1947
James Warren, Debra Allen, John Laurenz, Steve Brodie, Robert Clarke, Carol Forman, Rita Lynn, Harry Woods, Raymond Burr, Harry Harvey, Phil Warren, Emmett Lynn
A man and his daughter try to open an honest bank in the face of opposition from the corrupt town boss. However, two cowboys come to their aid. Fair.
Boa: novel by Zane Grey.
WES 55 min B/W
B,V KVD

## CODE, THE **
Jean Herman FRANCE/ITALY 15 1968
Alain Delon, Charles Bronson, Olga Georges-Picot, Brigitte Fresson
Following a stint of service in Algeria, two mercenaries return to Marseilles and team up to rob some company vaults, but fall out over the proceeds. Typical crime story that's nothing out of the ordinary.
Aka: ADIEU L'AMI; FAREWELL, FRIEND; HONOR AMONG THIEVES; SO LONG FRIEND
A/AD 90 min (ort 115 min)
V MANHAT; KRP

## CODENAME: BLACKFIRE **
Teddy Page HONG KONG 18 1986
Ron Kristoff, James Gaines, Anthony Carreon, Dick Isaac, Gerry Bailey, Ray Vernal, Charlotte Maine
A tough US Army sergeant is given the codename "Blackfire" and posted to San Sebastian as a military adviser. Once there he discovers that the local army captain is involved in a plot to illegally transport arms and equipment.
Aka: BLACKFIRE
A/AD 87 min
B,V TGP

## CODENAME: DANCER **
Buzz Kulik USA PG 1987
Kate Capshaw, Jeroen Krabbe, Cliff De Young

A married woman returns to her former life as a CIA agent and renews her friendship with one of Castro's top aides, in an attempt to free an agent being held in Cuba.
A/AD 90 min
B,V SONY

## CODENAME: EMERALD **
Jonathan Sanger USA PG 1985
Ed Harris, Max Von Sydow, Horst Buchholz, Helmut Berger, Eric Stoltz, Cyrielle Claire, Patrick Stewart, Graham Crowden
A double agent lands in France by parachute in order to rescue a captured American lieutenant who knows about the Allied plans for the D-Day landing. Plodding WW2 action tale rather let down by poor casting and an all too predictable story. The first theatrical feature produced by the NBC TV network. Scripted by Bass from his novel.
Aka: EMERALD
Boa: novel THe Emerald Illusion by Ronald Bass.
WAR 91 min
B,V MGM

## CODENAME: FOXFIRE –
## SLAY IT AGAIN SAM **
Corey Allen USA PG 1985
Joanna Cassidy, Sheryl Lee Ralph, Henry Jones, John McCook
Three women and a man form an undercover team, aided by a distinguished butler. They have to investigate the theft of a rocket with a nuclear warhead. Pilot for a short-lived TV series.
Aka: CODENAME: FIREFOX
THR 91 min (ort 99 min) Cut (35 sec) mTV
B,V CIC

## CODENAME: ICARUS **
Marilyn Fox UK U 1983
Barry Angel, Jack Galloway, Philip Locke
A boy who has made a scientific discovery has to prevent it falling into the wrong hands.
DRA 106 min mTV
B,V BBC

## CODENAME: RED DEVIL *
Bort Albertini ITALY PG
John Ireland, Guy Madison, Van Tenney, Anthony Steel, Pascale Petit
Standard Euro-adventure of intrigue, murder and mayhem. About as cliched as they come.
A/AD 97 min Cut (1 sec)
B,V CROWN; CERT

## CODENAME: ROBOTECH **
Robert Barron USA U 1985
This space adventure has the captain of a spaceship looking back over the last ten years of his career and recalling some nasty clashes with aliens. Hardly brilliant animation, but quite enjoyable.
CAR 72 min
V MAST; PARK

## CODENAME: THE SOLDIER **
James Glickenhaus USA 18 1982
Ken Wahl, Klaus Kinski, William Prince, Alberta Watson, Jeremiah Sullivan, Ron Harper, Joaquim De Almeida, Steve James, Peter Hooten, Ned Eisenberg, Alexander Spencer, Zeljko Ivanek, William Anagos, Bob Andrews, Lisa Cain
The world is on the brink of nuclear war, and a CIA super-agent and his band of super-heroes race against time to prevent damage to the West's oil supplies, in the form of a nuclear bomb planted by Soviet terrorists in a Saudi oil field. Cliched and violent actioner.
Aka: SOLDIER, THE
THR 83 min (ort 112 min) Cut (1 min 5 sec)
B,V,V2 EHE

## CODENAME: VENGEANCE ** 18
Maria Dante     ITALY     1987
*Robert Ginty, James Ryan, Cameron Mitchell, Kevin Brophy, Shannon Tweed, Don Gordon*
An ex-CIA agent, who for 12 years was incarcerated in a prison in the Middle East, agrees to undertake a perilous mission and rescue the wife and son of a shah.
A/AD     90 min
V     PRISM

## CODENAME: WILD GEESE ** 15
Anthony M. Dawson (Antonio Margheriti)
    ITALY/WEST GERMANY     1986
*Lewis Collins, Klaus Kinski, Ernest Borgnine, Lee Van Cleef, Mimsy Farmer, Manfred Lehmann*
Predictable film about a band of mercenaries, hired to close drug factories in the Golden Triangle area of South East Asia. A mindless action yarn that gives little scope to the good cast. The title bears no relation to those other films in the series that started with THE WILD GEESE.
A/AD     100 min
B, V/s     EIV

## COHEN AND TATE * 18
Eric Red     USA     1988
*Roy Scheider, Adam Baldwin, Harley Cross, Cooper Huckabee*
A boy is kidnapped by two professional killers who murdered his parents as part of a gang killing, and schemes to free himself by exploiting the tensions that arise between his two captors. Interesting ideas are sunk by a flaccid script and a lack of pace.
THR     82 min (ort 89 min)
B,V     GHV

## COLD BLOOD ** 18
Stephanie Weiss    NETHERLANDS     1988
*Rutger Hauer*
A pilot who has inadvertently become involved with the Mob attempts to break free in this formula actioner.
A/AD     76 min dubbed
V     VPD

## COLD COMFORT *** 15
Vic Sarin     CANADA     1989
*Maury Chaykin, Margaret Langrick, Paul Gross*
A travelling salesman crashes his car during a blizzard, but is saved from almost certain death by a passing trucker. However, his rescuer is not quite normal, and our salesman is taken home as a "present" for the man's nubile daughter. Swain's directorial debut is a bizarre thriller of considerable intensity.
Boa: play by James Garrard.
THR     90 min (ort 92 min)
V     PRISM L/A

## COLD FEET ** 15
Robert Dornhelm     USA     1989
*Sally Kirkland, Keith Carradine, Tom Waits, Rip Torn, Bill Pullman, Kathleen York, Vincent Schiavelli*
This weird comedy Western follows the exploits of three petty thieves out to smuggle a cache of emeralds from Mexico into the USA, having hidden it inside a horse that's being imported for stud purposes. Not all that funny, but certainly different. Co-scripted by Thomas McGuane, who worked on RANCHO DELUXE, but that earlier film is a lot funnier. Both McGuane and Jeff Bridges (who appeared in the first film) have small cameo parts.
WES     88 min (ort 94 min)
V     VIR

## COLD FRONT * 18
Paul Bnarbic (Allan S. Goldstein)
    CANADA     1989

*Martin Sheen, Michael Ontkean, Kim Coates, Beverly D'Angelo*
A terrorist with a penchant for murdering the wives of his intended victims is stalked by a Canadian Mountie and a US special agent, in this cheap looking and singularly uninspired thriller.
THR     96 min
V     SHAP

## COLD RIVER ** PG
Fred G. Sullivan     USA     1981
*Suzanne Weber, Pat Petersen, Richard Jaeckel, Robert Earl Jones, Brad Sullivan*
An experienced guide takes his two children on a long trek in the mountains but dies of a heart attack, leaving them to survive on their own in sub-zero temperatures. Nice locations in the Adirondack Mountains, but that's about all.
Boa: novel by William Judson.
A/AD    91 min (ort 94 min) Cut (1 min 2 sec)
B,V     CBS

## COLD ROOM, THE ** 15
James Dearden     USA     1984
*George Segal, Amanda Pays, Renee Soutendijk, Warren Clarke, Anthony Higgins, Elizabeth Spriggs, Clifford Rose, Ursula Howells, George Pravda, Lucy Hornack, Gertan Klauner, Tristram Wymark, Stuart Wolfe, Judich Melische*
A rebellious teenage girl goes with her father to East Berlin and becomes involved in a strange journey back in time when she discovers a dissident hiding in a secret chamber behind the furniture in her hotel room. A disjointed and bizarre thriller, let down by the muddled plot.
Boa: novel by Jeffrey Caine.
THR     95 min mCab
B,V     VFP L/A; HER

## COLD SASSY TREE, THE *** 15
Joan Tewkesbury     USA     1989
*Faye Dunaway, Richard Wydmark, Neil Patrick Harris, Frances Fisher, Lee Garlington, John Jackson*
At a conservative turn-of-the-century Southern town, where memories of the Civil War remain fresh, a recently widowed store-owner causes a scandal by marrying a colourful and individualistic woman from the North. Dunaway and Widmark work beautifully together in this charming romantic drama.
Boa: novel by Olive Ann Burns.
DRA     97 min (ort 100 min) mCab
V     TURNER

## COLD STEEL ** 18
Dorothy Ann Puzo     USA     1987
*Brad Davis, Jonathan Banks, Sharon Stone, Jay Acovone, Adam Ant, Eddie Egan*
A tough cop finds that his father has been murdered by a psycho, who holds the cop responsible for an accident that destroyed his vocal chords. He sets out to nail the criminal in a predictable and brutal drama, hampered by poor plotting and dialogue.
DRA     90 min
B,V     NDH

## COLD SWEAT ** 15
Terence Young     FRANCE/ITALY     1971
*Charles Bronson, James Mason, Liv Ullmann, Michel Constantin, Gabriele Ferzetti, Jill Ireland, Jean Topart, Yannick Delulle, Luigi Pistilli*
An American charterboat captain living in France, is forced to run drugs by a sinister crime baron, when his family is taken hostage. A predictable adaptation of Matheson's novel, watchable but lacking in tension.
Aka: DE LA PART DES COPAINS; L'UOMO DALLE DUE OMBRE
Boa: novel Ride The Nightmare by Richard Matheson.
THR     94 min
B,V     VPD

**COLDITZ STORY, THE \*\*\***                          U
Guy Hamilton                UK                 1954
*John Mills, Eric Portman, Frederick Valk, Denis*
*Shaw, Lionel Jeffries, Christopher Rhodes, Richard*
*Wattis, Ian Carmichael, Bryan Forbes, Theodore Bikel,*
*Eugene Deckers, Anton Diffring*
Nicely balanced and fairly realistic film, dealing with
the lives of the POWs held by the Germans in Colditz
Castle, in Saxony in 1940. A mixture of humour,
tension and factual incidents, set against the back-
ground of the boring routine of prison life. Screenplay
is by P.R. Read, Ivan Foxwell, William Douglas and
Guy Hamilton. A British TV series followed in 1972.
Boa: books The Colditz Story and The Latter Days by
P.R. Reed.
WAR                         93 min (ort 97 min) B/W
B,V                   TEVP L/A; WHV (VHS only)

**COLLECTOR, THE \*\***                              15
William Wyler              USA                 1965
*Terence Stamp, Samantha Eggar, Maurice Dallimore,*
*Mona Washbourne, William Beckley, Gordon Barclay,*
*David Haviland*
A remarkably flat attempt to film a fine novel, that
deals with a soulless man who collects butterflies until
a football pools win gives him freedom, whereupon he
decides to kidnap a girl to add to his collection.
Boa: novel by John Fowles.
DRA                         114 min (ort 119 min)
B,V                                            RCA

**COLLEGE GIRLS \*\***                               18
                           USA
*Sandra Dennesy, Charlene Mills, Sunshine Woods*
Some attractive female students take time off their
studies to enjoy more athletic pursuits, in this fairly
inane sex film.
A                                           80 min
V                                 MIDBLU/PLACE

**COLLISION COURSE \*\***                            18
Lewis Teague               USA                 1988
*Pat Morita, Jay Leno, Chris Sarandon, Al Waxman*
Two private detectives are rivals in their search for
the stolen prototype of a car turbocharger, but even-
tually join forces in an attempt to find it.
A/AD                                        96 min
V                                              PRES

**COLONEL REDL \*\*\***                              15
Istvan Szabo
        AUSTRIA/HUNGARY/WEST GERMANY 1985
*Klaus Maria Brandauer, Armin Muller-Stahl,*
*Gudrun Landgrebe, Jan Niklas, Hans-Christian*
*Blech, Laszlo Mensaros, Andras Balint*
An account of an ambitious homosexual career sol-
dier, whose working-class background does not hinder
his rise to high rank in the Austro-Hungarian army.
Eventually he is made head of the secret police, but
commits suicide just prior to WW1. Inspired by both
historical facts and John Osborne's play "A Patriot
For Me", this complex look at power politics has little
substance but much style, not least being Brandauer's
superb performance.
Aka: REDL EZREDES
DRA                                        144 min
B,V                                            RNK

**COLOR OF MONEY, THE \*\*\***                       15
Martin Scorsese            USA                 1986
*Paul Newman, Tom Cruise, Mary Elizabeth*
*Mastrantonio, Helen Shaver, John Turturo, Bill*
*Cobbs, Robert Agins, Keith McCready, Carol Messing,*
*Steve Mizerak, Bruce A. Young, Forest Whitaker*
A sharp and tense sequel to THE HUSTLER, with
Newman discovering a younger version of himself in
the shape of small-time pool hustler Cruise. They form
a partnership and through tutoring him, Newman
re-discovers his passion for the game. A flashy and

exciting film let down by a poor second half that fails
to deliver the expected climax. AA: Actor (Newman).
Boa: novel by Walter Trew.
DRA                                        115 min
B,V                                            RNK

**COLOR PURPLE, THE \*\*\*\***                       15
Steven Spielberg           USA                 1985
*Whoopi Goldberg, Danny Glover, Rae Dawn Chong,*
*Margaret Avery, Oprah Winfrey, Willard Pugh,*
*Akousa Busia, Desreta Jackson, Adolph Cesar, Dana*
*Ivey*
Sprawling epic tale looking at forty years in the life of
a Southern black woman, who is cruelly separated
from her sister and endures a lifetime of hardship,
until a blues singer enters her life and her real self
emerges. A beautifully made and acted tearjerker,
that piles on the sentiment all the way. Music is by
Quincey Jones, with screenplay by Menno Meyjes and
striking cinematography by Allen Daviau. Produced
and directed by Spielberg.
Boa: novel by Alice Walker.
DRA                                        148 min
B/sh, V/sh                                     WHV

**COLORADO CHARLIE \*\***
Robert Johnson (Roberto Mauri)
                           ITALY               1965
*Charlie Lawrence (Livio Loremon), Barbara Hudson*
*(Brunella Boro), Andrew Ray*
A sheriff wants to retire, but finds himself torn
between his peace-loving wife and the need to deal
with a gunman. Standard Italian offering.
WES                                         96 min
B,V,V2                                         VPD

**COLORS \*\*\***                                    18
Dennis Hopper              USA                 1988
*Sean Penn, Robert Duvall, Maria Conchita Alonso,*
*Randy Brooks, Grand Bush, Don Cheadle, Rudy*
*Ramos, Trinidad Silva*
An ageing cop near retirement, is assigned a rookie
partner, and together they are given the task of
cleaning the streets of urban gangs in L.A. A brutal
and realistic drama that lacks focus but works
surprisingly well, with Penn and Duvall both giving
believable and sympathetic portraits. The photography is by Haskell Wexler. An expanded 127 minute
version may also become available.
A/AD                        116 min (ort 120 min)
V                                              VIR

**COLT CONCERT \*\***
Lucio Fulci                ITALY               1966
*Franco Nero, George Hilton, Lyn Shane, Nino*
*Castelnuovo, John McDouglas, Rita Franchetti,*
*Aysanoa Runachaugua, Tchang Yu*
A man returns home and is eventually helped by his
brother to get rid of a corrupt gang who have seized
his ranch.
Aka: BRUTE AND THE BEAST, THE; TEMPO DI
MASSACRO
WES                                         90 min
B,V,V2                                         VPD

**COLUMBO GOES TO THE GUILLOTINE \*\*\***
Leo Penn                   USA                 1989
*Peter Falk, Anthony Andrews, Karen Austin, James*
*Greene, Alan Fudge, Dana Anderson, Robert*
*Constanzo, Anthony Zerbe*
One of several made-for-TV films that attempted to
revive the popular TV series "Columbo", with our
shabby police detective solving ingenious crimes by a
process of logical deduction. In this one, a stage
magician meets a gruesome death when a stunt goes
wrong. Average.
DRA                                    90 min mTV
V                                              CIC

## COLUMBO: GRAND DECEPTIONS **     PG
Sam Wanamaker     USA     1989
*Peter Falk*
Another one in this so-so 1980s series of detective
yarns, based on the popular TV series "Columbo". In
this tale, our sleuth investigates a murder which has a
military background. Average.
DRA     91 min mTV
V     CIC

## COLUMBO: MURDER, SMOKE AND SHADOWS
**     PG
James Frawley     USA     1988
*Peter Falk*
Our shabby police detective investigates a murder
that would appear to have a Hollywood connection,
the suspect being a special effects expert and young
prodigy film-maker. A well-made but overlong episode
(the first) from a new series of murder mysteries,
largely based on the popular TV series of 1970s.
Aka: MURDER, SMOKE AND SHADOWS
DRA     91 min mTV
V     CIC

## COLUMBO: SEX AND THE MARRIED     15
DETECTIVE *
James Frawley     USA     1989
*Peter Falk*
Another 1980s stab at reviving the popularity of the
1970s police detective series, with the plot revolving
around a sex therapist who murders her lover when
she discovers that he has been unfaithful. As with the
first of these episodes, the story is painfully drawn out
and strangely old-fashioned in form, and additionally
somewhat devoid of tension.
Aka: SEX AND THE MARRIED DETECTIVE
DRA     90 min mTV
V     CIC

## COMA ***     15
Michael Crichton     USA     1978
*Genevieve Bujold, Michael Douglas, Richard
Widmark, Elizabeth Ashley, Lois Chiles, Lance
LeGault, Harry Rhodes, Rip Torn*
Patients undergoing routine surgery in a hospital, are
being killed and their organs used. A woman doctor
defies her male superiors to investigate this. Bujold
and Widmark are excellent as opponents in a nasty
battle of wits, in which she risks her life to uncover
this sinister operation. The script is by Michael
Crichton.
Boa: novel by Robin Cook.
DRA     104 min
V     MGM

## COMANCHEROS, THE ***     PG
Michael Curtiz     USA     1961
*John Wayne, Stuart Whitman, Ina Balin, Lee Marvin,
Bruce Cabot, Nehemiah Persoff*
A Texas Ranger teams up with a gambler, to rid Texas
of renegade whites who sell guns and whisky to the
Indians. A likeable and rough Western, with some
good action sequences. Curtiz's last film.
Boa: novel by Paul I. Wellman.
WES     103 min (Cut at film release by 11 sec)
B,V     CBS

## COMBAT ACADEMY **     PG
Neal Israel     USA     1986
*Wally Ward, Keith Gordon, Jamie Farr, Robert Culp,
John Ratzenberger, George Clooney, Dana Hill,
Sherman Hemsley, Bernie Kopell, Richard Moll, Dick
Van Patten*
Two guys carry out a series of crazy pranks that result
in them being given a one year sentence, in a
state-sponsored programme for juvenile deliquents at
a military academy. However, once there they create
chaos in an effort to get expelled, in this simple-
minded comedy.

COM     93 min
V/h     NWV

## COMBAT KILLERS **  
Ken Loring     PHILIPPINES     1968
*Paul Edwards, Leopoldo Salcedo, Marlene Dauden,
Claude Wilson*
Battle weary soldiers find that their new commander
is a ruthless opportunist who is ready to sacrifice men
for his own glory. A standard war picture, no worse
than hundreds of others, but no better either.
WAR     91 min
B,V     REP/VPD

## COME AND GET IT ***     PG
William Wyler/Howard Hawks
    USA     1936
*William Wyler, Edward Arnold, Joel McCrea, Frances
Farmer, Walter Brennan, Andrea Leeds, Frank
Shields, Mandy Christians, Mary Nash*
An elaborate and entertaining tale set in the lumber
country of Wisconsin, with Arnold a capitalist out to
make his fortune. Farmer gives one of her best
performances playing two roles, but the Oscar went to
Brennan for his fine work. AA: S. Actor (Brennan).
Aka: ROARING TIMBER
Boa: novel by Edna Ferber.
DRA     95 min B/W
V     VGM

## COME AND LAY DOWN **     18
Joan Davis     ITALY
*Anne Libert, Malissa Longo*
An alluring invitation, but in this dismal sex film,
most of the cast need a little urging when it comes to
indulging in their favourite pursuit.
A     98 min
V     SWECOL

## COME AND PLAY *     18
Henri Sala     FRANCE     1974
*Anne Libert, Yann Keredec, Cherry Parker*
Routine sex fantasy with all the trimmings including
a minimal plot.
Aka: WE ARE NO VIRGINS (ACT or SHEP)
A 84 min; 69 min (ACT); 77 min (SHEP) Cut (2 min 28
sec)
B,V     ACT L/A; AVP L/A; SHEP

## COME BACK TO THE FIVE AND DIME JIMMY
DEAN, JIMMY DEAN **     15
Robert Altman     USA     1982
*Sandy Dennis, Karen Black, Sudie Bond, Kathy Bates,
Cher, Marta Heflin*
The reunion of a James Dean fan club is the occasion
for many personal and frank revelations. An attempt
to stretch a one-act play to a full length feature that
has good performances and lively direction, but is
seriously short of material to work with. Written by
Graczyk.
Boa: play by Ed Graczyk.
DRA     105 min
B,V     INT; MIA (VHS only); PARK (VHS only)

## COME NEXT SPRING ***     U
R.G. Springsteen     USA     1956
*Anne Sheridan, Steve Cochran, Walter Brennan,
Sherry Jackson, Richard Eyer, Sonny Tufts*
Story of a man who returns after leaving his wife and
children on their farm in Arkansas, determined to
turn over a new leaf. However, he has to win her trust
and respect. A well made, sensitive and unambitious
story. Music is by Max Steiner.
DRA     92 min
V     VMA; STABL

## COME PLAY WITH ME *     18
George Harrison Marks   UK     1977
*Irene Handl, Alfie Bass, George Harrison Marks,*

*Ronald Fraser, Ken Parry, Tommy Godfrey, Bob Todd,
Rita Webb, Cardew Robinson, Sue Longhurst, Jerry
Lorden, Mary Millington, Henry McGee, Norman
Vaughan, Queenie Watts*
Two counterfeiters pretending to be musicians, hide
out at a health farm staffed by sex-starved nurses. A
feeble and tedious sex romp boasting a cast of similar
attributes.
A                    90 min (ort 93 min) (Cut at film release)
B,V,V2                    VIDMOV/HOK; PHE (VHS only)

**COME PLAY WITH ME 3 ***                                18
Michael Thomas (Erwin C. Dietrich)
                        SWITZERLAND                    1980
*Brigitte Lahaie, Ella Rose, Jane Baker*
Ostensibly set in a girl's college, this is a badly clipped
together softcore account of sundry couplings, bearing
no relation to the original title film.
Aka: JULCHEN UND JETTCHEN: DIE
VERLIEBTEN APOTHEKERSTOECHTER
A   64 min (ort 90 min) Cut (1 min 25 sec in addition to
film cuts)
B,V                        PRI; SHEP; PHE (VHS only)

**COMEBACK ***                                          15
Christel Buschman
                        WEST GERMANY                   1982
*Eric Burdon, Julie Carmen, Michael Carenaugh,
Louisiana Red, Rosa King, Jorg Pfennigwerth, Bob
Lockwood, Julie Carmen*
Eric Burdon of the 1960s pop group "The Animals",
plays a pop singer who is attempting to make a
comeback, but is reluctant to adopt a more violent
hard rock image as advocated by his manager.
DRA                                                102 min
B,V                                            WOV; STABL

**COMEBACK KID, THE ***                                 PG
Peter Levin            USA                             1980
*John Ritter, Susan Dey, James Gregory, Doug
McKeon, Jeremy Licht, Rod Gist, Patrick Swayze*
Romantic comedy-drama about an ex-baseball player
who gets talked into coaching a gang of street kids,
and finds love into the bargain. A pleasant romantic
outing.
DRA                                            97 min mTV
B,V                                        DIPLO/VFP; IVS

**COMEBACK, THE ***                                     
Pete Walker            UK                              1977
*Jack Jones, Pamela Stephenson, David Doyle, Bill
Owen, Sheila Keith, Richard Johnson*
An American singer trying to make a comeback in the
UK is drawn into a series gruesome murders, in this
rubbishy effort.
Aka: DAY THE SCREAMING STOPPED, THE
HOR                                        100 min mTV
B,V                                                    DFS

**COMEBACK, THE ***                                     PG
Jerrold Freedman       USA                            1988
*Robert Urich, Chynna Phillips, Mitchell Anderson,
Ronny Cox, Brynn Thayer, Harvey Martin*
A former football star returns to his home town after
spending years living as a playboy, and attempts to
form a relationship with a son he barely knew.
Matters become complicated when the girlfriend of his
son falls for him, and he discovers that she is in fact
the daughter of a former associate who brought about
his early retirement. Standard soap opera tale, with a
football flavour.
DRA                                                90 min
V                                                     CBS

**COMEBACK, THE ***                                     15
Hall Bartlett          USA                            1983
*Michael Landon, Priscilla Presley, Moira Chen (Laura
Gemser), Jurgen Prochnow, Edward Woodward,
Gabriele Tinti, David Leonard, Cathy Bartlett,*

*William Kushner, Eric Miller, Dee Barough, Kurn
Ramivartan*
An account of a journalist's attempts to rescue his
Laotian girlfriend after Laos has been taken over by
the Communists. Based on the experiences of Australian journalist John Everingham, who spirited his
girlfriend to safety in 1978. The film experienced
many production difficulties before release, and "introduced" Indonesian actress Moira Chen, who was
later revealed to be Laura Gemser. Presley's TV
movie debut. Average.
Aka: LOVE IS FOREVER
DRA                                96 min (ort 150 min) mTV
B,V                                                    CBS

**COMEDY OF TERRORS, THE ***                            15
Jacques Tourneur       USA                            1963
*Vincent Price, Peter Lorre, Boris Karloff, Basil
Rathbone, Joyce Jameson, Joe E. Brown*
A firm of undertakers finds that the only way to
improve business is to help send people on their way.
This leads to complications, but little in the way of
real humour in this disappointing horror-spoof.
Scripted by Richard Matheson.
COM                                    82 min (ort 111 min)
B,V                            ORION/RNK; VIR (VHS only)

**COMES A HORSEMAN ***                                  15
Alan J. Pakula         USA                            1978
*Jane Fonda, James Caan, Jason Robards, George
Grizzard, Richard Farnsworth, Jim Davis, Mark
Harmon, Macon McCalman, Basil Hoffman, James
Kline, James Keach, Clifford A. Pellon*
Simple Western story set in 1940s Montana, which
tells of ranchers trying to save their land from an
oilman and an evil cattle baron. A low-key and often
ponderous melodrama, sullen and atmospheric, but
short on action.
WES                                                119 min
B,V                                                    WHV

**COMET QUEST ***                                       U
Will Vinton            USA                            1986
*Voices of: James Whitemore, Michele Mariana, Gary
Krug, Chris Ritchie, John Morrison, Carol Edelman,
Dallas McKennon, Herb Smith, Marley Stone, Wilbur
Vincent, Wally Newman, Tim Conner, Todd Tolces,
Billy Scream, Wilf Innton*
The critically acclaimed, first full-length feature film
in "claymation", the process of animating clay to
achieve life-like movement. Produced and directed by
the inventor of this process, this is a fantasy journey
in which Mark Twain carries some stowaways half-
way round the world in a fantastical flying-machine,
for a rendezvous with Halley's comet.
Aka: ADVENTURES OF MARK TWAIN, THE
CAR                                    82 min (ort 86 min)
B,V                                                    EIV

**COMFORT AND JOY ***                                   PG
Bill Forsyth           UK                             1984
*Bill Patterson, C.P. Grogan, Eleanor David, Alex
Norton, Patrick Malahide, Rikki Fulton, Roberto
Bernardi, George Rossi, Peter Rossi, Billy McElhaney,
Gilly Gilchrist, Caroline Guthrie, Oma McCracken,
Elizabeth Sinclair*
The life of a Glasgow D.J starts to fall apart, when his
girlfriend ditches him and he becomes involved in a
vendetta between warring Italian ice-cream families.
A disappointing film whose comic points fall flat, since
the humour is so dry as to be non-existent, and all the
mindless violence and stupidity appals rather than
amuses. Written and directed by Forsyth, who gave us
the superior GREGORY'S GIRL and LOCAL HERO.
COM                                    100 min (ort 106 min)
B,V                                            TEVP; WHV

**COMIC STRIP PRESENTS:**                               15
**DIDN'T YOU KILL MY BROTHER? ***

Bob Spiers               UK              1987
*Alexei Sayle, Beryl Reid, Peter Richardson, Graham*
*Crowden, Pauline Melvile*
A humorous episode from this uneven comedy series,
with the story revolving around the exploits of two
brothers – one a demented East End gangster and the
other a gentle no-hoper, who has emerged from prison
with over four hundred qualifications and taken on a
job as an "Unstructured Activities Co-ordinator" to a
group of juvenile delinquents.
Aka: DIDN'T YOU KILL MY BROTHER?
COM                                      55 min mTV
V                                        PAL

**COMIC STRIP PRESENTS:**                15
**MISTER JOLLY LIVES NEXT DOOR **
Stephen Frears           UK              1987
*Peter Cook, Adrian Edmondson, Rik Mayall, Peter*
*Richardson, Nicholas Parsons, Dawn French, Jennifer*
*Saunders*
An episode from the "Comic Strip" series with Mayall
and Edmondson a couple of tramps who run an escort
agency as a side-line. One day they intercept a
package sent to their lunatic hit-man neighbour, and
discover a message to "take out" the popular quizmas-
ter Nicholas Parsons. A coarse and vulgar effort,
whose occasional moments of humour tended to be
swamped in a feast of tastelessness.
Aka: MISTER JOLLY LIVES NEXT DOOR
COM                                      52 min mTV
B,V                                      PAL

**COMIC STRIP PRESENTS:**                15
**THE FUNSEEKERS ***
Simon Wright             UK              1987
*Nigel Planer, Keith Allen, Peter Richardson*
Another story from this popular TV series that
attempted to present crude parodies of events and
genres. In this tale some boozing slobs go on a
two-week holiday in Spain and cause general chaos.
Aka: FUNSEEKERS, THE
COM                                      52 min mTV
V/h                                      PAL

**COMIC STRIP PRESENTS: THE STRIKE ***  15
Peter Richardson         UK              1986
*Peter Richardson, Nigel Planer, Robbie Coltrane,*
*Keith Allen, Rik Mayall, Adrian Edmondson, Jennifer*
*Saunders, Alexei Sayle, Dawn French*
Another episode in this series. This one attempts to
provide a parody of the 1984 British miners' strike,
with overblown portraits of miners' leader Arthur
Scargill and others.
Aka: STRIKE, THE
COM                                      52 min; 59 min (VIR) mTV
V/h                                      PAL; VIR

**COMIC STRIP PRESENTS: THE YOB ***     15
Ian Emes                 UK              1987
*Keith Allen, Adrian Edmondson, Peter Richardson,*
*Gary Olson*
A parody of films of the 1950s, with a successful
director falling victim to a brain transplant experi-
ment and turning into a hooligan.
Aka: YOB, THE
COM                                      52 min mTV
V/h                                      PAL

**COMIC, THE ****                        18
Richard Driscoll         USA             1985
*Steve Munroe, Bernard Plant, Bob Flag, Jeff Pine,*
*Kym Stone, Simon Davies, Gary Twommey, Berdia*
*Timimi*
An interesting but not entirely successful psychologic-
al thriller, that's set ten years in the future. In a
dreary disease-ridden police state, comedians enter-
tain drugged audiences. One comic decides to use
murder in his act, but then finds himself the victim of

an evil and manipulative woman.
FAN                                      90 min
B,V                                      ABC

**COMING HOME ****                       18
Hal Ashby                USA             1978
*Jane Fonda, Jon Voight, Bruce Dern, Robert*
*Carradine, Robert Ginty, Penelope Milford*
A lonely wife whose husband is away fighting in the
Vietnam war, falls in love with a paralysed veteran.
An unusually mature examination of the Vietnam
War and its effects on people's lives, traces of mawkish
melodrama do not spoil it. AA: Actor (Voight), Actress
(Fonda), Screen (Orig) (Nancy Dowd/Waldo Salt/
Robert C. Jones).
Boa: book by Nancy Dowd.
DRA                                      90 min; 122 min (WHV)
B,V,V2                                   INT/CBS; WHV (VHS only)

**COMING OF ANGELS, A ****               
Joel Scott               USA             1977
*Annette Haven, Jamie Gillis, Amber Hunt, Leslie*
*Bovee, Abigail Clayton, Eric Edward*
Inspired in name only by the American TV series
"Charlie's Angels", which had three females fighting
crime, this film concentrates on the foolish tale of a
guy who can only experience orgasms as a voyeur.
Forgettable nonsense. A sequel called ANGELS came
in 1986.
A                                        87 min Cut
B,V                                      TCX L/A; ELV

**COMING OUT ALIVE ****
Don McBreeny             CANADA          1982
*Helen Shaver, Scott Heylands, Michael Ironside*
A divorced father kidnaps his handicapped son to use
as cover for a murder. Average.
THR                                      80 min
B,V                                      INT/CBS

**COMING OUT OF THE ICE ****
Waris Hussein            USA             1982
*John Savage, Ben Cross, Francesca Annis, Willie*
*Nelson, Frank Windsor, Peter Vaughan, Sylvia Kay,*
*John Malcolm, Bernice Stegers, Steven Berkoff,*
*Donald Eccles, Tom Chadbon, Clive Merrison,*
*Edward Burnham, David Hayman*
A film based on the true story of the unjust imprison-
ment and torture of Victor Herman, an American
citizen who was living in the Soviet Union in the
1930s, when he was arrested by the KGB on a
trumped-up spying charge. He endured nearly 20
years of suffering in Siberian labour camps before
being eventually released. An adequate biographical
drama.
Boa: book by Victor Herman.
DRA                                      93 min (ort 104 min) mTV
B,V,LV                                   SPEC/POLY

**COMING THROUGH ****                    PG
Peter Barber-Fleming     UK              1985
*Kenneth Branagh, Helen Mirren, Alison Steadman,*
*Philip Martin Brown, Norman Rodway*
An examination of D.H. Lawrence's relationship with
his eventual wife Frieda von Richthoper, that uses
flashbacks to explore the writer's early life, whilst at
the same time being rather awkwardly coupled to a
present-day tale of a young Lawrence scholar, and her
failure to relate to the work of the writer she is
studying. A dry lecture of a film, nice to look at but
coldly distant.
DRA                                      78 min
V                                        FUTUR

**COMING TO AMERICA ****                 15
John Landis              USA             1988
*Eddie Murphy, James Earl Jones, Madge Sinclair,*
*Arsenio Hall, Shari Headley, Paul Bates, Allison*
*Dean, Eriq LaSalle*

The prince of an African royal family decides to get wed, and comes to New York where he believes he will find the girls of his dreams. A sugary romantic comedy in the old style, with numerous in-jokes and a few amusing cameos.

| COM | 112 min |
|-----|---------|
| V/sh | CIC |

**COMING, THE *** **                                                18
Bert I. Gordon          USA                          1980
*Susan Swift, Albert Salmi, Guy Stockwell, Tisha Sterling, Beverly Ross, Dana Hardwick, David Rounds, Lauren Dowling, Frank Dolan, John Peters, Judd Dodd, Jennie Babo, Terese Giammarco, Janice Wayne, Harold Jackson*
Set at the height of the Salem witch-hunt in 1692, with a woman who has sent 20 innocent people to their deaths now branding a child of five a witch. Though her father has been burnt, his will to save his child carries him 300 years into the future to present day Salem. There he intends to find the reincarnation of this vengeful woman and save his child from death.

| HOR | 86 min Cut (1 min 11 sec) |
|-----|---------------------------|
| V | REP/VPD |

**COMMAND 5 *** **                                                 15
E.W. Swackhamer        USA                          1984
*Stephen Parr, Wings Hauser, John Matuszak, William Russ, Sonja Smits, Gregory Sierra, William Forsythe, Robert F. Lyons, Bruce Abbott, Arthur Adams, Marc Alaimo, Derek Barton, Lynn Benesch, Dennis Bowan, Chere Bryson*
An army captain recruits a group of misfits for a special mission, to free a town in Arizona from the control of a band of violent mercenaries. THE DIRTY DOZEN meet THE MAGNIFICENT SEVEN in this average offering. Pilot for a TV series.

| A/AD | 93 min (ort 104 min) mTV |
|------|--------------------------|
| B,V | CIC |

**COMMAND IN HELL *** **                                            15
Georg Stanford Brown    USA                          1987
*Suzanne Pleshette, Danny Aiello, Frank Converse, Georg Stanford Brown*
Violent urban action movie set in the south-east precinct of Los Angeles, where a tough lady cop is given the task of freeing the area from the grip of an assortment of thugs, drug-pushers and corrupt cops. Routine.

| A/AD | 94 min |
|------|--------|
| B,V | FUTUR |

**COMMANDER LAWIN *** **                                            18
                                                              198-
*Danny Varona*
Formula action tale of a tough Vietnam veteran who battles a corrupt regime.

| A/AD | 90 min |
|------|--------|
| B,V | TGP |

**COMMANDER, THE *** **                                             15
Anthony M. Dawson (Antonio Margheriti)
                        ITALY                        1988
*Lewis Collins, Lee Van Cleef, Donald Pleasence, Manfred Lehman, Brett Halsy, Chat Silayan, John Steiner*
Lightweight and corny actioner, with Collins leading an intrepid band of mercenaries into the steamy jungles of the Far East, in pursuit of a drugs baron who has come into possession of information that may tell him the identity of a mole working for the Drug Enforcement Agency. All the stock cliches are here, in a film of big guns, big trucks, lousy acting and a banal and convoluted script.

| A/AD | 84 min (ort 98 min) Cut (7 sec) |
|------|---------------------------------|
| B,V | EIV |

**COMMANDO *** **                                                  18
Mark L. Lester          USA                          1985

*Arnold Schwarzenegger, Dan Hedaya, Rae Dawn Chong, Vernon Wells, David Patrick Kelly, Alyssa Milano, James Olson, Bill Duke, Drew Snyder, Sharon Michael De Lano, Bob Minor, Mike Adams, Carlos Cervantes, Hank Celia*
A violent, comic-strip adventure, with Schwarzenegger a retired special agent who is forced to don his combat gear once more, when his beloved daughter is kidnapped as part of a plan to restore a Central American dictator to power. Occasional flashes of humour from the star do little to soften the film's mindless noise and violence.

| A/AD | 86 min (Cut at film release by 12 sec) |
|------|----------------------------------------|
| V | CBS |

**COMMANDO LEOPARD *** **                                          15
Anthony M. Dawson (Antonio Margheriti)
                        ITALY/WEST GERMANY           1985
*Lewis Collins, Klaus Kinski, John Steiner, Manfred Lehman, Cristina Donadio, Hans Leutenegger, Alan C. Walker*
An elite commando force is sent to overthrow a corrupt South American dictatorship, in this competent but uninspired action picture. Filmed in the Philippines.
Aka: KOMMANDO LEOPARD

| A/AD | 91 min |
|------|--------|
| B,V | EIV |

**COMMANDO SQUAD *** **                                            18
Fred Olen Ray           USA                          1987
*Brian Thompson, Kathy Shower, William Smith, Ross Hagen, Sid Haig, Robert Quarry, Mel Welles*
A former drug enforcement agent changes sides and becomes a ruthless cocaine dealer, and an expedition sent to nail him ends in disaster, with only one government agent surviving. In desperation he sends out an SOS and the authorities send his ex-partner, a female narcotics agent, to rescue him. A mindless and vacuous actioner, whose chief merit resides in the shapely form of agent Shower, Playboy Magazine's 1986 "Playmate of the Year".

| A/AD | 90 min |
|------|--------|
| B,V | MGM |

**COMMANDOS *** **                                                
Armando Crispino
                        ITALY/WEST GERMANY           1968
*Lee Van Cleef, Jack Kelly, Marino Mase*
Commandos have to capture an Italian base and hold it until the Allies land in North Africa. Average.

| WAR | 100 min |
|-----|---------|
| B,V,V2 | GHV |

**COMMON GROUND: PARTS 1 AND 2 *** **
Mike Newell              USA                          1990
*Jane Curtin, Richard Thomas, C.C.H. Pounder, James Farentino, George Emelin, Erika Anderson*
A look at the school "busing program" initiated by Boston in the 1960s and 1970s in a clumsy attempt to accelerate the pace of racial integration. The issue is very thoroughly examined, using three families to highlight the tensions this policy caused. Earnest and careful, but poor casting and awkward plotting dull its dramatic impact. Originally shown in two parts, though it was originally planned as a seven-hour mini-series.
Boa: book by J. Anthony Lukas.

| DRA | 186 min (ort 200 min) mTV |
|-----|---------------------------|
| V | WHV |

**COMMON-LAW CABIN *** **                                          18
Russ Meyer              USA                          1967
*Alaina Capri, Babette Bardot, Adele Rein, Jack Moran, Franklin Bolger, John Furlong, Ken Swofford, Andrew Hagara*
At a remote tourist spot, a man runs a game-hunting lodge with his young second wife, and daughter by his first marriage. A doctor and his wife arrive for a day of

shooting, but unknown to them an ex-cop turned robber is hiding out there. The doctor drops dead when his wife seduces the ex-cop. More deaths follow, but not before much sex and violence has come to pass in this typical Meyer offering.
Aka: HOW MUCH LOVING DOES A NORMAL COUPLE NEED?
A                                                   69 min
B,V                                      VSP L/A; ATLAN

**COMMUNION ✱✱**
Alfred Sole                    USA                  1976
*Brooke Shields, Tom Signorelli, Louisa Horton, Paula Sheppard, Mildred Clinton, Linda Miller, Lillian Roth*
A young girl preparing for her first communion is brutally murdered, and her twin sister, with whom she had a less than loving relationship, is suspected. Unpleasant and self-indulgent murder yarn, filmed on location in Paterson, New Jersey. Written by Rosemary Ritvo and Sole.
Aka: ALICE, SWEET ALICE; HOLY TERROR
HOR                                                103 min
B,V                                            VCL/CBS

**COMMUTER HUSBANDS ✱**
Derek Ford                     UK                   1973
*Gabrielle Drake, Robin Bailey, Jane Cardew, Heather Chasen, Dick Hayden, Claire Gordon, Dervis Ward, Dorothea Phillips, Brenda Peters, Mike Britton, Nicola Austine, Timothy Parkes, Yokki Rhodes, Robin Culver, George Selway*
A girl tells six stories to illustrate the predatory nature of Man, and all are illustrated by episodes in which men embark on woman-chasing forays. A feeble sex comedy.
Aka: SEX GAMES
COM                                83 min (ort 85 min)
B,V,V2                                       VFO L/A; VPD

**COMPANY OF WOLVES, THE ✱✱✱**              18
Neil Jordan                    UK                   1984
*David Warner, Angela Lansbury, Graham Crowden, Stephen Rea, Brian Glover, Kathryn Pogson, Tusse Silberg, Micha Bergese, Sarah Patterson, Georgia Slowe, Susan Porrett, Shane Johnstone, Dawn Archibald, Richard Morant*
A Freudian variant on the Red Riding Hood tale, with a set of eerie stories told by Granny to her ingenuous granddaughter, who begins to encounter wolves in all manner of guises. A visually powerful fantasy that's spoilt by fragmentary and disjointed development.
Boa: short stories by Angela Carter.
HOR                       95 min; 92 min (VES)
B,V                            PVG; VES (VHS only)

**COMPETITION, THE ✱✱**                     15
Joel Oliansky                  USA                  1982
*Richard Dreyfuss, Amy Irving, Sam Wanamaker, Lee Remick, Joseph Cali, Ty Henderson*
Two young pianists in a competition for the same prize fall in love. Nothing much in this romantic drama except some nice piano sequences. The directing debut for screenwriter Oliansky, who also wrote the script.
DRA                                                122 min
V                                                    RCA

**COMPLEAT RUTLES, THE ✱✱**                 15
Eric Idle/Gary Weiss           UK                   1980
*Eric Idle, Neill Innes, John Halsey, Mick Jagger, George Harrison, Ricky Fataar, Michael Palin, Bianca Jagger, John Belushi, Dan Aykroyd, Gilda Radner, Bill Murray, Paul Simon*
Unfunny and lacklustre attempt to parody the career of the pop group The Beatles, with an account of a fictitious group – "The Rutles". Worth seeing if only for the many songs that parody the style of the famous pop group, plus a few digs at some of their more esoteric interests. Well done, but it needs more than the one joke to sustain it.

Aka: ALL YOU NEED IS CASH; RUTLES, THE; RUTLES, THE: ALL YOU NEED IS CASH
COM                                 71 min (ort 78 min)
B,V                                                  PVG

**COMPROMISING POSITIONS ✱✱**              15
Frank Perry                    USA                  1985
*Susan Sarandon, Raul Julia, Anne De Salvo, Mary Beth Hurt, Joe Mantegna, Judith Ivey, Edward Herrman, Josh Mostel*
A woman decides to investigate the murder of her dentist and uncovers evidence to suggest a link with the distribution of pornography. An uneven black comedy that starts off well enough, but soon degenerates into feeble nonsense.
Boa: novel by Susan Isaacs.
COM                                                95 min
B,V                                                  CIC

**COMPUTER GHOSTS ✱✱**                      PG
Rob Stewart                    USA                  1987
*Nicholas Ryan, Emily Symonds, Peter Whitford, Noel Ferrier*
Crazy comedy revolving around a devious businessman who makes use of a spooky burglar alarm, to frighten home-owners and steal from them. When the "Chief Executive of the Hereafter" becomes aware of his actions, he sends some real ghosts to deal with him.
COM                                                82 min
V/s                                                  GHV

**COMPUTER KID, THE ✱✱**                    U
John Florea                    USA                  1977
*Henry Darrow, Kate Woodville, Guy Madison, Mark Gilpin, Rock Montano, Robert Clark, John Mitchum, Anthony Ganne*
An 8-year-old electronics wizard builds a device that causes no end of trouble for him, his father and the local sheriff. Lighthearted children's fare.
Aka: COMPUTER WIZARD; WHERE'S WILLIE? (VAL)
JUV                                                90 min
V                                       VAL L/A; NET

**COMPUTER WORE TENNIS SHOES, THE ✱✱**     U
Robert Butler                  USA                  1970
*Kurt Russell, Cesar Romero, Joe Flynn, William Schallert, Alan Hewitt, Richard Bakalayan*
A brilliant student is accidentally injected with the information stored in a computer and finds himself being chased by criminals. Formula Disney slapstick adventure, followed by NOW YOU SEE HIM, NOW YOU DON'T.
COM                                                87 min
B,V                                                  WDV

**COMRADES ✱✱✱**                            PG
Bill Douglas                   UK                   1987
*Vanessa Redgrave, James Fox, Michael Hordern, Barbara Windsor, Robin Soans, William Gaminara, Philip Davis, Stephen Bateman, Keith Allen, Patrick Field, Jeremy Flynn, Robert Stephens, Freddie Jones, Murray Melvin, Imelda Staunton*
An earnest, preachy and overlong look at the beginnings of trade unionism in Britain. Set in the 1820s, it follows the fortunes of a group of agricultural workers, who are transported to Australia in punishment for having attempted to form a trade union.
DRA          174 min (ort 183 min) (Cut at film release)
B,V                                                  VIR

**CON ARTISTS, THE ✱✱**                     PG
Serge Corbucci                 ITALY                1977
*Anthony Quinn, Corinne Clery, Capucine*
Two con-artists are thrown together by chance, and decide to work as a team. Average.
Aka: CON MEN, THE

COM                           89 min Cut (2 sec)
B,V,V2                        GOST/DFS; KRP/XTACY

## CONAN THE BARBARIAN ***                    15
John Milius            USA                   1982
*Arnold Schwarzenegger, Sandahl Bergman, James*
*Earl Jones, Gerry Lopez, Mako, Ben Davidson, Sven*
*Ole Thorsen, Max Von Sydow, Valerie Quennesen,*
*Cassandra Gaviola, William Smith*
Story of sword-and-sorcery revenge by a warrior in a
time of long ago, using characters drawn from the
"Conan" novels of Robert E. Howard. In this adven-
ture, our hero seeks revenge on the cult leader who
destroyed his village and enslaved him. A spectacular
and full-blooded treatment of pulp fiction. Sets are by
Ron Cobb, with music by Basil Pouledoris. Followed
by CONAN THE DESTROYER.
FAN                    121 min (Cut at film release)
B, V/sh, V2                          TEVP; WHV

## CONAN THE DESTROYER *                       15
Richard Fleischer      USA                   1984
*Arnold Schwarzenegger, Grace Jones, Wilt*
*Chamberlain, Mako, Sarah Douglas, Olivia D'Abo*
Second film based on the "Conan" books of Robert E.
Howard, that tries hard to please but ends up being
merely tiresome and ponderous.
A/AD                          96 min Cut (30 sec)
V                                            RCA

## CONCORDE AFFAIR **                          15
Roger Deodato (Ruggero Deodato)
                       ITALY                 1979
*James Franciscus, Mimsy Farmer, Van Johnson,*
*Joseph Cotten, Edmund Purdom, Mag Fleming, Mario*
*Maranzana, Venantino Venantini*
A Concorde plane crashes near Martinique, and a
reporter sent to investigate discovers that sabotage
was the cause. Average Euro-thriller.
Aka: CONCORDE AFFAIRE SEVENTY-NINE;
S.O.S. CONCORDE (VPD)
THR                                       93 min
B,V,V2                         EVC; VPD (VHS only)

## CONCRETE BEAT **                            PG
Robert Butler          USA                   1983
*John Getz, Kenneth McMillan, Darlanne Fluegel,*
*Rhoda Gemignani, Van Nessa L. Clarke, Dean*
*Santoro, Marla Adams, Ingrid Anderson, Thom Bray,*
*Gerry Gibson, Ray Girardin, Alexandra Johnson,*
*Terrence McNally, Patricia McPherson*
An investigative reporter who is totally dedicated to
his job, fights to clear a woman accused of murdering
her child. Pilot for a TV series. Average.
DRA                                  90 min mTV
B,V                                          EHE

## CONCRETE COWBOYS, THE **
Burt Kennedy           USA                   1979
*Jerry Reed, Tom Selleck, Morgan Fairchild, Claude*
*Akins, Gene Evans, Lucille Benson, Randolph Powell,*
*Roy Acuff, Barbara Mandrell, Ray Stevens, Red West,*
*Grace Zabriskie, Bob Hannah, Joseph Burke, Seidina*
*Reed*
Mystery about a couple of cowboys who get involved in
a complex blackmail scheme in Nashville. A light-
hearted mystery tale that formed the pilot for a
short-lived series.
DRA                                 100 min mTV
B,V                                          CBS

## CONCRETE HELL ***                           18
Eric Till              CANADA                1985
*Nicky Guadagni, Shirley Douglas, Anne Anglin,*
*Jackie Richardson, Bernard Behrens*
Account of a framed woman's struggle to survive the
horrors of the prison system, as she faces a seven-year
stretch for trying to smuggle drugs into Canada. For
once a realistic drama that doesn't slide into cliche,

with fine performances and an intelligent script.
Written by Judith Thompson.
Aka: TURNING TO STONE
Boa: novel by Judith Thompson.
DRA                                       98 min
V/h                                          CAN

## CONCRETE JUNGLE, THE *                      18
Tom De Simone         USA                    1982
*Jill St John, Tracy Bergman, Barbara Luna*
A girl is set up by her boyfriend and goes to jail for
smuggling cocaine. Once there, she is subjected to the
usual brutalities that seem to be largely the stock-in-
trade of women-in-prison movies. Written by Alan
Adler.
DRA       106 min; 96 min (INTMED); 94 min (MIA) Cut
(1 min 40 sec)
B,V                            VFP; INTMED; MIA

## CONDOR **                                   PG
Virgil L. Vogel       USA                    1986
*Ray Wise, Wendy Kilbourne, Vic Polizos, James Avery,*
*Cassandra Gava, Craig Stevens, Carolyn Seymour,*
*Shawn Michaels, Mario Roccuzzo, Barbara Beckley,*
*Catherine Battistone, Diana Bellamy, Gene Bicknell,*
*Myra Chason, Tony Epper*
The leading agent of an anti-terrorist organisation
teams up with an android in order to stop a super-
criminal. Set in the year 2001 and slightly reminis-
cent of Asimov's novel "The Caves Of Steel", this was
the pilot for a failed TV series.
FAN                                  90 min mTV
B,V                                          MGM

## CONDORMAN **                                 U
Charles Jarrott       UK                     1981
*Michael Crawford, Oliver Reed, Barbara Carrera,*
*James Hampton, Jean-Pierre Kalfon, Dana Elcar*
A writer of comic-book stories becomes his own hero
"Condorman", in order to help a Russian spy to defect,
in this example of Disney at its silliest.
Aka: CONDOR MAN
Boa: short story The Game Of X by Robert Sheckley.
COM                                       87 min
B,V                             RNK L/A; WDV

## CONDUCT UNBECOMING **                       PG
Michael Anderson      UK                     1975
*Michael York, Richard Attenborough, Trevor Howard,*
*Stacy Keach, Susannah York, Christopher Plummer,*
*James Faulkner, Michael Culver, James Donald,*
*Rafiq Anwar, Helen Cherry, Michael Fleming, David*
*Robb, David Purcell*
Old fashioned drama that follows the events arising
after an officer's wife of the Bengal Lancers is
indecently assaulted. A cadet is accused, but in reality
the culprit is someone quite different. A stuffy and
wooden adaptation of England's play, set in India
circa 1878.
Boa: play by Barry England.
DRA                                      107 min
B,V                                         TEVP

## CONFESSIONAL MURDERS, THE **               18
Pete Walker           UK                     1975
*Susan Penhaligon, Anthony Sharp, Stephanie*
*Beacham, Norman Eshley, Sheila Keith, Hilda Barry,*
*Stuart Bevan, Julia McCarthy, Jon Yule, Mervyn*
*Johns, Victor Winding, Kim Butcher, Bill Kerr, Jack*
*Allen, Andrew Sachs*
A demented priest embarks on a career of blackmail
and murder, employing the instruments of his calling
to achieve his ends (e.g. a poisoned communion wafer
or a tape recorder hidden in the confessional). A young
girl falls into his clutches, but eventually he gets his
just deserts. A grotesque and muddled attempt to use
the rites of Catholics in the service of a horror film.
Aka: CONFESSION AT DEATH'S DOOR, THE;
CONFESSIONAL, THE; HOUSE OF MORTAL SIN

HOR                          100 min (ort 104 min)
V                                              RCA

## CONFESSIONS FROM A HOLIDAY CAMP *      18
Norman Cohen          UK                    1977
*Robin Askwith, Anthony Booth, Bill Maynard, Doris
Hare, Sheila White, Colin Crompton, Liz Fraser, Linda
Hayden, John Junkin, Lance Percival, Nicholas Owen,
Mike Savage, Nicola Blackman, Caroline Ellis, Sue
Upton, David Auker*
Another ghastly British sex comedy. This one is set in
a holiday camp run by an ex-prison officer, whose
entertainments officer has taken to entertaining
himself with the ladies.
Boa: novel by Timothy Lea.
COM                           85 min (ort 88 min)
V                                              RCA

## CONFESSIONS FROM THE DAVID GALAXY    18
## AFFAIR *
Willy Roe             UK                    1979
*Alan Lake, Glynn Edwards, Anthony Booth, Diana
Dors, John Moulder-Brown, Milton Reid, Bernie
Winters, Kenny Lynch, Mary Millington, Sally
Faulkner, Jada Smith, Queenie Watts, Cindy Truman,
Vicky Scott, Alec Mango*
A girl is not fulfilled sexually until she meets a
superstud. And if that wasn't complex enough, he is
meanwhile being sought by the police who wish to
frame him for a murder.
Aka: SECRETS OF A SEXY GAME (KRP); STAR
SEX
Boa: novel by George Evans.
COM                           92 min (ort 96 min)
B,V,V2                                    HOK; MIG

## CONFESSIONS OF A BLUE MOVIE STAR **   18
Andrzej Kostenko
                      WEST GERMANY          1982
*Claudia Fielers*
Behind-the-scenes look at the world of pornographic
film-making, taking the real life example of a female
star who committed suicide.
Aka: BLUE MOVIE STAR
DRA              72 min (ort 89 min) (Cut at film release)
B,V                                INT L/A; PRI; SHEP

## CONFESSIONS OF A DRIVING INSTRUCTOR *   18
Norman Cohen          UK                    1976
*Robin Askwith, Anthony Booth, Sheila White, Doris
Hare, Bill Maynard, Liz Fraser, Windsor Davies, Irene
Handl, George Layton, Linda Bellingham, Avril
Angers, Maxine Casson, Ballard Berkeley, Suzy
Mandel, Peter Godfrey*
A "Carry On" type farce, with Askwith a dull-witted
guy who starts up a driving school with his brother,
and finds that women are his best customers if not
learners. A dull and coarse celebration of British
smut; the second one in the series.
Boa: novel by Timothy Lea.
A                                          90 min
B,V                          MOV L/A; PRV L/A; RCA

## CONFESSIONS OF A LADY COP *           PG
Lee H. Katzin         USA                   1988
*Karen Black, Eddie Egan, Don Murray, James
Whitmore Jr., Frank Sinatra Jr, Pat Crowley, A.
Martinez, Ron Masak, Donald May, Estrelita Lenore
Lopex, Herbert Jefferson Jr*
A tough lady cop is ordered to infiltrate a call-girl
ring, in this further entry to the "Police In Action"
series. A strictly routine look at the day-to-day life of a
busy cop, dealing with suicides, brutal murders and
the standard shoot-outs. As superficial as it is uncon-
vincing.
Aka: POLICE IN ACTION: CONFESSIONS OF A
LADY COP
A/AD                         94 min (ort 100 min) mTV
B,V                                            RCA

## CONFESSIONS OF A LESBOS HONEY **      18
Ilias Milosakos       ITALY
*Tina Spati, Magda Marci*
Dull exploits of a woman torn between her lesbian
lover and her boyfriend, that looks at two girls taking
on a variety of lovers in a quest to find sexual
fulfilment.
A                    81 min (ort 90 min) Cut (49 sec)
B,V   XTACY/KRP; 18PLAT/TOW; SHEP; PHE (VHS
only)

## CONFESSIONS OF A MALE ESCORT **       18
Alois Brummer   WEST GERMANY              1974
*Stefan Grey, Sandra Reni, Miriam Moor, Kurt
Grosskurth, Johan Buzalski, Eva Karinka, Daniela
Cinelli, Candy Holton*
A man who earns his living working as a stud, is
stricken by impotency and becomes desperate. An
organ transplant is contemplated.
Aka: OBSZÖNITATEN
A          74 min (TOW); 88 min (TCX); 67 min (SHEP)
(Cut at film release)
B,V                          18PLAT/TOW; TCX; SHEP

## CONFESSIONS OF A NAKED VIRGIN *       18
Ernst Hofbauer   WEST GERMANY            1976
*Evelyne Bugran, Erika Deuringer, Anna Duvier*
One of those enduringly tedious German sex films of
the 1970s, which the makers felt had to masquerade
as a documentary to be acceptable. This one looks at
the experiences of some young girls, in particular
17-year-old Martha who is willing to do anything to
get through her exams.
Aka: SCHULMADCHEN REPORT 11 TEIL:
PROBIEREN GEHT UBER STUDIEREN
A          50 min (PHE or GLOB); 55 min (SHEP) (ort
79 min) (Cut at film release)
B,V     IFS; 18PLAT/TOW; PHE (VHS only); GLOB;
SHEP

## CONFESSIONS OF A POLICE CAPTAIN **
Damiano Damiani       ITALY                 1971
*Martin Balsam, Franco Nero, Marilu Tolo, Claudio
Gora*
A dedicated cop becomes caught up in a web of
corruption, as he uses unorthodox methods to trap a
vicious gangster and bring him to justice. An absorb-
ing but heavy-handed drama.
DRA                                       100 min
B,V,V2                                         EHE

## CONFESSIONS OF A POP PERFORMER *      18
Norman Cohen          UK                    1975
*Robin Askwith, Anthony Booth, Bill Maynard, Doris
Hare, Sheila White, Bob Todd, Jill Gascoine, Peter
Cleall, Peter Jones, Carol Hawkins, Richard Warwick,
Maynard Williams, David Auker, Diane Langton,
Linda Regan*
More double entendres and farcical bedroom capers,
as Timothy Lea and Sid Noggit take on the task of
managing a talentless rock group, and end up causing
chaos at the London Palladium. The book was better
. . . slightly.
Boa: novel Confessions From The Pop Scene by
Timothy Lea.
COM                           87 min (ort 91 min)
V                                              RCA

## CONFESSIONS OF A PROSTITUTE **        18
Claude Mulot          FRANCE                1980
*Sylvie Dessarter (Sylvia Larno), Anna Perini, Anne
Fabien, Maurice Travail, Yves Jouffroy, Isabelle
Legentil*
A girl suffering from amnesia, discovers that she used
to be a prostitute in this routine sex film.
Aka: IMMORAL; L'IMORALE; L'IMORALLE
A    70 min (PHE); 86 min; 80 min (SHEP) (Cut at film
release)
B,V   18PLAT/TOW; VIP L/A; PHE (VHS only); SHEP

## CONFESSIONS OF A RIDING MISTRESS *  18
Vagelis Serdaris   GREECE   1977
*Anna Fonsou, John Argyris, Christo Spriopoulos,*
*Costa Carageorgis*
An artist hopes to regain his inspiration by seeing his
mistress and his son making love on horseback, in this
ludicrous effort.
Aka: LOVE ON A HORSE
A                                                    73 min
B,V                                       18PLAT/TOW; GLOB

## CONFESSIONS OF A SEX KITTEN *
Joseph W. Sarno  WEST GERMANY      1975
*Marie Forsa, Nadis Agnkowa, Brit Corvin*
Just as the title says – confessions of a sex kitten.
A                                                    78 min
B,V                                                      INT

## CONFESSIONS OF A SEX MANIAC *  18
Alan Birkinshaw      UK             1975
*Roger Lloyd-Pack, Vicki Hodge, Derek Royle,*
*Stephanie Marrian, Louise Rush, Candy Baker, Ava*
*Cadell, Cheryl Gilham, Jean Marsden, Carole*
*Hayman, John Aston, Bobbie Sparrow*
Forget the title. This one's about the difficulties a
young breast-obsessed architect faces, in designing a
new building. He finally solves his problem in a novel
way, designing a marina that resembles a giant pair
of breasts, in this dismal and cheap-looking effort.
Aka: DESIGN FOR LOVE; DESIGN FOR LUST;
MAN WHO COULDN'T GET ENOUGH, THE
(BLUES or INT)
A                              80 min; 75 min (BLUES)
B,V                                     ABC; BLUES; INT

## CONFESSIONS OF A SEXY PHOTOGRAPHER **18
Walter Boos        WEST GERMANY      1974
*Josef Mossholzer, Bertram Edelmann, Elke*
*Bitenhagen*
Routine softcore sex-comedy that follows the exploits
of the randy title character.
Aka: CHARLEYS NICHTEN
A                              78 min; 70 min (SHEP)
B,V,V2                             IFS L/A; SHEP

## CONFESSIONS OF A WINDOW CLEANER *  18
Val Guest         UK             1974
*Robin Askwith, Anthony Booth, Sheila White, Dandy*
*Nichols, Bill Maynard, Linda Hayden, John Le*
*Mesurier, Joan Hickson, Katya Wyeth, Richard Wattis,*
*Melissa Stribling, Anita Graham, Sam Kydd,*
*Christine Donna, Sue Longhurst*
A rude and childish early sex comedy, with an
apprentice window cleaner finding that he's irresisti-
ble to women – except in the case of the one he really
fancies. A silly sex romp that was a big moneyspinner.
Boa: novel by Timothy Lea.
COM                                                  90 min
B,V                                                     RCA

## CONFESSIONS OF AN ODD-JOB MAN *  18
John Sealey        UK             1975
*Barry Stokes, Gary Soper, Penny Meredith, Robert*
*Dorning, Sue Lloyd, Valerie Leon, Bob Todd, Chic*
*Murray, Olivia Syson, Ava Cadell, Julie Bond, John*
*Blythe, Nita Lorraine, Pauline Letts*
A feeble British comedy in which a newlywed handy-
man living in Surrey, finds that he has nothing but
female customers when he advertises his services.
Dross of the highest order.
Aka: UPS AND DOWNS OF A HANDYMAN, THE
A            94 min; 85 min (VPM or HER); 73 min (KMV)
B,V                         KMV L/A; VPM; HER; INT

## CONFESSIONS OF EMMANUELLE ***  18
Joe D'Amato (Aristide Massaccesi)
ITALY
*Laura Gemser, Karin Schubert, Kristine De Belle, Ivan*
*Rassimov, Don Powell, George Eastman (Luigi*

*Montefiore), Brigitte Petronio*
Big budget and colourful sex romp with Gemser
travelling across four continents to help a friend who's
been kidnapped by sex-slave traders.
Aka: EMMANUELLE: PERCHE VIOLENZA ALLE
DONNE?; SHE'S SEVENTEEN AND ANXIOUS
A               78 min (Cut at film release by 15 min 45 sec)
B,V                                       ROGUE; VPD

## CONFESSIONS OF THE SEX SLAVES **  18
Guy Gilbert (Erwin C. Dietrich)
FRANCE/SWITZERLAND      1977
*Gina Jansen, Erik Falk, Jack Stang, Monica Miller*
A story of white slavery, with extortion, violence and
drug addiction thrown in, to enliven the plot.
Aka: ISLAND OF THE SAVAGE SEX SLAVES;
NAKED STREET GIRLS; TANZERINNEN FUR
TANGER
A              69 min Cut (39 sec in addition to film cuts)
B,V,V2                          HOK L/A; PINK; MIG

## CONFIDENTIAL ***  18
Bruce Pittman      CANADA           1986
*August Shellenberg, Neil Munro, Chapelle Jaffe, Tom*
*Butler, Anthony Parr*
Done in the style of a 1940s detective yarn, this film
tells of a reporter who is given the task of investigat-
ing a murder that took place forty years ago. His
search for information leads him into a dangerous web
of intrigue, in this compelling thriller.
THR                              88 min (ort 95 min)
B,V                                                     RCA

## CONFIDENTIAL REPORT **  PG
Orson Welles       UK             1955
*Orson Welles, Michael Redgrave, Akim Tamiroff,*
*Katina Paxinou, Mischa Auer, Patricia Medina, Jack*
*Watling, Peter Van Eyck, Paola Mori, Robert Arden,*
*Gregoire Aslan, Suzanne Flon*
A long and rambling melodrama in which a wealthy
financier pays an American to seek out all the figures
from his past who either loved or hated him. The
limited budget seriously hampered the director's scope
and the film is never more than a loosely handled
collection of episodes.
Aka: MISTER ARKADIN
DRA                                                  100 min
V                                                    CONNO

## CONFLICT *  PG
Daniel Mann        USA             1965
*Sophia Loren, Peter Finch, Jack Hawkins, Hans*
*Verner, Andre Morell, Zharira Charifai*
An Austrian Jewess survives the death camps com-
pletely unscathed (with even her make-up intact) and
comes to Israel to participate in the hunt for her Nazi
war-criminal husband who denounced her. A mun-
dane and distasteful melodrama.
Aka: JUDITH
DRA                                                  101 min
V                                                 KSV; KRP

## CONFLICT **  PG
Curtis Bernhardt   USA     1943 (released 1945)
*Humphrey Bogart, Alexis Smith, Sidney Greenstreet,*
*Charles Drake, Rose Hobart, Grant Mitchell*
A husband plots to murder his wife in order to marry
her younger sister, and fakes a car accident. However,
clues keep appearing that seem to suggest she is still
alive. A complex and implausible thriller, made
watchable if not believable by the strong cast.
THR                                            83 min B/W
V                                                     WHV

## CONFLICT, THE ***  15
Jack Gold          UK             1973
*Trevor Howard, Martin Sheen, Raf Vallone, Cyril*
*Cusack, Andrew Keir, Godfrey Quigley, Michael*
*Gambon, Leon Vitale, Tom Jordan, John Kelly,*

*Richard Oliver, Patrick Long, Gilbert McIntyre,*
*Connor Evans, Seamus Healy*
Drama about the conflict between the simple forms of
worship practised in an ancient Irish monastery and
pressure exerted on it from an increasingly liberal
Vatican, with an emissary sent to the secluded
monastery as a herald of change. A wordy but
engrossing tale.
Aka: CATHOLICS, THE (IFS/CBS)
Boa: novel by Brian Moore.
DRA                      78 min; 84 min (SID) (ort 91 min) mTV
B,V                                              IFS/CBS; SID

## CONNECTING ROOMS *
Franklin Gollings       UK              1969
*Bette Davis, Michael Redgrave, Alexis Kanner, Kay*
*Walsh, Leo Genn, Olga Georges-Picot, Gabrielle*
*Drake, Richard Wyler, Brian Wilde, John Woodnutt,*
*Tony Hughes, Eyes of Blue, The Ladybirds*
Story of the strange relationships among the various
lodgers of a seedy boarding house in Bayswater, with
a dismissed teacher befriending a failed musician,
whilst a rebellious youth disrupts their relationship.
A dismal and tedious effort.
Boa: play The Cellist by Marion Hart.
DRA                                    99 min (ort 103 min)
B,V,V2                                            VCL

## CONNECTION, THE ***                          PG
Tom Gries               USA             1973
*Charles Durning, Ronny Cox, Zohra Lampert, Dennis*
*Cole, Heather MacRae, Dana Wynter, Howard Cosell,*
*Mike Kellin, Tom Rosqui, Richard Bright, Joe Keyes,*
*Christopher Allport, Norman Bush, Franlin Cover,*
*Dan Frazer, Frank Gio*
A daring jewel robbery leads to complex negotiations
between the thieves and the insurance company, with
Durning acting as the go-between. A complex and
fast-paced tale that culminates in an exciting high-
speed car chase through the streets of Manhattan.
Scripted by Albert Ruben.
THR                                           74 min mTV
B,V                                           NEON; VPD

## CONQUEROR OF MARACAIBO, THE **              PG
Jean Martin             ITALY/SPAIN      1961
*Hans Brody, Brigette Corey, Jan Clair*
An ex-pirate is welcomed as a hero after saving a
Spanish ship from pirates, and then proceeds to defend
the city of Maracaibo against attack, in this likeable
costumer.
Aka: IL CONQUISTATORE DI MARACALBO; LOS
CORSARIOS DEL CARIBE
A/AD                                          93 min
B,V                                    PRV L/A; CH5

## CONQUEST **
Lucio Fulci             ITALY/SPAIN      1984
*George Rivero, Sabrina Siani, Andrea Occhipinti,*
*Violeta Cela, Conrad San Martin*
Enjoyable space opera adventure with two rivals
chasing each other across the universe.
FAN                                    79 min (ort 92 min)
B,V                                    MERL/VCL L/A; APX

## CONQUEST OF SPACE **                         U
Byron Haskin            USA             1955
*Eric Fleming, Walter Brooke, Mickey Shaughnessy,*
*William Hopper, Ross Martin*
Set in 1980, this tells of an American space-station
that was built for a voyage to the moon, but is sent to
Mars instead. An interesting early SF film with good
effects, but severely hampered by pedestrian pacing
and flat dialogue. The rather peculiar emphasis on
religion is an annoyance too. A George Pal production.
Boa: novel by C. Bonestell and W. Ley/book The Mars
Project by Werner Von Braun. FAN        78 min
V                                             CIC

## CONQUEST OF THE EARTH *                       U
Sidney Hayers           USA             1980
*Lorne Greene, Kent McCord, Barry Van Dyke, Robert*
*Reed, Robyn Douglas*
A botched attempt to produce a film from various
episodes of the TV series "Battlestar Galactica".
Haven't we come this way before? This time our
heroes must foil a Cyclon attack against Earth. Barely
watchable. See also BATTLESTAR GALACTICA.
Aka: GALACTICA 3: CONQUEST OF THE EARTH
FAN                                           94 min mTV
B,V,LV                                        CIC

## CONQUEST OF THE PLANET OF THE APES **  15
J. Lee Thompson         USA             1972
*Roddy McDowall, Don Murray, Ricardo Montalban,*
*Natalie Trundy, Severn Darden*
This is the 4th in the series of monkey-movies and
tells of how the apes took over from the humans
following a conflict with their human masters. A limp
and disappointing effort, followed by BATTLE FOR
THE PLANET OF THE APES.
FAN                                           85 min
V                                             CBS

## CONSPIRACY **                                18
Christopher Barnard     USA             1989
*James Wilby, Glyn Houston, Kate Hardie, Steve Pacey,*
*Tony Caunter, Ann Tirard*
The US Defence Secretary's partiality for young girls
leads to the mother of one such girl committing
suicide. A security agent is sent to hush things up and
avert a political scandal. A muddled and murky
thriller.
THR                                           87 min
V                                             CBS

## CONSPIRACY **
Bob Kelljan             USA             1975
*Jesse Vint, Albert Salmi, Karen Carlson, Seymour*
*Cassel, Robert F. Lyons*
An inquisitive stuntman uncovers a plot to defraud
senior citizens of their land holdings, on the part of a
crooked sheriff and a mining company. An assembly-
line product with no surprises.
Aka: BLACK OAK CONSPIRACY
THR                                           92 min
B,V                                    CYC L/A; CBS

## CONSPIRACY OF TERROR **
John Llewellyn Moxey    USA             1975
*Michael Constantine, Barbara Rhoades, Mariclare*
*Costello, Roger Perry, David Opatoshu, Logan*
*Ramsey, Jon Lormer, Jed Allen, Arlene Martel,*
*Normann Burton, Eric Olson, Stewart Moss, Ken*
*Sansom, Paul Bryar, Beverly Bremers*
An ethnically mixed husband-and-wife detective
team, investigate a nasty case of Satanism in sub-
urbia, in this cute and contrived comedy-drama.
THR                                           78 min mTV
B,V                                    SPEC/POLY

## CONSTANCE **                                 15
Bruce Morrison          NEW ZEALAND     1984
*Donogh Rees, Shane Briant, Judie Douglass, Martin*
*Vaughan, Donald MacDonald, Mark Wignall*
A young woman growing up after WW2 dreams of
becoming an actress, but is frustrated by the res-
traints of her society. When she begins to act out some
of her movie fantasies the end result is tragedy. An
interesting idea fails to develop due to the unevenness
of the script.
DRA                                           98 min
B,V                                           MGM

## CONSTANTINE AND THE CROSS ***
Lionello de Felice      ITALY           1961
*Cornel Wilde, Belinda Lee, Christine Kaufmann, Elisa*
*Cegani, Massimo Serato*

Tells of the coming to power in the 3rd century AD of the Emperor Constantine and his subsequent edict which granted freedom of worship to the Christians in the 4th century A.D. A solid historical drama, albeit slightly overlong.
DRA                                              120 min
B,V                                                MEV

## CONSUMING PASSIONS *                          15
Giles Foster           UK/USA                      1988
*Vanessa Redgrave, Jonathan Pryce, Tyler
Butterworth, Sammi Davis, Freddie Jones, Prunella
Scales, Thora Hird, William Rushton, John Wells,
Timothy West, Mary Healey, Andrew Sachs, Bryan
Pringle*
A failing chocolate factory finds its products suddenly successful, when an accident adds three workers to the ingredients. Despite a cast of old comedy stalwarts, this one's a lot funnier to read about than to see.
Boa: play by Michael Palin and Terry Jones.
COM                                                90 min
V/sh                                               VES

## CONTAGION ***                                  18
Karl Zwicky            USA                          1987
*John Doyle, Ray Barrett, Nicola Bartlett, Nathy
Gaffney, Pamela Hawksford*
A basically decent man is corrupted by a millionaire recluse, who tempts him with offers of money and women, ultimately turning him into a deranged killer.
HOR          85 min (ort 87 min) Cut (1 min 37 sec)
B,V                                               SONY

## CONTAMINATION *                                18
Lewis Coates (Luigi Cozzi)
                       ITALY                        1981
*Ian McCulloch, Louise Monroe (Louise Marleau),
Siegfried Rauch, Marino Mase, Lisa Hahn, Carl Major
(Carl Money)*
Two astronauts returning from Mars bring back alien eggs, the contents of which cause people to explode. A badly dubbed and fairly witless mess, enlivened by recourse to the obligatory gory effects.
Aka: ALIEN CONTAMINATION
FAN                                90 min Cut dubbed
B,V                                       VIP L/A; ECF

## CONTEMPT ***                                   15
Jean-Luc Godard  FRANCE/ITALY                      1964
*Michel Piccoli, Jack Palance, Brigitte Bardot, Giorgia
Moll, Fritz Lang*
A wry look at the world of international moviemaking, in this tale of a scriptwriter whose marriage starts to break up while he is working on a film project in Rome. Lang plays himself as the director in charge of a project to film "The Odyssey", whilst Godard pops up as his assistant.
Aka: LE MEPRIS; IL DISPEZZO
Boa: novel A Ghost At Noon (Il Disprezzo) by Alberto Moravia.
DRA                                              103 min
B,V                                                EHE

## CONTINENTAL DIVIDE **                          PG
Michael Apted          USA                          1981
*John Belushi, Blair Brown, Allen Goorwitz (Garfield),
Carlin Glynn, Tony Ganios, Val Avery, Tim
Kazurinsky*
Story of a romance between a hard-bitten male journalist and a female naturalist, with the former invading the mountain retreat of the latter, who spends most of her time observing eagles in the Rockies. A pleasant enough amble, but lacking both focus and resolution.
DRA                                                99 min
B,V                                                CIC

## CONTRACT **
Fernando Di Leo        ITALY                        1972
*Barbara Bouchet, Lionel Stander, Mario Adorf*
Routine drama involving a coloured girl, a motorcyclist and hard drugs.
DRA                                                92 min
B,V                                            IFS; VPD

## CONTRACT, THE **                               15
Ian Toynton            UK                            1987
*Kevin McNally, Wilhelm Guttman, Bernard Hepton,
Hans Caninenberg*
The son of the Soviet Union's foremost rocket scientist fakes his own death to fool the KGB and flees to Britain where he is welcomed with open arms by MI5. A British agent is then sent persuade the man's father to defect as well and allow himself to be smuggled out of the country in a dangerous operation. Average espionage thriller.
THR                        105 min (ort 160 min) mTV
V                                                  CHV

## CONTROL **                                     15
Guiliano Montaldo      USA                          1987
*Zeudi Araya, Ben Gazzara, Erland Josephson, Kate
Nelligan, Burt Lancaster, Ingrid Thulin, Kate Reid*
Fifteen strangers volunteer to spend thirty days in a sophisticated nuclear shelter as part of an experiment, and soon find themselves embroiled in a series of personality clashes in this interesting drama.
DRA                           101 min; 97 min (VCC)
B,V                              CINE; VCC (VHS only)

## CONVERSATION PIECE **
Luchino Visconti  FRANCE/ITALY                      1976
*Burt Lancaster, Silvano Mangano, Helmut Berger,
Claudia Marsani, Claudia Cardinale*
An aged professor becomes involved with a group of young people who cause him to review the events of his life, and recognise his latent homosexuality and impending death. A wordy and often ponderous drama, but with a few rewarding moments.
Aka: GRUPPO DI FAMIGLIA IN UN INTERNO;
VIOLENCE ET PASSION
DRA                              112 min (ort 122 min)
B,V                                            VCL/CBS

## CONVERSATION, THE ****                         15
Francis Ford Coppola   USA                          1974
*Gene Hackman, John Cazale, Allen Garfield, Frederic
Forrest, Robert Duvall, Cindy Williams, Michael
Higgins, Elizabeth MacRae, Teri Garr, Harrison Ford,
Mark Wheeler, Robert Shields, Phoebe Alexander*
A surveillance expert makes the mistake of becoming personally involved with his work, only to find himself caught up in a web of conspiracy and murder. A brilliantly made film that makes a number of intelligent and chilling observations regarding the issue of privacy.
DRA                                              109 min
B,V,V2                                        ARENA/CIC

## CONVICTED ***                                  15
David Lowell Rich      USA                          1986
*Lindsay Wagner, John Larroquette, Carroll O'Connor,
Gary Grubbs, Jenny Lewis, Gabriel Damon, Alyson
Craft, Jamie McEnnan, Glenn Morrissey, Charles
Bartlett, Patricia Gaul, Laurie O'Brien, Caitlin
O'Heaney, Burton Gilliam*
Larroquette plays a man falsely convicted and imprisoned on a charge of rape, whilst his wife embarks on a five year struggle to have him exonerated. A strong drama that never goes over the top. Based to some extent on a real case.
DRA                           90 min (ort 104 min) mTV
B,V                                                NWV

## CONVOY **                                      15
Sam Peckinpah          USA                          1978

Kris Kristofferson, Ali MacGraw, Ernest Borgnine,
Burt Young, Franklyn Ajaye, Madge Sinclair, Brian
Davies, Seymour Cassel, Cassie Yates, Walter Kelly
Ludicrous story of a protest mounted by truckers
against police harassment, which turns into a mass
movement in the southwestern states of America.
Enjoyable in parts, boring in others and way over-the-
top throughout.

| A/AD | 105 min (ort 111 min) |
| B,V | TEVP; WHV (VHS only) |

## COOK, THE THIEF, HIS WIFE AND HER LOVER, THE ***    18

Peter Greenaway    UK    1989
Michael Gambon, Helen Mirren, Richard Bohringer,
Alan Howard
In an effort to improve his image, a gangster has
begun to invest in and patronise a superb French
restaurant. His presence there, together with that of
his wife and cronies, is reluctantly tolerated by the
chef. When one of the regular patrons embarks on an
affair with the gangster's wife, the chef tries to protect
them. A flashy and tangled allegory, made with
considerable style, but hampered by poor plotting and
characterisation.

| DRA | 120 min |
| V | PAL |

## COOKIE **    15

Susan Seidelman    USA    1988
Peter Falk, Emily Lloyd, Dianne Wiest, Michael V.
Gazzo, Jerry Lewis, Adrian Pasdar
A streetwise Brooklyn girl teams up with her criminal
father, who has just been released from jail. Together
they set out to obtain his share of the loot, owed to him
by his former partners. A fair little comedy, sustained
by the performances rather more successfully than by
the gags.

| COM | 93 min |
| V/sh | GHV |

## COOL BREEZE *    18

Barry Pollack    USA    1972
Thalmus Rasulala, Judy Pace, Jim Watkins, LIncoln
Kilpatrick, Sam Lewis, Raymond St Jacques
A gang of black crooks are rounded up to carry out a
daring diamond robbery. The third black remake of
"The Asphalt Jungle" (the other two were "The
Badlanders" and "Cairo"), updated in that the pro-
ceeds are to go to a black people's bank, but forgett-
able just the same.

| THR | 97 min B/W |
| B,V | MGM |

## COOL HAND LUKE ****    15

Stuart Rosenberg    USA    1967
Paul Newman, George Kennedy, Dennis Hopper,
Strother Martin, J.D. Cannon, Jo Van Fleet, Wayne
Rogers, Anthony Zerbe, Ralph Waite, Harry Dean
Stanton, Joe Don Baker, Clifton James, Lou Antonio,
Morgan Woodward
Splendidly offbeat story of a member of a prison chain
gang who becomes a hero to his fellow-convicts for
resisting the guards' attempts to break him. Full of
memorable moments and great performances but
slightly let down by the contrived and downbeat
ending. Written by Pearce and Frank R. Pierson and
with music by Lalo Schifrin. AA: S. Actor (Kennedy).
Boa: novel by Donn Pearce.

| DRA | 115 min |
| B,V | WHV |

## COOL IT CAROL! *    18

Pete Walker    UK    1970
Robert Askwith, Janet Lynn, Peter Elliot, Jess Conrad,
Stubby Kaye, Pearl Hackney, Martin Wyldeck, Chris
Sandford, Derek Aylward, Peter Murray, Eric Barker
A girl and her boyfriend come to London to make their

fortune, but find that things do not go as they planned,
and they get drawn into the seedier side of London
life.
Aka: OH, CAROL

| COM | 102 min |
| B,V | INT/CBS; KRP/XTACY |

## COP ***    18

James B. Harris    USA    1987
James Woods, Lesley Ann Warren, Charles Durning,
Charles Haid, Raymond J. Barry, Randi Brooks,
Annie McEnroe, Vicki Wauchope
A portrait of a conscientious cop, his strained marital
relationship and the tensions that come out during a
murder hunt for a crazed serial killer, who has been
murdering women for a decade. The far-fetched plot
leans heavily on a series of improbable coincidences,
but Woods' strong performance makes this one worth
watching.

| THR | 110 min |
| B,V | EIV |

## COP AND THE GIRL, THE **    18

Peter Keglevic
   AUSTRIA/WEST GERMANY    1986
Jurgen Prochnow, Annette von Klier, Daniel
Olbrychski, Stefan Meinke, Klaus Goschl, Krystyna
Janda
An 18-year-old girl who steals cars, is just one of the
problems faced by our tough cop hero in this gritty
formula actioner.
Aka: DER BULLE UND DAS MADCHEN

| A/AD | 88 min |
| B,V | KAS/ARF; KAS/CAST |

## COP AU VIN ***    15

Claude Chabrol    FRANCE    1984
Jean Poiret, Stephane Audran, Michel Bouquet, Jean
Topart, Lucas Belvaux, Pauline Lafont
A young mail boy lives at home with his invalid
mother, whilst a trio of nasties are harassing them in
order to get them to sell their property. The boy puts
sugar in the tank of one of them, causing him to crash
his car, and a tough French cop is sent to investigate
the murder. A well-paced and entertaining thriller,
but one with a disappointing and anti-climactic
resolution. Followed by "Inspector Lavardin".
Aka: POULET AU VINAIGRE

| THR | 109 min |
| B,V | PVG |

## COP IN BLUE JEANS ** 

Bruno Corbucci    ITALY    1976
Jack Palance, Tomas Milian, Maria Rosaria Omaggio,
Guido Mannari, Jack La Cayennie, Raf Luca, Benito
Stefanelli
An undercover cop in Rome, joins forces with a gang of
small-time crooks to stamp out street crime, and
encounters dishonesty at the highest level.
Aka: SQUADRA ANITSCIPPO

| THR | 100 min |
| B,V | SKY/VFP |

## COP KILLERS, THE **    18

Ted Dye    USA
Jason Williams, Bill Osco, Diane Keller
Two drug smugglers get involved in a shoot-out with
police in the desert, in this violent action thriller.

| THR | 83 min (ort 90 min) Cut (6 min 27 sec) |
| B,V | ARF |

## COP TARGET **    15

Tony Benett    USA    1990 (released 1991)
Robert Ginty, Charles Napier, Barbara Bingham,
Humphrey Humbert
A cop is entrusted with the task of escorting the widow
of a diplomat and her daughter to a Central American
country where she is to be presented with an award in
honour of her dead husband and his fight against the

drugs trade. When the daughter is kidnapped a vast ransom is demanded, and the cop has no choice but to pursue her abductors. A violent, low-budget actioner.

A/AD 89 min
V VPD

## COPACABANA ** U
Waris Hussein          USA          1985
*Barry Manilow, Annette O'Toole, Joseph Bologna, Ernie Sabella, Estelle Getty, Silvana Gallardo, James T. Callahan, Andra Akers, Cliff Osmond, Dwier Brown, Stanley Brock, Clarence Felder, Hamilton Camp, Hartley Silver*
Manilow makes his acting debut in a sort of acknowledgement of 1940s Hollywood musicals, with a plot based on one of his songs, all about a songwriter and his affair with a chorus girl in a nightclub. Sluggish and uninteresting, despite Manilow's engaging personality.

MUS 95 min mTV
V CBS

## COPS ** 18
Alexandre Arcady     FRANCE          1988
*Richard Berry, Patrick Bruel, Bruno Cremer, Claude Brasseur, Marthe Villalonga, Corinne Dacla, Amidou Said Amdis*
A Jew and an Arab are assigned to a narcotics case and eventually become firm friends as they tangle with a deadly terrorist organisation. A competent thriller that suffers badly from its atrocious dubbing.

THR 97 min dubbed
V/sh GHV

## COP'S HONOUR *** 18
Jose Pinheiro        FRANCE          1985
*Alain Delon, Jacques Perrin, Fiona Gelin, Eva Darlan, Stephane Ferrara, Jean-Francois Stevenin, Vincent Lindon, Sacha Gordine, J. Yves Chatelais, Bernard Atlan, Dominique Valera, J. Philippe Lafont*
Delon stars as an ex-cop who, following the murder of his wife, has chosen to live in exile in the Congo with his daughter. When she returns to France to continue her studies and is brutally murdered, Delon heads home seeking revenge.
Aka: COP OF HONOUR; PAROLE DE FLIC

THR 97 min
V/sh GHV

## COPTER KIDS, THE **
Ronnie Spender       UK          1976
*Sophie Neville, Sophie Ward, Jonathan Scott-Taylor, Paul Chambers, Kate Dorning, Robert Twitcher, Derek Fowlds, Edward Burnham, Peter Davidson, John Glyn-Jones, Michael Balfour, Vic Armstrong, Marc Boyle*
Children form a vigilante group to hunt down a gang of cattle rustlers, getting some help from helicopter pilots.

JUV 57 min
B,V RNK

## CORLEONE ** 15
Pasquale Squitieri   ITALY          1978
*Claudia Cardinale, Guiliano Gemma, Francisco Rabal, Stefano Satta Flores*
Two childhood friends grow up to find themselves on opposite sides of the law, as one joins the Mafia and the other leads the struggle to free local farmers from the grip of their Mafia bosses.
Aka: CORLEONE: FATHER OF THE GODFATHERS

DRA 110 min
B,V MGM

## CORMACK ** PG
                     USA
*Lynne Frederick, Lionel Stander*
A fearless lawman in the Canadian Rockies tracks down an escaped outlaw, in this routine Western adventure that's helped along by some nice outdoor locations.
Aka: CORMACK OF THE MOUNTIES

WES 94 min
B,V VTC L/A; VMA L/A; STABL

## CORNERED ***
Edward Dmytryck      USA          1946
*Dick Powell, Walter Slezak, Morris Carnovsky, Micheline Cheirel, Nina Vale, Edgar Barrier, Steven Geray, Jack La Rue, Luther Adler, Gregory Gay, Jean Del Val, Igor Dolgoruki, Ellen Corby, Louis Mercier, Jacques Lory*
A Canadian pilot released from a POW camp at the end of WW2, tracks down the Nazi war criminal who was responsible for the death of his wife and child. Powell is in fine form as the man seeking revenge, in a search that takes him to Buenos Aires. A high-tension drama.
Boa: story by John Wexley.

DRA 99 min B/W
B,V KVD

## CORONATION DEEP 1922 ***
                     SOUTH AFRICA          1984
*Jonathan Rands, Pamela Percy, Jane Sinclair*
True story of a gold miners' strike as seen through the eyes of one of the families involved. A well made but rather overlong drama.
Aka: 1922: A MINER'S STRIKE

DRA 330 min (3 cassettes)
B,V CASH/CAREY

## CORPSE GRINDERS, THE *
Ted V. Mikels        USA          1971
*Sean Kenney, Monika Kelly, Sanford Mitchell, J. Bryon Foster, Warren Ball*
Vicious moggies start attacking human beings, in film which could have been entitled Paws. Suspicion focuses on a new exotic catfood. An endearingly bad exercise in comedy-horror with a few funny moments in amongst the gore.

HOR 80 min
B,V,V2 VCL/CBS

## CORRIDORS OF BLOOD * 15
Robert Day           UK          1958 (released 1964)
*Boris Karloff, Christopher Lee, Betta St John, Finlay Currie, Adrienne Corri, Francis Matthews, Francis De Wolff, Nigel Green, Charles Lloyd-Pack*
Muddled story of a dedicated surgeon, who undertakes strange experiments in an attempt to find a way of easing the pain of patients undergoing surgery, and falls victim to the effects of his experiments.
Aka: DOCTOR FROM SEVEN DIALS

HOR 83 min (ort 87 min) B/W
V VGM; IFS; PARK

## CORRUPT ONES, THE **
James Hill
                FRANCE/ITALY/WEST GERMANY          1966
*Robert Stack, Elke Sommer, Nancy Kwan, Christian Marquand, Werner Peters, Maurizio Arena, Richard Haler, Dean Heyde, Ah-YueLou, Marisa Merlini, Heide Bohlen*
A photographer is befriended by a stranger, who gives him the key to an ancient Chinese treasure located in an emperor's burial tomb. He soon learns that two rival gangs are planning to steal it. A film of exotic locations and dull, uninspired direction.
Aka: DIE HOLLE VON MACAO; HELL TO MACAO; IL SIGILLO DI PECHINO; LES CORROMPUS; PEKING MEDALLION, THE
Boa: short story by Ladislas Fodor.

THR 87 min
B,V EHE

## CORSICAN BROTHERS, THE ***
Ian Sharp          USA          1985
*Trevor Eve, Geraldine Chaplin, Olivia Hussey,*
*Nicholas Clay, Jean Marsh, Benedict Taylor, Simon*
*Ward, Donald Pleasence, James Hazeldine, Patsy*
*Kensit, Margaret Tyzack, Mark Ryan, Kevork*
*Malikyan, Jennie Linden*
Remake of the Dumas story about twins who are
separated at birth but remain linked psychically. A
glossy and well mounted adaptation, scripted by
Robin Miller.
Boa: novel by Alexandre Dumas.
DRA          96 min mTV (ort 100 min)
B,V          VES/PVG

## CORVINI INHERITANCE, THE *
Gabrielle Beaumont    UK          1984
*David McCallum, Jan Francis, Terence Alexander,*
*Stephen Yardley, Paul Bacon*
Confused and disjointed attempt to tell of a collection
of Renaissance jewels which are put up for auction,
and seem to exert a strange influence on the head of
security of the auction house. A failed attempt to
combine supernatural and psychological elements in
one film.
Osca: LAST VIDEO AND TESTAMENT
HOR          70 min
B,V          BWV

## COSMOS CONQUEROR, THE **
Johnny T. Howard  HONG KONG       19890
Another animated space opera from the same studio
as CAPTAIN COSMOS. Here three youngsters with
special powers are contacted by the former leader of a
conquered planet, who sends them a robot warrior to
help defend the Earth from an attack by the evil
empire to his own planet has fallen. A colourful
fantasy of good ideas but rather cheap-looking animation techniques. See also FALCON 7.
CAR          70 min
V          VPD

## COTTER **
Paul Stanley       USA          1974
*Don Murray, Carol Lynley, Rip Torn, Sherry Jackson*
After a tragic accident in which a drunken rodeo rider
was killed, a rodeo clown tries to make a fresh start in
his home town, but only gets into more trouble. A fair
drama with a nice small-town atmosphere.
Osca: ISLAND OF LOST WOMEN
DRA          88 min (ort 94 min)
B,V          KVD

## COTTON CANDY *
Ron Howard         USA          1978
*Charles Martin Smith, Clint Howard, Leslie King,*
*Kevin Lee Miller, Manuel Padilla Jr, Dino Scofield,*
*Mark Wheeler, Alvy Moore, Joan Crosby, Ray LaPere,*
*Rance Howard, William H. Burkett, Connie Hearn,*
*Jessie Lee Fulton*
Story of some high school kids who form a rock band in
the 1970s. About as unmemorable as it is possible for
a film to be. Directed and co-written (with his brother
Clint) by Ron Howard.
MUS          100 min mTV
B,V          VTC

## COTTON CLUB, THE ***
Francis Ford Coppola   USA          1984
*Richard Gere, Gregory Hines, Bob Hoskins, Lonette*
*McKee, James Remar, Diane Lane, Nicolas Cage,*
*Allen Garfield, Fred Gwynne, Gwen Verdon, Maurice*
*Hines, Joe Dallesandro, Julian Beck, Jennifer Grey,*
*Lisa Jane Persky, Tom Waits*
An attempt to evoke the atmosphere of a famous New
York jazz club and the gangster-ridden era in which it
flourished. Set in Harlem during the time of prohibi-
tion, with Gere a rundown trumpet player who saves
the life of a powerful gangster, subsequently becoming
involved with the New York criminal element. This

colourful and episodic tapestry of a film visually
overwhelms, and has a great Duke Ellington soundtrack. All it needs is a stronger story.
DRA          123 min
B,V          EHE; CH5 (VHS only); POLY (VHS only)

## COUCH TRIP, THE **
Michael Ritchie      USA          1988
*Dan Aykroyd, Walter Matthau, Charles Grodin,*
*Donna Dixon, Richard Romanus, Mary Gross, David*
*Clennon, Ayre Gross*
An escaped prisoner takes a job as a replacement for
an overworked Beverly Hills psychiatrist, and
achieves media notoriety as a radio adviser. A few
good laughs in a featherweight tale that starts off
with promise, but soon degenerates into farce.
COM          94 min
V/h          VIR

## COUNT DRACULA'S GREAT LOVE **
Javier Aguirre       SPAIN          1972
*Paul Naschy (Jacinto Molina), Ingrid Garbo, Vic*
*Winner (Victor Alcazar), Julio Pena, Alvaro de Luna,*
*Haydee Politoff, Jose M. Martin, Susan Latur,*
*Rosanna Yanni*
A heavy box is delivered to a nursing home close to the
ruins of the Castle Dracula. This leads to complica-
tions . . .
Aka: CEMETERY GIRLS; DRACULA'S GREAT
LOVE; DRACULA'S LOVE; DRACULA'S VIRGIN
LOVERS; EL GRAN AMOR DEL CONDE
DRACULA
HOR          77 min Cut (1 min 29 sec); 66 min (SHEP:
abridged at release) (ort 91 min)
B,V          IFS L/A; 18PLAT/TOW L/A; VPD (VHS only);
SHEP

## COUNT OF MONTE-CRISTO, THE **
David Greene         UK          1975
*Richard Chamberlain, Trevor Howard, Louis*
*Jourdan, Tony Curtis, Donald Pleasence, Taryn*
*Power, Kate Nelligan, Angelo Infanti, Harold*
*Bromley, Carlo Puri, Alessio Orando, Dominic Guard,*
*Isabelle De Valvert, Ralph Michael*
Lavish adaptation of a much filmed Dumas classic,
with Chamberlain good as the swashbuckling
Edmond Dantes and Curtis suitably sinister as the
villain Mondego. An enjoyable costumed adventure,
adapted by Sidney Carroll.
Boa: novel by Alexandre Dumas.
A/AD          98 min mTV
B,V          PRV L/A

## COUNTDOWN ***
Robert Altman        USA          1967
*Robert Duvall, James Caan, Charles Aidman, Joanna*
*Moore, Steve Ihnat, Barbara Baxley, Ted Knight,*
*Michael Murphy*
The story of the first US moonshot and the strains it
imposed on the astronauts and their families, with the
plot largely following the race to the moon between
American and Soviet scientists. An earnest and
realistic drama, with the technology of the moonshot
the chief star.
Boa: novel The Pilgrim Project by Hank Searles.
DRA          101 min
B,V          WHV

## COUNTERFORCE **
Anthony J. Loma (Antonio De La Loma)
                MEXICO          1987
*George Rivero, George Kennedy, Andrew Stevens,*
*Louis Jourdan, Isaac Hayes, Kabir Bedi, Robert*
*Forster*
An elite fighting force is formed to protect the lives of
a deposed Middle Eastern ruler and his family. A
standard action yarn with no surprises.
A/AD          90 min dubbed
V/sh          MED

## COUNTESS DRACULA **

Peter Sasdy                          UK              1971              18

*Ingrid Pitt, Nigel Green, Sandor Eles, Maurice
Denham, Patience Collier, Peter Jeffrey, Lesley-Anne
Down, Leon Lissek, Jessie Evans, Andrea Lawrence,
Nike Arrighi, Charles Farrell, Hulya Babus*
Variation on the Dracula legend, the inspiration for
which was probably the notorious Countess Bathary.
In this tale an ageing countess needs the blood of
young virgins to preserve her youth, but the local
populace do not take so reasonable a view. Standard
Hammer Films offering, with little to distinguish this
one from a hundred others.
Boa: novel The Bloody Countess by V. Penrose. Osca:
VAMPIRE CIRCUS (VCC)
HOR                                        89 min (ort 93 min)
B,V                            RNK L/A; VCC (VHS only)

## COUNTRY ***

Richard Pearce                    USA                            PG
*Jessica Lange, Sam Shepard, Wilford Brimley, Matt
Clark, Therese Graham, Levi L. Knebel*
A perceptive and moving account of the hardships
faced by American farmers, with a modern farming
family theatened by foreclosure on a loan and the loss
of their land. A film that avoids all the usual
melodramatic cliches and has standout performances
from all concerned. Co-produced by Lange and
scripted by William D. Wittliff.
DRA                                                      108 min
B,V                                                          WDV

## COUNTRY BLUE *

Jack Conrad                        USA              1980              18
*Dub Taylor, Jack Conrad, Rita George, David
Huddleston*
A young bank robber, dissatisfied with his haul,
decides to go back for the rest. A pointless shoot-'em-
up type film with minimal plot.
A/AD                                                      89 min
B,V              AST L/A; MARKET/GOV L/A; WISE

## COUNTRY COMFORT ***

Bob Augustus                      USA              1981              R18
*Georgina Spelvin, Rhonda Jo Petty, Randy West, Drea,
Ginger, Tommy La Roc*
In this post-Civil War tale Martha runs a farm in the
south with the aid of her two daughters. Tom is a
soldier returning from the war, who arrives at the
farm with news of the death of both her husband and
son. All three women are attracted to Tom, and over
the course of his stay he makes love to them all, but
eventually chooses to marry Martha. A superior and
rather romantic sex film, strongly plotted and well
acted.
A                                                        68 min
B,V                                              EVI L/A; SHEP

## COUNTRY DIARY OF AN EDWARDIAN LADY, THE ***

U

Dirk Campbell                      UK                1988
*Pippa Guard, James Coombes*
A languid and quite pleasing adaptation of Holden's
bestseller, built around the life of the title character, a
young married woman, who observes the passage of
the seasons in rural Warwickshire. Filmed entirely in
this part of the country.
Boa: book by Edith Holden.
DRA                                                      90 min
V                                                            VGM

## COUNTRY GIRLS, THE **

Desmond Davis                    UK                1983              PG
*Sam Neill, Maeve Germaine, Jill Doyle*
Film version of a novel about two Irish convent girls
and their growing-up pains. A competent drama, with
screenplay by O'Brien from her novel. Made for
Channel 4 TV.

Boa: novel by Edna O'Brien.
DRA                            103 min (Cut: sound) mTV
B,V                                              SPEC/POLY

## COUNTRY NURSE ***

Alan W. Cools                    ITALY            1978              18
*Laura Gemser, Tony Raggetti, Aldo Ralli, Aldo
Sambrell, Lorna Green, Candice Kay, Gabriele Tinti*
Broad sex farce centred on the adventures of a young
nurse in a small Northern Italian town. A light-
hearted and bawdy romp.
Aka: CORNETTI A COLAZIONE; EMMANUELLE
IN THE COUNTRY
A                        73 min (ort 100 min) Cut (15 sec)
B,V                                  BLUMO; GOLD; CAN

## COUNTRYMAN **

Dickie Jobson                      UK                1982              15
*Countryman, Carl Bradshaw, Basil Keene*
Political thriller with mystic overtones, about a
Rastafarian who saves two American tourists from
being killed by gangsters in the pay of corrupt
politicians. Reggae soundtrack includes Bob Marley,
Toots and the Maytals, Aswad and others.
MUS            102 min; 97 min (CH5) Cut (1 min 32 sec)
B,V                            IAP L/A; CH5 (VHS only)

## COUPLES **

Claude Goddard                  USA                            1976
*Angel Barett, Gloria Haddit, Jamie Gillis, Cindy
Price, Gwen Fisher, Jeffrey Hurst, Rodney Farrell,
Mary Stewart, Lisa Love*
Two women are bored and sexually unsatisfied in
their marriages, and arrange with a former girlfriend
to take on some work as call-girls. Meanwhile, their
husbands are just as unhappy and contact a friend to
arrange some girls for them after work. Neither the
wives nor the husbands find their experiences satisfying but fortune smiles on them and in one last
encounter all four are brought together. A contrived
but mildly amusing tale.
A                                                        60 min
B,V                                                          VDX

## COURAGE *

Robert L. Rosen                  USA                            1984
*Ronny Cox, Louis Chiles, Art Hindle, M. Emmet
Walsh, Tim Maier, Lisa Sutton*
Three marathon runners are captured in the desert of
New Mexico by a group of soldiers on weekend
exercises. An inept and completely unbelievable tale.
Aka: RAW COURAGE
THR                                                      90 min
B,V                              VTC L/A; FTV L/A; IVS

## COURAGE ***

Jeremy Kagan                    USA                1986              15
*Sophia Loren, Billy Dee Williams, Hector Elizondo,
Val Avery, Ron Rifkin, Jose Perez, Mary McDonnell,
Richard Portnow, Gerry Bamman, Dan Hedaya, Corey
Parker, Michael Galardi, Robin Bartlett, Elizabeth
Lennie, Muget Moreau*
A New York city woman is drawn into the world of
drug smuggling when she learns of her son's addiction
to cocaine and heroin. She vows to fight the dealers,
becoming an undercover agent for the Drug Enforce-
ment Agency. A harsh and realistic drama, with
Loren excellent as the mother and housewife, driven
to do something positive to expiate her feelings of
guilt over her son's addiction. Based on a real case and
scripted by E. Neuman Jack.
Boa: story (from New York Magazine) Mother
Courage by Michael Daly.
A/AD                        134 min (ort 150 min) mTV
V/h                                                          NWV

## COURIER OF DEATH **

Tom Shaw                          USA                            1985
*Joey Johnson, Barbara Garrison, Mel Fletcher*

A courier whose job it is to carry bonds and other valuables, goes on the usual revenge rampage after crooks kill his family.
THR                                               89 min
B,V                                                  RCA

**COURAGE MOUNTAIN ***                          PG
Christopher Leitch FRANCE/USA                  1989
*Charlie Sheen, Leslie Caron, Juliette Caton, Nicola Stapleton, Jan Rubes, Jade Magri, Kathryn Ludlow, Yorgo Voyagis, Laura Betti, Urbano Barberini*
This bland attempt to update Johanna Spyri's "Heidi" has our heroine being sent off to an Italian boarding school just before the outbreak of WW1, and being rescued by her soldier boyfriend when the army takes it over. Sheen is unconvincing in his role, but as a piece of family entertainment the film is reasonably agreeable.
A/AD                                94 min (ort 98 min)
V                                                    EIV

**COURIER, THE ***                                15
Joe Lee/LeeFrank Deasy
                           EIRE                    1987
*Gabriel Byrne, Ian Bannen, Andrew Connelly, Michelle Houlden, Padraig O'Loingsigh, Cait O'Riordan, Patrick Bergin, Anne Enwright, Lucy Vigne Welsh, Ger Ryan, Owen Hyland, Martine Dunne*
A young man who works for a courier company, discovers by chance that his boss uses the company as a front for a drug running operation. The fact that the brother of his girlfriend died from drugs, prompts him to formulate a plan to hit back, in this instantly forgettable action film whose score, courtesy of Elvis Costello, is the best thing in it.
A/AD                                              85 min
V/h                                                  PAL

**COUSINS ***                                     15
Joel Schumacher            USA                 1989
*Ted Danson, Isabella Rossellini, Sean Young, William Petersen, Norma Aleandro, Lloyd Bridges, George Coe, Keith Coogan, Gina de Angelis*
A remake of the French film "Cousin/Cousine" that tells of two cousins by marriage who refuse to succumb to their mutual attraction, despite the fact that their respective spouses are having an affair. A little loosely plotted but beautifully acted, especially by Danson and Rossellini as the starcrossed lovers. The unusual locations are an additional attraction.
DRA                                              110 min
V/h                                                  CIC

**COUSINS IN LOVE ***                             18
David Hamilton
               FRANCE/WEST GERMANY            1980
*Thierry Tervini, Jean Rougerie, Anja Shute*
Soft-focus, softcore story of the sexual education of a 16-year-old boy, set against the approach of WW2. A typical offering from this director and not far removed from films such as BILITIS, but having a somewhat better story.
Aka: TENDRES COUSINES
Boa: novel by Pascal Laine.
A         90 min; 87 min (XTASY) (Cut at film release)
B,V                              INT/CBS L/A; XTASY

**COVER GIRL ***                                 R18
Alex De Renzy            USA                   1981
*Cheryl Hanson, John Leslie, David Morris, Joey Civera*
A top agent for photo-models is murdered under mysterious circumstances just before Cheryl arrives for an interview. But Cheryl has sex with the murderer, believing him to be the agent. Later she goes to use the shower and finds the dead agent hidden there. The rest of this utterly tedious film follows her search for the murderer – it appears that she cannot remember his face, only the fact that he had a tattoo on his thigh.

Aka: CHERYL HANSON: COVER GIRL (SHEP)
A              64 min (ort 82 min) Cut (1 min 21 sec)
B,V                                    EVI L/A; SHEP

**COVER GIRL MODELS ***                          18
Cirio H. Santiago
                      PHILIPPINES              1974
*John Kramer, Lindsay Bloom, Tara Stroheimer, Pat Anderson*
Three American fashion models inadvertently get caught up in an international spy ring, in this formula adventure.
THR                                               85 min
B,V                                    APX; INTMED

**COVER KILL ***                                 15
Don Medford               USA                  1976
*Wayne Rogers, Elaine Joyce, Philip Sterling, Clifton James, Diane Ladd, Meredith Baxter Birney, Laurence Luckinbill*
Set in 1934, this drama has a Los Angeles private eye investigating the mysterious circumstances surrounding the death of a newspaper columnist. He uncovers plans for a coup d'etat involving powerful figures in the armed forces and the worlds of business and politics.
Aka: CITY ON ANGELS; NOVEMBER PLAN, THE
DRA                            97 min (ort 103 min) mTV
V                                                   FILV

**COVER ME BABE ***                               15
Noel Black                USA                  1970
*Robert Foster, Sondra Locke, Susanne Benton, Robert S. Fields, Ken Kercheval, Sam Waterston, Regis Toomey*
A student film-maker will stop at nothing to win a contract, in this dismal and carelessly made offering.
DRA                                               86 min
B,V                                                  CBS

**COVERGIRLS ***                                  18
Jean-Claude Lord        CANADA                 1981
*Jeff Conaway, Irena Ferris, Kenneth Walsh, Cathie Shirrif, Roberta Leighton*
A model has to pay a heavy price for fame, in this glitzy and exploitative effort that follows a mannequin's rise up the career ladder, helped by an unscrupulous and hustling promoter.
Aka: COVERGIRL; DREAMWORLD
DRA                                               89 min
B,V                                                  CBS

**COVERT ACTION ***                               18
Romolo Guerrieri         ITALY                 1978
*David Janssen, Arthur Kennedy, Corinne Clery, Maurizio Merli, Stefano Satta Flores*
A former CIA operative finds that his life is in danger after writing a book about his old employers. When another operative who also intended to expose the CIA is murdered, Janssen is drawn into a web of murderous intrigue. A competent but somewhat paranoid thriller, filmed in Greece.
THR                                              100 min
B,V                                                  DFS

**COVERT ACTION ***                               18
J. Christian Ingvordsen
                           USA                 1988
*Rick Washburn, John Christian, Stuart Garrison Day, Amanda Zinsser*
An ex-CIA operative resorts to desperate action, when he discovers that he is to be made the fall guy in an international drugs conspiracy.
A/AD                                              90 min
B,V                                                  MED

**COWBOY ***                                      U
Jerry Jameson             USA                  1983
*James Brolin, Ted Danson, Annie Potts, Randy Quaid,*

George DiCenzo, Michael Pataki, Ed Holmes, Robert
Keith, Jerry Gatlin, Dan Doucette, Ben Scott
Brolin plays a teacher who is disillusioned with life in
the city, and decides to start anew as a rancher, hiring
a crippled ex-rodeo performer to teach him the ropes
and help run his ranch. He becomes the victim of a
plot cooked up between the sheriff, a banker and the
local land baron, who want to rob him of his land. A
contemporary Western that holds up well despite
offering few surprises.

| WES | 92 min mTV |
| B,V | MGM |

**COWBOY AND THE LADY, THE \*\***  U
H.C. Potter          USA          1938
Gary Cooper, Merle Oberon, Patsy Kelly, Walter
Brennan, Fuzzy Knight, Harry Davenport, Mabel
Todd, Henry Kolker, Emma Dunn, Walter Walker,
Berton Churchill, Charles Richman, Frederick
Vogeding, Arthur Hoyt, Ernie Adams
A rich city lady falls for a rodeo star, in this
lightweight comedy Western that's buoyed up by the
work of its stars. AA: Sound (Thomas T. Moulton).

| WES | 88 min (ort 91 min) |
| V | VGM |

**COWBOYS, THE \*\*\***  PG
Mark Rydell          USA          1971
John Wayne, Roscoe Lee Browne, Bruce Dern, Colleen
Dewhurst, Slim Pickens, A. Martinez, Alfred Barker
Jr, Nicholas Beauvy, Steve Benedict, Robert
Carradine, Norman Howells Jr, Stephen Hudis, Sean
Kelly, Clay O'Brien
An ageing rancher is deserted by his drovers and is
obliged to hire eleven youngsters to help him drive his
herd to market. A handsome film of violence and
bloodshed, with an old-fashioned and rather disagree-
able "eye for an eye" message.

| WES | 121 min Cut (1 min 30 sec) |
| V | WHV |

**CRACK CONNECTION, THE \*\***  18
Hajo Gies          WEST GERMANY          1987
Gotz George, Claudia Messner, Eberhard Feik, Hannes
Janicke, Wolfram Berger
A detective meets up with the daughter of a former
lover and discovers that she has become mixed up in
the local drug scene. Adopting a fatherly and caring
attitude towards her, he decides to mount a one-man
crusade against the local pushers.
Aka: SCHIMANSKI 2; ZABOU

| A/AD | 98 min |
| B,V | GHV |

**CRACK HOUSE \***  18
Michael Fischa          USA          1989
Gregg Gomez Thomsen, Jim Brown, Anthony Geary,
Angel Tompkins, Richard Roundtree, Clyde R. Jones,
Cheryl Kay
A former member of an L.A. street gang attempts to
go straight, but an attack on his cousin forces him to
take reprisals and he is sent to jail. However, he gets a
chance of freedom when he agrees to help trap a drugs
baron who has turned his ex-girlfriend into a junkie.
A grim and depressing movie, not all that well made,
and poorly acted for good measure.

| THR | 96 min |
| V | PATHE |

**CRACK IN THE MIRROR \*\***  18
Robby Benson          USA          1988
Robby Benson, Danny Aiello, Tawny Kitaen, Tony
Gillian, Alan Hunter, Kevin Gray, Judy Tenuta, Sally
Kirkland
A debt-ridden New Yorker with a drug addict for a
girlfriend, gets himself into deep trouble when he
agrees to look after a pusher's apartment. Interesting
drama, shot on high definition videotape.
Aka: DO IT UP

| DRA | 94 min |
| V | FUTUR |

**CRACK SHADOW BOXERS \*\*\***
Wan Yao Hua          HONG KONG          197-
Ku Feng, Chou Li Chung
Two fighters inadvertently become involved in a
village's struggle to stop the onslaught of a gang of
ruthless bandits. A satire on this genre with some
sight gags and even a little smut.

| MAR | 91 min |
| V | VIDRNG |

**CRACKDOWN \*\***  18
John Garwood          USA          1987
Chris Rose, Cynthia Killion, Chad Hayward, Seib
Seibl, Tyke Caravelli
A routine Vietnam actioner with two tough veterans
going back to the war zone in order to clean out the
pushers, and pay off an old debt.

| A/AD | 90 min |
| B,V | NOVA |

**CRACKERS \*\***  15
Louis Malle          USA          1984
Donald Sutherland, Jack Warden, Sean Penn, Wallace
Shawn, Larry Riley, Irwin Corey, Trinidad Silva,
Christine Baranski, Charlaine Woodard
Remake of a classic Italian comedy "Big Deal On
Madonna Street" that tells of a bungling gang who set
out to rob a San Francisco pawnshop. An offbeat little
comedy that's somewhat short on laughs.

| COM | 87 min (ort 92 min) |
| B,V | CIC |

**CRACKSHOT \***  PG
Josef Leytes          USA          1968
Jack Lord, Shirley Knight, Jack Weston, Charles
Drake, Joseph Wiseman, Don Hanmer, Robert Pine,
Mercedes McCambridge
An intelligence agent penetrates a counterfeiting
operation and faces a variety of dangers in this
cliche-ridden drama. An adaptation of a TV film "The
Faceless Man".
Aka: COUNTERFEIT KILLER, THE

| DRA | 90 min |
| B,V | AMBAS |

**CRACKSMAN, THE \*\***  U
Peter Graham Scott          UK          1963
Charlie Drake, George Sanders, Dennis Price, Nyree
Dawn Porter, Eddie Byrne, Finlay Currie, Percy
Herbert
An expert locksmith falls into the clutches of a gang of
safebreakers and is duped into assisting them. A
cheerfully daft vehicle for this popular comedian that
is diluted by overlength.

| COM | 108 min (ort 112 min) |
| V | WHV |

**CRACKUP \*\*\***
Irving Reis          USA          1946
Pat O'Brien, Claire Trevor, Herbert Marshall, Wallace
Ford, Ray Collins
An international gang decides to discredit a lecturer
in fine art who knows too much about how to detect
forgeries. An exciting thriller with more than a
passing resemblance to Hitchcock at his best.
Osca: I WALKED WITH A ZOMBIE

| THR | 90 min B/W |
| B,V | KVD |

**CRADLE WILL FALL, THE \*\***  15
John Llewellyn Moxey
                    USA          1983
Lauren Hutton, James Farentino, Ben Murphy,
Charita Bauer, Carolyn Ann Clark, Joe Ponazecki,
Elvera Roussel, Peter Simon, Jerry Ver Dorn, Doris
Belack, Michael Higgins, Ralph Byers, Debra Mooney,

*W.H. Macy, Frieda Bauer*
A woman lawyer investigating a mysterious death in
a hospital, uncovers a doctor who is performing some
very suspicious experiments in this adaptation of a
best-seller. Average.
Boa: novel May Higgins Clark.
DRA                                    100 min mTV
B,V                                    VFP L/A; HER

### CRANE FIGHTER, THE **                        18
                    HONG KONG
*Raymond Liu, Chia Ling, Chin Lang, Ting Hua
Chung, Chuen Yuan*
Formula martial arts offering.
MAR                                    90 min
B,V                                    VTEL

### CRASH AND BURN *                            15
                    USA                 1989
*Bill Moseley, Megan Ward, Ralph Waite*
In the year 2030 a powerful corporation has banned
the use of machinery, but is opposed by a group of
dissidents. When a girl's grandfather is murdered, she
receives help from a mysterious stranger, but the man
may not be quite as altruistic as he appears. A totally
derivative post-WW3 film that is as dull as it is
uninventive.
FAN                                    85 min
V                                      EIV

### CRASH OF FLIGHT 401, THE **
Barry Shear          USA                 1978
*William Shatner, Ron Glass, Adrienne Barbeau,
Eddie Albert, George Maharis, Brooke Bundy,
Christopher Connelly, Lloyd Bridges, Sharon Gless,
Lorraine Gary, Artie Shaw, Brett Halsey, Joyce
Jameson, Ed Nelson, Joe Silver*
True story of a baffling plane crash in the Florida
Everglades in 1972, and the heroic efforts mounted to
rescue the 73 survivors. This disaster also formed the
basis for an earlier TV film – "The Ghost Of Flight
401". Average.
Aka: CRASH
Boa: book by Rob Elder and Sarah Elder.
DRA                                    101 min mTV
B,V                                    VFP

### CRASH! *
Charles Band         USA                 1976
*Jose Ferrer, Sue Lyon, John Ericson, Leslie Parrish,
John Carradine*
Strange, confused film in which an evil spirit in a
trinket causes havoc, while a jealous husband tries to
kill his wife. A muddled mixture of mayhem and the
supernatural, that fails on both counts.
HOR                                    85 min
B,V,V2                                 VCL/CBS

### CRASHOUT ***                                15
Lewis R. Foster      USA                 1955
*William Bendix, Arthur Kennedy, Luther Adler,
William Talman, Gene Evans, Marshall Thompson,
Beverly Michaels*
Exciting drama about a prison breakout by 38 con-
victs, with Kennedy giving a nice performance as the
humane member of the gang. A low-budget effort, but
taut and well made.
DRA                                    90 min B/W
V                                      VMA; STABL

### CRAWLSPACE *                                18
David Schmoeller     USA/ITALY           1986
*Klaus Kinski, Talia Balsam, Barbara Whinnery, Sally
Brown, Carol Francis, Tane, Kenneth Robert Shippy*
The deranged son of a Nazi war criminal owns a block
of flats which he rents out to women. Unknown to
them he has cut an elaborate series of peepholes in the
crawlspace above their rooms, through which he spies
on them. As the mood takes him, he devises sinister

methods by which to trap and butcher them. A sick
imitation of PEEPING TOM that should never have
seen the light of day.
HOR                  76 min (ort 82 min) Cut (1 min 2 sec)
B,V                                    VES

### CRAZE *
Freddie Francis      UK                  1974
*Jack Palance, Julie Ege, Trevor Howard, Diana Dors,
Suzy Kendall, Michael Jayston, Edith Evans, Hugh
Griffith, Martin Potter, Percy Herbert, Kathleen Byron,
David Warbeck, Venecia Day, Marianne Stone, Anita
Sharp Bolster*
An antique dealer makes human sacrifices to an
African idol in order to obtain material benefits, when
he discovers that it will bring him wealth in return for
lives. A crude and forgettable shocker.
Aka: INFERNAL IDOL, THE
Boa: novel The Infernal Idol by Henry Seymour.
HOR                                    96 min
B,V                                    VFO L/A

### CRAZED *                                    18
Paul Leder           USA                 1972
*Zooey Hall, Joanne Moore-Jordan, Geri Reischl*
A psychotic woman-hater attacks women but cares for
a little girl, in this unpleasant little shocker.
Aka: I DISMEMBER YOU
HOR  80 min; 77 min (NET) (ort 98 min) Cut (5 min 12
sec)
V                                      ALPHA/INT; NET

### CRAZED **
Richard Cassidy      USA                 1982
*Laslo Papas, Belle Mitchell, Beverley Ross*
A young woman moves into a boarding house and
finds herself the object of a voyeur's unwelcome
attentions. His obsession with her is so total, that
when she drowns he steals her body, and kills all those
that might discover his secret, in this grisly horror
film.
HOR                                    85 min
B,V,V2                                 RNK; AMB/DFS

### CRAZY CAMPUS **                             15
Harry E. Kerwin      USA                 1977
*Rhonda Foxx, Patrice Michelle, Tom Leindecker*
Standard cheerleader campus comedy.
Aka: CHEERING SECTION
COM                                    84 min
V                                      KONTI

### CRAZY FOR YOU **                            15
Harold Becker        USA                 1985
*Matthew Modine, Linda Fiorento, Michael Schoeffling,
Ronny Cox, Harold Sylvester, Robert Blossom, Charles
Hallahan, Daphne Zuniga, Forest Whitaker,
Madonna, Raphael Sbarge*
A young man resorts to extreme action to get a girl to
fall in love with him. Standard growing-up type
movie. Madonna appears briefly singing, "Crazy for
You".
Aka: VISION QUEST
Boa: novel Vision Quest by Terry Davis.
DRA                                    105 min
V/sh                                   WHV

### CRAZY HORSE *                               15
Stephen Withrow      USA                 1988
*Daniel Stern, Sheila McCarthy, Damir Andrei, Page
Fletcher, Elias Koteas, Deborah Foreman*
A man is determined to win back his wife, who has
traded his obsessive love for a dull but safe rela-
tionship with her new boyfriend. This involves him in
some strange adventures and weird encounters, but
not unfortunately much humour in this chaotic and
unfunny screwball comedy.
COM                                    93 min
V                                      RCA

**CRAZY LEGS *** 15
Bill Berry            USA            1987
*Mark Neely, Terry Farrell, Jon Cypher, Clarence*
*Gilyard Jr, Barry Corbin, Norman Alden, Virginia*
*Capers*
Following an accident, a young athlete finds that his
legs have developed a will of their own, getting him
into some unbelievable and crazy adventures. An
attempt to produce a zany comedy that strains too
much for its few laughs.
Aka: OFF THE MARK
COM            88 min
B,V            TGP

**CRAZY MAMA *****
Jonathan Demme            USA            1975
*Cloris Leachman, Stuart Whitman, Ann Sothern, Jim*
*Backus, Donny Most, Linda Purl, Bryan Englund,*
*Merie Earle, Sally Kirkland*
Three generations of women go on a crime spree on
the way from California to Arkansas, to repossess the
family homestead that was sold off during the De-
pression. An absurd but high-spirited and campy
romp, set in 1958 and largely a celebration of 1950s
America.
A/AD            81 min
B,V            ATA

**CRAZY MOON ****
Allan Eastman            CANADA            1986
*Kiefer Sutherland, Peter Spence, Vanessa Vaughan,*
*Ken Pogue, Eve Napier*
A cliched HAROLD AND MAUDE-style yarn, in
which a wealthy high school misfit embarks on an
affair with a free spirited older woman who suffers
from a hearing disability. Painfully contrived at
times, this unoriginal tale offers warmth if not
inspiration.
Aka: HUGGERS
DRA            86 min
V            RCA

**CREATION OF THE HUMANOIDS ***
Wesley E. Barry            USA            1962
*Don Megowan, Erica Elliott, Frances McCann, Don*
*Doolittle*
Survivors of an atomic war, battle for survival against
robots that live on human blood. The title is the best
thing in this low-grade rubbish.
FAN            75 min
B,V            ATA

**CREATURE FROM BLACK LAKE, THE ****
Joy Houck Jr            USA            1976
*Jack Elam, Dub Taylor, Dennis Fimple, John David*
*Carson, Bill Thurman, Catherine McClenny*
Two students at the University of Chicago hear of
strange happenings in the swamps of Louisiana and
set off to investigate. Fairly enjoyable nonsense,
written by Jim McCullough Jr.
HOR            93 min
B,V            REP/VPD

**CREATURE FROM SHADOW LAKE, THE ****
Bill Rebane            USA            1984
*Glenn Scherer, Brad Ellingson, Karen McDiarmid,*
*Alan Ross, Julie Wheaton, Jerry Gregoris, Jim*
*Laquinta, Bruno Aclin, Michael J. Skewes*
There is an Indian legend that tells of a treasure
located at the bottom of a lake, guarded by a creature
called "Rana". An unmemorable horror yarn that
examines the fortunes of two groups drawn to the lake
– a party of female geologists who have come in
response to the discovery of a fossilised bone, and a
bunch of guys merely there on a treasure hunt.
Aka: RANA; RANA: THE LEGEND OF SHADOW
LAKE; RANA: CREATURE FROM SHADOW LAKE
HOR            90 min
B,V            MMA

**CREATURE FROM THE BLACK**            PG
**LAGOON, THE ****
Jack Arnold            USA            1954
*Richard Carlson, Julia Adams, Richard Denning,*
*Antonio Moreno, Nestor Paiva, Whit Bissell, Ricou*
*Browning (the creature)*
Originally made in 3-D, this tells of an expedition
down the Amazon and an encounter with a strange
lizard creature. Little in the way of a menacing
atmosphere, if anything the creature seems rather
likeable. The best thing in this one is the underwater
photography. Followed by "Revenge Of The Creature"
and "The Creature Walks Among Us".
HOR            79 min B/W
B,V            CIC

**CREATURES OF EVIL ****
Gerardo de Lyon
PHILIPPINES/USA            1970
*Amalia Fuentes, Eddie Garcia, Romeo Vasquez*
Screams reverberate through a stately home and a
man discovers that his mother is a vampire.
Aka: CURSE OF THE VAMPIRES
HOR            80 min
V            MMA

**CREATURES THE WORLD FORGOT *** 18
Don Chaffey            UK            1971
*Julie Ege, Tony Bonner, Robert John, Sue Wilson,*
*Marcia Fox, Rosalie Crutchley*
Another offering from the Hammer stable. This one is
a tedious story of the quarrels among rival tribes in
the Stone Age. A feeble follow-up to ONE MILLION
YEARS B.C and WHEN DINOSAURS RULED THE
EARTH, but this one doesn't even have any dinosaurs
to enliven it.
FAN            94 min
B,V            RCA

**CREEPER, THE ****            18
Wes Olsen            USA            198-
*James Moore, Wes Olsen, Sandy Schemmel, Dave*
*Bowling, Dan Myers*
A sequence of bizarre killings forces a police chief to
call on the assistance of a brilliant super-sleuth.
Aka: DARK SIDE OF MIDNIGHT, THE
HOR            90 min (ort 108 min)
B,V            AVR

**CREEPERS ****            18
Dario Argento            ITALY/USA            1985
*Donald Pleasence, Jennifer Connelly*
A girl uses her strange ability to communicate with
insects to hunt down a mad killer. Plenty of gore and
special effects in this low-grade nonsense. Not for the
squeamish.
Aka: PHENOMENA
HOR            80 min Cut (17 sec)
V            PAL

**CREEPOZOIDS ****            18
David De Coteau            USA            1987
*Linnea Quigley, Ken Abraham, Michael Aranda,*
*Richard Hawkins, Kim McKamy, Joi Wilson*
A bunch of survivors of a nuclear war take refuge in a
disused shelter in order to escape from the deadly acid
rain. However, they soon find that the shelter is not
unoccupied, in this routine chiller that inevitably
reminds one of ALIEN.
HOR            90 min; 67 min (CFD)
B,V            POLY; CFD

**CREEPSHOW *****            15
George Romero            USA            1982
*Hal Holbrook, Adrienne Barbeau, E.G. Marshall,*
*Leslie Nielsen, Fritz Weaver, Viveca Lindfors, Stephen*
*King, Carrie Nye, Ted Danson, Warner Shook, Robert*
*Harper, Elizabeth Regan, Gaylen Ross, Jon Lorner,*
*Don Keefer*

Collection of five separate stories that pay a kind of homage to those pulp comics of the 1950s and from which they draw their inspiration. The direction and acting are fine, but the Stephen King stories are shallow and predictable exercises in horror and grisliness, enlivened by flashes of humour. Each tale has a comic-book type introduction. Followed by CREEPSHOW 2 in 1987.
Boa: short stories by Stephen King.

| HOR | 115 min |
| B,V,V2 | INT/CBS; MAST |

## CREEPSHOW 2 **                                    18
Michael Gornick          USA          1987
*Lois Chiles, George Kennedy, Dorothy Lamour, Tom Savini, Domenick John, Frank S. Salsedo, Holt McCallany, Dan Kamin, Don Harvey, David Holbrook, Philip Dore, Daniel Bear, Jeremy Green, Page Hannah, Paul Satterfield*
Three more Stephen King horror tales are adapted for the screen, but this time the comic-book introduction is dispensed with, though the tales remain just as gruesomely heavy-handed as before (but slightly less stylish).
Boa: short stories by Stephen King.

| HOR | 85 min |
| B,V | NWV |

## CRIES AND WHISPERS ****
Ingmar Bergman          SWEDEN          1972
*Harriet Andersson, Liv Ullmann, Ingrid Thulin, Kari Sylwan, Erland Josephson, George Arlin, Henning Moritzen*
Another slab of the old doom 'n gloom from Bergman. This time we are treated to a story about the lives of a dying woman, her sisters and the servants. As beautifully made as ever but almost unbearably depressing.
AA: Cin (Sven Nykvist).
Aka: VISKINGAR OCH ROP

| DRA | 91 min |
| B,V | LNG/PVG |

## CRIME BUSTERS *                                   PG
E.B. Clucher (Enzo Barboni)
                          ITALY          1976
*Terence Hill (Mario Girotti), Bud Spencer (Carlo Pedersoli), Laura Gemser, Luciana Catanacci*
Unfunny spoof on all those cop movies in which two slobs plan a raid on a supermarket, but find themselves being recruited into the local police force. Filmed in Miami.
Aka: TWO SUPERCOPS

| COM | 109 min (ort 115 min) Cut (23 sec) dubbed |
| B,V | WHV |

## CRIME OF DEFEAT **                                15
Giuliano Montaldo
                 YUGOSLAVIA/ITALY          1969
*Franco Nero, Richard Johnson, Larry Aubrey, Michael Goodliffe, Bud Spencer (Carlo Pedersoli), Reija Basic, Helmut Schneider, Emilio Delle Piane, Enrico Osterman*
Follows the fortunes of a group of German soldiers, in Holland as WW2 draws to a close, with two German soldiers in an Allied POW camp being executed by their comrades for desertion.
Aka: DIO E CON NOI; FIFTH DAY OF PEACE, THE; GOTT MIT UNS

| WAR | 97 min |
| B,V | KSV |

## CRIME OF INNOCENCE **                             15
Michael Miller          USA          1985
*Andy Griffith, Ralphe Waite, Diane Ladd, Shawnee Smith, Steve Inwood, Tammy Lauren, Jordan Charney, Brent Spiner, Michael Champion, Alex McArthur, Brian Robbins, Michelle Rogers, Oceana Marr, Belita Moreno, Lynne Marta*
A harsh judge sentences two young girls to a night in the cells as a punishment for joyriding. When one of them is raped by a jailor, her parents take court action to enforce her civil rights. Average drama based on a true story.

| DRA | 86 min (ort 104 min) mTV |
| V/h | CBS |

## CRIME STORY ***                                   15
Abel Ferrara          USA          1985
*Dennis Farina, John Santucci, Anthony Dennison, William Smittrovich, Joseph Wiseman, Darlanne Fluegel, Jon Polito, Steve Ryan, Paul Butler, Bill Campbell, Stephen Lang*
Chicago of 1963 is carefully recreated in this police tale of a highly trained group of detectives who, led by their lieutenant, are relentlessly moving in on the city's major criminals. The emergence of a newer and more ruthless generation of crooks, poses a major problem for the police which can only be resolved by the use of similar methods. Followed by CRIME STORY parts 2 through to 6. The series was conceived and written by Chuck Adamson.

| A/AD | 91 min mTV |
| B,V | NWV |

## CRIME STORY: PART 2 –                             15
## THE MAFIA WAR **
Abel Ferrara          USA          1987
*Dennis Farina, Anthony Dennison*
Edited down and made up into separate stories, this is a further episode detailing the struggle between tough cop Frank Torello and his gangster opponent Ray Luca. In this tale Torello sets out to destroy Luca's Chicago operation.
Osca: CRIME STORY: PART 3 – BLOOD FEUD (asa)

| A/AD | 126 min; 240 min (2 film cassette) mTV |
| B,V | NWV |

## CRIME STORY: PART 3 – BLOOD FEUD **               15
Abel Ferrara          USA          1987
*Dennis Farina, Anthony Dennison*
A further episode in this well made crime series with our tough lieutenant out to nail mobster Ray Luca, this time helped by one of Luca's men who is ready to give evidence against his former boss.
Osca: CRIME STORY: PART 2 – THE MAFIA WAR (asa)

| A/AD | 130 min; 240 min (2 film cassette) mTV |
| B,V | NWV |

## CRIME STORY: PART 4 –                             15
## THE VEGAS CONNECTION **
Abel Ferrara          USA          1987
*Dennis Farina, Anthony Dennison*
A further episode from this gangster series in which Torello is still out to nail Luca, having followed him to Las Vegas, where the latter thought himself safe from his old enemy.
Osca: CRIME STORY: PART 5 – LUCA'S FALL (asa)

| A/AD | 140 min; 231 min (2 film cassette) mTV |
| B,V | NWV |

## CRIME STORY: PART 5 – LUCA'S FALL **              15
Abel Ferrara          USA          1987
*Dennis Farina, Anthony Dennison*
The continuation of this gangster tale sees Luca still operating in Las Vegas, despite the presence of his old enemy Lieutenant Torello, who has begun to despair of ever nailing him. However, when Luca makes a few mistakes he sows the seeds of his own destruction.
Osca: CRIME STORY: PART 4 – THE VEGAS CONNECTION (asa)

| A/AD | 91 min; 231 min (2 film cassette) mTV |
| B,V | NWV |

## CRIME STORY: PART 6 –                             15
## THE FINAL CHAPTER **
Colin Bucksey/Paul Krasny

USA 1987
*Dennis Farina, Anthony Dennison, Diahnne Abbott,*
*David Abrams*
In this final episode to a lengthly series, the action
takes place in Latin America, where our intrepid
police lieutenant corners his quarry for a final show-
down, thus concluding an extremely well-made series
that was often let down by clumsy editing.
A/AD                                              134 min mTV
B,V                                                        NWV

## CRIME ZONE ** 15
Luis Llosa          USA                               1988
*David Carradine, Peter Nelson, Sherilyn Fenn,*
*Michael Shaner, Orlando Sacha, Don Manor*
A couple face an uncertain destiny, in this nightmar-
ish tale of a future totalitarian society, when they are
recruited by an upper-caste citizen to commit crimes.
A well made low-budget fantasy that's let down by a
muddled plot. Filmed in Peru.
FAN                                                   92 min
B,V                                                      MGM

## CRIMEBUSTERS * 18
Michael Tarantini       ITALY                         1976
*Henry Silva, Antonio Sabato*
An army officer is asked to investigate the disappear-
ance of a consignment of guns. Forced into working
with the police, he is then subjected to many violent
attacks. Badly dubbed into English.
THR               88 min (ort 90 min) Cut (27 sec) dubbed
B,V                                            VTC L/A; MPV

## CRIMES OF PASSION ** 18
Ken Russell          USA                              1984
*Kathleen Turner, Anthony Perkins, John Laughlin,*
*Annie Potts, Bruce Davidson*
A married man has an affair with a fashion designer
who seems to spend her leisure hours as a high-class
prostitute. Less confused than some other work by this
director but still heavy-going. A fairly unmemorable
effort with Perkins giving his standard nutter per-
formance as he becomes increasingly obsessed with
Turner. Several minutes of kinky footage were removed on release.
DRA                              102 min (Cut at film release)
B,V                          ORION/RNK; VIR (VHS only)

## CRIMES OF THE HEART *** 15
Bruce Beresford       USA                             1987
*Diane Keaton, Jessica Lange, Sissy Spacek, Sam*
*Shephard, Tess Harper, David Carpenter, Beeson*
*Carroll, Jean Willard, Tom Mason, Gregory Travis,*
*Hurd Hatfield*
Three Southern sisters meet again in the family
home, after the youngest has just completed a prison
sentence, for shooting her husband because he beat up
her black lover. During their stay assorted family
secrets are revealed. A sad, funny and poignant drama
based on Henley's Pulitzer Prize-winning play, with
the screenplay by Henley.
Boa: play by Beth Henley.
DRA                                                  101 min
B,V                                                       CBS

## CRIMEWAVE * PG
Sam Raimi          USA                                1986
*Reed Birney, Sheree J. Wilson, Brion James, Paul*
*Smith, Louise Lasser, Edward R. Pressman, Bruce*
*Campbell, Julius Harris*
Two homicidal maniacs on the loose in Detroit,
indulge in a spate of compulsive killings in this crazy
and disjointed crime story. Written by Joel and Ethan
Coen who gave us BLOOD SIMPLE and RAISING
ARIZONA.
Aka: BROKEN HEARTS AND THE NOSES; XYZ
MURDERS, THE
COM                                                   83 min
B,V                                                 EHE; NELS

## CRIMSON ** 18
Jean Fortuny       FRANCE/SPAIN                       1985
*Paul Naschy, Sylvia Solar, Oliver Matthews, Evelyn*
*Scott, Richard Palmer, Yul Sanders*
A gangster whose head is grafted onto someone else's
body, becomes the usual rampaging monster we have
come to know and love. A predictable low-budget
shocker.
HOR               90 min; 82 min (CAREY) Cut (13 sec)
B,V                                     ASV L/A; CAREY

## CRITICAL CONDITION * 15
Michael Apted          USA                            1986
*Richard Pryor, Rachel Ticotin, Ruben Blades, Joe*
*Mantegna, Bob Dishy, Sylvia Miles, Joe Dallesandro,*
*Randall (Tex) Cobb, Garrett Morris*
A con-man takes charge of a prison hospital, in this
predictable and rather thin prison comedy. Pryor
gives a good performance, but the story is too limited
for comedy and too disorganised for drama.
COM                                                   94 min
V/h                                                       CIC

## CRITTERS * 15
Stephen Herek          USA                            1986
*Dee Wallace Stone, M. Emmet Walsh, Billy Green*
*Bush, Scott Grimes, Nadine Van Der Velde, Don*
*Opper, Terrence Mann*
Murderous alien criminals escape from their prison
planet and flee to Earth, where they proceed to feast
upon the occupants of an isolated Kansas farm. A
rubbishy horror yarn that has a few echoes of
GREMLINS though not its style. Followed by CRIT-
TERS 2.
HOR                                                   82 min
B,V                                                       RCA

## CRITTERS 2 ** 15
Mick Garris          USA                              1988
*Scott Grimes, Liane Curtis, Don Opper, Barry Corbin,*
*Tom Hodges, Sam Anderson, Lindsay Parker, Herta*
*Ware, Terrence Mann, Roxanne Kernohan*
Very much a re-run of the first film, set in the same
small Kansas town where, two years on, hatching
eggs once more give rise to the murderous title
creatures. Music is by Nicholas Pike.
Aka: CRITTER 2: THE MAIN COURSE
HOR                                      83 min (ort 87 min)
V                                                         RCA

## CROCODILE ** 
Sompote Sands/Herman Cohen
              HONG KONG/THAILAND                      1978
*Nat Puvanai, Tany Tim, Angela Wells, Kirk Warren*
A giant mutant crocodile is created by the fallout from
bomb tests and of course it decides to go on the
obligatory rampage killing dozens of people. Two
scientists attempt to track it down – no doubt to make
into handbags.
HOR                                                   83 min
B,V,V2                                                    INT

## CROCODILE DUNDEE *** 15
Peter Faiman       AUSTRALIA                          1986
*Paul Hogan, Linda Kozlowski, John Meillon, Mark*
*Blum, Michael Lombard, David Gulpilil, Irving*
*Metzman*
A New York reporter is intrigued by stories of an
Australian who tackles crocodiles in the outback, and
makes a journey through the bush in his company.
She entices him back to Manhattan, where muggers,
hookers and high society folk fall victim to his
easy-going charm. A humorous and happy old-
fashioned adventure story, co-written by Hogan; who
makes his screen debut. Followed by CROCODILE
DUNDEE 2.
A/AD                                     93 min Cut (23 sec)
V/sh                                                      CBS

**CROCODILE DUNDEE 2 ***           PG
John Cornell    AUSTRALIA/USA        1988
*Paul Hogan, Linda Kozlowski, John Meillon, Charles*
*Dutton, Hechter Ubarry, Juan Fernandez, Ernie*
*Dingo, Kenneth Welsh*
A pleasant sequel to the earlier film that starts off in
Manhattan and winds up in the bush. In between, our
laid-back charmer finds himself running foul of an
international drugs baron. Pace and tension are all
but eliminated in this leisurely journey, but as before,
Hogan's easy charm and ready wit carry him through.
Written by Hogan and his son Brett.
COM   107 min (ort 110 min) (Cut at film release by 1
sec)
V/sh                                 CIC

**CROMWELL ****                      PG
Ken Hughes         UK                1970
*Richard Harris, Alec Guinness, Robert Morley,*
*Dorothy Tutin, Frank Finlay, Stratford Johns,*
*Timothy Dalton, Patrick Wymark, Patrick Magee,*
*Nigel Stock, Charles Gray, Michael Jayston, Michael*
*Goodliffe, Stratford Johns*
A stuffy account of the rise to power of Oliver
Cromwell, with Harris badly miscast in the title role.
Excellent battle scenes and photography are com-
pensations in this cold and unmoving effort. AA: Cost
(Nino Novarese).
DRA                  134 min (ort 145 min)
V                                    RCA

**CROOKS ANONYMOUS ***              U
Ken Annakin        UK                1962
*Leslie Phillips, Stanley Baxter, Wilfrid Hyde White,*
*Julie Christie, James Robertson Justice*
A small-time crook joins an organisation for reform-
ing thieves, but finds himself succumbing to the
temptations of his trade once more. A clever and
mildly diverting comedy with an excellent cast. The
film debut for Christie, who plays a stripper.
COM              84 min (ort 88 min) B/W
V                                    WHV

**CROSS COUNTRY ****                18
Paul Lynch         CANADA            1983
*Richard Beymer, Nina Axelrod, Michael Ironside*
Standard mad-killer effort, with the boyfriend of a
murdered girl picking up some weird hitch-hikers on a
journey, whilst a cop who suspects him of the murders
is not far behind. A dull and pointless thriller.
Boa: novel by Herbert Kastle.
THR                                  95 min
B,V                                  TEVP

**CROSS CREEK ***                    U
Martin Ritt        USA               1983
*Mary Steenburgen, Rip Torn, Peter Coyote, Dana Hill,*
*Joanna Miles, Ike Eisenmann, Cary Guffey, Malcolm*
*McDowell*
This story tells of a woman who leaves her husband,
and moves to a remote home in the Florida backwoods
in order to "find" herself, and of her dealings with the
simple people around her. An absorbing drama,
loosely based on the exploits of Rawlings, who really
did take off to a remote cabin in 1928 in the hope of
producing a Gothic romance.
Boa: book by Marjorie Kinnan Rawlings.
DRA                                  119 min
B,V                                  TEVP

**CROSS MY HEART ****               18
Armyan Bernstein   USA               1987
*Martin Short, Annette O'Toole, Paul Reiser, Joanna*
*Kerns*
Two idealistic romantics are so tense on their first
date, that just about everything that can go wrong
does. However, after this shaky beginning they win
through to genuine affection for each other. Short and
O'Toole do their best in a film that makes a few nice

points but offers little of substance.
COM                                  87 min
V/sh                                 CIC

**CROSS OF FIRE ***                 15
Paul Wendkos       USA               1989
*John Heard, Mel Harris, Lloyd Bridges, David Morse,*
*Kim Hunter, George Dzundza, Donald Moffat, Keith*
*Szarabajka*
A first-rate re-enactment of the career of the man
responsible for reviving the flagging fortunes of the
Ku Klux Klan in Indiana in the 1920s, turning it from
an obscure fringe party into a potent political force.
Heard gives an outstanding performance in a power-
ful drama that charts the rise and fall of Klan Grand
Dragon D.C. Stephenson. Originally shown in two
parts.
DRA              180 min (ort 200 min) mTV
V                                    BRAVE

**CROSS OF IRON ***                 18
Sam PeckinpahUK/WEST GERMANY         1977
*James Coburn, Maximilian Schell, James Mason,*
*David Warner, Klaus Lowitsch, Roger Fritz, Vadim*
*Glowna, Fred Stillkraut, Burkhardt Driest, Dieter*
*Schidor, Senta Berger, Veronique Vendell*
A good solid account of the horrors of WW2 as seen
through the eyes of a German unit on the Russian
front, with competently handled battle sequences but
poor characterisation and gratuitous gore. The loosely
structured plot tells of a cowardly German officer who
is determined to win the Iron Cross. This was the
director's first war film. Followed by BREAK-
THROUGH.
Boa: novel Das Geduldige Fleisch by Willi Heinrich.
WAR                  127 min (ort 133 min)
B,V,V2         TEVP; WHV (VHS only)

**CROSSBONE TERRITORY ***          18
Danny Cabriera     1986
*Michael James, Don Gordon, Paul Vance, Mike Cohen,*
*Willie Williams, Peter Barker*
A small team of experienced soldiers are given the
task of destroying a key radar station perched in a
seemingly impregnable position atop a mountain.
On completion of their mission their only means of
escape is by way of a suicidal retreat through enemy
territory. A standard low-budget, high-decibel war
movie.
WAR              87 min (ort 90 min) Cut (27 sec)
B,V                                  APX

**CROSSFIRE ***                     PG
Edward Dmytryk     USA               1947
*Robert Ryan, Gloria Grahame, Robert Mitchum,*
*Robert Young, Paul Kelly, Sam Levene*
A Jewish hotel guest is murdered in a New York hotel
and three soldiers are suspected, one of whom is
violently anti-Semitic. A perfect example of how a
limited budget is no real handicap to a great director.
A tense and complex tale with the anti-Semitic aspect
handled with care and restraint. It is interesting to
note that in the original novel the victim was a
homosexual, but that this element was excluded from
the film. Scripted by John Paxton.
Boa: novel The Brick Foxhole by Richard Brooks.
DRA                          83 min B/W
B,V                        TEVP L/A; VCC

**CROSSING DELANCEY ***            PG
Joan Micklin Silver   USA            1988
*Amy Irving, Peter Riegert, Reizl Bozyk, Jeroen Krabbe,*
*Sylvia Miles, Suzzy Roche, George Martin, John*
*Bedford Lloyd, Claudia Silver, Rosemary Harris, Amy*
*Wright*
A gentle romantic comedy, with Irving as an upward-
ly mobile Jewish girl being fixed up with a down-to-
earth pickle-seller by her doting grandmother. The
film has considerable charm but the story stands in

need of development.
DRA                                    97 min
V/sh                                   WHV

**CROSSING THE MOB ***                 18
Steven H. Stern          USA           1988
*Jason Bateman, Maura Tierney, Patti D'Arbanville,*
*Louis Giambalvo, Evan Mirand, Michael Hanassery,*
*William Gallo, Joey Aresco, Frank Stallone*
Mob movie set on a New York waterfront, with
Bateman getting a job thanks to the local boss, but
trying to break his association and go straight as soon
as his wife gives birth. Average.
DRA                              132 min mTV
V                                      WHV

**CROSSOVER ***                        15
John Guillerman      CANADA
                   1980 (re-edited/re-released 1983)
*James Coburn, Kate Nelligan, Karen Black, Lois*
*Maxwell, Fionnula Flanagan, Les Carlson, Candy*
*Kane, Michael Kirby, Allan McRae, Jan Rubes, Hugh*
*Webster, Lynne Griffin, Charles Joliffe, Kenneth*
*Wickes, Tabitha Herrington*
A male nurse in a mental home begins to crack up
after the death of a patient. An over-complex drama of
little point or interest, though Coburn gives a good
performance.
Aka: MISTER PATMAN; PATMAN; SHADOWS OF
DARKNESS (KSV)
DRA                       90 min; 97 min (AVR)
B,V                           CAN; KSV; AVR

**CROSSROADS ***                       15
Walter Hill              USA           1986
*Ralph Macchio, Joe Seneca, Jami Gertz, Joe Morton,*
*Robert Judd, Harry Carey Jr*
A young musician traces a legendary bluesman to his
hospital bed in Harlem, and agrees to bring him back
to Mississippi if he will teach him some long lost
songs. This nice idea develops into a tacky morality
play, with the bluesman having sold his soul to the
devil – Macchio has to play like never before to win it
back. The backing score is by Ry Cooder.
A/AD                                   98 min
V/h                                    RCA

**CRUCIBLE OF TERROR ***               18
Ted Hooker               UK            1971
*Mike Raven, Mary Maude, James Bolam, Ronald*
*Lacey, Betty Alberge, John Arnatt, Beth Morris, Judy*
*Matheson, Melissa Stribling, Kenneth Keeling, Me Me*
*Lay*
A mad sculptor covers his beautiful models with wax
and then casts them in bronze, after having murdered
them. However, he is eventually killed by one of his
intended victims, who has become possessed by the
spirit of the first girl he murdered. An atmospheric
but disjointed film, and one that takes too long to get
going.
HOR                       85 min (ort 95 min)
B,V,V2                          VCL; VIR

**CRUEL PASSION ***                    18
Chris Boger              UK            1977
*Koo Stark, Lydia Lisle, Martin Potter, Hope Jackman,*
*Katherine Kath, Maggie Petersen, Barry McGinn,*
*Louis Ife, Ann Michele, Jason White, Alan Rebbeck,*
*David Masterman, Malou Cartwright, Barbara*
*Eatwell, Echo Strade*
Tedious erotic drama set in the last century, and
following the fortunes of two teenage sisters, who are
expelled from a convent and become prostitutes
working in a brothel.
Aka: JUSTINE; MARQUIS DE SADE'S JUSTINE
Boa: novel Justine by the Marquis De Sade.
A                         92 min (ort 97 min)
B,V,V2        INT L/A; NEWDIR/AVR; NET (VHS only)

**CRUEL SEA, THE ***                   PG
Charles Frend            UK            1953
*Jack Hawkins, Stanley Baker, Denholm Elliott, Moira*
*Lister, Donald Sinden, Virginia McKenna, John*
*Stratton, Liam Redmond, Meredith Edwards, Bruce*
*Seton, June Thorburn, Megs Jenkins, Glyn Houston,*
*Alec McCowen, John Warner*
Nicely balanced and faithful adaptation of Montsar-
rat's novel about the crew of a British corvette during
WW2. One of those typically British low-key and
workmanlike films of the 1950s.
Boa: novel by Nicholas Monsarrat.
WAR                 121 min (ort 126 min) B/W
B,V                    TEVP; WHV (VHS only)

**CRUEL SUMMER, OF PARACELSUS ***
Douglas Baker            UK            1985
*Philippe Madoc, Jeffrey Daunton, Leslie Pitt*
Story of a peasant uprising in Germany in 1524 and
its bloody suppression.
DRA                                    74 min
B,V                                    BRIF

**CRUISIN' HIGH ***                    18
John Bushelman           USA           1975
*David Kyle, Steve Bond, Kelly Yaegerman, Rhodes*
*Reason, Meegan King*
In the none-too-distant future rival gangs control the
city, in this average tale of teenage street gangs and
their warfare.
A/AD                                   94 min
V                             ATA L/A; TAKE2

**CRUISING ***                         18
William Friedkin         USA           1980
*Al Pacino, Paul Sorvino, Karen Allen, Richard Cox,*
*Don Scardino, James Sutorius (voice only)*
In order to investigate a series of killings, a cop goes
underground into the world of New York's homosex-
ual community. A distasteful film that plays up the
sleazy atmosphere for all it's worth, with the members
of the gay community unsympathetically portrayed.
Filmed in New York City at authentic locations.
Repellent, superficial and unjust. See also PART-
NERS.
Boa: novel by G. Walker.
THR            96 min (ort 106 min) Cut (54 sec)
B,V,LV        MGM; CINE (Betamax and VHS only)

**CRUSADE FOR LIFE ***                 PG
Glenn Jordan             USA           1982
*Marsha Mason, Robert Gunton, Penny Fuller, Roberta*
*Maxwell, Jeremy Licht, Louise Latham, James Ray,*
*Bianca Ferguson, Thomas Hill, Robert Picardo,*
*Priscilla Morill, Raleigh Bond, MacKenzie Astin,*
*Michael Flanagan*
A housewife becomes a crusading environmental
activist, when she discovers that the district of
Niagara Falls in which she lives, has been polluted by
the dumping of chemical waste. Mason's TV movie
debut is based on the work of this 1970s real-life
activist but the empty script gives her a poor role of
little substance.
Aka: LOIS GIBBS AND THE LOVE CANAL
DRA                              91 min mTV
B,V                    HER; INTMED (VHS only)

**CRUSOE ***                           15
Caleb Deschanel          USA           1988
*Aidann Quinn, Ade Sapara, Warren Clark, Hepburn*
*Grahame, Jimmy Nail, Tim Spall, Michael Higgins,*
*Shane Rimmer*
Cinematographer-turned-director Deschanel takes a
few liberties with Defoe's character, turning him into
an arrogant Virginian slave trader in the 19th
century, who learns the meaning of human dignity at
the hands of a native warrior, who proves to be more
than a match for him. The literate script, splendid
photography (courtesy of Tom Pinter) and luxurious

Seychelles locations add considerably to the film's other virtues.
Boa: novel Robinson Crusoe by Daniel Defoe.

| | 90 min |
|---|---|
| A/AD | |
| V | VIR |

## CRY BLOOD, APACHE *
Jack Starrett          USA          1972
*Jody McCrea, Dan Kemp, Marie Gahua, Don Henley, Robert Tessier, Joel McCrea*
Yet another one of those revenge yarns. This time it's a solitary Apache who survives a massacre of his village and sets out to have his revenge.

| WES | 82 min |
|---|---|
| B,V,V2 | CIN L/A; VPD |

## CRY DANGER ***
Robert Parrish          USA          1951
*Dick Powell, Rhonda Fleming, Richard Erdman, Regis Toomey, William Conrad*
Revenge yarn in which an ex-con hunts down those responsible for sending him to prison. A tough and effective story with lively performances from all concerned.

| THR | 75 min B/W |
|---|---|
| B,V | KVD; ODY |

## CRY FOR CINDY ***
                                   R18
Wendy Locke          USA          1975
*Amber Hunt, Mark McGuire, Mitzi Frazer*
The flashback story of a hooker, who puts her boyfriend through college but then becomes captured by the lure of easy money, becoming a high-class callgirl. Eventually she tries to escape from her pimp and commits suicide. A sad little moral sex-film with Hunt quite convincing in her role.

| A | 61 min (Abridged by distributor at film release) |
|---|---|
| B,V | EVI L/A; SHEP |

## CRY FOR HELP, A: THE TRACEY THURMAN STORY ***
                                   18
Robert Markowitz          USA          1989
*Nancy McKeon, Bruce Weitz, Dale Midkiff, Graham Jarvis, Yvette Heyden, Philip Baker Hall*
A harrowing but compelling drama, based on the real-life story of a battered Connecticut housewife, whose casual treatment following a near-fatal attack at the hands of her violent husband, led to a landmark trial and the adoption by the State of a new law. The script is by Beth Miller.

| DRA | 91 min (ort 100 min) mTV |
|---|---|
| V/h | ODY |

## CRY FOR JUSTICE, A **
                                   15
John Goldschmidt
          UK/WEST GERMANY          1985
*David Suchet, Maria Schneider, Laura Jensen*
Plodding and wooden attempt to fictionalise the true story of a drugs executive named Stanley Adams. His courageous decision to reveal his company's illicit trade practices with the EEC, resulted in him paying a very heavy price for his honesty. This film just does not do him justice.
Aka: CRIME OF HONOR; CRIME OF HONOUR; SONG FOR EUROPE, A; STRENG VERTRAULICH VERTRAULICH

| DRA | 95 min |
|---|---|
| B,V | PVG; VIR |

## CRY FOR THE STRANGERS **
                                   15
Peter Medak          USA          1982
*Patrick Duffy, Cindy Pickett, Lawrence Pressman, Claire Malis, Brian Keith, Robin Ignico, Shawn Carson, Jeff Corey, Taylor Lacher, Parley Baer, Anita Dangler, Martin Kove, J.V. Bradley, Josef James*
A psychiatrist is called in to help with an investigation into a series of murders at a Pacific coast resort, all of which were committed during thunderstorms. A muddled and unsuspenseful little yarn.

Aka: CRY FOR STRANGERS
Boa: book by John Saul.

| THR | 91 min mTV |
|---|---|
| B,V | MGM |

## CRY FREEDOM. ***
                                   PG
Richard Attenborough
          UK/ZIMBABWE          1987
*Kevin Kline, Penelope Wilton, Denzel Washington, Kevin McNally, John Thaw, Timothy West, Juanita Waterman, John Hargreaves, Alec McCowen, Zakes Mokae, Ian Richardson, Josette Simon*
A strong tale of the life of South African activist Steve Biko and his friendship with crusading editor Donald Woods. Following the death of Biko in police custody, Woods mounts a campaign for an inquest, and suffers government harassment as a result. The film runs down in the second half, with too much attention being paid to Woods and his family as they flee persecution. See also THE BIKO INQUEST.

| DRA | 151 min |
|---|---|
| V/sh | CIC |

## CRY IN THE DARK, A ****
                                   15
Fred Schepisi     AUSTRALIA/USA          1988
*Meryl Streep, Sam Neill, Bruce Myles, Charles Tingwell, Nick Tate, Neil Fitzpatrick, Maurie Fields, Lewis Fitz-gerald*
Drama based on the true story of Lindy Chamberlin, who was accused of murdering her baby whilst in the Outback, despite her protestations of innocence and claim that it was carried off by a dingo or wild dog. The couple suffered an ordeal by rumour, and fought for several years to clear their name. Written by Schepisi, this is an excellent account of those events. Streep won the Best Actress Award at the Cannes Film Festival.

| DRA | 117 min (ort 121 min) |
|---|---|
| V | PATHE |

## CRY IN THE NIGHT, A **
Frank Tuttle          USA          1956
*Edmond O'Brien, Brian Donlevy, Natalie Wood, Raymond Burr, Richard Anderson, Irene Hervey, Anthony Caruso*
Taut tale of a mentally unbalanced peeping Tom who is caught by a teenage couple and abducts the girl, leading to a hunt by both the police and her parents, in this well made but somewhat overblown drama.
Boa: novel All Through The Night by W. Masterson.

| DRA | 72 min B/W |
|---|---|
| B,V | KVD |

## CRY OF THE BANSHEE **
                                   15
Gordon Hessler          UK          1970
*Vincent Price, Elisabeth Bergner, Essy Persson, Hugh Griffith, Hilary Dwyer, Sally Geeson, Robert Hutton, Patrick Mower, Carl Rigg, Marshall Jones, Pamela Fairbrother*
A 16th century witch curses a magistrate and sends a devil after him to exact her revenge, in this confused yarn that fails to develop its interesting premise. Price gets to roll his eyes and snarl rather nicely, as the nobleman who's a witch-hunting magistrate in his spare time.

| HOR | 80 min (ort 87 min) |
|---|---|
| B,V,V2 | GHV |

## CRY OF THE BLACK WOLVES **
                                   PG
Harald Reinl     WEST GERMANY          1973
*Ron Ely, Raymond Harmstorf, Gila Weitershausen, Catherine Conti*
After being wrongly blamed for the death of another hunter, a trapper finds that the dead man's sister has hired a bounty hunter to bring him back dead or alive.
Aka: DER SCHREI DER SCHWARZEN WOLFE

| A/AD | 85 min Cut (28 sec) |
|---|---|
| V | MERC/VPD; VPD (VHS only) |

## CRY OF THE INNOCENT ***
Michael O'Herlihy    EIRE    1980
*Rod Taylor, Joanna Pettet, Nigel Davenport, Cyril
Cusack, Walter Gotell, Jim Norton, Alexander Knox,
Des Cave, Ronnie Walsh, Tom Jordan, Alison
McCormack, John Franklyn, Michael O'Sullivan,
James N. Healy, Fidelma Murphy*
An ex-commando vows vengeance on those responsi-
ble for a plane crash in which his family was killed.
He ends up going after the terrorists that were
responsible. An above-average thriller scripted by
Sidney Michaels.
Boa: story Cry Of The Innocent by Frederick Forsyth.
THR    105 min mTV
B,V,V2    VCL/CBS

## CRY UNCLE **
John G. Avildsen    USA    18   1971
*Allen Garfield, Madeleine de la Roux, Devin
Goldenberg. Pamela Gruen, David Kirk, Bruce
Pecheur, Sean Walsh, Deborah Morgan, Maureen
Byrnes, Melvin Stuart*
Private eye spoof in which our 'tec becomes involved
in the usual mixture of murder, blackmail and sex.
Aka: AMERICAN ODDBALLS; SUPER DICK
COM    87 min; 74 min (VIZ) Cut (1 min 10 sec)
B,V    FIFTH; MOV; GLOB; VIZ

## CRY WOLF **
John Davis    UK    1970
*Antony Kemp, Mary Burleigh, Martin Beaumont,
Judy Cornwell, Eileen Moore, Maurice Kaufmann,
John Trenaman, Alfred Bell, Pat Combs, Wilfrid
Brambell, Adrienne Corri, Ian Hendry, Janet Munro*
A boy with an overactive imagination stumbles across
a plot to kidnap a Commonwealth prime minister.
Nobody will believe him because of his earlier tales.
JUV    58 min
B,V    RNK

## CRY-BABY **
John Waters    USA    15   1990
*Johnny Depp, Amy Locane, Susan Tyrrell, Polly
Bergen, Iggy Pop, Ricki Lake, Traci Lords, Kim
McGuire, Troy Donahue, Mink Stole, Joe Dallesandro,
Joey Heatherton, David Nelson, Patricia Hearst,
Willem Dafoe*
Written and directed by Waters, this polished attempt
to remake HAIRSPRAY is set in 1950s Baltimore,
where a youngster from the wrong side of the tracks
falls for a classy debutante. A kind of parody of 1950s
juvenile delinquent films, full of amusing teen-movie
cliches and sarcastic insights, it's performed with
considerable vigour, but remains a flimsy vehicle at
best.
DRA    81 min (ort 85 min)
V    CIC

## CRY WOLF **
Peter Godfrey    USA    PG   1947
*Barbara Stanwyck, Errol Flynn, Richard Basehart,
Geraldine Brooks, Jerome Cowan*
A cliche-ridden thriller with Stanwyck having a nasty
time of it when she goes to the estate of her late
husband to untangle some family secrets.
Boa: novel by M.C. Carleton.
THR    80 min B/W
V    WHV

## CRYPT OF HORROR **
Camillo Mastrocinque    UK    15   1961
*Christopher Lee, Jose Campos, Ursula Davis*
A count and his daughter live in fear of an ancient
curse, meanwhile a series of inexplicable deaths have
occurred in the nearby village . . .
HOR    92 min B/W
B,V,V2    VDM; STABL

## CRYPT OF THE LIVING DEAD *
Ray Danton    SPAIN/USA    18   1973
*Andrew Prine, Mark Damon, Patty Sheppard,
Francisco Brana, Teresa Gimpera, Ihsan Genik,
Mariano Rey, Edward Walsh, John Alderman*
An archaeologist visits a Greek island (called Vam-
pire Island – so you can't say he wasn't warned) where
he excavates the tomb of a 700-year-old vampire
queen. She is still alive and all too ready to wreak the
usual havoc unless stopped in time. Dull, low-budget
horror.
Aka: HANNAH: QUEEN OF THE VAMPIRES; LA
TUMBA DE LA ISLA MALDITA; VAMPIRE
WOMEN; YOUNG HANNAH, QUEEN OF THE
VAMPIRES
HOR    81 min (ort 93 min)
B,V,V2    INT/CBS; APX (Betamax and VHS only)

## CRYSTAL FIST **
Pal Ming/Hwai Hung    HONG KONG    1979
*Billy Chong, Hau Chiu Sing, Simon Yuen, Sui Tin,
Kao Chuan, Chia Yu-Kue, Chu Tit Wo, David Woo,
Ma Shung Tak, Chaing Tao*
A veteran kung fu fighter who works as a cook, helps
out when the pupils at a martial arts academy are
attacked. A standard tale of fisticuffs and revenge.
Aka: JADE CLAW, THE
MAR    85 min
B,V,V2    VPD

## CRYSTAL HEART **
Gil Bettman    USA    15   1985
*Lee Curreri, Tawny Kitaen, Lloyd Bochner, Simon
Andreu, May Heatherly, Marina Saura*
A beautiful young rock 'n' roll singer falls in love with
a young man isolated inside a special glass room
because of a rare illness. A likeable if somewhat
predictable blend of music, drama and eroticism.
Reminiscent of the 1976 TV film "The Boy In The
Plastic Bubble".
DRA    102 min Cut (21 sec)
B/h, V/h    NWV

## CRYSTALSTONE ***
Antonio Pelaez    SPAIN    PG   1987
*Frank Grimes, Kamlesh Gupta, Laura Jane Goodwin*
An orphaned brother and sister having been aban-
doned by their father, run away from their village to
escape from a wicked guardian. They undertake a
journey in search of a magical gem that holds the key
to happiness. Pleasant fantasy adventure.
A/AD    95 min
V    VES

## CUBA CROSSING *
Chuck Workman    USA    1980
*Stuart Whitman, Robert Vaughn, Caren Kay, Sybil
Danning, Woody Strode, Albert Salmi, Michael Gazzo,
Raymond St Jacques, Marie-Louise Gassen*
Silliness in the extreme. The CIA and the Mafia get
together in a plot to invade Cuba and assassinate
Castro. Filmed in Key West, Florida.
Aka: ASSIGNMENT: KILL CASTRO; KILL
CASTRO; MERCENARIES, THE: SWEET VIOLENT
TONY
DRA    96 min
B,V    VCL

## CUJO *
Lewis Teague    USA    18   1983
*Dee Wallace, Danny Pintauro, Daniel Hugh-Kelly,
Christopher Stone, Ed Lauter, Mills Watson*
Nasty tale of a woman and her son who are trapped in
their broken-down car by a rabid dog. An unpleasant
film with little to recommend it apart from a few
chilling moments and a rather horrible climax.
Boa: novel by Stephen King.

HOR            87 min (ort 97 min)
B,V,V2          GHV; VCC (VHS only)

**CUL-DE-SAC \*\*\***          15
Roman Polanski    UK       1966
*Lionel Stander, Donald Pleasence, Francoise Dorleac,*
*Jack McGowran, Ian Quarrier, Renee Houston,*
*Geoffrey Sumner, Robert Dorning, Marie Kean,*
*William Franklyn, Jackie (Jacqueline) Bisset*
Two gangsters arrive at the home of a couple with the
intention of hiding there. Strange, offbeat film with
little plot but a strong undercurrent of menace and a
skilful use of location – Holy Island off the North-
umberland coast.
DRA 105 min; 100 min (STABL or ODY) (ort 111 min)
B/W
B,V,V2     VDM L/A; VMA L/A; STABL; ODY (VHS
only)

**CULPEPPER CATTLE COMPANY, THE \*\***
Dick Richards    USA      1972
*Gary Grimes, Bo Hopkins, Luke Askew, Billy "Green"*
*Bush, Geoffrey Lewis, Wayne Sutherlin, John*
*McLiam, Matt Clark, Raymond Guth, Anthony James,*
*Charles Martin Smith, Larry Finley, Bob Morgan, Jan*
*Burrell, Gregory Sierra*
Enjoyable but rather violent story of a young boy's
initiation into the world of the cattle drive and his
growth into manhood, with some harsh and brutal
lessons along the way.
WES             92 min Cut
B,V,V2,LV           CBS

**CULT OF THE DEAD \*\***      15
Juan Ibanez/Jack Hill
       MEXICO     1968
*Boris Karloff, Julissa, Charles (Carlos) East, Ralph*
*Bertram (Raphael Bertrand), Tongolele (Yolanda*
*Montes), Rafael Munoz (Santanon), Quintin Bulnes,*
*July Marichael, Yolanda Duhalt*
A demented scientist on a volcanic island in the
Pacific presides over cannibalistic witchcraft rituals
but is opposed by an army captain. Karloff assumes
two roles as both hero and villain in this routine
horror tale.
Aka: ISLAND OF THE SNAKE PEOPLE; ISLE OF
THE SNAKE PEOPLE; LA ISLA DE LOS
MUERTOS; LA MUERTE VIVIENTE; SNAKE
PEOPLE, THE
HOR             90 min
B,V              CINE

**CURIOSITY KILLS \*\***      15
Colin Bucksey    USA      1990
*C. Thomas Howell, Jeff Fahey, Rae Dawn Chong*
A youngster sets out to prove that the death of a
neighbour was not suicide, and enlists the help of a
female friend in his investigations.
THR             82 min
V               CIC

**CURIOUS CASE OF THE CAMPUS**    15
**CORPSE, THE \*\***
Douglas Curtis    USA      1977
*Jeff East, Brad David, David Hayward, Charles*
*Martin Smith*
An initiation stunt for a college fraternity goes wrong,
a student dies and a massive cover-up is mounted.
Aka: CAMPUS CORPSE, THE; HAZING, THE
COM            90 min
B,V            IVS; VES

**CURLEY AND HIS GANG IN THE**    U
**HAUNTED MANSION \*\***
Bernard Carr    USA      1947
*Larry Olsen, Eileen Janssen, Virginia Grey, Don*
*Castle, George Zucco, Whitford Kane, Claire Dubrey,*
*Grant Mitchell, Ardda Lynwood, Gerald Perreau*
*(Peter Miles), Dale Belding, Renee Beard, Donald King*

Curley and his gang investigate the strange dis-
appearance of a scientist following an explosion at his
home, and help out a friend accused of the man's
murder. A follow-up to THE ADVENTURES OF
CURLEY AND HIS GANG, the first film in this series
and one that formed part of the "Hal Roach Comedy
Carnival".
Aka: CURLEY AND HIS GANG; SINISTER HOUSE;
WHO KILLED DOC ROBBINS?
JUV        57 min; 51 min (MAST)
B,V      DFS L/A: MAST (VHS only)

**CURSE OF FRANKENSTEIN, THE \*\*\***    18
Terence Fisher    UK      1957
*Peter Cushing, Christopher Lee, Robert Urquhart,*
*Hazel Court, Valerie Gaunt, Noel Hood, Marjorie*
*Hulme, Melvyn Hayes, Sally Walsh, Paul Hardtmuth,*
*Fred Johnson, Claude Kingson, Henry Caine*
First of the Hammer horror series is a flashback
account of young Victor Frankenstein's experiments,
told as he awaits execution for the murder of his wife,
who in fact died in the struggle between him and the
monster. Stylish if somewhat gory, this film gave rise
to an interminable succession of lurid and increasingly cliched horror films. Loosely (and I mean loosely)
based on Mary Shelley's novel. REVENGE OF
FRANKENSTEIN was the next in line.
HOR     80 min (Cut at film release)
V               WHV

**CURSE OF SIMBA, THE \*\***      18
Lindsay Shonteff    UK      1964
*Dennis Price, Lisa Daniely, Bryant Halliday, Mary*
*Kerridge, Ronald Leigh Hunt, Jean Lodge, Dennis*
*Alaba Peters, Tony Thawnton, Andy Myers, Beryl*
*Cunningham, Bobby Breen Quintet*
A young American big game hunter is put under a
curse by an African tribe.
Aka: CURSE OF THE VOODOO
HOR           79 min B/W
B,V              KVD

**CURSE OF THE BLACK WIDOW \*\***    15
Dan Curtis    USA      1977
*Tony Franciosa, Donna Mills, Patty Duke Astin, Sid*
*Caesar, June Lockhart, June Allyson, Vic Morrow,*
*Roz Kelly, Jeff Corey*
A series of brutal murders takes place in L.A., with
the victims being found wrapped in a spider-like web.
A detective investigating these deaths discovers the
existence of a giant spider, linked by an ancient curse
to two mysterious sisters.
Aka: LOVE TRAP
HOR          97 min mTV
B,V              IVS

**CURSE OF THE CAT PEOPLE \*\*\***    U
Gunther Von Fritsch/Robert Wise
         USA      1944
*Robert Wise, Simone Simone, Kent Smith, Jane*
*Randolph, Elizabeth Russell, Ann Carter, Julia Dean*
This quirky follow-up to "Cat People" tells the moody,
atmospheric tale of a lonely little girl who conjures up
a vision of her father's first wife. Not a horror film, but
a strange, offbeat fantasy, with moments of genuine
power. Written by DeWitt Bodeen, this was Wise's
directing debut.
FAN          67 min B/W
V               VCC

**CURSE OF THE CRIMSON ALTAR \***
Vernon Sewell    UK      1968
*Boris Karloff, Christopher Lee, Rupert Davies, Mark*
*Eden, Barbara Steele, Michael Gough, Virginia*
*Wetherell, Rosemarie Reede, Derek Tansley, Denys*
*Peek, Millicent Scott*
An English country house is the setting for the usual
mixture of witchcraft, diabolism and mystery. Karloff
plays an expert on black magic and Steel a 300-year-

old witch (with a nice line in green make-up). A muddled, confused and laughable effort.
Aka: CRIMSON CULT, THE

| HOR | 87 min (ort 89 min) |
| B,V | VDM |

## CURSE OF THE DEVIL *
Charles Auted (Carlos Aured Alonso)
SPAIN/MEXICO 1973
*Paul Naschy (Jacinto Molina), Faye (Fabiola) Falcon, Vinc Molina (Antonio Vidal Molina), May Oliver (Maritza Olivares), Maria Silva, Ana Farra, Calvo, Patty Shepard, Santiago Rivero, Ines Morales*
A cursed wolf attacks people and drains them of blood, in this strictly routine horror yarn.
Aka: BLACK HARVEST OF COUNTESS DRACULA, THE; EL RETORNO DE WALPURGIS; RETURN OF WALPURGIS, THE

| HOR | 85 min |
| B,V | INT |

## CURSE OF THE MUMMY'S TOMB ** 15
Michael Carreras UK 1964
*Terence Morgan, Ronald Howard, Fred Clark, Jeanne Roland, George Pastell, Jack Gwillim, Dickie Owen (the mummy), John Paul, Jill Mai Meredith, Michael Ripper, Harold Goodwin*
The excavation of a pharoah's tomb, results in many deaths when the mummy of a dead king comes to life and begins to stalk the streets of Victorian London, in search of those who broke into the tomb. A well-mounted but predictable yarn that followed the 1959 film THE MUMMY without being a sequel to it. A Hammer film.

| HOR | 81 min |
| B,V | RCA |

## CURSE OF THE PINK PANTHER, THE * PG
Blake Edwards USA 1982 (released 1983)
*David Niven, Robert Wagner, Herbert Lom, Ted Wass, Joanna Lumley, Capucine, Robert Loggia, Leslie Ash, Harvey Korman, Burt Kwouk, Andre Maranne, Graham Stark, Peter Arne, Patricia Davis, Michael Elphick, Steve Franken, Ed Parker*
Niven's last film and what a pointless waste it is. A pathetic and unfunny attempt to keep the PINK PANTHER series going after the death of Sellers, with another bumbling detective selected to replace Inspector Clouseau, who appears to have vanished. Garbage of a very high order. See also THE TRAIL OF THE PINK PANTHER, which was filmed at the same time as this one.

| COM | 106 min (ort 110 min) |
| V | WHV |

## CURSE, THE *** 18
David Keith USA 1986
*Wil Wheaton, Claude Akins, Amy Wheaton, Malcolm Danare, Cooper Huckabee, John Schneider*
Actor David Keith makes a good directing debut in this striking horror yarn telling of a meteorite that brings a nasty parasite to Earth. Crashing near a farm, it soon has most of the inhabitants running about like raving loonies, as a young boy struggles to rescue his folk from the clutches of the aliens.
Aka: FARM, THE
Boa: short story The Colour Out Of Space by H.P. Lovecraft.

| HOR | 83 min (ort 92 min) |
| B,V | EIV |

## CURTAINS * 18
Jonathan Stryker (Richard Ciupka)
CANADA 1982
*John Vernon, Samantha Eggar, Linda Thorson, Anne Ditchburn, Lynne Griffin, Sandra Warren, Paul Naschy (Jacinto Molina)*
Six actresses attending a director's home where auditions are to be held, are menaced by a mad murderer. A disjointed and carelessly made muddle of a film.

| HOR | 89 min |
| B,V | APX; FTV; VSP |

## CUT ABOVE, A * 15
Thom Eberhardt USA 1989
*Matthew Modine, Daphne Zuniga, Christine Lahti, Todd Field, John Scott Clough, Alice Carter, Robert Desiderio, Zakes Mokae*
A cynical opportunist enrols at medical school in the hope of entering a lucrative profession, but without any intention of knuckling down to study for his degree. A medical variation on a theme explored in THE PAPER CHASE, but lacking that earlier film's depth. Lahti is especially good as the students' teacher, but her performance is largely wasted in this contrived dud.
Aka: GROSS ANATOMY

| COM | 105 min (ort 107 min) |
| V | TOUCH |

## CUT AND RUN ** 18
Ruggero Deodato ITALY 1985
*Lisa Blount, Leonard Mann, Michael Berryman, Willie Aames, Richard Lynch, Richard Bright, Karen Blake, Valentina Forte, Eriq Lasalle, Gabrielle Tinti, John Steiner, Barbara Magnolfi, Luca Barbareschi, Penny Brown*
Plenty of action in this story of a US news team who get involved with drug dealers in Latin America. Only the lack of a decent plot lets it down.
Aka: HELL, LIVE; INFERNO IN DIRETTA

| A/AD | 90 min |
| B,V | MED |

## CUTTER'S WAY ** 15
Ivan Passer USA 1981
*Jeff Bridges, John Heard, Lisa Eichhorn, Ann Dusenberry, Stephen Elliott, Nina Van Pallandt*
Yet another Vietnam vet story. This one's about a man who sets out to prove that an oil tycoon is guilty of murder. A low-key study that has a few good moments but is too sluggishly paced to really involve.
Aka: CUTTER AND BONE
Boa: novel Cutter And Bone by Newton Thornburg.

| THR | 106 min |
| B,V | WHV |

## CUTTING CLASS ** 18
Rospo Pallenberg USA 1988
*Donovan Leitch, Jill Schoelen, Brad Pitt, Roddy McDowall, Martin Mull*
A student who was committed to an asylum, turns up at his old high school and the despised vice chancellor is found murdered. Suspicion focuses on him but there are several other candidates who could be to blame. A murky and muddled horror-mystery with a few touches of gruesome humour.

| HOR | 88 min |
| B,V | VES |

## CYBORG * 18
Albert Pyun USA 1989
*Jean-Claude Van Damme, Vincent Klyn, Deborah Richter, Dayle Haddon, Alex Daniels, Blaise Loong, Rolf Muller*
The population of a world of the future has been decimated by evil creatures known as the Flesh Pirates, who have used plague to consolidate their rule. A female cyborg escapes with vital information that could eradicate the plague, but is recaptured. Luckily, a potential saviour is on hand to rescue her. A rather repulsive post-apocalyptic fantasy, with a foolish plot and worse dialogue.

| FAN | 80 min (ort 86 min) |
| V | PATHE |

**CYBORG 2087 ***                      15
Franklin Adreon          USA          1966
*Michael Rennie, Wendell Corey, Karen Steele, Warren*
*Stevens, Eduard Carey Jr, Adam Roarke, Chubby*
*Johnson, Tyler MacDuff, Dale Van Sickel, Troy*
*Melton, Jimmy Hibbard, Sherry Alberoni, Betty Jane*
*Royale, John Beck*
A humanoid escapes from a totalitarian society of the
future and travels back in time in order to persuade a
brilliant scientist not to continue work on a mind-
controlling device. Tedious, low-budget treatment
fails to do justice to a good idea.
FAN                                  86 min
B,V                          ITM L/A; GLOB

**CYCLES SOUTH ****
Don Marshall             USA          1971
*Vaughan Everly, Bobby Garcia, Don Marshall*
The adventures of three young men on a cycle trip
from Denver to Panama which passes through seven
countries. A pleasant action tale of no great depth.
A/AD                                 88 min
B,V,V2                                  VPD

**CYCLONE ****                         15
Rene Cardona     ITALY/MEXICO          1979
*Arthur Kennedy, Carroll Baker, Lionel Stander, Hugo*
*Stiglitz, Andress Garcia*
Routine survival epic in which a cyclone leaves a trail
of death and devastation behind it.
Aka: CICLON
DRA                                 100 min
B,V,V2                           DFS; XTASY

**CYCLONE *****                        18
Fred Olen Ray            USA          1987
*Jeff Combs, Teri Marshall, Martin Landau, Robert*
*Quarry, Dar Robinson, Ashley Ferrare, Heather*
*Thomas, Troy Donahue, Michael Reagan*
When the inventor of "Cyclone", a powerful computer
controlled motorcycle is murdered, his girlfriend
becomes responsible for his creation. Caught between
criminals and government agencies, she finds her life
in danger as she attempts to carry out her boyfriend's
wishes and deliver the invention to his friend. When
he too is killed, she must use her boyfriend's invention
to survive. Fast-paced but enjoyable nonsense.
A/AD                                 82 min
B,V                                     EIV

**CYCLONE ON HORSEBACK *****            U
Edward Killy             USA          1941
*Tim Holt, Marjorie Reynolds, Ray Whitley, Lee*
*"Lasses" White, Ted Donaldson, Dennis Moore, Harry*
*Worth, Monte Montague, John Dilson, Lew Kelly,*
*Terry Frost, Slim Whitaker*
Three cowboys come to the aid of a girl and her
brother, who are attempting to put up a telegraph
wire in order to win a contract, but are being hindered
by a gang. A well paced and intelligent film.
Osca: SON OF SINBAD plus one short
WES                          57 min B/W
B,V                                     KVD

**CYNARA ****                          PG
King Vidor               USA          1932
*Ronald Coleman, Kay Francis, Phyllis Barry, Henry*
*Stephenson, Paul Porcasi*
A London barrister has an affair with a working girl
while his wife is away, but when he returns to his
wife, the girl commits suicide. A competent but dated
melodrama, with Colman standing head and shoul-
ders above the shallow and contrived plot. Written by
Frances Marion and Lynn Starling.
Boa: novel An Imperfect Lover by Robert Gore Brown.
DRA                   75 min (ort 78 min) B/W
V                                       VGM

**CZECH MATE *****
John Hough               UK            1984
*Susan George, Patrick Mower, Michael Heffer, Peter*
*Vaughan, Sandor Eles*
Strange story of a woman TV researcher who goes to
Prague with her ex-husband. When he disappears
with both passports she is left in something of a
predicament. A good feeling of suspense is spoilt by a
rather lame ending.
Osca: IN POSSESSION
DRA                                  72 min
B,V                                     BWV

# D

**D.A.R.Y.L. ****                       PG
Simon Wincer             USA          1985
*Mary Beth Hurt, Michael McKean, Barret Oliver,*
*Colleen Camp, Kathryn Walker, Josef Sommer, Ron*
*Frazier, Steve Ryan, Danny Corkill, David Wohl, Amy*
*Linker, Ed L. Grady, Tucker McGuire, Richard*
*Hammatt, Charlie Gudger*
A couple fosters a small boy found abandoned in the
country and suffering from amnesia. Though over-
joyed to have a child in the house they find him to to be
quite unlike other boys of his age. When his real
"parents" arrive to claim him the truth is revealed; he
is in fact a sophisticated robot being eagerly sought by
the military. A sustained first half soon gives way to a
pointless chase and the film never explores any of the
ideas it raises.
Aka: DARYL
FAN                                  96 min
V/sh                                    RCA

**D.O.A. ****                          15
Rocky Morton/Annabel Jankel
                         USA          1988
*Dennis Quaid, Meg Ryan, Charlotte Rampling, Daniel*
*Stern, Jane Kaczmarek, Christopher Neame, Jay*
*Petterson*
An updated version of the 1949 classic study in
paranoia, telling of a college professor of English who
searches is for the person who has poisoned him in a
dispute over a prized fiction manuscript. Aided by a
pretty female student, his investigation throws up
numerous grim jokes and rather obvious red herrings
in à tongue-in-cheek, sardonic remake from the
creators of MAX HEADROOM. Written by C.E. Pogue
(who co-scripted the remake of THE FLY).
THR                                 100 min
V                                     TOUCH

**D.O.A. *****                         PG
Rudolf Mate              USA          1949
*Edmond O'Brien, Pamela Britton, Luther Adler,*
*Neville Brand, Henry Hart, Virginia Lee, Beverly*
*Campbell (Garland), Lyn Baggett*
A suspense-filled thriller in which O'Brien, as a
businessman on vacation in San Francisco, finds that
he has been given a slow-acting poison. With only a
few days to live unless he finds an antidote he sets out
to find out who has done this and why. Remade in
1969 as "Color Me Dead" and again in 1988.
THR            84 min B/W (VCC version is colourised)
V                                       VCC

**D-DAY THE SIXTH OF JUNE ****          PG
Henry Koster             USA          1956
*Robert Taylor, Richard Todd, Dana Wynter, Edmond*
*O'Brien, John Williams, Jerry Paris, Richard Stapley*
A British colonel and an American captain are in love
with the same girl, and they reminisce about her
whilst on their way to the Normandy invasion of 1944.
A flaccid and unremarkable romantic drama with a
few excellent action sequences providing some com-
pensation. The usual rose-tinted Hollywood depiction

of wartime London prevails.
Boa: novel by Lionel Shapiro.

| | |
|---|---|
| WAR | 106 min |
| V/h | CBS |

**DA ***
Matt Clark          USA          1988
*Barnard Hughes, Martin Sheen, Karl Hayden, Doreen
Hepburn, William Hickey, Hugh O'Conor, Ingrid
Craigie*
A successful Irish-born playwright living in New
York, returns to Ireland when his father dies. Once
there, his past life (and all its attendant problems) is
revealed in a series of flashbacks and encounters with
his father's quarrelsome ghost. A gentle and highly
unusual film that balances carefully between over-
sentimentality and excessive melodrama.
Boa: play by Hugh Leonard.

| | |
|---|---|
| DRA | 102 min |
| V | RCA |

**DAD ***                                          PG
Gary David Goldberg    USA          1989
*Jack Lemmon, Ted Danson, Olympia Dukakis, Kathy
Baker, Kevin Spacey, Ethan Hawke, Zakes Mokae,
Chris Lemmon, J.T. Walsh*
A man returns home to take care of his aged and frail
father when his mother suffers a heart attack and is
hospitalised. Appalled by the degeneration he finds in
his father, he attempts to revitalise him and re-kindle
their relationship, and eventually does the same with
his own son. A moving and warmhearted drama
slightly spoilt by an excess of sentiment and Lemmon's disappointing performance. Goldberg's feature
directing debut.
Boa: novel by William Wharton.

| | |
|---|---|
| DRA | 113 min (ort 117 min) |
| V | CIC |

**DADDY ***                                        15
John Herzfeld          USA          1987
*Dermot Mulroney, Patricia Arquette, John Karlen,
Tess Harper, Danny Aiello, Trey Adams*
A movie with a message, as Mulroney plays a high
school kid who has to abandon his lifetime ambition to
become a musician when he becomes a father instead.
Both he and his girlfriend are unprepared for the
realities of parenthood, in a perceptive but somewhat
preachy film, scripted by Herzfeld.

| | |
|---|---|
| DRA | 92 min mTV |
| B,V | BRAVE |

**DADDY'S BOYS *                                    18
Joe Minion          USA          1987
*Daryl Haney, Laura Burkett, Raymond J. Barry, Dan
Shor, Christian Clemenson*
A low-budget Roger Corman production all about an
ex-farmer and his two sons who go on a crime spree
during the era of the Depression. Said to be made in a
few weeks and it looks it too.

| | |
|---|---|
| COM | 83 min |
| B,V | RCA |

**DAD'S ARMY *                                      U
Norman Cohen          UK          1971
*Arthur Lowe, John Le Mesurier, Clive Dunn, Ian
Lavender, John Laurie, Arnold Ridley, James Beck,
Bill Pertwee, Liz Fraser, Bernard Archard, Derek
Newark, Frank Williams, Edward Sinclair, Pat
Coombs, Sam Kydd, Fred Griffiths*
Inspired by the popular TV series of the same name,
this tale is set in a small seaside town in 1939, and
follows the attempts of the locals to form a Home
Guard unit. Despite the presence of all the stars who
made the TV series such a hit, this over-stretched and
under-plotted film has little of the gentle self-mocking
humour of the original. Very disappointing.

| | |
|---|---|
| COM | 91 min (ort 95 min) |
| V | RCA |

**DAGGERS 8 **                                     PG
Cheung Sam/Wilson Tong
HONG KONG
*Meng Yuen Men, Lily Li, Wilson Tong, Chui Chung
Shun, Lee SA Ess*
Kung fu adventure in which the main character is
forbidden to study the martial arts, so he learns to kill
using eight daggers.

| | |
|---|---|
| MAR | 87 min Cut (3 sec) |
| B,V | VPD |

**DAIN CURSE, THE **                               15
E.W. Swackhamer     USA          1978
*James Coburn, Hector Elizondo, Jason Miller, Jean
Simmons, Paul Stewart, Beartrice Straight, Nancy
Addison, Tom Bower, David Canary, Beeson Carroll,
Martin Cassidy, Brian Davies, Roni Dengel, Paul
Harding, Karen Ludwig*
A complex story of an alleged family curse and
multiple murders, set against the background of
bogus religious cults. Watchable, but hampered by
uneven pacing.
Aka: PRIVATE EYE
Boa: novel by Dashiell Hammett.

| | |
|---|---|
| DRA | 118 min (ort 312 min) mTV |
| B,V,V2,LV | EHE |

**DAISY MILLER *                                    U
Peter Bogdanovich    USA          1974
*Cybill Shepherd, Cloris Leachman, Eileen Brennan,
Barry Brown, Mildred Natwick, Duilio Del Prete*
A slow and rather boring adaptation of a Henry James
work, which tells of a naive American girl who, while
on holiday in Rome in the 1880s with her mother and
brother, flaunts 19th century social conventions by
her reckless behaviour. A lifeless performance from
Shepherd as the girl, does not help. Filmed in Italy.
Boa: novel by Henry James.

| | |
|---|---|
| DRA | 87 min |
| B,V | CIC |

**DAKOTA **                                         U
Fred Holmes          USA          1988
*Lou Diamond Phillips, DeeDee Norton, Eli Cummins,
Jordan Burton, Steve Ruge, John Hawkes*
A troubled teenager goes on the run from his past and
takes a job at a farm, where he works off a debt
training horses and learns a little maturity at the
same time. An independently produced drama, undeniably sincere but a little lacking in the originality
department. The outstanding photography is its
strongest point.

| | |
|---|---|
| DRA | 92 min (ort 97 min) |
| V | RCA |

**DALLAS: THE EARLY YEARS ***                      PG
Larry Elikann        USA          1986
*Larry Hagman, Kevin Wixted, Hoyt Axton, David
Grant, Dale Midkiff, Molly Hagan, William
Frankfather, Wendel Meldrum, Joe Ranier, Marjie
Rynearson, Liz Keifer, Matt Mulhern, Joe Berryman,
Angie Bolling, Blue Deckert*
This spin-off from the American TV soap "Dallas",
tells of the rise to power of those oil tycoons the
Ewings. A lively prequel to the TV series, with a host
of new faces playing earlier incarnations of this
powerful oil family, from the Depresssion years
through to the 1950s. Written by David Jacobs, who
created the TV series.

| | |
|---|---|
| DRA | 141 min; 135 min (VCC) mTV |
| B,V | IVS; VCC (VHS only) |

**DAM BUSTERS, THE ***                             U
Michael Anderson     UK          1954
*Michael Redgrave, Richard Todd, Basil Sydney,
Ursula Jeans, Derek Farr, Ernest Clark, John Fraser,
Nigel Stock, Bill Kerr, George Baker, Robert Shaw,
Raymond Huntley, Anthony Doonan, Harold*

*Goodwin, Laurence Naismith*
Rather a Boy's Own treatment of the development and application of the bouncing bombs of Sir Barnes Wallace, which were used during WW2 in attacks on the Ruhr dams in 1943. Interestingly, security did not permit showing of the real bomb design, but despite its faults, this remains a competent work.
Boa: book Enemy Coast Ahead by Guy Gibson and Paul Brickhill.

| | |
|---|---|
| WAR | 120 min (ort 125 min) B/W |
| B,V | TEVP; WHV (VHS only) |

**DAMIEN: OMEN 2 \*\*** 18
Don Taylor          USA          1978
*William Holden, Lee Grant, Jonathan Scott-Taylor, Lew Ayres, Sylvia Sidney, Leo McKern, Robert Foxworth*
Sequel to DAMIEN with our Antichrist now fully grown and ready for world domination. An ineffective sequel that has a few good sequences but lacks the force of the earlier film.
Aka: OMEN 2

| | |
|---|---|
| HOR | 102 min |
| V/sh | CBS |

**DAMN YANKEES \*\*\*** U
George Abbott/Stanley Donen
          USA          1958
*Tab Hunter, Gwen Verdon, Ray Walston, Russ Brown, Shannon Bolin, Nathaniel Frey, Jimmie Komack, Rae Allen, Robert Shafer, Jean Stapleton, Albert Linville, Bob Fosse, Elizabeth Howell*
Inspired adaptation of the Broadway hit musical that ran for over 1,000 performances. A middle-aged baseball fan sells his soul to the Devil just to give his team a chance to beat the Yankees. The Devil however doesn't have things all his own way, and has to resort to some devious tricks to ensure the bargain is kept.
Aka: WHAT LOLA WANTS
Boa: play by George Abbott and Douglas Wallop/novel The Year The Yankees Lost The Pennant by Douglas Wallop.

| | |
|---|---|
| MUS | 106 min |
| V/h | WHV |

**DAMNATION ALLEY \*** PG
Jack Smight          USA          1977
*Jan-Michael Vincent, George Peppard, Dominique Sanda, Paul Winfield, Jackie Earle Haley*
Five survivors of a nuclear war, travel across country to New York to meet up with a community of fellow survivors. A flaccid SF adventure that rather mutilates Zelazny's novel.
Boa: novel by Roger Zelazny.

| | |
|---|---|
| FAN | 87 min |
| B,V,V2,LV | CBS |

**DAMNED, THE \*** 18
Luchino Visconti
          ITALY/WEST GERMANY          1969
*Dirk Bogarde, Ingrid Thulin, Helmut Berger, Helmut Griem, Charlotte Rampling, Florinda Bolkan*
Overblown and melodramatic tale of the break-up of a nasty family of German industrialists, set against the background of the Nazis' rise to power. The running time of domestic versions is 164 min.
Aka: GOTTERDAMMERUNG; LA CADUTA DEGLI DEI

| | |
|---|---|
| DRA | 148 min (ort 164 min) |
| B,V | WHV |

**DAMNED RIVER \*** 18
Michael Schroeder          USA          1989
*Stephen Shellen, Lisa Aliff, John Terlesky, Marc Poppel, Bradford Bancroft*
Four youngsters take a trip of a lifetime when they explore the white water rapids of the Zambezi River aboard a raft. However, they soon find that the guide they have hired is the biggest danger they are going to face. A tropical clone of DELIVERANCE – but done with none of that film's style.

| | |
|---|---|
| A/AD | 92 min (ort 95 min) |
| V | RCA |

**DAMNING, THE \*** 18
Jag Mundhra          USA          1987
*Hy Pyke, Gregory Scott Cummins, Katrina Garner, Carla Baron*
A man introduces his grandson to Satanism, with predictable results in the gore department.
Aka: DEATHMASK; HACK O'LANTERN

| | |
|---|---|
| HOR | 84 min Cut (8 sec) |
| B,V | IVS; BRAVE |

**DAMSEL IN DISTRESS, A \*\*\***
George Stevens          USA          1937
*Fred Astaire, George Burns, Gracie Allen, Joan Fontaine, Reginald Gardiner, Constance Collier, Montagu Love*
Musical comedy about an American dancer in London, who pursues an aristocratic British lady whom he thinks is a chorus girl. A fairly uninspired musical, redeemed by some bright and bouncy numbers. Numbers include "Foggy Day In London Town", "Nice Work If You Can Get It" and Pan's superb "Fun House" sequence. AA: Dance Dir ("Fun House" – Hermes Pan).
Boa: novel by P.G. Wodehouse. Osca: OLD MAN RHYTHM

| | |
|---|---|
| MUS | 87 min (ort 100 min) B/W |
| B,V | KVD |

**DANCE ACADEMY \*\*** PG
Ted Mathon          ITALY/USA          1986
*Galyn Gory, Paula Nichols, Scott Grossman, Eliska Krupka, Julie Newmar, Tony Deanfields*
When a school of classical ballet is taken over by a devotee of modern dance, the scene is set for a series of well choreographed routines, and all done to the pounding beat of a rock score. A formula dance movie that blends comedy, romance and action, and though not as slick as FAME, will be enjoyed by those who like films of this type.
Aka: BODY BEAT; SCUOLA DI BALLO

| | |
|---|---|
| MUS | 101 min |
| B,V | EIV |

**DANCE FEVER \*\*** PG
Riccardo Sesani          ITALY          1984
*Russell Spellman, Tom Hooker, Patricia More*
Two disc jockeys try to put on the biggest disco in the world.

| | |
|---|---|
| MUS | 63 min |
| B,V | MED |

**DANCE OF THE DWARFS \***
Gus Trikonis
          PHILIPPINES/USA          1983
*Peter Fonda, Deborah Raffin, John Amos, Carlos Palomino*
A female anthropologist looking for a tribe of lost pygmies, teams up with a drunken helicopter pilot and they encounter some strange creatures. A dim and dreary adventure yarn that turns somewhat nastier when they run into their monsters – unfortunately it remains just as boring.
Aka: JUNGLE HEAT
Boa: novel by G. Household.

| | |
|---|---|
| A/AD | 90 min |
| B,V | VIDMOV/HOK |

**DANCE OF THE VAMPIRES \*\*** 15
Roman Polanski          UK/USA          1967
*Jack MacGowran, Roman Polanski, Sharon Tate, Ferdy Mayne, Alfie Bass, Terry Downes, Fiona Lewis, Iain Quarrier, Jessie Robins, Ronald Lacey, Sydney*

*Bromley, Andreas Malandrinos*
Ponderous and unfunny spoof on vampire films, which nevertheless has some quite good moments. Polanski both directs and stars as the timid assistant to a vampire hunter, who has come to Transylvania to destroy a nest of these creatures.
Aka: FEARLESS VAMPIRE KILLERS OR: PARDON ME, BUT YOUR TEETH ARE IN MY NECK, THE
COM                                      124 min
B,V                                         MGM

## DANCE OR DIE *                              18
Richard W. Munchkin   USA                 1988
*Ray Kieffer, Rebecca Barrington, Georgia Neu, Jerry Cleary*
A drug-addicted Las Vegas choreographer finds his habit gets him into trouble with both mobsters and Federal agents. A lethargic little thriller of slight interest.
THR                                   90 min mVid
V                                            BOX

## DANCE PARTY **                              PG
Mark Rosenthal        USA                 1987
*Donovan Leitch, Jennifer Runyon, Scott Plank, Joe Pantoliano, Bruce Kirby, Wendy Gazelle, Page Hannah*
A student at an Ivy League college falls in love with a member of a group, whose musical taste and dancing skills make them popular. A teen-love tale set in 1965.
Aka: IN CROWD, THE
DRA                                       91 min
V                                 ORION/PVG; VIR

## DANCE WITH A STRANGER ***                   15
Mike Newell           UK                  1984
*Miranda Richardson, Rupert Everett, Ian Holm, Tom Chadbon, Jane Bertish, Matthew Carroll, David Troughton, Paul Mooney, Stratford Johns, Joanne Whalley, Susan Kyd, Lesley Manville, Martin Murphy, Michael Jenn, Ian Hurley*
Skilful story of the events leading up to the murder by Ruth Ellis of her lover. As the last woman to be hung in the UK, her death was instrumental in the eventual abolition of capital punishment. Reminiscent of "Yield To The Night", which attempted a similar story. Winner of the Cannes Best Picture Award of 1985.
DRA                         98 min (ort 102 min)
V/h                                          CBS

## DANCERS **                                  PG
Herbert Ross          USA                 1987
*Mikhail Baryshnikov, Leslie Browne, Alessandra Ferri, Thomas Rall, Lynn Seymour, Victor Barbee, Mariangela Melato, Julie Kent, Leandro Amato, Gianmarco Tognazzi, Desmond Kelly, Chrisa Keramidas, Amy Werba, Jack Brodsky*
A backstage saga of a ballet company on tour in Italy, with a world famous dancer being taught about unselfish love, by an innocent young ballerina with whom he has become infatuated whilst rehearsing for a screen version of "Giselle". A trite and shallow story, of little interest except for dedicated lovers of ballet.
DRA                          95 min (ort 99 min)
B/sh, V/sh                                   WHV

## DANCER'S TOUCH, THE **                       18
William A. Fraker     USA                 1988
*Burt Reynolds, Rita Moreno, Ossie Davis, Helen Shaver, David Hunt, Kristy Swanson, Abe Vigoda, Michael Smith, Alfie Wise*
Reynolds plays an ex-cop who is drawn into an investigation of a demented rapist, who abducts and ties up his victims, forcing them to watch him perform a dance before raping them. The case resembles a similar one he dealt with on his last investigation, and Reynolds finds himself working closely with the police psychologist. Another offering in the "Stryker" series.

See also CAROLANN, BLIND CHESS and DIRTY DIAMONDS.
Aka: B.L. STRYKER: THE DANCER'S TOUCH
THR                                   91 min mTV
B,V                                          CIC

## DANCIN' THRU THE DARK ***                    15
Mike Ockrent          UK                  1989
*Claire Hackett, Con O'Neill, Angela Clarke, Julia Deakin, Louise Duprey, Sandy Hendrickse, Mark Womack, Conrad Nelson, Simon O'Brien, Peter Watts, Andrew Naylor, Colin Welland*
Written by Willy Russell, and very much a typically bittersweet slice of Liverpudlian life, with a young couple about to be married celebrating separately with their respective friends, but inevitably ending up at the same club. Under the influence of drink, both parties begin to have second thoughts as they contemplate their future prospects. A blend of comedy and drama, a little stagebound and contrived, but quite engaging.
Boa: play by Willy Russell.
COM                                       95 min
V/h                                          PAL

## DANCING IN THE DARK ***                      15
Leon Marr             CANADA              1986
*Martha Henry, Rosemary Dunsmore, Neil Munro, Richard Manette*
A dedicated and obsessive housewife slowly changes on the way to a mental breakdown, lurching from devoted wife to icy murderess. The predictable and talky script is not a strong point, but Henry's obsessive performance as the housewife, for whom murder is just another mess to clean up, is hard to fault.
DRA                                       98 min
B/h, V/h                                     NWV

## DANCING PRINCESSES, THE **
Jon Scolfield         UK                  1978
*Jim Dale, Freddie Jones, Peter Butterworth, Jane Darling, Jane Winchester, Lesley Collier, Mo Willshire, Lavinca Lang, Loma Nathan*
Film version of the Brothers Grimm tale about a widowed king who has six beautiful daughters. He offers one in marriage to any suitor who can solve the mystery of how they all come to wear out a pair of dancing shoes each night.
Boa: short story by Jakob Ludwig Karl Grimm and Wilhelm Karl Grimm.
JUV                                   52 min mTV
B,V                                   PRV L/A

## DANCING YEARS, THE **
Richard Bramall       USA                 1979
*Anthony Valentine, Celia Gregory, Susan Skipper*
A competent updated version of the 1949 film of the Ivor Novello play, about a struggling composer who falls for a singer. She leaves him after a misunderstanding, but later bears him a son.
Boa: operetta by Ivor Novello.
MUS                                      143 min
B,V                                   PRV L/A

## DANGER ZONE 2: REAPER'S REVENGE ***          18
Geoffrey G. Bowers    USA                 1988
*Jason Williams, Robert Random, Jane Higginson, Alisha Das*
A sequel to the earlier film, with crazed biker "Reaper" getting out of jail on a technicality. Determined to settle a score with the cop who put him there, he joins up with his gang and kidnaps the cop's girlfriend. The chase is now on in a routine action yarn that culminates in a violent climax.
Aka: REAPER'S REVENGE
A/AD                       90 min Cut (1 min 4 sec)
B,V                                          RCA

## DANGER ZONE, THE ** 18
Henry Vernon          USA          1987
*Robert Canada, Jason Williams, Kriss Brixton, Dana
Dowell, David Friedman, Cynthia Gray, G. Cervi,
Mickey Elders, Jamie Ferreira, R.A. Mihailoff,
Michael Wayne, Suzanne Tara, Juanita Ranney*
A drug-smuggling biker gang captures a female rock
group when their car breaks down on the way to Las
Vegas. A grisly future beckons, but when a new
member joins the gang, the fate of the girls seems a
little less grim. Nasty action movie followed by a
sequel in 1988.
A/AD                        85 min Cut (13 sec)
B,V                                         RCA

## DANGEROUS AFFECTION ** PG
Larry Elikann          USA          1987
*Judith Light, Jimmy Smits, Audra Lindley, Michael
Parks, Billy Sullivan, Rhea Perlmann, Joseph Hacker*
A TV version of WITNESS, with Light a pregnant
mother whose young son becomes the target for a
killer when he witnesses a murder. A kind of comedy
thriller that's neither terribly amusing nor terribly
tense.
THR                               91 min mTV
B/h, V/h                                   NWV

## DANGEROUS CARGO ** PG
Boris Segal          USA          1975
*Nick Nolte, Jim Davis, Bo Hopkins*
Hijacking and smuggling along the Mississippi fea-
ture in this routine tale of adventure.
A/AD                                    69 min
B,V                                       POLY

## DANGEROUS COMPANY **
Lamont Johnson          USA          1982
*Beau Bridges, Carlos Brown, Karen Carlson, Jan
Sterling, Kene Holiday, Ralph Macchio, Max Wright,
Shizuko Hoshi, Dale Ishimoto, Chris Mulkey, Ward
Wood, Buck Taylor, Ray Johnson, Christopher Keane,
Tom Middleton, David McKnight*
True story of the 27 year career of a dangerous and
violent criminal and his eventual rehabilitation.
Bridges is outstanding in his role as Ray Johnson, the
man on whose life the film is based, but the sluggish
script tends to obscure the harsh picture of the
treatment he receives following his escape and recap-
ture.
Boa: book Too Dangerous To Be At Large by Ray
Johnson.
DRA                     98 min (ort 104 min) mTV
B,V                                   SPEC/POLY

## DANGEROUS CURVES ** PG
David Lewis          USA          1988
*Robert Stack, Leslie Nielsen, Robert Romanus, Martha
Quinn, Tate Donovan Robert Klein, Danielle Von
Zerneck, Elizabeth Ashley*
A young man agrees to deliver a Porsche to a
super-wealthy purchaser, but takes a little trip on the
side that brings him nothing but trouble. A light-
hearted and fairly mindless teen comedy.
COM                     90 min (ort 93 min)
B,V                                        VES

## DANGEROUS DAVIES:
## THE LAST DETECTIVE **
Val Guest          UK          1981
*Bernard Cribbins, Bill Maynard, Joss Ackland,
Bernard Lee, Frank Windsor, John Leyton, Maureen
Lipman*
Comedy about an accident prone detective constable
who is a one-man walking disaster area. In this film
he decides to reopen a 15-year-old murder case.
Average British comedy outing.
Boa: novel by Leslie Thomas.
COM                               105 min mTV
B,V                                   PRV L/A

## DANGEROUS GAME * 18
Stephen Hopkins     AUSTRALIA          1987
*Miles Buchanan, Marcus Graham, Steven Grives,
Sandie Lillington*
A thriller involving a psychotic cop, whose harass-
ment of some college kids leads to his dismissal.
Blaming the kids for his predicament he swears
vengeance and sets out to get even. A tedious revenger
that finally sees our college kids locked in a depart-
ment store with their ex-policeman friend, who has
armed himself with a crossbow. Written by Peter
West.
THR                                     97 min
V/h                                        MED

## DANGEROUS HOLIDAY **
Nicholas Barrows          USA          1937
*Ra Hould, Hedda Hopper, Guinn Williams, Jack La
Rue, Jed Prouty, Lynne Roberts, William Bakewell,
Fern Emmett, Virginia Sale, Franklin Pangborn,
Grady Sutton, William Newell, Thomas E. Jackson,
Olaf Hytten, Jack Mulhall*
A young kid who's a brilliant violinist, runs away
from home because he is tired of not being allowed to
play like other children. He finds his way to a criminal
gang who are eventually captured largely due to his
efforts.
Boa: story by Karen De Wolf and Barry Shipman.
DRA                               54 min B/W
B,V                                        ABA

## DANGEROUS LIAISONS **** 15
Stephen Frears          USA          1988
*Glenn Close, John Malkovich, Michelle Pfeiffer, Keanu
Reeves, Uma Thurman, Swoosie Kutz, Mildred
Natwick, Peter Capaldi*
An 18th century story of an unscrupulous woman who
enjoys manipulating and exploiting those around her
for her own amusement, being joined in this pursuit
by a count of similar tastes. An excellent and engros-
sing costume drama set in France, with Close quite
outstanding as the woman in question. AA: Art
(Stuart Craig/Gerard James), Screen (Adapt) (Christ-
opher Hampton), Cost (James Acheson). See also
WHEN A WOMAN IS IN LOVE.
Boa: novel Les Liaisons Dangereuses by Choderlos de
Laclos/play by Christopher Hampton.
DRA                     115 min (ort 120 min)
V/sh                                       WHV

## DANGEROUS LOVE * 18
Marty Ollstein          USA          1988
*Lawrence Monoson, Brenda Bakke, Teri Austin, Peter
Marc, Sal Landi, Anthony Geary, Elliott Gould*
A disagreeable and poorly made mess of a film that
revolves around the activities of a murderer who has
taken to killing the female members of a video-dating
club.
DRA                                     90 min
V/h                                        MED

## DANGEROUS MISSION ** 15
Louis King          USA          1954
*Victor Mature, Piper Laurie, William Bendix, Vincent
Price, Dennis Weaver*
A woman witness to a gangland murder in New York,
flees to the Glacier National Park out in the mid-
West, with both the cops and the Mob in hot pursuit.
Average.
Osca: IMPACT
THR                                     73 min
B,V                                        KVD

## DANGEROUS OBSESSION ** 18
Yuri Sivo          USA          1989
*Brian Benben, James Harper, Debrah Farentino,
James Sung*
When the leader of a evangelical organisation of

doubtful worth but proven financial success is murdered, the existence of the "Divine Church of the People" is threatened by the ensuing scandal. One of the church leaders hires a detective to reveal the culprit and prevent further bloodshed, but as the private eye probes further, he begins to untangle a complex web of greed and corruption. Adequate thriller in an unusual setting.

| THR | 90 min |
| V | BOX |

## DANGEROUS ORPHANS **                    18
John Laing     NEW ZEALAND          1987
*Peter Stephens, Michael Hurst, Jennifer Ward-Lealand, Ross Girven, Ian Mune, Peter Bland, Zoe Wallace, Grant Tilly*
An orphan plots with two friends to avenge his father's murder at the hands of gangsters. A bloody revenger that's well made but pretty standard in terms of its plot.

| A/AD | 87 min (ort 93 min) Colour and B/W |
| B,V | SCRN |

## DANGEROUS PURSUIT **
Sandor Stern     USA              1989
*Alexandra Powers, Brian Wimmer, Elena Stiteler, Gregory Harrison, Robert Prosky, Scott Valentine*
A happily married woman working as a secretary in Portland, finds her life turning into a nightmarish struggle for survival, when she recognises a man at her office she once used to know from her New York days. An above-average thriller, with a few good chase sequences and solid characterisation.

| THR | 89 min (ort 100 min) mTV |
| V | CIC |

## DANGEROUS SUMMER, A **                  15
Quentin Masters     AUSTRALIA      1981
*Tom Skerritt, Ian Gilmour, Wendy Hughes, James Mason, Ray Barrett, Guy Doleman*
A clumsy and implausible drama, with an American businessman building a summer resort in the Blue Mountains of Australia, all the time unaware of the fact that his psychotic, arsonist partner plans to burn it down in an insurance swindle. When a Lloyds agent is found murdered, another insurance man arrives to investigate.
Aka: BURNING MAN, THE

| DRA | 86 min (ort 100 min) |
| B,V | MED |

## DANGEROUS TRAFFIC **                     18
Don McDougall     USA              1979
*Joe Renteria, Shelley Novak*
Marijuana smugglers try to get one last shipment across the Texas/Mexico border. Standard action tale.
Aka: TOKE (GLOB)

| A/AD | 93 min Cut (10 sec) |
| B,V | VTC/CBS L/A; GLOB |

## DANGEROUSLY CLOSE *                       18
Albert Pyun     USA               1986
*John Stockwell, Carey Lowell, J. Eddie Peck, Bradford Bancroft, Madison Mason, Don Michael Paul, Thom Matthews, Jerry Dinome*
Confused account of a vigilante group inside a school, led by a teacher who is a Vietnam veteran. In their zeal to clean up their city they resort to brutality and murder. A simple-minded and unpleasant exploration of blind obedience, that raises some interesting issues, but does nothing to examine them.
Aka: CHOICE KILL

| THR | 91 min |
| B,V | RNK |

## DANIEL ***                                18
Sidney Lumet     USA              1983
*Timothy Hutton, Amanda Plummer, Mandy Patinkin, Lindsay Crouse, Edward Asner, Joseph Leon, Ellen*

*Barkin, Toviah Feldshuh, Joseph Leon*
Fictionalised account of the execution of the Rosenbergs for spying during the Cold War period of the 1950s. The film attempts to examine the effect this had on their children. A fine and thought-provoking adaptation.
Boa: novel The Book Of Daniel by E.L. Doctorow.

| DRA | 130 min |
| B,V | POLY |

## DANIEL AND NEBUCHADNEZZAR **
Charles Davis     USA             1979
*Donny Most, Hans Conreid, David Hedison, Jerry Houser, Linwood Boomer, Vic Morrow*
Part of the "Greatest Heroes of the Bible" series that presents this famous episode. Average.

| DRA | 48 min |
| B,V | VCL/CBS |

## DANIEL AND THE LION'S DEN **            U
              USA               1979
*Robert Vaughn, David Birney, Sherry Jackson, Nehemiah Persoff, Dean Stockwell*
Part of the "Greatest Heroes of the Bible" series that follows the career of this famous character. Average.

| DRA | 45 min |
| B,V | VCL; SCREL |

## DANISH BED AND BOARD **                  18
John Hibard     DENMARK           1972
*Oli Soltoft, Birte Tove, Annie Birgit Garde, Axel Stroby, Paul Hagen, Susanne Jagd*
A broad sex farce involving the bedroom antics of the head teacher at a boy's school, who finds himself in financial trouble and wants to admit girl students, fiercely opposed by the school governors. He hits on a scheme to turn the school into a summer hotel and it's a great success, not least because of the home-produced aphrodisiacs the pupils have started adding to the hotel food. One of a series of popular Danish lightweight sex-comedies.
Aka: BEDSIDE HEAD; REKTOR PA SENGEKANTEN

| A | 89 min |
| B,V | VOV/DARK L/A; SHEP |

## DANISH PILLOW TALK **                     18
John Hilbard     DENMARK          1973
*Birthe Tove, Annie Birgit Garde, Ole Soeltoft, Soeren Stroemberg*
A girl inherits a string of industrial concerns that stand to be bankrupted by inheritance tax unless she marries the son of the owner of a competing concern. As she ponders this prospect, she has sex with everyone in her firm from the secretary to the janitor, in a trite and lightweight Danish effort.
Aka: BEDSIDE ROMANCE; PILLOW TALK; ROMANTIK PAA SENGEKANTEN

| A | 92 min (ort 103 min) (Cut at film release) |
| B,V | PRI L/A; VOV/DARK BROS; PHE (VHS only); |
| SHEP | |

## DANNY **                                   U
Gene Feldman     USA              1979
*Janet Zarish, Gloria Maddox, Rebecca Page*
The story of a girl whose love and devotion turns a broken down horse into a champion jumper. Haven't we been this way before?

| DRA | 86 min (ort 89 min) |
| B,V,V2 | GHV |

## DANNY JONES **                            15
Jules Bricken     UK             1971
*Frank Finlay, Len Jones, Jane Carr, Jenny Hanley, Nigel Humphreys, Raymond Young, Andrea Lawrence, Philip Ross, Elizabeth Tyrell, Marianne Stone*

The story of a 17-year-old, his strained relationship with his strict and domineering father, and his seduction at the hands of a schoolgirl.
Aka: FIRES OF YOUTH (KRP)
Boa: novel Fires Of Youth by James Lincoln Collier.
DRA                          88 min (ort 91 min)
B,V                              CBS; FILV; KRP

## DANNY TRAVIS ***
Roy Boulting          USA              1981
*Richard Harris, Martin Landau, Karen Black*
A Los Angeles inventor refuses to be evicted from his home, and taking a cop hostage, resists every attempt to shift him, even one mounted by a crack police team. A TV reporter reveals high level political corruption behind the decision to demolish the building where he lives.
DRA                                  105 min
B,V,V2                                   VUL

## DANNY: THE CHAMPION OF THE WORLD *** U
Gavin Miller          UK               1989
*Jeremy Irons, Samuel Irons, Robbie Coltrane, Cyril Cusack, Jimmy Nail, Lionel Jeffries, Michael Hordern, Jean Marsh*
Set in the 1950s, this tells the story of Danny, a 9-year-old living with his father. When their tranquil life in a caravan is threatened by a local developer who has acquired all the surrounding land except their tiny plot, the boy hatches a scheme to teach him a lesson. A nicely made and wholesome kid's film.
JUV                                   94 min
V                                        COL

## DARBY O'GILL AND THE LITTLE PEOPLE **** U
Robert Stevenson      USA              1959
*Albert Sharpe, Janet Munro, Sean Connery, Jimmy O'Dea, Kieron Moore, Estelle Winwood*
An Irish caretaker tells so many tales that nobody believes him when he actually meets the King of the Leprechauns. A marvellously entertaining piece of whimsy with some splendid special effects. Based on the stories of H.T. Kavanagh.
FAN                                   93 min
B,V                                      WDV

## DAREDEVIL COMMANDOS **                18
R. Rapi (E.G. Bakker)  ITALY            1985
*Barry Prima, Harry Capri, Didier Hamel, Jonan Saimima*
Six highly trained men are sent to certain death when they are ordered to attack an entire company of enemy troops. Much violent action in a routine war film.
WAR                          82 min (ort 90 min)
B,V                                      AVR

## DAREDEVIL DRIVERS **
Stanley Wilson/Keitaro Miho
                      JAPAN             1978
*Linda Stayer, Howard Nishimura, Cheryl Waide*
A graphic account of a demolition derby between the USA and Japan, plus a love story with a Japanese man and a young American girl. Average.
Aka: MACH 78
DRA                                   93 min
B,V                                      MOV

## DAREDEVIL, THE *
Robert W. Stringer     USA              1972
*George Montgomery, Terry Moore, Gay Perkins, Cyril Poitier, Bill Kelly*
A top racing car driver works as a go-between for a drugs ring in this quirky but unlikeable effort. One point of interest is in the unusual role of Poitier as a black mortician and chief crook. Music is by The Brooklyn Bridge.
A/AD                                  90 min
B,V                                  MOG/CBS

## DAREDREAMER **                          15
Barry Caillier         USA              1989
*Tim Noah, Adam Eastwood, Alyce La Tourelle, Michael A. Jackson*
A high school Walter Mitty character becomes so involved with his fantasies that he is unable to concentrate on his forthcoming graduation. An imaginative musical-comedy, quite agreeable in a sugary and contrived way, despite the cliched finale. Filmed in Seattle.
COM                          104 min (ort 108 min)
V                                      FUTUR

## DARK AGE **                              18
Arch Nicholson    AUSTRALIA             1987
*John Jarratt, Max Phipps, David Gulpilil, Nikki Coghill, Burnam Burnam, Ray Meagher, Max Phipps*
A giant crocodile terrorises a town and proves to be a headache for the wildlife officer who has to capture it before poachers do. A competent and pleasant outdoors outing.
Boa: novel Numunwari by Grahame Webb.
THR                                   88 min
B,V                                      NELS

## DARK ANGEL ***                          18
M.S. Novack/Pablo Cairo/Peter Van Der Bilt
                      USA              1985
*Jamie Gillis, Desiree Lane, Don Fernando, Precious, Martina Brandt, Jon Martin, Chelsea Manchester, Gail Sterling, Lynx Cannon, Nick Nitler*
A wealthy man becomes obsessed with a mysterious woman that he is forever catching glimpses of but can never meet. Tormented sexually by his unfulfilled desires he allows himself to be dragged ever deeper into depravity until a final encounter, when he does indeed bed the woman, only to become convinced that he has slept with the Devil. A highly unusual but rather unpleasant tale. Cut before video submission by 24 min 39 sec.
A             60 min Cut (1 min 33 sec) (ort 86 min)
V                                    SCRN L/A

## DARK ANGEL ***                          18
Craig R. Baxley        USA             1989
*Dolph Lundgren, Brian Benben, Betsy Brantley*
A tough Houston vice cop (Lundgren) teams up with a rather square FBI agent to take on drug dealers who turn out to be aliens in this heady and surprisingly effective blend of SF and thriller genres.
Aka: I COME IN PEACE
FAN                                   88 min
V                                        EIV

## DARK ANGEL, THE ***                       U
Sidney Franklin        USA             1935
*Merle Oberon, Fredric March, Herbert Marshall, Janet Beecher, John Halliday Henrietta Crosman, Frieda Inescort, George Breakston, Claud Allister*
An officer blinded during WW1 tries to get his fiancee to marry another man without her discovering his reasons. Get out the Kleenex – this well made weepie is a three box affair. AA: Art (Richard Day).
DRA                                 106 min B/W
B,V                                      VGM

## DARK AUGUST ***                          15
Martin Goldman         USA             1976
*J.J. Barry, Carole Shelyne, Kim Hunter*
A New York artist walks out of his sterile marriage and starts life anew in a small Vermont town. Hoping to find peace there, he finds himself caught up in a web of supernatural terror after he accidentally kills a small girl and is cursed by her grandfather.
HOR                          95 min; 83 min (STABL)
B,V                              PMA L/A; STABL

## DARK COMMAND ***                          U
Raoul Walsh            USA             1940

John Wayne, Claire Trevor, Walter Pidgeon, Roy
Rogers, George "Gabby" Hayes, Porter Hall, Marjorie
Main, Raymond Walburn, Joseph Sawyer, Helen
MacKellar, J. Farrell MacDonald, Revor Bardette,
Harry Woods, Glenn Strange
At the end of the American Civil War, a number of
private armies ravaged the countryside. Pidgeon
plays one such man (loosely based on the 1860s
renegade Quantrill), who leads a band on raids but
eventually clashes with the newly elected marshal.
An enjoyable but patchy adventure.
Boa: novel Dark Command by W.R. Burnett.
WES                    59 min (ort 94 min) B/W
B,V,V2                      WOV L/A; VCC

### DARK CRYSTAL, THE ***                    PG
Jim Henson/Frank Oz    UK              1983
Voices of: Stephen Garlick, Lisa Maxwell, Billie
Whitelaw, Percy Edwards, Barry Dennen, Brian
Muehl, Michael Kilgarriff, Jerry Nelson, Steve
Whitmire, Thick Wilson, John Baddeley, David Buck,
Charles Collingwood, Sean Barrett
Puppet fantasy from the creators of "The Muppets". A
missing piece of a magical crystal must be found or
evil will engulf the world. The production is superb in
this incredibly ambitious puppet production, what lets
it down is the cliched and well-worn good-versus-evil
plot. A great pity – it could have been superb.
FAN                                  94 min
V/sh                                     RCA

### DARK HORSE *                            15
Robert Collins        USA              1984
Wings Hauser, James Whitmore Jr, Bo Hopkins,
Nicholas Campbell, Lenore Kasdorf, Randy Brooks
This failed pilot tells of a tough journalist who always
gets his story, not least owing to the fact that he is a
master of disguise. In this tale, he infiltrates a group
of extremists who are planning a coup in a South
American country. Short on action and long on
tedium, this dud is not helped by the lack of conviction
shown by all concerned.
A/AD                                70 min mTV
B,V                                      CIC

### DARK MIRROR, THE ***
Robert Siodmark       USA              1946
Olivia De Havilland, Lew Ayres, Thomas Mitchel,
Garry Owen, Richard Long, Charles Evans
A detective has to determine which one of a set of
identical twin girls was responsible for a murder. An
interesting film with de Havilland playing both girls.
Ayres as the psychologist, works in conjunction with
Mitchell as the detective to trap the culprit. Remade
for TV in 1984.
Boa: story by Vladimir Posner.
DRA                                 85 min B/W
B,V,V2                                INT/CBS

### DARK NIGHT OF THE SCARECROW, THE ***
Frank De Felitta     USA               1981
Charles Durning, Robert F. Lyons, Lane Smith,
Claude Earl Jones, Tonya Crowe, Larry Drake,
Jocelyn Brando, Tom Taylor, Richard McKenzie, Ivy
Jones, Jim Tartan, Ed Call, Alice Nunn, John
Steadman, Dave Adams, Ivy Bethune
The innocent friendship between a retarded man and
a young girl, leads to his brutal murder at the hands of
a group of self-appointed vigilantes. A well made if
rather predictable shocker.
Boa: story by J.D. Feigelson and Butler Handcock.
HOR                                108 min mTV
B,V,V2                                   VUL

### DARK OF THE SUN ***                     15
Jack Cardiff         UK                1968
Rod Taylor, Yvette Mimieux, Kenneth More, Jim
Brown, Andre Morell, Peter Carsten, Oliver Despax,
Guy Deghy, Bloke Modisane, Calvin Lockhart, Alan

Gifford, Murray Kash
A mercenary in the Belgian Congo in 1960 is ordered
to rescue the citizens of a besieged town, whilst
retrieving a fortune in gems at the same time. A taut
and gripping adventure tale and without doubt one of
Taylor's best films.
Aka: MERCENARIES, THE
Boa: novel by Wilbur Smith.
A/AD                                 101 min
B,V                                      MGM

### DARK PASSAGE ***                         15
Delmer Daves          USA              1947
Humphrey Bogart, Lauren Bacall, Agnes Moorehead,
Bruce Bennett, Bob Farber, Tom D'Andrea, Clifton
Young, Douglas Kennedy, Rory Mallinson, Houseley
Stevenson, Richard Walsh, Clancy Cooper, Pat McVey,
Dude Maschemeyer
A man imprisoned in San Quentin for the murder of
his wife, escapes and has his face altered by cosmetic
surgery, hiding out at Bacall's apartment while his
scars heal. She believes in his innocence and he falls
in love with her, but his new life is threatened by her
best friend, a woman with a guilty past. An uneven,
loose assembly of the incredible and the unbelievable,
but the splendid camerawork and acting are signi-
ficant compensations.
Boa: novel by David Goodis.
THR                                102 min B/W
V                                        WHV

### DARK PLACES **
Don Sharp           UK      1972 (released 1973)
Joan Collins, Christopher Lee, Herbert Lom, Robert
Hardy, Jane Birkin, Jean Marsh, Carleton Hobbs,
Jennifer Thanisch, Michael McVey, Martin Boddey,
Roy Evans, John Glyn Jones, John Levene
Strange happenings in an old manor house. The heir
to the estate (which belonged to a demented killer)
hears voices etc. and becomes possessed by his spirit,
killing those who stand between him and his inheri-
tance. A fair horror yarn, but one of no great force.
HOR                              87 min (ort 91 min)
B,V                                      CBS

### DARK POWER, THE **                       18
Phil Smoot           USA               1984
Anna Lane Tatum, Cynthia Bailey, Lash LaRue, Mary
Dalton, Paul Holman, Marc Matney, Cynthia
Farbman, Tony Shaw, Robert Bushyhead, Suzie
Martin, Dean Jones, Steve Templeton, Page Elizabeth
Ray, Eric Mikesell, Tony Ilwood
A Ranger sitting at the deathbed of his Indian friend
is told of the Ancient Toltec Sorcerers, cannibalistic
beings who buried themselves alive long ago and
continue to survive by feeding on the living. His
friend's dying request is that the Ranger attempts to
destroy these creatures, and our hero soon finds
himself obliged to protect a bunch of students who
have rented a house that's haunted by these beings.
Average.
Aka: DARK POWERS
HOR                               81 min Cut (7 sec)
B,V                                   ABC; NDH

### DARKROOM **                              18
Terence O'Hara        USA              1988
Aarin Teich, Jill Pierce, Jeffrey Allen Arbaugh, Sara
Lee Wade
A woman returns to her family's farm and learns of a
gruesome double murder that took place a few miles
away. As the members of her family begin to dis-
appear, she realises that she is meant to be one of his
victims. An adequate time-filler of reasonable quality
if not originality.
THR                                  82 min
V/h                                      GHV

**DARK SANITY ★★**
Martin Greene/Tim McWhorter/Martha Sudderth
USA                     1980
*Aldo Ray, Chuck Jamison, Kory Clark, Andy Gwyn,*
*Bobby Holt, Harry Carlson, Timothy McCormack,*
*Barry Ray Robinson, Dennis Barnett, Iris Bath,*
*Brenda Bennett, Toni Carleton, Roger Clark, Kevin*
*Downey, Rick Green, Ron Jennings*
A rehabilitated woman alcoholic, moves into a house
that was the scene of a mysterious and unsolved
murder, and begins to be haunted by sinister visions
of the event. Fair.
Aka: STRAIGHT JACKET
HOR                                    86 min
B,V                                    VIPCO

**DARK SIDE, THE ★★**                            18
Don Haldane            CANADA          1971
*Jack Creley, Jay Reynolds, Trudy Young, Gene*
*Tyburn, Hugh Webster, Terry Tweed, Rex Hagon,*
*Colin Fox, Anthony Kramreither, William McDermot,*
*Linda Houston, Stuart Gillard, Patrick Boxill, John*
*Kerr, Ron Hartmann*
A dying lawyer tries to recruit two new members to a
sinister cult that promises eternal life through rein-
carnation. A run-of-the-mill horror yarn.
Aka: REINCARNATE, THE (PYR or VDEL)
HOR            90 min; 96 min (PYR); (ort 122 min)
B,V              PYR L/A; GOV; VDEL

**DARK STAR ★★★★**                              PG
John Carpenter          USA            1974
*Dan O'Bannon, Brian Narelle, Cal Kuniholme, Dre*
*Pahich, Joe Sanders*
A highly-acclaimed tongue-in-cheek film all about a
sloppy bunch of misfits cruising space in their battered spaceship, blowing up unstable planets prior to
colonisation of space. They've been doing it for so long
now they hardly remember why. It all comes together
in this brilliantly inventive film, Carpenter's first
feature, which he expanded from a college short he
made with O'Bannon. Written by Carpenter and
O'Bannon.
FAN                      81 min; 84 min (HEND)
B, V/s, V2 IFS; WOV; HEND (VHS and Betamax only)

**DARK TOWER ★★**                               15
Ken Barnett              USA            1988
*Michael Moriarty, Jenny Agutter, Theodore Bikel,*
*Carol Lynley, Ann Lockhart, Kevin McCarthy*
This undeveloped but interesting idea for a horror film
has an evil presence existing within a skyscaper and
triggering off a series of inexplicable and deadly
events.
HOR                                    96 min
B,V                                    SONY

**DARK VICTORY ★★★**                            PG
Edmund Goulding         USA            1939
*Bette Davis, George Brent, Ronald Reagan, Humphrey*
*Bogart, Geraldine Fitzgerald, Cora Witherspoon,*
*Henry Travers*
Tear-jerker about a rich and spoiled society girl who
finds she is dying from a brain tumour and meets her
end with courage. Bogart as an Irishmen hits the only
jarring note, in this excellent and unashamedly
sentimental melodrama. Remade as "The Stolen
Hours" and then once more in 1976.
Boa: play by G.E. Brewer and B. Bloch.
DRA                                    102 min B/W
B,V                                    WHV

**DARK WATERS ★★**                              U
Andre De Toth           USA            1944
*Merle Oberon, Franchot Tone, Thomas Mitchell, Fay*
*Bainter, Rex Ingram, John Qualen, Elisha Cook Jr*
An orphan girl goes to live with her relatives in the
Southern swamplands, and is a victim of strange and
terrifying experiences, in this competent but confused

melodrama.
Boa: novel by Frank and Marian Cockrell.
DRA                                    86 min B/W
V                                      VCC

**DARK, THE ★★**                                15
John (Bud) Cardos       USA            1979
*William Devane, Cathy Lee Crosby, Richard Jaeckel,*
*Keenan Wynn, Vivian Blaine*
An alien zombie commits a series of terrifying mur-
ders in a Californian town. The father of a murdered
girl and a TV reporter try to track down the monster
in this well made but terribly predictable effort.
HOR                                    90 min
B,V,V2                                 GHV

**DARKER SIDE OF TERROR, THE ★**                15
Gus Trikonis            USA            1979
*Robert Foster, Adrienne Barbeau, Ray Milland, David*
*Sheiner, John Lehne, Denise DuBarry, Jack DeMave,*
*Thomas Bellin, Heather Hobbs, Eddie Quillan, Raye*
*Sheffield, Russell Shannon, Jim Nolan, Madeleine*
*Shaner, Johnny Hock*
Genetic cloning experiments lead to the creation of an
unstoppable monster but not unfortunately, to much
in the way of new ideas, in this strictly B-type horror
movie.
HOR                    91 min (ort 105 min) mTV
B,V                                    DIAM

**DARKROOM, THE ★★**                            18
Paul Harmon             AUSTRALIA       1981
*Alan Cassell, Svet Kovich, Anna Jemison*
A psychologically disturbed boy becomes obsessed
with his father's mistress in this absorbing thriller.
Aka: DARK ROOM
THR                    93 min (ort 96 min) Cut
V                                      MED

**DARLING ★★**                                  15
John Schlesinger        UK             1965
*Julie Christie, Dirk Bogarde, Laurence Harvey, Jose-*
*Luis De Villalong, Alex Scott, Roland Curram, Basil*
*Henson, Helen Lindsay, Tyler Butterworth, Hugo*
*Dyson, Pauline Yates*
A cynical portrait of a young London fashion model
who decides to climb the social ladder rather quickly,
by way of a few beds. Schlesinger's direction is
alternately flashy and perceptive, but Christie is
ravishing as the hard-bitten girl who winds up with
an Italian nobleman after a few false starts. AA:
Actress (Christie), Story/Screen (Frederic Raphael),
Cost (Julie Harris).
DRA    122 min (ort 127 min) (Cut at film release) B/W
V                                      WHV

**DARLINGS ★★**                                 18
Ruud van Memert NETHERLANDS            1984
*Akkemay, Peter Faber, Geert de Jong*
A mildly amusing satire on impossible children and
their beleaguered parents.
Aka: SCHATJES; SWEETHEARTS
COM                    99 min (ort 101 min) Cut (58 sec)
B,V                                    WHV

**DATE WITH AN ANGEL ★★**                       PG
Tom McLoughlin          USA            1987
*Michael E. Knight, Phoebe Cates, Emmanuelle Beart,*
*David Dukes, Phil Brock, Albert Macklin, Pete*
*Kowanko, Vinny Argiro, Bibi Besch, Cheryl A. Pollak,*
*Steven Banks, Charles Lane, J. Don Ferguson, Bert*
*Hogue, O'Clair Alexander*
An angel crashes to Earth and is befriended by a
musician, about to be wed and absorbed into his
father-in-law's cosmetics company. Beart is suitably
ethereal as the earthbound spirit who splashes into
his pool on the night of his bachelor party, but the
oh-so-cute sugary script offers little scope for comedy.

COM                                           102 min
B,V                                              CBS

## DAUGHTER OF EMMANUELLE **
Jean Luret        BELGIUM/FRANCE          1978
*Laurence Casey, Sarah Crystal, Greta Vayant, Mascha
Magall*
Emmanuelle's daughter takes over where her mother
left off, falling in love with a warped fashion designer
and an amnesiac GI (but not both at the same time).
Filmed in Paris and Greece.
DRA                                            84 min
B,V,V2                               HOK L/A; PINK

## DAUGHTER OF MATA HARI, THE *
Renzo Merusi          ITALY                  PG
                                              1955
*Frank Latimore, Ludmilla Tcherina, Erno Crisa,
Milly Vitale*
The daughter of the famous spy upholds the family
tradition by discovering the planned attack on Pearl
Harbour before it takes place. A mediocre and vacuous
effort.
Aka: MATA HARI'S DAUGHTER
DRA               83 min (ort 102 min) dubbed
B,V                                        PRV L/A

## DAUGHTER OF THE STREETS **
Ed Sherin             USA                     18
                                             1989
*Jane Alexander, Roxana Zal, John Stamos, Harris
Yulin, Luke Zimmerman, Martha Scott, Brandon
Maggart*
Teenage prostitution is the social evil on offer here in
this predictable TV drama that details the desperate
efforts made by a mother to save her daughter. A
preachy melodrama; earnest, intense and self-
righteous.
DRA                   90 min (ort 100 min) mTV
V                                              CBS

## DAUGHTERS OF DARKNESS ***
Harry Kuemel                               1971
    BELGIUM/FRANCE/ITALY/WEST GERMANY
*Paul Esser, John Karlen, Delphine Seyrig, Daniele
Ouimet, George Jamin, Andrea Rau, Joris Collet, Fons
Rademakers*
A female vampire and her companion come to a
Belgian seaside resort in the off-season, and become
erotically involved with a young couple. A mixture of
absurd humour and good photography place this a
notch or two above the average for this genre.
Aka: BLUT AN DEN LIPPEN; ERZEBETH; LA
ROUGE AUX LEVRES; LES LEVRES ROUGE;
PROMISE OF RED LIPS; RED LIPS, THE
HOR                      87 min (ort 96 min)
B,V                                  PRIME/CBS

## DAUGHTERS, DAUGHTERS **
Moshe Mizrahi         ISRAEL                1973
*Shai Ophir, Zarira Harifai, Joseph Shiloah*
Satire on Jewish family mores with a father who
wants a son getting nothing but daughters. Average.
Aka: ABU EL BANAT
COM                                            89 min
B,V                                              RNK

## DAVID AND GOLIATH *
Richard Pottier        ITALY                1960
*Orson Welles, Ivo Payer, Edward Hilton, Fernando
Baldi, Eleonora Rossi Drago, Giulia Rubini, Pierre
Cressoy, Furio Meniconi, Kronos, Dante Maggio, Luigi
Tosi, Umberto Fiz, Ugo Sasso, Carlo D'Angelo*
This less than brilliant attempt to turn the Biblical
story into an epic, is hampered by wooden acting and a
poor script – a mediocre and feeble effort.
Aka: DAVID E GOLIA
DRA                                            95 min
B,V                                              MEV

## DAVID AND GOLIATH **
                      USA                    1979
*Ted Cassidy, Jeff Corey, Roger Kern, John Dehner,
Hugh O'Brian, Daniel Travanti*
A competent if rather workmanlike rendition of this
biblical tale – one of several in the "Greatest Heroes of
the Bible" series.
DRA                                            41 min
B,V                                          VCL/CBS

## DAVID COPPERFIELD **
Alex Nicholas/Ian Mackenzie                   U
                                             1984
Fairly competent animated version of the famous
story.
Boa: novel by Charles Dickens.
CAR               -                            72 min
B,V                  RPTA/VSP; MSD (VHS only)

## DAVY CROCKETT ***
Norman Foster         USA                    1955
*Fess Parker, Buddy Ebsen, Basil Ruysdael, Hans
Conried, Nick Cravat, William Bakewell, Kenneth
Tobey*
Story of the famous Tennessee hunter and Indian
scout, who died during the fighting between Texas and
Mexico in the Battle of the Alamo. Originally made in
three 50 minute parts for a Disney TV show but later
released as a feature. A hugely enjoyable romp with
Parker making an admirable Crockett, and enjoying
numerous adventures in the company of his buddy
George Russel (Ebsen) before meeting his end at the
Alamo.
Aka: DAVID CROCKETT, KING OF THE WILD
FRONTIER
JUV                                      88 min mTV
B,V                                              WDV

## DAVY CROCKETT AND THE RIVER PIRATES ***
Norman Foster         USA                    1956
*Fess Parker, Buddy Ebsen, Jeff York, Kenneth Tobey,
Clem Bevans, Irvin Ashkenazy, Mort Mills, Paul
Newlan, Frank Richards, Walter Catlett, Douglas
Dumbrille, George Lewis, Troy Melton, Dick Crockett,
Hank Worden*
Feature film compiled from two TV shows. Our hero is
involved in a riverboat race in the first half and then
has to deal with Indian attacks in the second. A
lightweight fun film that provided a follow-up to
DAVY CROCKETT.
WES                                      81 min mTV
B,V                                              WDV

## DAWN OF THE MUMMY *
Frank Agrama      EGYPT/ITALY/USA           18
                                             1981
*Brenda King, Barry Sattels, George Peck, John Salvo,
Joan Levy, Diane Beatty, Victoria Johnson, Eileen
Falson*
A recently disturbed tomb in Egypt is used for a
fashion photographic session. This leads to our mum-
my going on the rampage, this time out to kill the
models involved – but you'll find it hard to care in this
yawn-inducing offering. The film was begun by
Armand Weston, but Agrama (who produced it) took
over.
HOR               87 min Cut (1 min 43 sec)
B,V                                        VSP; APX

## DAWN PATROL, THE ***
Edmund Goulding       USA                     U
                                             1938
*Errol Flynn, David Niven, Basil Rathbone, Donald
Crisp, Melville Cooper, Barry Fitzgerald, Carl Esmond*
An early remake of the 1930s classic, telling of the
exploits of a group of Royal Flying Corps officers
stationed in France during WW1. A solid wartime
action tale that uses much of the same footage as the
earlier film. Of the excellent cast, Rathbone as the
officer obliged to send up inexperienced flyers is
particularly memorable.

A/AD                          99 min (ort 103 min) B/W
V                                                    WHV

## DAWN: PORTRAIT OF A TEENAGE RUNAWAY* 15
Randal Kleiser           USA                         1976
*Eve Plumb, Bo Hopkins, Leigh J. McCloskey, George
Stanford Brown, Lynn Carlin, Marg DeLain, Joan
Prather, Anne Seymour, William Schallert, Anne
Ramsey*
A 15-year-old girl turns to prostitution when she is
unable to find a job after running away from home.
She discovers that life in L.A. can be really rough, in
this exploitative and superficial story. Followed by a
sequel entitled "Alexander: The Other Side Of Dawn".
DRA                                           100 min mTV
B,V                                          EMCO/VFP; HER

## DAWNING, THE **                                     PG
Robert Knights           UK                          1988
*Anthony Hopkins, Jean Simmons, Rebecca Pidgeon,
Trevor Howard, Hugh Grant, Tara MacGowran*
In Southern Ireland in 1920, an 18-year-old orphan
girl leaves her aunt and grandfather (Howard in his
last role), and comes to the aid of a mysterious
stranger she finds hiding in a beach hut. A well made
but rather strange drama of growing-up and change.
Boa: novel The Old Jest by Jennifer Johnston.
DRA                                                94 min
B,V                                                   MGM

## DAY AFTER, THE ***                                  15
Nicholas Meyer           USA                         1983
*Jason Robards, JoBeth Williams, Steve Guttenberg,
John Lithgow, John Cullum, Amy Madigan, Bibi
Besch, Lori Lethin, Jeff East, Georgann Johnson,
William Allen Young, Calvin Jung, Lin McCarthy,
Dennis Lipscomb, Clayton Day*
The effects of a full-scale nuclear war are seen
through the eyes of those living in a small Kansas
town. As a statement on the insanity of nuclear war
the film was a failure, for the effects of the war are so
sanitised as to leave no real trace of the true scale of
horror. Where the film is at its best is in the opening
stages, after which it's downhill all the way. See also
TESTAMENT and THE LAST WAR.
DRA                                           126 min mTV
B,V                                                   CBS

## DAY FOR NIGHT ***                                   PG
Francois Truffaut  FRANCE/ITALY                      1973
*Jacqueline Bisset, Valentina Cortese, Jean-Pierre
Leaud, Francois Truffaut, Jean-Pierre Aumont,
Alexandra Stewart*
This film, about the making of a romantic film in Nice,
cleverly explores all the behind-the-scenes clashes of
personality. Truffaut effectively plays himself. AA:
Foreign.
Aka: LA NUIT AMERICAINE
DRA                                                111 min
V                                                     WHV

## DAY OF JUDGEMENT, A **                            15/ʌ
C.D.H. Reynolds          USA                         1981
*William T. Hicks, Harris Bloodworth, Helen Tryon,
Careyanne Sutton, Carlton Bartell, Jerry Rushing,
Brownlee Davis*
A strange figure comes to a small town to punish the
inhabitants for their evil deeds in this routine chiller.
Aka: STORMBRINGER (TOW)
HOR          93 min (15 version); 100 min (18 version)
B,V                                                   TOW

## DAY OF THE ANIMALS **                               15
William Girdler          USA                         1977
*Christopher George, Leslie Nielsen, Richard Jaeckel,
Lynda Day George, Ruth Roman, Michael Ansara, Jon
Cedar, Paul Mantee, Walter Barnes, Susan Backlinie,
Andrew Stevens, Kathleen Bracken, Bobby Porter,
Michelle Stacy*

A bunch of campers out in the High Sierras find
themselves victims of attacks on the part of the
wildlife – depletion of the ozone layer having led to the
animals becoming crazed by excessive doses of the
sun's radiation. One by one the cast are killed off in a
feebly acted and dullish survival saga.
Aka: SOMETHING IS OUT THERE
DRA                                                98 min
B,V                                                   WHV

## DAY OF THE ASSASSIN **                              18
Brian Trenchard-Smith/Carlos Vasallo
                         AUSTRALIA                   1981
*Chuck Connors, Glenn Ford, Henry Silva, Richard
Roundtree, Andres Garcia, Jorge Rivero, Susana
Dosamantes*
The Shah of Iran's yacht is sabotaged and sunk,
taking to the bottom a vast treasure. Sundry adven-
turers gather and do battle over it but not, sadly, over
the cliched script.
THR                            96 min; 83 min (VIZ)
B,V                                         HEL L/A; VIZ

## DAY OF THE DEAD **                                  18
George Romero            USA                         1985
*Lori Cardile, Terry Alexander, Joseph Pilato, Jarlath
Conroy, Antone DiLeo Jr, Richard Liberty, Howard
Sherman*
Third and hopefully the last in a series of films that
tell of an Earth dominated by flesh-eating zombie
hordes. In this one a female scientist who's sheltering
with some army personnel in an underground bunker,
tries to study the creatures. A few heart-stopping
moments cannot compensate for sheer lack of ideas in
this wordy sequel. See also NIGHT OF THE LIVING
DEAD and ZOMBIES: DAWN OF THE DEAD.
HOR          96 min (ort 100 min) (Cut at film release)
B,V                                              MRD; EIV

## DAY OF THE DOLPHIN, THE **                          PG
Mike Nichols             USA                         1973
*George C. Scott, Trish Van Devere, Paul Sorvino, Fritz
Weaver, John Korkes, Edward Herrmann, John
Dehner*
A marine biologist who has spent his life working
with dolphins, and getting them to speak in the
process, discovers that one of his talking dolphins is
going to be used in a plot to assassinate the President
of the USA. A good idea spoilt by poor dialogue and
bad casting – Scott just does not convince. Scripted by
Buck Henry.
Boa: novel by Robert Merle.
DRA                                               104 min
B,V,LV                                 CBS; CH5 (VHS only)

## DAY OF THE EVIL GUN **                              PG
Jerry Thorpe             USA                         1968
*Glenn Ford, Arthur Kennedy, Dean Jagger, Paul Fix,
John Anderson, Nico Minardes, Royal Dano, (Harry)
Dean Stanton, Pilar Pellicer, Parley Baer, Barbara
Babcock, James J. Griffith*
Two bitter enemies join forces to rescue the wife and
kids of one of them, who have been abducted by
Indians. A big-budget outing with a few good mo-
ments but a routine script.
WES                                       90 min (ort 93 min)
B,V                                                   MGM

## DAY OF THE JACKAL **                                15
Fred Zinnemann    FRANCE/UK                          1973
*Edward Fox, Michel Lonsdale, Alan Badel, Eric
Porter, Donald Sinden, Timothy West, Jean Martin,
Tony Britton, Cyril Cusack, Delphine Seyrig, Derek
Jacobi, Ronald Pickup, Adrien Cayla-Legrand, Olga
Georges-Picot, Jean Sorel*
Incredibly wooden rendition of what could have been
quite gripping; the story of a lone killer who intends to
assassinate President de Gaulle, and the police opera-
tion that is mounted to prevent it. Interestingly, the

killer is shown getting a forged Danish passport but winds up with a name that could only be Swedish – Per Lundquist. So much for verisimilitude.
Boa: novel Day Of The Jackal by Frederick Forsyth.

| THR | 136 min (ort 142 min) |
| B,V | CIC |

## DAY OF THE PANTHER ** 18
Brian Trenchard-Smith
AUSTRALIA 1987
*Eddie Strazak, Linda Anderson, John Stanton, Jim Richards, Paris Jefferson, Michael Carman, Zale Daniel, Matthew Quartermaine*
A member of an elite martial arts unit goes on a revenge-seeking rampage after his female partner is killed. Followed by STRIKE OF THE PANTHER.

| A/AD | 83 min |
| B,V | GHV |

## DAY OF THE TRIFFIDS, THE * 15
Steve Sekely UK 1962
*Howard Keel, Janette Scott, Nicole Maurey, Kieron Moore, Mervyn Johns, Ewan Roberts, Alison Leggatt, Janita Faye, Alexander Knox, Geoffrey Matthews, Gilgi Hauser, Carol Ann Ford*
Plodding workmanlike adaptation of a science fiction tale about what happens when the world, with the bulk of humanity rendered blind, is taken over by semi-intelligent plants.
Boa: novel The Day Of The Triffids by John Wyndham.

| FAN | 94 min |
| B,V | QUA/VSP; CH5 (VHS only) |

## DAY OF THE WOLVES **
Ferde Grofe Jr USA 1972
*Richard Egan, Martha Hyer, Rick Jason, Jan Murray*
An ex-sheriff does battle with a gang of trained killers, who want to isolate a town for three days in order to pull off a perfect crime. An unusual and quite enjoyable thriller.
Osca: GANG BUSTERS

| THR | 87 min |
| B,V | KVD |

## DAY OF VIOLENCE **
ITALY
*Daria Norman, Mario Antoni, Ely Galleani*
Two young delinquents break every rule in the book and are hotly pursued by the police, in this deservedly obscure Italian crime thriller.

| THR | 120 min |
| B,V,V2 | VPD |

## DAY THE EARTH CAUGHT FIRE, THE ***
Val Guest UK 1961
*Edward Judd, Janet Munro, Leo McKern, Michael Goodliffe, Bernard Braden, Reginald Beckwith, Gene Anderson, Rene Asherson, Arthur Christianson, Austin Trevor, Edward Underdown*
A neat, low-key tale of the Earth being knocked off its axis by nuclear weapons tests, with a resultant rise in temperature that threatens all life. Unusual touch is that it is related through journalists and is sometimes too wordy on that account. Scripted by Wolf Mankowitz and Val Guest.

| FAN | 99 min B/W |
| B,V,V2 | INT/CBS |

## DAY THE EARTH MOVED, THE **
Robert Michael Lewis USA 1974
*Jackie Cooper, Stella Stevens, Cleavon Little, William Windom, Beverly Garland, Lucille Benson, Tammy Harrington, Kelly Thordsen, Ellen Blake, E.J. Andre, Sid Melton, Don Steele*
A pilot and a photographer discover a way of predicting earthquakes, but nobody will listen to their warning about a small town threatened by one, until it is almost too late. A fairly yawn-inducing treatment

of what might have been a rather good thriller.
Boa: story by Jack Turley.

| THR | 78 min mTV |
| B,V | GHV |

## DAY THE EARTH STOOD STILL, THE ***
Robert Wise USA 1951
*Michael Rennie, Patricia Neal, Hugh Marlowe, Billy Gray, Sam Jaffe, Lock Martin, Frances Bavier*
A well made and enjoyable film about an alien who arrives on Earth, to offer mankind the benefit of his race's wisdom, in the form of a powerful robot that can end all wars by punishing aggressors. Shot upon landing, he escapes from custody and hides out in a boarding house, befriending the young son of one of the lodgers. A rarity – an intelligent science fiction film. The script is by Edmund H. North and the score is by Bernard Herrmann.
Boa: story Farewell To The Master by Harry Bates.

| FAN | 88 min (ort 92 min) B/W |
| V/h | VDM |

## DAY THE EIFFEL TOWER RAN AWAY, THE
FRANCE
The Eiffel Tower gets lonely and goes off to meet other famous landmarks such as Big Ben, The Statue of Liberty etc. in a cute French animation.

| CAR | 56 min |
| B,V | VDM |

## DAY THE LOVING STOPPED, THE ** PG
Daniel Mann USA 1981
*Dennis Weaver, Valerie Harper, Dominique Dunne, James Canning, Ally Sheedy, Sam Groom, Stacey Glick*
Two young girls are in for a rough time when their parents decide to get divorced, in this sincere but cliched examination of the emotional trauma attached to divorce.

| DRA | 95 min (ort 104 min) mTV |
| B,V | VIDFOR; HER |

## DAY TIME ENDED, THE **
John (Bud) Cardos USA 1978
*Chris Mitchum, Jim Davis, Dorothy Malone, Marcy Lafferty, Scott Kolden, Natasha Ryan*
Strange things happen to a family whose remote house in the desert slips into another dimension, in this badly scripted mishmash of a fantasy. The reason for this happening is never made clear, and although the special effects of David Allen work well, the basic illogicality of the film serves only to undermine it.
Aka: VORTEX

| FAN | 80 min |
| B,V,V2 | INT/CBS L/A; HER |

## DAYBREAKERS, THE ***
Robert Totten USA 1979
*Glenn Ford, Tom Selleck, Sam Elliot, Jeffrey Osterhage, Ben Johnson, Gilbert Roland, John Vernon, Ruth Roman, Jack Elam, Gene Evans, L.Q. Jones, Paul Koslo, Mercedes McCambridge, Slim Pickens, Pat Buttram, James Gammon*
An overlong rambling Western saga, based on two Louis L'Amour novels and telling the tale of three brothers who set out to tame the post-Civil War West, seeking their fortunes and avenging a murder out in New Mexico. The first TV adaptation of L'Amour's work and the first half of the complete feature; the other section being known as "The Shadow Riders".
Aka: LOUIS L'AMOUR'S THE SACKETTS; SACKETTS, THE
Boa: novels The Daybreakers and Sackett by Louis L'Amour.

| WES | 106 min (ort 120 min) mTV |
| B,V | HOK |

## DAYDREAMER, THE *** U
Jules Bass USA 1966

*Ray Bolger, Jack Gilford, Margaret Hamilton, Paul O'Keefe. Voices of: Boris Karloff, Tallulah Bankhead, Burl Ives, Terry-Thomas, Victor Borge, Patty Duke, Hayley Mills*
A partly animated story of Hans Christian Anderson, who as a 13-year-old boy, meets many of the characters he is later to write about in his stories. A pleasant and warm-hearted kid's outing.

| JUV | | 94 min (ort 98 min) |
| B,V | | EHE; CH5 (VHS only) |

## DAYS OF HEAVEN *** PG
Terrence Malick    USA    1978
*Richard Gere, Brooke Adams, Sam Shepard, Linda Manz, Robert Wilke, Jackie Shultis, Stuart Margolin*
The story of a love triangle involving three young immigrants, from Chicago to the wheatfields of the mid-West. An engrossing and visually satisfying slice of early 20th century life, spoilt by a tendency towards symbolism. Shown originally in 70 mm; unfortunately TV will tend to minimise the fine photography of Alemandros. AA: Cin (Nestor Alemandros).

| DRA | 91 min |
| B,V,V2 | CIC |

## DAYS OF HELL ** 15
Anthony Richmond (Antonio Riccamonza)
ITALY    1985
*Conrad Nichols, Richard Raymond, Steve Elliott, Lawrence Richmond, Howard Ross, Kiwaku Havado*
Four skilled combat experts are given the task of rescuing a doctor and his daughter in Afghanistan, and have to face hostile Iranian rebels on their way there.

| A/AD | 88 min (ort 90 min) |
| B,V | MOG |

## DAYS OF THUNDER ** 15
Tony Scott    USA    1990
*Tom Cruise, Nicole Kidman, Robert Duvall, Randy Quaid, Cary Elwes, Michael Rooker, Fred Dalton Thompson*
From the makers of TOP GUN comes this similar film that takes a noisy, shallow and cliched tale, set in the world of stock car racing, with our obligatory kid from nowhere out to prove that he's the best. Good racing sequences are interspersed with the usual romantic sub-plot. The script is by Cruise and Robert Towne.

| A/AD | 103 min (ort 107 min) |
| V | CIC/CBSDIS |

## DAYTON'S DEVILS ** 
Jack Shea    USA    1968
*Rory Calhoun, Leslie Nielsen, Lainie Kazan, Hans Gudegast (Eric Braeden), Barry Sadler*
A gang plans to steal a two million dollar payroll from an Air Force base, being trained for this purpose by a former US Army colonel. Forgettable heist movie.

| A/AD | 103 min |
| B,V | VFP |

## DE SADE *
Cy Enderfield
USA/WEST GERMANY    1969
*Keir Dullea, Senta Berger, Lillie Palmer, Anna Massey, John Huston*
Fictionalised biography of the famous French writer who has become a victim of his own undeserved reputation. Don't expect anything stimulating, this is very dull stuff indeed.
Boa: novel by G. Lely.

| DRA | 113 min |
| B,V | RNK |

## DEAD AND BURIED ***
Gary A. Sherman    USA    1981
*James Farentino, Melody Anderson, Jack Albertson, Dennis Redfield, Nancy Locke Hauser, Lisa Blount*
Strange murders in a New England town become even

weirder when the dead come back to life in a seaside fishing town. Farentino plays the sheriff who has the task of coping with this. A bizarre and chilling horror yarn.

| HOR | 91 min |
| B,V | TEVP |

## DEAD BANG * 18
John Frankenheimer    USA    1988
*Don Johnson, Penelope Ann Miller, William Forsythe, Bob Balaban, Tim Reid, Frank Military, Tate Donovan, Michael Higgins, Evan Evans*
A Los Angeles homicide detective tracks down a cop killer, and uncovers a group of white supremacists in this factual but unpleasant effort.

| A/AD | 102 min |
| V | GHV |

## DEAD CALM *** 15
Phillip Noyce    USA    1989
*Sam Neill, Nicole Kidman, Billy Zane, Rod Mullinar*
A claustrophobic thriller set on the open seas. A couple go sailing in a bid to come to terms with the death of their young son in a road accident. When they spot a man in a dinghy who claims to be the remaining survivor of a bout of food poisoning onboard a nearby schooner, they pick him up and the husband rows out to investigate. Not a plausible film, but one that maintains a good sense of tension.

| THR | 92 min |
| V/sh | WHV |

## DEAD CAN'T LIE, THE ** 15
Lloyd Fonvielle    USA    1988
*Tommy Lee Jones, Virginia Madsen, Colin Bruce, Kevin Jarre, Denise Stephenson, Frederic Forrest*
A seedy private eye is hired by a wealthy man who, wants to get the ghost of his late wife to stop pestering him for money. A bizarre and unusual effort, often quite funny but a little too disjointed to really work.
Aka: GOTHAM

| HOR | 94 min (ort 100 min) mCab |
| V/sh | PATHE |

## DEAD EASY ** 18
Bert Deling    AUSTRALIA    1982
*Scott Burgess, Rosemary Paul, Max Phipps, Tim McKenzie*
A hustling prostitute and a policeman are caught up in a ruthless gang war triggered off by a hate-filled small-time bookie.

| DRA | 82 min (ort 92 min) Cut (31 sec) |
| B,V | VES/PVG |

## DEAD END **** PG
William Wyler    USA    1937
*Sylvia Sidney, Joel McCrea, Humphrey Bogart, Claire Trevor, Wendy Barrie, Marjorie Main, Huntz Hall, Leo Gorcey, Gabriel Dell, Ward Bond, Billy Halop, Bernard Punsley, Allen Jenkins*
Excellent study of slum life in New York, with Bogart playing a hoodlum who gets involved with a gang of street kids on a trip back to see his mother and girlfriend. The first film to introduce the "Dead End Kids" who appeared in the original Broadway production and later played in the classic ANGELS WITH DIRTY FACES. Scripted by Lillian Hellman with sets designed by Richard Day.
Aka: DEAD END: CRADLE OF CRIME
Boa: play by Sidney Kingsley.

| DRA | 88 min (ort 92 min) B/W |
| V | VGM |

## DEAD END CITY * 18
Peter Yuval    USA    1988
*Robert Z'dar, Dennis Cole, Gregg Cummins*
Vigilantes take on a vicious street gang, that has taken control of a city and imposed a reign of fear, in this action tale set in the near future. A murky and

laboured effort that doesn't even succeed as mindless entertainment.

A/AD 82 min (ort 90 min)
B,V AIP; BRAVE

## DEAD END DRIVE-IN ** 18
Brian Trenchard-Smith
AUSTRALIA 1985
*Ned Manning, Natalie McCurry, Peter Whitford, Wilbur Wilde, Ollie Hall, Jim Karangis, Lyn Collingwood, Nikki McWatters, Melissa Davis*
Silly, futuristic spoof revolving around the use of drive-in movie theatres as internment camps for society's outcasts, such as the ill and unemployed. Our hero is not content to stay in one and decides to break out.

FAN 87 min (ort 92 min) Cut (16 sec)
B,V NWV

## DEAD END STREET **
Yaki Yosha ISRAEL 1983
*Anath Atzmon, Yehoram Gaon, Gila Almager*
A TV producer asks a young prostitute for help in making a documentary. When broadcast it leads to tragedy for her. Average melodrama.
Aka: KVISH LELO MOTZA

DRA 86 min
B,V RNK

## DEAD HEAT * 18
Mark Goldblatt USA 1988
*Treat Williams, Joe Piscopo, Lindsay Frost, Darren McGavin, Vincent Price, Keye Luke, Clare Kirkconnell*
Two cops stumble on a lab that is creating zombie criminals, in this repulsive and dim-witted effort.

HOR 84 min
V NWV

## DEAD HEAT ** PG
Stefano Ferrari 1986
*Peter Lawrence, Donald Pleasence, Rochelle Redfield*
The son of a famous jockey comes to Italy to learn the truth about his father's death, but once there gets involved in an investigation into a smuggling ring. Average.

THR 83 min
B,V RCA

## DEAD MAN OUT *** 15
Richard Pearce USA 1989
*Danny Glover, Ruben Blades, Tom Atkins*
In keeping with a Supreme Court ruling that insane criminals cannot be executed, a psychiatrist is assigned to a Death Row prisoner who has gone mad whilst awaiting execution. This presents him with a difficult dilemma, since to cure him would be to sign his death warrant. An absorbing and literate drama that examines a thought-provoking issue with both skill and respect.

DRA 90 min mCab
V CASVIS

## DEAD MAN WALKING ** 18
Gregory Brown USA 1987
*Wings Hauser, Brion James, Jeffrey Combs, Pamela Ludwig*
Science fiction fantasy set in a post-plague world of the future where the population has been decimated. Hauser, though slowly dying of the disease himself, penetrates a plague-ridden stronghold to rescue a wealthy industrialist and his daughter from kidnappers. An unpleasant film to watch, though a few touches of satire make it slightly more palatable.

HOR 86 min (ort 90 min) Cut (25 sec)
B,V CINE

## DEAD MAN'S FLOAT *
Peter Sharp AUSTRALIA 1980
*Sally Boyden, Greg Rowe, Jacqui Gordon, Rick Ireland, Bill Hunter, Sue Jones, John Heywood*

Three children on their summer holidays become accidentally involved with drug smugglers, in this fast-paced but totally forgettable adventure.

A/AD 70 min
B,V,V2 VUL

## DEAD MAN'S FOLLY * PG
Clive Donner USA 1985
*Peter Ustinov, Jean Stapleton, Tim Pigott-Smith, Constance Cummings, Susan Wooldridge, Jonathan Cecil, Christopher Guard, Nicollette Sheridan, Jeff Yagher*
Another Agatha Christie whodunnit set (as always) in an English manor house. This one stars Ustinov as the famous sleuth "Hercule Poirot" who gets involved in a series of real murders that take place in the course of a "murder hunt" party being held by an American novelist. As tiresome as it is contrived.
Aka: AGATHA CHRISTIE'S DEAD MAN'S FOLLY
Boa: novel Dead Man's Folly by Agatha Christie.

DRA 90 min (ort 100 min) mTV
V/h WHV

## DEAD MEN DON'T DIE * PG
Malcolm Marmorsten USA 1990
*Elliott Gould, Melissa Anderson, Mark Moses, Philip Bruns, Jack Betts, Mabel King*
A TV news reporter is shot dead while investigating a story of drug dealers working from one of the company offices. However, he is brought back to life by his voodoo-practicing cleaning-lady. This sparks off a series of bizarre events in this inept and childish comedy. The script is by Marmorsten.

COM 84 min
V NWV

## DEAD MEN DON'T WEAR PLAID * PG
Carl Reiner USA 1982
*Steve Martin, Rachel Ward, Carl Reiner, Reni Santoni, George Gaynes, Frank McCarthy*
A private eye spoof, with a weak story helped slightly by clips from old 1940s thrillers. A kind of homage to the films of that period, but after the first five minutes the joke begins to wear thin. This was the last film for famed costume designer Edith Head.

COM 88 min; 84 min (CIC) B/W
B, V/h, V2 RNK; CIC (VHS only)

## DEAD OF NIGHT, THE ** 18
Deryn Warren USA 1987
*Julie Merrill, Kuri Browne, John Reno, J.K. Dumont*
A shy and innocent young girl who is afraid of men, dabbles in the occult when she comes across a book of ancient voodoo magic. This results in her body becoming possessed by the evil Empress Sura.

HOR 85 min
B,V MED

## DEAD OF WINTER *** 15
Arthur Penn USA 1987
*Mary Steenburgen, Roddy McDowall, Jan Rubes, William Russ, Ken Pogue, Wayne Robson, Mark Malone*
A gripping damsel-in-distress type thriller in which Steenburgen plays three parts. Her main role is that of an actress who's so desperate to obtain work, that she allows herself to be lured to a house where she has to give the performance of her life to avoid being killed. Predictable – but the tension never lets up. Based to some extent on a 1940s film "My Name Is Julia Rose".

THR 96 min
B,V MGM

## DEAD OR ALIVE ** 15
John Guillermin USA 1988
*Kris Kristofferson, Mark Moses, Scott Wilson, David Huddleston, Don Swayze*

A legendary gunfighter is trying to forget his violent past and make a new life for himself. However, a gang of crooks, led by a religious fanatic, break out of jail and go on a destructive rampage, forcing him to confront them.

WES                                            98 min
B,V                                            BRAVE

**DEAD PIGEON ON BEETHOVEN STREET *** 15**
Samuel Fuller    WEST GERMANY              1972
*Glenn Corbett, Christa Lang, Sieghardt Rupp, Anton Diffring, Alex D'Arcy, Anthony Ching, Eric P. Caspar*
An account of an American private detective in Bonn on a mission, and full of oblique references to other films of this genre. An enjoyable and rather tongue-in-cheek thriller.

THR                                            86 min
B,V                                            TEVP

**DEAD POETS SOCIETY ***                      PG**
Peter Weir              USA                    1989
*Robin Williams, Robert Sean Leonard, Ethan Hawke, Josh Charles, Gale Hansen, Dylan Kussman, Allelon Ruggiero, James Waterston, Norman Lloyd, Kurtwood Smith*
Set at a stuffy New England prep school in the 1950s, where a newly-arrived and unconventional English teacher inculcates a love of poetry and intellectual debate among his students, but not always with the most appropriate results. Melodramatic and over-wrought, but an impressive performance from Williams gives this contrived film its charm. AA: Screen (Orig) (Tom Schulman).

DRA                           110 min (ort 128 min)
V                                              TOUCH

**DEAD POOL, THE ***                           ***
Buddy Van Horn          USA                    1988
*Clint Eastwood, Patricia Clarkson, Evan C. Kim, Liam Neeson, David Hunt, Michael Currie, Michael Goodwin*
The fifth DIRTY HARRY movie in the series, has our tough police detective investigating a strange hit-list, with murder victims apparently linked to a bizarre bet among the members of a film crew. This well-tried formula puts our tough cop through his paces once more, in a predictable and well made thriller. Eastwood's screen persona as Harry Callahan does make it watchable for all that.

THR                           88 min (ort 91 min)
V/sh                                           WHV

**DEAD RECKONING **                            PG**
John Cromwell           USA                    1947
*Humphrey Bogart, Lizabeth Scott, Morris Carnovsky, William Prince, Wallace Ford, Charles Cane, Marvin Miller, James Bell*
Two WW2 veterans are on their way to Washington to be decorated when one of them disappears and is found murdered. Bogart as the tough ex-soldier investigating the death of his partner is excellent, but this is an example of film noir at its most opaque; a lighter touch was needed.

DRA                     96 min (ort 100 min) B/W
V                                              RCA

**DEAD RECKONING ***                           18**
Robert Michael Lewis    USA                    1989
*Rick Springfield, Cliff Robertson, Susan Blakely*
Tense thriller set on a yacht, with a wealthy man and his attractive younger wife taking a cruise in the company of a hired hand, who just happens to be the woman's old boyfriend.

THR                                            91 min
V                                     CIC/CBSDIS

**DEAD RINGER ***                              PG**
Paul Henreid            USA                    1964
*Bette Davis, Karl Malden, Peter Lawford, Philip*

*Carey, Estelle Winwood, Jean Hagen, George Macready, Cyril Delevanti*
Davis plays twin sisters, with the nasty one bearing a long-term grudge over a man and shooting her other half to settle the score. The remaining twin now takes over her erstwhile sister's identity, and hatches a complicated scheme to have her revenge against the man she feels wronged her. The implausible plot doesn't matter, this is Davis' film all the way. Remade for TV as "The Killer In The Mirror".

THR                     111 min (ort 115 min) B/W
V                                              WHV

**DEAD RINGERS ***                             18**
David Cronenberg        CANADA                 1988
*Jeremy Irons, Genevieve Bujold, Heidi Von Palleske, Barbara Gordon, Shirley Douglas, Stephen Lack*
A disquieting psychological thriller revolving round twin brothers (Irons in both roles) who work as doctors running a gynaecological clinic. They share every experience in life until a woman comes between them and disturbs a hitherto cosy set-up. Said to be based on a true story.

THR                           110 min (ort 117 min)
V                                              CBS

**DEAD TROUBLE **                              15**
Bill Norton             USA                    1989
*John Schneider, Paul Rodriguez, Susan Walters*
A former cop now working as a bounty hunter is offered a large sum to capture a dangerous jail breaker, but finds that his rival is also working on the case. However, when the baby of his latest girlfriend is kidnapped, our two bounty hunters join forces. A fairly mindless blend of humour and mayhem, followed by a sequel.

COM                                            90 min
V                                              NWV

**DEAD TROUBLE 2 **                            PG**
Bill L. Norton          USA                    1989
*John Schneider, Paul Rodriguez*
A production-line sequel to the first film that has our duo of modern bounty hunters swinging into action in a fast-paced comedy that makes the most of its shallow good-guys-chase-bad-guys plot.

COM                                            88 min
V/h                                            NWV

**DEAD WRONG **                                15**
Len Kowalewich          CANADA                 1982
*Britt Ekland, Winston Rekert, Jackson Davies*
Story of a gang that agrees to smuggle dope into Canada, but finds that the cargo is really cocaine and that an undercover agent is involved. Average.
Aka: COLUMBIA CONNECTION, THE; ENTRAPMENT (KRP)

THR                           93 min (ort 100 min)
B,V,V2                                  FILV; KRP

**DEAD ZONE, THE ***                           15**
David Cronenberg        USA                    1983
*Christopher Walken, Tom Skerritt, Herbert Lom, Martin Sheen, Brooke Adams, Anthony Zerbe, Colleen Dewhurst, Nicholas Campbell, Jackie Burroughs*
A man awakens after a four-year coma to discover that he has psychic powers with which he can predict the future. He drifts through life becoming a recluse, but is galvanised into action when he discovers that a man running for the Senate will one day initiate a nuclear war as US President. A film that mixes despair with tension, with Walken giving a performance of anguished sincerity. Abridged before video submission by 13 sec.
Boa: novel by Stephen King.

THR                                            99 min
B,V                                            TEVP

**DEAD-TIME STORIES: VOLUME 1 ***                18
Phillip Noyce/Carl Schenkel
                    CANADA                    1985
*Harry Hamlin, Deborah Lacey, Michael O'Keefe,*
*Jennifer Cooke, Tom Skerritt*
Three horror mystery tales: "The Curse", "Man's Best
Friend" and "True Believer". In the first a cop
investigates a haunted convent, in the second a man
exploits the savage nature of a dog and in the third
(the best tale) a callous landlord gets his just deserts
when he fails to repair a dangerous staircase. An
uninspired collection.
Aka: DEAD TIME STORIES
HOR                                        88 min mCab
B,V                                        IVS; BRAVE

**DEAD-TIME STORIES: VOLUME 2 ****                18
Ivan Nagy/Richard Rothstein
                    CANADA                    1987
*Shannon Tweed, Linda Smith, Gregg Henry, Audrey*
*Landers, Judy Landers, Bruce Greenwood, Alexandra*
*Stewart*
A trilogy of short horror tales – "Shattered Vows",
"Video Date" and "Split Decisions" – the last tale
telling of a young estate agent's experiences at the
hands of a pair of beautiful twins, who are in the habit
of dividing up everything they enjoy. As before, a fair
set of horror tales constrained by the short nature of
each story.
Aka: SCREAM SHOW (CINE)
HOR                                        72 min mCab
B,V                        CINE; BRAVE; VCC (VHS only)

**DEAD-TIME STORIES: VOLUME 3 ****                18
David Wickes/Paul Verhoeven
                    CANADA                    1986
*Robert Vaughn, Peter Coyote, Klaus Kinski, Sybil*
*Danning*
Three more variable quality tales of horror – "Face To
Face" looks at the experiences of an egocentric
cosmetic surgeon, "Last Scene" tells of an ambitious
director and "Love Sounds" is the tale of a virtuoso
musician.
Aka: DEAD EVEN (PACEV)
HOR                                        90 min mCab
B,V                        PACEV; VCC (VHS only)

**DEAD, THE *****                                U
John Huston
            UK/USA/WEST GERMANY            1987
*Angelica Huston, Donal McCann, Marie Kean, Donel*
*Donnelly, Helena Carroll, Cathleen Delany, Ingrid*
*Craigie, Rachael Dowling, Dan O'Herlihy, Frank*
*Patterson, Maria McDermottroe, Sean McClory,*
*Katherine O'Toole*
John Huston's last film as director is a slow, leisurely
and well-crafted look at the lives and hopes of family
and friends, gathered at a dinner party to celebrate
the Epiphany in Dublin of 1904. The insubstantial
nature of the narrative is less than important –
farewells are exchanged between the guests at the
film's end, toasts are drunk to absent friends and this
great director makes this film a fitting farewell of his
own.
Boa: short story by James Joyce.
DRA                                79 min (ort 83 min)
B,V                                            VES

**DEADLIEST SEASON, THE ****
Robert Markowitz        USA                    1977
*Michael Moriarty, Kevin Conway, Meryl Streep, Sully*
*Boyar, Jill Eikenberry, Walter McGinn, Andrew*
*Duggan, Patrick O'Neal, Mason Adams*
A brutal ice hockey player builds up a reputation for
viciousness, but goes too far when he injures another
player so badly he is charged with manslaughter. An
absorbing but violent drama. This was Streep's first
film role. Scripted by Ernest Kinoy.

DRA                                        98 min mTV
B,V                                            VFP

**DEADLINE ****                                18
Mario Azzopardi        CANADA                    1979
*Stephen Young, Sharon Masters, Cindy Hind,*
*Marvin Goldhar*
A horror film screenwriter, working on the ultimate in
terror movies, fails to see that his life is beginning to
resemble the scripts he writes, until the breakdown of
his family life leads to tragedy.
HOR                                        90 min
B,V                                AVP L/A; MPV

**DEADLINE AT DAWN ****
Harold Clurman        USA                    1946
*Susan Hayward, Paul Lukas, Bill Williams, Joseph*
*Calleia, Osa Massen, Lola Lane, Jerome Cowan,*
*Steven Geray*
A young sailor enjoying his shore leave in New York,
finds himself suspected of a murder in this confused
thriller. Hayward plays a woman who attempts to
clear him. Clurman's only film as director, with the
script adapted from the Woolrich novel by Clifford
Odets.
Boa: novel by William Irish (Cornell Woolrich). Osca:
STAGECOACH
THR                                        80 min B/W
B,V                                            KVD

**DEADLINE: MADRID ***                            PG
John Patterson        USA                    1987
*Leigh Lawson, Brynn Thayer, Joe Santos, J. Kenneth*
*Campbell, Andrew Rubin, Neva Patterson, Charles*
*Cioffi, Marta Dubois, Miriam Colon*
A foreign correspondent working in Madrid decides to
expose the work of a famine relief organisation that
has been supplying arms, and obtains a little help
from her former lover, a photo-journalist. Dull pilot
for a failed series.
Aka: DEADLINE MADRID
THR                            90 min (ort 100 min) mTV
B,V                                            CIC

**DEADLOCK ****                                15
James Dodson        USA                    1988
*Steffen Gregory Foster, Jeremy Slate, James Hong,*
*Ken Abraham, Maureen McVey, Karl Heinz Tauber*
Terrorists storm the compound of an arms supplier are
all killed, except for one, who takes two people
hostage. As he waits for the inevitable showdown, the
terrorist discovers that the arms supplier had a more
sinister operation.
A/AD                                87 min (ort 95 min)
B,V                                            CINE

**DEADLY ADDICTION ***                            18
Jack Vacek        USA                    1989
*Joseph Jennings, Michael Robbin, Alan Shearer, Trice*
*Schubert, Jack Vacek*
A Californian cop who uses unconventional methods
to tackle drug dealers takes in a young boy involved in
running drugs. The two eventually develop a close
relationship as the cop sets out to nail the local drug
baron. A dull film whose occasional car chases offer
some momentary relief. Written by Vacek.
A/AD                                        86 min
V                                            VES

**DEADLY AFFAIR, THE ****                        15
Sidney Lumet        UK                    1966
*James Mason, Maximilian Schell, Harriet Anderson,*
*Harry Andrews, Simone Signoret, Roy Kinnear,*
*Kenneth Haigh, Lynn Redgrave, Max Adrian, Robert*
*Fleming, Leslie Sands, Corin Redgrave, Les White,*
*June Murphy, David Warner*
Following the death of a Foreign Official official, an
agent refuses to believe the simple explanation of
suicide and eventually uncovers a complex espionage

intrigue. A bleak and murky spy thriller, that is sluggish in its development but takes great pains to generate a suitably sordid atmosphere. The script is by Paul Dehn.
Boa: novel Call For The Dead by John Le Carre.
THR                              102 min (ort 106 min)
V                                                 RCA

## DEADLY BLESSING **                          18
Wes Craven              USA                    1981
*Maren Jensen, Susan Buckner, Ernest Borgnine,*
*Sharon Stone, Lois Nettleton, Jeff East, Lisa Hartman*
A strict religious sect in Pennsylvania is the scene for a sequence of gruesome murders that are eventually found to be the work of an incubus. A not altogether successful attempt at a Gothic horror yarn, that's basically no more than a series of nasty shocks, as the murderous creature goes about its business. However, Borgnine gives a compelling performance as a sinister member of the community on whom suspicion first falls.
HOR                                            98 min
B,V,V2            SPEC/POLY; CH5 (VHS only)

## DEADLY BREED *                              18
Charles T. Kanganis    USA                    1989
*William Smith, Addison Randall, Blake Bahner,*
*Mitchell Berger, Joe Vance, Rhonda Grey*
A disagreeable and shallow re-working of an idea explored in MAGNUM FORCE, but this time round our maverick vigilante cops are all members of a violent neo-Nazi cult.
A/AD                                           90 min
V                                                CINE

## DEADLY CARE *                               15
David Anspaugh         USA                     1987
*Cheryl Ladd, Jason Miller, Jennifer Salt, Belinda*
*Balaski, Peggy McKay, Ann Hearn, Silvana Gallardo,*
*Richard Evans, Joe Dorsey*
A stressed nurse working in an intensive-care unit, develops a dangerous dependency on drink and drugs in order to cope with the pressures of her job. Ladd is seriously miscast in this failed attempt to address what has become a serious social issue. Well below average.
DRA                                    90 min mTV
B,V                                               CIC

## DEADLY CHASE **
Franco Prosperi        ITALY                   1978
*Luc Merenda, Janet Agren, Maria Baxa*
The story of an unorthodox police inspector who investigates a series of violent crimes that have been masterminded by a baron. Fairly typical Continental crime story of little memorability.
Aka: IL COMMISSARIO VERRAZZANO
DRA                                            90 min
B,V,V2                                           VPD

## DEADLY DECEPTIONS ***                       15
John Llewellyn Moxey
                       USA                     1987
*Matt Salinger, Lisa Eilbacher, Bonnie Bartlett,*
*Mildred Natwick, James Noble, Christopher Allport,*
*Robert Harper*
A psychological drama that examines the inability of a man to come to terms with the apparent suicide of his wife, whilst at the same time conducting a frantic search for his missing baby son, presumed dead. Well made and taut, with Natwick giving a splendid performance in a one-scene cameo.
Aka: DEADLY DECEPTION
DRA                           88 min (ort 100 min) mTV
B,V                                               CBS

## DEADLY DREAMS ***                           18
Kristine Peterson      USA                     1988

*Mitchell Anderson, Juliette Cummins, Xander*
*Berkeley*
A writer is haunted by the brutal murder of his parents and becomes convinced the killer is out to get him too. A set of neat plot twists and careful direction help make the most of this horror-thriller's low budget.
THR                              76 min (ort 79 min)
V                                                CINE

## DEADLY EMBRACE *                            18
Ellen Cabot            USA                     1988
*Jan-Michael Vincent, Jack Carter, Ty Randolph,*
*Linnea Quigley, Michelle Bauer, Ken Abraham*
A wealthy man wishes to ditch his mentally ill wife but she has other plans. When the husband engages a new houseboy in order to entice her into a relationship that will give him grounds for divorce, she is driven over the edge into violence. A cheap exercise in titillation that was promoted as an erotic thriller, but is neither thrilling nor erotic.
THR                                            90 min
V                                                CINE

## DEADLY FORCE *                              18
Paul Aaron             USA                     1983
*Wings Hauser, Joyce Ingalls, Paul Shenar, Al Ruscio,*
*Arlen Dean Snyder, Lincoln Kilpatrick*
An ex-cop is on the trail of a psychotic killer who has killed 17 times. He is harassed by a former colleague and has problems trying to get together again with his wife. Mediocre rubbish that contains just about every cliche going.
THR                                            92 min
B,V                                               EHE

## DEADLY FRIEND **                            18
Wes Craven             USA                     1986
*Matthew Laborteaux, Anne Twomey, Kristy Swanson,*
*Michael Sharrett, Richard Marcus, Anne Ramsey,*
*Russ Martin, Lee Paul, Andrew Roperto, Robin*
*Nyuen, Frank Cavastani, Merritt Olsen, William H.*
*Faeth, Joel Hile*
The robot creation of a young genius is destroyed, and his girlfriend is accidentally killed by her violent father. He decides to implant his robot's brain in the body of his dead friend, thereby re-animating her. The results are far from what he expected, in this laughable but perversely entertaining shocker.
Boa: novel Friend by Diana Henstell.
HOR                                            87 min
B,V                                               WHV

## DEADLY GAME ***                             PG
Marshall Brickmann     USA                     1986
*John Lithgow, Christopher Collett, Cynthia Nixon, Jill*
*Eikenberry, John Mahoney, Paul Austin, Sully Boyar*
A precocious kid steals some plutonium from a top-secret plant and builds his own nuclear reactor to show how smart he is. Needless to say, the security authorities do not see it this way and he soon finds himself in trouble. A slick and well acted effort, but one that inevitably annoys by its very lack of responsibility, with our irritating kid ready to risk a nuclear catastrophe just to make a point.
Aka: MANHATTAN PROJECT, THE;
MANHATTAN PROJECT, THE: THE DEADLY GAME
A/AD                             108 min (ort 120 min)
V                                                WHV

## DEADLY GAME, THE **                         PG
Lane Slate             USA                     1977
*Andy Griffith, Mitzi Hoag, Claude Earl Jones, Sharon*
*Spelman, James Cromwell, Hunter Von Leer, Dan*
*O'Herlihy, Rebecca Balding, Morgan Woodward,*
*Eddie Foy Jr, Fran Ryan, Med Flory, John Perak,*
*Steffen Zacharias*
A small-town sheriff races against time to prevent

death and injury when a tanker carrying nerve gas is ambushed. A sequel to THE GIRL IN THE EMPTY GRAVE. Average.

THR                          90 min (ort 100 min) mTV
B,V                                              MGM

## DEADLY GAMES **
Scott Mansfield          USA                       1979
*Sam Groom, Steve Railsback, Jo Ann Harris, Denise Galik, Dick Butkus, June Lockhart, Alexandra Morgan, Colleen Camp, Christine Tudor*
A maniacal masked killer stalks attractive women in a small town, playing deadly games with his victims in this remarkably unmoving horror tale, whose title refers to a video game played by some of the characters. The final stupid resolution is a fitting comment on the whole.
Aka: ELIMINATOR, THE
HOR                                              92 min
B,V,V2                                         INT/CBS

## DEADLY HERO ***                                   18
Ivan Nagy               USA                       1976
*Don Murray, Diahn Williams, James Earl Jones, Lilia Skala, George S. Irving, Conchata Ferrell, Charles Siebert, Dick A. Williams, Joshua Mostel, Treat Williams, Danny DeVito*
A brutal cop saves a woman's life by killing her attacker. When she begins to say that her attacker was not armed with a knife, she finds herself being harassed. A violent drama with an intriguing premise. Treat Williams' film debut.
DRA                                             102 min
B,V,V2                                             EHE

## DEADLY HUNT, THE **
John Newland            USA                       1971
*Jim Hutton, Anjanette Comer, Tony Franciosa, Peter Lawford, Tim McIntire, Tom Hauff, Bob George, Ivor Harries, Wally McSween, Bill Barringer, David Glyn-Jones, Derek Glyn-Jones, Dennis Robertson, Mallie Boman, Alex Louie*
A wealthy playboy hires two killers, so that he can gain control of his wife's business empire in this competent thriller. The script is by Jerrold Ludwig and Eric Bercovici.
Boa: novel Autumn Of A Hunter by Pat Stadley.
THR                                          72 min mTV
B,V                                           VCL/CBS

## DEADLY ILLUSION **                                15
William Tannen/Larry Cohen
                        USA                       1988
*Billy Dee Williams, Vanity, Morgan Fairchild, John Beck, Joseph Cortese, Joe Spinell, Dennis Hallahan*
An over-the-top private eye film, with a detective being hired to kill the wife of a Wall Street tycoon only to find that he is framed for murder. A few touches of humour add some sparkle to a preposterous tale. Scripted by Cohen.
Aka: LOVE YOU TO DEATH
A/AD                            87 min (ort 90 min)
B,V                                               VES

## DEADLY IMPACT **                                  15
Larry Ludman (Fabrizio de Angelis)
                        ITALY                     1983
*Bo Svenson, Fred Williamson, Marcia Clingan, John Morghen, Vincent Conte*
Implausible crime caper in which some crooks try to use a computer to tap into the casino information networks at Las Vegas, in order to discover when the slot machines are about to pay out.
DRA                                              84 min
B,V                                               EIV

## DEADLY INTENT **                                  18
Nigel Dick              USA                       1988
*Lisa Eibacher, Steve Railsback, Maud Adams, Lance*

*Henriksen, Fred Williamson, Persis Khambatta*
A man returns from an expedition to the South American jungle with a valuable gem, but insists to his employer that he returned with nothing, and that the other expedition members all perished. However, this is untrue and when they return for a share of the spoils he is found murdered, and a race ensues between them to find the jewel. A mediocre thriller with a few lively sequences.
THR                            82 min (ort 96 min)
V                                                SONY

## DEADLY INTENTIONS **                              18
Noel Black              USA                       1985
*Michael Biehn, Madolyn Smith, Morgana King, Jack Kruschen, Kevin McCarthy, Cliff De Young, Cloris Leachman, Susan Wheeler Duff, Edward Edwards, Bruce French, Arthur Rosenberg, Kimberly Beck, Matthew Faison, Robert Clarke*
A woman's life turns into a nightmare when she discovers that her doctor husband is a dangerous psychotic. Cut down from a mini-series of 240 minutes and originally shown in two parts. Based on a true story and adapted from Stevens' book by Andrew Peter Martin. An overlong and sluggish thriller with a few chilling moments.
Boa: book by William Randolph Stevens.
THR        181 min (2 cassettes – ort 240 min) mTV
B,V                                               CBS

## DEADLY INTRUDER, THE **                           18
John McCauley           USA                       1984
*Stuart Whitman, Chris Holder, Molly Cheek, Tony Crupi, Danny Bonaduce, Laura Melton*
The usual nutter-on-the-loose-in-small-town story, with all the expected incidents. Average.
HOR                             83 min Cut (44 sec)
B,V                                         IVS; BRAVE

## DEADLY NIGHTMARES ***                             18
Carl Schenkel/Chris Leitch/Roger Vadim
                        CANADA                    1988
*Jenny Seagrove, Patrick Houser, Edward Albert, Penelope Milford, Belinda Montgomery, Michael Medsen, Susan Anspach*
Three horror tales taken from a Canadian series entitled "The Hitchhiker". In "The Killer", a wheelchair-bound girl finds herself trapped in a house with a demented psycho, in "Dead Man's Curve" a woman confronts a ghost from her past, and in "Man At The Window" a burnt-out Hollywood scriptwriter discovers a new source of inspiration when he becomes a voyeur. Extremely well made and enjoyable.
HOR                                          81 min mCab
B,V                                             BRAVE

## DEADLY OBSESSION *                                18
Jeno Hodi               USA                       1988
*Jeffrey Iorio, Joe Paradise, Darnell Martin*
A psycho decides to get even with the college that rejected his application, and sets out to poison the students with a tub of contaminated ice cream. However, one of his victims survives and is forced to play a deadly cat-and-mouse game with her tormentor. A repulsive film that blends sadism and voyeurism in equal degrees.
HOR                                              93 min
V/h                                               NWV

## DEADLY PASSION *                                  18
Larry Larson            USA                       1985
*Brent Huff, Ingrid Boulting, Harrison Coburn, Lyn Maree, Eric Flynn, Michael McAbe, Jon Maytham, Gabrielle Lomberg, Erica Rogers*
A private detective becomes heavily involved with a beautiful young widow, who stands to inherit a fortune following the death of her elderly husband. However, her intention is merely to use him as a tool, in a scheme to outsmart her late husband's business

manager, who is trying to block her legacy. A sluggish and unconvincing thriller.

THR            95 min (ort 100 min) Cut (6 sec)
B,V                                          VES

## DEADLY PREY **                                    18
David A. Prior            USA                    1987
*Cameron Mitchell, Ted Prior, Troy Donahue, Fritz Matthews, David Campbell, Dawn Abraham*
At a secret training camp for mercenaries, live people are used for target practice. A hardened killer takes on the entire mercenary band, with only his bare hands and feet for weapons, in this violent but empty film.

A/AD                                         90 min
B,V                                             AVA

## DEADLY PURSUIT ***                                15
Roger Spottiswoode        USA                    1987
*Sidney Poitier, Tom Berenger, Kirstie Alley, Clancy Brown, Richard Masur, Andrew Robinson, Kevin Scannell, Frederick Coffin, Michael McRae, Robert Lesser*
A smart FBI agent from the big city, pursues a killer who has fled to a remote mountain range in the Pacific Northwest. Now on unfamiliar terrain, he is forced to rely on an expert mountain guide with whom he forms an uneasy partnership, this latter man having had his girlfriend taken hostage by the killer.
Aka: SHOOT TO KILL

A/AD                                        110 min
B,V                                           BUENA

## DEADLY REACTOR *                                  18
David Heavener            USA                    1988
*Stuart Whitman, David Heavener*
The minister of a small town, resorts to violence to deal with a biker gang that is terrorising the locals. Set in a post-WW3 world that seems remarkably unscathed by nuclear destruction.

A/AD                          86 min; 90 min (VPD)
B,V                                           BRAVE

## DEADLY REVENGE **
Roberto E. Montero
                    AUSTRIA/ITALY                1971
*Van Johnson, Klaus Kinski, Lucrezia Love*
A gang member is captured during a daring robbery in Vienna. He is sprung from prison, and begins to hunt his accomplices and the loot.
Aka: DAS AUGE DER SPINNE; EYE OF THE SPIDER; L'OCCHIO DEL RAGNO

THR                                          90 min
B,V,V2                                         VPD

## DEADLY SILENCE **                                 15
John Patterson            USA                    1989
*Mike Farrell, Bruce Weitz, Heather Fairfield, Charles Haid, Richard Portnow, Sally Struthers, Wally Ward*
A sexually abused teenager resorts to extremes when she hires a classmate to murder her obnoxious father. Listless and clinical, this fact-based film fails to breathe life into the tale of Cheryl Pierson, as detailed in the book by New York Times reporter Kleiman. The adaptation is by Jennifer Miller.
Boa: book by Dena Kleiman.

DRA                      90 min (ort 100 min) mTV
V                                            CASPIC

## DEADLY SNAKE VERSUS KUNG FU KILLERS **
                    HONG KONG
*Chow Cheung Fook, Tony Wong, Candice Yu, Nu Tzin Mai*
An offbeat martial arts fantasy in which a lone fighter is befriended by three fairies, falling in love with and marrying one of them. He and his bride are then obliged to face some strange forces that may destroy them.
Aka: DEADLY SNAIL VERSUS KUNG FU KILLERS

MAR                                          90 min
B,V                                       SPEC/POLY

## DEADLY SPAWN, THE *                               18
Douglas McKean            USA                    1983
*Charles George Hildebrandt, Tom de Franco, Jean Taffler, Richard Lee Porter*
A meteorite brings a germ to Earth which grows into a three-headed monster and proceeds to gobble up humans. Amateurishly made film, originally shot in 16 mm.
Aka: RETURN OF THE ALIEN'S DEADLY SPAWN

HOR              80 min; 78 min (CERT) (ort 90 min)
B,V                              VIP; THV; CERT

## DEADLY STRANGER **                                15
Max J. Kleven             USA                    1988
*Darlanne Fluegel, John Vernon, Michael J. Moore*
A drifter gets into trouble in a small farming community, and pays off his fines by working for some corrupt farmers, but in reality he is an undercover cop gathering evidence for a prosecution.

THR                                          90 min
V                                               RCA

## DEADLY STRIKE, THE **                             18
Huang Lung              HONG KONG              1979
*Bruce Li (Ho Tsung-Tao), Chen Hsing, Tang Wei, Lung Fei*
Kung fu Western with a new law officer recruiting his men from the local jail, in order to break up a criminal gang. Fair.

MAR          87 min (ort 90 min) Cut (1 min 23 sec)
B,V                                            VPD

## DEADLY TRACKERS, THE *                            15
Barry Shear               USA                    1973
*Richard Harris, Rod Taylor, Al Lettieri, Neville Brand, William Smith, Isela Vega, Paul Benjamin, Pedro Armendariz Jr, Kelly Jean Peters, Sean Marshal, Red Morgan, William Bryant*
The sheriff of a small Texan town tracks a gang of bank robbers to Mexico to avenge the death of his wife and son. A lacklustre tale that dwells on violence at the expense of the plot. Sam Fuller was the original director for this dud and also wrote the story.
Aka: KILLBRAND; RIATA

WES                     101 min (Cut at film release)
B,V                                            WHV

## DEADLY TRAP, THE *
Rene Clement   · FRANCE/ITALY                    1971
*Faye Dunaway, Frank Langella, Barbara Parkins, Karen Glanguernon, Maurice Ronet*
A gang of industrial spies tries to force a former member, a brilliant mathematician, to work for them by harassing his neurotic wife and abducting his kids. Quite well made, but almost totally suspense-free.
Aka: DEATH SCREAM
Boa: novel The Children Are Gone by A. Cavanaugh.

THR                      92 min (ort 100 min)
B,V                                           POLY

## DEADLY VENGEANCE **                               18
A.C. Quamer               USA                    1985
*Arthur Roberts, Alan Marlow, Grace Jones*
A woman takes a razor-sharp vengeance on the gang who murdered her lover. Don't expect any surprises in this unpleasant slasheroo.

A/AD                                 84 min Cut (41 sec)
B,V                                     ALLAM/MOG

## DEADLY VOWS ***                                   15
Jerrold Freedman          USA                    1988
*Patrick Duffy, Charles Durning, Lisa Blount, Michael O'Keefe*
A detective is assigned to a case in which a young woman was killed by a hit-and-run driver. Prompted by the woman's aunt who insists she was murdered, he uncovers a nasty criminal conspiracy.

THR                                    96 min mTV
B,V                                         WATER

## DEADLY WEAPON *** 15
Michael Miner          USA              1988
Rodney Eastman, Kim Walker, Gary Frank, Gary
Kroeger, Michael Horse, Joe Regalabuto, William
Sanderson
A bullied teenager is satisfy his desire for revenge
when he comes into possession of a newly-developed
and highly experimental secret weapon. A low budget
re-working of LASERBLAST, surprisingly effective
and inventive.
FAN                          86 min (ort 90 min)
V                                            PRES

## DEADLY WEAPONS ** 18
Doris Wishman          USA              1974
Zsa Zsa (Doris Wishman, also known as "Chesty
Morgan"), Harry Reems, Saul Meth
Routine gangster melodrama only memorable because
of Wishman's 73 inch bust which she uses to good
effect in disposing of various unsavoury characters.
See also DOUBLE AGENT '73 in which Doris pops up
(perhaps we should say pops out) again.
Aka: INCREDIBLE CHESTY (72-32-36) MORGAN
AND HER DEADLY WEAPONS, THE
A                    71 min (ort 73 min) Cut (24 sec)
B,V        INT L/A; WESTRUM L/A; PICPAL; XTASY

## DEADRINGER ** 
Teddy Page             USA              1985
Max Thayer, Mike Cohen, Christine Lassiter, Nick
Nicholson, Mike Monty
A case of mistaken identity leads to violence as a man
takes revenge for the murder of his mother and
girlfriend. Average violent revenger.
DRA                                        90 min
B,V                                          CAN

## DEAF SMITH AND JOHNNY EARS ** 15
Paolo Cavara           ITALY            1973
Anthony Quinn, Franco Nero, Pamela Tiffin, Ira
Furstenberg, Franco Grazios, Renato Romano, Adolfo
Castretti
Two men try to prevent an ex-army general from
overthrowing the government of Texas and stopping it
from joining the Union in 1834. Fairly unmemorable
"buddy Western" with nice interplay between Quinn
(a deaf-mute) and Nero plus superb photography by
Tonino Delli Colli.
Aka: LOS AMIGOS
WES                  87 min (ort 97 min) Cut (8 sec)
B,V                                          MGM

## DEAL OF THE CENTURY * 15
William Friedkin       USA              1983
Chevy Chase, Sigourney Weaver, Gregory Hines, Vince
Edwards, Richard Libertini, William Marquez,
Eduard Ricard, Wallace Shawn
Feeble satire on the international arms trade, with an
arms dealer being urged not to sell a powerful new
weapon to a warmongering dictator. Despite a promis-
ing start this one rapidly degenerates into a fairly
mindless and disjointed farce. Scripted by Paul
Brickman.
COM                                        99 min
V/sh                                         WHV

## DEALERS ** 15
Colin Bucksey          UK               1989
Paul McGann, Rebecca DeMornay, Derrick O'Connor
A high-flying businessman loses his position in the
company, and as he fights to save his career he
discovers that he is no more than a pawn in a power
struggle. Fair.
A/AD                        88 min (ort 110 min)
V                                            MGM

## DEAREST LOVE **** 
Louis Malle
            FRANCE/ITALY/WEST GERMANY   1971
Lea Massari, Benoit Ferreux, Daniel Gelin, Fabien
Ferreux, Marc Winocourt, Michel Lonsdale, Jacqueline
Chauveau
An affectionate and satirical examination of the
lifestyle of the French upper-class, as a precocious
14-year-old boy begins to experience the first onset of
sexuality and the possibility of his mother becoming
his tutor arises. This delicate comedy of manners
manages to say something fresh, witty and perceptive
about love, relationships and social conventions.
Aka: LE SOUFFLE AU COEUR; MURMUR OF THE
HEART; NOW IS THE TIME
DRA                                        118 min
V                                            INT

## DEATH AT LOVE HOUSE ** 15
E.W. Swackhamer        USA              1976
Robert Wagner, Kate Jackson, Sylvia Sidney, Joan
Blondell, Dorothy Lamour, John Carradine, Bill
Macy, Marianna Hill, Joseph Bernard, John A. Zee,
Robert Gibbons, Al Hansen, Crofton Hardester
A young writer comes to the deserted mansion of a
long-dead movie star who once had an affair with his
father, in order to work on a biography of her.
However, strange forces are at work and her spirit
reaches out to him in this creepy but implausible tale.
Filmed at the magnificent estate of Harold Lloyd.
HOR                                    72 min mTV
B,V                                          GHV

## DEATH AT ORWELL ROCK ** 15
George Lincoln (Riccardo Fredo)
                         ITALY           1967
Mark Damon, Stephen Forsyth, Alan Collins, Pamela
Tudor, Pedro Sanchez
The son of a murdered army major returns to the town
where his father was killed. He is reluctant to get
involved in a vendetta against the family responsible,
but soon finds that he has no choice.
Aka: LA MORTA NON CONTA I DOLARI
WES                      85 min Cut (22 sec)
B,V                                          VPD

## DEATH BEFORE DISHONOR ** 18
Terry J. Leonard       USA              1987
Fred Dryer, Brian Keith, Joanna Pacula, Paul
Winfield, Kasey Walker, Rockne Tarkington
Former stuntman Leonard's directorial debut, is this
cliched story of a tough Marines sergeant who takes
on a bunch of Middle-East terrorists when they launch
an attack and take two American diplomats hostage.
Good stunts; shame about the plot.
A/AD                         89 min Cut (9 sec)
B,V                                          NWV

## DEATH BLOW ** 
Tim Spring             USA              1983
Willie Van Rensburg, Duane Bobick, Tulio Moneta
A boxer takes a bloody revenge on the men who raped
his girlfriend in this formula revenger.
DRA                                        90 min
B,V                                          ARF

## DEATH BY DIALOGUE ** 18
Tom Dewier             USA              1988
Ken Sagoes, Lenny Delduca, Kelly Sullivan, Laura
Albert
A bunch of brainless teens find a haunted screenplay
and begin to read it. In doing so, they come across
passages predicting their own deaths, and a murderous demon is released. Trapped in a remote mansion,
they learn that the ending must be rewritten if they
are to survive. A good premise receives a poor
treatment.
HOR                                        90 min
B,V                                          CFD

## DEATH CAR ON THE FREEWAY ** 
Hal Needham          USA          1979          PG
*Shelley Hack, George Hamilton, Frank Gorshin, Peter
Graves, Harriet Nelson, Barbara Rush, Dinah Shore,
Abe Vigoda, Alfie Wise, Tara Buckman, Morgan
Brittany, Robert F. Lyons, Nancy Stephens, Gloria
Stroock, Hal Needham*
A female TV reporter is sent to investigate a deranged
driver in L.A. who is terrorising women alone on the
freeway in their cars, forcing them off the road with
his van. An average TV action-thriller whose poor
acting is compensated for by the good stunt driving.
Shore's TV movie debut.
Aka: DEATH CAR; DEATH CARS; DEATH ON THE
FREEWAY; WHEELS OF DEATH (AMBAS or
VDEL)
A/AD          92 min; 95 min (GLOB) (ort 100 min) mTV
B,V          PRV L/A; VFP; GLOB; AMBAS; VDEL

## DEATH CHASE * 
                     USA
*Peter Brown, William Smith, Anna Capri*
An Amazonian expedition is threatened by a man's
strange behaviour in this obscure and eminently
forgettable adventure yarn.
A/AD          86 min
B,V          VCL/CBS

## DEATH CODE: NINJA **          18
*John Wilford, Mike Abbott, Edgar Fox, Judy Barnes,
Ivan Tin, Julie Lik, Kent Poon, Peter Sung*
A secret war map is eagerly sought by agents working
for several world powers in this routine high-kicking
adventure.
MAR          83 min Cut (2 min 51 sec)
V          HBL L/A; HILL

## DEATH COLLECTOR **          18
Ralph De Vito          USA          1975
*Joseph Cotten (Joseph Cortese), Jack Ramage, Amos
Johns, Keith Davis, Lou Christopher (Lou Criscoulo),
Joe Peters (Joe Pesci), Bobby Alton (Bobby Alto),
Frank Vincent*
A young man embarks on a violent career as a debt
collector for the Mafia, in this formula effort.
Aka: ENFORCER 2; FAMILY ENFORCER, THE
DRA          91 min; 85 min (VTC); 76 min (DRUM)
B,V          COU L/A; VTC L/A; DRUM

## DEATH CRUISE **          PG
Ralph Senensky          USA          1979
*Richard Long, Polly Bergen, Edward Albert Jr, Kate
Jackson, Celeste Holm, Tom Bosley, Michael
Constantine, Cesare Danova*
Three couples win a free, all expenses paid cruise
holiday, only to find that they have been chosen as
potential murder victims. Well cast and quite well
acted, but let down by cliched development. However,
the unexpected ending compensates.
THR          71 min (ort 78 min) mTV
B,V,V2          GHV; MSD (VHS only)

## DEATH CURSE OF TARTU **          15
William Grefe          USA          1966
*Fred Pinero, Babette Sherril, Mayra Cristine,
Sherman Hayes, Gary Holtz, Doug Hobart, William
Marcos*
A group of archaeology students in the Florida
Everglades accidentally disturb the grave of a Semi-
nole medicine man wherupon he springs back into life,
taking up various guises in a bloody quest for revenge.
HOR          87 min
B,V          FIFTH

## DEATH DEALER, THE **          18
Raymond Danton          USA          1975
*Jim Hutton, Julie Adams, Paul Burke, Aldo Ray,
Neville Brand, Whit Bissell, Nehemiah Persoff, Rod*

*Cameron, Della Reese*
A mental patient gains psychic powers and uses them
in a violent quest for revenge.
Aka: PSYCHIC KILLER (VIPCO)
HOR          85 min Cut (9 sec)
B,V          THV L/A; VIPCO; CERT

## DEATH DIMENSIONS *          18
Al Adamson          USA          1980
*Jim Kelly, Aldo Ray, George Lazenby, Harold Sakata,
Myron Bruce Lee, Terry Moore*
A mad scientist has developed a sinister bomb that
can revolutionise warfare. It takes the form of a
microdot that is implanted under a woman's skin. She
becomes the prey of agents from several countries that
want to get their hands on this. Not as silly as it
sounds . . . . sillier.
Aka: BLACK ELIMINATOR, THE; DEATH
DIMENSION; FREEZE BOMB; KILL FACTOR, THE
THR          90 min
B,V          INT/CBS; APX

## DEATH DOLL **          18
William Mims          USA          1989
*Andrea Walters, William Dance, Jennifer Davis,
Desiree Pennoyer*
When a couple acquire an antique fortune-telling
device, they decide to see what the future holds for
them, but learn that they are to die soon after the
birth of their child. An intriguing film that never
fulfils its early promise.
HOR          90 min
V          BOX

## DEATH DRIVE **          18
Pasquale Festa Campanile
                     ITALY          1976
*Franco Nero, Corinne Clery, David Hess, Carlo Puri*
An Italian reporter and his wife try to patch up their
marriage by taking a caravan trip through California.
However, this turns into a nightmare when they pick
up a hitch-hiker and discover that he is a bank-robber
on the run.
Aka: AUTOSTOP ROSSO SANGUE; HITCH-HIKE
(VTC)
DRA          104 min; 93 min (REN); 99 min (VIDAGE)
B,V          VTC L/A; DFS; REN; VIDAGE

## DEATH DRIVER *          PG
Jimmy Huston          USA          1979
*Earl Owensby, Mike Allen, Patty Shaw, Mary Anne
Hearn*
Car chases form the basis of this action film all about a
stunt car driver.
Aka: HELL RACER (ECF); HELL RACERS
A/AD          90 min
B,V          ECF; ITL L/A

## DEATH FLASH **          18
Tony Zarindist          USA
*Jeremy Ney, Doreen Alderman, David Lewis,
Kimberley Evans, Cherry Williams, Brodie Greer,
Myron Natwick*
When a tough vice cop discovers his pretty wife has a
lover, he takes the law into his own hands and is
imprisoned on a murder charge. Learning that his
young daughter has become involved in prostitution
drives him to break out of jail and try to reach her.
Average.
A/AD          94 min Cut (3 sec)
B,V          MED

## DEATH FLIGHT *          1977
David Lowell Rich          USA
*Barbara Anderson, Bert Convy, Peter Graves, Lorne
Greene, Season Hubley, Tina Louise, George Maharis,
Burgess Meredith, Doug McClure, Martin Milner,
Brock Peters, Robert Reed, Susan Strasberg, Billy
Crystal, Misty Rowe*

Terror strikes the inaugural flight of the first American supersonic aircraft as a highly contagious sample of an influenza virus is released. One of those tedious airborne disaster movies weighed down with a host of celebrities and a minimum of ideas.
Aka: SST: DEATH FLIGHT; SST: DISASTER IN THE SKY
Boa: story by Guerdon Trueblood.
A/AD                                    97 min (ort 106 min) mTV
B,V                                                            VFP

## DEATH FORCE **
Cirio H. Santiago
                    PHILIPPINES/USA                1979
James Iglehart, Leon Isaac Kennedy, Jayne Kennedy
Two US soldiers try to kill a third who has refused to become involved in their criminal plans. He survives their attack and begins a one-man crusade to destroy their criminal empire.
Aka: FORCE OF DEATH (ARCTIC)
THR                                                         90 min
B,V                                                          ARCTIC

## DEATH FORCE **                                            15
Frans Nel                   USA                      1989
John Barrett, Kryska Witowska, Robin Smith
A private detective is plunged into a web of corruption and murder when he takes a case that involves him in the world of racing.
A/AD                                                       90 min
V                                                           CASVIS

## DEATH GAME *
Peter S. Traynor          USA      1974 (released 1977)
Sondra Locke, Colleen Camp, Seymour Cassel, Beth Brickell, Ruth Warshawsky, Michael Kalmansohn
Hateful film about two mad lesbians who tease and torture a man in his own home for no apparent reason. Should please the militant feminist lobby.
Aka: MRS MANNING'S WEEKEND; SEDUCERS, THE
HOR                                                       89 min
B,V                                                       INT L/A

## DEATH GAMES **                                            18
William Vanderkloot      USA                         1987
Ed Marinaro, Isaac Hayes, Darrell Larson, Cassandra Gava, John Hancock, William Sanderson, Corbin Bensen, Harry Goz, William Windom
A tough cop is transferred from the vice squad because of his harsh methods. However, when a number of strippers are brutally murdered, he is drawn into a sinister drugs and espionage plot that involves both the KGB and the FBI, and when some of his colleagues are killed he finds himself back in favour, and is given a free hand to solve these crimes.
Aka: MACE
THR                                            87 min Cut (7 sec)
B,V                                                          SONY

## DEATH HUNT **                                             18
Peter R. Hunt             USA                        1981
Charles Bronson, Lee Marvin, Andrew Stevens, Angie Dickinson, Carl Weathers, Ed Lauter
A man who is innocent of a murder charge is pursued through the icy wastes of Canada by a tough Mountie. Some good action sequences are all that's worth watching in this lacklustre adventure. Loosely based on a real manhunt that took place in the 1930s, when a trapper named Albert Johnson was allegedly framed for murder.
A/AD                                                       97 min
B,V,V2,LV                                                     CBS

## DEATH IN CALIFORNIA, A ***                                18
Delbert Mann             USA                         1985
Cheryl Ladd, Sam Elliott, Alexis Smith, Fritz Weaver, Barry Corbin, Kerrie Keane, John Ashton, Jim Haynie, George Wyner, Granville Van Dusen, Bill Lucking, Joel Polis, Chad Allen, Michael Cavanaugh, Tom Fuccello
A woman's boyfriend is killed in front of her, yet she somehow evolves a strange, ambivalent rapport with his killer, who for good measure also rapes her. Supposedly based on a true case and a lot better than the unpleasant premise would have led one to expect. Adapted from Barthel's best-seller by E. Jack Neuman and originally shown in two parts.
Boa: novel by Joan Barthel.
DRA              182 min (2 cassettes – ort 200 min) mTV
B,V                                                          GHV

## DEATH IN VENICE **                                        15
Luchino Visconti          ITALY                      1971
Dirk Bogarde, Mark Burns, Marisa Berenson, Silvana Mangano, Bjorn Andreson, Luigi Battaglia
Beautifully filmed slow-moving account of the last days of a composer who falls in love with a young boy, and stays in Venice too long to escape the epidemic that is sweeping the city. A section of Mahler's Fifth Symphony is a high-spot in a lavish but quite vacuous film. Written by Visconti and Nicola Bandalucco.
Aka: MORTE A VENEZIA
Boa: novella by Thomas Mann.
DRA                                          125 min (ort 130 min)
B,V                                                          WHV

## DEATH JOURNEY **                                          18
Fred Williamson          SPAIN                       1975
Fred Williamson, Bernard Kuby, Heidi Dobbs, D'Urville Matin
The New York D.A. hires a private detective to take a female witness from coast to coast by train in 48 hours, but the Mafia have sent a hit squad to silence her. Average.
Aka: JORNADA DE MUERTE
A/AD                                           72 min (ort 96 min)
B,V                                       CHM/PPL L/A; NET

## DEATH KISS, THE ***
Edwin L. Marin            USA                        1933
Bela Lugosi, David Manners, Adrienne Ames, John Wray, Vince Barnett, Edward Van Sloan, Wade Boteler, Vince Barnett, Alexander Carr, Harold Minjir, Al Hill, Barbara Bedford, Alan Roscoe, Mona Maris, Edmund Burns, Jimmy Donlin
Low-budget mystery thriller with an actor killed on the film set whilst making a gangster film. Pretty much par for the course but the scenes of a 1930s film set at work add a degree of interest. The film contains some hand-coloured sequences.
Boa: novel by Madelon St. Dennis.
THR                                      60 min (ort 75 min) B/W
V                                                            HVS

## DEATH LINE **                                             18
Gary Sherman             UK                          1972
Donald Pleasence, David Ladd, Sharon Gurney, Christopher Lee, Norman Rossington, Hugh Armstrong, James Cossins, June Turner, Heather Stoney, Hugh Dickson, Clive Swift, Suzanne Winkler, Ron Pember, Jack Woolgar
A far-fetched story of strange cannibalistic being that lives in the bowels of the London Underground system. Quite atmospheric (filmed on location at Russell Square Station) and surprisingly sensitive and poignant in places, but gruesomely overdone.
Aka: RAW MEAT
HOR                                      84 min; 88 min (MIA)
B,V                                       RNK; MIA (VHS only)

## DEATH MACHINES *                                       18/15
Paul Kyriazi             USA                         1976
Mari Honjo, Ron Marchini, Michael Chong, Ron Ackerman, Joshua Johnson, Chuck Katzaian
A female gangster and her associates provide a contract killer service in this exploitative and dreary offering.

Aka: NINJA MURDERS (MPV)
A/AD    89 min (ort 92 min) (VIZ: 18 version; MPV: 15 version – cut at film release)
B,V                              VTC L/A; VIZ; MPV

## DEATH MOON *

Bruce Kessler          USA              1978
*France Nuyen, Robert Foxworth, Joe Penny, Barbara Trentham, Debralee Scott*
An executive on holiday in Hawaii becomes involved with both a demented killer possessed by an Indian spirit and a woman with supernatural powers. Pedestrian horror yarn of few chills but much tedium.
HOR                              89 min mTV
B,V                              VES/PVG

## DEATH OF A CENTREFOLD *          15

Gabrielle Beaumont     USA              1981
*Jamie Lee Curtis, Bruce Weitz, Robert Reed, Mitchell Ryan, Mark Withers, Tracy Reed, Bibi Besch, Hugh Gillin, Gloria Gifford, Luca Bercovici, Karlene Crockett, Steven Hirsch, Jim Boeke, Linda Brooks, Kale Browne, Robert Burgos*
Supposedly based on a true story, this tells of the tragic end of a teenage girl who achieves fame via the centre pages of Playboy Magazine. A highly depressing and exploitative tale. The script by Donald Stewart also formed the basis for the Bob Fosse film – STAR 80.
Aka: DEATH OF A CENTREFOLD: THE DOROTHY STRATTEN STORY; DOROTHY STRATTEN STORY, THE; DOROTHY STRATTEN: UNTOLD STORY
DRA                92 min (ort 95 min) Cut mTV
B,V                              MGM

## DEATH OF A HOOKER **

Ernie Pintoff          USA              1971
*Red Buttons, Alice Playten, Sylvia Miles, Sam Waterston, Conrad Bain, Donald Marye, Dick Williams, Norman Rose, David Doyle, Ellen Gurin, Gilbert Lewis, Ron Carey, Earl Hindman, Antony Page, Sally Birkhead, Sella Longo*
An ex-boxer decides to find the murderer of an obscure New York hooker when everyone else has given up. Average murder mystery of no great merit, but quite well acted.
Aka: WHO KILLED MARY MAGDELENE; WHO KILLED MARY WHAT'S 'ER NAME?
DRA                86 min (ort 90 min)
B,V,V2                           INT/CBS

## DEATH OF A SALESMAN ***          PG

Volker Schlondorff     USA              1985
*Dustin Hoffman, Kate Reid, Charles Durning, Stephen Lang, John Malkovich, Louis Zorich, David S. Chandler, Kathy Rossetter, Jon Polito, Anne McIntosh, Tom Signorelli, Linda Kozlowski, Karen Needle, Michael Quinlan*
A stylised but excellent production of the 1984 Broadway version of this classic Pulitzer prize-winning play. Most of the cast from the stage play appear in this fine story, of a middle-aged salesman whose life no longer has purpose or meaning. This powerful study of emotional disintegration is enhanced by the skilful use of flashbacks and the fact that it was filmed within the confines of a Broadway theatre – thereby enhancing its intimacy.
Boa: play by Arthur Miller.
DRA                              133 min mTV
B,V                              WHV

## DEATH OF A SNOWMAN **           15

Christopher Rowley     USA              1972
*Nigel Davenport, Ken Gampu, Peter Dynely, Bima Stagg, Madala Mphahlele*
A hit-man wants a piece of the action on the streets of New York and organises the Harlem gangs to fight the Mafia.

Aka: BLACK TRASH
THR                              84 min
B,V,V2                           INT L/A; SID

## DEATH OF A SOLDIER **           18

Philippe Mora          AUSTRALIA        1985
*James Coburn, Bill Hunter, Reb Brown, Maurie Fields, Max Fairchild, Belinda Davey, Randall Berger, Michael Pate, Oscar Sherl, Richard Tanner*
In Melbourne during May of 1942 three girls are murdered in the space of a week. Australian police and American forces join in a giant manhunt and eventually track down the killer, a deranged 24-year-old GI. His court martial develops into a duel between his defence lawyer and the American authorities, who are determined that he must hang. Based on true events but nothing like as taut as it could have been.
DRA                              92 min
B,V                              VES

## DEATH OF ADOLF HITLER **        PG

Rex Firkin             UK               1973
*Frank Finlay, Caroline Mortimer, Ed Devereaux, Michael Sheard*
Competent portrayal of the last ten days of Hitler's life.
DRA                              107 min
B,V                TEVP L/A; GMH (VHS only)

## DEATH OF THE INCREDIBLE HULK, THE *   PG

Bill Bixby             USA              1990
*Bill Bixby, Lou Ferrigno, Elizabeth Gracen, Philip Sterling, Barbara Tarbuck, Anna Katerina*
The monstrous green one meets his end (or does he?) when he clashes with terrorists who are out to discover the secret Hulk formula. Aimed fairly and squarely at cult followers of the popular TV series, and embellished by a romantic sub-plot, this juvenile re-hash of the old and familiar has little to offer in the way of solid entertainment.
FAN                95 min (ort 100 min) mTV
V                                NWV

## DEATH ON THE NILE **            PG

John Guillermin        UK               1978
*Peter Ustinov, Jane Birkin, Lois Chiles, Bette Davis, Mia Farrow, David Niven, Jon Finch, Olivia Hussey, Maggie Smith, Angela Lansbury, George Kennedy, Jack Warden, Simon MacCorkindale, Jane Birkin, Harry Andrews*
One of those typical adaptations of an Agatha Christie novel which totally fails to be anything other than a turgid and static production, in spite of (or possibly because of), a star-studded cast. In this tale, Hercule Poirot is presented with a boatload of suspects after Chiles is murdered on a cruise up the Nile. Visually impressive, but difficult to sit through. The script is by Anthony Shaffer. AA: Cost (Anthony Powell).
Boa: novel by Agatha Christie.
DRA                              134 min (ort 140 min)
B,V,V2              TEVP; WHV (VHS only)

## DEATH PROMISE **               18

Robert Warmflash       USA              1978
*Charles Bonet, Speedy Leacock, Bill Laurie, Vincent Van Lynn, Thomson Kaokang, Abe Hendy, Monica Germaine*
Young men train in the martial arts in order to fight back against a ruthless landlord who keeps raising their rent without making any improvements to their slum-dwellings. A tough and simple-minded action story.
Aka: PAY-OFF TIME (VIDAGE)
A/AD               89 min Cut (1 min 25 sec)
B,V,V2                           QLV/VTC; VIDAGE

## DEATH RACE 2000 **             18

Paul Bartel            USA              1975
*David Carradine, Simone Griffith, Sylvester Stallone,*

*Louisa Moritz, Mary Woronov, Don Steele, Joyce Jameson, Fred Grandy*
In the year 2000 the national sport is cross-country racing, with points scored for knocking down pedestrians. A fast and furious spoof on all those car-race films, spoilt by too much concentration on gore. Followed by DEATHSPORT.
Boa: story by Ib Melchior.
FAN                                              80 min
B,V                                   ORSCO; BWV/VSP

## DEATH RAIDERS **                              18
Segundo Ramos
*Johnny Wilson, George Pallance, George Regan, Ramen Zamora, Robert Lee, June Artiston*
When a provincial president and his two daughters are kidnapped by ruthless terrorists an elite commando squad is sent to rescue them, in this obscure and violent actioner.
A/AD                                             77 min
B,V                                              TEVP

## DEATH RIDE TO OSAKA *                         18
Jonathan Kaplan        USA                       1983
*Jennifer Jason-Leigh, Ann Jillian, Thomas Byrd, Mako, Carolyn Seymour, Richard Narita, Soon-Teck Oh, Philip Charles MacKenzie, Yvonne McCord, Leslie Wing, John Hancock, Lionel Decker, Eda Reiss Merin, Isabell Monk*
A young woman takes a job as a singer in a Japanese night-club and finds herself at the mercy of white slavers, in this sleazy and exploitative effort.
Aka: GIRLS OF THE WHITE ORCHID
Boa: story Girls Of The White Orchid by Tom Allard.
DRA                    94 min (ort 100 min) mTV
B,V                                              ODY

## DEATH SENTENCE *                              PG
E.W. Swackhamer        USA                       1974
*Cloris Leachman, Laurence Luckinbill, Nick Nolte, Alan Oppenheimer, William Schallert, Yvonne Wilder, Herbert Voland, Hope Summers, Peter Hobbs, Doreen Lang, Murray MacLeod, Bing Russell, Meg Wyllie, Lew Brown, C.J. Hincks*
A woman sitting on the jury at a murder trial, gradually becomes aware that the evidence points to her own husband as the killer in this implausible tale.
Boa: novel After The Trial by Eric Roman.
DRA                                         78 min mTV
B,V                                              GHV

## DEATH SHIP *                                  18
Alvin Rakoff           CANADA/UK                 1980
*George Kennedy, Richard Crenna, Nick Mancuso, Sally Ann Howes, Kate Reid, Victoria Burgoyne, Jennifer McKinney, Danny Higham, Saul Rubinek, Lee Murray, Doug Smith*
A mysterious ship collides with a cruise ship in the Caribbean and the survivors climb aboard, only to discover that the vessel is a former SS torture ship which seems to be intent on killing them. About as stupid as it sounds.
HOR                         87 min (ort 91 min)
B,V                                              TEVP

## DEATH SQUAD, THE *                            15
Harry Falk             USA                       1973
*Robert Forster, Michelle Phillips, Claude Akins, Mark Goddard, Melvyn Douglas, Kenneth Tobey, George Murdock, Jesse Vint, Stephen Young, Julie Cobb, Bert Remsen, Dennis Patrick, Janis Hansen, Nate Esformes, Sidney Clute*
A tough cop is given a tough assignment, to root out a self-appointed hit squad within the police force who take the law into their own hands by executing criminals released on technicalities. A sub-standard MAGNUM FORCE clone.
THR                                         78 min mTV
B,V,V2                                           GHV

## DEATH THREAT **
Jack Starrett          USA                       1976
*William Smith, Don Stroud, Judy Farese, James Ryan*
A film-maker who is both an actor and director is obsessed with films and filming and finds that his life is in danger because of his latest project.
Aka: NO ONE CRIES FOREVER
DRA                                              86 min
B,V,V2                                       VCL/CBS

## DEATH VALLEY *                                18
Dick Richards          USA                       1982
*Paul Le Mat, Catherine Hicks, Stephen McHattie, A. Wilford Brimley, Edward Herrmann*
A boy from the city visiting his mother in Arizona, finds himself being pursued by a psychotic maniac in this tedious chiller.
HOR                                              90 min
B, V, V2, LV                                     CIC

## DEATH VENGEANCE **                            18
Lewis Teague           USA                       1982
*Tom Skerritt, Michael Sarrazin, Patti LuPone, Yaphet Kotto, David Rasche, Ted Ross, Pat Cooper*
A man whose wife and mother are attacked, decides to form a vigilante group to combat crime in his neighbourhood. At first he gets some support from the police and business community but starts to use increasingly violent methods. A well made and fairly unpleasant DEATHWISH clone.
Aka: FIGHTING BACK
DRA                          92 min (ort 99 min)
B,V,V2                                           TEVP

## DEATH WARMED UP *                             18
David Blyth       NEW ZEALAND                    1984
*Michael Hurst, Margaret Umbers, Bruno Lawrence, David Letch, Norelle Scott, William Upjohn, Gary Day, Geoff Snell, Ian Watkin, David Weatherly, Tina Grenville, Nat Lees, Judy McIntosh, Ken Harris, Karam Haas, Jonathan Hardy*
Horror spoof about a mad surgeon and the results of his experiments in neurosurgery. After being treated by the doctor, a young man slaughters his parents. The surgeon now retreats to an island haven, where he sets about creating an army of murderous mutants, but the youngster upon whom he first experimented finds his abode and destroys him. A technically competent but remarkably unappealing work.
HOR                    78 min (ort 85 min) Cut (54 sec)
V/s                                              MED

## DEATH WEEKEND *
William Fruet          CANADA                    1977
*Brenda Vaccaro, Don Stroud, Chuck Shamata, Richard Ayres, Kyle Edwards*
Nasty film in which four thugs invade a lovers' country cottage and subject them to a reign of terror. A vacuous shocker that largely sacrifices a plot for gratuitous unpleasantness, with rape and murder the main items on the agenda.
Aka: HOUSE BY THE LAKE, THE
HOR                                              89 min
B,V                          VIPCO; BWV/VSP; VDM

## DEATH WISH **
Michael Winner         USA                       1974
*Charles Bronson, Vincent Gardenia, Hope Lange, Stuart Margolin, William Redfield, Steven Keats, Stephen Elliott, Kathleen Tolan, Jack Wallace, Fred Scollay, Chris Gampel, Robert Kya-Hill, Ed Grover, Jeff Goldblum*
Charles Bronson gives a totally wooden performance as a man who turns into a vigilante after his wife and daughter are so brutally raped that the former dies. An unconvincing and predictable film that has spawned a series of sequels and several imitations. Music is by Herbie Hancock. Look out for Jeff Goldblum in his screen debut as one of the muggers.

Boa: novel by Brian Garfield.
A/AD                                        93 min
B,V,V2,LV                                      CIC

## DEATH WISH 2 *                              18
Michael Winner        USA              1982
*Charles Bronson, Jill Ireland, Ben Frank, Vincent
Gardenia, J.D. Cannon, Anthony Franciosa*
Predictable sequel to DEATH WISH with our lone
vigilante back in action on the streets of L.A., after
the gang rape and murder of his housekeeper and the
suicide of his daughter. Poor Bronson just doesn't
seem to have much luck, but he makes someone pay in
a sequel that's a little more bloody and a great deal
more shallow. Now move on to DEATH WISH 3.
Boa: novel by B. Garfield.
A/AD          85 min (ort 93 min) (Cut at film release)
B,V                              RCA; PREST (VHS only)

## DEATH WISH 3 *                              18
Michael Winner        USA              1985
*Charles Bronson, Ed Lauter, Deborah Raffin, Martin
Balsam, Gavin O'Herlihy*
Third time round and Bronson creaks into action as
the lone vigilante in this yet more stylised, violent
and unrealistic sequel – culminating in a quite
remarkable set-piece battle in which a street gang are
blown to pieces with weapons that include sub-
machine guns and a missile-launcher. And who can
blame him, as assorted rapists, muggers and murderers conspire to attack all his friends? (Perhaps he
should move to an island.)
A/AD              86 min (ort 92 min) Cut (13 sec)
B,V                          GHV; VCC (VHS only)

## DEATH WISH 4: THE CRACKDOWN *             18
J. Lee Thompson       USA              1987
*Charles Bronson, Kay Lenz, John P. Ryan, Perry
Lopez, George Dickerson, Soon-Teck Oh, Dana Barron,
Jesse Dabson*
A flabby sequel to the earlier film with a different
director but much the same "shoot 'em up" vigilante
plot. This time round Bronson is galvanised into
action (if not into acting) by the death of his girl-
friend's daughter from drugs. He now attempts a
wholesale wipe-out for L.A.'s drug dealers.
A/AD       94 min (ort 98 min) (Cut at film release by 54
sec)
B,V                                        CAN

## DEATH ZONE **                              18
Juan Antonio Bardem
              ITALY/SPAIN/USA            1969
*George Maharis, Maria Perschy, James Philbrook,
Gerard Herter, Gustavo Rojo, Aldo Ray*
An American unit in the closing days of WW2, battles
crack SS troops in order to capture a famous German
scientist before he is killed by the Nazis. A standard
war tale, filmed in Spain.
Aka: EL ULTIMO DIA DE LA GUERRA; LAST DAY
OF THE WAR, THE
WAR                                        96 min
B,V                          HVM L/A; VUL L/A; TWF

## DEATH-HEAD VIRGIN, THE **
                                          1974
*Jock Gaynor, Larry Ward, Diane McBain, Vic Diaz,
Kim Ramos, Manny Ojeda, Iraida Arambulo*
A strange amulet found at the bottom of the sea bears
a curse. When it is stolen by two men they incur the
enmity of the supernatural creature that is its guar-
dian.
HOR                                        90 min
B,V                                     INT/CBS

## DEATHCHEATERS **
Brian Trenchard Smith
              AUSTRALIA                  1976
*Grant Page, Margaret Gerard, Noel Ferrier*

Two professional stuntmen are contacted by an intelligence network for an "impossible" mission – to land on
an island in the Philippines, break into a secret base
and get out again.
A/AD                                       83 min
B,V                                        GHV

## DEATHDREAM ***
Bob Clark             CANADA             1972
*Lynn Carlin, John Marley, Richard Backus,
Henderson Forsythe, Anya Ormsby, Jane Daly,
Michael Mazes, Arthur Bradley*
A boy who has been reported as killed in action, comes
back to his family as a vampire in this gruesome
chiller.
Aka: DEAD OF NIGHT (INT); KILL; NIGHT ANDY
CAME HOME, THE; NIGHT WALK; VETERAN,
THE
HOR            88 min; 78 min (INT) (ort 90 min)
B,V,V2                        INT; PMA L/A; VPD

## DEATHGAME **
Jerry Jameson         USA
*Michael Forrest, Michael Pataki, Paul Carr, Jo Anne
Meredith, Nancy Harris*
Bikers wreak havoc as only they can in this little-
known actioner.
Aka: DEATH GAME
A/AD                                       85 min
B,V                 KRP L/A; VFM L/A; PRIME/CBS

## DEATHLINE *                                 18
Douglas F. O'Neans    USA              1984
*Vince Edwards, Paul Smith, Jane Wilkinson, Phil
Foster, Louis Guss, Carey Clark*
Violent account of underworld drug dealing and
gambling, with a corrupt Texas D.A. finding that the
Mob are trying to take over his cocaine operation. A
disjointed and confusing exercise in tedium, set off by
some remarkably poor acting.
Aka: SNO-LINE
A/AD                  88 min Cut (1 min 9 sec)
B,V                                        VES

## DEATHMASK **                                18
Richard S. Friedman   USA              1984
*Farley Granger, Lee Bryant, John McCurry, Arch
Johnson, Barbara Bingham, Danny Aiello, Ruth
Warrick*
A medical investigator, haunted by the drowning of
his own daughter, becomes obsessed with discovering
the identity of a dead 4-year-old boy found in a
cardboard box. A confusing and disjointed tale which
fails to develop the opening mystery.
THR                                 90 min mTV
B,V                                        TGP

## DEATHROW GAMESHOW **                        18
Mark Pirro            USA              1987
*John McCafferty, Robyn Blythe, Beano, Mark Lasky,
Darwyn Carlson, Kent Butler, Debra Lamb, Paul
Farbman*
A misfire of a black comedy in which killers waiting
on deathrow can take part in a new TV quiz show.
They stand to either win their freedom or have their
sentence of death carried out.
COM                                        80 min
B,V                                        CHV

## DEATHSPORT *
Henry Suso/Allan Arkush
              USA                      1978
*Allan Arkush, David Carradine, Claudia Jennings,
Richard Lynch, David McLean, Jesse Vint*
A kind of follow-up to DEATHRACE 2000 but set
1,000 years in the future where there are good
gladiators who ride horses and carry lances, and
baddies who prefer to stick to motorcycles. A feeble

sequel with little going for it.

| FAN | 87 min Cut |
| B,V | WHV |

## DEATHSTALKER *                                    18
John Watson     ARGENTINA/USA                   1983
*Richard Hill, Barbi Benton, Richard Brooker, Lana Clarkson, Victor Bo, Bernard Erhard*
Sword-and-sorcery tale with a warrior sent to rescue a princess from an evil wizard. Like so many of these, the title may change but the plot remains the same. Filmed in Argentina and followed by a sequel in 1987.
Aka: DEATH STALKER; EL CAZADOR DE LA MUERTE

| FAN | 77 min |
| B,V | VTC L/A; STABL; PALAN |

## DEATHSTALKER 2 *                                  18
Jim Wynorski     USA                            1985
*John Terlesky, Monique Gabrielle, John La Zar, Toni Naples, Maria Socas, Marcos Wolinsky, Jake Arnt, Carina Davi, Arch Stanton, Douglas Mortimer, Maria Luisa Carnivani, Nick Sardansky, Leo Nichols, Frank Sisty*
Sequel to the 1983 film with the same elements as before. A princess in exile is aided in her attempts to regain her throne by a soldier of fortune who must battle the forces of evil and save a kingdom. A medieval fantasy adventure just like the earlier film and with just as poor a plot. Filmed on the cheap in Argentina and released directly to video. DEATHSTALKER 3 soon followed.
Aka: DEATHSTALKER 2: DUEL OF THE TITANS; DUEL OF THE TITANS

| A/AD | 85 min Cut (22 sec) |
| B,V | NDH; MED |

## DEATHSTALKER 3 **                                 15
Alfonso Corona                                  1989
*John Allen Nelson, Carla Hert, Thom Christopher, Terri Treas*
A further fantasy-adventure in the DEATHSTALKER series, with a princess who has been entrusted with a valuable jewel from a lost city, claiming the protection of this warrior. Together they set out to recover the remaining jewels and have many adventures, not least being a battle between our hero and an evil wizard.
Aka: DEATHSTALKER 3: THE WARRIORS FROM HELL

| A/AD | 82 min |
| V | VES |

## DEATHSTONE *                                      18
Andrew Prowse     USA                           1989
*Jan-Michael Vincent, R. Lee Ermey, Nancy Everhard*
A woman journalist investigating a wave of murders in Manila teams up with a former boyfriend and ex-soldier to clear a US soldier who has been accused. A supernatural sub-plot and clashes with local triads help pad out this unappealing trifle.

| A/AD | 90 min |
| V | BANO |

## DEATHTRAP **                                      PG
Sidney Lumet     USA                            1982
*Michael Caine, Dyan Cannon, Christopher Reeve, Irene Worth, Henry Jones, Joe Silver*
A playwright finds that he can no longer write, so he decides to remedy this by murdering a brilliant young talent and stealing his latest work. Overlong and fairly boring murder thriller, adapted from Levin's successful play by Jay Presson Allen.
Boa: play by Ira Levin.

| THR | 113 min |
| B,V | WHV |

## DEATHWATCH ***                                    15
Bertrand Tavernier
                FRANCE/WEST GERMANY             1979
*Harvey Keitel, Romy Schneider, Max Von Sydow, Harry Dean Stanton, Therese Liotard, Bernhard Wicki, Caroline Langrise, William Russell*
In a future society dominated by television, a terminally ill woman with only three weeks to live is persuaded to have her last days filmed for broadcasting. A bitter and harsh examination of the ways in which mass media can be used to abuse the rights of individuals.
Aka: DEATH IN FULL VIEW; DEATH WATCH; LA MORTE EN DIRECT
Boa: novel The Continuous Katherine Mortenhoe by David Compton.

| FAN | 128 min |
| B,V,V2 | VTC; VIZ |

## DEATHWAVE *                                        18
Frank Shields     USA                           1986
*Gary Day, Gosia Dobrowolska*
A cop who took early retirement goes to meet an old friend at a late night rendezvous, and becomes embroiled in a complex web of murder and blackmail when his friend is shot dead at the meeting. When further murders occur he is forced to go on the run. A sluggish and uninteresting yarn, with a plot as predictable as it is hackneyed.

| A/AD | 89 min |
| B,V | EHE |

## DEBBIE DOES DALLAS **                             
Jim Clark     USA                               1978
*Bambi Woods, Richard Bolla, Arcadia Lake, Eric Edwards*
A woman joins a cheerleading team and inspires them to raise money by providing sexual services. Followed by two sequels and many imitations, this lighthearted plot-empty sex film had considerable success on release, coming second in popularity to the 1980 film "Deep Throat".

| A | 90 min |
| V | RIP |

## DECAMERON, THE ***                                18
Pier Paolo Pasolini
                FRANCE/ITALY/WEST GERMANY       1970
*Franco Citti, Ninetto Davoli, Angela Luce, Patrizia Capparelli, Jovan Jovanovic, Silvana Mangano, Pier Paolo Pasolini*
Lavishly made film version of eight tales from Boccaccio's 14th century collection of stories. A colourful and rumbustious film with music by Ennio Morricone and Pasolini. The first work in a trilogy of medieval tales from the director – "The Canterbury Tales" and "The Arabian Nights" followed. Screenplay was by Pasolini.
Aka: IL DECAMERONE
Boa: tales by Boccaccio.

| DRA | 107 min (ort 111 min) Cut (22 sec) |
| B,V | WHV |

## DECEIT *                                           18
Albert Pyun                                     1989
*Norbert Weisser, Samantha Phillips, Scott Paulin*
Silly SF-comedy in which an alien sex fiend joins three travellers, having made plans to make love to one earthling an hour before blowing the planet up with a nuclear device.

| COM | 90 min |
| V | CASPIC |

## DECEIVERS, THE **                                 15
Nicholas Meyer     INDIA/UK                     1988
*Pierce Brosnan, Shashi Kapoor, Saeed Jaffrey, Helena Michell, Keith Michell, David Robb, Tariq Yunis*
Period adventure set in 1820s India, where Brosnan plays a British officer given the job of infiltrating the

murderous Thuggee cult. Hampered by uneven direction and pacing, what could have been an intriguing tale remains curiously flat and undeveloped, though it does have its moments.
Boa: novel by John Masters.

| A/AD | 100 min (ort 112 min) |
|---|---|
| V | VES |

## DECEPTION **
Maximilian Schell
                    ITALY/WEST GERMANY          1975
*Jon Voight, Jacqueline Bisset, Robert Shaw*
A fairly competent thriller, in which a police inspector is charged with the investigation of a murder case where the murderer is an establishment figure with whom he has been previously associated.
Aka: DER RICHTER UND SEIN HENKER; END OF THE GAME; GETTING AWAY WITH MURDER; IL GIUDICE E I SUO BOIA
Boa: novel by Friedrich Durrenmatt.

| THR | 96 min |
|---|---|
| B,V,V2 | VIPCO; WHV |

## DECEPTION ****                                    PG
Irving Rapper          USA                    1946
*Bette Davis, Paul Henreid, Claude Rains, John Abbott, Benson Fong*
At the end of WW2 a European musician returns to the USA only to find that he has lost his one-time girlfriend to a wealthy man. Davis must now choose between her old flame and rich composer Rains, who has been keeping her in a style to which she would like to grow accustomed. A powerful soap opera style film with Rains quite wonderful as the jealous benefactor and Davis equally good.
Boa: play Monsieur Lamberthier by Louis Verneuil.

| DRA | 107 min B/W |
|---|---|
| V | WHV |

## DECEPTIONS *                                      PG
Robert Chenault/Melville Shavelson
                    USA                        1985
*Stefanie Powers, Barry Bostwick, Jeremy Brett, Sam Wanamaker, Gina Lollobrigida, Brenda Vaccaro, Joan Sims, Fabio Testi, James Faulkner*
Silly and contrived film about twin sisters whose plan to change places for a week creates unexpected difficulties when one of them is killed. Full of endless padding such as an interminable disco-dancing sequence and a stupid sub-plot. Stefanie Powers plays both roles. Very much a TV film and originally shown in two parts. Screenplay was by Shavelson.
Boa: novel by Judith Michael (Judith Bernard and Michael Fain).

| DRA | 188 min (2 cassettes) mTV |
|---|---|
| B,V | EHE |

## DECLINE OF THE AMERICAN EMPIRE, THE *** 18
Denys Arcaud          CANADA                  1986
*Dominique Michel, Louise Portal, Dorothee Berryman, Pierre Curzi, Genevieve Rioux, Remy Girard, Yves Jacques, Daniel Briere, Gabriel Arcand*
An amusing and perceptive examination of male/female relationships and the differences between the sexes in terms of their aspirations and desire for happiness. The story focuses on a group of friends who have arranged a dinner party; whilst the women work out at a health club the men prepare the meal. Winner of the Critics Award at the Cannes Film Festival.

| COM | 101 min |
|---|---|
| V/h | NWV |

## DEEP END ***
Jerzy Skolimowski
                    UK/WEST GERMANY           1970
*John Moulder-Brown, Jane Asher, Diana Dors, Karl Michael Vogler, Christopher Sanford*
Tragedy of obsessive love between a 15-year-old boy and a 20-year-old girl, both of whom work as atten-

dants at a public baths. A well made and sad little tale. Music is by Cat Stevens.

| DRA | 88 min |
|---|---|
| B,V | CAB |

## DEEP FEELINGS **                                  R18
                    USA                        1982
*Ron Jeremy, Pamela Mann, Kitten Natividad, Estevee Lane*
The owner of The Blue Fox – a seedy dive in Mexico, imports three young girls to entertain the customers. A classic American hardcore film built around the girls' sexy stage acts and the audience participation.

| A | 97 min |
|---|---|
| B,V | ELV |

## DEEP IN MY HEART ***                              U
Stanley Donen          USA                    1954
*Jose Ferrer, Merle Oberon, Henry Traubel, Doe Avedon, Tamara Toumanova, Paul Stewart, Douglas Fowley, Jim Backus, Walter Pidgeon, Paul Henreid, Rosemary Clooney, Gene Kelly, Jane Powell, Vic Damone, Ann Miller, Cyd Charisse*
No insights in this very Hollywood account of the life of the famous songwriter Sigmund Romberg with a host of guest stars and several good numbers; highlights being a dance number featuring Cyd Charisse and James Mitchell and a sequence where Ferrer performs an entire show himself.
Boa: book by Elliott Arnold.

| MUS | 132 min |
|---|---|
| B,V | MGM |

## DEEP RIVER SAVAGES **
Umberto Lenzi          ITALY                  1972
*Ivan Rassimov, Me Me Lay, Pratitsak Singhara, Sulallewan Suwantat, Ong Ard, Prapas Chindang, Tuan Tevan*
A tale of tribal savagery and cannabalism deep in the heart of the jungles of South-East Asia.
Aka: EL PAESE DEL SESSO SELVAGGIO; MAN FROM DEEP RIVER, THE; MONDO CANNIBALE

| HOR | 88 min (ort 94 min) |
|---|---|
| B,V,V2 | DFS |

## DEEP SIX, THE ***
Rudolph Mate          USA                    1958
*Alan Ladd, Dianne Foster, William Bendix, Efrem Zimbalist Jr, Keenan Wynn, James Whitmore, Joey Bishop, Barbara Eiler, Ross Bagdasarian, Walter Reed, Jeanette Nolan, Peter Hansen, Richard Crane, Morris Miller, Perry Lopez*
When a WW2 naval officer who is also a Quaker loses the respect of the men he commands by his past inaction, he is obliged to head a dangerous shore mission in order to regain it. A competent, solid film built around a simple idea.
Boa: novel by Martin Dibner.

| THR | 108 min |
|---|---|
| B,V | PACVI L/A; GHV |

## DEEP SPACE **                                     18
Fred Olen Ray          USA                    1987
*Charles Napier, Ann Turkel, Ron Glass, James Booth, Anthony Eisley, Bo Svenson, Norman Burton, Julie Newmar*
An alien, human-eating monster terrorises a small town and is eventually killed by two police officers, but more horror is in store since it has spawned some offspring.

| HOR | 87 min |
|---|---|
| B,V | EIV |

## DEEP THOUGHTS *
Jack Regis          ITALY                    1981
*Loise Lovelace, Ajita Wilson, John C. Holmes*
A softcore look at love, with a contribution from American hardcore star Holmes.
Aka: PENSIERI MORBOSI

A 81 min
B,V XTACY/KRP

**DEEP, THE *** 15
Peter Yates USA 1977
*Robert Shaw, Nick Nolte, Jacqueline Bisset, Eli Wallach, Louis Gossett Jr, Robert Tessier*
An overlong and flat version of a novel about a couple who become innocently involved in drug smuggling off Bermuda. A good-looking but almost unbearably tedious effort, with lashings of gratuitous violence that adds nothing whatsoever to the thin and implausible plot. Written by Benchley and Tracy Keenan Wynn.
Boa: novel by Peter Benchley.
THR 116 min (ort 123 min)
V/sh RCA

**DEEPSTAR SIX *** 15
Sean S. Cunningham USA 1988
*Greg Evigan, Nancy Everhard, Cindy Pickett, Miguel Ferrer, Taurean Blacque, Marius Weyers, Nia Peeples, Matt McCoy, Elya Baskin, Thom Bray, Ronn Carroll*
Set in the near future, this tells of an underwater research base that's threatened by a monster crustacean. A waterlogged and talky yarn with little to recommend it.
FAN 94 min (ort 100 min)
V GHV

**DEER HUNTER, THE ***** 18
Michael Cimino USA 1978
*Robert De Niro, John Savage, John Cazale, Meryl Streep, Christopher Walken, George Dzundza, Chuck Aspegren*
This story of Pennsylvanian steelworkers before, during and after the Vietnam War is visually quite remarkable and is strongest when concentrating on the emotions and thoughts of the protagonists. Less a direct examination of the war, it is more a study of its effect on their mutual relationships. The beautiful score is by John Williams. AA: Pic, Dir, S. Actor (Walken), Edit (Peter Zinner), Sound (William McCaughey/Aaron Rochin/Darin Knight).
Boa: novel by E.M. Corder.
WAR 175 min
B,V,V2 TEVP; WHV (VHS only)

**DEERSLAYER, THE *** 1978
Dick Friedenberg USA 1978
*Steve Forrest, Ned Romero, John Anderson, Victor Mohica, Joan Prather, Charles Dierkop, Brian Davies, Ted Hamilton, Madeline Stowe, Ruben Moreno, Betty Ann Carr, Alma Bettran, Rosa Maria Hudson, Andrew William Lewis*
More recent version of James Fenimore Cooper's novel of early American life during the French and Indian wars. A frontiersman and his Indian companion set out to save an Indian chief's daughter after she has been kidnapped. A companion piece to THE LAST OF THE MOHICANS and done in the same bland "Classics Illustrated" style.
Boa: novel by James Fenimore Cooper.
WES 74 min (ort 98 min) mTV
B,V HVP/VSP L/A

**DEERSLAYER, THE *** 
Kurt Neumann USA 1957
*Lex Barker, Forrest Tucker, Cathy O'Donnell, Rita Moreno, Jay C. Flippen, Carlos Rivas, John Halloran, Joseph Vitale, Rocky Shahan, Carol Henry*
The third version of Cooper's classic novel that follows the adventures of a white man who's raised by Indians. A flat and lifeless acount, rendered more so by the indoor sets and clumsy back-projection. Made twice before, in 1923 by Arthur Wellin and in 1943 by Lew Landers.
Boa: novel by James Fenimore Cooper.

WES 77 min
B,V MEV

**DEF-CON 4 *** 15
Paul Donovan CANADA 1983
*Lenore Zann, Maury Chaykin, Tim Choate, Kate Lynch*
Another post-nuclear holocaust film, with nasty things happening to the crew of an armed space station who land on Earth after hostilities have ceased. An average tale of cannibalism and other assorted delights.
Aka: DEFENSE CONDITION FOUR
FAN 85 min
B,V CBS

**DEFENCE OF THE REALM *** PG
David Drury UK 1985
*Gabriel Byrne, Greta Scacchi, Denholm Elliott, Ian Bannen, Bill Paterson, Fulton Mackay, David Calder, Frederick Treves, Robbie Coltrane, Annabel Leventen, Graham Fletcher Cook, Steven Woodcock, Alexei Jawdokimov*
An intrepid Fleet Street reporter investigates the relationship between a British MP and a Russian agent, but finds there is more to the case than he first suspected. A competent political thriller, whose many diverse strands are not resolved until the end.
DRA 93 min (ort 96 min)
V RNK

**DEFENDERS OF THE EARTH: BATTLEGROUND*** U
USA 1986
One in a series of animations inspired by the "Flash Gordon" episodes, this tells of a plot by Ming the Merciless to enslave the human race, using some creatures he has created. Fortunately, the Defenders team are on hand to oppose him.
CAR 65 min
V VGM

**DEFENDERS OF THE EARTH: THE MOVIE *** U
USA 1986
A feature-length animation inspired by the "Flash Gordon" adventures, with a gallant band of heroes led by Flash, out to prevent Ming the Merciless from enslaving the Earth.
CAR 94 min
V VGM

**DEFENDERS OF THE EARTH: NECKLACE OF OROS *** U
1986
Were a magical necklace to fall into the hands of Ming, it would enable him to conquer Earth. Fortunately Flash and Prince Barin are on hand to foil his evil plans for world domination. One in a series of generally mediocre cartoon animations.
CAR 90 min
V VGM

**DEFENSE PLAY *** PG
Monte Markham USA 1987
*David Oliver, Susan Ursitti, Eric Gilliom, Monte Markham, Patch Mackenzie*
The father of a young boy's girlfriend is mysteriously killed whilst working on a top secret American Air Force project. Together with a friend, he finds himself drawn into a Soviet plot to sabotage a rocket launch and steal a high-tech helicopter.
A/AD 90 min
B,V VIR

**DEFIANCE *** 15
John Flynn USA 1980
*Jan-Michael Vincent, Art Carney, Theresa Saldana, Danny Aiello, Lee Fraser, Don Blakely, Frank Pesce,*

*Rudy Ramos*
A drop-out seaman tries single-handededly to deal with a vicious New York street gang when they begin to threaten the neighbourhood. A routine urban violence tale; tough, moody and fairly predictable.
DRA                               103 min
B,V                           ORION/RNK

**DEFIANT ONES, THE ***
David Lowell Rich
                USA                   1985
*Robert Urich, Carl Weathers, Barry Corbin, Ed Lauter, Laurence O'Brien, Thalmus Rasulala*
A poor remake of the 1958 classic, with two prisoners who are shackled gother, one black and one white, escaping and going on the run. A carefully made film that follows the earlier classic almost scene for scene, but never really comes to life on its own terms. Adapted by James Lee Barrett.
DRA              95 min (ort 100 min) mTV
B,V                              MGM

**DEJA VU ***                         15
Anthony Richmond      UK              1984
*Jaclyn Smith, Shelley Winters, Nigel Terry, Claire Bloom, Richard Kay, Frank Gatliff, Michael Ladkin, David Lewin, Marianne Stone, Virginia Guy, David Adams, Josephine Buchan, Richard Graydon, Claire Bayliss*
A couple discover that events that took place in the 1920s are shaping their lives, as they live through a love affair they experienced in an earlier incarnation. A muddled film that starts off as a supernatural thriller and then changes into a clumsy mystery yarn.
Aka: ALWAYS
Boa: novel Always by Trevor Meldal-Johnson.
DRA                                94 min
B,V                                GHV

**DELIBERATE STRANGER, THE:         18
PARTS 1 AND 2 ***
Marvin J. Chomsky      USA            1986
*Mark Harmon, Frederic Forrest, George Grizzard, Ben Masters, Glynnis O'Connor, M. Emmet Walsh, John Ashton, Bonnie Bartlett, Billy Green Rush, Frederick Coffin, Deborah Goodrich, Lawrence Pressman, Macon McCalman*
The story of Ted Bundy – a charismatic law student who was convicted and sentenced to death for three murders in Florida, and was suspected of being responsible for the murder of a further 25 women across six states. Harmon makes the most of his role in this glossy and absorbing drama.
Boa: book Bundy: The Deliberate Stranger by Richard W. Larsen.
DRA              179 min (ort 240 min) mTV
B,V                               CBS

**DELINQUENTS ***                     18
Gregory Corarito      USA             1984
*Michael Pataki, Bob Miner, Stephen Stucker*
Three men escape from a state mental home and break into a nearby female prison in order to fulfil all their perverted sexual desires, but find they get more than they bargained for.
DRA          49 min (ort 89 min) Cut (9 min 44 sec)
B,V                               SAT

**DELINQUENTS, THE ***               15
Chris Thomson      AUSTRALIA          1989
*Kylie Minogue, Charlie Schlatter, Angela Punch-McGregor, Bruno Lawrence*
Soap actress turned pop singer Minogue makes her feature film debut in this lightweight melodrama from Down Under that has a couple of teenage starcrossed lovers fighting to keep their love alive in 1950s Queensland. A glossy, production-line effort, as lacking in impact as it is in interest.
Boa: novel by Criena Rohan.

DRA                               101 min
V/sh                              WHV

**DELIRIUM ***                        18
Peter Maris            USA            1977
*Turk Cekovsky, Debi Shaney, Terry Ten Brock, Barron Winchester, Bob Winters, Nick Panousis, Garrett Bergfeld, Harry Gorsuch, Chris Chronopolis, Lloyd Schattyn, Jack Garvey, Mike Kallist, Myron Kozman*
A Vietnam veteran escapes from a mental hospital and goes berserk, killing at random. He's hunted by two further vets who head a vigilante-style society set up to kill off criminals found innocent by the law. A brutal action drama of little merit but much bloodshed.
Aka: PSYCHO PUPPET (VIZ or VIDAGE)
DRA          84 min (ort 94 min) Cut (16 sec)
B,V                    VTC L/A; VIZ; VIDAGE

**DELIVER US FROM EVIL ***
Boris Sagal            USA            1973
*George Kennedy, Jan-Michael Vincent, Bradford Dillman, Jack Weston, Jim Davis, Charles Aidman, Allen Pinson*
Five buddies are on a camping trip in the Oregon wilderness accompanied by a guide. They inadvertently stumble across a dead skyjacker who was injured when he parachuted out of a plane after being paid a $600,000 ransom. The men decide to divide up his loot but eventually fall out over their shares. A tense story of greed and dishonesty with the spectacular scenery of Oregon adding to the film's merits.
HOR                           78 min mTV
B,V                             ATA L/A

**DELIVERANCE ***                     18
John Boorman           USA            1972
*John Voight, Burt Reynolds, Ned Beatty, Ronny Cox, Billy McKinney, Herbert Coward, James Dickey*
Menacing and well made film about four businessmen whose weekend canoeing trip turns into a nightmare when they are terrorised by two of the more degenerate local inhabitants. Good performances all-round. Contains the famous "Guitars Duelling" sequence – one of the more lighthearted sections of the film. Film debuts for Beatty and Cox, and scripted by Dickey (who appears briefly as a local sheriff).
Boa: novel by James Dickey.
DRA              100 min (ort 109 min)
B,V                              WHV

**DELIVERY BOYS ***                   18
Ken Handler            USA            1984
*Joss Marcano, Tom Sierchio, Jim Soriero, Nelson Vasquez, Jody Oliver, Mario Van Peebles*
Two groups compete to win a breakdance competition. With a prize of $10,000, it's no holds barred time in this amateurish and almost totally uninteresting nonsense.
MUS                                90 min
B,V                               POLY

**DELOS FILE, THE ***                 15
Joseph Purcell         USA            1986
*Roger Kern, Jenny Neumann, Kurtwood Smith, E.J. Castillo, Kevin Brophy, Al Mancini, Charles Lanyer, James Higgins, Kathryn Noble, Sands Hall, Dava Villalprando, Steve Frohardt*
While installing a satellite-fed buoy system on a remote island in South America, a demolition expert and a woman geologist unearth a secret Soviet military operation. Refused aid by the US government, they face great danger from a crack team of Soviet commandos and have to fight for their lives unaided.
Aka: DELOS ADVENTURE, THE
THR                                99 min
B,V                                IVS

## DELTA FACTOR **
Tay Garnett            USA            1970
*Christopher George, Yvette Mimieux, Diane McBain,*
*Ralph Taeger, Yvonne de Carlo, Sherri Spillane, Ted*
*de Corsia, Rhodes Reason, Joseph Sirola, Richard*
*Ianni, George Ash, Fred Marsell*
An escaped prisoner has to choose between going back
to jail or taking part in a CIA mission to rescue a
scientist from an impregnable island fortress. Quite
an enjoyable adventure yarn.
Boa: novel by Mickey Spillane.
A/AD                                    90 min
B,V                                  VCL/CBS

## DELTA FORCE COMMANDO **            18
Frank Valenti          USA            1987
*Brett Clark, Fred Williamson, Bo Svenson, Mark*
*Gregory*
Two US fighter pilots fight terrorists in the jungles of
Nicaragua, whilst waiting for the crack Delta Force to
come to their aid.
WAR                           89 min Cut (52 sec)
B,V                                      VPD

## DELTA FORCE, THE ***               18
Menahem Golan          USA            1985
*Chuck Norris, Lee Marvin, Martin Balsam, Joey*
*Bishop, Robert Forster, Lainie Kazan, George*
*Kennedy, Hanna Schygulla, Susan Strasberg, Bo*
*Svenson, Robert Vaughn, Shelley Winters*
The story of the creation of a special squad to free the
hostages of the real-life 1985 TWA Athens hijack. A
simple and unadorned account that works quite well,
despite unevenness and poor characterisation. Filmed
in Israel.
A/AD                                   124 min
B,V                                      RNK

## DELTA FOX **                        18
Beverly C. Sebastian/D. Ferd Sebastian
                       USA            1977
*Richard Lynch, Stuart Whitman, John Ireland,*
*Richard Jaeckel, Priscilla Barnes*
A convict is released on condition that he helps in a
plan to trap a corrupt official in this formula action
story.
A/AD                                    89 min
B,V                                      CIC

## DELUGE, THE **
James L. Conway        USA            1979
*Lew Ayres, Robert Emhardt, Ed Lauter, Eve Plumb,*
*Rita Gam*
Story of Noah and his Ark in this part of the "Greatest
Heroes of the Bible" series. Average.
Aka: NOAH
DRA                                     42 min
B,V                                  VCL/CBS

## DEMENTED *                          18
Arthur Jeffreys        USA            1980
*Sallee Elyse, Bruce Gilchrist, Deborah Alter*
One of those sick-ploitation films in which a woman is
brutally raped by four men and has her revenge by
murdering them in a variety of revolting ways.
Similar to "I Spit On Your Grave" only this one hasn't
been banned.
HOR      92 min; 86 min (ACAD or APX) Cut (1 min 19
sec)
B,V                            VPD; ACAD; APX

## DEMETRIUS AND THE GLADIATORS **    PG
Delmer Daves           USA            1954
*Victor Mature, Susan Hayward, Michael Rennie,*
*Debra Paget, Anne Bancroft, Richard Egan, Ernest*
*Borgnine*

A sequel to THE ROBE with the Emperor Caligula
searching for the robe of Christ, which he believes to
possess magical powers. Spectacle aplenty with some
nice scenes where gladiators get to perform in the
arena; a shame about Mature's performance out of it.
DRA                             97 min (ort 101 min)
V/h                                      CBS

## DEMON **
Larry Cohen            USA            1976
*Tony Lo Bianco, Sandy Dennis, Sylvia Sidney,*
*Deborah Raffin, Sam Levene, Richard Lynch, Mike*
*Kellin*
A New York cop investigates a spate of seemingly
senseless murders committed by people possessed by a
Christ-like demon. A bizarre and occasionally shock-
ing horror yarn.
Aka: GOD TOLD ME TO
HOR                             87 min (ort 95 min)
B,V                                      VTC

## DEMON MURDER CASE, THE **          15
Billy Hale             USA            1983
*Kevin Bacon, Liane Langland, Andy Griffith, Eddie*
*Albert, Cloris Leachman, Richard Masur, Ken*
*Kercheval, Joyce Van Patten, Charlie Fields*
A demonologist, a psychic and a priest attempt an
exorcism on a young boy in this so-so story.
Aka: RHODE ISLAND MURDERS, THE
HOR                                    100 min mTV
B,V                      VIDFOR L/A; HER L/A; MRD

## DEMON OF PARADISE *                 15
Cirio H. Santiago      USA            1987
*Kathryn Witt, William Steis, Lesley Huntly, Laura*
*Banks*
A carnivorous lizard-man is disturbed by fishermen
using dynamite on the island of Hawaii, and rises to
the surface to terrorise all and sundry. A cross
between JAWS and THE CREATURE FROM THE
BLACK LAGOON with too little of the monster and
too much in the way of sub-plots. Very poor.
HOR                                     84 min
B,V                                      NDH

## DEMON SEED **                       15
Donald Camell          USA            1976
*Julie Christie, Fritz Weaver, Gerrit Graham, Berry*
*Kroeger, Lisa Lu, Robert Vaughn (voice only)*
A super-computer takes over the computer controlling
the house where the wife of a scientist lives. She is
held prisoner, for it has decided to take over the world
by cloning a child from her. Some good effects and
rather scary moments cannot rescue the film from the
dullness of the script and its utterly ludicrous ending.
Pity.
Boa: novel by Dean R. Koontz.
FAN                                     90 min
B,V                                  MGM; VPD

## DEMON WIND **                       18
Charles Philip Moore   USA            1990
*Francine Lapensee, Eric Larson, Rufus Norris*
Accompanied by his girlfriend and several others, a
man ignores warnings from the locals, and visits the
home of his grandparents, the scene of their mysterious disappearance back in 1929. The party soon fall
victim to an evil force and eventually only the man
and his girlfriend are left to battle a hideous monster.
A few chilling special effects are about all there is in
this offering.
HOR                                     94 min
V                                        RCA

## DEMON, THE **                       18
Percival Rubens
             NETHERLANDS/SOUTH AFRICA    1981
*Cameron Mitchell, Jennifer Holmes, Moira Winslow,*
*Zola Markey, Craig Gardner, Mark Tanous*

A demonic maniac terrorises a small town, preying on the inhabitants and drinking their blood, and a well-to-do family are besieged in their country home by this misshapen creature. Standard horror feast.

| | |
|---|---|
| HOR | 90 min |
| B,V,V2 | FTV; ACAD (Betamax and VHS only) |

## DEMONOID, MESSENGER OF DEATH *
Alfred Zacharias    USA    1981
*Samantha Eggar, Stuart Whitman, Roy Cameron Jenson, Narisco Busquets, Erika Carlsson, Lew Saunders*
A couple working an old Mexican mine come across a hand which contains an evil presence and takes possession of the husband. A number of murders are the result in this insipid and low-budget effort.
Aka: DEMONOID; MACABRA

| | |
|---|---|
| HOR | 85 min |
| B,V,V2 | VPD |

## DEMONS **
Lamberto Bava    ITALY    1985
*Natasha Hovey, Fiore Argento, Urbano Barberini, Paolo Cozza, Bobby Rhodes*
Horror spoof in which the patrons of a Berlin cinema watching a film about zombies become victims of the real thing, as the creatures stream out of the screen and slash the audience to pieces. An utterly over-the-top celebration of gore, well directed but about as illogical as they come.
Aka: DEMONI; DEMONS 1

| | |
|---|---|
| HOR | 84 min Cut (1 min 5 sec) |
| B,V | AVA |

## DEMONS 2 **
Lamberto Bava    ITALY    1987
*David Knight, Nancy Brilli, Coralina Cataldi Tassani, Dario Casalini, Bobby Rhodes, Asia Argento, Virginia Bryant, Anita Bartolucci, Antonio Cantafara, Luisa Passega, Davide Marotta, Marco Vivio, Michele Mirabella*
Sequel to the earlier film, with our lovable bloodthirsty creatures coming out of TV sets this time and turning a young girl's sixteenth birthday party into a most unpleasant affair.
Aka: DEMONI 2; DEMONS 2: THE NIGHTMARE BEGINS; DEMONS 2: THE NIGHTMARE CONTINUES

| | |
|---|---|
| HOR | 87 min (ort 95 min) |
| B,V | AVA |

## DEMONS 3 **
Lamberto Bava    ITALY    1988
*Virginia Bryant, David Flosey*
An American writer, staying at a villa with her husband and young son, discovers that a figure out of one of her childhood nightmares is present in reality, and is lurking in the basement of the house. Her husband refuses to believe her until their babysitter is killed and the child taken. A film of effective sequences and rather slow development.
Aka: OGRE, THE

| | |
|---|---|
| HOR | 90 min |
| B,V | TGP |

## DEMONS OF LUDLOW, THE *
Bill Rebane    USA    1983
*Paul Von Hausen, Stephanie Cushna, James Robinson, Carol Perry, C. Dave Davis, Debra Dulman, Angailice*
At the 200th anniversary of a small town, a pianist inadvertently conjures up demons out of the past by playing on an old piano, said demons seeking a bloody revenge in this low-budget shocker of few thrills.

| | |
|---|---|
| HOR | 89 min |
| B,V | PYRAM/CBS; 21ST; HOMCO |

## DEMONS OF THE MIND **
Peter Sykes    UK    1972

*Paul Jones, Patrick Magee, Gillian Hills, Robert Hardy, Michael Hordern, Shane Briant, Yvonne Mitchell, Kenneth J. Warren, Robert Brown, Virginia Wetherell, Deidre Costello, Barry Stanton, Sidonie Bond, Sheila Raynor*
In 19th century Austria a baron keeps his son and daughter as virtual prisoners, for he is convinced that insanity runs in the family. A garbled and cliched mess of chases, intrigues and murders.
Aka: BLOOD EVIL; BLOOD WILL HAVE BLOOD; NIGHTMARE OF TERROR

| | |
|---|---|
| HOR | 89 min |
| B,V | TEVP |

## DEMONS, THE **    18
Clifford Brown (Jesus Franco)
    FRANCE/PORTUGAL    1972
*Anne Lipert (Josiane Gibert), Britt Nichols, Doris Thomas, Karen Field, John Foster, Luis Barboo, Alberto Dalbes*
A condemned witch curses a judge and his companions, leaving vengeance to her daughters and their sexual and magical powers.
Aka: LES DEMONS; LES DEMONS DU SEXE; OS DEMONIOS; SEX DEMONS, THE

| | |
|---|---|
| HOR | 84 min |
| B,V | GOV; AVA |

## DEMONWARP ***    18
Emmett Alston    USA    1988
*George Kennedy, Hank Stratton, David Michael O'Neill, Pamela Gilbert, Billy Jacoby, Colleen McDermott, Hank Stratton, Michelle Bauer, Shannon Kennedy, John Durbin, Joe Praml, Jill Mern*
Horror yarn in which a man hunts for his daughter, who has been abducted along with five others by a beastlike creature. His search takes him into a world of horror as he encounters even nastier creatures along the way.

| | |
|---|---|
| HOR | 88 min (ort 96 min) Cut (1 min 7 sec) |
| B,V | TGP |

## DEMPSEY **    15
Gus Trikonis    USA    1984
*Treat Williams, Sam Waterston, Sally Kellerman, Victoria Tennant, Peter Mark Richman, Jesse Vint, Robert Harper, John McLiam, Bonnie Bartlett, James Noble, John Lehne, Cliff Emmich, Michael McManus, Mark L. Taylor*
Biopic on the career of this famous boxer and his marriage to Estelle Taylor, a star of the silent screen. Realistic fight scenes, but the pedestrian pacing and lack of warmth are drawbacks. Scripted by Edward DiLorenzo.
Boa: book by Jack and Barbara Piattelli Dempsey

| | |
|---|---|
| DRA | 109 min mTV |
| B,V | MRD; HER |

## DEMPSEY AND MAKEPEACE: THE MOVIE **    PG
Tony Wharmly    USA    1985
*Michael Brandon, Glynis Barter, Ray Smith*
A tough, straight cop is shipped across the ocean in an exchange program with Scotland Yard, where he is teamed up with a streetwise female detective. High-tech action is combined with low-tech acting in a totally contrived formula film. Pilot for a crime-busting duo TV series.

| | |
|---|---|
| DRA | 105 min mTV |
| V | VCC |

## DENNIS: THE MOVIE – MEMORY MAYHEM *** U
    USA    1987
Enjoyable kiddie's animation with Dennis riding his bike into Mr Wilson and causing him to lose his memory. Together with a friend and his dog Ruff, he tries to figure out a way to help him get his memory back.
Aka: DENNIS THE MENACE MOVIE
EXCLUSIVES: MEMORY MAYHEM

CAR                                    69 min
V                                         MSD

## DENTIST ON THE JOB *                PG
C.M. Pennington-Richards
                    UK                   1961
*Bob Monkhouse, Kenneth Connor, Shirley Eaton, Eric
Barker, Richard Wattis, Ronnie Stevens, Reginald
Beckwith, Charles Hawtrey*
Here we go again – it's another dire British comedy
whose deliberately misleading and titillating title
refers to nothing more than the efforts made by two
student dentists to promote a new brand of toothpaste.
As unfunny as a trip to the dentist, but not quite as
useful.
Aka: CARRY ON TV; GET ON WITH IT!
COM                 85 min (ort 88 min) B/W
V                                         WHV

## DENTIST ON THE JOB **               18
John Hilbard        DENMARK              1971
*Ole Soltroft, Annie Birgit Garde, Paul Hagen, Karl
Stegger, Soren Stromberg, Susanne Jagd, Carl
Ottosen*
A shy trainee dentist has difficulty with his love life,
unlike his fellow students, but help is at hand from an
aunt who wants him to prove his virility before he is
allowed to take up a good job in the company firm. An
innocent little comedy, one in a popular Danish series
that was a box-office hit in Scandinavia.
Aka: DANISH DENTIST ON THE JOB;
TANDLAEGE PA SENGEKANTEN
COM          91 min (ort 103 min) (Cut at film release)
B,V                  VOV/DARK; PRI L/A; SHEP

## DERANGED **                         18
Chuck Vincent       USA                 1987
*Jane Hamilton, James Gillis*
A pregnant woman kills an intruder when he tries to
rape her, but is unhinged by her ordeal in this
disturbing and unpleasant film.
HOR                                    80 min
V                                         HER

## DERBY DAY **                        U
Herbert Wilcox      UK                  1952
*Michael Wilding, Anna Neagle, John McCallum,
Googie Withers, Peter Graves, Suzanne Cloutier,
Gordon Harker, Edwin Styles, Gladys Henson, Nigel
Stock, Ralph Reader, Tom Walls Jr, Josephine
Fitzgerald, Alfie Bass*
The varied adventures of four people who make their
way to the Epsom races. A skilfully blended mixture
of comedy and pathos, undeniably effective but a little
too class-conscious for modern tastes.
Aka: FOUR AGAINST FATE
DRA                 82 min (ort 84 min) B/W
V                                         WHV

## DESERT BLOOM ***                    PG
Eugene Corr         USA                 1986
*Jon Voight, JoBeth Williams, Ellen Barkin, Annabeth
Gish, Allen Garfield, Jay D. Underwood*
Set at the time of the first atom bomb tests in 1951,
this powerful drama examines the lives of a strug-
gling middle-class Nevada family, seen through the
eyes of teenager Gish, who has to live with the
explosions going on in the desert as well as those
going on in her family.
Boa: short story by Eugene Corr and Linda Remy.
DRA                                    104 min
V                                         RCA

## DESERT COMMAND **
Umberto Lenzi
          FRANCE/ITALY/WEST GERMANY    1967
*Ken Clark, Horst Frank, Jeanne Valerie*
German commandos attempt to assassinate Churchill,

Stalin and Roosevelt at the Casablanca Conference.
Another formula war movie.
Aka: ATTENTATO AI TRE GRANDI; FUNF GEGEN
CASABLANCA; LES CHIENS VERTS DU DESERT
WAR                                    99 min
B,V,V2                                    FFV

## DESERT FOX, THE ***                 PG
Henry Hathaway      USA                 1951
*James Mason, Cedric Hardwicke, Jessica Tandy,
Luther Adler, Desmond Young, Leo J. Carroll, Everett
Sloane, Richard Boone*
Film account of the career of Field Marshal Rommel,
his military defeat in Africa in the course of WW2,
and eventual return to Germany and implication in
the plot to assassinate Hitler. A competent war film
with an interesting portrayal of Hitler by Adler.
Mason played Rommel once again in the 1953 film
THE DESERT RATS.
Aka: ROMMEL: THE DESERT FOX
Boa: book by Desmond Young.
WAR                 85 min (ort 90 min) B/W
V/h                                       CBS

## DESERT HEARTS **                    18
Donna Deitch        USA                 1985
*Helen Shaver, Patricia Charbonneau, Audra Lindley,
Andra Akers, Dean Butler, Gwen Welles, James
Stanley, Jeffrey Tambor*
A woman in Reno to get a "quickie" divorce, embarks
on a passionate lesbian love affair following her
pursuit by a young woman who has become ena-
moured of her. This debut for writer-director Deitch
has moments of interest, but is too uneven to really
work.
Boa: novel Desert Of The Heart by J. Rule.
DRA                                    90 min
B,V                                       VES

## DESERT LOVERS **                    18
Michel Leblanc      FRANCE              1985
*Michael Leska, Andre Kay, Christophe Gil, Michelle
Davy, Jessy Gory, Bertrand Corne, Linda Parker*
A girl joins an expedition of illegal immigrants being
smuggled out of an African country. However, their
Land Rover breaks down in the desert and she
eventually comes to an oasis where a bedouin and his
wives use her as a sex slave. A weak plot serves as a
backdrop for scenes of sensuality in this softcore sex
film.
A                   75 min (ort 81 min)
B,V                          CASS/IVS; GLOB

## DESERT RATS *                       PG
Tony Wharmby        USA                 1988
*Scott Plank, Scott Paulin, Dietrich Bader, Mark
Thomas Miller, Geoffrey Lewis, Shanna Reed*
Pilot for a failed TV series that was to have been a
kind of modern-day Western. In this tale a local rebel
inadvertently foils a bank robbery and gets to be made
sheriff. Very poor.
A/AD                68 min (ort 78 min) mTV
V                                         CIC

## DESERT RATS, THE ***
Robert Wise         USA                 1953
*Richard Burton, James Mason, Robert Douglas, Torin
Thatcher, Robert Newton, Chips Rafferty, Charles
Tingwell, Charles Davis, Ben Wright, James Lilburn,
John O'Malley, Ray Harden, John Alderson*
Made to cash in on the success of THE DESERT FOX,
this excellent war film concerns a British captain who
takes charge of an Australian company, and has to
win their respect if not their affection with his cold,
professional manner. Mason adds strong support,
repeating his role as Rommel from the earlier film.
WAR                                    88 min B/W
V                                         CBS L/A

## DESERT SONG, THE ***
Bruce Humberstone    USA    1953
*Kathryn Grayson, Gordon MacRae, Steve Cochran,*
*Raymond Massey, Dick Wesson, Allyn McLerie, Ray*
*Collins, Paul Picerni, William Conrad*
This third version of the Sigmund Romberg operetta
set in Africa runs along pretty conventional lines.
MacRae as the secret leader of good natives in the
battle against nasty ones, still finds time to sing of his
love. Filmed before in 1929 and 1944. Highspots are
the songs "The Riff Song" and "One Alone". Fair.
Boa: play by Otto Harbuch, Lawrence Schwab and
Frank Mandel/operetta by Sigmund Romberg.
MUS                                          110 min
V                                               WHV

## DESERT TIGERS **
Ivan Kathansky    SPAIN
*Gordon Mitchell, Richard Harrison, Lea Lander, John*
*Brown*
Survivors of a daring raid on a German oil depot in
North Africa end up in the hands of a sadistic German
prison camp commander. Escaping from this POW
camp, they face a battle for survival in the North
African desert.
Aka: LOS TIGROS DEL DESIERTO
WAR                                           92 min
B,V,V2                                           VPD

## DESERT WARRIOR *                              18
Enzo G. Castellari
            ISRAEL/ITALY/SPAIN      1984
*Mark Hamon, Paolo Malco, Antonio Sabato*
An army unit violates desert hospitality by killing an
honoured guest and must pay the price of tribal
vengeance.
Aka: TUAREG: THE DESERT WARRIOR; TUAREG
IL GUERRIERO DEL DESERTO
A/AD                                          91 min
B,V                                             MED

## DESERTER, THE *                               15
Burt Kennedy
            ITALY/YUGOSLAVIA/USA      1971
*Bekim Fehmiu, Richard Crenna, John Huston, Chuck*
*Connors, Ricardo Montalban, Ian Bannen, Brandon*
*de Wilde, Slim PIckens, Woody Strode, Patrick Wayne*
A US Cavalry captain becomes a one-man killing
machine after his wife is killed by the Apaches.
Routine spaghetti.
Aka: DJAVOLJA KICMA; IL DISERTORE; LA
SPINA DORSALE DEL DIAVOLO; PRELAZ PREKO
DJAVOLJE KICME
WES                                           99 min
B,V                                             CIC

## DESIREE *                                     PG
Henry Koster    USA    1954
*Marlon Brando, Jean Simmons, Merle Oberon,*
*Michael Rennie, Cameron Mitchell, Elizabeth Sellars,*
*Cathleen Nesbitt, Isobel Elsom*
An elaborate but stuffy costume drama presenting a
fictionalised account of one of Napoleon's mistresses
before he became Emperor. Both Simmons as the
mistress and Oberon as the Empress Josephine are
suitably ravishing, but Brando looks distinctly out of
place in this muddled epic.
Boa: novel by Annemarie Selinko.
DRA                               102 min (ort 110 min)
V/sh                                            CBS

## DESIRES WITHIN YOUNG GIRLS ***             18
Ramsay Karson    USA    1977
*Georgina Spelvin, Clair Dia, Abigail Clayton, Annette*
*Haven, Sabrina, John Leslie, John Seeman, Paul*
*Thomas, Stacy Evens*
A woman whose second husband died (making love in
the saddle) tries to get rich husbands for her two
teenage daughters in this amusing and occasionally

romantic sex film. Ultimately, she winds up marrying
the millionaire her daughters rejected.
A    57 min (ort 97 min) Cut (45 sec in addition to film
cuts)
B,V                                        PRI; PHE

## DESPAIR ***                                   15
Rainer Werner Fassbinder
            FRANCE/WEST GERMANY      1978
*Dirk Bogarde, Andrea Ferreol, Klaus Lowitsch, Volker*
*Spengler*
Strange story of a Russian emigre running a chocolate
factory in Germany in the late 1930s. Tired of his life,
he plans to murder a tramp so as to assume his
identity. Adaptation of the novel is by Tom Stoppard.
Aka: EINE REISE INS LICHT
Boa: novel by Vladimir Nabokov.
DRA                                          108 min
B,V                                            TEVP

## DESPERADO **                                  15
Virgil W. Vogel    USA    1987
*Alex McArthur, Lise Cutter, David Warner, Robert*
*Vaughn, Yaphet Kotto, Donald Moffat, Gladys Knight,*
*Stephen Davies, Pernell Roberts, Sydney Walsh*
This pilot for a TV Western has a moody and silent
cowboy taking on the corrupt folk who control a
mining town. Knight makes her TV movie debut as a
good-hearted madam – one of the few bright points in
this sullen and slack story. Followed by A TOWN
CALLED BEAUTY.
WES                          93 min (ort 100 min) mTV
B,V                                             CIC

## DESPERADOS, THE ***                           15
Henry Levin    USA    1969
*Vince Edwards, Jack Palance, George Maharis,*
*Neville Brand, Sylvia Sims, Kate O'Mara*
Civil War deserters turn outlaw and go on the
rampage in this fairly enjoyable but simple-minded
effort.
WES                          86 min (Cut at film release)
V                                               RCA

## DESPERATE CHARACTERS **
Frank Gilroy    USA    1971
*Shirley MacLaine, Kenneth Mars, Gerald O'Loughlin,*
*Sada Thompson, Jack Somack*
Study of a couple living in a decaying part of New
York and unable to move out. An overblown and
overwrought effort, rescued by some fine acting.
Boa: novel by Paula Fox.
DRA                                           88 min
B,V                                          PRV L/A

## DESPERATE JOURNEY ***                         PG
Raoul Walsh    USA    1942
*Errol Flynn, Raymond Massey, Ronald Reagan,*
*Nancy Coleman, Alan Hale, Arthur Kennedy, Albert*
*Basserman, Ronald Sinclair, Sig Rumann, Ilka*
*Gruning, Pat O'Moore*
An exciting acount of the struggles three American
pilots face in making their way back to freedom after
they escape from a POW camp. One of those wartime
efforts in which Flynn wins the war singlehandedly;
despite the clumsy propaganda this is a rousing and
enjoyable adventure.
WAR                        103 min (ort 107 min) B/W
V                                                HV

## DESPERATE LIVES **
Robert Lewis    USA    1982
*Diana Scarwid, Doug McKeon, Helen Hunt, William*
*Windom, Art Hindle, Tom Atkins, Sam Bottoms,*
*Diane Ladd, Joyce Brother*
One of those films-with-a-message. This one is aimed
at high school kids and focuses on the dangers of
drug-taking, telling of a brother and sister who

become involved with drugs at their high school. Okay if you like being preached at.

DRA | 96 min mTV
B,V | POLY/SPEC

## DESPERATE LIVING *
John Waters          USA          1974
Liz Renay, Mink Stole, Edith Massey, Susan Lowe, Mary Vivian Pearce, Jean Hill
Revolting trash comedy starring an overweight female pervert who rules over the depraved town of Montville. Full of all the usual Waters excesses and not surprisingly, now something of a cult film.

COM | 90 min
B,V | PVG

## DESPERATE ONES, THE **
Alexander Ramati   SPAIN/USA          1967
Maximilian Schell, Raf Vallone, Irene Papas, Theodore Bikel
Two Polish brothers escape from a Siberian labour camp, and meet two women on the way to the Afghan border in this adequate time-filler.
Boa: novel Beyond The Mountains by Alexander Ramati.

WAR | 103 min
B,V,V2 | RNK

## DESPERATE WOMEN **
Earl Bellamy          USA          1978
Susan St James, Dan Haggerty, Ronee Blakley, Ann Dusenberry, Max Gail
Three female prisoners team up with a gunfighter so as to outsmart a gang of bandits, in this scrappy and muddled comedy Western.

WES | 97 min mTV
B,V | POLY

## DESPERATELY SEEKING SUSAN ***          18
Susan Seidelman          USA          1985
Aidan Quinn, Madonna, Rosanna Arquette, Max Blum, Robert Joy, Laurie Metcalf, Steven Wright, Richard Hell, Ann Magnuson, Richard Edson, John Laurie, Anne Carlise, John Turturro
A bored housewife becomes involved at a distance with a young girl who lives a sort of rootless semi-criminal life in New York. Many twists and turns of the plot ensue before the final climax. Offbeat and sometimes amusing.

COM | 99 min
B,V | RNK

## DESTINATION AMERICA **          PG
Corey Allen          USA          1987
Bruce Greenwood, Rip Torn, Corinne Bohrer, Joe Pantoliano, Alan Autry
An upper-class guy gives up the blue-collar life he chose out of spite and returns to the family fold, only to find that he is the prime suspect in the murder of his estranged father. Torn is excellent in the role of the cold and aloof patrician in an otherwise average film. Pilot for a TV series.

DRA | 94 min (ort 104 min)
B,V | EIV

## DESTINATION INNER SPACE **
Francis D. Lyon          USA          1966
Scott Brady, Sheree North, Gary Merrill, John Howard
A team of marine scientists isolated in an underwater lab have to fight for survival against aliens who are trying to take over the Earth. A flat and unscary offering.
Osca: WIZARD OF MARS, THE

FAN | 81 min
B,V | VFP

## DESTINATION MOON **
Irving Pichel          USA          1950
John Archer, Warner Anderson, Tom Powers, Dick Wesson, Erin O'Brien-Moore
Story of a race between the USA and the USSR to reach the Moon. A simple and fairly modest effort, produced by George Pal with Heinlein co-scripting the film from his novel. AA: Effects (George Pal).
Boa: novel Rocketship Galileo by Robert A. Heinlein.

FAN | 91 min
B,V | PVG

## DESTINATION TOKYO ***          U
Delmer Daves          USA          1944
Cary Grant, John Garfield, Dane Clark, Robert Hutton, Alan Hale, John Ridgely, Tom Tully, Whit Bissell, Warner Anderson, William Prince, Peter Whitney, Faye Emerson, John Forsythe
A suspense-filled drama of a US submarine sent into a Tokyo harbour, to prepare a mission in which an attack is to be mounted on a Japanese aircraft carrier. Well made and acted despite the implausible plot and excessive length. John Forsythe makes his screen debut in this one.
Boa: novel by S.G. Fisher.

WAR | 130 min B/W
V | WHV

## DESTINY TO ORDER ***          18
Jim Purdy          USA          1988
Stephen Ouimette, Michael Ironside, Alberta Watson
A reworking of the theme of Pirandello's "Six Characters In Search Of An Author" in this tale of a blocked writer whose creations, tired of his inactivity, come to life and proceed to take matters into their own hands. A neat and carefully realised comedy-thriller.

COM | 90 min
V | CFD

## DESTROYERS, THE **          15
Cirio H. Santiago          USA          1985
Richard Hill, Katt Shea, Crofton Harvester
A Vietnam veteran rounds up his old buddies, to avenge the death of their former commander at the hands of drug-dealers. A cliched actioner.
Aka: DESTROYER

A/AD | 90 min
B,V | MED

## DESTRUCTION OF HERCULANEUM, THE *          U
Gianfranco Parolini
FRANCE/ITALY          1962
Susan Paget, Brad Harris, Maru Lane, Carlo Tamberlini, Scilla Gabel
The spectacular destruction of Herculaneum forms the background for this standard Euro-costumer.
Aka: 79 A.D. – THE DESTRUCTION OF HERCULANEUM; ANO 79 DOPO CRISTO

DRA | 131 min
B,V | PRV

## DESTRUCTORS, THE **
Francis D. Lyon          USA          1968
Richard Egan, Patricia Owens, John Ericson, Michael Ansara, Joan Blackman
Federal agents investigate the theft of laser rubies from an optical company, following a bombing in this contrived nonsense.

THR | 97 min
B,V | SKY/VFP L/A; HER

## DETECTIVE KID, THE **          15
Joseph Manduke          USA          1989
Jay Underwood, Tracy Scoggins, Vince Edwards
A young fellow who has inherited a share in his uncle's detective agency finds himself plunged into a world of intrigue when he sets out to make a go of

running the business. Average.

| COM | 90 min |
|---|---|
| V | FUTUR |

**DETECTIVE SCHOOL DROP-OUTS ***     PG
Filippo Ottoni     ITALY     1985
*David Landsburg, Lorin Dreyfuss, Christian De Sica*
Two numbskull investigators manage to solve their assignments, despite having the odds piled up against them in this dumb comedy.

| COM | 87 min (ort 92 min) |
|---|---|
| B,V | RNK |

**DETECTIVE, THE ** **     15
Gordon Douglas     USA     1968
*Frank Sinatra, Lee Remick, Ralph Meeker, Jacqueline Bisset, William Windom, Al Freedman, Tony Musante, Jack Klugman, Robert Duvall*
A beautiful woman hires a detective to find her husband's killer and the latter finds himself embroiled in the world of homosexuals. Good acting and direction rescue the film from its poor script.
Boa: novel by Roderick Thorpe.

| DRA | 114 min |
|---|---|
| B,V | CBS |

**DETROIT 9000 ***     18
Arthur Marks     USA     1973
*Alex Rocco, Hari Rhodes, Vonetta McGee*
Cops vesus jewel thieves in a story set against a background of racial disturbances in Detroit. Another blaxploitation movie, with violence and tedium mixed in equal proportions.
Aka: POLICE CALL 9000

| DRA | 106 min |
|---|---|
| B,V | VUL L/A; ODY |

**DEVIL AND LEROY BASSETT, THE *** 
Robert E. Pearson     USA     1973
*Cody Bearpaw, John Golf, George Flower*
Three brothers rescue a murderer who is to be extradited to his home state. All four of them then hide out in the home of a family who have a deaf-mute daughter.

| DRA | 89 min |
|---|---|
| B,V | PRV L/A |

**DEVIL AND MAX DEVLIN, THE ** **     PG
Steven Hilliard Stern
    USA     1981
*Elliot Gould, Bill Cosby, Susan Anspach, Adam Rich, Julie Budd, David Knell*
A dead man makes a pact with the devil in which he will be restored to life if he can persuade three people to sell their souls. Likeable Disney comedy that would have been improved with more work on the script.

| COM | 96 min |
|---|---|
| B,V | WDV |

**DEVIL AND MISS JONES, THE *** **     U
Sam Wood     USA     1941
*Jean Arthur, Charles Coburn, Robert Cummings, Spring Byington, S.Z. Sakall, William Demarest*
A millionaire store-owner takes a job as a sales assistant in his own store, as a way of checking out the complaints of his employees. A charming and witty social comedy, scripted by Norman Krasna.

| COM | 92 min; 88 min (STABL) B/W |
|---|---|
| V | VNET; VMA; STABL |

**DEVIL DOG: HOUND OF HELL *** 
Curtis Harrington     USA     1978
*Richard Crenna, Yvette Mimieux, Kim Richards, Ken Kercheval, Ike Eisenmann, Victor Jory, Martine Beswick*
A family is given a puppy whose mother mated with the devil. This leads to complications beyond the scope of the local vet. Written by Steven and Elinor Karpf.

| HOR | 92 min mTV |
|---|---|
| B,V | VTC |

**DEVIL DOLL *** **     18
Lindsay Shonteff     UK     1963
*William Sylvester, Bryant Halliday, Yvonne Romain, Sandra Dorne, Nora Nicholson, Karel Stepanek, Francis De Wolff, Philip Ray, Alan Gifford, Heidi Erich*
Chilling story of a sinister ventriloquist's doll which is locked away in a cage every night, with Halliday a hypnotist/ventriloquist attempting to transfer Romain's soul into that of the dummy, as he did once before with a former assistant.
Osca: CURSE OF SIMBA, THE

| HOR | 77 min (ort 80 min) B/W |
|---|---|
| B,V | KVD |

**DEVIL HUNTER, THE *** 
    ITALY
*Al Cliver (Pier Luigi Conti), Gisela Hahn, Robert Foster*
A model on assignment in South America is kidnapped by a primitive savage tribe. Unlikely to be available in an uncut form in the UK.
Aka: TREASURE OF THE WHITE GODDESS

| HOR | 80 min |
|---|---|
| B,V,V2 | VPD |

**DEVIL IN MISS JONES PART 2 *** **     18
Henri Pachard     USA     1982
*Georgina Spelvin, Samantha Fox, Jacqueline Lorians, Jack Wrangler, Joanna Storm, Anna Ventura, Bobby Astyr, Alan Adrian, Michael Bruce, Ron Jeremy, Richard Bolla, Joey Civera*
A sequel to the first film with the Devil returning our heroine to Earth, where she inhabits various bodies as a reward for bringing him to a climax. As she moves from body to body and encounter to encounter, Lucifer watches jealously, all the while discussing her with his Advocate. Finally, even he can stand it no longer and abdicates his throne, appearing in her bedroom. A crazy sex comedy of wild inventiveness and fairly witty dialogue.

| A | 73 min (ort 84 min) (Cut at film release) |
|---|---|
| B,V | EIV |

**DEVIL IN THE FLESH ** **     18
Scott Murray     AUSTRALIA     1985
*Katia Caballero, Keith Smith, John Morris, Jim Foster, Colin Duckworth, Reine Lavoie*
During WW2, a married woman has an affair with a 17-year-old. So-so remake of the 1946 French film by Claude Autant-Lara. Filmed once more in 1986.
Boa: novel Le Diable Au Corps by Raymond Radiguet.

| DRA | 100 min |
|---|---|
| B,V | MOG |

**DEVIL INSIDE HER, THE *** **     
Leon De Leon     USA     1978
*Rod Dumont, Zebedy Colt, Terri Hall, Jodi Maxwell*
Set in England in 1826, this follows the fortunes of two daughters and their religious zealot father. Both girls are in love with the hired hand, but one is rejected in favour for the other. Invoking the Devil so as to have him, she instantly inherits a grotesque demon. The story now becomes one of general possession as mothers, fathers and sisters perform horrible acts with each other in this lewd and powerful mixture of sex and horror genres.

| A | 90 min |
|---|---|
| V | RIP |

**DEVIL RIDER, THE ***     18
Victor Alexander     USA
*Rick Groat, Deborah Norris, David Campbell, Wayne Douglass, Tag Groat*
The ghost of a dead outlaw returns to cause fresh misery.

HOR                          90 min (ort 100 min)
V                                      CAST; CFD

## DEVIL RIDERS, THE **
Sam Newfield            USA              1943
*Buster Crabbe, Al St John, Patti McCarthy, Charles
King, John Merton, Frank LaRue, Kermit Maynard,
Jack Ingram, George Chesebro, Ed Cassidy, Frank
Ellis, Al Ferguson, Bert Dillard, Bud Osborne, Artie
Ortego, Herman Hack*
Fair film in the "Billy The Kid" series, with a crooked
lawyer and his friend out to get land designated by the
government for a stage route. Billy comes to the aid of
the beleaguered stage company owner.
Osca: AFFAIRS OF PIERRE, THE
WES            59 min; 160 min (2 film cassette) B/W
V                                          WOOD

## DEVIL TIMES FIVE *                         18
Sean McGregor           USA              1974
*Gene Evans, Sorrel Brooke, Shelley Morrison, Dawn
Lyn, Leif Garrett, Taylor Lacher, Carolyn Steller*
Charming film about six adults stranded in an
isolated mansion, with five children who have escaped
from a mental home. The children take revenge on the
adults in a variety of gruesome ways. Not badly made,
but hardly an edifying experience.
Aka: HORRIBLE HOUSE ON THE HILL, THE;
PEOPLE TOYS; PEOPLETOYS; TANTRUMS (MPV)
HOR           83 min (ort 87 min) Cut (1 min 9 sec)
B,V                                   INT/CBS; MPV

## DEVIL WITHIN HER, THE *                     18
Peter Sasdy             UK                1975
*Joan Collins, Ralph Bates, Donald Pleasence, Eileen
Atkins, Caroline Munro, Hilary Mason, John Steiner,
George Claydon, Janet Key, Judy Buxton, Derek
Benfield, Stanley Lebor, John Moore, Floella
Benjamin, Suzie Lightning*
Rip-off of ROSEMARY'S BABY with an ex-stripper
giving birth to a monster that goes on the obligatory
rampage. Re-released in 1982 as "The Monster".
Aka: BABY, THE; I DON'T WANT TO BE BORN; IT
LIVES WITHIN HER (ARCTIC); MONSTER, THE;
SHARON'S BABY
HOR                          89 min (ort 100 min)
B,V               RNK L/A; ARCTIC; MIA (VHS only)

## DEVIL WITHIN HER, THE *
Oliver Hellman (Ovidio Assonitis)
                        ITALY/USA        1974
*Juliet Mills, Richard Johnson, Elizabeth Turner,
David Colin Jr*
A rip-off of the THE EXORCIST with the story of a
woman who becomes pregnant by the Devil. A verit-
able feast of regurgitations, contortions and even a
Mercedes McCambridge-style voice-over; not surpri-
singly Warner Brothers took legal action for plagiar-
ism. Followed in 1977 by SHOCK.
Aka: BEHIND THE DOOR; BEYOND THE DOOR;
CHI SEI?
HOR                                     94 min
B,V                                VSP L/A; APX

## DEVIL'S ADVOCATE, THE **                    15
Guy Green          WEST GERMANY          1977
*John Mills, Stephanie Audran, Jason Miller, Timothy
West, Patrick Mower, Paola Pitagora, Daniel Massey,
Leigh Lawson, Raf Vallone, Jack Hedley*
A dying priest is called to Rome to investigate the case
for the canonisation of a local Italian miracle-worker.
An earnest and sincere effort that is hampered by a
distinct lack of thrust to the narrative.
Boa: novel by Morris West.
DRA                                    109 min
B,V,V2                                   TEVP

## DEVIL'S ADVOCATE, THE ***                   15
Brian Stuart            USA              1982

*Leigh Harris, Lynette Harris, Bob Nelson, David
Millbern, Ana De Sade, Bruno Rey, Robert Ballesteros,
Douglas Sanders, Tony Stevens, Martin LaSalle,
Silvia Masters, William Arnold, Teresa Conway, Lucy
Jensen, Michael Fountain*
This fair sword and sorcery epic has two sisters with
supernatural powers seeking out the wizard who
murdered their mother.
Aka: SORCERESS
HOR                     79 min (ort 92 min) Cut (23 sec)
B,V                                      VDEL

## DEVIL'S ANGELS *
Daniel Haller           USA              1967
*John Cassavetes, Mimsy Farmer, Beverly Adams, Leo
Gordon*
A murderous band of Hell's Angels head for an outlaw
sanctuary, mowing down everything in their way and
causing mayhem at a local seaside resort. A low-
budget exercise in lurid violence.
HOR                                     83 min
B,V                                  ORION/RNK

## DEVIL'S CANYON **
Alfred L. Werker        USA              1953
*Dale Robertson, Virginia Mayo, Stephen McNally,
Arthur Hunnicutt*
A female stagecoach robber is the only woman among
550 men in an Arizona prison. A former US marshal is
sent to join her and becomes the target for murder.
Average.
Osca: CRY IN THE NIGHT, A
WES                          88 min (ort 92 min)
B,V                                      KVD

## DEVIL'S GARDEN, THE **                      18
                        USA
*Sandra Carey, Lawrence Edwards, Paula Temple,
Henry Saunders McGuire, Helene De Sade*
A mixture of sex and witchcraft in this tale of a
woman who goes to a Caribbean island in search of
her husband who disappeared there. On arriving she
falls into the hands of a decadent couple who control a
strange voodoo cult. Cut before video submission by 11
min 6 sec.
A                                       55 min
B,V                              CRAW; BLUES/DOV

## DEVIL'S GIFT *
Ken Barton              USA              1984
*Bob Mendelsohn, Vicki Saputo, Struan Robertson*
A boy is given a toy monkey that is possessed by an
evil spirit in this obscure and fairly unmemorable
horror yarn.
HOR                                     90 min
B,V                                   CAP/CBS

## DEVIL'S MEN, THE **                         18
Costa Carayiannis
                        UK/USA           1976
*Donald Pleasence, Luan Peters, Nikos Verlakis, Costas
Skouras, Peter Cushing, Vanna Revilli, Bob Behling,
Fernando Bislani, Anna Mentgosrani, Christina,
Meira, Jane Lyle, Jessica*
An archaeologist uncovers a baron's cult of Minoan
devil-worshippers on a Greek island. The cult kidnaps
some tourists and the local priest steps in to try and
save them, in this slow and tedious effort.
Aka: DEVIL'S PEOPLE, THE; LAND OF THE
MINOTAUR; MINOTAUR
HOR                          89 min (ort 93 min)
B,V                                      CBS

## DEVIL'S NIGHTMARE **
Jean Brismee
                        BELGIUM/ITALY    1971
*Erika Blanc, Jean Servais, Daniel Emilfolk*
In a spiteful attempt to hurt his wife, a lovesick

German general murders their young child. Years later the Devil pays him a visit.
Aka: AU SERVICE DU DIABLE; LA PLUS LONGUE NUIT DU DIABLE; VAMPIRE PLAYGIRLS
HOR                                               90 min
B,V,V2                                            GOV

## DEVILS OF DARKNESS *
Lance Comfort        UK              1965
William Sylvester, Hubert Noel, Tracy Reed, Carole Gray, Diana Decker, Rona Anderson, Peter Iling, Gerard Heinz, Victor Brooks, Avril Angers, Julie Mendes
A vampire disguises himself as a French count (a most original disguise), in order to prey on young girls in this tale of vampirism and black magic. Generally shoddy despite a couple of good scenes.
HOR                                               90 min
B,V,V2                                            DFS

## DEVILS OF MONZA **                             18
Luciano Odoriso      ITALY           1986
Myriam Roussel, Alessandro Gassman, Alina De Simon
Just one more tale of obsessed nuns and their stifled and claustrophobic lives.
DRA                                              104 min
B,V                                              CINE

## DEVIL'S PARADISE, THE ***                      15
Vadim Glowna    WEST GERMANY          1987
Jurgen Prochnow, Sam Waterston, Suzanna Hamilton, Mario Adorf, Dominique Pinon, Ingrid Caren
Set in South-East Asia just prior to WW2, this has Prochnow managing a coal mine on a remote Indonesian island. When his partner is murdered he goes to the mainland to clear up his affairs, and meets a pretty girl who plays in a female band. He takes her back to his island, but a crook who also has an interest in her soon follows. An atmospheric and generally effective thriller.
Aka: DES TEUFELS PARADIES
THR                                               90 min
B,V                                               GHV

## DEVIL'S POSSESSED, THE **                      15
Leon Klimovsky       SPAIN
Paul Naschy, Norma Sebre, Vidal Molina
Story of a cruel 17th century French aristocrat who becomes an evil tyrant. A standard costumer with horror elements.
HOR                                               85 min
B,V,V2                                            VPD

## DEVIL'S SWORD **                               18
R. Timoer                            1984
Barry Prima, Rita Christina, Cubby Sinatra
One more in a long line of forgettable sword and sorcery adventures.
FAN                                               93 min
B,V                                          ECF/VIDLNE

## DEVIL'S WIDOW, THE **
Roddy McDowall        UK              1971
Ava Gardner, Ian MacShane, Cyril Cusack, Stephanie Beacham, Richard Wattis, David Whitman, Madeline Smith
A middle-aged widow has a satanic effect on young people around her, with a young man being sacrificed every seven years as a "tithe to Hell". An arty and uneven directing debut for McDowall.
Aka: BALLAD OF TAM-LIN, THE; TAM-LIN
HOR                                              106 min
B,V                                               VFP

## DEVILS, THE **                                 18
Ken Russell          UK              1971
Oliver Reed, Vanessa Redgrave, Dudley Sutton, Max Audrian, Gemma Jones, Murray Melvin, Michael Gothard, Georgina Hale, Brian Murphy, Christopher Logue, Graham Armitage, John Woodvine, Andrew Faulds, Kenneth Colley
Overblown and over-rated account of the alleged demonic possession of a number of nuns in 17th century France. Concentration on the visual aspects of death and horror to the exclusion of everything else, results in a failure to capture any of the psychological aspects of mass-hysteria. Shallow.
Boa: book The Devils Of Loudoun by Aldous Huxley/play by John Whiting.
DRA         103 min (ort 111 min) (Cut at film release)
B,V                                               WHV

## DEVONSVILLE TERROR, THE **                     18
Ulli Lommel          USA             1983
Suzanna Love, Robert Walker Jr, Donald Pleasence, Paul Wilson
An outbreak of strange happenings takes place not long after the arrival of a new school-teacher to a town with a history of witchcraft, haunted by the curse of a witch who was killed 300 years ago. Formula horror tale that builds up to a RAIDERS OF THE LOST ARK-style climax.
HOR                                               82 min
B,V                                         VTC; XTASY

## DEVOURING WAVES **                             18
John Old Jr (Lamberto Bava)
                     FRANCE/ITALY    1984
Michael Sopkiw, Lawrence Morgant, Cinthia Stewart, Gianni Garko, William Berger, Dagmar Lassander, Valentine Monnier, Iris Peynard, Paul Branco
A prehistoric sea-creature rises from the deep to wreak havoc on all and sundry, but not, unfortunately, on the producers of this undistinguished dross.
Aka: DEVIL FISH; MONSTER SHARK
HOR                                               89 min
B,V                                               MED

## DIAGNOSIS MURDER ***
Sidney Hayers        UK              1974
Jon Finch, Judy Geeson, Christopher Lee, Tony Beckley, Dilys Hamlett, Jane Merrow, Colin Jeavons, David Trevina, Adrian Cairns, Daphne Neville, Hugh Smith-Marriott
When the wife of a psychiatrist disappears, he becomes the prime suspect and the victim of the unorthodox methods of an extremely offensive C.I.D. police officer. An unambitious but quite effective thriller.
THR                                               90 min
B,V                                               ARF

## DIAL HELP **                                   18
Ruggero Deodato      ITALY           1988
Charlotte Lewis, Marcello Modugno, Mattia Sbragia
A young, beautiful model with a decadent lifestyle, pours her heart out to what she thinks is her ex-lover's answering machine when their affair ends. However, she soon discovers that she dialed the wrong number and in the days that follow receives strange calls begging for her love. When two of her friends are found murdered, the situation takes a more sinister turn, in this ludicrous but undeniably imaginative tale. Filmed in English.
THR                                    90 min (ort 94 min)
V                                                 CHV

## DIAL M FOR MURDER **
Boris Sagal          USA             1981
Angie Dickinson, Christopher Plummer, Anthony Quayle, Michael Parks, Ron Moody, Gerry Gibson
A remake of the classic Hitchcock film from 1954, with

the same plot of an ageing tennis star planning to murder his wife, but little of the original's tension, despite a few carefully recreated Hitchcock touches.
Boa: play by Frederick Knott.

| THR | 100 min mTV |
| B,V,V2 | VTC |

### DIAL M FOR MURDER ***
Alfred Hitchcock   USA   1954
*Ray Milland, Grace Kelly, Robert Cummings, John Williams, Anthony Dawson*
An ageing tennis champion plots to kill his wife in the perfect crime. Most of the action takes place in one room and although the cast try hard, the film never really convinces, despite a few moments of genuine tension. Remade for TV in 1981.
Boa: play by Frederick Knott.

| DRA | 100 min (ort 103 min) |
| B,V | WHV |

### DIAMOND HORSESHOE **
George Seaton   USA   1945
*Betty Grable, Dick Haymes, Phil Silvers, William Gaxton, Beatrice Kay, Carmen Cavallaro, Margaret Dumont*
A flashy comedy-musical set in a famous cabaret, where a nightclub singer gives up her career for a her love of a medical student. A colourful vehicle for Grable; efficient rather than appealing. Written and directed by Seaton. Songs include "The More I See You".
Aka: BILLY ROSE'S DIAMOND HORSESHOE
Boa: play The Barker by Kenyon Nicholson.

| MUS | 100 min (ort 104 min) |
| V/h | CBS |

### DIAMOND HUNTERS *
Dirk de Villiers
SOUTH AFRICA   1975
*Hayley Mills, David McCallum, Jon Cypher*
The head of a diamond empire is forced by illness to hand over the reins of power but there are three rivals for his job.

| A/AD | 86 min (ort 95 min) |
| B,V | PRV L/A; CH5 |

### DIAMOND MERCENARIES, THE **
Val Guest
EIRE/SOUTH AFRICA/SWITZERLAND   1975
*Telly Savalas, Peter Fonda, Hugh O'Brian, Christopher Lee, Maud Adams, O.J. Simpson, Ian Yule*
Mercenaries attempt to rob a syndicate's diamond mine in South Africa in this convoluted and over-complex caper.
Aka: DIE SOELDNER; KILLER FORCE; LES MERCENAIRES

| A/AD | 98 min (ort 101 min) |
| B,V,V2 | VIPCO |

### DIAMOND NINJA FORCE **
18
HONG KONG   1986
*Richard Harrison, Melvin Pitcher, Andy Chrorowsky, Clifford Aiken, Pierre Trembley, Donald Kong, Maria Francesca*
Battling Ninja clans fight a bloody feud in this standard Ninja nonsense.

| A/AD | 85 min Cut (1 min 22 sec) |
| B,V | VPD |

### DIAMOND QUEEN, THE **
John Brahm   USA   1953
*Fernando Lamas, Arlene Dahl, Gilbert Roland, Michael Ansara*
Costume drama set in India where a merchant and a soldier are sent by King Louis XIV to recover a famous diamond from Nepal.

| A/AD | 80 min |
| V | VMA; STABL |

### DIAMONDS **
Menahem Golan   PG
ISRAEL/USA   1975
*Robert Shaw, Richard Roundtree, Shelley Winters, Barbara (Hershey) Seagull, Shai K. Ophir*
A diamond merchant masterminds an attempt to rob the Israeli Diamond Exchange, in this rather unin-spired crime thriller. Some good location scenes in Tel Aviv and Jerusalem partially rescue it.

| THR | 104 min |
| B,V,V2 | EHE |

### DIAMONDS ARE FOREVER **
Guy Hamilton   UK   PG   1971
*Sean Connery, Jill St John, Charles Gray, Jimmy Dean, Lana Wood, Bruce Cabot, Putter Smith, Bruce Glover, Norman Burton, Joseph Furst, Bernard Lee, Desmond Llewellyn, Leonard Barr, Lois Maxwell, Margaret Lacey, Joe Robinson*
James Bond versus the villain, who this time is trying to corner the world's diamond supply. A fast-moving and colourful adventure, set in Las Vegas, but spoilt by some rather unnecessary touches of viciousness. Number seven in this long-running series, and fol-lowed by LIVE AND LET DIE, in which Roger Moore took over from Connery.
Boa: novel by Ian Fleming.

| A/AD | 115 min (ort 120 min) |
| B,V | WHV |

### DIAMONDS ON WHEELS **
Jerome Courtland   UK   U   1972
*Patrick Allen, George Sewell, Derek Newark, Peter Firth, Dudley Sutton, Barry Jackson, Christopher Malcolm, Richard Wattis, Allan Cuthbertson, Spencer Banks, Cynthia Lund, George Woodbridge, Ambrosine Philpotts*
A trio of teeanage car fanciers find an abandoned sports car and proceed to restore it, unaware that some crooks have hidden their loot in the seat. A dull Disney adventure of little worth.
Boa: novel Nightmare Rally by Pierre Castex.

| JUV | 85 min |
| B,V | WDV |

### DIARY OF A CHAMBERMAID, THE **
Jean Renoir   USA   U   1946
*Paulette Goddard, Hurd Hatfield, Francis Lederer, Burgess Meredith, Irene Ryan, Reginald Owen, Florence Bates, Almira Sessions*
A maid causes all sorts of problems for the families who employ her in this drama set in the 19th century. An artificial and utterly stilted rendition of a minor classic, remade in 1964. Screenplay is by Burgess Meredith.
Boa: novel A Chambermaid's Diary by Octave Mirbeau/play by Andre Heuse, Andre de Lorde and Thielly Nores.

| DRA | 86 min (ort 98 min) B/W |
| B,V | VMA; STABL |

### DIARY OF ANNE FRANK, THE ***
George Stevens   USA   1959
*Millie Perkins, Joseph Schildkraut, Shelley Winters, Richard Beymer, Lou Jacobi, Diane Baker, Ed Wynn*
The true story of the fate of a group of Dutch Jews who hid from the Nazis in an Amsterdam attic, based on Frank's diary and a stage play. Despite poor casting of Perkins as the title character, this film makes a brave attempt to bring her story to the screen. Written by Goodrich and Hackett and remade for TV in 1980. AA: S. Actress (Winters), Cin (William C. Mellor), Art/Set (Lyle R. Wheeler and George W. Davis/Walter M. Scott and Stuart A. Reiss).
Boa: the diary of Anne Frank/play by Frances Goodrich and Albert Hackett.

| DRA | 150 min (ort 156 min) |
| B,V | CBS L/A |

## DICK DEADEYE OR DUTY DONE ***    PG
Bill Melendez          UK          1975
*Voices of: Victor Spinetti, Miriam Karlin, Peter
Gilmore, Barry Cryer, Casey Kelly, Linda Lewis, John
Baldry, George A. Cooper, Liza Strike, Ian Samwell*
Drawings by Ronald Searle are used in this anima-
tion, which combines the elements of several Gilbert
and Sullivan musicals into one story. A naval officer is
charged by Queen Victoria with the recovery of the
Ultimate Secret from the Wicked Sorcerer. Imagina-
tive but not altogether successful.
CAR                              81 min
B,V               IFS L/A; VMA; STABL

## DICK TRACY ***    PG
Warren Beatty          USA          1990
*Warren Beatty, Madonna (Madonna Ciccone), Charlie
Korsmo, Al Panino, Glenne Headly, Mandy Patinkin,
Charles Durning, Paul Sorvino, William Forsythe,
Seymour Cassel, Dustin Hoffman, Dick Van Dyke,
Catherine O'Hara*
An incredibly ambitious attempt to adapt Chester
Gould's comic strip character for the screen, and yet
retain the flavour of a comic – the use of a restricted
range of colours in producing the film was a master-
stroke. The simple story parades a variety of grotes-
que villains across the screen for our square-jawed
and resolute hero to deal with. Not so much a straight
movie as an overblown parody. Pacino as "Big Boy
Caprice" is a delight.
A/AD                101 min (ort 104 min)
V                                  TOUCH

## DICK TRACY MEETS GRUESOME ***    PG
John Rawlins          USA          1947
*Ralph Byrd, Boris Karloff, Anne Gwynne, Edward
Ashley*
Byrd gives a repeat performance of the role he
popularised at Republic Studios, when he plays the
famous sleuth, this time out to capture a set of bank
robbers who use a special kind of paralysing gas to
carry out their robberies. A fast-paced comic-style
adventure; the title villain is played with considerable
panache by Karloff.
A/AD                          65 min B/W
V                                  PARK

## DICK TRACY VERSUS CUEBALL **    PG
Gordon Douglas          USA          1946
*Morgan Conway, Anne Jeffreys, Lyle Latell, Rita
Corday, Dick Wessel*
Tracy is out to break up a gang of jewel thieves, but
finds that a bald-headed strangler whom the gang
double-crossed, keeps beating him to it and murdering
them. This low budget Tracy adventure has Wessel
well cast as Cueball, but Conway is no more than
adequate as the sleuth.
A/AD                          62 min B/W
V                                  PARK

## DICK TRACY'S DILEMMA **    PG
John Rawlins          USA          1947
*Ralph Byrd, Lyle Latell, Kay Christopher, Jack
Lambert, Ian Keith*
Tracy comes up against a crazed killer known as "The
Claw", whose penchant it is to murder his victims
with an iron hook. A fast-paced formula adventure,
entirely predictable but reasonably entertaining.
A/AD                          62 min B/W
V                                  PARK

## DICK TRACY: THE SPIDER STRIKES *    PG
                      USA          1937
*Ralph Byrd, Morgan Conway, Francis X. Bushman*
Tracy teams up with his pals Mike McGurk and Gwen
Andrews to take on master criminal The Spider in this
generally forgettable adventure compiled from epi-
sodes of a long-running and somewhat variable series.

A/AD                          57 min B/W
V                                  SIMIT

## DIE HARD ***    18
John McTiernan          USA          1988
*Bruce Willis, Bonnie Bedelia, Paul Gleason, William
Atherton, Hart Bochner, Alan Rickman, Alexander
Gudonov, Reginald Veljohnson, De'voreaux White,
Robert Davi, James Shigeta*
Tough action thriller, about a cop who happens to be
attending a Christmas party on the top of a skyscrap-
er, when terrorists burst in and take the guests
hostage. Worth seeing for its good action stunts and
sequences, though its excessive length is a handicap.
A/AD                126 min (ort 132 min)
V                                  CBS

## DIE HARD 2 ***    15
Renny Harlin          USA          1990
*Bruce Willis, Bonnie Bedelia, William Atherton,
Reginald Veljohnson, Franco Nero, William Sadler,
John Amos*
Formula sequel made to trade on the success of the
first film. A gang of terrorists seizes an airport to
rescue a drug baron and Detective McClane, there to
meet his wife, has to do battle with all and sundry.
Meanwhile, his wife's plane is running low on fuel. A
film that's very strong on action sequences if not on
plausibility.
Boa: novel 58 Minutes by Walter Wager.
A/AD                              118 min
V                                  CBS

## DIE LAUGHING *    PG
Jeff Werner          USA          1980
*Robby Benson, Linda Grovenor, Charles Durning,
Elsa Lanchester, Bud Cort, Peter Coyote*
Black comedy about the murder of a nuclear scientist,
in which a young musician and a cab driver are
implicated. Benson is co-author and co-producer of
this witless and unfunny effort, though Cort has a nice
part as a fascist villain.
COM                108 min Cut (1 min 59 sec)
B,V                                WHV

## DIE SCREAMING MARIANNE *
Peter Walker          UK          1973
*Susan George, Barry Evans, Christopher Sandford,
Leo Genn*
A woman on the run from her father, has a casual
romance which develops some unpleasant side effects.
HOR                              99 min
B,V                                DFS

## DIE SISTER DIE *
Randall Hood          USA          1974
*Jack Ging, Edith Atwater, Kent Smith*
A man hires a maid to encourage his sister to commit
suicide, but his plans go awry.
Aka: DIE, SISTER DIE!
HOR                              82 min
B,V                                VFP

## DIE, MONSTER, DIE! ***    15
Daniel Haller          USA          1965
*Boris Karloff, Nick Adams, Freda Jackson, Suzan
Farmer, Terence De Marney, Patrick Magee*
A pretty fair adaptation of Lovecraft's classic tale of a
sinister meteorite, that crashes to earth and poisons
everything that comes into contact with it, causing
plants to grow huge and humans to mutate. Karloff
plays the scientist who attempts to find a way of
combating its menace.
Aka: HOUSE AT THE END OF THE WORLD, THE;
MONSTER OF TERROR
Boa: short story The Color Out Of Space by H.P.
Lovecraft.
HOR                              75 min
B,V                                RCA

## DIFFERENT STORY, A ** 15
Paul Aaron          USA          1978
*Perry King, Meg Foster, Valerie Curtin, Peter Donat,*
*Richard Bull, Barbara Collentine*
A homosexual and a lesbian marry so as to prevent his
deportation, and then proceed to fall in love. Not as
bad as it sounds, though as the film progresses it
slowly runs out of steam, despite a great performance
from Foster.
COM                                107 min
B,V                 VTC L/A; VMA; STABL

## DIGITAL DREAMS * PG
Robert Dornhelm     UK           1983
*Bill Wyman, Stanley Unwin, Richard O'Brien*
Musical fantasy consisting of a blend of comedy,
drama and animation.
MUS                                72 min
B,V                                MGM

## DILLINGER *** PG
Max Nosseck         USA          1945
*Edmund Lowe, Anne Jeffreys, Lawrence Tierney,*
*Eduardo Ciannelli, Elisha Cook Jr, Marc Lawrence*
A biopic on the life of one of America's most notorious
gangsters, who was shot by the police in 1934. One of
Monogram's low-budget gangster movies, an effective
B picture of its type, despite the inclusion of footage
from Lang's "You Only Live Once" for a key bank
robbery sequence. The score is by Dmitri Tiomkin.
A/AD                 66 min (ort 70 min) B/W
V/h                                CBS

## DILLINGER *** 18
John Milius          USA          1973
*Warren Oates, Ben Johnson, Cloris Leachman,*
*Richard Dreyfuss, Harry Dean Stanton, Michelle*
*Phillips, Steve Kanaly*
Romanticised and inaccurate account of the latter half
of the notorious gangster's career up to his death in a
police ambush outside the Biograph Theatre. Con-
tains some of the most violent gunfights put on film.
See also THE WOMAN IN RED.
DRA                                106 min
V/h                  RNK; VIR (VHS only)

## DIM SUM *** PG
Wayne Wang          USA          1985
*Laureen Chew, Kim Chew, Victor Wong, Ida F.O.*
*Chung, Cora Miao, John Nishio, Amy Hill, Keith*
*Choy, Mary Chew, Nora Lee, Joan Chen, Rita Yee,*
*George Wu*
A warm and loving look at three generations of San
Francisco Chinese, and especially at the relationships
between parents and children. This gentle and often
comical tale focuses on an old-fashioned mother whose
modern and free-spirited daughter yearns to leave
home for a life of her own. Slow in places, with long
leisurely shots of empty rooms, but most definitely
worth seeing.
Aka: DIM SUM: A LITTLE BIT OF HEART
DRA    89 min (English and Cantonese with Mandarin
subtitles)
V                                   PAL

## DINER *** 15
Barry Levinson      USA          1982
*Steve Guttenberg, Daniel Stern, Mickey Rourke, Kevin*
*Bacon, Ellen Barkin, Timothy Daley, Paul Reiser,*
*Michael Tucker, Kathryn Dowling, Jessica James*
An evocation of the problems of growing, up experi-
enced by a bunch of 1950s kids who hang out in a
Baltimore diner, looking forward to Christmas and a
big ball game, and wondering what life is all about
along the way. A warm and quite touching film and
the directorial debut for Levinson, who also wrote the
script.
COM                 105 min (ort 110 min)
V                                   MGM

## DINNER AT EIGHT ** 15
Ron Lagomarsino     USA          1989
*Lauren Bacall, Harry Hamlin, Charles Durning, John*
*Mahoney, Ellen Greene, Marsha Mason, Joel Brooks,*
*Tim Kazurinsky*
An updated version of the classic 1930s comedy-
drama, in which a variety of characters attend a
swanky dinner party, held by a pulp novelist who has
social climbing pretensions. A varied collection of
sub-plots offers some interest despite the lack of a
coherent story, and the strong cast do their best with
the flimsy material.
Boa: play by George Kaufman and Edna Ferber.
DRA                 94 min (ort 100 min) mCab
V/sh                               TURNER

## DINNER AT EIGHT **** PG
George Cukor        USA          1933
*Jean Harlow, John Barrymore, Marie Dressler, Lionel*
*Barrymore, Wallace Beery, Lee Tracy, Billie Burke,*
*Edmund Lowe, Madge Evans, Jean Hersholt, Karen*
*Morley, Phillips Holmes, May Robson*
Story of the guests at a dinner party who are drawn
from various levels of society. Polished, sophisticated
and witty; a Hollywood classic. The script is by
Herman Mankiewicz, Frances Marion and Donald
Ogden Stewart.
Boa: play by Edna Ferber and George Kaufman.
COM                 107 min (ort 113 min) B/W
V                                   MGM

## DINOSAURUS! **
Irvin S. Yeaworth Jr
                    USA          1960
*Ward Ramsey, Paul Lukather, Kristina Hanson, Alan*
*Roberts*
Cavemen and two prehistoric monsters are accidental-
ly unearthed on an isolated tropical island in this
dated minor fantasy yarn.
FAN                 80 min (ort 85 min)
B,V                                 MOV

## DIRECTORS, THE *
Mark Haggard/Bruce Kimmel
                    USA          1976
*Stephen Nathan, Cindy Williams, Bruce Kimmel,*
*Leslie Ackerman, Alan Abelew, Diana Canova,*
*Alexandra Morgan, Frank Doubleday, Kathleen*
*Hietala, Hy Pyke, Art Marino, Rene Hall, Greg Finley,*
*Vernon Joyce, Nancy Chadwick*
A Hollywood director reduced to making sex films
plans a porno musical complete with appropriate
dancing numbers – "Dancing Dildos" being one of the
film's choice treasures. A one-joke film that gets very
tiresome very quickly. Scripted by Kimmel who also
wrote most of the songs.
Aka: FIRST NUDIE MUSICAL, THE; NYMPHO
SUPERSTARS
COM          90 min; 83 min (KRP) (ort 100 min)
B,V                 KRP L/A; BLAC/VFM

## DIRT BIKE KID, THE ** PG
Hoite C. Castan     USA          1986
*Peter Billingsley, Stuart Pankin, Anne Bloom, Patrick*
*Collins, Danny Breen, Sage Parker, Chad Sheets*
A kid has a motor bike with a mind of its own which
comes in handy whenever he is in a tight corner. A
two-wheeled re-working of a theme handled in all
those "Herbie" films and about as memorable.
A/AD                87 min (ort 90 min) Cut (9 sec)
B,V                                 MED

## DIRTY DANCING ** 15
Emile Ardolino      USA          1987
*Patrick Swayze, Jennifer Grey, Cynthia Rhodes, Jerry*
*Orbach, Jack Weston, Jane Brucker, Kelly Bishop,*
*Lonny Price, Charles "Honi" Coles, Bruce Morrow*
A naive 17-year-old girl on holiday with her parents
in the Catskills in the early 1960s, meets the local

dance instructor and becomes infatuated with him, embarking on a passionate affair. A pleasant if superficial story held together by some great dance numbers and later followed by a TV series. AA: Song ("(I've Had) The Time Of My Life" – Franke Previte, John Denicola and Donald Markowitz – music/ Frankie Previte – lyrics).

DRA                                              100 min
B,V                                              VES

### DIRTY DIAMONDS **                            15
USA                                              1989
*Burt Reynolds, Maureen Stapleton, Douglas Fairbanks Jr*
Another film in the "Stryker" series, in which Reynolds plays a private eye who attends a party given by his aunt who lives in a retirement home. After being attacked and warned to stay away from the home, he discovers a link between it and a smuggling operation and sets out to help his aunt. A fairly enjoyable film for its type, though hardly demanding. See also BLIND CHESS, CAROLANN and THE DANCER'S TOUCH.

THR                                           90 min mTV
V                                                CIC

### DIRTY DINGUS MAGEE **                        PG
Burt Kennedy          USA                        1970
*Frank Sinatra, George Kennedy, Anne Jackson, Lois Nettleton, Jack Elam, Michele Carey, John Dehner, Henry Jones, Harry Carey Jr, Paul Fix*
Western spoof about a hopeless outlaw who just cannot do anything right, and fortunately the sheriff he comes up against is equally inept. A broad and sluggish farce that has a number of good moments, but not too many of them. Co-written by Joseph Heller.
Boa: novel The Ballad Of Dingus Magee by D. Markson. Osca: HEAVEN WITH A GUN

WES                                  87 min (ort 90 min)
B,V                                              MGM

### DIRTY DOZEN, THE ***                         15
Robert Aldrich        USA                        1967
*Lee Marvin, Telly Savalas, Jim Brown, Ernest Borgnine, Robert Ryan, Charles Bronson, Donald Sutherland, John Cassavetes, Clint Walker, Richard Jaeckel, George Kennedy, Ralph Meeker, Trini Lopez, Robert Webber*
Fairly competent action film with twelve prisoners being recruited for a suicide mission during WW2. Well-acted and highly entertaining. The inevitable parade of sequels followed. AA: Effects (Aud) (John Poyner).
Boa: novel by E.M. Nathanson.

WAR                                 146 min (ort 150 min)
V                                                MGM

### DIRTY DOZEN, THE: THE DEADLY MISSION ** 15
Lee H. Katzin         USA                        1987
*Telly Savalas, Ernest Borgnine, Vince Edwards, Gary Graham, James Van Patten, Vincent Van Patten, Bo Svenson*
Second sequel to THE DIRTY DOZEN, with a bunch of army convicts being assembled once again, this time to go on a dangerous mission behind the German lines. Their task is to destroy a deadly nerve gas factory and rescue the scientists who are being forced to work there. Adequate, but only just.
Aka: DIRTY DOZEN 3: THE DEADLY MISSION; DEADLY MISSION, THE

WAR                                90 min (ort 96 min) mTV
B,V                                              MGM

### DIRTY DOZEN, THE: THE NEXT MISSION **        PG
Andrew V. McLaglen
USA                                              1985
*Lee Marvin, Ernest Borgnine, Ken Wahl, Richard Jaeckel, Larry Wilcox, Sonny Landham, Wolf Kahler,*

*Gavin O'Herlihy, Ricco Ross, Stephen Hattersley, Rolf Saxon, Jay Benedict, Michael John Paliotti, Paul Herzberg, Jeff Harding*
We could have done without this flawed attempt to recapture some of the excitement of the first film. Our heroes are coerced into a mission to bump off a German general, who wants to assassinate Adolf and thus prolong the war. A fine example of how the total amounts to less than the sum of the parts – all the necessary action elements are there but the foolish script causes the whole film to sag badly. Followed by two mediocre sequels.

WAR                              92 min (104 min) mTV
V                                                MGM

### DIRTY DOZEN: THE FATAL MISSION **            PG
Lee H. Katzin         USA                        1988
*Telly Savalas, Ernest Borgnine, Erik Estrada, Robert Vaughn, Heather Thomas, Jeff Conaway, Alex Cord, Hunt Block, Ray Mancini*
The third TV sequel, with our ever changing group of WW2 misfits out to stop Adolf starting up a Fourth Reich in the Middle East. Set on the Orient Express, where they have to discover which of their members is a spy. Could it be their latest recruit – a woman? Poor fare indeed.

WAR                                91 min (ort 96 min) mTV
B,V                                              MGM

### DIRTY FINGERS **                             18
Arne Mattson          SWEDEN                      1973
*Frank Sundstrom, Barbella Kaliff, Peder Kinberg, Ulf Brunnberg, Hein Hopf, Babro Hiort af Ornas, Lena Bergqvist, Jim Steffe, Ulf Palme*
The brother of a girl murdered by drug traffickers is out to have his revenge, in this journey into the world of drugs, brothels, photo studios and sex. A fairly routine gangster story spiced up by its sexual content.
Aka: SMUTSIGA FINGRAR
Osca: HOT AND NAKED (NET/TCX)
A   77 min (ort 102 min) Cut (43 sec in addition to cuts to abridged film)
B,V                      ACT L/A; NET/TCX; SHEP

### DIRTY GAMES **                               15
Gray Hofmeyr                                     1989
*Valentine Vargas, Jan-Michael Vincent*
A woman sees her father killed by terrorists and swears to avenge his death. Six years later she has gone undercover and is in a position to do so, and now learns that the terrorists are planning an action against a nuclear installation that could have catastrophic consequences.

THR                                              96 min
V                                                BRAVE

### DIRTY GANG **                                18
ITALY
*Luc Merenda, Thomas Milian*
Another tough but ultimately forgettable gangster thriller.
Aka: DESTRUCTION FORCE (SAT)
A/AD                                             85 min
B,V,V2                                   FFV L/A; SAT

### DIRTY HARRIET **                             18
Sig Shore             USA                        1985
*Denise Coward, Frank Runyeon, James Tirelli, Rebecca Hollen*
A beautiful career woman is raped and turns into a brutal DEATHWISH-style killing machine. A worthy successor to the trend initiated by LIPSTICK and just as exploitative and superficial.

DRA             84 min (ort 90 min) Cut (2 min 32 sec)
B,V                                              VES

### DIRTY HARRY ***                              18
Don Siegel            USA                        1971
*Clint Eastwood, Harry Guardino, John Vernon, Reni*

*Santoni, John Larch, Andy Robinson*
Nice tense thriller in which a tough San Francisco cop breaks all the rules in order to catch a psychotic killer. Dialogue is somewhat contrived but the action sequences are very well handled. Followed by a number of sequels, beginning with MAGNUM FORCE.
THR                                    98 min (ort 102 min)
V                                                          WHV

### DIRTY HEROES, THE **
Alberto De Martino
                        ITALY                    1969
*Frederick Stafford, John Ireland, Curt Jurgens, Daniela Bianchi, Adolfo Celi, Helmut Schneider, Michael Constantine, Faida Nicols, Howard Ross (Renato Rossini), Anthony Monod, Tom Felleghi, Valentino Macchi*
A rip-off of THE DIRTY DOZEN with a band of ex-cons turned GIs fulfilling a mission behind enemy lines. This time the action takes place in Holland in 1945 with our ex-cons out to beat the Nazis to a hidden fortune. Average.
Aka: DALLE ARDENNE ALL'INFERNO
WAR                                              105 min
B,V                                     SVC; VFO; VIP

### DIRTY LAUNDRY **                              15
William Webb          USA               1987
*Leigh McCloskey, Jeanne O'Brien, Frankie Valli, Sonny Bono, Nicholas Worth, Robbie Rist, Edy Williams, Carl Lewis, Greg Louganis*
The story of an innocent man who becomes involved with gangsters when a satchel full of drugs gets switched with his laundry. The odd cast (including Olympic athletes Lewis and Louganis) add a little sparkle to the basically routine script.
COM                                               80 min
B,V                                                    VPD

### DIRTY LILLY **
Mark Ubell            USA               1979
*Eric Edwards, Beth Anna, Sharon Mitchell*
A happy, sappy moron of a girl has sex with a variety of guys, eventually taking on five Satanists in this hammy pointless offering.
A                                                  90 min
V                                                    CARN

### DIRTY LOOKS ***                               PG
Martin Davidson       USA               1978
*Lee Purcell, Tim Matheson, John Frederick, Didi Conn, Thomas Carter, David Wilson, Petronia Paley, Sherry Hursey, Harvey Lewis*
High school teen-comedy with the usual end-of-term frolics, and a look at the crooked politics surrounding a school election to the student council. A bright and breezy comedy, witty and cheerful if not over-burdened with subtlety.
Aka: ALMOST SUMMER
COM                                               83 min
V                                                MANHAT

### DIRTY LOVE **                                 18
Joe D'Amato (Aristide Massaccesi)
*Valentine Demy, Susan Little, Thomas Russell, Frederick Thompson*
A girl sets off from the suburbs of New York City to seek her fortune as a dancer on Broadway and has numerous sexual encounters in the process.
A                                                  90 min
B,V                                                   CINE

### DIRTY LOVE 2 *                                18
Joe D'Amato (Aristide Massaccesi)
                        ITALY
*Peter Marc, Josie Bisset, Courtney Allen*
The story of a naive American girl who falls victim to

some very lecherous men. A dull, glossy travelogue of a movie.
A                                    90 min (ort 96 min)
V                                               PRISM L/A

### DIRTY MARY, CRAZY LARRY ***                   15
John Hough            USA               1974
*Peter Fonda, Susan George, Roddy McDowall, Vic Morrow*
A couple extort $150,000 from a supermarket and are then hunted through rural California, as racing driver Fonda plus mechanic McDowall proceed to demolish every car in sight. George plays a thrill crazy girl just along for the ride, her part being an unnecessary distraction to a fast and furious film, spoilt by a contrived downbeat ending.
Boa: novel The Chase by R. Unekis.
THR                                               92 min
B,V                                                    CBS

### DIRTY MIND OF YOUNG SALLY, THE **            18
Harry Novak           USA               1972
*Sharon Kelly, James Mathers, C.D. la Fleure, Angela Carnon*
A bored secretary decides to liven up the broadcasts of a mobile pirate radio station by talking dirty over the air-waves.
Aka: INNOCENT SALLY
A                          62 min (ort 84 min) Cut (19 sec)
B,V                              TCX; 18PLAT/TOW; ECF

### DIRTY MONEY **
Frances Megahy        UK                1979
*Ian McShane, Warren Clarke, Stephen Greif, Nigel Humphreys, Christopher Malcolm*
Film about a daring robbery that took place in France in 1976 when a bank in Nice was robbed. Based on the exploits of Albert Spaggiari, whose gang got into the bank from the sewers beneath. This overlong caper has everyone sounding as if they've been dubbed, in a clumsy attempt to convey the idea of British actors playing Frenchmen. Very poor.
Aka: GREAT RIVIERA BANK ROBBERY, THE; SEWERS OF GOLD
THR                                          102 min mTV
B,V                                               PRV L/A

### DIRTY MONEY **                                15
Carl Workman          USA               1975
*Lawrence Luckinbill, Graham Beckel, Regina Baff, Elizabeth Richards, Sam Leverne, Danny DeVito*
A moral tale about how money and the need for it influences the behaviour and attitudes of people. Average.
Aka: MONEY, THE
DRA                                               87 min
B,V                                                  CAB2

### DIRTY MONEY **
Jean-Pierre Melville
                        FRANCE                   1972
*Alain Delon, Richard Crenna, Catherine Deneuve, Ricardo Cucciolla, Michael Conrad, Andre Pousse, Paul Crauchet, Simon Valere, Jean De Sailly*
Pedestrian thriller about a bank robbery and drug trafficking, with a police inspector out to smash a drugs racket, even to the extent of endangering his friend's life.
THR                                               95 min
B,V                                                   POLY

### DIRTY ROTTEN SCOUNDRELS ***                   PG
Frank Oz              USA               1988
*Steve Martin, Michael Caine, Glenne Headly, Anton Rodgers, Barbara Harris, Ian McDiarmid, Dana Ivey*
A successful con artist who makes a career of fleecing wealthy women on the French Riviera, faces competition from a crass new arrival. In an effort to decide who is to remain, they make a wager to see who can be

the first to get a foolish soap heiress to part up with $50,000. Something of an improvement of "Bedtime Story" (1964), with both Martin and Caine engaging in countless double-crosses as each one tries to outsmart the other.

COM 105 min (ort 110 min)
V/sh VIR

## DIRTY TRICKS *
Alvin Rakoff USA/CANADA 1980
Elliott Gould, Kate Jackson, Rich Little, Arthur Hill, Nick Campbell, Angus McInnes
A Harvard professor clashes with criminals, over the theft of a letter written by George Washington in this ponderous and pretentious effort at a comedy-thriller.
Boa: novel The Glendower Legacy by T. Clifford.
THR 91 min
B,V,V2 GHV

## DIRTY TWO, THE **
Teodoro Ricci ITALY 1969
Klaus Kinski, George Hilton, Rai Sanders, Betsy Bell, Lanfranco Cobianci, Enrico Pugano, Piero Mazzinghi, Bruno Adinolfi, Umberto Ceceoni
Two condemned GIs fight to win a reprieve by liberating an Italian village from the Germans in this formula war film.
Aka: AD OGNI CESTO OGNANO PER SE; BADGE OF COURAGE; GRAND SLAM; IL DITO NELLA PIAGA
WAR 93 min
B,V ITM; PHE (VHS only)

## DIRTY WAR **
18
Alfred Cassatas (Alfredo Cassado)
SPAIN 1984
Pierre Oudin, Carol Fuljames, Frank Brana, Lili Murati, Alito Rogers, Monica Breckenridge, Lone Fleming, Vidal Molina, Alice Principe, William Anton, Frank Susman, Oscar Simon, Emil Linder
International thriller about criminals who are after a cargo of plutonium. The usual anti-hero super-agent is sent to thwart their plans.
Aka: GUERRA SUCIA
A/AD 83 min (ort 90 min) Cut (40 sec)
B,V MGM

## DIRTY WESTERN, A ***
David Fleetwood USA 1975
Richard O'Neal, Geoffrey Parker, Dick Payne, Barbara Bourbon, Verne Rossi, Simone
Set in the 1890s this tells of three convicts who escape after seven years in jail and go on a nasty orgy of violence. Having raped a rancher's wife in front her daughters, they abduct the three girls and the youngest is raped in a most unpleasant scene. Eventually the posse catches up with them and the rancher's wife discharges her shotgun full in the face of the one who raped her daughter. A well made, disturbing and extremely brutal film.
A 60 min
V RIP

## DISAPPEARANCE, THE *
15
Stuart Cooper CANADA/UK 1977
Donald Sutherland, David Hemmings, Francine Racette, John Hurt, David Warner, Peter Bowles, Virginia McKenna, Christopher Plummer, Michele Magny, Duane Howard, Robert Korne, Michael Kramer, Patricia Hodge, Danny Galivan
A top hit-man becomes preoccupied with the disappearance of his wife to such an extent that it interferes with his latest contract. Despite a strong performance from Sutherland, this one is badly let down by the flawed script.
Boa: novel Echoes Of Celandine by Derek Marlow.
DRA 90 min; 87 min (VIR) (ort 102 min)
B,V,V2 VCL; VIR (Betamax and VHS only)

## DISASTER AT SILO 7 **
PG
Larry Elikann USA 1988
Perry King, Ray Baker, Peter Boyle, Patricia Charbonneau, Michael O'Keefe, Joe Spano, Dennis Weaver
A routine maintenance operation at a Texas missile silo damages a fuel tank leading to a nuclear missile, and a US Air Force technician has to race against time to avert a catastrophe. Very loosely based on a true 1980 incident, this fictionalised account has a wealth of technical detail, but the lack of convincing characterisation is a serious flaw.
THR 92 min (ort 100 min) mTV
V RCA

## DISASTER ON THE COASTLINER ***
U
Richard Sarafian USA 1979
Lloyd Bridges, Raymond Burr, Pat Hingle, Robert Fuller, E.G. Marshall, Yvette Mimieux, William Shatner, Paul L. Smith, Arthur Malet, Harry Caesar, Jacques Lynn Colton, Michael Pataki, Peter Jason, Jerry Ayres, Julie Mannix
Two trains are set on a collision course by a deranged engineer, as an act of vengeance for the death of his wife and daughter. A gripping if somewhat implausible thriller.
THR 97 min (ort 100 min) mTV
B,V VFP L/A; HER

## DISCO DYNAMITE *
USA 198-
Boney M, Eruption, La Bionda
A story of young people and their lives set to the pounding of a disco beat. Not for people prone to migraine or those who like a reasonable amount of plot in their films.
MUS 79 min
B,V,V2 HOK

## DISCONNECTED *
18
Gorman Bechard USA 1984
Francis Raines, Mark Lyall, Carl Koch, Mark Walker, William A. Roberts, Carmine Capobianco, Ben Page
Twin sisters fall out over a man and one of them takes up with a suspected "maniac-slasher", just to give the plot an excuse for a little blood-letting.
HOR 80 min (ort 90 min) Cut (25 sec)
B,V STUD L/A; BRO

## DISORDERLIES **
PG
Michael Schultz USA 1987
The Fat Boys, Ralph Bellamy, Anthony Geary, Mark Morales, Dannon Wimbley, Tony Plana, Helen Reddy, Ray Parker Jr, Darren Robinson
Bellamy plays an elderly Palm Beach millionaire with a scheming nephew who, assisted by a valet, has cooked up a plan to kill him off and get his hands on the estate. He hires three incompetents – to look after and hopefully kill off uncle – the well-named rap group "The Fat Boys", who rely on their girth to raise laughs. A tired attempt to squeeze some more mileage out of a basically cliched and well-worn idea.
COM 83 min
B,V WHV

## DISORGANIZED CRIME *
15
Jim Kouf USA 1989
Corbin Bernsen, Hoyt Axton, Ruben Blades, Lou Diamond Phillips, Fred Gwynne, Ed O'Neill, Daniel Roebuck, William Russ, Marie Butler Kouf
A silly crime caper in which five ex-cons plan a bank robbery at a small Montana town but experience a series of misadventures when their leader is arrested. They hide out in a Montana cabin and await his arrival. This restrained farce hovers uneasily between comedy and action, and neither thrills nor amuses.
COM 92 min (ort 101 min)
V TOUCH

**DISTANT SCREAM, A ***
John Hough            UK              1984
*David Carradine, Stephanie Beacham, Stephen Greif,*
*Lesley Dunlop, Fanny Carby*
A married woman on holiday in Cornwall with her
lover is haunted by the vision of an old man. Good idea
ruined by the usual heavy-handed direction.
Osca: BLACK CARRION
HOR                                  72 min
B,V                               BWV/VSP

**DISTANT THUNDER ***
Rick Rosenthal      CANADA/USA        1988
*John Lithgow, Ralph Macchio, Kerrie Keane, Reb*
*Brown, Janet Margolin, Dennis Arndt, Jamey*
*Sheridan, Tom Bower*
The story of a disturbed Vietnam veteran who has
taken to living in the wilds, and whose son decides to
visit him, despite having been abandoned by him
years ago. A likeable but rather contrived drama,
saved by good performances, especially Lithgow's as
our unsociable Vietnam vet.
DRA                  109 min (ort 114 min)
B,V                                    CIC

**DISTANT VOICES, STILL LIVES ***          15
Terence Davies       UK               1988
*Freda Dowie, Peter Postlethwaite, Angela Walsh, Dean*
*Williams, Lorraine Ashbourne, Sally Davies, Nathan*
*Walsh, Susan Flanagan, Michael Starke, Vincent*
*Maguire, Antonia Mallen, Debi Jones, Chris Darwin,*
*Marie Jelliman*
A musical saga of working class Liverpool life in the
years just after WW2, told almost entirely through
songs with little spoken dialogue. It presents a
convincing and depressing picture of people crippled
and restricted by their upbringing and social cir-
cumstances, but lacks a coherent story with well-
developed characters and understandable motivations.
DRA                    80 min (ort 87 min)
V                                      VIR

**DISTORTIONS ***                           18
Armand Mastroianni   USA              1986
*Eddie Albert, Olivia Hussey, Steve Railsback, Piper*
*Laurie, June Chadwick, Rita Gam, Terence Knox*
A tale of murder and mystery, with Hussy playing a
woman whose husband meets his death in a car
accident under strange circumstances. Overwhelmed
by her feelings of guilt, she begins to doubt her sanity
when she finds herself being haunted by her dead
husband. There is of course a perfectly rational
explanation, in a cliched horror yarn that wastes
several fine performances.
THR                                  95 min
B,V                                    VIR

**DIVA ***                                   15
Jean-Jacques Beineix   FRANCE         1981
*Frederic Andrei, Roland Bertin, Richard Bohringer,*
*Wilhelmenia Wiggins Fernandez, Thuy An Luu,*
*Jacques Fabbri*
A young mailboy makes a pirate recording of an opera
star who has never agreed to be recorded, and finds
himself drawn into a nasty web of murder, when his
tape gets mixed up with one made by a prostitute in
order to incriminate a gangster. From this fairly
straightforward beginning the film develops into a
flashy, pretentious and only occasionally gripping
thriller. The directorial debut for Beineix.
THR       120 min; 112 min (PAL-dubbed) (ort 123 min)
B,V                                PVG; PAL

**DIVE BOMBER ***
Michael Curtiz       USA              1941
*Errol Flynn, Fred MacMurray, Ralph Bellamy, Alexis*
*Smith, Robert Armstrong, Regis Toomey, Allen*

*Jenkins, Gig Young, Charles Drake, William Hopper,*
*Craig Stevens, Ann Doran*
A solid and well-paced aviation story of the experi-
ments conducted to research and eliminate pilot-
blackout during WW2.
WAR                                 133 min
V                                      WHV

**DIVE, THE ***                              15
Tristan De Vere Cole   NORWAY/UK      1989
*Bjorn Sundquist, Michael Kitchen, Eindride Eidsvold,*
*Sverre Anker Ousdal, Frank Grimes*
Two men in a diving-bell are lowered to the sea bed in
an attempt to stop a net from fouling an undersea
pipeline, but their bell becomes trapped and they face
a slow death from suffocation unless they can make it
to the surface before their air is exhausted. A tense
and claustrophobic film that makes the most of its
restricted setting.
Aka: DYKKET
THR                                  95 min
V/h                                    PAL

**DIVIDED LOYALTIES ***
Harvey Hart          USA              1985
*Janet Eilber, Granville Van Dusen, Greg Mullarey*
Okay melodrama telling of a woman who, torn
between her career and her baby daughter, finds
herself being pursued by the brother of a murderer she
condemned in her news programme.
DRA                                  90 min
B,V                                   POLY

**DIVORCE HIS, DIVORCE HERS ***            PG
Waris Hussein        USA              1972
*Richard Burton, Elizabeth Taylor, Carrie Nye, Barry*
*Foster, Gabriele Ferzetti, Daniela Surina, Rudolph*
*Walker, Mark Colleano, Eva Griffith, Rosalyn Landor,*
*Thomas Baptiste, Ronald Radd, Marietta Schupp*
The dissection of a marital breakdown seen from the
point of view of both partners and done in two
sections. In the first part the breakdown is seen from
the point of view of the husband and in the second
from that of the wife, who has found herself a new
lover. Despite good performances the clumsy script
remains a major handicap.
DRA                    148 min (2 cassettes) mTV
B,V                      RNK; TELS (VHS only)

**DIXIE DYNAMITE ***
Lee Frost            USA              1976
*Warren Oates, Jane Anne Johnstone, Christopher*
*George, Kathy McHaley, Wes Bishop, Mark Miller,*
*R.G. Armstrong, Stanley Adams*
The two daughters of a moonshiner who was cheated
out of his property, wreak havoc on the town after he
is killed by the deputy, in this over-familiar and
uninspired melodrama.
DRA                                  89 min
B,V,V2                                 TEM

**DIXIE: CHANGING HABITS ***               PG
George Englund       USA              1983
*Suzanne Pleshette, Cloris Leachman, Kenneth*
*McMillan, Susan Kellerman, John Considine,*
*Geraldine Fitzgerald, Judith Ivey, Maureen Silliman,*
*Richard Hamilton, Monique Van De Ven, Robert*
*Picardo, Becki Davis, Eric Bethancourt*
A woman found guilty of running a brothel is
sentenced to spend 90 days in a convent in an effort to
rehabilitate her. There she comes into conflict with
the Mother Superior in this sharp and amusing farce.
Written by actor John Considine.
COM                                100 min mTV
B,V                             VDM/GHV; HER

## DJANGO **
Sergio Corbucci
          ITALY/SPAIN       1965
*Franco Nero, Loredana Nusciak, Angel Alvarez, Jose Bodalo, Eduardo Fajardo, Jimmy Douglas, Simone Arrag, Ivan Scratuglia*
Average Italian Western with plenty of action and violence. The first in the "Django" series, this has a mysterious stranger arriving at a town at the height of a battle between American and Mexican soldiers, and taking off with gold belonging to the Mexican army.
Aka: IL MERCENARIO; MERCENARY, THE; PROFESSIONAL GUN, A
WES                              100 min
B,V                  GOV L/A; VPD

## DJANGO KILL (IF YOU LIVE SHOOT) *
Giulio Questi     ITALY/SPAIN     1968
*Tomas Milian, Marilu Tolo, Piero Lulli*
A shipment of gold changes hands when a gang of bandits are killed, but the new owners soon fall out. A mediocre and predictable Western, one in a series of "Django" films.
Aka: ORO MALDITO; SE SEI VIVO SPARA
WES                              110 min
B,V                               FFV

## DJANGO SHOOTS FIRST **
Alberto De Martino
              ITALY           1966
*Glenn Saxon, Evelyn Stewart (Ida Galli), Lee Burton, Fernando Sancho, Alberto Lupo, Nando Gazzolo, Erika Blanc*
When a crooked banker frames his partner for a crime he did not commit, the latter is shot by a bounty hunter and the son sets out to have his revenge. Another film in the "Django" series.
Aka: DJANGO SPARA PER PRIMO; HE WHO SHOOTS FIRST
WES                95 min; 90 min (INT)
B,V                         VPD; INT

## DJANGO STRIKES AGAIN **       18
Ted Archer       ITALY          1987
*Franco Nero, Christopher Connolly, Licia Lee Lyon, Donald Pleasence, William Berger*
Another film in the "Django" series of Italian Westerns – the mixture of blood and bullets is as before.
Aka: IL GRANDE RITORNO DI DJANGO
WES                              86 min
B,V                               TGP

## DJANGO'S CUT PRICE CORPSES **
              ITALY           197-
*Jeff Cameron, John Desmont, Esmeralda Barros*
Yet another spaghetti Western revolving around the character of Django, the mysterious stranger who always rides into town when needed but never stays longer than necessary.
WES                              81 min
B,V,V2                             FFV

## DO THE RIGHT THING ***       18
Spike Lee        USA          1989
*Spike Lee, Danny Aiello, Ruby Dee, Ossie Davis*
An engrossing comedy-drama that follows 24 hours in the life of a pizza delivery-man, who is always ready to calm the frequent disputes that occur between the various ethnic groups that inhabit his neighbourhood. However, some trivial disagreements cause a riot and the film rapidly moves from comedy to sharp social comment.
DRA                              115 min
V                                 CIC

## DO YOU KNOW THE MUFFIN MAN? ***  15
               USA          1989
*John Shea, Pam Dawber*
A well-balanced and sensitively handled examination of child sex abuse, made all the more shocking by the fact that the culprits are several schoolteachers. When a family discover that their young son has been a victim they face an uphill struggle in getting the authorities to believe them and take the appropriate action.
DRA                              90 min
V                                 ODY

## DO YOU REMEMBER LOVE ****     PG
Jeff Bleckner       USA          1985
*Joanne Woodward, Richard Kiley, Geraldine Fitzgerald, Jim Meltzer, Jordan Charney, Marilyn Jones, Carolyn Lagerfelt, Charles Levin, Craig Richard Nelson, Ron Rifkin, Duncan Ross, Rose Gregorio, Susan Ruttan, Sue Giosa*
A middle-aged woman teacher of English starts to suffer from strange lapses of memory and encroaching forgetfulness which is eventually diagnosed as Alzheimer's disease. A sensitive and unsentimental treatment of how this complaint affects every aspect of a person's life, especially their personal relationships. Emmys went to Woodward as Outstanding Actress, to Vickie Patik for the script and to the film itself as Outstanding Drama.
DRA                        92 min mTV
V                                 VCC

## DOC **                         15
Frank Denny        USA          1971
*Stacy Keach, Harris Yulin, Faye Dunaway, Mike Witney, Denver John Collins, Dan Greenburg, Penelope Allen, Hedy Sontag, Bruce M. Fisher, James Green, Richard MacKenzie, John Scanlon, Antonia Rey, John Bottoms, Philip Shafer*
In this thorough re-assessment of the Earp-Holliday myth, our good Doctor is constantly incapacitated by spasms of coughing whilst poor Earp gets his face bashed in. A well made anti-Western look at the OK Corral showdown that strives hard for realism but often just delivers plain nastiness.
WES             92 min (ort 96 min) Cut (5 sec)
B,V                              WHV

## DOC SAVAGE: THE MAN OF BRONZE **  PG
Michael Anderson   USA          1975
*Ron Ely, Darrell Zwerling, Michael Miller, Pamela Hensley, Paul Wexler, Robyn Hilton, William Lucking, Paul Gleason, Eldon Quick, Janice Heiden*
An attempt to bring a pulp fiction character to the screen that becomes a parody of what was originally a straightforward series of adventure stories. Doc and his associates go to South America to investigate the murder of his father. Based on the "Doc Savage" novels of Kenneth Robeson. The last film for producer George Pal.
A/AD                      96 min (ort 100 min)
B,V                              WHV

## DOCTOR ALIEN **             18
Dave De Coteau     USA          1988
*Judy Landers, Billy Jacoby, Linnea Quigley, Olivia Brash, Troy Donahue*
A female alien masquerades as a biology professor and experiments with campus freshmen, turning one of the wimps into a gorgeous hunk no-one can resist, including herself. A juvenile comedy, but a sprinkling of one-liners keeps it afloat.
COM                              90 min
B,V                               CFD

## DOCTOR AND THE DEVILS, THE *    15
Freddie Francis    UK          1985
*Timothy Dalton, Jonathan Pryce, Julian Sands, Stephen Rea, Phyllis Logan, Beryl Reid, Nichola McAuliffe, Sian Phillips, Twiggy (Lesley Hornby)*
Based on a 1940s screenplay by Dylan Thomas and

inspired by the real-life exploits of the famed graverobbers Burke and Hare, this Gothic style tale follows the exploits of a doctor, who hires a pair of thugs to supply him with corpses for medical research, being content not to ask too many questions about their sources. Made with a good deal of care but generally unmoving and unsuccessful.

THR                                  88 min (Cut at film release by 9 sec)
B,V                                                                    CBS

## DOCTOR AT LARGE *                                                     U
Ralph Thomas          UK                                              1957
*Dirk Bogarde, Muriel Pavlow, Donald Sinden, James Robertson Justice, Shirley Eaton, Derek Farr, Michael Medwin, Edward Chapman, George Colouris, Gladys Henson, Ann Heywood, Lionel Jeffries, Mervyn Johns, Geoffrey Keen*
Continuation of a ghastly series. A doctor tries two country practices but returns to medical college. Epitomises everything bad in British comedy films of this period with all the expected stereotypes and stock situations.
Boa: novel by Richard Gordon.
COM                                       104 min; 94 min (VCC)
B,V                                          RNK; VCC (VHS only)

## DOCTOR AT SEA **                                                     PG
Ralph Thomas          UK                                              1955
*Dirk Bogarde, Brenda de Nanzie, Brigitte Bardot, James Robertson Justice, Maurice Denham, Michael Hordern, Hubert Gregg, James Kenney, Raymond Huntley, Geoffrey Keen, George Colouris, Noel Purcell, Jill Adams, Joan Sims*
The second in this interminable series of dreadful medical farces. Our doctor now becomes medical officer on a cargo steamer. This one does have a few funny moments however.
Boa: novel by Richard Gordon.
COM                                        93 min; 89 min (VCC)
B,V                                          RNK; VCC (VHS only)

## DOCTOR DETROIT **                                                    15
Michael Pressman      USA                                            1983
*Dan Aykroyd, Howard Hesseman, Donna Dixon, T.K. Carter, Lynn Whitfield, Lydia Lei, Fran Drescher, Kate Murtagh, George Furth, Andrew Duggan, James Brown*
A quiet professor becomes involved with criminals and prostitutes and develops a completely different side to his personality. An insipid and only occasionally amusing comedy, scripted by Bruce Jay Friedman.
COM                                       86 min (ort 89 min)
B,V                                                            CIC

## DOCTOR DOLITTLE *                                                     U
Richard Fleischer     USA                                            1967
*Rex Harrison, Samantha Eggar, Anthony Newley, Richard Attenborough, Peter Bull, Geoffrey Holder, William Dix*
Unsuccessful attempt to transfer to the screen Hugh Lofting's books, about a 19th century doctor who is an expert in animal languages. It was a serious mistake to make the film as a musical, as this trivialises a rather fascinating idea. In any case the songs are nearly all mediocre. AA: Song ("Talk To The Animals" – Leslie Bricusse), Effects (Vis) (L.B. Abbott).
MUS                                        138 min (ort 144 min)
B,V,LV                                                         CBS

## DOCTOR FAUSTUS *
Richard Burton        UK                                            1967
*Richard Burton, Andreas Teuber, Elizabeth Taylor, Ian Marter, Elizabeth O'Donovan, David McIntosh, Jeremy Eccles, Ram Chopra, Richard Carwardine, Hugh Williams, Nevill Coghill, Ambrose Coghill, Bridget Coghill*
Flabby adaptation of Marlowe's marvellous play about a man who sells his soul to the Devil in return for

24 years of power and gratification. Little to recommend it except the dialogue.
Boa: play The Tragical History Of Doctor Faustus by Christopher Marlowe.
DRA                                                              92 min
B,V                                                                 RNK

## DOCTOR FISCHER OF GENEVA **                                          PG
Michael Lyndsay-Hogg                                                1984
*James Mason, Alan Bates, Greta Scacchi, Cyril Cusack, Barry Humphries, Clarissa Kaye*
A wealthy Swedish industrialist holds parties to allay his boredom, and enjoys observing the reactions of his guests as he lays out a set of tests to reveal their weaknesses and foibles.
DRA                                                              97 min
V                                                                   VCC

## DOCTOR GOLDFOOT AND THE
## BIKINI MACHINE *
Norman Taurog         USA                                            1965
*Vincent Price, Fred Clark, Frankie Avalon, Jack Mullaney, Susan Hart, Dwayne Hickman*
A mad scientist hatches a crazy plan for fleecing wealthy men of their money by creating a bevy of attractive "female" robots. A tasteless and stupid farce.
COM                                                              85 min
V                                                                   RCA

## DOCTOR HACKENSTEIN **                                                18
Richard Clark         USA                                            1989
*David Muir, Anne Ramsey, Logan Ramsey*
A brainless comedy in the style of YOUNG FRANKENSTEIN with a doctor keeping his dead wife's head alive whilst trying to find her a new body. When three beautiful stranded women turn up at his mansion asking for a bed for the night, he gets his operating theatre ready. A clumsy misfire that mixes comedy and horror genres and comes up with nothing new.
HOR                                                              90 min
B,V                                                                 CHV

## DOCTOR IN CLOVER *                                                    PG
Ralph Thomas          UK                                            1966
*Leslie Phillips, James Robertson Justice, Shirley Ann Field, John Fraser, Joan Sims, Arthur Haynes, Elizabeth Ercy, Fenella Fielding, Jeremy Lloyd, Noel Purcell, Robert Hutton, Eric Barker, Terry Scott, Alfie Bass*
Sixth in this series of dated and geriatric medical farces with our medic being sent on a refresher course and falling for a french physiotherapist.
Aka: CARNABY, M.D.
Boa: novel by Richard Gordon.
COM                        97 min (ort 101 min) (Cut at film release)
B,V                                          RNK; VCC (VHS only)

## DOCTOR IN DISTRESS **                                                PG
Ralph Thomas          UK                                            1963
*Dirk Bogarde, Samantha Eggar, James Robertson Justice, Mylene Demongeot, Donald Houston, Barbara Murray, Dennis Price, Leo McKern, Jessie Evans, Ann Lynn, Fenella Fielding, Jill Adams, Michael Flanders, Frank Finlay*
Another in the "Doctor" series. Here our hero returns to his old medical college to work under his former professor, who just happens to be in love (for the first time). Slightly more entertaining than the usual run of these comedies with Bogarde giving his last performance as Dr Sparrow.
COM                        98 min (ort 112 min) (Cut at film release)
B,V                                          RNK; VCC (VHS only)

## DOCTOR IN LOVE *                                                      PG
Ralph Thomas          UK                                            1960
*Michael Craig, James Robertson Justice, Virginia Maskell, Carole Lesley, Leslie Phillips, Reginald*

*Beckwith, Joan Sims, Liz Fraser, Nicholas Phippotts, Irene Handl, Fenella Fielding, Nicholas Parsons, Moira Redmond*
The amorous adventures of two doctors form the basis for this addition to the "Doctor" series with Craig taking over the role played by Bogarde in the earlier films. A worthy addition to a worthless series.
Boa: novel by Richard Gordon.
COM                              97 min; 93 min (VCC)
B,V                              RNK; VCC (VHS only)

## DOCTOR IN THE HOUSE *                              U
Ralph Thomas          UK                              1954
*Dirk Bogarde, Muriel Pavlow, Kenneth More, Kay Kendall, James Robertson Justice, Donald Houston, Suzanne Cloutier, Geoffrey Keen, George Colouris, Harry Locke, Ann Gudrun, Joan Sims, Shirley Eaton, Nicholas Phipps*
The first film in a series that spawned several sequels and a TV show. This one purports to tell of the life and pranks of a group of immature medical students. Not funny, merely tiresome, despite an engaging perform-ance from Justice as the pompous Sir Lancelot Spratt (a role he was to repeat throughout the series). Scripted by Gordon, Ronald Wilkinson and actor Nicholas Phipps.
Boa: novel by Richard Gordon.
COM                              88 min (ort 91 min)
V                                RNK L/A; VCC (VHS only)

## DOCTOR IN TROUBLE *                              PG
Ralph Thomas          UK                              1970
*Leslie Phillips, Harry Secombe, Angela Scoular, Irene Handl, Simon Dee, Robert Morley, Freddie Jones, James Robertson Justice, Joan Sims, John Le Mesurier, Graham Stark, Janet Mahoney, Graham Chapman, Fred Emney*
Last in the series, with our accident prone doctor stowing away on a cruise liner. Despite good work from the cast this one never rises above the level of a mediocre farce.
Boa: novel Doctor On Toast by Richard Gordon.
COM          87 min (ort 90 min) (Cut at film release)
B,V                              RNK; VCC (VHS only)

## DOCTOR JEKYLL AND MISTER HYDE *
David Winters          USA                              1973
*Kirk Douglas, Susan Hampshire, Susan George, Michael Redgrave*
A musical (yes really!) version of this classic tale of a doctor whose experiments lead to tragedy.
MUS                              90 min
B,V,V2                           VCL/CBS

## DOCTOR JEKYLL AND MISTER HYDE **          15
Alastair Reid          UK                              1981
*David Hemmings, Lisa Harrow, Ian Bannen*
BBC dramatisation of the classic tale with many invented scenes. Not bad but very much a TV production and a stilted one at that.
Boa: novella The Strange Case Of Dr Jekyll And Mr Hyde by Robert Louis Stevenson.
DRA                              107 min (ort 115 min) mTV
B,V                              BBC

## DOCTOR JEKYLL AND MISTER HYDE **
Charles B. Griffith          USA                              1980
*Oliver Reed, Jackie Coogan, Mel Wells*
Comic version of the Jekyll and Hyde story, with Jekyll drinking a potion in order to commit suicide, but finding that it turns him into a handsome murderer instead.
COM                              96 min
B,V                              RNK

## DOCTOR JEKYLL AND MISTER HYDE ***
John S. Robertson          USA                              1920
*John Barrymore, Martha Mansfield, Brandon Hurst, Nita Naldi, Charles Lane, Louis Wolheim*

A silent version of the famous tale of split-personality, with Barrymore giving a great performance as the doctor whose thirst for knowledge drives him to experiment upon himself. Some of Barrymore's trans-formations to the evil Mr Hyde are done by facial contortion in this well-paced and often quite gripping version.
Boa: novella The Strange Case Of Dr Jekyll And Mr Hyde by Robert Louis Stevenson.
HOR                              63 min B/W silent
B,V                              POLY

## DOCTOR JEKYLL AND SISTER HYDE **
Roy Ward Baker          UK                              1971
*Ralph Bates, Martine Beswick, Gerald Sim, Lewis Fiander, Dorothy Alison, Neil Wilson, Ivor Dean, Paul Whitsun-Jones, Philip Madoc, Tony Calvin, Susan Broderick, Dan Meaden, Virginia Wetherell, Irene Bradshaw, Anna Brett*
Novel twist to the classic Robert Louis Stevenson story. This time round Dr Jekyll finds that his potion turns him into a beautiful woman, who in her turn kills prostitutes so as to provide corpses for the doctor's experiments. Not the least bit scary but quite watchable.
HOR                              94 min (ort 97 min)
B,V                              TEVP

## DOCTOR MABUSE: THE GAMBLER ***
Fritz Lang          GERMANY                              1922
*Rudolf Klein-Rogge, Alfred Abel, Gertrude Welcker, Lil Dagover, Paul Richter*
Celebrated film about a master criminal who uses hypnotism and blackmail in his attempt to rule the world. He is finally cornered and defeated whereupon he reveals himself as a lunatic. Unintentionally funny in parts, fascinating in others, this angst-ridden journey through post-WW1 German cinema takes the form of a Fu Manchu type thriller. Originally made in two halves (153 min and 112 min) and followed by several sequels.
Aka: DOCTOR MABUSE: THE FATAL PASSION; DOKTOR MABUSE: DER SPIELER
Boa: novel by Norbert Jacques.
DRA                          95 min (ort 265 min) B/W silent
B,V                              TEVP

## DOCTOR MINX *
Hikmet Avedis          USA                              1975
*Edy Williams, Randy Boone, Harvey Jason, Marlene Schmidt, William Smith, Alvy Moore*
A woman doctor is unwittingly involved in the murder of her husband by her unscrupulous lover, in this overwrought and contrived melodrama.
DRA                              72 min (ort 94 min)
B,V                              STV

## DOCTOR NO ***                              PG
Terence Young          UK                              1962
*Sean Connery, Ursula Andress, Bernard Lee, Joseph Wiseman, Jack Lord, Lois Maxwell, Eunice Gayson, Anthony Dawson, Zena Marshall, John Kitzmiller, Lester Prendergast*
Reasonably straight and competent adaptation of one of Ian Fleming's "James Bond" adventures, with our secret agent investigating strange happenings in Jamaica and coming up against a criminal master-mind. This one was the first film in the series and, although by no means the best, doesn't exhibit the irritating reliance on gadgetry that so marred the later entries. Followed by FROM RUSSIA WITH LOVE.
Boa: novel Dr No by Ian Fleming.
A/AD                              105 min (ort 111 min)
V                                WHV

## DOCTOR OTTO AND THE RIDDLE OF          PG
## THE GLOOM BEAM **
John Cherry          USA                              1985

*Jackie Welch, Jim Varney, Esther Huston*
Spoof on the theme of the mad scientist out to gain
world domination.
COM                                           90 min
B,V                                        AVA; CAN

## DOCTOR PHIBES RISES AGAIN ***          15
Robert Fuest              UK                 1972
*Vincent Price, Robert Quarry, Valli Kemp, Fiona
Lewis, Peter Cushing, Beryl Reid, Terry-Thomas,
Hugh Griffith, Peter Jeffrey, John Cater, Gerald Sim,
John Thaw, Keith Buckley, Lewis Fiander, Milton
Reid*
In this sequel to THE ABOMINABLE DOCTOR
PHIBES, our dotty doctor is revived from death and
travels to Egypt with his assistant, in search of an
elixir that will revive his dead wife. He is not alone in
his quest but has a rival for the potion and is
consequently forced to employ some novel ways of
killing off the competition. Price is good in an uneven
and decidedly campy sequel.
HOR          84 min (ort 89 min) (Cut at film release)
V                                              VIR

## DOCTOR STRANGE *                          U
Philip DeGuere            USA                 1978
*Peter Hooten, Jessica Walter, John Mills, Clyde
Kusatsu, Eddie Benton, Philip Sterling, June Barrett,
Sarah Rush, David Hooks, Diana Webster, Blake
Marion, Bob Delegall, Frank Catalano, Larry
Anderson, Inez Pedroza*
A comic strip hero from Marvel comics, Dr Strange is
a "Master of the Mystic Arts". He is brought to life in
this pilot for a series, where he becomes the protege of
another sorcerer (Mills) in order to foil Walter's plans
to enlarge her collection of souls. A pathetic effort that
strips a lively and imaginative comic strip of its
essential mystic qualities, leaving a series of clumsy
battles and endless footage of Hooten at work in his
hospital.
FAN                       89 min (ort 100 min) mTV
B,V                                            CIC

## DOCTOR STRANGELOVE ****                   PG
Stanley Kubrick           UK                 1963
*Peter Sellers, Sterling Hayden, Slim Pickens, George
C. Scott, Keenan Wynn, James Earl Jones, Tracy Reed,
Peter Bull, Tracy Reed, Jack Creley, Frank Berry,
Glenn Beck, Shane Rimmer, Paul Tamarin, Gordon
Tanner*
A demented American general launches a flight of
B-52 bombers at the Soviet Union with the intention
of wiping it off the face of the earth. Since he is the
only person who knows the code that can recall them
the President is faced with a tricky problem. A biting
black comedy that dares to think the unthinkable and
is more effective than any straight treatment of the
subject to date. One of Kubrick's best films with
Sellers splendid in three roles.
Aka: DOCTOR STRANGELOVE, OR HOW I
LEARNED TO STOP WORRYING AND LOVE THE
BOMB
Boa: novel Red Alert (also known as Two Hours To
Dream) by Peter George.
COM                       91 min (ort 94 min) B/W
B,V                                            RCA

## DOCTOR SYN: ALIAS THE SCARECROW ***
James Neilson             UK                 1962
*Patrick McGoohan, George Cole, Tony Britton,
Michael Hordern, Geoffrey Keen, Kay Walsh, Eric
Pohlmann, Patrick Wymark, Alan Dobie, Sean Scully,
Eric Flynn, David Buck, Richard O'Sullivan*
In 1775 the vicar of Dymchurch rides by night as a
smuggler and pirate, and helps the peasants resist the
oppressive rule of the King. A lively and spirited
remake of the 1937 film with McGoohan particularly
well cast as the hero. Re-issued in 1976 with 23
minutes cut.

Aka: DOCTOR SYN
Boa: novel Christopher Syn by William Russell
Thorndike.
A/AD                          94 min (ort 98 min)
B,V                                           TEVP

## DOCTOR WHO AND THE DALEKS *              U
Gordon Flemyng            UK                 1965
*Peter Cushing, Roy Castle, Jennie Linden, Roberta
Tovey, Barrie Ingham, Michael Coles, Geoffrey Toone,
Mark Peterson, John Brown, Yvonne Antrobus*
More of the same from the long running BBC TV
series that outlived its ideas. Three children and their
grandfather travel in his time machine to a planet
ruled by the evil Daleks. A rubbishy film that does not
even try to do justice to one of the early "Dr Who"
adventures, on which it is based.
JUV                           78 min (ort 83 min)
B,V                         BBC; WHV (VHS only)

## DOCTOR WHO AND THE REVENGE OF          U
## THE CYBERMEN *
Michael E. Briant         UK                 1975
*Tom Baker, Elisabeth Sladen, Ian Martin, Ronald
Leigh-Hunt, Alec Wallis, Jeremy Wilkin, William
Marlowe, David Collins, Michael Wisher, Christopher
Robbie, Melville Jones, Kevin Stoney, Brian Grellis*
Compilation of the TV series with the good doctor
battling the evil Cybermen – half man and half
machine. A dire attempt at SF cobbled together from a
series that had long since outlived its inspiration.
Aka: DOCTOR WHO: REVENGE OF THE
CYBERMEN
JUV                                   90 min mTV
V/h                                            BBC

## DOCTOR WHO: DEATH TO THE DALEKS **      U
Michael Briant            UK                 1974
*Jon Pertwee, Arnold Yarrow, Roy Heymann, John
Abineri, Duncan Lamont, Julia Fox, Joy Harrison,
Neil Seiler, Mostyn Evans, Terry Walsh, Steven Ismay,
John Scott Martin, Murphy Grumbar, Cy Town*
Feature cobbled together from episodes of the popular
children's TV series in which a time-travelling adven-
turer faced a multitude of menaces both human and
otherwise. Enjoyable in a clumsy and inept sort of
way, this is science fiction for seven-year-olds. In this
adventure the good Doctor faces one of his deadliest
enemies – those irascible and somewhat hysterical
robots known as the Daleks.
JUV                                   90 min mTV
V/h                                            BBC

## DOCTOR WHO: INVASION EARTH 2150 A.D. *  U
Gordon Flemyng            UK                 1966
*Peter Cushing, Bernard Cribbins, Ray Brooks, Jill
Curzon, Roberta Tovey, Andrew Keir, Godfrey
Quigley, Roger Avon, Keith Marsh, Geoffrey Cheshire,
Steve Peters, Robert Jewell*
Spin-off from a long-running BBC TV series. The
Doctor and his friends join the survivors of a Dalek
occupation of the Earth in the ruins of a devastated
London. Tedious tripe, made without care or interest.
Aka: DALEKS: INVASION EARTH 2150 A.D.;
INVASION EARTH 2150 A.D.
JUV                           80 min (ort 84 min)
B,V                              TEVP L/A; WHV

## DOCTOR WHO: SPEARHEAD FROM SPACE **    U
Derek Martinus            UK                 1970
*Jon Pertwee, Hugh Burden, Neil Wilson, John Breslin,
Anthony Webb, Helen Doward, Talfryn Thomas,
George Lee, Iain Smith, Tessa Shaw, Ellis Jones,
Allan Mitchell, Prentis Hancock, Derek Smee, John
Woodnutt, Betty Bowden*
Another cobbled up TV feature with Doctor Who and
friends out to foil an alien take-over of the planet.
JUV                                   91 min mTV
V/h                                            BBC

## DOCTOR WHO: TERROR OF THE ZYGONS ** PG
Douglas Camfield        UK        1075
*Tom Baker, John Woodnutt, Hugh Martin, Tony
Sibbald, Angus Lennie, Bruce Wightman, Lilias
Walker, Bernard G. High, Peter Symonds, Keith
Ashley, Ronald Gough*
As the "Doctor Who" TV series progressed old Doctors
"retired" as new actors took their place. Now we have
another made-up feature with Baker as the Doctor
investigating an outbreak of monstrous attacks in the
North Sea. And oh yes, there's a link with the Loch
Ness monster.
JUV        92 min mTV
V/h        BBC

## DOCTOR WHO: THE ARK IN SPACE ** U
Rodney Bennett        UK        1974
*Tom Baker, Elisabeth Sladen, Ian Marter, Wendy
Williams, Kenton Moore, Richardson Morgan, Stuart
Fell, Nick Hobbs, Christopher Masters*
This 4-part story has the Doctor visiting a space
station of the future, where a race of insect-like
creatures threatens to destroy the human beings held
in cryogenic suspension aboard the vessel. Average.
JUV        94 min mTV
V/h        BBC

## DOCTOR WHO: THE BRAIN OF MORBIUS ** U
Christopher Barry        UK        1976
*Tom Baker, Elisabeth Sladen, Colin Fay, Philip
Madoc, Gilly Brown, Cynthia Grenville, Stuart Fell,
John Scott Martin, Sue Bishop, Janie Kells, Veronica
Ridge, Gabrielle Mowbray, Michael Spice (voice of
Morbius)*
Compilation from a four part TV serial with an exiled
Time Lord attempting to implement an evil plan so as
to take power.
JUV        59 min mTV
B,V        BBC

## DOCTOR WHO: THE DALEK INVASION OF
## EARTH – PARTS 1 AND 2 *** PG
Richard Martin        UK        1964
*William Hartnell, Carole Ann Ford, William Russell,
Jacqueline Hill, Bernard Kay, Peter Fraser, Alan
Judd, Ann Davies, Graham Rigby, Nicholas Smith,
Martyn Huntley, Peter Badger*
Compilation of a 6-part story from the popular SF
series. Having landed on Earth in the year 2167 AD
the Doctor finds that the Daleks have invaded the
planet and are now in control. However, a small band
of freedom fighters struggles to overthrow their rule.
One of the most ambitious stories in the series, that
was remade as the film DALEKS: INVASION
EARTH 2150 AD.
JUV        151 min (2 cassettes) mTV B/W
V/h        BBC

## DOCTOR WHO: THE DALEKS *** U
Christopher Barry/Richard Martin
        UK        1963
*William Hartnell, Carole Ann Ford, William Russell,
Jacqueline Hill, Alan Wheatley, Philip Bond, John
Lee, Marcus Hammond, Gerald Curtis, Virginia
Wetherell, David Graham (Dalek voice only), Peter
Hawkins (Dalek voice only)*
Compilation of an early 7-part Doctor Who adventure
that introduced the Daleks. When the TARDIS lands
on the Planet Skaro the Doctor finds himself involved
in a conflict between the human-like Thal and the
mutated Daleks, both representing the very different
survivors of a neutronic war. Writer Terry Nation's
irascible Daleks proved to be too good an idea to
abandon, and popped up in several other episodes as
well as a feature film in 1965.
JUV        174 min (2 cassettes) mTV
V/h        BBC

## DOCTOR WHO: THE DAY OF THE DALEKS ** U
Paul Bernard        UK        1972
*Jon Pertwee, Katy Manning, Jean McFarlane, Wilfrid
Carter, Tim Condreen, John Scott Martin, Oliver
Gilbert, Aubrey Woods, Deborah Brayshaw, Gypsie
Kemp, Anna Barry, Jimmy Winston, Scott Fredericks,
Valentine Palmer*
In this compilation of the TV series our hero has to do
battle with the evil Daleks.
JUV        90 min mTV
V/h        BBC

## DOCTOR WHO: THE DOMINATORS ** U
Morris Barry        UK        1968
*Patrick Troughton, Frazer Hines, Wendy Padbury,
Ronald Allen, Kenneth Ives, Arthur Cox, Felicity
Gibson, Giles Block, Johnson Bayly, Walter Fitzgerald*
Five-part compilation from the popular and long-
running TV series. This adventure deals with a
holiday the Doctor plans on the planet Dulkis, which
he soon discovers has been taken over by the cruel
Dominators and their robot servitors, their intention
being to turn the planet into a radioactive power
source.
JUV        122 min mTV B/W
V/h        BBC

## DOCTOR WHO: THE FIVE DOCTORS * U
Peter Moffatt        UK        1983
*Jon Pertwee, Peter Davidson, Patrick Troughton, Tom
Baker, Richard Hurndall, Janet Fielding, Nicholas
Courtney, David Savile, Ray Float, Lalla Ward,
Elisabeth Sladen, Philip Latham, Dinah Sheridan,
Carol Ann Field*
A specially designed episode to celebrate the 20th
anniversary of the British TV series, in which the five
incarnations of "Doctor Who" are brought together to
face a motley collection of their enemies. A strictly
average entry to a fairly undistinguished series.
JUV        89 min mTV
B,V        BBC

## DOCTOR WHO: THE MIND ROBBER * U
David Maloney        UK        1969
*Patrick Troughton, Frazer Hines, Wendy Padbury,
Emrys Jones, Bernard Horsfall, Christina Pirie, Sue
Pulford, Christopher Robbie, John Greenwood*
In this 5-part story the Doctor and his friends find
themselves in a strange region of mythological crea-
tures and fictional characters, and the Doctor is
offered the rule of this kingdom by its ancient ruler.
JUV        101 min mTV
V        BBC

## DOCTOR WHO: THE PYRAMIDS OF MARS ** U
Paddy Russell        UK        1975
*Tom Baker, Vik Tablian, Elisabeth Sladen, Bernard
Archad, Gabriel Woolf, Peter Copley, Peter Maycock,
Michael Bilton, Michael Sheard, George Tovey, Nick
Burnell, Melvyn Bedford, Kevin Selway*
A feature-length compilation of that long-running TV
series that died a long time ago but refused to lay
down. Here the Doctor fights against an ancient
Egyptian enemy when he returns to Earth in the year
1911.
Aka: PYRAMIDS OF MARS, THE
JUV        90 min mTV
B, V/h        CIC, BBC (VHS only)

## DOCTOR WHO: THE ROBOTS OF DEATH ** U
Michael E. Briant        UK        1977
*Tom Baker, Louise Jameson, Rob Edwards, Russell
Hunter, Pamela Salem, David Bailie, Brian Croucher,
Tariq Yanus, David Collins, Tania Rogers, Miles
Fothergill, Gregory De Polnay, Mark Blackwell Baker*
Compilation feature from the British "Doctor Who"
series with Doc and his assistant doing battle with a
power mad scientist and his array of killer gadgets.

JUV 90 min mTV
V/h BBC

## DOCTOR WHO: THE SEEDS OF DEATH * U
Michael Ferguson UK 1969
*Patrick Troughton*
A dreadful compilation of a once imaginative TV series in which a time traveller runs into all sorts of adventures in different worlds and times. Here our good doctor battles the "Ice Warriors".
JUV 136 min B/W mTV
V/h BBC

## DOCTOR WHO: THE TALONS OF WENG-CHIANG ** PG
David Maloney UK 1977
*Tom Baker, John Bennett, Deep Roy, Michael Spice, Trevor Baxter, Christopher Benjamin, Tony Then, Alan Butler, Chris Cannon, John Wu, Conrad Asquith, David McKail, Patsy Smart, Judith Lloyd, Vaune Craig-Raymond, Penny Lister*
Another feature-length compilation with Doctor Who now in the heart of Victorian London, where he battles giant creatures from the sewers, and others who wish him ill. Laughable space opera nonsense pitched at kiddie-level.
JUV 134 min Cut (10 sec) mTV
V/h BBC

## DOCTOR WHO: THE TIME WARRIOR ** U
Alan Bromly UK 1973
*Jon Pertwee, Elisabeth Sladen, David Daker, John J. Carney, Sheila Fay, Kevin Lindsay, Donald Pelmear, June Brown, Alex Rowe, Jeremy Bulloch*
This compilation of a 4-part story sees a girl stowaway travelling with the Doctor back to the Middle Ages, where he hopes to find some missing scientists, but instead meets an alien warrior.
JUV 91 min mTV
V/h BBC

## DOCTOR WHO: THE WAR GAMES ** U
David Maloney UK 1969
*Patrick Troughton, Jane Sherwin, David Savile, John Livesby, Bernard Davies, Brian Forster, Terence Buyler, Noel Coleman, Hubert Rees, Esmond Webb, Richard Steele, Peter Stanton, Pat Gorman, Tony McEwan, David Valla*
Compilation of a 10-part story that has the intrepid Doctor and his companions trapped on a planet where aliens play out a series of war games using soldiers they have captured from different periods in Earth's history. When the Doctor calls in the Time Lords to end these games he is put on trial for "intervention" and exiled to Earth. A fair entry in the series that ended Troughton's run as the Doctor.
JUV 243 min (2 cassettes) mTV
V/h BBC

## DOCTOR WHO: THE WEB PLANET – PARTS 1 AND 2 ** U
Richard Martin UK 1965
*William Hartnell, Carole Ann Ford, William Russell, Jacqueline Hill, Maureen O'Brien, Roslyn de Winter, Arne Gordon, Jolyon Booth, Jocylyn Birdsall, Martin Jarvis*
Originally a six-part story that takes the Doctor to the planet Vortis, where a war between the ant-like Zarbi and the butterfly-like Menoptra is raging.
JUV 148 min mTV B/W
V BBC

## DOCTOR ZHIVAGO ** 15
David Lean USA 1965
*Omar Sharif, Julie Christie, Rod Steiger, Alec Guinness, Ralph Richardson, Geraldine Chaplin, Tom Courtenay, Rita Tushingham*
Pasternak's epic tale of the Russian Revolution and its effect on a group of people, is transformed into a visually handsome but stilted and lifeless effort. The dialogue is wooden and Omar Sharif is totally unconvincing as a Russian. Now remembered chiefly for Jarre's beautiful melodies. AA: Screen (Adapt) (Robert Bolt), Cin (Freddie Young), Art/Set (John Box and Terry Marsh/Dario Simoni), Cost (Phyllis Dalton), Score (Orig) (Maurice Jarre).
Boa: novel by Boris Pasternak.
DRA 185 min
V/sh MGM

## DOCTORS' WIVES * 18
George Schaefer USA 1971
*Dyan Cannon, Richard Crenna, Gene Hackman, Janice Rule, Carroll O'Connor, Rachel Roberts, Diana Sands, Cara Williams, Ralph Bellamy*
Soap opera about a doctor who shoots his unfaithful wife and the effect this has on his colleagues. A glossy, empty and unconvincing time-filler, scripted by Daniel Taradash.
Boa: novel by F.G. Slaughter.
DRA 98 min (ort 100 min)
B,V WDV; RCA (VHS only)

## DODGE CITY *** 
Michael Curtiz USA 1939
*Errol Flynn, Olivia de Havilland, Ann Sheridan, Bruce Cabot, Frank McHugh, Alan Hale, John Litel, Victor Jory, Ward Bond, Cora Witherspoon, Henry Travers, Henry O'Neill, Guinn Williams, William Lundigan, Gloria Holden*
Nothing less than a Western swashbuckler in which a dashing rancher and soldier of fortune gets elected as sheriff of Dodge City, and proceeds to take on the bad guys and make the town fit for decent folks. A simple value-for-money film with ample action packed into a meagre plot.
WES 100 min (ort 105 min) B/W
V WHV

## DOG DAY ** 18
Yves Boisset FRANCE 1983
*Lee Marvin, David Bennett, Miou-Miou, Victor Lanoux, Jean Carmet, Bernadette Lafont, Jean-Pierre Kalfon, Pierre Clementi, Tina Louise*
An American gangster is running for his life after a wages robbery and hides out in a farmhouse in France, where he meets some very strange characters. An engaging homage to the gangster genre that is spoilt by some unpleasant and unnecessary violence.
Aka: CANICULE; DOGSDAY
DRA 99 min (ort 101 min)
B,V VES/PVG

## DOG DAY AFTERNOON *** 15
Sidney Lumet USA 1975
*Al Pacino, John Cazale, Charles Durning, James Broderick, Sully Boyar, Penny Allen, Carol Kane*
A tense and gritty story about a loser who holds up a bank so that his homosexual lover will have the money for a sex-change operation. However, his simple robbery goes badly wrong and develops into a major incident. An enjoyable film of much atmosphere and little plot. AA: Screen (Orig) (Frank Pierson).
DRA 119 min (ort 130 min)
V WHV

## DOG TAGS *** 18
Romano Scavolini ITALY 1986
*Clive Woods, Baird Stafford, Robert Haufrecht*
Standard tale of warfare in a South-East Asian jungle. A crack squad of Marines is sent to Vietnam on a suicide mission to rescue POWs and recover some boxes of military documents. They discover that most of the POWs are already dead and that the boxes actually contain a fortune in gold, disguised as dog tags. As they struggle back home they have to contend with numerous attacks in this extremely well made but gore-laden adventure.

WAR                                              86 min
B,V                                              RNK

**DOG WHO STOPPED THE WAR, THE \*\*\***          U
Andre Melancon      CANADA                       1986
*Cedric Jourde, Julien Elie, Maripierre Arseneau
D'Amour, Doc Minh Vu, Maryse Cartwright, Luc
Boucher, Nathalie Gagnon, Olivier Monette, Gilbert
Monette, Mathieu Savard, Patrick Periz, Jean-
Francois Leblanc, Steve Savage*
A local gang leader organises a snowball fight which
is destined to turn into a neighbourhood battle.
However, his plans are thwarted by a boy and his dog
when the latter outsmarts both sides in this enjoyable
little romp.
Aka: DOG THAT STOPPED THE WAR, THE; LA
GUERRE DES TUQUES; LE CHATEAU DE NEIGE
JUV                                              84 min
B/h, V/h                                         NWV

**DOGS IN SPACE \***                             18
Richard Lowenstein
                    AUSTRALIA                     1986
*Michael Hutchence, Saskia Post, Nique Needles, Chris
Haywood, Deanna Bond, Tony Helou*
A group of young people enjoy the summer of 1978 in
the belief that they will never grow up and join the
world of adult squares. An examination of teen pop
culture largely intended as a vehicle for Hutchence –
lead singer with the Aussie group INXS. The title
refers to the epoch-making early space flights, especially those Soviet ones with dogs. Noisy and unbearably tiresome.
COM                                              109 min
V                                                COL

**DOGS OF WAR, THE \*\***                        15
John Irvin          UK                           1980
*Christopher Walken, Tom Berenger, Colin Blakely,
Hugh Millais, Paul Freeman, Robert Urquhart,
JoBeth Williams, Jean-Francois Stevenin, Winston
Ntshona, Pedro Armendariz Jr, Harlen Carey Pope,
Ed O'Neill, Isabel Grandin*
A sombre adaptation of Forsyth's bestseller, with a
cynical and disenchanted mercenary, plotting to over-
throw a nasty Amin-like dictator of a poverty stricken
African state, and seize power himself. Lacking in
surprises if not in brutality this tough action film now
seems very dated.
Boa: novel by Frederick Forsyth.
A/AD                114 min (ort 118 min) Cut (5 sec)
B,V,V2                    WHV; HOLLY (VHS only)

**DOGS TO THE RESCUE \*\***
Paul Fritz-Nemeth
                    CANADA/ROUMANIA               1972
*Tony Kramreither, Dorine Dron, Draga Olteanu,
Gheorges Gima*
Two Alsatians rescue two children from their uncle
who, having killed their father is now planning their
demise in order to seize the family fortune. An
enjoyable kid's adventure of no great depth.
JUV                                              70 min
V                                                INT

**DOGS, THE \***
Burt Brinckerhoff   USA                          1977
*David McCallum, Sandra McCabe, Eric Server, Linda
Grey, George Wyner, Holly Harris, Sterling Swanson,
Barry Greenberg, Dean Santoro, Cathy Austin, Lance
Hool, Debbie Davis, Jim Stathis, Paul Paolasso,
Michael M. Davis*
A professor tries to discover why packs of dogs are
attacking people in this dreary and yawn-inducing
low-budget effort.
Aka: SLAUGHTER
HOR                                              91 min
B,V                                              DFS

**DOIN' TIME \***                                15
George Mendeluk     USA                          1983
*Richard Mulligan, Dey Young, Jeff Altman, John
Vernon, Colleen Camp, Melanie Chartoff, Graham
Jarvis, Pat McCormick, Eddie Velez, Jimmie Walker,
Judy Landers, Mike Mazurki, Muhammad Ali*
A crazy prison comedy in which the arrival of a new
governor threatens the cosy life enjoyed by warders
and inmates alike. Despite one or two funny moments,
this one is simply too low-brow and simple-minded for
its own good.
Aka: BIG HOUSE, THE
COM                           81 min; 76 min (VIR)
V/sh                          PVG; VIR (VHS only)

**DOIN' TIME ON PLANET EARTH \*\***              15
Charles Matthau     USA                          1987
*Andrea Thompson, Adam West, Hugh Gillin, Candice
Azzara, Roddy McDowall, Maureen Stapleton, Hugh
O'Brian, Nicholas Strouse, Matt Adler, Timothy
Patrick Murphy*
The tale of a youngster who feels really alienated from
his folks and meets up with a couple of weirdos who
convince him that he really is an alien. A cheerfully
wacky tale that is hampered by its lack of direction.
COM                           80 min (ort 83 min)
B,V                                              WHV

**DOING LIFE \*\*\***                            15
Gene Reynolds       USA                          1986
*Tony Danza, John De Vries, Alvin Epstein, Mitchell
Jason, Lisa Langlois, Rocco Sisto, Dawn Greenhalgh,
Dan Luria, Kenneth Pogue, Allan Royal, John
Randolph Jones, Reginald Vel Johnson, Mara Hobel,
Frank Pesce*
A dramatised account of the horrors of prison life as
faced by a convicted cop-killer whose sentence has
been commuted to life imprisonment. Said to be
inspired by the real-life story of Jerry Rosenberg, who
escaped the death sentence and became a spokesman
for his fellow inmates during the Attica riots. Adapted
by Bello from his book.
Boa: book by Steve Bello.
DRA                                              104 min mTV
B,V                                              ODY

**DOLL SQUAD, THE \***
Ted V. Mikels       USA                          1974
*Michael Ansara, Francine York, John Carter, Anthony
Eisley, Rafael Campos, Lisa Todd*
An all-female band battles an ex-CIA agent for world
domination in this shoddy and uneventful actioner.
Aka: HUSTLER SQUAD
A/AD                          90 min (ort 101 min)
B,V,V2                                           VCL/CBS

**DOLLARS \*\*\***                               15
Richard Brooks      USA                          1972
*Warren Beatty, Goldie Hawn, Gert Frobe, Scott Brady,
Robert Webber, Arthur Bliss*
A security consultant installing a new system in
Hamburg sets up an elaborate scheme to rob it, ably
assisted by his blonde (but by no means dumb)
girlfriend. Pacing is slow but there are some splendid
moments of tension in an entertaining crime caper
spoilt by an interminable car chase that goes on ad
nauseum. The nice, catchy score is by Quincy Jones.
Aka: HEIST, THE
THR                                              116 min
V                                                RCA

**DOLLMAKER, THE \*\*\***                        PG
Daniel Petrie       USA                          1983
*Jane Fonda, Levon Helm, Amanda Plummer, Susan
Kingsley, Geraldine Page, Ann Hearn, Robert Swann,
Nikki Creswell, David Dawason, Starla Whaley, David
Wilson, Jason Yearwood, Ray Serra, Dan Hedaya,
Christine Ebersole*
A wife and mother tries to overcome the pressures of

WW2 by concentrating on her hobby of making dolls, after she moves with her family from Kentucky to the big city. A charming little drama with Fonda giving an Emmy-winning performance in her TV movie debut. The script is by Susan Cooper and Hume Cronyn.
Boa: novel by Hariette Arrow.
DRA                              135 min (ort 150 min) mTV
B,V,V2                                                POLY

## DOLLS **                                           18
Stuart Gordon          USA               1986
*Ian Patrick Williams, Carolyn Purdy-Gordon, Carrie Lorraine, Guy Rolfe, Hilary Mason, Bunty Bailey, Cassie Stuart, Stephen Lee*
Some travellers shelter at a sinister mansion during a storm, that's owned by an elderly couple who make beautiful handcrafted dolls. They stay the night only to find to their cost that the dolls are in the habit of attacking people they dislike. A grisly but unmemorable offering from the director of RE-ANIMATOR.
Aka: DOLL, THE
HOR                                          74 min
B,V                                             VES

## DOLL'S HOUSE, A **
Joseph Losey          FRANCE/UK          1973
*Jane Fonda, David Warner, Trevor Howard, Delphine Seyrig, Edward Fox, Anna Wing, Pierre Oudrey, Frode Lien, Tone Floor, Morten Floor, Ingrid Natrud, Freda Krogh, Ellen Holm, Dagfinn Hertzberg*
A film version of a play about a woman who finally rebels against being treated like a doll by her father and then her husband. Fonda is more interesting than convincing as a liberated woman of the 19th century, but Howard's performance as Dr Rank really stands out. Filmed in Norway.
Boa: play by Henrik Ibsen.
DRA                              102 min (ort 106 min)
B,V                                             RNK

## DOMINIQUE **
Michael Anderson       UK                1978
*Cliff Robertson, Jean Simmons, Jenny Agutter, Judy Geeson, Simon Ward, Flora Robson, Ron Moody, Michael Jayston, David Tomlinson, Jack Warner, Leslie Dwyer*
A lame woman is driven to suicide by her husband, in a ruthless attempt to gain control of her money. Events take an unpleasant turn when he finds himself apparently being haunted by her ghost. A sluggish British attempt at a ghost yarn, not helped by wooden acting and interminable use of the "let's make it look like night" blue lens filter. The twist at the end is entirely predictable in this tedious effort. Written by Edward and Valerie Abraham.
Aka: DOMINIQUE IS DEAD
Boa: story What Beckoning Ghost by Harold Lawlor.
DRA                              98 min (ort 100 min)
B,V,V2                                          GHV

## DOMINO *                                           18
                       ITALY               1988
*Brigitte Nielsen*
An empty exercise in tedium in which Nielsen, as a maker of music videos, has embarked on one about Billie Holiday but at the same time is being plagued by phone calls from a man promising her total fulfilment. Unfortunately, this muddled and pretentious dud offers the viewer a good deal less.
DRA                                          95 min
V                                               VIR

## DOMINO KILLINGS, THE *                             15
Stanley Kramer         USA               1977
*Gene Hackman, Candice Bergen, Richard Widmark, Mickey Rooney, Edward Albert, Eli Wallach*
A convict serving twenty years is promised his freedom in return for assassinating a national figure

in this clumsy and rather muddled yarn.
Aka: DOMINO PRINCIPLE, THE
Boa: novel The Domino Principle by Adam Kennedy.
THR                              95 min (ort 97 min)
V                                               CH5

## DON IS DEAD, THE *                                 18
Richard Fleischer      USA               1973
*Anthony Quinn, Frederic Forrest, Al Litteri, Robert Forster, Ina Balin*
Rival gangs fall out over the choice of the successor to a gangland boss. A run-of-the-mill ganster saga with all the expected cliches and characterisations.
Aka: BEAUTIFUL BUT DEADLY
Boa: novel by Marvin H. Albert.
DRA                                          115 min
B,V                                             CIC

## DONA FLOR AND HER TWO HUSBANDS **                  18
Bruno Barreto          BRAZIL            1978
*Sonja Braga, Jose Wilker, Mauro Mendonca, Dinorah Brillanti, Nelson Xavier*
A widow who remarries is visited by the ghost of her first husband and finds her loyalty torn between the two. Despite an unquestionably sexy performance from Braga, this one-joke story has too little material to work with and has more in common with softcore films than romantic fantasies. Later remade as KISS ME GOODBYE.
Aka: DONA FLOR E SEUS DOS MARIDOS
Boa: novel by Jorge Amado.
COM                              105 min Cut (34 sec)
V                                               RCA

## DONKEYS' YEARS *                                   PG
Kenneth Ives           UK                1979
*Penelope Keith, Colin Blakely, Denholm Elliott*
Dull film version of a play about a college reunion.
Boa: play by Michael Frayn.
DRA                                          80 min
B,V                                    PRV L/A; CH5

## DONOVAN'S KID *                                    U
Bernard McEveety       USA               1978
*Darren McGavin, Mickey Rooney, Shelley Fabares, Murray Hamilton, Michel Conrad, Ross Martin*
A con-man discovers that he has a child in San Francisco and goes there to try to re-unite his family against the opposition of a dominant and overbearing uncle. Dismal Disney fare, made to the same tired and sad formula.
JUV                              91 min (ort 104 min)
B,V                                             WDV

## DON'S PARTY ***
Bruce Beresford
                       AUSTRALIA          1976
*John Hargreaves, Graham Kennedy, Pat Bishop, Ray Barrett, Veronica Lang, Claire Binney, Jeannie Drynan, Candy Raymond, Harold Hopkins*
A look at the wife-swapping mores of the middle-class inhabitants of a Sydney suburb, who hold a get-together to watch election returns and have a little fun at the same time. A sharp and biting black comedy, based on a script by Williamson.
Boa: play by David Williamson.
COM                                          90 min
B,V,V2                                         HOME

## DON'T ANSWER THE PHONE *
Robert Hammer          USA               1980
*James Westmoreland, Flo Gerrish, Ben Frank, Nicholas Worth, Pamela Bryant, Stan Haze, Paul Warner, Gail Jensen, Denise Galik, Dale Kalberg, Susanne Severeid*
Some girls who live alone and the patients of a doctor are being brutally murdered by a crazy and sadistic Vietnam veteran. An exploitative shocker.

Aka: HOLLYWOOD STRANGLER, THE
HOR                                    90 min
B,V,V2                                    WOV

## DON'T BE AFRAID OF THE DARK **
John Newland          USA            1973
*Kim Darby, Jim Hutton, Barbara Anderson, Pedro
Armendariz Jr, William Demarest, Lesley Woods,
Robert Cleaves, Sterling Swanson, J.H. Lawrence,
William Sylvester, Don Mallon, Celia Kaye, Ted
Swanson, Felix Silla*
A young couple inherit a house that is haunted by
strange entities whose aim is to possess the wife.
Despite a promising start the flaccid script never
allows any tension to develop.
HOR              72 min (ort 74 min) mTV
B,V                                SPEC/POLY

## DON'T BOTHER TO KNOCK ***            PG
Roy Ward Baker        USA            1953
*Marilyn Monroe, Richard Widmark, Anne Bancroft,
Jim Backus, Elisha Cook Jr, Donna Corcoran, Jeanne
Cagney, Lurene Tuttle, Gloria Blondell*
A young girl taken on as a babysitter proves to be
mentally unbalanced in this gripping example of film
noir. Monroe is excellent as the girl who's saved from
harming both herself and her charges by the interven-
tion of Widmark, whom she envisions as her dead pilot
boyfriend. Bancroft's film debut.
Boa: novel Mischief by Charlotte Armstrong.
THR              73 min (ort 76 min) B/W
V                                      CBS

## DON'T GO IN THE HOUSE *               18
Joseph Ellison        USA            1980
*Dan Grimaldi, Robert Osth, Ruth Dardick, Charles
Bonet, Bill Ricci, Dennis M. Hunter, John Hedburg,
Johanna Brushey, Darcy Shean, Mary Ann Chin*
A pyromaniacal woman-hater abused by his mother
as a child, lures his victims to a horrifying death in
this sickening rubbish.
Aka: BURNING, THE
HOR          76 min (ort 82 min) Cut (3 min 7 sec)
B,V                              VSP L/A; APX

## DON'T GO IN THE WOODS . . . ALONE **
Jim Bryan             USA            1981
*Nick McClelland, Mary Gail Artz, Ken Carter, James
P. Hayden*
Four young campers in the mountains are attacked by
a machete-wielding maniac, in this violent and unim-
aginative shocker. Unlikely to be available in an
uncut form in the UK.
Aka: DON'T GO IN THE WOODS
HOR                                    88 min
B,V                                      RNK

## DON'T GO NEAR THE PARK *
Lawrence D. Foldes    USA            1981
*Aldo Ray, Meeno Peluce, Tamara Taylor, Barbara
Monke, Crackers Phinn, Linnea Quigley, Chris Riley,
Lara Moran, Earl Statler, Cambra Foldes, K.L.
Garber, David Ariniello, Steven Lovy, Janet Giglio,
Doug White*
An obscure and fairly unmemorable horror yarn, in
which two flesh-eating vampires terrorise Los Angeles
in their hunt for food.
Aka: NIGHTSTALKER
HOR                          80 min (ort 90 min)
B,V                                  INT/CBS

## DON'T JUST LIE THERE, SAY SOMETHING *   PG
Andrew Mitchell       UK             1973
*Brian Rix, Leslie Phillips, Joanna Lumley, Joan Sims,
Derek Griffiths, Diane Langton, Derek Royle, Peter
Bland, Myra Frances, Katy Manning, Barry Gosney,
Nicola Rowley, Arnold Diamond, Corbet Woodall,
Aubrey Woods, Anita Graham*

Wildly unfunny farce about a politician who finds
himself in a situation of great personal and political
embarrassment.
Boa: play by Michael Pertwee.
COM                                    90 min
V                                        MIA

## DON'T LOOK IN THE BASEMENT *
S.F. Brownrigg        USA            1973
*William McGhee, Annie MacAdams, Rosie Holotik,
Jessie Lee Fulton, Camilla Carr, Gene Ross*
The inmates of a Florida asylum stage a bloody
takeover in this shoddy and rather poorly made
shocker.
HOR                                    95 min
B,V,V2                                    DFS

## DON'T LOOK NOW ***                    18
Nicolas Roeg          UK             1973
*Donald Sutherland, Julie Christie, Hilary Mason,
Celia Matania, Massimo Serrato, Renato Scarpa,
Giorgio Trestini, Leopoldo Trieste, David Tree, Ann
Rye, Nicholas Salter, Sharon Williams, Adelina Poerio*
A short story serves as the basis for this broodingly
atmospheric film about a young couple who go to
Venice shortly after one of their children is drowned.
The husband has the gift of second sight and sees
things that cannot be explained, but all is resolved in
a chilling climax.
Boa: short story by Daphne Du Maurier.
DRA              110 min; 105 min (WHV)
B,V                      TEVP; WHV (VHS only)

## DON'T OPEN TILL CHRISTMAS *           18
Edmund Purdom         UK             1984
*Edmund Purdom, Gerry Sandquist, Mark Jones,
Belinda Mayne, Alan Lake, Caroline Munro, Kevin
Lloyd, Kelly Baker, Pat Ashley, Des Dolan*
Routine slasher in which a demented killer has it in
for Santa and consequently has a pretty busy time at
Christmas. The directorial debut for actor Purdom.
HOR          80 min (ort 89 min) Cut (2 min 13 sec)
B,V                                      VES

## DON'T PANIC ***                       18
Ruben Galindo Jr      USA            1987
*John Michael Bischof, Helen Rojo, George Luke*
A shy high school student gets a Ouija board for his
seventeenth birthday, and inadvertently causes the
release of a murderous demon. To prevent more
bloodshed he must find a sacrificial dagger and plunge
it into the demon's heart. An enjoyable if rather
low-budget horror tale whose lack of expensive effects
is more than made up for by the performances and
direction.
HOR                                    90 min
B,V                                      CFD

## DON'T PLAY WITH FIRE **
Tuis Hark             HONG KONG      1980
*Lo Lieh, Lin Chen-Chi, Albert Au*
Three young men are blackmailed into working for
the Hong Kong underworld.
Aka: DANGEROUS ENCOUNTERS OF THE FIRST
KIND; DIYI LEI YING WEIXIAN
A/AD                                   90 min
B,V,V2                                INT/CBS

## DON'T RAISE THE BRIDGE, LOWER THE
RIVER *                                   U
Jerry Paris          USA             1968
*Jerry Lewis, Terry-Thomas, Jacqueline Pearce,
Bernard Cribbins, Patricia Routledge, Nicholas
Parsons, Michael Bates*
An American whose get-rich-quick scheme involves
turning the home of his English wife into a discothe-
que, finds himself facing the prospect of divorce. A
dismal Lewis vehicle; the star is a little less zany than
usual but is just as unfunny. The script is by Wilk.
Boa: novel by Max Wilk.

COM                          96 min (ort 100 min)
V                                              RCA

## DOOMED TO DIE **
William Nigh              USA            1940
*Boris Karloff, Grant Withers, Marjorie Reynolds,*
*Melvin Lang, Guy Usher*
One in a set of second features starring Karloff as a
Chinese detective. In this film he is asked to clear the
son of a shipping magnate accused of the murder of a
business rival. This was number five in the "Mister
Wong" series based on the stories of Hugh Wiley.
Average.
THR                                   65 min B/W
B,V,V2                                     VCL/CBS

## DOOMWATCH *
Peter Sasdy              UK             1972
*Ian Bannen, Judy Geeson, John Paul, Simon Oates,*
*George Sanders, Percy Herbert, Geoffrey Keen, Joseph*
*O'Conor, Shelagh Fraser, Jean Trend, Joby*
*Blanshard, George Woodbridge, Brian Anthony, Rita*
*Davies, James Cosmo*
Tedious spin-off from a TV series about ecological
hazards. The inhabitants of a remote British island
are being affected by a strange disease, caused by the
illegal dumping of nuclear waste. A good idea is given
a stilted and stagey treatment.
FAN                                       92 min
B,V                                          GHV

## DOOR TO DOOR **                           PG
Patrick Bailey           USA             1984
*Ron Leibman, Arliss Howard, Jane Kaczmarek, Mimi*
*Monce*
Two inept door-to-door salesmen hustle their way
across the country in this average comedy.
COM                                       93 min
B,V                                        PACEV

## DOORMAN *                                  18
Tony LoBianco            USA             1982
*Mike Connors, Anne Archer, Leon Isaac Kennedy,*
*John Heard, Ian McShane, Ruth Ford, Maureen*
*O'Sullivan, Carrie Nye, Murray Hamilton, Ken Norris,*
*Sully Boyar, Val Avery, Chet Doherty, Karen*
*Rushmore, Rony Clanton, Fred Ford*
The doorman of a fashionable block of Manhattan flats
becomes the prime suspect when a number of female
tenants are murdered. A lacklustre and disappointing
effort that never really gets going.
Aka: TOO SCARED TO SCREAM
THR                          95 min (ort 104 min)
B,V                                          MGM

## DOORMAN **                                 PG
Gary Youngman            USA             1985
*Brad Whitfield, Sharon Schlarth, Bruce Taylor, San*
*Lou, Dan Biggers, Don Devendorf*
After a number of New York doormen are killed, the
daughter of one of the victims and a witness try to trap
the killer.
Aka: DEAD AS A DOORMAN
THR                                       85 min
B,V                                          AVA

## DORIAN GRAY *
Massimo Dallamano                        1970
     ITALY/LICHTENSTEIN/WEST GERMANY
*Helmut Berger, Richard Todd, Herbert Lom, Marie*
*Liljedahl, Margaret Lee*
A poor and unimaginative remake of the original 1945
film version of Wilde's famous story, updated to the
present time but still following the exploits of a vain
young man whose portrait ages instead of him.
Aka: SECRET OF DORIAN GRAY, THE
Boa: novel The Picture Of Dorian Gray by Oscar
Wilde.

DRA                           86 min (ort 93 min)
B,V                                          VFP

## DOT AND SANTA CLAUS ***                    Uc
Yoram Gross          AUSTRALIA          1979
Sequel to DOT AND THE KANGAROO in which Dot
meets Santa Claus and together they set out in search
of a lost baby kangaroo. As in the original, both live
action and animation are used to good effect.
Aka: AROUND THE WORLD WITH DOT; DOT
AROUND THE WORLD
JUV                                       80 min
B,V                                          GHV

## DOT AND THE BUNNY ***                      Uc
Yoram Gross          AUSTRALIA          1982
*Drew Forsythe, Barbara Frawley, Ron Haddrick, Anne*
*Haddy, Ross Higgins, Robyn Moore*
Continuation of the Dot Saga. In this one Dot
continues her search for a baby kangaroo called Joey.
As before, this quality cartoon employs live action and
animation.
JUV                                       79 min
B,V                                          GHV

## DOT AND THE KANGAROO ***                   Uc
Yoram Gross          AUSTRALIA          1976
Adventure story with cartoon animals set against live
action shots of the Australian bush. A little girl gets
lost in the bush but makes friends with a kangaroo
who helps her find her way home. Artwork is by Spike
Milligan. Followed by DOT AND SANTA KLAUS.
JUV                                       80 min
B,V                                          GHV

## DOT AND THE KOALA ***                       U
Yoram Gross          AUSTRALIA          1986
*Robyn Moore, Keith Scott*
Another in this famous series of animated/live action
adventures from Australia. Here Dot and a koala stop
the bush from being destroyed by a scheme that
involves the building of a dam.
JUV                          67 min (ort 75 min)
B,V                                          VGM

## DOUBLE AGENT '73 **                        18
Doris Wishman            USA             1974
*Chesty Morgan (Doris Wishman), Saul Meth, Jill*
*Harris*
An over-endowed woman agent (73 is her bust size in
inches) infiltrates a heroin ring with a secret camera
implanted in one of her breasts. A film as silly as it
sounds, with the same star who appeared in DEADLY
WEAPONS doing her best in this confused and
unintentionally hilarious sex romp.
A                    69 min (ort 77 min) Cut (26 sec)
B,V,V2                                       VPD

## DOUBLE CROSSERS, THE **
Cheng Chang-Wa
               HONG KONG/INDONESIA      1975
*Chen Hsing, Shin Il-Lung, Tuty Kirana*
In Singapore a policeman investigating his father's
murder discovers that he was a member of a gang of
smugglers. He sets out to avenge himself against his
father's partner, whom he believes was responsible for
his death.
THR                                       96 min
B,V                                          RNK

## DOUBLE DEAL *                              15
Brian Kavanagh      AUSTRALIA          1981
*Louis Jourdan, Angela Punch-McGregor, Diana*
*Craig, Warwick Comber, Peter Cummins*
The wife of a businessman is bored and sexually
frustrated so she takes up with a drifter who involves
her in various crimes. A trashy drama of implausible
development and unconvincing dialogue.

DRA                           86 min (ort 90 min) Cut
V                                              MED

## DOUBLE DRAGON IN LAST DUEL *          18
Key Nam Nam     HONG KONG                   1985
*Kang Ho, Mae Li, Jum Soon Park, Bong Choi*
Two black-suited fighters save the day in this dis-
jointed tale of kung fu plotting and revenge.
Aka: REVENGE
MAR                                      90 min
B,V                                         SAT

## DOUBLE DYNAMITE *
Irving Cummings     USA                     1951
*Frank Sinatra, Jane Russell, Groucho Marx, Don
McGuire, Howard Freeman*
Two engaged bank tellers become prime suspects
when their bank is robbed, because one of them
accepted a reward for having saved the life of a
gangster. A disappointingly inane comedy with none
of the stars being shown to their best advantage. A
few one-liners from Groucho cannot save it.
Aka: IT'S ONLY MONEY
COM                       78 min (ort 80 min) B/W
B,V                                         KVD

## DOUBLE EXPOSURE *
William Webb     UK                         1976
*Anouska Hempel, David Baron, Alan Brown, Robert
Russell, Julia Vidler, Dean Harris, Alan Hay, Deacon
Mulholland, Graham Mallard, Hugh Martin, Mary
Maude, Trevor Ainsley, Ali Baba, Hazel O'Connor*
A top photographer falls in love with the mistress of a
powerful and wealthy man and this causes him
considerable trouble.
DRA                                      80 min
B,V,V2                                      INT

## DOUBLE EXPOSURE **                        18
William Byron Hillman
                  USA                       1982
*Michael Callan, Joanna Pettet, James Stacy, Pamela
Hensley, Seymour Cassell, Cleavon Little*
A young photographer's violent nightmares become
the next day's headlines. Well acted and quite compe-
tent, but lacking in tension.
THR              91 min (ort 95 min) Cut (10 sec)
B,V                                        TEVP

## DOUBLE JEOPARDY **                        18
Ulli Lommel     USA                         1983
*Robert Walker, Suzanna Love, Bibbe Hansen*
A woman avenges the murder of her mother, which
took place when she was a child.
Aka: BEYOND THE BRIDGE; FACES OF FEAR;
OLIVIA
DRA                                      81 min
B,V                                       VIPCO

## DOUBLE LIFE, A ****
George Cukor     USA                        1947
*Ronald Colman, Signe Hasso, Edmond O'Brien,
Shelley Winters, Ray Collins, Millard Mitchell*
Colman gives a powerful and moving performance in
this fine story of the mental disintegration of an actor,
no longer able to separate his roles from his real-life
actions. Look out for Shelley Winters in an early role
playing Desdemona to Colman's deranged Othello. A
superb film. AA: Actor (Colman), Score (Miklos
Rozsa).
Aka: DOUBLE TROUBLE
DRA                                  103 min B/W
B,V                                    INT/CBS

## DOUBLE MAN, THE **                        PG
Franklin J. Schaffner     UK                1967
*Yul Brynner, Britt Ekland, Clive Revill, Anton
Diffring, Moira Lister, Lloyd Nolan, George Mikell,
Brandon Brady, Julia Arnall, Kenneth J. Warren,
Franklin J. Schaffner*
A dreary spy thriller about an agent who is lured to
the Austrian Tyrol, to investigate the death of his son
in a suspicious skiing accident. Brynner plays both a
CIA agent and an East German lookalike. Photogra-
phy is by Denys Coop.
Boa: novel Legacy For A Spy by Henry S. Maxfield.
THR                          100 min (ort 105 min)
B,V                                         WHV

## DOUBLE McGUFFIN, THE ***                  PG
Joe Camp     USA                            1979
*Ernest Borgnine, George Kennedy, Elke Sommer, Rod
Browning, Dion Pride, Lisa Whelchel, Ed Jones, Jeff
Nicholson, Michael Gerard*
Boys from a prep school uncover clues pointing to an
international murder plot but no-one will believe
their story. A pleasant family-style thriller from the
creator of BENJI. Orson Welles explains the film title
at the beginnning.
A/AD                   94 min Cut (1 min 29 sec)
V                                           VES

## DOUBLE NEGATIVE *
George Bloomfield     CANADA                1980
*Michael Sarrazin, Susan Clark, Anthony Perkins,
Howard Duff, Kate Reid, Al Waxman, Elizabeth
Shepherd*
A photo-journalist tries to find out who murdered his
wife and gets a nasty surprise in this muddled and
confusing thriller, which is not helped by an uncon-
vincing performance from Sarrazin.
Boa: novel The Three Roads by Ross MacDonald.
DRA                                      96 min
B,V                                         VTC

## DOUBLE NICKELS *
Jack Vacek     USA                          1977
*Jack Vacek, Patrice Schubert, Ed Abrams, Heidi
Schubert, Mick Brennan*
A highway patrolman gets involved in a car reposses-
sion racket. If you like noisy footage of speeding cars
you'll enjoy this one, otherwise skip it.
A/AD                                     89 min
B,V                                   SPEC/POLY

## DOUBLE PLAY *                              15
Karoly Makk
                  HUNGARY/USA               1984
*Maggie Smith, Christopher Plummer, Elke Sommer,
Adolph Green, Szabo Sandor*
A married couple fall out when the playwright wife
says her arrogant actor husband is unsuited for the
lead role in the screenplay she's written. He dresses
up as an Italian to court and test his wife in this poor
adaptation of Molnar's classic play of jealousy. First
made in 1931 as "The Guardsman" and then again in
1941 as "The Chocolate Soldier", this latest attempt is
by far the worst. Molnar was not even credited in this
one.
Aka: FITZ AND LILY; JATSZANI KELL; LILY IN
LOVE; LOVES OF LILY, THE; PLAYERS;
PLAYING FOR KEEPS
Boa: play The Guardsman by Ferenc Molnar.
COM                                     108 min
B,V                                         EHE

## DOUBLE REVENGE **                         18
Armand Mastroianni     USA                  1988
*Joe Dallesandro, Leigh McCloskey, Theresa Saldana,
Richard Rust*
A man is taking his wife out for an anniversary meal
when a robbery occurs at the local bank, and she is
taken hostage and deliberately shot by one of the
robbers. However, when the murderer is freed on a
technicality, the dead woman's husband sets out to
have his own revenge, in this formula effort.
THR                                      92 min
V                                           MED

## DOUBLE SWITCH *
David Greenwalt          USA          1986

U

*George Newbern, Elisabeth Shue, Michael Des Barres,
Mariclare Costello, Barbara Rhoades, John Lawlor*
Another identity-switching comedy as a rock star
decides to change places with the winner of a competition to find his double. That way our jaded pop star can
get some privacy and our ordinary teenager can
experience the fame and adulation of his idol. Mawkish, shallow and bland, this Disney comedy continues a long tradition of empty teen films of sugary
simplicity.

COM                       88 min (ort 100 min) mTV
B,V                                            WDV

## DOUBLE TROUBLE *
E.B. Clucher (Enzo Barboni)
                         ITALY          1984

PG

*Terence Hill (Mario Girotti), Bud Spencer (Carlo
Pedersoli), April Gough, Harold Bergman, C.V. Wood
Jr, Dary Reiz, Nello Pazzafini, Jose Van De Kamp,
Dennis Rourke, Roberto Ronery, Ataide Arcoverde,
Nollo Pazzafini*
An agency specialises in the supply of "doubles" for
people who need to be in two places at once. Two of its
staff have to impersonate Latin American millionaires and find themselves involved with crooks.
Crude, Italian slapstick without an ounce of redeeming comedy.
Aka: IO, TU, LORO E GLI ALTRI

COM                      100 min Cut (10 sec)
V                                              RCA

## DOVE, THE ***
Charles Jarrott          USA          1974

*Joseph Bottoms, Deborah Raffin, John McLiam,
Dabney Coleman*
A film account of the true story of a 16-year-old boy's
journey around the world in a 24-foot sloop accompanied by his cat. A likeable family outing, filmed on
location and produced by Gregory Peck.
Boa: book by R.L. Graham and D. Gill.

A/AD                     100 min (ort 105 min)
B,V                                           TEVP

## DOWN AMONG THE Z-MEN *
MacLean Rogers           UK            1952

U

*Peter Sellers, Spike Milligan, Michael Bentine, Harry
Secombe, Carol Carr, Clifford Stanton, Graham Stark,
Miriam Karlin*
Daft tale of MI5 and atomic research, from the stars of
the popular radio series of the 1950s "The Goons". The
plot (if we may use that term) has a group of criminals
visiting a small town, with the intention of stealing a
professor's secret atomic formula. Sellers does some
nice impressions but the whole thing is so creakingly
contrived that it rapidly becomes rather painful to
watch.
Aka: GOON SHOW MOVIE, THE; STAND EASY

COM                      67 min (ort 82 min) B/W
B,V                      CEN L/A; CH5 (VHS only)

## DOWN AND OUT IN BEVERLY HILLS ***          15
Paul Mazursky            USA          1985

*Nick Nolte, Bette Midler, Richard Dreyfuss, Tracy
Nelson, Richard Penniman, Little Richard, Evan
Richards, Valerie Curtin, Mike the Dog*
A tramp saved from drowning upsets the neurotic
lives of an over-rich Californian family, exposing the
emptiness of their existence. A slick and often funny
reworking of the 1932 French film "Bondu Sauve Des
Eaux". Later a TV series.

COM                      103 min; 99 min (WDV)
B,V                               RNK; WDV

## DOWN BY LAW ***          15
Jim Jarmusch             USA          1986

*Tom Waits, John Lurie, Robert Benigni, Nicoletta
Braschi, Ellen Barkin, Nicoletta Braschi, Billie Neal,*

*Rockets Redglare, Vernel Bagneris*
Comical jailhouse tale in which two down-and-outs
get framed and thrown into a Louisiana jail where
they meet Benigni, all three deciding to make a break
for it. Slow to get going, but the arrival of Benigni
heralds the start of a lively comedy. Witten by
Jarmusch and photographed by Robby Muller on
location in Louisiana. Lurie and Waits provide the
music soundtrack.

COM                      106 min B/W
B,V                                PAL

## DOWN THE LONG HILLS ***
Burt Kennedy             USA          1987

U

*Bruce Boxleitner, Bo Hopkins, Michael Wren, Don
Shanks, Ed Bruce, Buck Taylor, Thomas Wilson
Brown, Lisa MacFarlane, Jack Elam, Dave Cass,
Peggy Matheson, Beverly Rowland, Michael Rudd,
Corry Randall, Roy J. Cohoe*
A Disney family adventure telling of the struggles a
teenage boy and girl face when, following a wagon
train massacre, they attempt to make their way
through the Utah wilderness with their red stallion.
As they travel they are obliged to keep one jump
ahead of a fierce grizzly bear, a couple of horse thieves
and an Indian. Conventional but entertaining tale
filmed entirely in Utah's Wasatch and Uinta Mountains and Heber Valley.
Aka: LOUIS L'AMOUR'S DOWN THE LONG HILLS
Boa: novel by Louis L'Amour.

A/AD                     89 min (ort 104 min) mTV
B,V                                           WDV

## DOWNHILL RACER **
Michael Ritchie          USA          1969

PG

*Robert Redford, Gene Hackman, Camilla Sparv, Karl
Michael Vogler, Jim McMullan, Christian Doermer,
Dabney Coleman*
A man is chosen for the US Olympic ski-team but his
ego keeps getting in the way. Really no more than a
character study, with Redford playing an empty and
disagreeable person, this lack of sympathy for the
central character is the film's chief failing. The ski
sequences are however, excellent.
Aka: DOWNHILL RACERS, THE
Boa: novel The Downhill Racers by O. Hall.

A/AD                     102 min
B,V                              CIC

## DOWNPAYMENT ON MURDER **          15
Waris Hussein            USA          1987

*Ben Gazzara, Connie Selleca, David Morse, Jonathan
Banks, G.W. Bailey, John Karlen, Sheila Larkin*
The battered wife of a psychotic real-estate dealer
finally plucks up the courage to leave, taking their
kids with her. His efforts to get the children back
involve hiring a hit-man to murder her, in this
conventional tale largely redeemed by Gazzara's
chilling performance.

THR                      95 min (ort 100 min) mTV
B,V                                           CBS

## DOWNTOWN *          18
Richard Benjamin         USA          1990

*Anthony Edwards, Forest Whitaker, Penelope Ann
Miller, Joe Pantoliano, David Clennon, Art Evans,
Kimberly Scott, Rick Aiello*
An inexperienced Philadelphia cop makes some
powerful enemies and finds himself transferred to
duty in a rundown neighbourhood, where his new
partner is a solitary and sullen black officer. With the
look of a pilot TV movie, this "odd couple" tale blends
elements of comedy, melodrama and action with
neither skill nor originality.

DRA                      91 min (ort 96 min)
V                                          CBS

## DOWNTWISTED **          15
Albert Pyun             USA          1987

*Carey Lowell, Charles Rocket, Trudi Dochtermann,*
*Thom Matthews, Norbert Weisser, Linda Kerridge,*
*Nicholas Guest*
An over-complex caper yarn that finds a young woman
being pursued by crooks who are convinced she's in
possession of a priceless artifact. Leans heavily on
numerous other comedy-thrillers of this type without
adding anything new.

| COM | 85 min |
|-----|--------|
| V/sh | WHV |

### DRACULA *** 15
John Badham          UK          1979
*Frank Langella, Laurence Olivier, Kate Nelligan,*
*Donald Pleasence, Trevor Eve, Jan Francis,*
*Janine Duvitski, Tony Haygarth, Teddy Turner,*
*Sylvester McCoy, Kristine Howarth, Joe Belcher,*
*Gabor Vernon*
A more lush and romantic version of the familiar
vampire story with good performances all round and
some genuinely horrific moments. Let down by rather
meandering plot development that weakens any sense
of tension, plus Olivier's dreadful over-acting. Worth a
look for Langella's remarkable and acclaimed stage
characterisation – his vampire is both sinister and
sexual, but the trendy and overblown effects swamp
him. Filmed in England.
Boa: novel by Bram Stoker/play by John L. Balderston
and Hamilton Deane.

| HOR | 109 min (ort 112 min) |
|-----|------------------------|
| B,V | CIC |

### DRACULA *** PG
Tod Browning          USA          1931
*Bela Lugosi, Helen Chandler, David Manners,*
*Edward Van Sloan, Dwight Frye, Herbert Bunston,*
*Frances Dade*
A classic horror film telling of a Transylvanian
vampire count who comes to London and unleashes a
wave of terror until he is destroyed. Lugosi's fine
performance is rightly considered to be the definitive
interpretation, but unfortunately, the strengths of the
novel are diluted by the weaknesses of the play, from
which the film draws much of its stilted dialogue.
Followed by DRACULA'S DAUGHTER and countless
remakes and spin-offs.
Boa: play by Hamilton Deane and John Balderstone/
novel by Bram Stoker. Osca: DRACULA'S
DAUGHTER (asa)

| HOR | 73 min (ort 75 min); 139 min (2 film cassette) |
|-----|--------|
| B/W | |
| V/h | CIC |

### DRACULA ***
Dan Curtis          USA          1973
*Jack Palance, Simon Ward, Nigel Davenport, Pamela*
*Brown, Fiona Lewis, Murray Brown, Penelope Horner,*
*Sarah Douglas, Virginia Wetherall, Barbara Lindley,*
*George Pravda, Hanna-Maria Pravda, Reg Lye, Fred*
*Stone, Sandra Caron*
Another version of the famous legend, with Palance
giving an interesting interpretation of the Count, who
is now largely shown as a victim of fate. The
intelligent script of Richard Matheson and the photo-
graphy of Oswald Morris put some life into the now
over-familiar story.
Boa: novel by Bram Stoker.

| HOR | 97 min mTV |
|-----|------------|
| B,V,V2 | GOV |

### DRACULA A.D. 1972 * 18
Alan Gibson          UK          1972
*Peter Cushing, Christopher Lee, Stephanie Beacham,*
*Michael Coles, William Ellis, Christopher Neame,*
*Marsha Hunt, Philip Miller, Michael Kitchen, David*
*Andrews, Caroline Munro, Janet Key, Lally Bowers*
Dracula comes to swinging London of the 1970s and
stays at trendy Chelsea. Forgettable, confusing and
unconvincing, in roughly that order. Followed by THE
SATANIC RITES OF DRACULA, another film from

the Hammer stable.
Aka: DRACULA TODAY

| HOR | 92 min (ort 100 min) |
|-----|----------------------|
| B,V | WHV |

### DRACULA EXOTICA ***
Warren Evans          USA          1981
*Jamie Gillis, Samantha Fox, Vanessa Del Rio, Mark*
*Dexter, Eric Edwards, Bobby Astyr*
An erotic version of the Dracula story updated to the
twentieth century. He arrives in New York aboard a
freighter but, having lived behind the Iron Curtain, is
investigated by the FBI. The plot now gets lost amid a
welter of sexual encounters with the Count and
various luscious female vampires biting everyone in
sight. Before this film is done everyone has fangs, in a
kinky and enjoyable romp through the famous legend,
both well-acted and produced.

| A | 78 min |
|---|--------|
| B,V | TCX |

### DRACULA HAS RISEN FROM THE GRAVE ** 15
Freddie Francis          UK          1968
*Christopher Lee, Rupert Davies, Veronica Carlson,*
*Barbara Ewing, Barry Andrews, Ewan Hooper,*
*Marion Mathie, Michael Ripper, George A. Cooper*
But the tired old script stays dead and buried. Another
tale from Transylvania circa 1905, with our Count
pursuing the pretty niece of a small-town priest.
Followed by TASTE THE BLOOD OF DRACULA.

| HOR | 88 min (ort 92 min) |
|-----|---------------------|
| V | WHV |

### DRACULA SAGA, THE ** 18
Leon Klimovsky          SPAIN          1972
*Tina Saenz, Tony Isbert, Maria Kost, Helga Line, Neal*
*Franklin Menta, Narcisco-Ibanez Menta, Christiana*
*Suriani, J.J. Paladino, Betsabe Ruiz, Luis Ciges*
Run-of-the-mill vampire movie with the Count's pre-
gnant granddaughter and husband arriving at the
castle, where she gradually becomes aware of the
plans the family have for her unborn child. A
low-budget attempt to inject some new life into an old
tale.
Aka: DRACULA: THE BLOODLINE CONTINUES;
DRACULA'S SAGA; LA SAGA DE LOS DRACULA;
SAGA OF DRACULA, THE; SAGA OF THE
DRACULAS, THE

| HOR | 88 min (ort 102 min) |
|-----|----------------------|
| B,V | VPD |

### DRACULA SUCKS * 18
Philip Marshak          USA          1979
*Jamie Gillis, Annette Haven, John C. Holmes, John*
*Leslie, Serena*
Erotic version of the famous legend, that's essentially
a series of episodes mixing stilted dialogue, sexual
activity and nauseating gore in roughly equal proportions. An unpleasant film that even became available
in the USA in an edited softcore version. Cut before
video submission by 7 min 11 sec.
Aka: DRACULA'S BRIDE; LUST AT FIRST BITE

| A | 72 min (ort 91 min) Cut (2 min 26 sec) |
|---|--------|
| B,V | HOK L/A; ELV |

### DRACULA VERSUS FRANKENSTEIN * 15
Al Adamson          USA          1971
*J. Carrol Naish, Lon Chaney Jr, Zandor Vorkov,*
*Anthony Eisley, Regina Carroll, Russ Tamblyn, Jim*
*Davis*
Dracula and Frankenstein (the monster that is), make
a deal to keep them both supplied with blood. A
pretentious black comedy that wastes a good cast on a
muddled script that is neither funny nor chilling. The
last film for both Naish and Chaney.
Aka: BLOOD OF FRANKENSTEIN; REVENGE OF
DRACULA (DIAM)

| HOR | 89 min; 87 min (DIAM) |
|-----|------------------------|
| B,V | MOV; CINV; DIAM |

## DRACULA'S DAUGHTER ***
Lambert Hillyer    USA    PG    1936
*Gloria Holden, Otto Kruger, Edward Van Sloan,*
*Irving Pichel, Hedda Hopper, Marguerite Chuchill,*
*Claud Allister, Nan Grey, E.E. Clive, Gilbert Emery,*
*Billy Bevan, Halliwell Hobbes, Eily Malyon, Christian*
*Rub, Guy Kingsford*
A logical progression from the 1931 original, with the
Count's daughter longing to be free of her affliction.
However, when she falls in love with a man about to
be married, she's not above putting a spell on his
fiancee. This sequel is interesting rather than chill-
ing, though Holden is rather good in the title role.
Boa: story Dracula's Guest by Bram Stoker. Osca:
DRACULA
HOR    72 min; 139 min (2 film cassette) B/W
V/h    CIC

## DRACULA'S LAST RITES *
Domonic Paris    USA    1979
*Patricia Lee Hammond, Gerald Fielding, Victor Jorge,*
*Michael Lally, Mimi Weddell*
A housewife and mother fall victim to the vampire
mortician in this utterly dire effort.
Aka: LAST RITES
HOR    84 min (ort 88 min)
B,V    RNK

## DRAGNET **
Tom Mankiewicz    USA    PG    1987
*Dan Aykroyd, Tom Hanks, Harry Morgan, Dabney*
*Coleman, Elizabeth Ashley, Alexandra Paul,*
*Christopher Plummer, Jack O'Halloran*
Aykroyd plays Sergeant Joe Friday's bumbling
nephew, the role formerly taken by Jack Webb, in this
spoof on the popular TV series of the same name. The
plot revolves around an investigation pursued by
Aykroyd and partner into the activities of a TV
preacher and a porno magazine king, who are suspected of running a criminal cult. A comedy that runs
out of steam very early on and stays like that until the
end, although the punchline is pretty funny.
COM    101 min (ort 106 min) (Cut at film release by 14
sec)
V/sh    CIC

## DRAGON BRUCE LEE **
HONG KONG    18
*Bruce Le (Hunag Kin Lung), Richard Harrison, Wang*
*Jang Lee, May Hong, Dick Randall, Bradford Harris,*
*Naduska*
A Hong Kong policeman and kung fu expert, has to
find some murderous Japanese army in the pay of
Chinese warlords, as they hide out in the colony's
slums. A crime thriller with a martial arts slant
revolving around the theft of a top secret formula. An
average kick 'n' punch offering.
Aka: CHALLENGE OF THE TIGER (STABL)
MAR    85 min (ort 90 min) Cut (2 sec)
B,V    SPEC L/A; XTASY; STABL

## DRAGON BRUCE LEE: PART 2 **
HONG KONG    18
*Bruce Le (Huang Kin Lung)*
The further adventures of this Hong Kong cop and
kung fu expert.
MAR    88 min
B,V    STABL

## DRAGON DIES HARD, THE **
Lee Koon-Cheng    HONG KONG    1976
*Bruce Li (Ho Tsung-Tao), Lei Hsiao Lung, Lung Fei*
Kung fu action involving a plot to cash in on a
fighter's remarkable resemblance to Bruce Lee. Is
there no end to these Bruce Lee spin-offs?
Aka: BRUCE LEE, WE MISS YOU; CHIN-SE TAI
YANG
MAR    90 min
B,V,V2    VPD

## DRAGON FIGHTER **
HONG KONG    18
Beneath the Castle of Ching is a secret gold mine
where people are abducted and forced to work as
slaves. One worker revolts and for his pains his hands
are broken. But this only fuels his determination to
destroy the Castle and its keepers, and to this end he
sets about learning the "Heaven Legs" technique.
Fair.
MAR    92 min Cut (28 sec)
B,V    VPD

## DRAGON FIST **
Lo Wei    HONG KONG    18    1985
*Jackie Chan, James Tien*
Plot: revenge for death of master. 'Nuff said?
MAR    92 min
V    CLOK; TGP; VIDMQ

## DRAGON FORCE **
Michael King (Key Nam Nam)    18
HONG KONG    1982
*Bruce Baron, Mandy Moore, James Barnett, Jovy*
*Couldry, Frances Fong, Olivia Jeng, Randy Channel,*
*Sean Blake, Bruce Li (Ho Tsung-Tao), Kangjo Lee*
Kung fu epic set in the 1930s, when Korean fighters
use their skills against the Japanese occupation
forces.
MAR    89 min (ort 101 min) Cut (28 sec)
B,V    MONTE L/A; VPD

## DRAGON FROM SHAOLIN, THE **
HONG KONG    18
*Richard Kong, Li Ying Ying, Bruce Cheung, Steve*
*Chen, Nam Chi I, Debbie Ling*
Martial arts tale set in the Ming Dynasty that sees the
winner of a kung fu contest having his family
murdered when he refuses to work for the man who
organised it. But the man's young daughter escapes
and over the next 20 years becomes proficient in the
fighting arts, awaiting the day she can have her
revenge. Better than average fight sequences enliven
the painfully predictable plot.
MAR    82 min (ort 90 min)
B,V    VPD

## DRAGON LIVES AGAIN, THE **
HONG KONG    1979
*Bruce Leong, Alexander Grand*
A kung fu expert clashes with an underworld boss in
this standard martial arts tale.
MAR    87 min
B,V,V2    VCL/CBS

## DRAGON LORD **
Jackie Chan    HONG KONG    18    1982
*Jackie Chan, Chen Hui-Min, Sidney Yim, Whang*
*In-Sik, Mars*
A master of the martial arts and his friend fight to
prevent the sale of treasures from the Forbidden City
in this fairly routine martial arts actioner.
MAR    86 min (ort 93 min)
B,V,V2    GHV L/A; VCC (VHS only)

## DRAGON ON FIRE **
Chiang Hung/Ho Chih-Chiang
HONG KONG    198-
*Bruce Lei, Bruce Lea, Bruce Li (Ho Tsung-Tao)*
Bruce Lee clones battle it out in yet another martial
arts spectacular.
MAR    88 min
B,V    PAE

## DRAGON THAT WASN'T ... OR WAS
HE?, THE **    U
NETHERLANDS    1983
A boy gets a baby dragon as a pet, but when it grows
too big for his home, he is forced to return it to its
natural habitat, the land beyond the mountains. On

the way there, they face many dangers together.
Aka: DRAGON THAT WASN'T (OR WAS HE?), THE
CAR                              82 min (ort 96 min)
B,V                                            CIC

## DRAGON, THE HERO, THE **                    18
Godfrey Ho          HONG KONG              1981
*John Liu, Dragon Lee, Tino Wong, Philip Ku, Yang
Sze*
Two masters of the "Stone Fist" – a powerful fighting
style, quarrel, and one of them dies in the fight.
Twenty years later their sons meet by chance and
Tong, the dead man's son, plots his revenge. His
opponent is superior to him and easily defeats him,
but when they find that they have the same enemies,
they decide to join forces and fight together as their
fathers once did.
MAR                        80 min Cut (2 min 59 sec)
B,V                                            VPD

## DRAGON, THE YOUNG MASTER, THE **           18
Godfrey Ho          HONG KONG
*Dragon Lee*
Routine kung fu adventure revolving round a hunt for
stolen jewellery that has been hidden in the Snow
Mountain.
MAR                              84 min Cut (2 sec)
B,V                                            VPD

## DRAGONS **                                  15
Curtis Hanson        USA                   1980
*Ann Southern, Chris Peterson, Sally Boyden, Pat
Peterson, Rick Lenz, Sharon Webber, Joe Spinell,
Charles Lane, John Chandler, Clifford Dellow*
Two vacationing karate students become involved in
solving a kidnapping and eventually rescue a family
being held by hillbillies. A juvenile family adventure
for all ages.
Aka: LITTLE DRAGONS, THE
A/AD                                       86 min
B,V                                            PVG

## DRAGONS FOREVER ***                         18
Samo Hung           HONG KONG              1988
*Jackie Chan, Samo Hung, Yuen Biao, Crystal Kwok,
Deannie Yip, Pauline Yeung*
The waste from a chemical plant is destroying the
local fish farming. When the attractive owner of a
farm threatens to go to court, the plant hires Chan, a
wily lawyer, to fight her. However, he falls for her star
witness and his buddy falls for her. Events take a
sinister turn when it transpires that the plant is a
disguised drugs plant. The two sides now unite in an
effort to smash the drugs ring running it.
A/AD                                       90 min
V                                              VPD

## DRAGONSLAYER ***                            PG
Mathew Robbins       USA                   1981
*Peter MacNicol, Caitlin Clarke, Ralph Richardson,
John Hallam, Peter Eyre, Albert Salmi*
A sorcerer's apprentice finds that he has bitten off
more than he can chew, when he accepts a challenge
to slay a dragon in this lively and enjoyable fantasy.
Filmed in England, Scotland and Wales. The score is
by Alex North.
Aka: DRAGON'S SLAYER, THE
FAN        104 min (ort 108 min) (Cut at film release)
B,V                                            WDV

## DRAGOON WELLS MASSACRE ***                  PG
Harold Schuster      USA                   1957
*Barry Sullivan, Dennis O'Keefe, Mona Freeman, Katy
Jurado, Sebastian Cabot, Jack Elam, Trevor Bardette,
Hank Worden, Warren Douglas, John War Eagle*
Outlaws and the law join together to fight off attacks
by Apaches. A well made action tale, extremely
competent if not outstanding.

WES                  83 min (ort 88 min) Cut (12 sec)
B,V                                 VMA L/A; STABL

## DRAUGHTSMAN'S CONTRACT, THE **             15
Peter Greenaway      UK                    1982
*Anthony Higgins, Janet Suzman, Anne Louise
Lambert, Neil Cunningham, Hugh Fraser, Dave Hill,
David Gant, David Meyer, Tony Meyer, Nicolas Amer,
Suzan Crowley, Lynda Marchal, Michael Feast,
Alastair Cummings, Steve Ubels*
Unusual seventeenth century drama about a young
draughtsman whose commission includes sexual
favours from his female employer. A lavish and
complex tale, full of symbols and hidden meanings,
but let down by a cold and unmoving script. The music
is by Michael Nyman. Made for TV but released
theatrically.
DRA                 102 min (ort 108 min) mTV
B,V,LV                           GHV; VCC (VHS only)

## DRAW! **                                    15
Steven Hilliard Stern
                     CANADA/USA            1984
*Kirk Douglas, James Coburn, Alexandra Bastedo,
Graham Jarvis, Derek McGrath, Len Birman, Jason
Michas, Maurice Brand, Graham McPherson,
Vladimir Valenta, Linda Sorenson, Gerald Parkes,
Richard Donat, Frank Adamson*
After killing the town sheriff a legendary gunman
takes refuge in a hotel and another gunman is sent
for, but unforeseen complications arise. Average.
WES                       94 min (ort 98 min) mCab
B,V                              POLY; CH5 (VHS only)

## DREAM A LITTLE DREAM *                      15
Marc Rocco           USA                   1989
*Jason Robards, Corey Feldman, Piper Laurie,
Meredith Salenger, Harry Dean Stanton, Corey Haim,
Susan Blakely, William McNamara, Matt Adler,
Victoria Jackson, Alex Rocco*
Another body-switching comedy as a couple's experi-
ments with transcendental meditation lands them in
the bodies of a couple of teenagers. Fairly predictable
and most unfunny.
COM                                       110 min
V                                              VES

## DREAM BREAKERS **                           15
Stuart Millar        USA                   1989
*Robert Loggia, Kyle MacLachlan, D.W. Moffett,
Charles Cioffi, John McIntire, Hal Linden*
Drama following the lives of a Chicago building
contractor and his two sons, one a dedicated priest and
the other a gifted business graduate. The latter has
just taken a job with a corrupt and power-hungry land
developer, a former partner of his father's. Eventually, all three unite to oppose the man's crooked
schemes. Interesting casting is the best feature in this
cliched and curiously old-fashioned family saga.
THR                 90 min (ort 100 min) mTV
V                                              CBS

## DREAM CHASERS ***                           U
David E. Jackson/Arthur Dubbs
                     USA                   1984
*Harold Gould, Justin Dana, Wesley Grant*
A boy who is dying of cancer, makes one last journey
with an elderly friend rather than his father, who has
shunned him as he is unable to come to terms with his
son's imminent death. The unlikely pair take off and
act out a cowboy fantasy together.
DRA                        90 min (ort 97 min)
B,V                                            EIV

## DREAM DEMON ***                             18
Harley Cokliss       UK                    1988
*Kathleen Wilhoite, Jemma Redgrave, Jimmy Nail,
Timothy Spall, Annabelle Lanyon, Susan Fleetwood,
Mark Green Street, Nikolaus Grace, Patrick O'Connell,*

*Andrew Jones, Richard Warner*
A rich heiress about to be married, starts to suffer from horrific nightmares that draw her into a world where reality and dreams meet. In this fantasy world she finds herself constantly hounded by two reporters who become more grotesque with each encounter. A downright peculiar horror yarn with quite a few touches of grisly humour.

HOR                                      89 min (ort 99 min)
V/h                                                   PAL

## DREAM FOR CHRISTMAS, A ***
Ralph Senensky            USA                      1973
*Hari Rhodes, George Spell, Beah Richards, Lynn Hamilton, Marlin Adams, Joel Fluellen, Robert DoQui, Ta-Ronce Allen, Juanita Moore, Bebe Redcross, Clarence Muse, Dorothy Meyer, Sarina C. Grant, Maidie Norman, Dennis Hines*
A black churchman and his family move from Arkansas to Los Angeles, where they restore a dilapidated church and revive its poor congregation, in this engaging tale.
Boa: story by Earl Hamner Jr.

DRA                          97 min (ort 100 min) mTV
B,V                                          SPEC/POLY

## DREAM LOVER *
Alan J. Pakula            USA                      1986
*Kirsty McNichol, Ben Masters, Ben Gardner, Paul Shenar, Justin Deas, John McMartin, Gayle Hunnicutt*
After killing her attacker, a young girl begins to suffer from a series of dreams which totally changes her life.

HOR                                              108 min
B,V                                                   MGM

## DREAM NO EVIL ***
John Hayes                USA                      1974
*Edmond O'Brien, Mark Lawrence, Brooke Mills, Arthur Franz*
Horrific tale of a mentally disturbed woman who is obsessed with the idea of finding the father she never knew. She commits a series of strange murders to protect an imaginary family her warped mind has created.
Osca: THIRSTY DEAD, THE

HOR                                               84 min
B,V                                                   AVR

## DREAM OF PASSION, A *
Jules Dassin              GREECE                    1978
*Melina Mercouri, Ellen Burstyn, Andreas Voutsinas, Despo Diamantidou, Dimitris Papa-Michael*
An American mother in Greece kills her three children when her husband leaves her, in this unclear parallel to the Medea legend. Burstyn is entirely wasted in this clumsy and uninteresting melodrama. Mercouri plays an actress who sets out to fight a legal battle on her behalf.

DRA                                              106 min
B,V                                          SPEC/POLY

## DREAM TEAM, THE ***
Howard Zeiff              USA                      1989
*Michael Keaton, Peter Boyle, Christopher Lloyd, Stephen Furst, Dennis Boutsikaris, Lorraine Bracco, Milo O'Shea, Philip Bosco, James Remar*
A psychiatrist takes four mental patients on a trip to New York's Yankee Stadium, but the doctor inadvertently witnesses a murder, is injured and hospitalised, leaving his charges to survive as best they can. Their growing sense of co-operation and a strong set of performances, make this uneven farce a lot more enjoyable than it might have been.

COM                          108 min (ort 113 min)
V                                                     CIC

## DREAM TO BELIEVE **                                15
Paul Lynch                USA                      1985
*Olivia D'Abo, Rita Tushingham, Keanu Reeves*
Silly teen drama with a gymnastics enthusiast being refused a place on the school team and practising day and night to gain acceptance. A real Girls' Own Paper style movie with our heroine overcoming the additional problems of a broken home, a bitchy sister and a wicked stepfather. Gymnastics fans will enjoy this FLASHDANCE on the parallel bars, but others may find the film's basic contrived shallowness irritating.

DRA                                               98 min
B,V                                                   RNK

## DREAMCHILD ***                                     PG
Gavin Millar              UK                        1985
*Ian Holm, Coral Browne, Jane Asher, Peter Gallagher, Nigel Hawthorne, Caris Corfman, Nicola Cowper, Amelia Shankley, Shane Rimmer*
Fantasy adaptation of "Alice in Wonderland" with the story set against a trip to New York in the 1930s by the 83-year-old woman who, as a girl provided Lewis Carroll with the inspiration for his stories. An absorbing intellectual exercise flawed by an unnecessary romantic sub-plot. Scripted by Dennis Potter with the Wonderland characters supplied by Jim Henson of Muppets fame.

DRA                          90 min (ort 94 min)
B,V                                          TEVP; CAN

## DREAMER, THE **                                    PG
Dan Wolman                ISRAEL                    1970
*Leora Rivlin, Tuvia Tavi, Berta Litvina*
A young man working at an Israeli home for the aged neglects his duties when he becomes interested in a beautiful girl. Fair melodrama.
Aka: HATIMOHNI

DRA                          83 min; 87 min (HER)
B,V                                          RNK; HER

## DREAMING, THE **                                   18
Mario Andreacchio AUSTRALIA                        1988
*Arthur Dignam, Penny Cook, Gary Sweet*
A psychological chiller, telling of an Aboriginal curse and a series of bizarre events that lead a doctor to uncover an ancient mystery. Written by Rob George and Stephanie McCarthy.

HOR                                               86 min
V/h                                                   MED

## DREAMS ***
Akira Kurosawa            JAPAN                     1990
A remarkable effort from writer-director Kurosawa, this is a collection of eight diverse tales that range from charming fairytales to visions of apocalyptic doom. Beautifully photographed and with music that matches each piece's mood, but lacking the coherence of artistic vision that generally typifies the work of this master director.

FAN                                              119 min
V/sh                                                  WHV

## DREAMS COME TRUE ***                               18
Max Kalmanowicz          USA                        1984
*David Platt, Michael Sanville, Nancy Baldwin, Stephanie Shuford, Richard France, Bert Kenyon, Catherine Heenan, Robert Heise, Jim Lehnedorf, Mark Schumerth, Don Braun, Virginia Cox, Gay Strandemo, Ken Charlton*
A young teenage couple discover the secret of astral projection and live out their fantasies in this decidedly offbeat and unusual comedy.

COM                          85 min (ort 95 min)
B,V                                                   MED

## DREAMS LOST, DREAMS FOUND **                       PG
Willi Patterson          UK/USA                     1987
*Kathleen Quinlan, David Robb, Betsy Brantley, Colette O'Neil, Charles Gray, Tom Watson, Kay Gallie, Anne*

*Kristen, Fiona Mollison, Tom Mannion, Anne Downie, Raymond Ross, Gary Denis*
An American widow sells her art gallery and moves to Scotland where she has bought an ancient castle. Newly arrived, she embarks on a tempestuous relationship with the local aristocrat. Another dull entry in the Harlequin Romance series, barely enlivened by attempts to incorporate a supernatural element in the form of a legend of tragic lovers.
Boa: novel by Pamela Wallace.
DRA                                           97 min mTV
V                                                      CIC

## DREAMS OF THIRTEEN *
Nicholas Ray et al.
          NETHERLANDS/WEST GERMANY   1974
*Nicholas Ray, Dawn Cumming, Rob Van Reijn*
Tedious compilation of the erotic fantasies of thirteen directors, some of whom dropped out.
Aka: WET DREAMS
A                                                   68 min
B,V                                                   WOV

## DREAMSCAPE **
Joseph Ruben            USA                    1984
*Dennis Quaid, Christopher Plummer, Max Von Sydow, Kate Capshaw, Eddie Albert, George Wendt, David Patrick Kelly*
A man with telepathic ability, is hired by an organisation that has built a device enabling people such as him to enter the dreams of others. As he begins work as a therapist, helping disturbed individuals through their dreams, he finds himself caught up in a plot to harm the US President. A film that's at its best during the dream sequences, which to some extent compensate for the contrived and inadequate plot.
FAN        94 min (ort 99 min) (Cut at film release)
B, V/sh   -              TEVP L/A; WHV (VHS only)

## DREAMSLAYER **
Alan J. Levi            USA                    1974
*Richard Jaeckel, Dane Clark, Donna Wilkes, Frankie Avalon, Antoinette Bower, William Kirby, Jennifer Kaeckel, Victor Izxay, Noelle North, Lenny Montana, Christopher Scarano, David Arndt, Joseph Stanfill, Norman Brecke*
A woman finds her life turning into a nightmare, as she becomes the prey of a mental patient who has murdered his attendant, and now prowls on the loose, announcing his murderous intentions by playing a mournful dirge on a flute.
Aka: DREAM SLAYER; HUNTERS, THE
HOR                                                88 min
B,V                       IFS/CBS L/A; AVR; NET

## DRESSED TO KILL ***                              18
Brian De Palma         USA                    1980
*Michael Caine, Angie Dickinson, Nancy Allen, Keith Gordon, Ennis Franz, David Marguiles, Brandon Maggart, Fred Weber, Susanna Clemm, Ken Baker, Robert Lee Rush, Bill Randolph, Sean O'Rinn, Mary Davenport*
Having told her psychiatrist that her husband is useless sexually, suburban housewife Dickinson finds herself in peril from a sinister figure stalking both her and a streetwise prostitute. When she is killed the hooker teams up her son to catch the murderer, in this tense and absorbing thriller. Written by De Palma, this film plays on emotion rather than logic, utilising a fine cast and some film-making flashy techniques. The score is by Pino Donaggio.
THR                         104 min; 100 min (VIR)
B,V,V2                 GHV L/A; VCC; VIR (VHS only)

## DRESSER, THE ****                                PG
Peter Yates            UK                      1983
*Albert Finney, Tom Courtenay, Edward Fox, Zena Walker, Eileen Atkins, Michael Gough, Cathryn Harrison, Betty Marsden, Sheila Reid, Lockwood West,*

*Donald Eccles, Llewellyn Rees, Guy Manning, Anne Mannion, Kevin Stoney*
Acutely observed study of the relationship between an ageing actor and his devoted dresser, who lives his life through the performances of his master. A superb character study that perfectly captures the atmosphere of wartime England, the period in which the tale is set.
Boa: play by Ronald Harwood.
DRA                          113 min (ort 118 min)
V                                                      RCA

## DRESSMAKER, THE ***                              15
Jim O'Brien            UK                      1988
*Joan Plowright, Billie Whitelaw, Peter Postlethwaite, Jane Horrocks, Tim Ransom*
Two sisters share the same household with their niece in this story set in war-time Liverpool. Their cosy lives are disrupted when the niece brings home an American soldier. The girl is unwilling to go to bed with him so he has a fling with the younger aunt, but their short-lived affair ends in tragedy. The gruesome and wholly unexpected climax may well shock, but in terms of both realism and acting this film is hard to fault.
Boa: novel by Beryl Bainbridge.
DRA                                                89 min
V                                                      MGM

## DRIBBLE **
Michael De Gaetano     USA
*Charles Fatone, Freya Crane, Pete Maravich*
The saga of a professional women's basketball team which has seen better days. Average.
COM                                                92 min
B,V,V2                                                VUL

## DRIFTER, THE **                                  18
Larry Brand            USA                     1988
*Kim Delaney, Timothy Bottoms, Al Shannon, Miles O'Keeffe, Loren Haines, Thomas Wagner, Larry Brand*
A businesswoman has a casual fling with a handsome stranger who cannot accept the fact that he was just a one-night stand. He rapidly becomes obsessive, refusing to leave her alone. To compound her problems, he may also be resposible for the murder of her best friend, in a neat little thriller that entertains in a rather undemanding way.
THR        82 min (ort 90 min) Cut (2 min 44 sec)
B,V                                                   MGM

## DRIFTWOOD ***                                    U
Allan Dwan             USA                     1947
*Ruth Warrick, Walter Brennan, Natalie Wood, Dean Jagger, Charlotte Greenwood, Jerome Cowan, H.B. Warner, Margaret Hamilton*
Family drama about an orphan adopted by a doctor, the former being a young girl who has never experienced the benefits of civilisation before. A wholesome family film with a great performance from Wood.
DRA                                         90 min B/W
V                                          VMA; STABL

## DRIVER, THE ***                                  15
Walter Hill            USA                     1978
*Ryan O'Neil, Bruce Dern, Isabelle Adjani, Matt Clark, Ronee Blakley, Felice Orlandi*
A tough cop and a professional getaway-driver fight a battle of wits in this somewhat convoluted but enjoyable and tense thriller. The car chases are well-handled and Dern gives an intense portrayal of a cop who has carried his desire to uphold the law to the point of obsession. Hill's directorial debut.
A/AD                           88 min (ort 90 min)
B,V,V2                 TEVP; WHV (VHS only)

## DRIVING ACADEMY *                                PG
Oz Scott               USA                     1987
*Charlie Robinson, Jackee Harvey Korman, Dick*

*Butkus, Ray Walston*
A boring film that is quite difficult to sit through, this follows the very unfunny antics of a bunch of kids who have to pass a preliminary driving test, before being allowed to graduate from the title academy. All the usual stereotyped characters are here, in this tired and hackneyed effort.

COM                                    95 min
B,V                                       VIR

**DRIVING FORCE ***                         15
Andrew J. Prowse   AUSTRALIA               1989
*Sam J. Jones, Catherine Bach, Don Swayze*
A truck owner faces trouble on two fronts from both his ruthless business rivals and the family of his estranged wife, who are trying to get custody of his young daughter. A formula action story with the usual blend of mayhem and revenge.

A/AD                                   90 min
V                                         MED

**DRIVING MISS DAISY ***                       U
Bruce Beresford        USA                 1989
*Morgan Freeman, Jessica Tandy, Dan Aykroyd, Patti LuPone, Esther Rolle*
An uneducated but wily black man is hired to work as chauffeur to a peevish old Southern woman, and over 25 years the two become inseparable. A polished film of great charm, it covers the period from the 1940s to the 1960s, says next to nothing about race relations, and yet for all its contrived warmth is undeniably entertaining. AA: Pic, Actress (Tandy), Screen (Adapt) (Alfred Uhry), Make (Manlio Rocchetti/Lynn Barber/Kevin Haney).
Boa: play by Alfred Uhry.

COM                       95 min (ort 99 min) subH
V/sh                                       WHV

**DROWNING BY NUMBERS ***                      18
Peter Greenaway
              NETHERLANDS/UK               1987
*Bernard Hill, Joan Plowright, Juliet Stevenson, Joely Richardson, Jason Edwards, Bryan Pringle, Trevor Cooper, David Morrissey, John Rogan, Paul Mooney, Jane Gurrett, Kenny Ireland, Michael Percival, Joanna Dickens*
An absurd over-intellectual tale of three generations of women, who all drown their unwanted husbands, eventually coming up against an obsessive coroner. Excellent photography is a compensation in this bizarre tale.

COM                       113 min (ort 119 min)
V/h                                       PAL

**DRUG WARS ***                                15
Brian Gibson           USA                 1989
*Steven Bauer, Craig T. Nelson, Treat Williams, Elizabeth Pena*
Another look at the fight against drugs that has an American narcotics agent being kidnapped and murdered and his colleagues' efforts to apprehend those responsible being stymied by a deep-rooted web of corruption in both the US and Mexican governments. A compelling drama that attempts a more realistic appraisal of the complexities of combating the drugs trade.

A/AD                                  129 min
V/sh                                      WHV

**DRUGSTORE COWBOY ****                        18
Gus Van Sant Jr        USA                 1989
*Matt Dillon, Kelly Lynch, James Remar, James Le Gros, Heather Graham, Beah Richards, Grace Zabriskie, Max Perlich, William S. Burroughs*
A harsh look at the lives of a group of 1970s drug addicts, who support their addiction by robbing drugstores until the day their luck runs out. The pointlessness of their lives is well captured in a film that delivers no sermons or cliches. Dillon and Lynch are

totally convincing as a junkie couple. The screenplay is by Van Sant and Daniel Yost.
Boa: novel (unpublished) by James Fogle.

DRA                        97 min (ort 100 min)
V                                         VIR

**DRUM ***                                      18
Steve Carver           USA                 1976
*Warren Oates, Ken Norton, Yaphet Kotto, Isela Vega, Pam Grier, John Colicos*
Steamy tale of a New Orleans bordello house slave and the sexual harassment he faces. A dull and plodding follow-on to MANDINGO.
Boa: novel by Kyle Onstott.

DRA                        100 min (ort 110 min)
B,V,V2                                     GHV

**DRUM, THE ***                                 U
Zoltan Korda           UK                  1938
*Sabu, Raymond Massey, Valerie Hobson, Roger Livesey, David Tree, Desmond Tester, Francis L. Sullivan, Archibald Batty, Frederick Culley, Edward Lexy, Amid Taftazani, Roy Emerton, Martin Walker, Charles Oliver, Julien Mitchell*
Fairly competent tale set on the Indian Northwest frontier in the days of British rule. Military action by the British against hostile tribesmen forms the backdrop for a story of the friendship between an Indian prince (Sabu) and a drummer (Tester), who shows him how to play the drum. Massey makes a fine villain.
Aka: DRUMS
Boa: novel by A.E.W. Mason.

A/AD                        90 min (ort 104 min)
B,V              SPEC/POLY; SCREL; PICK

**DRUMBEAT ***                                 1954
Delmer Daves           USA
*Alan Ladd, Audrey Dalton, Marisa Pavan, Robert Keith, Charles Bronson, Rodolfo Acosta, Warner Anderson, Elisha Cook Jr, Anthony Caruso, Richard Gaines, Edgar Stehli, Hayden Rorke, Frank DeKova, Isabel Jewell, Perry Lopez*
An Indian fighter is ordered to negotiate peace with a band of warring Indians. A solid action film with Bronson well-cast as the Indian leader.
Osca: TO BEAT THE BAND

WES                        105 min (ort 111 min)
B,V                                       KVD

**DRUMMER OF VENGEANCE ***
Robert Paget (Mario Gariazzi)
              ITALY/UK                     1974
*Ty Hardin, Rossano Brazzi, Craig Hill, Gordon Mitchell, Edda Di Benedetta, Rosaldo Neri, Lee Burton, Umberto Raho, Jenny Atkins, Andrew Robertson, Patricia Patterson, Peter Martin, Tony Stevens, Robert Whitman*
A man sets out to have revenge on the gang of former Confederates who killed his Indian wife, but finds that their leader has now become a sheriff. A fair co-production in which the acting outshines the cliched plot.

WES                                    89 min
B,V                                       DFS

**DRUNKEN MASTER ***                           15
Yuen Woo Ping      HONG KONG
*Jackie Chan*
A student learns a special style of combat in this martial arts movie of enjoyable but uninspired action.

MAR                        106 min (ort 113 min)
B,V                                       RNK

**DRUNKEN SWORDSMAN, THE ***                   18
Chang Jen-Tsei     HONG KONG
*Yo Hua, Shih Rong, Lung Fei, Yen Han Se, Lo Lieh, Chen Chiang-Lung, Chen Yun-Ching*
A foolish imposter poses as the title hero but soon wishes he hadn't when the real swordsman turns up.

Some touches of humour enliven an otherwise formula kung fu story.

MAR        80 min
B,V        VTEL

## DRY WHITE SEASON, A ***    15
Euzhan Palcy     USA     1989
*Donald Sutherland, Janet Suzman, Jurgen Prochnow, Zakes Mokae, Susan Sarandon, Marlon Brando, Winston Ntshona, Thoko Ntshinga, Susannah Harker, Rowan Elmes*
An absorbing drama written by Colin Welland and Palcy, and telling of a well-meaning but naive white schoolteacher who receives a harsh lesson in the realities of apartheid, and its implications for his black fellow citizens. Brando is outstanding as a clever lawyer who has resigned himself to the system, and the film is quite memorable, despite contrived plotting and an excess of melodramatics.
Boa: book by Andre Brink.

DRA      103 min (ort 107 min)
V       MGM

## DUCHESS AND THE DIRTWATER FOX, THE ** PG
Melvin Frank     USA     1976
*George Segal, Goldie Hawn, Conrad Janis, Thayer David, Roy Jenson, Jennifer Lee, Pat Ast, Sid Gould, Bob Hoy, E.J. Andre, Richard Farnsworth, John Alderson, Prentiss Rowe, Jerry Gatlin*
A card-sharp teams up with a dancehall girl and have various adventures in the Old West, in this uneven and rather simple-minded comedy. A few good scenes build some atmosphere that is soon dissipated by the tiresome song interludes.

WES      100 min (ort 103 min)
B,V,LV      CBS

## DUDES *    15
Penelope Spheeris     USA     1988
*Jon Cryer, Daniel Roebuck, Catherine Mary Stewart, Flea, Lee Ving, Billy Ray Sharkey, Glenn Withrow, Michael Melvin, Axxel G. Reese, Marc Rude, Calvin Bartlett, Pete Wilcox, Vance Colvig, Pamela Gidley*
Three New York punks head West in search of a new open-air lifestyle, but find themselves running foul of a gang of murderous rednecks in Montana, and get drawn into a revenge-seeking conflict. A repulsive and rather incoherent formula revenger of much violence but little merit.

A/AD      86 min
V/h      CBS

## DUEL ****    PG
Steven Spielberg     USA     1971
*Dennis Weaver, Tim Herbert, Charles Peel, Eddie Firestone, Shirley O'Hara, Lucille Benson, Alexander Lockwood, Amy Douglass, Gene Dynarski, Cary Loftin*
Spielberg's debut was this well made story of a businessman on a trip who begins to realise that the driver of a lorry is out to kill him. The tension is maintained right to the very end in a film that is pared down to the bone. Script is by Richard Matheson. Additional footage was added for cinema release, hence the longer running time.
Boa: story by Richard Matheson.

DRA      85 min (ort 92 min) mTV
B,V      ARENA/CIC

## DUEL AT DIABLO ***    15
Ralph Nelson     USA     1966
*James Garner, Sidney Poitier, Bibi Andersson, Dennis Weaver, Bill Travers, William Redfield, John Hoyt, John Crawford, John Hubbard, Kevin Coughlin, Jay Ripley, Jeff Cooper, Ralph Bahnsen, Bobby Crawford, Richard Lapp*
A mixed bunch travel through the desert with a convoy of munitions, and face the constant threat of Indian attack. A simple tale, told with style and verve with excellent performances from Garner, as an

Indian scout out to avenge the death of his wife, and Poitier as an ex-Army sergeant.
Boa: novel Apache Rising by M. Albert.

WES      101 min
V      WHV

## DUEL IN THE JUNGLE *    PG
George Marshall     UK     1954
*Dana Andrews, Jeanne Crain, David Farrar, George Coulouris, Wilfrid Hyde White, Patrick Barr*
An insurance investigator attempts to track down a man who is alleged to have died in Africa, but has in fact staged a fraud, setting traps for his pursuer. A strong cast do their best with this dreary and studio-bound jungle adventure.

A/AD      97 min (ort 101 min)
V      WHV

## DUEL IN THE SUN **    PG
King Vidor     USA     1946
*Jennifer Jones, Joseph Cotten, Gregory Peck, Lionel Barrymore, Walter Huston, Herbert Marshall, Butterfly McQueen, Charles Bickford, Lillian Gish, Joan Tetzel, Tilly Losch, Harry Carey, Otto Kruger, Sidney Blackmer*
Sprawling overlong Western with little plot and a strange ending that tells of a half-breed girl torn between two brothers. Lavish, detailed and rather disjointed, despite a number of scenes of undoubted power.
Boa: novel by Niven Busch.

WES      125 min (ort 130 min)
V      STRAND L/A; VCC

## DUEL OF CHAMPIONS **    PG
Terence Young (Ferdinado Baldi)
     ITALY/SPAIN     1961
*Alan Ladd, Franca Bettoja, Robert Keith, Franco Fabrizi, Luciano Marin, Mino Doro, Jacques Sernas, Audrea Aureli, Osvaldo Ruggeri, Jacqueline Derval, Pieor Palmeri, Umberto Raho, Alfredo Varelli, Nando Agelini, Francesca Bett*
Historical epic about the power struggle between the cities of Rome and Alba, with Ladd looking distinctly out of place as the Roman leader who challenges the forces of Alba. A stilted and stodgy costumer.
Aka: ORAZI E CURIAZI

DRA      86 min (ort 105 min) Cut (4 sec)
B,V,V2      VDM L/A; VMA L/A; STABL

## DUEL OF THE BRAVE ONES **    18
     HONG KONG
*Chang Wu Lang, Yan Kego Hom, Tong Wai Shing*
A convicted thief is freed from prison and exacts revenge on a master criminal who cheated him in this routine punch 'n' kicker.

MAR      85 min (ort 87 min) Cut (1 min 21 sec)
B,V      VPD

## DUEL OF THE IRON FIST ** 
Chang Chech     HONG KONG     1971
*Ti Lung, David Chiang, Yu Hui, Wang Ping, Ku Feng, Wang Chung, Cheng Lei, Chen Yuan, Yang Chih Ching, Cheng Kan Yeh, Hsia Hui*
Two heroes battle a horde of villains in a Shaw Brothers offering which has better than average sets and production values, although these do little to improve the mediocre plot.

MAR      98 min
B,V      VCD

## DUEL OF THE MASTERS ** 
Tang Wei Cheng     HONG KONG
*Hsu Shao Chiang, Sunny Yu Huan Chung*
Two skilled combatants engage in one final battle. At stake are both their lives and their honour. Average.

MAR      85 min
B,V      MMA

## DUEL OF THE TOUGH *
Ho Chih-Chiang    HONG KONG                    1982
*Jackie Chow, Steve Mak, Howard Ki*
A formula kung fu movie for punch 'n' kick fans.
MAR                                          86 min
B,V                                            PAE

## DUELLISTS, THE **                            PG
Ridley Scott          USA                      1977
*Keith Carradine, Harvey Keitel, Edward Fox, Cristina
Raines, Robert Stephens, Diana Quick, Tom Conti,
Albert Finney*
Two officers in Napoleon's army fall out over a woman
and fight a series of duels stretching over thirty years,
in this strangely pointless but highly atmospheric
film. Scott's directorial feature debut.
Boa: short story The Point of Honour (also known as
The Duel) by Joseph Conrad.
DRA                        96 min (ort 101 min)
B,V                                            CIC

## DUET FOR ONE ***                              15
Andrei Konchalovsky    USA                     1986
*Julie Andrews, Alan Bates, Max Von Sydow, Rupert
Everett, Cathryn Harrison, Margaret Courtenay,
Macha Neill, Liam Neeson*
A world famous concert violinist is stricken with
multiple sclerosis whilst in her prime. As her illness
progresses she is forced to come to terms with her
inability to play and her husband's mounting infide-
lities. Kempinski's acclaimed two-act play (with just
virtuoso and psychiatrist) is expanded for the screen
and in the process its power is diluted, but it is
Andrews' remarkable performance that saves it.
Filmed in England.
Boa: play by Tom Kempinski.
DRA                        102 min (ort 107 min)
B,V                                            GHV

## DUMB WAITER, THE ***                          PG
Robert Altman          USA
*John Travolta, Tom Conti*
In a basement two hired killers await the arrival of
their victim whilst being harassed by a dumb-waiter.
It then transpires that one man has been deputed to
kill the other in this competent adaptation of Pinter's
one-act play of ambiguity and intrigue.
Boa: play by Harold Pinter.
DRA                                          58 min
V                                              IVA

## DUMBO ****                                    Uc
Ben Sharpsteen         USA                     1941
*Voices of: Sterling Holloway, Edward Brophy, Verna
Felton, Herman Bing, Cliff Edwards*
A marvellous cartoon feature about a baby elephant
whose ears are so enormous that he is able to use them
to fly. The film contains a remarkable scene, one of
Disney's finest, in which Dumbo has a nightmare. AA:
Score (Frank Churchill/Oliver Wallace).
Boa: story by H. Aberson and H. Pearl.
CAR                                          90 min
V                                              WDV

## DUNDERKLUMPEN ***
Per Ahlin              SWEDEN                   1974
*Beppe Wolgers, Jens Wolgers, Kerstin Wolgers,
Camilla Wolgers*
Mixture of animation and live action in a tale of a
strange woodland creature that sneaks into a girl's
room, steals her dolls and brings them to life.
CAR                                         100 min
B,V                                            ART

## DUNE **                                        15
David Lynch            USA                     1984
*Kyle MacLachlan, Francesca Annis, Brad Dourif, Jose
Ferrer, Linda Hunt, Freddie Jones, Jurgen Prochnow,
Richard Jordan, Everett McGill, Kenneth McMillan,*

*Sting (Gordon Sumner), Silvana Mangano, Jack
Nance, Max Von Sydow*
Though generally acknowledged as a failure in its
attempt to bring Frank Herbert's fantasy to the
screen, this film still has some memorable special
effects. It tells of a futuristic galactic empire, whose
very existence is dependent on supplies of a strange
spice found only on one planet. Complex and multi-
layered, its greatest failings are the lack of a coherent
narrative and the assumption of familiarity with
Herbert's novel.
Boa: novel by Frank Herbert.
FAN                                         131 min
B, V/sh           TEVP L/A; WHV (VHS only)

## DUNERA BOYS, THE **                            15
Ben Lewin             AUSTRALIA                1985
*Bob Hoskins, Joseph Spano, Warren Mitchell, Joseph
Furst, Simon Chilvers*
In the first wave of hysteria following the German
victories in Europe, two Jewish refugees find themselves transported to an Australian outback prison
camp, along with a motley assortment of aliens,
refugees and suspected collaborators. They become
friendly with the guards and are eventually recruited
to fight in the army in this offbeat and uneven tale.
DRA                        149 min (ort 230 min) mTV
V                                            FUTUR

## DUNWICH HORROR, THE **                         18
Daniel Haller          USA                     1970
*Sandra Dee, Dean Stockwell, Ed Begley, Lloyd
Bochner, Sam Jaffe, Joanna Moore, Talia Coppola
(Shire)*
This mangled adaptation of an H.P. Lovecraft short
story bears little relation to the original, instead
dealing with the sinister plans a Satanist has for a
young girl. Occasionally effective, but badly let down
by the poor ending.
Boa: short story The Shuttered Room by H.P.
Lovecraft.
HOR                        86 min (ort 90 min)
B,V,V2                                         GHV

## DUTCH GIRLS *                                  15
Giles Foster           UK                      1985
*Bill Paterson, Colin Firth, Timothy Spall, Gusta
Gerritsen, John Wells*
The boys of a public school go to Holland to play in a
series of hockey matches and the lads are of course
eager for female company. A limp and fairly mirthless
jaunt.
COM                                       83 min mTV
B,V                                           TEVP

## DUTCH TREAT **                                 15
Boaz Davidson          USA                     1986
*David Landesman, Lorin Dreyfuss, The Dolly Dots*
Two bumbling nerds get into deep water when they
meet an attractive all-girl band and are inspired to
pretend to be hot-shot record promoters. The cute
"Dolly Dots" add a little glamour to a dreary comedy,
whose shortage of ideas hides behind a desperately
zany search for laughs.
COM                        91 min (ort 95 min)
B,V                                            RNK

## DYING TIME **                                  18
Allan Kuskowski        USA                     1990
*Jimmy Stathis, Deborah Downey, Paul Drake*
A Federal Agent takes on a case that involves a series
of Satanic murders, but when the chief of the Los
Angeles Homicide Division is kidnapped the pressure
really begins to mount to crack the case.
THR                                          89 min
V                                           BIGPIC

## DYNAMITE **
William H. Pine        USA                     1949

*William Gargan, Virginia Welles, Richard Crane, Irving Bacon, Mary Newton, Frank Ferguson*
Love triangle drama set in a dynamite factory where an ex-GI comes into conflict with an older man as they vie for the attentions of the same girl.
DRA 68 min B/W
B,V MARKET/GOV

## DYNAMITE BROTHERS, THE *
Al Adamson USA 1974
*Alan Tang, Timothy Brown, James Hong, Aldo Ray, Carolyn Ann Speed, Don Oliver*
The story of violent clashes between rival Chinese gangs in Los Angeles.
Aka: STUD BROWN
MAR 83 min
B,V,V2 INT/CBS

## DYNAMITE JOHNSON ** 15
Bobby A. Stuart (Bobby A. Suarez)
HONG KONG/PHILIPPINES 1978
*Maria Lee, Ken Metcalfe, Johnson Yap, Joseph Zucchero, Alex Pecate, Joe Sison, Johnny Wilson, Chito Guerrero*
A sequel to "The Bionic Boy" (1977) in which our little martial arts hero and his equally resolute aunt, battle an ex-Nazi who plans to take over the world from his base in the Philippines, where he has enslaved the local inhabitants. Fairly ludicrous but quite good fun.
Aka: NEW ADVENTURES OF THE BIONIC BOY, THE; RETURN OF THE BIONIC BOY, THE; TWELVE MILLION DOLLAR BOY, THE
A/AD 98 min
B,V MOV; CAB2

## DYNAMITE SHAOLIN HEROES ** 15
Godfrey Ho HONG KONG
*Lo Lieh, Sam Kuen, Willie Wong, Tim Ming, Carlo Kim, Roman Lee, Man Yeung*
The prince of a fallen Ming Dynasty is to be used as nothing more than a tool in an ambitious government official's power-struggle. However, the intervention of a mysterious Shaolin master with superb skills thwarts his evil plans.
MAR 78 min
B,V VPD

## DYNAMITE TRIO *
Cheng Yu-Wen HONG KONG 1982
*Dragon Lung, Jacky Chek, Lung Fei*
A book containing ancient martial arts secrets is not surprisingly sought by a number of people.
Aka: CH'I-SOU SHIN ERH TAO
MAR 89 min
B,V PAE; CCV

## DYNAMO **
Hwa I Hung HONG KONG
*Bruce Li (Ho Tsung-Tao), Ma Li, Ku Feng, Chaing Tao, Mary Kan*
Another kung fu movie which makes use of a clone of the late Bruce Lee. A fighter taking part in a tournament must lose in order to save his girlfriend.
MAR 96 min
B,V,V2 VPD

# E

## E.T. THE EXTRA-TERRESTRIAL **** U
Steven Spielberg USA 1982
*Dee Wallace, Henry Thomas, Peter Coyote, Robert MacNaughton, Drew Barrymore, K.C. Martel, Sean Frye, C. Thomas Howell*
A modern fairytale for adults and kids alike as a young boy befriends an alien creature stranded on

Earth, who for once is shown as benign in sharp contrast to the cold, clinical forces of the state. A captivating fantasy. AA: Score (Orig) (John Williams), Sound (Robert Knudson/Robert Glass/Don Digirolamo/Gene Cantamessa), Effects (Aud) (Charles L. Campbell/Ben Burtt), Effects (Vis) (Carlo Rambaldi/Dennis Muren/Kenneth F. Smith).
FAN 109 min (ort 115 min)
V/sh CIC

## EACH DAWN I DIE *** PG
William Keighley USA 1939
*James Cagney, George Bancroft, George Raft, Jane Bryan, Maxie Rosenbloom, Thurston Hall, Stanley Ridges, Alan Baxter, Victor Jory*
A reporter is framed for manslaughter and sent to prison where the tough conditions make him into a hardened con. Enjoyable prison drama kept afloat by the three stars though the unbelievable and contrived second half does let it down considerably.
Boa: novel by Jerome Odlum.
DRA 88 min (ort 113 min) B/W
V WHV

## EAGLE CLAWS CHAMPION **
HONG KONG
*Conan Han, Seaman Kim, Sho Kosugi*
A young student accidentally kills his best friend's brother and after his release from jail has to face his erstwhile friend in a duel to the death.
MAR 90 min
B,V VTC

## EAGLE HAS LANDED, THE *** 15
John Sturges UK 1976
*Michael Caine, Donald Sutherland, Robert Duvall, Jenny Agutter, Anthony Quayle, Donald Pleasence, Jean Marsh, Sven-Bertil Taube, John Standing, Judy Geeson, Larry Hagman, Maurice Reeves, Treat Williams, Siegfried Rauch*
WW2 story with German commandos parachuting into England where they infiltrate a small English village in a bungled attempt to kill Churchill. An imaginative and exciting film with a convoluted and twist-laden plot.
Boa: novel by Jack Higgins.
WAR 118 min (ort 135 min)
B,V PRV L/A; CH5 (VHS only); POLY (VHS only)

## EAGLE IN A CAGE ***
Fielder Cook UK/YUGOSLAVIA 1970
*John Gielgud, Ralph Richardson, Billie Whitelaw, Ferdy Mayne, Lee Montague, Kenneth Haigh, Moses Gunn*
Napoleon's last days as a prisoner on St. Helena courtesy of the British are examined in this excellent drama. Haigh is outstanding as Napoleon and the intelligent script is by Millard Lampell.
DRA 98 min
B,V INT/CBS

## EAGLE ISLAND *** 18
Mats Helge (Mats Helge Olsson)
SWEDEN 1987
*Tom O'Rourke, Terry D. Seago, Summer Lee Thomas*
Action tale set on a Northern European island where a top secret US Army post is used for storing the secrets of the US rocket defence system. After a security breach Captain Eddie Foster is dismissed, but he is determined to return to keep the secrets from falling into Russian hands.
A/AD 90 min
B,V IVS

## EAGLE SHADOW FIST *** 18
Hdeng Tsu HONG KONG 198-
*Jackie Chan*
Martial arts tale set during WW2 with a famous actor of the Chinese theatre leaving the stage to become a

resistance fighter against the Japanese.
MAR                                85 min Cut (1 min 44 sec)
V                                                    TGP

**EAGLE VERSUS SILVER FOX ** **                    18
Godfrey Ho          HONG KONG
*Wang Chen Li, Jacky Lee, Sam Yuen, Stan Yuen*
Set during the time of the Manchu Dynasty with a
powerful fighter being chosen by the kung fu schools
to lead the battle against a sinister warrior and his
followers.
MAR                                    83 min Cut (5 sec)
B,V                                                  VPD

**EAGLE WARRIORS ***                                PG
John Peyser          USA                            1967
*James Drury, Robert Pine, Hank James, Tim Nolan,*
*Norman Fell, Jeff Salt, Steve Carlson, Michael*
*Stanwood, Jonathan Daly*
Very loosely based on a Matheson's novel (he also did
the screenplay), this cliched WW2 story takes a very
superficial look at the effect the war has on young
men. Shot entirely on studio backlots, this low-budget
effort is about as stereotyped as they come. Some good
camerawork is a slight compensation.
Aka: YOUNG WARRIORS, THE
Boa: novel Beardless Warriors by Richard Matheson.
WAR                                  88 min (ort 93 min)
V                                                    EAG

**EAGLE, THE ***                                    PG
Clarence Brown       USA                            1925
*Rudolf Valentino, Louise Dresser, Vilma Banky,*
*Albert Conti*
Valentino plays a Cossack lieutenant who becomes a
bandit when his father's lands are annexed and has
numerous adventures, including an encounter with
Catherine the Great where he spurns her advances.
An enjoyable costumed romp with the star at his best.
Boa: novel Dubrovsky by Alexander Pushkin.
DRA          44 min (1949 UK cinema version – ort 80 min
at 24 fps) B/W silent
V                                                    VIR

**EAGLES ATTACK AT DAWN ****
Menahem Golan        ISRAEL                         1974
*Rick Jason, Peter Brown, Joseph Shiloal*
The story of the escape of Israeli POWs from captivity
in Syria. A fair but unimaginative actioner.
A/AD                                             101 min
B,V                                                  RNK

**EAGLE'S WING ***                                  PG
Anthony Harvey       UK                             1979
*Martin Sheen, Sam Waterson, Caroline Langrishe,*
*Harvey Keitel, Stephane Audran, John Castle, Jorge*
*Luke, Jorge Russek, Manuel Ojeda, Pedro Damian,*
*Claudio Brook, Jose Carlos Ruis, Cecilia Camacho,*
*Julio Lucena*
Deadly dull but beautifully photographed British-
made Western dealing with a contest between an
Indian warrior and a trapper for a prize white stallion
which the latter has stolen. Derivative of a hundred
other films with hardly an original scene of its own.
The photography is by Billy Williams with screenplay
by John Briley (of GANDHI).
WES                                100 min (ort 111 min)
B,V                                                  RNK

**EARLY BIRD, THE ***
Robert Asher         UK                             1965
*Norman Wisdom, Edward Chapman, Jerry*
*Desmonde, Paddie O'Neil, Bryan Pringle, Richard*
*Vernon, John Le Mesurier, Penny Morell, Frank*
*Thornton, Harry Locke, Dandy Nichols, Imogen*
*Hassall, Eddie Leslie*
A milkman gets involved in a feud between a large
dairy company and a tiny one-horse outfit. A stiff and
unfunny waste of Wisdom's talents.

Aka: NORMAN WISDOM: THE EARLY BIRD
COM                                95 min (ort 98 min)
B,V                                                  RNK

**EARLY FROST ***                                   18
Terry O'Connor       AUSTRALIA                      1982
*Diana McLean, Jon Blake, David Franklin, Janet*
*Kingsbury*
A private detective investigating a death, suspects
that he is dealing with murder as a large number of
mothers are meeting with similar "accidents".
DRA                                87 min (ort 90 min) Cut
B,V,V2                                               MED

**EARLY FROST, AN ****                              15
John Erman          USA                             1985
*Ben Gazzara, Gena Rowlands, Aidann Quinn, Sylvia*
*Sydney, John Glover, Sydney Walsh, D.W. Moffett,*
*Terry O'Quinn, Bill Paxton, Cheryl Anderson, Sue*
*Ann Gilfillan, Christopher Bradley, Don Hood,*
*Barbara Iley, Scott Jacek*
Quite a powerful drama, in which a son attending his
parents' wedding anniversary has to tell them them
that he is both homosexual and an AIDS sufferer.
Despite the temptation to sink into sentimentality
this one never succumbs. Daniel Lipman won an
Emmy for his script.
Boa: story by Sherman Yellen.
DRA                               97 min (ort 100 min) mTV
V                                                    RCA

**EARTH GIRLS ARE EASY ****                         PG
Julien Temple        USA                            1989
*Geena Davis, Jim Carrey, Damon Wayams, Jeff*
*Goldblum, Julie Brown, Michael McKean, Charles*
*Rocket, Larry Linville, Rick Overton, Angelyne*
Three furry aliens crash-land in a swimming pool
belonging to a San Fernando manicurist who's a little
short-changed in the brains department. Having
shaved the aliens and discovered them to be gorgeous
hunks, the girl and her friend take them out for a tour
of what L.A. has to offer in the way of fun. A wacky
musical-comedy of infectious appeal, its lack of a
strong plot and relentless cheerfulness grows just a
little tiresome.
COM                                             100 min
V                                                    MGM

**EARTH STAR VOYAGER ****                           PG
James Goldstone      USA                            1988
*Duncan Regehr, Brian McNamara, Julia*
*Montgomery, Jason Michas, Peter Donat, Tom*
*Breznahan, Margaret Langrick, Sean O'Byrne*
Enjoyable fantasy about a group of young space cadets
who leave the dying planet Earth and embark on an
interstellar voyage that will last 25 years in search of
the planet Demeter. Originally shown in two parts
this pilot for a TV series is done very much in the
STAR TREK mould.
FAN                                           120 min mTV
B,V                                                  RNK

**EARTH TWO ***                                     U
Tom Gries            USA                            1971
*Gary Lockwood, Anthony Franciosa, Scott Hylands,*
*Hari Rhodes, Lew Ayres, Mariette Hartley, Gary*
*Merrill, Inga Swenson, Brian Dewey, Edward Bell,*
*Bart Burns, Diana Webster, John Carter, Herbert*
*Nelson, Serge Tschernisch*
The adventures of the first manned space station and
its day-to-day operation form the basis of this film.
Unfortunately the film has nowhere to go. Very dull.
Aka: EARTH 2
FAN                               93 min (ort 100 min) mTV
B,V                                                  MGM

**EARTH VERSUS THE FLYING SAUCERS ****             U
Fred F. Sears        USA                            1956
*Hugh Marlowe, Joan Taylor, Donald Curtis, Morris*

*Ankrum, Tom Browne Henry, Paul Frees (voice only)*
Alien invaders threaten dire consequences if their
attempt to take over the Earth is opposed. A low-key
and somewhat matter-of-fact story, given an occasional boost by some competent Ray Harryhausen special
effects.
Boa: story by Curt Siodmak.
FAN                          80 min (ort 82 min) B/W
V                                             RCA

**EARTHLING, THE **                              PG
Peter Collinson    AUSTRALIA                    1980
*William Holden, Ricky Schroder, Jack Thompson,*
*Olivia Hamnett, Alwyn Kurts*
A lost orphan learns how to survive in the Outback
from a man who is terminally ill. A competent
outdoors adventure with an appeal largely restricted
to kids, though the nature scenes are nice.
A/AD                         97 min (ort 102 min)
B,V                                           RNK

**EARTHQUAKE ***                                 PG
Mark Robson        USA                          1974
*Charlton Heston, Richard Roundtree, Lorne Greene,*
*Ava Gardner, George Kennedy, Genevieve Bujold,*
*Walter Matthau, Lloyd Nolan, Victoria Principal*
Disaster epic with a star-studded cast about the
destruction of Los Angeles, as the most catastrophic
earthquake of all time rips through Southern Califor-
nia, affecting the lives of all who live there. Excellent
special effects (which will lose impact on TV) make up
for the tedious and cliched plot. AA: Sound (Ronald
Pierce/Melvin Metcalf Sr), Spec Award (Frank Bren-
del/Glen Robinson/Albert Whitlock for Visual
Effects).
A/AD                         116 min (ort 129 min)
B,V                               CIC (VHS only)

**EAST OF EDEN ***                               15
Harvey Hart        USA                          1980
*Jane Seymour, Timothy Bottoms, Bruce Boxleitner,*
*Soon-Teck Oh, Karen Allen, Hart Bochner, Sam*
*Bottoms, Warren Oates, Howard Duff, Anne Baxter,*
*Richard Masur, Nicholas Pryor, Lloyd Bridges, Nellie*
*Bellflower, M. Emmet Walsh*
A competent remake of the earlier classic, that covers
far more ground than the 1955 James Dean film, and
follows the changing fortunes of the Trask family and
the two half-brothers who compete for the affection of
their father. The film won Emmy Awards for art
direction and set decoration. Originally shown in
three parts.
Aka: JOHN STEINBECK'S EAST OF EDEN
Boa: novel by John Steinbeck.
DRA    248 min; 199 min (BRAVE) (ort 640 min) mTV
B,V                      VFP L/A; BRAVE (VHS only)

**EAST OF EDEN ****                              PG
Elia Kazan         USA                          1955
*James Dean, Raymond Massey, Jo Van Fleet, Julie*
*Harris, Burl Ives, Richard Davalos, Albert Dekker*
A modern Cain and Abel story with two brothers as
arivals for the love of their father. Full of moments of
power this is deservedly recognised as a classic. It also
gave Dean his first starring role. Remade some years
later as a TV mini-series. AA: S. Actress (Van Fleet).
Boa: novel by John Steinbeck.
DRA                          110 min (ort 115 min)
V                                             WHV

**EAST OF ELEPHANT ROCK **
Don Boyd           UK                           1976
*John Hurt, Jeremy Kemp, Judi Bowker, Christopher*
*Cazenove, Anton Rodgers, Tariq Yunus, Vajira, Sam*
*Poythress, Geoffrey Hale*
Steamy drama of a young civil servant and his jealous
mistress set against the unrest in Malaya in 1948. The
Sri Lankan locations are nice but this clumsily made
film never gets to grips with its material, some of
which is cribbed from the 1940 film THE LETTER.

DRA                                          93 min
B,V,V2                                    PRV L/A

**EAST OF SUDAN **                               U
Nathan Juran       UK                           1964
*Anthony Quayle, Sylvia Sims, Jenny Agutter, Derek*
*Fowldes, Johnny Sekka, Joseph Layode, Harold*
*Coyne, Derek Blomfield*
A British soldier leads an English governess and
others to safety from one of General Gordon's outposts
following an Arab attack in the 1880s. An object
lesson in how to make a shoddy film, with footage
stolen from THE FOUR FEATHERS (and an un-
known safari film), a plot loosely derivative of THE
AFRICAN QUEEN, plus a dozen gloriously bad
moments where the director delights in the clumsy
use of back projection or studio-bound settings.
A/AD                                         85 min
V                                             RCA

**EAST SIDE HUSTLE **                            18
Frank Vitale       USA                          1976
*Anne Marie Provenchev, Man Moyle*
Prostitutes decide to quit the game but meet with
violent resistance from their pimp in this tough, mean
story of violence and revenge.
DRA                          87 min Cut (5 sec)
B,V                                           VPD

**EASTER PARADE ****                             U
Charles Walters    USA                          1948
*Judy Garland, Fred Astaire, Peter Lawford, Ann*
*Miller, Jules Munshin*
Irving Berlin musical about a dancer trying to forget
his ex-partner while finding a new one. Bright, breezy
and great fun. Songs include "A Couple Of Swells",
"Stepping Out With My Baby" and "Shaking The
Blues Away". AA: Score (Johnny Green/Roger Edens).
MUS                          100 min (ort 103 min)
B,V                                           MGM

**EASY ***                                       
Anthony Spinelli   USA                          1978
*Jesie St James, Jack Wright, Georgina Spelvin, John*
*Wilson, Desiree Cousteau*
A female high school teacher has a reputation as
being "easy" – not because she wants to be but simply
because she cannot resist her powerful urges. Having
already lost her husband to another teacher, she
embarks on a rapid series of encounters with just
about anyone who's available. Finally she meets a
man she does fall for, but he is already married. A
well-acted and rather forlorn little tale.
A                                            84 min
B,V,V2                                    CAL; PPL

**EASY LIVING ***                                PG
Jacques Tourneur   USA                          1949
*Victor Mature, Lizabeth Scott, Lucille Ball, Sonny*
*Tufts, Lloyd Nolan, Paul Stewart, Jeff Donnell, Jack*
*Paar, Art Baker*
An ageing football star cannot face up to the fact that
he is due to retire very soon. An absorbing drama in
which Mature gives one of his better performances.
Boa: story by Irwin Shaw. Osca: CAREFREE (KVD)
DRA                          74 min (ort 77 min) B/W
B,V                                  KVD L/A; STABL

**EASY MONEY ***                                 15
James Signorelli   USA                          1983
*Rodney Dangerfield, Joe Pesci, Candy Azzara,*
*Geraldine Fitzgerald, Jennifer Jason-Leigh, Tom*
*Ewell, Tom Noonan*
An undisciplined character must reform by overcom-
ing all his bad habits within one year, in order to gain
an inheritance. A likeable comedy with a number of
good gags. Dangerfield is in good form in his first
starring comedy vehicle.
COM                                          95 min
B,V                                           RNK

**EASY PREY \*\*** 15
Sandor Stern            USA            1986
*Gerald McRaney, Sean McCann, Susan Hogan, Kate
Lynch, Barry Flatman, Neil Clifford, Jessica Steen,
Shawnee Smith, Philip Akin, Laurie Paton, Brian
Taylor, Jeremy Ratchford, Alan Fawcett, Teddy
Moore, Denise Ferguson*
Based on a true story, this has Smith as a naive
sixteen-year-old who falls into the clutches of a
wealthy Australian racing driver who has become a
cold-blooded serial killer. As the FBI launch a nation-
wide manhunt, the girl is forced to endure a terrifying
ordeal of cross-country travel with her vicious companion. A repulsive and vicious film of compelling
vacuity.
THR            90 min mTV
B,V            NWV

**EASY RIDER \*\*\*** 18
Dennis Hopper            USA            1969
*Peter Fonda, Dennis Hopper, Jack Nicholson, Karen
Black, Luke Askew, Luana Anders, Robert Walker,
Phil Spector*
Now a cult film, this was one of the most influential
films of the 1960s. It tells of two hippy bikers who go
on a long journey of exploration through America.
Memorable for an excellent backing of rock songs, it
has some good moments and an extremely violent
ending. The photography is by Laszlo Kovacs. Fea-
tures music by: Hendrix, The Byrds, Steppenwolf,
Roger McGuinn and others. Written by Hopper, Peter
Fonda and Terry Southern.
DRA            94 min
B,V            RCA

**EAT A BOWL OF TEA \*\*\*** 15
Wayne Wang            USA            1989
*Cora Miao, Russell Wong, Victor Wong, Lau Siu Ming,
Eric Tsang Chi Wai*
Ethnic comedy set in New York's Chinatown in 1949,
when the authorities first permitted the immigration
of Chinese women into the US (there being a ban in
place from 1924 until then). A young Chinese-
American war veteran visits China and returns with a
Chinese-born wife, but his elders, having been with-
out women for so long, can give him little help as to
what marriage involves. A charming little tale,
scripted by Judith Rascoe.
Boa: novel by Louis Chu.
COM            99 min (ort 104 min)
V            RCA

**EAT AND RUN \*\*** 15
Christopher Hart            USA            1986
*Ron Silver, R.L. Ryan, Sharon Schlarth, John F.
Fleming, Derek Murcott*
A huge alien lands on Earth and gobbles up an Italian
sausage-maker, developing a taste for "Italian food" in
this bizarre and mildly amusing SF spoof.
Aka: MANGIA; MANIA
COM            80 min
B,V            NWV

**EAT MY DUST! \*\*** 15
Charles Griffith            USA            1976
*Ron Howard, Christopher Norris, Warren
Kemmerling, Dave Madden, Rance Howard, Clint
Howard, Corbin Bernsen*
A boy steals a car to impress a girl and starts a hell of
a chase in this simple-minded comedy whose appeal
will be largely restricted to speed freaks.
COM            90 min
B,V            PRIME/CBS

**EAT THE PEACH \*\*\*** PG
Peter Ormrod            EIRE            1986
*Stephen Brennan, Eamon Morrissey, Niall Toibin,
Catherine Byrne, Joe Lynch, Tony Doyle*
Two friends in rural Ireland lose their jobs, but

inspired by ROUSTABOUT, the film in which Presley
rides a "Wall of Death", they decide to build one near
their homes. As their money runs out they are forced
to raise more by dubious means and encounter some
strange characters. An engaging and quirky tale
written by Ormrod and producer John Kelleher and
based on a true story.
COM            91 min
B,V            RCA

**EAT THE RICH \*** 15
Peter Richardson            UK            1987
*Ronald Allen, Sandra Dorne, Jimmy Fagg, Lemmy
Lanah Pellay, Nosher Powell, Fiona Richmond, Ton
Tarr, Paul McCartney, Bill Wyman, Koo Stark, George
Harrison, Sandy Shaw*
An utterly tasteless black comedy with Pellay getting
fired from his job in a restaurant and returning with a
bunch of revolutionaries to serve up human flesh on
the menu. A misfire of a satire with a succession of
pointless cameos and a pounding score from Motor-
head.
COM            89 min
B,V            CBS

**EATEN ALIVE \*\*** 18
Umberto Lenzi            ITALY            1980
*Robert Kerman, Ivan Rassimov, Mel Ferrer, Janet
Agren, Paola Senatore, Me Me Lai, Meg Fleming,
Franco Fantasia, Michele Schmiegelm, Gianfranco
Coduti, Alfred Joseph Berry*
A young girl goes to New Guinea in search of a sister
who has disappeared after becoming a member of a
strange sect. A cannibalism story incorporating some
elements of the notorious mass-suicide when the
followers of demented self-styled messiah Jim Jones
took their lives in the Guyanan jungle. See also
GUYANA: CRIME OF THE CENTURY.
Aka: CANNIBALS; DEFY TO THE LAST
PARADISE; DOOMED TO DIE; EATEN ALIVE BY
THE CANNIBALS; MANGIATI VIVI; MANGIATI
VIVI DAI CANNIBALI
HOR            82 min Cut (1 sec in addition to film cuts)
B,V            VDM/GHV; GOV; ELE

**EATING RAOUL \*\*\*** 
Paul Bartel            USA            1982
*Paul Bartel, Mary Woronov, Robert Beltran, Susan
Saiger, Buck Henry, Dick Blackburn, Edie McClurg,
Ed Begley Jr, John Paragon, Hamilton Camp*
Amusing black comedy about a couple who hit on a
novel way of financing their restaurant business by
luring wealthy swingers to their apartment, then
killing and robbing them.
COM            87 min
B,V            PVG

**EBONY TOWER, THE \*\*** 15
Robert Knights            UK            1984
*Laurence Olivier, Toyah Wilcox, Greta Scacchi, Roger
Rees*
Ponderous rendering of a novel about an ageing
painter and his strange relationship with two young
female students, with whom he shares an idyllic
existence until the arrival of a young artist.
Boa: novel by John Fowles.
DRA            79 min (ort 120 min) mTV
B,V            GRN

**EBONY, IVORY AND JADE \*\*** PG
John Llewellyn Moxey   USA            1979
*Bert Convy, Debbie Allen, Martha Smith, Donald
Moffat, Nina Foch, Clifford David, Nicolas Coster,
Lucille Benson, Ji-Tu Cumbuka, Claude Akins, David
Brenner, Frankie Valli, Ted Shackelford, Bill Lane,
Ray Guth, Cletus Young*
A performer and two showgirls in Las Vegas work
undercover to protect a scientist from a terrorist. Pilot
for a series that never got off the ground. Average.

THR                 68 min (ort 78 min) Cut (25 sec) mTV
B,V                                         VFP L/A; HER

## ECHO PARK **                                    15
Robert Dornhelm    AUSTRIA/USA                   1985
*Thomas Hulce, Susan Dey, Michael Bowen,*
*Christopher Walker, Richard Marin, Cassandra*
*Peterson, Timothy Carey, Shirley Jo Finney, Heinrich*
*Schweiger, John Paragon*
The title refers to a small area of L.A. inhabited by a
motley collection of misfits, and the film concentrates
on the lives of three of them: a single mother who
aspires to be an actress, a pizza delivery man who
writes poetry and an Austrian weightlifter who
dreams of breaking into TV. A slightly interesting
drama of no great depth.
DRA                            84 min (ort 92 min)
B,V                                              VES

## ECHOES IN THE DARKNESS: PARTS 1 & 2 ***  15
Glenn Jordan       USA                           1987
*Robert Loggia, Stockard Channing, Treat Williams,*
*Peter Coyote, Cindy Pickett, Peter Boyle, Gary Cole,*
*Zeljko Ivanek, Alex Hyde-White, Vincent Irizarry,*
*Philip Bosco, Brenda Bazinet, Eugene A. Clark,*
*Richard Comar*
A solid recreation of the bizarre 1979 "Main Line"
murder case, that involved two teachers from an
exclusive Philadephia school, the killing of a col-
league and the disappearance of her two children. An
overlong account but well-acted with Coyote excellent
as the devious professor and Loggia good as the
unconventional principal. The adaptation is by Wambaugh.
Boa: book by Joseph Wambaugh.
DRA                           235 min (2 cassettes)
B,V                                              NWV

## ECSTASY *                                        18
Bud Townsend       USA                           1983
*Britt Ekland, Tiffany Bolling, Franc Luz*
A female photographer gets caught up in an erotic
film. Routine smut made for the US Playboy Channel
with Ekland giving her usual stab at acting.
Aka: LOVESCENE; LOVE SCENES
A                              86 min Cut (31 sec)
B,V                                      VTM L/A; MGM

## ECSTASY GIRLS, THE **
Robert McCallum    USA                           1979
*Jamie Gillis, John Leslie, Paul Thorpe, Nancy Sutter,*
*Desiree Cousteau, Georgina Spelvin, Serena, Leslie*
*Bovee*
Sex film about a plot to disinherit five women by
filming their more intimate moments and showing the
results to their puritanical father. Not a badly made
film but about as contrived as one of these films can
get.
A                                            90 min
V                                                RIP

## EDDIE AND THE CRUISERS *                        PG
Martin Davidson    USA                           1983
*Tom Berenger, Michael Pare, Joe Pantoliano, Matthew*
*Laurance, Helen Schneider, Ellen Barkin*
A TV reporter tries to get at the truth behind the
demise of a rock band after its lead singer dies in a car
crash. Despite the promising start (CITIZEN KANE
in a rock 'n' roll genre), the film badly sags after the
first 30 minutes. The score is by Kenny Vance. A
sequel followed.
DRA                                          92 min
B,V                                  VFP L/A; MRD; EIV

## EDDIE AND THE CRUISERS 2: EDDIE LIVES! *  PG
Jean-Claude Lord   USA                           1989
*Michael Pare, Marina Orsini, Bernie Coulson,*
*Matthew Laurance, Michael Rhoades, Anthony*
*Sherwood*

A sequel to the first film, this has rock star Eddie
Wilson alive and well (not having died in a New
Jersey car accident as widely believed) and living in
Montreal incognito where he earns a living as a
construction worker. When interest in Eddie revives,
a concept album is mooted, but the master tape is
stolen and the singer's old collaborator has to retrieve
it. Songs (supplied by John Cafferty) are only so-so,
and this dull tale is a big letdown.
DRA                            99 min (ort 103 min)
V                                                MED

## EDDIE MACON'S RUN **                            15
Jeff Kanew         USA                           1983
*Kirk Douglas, John Schneider, Lee Purcell, Leah*
*Ayres, Lisa Dunsheath, Tom Noonan*
A wrongly convicted man escapes from prison and is
pursued by the law while trying to make it to Mexico
in this fast-paced chase movie that is spoilt by
unnecessary violence.
Boa: novel by James McLendon.
DRA                            91 min (ort 95 min)
B,V                                              CIC

## EDGE OF DARKNESS ****                           PG
Lewis Milestone    USA                           1943
*Errol Flynn, Ann Sheridan, Walter Huston, Nancy*
*Coleman, Judith Anderson, Ruth Gordon, Helmut*
*Dantine, John Beal, Roman Bohnen*
A compelling drama examines the conditions faced by
the Norwegian resistance movement in opposing the
Nazi occupation of their country during WW2. The
superb camerawork is nicely balanced by the equally
fine performances.
WAR                   115 min (ort 120 min) B/W
V                                                WHV

## EDGE OF DARKNESS: PARTS 1 AND 2 *               15
Martin Campbell    UK                            1985
*Joe Don Baker, Joanne Whalley, Bob Peck*
An over-the-edge attempt at a complex thriller, where
the justified worries over nuclear power and weapons
degenerate into a confused and unbelievable story.
Especially annoying is the persistent anti-American
tone (more so since Chernobyl). Originally a TV
series, screened in November 1985.
THR                           307 min (2 cassettes) mTV
V/h                                              BBC

## EDGE OF HELL, THE **                            18
John Fasano        CANADA                        1987
*Jon-Mikl Thor, Teresa Simpson, Paola Francescatto,*
*Jesse D'Angelo, Dave Lane, Rusty Hamilton, Jim*
*Cirile, Jillian Perri, Frank Dietz*
A rock group on vacation with their girlfriends at an
isolated farm are attacked by murderous demons in
this unpleasant nonsense.
Aka: ROCK 'N' ROLL NIGHTMARE
HOR                                          90 min
B,V                                              IVS

## EDGE OF POWER ***                               18
Henri Safran       AUSTRALIA                     1986
*Henri Szeps, Anna Maria Monticelli, Ivor Kants,*
*Katherine Thompson, Sheree Da Costa*
A political thriller in which a journalist circulates a
false rumour that threatens to destroy a politician's
career. Following the murder of the leader of a radical
group he is obliged to act swiftly to bring the killers to
justice in this tense and well-plotted drama.
DRA                                          93 min
V                                                GHV

## EDGE OF SANITY **                               18
Gerard Kikoine     USA                           1988
*Anthony Perkins, Glynis Barber, David Lodge, Sarah*
*Maurthorp, Ben Cole, Lisa Davis, Kay Jewers, Harry*
*Landis, Briony McRoberts*

A doctor experiments with cocaine, bringing out his murderous alter ego in this rather cliched low-budget adaptation of the Jekyll and Hyde story. Not very different from the 1960s Hammer films of this type, Perkins is in good form in a role similar to his demented CRIMES OF PASSION preacher but Barber as his sexually repressed wife is unconvincing. A film of atmosphere let down by lack of imagination, lack of money and an utterly daft ending.

HOR                                            90 min
B,V                                              PAL

### EDGE OF TERROR, THE **                       15
Nico Mastarakis          USA              1986
*Meg Foster, Wings Hauser, David McCallum, John Michaels, Summer Thomas, Tracy Young, Robert Morley, Steve Railsback, Michael Yannatos*
A female thriller writer goes to an isolated Greek town to spend three weeks on a book, but she soon finds herself confronting an unknown terror in this low-budget horror spoof of little value.
Aka: TERROR'S EDGE; WIND, THE
HOR                                            95 min
B,V                                        POLY/SPEC

### EDGE OF THE AXE **                            18
Joseph Braunstein        USA              1987
*Barton Faulks, Christina Marie Lane, Page Moseley, Fred Hollyday*
The residents of a small town find themselves being terrorised by an axe-wielding escaped mental patient. When a young computer hacker breaks into the mental hospital records, he discovers a common link between all the victims of the attacker, and learns that his girlfriend is to be a likely target.
HOR                                            90 min
V                                                BOX

### EDNA, THE INEBRIATE WOMAN ***
Ted Kotcheff             UK               1971
*Patricia Hayes, Barbara Jefford, Pat Nye*
Hayes is excellent in this play about a woman tramp who lives out her life in a kind of twilight semi-existence. A profoundly depressing but undeniably absorbing story.
DRA                                        90 min mTV
B,V                                              BBC

### EDUCATING JULIE **                            15
Gale Hardman             UK               1985
*Gail Ward, Miles Taylor, Phil Benyard, Anthony Shaefer, Gary Willock*
A girl is given the task of researching nudism by her professor as part of her course of study. Initially repelled by the idea she soon becomes fascinated by the subject and after some opposition, so does her boyfriend. Made by the Central Council for British Nudism, this innocent little documentary style film is reminiscent of those naturist films made in the 1950s.
A                                             108 min
B,V                                            HERIT

### EDUCATING NINA *                             R18
Juliet Anderson          USA              1984
*Juliet Anderson, Nina Hartley, Karen Summer, Lili Marlene, Don Hart, Dan T. Mann, Nick Hunter*
This thin plot has a woman researching the effects of living out sexual fantasies as part of her Master's thesis. With a group of subjects and her old chums from drama school, fantasies dealing with seduction, infidelity and general debauchery are presented for our boundless edification. The girls are pleasing enough, but the script, dialogue and acting leave much to be desired. Distinctly amateurish.
A                                  70 min Cut (10 sec)
V                                              SHEP

### EDUCATING RITA **                             15
Lewis Gilbert            UK               1983
*Michael Caine, Julie Walters, Michael Williams, Maureen Lipman, Jeananne Crowley, Malcolm Douglas, Godfrey Quigley, Dearbhla Molloy, Pat Daly, Kim Fortune, Philip Hurdwood, Hilary Reynolds, Jack Walsh, Christopher Casson*
A young working-class girl wants to broaden her horizons and signs on as a student at the Open University, where she meets her alcoholic tutor. A depressing reworking of the "Pygmalian" theme, though Caine does give one of his best performances. Walters' film debut.
Boa: play by Willy Russell.
DRA                             108 min (ort 110 min)
V                                              RNK

### EDUCATION OF ALLISON TATE, THE **             15
Paul Leder               USA              1986
*Barbara Bosson, Hank Cheyne, Sondra Currie, Leslie Hope, Joe Santos, Donovan Letch, Greg Mullavey, Bernie White*
A spoilt rich girl and three other teenagers are kidnapped by some Indians who are fighting for their land rights, and as time goes on find themselves becoming sympathetic to the plight of their captors.
A/AD                                           88 min
B,V                                              MED

### EDUCATION OF SONNY CARSON, THE ***            18
Michael Campus           USA              1974
*Rony Clanton, Don Gordon, Joyce Walker, Paul Benjamin, Ram John Holder*
Over-wrought but compelling story of a defiant black youth and his childhood in the 1950s and 1960s in a Brooklyn slum, when the only escape seems to be via a life of crime. A rambling tale, well-acted and still of considerable relevance.
Boa: book by Sonny Carson.
DRA                                           104 min
B,V                                              IVS

### EDWARD AND MRS SIMPSON: PARTS 1               U
AND 2 ***
Waris Hussein            UK               1979
*Edward Fox, Cynthia Harris, Peggy Ashcroft, Maurice Denham, Marius Goring, Nigel Hawthorne, Cherie Lunghi, Jessie Matthews, David Waller*
A lavish and absorbing account of the events that led up to the abdication of Edward VIII. No expense was spared to make this a realistic and convincing portrayal, and the film captures the atmosphere of the period splendidly. Originally shown in six 50-minute episodes.
DRA                            300 min (2 cassettes) mTV
B,V                              TEVP; VCC (VHS only)

### EIGER SANCTION, THE **                        15
Clint Eastwood           USA              1975
*Clint Eastwood, George Kennedy, Jack Cassidy, Vonetta McGee, Thayer David, Dan Howard, Heidi Bruhl, Reiner Schoene, Brenda Venus*
Long boring spy story with Eastwood playing a college lecturer who has retired from Intelligence work until forced to return in order to expose a spy. Enjoyable for its action sequences that take place during an ascent of the Eiger.
Boa: novel by John Trevanian.
THR                             113 min (ort 125 min)
V/h                                              CIC

### EIGHT MASTERS, THE *                          18
Joseph Kuo           HONG KONG            1974
*Carter Huang, Chi Ling*
Yet another standard kung fu tale of honour, revenge etc.
Osca: JAWS OF THE DRAGON (TURBO)
MAR                                            89 min
B,V                                 AVP L/A; TURBO

## EIGHT MEN OUT ***
USA         15
    1989
*John Cusack, Clifton James, Michael Lerner,*
*Christopher Lloyd, Charlie Sheen, David Strathairn,*
*D.B. Sweeney*
A recreation of a true incident from 1919 when
members of the Chicago White Sox baseball team
were accused of accepting bribes in return for throw-
ing the World Series. The film carefully probes their
motivations and the all-pervading atmosphere of
corruption that infested the game.
DRA     114 min
V     VIR

## EIGHT MILLION WAYS TO DIE **
Hal Ashby     USA     18
    1985
*Jeff Bridges, Rosanna Arquette, Alexandra Paul,*
*Andy Garcia, Randy Brooks*
An alcoholic cop is booted off the force and tries to
redeem himself and salvage some self-respect by
hunting down the killer of a hooker who sought his
protection. In doing so he finds himself sucked down in
the underworld in a squalid and confusing thriller full
of noise and nastiness, the film not being helped by the
fact that the director was fired after the main filming
and took no part in the editing.
Boa: novel by Lawrence Block.
THR     115 min
B,V     CBS

## EIGHT TO FOUR **
Louie Lewis     USA     R18
    1981
*Annette Haven, Veronica Hart, Juliet Anderson,*
*Hubert Savage, Loni Sanders, Paul Thomas, Lisa De*
*Leeuw*
Adult rip-off of NINE TO FIVE with no real plot and
little in common with that film except the title. All the
women are sex-starved experts in lovemaking at the
Osborne Insurance Agency and a top woman official
likes to try out the men she hires. A heavily cliched
film with all the usual sex jokes and escapades
presented without any attempt being made to inte-
grate them into a story.
Aka: 8 TO 4
Osca: CANDY GOES TO HOLLYWOOD (TCX)
A     81 min (Cut at film release)
B,V     TCX L/A; HAR

## EIGHTEEN AGAIN! ***
Paul Flaherty     USA     PG
    1988
*George Burns, Tony Roberts, Charlie Schlatter, Anita*
*Morris, Red Buttons, Miriam Flynn, Jennifer Runyon*
"Vice Versa" once more with an 81-year-old entrepreneur making a wish to be the same age as his
grandson when he blows out his birthday candles. On
the way home a car crash puts them both in hospital
and, guess what, they swap bodies. A fair movie that
treads a distinctly worn-looking path and contains the
expected complications as both individuals re-adjust
to their new identities – Schlatter in particular doing
a passable impression of Burns.
Aka: 18 AGAIN!
COM     96 min (ort 100 min)
B,V     NWV

## EIGHTEEN BRONZE GIRLS OF SHAOLIN, THE ** 15
Chien Lai Yen     HONG KONG     1983
*Lung Chung Er, Kinh Kong, Tung Fang Yu*
Standard martial arts mayhem with plenty of action
but a rather shallow and formula plot.
Aka: 18 BRONZE GIRLS OF SHAOLIN, THE;
BRONZE GIRLS OF SHAOLIN
MAR     89 min
B,V     MART L/A; NINCOL; NET

## EIGHTY-FOUR CHARING CROSS ROAD ***   U
David Jones     USA     1986
*Anne Bancroft, Anthony Hopkins, Judi Dench, Jean*
*De Baer, Maurice Denham, Eleanor David, Mercedes*
*Ruehl, Daniel Gerroll*
Bancroft stars as a New York collector of rare books
who begins a 20 year correspondence with the staff of
a London bookshop, little dreaming that this will lead
to a love-affair conducted by mail but with her
unfortunately failing to make the trip over to London
before her pen-friend dies. Filmed once before as a
BBC TV play, this low-key and detailed film is
lovingly made but essentially episodic and lacking in
drama.
Aka: 84 CHARING CROSS ROAD
Boa: book by Helen Hanff.
DRA     96 min
B,V     RCA

## EIGHTY-FOUR CHARLIE MOPIC ***   18
Patrick Duncan     USA     1989
*Jonathan Emerson, Richard Brooks, Christopher*
*Burgard, Nicholas Cascone, Glenn Morshower, Jason*
*Tomlins, Byron Thomas*
A low-budget and unusual look at life on the front line
in Vietnam, where a reconnaissance patrol sets off on
a routine mission into the interior, complete with an
army motion picture (or MOPIC) cameraman. Howev-
er, what starts off as a simple mission rapidly develops
into a battle to survive and despite a few plot lulls, the
film (seen entirely through the single hand-held
camera) remains totally absorbing. The script is by
Duncan.
WAR     90 min (ort 95 min)
V     VIR

## EIGHTY-THOUSAND SUSPECTS **
Val Guest     UK     1963
*Claire Bloom, Richard Johnson, Michael Goodliffe,*
*Yolande Donlan, Cyril Cusack, Mervyn Johns, Kay*
*Walsh, Norman Bird, Basil Dignam, Andrew*
*Crawford, Ray Barrett, Norman Chappell, Arthur*
*Christiansen, Vanda Godsell*
A smallpox epidemic threatens the city of Bath and
imposes a terrible strain on two doctors' marriages in
this solid if unimaginative drama.
Aka: 80,000 SUSPECTS
Boa: novel The Pillars Of Midnight by Elleston
Trevor.
DRA     96 min (ort 113 min) B/W
B,V     RNK

## EJECTION *
Chuck Vincent     USA     18
    1977
*Joan Summer, W.R. Dremak, Marlowe Ferguson, Jeff*
*Alin, David Houseman, Leta Binder, Joe Piscopo, Jane*
*Dentinger, Bev Lubin, Tyrone Quinn, Zuleyka Reyes,*
*Kathy Hickman, Paulette Sanders, Michael Dattore,*
*Arthur Epstein*
A crazy and crude sex comedy consisting of a series of
sketches linked to a phoney and bizarre awards
ceremony. Very dull.
Aka: AMERICAN TICKLER OR THE WINNER OF
10 ACADEMY AWARDS; DRAWS
COM     73 min (ort 77 min)
B,V     WOV; FILV

## EL CID ***
Anthony Mann     SPAIN/USA     U
    1961
*Charlton Heston, Sophia Loren, Raf Vallone,*
*Genevieve Page, Herbert Lom, Hurd Hatfield, John*
*Fraser, Gary Raymond, Massimo Serato, Michael*
*Hordern, Andrew Cruickshank, Douglas Wilmer,*
*Frank Thring*
Highly fictionalised account of the 11th century figure
who fought to expel the Moors from Spain. If not true
to the past, it remains highly enjoyable for its
numerous action sequences and skilful direction. A
superior epic of considerable opulence if not veracity.
(Look out for the sequence where Heston rides from
Valencia to Burgos and back again in a single day.)
The score is by Miklos Rosza.

DRA                    180 min; 172 min (VCC)
B,V,V2,LV            INT/CBS L/A; VCC (VHS only)

## ELECTRA GLIDE IN BLUE ****                    18
James William Guercio   USA                    1973
*Robert Blake, Billy "Green" Bush, Mitchell Ryan,*
*Jeannine Riley, Elisha Cook Jr, Royal Dano*
A slick and incredibly stylish look at the life of an
undersized motorcycle cop and his partner. Serious at
times, the film has some wry moments as it examines
his progress from patrol cop to plainclothes detective
working on a strange murder case. Now something of
a cult film.
A/AD                                           108 min
V/sh                                              WHV

## ELECTRIC DREAMS: THE MOVIE **                 PG
Steve Barron            UK/USA                  1984
*Lenny Von Dohlen, Virginia Madsen, Maxwell*
*Caulfield, Don Fellows, Bud Cort (voice only)*
A computer freak has a computer which falls for the
girl upstairs in this bizarre love-triangle tale that
starts off well enough but never amounts to anything
of substance.
COM                        112 min; 92 min (VIR)
B, V/s                                      PVG; VIR

## ELECTRIC HORSEMAN, THE **                     PG
Sydney Pollack          USA                    1980
*Robert Redford, Jane Fonda, Valerie Perrine, Willie*
*Nelson, Nicolas Coster, John Saxon, Allan Arbus,*
*Wilford Brimley, Will Hare, Basil Hoffman, Timothy*
*Scott, James B. Sikking, James Kline, Frank Speiser,*
*Quinn Redexer*
A rodeo rider reduced to advertising breakfast cereals
suddenly decides that he has had enough of corporate
greed and rides off with his $12,000,000 thoroughbred
horse out of Las Vegas and into the hills and freedom.
A long, meandering journey through some spectacular
scenery, with Fonda and Redford displaying their
limited acting range; all wrapped up in the slick
sentimentality of a happy end.
Boa: story by Shelly Burton.
DRA                         114 min (ort 120 min)
B,V,LV                                            CIC

## ELENI: A SON'S REVENGE **                     PG
Peter Yates             USA                    1985
*Kate Nelligan, Linda Hunt, John Malkovich, Oliver*
*Cotton, Ronald Pickup, Rosalie Crutchely, Dimitra*
*Arliss*
A New York Times reporter takes a job in Athens in
order to uncover the circumstances surrounding the
murder of his Greek mother at the hands of Commun-
ist partisans during the Civil War. The script by Steve
Tesich is based on Gage's book and life but the film
remains flat and uninspiring for most of the time,
though Nelligan as Gage's mother (seen in a series of
flashbacks) performs well. A thoroughly disappointing
effort.
Aka: ELENI
Boa: novel Eleni by Nicholas Gage.
DRA                                            111 min
B,V                                               EHE

## ELEPHANT BOY ***
Robert Flaherty/Zoltan Korda
                        UK                     1937
*Sabu, Walter Hudd, Walter E. Holloway, Wilfrid*
*Hyde-White, Allan Jeayes, Bruce Gordon, D.J.*
*Williams*
This film made an international star of Sabu whose
portrayal of the title character is outstanding. The
story revolves around his efforts to help conservation-
ists and his insistence that he knows of the elephant's
burial ground. Dated and rather slow, but the outdoor
locations are excellent and the film has some memorable moments.
Boa: novel Toomai Of The Elephants by Rudyard
Kipling.

DRA                             76 min (ort 80 min) B/W
B,V                                         SPEC/POLY

## ELEPHANT CALLED SLOWLY, AN **
James Hill              UK                      1970
*Bill Travers, Virginia McKenna, George Adamson*
A thinly-disguised wildlife documentary where the
human actors play themselves. Average.
A/AD                                            86 min
B,V                                               TEVP

## ELEPHANT MAN, THE **
Jack Hofsiss            USA                     1981
*Philip Anglim, Kevin Conway, Penny Fuller, Glenn*
*Close, David Rounds*
The story of John Merrick, a man so grotesquely
deformed that he lived by exhibiting himself in
sideshows. This TV version of a Broadway production
covers much the same story as dealt with in the more
widely known film of David Lynch and is generally
inferior to that film.
Boa: book The Elephant Man And Other Curiosities
by Sir Frederick Treves and play by Bernard
Pomerance.
DRA                                        97 min mTV
B,V                                          PRV L/A

## ELEPHANT MAN, THE ***                         PG
David Lynch             UK                      1980
*Anthony Hopkins, John Hurt, John Gielgud, Freddie*
*Jones, Wendy Hiller, Anne Bancroft, Michael Elphick,*
*Hannah Gordon, Helen Ryan, John Standing, Dexter*
*Fletcher, Lesley Dunlop, Phoebe Nicholls, Pat Gorman,*
*Claire Davenport*
Beautifully made but rather sentimental story of a
hideously deformed man who lived in Victorian
England. Rescued from a miserable existence as a
circus freak he is taken to live in the London Hospital.
(His skeleton is on display there; for those interested
he suffered from neurofibromatosis.)
Boa: book The Elephant Man And Other Curiosities
by Sir Frederick Treves.
DRA                     118 min (ort 125 min) B/W
B, V/sh                        TEVP; WHV (VHS only)

## ELEVATOR, THE *                               15
Jerry Jameson           USA                     1974
*James Farentino, Roddy McDowall, Craig Stevens,*
*Myrna Loy, Teresa Wright, Carol Lynley, Don Stroud,*
*Arlene Golonka, Barry Livingston, Jean Allison, Bob*
*Fisher, Paul Sorenson, Ed Deemer, Will J. White, Jack*
*Griffin*
A motley group of individuals are thrown together
when a lift stops between floors in a skyscraper. A
good cast is wasted in a disappointingly dull film.
THR                                        89 min mTV
B,V                              EAG; CIC (VHS only)

## ELEVEN DAYS ELEVEN NIGHTS **                  18
Joe D'Amato (Aristide Massaccesi)
                        ITALY                   1987
*Jessica Moore, Mary Sellers, Joshua McDonald, Tom*
*Mojack*
A man due to marry in eleven days has a chance
meeting with a female writer that threatens to upset
all his plans. She is near completion of a book
detailing her 100 lovers and he is about to become her
final conquest for inclusion in "Sarah Asproah And
Her One Hundred Men".
Aka: UNDICI GIORNI, UNDICI NOTTI
A                                              93 min
B,V                                               AVA

## ELEVEN DAYS ELEVEN NIGHTS: PART 2 *           18
Joe D'Amato (Aristide Massaccesi)
                        ITALY                   1988
*Jessica Moore, Ale Dugas, James Sutterfield*

Italian-made rip-off of NINE AND A HALF WEEKS, with Moore researching for a book on prostitution and getting drawn into a world of erotic abandon.
Aka: TOP MODEL
DRA                          84 min (ort 90 min)
B,V                                          CFD

## ELEVEN DAYS ELEVEN NIGHTS: PART 3 **   18
Joe D'Amato (Aristide Massaccesi)
                    ITALY                    1988
*Valentine Demy, Allen Cort*
A reporter is assigned to a case involving a woman who lost her husband in a strange voodoo ritual. He goes to New Orleans to investigate, but rather unwisely takes his wife along. An erotic thriller.
Aka: 11 DAYS 11 NIGHTS: PART 3 – THE FINAL CHAPTER
THR                                       92 min
V                                            TGP

## ELEVENTH COMMANDMENT, THE ***   15
Michael Anderson   CANADA/UK            1986
*Steven Bauer, Robert Joy, Leslie Hope, Laurent Malet, Peter Dvosky, Rod Steiger, Colleen Dewhurst, Michael York, John Hirsch, Linda Griffiths, Lino Ventura, Cyrielle Claire, Eric Gaudry, Audi Levy, Hrant Alianak, Miro Wahba*
The story of an anti-terrorist team picked to avenge the massacre of Israeli athletes during the Munich Olympics. A well-made and literate film with Dewhurst giving an interesting portrayal of Golda Meir
Aka: MUNCHEN STRIKE, THE; SWORD OF GIDEON
Boa: book Vengeance by George Jonas.
A/AD                     145 min (ort 148 min) mCab
B,V                     CINE; BRAVE (VHS only)

## ELIMINATOR, THE *
Alexandre Alov/Vladimir Naoumov
                    FRANCE/USSR             1981
*Alain Delon, Curt Jurgens, Claude Jade*
A confusing attempt to tell the story of a German plot to assassinate the Allied leaders at the Teheran Conference held in Persia in 1943.
Aka: LE NID D'ESPIONS; TEHERAN '43
WAR                                      104 min
B,V                                          VFP

## ELIMINATORS **                         15
Peter Manoogian       USA                1986
*Andrew Prine, Denise Crosby, Patrick Reynolds, Conan Lee, Roy Dotrice*
Clone of THE TERMINATOR in which the android (cast here as a goodie) and his companions are out to stop his megalomaniacal creator from dominating the world.
A/AD                    91 min (ort 96 min) Cut (31 sec)
B,V                                          EIV

## ELITE KILLER, THE **                   PG
Robert Mulligan       USA                1969
*Gregory Peck, Eva Marie Saint, Robert Forster, Nolan Clay, Russell Thorsen, Frank Silvera, Lonny Chapman, Lou Frizzell, Henry Beckman, Charles Tyner, Richard Bull, Sandy Wyeth, Joaquin Martinez, Boyd "Red" Morgan*
A US Army scout helps a young white woman who has lived with the Apaches escape, together with her young son. They settle down on the man's New Mexico ranch but the boy's father comes after them. An unmemorable tale, flatly directed and of little suspense, though the photography of Charles Lang helps to relieve the tedium.
Aka: STALKING MOON, THE
WES                                      104 min
V                                           SCAN

## ELIZA FRASER **
Tim Burstall       AUSTRALIA               1976

*Susannah York, Trevor Howard, Rory McBride, Noel Ferrier*
A nineteenth century seafarer and his wife journey to Australia, the crew mutiny and they are captured by Aborigines. The husband is killed and the wife has many adventures before returning home. A lively historical romp that is too uneven to hold up well.
A/AD                                     130 min
B,V,V2                                 CBS; 21ST

## ELLIE ***                               15
Peter Wittman         USA                1985
*Shelley Winters, Sheila Kennedy, Eddie Albert, Pat Paulsen, George Gobel*
A "professional widow" is in the habit of marrying old men and disposing of them once their wills have been changed in her favour. The step-daughter of one of her recently deceased husbands plots to have her revenge in this broad black comedy.
COM                                       90 min
B,V                                     VES/PVG

## ELLIS ISLAND ***                        15
Jerry London          USA                1984
*Peter Riegert, Greg Martyn, Claire Bloom, Judi Bowker, Kate Burton, Joan Greenwood, Ann Jillian, Lila Kaye, Stubby Kaye, Alice Krige, Cherie Lunghi, Melba Moore, Milo O'Shea, Emma Samms, Ben Vereen, Faye Dunaway*
The story of the gateway to the USA, through which countless immigrants passed, and how some of them fared in their new homeland. A sprawling, colourful epic. Look out for Richard Burton, who has a small part as a senator.
Boa: novel by Fred Mustard Stewart.
DRA                     313 min (3 cassettes) mTV
B,V                                 VFP L/A; HER

## ELM-CHANTED FOREST, THE ***            U
Milan Blazekovic                         1986
Charming full-length animation with a young artist falling asleep beneath an enchanted elm tree and acquiring the ability to paint magical pictures and talk to animals. When the forest is threatened by dark forces he is obliged to come to the aid of his friends.
CAR                                       83 min
B,V                                          CHV

## ELMER GANTRY ****                       15
Richard Brooks        USA                1960
*Burt Lancaster, Jean Simmons, Dean Jagger, Shirley Jones, Arthur Kennedy, Patti Page, Edward Andrews, Hugh Marlowe, John McIntire, Rex Ingram*
An Oscar-winning portrayal of an evangelist in the American mid-West of the 1920s who cynically exploits his talents for commercial gain. Lancaster gives one of his finest performances in this fascinating and literate film. AA: Actor (Lancaster), S. Actress (Jones), Screen (Adapt) (Richard Brooks).
Boa: novel by Sinclair Lewis.
DRA                      142 min (ort 145 min)
B,V                                          WHV

## ELSA, FRAULEIN SS **
Mark Stern (Mark Staow)
                    FRANCE                  1977
*Malisa Longo, Olivier Mathot, Pamela Stanford*
A bordello on a train is arranged to improve the morale of front-line German officers during WW2.
A                                         82 min
B,V                                          MOV

## ELVES **                                18
Jeff Mandel           USA                1989
*Dan Haggerty, Deanna Lund, Ken Carpenter, Julie Austin, Borah Silver*
Neo-Nazis hatch an ambitious scheme to re-establish the Third Reich by re-creating Hitler with the help of an elf who carries the secret of his genetic code.

Certainly unusual, but this bizarre tale has little to offer.

HOR                                              89 min
V                                                HIFLI

## ELVIRA: MISTRESS OF THE DARK **                15
James Signorelli         USA                     1988
*Elvira (Cassandra Peterson), W. Morgan Sheppard,*
*Daniel Greene, Susan Kellerman, Jeff Conaway*
Feature film built around the personality (and impressive bust) of TV horror show personality "Elvira". The shallow plot, involving a conflict with some small-town conservatives and the hunt for a magic book, is no more than an excuse for a series of risque jokes in this campy and only marginally amusing comedy. A pity, because Peterson has an engaging personality.

COM                                              96 min
V                                                NWV

## ELVIS AND ME **                                15
Larry Peerce             USA                      1987
*Dale Midkiff, Susan Walters, Billy Green Bush, Linda*
*Miller, Jon Cypher, Anne Haney, Marshall Teague*
A portrait of Elvis and the women he loved, largely based on his wife's book (she was one of the executive producers). Despite a good performance from Midkiff the film leaves us no wiser about this rock legend. Songs are performed by Ronnie McDowell. See also ELVIS: THE MOVIE and THIS IS ELVIS.
Boa: book by Priscilla Presley.

DRA                          178 min (ort 200 min) mTV
B,V                                              NWV

## ELVIS PRESLEY: BLUE HAWAII **                  PG
Norman Taurog            USA                      1962
*Elvis Presley, Stella Stevens, Angela Lansbury, Joan*
*Blackman, Jenny Maxwell, Roland Winters, John*
*Archer, Howard McNear, Iris Adrian*
This story of a returning GI who comes home to Honolulu and becomes a beachcomber, serves as a vehicle for Elvis' star talent. Pleasant and quite entertaining if hardly memorable, but Elvis does get to perform one of his best hits – "Can't Help Falling In Love". The exotic locations are a big asset.
Aka: BLUE HAWAII

MUS                               101 min; 97 min (CH5)
B,V,LV                    CBS; HER; CH5 (VHS only)

## ELVIS PRESLEY: CLAMBAKE *                      U
Arthur H. Nadel          USA                      1967
*Elvis Presley, Will Hutchins, Bill Bixby, Shelley*
*Fabares, Gary Merrill, James Gregory*
Elvis appears as the son of an oil baron, who switches identities with a motorcyclist to work as a water-ski instructor in Miami, and learns all about life. One of the star's weakest vehicles.
Aka: CLAMBAKE

MUS                               95 min (ort 97 min)
V/h                                              WHV

## ELVIS PRESLEY: DOUBLE TROUBLE **              U
Norman Taurog            USA                      1967
*Elvis Presley, Yvonne Romain, Annette Day, John*
*Williams, The Wiere Brothers, Chips Rafferty*
Typical vehicle for Presley's musical talents. This time round he plays a nightclub singer for whom a teenage heiress falls when he performs in England. (An irony not lost on Presley fans is that in real life he never did perform there.) Songs include "Long Legged Girl", one of the star's best numbers.
Aka: DOUBLE TROUBLE

MUS                               88 min (ort 90 min)
V                                                MGM

## ELVIS PRESLEY: FLAMING STAR, THE ***           PG
Don Siegel               USA                      1960
*Elvis Presley, Barbara Eden, Steve Forrest, Dolores*
*Del Rio, John McIntire, Rodolfo Acosta*

A half-breed must choose sides when the Indians go on the warpath. There are no songs after the first ten minutes but a surprisingly strong performance from the star and good action sequences make this one of his best films.
Aka: FLAMING STAR
Boa: novel by Clair Huffaker.

WES                              88 min (ort 110 min)
V                                                CBS

## ELVIS PRESLEY: FOLLOW THAT DREAM **           U
Gordon Douglas           USA                      1962
*Elvis Presley, Arthur O'Connell, Anne Helm, Joanna*
*Moore, Jack Kruschen, Simon Oakland*
Easy-going Presley comedy with our star and his family moving to southern Florida with the intention of running a small homestead. No great shakes as a movie but Presley does get to sing "Home Is Where The Heart Is" and "On Top Of Old Smokey".
Aka: FOLLOW THAT DREAM
Boa: novel Pioneer Go Home by Richard Powell.

MUS                                              106 min
V/h                                              WHV

## ELVIS PRESLEY: FRANKIE AND JOHNNY **           U
Frederick De Cordova     USA                      1966
*Elvis Presley, Donna Douglas, Harry Morgan, Sue*
*Anne Langdon, Nancy Kovack, Audrey Christie,*
*Jerome Cowan*
An old saloon song is reworked into a suitable vehicle for Presley, with him cast as a singing riverboat gambler down on his luck and afflicted with girl troubles. Now best remembered for songs such as "When The Saints Go Marching In" and "Down By The Riverside". A colourful time-filler.
Aka: FRANKIE AND JOHNNY

MUS                                              84 min
V/h                                              WHV

## ELVIS PRESLEY: FUN IN ACAPULCO **              U
Richard Thorpe           USA                      1963
*Elvis Presley, Ursula Andress, Paul Lukas, Alejandro*
*Rey*
Another typical Presley vehicle but with superior scenery as our star works as a lifeguard and entertainer in this Mexican resort and finds himself the object of the affections of a lady bullfighter. Song include "No Room To Rhumba In A Sports Car", "Bossa Nova Baby" and "You Can't Say No In Acapulco".
Aka: FUN IN ACAPULCO

MUS                               97 min; 93 min (CH5)
B,V                  VFP L/A; HER; CH5 (VHS only)

## ELVIS PRESLEY: G.I. BLUES **                   U
Norman Taurog            USA                      1960
*Elvis Presley, Juliet Prowse, James Douglas, Robert*
*Ivers, Leticia Roman, Ludwig Stossel, Arch Johnson*
Three soldiers in West Germany fall in love with the same cabaret dancer in this routine Presley movie. A spirited performance from Prowse as the dancer compensates for the banality of the script. Songs include "Tonight Is So Right For Love", "Wooden Heart", "Blue Suede Shoes" and the title song.
Aka: G.I. BLUES

MUS                                              104 min
B,V                                              HER; CH5

## ELVIS PRESLEY: GIRL HAPPY *                    PG
Boris Sagal              USA                      1965
*Elvis Presley, Harold J. Stone, Shelley Fabares, Gary*
*Crosby, Joby Baker, Nita Talbot, Mary Ann Mobley,*
*Chris Noel, Jackie Coogan*
A nightclub entertainer in Fort Lauderdale finds himself acting as chaperone to a group of college girls, one of whom is the daughter of a gangster. A slick and entirely predictable star vehicle, as forgettable as it is innocuous.
Aka: GIRL HAPPY

MUS                           93 min (ort 96 min)
V                                          MGM

## ELVIS PRESLEY: GIRLS! GIRLS! GIRLS! *        U
Norman Taurog          USA              1962
*Elvis Presley, Stella Stevens, Laurel Goodwin, Jeremy
Slate, Robert Strauss, Benson Fong, Ginny Tiu*
Presley vehicle with the singer running a fishing boat
as a hobby and being chased by a crowd of girls, most
of his troubles arising from his inability to decide
which one he likes the most. A host of largely
forgettable songs follow, but our star does get to sing
one classic number, "Return To Sender".
Aka: GIRLS! GIRLS! GIRLS!
MUS                           106 min; 94 min (CH5)
B,V                            HER; CH5 (VHS only)

## ELVIS PRESLEY: HAREM HOLIDAY *             U
Gene Nelson            USA              1965
*Elvis Presley, Michael Ansara, Mary Ann Mobley,
Fran Jeffries, Jay Novello, Theo Marcuse, Philip Reed,
Theo Marcuse, Billy Barty*
Dull Presley vehicle set in the Middle East with a
singer/star kidnapped on his way to a premiere of his
latest film and finding himself involved in a plot to
murder a king. Lots of boring back-lot "desert"
locations and a clutch of forgettable songs make this
one a must to avoid.
Aka: HAREM HOLIDAY; HARUM SCARUM
MUS                           81 min (ort 95 min)
V                                          MGM

## ELVIS PRESLEY: IT HAPPENED AT THE        PG
## WORLD'S FAIR **
Norman Taurog          USA              1962
*Elvis Presley, Joan O'Brien, Gary Lockwood, Yvonne
Craig, Ginny Tiu, Kurt Russell*
Presley does his thing at the Seattle World's Fair, in
this tale of two crop-dusting pilots who enjoy a little
fun and romance. A bright and cheerful musical with
songs including "One Broken Heart For Sale", "A
World Of Our Own" and "Happy Ending". Look out for
young Kurt Russell, who played the star in ELVIS in
the 1979 TV movie.
Aka: IT HAPPENED AT THE WORLD'S FAIR
MUS                           100 min (ort 105 min)
B,V                                        MGM

## ELVIS PRESLEY: JAILHOUSE ROCK ***         U
Richard Thorpe         USA              1957
*Elvis Presley, Judy Tyler, Dean Jones, Vaughn Taylor,
Mickey Shaughnessy, Jennifer Holden*
One of the best of Elvis' films in which he plays a
convict sent to jail for accidentally killing a man in a
brawl. Here he learns to play the guitar and becomes a
star when he gets out, but finds that his ex-cellmate
wants to share his success. Has the memorable
"Jailhouse Rock" sequence in which Elvis (who
choreographed the steps) can be seen at his very best.
Score is by Leiber and Stoller.
Aka: JAILHOUSE ROCK
MUS                           92 min B/W
B,V                                        MGM

## ELVIS PRESLEY: KID GALAHAD **             PG
Phil Karlson           USA              1962
*Elvis Presley, Lola Albright, Gig Young, Joan
Blackman, Charles Bronson, Ned Glass, David Lewis,
Robert Emhardt*
This musical remake of the 1937 film lacks the punch
of its predecessor and casts Presley as a peaceable
garage mechanic who gets inadvertently drawn into
the world of boxing. Presley turns in a rather good
performance and sings six unmemorable songs in a
film that hardly does him justice. Average.
Aka: KID GALAHAD
Boa: novel by F. Wallace.
MUS                           93 min
V/h                                        WHV

## ELVIS PRESLEY: KING CREOLE **              PG
Michael Curtiz         USA              1958
*Elvis Presley, Carolyn Jones, Walter Matthau, Dolores
Hart, Dean Jagger, Paul Stewart, Vic Morrow,
Raymond Bailey*
A failed student gets involved with criminals and a
hold-up, but later becomes a big hit when he is forced
to start work singing at a gangster's nightclub. A
very, very loose adaptation of the Robbins novel which
was co-scripted by Michael V. Gazzo. Songs include
"Hard Headed Woman", "Trouble" and the title num-
ber. Not one of the star's best films, but his perform-
ance carries it along.
Aka: KING CREOLE
Boa: novel A Stone For Danny Fisher by Harold
Robbins.
MUS                           115 min; 111 min (CH5) B/W
B,V                            VIPCO L/A; HER; CH5 (VHS only)

## ELVIS PRESLEY: KISSIN' COUSINS *          U
Gene Nelson            USA              1964
*Elvis Presley, Arthur O'Connell, Glenda Farrell,
Pamela Austin, Yvonne Craig, Jack Albertson*
Some of the locals attempt to thwart plans by the US
Air Force to build a missile base on Smokey Moun-
tain, and the military man sent to win them over
discovers that one of the hillbillies is his double. A
feeble effort with the star given a double role and a
collection of generally unremarkable songs.
Aka: KISSIN' COUSINS
MUS                           93 min (ort 96 min)
V                                          MGM

## ELVIS PRESLEY: LIVE A LITTLE,            PG
## LOVE A LITTLE **
Norman Taurog          USA              1968
*Elvis Presley, Michele Carey, Don Porter, Rudy Vallee,
Dick Sargent, Eddie Hodges, Sterling Holloway*
Standard Presley film with our singer playing a
pin-up photographer who manages to land two jobs
and does both by running back and forth between
offices. An inconsequential film that could have done
with a few more songs, there are only four.
Aka: LIVE A LITTLE, LOVE A LITLE
MUS                           89 min
V                                          MGM

## ELVIS PRESLEY: LOVE ME TENDER **          U
Robert D. Webb         USA              1956
*Richard Egan, Debra Paget, Elvis Presley, Robert
Middleton, Neville Brand, William Campbell, Mildred
Dunnock, Bruce Bennett, James Drury, Russ Conway,
Ken Clark, Barry Coe, L.Q. Jones, Paul Burns, Jerry
Sheldon, James Stone*
Civil War Western which started Presley's film
career. The story is one of conflicting politics in a
Southern family and of two sons and their mutual love
for Paget. Of interest mainly for Presley's singing of
several ballads (complete with anachronistic hip
swiveling), rather than any strengths of plot or
dialogue. "The Brothers Reno" was the title this film
was to have had.
Aka: LOVE ME TENDER
Boa: novel The Brothers Reno by Maurice Geraghty.
MUS                           86 min (ort 89 min) B/W
V                                          CBS

## ELVIS PRESLEY: LOVING YOU **
Hal Kanter             USA              1957
*Elvis Presley, Lizabeth Scott, Wendell Corey, Dolores
Hart, James Gleason*
A publicist discovers hillbilly Elvis working at a
petrol station and signs him up to sing with her
husband's band in this glossy but vacuous star
vehicle. Forget the plot, shut your eyes, and enjoy the
music. Songs include "Teddy Bear" and the title
number.
Aka: LOVING YOU

MUS　　　　　　　　　90 min (ort 101 min)
B,V　　　　STARX/SEL; SEL; VCC (VHS only)

## ELVIS PRESLEY: PARADISE, HAWAIIAN　　U
## STYLE *
Michael Moore　　　　USA　　　　1966
*Elvis Presley, Suzanna Leigh, James Shigeta, Donna
Butterworth, Irene Tsu, Marianna Hill, Julie Parrish,
Philip Ahn, Mary Treen, Linda Wong*
Another vehicle for the talents of Presley (unfortu-
nately he has little chance to show his true worth)
that's essentially a rehash of BLUE HAWAII with our
star a pilot who returns to Hawaii to set up a charter
helicopter service. Good-looking but empty.
Aka: PARADISE, HAWAIIAN STYLE
MUS　　　　　　91 min; 87 min (CH5)
B,V　　　　　　　HER; CH5 (VHS only)

## ELVIS PRESLEY: ROUSTABOUT *
John Rich　　　　USA　　　　1964
*Elvis Presley, Barbara Stanwyck, Joan Freeman, Leif
Erickson, Sue Ann Langdon, Raquel Welch*
A roving singer joins a carnival, works hard and finds
true love in this Presleyscope offering. Despite good
work from the support cast, this is a dull and dismal
effort. The song "Little Egypt" offers the one high-
light.
Aka: ROUSTABOUT
MUS　　　　　　101 min; 95 min (CH5)
B,V　　　　　　HER; CBS; CH5 (VHS only)

## ELVIS PRESLEY: SPEEDWAY **　　U
Norman Taurog　　　USA　　　　1968
*Elvis Presley, Nancy Sinatra, Bill Bixby, Gale Gordon,
William Schallert, Carl Ballantine, Ross Hagen*
Routine Presley film set in the world of stock car
racing with our star a good-natured racing driver and
Sinatra the tax inspector he falls for.
Aka: SPEEDWAY
MUS　　　　　　　90 min (ort 94 min)
V　　　　　　　　　　　MGM

## ELVIS PRESLEY: SPINOUT **　　U
Norman Taurog　　　USA　　　　1966
*Elvis Presley, Shelley Fabares, Diane McBain,
Deborah Walley, Cecil Kellaway, Una Merkel, Warren
Berlinger, Jack Mullaney, Will Hutchins, Carl Betz*
A happy-go-lucky singer is persuaded to test-drive an
experimental car in a motor race and finds himself
having to fend off the usual admirers. A bland Presley
musical with nice open air locations and some of his
poorer numbers. Songs include "Beach Shack", "Adam
And Evil" and "Smorgasbord".
Aka: CALIFORNIA HOLIDAY; SPINOUT
MUS　　　　　　　　　　90 min
V　　　　　　　　　　　MGM

## ELVIS PRESLEY: STAY AWAY, JOE *　　U
Peter Tewksbury　　　USA　　　　1968
*Elvis Presley, Burgess Meredith, Joan Blondell, Katy
Jurado, Thomas Gomez, Henry Jones, L.Q. Jones,
Quentin Dean, Anne Seymour, Angus Duncan,
Douglas Henderson, Michael Lane, Susan Trustman,
Warren Vanders, Buck Kartalian*
A half-breed Indian rodeo rider returns to his reserva-
tion to help his people set up as cattle ranchers as part
of a government rehabilitation scheme. An unusual
setting does little for the star in this lacklustre and
dreary offering. Written by Michael A. Hoey.
Aka: STAY AWAY, JOE
Boa: novel by Dan Cushman.
MUS　　　　　　　97 min (ort 102 min)
V　　　　　　　　　　　MGM

## ELVIS PRESLEY: THE TROUBLE WITH GIRLS *** U
Peter Tewksbury　　　USA　　　　1969
*Elvis Presley, Marlyn Mason, Nicole Jaffe, Sheree
North, Edward Andrews, John Carradine, Vincent
Price*

Presley vehicle with him playing the manager of a
travelling medicine show in the 1920s and finding
himself involved in murder. Written by Arnold and
Lois Peyser this is a superior Presley film with a nice
feel for the period and a better than average script.
Aka: TROUBLE WITH GIRLS, THE
Boa: novel The Chautauqua by Day Keene and
Dwight Babcock.
MUS　　　　　　　95 min (ort 104 min)
B,V　　　　　　　　　　MGM

## ELVIS PRESLEY: VIVA LAS VEGAS **　　U
George Sidney　　　USA　　　　1963
*Elvis Presley, Ann-Margret, Cesare Danova, William
Demarest, Jack Carter, Nicky Blair*
Elvis plays a sports car racing driver with the action
being set in the gambling resort of Las Vegas. A
routine journey for all concerned, though the colourful
locations make it bearable.
Aka: LOVE IN LAS VEGAS; VIVA LAS VEGAS
MUS　　　　　　　81 min (ort 86 min)
B,V　　　　　　　　　　MGM

## ELVIS PRESLEY: WILD IN THE COUNTRY *　　PG
Philip Dunne　　　USA　　　　1961
*Elvis Presley, Tuesday Weld, Hope Lange, John
Ireland, Gary Lockwood, Millie Perkins, Rafer
Johnson, Christina Crawford, Jason Robards Sr*
A strange vehicle for Presley in which he plays a
country boy with ambitions to be a writer who gets
involved with various women and is saved from
delinquency by the efforts of a female social worker.
Earnest, boring and pointless, with a clutch of good
performances largely wasted on the cliched script.
Written by Clifford Odets.
Aka: WILD IN THE COUNTRY
Boa: novel The Lost Country by J.R. Salamanca.
DRA　　　　　110 min (ort 114 min) B/W
V　　　　　　　　　　　CBS

## ELVIS: THAT'S THE WAY IT IS ***　　U
Denis Sanders　　　USA　　　　1970
*Elvis Presley*
An absorbing look at Presley that follows him as he
prepares for an opening-night performance at a
nightclub during his second Las Vegas season following his return to the stage in 1969. Hardly an in-depth
examination of the star, and the interviews with his
followers add nothing of interest to the film, but worth
a look if only to capture the flavour of his performance.
Aka: THAT'S THE WAY IT IS
DOC　　　　　　104 min (ort 108 min)
V　　　　　　　　　　　MGM

## ELVIS: THE MOVIE ***　　U
John Carpenter　　　USA　　　　1979
*Kurt Russell, Shelley Winters, Season Hubley, Pat
Hingle, Bing Russell, Ed Begley Jr, Melody Anderson,
James Canning, Charles Cyphers, Peter Hobbs, Les
Lannom, Elliott Street, Will Jordan, Joe Mantegna,
Galen Thompson*
The story of Presley up to 1969 is retold in a believable
way with effective performances, especially from
Russell in the title role (though the songs were dubbed
by Ronnie McDowell who later worked on ELVIS
AND ME). The script is by Anthony Lawrence. See
also THIS IS ELVIS.
Aka: ELVIS
MUS　　　　120 min; 164 min (VCC) mTV
B,V　　　　　　VCL/CBS; VCC (VHS only)

## EMANON *　　PG
Stuart Paul　　　USA　　　　1986
*Stuart Paul, Cheryl M. Lynne, Jeremy Miller, Patrick
Wright, William F. Collard, Joanne Jackson*
A clumsy allegorical saga in which the crippled son of
a struggling young widow befriends a strange Christ-
like tramp, who appears to have the power to bring
happiness to all those about him. What must have

seemed a promising idea on paper never comes to life on screen.

DRA 98 min
B,V EHE

## EMBASSY **
Gordon Hessler UK/USA 1972
*Richard Roundtree, Chuck Connors, Max Von Sydow, Broderick Crawford, Ray Milland, Marie-Jose Nat, David Bauer, Larry Cross, David Healy, Kate Heid, Sarah Marshall, Dee Pollock, Leila Buheiry, David Parker, Dean Turner*
A spy thriller about an attempt to smuggle out a Soviet defector under the noses of the KGB. Uneven and contrived, with too little action to work well as a thriller.
Boa: novel by Stephen Coulter.

THR 90 min
B,V VCL/CBS

## EMBRYO **
Ralph Nelson USA 1976
*Rock Hudson, Diane Ladd, Roddy McDowall, Barbara Carrera, Anne Schedeen*
A scientific experiment gets out of hand as a foetus grows into an adult woman in just four and a half weeks. An unpleasant fantasy that borrows heavily from the genre of horror films, especially with regard to the repulsive effects.
Aka: CREATED TO KILL

FAN 110 min
B,V VFP L/A; HER

## EMERALD CITY OF OZ, THE **          U
USA 1987
*Narrated by Margot Kidder*
Last of a four-part animated Oz series. In this tale Dorothy and her friends must defeat the invasion plans of the Gnome King. Average.

CAR 92 min
V RCA

## EMERALD FOREST, THE ***          15
John Boorman UK 1985
*Powers Boothe, Meg Foster, William Rodriguez, Yara Vaneau, Estee Chandler, Charley Boorman, Dira Paes, Eduardo Conde, Ariel Coelho, Peter Marinker, Mario Borges, Atilia Lorio, Babriel Archanjo, Gracindo Junior, Chico Terto*
A young boy is kidnapped by South American rain-forest Indians from his engineer father who then spends the next fifteen years searching for him. An absorbing look at a vanishing way of life, though the lack of a strong storyline is a handicap. Scripted by Rospo Pallenberg and with a score by Junior Homrich.
A/AD 114 min; 109 min (CH5)
B,V EHE; CH5 (VHS only)

## EMIL AND THE DETECTIVES **          U
Peter Tewksbury USA 1964
*Bryan Russell, Walter Slezak, Roger Mobley, Heinz Schubert, Peter Ehrlich, Cindy Cassell*
Based on a famous Children's classic, this tells of how a boy has his bag stolen on the way to visit his aunt. Instead of calling the police, he enlists the aid of some young friends and in doing so uncovers plans to rob a bank. A remake of the exciting 1931 German classic, reduced to mediocrity by the usual bland process of Disneyfication. Filmed in Germany. Average.
Boa: novel by Erich Kastner.

JUV 93 min
B,V WDV

## EMISSARY, THE **          15
Jan Sholtz USA 1988
*Ted Leplat, Terry Norton, Andre Jacobs, Patrick Mynhardt, Greg Latter, Robert Vaughn, Jonathan Taylor, Colin Sutcliffe, Hans Strydom*
In an attempt to capture secret codes, the KGB resort to blackmailing an American politician and his wife.

THR 92 min
B,V CIC

## EMMA, QUEEN OF THE SOUTH SEAS *          15
John Banas USA 1988
*Barbara Carrera, Hal Holbrook, E.G. Marshall, Steve Bisley, Rebecca Rigg, Andrew Tighe*
A stuffy and overlong TV movie based on the exploits of an important woman in the colonial struggles of nineteenth-century Samoa. Carrera is nice to look at but the film really has nothing of interest to say. Very poor.

DRA 180 min (available as 2 cassettes) mTV
B,V CINE

## EMMANUELLE ***
Just Jaeckin FRANCE 1974
*Sylvia Kristel, Alain Cuny, Marika Green, Daniel Sarky, Jeanne Colletin, Christine Boisson*
Supposedly based on Arsan's own experiences, this early softcore film has had many sequels. The story opens in Bangkok, where Emmanuelle arrives with her diplomat husband after his transfer there. Believing that his wife should experience the full range of sexuality, her husband encourages her to embark on some extramarital affairs. She does so in a beautifully made but utterly empty and loveless study of sexuality and decadence.
Boa: book by Emmanuelle Arsan.

A 92 min
B,V BWV/GHV

## EMMANUELLE 2 **
Francis Giacobetti FRANCE 1975
*Sylvia Kristel, Umberto Orsini, Catherine Rivet, Frederic La Gache, Henry Czarniak, Marion Womble*
Bangkok is replaced by Hong Kong and Bali in the further adventures of our erotically obsessed heroine. After some encounters on the steamer she gets off at Hong Kong and quickly embarks on a rapid succession of liaisons, mostly with just about anyone who's available. Made with some care, this largely plotless film explores a philosophy of sex totally divorced from notions such as love – the result is a glossy exercise in sleaze.
Aka: EMMANUELLE, THE JOYS OF A WOMAN
A 76 min (ort 100 min)
B,V,V2 TEVP

## EMMANUELLE 3 **          18
FRANCE
*Silvia Castell, Brigitte Lahaie, Jean-Marie Pallady*
A glamour photographer gets an assignment that takes him to the Orient with two beautiful French models. However, all is not really as it appears to be, for our photographer is in reality a spy. A turgid softcore film not really related to the others in the series.
A 78 min; 72 min (NET)
B,V,V2 HOK L/A; ABC; NET; TCX

## EMMANUELLE 4 *          18
Francis Giacobetti FRANCE 1984
*Sylvia Kristel, Mia Nygren, Deborah Power, Patrick Bauchau, Sophie Berger, Sonia Martin*
One of those endless EMMANUELLE films with our queen of love fleeing from a cruel lover and undergoing cosmetic surgery to emerge with a completely new identity (played by a younger actress). If only she could emerge with a new script. A ludicrous softcore exercise in credibility-stretching.
A 85 min (ort 89 min) Cut (10 sec in addition to film cuts)
B,V TEVP

## EMMANUELLE 5 **          18
Walerian Borowczyk FRANCE 1986
*Monique Gabrielle, Alex Cunningham, Crofton*

*Hardester, Yaseen Khan, Dana Burns Westberg*
Action erotic thriller set against the backdrop of
Cannes and the Far East. After a screening of
Emmanuelle's latest film – "Love Express" – she is
hounded by the press and runs away with millionaire
playboy Charles Foster. Then she is kidnapped by the
sinister Rajid, who sets her up as part of his harem.
Can Foster rescue her? Now read on . . .

| A | 76 min (ort 85 min) Cut (2 min 41 sec) |
|---|---|
| B,V | VES |

## EMMANUELLE 6 *

| | 18 |
|---|---|
| Bruno Zincone | 1989 |

*Natalie Uher, Jean Rene Gossart*
After suffering a variety of hardships in the Amazonian jungle, Emmanuelle receives therapy at a private clinic in a bid to help her regain her memory.
This most insubstantial of plots serves as little more
than a vehicle for the usual repetitive softcore encounters, all beautifully photographed in a style that
resembles nothing so much as a TV commercial.

| A | 73 min |
|---|---|
| V | VPD |

## EMMANUELLE GOES TO CANNES **

| | 18 |
|---|---|
| Jean-Marie Pallardy  FRANCE | 1984 |

*Gabriel Pontello, Paola Farrow, Olinka Richter, Jean-
Marie Pallardy, Pino Curia, Mike Monty, Bruno
Ramagnoli, Georges Delerno, Glynis Whitman*
Young Emmanuelle is now a stripper but she escapes
the clutches of her ruthless manager and heads for
Cannes and the film festival, in search of fame and
fortune whilst sleeping with all and sundry. She also
gets involved in a kidnapping by way of a sub-plot in
this confused softcore story. The scenery is rather nice
though.
Aka: ELEMENTARY STUD, THE (18CAR)

| A | 80 min; 42 min (18CAR); 76 min (SEX) Cut (14 sec |
|---|---|
| in addition to film cuts) | |
| B,V | XTACY/KRP; NET (VHS only); 18CAR; SEX |

## EMMANUELLE IN AMERICA ***

| | 18 |
|---|---|
| Joe D'Amato (Aristide Massaccesi) | |
| ITALY | 1979 |

*Laura Gemser, Gabriele Tinti, Roger Browne,
Riccardo Salvino, Lars Bloch, Paola Senatore, Maria
Piera Begoli, Giulio Bianchi, Efrem Appel, Matilde
Dall'Anglio, Carlo Foschi, Maria Renata Franco,
Giulio Massimini*
In this well made EMMANUELLE sequel Gemser
replaces Kristal, playing a photographer and investigative journalist. In her first encounter she uncovers
a drug dealer who runs a private harem and later she
moves on to Venice, where she meets a count who
deals in art forgeries. Other adventures follow, and in
each one D'Amato treats us to a strong dose of
sexuality and decadence. Cut before video submission
by 13 min 3 sec.

| A | 79 min Cut (5 min 49 sec) |
|---|---|
| B,V | ROGUE |

## EMMANUELLE IN DENMARK **

| | 18 |
|---|---|
| Werner Hedman  DENMARK | 1977 |

*Ole Soltoft, Anna Bergman, Soren Stromberg*
Routine softcore story of a Danish Secret Service
agent and her amatory exploits in intercepting a roll
of microfilm before it reaches Germany. A standard
series of sexy frolics with a flimsy espionage plot.
Aka: AGENT 69 (DAPON); AGENT 69 JENSEN I
SKYTTENS TEGN; I SKYTTENS TEGN

| A | 75 min; 59 min (DAPON) Cut (49 sec in addition to |
|---|---|
| film cuts) | |
| B,V | DAPON L/A; CTY L/A; 18PLAT/TOW; PHE; |
| SHEP | |

## EMMANUELLE IN SOHO **

| | 18 |
|---|---|
| David Hughes  UK | 1981 |

*Mandy Miller, Julie Lee, John M. East, Kevin Fraser,
Gavin Clare, Tim Blackstone, Geraldine Hooper, Anita*

*Desmarais, Georges Waser, Erika Lea, Cathy Green,
Suzanne Richens, John Roach, Louise London,
Samantha Devonshire*
Feeble and dull sex comedy that purports to be a look
at the seamier side of London's Soho. A young
sex-obsessed French girl gets involved with a porno
photographer and appears in some rather risque
productions. Bears no relation to those other generally
well made "Emmanuelle" films except the title.

| A | 65 min (ort 90 min) Cut |
|---|---|
| B,V | ABC; NET; TCX |

## EMMANUELLE: QUEEN OF THE SADOS **

| | |
|---|---|
| Ilias Mylonakos  CYPRUS/GREECE | 1979 |

*Laura Gemser, Livia Russo, Gabriele Tinti, Harris
Stevens, Nadia Nero, Vagelis Vatran, Gordon
Mitchell, Pantelis Agelopu*
Emmanuelle's husband has taken to beating and
torturing her as a prelude to his lovemaking so she is
obliged to hire a killer (who it would appear is also her
lover) to bump him off. With the death of her husband
she inherits his wealth and gets custody of his
15-year-old girl. However, the killer now begins to
blackmail her and in one nasty scene, rapes the girl.
Emmanuelle responds by shooting him in this well
made but thoroughly unpleasant film.
Aka: EMMANUELLE QUEEN BITCH;
EMMANUELLE'S DAUGHTER

| A | 93 min |
|---|---|
| B,V,V2 | HOK L/A; PINK |

## EMMANUELLE'S SILVER TONGUE **

| | 18 |
|---|---|
| Mauro Ivaldi  ITALY | 1980 |

*Carmen Villani, Nadia Cassini, Roberto Cenci*
Sex comedy based on the amatory exploits of our title
heroine.
Aka: LINGUA D'ARGENTO

| A | 92 m.n; 86 min (SHEP) |
|---|---|
| B,V | 18PLAT/TOW; SHEP |

## EMMA'S WAR **

| | PG |
|---|---|
| Clytie Jessop  USA | 1989 |

*Lee Remick, Miranda Otto*
Set in Australia in 1942, this tells of a woman who is
unable to face both the absence of her husband and the
WW2 bombing of Sydney. Eventually, she takes her
two children to the mountains in search of a new life,
but finds danger there too. Average.

| THR | 92 min |
|---|---|
| V | VIR |

## EMPEROR OF THE NORTH ***

| | |
|---|---|
| Robert Aldrich  USA | 1973 |

*Lee Marvin, Ernest Borgnine, Keith Carradine,
Charles Tyner, Harry Caesar, Malcolm Atterbury,
Simon Oakland, Matt Clark, Hal Baylor, Elisha Cook
Jr, Joe Di Reda, Liam Dunn, Daine Dye, Robert Foulk,
James Goodwin*
A duel to the death between a sadistic train conductor
who kills any hobo trying to steal a free ride on his
train, and a legendary tramp who claims that he will
be the first to succeed and live to tell the tale.
Surprisingly effective, with great photography by
Joseph Biroc. The script is by Christopher Knopf.
Filmed in Oregon.
Aka: EMPEROR OF THE NORTH POLE

| A/AD | 120 min Cut |
|---|---|
| B,V,LV | CBS |

## EMPEROR'S NEW CLOTHES, THE ***

| | U |
|---|---|
| David Irving  USA | 1987 |

*Sid Caesar, Clive Revill, Robert Morse, Jason Carter*
Caesar stars in this lively adaptation of the famous
Brothers Grimm tale in which a vain and foolish
emperor is taken by two rogues who persuade him to
part with his money for some non-existent robes.
Aka: CANNON MOVIE TALES: THE EMPEROR'S
NEW CLOTHES
Boa: short story by Hans Christian Andersen

Wilhelm Karl Grimm.
JUV                                81 min
V/sh                               WHV

## EMPIRE OF ASH *                    18
Lloyd Simandl/Michael Mazo
                 USA              1987
*Melanie Kilgour, Thom Scholer, Frank Wilson, James*
*Stevens, Sandy MacKenzie, Michelle Chipanski*
Yet another post-holocaust tale set in a violent and
brutal world, and one in which the destruction was
wrought by plague rather than by nuclear weapons. A
low-budget MAD MAX clone of inane dialogue,
minimal plotting and mindless action.
FAN                                92 min
B,V                                MOG

## EMPIRE OF THE ANTS *
Bert I. Gordon        USA         1977
*Joan Collins, Robert Lansing, Albert Salmi, John*
*David Carson, Robert Pine, Jacqueline Scott*
Giant ants go on the rampage in Florida and threaten
holidaymakers on vacation on an isolated island in
this ineffective yarn.
Boa: short story by H.G. Wells.
HOR                                91 min
B,V                                RNK

## EMPIRE OF THE SUN **               PG
Steven Spielberg      USA         1987
*Christian Bale, John Malkovich, Miranda*
*Richardson, Nigel Havers, Leslie Phillips, Joe*
*Pantoliano, Masato Ibu, Emily Richard, Rupert*
*Frazer, Ben Stiller, Robert Stephens, Burt Kwouk*
A British boy living a comfortable life in Shanghai is
separated from his parents following the Japanese
invasion of China at the start of WW2 and winds up in
an internment camp where he has to fend for himself.
This good opening develops into a confused and
manipulative tale full of melodramatic set-pieces and
emotion-charged episodes. The over-bearing score is
by John Williams in this irritating adaptation of
Ballard's autobiographical novel.
Boa: novel by J.G. Ballard.
DRA                               146 min
B/sh, V/sh                         WHV

## EMPIRE STATE **                    18
Ron Peck              UK          1986
*Ray McAnally, Cathryn Harrison, Ian Sears, Martin*
*Landau, Lorcan Cranitch, Lee Drysdale, Emily Bolton,*
*Jason Hoganson, Elizabeth Hickling, Jamie Foreman*
A story of London's underworld with a young Amer-
ican coming to London where he is drawn to the
Empire State, a nightclub in the East End docklands
and a favoured haunt of gangsters and thugs. A dull
dud of a film which promises much but delivers little,
nothing happening until the violent shoot-out at the
end.
THR                    98 min (ort 102 min)
B,V                                VIR

## EMPIRE STRIKES BACK, THE ****      U
Irvin Kershner        USA         1980
*Mark Hamill, Harrison Ford, Carrie Fisher, Billy Dee*
*Williams, Dave Prowse, Anthony Daniels, Peter*
*Mayhew, Kenny Baker, Alec Guinness, Jeremy*
*Bulloch, Frank Oz, James Earl Jones (voice only)*
First sequel to STAR WARS but this time the tone is a
lot more serious in a film that is both sadder and more
mature in its development of this saga, though it does
assume one has seen the first film. Followed by
RETURN OF THE JEDI. AA: Sound (Bill Varney/
Steve Maslow/Gregg Landaker/Peter Sutton), Spec
Award (Brian Johnson/Richard Edlund/Dennis
Muren/Bruce Nicholson for visual effects).
FAN                   119 min (ort 124 min)
B,V,V2                             CBS

## EMPTY BEACH, THE **                18
Chris Thomson     AUSTRALIA       1985
*Bryan Brown, Anna Jenison (Maria Monticelli), Roy*
*Barrett, Belinda Giblin, Kerry Mack, John Wood, Peter*
*Collingwood, Nick Tate, Joss McWilliams, Sally*
*Cooper*
A woman hires a private eye to see if her black market
racketeer husband really is dead, although he was
supposedly drowned two years earlier. As his inves-
tigations proceed the detective finds himself getting
drawn into the murky and unpleasant world of
Sydney's criminal fraternity.
Boa: novel by Peter Corris.
THR                                87 min
B,V                                SONY

## ENCHANTED ISLAND **
Allan Dwan            USA         1958
*Dana Andrews, Jane Powell, Don Dubbins, Arthur*
*Shields*
Two sailors desert from their whaling ship and settle
on a South Sea island with Andrews falling for native
girl Powell. Nice settings cannot disguise poor casting
and the lack of pace.
Boa: novel Typee by Herman Melville. Osca:
WESTWARD PASSAGE
A/AD                   90 min (ort 94 min)
B,V                                KVD

## ENCOUNTER AT RAVEN'S GATE *         15
Rolf De Heer      AUSTRALIA       1990
*Celine Guiltin, Steven Vidler, Ritchie Singer*
Atmospheric but leaden and confusing account of
strange events in the Outback. Power supplies come
and go, family pets savage their owners and both
murder and madness is rife, but in the end nothing is
explained or resolved. A poor effort indeed.
HOR                                85 min
V                                 CASPIC

## ENCOUNTERS IN THE DEEP **           PG
Tonino Ricci      ITALY/SPAIN     1978
*Gianna Garcia, Manuel Zarzo, Olga Bustillo, Andres*
*Garcia, Carole Andre, Alfredo Mayo*
The daughter of a wealthy businessman vanishes in
the Bermuda Triangle whilst on her honeymoon
cruise. He finds himself forced to organise a search
party, unaware that supernatural forces are at work
in this region.
Aka: ENCUENTRO EN EL ABISMO
HOR                                82 min
B,V                                ELE

## END OF AUGUST, THE **
Bob Graham            USA         1981
*Sally Sharp, Lilia Skala, David Marshall Grant,*
*Kathleen Widdoes, Paul Roebling, Paul Shenar*
In 1900 a bored young wife starts an affair with a man
from a lower social class. Good on period detail and
attractive to look at but generally fairly uninspiring.
The script is by Eula Seaton and Leon Haller.
Boa: novel The Awakening by Kate Chopin.
DRA                               107 min
B,V                                RNK

## END OF SAINT PETERSBURG, THE ***    PG
Vsevolod I. Pudovkin  USSR        1927
*Ivan Chuvelov, Vera Baranovskaya, A.P. Chistiakov,*
*V. Obolenski*
A peasant comes to Saint Petersburg in 1914 and
becomes a strike-breaker during a dispute, but even-
tually comes to side with the workers and takes part
in the Revolution. A stirring propaganda piece
officially commissioned to mark the tenth anniversary
of the October Revolution.
Aka: KONYETS SANKT-PETERBURGA
DRA           69 min (ort 106 min) B/W silent
V                                 HEND

## END OF THE LINE **  PG
Jay Russell          USA          1987
*Wilford Brimley, Levon Helm, Mary Steenburgen,*
*Barbara Barrie, Kevin Bacon, Holly Hunter, Bob*
*Balaban, Clint Howard, Rita Jenrette, Howard*
*Morris, Bruce McGill, Trey Wilson*
Two buddies lose their jobs on the Southern railroads
when their parent company moves over to air freight,
so they take off for the corporate headquarters in
Chicago in a stolen engine. An offbeat comedy-drama
that quickly runs off its own rails, degenerating into
little more than a silly farce.
DRA                               105 min
B,V                                 BOX

## END OF THE WORLD **
John Hayes          USA          1977
*Christopher Lee, Sue Lyon, Kirk Scott, Lew Ayres,*
*Macdonald Carey, Dean Jagger, Liz Ross*
A strange tale about an invasion of the world by
aliens, with Lee playing both a priest and his
malevolent "double". A promising start is very soon
wasted.
FAN                                88 min
B,V,V2                           INT/CBS

## END, THE **  15
Burt Reynolds          USA          1978
*Burt Reynolds, Sally Field, Dom DeLuise, Joanne*
*Woodward, Carl Reiner, Robby Benson, David*
*Steinberg, Norman Fell, Pat O'Brien, Myrna Loy,*
*Kristy McNichol, Strother Martin, Jock Mahoney*
A man who is dying decides to get the affairs of his life
sorted out to his satisfaction before committing
suicide in this outrageous but only partially successful
black comedy.
COM                               100 min
B,V                                 WHV

## ENDANGERED SPECIES *  15
Alan Rudolph          USA          1982
*Robert Urich, JoBeth Williams, Paul Dooley, Hoyt*
*Axton, Peter Coyote, Marin Kanter, Dan Hedaya,*
*Harry Carey Jr, John Considine*
The strange story of cattle being mutilated in Wyom-
ing. Though based on a true story the point of it all is
never made clear.
FAN                     93 min (ort 97 min)
B,V,V2                              MGM

## ENDGAME **  18
Steven Benson          ITALY          1983
*Joe Spencer, Moira Chen, Jill Elliott, Al Cliver (Pier*
*Luigi Conti), George Eastman (Luigi Montefiore), Jack*
*Davis, Al Yamanouchi, Mario Pedone, Gordon*
*Mitchell, Gus Stone, Al Waterman, Bobby Rhodes, Nat*
*Williams, David Brown*
Another post-nuclear holocaust film set in New York
where a group of mutants try to escape to join a new
civilisation.
Aka: ENDGAMES
DRA          92 min (ort 94 min) Cut (41 sec)
B,V,V2                      VTC L/A; STABL

## ENDLESS LOVE *  15
Franco Zeffirelli          USA          1981
*Brooke Shields, Martin Hewitt, Shirley Knight, Don*
*Murray, Richard Kiley, Beatrice Straight, James*
*Spader, Robert Moore, Penelope Milford, Jan Miner,*
*Tom Cruise, Jami Getz*
The doomed love affair between a high school student
and a 15-year-old girl forms the basis of this highly
melodramatic version of a novel. Trashy and exploita-
tive with not one memorable scene in the whole film.
This was the film debut of Cruise (fortunately it
doesn't appear to have harmed his career).
Boa: novel by Scott Spencer.
DRA                               110 min
B,V,V2,LV                 SPEC/POLY; CH5

## ENDLESS NIGHT **  15
Sidney Gilliat          UK          1971
*Hayley Mills, Hywel Bennett, Britt Ekland, George*
*Sanders, Per Oscarsson, Lois Maxwell, Peter Bowles,*
*Aubrey Richards, Ann Way, Patience Collier, Madge*
*Ryan, Walter Gotell, Helen Horton, David Bauer,*
*Geoffrey Chater*
A chauffeur marries a rich American heiress and they
move into a stately home only to find it turning into a
nightmare mansion. A creaky British thriller of weak
plotting and worse characterisation.
Aka: AGATHA CHRISTIE'S ENDLESS NIGHT
Boa: novel by Agatha Christie.
THR                                98 min
V                                   WHV

## ENEMIES, A LOVE STORY ****  15
Paul Mazursky          USA          1989
*Anjelica Huston, Ron Silver, Lena Olin, Margaret*
*Sophie Stein, Alan King, Judith Malina, Rita Karlin,*
*Phil Leeds, Elya Baskin, Paul Mazursky*
A Jewish intellectual who escaped the Holocaust lives
a strange double life, being married to his wartime
protector and yet carrying on a relationship with
another woman. The re-appearance of his first wife,
whom he thought dead, complicates matters some-
what further. Set in New York in 1949, this strange
blend of comedy, pathos and drama is as poignant as it
is unusual. The script is by Mazursky and Roger L.
Simon with music by Maurice Jarre.
Boa: novel by Isaac Bashevis Singer.
DRA                 114 min (ort 119 min)
V                                 20VIS

## ENEMY BELOW, THE ***  PG
Dick Powell          USA          1957
*Robert Mitchum, Curt Jurgens, Theodore Bikel, Doug*
*McClure, Russell Collins, David Hedison*
An American destroyer on an anti-submarine patrol
in the South Atlantic plays a cat-and-mouse game
with a U-boat commanded by a wily German. An
excellent WW2 action film, tense, literate and well
directed. The underwater effects won a well deserved
Oscar. AA: Effects (Walter Rossi).
Boa: novel Escort by Commander D.A. Rayner.
WAR                                98 min
B, V/h, LV                         CBS

## ENEMY MINE ***  15
Wolfgang Peterson          USA          1985
*Dennis Quaid, Louis Gossett Jr, Brion James, Richard*
*Marcus*
An Earthman and his alien enemy are both stranded
on a hostile planet, where they are gradually forced to
abandon their struggle in order to survive. Reminiscent of HELL IN THE PACIFIC with considerable
effort being made to portray the alien as an intelligent
sentient being rather than a monster. A workmanlike
and original film with good special effects its best
feature.
FAN                    89 min (ort 108 min)
V/sh                               CBS

## ENEMY OF THE PEOPLE, AN ***  U
George Schaefer          USA          1977
*Steve McQueen, Charles Durning, Bibi Andersson,*
*Richard Bradford, Eric Christmas, Robin Pearson*
*Rose, Richard A. Dysart*
A small-town doctor risks his livelihood when he
reveals that the water in the local spa has been
contaminated by waste from a tannery, a fact the town
council is keen to conceal. Adapted from the play by
Henry Miller, this sincere and plodding film has a fine
performance from McQueen let down by the stilted
manner in which it develops. Nevertheless, as an
example of one of McQueen's more interesting roles it
certainly deserves a look.
Boa: play by Henrik Ibsen.
DRA                               102 min
B,V                                 WHV

## ENEMY TERRITORY *                    18
Peter Manoogian        USA              1987
*Gary Frank, Ray Parker Jr, Jan-Michael Vincent,*
*Tony Todd, Peter Teschner*
A vicious and fairly mindless look at what happens
when a white insurance salesman annoys a nasty
black gang on a visit to their ghetto and finds himself
trapped in a building by them.
THR                                    85 min
B,V                                    EIV

## ENEMY UNSEEN **                     15
Elmo DeWitt                            1989
*Vernon Wells, Angela O'Neill, Stack Pierce*
An heiress and her photographer disappear while
exploring an isolated valley in Africa that has a
sinister reputaion, and later the mutilated body of the
photograpgher is recovered. The girl's father organises a search party comprising crack mercenaries all
prepared to brave the unknown dangers that lie
ahead. A standard jungle-action yarn with all the
expected elements.
A/AD                                   87 min
V                                      MED

## ENFORCER FROM DEATH ROW **          18
Efron C. Pinon/Marshall M. Bordon      1978
*Cameron Mitchell, Leo Fong, Darnell Garcia, Gene*
*Wisner, Lotus Key*
A man is saved from Death Row by an international
peacekeeping organisation which in the interests of
world peace, gives him the task of tracking down and
eliminating a gang of spies.
A/AD          76 min (ort 87 min) Cut (1 min 39 sec)
V                                      BUDPAC

## ENFORCER, THE **                    18
James Fargo            USA             1976
*Clint Eastwood, Tyne Daly, Harry Guardino, Bradford*
*Dillman, John Mitchum, DeVeren Bookwalter, John*
*Crawford, Albert Popwell*
The second sequel to DIRTY HARRY, with our tough
cop coping with a female partner as well as an
underground terrorist group. A violent and simplistic
celebration of macho cops and big guns, but undeni-
ably slick. Followed by SUDDEN IMPACT.
A/AD                          92 min (ort 96 min)
V                                      WHV

## ENFORCER, THE ***                   PG
Bretaigne Windust      USA             1950
*Humphrey Bogart, Zero Mostel, Ted De Corsia, Everett*
*Sloane, Roy Roberts*
Bogart plays a crusading D.A. out to crush a criminal
gang led by Sloane in this gritty and realistic gangster
movie that is without doubt one of the director's best
efforts.
THR                                    87 min B/W
V                                      VIR

## ENGLAND MADE ME ***                 15
Peter Duffell          UK              1972
*Peter Finch, Michael York, Hildergarde Neil, Michael*
*Hordern, Joss Ackland, Tessa Wyatt, Michael Sheard,*
*Basil Baskiville, Demeter Bitenc, Mira Nikolic,*
*Vladimir Bacic, Maja Papandopulo*
A young Englishman becomes involved with a power-
ful German financier through his sister in Nazi
Germany of 1935. A powerful and absorbing tale, not
appreciated when first released but now well re-
garded. Filmed in Yugoslavia.
Aka: RAPE OF THE THIRD REICH, THE
Boa: novel by Graham Greene.
DRA                          90 min (ort 100 min)
B,V,V2                                 VCL/CBS

## ENGLISHMAN ABROAD, AN ****          PG
John Schlesinger       UK              1985
*Alan Bates, Coral Browne*

Alan Bennett's recreation of actress Coral Browne's
encounter with former spy and traitor Guy Burgess
while she was on tour with the Royal Shakespeare
Company in Moscow is an outstanding piece of drama.
Bates is quite superb as the misguided traitor,
anxious for gossip (and clothes) from England, but not
regretting his treachery for a moment. Browne plays
herself.
DRA                                    63 min mTV
V/h                                    BBC

## ENIGMA *                            15
Jeannot Szwarc    FRANCE/UK            1982
*Martin Sheen, Brigitte Fossey, Sam Neill, Derek*
*Jacobi, Michel Lonsdale, Frank Finlay, David Baxt,*
*Kevin McNally, Michael Williams, Warren Clarke,*
*Vernon Dobtcheff*
The KGB send five of their top killers to silence five
Soviet dissidents and a CIA agent tries to stop them.
Never more than mediocre, though an excellent cast
do their best. The script is by John Briley.
Boa: novel Enigma Sacrifice by Michael Barak.
THR                          97 min (ort 122 min)
V                                      GHV

## ENIGMA OF KASPAR HAUSER, THE ****
Werner Herzog    WEST GERMANY          1975
*Bruno S, Walter Ladengast, Brigitte Mira*
In the 1820s a man appeared outside the gates of
Nuremberg who stated that he had been kept in
confinement from an early age. This mystery has
never been solved though it is thought that he may
have been of royal birth. This film is an engrossing
look at the world as seen through his eyes.
Aka: EVERY MAN FOR HIMSELF AND GOD
AGAINST ALL; JEDER FUR SICH UND GOTT
GEGEN ALLE; KASPAR HAUSER; LEGEND OF
KASPAR HAUSER, THE; MYSTERY OF KASPAR
HAUSER, THE
DRA                                    110 min
B,V                                    PVG

## ENOLA GAY **
David Lowell Rich       USA            1980
*Billy Crystal, Kim Darby, Patrick Duffy, Gary Frank,*
*Gregory Harrison, Stephen Macht, Walter Olkewicz,*
*Robert Pine, James Shigeta, Robert Walden, Richard*
*Venture, Richard Herd, Henry Wilcoxon, Stephen*
*Roberts, Than Wyenn*
The story of the aircrew who were given the task of
dropping the first atomic bomb on Japan during WW2,
largely based on the reminiscences of Paul Tibbets,
who led the mission. A disappointing effort. Scripted
by James Poe and Millard Kaufman.
Aka: ENOLA GAY: THE MEN, THE MISSION, THE
ATOMIC BOMB
Boa: book by Max Morgan-Witts and Gordon Thomas.
DRA                                    156 min mTV
B,V                              VFP L/A; HER

## ENTER THE DEVIL **                  18
Frank Q. Dobbs/David Cass
                       USA             1971
*David Cass, Irene Kelly, Josh Bryant, Carle Benson,*
*Linda Rascoe, John Martin, Norris Dominique,*
*Wanda Wilson, Ed Geldert, Happy Shahan, Carla*
*Bensen, Robert John Allen, Ray Demney, Bryan*
*Quesenberry, Willie Gonzales*
A deputy sheriff and a lady professor of the occult
become involved with Satanists.
Aka: DISCIPLES OF DEATH
HOR                                    83 min
B,V                              VPD; GLOB

## ENTER THE DRAGON ***                18
Robert Clouse   HONG KONG/USA          1973
*Bruce Lee, John Saxon, Jim Kelly, Ahna Capri, Yang*
*Tse, Angela Mao*
A martial arts fighter infiltrates a tournament to be

held on an island in an attempt to prevent opium smuggling on behalf of British Intelligence. The foolish plot is best ignored in the face of some excellent martial arts sequences. This was Lee's last complete film role.

MAR 93 min (ort 97 min) Cut (1 min 45 sec)
B,V WHV

### ENTER THE INVINCIBLE HERO ** 18
HONG KONG
*Dragon Lee*
A young drifter starts work at a security firm only to discover that it is a front for criminal operations.

MAR 86 min Cut (6 sec)
B,V VPD

### ENTER THE NINJA ** 18
Menahem Golan USA 1981
*Franco Nero, Susan George, Sho Kosugi, Alex Courtney, Will Hare, Zachi Noy, Dale Ishimoto, Christopher George*
Typical kung fu action film with Nero battling it out with a couple of old enemies. Fairly mediocre. NINJA 2: THE REVENGE OF THE NINJA followed.

MAR 91 min (ort 94 min) (Cut at film release)
B,V RCA

### ENTER THE STREETFIGHTER ** 
S. Ozawa JAPAN
*Sonny (Shinichi) Chiba, Gerald Yamada, Doris Nakajima, Tony Setera*
A kung fu expert battles corruption and evil in this routine martial arts tale. One of several "Street-fighter" films. See also THE STREETFIGHTER'S LAST REVENGE.

MAR 76 min
B,V,V2 VTC L/A

### ENTERTAINER, THE **** PG
Tony Richardson UK 1960
*Laurence Olivier, Joan Plowright, Roger Livesey, Brenda De Banzie, Alan Bates, Albert Finney, Thora Hird, Shirley Ann Field, Daniel Massey*
Olivier gives a remarkable performance in this depressing tale of an obnoxious seaside music-hall entertainer, whose pathetic attempts to stave off the end of his career are doomed to failure. A stilted but poignant character study, with the star repeating his earlier stage success. The screenplay is by Osborne. Remade for TV (with Jack Lemmon in the title role) in 1975.
Boa: play by John Osborne.

DRA 93 min (ort 96 min) B/W
V CASPIC

### ENTERTAINING MISTER SLOANE *** 15
Douglas Hickox UK 1969
*Beryl Reid, Harry Andrews, Peter McEnery, Alan Webb*
Sparkling black comedy about a young lodger who becomes inveigled into an amorous relationship with both the middle-aged daughter and son of an old man he has murdered. Suffers from uneven adaptation but a treat for all that.
Boa: play by Joe Orton.

COM 90 min (ort 94 min)
B,V TEVP; WHV (VHS only)

### ENTITY, THE ** 18
Sidney J. Furie USA 1981
*Barbara Hershey, Ron Silver, Jacqueline Brooks, David Lablosa, George Coe, Sho Kosugi, Alex Courtney, Will Hare, Zachi Noy, Dale Ishimoto, Christopher George, Margaret Blye, Alex Rocco*
A young woman is raped by a strange invisible entity and at first no-one will believe her and she is referred to a psychiatrist. However, university parapsychologists eventually isolate the creature. An occasionally effective piece of nonsense.

Boa: novel by Frank DeFelitta.

HOR 119 min
V/sh CBS

### EPITAPH *** 18
Joseph Merhi USA 1986
*Richard Pepin, Red Horton, Constance J. Damron, Natasha Pavlova, Jim Williams*
A chilling psychological thriller about the supervisor of the Los Angeles Police detective department who spends all his time trying to cover up the gruesome axe murders committed by his own wife.

THR 90 min
B,V IVS

### EQUALISER, THE: BLOOD AND WINE ** 15
Alan Metzger USA 1987
*Edward Woodward, Telly Savalas, William Atherton, Keith Szarabaja, Moira Harris, Tom Atkins, Christopher Murray, Elizabeth Franz*
A feature-length episode from the TV series of the same name, with tough private eye Robert McCall joining forces with a priest when a psychotic and deadly terrorist threatens to bring New York to a standstill.
Aka: BLOOD AND WINE

A/AD 93 min mTV
B,V CIC

### EQUALISER, THE: THE MYSTERY OF 15
MANON **
Bradford May USA 1988
*Edward Woodward, Anthony Zerbe, Keith Szarabajka, Anne Heywood, Melissa Anderson, Lawrence Dane, William Zabka, Mark Margolis*
One more feature-length episode from the popular TV series, in which our tough former agent turned private detective, meets up with an old friend who is convinced his wife (also a former agent) is still alive. With the arrival of the man's daughter the plot thickens. Average.
Aka: MYSTERY OF MANON, THE

A/AD 88 min mTV
B,V CIC

### EQUALIZER 2000 ** 18
Cirio H. Santiago ITALY 1986
*Richard Norton, Corrine Wahl, Robert Patrick, William Steis*
Yet another bleak post-WW3 survival epic, in which a man is double-crossed by his government and finds himself in the hands of an opposing faction. He escapes and acquires the Equalizer 2000, a weapon so powerful that it can be used to decide which faction shall gain control of the scattered remnants of humanity. Average action fantasy yarn.

FAN 85 min
B,V MED; NDH/GHV

### EQUINOX * 
Jack Woods USA 1969
*Edward Connell, Barbara Hewitt, Frank Boers Jr (Frank Bonner), Robin Christopher, Jack Woods, Fritz Leiber*
Archaeology students get involved with Satanism and mutant monsters while looking for a lost professor. Generally inept, despite some good effects and made over several years, with both the cast and the script suffering in consequence.
Aka: BEAST, THE

HOR 78 min (ort 80 min)
B,V MOV

### EQUUS *** 15
Sidney Lummet UK 1977
*Richard Burton, Peter Firth, Colin Blakely, Joan PLowright, Harry Andrews, Jenny Agutter, Eileen Atkins, Kate Reid, John Wyman, Elva Mai Hoover, Ken James, Patrick Brymer*

A psychiatrist investigates the case of a boy who blinded six horses and finds himself questioning his own life and values as he penetrates to the core of his patient's madness. A static and stagebound film, yet not without a certain spellbinding power, rendered thus primarily by the superb acting of the two leads and the poetry of the dialogue.
Boa: play by Peter Shaffer.
DRA 132 min (ort 137 min)
B,V WHV

## ERASERHEAD ** 18
David Lynch USA 1976
*John Nance, Charlotte Stewart, Allen Joseph*
An unpleasant surrealistic film that is almost impossible to watch. It consists of a series of nightmarish images loosely tied to the story of an introverted young man whose girlfriend has given birth to a grotesquely repulsive mutant. She leaves him to look after it. The work is not without moments of considerable power, and now has a degree of cult status.
HOR 100 min B/W
B,V PVG; CH5 (VHS only)

## ERIC *** 
James Goldstone USA 1975
*Patricia Neal, John Savage, Claude Akins, Sian Barbara Allen, Mark Hamill, Nehemiah Persoff, Tom Clancy, John Savage, James G. Richardson, Eileen McDonough, Katherine Squire, Harry Basch, Nancy Wolfe, Ron Joseph*
A young man who is terminally ill refuses to give up his athletic pursuits just because he is dying. A touching film based on Lund's memoirs of her son's last year, undeniably weepy in parts but Savage's fine performance as the boy and Neal's as his valiant mother give it dignity.
Boa: book by Doris Lund.
DRA 95 min mTV
B,V SPEC/POLY

## ERIK THE VIKING ** 15
Terry Jones USA 1989
*Tim Robbins, Gary Cady, Terry Jones, Eartha Kitt, Mickey Rooney, John Cleese, Tsutomu Sekine, Antony Sher, Gordon John Sinclair, Imogen Stubbs, Freddie Jones*
Written by ex-Monty Python member Jones, this spoof Viking saga follows the exploits of Erik, a man who abhors rape and pillage, instead choosing to sail off in search of the home of the gods. Cheap looking and dreadfully unfunny to start with, the film eventually delivers a couple of laughs if one is patient.
COM 89 min (ort 104 min)
V CBS

## ERNEST GOES TO CAMP ** PG
John R. Cherry III USA 1987
*Jim Varney, Victoria Racimo, John Vernon, Iron Eyes Cody, Lyle Alzado, Gailard Sartain, Daniel Butler, Hakeem Abdul-Samad*
Based on a character created in a spate of TV commercials, this tells of a dimwitted and obnoxious fellow who gets his wish to become a summer camp counsellor. He quickly finds his hands full with problems ranging from juvenile delinquency to a takeover by a mining company. A lacklustre and exploitative comedy.
COM 89 min
B,V RNK

## ERNEST SAVES CHRISTMAS ** U
John Cherry USA 1988
*Jim Varney, Noelle Parker, Douglas Seale, Oliver Clark, Robert Lesser, Gailard Sartain, Billie Bird*
Another Ernest adventure that offers a slight improvement on ERNEST GOES TO CAMP, following the exploits of our irritating hero who this time round has the task of helping Santa find a successor, without

which there will be no more Christmases. Mildly amusing in a soppy and over-sentimental way. "Ernest Goes To Jail" followed.
COM 88 min
V TOUCH

## EROTIC ADVENTURES OF CANDY, THE *** 
Gail Palmer USA 1978
*Carol Connors, John C. Holmes, Georgina Spelvin, Turk Lyon, Paul Thomas*
This film preceded CANDY GOES TO HOLLYWOOD and follows a young girl and her sexual adventures with all and sundry. Not terribly well-plotted (though the makers claim Voltaire's "Candide" as inspiration), but lighthearted and quite good fun.
Osca: LADIES' NIGHT (asa)
A 85 min
B,V HAR

## EROTIC ADVENTURES OF PINNOCHIO ** 18
Coren Allen USA 1970
*Alex Roman, Karen Smith, Dyanne Thorne, Eduardo Ranez*
Nude sex comedy bearing little similarity to the famous fairytale.
A 75 min
B,V VCL L/A; ELV

## EROTIC ADVENTURES OF ROBINSON 18
## CRUSOE ** 
Ken Dixon USA 1975
*Lawrence Casey, Eva Carson, Dan Harrison, Malisa Longo, Paolo Macolini, Colette Descombe*
A shipwrecked sailor finds himself slap bang in the middle of a softcore movie when he gets washed up on a desert isle populated almost exclusively by sex-starved ladies.
A 81 min Cut (58 sec)
B,V ABC; NET; TCX

## EROTIC ADVENTURES OF ZORRO, THE ** 18
Robert Freeman
FRANCE/USA/WEST GERMANY 1972
*Douglas Frey, Robyn Whitting, Penny Boran, John Alderman, Lynn Harris Michelle Simer*
An attempt to produce an erotic version of the legend of this masked avenger, with Don Diego, Spain's greatest horseman, swordsman and lover, being summoned to a little town to rid the townsfolk of their lecherous mayor and his henchmen. During the day Diego minces about as a laughable fop, but at night he becomes the masked avenger Zorro. Occasionally amusing but generally a little too overblown to be effective.
COM 84 min Cut
B,V,V2 DFS; XTACY/KRP

## EROTIC EVA * 18
Joe D'Amato (Aristide Massaccesi)
ITALY 1976
*Jack Palance, Laura Gemser, Gabriele Tinti, Michele Stark, Ely Galleani, Sigrid Zanger, G. Mariotti*
Sex and sexuality in Hong Kong form the basis for this dull effort.
Aka: EVA NERA
A 83 min (ort 86 min) (Abridged at film release)
B,V 18PLAT/TOW; PRI; SHEP

## EROTIC FANTASIES * 18
Derek Ford/Paul Selway
ITALY 1978
*Ajita Wilson, Karin Wells, Vivienne Sultan, Anna Valentino, Monty Duro, Zaira Zoccheddu*
Dialogue free sexploiter with parts of "Rip Off" – the Paul Raymond musical. A big drum player in an orchestra fantasises sexually to a series of classical pieces.
A 70 min (ort 96 min) (Abridged at film release)
B,V 18PLAT/TOW; PRI; PHE; SHEP

**EROTIC INFERNO** ** 18
Trevor Wrenn            UK            1975
*Jenny Westbrook, Chris Chittell, Michael Watkins,*
*Karl Larchbury, Jeannie Collings, Heather Deely,*
*Lindy Benson, Monika Ringwald, Michael Sheard*
All the beneficiaries in a businessman's will spend a
dirty weekend together as they wait for it to be read.
However, the whole thing is a pretence set up to give
the man the opportunity to see how his two sons
behave once they think he's dead. A dated and
unfunny attempt at a sex comedy.
Aka: ADAM AND NICOLE; NAKED AND WILLING
A              78 min (ort 80 min) (Cut at film release)
B,V,V2        NET L/A; TCX L/A; ATLAS L/A; SHEP

**EROTIC ODYSSEY** * 18
Nick Milas            GREECE            1976
*Natalie Danck, G. Stratigakis, A. Vlachos, George*
*Louikas, Cathy Mandely*
A wealthy family indulge themselves with the ser-
vants.
Aka: ROXANA
A          84 min; 75 min (TOW) (ort 100 min) Cut (52 sec)
B,V                    ILV L/A; ROXY L/A; TOW

**EROTIC PLEASURES: THE BODIES DESIRE** *** 18
Francis Le Roi            FRANCE            1976
*Maryline Guillaume, Siegfried Cellier, Chris Martin,*
*Herve Amalou, Jack Gatteau, Louison Boutin, Rene*
*Douglas, Jean-Baptiste Ory, Gilles Keruizic, Dolores*
*Manta, Bernard Talbin, Guy Roger, Dominique*
*Aveline*
The story of three French ladies who live in the same
apartment block and their sexual escapades. Martine
decides to cheat on her husband and does so, visiting
an old boyfriend with this in mind. Joelle is a
schoolgirl who encounters great difficulty losing her
virginity. Finally there is Arlene, a rich woman who
usually hires gigolos for sex but now searches in vain
for a deeper relationship. A sophisticated, romantic
and often very funny film.
Aka: EROTIC PLEASURES; LES PLAISIRS
SOLITAIRES; LONELY PLEASURES
A              71 min (ort 90 min) Cut (12 min 16 sec)
B,V                    ELV; INT; TAR

**EROTIC RADIO WSEX** *** 18
Bob Augustus            USA            1984
*Herschel Savage, Renee Summers, Tanya Lawson,*
*Ron Jeremy, Desiree Lane, Bunny Bleu, Brian Curtis,*
*Kay Parker, Scott Irish, Mark Harris, William*
*Margold*
Sex comedy set in San Fernando Valley and telling of
a late-night disc jockey who is so popular with the
ladies that they often ring him to give their addresses.
Eventually our D.J. gets fired for making love on the
air but his job is saved by a woman who manufactures
and sells cosmetics from door to door. She wants to
advertise on Radio WSEX because she knows he
reaches the ladies. The station needs the money – he
gets his job back.
Aka: EROTIC RADIO WSSX
A                              55 min
B,V                            VEXCEL

**EROTIC TALES** ** 18
Regine Deforges    FRANCE/ITALY            1980
*Francoise Gayat, Carina Barone, Salina Gardel, Zora*
*Kerowa*
Three undistinguished stories on a sexual theme.
Aka: CONTES PERVERS; PERVERSE TALLES;
TALES OF EROTIC FANTASIES (ROXY)
A                              84 min Cut
B,V                    INT; ROXY; XTACY/KRP

**EROTIC WORLD OF ANGEL CASH** ** 
Howard A. Howard        USA            1982
*Angel Cash, Jim Sims, Juliet Anderson, Danielle,*
*Bunny Hatton, David Ambrose, Felix Krull*

"All I can think about is sex" says lovely Angel as she
wanders half-naked around her houseboat. She then
sets out to prove it in a series of encounters with guys
from an all-male chorus, in this hardcore and thoroughly uncompromising sex film. In a minor role as
the mistress of the ballet school Angel attends,
Anderson also gets a chance to do likewise.
A                      80 min (ort 89 min)
B,V                            XTACY/KRP

**EROTIC YOUNG LOVERS** * 18
Ernst Hofbauer  WEST GERMANY            1973
Another one of those tiresome German sex-farces from
the 1970s. This one is set on a college campus.
Aka: SCHULMADCHEN REPORT 6 TEIL: WAS
ELTERN GERN VERTUSCHEN MOCHTEN
A          71 min; 69 min (SHEP) (Cut at film release)
B,V                    IFS; 18PLAT/TOW; SHEP

**EROTICA** * 
Brian Smedley-Aston      UK            1980
*Brigitte Lahaie, Paul Raymond, Diana Cochran*
Story set around Paul Raymond's famous Revuebar in
London with a sex-mad French photographer even-
tually becoming one of Raymond's performers. More
or less a simple plug for this establishment.
Aka: PAUL RAYMOND'S EROTICA
A                              86 min
B,V,V2                        ELV

**EROTICIST, THE** *** 18
Lucio Fulci        FRANCE/ITALY            1971
*Lionel Stander, Lando Buzzanca, Anita Strindberg*
A US senator running for President just cannot keep
his hands off women in this amusing sex farce.
Aka: ALL'ONOREVOLE PIACCIONO LE DONNE
A                              85 min
B,V                            VPD

**ERRAND BOY, THE** ** U
Jerry Lewis            USA            1961
*Jerry Lewis, Brian Dunlevy, Fritz Feld, Howard*
*McNear, Sig Rujman, Iris Adrian, Kathleen Freeman,*
*Joe Besser, Mike Mazurki*
Frenetically paced account of a bumbling idiot who
masquerades as an errand boy but has in reality been
hired by a studio mogul to uncover waste and
inefficiency. Has a few funny moments but most gags
misfire.
COM                            92 min B/W
V                              COL

**ERUPTION** *** 18
Stanley Kurlan            USA            1978
*John C. Holmes, Leslie Bovee, Susan Hart, Eric Evol,*
*Gene Clayton*
Filmed entirely on location in Hawaii, this tells of a
wealthy woman who conspires with her con-man lover
to murder her husband and collect a large insurance
sum. However, her young daughter has other ideas,
and she sets out to ensnare her mother's lover to
create a love triangle. A well-acted and produced
erotic version of DOUBLE INDEMNITY. Cut before
video submission by 11 min 54 sec.
A                      59 min; (ort 90 min)
B,V,V2                    CRAW L/A; GOLD

**ESCALIER C** *** 15
Jean-Charles Tacchella
                        FRANCE            1985
*Robin Renucci, Jean-Pierre Bacri, Catherine Leprince,*
*Jacques Bonaffre, Jacques Weber, Claude Rich, Michel*
*Aumont, Hugues Quester, Catherine Frot, Florence*
*Giorgietti, Fiona Gelin, Gilles Gaston-Dreyfus, Mony-*
*Rey*
The story of passions and stormy relationships written
around the lives of some of the residents of a set of
apartments in suburban Paris: a writer, an alcoholic,

a lonely old lady, a teacher and her daughter, and a cynical art critic. Quite an absorbing drama, with moments of humour and sadness.
Aka: STAIRCASE C
DRA                                            98 min
B,V                                             RNK

## ESCAPADE IN JAPAN **
Arthur Lubin            USA               1957
*Cameron Mitchell, Teresa Wright, Jon Provost, Roger Nakagawa, Philip Ober, Clint Eastwood*
A 7-year-old boy who survives a plane crash in Japan runs away because he thinks the police are after him. The location filming in Japan is the most memorable aspect of an otherwise forgettable adventure yarn. Look out for Eastwood in an early role as a serviceman.
Osca: GIFT FOR HEIDI, A
A/AD                                           89 min
B,V                                             KVD

## ESCAPE *                                    18
Eddie Romero      PHILIPPINES/USA         1972
*John Ashley, Sid Haig, Laurie Rose, Lisa Todd, Eddie Garcia, Charlene Jones, Pat Woodell*
A rotten and exploitative version of "The Most Dangerous Game", with kidnapped women being used as prey. Todd is particularly unendearing as a black-clad lesbian sadist in this dull and trashy effort.
Aka: WOMAN HUNT, THE (MEDPER)
FAN                                            72 min
B,V                                    MEDPER; APX

## ESCAPE 2000 *                               18
Brian Trenchard-Smith
                        AUSTRALIA          1981
*Steve Railsback, Olivia Hussey, Michael Craig, Noel Ferrier, Lynda Stoner, Carmen Duncan, Roger Ward, Michael Petrovich, John Ley, Gus Mercurio, Steve Rackman, Billy Young, John Godden, Oriana Panozzo*
In a future society deviants and political undesirables are hunted to death as a way of controlling crime. A violent and repellent version of "The Most Dangerous Game" with an unending stream of whippings, burnings and gruesome decapitations.
Aka: TURKEY SHOOT (GHV)
FAN        84 min (ort 88 min) (Cut at film release)
B,V                                     EHE L/A; GHV

## ESCAPE ARTIST, THE **                       PG
Caleb Deschanel          USA              1982
*Griffin O'Neal, Raul Julia, Teri Garr, Joan Hackett, Desiderio (Desi) Arnaz Sr, Gabriel Dell, M. Emmet Walsh, Jackie Coogan, Huntz Hall*
The orphan son of an escape artist employs magic to get to the truth behind his father's death and reveal local corruption. A muddled tale of intrigue and exploitation partially redeemed by the pleasant screen presence of O'Neal, the son of Ryan.
Boa: novel by D. Wagoner.
DRA                                            96 min
B,V,V2                                    POLY; CH5

## ESCAPE FROM ALCATRAZ ***                    15
Don Siegel               USA              1979
*Clint Eastwood, Patrick McGoohan, Paul Benjamin, Fred Ward, Roberts Blossom, Jack Thibeau, Danny Glover*
Retells the true story of a breakout in 1962 from this infamous maximum security prison. A film with hardly any dialogue but held together by a profound sense of tension coupled with some good acting.
Boa: book by J. Campbell Bruce.
THR                                           112 min
B,V,V2,LV                                       CIC

## ESCAPE FROM ANGOLA **
Leslie Martinson         USA              1976

*Stan Brock, Anne Collings, Ivan Tors, Steven Tors, Peter Tors, David Tors, Mackson Ngobeni*
Adventure story about a family struggling to survive in the vast African bush. Pleasant and undemanding.
Aka: RETURN TO AFRICA
A/AD                              85 min (ort 95 min)
B,V                                             MEV

## ESCAPE FROM DS-3 **                         15
Allen Sandler/Robert Emenegger
                        USA               1981
*Bubba Smith, Jackson Bostwick, Channing Mitchell*
A man is wrongly imprisoned in a satellite jail and plots his escape in this fantasy adventure.
FAN                             86 min Cut (28 sec)
B,V                                        SAT; QUA

## ESCAPE FROM EL DIABLO **
Gordon Hessler    SPAIN/UK/USA           1983
*John Ethan Wayne, Patrick Mower, Suzanne Danielle, Jimmy McNichol*
Adventure set against the background of an American youngster imprisoned in a Mexican fortress, and telling of an attempt to rescue him. Fair.
A/AD                             86 min (ort 92 min)
B,V                                      ARCADE/VSP

## ESCAPE FROM GALAXY 3 *
Ben Norman               ITALY            1986
*Cheryl Buchanan, James Milton, Don Powell*
Story of a cosmic war and the struggle between the forces of good and evil in a distant galaxy. An unmemorable space opera.
FAN                                            85 min
B,V,V2                                      VCL/CBS

## ESCAPE FROM NEW YORK **                     15
John Carpenter           USA              1981
*Kurt Russell, Lee Van Cleef, Isaac Hayes, Ernest Borgnine, Donald Pleasence, Harry Dean Stanton, Adrienne Barbeau, Season Hubley*
In 1997 the island of Manhattan has been transformed into a maximum security prison with millions of inmates. The President's plane crashes there and a convicted felon is given the job of going in and rescuing him. A large-scale film of many ideas, but over-complex and excessively grim.
A/AD                            106 min; 95 min (CH5)
B,V,V2,LV       EHE; CH5 (VHS only); POLY (VHS
                                                only)

## ESCAPE FROM SOBIBOR ***                     15
Jack Gold
                 UK/USA/YUGOSLAVIA        1987
*Alan Arkin, Rutger Hauer, Joanna Pacula, Jack Shepherd, Emil Wolk, Harmut Becker, Kurt Raab, Patti Love, Sara Sugarman, Simon Gregor, Linal Haft, Jason Norman, Robert Gwilyn, Eli Nathenson, Eric P. Caspar, Hugo Bower*
Horrifyingly true story of the Nazi's inhumane treatment of Jews at a secluded death camp. Dspite the terrible odds, a number of emaciated prisoners successfully organised an escape resulting in the setting loose of over 600 inmates, some 320 actually getting to freedom. Based on two books and Blatt's as yet unpublished manuscript. The script is by Reginald Rose.
Boa: book by Richard Rashke/book Inferno In Sobibor by Stanislaw Szmajner/ book From The Ashes Of Sobibor by Thomas Blatt.
DRA                          142 min (ort 165 min) mTV
B,V                                            SONY

## ESCAPE FROM THE DARK ***                    U
Charles Jarrott          USA              1976
*Alastair Sim, Peter Barkworth, Susan Tebbs, Prunella Scales, Joe Gladwin, Maurice Colbourne, Andrew Harrison, Chloe Franks*
Three children in England at the turn of the century,

struggle to save pit ponies from the slaughterhouse in this effective family outing.
Aka: LITTLEST HORSE THIEVES, THE

| JUV | 104 min |
| B,V | WDV |

## ESCAPE FROM THE PLANET OF THE APES ** 15
Don Taylor     USA     1971
*Roddy McDowall, Kim Hunter, Bradford Dillman, Natalie Trundy, Eric Braeden, William Windom, Sal Mineo, Ricardo Montalban*
Third in the series has three of the apes travelling back in time to present day Los Angeles. Human hospitality turns sour however when it is revealed that one day the world will be ruled by apes. Fairly predictable and hampered by a few clumsy touches of humour.

| FAN | 97 min |
| V | CBS |

## ESCAPE IN THE SUN **
George Breakston     UK     1955
*John Bentley, Vera Fusek, Martin Boddey, Alan Tarlton*
Love triangle drama set in Kenya, with a millionaire taking his wife on an elephant hunt since he knows that she and their guide are lovers. Although he has planned to hunt them down, he foolishly allows them a head start and they turn the tables on him. A so-so variant on a theme explored in "The Hounds Of Zaroff".

| A/AD | 85 min |
| B,V | GVI L/A |

## ESCAPE TO ATHENA ** PG
George Pan Cosmatos     UK     1979
*Roger Moore, Telly Savalas, David Niven, Elliott Gould, Sonny Bono, Claudia Cardinale, Richard Roundtree, Stefanie Powers, William Holden, Anthony Valentine, Siegfried Rauch, Michael Sheard, Richard Wren, Philip Locke*
Allied POWs held on a Greek island plan their escape and the theft of some art treasures at the same time. Little more than a standard time-filler.

| WAR | 114 min (ort 125 min) |
| B,V | PRV L/A; CH5 |

## ESCAPE TO VICTORY * PG
John Huston     USA     1981
*Sylvester Stallone, Michael Caine, Max Von Sydow, Pele, Carole Laure, Daniel Massey, Bobby Moore*
Allied POWs in 1943 are tricked into playing football against a German side, but turn this encounter into a chance to escape. A long boring waste of film, watchable if only to appreciate Pele's footballing prowess.
Aka: VICTORY

| WAR | 116 min; 111 min (VCC) (ort 120 min) |
| B,V,V2,LV | GHV; VCC (VHS only) |

## ESCAPE TO WITCH MOUNTAIN *** U
John Hough     USA     1974
*Ray Milland, Eddie Albert, Kim Richards, Ike Eisenmann, Donald Pleasence*
Two children with strange powers try to discover the secret of their origin while being pursued by a millionaire who wants to use them for his own evil ends. A fine Disney fantasy slightly marred by poor scripting. Followed by RETURN FROM WITCH MOUNTAIN.
Boa: novel by Alexander Key.

| JUV | 97 min |
| B,V | WDV |

## ESCORT GIRLS * 18
Donovan Winter     UK     1974
*David Dixon, Maria O'Brien, Marika Mann, Gil Barber, Helen Christie, Richard Wren, David Brierly, James Hunter, Teresa Van Ross, Veronica Doran,*

*Brian Jackson, Barbara Wise*
A behind-the-scenes look at the escort business following the exploits of several of the girls. Another tired and dated attempt at titillation.

| A | 90 min (ort 101 min) |
| B,V | INT L/A |

## ESCORT GIRLS *** 18
John Hilbard     DENMARK     1976
*Ole Soltoft, Vivi Rau, Soren Stromberg, Karl Stegger, Annie Birgit Garde*
Sex farce. Promised a commission on any trade he can produce for his girlfriend's escort agency, Axel supplies girls to prospective clients of the design engineering firm he works for.
Aka: DANISH ESCORT GIRLS (PRI or SHEP); HOPLA PA SENGEKANTEN; JUMPIN' AT THE BEDSIDE

| A | 93 min (ort 101 min) Cut (4 sec in addition to film cuts) |
| V | PRI; VOV/DARK; SHEP |

## ESKIMO NELL * 18
Martin Campbell     UK     1974
*Michael Armstrong, Terence Edmond, Christopher Timothy, Roy Kinnear, Diane Langton, Gordon Tanner, Beth Porter, Richard Caldicott, Prudence Drage, Jeremy Hawke, Rosalind Knight, Katy Manning, Lloyd Lamble, Anna Quayle*
Smutty comedy about four different versions of an "Eskimo Nell" film, being made to trick those who have provided the finances for the film. A mediocre offering.

| COM | 82 min (ort 85 min) |
| B,V | MOV L/A; SHEP |

## ESPIONAGE ** 18
Alan Smithee (Ramzi Thomas)
    USA     1988
*Ben Masters, Elyssa Davalos*
A former FBI agent comes out of hiding to save his father's chateau in the South of France. However, his action reveals him to enemies determined to assassinate him. Standard espionage thriller.

| THR | 80 min |
| B,V | TGP |

## ETERNAL EVIL ** 18
George Mihalka     CANADA     1985
*Karen Black, Winston Rekert, Patty Talbot, Andrew Bednarski, Vlasta Vrana, John Novak, Tom Rack, Joanne Cote, Bronwen Booth, Philip Spensley, Ron Lea, Len Watt, Anthony Sherwood, Walter Massey, Roger Garand, Dean Hagopian*
A young television director finds that his life has become rather humdrum. However, when he meets a devotee of the occult he learns the art of astral projection, but this gift soon propels him into a world of nightmarish encounters.
Aka: BLUE MAN, THE

| HOR | 81 min |
| B,V | VES |

## EUREKA ** 18
Nicholas Roeg     UK/USA     1983
*Gene Hackman, Rutger Hauer, Theresa Russell, Jane Lapotaire, Mickey Rourke, Ed Lauter, Joe Pesci, Helena Kallianiotes, Corin Redgrave, Cavan Kendall, Joe Spinell, Frank Peske, Michael Scott Addis, Norman Beaton, Emrys James*
Film based on the true tale of the unsolved murder of a rich gold prospector living on a Caribbean island. The melodramatic plot has personal problems, such as his daughter's affair with an adventurer, flung into the main story in which he watches his thirty-year-old empire collapse as thugs from Miami converge on him. An unusual foray for Roeg, whose flashy style keeps this one going even after one's interest in the characters has evaporated.

Boa: book Who Killed Sir Harry Oakes? by Marshall
Houts.
THR                                 124 min (ort 129 min) Cut
B,V                                                    WHV

## EUREKA STOCKADE **                                   PG
Rod Hardy            AUSTRALIA                          1983
*Bryan Brown, Brett Cullen, Penelope Stewart*
Remake of a 1948 film dealing with four Australian
gold prospectors who join forces to get rid of a despotic
governor, in the biggest uprising in Australia's his-
tory. Average.
DRA                                                204 min
B,V,V2                                               TEVP

## EUROPEANS, THE ***
James Ivory          UK                                1979
*Lee Remick, Robin Ellis, Wesley Addey, Tim Choate,*
*Lisa Eichhorn, Tim Woodward, Kristin Griffith*
A European baroness goes to Boston to see her cousins
and to find herself a husband in this tale set in the
1850s. An engaging period-piece, splendidly recreated
and photographed, but rather slow to develop.
Boa: novel by Henry James.
DRA                                  83 min (ort 90 min)
B,V                                                    PVG

## EVA **
Franci Slak          YUGOSLAVIA                        1982
*Pierre Clementi, Katya Berger, Miranda Caharija*
A beautiful woman discovers that she can use her
body to get what she wants in this well made but
rather forgettable story.
A                                                   86 min
B,V,V2                                              AVA/CBS

## EVASION ***                                           PG
Vince Edwards        USA                               1973
*Ben Gazzara, Richard Basehart, Sheree North, Kip*
*Niven, Laurette Sprang, Claire Brennan, Stewart*
*Raffill, Lou Farragher, Jerry Fitzpatrick*
Four holidaymakers have to contend with more than
their fair share of danger, from man-eating tigers set
on them by a deranged animal trainer, in this tense
thriller. Written and directed by Edwards.
Aka: MANEATER
Boa: story by Vince Edwards.
THR                           90 min; 69 min (EAG) mTV
B,V                                             FOX L/A; EAG

## EVASIVE PEACE **                                      PG
Melville Shavelson   USA                               1966
*Kirk Douglas, John Wayne, Frank Sinatra, Yul*
*Brynner, Senta Berger, Angie Dickinson, James*
*Donald, Chaim Topol, Luther Adler*
Biopic of Colonel Mickey Marcus of the US Army who
helped the newly formed State of Israel in her war of
independence. Good battle scenes but no real sense of
purpose or direction produce a film that wastes the
talents of its actors.
Aka: CAST A GIANT SHADOW
Boa: book by Ted Berkman.
WAR                                 131 min (ort 142 min)
B,V                                             AMBAS; KRP

## EVEN DWARFS STARTED SMALL *
Werner Herzog   WEST GERMANY                           1969
*Helmut Doring, Gerd Gickel*
A supposedly comic account of a failed revolution,
where all the roles are played by dwarfs. Not much of
a comedy but certainly a curiosity. See also THE
TERROR OF TINY TOWN.
COM                                                 96 min
B,V                                                    PVG

## EVERGREEN ***                                         PG
Fielder Carr         USA                               1984
*Lesley Anne Warren, Armand Assante, Ian McShane,*

Betty Buckley, Brian Dennehy, Robert Vaughn,
Patricia Barry, Ron Rifkin, Katherine Borowitz, Joan
Allen, Kate Burton, Tony Soper, Jan Triska, Mark
Keyloun, Cecile Callan
Saga that stretches over many years, and tells of a
Jewish woman who arrives in New York in 1909 and
proceeds to make her way in the world. A lush and
expensive effort, filmed in Toronto and Israel. The film
won Emmy Awards for art and set decoration.
Boa: novel by Belva Plain.
DRA                              285 min (3 cassettes) mTV
B,V                                             VFP L/A; HER

## EVERLASTING CHIVALRY **                               18
                    HONG KONG
*Meng Fei, Long Tiun Erl, Doris Chen*
Standard kung fu tale of honour, revenge and daring.
Average.
MAR                                                 91 min
B,V                                                    VTEL

## EVERY HOME SHOULD HAVE ONE *
James Clerk          UK                                1970
*Marty Feldman, Shelley Berman, Julie Ege, Patrick*
*Cargill, Jack Watson, Judy Cornwell, Patience Collier,*
*Penelope Keith, Dinsdale Landen, John McKelvey,*
*Sarah Bedel, Dave Dee, Hy Hazell, Judy Huxtable,*
*John Wells*
An ad-man is using sex to sell frozen porridge while
his wife has joined a clean-up TV campaign in this
dreary piece of smut. The script is by Marty Feldman.
Aka: THINK DIRTY
COM                                  90 min (ort 94 min)
B,V                                                    TEVP

## EVERY TIME WE SAY GOODBYE ***                         15
Moshe Mizrahi        ISRAEL                            1986
*Tom Hanks, Cristina Marsillach, Benedict Taylor,*
*Anat Atzmon, Gila Almagor*
A simple and straightforward romantic drama set in
Israel during WW2. This tells of an American officer
commissioned in the RAF and of his courtship of a
Jewish girl. As the son of a Protestant minister, he
finds his family set against the union, the film story
largely examining this clash of cultures. An engaging
but rather cliched film of charm if not inventiveness.
DRA                                                 94 min
B,V                                                    VES

## EVERY WHICH WAY BUT LOOSE **                          15
James Fargo          USA                               1978
*Clint Eastwood, Sondra Locke, Geoffrey Lewis, Ruth*
*Gordon, Beverly D'Angelo*
Simple-minded knockabout story of a Los Angeles
trucker who, after winning an orang-utan in a fight,
has further comic adventures with him. Followed by
ANY WHICH WAY YOU CAN.
Boa: novel by J.J. Kronberg.
COM                                 110 min (ort 114 min)
B,V                                                    WHV

## EVERYBODY'S ALL-AMERICAN **                           15
Taylor Hackford      USA                               1988
*Jessica Lange, Dennis Quaid, Timothy Hutton, John*
*Goodman, Carl Lumbly, Ray Baker, Savannah Smith*
*Boucher, Patricia Clarkson*
The 25-year-old marriage between two rather un-
appealing individuals: a beauty queen and a college
football player, is put under the microscope in this
contrived and shallow drama of little poignancy or
wit. A fine performance from Lange is all but wasted.
Boa: novel by Frank Deford.
DRA                                 121 min (ort 127 min)
V/sh                                                   WHV

## EVERYTHING GOES **                                    18
Georges Fleury       FRANCE                            1975
*Marilyn Gule, Charles Schreiner, Erica Cool,.*

*Elizabeth Buret*
A well-endowed married man finds himself unable to keep his hands off other women. Eventually he leaves his wife and goes off to live in a seedy hotel. After some persuasion his wife decides to become a swinger too, much to the disgust of the husband in a film whose lack of originality is more than made up for by a surfeit of sexual activity.

A 78 min (ort 95 min) Cut (12 min 19 sec)
V ELV; TAR

## EVERYTHING YOU ALWAYS WANTED TO KNOW ABOUT SEX (BUT WERE AFRAID TO ASK) *** 18
Woody Allen USA 1972
*Woody Allen, John Carradine, Lou Jacobi, Louise Lasser, Anthony Quayle, Lynn Redgrave, Tony Randall, Burt Reynolds, Gene Wilder, Meredith MacRae, Regis Philbin, Geoffrey Holder*
A very uneven series of sketches whose inspiration was a best-selling sex manual by Dr David Reuben. Each sketch is self-contained and purports to examine a particular aspect of sexuality, though all too often never rising above simple farce. Of the seven, Jacobi's contribution on transvestism and Wilder's on bestiality are the funniest.
COM 84 min
V WHV

## EVICTORS, THE * 18
Charles B. Pierce USA 1979
*Vic Morrow, Michael Parks, Jessica Harper, Sue Anne Langdon, Dennis Fimple, Bill Thurman*
Undistinguished haunted house of horror film in which a family move into their new house unaware (as usual) of just what's in store for them.
HOR 88 min (ort 92 min)
B,V ORION/RNK

## EVIL ALTAR ** 18
Jim Winburn USA 1987
*William Smith, Pepper Martin, Robert Z'dar, Teresa Cooney, John Powers*
An evil necromancer has made a pact with the Devil that will grant him immortality in return for the sacrifice of 103 lives. For years children visiting a small town have disappeared as sacrifices, and the time fast approaches when he will have fulfilled his bargain.
HOR 89 min Cut (3 sec)
B,V BRAVE

## EVIL BELOW, THE ** 15
Wayne Crawford USA 1989
*June Chadwick, Wayne Crawford, Ted LePlatt, Graham Clarke, Brian O'Shaunessy*
A man and woman set out to recover treasure on board a sunken wreck, but their operation disturbs an evil force.
HOR 90 min
V CINE

## EVIL COME EVIL GO * 
Walt Davis USA
*Cleo O'Hara, Sandra Henderson, Gerard Broulard, Jacqueline Lisette, Gina Dair, Jane Louise, Margot Deuletian*
An apparently Godfearing woman embarks on a religious mission aimed at redeeming "sinners", and with the help of a female assistant seduces and then murders a succession of men. The script is by Davis.
HOR 72 min
B,V VPD

## EVIL DEAD, THE ** 18
Sam M. Rami USA 1980 (released 1983)
*Bruce Campbell, Ellen Sandweiss, Sarah York, Betsy Baker, Hal Delrich*
Five college students on holiday in the backwoods of Tennessee release the spirits of the dead who proceed to take over the bodies of the living, resulting in the students turning into hideous killers. A wild over-the-top horror yarn with lashings of gore, best appreciated by those with very strong stomachs. Followed by EVIL DEAD 2.
HOR 90 min
B,V PVG; PAL (VHS only)

## EVIL DEAD 2 ** 18
Sam M. Raimi USA 1987
*Bruce Campbell, Sarah Berry, Dan Hicks, Kassie Wesley, Theodore Raimi, Denise Bixler, Richard Domeier*
A sequel to THE EVIL DEAD, which is the continuing story of one man's efforts to defeat these gruesome creatures who haunt the cabin in the woods and take possession of those that enter it. Much the same formula as the original film, with no shortage of gore and special effects.
HOR 81 min (ort 85 min) (Cut at film release by 2 sec)
B,V PAL

## EVIL IN CLEAR RIVER ** PG
Karen Arthur USA 1987
*Randy Quaid, Lindsay Wagner, Michael Flynn, Thomas Wilson Brown, Stephanie Dees, Carolyn Croft*
Fictionalised drama that follows the exploits of a real-life small-town housewife in Canada who discovers that her hockey star son is being taught to hate by an anti-Semitic history teacher he reveres. Quaid is good as the bigoted teacher who is also the hockey coach and town's mayor but this overwrought drama has a cliched and unimaginative script. See also SCANDAL IN A SMALL TOWN.
DRA 94 min mTV
B,V SONY

## EVIL SENSES ** 18
Gabrielle Lavia ITALY 1987
*Gabrielle Lavia, Monica Guerritore*
A professional killer makes a serious mistake when he steals his victim's brief case and finds it to contain sensitive documents and details of blackmail victims. From this moment he finds himself in danger from gangsters who have decided he must be eliminated.
THR 95 min
B,V AVA

## EVIL THAT MEN DO, THE * 18
J. Lee Thompson USA 1984
*Charles Bronson, Theresa Saldana, Joseph Maher, Jose Ferrer, Rene Enriquez, John Glover, Raymond St Jacques, Antoinette Bower*
A professional assassin is brought out of retirement for one last job, to kill a sadistic torturer holed-up in a fortress somewhere in Latin America. A standard Bronson offering with the star beginning to show his age.
Boa: novel by R.L. Hill.
THR 85 min (ort 89 min) Cut (10 sec in addition to film cuts)
B,V,V2 PRV L/A; HER; CH5 (VHS only)

## EVIL TOWN ** 18
Edward Collins/Peter S. Traynor/Larry Spiegel USA 1977
*James Keach, Dean Jagger, Robert Walker, Michele Marsh, Scott Hunter, Doria Cook*
A mad doctor has created an army of zombies and taken over an entire town, in this formula zombie horror yarn.
HOR 81 min (ort 88 min)
B,V MOG

## EVIL UNDER THE SUN * PG
Guy Hamilton UK 1982
*Peter Ustinov, Jane Birkin, Colin Blakely, Roddy McDowall, James Mason, Nicholas Clay, Sylvia Miles,*

*Dennis Quilley, Diana Rigg, Maggie Smith, Emily Hone, John Alderson, Paul Antrim, Cyril Conway, Barbara Hicks*
Another ponderous adaptation of an Agatha Christie murder mystery, this time set in a resort hotel. Glossy and undeniably well put together but excruciatingly dull. The script is by Anthony Shaffer.
Boa: novel by Agatha Christie.

| DRA | 111 min (ort 117 min) |
| B,V,V2 | TEVP; WHV (VHS only) |

**EVIL, THE \*\***                                    18
Gus Trikonis          USA          1978
*Richard Crenna, Joanna Pettet, Andrew Prine, Victor Buono, Mary Louise Weller, Robert Viharo, Milton Selzer*
A doctor rents a crumbling mansion to use as a clinic, but finds that he and his colleagues are terrorised by the powers that inhabit it. A low-budget film that moves slowly and delivers a few chills.
Aka: CRY DEMON; FORCE BEYOND, THE; HOUSE OF EVIL

| HOR | 96 min |
| B,V | VFO L/A; MKR |

**EVILSPEAK \***                                    18
Eric Weston          USA          1982
*Clint Howard, R.G. Armstrong, Joseph Cortese, Charles Tyner, Lynn Hancock, Don Stark, Lou Gravance, Claude Earl Jones, Haywood Nelson, Lauren Lester*
A victim of bullying at a US military academy finds a way of getting even with his tormentors with the aid of a computer and some black magic, when he stumbles on a secret temple beneath the academy chapel. Unlikely to be available in an uncut form in the UK.

| HOR | 89 min; 96 min (APX) Cut (3 min 34 sec). |
| B,V | VSP L/A; APX |

**EWOKS: THE BATTLE FOR ENDOR \*\***                 U
Jim Wheat/Ken Wheat  USA          1986
*A. Wilford Brimley, Warwick Davis, Aubree Miller, Sian Phillips, Carel Struycken, Niki Bothelo, Erick Walker, Marianne Horine, Daniel Frishman, Tony Cox, Pam Grizz, Roger Johnson, Johnny Weissmuller Jr*
An expensive, flashy but unsatisfying sequel to CARAVAN OF COURAGE: AN EWOK ADVENTURE, telling of an old hermit who joins a girl and her Ewok pal in a quest to rescue an Ewok family held captive by an evil king. Average.
Boa: story by George Lucas.

| JUV | 93 min mTV |
| B,V | MGM |

**EXCALIBUR \*\*\***                                 15
John Boorman         UK/USA        1981
*Nicol Williamson, Nigel Terry, Helen Mirren, Nicholas Clay, Cherie Lunghi, Corin Redgrave, Paul Geoffrey*
Colourful version of the legend of King Arthur that concentrates on visual imagery to the exclusion of nearly everything else. Williamson gives a strange offbeat performance as Merlin that is probably the best thing in the film. Much of the visual impact will be lost on the small screen.
Boa: poem Le Morte d'Arthur by Thomas Malory.

| DRA | 140 min |
| B,V,V2 | WHV |

**EXECUTION, THE \*\***                              PG
Paul Wendkos         USA          1984
*Loretta Swit, Rip Torn, Jessica Walter, Barbara Barrie, Sandy Dennis, Peter White, Valerie Harper, Martin E. Brooks, Michael Lerner, Allan Miller, Alan Oppenheimer, John Randolph, Robert Hooks, Rita Zohar, Jared Barclay*

Five female survivors of the Birkenau death-camp now living in L.A. discover that the camp doctor who tormented them is also living there, working as a successful restaurateur. As he served only a year for his crimes, they decide to exact their own revenge. A cheap, exploitative film that's as unconvincing as the actresses' accents.
Boa: novel by Oliver Crawford.

| DRA | 89 min mTV |
| B,V | VIPCO L/A; HER |

**EXECUTIONER, THE \***                             PG
Sam Wanamaker        UK           1970
*Joan Collins, George Peppard, Judy Geeson, Oscar Homolka, Charles Gray, Nigel Patrick, Keith Michell, George Baker, Alexander Scourby, Peter Bull, Peter Dyneley*
A British spy suspects his colleague of being a double agent in this lacklustre formula espionager.

| THR | 106 min (ort 111 min) |
| B,V | RCA |

**EXECUTIONER, THE \***                             18
James Bryant         USA          1984
*Christopher Mitchum, Aldo Ray, Renee Harmon, Antoine John Mottet, Jim Dratfield, Dan Bradley*
Urban drama set in Los Angeles when two Vietnam veterans return and end up on opposite sides of the law and homicide cop Mitchum now has the task of hunting down a vigilante murderer. A trashy film, badly acted and directed and bearing no relation to the 1970 Sam Wanamaker film.
Aka: EXECUTIONER 2; EXECUTIONER, PART 2

| THR | 105 min |
| B,V | 21ST L/A; APX; SCAN |

**EXECUTIONER, THE \*\***                            18
Duke Mitchell        USA          1978
*Dominic Miceli, Vic Caesar, John Strong, Jim Williams*
The grim tale of a bloody feud that erupts between rival factions of the Mafia. Based on a true story and something of an exercise in violence and gore.

| A/AD | 90 min |
| B,V | TGP |

**EXECUTIONER, THE \*\***
Luigi Capuano        ITALY         1963
*Lex Barker, Guy Madison, Sandra Panaro*
An unmemorable historical costume drama.
Aka: EXECUTIONER OF VENICE, THE; IL BOIA DI VENEZIA

| DRA | 84 min (ort 90 min) |
| B,V | HEL L/A; MEV |

**EXECUTIONERS FROM SHAOLIN \*\***                   15
Liu Chia-Ling        HONG KONG     1977
*Chen Kuan-Tai, Lo Lieh, Wang Yue, Lily Li, Cheng Kang Yeh, Tien Ching*
Monks are besieged by troops loyal to a despot, and when a young man's father is killed he swears to have his revenge.

| MAR | 100 min Cut (27 sec) |
| V | WHV |

**EXECUTIONER'S SONG, THE \*\*\***
Lawrence Schiller    USA          1982
*Tommy Lee Jones, Rosanna Arquette, Eli Wallach, Christine Lahti, Jordan Clark, Steven Keats, Richard Venture, Michael LeClair, Walter Olkewicz, Pat Curley, Jenny Wright, Grace Zabriskie, Pat Corley, Mark Gregory*
The true story of convicted murderer Gary Gilmore and his fight to get the State of Utah to carry out his death sentence. This exploitative drama, with a screenplay by Mailer from his book, looks largely at the character of Gilmore and at the legal complexities

that stood in the way of his wish to face execution and thus end his incarceration. Jones is electrifying in a dull and downbeat documentary-style story.
Boa: book by Norman Mailer.
DRA 200 min mTV
V PVG

### EXECUTIVE ACTION *
David Miller     USA     PG 1973
Burt Lancaster, Robert Ryan, Will Geer, John Anderson, Gilbert Green
An attempt to explain the events that led up to the assassination of John F. Kennedy with the writers of the book on which the film is based attempting to demonstrate that the president was assassinated by a powerful clique that included high-ranking CIA operatives. Painfully slow and boring, this was Ryan's last film.
Boa: book Rush To Judgement by Donald Freed and Mark Lane.
DRA 91 min
B,V WHV

### EXILE **
David Greenwalt     USA     15 1989
Corey Feldman, Chris Lawford, Mike Preston
The story of a group of American students who find themselves stranded on a remote South Pacific island with neither supplies nor a means of escaping.
A/AD 86 min
V BUENA

### EXIT THE DRAGON, ENTER THE TIGER *
Lee Tse Nam     HONG KONG     1976
Bruce Li (Ho Tsung-Tao), Loong Fei, San Moo
A martial arts teacher sets out to discover the truth about the death of Bruce Lee, in this tedious formula spin-off.
MAR 84 min
B,V VPD

### EXODUS **
Otto Preminger     USA     PG 1960
Paul Newman, Eva Marie Saint, Sal Mineo, Ralph Richardson, Lee J. Cobb, Hugh Griffith, Peter Lawford, John Derek, Jill Haworth, Gregory Ratoff, Felix Aylmer, David Opatoshu, Alexander Stewart, Martin Benson, Martin Miller
Overlong and strangely lifeless account of the events that led up to the founding of the modern state of Israel. The film rapidly degenerates into an episodic series of clashes, with Newman and Saint utterly miscast and the supporting actors merely providing stereotyped portrayals. AA: Score (Ernest Gold).
Boa: novel by Leon Uris.
DRA 213 min
B,V WHV

### EXORCISM **
Juan Bosch     SPAIN     1974
Maria Perschy, Paul Naschy (Jacinto Molina), Maria Kosti, Grace Mills, Jorge Torras, Marta Avile, Roger Leveder
The beautiful daughter of an aristocrat is anxious for new thrills and dabbles in black magic with the usual results.
Aka: EXORCISMO
HOR 86 min dubbed
B,V,V2 VPD

### EXORCIST 2: THE HERETIC *
John Boorman     USA     18 1977
Linda Blair, Max Von Sydow, Richard Burton, Louise Fletcher, Paul Henreid, James Earl Jones, Kitty Winn, Ned Beatty
Sequel to the 1973 film which falls quite flat despite good special effects. In this one Burton plays a priest out to discover the mystery of the demons that still inhabit Blair.

Aka: HERETIC, THE
HOR 98 min (ort 117 min)
V WHV

### EXORCIST 3, THE: CRIES AND SHADOWS **  18
Frank C. Lucas (Elo Pannaccio)
    ITALY     1975
Richard Conte, Francoise Prevost, Jean-Claude Verne, Mimma Monticeli, Elena Svevo, Sonia Viviami, Patrizia Gori
Routine rip-off of THE EXORCIST with a nun having to help her brother who has become possessed.
Aka: L'ESORCISTA N.2; NAKED EXORCISM (IFS); UN URLO DALLE TENEBRA
HOR 84 min (ort 88 min)
B,V IFS; HBL; HILL

### EXPECTATIONS **  R18
Arvid Beller     USA
Desiree West, Delania Ruffino, Suzette Holland, Joey Civera, Suzanne Wright, Jack Wright
Thinly plotted story of a group of women who exchange both apartments and lovers and enjoy a succession of encounters.
A 56 min Cut (46 sec)
B,V EVI; PRI; VEXCEL

### EXPENDABLES, THE **  18
Cirio H. Santiago     1988
Anthony Finetti, Peter Nelson, Loren Haynes, William Steis, Kevin Duffis
Another assembly-line B-movie set in war-torn Southeast Asia, where a new battalion of raw recruits lacking battle experience is sent on a suicide-mission behind enemy lines. A film of ample action but little else.
A/AD 86 min
V CINE

### EXPERTS, THE *  15
Dave Thomas     USA     1987 (released 1989)
John Travolta, Ayre Gross, Charles Martin Sheen, Kelly Preston, Deborah Foreman, James Keach, Jan Rubes, Brian Doyle Murray, Rich Ducommun
This tepid comedy, has two cool New Yorkers supposedly being hired to open a nightclub in a small Nebraska town. In reality, they are abducted to the USSR where they arrive at a Soviet copy of a typical American town, the intention being to use their "expertise" in the training of spies. A flimsy and sentimental mess, as silly as it is contrived. Filmed in Canada.
COM 89 min
V CIC

### EXPLORERS **  U
Joe Dante     USA     1985
Ethan Hawke, River Phoenix, Jason Presson, Amanda Peterson, Dick Miller, Robert Picardo, Mary Kay Place
Three children go on a fantastic adventure in a home-made spaceship, courtesy of their genius chum. An excellent beginning is sadly thrown away as the film degenerates into a mere spoof, with our kids encountering an alien civilisation who have based their culture on intercepted TV programmes.
FAN 105 min (ort 109 min)
B,V CIC

### EXPLOSION *  15
Jules Bricken     CANADA     1969
Richard Conte, Don Stroud, Cec Linder, Gordon Thomson, Michele Chicoine, Robin Ward, Sherry Mitchell, Olga Kaya, Murray Matheson, Ann Sears, Lloyd Berry, Ted Stidder, Bud Browning, William Buckingham, Barney O'Sullivan
Two Vietnam draft-dodgers in Canada get drawn into a life of violent crime in this ponderous and pointless melodrama.
A/AD 92 min (ort 96 min) Cut (11 sec)
B,V TWE; VPD

## EXPOSE ***
James Kenelm Clarke  UK  1975
*Udo Kier, Linda Hayden, Fiona Richmond, Patsy Smart, Vic Armstrong, Karl Howman, Sydney Knight*
A wealthy and egotistical author, having made a fortune from his first novel, hires a girl to work as his typist while he produces his second book at his remote country estate. It transpires however, that he never wrote the first book and the girl is the true author's widow and plans to revenge her husband. A low-budget mixture of horror and sex, incoherent but absorbing. Unlikely to be available in an uncut form in the UK.
Aka: HOUSE ON STRAW HILL, THE; TRAUMA
A  86 min (ort 117 min)
B,V,V2  INT/CBS

## EXPOSE ME LOVELY ***
Armand Weston  USA  R18 1976
*Jennifer Welles, Ras Kean, Cary Lacy, Katherine Burgess, Annie Sprinkles, Bobby Astyr, Jody Maxwell, Iminu, Eve Adams*
A private detective is hired by a wealthy woman to find her brother. As he pursues the clues leading to the missing brother he enjoys a variety of encounters but becomes involved in a deepening mystery. The search finally takes him back to his ex-wife where he finds the answer to the disappearance in a carefully thought out and absorbing adult mystery.
A  90 min
B,V  TCX

## EXPOSE ME NOW ***
Joe Sherman  USA  1982
*Danielle Martin, Herschel Savage, Ron Jeremy, Angel Burgon, Lynx Cannon, Richard Pacheco, Paul Thomas*
Abel is a bad guy whilst his brother, Shane is not. Their rich uncle dies, leaving his entire estate to Shane on the condition that he devotes his evenings from 6.00 to 9.00 to good deeds. Whilst Shane is out and about spreading happiness, Abel hires some women to sell their uncle's mansion out from under his brother. But his plot fails and this silly but likeable tale concludes with our brothers both married and friends once more.
Osca: CHINA GIRL (asa)
A  75 min
B,V  HAR

## EXPOSED *
James Toback  USA  15 1983
*Nastassia Kinski, Rudolph Nureyev, Harvey Keitel, Ian McShane, Bibi Andersson, Ron Randell, Pierre Clementi, James Russo*
A girl from the American Midwest leaves home for New York where she gets a job as a model, and then becomes involved in a strange struggle between a terrorist group and their opponents. A difficult film to follow, it looks like several movies rolled into one, but none of them are worth watching.
THR  96 min (ort 100 min)
B,V  WHV

## EXPOSED **
Jeffrey Fairbanks  USA  1980
*John Leslie, Shirley Woods, Georgina Spelvin, Kitty Shayne, Jon Martin, Lynn Lucan, Kelly Stuart, Sharon Cain*
A male porno star quits the business when he gets married but is blackmailed into making one last sex film.
A  86 min
B,V  ROXY

## EXPRESSO BONGO ***
Val Guest  UK  PG 1959
*Laurence Harvey, Sylvia Syms, Cliff Richard, Yolande Donlan, Meier Tzelniker, Ambrosine Philpotts, Eric Pohlmann, Gilbert Harding, Hermione Baddeley, Reginald Beckwith, Wilfrid Lawson, Martin Miller, Kenneth Griffith*
The story of an over-ambitious talent agent who tries to exploit his latest discovery and make him into a star. Harvey gives a vigorous performance as a Soho hustler and Tzelniker as the agent is also good but an attempt to capture the sleazy suide of Soho does not convince. Worth watching anyhow.
Boa: play by Wolf Mankowitz.
DRA  101 min (ort 109 min) B/W
B,V  VDM L/A; VMA; STABL

## EXTERMINATOR, THE ***  18
James Glickenhaus  USA  1980
*Robert Ginty, Christopher George, Samantha Eggar, Steve James, Tony Di Benedetto*
Two Vietnam veterans, one black and one white, work in a warehouse. One is deliberately paralysed in revenge after he foils a robbery attempt by some local thugs. After dealing with the gang his buddy decides to become a lone vigilante and clean up the city. A tough, violent and uncompromising film with a stomach-churning opening sequence that will not survive the UK censor. Followed by a sequel.
DRA  90 min (ort 101 min) Cut (2 min 54 sec in addition to film cuts)
B,V,V2,LV  INT/CBS L/A; MAST (VHS only)

## EXTERMINATOR 2 *  18
Mark Buntzman  USA  1985
*Robert Ginty, Deborah Geffner, Mario Van Peebles, Frankie Faison, Scott Randolph*
A sequel to the first film with a similar theme as our vigilante goes back into action, complete with blowtorch. Low-grade rubbish with none of the believable characterisation that was present in the first film.
A/AD  83 min (ort 88 min)
B,V  GHV; VCC (VHS only)

## EXTERMINATORS OF THE YEAR 3000, THE *  18
Jules Harrison  ITALY/SPAIN  1983
*Alan Collins, Beryl Cunningham, Robert Jannucci, Luca Venantini, Fred Harris*
In a post-WW3 world, desperate groups of survivors look for water while fighting off evil marauding gangs. Yet another offering on this tired old theme, with no new insights or ideas.
FAN  87 min (ort 90 min) Cut (8 sec)
B,V,V2  MED

## EXTRA GIRL, THE **
Mack Sennett  USA  1923
*Mabel Normand, Max Davidson, Ralph Graves, George Nicholls*
A girl from a small town wins a beauty contest through a misunderstanding and goes off to Hollywood. A minor comedy with the star in good form.
COM  65 min B/W silent
B,V  SPEC/POLY

## EXTRA TERRESTRIAL VISITORS **  15
Juan Piquer Simon  SPAIN  1983
*William Anton, Oscar Martin, Ian Sera, Nina Ferrer, Emil Linder, Concha Cuetos, M. Pereiro, Frank Brana, Susi Blasques*
Aliens land in a mountainous region in the USA and kill three hunters whose bodies they take over in this low-budget science fiction yarn.
Aka: LOS NUEVOS EXTRA TERRESTRES
FAN  80 min
B,V  AVR

## EXTREME CLOSE-UP ****  18
Charles De Sante  USA  1981
*Gloria Leonard, John C. Holmes, Jamie Gillis, Felania Raffino, Denise Deneuve, Diane Deneuve*
A beautiful writer travels to France to visit a woman famed for producing bizarre sado-erotic photographs. Despite being happily married she quickly falls under

the spell of the erotic environment in which she finds herself and embarks on an affair with the woman's lover. Finally, she returns home more than a little confused in this exceptionally well made and sophisticated story. Cut before video submission by 22 min 24 sec.

A                                  39 min (ort 80 min) Cut
B,V     TCX L/A; 18PLAT/TOW L/A; NET; EVI; SHEP

### EXTREME PREJUDICE **                    18
Walter Hill            USA                 1986
*Nick Nolte, Powers Boothe, Maria Conchita Alonso, Michael Ironside, Clancy Brown, Rip Torn, William Forsythe, Matt Mulhern, Larry B. Scott, Dan Tullis Jr*
A tough Texas ranger stands on one side of the border and aims to clean up the drugs traffic from Mexico. On the other side is a former boyhood friend who's now a ruthless narcotics dealer. Nolte as the ranger decides to go after him in a film of excesses – excesses of characterisation, of violence and of music. A few tongue-in-cheek touches make it more bearable but the plot – the work of four screenwriters, suffers badly from over-complexity.
A/AD                               100 min (ort 104 min)
V/sh                                       GHV

### EXTREMITIES *                            18
Robert M. Young        USA                 1986
*Farrah Fawcett, James Russo, Diana Scarwid, Alfred Woodard, Sandy Martin*
A woman menaced by a rapist manages to turn the tables on him and gain the upper hand when she traps him in her own home. Fawcett is no more than adequate in this clumsy drama. Adapted by Mastrosimone from his play.
Boa: play by William Mastrosimone.
DRA                                        90 min
B,V                                         EIV

### EYE FOR AN EYE, AN **                    18
Steve Carver           USA                 1981
*Chuck Norris, Christopher Lee, Richard Roundtree, Mako, Terry Kiser*
An ex-cop mounts a one-man vendetta against the drug peddlars who killed his partner and his girlfriend, making use of his skill in the martial arts for this purpose. A predictable revenger – short on acting but long on fisticuffs.
A/AD                               106 min; 100 min (CH5)
B,V,V2,LV        WOV L/A; EHE; CH5 (VHS only)

### EYE OF THE EAGLE *                       18
Cirio H. Santiago                          1987
*Brett Clark, Robert Patrick, William Steis, Nick Nicholson, David Light*
Vietnam actioner, in which a group of renegade soldiers become involved in a cover-up, when they shoot a GI who sees them terrorise a small village. However, they find themselves having to deal with his brother, who has been sent to Vietnam, as the leader of a squad given the task of blowing up a bridge. Mindless, tedious violence, with banal dialogue and worse acting. Filmed in the Philippines.
WAR                                82 min Cut (8 sec)
B,V                                        CBS

### EYE OF THE EAGLE 2 **                    18
Carl Franklin          USA                 1988
*William Field, Andy Wood, Ken Jacobson, Ronald Lawrence*
Vietnam action tale with one soldier, the only survivor of an ambush in a Vietnamese village being helped by a beautiful refugee. When a rogue major kidnaps her for prostitution he decides to rescue her and settle his score with the officer at the same time.
Aka: EYE OF THE EAGLE 2: INSIDE THE ENEMY; KIA
A/AD                                       75 min
V                                          RCA

### EYE OF THE NEEDLE ***                    15
Richard Marquand       UK                  1981
*Donald Sutherland, Kate Nelligan, Ian Bannen, Christopher Cazenove, Philip Martin Brown, George Belpin, Faith Brook, George Lee, Arthur Lovegrove, Colin Rix, Barbara Ewing, Patrick Connor, Rupert Frazer, Alex McCrindle*
A German agent on a mission in Britain in 1940, plays a cat-and-mouse game with a lonely woman on a Scottish island in this gripping thriller.
Boa: novel by Ken Follett.
THR                               108 min (ort 112 min)
B,V                                        WHV

### EYE OF THE TIGER **                      18
Richard Sarafian       USA                 1986
*Gary Busey, Yaphet Kotto, Seymour Cassel, William Smith, Kimberlin, Ann Brown, Bert Ramsen, Denise Galik, Judith Barsi*
Busey plays a Vietnam veteran who clashes with a violent motorcycle gang when they invade his town and sadistically murder his wife. In a one-man bid to wipe them out, he attacks their secret desert hide-out at the wheel of a powerful, customised truck. DEATH-WISH meets DUEL in this average actioner of blood and gore.
DRA                                        88 min
V/sh                                       MED

### EYE ON THE SPARROW ***                   PG
John Korty             USA                 1987
*Keith Carradine, Mare Winningham, Sandy McPeak, Kaaren Lee, Conchata Ferrell, Bianca Rose*
The story of a blind couple whose desire to adopt is opposed by bureaucratic red tape. Carradine and Winningham give nice dignified portrayals of this real-life couple whose fight against discrimination of the handicapped was the inspiration for the film. Written by Barbara Turner.
DRA                               96 min (104 min) mTV
V                                          VIR

### EYES BEHIND THE STARS *
Roy Garett (Mario Gariazzo)
                       ITALY               1977
*Robert Hoffman, Nathalie Delon, Martin Balsam*
A ludicrous attempt at a fantasy mystery. The alien menace is never clearly defined and the film gradually degenerates into a meaningless shoot-out.
Aka: EYES BEYOND THE STARS; OCCHI D'ALLE STELLE
FAN                                        90 min
B,V                                     INT/CBS

### EYES OF A STRANGER, THE *                18
Ken Wiederhorn         USA                 1981
*Lauren Tewes, John DiSanti, Jennifer Jason Leigh, Peter DuPre, Gwen Lewis*
Usual story of a psycho who attacks and kills women, but in the end gets his just deserts when Tewes tracks him down. Gory trash.
THR   80 min (ort 85 min) Cut (Cut at film release by 1 min 25 sec)
B,V                                        WHV

### EYES OF FIRE **                          18
Avery Crounse          USA                 1984
*Dennis Lipscomb, Rebecca Stanley, Sally Klein, Fran Ryan, Rob Paulsen, Guy Boyd*
People living in an isolated valley are terrorised by evil forces in this unusual tale set on the American frontier during the 18th century. The effects heavily outweigh the story.
Aka: CRYING BLUE SKY
HOR                               86 min; 81 min (VCC)
B,V                               IVS; VCC (VHS only)

### EYES OF LAURA MARS, THE **               15
Irvin Kershner         USA                 1978

Faye Dunaway, Tommy Lee Jones, Brad Dourif, Rene
Auberjonois, Raul Julia, Frank Adonis, Michael
Tucker
A fashion photographer seems to have a bizarre
ability to predict the future and forsees some grisly
murders. A detective investigates. Co-written by John
Carpenter. What tension there is is dissipated by a
series of silly red herrings and a stupid ending.

| THR | 99 min |
|-----|--------|
| V | RCA |

## EYES OF THE DRAGON **
USA                              1981
Christopher Mitchum
A US agent must find a missing Soviet scientist who
has a formula that could alter the balance of world
power in this routine thriller.

| THR | 80 min |
|-----|--------|
| B,V | HVH |

## EYES WITHOUT A FACE ***
George Franju      FRANCE/ITALY            1959
Pierre Brasseur, Alida Valli, Edith Scob, Francois
Guerin
A mad surgeon murders young girls in an attempt to
repair the face of his daughter who was mutilated in a
car accident. An unpleasant but undeniably powerful
horror yarn that over the years has achieved cult
status.
Aka: HORROR CHAMBER OF DR FAUSTUS; LES
YEUX SANS VISAGE

| HOR | 90 min B/W |
|-----|-----------|
| B,V | TEVP |

## EYEWITNESS **
John Hough          UK                    1970
Mark Lester, Lionel Jeffries, Susan George, Tony
Bonner, Jeremy Kemp, Peter Vaughan, Peter Bowles,
Betty Marsden, Anthony Stamboulish, John Allison,
Tom Eytle, Joseph Furst, Robert Russell, Maxine
Kalil, David Lodge, Jeremy Young
A young boy on a Mediterranean island is a witness to
a political murder but nobody will believe him
because of his habit of telling fanciful tales. A kind of
sub-Hitchcock thriller with all the usual cliches, but
quite well done.
Aka: SUDDEN TERROR
Boa: novel Eye-Witness by Mark Hebden.

| THR | 88 min (ort 91 min) |
|-----|---------------------|
| V | WHV |

## EYEWITNESS TO MURDER **                  18
Jag Mundhra                                1989
Sherilyn Wolter, Andrew Stevens, Adrian Zmed
An apparent eyewitness to a murder become a target
for the killers, who are unaware that their intended
victim has lost her sight and poses no threat to them.
An absorbing little thriller, slightly marred by an
unconvincing performance from the lead.

| THR | 82 min |
|-----|--------|
| V | RCA |

## F

## FABLES OF THE GREEN FOREST **           U
USA
Characters created by Thornton W. Burgess are
brought to life in this pleasant, animated feature.

| CAR | 43 min (ort 86 min) |
|-----|---------------------|
| V | JVC L/A; MARKET/GOV L/A; SAT |

## FABULOUS DORSEYS, THE *                  U
Alfred E. Green      USA                   1947
Tommy Dorsey, Jimmy Dorsey, Janet Blair, Paul
Whiteman, William Lundigan
Should have been retitled The Fighting Dorseys, for in
between songs that's what they do. Only the music

makes this flat biopic watchable. Songs include
"Marie" and "Green Eyes".

| MUS | 88 min; 84 min (DIAM) B/W |
|-----|--------------------------|
| B,V | MOV L/A; DIAM |

## FABULOUS BAKER BOYS, THE ***            15
Steve Kloves         USA                   1989
Jeff Bridges, Michelle Pfeiffer, Beau Bridges, Elie
Raab, Jennifer Tilly
Written by Kloves, this well-crafted tale explores the
formation of an unusual love triangle, when two
singing brothers hire a cynical hooker to act as
vocalist and spice up their act. However, she is both
the catalyst for their success and jealous rivalry. A
polished and confident directing debut for Kloves, this
romantic drama is atmospheric, detailed and simplistic, but Pfeiffer is ideally cast as the sexy singer.

| DRA | 109 min (ort 113 min) subH |
|-----|---------------------------|
| V | MGM |

## FACE OF FU MANCHU, THE **
Don Sharp            UK                     1965
Christopher Lee, Nigel Green, Tsai Chin, James
Robertson Justice, Howard Marion-Crawford,
Joachim Fuchsberger, Karin Dor, Walter Rilla, Harry
Brogan, Poulet Tu, Peter Mossbacher, Edwin Richfield
Story of a Chinese criminal mastermind who plots to
take over the world with the aid of poison gas. An
occasionally entertaining spoof set in the 1920s and
based on the character created by Sax Rohmer in the
1911 novel. "The Brides Of Fu Manchu" followed.

| THR | 96 min |
|-----|--------|
| B,V | TEVP |

## FADE TO BLACK *                          18
Vernon Zimmerman     USA                    1980
Tim Thomerson, Mickey Rourke, Dennis Christopher,
Linda Kerridge, Norman Burton, Morgan Paull,
Marya Small, Gwynne Gilford, James Luisi, Eve Brent
Ashe, John Steadman, Marcie Barkin
A film buff is unable to between distinguish film and
reality, and takes a terrible revenge on his enemies
whilst dressed in the clothes of his favourite cinema
villains. A great idea goes nowhere in this violent and
sterile film.

| HOR | 100 min; 98 min (PARA) |
|-----|------------------------|
| B,V,V2 | VPD; PARA (Betamax and VHS only) |

## FAIL SAFE ***                           PG
Sidney Lumet         USA                    1963
Henry Fonda, Dan O'Herlihy, Walter Matthau, Frank
Overton, Edward Binns, Fritz Weaver, Sorrell Brooke,
Larry Hagman, Dom DeLuise
A computer system designed to make it impossible for
a malfunction to start a nuclear attack malfunctions
itself. Because of unforeseen circumstances the un-
thinkable happens and Moscow is destroyed. The US
President is now faced with an appalling decision in
order to appease the Soviets and avoid WW3. A taut
drama that succeeds where other more ambitious
ventures would not. Written by Walter Bernstein.
Boa: novel by Eugene Burdick and Harvey Wheeler.

| DRA | 108 min B/W |
|-----|-------------|
| V | RCA |

## FAIR GAME *                             18
Mario Andreacchio  AUSTRALIA               1986
Cassandra Delaney, Peter Ford, Gary Who, David
Sandford
A woman living alone on a remote farm, takes a
gruesome revenge for the indignities she suffered at
the hands of a gang of crazed criminals in this squalid
exploiter.

| DRA | 81 min Cut (57 sec) |
|-----|---------------------|
| V | EHE |

## FAIR GAME **                            15
Mario Orfini         USA                    1988

*Trudie Styler, Gregg Henry*
A woman whose ex-husband is determined to punish
her for rejecting him, traps her in her house with a
deadly Black Mamba snake, in this tense but cliched
thriller.
THR                                          81 min
V                                             MED

**FAIR WIND TO JAVA ***                        PG
Joseph Kane          USA                       1952
*Fred MacMurray, Vera Ralston, Victor McLaglen,*
*Robert Douglas, Philip Ahn*
A sea captain goes on a hunt for jewels in the South
Seas with his mutinous crew in this pleasant adven-
ture. The highlight is a climactic volcano explosion.
Boa: novel by Garland Roark.
A/AD                            88 min (ort 92 min)
V                                             VCC

**FAKE OUT ***
Matt Cimber (Matteo Ottaviano)
                     USA                       1982
*Pia Zadora, Telly Savalas, Desi Arnaz Jr*
A gangster's moll is under pressure to testify against
him and a tough cop is assigned to protect her. An
inconsequential little melodrama.
DRA                             89 min (ort 96 min)
B,V                                          TEVP

**FALCON 7 ***                                  PG
Roy Thomas     HONG KONG                        1989
A space opera-style animation from the makers of
CAPTAIN COSMOS and THE COSMOS CON-
QUEROR. The Earth Defence Force must undertake a
perilous mission to save a planet and a missing
inventor from the ruthless Zoic Empire and its evil
Empress. Watchable but not especially well-mounted
or scripted.
CAR                                          63 min
V                                             VPD

**FALCON AND THE SNOWMAN, THE ***              15
John Schlesinger     USA                       1984
*Timothy Hutton, Sean Penn, David Suchet, Lori*
*Singer, Pat Hingle, Dorian Harewood, Mady Kaplan,*
*Richard Dysart, Chris Makepeace*
Based on true events, this tells of two young men who
became involved in spying for the Russians. An
intriguing film that unfortunately never really ex-
amines the inner motivations of the two characters,
though Penn's performance is outstanding.
Boa: book by Robert Lindsay.
DRA                            126 min (ort 131 min)
B,V           RNK; ORION/PVG; VIR (VHS only)

**FALL AND RISE OF REGINALD PERRIN, THE ** PG
John Howard Davies    UK              1976/1980
*Leonard Rossiter, Pauline Yates, John Barron*
Compilation of twenty 30 minute episodes of a TV
series, telling the story of a well-paid executive who
one day cracks up from boredom and drops out.
Rossiter is good in this compilation comedy but the
lack of material and the tendency to rely on the same
gags lets it down badly. Written by David Nobbs.
COM                      107 min (2 cassettes) mTV
B, V/h, LV                                    BBC

**FALL OF THE HOUSE OF USHER, THE ***          15
Roger Corman         USA                       1960
*Vincent Price, Mark Damon, Myrna Fahey, Harry*
*Ellerbe*
A Corman low-budget mangling of a fine Poe story
about an ancient house inhabited by a man who is the
last of his line. Dull, boring and cheap, all those things
that have given Corman cult status as a director.
Filmed twice before in 1928 and 1949 and made for TV
in 1978.
Aka: HOUSE OF USHER

Boa: short story by Edgar Allan Poe.
HOR                          85 min; 76 min (VCC)
B,V,V2              GHV; VCC (VHS only)

**FALL OF THE HOUSE OF USHER, THE ***          15
James L. Conway      USA                       1982
*Martin Landau, Robert Hays, Charlene Tilton, Ray*
*Walston, Dimitra Arliss, Peg Stewart*
The story of the mystery surrounding an ancient
house and family. The most well known was Corman's
1960 version but in fact this was filmed in 1928 and
1949 as well. This "Classics Illustrated" version is well
below average.
Boa: short story by Edgar Allan Poe.
HOR                         76 min (ort 95 min) mTV
B,V                            HOM L/A; VCC

**FALL OF THE ROMAN EMPIRE, THE ***             U
Anthony Mann         USA                       1964
*Alec Guinness, James Mason, Sophia Loren, Stephen*
*Boyd, John Ireland, Christopher Plummer, Anthony*
*Quayle, Mel Ferrer, Omar Sharif, Eric Porter*
Long-winded account of the events leading up to the
end of the Roman Empire chaos after the poisoning of
Emperor Aurelius by his mad son Commodus. A film
that starts off intelligently enough but degenerates
into a boring epic, only a parade of spectacular events
keeps us watching.
DRA                          178 min; 172 min (VCC)
B,V,V2,LV            INT/CBS; VCC (VHS only)

**FALLEN ANGEL ***                              15
Robert Michael Lewis    USA                    1981
*Richard Masur, Melinda Dillon, Dana Hill, Ronny*
*Cox, David Hayward, Virginia Kiser, Shelby*
*Leverington, Adam Gunn, Ron Joseph, David Rode,*
*Arthur Rosenberg, Sherrie Wills, Ed Call*
Unsavoury story of a child pornographer who lures
children into posing for him. Fairly mundane but
owing to the nature of the subject matter this one
received a huge rating on its first showing. Rather
surprisingly the film won an Emmy as Outstanding
Drama Special. Written by Lew Hunter.
DRA                         92 min (ort 100 min) mTV
B,V                                           RCA

**FALLEN IDOL, THE ***
Carol Reed           UK                        1948
*Ralph Richardson, Michele Morgan, Bobby Henrey,*
*Sonia Dresdel, Denis O'Dea, Jack Hawkins, Dora*
*Bryan, Walter Fitzgerald, Bernard Lee, Karel*
*Stepanek, Joan Young, Geoffrey Keen, James Hayter,*
*Dandy Nichols, George Woodbridge*
A small boy hero-worships his friend, a butler, and
lies to protect him when he is accused of murdering
his wife. Scripted by Graham Greene from a short
story by him.
Boa: short story The Basement Room by Graham
Greene.
DRA                          91 min (ort 94 min) B/W
B,V                                          TEVP

**FALLING IN LOVE ***                           PG
Ulu Grossbard        USA                       1984
*Robert De Niro, Meryl Streep, Jane Kaczmarek,*
*Harvey Keitel, Dianne Wiest, George Martin, David*
*Clennon, Victor Argo, Wiley Earl, Jesse Bradford,*
*Chevi Coltron, Richard Gizza, Frances Conroy, James*
*Ryan, Sonny Abagnale*
Two Long Island commuters who are both married,
meet and fall in love. A glossy, one-dimensional story
set in the comfortable world of professional people who
can afford to indulge their emotional whims to the
full. Not helped any by totally unsuitable and ulti-
mately irritating theme music.
DRA                            102 min (ort 106 min)
V                                             CIC

## FALLING IN LOVE AGAIN *  15
Steven Paul      USA      1980
*Elliott Gould, Susannah York, Michelle Pfeiffer, Stuart Paul, Kaye Ballard, Robert Hackman, Steven Paul*
A husband and wife experience trouble in their marriage when he is unable to stop idolising his youthful days in the Bronx. An inept and contrived feature debut for writer-actor-producer-director Paul.
DRA      103 min
B,V,V2      CBS; VGM (VHS only)

## FALSE WITNESS **  15
Arthur Allan Seidelman
     USA      1988
*Phylicia Rashad, Philip Michael Thomas*
When the hostess of a popular chat show is murdered, an investigator and his Assistant D.A. girlfriend set out to catch those responsible. However, this murder hunt puts their relationship under great strain. A standard thriller, scripted by Bill Driskill.
Boa: novel by Dorothy Uhnak.
THR      95 min
V      NWV

## FALSE WITNESS **  PG
Richard A. Colla      USA      1970
*George Kennedy, Anne Jackson, Eli Wallach, Steve Ihnat, Joan Tompkins, William Marshall, Joe Maross*
A terminally ill man plans to provide for his family after his death by pinning a murder on himself so that his family will collect the insurance money. However, his plans go awry in this fairly competent drama.
Aka: ZIGZAG
DRA      99 min (ort 105 min)
B,V      MGM

## FAME: THE MOVIE ***  15
Alan Parker      USA      1980
*Irene Cara, Lee Curreri, Eddie Barth, Laura Dean, Paul McCrane, Barry Miller, Gene Anthony Ray, Maureen Teefy, Antonio Franceschi, Anne Meara, Albert Hague*
A rather episodic look at the lives and loves of the students at New York's School for the Performing Arts. Despite vigorous performances from all concerned, the lack of any real story lets one's interest evaporate. A considerably better TV series followed. Written by Michael Gore. AA: Song ("Fame" – Michael Gore – music/Dean Pritchard – lyrics), Score (Orig) (Michael Gore).
Aka: FAME
MUS      128 min (ort 134 min)
V      MGM

## FAMILY AND HONOUR **  18
Meir Zarchi
*Joe Pesci, Jeannine Lemay, Jack Gurli, Peter Sapienza*
A man's one-night stand with an exotic dancer causes serious repercussions when he finds his wife and her relatives not taking too kindly to this extra-marital adventure.
DRA      86 min
B,V      AVA

## FAMILY BUSINESS ***  15
Sidney Lumet      USA      1989
*Sean Connery, Dustin Hoffman, Matthew Broderick, Rosana DeSoto, Janet Carroll, Victoria Jackson, Bill McCutcheon, Deborah Rush*
An unusual drama with three generations of crooks: a professional thief, his reformed son, and his bright and ambitious grandson. When the grandson decides to plan a perfect crime, he enlists the help of his grandfather in order to entice his father, from whom he is estranged, into the robbery. A clever drama, scripted by Patrick, and if not quite believable, sustained by a set of great performances from the leads.

Boa: novel by Vincent Patrick.
DRA      109 min (ort 115 min)
V      BRAVE/MGM

## FAMILY LIFE ***
Ken Loach      UK      1971
*Sandy Ratcliff, Bill Dean, Grace Cave, Malcolm Tierney, Hilary Martyn, Michael Riddall, Alan McNaughton, Johnny Gee, David Markham*
A brilliant but harrowing look at the gradual descent of a withdrawn young girl into madness. Both her parents and medical staff fail her, and their clumsy attempts to help only exacerbate her condition, her mental state at the end of the film having the horror of finality.
Aka: WEDNESDAY'S CHILD
Boa: play In Two Minds by David Mercer.
DRA      102 min (ort 108 min)
B.V      TEVP

## FAMILY PLOT ***  PG
Alfred Hitchcock      USA      1976
*Karen Black, Bruce Dern, William Devane, Barbara Harris, Ed Lauter, Cathleen Nesbitt, Katherine Helmond, Warren J. Kemmerling, Edith Atwater, William Prince, Nicholas Colasanto, Madge Redmond, John Lehne, Charles Tyner*
Hitchcock's last film is not one of his best although it shows a return to the tongue-in-cheek direction of his pre-war films. This is his 54th film and tells of a phoney medium and his girlfriend who are searching for a missing heir but become entangled with a sinister couple planning a kidnappping. A mildly entertaining film, but one in which credibility is stretched rather too far. Scripted by Ernest Lehman.
Boa: novel The Rainbird Pattern by Victor Canning.
THR      120 min
B,V      CIC

## FAMILY REUNION **  18
Michael Hawes      CANADA      1989
*Mel Novak, Pam Phillips, John Andes*
Forty years after he was rescued from the clutches of a murderous Satanic cult, a man finds himself and his family at risk once more.
HOR      85 min
V      BIGPIC

## FAMILY SECRETS **  PG
Jack Hofsiss      USA      1984
*Stefanie Powers, Maureen Stapleton, Melissa Gilbert, Gary Dontzig, Marion Ramsey, James Spader, Irene Tedrow, Kimmy Robertson, Gary Sinisie, Marlena Giovi*
Three generations of women in a family fall out when certain closely guarded secrets threaten to come out during a weekend together at the grandmother's house. Powers gives a nice performance as a hard-pressed advertising executive, unable to communicate with either mother or daughter in this otherwise forgettable drama.
Boa: story by Stefanie Powers.
DRA      120 min mTV
B,V      PRV

## FAMILY SINS ***  15
Jerrold Freedman      USA      1987
*James Farentino, Jill Eikenberry, Andrew Bednarski, Mimi Kuzyk, Brent Spiner, Michael Durrell, Tom Bower*
The study of a family crisis with strict father Farentino favouring one son over the others and thereby causing a tragedy. Good performances from both Farentino and Eikenberry as the mother.
DRA      93 min mTV
B,V      VIR

## FAMILY WAY, THE **  15
John Boulting/Roy Boulting

UK 1966
*Hywel Bennett, Hayley Mills, John Mills, Marjorie Rhodes, Wilfred Pickles, Murray Head, Barry Foster, Liz Fraser, Avril Angers, John Comer, Colin Gordon, Robin Parkinson, Andrew Bradford, Harry Locke, Thorley Walters*
Laboured British comedy-drama about the problems a pair of newlyweds face, not least being the fact that they are obliged to continue living in the boy's parents' house and that Bennett as the husband is suffering from impotence. A conspiracy of circumstances prevents consummation but by the time the husband does succeed one no longer cares. A film seen as controversial in its day may now be seen for what it really is: dull.
Boa: play Honeymoon Deferred (also known as All In Good Time) by Bill Naughton.
DRA 114 min
V WHV

## FAMILY-NESS, THE **
Uc
UK 1984
Compiled feature about a family of monsters who live in Loch Ness. Average.
CAR 58 min
B,V BBC

## FAMOUS FIVE: FIVE ARE TOGETHER AGAIN ** Uc
UK 1983
*Michelle Gallagher, Gary Russell, Marcus Harris, Jenny Thanisch, Toddy Woodgate, Michael Hinz, Sue Best*
Children's adventure based on an Enid Blyton book. When Quentin Kirrin and his wife are put into quarantine because of scarlet fever, the children are sent to stay with Professor Hayling and his son Tinker. Their adventures start with the arrival of a circus near the Professor's home and the theft of some notes from his study.
Boa: novel by Enid Blyton.
JUV 47 min mTV
V PICK; LNG

## FAMOUS FIVE: FIVE FALL INTO
Uc
## ADVENTURE **
UK 1983
*Michelle Gallagher, Gary Russell, Marcus Harris, Jenny Thanisch*
Another adventure in this series, with our kids finding themselves trapped after investigating some peculiar events and a strange theft. Average.
Boa: novel by Enid Blyton.
JUV 46 min mTV
V PICK

## FAMOUS FIVE: FIVE GET INTO TROUBLE ** Uc
UK 1983
*Michelle Gallagher, Gary Russell, Marcus Harris, Jenny Thanisch*
Our five kids are now on a cycling holiday, when they are joined by the son of wealthy parents and foil an attempt to kidnap their new friend. However, when one of the other kids is kidnapped by mistake, our young sleuths are obliged to mount a rescue.
Boa: novel by Enid Blyton.
JUV 48 min mTV
V PICK

## FAMOUS FIVE: FIVE GO DOWN TH THE SEA ** Uc
UK 1983
*Michelle Gallagher, Gary Russell, Marcus Harris, Jenny Thanisch, Toddy Woodgate, Michael Hinz, Sue Best*
Another adventure in this passable children's series based on the works of Enid Blyton.
Boa: novel by Enid Blyton.
JUV 44 min mTV
V PICK

## FAMOUS FIVE: FIVE GO TO MYSTERY MOOR/
## FIVE GO OFF TO CAMP **
Uc
UK 1983
*Michelle Gallagher, Gary Russell, Marcus Harris, Jenny Thanisch, Toddy Woodgate, Michael Hinz, Sue Best*
Two more children's adventures in the series. Average.
Boa: novels by Enid Blyton.
JUV 71 min mTV
V LNG

## FAMOUS FIVE: FIVE GO TO SMUGGLER'S TOP
## FIVE GO OFF IN A CARAVAN **
Uc
UK 1983
*Michelle Gallagher, Gary Russell, Marcus Harris, Jenny Thanisch, Toddy Woodgate, Michael Hinz, Sue Best*
Two adventures in the series.
Boa: novels by Enid Blyton.
JUV 72 min mTV
V PICK; LNG

## FAMOUS FIVE: FIVE GO TO THE
## DEMON'S ROCK **
Uc
UK 1983
*Michelle Gallagher, Gary Russell, Marcus Harris, Jenny Thanisch, Toddy Woodgate, Michael Hinz, Sue Best*
In this "Famous Five" adventure, the children go treasure hunting after they hear rumours of hidden gold near the Demon's Rock. They find an old gold coin but soon discover that they are not the only ones searching for the treasure.
Boa: novel by Enid Blyton.
JUV 44 min mTV
V LNG L/A; PICK

## FAMOUS FIVE: FIVE ON KIRRIN ISLAND/
## FIVE GO ADVENTURING AGAIN **
Uc
UK 1983
*Michelle Gallagher, Gary Russell, Marcus Harris, Jenny Thanisch, Toddy Woodgate, Michael Hinz, Sue Best*
Two adventures in this passable series for children.
Boa: novels by Enid Blyton.
JUV 69 min mTV
V PICK; LNG

## FAN, THE *
18
Edward Bianchi USA 1981
*Lauren Bacall, Michael Biehn, Maureen Stapleton, James Garner, Hector Elizondo, Anna Maria Horsford, Kurt Johnson, Griffin Dunne*
A Broadway actress is threatened by a psychotic lovestruck fan who feels rejected by her in this disagreeable adaptation of Randall's novel. Sad to see someone as talented as Bacall in something as low-grade as this.
Boa: novel by Bob Randall.
DRA 95 min
B,V,LV CIC

## FANDANGO ***
15
Kevin Reynolds USA 1984
*Kevin Costner, Judd Nelson, Sam Robards, Chuck Bush, Brian Cesak, Suzy Amis, Marvin J. McIntyre*
Study of several college buddies who graduate and have to face the prospect of the Vietnam War. To forget things they go on one last wild weekend. A fresh and likeable if rather uneven story. Based on "Proof", a student film made by Reynolds and then expanded under the sponsorship of Steven Spielberg.
COM 87 min
V/h WHV

## FANNY BY GASLIGHT **
PG
Anthony Asquith UK 1944

*James Mason, Phyllis Calvert, Stewart Granger,*
*Wilfred Lawson, John Laurie, Margaretta Scott, Jean*
*Kent, Stuart Lindsell, Nora Swinburne, Amy Veness,*
*Ann Wilton, Helen Haye, Cathleen Nesbitt, Ann*
*Stephens, Gloria Sydney*
A psychotic aristocrat tries to dominate the lives of
others and seduces the illegitimate daughter of a
cabinet minister. An elaborate mystery drama whose
slow and ponderous development hampers its effec-
tiveness.
Aka: MAN OF EVIL
Boa: novel by Michael Sadleir.
DRA                                       106 min B/W
B,V                                             VCC

## FANNY HILL **                                   18
Gerry O'Hara          UK                        1983
*Lisa Raines, Oliver Reed, Shelley Winters, Wilfrid*
*Hyde-White, Alfred Marks, Jonathan York, Paddie*
*O'Neil, Maria Harper, Angie Wick, Susie Silvey,*
*Lorraine Doyle, Harry Fowler, Howard Goorney,*
*Fanny Carby, Tracy Dixon*
Film version of a classic novel based on the memoirs of
a woman-of-pleasure of the 18th century. A competent
but uninspired romp.
Boa: novel by John Cleland.
A   86 min (ort 92 min) Cut (1 min 34 sec in addition to
film cuts)
B,V,V2              BWV/GHV; INTMED (VHS only)

## FANTASIES *                                     15
John Derek            USA                        1976
*Bo Derek, Peter Hooten, Anna Alexiadis, Phaedon*
*Gheorghitis, Therese Bohlin*
The efforts of two men to turn a Greek island into a
tourist resort are just a vehicle for displaying Bo
Derek plus her minimal acting ability. Another
homage by the director to the charms of Derek, who
was sixteen when this amateurish nonsense was
made.
Aka: AND ONCE UPON A LOVE
A                            87 min; 75 min (VDEL)
B,V                 MMA; TEM L/A; VDEL; BLUES

## FANTASIST, THE ***                              18
Robin Hardy           EIRE                       1986
*Christopher Cazenove, Timothy Bottoms, John*
*Kavanagh, Moira Harris, Mick Lally, Dairbre Noi*
*Chaoimh, James Bartey, Deirdre Donnelly, Liam*
*O'Callahan*
A murderous psychotic is in the habit of talking his
way into the homes of beautiful women and then
murdering them. Harris plays one of his potential
victims, new to Dublin and friends with all the men
who may or may not be responsible for these murders.
The plot unfolds carefully and though the film lacks
the style or chills of some of its more expensive rivals,
it's never less than watchable.
Boa: novel Goosefoot by Patrick McGinley.
THR                            95 min (ort 98 min)
B,V                                            POLY

## FANTASTIC ARGOMAN **
Terence Hathaway (Sergio Grieco)
                      ITALY                      1967
*Roger Browne, Edward Douglas, Dick Palmer,*
*Dominique Boschero, N. Marlowa*
Adventures of a super-hero, and his battle to save the
world from the schemes of a wicked master criminal.
Fairly enjoyable but mindless nonsense.
Aka: ARGOMAN SUPERDIABOLICO; ARGOMAN
THE FANTASTIC SUPERMAN; COME RUBARE
LA CORONA D'INGHILTERRA; HOW TO STEAL
THE CROWN OF ENGLAND
A/AD                                       94 min
B,V                                             VPD

## FANTASTIC VOYAGE **                              U
Richard Fleischer     USA                        1966

*Stephen Boyd, Edmond O'Brien, Raquel Welch,*
*Donald Pleasence, Arthur O'Connell, William*
*Redfield, Arthur Kennedy, James Brolin*
When a famous scientist is shot, a highly ex-
perimental technique is used in order to save him. A
medical team is placed aboard a submarine, reduced
to microscopic size and injected into his bloodstream to
remove a blood clot on his brain. An interesting film of
good special effects (largely wasted on TV) but poor
acting and dialogue. Script is by Harry Kleiner. AA:
Art/Set (Smith and Hennesy/Scott and Reiss), Effects
(Vis) (Cruickshank).
Boa: novel by Otto Klement and Jay Lewis Bixby.
FAN                                          96 min
V/h                                             CBS

## FANTASY GIRLS **                                 18
Alex De Renzy         USA                        1976
*Sharon Thorpe, Bonnie Holiday, Laura Fujiyama,*
*Carol Bigby*
A story revolving around a massage parlour and the
lives of the women who work there, both on duty and
off.
A                         54 min (ort 80 min) Cut
B,V                              ELV L/A; ATLAN

## FANTASY MISSION FORCE **                         15
Chu Yen Ping       HONG KONG                     1984
*Jackie Chan*
Story of resistance against the Japanese in WW2,
when a commando squad is formed to recover money
stolen by the enemy.
MAR                          85 min (ort 90 min)
V                                               TGP

## FANTASY WORLD **                              R18/18
Bob Chinn/Jeffrey Fairbanks
                      USA                        1979
*Jesie St James, Laurien Dominique, Sharon Cain, Jon*
*Martin, James Price, Paul Thomas*
Three sailors arrive at a nightclub that turns out to be
a hardcore sex show where the members of the
audience are expected to participate. They find themselves sitting next to three girls at the club and in the
course of the evening all parties concerned have their
sexual fantasies fulfilled. The 18 version was cut
before video submission by 22 min 15 sec.
Osca: NAKED CAME THE STRANGER
A    34 min (18 version); 54 min (R18 version); 83 min
(2 film cassette)
B,V,V2                          TCX; PHV; SHEP

## FAR FROM HOME *                                  18
Meiert Avis           USA                        1989
*Matt Frewer, Drew Barrymore, Richard Masur, Karen*
*Austin, Susan Tyrrell, Anthony Rapp, Jennifer Tilly,*
*Andras Jones, Dick Miller*
A girl and her father go on vacation and stop at a
trailer park, where the girl seems destined to fall
victim to a demented serial killer. This formula
offering has a few black comedy touches and starts off
well, but rapidly goes downhill.
THR                                          87 min
V                                               VES

## FAR FROM THE MADDING CROWD ***
John Schlesinger      UK                         1967
*Julie Christie, Alan Bates, Terence Stamp, Peter*
*Finch, Prunella Ransome, Fiona Walker, Alison*
*Leggatt, Paul Dawkins, Julian Somers, Freddie Jones,*
*Brian Rawlinson, Denise Coffey*
The story of a beautiful female landowner and her
relationship with the three men in her life in Dorset of
1866. Overlong and carefully made, but with little
feeling for an England long since gone, perhaps
largely because Christie is too much of a modern miss
to bring conviction to her part. The excellent photography is by Nicolas Roeg, with a score by Richard
Rodney Bennet and a script by Frederic Raphael.

Boa: novel by Thomas Hardy.
DRA     159 min (ort 169 min)
B,V     TEVP

## FAR NORTH ***                                    15
Sam Shepard     USA     1987
*Jessica Lange, Charles Durning, Tess Harper, Donald
Moffat, Ann Wedgeworth, Patricia Arquette, Nina
Draxton*
A restrained drama with a few touches of comedy, that
follows the changing fortunes of a Minnesota farming
family, where three generations interract and are
soon to see the demise of their way of life. When the
wayward daughter returns to see her badly injured
father, she is given the job of shooting the wild horse
that nearly caused his death in a wagon accident.
Written by Shepard, this is an impressive directing
debut.
DRA     85 min (ort 90 min)
V     VES

## FAR OUT MAN *                                     15
Thomas Chong     USA     1989
*Tommy Chong, Rae Dawn Chong, Shelby Chong,
Paris Chong, C. Thomas Howell, Martin Mull, Judd
Nelson*
A ghastly vanity vehicle for Chong, who stars as a
burnt-out 1960s hippie, who is trying to return to his
estranged girlfriend and child, but finds the task made
difficult by the fact that he is permanently stoned.
Badly scripted and acted, and with a host of cameos
(Cheech Marin appears briefly) that do nothing for it.
COM     85 min (ort 91 min)
V     VES

## FAR PAVILIONS, THE **                             PG
Peter Duffell     UK     1984
*Ben Cross, Amy Irving, Omar Sharif, Christopher Lee,
Benedict Taylor, Saeed Jaffrey, John Gielgud,
Rossano Brazzi, Robert Hardy, Sneh Gupta, Jennifer
Kendal, Felicity Dean, Rupert Everett, Mary Peach,
Adam Bareham*
A long wallow in nostalgia for the days of the British
Raj in this tale of a
19th century officer who is torn between love of his
country and his Hindu upbringing. Lavish and incred-
ibly detailed, but the cliched script is a serious flaw.
Originally shown in three 96 minute episodes.
Boa: novel by M.M. Kaye.
DRA     108 min (ort 288 min) Cut (12 sec) mTV
B,V     TEVP; WHV (VHS only)

## FAR SIDE OF PARADISE, THE **                      15
Arturo Ripstein
    MEXICO/SWITZERLAND     1976
*Peter O'Toole, Charlotte Rampling, Max Von Sydow,
Jorge Luke, Helen Rojo, Claudio Brook*
A man and his wife leave Rumania just before WW2
for an island paradise, but become caught up in a web
of love, hate and revenge in this superficial and
cliched drama. Filmed in Mexico. Additional sex
footage was added for the version entitled "The Other
Side Of Paradise".
Aka: FOXTROT; OTHER SIDE OF PARADISE, THE
DRA     91 min
B,V     VDB L/A; ODY

## FAREWELL TO ARMS, A **                            15
Charles Vidor     USA     1957
*Rock Hudson, Jennifer Jones, Vittorio De Sica, Oscar
Homolka, Alberto Sordi, Mercedes McCambridge,
Elaine Stritch*
An inferior remake of the 1932 film of the same name
that suffers badly from poor casting and excessive
length, treating Hemingway's WW1 love story with a
surprising lack of feeling.
Boa: novel by Ernest Hemingway.
WAR     146 min (ort 152 min)
V/h     CBS

## FAREWELL TO ARMS, A ***
Frank Borzage     USA     1932
*Gary Cooper, Helen Hayes, Mary Philips, Adolphe
Menjou, Jack LaRue, Blanche Frederici*
The story of the romance between a wounded Amer-
ican ambulance driver and his nurse in WW1. Avoids
all of the deeper issues raised in the novel on which it
is based but works perfectly as a simple love story. An
inferior remake followed in 1957. AA: Cin (Charles
Bryant Lang Jr), Sound (Franklin B. Hansen).
Boa: novel by Ernest Hemingway.
WAR     75 min (ort 78 min) B/W
B,V,V2     VCL/CBS; VIR (VHS only)

## FAREWELL TO THE KING ***                          PG
John Milius     USA     1988
*Nick Nolte, Nigel Havers, Frank McRae, Gerry Lopez,
Marilyn Tokuda, Choy Chang Wing, Aki Aleong,
Marius Weyers, William Wise, Wayne Pygram,
Richard Morgan, Elan Oberon, James Fox, Michael
Nissman, John Bennett Perry*
Action wartime adventure set in the exotic jungles of
Borneo where a British commando has parachuted
into the jungle with the intention of leading a native
rebellion against the Japanese. Three years before, a
US sergeant turned his back on the war and now lives
with a native tribe as their ruler. He is about to find
the peace of his haven destroyed in this colourful and
exciting adventure, written and directed by Milius.
Boa: novel L'Adieu Au Roi by Pierre Schoendoerffer.
A/AD     112 min
B,V     VES

## FAREWELL, MY LOVELY ***                           15
Dick Richards     USA     1975
*Robert Mitchum, Charlotte Rampling, John Ireland,
Anthony Zerbe, Sylvia Miles, Sylvester Stallone, Harry
Dean Stanton*
The third version of a classic detective story with a
confusing and incomprehensible plot about a private
eye and his search for an ex-con's missing girlfriend.
Mitchum is well chosen to play the cynical and world
weary Marlowe. Followed by THE BIG SLEEP in
1978.
Boa: novel by Raymond Chandler.
DRA     91 min (ort 97 min)
B,V     PRV; POLY (VHS only)

## FARMER'S DAUGHTER, THE ****
H.C. Potter     USA     1947
*Loretta Young, Joseph Cotten, Ethel Barrymore,
Charles Bickford, Rose Hobart, Harry Davenport, Lex
Barker, James Aurness (Arness), Keith Andes*
A Congressman's Swedish maid enters politics and
has to fight both her boss and her boyfriend in this
charming and witty comedy. The adaptation of Terva-
ta's play is by Allen Rivkin and Laura Kerr. A TV
series followed later. AA: Actress (Young).
Boa: play Hulda, Daughter Of Parliament by Juhni
Tervataa.
COM     97 min B/W
B,V     GHV; VCC

## FARRELL FOR THE PEOPLE **                         15
Paul Wendkos     USA     1982
*Valerie Harper, Ed O'Neill, Gregory Sierra, Judith
Chapman, Steve Inwood, Kene Holliday, Dennis
Lipscomb, Richard T. Herd, Eugene Roche, Frank
McCarthy, Millie Slavin, Calvin Jung, Alba Oms,
Celia Perry, Floyd Levine*
An ambitious district attorney fights to secure a
conviction of an ex-con accused of murder whilst
having to battle the man's celebrity author sponsor as
well. A failed pilot inspired by the real-life case of
convict Jack Henry Abbott and writer Norman
Mailer.
DRA     92 min (ort 104 min) mTV
B,V     MGM

## FASCINATION ** 18
Gerard Damiano USA 1978
*Georgina Spelvin, Kyoto Sun, Brooke West, Paul*
*Thomas, David Morris, Nicolle O'Neal*
A kind of spoof on the TV series "Fantasy Island" and
consisting of a series of unrelated vignettes in which a
group of people, mostly women, explore their sexual
fantasies. Cut before video submission by 25 min 29
sec.
Aka: FANTASY (RIP); THAT PRICKLY FEELING
Osca: JACK 'N' JILL
A          50 min (ort 90 min) (2 film cassette) Cut (3 sec)
B,V                                       TCX; PHV; RIP; SHEP

## FAST CARS, FAST WOMEN *** R18
Scott McHaley USA 1979
*Kay Parker, Lisa Lane, Carolyn Jackson, Ken Gibson,*
*Al Chiurrizzi, Ron Jeremy*
This motor racing tale follows the adventures of a
wealthy woman who owns a string of racing cars. One
of her female drivers was killed in a race after her car
was tampered with so she hires a new girl to race for
her. Various sexual encounters follow, it being the
habit of the new driver to use sex to get what she
wants. Meanwhile the crooks are getting ready to fix
her car too but their plans are foiled by the good guys
and all ends happily.
Aka: FAST CARS
A                               74 min Cut (1 min 4 sec)
B,V                                           EVI; SHEP

## FAST COMPANY *
David Cronenberg CANADA 1978
*John Saxon, William Smith, Claudia Jennings,*
*Nicholas Campbell, Cedric Smith, Judy Foster, George*
*Buza, Robert Haley, David Graham, Don Franks,*
*David Petersen, Chuck Chandler, Cheri Hilsabeck,*
*Sonya Ratke, Michael Bell*
A drag racing driver becomes involved with some very
tough competition, in this forgettable effort.
DRA                                              90 min
B,V                                                 VTC

## FAST FORWARD ** PG
Sidney Poitier USA 1984
*Monique Cintron, John Scott Clough, Don Franklin,*
*Noel Conlon, Tamara Mark, Tracy Silver, Cindy*
*McGee, Gretchen F. Palmer, Irene Worth, Constance*
*Towers*
Eight singers and dancers go to New York for a talent
contest in this corny and unimaginative musical.
MUS         105 min (ort 109 min) Cut (1 min 13 sec)
B,V                                                 RCA

## FAST LADY, THE * PG
Ken Annakin UK 1962
*James Robertson Justice, Leslie Phillips, Stanley*
*Baxter, Kathleen Harrison, Julie Christie, Eric Barker,*
*Allan Cuthbertson, Oliver Johnston, Esma Cannon,*
*Dick Emery, Derek Guyler, Victor Brooks, Terence*
*Alexander*
A civil servant has to buy a Bentley to impress his
car-mad girlfriend. A flat and insipid farce directed
mainly at car buffs.
Boa: story by Keble Howard.
COM                                              94 min
B,V                                         RNK; STRAND

## FAST LANE FEVER **
John Clark AUSTRALIA 1982
*Terry Sergio, Vagelis Mourikis, Debbie Conway*
A young factory worker starts to woo the girlfriend of
a champion drag racer and is obliged to compete
against the champ for her favour, in this cliched
formula offering.
Aka: RUNNING ON EMPTY; WILD WHEELS
A/AD                              86 min (ort 94 min)
B,V                                        FTV L/A; IVS

## FAST TALKING * 18
Ken Cameron AUSTRALIA 1983
*Rod Zuanic, Steve Bisley, Peter Collingwood, Tony*
*Allaylis, Chris Truswell, Gail Sweeney*
A 15-year-old finds that his mouth has to be as quick
as his wits, if he is to survive when he gets into trouble
in this aimless and rather downbeat tale.
DRA                                              98 min
B,V                                                 EHE

## FAST TIMES AT RIDGEMONT HIGH *** 18
Amy Heckerling USA 1982
*Sean Penn, Jennifer Jason Leigh, Phoebe Cates, Judge*
*Reinhold, Ray Walston, Robert Romanus, Hallie*
*Eckstein, Brian Backer, Forest Whitaker, James*
*Russo, Pamela Springsteen, Martin Brest, Eric Stoltz,*
*Anthony Edwards*
Students at a school in California try various ploys to
lose their virginity in this engaging and surprisingly
funny comedy, helped along by some great perform-
ances. The film debuts for Stoltz and Edwards. A TV
series followed.
Aka: FAST TIMES
Boa: novel by Cameron Crowe.
COM                              86 min (ort 92 min)
V/h                                                 CIC

## FAST-WALKING ** 18
James B. Harris USA 1981
*James Woods, Tim McIntire, Kay Lenz, Robert Hooks,*
*M. Emmet Walsh, Timothy Carey, Susan Tyrrell*
Story of two men who are old friends and end up on
either side of prison bars with Woods playing a prison
guard who is hired to assassinate a politician. An
offbeat and mostly unpleasant prison drama with a
few touches of black humour.
Boa: novel The Rap by Ernest Brawley.
DRA                              111 min (ort 115 min)
B,V,V2                                              GHV

## FASTER PUSSYCAT, KILL . . . KILL *
Russ Meyer USA 1966
*Tura Santana, Haji, Lori Williams, Stuart Lancaster,*
*Paul Trinka, Dennis Busch, Hay Barlow, Linda*
*Bernard*
Cheap and nasty Meyer offering, with wicked Varla
the tough leader of a gang of three women on the
lookout for thrills. Varla challenges the boyfriend of a
girl to a car race and when he loses she kills him. They
tie the girl up and drive off to a remote shack where an
old man and his retarded son live. More gratuitous
violence and killing follows but Varla finally meets a
fitting end, being left to die in the desert. A mindless
and sick anti-film.
Aka: LEATHER GIRLS; MANKILLERS
A                                         83 min B/W
B,V                                                 VSP

## FAT GUY GOES NUTZOID ** 15
John Golden USA 1986
*Tibor Golden, Peter Linari, John Mackay, Douglas*
*Stone, Max Alexander*
Following his escape from an asylum, a fat slob with a
Mohican hair style is befriended by two rich kids who
provide him with romance and adventure as they
introduce him to the good life. Score is by Leo Kottke.
Aka: ZEISTERS
COM                              76 min (ort 83 min)
B,V                                                 AVR

## FATAL ATTRACTION * 18
Michael Grant CANADA 1980
                                    (re-released 1985)
*Sally Kellerman, Lawrence Dane, John Huston,*
*Stephen Lack, John Peter Linton, Patrick Crean,*
*Marty Galin, Joanna McIntyre, Sheilah Currie,*
*Sandra Scott, Harry Kumano, Kunio Suyama, Hadley*
*Kay, Mina E. Mina, Al Bernardo*
A couple meet after their cars collide and gradually

begin to play strange sexual games in which they act out each other's fantasies. A dark film in many respects both for the passions unleashed and the fact that much of the story unfolds at night. The leading players perform well, but the story never really convinces, and the ending is pure contrivance.
Aka: HEAD ON (AFE)
THR                86 min; 83 min (VES) (ort 98 min)
B,V                                        AFE; VES

## FATAL ATTRACTION ***                                18
Adrian Lyne            USA                    1987
Michael Douglas, Glenn Close, Anne Archer, Ellen Hamilton Latzen, Stuart Pankin, Ellen Foley, Fred Gwynne, Meg Mundy, Tom Brennan, Lois Smith, Mike Nussbaum, J.J. Johnston, Michael Arkin, Sam J. Coppola, Eunice Prewitt
A successful lawyer has a quick fling with an attractive woman not knowing she is unbalanced. When he tries to say goodbye she refuses to accept this and pursues him with obsessive rage, turning his family's life into a living hell. A slick and well-acted thriller of considerable tension spoilt by a climax that would be more appropriate to a Stallone film (the original subtler ending having been dropped after an unsuccessful preview).
THR                                        114 min
V/sh                                           CIC

## FATAL BEAUTY *                                      18
Tom Holland            USA                    1987
Whoopi Goldberg, Sam Elliott, Ruben Blades, Jennifer Warren, Harris Yulin, John P. Ryan, Brad Dourif, Mike Jolly, Charles Hallahan, Neil Barry, Richard (Cheech) Marin, Ebbe Roe Smith
A violent and incoherent attempt to cash in on the success of BEVERLY HILLS COP with Goldberg playing an undercover cop out to track down the dealers responsible for pushing poisoned cocaine in L.A. The anti-drugs message comes through loud and clear but this dreadful mess of a film carries such a weight of dross (not least being the awful dialogue) that it fails on all counts.
A/AD                                       100 min
B,V                                            MGM

## FATAL CLAWS AND DEADLY KICKS ***                    18
HONG KONG
Hsia Kuang-Li, Peng Kang, Wang Chi-Sheng, Liu Shan, Chang Kuan-Lung, Tai Chi-Hsia, Lu Yi-Lung
Returning home with his wife, a famous escort guard chief is attacked by four bandits who murder him and rape his wife. Rescued by a nun who is skilled in the martial arts, she swears vengeance and spends the next three years training until the time comes for her to track down her assailants and take her revenge. Formula martial arts revenger with some nicely choreographed sequences.
MAR                        89 min Cut (1 min 1 sec)
V                                              VPD

## FATAL FLYING GUILLOTINE, THE **                     18
HONG KONG
Cheng Hsang, Chia Ta
Standard martial arts fisticuffs revolving around the use of an unusual and deadly technique.
MAR                                        88 min
B,V                                       KFM; VTEL

## FATAL VISION ****                                   15
David Greene           USA                    1984
Karl Malden, Eva Marie Saint, Gary Cole, Barry Newman, Andy Griffith, Gary Grubbs, Mitchell Ryan, Albert Salmi
An excellent fact-based drama that explores the events surrounding the trial of ex-Green Beret Jeffrey MacDonald, who in 1970 was convicted of murdering his pregnant wife and their two daughters. Despite repeatedly protesting his innocence, his conviction

was assured by his father-in-law, who, having had his suspicions aroused, was remorseless in his fight for justice. Malden as the father-in-law won a well-deserved Emmy. The script was by John Gay.
Boa: book by Joe McGinniss.
DRA                        174 min (ort 200 min) mTV
V                                              VCC

## FATE OF THE HUNTER **                               15
Paul Almond            USA                    1987
Noriyuki "Pat" Morita, Chris Makepeace, Mari Sato, Michael Sarrazin, Seth Sakai
Two American airmen are shot down over northern Japan during WW2 and held prisoner at a remote mountain village. One of the men falls in love with a Japanese woman in this simplistic and cliched tale.
Aka: CAPTIVE HEARTS
DRA                               92 min (ort 97 min)
B,V                                            MGM

## FATHER GOOSE **                                      U
Ralph Nelson           USA                    1964
Cary Grant, Leslie Caron, Trevor Howard, Jack Good, Nicole Felsette
A layabout on an island in the South Seas is redeemed by a schoolteacher and her girls who find shelter with him after fleeing the Japanese during WW2. A modest and fairly enjoyable tale. AA: Story/Screen (S.H. Barnett/Peter Stone/Frank Tarloff).
DRA                             112 min (ort 115 min)
V                                              VCC

## FATHERLAND ***                                      15
Ken Loach
FRANCE/UK/WEST GERMANY            1986
Gerulf Pannach, Christine Rose, Fabienne Babe
The story of an East German "Liedermacher" whose political songs put him out of favour with the authorities. He reluctantly accepts a one-way ticket to the West, where his "voice of dissent" becomes a marketable commodity. But what he really wants is to find his father, a classical musician who defected years earlier. A French journalist, who has her own reasons for wanting to find his father, helps him in his search.
DRA          106 min (subtitles with German dialogue)
B,V                                            PAL

## FATHER'S REVENGE, A **                              18
John Herzfeld          USA                    1988
Brian Dennehy, Joanna Cassidy, Ron Silver, Anthony Valentine, Christoph M. Ort, Claudia Matschulla
A father hires a bunch of mercenaries to help him find his daughter who has been snatched by terrorists in West Germany. A good performance from Dennehy rescues the film from the pure contrivance of its script.
Aka: FATHER'S REVENGE, A: THE TERRORISTS
A/AD                                     96 min mTV
B,V                               IVS; BRAVE (VHS only)

## FATSO *
Anne Bancroft          USA                    1980
Dom DeLuise, Anne Bancroft, Ron Carey, Candice Azzara, Michael Lombard, Sal Viscuso
An overweight Italian man decides to slim down after his cousin dies from a heart attack but unfortunately finds himself lacking in will-power. A crude and fairly unamusing effort from Bancroft in her first feature as writer-director.
COM                                        98 min
B,V                                            CBS

## FBI MURDERS, THE ***                                18
Dick Lowry             USA                    1988
David Soul, Michael Gross, Ronny Cox, Doug Sheehan, Bruce Greenwood
Based on a true story, this tells of the six month investigation mounted by the FBI into a wave of bank robberies that took place in Miami during 1986. The

crimes are eventually traced to two men, both of whom lead seamingly normal middle-class lives but are in reality ruthless criminals. A tough action film culminating in the obligatory shoot-out.

| A/AD | 92 min |
|---|---|
| V | CIC |

**FBI STORY, THE ** PG**
Mervyn LeRoy          USA                1959
*James Stewart, Vera Miles, Nick Adams, Murray Hamilton, Larry Pennell, Diane Jergens, Joyce Taylor*
An FBI agent looks back at his career in this one-sided and totally fictional account of what the FBI was really like under J. Edgar Hoover. Good performances paper over the candyfloss script that tells us nothing of substance.
Boa: book by D. Whitehead.

| DRA | 144 min (ort 149 min) |
|---|---|
| B,V | WHV |

**FEAR *** 18
Robert A. Ferretti          USA                1988
*Cliff De Young, Kay Lenz, Frank Stallone, Robert Factor, Scott Schwartz, Geri Betzler*
A vacationing family are taken hostage by a psychotic Vietnam vet in one of those standard you've-seen-it-all-before movies.

| A/AD | 92 min |
|---|---|
| B,V | VIR |

**FEAR CITY *** 18
Abel Ferrara          USA                1984
*Tom Berenger, Billy Dee Williams, Melanie Griffith, Rossano Brazzi, Jack Scalia, Rae Dawn Chong, Joe Santos, Michael V. Gazzo, Jan Murray, Ola Ray*
Another one of those psychotic slashers is on the prowl and this time he's attacking showgirls. Violent and unappealing in equal measure.

| HOR | 91 min (ort 96 min) (Cut at film release) |
|---|---|
| B, V/h | TEVP L/A; WHV (VHS only) |

**FEAR EATS THE SOUL *****
Rainer Werner Fassbinder
          WEST GERMANY          1973
*El Hedi Ben Salem, Brigitti Mira, Barbara Valentin, Rainer Werner Fassbinder*
When a Moroccan guest-worker marries a German woman twice his age, their relationship is marred by the racist attitudes of those around them. A touching and sensitive study of a doomed love affair.
Aka: ALI: FEAR EATS THE SOUL; DIE ANGST ESSEN SEELE AUF

| DRA | 93 min |
|---|---|
| B,V | PVG |

**FEAR IN THE CITY *****          18
Gianni Manera          ITALY                1977
*James Mason, Fred Williamson, Maurizio Merli, Raymond Pellegrin, Michael Constantin, Gianni Manera*
A gang leader and some of his underlings escape from jail and return to a life of violent crime. In a desperate bid to recapture them, a suspended police captain notorious for his brutal methods is reinstated and sent after them.
Aka: HOT STUFF; LA PAURA IN CITTA

| THR | 93 min |
|---|---|
| B,V | ELE |

**FEAR IN THE NIGHT *****
Jimmy Sangster          UK                1972
*Judy Geeson, Joan Collins, Peter Cushing, Ralph Bates, Gillian Lind, James Cossins, John Brown, Brian Grellis*
Horror shocker about a nervous woman who marries a prep school master and goes to live with him. Strange things begin to happen to her in a school as deserted in term time as it is during the school holidays. A competent yarn with several inventive touches.

Aka: DYNASTY OF FEAR

| HOR | 82 min (ort 93 min) |
|---|---|
| B,V | TEVP |

**FEAR IS THE KEY *****
Michael Tuchner          UK                1972
*Barry Newman, Suzy Kendall, John Vernon, Ben Kingsley, Dolph Sweet, Ray McAnally, Peter Marinker, Elliott Sullivan, Roland Brand, Tony Anholt*
Confusing story of a man out for revenge on those who were responsible for the death of his wife and family in a plane crash. The debut for Kingsley, his only film prior to GANDHI.
Boa: novel by Alistair MacLean.

| THR | 101 min (ort 108 min) |
|---|---|
| B,V | TEVP |

**FEAR NO EVIL *****
Frank Laloggia          USA                1981
*Stefan Arngrim, Elizabeth Hoffman, Kathleen Rowe McAllen, Frank Birney, Daniel Eden*
Classic conflict between good and evil in the shape of two high school students with one of them turning out to be an incarnation of Satan. Fortunately he is opposed by a couple of angels.

| HOR | 87 min (ort 96 min) |
|---|---|
| B,V,V2 | EHE |

**FEARLESS DRAGONS *****          15
          HONG KONG
*Philip Ko, Leung Ka You*
Another martial arts battle for honour and revenge, this time featuring two of the screen's best exponents.

| MAR | 83 min |
|---|---|
| B,V | VPD |

**FEARLESS FUZZ *****
Stelvio Massi          AUSTRIA/ITALY          1978
*Joan Collins, Franco Reddel, Gastone Moschin, Maurizio Merli*
An Italian private eye has to locate the daughter of an Austrian banker who has been kidnapped. A poorly dubbed co-production.
Aka: FEARLESS

| THR | 95 min dubbed |
|---|---|
| B,V | VIDMOV/HOK |

**FEARLESS HYENA, THE *****          18
Jackie Chan          HONG KONG          1979
*Jackie Chan, Yen Si Kuan, Li Kuen*
Story of a martial artist and his quest for revenge for the murder of his grandfather. Set in the days of the Ching Dynasty but don't let that put you off, the film is actually well made and enjoyable. Followed by a sequel in 1985.

| MAR | 93 min |
|---|---|
| B,V | AVR; TGP (VHS only) |

**FEARLESS HYENA 2 *****          18
Jackie Chan          HONG KONG          1985
*Jackie Chan*
Sequel to the first film with Chan and his brother out to avenge the death of their father in this continuing story of the clash between rival gangs the "Ying/Yang" and the "Heaven and Earth".

| MAR | 91 min |
|---|---|
| V | TGP |

**FEARSTALK *****          18
Larry Shaw          USA                1990
*Jill Clayburgh, Steven Macht, Lynne Thigpen, Sada Thompson*
A woman has her purse stolen but the thief, not content with this, subjects her to a constant campaign of torment, using the knowledge he has gained from her belongings to terrorise both her and her family. Eventually she is driven so far that she embarks on

her own campaign of vengeance. An absorbing but rather disagreeable thriller.

THR                                    93 min
V/sh                                   NWV

**FEDORA \*\***                        PG
Billy Wilder
                FRANCE/WEST GERMANY    1978
*William Holden, Marthe Keller, Hildegarde Knef, Jose Ferrer, Francis Sternhagen, Henry Fonda, Michael York, Mario Adorf*
A film producer tries to lure an ageing legendary film star of Hollywood out of her retirement on a Greek island in this glossy but heavy-going effort.
Boa: novel Crowned Heads by Thomas Tryon.

DRA                      108 min (ort 114 min)
B,V                                    TEVP

**FEDS \***                            15
Dan Goldberg          USA              1988
*Rebecca DeMornay, Mary Gross, Fred Dalton Thompson, Ken Marshall, Larry Cedar*
A pointless and largely humourless stab at comedy following the fortunes of a couple of female students at the FBI Academy. Despite one or two funny moments, this crude and low-grade attempt at a POLICE ACADEMY-style film has little going for it.

COM                       80 min (ort 91 min)
V/sh                                   WHV

**FEEL THE HEAT \***                   18
Joel Silberg          USA              1986
*Tiana Alexandra, David Dukes, Rod Steiger, Brian Thompson, Jorge Martinez, John Hancock, Brian Libby, Toru Tanaka, Jessica Schultz*
A drugs baron uses beautiful women couriers to smuggle narcotics inside their bodies, but finally gets his just deserts at the hands of an undercover lady cop who poses as an exotic dancer and for good measure, is a martial arts expert. Fast, violent and predictable.
Aka: CATCH THE HEAT

A/AD                      84 min (ort 95 min)
V                                      EIV

**FELICITY \*\*\***
John D. Lamond    AUSTRALIA           1979
*Gloria Annen, Toni Flynn, Christopher Milne, Jody Hansen*
A fun-loving schoolgirl travels to the Far East and stays with her permissive aunt and uncle, who insist on teaching her everything they know about sex. A lavish and picturesque sex movie in which our heroine has numerous sexual encounters but eventually meets the man of her dreams.

A                                      93 min
B,V                          ARI L/A; CASS/IVS;

**FELLINI'S SATYRICON \*\*\***         18
Federico Fellini
                FRANCE/ITALY           1969
*Martin Potter, Hiram Keller, Salvo Randone, Max Born, Capucine*
Lavish if somewhat self-indulgent account of the adventures (mostly sexual) of a young student as he encounters various types of people in Roman society. The screenplay is by Fellini.
Aka: SATYRICON
Boa: book Satyricon by Petronius.

DRA                      124 min (ort 129 min)
B,V                                    WHV

**FELLOW TRAVELLER \*\*\***
Philip Saville       UK/USA            1989
*Ron Silver, Imogen Stubbs, Hart Bochner, Daniel J. Travanti, Katherine Borowitz*
An interesting political thriller set during the period of the McCarthy witch-hunts, with Silver starring as a blacklisted screenwriter who flees to England rather than testify before the House Committee on Un-American Activities, after his best friend, a black-listed movie star, commits suicide after having implicated him in his HCUA testimony. A highly unusual work that unfortunately fails to maintain its momentum.

THR                                    97 min
V                                      CONNO

**FEMALE BUNCH, THE \*\***            18
Al Adamson           USA              1978
*Russ Tamblyn, Jennifer Bishop, Lon Chaney Jr*
A man and a woman are held prisoner on a ranch by a strange gang of women.

A                                      85 min
B,V                            INT/CBS; MPV

**FEMALE FANTASIES \***
                     USA
*Georgina Spelvin, Samantha Fox*
A pretentious look at two oversexed women and their erotic fantasies.
Osca: CHORUS CALL/MARY! MARY! (asa)

A                                      68 min
B,V                                    HAR

**FEMALE TROUBLE \***                 18
John Waters          USA              1978
*Rosie Divine (Glenn Milstead), Mink Stole, Edith Massey, Mary Vivian Pearce, Cookie Miller*
An outrageous account of the career of a notorious female transvestite all the way to the electric chair. Another "revolting" John Waters film that has (like so much of his work) achieved cult status. The occasional flashes of wit tend to be swamped in a welter of unpleasantness.

COM            90 min; 92 min (PAL) Cut (3 sec)
B,V                        PVG; PAL (VHS only)

**FER-DE-LANCE \***                    PG
Russ Mayberry        USA              1974
*David Janssen, Hope Lange, Ivan Dixon, Jason Evers, Dominic Frontiere, Russ Mayberry, Ben Piazza, Charles Robinson, Leslie Stevens*
A submarine is trapped on the sea-bed, but the main peril the passengers face is a cargo of deadly snakes. An utterly ridiculous thriller, that offers boredom and nonsensical plotting in equal measure.

THR                     74 min (ort 100 min) mTV
V                                      CASPIC

**FERRIS BUELLER'S DAY OFF \*\***     15
John Hughes          USA              1986
*Matthew Broderick, Mia Sara, Alan Ruck, Jennifer Grey, Jeffrey Jones, Cindy Pickett, Lyman Ward, Edie McClurg, Charlie Sheen, Del Close*
The story of a youngster's day of crazy adventures whilst taking the day off school. Starts off brilliantly but suffers from uneven development, sagging badly halfway as the film develops an introspective streak. The script is by John Hughes.

COM                      99 min (ort 103 min)
V/sh                                   CIC

**FERRY TO HONG KONG \*\***            U
Lewis Gilbert        UK               1961
*Curt Jurgens, Orson Welles, Sylvia Sims, Noel Purcell, Jeremy Spenser, Margaret Withers, John Wallace, Milton Reid, Roy Chiao, Shelley Shen*
An Austrian drunk is not allowed to land at either Hong Kong or Macao and spends all his time on board a ferry travelling between these two ports. He eventually proves his worth when the area is struck by a typhoon.
Boa: novel by Max Catto.

A/AD                 113 min; 98 min (VCC)
B,V                      RNK; VCC (VHS only)

**FEVER PITCH \***                     15
Richard Brooks       USA              1985

*Ryan O'Neal, Catherine Hicks, Giancarlo Giannini, Bridgette Andersen, Chad Everett, John Saxon, William Smith*
A journalist investigating gambling becomes addicted and spends most of his time dodging bookmakers' thugs. A poor script is nicely complemented by mediocre acting.
DRA     91 min (ort 96 min)
B,V     MGM

## FEVERHOUSE, THE **    15
Howard Walmsley    UK    1984
*Graham Massey, Joanne Hill, Patrick Nyland*
Three characters in a strange establishment share shifting relationships of power and attraction in this unusual tale.
DRA     45 min
B,V     IKON

## FICTION MAKERS, THE **    PG
Roy Ward Baker    UK    1967
*Roger Moore, Sylvia Syms*
A private detective is hired to protect a beautiful novelist who is being threatened by an underworld crime syndicate. A spin-off from the TV series "The Saint", which in turn was based on the "Saint" novels of Leslie Charteris.
A/AD     100 min
B,V     PRV; CH5 (VHS only)

## FIDDLER ON THE ROOF ****    U
Norman Jewison    USA    1971
*Chaim Topol, Norma Crane, Molly Picon, Candice Bonstein, Leonard Frey, Paul Mann, Rosalind Harris, Paul Michael Glaser, Michele Marsh, Neva Small*
A brilliant version of a Broadway musical based on the writings of Sholem Aleichem. Made with enormous care, and though entertaining in its portrayal of life for the Jews in a small village in the Pale, it has a deeper and serious side in examining the sufferings of Jews in Tsarist Russia. Songs are by Sheldon Harnick and Jerry Bock. AA: Cin (Oswald Morris), Score (John Williams), Sound (Gordon K. McCallum/David Hildyard).
Boa: short story Tevye And His Daughters by Sholem Aleichem/stage musical by Josef Stein.
MUS     172 min
V/sh     WHV

## FIELD OF DREAMS ****    PG
Phil Alden Robinson    USA    1988
*Kevin Costner, Amy Madigan, Gaby Hoffman, Ray Liotta, Timothy Busfield, James Earl Jones, Burt Lancaster, Frank Whaley, Dwier Brown*
An Iowan farmer hears a disembodied voice, and is inspired to build a baseball pitch in the middle of a cornfield. This proves to be what was needed to bring a legendary baseball star, unfairly disgraced in a famous scandal, back to Earth to play one more game. An uplifting and magical fantasy, telling of faith, hope and ultimate redemption. Written by Robinson, and with a fine score by James Horner.
Boa: novel Shoeless Joe by W.P. Kinsella.
FAN     106 min
V/sh     GHV

## FIELD OF HONOR **    18
Hans Scheepmaker    USA    1986
*Everett McGill, Ron Brandsteder, Hey Young Lee, Min Yoo, Dong Hyun Kim*
The story of a Dutch infantryman and his experiences serving with the UN forces during the Korean War. Our soldier finds himself stranded behind enemy lines when his platoon is wiped out. With only a dog for company, he attempts to make his way back to his unit, picking up two Korean kids along the way. A graphically realistic film – crude, bloody and devoid of

humour. This one says nothing new.
Aka: FIELD OF HONOUR
WAR     89 min
B,V     RNK

## FIEND WITHOUT A FACE, THE * 
Arthur Crabtree    UK    1957
*Marshall Thompson, Kim Parker, Kynaston Reeves, Stanley Maxted, Terence Kilburn, James Dyrenforth, Peter Madden, Gilbert Winfield, Michael Balfour*
A scientist conducting experiments in mental power, triggers a series of inexplicable killings when monsters materialise out of his own subconscious. A dull shocker that is slightly memorable for its unusual "crawling brain" monsters that inject a much-needed note of hilarity into this tale.
Boa: short story The Thought Monster by Amelia Reynolds Long. Osca: GRIP OF THE STRANGLER
FAN     71 min (ort 73 min) B/W
B,V     KVD

## FIEND, THE * 
Robert Hartford-Davis    UK    1972
*Ann Todd, Patrick Magee, Tony Beckley, Madeleine Hinde, Percy Herbert, Suzanna Leigh, David Lodge, Ronald Allen, Maxine Barrie, Janet Wild, Diana Chappell, Suzanna East*
The strange tale of a weird religious sect of psychotics and the woman journalist who begins to investigate them. Unusual and fairly unappealing.
DRA     87 min
B,V     DFS

## FIENDISH PLOT OF DR FU MANCHU, THE *    PG
Piers Haggard    USA    1980
*Peter Sellers, Helen Mirren, Stratford Johns, David Tomlinson, Sid Caesar, Simon Williams, Steve Franken*
A weak spoof on the return of the evil Fu Manchu who was thought to be dead but is now masterminding a series of diamond thefts. Sellers' last film.
COM     96 min (ort 108 min)
B,V     WHV

## FIFTEEN STREETS, THE **    15
David Wheatley    UK    1989
*Owen Teale, Clare Holman, Ian Bannen, Sean Bean, Billie Whitelaw, Frank Windsor, Jane Horrocks*
In turn-of-the-century Newcastle, two lovers are separated by the social divide to which the title alludes.
Boa: novel by Catherine Cookson.
DRA     105 min mTV
V     CHEREN

## FIFTH FLOOR, THE * 
Howard Avedis    USA    1980
*Bo Hopkins, Dianne Hull, Patti D'Arbanville, Mel Ferrer, Sharon Farrell, Julie Adams, John David Carson*
A college disco dancer is wrongly committed to a mental home and neither her boyfriend nor her doctors believe her when she says she shouldn't be there. Unappealing nonsense.
THR     90 min
B,V     HOK

## FIFTH MISSILE, THE *    PG
Larry Peerce    USA    1986
*Robert Conrad, Sam Waterston, Richard Roundtree, Jonathan Banks, Dennis Holahan, Art LeFleur, Sergio Fantoni, Yvette Mimieux, David Soul, Ed Bishop, Michael Aronin, William Berger, David Gilliam, Trevor Thomas, David Lema*
A nuclear war exercise aboard a US submarine goes wrong due to toxic paint fumes and threatens to start WW3. The lame and overlong plot develops an occasional flash of tension, but no more than that.

Boa: novel The Gold Crew by Thomas N. Scortia and
Frank M. Robinson.
DRA                         139 min (ort 156 min) mTV
B,V                                              MGM

## FIFTH MUSKETEER, THE ***
Ken Annakin      AUSTRIA/UK              1978
*Beau Bridges, Sylvia Kristel, Rex Harrison, Ursula
Andress, Cornel Wilde, Jose Ferrer, Ian McShane,
Lloyd Bridges, Alan Hale Jr, Helmut Dantine, Olivia
De Havilland*
A virtual remake of "The Man In The Iron Mask"
about the struggle between Louis XIII and his twin
brother for the throne of France. This one has little
new to offer but the Austrian locations and support
from a strong cast of veterans are compensations.
Written by David Ambrose.
Boa: novel The Man In The Iron Mask by Alexandre
Dumas.
A/AD                       103 min (ort 120 min)
B,V,V2                                           GHV

## FIFTH OFFENSIVE, THE **                     PG
Stipe Delic        YUGOSLAVIA            1973
*Richard Burton, Ljuba Tadic, Irene Papas*
An epic account of the struggle of the Yugoslav
partisans during WW2. Somewhat overlong but
generally effective.
Aka: SUTJESKA
WAR                         105 min Cut (7 sec)
B,V,V2                                   VDM; STABL

## FIFTH SEASON, THE **
Gordon Vorster    SOUTH AFRICA          1981
*Martin Freyer, Louise Roux*
A girl who is in danger of going blind falls in love with
a rally motorcyclist who has served a prison sentence
for manslaughter. Average.
DRA                                      100 min
B,V                                      CYC; CIN

## FIFTY-FIVE DAYS IN PEKING **              U
Nicholas Ray       SPAIN/USA             1962
*Charlton Heston, Ava Gardner, David Niven, Flora
Robson, Leo Genn, Robert Helpmann, Harry Andrews,
Paul Lukas, John Ireland, Elizabeth Sellars, Massimo
Serrato, Jacques Sernas, Geoffrey Bayldon*
This overlong star-studded account of the Chinese
Boxer uprising of 1900 fails to give a clear insight into
the causes of the rebellion, such as the resentment felt
by the Chinese at their treatment by the Western
powers. A colourful feast of star names, with Robson
playing the Dowager Empress who encourages the
rebels to take over Peking.
Aka: 55 DAYS AT PEKING
Boa: book 55 Days At Peking by S. Edwards.
DRA   150 min; 147 min (VCC) (ort 154 min) (Cut at
film release)
B,V,V2,LV                   INT/CBS; VCC (VHS only)

## FIFTY-TWO PICK-UP **                       18
John Frankenheimer  USA                 1986
*Roy Scheider, Ann-Margret, Vanity, John Glover,
Robert Trebor, Lonny Chapman, Kelly Preston, Doug
McClure, Clarence Williams III*
A wealthy industrialist is blackmailed when he has
an affair and is forced to re-examine how he feels
about his wife, as he struggles to free himself from the
grip of these squalid extortionists. A confused and
disjointed thriller, heavy on sleazy atmosphere, but
without the benefit of a coherent plot. See also THE
AMBASSADOR.
Aka: 52 PICK-UP
Boa: novel 52 Pick-Up by Elmore Leonard.
THR        104 min (Cut at film release by 1 min 36 sec)
B,V                                              RNK

## FIGHT FOR GLORY **                          18
Hu Sin Yue        HONG KONG

*David Kun, Tsui Sen Keng, Lau Sheung Hiou, Jan Li*
Formula martial arts tale of revenge etc. with no
surprises but one or two well choroegraphed combat
sequences.
MAR                                       78 min
B,V                                              VTEL

## FIGHT FOR JENNY, A **                        PG
Gilbert Moses      USA                   1986
*Philip Michael Thomas, Lesley Anne Warren, Jaclyn-
Rose Lester, William Atherton, Drew Snyder, Jean
Smart, Lynne Moody, Barbara Montgomery, Chip
Arnold, Matthew Faison, Kenneth Kimmins, James
Staley, Wally Taylor*
A divorcee meets a black man and they fall in love and
marry. Though he is ideal as a stepfather to her
daughter from a previous marriage, her bigoted
ex-husband attempts to use the courts to gain custody
of his daughter. A drama based on a real custody
battle fought by a similar couple through the southern
courts.
DRA                        95 min (ort 100 min) mTV
B,V                                              APOL

## FIGHT FOR LIFE *                             PG
Elliott Silverstein   USA                1986
*Jerry Lewis, Morgan Freeman, Patty Duke, Jaclyn
Bernstein, Gerard Parkes, Barry Morse*
Dull tearjerker set in the 1970s following the plight of
parents with an epileptic child. A drug available in
Europe cannot be obtained in the US as it has not yet
been tested. The film highlights the struggle of the
parents to obtain this drug in the face of bureaucratic
obstacles, at the same time the simplistic message
appears to be that drug testing costs lives. A mawkish,
tedious and sentimental melodrama.
DRA                                       94 min
B,V                                              VIR

## FIGHT TO WIN                                 18
Leo Fong          HONG KONG             1988
*Cynthia Rothrock, Richard Norton*
Following his defeat at the hands of a rival, a karate
student must regain a priceless statue and his honour,
and calls in Rothrock to assist him. A competent
martial arts vehicle for the female star of ABOVE
THE LAW and CHINA O'BRIEN.
MAR                                       77 min
V                                              BRAVE

## FIGHTER, THE **                             15
David Lowell Rich   USA                 1983
*Gregory Harrison, Glynnis O'Connor, Pat Hingle,
Steve Inwood, Susan Kellerman, Justin Lord, Susan
Krebs, Roxanne Reese, Robert Englund, Craig Ashley,
Darlene Conley, Peggy Kaye Fury, Lindy Nesbitt,
Susan Ruttan*
An unemployed Vietnam veteran takes up boxing to
make a few bucks but his wife is against this. A
run-of-the-mill boxing tale with all the attendant
cliches.
DRA                        96 min (ort 104 min) mTV
B,V                           VFP; INTMED (VHS only)

## FIGHTING 69TH ***
William Keighley    USA                 1940
*James Cagney, George Brent, Pat O'Brien, Alan Hale,
Jeffrey Lynn, Frank McHugh, Dennis Morgan*
Corny war drama mixing comedy, pathos and action
in a tale that follows the exploits of a famous Irish
regiment. About as unrealistic as they come but
entertaining nonetheless. A computer coloured ver-
sion has become available in the States.
WAR                                       89 min B/W
V                                              WHV

## FIGHTING CHOICE, A **                        PG
Ferdie Fairfax      USA                 1986
*Beau Bridges, Karen Valentine, Patrick Dempsey,*

*Frances Lee McCain, Lawrence Pressman, Danielle Von Zerneck, Allan Arbus, Alice Hirson, Parker Jacobs, Allen Williams, Phillip Linton, Robin Thomas, Charles Lanyer, Nina Henderson*
A 16-year-old boy takes his parents to court in order to be allowed to undergo a risky operation that offers him a chance of curing his epilepsy. A standard sugary Disney offering, treating a good subject with the expected superficiality.
DRA 80 min (ort 91 min) mTV
B,V WDV

## FIGHTING DRAGON, THE *
Peng Chien HONG KONG 1980
*Bruce Liang, Soji Kurata, Yang Sze*
A man out for revenge helps to round up a criminal gang in this dull offering that has too few fight sequences to make it worth seeing.
MAR 90 min
B,V OCEAN

## FIGHTING FIST, THE ** 15
Chin Sheng En HONG KONG 1977
A martial arts fighter disregards the advice of a fortune-teller and nearly loses his life in an encounter with two underworld figures. Following this defeat, he seeks out a master he believes can teach him enough techniques to make him virtually unbeatable. Average.
MAR 83 min
B,V VPD

## FIGHTING FISTS OF SHANGHAI JOE, THE **
Mario Caiano ITALY 1973
(released in USA 1975)
*Robert Hundar, John Stuart (Giacomo Rossi), Gordon Mitchell, Klaus Kinski, Chen Lee, Pancho del Rio, Carla Romanelli, Piero Lulli, Umberto D'Orsi, Dante Maggio, Rick Boyd, Martha Colatriano, Andre Aurelli, Carla Mancini*
A young Chinaman comes into conflict with some unsavoury types when his desire to become a cowboy takes him to the Wild West. An obscure and violent Western, partially redeemed by an unusual premise.
Aka: IL MIO NOME SHANGHAI JOE; MEZZOGIORNO DE FUCCO PER AN HAO; SHANGHAI JOE; TO KILL OR TO DIE
WES 94 min (ort 98 min)
B,V,V2 FFV

## FIGHTING JUSTICE *** 15
Joseph Rubin USA 1988
*James Woods, Robert Downey Jr, Yuji Okumoto, Kurtwood Smith, Margaret Colin*
A defence attorney fallen on hard times and saddled with an idealistic, hero-worshipping assistant, takes on the case of a criminal who killed a fellow-prisoner in self-defence. To bolster a somewhat weak case, he probes the circumstances that surround the man's original conviction and uncovers corruption in high places. A slick, well-acted and tightly-directed court-room drama that maintains tension throughout.
Aka: TRUE BELIEVER
DRA 104 min subH
V 20VIS

## FIGHTING OF SHAOLIN MONKS, THE ** 18
HONG KONG
*Chen Hsing*
Routine martial arts combat with a Shaolin slant.
Aka: FIGHTING OF SHAOLIN MONK, THE
MAR 83 min
V TAMO

## FIGHTING PRINCE OF DONEGAL, THE *** U
Michael O'Herlihy USA 1966
*Susan Hampshire, Peter McEnery, Gordon Jackson, Tom Adams, Andrew Keir, Donal McCann, Norman Woolland, Richard Leech*
A prince tries to unite the clans of Northern Ireland against the British, in this spirited and vivid romp. Jackson makes a good villain.
A/AD 106 min (ort 112 min)
B,V WDV

## FIGHTING SEABEES, THE *** U
Edward Ludwig USA 1944
*John Wayne, Susan Hayward, Dennis O'Keefe, William Frawley, Duncan Renaldo*
A story following the work of the C.B.s or Construction Battalion, as tough foreman Wayne and Navy man O'Keefe organise repairs to installations close to the Japanese lines, whilst stationed on an island in the South Pacific. In between they find time to fight for the affections of Hayward, and Wayne goes into battle at one point with a line of construction vehicles. An overblown, melodramatic but rousing war film.
WAR 95 min B/W
V VCC

## FINAL ASSIGNMENT *
Paul Almond CANADA 1980
*Genevieve Bujold, Michael York, Burgess Meredith, Colleen Dewhurst, Alexandra Stewart*
A Canadian female reporter becomes involved in a plot to smuggle the granddaughter of a Russian dissident to the West for medical treatment and discovers that the Russians are carrying out medical experiments on children. Unadulterated garbage with Montreal standing in for Moscow.
DRA 80 min (ort 100 min)
B,V,V2 GHV

## FINAL COMEDOWN *
Oscar Williams USA 1972
*Billy Dee Williams, D'Urville Martin, Celia Kaye*
Black militants clash violently with the police in this predictable effort.
THR 83 min
B,V ATA L/A; APX

## FINAL CONFLICT, THE: OMEN 3 * 18
Graham Baker USA 1981
*Sam Neill, Rossano Brazzi, Don Gordon, Lisa Harrow, Mason Adams, Robert Arden*
The last part of THE OMEN cycle with a final battle between Christ and the Antichrist taking place. The latter is now 32 and an American ambassador in London. A tired and dispirited sequel.
Aka: FINAL CONFLICT, THE; OMEN 3: THE FINAL CONFLICT; OMEN 3
DRA 109 min
V/sh CBS

## FINAL COUNTDOWN, THE ** PG
Don Taylor USA 1980
*Kirk Douglas, Martin Sheen, Katherine Ross, James Farentino, Ron O'Neal, Charles Durning*
A strange storm carries an American aircraft carrier back in time to the eve of the battle of Pearl Harbour in this interesting fantasy yarn that is marred by an opaque ending.
FAN 98 min (ort 104 min) Cut (6 sec)
V/sh WHV

## FINAL CUT ** 18
Larry G. Brown USA 1986
*J. Don Ferguson, Joe Rainer, Jordan Williams, Brett Rice, T.J. Kennedy, Carla De Lane, Deborah Morehart*
While a film is being shot in the Tournee swamp, an actor and a local girl disappear. The plot quickly develops into a life or death struggle to unravel a sinister scheme; the brainchild of the local sheriff.
A/AD 88 min
B,V CAB L/A; PACEV; TOW

**FINAL CUT ***   18
Frans Nel              USA                    1989
*John Barrett, Matthew Stewardson*
A boy witnesses a "snuff" movie being made at a
deserted warehouse and flees for his life, but having
been identified risks being murdered along with his
mother. Enter our hero, an unemployed sleuth with a
nice line in violent action. Despite the limitations of
its budget, this is a competent thriller. Barrett is
better known as a stuntman, having worked with
Chuck Norris as his fight co-ordinator.
THR                                       90 min
V                                          NWV

**FINAL EXAM ***   18
Jimmy Huston           USA                    1981
*Cecile Bagdadi, Joel S. Rice, Ralph Brown, Deanna
Robbins, Sherry Willis-Burch*
A psychotic killer hunts and kills kids at exam time.
Don't expect any surprises, although this one is
mercifully fairly gore-free.
HOR                                       90 min
B,V,V2,LV                                  EHE

**FINAL EXECUTIONER ***
Anthony M. Dawson (Antonio Margheriti)
                       ITALY                  1984
*Woody Strode, Harrison Muller, David Warbeck,
William Mang, Maria Costa*
In a post-nuclear holocaust world the survivors amuse
themselves by hunting human prey. A dreary and
unappealing effort.
Aka: FINAL EXECUTOR
FAN                                       90 min
B,V                              AVP L/A; MED

**FINAL JEOPARDY, THE ****   15
Michael Pressman       USA                    1985
*Richard Thomas, Mary Crosby, Jeff Corey, Jonathan
Goldsmith, Joey Sagal, Michael Cavanaugh, Jaime
Alba, Travis McKenna, Johnny Venocur, Jordan
Charney, John Malloy, Dennis Farina, Lycia Maff,
Sharon Wyatt, Kim Joseph*
A businessman takes his wife with him on a trip to
Detroit that turns into a terrifying nightmare.
Average.
DRA                      86 min (ort 100 min) mTV
B,V                                        GHV

**FINAL JUSTICE ***   18
Greydon Clark          USA                    1985
*Joe Don Baker, Rossano Brazzi, Bill McKinney,
Patrizia Pellegrino, Venantino Venantini*
A Texan law enforcement officer goes to Europe to get
revenge for the murder of his partner. A violent
actioner whose plot unwinds like a clockwork toy,
with acting to match.
Aka: MALTESE CONNECTION, THE; MALTESE
PROJECT, THE
A/AD                     86 min (ort 90 min) Cut (38 sec)
B,V                                        VES

**FINAL MISSION, THE ***   18
Cirio H. Santiago   PHILIPPINES               1984
*Robert Young, John Dresden, Kaz Gavas*
A former Los Angeles police SWAT team member sees
his family slaughtered and embarks on a mission of
vengeance. This takes him to Laos where he eventually catches up with the killers. Yet another Vietnam
revenger with the usual lashings of gore and minimal
plot.
DRA                      97 min (ort 100 min) Cut (7 sec)
B,V                                        TEVP

**FINAL NOTICE ****   15
Steven Hilliard Stern   USA                   1989
*Gil Gerard, Robert Urich, Melody Anderson, Jackie
Burroughs, Kevin Hicks, Louise Fletcher, David
Ogden Stiers, Steve Landesburg*
A woman-hating murderer foreshadows his crimes by
slashing pictures of women in library books, and then
repeating his actions in reality. The detective
assigned to the case teams up with a female librarian,
and they begin to search for the killer. Competently
adapted by John Gay, this thriller is no better than
average.
Boa: novel by Jonathan Valin.
THR                      88 min (ort 100 min) mCab
V                                          CIC

**FINAL PROGRAMME, THE ****   
Robert Fuest           UK                     1973
*Jon Finch, Jenny Runacre, Sterling Hayden, Patrick
Magee, Hugh Griffith, Harry Andrews, Julie Ege,
Graham Crowden, George Coulouris, Basil Henson,
Derrick O'Connor, Gilles Millinaire, Ronald Lacey,
Sandy Ratcliffe*
Strange tongue-in-cheek story of the attempts to
create a new race of men as the end of the world
approaches. Glossy and mildly appealing but far too
opaque to really work.
Aka: LAST DAYS OF MAN ON EARTH, THE
Boa: novel by Michael Moorcock.
FAN                      85 min (ort 89 min)
B,V                                        TEVP

**FINAL TACTIC ***   PG
Walter Grauman         USA                    1975
*Gerald Gordon, Nicholas Pryor, James Hampton, Roy
Jenson, Bill Lucking, Bradford Dillman, David
Spielberg, Leif Erickson, Normann Burton, Victor
Argo, Lee Paul, Belinda Balaski, Rod Haase, Nancy
Belle Fuller, George Loros*
Three ex-cons on parole are sent on a dangerous
crime-busting mission in this below-average clone of
THE DIRTY DOZEN.
Aka: FORCE FIVE
DRA                      68 min (ort 90 min) mTV
B,V                                        EAG

**FINAL TERROR, THE ***   18
Andrew Davis           USA                    1981
*John Friedrich, Adrian Zmed, Daryl Hannah, Rachel
Ward, Mark Metcalf*
Teenagers camping in the forest are menaced by a
lurking killer. Another low-grade chiller of minimal
interest.
Aka: CAMPSITE MASSACRE
HOR                      80 min (ort 82 min) Cut (27 sec)
B,V                                        TEVP

**FINAL TEST, THE ****   U
Anthony Asquith        UK                     1953
*Jack Warner, Robert Morley, George Relph, Brenda
Bruce, Richard Wattis, Adrianne Allen*
A champion batsman looking forward to his last test
match is dismayed to learn that his son is more
interested in being a poet than in seeing him play. A
minor comedy-drama, held back by the lack of
momentum and unnecessarily padded out with real-
life cricketing stars. Scripted by Rattigan.
Boa: TV play by Terence Rattigan.
DRA                      88 min (ort 91 min) B/W
V                                          ODY

**FINALLY SUNDAY ****   PG
Francois Truffaut   FRANCE                    1983
*Fanny Ardent, Jean-Louis Trintignant, Phillip
Laudenbach, Caroline Sihol, Philippe Morier-Genoud,
Xavier Saint Macary*
A wife and her lover are found murdered. Suspicion
falls on her estate agent husband whose loyal secret-
ary tries to prove his innocence. A mildly diverting
Hitchcock style thriller with a few touches of humour.
The excellent photography is by Nestor Almendros.
Aka: CONFIDENTIALLY YOURS; VIVEMENT
DIMANCHE
Boa: novel The Long Saturday Night by Charles

Williams.
THR 107 min (ort 111 min) B/W
B,V TEVP

**FIND A PLACE TO DIE ** ** 15
Anthony Ascott (Giuliano Carmineo)
ITALY 1968
*Jeffrey Hunter, Pascale Petit, Piero Lulli, Daniela
Giordano, Gianni Pallavicini, Nello Pazzafini, Aldo
Lastretti, Reza Fahzeli*
A young geologist and his wife are attacked by bandits
after they have discovered gold. The man is injured
and his wife goes for help to the nearby town, which is
infested by thieves and cut-throats. An extremely
violent tale of revenge and sudden death.
Aka: CERCATI UN POSTO PER MORIRE; JOE,
CERCATI UN POSTO PER MORIRE
WES 96 min (ort 100 min)
B,V GOST L/A; DFS; KRP/XTACY

**FIND THE LADY *** ** PG
John Trent CANADA 1976
*Lawrence Dane, John Candy, Dick Emery, Mickey
Rooney, Peter Cook, Alexandra Bastedo, Richard
Monette, Bob Vinci, Ed McNamara, Tim Henry,
Robert McHeady, Harry Spiegel, Laurie Seto, Michael
Kirby, Rummy Bishop*
A bumbling and accident-prone detective is assigned
to keep a watch on an inept gangster who has been
hired to kidnap a beautiful socialite. As the clumsy
detective staggers from one mishap to the next, the
complications begin to mount up in this slapstick
comedy of kidnapping and mistaken identity.
COM 90 min
B,V INT/CBS; MPV

**FINDERS, KEEPERS ** ** 15
Richard Lester USA 1984
*Michael O'Keefe, Beverly D'Angelo, Louis Gossett Jr,
Ed Lauter, David Wayne, Brian Dennehy, Pamela
Stephenson, John Schuck, Timothy Blake, Jim Carrey,
Jack Riley*
A crazy comedy about $5,000,000 hidden in a coffin on
a train with con-artists, hit-men and assorted weirdos,
that could have been very funny indeed but remains
undeveloped.
Aka: FINDERS KEEPERS
Boa: novel The Next-To-Last Train Ride by C. Dennis.
COM 91 min (ort 96 min)
B,V CBS

**FINE GOLD ** ** 15
Anthony J. Loma USA 1987
*Stewart Granger, Lloyd Bochner, Ted Wass, Jane
Badler*
The rivalry between two winegrowing families over
the production of a perfect vintage results in much
suffering for all concerned, but love later finds a way
for them to settle their differences. An unoriginal
yarn, adequately handled, but no more than passable.
DRA 96 min
V/sh CBS

**FINE MESS, A *** PG
Blake Edwards USA 1985
*Ted Danson, Stuart Margolin, Howie Mandel, Richard
Mulligan, Jennifer Edwards, Paul Sorvino, Maria
Conchita Alonso*
A zany comedy set at a race-course, involving an
incompetent film-maker who accidentally discovers a
doping plot and attempts to cash in on it. One of
Edwards' slapstick sagas, with the laughs spread out
sparingly.
COM 87 min (ort 100 min)
B,V RCA

**FINGERS *** ** 18
James Toback USA 1978

Harvey Keitel, Tisa Farrow, Jim Brown, Michael V.
Gazzo, Tanya Roberts, Marian Seldes, Carol Francis
A man who dreams of becoming a concert pianist is
forced to moonlight as a strong-arm Mafia debt
collector for his overbearing gangster father. When he
meets a prostitute he finds himself torn between two
worlds in this harsh and sombre drama.
DRA 90 min
B,V CINE

**FINISH LINE *** ** 15
John Nicolella USA 1988
*James Brolin, Josh Brolin*
A former track star coaches his son, forcing him to
excel in track and field events and in the process
driving him into a dangerous dependency on drugs.
DRA 90 min (ort 96 min)
V CHV

**FINISHING OUT *** 18
Bruce Seven USA
*Heather Wayne, Sharon Mitchell, Erica Boyer, Tom
Byron*
A father sends his unruly daughter to finishing school
in the hope that she will acquire manners and a little
refinement, but her behaviour there can hardly be
described as ladylike. Another silly softcore romp.
A 40 min Cut (17 sec)
V GENT; KRP

**FINISHING SCHOOL *** *
Alois Brumme WEST GERMANY 1969
*Elke Hagen, Jutta Dorn, Gabrielle Pappel*
Dated sex comedy set in a girls school.
Aka: GEFAHRLICHE SEXFRUREIFE MADCHEN
A 84 min
B,V VCL/CBS

**FIRE AND ICE ** ** PG
Ralph Bakshi USA 1982
*Voices of: Susan Tyrrell, Maggie Roswell, William
Ostrander, Stephen Mendel*
Animated feature about the struggle between Good
and Evil with a sword wielding hero and a buxom
heroine. Passable but not inspired, this cartoon does
not compare well to Bakshi's earlier works such as
FRITZ THE CAT or WIZARDS. In this one the
animations were traced from live-action footage, and
benefited from the design work of illustrator Frank
Frazetta. Written by Roy Thomas and Jeff Conway.
CAR 81 min
B,V,V2 TEVP

**FIRE AND RAIN ** ** 15
Jerry Jameson USA 1989
*Charles Haid, John Beck, Tom Bosley, Penny Fuller,
Robert Guillaume, David Hasselhoff, Dean Jones,
Patti LaBelle, Lawrence Pressman, Susan Ruttan,
Angie Dickinson*
A true-life tale of an aircraft in distress, with a host of
stars in minor roles, doing little to enliven this
formula account of the 1985 Delta Airlines disaster,
when Flight 191 crashed in Dallas. As ever, Holly-
wood demonstrates its addiction to disaster themes as
a source of inspiration.
THR 83 min (ort 100 min) mCab
V CIC

**FIRE FIGHT *** 18
Scott Pfeiffer USA 1987
*James Pfeiffer, Janice Carraher, Mark Chaet, Jack
Tucker*
Post-WW3 saga in which a vicious gang attempts to
control what's left of the country after a catastrophic
Soviet attack. Meanwhile, the gangleader's ex-wife
plots with others to bring about his downfall.
A/AD 86 min
V WATER

## FIRE IN THE NIGHT ** 15
John Steven Soet          USA          1985
*John Martin, Patrick St Esprit, Muni Zano, Burt Ward, Graciela Casillas*
A wealthy executive and karate expert who has a stranglehold over a small town, is challenged to a duel by a young girl, in a brave but foolhardy attempt to rid the town of his baleful influence.
A/AD          85 min (ort 90 min) Cut (8 sec)
B,V          CAN; ARC

## FIRE IN THE SKY, A *** PG
Jerry Jameson          USA          1978
*Richard Crenna, Elizabeth Ashley, David Dukes, Joanna Miles, Lloyd Bochner, Andrew Duggan, Nicolas Coster, Merlin Olsen, Maggie Wellman, Marj Dusay, John Larch, Kip Niven, William Bogart, Jenny O'Hara, Michael Biehn, Al White*
An overlong and vastly expensive disaster movie, in which a comet is seen to be heading for Phoenix, Arizona. Warnings of impending doom from an anxious astronomer are ignored by the town council who dither over evacuation plans until it is almost too late. The tedious multi-character plot is best ignored in favour of the excellent special effects and miniature work, plus the well-handled crowd scenes.
Boa: story by Paul Gallico.
A/AD          140 min (ort 150 min) mTV
V          RCA

## FIRE IN THE WIND ** 18
USA          198-
*Stephen Sander, Richard Tarkington, Michael Lane, Michael Prichard, Rockne Tarkington, Heidi Vaughn, Ron Thompson, Daniel Booth*
Another post-Vietnam POW rescue epic on the same lines as all those other "Rambo" type sagas.
WAR          90 min
B,V          VDM; KES

## FIRE OVER ENGLAND *** 15
William K. Howard          UK          1936
*Laurence Olivier, Flora Robson, Vivien Leigh, Leslie Banks, Raymond Massey, Tamara Desni, Morton Selten, Lyn Harding, George Thirlwell, James Mason, Henry Oscar, Robert Newton, Donald Calthrop, Charles Carson*
A fine cast coupled with good acting make this historical drama dealing with England's struggle against the Spanish Armada a most enjoyable film. Flora Robson's performance as Queen Elizabeth I is considered a gem, and rightly so. Look out for Mason in an early (and unbilled) small part.
Boa: novel by A.E.W. Mason.
DRA          91 min B/W
B,V,V2          PRV; VDM/GHV

## FIRE WITH FIRE ** 15
Duncan Gibbins          USA          1986
*Craig Sheffer, Virginia Madsen, Jon Polito, Jeffrey Jay Cohen, Kate Reid, Jean Smart*
A young teenage girl at a Catholic school falls for a boy serving a sentence at a juvenile detention centre, but their love affair has serious consequences. A film that sails along pleasantly enough until the ridiculous ending.
Aka: CAPTIVE HEARTS
DRA          105 min
B,V          CIC

## FIREBACK * 18
Teddy Page          USA          1978
*Richard Harrison, Bruce Baron, Gwendolyn Hung, James Gaines, Ruel Vernal, Ann Milhench, Dove Anderson, Ronnie Patterson*
Vietnam-veteran-vengeance once more. Oh yes, this time round our vet is equipped with a massive superweapon and is out to avenge the death of his wife.

A/AD          85 min
B,V          APX; INTMED: MPI

## FIREBIRD 2015 A.D. **
David M. Robertson          USA          1980
*Doug McClure, Darren McGavin, George Touliatos*
In the 21st century oil shortages have led to the total prohibition of private motoring, and driving is a capital crime. This does not deter two hot-rod enthusiasts, who hide their cars in the desert.
A/AD          97 min
B,V          HER

## FIRECHASERS, THE **
Sidney Hayers          UK          1970
*Chad Everett, Anjanette Comer, Keith Barron, Rupert Davies, Joanne Dainton, James Hayter, Robert Flemyng, Roy Kinnear, Allan Cuthbertson, John Loder*
An insurance investigator is after the arsonist responsible for a series of fires in this solid, workmanlike drama.
DRA          100 min
B,V          PRV

## FIREFIST OF INCREDIBLE DRAGON ** 18
Jimmy Tseng          HONG KONG          1980
*Maple Lin, Jerry Young, Keith Lee*
Another formula martial arts adventure.
MAR          76 min (ort 90 min) Cut (51 sec)
B,V          VPD

## FIREFOX ** 15
Clint Eastwood          USA          1982
*Clint Eastwood, Freddie Jones, David Huffman, Ronald Lacy, Warren Clarke, Stefan Schnabel, Kenneth Colley, Nigel Hawthorne*
An ex-US pilot is persuaded to undertake a mission to the USSR to steal a supersonic jet fighter that is invisible to radar. Terribly slow and dull plot development mars and ultimately overpowers the exciting flying sequences. Eastwood as the Russian speaking US pilot does little to convince.
Boa: novel by Craig Thomas.
THR          121 min (ort 137 min)
V          WHV

## FIREHOUSE * 15
J. Christian Ingvordsen
USA          1986
*Gianna Rains, Martha Peterson, Renee Raiford, Gideon Fountain, Peter MacKenzie*
A tepid clone of POLICE ACADEMY, that's set in a firehouse where the first batch of female graduates are out to prove they're as good as the men.
COM          86 min
B,V          CINE

## FIREHOUSE ** 15
Alex March          USA          1972
*Richard Roundtree, Vince Edwards, Richard Jaeckel, Andrew Duggan, Sheila E. Frazier, Val Avery, Paul Le Mat, Michael Lerner, Mel Scott, Howard Curtis, Joshua Shelley, Alma Beltran, Mwako Cumbuka, Ty Henderson, Dewayne Jessie*
A young black trainee joins an all-white team of fire fighters. He has to face plenty of racial harassment at the same time as a series of deliberate fires breaks out in a black area of the city. A fairly average pilot for a TV series.
Aka: NIGHT WATCH
DRA          74 min (ort 90 min) mTV
B,V,V2          IFS L/A; VDEL

## FIREPOWER * 15
Michael Winner          UK          1979
*Sophia Loren, James Coburn, Eli Wallach, Anthony Franciosa, O.J. Simpson, George Grizzard, Vincent*

Gardenia, Fred Stuthman, Richard Caldicot, Frank
Sanguineau, George Touliatos, Hank Garrett, Conrad
Roberts, Billy Barty
A chemist is murdered by an international crime
syndicate and his wife sets out to nail those responsi-
ble, in this glossy and convoluted yarn of pleasant
locations and insipid dialogue.
A/AD            99 min (ort 104 min) Cut (15 sec)
B,V,V2                         PRV L/A; CH5

**FIRESTARTER ***                                    15
Mark L. Lester          USA                        1984
David Keith, Drew Barrymore, Freddie Jones, George
C. Scott, Martin Sheen, Heather Locklear, Art Carney,
Louise Fletcher, Moses Gunn, Antonio Fargas
A little girl has strange psychic powers and is able to
set fire to anything at will, and the government
decides that she could be useful as a weapon. A
muddled fantasy yarn with a few good effects but little
else of note. Written by Stanley Mann.
Boa: novel by Stephen King.
HOR                         109 min (ort 115 min)
B,V                       TEVP; WHV (VHS only)

**FIREWALKER ***                                     15
J. Lee Thompson         USA                        1986
Chuck Norris, Louis Gossett Jr, Melody Anderson,
Will Sampson, Sonny Landham, John Rhys-Davies,
Ian Abercrombie
After a series of unsuccessful expeditions, two inept
adventurers meet a young woman with a map that
will lead them to forgotten Aztec treasure buried deep
in Guatemala. A dire adventure film done in the style
of RAIDERS OF THE LOST ARK but with none of
that film's verve.
A/AD                        101 min (ort 104 min)
B,V                                            RNK

**FIRING SQUAD ***                                   15
Michel Andrieu          USA                        1989
Stephen Quimette, Robin Renucci, Cedric Smith,
Charley Boorman
An absorbing WW2 drama based on McDougall's
award-winning play in which a soldier finds his career
in jeopardy because of a moment of cowardice in the
heat of battle. In order to clear his name he is obliged
to order a firing squad to execute a fellow soldier, but a
few hours before the execution learns that the conde-
mned man is innocent.
Boa: play by Colin McDougall.
DRA                                           89 min
V                                                BCB

**FIRST AMONG EQUALS: PARTS 1 TO 4 ***              15
John Gorrie/Brian Mills/Sarah Harding
                        UK                         1986
David Robb, Tom Wilkinson, James Faulkner, Jeremy
Child, Diana Hardcastle, Anita Carey, Joanna David
Competent political drama based on Archer's novel,
that deals with the careers of four politicians, all of
whom have an overwhelming desire to be Prime
Minister. Fair.
Boa: novel by Jeffrey Archer.
DRA                 484 min (4 cassettes) mTV
V                                           CASPIC

**FIRST BLOOD ***                                    15
Ted Kotcheff           USA                         1982
Sylvester Stallone, Richard Crenna, Brian Dennehy,
David Caruso, Jack Starrett
An ex-Green Beret gets into trouble with the local
police, escapes and uses his military skills to defeat
his pursuers. Stallone mumbles and stumbles through
this lame-brained actioner, spreading mayhem all
about him yet never suffering more than a scratch
himself. Followed by RAMBO: FIRST BLOOD, PART
2.
Boa: novel by David Morrell.

A/AD                        89 min (ort 97 min)
V/sh                      TEVP; GHV (VHS only)

**FIRST DEADLY SIN, THE ***                          15
Brian G. Hutton        USA                         1980
Frank Sinatra, Faye Dunaway, David Dukes, Brenda
Vaccaro, Anthony Zerbe, Martin Gabel, James
Whitmore
A New York cop tracks down a vicious homicidal
maniac whilst his wife is dying in hospital. Dunaway
has little to do except act comatose in this film, but the
atmospheric script and a convincing performance from
Sinatra do much to make this one of his better movies.
The score is by Gordon Jenkins.
Boa: novel by Lawrence Sanders.
DRA                         108 min (ort 112 min)
B,V                                            WHV

**FIRST FAMILY ***                                   15
Buck Henry             USA                         1980
Bob Newhart, Gilda Radner, Madeline Kahn, Richard
Benjamin, Bob Dishy, Harvey Korman, Rip Torn,
Austin Pendleton, Fred Willard, Julius Harris, Buck
Henry
Political satire about the strange members of the US
President's family. One or two flashes of wit are lost in
the generally heavy-handed script.
COM                          96 min (ort 104 min)
B,V                                            WHV

**FIRST GREAT TRAIN ROBBERY, THE ***                15
Michael Crichton       UK                          1978
Sean Connery, Donald Sutherland, Lesley-Anne
Down, Alan Webb, Malcolm Terris, Robert Lang,
Michael Elphick, Wayne Sleep, Pamela Salem,
Gabrielle Lloyd, George Downing, James Cossins,
John Bett, Janine Duvitski
In 1855 a gang of crooks plan to rob an express train of
a cargo of gold bullion. Uneven in places but generally
well-paced and atmospheric, with the story holding up
quite well. Scripted by Michael Crichton.
Aka: GREAT TRAIN ROBBERY, THE
Boa: novel The Great Train Robbery by Michael
Crichton.
A/AD                 106 min (ort 111 min) Cut (12 sec)
V                                              WHV

**FIRST LOVE ***                                     15
Joan Darling           USA                         1977
William Katt, Susan Dey, John Heard, Beverly
D'Angelo, Robert Loggia, Swoosie Kurtz
A young man falls for a girl who is more interested in
a married man in this soggy and unsatisfying melod-
rama.
Boa: short story A Sentimental Education by Harold
Brodkey.
DRA                                           92 min
B,V                                            CIC

**FIRST LOVE ***                                     15
Maximilian Schell
                  FRANCE/SWITZERLAND/UK           1970
Dominique Sanda, John Moulder-Brown, Maximilian
Schell, John Osborne
A son falls in love with his father's mistress and all
the expected complications result. Uneven direction
and sudden inexplicable shifts in mood rather spoil
the intelligent script.
Boa: novella by Ivan Turgenev.
DRA                                           96 min
B,V                                  VFP L/A; HER

**FIRST MEN IN THE MOON, THE ***                     U
Nathan Juran           UK                          1964
Edward Judd, Lionel Jeffries, Martha Hyer, Erik
Chitty, Marne Maitland, Hugh McDermott, Miles
Malleson, Gladys Henson, Gordon Robinson, Sean

*Kelly, Betty McDowall, John Murray Scott, Lawrence Herder, Paul Carpenter, Peter Finch*
A lavish but uneven adaptation of Wells' story of a Victorian inventor who discovers a material impervious to gravity and uses it to construct a spaceship for a voyage to the moon. The addition of some comic elements turns the film into something of a lark but despite this it remains a worthy and enjoyable experience. Special effects are by Ray Harryhausen.
Boa: novel by H.G. Wells.
FAN                                    99 min (ort 103 min)
V                                                    RCA

**FIRST MISSION, THE ***                       18
Samo Hung          HONG KONG          198-
*Jackie Chan, Samo Hung*
Chan stars as a policeman who looks after his mentally retarded brother Samo. When Samo is innocently caught up in a gangland fight over some stolen jewels he is taken prisoner and held hostage in order to force Chan to hand over a police informer. A fast-paced and spirited kung fu adventure.
Aka: HEART OF DRAGON
A/AD                                              87 min
B,V                                                  VPD

**FIRST MONDAY IN OCTOBER ****               15
Ronald Neame          USA          1981
*Walter Matthau, Jill Clayburgh, Barnard Hughes, Jan Sterling, James Stephens, Joshua Bryant*
The first female member of the Supreme Court (a real conservative) clashes with her more liberal male colleagues but eventually wins them over to her point of view. Mildly amusing but seriously deficient in pace and direction.
Boa: play by Jerome Lawrence and Robert E. Lee.
COM                                    93 min (ort 99 min)
B,V                                                  CIC

**FIRST MRS FRASER, THE ****
Sinclair Hill          UK          1932
*Joan Barry, Henry Ainley, Dorothy Dix, Harold Huth, Richard Cooper, Gibb McLaughlin, Hargrave Pawson, Henry Hewitt, Arnold Riches, Ivan Brandt, Oriel Ross, Millicent Wolff, Eileen Peel, Naunton Wayne, Frances Day, Noel Leyland*
A divorced woman who still loves her husband discovers that his second wife is plotting to divorce him in order to marry a peer. All ends happily with the husband returning to his first wife in this dated but enjoyable melodrama.
Boa: play by St J. Ervine. Osca: GLORIFYING THE AMERICAN GIRL
DRA                                              95 min B/W
V                                                    WOOD

**FIRST OF THE FEW, THE ****                    U
Leslie Howard          UK          1942
*Leslie Howard, David Niven, Rosamund John, Roland Culver, David Horne, Anne Firth, John H. Roberts, Derrick De Marney, Rosalyn Boulter, Tonie Edgar Bruce, Gordon McLeod, Erik Freund, Filippo Del Guidice, Brefni O'Rorke*
Fine biographical drama about R.J. Mitchell who foresaw the advent of WW2 and developed the Spitfire. A restrained account that makes the most of its limited budget. Howard's last screen appearance.
Aka: SPITFIRE; SPITFIRE: THE FIRST OF THE FEW
DRA                           117 min; 107 min (ODY) B/W
B,V                                      PRV; ODY (VHS only)

**FIRST REBEL, THE ****                         U
William A. Seiter          USA          1939
*John Wayne, Claire Trevor, Brian Donlevy, George Sanders, Robert Barrat, John F. Hamilton, Moroni Olsen, Eddie Quillan, Chill Wills, Ian Wolfe, Wallis Clark, Monte Montague, Eddy Waller, Clay Clement, Olaf Hytten*

Wayne plays frontiersman James Smith, who leads a band of men against a tyrannical British captain in pre-revolutionary American colonies as he sets out to smash liquor trafficking with the Indians. A simple and unpretentious tale with a nice performance from Trevor as the girl who's sweet on Wayne.
Aka: ALLEGHENY UPRISING
Boa: novel N.H. Swanson. Osca: BACK FROM ETERNITY (KVD); SHE WORE A YELLOW RIBBON (VCC)
WES        70 min; 169 min (2 film cassette – VCC) B/W
B,V                                      KVD; VCC (VHS only)

**FIRST TIME, THE ****                         15
Noel Nosseck          USA          1982
*Susan Anspach, Jennifer Jason Leigh, Peter Barton, Edward Winter, Michael Mackenzie, John Anderson, Krita Errickson, Harriet Nelson*
A mother and daughter disagree over sexual morality and find it difficult to reconcile their conflicts. When the daughter runs off to San Diego with her boyfriend, the girl's mother comes after her. However, though frustrated herself, she still refuses to recognise her daughter's needs. This competent examination of the generation gap says nothing new.
DRA                                              96 min
B,V                                      HER L/A; POLY

**FIRST TIME, THE ****                         15
Charlie Loventhal          USA          1983
*Tim Choate, Krista Errickson, Wallace Shawn, Marshall Efron, Wendie Jo Sperber, Wendy Fulton, Raymond Patterson, Cathryn Damon*
A first-year college student is still a virgin, but he's looking for love and not just sex in this warmhearted and articulate tale. Set in a college where the women outnumber the men, this has Choate making up for his lack of sexual experience by his expertise in film-making. Contains many funny moments as college life in general and film-school life in particular are both lampooned unmercifully. Loventhal's directorial debut.
COM                                              92 min
B,V                              VTC L/A; FIFTH; GLOB

**FIRST TRAVELING SALESLADY, THE ***
Arthur Lubin          USA          1956
*Ginger Rogers, Carol Channing, Barry Nelson, James Arness, David Brian, Robert F. Simon, Frank Wilcox, Dan White, Harry V. Cheshire, Clint Eastwood, Ed Cassidy, Fred Essler*
Two saleswomen wander around the Wild West and are forced to sell barbed wire instead of corsets in this dismal and laboured comedy. Originally this one was written for Mae West.
Osca: LADY TAKES A CHANCE, A (KVD – asa)
COM             90 min; 88 min (VCC) (ort 92 min)
B,V                                      KVD; VCC (VHS only)

**FIRST TURN ON, THE ***                       18
Michael Herz/Samuel Weil
                               USA          1983
*Georgina Havrell, Michael Sanville, Googy Gress*
Campers trapped in a cave by a rockfall, pass the time until they find a way out by recounting true and imaginary accounts of their sexual initiation.
COM                                          85 min Cut
B,V,V2                                            MED

**FISH CALLED WANDA, A ******                  15
Charles Crichton          USA          1988
*John Cleese, Michael Palin, Kevin Kline, Jamie Lee Curtis, Maria Aitken, Tom Georgeson, Patricia Hayes, Geoffrey Palmer*
A motley collection of jewel thieves have just pulled off a big robbery in London's Hatton Garden. Only the brains behind the robbery knows where the jewels have been hidden and he's now in prison. The gang's sexy member plans to seduce his defence counsel and

obtain the loot for herself. A hilarious farce replete with bad taste jokes (some involving squashed animals) and a witty script written by Cleese and Crichton. AA: S. Actor (Kline).

COM                                    109 min
V                                        MGM

## FISH THAT SAVED PITTSBURGH, THE *
Gilbert Moses              USA              1979
*Julius Erving, James Bond III, Stockard Channing, Jonathan Winters, Margaret Avery, Jack Kehoe, Meadowlark Lemon, Nicholas Pryor, Flip Wilson, Kareem Abdul-Jabbar*
A basketball team changes its name and uses astrology to win the championship in this simple-minded comedy. The disco soundtrack is an annoyance, but less of one than the sheer lack of laughs.

COM                                    103 min
B,V,V2                                    GHV

## FIST **
Norman Jewison             USA              1978
*Sylvester Stallone, Rod Steiger, Peter Boyle, Melinda Dillon, David Huffman, Tony LoBianco, Kevin Conway, Cassie Yates, Henry Wilcoxon, Brian Dennehy, Peter Donat*
The story of the rise and fall of a power-mad union boss loosely based on the life of Jimmy Hoffa. A good script is largely wasted by poor casting, especially with regard to Stallone, who was well and truly out of his depth in this one.
Aka: F.I.S.T.
Boa: novel by Joe Eszterhas.
DRA                        125 min (ort 145 min)
B,V                                       WHV

## FISTFIGHTER **                            18
Frank Zuniga               USA              1989
*George Rivero, Matthias Hues, Edward Albert, Brenda Bakke, Mike Connors, Simon Andreu, Tony Isbert, Gus Rethwisch, Billy Graham*
A man plunges into the brutal world of bare-fist fighting in order to avenge the murder of his brother by one of the champions of this sport. However, before he can put his plan into action, he is obliged to demonstrate his skill against other fighters and his success in the ring leads to unforeseen consequences. Violent, witless and largely forgettable.
Aka: FIST FIGHTER
A/AD                        92 min (ort 99 min)
V                                   CBS; CASPIC

## FISTFUL OF DEATH, A **                     15
                           USA
*Lincoln Tate, William Berger, Perry Dell, Dean Stratford, Richard Melvill*
The story of a ruthless gunslinger and those foolish enough to cross him. Average.
WES                                     84 min
B,V                                       VPD

## FISTFUL OF DOLLARS, A ***                  15
Sergio Leone
              ITALY/SPAIN/WEST GERMANY     1964
*Clint Eastwood, Gian Maria Volonte, Marianne Koch, Wolfgang Lukschy, S. Rupp, Antonio Prieto, Pepe Clavo, Benny Reeves, Mario Brega, Carol Brown*
One of the first and best of the spaghetti Westerns, loosely based on Kurosawa's YOJIMBO. A mysterious stranger rides into a town that is divided between two warring families and proceeds to play one side off against the other. The excellent score is by Ennio Morricone. Followed by FOR A FEW DOLLARS MORE and THE GOOD, THE BAD AND THE UGLY.
Aka: PER UN PUGNO DI DOLLARI
WES                                     96 min
B,V                                       WHV

## FISTFUL OF DYNAMITE, A **                  18
Sergio Leone               ITALY            1971
*Rod Steiger, James Coburn, Romolo Valli, Maria Monti, Rik Battaglia, Franco Graziosi, Domingo Antoine, Goffredo Pistoni, Roy Bosier, John Frederick*
A fugitive IRA man and a Mexican bandit team up to rob a bank which is also a jail holding political prisoners in a story set at the time of the 1913-1914 Mexican Revolution. A vastly over-long and over-inflated saga that would have worked well enough with half the running time. The score is by Ennio Morricone.
Aka: DUCK, YOU SUCKER!; GIU LA TESTA
WES                       132 min (ort 158 min)
B,V                                       WHV

## FISTS AND GUTS **                          15
                        HONG KONG
*Lau Ka-Wing, Lau Ka Fei, Lo Lieh*
Routine martial arts thriller.
MAR                     87 min Cut (3 min 11 sec)
V                                        OCEAN

## FISTS OF FURY ***                          18
Lo Wei                  HONG KONG           1971
*Bruce Lee, Miao Ker Hsiu, Nora Miao, James Tien, Maria Yi, Han Ying Chieh, Tony Liu, Li Hua Sxe, Robert Baker*
A kung fu student returns to Shanghai in 1908 for his master's funeral and takes an oath to refrain from using his skills. He takes a job at a Bangkok ice factory but following the mysterious disappearance of his cousins, discovers it to be no more than a front for a drug smuggling ring. Refusing to be bribed, he sets out to smash the operation. A simple plot is combined with dazzling fight sequences in Bruce Lee's first martial arts film.
Aka; BIG BOSS, THE; FIST OF FURY
MAR              99 min (ort 103 min) Cut (2 min 51 sec)
B,V,V2                                     RNK

## FISTS OF FURY 2 ***
Li Tso-Nan (To Lo Po)
                        HONG KONG           1976
*Bruce Li (Ho Tsung-Tao), Lo Lieh, Tien Fong, Ku Feng, Tong Yim Chen, Mgai Ping O, Shum Shim Po*
Kung fu movie set in Shanghai in the 1920s where a man battles a sinister criminal organisation and goes all out for revenge when his mother is murdered.
Aka: CHING-WU MEW SU-TSI; FIST OF FURY PART 2
MAR                                     98 min
B,V,V2                                    HOK

## FISTS OF SHAOLIN **                        18
Li Hsun                 HONG KONG           1973
*Pai Ying, Han Ying Chieh, Wan Chung Shan*
A man hears of a plot to murder his family and rushes home to defend them. He arrives too late finding them massacred and the family's sacred emblem, a Shaolin Fighting Stick, stolen. Honour must be avenged etc.
Aka: FIST OF SHAOLIN
MAR                     83 min Cut (5 min 34 sec)
V                                  IVC L/A; VPD

## FISTS OF STEEL **                          18
Martin Dolman              ITALY            1985
*Daniel Greene, Janet Agren, Claudio Cassinelli*
A tale set in the near future, with the Earth severely polluted and an ecologist preparing to expose the activities of a powerful corporation. A cyborg is sent to kill him but it baulks at its mission, and takes refuge in a desert saloon, where a conflict ultimately erupts when two hit-men are sent after it. A kind of mediocre clone of THE TERMINATOR.
FAN                    85 min; 89 min (VES) Cut (1 sec)
B,V                                VES/CBS; VES

## FISTS OF VENGEANCE, THE *
Cheng Hung Man   HONG KONG   1973
*Kung Bun, Tung Chi, Shoji Kurata, Lu Pi Chen, Tsao
Chien, Lu Ping, Chen Hui Lou, Yong Lung, Pai I Feng,
Tang Hsin, Has Su, Chiang Chih Yang, Yu Sung
Chao*
A Japanese fighter is sent to escort a shipment of red
sand, that is used in the making of high-grade steel
and has the usual conflicts, in this early and unsoph-
isticated effort.
Aka: FIST OF VENGEANCE; TWO FISTS VERSUS
SEVEN SAMURAI
MAR                                  77 min
B,V,V2              ICV L/A; NELS/CBS

## FITZCARRALDO ***                        PG
Werner Herzog   WEST GERMANY   1982
*Klaus Kinski, Claudia Cardinale, Jose Lewgoy, Paul
Hittscher, Miguel Angel Fuentes, Grande Othelo*
At the turn of the century, an eccentric Irishman is
obsessed by the idea of building an opera house in the
Peruvian jungle and is forced to drag his boat over the
mountains from one river to another. A hauntingly
beautiful film; pointless but undeniably hypnotic.
DRA                     160 min; 150 min (PAL)
B,V                                PVG; PAL

## FIVE CORNERS **                          15
Tony Bill              USA              1987
*Jodie Foster, Tim Robbins, Catherine De Prume, Todd
Graff, John Turturo*
A messy and incoherent look at teenagers and their
life in the Bronx in the 1960s, mostly dealing with the
cat-and-mouse game played between Foster and a
psychotic rapist she helped convict who has just been
released. Lots of good ideas swim about in this one but
never come together to form a clear story.
THR                                  91 min
V                                     PATHE

## FIVE DAYS FROM HOME ***
George Peppard         USA              1978
*George Peppard, Neville Brand, Savannah Smith,
Sherry Boucher, Victor Campos, Robert Donner*
An ex-cop who is serving a prison sentence for having
killed his wife's lover has only six days left to serve.
However, when his son is critically injured in an
accident he breaks out of jail in Louisiana and heads
for Los Angeles to see him by Christmas Eve. A
spirited but unlikely tale.
THR                                 107 min
B,V,V2                                  GHV

## FIVE DAYS ONE SUMMER **                  PG
Fred Zinnemann
                    AUSTRALIA/USA     1982
*Sean Connery, Betsy Brantley, Lambert Wilson,
Jennifer Hilary, Isabel Dean, Anna Massey, Gerald
Buhr*
In 1932 a middle-aged doctor takes a young woman,
who poses as his wife but is really his mistress, on a
mountain-climbing expedition in Switzerland, where
she falls in love with a guide. Stilted and rather
ponderous, despite marvellous attention to detail and
splendid photography. The score is by Elmer Bern-
stein.
Boa: short story Maiden, Maiden by Kay Boyle.
DRA                                 108 min
B,V                                    WHV

## FIVE DESPERATE WOMEN **
Ted Post               USA              1971
*Anjanette Comer, Bradford Dillman, Joan Hackett,
Stefanie Powers, Denise Nicholas, Julie Sommars,
Robert Conrad, Connie Sawyer, Beatrice Manley,
Patrick Waltz*
Five female college graduates hold a reunion in a
rented mansion on an island and are menaced by an
escaped lunatic. A standard production-line thriller.

Boa: story by Lawrence Gordon.
THR              73 min (ort 90 min) mTV
B,V                                    GHV

## FIVE FINGERS OF STEEL **                 18
                    HONG KONG
A criminally-minded martial artist starts up a kung
fu school with his nephew, but only in order to front
his less honest activities. Their dominance is brought
to an end when they kill an old boxer and incur the
wrath of one man. Average.
MAR                                  88 min
B,V                                    VPD

## FIVE FOR HELL **
Frank Kramer (Gianfranco Pardini)
                    ITALY              1968
*Klaus Kinski, John Garko, Margaret Lee, Nick
Jordan, Sal Borgese, Luciano Rosi, Sam Burke*
A five-man group of American commandos, each
possessing a special skill, goes behind enemy lines to
obtain information on a German WW2 offensive.
Aka: CINQUE PER L'INFERNO
WAR                                  88 min
B,V                                    VPD

## FIVE GUNS WEST **
Roger Corman           USA              1955
*Touch (Mike) Connors, John Lund, Dorothy Malone,
Paul Birch, Jonathan Haze, Jack Ingram, Larry Thor*
The Confederate army enlists the help of five crimin-
als to steal some Union gold and trap a traitor. The
plot is reminiscent of THE DIRTY DOZEN. This was
Corman's directorial debut.
WES                                  78 min
B,V                                    RNK

## FIVE MILE CREEK **                        U
George Miller          AUSTRALIA        1984
*Louise Claire Clark, Rod Mullinar, Ray Meagher,
Charito Ortez, Liz Birch, Paul Sonkkila, Michael
Caton*
An American woman searches the Australian outback
for her husband. Cut down feature cobbled together
from a 20-episode TV serial. Average.
DRA                             91 min mTV
B,V                                    WDV

## FIVE PATTERN DRAGON CLAWS **            18
Godfrey Ho            HONG KONG
*Wong Cheung Li, Dragon Kitty Chui*
Another martial arts adventure with a minimal
"honour must be avenged" type plot.
MAR                                  86 min
B,V                                    DIAM

## FIVE SUPERFIGHTERS **                    15
Lo Mar                HONG KONG          1979
*How Chao-Sheng, Hsung Kang, Huiten-Chi*
An old man is beaten up by an aggressive martial arts
fighter and the man's three apprentices decide to
brush up their fighting skills in a bid to restore the old
man's honour.
MAR                                  96 min
V                                     WHV

## FIVE-MAN ARMY, THE **                    15
Don Taylor            ITALY              1970
*Peter Graves, James Daly, Bud Spencer (Carlo
Pedersoli), Tetsuro Tamba, Nino Castelnuovo, Daniela
Giordano, Marc Lawrence, Claudio Gora, Annabella
Andreoli, Carlo Alighiero, Jack Stuart (Giancorno
Rossi-Stuarti)*
In 1914 five adventurers try to rob the Mexican
government of a fortune in gold, but one of the gang
wants it for the Mexican Revolution. Adequate.
WES                    101 min (ort 107 min)
B,V                                    MGM

## FLAME **
Richard Loncraine          UK          1974
*Tom Conti, Alan Lake, Dave Hill, Noddy Holder, Don Powell, Johnny Shannon, Kenneth Colley, Sara Clee, Anthony Allen, Tommy Vance, Mike Pasternak, John Dicks, Michael Coles, Nina Thomas, A.J. Brown, Susan Tebbs, John Steel*
A look at the ruthless world of the music business, that's set in 1965 and follows the changing fortunes of a group being promoted by a smart advertising executive.
DRA                          86 min (ort 91 min)
B,V                                     3MVID/PVG

## FLAME OF THE BARBARY COAST **          U
Joseph Kane          USA          1945
*John Wayne, Ann Dvorak, Joseph Schildkraut, William Frawley, Virginia Grey, Russell Hicks, Jack Norton, Paul Fix, Manart Kippen, Eve Lynne, Butterfly McQueen, Marc Lawrence, Rex Lease, Hank Bell, Al Murphy, Adele Mara*
A saloon singer is pursued by both a rancher and a sophisticate with the former opening his own gambling hall. However, all complications are nicely resolved by a well-timed earthquake. An adequate time-filler in which Wayne played a character named Duke, thus giving rise to his lifelong nickname.
Osca: RIO GRANDE
WES          91 min; 189 min (2 film cassette) B/W
V                                             VCC

## FLAME TO THE PHOENIX, A **          15
                                   USA          1985
*Paul Geoffrey, Ann Firbank*
A standard high-action WW2 film, set on the eve of the German invasion of Poland and the outbreak of war.
WAR                          75 min (ort 80 min)
V                                             GRN

## FLAME TREES OF THIKA, THE: PARTS 1          PG
AND 2 **
Roy Ward Baker          UK          1981
*Hayley Mills, David Robb, Holly Aird, Ben Cross, Nicholas Jones, Sharon Maughan*
Story of the fortunes of a family of coffee planters in Kenya in 1914. A competent family drama with a lack of action but some pleasant locations. Originally shown in seven 50-minute episodes. Huxley's novel is to some extent autobiographical.
Boa: novel by Elspeth Huxley.
DRA                          350 min (2 cassettes) mTV
B,V                   THAMES/TEVP; VCC (VHS only)

## FLAMING BULLETS **
Harry Fraser          USA          1945
*Tex Ritter, Dave O'Brien, Guy Wilkerson, Patricia Knox, Charles King, Bud Osborne, I. Stanford Jolley, Kermit Maynard, Richard Alexander, Bob Duncan, Dan White*
The Texas Rangers are given the task of catching a master criminal, and a lawman pretends to be an outlaw in order to capture his gang, which specialises in killing wanted criminals for the reward money. A fair vehicle for Ritter in which he even gets to sing a couple of tunes.
WES                                   59 min
B,V,V2                                   WOV

## FLAMINGO KID, THE ***          15
Garry Marshall          USA          1984
*Matt Dillon, Richard Crenna, Jessica Walter, Hector Elizondo, Fisher Stevens, Janet Jones, Bronson Pinchot*
A young man grows up on Long Island in the first half of the 1960s and experiences the usual family conflicts. A perceptive coming-of-age film that benefits

from the intelligent Neal Marshall script.
DRA                                   100 min
B,V                                      PVG

## FLARE UP **          15
James Neilson          USA          1969
*Raquel Welch, James Stacy, Luke Askew, Don Chastain, Ron Rifkin, Jeane Byron*
A man kills his wife and stalks her friend, a go-go dancer, because he blames her for the break-up of his marriage. A fast and furious melodrama.
DRA                          94 min (ort 100 min)
B,V                                      MGM

## FLASH AND THE FIRECAT *          15
Beverly C. Sebastian/D. Ferd Sebastian
                                   USA          1975
*Roger Davis, Tricia Sembera, Dub Taylor, Richard Kiel, Joan Shawlee, Philip Bruns*
A couple kidnap a banker's son and run from the police, in this flat and insipid comedy.
COM                          81 min (ort 84 min)
B,V                                      CIC

## FLASH GORDON **          PG
Michael Hodges          UK          1980
*Sam J. Jones, Melody Anderson, Chaim Topol, Max Von Sydow, Ornella Muti, Timothy Dalton, Brian Blessed, Peter Wyngarde, Mariangela Melato, John Osborne, Richard O'Brien, John Hallam, Philip Stone, Suzanne Danielle*
An updated version of the old serial from Republic. An evil emperor from another planet tries to conquer the Earth but is opposed by Flash and his pals, who have been brought to the planet Mongo. A visually remarkable film with superb sets and costumes, but seriously deficient in characterisation and with Jones making a woefully inadequate hero. The rock score soundtrack is by Queen.
FAN                          109 min (ort 115 min)
B,V                                      TEVP

## FLASH GORDON **          U
                                   USA          198-
Children's animated adventure based on the popular character from the 1930s. In this tale Flash and friends have to stop the wicked Ming the Merciless from destroying Arborea and taking over the world. Average.
CAR                                   56 min
V                                         PARK

## FLASH GORDON: A PLANET IN PERIL **          U
                                   USA          1989
A further animated adventure based on the popular 1930s character, with Flash and friends once more doing battle with that wicked tyrant Ming the Merciless, the cruel ruler of the planet Mongo.
CAR                                   60 min
V                                         HEND

## FLASH GORDON: TO SAVE THE EARTH **          U
                                                1989
Another animated adventure in the series, telling of Flash's attempts to save the world from destruction at the hands of the ruthless Ming, whose planet Mongo is on a collision course with the Earth.
CAR                                   60 min
V                                         HEND

## FLASH PANTS **          R18
Eve Milan          USA          1984
*Tanya Lawson, Christie Williams, Michele Morgen, Alexis X, Athena Star, George Payne, Jerry Butler*
Sex film set in a high school with the school prom coming up at the same time as a "Flashpants" contest which, despite the wishes of the parents, many of the kids intend to enter. There follow some amusing episodes that examine the kids and their attitudes to

sexuality but on the whole the film remains a fairly mindless mess.

A 49 min
B,V TCX; SHEP

## FLASHBACK ** 15
Franco Amurri USA 1989
*Dennis Hopper, Kiefer Sutherland, Carol Kane, Cliff De Young, Paul Dooley, Michael McKean, Richard Masur*
A young and rather straightlaced FBI agent is given the job of taking a hippie fugitive to Oregon, where he is to stand trial for subversive political activities in the 1960s, when he disrupted a Spiro Agnew rally. One that will undoubtedly appeal to old hippies, as the film is full of music and memories of the period, and the interplay between the two leads is quite good fun, yet for all that the plotting could use some inspiration.
COM 103 min (ort 108 min)
V CIC

## FLASHDANCE ** 15
Adrian Lyne USA 1983
*Jennifer Beals, Michael Nouri, Lilia Skala, Sunny Johnson, Kyle T. Heffner, Belinda Bauer*
A young female welder dreams of becoming a ballerina. A sort of overlong video with plenty of music and some high octane dance sequences (most of which were actually performed by uncredited French dancer Marine Jahan). AA: Song ("What A Feeling" – Giorgio Moroder – music/Keith Forsey and Irene Cara – lyrics).
MUS 91 min
B,V CIC

## FLASHPOINT ** 15
William Tannen USA 1984
*Kris Kristofferson, Rip Torn, Treat Williams, Kevin Conway, Miguel Ferrer, Jean Smart, Robert Blossom, Tess Harper*
Two border patrolmen are in deep trouble when they discover some evidence linked to the assassination of Kennedy. This promising start never develops into anything of note.
A/AD 90 min; 89 min (WHV) (ort 94 min)
B,V TEVP; WHV (VHS only)

## FLASHPOINT AFRICA **
Francis Megahy
SOUTH AFRICA/WEST GERMANY 1978
*Gayle Hunnicut, Trevor Howard, James Faulkner*
A television team go into the African jungle to make a programme about a rebel leader.
Aka: DIE REBELLEN; ONE TAKE TWO
A/AD 97 min
B,V VCL

## FLAT TOP *** 
Lesley Selander USA 1952
*Sterling Hayden, Richard Carlson, Keith Larsen, Bill Phipps*
An account of the struggle for air supremacy in the Pacific during WW2, that concentrates on the training of aircraft-carrier fighter pilots. A solid little film.
WAR 89 min
B,V MEV

## FLATFOOT *
Steno ITALY/WEST GERMANY 1978
*Bud Spencer (Carlo Pedersoli), Joe Stewardson, Werner Pochat, Enzo Cannavale, Bodo, Dagmar Lassander, Raymond Pellegrin*
An over-the-top knockabout cop comedy, detailing the exploits of tough-guy Spencer as he uses his own methods in dealing with drug smugglers. A silly comic strip with live actors that signals its slapstick humour well in advance.

Aka: KNOCK OUT COP, THE
A/AD 103 min Cut (13 sec)
B,V VPD

## FLESH **
Paul Morrissey USA 1969
*Joe Dallesandro, Geraldine Smith, Maurice Bradell, Candy Darling, Louis Waldon, Geri Miller, Jackie Curtis, Patti Darbanville*
A bizarre film about a young hustler in New York (from a graduate of Andy Warhol's film factory), that follows his exploits as he tries to raise the money to pay for an abortion for his wife's girlfriend. A difficult film to follow, but there are a good number of potent observations in there.
A 86 min (ort 105 min)
B,V PVG

## FLESH AND BLOOD ** 18
Paul Verhoeven USA 1985
*Rutger Hauer, Jennifer Jason Leigh, Tom Burlinson, Jack Thompson, Susan Tyrell, Ronald Lacey, Brion James, Bruno Kirby*
A medieval epic with knights in armour, damsels in distress and all the other trappings one expects, shown with a heavy emphasis on the seamier side of life rather than its romantic aspects, with a young bride-to-be kidnapped and raped but growing to like her captor.
A/AD 122 min (ort 126 min) (Cut at film release)
B,V RNK; VIR (VHS only)

## FLESH AND BLOOD SHOW, THE *
Peter Walker UK 1972
*Ray Brooks, Jenny Hanley, Luan Peters, Judy Matheson, Candace Glendinning, Robin Askwith, Tristan Rogers, Penny Meredith, Patrick Barr, David Howey, Elizabeth Bradley, Raymond Young, Brian Tulley, Rodney Diak, Sally Lahee*
A group of actors is hired to perform a Grand Guignol play for a mysterious employer they have never met. Their employer turns out to be a deranged ex-actor, whose hatred for his former profession is so strong that he sets out to decimate the troupe as they rehearse. A clumsy horror yarn, with some ill-advised touches of humour and uncertain direction.
HOR 97 min
B,V VDM/GHV

## FLESH AND LACE: PART 1 ** R18
Troy Benny (Carlos Tobalina)
USA 1983
*Jamie Gillis, Tamara Longley, Colleen Applegate, Jesie St James, Rose Lynn, Sparky, Joey Silvera, William Margold, Carlos Tobalina*
From his hospital deathbed a millionaire calls together his three sons and daughter to tell them that his estate will go to whoever has the most active sex life. He has arranged to have their homes monitored with TV cameras and can thus watch them at work and decide for himself. In between watching his kids he finds time to enjoy some nurses, eventually being told (in Part 2, made separately), that he's well enough to go home.
A 59 min (ort 95 min) Cut (23 min 39 sec)
B,V,V2 ELV

## FLESH GORDON * 18
Michael Benveniste/Howard Ziehm
USA 1974
*Jason Williams, Suzanne Fields, John Hoyt, William Hunt, Joseph Hudgins*
This semi-porno version of FLASH GORDON has little to recommend it. A sex ray is causing chaos on Earth and Flesh blasts off to the Planet Porno, where the ray emanates from, in order to do battle. Most of the original graphic sex scenes are cut.
COM 84 min (ort 90 min) Cut (1 min 16 sec)
B,V VPD L/A; EIV

**FLESHBURN \***                                    15
George Gage            USA            1984
*Steve Kanaly, Macon McCalman, Karen Carlson,*
*Robert Chimento, Sonny Landham, Duke Stroud,*
*Robert Alan Browne*
A Vietnam veteran has his revenge on the psychiat-
rists who were responsible for placing him in an
institution by leaving them to die in the desert, in this
sterile revenger.
Boa: novel Fear In A Handful Of Dust by Brian
Garfield.
DRA                                        90 min
B,V                                        CBS

**FLESHDANCE \*\***
Ken Gibb               USA            1984
*Shanna Evans, Herschel Savage, Desiree Lane, John*
*Leslie, Rachel Ashley, Tanya Lawson (Tanya*
*Larsson), Kimberly Carson, Ron Jeremy*
A porno version of FLASHDANCE, that follows a
pretty black dancer whose ambition is to appear as
one of the performers at the popular "All-Nude Girl's
Club" owned by Savage. Eventually she gets to
perform there as one of the dancers in a competition
designed to put new life into the club and wins the
contest.
A                                          80 min
B,V                                        EVI

**FLETCH \*\***                                    PG
Michael Ritchie        USA            1985
*Chevy Chase, Tim Matheson, Dana Wheeler-*
*Nicholson, Joe Don Baker, Richard Libertini, Geena*
*Davis, M. Emmet Walsh, George Wendt, Kenneth Mars*
A reporter adopts various disguises in his investiga-
tions and becomes involved with a vast drugs-running
conspiracy. Okay in small doses but after a while the
constant stream of wisecracks begins to irritate.
Scripted by Andrew Bergman and followed by
FLETCH LIVES.
Boa: novel by Gregory McDonald.
COM                            94 min (ort 96 min)
V/sh                                       CIC

**FLETCH LIVES \***                                PG
Michael Ritchie        USA            1989
*Chevy Chase, Hal Jolbrook, Julianne Phillips, Cleavon*
*Little, R. Lee Emery, Richard Libertini, Randall (Tex)*
*Cobb, George Wyner, Patricia Kalember, Geoffrey*
*Lewis, Richard Belzer*
This sequel to FLETCH has our identity-changing
reporter now on a trip to Louisiana where he has to
deal with the expected stock characters. Even less
funny than the earlier film.
COM                            91 min (ort 95 min)
V                                          CIC

**FLIGHT 90: DISASTER ON THE POTOMAC \*\*\*** PG
Robert Michael Lewis   USA            1984
*Jeanetta Arnette, Barry Corbin, Stephen Macht, Dinah*
*Manoff, Richard Masur, Donnelly Rhodes, Jamie*
*Rose, Richard Beauchamp, K. Callan, Jane*
*Kaczmarek, Kerrie Keane, Ken Olin, James Whitmore*
*Jr, Richard Backus, Steve Tannen*
An account of a fatal plane crash in Washington D.C.
in 1982, that steers clear of the over-reliance of a
parade of star cameos so typical of these disaster-in-
the-air movies and is all the better for it.
DRA                    92 min (ort 100 min) mTV
B,V,V2                                     MED

**FLIGHT OF THE ANGRY DRAGON \*\***               18
Foong Wu Ma    HONG KONG              1986
*Lo Lieh, Yueh Tua, Tsk Kun Chu*
A hired assassin clashes with a Ninja warrior.
MAR                                        90 min
B,V                                        CLOK

**FLIGHT OF THE COUGAR \*\***                       U
Jack B. Hively         USA            1976
*Robert Bray, Merry Anders, Lee Brown Jr*
Lassie protects a wild cougar unfairly blamed for
killings that are due to a mad dog. A mediocre feature
clipped together from episodes of a TV series.
JUV                                        75 min mTV
B,V                                        MGM

**FLIGHT OF THE DOVES \*\***                        U
Ralph Nelson           UK             1971
*Ron Moody, Jack Wild, Dorothy McGuire, Stanley*
*Holloway, Helen Raye, William Rushton, Dana, John*
*Molloy, Barry Keegan, Brenda O'Reilly, Noel Purcell,*
*Thomas Hickey, Nial Tobin*
Two Liverpool kids run away to Ireland to escape their
cruel stepfather and visit their grandmother, but find
their problems have only just begun. A cute and
whimsical effort that never develops into anything
substantial.
Boa: novel by Walter Macken.
JUV                            97 min (ort 105 min)
B,V                                        RCA

**FLIGHT OF THE DRAGON, THE \*\***                  U
Arthur Rankin Jr/Jules Bass
                       USA            1982
*Voices of: James Earl Jones, Harry Morgan, Victor*
*Buono, James Gregory*
Animated fantasy about a group of wizards, who bring
a man back from modern times to their world of
magic, knights and dungeons and send him on a
heroic mission.
Aka: FLIGHT OF DRAGONS
CAR                            85 min (ort 98 min)
B,V                                ODY L/A; CH5

**FLIGHT OF THE GREY WOLF, THE \*\***               U
Frank Zuniga           USA            1976
*Jeff East, Bill Williams, Barbara Hale, William*
*Bryant, Eric Server*
A tame wolf is mistakenly thought to be a killer and
runs away to the wilderness to escape the hunters, in
this typical Disney film for kids.
JUV                        81 min Cut (1 min 24 sec)
B,V                                        WDV

**FLIGHT OF THE NAVIGATOR \*\***                    U
Randall Kleiser        USA            1986
*Joey Cramer, Veronica Cartwright, Cliff De Young,*
*Howard Hesseman, Sarah Jessica Parker, Matt Adler,*
*Robert Small, Albie Whitaker, Paul Reubens (voice*
*only)*
This kid's adventure begins with a 12-year-old exploring a ravine in the woods and falling in. On waking up
he returns home only to find that eight years have
passed, his parents have moved but he hasn't aged a
single day. He soon discovers a link between his
disappearance and a spacecraft when a strange robotic
creature summons him to help it steer its craft home.
An interesting but excessively cute fantasy aimed
rather too pointedly at kids.
FAN                                        87 min
V/h                                        CBS

**FLIGHT OF THE PHOENIX \*\*\*\***
Robert Aldrich         USA            1965
*James Stewart, Richard Attenborough, Hardy Kruger,*
*Peter Finch, Dan Duryea, Ernest Borgnine, George*
*Kennedy, Ian Bannen, Ronald Fraser, Christian*
*Marquand*
A beautifully balanced portrayal of the efforts made
by the survivors of a plane crash in the desert to
escape from their predicament, finally being per-
suaded by one of their number that their only hope
lies in trying to rebuild their shattered aeroplane. A
superb film that avoids all the usual Hollywood heroic
cliches.
Boa: novel by Elleston Trevor.

DRA 149 min
B,V CBS

**FLIGHT TO HOLOCAUST \***
Bernard Kowalski  USA  1977
*Patrick Wayne, Christopher Mitchum, Desi Arnaz Jr,*
*Fawne Harriman, Sid Caesar, Rory Calhoun, Greg*
*Morris, Lloyd Nolan, Paul Williams, Robert Patten,*
*Anne Schedeen, Bill Baldwin, Katherine Baumann,*
*Shirley O'Hara*
Professional troubleshooters have to rescue the pas-
sengers of a private plane that has crashed into the
side of a skyscraper and is now lodged there. A
formula disaster movie with all the attendant cliches.
Boa: story by Robert Heverly.
A/AD 90 min (ort 100 min) mTV
B,V VCL/CBS

**FLIGHT TO MARS \*\***
Lesley Selander  USA  1951
*Cameron Mitchell, Marguerite Chapman, Virginia*
*Huston, Arthur Franz, John Litel*
An expedition to Mars crash-lands on the planet and
discovers an advanced civilisation. An early science
fiction film that seems very amateurish by today's
standards, mainly due to limitations imposed by the
restricted budget.
FAN 75 min
B,V VFP L/A; HER

**FLINTSTONES: A FLINTSTONE CHRISTMAS \*\* U**
Charles A. Nichols  USA  1977
Short feature spin-off based on the popular children's
TV series. In this story Santa Claus breaks his ankle
and it looks as if kids the world over are going to be in
for a big disappointment. However, Fred and Barney
save the day even if things don't turn out quite as
planned. Average animation from Hanna-Barbera.
Aka: FLINTSTONE CHRISTMAS, A
CAR 49 min
V VCC

**FLINTSTONES: MEET ROCKULA AND** U
**FRANKENSTONE \*\***
USA  1977
Flintstones cartoon adventure based on the popular
Hanna-Barbera series. The Flintstones and the Rub-
bles are winners on a quiz show and the prize is a trip
to Count Rockula's castle in Rocksylvania. Neither
couple bargains for what happens when the Count is
accidentally woken from his 500 year sleep.
CAR 50 min
B,V VCC

**FLINTSTONES: THE JETSONS MEET THE** U
**FLINTSTONES \*\***
Don Lusk  USA  1987
*Voices of: Jon Bauman, Mel Blank, Daws Butler,*
*Hamilton Camp, Henry Carden, Julie Dess, Don*
*Messick, George O'Hanlon, Penny Singleton, John*
*Stephenson, Brenda Vaccaro, Jean Vander Pyl, Janet*
*Waldo, Frank Weller, Patric Zimmerman*
A recent "Flintstones" feature, inspired by the popular
but patchy TV series, that followed the exploits of a
Stone Age couple. In this tale, Fred and Wilma meet a
family of time travellers from the distant future, and
go back there for a visit. Average.
Aka: JETSONS MEET THE FLINTSTONES, THE
CAR 92 min (ort 100 min)
V VCC

**FLORIDA CONNECTION, THE \*** 15
William Grefe  USA  1974
*Dan Pastorini, June Wilkinson, Robert Enery, Massey*
*Creamer, Jeremy Slate, Willie Patrano, Steve Alaimo,*
*Ceci Stone, John David Chandler, Socrates Ballis,*
*Walter Philbin, Milton Smith*
An action thriller about drug smuggling in the
Florida swamps, with corrupt Miami cops incurring
the wrath of the Mafia when they attempt to steal a
cache of drugs aboard a sunken yacht.
Aka: ALLIGATOR ALLEY; EVERGLADE
KILLINGS, THE (MPV); HOOKED GENERATION,
THE
THR 107 min; 85 min (MPV)
B,V,V2 CHM/PPL L/A; INT/CBS; MPV

**FLORIDA STRAITS \*\*** 15
Mike Hodges  USA  1986
*Raul Julia, Fred Ward, Daniel Jenkins, Antonio*
*Fargas, Daniel Jenkins, Jaime Sanchez, Victor Argo,*
*Ilka Tanya Payan, Jesse Corti, Raul Davila, Simon*
*Frederick, Olivia Grieco, Ed L. Grady, Mario R.*
*Grieco, Dani Gulledge*
A Cuban recently released after 20 years in prison for
his part in the Bay of Pigs debacle, teams up with two
others on a perilous treasure hunt for a fortune in gold
he buried in the Cuban jungle. A lifeless adventure of
little excitement, filmed at Mytle Beach, California.
A/AD 94 min mCab
B,V RNK

**FLOWERS IN THE ATTIC \*\*** 15
Jeffrey Bloom  USA  1987
*Louise Fletcher, Victoria Tennant, Jeb Stuart Adams,*
*Kristy Swanson, Ben Granger, Lindsay Parker,*
*Marshall Colt*
Silly, tedious tale adapted from a bestseller that tells
of four youngsters kept locked in the attic of the
family mansion by their widowed mother as part of a
plan to win favour with the wealthy parents that
disowned her. The film tones down the novel's sado-
masochistic and incestuous aspects and adds little of
its own, but good casting generally keeps it going
right up to its ludicrous climax. Written by Bloom.
Boa: novel by V.C. Andrews.
THR 88 min
B,V NWV

**FLUSH \*\*** 15
Andrew J. Kuehn  USA  1981
*William Calloway, William Bronder, Jeannie Linero*
Treasure hunt with no holds barred for the fortune
which an eccentric millionaire has buried, complete
with various clues to be followed after his death.
Another film in the IT'S A MAD, MAD, MAD, MAD
WORLD mould and about as tediously contrived.
COM 75 min
B,V VTC L/A; VMA; STABL

**FLUTEMAN, THE \*** U
Peter Maxwell  AUSTRALIA  1982
*John Jarratt, Emil Minty, Aileen Britton*
A man with a flute offers to relieve a town of the
drought it is suffering from, in this obscure and
uncertain tale.
DRA 84 min
B,V ALPHA/INT; XTASY

**FLY, THE \*\*** 15
Kurt Neumann  USA  1958
*Al (David) Hedison, Patricia Owens, Herbert*
*Marshall, Vincent Price, Kathleen Freeman*
A scientist invents a method of transmitting matter
and tries it out on himself, but something goes terribly
wrong when a fly gets into the transmission chamber.
A stilted and wooden film with little but one good idea
to hold the interest. A sequel THE RETURN OF THE
FLY followed. Remade in 1986.
Boa: short story by George Langelaan.
HOR 91 min (ort 94 min)
V/h CBS

**FLY, THE \*\*\*** 18
David Cronenberg  USA  1986
*Jeff Goldblum, Geena Davis, John Getz, Joy Boushel,*

*Les Carlson, George Chuvalo*
A gory remake of the 1958 film of the same name, telling of a brilliant scientist who develops a matter transporter and falls prey to some hideous changes when he uses. Goldblum is perfectly cast as the eccentric scientist whose gradual evolution into a human fly is handled with some style and wit but leans too heavily on the repulsive effects. Written by Cronenberg and Edward Pogue. AA: Make (Chris Walas/Stephan Dupuis).

| HOR | 92 min (ort 100 min) |
| V/h | CBS |

**FLY 2, THE \***  18
Chris Walas          USA          1989
*Eric Stoltz, Daphne Zuniga, Lee Richardson, John Getz, Frank Turner, Ann Marie Lee, Gary Chalk, Saffron Henderson, Harley Cross, Matthew Moore*
Knowing little of his father, Brundle Jr continues the scientific work of the former, unaware of the reasons behind his rapid growth to adulthood. Meanwhile, the scientists in whose care he has been placed are content to exploit his gifts. This messy sequel jettisons the human elements of the story in favour of repulsive effects. Despite the gruesome ending (not recommended for the squeamish), this is a dull and inept work.

| HOR | 100 min (ort 104 min) |
| V | CBS |

**FLY ME \*\***  18
Cirio Santiago          ITALY          1973
*Richard Young, Naomi Stevens, Richard Miller, Buzz Albert*
Airline stewardesses and their boyfriends get involved in a series of wild encounters in this adult comedy.

| COM | 70 min |
| B,V | ED; APX |

**FLYING DOWN TO RIO \*\*\***  U
Thornton Freeland          USA          1933
*Dolores Del Rio, Gene Raymond, Ginger Rogers, Fred Astaire, Franklin Pangborn, Raul Roulien, Blanche Frederici, Eric Blore*
Fun musical memorable mainly for its scenes of girls dancing on the wings of an aeroplane. The start of a long and fruitful Astaire-Rogers partnership.
Osca: GAY DIVORCEE, THE (asa)

| MUS | 86 min (ort 89 min); 186 min (2 film cassette) |
| B/W |  |
| V | VCC |

**FLYING HIGH \***  PG
Peter Hunt          USA          1978
*Kathryn Witt, Patricia Klous, Connie Sellecca, Howard Platt, Marcia Wallace, Jim Hutton, David Hayward, Martin Speer, Val Bisoglio, Lynn Marie Johnston, Richard Hack, Casey Biggs, Carmen Zapata, Lilyan Chauvin, Louis Zito*
Witless comedy about three newly trained air hostesses and the men in their lives. Gave rise to a brief TV series.

| COM | 97 min (ort 104 min) mTV |
| B,V | IMPACT/ODY |

**FLYING LEATHERNECKS \*\***  PG
Nicholas Ray          USA          1951
*John Wayne, Robert Ryan, Jay C. Flippen, Janis Carter, Don Taylor, William Harrigan, James Bell*
WW2 drama about a tough Marine flying corps major who's disliked by his men because of his excessive strictness. All is forgotten in war however, in this solid but unimaginative actioner. Highspots are the good aerial battle scenes but the film's slow pace is a handicap.
Osca: BEYOND A REASONABLE DOUBT (KVD)

| WAR | 102 min; 98 min (VCC) |
| B,V | KVD; VCC (VHS only) |

**FLYING MISFITS, THE \***  U
Russ Mayberry          USA          1976
*Robert Conrad, Dirk Blocker, Simon Oakland, George Gaynes, Jeff Mackay, Dana Elcar, Anthony Charnotta*
A pilot for the TV series "Baa Baa Blacksheep", this comedy-action tale is a kind of aerial version of THE DIRTY DOZEN and follows the exploits of a bunch of misfits recruited by an unconventional major to form a crack fighter squadron in the Pacific. Sequences of real flying footage are clumsily intercut with studio ones, and on the whole this shoddy and inept effort is best avoided.
Aka: BAA BAA BLACKSHEEP
Boa: book by Major Gregory Boyington.

| A/AD | 94 min mTV |
| V/h | CIC |

**FLYING SEX \***  18
Frank Martin          ITALY          1980
*Al Cliver (Pier Luigi Conti), Eveline Barnett, Franz Muller*
A newly married woman has sex problems – she is only aroused by aircraft, so she becomes a stewardess. A puerile sex comedy.
Aka: SESSO PROFONDO

| COM | 91 min |
| B,V | VDM/GHV; STABL |

**FLYING TIGERS \*\***  PG
David Miller          USA          1942
*John Wayne, John Carroll, Anna Lee, Paul Kelly, Mae Clarke, Gordon Jones*
A solid WW2 epic set among an American fighter squadron bssed in China. Full of the expected heroics and dogfight sequences, but quite adequately put together.
Osca: SANDS OF IWO JIMA (asa)

| WAR | 98 min (ort 102 min); 199 min (2 film cassette) |
| B/W |  |
| V | VCC |

**FOG, THE \*\*\***  15
John Carpenter          USA          1979
*Adrienne Barbeau, Hal Holbrook, John Houseman, Janet Leigh, Jamie Lee Curtis, Tom Atkis, Nancy Loomis, Charles Cyphers*
A small town in California is attacked by the ghosts of mariners who take a grisly revenge on the descendants of the six people who lured their ship onto the rocks 100 years ago. A well-directed film of occasionally scary moments as the remarkably substantial ghosts proceed to hack and club their way to revenge under cover of a dense, sinister fog. A kind of ghostly but equally gory follow-up to HALLOWEEN.

| HOR | 86 min |
| B,V,V2,LV | EHE; CBS; CH5 (VHS only); POLY (VHS only) |

**FOLLOW ME QUIETLY \*\*\***  
Richard Fleischer          USA          1949
*William Lundigan, Dorothy Patrick, Jeff Corey, Nestor Paiva, Charles D. Brown, Paul Guilfoyle*
The police have to trap a self-righteous psychopathic killer who becomes obsessed with murder whenever it rains. A fine little example of film noir.
Osca: FUGITIVE, THE

| DRA | 58 min B/W |
| B,V | KVD |

**FOLLOW ME, BOYS! \*\***  U
Norman Tokar          USA          1966
*Fred MacMurray, Vera Miles, Lillian Gish, Charlie Ruggles, Elliott Reid, Kurt Russell*
Story of a man in a small town in the 1930s who devotes all his time to running a scout troop. A sentimental and patriotic saga done with a lot of flair.
Boa: novel God And My Country by Mackinlay Kantor.

DRA 116 min (ort 131 min)
B,V WDV

## FOLLOW THAT BIRD *
Ken Kwapis USA 1985
U
*Carroll Spinney, John Candy, Sandra Bernhard,*
*Chevy Chase, Joe Flaherty, Jim Henson, Frank Oz,*
*Paul Bartel, Waylon Jennings, Dave Thomas*
The Big Bird from "Sesame Street" returns to New
York after being sent to join its Dodo family in
Illinois. An attempt to squeeze some more mileage out
of the characters that featured in the above series and
also "The Muppets".
Aka: SESAME STREET PRESENTS FOLLOW
THAT BIRD
JUV 85 min
B/sh, V/sh WHV

## FOLLOW THE FLEET ***
Mark Sandrich USA 1936
U
*Fred Astaire, Ginger Rogers, Randolph Scott, Betty*
*Grable, Harriet Hilliard (Nelson), Astrid Allwyn,*
*Lucille Ball*
An enjoyable Hollywood musical about two sailors
and their girlfriends. The memorable songs are by
Irving Berlin and feature numbers such as: "Let's
Face The Music And Dance", "Let Yourself Go" and
"We Saw The Sea". Borrows heavily from "Shore
Leave (1925) and "Hit The Deck" (1930).
MUS 106 min (ort 110 min) B/W
V VCC

## FOOD OF THE GODS, THE *
Bert I. Gordon USA 1976
18
*Marjoe Gortner, Pamela Franklin, Ida Lupino, Ralph*
*Meeker, John McLiam, John Cypher, Belinda Belaski*
A strange substance oozing out of the ground on a
remote island causes small animals and insects to
grow to giant proportions. A poorly realised attempt to
get some mileage out of the classic Wells story. Filmed
11 years before by Gordon as VILLAGE OF THE
GIANTS.
Boa: short story by H.G. Wells.
FAN 84 min
V RNK

## FOOD OF THE GODS: PART 2 **
Damian Lee USA 1988
18
*Paul Coufos, Lisa Schrage, Jackie Burroughs, Michael*
*Copeman, Colin Fox, Frank Pellegrino, Frank Moore,*
*David B. Nichols, Real Andrews, Stuart Hughes*
In name only remake of the 1976 film that uses an
entirely different story, in which an experiment with
growth hormones goes wrong and leads to a boy
becoming 12 feet tall. Attempts to find an antidote to
restore him to normal size result in the the escape of
giant man-eating rats. A predictable and low-grade
affair of poor special-effects and plotting; a few
touches of humour make it slightly more palatable.
HOR 83 min
V GHV

## FOOL FOR LOVE *
Robert Altman USA 1985
15
*Sam Shephard, Kim Basinger, Harry Dean Stanton,*
*Randy Quaid*
Story of the complex and self-destructive love-hate
relationship between a pair of lovers, set against the
harsh surroundings of a seedy New Mexico motel. A
profoundly depressing experience.
Boa: play by Sam Shephard.
DRA 103 min (ort 106 min)
B,V RNK

## FOOLIN' AROUND *
Richard T. Heffron USA 1979
PG
*Gary Busey, Eddie Albert, Annette O'Toole, Cloris*
*Leachman, Tony Randall, John Calvin*
A country boy wins the heart of a runaway heiress
despite the fact that she is already engaged. A
scatterbrained slapstick comedy that attempts to
incorporate some of the style of a 1950s comedy but
generally fails.
COM 101 min; 97 min (APX) (ort 111 min)
B,V VCL; APX

## FOOLS OF FORTUNE ***
Pat O'Connor UK 1989
15
*Mary Elizabeth Mastrantonio, Iain Glen, Julie*
*Christie, Michael Kitchen, Niamh Cusack, Sean T.*
*McClory, Catherine McFadden*
A portrait of shattered lives during the aftermath to
Irish independence in the 1920s. An attack on a
peaceful, Protestant family by the pro-British irregu-
lars, the Black & Tans, leaves the father and two
sisters dead and the only son with a bitter thirst for
revenge. Distinguished by its visual power, this fine
drama is marred by its elaborate flash-forwarding
structure that seriously hampers its narrative flow.
Boa: novel by William Trevor.
DRA 110 min
V/h PAL

## FOOTLIGHT PARADE ****
Lloyd Bacon USA 1933
U
*James Cagney, Joan Blondell, Ruby Keeler, Dick*
*Powell, Guy Kibbee, Ruth Donnelly, Hugh Herbert,*
*Frank McHugh, Claire Dodd, Herman Bing*
Cagney plays a producer of live stage shows that
feature between films, and runs into trouble when he
tries to outdo himself staging some ambitious num-
bers. A fascinating backstage musical whose straight
parts are every bit as entertaining as the musical
numbers. Ends with three superb Busby Berkley
numbers: "Honeymoon Hotel", "By A Waterfall" and
"Shanghai Lil".
MUS 99 min
V/h WHV

## FOOTLOOSE **
Herbert Ross USA 1984
15
*Kevin Bacon, Lori Singer, John Lithgow, Dianne*
*Wiest, Christopher Penn, Sarah Jessica Parker, John*
*Laughlin, Elizabeth Gorcey, Frances Lee McCain*
A big-city kid moves to a small town where dancing
has been banned due to the efforts of a hellfire
preacher. He decides to convert the town to his way of
thinking. It's hard to know what point this film is
trying to make but at least the dance sequences are
well handled. The script is by Dean Pritchford, who
also worked on FAME: THE MOVIE and SING.
MUS 103 min (ort 107 min)
B,V,V2 CIC

## FOR A FEW DOLLARS MORE ***
Sergio Leone
ITALY/SPAIN/WEST GERMANY 1965
15
*Clint Eastwood, Lee Van Cleef, Gian Maria Volonte,*
*Jose Egger, Mara Krup, Rosemarie Dexter, Klaus*
*Kinski, Mario Brega, Aldo Sambrell, Luigi Pistilli,*
*Robert Camardiel, Benito Stefanelli, Luis Rodriguez,*
*Panos Papadopulos*
An excessively drawn out sequel to A FISTFUL OF
DOLLARS. In this one the "man with no name" teams
up with a bounty hunter to track down an outlaw
gang. Vague and ponderous in places, but enlivened
by the occasional flash of humour and a nice pairing of
Eastwood and Van Cleef. The score is by Ennio
Morricone.
Aka: PER QUAICHE DOLLARO IN PIU
WES 127 min (ort 133 min)
B,V WHV

## FOR BETTER OR FOR WORSE **
Gene Quintano USA 1989
15
*Kim Cattrall, Robert Hays, Christopher Lee*

A slight, romantic-comedy about an ordinary guy who pursues and marries a glamorous woman after a whirlwind courtship, blissfully unware that she has a double life and in reality is a spy. Complications abound as the couple go on their honeymoon in this tongue-in-cheek and implausible effort.

COM                                                    89 min
V                                                        EIV

**FOR LADIES ONLY ***
Mel Damski            USA                              1981
*Gregory Harrison, Marc Singer, Patricia Davis, Viveca Lindfors, Steven Keats, Dinah Manoff, Louise Lasser, Lee Grant, Richard Charles Barsch, Melvin Bernhardt, Max Wright, Vivian Matalon, Charles Kimbrough*
A young actor in New York works as a male stripper to make ends meet while waiting for his big chance. The TV film debut for Davis. Average.

DRA                              95 min (ort 100 min) mTV
B,V,V2                                 FTV L/A; INT/CBS

**FOR LOVE AND HONOR ***                               15
Gary Nelson          USA                              1983
*Cliff Potts, Yaphet Kotto, Amy Steel, Gary Grubbs, Rachel Ticotin, David Caruso, Pete Kowanko, Eddie Velez, Keenan Ivory Wayans, Tony Becker, John Mengatti, Kelly Preston, Shanna Reed*
This story of the US Army and its 88th Airborne Division was the pilot for an unsuccessful soap opera type series. In this feature attention focuses on the events following the death of a young recruit whose parachute failed to open during a night jump.

A/AD                             88 min (ort 104 min) mTV
B,V                                                     MGM

**FOR LOVE OF IVY ***
Daniel Mann          USA                              1968
*Sidney Poitier, Abbey Lincoln, Beau Bridges, Leon Bibb, Nan Martin, Lauri Peters, Carroll O'Connor*
A family does not want to lose the services of their coloured maid so they find her a boyfriend. A laboured and stale comedy with precious few jokes and a patronising script. Of slight historical interest.

COM                                                   102 min
B,V                                                     GHV

**FOR LOVE OR MONEY ***                                 PG
Terry Hughes         USA                              1984
*Suzanne Pleshette, Gil Gerard, Jamie Farr, Ray Walston, Lawrence Pressman, Barney Martin, Lori Lethin, Ray Buktenica, Mary Kay Place, Michael Pasternak, Squire Fridell, Nedra Volz, Ray Young, Donna Mitchell*
A TV game show comedy that focuses on the greed of the contestants who are ready to do anything in order to win. A film that leaves no lasting impression despite one or two good performances.

COM                                               96 min mTV
B,V                                                     ARF

**FOR LOVERS ONLY ***                                   PG
Claudio Guzman       USA                              1982
*Deborah Raffin, Andy Griffith, Robert Hegyes, Katherine Helmond, Gordon Jump, Jane Kaczmarek, Sally Kellerman, Anna Garduno, Alan North, Christopher Wells, Charlie White, Cindy Perlman, Dick Bocelli, James S. Henerson*
Silly comedy account of a honeymoon resort and the assorted strange couples who stay there. A good time-filler, but only if you have absolutely nothing more worthwhile to do.

COM                              91 min (ort 100 min) mTV
B,V                                                     MGM

**FOR PETE'S SAKE ***                                   PG
Peter Yates          USA                              1974
*Barbra Streisand, Michael Sarrazin, Estelle Parsons, Molly Picon, William Redfield*

Boring attempt at comedy with a cab-driver's devoted wife borrowing money from the underworld and then finding that she has some problems. Streisand is great in this one but the feeble script gives her little to work with. Written by Stanley Shapiro and Maurice Richlin.

COM                               86 min (ort 90 min)
B,V                                                     RCA

**FOR QUEEN AND COUNTRY ***                             15
Martin Stellman      UK/USA                           1988
*Denzel Washington, Dorian Healy, Amanda Redman, Sean Chapman, Bruce Payne, George Baker*
The story of a black Falklands War hero who returns to his run-down council housing estate after nine years. Still encountering rejection and hostility, and with few opportunities to make good, he eventually snaps when informed by the immigration authorities that his application to renew his British passport is to be denied. An ambitious but disappointing film that trades on contemporary violence and is let down by a ludicrous final shoot-out.

DRA                              100 min (ort 106 min)
V                                                      SONY

**FOR SERVICES RENDERED ***                             18
                     USA
*Cyndee Summers, Bridgette Monet, Ian MacGregor, Dave Cannon, Rick Cassidy, Maria Tortuga*
Adult spy spoof inspired by those countless James Bond films with our hero going to Russian and enjoying various encounters as he tracks down some sexy female spies in the search for an incriminating microfilm.

A                             69 min Cut (12 min 48 sec)
B,V                                                     ELV

**FOR THE LOVE OF ADA ***
Ronnie Baxter        UK                               1973
*Wilfred Pickles, Irene Handl, Barbara Mitchell, Jack Smethhurst, Arthur English, Andrea Lawrence, Larry Martyn, Hilda Braid, John Boxer, Duggie Brown, Johnny Wade, Nancy Nevinson, Gareth Hunt, Donald Bissett*
A well-organised wedding anniversary party ends in chaos, mishap, mayhem and misunderstanding. A spin-off from a TV series of the same name. Average.

COM                               86 min (ort 88 min)
B,V,V2                                                  HOK

**FOR THE LOVE OF BENJI ***                              U
Joe Camp             USA                              1977
*Cynthia Smith, Patsy Garrett, Ed Nelson, Allen Fiuzat, Peter Bowles, Bridget Armstrong*
Sequel to BENJI in which our canine hero is taken on vacation to Athens but becomes involved in international espionage when he is abducted to be used to smuggle out a secret formula that's stamped onto his paw. He soon gives the bad guys the slip and the chase is on in a likeable and diverting family adventure. Followed by OH HEAVENLY DOG!

A/AD                                                  84 min
V                                                      VES

**FOR THE LOVE OF IT ***                                PG
Hal Kanter           USA                              1980
*Deborah Raffin, Jeff Conaway, Barbi Benton, Tom Bosley, William Christopher, Norman Fell, Henry Gibson, Lawrence-Hilton Jacobs, Adrian Zmed, Adam West, Pat Morita, Don Rickles, Jack Carter, Tony Epper, Abbe Kanter, Gil Lamb*
A model's best friend is murdered and she is drawn into a strange Cold War conspiracy when she accidentally gets hold of some Soviet plans. A frantic and frothy comedy that never pauses for breath long enough to establish itself.

COM                                               100 min mTV
B,V                                                     HER

## FOR THE LOVE OF PLEASURE *** R18
Edwin S. Brown  USA  1980
*Annette Haven, Jamie Gillis, Samantha Fox, Suzanne Nero, Veri Knotty, Serena*
A down-and-out steals a car and breaks into an apartment. He's about to get away with his loot when the lights are turned on and a woman with a gun tells him to strip. However, with the arrival of her husband she decides to shoot him dead. In the afterlife an "angel" instructs him in sex and he enjoys a series of non-stop sexual encounters. Eventually he tires and only then discovers that he is in fact in hell. Well made and quite witty.
A  71 min; 78 min (SHEP) Cut (1 min 36 sec)
B,V  TCX; SHEP

## FOR THOSE I LOVED *** 15
Roberto Enrico  CANADA/FRANCE  1983
*Michael York, Brigitte Fossey, Jacques Penot, Macha Meril, Helen Hughes, Wolfgang Muller, Jean Bouise, Boris Bergman, Bernard Freyd, Dominique Frot, Jean Lescot, Guy Matachoro, Eugeniusz Priwieziencew*
The story of a survivor of the Warsaw Ghetto Uprising who becomes a powerful property developer but finds that anti-Semitism is far from dead. The cinema version was cut to 150 minutes.
Aka: AU NOM DE TOUS LES MIENS
Boa: novel by Martin Gray.
DRA  350 min (3 cassettes)
B,V  VFP L/A; HER

## FOR WHOM THE BELL TOLLS *** PG
Sam Wood  USA  1943
*Gary Cooper, Ingrid Bergman, Akim Tamiroff, Arturo de Cordova, Joseph Calleia, Katina Paxinou, Vladimir Sokoloff, Mikhail Rasumny, Fortunio Bonanova*
Romance between an orphan girl and an American school-teacher set against the background of the Spanish Civil War. Cooper joins the Partisans and falls for Bergman as a refugee before going on a suicide mission. Good photography, but the static and sombre story just doesn't generate any realism. The score is by Victor Young. AA: S. Actress (Paxinou).
Boa: novel by Ernest Hemingway.
DRA  128 min (ort 170 min)
B,V  CIC

## FOR YOUR EYES ONLY *** PG
John Glen  UK  1981
*Roger Moore, Carole Bouquet, Chaim Topol, Lynn-Holly Johnson, Julian Glover, Cassandra Harris, Jill Bennett, Michael Gothard, John Wyman, Jack Hedley, Lois Maxwell, Desmond Llewellyn, Geoffrey Keen, Walter Gotell*
A nuclear submarine activating device has been lost in a sea crash and agent 007 races against time to prevent it falling into the wrong hands. Not one of the best James Bond films, but the plot is quite plausible and Moore gives a nice relaxed performance. This was number twelve in a long-running series that started with DOCTOR NO. The next one in line was OCTOPUSSY.
A/AD  123 min (ort 128 min)
V/sh  WHV

## FOR YOUR LOVE ONLY ** 18
Wolfgang Peterson
WEST GERMANY  1976
(cinema release 1982)
*Nastassia Kinski, Christian Quadflieg, Judy Winter, Klaus Schwartzkopf*
A 17-year-old schoolgirl has an affair with her teacher, but is forced into murder when one of her classmates discovers their relationship and tries to blackmail her. A turgid and dull soap opera type story.
DRA  99 min mTV
B,V,V2  GHV

## FORBIDDEN ** PG
Anthony Page
UK/USA/WEST GERMANY  1984
*Jacqueline Bisset, Jurgen Prochnow, Irene Worth, Peter Vaughan, Robert Dietl, Avis Bunnage, Malcolm Kaye, Georg Tryphon, Annie Leon, Amanda Cannings, Osman Ragheb, Herta Schwartz, Ulli Kinalzik, Gerhard Frey*
Hollywood retells the true story of a German countess who hid her Jewish lover from the Nazis during WW2. Prochnow as her lover is convincing but Bisset (in her TV movie debut) really doesn't convince.
Aka: VERSTECKT
Boa: novel The Last Jews In Berlin by Leonard Gross.
DRA  105 min; 109 min (VGM) (ort 116 min) mCab
B,V  ODY; VGM (VHS only)

## FORBIDDEN JUSTICE ** 18
Robert W. Young  USA
*Bruce Davidson, Jose Perez, Nathan George, Don Blakely, Miguel Pinero, Tito Gaya, Freddie Fender*
Routine tough prison drama.
DRA  90 min
B,V  WARAD

## FORBIDDEN LOVE * U
Steven H. Stern  USA  1982
*Yvette Mimieux, Andrew Stevens, Lisa Lucas, Jerry Houser, Randy Brooks, Lynn Carlin, Hildy Brooks, John Considine, Dana Elcar, Jack Fletcher, Robbi Morgan, Eb Lottimer, Jill Jacobson, Bryan O'Bryne, John Petlock*
The story of a romance between an older woman and a younger man that ploughs the same old furrow and turns up nothing new.
DRA  100 min mTV
B,V  POLY

## FORBIDDEN PLANET *** U
Fred McLeod Wilcox  USA  1956
*Walter Pidgeon, Leslie Nielsen, Anne Francis, Warren Stevens, Jack Kelly, Earl Holliman*
One of the all-time best science fiction films. A highly intelligent account of a mission to the planet Altair 4 in 2200 A.D. One scientist lives alone with his daughter and Robby, a robot servant, all other members of the settler ship having died. The remains of a powerful non-human civilisation are to be found buried beneath the planet's surface. The sluggish script and poor dialogue are handicaps. Allegedly based on Shakespeare's "The Tempest".
FAN  98 min
V  MGM

## FORBIDDEN PLEASURES ** 18
Michel Leblanc  SWITZERLAND  1986
*Andre Kay, Amanda Shell, Marilyn Jess, Tina Loren, Jean-Pierre Armand, Valerie Vinal, Faby Verneuil*
Two fun-loving women indulge in a wild hunt for pleasure in this glossy European hardcore offering.
A  80 min
B,V  AVR

## FORBIDDEN WORLD ** 18
Allan Holzman  USA  1982
*Jesse Vint, Dawn Dunlap, June Chadwick, Linden Chiles, Fox Harris*
An ALIEN rip-off from the Corman studio. The lives of the researchers at a genetic research station are threatened by an organism they have created which is capable of changing its form as it grows. Lashings of gore take the place of big-budget special effects. Preceded by GALAXY OF TERROR which had a somewhat similar plot.
Aka: MUTANT
FAN  74 min (ort 82 min)
B,V,V2  EHE

## FORCE OF DARKNESS ** 18
Alan Hauge     USA     1985
*Mel Novak, Douglas Alan Shanklin, Loren Cedar, Mark Milan*
The story of a group of people living in Alcatraz prison, now disused, who become victims of a strange evil force.
HOR     89 min
B,V     CAN; ARC; GLOB

## FORCE OF EVIL ** 15
Richard Lang     USA     1977
*Lloyd Bridges, Pat Crowley, Eve Plumb, William Watson*
A recently paroled ex-convict returns to terrorise the family of a doctor, whose testimony led to his conviction for rape and murder years before. Routine thriller.
THR     100 min mTV
B,V     ACAD

## FORCE OF ONE, A ** 15
Paul Aaron     USA     1979
*Chuck Norris, Jennifer O'Neill, Clu Gulager, Bill Wallace, Ron O'Neal, James Whitmore Jr, Clint Ritchie, Pepe Serna*
A six times undefeated world karate champion helps a Californian town combat a drugs racket after a number of narcotics agents are murdered. A sound action film without any deep meanings.
MAR     86 min (ort 90 min) Cut (1 min 2 sec)
B,V     VTC L/A; VMA; VCC (VHS only); MAST (VHS only)

## FORCE TEN FROM NAVARONE * 15
Guy Hamilton     UK     1978
*Robert Shaw, Harrison Ford, Edward Fox, Franco Nero, Barbara Bach, Richard Kiel, Carl Weathers, Alan Badel, Angus MacInnes, Michael Byrne, Philip Latham, Petar Buntic, Michael Sheard, Paul Humpoletz, Dicken Ashworth*
An attempt to create a sequel to THE GUNS OF NAVARONE in which the target this time is a bridge and dam in Yugoslavia. A sluggish and implausible tale that has absolutely nothing in common with the earlier film, although the cast give of their best.
Boa: novel by Alistair MacLean.
WAR     114 min (ort 118 min)
B,V     RCA

## FORCED IMPACT * 18
Franco Mardinenni     ITALY     1975
*Richard Conte, Maurizio Merli, John Steiner, Ray Lovelock*
A policeman carries on a one-man vigilante struggle against crime, in this low-grade and derivative offering.
THR     84 min (ort 86 min) Cut (1 min 22 sec)
B,V     VPD

## FORCED VENGEANCE * 18
James Fargo     USA     1982
*Chuck Norris, Mary Louise Weller, Camilla Griggs, Michael Cavanaugh, David Opatoshu, Seiji Sakaguchi*
A Vietnam veteran who now works as a casino security chief finds himself caught up in a power struggle between two Hong Kong crime syndicates. A formula-ridden martial arts caper which has little going for it.
MAR     86 min Cut (50 sec)
V     MGM

## FORCED WITNESS ** 18
Raphael Rebibo     ISRAEL     1984
*Anath Atzmon, Uri Gavriel, Tzadok Tzarum, Moscu Alkalay, Irith Frank*
A woman witnessing a rape case is terrorised by the culprit's brother. Average.
Aka: EDUT ME ONESS

THR     88 min (ort 103 min) Cut (2 min 42 sec)
V     CAN

## FORD * PG
Allan Eastman     USA     1987
*Cliff Robertson, Hope Lange, R H. Thompson, Michael Ironside, Chris Wiggins, Heather Thomas*
A plodding and episodic adaptation of Lacey's book telling of the life and times of Henry Ford with more than a little attention focusing on his family and mistress troubles. A deadly dull dud.
Aka: FORD: HIS MISTRESS AND HIS MACHINE – PARTS 1 AND 2; FORD: THE MAN AND THE MACHINE
Boa: book by Robert Lacey.
DRA     200 min mTV
B,V     CINE

## FOREIGN BODY *** 15
Ronald Neame     UK     1986
*Victor Banerjee, Trevor Howard, Warren Mitchell, Geraldine McEwan, Amanda Donohoe, Dennis Quilley, Eve Ferret, Stratford Johns, Anna Massey, Stratford Johns, John Laurie*
A young Indian bus driver quits his job and sets up as a bogus physician, acquiring an impressive list of patients thanks to his bedside manner. A likeable 1950s-style sex comedy.
COM     107 min
B,V     RCA

## FOREIGN CORRESPONDENT **** PG
Alfred Hitchcock     USA     1940
*Joel McCrea, Laraine Day, Herbert Marshall, George Sanders, Edmund Gwenn, Albert Basserman, Eduardo Ciannelli, Barbara Pepper, Eddy Conrad, Robert Benchley, Harry Davenport, Charles Wagenheim, Martin Kosleck*
A journalist gets involved in a mysterious espionage plot that unfolds at a furious pace when he is sent to Europe in 1938. Despite a few rambling moments this film builds up to a great climax, with several memorable scenes along the way. One of Hitchcock's best films. Scripted by Charles Bennett and Joan Harrison and with dialogue by James Hilton and Robert Benchley.
Boa: book Personal History by Vincent Sheean.
THR     115 min (ort 119 min) B/W
V     VCC

## FOREPLAY * 18
John Eastway     AUSTRALIA     1984
*Gerry Sont, Tina Bursill, Lenita Psillakis, Jon Finlayson*
A further sequel to the Australian sex comedy "Alvin Purple", and telling of a young boy who inherits his father's way with women.
Aka: GIRL-TOY; MELVIN: SON OF ALVIN; PRESIDENT'S WOMAN, THE
COM     90 min
B,V     MED

## FOREPLAY * R18
Robert J. McCarty/Bruce Malmuth/John G. Avildsen/Vinnie Ross     USA     1975 (re-released 1982)
*K.C. Valentine, Paul Thomas, Ron Jeremy, Pat Paulsen, Cara Lott, Starbuck, Julian Michel, Zero Mostel, Estelle Parsons, Jerry Orbach, George S. Irving, Andrew Duncan*
Sex film that was originally intended to be four short sketches. One was too explicit for release, the remaining three were cobbled together to form an incoherent whole. This tells of a shy virgin who takes a job in a hotel and decides to install two-way mirrors and intercoms in the rooms in order to get a sex education. She enjoys watching various exploits and ultimately discovers that the "hotel" is used by people to live out their fantasies.

A                                66 min (ort 100 min) Cut (55 sec)
B,V                              TCX L/A; PRI L/A; SHEP

## FOREPLAY: THE PREQUEL *                    18
Tim Burstall          USA                     1973
*Graeme Blundell, Noel Ferrier*
A sequel to "Alvin Purple", that follows the exploits of
a young chap who is totally irresistible to women.
Unfortunately, his exploits make for a totally resisti-
ble comedy.
Aka: ALVIN RIDES AGAIN
COM                                           87 min
B,V                                           SCRN

## FOREST, THE **                             18
Don Jones             USA                     1981
*Dean Russell, Michael Brody, Elaine Warner, John
Batis, Ann Wilkinson*
Two couples go on a hiking holiday and meet a mad
and murderous hermit in a fairly routine slasher tale
with a supernatural slant. Unmemorable except for
an interesting feminist angle that allows Warner to
demonstrate heroics while Russell contents himself
with supplying general hysteria.
HOR                    82 min (ort 85 min) Cut (22 sec)
B,V                    PYR L/A; 21ST L/A; COBRA

## FOREVER AND BEYOND **                      PG
Thomas Flood          USA                     1982
*Terence O'Connor, John Snee, Dixie Wade*
A mawkish story of a 7-year-old boy who is dying of
leukaemia and meets a mystical messenger from God.
DRA                                           100 min
B,V                                   INT L/A; NET

## FOREVER LULU *                             18
Amos Kollek          USA                      1986
*Hanna Schygulla, Deborah Harry, Alec Baldwin, Paul
Gleason, Annie Golden, Paul Gleason, Ruth
Westheimer, Amos Kollek*
Schygulla plays a would-be New York novelist who
has fallen on hard times and finds herself involved in
a real-life gangster mystery of drugs and murder. A
kind of DESPERATELY SEEKING SUSAN clone, of
leaden pace and lousy direction.
COM                                           86 min
B,V                                           VES

## FOREVER YOUNG ***                          15
David Drury           UK                       1983
*James Aubrey, Nicholas Gecks, Karen Archer, Jason
Carter, Julian Firth, Liam Holt, Alex McCowen*
Two friends meet again after a long separation but
their attempts to re-establish their friendship founder
on their need to settle old scores, in this thoughtful
and perceptive tale.
DRA                                           84 min mTV
B,V                                           TEVP

## FORGOTTEN MAN, THE **
Walter Grauman        USA                     1971
*Dennis Weaver, Lois Nettleton, Anne Francis, Andrew
Duggan, Percy Rodrigues, Pamelyn Ferdin, Robert
Doyle, James Hong, Byron Morrow, Carl Reindel,
John S. Ragin, Vernon Weddle*
An American POW escapes from captivity in Vietnam
and returns home only to find that his wife has
remarried, his business has been sold and his daugh-
ter has been adopted. Not surprisingly, he suffers a
breakdown. Weaver gives a vigorous performance, but
the cliched script and implausible climax are serious
flaws.
DRA                                           71 min mTV
B,V                                           RNK

## FORGOTTEN PARALLEL, THE **                 18
Lyndon Swift          USA
*Lawrence Day, Luis Manuel, Tom Pollard, Chris
Munke, Daniel Foley, Garramy Quatro*

Formula war film set in Vietnam.
Aka: HOW SLEEP THE BRAVE
WAR                                           90 min
B,V                                           WARAD

## FORGOTTEN WARRIOR, THE **                  18
Nick Cacas/Charles Ordonez                    1986
*Ron Marchini, Quinn Frazier, Marilyn Bauista, Sam
T. Lapuz, Mike Cohen, Sonny Villanueva, Vilma Vitug*
An American soldier in Vietnam witnesses the mur-
der of his superior and is shot and left for dead. Nursed
back to health by a village girl, he still finds his life in
danger from the murderer who intends to silence him
for good.
A/AD                   77 min (ort 90 min) Cut (10 sec)
B,V                                  ARIES L/A; APX

## FORGOTTEN, THE **                          15
James Keach          USA                      1989
*Keith Carradine, Steve Railsback, Stacy Keach,
William Lucking, Pepe Serna, Mimi Maynard,
Richard Lawson*
When six Green Berets return to the USA after 17
years as prisoners of the Vietnamese they find them-
selves being stalked by sinister government agents.
An implausible thriller, co-written by Keach in his
directing debut.
THR                            92 min (ort 100 min) mCab
V                                             CIC

## FORMATORS: ATTACK OF THE XELANS **         U
Jim Terry            JAPAN
Earth is attacked by evil aliens in this animated space
adventure. Average.
CAR                                           50 min
B,V                                           KRP

## FORMATORS: EARTH'S DEFENCE **              U
Jim Terry            JAPAN
Another episode in "The Formators" space epic.
Aka: EARTH'S DEFENCE
CAR                                           45 min
V                                             KRP

## FORMULA, THE **                            15
John G. Avildsen     USA                      1980
*Marlon Brando, George C. Scott, Marthe Keller, John
Gielgud, G.D. Spradlin, Beatrice Straight, Richard
Lynch, John Van Dreelen*
A Los Angeles policeman's life is in danger, when he
discovers that a friend's murder is linked to a
conspiracy involving a formula for synthetic fuel.
Scott and Brando give great performances, but this
humdrum thriller is too predictable to build up any
tension. Written by Steve Shagan.
Boa: novel by Steve Shagan.
THR                            112 min (ort 117 min)
B,V,V2                                        MGM

## FORSYTE SAGA, THE **                       PG
David Giles/James Cellan Jones
                      UK                       1967
*Nyree Dawn Porter, Kenneth More, Eric Porter, Susan
Hampshire, Martin Jarvis*
Long and rambling adaptation of a series of novels
dealing with the fortunes of a single family of London
merchants, from the 1870s to the 1920s. A competent
and workmanlike account, that spared no expense and
was immensely popular, yet for all that was curiously
lifeless. Originally shown as a set of twenty-six
60-minute episodes.
Boa: the "Forsyte" novels by John Galsworthy.
DRA               1,300 min (12 cassettes) B/W mTV
B,V                                           BBC

## FORT APACHE **                             U
John Ford             USA                     1948
*Henry Fonda, John Wayne, Shirley Temple, Pedro
Armendariz, Ward Bond, Victor McLaglen, John*

*Agar, Irene Rich, George O'Brien, Anna Lee, Dick*
*Foran, Jack Pennick, Guy Kibbee, Grant Withers,*
*Miguel Inclan, Mae Marsh, Francis Ford*
Story of the conflict between the US Cavalry and the
Indians. Fonda plays a martinet who has troubles
with his family as well as the Indians. Not up to Ford's
usual standard but entertaining with a fine cast and a
couple of good action sequences.
WES                                112 min; 122 min (CH5) B/W
B,V                                TEVP; HER; CH5 (VHS only)

## FORT APACHE, THE BRONX **
Daniel Petrie            USA                         1980
*Paul Newman, Edward Asner, Ken Wahl, Pam Grier,*
*Kathleen Beller, Rachel Ticotin, Kathleen Beller*
A tough police drama about the hazards of working in
the "war zone" of the South Bronx. Gripping and often
tense, with Newman giving one of his best perform-
ances, but gratuitously violent and contrived.
Boa: novel by Heywood Gould.
DRA                                120 min (ort 125 min)
B,V                                                    VTC

## FORTRESS **                                          15
Arch Nicholson      AUSTRALIA                         1985
*Rachel Ward, Sean Garlick, Rebecca Rigg, Robin*
*Mason, Marc Gray, Beth Buchanan, Asher Keddie,*
*Bradley Meehan, Anna Crawford, Richard Terrill,*
*Peter Hehir, Roger Stephen, Vernon Wells, David*
*Bradshaw, Elaine Cusick*
A teacher and her class of nine are kidnapped by a
gang of four vicious thugs wearing grotesque masks.
The victims plot to escape by outwitting their captors.
A violent film, but one that tends to hold the interest.
DRA                                            85 min mCab
B,V                                                    CBS

## FORTUNATE PILGRIM, THE **                            15
Stuart Cooper            USA                         1987
*Sophia Loren, Edward James Olmos, Hal Halbrook,*
*John Turturro, Lucia Angeluzzi, Anna Strasberg,*
*Yorgo Voyagis, Roxann Biggs, Ed Wiley, Mirjana*
*Karanovic, Ron Marquette*
A turn-of-the-century story, telling of an Italian
immigrant who experiences poverty and the tragic
loss of her two husbands, struggling for years to give
her five children a better life. A sprawling, melod-
ramatic exercise, strong on atmosphere and detail
(despite using Belgrade for New York), but far too
long. The opera-style soundtrack is an annoyance.
Scripted by John McGreevey and photographed by
Reginald Morris. First shown in two parts.
Aka: MARIO PUZO'S THE FORTUNATE PILGRIM
Boa: novel by Mario Puzo.
DRA                         144 min (ort 250 min) mTV
V                                                    GHV

## FORTUNE COOKIE, THE **                                U
Billy Wilder             USA                         1966
*Jack Lemmon, Walter Matthau, Ron Rich, Cliff*
*Osmond, Judi West, Lurene Tuttle*
A TV cameraman is slightly injured filming a football
game but falls under the influence of his brother-in-
law who is a totally unscrupulous lawyer. His inten-
tion is to make these injuries appear to be so serious
that he will get a million-dollar compensation. Matth-
au as the lawyer is great, but he's wasted in a film that
lacks both gags and plot development. AA: S. Actor
(Matthau).
Aka: MEET WHIPLASH WILLIE
COM                                121 min (ort 125 min) B/W
B,V                                                    WHV

## FORTUNE DANE **                                      15
Nicholas Sgarro/Charles Corell
                         USA                         1986
*Carl Weathers, Sonny Landham, Adolphe Caesar,*
*Daphne Ashbrook*
A former college athlete now works as a policeman in

his home town and is respected by all. However,
following the murder of several people by a contract
killer, a link is established between this event and the
bank where his father works, which is found to
launder Mob money. Our cop resigns from the force
and sets out to regain the family honour. A better-
than-average police tale that formed the pilot for a TV
series.
DRA                                            84 min mTV
B,V                                                    SONY

## FORTY CARATS ***                                     PG
Milton Katselas          USA                         1973
*Liv Ullmann, Edward Albert, Gene Kelly, Binnie*
*Barnes, Deborah Raffin, Billy Green Bush, Nancy*
*Walker*
A middle-aged New York woman has a holiday
romance in Greece with young boy of 20. He follows
her home however, and she agonises over whether
there is any future in their relationship. Glossy and
mildly amusing, but miscasting of Ullmann in a comic
role seriously undermines it. A screen version of a
well-received Broadway comedy that was adapted in
turn from a French farce. The script is by Leonard
Gershe.
Aka: 40 CARATS
Boa: play by Pierre Barillet.
COM                                                104 min
B,V                                                    RCA

## FORTY DEUCE *
Paul Morrissey           USA                         1982
*Orson Bean, Kevin Bacon, Mark Keyloun, Harris*
*Laskaway, Tommy Citera*
A teenage hustler attempts to sell a runaway boy to a
wealthy man, but things become complicated when
the boy dies of a heroin overdose. A sombre and
uninteresting melodrama of minimal value.
Boa: play by Alan Browne.
DRA                                                89 min
B,V                                                    PVG

## FORTY MILLION BUCKS **
Henry Levin              USA                         1978
*Rod Taylor, Stuart Whitman, Elke Sommer, Keenan*
*Wynn, Jeremy Kemp*
A search by two old friends for sunken treasure
involves them with a double-dealing crook, in this
formula action yarn.
Aka: CONTRABAND (KES); FORTY MILLION
BUCKS ON A DEAD MAN'S CHEST; FORTY
MILLION DOLLARS; GOLD; JAMAICAN GOLD;
TREASURE OF DEATH (MARKET); TREASURE
SEEKERS, THE
A/AD                                               82 min
B,V                         DFS L/A; KES; MARKET

## FORTY-EIGHT HOURS ***                                15
Walter Hill              USA                         1982
*Eddie Murphy, Nick Nolte, James Remar, Annette*
*O'Toole, Frank McRae, James Remar, David Partrick*
*Kelly, Sonny Landham, Brion James, Kenny*
*Sherman, Jonathan Banks, James Keane, Tara King,*
*Agneta Blackburn, Margot Rose*
A hard-nosed cop enlists the aid of a jailed robber to
help him nab a pair of escaped killers, one of whom
being Murphy's former partner. With only two days of
freedom for Murphy, this unlikely duo find themselves
in a number of tricky situations as they comb the
streets in their search. Murphy's screen debut is a
high-energy performance in this sometimes funny,
sometimes noisy, but often downright unpleasant
mixture of comedy and action.
A/AD                                89 min (ort 97 min) Cut
B,V                                                    CIC

## FORTY-NINTH PARALLEL, THE ***
Michael Powell/Emeric Pressburger
                         UK                          1941

Leslie Howard, Raymond Massey, Eric Portman, Laurence Olivier, Anton Walbrook, Glynis Johns, Niall MacGinnis, Finlay Currie, Raymond Lovell, John Chandos, Basil Appleby, Eric Clavering, Charles Victor, Ley On
Five sailors from a sunken U-boat try to escape to the USA from Canada. Generally effective, this strong propaganda piece allows a fine cast the chance to display their talents. AA: Story (Orig) Emeric Pressburger.
Aka: INVADERS, THE
DRA                    121 min (ort 123 min) B/W
B,V                                          RNK

**FORTY-SECOND STREET ****                   U
Lloyd Bacon          USA             1933
Warner Baxter, Ginger Rogers, Ruby Keeler, Bebe Daniels, Dick Powell, George Brent, Una Merkel, Guy Kibbee, Ned Sparks, George E. Stone, Allen Jenkins
Problems of an ailing director who has to put on a musical with sensational Busby Berkley numbers. The leading lady is indisposed and a chorus girl takes her role and becomes a star. Performed with great zest with highly enjoyable songs and some great dancing. This definitive Hollywood musical has formed the standard by which later ones are judged. Some colourised versions are available – avoid them if possible. Music is by Al Dubin.
Aka: 42ND STREET
Boa: novel Bradford Ropes by Rian James.
MUS                                  89 min B/W
B, V/h                                 WHV; CIC

**FOUL PLAY ***                              PG
Colin Higgins        USA             1978
Goldie Hawn, Chevy Chase, Burgess Meredith, Dudley Moore, Rachel Roberts, Eugebe Roche, Marilyn Sokol, Billy Barty, Marc Lawrence, Brian Dennehy
An innocent woman becomes unwittingly embroiled in a murder plot and there are several attempts on her life, but no-one will believe her except a young detective. A tasteless and fairly unamusing comedy with a few Hitchcock touches but little else. Later followed by a brief TV series.
COM                       111 min (ort 116 min)
V/h                                          CIC

**FOUR DEUCES, THE ****
William H. Bushnell Jr  USA          1975
Jack Palance, Carol Lynley, Adam Roarke, Warren Berlinger, E.J. Peaker, Gianni Russo
Drama set in the Prohibition Era about a gang leader, his girl and his casino. A mixture of action and comedy elements that generally does justice to neither.
DRA                                    87 min
B,V                                          RNK

**FOUR FEATHERS, THE ****                    U
Don Sharp            UK              1977
Beau Bridges, Simon Ward, Robert Powell, Richard Johnson, Jane Seymour, Harry Andrews, David Robb, Richard Beale, Robin Bailey, John Hallam, Julian Barnes, Mary Maude, Frank Gatliff, Robert Flemyng, Robert James
A young army officer refutes charges of cowardice levelled at him by going off to fight in the Sudan. Fifth time around for this story of the Dervish revolt in the Sudan and the fighting that took place when the British army ended the rule of the Dervishes. Well above average with a lively script by Gerald DiPego.
Boa: novel by A.E.W. Mason.
A/AD                      96 min (ort 110 min) mTV
B,V                                          TEVP

**FOUR FEATHERS, THE ****                    U
Zoltan Korda         UK              1939
John Clements, Ralph Richardson, C. Aubrey Smith,

June Duprez, Clive Baxter, Allan Jeayes, Jack Allen, Donald Gray, Frederick Culley, Clive Barker, Derek Elphinstone, Robert Rendel, Archibald Batty, Hal Walters, Norman Pierce
Brilliant account of a British stay-at-home who refutes charges of cowardice (he received four feathers after resigning his commission) by going off to help his comrades in the army put down an uprising in the Sudan. Highly atmospheric and boasting some memorable battle scenes. Remade for TV in 1977.
Boa: novel by A.E.W. Mason.
A/AD                      109 min (ort 115 min)
B,V              SPEC/POLY; SCREL; CENTVID

**FOUR INFERNOS TO CROSS ****
                     HONG KONG
Musung Kwak, Kyhee Kim
Martial arts film set in Korea before WW2 and dealing with the Korean resistance to Japanese occupation. Average.
MAR                                    90 min
B,V                                          SAT

**FOUR MUSKETEERS, THE ****                  PG
Richard Lester
                   PANAMA/SPAIN       1975
Oliver Reed, Faye Dunaway, Raquel Welch, Richard Chamberlain, Frank Finlay, Michael York, Christopher Lee, Jean-Pierre Cassel, Geraldine Chaplin, Simon Ward, Charlton Heston
Second half of this version of the Dumas novel is a little too much of a spoof to do justice to it and tends to degenerate into slapstick. Made at the same time as the 1973 version of THE THREE MUSKETEERS, this is in effect the continuation of the first film with the same mixture of visual gags, damsels in distress and acts of bravery.
Aka: FOUR MUSKETEERS, THE: THE REVENGE OF MILADY
Boa: novel The Three Musketeers by Alexandre Dumas.
DRA                                   102 min
B,V                                          TEVP

**FOUR SEASONS, THE ****                     15
Alan Alda            USA             1981
Alan Alda, Sandy Dennis, Carol Burnett, Rita Moreno, Jack Weston, Len Cariou, Bess Armstrong
The various stages or "seasons" in the relations between three married couples are examined in this rather low-key drama which later became a TV series. Mildly amusing in places but generally smug and superficial. Written by Alda. who made his feature directing debut with this film.
DRA                       103 min (ort 107 min)
V/h                                          CIC

**FOUR SHAOLIN CHALLENGERS, THE ****        18
                     HONG KONG
Wong Yuen, Sun Leung, Shiu Loung, Pai Bei, Wing Fat
Four brothers fight against the odds to rescue their sister who has been sold into prostitution. Another run-of-the-mill martial arts adventure.
MAR                                    95 min
B,V                                    ACE; VTEL

**FOURTEEN GOING ON THIRTY ****              U
Paul Schneider       USA             1988
Steve Eckholdt, Rick Rossovich, Loretta Swit, Patrick Duffy, Daphne Ashbrook, Adam Carl, Gabey Olds, Harry Morgan, Alan Thicke, Dick Van Patten, Rick Rossovich
This Disney reversal of the PEGGY SUE GOT MARRIED comedy has a love-sick teenager getting to be an adult overnight and making a play for the affections of his pretty teacher, thus preventing her from marrying an obnoxious gym instructor. A

pleasant, silly, sugary Disney offering.
Aka: 14 GOING ON 30
COM                          81 min (ort 100 min) mTV
B,V                                                    WDV

## FOURTH MAN, THE *** 18
Paul Verhoeven   NETHERLANDS           1979
                          (released in USA 1984)
*Renee Soutendijk, Jeroene Krabbe, Thom Hoffman,
Dolf De Vries, Geert De Jong*
A homosexual lecturer becomes involved with a young
woman and her fiance and becomes increasingly
disturbed as he begins to suspect that she may have
murdered several previous husbands. A flashy and
fairly stylish black comedy.
Aka: DE VERDE MAN
COM                 95 min (ort 98 min) Cut (1 sec)
B,V                                                    EHE

## FOURTH PROTOCOL, THE *** 15
John Mackenzie         UK                    1986
*Michael Caine, Pierce Brosnan, Joanna Cassidy, Ned
Beatty, Michael Gough, Julian Glover, Ray McAnally,
Ian Richardson*
Secret agent Caine has to foil a Soviet plan to detonate
one of the nuclear bombs kept by America at an air
base in the UK, it being their intention to thus cause
the collapse of NATO. A pretty enjoyable if rather
predictable spy caper. Brosnan is good as a Russian
agent but Caine gives a wooden and unconvincing
performance.
Boa: novel by Frederick Forsyth.
A/AD                                            117 min
B,V                                                    RNK

## FOURTH WAR, THE ** 15
John Frankenheimer     USA               1988
*Roy Scheider, Jurgen Prochnow, Tim Reid, Lara
Harris, Harry Dean Stanton, Dale Dye*
An American colonel cannot adjust to the new peace-
time role of the army, and when he finds himself
confronted by a like-minded Soviet colonel, the two
are able to engage in a private little war of their own.
Strong performances are let down by the mediocre
script in this unimaginative Cold War tale.
Boa: novel by Stephen Peters.
THR                             87 min (ort 91 min)
V/sh                                                   GHV

## FOURTH WISE MAN, THE * U
Michael Ray Rhodes     USA               1985
*Martin Sheen, Alan Arkin, Eileen Brennan, Ralph
Bellamy, Lance Kerwin, Harold Gould*
An unknown wise man who was delayed by helping
others when his colleagues followed the star to
Bethlehem, spends the next thirty years searching for
Christ. A soggy adaptation of a rather beautiful tale,
done in suitably evangelical style.
Boa: novel by Henry Van Dyke.
DRA                                       73 min mTV
B,V                                                    VES

## FOX ***
Rainer Werner Fassbinder
              WEST GERMANY                    1975
*Rainer Werner Fassbinder, Peter Chatel, Karl-Heinz
Boehm, Ulla Jacobsen, Adrian Hoven*
The lives and loves of a not very endearing group of
West German homosexuals are examined in this tale
that largely focuses on the declining fortunes of a
sideshow performer. Heavily ironic in tone and cer-
tainly memorable, but far too long.
Aka: FOX AND HIS FRIENDS
DRA                                             123 min
B,V                                                    PVG

## FOXEHOLE IN CAIRO **
John Moxey             UK                    1960

*James Robertson Justice, Adrian Hoven, Gloria
Mestre, Albert Lieven, Niall MacGinnis, Robert
Urquhart, Peter Van Eyck, Fenella Fielding, John
Westbrook, Lee Montague, Henry Oscar, Howard
Marion Crawford*
The story of a counter intelligence agent at work
during WW2 in Egypt who supplies Rommel with
false information. Quite diverting but rather muddled
and inconsistent.
Boa: book The Cat And The Mice by Leonard Moseley.
THR                                              80 min
B,V,V2                                             INT/CBS

## FOXES * 15
Adrian Lyne            USA                    1980
*Jodie Foster, Cherie Currie, Marilyn Kagan, Kandice
Stroh, Scott Baio, Sally Kellerman, Randy Quaid, Lois
Smith*
Four teenage girls find that growing up is a traumatic
experience in this sincere but eminently forgettable
melodrama.
DRA                             102 min (ort 106 min)
B,V                                                    WHV

## FOXTRAP * 18
Fred Williamson     ITALY/USA             1986
*Fred Williamson, Christopher Connelly, Beatrice
Palme, Donna Owen, Leia Rochon, Arlene Golonka,
Cleo Sebastian, Lela Rochon*
A strong-arm private eye is hired by an uncle to find
his missing niece but unfortunately he is not told the
whole truth by his client and this leads to tragic
results. A low-budget offering that is not much more
than a vehicle for Williamson.
THR                             85 min (ort 88 min)
B,V                                                PEGA/MED

## FOXY BROWN * 18
Jack Hill              USA                    1974
*Pam Grier, Peter Brown, Terry Carter, Kathryn Loder*
A black nurse takes a routine revenge when her
boyfriend, an undercover narcotics agent, is killed by
the Mob. A standard revenger.
A/AD           85 min (ort 94 min) Cut (2 min 48 sec)
B,V,V2                                                GHV

## FRAGMENT OF FEAR ** 15
Richard C. Sarafian    UK                    1970
*David Hemmings, Gayle Hunnicutt, Wilfrid Hyde-
White, Flora Robson, Adolfo Celi, Roland Culver,
Daniel Massey, Mona Washbourne, Mary Wimbush,
Glynn Edwards, Derek Newark, Arthur Lowe, Yootha
Joyce, Bernard Archard*
A writer and former drug addict attempts to make
sense of some bizarre events, such as the murder of an
aunt, but is slowly driven to the conclusion that he
may be insane. A murky and ponderous thriller that
shows great style, but is hampered by a lack of depth.
Written by Paul Dehn and photographed by Oswald
Morris.
Boa: novel by John Bingham.
THR                             92 min (ort 95 min)
V                                                     RCA

## FRAMED * 18
Phil Karlson           USA                    1974
*Joe Don Baker, Conny Van Dyke, Gabriel Dell, John
Marley, Brock Peters, Roy Jenson*
A man vows revenge on the crooked and corrupt cops
who framed him and sent him to prison after he
inadvertently killed a sheriff. Of interest if your tastes
run towards gratuitous violence, otherwise forget it.
Boa: novel by A. Powers and M. Misenheimer.
DRA        100 min (ort 106 min) (Cut at film release by
                                          1 min 11 sec)
B,V                                                    CIC

## FRANCES ***
Graeme Clifford      USA      15    1982
*Jessica Lange, Sam Shephard, Kim Stanley, Bart Burns, Jeffrey DeMunn, Jordan Charney, Lane Smith, Kevin Costner*
An aspiring young female filmstar suffers from self-destructive tendencies and has an eventual nervous breakdown, spending some time in a mental home. A biography of the 1930s star Frances Farmer which chronicles her tragic life in some detail. See also WILL THERE REALLY BE A MORNING?
DRA      113 min (ort 140 min)
B,V      TEVP; WHV (VHS only)

## FRANK AND I *
Gerard Kikoine      18
     CANADA/FRANCE/USA      1983
*Jennifer Inch, Christopher Pearson, Sophie Favier*
A sort of "Fanny Hill" story of debauchery set in Victorian times.
Aka: LADY LIBERTINE
DRA      78 min (ort 81 min) (Cut at film release)
B,V      GHV

## FRANKENHOOKER ***
Frank Henenlotter      USA      18    1990
*James Lorinz, Patty Mullen, Charlotte Helmkamp, Shirley Stoler, Louise Lasser*
A biting and surreal adaptation of the Frankenstein legend from the director of BASKET CASE, in which a beautiful female monster is created from body parts obtained from dead prostitutes, and causes considerable trouble for the patrons of Times Square.
COM      81 min (ort 90 min)
V      MED

## FRANKENSTEIN ****
James Whale      USA      PG    1931
*Boris Karloff, Mae Clark, Colin Clive, John Boles, Edward Van Sloan, Dwight Frye, Frederick Kerr, Lionel Belmore*
This is the daddy of them all, the original classic tale which though dated is well worth seeing. A scientist creates a monster out of parts of bodies and brings it to life with electricity. It then goes on a rampage. This film (which bears little resemblance to the novel) has spawned hundreds of imitations and spin-offs. Followed by THE BRIDE OF FRANKENSTEIN.
Boa: novel Frankenstein; Or, The Modern Prometheus by Mary Shelley. Osca: BRIDE OF FRANKENSTEIN, THE
HOR      69 min (ort 71 min); 134 min (2 film cassette)
B/W
V/h      CIC

## FRANKENSTEIN MEETS THE WOLF MAN *** PG
Roy William Neill      USA      1943
*Lon Chaney Jr, Patric Knowles, Ilona Massey, Bela Lugosi, Lionel Atwill, Maria Ouspenskaya, Dennis Hoey, Rex Evans, Dwight Frye*
A sequel to both "The Ghost Of Frankenstein" and THE WOLF MAN, with Chaney discovering that Baron Frankenstein is dead when he comes to him for help. However, he soon finds that the Baron's monster is alive and well. Lugosi is miscast as the monster in his only attempt at the role. Followed by "House Of Frankenstein".
Osca: WOLF MAN, THE
HOR      72 min; 140 min (2 film cassette) B/W
V      CIC

## FRANKENSTEIN MUST BE DESTROYED **
Terence Fisher      UK      1969
*Peter Cushing, Simon Ward, Veronica Carlson, Maxine Audley, Thorley Walters, Freddie Jones, George Pravda, Geoffrey Bayldon, Colette O'Neill, Peter Copley*
Hammer's fifth outing for the Frankenstein legend has Cushing doing his usual bit with brain trans-

plants and inevitable rampaging monsters. Followed by THE HORROR OF FRANKENSTEIN, but the real horror is the sameness of these films, this undistinguished effort being a case in point.
HOR      97 min
V      WHV

## FRANKENSTEIN'S ISLAND *
Jerry Warren      USA      PG    1982
*John Carradine, Cameron Mitchell, Andrew Duggan, Robert Clarke, Steve Brodie, Tain Bodkin, Laurel Johnson*
Four balloonists are caught in a storm and drift ashore on a strange island where they are the unwilling guests of Frankenstein's great-great-granddaughter. A dismal affair indeed.
Aka: FRANKENSTEIN ISLAND
HOR      91 min
B,V,V2      DFS; KRP/XTACY

## FRANTIC ***
Roman Polanski      USA      15    1987
*Harrison Ford, Emmanuelle Seigner, Betty Buckley, John Mahoney, Jimmy Ray Weeks, Yorgo Voyagis, David Huddleston, Gerard Klein*
An American heart surgeon arrives in Paris to attend a convention, only to have his wife suddenly disappear without trace. An intriguing suspense tale that happily never becomes overblown, as so many films of this genre are apt to.
THR      115 min (ort 120 min)
V/sh      WHV

## FRAT HOUSE *
Sven Conrad      USA      1979
*Randy Allen, Aimee Leigh, Lisa De Leeuw*
A puerile and slapstick series of sexual jokes, revolving around the antics of a bunch of randy college kids at a university where sex is a way of life for the students. As tiresome as it is witless, this is something of a down-market ANIMAL HOUSE.
A      90 min
V      RIP

## FRATERNITY VACATION **
James Frawley      USA      15    1985
*Stephen Geoffreys, Sheree J. Wilson, Cameron Dye, Leigh McCloskey, Tim Robbins, John Vernon, Britt Ekland, Nita Talbot*
Five college lads go to Palm Springs to try to get a little sexual experience for one of their number. A typical teen-oriented comedy with little of lasting value but a few nice performances.
COM      85 min (ort 89 min)
B,V      POLY; CH5 (VHS only)

## FRAUD *
Donald Monat      SOUTH AFRICA      1974
*Brian O'Shaugnessy, Michael McCabe, Anabel Linder*
In two unrelated companies, senior executives commit suicide after share frauds, in this unsatisfactory and muddled drama.
DRA      88 min
B,V      RNK

## FRAULEINS IN UNIFORM **
Erwin C. Dietrich WEST GERMANY      1972
*Brigitte Bergen, Karen Heske, Elizabeth Felchner*
In Germany during WW2 a volunteer force of young girls is formed to fight at the front. A humane doctor who reveals much of the sexual degradation beneath the apparent glamour, is sent to the Russian front as a punishment.
DRA      97 min
B,V      DFS

## FREAKY FAIRY TALES *
Jeffrey S. Delman      USA      18    1985
*Nicole Picard, Scott Valentine, Catheryn le Prume*

A trio of horror tales that are all versions of familiar fairy tales, provide the material for this tongue-in-cheek effort.
Aka: DEAD TIME
HOR                    88 min Cut (29 sec)
B,V                                        EIV

## FREAKY FRIDAY **                        U
Gary Nelson          USA              1976
Jodie Foster, Barbara Harris, John Astin, Patsy Kelly,
Dick Van Patten, Sorell Brooke, Marie Windsor,
Charlene Tilton
Inspired by the 1947 British film "Vice Versa" in which a boy and his dad swap minds, this one looks at a mother-and-daughter exchange that takes place due to a magic amulet. A standard Disney comedy somewhat enlivened by winning performances from Foster and Harris. The script is by Mary Rodgers. See also EIGHTEEN AGAIN!
Boa: story by Mary Rodgers.
COM                                    94 min
B,V                                       WDV

## FREDDY'S NIGHTMARES 2 ***            18
Ken Wiederhorn       USA              1988
Robert Englund
Two episodes from the gruesome TV series featuring the devilish character of "Freddy Krueger" from A NIGHTMARE ON ELM STREET. In "Sister's Keeper" Freddy fights a battle of wits when he returns to Springwood to confront the twins whose father supposedly burnt him to death years ago. In "Freddy's Tricks Or Treats" our lovable rogue has some fun with a sexually repressed girl who is working late at the the school science labs on the eve of Halloween
HOR                              90 min mTV
B,V                                     BRAVE

## FREDDY'S NIGHTMARES:                 18
## A NIGHTMARE ON ELM STREET ***
Tobe Hooper/Tom McLoughlin
                     USA              1988
Robert Englund, Gry Park, Hili Park, Ian Williams,
William Frankfather, Lori Petty, Yvette Nifar, Lee
Kessler, Kane Picoy, Anthony Barton
A spin-off from A NIGHTMARE ON ELM STREET with the unpleasant razor-fingered character of Freddy Krueger giving his account of the Elm Street child murders and his own "death" at the hands of their horrified parents. Now Freddy is back to have his revenge in this unpleasant and stomach-churning tale. The pilot for a TV series.
HOR                              90 min mTV
B,V                      CHV; VCC (VHS only)

## FREDDY'S NIGHTMARES: SIX PACK ***    18
                     USA              1988
Robert Englund
Six 90 minute videos, each featuring Englund in an episode from his popular horror series inspired by the numerous "Nightmare On Elm Street" films. Episodes are: "Safer Sex", "It's A Miserable Life", "Freddy's Mother's Day", "Nightmare Fever", "Rock Me, Freddy" and "Do Dreams Bleed?". The mixture of gruesome humour and ghoulish horror is as before, as the citizens of Springwood find the devilish Freddy Krueger invading their dreams.
HOR                     540 min (6 cassettes) mTV
V                                       BRAVE

## FREE RIDE *                          15
Tom Tribovich        USA              1986
Gary Hershberger, Reed Rudy, Dawn Schneider, Peter
DeLuise, Brian MacGregor, Warren Berlinger, Mami
Van Doren, Frank Campanella
A high school kid takes a girl for a ride in a sports car he pretends to own in order to impress her, but soon finds that he is being chased by the Mafia as the car is full of stolen money. The rest can be guessed at in this silly by-numbers caper.
COM                          85 min (ort 92 min)
B,V                              NDH/MED; MED

## FREEBIE AND THE BEAN **              18
Richard Rush         USA              1974
Alan Arkin, James Caan, Loretta Swit, Valerie
Harper, Jack Kruschen, Mike Kellin, Alex Rocco
Two somewhat happy-go-lucky cops almost destroy the city of San Francisco in an attempt to trap a gangster who runs an illegal gambling racket. Caan and Arkin work well together in a frantic, frenetic, noisy failure of a comedy whose highspots are its car crashes rather than its humour. Later the basis for a short-lived TV series.
COM    108 min (ort 111 min) (Cut at film release by 29 sec)
B,V                                       WHV

## FREEDOM FIGHTERS **                  18
Riki Shelach         USA              1987
Peter Fonda, Reb Brown, Ron O'Neal, James Mitchum
Action story of a mercenary in the pay of a nasty dictatorship, who has a change of heart in the process of putting down a tribal rebellion when he meets a white nurse who convinces him that he's fighting on the wrong side. Mediocre.
A/AD                                    89 min
B,V                                       CAN

## FREEDOM FORCE, THE ***                U
                     USA              1978
Likeable animated story of magical freedom fighters.
CAR                                    52 min
B,V                              SEL L/A; HER

## FREEDOM ROAD **
Jan Kadar            USA              1979
Muhammad Ali, Kris Kristofferson, Ron O'Neal,
Edward Herrmann, John McLiam, Barbara O. Jones,
Sonny Jim Gaines, Joel Fluellin, Jean Renee Foster,
Grace Zabriskie, Bill Mackey, Earl Smith, Alfre
Woodard, Ossie Davis (narration)
Story of an emancipated slave who eventually becomes a senator for Southern Carolina, during the Reconstruction period following the Civil War, plus a look at the rise of the Ku Klux Klan during that same period. An earnest, plodding and painfully slow adaptatation of Fast's novel, heavily hampered by Ali's lack of screen presence. Kadar died just after completion. First shown in two parts and the TV debuts for both Ali and Kristofferson.
Boa: novel by Howard Fast.
DRA                        200 min (ort 240 min) mTV
B,V                              VFP L/A; HER

## FREELANCE **
Francis Megahy       UK               1970
Ian McShane, Gayle Hunnicut, Keith Barron, Alan
Lake, Peter Gilmore, Charles Hyatt, Luan Peters, John
Hollis, David Graham, Peter Birrell
A small-time crook is witness to the murder of an old man, and finds himself on the murderer's hit-list. Fair.
THR                                    95 min
B,V                                       DFS

## FREEWAY **                           18
Francis Delia        USA              1988
Darlanne Fluegel, James Russo, Richard Belzer,
Michael Callan, Billy Drago
A publicity-seeking serial killer and religious nutter is in the habit of ringing a chat show to give away clues about his next intended victim. Meanwhile Fluegel, whose husband was picked off by a sniper a few months ago, teams up with a suspended cop to catch him. A glossy, slickly directed and thoroughly

unpleasant thriller whose air of menace is enhanced by the constant stream of weirdos Fluegel encounters in her quest.

THR | 87 min
B,V | EIV; NWV

## FREEWAY KILLINGS, THE ** | 15
William A. Graham    USA | 1987
*Angie Dickinson, Ben Gazzara*
Dickinson and Gazzara play Los Angeles cops out to catch some torture-loving murderers of women whose use of the massive freeway system is terrorising an entire city. Average.

THR | 139 min
B,V | MGM

## FRENCH BLUE ** | 18
Jean-Claude Laureux FRANCE | 1975
*Francoise Brion, Corinne O'Brian, Jacqueline Staup, Elizabeth Graine*
The tale of a young widow and her daughter out for a share of the family fortune.
Aka: FAMILY JEWELS; LES BIJOUX DE FAMILLE
A | 74 min; 80 min (VIDMID)
B,V | ALPHA/CBS; VIDMID

## FRENCH CONNECTION, THE **** | 18
William Friedkin    USA | 1971
*Gene Hackman, Roy Scheider, Fernando Rey, Tony LoBianco, Marcel Bozzuffi*
Fast and well-paced story of a hard-headed New York cop who, together with his buddy is assigned to a serious narcotics case. Fine action sequences such as an excellent car chase combine with a sense of real tension as they stake-out their quarry, an international heroin smuggling king. A sequel, lacking the tension and pace of the first film, followed. AA: Pic, Dir, Actor (Hackman), Screen (Adapt) (Ernest Tidyman), Edit (Jerry Greenberg).
Boa: novel by Robin Moore.

THR | 99 min
V | CBS

## FRENCH CONNECTION 2, THE ** | 18
John Frankenheimer    USA | 1975
*Gene Hackman, Fernando Rey, Charles Millot, Bernard Fresson, Jean-Pierre Castaldi, Cathleen Nesbitt*
In this sequel Popeye Doyle, the cop from the previous film, pursues his quarry to Marseilles intent on smashing the drugs ring. Has none of the tension and pace of the first film and is marred by a long and tormenting drugs sequence halfway through. Hackman is as good as ever though.

A/AD | 114 min (ort 119 min)
V | CBS

## FRENCH CONSPIRACY, THE * | PG
Yves Boisset
    FRANCE/ITALY/WEST GERMANY | 1973
*Jean-Louis Trintignant, Jean Seberg, Roy Scheider, Gian Maria Volonte, Nigel Davenport, Philippe Noiret, Michel Piccoli*
A left-wing reporter becomes a pawn in a plot to assassinate a Third World leader in this realistic but ponderous effort.

DRA | 124 min; 93 min (TURBO)
B,V | VTC; TURBO

## FRENCH EROTIC FANTASIES ** | 18
Burd Tranboree (Claude Bernard-Aubert)
    FRANCE | 1978
*Brigitte Lahaie, Ursula White, Jean-Louis Vattier*
Cut sex film with the usual minimal plot revolving around a search for pleasure.
Aka: LES GRANDES JOUISSEUSES
A | 69 min; 64 min (TAR) (ort 90 min) Cut (24 min 16 sec)
B,V | MOV; TAR

## FRENCH LIEUTENANT'S WOMAN, THE *** | 15
Karel Reisz    UK | 1981
*Jeremy Irons, Meryl Streep, Leo McKern, Lynsey Baxter, Patience Collier, Hilton McRae, Emily Morgan, Peter Vaughan, Penelope Wilton, David Warner, Charlotte Mitchell, Jean Faulds, Colin Jeavons, Liz Smith, John Barrett*
The relationship between a gentleman and a jilted mistress in Victorian times is paralleled by a modern affair between an actor and an actress playing these roles in a film. After an uncertain start, this diverting film gets better as it develops, helped in no small measure by Harold Pinter's literate script. The storyline does however, still remain painfully thin.
Boa: novel by John Fowles.

DRA | 121 min (ort 124 min)
B,V,V2 | WHV

## FRENCH LINE, THE ** | U
Lloyd Bacon    USA | 1953
*Jane Russell, Gilbert Roland, Arthur Hunnicutt, Mary McCarty, Craig Stevens, Steven Geray, Joyce McKenzie, Paula Corday, Scott Elliot*
A Texan oil heiress changes places with a model and goes on a cruise to France. A lightweight musical of slight interest.
Osca: TOUGH GUY or three shorts

MUS | 97 min (ort 102 min)
B,V | KVD

## FRENCH LOVERS, THE ** | 18
Max Pecas    FRANCE | 1979
*Sylvain Green, Caroline Lawrence*
Two boys about to do their military service have one last fling when they go off to the Mediterranean and work their way through a succession of girls in this adult comedy romp.

A | 84 min
B,V | VPD; NET; TCX

## FRENCH MISTRESS, A ** | PG
Roy Boulting    UK | 1960
*James Robertson Justice, Cecil Parker, Raymond Huntley, Ian Bannen, Agnes Laurent, Thorley Walters, Edith Sharpe, Athene Seyler, Kenneth Griffith*
Complications arise with the arrival of an attractive French teacher at a public boys' school, where the headmaster comes to believe that the girl is his illegitimate daughter. A haphazard and unfocused romp, with a competent cast of comedy stalwarts giving of their best.
Boa: play by Robert Munro (Sonnie Hale).

COM | 94 min (ort 98 min) B/W
V | CBS

## FRENCH POSTCARDS ** | 15
Willard Huyuck    USA | 1979
*Miles Chapin, Valerie Quennessen, David Marshall Grant, Blanche Baker, Debra Winger, Mandy Patinkin, Marie-France Pisier, Jean Rochefort*
The romantic adventures of a group of American college students spending a year abroad in Paris, form the basis for this amiable but hardly memorable comedy, made as something of a follow-up to "American Graffiti".

COM | 90 min (ort 92 min)
V/h | CIC

## FRENCH QUARTER *** |
Dennis Kane    USA | 1977
*Bruce Davidson, Virginia Mayo, Lindsay Bloom, Alisha Fontaine, Lance LeGault, Ann Michelle, Laura Misch Owens, Becky Allen, Barry Sullivan, William Sims*
The tale of a New Orleans prostitute at the turn of the century is mirrored by a similar story set in the present day, both elements of this convoluted plot being linked by a voodoo theme. A bizarre film that is unexpectedly entertaining.

DRA                              101 min
B,V                              VCL/CBS

## FRENCH QUARTER UNDERCOVER **    18
Joseph Catalanatto/Patrick C. Poole
                    USA            1985
*Michael Parks, Bill Holliday, John Wilmet, Lew
Weinberg, Suzanne Regard, Becky Allen, Layton
Martens*
Two agents race against time to stop Castro and the
KGB from ruining the New Orlean's World's Fair by
contaminating the town's water supply. Average.
THR                               80 min
B,V                               CAN

## FRENCH SHAMPOO **
Phillip T. Drexler     USA         1978
*Darby Lloyd Rains, Kim Pope, Helen Madigan, Annie
Sprinkles, Bobby Astyr, Mark Stevens, Alan Mario*
An Arab sheikh has a daughter so ugly that he has
offered $1,000,000 to a woman who runs a Fifth
Avenue beauty salon if she can make her marriage-
able. She contacts a man whose sexual prowess is such
that he can transform any woman and the tale ends
with the girl so attractive that even her father cannot
resist her charms.
A                                 90 min
V                                 RIP

## FRENCH WAY, THE **
Michel Deville     FRANCE/ITALY    1974
*Jean-Louis Trintignant, Jean-Pierre Cassel, Romy
Schneider, Jane Birkin, Florinda Bolkan, Georges
Wilson*
An unsuccessful crippled novelist lives life through
the experiences of his handsome bank clerk friend,
who takes lessons in the art of seduction as a means of
sleeping with lots of women and becoming rich and
powerful. A slick, untidy and superficial film whose
early promise soon gives way to a vacuous plot.
Aka: LE MOUTON ENRAGE; LOVE AT THE TOP;
SEDUCER, THE
DRA                               90 min
B,V                               VCL/CBS; VPD

## FRENCHMAN'S FARM **            15
Ron Way     AUSTRALIA              1986
*Ray Barrett, Tracey Tainsh, David Reyne, John
Mullion, Norman Kaye*
A woman has a paranormal experience whilst out
driving, and finds herself momentarily in the past
where she witnesses a murder. She reports her
experience to the police who fail to believe her, but
eventually the mystery is resolved in this intriguing
little thriller.
THR                               96 min
B,V                               AVA

## FRENZY **                      18
Alfred Hitchcock     UK            1972
*Jon Finch, Alec McGowen, Barry Foster, Barbara
Leigh-Hunt, Anna Massey, Vivien Merchant, Bernard
Cribbens, Billie Whitelaw, Michael Bates, Jimmy
Gardner, Rita Webb, Clive Swift, Jean Marsh, Madge
Ryan, George Tovey*
Hitchcock is at his most stilted with a crazed killer
who uses neckties to strangle girls, escaping suspicion
whilst an innocent man is suspected. Some good
camerawork and good casting of Foster as the maniac,
but a sense of tension is just not maintained. The
script is by Anthony Shaffer.
Boa: novel Goodbye Piccadilly, Farewell Leicester
Square by Arthur La Bern.
DRA          111 min (ort 116 min) Cut (19 sec)
B,V                               CIC

## FRESH HORSES **                15
David Anspaugh     USA             1988
*Molly Ringwald, Andrew McCarthy, Patti*

*D'Arbanville, Molly Hagan, Doug Hutchison, Ben
Stiller, Leon Russom, Viggo Mortensen*
This adult version of PRETTY IN PINK casts Ringwald as a backwoods girl from the wrong side of the
tracks, and McCarthy as the middle-class college boy
who falls for her. Not a very effective or interesting
drama, though the fine Midwest locations are some
compensation.
DRA              99 min (ort 105 min)
V                                 20VIS

## FRESH KILL **                  18
Joseph Merhi     USA              198-
*Flint Keller, Patricia Parks, Robert Z'dar*
A Chicago boy on his way to Hollywood has his
dreams of fame shattered when he accidentally be-
comes involved with drugs and murder.
DRA          83 min Cut (1 min 29 sec)
V                                 TGP

## FRESH, YOUNG AND SEXY *        18
Eberhard Schroeder
                    WEST GERMANY   1971
*Sascha Hehn, Astrid Snyder, Mara Raber, Hans
Bergmann, Joseph Moosholzer, Edgar Wenzel, Dunja
Lock, Jo Frohlich, Uli Steiberg, Astrid Boner, Felix
Frauchy, Hans Kern, Masso Preiss, Elisabeth
Volkmann, Thomas Brendl*
A series of episodes to illustrate how swinging Ger-
man girls can be. Utter garbage.
Aka: SCHUELER-REPORT-JUNGE, JUNGE WAS
DIE MADCHEN ALLES VON UNS WOLLEN!
A     59 min (ort 84 min) Cut (15 sec of abridged film
release)
B,V                               18PLAT/TOW

## FRESNO: PARTS 1 AND 2 *        15
Jeff Bleckner     USA              1986
*Carol Burnett, Dabney Coleman, Gregory Harrison,
Teri Garr, Charles Grodin, Jeffrey Jones, Luis Avalos,
Pat Corley, Valerie Mahaffey, Melanie Chartoff,
Anthony Heald, Teresa Ganzel, Bill Paxton, Jerry Van
Dyke, Charles Keating*
Awful, leaden and unfunny parody of TV soap operas
set in the USA's raisin-growing district. This lavish
and tiresome mess revolves around two families who
make a living out of producing raisins, and are
feuding over control of the water needed for irrigation.
COM      259 min (2 cassettes) (ort 360 min) mTV
B,V                               PACEV; BRAVE

## FRIDAY FOSTER *                18
Arthur Marks     USA              1975
*Pam Grier, Yaphet Kotto, Godfrey Cambridge,
Thalmus Rasulala, Eartha Kitt, Jim Backus, Scatman
Crothers, Ted Lange, Carl Weathers*
A black fashion photographer tries to foil an assas-
sination plot directed at a black politician in this
tiresome black exploitation movie.
DRA              86 min (ort 90 min)
B,V                               RNK

## FRIDAY THE 13TH **             18
Sean S. Cunningham     USA         1980
*Betsy Palmer, Adrienne King, Harry Crosby, Laurie
Bartram, Mark Nelson, Jeannine Taylor, Kevin Bacon*
Grisly murders occur again when a summer camp is
opened after many years. A film whose only reason for
being is to deliver a series of well timed shocks – but it
does that very well. The film grossed $17,000,000 and
has led to a veritable industry churning out a range of
sequels and spin-offs.
HOR              91 min (ort 95 min)
V/h                               WHV

## FRIDAY THE 13TH, PART 2 *      18
Steve Miner     USA                1981
*Amy Steel, Adrienne King, John Furey, Betsy Palmer,*

*Kirsten Baker, Stu Charno, Warrington Gillette*
Sequel in which the sole survivor of the first slaughter
is killed and the murders start all over again. This
time round the villain is the son of the woman who
committed the first lot of killings.
HOR 83 min (ort 87 min)
V/h CIC

## FRIDAY THE 13TH, PART 3 * 18
Steve Miner USA 1982
*Dana Kimmell, Paul Kratka, Tracie Savage, Jeffrey
Rogers, Catherine Parks, Larry Zerner*
Some years have passed since Jason gave his first
group of happy campers a holiday to remember.
Unaware of the latest spate of murders at Crystal
Lake, a group of friends decide to spend the weekend
at a lakeside cottage. They ignore the warnings of a
local and settle in only to find themselves threatened
by a motorcycle gang, but receive help rather unex-
pectedly. Slightly less gory than its predecessor, but
the basic recipe is unchanged.
HOR 91 min (ort 96 min) Cut (4 sec)
V/h CIC

## FRIDAY THE 13TH, PART 4: 18
## THE FINAL CHAPTER *
Joseph Zito USA 1984
*Kimberly Beck, Corey Feldman, Crispin Glover,
Barbara Howard, Ted White, Bruce Mahler, E. Erich
Anderson, Joan Freeman, Lawrence Monoson
Monoson*
Our lovable maniac Jason, dispatches yet more teens
in his own inimitable style in this gruesome sequel.
And oh yes, at the end he gets his comeuppance, only
don't bank on that keeping him from making a sequel.
HOR 87 min Cut (27 sec)
V/h CIC

## FRIDAY THE 13TH, PART 5: 18
## A NEW BEGINNING *
Danny Steinmann USA 1985
*John Shepard, Melanie Kinnaman, Shavar Ross,
Richard Young, Carol Lacatell*
Psychopath Jason Voorhees is dead at last but the
killings continue, with inmates of an institute of
mental health succumbing this time round. Did I hear
you ask about a new plot? Why change a winning
formula?
HOR 87 min Cut (1 min 22 sec in addition to film cuts)
B,V CIC

## FRIDAY THE 13TH, PART 6: JASON LIVES * 18
Tom McLoughlin USA 1986
*Thom Mathews, Jennifer Cooke, David Kagan, Renee
Jones, Kerry Noonan, C.J. Graham, Tom Fridley,
Darcy Demoss, Vincent Gustaferro, Tony Goldwyn,
Nancy McLoughlin, Ron Palillo*
Now, young Tommy, as you may recall, finally put
paid to psycho killer Jason Vorhees. However, he
begins to suspect that Jason is not really dead and
persuades a friend to help him dig up the body. And
instead of the rotting corpse they expected to find?
Well I won't spoil this one for you.
Aka: JASON LIVES: FRIDAY THE 13TH PART 6
HOR 87 min
V/sh CIC

## FRIDAY THE 13TH, PART 7: 18
## THE NEW BLOOD *
John Carl Buechler USA 1988
*Lar Parc-Lincoln, Kevin Blair, Susan Blu, Terry
Kiser, Jennifer Banko, John Otrin, Susan Jennifer
Sullivan, Heidi Kozak, Kane Hodder*
A young girl with telekinetic powers accidentally
releases Jason from his grave and the killing com-
mences. Unfortunately, nothing can levitate this film
to the level of the merely mediocre.
HOR 85 min (ort 88 min) (Cut at film release by 8 sec)
B,V CIC

## FRIDAY THE 13TH, PART 8: JASON TAKES
## MANHATTAN ** 18
Rob Hedden USA 1989
*Jensen Daggett, Kane Hodder, Peter Mark Richman,
Scott Reeves, Barbara Bingham, V.C. Dupree,
Sharlene Martin*
Yet another slasher film in this series, though this one
offers a little imagination, with most of the action
taking place on a cruise ship (we only reach Manhat-
tan in the last 15 minutes) where the usual bunch of
unfortunate teens meet grisly ends. Written by Hed-
den, this overlong shocker is one of the best ones in the
series, but that isn't saying much.
HOR 97 min (ort 100 min)
V CIC

## FRIDAY THE 13TH: THE LEGACY – 18
## THE INHERITANCE/CUPID'S QUIVER **
William Fruet USA 1987
*Christopher Wiggins, John D. LeMay*
Spin-off from those innumerable FRIDAY THE 13TH
films with two young cousins less than pleased to find
that they've inherited their late uncle's antique shop.
They are even less pleased when they discover that
Uncle Lewis made a pact with Satan that involved
him taking over the stock. More grisly and ludicrous
nonsense in two tales from the FRIDAY THE 13TH
team.
HOR 88 min
B,V CIC

## FRIDAY'S CURSE 4: QUILT OF HATHOR/ 15
## THE AWAKENING **
Timothy Bond/Frank Mancuso/Atom Egoyan
USA 1987
*Christopher Wiggins, Cliff Gorman, Robey*
Two more tales following the adventures of cousins
Micki and Ryan as they attempt to take over the
antique shop dear old Uncle Lewis left them. Not an
easy task when he gave all his stock to Satan. In the
first story they enter the closed world of a sinister
religious sect when they attempt to retrieve an old
patchwork quilt.
Aka: QUILT OF HATHOR
HOR 88 min Cut (1 min 31 sec) mTV
V/sh CIC

## FRIDAY'S CURSE 5: THE ELECTROCUTIONER/ 18
## FAITH HEALER **
Rob Heddon/David Cronenberg
USA 1988
*John D. Le May, Christopher Wiggins, Robey*
Another two episodes following our cousins as they
attempt to retrieve some of those diabolical objects
sold by their late uncle from his demonic antiques
shop. Cronenberg adds his usual light touch to the
second of these two stories.
HOR 90 min mTV
B,V CIC

## FRIDAY'S CURSE: DOCTOR JACK/ 15
## SHADOW BOXER **
Lyndon Chubbock/William Fruet
USA 1987
*Chris Wiggins, Cliff Gorman, John D. Le May*
Another two tales inspired (if that's the right word) by
all those FRIDAY THE 13TH films. These two stories
focus on two objects for sale in a New Orleans antique
shop: a surgeon's knife and a pair of boxing gloves.
These are no ordinary articles folks, for if you've been
keeping up with the series you'll know that before he
died, Uncle Lewis got Satan to take over all his stock,
so be warned.
HOR 88 min mTV
B,V CIC

## FRIDAY'S CURSE: TALES OF THE UNDEAD/ SCARECROW **   15
Lyndon Chubbock/William Fruet
USA                   1987
*John D. Le May, Chris Wiggins*
Two further tales in the series following the attempts
of cousins Micki and Ryan to retrieve some of the
demonic objects sold by their late uncle from his
antique shop. "Tales Of The Undead" tells of a
valuable edition of a comic book with strange powers,
whilst "Scarecrow" tells the story of a cursed
scarecrow which performs strange rituals.
HOR                   90 min mTV
B,V                       CIC

## FRIEND OR FOE **                     U
John Krish          UK          1981
*Mark Luxford, John Holmes, Stacy Keach, John
Bardon, Jennifer Piercey, Valerie Lush, Jasper Jacobs,
Robin Hayter, Philip Manikum, Edward Burnham,
Len Marten, David Cunningham, Prentis Hancock*
In wartime Britain the pilot of a crashed German
plane saves a boy from drowning. An average kid's
drama with good performances.
Boa: novel by Michael Morpurgo.
JUV                   68 min (ort 70 min)
B,V                       RNK

## FRIENDLY FIRE ****
David Greene        USA          1979
*Ned Beatty, Carol Burnett, Sam Waterson, Dennis
Erdman, Timothy Hutton, Fanny Spiess, Sherry
Hursey, Michael Flanagan, Hilly Hicks, William
Jordan, Vernon Weddle, Jack Rader, Robert Wahler,
David Keith*
An American couple are told that their son's death in
Vietnam was due to friendly fire. They try to find out
more about what really happened. A most moving and
sensitive portrayal which, if somewhat overlong, is
never less than totally absorbing. Based to some
extent on the real-life story of activist Peg Mullen and
scripted by Fay Kanin.
Boa: book by C.D.B. Bryan.
DRA               140 min (ort 146 min) mTV
B,V                       PRV

## FRIENDS *                           15
Lewis Gilbert       UK          1971
*Anicee Alvina, Sean Bury, Pascale Roberts, Sady
Rebbot, Ronald Lewis*
Two misunderstood teenagers run away and set up
home together, then proceed to have a child. Sen-
timental tripe that was, believe it or not, followed by a
sequel – "Paul And Michelle".
DRA            97 min (ort 102 min) Cut (11 sec)
B,V                       CIC

## FRIENDSHIP IN VIENNA **             PG
Arthur Allan Seidelman  USA      1988
*Edward Asner, Jane Alexander, Stephen Macht,
Jenny Lewis, Kamie Harper, Rosemary Forsyth,
Ferdinand Mayne, Jean Simmons (narration)*
A Viennese Jewish teenager is aided in her escape
from the Nazis by her Christian best friend and the
family of the latter. A competent family drama from
Disney that inevitably skates over the true horror of
the period it attempts to depict.
Boa: novel Devil In Vienna by Doris Orgel.
DRA               96 min (ort 100 min) mCab
V                       FUTUR

## FRIGHT *
Peter Collinson     UK          1971
*Susan George, Honor Blackman, Ian Bannen, John
Gregson, George Cole, Dennis Waterman, Tara
Collinson, Maurice Kaufman, Michael Brennan, Roger
Lloyd Pack*
A young babysitter alone in a country house is

threatened by a psychotic who has escaped from an
asylum. A disagreeable yarn that starts badly and
never gets any better.
HOR                   84 min (ort 87 min)
B,V                       TEVP

## FRIGHT NIGHT ***                    18
Tom Holland         USA          1985
*William Ragsdale, Chris Sarandon, Roddy McDowall,
Amanda Bearse, Stephen Geoffreys, Jonathan Stark*
A young horror-film fan discovers that his new
neighbour is a vampire but of course no-one will
believe him. Intelligent handling and some fresh ideas
redeem a tired theme. The remarkable special effects
are by Richard Edlund. Holland both wrote and
directed. A sequel followed.
HOR                   102 min (ort 105 min)
V/sh                       RCA

## FRIGHT NIGHT 2 *                    18
Tommy Lee Wallace   USA          1988
*Roddy McDowall, William Ragsdale, Traci Lin, Julie
Carmen, Jonathan Gries, Russell Clark, Brian
Thompson, Merritt Butrick, Ernie Sabella*
A young man meets the girl of his dreams but finds
that it is his blood she wants in this slack and
disappointing sequel to the first film.
HOR                   99 min (ort 108 min)
V                       PRES

## FRINGE BENEFITS *
Pendulous Productions (Al Gordon/Ed Reese)
USA                   1973
*Georgina Spelvin, Eric Edwards, Kevin Andre,
Kenneth Angle, Michelle Magazine, Angel Street*
Spelvin is the head of the Tighttwat Institute for
Sexual Research and the film follows the treatment
for impotence undergone by one Harry Flatout. This
one just goes on and on, as various methods are tried
out on poor Harry until he is successfuly cured;
becoming such a hit with the ladies that he is made
vice president of his company. A childish and tedious
effort; very juvenile, very 1970s. See also SLIP UP.
A                     76 min
B,V                   UNIV L/A

## FRISCO KID, THE **                  PG
Robert Aldrich      USA          1979
*Gene Wilder, Harrison Ford, Ramon Bieri, Val
Bisoglio, George Ralph DiCenzo, Leo Fuchs, Penny
Peyser, William Smith, Jack Somack, Cliff Pellow,
Allan Rich*
A Polish rabbi travelling across the USA to San
Francisco in the 1850s makes friends with an outlaw.
An unsuccessful effort that is too episodic to work as a
coherent comedy, but is best enjoyed as a series of
mildly amusing vignettes instead.
COM                   113 min (ort 122 min)
B,V                       WHV

## FRITZ THE CAT ****
Ralph Bakshi        USA          1971
*Voices of: Skip Hinnant, Rosetta Le Noire, John
McCurry, Judy Engles, Phil Seuling*
Inventive and comical story of an alley-cat student
and his adventures in New York. All the parts are
played by animals with different peoples being repre-
sented by different species (for example, the cops are
all pigs). A rarity in that the cartoon was X-rated for
its graphic sexuality. Largely based on the cartoons of
Robert Crumb drawn for an underground magazine
The vastly inferior sequel THE NINE LIVES OF
FRITZ THE CAT followed.
CAR                   78 min
B,V,V2                     TEVP

## FROG PRINCE, THE **                 15
Brian Gilbert       UK          1985
*Jane Snowden, Alexandre Sterling, Jacqueline Doyen,*

*Raoul Delfosse, Jeanne Herivale, Francoise Brion, Pierre Vernier, Diana Blackburn, Oystein Wilk, Fabienne Tricottet, Jean-Marc Barr, Arabella Weir, Lucy Durham-Matthews*
Set in the 1960s, this tells of a young girl studying at the Sorbonne who embarks on an affair with a French architect, but eventually finds a more lasting relationship.
Aka: FRENCH LESSON
Boa: novel by N. Rootes.
DRA 87 min (ort 90 min)
V/sh WHV

**FROG PRINCE, THE \*\*\*** U
Jackson Hunsicker USA 1987
*Aileen Quinn, John Paragon, Clive Revill, Helen Hunt*
A nice adaptation of a Brother's Grimm tale in which Quinn, as the little Princess Zora, drops a golden ball down a well, encountering a talking frog who promises to retrieve it if she will take him into her home as her companion.
Boa: short story by Jakob Ludwig Karl Grimm and Wilhelm Karl Grimm.
JUV 83 min
V/h WHV

**FROGS \***
George McCowan USA 1972
*Ray Milland, Joan Van Ark, Sam Elliott, Adam Roarke, Judy Pace*
A house on a remote island is over-run by frogs and other creatures who take revenge on the owner for his destruction of the local wildlife. An utterly silly film that just cannot be taken seriously on any level. The frogs (and other assorted reptiles) kill everyone in sight and in a gloriously ludicrous final scene, the lights of the house are seen to go out one at a time – switched off by the frogs no doubt. Croak! Croak!
HOR 91 min
B,V,V2 GHV

**FROM A FAR COUNTRY: POPE JOHN PAUL II \*\***
Krzysztof Zanussi
ITALY/POLAND/UK 1982
*Sam Neill, Christopher Cazenove, Warren Clarke, Lisa Harrow, Maurice Denham, Cezary Morawski, Jonathan Blake, John Franklyn-Robbins, Philip Latham, Erna Relph, John Welsh, Susan Dutton*
Dull biopic on the life of Karol Wojtyla from his boyhood and through WW2. See also POPE JOHN PAUL II.
DRA 138 min (ort 140 min) mTV
B,V PRV

**FROM A WHISPER TO A SCREAM \*\*** 18
Jeff Burr USA 1986
*Vincent Price, Clu Gulager, Terry Kiser, Harry Caesar, Rosalind Cash, Susan Tyrrell, Cameron Mitchell, Martin Beswicke*
Price's last horror movie in which he plays a small-town librarian who tells four tales of horror that took place there. The stories range from the weak to the repulsive and include the tale of a psychopath whose evil lust gives rise to a deadly offspring, and the story of a circus freak who pays a heavy price for his bizarre talent.
Aka: OFFSPRING, THE
HOR 94 min (1 min 45 sec)
B,V MED

**FROM BEYOND \*\*** 18
Stuart Gordon USA 1986
*Jeffrey Combs, Barbara Crompton, Ken Foree, Ted Sorel, Carolyn Purdy-Gordon, Bunny Summers, Bruce McGuire*

A beautiful psychiatrist is called upon to investigate Dr Pretorious, a mad scientist who has created a device that activates a deadly sixth sense in humans, and is attacked by terrifying creatures from another dimension. The title (if nothing else) is taken from a short story by H.P. Lovecraft.
HOR 81 min (ort 90 min) Cut (10 sec)
B,V VES

**FROM HELL TO VICTORY \*\*** 15
Hank Milestone (Umberto Lenzi)
FRANCE/ITALY/SPAIN 1979
*George Peppard, George Hamilton, Horst Bucholz, Anny Duprey, Sam Wanamaker, Jean Pierre Cassel, Capucine*
Routine war film set in Europe during WW2, and telling of the effect the conflict has on a group of friends of different nationalities. A shallow and undistinguished tale.
Aka: DA DUNKERQUE ALLA VITTORIA; FORTRESS EUROPE (KRP)
WAR 98 min (ort 100 min)
V KRP

**FROM HERE TO ETERNITY \*\*\*\*** PG
Fred Zinnemann USA 1953
*Burt Lancaster, Deborah Kerr, Montgomery Clift, Frank Sinatra, Donna Reed, Ernest Borgnine, Philip Ober, Mickey Shaughnessy, Jack Warden, Claude Akins, George Reeves*
Despite the loss of the novel's harsh criticism of the US Army and its more interesting passages, this remains an excellent account of life at an army base on Hawaii just before the attack on Pearl Harbour. Brilliantly acted throughout. Remade for TV as a six hour mini-series in 1979. AA: Pic, Dir, S. Actor (Sinatra), S. Actress (Reed), Cin (Burnett Guffey), Screen (Daniel Taradash), Edit (William A. Lyon), Sound (John P. Livadary).
Boa: novel by James Jones.
DRA 114 min B/W
V RCA

**FROM NOON TILL THREE \*** 15
Frank D. Gilroy USA 1976
*Charles Bronson, Jill Ireland, Douglas V. Fowley, Stan Haze, Bert Williams, Damon Douglas, Anne Ramsey, Hector Morales, Howard Brunner*
A strictly second-rate bank robber becomes a legend after he is mistakenly thought to have been gunned down, and a former girlfriend publishes a colourful but highly inaccurate account of his life and times. A strange, lame spoof that never really gets going.
Boa: novel by Frank D. Gilroy.
WES 95 min (ort 99 min)
V WHV

**FROM RUSSIA WITH LOVE \*\*\*** PG
Terence Young UK 1963
*Sean Connery, Robert Shaw, Pedro Armendariz, Daniela Bianchi, Lotte Lenya, Bernard Lee, Eunice Gayson, Walter Gotell, Francis De Wolff, Lois Maxwell, George Pastell, Nadja Regin*
One of the best of the James Bond adventures, made before the gadgets and special effects had taken over completely. Agent 007 is sent to steal a coding machine from the Russkies and has plenty of narrow escapes. The music is by John Barry. Followed by GOLDFINGER.
Boa: novel by Ian Fleming.
A/AD 111 min (ort 118 min) (Cut at film release)
V WHV

**FROM THE DEAD OF NIGHT \*\*\*** 15
Paul Wendkos USA 1989
*Lindsay Wagner, Bruce Boxleitner, Diahann Carroll, Robin Thomas, Robert Prosky, Merritt Butrick, Joanne Linville*

A fashion designer narrowly escapes being killed and then finds herself being stalked by dead people who feel envious of her lucky escape and want to make her one of their number. An overlong shocker, but quite frightening in places. The script is by William Bleich. Originally shown in two parts.
Boa: novel Walkers by Gary Bradner.

| HOR | 138 min |
| V | BRAVE |

### FROM THE EARTH TO THE MOON **
Byron Haskin          USA          1958
*Joseph Cotten, George Sanders, Henry Daniell, Carl Esmond, Melville Cooper, Debra Paget*
An armaments millionaire makes use of a new explosive invented by a scientist to send a manned projectile to the Moon. A predictable and rather typical 1950s science fiction adventure in which the passable acting must take second place to the special effects.
Boa: novel by Jules Verne. Osca: JACK AND THE BEANSTALK

| FAN | 96 min (ort 100 min) |
| B,V | KVD |

### FROM THE EARTH TO THE MOON **
1979
Passable animated version of the classic Jules Verne tale.
Boa: novel by Jules Verne.

| CAR | 45 min |
| B,V | VCL/CBS |

### FROM THE HIP *
15
Bob Clark          USA          1986
*Judd Nelson, Elizabeth Perkins, John Hurt, Darren McGavin, Ray Walston, Dan Monahan, David Alan Grier, Nancy Marchand, Allan Arbus, Edward Winter*
A young lawyer finds his unconventional approach to defence methods makes him an overnight media sensation, when he undertakes the defence of a cold but brilliant man accused of murder. An irritating film that tries hard to amuse but succeeds in being merely outrageous.

| COM | 108 min (ort 112 min) |
| B,V | PRES |

### FROM THE LIFE OF THE MARIONETTES ***
Ingmar Bergman WEST GERMANY          1980
*Robert Atzorn, Christine Buchegger, Martin Benrath, Rita Russek, Lola Muethel, Walter Schmidinger, Heinz Bennent*
Typical Bergman gloomy film set in Germany and revolving around the reasons why a businessman killed a prostitute. Undeniably powerful but far too sombre to find an appreciative audience.

| DRA | 99 min B/W and Colour |
| B,V | PRV |

### FRONT, THE ****
15
Martin Ritt          USA          1976
*Woody Allen, Zero Mostel, Michael Murphy, Herschel Bernardi, Remak Ramsay, Andrea Marcovicci, Joshua Shelley, Lloyd George*
During the McCarthy witch-hunt era of the 1950s, blacklisted writers use a bookmaker as a "front" so that they can get their work published. Various complications arise in a refreshing and witty comedy, that makes a number of salient points. A highlight is a performance from Mostel as a blacklisted comedian fighting to get work. The script is by Walter Bernstein who was blacklisted in reality (as were Ritt, Mostel, Bernardi, Shelley and Gough).

| COM | 94 min |
| B,V | RCA |

### FROZEN SCREAM **
Frank Roach          USA          1980
*Renee Harman, Lynne Kocol, Thomas Gowen, Lee James, Sunny Bartholemew*
A haunted house and strange hooded figure feature in this cliched horror story.

| HOR | 77 min |
| B,V | INT/CBS |

### FRUIT MACHINE, THE ***
15
Philip Saville          UK          1987
*Emile Charles, Tony Forsyth, Robert Stephens, Robbie Coltrane, Clare Higgins, Bruce Payne*
Two 16-year-old boys – one a streetwise "rent boy" and the other a naive and confused daydreamer – are drawn together by their mutual distrust of society and take to frequenting a local nightclub run by a transvestite. When they witness his murder they flee to Brighton but soon find the killers not far behind. A strange, surreal, but not altogether successful effort, that makes a few interesting observations but suffers from a self-indulgent script.

| THR | 103 min |
| B,V | VES |

### FUGITIVE ALIEN **
PG
Minoru Kanaya/Kiyosumi Kukazawa          JAPAN
*Tatsuya Azuma, Miyuki Tamigawa, Choei Takahashi, Joe Shisido*
Dullish fantasy following the adventures of an alien on Earth.

| FAN | 103 min |
| V | XTASY |

### FUGITIVE FAMILY **
Paul Krasny          USA          1980
*Richard Crenna, Diane Baker, Eli Wallach, Don Murray, Ronny Cox, Mel Ferrer, Robin Dearden, K.C. Martel, William Kirby Cullen, Paul Mantee, Felice Orlandi, Sidney Clute, Judy Farrell, Bobby Rolofson, Ken Hill, Burt Marshall*
A government witness is forced to go into hiding with his family and take on a new identity after testifying at the trial of a mobster. Predictable and tame crime melodrama.
Boa: story by James G. Hirsch.

| DRA | 100 min mTV |
| B,V | VTC |

### FUGITIVE, THE ***
John Ford          USA          1947
*Henry Fonda, Dolores Del Rio, Pedro Armendariz, J. Carrol Naish, Ward Bond, Leo Carrillo*
Fonda plays a priest on the run in a Latin American country taken over by an anti-clerical dictatorship. He is eventually betrayed and shot. A rather boring plot is strengthened by references to the betrayal of Christ, a fine cast and some excellent photography. Not brilliant, but it might nearly have been. The photography is by Gabriel Figueroa.
Boa: novel The Power And The Glory by Graham Greene. Osca: FOLLOW ME QUIETLY

| DRA | 86 min B/W |
| B,V | KVD |

### FUGITIVE, THE: THE JUDGEMENT **
U
Don Medford          USA          1966
*David Janssen, Barry Morse*
The conclusion to a long-running TV series in which Janssen played a man forced to go on the run when he is suspected of the murder of his wife. In this episode all the loose ends are neatly tied up and the "one-armed man" is finally located. Average.

| DRA | 103 min mTV |
| V | CASVIS |

### FULL METAL JACKET ***
18
Stanley Kubrick          USA          1987
*Matthew Modine, Adam Baldwin, Vincent D'Onofrio, Lee Ermey, Dorian Harewood, Arliss Howard, Kevyn Major Howard, Ed O'Ross*
A story following a Marine private, from his tough

training through to his involvement in the Vietnam War and the heavy fighting of the 1968 Tet offensive. Kubrick's first film for seven years was shot entirely on location in South London and the unmistakably English light coupled with the unreality of the sets does not make for great realism. However, as a stylised statement on the meaningless of war it largely succeeds.
Boa: novel The Short Timers by Gustav Hasford.

| WAR | 112 min (ort 116 min) |
| B,V | WHV |

## FULL MOON HIGH ** 15
Larry Cohen          USA          1981
*Adam Arkin, Ed McMahon, Roz Kelly, Elizabeth Hartman, Bill Kirchenbauer, Kenneth Mars, Joanne Nail, Alan Arkin*
A high school football star goes to Transylvania for a holiday and suffers a minor injury that turns him into a werewolf. A silly but fairly enjoyable teen werewolf comedy.

| COM | 91 min (ort 94 min) |
| B,V | STABL |

## FULL MOON IN BLUE WATER *** 15
Peter Masterson          USA          1988
*Gene Hackman, Teri Garr, Burgess Meredith, Elias Koteas*
The owner of a seedy bar in the South is obsessed with locating his wife, who vanished a year ago. He spends most of his time watching home movies whilst his girlfriend tries to keep the business running. When a crooked estate agent moves in and tries to get him to sell his business, an intriguing mystery develops.

| DRA | 91 min |
| B,V | EIV |

## FULLER REPORT * 15
Terence Hathaway (Sergio Grieco)
FRANCE/ITALY          1968
*Ken Clark, Lincoln Tate, Bebi Loncar, Sarah Ross*
A racing driver is chased by spies who believe him to have documents in his possession which could alter the fate of the world.
Aka: RAPPORTO FULLER BASE A STOCCOLMA; SVETLAWA UCCIDERA IL 28 SETTEMBRE; TRAHISON A STOCKHOLM

| A/AD | 91 min (ort 96 min) |
| B,V | VPD |

## FUNERAL IN BERLIN *** PG
Guy Hamilton          USA          1967
*Michael Caine, Hugh Burden, Oscar Homolka, Eva Renzi, Rachel Gurney, Guy Doleman, Thomas Holtzman, Gunter Meisner, Heinz Schibert, Wolfgang Volz, Klaus Jepsen, Herbert Fux, Rainer Brandt, Ira Hagen*
Second outing for cockney secret agent Harry Palmer following THE IPCRESS FILE, with Caine being sent to Berlin to oversee arrangements for the defection of a Russian colonel in charge of Berlin war security. Sluggish and over complex, with a good many superfluous twists to a plot that never really comes to life. Followed by BILLION DOLLAR BRAIN, the last film in the series.
Aka: HARRY PALMER RETURNS
Boa: novel The Berlin Memorandum by Len Deighton.

| A/AD | 100 min |
| V | CIC |

## FUNHOUSE, THE ** 18
Tobe Hooper          USA          1981
*Elizabeth Berridge, Cooper Huckabee, Miles Chapin, Largo Woodruff, Sylvia Miles, Shawn Carlson, William Finley, Kevin Conway*
Four teenagers decide to stay the night at a carnival funhouse, but get more than they bargained for as they fall victim to a variety of nasty surprises, in this stylish, but patchy and somewhat disjointed horror tale.
Aka: CARNIVAL OF TERROR

| HOR | 89 min (ort 96 min) |
| V/h | CIC |

## FUNLAND * 15
Michael A. Simpson          USA          1986
*William Windom, David Lander, Bruce Mahler, Robert Sacchi, Lane Davies, Mike McManus, Jan Hooks, Susan Ursitti*
An amusement park provides the setting for this failed attempt at a zany comedy. A mishmash of a comedy with elements of MAGIC, POLICE ACADEMY and PLAY IT AGAIN, SAM thrown together in a disjointed and clumsy way.

| COM | 83 min (ort 105 min) |
| V | SONY |

## FUNNY FARM *** PG
George Roy Hill          USA          1988
*Chevy Chase, Madolyn Smith, Joseph Maher, Jack Gilpin, Brad Sullivan, MacIntyre Dixon*
A New York sportswriter and his wife take up the country life but they find things are far from simple in this episodic, uneven but engaging comedy. A film that tends to get better as it goes along, being helped considerably by the photography of Miroslav Ondricek.

| COM | 97 min Cut (3 sec) |
| V/sh | WHV |

## FUNNY FARM, THE * PG
Ron Clark          CANADA          1982
*Miles Chapin, Eileen Brennan, Jack Carter, Tracy Bregman, Howie Mandel, Marjorie Gross, Lou Dinos, Peter Aykroyd*
A young man from Ohio tries to make it in L.A. as a stand-up comic. A slow and disjointed film largely consisting of a sequence of comedy turns and little else.

| COM | 95 min; 97 min (WHV) |
| B,V | VFP L/A; HER; WHV |

## FUNNY GIRL *** U
William Wyler          USA          1968
*Barbra Streisand, Omar Sharif, Kay Medford, Anne Francis, Walter Pidgeon, Lee Allen, Gerald Mohr, Frank Faylen*
Streisand is a knockout in this long, lively biopic devoted to the career of comedienne Fanny Brice. The musical numbers are great but the drama tends to drag, especially the account of her troubled first marriage to gambler Nicky Arnstein (Sharif gloriously miscast). Bad as biography, but great as a musical; the score is by Bob Merrill and Jule Styne. Followed by FUNNY LADY. AA: Actress (Streisand – she tied with Hepburn for THE LION IN WINTER).
Boa: play by Isobel Lennart.

| MUS | 141 min (ort 151 min) |
| V/sh | RCA; PREST |

## FUNNY LADY ** PG
Herbert Ross          USA          1974
*Barbra Streisand, James Caan, Roddy McDowall, Omar Sharif, Ben Vereen, Carole Wells, Larry Gates*
This sequel to FUNNY GIRL has Fanny Brice at the height of her career, meeting and marrying ambitious showman Billy Rose. Unfortunately, tiresome bouts of domestic turmoil get in the way of the good moments, these latter being mainly the highly effective musical set-pieces. An uneven, cliched effort that fails to recapture the sparkle of the earlier film.

| MUS | 133 min |
| V/sh | RCA |

## FUNNY MONEY **
James Kenelm Clarke          UK          1983

Gregg Henry, Elizabeth Daily, Gareth Hunt, Derren
Nesbitt, Annie Ross, Joe Prami, Rose Alba, Stephen
Yardley, Nigel Lambert, Bill McAllister, Lyndam
Gregory, Carol Cleveland, Mildred Shay, Alan
Campbell, Rai Bartonious
A girl arrives in London with a load of stolen credit
cards, and starts looking for a partner to help her use
them.
DRA                                      92 min (ort 97 min)
B,V                                               EIV

### FUNNY THING HAPPENED ON THE WAY TO THE FORUM, A **
Peter Lester            USA               PG
                                          1966
Zero Mostel, Phil Silvers, Jack Gilford, Buster Keaton,
Michael Crawford, Michael Hordern, Annette Andre,
Patricia Jessel, Leon Greene, Beatrix Lehmann
An over-excited adaptation of a bawdy Broadway
musical set in ancient Rome and telling of a cunning
slave who connives to win his freedom. Fast and
furious but the film tries too hard to be funny, though
the slapstick finale is a highlight. Music and lyrics are
by Stephen Sondheim. AA: Score (Adapt) (Ken
Thorne).
Boa: musical comedy by Bert Shevelove and Larry
Gelbart.
COM                                      93 min (ort 99 min)
V                                               WHV

### FUR TRAP, THE **
                        USA               1978
Colleen Anderson, Bill Berry, Richard Bolla, Marc
Baramy, Kelly Mint, Marlene Willoughby
A man who works for an advertising agency has let
his worries about work spoil his performance in bed so
his disgruntled wife decides to go out to work. After a
brief stint at a furriers she takes a one-night job, and
with a female friend pops out of a cake at a stag party
her husband is attending. A general orgy develops and
heralds the end of this contrived and rather silly tale.
Aka: LUSTFUL DESIRES
A                                        55 min (ort 72 min)
B,V                                         KTC L/A; PPL

### FURY AT SUNDOWN ***
Gerd Oswald            USA               1957
John Derek, John Smith, Carolyn Craig, Nick Adams,
Gage Clarke, Robert Griffin, Malcolm Atterbury, Rusty
Lane, Frances Morris, Tyler McDuff, Robert Adler,
Norman Leavitt, Ken Christy
A former outlaw is branded a coward for refusing to
use his gun, but when an outlaw takes his girl as an
escape hostage he comes to her defence. A good, solid
story with nice performances all round.
WES                                      75 min B/W
B,V                                               MAR

### FURY IN ISTANBUL **
Terence Hathaway (Sergio Grieco)
                    FRANCE/ITALY/SPAIN    1965
Ken Clark, Helga Line, Phillipe Hersent, Fabienne
Dali, Margaret Lee, Vittorio Sanipoli
A tedious and totally forgettable film in a series of
European formula agent films. See also MISSION
BLOODY MARY and SPECIAL MISSION LADY
CHAPLIN.
Aka: 077: FURY IN ISTANBUL; AGENTE 077
DALL'ORIENTE CON FURORTE; FROM THE
ORIENT WITH FURY; FUREUR SUR LE
BOSPHORE; PARIS-ESTAMBUL SIN REGRESO
A/AD                                      102 min
V                                          IOVID; VPD

### FURY IN SHAOLIN TEMPLE **
Godfrey Ho        HONG KONG               15
Liu Chia Hui                              198-
A kung fu master catches a thief stealing secrets from
his temple but takes him on as a student instead of
punishing him.

MAR                                      83 min
B,V                                               VPD

### FURY OF HERCULES, THE *
V. Scega            ITALY                 PG
                                          1961
Brad Harris, Brigitte Corey, Mara Berni, Carlo
Tamberlani, Serge Gainsbourg
Hercules fights the tyrannical Queen of Thebes, in
this plodding and painfully dull Italian costume saga.
A/AD                                      95 min
B,V                                         PRV L/A

### FURY OF SHAOLIN FIST **
Li Chih Sho/Liu Yeh
                    HONG KONG             1977
Chen Jung Li, Shik Chuan, Chen-I, Chiang Pin, Chiao
Chiao, Meng Li, Wang Lai, Miao Tien, Liang Feng,
Sung Ling, Li Chiang
Routine good guys versus bad guys story, with one of
the latter making good use of a whip.
MAR                                      90 min
B,V                                         OCEAN

### FURY OF THE DRAGON **
William Beaudine        USA               1966
Bruce Lee, Van Williams
The Green Hornet is a crimebuster by night and a
publisher by day. Together with his bodyguards
(proof-readers by day?), he fights urban crime. A silly
but endearing piece of nonsense, compiled from epi-
sodes of a TV series and mainly of interest for showing
Bruce Lee in an early role.
Aka: GREEN HORNET, THE
MAR                                      93 min mTV
B,V                                               EIV

### FURY ON WHEELS *
Joe Manduke            USA               PG
                                          1971
Judd Hirsch, Tom Ligon, Colin Wilcox-Horne
A young man leaves college and becomes a racing
driver, in this largely plotless tale of car smash-ups
and driving stunts.
Aka: JUMP
THR                                      85 min (ort 89 min)
B,V,V2                                   CBS; MPV; GLOB

### FURY TO FREEDOM *
Erik Jacobson            USA             15
                                          1985
Tom Silardi, Joy Vogel, John Quade, Gil Gerard
It's REBEL WITHOUT A CAUSE 1980s-style, with a
punk getting his girlfriend pregnant so her snooty
folks will have to let them get married. Taking up the
martial arts, he eventually winds up in jail and gets
shipped off to Vietnam. He returns disabled and
drives his wife to leave him, whereupon our by now
hate-filled kid makes plans for her demise but has a
sudden change of heart and starts preaching the
gospel. As implausible as it is unwatchable.
DRA                                      78 min
B,V                                               RCA

### FURY, THE *
Brian De Palma            USA            18
                                          1978
Kirk Douglas, John Cassavetes, Carrie Snodgress,
Amy Irving, Fiona Lewis, Andrew Stevens, Charles
Durning, Gordon Jump, Daryl Hannah
The head of a government unit tries to prevent his son
(who has psychic powers) from being kidnapped by
terrorists who want to make use of him. A violent and
gory film, quite well made in its way but trashy and
painfully contrived. This was Hannah's film debut.
Boa: novel by John Farris.
A/AD                                      118 min
B,V,V2,LV                                   CBS

### FUTTOCK'S END *
Bob Kellett            UK                 1969
Ronnie Barker, Michael Hordern, Roger Livesey,
Julian Orchard, Kika Markham, Mary Merrall, Hilary

*Pritchard, Richard O'Sullivan*
Set in a country house, this is the story of several people who spend the weekend there. It's merely a collection of visual gags without any real dialogue that gets pretty tiresome after a while. Written by Ronnie Barker.
COM                              47 min (ort 49 min)
B,V                                            RNK

**FUTURE HUNTERS \*\*\***                              18
Cirio H. Santiago      ITALY              1985
*Robert Patrick, Linda Carol, Ed Crick, Bob Schott, Ursula Marquez, Elizabeth Oropesa, Richard Norton*
Adventure story set in one of those familiar post-WW3 devastated worlds where a warrior seeks a magic spear. Guns blaze, fists fly, strange vehicles and stranger people appear at every opportunity, in a crazy, disjointed and altogether breathless fantasy tale; not a million miles away from all those "Indiana Jones" films. A watchable and enjoyable piece of nonsense.
FAN                              95 min Cut (53 sec)
B,V                                             VES

**FUTURE PAST \*\*\***                              PG
Bob Stewart           USA
*Nicholas Ryan, Gary Down, Imogen Annersley, John Ley, Cornelia Frances*
A man constantly plays with his computer as a way of escaping his humdrum existence. One day an experiment with holograms leads to a visit on the part of a character from the future, in this intriguing fantasy comedy.
COM                                         83 min
B,V                                             GHV

**FUTUREWORLD \*\*\***                              PG
Richard T. Heffron     USA              1976
*Peter Fonda, Blythe Danner, Arthur Hill, Yul Brynner, Stuart Margolin, John Ryan*
A sequel to WESTWORLD. The robot complex is repaired but there is a sinister purpose behind it with visitors to the complex being exchanged for robot duplicates in a nasty plan for world domination. A kind of robotic answer to INVASION OF THE BODY-SNATCHERS.
FAN                                        104 min
B,V,V2                         GHV; VCC (VHS only)

**FUZZ \*\***                                        18
Richard A. Colla       USA              1972
*Burt Reynolds, Raquel Welch, Jack Weston, Yul Brynner, Tom Skerritt, Peter Bonerz, Steve Ihnat, James McEachin, Bert Remsen*
A police spoof about the detectives at a police station in Boston who try to catch a rapist. A fast-paced black comedy whose barbs occasionally hit home. Scripted by Evan Hunter from one of his "87th Precinct" stories.
Boa: novel by Ed McBain (Evan Hunter).
COM                                         98 min
B,V                                            WHV

**FX: MURDER BY ILLUSION \*\*\***                   15
Robert Mandel         USA              1986
*Bryan Brown, Brian Dennehy, Diane Venora, Cliff De Young, Mason Adams, Jerry Orbach, Joe Grifasi, Martha Gehman*
An expert who creates special effects for films is contacted by the Justice Department to fake the killing of a gangster who has turned squealer. He discovers that he is to be the scapegoat in a murder conspiracy and has to use his specialised skills to save his life. A modest and entertaining thriller whose unusual premise gives rise to some clever moments, but one that's let down by innumerable loose ends and a contrived ending.

Aka: F/X
THR                                        104 min
V/sh                                           RCA

**FYRE \***
Richard Grand         USA              1978
*Lynn Theel, Allen Goorwitz, Frank Sivero, Tom Baker, Cal Haynes, Bruce Kirby, Donna Wilkes*
A 17-year-old girl is raped and the following day her family drive off a cliff. Eight years later we find her working as a prostitute in Los Angeles and desperate to break free of her squalid lifestyle. In between we are offered glimpses of drug taking, lesbianism and general nastiness in this low-grade and exploitative dud.
DRA                                         90 min
B,V                                   MED L/A; VPD

# G

**G-STRING MURDERS, THE \*\*\***                   PG
William Wellman       USA              1943
*Barbara Stanwyck, Michael O'Shea, J. Edward Bromberg, Iris Adrian, Marion Martin, Pinky Lee, Frank Conroy, Gloria Dickson, Charles Dingle*
Strippers are being systematically murdered and one of them decides to investigate in an attempt to find the killer. A competent murder mystery with a few enlivening touches of humour.
Aka: LADY OF BURLESQUE (DIAM); STRIPTEASE LADY
Boa: novel The G-String Murders by Rose Lee.
THR                              86 min (ort 91 min) B/W
B,V                              GOV L/A; DIAM; MMA

**G.I. EXECUTIONER \*\***                            18
Joel M. Read          USA              1971
*Tom Kenna, Victoria Racimo, Angelique Pettyjohn, Janet Wood, Brian Walden, Peter Genert*
A former Vietnam veteran turned bar owner, tracks down a Red Chinese scientist who may have been abducted by the Tongs in this formula action yarn. Filmed in Singapore.
Aka: DRAGON LADY; WIT'S END
A/AD                   82 min (ort 86 min) Cut (1 min 10 sec)
V                                               VES

**GABY: A TRUE STORY \*\*\***                       15
Luis Mandoki          USA              1987
*Rache Levin, Liv Ullmann, Norma Aleandro, Robert Loggia, Lawrence Monoson, Robert Beltran, Beatriz Sheridan*
The story of Gaby Brimmer, a woman born with cerebral palsy to wealthy refugee parents in Mexico. Though almost completely paralysed, she overcame this handicap, eventually becoming a successful author after she was taught to communicate using her left foot. Levin gives a remarkable performance in this often harrowing but moving story of persistence and courage. Brimmer was the executive producer. See also MY LEFT FOOT.
DRA                                        110 min
V                                              RCA

**GALAXINA \***
William Sachs         USA              1980
*Dorothy R. Stratton, Stephen Macht, Avery Schreiber, James David Hinton, Ronald Knight*
Spoof SF tale set in the 31st century where a beautiful female robot has been given the capacity to feel human emotions. A cheap and tedious effort that is severely limited by its low budget.
FAN                                         96 min
B,V,V2                                         GHV

**GALAXY OF TERROR \***                              18
B.D. Clark            USA              1981

*Edward Albert, Erin Moran, Ray Walston, Bernard Behrens, Sid Haig, Zalman King, Grace Zabriskie*
Astronauts on a mission to rescue a stranded space vessel, are killed off by a monster in this cheap rip-off of ALIEN. Followed by FORBIDDEN WORLD.
Aka: MINDWARP: AN INFINITY OF TERROR; PLANET OF HORRORS
FAN                     78 min (ort 80 min) Cut (14 sec)
V/h                                                    WHV

## GALLAGHER'S TRAVELS **                          PG
Michael Caulfield    AUSTRALIA               1986
*Ivar Kants, Joanne Samuels, Stuart Campbell, Francis Yin, Jennifer Hogan, Sylvester Iwinski*
A sort of home-grown riposte to the highly successful CROCODILE DUNDEE. An Australian reporter goes to London and becomes involved in the hunt for a gang of wildlife smugglers.
COM                              90 min Cut (10 sec)
B,V                              PACEV L/A; APOL

## GALLANT HOURS, THE ***                         PG
Robert Montgomery     USA                     1960
*James Cagney, Dennis Weaver, Ward Costello, Richard Jaeckel, Carl Benton Reid*
Cagney gives a nice performance in this low-key, documentary-style biopic on Admiral Frederick Halsey Jr, one of the key naval commanders in the Pacific during WW2. A solid if uninspired war film.
WAR                                    111 min B/W
V                                                   WHV

## GALLIPOLI ***                                   PG
Peter Weir           AUSTRALIA               1981
*Mark Lee, Mel Gibson, Bill Hunter, Bill Kerr, Robert Grubb, David Argue, Tim McKenzie*
The story of two young boys who join up to fight in WW1 and become part of the ill-fated Gallipoli landing. An absorbing drama that pays great attention to detail without ever swamping the human element.
WAR                               106 min (ort 110 min)
B, V/h, V2, LV                                       CIC

## GALYON **                                       15
Ivan Tors            USA
*Lloyd Nolan, Ron Hayes, Stan Brock, Ina Balin*
Standard action yarn in which a squad of PLO terrorists have sabotaged an oil well in the middle of an energy crisis, and taken two Americans hostage. A tough and ruthless mercenary goes after them.
Aka: GALYON: THE INDESTRUCTIBLE MAN
A/AD                             86 min Cut (20 sec)
V                                                   ARF

## GAMBLER, THE **                                 18
Karel Reisz          USA                      1974
*James Caan, Paul Sorvino, Lauren Hutton, Morris Carnovsky, Burt Young, Jacqueline Brookes, Carmine Caridi, Vic Tayback, Steven Keats, London Lee, M. Emmett Walsh, James Woods, Stuart Margolin*
Dull story of a college professor who is a compulsive gambler, made at about the same time as "California Split" but considerably inferior. The script is by James Toback – possibly very slightly inspired by the Dostoevsky story.
DRA                                          106 min
B,V                                                 CIC

## GAMBLER, THE ***                                PG
Dick Lowry           USA                      1980
*Kenny Rogers, Bruce Boxleitner, Harold Gould, Christine Belford, Lance LeGault, Clu Gulager, Lee Purcell, Ronnie Scribner, Noble Willingham, Bruce M. Fischer, Borah Silver, Lew Brown, Lee Paul, Robert Lussier*
A gambler discovers that he has a son and resolves to

go and see him, having various adventures along the way. An amiable Western with Rogers in his first starring role. Inspired by a similarly titled song by Rogers and followed by a couple of sequels.
Aka: KENNY ROGERS AS THE GAMBLER
WES                   92 min (ort 94 min) Cut (1 sec) mTV
V                                                   VPD

## GAMBLER, THE: PART 2 **                         PG
Dick Lowry           USA                      1983
*Kenny Rogers, Bruce Boxleitner, Linda Evans*
The further adventures of our gambler, who tries to give up his dangerous profession but is forced to make a risky decision, when his son is kidnapped by outlaws who demand a shipment of gold bullion in return for his life.
Aka: KENNY ROGERS AS THE GAMBLER: PART 2
WES                                     220 min mTV
V                                                 CASPIC

## GAMBLER, THE: PART 3 **                         PG
Dick Lowry           USA                      1987
*Kenny Rogers, Linda Gray, Bruce Boxleitner*
More adventures for Rogers as the colourful gambling hero of this popular TV series, who this time becomes involved with a woman who took the part of Indians over a land dispute.
Aka: KENNY ROGERS AS THE GAMBLER: PART 3
WES                                     220 min mTV
V                                                 CASPIC

## GAME FOR VULTURES, A *                          18
James Fargo          UK                       1979
*Richard Harris, Richard Roundtree, Ray Milland, Joan Collins, Denholm Elliott, Sven-Bertil Taube, Jana Cilliers, John Parsonson, Tony Oscoba, Alibe Parsons, Neil Hallett, Ken Gampu, Victor Melleny, Graham Armitage*
Violent story of a sanctions-buster and a black nationalist guerilla, set in Rhodesia. An unpleasant and pretentious piece of nonsense.
Boa: novel by Michael Hartmann.
A/AD                                         106 min
B,V                                                 RCA

## GAME OF DEATH ***                               18
Robert Clouse        HONG KONG                1979
*Bruce Lee, Kim Tai Jong, Gig Young, Hugh O'Brian, Dean Jagger, Chuck Norris, Colleen Camp, Kareem Abdul-Jabbar, Danny Inosanto, Mel Novak*
Released six years after Lee's death and completed using a double, this is a standard fists and feet kung fu movie, in which a young actor fakes his own death to outwit a gang threatening his career. Fairly mundane until the explosive final half hour. See also TRUE GAME OF DEATH.
Aka: BRUCE LEE: GAME OF DEATH
MAR                   92 min (ort 102 min) Cut (2 sec)
V                                                   RNK

## GAME OF DEATH 2 ***                             18
Ng See-Yuan          HONG KONG                1981
*Bruce Lee (Hah), Tang Lung (Kim Tai Ching), Huang Chen-Li, Cassanova Wong, Miranda Austia, Mun Ping, Lung Fei, Kuslai, Sandus*
Exploitative martial arts tale built around some out-takes of Bruce Lee from ENTER THE DRAGON. A fighter is suspicious of the death of a friend and at his funeral meets his own death when he tries to prevent a helicopter from carrying off the coffin. These bizarre events send the fighter's brother out to confront those responsible, leading to an exciting climax when he fights an evil drug baron. Good action, poor plot.
Aka: NEW GAME OF DEATH, THE
MAR                                   96 min dubbed
B,V                                                 RNK

## GAME OF LOVE, THE ** 15
Bobby Roth    USA    1987
*Ed Marinaro, Belinda Bauer, Tracy Nelson, Max Gail*
A yawn-inducing story built around singles bars and
the people that frequent them. Intercut with Marinaro's search for a soulmate are some formula tales,
such as the one telling of a divorced airline pilot and
another examining the experiences of a shy computer
operator. A contrived and shallow piece of nonsense.
DRA    94 min
B,V    SONY

## GAMES OF SURVIVAL ** 18
Armand Gazarian    1988
*Nikki Hill, Cindy Coatman*
A man who is taking part in a galactic game of
survival, travels to Earth in search of an artefact that
will ensure his success.
FAN    90 min
V    BOX

## GAMES THAT LOVERS PLAY *
Malcolm Leigh    UK    1970
*Joanna Lumley, Penny Brahms, Richard Wattis,
Jeremy Lloyd, Diane Hart, Nan Munro, John Gatrell,
Charles Cullum, Leigh Anthony, George Belbin, June
Palmer*
Two of London's greatest brothel-keepers compete to
see who has the best girls in this stupid sex comedy set
in the 1920s.
A    90 min
B,V,V2    VCL/CBS

## GAMES WOMEN PLAY **
Chuck Vincent    USA    1980
*Samantha Fox, Roger Caine, Jack Wrangler, Leslie
Bovee, Merle Michael, Kelly Nichols, Veronica Hart,
Frank Adams*
Fairly plotless film following the sexual encounters of
a group of married and single women, the linking
strand the fact that they generally wind up making
love to each other or each other's husbands or
boyfriends. A kind of interminable sexual soap opera.
A    87 min
B,V    EVI

## GAMES, THE ** PG
Michael Winner    UK    1969
*Stanley Baker, Michael Crawford, Ryan O'Neal,
Charles Aznavour, Jeremy Kemp, Elaine Taylor, Athol
Compton, Fritz Wepper, Kent Smith, Sam Elliott, Reg
Lye, Mona Washbourne, June Jago, Karel Stepanek*
Story of four runners from different countries and
their preparations for participation in the 26 mile
Olympic Marathon. Dull and episodic treatment of
what could have been an interesting subject, partially
redeemed by a good race sequence at the end.
Boa: book by Hugh Atkinson.
DRA    95 min
B,V,LV    CBS

## GANDHI **** PG
Richard Attenborough  UK    1982
*Ben Kingsley, Candice Bergen, Edward Fox, John
Gielgud, Trevor Howard, John Mills, Martin Sheen,
Ian Charleson, Athol Fugard, Gunter Maria Halmer,
Geraldine James, Amrish Puri, Saeed Jaffrey, Alyque
Padamsee, Roshan Seth*
Biopic on the life of the man who led India's campaign
for independence. Though inclined to sluggishness at
times, this excellent recreation is carried along by
Kingsley's superb portrayal. The script is by John
Briley. AA: Pic, Dir, Actor (Kingsley), Screen (Orig)
(John Briley), Cin (Billy Williams/Ronnie Taylor),
Art/Set (Stuart Craig and Bob Laing/Michael Seir-
ton), Cost (John Mollo/Bhanu Athaiya), Edit (John
Bloom).

DRA    180 min (ort 188 min)
V/sh    RCA

## GANG BUSTERS **
Bill Karan    USA    1955
*Myron Healey, Don C. Harvey, Sam Edwards, Frank
Gerstle*
A gangster: Public Enemy No. 4 no less, escapes from
prison with his cellmates and is hunted by the police
in this routine prison story.
Osca: DAY OF THE WOLVES
THR    68 min (ort 78 min) B/W
B,V    KVD

## GANG THAT COULDN'T SHOOT 15
STRAIGHT, THE *
James Goldstone    USA    1971
*Jerry Orbach, Lionel Stander, Joe Santos, Robert De
Niro, Jo Van Fleet, Leigh Taylor-Young, Herve
Villechaize*
Some tenth-rate New York crooks attempt to make
the big time by organising a cycle race, but their
efforts are crowned with disaster. A limp and totally
unfunny comedy, in which there's a lot of shouting but
precious little humour.
Boa: novel by Jimmy Breslin.
COM    93 min (ort 96 min)
B,V    MGM

## GANGLAND: THE VERNE MILLER STORY ** 15
Rod Hewitt    USA    1987
*Scott Glenn, Thomas G. Waites, Andrew Robinson,
Richard Bright, Ed O'Ross, Barbara Stock, Sonny
Carl Davis, Lucinda Jenney*
The true account of Verne Miller, who was Capone's
trusted assassin until he was disowned by the Mob,
following a botched attempt to rescue one of Capone's
book-keepers. This story follows his career, which
ended with his death by an unknown assailant after
having been hunted across Kansas by mobsters sent
after him. A fragmented and uneven movie that
largely wastes a powerful performance by Glenn in
the title role.
Aka: VERNE MILLER
DRA    90 min
B,V    EIV

## GANGSTER WARS ** 15
Richard C. Sarafian  USA    1981
*Michael Nouri, Brian Benben, Joe Penny, Markie Post,
Richard Castellano, George DiCenzo, Alan Arbus,
Madeline Stowe*
The first part of a compilation film, condensed from
episodes of "The Gangster Chronicles", a saga telling
of the rise to power of gangsters Lucky Luciano, Bugsy
Siegel and Co. The original TV series was shown in
thirteen 50-minute episodes; this detailed account was
trimmed considerably from that ponderous original,
but shows little improvement.
DRA    103 min mTV
B,V    CIC

## GANGSTER WARS 2 ** 15
Richard C. Sarafian  USA    1981
*Michael Nouri, Brian Benben, Joe Penny*
A continuation of the story of GANGSTER WARS,
that's really a condensed version of a much longer TV
series. This tale largely revolves around the efforts
made by various gangs to control the 1930s trade in
illicit alcohol.
DRA    86 min (ort 100 min) mTV
B,V    CIC

## GANGSTERS **
Joseph Warren (Giuseppe Vari)
    ITALY    1977

*Antonio Sabato, Max Delys, Giampiero Albertini*
Gangsters virtually hold a city to ransom with their extortion rackets, and a special squad tries to fight them but finds the odds stacked against them.
Aka: RETURN OF THE 38 GANG, THE; RITORNANO QUELLI DELLA CALIBRO 38
DRA                                              120 min
B,V,V2                                              VPD

### GANGSTERS' LAW **                               15
Siro Marcellini        ITALY                        197-
*Klaus Kinski, Maurice Poli, Suzy Anderson, Max Delys, Helen Chanel*
The sleazy account of the downfall of a gang leader, who goes on the run and faces betrayal at every turn. Not quite the example of film noir its makers intended, this slack and undistinguished affair is barely worth a look.
THR                                               89 min
B,V                                                MOG

### GAPPA THE TRIFIBIAN MONSTER ***               U
Haruyasu Noguchi       JAPAN                        1967
*Tamio Kawaji, Yoko Yamamoto, Yuji Okada, Koji Wada, Tatsuya Fuji*
An expedition to a remote island to collect tropical birds, returns to Japan with the huge egg of a prehistoric monster. Two giant monsters go after them to get back their offspring. This tongue-in-cheek parody of the genre has many effective moments, and of course the obligatory earthquake, tidal wave and volcanic eruption.
Aka: DAIKYOJU GAPPA; MONSTER FROM A PREHISTORIC PLANET
FAN                                               81 min
B,V,V2                          DFS L/A; VMA; STABL

### GARAGE GIRLS ***
Robert McCallum (Robert Neeallum)
                       USA                          1980
*Georgina Spelvin, John Leslie, Lisa De Leeuw, John Seeman, Jon Martin, Dorothy Le May, Chris Cassidy, Brooke West, Susanne Nero, Dewey Alexander*
Bawdy sex comedy about four girls who open a garage and provide a few extra services not available from their competitors. A crazy and unashamedly coarse tale, with poolroom encounters, attempts to blow up the garage, a Bonnie and Clyde-style car chase and a hilarious sequence detailing the exploits of a bunch of sex-crazed Youth Campers.
A                                                 81 min
B,V                                                CAL

### GARBAGE PAIL KIDS' MOVIE, THE *                PG
Rod Amateau            USA                          1987
*Anthony Newley, Mackenzie Astin, Katie Barberi, Ron MacLachlan, Kevin Thompson, Phil Fondacaro, Robert Bell, Larry Green, Arturo Gil, Debbie Lee Carrington, Sue Rossitto, J.P. Amateau, Marjory Graue, John Cade*
Crude and badly-made movie inspired by the obnoxious characters of a series of nauseating bubble-gum cards. "Greaser Greg", "Valerie Vomit" and friends all live happily in a garbage pail but are released to enjoy themselves in various adventures, when the magic bucket in which they live is kicked over by an antiques shop-owner.
JUV                    92 min (ort 100 min) Cut (26 sec)
B,V                                                EIV

### GARBO TALKS **                                 15
Sidney Lumet           USA                          1984
*Anne Bancroft, Ron Silver, Carrie Fisher, Catherine Hicks, Steven Hill, Howard da Silver, Dorothy London, Harvey Fierstein, Hermione Gingold*
A woman film buff who is dying from cancer, dreams of meeting Garbo before it is too late, and sends her son off to try to arrange a meeting. A contrived and pretentious drama with a few good vignettes, but

acres of tedium in between.
DRA                                    90 min (ort 103 min)
V/h                                                WHV

### GARDEN OF ALLAH, THE **                        PG
Richard Boleslawski    USA                          1936
*Marlene Dietrich, Charles Boyer, Basil Rathbone, Tilly Losch, C. Aubrey Smith, Joseph Schildkraut, Lucille Watson, Henry Kleinbach (Henry Brandon), John Carradine*
A Trappist monk and a disillusioned socialite fall in love in the desert, in a film that is nothing more than an interesting star vehicle, albeit a gorgeously photographed one – the cameramen were Howard Greene and Harold Rosson. Spec Award (for colour cinematography).
Boa: novel by Robert Hichens. Osca: INTERMEZZO (VCC)
DRA          85 min; 156 min (VCC – 2 film cassette)
B,V                            GHV; VCC (VHS only)

### GARDEN OF DEATH *                              15
James H. Kay III       USA                          1974
*Katherine Houghton, Rita Gam, Joe Dallesandro, James Congdon, Anne Meacham, Theodorina Bello*
A gardener who possesses the ability to turn into a tree feeds all his plants on human flesh. A low-grade shocker, filmed in Puerto Rico.
Aka: GARDENER, THE; SEEDS OF EVIL, THE
HOR                                     79 min (ort 97 min)
B,V              CHM/PPL L/A; AVA/CBS; AVR; NET

### GARDENIA **
Domenico Paolella      ITALY                         1979
*Martin Balsam, Franco Califano, Robert Webber*
One man fights against drug pushers and suffers greatly in the process, in this cliche-ridden gangster saga.
A/AD                                              90 min
B,V                                                HER

### GARDENS OF STONE *                             15
Francis Ford Coppola   USA                          1987
*James Caan, Anjelica Huston, James Earl Jones, D.B. Sweeney, Mary Stuart Masterson, Dean Stockwell, Dick Anthony Williams, Lonette McKee, Sam Bottoms, Larry Fishburne*
Another failed attempt to address the issues of the Vietnam War, seen here in the story of a sergeant in charge of the ceremonial troop of honour at Arlington National Cemetery, at the height of the fighting. Some good performances, but overall a disappointing film.
DRA                                    107 min (ort 111 min)
B,V                                                CBS

### GARTERS AND LACE **                            R18
Chuck Vincent          USA                          1981
*Randy West, Robin Byrd, Erica Richardson*
Routine sex film bearing no relation to a 1975 sex film of the same title.
A                                                 69 min
B,V                             EVI L/A PRI; SHEP

### GAS ***                                        18
Roger Corman           USA                          1970
*Robert Corff, Elaine Giftos, Bud Cort, Talia Coppola (Shire), Ben Vereen, Cindy Williams, Alex Wilson, Lou Oricopio, George Armitage, Country Joe and the Fish*
The accidental release of a nerve gas from a defence plant in Alaska, kills everyone over thirty in this meandering, disjointed, insane but often very funny story. See also CITY LIMITS.
Aka: GAS-S-S-S; GAS . . . OR IT MAY BECOME NECESSARY TO DESTROY THE WORLD IN ORDER TO SAVE IT
COM                                    74 min (ort 79 min)
B,V                                                RCA

## GAS PUMP GIRLS **
Joel Bender  USA  1979
*Kristen Baker, Dennis Bowen, Huntz Hall, Steve Bond,*
*Sandy Johnson, Leslie King, Joe E. Ross, Mike*
*Mazurki, Linda Lawrence, Rikki Martin, Bill Smith*
Five girls manage a petrol station and use their
charms to such good effect that their increase in
business threatens the viability of a rival station.
When they incur the wrath of a shady oil sheikh, they
are forced to go all out in a struggle over which of the
two stations is to survive, in this lightweight comedy
with sexual overtones.
COM  102 min
B,V  RNK

## GASLIGHT ***  PG
George Cukor  USA  1944
*Ingrid Bergman, Charles Boyer, Joseph Cotten, Dame*
*May Whitty, Barbara Everest, Angela Lansbury, Terry*
*Moore*
Atmospheric period piece with Boyer attempting to
drive his wife insane, in order to have a free hand in a
search of their attic whilst preserving a guilty secret.
This gave Bergman her first Oscar. Lansbury's film
debut. Originally filmed in 1939. AA: Actress (Berg-
man), Art/Int (Cedric Gibbons and William Ferrari/
Edwin B. Willis and Paul Huldschinsky).
Boa: play Angel Street by Patrick Hamilton.
DRA  110 min (ort 114 min) B/W
V  MGM

## GATE, THE **  15
Tibor Takacs  USA  1987
*Stephen Dorff, Louis Tripp, Christa Denton, Kelly*
*Rowan, Jennifer Irwin, Deborah Grover, Scot Denton*
A bored young lad is messing about in his backyard
with a pal whilst the parents are away, when they
inadvertently smash some rocks and open a gateway
to Hell in their backyard. Some good special effects
enliven a fairly undemanding horror yarn. A sequel
followed.
HOR  84 min (ort 92 min)
B,V  MED

## GATE 2 **  15
Tibor Takacs  1989
*Louis Tripp, James Villemaire, Pamela Segall*
Having paid a visit to the burnt-out remains of his
friend's house, where a demonic battle took place
years before, a man summons up a demon from Hell in
an effort to solve his problems, but soon finds himself
locked in a battle of his own.
HOR  89 min
V  BRAVE/MGM

## GATLING GUN **  15
Paolo Bianchini  ITALY/SPAIN  1968
*Robert Woods, John Ireland, Ida Galli*
Various groups compete to gain control over Gatling's
new weapon during the American Civil War. Average.
Aka: LA AMETRALLADORA; QUEL CALDO MALE
DETTO GIORNO DI FUOCO
WES  93 min
B,V  VDUP L/A; VPD

## GATLING GUN, THE ***  15
Robert Gordon  USA  1972
*Guy Stockwell, Robert Fuller, Woody Strode, Patrick*
*Wayne, John Carradine, Phil Harris*
A man steals a gatling gun from the US Army to sell
to the Indians, but is captured and has to be escorted
back to the fort through Apache territory whilst the
Indians make plans to retrieve it. Fair action
Western.
Aka: KING GUN; SERGEANT BLUE
WES  84 min
B,V  VIP

## GATOR *  15
Burt Reynolds  USA  1976
*Burt Reynolds, Lauren Hutton, Jack Weston, Jerry*
*Reed, Alice Ghostly, Dub Taylor, Michael Douglas*
An ex-con moonshiner is blackmailed by the Justice
department into becoming an undercover man in a
hoodlum's gang, in an attempt to grapple corruption.
A sequel to the 1973 film WHITE LIGHTNING in
which action is heavily outweighed by tedium.
Reynolds' directing debut.
COM  114 min (ort 116 min)
B,V  WHV

## GATOR BAIT *  18
Beverly C. Sebastian/D. Ferd Sebastian
  USA  1973
*Claudia Jennings, Sam Gilman, Clyde Ventura, Doug*
*Dirkson, Sam Gilman, Bill Thurman*
A sexy swamp girl becomes involved in murder in this
unpleasant and violent tale. Followed by a sequel.
Aka: SWAMP BAIT (ACN)
DRA  81 min (ort 93 min) Cut (3 min 8 sec)
B,V  ACN; CIC

## GATOR BAIT 2 **
Beverly C. Sebastian/D. Ferd Sebastian
  USA  1988
*Jan MacKenzie, Tray Loren, Paul Muzzcat*
Sequel to the original film, with a gang of human
low-lifes descending upon a peaceful Cajun wedding
ceremony, in search of revenge on the groom and his
new bride.
THR  99 min
V  CIC

## GAUGIN: THE SAVAGE *
Fielder Cook  USA  1980
*David Carradine, Lynn Redgrave, Barrie Houghton,*
*Michael Hordern, Flora Robson, Ian Richardson,*
*Carmen Matthews, Emrys James, Bernard Fox, Alan*
*Caillou, Christopher Cary, Fiona Fullerton, Alex*
*Hyde-White, Vanessa Paine*
A look at the life of this famous French painter, who
went to Tahiti to escape Western civilisation. Bad
casting, with Carradine quite unbelievable in the title
role, is complemented by sluggish development to
produce a film that falls quite flat. Scripted by J.P.
Miller.
DRA  116 min (ort 125 min) mTV
B,V,V2  CAREY

## GAUNTLET, THE **  18
Clint Eastwood  USA  1977
*Clint Eastwood, Sondra Locke, Pat Hingle, William*
*Prince, Mara Corday, Bill McKinney*
A cop has to escort a prostitute to the trial of a corrupt
official where she is a chief witness, and together they
run the gauntlet of the Mob who are determined to
prevent her testifying. A generally exciting tale if
somewhat unbelievable and excessively violent.
THR  104 min (ort 109 min)
V  WHV

## GAY DIVORCEE, THE ***  U
Mark Sandrich  USA  1934
*Fred Astaire, Ginger Rogers, Alice Brady, Edward*
*Everett Horton, Eric Blore, Erik Rhodes, Lillian Miles,*
*Betty Grable*
Routine 1930s musical with the Astaire-Rogers dance
duo. The thin plot has a would-be divorcee staying in a
hotel where she mistakes an author who is in love
with her, for a professional co-respondent. Dated but
still retaining considerable zest and a number of still
comical routines. AA: Song ("The Continental" – Con
Conrad – music/Herb Magidson – lyrics).
Osca: FLYING DOWN TO RIO (asa)
MUS  100 min (ort 107 min); 186 min (2 film cassette)
B/W
V  VCC

**GAYLON ** **                                              15**
Ivan Tors                    USA           1978
*Lloyd Nolan, Ron Hayes, Stan Brock, Ina Balin*
Terrorists sabotage an oil well and take two Amer-
icans hostage. A mercenary is sent in to rescue them.
A/AD                         97 min (ort 100 min)
B,V                                          ARF

**GEEK ** **                                                18**
Dean Crow                    USA           1986
*Brad Armacost, Christina Noonan, Jack O'Hara, Dick*
*Kreuser*
A young doctor and his wife are out on a camping trip
when they come across a hillbilly child accidentally
shot by her father. They return with the child to the
man's cabin, where they discover that he has a
dangerous retard for a son he keeps locked up in the
woodshed. Having taken a fancy to the doctor's wife,
said son breaks out and comes after her in this
predictable and boring attempt at a shocker.
Aka: BACKWOODS
HOR                                          90 min
B,V                                        SHEER

**GENERAL LINE, THE ***                             PG**
Sergei Eisenstein/Grigori V. Alexandrov
                             USSR          1929
*Marfa Lapkina, Vasya Buzenkov, Kostya Vasiliev,*
*Chukhamarev*
Eisenstein's last silent film tells of a peasant woman
who is converted to communism and helps a village
start up a co-operative. Despite his efforts to avoid
trouble over this offering, the director's satirical
touches offended the authorities. A mixture of art and
propaganda in equal degrees; the famous montage
sequence demonstrating the operation of a cream
separator is one of the film's highlights.
Aka: GENERALNAYA LINYA; OLD AND NEW;
STAROYE I NOVOYE
DRA                          97 min (ort 90 min) B/W silent
V                                           HEND

**GENERATION, A ***                                         **
Andrzej Wajda        POLAND              1954
*Tadeusz Lomnicki, Ursula Mordzynska, Roman*
*Polanski, Tadeusz Janczar, Zbigniew Cybulski.*
First part of the Wajda trilogy dealing with young
Poles and their attitudes towards the German occupa-
tion of Poland, particularly exploring the role of the
Polish Resistance during WW2, with a young man
falling in love with the woman leader of a Resistance
group. An absorbing and perceptive study, followed by
KANAL and then ASHES AND DIAMONDS.
Aka: POKOLENIE
Boa: novel by Bohdan Czeszko.
DRA                          86 min B/W
B,V                                         TEVP

**GENEVIEVE ***                                          U**
Henry Cornelius             UK            1954
*Kenneth More, Kay Kendall, John Gregson, Dinah*
*Sheridan, Geoffrey Keen, Reginald Beckwith, Arthur*
*Wontner, Joyce Grenfell, Michael Medwin, Leslie*
*Mitchell, Michael Balfour, Edie Martin, Harold*
*Siddons*
A dose of typical 1950s whimsy about the rivalry
between the contestants in the London-to-Brighton
veteran car race. The music was composed and played
by Larry Adler.
COM                          83 min (ort 86 min)
V                                            RNK

**GENGHIS KHAN ** **                                    PG**
Henry Levin                              1965
       UK/USA/WEST GERMANY/YUGOSLAVIA
*Omar Sharif, Stephen Boyd, James Mason, Eli*
*Wallach, Francoise Dorleac, Telly Savalas, Robert*
*Morley, Yvonne Mitchell, Woody Strode.*
Loose, untidy spectacle following the career of this

warlord as he grows up to take revenge on the rival
chieftain who murdered his father. There is no fine
sweep of history here, just poor casting, a pathetic
script and a few spectacular moments by way of
compensation.
A/AD        119 min (ort 124 min) Cut (1 min 3 sec in
                                addition to film cuts)
V                                            RCA

**GENTLE SAVAGE ** **                                   18**
Sean MacGregor              USA          1976
*William Smith, Gene Evans, Joe Flynn, Kevin Hagen,*
*Barbara Luna*
An Indian in a small Arizona town, is wrongly accused
of rape by the local racists and escapes from jail to
clear his name and get his revenge.
DRA                                          82 min
B,V                                          RNK

**GENTLE SINNERS ** **                                  15**
Eric Till              CANADA            1984
*Christopher Earle, Charlene Seniuk, Ed McNamara,*
*Jackie Burroughs*
Set in the 1950s, this is an account of a young man
who leaves his religious home in rural Manitoba to go
and live with his uncle.
DRA                          101 min (ort 105 min)
B,V                                          CBS

**GENTLEMAN BANDIT, THE ** **                             **
Jonathan Kaplan             USA          1981
*Ralph Waite, Julie Bovasso, Jerry Zaks, Estelle*
*Parsons, Joe Grifasi, Tom Aldredge, Arthur French,*
*Ed Van Nuys, Joe Ponazecki, Frances Chaney, Sheila*
*K. Adams, Joyce Reehling, Charley Lang, Marta*
*Heflin, Scotty Bloch*
A Catholic priest with a busy parish, is mistakenly
suspected of being involved in a series of murders.
Based on the true story story of Father Bernard
Pagano.
DRA                          100 min mTV
B,V,V2                                    AFE; IFS

**GENTLEMAN JIM ***                                     U**
Raoul Walsh                 USA          1942
*Errol Flynn, Alexis Smith, Jack Carson, Alan Hale,*
*John Loder, William Frawley, Minor Watson, Ward*
*Bond, Arthur Shields*
Biopic about Jim Cobbett, an early prizefighter. Flynn
as Corbett is good and the fight scenes are handled
extremely well. Scripted by Vincent Lawrence and
Horace McCoy.
Boa: book The Roar Of The Crowd by James J.
Corbett.
DRA                          101 min (ort 104 min) B/W
B,V                                          WHV

**GENTLEMEN PREFER BLONDES ** **                        U**
Howard Hawks                USA          1953
*Marilyn Monroe, Jane Russell, Charles Coburn,*
*Tommy Noonan, Elliott Reid, George "Foghorn"*
*Winslow*
Two showgirls go to Paris in search of rich husbands,
in this musical comedy which is only memorable for
the score, and songs such as "Diamonds Are A Girl's
Best Friend". Followed by "Gentlemen Marry
Brunettes".
Boa: story by Anita Loos.
MUS                          89 min (ort 91 min)
V                                            CBS

**GEORGE ** **                                            **
Wallace C. Bennett
                     SWITZERLAND/USA     1970
*Marshall Thompson, Kack Mullaney, Inge Schoner*
A carefree, unmarried pilot finds that the gift of an
oversize St Bernard dog from his eccentric aunt turns
his life upside down. A mediocre comedy.

COM 81 min (ort 87 min)
B,V,V2 VPD

## GEORGE AND MILDRED * 15
Peter Frazer-Jones UK 1980
*Yootha Joyce, Brian Murphy, Stratford Johns,
Norman Eshley, Sheila Fearn, Kenneth Cope, David
Barry, Sue Bond, Nicholas Bond-Owen, Neil
McCarthy, Dudley Sutton, Garfield Morgan, Harry
Fowler, Suzanne Owens, Roger Avon*
TV spin-off of a popular but pretty feeble British
sit-com. Gangsters mistake George for a contract
killer when our loving couple go to a hotel to celebrate
their wedding anniversary. Embarrassingly bad in a
way that so much of British comedy is. In other words,
pathetic.
COM 89 min (ort 93 min)
B,V PRV; CH5 (VHS only); POLY (VHS only)

## GEORGE McKENNA STORY, THE *** 15
Eric Laneuville USA 1986
*Denzel Washington, Lynn Whitfield, Akosua Busia,
Richard Masur, Virginia Capers, Ray Buktenica,
Barbara Townsend, Israel Juarbe, J.A. Preston, Bill
Henderson, Earl Billings, Brent Jennings, Terrance
Ellis, Ken Sagoes*
A high school principal turns a run-down and gang-
ridden school in the poorer part of Los Angeles into a
well-run place of learning. A simple and inspiring
drama based on the experiences of this real-life
principal. The script is by Charles Eric Johnson.
Ironically, the film was actually shot on location in
Houston, Texas.
DRA 94 min (ort 100 min) mTV
B,V VIR

## GEORGIA * 15
USA 1989
*Judy Davis, John Bach, Julia Blake*
A woman lawyer discovers that her real mother is
somebody entirely different and despite the fact that
she is now dead, she becomes obsessed with the need
to learn all she can about her. An obscure and
slow-moving drama that suffers badly from a lack of
direction and an indifferent script.
DRA 90 min
V MED

## GEORGIA *** 15
Arthur Penn USA 1981
*Craig Wasson, Jodi Thelen, Jim Metzler, Michael
Huddleston, Lois Smith, Reed Birney, James Leo
Herlihy*
A study of the relationship between four friends, three
boys and a girl, growing up in Indiana of the early
1960s, and largely revolving around the experiences
of one, a Yugoslavian immigrant. Scripted by Steve
Tesich and based to some extent on his own experi-
ences.
Aka: FOUR FRIENDS; GEORGIA'S FRIENDS
DRA 113 min (ort 115 min)
B,V RNK; ORION

## GEORGY GIRL ** 15
Silvio Narizzano UK 1966
*Lynn Redgrave, James Mason, Alan Bates, Charlotte
Rampling, Bill Owen, Clare Kelly, Rachel Kempson,
Denise Coffrey, Dorothy Alison, Peggy Thorp-Bates,
Dandy Nichols*
Dated black comedy about a dowdy English girl and
her involvement with men, in particular wealthy
married man Mason, who wants her for his mistress.
Considered in its day to be controversial, this "swing-
ing London" comedy now has the appearance of a film
that's been kept in mothballs.
Boa: novel by Margaret Forster.
COM 95 min (ort 99 min) B/W
V PREST

## GESTAPO'S LAST ORGY * 
Cesare Carnevari ITALY 1977
*Marc Loud, Daniele Levy, Maristella Greco*
One of a series of films made to cash in on the success
of THE NIGHT PORTER, through its crude exploita-
tion of the unspeakable sufferings of women prisoners
at the hands of the Nazis. Unlikely to be available in
an uncut form in the UK.
Aka: L'ULTIMA ORGIA DEL III REICH
WAR 80 min
B,V VFP

## GET CRAZY *** 18
Allan Arkush USA 1983
*Malcolm McDowell, Daniel Stern, Gail Edwards,
Allen Goorwitz (Garfield), Ed Begley Jr, Miles Chapin,
Lou Reed, Stacey Nelkin, Bill Henderson, Franklin
Ajaye, Bobby Sherman, Fabian Forte, Lori Eastside,
Lee Ving*
A New York theatre-owner decides to stage the
world's largest rock-and-roll concert but finds that
things do not go smoothly, in this fast-paced and witty
comedy.
COM 88 min (ort 92 min)
B,V HER

## GET MEAN ** 
Fernando Baldi ITALY 1976
*Tony Anthony, Lloyd Battista*
A hired killer is promised a golden treasure, in return
for stopping the advance of a murderous barbarian
horde in this formula adventure.
Aka: VENGEANCE OF THE BARBARIANS
A/AD 90 min
B,V,V2 VCL/CBS; DFS

## GET SMART, AGAIN! ** PG
Gary Nelson USA 1989
*Don Adams, Barbara Feldon, Bernie Kopell, Dick
Gautier, Robert Karvelas, King Moody, Harold Gould,
Kenneth Mars, Roger Price, Fritz Feld*
Another reunion movie following THE NUDE BOMB,
in which our idiotic secret agent from the 1960s TV
series "Get Smart", is brought out of retirement to face
his old opponents from KAOS once more. Average.
COM 93 min (ort 100 min) mTV
B,V BRAVE

## GETAWAY, THE *** 18
Sam Peckinpah USA 1972
*Steve McQueen, Ali MacGraw, Ben Johnson, Slim
Pickens, Sally Struthers, Al Lettieri*
A crook leaves prison to join his wife in planning and
carrying out a bank robbery, which does not go as
planned. Plenty of car chases and violent action help
make up for the deficiencies of the plot. Written by
Walter Hill.
Boa: novel by Jim Thompson.
THR 123 min
B,V WHV

## GETTING EVEN ** 15
Harvey Hart CANADA 1981
*Robert Hays, Brooke Adams, John Marley, James
Blendick, Lee Brooker, Helen Burns, Benjamin
Gordon, John-Peter Linton, Jan Rubes, Helene
Winston, Steve Pernie, Toby Tarnow, Don Lamont,
Jane Mallet, Shelby Gregory, Margaret Pacsu*
A social worker sets out to get even with the utility
companies who cut off supplies when the poor are
unable to meet their bills, in this undeveloped and
limp attempt at a social satire.
Aka: UTILITIES
COM 92 min; 89 min (MAST)
B,V VTC; STABL; MAST (VHS only)

## GETTING IT ON ** 18
William Olsen USA 1983
*Martin Yost, Jeff Edmond, Kathy Brickmeier, Heather*

*Kennedy, Mark Alan Ferri, Charles King Bibby*
Two teenagers acquire video equipment and use it to
spy on girls in various states of undress in this witless
sex comedy.
Aka: AMERICAN VOYEUR

| | |
|---|---|
| A | 92 min (ort 96 min) |
| B,V | ODY; BLUES |

## GETTING IT RIGHT **   15
Randal Kleiser   UK   1988
*Jesse Birdsall, Lynn Redgrave, Helena Bonham-Carter, Peter Cook, John Gielgud, Jane Horrocks*
A wimpish man who lives with his parents is taken in
hand by his friends who drag him off to a party where
he enjoys several romantic encounters before finally
succumbing to true love. A pleasant and undemanding time-filler.
Boa: novel by Elizabeth Jane Howard.

| | |
|---|---|
| COM | 94 min |
| V | MED |

## GETTING L.A.'D **   R18
Miles Kidder   USA   1986
*Jamie Gillis, Amber Lynn, Nina Hartley, Jerry Butler, Kari Foxx, Ron Jeremy, Bunny Bleu, Kristara Barrington, Buck Adams, Don Frederico, Troy Tanier*
This film opens with Hartley making love to Gillis,
who works as some kind of undercover agent. A phone
call sends him off on an assignment and he is never
seen again, but as for Hartley, she spends the rest of
the film sleeping around in an effort to forget him.

| | |
|---|---|
| A | 60 min |
| V | SHEP |

## GETTING LUCKY *   18
Michael Paul Girard   USA   1989
*Steven Cooke, Lezlie Z. McGraw, Rick McDowell*
A brainless high school nerd has never had a date, but
when a leprechaun shrinks him to the size of a flea he
gets the chance to have a close relationship with a
pretty cheer-leader.

| | |
|---|---|
| COM | 90 min |
| V | BCB |

## GETTING OF WISDOM, THE ***
Bruce Beresford   AUSTRALIA   1977
*Susannah Fowle, Hilary Ryan, Alix Longman, Sheila Helpmann, Barry Humphries, Laura Rambotham, Patricia Kennedy, John Waters, Kerry Armstrong*
A girl from the outback goes to a snobbish Victorian
ladies' college, but refuses to share its values and
customs. An engaging period drama that is slightly
spoilt by the bad casting of Fowle, but generally
succeeds on all counts.
Boa: novel by Henry Handel Richardson.

| | |
|---|---|
| DRA | 100 min |
| B,V | GHV |

## GETTING WASTED *
Paul Frizler   USA   1980
*Brian Kerwin, Stephen Furst, Cooper Huckabee, Wendy Ratstatter*
A military academy is turned upside down when the
cadets meet some hippies. Set in 1969 and looking as
dated as if it had been made in the 1960s.

| | |
|---|---|
| COM | 98 min |
| B,V,LV | MOG; CBS |

## GHETTO BLASTER, THE **   18
Alan L. Stewart   USA   1987
*Richard Hatch, R.G. Armstrong, Richard Jaeckel, Harry Caesar, Del Zamora, Diane Moser, Kamar Reyes, Rosie Marie*
Rival drug-dealing gangs turn a local neighbourhood
into a battleground and the police are reluctant to
interfere. The residents finally take the law into their
own hands, being led by a Vietnam veteran who sets
out to avenge the death of his daughter from drugs.
Average.

| | |
|---|---|
| A/AD | 84 min (ort 86 min) |
| V | BRAVE |

## GHETTO WARRIORS *   18
Lee Frost   USA   1986
*Rod Perry, Charles P. Robinson*
A social welfare organisation helping alcoholics and
drug addicts in the slums, takes to violence when a
nurse is attacked and raped. An unpleasant, mind-numbing and violent exploiter.
Aka: BLACK GESTAPO

| | |
|---|---|
| DRA | 81 min Cut (4 min 8 sec) |
| B,V | AVR L/A; NET |

## GHIDRAH: THE THREE-HEADED DRAGON *
Inoshiro Honda   JAPAN   1965
*Yosuke Natsuki, Yuriko Hoshi, Hiroshi Koizumi, Emi Ito*
The title monster menaces Tokyo in this further
dollop of low-budget Japanese garbage. Three of our
favourite schlock-monsters, Mothra, Rodan and Godzilla, are called in to see the monster off. (King Kong
wasn't in when they phoned.) One of those films that
improves after a few beers (but only slightly).
Aka: GHIDRAH: THE THREE-HEADED MONSTER

| | |
|---|---|
| FAN | 85 min |
| B,V | MOV |

## GHOST CHASE ***   PG
Roland Emmerich   USA   1988
*Jason Lively, Jill Whitlow, Tim McDaniel, Paul Gleeson*
A young maker of horror films inherits some relics
from his grandfather, who owned a Hollywood film
studio. One of the articles is a strange clock which
upon striking midnight, causes the ghost of his
grandfather's dead butler to take over a special effects
figure, and help the grandson fight a powerful movie
mogul who is trying to take over the grandfather's
studio. A lively piece of implausible nonsense.

| | |
|---|---|
| FAN | 90 min |
| V/sh | MED |

## GHOST FEVER **   15
Alan Smithee (Ramzi Thomas)
   MEXICO/USA   1984 (released 1987)
*Sherman Hemsley, Luis Avalos, Jennifer Rhodes, Deborah Benson, Diana Brookes, Myron Healey, Pepper Martin, Joe Frazier*
Two New York policemen find themselves serving a
summons for non-payment of taxes, on the ghost of an
evil plantation owner who is suffering a curse of
eternal restlessness, placed on him by his hapless
slaves. The ghost's beautiful great-great-granddaughter persuades them to undertake the task
of exorcising his tormented spirit. An uneven black
comedy.

| | |
|---|---|
| COM | 89 min |
| B,V | VIR |

## GHOST IN THE INVISIBLE BIKINI, THE *   PG
Don Weis   USA   1966
*Tommy Kirk, Deborah Walley, Aron Kincaid, Quinn O'Hara, Nancy Sinatra, Claudia Martin, Harvey Lembeck, Jesse White, Susan Hart, Basil Rathbone, Boris Karloff, Patsy Kelly, Francis X. Bushman, Benny Rubin*
A bunch of bikers get mixed up with a rejuvenated
corpse when they pay a visit to a haunted mansion in
this scatterbrained, knockabout comedy, the seventh
in the "Beach Party" (1963) series.

| | |
|---|---|
| COM | 80 min (ort 82 min) |
| V | RCA |

## GHOST IN THE NOONDAY SUN *
Peter Medak   UK   1974
*Peter Sellers, Anthony Franciosa, Spike Milligan, Peter Boyle, Clive Revill, Richard Willis, James Villiers, Rosemary Leach*

The cook kills the captain of a pirate ship and sets out to look for buried treasure, in this rubbishy pirate comedy that was deservedly never put on general release.
COM 90 min
B,V RNK

**GHOST OF A CHANCE ** PG**
Don Taylor USA 1986
*Dick Van Dyke, Redd Foxx, Geoffrey Holder, Brynn Thayer, Richard Romanus*
A piano player is shot accidentally by a trigger-happy cop, but gets a reprieve because it's not yet his time to die. The pilot for a prospective series, with Foxx in his TV movie debut. Sometimes amusing but generally just rather dull.
COM 92 min (ort 100 min) mTV
B,V GHV

**GHOST OF CYPRESS SWAMP, THE *** U**
Vincent McEveety USA 1977
*Vic Morrow, Jacqueline Scott, Noah Beery, Jeff East, Louise Latham, Tom Simcox, Cindy Eilbacher*
The first TV film from Disney is a pleasant adventure in which East tracks a wounded panther through a forest and meets a mysterious hermit who lives there.
A/AD 92 min (ort 106 min) mTV
B,V WDV

**GHOST OF WOLFPACK, THE ** PG**
Don Chaffey UK 1968
*Richard Johnson, Honor Blackman, Jeremy Kemp, Peter Vaughan, Roy Dotrice, Clifford Evans, Guy Doleman, Jack May, Kenneth Cope*
A pretty forgettable yarn, with Johnson an ex-submarine commander leading a bunch of smugglers on an expedition for diamonds.
Aka: TWIST OF SAND, A
Boa: novel A Twist Of Sand by Jeffrey Jenkins.
A/AD 85 min (ort 90 min)
V INTCON

**GHOST SHIP ** 18**
Vernon Sewell UK 1952
*Dermot Walsh, Hazel Court, Hugh Burden, John Robinson, Joss Ambler, Joan Carol, Joss Ackland, John King Kelly*
Despite a warning, a couple go ahead with their purchase of a yacht, only to find that it's haunted by the ghost of the former owner. A dull second feature, with very little to offer despite the unusual premise. The script is by Sewell.
HOR 69 min B/W
V WHV

**GHOST SHIP, THE ****
Mark Robson USA 1943
*Richard Dix, Russell Wade, Edith Barrett, Ben Bard, Lawrence Tierney, Edmund Grover, Skelton Knaggs*
A young officer on a merchant vessel is worried by his captain's increasingly irrational behaviour. An intriguing and atmospheric film that is spoilt by an unsatisfying ending. Despite the title, there is in fact no supernatural element.
Osca: MISTER KINGSTREET'S WAR
DRA 66 min (ort 69 min) B/W
B,V KVD

**GHOST STORY ** 18**
John Irvin USA 1981
*Fred Astaire, Melvyn Douglas, John Houseman, Douglas Fairbanks Jr, Craig Wasson, Alice Krige, Patricia Neal, Jacqueline Brooks*
Four elderly men pass the time by telling each other ghost stories, but all share a guilty secret from the past. An unusual film for the four stars, that gradually flounders as it runs out of steam. This was Astaire's last movie.
Boa: novel by Peter Straub.

HOR 106 min (ort 110 min)
B,V,V2 CIC

**GHOST TOWN *** 18**
Richard Governor USA 1988
*Frank Luz, Jimmie F. Skaggs, Catherine Hickland, Bruce Glover, Michael Aldredge*
Hunting for a missing girl, a policeman searches in a dusty ghost town in Arizona that holds a dark secret – a bunch of zombie gunslingers. A stylish and eerie combination of Western and horror genres.
HOR 81 min
B,V EIV

**GHOST TRAIN, THE ** U**
Walter Forde UK 1941
*Arthur Askey, Richard Murdoch, Kathleen Harrison, Morland Graham, Linden Travers, Peter Murray Hill, Carole Lynn, Herbert Lomas, Raymond Huntley, Betty Jardine, Stuart Latham, D.J. Williams, George Merritt*
A detective poses as a passenger in order to catch spies who are using an abandoned track. A so-so remake of the 1931 film, with the leading role rather ill-advisedly split into two characters. See OH! MR PORTER which also made use of the plot from the earlier film.
Boa: play by Arnold Ridley.
COM 83 min B/W
B,V RNK; VCC

**GHOSTBUSTERS ** PG**
Ivan Reitman USA 1984
*Dan Aykroyd, Bill Murray, Harold Ramis, Sigourney Weaver, Rick Moranis, Annie Potts, Ernie Hudson, William Atherton*
When three scientists lose their research funding they decide to make use of their knowledge of the paranormal, hiring themselves out as a team able to rid buildings of unwanted supernatural phenomena. A brash film that hovers uneasily between comedy and the supernatural, developing eventually into a silly duel between the forces of Good (our three scientists), and those of Evil. Special effects are by Richard Edlund. Written by Aykroyd and Ramis.
COM 105 min
V/sh RCA

**GHOSTBUSTERS 2 *** PG**
Ivan Reitman USA 1988
*Dan Aykroyd, Bill Murray, Harold Ramis, Ernie Hudson, Sigourney Weaver, Rick Moranis, Annie Potts, Ernie Hudson, William Atherton*
A likeable sequel to the earlier film that offers little in the way of new ideas, but has our ghostbusting team re-assembled to save New York from an attack by a sea of slime, that's been nourished by the city's famous negative vibes. A loosely plotted comedy, sustained by nice interplay between the leads and some good jokes about the quality of life in the Big Apple. Written by Ramis and Aykroyd.
Osca: GHOSTBUSTERS (asa)
COM 100 min (ort 102 min); 204 min (2 film cassette)
subH
V RCA

**GHOSTHOUSE ** 18**
Humphrey Hubert (Umberto Lenzi)
ITALY 1987
*Lara Wendel, Greg Scott, Mary Sellers, Kate Silver, Ron Houck*
A man too poor to buy his little girl a birthday present, steals a doll from the coffin of a witch. Under its influence the girl murders her parents and then commits suicide. The story now moves forward eight years to a bunch of teen radio hams who are having a session at the now deserted house. Our girl returns in spirit form and proceeds to chop, hack and stab her

way through their number in this entirely predictable effort.

HOR 93 min
B,V CFD

## GHOSTHOUSE 2 ** 18
Martin Newlin ITALY 1988
*Linda Blair, David Hasselhoff, Catherine Hickand, Annie Ross, Richard Farnsworth, Michael Leemanchester, Robert Champagne, Hildegarde Knef*
A ramshackle old hotel is situated on a remote New England island and is the property of the greedy Brooks family, who arrive by ferry to look it over, prior to selling it off to developers. They encounter a photographer and his girlfriend who are staying there, but unknown to all parties the house is haunted by the spirit of an evil witch. One by one they fall victim to evil as various grisly happenings now take place in this gory, formula shocker.
Aka: WITCHERY; WITCHCRAFT

HOR 89 min (ort 96 min)
B,V CFD

## GHOSTKEEPER ** 18
James Makichuk CANADA 1980
*Riva Spier, George Collins, Murray Ord, Sheri McFadden, Bill Grove, Les Kimber, John MacMillan, James Hutchison*
There is an Indian legend of the "Wendigo", a creature that eats human flesh and lives in the Rocky Mountains. A group of people on a holiday trip fall victim to it.

HOR 87 min; 83 min (APX)
B,V,V2 INT; APX

## GHOSTRIDERS ** 15
Alan L. Stewart USA 1986
*Bill Shaw, Jim Peters*
In 1888 a vicious desperado shouts an evil curse on the town preacher, just as he and his gang are dying on the gallows. A hundred years later they return from the grave, to take revenge on the descendants of those who condemned them. Fair.

HOR 88 min
B,V IVS

## GHOSTS CAN'T DO IT * 18
John Derek USA 1990
*Bo Derek, Anthony Quinn, Don Murray, Leo Damian*
Shallow, dreary vehicle for Derek, in which an invalid billionaire commits suicide, but is obliged by an angel to stay on Earth a while longer. Our frustrated tycoon hatches a plan with his young wife to circumvent the angel's ruling.

COM 83 min
V EIV

## GHOSTS OF BUXLEY HALL, THE *** U
Bruce Bilson USA 1980
*Dick O'Neill, Victor French, Louise Latham, Monte Markham*
Gentle, supernatural kid's comedy in which an old military academy is forced to merge with a school for girls when it falls on hard times. The academy's resident ghosts are outraged by this change and attempt to do something to bring back respect for tradition.

COM 93 min
B,V WDV

## GHOUL, THE * 18
Freddie Francis UK 1974
*Peter Cushing, Alexandra Bastedo, John Hurt, Gwen Watford, Veronica Carlson, Don Henderson, Ian McCulloch, Stewart Bevan, John D. Collins, Dan Meaden*
A group of stranded travellers are attacked by something that lurks in the house of a former clergyman, in this horror yarn set in the 1920s. (I won't spoil the film

for you by revealing that the creature is the cleric's cannibalistic son.)
Aka: THING IN THE ATTIC, THE

HOR 84 min (ort 87 min) (Cut at film release)
B,V RNK

## GHOULIES * 15
Luca Bercovici USA 1985
*Peter Liapis, Lisa Pelikan, Michael Des Barres, Jack Nance, Peter Risch, Tamara de Treux*
Nasty little monsters start popping up after a boy and his friends mess about with some magic spells. A boring and rather repulsive GREMLINS clone.

COM 77 min (ort 84 min)
V EIV

## GHOULIES 2 ** 15
Albert Band USA 1987
*Damon Martin, Royal Dano, Phil Fondacaro, J. Downing, Kerry Remsen*
Just when Larry is ready to give up running his carnival show — "Satan's Den" — some unexpected visitors arrive and make their home there, proving a big hit with the paying customers. Unfortunately, our demonic imps cause considerable trouble in the process, not to mention a few gruesome murders, in this unsubtle and entirely inevitable sequel.

COM 86 min Cut (55 sec)
B,V EIV

## GHOULIES 3 * 15
John Carl Buechler USA 1990
*Kevin McCarthy, Evan Mackenzie, Griffin O'Neal*
Second sequel to the original film that sticks strictly to the level of POLICE ACADEMY and the like, with our adorable little nasties being summoned up by a college professor in order to deal with the antics of two rival gangs during the college's annual week of pranks. Apart from a few traces of black humour, this is a very dull effort indeed.
Aka: GHOULIES GO TO COLLEGE

HOR 90 min
V VES

## GIANT ** PG
George Stevens USA 1956
*Rock Hudson, Elizabeth Ta, Mercedes McCambridge, James Dean, Carroll Baker, Chill Wills, Jane Withers, Dennis Hopper, Sal Mineo, Rodney (Rod) Taylor, Earl Holliman*
A flat, overlong and boring study, telling of the changing fortunes of several generations on a Texan farm, that's only enlivened by the occasional appearances of Dean. A film that's unaccountably highly regarded by the critics, almost certainly due to the presence of Dean in what was his last movie. It picked up an Oscar but one has to struggle to see why. AA: Dir.
Boa: novel by Edna Ferber.

DRA 201 min
B,V WHV

## GIANT SPIDER INVASION, THE *
Bill Rebane USA 1975
*Steve Brodie, Barbara Hale, Leslie Parrish, Alan Hale, Robert Easton, Bill Williams*
Nuclear fallout results in a rampage by giant spiders. A re-run of 1950s movies like "Tarantula" and others of that ilk.
Aka: GREAT SPIDER INVASION, THE

FAN 73 min (ort 82 min)
B,V VCL/CBS

## GIDEON'S TRUMPET **** U
Robert Collins USA 1980
*Henry Fonda, Jose Ferrer, John Houseman, Fay Wray, Sam Jaffe, Dean Jagger, Nicholas Pryor, William Prince, Lane Smith, Richard McKenzie, Dolph Sweet, Ford Rainey, David Sheiner, Pat McNamara, Les*

*Lannom, Malcolm Groom*
A down-and-out charged with breaking and entering,
changed the course of American legal history in the
1960s by being the first defendant to be provided with
the services of a defence lawyer. Fonda gives a
brilliant performance as a semi-literate drifter in this
powerful drama. The script is by David W. Rintels.
Boa: book by Anthony Lewis.
DRA                                      104 min mTV
B,V                                        HER; CBS

## GIDEON'S WAR **
USA                1989
*Louis Gossett Jr*
An inquisitive professor who is in the West Indies for
a conference, finds himself drawn into a nasty crime
involving the murder of some tourists, and becomes
increasingly involved in trying to uncover the truth,
learning of some dubious plans being hatched by a
corrupt government. One in a series of films starring
Gossett in this role. See also SLEEP WELL, PROFES-
SOR OLIVER and TONGS.
A/AD                                      90 min mTV
V                                              CIC

## GIFT FOR HEIDI, A **
                                                U
George Templeton      USA            1958
*Douglas Fowley, Sandy Descher, Van Dyke Parks*
Heidi learns the meaning of faith, hope and charity
through the gift of three woodcarvings, in this
pleasant and undemanding yarn, inspired by Johanna
Spyri's famous tale.
Osca: ESCAPADE IN JAPAN
JUV                                         72 min
B,V                        KVD; MAST (VHS only)

## GIGI ****
                                              PG
Vincente Minnelli      USA            1958
*Leslie Caron, Maurice Chevalier, Louis Jourdan,*
*Hermione Gingold, Jacques Bergerac, Eva Gabor,*
*Isabel Jeans, John Abbott*
Set in Paris at the turn of the century, this famous
musical tells of a young tomboy who grows up into a
beautiful woman and is trained to be a courtesan. A
colourful joyful romance. AA: Pic, Dir, Cin (J. Rutten-
berg), Edit (A. Fazan), Art/Set (W.A. Horning and P.
Ames/F.K. Gleason and H. Grace), Screen (Adapt)
(A.J. Lerner), Cost (C. Beaton), Score (A. Previn),
Song ("Gigi " – F. Loewe – music/A.J. Lerner – lyrics).
Boa: novel by Colette.
MUS                                        111 min
V/sh                                          MGM

## GIGI AND THE FOUNTAIN OF YOUTH ***
Pleasant children's story in which Gigi is a princess
sent to Earth to learn its ways before she can inherit
her parent's kingdom on another world. On Earth she
meets Peter, who controls the magical Fountain of
Youth and together they embark on a struggle to stop
it falling into the wrong hands.
CAR                                         77 min
V                                              VGM

## GILDA ***
                                              PG
Charles Vidor      USA                1946
*Rita Hayworth, Glenn Ford, George Macready, Steven*
*Geray, Joseph Calleia, Joe Sawyer, Gerald Mohr,*
*Ludwig Donath*
In South America, a drifter gets taken on as a casino
owner's right-hand man and becomes unwillingly
involved with the latter's glamorous young wife,
having known her before her marriage. An entertain-
ing example of film noir, with good moments of
tension but spoilt by a clumsily contrived ending. A
highspot is Hayworth singing "Put The Blame On
Me".
DRA                                    105 min B/W
V                                              RCA

## GIMME AN "F" *
                                              15
Paul Justman      USA                 1984
*Steve Shellen, John Karlen, Mark Keyloun, Daphne*
*Ashbrook, Beth Miller, Jennifer C. Cooke, Karen Kelly,*
*Sarah M. Miles*
Undistinguished teen comedy about a cheerleaders'
contest with the inevitable high school frolics. Don't
they ever do any schoolwork?
COM                             96 min (ort 103 min)
B,V                                            CBS

## GINGER IN THE MORNING **
                                              PG
Gordon Wiles      USA                 1973
*Sissy Spacek, Monte Markham, Mark Miller, Susan*
*Oliver, Slim Pickens*
A lonely divorced salesman picks up a young female
hitch-hiker, but his relationship with her is compli-
cated by his best friend. A variable romantic comedy
that remains largely unfocused and undeveloped.
COM                                         89 min
B,V                                            PRV

## GIRL CALLED JULES, A ***
                                              18
Tonino Valeril      ITALY             1970
*Silvia Dionisio, Gianni Maechia, Anna Moffo, Malissa*
*Longo, John Steiner, Livio Barbo, Roberto Chevalier,*
*Raul Martinez, Riccardo Garrone, Nino Niki*
A teenage girl seduced by her governess finds it
difficult to form a lasting relationship with a man. She
has many affairs but none provide her with lasting
satisfaction, until she meets a successful artist and
embarks on a passionate affair.
Aka: GIRL NAMED JULIUS, A; LA RAGAZZA DI
NOME GIULIO; MODEL LOVE (ROXY)
A                                           81 min
B,V                   DFS: XTACY/KRP; ROXY; GOST

## GIRL CAN'T HELP IT, THE ***
                                                U
Frank Tashlin      USA                1956
*Jayne Mansfield, Edmond O'Brien, Tom Ewell, Henry*
*Jones, John Emery, Julie London, Ray Anthony, Fats*
*Domino, Little Richard, The Platters, Gene Vincent*
A gangster prevails upon a theatrical agent to groom
the former's dumb girlfriend for stardom. A mixture of
scatterbrained plotting, good sight gags and an end-
less series of jokes regarding the star's ample bosom.
Worth a look for a set of classic performances from
Fats Domino and friends. Songs include "Blue Mon-
day", "You'll Never Know", "BeBop A Lula", "She's
Got It" and the title song.
Boa: story Do Re Mi by Garson Kanin.
COM                             97 min (ort 99 min)
V/h                                            CBS

## GIRL FROM TRIESTE, THE **
Pasquale Festa Campanile
                      ITALY           1983
*Ben Gazzara, Ornella Muti, Mimsy Farmer*
A cartoonist wants to get away from it all on holiday
in Trieste. There he meets and has an affair with a
local girl who's a voluntary patient at a psychiatric
clinic.
Aka: LA RAGAZZA DI TRIESTE
DRA                                        103 min
B,V                                       APX; VFP

## GIRL IN A SWING, THE *
                                              18
Gordon Hessler      UK/USA            1989
*Meg Tilly, Rupert Frazer, Nicholas Le Prevost, Elspet*
*Gray, Lorna Heilbron, Helen Cherry*
Overblown adaptation of the Adams novel in which a
foolish antique dealer develops a passion for a mysterious German femme fatale, and pursues her to the
point of marriage. He then has to suffer the consequences of his hasty action when he is forced to contend
with her disturbed behaviour. A good deal of softcore
coupling fails to enliven this shallow and deadening
melodrama.
Boa: novel by Richard Adams.

DRA                          104 min (ort 112 min)
V                                         FUTUR

## GIRL IN EVERY PORT, A *
Chester Erskine          USA                1952
*Groucho Marx, William Bendix, Marie Wilson, Don
DeFore, Gene Lockhart, Dee Hartford*
Two sailors are tricked into buying a useless race-
horse which they attempt to hide on their ship, while
trying to win a race with an identical horse. A dated
and contrived romp that wastes the considerable
comic talents of a fine cast.
Osca: RETURN OF THE BADMEN
COM                      84 min (ort 86 min) B/W
B,V                                          KVD

## GIRL IN GOLD BOOTS **
Ted V. Mikels            USA                1968
*Jody Daniel, Leslie McRae, Tom Pace, Bara Byrnes,
Rafael Campos, Mark Herron, Bill Bagdad, Victor
Izay, Harry Lovejoy, James Victor, Rod Wilmoth,
Chris Howard, Mike Garrison, Michael Derrick,
Sheila Roberts*
A low-budget look at the 1960s guitar culture com-
plete with lashings of music, sex and drugs. A girl
dreams of stardom and takes the first step on this road
by becoming a go-go dancer, only to find that fame has
a bitter price.
MUS                                       90 min
V                                            VCL

## GIRL IN THE EMPTY GRAVE, THE *            U
Lou Antonio              USA                1977
*Andy Griffith, James Cromwell, Mitzi Hoag, Sharon
Spelman, Hunter Von Leer, Claude Earl Jones, Jenny
Neumann, Edward Winter, Jonathan Banks, George
Gaynes, Byron Morrow, Mary-Robin Redd, Deborah
White, Robert F. Simon*
Third and failed attempt to build a TV series around
the character of a small-town sheriff. Here, he is
called upon to solve the mystery of a "dead" woman
who suddenly reappears among the living. Well below
average. Followed by THE DEADLY GAME.
DRA                     87 min (ort 100 min) mTV
B,V                                          MGM

## GIRL IN THE PICTURE, THE **                15
Cary Parker              UK                 1985
*David McKay, John Gordon-Sinclair, Irina Brook,
Gregor Fisher, Paul Young, Caroline Guthrie, Simone
Lahbib, Kathy Hale, Benny Young, Joyce Deans, Rikki
Fulton, John Christie, Walter Carr, William Elliott,
Jonathan Watson*
Trio of romantic tales set against the background of a
Glasgow photographer, his studio and his desire to
break up his relationship with his live-in girlfriend.
When she does finally leave him, he discovers that he
cannot live without her, in this palatable but trivial
romantic comedy.
COM                          85 min (ort 91 min)
B,V                                          RNK

## GIRL IN THE RED VELVET SWING, THE **      PG
Richard Fleischer        USA                1955
*Joan Collins, Ray Milland, Farley Granger, Cornelia
Otis Skinner, Glenda Farrell, Luther Adler*
A glossy, soap opera-style reconstruction of the
famous murder case in the early 1900s when mil-
lionaire Harry K. Thaw killed famed playboy
architect Stanford White over his affair with his wife.
Despite having a good cast, the deficiencies of the
script dispel any impact the story might have de-
veloped.
DRA                                      109 min
V                                            CBS

## GIRL MOST LIKELY, THE **                   U
Mitchell Leisen          USA                1956
*Jane Powell, Cliff Robertson, Keith Andes, Kaye
Ballard, Tommy Noonan, Una Merkel*
In this musical entertainment a girl has to choose who
she wants to marry from among three men, one of
whom is a millionaire. A boring remake of TOM,
DICK AND HARRY that's partially redeemed by
some fair songs.
MUS                          94 min (ort 98 min)
B,V                           KVD; VCC (VHS only)

## GIRL OF PASSION **                         18
Omiros Efstratiadis    GREECE              198-
*Maria Vassilou, Dimitra Galani, Nicolas Galanos,
Costas Caragiorgis*
Routine sex film severely pruned from its hardcore
original.
A      70 min; 80 min (SHEP) (ort 112 min) Cut (50 sec)
B,V                     18PLAT/TOW; SHEP

## GIRL ON A MOTORCYCLE                       18
Jack Cardiff          FRANCE/UK            1968
*Marianne Faithfull, Alain Delon, Roger Mutton,
Marius Goring, Catherine Jourdan, Jean Leduc,
Jacques Marin, John G. Heller*
One of the dullest and most pointless films ever made.
A woman leaves her husband and goes on her
motorbike to see her lover. The film consists of an
interminable series of her recollections which take
place along the journey. The sudden end is meant to
shock but instead comes as a blessed relief.
Aka: LA MOTORCYCLETTE; NAKED UNDER
LEATHER
Boa: novel La Motocyclette by Pieyre de Mardiargues.
DRA                                       91 min
V                                         CASPIC

## GIRL TO KILL FOR, A *                      18
Richard Oliver           USA                1989
*Karen Medak, Sasha Jenson*
Story of a girl called Sue, so voluptuous that men
might kill for a date with her. And some do just that,
in this low-grade exercise in exploitative nonsense.
THR                                       85 min
V                                            EIV

## GIRL TROUBLE *                             PG
Menahem Golan            UK                 1969
*Norman Wisdom, Sally Geeson, Terence Alexander,
Sarah Atkinson, Sally Bazeley, Derek Francis, David
Lodge, Paul Whitsun-Jones, George Meaton, The
Pretty Things*
A banker on his way to a conference, falls for a a
teenage hitch-hiker he gives a lift to in this feeble sex
comedy. Written by Wisdom.
Aka: NORMAN WISDOM: GIRL TROUBLE;
WHAT'S GOOD FOR THE GOOSE
COM                     94 min; 84 min (KRP) (ort 105 min)
B,V                     HOK L/A; FOX L/A; KRP

## GIRL WHO COULDN'T SAY NO, THE **
Franco Brusati         ITALY               1968
*George Segal, Virna Lisi, Lila Kedrova, Akim
Tamiroff, Paola Pitagora, Felicity Mason*
An eccentric girl and a medical assistant enjoy a
relationship that has more than its fair share of ups
and downs. A mild romantic comedy of no great merit.
Aka: IL SUO MODO DI FARE
COM                          80 min (ort 104 min)
B,V                                      VCL/CBS

## GIRL WHO SPELLED FREEDOM, THE ***          U
Simon Wincer             USA                1986
*Wayne Rogers, Mary Kay Place, Kieu Chinh, Kathleen
Sisk, Margot Pinvidic, Susan Walden, Blu Mankuma,
Jade Chinn, Diana Ung, Linda Wong, Jasmin Tam,
Wilson Lo, Raymond Lau*
An American couple sponsor a refugee family for
re-settlement in the USA, where they face the painful
process of coming to terms with a completely new
language and way of life. A surprisingly enjoyable

story based on the real-life experiences of a Cambodian refugee who arrived in the USA in 1979, speaking hardly any English, and won a national spelling competition four years later. Scripted by Wincer, Christopher Knopf and David A. Simons.

DRA                                 91 min (ort 100 min) mTV
B,V                                                              WDV

## GIRL WITH THE GREEN EYES, THE **

Desmond Davis              UK                    1964
Rita Tushingham, Peter Finch, Lynn Redgrave, T.P. McKenna, Julian Glover, Marie Kean, Arthur O'Sullivan, Lislott Goettinger, Eileen Crowe, Harry Brogan, Patrick Laffan
An innocent Irish girl falls madly in love with an older man, in this minor romance that's helped along by nice Dublin locations.
Aka: GIRL WITH GREEN EYES
Boa: novel The Lonely Girl by Edna O'Brien.

DRA                           89 min (ort 91 min) B/W
B,V                                                             TEVP

## GIRL/BOY *

Bob Kellett                 UK                    1972
Joan Greenwood, Michael Horden, Clive Francis, Patricia Routledge, Peter Bull, Rudolph Walker, Elizabeth Welch, Roberta Gibbs, Jonathan Kramer, Diana Hodinott
The son of a headmaster is constantly at odds with his parents. One day he comes home with a new friend who is both black and of indeterminate sex, in this peculiar one-joke comedy that revolves around the efforts his parents make to determine the identity of their guest. A ghastly and severely over-extended tale that might have worked well enough as a ten-minute sketch, though even that would have been nine minutes too long.
Aka: GIRL STROKE BOY
Boa: play Girlfriend by David Percival.

COM                          84 min (ort 88 min)
B,V,V2                                             VCL/CBS

## GIRL, THE *                                     18

Arne Mattsson          SWEDEN                    1987
Franco Nero, Christopher Lee, Bernice Stegers, Clare Powney, Frank Brennan, Mark Robinson, Clifford Rose, Lenore Zann
A married lawyer embarks on an affair with a precocious 14-year-old, with tragic and violent consequences. An inane and tedious softcore drama that goes on long past the point where all interest in the characters has evaporated.

A/AD                        103 min (ort 108 min) Cut (9 sec)
B,V                                                              RCA

## GIRLFRIEND FROM HELL **                         18

Daniel M. Peterson      USA                    1989
Liane Curtis, Dana Ashbrook, Leslie Deane, James Doughton
A comedy-horror yarn directed at the teen end of the market, with a boring and unattractive woman becoming possessed by the Devil and turning into a beguiling siren. However, she now embarks on an orgy of self-fulfilment and destruction, and a demon hunter sets out to put a stop to her shenanigans.

COM                                               89 min
V                                                              FUTUR

## GIRLFRIENDS *

Alex De Renzy            USA                    1983
Janey Robbins, Lili Marlene, Taire Aire, John Leslie, Jamie Gillis, Ron Jeremy, Genoa
A series of unrelated cameos strung together to form a film whose explicit content will be toned down to comply with UK legislation. The film opens with a lesbian encounter, moves on to a sex contest and then continues with more of the same. A tedious and incoherent mess.

A                                                 85 min
B,V,V2                                                          TCX

## GIRL'S BEST FRIEND, A ***

Henri Pachard            USA                    1981
Juliet Anderson, Veronica Hart, Bobby Astyr, Ron Jeremy, Richard Bolla, Samantha Fox, Jody Maxwell, Merle Michaels
Sex comedy about a mother and son who work as jewel thieves, only stealing from the super-rich. Whilst Mom keeps a count occupied, her son searches for a priceless diamond to add to their collection. They follow the gem to New York and the home of a wealthy importer, to whom the count sold it. But his maid steals the diamond and then goes after their collection too. However, both mother and son catch her and all three end up as lovers.

A                                                 84 min
B,V                                              XTACY/KRP

## GIRLS COME FIRST *

Joseph McGrath (Croisette Meuble)
                          UK                    1975
John Hamil, Bill Kerr, Burt Kwouk, Sue Longhurst, Rikki Howard, Cherly Gilham, Hazel O'Connor, Bobbie Sparrow, Heather Dealey
Sex comedy in which a porno magazine publisher hires an artist to draw the hostesses at his nightclub. A very dull effort with a deliberately misleading title.

A                                42 min (ort 45 min)
B,V                                                             WOV

## GIRLS FOR RENT *

Al Adamson               USA                    1974
Georgina Spelvin, Susan McIver, Rosalind Miles, Preston PIerce, Kent Taylor, Robert Livingston
Low-budget chase thriller about a female contract killer that is little more than an attempt to cash in on Spelvin's success in the porno classic THE DEVIL IN MISS JONES.

THR                             86 min (ort 92 min)
B,V                                               INT/CBS

## GIRLS IN THE OFFICE, THE **

Ted Post                 USA                    1979
Barbara Eden, Susan St James, Tony Roberts, Robyn Douglass, Penny Peyser, Joe Penny, Jonathan Goldsmith, David Wayne, Jaki Morrison, Hugh Gorian, Nik Hagler, Gretana Campbell, Yvonne McCord, David Wurst, Eddie Hinton
Three women begin work at a department store in Texas, and use various methods to advance their careers in this predictable romantic comedy.
Boa: book by Jack Olsen.

COM                           97 min (ort 104 min) mTV
B,V                                           VFP L/A; HER

## GIRLS JUST WANT TO HAVE FUN: THE MOVIE
**                                                PG

Alan Metter              USA                    1985
Sarah Jessica Parker, Lee Montgomery, Morgan Woodward, Biff Yeager, Shannon Doherty, Jonathan Silverman, Helen Hunt, Holly Gagnier, Ed Lauter, Ian Giatti, Margaret Howell, Terence McGovern, Richard Blade, Kristi Somers
Three girls enter a musical competition for a cable TV station. A fairly cliche-ridden comedy that's saved by good performances from Parker and Hunt.

COM                          83 min (ort 89 min) Cut (33 sec)
B,V                                       POLY; CH5 (VHS only)

## GIRLS OF GODIVA HIGH, THE **

Jim Clark                USA                    1981
Kitsy Storme, Mae East, Meryl Michaels, Richard Bolla, Bob Presley, Daphne, Danielle, Susan De Angelis, Ron Jeremy
The girls of Godiva School all sleep in a barracks-style dormitory and are all virgins. What story there is, involves the middle-aged school handyman who teaches the girls all about sex. By way of a sub-plot there is a ban on the girls having a disco graduation

party, but they use their ingenuity to get round this.
Aka: GODIVA GIRLS; GOOD GIRLS OF GODIVA
HIGH, THE
A                                                89 min
B,V                                              RIP

## GIRL'S SCHOOL SCREAMERS *                     18
John P. Finegan          USA             1986
*Mollie O'Mara, Sharon Christopher, Mari Butler, Beth
O'Malley, Karen Krevitz*
Seven girls spend a weekend in a deserted house to
catalogue works of art prior to auction, and become
prey to supernatural forces, screaming their heads off
in this laughable effort.
Aka: DEATH LEGACY; GIRL SCHOOL
SCREAMERS (PALAN); PORTRAIT, THE
HOR                                              87 min
B,V                                     PVG; PALAN

## GISELLE **
Victor di Mello         BRAZIL           1981
*Alba Valeria, Maria Lucia Dahl, Carlo Mossey*
Story of a young girl's sexual adventures with all and
sundry.
Aka: HER SUMMER VACATION
A                                                92 min
B,V                                       LOTUS/CBS

## GITANOS: ESCAPE FROM APARTHEID **             15
Sidney Hayers           USA              1976
*Elke Sommer, Patrick Mower, Dean Stockwell,
Bradford Dillman, Roberta Durrant*
A gypsy, serving a sentence in a South African prison
camp for avenging his girlfriend's rape, escapes across
the veldt; helped by his two brothers, who make good
use of their motorcycling skills in plotting his escape.
Aka: ESCAPE FROM APARTHEID; ONE AWAY
THR                                              96 min
B,V                              VUL L/A; VID L/A; FOX

## GIVE MY REGARDS TO BROAD STREET *      PG
Peter Webb              UK               1984
*Paul McCartney, Bryan Brown, Ringo Starr, Linda
McCartney, Ralph Richardson, Barbara Bach, Tracey
Ullman, George Martin, Ian Hastings, John Bennett,
Luke McMasters, Philip Jackson, Marie Colett, John
Harding, Mark Baldwin*
Musical fantasy revolving around the theft of McCart-
ney's tapes for his latest album. A silly vanity vehicle
that is worth listening to if not watching. Songs
include "Ballroom Dancing" and "No More Lonely
Nights".
MUS                          104 min (ort 108 min)
B,V                                             CBS

## GLADIATOR, THE **                            15
Abel Ferrara            USA              1986
*Ken Wahl, Nancy Allen, Robert Culp, Stan Shaw,
Rosemary Forsyth, Linda Thorson, Bart Braverman,
Brian Robbins, Rick Dees, Michael Young, Harry
Beer, Gary Goodrow, Gary Lev, Georgie Paul, Mort
Sertner, Mary Baldwin*
Los Angeles is the setting for this tale of a homicidal
maniac called "The Skull", who drives round town in
his "death car" killing people at random. Wahl plays a
mechanic who becomes obsessed with ideas of revenge
when his younger brother becomes one of the victims.
He sets about converting his truck into an armoured
car.
A/AD                                       94 min mTV
B,V                                             NWV

## GLASS HOUSE, THE ***                         15
Tom Gries               USA              1972
*Alan Alda, Vic Morrow, Dean Jagger, Billy Dee
Williams, Clu Gulager, Scott Hylands, Tony Mancini,
Kristoffer Tabori*
A view of life in a state prison seen from the inside,
and following two newcomers, one a college professor

who has committed manslaughter and the other an
idealistic warder. This harsh and convincing look at
prison life follows one prisoner and his brave attempts
to get involved in prison reform. The script is by Tracy
Keenan Wynn.
Aka: TRUMAN CAPOTE'S THE GLASS HOUSE
Boa: short story by Truman Capote and Wyatt Cooper.
DRA                                        73 min mTV
B,V                                 ODY; CH5 (VHS only)

## GLASS JUNGLE, THE **                         18
Joseph Merhi            USA              1988
*Lee Canalito, Diana Frank, Frank Scala, Mark High,
Joe Filbeck, Richard Pepin, Paul Volk, Red Horton,
Judy Yonemoto*
Terrorists threaten massive destruction of L.A. unless
they get a $5,000,000 ransom and an innocent cab-
driver gets caught up in the confrontation. Average.
A/AD                                 82 min Cut (1 sec)
V                                               BOX

## GLASS MENAGERIE, THE ***                     PG
Paul Newman             USA              1987
*Joanne Woodward, Karen Allen, John Malkovich,
James Naughton*
Depression-era Southern drama with Woodward the
domineering matriarch whose memories of her happy
youth as a Southern belle are her only means of escape
from her cramped existence in a St Louis apartment.
Sharing her home with her crippled daughter and
rebellious son, she attempts to arrange a date for the
girl, but one night the arrival of a "gentleman caller"
brings some bitter truths out into the open. A well
made and powerfully acted drama.
Boa: play by Tennessee Williams.
DRA                                            129 min
B,V                                             RCA

## GLEAMING THE CUBE **                         PG
Graeme Clifford         USA              1988
*Christian Slater, Steven Bauer, Ed Lauter, Micole
Mercurio, Richard Herd, Charles Cyphers, Le Tuan,
Minh Luong, Kieu Chinh*
A competent murder mystery that's clearly aimed at
the teen set, with a rebellious skateboarding youngs-
ter out to solve the death of his adopted Vietnamese
brother, getting some help along the way from a smart
detective. A series of spectacular skateboarding stunts
and the pleasing performances keep the film rolling
despite the thin storyline.
A/AD                                           104 min
V                                               MGM

## GLEN AND RANDA *
Jim McBride             USA              1971
*Steven Curry, Shelley Plimpton, Woodrow Chambliss,
Garry Goodrow, Roy Fox*
Twenty-five years after a nuclear war, two young
people set out in search of a legendary city where life
has been unaffected by the war. On their journey they
ponder on the destruction of human civilisation.
Tiresome and pompous.
FAN                                             94 min
B,V                                             VFP

## GLENN MILLER STORY, THE ***                  U
Anthony Mann            USA              1954
*James Stewart, June Allyson, Henry Morgan, Charles
Drake, George Tobias, Frances Langford, Louis
Armstrong, Gene Krupa*
An excellent account of the life of this unforgettable
band leader, in which the over-sentimental plot takes
very much second place to Miller's great music.
MUS                          108 min (ort 116 min)
V/sh                                            CIC

## GLITCH! **                                   15
Nico Mastorakis        USA              1987

Steve Donmeyer, Julia Nickson, Terry Weigel, Ted
Lange, Dick Gautier, Willi Egan, Ji Tu Kambuka
Softcore sex farce with two inept burglars being
mistaken for film tycoons when they raid a Hollywood
mansion. Thereafter they find themselves forced to
continue the charade, auditioning a bevy of girls.
Their pleasure is somewhat muted when they learn
that the Mob has put a price on their head, in this
mildly amusing but incoherent tale.
COM                              86 min Cut (44 sec)
B,V                                             MED

## GLITTER DOME, THE ** 18
Stuart Margolin        USA               1984
James Garner, John Lithgow, Margot Kidder, Colleen
Dewhurst, John Marley, Stuart Margolin, Paul Koslo,
Alex Diakun, Billy Kerr, William Taylor, Dusty
Morean, Christianne Hirt, Tom McBeath, Dixie Seatle,
Dale Wilson, Sal Lopez
Two tired and cynical Hollywood vice-cops, investi-
gate the murder of a studio head and uncover a really
nasty business. Co-produced by Margolin who also
wrote the music. Average.
Boa: novel by Joseph Wambaugh.
DRA                                       90 min mCab
B,V                              TEVP; WHV (VHS only)

## GLITTERBALL, THE ** U
Harley Cokliss         UK                1977
Ben Buckton, Keith Jayne, Ron Pember, Marjorie
Yates, Andrew Jackson, Barry Jackson
The children of an RAF sergeant find a crashed UFO
from the planet Starga and rescue the injured alien,
but find that it has an insatiable appetite for human
food.
FAN                               53 min (ort 56 min)
B,V                                             RNK

## GLITZ * 15
Sandor Stern           USA               1989
Jimmy Smits, Markie Post, John Diehl, Madison
Mason, Ken Foree, Geno Silva, James Purcell, Robin
Strasser
A tough Miami cop hunts the killer of his girlfriend in
this mundane and forgettable adaptation of Leonard's
novel.
Boa: novel by Elmore Leonard.
A/AD                       95 min (Ort 100 min) mTV
V                                               WHV

## GLO FRIENDS SAVE CHRISTMAS, THE ** U
1986
Story of little luminous creatures, who fight a wicked
witch plotting to stop Santa Claus and his reindeer in
their tracks. They leave their celebration preparations in Gloland and come to the rescue.
CAR                                          44 min
V                                               VGM

## GLO FRIENDS: THE MOVIE – THE QUEST *** U
1987
Animated feature based on the popular Hasbro soft
toy characters, with our little luminous friends discovering that they are running out of Moondrops, so
they set off to find the Moondrop Lake and replenish
their stock. On the way they have various adventures
and face danger from Rook and the nasty Moligans.
Aka: GLO FRIENDS: THE QUEST
CAR                                          93 min
V                                               MSD

## GLORIA *** 15
John Cassavetes        USA               1980
Gena Rowlands, Buck Henry, John Adames, Julie
Carmen, Lupe Guarnica
An ex-gangster's moll protects a young boy after his
parents have been killed by the Mob, but finds that
she has to resort to violence. Generally entertaining
but seriously overlong. There is a point being made in

there but one cannot be sure what it is. Written by
Cassavetes.
DRA                        116 min (ort 121 min)
B,V                                    XTASY; RCA

## GLORIFYING THE AMERICAN GIRL ***
Milliard Webb/John Harkrider
                        USA               1929
Mary Eaton, Edward Crandall, Eddie Cantor, Helen
Morgan, Rudy Vallee, Adolph Zucker, Florenz
Ziegfeld, Jimmy Walker, Johnny Weissmuller, Otto
Kahn, Texas Guinan, Noah Beery, Norman
Brokenshire, Charles Dillingham
Early Ziegfeld-produced talkie musical, revolving
around the flimsy plot of a girl who wants to make it
in showbiz – this routine story is no more than an
excuse to parade a series of dazzling, bizarre and often
still impressive numbers. Some two-colour Technico-
lor sequences were shot for a number in the last reel,
but no prints appear to have survived.
Osca: FIRST MRS FRASER, THE
MUS                        80 min (ort 87 min) B/W
V                                              WOOD

## GLORIOUS MUSKETEERS, THE **
John Halas       FRANCE/ITALY/UK          1974
Voices of: John Fortune, Maurice Denham, Roy
Kinnear, Adrienne Corri
Satisfactory animated adventure film based on this
Dumas famous legend.
Aka: D'ARTAGNAN L'INTREPIDE
CAR                                          67 min
V                                             VIPCO

## GLORY **** 15
Edward Zwick           USA               1989
Matthew Broderick, Denzel Washington, Cary Elwes,
Morgan Freeman, Jihmi Kennedy, Andre Braugher,
John Finn, Donovan Leitch, John David Cullum, Bob
Gunton, Cliff De Young
An anti-war film with a difference, that focuses on the
role played by black soldiers in the American Civil
War, when a naive Northerner is given the job of
training the Union Army's first black unit. Partly
based on the letters written by the unit's young
commander, this outstanding story is performed with
complete conviction and directed with consummate
skill. Screenplay is by Kevin Jarre. AA: S. Actor
(Washington), Cin (Freddie Francis).
DRA                                         128 min
V                                               RCA

## GLORY BOYS, THE * 15
Michael Ferguson       UK/USA            1982
Rod Steiger, Joanna Lumley, Alfred Burke, Anthony
Perkins, Gary Brown, Aaron Harris
A spy thriller originally shown on TV in three
60-minute episodes, in which IRA and Arab terrorists
join forces in order to assassinate a scientist visiting
London. Bad casting and hammy production values
resulted in a film that sank without trace.
Boa: novel by Gerald Seymour.
THR                        105 min (ort 180 min) mTV
V                                               VCC

## GLOVE, THE *
Ross Hagen             USA               1978
John Saxon, Rosey Grier, Joanna Cassidy, Joan
Blondell, Jack Carter, Aldo Ray, Keenan Wynn
An ex-con armed with a steel glove who is out for
revenge, tangles with a world-weary bounty hunter. A
routine actioner that is little more than a vehicle for a
series of violent battles.
A/AD                                         91 min
B,V                                         INT/CBS

## GNOMEMOBILE, THE ** U
Robert Stevenson       USA               1967
Walter Brennan, Matthew Garber, Karen Dotrice,

*Richard Deacon, Ed Wynn, Sean McClory, Tom Lowell, Cami Sebring*
A businessman and his relatives come across two lost gnomes in a forest, and try to protect them from freak-show owners and land developers. A lively Disney candyfloss of a film with good effects and broad comedy.
Boa: novel by Upton Sinclair
COM                                            90 min
B,V                                             WDV

### GNOMES ***
                                                1980
Delightful animated fantasy, based on the books of Wil Huygen and Rien Poortlivet, in which a group of gnomes are harassed by their evil adversaries, the over-sized trolls, but win through in the end. Not the most exciting animation, perhaps, but distinctive figures and a good plot make this an enjoyable film for kids of all ages.
Boa: novel by Wil Huygen.
CAR                                            47 min
V                                               RCA

### GO FOR BROKE ***                            U
Paul Aaron            USA
*Cindy Williams, Tony Randal, Catherine Helmond*
High-spirited Disney comedy with a penniless and down-on-her-luck actress landing a job and earning enough money to pay for an operation for her dog. She soon gets embroiled in a series of comic mishaps and gets mixed up in a bank raid.
COM                                            90 min
V                                               WDV

### GO FOR GOLD **                              15
Stuart F. Fleming SOUTH AFRICA                  1984
*Cameron Mitchell, Sandra Horne, Tamara Franke, James Ryan, M'Zwandile*
A long-distance runner has to choose between staying honest or accepting the help of criminals in his bid for success.
A/AD                                           95 min
B,V                                             VES

### GO FOR IT **                                15
E.B. Clucher (Enzo Barboni)
                    ITALY/USA                   1983
*Terence Hill (Mario Girotti), Bud Spencer (Carlo Pedersoli), David Huddleston*
Our two heroes are mistaken for secret agents and are chased by villains. Another formula Hill-Spencer pairing, with the usual slapstick antics and broad comedy.
COM               104 min (ort 109 min) Cut (34 sec)
B,V                                             WHV

### GO HOG WILD **
Les Rose              USA                       1979
*Patti D'Arbanville, Michael Biehn, Tony Rosato, Angelo Rizacos, Martin Doyle, Claude Philippe, Matt Craven, Jack Blum, Keith Knight, Michael Zelniker, Robin McCulloch, Sean McCann, John C. Ritter, Bronwen Mantel*
A juvenile comedy about a motorcycle gang coming into conflict with college students.
Aka: HOG WILD
COM                                            93 min
B,V,V2                                          VPD

### GO KIDS, THE **                             PG
Brian Trenchard Smith
                    AUSTRALIA                   1985
*Henry Thomas, Tony Barry, David Ravenswood, John Ewart, Rachel Friend*
A young boy investigates an Aborigine legend, and stumbles into an exciting adventure in this appealing kid's film.
Aka: FROG DREAMING

JUV                                            89 min
B,V                                             PVG

### GO TELL THE SPARTANS ***                    15
Ted Post              USA                       1978
*Burt Lancaster, Craig Wasson, Jonathan Goldsmith, Marc Singer, Joe Unger, David Clennon, Dolph Sweet, James Hong*
In Vietnam an experienced commander has to rescue a platoon of raw recruits from a Vietcong ambush. A realistic war story that is far better than one would have expected, mainly thanks to Wendell Mayes' literate and often caustic script.
Boa: novel Incident At Muc Wa by Daniel Ford.
WAR                                            114 min
B,V                                             WHV

### GO TO BLAZES *                              U
Michael Truman        UK                        1962
*Dave King, Daniel Massey, Norman Rossington, Wilfrid Lawson, Maggie Smith, Robert Morley, Coral Browne*
With the help of an arsonist a bunch of former convicts pose as firemen, but only in order to use their fire engine to rob a bank. A very tame effort indeed; the unnecessary use of Cinemascope (lost on TV) was more of a distraction than an asset.
COM                             90 min (ort 84 min)
V                                               WHV

### GO TOWARD THE LIGHT **                      PG
Mike Robe             USA                       1989
*Linda Hamilton, Richard Thomas, Ned Beatty, Piper Laurie, Joshua Harris, Brian Bonsall, Rosemary Dunsmore*
A sincere but sombre tale of a family who have to live with the certain knowledge that their haemophiliac child has contracted AIDS and is soon to die. The film does what it can with the material, but the constant note of gloom makes it difficult to watch.
Aka: GO TO THE LIGHT
DRA                         92 min (ort 100 min) mTV
V                                               PRISM

### GO-BETWEEN, THE **
Joseph Losey          UK                        1970
*Julie Christie, Alan Bates, Michael Redgrave, Dominic Guard, Edward Fox, Margaret Leighton, Michael Gough, Richard Gibson, Simon Hume-Kendall, Amaryllis Garnett, Roger Lloyd Pack*
A 12-year-old boy is used to carry messages between his friend's sister and a poor tenant farmer. A rather ponderous and over-rated recreation of the life and times of Edwardian gentry. Scripted by Harold Pinter.
Boa: novel by L.P. Hartley.
DRA                         112 min (ort 116 min)
B,V                      TEVP; WHV (VHS only)

### GOBOTS: BATTLE OF THE ROCK LORDS *          PG
Don Lusk/Ray Patterson/Alan Zaslove
                    USA                         1986
*Voices of: Margot Kidder, Roddy McDowall, Michael Nouri, Telly Savalas*
Animated feature in which our robot heroes battle strange rocklike creatures that can transform themselves into humanoid form. As ever, the fate of galaxies hangs on the outcome. Both plot and animation are sadly devoid of imagination in this lavish Hanna-Barbera production, inspired by a TV series.
CAR                                            74 min
B,V                                             EIV

### GOBOTS: THE ORIGINAL FULL LENGTH            U
### STORY **
                    USA                         1986
Animated feature based on robot toys – in this story our robot guardians from the planet Gobotron must once more do battle with evil renegades in order to save the Earth from destruction.

CAR                                    100 min
B,V                                       VCC

## GOD BLESS THE CHILD ***                    15
Larry Elikann          USA                1988
*Mare Winningham, Dorian Harewood, Grace*
*Johnston, Charlaine Woodard, Obba Babatunde, L.*
*Scott Caldwell*
The story of a homeless single mother who is caught
with her young daughter in a poverty trap. A rarity –
a film with a social conscience that does not preach.
The script is by Dennis Nemec.
DRA                    93 min (ort 96 min) mTV
B,V                                      SONY

## GODDESS OF LOVE, THE ***                   15
James R. Drake         USA                1988
*Vanna White, David Naughton*
On the night of his bachelor party a young man slips
his wedding ring on a stone statue of Venus for a joke.
The statue is transformed into a real live goddess, who
is determined to take him back with her to Mount
Olympus to be her lover. Now torn between two
women, his troubles are exacerbated when he finds
himself being pursued by two crooks who had original-
ly stolen the statue from a museum.
COM                                     90 min
B,V                                       CHV

## GODFATHER, THE ****                        18
Francis Ford Coppola   USA                1971
*Marlon Brando, Al Pacino, Robert Duvall, James*
*Caan, Diane Keaton, Sterling Hayden, Richard*
*Castellano, John Cazale, Talia Shire, Richard Conte,*
*John Marley, Al Lettieri, Abe Vigoda, Morgana King,*
*Alex Rocco*
A superb evocation of the life of a Mafia family and the
problems that arise when one of the sons takes over as
head on the death of his father. Not so much a sequel
as a closer examination of the story followed soon
after. The script is by Francis Ford Coppola and Mario
Puzo. AA: Pic, Actor (Brando), Screen (Adapt) (Mario
Puzo/Francis Ford Coppola).
Boa: novel by Mario Puzo.
DRA                    167 min (ort 175 min)
B,V                                       CIC

## GODFATHER OF HONG KONG *
Roc Tien              HONG KONG            1972
*Roc Tien, Chen Hung-Lieh, Tien He*
Two police agents break up a Japanese-run opium
ring.
Aka: NOTORIOUS BANDIT, THE; TA E KOU
MAR                                     89 min
B,V                                   INT/CBS

## GODFATHER PART 2, THE ****                 18
Francis Ford Coppola   USA                1974
*Al Pacino, Robert De Niro, Robert Duvall, Diane*
*Keaton, Lee Strasberg, Talia Shire, John Cazale,*
*Michael V. Gazzo, G.D. Spradlin, Morgana King,*
*Mariana Hill, Troy Donahue, Joe Spinell, Abe Vigoda,*
*Fay Spain, Harry Dean Stanton*
A sequel that alternates between the early days of the
title character and the problems experienced by his
son and successor. Somewhat convoluted and hard to
follow, but full of memorable moments and thoroughly
entertaining. AA: Pic, Dir, S. Actor (De Niro), Screen
(Adapt) (Francis Ford Coppola/Mario Puzo), Art/Set
(Dean Tavoularis and Angelo Graham/George R.
Nelson), Score (Orig) (Nino Rota/Carmine Coppola).
Boa: novel by Mario Puzo.
DRA                    190 min (ort 200 min)
B,V                                       CIC

## GODMOTHERS, THE **
William Grefe          USA
*Mickey Rooney, Jerry Lester, Frank Fontaine*
Fatuous, giddy Mafia spoof that attempts to make fun

of gangster movies.
COM                                     80 min
B,V,V2                                    VPD

## GOD'S GUN **                               18
Frank Kramer (Gianfranco Parolini)
                       ITALY              1976
*Richard Boone, Lee Van Cleef, Jack Palance,*
*Christopher George, Lynda Day George, Leif Garnett,*
*Robert Lipton, Cody Palance*
A former gunslinger avenges the killing of a preacher
and stands up to a six-man gang. A moderate action
tale filmed in Israel.
WES                                     89 min
B,V                                       RNK

## GODS MUST BE CRAZY, THE ***                PG
Jamie Uys             BOTSWANA            1981
*N!xau, Marius Weyes, Sandra Prinsloo, Louw Verwey,*
*Jamie Uys, Michael Thys, Nic de Jager*
A Coca Cola bottle dropped from a plane, brings havoc
to the life of a tribe of Kalahari bushmen. An
unexpectedly engaging comedy that after a slow start
parades a sequence of slapstick incidents and catas-
trophes. Written by Uys and followed by a sequel.
COM                                     108 min
B,V                                  GHV; CBS

## GODS MUST BE CRAZY 2, THE ***              PG
Jamie Uys          BOTSWANA/USA
                        1989 (released 1990)
*N!xau, Lena Farugia, Hans Strydom, Eiros, Nadies,*
*Erick Bowen*
A charming and gently amusing sequel to the first
film that follows the exploits of our bushman N!xau,
who has to retrieve his two children when they are
inadvertently carried off to civilisation in the back of a
poacher's truck. The film began production in 1985
but completion and release were delayed for several
years.
COM                    93 min (ort 97 min)
V                                         CBS

## GODS MUST WAIT, THE **                     15
Ted Post               USA                1972
*Jan-Michael Vincent, Gary Crosby, Bonnie Bedelia,*
*Herschel Bernardi, Mariette Hartley, Loretta Leversee,*
*Lloyd Gough, William Long Jr, William Hansen,*
*Mimi Davis, Dick Valentine, Jody Hauber*
The spirit of a young man killed in a car crash returns
to Earth, and embarks on a supernatural romance
with a lonely young woman. The first TV movie shot
using a single-camera videotape system and then
transferred to film. Average.
Aka: SANDCASTLES
DRA                                  91 min mTV
B,V                                       SID

## GODSEND, THE **                            15
Gabrielle Beaumont     UK                 1979
*Cyd Hayman, Malcolm Stoddard, Angela Pleasence,*
*Patrick Barr, Wilhelmina Green, Joanne Boorman,*
*Angela Deamer, Clarissa Young, Lee Gregory, Piers*
*Eady, Anna Wing, Artro Morris, Hilary Minster,*
*Corinne Skinner-Garter*
A little girl is left at a family farm by a strange
woman, and sundry nasty things happen to the family
over the next few years, in this competent little
thriller.
Boa: novel by Bernard Taylor.
THR                    84 min (ort 93 min)
B,V                                       RNK

## GODZILLA VERSUS THE COSMIC MONSTER *
Jun Fukada            JAPAN               1974
*Masaaki Daimon, Kazuya Aoyama, Akihiko Hirata,*
*Reiko Tajima, Barbara Lynn, Hiroshi Koizumi, Masao*
*Imafukuu, Mori Kishida, Kenji Sahara*
Aliens attempt to invade Earth using a steel replica of

Godzilla. The real flesh-and-scales monster comes to the rescue, but finds he needs help from an Okinawan monster spirit in order to vanquish his opponent, who is out to destroy the world. Delightfully insane rubbish, badly made, badly dubbed and badly acted. One of a series.
Aka: GODZILLA VERSUS THE BIONIC MONSTER; GODZILLA VERSUS MECHAGODZILLA; GOJIRA TAI MEKA GOJIRA
FAN                                  80 min dubbed
B,V,V2                                         HOK

### GODZILLA: THE LEGEND IS REBORN *          PG
Kohji Hashimodo/R.J. Kizer
                         JAPAN                  1985
Raymond Burr, Keiju Kobayashi, Ken Tanaka, Yasuko Sawaguchi, Yusuke Natsuki, Shin Takuma, Eitaro Ozara, Teketoshi Naito, Takeshi Katoh, Nobuo Kaneko
Thirty years after wrecking Tokyo in 1956, Godzilla returns, proving that a lack of fresh ideas is not restricted to Hollywood.
Aka: GODZILLA; GODZILLA 1985; GOJIRA
FAN                                          91 min
B,V                                             NWV

### GOIN' ALL THE WAY *
Robert Freedman        USA                     1982
Dan Waldman, Deborah Van Rhyn, Joshua Cadman, Sheri Miller, Joe Colligan
Every girl on the campus wants to sleep with a guy except his girlfriend, in this juvenile teen comedy.
COM                                          93 min
B,V,V2                                         POLY

### GOIN' COCONUTS *
Howard Morris          USA                     1978
Donny Osmond, Marie Osmond, Herbert Edelman, Kenneth Mars, Marc Lawrence, Chrystin Sinclaire, Ted Cassidy, Khigh Dhiegh, Harold Sakata
Osmond pop vehicle. The plot: the bad guys try to steal Marie Osmond's necklace in Hawaii. Donny and Marie play themselves . . . badly.
COM                                         110 min
B,V                                    VFP L/A; HER

### GOIN' SOUTH **                            PG
Jack Nicholson         USA                     1978
Jack Nicholson, Mary Steenburgen, Christopher Lloyd, Veronica Cartwright, John Belushi, Richard Bradford, Lucy Lee Flippen, Jeff Morris, Danny DeVito, Tracey Walter, Gerald H. Reynolds, Luana Anders, George W. Smith
An outlaw is saved from hanging by agreeing to marry, but his wife has far from romantic notions about what his obligations towards her are. An offbeat and mildly diverting comedy Western.
WES                                         105 min
B,V                                             CIC

### GOING BANANAS ***                         U
Boaz Davidson          USA                     1987
Dom DeLuise, Jimmy Walker, David Mendenhall, Deep Roy, Herbert Lom
A slapstick kiddie's comedy, in which the young son of a millionaire and his over-protective companion in-adventently return from a trip to a safari park with a rather special chimp. The chimp is soon a big hit with all and sundry, and they have to fight hard to save it from the clutches of a corrupt police chief, who wants it to perform in a local circus.
Aka: MY AFRICAN ADVENTURE (RNK)
JUV                                          90 min
B, V/sh                              RNK; CAN; PATHE

### GOING BERSERK *                           15
David Steinberg        CANADA                  1983
John Candy, Joe Flaherty, Eugene Levy, Alley Mills, Pat Hingle, Richard Libertini, Paul Dooley, Murphy

Dunne, Dixie Carter, Ernie Hudson
A young man sets out to marry a politician's daughter but finds the path of true love strewn with hazards. An unfunny and muddle-headed comedy.
COM                    81 min (ort 85 min) Cut (15 sec)
B,V                                             CIC

### GOING DOWN ***
Hadyn Keenan          AUSTRALIA                1982
Tracey Mann, Vera Pleunik, Julie Barry
Covers 24 hours in the lives of four friends. All are facing dead-ends in their lives and each person chooses a different means of overcoming this problem, in this interesting Aussie drama.
DRA                                          92 min
B,V                               KRP L/A; PRIME/CBS

### GOING FOR THE GOLD: THE BILL              U
### JOHNSON STORY **
Don Taylor             USA                     1985
Anthony Edwards, Sarah Jessica Parker, Deborah Van Valkenburgh, Wayne Northrop, Dennis Weaver, Ed Bishop, David Lema, Jean-Marc Barr, Sam DeFazio, Dan Pinto, Roman Muller, Paul Sinclair, Michael John Paliotti, Vicko Ruic
The story of a young man determined to make the Winter Olympic skiing team, that traces the career of Bill Johnson from Oregon to Sarajevo, Yugoslavia, for the 1984 competition. Average.
Aka: BILL JOHNSON STORY, THE
Boa: story by Maxwell Pitt.
DRA                             90 min (ort 100 min) mTV
B,V                                             PRV

### GOING IN STYLE **                         PG
Martin Brest           USA                     1979
George Burns, Art Carney, Lee Strasberg, Charles Hallahan, Pamela Payton-Wright
Three pensioners decide to rob a Manhattan bank but find that things do not go all that smoothly. A meandering comedy that relies heavily on the talents of Burns and the rest of the cast, who work hard to make something out of the thin storyline.
COM                                          96 min
B,V                                             WHV

### GOING ON 40 *                             15
John Trent             CANADA                  1979
Bruce Dern, Ann-Margret, Eric Christmas, Deborah Wakeham, Graham Jarvis, Helen Hughes, Geoffrey Bowes, Michael Kane, Diane Dewey, Vivian Reis, Ann Lantuch, Patricia Hamilton, Gina Dick, Thomas Baird
A middle-aged man embarks on one last fling as he rapidly approaches his fortieth birthday. No surprises here in this production-line drama.
Aka: MIDDLE AGE CRAZY; PRIME 40
DRA                             90 min (ort 95 min)
V                                         CBS; KRP

### GOING SANE ***                            15
Michael Robertson     USA                      1986
John Waters, Judy Morris, Frank Wilson, Kate Raison, Linda Cropper
An unhappy mining engineer becomes obsessed with the passage of time and lies down in a derelict warehouse to die. He is found and taken to a hospital where he meets a woman who helps him overcome his obsession.
DRA                                          87 min
V                                             RCA

### GOING STEADY *                            18
Boaz Davidson
                 ISRAEL/WEST GERMANY           1979
Yiftach Katzur, Yvonne Michaels, Zachi Noy, Rachel Steiner, Jonathan Segal, Daphna Armoni
The first sequel in the LEMON POPSICLE series of minimally-plotted Israeli teen comedies. Here our

boys clash with the local bike gang over some girls. Followed by HOT BUBBLEGUM.
Aka: YOTZ'IM KAVUA
COM                              84 min (ort 90 min)
B,V,V2                                 HOK L/A; TAKE2

## GOKE: BODYSNATCHER FROM HELL **   15
Hajime Sato          JAPAN               1967
*Hideo Ko, Teruo Yoshida, Tomomi Sato, Eiko Kitamura, Masaya Takahashi, Cathy Horlan, Kazuo Kato, Yuko Kusunoki*
One of those cheerfully silly Japanese SF films. In this one an aeroplane passes through a strange cloud and crash-lands in the desert. Under the influence of said cloud, everyone onboard becomes a vampire except the captain and the stewardess, who escape only to discover that an invasion is well under way. Worth seeing if only to enjoy the ludicrousness of it all.
Aka: GOKE THE VAMPIRE; KYUKETSUKI GOKEMIDORO
FAN                        80 min; 78 min (SHEP)
B,V                                   JVI L/A; SHEP

## GOLD ***
Peter Hunt            UK                  1974
*Roger Moore, Susannah York, Ray Milland, Bradford Dillman, John Gielgud, Tony Beckley, Simon Sabella, Marc Smith, John Hussey, Bernard Horsfall, Norman Coombes, Dennis Smith*
A mining engineer falls in love with the boss's granddaughter, and prevents a conspiracy to control the price of gold on the world markets by destroying a South African mine. An overlong film that's at its best during the gripping underground sequences. The music is by Elmer Bernstein.
Boa: novel Gold Mine by Wilbur Smith.
A/AD                     122 min (ort 124 min)
B,V,V2                                  VCL/CBS

## GOLD AND THE GLORY, THE ***   15
Igor Auzins          AUSTRALIA           1983
*Joss McWilliams, Colin Friels, Nick Tate, Robyn Nevin, Josephine Smulders*
A colourful story set on Queensland's Gold Coast, with two brothers, one a promising athlete and the other something of an underdog, falling out over a girl. They both enter a tough run, swim and ski marathon – "The Coolangatta Gold" – as a way of resolving their conflict.
Aka: COOLANGATTA GOLD, THE
DRA                       97 min (ort 100 min)
B,V                                         GHV

## GOLD DIGGERS OF 1933 ****   U
Mervyn Le Roy        USA                 1933
*Joan Blondell, Dick Powell, Ginger Rogers, Ruby Keeler, Aline MacMahon, Warren Williams, Guy Kibbee, Ned Sparks, Clarence Nordstrom, Sterling Holloway*
Flamboyant Busby Berkeley musical built around the attempts of showgirls to help a songwriter save his show. Contains numerous fine song and dance numbers such as: "Remember My Forgotten Man", "We're In The Money" and the "Shadow Waltz". A few slight sub-plots such as the affair between Powell and Keeler are added for good measure, but this one stands or falls by its superb musical sequences.
MUS                               96 min B/W
V                                          WHV

## GOLD DIGGERS OF 1935 ****   U
Busby Berkeley       USA                 1935
*Dick Powell, Adolphe Menjou, Gloria Stuart, Alice Brady, Glenda Farrell, Frank McHugh, Winifred Shaw, Hugh Herbert, Grant Mitchell*
Berkeley's first solo as choreographer and director is a flashy big-scale musical with the usual flimsy plot (a socialite wants to stage a show at her country seat) providing a few laughs in between the superb preci-

sion numbers such as: "The Words Are In My Heart" and the Oscar-winning classic "Lullaby Of Broadway" that's sung by Shaw. AA: Song ("Lullaby Of Broadway" – Harry Warren – music/Al Dubin – lyrics).
MUS                               91 min B/W
V                                          WHV

## GOLD OF THE AMAZON WOMEN *   PG
Mark L. Lester       USA                 1979
*Bo Svenson, Anita Ekberg, Donald Pleasence, Richard Romanus, Robert Minor, Maggie Jean Smith, Bond Gideon, Susan E. Miller, Yasmine, Mary Peters, Ian Edward, Sarita Butterfield, Charles Reynolds, John Anthony Sarno, Carl Low*
Two fortune-hunters stumble across a tribe of female warriors in the South American jungle, and the latter follow our fortune hunters back to the big city. Forgettable.
Aka: QUEST FOR THE SEVEN CITIES (AMB or KRP)
A/AD        100 min (GHV); 94 min (AMB or KRP) mTV
B,V,V2                          GHV L/A; AMB; KRP

## GOLD RAIDERS **   18
D.P. Chalong         THAILAND            1982
*Robert Ginty, Sarah Langenfeld, William Stevens*
Actioner telling of the hardships endured by a military mission to salvage a shipment of US gold, that was on a plane shot down over Laos. Mediocre.
A/AD                                   105 min
B,V                                  IMPACT/ODY

## GOLD ROBBERS ***   PG
Jacques Besnard      FRANCE
*Frederick Stafford, Jean Seberg, Maria Rodriguez, Fernand Bellan, Paul Crauchet, Serge Gainsbourg*
A corrupt politician plots with revolutionaries to steal gold bullion from his country's dictator, and thereby seize power himself.
Aka: LOOTERS, THE
A/AD                        90 min; 98 min (KRP)
B,V                                    KES; KRP

## GOLDEN CHILD, THE *   PG
Michael Ritchie      USA                 1986
*Eddie Murphy, Charlotte Lewis, Charles Dance, Randall "Tex" Cobb, Victor Wong, James Hong, J.L. Reate, Shakati, Tau Logo, Tiger Chung Lee, Pons Marr, Peter Kwong*
A social worker who specialises in tracing missing kids is given the job of tracking down a "perfect child" who, despite magical powers that an oracle predicts will be used to save the world from evil, has been kidnapped. An insufferable piece of hokum built around Murphy's smart wisecracking flair for comedy and Lewis' non-acting.
COM                                    89 min
V/sh                                        CIC

## GOLDEN DRAGON, SILVER SNAKE **   18
Godfrey Ho           HONG KONG
*Dragon Lee, Johnny Chan*
A fighter known as the "Golden Dragon" teams up with one known as the "Silver Snake" to avenge the murder of his brother.
MAR                                    85 min
V                                          VPD

## GOLDEN GATE MURDERS, THE ***   PG
Walter Grauman       USA                 1979
*David Janssen, Susannah York, Lloyd Bochner, Paul Coufos, Tim O'Connor, Kim Hunter, Alan Fudge, Regis J. Cordic, Richard O'Brien, Kenneth Tigar, Sandy Ward, Lee Paul, Jon Lormer, Jason Wingreen, Hank Brandt, Byron Morrow*
A gruff detective investigating the apparent suicide of a priest who is said to have jumped from the Golden Gate Bridge, teams up with a pretty nun in an attempt to prove that he was in fact murdered.

Despite a bad studio recreation of the San Francisco landmark and the implausible basic premise, this is quite a watchable if uninventive crime drama.
Aka: SPECTER ON THE BRIDGE
DRA                                        92 min mTV
B,V                                              CIC

## GOLDEN LADY, THE **
Jose Larraz        HONG KONG/UK              1974
Christina World, June Chadwick, Anika Pavel,
Suzanne Danielle, Stephan Chase, Edward De Souza,
David King, Patrick Newell, Richard Oldfield, Ava
Cadell, Terry Downes, Desmond Llewellyn, Michael
Stock, Seymour Green
Female agents foil a plot to assassinate the ruler of an
oil-producing country. Average.
THR                               90 min (ort 94 min)
B,V,V2                                       VCL/CBS

## GOLDEN MOMENT, THE *                          PG
Richard Sarafian        USA                 1980
Stephanie Zimbalist, David Keith, Richard Lawson,
Victor French, Merlin Olsen, Ed McMahon, Salome
Jens, Robert Peirce, Jack Palance, James Earl Jones,
Bryant Gumbel, Charlie Jones, O.J. Simpson, Dick
Enberg, Bruce Jenner
An American athlete falls for a Russian gymnast at
the 1980 Olympics (from which the USA withdrew!).
A badly timed filmed if ever there was one, but the
cliched and over-sentimental plot probably would
have finished it off anyway.
Aka: GOLDEN MOMENT, THE: AN OLYMPIC
LOVE STORY
Boa: story by Douglas Wolfe and Don Ohlmeyer.
DRA                    200 min; 117 min (VGM) mTV
B,V,V2                 ARCADE/VSP; VGM (VHS only)

## GOLDEN NEEDLES *
Robert Clouse        USA                    1974
Joe Don Baker, Jim Kelly, Burgess Meredith,
Elizabeth Ashley, Ann Sothern
A golden statue showing seven acupuncture points
and containing needles that restore youth, is sought
by several factions. A foolish blend of martial arts and
James Bond-style action movies.
Aka: CHASE FOR THE GOLDEN NEEDLES, THE
A/AD                                       92 min
B,V                                              RNK

## GOLDEN NINJA WARRIOR **                       18
Joseph Lai        HONG KONG                  1986
Donald Owen, Queenie Yang, Richard Harrison,
Morna Lee, David Chan, Nancy Cheng, Mike Tien
Another assembly-line martial arts caper featuring
the familiar figure of the Ninja. In this tale the
followers of the Red Ninja Empire are out to pinch a
priceless gold statue owned by the Golden Ninja.
Aka: GOLDEN NINJA WARRIORS
MAR        79 min (ort 92 min) Cut (5 min 58 sec)
B,V                                         NINJ/VPD

## GOLDEN RENDEZVOUS *                           15
Ashley Lazurus        USA                   1977
Richard Harris, Ann Turkel, David Janssen, Gordon
Jackson, John Vernon, Robert Beatty, Burgess
Meredith, Keith Baxter, Dorothy Malone, John
Carradine, Robert Flemyng, Leigh Lawson
A ship is taken over by terrorists who have failed to
reckon with the courage of its first officer. A pointless
feast of noise and violence with not much of a plot to
sustain it.
Aka: NUCLEAR TERROR
Boa: novel by Alistair MacLean.
DRA                              99 min (ort 103 min)
B,V                          RNK; VCC (VHS only)

## GOLDEN SEAL, THE **                           PG
Frank Zuniga        USA                     1983
Steve Railsback, Michael Beck, Penelope Milford,

Torquil Campbell, Seth Sakai
A father comes into conflict with his young son, over a
seal with a rare golden pelt which the latter wishes to
preserve from extinction. A satisfying if rather thin
tale, that is helped considerably by its Aleutian
Islands location.
Boa: novel A River Ran Out Of Eden by James Vance
Marshall.
A/AD                                       94 min
B,V                                              TEVP

## GOLDEN TRIANGLE, THE **
Lee Lo        HONG KONG                      1980
Lo Lieh, Sombat Metanee, Tien Nee
Rival gangs struggle for control of the opium trade.
A/AD                                      100 min
B,V,V2                                           VPD

## GOLDEN VOYAGE OF SINBAD, THE ***            U
Gordon Hessler        UK                    1973
John Phillip Law, Tom Baker, Caroline Munro,
Douglas Wilmer, Gregoire Aslan, Kurt Christian,
Takis Emmanuel, John D. Garfield Jr
Enjoyable 1950s-style rehash of all those earlier
Sinbad adventures, with Sinbad and crew encounter-
ing one danger after another as they sail to the
mysterious island of Lemuria in search of a golden
crown. Highlights are the jerky but entertaining
effects of Ray Harryhausen, such as a duel with the
six-armed statue of a goddess. See also SINBAD AND
THE EYE OF THE TIGER.
A/AD                             102 min (ort 105 min)
V                                              PREST

## GOLDENGIRL *                                  15
Joseph Sargent        USA                   1979
Susan Anton, Curt Jurgens, Robert Culp, Leslie
Caron, Harry Guardino, Jessica Walter
A female athlete is virtually turned into a robot in
order to win in the Moscow Olympics, in this pro-
foundly uninteresting saga.
Aka: GOLDEN GIRL
Boa: book by Peter Lear.
DRA                          101 min (ort 192 min) mTV
B,V,V2,LV                                        EHE

## GOLDFACE *                                    15
Stanley Mitchell (Adalberto Albertini)
                    ITALY/SPAIN             1968
Robert Anthony, Manuel Monroy, Big Matthews
A superhero goes after a terrorist group who threaten
the local petrol and mining companies. Mediocre
action nonsense.
Aka: GOLDFACE, IL FANTASTICO SUPERMAN;
GOLDFACE THE FANTASTIC SUPERMAN
A/AD                                       93 min
B,V                                              PRV

## GOLDFINGER ***                               PG
Guy Hamilton        UK                      1964
Sean Connery, Honor Blackman, Gert Frobe, Shirley
Eaton, Bernard Lee, Harold Sakata, Tania Mallett,
Martin Benson, Cec Linder, Austin Willis, Lois
Maxwell, Bill Nagy, Nadja Regin
The third of the "James Bond" films is a well-plotted
and exciting film, about our secret agent's attempt to
foil a gold robbery planned by a criminal mastermind.
Unfortunately, many of the strengths and interesting
sub-plots of the novel are lost in an adaptation that
gets bogged down in gadgetry and fisticuffs. Music is
by John Barry with the title song sung by Shirley
Bassey. THUNDERBALL followed. AA: Effects (Aud)
(Norman Wanstall).
Boa: novel by Ian Fleming.
A/AD        105 min (ort 112 min) (Cut at film release)
B,V                                              WHV

## GOLDILOCKS ***                               Uc
Gilbert Cates        USA                    1985

*Tatum O'Neal, Hoyt Axton, John Lithgow, Alex Karras, Brandis Kemp, Donovan Scott, Carole King*
Film version of the classic tale from the Faerie Tale Theatre, in which a little girl learns to respect the property of others – in this case a rather tetchy family of bears.
Aka: GOLDILOCKS AND THE THREE BEARS
JUV                                    48 min (ort 60 min)
V                                                          MGM

## GOLDRUNNER ** 15
Richard Losee          USA
*Richard Losee, Kristin Kelly, David Fitzen, Roger Clarc, Tony Chase, Gary Kalpakott, Vic Deauvonov*
A man hatches a perfect plan for revenge against an ex-business partner, in this routine action story.
Aka: RANSOM RUNNER (KSV)
A/AD                                                  90 min
B,V,V2                                    VUL L/A; KSV

## GOLDWING *** U
David Thornton                                      1980
Animated feature in which a boy is given superhuman powers and changed into the superhero "Goldwing" by a dying Interplanetary Peace Enforcer. He now has to continue the fight against the dark forces of Evil Planet and defeat their attempts to invade Earth.
Aka: GOLD WING
CAR                                                    90 min
B,V                                             PRV; MIA

## GOLDWYN FOLLIES, THE ** U
George Marshall          USA                      1938
*Adolphe Menjou, Andrea Leeds, Kenny Baker, The Ritz Brothers, Vera Zorina, Helen Jepson, Bobby Clark, Edgar Bergen and Charlie McCarthy, Phil Baker, Ella Logan, Jerome Cowan, Nydia Westman*
A producer engages a woman to comment on his films from the standpoint of an ordinary person. This flimsy plot is merely an excuse for a repertoire of musical numbers by George and Ira Gershwin. A mixed bag of comedy and song and dance routines, with The Ritz Brothers the main highlight of the film.
MUS                                    111 min (ort 115 min)
V                                                          VGM

## GOLDY: THE LAST OF THE GOLDEN BEARS ** U
Trevor Black          USA                          1984
*Jeff Richardson, Jessica Black*
Set in California, this tale follows the friendship between a young orphaned girl and a lone prospector, and tells of their contact with a rare golden bear. A pleasant outdoors adventure.
A/AD                                                  91 min
V                                                          VES

## GOLDY 2: THE SAGA OF THE GOLDEN BEAR * U
Trevor Black          USA                          1986
*Jessica Black*
This sequel to GOLDY: THE LAST OF THE GOLDEN BEARS is a witless film of flat characterisation and over-cute scripting, that tells of a rescue mission that's mounted to save the title creature from the clutches of a wicked circus-owner.
JUV                                                    91 min
V                                                          VES

## GOLIATH AGAINST THE GIANTS * PG
Guido Malatesta          ITALY                    1961
*Brad Harris, Gloria Milland, Barbara Carrol, Fernando Rey*
Goliath has to fight sea creatures, Amazons, and the man installed as temporary regent who has become a power-crazed tyrant. Standard adventure fare with an appeal largely resticted to kids (young ones).
A/AD                                                  90 min
B,V                                                      PRV

## GOLIATH AND THE BARBARIANS ** 15
Carlo Campogalliani          ITALY              1960
*Steve Reeves, Bruce Cabot, Giulia Rubini, Chelo Alonso, Arturo Dominici, Gino Scotti*
Strongman Reeves fights off hordes of barbarians trying to invade Italy. (I do hope he remembers to let the tourists in.) Average.
A/AD                                                  90 min Cut
B,V                                                      MED

## GONE ARE THE DAYES ** U
Gabrielle Beaumont          USA                  1984
*Harvey Korman, Susan Anspach, Robert Hogan, Bibi Besch*
The family of a man who is appearing as a government witness has to be given police protection but its members are determined to get away from both the gangsters and their police protectors. A pleasant little chase comedy that leaves no lasting impression.
COM                                    87 min (ort 90 min) mCab
B,V,V2                                                  WDV

## GONE IN 60 SECONDS * 
H.B. Halicki          USA                          1974
*H.B. Halicki, Marion Busia, J.C. Agajanian, Jerry Daugirda, James McIntire, George Cole, Parnelli Jones, Gary Bettenhausen*
A professional car thief has to fulfil a contract, but the last car causes him lots of problems. A film that's just an excuse for an orgy of car chases and spectacular smashes. A sequel followed.
A/AD                                                  103 min
B,V,V2                                                  VPD

## GONE IN 60 SECONDS 2 ** PG
H.B. Halicki          USA                          1982
*H.B. Halicki, Christopher Stone, Hoyt Axton, Susan Shaw, Lang Jeffries, Judi Gibbs, Lynda Day George, George Barris, Freedy Cannon, The Belmonts*
About 150 cars were smashed up making this sequel. The plot (such as it is) involves the making of a film which is to be used as a cover-up for a crime. As enjoyable as a Banger Derby but with a slightly less complex plot.
Aka: JUNKMAN, THE
A/AD                                    89 min (ort 96 min)
B,V                          VTC; XTACY/KRP; MAST (VHS only)

## GONE WITH THE WEST ** 
Bernard Girard          USA                        1969
*James Caan, Sammy Davis Jr, Stefanie Powers, Aldo Ray, Barbara Werle, Robert Walker Jr, Mike Lane, Michael Conrad, Kenny Adams, Fred Book, Anne Barton, Paul Bergen, Fabian Dean, Noel Drayton, Anthony Gordon*
A man and a girl team up to destroy an outlaw team in this episodic comedy.
Aka: BRONCO BUSTERS; LITTLE MOON AND JUD GRAW; MAN WITHOUT MERCY
COM                                                    92 min
B,V,V2                                            VCL/CBS

## GONE WITH THE WIND **** PG
Victor Fleming          USA                        1939
*Clark Gable, Vivien Leigh, Olivia De Havilland, Leslie Howard, Thomas Mitchell, Hattie McDaniel, Barbara O'Neil, Victor Jory, Laura Hope, Crews, Ona Munson, Harry Davenport, Ann Rutherford, Evelyn Keyes, Carroll Nye*
An all-time movie classic telling of the turbulent love affair and marriage of a Southern belle during the time of the Civil War. The memorable score is by Max Steiner. MacDaniel was the first black actress to win an Oscar. AA: Pic, Dir, Actress (Leigh), S. Actress (McDaniel), Screen (Sidney Howard), Cin (Ernest Haller/Ray Rennahan), Art (Lyle Wheeler), Spec Award (William Cameron Menzies for the use of colour in the enhancement of dramatic mood).
Boa: novel by Margaret Mitchell.

DRA                211 min (ort 222 min)
V/s                              MGM

## GONKS GO BEAT                        U
Robert Hartford-Davis    UK          1965
*Kenneth Connor, Jerry Desmonde, Reginald Beckwith*
An utterly awful attempt to produce a film that it was
mistakenly thought would appeal to the "young set" of
the time – and how dated it all looks now! With the
Earth in turmoil over a pop music contest between
Beatland and Balladisle, a Martian emissary arrives
to help bring about a peaceful resolution. Of slight
historical interest for appearances by a few popular
groups of the time, such as The Nashville Teens, Lulu
And The Luvvers etc.
MUS                                88 min
V                                   WHV

## GOOD DIE FIRST FOR A HANDFUL OF SILVER, THE **                              15
Giorgio Stegani    ITALY              1968
*Lee Van Cleef, Anthony Sabato, Bud Spencer (Carlo
Pedersoli), Ann Smyrner, Lionel Stander, Graziella
Granata, Herbert Fox, Carlo Gaddi, Gordon Mitchell,
Enzo Fiermonte, Hans Elwenspoek*
A bandit and his comrades rob a stagecoach but later
he befriends a man who saves his life and in an career
change, becomes the sheriff of a small town. An
extremely violent but well made spaghetti Western.
Aka: AL DI LA DELLA LEGGE; BEYOND THE
LAW
WES                                90 min
B,V                               WARAD

## GOOD DIE YOUNG, THE *
Lewis Gilbert      UK                 1954
*Laurence Harvey, Richard Basehart, Gloria Grahame,
Joan Collins, John Ireland, Rene Ray, Stanley Baker,
Margaret Leighton, Robert Morley, Freda Jackson,
James Kenney, Susan Shaw, Lee Patterson, Sandra
Dorne*
Four crooks with private problems plan and execute a
mail-van robbery in this fairly mediocre heist yarn.
Boa: novel by Richard Macauley.
DRA              95 min (ort 100 min) B/W
B,V                                 CBS

## GOOD EARTH, THE ****
Sidney Franklin/George Hill
                   USA                1937
*Paul Muni, Luise Rainer, Charely Grapewin, Walter
Connolly, Tilly Losch, Jesse Ralph, Soo Young, Keye
Luke, Roland Lui, Harold Huber*
An effective if dated adaptation of Buck's mammoth
novel about the life of a Chinese peasant couple, and
how greed ruins a farmer's marriage. Excellent
special effects and flawless acting are among this
film's major virtues. The screenplay was written by
Talbot Jennings, Tess Slesinger and Claudine West.
AA: Actress (Rainer), Cin (Karl Freund).
Boa: novel by Pearl S. Buck/play by Owen Davis and
Donald Davis.
DRA                               138 min
V                              MGM L/A

## GOOD FATHER, THE ***                  15
Mike Newell        UK                 1986
*Anthony Hopkins, Jim Broadbent, Harriet Walter,
Joanne Whalley, Simon Callow, Fanny Viner, Michael
Byrne*
The story of two recently separated men, and their
feelings of rage and resentment at their estrangement
from their children. A low-key typically British
production.
Boa: novel by Peter Prince.
DRA                 86 min (ort 90 min) mTV
B,V                                 VIR

## GOOD GIRL, BAD GIRL *                  18
Art Ben            USA                1984
*Joey Silvera, Colleen Brennan, Taija Rae, George
Payne, Sharon Mitchell, Carol Cross, Paula Meadows,
Sandra King, Eric Monti, Jeremy Butler*
Mystery surrounds the death of a beautiful actress,
but the search for her killer is a mere excuse for
another boring hardcore sex film.
Aka: GOOD GIRLS, BAD GIRLS
A             49 min (ort 81 min) Cut (6 min 40 sec)
B,V                            IVS L/A; ECF

## GOOD GUYS WEAR BLACK **
Ted Post           USA                1979
*Chuck Norris, Anne Archer, James Franciscus, Dana
Andrews, Lloyd Haynes, Jim Backus*
A quiet professor uses the skills he learnt as leader of
a commando unit in Vietnam, to stay alive when he
discovers that he is on a CIA hit list. A fast and
furious display of Norris' athletic prowess; too bad
about the storyline. Followed by A FORCE OF ONE.
A/AD                               96 min
B,V                                 VTC

## GOOD LIFE, THE **                      U
John Howard Davies   UK               1975
*Richard Briers, Felicity Kendal, Penelope Keith, Paul
Eddington*
Pilot episode from a long-running TV series about a
suburban couple who suddenly decide to become
self-sufficient farmers, with no more than their back
garden. Average.
COM                             55 min mTV
B,V                                 BBC

## GOOD LUCK, MISS WYCKOFF *              18
Marvin J. Chomsky  USA                1979
*Anne Heywood, Donald Pleasence, Robert Vaughn,
Carolyn Jones, Dorothy Malone, Ronee Blakley, John
Lafayette, Earl Holliman*
A schoolteacher is introduced to sex by being raped, in
this uneven and ineffective adaptation of Inge's novel.
Aka: SHAMING, THE (SCRN); SIN, THE
Boa: novel by William Inge.
DRA   90 min (ort 105 min) Cut (2 min 31 sec of abridged
film)
B,V              VUL L/A; CAREY L/A; SCRN

## GOOD MORNING, BABYLON ***            15
Paolo Taviani/Vittorio Taviani
                FRANCE/ITALY/USA     1986
*Vincent Spano, Greta Scacchi, Joaquim De Almeida,
Charles Dance, Desiree Becker, Omero Antonutti,
David Brandon*
The story of two Italian brothers who come to America
hoping to make their fortune and wind up working on
D.W. Griffith's epic film INTOLERANCE. A homage
to the early days of film-making, rather simplistic but
quite charming.
Aka: GOOD MORNING, BABYLONIA
DRA                               116 min
B,V                                 PAL

## GOOD MORNING, BOYS ***                 U
Marcel Varnel      UK                 1937
*Will Hay, Lilli Palmer, Martita Hunt, Peter
Gawthorne, Graham Moffatt, Mark Daly, Fewlass
Llewellyn, Peter Godfrey, C. Denier Warren, Charles
Hawtrey, Will Hay Jr, Basil MacGrail, Jacques Brown*
A school trip to Paris becomes complicated when the
pupils get involved in an art theft. An engaging
comedy in which Hay gives full rein to his comic
schoolmaster persona that had been several years in
the making. Remade as "Top Of The Form".
Aka: WHERE THERE'S A WILL
COM                            79 min B/W
B,V                                 RNK

## GOOD MORNING, VIETNAM ***  15
Barry Levinson          USA          1988
*Robin Williams, Forest Whitaker, Tung Tuanh Tran,*
*Chintara Sukapatana, Bruno Kirby, Robert Wuhl, J.T.*
*Walsh, Noble Willingham, Floyd Vivino*
An anarchic, manic anti-establishment DJ blasts the
airwaves on the American Forces radio in Saigon in
1965. Williams gets plenty of opportunity to indulge
his gift for improvisation in a never-ending stream of
monologues, but the thin story fails to make any clear
statement about the rights or wrongs of US involvement in this conflict. A comical, insane, fast trip
nowhere, based to some extent on real-life DJ Adrian
Cronauer.
COM                                    116 min
B,V                                    BUENA

## GOOD SOLDIER, THE ***  PG
Kevin Billington          UK          1981
*Robin Ellis, Susan Fleetwood, Jeremy Brett, Vickery*
*Turner, Elizabeth Garvie*
In the twilight of the Edwardian age, just before
WW1, two couples meet regularly at a German spa
and develop a strange relationship. An engrossing
character study.
Boa: novel by Ford Madox Ford.
DRA                     105 min (ort 120 min) mTV
B,V                                    GRN

## GOOD TIMES ***  PG
William Friedkin          USA          1967
*Sonny Bono, Cher, George Sanders, Norman Alden,*
*Larry Duran*
An enjoyable musical vehicle for this former singing
duo, in which Sonny gets to fantasise about various
roles and Cher sings "I Got You, Babe". Cher's first
film role and Friedkin's directorial debut.
MUS                     88 min (ort 91 min) Cut (5 sec)
B,V                                    RNK; VGM

## GOOD TO GO **  15
Blaine Novak          USA          1986
*Art Garfunkel, Harris Yulin, Robert Doqui, Michael*
*White, Reginald Daughtry, Richard Brooks, Hattie*
*Winston, Paula Davis*
A local journalist investigates the rape and murder of
a nurse by a drummer, and finds the police less than
co-operative, so he is forced to enlist the help of black
slum kids. Really a youth musical in disguise, where
the black "go-go" sound plays the major role, little else
mattering.
Aka: SHORT FUSE
A/AD                                   86 min
B,V                                    CBS

## GOOD WIFE, THE ***  15
Ken Cameron          AUSTRALIA          1986
*Rachel Ward, Bryan Brown, Sam Neill, Steven Vidler,*
*Jennifer Clair, Bruce Barry, Clarissa Kaye-Mason*
A lumberjack's wife breaks the restraints of her
stifling marriage and takes up with the new man in
town. Slow to get going but generally worth staying
with.
Aka: UMBRELLA WOMAN, THE
DRA                                    94 min
B,V                                    EIV

## GOOD-TIME OUTLAWS, THE ***
Alex Grashoff          USA          1978
*Slim Pickens, Dianne Shevril, Jesse Turner, Dennis*
*Temple, Dennis Fimple, Sully Boyar*
Two ranch-hands lose their jobs and set off on a 2,000
mile journey to Nashville, to try their hand at
becoming Country an Western singers, in this light-
weight but easy-going comedy.
Aka: SMOKEY AND THE GOOD-TIME OUTLAWS
(TEM)
COM                                    89 min
B,V,V2                        TEM L/A; DFS; APX

## GOOD, THE BAD, AND THE UGLY, THE ***  18
Sergio Leone          ITALY/SPAIN          1966
*Clint Eastwood, Eli Wallach, Lee Van Cleef, Rada*
*Rassimov, Mario Brega, Aldo Giuffre, Chelo Alonso,*
*Silvana Bacci, Luigi Pistilli, Enzo Petito, Al Mulloch*
This is the third and most colourful of the three "man
with no name" films of Leone. Set against the
background of the Civil War, Eastwood and Wallach
form an uneasy partnership in a hunt for the proceeds
of a bullion robbery. As before, Ennio Moricone
provides an excellent score. Look out for the sequence
in which Eastwood obtains his poncho, thus becoming
the character of the two earlier films.
Aka: IL BUONO, IL BRUTO, IL CATTIVO
WES                 120 min; 155 min (WHV) (ort 180 min)
B,V                      INT/CBS; WHV (VHS only)

## GOODBYE CRUEL WORLD **  15
David Irving          USA          1982
*Dick Shawn, Cynthia Sikes, Chuck Mitchell, Nicholas*
*Niciphor*
Before committing suicide, a TV anchorman decides to
film his relatives who have driven him to take such a
desperate measure. An offbeat comedy misfire.
Aka: UP THE WORLD (ATLA)
COM                     78 min (ort 90 min)
B,V                      FFV L/A; ATLAS

## GOODBYE EMMANUELLE *  18
Francois Leterrier          FRANCE          1977
*Sylvia Kristel, Umberto Orsini, Alexandra Stewart*
The setting is the Seychelles this time, and our
heroine is now married to an architect in yet another
glossy, empty, interminable EMMANUELLE sequel.
Hopefully this time it's good riddance.
A                     95 min (ort 100 min) (Cut at film release)
B,V                      STABL; RCA (VHS only)

## GOODBYE GIRL, THE***  PG
Herbert Ross          USA          1977
*Richard Dreyfuss, Marsha Mason, Paul Benedict,*
*Quinn Cummings, Barbara Rhoaes, Theresa Merritt,*
*Michael Shawn, Nicol Williamson*
Mason is a dancer whose husband has skipped off,
deserting her and their 10-year-old daughter, and at
the same time selling their apartment lease to an
actor. In the resulting confusion Dreyfuss and Mason
find themselves sharing the same apartment, in this
warm and funny exploration of their growing, albeit
initially reluctant friendship. A succession of funny
one-liners sustains the thin plot. Scripted by Simon.
AA: Actor (Dreyfuss).
Boa: play by Neil Simon.
COM                                    110 min
B,V                                    WHV

## GOODBYE PARADISE **
Carl Schultz          AUSTRALIA          1981
*Ray Barrett, Robyn Nevin, Guy Doleman*
An ex-policeman investigates the disappearance of a
politician's daughter and uncovers a nasty plot, in this
competent thriller.
THR                                    121 min
B,V,V2                                 PRV

## GOODBYE PORK PIE **
Geoff Murphy          NEW ZEALAND          1980
*Tony Barry, Kelly Johnson, Claire Oberman*
Three young people are chased by the cops up and
down New Zealand's freeways at great speed, and are
arrested one by one in this good-looking but rather
pointless tale.
A/AD                                   105 min
B,V                                    BWV/VSP

## GOODBYE, BRUCE LEE *
Lin Ping          HONG KONG          1975
*Ronald Brown, Johnny Floyd, Mun Ping*
Footage of Lee plus interviews with some of his

friends, starts off a tale of a fighter who unwittingly gets drawn into the underworld. An unashamed and exploitative attempt to cobble together a film that trades on the presence of the late star.
Aka: GOODBYE BRUCE LEE: HIS LAST GAME OF DEATH; LEGEND OF BRUCE LEE, THE
MAR                                                    84 min
B,V,V2                                            INT/CBS

### GOODBYE, FRANKLIN HIGH ***     15
Mike MacFarland          USA                       1978
*Lane Caudell, Ann Dusenberry, Darby Hinton, Julie Adams, William Windom*
A young man at high school finds his life and choice of future career are complicated when he falls in love, in this unambitious but enjoyable little drama.
DRA                                        89 min (ort 94 min)
B,V                                                   POLY

### GOODBYE, NEW YORK **     15
Amos Kollek          ISRAEL/USA                    1985
*Julie Hagerty, Amos Kollek, David Topaz, Aviva Ger, Shmuel Shiloh, Jennifer Babtist, Christopher Goutman, Hanan Goldblat, Mosku Alkalay, Yaacov Ben Sira, Chaim Banai, Irit Ben Zur, Chaim Girafi, Bella Ben David*
A woman oversleeps on a Paris flight and arrives in Israel where she has to cope as best she can, eventually getting to live on a kibbutz and starting a relationship with a part-time soldier. A cute little comedy of no great depth.
COM                                                 90 min
B,V                                                   GHV

### GOODBYE, NORMA JEAN *     18
Larry Buchanan          USA                        1976
*Misty Rowe, Norma Jean Baker, Terence Locke, Preston Hanson, Patch Mackenzie*
The story of Marilyn Monroe's early years and her climb to stardom, with centrefold Rowe playing the title role in this depressing and seedy effort.
DRA                                        91 min (ort 95 min)
B,V                              INT/CBS; VGM (VHS only)

### GOONIES, THE **     PG
Richard Donner          USA                        1985
*Sean Austin, Josh Brolin, Jeff Cohen, Corey Feldman, Kerri Green, Robert Davi, Martha Plimpton, Ke Huy Quan, John Matuszak, Anne Ramsey, Mary Ellen Trainor, Joe Pantoliano, Lupe Ontiveros, Keith Walker, Curtis Hanson*
A group of boys living in a small Oregon town, discover a pirate treasure map and embark on a wild adventure, in an attempt to save their home from land developers. A lively, noisy and badly-articulated film, aimed well and truly at kids, and based on a Steven Spielberg story as well as being produced by him.
JUV                               109 min (Cut – sound only)
V/sh                                                  WHV

### GOOSE BOXER, THE ** 
Dai Shifu          HONG KONG
*Charles Heung, Kao Fei, Li Hai Sheng, Tian Qing, Dai Hsiao Yan*
The owner of a market stall selling roast goose, develops his own powerful fighting style after thugs smash up his stall, and causes quite a few feathers to fly in this standard punch 'n' kicker.
MAR                                                 90 min
B,V                                              SPEC/POLY

### GOR **     15
Fritz Kiersch          ITALY                        1987
*Urbano Barberini, Rebecca Ferratti, Jack Palance, Paul L. Smith, Oliver Reed*
Following a car crash, a New England professor is catapulted into a parallel universe by a strange ring, and finds himself on Gor, a primitive planet ruled over

by a barbaric tyrant. In order to return home he has to lead the rebels in an attack on the tyrant's domain. A cheap and nasty version of a rather good yarn from Norman's "Gor" series, and one more attempt to revive the fading interest in sword-and-sorcery films. Followed by OUTLAW OF GOR.
Boa: novel Tarnsman Of Gor by John Norman.
FAN                                                 91 min
B,V                                                   WHV

### GORDON THE BLACK PIRATE **     U
Mario Costa          ITALY                          1964
*Ricardo Montalban, Vincent Price*
Routine swashbuckler with the valiant "Black Pirate" attempting to put an end to slavery and encountering opposition from the evil "Tortuga".
A/AD                                                83 min
V                                                     ELE

### GORGON, THE **     15
Terence Fisher          UK                          1964
*Peter Cushing, Christopher Lee, Barbara Shelley, Richard Pasco, Michael Goodliffe, Patrick Troughton, Joseph O'Conor, Prudence Hyman, Jack Watson, Redmond Phillips, Jeremy Longhurst, Toni Gilpin*
A castle ruin near a German village houses a girl whose gaze turns people to stone. Fairly atmospheric though lacking in any real power, and with the title creature barely glimpsed. (Perhaps they wanted to protect us.)
HOR                                                 83 min
B,V                                                   RCA

### GORILLAS IN THE MIST ***     15
Michael Apted          USA                          1988
*Sigourney Weaver, Bryan Brown, Julie Harris, John Omirah Miluwi, Iain Cuthbertson, Constantin Alexandrov, Waigwa Wachira*
A biopic on the life of Dian Fossey, who embarked on a twenty year mission to save the mountain gorilla from extinction, from the time of her arrival in Rwanda up to her death in 1965. The tacked on human interest drama is of little value, but Weaver's committed performance, and the sequences that show her gradually establishing communication with these shy creatures, are the film's best points.
DRA                                       124 min (ort 129 min)
V/sh                                                  WHV

### GORKY PARK ***     15
Michael Apted          USA                          1983
*William Hurt, Lee Marvin, Brian Dennehy, Ian Bannen, Joanna Pacula, Michael Elphick, Richard Griffiths, Rikki Fulton, Alexander Knox, Alexei Sayle, Ian McDiarmid, Niall O'Brian, Henry Woolf, Tusse Silberg, Patrick Field*
A Moscow detective investigates the strange case of three bodies buried in Gorky Park. In an attempt to hide their identities their faces and fingerprints have been mutilated. A strongly atmospheric rendition of Smith's novel, that is severely handicapped by the lack of real Moscow locations (once again Helsinki stands in for Moscow) and the basically conventional nature of the plot.
Boa: novel by Martin Cruz Smith.
DRA                                       124 min (ort 128 min)
B,V,V2                                               RNK

### GOSSIP FROM THE FOREST ***     PG
Brian Gibson          UK                            1979
*Michael Jayston, John Shrapnel, Hugh Burde*
An adaptation of a novel describing the ill-fated negotiations that took place in 1918 in a railway carriage in the woods of Compiegne, and which brought WW1 to an end, but created the conditions that led to the rise of Nazism and WW2. An absorbing drama that contains no great insights but is well-directed and atmospheric.
Aka: GOSSIP FROM THE FRONT

Boa: novel by Thomas Keneally
DRA                                    90 min mTV
B,V                                         GRN

## GOT IT MADE *
James Kenelm Clarke    UK              1974
*Lalla Ward, Michael Latimer, Douglas Lambert,*
*Katya Wyeth, Michael Feast, Fabia Drake, Barbara*
*Markham, Michael Lees, Joh Warner, Richard Leech,*
*Leslie Anderson, Erith Kent, Marilyn Sandford*
A young girl's wedding plans are radically altered
when she meets a rock star, in this trivial little sex
comedy.
Aka: COLORADO STONE; SWEET VIRGIN
COM                            77 min (ort 85 min)
B,V                                      INT/CBS

## GOTCHA! **                                   15
Jeff Kanew             USA             1985
*Anthony Edwards, Linda Fiorentin, Nick Corri, Alex*
*Rocco, Klaus Lowitsch, Marla Adams, Christopher*
*Rydell, Christie Cladige, Brad Cowgill, Kar Lizer,*
*David Wohl, Irene Olga Lopez, Bernard Speigel,*
*Muriel Dubrule*
A student's prowess at a college espionage game called
"Gotcha", eventually leads him into espionage entang-
lements when he is initiated into sex by a mysterious
woman, who has links with European spies. A lame
and concocted attempt to add a little spice to a simple
teen story of loss of virginity and innocence.
Boa: story by Paul G. Hensler.
DRA                                       96 min
V/h                                         CIC

## GOTHIC ***                                   18
Ken Russell            UK              1986
*Gabriel Byrne, Julian Sands, Natasha Richardson,*
*Myriam Cyr, Timothy Spall*
A recreation of the night in 1816 when Mary Shelley
and Dr Polidori were inspired to write their Gothic
horror classics, "Frankenstein" and "The Vampyre"
respectively. A vivid and enjoyable fantasy full of the
usual Russell touches, only this time they add some-
thing to the film. The screen debut for Richardson.
Remade two years later as HAUNTED SUMMER.
HOR                            83 min (ort 90 min)
B,V                                         VIR

## GRACE KELLY STORY, THE **                     U
Anthony Page           USA             1983
*Cheryl Ladd, Lloyd Bridges, Diane Ladd, Alejandro*
*Rey, Ian McShane, William Schallert, Marta DuBois,*
*Salome Jens, Ryan MacDonald, Donna Martel, David*
*Paymer, Paul Lieber, Paul Lambert, Boyd Holister,*
*Scott Edmund Lane*
Biopic about the late Princess Grace Rainier of
Monaco, born Grace Kelly. A laughably superficial
and sugar-coated film that tells us nothing at all, but
is of minor interest if only to see a succession of
Hollywood stars of former days being impersonated.
Scripted by Cynthia Mandelberg.
Aka: GRACE KELLY
DRA                        99 min; 95 min (CH5) mTV
B,V,V2                           EHE; CH5 (VHS only)

## GRACE QUIGLEY *                               15
Anthony Harvey         USA             1984
*Katharine Hepburn, Nick Nolte, Kit Le Fever,*
*Elizabeth Wilson, Chip Zien, William Duell, Walter*
*Abel*
Black comedy about an old woman who develops a
strange relationship with a contract killer after she
asks him to kill her. A highly insulting and patronis-
ing look at old age and extremely dull to boot.
Aka: ULTIMATE SOLUTION OF GRACE
QUIGLEY, THE
COM                           87 min (ort 102 min)
B,V                                         GHV

## GRADUATE, THE ****                            15
Mike Nichols           USA             1967
*Dustin Hoffman, Anne Bancroft, Katherine Ross,*
*Murray Hamilton, William Daniels, Elizabeth Wilson,*
*Brian Avery, Norman Fell, Marion Lorne, Alice*
*Ghostley*
The film that made Hoffman. A wry look at what
happens when a young graduate embarks on a
loveless affair with one of his mother's friends but
then falls in love with her daughter. The brilliant
score is by Simon and Garfunkel. Scripted by Buck
Henry (who plays the hotel desk clerk) and Calder
Willingham. AA: Dir.
Boa: novel by Charles Webb.
DRA                                       106 min
B,V        WHV; CH5 (VHS only); POLY (VHS only)

## GRADUATION DAY *                              18
Herb Freed             USA             1981
*Christopher George, Patch MacKenzie, E. Danny*
*Murphy, Michael Pataki, E.J. Peaker, Vanna White*
Members of a college track team are murdered one by
one, in this carbon copy of FRIDAY THE 13TH.
HOR                            85 min (ort 92 min)
B,V,V2             IFS L/A; NET; TRACKS; GLOB

## GRAND HOTEL ***                                U
Edmund Goulding        USA             1932
*Greta Garbo, John Barrymore, Joan Crawford,*
*Wallace Beery, Lionel Barrymore, Lewis Stone, Jean*
*Hersholt*
An ambitious vehicle for a collection of stars, built
around the hopes and fears of a group of guests at a
plush Berlin hotel, whose lives become intertwined.
Faded and certainly stagebound, but containing
several fine performances; John Barrymore as a jewel
thief, Garbo as a lonely ballerina and Lionel Barry-
more as a dying man are particularly memorable.
Later a Broadway musical and used as the plot for
several films. AA: Pic.
Boa: novel by Vicki Baum.
DRA                                   112 min B/W
V                                           MGM

## GRAND LARCENY ***                              U
Jeannot Szwarc                         1988
*Omar Sharif, Ian McShane, Marilu Henner, Louis*
*Jourdan*
A master criminal made his fortune by returning
stolen articles to their original owners. His dying wish
is that his daughter should carry on in this work, and
to encourage her, she is given the task of recovering a
priceless horse that has been kidnapped. By way of an
incentive, the estate will pass to the father's life-long
friend should she fail. A colourful story set in the Cote
d'Azur.
A/AD                                      90 min
V                                           VGM

## GRAND SLAM **                                 15
John Hefin             UK              1978
*Hugh Griffith, Windsor Davies, Davi Morris*
A group of Welsh rugby fans go to Paris for a
championship match, and create the expected
mayhem in this boozy comedy.
COM                                    60 min mTV
B,V,V2                                      BBC

## GRAND THEFT AUTO *                            PG
Ron Howard             USA             1977
*Ron Howard, Nancy Morgan, Marion Ross, Pete*
*Isacksen, Barry Cahill, Clint Howard, Don Steele*
The usual car-crash story, where the machines out-act
the humans. The directorial debut for Howard who
co-wrote the script (such as it is).
A/AD                           81 min (ort 85 min)
B,V                                         WHV

## GRANDMA'S HOUSE **                            18
Peter Rader            USA             1988

*Eric Poster, Kim Valentine, Ida Lee, Brinke Stevens,*
*Len Lesser*
Following the death of their parents, two youngsters
are sent to live with their grandmother, and this
heralds the start of a most unpleasant stay as they
find themselves threatened by insanity and murder.
An efficient little low-budget yarn with the gore
mercifully kept to a minimum.
Aka: GRANDMOTHER'S HOUSE

| | |
|---|---|
| HOR | 86 min |
| B,V | GHV |

## GRANDVIEW, USA **                                    15
Randal Kleiser          USA                      1984
*Jamie Lee Curtis, John Cusack, Michael Winslow, C.*
*Thomas Howell, Patrick Swayze, Troy Donahue,*
*Jennifer Jason Leigh, William Windom, Carole Cook,*
*Elizabeth Gorcey*
An account of a small-town demolition derby and its
participants in a small town, serves as the basis for a
look at life in the Midwest. So-so.

| | |
|---|---|
| DRA | 97 min |
| B,V | CBS |

## GRAPES OF WRATH, THE ****                          PG
John Ford          USA                           1940
*Henry Fonda, John Carradine, Jane Darwell, Charley*
*Grapewin, Dorris Bowden, Russell Simpson, Zeffie*
*Tilbury, O.Z. Whitehead, John Qualen, Eddie Quillan,*
*Grant Mitchell*
A superb screen adaptation of Steinbeck's tale of
destitute Oklahoma farmers forced to leave their
dustbowl-ruined lands during the Depression in the
hope of a better life in California. Despite the omission
of the novel's ending (which would never have passed
the censor) this is a splendid film, made with infinite
love and care. Scripted by Nunnally Johnson. AA: Dir,
S. Actress (Darwell).
Boa: novel by John Steinbeck.

| | |
|---|---|
| DRA | 129 min B/W |
| V/h | CBS |

## GRASS IS GREENER, THE **                            U
Stanley Donen          UK                        1960
*Cary Grant, Deborah Kerr, Jean Simmons, Robert*
*Mitchum, Moray Watson*
An earl and his wife open up their stately home to
tourists in order to make ends meet. However, an
American millionaire turns up and proceeds to have
an affair with the lady of the house. A stilted film
version of a lightweight West End play.
Boa: play by Hugh and Margaret Williams. Osca:
THAT TOUCH OF MINK (VCC)

| | |
|---|---|
| COM | 105 min; 100 min (VCC) |
| B,V | BBC L/A; VCC (VHS only) |

## GRASS IS SINGING, THE ***
Michael Raeburn  SWEDEN/ZAMBIA           1981
*Karen Black, John Thaw, John Kani, John Moulder*
*Brown, Patrick Mynhardt*
A woman marries a farmer but cannot adjust to life in
the bush and eventually cracks up. A vivid and quite
moving drama, filmed in Zambia.
Aka: KILLING HEAT, THE
Boa: novel by Doris Lessing.

| | |
|---|---|
| DRA | 110 min |
| B,V,V2 | 3MVID/PVG |

## GRASSCUTTER, THE **                                 15
Ian Mune          UK                             1988
*Ian McElhinney, Frances Barber, Judy McIntosh*
A former member of the Ulster Volunteer Forces tires
of the mindless violence and turns Queen's Evidence,
leading to the jailing of 23 men. In return, he is given
a new identity and re-settled in New Zealand, where
he leads a tranquil life as a landscape gardener.
Unfortunately, his past catches up with him when a
hit-squad is sent to kill him and his family.

| | |
|---|---|
| DRA | 104 min |
| V | FUTUR |

## GRAVE OF THE VAMPIRE **                             18
John Hayes          USA                          1973
*William Smith, Michael Pataki, Kitty Vallacher*
A girl raped by a vampire gives birth to a monster
which she feeds with her blood in order to sustain it,
the son eventually growing up to have his revenge on
his father. A convoluted low-budget shocker that
starts off with great verve but gradually runs down.

| | |
|---|---|
| HOR | 91 min |
| B,V | GHV |

## GRAVEYARD DISTURBANCE *                             18
Lamberto Bava          ITALY                     1987
*Karl Zinny, Beatrice Ring*
A bunch of reckless teenagers on a shoplifting trip
make an ill-advised detour into a haunted cemetery,
when they are told at a spooky tavern that untold
wealth awaits whoever can spend a night in a musty
crypt. A largely comical tale of ghoulishness and
assorted zombie nastiness, is now unleashed in a film
as brainless as its central characters.

| | |
|---|---|
| HOR | 93 min |
| B,V | AVA |

## GRAVEYARD SHIFT ***                                 18
Gerard Ciccoritti          USA                   1985
*Silvio Oliviero, Helen Papas, Cliff Stoker, Dorin Ferber*
A 350-year-old vampire reduced to driving a cab in
New York falls, in love with a woman who reminds
him of his beloved, to whom he was betrothed three
centuries earlier. An unusual and rather tongue-in-
cheek yarn, followed by a sequel.

| | |
|---|---|
| HOR 86 min (ort 90 min) (Cut at film release by 16 sec) | |
| B,V | MED |

## GRAVEYARD SHIFT 2 **                                18
Gerard Ciccoritti          USA                   1988
*Wendy Gazelle, Mark Soper, Silvio Oliviero, Ilse Von*
*Glatz*
A weak follow-up to the first tale, with our vampire in
search of fresh blood.
Aka: UNDERSTUDY, THE

| | |
|---|---|
| HOR | 90 min |
| V | ACDV |

## GRAY LADY DOWN *                                    PG
David Greene          USA                        1978
*Charlton Heston, Stacy Keach, David Carradine, Ned*
*Beatty, Ronny Cox, Rosemary Forsyth, Stephen*
*McHattie, Christopher Reeve*
A nuclear submarine collides with a freighter and is
damaged, becoming stuck in an underwater crevice. A
rescue mission is mounted but it's the script that
really needs salvaging in this yawn-inducing tale.
Boa: novel by David Lavallee.

| | |
|---|---|
| DRA | 105 min (ort 111 min) |
| B,V | CIC |

## GRAYEAGLE **                                        PG
Charles B. Pierce          USA                   1978
*Ben Johnson, Alex Cord, Lana Wood, Iron Eyes Cody,*
*Jack Elam, Paul Fix, Jacob Daniels, Charles B. Pierce*
A man tracks down the Indian who has kidnapped his
daughter in this retread of THE SEARCHERS that is
badly flawed by poor pacing. Written and directed by
Pierce, who also pops up very briefly in the film.

| | |
|---|---|
| WES | 99 min (ort 104 min) |
| B,V,V2 | GHV |

## GREASE ***                                          PG
Randal Kleiser          USA                      1978
*John Travolta, Olivia Newton-John, Eve Arden,*
*Stockard Channing, Sid Caesar, Jeff Conaway, Didi*
*Conn, Jamie Donnelly, Dinah Manott, Barry Pearl,*
*Kelly Ward*
Film version of a Broadway musical looking at the

lives and loves of kids in a 1950s high school. An amusing pastiche of 1950s films and manners, in which nothing and nobody is to be taken seriously. The lively dance routines were choreographed by Patricia Birch. Followed by GREASE 2 – one of those sequels that's best forgotten.
Boa: musical by Jim Jacobs and Warren Casey.
MUS                                                      110 min
B, V/h, V2                                                   CIC

**GREASE 2 ***                                              PG
Patricia Birch              USA                           1982
*Maxwell Caulfield, Michelle Pfeiffer, Adrian Zmed, Lorna Luft, Eve Arden, Didi Conn, Sid Caesar, Dody Goodman, Leif Green, Tab Hunter, Connie Stevens*
An attempt to cash in on the success of the first movie, but this time round the story is one of a British boy who joins the senior high school class. Clumsy, muddled and lacking in good numbers, a dud on all counts. Birch's directorial debut.
MUS                                      109 min (ort 114 min)
V                                                            CIC

**GREASED LIGHTNING ***                                    PG
Michael Schultz            USA                            1977
*Richard Pryor, Beau Bridges, Pam Grier, Cleavon Little, Vincent Gardenia, Richie Havens, Julian Bond*
A dull biopic about Wendell Scott, the first black racing-car driver. Episodic and sluggish and uninteresting, despite the best efforts of a good cast.
DRA                                                       94 min
B,V                                                        WHV

**GREAT AMERICAN TRAFFIC JAM, THE ***
James Frawley              USA                            1981
*Desi Arnaz Jr, John Beck, Noah Beery, Rene Enriquez, James Gregory, Shelley Fabares, Phil Foster, Lisa Hartman, Michael Lerner, Rue McClanahan, Ed McMahon, Christopher Norris, Al Molinaro, Allen Sues, Vic Tayback*
Comedy involving a vast traffic jam that blocks the L.A. freeway system. Quite well done if you like that sort of thing, which in this movie, largely results in acres of hooting cars.
Aka: GRIDLOCK
COM                                              110 min mTV
B,V                                               SPEC/POLY

**GREAT AMERICAN TRAGEDY, A ***
J. Lee Thompson           USA                             1972
*George Kennedy, Vera Miles, William Windom, Sallie Shockley, Kevin McCarthy, Hilary Thompson, James Woods, Natalie Trundy, Nancy Hadley, Robert Mandan, Tony Dow, Marcia Mae Jones*
A family falls on hard times when the father, an aerospace engineer, is made redundant. A fairly straightforward tale with a simple message and a hopeful ending.
DRA                                               73 min mTV
B,V                                                        IFS

**GREAT BALLOON ADVENTURE, THE ***
Richard A. Colla          USA                             1978
*Katharine Hepburn, Kevin McKenzie, Dennis Dimster, George Kennedy, Vera Peter Kilman, Vera Miles, William Windom*
A boy wants to follow in his grandfather's footsteps by flying a circus balloon and performing aerial stunts at fairs. Hepburn plays a colourful junk dealer who befriends him and his friend, helping them realise this ambition in a forgettable story, with a script as light as the hot-air balloon they eventually fly in.
Aka: OLLY OLLY OXEN FREE
A/AD                                          84 min (ort 89 min)
B,V,V2                                                   INT/CBS

**GREAT BALLS OF FIRE! ****                                 15
Jim McBride               USA                             1989
*Dennis Quaid, Winona Ryder, Trey Wilson, Lisa*

*Blount, Alec Baldwin, Stephen Tobolowsky, John Doe, Steve Allen*
Quaid is outstanding in this flashy and stylised account of the rise and fall of rock 'n' roller Jerry Lee Lewis, a thrice married and hard living singer who suffered a temporary setback in his career following his marriage to his third wife, a 13-year-old cousin. Lewis' voice is dubbed in, but that's Quaid playing the piano. Entertaining if a trifle clumsily edited. Look out for Baldwin as evangelist Jimmy Swaggart, Lewis' famous cousin.
Boa: book by Myra Lewis.
DRA                                                      103 min
V                                                           VIR

**GREAT BOOKIE ROBBERY, THE ***                            15
Marcus Cole/Mark Joffe
                    AUSTRALIA                             1985
*John Bach, Catherine Wilkin, Gary Day, Bruno Lawrence, Paul Sonkkila, Dennis Moore, Andy Anderson, George Spartels, Ray Meagher, Scott Burgess, Gary Sweet, Frank Gallagher, Gary Files, Tim McKenzie, Madelaine Blackwell*
The story of a 1976 robbery in Melbourne in which an armed gang relieved the local bookies of over three million Australian dollars forms the background to an undistinguished crime drama. The last third describes the difficulties faced by the crooks afterwards from greedy fellow criminals and the police alike, and the latter emerge with little glory, being depicted as slow-witted, inefficient and corrupt.
THR          262 min (ort 270 min) (3 cassettes) Cut (2 sec)
B,V                                              CAN; CAREY

**GREAT CARUSO, THE ****                                     U
Richard Thorpe            USA                             1950
*Mario Lanza, Ann Blyth, Dorothy Kirsten, Jarmila Novotna, Carl Benton Reid, Eduard Franz, Richard Hageman, Ludwig Donath, Alan Napier*
The rags-to-riches story of Enrico Caruso, one of the world's greatest opera singers. Largely fictional in content, and fairly well-supplied with the standard Hollywood cliches, but generally enjoyable and skilfully put together. AA: Sound (Douglas Shearer).
MUS                                104 min (ort 109 min) B/W
V                                                          MGM

**GREAT DAY IN THE MORNING ***
Jacques Tourneur          USA                             1955
*Virginia Mayo, Robert Stack, Ruth Roman, Alex Nicol, Raymond Burr, Leo Gordon, Regis Toomey, Peter Whitney, Dan White, Donald McDonald*
Western set in pre-Civil War Colorado, with clashes between gold prospectors and secessionists. A formula story lacking in excitement, but considerably helped by the nice locations.
Boa: novel by Robert Hardy Andrews. Osca: SECOND CHANCE
WES                                          89 min (ort 92 min)
B,V                                                        KVD

**GREAT DIAMOND ROBBERY, THE ***
Michele Lupo           ITALY/SPAIN                        1967
*Richard Harrison, Margaret Lee, Adolfo Celi*
An actor is asked to take part in a diamond robbery because of his striking resemblance to the head of security at the diamond company. Average.
Aka: COLPO MAESTRO AL SERVIZIO DI SUA MAESTA BRITANNICA; GRAN GOPLE AL SERVICIO DE SU MAJESTAD BRITANICA
THR                                                      101 min
B,V                                                        VPD

**GREAT ESCAPE, THE ****                                    PG
John Sturges              USA                             1963
*Steve McQueen, James Garner, Donald Pleasence, David McCallum, James Coburn, Richard Attenborough, Charles Bronson, Gordon Jackson, James Donald, John Leyton*

The true story of an Allied breakout from a German prison camp is shown in considerable detail, with the major portion of the film devoted to the preparations. Steve McQueen supplies the comic element as the "Cooler King". Entertaining if overlong, but with an unexpectedly depressing ending. The script is by James Clavell and W.R. Burnett. A TV sequel followed twenty-five years later.
Boa: book by Paul Brickhill.
WAR                          165 min (ort 168 min)
V                                                    WHV

**GREAT ESCAPE 2, THE ** **                    PG**
Paul Wendkos          USA              1988
*Christopher Reeve, Michael Nader, Ian McShane,*
*Donald Pleasence, Judd Hirsch, Arthur Dennison,*
*Charles Haid*
Another clear manifestation of the shortage of new ideas in Hollywood, is this ill-conceived attempt to produce a version of the original film. This one is in two parts, with the first half an examination of the planning and execution of this famous WW2 Allied escape, and the second a look at the tragically brutal consequences. Well made, but a film that adds very little to the earlier version of this tale.
Aka: GREAT ESCAPE 2, THE: THE UNTOLD STORY – PARTS 1 AND 2
WAR                          180 min (2 cassettes)
V                                                    RCA

**GREAT EXPECTATIONS ** **                      U**
Joseph Hardy          UK/USA            1974
*Michael York, Sarah Miles, James Mason, Margaret*
*Leighton, Robert Morley, Anthony Quayle, Joss*
*Ackland, Rachel Roberts, Heather Sears, Andrew Ray,*
*Simon Gipps-Kent, James Faulkner, Peter Bull, Sam*
*Kydd, John Clive*
Very much an average attempt at remaking the 1946 film, that was to have been produced as a musical, but had the songs deleted.
Boa: novel by Charles Dickens.
DRA                          119 min (ort 124 min) mTV
B,V                                                  PRV

**GREAT EXPECTATIONS ** **                      U**
Jean Tych          AUSTRALIA            1982
Competent animated version of the Dickens story.
Boa: novel by Charles Dickens.
CAR                                             72 min
B,V                          RPTA/VSP; MSD (VHS only)

**GREAT EXPECTATIONS **** **                    PG**
David Lean          UK                  1946
*John Mills, Valerie Hobson, Bernard Miles, Francis L.*
*Sullivan Finlay Currie, Martita Hunt, Anthony*
*Wager, Jean Simmons, Alec Guinness, Ivor Bernard,*
*Freda Jackson, Torin Thatcher, Eileen Erskine, Hay*
*Petrie*
The second sound version of the story of a young boy, befriended from afar by an escaped convict he once helped. One of the best films to ever come out of the British cinema; beautifully acted, superbly designed and wonderfully directed. Remade for TV in 1974. AA: Cin (Guy Green), Art/Set (John Bryan/Wilfred Singleton).
Boa: novel by Charles Dickens.
DRA                          113 min (ort 118 min) B/W
V                                                    RNK

**GREAT GATSBY, THE *** **                      PG**
Jack Clayton          USA              1974
*Robert Redford, Mia Farrow, Karen Black, Scott*
*Wilson, Sam Waterston, Lois Chiles, Bruce Dern,*
*Howard da Silva, Edward Herrmann, Patsy Kensit*
Second attempt to film the Scott Fitzgerald story, about a mysterious young millionaire who breaks into Long Island society in the 1920s. A vivid recreation of the period that stays faithful to the book but never develops into anything substantial, remaining a

frothy jazz-age celebration. The script is by Francis Ford Coppola. AA: Score (Nelson Riddle), Cost (Theoni V. Aldredge).
Boa: novel by F. Scott Fitzgerald.
DRA                          135 min (ort 144 min)
B,V                                                  CIC

**GREAT GOLD SWINDLE, THE ** **                 15**
John Power          AUSTRALIA            1984
*John Hargreaves, Robert Hughes, Tony Rickards,*
*Chris Haywood, Brian Marshall*
Formula action yarn of little complexity.
A/AD                                           97 min
B,V                                                  MPV

**GREAT GUNDOWN, THE ** **
Paul Hunt          USA                  1971
*Robert Padilla, Richard Rust, Mihita St David, El*
*Salvejo, Stanley Adams, Rita Rogers, Steven Oliver,*
*David Eastman, Rockne Tarkington, Michael*
*Christina, Owen Orr, Michael Green, Dirk Peno*
An outlaw gang raids a small Mexican town and carries off a priceless gold cross, but is then pursued by the Mexican army. A general bloodbath ensues in this violent story. Filmed in Arizona.
Aka: EL SALVEJO; FORTY GRAVES FOR FORTY GUNS; MACHISMO; MACHISMO: FORTY GRAVES FOR GUNS; SAVAGE, THE
WES                          83 min (ort 95 min)
B,V,V2                                               VCL/CBS

**GREAT GUY ** **
John G. Blystone          USA            1936
*James Cagney, Mae Clarke, Edward Brophy, James*
*Burke, Henry Kolker, Edward McNamara, Bernadene*
*Hayes*
An ex-prize fighter becomes an inspector of weights and measures and fights corruption in the meat trade. Typical Cagney, with Cagney playing Cagney, and this is the film's chief fault.
Aka: PLUCK OF THE IRISH
DRA                                       77 min B/W
B,V,V2                                               EVC

**GREAT HOUDINI, THE *** **
Melville Shavelson          USA          1976
*Paul Michael Glaser, Vivian Vance, Ruth Gordon,*
*Sally Struthers, Peter Cushing, Adrienne Barbeau,*
*Bill Bixby, Jack Carter, Nina Foch, Maureen*
*O'Sullivan, Wilfrid Hyde-White, Clive Revill, Geoffrey*
*Lewis, Jerome Thor*
Good biopic of the famous escapologist who seemed obsessed with the occult. Well-paced and articulate, with Gordon giving a strong performance as the illusionist's possessive mother.
Aka: GREAT HOUDINIS, THE
DRA                          96 min (ort 108 min) mTV
B,V                                                  GHV

**GREAT ICE RIP-OFF, THE ** **
Dan Curtis          USA                  1974
*Lee J. Cobb, Gig Young, Robert Walden, Grayson Hall,*
*Matt Clark, Geoffrey Lewis, Hank Garrett, Bill Smillie,*
*Orin Cannon, Norman Honath, Jerry August, Edgar*
*Daniels, Jason Dunn, Al Hansen, John Hart, Marcia*
*Lewis, Robert Nadder*
A retired cop enjoys a battle of wits with a jewel thief, during a bus journey from Seattle to San Diego. A lightweight and mildly enjoyable outing.
COM                                        78 min mTV
B,V                                                  RNK

**GREAT KIDNAPPING, THE ** **                   PG**
Roberto Infascelli          ITALY        1973
*Lee J. Cobb, Jean Sorel, Laura Belli*
A detective is assigned to a case of blackmail and has his son kidnapped by the blackmailers. Fair.
Aka: LA POLIZIA STA A GUARDERE

DRA 92 min
B,V TEVP; SCRN

## GREAT LAND OF SMALL, THE ***   U
Vojta Jasny   CANADA   1986
*Karen Elkin, Michael Blouin, Michael Anderson, Ken
Roberts, Lorraine Desmarais, Gilles Pelletier, Michele
Elaine Turmel, Jack Lanbedijk, Francoise Gratton*
A couple of New York kids visit the grandparents in
rural Quebec, and grandpa tells them about the
invisible creatures who live at the end of a rainbow.
This heralds the start of an enjoyable fantasy adven-
ture, as the two kids meet a leprechaun-like creature
and help him recover his bag of fairy gold dust.
A/AD 86 min
B,V NWV

## GREAT LOCOMOTIVE CHASE, THE ***   U
Frances D. Lyon   USA   1961
*Fess Parker, Jeffrey Hunter, Jeffrey York, John
Lupton, Don Megowan, Eddie Firestone, Claude
Jarman Jr, Harry Carey Jr, Slim Pickens, Kenneth
Tobey, Lennie Geer, Stan Jones, Morgan Woodward,
Harvey Hester*
Adventure story based on a true Civil War incident
when a Union spy led a band of rowdy volunteers on a
dangerous mission behind Confederate lines to steal a
Union train and destroy some strategically important
bridges. Parker is imposing as the famous spy in this
colourful and exciting story of the "Andrews' Raiders",
filmed once before by Buster Keaton as THE
GENERAL.
Aka: ANDREWS' RAIDERS
A/AD 72 min (ort 85 min)
B,V WDV

## GREAT McGONAGALL, THE *
Joseph McGrath   UK   1975
*Spike Milligan, Peter Sellers, Julia Foster, Julian
Chagrin, John Bluthal, Valentine Dyall, Clifton Jones,
Victor Spinetti, Charlie Atom, Janet Adair*
Set in Dundee 1890, this fictitious comedy was
inspired by the life of one of Britain's worst poets,
William McGonagall, who dreams of being made Poet
Laureate and saves the Queen from assassination. A
feeble effort.
COM 89 min (ort 95 min)
B,V,V2 VDM/GHV

## GREAT MONKEY RIP-OFF, THE **
Tom Stobart   USA   1979
*Alan Hale Jr, Robert J. Wilke, Ashay Chtire*
An animal trader plans to steal some sacred temple
monkeys, but his plans are upset by the temple
overseer.
COM 87 min
B,V,V2 INT/CBS

## GREAT MUPPET CAPER, THE **
Jim Henson   UK   1981
*Diana Rigg, Charles Grodin, John Cleese, Robert
Morley, Peter Usinov, Jack Warden, Erica Creer, Kate
Howard, Della Finch, Michael Robbins, Joan
Sanderson, Tommy Godfrey, Katia Borg, Valli Kemp,
Michele Ivan-Zadeh*
Feature film written around the puppet characters
from a TV series; "The Muppets". Here Kermit and
Fozzie are newspaper reporters assigned to cover a
jewel robbery. A large collection of guest stars make
appearances and help buoy up this somewhat thin
story.
COM 98 min
B,V,V2,LV PRV

## GREAT NORTHFIELD MINNESOTA RAID, THE
***
Philip Kaufman   USA   1972

*Robert Duvall, Cliff Robertson, Luke Askew, R.G.
Armstrong, Dana Elcar, Elisha Cook Jr, Royal Dano,
Donald Moffatt, John Pearce, Matt Clark, Barry
Brown, Wayne Sutherlin, Robert H. Harris, Jack
Manning, Mary-Robin Redd*
Two sets of criminal brothers, the Youngers and the
James, plan a raid on a well-guarded bank in
Minnesota. Good in the way it shows the seamy side of
this famous ill-fated robbery, but the muddled script
and quirky direction, hamper its development.
DRA 91 min
V CIC

## GREAT OUTDOORS, THE *   PG
Howard Deutch   USA   1988
*Dan Aykroyd, John Candy, Stephanie Faracy, Annette
Bening, Chris Young, Ian Giatti, Hilary Gordon,
Rebecca Gordon, Robert Prosky*
A family's vacation is ruined when the husband's
brother-in-law and his uncouth crowd invite them-
selves along. An unpleasant comedy that fires off its
jokes in all directions, without ever engaging one's
interest. Scripted by John Hughes.
Aka: BIG COUNTRY
COM 87 min (ort 90 min)
V/sh CIC

## GREAT RACE, THE **   U
Blake Edwards   USA   1965
*Jack Lemmon, Tony Curtis, Natalie Wood, Peter Falk,
Keenan Wynn, Larry Storch, Dorothy Provine, Arthur
O'Connell, Vivian Vance, Ross Martin, George
Macready*
Overlong and unfunny account of a 1908 car race
across three continents from New York to Paris.
Over-elaborate and sometimes spectacular, this long
and laboured comedy has a few good moments, but
most of them occur in the first half. AA: Effects (Aud)
(Tregoweth Brown).
COM 147 min (ort 163 min)
B,V WHV

## GREAT RIDE, A ***   15
Donald Hulette   USA   1977
*Perry Lang, Michael Sullivan, Michael MacRae*
Echoes of DUEL with two young dirt-riders crossing
America on their way from Mexico to Canada, and
being menaced by a strange vehicle; a high-tech
pick-up truck driven by an irate father, who wrongly
blames them for the death of his child.
Aka: GREAT RIDE, THE; NIGHTMARE TRACKS
DRA 90 min
B,V VUL L/A; FOX

## GREAT ROCK 'N' ROLL SWINDLE, THE **   18
Julian Temple   UK   1980
*Malcolm McLaren, Sid Vicious, Johnny Rotten, Steve
Jones, Paul Cook, Ronald (Ronnie) Biggs, Mary
Millington, Irene Handl, Eddie Tudor, Helen of Troy,
Sue Catwoman, Liz Fraser, Jess Conrad, Julian
Holloway, Dave Dee, Day D'Arcy*
A fictionalised account of the career of the punk rock
group "The Sex Pistols", that is alternately fascinat-
ing and repulsive. See also SID AND NANCY.
Aka: ROCK 'N' ROLL SWINDLE, THE
DRA 100 min (ort 105 min) (Cut at film release)
B,V PVG; VIR

## GREAT SANTINI, THE ***   PG
Lewis John Carlino   USA   1979
*Robert Duvall, Blythe Danner, Michael O'Keefe, Lisa
Jane Persky, Stan Shaw, Theresa Merritt, David Keith*
A Marine pilot has problems in adjusting to civilian
life, as well as in his relationship with his teenage son.
A vivid character study, with great performances but
little direction. Adapted from Conway's novel by
Carlino.
Aka: ACE, THE; GIFT OF FURY

Boa: novel by Pat Conway.

DRA    111 min (ort 115 min)
B,V    WHV

## GREAT SKYCOPTER RESCUE, THE **    18
Lawrence D. Foldes    USA    1982
*William Marshall, Aldo Ray, Russell Johnson, Terry Michos, Terri Taylor, Alex Manner, Richard C. Adams*
Two men run a skycopter business. They use this device, a combination of helicopter and hang-glider, to save their town from both Hell's Angels and an oil prospector. Average.

A/AD    74 min; 92 min (MGM) Cut (11 sec)
B,V    HVH L/A; MGM

## GREAT SMOKEY ROADBLOCK, THE **    15
John Leone    USA    1976
*Henry Fonda, Eileen Brennan, John Byner, Joseph Sergent, Dub Taylor, Susan Sarandon, Melanie Mayron, Austin Pendleton*
A terminally ill trucker makes one last cross-country run, this time his load is a brothel complete with occupants and fittings, with the police in hot pursuit. A few nice performances float about in there, but the overall impression is one of unremitting blandness. Co-produced by Sarandon.
Aka: LAST OF THE COWBOYS, THE

A/AD    106 min; 85 min (MAST)
B,V    VTC L/A; VMA; MAST (VHS only)

## GREAT ST TRINIANS TRAIN ROBBERY, THE *    U
Frank Lauder/Sidney Gilliat
    UK    1966
*Frankie Howerd, Dora Bryan, George Cole, Reg Varney, Raymond Huntley, Richard Wattis, Portland Mason, Terry Scott, Eric Barker, Godfrey Winn, Desmond Walter-Ellis, Colin Gordon, Barbara Couper, Elspeth Duxbury*
Filmed three years after the real Great Train Robbery, this tale follows the exploits of a bunch of criminals who hide their loot on a site that is used for building this notorious girls' school, forcing them to infiltrate the staff, in an attempt to regain it. The usual madcap capers and laboured comic moments ensue. Yet another sequel to THE BELLES OF ST TRINIANS, this dismal farce was followed by THE WILDCATS OF ST TRINIANS.

COM    94 min
V    WHV

## GREAT TELEPHONE ROBBERY, THE **
Menahem Golan    ISRAEL    197-
*Gadi Yagil, Bomba Tzur, Shai Ophir*
A bank clerk's mother is kidnapped and he plans a robbery to raise the ransom in this predictable offering.

COM    98 min
B,V    RNK

## GREAT TEXAS DYNAMITE CHASE, THE *    18
Michael Pressman    USA    1976
*Claudia Jennings, Jocelyn Jones, Johnny Crawford, Chris Pennock, Tara Strohmeir*
Two young women drive across Texas, leaving a trail of robbed banks behind them in this cliche-ridden, and all too predictable actioner.
Aka: DYNAMITE WOMEN

A/AD    85 min (ort 92 min) Cut (5 sec)
B,V    WHV

## GREAT WALDO PEPPER, THE ***    PG
George Roy Hill    USA    1975
*Robert Redford, Bo Svenson, Susan Sarandon, Geoffrey Lewis, Margot Kidder, Bo Brundin, Edward Herrmann, Scott Newman*
WW1 flying aces are forced to make a living by giving stunt shows. An interesting film that hovers between drama and comedy, without ever coming to land at either point. However, the flying stunts are superb, as is the photography (by Robert Surtees). The music is by Henry Mancini.

A/AD    102 min (ort 107 min)
B,V    CIC

## GREAT WALL, A **    PG
Peter Wang    CHINA/USA    1986
*Peter Wang, Sharon Iwai, Kelvin Han Yee, Li Qinqin, Hu Xiaoguang, Shen Guanglan, Wang Xiao, Xiu Jian, Ran Zhiluan, Han Tan, Jeanette Pavini, Howard Frieberg, Bill Neilson, Teresa Roberts*
A wry comedy about an American computer expert visting his relatives in Peking, and the resulting clash of cultures that occurs, as this Americanised family encounters life in the People's Republic. Likeable enough, but hardly great comedy. Wang's first feature as co-writer, star and director.
Aka: GREAT WALL, THE; GREAT WALL IS A GREAT WALL, THE

COM    100 min
V    PAL

## GREAT WHITE HOPE, THE ***    15
Martin Ritt    USA    1970
*James Earl Jones, Jane Alexander, Chester Morris, Lou Gilbert, Joel Fluellin, Robert Webber, R.G. Armstrong, Hal Holbrook, Beah Richards, Moses Gunn*
The story of the first black heavyweight boxing champion and the racial hatred he encountered. A strong character study of Jack Johnson (called Jefferson) that has serious deficiencies in the dramatic department, but is hard to fault in terms of acting, or authentic-looking period detail. Set in 1910.
Boa: play by Howard Sackler.

DRA    100 min
B,V,LV    CBS

## GREATEST AMERICAN HERO, THE **    PG
Rod Holcomb    USA    1981
*William Katt, Robert Culp, Connie Sellecca, Michael Pare, Faye Grant, Jesse D. Goins, Don Cervanties*
This pilot for a series that lasted from 1981 to 1983, is a super-hero spoof in which a young teacher is given a flying suit by aliens, that endows him with many powers. Unfortunately, he loses the instruction manual that comes with it, thereby restricting his usefulness to a neurotic FBI agent who wants to employ him as a crimefighter.

COM    91 min mTV
V    CIC

## GREATEST ATTACK, THE **    18
Pierre Granier-Deferre
    FRANCE    1979
*Alain Delon, Veronique Jannot, Bernard Giraudeau, Francine Berge*
A love story about an army doctor and a nurse on the eve of WW3.
Aka: HARMONIE; LE TOUBIB; MEDIC, THE; PRELUDE TO APOCALYPSE (VIZ or GLOB)
Boa: novel Harmonie Ou Les Horreurs De La Guerre by Jean Frustie.

DRA    90 min; 92 min (VIDAGE)
B,V    VTC L/A; VIDAGE; VIZ; GLOB

## GREATEST SHOW ON EARTH, THE ***    U
Cecil B. De Mille    USA    1952
*Charlton Heston, Betty Hutton, Cornel Wilde, James Stewart, Dorothy Lamour, Gloria Grahame, Henry Wilcoxon, Lawrence Tierney, Lyle Bettger, Emmett Kelly, John Kellogg, John Ringling North*
A long epic about life under the big-top, where various dramatic situations are played out. Everything is here: cliches in abundance, spectacular disasters, the excitement of the big-top, and the lives and loves of the people in it. Not so much a film as a parade of stars

and situations, but all very impressively done. AA: Pic, Story (Fredrick M. Frank/Theodore St John/ Frank Cavett).

DRA 147 min (ort 153 min)
B,V CIC

## GREATEST, THE ** PG
Tom Gries USA 1977
*Muhammad Ali, Ernest Borgnine, John Marley, Lloyd Haynes, Robert Duvall, James Earl Jones, Dina Merrill, Paul Winfield, Roger E. Mosley, Ben Johnson, Malachi Thorne, David Huddleston*
Ali plays himself in this bland, unfocused and boring mess that attempts to chart the rise of this brilliant boxer from rags to riches, but succeeds only in being ponderous and dull. Ali's acting is adequate, but it's Mosley, as former champ Sonny Liston, who engages our attention. Written by Ring Lardner Jr.
Boa: book by Muhammad Ali, Herbert Muhammad and Richard Durham.

DRA 98 min
V RCA

## GREEK CONNECTION, THE **
Dacosta Caragan GREECE 1974
*John Miller, Rita Adler, Fernando Bislani*
A safe-cracker is forced by an Athens underworld leader into taking part in a robbery in this formula time-filler.

DRA 77 min
B,V PRV

## GREEK TYCOON, THE * 15
J. Lee Thompson USA 1978
*Anthony Quinn, Raf Vallone, Jacqueline Bisset, Charles Durning, Camilla Sparv, Edward Albert, James Franciscus*
The romance and marriage of a President Kennedy's widow and Greek shipping tycoon Aristotle Onassis, form the basis for this pointless film. The beautiful settings only serve to highlight the painful emptiness of the script.

DRA 112 min
B,V CIC

## GREEN BERETS, THE * PG
John Wayne/Ray Kellogg
USA 1968
*John Wayne, David Janssen, Ray Kellogg, Jim Hutton, Aldo Ray, Raymond St Jacques, Bruce Cabot, George Takei, Jack Soo, Patrick Wayne, Mike Henry*
Story of the Special Forces in Vietnam. The final scene has the sun setting in the East, a nice comment on the credibility of the whole film.
Boa: novel by Robin Moore.

WAR 136 min (ort 141 min)
B,V WHV

## GREEN EYES ***
John Erman USA 1976
*Paul Winfield, Rita Tushingham, Jonathan Lippe, Victoria Racimo, Lemi, Royce Wallace, Robert DoQui, Fred Sadoff, Dabbs Greer, Claudia Bryar, Joseph Hieu, Ric Mancini*
A black ex-GI returns to Vietnam to look for his common-law wife and child, and has a tragic reunion in this engrossing drama.
Boa: story by David Seltzer and Eugene Logan.

DRA 100 min mTV
B,V POLY

## GREEN HORIZONS **
Susumu Hani JAPAN 1981
*James Stewart, Philip Sayer, Eleonora Vallone*
The survivor of a plane crash is taken care of by a recluse and his young granddaughter, who live a secluded life in the wilderness.
Aka: AFURIKA MONOGATARI; GREEN HORIZON, THE; TALE OF AFRICA, A

DRA 97 min
B,V VFP

## GREEN ICE * 15
Ernest Day UK 1981
*Ryan O'Neal, Anne Archer, Omar Sharif, Domingo Ambriz, John Larroquette, Philip Stone, Michael Sheard, Enrique Lucero, Manuel Ojeda, Tara Fellner, Sandra Kerns, Raul Martinez, Deloy White*
An electronics engineer becomes involved in a plot to steal a cache of emeralds. A yawn-inducing caper that has one good moment – the use of a balloon to commit the theft.
Boa: novel by Gerald Browne.

A/AD 112 min; 105 min (CH5) (ort 115 min)
B,V,LV PRV; CH5 (VHS only)

## GREEN MAN, THE ***
Robert Day UK 1957
*Alastair Sim, George Cole, Terry-Thomas, Jill Adams, Dora Bryan, Raymond Huntley, Avril Angers, Eileen Moore, John Chandos, Colin Gordon, Cyril Chamberlain, Doris Yorke, Vivienne Wood, Arthur Brough, Marie Burke*
A seemingly timid clockmaker much prefers his part-time job as paid assassin, and encounters unforeseen obstacles when he takes on an assignment to kill a politician, who's staying at a country inn. A droll and quirky little comedy with Sim quite delightful, in a role that's both wicked and hilarious.
Boa: play Meet A Body by Frank Launder and Sidney Gilliat.

COM 80 min B/W
V WHV

## GREENGAGE SUMMER, THE ** PG
Lewis Gilbert UK 1961
*Kenneth More, Susannah York, Danielle Darrieux, Jane Asher, Maurice Denham, Claude Nollier, Elizabeth Dear, Richard Williams, David Saire, Raymond Gerome, Andre Maranne, Harold Kasket, Jacques Brunuis, Joy Shelton, Balbina*
A young girl, staying at a hotel on the Continent, has a love affair with a jewel thief.
Aka: LOSS OF INNOCENCE
Boa: novel by Rumer Godden.

DRA 99 min
V RCA

## GREETINGS *** 18
Brian De Palma USA 1968
*Jonathan Warden, Robert De Niro, Gerrit Graham, Richard Hamilton, Megan McCormick, Allen Garfield*
An improvised and haphazard satire revolving around draft-dodgers, sex and 60s sub-culture, with a guy trying every trick in the book to get himself exempted. A mixture of funny gags, faded ideas and self-indulgence, it has a dated 60s feel all of its own. Not so much a film as a time-capsule. Written by Charles Hirsch and De Palma, and followed by "Hi, Mom!".

COM 88 min
V CASPIC/TERRY

## GREGORY'S GIRL ** PG
Bill Forsyth UK 1980
*Gordon John Sinclair, Dee Hepburn, Jake D'Arcy, Clare Grogan, Robert Buchanan, William Greenlees, Alan Love, Caroline Guthrie, Carl Macartney, Douglas Sannachan, Allison Foster, Chic Murray, Alex Norton, John Bett*
Over-rated comedy about a young teenager who falls for a girl at his school, but is too bashful to ask her out. After several false starts he finds himself taking out the girl who really does fancy him. A mildly engaging comedy with a few nice cameos, but little else.

COM 91 min; 89 min (PICK)
B,V HOK; PICK (VHS only)

## GREMLINS **
Joe Dante     USA     1984
*Zach Galligan, Phoebe Cates, Hoyt Axton, Frances Lee McCain, Polly Holliday, Judge Reinhold, Corey Feldman, Glynn Turman, Dick Miller, Keye Luke, Scott Brady, Jackie Joseph*
A boy is given a strange animal as a Christmas present, and ignores the injunction against allowing it to come in contact with water, whereupon it gives rise to a host of murderous creatures that go on a rampage. A spoofy horror yarn, full of film-buff in-jokes, it would have been far better as a a straight horror tale. Look out for several cameos, not least one featuring executive producer Steven Spielberg.
HOR     102 min (ort 111 min)
V/sh     WHV

15

## GREMLOIDS ***
Todd Durham     USA     1986
*Alan Marx, Paul Poundstone, Chris Elliott, Robert Bloodworth*
A one-joke film, spoofing all those expensive science fiction movies with the title characters being a bunch of midgets, who scurry about their evil but not terribly powerful leader. Despite a number of funny skits on famous earlier films, this one is too episodic to work as a movie, but as a series of low-budget parodies, it's fine.
Aka: HYPERSPACE
FAN     86 min
B,V     PVG; CERT

PG

## GREVIOUS BODILY HARM ***
Mark Joffre     AUSTRALIA     1988
*Colin Friels, John Waters, Bruno Lawrence, Joy Bell*
An investigative reporter discovers a link between a man's obsessive belief that his apparently dead wife is really alive, and a series of inexplicable murders. A complex and carefully thought out thriller.
Aka: GBH: GREVIOUS BODILY HARM (WOV)
THR     90 min
V     WOV L/A; CHV

18

## GREY FOX, THE ***
Philip Borsos     CANADA     1982
*Richard Farnsworth, Jackie Burroughs, Wayne Robson, Ken Pogue, Timothy Webber, Gary Reineke, David Peterson, Don McKay, Samantha Langevin, James McLarty, Tom Heaton, George Dawson, Ray Michal, Stephen E. Miller*
After 33 years in jail, a robber switches from stage-coaches to trains, rather than retire from the only work he knows. An unusual and entertaining film based on the life of Bill Miner, who really did start robbing again soon after his release. Farnsworth gives a nice performance, a highlight is the sequence which has him watching "The Great Train Robbery".
DRA     92 min
B,V     PVG

PG

## GREYFRIARS BOBBY **
Don Chaffey     UK/USA     1960
*Donald Crisp, Laurence Naismith, Alexander Mackenzie, Kay Walsh, Andrew Cruickshank, Gordon Jackson, Freda Jackson, Duncan Macrae, Vincent Winter, Rosalie Crutchley*
A dog keeps watch over its master's grave, and is eventually given the Freedom of Edinburgh, in this Disney remake of "Challenge To Lassie". Based on the real-life tale of a 19th century Skye terrier. A film of some charm, but handicapped by slow development. Crisp played the dog's master in the earlier film.
Boa: novel by Eleanor Atkinson.
DRA     91 min
B,V     WDV

U

## GREYSTOKE: THE LEGEND OF TARZAN, LORD OF THE APES **
Hugh Hudson     USA     1984

PG

*Christopher Lambert, Andie McDowell, Ian Holm, Ralph Richardson, James Fox, Cheryl Campbell, Ian Charleson, Nigel Davenport*
A flawed attempt to make a more authentic version of the "Tarzan" stories of Edgar Rice Burroughs. Here the boy is discovered by a Belgian explorer, after having been brought up by apes (of an indeterminate species), and taken back to civilisation and his grandfather's estate. A faintly absurd film, that adopts an irritating moral tone. McDowell's voice was dubbed over by Glenn Close. This was Richardson's last film.
Aka: GREYSTOKE
Boa: novel Tarzan Of The Apes by Edgar Rice Burroughs.
DRA     129 min
V/sh     WHV

## GRIFFIN AND PHOENIX: A LOVE STORY ***
Daryl Duke     USA     1976
*Peter Falk, Jill Clayburgh, John Lehne, Dorothy Tristan, George Chandler, Milton Parsons, Ben Hammer, John Harkins, Randy Faustino, Charone, Stephen Rogers, Rod Hasse, Ken Sansom, Sally Kirkland, Russell Shannon*
Two doomed people enjoy a brief affair before they both succumb to their terminal illnesses, in this sentimental tearjerker that is redeemed by a couple of fine performances.
Aka: TODAY IS FOREVER
DRA     100 min mTV
B,V     RNK

## GRIP OF THE STRANGLER **
Robert Day     UK     1958
*Boris Karloff, Elizabeth Allan, Jean Kent, Vera Day, Anthony Dawson, Tim Turner, Diane Aubrey, Dorothy Gordon, Leslie Perrins, Derek Birch*
A crime-writer re-opens an old murder case, but finds that he was in fact the "Haymarket strangler" who was hanged twenty years ago. An effective if somewhat predictable thriller.
Aka: HAUNTED STRANGER, THE
Osca: FIEND WITHOUT A FACE
THR     70 min (ort 81 min) B/W
B,V     KVD

## GRISSOM GANG, THE **
Robert Aldrich     USA     1971
*Scott Wilson, Kim Darby, Tony Musante, Irene Dailey, Ralph Waite, Robert Lansing, Connie Stevens, Robert Lansing, Wesley Addy*
This remake of the 1948 British film "No Orchids For Miss Blandish", tells of an heiress who is kidnapped by a gang, but falls in with them when she acquires a taste for the life they lead. Violent and generally unpleasant but occasionally redeemed by sparks of black humour.
Boa: novel No Orchids For Miss Blandish by James Hadley Chase.
DRA     128 min
B,V     GHV

## GRIZZLY ***
William Girdler     USA     1976
*Christopher George, Andrew Prine, Richard Jaeckel, Joan McCall, Joe Dorsey, Vicki Johnson, Harvey Flaxman, Kermit Echols, Charles Kissinger, Tom Arcuragi*
A giant 2,000 lb grizzly bear goes on a rampage, attacking campers at a popular national park and forcing the park commission to send in troops to tackle it. A fair thriller with some good moments.
Aka: KILLER GRIZZLY
THR     92 min
B,V     RCA

15

## GROUND ZERO *
James T. Flocker     USA     1973

15

*Ron Casteel, Melvin Belli, John Waugh, Yvonne
D'Angiers*
San Francisco is held to ransom by a gang that
threatens to detonate a nuclear bomb in this predict-
able thriller.
THR                                                87 min
B,V                                     DFS; KRP/XTACY

### GROUND ZERO ***                                15
Michael Pattinson/Bruce Myles
                 AUSTRALIA                       1987
*Jack Thompson, Colin Friels, Donald Pleasence,
Natalie Bate, Simon Chilvers, Neil Fitzpatrick, Bob
Maza, Peter Cummins*
A cameraman learns that his father was a witness to
much of the British A-bomb testing that took place in
Australia in the 1950s, and may have been murdered
because of this. A slow-moving political thriller that
generates a good sense of paranoia, successfully
incorporating a host of issues regarding Aborigines,
political intrigue and genocide, but failing to hit most
of the targets it aims for.
THR                                                96 min
V                                                   VIR

### GROUP MARRIAGE ***
Stephanie Rothman        USA                     1972
*Victoria Vetri, Claudia Jennings, Aimee Eccles, Zack
Taylor, Jeff Pomerantz, Jayne Kennedy, Milt Karmen*
A group of young people in California set up a
commune, much to the displeasure of their neigh-
bours. An attractive cast make the most of the thin
plot, producing an enjoyable comedy.
COM                                                88 min
B,V                                             INT/CBS

### GROUPIE GIRL **
Derek Ford               UK                      1970
*Esme Johns, Billy Boyle, Donald Sumpter, Richard
Shaw, Neil Hallett, Charles Finch, Eliza Terry*
The dull story of a young groupie girl who runs away
from home to live with drug-taking pop groups. More
of a drama than a sex film, but not terribly interesting
on either score.
A                                                  87 min
B,V                                    MOV L/A; PORVI

### GRUNT *                                        15
Allan Holzman            USA                     1985
*Jeff Dial, Robert Glaudini, Marilyn Dodds Farr, Greg
Magic Schwartz, Wally Greene, Dick Murdoch, Steven
Cepello, John Tolos*
A documentary film-maker investigates a wrestler,
alleged to have decapitated an opponent in a bout in
1979. A dismal spoof that lands on the ropes in the
first round.
Aka: GRUNT! THE WRESTLING MOVIE
COM                                                91 min
B,V                                                 NWV

### GUARDIAN OF THE ABYSS **
Don Sharp                UK                      1984
*Ray Lonnen, Rosalyn Landor, John Carson, Paul
Darrow, Caroline Langrishe, Sophie Thompson,
Susan Fussey, Barry McDonald, Barbara Ewing*
An antiques dealer buys a mirror that possesses
strange powers in this unusual horror yarn.
Osca: CARPATHIAN EAGLE, THE
HOR                                                52 min
B,V,V2                                              PRV

### GUARDIAN, THE ***                              18
David Greene             USA                     1984
*Martin Sheen, Louis Gossett Jr, Arthur Hill, Tandy
Cronyn, Simon Reynolds, Tom Harvey, Maury
Chaykin, Anthony Sherwood, Taborah Johnson, Kate
Lynch, Dinah Christie, Shaaun Taylor, Bathsheba
Grant, Hadley Kay, Sean McCann*
The inhabitants of a New York building hire a

Vietnam veteran for protection after a murder and
rape have been committed there, but find that they
made a bad mistake. Thought provoking and generally effective if somewhat contrived.
DRA        97 min; 93 min (CH5) (ort 102 min) mCab
B,V                         VFP L/A; HER L/A; CH5

### GUARDIAN, THE **                               18
William Friedkin         USA                     1990
*Jenny Seagrove, Dwier Brown, Carey Lowell, Brad
Hall, Miguel Ferrer, Natalia Nogulich, Pamela Brull,
Gary Swanson*
Friedkin's first horror film since "The Exorcist" fea-
tures a malevolent nanny who is hired by a middle-
class couple to act as the nanny for their child.
However, she delights in sacrificing her young
charges to a Druidic tree god. A patchy film that
manages to maintain tension up to the point where
her true nature is revealed, after which the special
effects takes over and the film rapidly degenerates.
Co-scripted by the director.
Boa: novel The Nanny by Dan Greenburg.
HOR                                                89 min
V                                            CIC/CBSDIS

### GUERRILLAS IN PINK LACE *
George Montgomery        USA                     1964
*George Montgomery, Valerie Varda, Joan Shawlee,
Roby Grace*
A man on the run from the Japanese occupation of
Manila becomes involved with a group of showgirls, in
this insipid yarn whose best asset is its daft title.
COM                              80 min (ort 96 min)
B,V,V2                                          VCL/CBS

### GUESS WHAT HAPPENED TO COUNT
DRACULA? **
Laurence Merrick         USA                     1971
*Des Roberts, Claudia Barron, John Landon*
Count Dracula is alive and well and living in Holly-
wood, in this not entirely successful but occasionally
amusing spoof.
COM                                                80 min
B,V                                                 PRV

### GUESS WHAT WE LEARNT IN SCHOOL TODAY?
**
John G. Avildsen         USA                     1970
*Richard Carballo, Yvonne McCall, Jane McLeod,
Devin Goldberg*
A young woman teacher is accused of undermining
young people's morality because of her sex education
lessons, in this trite sex comedy set in a conservative
suburban community.
Aka: GUESS WHAT!?!/I AIN'T NO BUFFALO
A                                                  87 min
B,V,V2                                          INT/CBS

### GUESS WHO'S COMING TO DINNER ***          PG
Stanley Kramer           USA                     1965
*Spencer Tracy, Katharine Hepburn, Sidney Poitier,
Katherine Houghton, Cecil Kellaway, Beah Richards,
Roy E. Glenn Sr, Isabell Sanford, Virginia Christine*
A glossy and contrived tale of a white, liberal couple,
whose daughter announces her intention to marry a
man who would be anyone's choice, but for the fact
that he is a Negro. This gives rise to serious misgiv-
ings on their behalf, which are shared by his parents.
A stilted and superficial look at bigotry and mixed
marriage, well-acted but filmed like a stage play. This
was Tracy's last film. AA: Actress (Hepburn), Story/
Screen (William Rose).
DRA                            103 min (ort 108 min)
V                                                  RCA

### GUESS WHO'S SLEEPING IN MY BED? ***
Theodore Flicker         USA                     1973
*Barbara Eden, Dean Jones, Kenneth Mars, Susanne*

*Benton, Reta Shaw, Todd Lookinland, Diana Herbert, Walter Beakel*
A man too lazy to work, takes his new wife, young baby and Great Dane to stay at his ex-wife's home. A surprisingly engaging comedy despite the foolishness of the basic premise.
Boa: play Six Weeks In August by Pamela H. Chains
COM                       74 min (ort 90 min) mTV
B,V                                          GHV

### GUIDE FOR THE MARRIED MAN, A ****     PG
Gene Kelly            USA                1967
*Walter Matthau, Robert Morse, Inger Stevens, Sue Ann Langdon, Claire Kelly, Elaine Devry. Guest stars: Lucille Ball, Jack Benny, Polly Bergen, Joey Bishop, Sid Caesar, Art Carney, Wally Cox, Jayne Mansfield, Hal March*
A man's friend tries to teach him how to be an unfaithful husband, much against his own inclinations in this consistently funny adult comedy. A host of guest stars (eighteen in all) make appearances to teach the basics of adultery to faithful husband Matthau, and to demonstrate Morse's theories.
Boa: book by F. Tarloff.
COM                                     91 min
B,V                                       CBS

### GULAG ***                             18
Roger Young          UK                  1984
*David Keith, Malcolm McDowell, Warren Clarke, Nancy Paul, Brian Pettifer, David Suchet, John McEnery, Shane Rimmer, Bruce Boa, Eugene Lipinski, George Pravda, Alexei Jawdokimov, David Wozniak, Angela Pleasence, Barrie Houghton*
An American sportscaster is arrested on false charges whilst in the USSR, and is given ten years in a labour camp, in this often harrowing prison thriller covering similar ground to COMING OUT OF THE ICE. With a small group of his fellow prisoners, he plans an ingenious escape. The script is by Dan Gordon.
Boa: story by Dan Gordon, Raphael Shauli and Yehousha Ben-Porat.
THR                      114 min (ort 129 min) mCab
B,V                                       HER

### GULLIVER IN LILLIPUT **               U
Barry Letts     AUSTRIA/UK/USA           1981
*Elisabeth Sladen, Linda Polan, Jonathan Cecil, Andrew Burt, George Little*
A compilation of a drama serial telling of Gulliver's adventures among the tiny people of Lilliput, that attempts to restore some of the caustic wit to be found in the novel.
Boa: novel by Jonathan Swift.
A/AD                                 105 min mTV
B,V                                       BBC

### GULLIVER'S TRAVELS *                   U
Peter R. Hunt    BELGIUM/UK              1976
*Richard Harris, Catherine Schell, Norman Shelley, Meredith Edwards. Voices of: Michael Bates, Denise Bryer, Julian Glover, Stephen Jack, Bessie Love, Murray Melvin, Nancy Nevinson, Robert Rietti, Vladek Sheybal, Graham Stark*
A live-action and animation version of this famous tale that, is about as ineffective an adaptation as any ever made. Dreary songs are complemented by poor animations.
Boa: novel by Jonathan Swift.
JUV                  78 min; 74 min (STABL) (ort 81 min)
B,V                                RNK; STABL

### GULLIVER'S TRAVELS **                  U
                     USA
A competent but by no means inspired Hanna-Barbera production, following Gulliver's adventures in Lilliput.
Boa: novel by Jonathan Swift.

CAR                                     47 min
B,V                        MOV L/A; VCC (VHS only)

### GULLIVER'S TRAVELS ***                 Uc
Dave Fleischer       USA                 1939
*Voices of: Lanny Ross, Jessica Fragonette*
Cartoon animation of this famous tale, dealing with Gulliver's adventures in Lilliput only. A weak and aloof story that never really comes to life, is helped slightly by a few pleasant songs and fair animation.
Boa: novel by Jonathan Swift.
CAR                                     74 min
B, V/h, V2, LV    DFS L/A; VCL L/A; VMA; BBC (VHS only)

### GULLIVER'S TRAVELS PART 2 **           U
Cruz Delgado         SPAIN               1983
Fair Spanish animation following Gulliver's second adventure among the giant Brobdignagians.
Aka: LAND OF THE GIANTS: GULLIVER'S TRAVELS PART 2 (MOG)
Boa: novel by Joanthan Swift.
CAR                                     90 min
B,V                                       MOG

### GUMBALL RALLY, THE ***                 PG
Chuck Bail           USA                 1976
*Michael Sarrazin, Normann Burton, Gary Busey, Tim McIntire, Raul Julia, Nicholas Pryor, Susan Flannery, Steven Keats, J. Pat O'Malley, Harvey Jason, Joanne Nail, Vaughn Taylor, Tricia O'Neil, Med Flory*
The first of the cross-country road race films, with a variety of vehicles taking part in a race from New York to Long Beach, California. The best of the madcap car race movies so far, but it's the stunts that really score over the humour, though there are a couple of nice cameos. Almost certainly provided the inspiration for the CANNONBALL RUN series.
COM                     102 min (ort 107 min)
B,V                                       WHV

### GUMS *
                     USA                 198-
*Terri Hall, Brother Theodore*
The story of a beautiful mermaid, who lures sailors to their doom by offering oral sex. Dull and exploitative attempt at titillation of no great merit.
A                                       64 min
B,V                        MOV L/A; PORVI

### GUMSHOE **                             15
Stephen Frears       UK                  1971
*Albert Finney, Billie Whitelaw, Frank Finlay, Janice Rule, Carolyn Seymour, Fulton Mackay, Billy Dean, George Innes, George Silver, Wendy Richard, Maureen Lipman, Neville Smith, Oscar James, Joey Kenton, Chris Cunningham*
A bingo caller fantasises about being a private eye, and suddenly becomes stuck with a murder case. A fairly effective spoof that is nothing like as funny as it could have been. Produced by Finney.
COM                     82 min (ort 88 min)
V                                         RCA

### GUN IN THE HOUSE, A **
Ivan Nagy            USA                 1981
*Sally Struthers, David Ackroyd, Dick Anthony Williams, Jeffrey Tambor, Allen Rich, Millie Perkins, Joel Bailey, Frank Koppala, Belita Moreno, Missy Francis, Valorie Armstrong, Max Showalter, Gary Wood, Matthew Faison*
A woman takes firearm lessons, and eventually shoots and kills an intruder in her home. However, the police refuse to accept she acted in self-defence, and prosecute her, thus treating us to a tedious lecture on the pros and cons of self-defence and firearms legislation.
DRA                     92 min (ort 100 min) mTV
B,V                                SPEC/POLY

**GUN LAW ★★**                                    15
Tonino Valerii         ITALY              1969
*Lee Van Cleef, Walter Rilla, Giuliano Gemma, Christa*
*Linder, Ennio Balbo, Lukas Ammann, Andrea Bosic,*
*Pepe Calvo, Giorgio Gargiullo, Anna Orso, Benito*
*Stefanelli*
A ruthless gunfighter befriends a young man and
teaches him how to handle a gun, but the latter
eventually comes to reject a life of violence, and the
two of them face a final showdown. A callous and
brutal actioner of no great merit.
Aka: DAY OF ANGER; DAY OF WRATH; DAYS OF
WRATH; I GIORNI DELL'IRA
WES                      81 min (ort 109 min)
B,V              WARAD L/A; FFV L/A; KRP

**GUN OF APRIL MORNING, THE ★★**          15
Alexander Singer      SPAIN/USA          1971
*Lee Van Cleef, Carroll Baker, Stuart Whitman, Elisa*
*Montes, Percy Herbert, Tony Vogel, Charles Stalnaker,*
*Charlie Bravo, Faith Clift, Dan Van Husen, D. Pollock,*
*Hugh McDermott, George Margo, Jose Bodalo*
A violent tale of the Old West, full of sound and fury
but little else. An Apache Indian serving with the US
Army Intelligence is assigned to investigate the
murder of an Indian commissioner and has to track
down a gun-runner.
Aka: CAPTAIN APACHE (VCL)
Boa: novel Captain Apache by S.E. Whitman.
WES        88 min (ort 95 min) (Cut at film release)
B,V                             VCL L/A; SCAN

**GUN THAT SHOOK THE WEST, THE ★**        PG
Andrew V. McLaglen     USA               1971
*Dean Martin, Brian Keith, Honor Blackman, Carol*
*White, Ben Johnson, Albert Salmi, Don Knight, Joyce*
*Van Patten, Denver Pyle, Merlin Olsen, Robert*
*Donner, Harry Carey Jr, Judi Meredith, Edward*
*Faulkner, Paul Fix, Bob Steele*
A big-budget waste of time and money, with bandits
battling each other for possession of a Gatling gun
during the Mexican War.
Aka: SOMETHING BIG
WES                      83 min (ort 108 min)
V                                       SCAN

**GUN, THE ★★★**                            PG
John Badham            USA               1974
*Stephen Elliott, Jean LeBouvier, Wallace Rooney,*
*David Huffman, Pepe Serna, Edith Diaz, Felipe*
*Turich, Val De Vargas, Ramon Bieri, Michael*
*McGuire, Ron Thompson, John Sylvester White,*
*Richard Bright, Mariclare Costello*
Follows the fate of a .38 Police Special handgun, from
the day it comes off the production line, through its
various owners; never being fired until the end, when
it is the instrument of a tragedy. Inevitably episodic,
but utterly absorbing.
Boa: story by Richard Levinson, William Link and Jay
Benson.
DRA                      71 min (ort 78 min) mTV
B,V                                      CIC

**GUNBUS ★★**                               PG
Zoran Perisic          UK                1986
*Scott McGinnis, Jeff Osterhage, Miles Anderson,*
*Ronald Lacey, Ingrid Held, Valerie Steffen, Keith*
*Buckley, Terrence Harvey, Nicholas Lyndhurst*
A pair of cowboy bank robbers are caught after
robbing their umpteenth bank and opt to serve in the
trenches of WW1 rather than go to jail. However, they
soon tire of this and join a suicide squadron of the
Royal Flying Corps and capture an enemy blimp. A
plethora of special effects and action sequences makes
up for the simple-mindedness of the script.
Aka: SKY PIRATES
COM                                     90 min
B,V                                      EIV

**GUNFIGHT AT THE OK CORRAL ★★★**          PG
John Sturges           USA               1957
*Burt Lancaster, Kirk Douglas, Jo Van Fleet, Rhonda*
*Fleming, John Ireland, Lyle Bettger, Frank Faylen,*
*Earl Holliman, Ted De Corsia, Dennis Hopper, Martin*
*Milner, Whit Bissell, George Matthews, John Hudson,*
*Olive Carey*
Excellent account of the events that led up to a famous
gunfight, when Wyatt Earp teamed up with Doc
Holliday, and shot it out with the Clanton gang. A
little slow getting there, but the final shoot-out is
worth waiting for. Written by Leon Uris with Frankie
Laine singing the title song.
WES                117 min (ort 121 min) B/W
V                                        CIC

**GUNFIGHT, A ★★★**
Lamont Johnson         USA               1970
*Kirk Douglas, Johnny Cash, Jane Alexander, Raf*
*Vallone, Karen Black, Eric Douglas, Dana Elcar,*
*Robert Wilke, Keith Carradine, Paul Lambert, Philip*
*L. Mead, John Wallwork*
Two gunfighters agree to stage a gunfight, and sell
tickets in an attempt to raise money for their shoot-
out. A spare and sombre mood piece, with Cash giving
a good performance in his debut. The film climaxes
with two possible endings.
WES                      87 min (ort 90 min)
B,V                                      RNK

**GUNG HO! ★★★**                           15
Ron Howard             USA               1986
*Michael Keaton, Gedde Watanabe, George Wendt,*
*Mimi Rogers, John Turturro, Soh Yamamura, Sab*
*Shimono, Clint Howard, Michelle Johnson*
A Japanese company is persuaded by Keaton to
re-open a Tennessee auto plant that closed down in his
depression-hit home town. The owners of the company
are totally unprepared for the ensuing clash of
cultures, especially the somewhat happy-go-lucky
attitude to work on the part of the local labour force. A
lightweight but enjoyable satire making few sharp
points on the differences between American and
Japanese work attitudes. Later a TV series.
COM                     108 min (ort 111 min)
B,V                                      CIC

**GUNGA DIN ★★★★**                          U
George Stevens         USA               1939
*Cary Grant, Douglas Fairbanks Jr, Sam Jaffe, Victor*
*McLaglen, Joan Fontaine, Eduardo Ciannelli,*
*Montagu Love, Abner Biberman, Robert Coote*
Exciting adventure set on the North-West Frontier,
and revolving around three army veterans who fight
the local tribesmen and chase women with equal
enthusiasm. Jaffe plays the title character, a water
carrier who has a moment of glory as he saves a
column of British soldiers from ambush. The script is
by Ben Hecht and Charles MacArthur.
A/AD               112 min (ort 117 min) B/W
V                                        VCC

**GUNPOWDER ★**                             PG
Norman J. Warren       UK                1985
*Gordon Jackson, Martin Potter, David Gilliam,*
*Anthony Schaeffer*
Two Interpol agents are given the task of saving
Western currencies from collapse, as the price of gold
plummets due to the sudden release of a vast stock by
criminal mastermind Dr Vache. A sub-Bond epic that
sounds and looks like an echo from the 1960s and is
not one jot better.
A/AD                                    81 min
B,V                                      VES

**GUNRUNNER, THE ★★**                       15
Nardo Castillo         CANADA            1984
                              (re-released 1989)
*Kevin Costner, Sara Botsford, Paul Soles, Gerard*

Parkes, Ron Lea, Mitch Martin, Larry Lewis, Aline
Van Dine, Ruth Dahan
A young man seeking guns to help the Chinese
rebellion of the 1920s, returns to Canada, and gets
involved in smuggling spirits with his brother, but
they are betrayed and his brother is killed. A dreary
gangster yarn with a few good moments, that was
shelved after being made, until Costner's stardom
prompted its release.

| A/AD | 90 min |
| B,V | NWV |

## GUNS AND THE FURY, THE **  PG
Tony Zarindast          USA          1981
Peter Graves, Cameron Mitchell, Michael Ansara,
Albert Salmi, Shaun Curry, Barry Stokes, Ben
Feitelson, Monique Vermeer, Ahmed Mazhar, Derren
Nesbitt, Amr Sahm, John Collin, Magdy Wahba
Two Americans drilling for oil in Persia in 1900,
become caught up in the struggle between the British,
the Russians and the locals. A cinema version of a TV
mini-series. The script is by Donald P. Fredette.
Average.
Aka: GUNS AND FURY

| A/AD | 96 min (ort 118 min) mTV |
| B,V,V2 | GHV |

## GUNS DON'T ARGUE **
Bill Karn/Richard G. Kaln
                        USA          1955
Myron Healy, Jean Harvey, Richard Crane
A re-enacted documentary on the lives of famous
American gangsters.
Osca: PROJECTED MAN, THE

| DRA | 87 min B/W |
| B,V | KVD |

## GUNS FOR SAN SEBASTIAN *  PG
Henri Verneuil
                FRANCE/ITALY/MEXICO          1968
Anthony Quinn, Charles Bronson, Anjanette Comer,
Sam Jaffe, Silvia Pinal, Jorge Martinez de Hoyos,
Jaime Fernandez, Pedro Armendariz Jr, Rosa
Furman, Leon Askin, Ivan Desny
A bandit is mistaken for a priest, and helps a Mexican
village fight off an Indian attack in this action-filled
but forgettable yarn, set in 1746.
Aka: GUNS OF SAN SEBASTIAN

| WES | 107 min (ort 111 min) |
| B,V | MGM |

## GUNS IN THE HEATHER **  U
Robert Butler          USA          1968
Kurt Russell, Glen Corbett, Alfred Burke, Patrick Barr
Espionage thriller for kids set in Ireland. A boy's
holiday lives livens up when he discovers that his
older brother is a CIA agent. Standard Disney non-
sense, competently put together. The script is by
Herman Groves.
Aka: SPY BUSTERS
Boa: novel by L. Amerman.

| JUV | 85 min |
| B,V | WDV |

## GUNS OF DIABLO, THE **  PG
Boris Sagal          USA          1964
Charles Bronson, Susan Oliver, Kurt Russell, Jan
Merlin, John Fielder, Douglas Fowley, Raymond
Barnes, Morris Ankrum, Russ Conway
A routine oater with the head of a wagon train
stopping at a small town and finding himself
embroiled in a conflict with a former adversary. A
feature compiled from a TV Western "The Travels Of
Jamie McPheeters" (1963-1964), but with some extra
footage added. Interestingly, Bronson gives a much
better performance in this one than in just about any
of his later films.
Aka: DAY OF RECKONING
Boa: novel The Travels Of Jamie McPheeters by R.L.

Taylor.

| WES | 77 min (ort 79 min) |
| B,V | MGM |

## GUNS OF NAVARONE, THE ***  PG
J. Lee Thompson          UK/USA          1961
Gregory Peck, David Niven, Stanley Baker, Anthony
Quinn, Anthony Quayle, Irene Papas, James Darren,
Gia Scala, James Robertson Justice, Richard Harris,
Bryan Forbes, Allan Cuthbertson, Albert Lieven,
Walter Gotell
Overlong story of a mission to blow up two massive
German guns, set atop an all but impregnable fortress
on an occupied Greek island in 1943. A nicely
balanced mixture of drama, tension and intrigue, and
if a trifle slow still highly enjoyable. Written by Carl
Foreman and followed by the inferior FORCE TEN
FROM NAVARONE. AA: Effects (Bill Warrington/
Vivian C. Greenham).
Boa: novel by Alistair MacLean.

| WAR | 157 min |
| V | RCA |

## GUNSLINGER *  PG
Roger Corman          USA          1956
John Ireland, Beverly Garland, Allison Hayes, Martin
Kingsley, Jonathan Haze, Chris Alcaide, Dick Miller,
Bruno Ve Sota, William Schallert, Margaret Campbell
An obscure little Western, in which a woman takes
over as sheriff in a small town after her sheriff
husband is gunned down, but discovers that the
baddies have sent for a gunslinger. A Corman quickie,
of poor scripting and low production values.

| WES | 75 min (ort 83 min) |
| B,V | RNK |

## GUNSMOKE: RETURN TO DODGE **  15
Vincent McEveety          USA          1987
James Arness, Amanda Blake, Buck Taylor, Fran
Ryan, Earl Holliman, Ken Olandt, W. Morgan
Sheppard, Patrice Martinez, Tantoo Cardinal, Steve
Forrest, Vincent McEveety
Once again, an ancient TV series is relaunched, as
part of a spate of films in the late 1980s that
attempted to re-establish the Western. The stories in
the series "Gunsmoke" followed the career of Marshal
Matt Dillon, as he upheld law and order at Dodge
City. In this tale the marshal is now retired, but
discovers that an old enemy is out to kill him when a
friend breaks out of jail to warn him. Average.

| WES | 90 min mTV |
| B,V | CBS |

## GUNSMOKE: THE LAST APACHE *  PG
Charles Correll          USA          1990
James Arness, Richard Kiley, Michael Learned, Amy
Stock-Poynton, Geoffrey Lewis, Joe Lara, Joaquin
Martinez, Hugh O'Brian, Amanda Blake
This misconceived attempt to revive a once-popular
TV series brings former US Marshall, Matt Dillon, out
of retirement to rescue a daughter he never knew he
had, when he visits an old flame and learns that the
girl has just been kidnapped by an Apache brave. A
mixture of dull plotting, mawkish sentimentality and
unrealistic characterisation.

| WES | 90 min mTV |
| V | CBS |

## GUS **  U
Vincent McEveety          USA          1976
Edward Asner, Don Knotts, Gary Grimes, Tim
Conway, Harold Gould, Dick Van Patton, Bob Crane,
Liberty Williams, Johnny Unitas, Dick Butkus, Tom
Bosley
A no-hope football team discovers a mule with a
powerful kick, and tries to keep him on their side.
When crooks attempt to kidnap him, the obligatory
madcap Disney chase ensues. Entertaining enough in
its way, but somewhat deficient in the new ideas

department.
COM 93 min (ort 96 min)
B,V WDV

## GUTS AND GLORY: THE RISE AND FALL OF OLIVER NORTH ** PG
Mike Robe USA 1989
*David Keith, Annette O'Toole, Barnard Hughes, Peter Boyle, Bryan Clark, Amy Stock-Poynton, Donald Craig*
A fact-based drama, following the career of the title character, from his military days to his work in the National Security Council and final downfall following the Iran-Contra scandal. This fairly straightforward tale is reasonably absorbing, despite some clumsy attempts to give a more "balanced" account of the events that led to North's resignation. Originally shown in two parts.
DRA 113 min (ort 200 min) mTV
V CIC

## GUYANA TRAGEDY: THE STORY OF JIM JONES ***
William A. Graham USA 1980
*Powers Boothe, Ned Beatty, Irene Cara, Veronica Cartwright, Rosalind Cash, Brad Dourif, Meg Foster, Diane Ladd, Randy Quaid, Ron O'Neal, Diana Scarwid, Madge Sinclair, LeVar Burton, James Earl Jones, Colleen Dewhurst, Ed Lauter*
Above-average recreation of the sordid tale of the growth of the cult led by the Rev. Jim Jones, and its tragic end, in the jungles of Guyana in November of 1978. Boothe won an Emmy for his powerful performance. The script is by Ernest Tidyman. See also GUYANA: CRIME OF THE CENTURY.
Boa: book Guyana Massacre: The Eyewitness Account by Charles A. Krause and The Washington Post staff.
DRA 192 min (ort 240 min) mTV
B,V SPEC/POLY

## GUYANA: CRIME OF THE CENTURY *
Rene Cardona Jr
MEXICO/PANAMA/SPAIN 1979
*Stuart Whitman, Gene Barry, John Ireland, Joseph Cotten, Bradford Dillman, Jennifer Ashley, Yvonne De Carlo*
A strange title for a film looking at the mass suicide of the Reverend Jim Jones and his followers, in a Guyanan jungle in November 1978. This insipid, uninspired drama compares badly with GUYANA TRAGEDY: THE STORY OF JIM JONES.
Aka: GUYANA: CULT OF THE DAMNED
DRA 108 min
B,V,V2 PRV

## GUYS AND DOLLS **** U
Joseph L. Mankiewicz USA 1955
*Frank Sinatra, Marlon Brando, Jean Simmons, Vivian Blaine, Stubby Kaye, B.S. Pully, Veda Ann Borg, Sheldon Leonard, Regis Toomey*
With dialogue drawn straight from Runyon, and some great numbers, this has to be one of the best musicals ever. Set in the underworld of small-time New York petty criminals and gamblers, it tells of one Sky Masterson, who is tricked into a bet that he cannot make a date with a girl from the Salvation Army. Songs (by Frank Loesser) include: "If I Were A Bell", "Luck Be A Lady", "Adelaide's Lament" and "Sit Down, You're Rockin' The Boat".
Boa: short stories by Damon Runyon.
MUS 150 min; 143 min (VGM)
B,V CBS; VGM (VHS only)

## GWENDOLINE ** 18
Just Jaeckin FRANCE 1984
*Tawny Kitaen, Brent Huff, Zabou, Bernadette LaFont, Jean Rougerie*
In the company of another girl and a man, Kitaen goes off in search of her long-lost father, and all three are captured by a tribe of warrior women out in the East and enjoy many adventures. A juvenile sex adventure, based on a French erotic comic strip with lots of nudity but not much else.
Aka: PERILS OF GWENDOLINE, THE; PERILS OF GWENDOLINE IN THE LAND OF THE YIK-YAK, THE
A 95 min; 97 min (EHE) Cut (2 min 51 sec)
B,V,V2 EHE; NELS

## GYMKATA * 18
Robert Clouse USA 1985
*Kurt Thomas, Tetchie Agbayani, Richard Norton, Edward Bell, Conan Lee*
A gymnast is sent to a Balkan country to take part in a martial arts contest, in this utterly inconsequential offering shot in Yugoslavia.
Boa: novel The Terrible Game by Dan Tyler Moore.
MAR 86 min (ort 90 min)
V MGM

## GYPSY MOTHS, THE *** 15
John Frankenheimer USA 1969
*Burt Lancaster, Deborah Kerr, Gene Hackman, Scott Wilson, Sheree North, Bonnie Bedelia, William Windom*
The story of a group of aerial stunt men who travel the USA putting on aerial displays, forms the basis for this exciting tale that tends to get bogged down in sentiment, once it's on the ground.
Boa: novel by James Drought.
DRA 103 min (ort 110 min)
B,V VFP L/A; MGM

## GYPSY WARRIORS, THE ** U
Lou Antonio USA 1978
*James Whitmore Jr, Tom Selleck, Joseph Ruskin, Lina Raymond, Michael Lane*
Set in 1940, this war drama tells of two US Army captains who are faced with a dangerous assignment: to parachute into occupied France to either retrieve a deadly toxin capable of killing millions, or destroy the laboratory it is housed in. They are helped in their mission by a friendly gypsy family.
WAR 75 min mTV
B,V CIC

## GYPSY, THE ** 
Jose Giovanni FRANCE/ITALY 1975
*Alain Delon, Annie Giradot, Paul Meurisse*
A gypsy escapes from prison to take his revenge on society for scorning and imprisoning him.
Aka: LE GITAN; LO ZINGARO
DRA 100 min
B,V,V2 VCL/CBS

# H

## H-BOMB ** 
P. Chalong THAILAND 1976
*Olivia Hussey, Christopher Mitchum, Krung Srmial*
A power-mad Cambodian general, teams up with the Bangkok underworld to steal an American nuclear missile, in a bid to dominate South East Asia. The CIA, the KGB and a group of terrorists go all out to get it in this formula action tale.
A/AD 93 min
B,V RNK

## H.O.T.S. ** 18
Gerald Seth Sindell USA 1979
*Susan Kiger, Lisa London, Pamela Jean Bryant, Kimberly Cameron, Lindsay Bloom, Mary Steelsmith, Steve Bond, H.C. Winkler, Angela Aames, Danny Bonaduce, Ken Olfson*
No holds are barred when two American college sororities fight it out to see which one of them is the

best, settling their differences with a strip football game. A trite and coarse spin-off from NATIONAL LAMPOON'S ANIMAL HOUSE, quite well made for this type of film.
Aka: HOTS

| COM | 97 min |
|---|---|
| B,V,V2 | SVC; ADB L/A; APX |

**H.O.T.S. 2 ***                                18
                    USA
*Coleen Camp, Jo Johnston, Rainbeaux Smith,*
*Rosanne Katon*
More of the same in this witless sequel to the first sorority sex-comedy and just as raucous and dim-brained.
Aka: HOTS 2

| COM | 88 min |
|---|---|
| B,V | SVC |

**H.R. PUFNSTUF ***                              U
Hollingsworth Morse     USA          1970
*Jack Wild, Billie Hayes, Martha Raye, "Mama" Cass*
*Elliott, Roberto Gamonet, Sharon Baird, Johnny*
*Silver, Andrew Ratoucheff, Billy Barty, Felix Silver,*
*Joy Campbell, Jane Dulo, Jan Davis, Princess*
*Livingston, Angelo Rossitto*
Animated puppet story of Living Island, where trees, houses etc. are all Mixed live-action and puppet animation tale of "Living Island", where tress, houses etc. are alive and a young boy is brought to the island by means of a magic flute. A film version of a popular TV show that's OK for kids of about seven and under.
Aka: PUFNSTUF

| JUV | 60 min (ort 98 min) |
|---|---|
| B,V | EHE |

**HAIR ***                                      15
Milos Forman          USA            1979
*Treat Williams, John Savage, Beverly D'Angelo, Annie*
*Golden, Dorsey Wright, Don Dacus, Cheryl Barnes,*
*Nicholas Ray, Charlotte Rae*
Film version of a 1960s Broadway musical, which was a kind of celebration of the hippy sub-culture. Many memorable scenes and good songs are woven around the story of a rich girl, a group of hippies and a boy waiting to be sent to fight in Vietnam. As a period piece its impact will be minimal, but still enjoyable for the vigour of its performances if not its freshness. The choreography is by Twyla Tharp.
Boa: musical by Galt MacDermot, Gerome Ragni and James Rado.

| MUS | 118 min (ort 121 min) |
|---|---|
| B,V,V2 | INT/CBS; WHV |

**HAIRSPRAY ***                                 PG
John Waters           USA            1988
*Divine (Glenn Milstead), Michael St Gerard, Ricki*
*Lake, Debbie Harry, Pia Zadora, Jerry Stiller, Ruth*
*Brown, Sonny Bono, Colleen Fitzpatrick, Shawn*
*Thompson, Ric Ocasek, John Waters*
After an absence, Waters marked his return to the screen with this nostalgic and spirited look at the 1960s, by way of a gleeful and sharp parody on all those 1950s and 1960s teen movies. Contains some wonderfully tacky moments and inspired casting, not least being Lake as hefty Tracy Turnblad, and an appearance by female impersonator Divine in his last role. The slight plot is built around an integrated teen-dance in Baltimore of 1962.

| COM | 88 min |
|---|---|
| V/sh | RCA |

**HALF A HOUSE ***                                1979
Brice Mack            USA            1979
*Anthony Eisley, Pat Delaney, Francine York, Kaz*
*Garas, Angus Duncan, Mary Grace Canfield*
A happily married couple fall out after their house-warming party and divide their possessions in this silly comedy.

| COM | 77 min |
|---|---|
| B,V,V2 | VCL/CBS |

**HALF A LOAF OF KUNG FU ***                      18
Chen Chi Hwa     HONG KONG           1985
*Jackie Chan*
Comedy martial arts film in which a group of body-guards entrusted with the safe delivery of a jade treasure, find themselves heavily outnumbered by bandits.

| MAR | 91 min (ort 96 min) Cut (3 min 7 sec) |
|---|---|
| B,V | VIDMQ; CLOK; TGP (VHS only) |

**HALF MOON STREET ***                            18
Bob Swaim             USA            1986
*Michael Caine, Sigourney Weaver, Keith Buckley,*
*Patrick Kavanagh, Nadim Sawalha, Angus MacInnes,*
*Faith Kent*
A woman working on a research fellowship in London, supplements her income by working as a professional escort, and is introduced to a powerful British diplomat in this stuffy and tiresome thriller. Adapted from "Doctor Slaughter", the first half of Theroux's book.
Boa: novella by Paul Theroux.

| THR | 86 min (ort 90 min) |
|---|---|
| B,V | EHE |

**HALF THE ACTION ***
B. Ron Eliot          USA            1980
*Mike Ranger, Ron Jeremy, Becky Bitter, Donna Jones,*
*Terri Galko*
A man kicks out his girlfriend of several years but she returns for half of everything he owns, even taking off with one of his new girlfriends in his 50-foot ketch. Together the girls turn the boat into a floating whorehouse, and charge $1,000 for a tour of the islands. Of course our man gets his boat back eventually, but the best thing in this film is the scenery.
Osca: MISTY BEETHOVEN (asa)

| A | 80 min |
|---|---|
| B,V | HAR |

**HALFBREED, THE ***                             1952
Stuart Gilmore        USA            1952
*Robert Young, Janis Carter, Jack Beutel, Barton*
*MacLane, Reed Hadley, Porter Hall, Connie Gilchrist*
A gambler and a half-breed help to stop a massacre by the Apaches, when an unscrupulous profiteer tries to incite an Indian attack.
Osca: WALK SOFTLY, STRANGER

| WES | 78 min (ort 81 min) |
|---|---|
| B,V | KVD |

**HALLELUJAH TRAIL, THE ***                       U
John Sturges          USA            1965
*Burt Lancaster, Lee Remick, Martin Landau, Jim*
*Hutton, Brian Keith, Donald Pleasence, Pamela Tiffin,*
*John Anderson, Tom Stern, Robert Wilke, John*
*Dehner (plus narration), Jerry Gatlin, Larry Duran,*
*Jim Burk, Dub Taylor*
A temperance leader plans to stop a cavalry-guarded shipment of whisky reaching thirsty Denver miners. Meanwhile, the Indians have their eyes on the shipment too. An easy-going and likeable comedy Western that just goes on for far too long. Originally released in Cinerama.
Boa: novel by B. Gullick.

| WES | 140 min (ort 165 min) |
|---|---|
| V | WHV |

**HALLELUJAH, I'M A TRAMP ***
Lewis Milestone       USA            1933
*Al Jolson, Harry Langdon, Frank Morgan, Madge*
*Evans, Chester Conklin, Tyler Brooke, Edgar Conner*
The leader of a troupe of tramps living in Central Park, smartens himself up when he falls in love with a girl who has lost her memory. The witty and intelligent script is by Ben Hecht and S.N. Behrman, with

songs by Rodgers and Hart. A shortened version was re-issued as "The Heart Of New York", and the British version has unfortunately been cut and redubbed.
Aka: HALLELUJAH, I'M A BUM; LAZY BONES
MUS                                77 min (ort 82 min) B/W
B,V,V2                                            INT/CBS

## HALLOWEEN ***                                        18
John Carpenter            USA                        1978
*Donald Pleasence, Jamie Lee Curtis, P.J. Soles, Nancy Loomis, Charles Cyphers, Kyle Richards*
A killer escapes from the state mental home in Illinois, and goes on a bloody rampage at Halloween in his home town, reliving the crime that got him put away 15 years earlier. As a horror film it's excellent, but the end, with its hint of the supernatural, fails to make any real sense. Numerous sequels and spin-offs have followed.
HOR                              92 min; 90 min (CH5)
B,V                              VPD; CH5 (VHS only)

## HALLOWEEN 2 **
Rick Rosenthal            USA                        1981
*Jamie Lee Curtis, Donald Pleasence, Charles Cyphers, Jeffrey Kramer, Lance Guest, Pamela Susan Shoop*
Sequel to the first film, with our mad killer doing his slash and stab act, as he stalks Curtis in this unpleasant and bloody effort. The script is by John Carpenter and Debra Hill.
HOR                                              88 min
B,V                                                TEVP

## HALLOWEEN 3: SEASON OF THE WITCH *        15
Tommy Lee Wallace         USA                        1983
*Tom Atkins, Stacey Nelkin, Dan O'Herlihy, Ralph Strait, Michael Currie*
A maniacal toymaker intends to murder millions of children on Halloween as a vast human sacrifice. The title is not related to any of those other HALLOWEEN films but has more in common with THE INVASION OF THE BODYSNATCHERS. Abridged before video submission by 2 min 6 sec.
HOR                              92 min (ort 96 min)
B,V                              TEVP; WHV (VHS only)

## HALLOWEEN 4: THE RETURN OF               18
## MICHAEL MYERS **
Dwight H. Little          USA                        1988
*Donald Pleasence, Ellie Cornell, Danielle Harris, George P. Wilbur, Michael Pataki, Beau Starr, Kathleen Kinmont*
Ten years after he went on a bloodthirsty rampage, a demented killer emerges from his coma and sets out for his home town, intending to murder his niece, plus any other folk unfortunate enough to get in his way. A gory sequel that follows on from the first HALLO-WEEN film, just as if sequels 1 and 2 had never been made. Technically competent, but totally lacking in surprises or fresh ideas.
HOR                              85 min (ort 88 min)
V                                                 BRAVE

## HAMBURGER HILL **                                18
John Irvin                USA                        1987
*Anthony Barrile, Michael Patrick Boatman, Tim Quill, Courtney B. Vance, Don Cheadle, Michael Dolan, M.A. Nickles*
Clinical recreation of a bloody engagement that took place at the base of Hill 937 in the Ashau Valley in the course of the Vietnam War, when troops of the 101st Airborne Division encountered stiff enemy opposition. Realistic, gory and quite unmoving. Scripted by Jim Carabatsos.
WAR                                             110 min
V                                                    VES

## HAMBURGER: THE MOTION PICTURE *          18
Mike Marvin               USA                        1985

*Leigh McCloskey, Dike Butkus, Chuck McCann, Sandy Hackett, Deborah Blee, Randi Brooks, Jack Blessing, Charles Tyner*
Juvenile farce with a boy who has been kicked out of every college in the land starting up a "university" for future hamburger franchise operators, in a bid to get a degree and so fulfil the conditions laid down in an inheritance. As tasteless as junk food and just as indigestible.
COM                                90 min (ort 99 min)
B,V                                                  AVA

## HAMLET **                                         U
Tony Richardson           UK                         1969
*Nicol Williamson, Judy Parfitt, Anthony Hopkins, Marianne Faithfull, Mark Dignam, Michael Pennington, Gordon Jackson, Ben Aris, Clive Graham, Peter Gale, Roger Livesey*
Competent screen version of the famous play, that relies rather too heavily on the use of close-ups, but the unusual casting of Faithfull as Ophelia is an asset.
Boa: play by William Shakespeare.
DRA                              114 min (ort 117 min)
B,V                                                  RCA

## HAMLET ***                                        U
Laurence Olivier          UK                         1948
*Laurence Olivier, Eileen Herlie, Basil Sydney, Jean Simmons, Norman Wooland, Felix Aylmer, Terence Morgan, Stanley Holloway, John Laurie, Esmond Knight, Anthony Quayle, Niall McGinnis, Harcourt Williams, Peter Cushing*
Famous version of Shakespeare's play of the tragic Danish prince, that's beautifully photographed in Denmark. Only Olivier's tendency to over-act mars this one, but that is more a reflection of his stage origins (where a different style of acting is called for) than a criticism of his failings as an actor. AA: Pic, Actor (Olivier), Art/Set (Roger K. Furse/Carmen Dillon), Cost (Roger K. Furse).
Boa: play by William Shakespeare.
DRA                                          155 min B/W
B,V                                                  RNK

## HAMLET, PRINCE OF DENMARK ***            U
                                                      UK
*Derek Jacobi, Ian Charleson*
A good TV adaptation of this famous play.
Boa: play by William Shakespeare.
DRA                              217 min (2 cassettes) mTV
V/h                                                  BBC

## HAMMERHEAD JONES: DEATH MATCH **        15
Robert Michael Ingria
*Ted Vernon, Anthony Albarino, R.S. King*
Tough action thriller with a champ meeting his match in an arena. Screenplay is by Manny Diez.
THR                              81 min (ort 88 min) Cut (12 sec)
B,V                                                  VPD

## HAMMERSMITH IS OUT *
Peter Ustinov             USA                        1972
*Richard Burton, Elizabeth Taylor, Peter Ustinov, Beau Bridges, Leon Askin, Leon Ames, John Schuck, George Raft*
Larger than life reworking of the Faust legend. Burton plays a mental patient who escapes with the aid of a male nurse and becomes an extremely powerful person. A silly film that is all form and no substance.
DRA                                             114 min
B,V                                             BWV/VSP

## HAMMETT ***
Wim Wenders               USA                        1982
*Frederic Forrest, Peter Boyle, Marilu Henner, Elisha Cook, R.G. Armstrong, Sylvia Sidney, Samuel Fuller, Roy Kinnear, Royal Dano, Richard Bradford, Lydia Lei*

Crime thriller involving a real-life crime writer who is asked to find a missing Chinese girl. His experiences provide the basis for a new book. An excellent effort that recreates feel of the 1930s and was several years in the making.
Boa: novel by Joe Gores.
DRA 93 min (ort 97 min)
B,V 3MVID

## HANCOCK: THE PUNCH AND JUDY MAN *** U
Jeremy Summers UK 1962
*Tony Hancock, Sylvia Sims, Ronald Fraser, Barbara Murray, John Le Mesurier, Hugh Lloyd, Mario Fabrizi, Pauline Jameson, Norman Bird, Walter Hudd, Eddie Byrne, Peter Myers, Hattie Jacques*
A nicely observed, bittersweet comedy, with Hancock playing a seaside Punch and Judy man who tries, and fails, to become part of the snobby social set. Written by Philip Oakes and Tony Hancock.
Aka: PUNCH AND JUDY MAN, THE
Osca: HANCOCK: THE REBEL (TEVP)
COM 96 min; 88 min (WHV) B/W
B,V TEVP; WHV (VHS only)

## HANCOCK: THE REBEL *** U
Robert Day UK 1960
*Tony Hancock, George Sanders, Irene Handl, Paul Massie, Margit Saad, Dennis Price, Gregoire Aslan (Krikor Aslanian), Mervyn Johns, John Le Mesurier, Liz Fraser, Nanette Newman, Peter Bull, John Wood*
A clerk with delusions of artistic grandeur, goes to Paris in order to achieve fame as a painter, and eventually does so, but thanks only to the work of someone else. Enjoyable feature length spin-off from the popular TV comedy series "Hancock's Half Hour" and written by the same team; Ray Galton and Alan Simpson.
Aka: CALL ME GENIUS; REBEL, THE
Osca: HANCOCK: THE PUNCH AND JUDY MAN (TEVP)
COM 101 min (ort 105 min)
V TEVP; WHV

## HAND, THE * 18
Oliver Stone USA 1981
*Michael Caine, Andrea Marcovicci, Annie McEnroe, Bruce McGill, Viveca Lindfors, Rosemary Murphy, Mara Hobel, Pat Corley, Nicholas Hormann, Ed Marshall, Charles Fleischer, John Stinson, Richard Altman, Sparky Watt*
A successful cartoonist has his hand severed in a car accident, it then disappears, taking on a life of its own and killing his enemies. This poor imitation of THE BEAST WITH FIVE FINGERS has Caine well and truly miscast as the cartoonist. A flabby script doesn't help much either.
Boa: novel The Lizard's Tail by Marc Brandel.
HOR 105 min
B,V WHV

## HANDFUL OF DUST, A **** PG
Charles Sturridge UK 1988
*James Wilby, Kristen Scott Thomas, Rupert Graves, Anjelica Huston, Judi Dench, Alec Guinness, Pip Torrens, Cathryn Harrison*
A handsome adaptation of Waugh's 1930s novel looking at the life of an upper-class couple whose marriage is on the rocks, and at the inevitable break-up of their relationship, brought on by the death of their son. This detailed and sharp examination of the stifling social conventions of 1930s Britain, has some beautiful performances and an excellent script by Tim Sullivan, Derek Granger and Sturridge.
Boa: novel by Evelyn Waugh.
DRA 115 min
B,V CASVIS

## HANDGUN ** 18
Tony Garnett USA 1982

*Karen Young, Clayton Day, Ben Jones, Suzie Humphreys*
After her rape, a young girl joins a gun club in order to have her revenge on the man responsible. A dull exploitation movie, masquerading as one of those "films with a message".
Aka: DEEP IN THE HEART
THR 95 min
B, V/h, V2 TEVP; WHV (VHS only)

## HANDS OF A STRANGER: PARTS 1 AND 2 *** 15
Larry Elikann USA 1987
*Armand Assante, Blair Brown, Beverly D'Angelo, Michael Lerner, Phillip Casnoff, Arliss Howard, Patricia Richardson, Sam McHoward, Ben Affleck*
An ambitious narcotics detective obsessed with finding the man who raped his wife, becomes romantically involved with a female assistant D.A. A film that promises much excitement but very quickly runs out of steam. Adapted from Daley's novel by playwright Arthur Kopit and originally shown in two parts.
Boa: novel by Robert Daley.
DRA 180 min (2 cassettes) (ort 240 min) mTV
B,V CBS

## HANDS OF DEATH: JACKSON'S BACK * 18
Anders Palm USA 1988
*Gregory Cox, Fiona Evans, Edward Brayshaw*
Silly and tasteless spoof about an insane serial killer called Jackson, who attempts to go straight after he falls in love with a blind girl who shares his passion for the poetry of Byron. However, he is on the verge of finding that his congenital madness is about to rear its head once more.
HOR 90 min
V CFD

## HANDS OF THE RIPPER ** 15
Peter Sasdy UK 1971
*Eric Porter, Jane Merrow, Angharad Rees, Dora Bryan, Keith Bell, Derek Godfrey, Marjorie Rhodes, Lynda Baron, Norman Bird, Margaret Rawlings, Marjie Lawrence, Elizabeth MacLennan, Barry Lowe, A.J. Brown, April Wilding*
The daughter of Jack the Ripper grows up a murderess, as a result of seeing her father kill her mother, and an early follower of the teachings of Freud tries to help her. Another Hammer House of Horror offering that takes an interesting idea and does nothing with it.
Boa: story by Edward Spenser Shew.
HOR 85 min; 81 min (MIA)
B,V,LV RNK; MIA (VHS only)

## HANG 'EM HIGH *** 18
Ted Post USA 1967
*Clint Eastwood, Inger Stevens, Ed Begley, Pat Hingle, Arlene Golonka, James MacArthur, Ben Johnson, Bruce Dern, Charlie McGraw, L.Q. Jones, Ruth White, Bob Steele, Arlene Golonka, Alan Hale Jr, Dennis Hopper*
A cowboy survives a lynching and plans his revenge on those responsible in this brutal but well made Hollywood stab at a spaghetti Western.
WES 110 min (ort 114 min)
V WHV

## HANGAR 18 ** 
James L. Conway USA 1980
*Robert Vaughn, Gary Collins, Philip Abbott, James Hampton, Joseph Campanella, Darren McGavin, William Schallert, Cliff Osmond, Tom Hallick, Pamela Bellwood, Steven Keats*
A UFO crashes and the American government tries to keep it a secret by keeping the spacecraft and the dead bodies of its crew hidden away in a hangar. A flashy but implausible piece of nonsense, re-released for TV as "Invasion Force" with a new ending that did nothing to improve it.

Aka: INVASION FORCE
FAN                                          99 min
B,V                              VFP L/A; HER

**HANGING WOMEN, THE ***                     18
John Davidson        SPAIN              1982
*Stanley Cooper, Vickie Nesbitt, Paul Naschy (Jacinto*
*Molina), Marcella Wright, Gerald Tichy, Carl*
*Mansion, Charles Fay, Catherine Gilbert, Charles*
*Quince, Janis Brown, Harold Stancey, Joseph Carter*
The dead rise up and slaughter the living in this
low-budget and low-brow zombie offering.
HOR                                          90 min
B,V                                        TURBO

**HANGMEN ****                               18
J. Christian Ingvordsen USA            1987
*Rick Washburne, Jake LaMotta, Dog Thomas, Kosmos*
*Vinyl, Keith Bogart*
A young man who secretly admires his estranged
father, a former special commando, gets his chance to
emulate his lifestyle when a splinter group within the
CIA murders his mother and stepfather, and a special
unit his father once commanded is reformed. A loud,
noisy action tale.
A/AD          81 min (ort 88 min) Cut (5 min 35 sec)
B,V                                          MED

**HANKY PANKY ****                           15
Sidney Poitier       USA               1982
*Gene Wilder, Gilda Radner, Kathleen Quinlan,*
*Richard Widmark, Robert Prosky, Josef Sommer,*
*Johnny Sekka*
A female spy involves an architect in her mission and
together they are chased by spies, cops etc. in this
predictable spoof of NORTH BY NORTHWEST. Writ-
ten by Henry Rosenbaum and David Taylor and
originally intended to be a follow-up to STIR CRAZY,
but Pryor's part was rewritten for Radner.
COM                          103 min (ort 110 min)
V                                            RCA

**HANLON: IN DEFENCE OF MINNIE DEAN ***** 15
Wayne Tourell     NEW ZEALAND          1984
*David Gwillim, Robyn Nevin, Sylvia Rands, Philip*
*Holder, Alma Woods, Jim MacFarlane*
Pilot for a six-part mini-series that describes the
career of a real defence lawyer. In this film he sets out
to defend a woman baby-minder charged with infanti-
cide.
Aka: DEFENCE OF MINNIE DEAN, THE;
HANLON
DRA                                       94 min mTV
B,V                                          CIC

**HANNAH AND HER SISTERS ******            15
Woody Allen          USA               1986
*Woody Allen, Michael Caine, Mia Farrow, Carrie*
*Fisher, Barbara Hershey, Lloyd Nolan, Maureen*
*O'Sullivan, Daniel Stern, Max Von Sydow, Dianne*
*Wiest, Tony Roberts, Sam Waterston, Julie Kavner,*
*Bobby Short*
This examination of three sisters whose lives intert-
wine is a sharp, witty and affectionate look at their
loyalties, conflicts and neurotic tendencies. The thin
plot of an affair between Hannah's husband and the
youngest sister is nothing more than a vehicle to
support a perceptive and often funny look life, with
Allen himself in top form as Farrow's hypochondriac
ex-husband. AA: S. Actor (Caine), S. Actress (Wiest),
Screen (Orig) (Allen).
COM                                         102 min
V                                            RNK

**HANNA'S WAR ***                            15
Menahem Golan        USA               1988
*Ellen Burstyn, Anthony Andrews, David Warner,*
*Donald Pleasence, Maruschka Detmers, Denholm*
*Elliott, Vicenzo Ricotta, Ingrid Pitt*

Biopic on the life of Hanna Senesh, a Hungarian
Jewess who emigrated to Palestine and assisted the
British during WW2. An overlong and jumbled mess
of a film, said to be based in part on her diaries. The
script is by Golan and Stanley Mann.
THR                          145 min (ort 148 min)
B,V                                        PATHE

**HANNIBAL ***                               PG
Edgar G. Ulmer       ITALY/USA         1960
*Victor Mature, Rita Gam, Gabriele Ferzetti, Milly*
*Vitale, Rik Battaglia*
A paper-thin and poorly mounted costumer with
Mature giving a more than usually wooden perform-
ance as the famous Carthaginian foe of the Romans in
a film in which poor acting competes with historical
inaccuracy.
A/AD                                        103 min
B,V                                        COLISS

**HANNIE CAULDER ****                        15
Burt Kennedy         UK                1971
*Raquel Welch, Robert Culp, Ernest Borgnine, Jack*
*Elam, Strother Martin, Christopher Lee, Diana Dors*
A woman takes revenge on the outlaw who raped her
and killed her husband, after getting shooting lessons
at the hands of a bounty hunter, in this gory and
offbeat tale.
WES                           81 min (ort 85 min)
B,V              HOK; HOLLY (VHS only); MIA

**HANOI HILTON, THE ***                      15
Lionel Chetwynd      USA               1987
*Michael Moriarty, Jeffrey Jones, Paul Le Mat,*
*Lawrence Pressman, David Soul, Stephen Davies, Rick*
*Fitts, Aki Aleong, Gloria Carlin*
One in a spate of recent films that indicated the
industry's belated interest in the Vietnam War. This
one focuses on POW experiences in Hanoi's Hao Lo
prison. Dull, overlong and preachy.
DRA                          121 min (ort 130 min)
B/sh, V/sh                                   WHV

**HANOVER STREET ****                        PG
Peter Hyams          UK                1979
*Harrison Ford, Lesley-Anne Down, Christopher*
*Plummer, Alex McCowen, Richard Masur, Michael*
*Sacks, Patsy Kensit, Max Wall, Shane Rimmer, Keith*
*Buckley, Sherrie Hewson, Cindy O'Callaghan, Di*
*Trevis, Suzanne Bertish, Jay Benedict*
In 1943 an American bomber pilot meets a married
English nurse, but their budding relationship is
abruptly interrupted when he is sent on a secret
mission. Quite well made, but the contrived nature of
the script (written by Hyams) is a serious drawback.
DRA                                         109 min
B,V                                          RCA

**HANS BRINKER *****                         U
Robert Scheerer.     USA               1979
*Eleanor Parker, Richard Basehart, Rony Zeander,*
*Karin Rosshy, Roberta Torey, John Gregson, Robin*
*Askwith, Cyril Ritchard*
The story of a poor Dutch boy who plans to win a pair
of silver skates in a skating competition, so as to help
his seriously ill father pay for the treatment he needs.
Aka: HANS BRINKER AND THE SILVER SKATES;
HANS BRINKER OF THE SILVER SKATES;
SILVER SKATES, THE
Boa: story by Mary Mapes Dodge.
MUS                          86 min (ort 103 min) mTV
B,V                                          WDV

**HANS CHRISTIAN ANDERSEN ****              U
Charles Vidor        USA               1952
*Danny Kaye, Farley Granger, Zizi Jeanmaire, Roland*
*Petit, John Qualen, Joey Walsh*
This biography has little to do with the life of this
great writer, but has some fine songs by Frank

Loesser and Richard Day, that compensate for the emptiness of the script.

MUS                                    105 min (ort 120 min)
V                                                POLY; VGM

## HANSEL AND GRETEL **
                    USA                    1954
Voices of: Anna Russell, Mildred Dunnock
Animated puppet version of this famous fairytale. Average.
Boa: short story by Jakob Ludwig Karl Grimm and Wilhelm Karl Grimm.
CAR                                                    82 min
B,V,V2                                                    VPD

## HANSEL AND GRETEL **                            Uc
James Frawley          USA                    1982
Joan Collins, Paul Dooley, Ricky Schroder, Bridgette Anderson
A film version of the famous fairytale from the Faerie Tale Theatre.
Boa: short story by Jakob Ludwig Karl Grimm and Wilhelm Karl Grimm.
JUV                                    48 min (ort 60 min)
V                                                        MGM

## HANSEL AND GRETEL ***                            U
Len Talan          ISRAEL/UK                    1987
Cloris Leachman, David Warner, Nicola Stapleton, Hugh Pollard
A newer version of this famous tale that is often dull in plot but never less than striking visually. The music of Humperdinck is replaced by a bland and forgettable score, but despite this and other defects, this is one of the best versions yet, and one with a sense of humour.
Boa: short story by Jakob Ludwig Karl Grimm and Wilhelm Karl Grimm.
MUS                                                    82 min
V/sh                                                    WHV

## HAPPIEST MILLIONAIRE, THE **
Norman Tokar          USA                    1967
Fred MacMurray, Tommy Steele, Geraldine Page, Greer Garson, Gladys Cooper, Hermione Baddeley, Lesley Anne Warren, John Davidson
Musical about the problems of the family in the household of an eccentric Philadelphia millionaire in 1916, and somewhat loosely based on the recollections of Cordelia Drexel Biddle, as told to the writer Kyle Crichton. A high-spirited and glossy story, but only slightly interesting.
Boa: book by Kyle Crichton.
COM                                    155 min (ort 164 min)
B,V                                                    WDV

## HAPPILY EVER AFTER **
Robert Scheerer          USA                    1978
Suzanne Somers, Bruce Boxleitner, Eric Braeden, John Rubinstein, Ron Hayes
A female singer is torn between her own success and the man she loves, in this formula soap opera style tale. This was Somers' first starring role.
DRA                          95 min (ort 104 min) mTV
B,V                                            VTC L/A; VES

## HAPPY BIRTHDAY TO ME *                            18
J. Lee Thompson    CANADA                    1980
Melissa Sue Anderson, Glenn Ford, Lawrence Dane, Sharon Acker, Jack Blum, Tracy Bregman, Lisa Langlois, Frances Hyland, Lenore Zann, David Eisner, Michel Rene LaBelle, Richard Rabiere, Lesleh Donaldson, Alan Katz
Senior students at a college are being murdered one by one. The killer is one of them in this drearily familiar campus-carnage movie.
HOR                                    106 min (ort 108 min)
V                                                        RCA

## HAPPY ENDINGS **                            15
Noel Black          USA                    1983
John Schneider, Catherine Hicks, Ana Alicia, Bibi Osterwald, Joseph Hacker III, Matthew Faison, Murphy Cross, Jonathan Perpich, Robin Tilghman, Frantz Turner, Al Fann, Erik Holland, James Hornbeck, Candace McKendree
This attempt at a light romantic comedy, only succeeds in being light. The paper-thin and rather empty story tells of two people living in San Francisco who, each suffering from a broken romance, form a relationship with each other to forget their pain.
COM                                        96 min mTV
B,V                                                        HER

## HAPPY EVER AFTER ***                            U
Mario Zampi          UK                    1954
David Niven, Yvonne De Carlo, A.E. Matthews, Michael Shepley, George Cole, Barry Fitzgerald
The new squire of an Irish village makes himself so unpopular that the locals decide to draw lots for the task of murdering him. A funny black comedy helped along by vigorous direction and a strong cast.
Aka: TONIGHT'S THE NIGHT
COM                                    85 min (ort 91 min)
V                                                        WHV

## HAPPY GO LOVELY *
Bruce Humberstone          UK                    1951
David Niven, Vera-Ellen, Cesar Romero, Bobby Howes, Diane Hart, Gordon Jackson, Barbara Couper, Gladys Henson, Joyce Carey
In Britain for the Edinburgh Festival and hoping to produce a show, an American producer hires a chorus girl in the hope that her millionaire boyfriend will invest his money in the show. A forgettable and boring musical comedy that served as a kind of semi-official effort in celebration of the Festival of Britain, and containing very little of note.
MUS                                    93 min (ort 97 min)
V                                                        WHV

## HAPPY HOLIDAY *
Jon Sanderson.                                        1978
Olinka Johnsson, Nina Lund, Karen Karlsson, Karl Blake, Stephen Roberts
An irritating film done in the style of a tourist guide, that opens with a tour of London and offers comments on the action throughout. A girl who lives with her boyfriend in London, leaves for Hamburg to visit her father and stepmother, who collect pornography and run a stud service respectively. Various encounters take place in this tedious and dated effort.
A                                                    60 min
B,V                                                        RIP

## HAPPY HOOKER, THE **                            18
Nicholas Sgarro          USA                    1975
Lynn Redgrave, Jean-Pierre Aumont, Lovelady Powell, Nicholas Pryor, Tom Poston, Elizabeth Wilson, Conrad Janis, Mason Adams, Anita Morris
The story of an office girl who changes her job and becomes a prostitute, and then a society madam. An anaemic effort that's funny in one or two places, but has little of the flavour of Hollander's book. Followed by two fictitious sequels. See also MY PLEASURE IS MY BUSINESS.
Boa: book by Xaviera Hollander.
COM                          87 min; 93 min (CAN) (ort 98 min)
B,V,V2                                        INT/CBS; CAN

## HAPPY HOOKER GOES TO HOLLYWOOD, THE*    18
Alan Roberts          USA                    1979
Martine Beswicke, Chris Lemmon, Adam West, Phil Silvers, Richard Deacon, Lindsay Bloom, Army Archerd, Edie Adams
Sequel to THE HAPPY HOOKER, with the protagonist going to the rescue of a film studio that is riddled

with corruption. Trite, tiresome and unfunny.
COM                              83 min (ort 85 min)
B,V                                           RNK

## HAPPY HOOKER GOES TO WASHINGTON, THE *
William A. Levey        USA              1977
*Joey Heatherton, George Hamilton, Ray Walston, Jack Carter, Phil Foster, Rip Taylor, Larry Storch, Billy Barty*
Sequel to THE HAPPY HOOKER which was based on the autobiography of Xaviera Hollander. This time round our high-class madam has to appear before a Congressional committee and gets involved with the CIA. A foolish romp that scatters a few laughs here and there. Written by Bob Kaufman, who went on to work on an infinitely better film – LOVE AT FIRST BITE.
COM                              86 min (ort 89 min)
B,V                                        INT/CBS

## HAPPY NEW YEAR ***                           15
John G. Avildsen        USA              1986
*Peter Falk, Charles Durning, Tom Courtenay, Wendy Hughes, Joan Copeland, Claude Lelouch*
Two men team up to pull off a jewel robbery, but when one of them meets a beautiful woman, the outcome looks uncertain. A slick remake of Claude Lelouch's 1973 film, with this director making a cameo appearance in the opening scene.
COM                                      85 min
B,V                                           RCA

## HAPPY SINCE I MET YOU **                      15
Baz Taylor              UK               1981
*Julie Walters, Duncan Preston, Kathryn Apanowicz, Tracey Ullman, Jim Bowen*
A comedy-drama in which a female teacher who has, up till now, been happily single, meets an actor and develops a relationship but is unwilling to give up her free and uncommitted lifestyle.
DRA                                   60 min mTV
B,V                                           GRN

## HARD CHOICES ***                              18
Rick King         USA        1984 (released 1986)
*Margaret Klenck, John Seitz, Gary McCleery, John Sayles, John Snyder, Martin Donovan, Spalding Gray*
Story of a teenager who is unjustly jailed, after getting unwittingly involved in a robbery, and is befriended by a female social worker. An absorbing tale somewhat hampered by an uneven script.
A/AD                                     90 min
B,V                                           MED

## HARD CONTRACT **
S. Lee Pogostin         USA              1969
*James Coburn, Lee Remick, Lilli Palmer, Burgess Meredith, Patrick Magee, Sterling Hayden, Karen Black*
A contract killer begins to have doubts about his profession when he meets a woman who exerts a more positive influence on him. An interesting idea is spoilt by an earnest and preachy treatment.
A/AD                                    107 min
B,V                                           CBS

## HARD COUNTRY **
David Greene            USA              1981
*Jan-Michael Vincent, Kim Basinger, Michael Parks, Gailard Sartain, Tanya Tucker, Ted Neeley, Daryl Hannah, Richard Moll*
A woman decides to leave her boyfriend and the small Texas town where they live, in this conventional romance in a Country and Western setting. The film debuts for Basinger and Nashville singer Tucker.
DRA                              97 min (ort 104 min)
B,V                                           PRV

## HARD KNUCKLE **                               18
Lex Marinos        AUSTRALIA            1987
*Steven Bisley, Paul Chubb, Gary Day*
A down-market version of THE COLOR OF MONEY, with a top pool player hitting the bottle and going rapidly downhill. After a while he tries to make a comeback and hires an agent, only to find that it's not going to be easy, as a new champ has taken over in his absence.
DRA                                      88 min
B,V                                           GHV

## HARD ROCK ZOMBIES *                           18
Krishna Shah            USA              1980
*E.J. Curcio, Geno Andrews, Sam Mann*
A rock band play a small town and are turned into zombies by the local crazies in this inept, low-budget offering.
HOR              89 min (ort 95 min) Cut (3 min 29 sec)
B,V                               CBS L/A; CAREY/PVG

## HARD SOAP, HARD SOAP **
Bob C. Chinn            USA              1977
*Laurien Dominique, John C. Holmes, Candida Royalle*
Silly, funny satire on soap operas, telling of an impotent psychoanalyst who cannot satisfy his sexy wife, and of the various ploys she is obliged to use in her search for fulfilment.
Aka: HARD SOAP
A                                        78 min
B,V,V2                                        CAL

## HARD TICKET TO HAWAII **                      18
Andy Sidaris            USA              1987
*Dona Speir, Hope Marie Carlton, Ronn Moss, Harold Diamond, Rodrigo Oberon, Cynthia Brimhall, Wolf Larson, Kiram Hi Lam, Rustam Branaman, Peter Browmilow*
A sequel to MALIBU EXPRESS, with two female undercover Federal agents using the front of an inter-island cargo service for their investigations. When they stumble on a cache of diamonds, they soon find themselves menaced by a drug dealer's contract killer. A picturesque but forgettable trip round some of Hawaii's more colourful islands.
A/AD                          91 min Cut (1 min 13 sec)
V                                             RCA

## HARD TIMES: PARTS 1 AND 2 ***                 PG
John Irvin              UK               1977
*Patrick Allen, Timothy West, Alan Dobie, Edward Fox, Michelle Dibnah, Jacqueline Tong, Ursula Howells*
In Victorian England an abandoned circus girl is taken in by a stuffy northern industrialist and made into his ward. A strong cast and good attention to detail make this rather talkative Dickens adaptation quite entertaining. Originally shown as four 50-minute episodes.
Boa: novel by Charles Dickens.
DRA                         220 min (2 cassettes) mTV
V                                     CASPIC/TERRY

## HARD TO HOLD *                                15
Larry Peerce            USA              1984
*Rick Springfield, Patti Hansen, Albert Salmi, Janet Eilber, Gregory Itzin, Bill Mumy*
A pop star falls in love with a girl when he crashes her car. A tiresome vehicle for teen idol Springfield.
DRA                                      93 min
B,V                                           CIC

## HARD TO KILL **
Bruce Malmuth           USA              1990
*Steven Seagal, Kelly LeBrock, Bill Sadler, Frederick Coffin, Bonnie Burroughs, Zachary Rosencrantz, Dean Norris*
A martial arts-trained police detective uncovers poli-

tical corruption and is shot and left for dead, but survives in a 7-year coma. Awakening from this he sets out to have his revenge. Tight direction and well handled chase sequences enliven this otherwise fairly standard action-and-revenge tale.

A/AD                                    92 min (ort 95 min)
V/sh                                                    WHV

## HARD TRAVELING ***                                  PG
Dan Bessie            USA                             1988
Ellen Geer, J.E. Freeman, Barry Corbin, James
Gammon, Jim Haynie, W. Scott De Venney, Joe
Miksak, William Peterson, Al Blair
A gentle, decent but illiterate drifter finds hope and happiness with a farmer's widow, but tragedy strikes when he commits a murder in the course of a robbery, which he foolishly embarked on in a forlorn attempt to support her. A touching but poorly realised account of the 1930s Depression era, spoilt by too much reliance on flashbacks.
Boa: novel Bread And A Stone by Alvah Bessie.
DRA                                                94 min
V/h                                                   NWV

## HARD WAY, THE *
Michael Dryhurst      EIRE/UK                         1979
Patrick McGoohan, Edna O'Brien, Lee Van Cleef,
Donal McCann, Michael Muldoon
A mercenary faces problems when he tries to retire and is forced into one last job by his employer. A depressing and murky drama which ends with both men gunning each other down, a suitable comment on the whole affair.
Boa: story by Edna O'Brien.
DRA                          85 min (ort 100 min) mTV
B,V                                                   PRV

## HARDBODIES *                                        18
Mark Griffiths        USA                             1984
Teal Roberts, Gary Wood, Grant Cramer, Roberta
Collins, Cindy Silver, Kristi Somers, Michael Rapport,
Sorrells Pickard, Joyce Jameson
Sun and surf comedy about three men in their forties, who hire a beach-house for their amorous adventures, and hire a young stud to teach them how to score with girls. Mindless nonsense, followed by HARDBODIES 2. Written by Steve Greene and Eric Alter.
COM                                          86 min mCab
B,V                                                   RCA

## HARDBODIES 2 *                                      15
Mark Griffiths        USA                             1986
Brad Zutaut, Fabiano Udinio, James Karen, Alba
Francesca, Roberta Collins, Sorrells Pickard, Brenda
Bakke, Sam Temeles, Louise Baker
Two of the three middle-aged lechers from HARD-BODIES jump at the chance of acting in a film opposite a load of scantily clad young girls, and as expected, cannot keep their minds on the job (the film that is). A dismal bottom-of-the-barrel attempt to wring a few laughs out of a tired script.
COM                                                84 min
B,V                                                   VES

## HARDCASE AND FIST **
Tony Zarindast        USA                             1989
Ted Prior, Carter Wong, Maureen Lavette
A cop framed by a gang leader sets out to get his revenge, with the help of a friend he made in prison after the two of them escape. A mediocre tale of murder and mayhem.
A/AD                                               93 min
V                                                   BRAVE

## HARDCORE **                                         18
Paul Schrader         USA                             1978
George C. Scott, Peter Boyle, Season Hubley, Dick
Sargent, Ed Begley Jr, Leonard Gaines, David Nichols

A religious man of the Calvanist persuasion explores the sleazy world of porno films, in a search for his daughter who has taken to acting in them. A sad and poignant story, spoilt by an implausible climax. The script is by Schrader.
Aka: HARDCORE LIFE, THE
DRA                                   103 min (ort 108 min)
V                                                     RCA

## HARDCORE **                                         18
James Kenelm Clarke   UK                              1977
Fiona Richmond, Anthony Steel, David Cole, Neil
Cunningham, Donald Sumpter, Arthur Howard,
Murray Brown, Patricia Bourdel, Linda Regan,
Ronald Fraser, Harry H. Corbett, Roland Curram,
John Clive, Norman Bacon, Joan Bentham
A lightly fictional autobiography, in which Fiona Richmond relates her sexy life to a reporter. Set in France.
A                             79 min (ort 92 min) Cut (3 sec)
B,V                            INT L/A; NEWDIR/AVR

## HARDCOVER **                                        18
Tibor Takacs          USA                             1988
Jenny Wright, Clayton Rohner
A young actress who enjoys reading horror stories, becomes the victim of a fictional demon that crosses over into the real world. An intriguing idea, but an unsatisafactory development.
HOR                                                85 min
V                                                     EIV

## HARDER THEY COME, THE ***
Perry Henzell         JAMAICA                         1973
Jimmy Cliff, Janet Barkley, Ras Daniel Hartman,
Carl Bradshaw, Bobby Charlton, Basil Keame
Jamaica's first feature film is a story of a country boy who comes to Kingston to become a singer, but has to resort to crime in order to become a success. A simple tale of considerable vigour, now something of a cult film.
DRA                                               100 min
B,V                                                  TEVP

## HARDER THEY FALL, THE ****                          15
Mark Robson           USA                             1956
Humphrey Bogart, Rod Steiger, Jan Sterling, Mike
Lane, Max Baer, Edward Andrews, Harold J. Stone
In his last performance, Bogart plays a cynical press agent and former sportswriter who sets out to expose the ruthless exploitation of prizefighters by their managers. A powerful and often brutally honest expose of the less endearing aspects of the fight game. Scripted by Philip Yordan and photographed by Burnett Guffey (for which he obtained an AAN).
Boa: novel by Budd Schulberg.
DRA                                           105 min B/W
V                                                     RCA

## HARDWARE ***                                        18
Richard Stanley       UK                              1989
Dylan McDermott, Stacey Travis, John Lynch,
William Hootkins, Carl McCoy, Iggy Pop
Writer-director Stanley makes his directorial debut with this futuristic fantasy, in which the remains of a scrapped killer-robot is foolishly given to a female scuptress as a present. When the device re-activates itself her apartment is turned into a combat zone as the robot sets out to kill her and any other living things in its path. A flashy and gruesome blend of ALIEN and THE TERMINATOR.
FAN                                                95 min
V                                                     PAL

## HAREM *                                             15
Arthur Joffe          FRANCE                          1985
Nastassja Kinski, Ben Kingsley, Dennis Goldson,
Zohra Segal, Michel Robin, Juliette Simpson
An OPEC oil minister visiting New York, falls for a

beautiful stockbroker. He arranges for her to be kidnapped and brought to his own country, where she becomes the latest addition to his harem. French cinema at its most international and its most inane. A flat and boring tale dressed up in beautiful sets and exquisite photography but going absolutely nowhere.
Aka: D'ARDENELLE
DRA                              94 min (ort 114 min)
B,V                                              RNK

## HAREM: PARTS 1 AND 2 **                    PG
Billy Hale            USA                     1986
Omar Sharif, Ava Gardner, Sarah Miles, Nancy Travis, Yaphet Kotto, Art Malik, Julian Sands, Cherie Lunghi, Georgine Anderson, Shirley Cain, George Camiller, Jojo Cole, James Coyle, Sarah Crowden, Caroline Dorian
A whirlwind action tale set in the 1900s and telling of an American beauty kidnapped and bought by a sultan as the latest addition to his harem. There she finds enmity and intrigue in the shape of wife no. 1 but eventually gets rescued. Expensively mounted but sprawling and unsatisfactory. Originally shown in two parts.
Aka: HAREM: THE LOSS OF INNOCENCE
DRA            186 min (2 Cassettes) (ort 240 min) mTV
B,V                                              NWV

## HARLEM NIGHTS **                            18
Eddie Murphy          USA                     1989
Eddie Murphy, Richard Pryor, Redd Foxx, Danny Aiello, Arsenio Hall, Berlinda Tolbert, Della Reese, Jasmine Guy, Michael Lerner
Written and produced by Murphy in his directorial debut, this is a fairly enjoyable and somewhat old-fashioned gangster tale in which a black 1930s Harlem club-owner takes a stand against a white mobster who is out for a slice of their business. Short on plotting and long on profanity, this film never quite develops the expected impact. Music is by Herbie Hancock.
DRA                              111 min (ort 115 min)
V                                                CIC

## HAROLD AND MAUDE ****                       15
Hal Ashby             USA                     1971
Ruth Gordon, Bud Cort, Vivian Pickles, Cyril Cusack, Charles Tyner, Ellen Geer
Brilliant black comedy following the partnership of a 20-year-old youth obsessed with death and a vital and lively 80-year-old woman. A film that has achieved cult status. Highspots are Cort's phony suicides. The music is by Cat Stevens.
Boa: story by Colin Higgins.
COM                                        90 min
B,V                                           CIC

## HAROLD LLOYD: SAFETY LAST ****              U
Fred Newmayer/Sam Taylor
                      USA                     1923
Harold Lloyd, Mildred Davis, Bill Strother, Noah Young
A go-getter comes to the big city determined to make good, in this visually inventive and hilarious Lloyd silent. Contains the famous sequence where our hero climbs the face of a building.
Aka: SAFETY LAST
COM                               82 min B/W silent
V                                                VIR

## HAROLD LLOYD: THE FRESHMAN ****             U
Sam Taylor/Fred Newmeyer
                      USA                     1925
Harold Lloyd, Jobyna Ralston, Brooks Benedict, James Anderson, Hazel Keener
Lloyd plays a college guy who'll do anything to win popularity, blissfully unaware that his best efforts are giving rise to much mirth behind his back. The football game finale is one of several great highlights.

Aka: FRESHMAN, THE
COM                               75 min B/W silent
V                                                VIR

## HAROLD LLOYD: THE KID BROTHER ****          U
Ted Wilde/J.A. Howe     USA                   1927
Harold Lloyd, Jobyna Ralston, Leo Willis, Olin Francis
Lloyd plays a Cinderella-type kid brother in a tough all-male family, who finally gets to show his stuff in a hilarious finale in which he subdues a burly opponent.
Aka: KID BROTHER, THE
COM                               84 min B/W silent
V                                                VIR

## HARPER VALLEY PTA *
Richard Bennett       USA                     1978
Barbara Eden, Ronny Cox, Nanette Fabray, Susan Swift, Ron Masak, Louis Nye, Pat Paulsen, Audrey Christie, John Fiedler, Bob Hastings
A small-town widow is ostracised for her free lifestyle, and plots an elaborate revenge to expose local hypocrisy. Inspired by a hit song by Jeannie C. Riley and later made into a TV series. An empty-headed and inconsequential comedy.
COM                              90 min (ort 102 min)
B,V                                             STUD

## HARRAD EXPERIMENT, THE **
Ted Post              USA                     1973
Don Johnson, James Whitmore, Tippi Hedren, Robert Middleton, Victoria Thompson, Bruno Kirby, Laurie Walters
Story of a co-educational college that pursues a policy of sexual freedom, with the film largely exploring the effect this has on two sets of relationships. An offbeat but rather inane tale, followed HARRAD SUMMER.
Boa: novel by Robert H. Rimmer.
DRA                                        95 min
V2                                           AST L/A

## HARRAD SUMMER **                            15
Steven H. Stern      USA                     1974
Richard Doran, Victoria Thompson, Laurie Walters, Robert Reiser, Bill Dana, Marty Allen
A sequel to THE HARRAD EXPERIMENT made in 1973, in which students at an experimental college attempt to practice the sex education theories they've been taught, at home during the summer holiday. A banal and dated work.
Aka: STUDENT UNION
DRA                              101 min (ort 103 min)
B,V                                   WIZ/VPD; WIZ

## HARRIS DOWN UNDER **                        PG
Russ Mayberry        USA                     1988
Lee Majors, Rebecca Gilling, Martin Vaughn, William Wallace, Bruce Hughes, Morgan Lewis, Paul Chubb
Antipodean action adventure involving an American rancher who runs a horse breeding business in New South Wales.
Aka: DANGER DOWN UNDER
A/AD                                   97 min mTV
B,V                                              EIV

## HARRY AND SON **                            15
Paul Newman          USA                     1984
Paul Newman, Robby Benson, Joanne Woodward, Ellen Barkin, Ossie Davis, Wilford Brimley, Judith Ivey, Morgan Freeman
This film examines the relationship between a widower who has just lost his job and his son who has not yet managed to straighten out his life. A contrived and treacly effort, co-written and co-produced by Newman.
DRA                                        117 min
B,V                                              RNK

## HARRY AND WALTER GO TO NEW YORK **          U
Mark Rydell          USA                     1976

*James Caan, Elliott Gould, Michael Caine, Diane
Keaton, Charles Durning, Lesley Anne Warren, Val
Avery, Jack Gilford, Carol Kane*
In New York of the 1890s, two entertainers become
involved with a master criminal and try their luck as
safebreakers, in this likeable but uneven comedy.
Written by John Byrum and Robert Kaufman.
COM                                      123 min
B,V                                         RCA

## HARRY TRACY: DESPERADO ***
William A. Graham   CANADA              1982
*Bruce Dern, Helen Shaver, Michael C. Gwynne,
Gordon Lightfoot*
The story of a modern day Robin Hood who robs banks
and trains. Implausible and often unconvincing, but
Dern's strong performance carries it off.
Aka: HARRY TRACY
DRA                          91 min (ort 111 min)
B,V,V2                                   INT/CBS

## HARRY'S GAME ***                          15
Lawrence Gordon Clark  UK                1984
*Ray Lonnen, Derek Thompson, Gil Braley, Margaret
Shelvin, Benjamin Whitrow*
A Cabinet minister is murdered by the IRA, and a
British agent is sent to work undercover in Northern
Ireland, to infiltrate the IRA unit responsible and
track down the killers. Adapted from a three-part TV
serial.
Aka: BELFAST ASSASSIN, THE; HARRY'S GAME:
THE MOVIE
Boa: novel by Gerald Seymour.
DRA            150 min; 130 min (CASVIS) mTV
B,V                     GHV; CASVIS (VHS only)

## HAUNTED **                                PG
John Glenister/Gordon Flemying
                      UK                 1982
*Joanna David, Norma West, Ian Collier, Roger
Llewellyn, Harry Littlewood, Charlotte Mitchell, Clive
Duncan, Jane Brown, Jeremy Kemp, Carol Royle,
Joanna Van Gyseghem, Peter Mackin, Heather Chasen*
Two ghostly tales of the supernatural: "The Lady's
Maid's Bell" and "Feet Foremost". Average.
Boa: short stories by Edith Wharton and L.P. Hartley
respectively.
DRA                               105 min mTV
B,V                                         GRN

## HAUNTED HONEYMOON *                       PG
Gene Wilder         USA                  1986
*Gene Wilder, Gilda Radner, Paul L. Smith, Dom
DeLuise, Jonathan Pryce, Peter Vaughan, Bryan
Pringle*
A comedy-horror spoof, with a man on his honeymoon
being stalked by a killer while his relatives are trying
to scare him out of an anxiety attack. A disappointing
effort for all concerned, inspired by all those early Bob
Hope haunted house comedies.
COM                          80 min (ort 89 min)
V/sh                                        RCA

## HAUNTED HOUSE OF HORROR, THE
Michael Armstrong   UK                   1969
*Frankie Avalon, Jill Hayworth, Dennis Price, Mark
Wynter, George Sewell, Gina Warwick, Richard
O'Sullivan, Carl Dilworth, Julian Barnes, Veronica
Doran, Robin Stewart, Jan Holden, Clifford Earl,
Robert Raglan*
Nasty things happen to a group of teenagers who
spend the night in a haunted house. A sad and slack
effort, memorable as one of the very worst films of this
genre.
Aka: HORROR HOUSE
HOR                                      91 min
B,V                                         VDM

## HAUNTED PALACE, THE ***                   18
Roger Corman        USA                  1963
*Vincent Price, Debra Paget, Lon Chaney Jr, Frank
Maxwell, Leo Gordon, Elisha Cook Jr, John Dierkes*
A man inherits a mansion in New England in 1875,
that is located in a town peopled by strange mutants.
His ancestor was burnt as a male witch in 1765 but
soon takes possession of him to have his revenge. A
fairly competent effort from Corman's supernatural
period, very loosely based on a Lovecraft tale. The
screenplay is by Charles Beaumont.
Boa: short story The Case of Charles Dexter Ward by
H.P. Lovecraft.
HOR                        85 min; 83 min (VIR)
B,V                          RNK; VIR (VHS only)

## HAUNTED SUMMER **                         18
Ivan Passer         USA                  1988
*Eric Stoltz, Laura Dern, Philip Anglim, Alice Krige,
Alex Winter*
Another look at the events of the summer of 1816,
when Byron and Shelley and their lovers and friends,
stayed at the Villa Deodati in Italy. Extremely well
made and pleasing to look at, but stilted and uncon-
vincing. See also GOTHIC for Ken Russell's attempt.
Boa: novel by Anne Edwards.
DRA                         101 min (ort 106 min)
V                                          PATHE

## HAUNTING FEAR *                           18
Fred Olen Ray       USA                  1989
*Jan-Michael Vincent, Della Sheppard, Michael
Berryman, Karen Black, Brinke Stevens, Jay
Richardson, Robert Quarry*
A woman is plagued by nightmares in which she is
buried alive and seeks help from a hypnotist. Her
fears become a reality when her husband, desperate to
pay off a loan shark, tries to kill her for her money by
burying her alive in their cellar. However, her
psychiatric treatment has made her strong enough to
get free, but in the process she becomes a homicidal
maniac. Not an edifying film.
HOR                                      87 min
V                                          HIFLI

## HAUNTING OF HARRINGTON HOUSE, THE ** PG
Murray Golden       USA                  1982
*Dominique Dunne, Edie Adams, Roscoe Lee Browne,
Phil Leeds, Vitto Scotti*
A young girl decides to uncover the mystery surround-
ing a strange house that is reputed to be haunted.
A/AD                                     45 min
V                                          PICK

## HAUNTING OF JULIA, THE **
Richard Loncraine  CANADA/UK             1976
*Mia Farrow, Jill Bennett, Tom Conti, Keir Dullea,
Cathleen Nesbitt, Robin Gammell, Mary Morris,
Edward Hardwicke, Anna Wing, Pauline Jameson,
Peter Sallis, Sophie Ward, Samantha Gates*
After her small daughter dies, a woman goes to live in
a large old house in London, that is haunted by the
evil spirit of another child that died many years
before. A good start is soon spoilt by predictability.
Scripted by Straub from his novel.
Aka: FULL CIRCLE
Boa: novel Julia by Peter Straub.
DRA                                      96 min
B,V,V2                                   MED; VPD

## HAUNTING OF M, THE ***
Anna Thomas         USA                  1979
*Sheelagh Gilbey, Nini Pitt, Alan Hay, Evie Garrett, Jo
Scott Matthews, Isolde Cazalet, William Bryan, Peter
Austin, Peter Stenson, Varvara Pepper, Ernest Bale,
Jenny Greenaway, Gwen Williams, Ruby Melvin,
William Payne*
Gothic horror yarn of a young girl who goes to the

family mansion for her sister's coming-out party and becomes obsessed by a stranger pictured in a photograph of the party. Interesting idea that is never really developed sufficiently to have enough impact.

DRA 90 min
B,V TEM L/A; APX

### HAUNTING OF SARAH HARDY, THE *** 15
USA 1989
*Polly Bergen, Sela Ward, Michael Woods, Morgan Fairchild*
A woman who is haunted by the suicide of her mother finds herself plagued by visions, after returning from her honeymoon to live with her husband at the family home. A rather neat psychological thriller with an unexpected ending.

DRA 88 min
V CIC

### HAUNTING PASSION, THE ** 15
John Korty USA 1983
*Jane Seymour, Gerald McRaney, Millie Perkins, Ruth Nelson, Paul Rossilli, Ivan Bonar*
A woman lives with her husband in a house by the sea, and finds herself the object of a ghostly passion. An excellent idea is spoilt by a descent into sentimentality halfway through.

DRA 93 min (ort 104 min) mTV
B,V PRV

### HAUNTS ***
Herb Freed USA 1977
*May Britt, Cameron Mitchell, Aldo Ray, William Gray Espy, Susan Nohr*
The peaceful life of a small coastal town is destroyed by a series of murders in the surrounding countryside, and a lonely woman at a farm finds her own sexuality more than she can cope with in this slow but gripping thriller. Scripted by Anne Marisse and Herb Freed, with an outstanding performance from Britt.

THR 85 min (ort 97 min)
B,V DFS

### HAVE A NICE WEEKEND! ** 15
Michael Walters USA 1975
*M.B. Miller, Peter Dompe, Valerie Shephard, Nikki Counselman, Pat Joyce, Colette Bablon*
A standard suspense thriller with the usual mysterious killer on the prowl.

THR 90 min
B,V DFS L/A; FNF

### HAVING IT ALL! * R18
Edward Zwick USA 1982
*Dyan Cannon, Barry Newman, Hart Bochner, Melanie Chartoff, Sylvia Sidney, Herb Walker, Gay Hagen, Frank Delsi, Andra Millican, Richard Hochberg, Heather Hobbs, Cynthia Kanai*
A woman has two husbands, one in Los Angeles and the other in New York. Unfortunately what she doesn't have is a good script.
Boa: story by Elizabeth Gill.

COM 60 min (ort 95 min) Cut (9 sec) mTV
B,V VSP L/A; VEXCEL

### HAWAIIAN HEAT ** PG
Mike Vejar USA 1984
*Robert Ginty, Jeff McCracken, Mako*
Two Chicago cops pull up stakes and go to Hawaii only to discover that even in a sunshine paradise, a policeman's lot is not a happy one. Pilot for a TV series.

DRA 93 min (ort 101 min) mTV
B,V CIC

### HAWK THE SLAYER * PG
Terry Marcel UK 1980
*Jack Palance, John Terry, Bernard Bresslaw, Ray Charleson, Peter O'Farrell, Morgan Sheppard,*

*Patricia Quinn, Cheryl Campbell, Annette Crosbie, Catriona McColl, Shane Briant, Harry Andrews, Christopher Benjamin, Roy Kinnear*
A British attempt at a sword-and-sorcery epic, with two brothers, one good and the other not so good, battling it out for possession of a magic sword. A tedious and clumsy effort.

FAN 90 min (ort 94 min)
B,V,V2,LV PRV L/A; CH5 (VHS only)

### HAWKS *** 15
Robert Ellis Miller UK 1988
*Timothy Dalton, Anthony Edwards, Janet McTeer, Jill Bennett, Sheila Hancock, Connie Booth*
The story of two terminally ill young men; a cynical but brave British lawyer and an American football player. They meet in hospital where the former faces his imminent death with wry humour whilst the latter is more than a little fearful. The lawyer persuades the ex-footballer to fight back and when remission comes they steal an ambulance and have several amusing encounters. A poignant, sad, funny but not altogether successful film.

COM 105 min (Cut at film release)
V/sh WHV

### HAWMPS! * PG
Joe Camp USA 1976
*James Hampton, Christopher Connelly, Slim Pickens, Jack Elam, Denver Pyle, Gen Conforti, Mimi Maynard, Lee DeBroux, Herbert Vigran, Jesse Davis, Frank Inn, Mike Travis, Larry Swartz, Tiny Wells, Dick Drake, Henry Kendrick*
Based on a true incident, this is the story of an attempt by the US Army to use camels as mounts, and follows their training among the sand dunes of the Texas desert. A one-joke film.

COM 113 min (ort 127 min)
B,V PVG; VES

### HAZARD OF HEARTS, A * PG
John Hough UK 1987
*Helena Bonham-Carter, Edward Fox, Fiona Fullerton, Gareth Hunt, Diana Rigg, Stewart Granger, Anna Massey, Neil Dickson, Marcus Gilbert*
A glossy and totally superficial romantic drama telling of a spoilt young virgin who is lost in a game of cards by her wealthy father to a lecherous nobleman, but falls under the spell of a mysterious marquis. A big-budgeted Lew Grade production of considerable splendour and vast tedium.
Boa: novel by Barbara Cartland.

DRA 92 min
B,V MGM

### HE KNOWS YOU'RE ALONE * 18
Armand Mastroianni USA 1980
*Don Scardino, Caitlin O'Heaney, Elizabeth Kemp, Lewis Arlt, James Rebhorn, Tom Rolfing, Patsy Pease, Tom Hanks, Dana Barron, Paul Gleason, Joseph Leon*
Brides-to-be are the victims of a sex-starved homicidal maniac armed with a knife. Not as gory as many similar efforts, but just as cliched. Hanks' film debut.

HOR 90 min (ort 94 min)
B,V,V2 MGM

### HE-MAN AND SHE-RA: A CHRISTMAS SPECIAL ** U
Frank Hayes USA 1986
Cartoon tale based on these popular characters, with Orko rescuing two kids from Earth and taking them to Eternia. When evil Lord Skeletor discovers that they carry the spirit of Christmas, he joins forces with Hordak to capture them and stop the spread of goodwill.

CAR 44 min
V VCC

## HE-MAN AND SHE-RA: THE SECRET OF   U
## THE SWORD **
Ed Friedman/Lou Kachivas/Marsch Lamore/Bill
Reed/Gwen Wetzler     USA         1985
*Voices of: John Erwin, Melandy Britt, George Dicenzo,*
*Linda Gary, Ericka Scheimer, Erik Gunden, Alan*
*Oppenheimer*
Full-length animated adventure feature with He-Man
and She-Ra and the inevitable struggle against the
forces of evil. This story introduces She-Ra, who is
He-Man's long lost sister but is unaware of her
identity.
Aka: SECRET OF THE SWORD, THE
CAR                     91 min
B,V              IVS; VCC (VHS only)

## HEAD ***                 PG
Bob Rafelson     USA         1968
*Mickey Dolenz, Peter Tork, Michael Naismith, David*
*Jones, Terry (Teri) Garr, Vito Scotti, Timothy Carey,*
*Logan Ramsey, Annette Funicello, Frank Zappa, Jack*
*Nicholson*
Written by Nicholson and Rafelson, this 60s extrava-
ganza of a film tried to do for The Monkees what A
HARD DAY'S NIGHT did for The Beatles but though
endearing in many respects, is too incoherent for its
own good. A wild collection of crazy ideas, old film
clips, good songs and bizarre guest appearances (look
out for Sonny Liston and Victor Mature). The debut
for both Rafelson and Garr.
MUS             82 min (ort 86 min)
V                      RCA

## HEAD OFFICE **         15
Ken Finkleman     USA       1986
*Judge Reinhold, Jane Seymour, Danny DeVito, Eddie*
*Albert, Rick Moranis, Don Novello, Michael*
*O'Donaghue, Richard Masur, Don King, Wallace*
*Shawn, Lori-Nan Engler*
The corruption of innocence is the theme of this lame
comedy about a wide-eyed college graduate, who lands
a job with a powerful multinational, thanks to his
father's efforts behind the scenes, and soon learns how
to succeed in business. Some funny moments in an
episodic and disjointed tale.
COM                  86 min
B, V/s         CAN; WHV (VHS only)

## HEADHUNTER **         18
Francis Schaeffer     USA     1988
*Wayne Crawford, Kay Lenz, Steve Kanaly, June*
*Chadwick*
A series of gruesome murders have taken place in
Boston and terrorised the inhabitants. Two detectives
are assigned to the case, and discover that the
murders are the work of a supernatural creature of
immense power, who must hunt down and destroy
three more victims to achieve immortality. They have
to find the creature whilst it can still be stopped, in a
film whose scary ideas are soon frittered away by a
plodding and unfocused script.
HOR                 90 min
B,V                   CINE

## HEADIN' FOR BROADWAY *     PG
Joseph Brooks     USA       1980
*Rex Smith, Terr Treas, Vivian Reed, Paul Carafotes,*
*Gene Foote, Gary Glendell*
Follows four young couples who are all auditioning for
a part in a Broadway musical. An inconsequential
little film that should be retitled "Heading Nowhere".
Written, produced, composed and directed by Brooks.
Aka: HEADING FOR BROADWAY
DRA                 90 min
B,V          VUL L/A; KRP; MPV

## HEALTH SPA, THE **       18
Clair Dia         USA        1978

*Kay Parker, Abigail Clayton, John Seeman, Robert*
*Girard*
A sexually-repressed female reporter decides to expose a health club that uses sex as part of a weight
reduction plan. A plotless, female-directed tale exploring the sexual activities of the clientele, who are not
averse to using any piece of equipment on offer as an
aid to their enjoyment.
A         55 min (ort 81 min) Cut (1 min 55 sec)
B,V               EVI L/A; SHEP

## HEAR NO EVIL **         15
Harry Falk       USA       1982
*Gil Gerard, Bernie Casey, Wings Hauser, Mimi*
*Rogers, Christina Hart, Brion James, Ron Karabatos*
A tough cop completely loses his hearing in a bomb
explosion and has to readjust to living with this
handicap, while still trying to prove he can work in
the field. Does not always avoid cliches, especially
romantic ones, but is still well made and watchable.
Pilot for a prospective series.
DRA        93 min (ort 104 min) mTV
B,V                   MGM

## HEARSE, THE **          15
George Bowers     USA       1980
*Joseph Cotten, Trish Van Devere, Perry Lang, Donald*
*Hotton, David Gautreaux, Med Flory, Donald Petrie*
A woman schoolteacher finds herself threatened by a
haunted house and a black hearse. Interesting now
and then, but contrived and unimaginative.
HOR     97 min; 95 min (ACAD) (ort 100 min)
B,V,V2     VPD; ACAD (Betamax and VHS only)

## HEART **              15
James Lemmo     USA       1987
*Brad Davis, Jesse Doran, Gary Warner, Sam Gray,*
*Steve Buscemi, Robinson Frank Adu, Frances Fisher*
Dreary and depressing tale of a burnt-out boxer who
avidly accepts the chance to make a comeback, even
though he knows that the fight will be fixed and that
his opponent is ten years younger.
DRA           90 min Cut (21 sec)
B,V                   NWV

## HEART BEAT *           18
John Byrum     USA       1979
*John Heard, Nick Nolte, Sissy Spacek, Ray Sharkey,*
*Anne Dusenberry, Tony Bill, Steve Allen, Margaret*
*Fairchild, Ken Williams, Stephen Davies*
Charts the relationship between the beat poet Jack
Kerouac and a young couple. Largely fictional in
content and far from a true story, let down by a
disjointed script. However, Jack Nitzche's period-
flavour score is a small compensation.
Aka: HEARTBEAT
Boa: novel by C. Cassady.
DRA                 109 min
B,V               WHV; CBS

## HEART IS A LONELY HUNTER, THE ***   PG
Robert Ellis Miller     USA     1968
*Alan Arkin, Stacy Keach, Sondra Locke, Laurinda*
*Barrett, Cicely Tyson, Chuck McCann*
The moving story of a lonely deaf mute living in a
small Southern town. Arkin gives one of the best
performances of his career, and if the story is some-
what over-sentimental, it's held together by fine
performances from all concerned. The film debuts of
Locke and Keach.
Boa: novel by Carson McCuller.
DRA                 123 min
B,V                   WHV

## HEART LIKE A WHEEL **     PG
Jonathan Kaplan     USA     1983
*Bonnie Bedelia, Beau Bridges, Leo Rossi, Hoyt Axton,*
*Bill McKinney, Anthony Edwards, Dean Paul Martin,*
*Paul Bartel, Dick Miller, Terence Knox*

Story of a female racing car driver, who has to face male prejudice and the conflict of a career versus marriage, in her fight to reach the top. Despite a fine performance from Bedelia, this loose and episodic effort fails to ever come to life.

DRA                                                          112 min
B,V                                                          EHE

## HEART OF A CHAMPION: THE RAY MANCINI
STORY **                                                      PG
Richard Michaels          USA                               1985
*Doug McKeon, Robert Blake, Mariclare Costello, Curtis Conway, Tony Burton, Ray Buktenica, James Callahan*
This TV movie focuses on the challenge by Mancini for the lightweight boxing title, his quest being given added impetus by the certain knowledge that his father would have won it had not WW2 cut short his career. The film's executive producer was Sylvester Stallone, who choreographed the boxing sequences, but these do little to enliven a shallow offering.

DRA                               90 min (ort 100 min) mTV
V                                                            CBS

## HEART OF DIXIE *                                            15
Martin Davidson          USA                                1989
*Ally Sheedy, Virginia Madsen, Phoebe Cates, Treat Williams, Don Michael Paul, Kyle Secor, Francesca Roberts, Kurtwood Smith, Richard Bradford, Barbara Babcock*
A period drama set around a 1950s Alabama college sorority, with a young girl becoming aware of the civil rights movement and the plight of blacks in the South, and using her post as a college newspaper reporter to write on this issue. Meanwhile, other Southerners enjoy their way of life while it lasts. An intensely self-righteous and irritating film, that never gets to grips with the problems it purports to examine.

DRA                                91 min (ort 95 min)
V                                                            VIR

## HEART OF MIDNIGHT ***                                       18
Matthew Chapman          USA                                1988
*Jennifer Jason Leigh, Peter Coyote, Frank Stallone, Brenda Vaccaro*
Bizarre tale of a young woman hovering on the edge of a mental breakdown, who inherits a dilapidated former nightclub on the death of her uncle. She moves into it and workmen begin the process of renovation. Her troubles start when she finds that her uncle used it to satisfy his perversions. Later she is raped by one of the workmen, but on reporting this merely finds herself drawn into a murderous web of intrigue. Scripted by Chapman.

THR                                                          105 min
B,V                                                          VES

## HEARTACHES **                                               15
Donald Shebib          CANADA                               1981
*Margot Kidder, Annie Potts, Robert Carradine, Winston Rekert, George Touliatos, Guy Sanvido*
A pregnant woman leaves her husband, and falls in with a man-hunting swinger in this slight and rather forgettable comedy.

COM                                                          98 min
B,V,V2                                                       GHV

## HEARTBEEPS **                                               U
Allan Arkush          USA                                   1981
*Andy Kaufman, Bernadette Peters, Randy Quaid, Richard B. Schull, Melanie Mayron, Dick Miller, Kathleen Freeman, Mary Woronov, Paul Bartel, Anne Wharton, Barry Diamond, Stephanie Faulkner, Jack Carter (voice only)*
Futuristic comedy about two robots who fall in love and decide to run away together. A downright peculiar comedy that is more weird than funny, though it does have some amusing ideas. The make-up is by Stan Winston.

COM                                     76 min (ort 88 min)
V/h                                                          CIC

## HEARTBREAK GIRL, THE *                                      R18
                         USA
*Heather Wayne, Gina Valentino*
The story of three girls and their various lovers.

A                                                            42 min
V                                                            VTEL

## HEARTBREAK HOTEL **                                         15
Chris Columbus          USA                                 1988
*David Keith, Tuesday Weld, Charlie Schlatter, Jacque Lynn Colton, Angela Goethals, Chris Mulkey, Karen Landry*
A bizarre comedy set in 1972 in which a teenager kidnaps Elvis Presley and brings him home to see his divorced mother, who has been a lifelong fan of his. A basic premise such as this creates too many improbabilities for the film to really hold together, but there are one or two very funny moments (most of which are unintentional).

COM                                                          96 min
V                                                            TOUCH

## HEARTBREAK KID, THE **                                      PG
Elaine May          USA                                     1972
*Charles Grodin, Cybill Shepherd, Jeannie Berlin, Edward Albert, William Prince*
A Jewish boy regrets his marriage during his honeymoon and plans to drop his wife in favour of a cool blonde. A modern social comedy somewhat reminiscent of THE GRADUATE, but lacking in warmth. Screenplay is by Neil Simon.
Boa: story A Change Of Plan by Bruce Jay Friedman.

COM                               101 min; 102 min (CH5)
B,V                               CBS; CH5 (VHS only)

## HEARTBREAK RIDGE ***                                        15
Clint Eastwood          USA                                 1986
*Clint Eastwood, Marsha Mason, Everett McGill, Eileen Heckart, Moses Gunn, Bo Svenson, Mario Van Peebles, Arlen Dean Snyder, Roman Franco*
One of those formula films in which a tough marine sergeant whips a bunch of raw recruits into shape, before sending them off to battle. Overlong and predictable, but rescued by Eastwood's vigorous performance.

A/AD                              124 min (ort 130 min) Cut (15 sec)
V/sh                                                         WHV

## HEARTBREAKER *                                              18
Frank Zuniga          USA                                   1983
*Fernando Allende, Dawn Dunlap, Peter Gonzales Falcon, Michael D. Roberts, Miguel Ferrer, Pepe Serna, Rafael Campos, Patty (Apollonia) Kotero*
A boy from a Spanish-speaking background falls in love with a WASP girl, in this superficial and boring tale.

DRA                                                          90 min
B,V                               MEGA L/A; BLAC/VFM

## HEARTBREAKERS ***                                           18
Bobby Roth          USA                                     1984
*Peter Coyote, Nick Mancuso, Carol Wayne, Kathryn Harrold, Max Gail, James Laurenson, Carole Laurie, Jamie Rose, George Morfogen, Jerry Hardin, Henry Sanders, Walter Olkewicz, Terry Wills, Annoe O'Neill, Michelle Davidson*
The story of two male friends looking for creative and sexual fulfilment as they sample the trendy L.A. scene. A personal and intense statement on human relationships, making good use of L.A. locations and some excellent performances.

DRA                                                          95 min
B,V                                                          RNK

## HEARTBURN ***                                               15
Mike Nichols          USA                                   1986
*Jack Nicholson, Meryl Streep, Maureen Stapleton, Jeff*

*Daniels, Stockard Channing, Richard Musur,*
*Catherine O'Hara, Steven Hill, Milos Forman, Karen*
*Akers, Anna Maria Horsford, Mercedes Ruehl, Joanna*
*Gleason, Yakov Smirnoff*
Bittersweet comedy with Streep a divorced cookery
writer, meeting Nicholson, a Washington columnist at
a friend's wedding. There follows a marriage, a baby,
an affair, a separation and finally, a reconciliation.
Though this poignant look at modern marriage lacks
the cutting edge of Ephron's autobiographical best-
seller, fine performances hold it together. Director
Foreman makes his acting debut.
Boa: novel by Nora Ephron.
COM                            105 min (ort 108 min)
V/h                                             CIC

**HEARTLAND ****
Richard Pearce          USA               1979
*Conchata Ferrell, Rip Torn, Lilia Skala, Barry*
*Primus, Megan Folson, Amy Wright*
Beautifully made reconstruction of the life of a woman
housekeeper and a dour Scots rancher in Wyoming at
the end of the last century. Every performance is a
gem, and not a single cliche as far as the eye can see.
Recommended viewing. Based on the actual diaries of
a pioneer woman.
DRA                                        95 min
B,V                                          TEVP

**HEARTS AND ARMOUR ****                       18
Giancomo Battiato   ITALY/USA             1982
*Barbara De Rossi, Tanya Roberts, Ron Moss, Leigh*
*McCloskey, Rick Edwards, Giovanni Visentin, Zeudi*
*Araya*
Epic set in 8th century Spain and depicting French
knights and their bitter struggle against the Moors.
De Rossi is a sexy warrior who wears knight's armour
and takes part in the battles. A well-mounted but
confusing film, loosely based on a classic fantasy of
1516.
Aka: HEARTS IN ARMOUR; I PALADINI: STORIA
D'ARMI E D'AMORI; LE ARMI ES GLI AMORI
Boa: story Orlando Furioso by Ludovico Ariosto.
A/AD             96 min (ort 101 min) Cut (21 sec)
V/sh                                          WHV

**HEARTS OF FIRE ****                          15
Richard Marquand        USA               1986
*Fiona Flanagan, Rupert Everett, Bob Dylan, Suzanne*
*Bertish, Julian Glover, Susannah Hoffman, Larry*
*Lamb, Maury Chaykin, Tony Rosato, Richie Havens,*
*Tim Cappello, Ian Dury*
Standard, cliched rock 'n' roll fantasy with the story of
three rock stars; one on the way up, one on the way
down and one just starting out. The stars sing OK
(especially Dylan), but the dramatic aspects leave a
lot to be desired.
DRA                             91 min (ort 95 min)
V/sh                                          GHV

**HEARTS OF THE WEST ****                      PG
Howard Zieff            USA               1975
*Jeff Bridges, Andy Griffith, Donald Pleasence, Blythe*
*Danner, Alan Arkin, Richard B. Shull, Herb Edelman*
A young man goes to Hollywood in the 1930s to
become a writer but ends up acting in cowboy films
instead, in this minor but engaging drama.
Aka: HOLLYWOOD COWBOY
DRA                            98 min (ort 102 min)
B,V                                          MGM

**HEARTSOUNDS ****                             15
Glenn Jordan            USA               1984
*James Garner, Mary Tyler Moore, Sam Wanamaker,*
*Wendy Crewson, David Gardner, Carl Marotte*
When a middle-aged doctor has a heart attack, he
finds out just what it's like being a patient under
treatment by his own profession, in this highly
regarded and well acted tearjerker. Written by Fay

Kanin.
Boa: novel by Martha Weinman Lear.
DRA                            126 min (ort 135 min) mTV
B,V                            EHE; CH5 (VHS only)

**HEAT ***                                     18
R.M. Richards          USA                1986
*Burt Reynolds, Karen Young, Peter MacNicol, Howard*
*Hesseman, Neill Barry, Diana Scarwid, Joe Mascolo,*
*Alfie Wise*
A messy and unpleasant actioner, with Reynolds
playing a freelance bodyguard who, whilst teaching
his "protege" MacNichol all he knows, takes on a case
to protect a battered wife and finds himself caught up
in some tricky situations.
A/AD                            97 min (ort 103 min)
B,V                                          WHV

**HEAT ****                                    
Paul Morrissey          USA               1972
*Sylvia Miles, Joe Dallesandro, Andrea Feldman, Pat*
*Ast, Ray Vestal*
An unemployed actor who has come to Hollywood to
become a star, involves himself with the usual
outcasts and takes up with a faded star. An intense,
moody and offbeat film, with the plot lifted from
SUNSET BOULEVARD.
DRA                                       100 min
B,V                                          PVG

**HEAT AND DUST ****                           15
James Ivory             UK                1982
*Julie Christie, Christopher Cazenove, Shashi Kapoor,*
*Greta Scacchi, Julian Glover, Madhur Jaffrey, Barry*
*Foster, Susan Fleetwood, Nickolas Grace, Zakir*
*Hussain, Jennifer Kendal, Amanda Walker, Sudha*
*Chopra, Sajid Khan*
A woman researcher at the BBC goes to India to find
out more about her aunt and the scandalous life she is
supposed to have led there. Her story unfolds in
parallel with that of her aunt's, half a century earlier.
An engrossing drama with a literate script by Jhabva-
la, from her novel.
Boa: novel by Ruth Prawer Jhabvala.
DRA                            124 min (ort 133 min)
B,V,V2             3MVID; HOLLY (VHS only); MIA

**HEATED VENGEANCE ****                        18
Edward Murphy          USA                1984
*Richard Hatch, Michael J. Pollard, Dennis Patrick,*
*Mills Watson, Cameron Dye, Ron Max, Jolina*
*Mitchell-Collins, Robert Walker*
A man returns to Vietnam looking for the woman he
left behind thirteen years earlier, but soon discovers
he's in trouble with a nasty bunch of deserters.
A/AD                            87 min (ort 91 min)
V                                            CBS

**HEATHCLIFF MOVIE, THE: HEATHCLIFF**          U
**AND ME ****
Bruno Bianchi           USA               1986
*Voice of Mel Blanc*
Feature-length story of this feline hero in which our
cat tells his nephew of his many adventures.
Aka: HEATHCLIFF: THE MOVIE
CAR                                        89 min
V                                            MSD

**HEATHERS ****                                18
Michael Lehmann         USA               1989
*Winona Ryder, Christian Slater, Shannon Doherty,*
*Kim Walker, Lisanne Falk, Penelope Milford, Glenn*
*Shadix, Lance Fenton*
A sharp black comedy that examines a variety of
issues of interest to the high school set, most notably
peer group pressure and sexuality. Largely built
around the tale of a girl who finds herself unable to fit
in with the reigning college clique. Witty, irreverent
and often quite tasteless, the lack of a strong plot

weakens its impact. The feature debut for Lehmann.
Aka: LETHAL ATTRACTION
COM                                    98 min (ort 102 min)
V                                                    20VIS

### HEATWAVE ***                                    15
Phillip Noyce        AUSTRALIA              1982
*Judy Davis, Richard Moir, Bill Hunter, John Mellon,*
*John Gregg, Chris Haywood, Anna Jemison*
A property development company resorts to violence
during the Christmas heatwave in Sydney, to push
through the construction of a new apartment block. A
kind of Australian answer to CHINATOWN, polished
but melodramatic.
DRA                                      95 min (ort 99 min)
B,V,V2                                             GHV

### HEAVEN CAN WAIT **                              PG
Warren Beatty/Buck Henry
                 USA                        1978
*Warren Beatty, Julie Christie, Dyan Cannon, Jack*
*Warden, Charles Grodin, James Mason, Buck Henry,*
*Vincent Gardenia, Joseph Maher, Hamilton Camp,*
*Arthur Malet, Stephane Faragy, Jeannie Unero, Harry*
*D.K. Wong*
A football player is called to Heaven too soon and
returns to Earth in another man's body. Remake of
the 1941 film "Here Comes Mr Jordan" that despite its
talented cast, feels lifeless and uninspired, with a
total lack of wit and listless, uninspired direction. AA:
Art/Set (Paul Sylbert and Edwin O'Donovan/George
Gaines).
COM                                            100 min
B,V,LV                                             CIC

### HEAVEN WITH A GUN **                            18
Lee H. Katzin        USA                    1969
*Glenn Ford, Carolyn Jones, Barbara Hershey, David*
*Carradine, J.D. Cannon, Noah Beery Jr*
A gunfighter gives up his profession and becomes a
preacher, but is forced by events to take up his gun
again, in this solid if uninspired Western.
WES                                            101 min
B,V                                               MGM

### HEAVENLY BODIES *                               15
Lawrence Dane        CANADA                1983
*Cynthia Dale, Richard Rebiere, Walter George Alton,*
*Laura Henry, Stuart Stone*
A young girl who starts a health and fitness institute
runs into trouble when she turns down the advances of
a famous sports star. A kind of aerobics musical, best
left in the obscurity it deservedly achieved.
DRA                                      88 min (ort 99 min)
B,V                                               CBS

### HEAVENLY DESIRE **
Jaacov Jaacovi       USA                    1979
*Serena, Johnnie Keyes, Seka, Jamie Gillis*
The story begins in the Old West, when a shortsighted gunslinger and his two girlfriends are killed
at high noon. Moving to modern times, they return as
ghosts to a sorority house that has been built on the
site of their old bordello, and using their influence,
encourage all the kids to have a good time.
A                                               88 min
B,V,V2                                             CAL

### HEAVENLY KID **                                 15
Cary Medoway         USA                    1985
*Lewis Smith, Jane Kaczmarek, Jason Gedrick,*
*Richard Mulligan, Mark Metcalf, Nancy Valen, Anne*
*Sawyer*
After getting himself killed in a car race, a greasy
1960s teenager finds that he cannot get into Heaven
until he performs the obligatory Good Deed. In his
case this is to help out a young nerd of the 1980s who
is having girl problems. An inconsistent and amateur-

ish fantasy-comedy with a few good moments – but
they come mainly at the end.
Aka: ANGEL, THE
COM                                             88 min
B,V                                               RNK

### HEAVENLY PURSUITS *                             15
Charles Gormley      UK                     1986
*Tom Conti, Helen Mirren, Brian Pettifer, David*
*Anderson, David Hayman, Jennifer Black*
A Glaswegian schoolteacher seems to gain miraculous
powers after saving a pupil from a fall. A waste of the
talents of a good cast.
Aka: GOSPEL ACCORDING TO VIC, THE; JUST
ANOTHER MIRACLE
COM                                             91 min
B,V                                               CBS

### HEAVENS ABOVE! **
John Boulting/Roy Boulting
                 UK                         1963
*Peter Sellers, Ian Carmichael, Irene Handl, Cecil*
*Parker, Isabel Jeans, Eric Sykes, Bernard Miles, Brock*
*Peters, Roy Kinnear, Miriam Karlin, Joan Miller,*
*Miles Malleson, Eric Barker, William Hartnell, Joan*
*Hickson, Mark Eden*
A down-to earth parson is appointed to a snobby
parish and manages to turn the entire area upside
down. A typical Boulting Brothers satire, which waits
until the end, and then pulls its punches.
COM       105 min; 113 min (WHV) (ort 118 min) B/W
B,V                         TEVP; WHV (VHS only)

### HEAVEN'S GATE **                                18
Michael Cimino       USA                    1980
*Kris Kristofferson, Isabelle Huppert, Christopher*
*Walken, Jeff Bridges, John Hurt, Brad Dourif,*
*Richard Masur, Joseph Cotten, Sam Waterston,*
*Geoffrey Lewis, Terry O'Quinn, Mickey Rourke*
A vast overblown Western that cost $44,000,000 to
make. It is supposed to recreate the period of the
Johnson County War, when cattlemen tried to force
out new settlers. Wonderfully photographed with
magnificent locations and sets, but utterly destroyed
by the lack of a clear story.
WES    207 min (ort 220 min) (Cut at film release by 1
                                        min 14 sec)
B,V                                               WHV

### HEAVEN'S HEROES **                              PG
                 USA                        1986
*David Ralphe, James O'Hagen*
A low-budget film shot on 16 mm, that tells the
true-life story of a Des Moines police officer who was
killed in the line of duty, but not before he had
converted his partner to an active belief in Christian-
ity. Quite a well made and acted film, but little more
than a vehicle for the preachy message.
DRA                                             72 min
B,V                                               MKIV

### HEAVEN'S TOUCH **                               R18
Warren Evans         USA                    1983
*Kelly Nichols, Sharon Kane, Ron Jeremy, Gayle*
*Sterling, Joanna Storm, Michael Knight*
An executive spends most of his time having sex with
every young woman in the company. Finally he drops
dead and arrives in Heaven, but only to discover that
he died before his time. A friendly angel sends him
back to Earth and he takes over the body of Barry,
who owns the company he worked for. But Barry's
wife wants her husband dead and has hired a woman
to accomplish this. A ridiculous and overdone porno
version of HEAVEN CAN WAIT.
A                                               81 min
B,V                                               ELV

## HEAVY TRAFFIC ** 18
Ralph Bakshi            USA                 1973
*Voices of: Joseph Kaufman, Beverly Hope Atkinson,*
*Frank De Kova, Terri Haven, Mary Dean Lauria*
Animated X-rated satire about the sexual and other
adventures of a young New Yorker. Bakshi made this
one on the strength of his success with FRITZ THE
CAT. Intercut with a number of pointless live-action
sequences and let down by lack of story development.
See also WIZARDS, HEY GOOD-LOOKIN' and FIRE
AND ICE, three other films by this director.
CAR                                      76 min
B,V                                       TEVP

## HECTOR THE MIGHTY * 15
Enzo G. Castellari
            FRANCE/ITALY/SPAIN           1972
*Mike Forrest, Philipp Leroy*
Updated version of Helen of Troy with the action
taking place in a brothel and Hell's Angels taking the
place of Greek troops. (Do I see a wooden motorbike?)
Aka: ETTORE LO FUSTO; EL RAPTO DE ELENA,
LA DELENTE ITALIANA; HECTOR LE FORTICHE;
LES PROXENETES
COM                                     103 min
B,V                                        VPD

## HEDDA ** PG
Trevor Nunn             UK                  1975
*Glenda Jackson, Timothy West, Peter Eyre, Patrick*
*Stewart, Jennie Linden, Constance Chapman, Pam St*
*Clement*
Flat and dull version of a fine play, with Jackson as an
unhappy wife who takes pleasure in manipulating
others, but comes unstuck when she hatches a plan to
take revenge on a former lover. A Royal Shakespeare
Company production that is sustained if not redeemed
by Jackson's strong performance.
Boa: play Hedda Gabler by Henrik Ibsen.
DRA                                     102 min
V                                        HOLLY

## HEIDI ** U
June Wyndham-Davis  UK                     1974
*Emma Blake, Flora Robson, Hans Meyer*
A TV version of the Spyri story, originally shown in
six episodes. Fair.
Boa: novel by Johanna Spyri.
JUV                                    112 min mTV
B,V                                        BBC

## HEIDI ** U
Delbert Mann            USA                 1968
*Maximilian Schell, Jean Simmons, Michael Redgrave,*
*Walter Slezak, Peter Van Eyck, Jennifer Edwards*
A more recent version of the classic story, made for
NBC TV in the USA. A well-made version, with
strong performances and a good script by Earl Ham-
ner Jr. Edwards is the daughter of director Blake
Edwards.
Boa: novel by Johanna Spyri.
JUV                                    100 min mTV
B,V                                        SEL

## HEIDI *** U
Allan Dwan              USA                 1937
*Shirley Temple, Jean Hersholt, Arthur Treacher,*
*Helen Westley, Pauline Moore, Mary Nash, Thomas*
*Beck, Sidney Blackmer, Mady Christians, Sig*
*Rumann, Marcia Mae Jones, Christian Rub*
Film version of a famous children's classic about a
young orphan sent to live with her gruff grandfather
in the Swiss Alps. A classic children's story that forms
a useful vehicle for the talents of Temple. Written by
Walter Ferris and Julian Josephson.
Boa: novel by Johanna Spyri.
JUV                       84 min (ort 88 min) B/W
V                                          CBS

## HEIDI'S SONG ** U
Robert Taylor           USA                 1982
*Voices of: Lorne Greene, Sammy Davis Jr, Margaret*
*Gray, Michael Bell, Peter Cullen*
A young girl is forced to leave her mountainside home
to live in Frankfurt. Unused to urban life, she seeks a
way of returning home. A Hanna-Barbera cartoon
based on a famous tale. Despite songs by Sammy Cahn
and Burton Lane, lifeless animation and an excess of
cuteness make this a dismally ordinary offering.
Boa: novel Heidi by Johanna Spyri.
CAR                                      91 min
V                                          RNK

## HEIST, THE *** 15
Stuart Orme             USA       1989 (released 1990)
*Pierce Brosnan, Tom Skerritt, Wendy Hughes, Robert*
*Prosky, Noble Willingham*
Brosnan plays an ex-con who was framed by his
former partner over an emerald-smuggling job, but
plans a complex racetrack robbery to have his re-
venge. A violent action tale with a strong cast and
enough twists in the plot to sustain interest.
A/AD               93 min (ort 97 min) mCab
V                                          CIC

## HELL BELOW ** 15
            FRANCE
*Michel Constantin, Serge Reggiani, Juliet Berto, Jean*
*Borise, Robert Enrico*
A group of bank robbers on a job become trapped in
the vaults, in this fairly tense but cliched crime
thriller.
THR                    86 min (Cut at film release)
V                                  MANHAT; KRP

## HELL BOATS *** PG
Paul Wendkos            UK                  1969
*James Franciscus, Elizabeth Shephard, Ronald Allen,*
*Reuven Bar-Yotam, Inigo Jackson, Mark Hawkins,*
*Drewe Henley, Magda Kunopka, Takis Emmanuel*
A Royal Navy commander engaged in the defence of
Malta, plans a raid on a German base in Sicily, using
a captured German motor torpedo boat. Solid British
war film displaying those typical virtues common to
films of this period.
Aka: M.T.B.; MTB: MALTA WORLD WAR 2 (GLOB)
WAR                       89 min (ort 95 min)
B,V                                 AMBAS; GLOB

## HELL CAMP ** 18
Eric Karson             USA                 1986
*Tom Skerritt, Lisa Eichhorn, Anthony Zerbe, John*
*Considine, Robert Wightman, Richard Roundtree*
An experiment, in training air force personnel to
withstand torture as POWs, is being staged on a
Pacific island, but it goes horribly wrong when the
base commander goes insane, in this tense but
ultimately disappointing tale.
Aka: OPPOSING FORCE
A/AD                                     96 min
B,V                                        RCA

## HELL COMES TO FROGTOWN ** 15
R.J. Kizer/Donald G. Jackson
            USA                             1987
*Roddy Piper, Sandahl Bergman, Rory Calhoun, Cec*
*Verrell, William Smith, Nicholas Worth, Edye Byrde,*
*Kridsit Somers, Brian Frank, Cliff Bemis, Danielle*
*Hand, Suzanne Solari*
Another in the seemingly endless parade of low-
budget, poorly realised sagas of a post-WW3 world.
Here one of the few remaining fertile men goes on a
hazardous mission, to rescue eight female captives
being held by the mutants of "Frogtown", whilst
finding time to fertilise as many women as possible for
the all-female government.
A/AD                                     82 min
B,V                                        NWV

## HELL DRIVERS ***
Cy Endfield                UK                    PG
                                                1957
*Stanley Baker, Patrick McGoohan, Herbert Lom,*
*Peggy Cummins, Jill Ireland, Sidney James, Gordon*
*Jackson, William Hartnell, David McCallum, Sean*
*Connery, Wilfrid Lawson, Alfie Bass, Marjorie*
*Rhodes, Vera Day, Robin Bailey*
Extremely competent thriller set in a second-rate
haulage firm. An ex-con gets a job there, comes into
conflict with the top driver and discovers that the firm
runs a profitable racket. McGoohan as the somewhat
unbalanced trucker with a murderous temper, gives
one of his best performances.
Boa: story by John Kruse.
THR                          106 min (ort 108 min) B/W
B,V                    _              RNK; STRAND

## HELL FIRE **
William Murray          USA                    1986
*Sharon Mason, Kenneth McGregor, Julie Miller*
In 1997, a new kind of fuel is in use and a private eye
is given the job of investigating the corporation that
produces it.
Aka: PRIMAL SCREAM
FAN                                             90 min
B,V                                                AVA

## HELL HOLE *
                                                  18
Pierre De Moro          USA                    1985
*Judy Landers, Ray Sharkey, Marjoe Gortner, Edy*
*Williams, Terry Moore, Mary Woronov, Richard Cox*
A young girl is sent to a sinister mental home, to
prevent her revealing the location of evidence that a
drugs company would like to suppress, in this un-
pleasant and muddled effort.
DRA                                             88 min
B,V                                                MGM

## HELL HOUNDS OF ALASKA, THE **
                                                  PG
Harald Reinl
          WEST GERMANY/YUGOSLAVIA          1973
*Doug McClure, Harold Leipnitz, Angela Ott*
A gold shipment in Alaska is ambushed by a gang. A
man tries to track them down, but his efforts are
hampered by the presence of an injured boy who needs
immediate medical attention.
Aka: DIE BLUTIGEN GEIER VON ALASKA;
KRVAVI JASTREBOVI ALJASKE
A/AD                                            91 min
V                                                  VPD

## HELL IN THE PACIFIC ***
                                                  PG
John Boorman            USA                    1969
*Lee Marvin, Toshiro Mifune*
During WW2, an American pilot and a Japanese
naval officer find themselves alone on a Pacific island
and confront each other. From an initial desire to
murder each other, their relationship goes through a
number of phases as they realise the value of co-
operation. An engrossing character study spoilt by the
contrived ending.
Osca: RELUCTANT HEROES, THE (VCC)
WAR               102 min; 168 min (2 film cassette)
B,V                            GHV; VCC (VHS only)

## HELL IS EMPTY **
John Ainsworth/Bernard Knowles
          CZECHOSLOVAKIA/UK                1967
*Martine Carol, Anthony Steel, Shirley-Anne Field,*
*James Robertson Justice, Isa Miranda, Carl Mohrer,*
*Jess Conrad, Anthony Dawson, Catherine Von Schell,*
*Irene Von Meyendorff, Patricia Viterbo, Anna Gael,*
*Eugene Deckers*
A gang hides out in an island mansion and holds its
occupants hostage, after committing a robbery in
which the guards were killed.
Boa: novel by J.F. Straker.
DRA                          90 min (ort 109 min)
B,V                               MARKET; DFS

## HELL ISLAND **
                                                  18
Dimitri Logothetis      USA                    1986
*Tom Reilly, Donna Denton, Nicholas Celozzi, Toni*
*Basil, Hope Marie Carlton, Tamara Hyler, Steven*
*Brian Smith, Ty Miller*
A college student suffers from nightmares that are
literally deadly, and threaten his life. A dream
specialist is called in to help before it is too late, in this
rip-off reworking of the "Freddy" theme of all those
NIGHTMARE ON ELM STREET movies.
Aka: SLAUGHTERHOUSE ROCK
HOR                   80 min (ort 82 min) Cut (1 min 14 sec)
V/sh                                               MGM

## HELL NIGHT *
                                                  18
Tom De Simone          USA                    1981
*Linda Blair, Vincent Van Patten, Peter Barton, Jenny*
*Neumann, Kevin Brophy, Suki Goodwin, Jimmy*
*Sturtevant*
A group of young college students have to spend a
night in a haunted house, as part of their initiation
into the college fraternity. There is however, no ghost,
just a crazed killer. Dull.
HOR                        98 min (ort 101 min) Cut (1 sec)
B,V                            VPD; ACAD; APX

## HELL ON FRISCO BAY ***
                                                  15
Frank Tuttle            USA                    1955
*Alan Ladd, Edward G. Robinson, Joanne Dru,*
*William Demarest, Fay Wray, Jayne Mansfield, Paul*
*Stewart*
An ex-cop, framed for manslaughter, comes out of
prison and goes after the crook who put him there, in
this gripping 1930s-style gangster yarn.
Boa: novel Darkest Hour by W.P. McGivern. Osca:
MAD MISS MANTON, THE
THR                          94 min (ort 98 min)
B,V                                                KVD

## HELL ON THE BATTLEGROUND ***
                                                  18
David Prior             USA                    1988
*Ted Prior, Fritz Matthews, William Smith*
Vietnam War story of two NCO Army Rangers, who
get caught in enemy crossfire with little hope of being
rescued. Making their own way back to their lines and
stealing some tanks in the process, they are rewarded
by being given an assignment to take a new platoon
through non-hostile territory. The platoon is
ambushed by Russian troops, and as the less experienced soldiers are picked off, the two have to decide
which one is to go for help.
WAR                          82 min (ort 91 min)
V                                                BRAVE

## HELL ON WHEELS *
Will Zens               USA                    1967
*Marty Robbins, John Asley, Gigi Perreau*
A man is a stock car racer by day and a recording
artist by night in this pointless tale.
DRA                                             97 min
B,V                                           VCL/CBS

## HELL PRISON **
                                                  18
Rino Di Silvestro       ITALY
*Anita Strindberg, Eve Czemerys*
Exploitative sex film set in a woman's prison, where a
young woman has to endure various encounters after
being sentenced for drug smuggling.
A     80 min; 85 min (SHEP) (ort 88 min) Cut (3 min 46
sec)
B,V                    KMV L/A; PRI; GLOB; PHE

## HELL RAIDERS **
                                                  18
Gope Samtani            PHILIPPINES            1985
*Barry Prima, Roy Marten*
After a Pacific island is invaded and most of its
defenders killed, the survivors band together into

resistance groups.

| | |
|---|---|
| WAR | 125 min Cut (4 sec) |
| B,V | ARF |

## HELL SQUAD *

Kenneth Hartford    USA    15
1984
*Tina Ledermann, Glen Hartford, Bainbridge Scott*
The son of an American ambassador is kidnapped in the Middle East and a troupe of showgirls is trained so that a rescue mission can be mounted. Low-grade nonsense.

| | |
|---|---|
| A/AD | 83 min (ort 87 min) |
| B,V | GHV |

## HELLBENDERS, THE **

Sergio Corbucci    ITALY/SPAIN    1966
*Joseph Cotten, Norma Bengell, Julian Mateos, Aldo Sambrell, Angel Aranda, Gino Pernice, Claudio Gora, Maria Martin*
Civil War story shot in Spain, and involving a plot to steal money from the Union forces with which to rebuild the South. Average.
Aka: I CRUDELI

| | |
|---|---|
| WES | 92 min dubbed |
| B,V | EHE |

## HELLBOUND: HELLRAISER 2 **

Tony Randel    UK    18
1988
*Ashley Laurence, Kenneth Cranham, Clare Higgins, Imogen Boorman, Sean Chapman, Doug Bradley, William Hope*
A film that begins where the earlier HELLRAISER left off, with our young heroine from the first film being forced to do battle with the psychiatrist in charge of the mental hospital to which she has been confined, and taking a trip to Hell in the hope of rescuing her father. As ever, the nasty Cenobites are out to cause misery, in a thinly-plotted film that's all but overwhelmed by its gruesome effects.

| | |
|---|---|
| HOR | 91 min (ort 97 min) |
| V | 2020 |

## HELLCATS OF THE NAVY ***

Nathan Juran    USA    U
1957
*Ronald Reagan, Nancy Davis (Reagan), Arthur Franz, Robert Arthur, William Leslie, William Phillips*
Set during WW2 aboard a US submarine, this story tells of the ship's captain who is ordered to undertake a dangerous mission, which takes him to the heavily mined waters off the Asiatic mainland. A standard war film with some good action sequences.
Boa: novel Hellcats Of The Sea by C.A. Lockwood and H.C. Adamson.

| | |
|---|---|
| WAR | 78 min (ort 82 min) B/W |
| V | RCA |

## HELLFIGHTERS **

Andrew V. McLaglen    USA    PG
1969
*John Wayne, Vera Miles, Katherine Ross, Jim Hutton, Bruce Cabot, Barbara Stuart*
Adventure tale of the men who have the dangerous job of fighting oil-well fires. The action sequences and special effects are fine in themselves, and the cast play their parts well, but the thin plot cannot sustain the dramatic situations or plausibly handle an examination of their personal relationships or family lives.

| | |
|---|---|
| A/AD | 115 min |
| V | CIC |

## HELLGATE ***

William A. Levey    USA    18
1988
*Ron Pallilo, Abigail Wolcott, Carel Trichardt*
In an old abandoned mining town a grief-stricken father is the only inhabitant, kept there by the memory of his daughter who was murdered years ago. He finds a strange crystal that has the power to restore life, and uses it to resurrect his daughter and then lure strangers to the town, where they are murdered and then resurrected as zombies. A foolish

idea, but quite chilling.

| | |
|---|---|
| HOR | 92 min |
| B,V | NWV |

## HELLO AGAIN **

Frank Perry    USA    PG
1987
*Shelley Long, Judith Ivey, Gabriel Byrne, Corbin Bernsen, Madeleine Potter, Sela Ward, Austin Pendleton, Carrie Nye, Robert Lewis, Thor Fields, Tony Sivic, John Cunningham, Mary Fogarty, Elkan Abramawitz, Shirley Rich*
A Long Island woman chokes to death, but is resurrected a year later by her witch sister. She soon finds that she's unable to pick up her life again where she left off – her husband has remarried and is none too thrilled at her return. A contemporary social comedy that does little with the basic premise, except scatter a few laughs in different directions.

| | |
|---|---|
| COM | 92 min |
| B,V | BUENA; WDV |

## HELLO, DOLLY! ***

Gene Kelly    USA    U
1969
*Barbra Streisand, Walter Matthau, Michael Crawford, Tommy Tune, E.J. Peaker, Louis Armstrong, Marianne MacAndrew, David Hurst*
Overlong and somewhat tedious film version of a smash hit musical about a celebrated matchmaker who decides it's time to get hitched herself. Some good songs, a vigorous performance from Streisand, and wonderful costumes, make it bearable. AA: Art/Set (John DeCuir, Jack Martin Smith and Herman Blumenthal/Walter M. Scott, George Hopkins and Raphael Bretton), Score (Adapt) (Lennie Hayton/ Lionel Newman), Sound (Jack Solomon/Murray Spivack).
Boa: musical by Jerry Herman and Michael Stewart/ play The Matchmaker by Thornton Wilder.

| | |
|---|---|
| MUS | 139 min (ort 146 min) |
| V | CBS |

## HELLRAISER ***

Clive Barker    UK/USA    18
1987
*Andrew Robinson, Clare Higgins, Ashley Lawrence, Sean Chapman, Oliver Smith, Robert Hines*
Larry and Julia move into Larry's childhood home where the remains of Frank, his brother and Julia's ex-lover, lie upstairs in the attic. The victim of some macabre experiments with demons from another world, he is accidentally brought back to life when Larry cuts himself. Julia now agrees to lure men into the home and murder them in order to provide the blood he requires. A gruesome but slick debut for writer Barker. A sequel followed.
Boa: novella The Hellbound Heart by Clive Barker.

| | |
|---|---|
| HOR | 89 min (ort 93 min) Cut (4 sec) |
| B,V | NWV |

## HELL'S ANGELS ON WHEELS **

Richard Rush    USA    18
1967
*Adam Roarke, Jack Nicholson, Sabrina Scharf, Jana Taylor, John Garwood, Sonny Barger, Richard Anders*
Exploits of a bunch of Hell's Angels on a violent trip across America. A tough but trashy film, watchable chiefly thanks to the excellent work of photographer Laszlo Kovacs.
Aka: LEADER OF THE PACK, THE

| | |
|---|---|
| A/AD | 80 min (ort 95 min) Cut (10 min 59 sec) |
| B,V | TURBO L/A; MIA (VHS only) |

## HELL'S HIGHWAY **

Rowland Brown    USA    1932
*Richard Dix, Rochelle Hudson, Tom Brown, Louis Carter, C. Henry Gordon*
A brutal study of appalling prison conditions in America in the 1930s, with a convict plotting to escape. An effective but unremittingly harsh tale. The

screenplay is by Samuel Ornitz.
Osca: OUT OF THE PAST
DRA                                             59 min B/W
B,V                                                   KVD

## HELP WANTED: KIDS **                                U
David Greenwalt         USA               1986
Cindy Williams, Bill Hudson, Chad Allen, Hillary
Wolf, John Dehner, Joel Brooks, Miriam Flynn, Billie
Bird, Carol Morley, Ebbe Roe Smith, Cecily
Thompson, Joseph Chapman, Kenneth Kimmins, Hap
Lawrence, Toni Attell
A New York business executive and his wife find
themselves having to engage two street kids to
impersonate their own offspring, so as to pander to the
whims of his new boss who expects his employees to
represent "perfect families". An intermittently engag-
ing Disney floss.
COM                              90 min (ort 104 min) mTV
B,V                                                   WDV

## HELTER SKELTER ***                                  18
Tom Gries              USA               1976
Georg DiCenzo, Steve Railsback, Nancy Wolfe,
Marilyn Burns, Christina Hart, Cathey Paine, Alan
Oppenheimer, Rudy Ramos, Sondra Blake, George
Garro, Vic Werber, Howard Caine, Jason Ronard,
Skip Homeier, Marc Alaimo, Bill Durkin
Story of the hunt and trial of Manson and his "family"
after their savage murder of a number of people. The
prosecutor co-wrote the bestseller on which the film is
based. An intense and chilling tale, with a powerful
performance from Railsback as the crazed hippie
leader.
Boa: book by Vincent Bugliosi and Curt Gentry.
DRA                             115 min (ort 194 min) mTV
B,V                                                   CBS

## HENDERSON MONSTER, THE **                           U
Waris Hussein          USA               1980
Stephen Collins, Larry Gates, Christine Lahti, Jason
Miller, Nehemiah Persoff, David Spielberg, Josef
Sommer, Peter Evans, Kenneth Kimmins, Mark
Hulcher, Andrew Early, Glenn Crone, Lalla Rolfe,
David Kilgore
A Nobel Prize-winning scientist is doing research
work into genetics that poses a great threat to
humanity. An absorbing idea is thrown away in a
hotchpotch of romantic-triangle distractions. Scripted
by Ernest Kinoy.
FAN                              99 min (ort 105 min) mTV
B,V                                                   PRV

## HENNESSY **                                         15
Don Sharp              UK                1975
Rod Steiger, Lee Remick, Trevor Howard, Richard
Johnson, Peter Egan, Eric Porter, Stanley Lebor, Ian
Hogg, John Hallam, Patrick Stewart, David Collings,
John Shrapnel, Hugh Moxey, Peter Copley, Diana
Fairfax, Alan Barry
A demolition expert, angered at the fatal shooting of
his wife and child by British soldiers in Belfast,
swears vengeance against the British, embarking on a
plan to bomb Parliament. A disagreeable thriller,
slackly directed and of limited interest.
Boa: story by Richard Johnson.
DRA                             100 min (ort 103 min)
B,V                                                   RNK

## HENRY IV: PARTS 1 AND 2 ***                         U
David Giles            UK                1979
Jon Finch, Anthony Quayle, David Gwillim, Michele
Dotrice, Robert Eddison, Brenda Bruce, Frances Cuka
Competent and well-acted TV version of this famous
play, originally shown in two parts. Part 1 examines
the monarch's change from dissolute heir apparent to
responsible prince, whilst Part 2 explores his conflict
with his father and his final transition to ruler.
Boa: play by William Shakespeare.

DRA                             301 min (2 cassettes) mTV
V/h                                                   BBC

## HENRY V ***                                         U
David Giles            UK                1979
David Gwillim, Alec McCowen, Jocelyne Boisseau,
Martin Smith, Rob Edwards, Roger Davenport,
Clifford Parrish, Derek Hollis, Robert Ashby, David
Buck, Rod Beacham, Trevor Baxter, John Abineri
One in a series of BBC adaptations, with Gwillim
effective in the title role and ably supported by a
strong cast.
Boa: play by William Shakespeare.
DRA                                          165 min mTV
V/h                                                   BBC

## HENRY V ****                                        U
Laurence Olivier       UK                1944
Laurence Olivier, Robert Newton, Leslie Banks, Renee
Asherson, Esmond Knight, Leo Genn, George Robey,
Ernest Thesiger, Ivy St Helier, Ralph Truman,
Harcourt Williams, Max Adrian, Valentine Dyall,
Felix Aylmer
Excellent film version of the famous play, with superb
acting and some unforgettable battle scenes. An
outstanding film in many ways, stirring, stylised and
utterly absorbing. The film opens and closes with a
typical performance at the Globe Theatre, set in the
year 1603. The splendid score is by William Walton.
AA: Spec Award (Laurence Olivier for outstanding
achievement as actor, producer and director).
Boa: play by William Shakespeare.
DRA                                              137 min
V                                                     RNK

## HENRY V ****                                        PG
Kenneth Branagh        UK                1989
Kenneth Branagh, Derek Jacobi, Paul Scofield, Judi
Dench, Emma Thompson, Alec McCowen, Ian Holm,
Robbie Coltrane, Brian Blessed, Richard Briers,
Robert Stephens, Christian Bale, Michael Maloney,
Geraldine McEwan
In this remarkable directorial debut, Branagh has
succeeded in creating a stunning and highly original
rendition of Shakespeare's famous play of the warrior-
king and his war against France. Quite different in
feel from the famous Olivier film, this interpretation
is no less visually impressive, and yet offers an
intimacy and warmth absent from that earlier classic.
AA: Cost (Phyllis Dalton).
Boa: play by William Shakespeare.
DRA                             130 min (ort 137 min)
V                                                     20VIS

## HENRY VIII AND HIS SIX WIVES ***
Waris Hussein          UK                1972
Keith Michell, Frances Cuka, Charlotte Rampling,
Donald Pleasence, Jane Asher, Lynne Frederick,
Barbara Leigh-Hunt
The story of one of England's most degenerate and
bloodthirsty monarchs, seen as a series of flashbacks
on his deathbed. A generally well made TV drama,
with Michell giving one of his best performances as
the monarch. See also THE SIX WIVES OF HENRY
VIII.
DRA                                          120 min mTV
B,V                                                   TEVP

## HER ALIBI **                                        PG
Bruce Beresford        USA               1988
Tom Selleck, Paulina Porizkova, William Daniels,
James Farentino, Hurd Hatfield, Patrick Wayne, Tess
Harper, Joan Copeland
A comedy thriller, in which a successful writer of
mysteries hopes to cure himself of a temporary slump
in his writing, by providing a false alibi for an accused
murderess and taking her back home to observe her.
Neither tense nor particularly funny, this strange film
is a dud on both counts. Likeable performances

partially rescue it.
THR                                    91 min (ort 94 min)
V                                                    WHV

## HER FIRST AFFAIR **
Alan Dwan                  USA                    1932
*Ida Lupino, George Curzon, Harry Tate*
A girl is infatuated with a writer of adventure stories,
but he rejects her advances and tries to teach her a
lesson.
DRA                                            65 min B/W
B,V,V2                                          VCL/CBS

## HER LIFE AS A MAN ***                           PG
Robert Ellis Miller        USA                    1983
*Robyn Douglass, Marc Singer, Robert Culp, Laraine
Newman, Miriam Flynn, Joan Collins, Anthony
Holland, Patricia Barry, Malcolm Campbell, Steve
Fogel, Dino Gigante, Debbie Gilbert, loretta
Greenwood, Bobby Hosea, Suze Lanier*
A female reporter has to disguise herself as a man, in
order to land a job as a sportswriter. A likeable and
amusing addition to films such as TOOTSIE and
VICTOR/VICTORIA. The adaptation (based on a true
story) is by Joanna Crawford. See also JUST ONE OF
THE GUYS.
Boa: magazine article in "The Village Voice" by Carol
Lynn Mithers.
COM                         92 min (ort 100 min) mTV
B,V                                          IPC/VSP; CBS

## HERBIE GOES BANANAS *                            U
Vincent McEveety          USA                     1980
*Cloris Leachman, Charles Martin-Smith, John
Vernon, Steven W. Burns, Harvey Korman, Elyssa
Davalos, Fritz Feld, Richard Jaeckel, Joaquin Garay
III, Alex Rocco*
The fourth in the series of THE LOVE BUG comedies,
about a Volkswagen with a life of its own. This time it
takes its owners on a motoring holiday in South
America. Thankfully this was the last one in an
increasingly dreary chain of sequels. However, a TV
series soon followed in the States.
JUV                                              100 min
B,V                                                 WDV

## HERBIE GOES TO MONTE CARLO **                    U
Vincent McEveety          USA                     1977
*Dean Jones, Don Knotts, Julie Sommers, Roy Kinnear,
Jacques Marin*
One of an endless series of sequels to THE LOVE
BUG, with our car entering the Monte Carlo Rally
where a spy ring hides diamonds in its petrol tank.
Followed by HERBIE GOES BANANAS.
JUV                                    91 min (ort 104 min)
B,V                                                 WDV

## HERBIE RIDES AGAIN ***                           U
Robert Stevenson          USA                     1974
*Helen Hayes, Ken Berry, Stefanie Powers, Keenan
Wynn, John McIntire, Huntz Hall, Ivor Barry, Dan
Tobin, Vito Scotti, Raymond Bailey, Liam Dunn,
Elaine Devry, Chuck McCann, Richard X. Slattery,
Hank Jones, Rod McCary*
First sequel to THE LOVE BUG. The Volkswagan
Beetle with a mind of its own, saves its owner from the
attentions of a greedy property developer. Fairly
typical Disney slapstick, good fun in a mindless sort of
way. Followed by HERBIE GOES TO MONTE
CARLO.
JUV                                               88 min
B,V                                                 WDV

## HERCULES *                                       PG
Lewis Coates (Luigi Cozzi)
                          ITALY                   1983
*Lou Ferrigno, Sybil Danning (Sybelle Danninger),
Ingrid Anderson, Mirella D'Angelo, Brad Harris,
William Berger, Rossana Podesta*

A sort of SF version of the Hercules story, with our
hero trying to rescue an abducted princess. Despite
good casting of Ferrigno, this foolish fantasy adventure soon comes adrift and substitutes special effects
for a decent script.
FAN                                               98 min
B,V                                                 GHV

## HERCULES **                                       U
Pietro Francisci           ITALY                  1957
*Steve Reeves, Sylva Koscina, Fabrizio Mione, Ivo
Garrani, Gina Rovere, Gianna Maria Canale,
Lucianna Paoluzzi (Paluzzi)*
One of the earliest of the Hercules films, this purports
to be a tale of his labours for the hand of the woman he
loves. Followed by HERCULES UNCHAINED. Fair.
Aka: LE FATICHE DI ERCOLE
A/AD                            107 min; 99 min (VGM)
B,V                              INT/CBS L/A; VGM

## HERCULES AGAINST THE SONS OF THE SUN** U
Osvaldo Civirani          ITALY                   1963
*Mark Forest, Anna Pace, Andrea Rhu, Giuliano
Gemma*
Hercules is the sole survivor of a devastating storm,
and is washed ashore in the Land of the Incas, where
he is befriended by Prince Mika. He promises to use
his strength to save the prince's sister from sacrifice in
this production-line adventure.
A/AD                                              91 min
B,V                                            DFS; PIR

## HERCULES CHALLENGE **
Giorgio Ferroni           ITALY                   1963
*Gordon Scott, Alessandra Panaro, Rosalba Neri*
Hercules saves the people of Mycenae from the
tyranny of Prince Moloch, in this amiable costume
adventure.
Aka: CONQUEST OF MYCENAE, THE
A/AD                                              95 min
B,V,V2                                             VPD

## HERCULES CONQUERS ATLANTIS **                   PG
Victorri Cottafavi
                          FRANCE/ITALY            1961
*Reg Park, Fay Spain, Ettore Manni, Luciano Marin,
Ivo Garrani, Laura Allan, Mario Petri, Mimmo
Palarma, Enrico-Maria Salerno, Salvatore Furnari,
Mario Valdermarin, Gianmaria Volonte, Allesandro
Sperli, Maurizio Caffarelli*
Greece is menaced by the sinister power of Atlantis,
and even the great Hercules appears powerless to stop
the Atlantean onslaught. A lightweight mythological
epic.
Aka: ERCOLE ALLA CONQUISTA DI ATLANTIDE;
HERCULE A LA CONQUETE DE L'ATLANTIDE;
HERCULES AND THE CAPTIVE WOMEN;
HERCULES AND THE CONQUEST OF ATLANTIS
A/AD                                  80 min (ort 84 min)
V                          VFP L/A; HER; PARA; INTMED

## HERCULES IN NEW YORK *                           PG
Audrey Wiseberg/Arthur Seidelman
                          USA                     1970
*Arnold Schwarzenegger, Arnold Stang, Deborah
Loomis, Taina Elg, James Karen*
Hercules is bored with his life among the Gods on
Mount Olympus and ends up on a visit to New York. A
weak attempt at spoofing the many films based on this
heroic character.
Aka: HERCULES GOES BANANAS; HERCULES
THE MOVIE
COM                                               86 min
V                                                   VPD

## HERCULES IN THE CENTRE OF THE EARTH *
Mario Bava                ITALY                   1961
*Reg Park, Leonora Ruffo, Giorgio Ardisson,
Christopher Lee, Ely Draco, Milton Reid, Ida Galli,*

*Marisa Belli*
Hercules fights evil forces and saves a beautiful woman, when he goes on a trip to the Earth's centre. Too bad he didn't stay there.
Aka: ERCOLE AL CENTRO DELLA TERRA; HERCULES AND THE HAUNTED WORLD; HERCULES AT THE CENTRE OF THE WORLD; HERCULES IN THE HAUNTED WORLD
A/AD 80 min
B,V VFP L/A; HER

## HERCULES UNCHAINED ** U
Pietro Francisci FRANCE/ITALY 1959
*Steve Reeves, Sylva Koscina, Primo Carnera, Sylvia Lopez*
Sequel to HERCULES, with Reeves having many adventures as he tries to rescue his bride-to-be.
Aka: ERCOLE E LA REGINA DI LIDIA
A/AD 97 min; 93 min (VGM) (ort 101 min)
B,V,V2 INT/CBS L/A; VGM

## HERE COMES THE BRIDE **
USA
*David Morris, Joey Civera, Samantha Fox, Colleen Anderson, Clea Carson*
Story of a nymphomaniac who has a hard time adapting to married life.
A 60 min
V RIP

## HERO AND THE TERROR ** 15
William Tannen USA 1988
*Chuck Norris, Steve James, Brynn Thayer, Jack O'Halloran*
A cop tracks down a demented killer he once caught years ago. A film that marks a change for Norris, from fairly non-stop martial arts action, to some attempt at characterisation, a change which is not entirely successful.
A/AD 93 min
B, V/sh CAN; PATHE

## HERO AT LARGE ** PG
Martin Davidson USA 1980
*John Ritter, Anne Archer, Bert Convy, Kevin McCarthy, Harry Bellaver, Anita Dangler, Kevin Bacon*
A man dressed up as a super-hero to promote a new film, actually foils a robbery and becomes a hero. Politicians then try to cash in on his popularity in this engaging if implausible comedy.
COM 95 min (ort 98 min)
V MGM

## HERO BUNKER **
George Andrews GREECE 1971
*John Miller, Maria Xenia, Anna Maggi*
A Greek battleship is torpedoed during WW2 but the crew decide to fight on regardless.
WAR 86 min (ort 93 min)
B,V,V2 GOV

## HERO COMMANDOS ** 15
Andy Rosenberg USA
*Max King, Lewis West, Bruce Orr, Carter Link, Susan Man*
Routine war film set in China at the time of the Japanese invasion.
WAR 87 min
B,V DIAM

## HERO IN THE FAMILY ** U
Mel Damski. USA 1986
*Christopher Collett, Cliff De Young, Annabeth Gish, Darleen Carr, Keith Dorman, David Wohl, M. Emmet Walsh, Jay Brazen, Bernard Cuffling, Don Davis, Bill Down, Deryl Hayes, Max Margolin, Alicia Michelle, Stephen E. Miller*

An astronaut is sent on a space mission together with a chimp, but they discover a crystal there that results in an exchange of personalities. A standard Disney "swap-over" comedy.
JUV 87 min (ort 100 min) mTV
B,V WDV

## HEROES ** 15
Jeremy Paul Kagan USA 1977
*Henry Winkler, Sally Field, Harrison Ford, Val Avery, Olivia Cole, Hector Elias*
A Vietnam veteran who has been in and out of mental hospitals, has to choose between his dreams of wealth and the woman he loves, in this disappointing effort that gave Winkler his first starring role.
DRA 108 min (ort 113 min)
B,V CIC

## HEROES OF TELEMARK, THE *** U
Anthony Mann UK 1965
*Kirk Douglas, Richard Harris, Ulla Jacobsson, Michael Redgrave, Mervyn Johns, Anton Diffring, David Weston, Roy Dotrice, Eric Porter, Jennifer Hilary, Barry Jones, Ralph Michael, Geoffrey Keen, Maurice Denham*
Low-key and realistic tale of Norwegian resistance to the German occupation in WW2, and how they helped destroy a heavy water plant that was to be used in the development of an atomic bomb. Good action sequences but not a very exciting film as a whole.
Boa: books But For These Men by J.D. Drummond/ Skies Against The Atom by Knut Haukelid.
WAR 126 min; 124 min (VCC) (ort 131 min)
B,V RNK; VCC (VHS only)

## HEROES STAND ALONE ** 18
Mark Griffiths USA 1988
*Chad Everett*
A secret recording device is lost from an American spy plane, and a soldier leads a group of specialists into the jungle to recover it. Average.
A/AD 79 min
V MGM

## HEROES WITHOUT GLORY ** 15
1989
*Jeff Cameron*
Standard war heroics in North Africa circa 1942, where a British major is given the job of assembling a crack strike-force for the dangerous mission of destroying Rommel's fuel dumps. Against all the odds his force wins through in this utterly undistinguished effort.
WAR 88 min
B,V VPD

## HERO'S TEARS, A *** 18
Li Tan Yeong HONG KONG
*Chung Hwa, Lin Yin, Lung Chung-Erl, Bor Shing Fon, Lee Li-Li*
A rather unusual martial arts tale in which a famous hired killer endures many dangers in his search for the medicine that he hopes will cure his sister's blindness.
MAR 96 min
B,V VTEL

## HE'S MY GIRL *** 15
Gabrielle Beaumont USA 1987
*T.K. Carter, David Hallyday, Misha Mack, Jennifer Tilly, David Clennon, Warwick Sims, Monica Parker*
An aspiring rock star and his manager win a trip to Hollywood, but discover that the contest is open to couples only, so Carter reluctantly agrees to masquerade in drag as a companion for Hallyday. A funny little farce with numerous plot twists and a great performance from black comedian Carter.
COM 100 min
B,V MED

## HEY GOOD-LOOKIN' ** 18
Ralph Bakshi          USA          1975 (re-edited
                                   for release in 1982)
*Voices of: Richard Romanus, David Proval, Jesse*
*Welles, Tina Bowman*
Film animation set in the 1950s and based on the
director's own youth in Brooklyn, largely telling of the
exploits of two young womanizers. An ambitious stab
an a youth culture film via animation; interesting but
not all that effective. Written by Bakshi, whose other
films include FRITZ THE CAT, WIZARDS, FIRE
AND ICE and HEAVY TRAFFIC.
CAR                              74 min (ort 87 min)
B,V                                  VTC L/A; XTASY

## HEY THERE, IT'S YOGI BEAR ** U
William Hanna/Joseph Barbera
                      USA          1963
*Voices of: Mel Blanc, J. Pat O'Malley, Julie Bennett,*
*Daws Butler, James Darren, Don Messick*
Animated feature with our hero rescuing Candy Bear
from a wicked circus owner who wants to make her
perform tricks on a high wire. A pleasant and fairly
enjoyable cartoon, the first full-length animation from
the Hanna-Barbera studio.
CAR                              86 min (ort 89 min)
V                                        VCC

## HICKEY AND BOGGS ** 15
Robert Culp            USA          1972
*Bill Cosby, Robert Culp, Rosalind Cash, Sheila*
*Sullivan, Isabel Sanford, Lou Frizzell, Ta-Ronce Allen*
Two hard-boiled private eyes become involved in a
violent search for a missing girl, and $500,000 from a
robbery, but seem to bring death to everyone they
come into contact with. Well made, but excessively
violent and depressing. A few moments of humour
help.
THR                            107 min (ort 111 min)
B,V                                      WHV

## HIDDEN FEAR ** 15
Mark Stouffer          USA          1986
*Robert Logan, Kathleen Quinlan, Levon Helm,*
*Bradford Dillman*
Arriving home to find his house burnt down and his
wife killed, a man takes off and sets up home deep in
the woods, where he lives as a hermit. Years later he
is discovered by a sociology student and a lady teacher
starts to take an interest in him. However, when a
young boy goes missing, suspicion falls on him rather
than the true culprit. A film that contains the
elements of a good story, but does very little with
them.
Aka: MAN OUTSIDE
A/AD                                   93 min
B,V                                     POLY

## HIDDEN THOUGHTS ** 18
Jeff Kanew             USA          1979
*Hal Holbrook, Viveca Lindfors, Louis Fletcher, Jose*
*Ferrer, Patricia Eliot, Peter Armstrong, Beth Berridge,*
*Steve Austin*
A successful publisher wakes up one day with a
bizarre compulsion to murder his family in this
bizarre oddity, written and directed by Kanew.
Aka: NATURAL ENEMIES
Boa: novel by Julius Horwitz.
DRA                         95 min; 100 min (HOK)
B,V,V2              HOK; KES (Betamax and VHS only)

## HIDDEN, THE * 18
Jack Sholder      CANADA/USA        1987
*Michael Nouri, Kyle McLachlan, Ed O'Ross, Clu*
*Gulager, Claudia Christian, Clarence Felder, William*
*Boyett, Richard Brooks, Catherine Cannon*
An alien creature moves from the body of one victim to
the next, causing each host to commit acts of violence.
Nouri plays a Los Angeles cop who is given the task of

investigating a bizarre wave of violence, fortunately
he receives a little help from one of the good aliens in
the shape of McLachlan. A flawed marriage of fantasy
and urban violence genres that does justice to neither.
HOR                              94 min (ort 96 min)
B,V                                      CBS

## HIDE AND SHRIEK * 18
John Hough             USA          1987
*Rod Steiger, Yvonne De Carlo, Michael J. Pollard,*
*Fiona Hutchinson, Sarah Torgov, Janet Wright,*
*William Hootkins*
Three couples go off for an island weekend off the
Seattle coast, but are forced to land on an unknown
island inhabited by a murderous family of degener-
ates, in this obnoxious and low-grade rubbish.
Aka: AMERICAN GOTHIC
HOR                              84 min Cut (58 sec)
B,V                                      VIR

## HIDE IN PLAIN SIGHT ** PG
James Caan             USA          1980
*James Caan, Jill Eikenberry, Robert Viharo, Joe*
*Grifasi, Barbra Rae, Thomas Hill, Kenneth McMillan,*
*Josef Sommer, Danny Aiello*
A divorced man discovers that his children have
disappeared, because their new father is a govern-
ment witness who has been given a new identity. A
cliched melodrama whose unusual plot premise offers
something by way of compensation.
Boa: novel by Leslie Waller.
DRA                                    98 min
B,V,V2                                   MGM

## HIDEAWAYS, THE ** 1973
Fielder Cook           USA          1973
*Ingrid Bergman, Sally Prager, Johnny Doran,*
*Madeline Kahn, George Rose, Georgann Johnson,*
*Richard Mulligan*
Two New Jersey kids hide out in New York's Metropo-
litan Museum and create a private world of their own,
meeting and befriending an art-collector recluse. A
good idea let down by disappointing development,
though the brief appearance of Bergman provides a
welcome spark of brightness. Adapted by Blanche
Hanalis from Konigsburg's novel.
Aka: FROM THE MIXED-UP FILES OF MR BASIL
E. FRANKWEILER
Boa: novel From The Mixed-Up Files Of Mr Basil E.
Frankweiler by E.L. Konigsburg.
DRA                                   105 min
B,V                                      VUL

## HIDER IN THE HOUSE *** 18
Matthew Patrick        USA          1989
*Gary Busey, Mimi Rogers, Michael McKean*
A disturbed killer is released despite the doubts of his
psychiatrist and takes up residence in the attic of a
recently renovated house, from which vantage point
he spies on the lives of its occupants, occasionally
intervening directly. A skilfully-handled and original
psychodrama that unfortunately falls back into using
all the standard cliches towards the climax.
THR                                   108 min
V                                        VES

## HIDING OUT ** 15
Bob Giraldi            USA          1987
*Jon Cryer, Keith Coogan, Annabeth Gish, Oliver*
*Cotton*
A silly, contrived comedy with Cryer playing a
stockbroker on the run from mobsters and hiding out
as a high school senior.
COM                                    99 min
B,V                                      PRES

## HIGH AND LOW *** 1962
Akira Kurosawa        JAPAN        1962
*Toshiro Mifune, Kyoko Kagawa, Tatsuya Nakadai,*

*Tsutomu Yamakazi, Tatsuya Mihashi, Yatuka Sada,*
A businessman is financially ruined when he pays a
ransom for his chauffeur's son who was kidnapped by
mistake. A gloomy adaptation of a lightweight Amer-
ican thriller, with the director once again giving us a
lesson in how a film should be made.
Aka: TENGOKU TO JIGOKU
Boa: novel The King's Ransom by Ed McBain.
DRA                    142 min B/W (plus a colour sequence)
B,V                                                    PVG

## HIGH ANXIETY **                                    15
Mel Brooks            USA                    1977
*Mel Brooks, Madeline Kahn, Cloris Leachman, Harvey
Korman, Ron Carey, Howard Morris, Dick Van Patten,
Murphy Dunne, Jack Riley, Charlie Callas*
A spoof of Hitchcock films about a psychiatrist who
gets into trouble when he takes charge of a sanator-
ium. An affectionate pastiche of a hundred other films,
with several isolated moments of brilliance strung
together in a haphazard fashion.
COM                                           94 min
B,V,V2,LV                                        CBS

## HIGH BALLIN' **                                    15
Peter Carter          CANADA/USA             1978
*Peter Fonda, Helen Shaver, Jerry Reed, Chris
Wiggins, David Ferry, Chris Langevin*
A truck-driving duo have to fight an unscrupulous
rival, to stay on the road and in business. The truck
acts OK but is let down by the rest of the film.
A/AD                           98 min (ort 100 min)
B,V                                              RNK

## HIGH CRIME **
Enzo G. Castellari    ITALY                  1973
*Franco Nero, James Whitmore, Fernando Rey, Delia
Boccardo, Duilio Del Prete*
An Italian drugs agent pits his wits against a Mafia
boss, in this routine thriller that's enlivened by fair
action sequences.
THR                            97 min (ort 100 min)
B,V                                              ABA

## HIGH DESERT KILL ***                               15
Harry Falk            USA                    1989
*Anthony Geary, Marc Singer, Chuck Connors, Micah
Grant, Vaughn Armstrong*
Four men on a hunting trip to the New Mexico desert
fall prey to a strange entity that takes them over
completely. A neat and unusual SF yarn, penned by
T.S. Cook, who also wrote THE CHINA SYNDROME.
HOR                            88 min (ort 100 min) mCab
V                                                CIC

## HIGH FLYING SPY **                                  U
Vincent McEveety      USA                    1972
*Stuart Whitman, Vincent Van Patten, Darren
McGavill*
During the American Civil War, two rival balloonists
come together to work for the Union side. A formula
Disney offering with a slightly unusual premise.
JUV                                          127 min
B,V                                              WDV

## HIGH HOPES ***                                     15
Mike Leigh            UK                      1988
*Philip Davies, Ruth Sheen, Edna Dore, Philip
Jackson, Heather Tobias, Lesley Manville, David
Bamber, Jason Watkins*
Mike Leigh's first cinema feature since "Bleak Mo-
ments" seventeen years ago, is a semi-farcical tale of a
good-natured working-class couple's involvement
with a suburban moron, a near-senile mother,
nouveau-riche relations and some appalling, over-the-
top yuppie neighbours. Scripted by Leigh.
COM                            108 min (ort 112 min)
V/h                                              PAL

## HIGH ICE **
Eugene S. Jones       USA                    1980
*David Janssen, Tony Musante, Madge Sinclair,
Gretchen Corbett, James G. Richardson, Allison Argo,
Dorian Harewood, Warren Stevens, Katherine
Cannon, James Canning, James Kaufman, Dan
Chambers, Byron Patt, Jeffrey Prather*
An account of the rescue attempts to save a group of
climbers trapped on a narrow ledge, with a veteran
ranger coming into conflict with a stolid and obstinate
colonel. Average.
Boa: story by Eugene S. Jones and Natalia R. Jones.
DRA                                           96 min mTV
B,V,V2,LV                                    SPEC/POLY

## HIGH MIDNIGHT **                                    15
Daniel Haller         USA                    1979
*David Birney, Mike Connors, Christine Belford,
Granville Van Dusen, George DiCenzo, Marc Alaimo,
Victor Campos, John Durren, Edward Grover,
Kathleen Lloyd, Larry Bishop, Ben Gerard, Jeri Lea
Ray, Virginia Hawkins, Ben Frank*
A drugs raid goes terribly wrong, resulting in the
death of a man's wife and child. The child's father
swears vengeance and stalks the ambitious narcotics
cop responsible for the tragedy. Average.
THR                            94 min (ort 100 min) mTV
B,V                                              CIC

## HIGH MOUNTAIN RANGERS **                            PG
Robert Conrad         USA                    1987
*Robert Conrad, Tom Towles, Christian Conrad, Shane
Conrad, Tony Acierto, P.A. Christian, Timothy
MacLachlan, Roy Conrad*
Conrad plays a former mountain ranger who helps
round up some escaped prisoners, one of whom is an
old enemy of his. Average pilot for a series looking at
the work of a group of special rangers, working in the
High Sierras of the USA.
A/AD                                          89 min mTV
V/h                                              NWV

## HIGH NOON ****                                      U
Fred Zinnemann        USA                    1952
*Gary Cooper, Grace Kelly, Lloyd Bridges, Thomas
Mitchell, Katy Jurado, Otto Kruger, Lon Chaney Jr,
Henry Morgan, Ian MacDonald, Eve McVeagh, Harry
Shannon, Lee Van Cleef, Robert Wilke, Sheb Wooley,
Tom London, Ted Stanhope*
A sheriff has to save the selfish townsfolk of a town
from a gang of outlaws who have been freed from
prison. Cooper plays the ageing sheriff with great
style, alone in a town where nobody is prepared to
help him. A classic film. AA: Actor (Cooper), Edit
(Elmo Williams/Harry Gerstad – note how the tale
unfolds in "real-time"), Song ("Do Not Forsake Me, Oh
My Darlin'" – Dmitri Tiomkin – music/Ned Washing-
ton – lyrics) and Score (Tiomkin).
Boa: novel The Tin Star by John W. Cunningham.
Osca: AMERICANO, THE (VCC)
WES                            81 min (ort 84 min) B/W
B,V,V2                             BBC; VCC (VHS only)

## HIGH NOON PART 2: THE RETURN OF
## WILL KANE **
Jerry Jameson         USA                    1980
*Lee Majors, David Carradine, J.A. Preston, Pernell
Roberts, M. Emmet Walsh, Michael Pataki, Katherine
Cannon, Frank Campanella, Tracey Walter, Britt
Leach, Charles Benton, Sanford Gibbons, Stonewall
Jackson, Francesca Jarvis*
An unnecessary and feeble attempt to cash in on the
cult status of the original, which begins where the
earlier classic ended, with our former marshal being
forced to face the man who replaced him. Average.
WES                            96 min (ort 100 min) mTV
B,V                                              VIPCO

**HIGH PLAINS DRIFTER ***                    18
Clint Eastwood            USA              1973
*Clint Eastwood, Verna Bloom, Marianna Hill,
Mitchell Ryan, Jack Ging, Stefan Gierasch, Billy
Curtis, Ted Hartley, Geoffrey Lewis, Walter Barnes,
Paul Brinegar, Dan Vadis, Jack Kosslyn, Belle
Mitchell, John Mitchum, Pedro Regas*
A town hires a mysterious stranger, to protect them
from outlaws who have just been released from prison.
Skilful use of intercut sequences show us how the
original sheriff met his death, whilst the townsfolk
looked on. His replacement bears an uncanny re-
semblance in all but features to the murdered man. A
compelling film, both under-stated and atmospheric,
that demonstrated Eastwood's abilities as a director.
WES                                      105 min
V/h                                        CIC

**HIGH RISK ****
Stewart Raffill           USA              1981
*James Brolin, Lindsay Wagner, Cleavon Little,
Anthony Quinn, James Coburn, Ernest Borgnine,
Bruce Davidson, Chick Vennera*
A group of Americans parachute into the jungle to
steal $5,000,000 from the head of a drug-smuggling
ring. A high-action tale that rarely pauses long
enough to give one a chance to see the numerous holes
in the plot.
A/AD                                      93 min
B,V,V2,LV                                  GHV

**HIGH ROAD TO CHINA ***                    PG
Brian G. Hutton           USA              1983
*Tom Selleck, Bess Armstrong, Jack Weston, A. Wilford
Brimley, Robert Morley, Brian Blessed, Cassandra
Gava*
An ex-WW1 ace pilot is hired by an heiress to find her
missing father, in this mediocre RAIDERS OF THE
LOST ARK-style adventure yarn. Armstrong is suit-
ably obnoxious and Selleck admirably taciturn, but
they can do nothing with the lousy dialogue they are
given. Selleck's first starring feature.
Boa: novel by Jon Cleary.
A/AD                          100 min (ort 120 min)
B,V,V2                       GHV; MSD (VHS only)

**HIGH SCHOOL SPIRITS ****                   15
Michael L. Schaertl       USA              1988
*Neil La Bute, Wayne Gilbert*
Teen-oriented comedy, with two college kids reluc-
tantly agreeing to exorcise the ghost from Fulton
House, one of the college's less popular buildings. The
usual comic mishaps and bizarre occurrences take
place until they achieve their aim.
COM                                       87 min
B,V                                PARK; CINE

**HIGH SCHOOL, USA ****                      PG
Rod Amateau               USA              1983
*Michael J. Fox, Nancy McKeon, Todd Bridges, Lauri
Hendler, Dana Plato, Bob Denver, Angela Cartwright,
Dwayne Hickman, Crystal Bernard, Anthony
Edwards, Frank Bank, Elinor Donahue, Tony Dow,
Steve Franken, David Nelson*
A young high school student falls in love with the
girlfriend of the local bully, and has to work hard to
prove his worth. Okay for the teen-set, otherwise
strictly formula stuff.
COM                          92 min (ort 100 min) mTV
B,V                                        ARF

**HIGH SEASON ****                           15
Clare Peploe              UK                1987
*Jacqueline Bisset, James Fox, Irene Papas, Sebastian
Shaw, Kenneth Branagh, Lesley Manville, Robert
Stephens*
A look at the effects of tourism on a small Greek
island, with Bisset a female photographer whose
peaceful life on Rhodes, is shattered by the arrival of a

pair of obnoxious tourists, a spy and her self-centred
husband. A fluffy romantic comedy of little substance
but pretty locations.
COM                          90 min (ort 101 min)
B,V                                        VIR

**HIGH SIERRA ***                            PG
Raoul Walsh               USA              1941
*Humphrey Bogart, Ida Lupino, Joan Leslie, Alan
Curtis, Arthur Kennedy, Henry Hull, Henry Travers,
Barton MacLane, Jerome Cowan, Cornel Wilde*
Bogart stars as a gangster on the run from the police,
who befriends a lame girl and pays for her to have an
operation. Eventually his luck runs out and he is shot
and wounded, hiding in the mountains for a final
showdown. A sombre gangster movie that gave the
star his first good role (George Raft turned the part
down). Scripted by John Huston and W.R. Burnett.
Remade as "I Died A Thousand Times" and as the
Western, "Colorado Territory".
Boa: novel by W.R. Burnett.
A/AD                      96 min (ort 100 min) B/W
V                                          WHV

**HIGH SOCIETY ****                          U
Charles Walters           USA              1956
*Bing Crosby, Frank Sinatra, Grace Kelly, Celeste
Holm, Louis Calhern, Louis Armstrong, Sidney
Blackmer, Margalo Gillmore, Lydia Reed, John Lund*
A lightweight and clinical remake of the 1940 film
"The Philadelphia Story" in which a rich socialite is
about to re-marry when her former husband arrives
on the scene. Songs include: "True Love", "Did You
Evah?", "You're Sensational" and "Now You Have
Jazz". The last acting role for Kelly.
Boa: play The Philadelphia Story by Philip Barry.
MUS                          103 min (ort 107 min)
V                                          MGM

**HIGH SPIRITS ***                           15
Neil Jordan               USA              1988
*Daryl Hannah, Peter O'Toole, Steve Guttenberg,
Beverly D'Angelo, Jennifer Tilly, Liam Neeson*
The soused debt-ridden owner of an Irish castle
decides to open it as a haunted bed-and-breakfast, and
gets his staff to dress up in sheets in order to scare the
guests. Events take an unexpected turn however,
when the former, now deceased residents, decide to
join in the fun.
COM                                       92 min
V/h                                        PAL

**HIGH STAKES ***                            15
Larry Kent                CANADA            1986
*David Foley, Roberta Weiss, Jackson Davies, Winston
Reckert*
An inept comedy-thriller in which an accident-prone
youngster enjoys a whole series of mishaps and crazy
encounters with assorted gangsters and eccentrics,
and finds himself embroiled in a plot to obtain a
hidden hoard of Nazi loot. As brainless as it is
unfunny.
COM                                       85 min
B,V                                        SHEER

**HIGH STAKES ***                            18
Amos Kolleck              USA              1989
*Sally Kirkland, Robert LuPone, Richard Lynch, Sarah
Gellar, Kathy Bates, W.T. Martin*
A housewife-turned-hooker tries to rescue her daugh-
ter from the clutches of mobsters, but at the same time
falls for a Wall Street broker who is in the throes of his
own difficulties. A sleazy little thriller of much talk
and little action.
Aka: MELANIE ROSE
THR                          85 min (ort 102 min)
V                                          NWV

**HIGH VELOCITY ** **
Remi Kramer            USA              1977
*Ben Gazzara, Britt Ekland, Alejandro Rey, Paul*
*Winfield, Keenan Wynn, Victoria Racimo*
Tough Vietnam veterans are sent on a mission to
rescue a kidnapped executive from a tropical country.
A standard action piece with the usual fisticuffs and
assorted mayhem, but little else.
A/AD                                   106 min
B,V                                       GHV

**HIGHER AND HIGHER ** ***
Tim Whelan             USA              1943
*Michele Morgan, Jack Haley, Frank Sinatra, Leon*
*Errol, Victor Borge, Mel Torme, Marcy McGuire, Mary*
*Wickes, Barbara Hale, Elizabeth Risdon*
Servants plan to help their master restore the family
fortune in this bright and enjoyable musical with a
plot that's if anything even more insubstantial than is
usual for these films. Songs (by Jimmy McHugh and
Harold Adamson) include: The Music Stopped" and "I
Couldn't Sleep A Wink Last Night". This was Sinat-
ra's first starring role.
Osca: STRICTLY DYNAMITE
MUS                                 90 min B/W
B,V                                       KVD

**HIGHER EDUCATION ** **              15
John Sheppard          USA              1987
*Kevin Hicks, Lori Hallier, Steven Black, Richard*
*Monette, Isabelle Mejias*
A small-town boy wins a place at an art college and
embarks on the usual frolics and amorous pursuits,
including a passionate affair with a pretty art teacher.
An easygoing but insubstantial film, short on laughs
but long on an intrusive rock score and some rather
silly sound effects.
COM                                     84 min
B,V                                      SHEER

**HIGHEST HONOUR, THE: A TRUE STORY ** **   15
Peter Maxwell
                AUSTRALIA/JAPAN          1983
*John Howard, Stuart Wilson, Atsuo Nakamura, Steve*
*Bisley*
An Allied undercover sabotage team is finally cap-
tured by the Japanese, after a series of successful
raids on enemy bases in the South Pacific.
Aka: HIGHEST HONOUR, THE; SOUTHERN
CROSS
WAR                                    105 min
V                              NELS/CBS L/A; CH5

**HIGHLANDER ** *                         15
Russell Mulcahy        UK/USA            1986
*Christopher Lambert, Sean Connery, Clancy Brown,*
*Alan North, Beatie Edney, Sheila Gish, Roxanne Hart*
Two immortal beings fight it out across time and
space, as a 14th century Scotsman discovers that his
old enemy has pursued him to 20th century Manhattan. An interesting idea is thrown away by flashy
direction and ridiculous plotting. As much of a pain to
listen to as it is to watch (the director started out
making rock videos).
FAN                                    111 min
V/sh                            CAN L/A; WHV

**HIGHPOINT ** *                          PG
Peter Carter        CANADA  1979 (released 1984)
*Richard Harris, Christopher Plummer, Beverly*
*D'Angelo, Kate Reid, Peter Donat, Saul Rubinek*
An accountant becomes involved in a plot involving
the Mafia, the FBI and $10,000,000. The obligatory
chase sequences provide the highlights in this con-
fused and tiring comedy thriller.
THR                  87 min (ort 88 min) Cut (10 sec)
B,V,V2                      INT/CBS; MIA (VHS only)

**HIGHWAY TO HELL ** *
Mark Griffiths         USA              1983
*Eric Stolz, Monica Carrico, Stuart Margolin*
A prisoner under sentence of death escapes with the
help of his female pen-friend.
THR                                     90 min
B,V                                   VDM/GHV

**HIJACK ** **
Michael Forlong        UK               1975
*Richard Morant, James Forlong, Tracey Peel, Sally*
*Forlong, David Hitchen, Richard Kerrigan, Derek*
*Bond, Robert Swales*
Three children are forced to put to sea in their father's
yacht, by an armed man who wants to flee to France.
A fairly exciting kid's adventure.
JUV                                     59 min
B,V                                       RNK

**HIJACK! ** **                            U
Leonard Horn           USA              1973
*David Janssen, Keenan Wynn, Lee Purcell, Jeanette*
*Nolan, William Schallert, Tom Tully, Ron Feinberg,*
*John A. Zee, William Mims, James Gavin, Dallas*
*Mitchell, Morris Buchanan, James Burke, Walter*
*Wyatt, Robert Golden*
Two truck drivers are chased by criminals who want
to get hold of the cargo they are carrying, in this
strictly formula actioner.
Boa: story by Michael Kelly.
A/AD                        71 min (ort 90 min) mTV
B,V,V2                                MSD; GHV

**HIJACK TO HELL ** **                     15
John Power           AUSTRALIA           1986
*John Waters, Rosey Jones, Esben Storm, Steve Jacobs,*
*Swabomir Wabik*
A bungled robbery in which a priceless opal necklace
is stolen and two men killed, leads to the secretion of
said necklace in the luggage of a woman who is on her
way to a tiny mission hospital. Our crooks follow and
take both her and her tough trucker companion
hostage in this formula yarn.
Boa: novel by Evan Green.
A/AD                                    186 min
B,V                                       CIC

**HIJACKERS, THE ** **
James O'Connolly       UK               1963
*Anthony Booth, Jacqueline Ellis, Derek Francis,*
*Patrick Cargill, Glynn Edwards, David Gregory,*
*Harold Goodwin, Arthur English, Anthony Wager*
A criminal gang specialises in robbing long distance
lorries, and a divorcee helps a haulage contractor
expose his partner as the head of the gang. Fair.
Osca: NIGHT CALLER, THE and ECHOES
DRA                                 69 min B/W
B,V                                       DFS

**HIJACKING OF THE ACHILLE LAURO, THE ** *** PG
Robert Collins         USA              1988
*Karl Malden, Lee Grant, E.G. Marshall, Christina*
*Pickles*
Competent recreation of the hijacking of this liner, off
the coast of Egypt in 1985, when PLO terrorists
boarded the ship, threatening the lives of the 380
passengers and murdering wheelchair-bound Leon
Klinghoffer.
Aka: TERROR SQUAD (TGP)
DRA                                     91 min
V                                  BRAVE; TGP

**HILL 171: TOUR OF DUTY ** **             18
                    USA
*Robert Miller, David Light*
Foiled by their attempts to destroy a secret group of

terrorists, the US government calls on the services of a bunch of mercenaries, in an attempt to infiltrate their base. Finding the terrorists more powerful than they expected, our mercenaries are forced into a bloody battle to the death, in this standard action tale.
Aka: HILL 171

| A/AD | | 83 min |
| B,V | | TGP |

## HILL'S ANGELS **
U
Bruce Bilson          USA          1979
*Edward Herrmann, Barbara Harris, Susan Clark, Cloris Leachman, Karen Valentine, Michael Constantine, Patsy Kell, Virginia Capers, Douglas Fowley, Alan Hale Jr*
A new parson and six of the women in his congregation, get together to fight crime in the town where they live. An innocuous Disney comedy, that starts off well enough but soon degenerates into cliche, with the obligatory chase and car smash-up sequences.
Aka: NORTH AVENUE IRREGULARS, THE
Boa: novel by the Rev. Albert Fay Hill.

| COM | | 95 min |
| B,V | | WDV |

## HILLS HAVE EYES, THE ***
18
Wes Craven          USA          1977
*Susan Lanier, Robert Houston, Martin Speer, Virginia Vincent, Russ Grieve, Michael Berryman, Dee Wallace, James Whitworth, John Steadman, Janus Blythe, Lance Gordon*
A family crossing the Californian desert is attacked by a ghastly family of cannibalistic mutants. A gory low-grade shocker that is undeniably well made and has several complex plot twists and unpleasant surprises. Now a cult film. A trashy sequel followed in 1983.

| HOR | 86 min; 90 min (PAL) Cut (2 sec in addition to film cuts) |
| B,V,V2 | WOV; PAL (VHS only) |

## HILLS HAVE EYES PART 2, THE *
18
Wes Craven          UK/USA    1983 (released 1985)
*Michael Berryman, John Bloom, John Laughlin, Tamara Stafford, Janus Blythe, Kevin Blair*
A sequel to the previous film. This time a group of teenagers run out of petrol in the desert and are attacked by the local mutant family. Gruesome, unadulterated rubbish, with numerous flashback sequences that borrow footage from the earlier (and superior) effort, including an unintentionally funny episode that is meant to represent the recollections of a dog.

| HOR | | 86 min |
| B,V,V2 | | TEVP; WHV (VHS only) |

## HINDENBURG, THE **
PG
Robert Wise          USA          1975
*George C. Scott, Anne Bancroft, Burgess Meredith, William Atherton, Roy Thinnes, Gig Young, Charles Durning, Robert Clary, Rene Auberjonois, Richard A. Dysart, Katherine Helmond*
Advances the theory that the crash of the Hindenburg airship in New York in 1937, was due to sabotage by anti-Nazis. A drawn out and lightweight tale with some ludicrous characterisations and an anti-climactic ending. Some use of original newsreel footage adds a little interest, to this over-long and stilted yarn. AA: Spec Award (Peter Berkos for sound effects), Spec Award (Glen Robinson/Albert Whitlock for visual effects).
Boa: novel by Michael M. Mooney.

| DRA | | 110 min (ort 125 min) |
| B,V | | ARENA/CIC |

## HIRED HAND, THE ***
15
Peter Fonda          USA          1971
*Warren Oates, Peter Fonda, Robert Pratt, Verna Bloom, Severn Darden, Ted Markland, Rita Rogers, Megen Denver*
A man runs out on his wife to go gold prospecting in California with two companions. When he returns seven years later, she will only take him back as a paid worker. However, he is soon obliged to leave once more, when a buddy is taken prisoner by bandits. A quirky and uneven story, aided by excellent acting and photography.

| WES | | 86 min (ort 98 min) |
| B,V | | CIC |

## HIRELING, THE **
PG
Alan Bridges          UK          1973
*Sarah Miles, Robert Shaw, Peter Egan, Elizabeth Sellars, Caroline Mortimer, Patricia Lawrence, Petra Markham, Ian Hogg, Christine Hargreaves, Lyndon Brook, Alison Leggatt, Ernest Jennings*
A WW1 widow is helped over her depression by her loyal chauffeur, who conceals his feelings for her beneath a professional facade. A fairly elegant drama with good dialogue but little development. The script is by Wolf Mankowitz.
Boa: novel by L.P. Hartley.

| DRA | | 103 min (ort 108 min) |
| V | | RCA |

## HIROSHIMA ***
15
USA          1990
*Brian Dennehy, Michael Tucker*
A TV film that traces the development of the A-bomb and, thanks to its length, gives a more detailed account of this complex process as well as the tangled chain of events that led to its use on Hiroshima and Nagasaki during WW2. See SHADOW MAKERS for another look at this subject.

| DRA | | 180 min mTV |
| V | | PRISM |

## HISTORY MAN, THE ***
15
Robert Knights          UK          1981
*Isla Blair, Nigel Stock*
An entertaining look at the intrigues and rivalries of university life, with the central character a scheming left-wing sociology lecturer at one of the 1970s-built "modern" universities. Originally shown in four 75 minute parts.
Boa: novel by Malcolm Bradbury.

| DRA | 165 min (Abridged version – 300 min) mTV |
| V | BBC |

## HISTORY OF THE WORLD: PART 1 **
15
Mel Brooks          USA          1981
*Mel Brooks, Madeline Kahn, Harvey Korman, Gregory Hines, Pamela Stephenson, Dom DeLuise, Shecky Greene, Jack Carter, Jan Murray, Sid Caesar, Jackie Mason, Cloris Leachman, Ron Carey, Spike Milligan, Orson Welles (narration)*
Episodic comedy ranging from the Stone Age to the French Revolution. Despite the best efforts of a talented cast, this frenzied, frenetic scattershot comedy fails to sustain the momentum of its opening, and soon degenerates into a series of one-line gags. The few funny moments (such as Caesar's role as a caveman in the opening) could have been compressed into a 30-minute short.

| COM | | 92 min |
| B,V,V2,LV | | CBS; HOLLY (VHS only) |

## HIT AND RUN **
PG
Charles Braverman          USA          1982
*Paul Perri, Claudia Cron, Will Lee, Bart Braverman, E. Brian Dean, Donald Symington*
A New York cabbie tries to find out who is behind the accident that killed his wife, but becomes involved in a murder hunt. A flashy and unconvincing thriller that offers nothing of substance.
Aka: REVENGE SQUAD; TAXI

THR                                  96 min
B,V                          AVP L/A; FILV

**HIT LADY ** **                              PG
Tracy Keenan Wynn     USA           1974
*Yvette Mimieux, Joseph Campanella, Clu Gulager,
Dack Rambo, Keenan Wynn, Roy Jensen, Paul Genge,
Del Monroe, Mitzi Hoag, Sam Edwards, Francisco
Ortega, Leslie McRay*
A successful female artist is really a successful
contract killer for the Mob, in this average gangster
movie. Wynn's directorial debut. The script was by
Mimieux.
THR               69 min (ort 78 min) mTV
B,V,V2                                 GHV

**HIT LIST *** **                              18
William Lustig       USA            1988
*Jan-Michael Vincent, Leo Rossi, Lance Henriksen,
Charles Napier, Rip Torn*
A Mafia gangster is on trial, and makes arrangements
with a hitman to kill all the witnesses willing to
testify against him. However, a blunder leads to the
wrong house being struck, and the son of a person
uninvolved in the trial being abducted. The boy's
father now swears revenge and finds an unexpected
ally in the form of a mobster, who is to give evidence
at the trial.
THR                                  84 min
V/sh                                   WHV

**HIT MAN, THE ** **                          18
George Armitage     USA             1972
*Bernie Casey, Pamela Grier, Lisa Moore, Don
Diamond*
Crime story involving a gang killing, with the victim's
brother being helped in his quest for revenge by a
porno star. A kind of black version of "Get Carter" but
with nothing of the style of that earlier film.
Aka: STREET WARRIOR
DRA            86 min (ort 90 min) Cut (36 sec)
B,V                              MGM; MPV

**HIT TEAM, THE ** **                         PG
Jerry Thorpe        USA             1970
*Ray Milland, Van Johnson, John Saxon, Brian Kelly,
Fritz Weaver, Susan Oliver, Clu Gulager, Diana Lynn,
Robert Middleton, Terry Carter*
A businessman in financial difficulties, hires a con-
tract killer in a desperate attempt to avoid ruination.
However, this scheme backfires when a patrolman is
gunned down, and the killer finds himself forced to
hide from both the police and his fellow mobsters. A
tense thriller that never really gets to grips with its
material.
Aka: COMPANY OF KILERS
THR                                  83 min
B,V                                    AMB

**HIT! *** **
Sidney J. Furie      USA            1973
*Billy Dee Williams, Paul Hampton, Richard Pryor,
Gwen Welles*
A black narcotics agent goes after the drug bosses in
Marseilles when his daughter dies. An exciting,
detailed but rather overlong thriller.
THR                                 134 min
B,V                                    CIC

**HIT, THE *** **                             18
Stephen Frears       UK             1984
*John Hurt, Tim Roth, Laura Del Sol, Terence Stamp,
Bill Hunter, Brian Royal, Abie Woodington, Willoughby
Searl, Gray, Jim Broadbent, Manuel De Benito, Joan Calot*
A supergrass who has been hiding away in Spain for
ten years, finds that the past has caught up with him
in the shape of two hit-men. An old-fashioned gangs-
ter movie with some 1980s-style violence but general-

ly quite gripping. Written by Peter Prince, and with
theme music by Eric Clapton.
THR         98 min; 93 min (CH5) (ort 105 min)
B,V,V2                   PVG; CH5 (VHS only)

**HITCHER, THE ** **                          18
Robert Harmon       USA             1986
*Rutger Hauer, C. Thomas Howell, Jennifer Jason
Leigh, Jeffrey DeMunn, John Jackson, Bill
Greenbush, Jack Thibeau, Armin Shimerman, Eugene
Davis*
Unbelievable tale of mass-murder, with the story of a
psychotic hitch-hiker who doggedly keeps reappearing
in a man's life. Occasionally intriguing but generally
disagreeable.
DRA               93 min (ort 97 min)
B, V/sh                CAN; WHV (VHS only)

**HITLER: THE LAST TEN DAYS ** **
Ennio de Concini    ITALY/UK        1973
*Alec Guinness, Simon Ward, Adolfo Celi, Diane
Cilento, Dori Kuntsmann, Eric Porter, Gabriele
Ferzetti, Joss Ackland, John Bennett, John Barron,
Sheila Gish, Barbara Jefford, Julian Glover, Michael
Goodliffe, Mark Kingston*
The last ten days of the Reich as seen from within
Hitler's bunker. A muddled and unconvincing recon-
struction, with this great actor looking distinctly
uncomfortable in his role. See also THE BUNKER.
Aka: LAST TEN DAYS, THE
Boa: book The Last Days Of The Chancellery by
Gerhardt Boldt.
DRA              103 min (ort 108 min)
B,V                                    RNK

**HITLER'S SS: PORTRAIT OF EVIL * **          18
Jim Goddard         USA             1984
*John Shea, Bill Nighy, Lucy Gutteridge, David
Warner, Warren Clarke, Michael Elphick, Stratford
Johns, Robert Urquhart, Jose Ferrer, Carroll Baker,
Tony Randall, John Normington, Derek Newark, Paul
Brooke, Colin Jeavons*
Two brothers become drawn into the SS only to realise
too late what this entails. One or two good cameos
(such as Randall in a role akin to Joel Grey's in
CABARET) cannot rescue this unremittingly dull
effort.
Aka: HITLER'S SS: PORTRAIT IN EVIL
DRA              129 min (ort 156 min) mTV
B,V                             IMPACT; ODY

**HITTER, THE ** **                           18
Christopher Leitch   USA            1978
*Ron O'Neal, Sheila Frazier, Adolph Caesar*
The story of a boxer who has to fight illegally after
being banned from professional fights for having used
too much force against an opponent. He teams up with
a down-at-heel boxing promoter in this mediocre fight
drama.
DRA                                  94 min
B,V                            HEL L/A; APX

**HOAX * **
Robert Anderson      USA            1972
*Bill Ewing, Frank Bonner, Jacques Aubuchan*
Two young men find a lost H-bomb and decide to hold
L.A. to ransom, in this tasteless and unfunny effort.
COM                                  90 min
B,V,V2                             VCL/CBS

**HOBO'S CHRISTMAS, A ** **                    U
William Mackenzie    USA            1987
*Barnard Hughes, William Hickey, Gerald McRaney,
Wendy Crewson, Helen Stenborg, Lee Weaver*
Treacly story of a hobo who makes a trip back to see
the son he deserted twenty years before, arriving in
time for a Christmas reunion. Hughes gives a nice
performance, but the cute and happy script muffles
any impact this tale might have had. A film as pretty

as candyfloss and a lot less substantial.

DRA                          93 min mTV
B,V                          NWV

## HOBSON'S CHOICE ****                    U
David Lean           UK              1953
*Charles Laughton, John Mills, Brenda De Banzie,*
*Daphne Anderson, Prunella Scales, Richard Wattis,*
*Derek Blomfield, Helen Haye, Julien Mitchell, Joseph*
*Tomelty, Gibb McLaughlin, Dorothy Gordon, John*
*Laurie, Raymond Huntley*
A tyrannical Lancashire bootmaker is brought to heel
by his eldest daughter when she marries his boothand
in the face of his opposition, and sets about starting up
their own business. Laughton is a delight to watch, as
the tyrant in this fine period comedy. Scripted by
Norman Spencer from the play. Remade for TV in
1983.
Boa: play by Harold Brighouse.

COM                  102 min (ort 107 min) B/W
B,V                          TEVP; WHV (VHS only)

## HOFFMAN **
Alvin Rakoff         UK              1970
*Peter Sellers, Sinead Cusack, Ruth Dunning, Jeremy*
*Bulloch*
A middle-aged creep blackmails a typist about to be
married, into spending a dirty weekend with him. A
bizarre character study that is occasionally funny but
more often just tiresome.
Boa: novel/play Shall I Eat You Now? by Ernest
Gebler.

COM                  109 min (ort 116 min)
B,V                          TEVP

## HOLCROFT COVENANT, THE *              15
John Frankenheimer   UK              1985
*Michael Caine, Anthony Andrews, Victoria Tennant,*
*Lilli Palmer, Mario Adorf, Michael Lonsdale, Bernard*
*Hepton, Richard Munch, Carl Rigg, Andre Penvern,*
*Andrew Bradford, Shane Rimmer, Alexander Kerst,*
*Michael Wolf, Hugo Bower*
Caine finds that he is executor for a Nazi fortune that
is to be used to help the victims of Nazism that was
left behind by his late father (one of Hitler's pals) as a
way of making amends for his evil. He is obliged to
embark on a mission to ensure that it doesn't fall into
the wrong hands. A clumsy and contrived thriller that
is never able to shake off the ludicrous premise upon
which the film is built.
Boa: novel by Robert Ludlum.

THR                  107 min (ort 112 min)
B,V                          TEVP

## HOLD MY HAND, I'M DYING **            15
Terence Ryan     SOUTH AFRICA        1988
*Christopher Cazenove, Oliver Reed, Patrick Shai*
One of the last tasks facing a Colonial Commissioner
before an African state gains its independence, is to
convince the people of a tribal village to move from
their homes before they are flooded out by an ambitious dam project. Complications arise when he tries
to prevent terrorists from stirring up the villagers. A
long and rambling melodrama that strays from the
main storyline rather too often, but has some nice
location work.

DRA                          105 min
B,V                          WATER

## HOLD THE DREAM: PARTS 1 AND 2 **      15
Don Sharp            UK              1986
*Jenny Seagrove, Stephen Collins, Deborah Kerr,*
*James Brolin, Claire Bloom, Fiona Fullerton, Paul*
*Daneman, Suzanna Hamilton, Nigel Havers, John*
*Mills, Liam Neeson, Pauline Yates, Valentina Pelka,*
*Sarah-Jane Varley*
A sequel to A WOMAN OF SUBSTANCE, in which
our elderly heroine struggles to retain control of her
commercial empire, although she ultimately intends

to hand it over to her favourite granddaughter. A
glossy and inferior sequel, scripted by Barbara Taylor
Bradford.
Aka: HOLD THAT DREAM
Boa: novel A Woman Of Substance by Barbara Taylor
Bradford.

DRA 180 min; 194 min (VCC or BRAVE) (ort 200 min)
mTV
B,V           IVS; VCC (VHS only); BRAVE (VHS only)

## HOLIDAY INN ***                        U
Mark Sandrich        USA              1942
*Bing Crosby, Fred Astaire, Marjorie Reynolds, Walter*
*Abel, Virginia Dale, Louise Beavers, Irving Bacon,*
*James Bell*
The two owners of a country inn that's only open on
holidays, fall for the same girl, in this flimsy romantic
triangle plot that serves simply as a vehicle for some
great Irving Berlin songs, including the famous
"White Christmas". A breezy fun-filled musical, super-
ior to that partial remake WHITE CHRISTMAS.

MUS                          100 min B/W
V                            CIC

## HOLIDAY ON THE BUSES *
Bryan Izzard         UK              1973
*Reg Varney, Doris Hare, Stephen Lewis, Anna Karen,*
*Michael Robbins, Bob Grant, Wilfrid Brambell, Kate*
*Williams, Arthur Mullard, Queenie Watts, Henry*
*McGee, Adam Rhodes, Michael Sheard, Franco*
*Derosa, Gigi Gatti, Eunice Black*
Third in this series of spin-offs from a TV series about
the adventures of the crew of a bus company. This
time round the family goes on holiday, but ends up
driving for a holiday camp. Another one of those
dismal and dated British comedies inspired by the
somewhat better series "On The Buses". See also ON
THE BUSES and MUTINY ON THE BUSES.

COM                          83 min (ort 85 min)
B,V                          TEVP

## HOLLOW POINT ***                      15
Bruce Seth Green     USA              1987
*Linda Purl, Yaphet Kotto*
A therapist agrees to testify against a murderer, who
is then freed and begins a campaign of intimidation
against her. As her work begins to suffer, she is driven
to taking drastic action in this competent thriller.

THR                          90 min
B,V                          SONY

## HOLLYWOOD AIR FORCE **                15
Bert Convy           USA              1986
*Chris Lemmon, Lloyd Bridges, Graham Jarvis, Brian*
*Bradley, Alan Campbell, Marty Cohen, Danny Greene,*
*Art Kimbo, Matt McCoy, Jeff Mayer, Juney Smith,*
*Frank Mugavero, Tom Villiard, Vic Tayback*
In 1961 a group of young film studio workers join the
National Guard, as a means of dodging the draft. A
simple-minded and fairly unfunny comedy outing,
with all the expected capers and pranks. Convy's
directorial debut.
Aka: WEEKEND WARRIORS

COM                          88 min
B,V                          NDH

## HOLLYWOOD BOULEVARD **                18
Joe Dante/Allan Arkush
                     USA              1976
*Allan Arkush, Candice Rialson, Mary Woronov, Rita*
*George, Jeffrey Kramer, Jonathan Kaplan, Charles B.*
*Griffith, Joe McBride, Commander Cody and his Lost*
*Planet Airmen*
A low-budget comedy that splices footage from various
Corman films into the story (if that is the correct
description) of a young aspiring actress who goes to
work for some schlock film-makers. A scattering of
funny gags and an endearing silliness are not enough
to make this one work.

COM 79 min (ort 83 min) Cut (24 sec)
B,V WHV

## HOLLYWOOD BOULEVARD 2 * 18
Steve Barnett USA 1989
*Kelly Monteith, Ginger Lynn Allen*
The head of a second-rate film studio keeps losing all
his leading ladies, and desperately needs someone to
play the female lead in his forthcoming masterpiece –
"Barbarian Goddess Of The Amazon".
COM 78 min
V 20VIS

## HOLLYWOOD CHAINSAW HOOKERS * 18
Fred Olen Ray USA 1988
*Linnea Quigley, Gunnar Hansen, Dawn Wildsmith,
Michelle Bauer*
A nasty piece of sleaze, with a private eye hired to
locate a missing teenage girl, discovering that she has
been kidnapped by a strange sect of hookers who
worship chainsaws, their intention being to make her
a virgin sacrifice to their leader. A grisly black
comedy, inspired by the repulsive low-budget 1960s
films of Herschell Gordon Lewis and equally full of
gore and mutilation. Hansen was "Leatherface" in
THE TEXAS CHAINSAW MASSACRE.
Aka: HOLLYWOOD HOOKERS
HOR 70 min (ort 90 min) Cut (1 min 6 sec)
B,V CFD

## HOLLYWOOD COP * 18
Amir Shervan USA 1988
*Jim Mitchum, Cameron Mitchell, David Goss, Julie
Schonhofer, Lincoln Fitzpatrick*
When a woman's former husband steals several
million dollars from the Mafia, her young son is
kidnapped, but a tough cop and a bunch of Hell's
Angels set out to rescue him. A fairly mindless action
tale, written by Shervan.
A/AD 100 min
V VPD

## HOLLYWOOD DETECTIVE, THE ** 
Kevin Connor USA 1989
*Telly Savalas, Helen Udy, George Coe, Joe
Dallesandro, Tom Reese, James Green, Donald
Hotton, William H. Bassett*
A once popular TV detective and now fading star, gets
involved in a real life mystery when a girl asks him to
locate her missing fiance. Unfortunately for him,
events take a turn for the worse when the man is
found murdered and our 'tec becomes a prime suspect.
A good opening premise for a film that never delivers
what it promises.
THR 98 min (ort 100 min) mTV
V CIC

## HOLLYWOOD DREAMING ** 15
Jim Marshall USA 1986
*Ben Glass, Orson Bean, Natasha Kautsky, Anthony
Alda, Kerry Remsen, Orson Bean, Lucinda Crosby,
David Hedison, Bill Henderson, Zsa Zsa Gabor*
A chronicle of the frustrations facing an eccentric
aspiring film-maker, as he attempts to find the money
to finance his ambition. A dullish and rather stupid
comedy.
Aka: MOVIE MAKERS, THE; SMART ALEC
COM 87 min
B,V CBS

## HOLLYWOOD HOT TUBS ** 15
Chuck Vincent USA 1984
*Donna McDaniel, Michael Andrew, Paul Gunning,
Edy Williams, Michael Andrews, Katt Shea*
A cheerful and bawdy sex comedy about a Hollywood
plumber.
A 99 min (ort 103 min) Cut (49 sec)
B,V EIV; MRD

## HOLLYWOOD PINK ** R18
USA
*Bunny Bleu, Kathleen Kelly, Studley Doright*
Sexual parody of Hollywood's gossip magazines re-
volving around the sexual exploits of three publishers.
A 41 min
V VEXCEL

## HOLLYWOOD SHUFFLE *** 15
Robert Townsend USA 1987
*Robert Townsend, Anne-Marie Johnson, Starletta
Dupois, Helen Martin, Craigus R. Johnson, Domenick
Irrera*
A look at the struggles of a black aspiring actor to get
parts. As he goes after yet another stereotyped "cool
cat" or "butler" role, he dreams of fame and a real part
in a Hollywood film. He does eventually get a part, but
only because the directors were looking for an Eddie
Murphy lookalike. A most enjoyable and perceptive
story, that's by turns gleeful, affectionate and percep-
tive. Written by Townsend and Keenan Ivory Wayans.
COM 78 min
B,V VIR

## HOLLYWOOD SUPERSTAR ** 18
Gene Nash USA 1970
*Andy Davis, Vitra Videt, Joe Taylor, Reid Smith, Ray
Foster, Matt Bennett, Jeremy Stockwell*
A male actor dresses in drag in order to create a career
and has to continue playing his female role. The same
idea was used in a later film: TOOTSIE.
Aka: DINAH EAST (POR)
DRA 89 min (ort 96 min)
B,V,V2 VSP L/A; POR; SQUIR

## HOLLYWOOD VICE SQUAD * 18
Penelope Spheeris USA 1986
*Trish Van Devere, Ronny Cox, Carrie Fisher, Frank
Gorshin, Leon Isaac Kennedy, Ben Frank, Robin
White, Joey Travolta*
A distraught mother tries to save her daughter from a
life on the street and enlists police help. The trouble
with this film is that is neither an effective parody of
the TV series "Miami Vice" that inspired it, nor a
particularly engaging action film in its own right. The
comic moments don't amuse and the dramatic mo-
ments don't convince.
A/AD 97 min (ort 100 min)
B,V MED

## HOLLYWOOD WIVES * 15
Robert Day USA 1985
*Anthony Hopkins, Angie Dickinson, Candice Bergen*
The story of the bed-hopping adventures and other
activities of some of the women in celluloid city. Dross
of a high order, based on a trashy novel of similar
merits.
Boa: novel by Jackie Collins.
DRA 360 min (3 cassettes)
B,V WHV

## HOLLYWOOD ZAP ** 15
David Cohen USA 1986
*Ben Frank, Neil Flanagan, Ivan E. Roth, Chuck
Mitchell, De Waldron, Annie Gaybis, Claude Earl
Jones, Stan Ross, Helen Verbit*
A youngster sets out for Hollywood in search of his
father, and meets up with a drifter who is a video
games freak. Together this unlikely pair have a
number of strange adventures, and meet some very
weird characters.
COM 82 min (ort 93 min) Cut (14 sec)
B,V AVR

## HOLOCAUST * 
Marvin Chomsky USA 1978
*Tom Bell, Joseph Bottoms, Tovah Feldshuh, Marius
Goring, Rosemary Harris, Anthony Haygarth, Ian
Holm, Lee Montague, Michael Moriarty, Deborah*

*Norton, George Rose, Robert Stephens, Meryl Streep,
Sam Wanamaker, David Warner*
Reduces the story of the destruction of European
Jewry to the level of a bad soap opera, proving that
where a fast buck is concerned, Hollywood will stop at
nothing.
DRA                              482 min (3 cassettes) mTV
B,V,V2                                                  GHV

## HOLOCAUST 2000 *
Alberto De Martino
                    ITALY/UK                        1977
*Kirk Douglas, Simon Ward, Anthony Quayle,
Agostina Belli, Virginia McKenna, Spiros Focas, Ivo
Carrani, Alexander Knox, Adolfo Celi, Romolo Valli,
Geoffrey Keen, Massimo Foschi, Penelope Horner*
An executive in charge of a nuclear plant discovers
that his son is the anti-Christ. A muddled attempt to
cash in on the success of films such as THE OMEN,
that fails in just about every department except with
regard to the Ennio Morricone score.
Aka: CHOSEN, THE
HOR                              99 min (ort 105 min)
B,V                                                    RNK

## HOMBRE ***                                          PG
Martin Ritt                USA                      1967
*Paul Newman, Fredric March, Martin Balsam,
Richard Boone, Diane Cilento, Cameron Mitchell,
Barbara Rush, Margaret Blye, Peter Lazer, Skip Ward,
Frank Silvera, Val Avery, David Canary*
A strange silent man, raised by the Indians, joins the
passengers of an Arizona stagecoach in the 1880s.
They soon come to despise him, but when they are
trapped by outlaws, find that it is their own actions
and thoughts that are worthy of contempt. An enter-
taining Western, with Newman as the half-breed,
playing a dangerous cat-and-mouse game with Boone,
as the leader of the outlaws.
Boa: novel by Elmore Leonard.
WES                                              111 min
B,V                                                    CBS

## HOME BEFORE MIDNIGHT **
Pete Walker                UK                        1978
*James Aubrey, Alison Elliot, Mark Burns, Richard
Todd, Debbie Linden, Juliet Harmer, Andy Foray,
Chris Jagger, Ian Sharrock, Sharon Maughan,
Leonard Kavanagh, Joan Pendleton, Antonia
Pendleton, Ivor Roberts, Faith Kent*
A songwriter who picks up a young girl hitch-hiker,
falls in love with her but gets into trouble as she is
only fourteen.
DRA                                              115 min
B,V                                                    HVH

## HOME MOVIES ***
Brian De Palma             USA                      1979
*Keith Gordon, Kirk Douglas, Nancy Allen, Gerrit
Graham, Vincent Gardenia, Mary Davenport*
A farce about a young man who gets "star therapy" at
the hands of an egomaniacal film director (who has his
own life filmed constantly) in an effort to stop him
feeling that he's "just an extra in his own life". An
uneven, wacky and often very funny comedy, that's
original in conception if somewhat less so in execution.
COM                                               93 min
B,V,V2                                                 GHV

## HOME SWEET HOME *                                   18
Nettie Pena                USA                      1980
*Jake Steinfeld, Sallee Elyse, Peter de Paula, Colette
Trygg, Vanessa Shaw*
A maniacal killer on the loose on Thanksgiving Day
brings horror to a family, butchering them one-by-one
as they are gathered to celebrate Thanksgiving. A

repulsive and dreary shocker.
HOR                      90 min; 83 min (ACAD)
B,V,V2              VPD; ACAD (Betamax and VHS only)

## HOME TO STAY ***
Delbert Mann               USA                      1978
*Henry Fonda, Michael McGuire, Kirsten Vigard,
Frances Hyland, David Stambaugh, Pixie Bigelow,
Louis Del Grande, Trudy Young, Doris Petrie, Eleanor
Beecroft, Dave Thomas, David Hughes, Judy Sinclair,
Len Doncheff*
A high-spirited teenager goes off on a trip with her
aged grandfather, in an effort to keep him from being
sent to an old people's home by his son, who feels
unable to look after him after the old man had a
stroke. A sentimental but quite touching piece of
whimsy, filmed in Canada.
Boa: novel Grandpa And Frank by Janet Majerus.
DRA                                               74 min mTV
B,V,V2                                                 VTC

## HOMEBODIES **
Larry Yust                 USA                      1974
*Frances Fuller, Ian Wolfe, Ruth McDevitt, Paula
Trueman, Peter Brocco, Linda Marsh, William
Hansen, Douglas Fowley, Kenneth Tobey, Wesley Lau*
The elderly tenants of a condemned building go a little
too far in their efforts to avoid eviction, resorting to
murder in this weird black comedy.
COM                              94 min (ort 96 min)
B,V,V2                                                 EHE

## HOMEBOY **                                          15
Michael Seresin            USA                      1988
*Mickey Rourke, Christopher Walken, Debra Feuer*
A young boxer who dreams of the big time finds that
his unscrupulous manager has made a crooked deal
that could ruin his career.
DRA                                              111 min
V                                                    BRAVE

## HOMEFRONT **                                        PG
Alan Smithee (Ramzi Thomas)
                           USA                      1987
*Lynn Redgrave, Jon Cryer, Paul Gleason, Nicholas
Pryor, Viveka Davis*
An aspiring candidate in an American election,
usually keeps his son at a boarding school so that he
and his wife can devote their energies fully to
campaigning. When they realise that it will be
advantageous to appear as a close-knit family, they
invite their son home for a while, but find that things
do not go according to plan.
COM                                               88 min
B,V                                                    VES

## HOMETOWN USA *                                      15
Max Baer                   USA                      1979
*Gary Springer, David Wilson, Brian Kerwin, Pat
Delaney, Julie Parsons, Sally Kirkland*
Nostalgic nonsense about teenage life in the 1950s in
California, when all that mattered was girls and fast
cars. A soggy and plotless clone of "American Graffiti".
COM                              93 min Cut (12 sec)
V                                                    ARF

## HOMEWORK *                                          18
James Beshears             USA                      1979
*Joan Collins, Michael Morgan, Shell Kepler, Lanny
Horn, Lee Purcell, Carrie Snodgress, Wings Hauser,
Mel Welles, Beverly Todd, Betty Thomas*
A 16-year-old boy can't make it with girls his own age,
so he tries an older woman. Despite some clumsy
attempts to simulate nude scenes with Joan Collins,
this dismal dud (promoted as a comedy) is best
avoided. See PRIVATE LESSONS or MY TUTOR,
that at least attempted to inject some style into this
theme.

Aka: GROWING PAINS
DRA                                   88 min (ort 90 min)
V/h                                                   CIC

**HONEY \*\***                                        18
Gianfranco Angelucci
                          ITALY/SPAIN              1981
*Clio Goldsmith, Fernando Rey, Catherine Spaak,*
*Donatella Damiani, Susan Scott, Luc Merenda*
A female writer forces a publisher at gunpoint, to read
her manuscript about the erotic awakening of a young
girl.
A                                                 89 min
B,V                                                   CBS

**HONEY, I SHRUNK THE KIDS \*\*\***                    U
Joe Johnston            USA                       1989
*Rick Moranis, Matt Frewer, Marcia Strassman, Amy*
*O'Neill, Jared Rushton, Kristine Sutherland, Thomas*
*Brown, Robert Oliveri*
An old-fashioned Disney fantasy-comedy done in the
style of THE ABSENT-MINDED PROFESSOR, that
sees a scientist inventing a shrinking machine and
then being forced to mount a frantic search when it
accidentally causes his own kids and those of a
neighbour to shrink to the size of ants. An entertaining family film, somewhat bland, but enlivened by the
excellent special effects.
COM                                   90 min (ort 93 min)
V                                                     WDV

**HONEYBOY \*\***                                     PG
John Berry              USA                       1982
*Erik Estrada, Morgan Fairchild, Hector Elizondo,*
*James McEachin, Roberto Costanzo, Yvonne Wilder,*
*Phillip R. Allen, Robert Alan Browne, Jill Jaress, Bill*
*Baldwin, Jem Echollas, Sugar Ray Robinson, Fred*
*Dennis, Lydia Nicole*
A look at the sad and sleazy world of a young boxer
and his relationship with his family and girlfriend.
Estrada tries to box his way to fame and fortune in
this mediocre and cliched exercise.
Aka: HONEY BOY
DRA                                               95 min mTV
B,V                                                   VPD

**HONEYBUN \*\*\***                                    18
Ruud Van Hemert
                          NETHERLANDS             1988
*Nadia Van Nie, Marc Hazelwinkel, Hans Man In't*
*Weld, Marijke Merckens*
Tempted by romantic fiction, a naive convent school-
girl heads for the bright lights of the city, and has a
variety of encounters, as various individuals try to
either exploit or shelter her. Meanwhile, her parents
believe she has been kidnapped and have got the
police out looking for her. A pleasant and relaxed
comedy.
Aka: HONEYBUNCH
COM                                               93 min
B,V                                           CAN; PATHE

**HONEYMOON \*\*\***                                   15
Patrick Jamain  CANADA/FRANCE                     1986
*Nathalie Baye, John Shea, Richard Berry, Peter*
*Donat, Maria Lukovsky, Gregg Ellwand, Arthur*
*Grosser, Alf Humphreys, Cec Linder, Michel Beauline,*
*Morris Rosengarten, Irene Kessler, Shirley Merovitz,*
*Tyrone De Costa Benskin*
A young French girl goes to New York to be with her
boyfriend, but when he's arrested on a drugs charge
she's left to fend for herself. Not wanting to return to
France, and short of cash, she makes a marriage of
convenience when assured that she need never meet
her husband. But her new husband is a psycho and
turns up at her apartment to claim her. Her rejection
drives him into a fury, in this generally well-balanced
but rather slow-paced thriller.

Aka: LUNE DE MIEL
THR                                  98 min (ort 100 min)
B,V                                                   VES

**HONEYMOON IN PARADISE \***                          18
Michel Lemoine (Michel Leblanc)
                          FRANCE                  1985
*Andre Kay, Michelle Davy, Christopher Gill, Jessy*
*Gory, Michele Leska*
An inhibited couple of newlyweds, see nothing but
couples making love wherever they go whilst on their
honeymoon. Pretty soon they join in, but don't expect
to see too much in this cut version.
A                                    74 min (ort 80 min) Cut
B,V                                         CASS/IVS; GLOB

**HONEYMOON KILLERS, THE \*\*\***                      18
Leonard Kastle          USA                       1970
*Shirley Stoler, Tony LoBianco, Mary Jane Higby,*
*Doris Roberts, Dotha Duckworth*
A ruthless couple murder lonely old women for their
money. Based on the true story of multiple murderers
Martha Beck and Raymond Fernandez, who were
executed in 1951. The chilling script is by Kastle.
DRA                                           108 min B/W
B,V                                                   PVG

**HONEYMOON SWEDISH STYLE \***                        18
Andrew Whyte (Andre Feher)
                          SWEDEN                  1982
*Barbi Andersson, Jean Laporte, Isabelle Dior*
A Swedish couple on honeymoon in France enjoy the
usual activities.
Aka: PILSKA JULIA PA BROLLOPSRESAN
A                                    74 min (ort 105 min) Cut (16 sec)
B,V                                  SFI; 18PLAT/TOW; ACTION

**HONEYSUCKLE ROSE \*\*\***                            15
Jerry Schatzberg        USA                       1980
*Willie Nelson, Dyan Cannon, Slim Pickens, Amy*
*Irving, Joey Floyd, Charles Levin, Mickey Rooney Jr,*
*Priscilla Pointer, Diana Scarwid*
A Country music star finds that his life is falling to
pieces and that he can no longer cope with the
pressures of life on the road, when he embarks on an
affair with the young daughter of one of his col-
leagues. A restrained account (said to be based on
INTERMEZZO, but I have my doubts) that has some
fine music and lively performances.
Aka: ON THE ROAD AGAIN
DRA                                              119 min
B,V                                                   WHV

**HONKY TONK FREEWAY \*\***                            15
John Schlesinger        USA                       1981
*William Devane, Beverly D'Angelo, Beau Bridges,*
*Jessica Tandy, Hume Cronyn, Geraldine Page, George*
*Dzundza, Teri Garr, Joe Grifasi, Deborah Rush,*
*Howard Hesseman, Paul Jabara*
A satire on the American love affair with the car, with
assorted car freaks assembling, in a tiny town deter-
mined to keep its tourist trade despite being bypassed
by a motorway. An expensive and flashy farce that has
some nice cameos but no real story to get one's teeth
into.
COM                                  102 min (ort 107 min)
B,V                                           TEVP; WHV

**HONKYTONK MAN \*\***                                 15
Clint Eastwood          USA                       1982
*Clint Eastwood, Kyle Eastwood, John McIntire, Alexa*
*Kenin, Verna Bloom, Matt Clark, Barry Corbin*
Eastwood and his son team up, in this story of a
Depression-era Country singer dying of cancer, and
his relationship with his young nephew, who has
tagged along with him on one last singing trip. A
touching but overlong and contrived story, with
Eastwood coming across well as the singer, but having
too little material to work with. Features appearances

by some of the greats of Country music, such as Marty Robbins, who died just before film release.
Boa: novel by C. Carlile.
DRA 119 min (ort 123 min)
B,V WHV

## HONORARY CONSUL, THE * 18
John MacKenzie UK 1983
*Michael Caine, Richard Gere, Bob Hoskins, Elpidia Carrillo, Joaquim De Almeida, A. Martinez, Staphanie Cotsirilos, Domingo Ambriz, Eric Valdez, Nicholas Jasso, Geoffrey Palmer, Leonard Maguire, Jorge Russek*
A British doctor living in a South American country, gets drawn into a plot by terrorists to kidnap the British consul there. A muddled and maudlin drama, with Caine as the alcoholic diplomat doing his best, but with Gere as the naive doctor, well and truly miscast.
Aka: BEYOND THE LIMIT
Boa: novel by Graham Greene.
DRA 104 min; 99 min (WHV)
B,V,V2 TEVP; WHV (VHS only)

## HOOCH *
Edward Mann USA 1976
*Gil Gerard, Erika Fox, Melody Rangers, Mike Allen, Ray Serra, Danny Aiello*
A moonshiner has to prevent Eastern hoods from taking over his operation.
A/AD 99 min
B,V MOV

## HOODWINK ** 15
Claude Whatham AUSTRALIA 1981
*John Hargreaves, Wendy Hughes, Kim Dencon*
A bank robber fakes blindness to get a lighter sentence, and falls in love with a religious prison visitor.
DRA 93 min
B,V,V2,LV PRV

## HOODWINKED * 15
Lee H. Katzin USA 1989
*Ernest Borgnine, Robert Mitchum*
A retired detective is hired by a man he sent to prison for 25 years, as the latter wants help in tracing his kidnapped grand-daughter, who it transpires has become a drug dealer.
A/AD 93 min
V FUTUR

## HOOK, LINE AND SINKER * U
George Marshall USA 1968
*Jerry Lewis, Anne Francis, Peter Lawford, Pedro Gonzales, Jimmy Miller, Kathleen Freeman*
Having been told he has only two months to live, an insurance salesman goes on a trip around the world, running up debts of $100,000 in the process. He then learns that he is perfectly healthy and has to avoid his creditors. A trite and plodding Lewis comedy vehicle; a few frantic chase sequences do nothing but highlight the feebleness of it all.
COM 88 min (ort 91 min)
V RCA

## HOOPER ** PG
Hal Needham USA 1978
*Burt Reynolds, Jan-Michael Vincent, Sally Field, Brian Keith, John Marley, Robert Klein, Adam West, James Best, Alfie West*
An ageing ace stunt-man has to face the threat from a younger challenger, and is tempted to try the toughest stunt of his career. Though there are some good moments, this film is seriously deflated by the lack of narrative thrust.
COM 86 min (ort 100 min)
B,V WHV

## HOPE AND GLORY *** 15
John Boorman UK 1986
*Sarah Miles, David Hayman, Sebastian Rice-Edwards, Ian Bannen, Derrick O'Connor, Susan Wooldridge, Sammi Davis, Geraldine Muir, Jean-Marc Barr, Annie Leon, Jill Baker, Amelda Brown, Katrine Boorman, Colin Higgins*
Story drawn from the director's experiences as a child, living through the wartime London Blitz, and drawn around the experiences of a nine-year-old boy, for whom the war was a time of great excitement. An affectionate and carefully drawn tale, full of rich performances and striking period detail.
DRA 108 min (ort 112 min)
V/sh RCA

## HOPPITY GOES TO TOWN *** Uc
Dave Fleischer USA 1941
Good-looking cartoon, telling of a village of bugs threatened by the humans and their building work. Grasshopper "Hoppity" takes them on a long Exodus to safety, atop a new apartment block. The thin storyline and forgettable songs (courtesy of Frank Loesser and Hoagy Carmichael) are serious flaws in an otherwise imaginative and lively animation.
Aka: MISTER BUG GOES TO TOWN
CAR 74 min
B,V,V2 IVC L/A; ITM L/A; BBC

## HOPSCOTCH *** 15
Ronald Neame USA 1980
*Walter Matthau, Glenda Jackson, Ned Beatty, Sam Waterston, Herbert Lom*
A seasoned CIA man teaches his idiotic superior a lesson by publishing some highly revealing memoirs. Despite a somewhat thin plot, this is an enjoyable and well made comedy. Co-written by Garfield from his novel.
Boa: novel by Brian Garfield.
COM 104 min
B,V TEVP

## HORRIBLE SEXY VAMPIRE, THE **
Jose Luis Madrid SPAIN 1970
*Waldemar Wohlfahrt, Patricia Loran, Barta Barry*
One of those typical Euro horror films, with a strong sexual element. No more than average, despite the promise inherent in the title.
Aka: EL VAMPIRO DE LA AUTOPISTA
A 85 min
B,V VPD

## HORROR EXPRESS *** 
Eugenio Martin SPAIN/UK 1972
*Christopher Lee, Peter Cushing, Telly Savalas, Silvia Tortosa, Jorge Rigaud, Helga Line*
A turn-of-the-century horror yarn, with a long-frozen monster being discovered by an anthropology professor who thinks he has found the missing link. He loads his discovery onto a train to take it from Asia to the West, thus giving it a chance to thaw out and make use of its ability to turn humans into zombies, in this superior horror tale.
Aka: PANIC ON THE TRANS-SIBERIAN EXPRESS
HOR 88 min
V INT

## HORROR OF FRANKENSTEIN, THE *
Jimmy Sangster UK 1970
*Ralph Bates, Kate O'Mara, Veronica Carlson, Dennis Price, Joan Rice, Bernard Archard, Graham James, Dave Prowse*
Frankenstein's son takes over on the death of his father. When not making monsters, he chases women instead. One of the last in the Hammer series and an attempt at black comedy that is certainly laughable if nothing else. Followed by "Frankenstein And The Monster From Hell".

HOR                          93 min (ort 95 min)
B,V                                        TEVP

## HORROR OF PARTY BEACH, THE *
Del Tenney            USA              1964
*John Scott, Alice Lyon, Allen Laurel, Marilyn Clark,*
*Eulabelle Moore*
The dumping of radioactive waste offshore, results in
the creation of nasty scaly monsters that spoil the
enjoyment of some simple-minded beach types. Low-
grade nonsense, with poor effects and worse acting.
HOR                                 82 min B/W
B,V                                         GHV

## HORSE IN THE GREY FLANNEL SUIT, THE *    U
Norman Tokar          USA              1969
*Dean Jones, Diane Baker, Lloyd Bochner, Fred Clark,*
*Ellen Janov, Kurt Russell, Lurene Tuttle, Morey*
*Amsterdam*
An advertising man uses his daughter's interest in
horses in a client's campaign to advertise a stomach
pill. A yawn-inducing and interminable kiddie com-
edy, badly in need of a pill of its own.
Boa: novel The Year Of The Horse by Eric Hatch.
COM                                    112 min
B,V                                         WDV

## HORSE SOLDIERS, THE **                    PG
John Ford             USA              1959
*John Wayne, William Holden, Constance Towers,*
*Althea Gibson, Hoot Gibson, Anna Lee, Russell*
*Simpson, Stan Lee, Carleton Young, Basil Ruysdael,*
*Willis Bouchey, Ken Curtis, O.Z. Whitehead, Judson*
*Pratt, Denver Pyle, Hank Worden*
Big-budget Civil War Western, about the daring
exploits of a troop of Union soldiers led by a pair of
bickering officers, who penetrate 300 miles behind
Confederate lines to destroy a railroad junction, and
thus disrupt the enemy's communication and trans-
port lines. Based on some true incidents and Ford's
only film set in the Civil War period, but this is little
more than a sprawling and overlong affair.
Boa: novel by Harold Sinclair.
WES                          115 min (ort 119 min)
V                                          WHV

## HOSPITAL, THE **                           15
Arthur Hiller         USA              1971
*George C. Scott, Diana Rigg, Barnard Hughes, Nancy*
*Marchand, Richard Dysart, Stephen Elliott, Robert*
*Blossom, Robert Walden, Lenny Baker, Frances*
*Sternhagen, Stockard Channing*
Black medical farce about mishaps at a hospital, that
are really the work of a deranged killer, with Scott
giving an unappealing performance as a cynical
doctor battling chaos and apathy. Supposedly a mad-
cap comedy, but the note of bitterness injected by the
central character makes the whole affair rather
unrewarding. AA: Story/Screen (Paddy Chayefsky).
COM                                    103 min
B,V                                         WHV

## HOSTAGE **                                 18
Frank Shields
           AUSTRALIA/WEST GERMANY      1983
*Kerry Mack, Ralph Schicha, Judy Nunn, Clare*
*Binney, Lydia Greibohm*
A young girl who has been blackmailed into marriage
to an unpleasant Nazi type, becomes the hostage of a
robber on the run. Based on a true story, but muddled
and fairly uninteresting.
Aka: HOSTAGE: THE CHRISTINE MARESCH
STORY; SAVAGE ATTRACTION
DRA                                     89 min
B,V                                         MED

## HOSTAGE **                                 18
Hanro Mohr            USA              1986

*Karen Black, Wings Hauser, Kevin McCarthy, Nancy*
*Locke (Hauser), Robert Whitehead, Gerhard*
*Hametner, Billy Second,*
A planeload of people are kidnapped by Arab terror-
ists, in a bid to gain the release of a religious zealot.
Hauser and McCarthy enlist the aid of some ex-
soldiers to mount a rescue mission. Filmed in South
Africa.
THR                                     97 min
B,V                                         VES

## HOSTAGE DALLAS **                          18
Dwight H. Little      USA              1986
*Edward Albert, Audrey Landers, Joe Don Baker, Ron*
*Pilloud, Billy Streater, Blue Deckert, Caroline*
*Williams*
Dallas is held hostage by a gang of criminals, who
have stolen containers of deadly gas and are deman-
ding a ransom of $50,000,000. A few good helicopter
stunts are about all there is, in this predictable and
implausible tale.
Aka: GETTING EVEN
THR                          86 min (ort 90 min)
B,V                                         VIR

## HOSTAGE FLIGHT **                          15
Steve Hilliard Stern   USA             1985
*Ned Beatty, Barbara Bosson, Jack Gilford, Frank*
*McRae, Rene Enriquez, John Karlen, Dee Wallace*
*Stone, Mitchell Ryan, Kristina Wayborn, Ina Balin,*
*Kim Ulrich, Frank M. Benard, Frank Annesse,*
*Michael Alldredge, Allan Miller*
A plane is hijacked by terrorists, who threaten to
execute their hostages, but they are surprised by the
reactions of the passengers. Fairly average sky-
drama, made with two different endings, the more
radical of which was added for overseas release.
Boa: story by Howard Koch and Harry Essex.
DRA                         92 min (ort 104 min) mTV
B,V                                         CBS

## HOSTAGE TOWER, THE **                      PG
Claudio Guzman        USA              1980
*Peter Fonda, Billy Dee Williams, Keir Dullea, Maud*
*Adams, Celia Johnson, Rachel Roberts, Douglas*
*Fairbanks Jr, Jack Lenoir, Andre Oumansky, Jacques*
*Maury, Nicholas Vogel, Britt Ekland, Daniel Perche,*
*Hubert Noel*
Criminals capture the Eiffel Tower, and hold the US
President's mother as hostage for a $30,000,000
ransom. Unbelievably silly, but made with enough
care for it to nearly convince. Scripted by Robert
Carrington.
Boa: story by Robert Carrington and Alistair
MacLean.
THR                                   105 min mTV
B,V                                         WHV

## HOSTILE WITNESS **                         PG
Jeff Bleckner         USA              1987
*Sam Waterston, Robert Davi, Ron Leibman*
Under a new Federal statute, murder of US citizens
overseas is declared a felony. The film revolves around
the kidnap of an Arab terrorist in West Beirut, who is
taken back to the US to stand trial, but insists in court
that his actions are political not criminal. An interesting but contrived attempt to examine the issue of
terrorism as it relates to criminal law.
DRA                                    129 min
B,V                                        BRAVE

## HOT ACTS OF LOVE **                        18
Jean-Marie Pallardy  FRANCE            1974
*Michel Lemoine, Corinne Marchand, Jean Luisi,*
*Willeke von Ammelrooij*
Two brothers scheme to take over the family newspap-
er following the death of their father. One brother is

killed in a mysterious accident and the other finds his efforts hampered by a sexy aunt, his brother's wife and his late father's mistress.
Aka: ADULTERESS IN LOVE; L'AMOUR AUX TROUSSES
A                    73 min (ort 80 min) Cut (1 min 55 sec)
B,V                                              NET; TCX

### HOT AND BLUE **                                        18
Georges Fleury        FRANCE              1972
Pierre Rousseau, Daniele Vlamink, Sophie Knudde, Michel David
A couple find that the husband's work on an erotic ad campaign, does wonders for their marriage.
Aka: EXECUTIVE HOUSEWIVES; HOT BLUE (VIDMID); JEUX POUR COUPLES INFIDELES
A                          73 min; 90 min (VIDMID)
B,V                               INT; VIDMID; ROXY

### HOT AND NAKED **                                       18
Guy Maria             FRANCE              1973
Bob Asklof, Jean-Michel Dhermay, Anne Kerylynne, Marie-Georges Pascale
Sex story set at the racing tracks, with two stunt drivers competing for the same woman, in a ruthless struggle that leads one into committing a crime in order to discredit the other.
Aka: LES DECHAINEES; THRILL SEEKERS
Osca: DIRTY FINGERS (NET/TCX)
A              73 min; 80 min (SHEP) Cut (8 min 20 sec)
B,V                          ACT L/A; NET/TCX; SHEP

### HOT BOX, THE **                                        18
Joe Viola             PHILIPPINES/USA    1972
Laurie Rose, Ricky Richardson, Carmen Argenziano, Andrea Cagan, Margaret Markov, Charles Dierkop
Four nurses sent to work in a South American republic, are kidnapped by guerillas and discover that their captors are in fact more humane than the government forces. They begin to sympathise with the struggle and when they find that arrangements are made to get them back home, one decides to stay. A well-paced but cliched action film, spiced up with a few gratuitous sex sequences. Co-written and produced by Jonathan Demme.
THR                  81 min (84 min) Cut (3 min 30 sec)
B,V                                       TURBO; XTASY

### HOT BUBBLEGUM *                                         18
Boaz Davidson
           ISRAEL/WEST GERMANY          1981
Jonathan Segal, Zachi Noy, Yftach Katzur
A 1950s look at teen life and culture but set in Israel. One in a series of mindless LEMON POPSICLE films. The next one in line was PRIVATE POPSICLE.
Aka: LEMON POPSICLE 3; SHIFSHUF NAIM
COM                                              95 min
B,V,V2,LV                                           RNK

### HOT CHILD IN THE CITY **                               18
John Florea           USA                1987
Leah Ayres Hendrix, Shari Shattuck, Will Bledsoe, Anthony Alda, Geof Prysirr
A girl from Kansas goes to visit her successful sister in Hollywood, and is shocked to discover that she has been murdered. Following her funeral, she decides to infiltrate the underworld to find the truth. A disjointed and noisy story, that often resembles little more than a badly made music video.
THR                                              82 min
B,V                                                CINE

### HOT CHILI *                                            18
William Sachs         USA                1985
Victoria Barrett, Charles Schillaci, Allan J. Kayser, Joe Rubbo, Chuck Hemingway, Louisa Moritz
Four boys work at a top resort hotel and enjoy the usual pranks. A silly, light and brainless comedy.
Aka: HOT SUMMER

COM                                              86 min
B,V                                                RNK

### HOT DOG: THE MOVIE *                                   18
Peter Markle          USA                1984
David Naughton, Tracy N. Smith, Patrick Houser, Frank Koppola, John Patrick Reger, Shannon Tweed
Film about "hot-dogging", i.e., suicide-style ski stunts. The story involves two rival teams fighting for control of the slopes. An empty-headed change from all those empty-headed teen college comedies, but just as boring.
COM                                              98 min
B,V                                                 EIV

### HOT LEAD AND COLD FEET ***                             U
Robert Butler         USA                1978
Jim Dale, Darren McGavin, Karen Valentine, Jack Elam, Don Knotts, Warren Vanders, John Williams, Debbie Lytton, Michael Sharrett, Dave Cass, Richard Wright, Don Barry, Jimmy Van Patten, Gregg Palmer, Ed Bakey
Over-the-top Western spoof in which Dale plays no less than three parts: a tough old patriarch, his gunfighter son and his other Salvation Army son, both of whom are competing for control of the town.
COM                          86 min (ort 90 min)
B,V                                                WHV

### HOT LEGS **                                           R18
Bob C. Chinn          USA                1980
Jesie St James, Dewey Alexander, Jennifer Wolfe, Paul Thomas, Laurien Dominique, Sharon Cain
Silly porno movie set in the garter and stocking industry, where "Hot Legs" are a brand of stockings being promoted in an advertising campaign. This shallow plot provides the framework for a film that consists of little more than a sequence of romantic sexual encounters.
A                          70 min (ort 83 min) Cut (2 sec)
B,V,V2                                              TCX

### HOT LUNCH **                                           18
Harold Perkins        USA
Desiree Cousteau, Jerry Heath, Brigit Olsen, Christine De Schaffer
A country couple decide to look for opportunities in the big city. Full of optimism they rent a rundown flat, but after failing to find jobs and using up their savings, they are forced to find other ways of paying the rent.
A              52 min (ort 66 min) Cut (2 min 37 sec
                               in addition to film cuts)
B,V,V2                                              HAR

### HOT MOVES **                                           18
Jim Sotos             USA                1984
Michael Zorek, Adam Silbar, Debi Richter, Jeff Fishman, Johnny Timko, Jill Schoelen
Standard teenage comedy about how three boys try to lose their virginity in a variety of more or less successful ways.
COM                                              85 min
B,V                                            VES/PVG

### HOT ONE, THE **                                        15
Matthew Robbins      USA                1979
Mark Hamill, Annie Potts, Eugene Roche, Kim Milford, Richard McKenzie, William Bryant
The title refers to a souped-up Corvette, which is stolen after having been lovingly restored by a high school kid and his classmates. Hamill takes off in pursuit and has a number of adventures in and around Las Vegas, in this mundane comedy.
Aka: CORVETTE SUMMER
COM                          100 min (ort 107 min)
B,V                                                MGM

**HOT PAINT ** **                                    PG
Sheldon Larry            USA              1987
*Gregory Harrison, John Larroquette, John Glover,
Cyrielle Claire, Jonathan Cecil, Julie Bovasso*
A pair of inept hustlers inadvertently steal a Renoir
belonging to the Mafia, and then spend the rest of the
movie trying to return it, without being killed in the
process. Amusing in fits and starts, but mostly dull.
COM                    88 min (ort 90 min) mTV
B,V                                            MGM

**HOT POTATO ***                                  15
Oscar Williams           USA              1976
*Jim Kelly, George Memmoli, Geoffrey Binney, Irene
Tsu, Judith Brown*
Three martial arts mercenaries are engaged to snatch
the daughter of a US senator from captivity in the Far
East. Simple-minded fare that was filmed in Thailand.
Remade as "Force Five" in 1981.
MAR                                         87 min
B,V                                            WHV

**HOT PURSUIT ** **                                15
Steven Lisberger         USA              1987
*John Cusack, Robert Loggia, Wendy Gazelle, Jerry
Stiller, Monte Markham, Shelley Fabares, Terence
Cooper*
Owing to his bad grades, a student is prevented from
going on vacation with his girlfriend and her wealthy
family. A last minute reprieve from one of his teachers
enables him to set off in pursuit. Once he arrives at
their tropical island holiday resort, he encounters
some desperate hijackers and faces other perils, in this
foolish formula comedy.
COM                                         90 min
B,V                                            VES

**HOT PURSUIT *** **                              18
Stanley Forrest
                    NETHERLANDS/USA       1983
*Annette Haven, Sidney Derko, Jackie Jowes, Sandy
Lane, Tanya Taylor, Lola James, Abel Caine, Mary
Van Cleef, Michelle Norris, Sam Arthur, John Mann,
Mark Raymond*
Set in Amsterdam, this film tells of a wealthy pop
singer who has made her fortune from innocent and
virginal songs. However, she once made a porno film
years ago that could ruin her career. In desperation
she hires a detective to find it, and his search leads
him to some of the brothels and dives of the city. A
complex and often incoherent tale that sometimes
loses its thread, but is held together by a convincing
performance from Haven.
Aka: HEAVEN CAN'T WAIT; YAB-YUM OP
STELTEN
A       61 min (ort 93 min) Cut (2 min 1 sec in addition
                                        to film cuts)
B,V                            TCX; VES; ELV; HAR

**HOT RACKETS ** **
Robert McCallum          USA              1979
*Candida Royalle, Jon Martin, Laurien Dominique,
Mike Ranger, Desiree Clearbranch, Chris Cassidy,
Mike Fairmont, Turk Lyon*
A wealthy tennis addict has an unsatisfactory sex life
with his frigid wife, but spends most of his time at his
tennis club. When she learns that the club employs a
female masseuse she pays it a visit, and loses some of
her hangups in the process – for the club is full of
swingers who play in the nude and make love between
sets. A healthy outdoors-type sex film, not all that far
removed from innocent films promoting nudism.
A                                           81 min
B,V,V2                                         CAL

**HOT RESORT ***                                  18
John Robins              USA              1984
*Tom Parsekian, Michael Berz, Bronson Pinchot,
Daniel Schneider, Debra Kelly, Samm-Art Williams,*

*Victoria Barrett, Frank Gorshin, Dana Kaminsky, Mae
Questel*
Teenage sex comedy set in a luxury hotel in a
Caribbean resort, where three young boys get a
summer job helping out. A low-brow and fairly crude
effort, with nice locations but not much comedy.
COM                              87 min (ort 91 min)
B,V                                            GHV

**HOT ROCK, THE *** **                            PG
Peter Yates              USA              1972
*Robert Redford, George Segal, Zero Mostel, Ron
Leibman, Paul Sand, Moses Gunn, William Redfield,
Charlotte Rae, Topo Swope*
Four inept crooks plan to steal a valuable diamond
from a museum, but commit a series of blunders every
step of the way in this engaging crime caper. Most of
the film is taken up, not with the robbery, but with
their bungling attempts to get back the gem after
having lost it. Screenplay is by William Goldman.
Followed by BANK SHOT.
Aka: HOW TO STEAL A DIAMOND IN FOUR
UNEASY LESSONS
Boa: novel by Donald Westlake.
COM                             97 min (ort 105 min)
B,V                                            CBS

**HOT SEX IN BANGKOK *** **
Michael Thomas (Erwin C. Dietrich)
                    SWITZERLAND           1974
*Claude Martin, Michael Jacot, Silver Moon, Steve
Marachuk*
The story of eight guys who go off to Bangkok in
search of some romance and to enjoy the charms of the
beautiful Thai women. The entire film was shot in the
city, and its canals, nightclubs and bars, and although
the plot merely follows each guy and his encounters,
the film as a whole has a simple innocence and appeal
that is generally absent from later sex films.
Aka: HEISSE SEX IN BANGKOK
A                                           60 min
B,V                                            CAL

**HOT SHOTS *** **                                R18
                         USA
*Jennifer Jordan, Helen Willis, Annette Haven, Kelly
Nichols, Chelsea Blake, Cassandra Leigh, Paul
Thomas*
A crusading Congressman who defends women's
rights, is actually a sex-mad chauvinist behind closed
doors, and forces his secretary to serve his desires.
Needless to say, he gets his come-uppance.
A                           71 min Cut (4 min 4 sec)
B,V                                            ELV

**HOT SPLASH ** **                                18
James Ingrassia          USA              1987
*Richard Steinmetz, Rebecca Thompson, Jeremy
Wheelan, Richard Steele*
Four Florida teenagers make plans to hold a wild
surfing party, but run into trouble from a local
gangster, in this bright and brainless teen comedy.
COM                                         89 min
V                                              RCA

**HOT STUFF ** **                                 15
Dom DeLuise              USA              1979
*Dom DeLuise, Suzanne Pleshette, Jerry Reed, Luis
Avalos, Ossie Davis, Marc Lawrence*
Four Miami cops set up their own operation to fence
stolen goods, and thereby improve their arrest record,
by pretending to be fences and then arresting thieves
at the end of the operation. Amiable and mildly
diverting, with good characterisations. Written by
Michael Kane and Donald Westlake.
COM                                         87 min
V                                              RCA

## HOT SUMMER IN BAREFOOT COUNTY **
Will Zens            USA              1974
*Don Jones, Sherry Robinson, Tonia Bryan, Charles*
*Elledye, Jeff Mackay, Ned Austin, Larry Lambeth,*
*Valerie Putney, Dick Smith*
An undercover agent is sent in to smash a moonshin-
ing racket but is faced with a moral quandry when he
falls in love with one of the moonshiners. Average.
A/AD                                 92 min
B,V                                   MMA

## HOT T-SHIRTS **
Chuck Vincent (Mark Ubell)
               USA                   1979
*Ray Holland, Stephanie Lawlor, Pauline Rose,*
*Corinne Alpen, Glenn Mure*
A bar owner dresses his barmaids in clinging wet
T-shirts to pull in the punters in this cheerfully inane
offering.
COM                                  84 min
B,V                                   RNK

## HOT TARGET **                        18
Denis Lewiston   NEW ZEALAND          1985
*Simone Griffeth, Steve Marachuk, Bryan Marshal,*
*Peter McCauley*
An American woman plans to get rid of her husband
with the aid of her lover, who unknown to her is in fact
a ruthless jewel thief who's setting her up for a
robbery. A competent if uninventive thriller, with a
twist ending that's all too predictable.
THR                           91 min Cut (14 sec)
B,V                                 PARK; RCA

## HOT TIMES *                           18
Jim McBride           USA             1974
*Henry Cory, Gail Lorber, Amy Farber, Bob Lesser,*
*Steve Curry*
American teenage comedy about a sex-mad boy whose
urges take him to New York's Times Square. Said to
have been made for $5,000 but looks a good deal
cheaper.
Aka: ADVENTURES OF ARCHIE, THE
COM                                  77 min
B,V                             CAP L/A; TAKE2

## HOT TO TROT *
Michael Dinner        USA             1988
*Bobcat Goldthwait, Jim Metzler, Virginia Madsen,*
*Dabney Coleman, Mary Gross, John Candy (voice*
*only)*
A talented cast do their best in this utterly stupid
comedy revolving around a talking horse. Just as
stupid as that "Francis The Talking Mule" series from
the 1950s, but even less funny.
COM                                  80 min
V/sh                                  WHV

## HOT TOUCH, THE **
Roger Vadim          CANADA           1982
*Marie-France Pisier, Wayne Rogers, Lloyd Bochner,*
*Samantha Eggar, Patrick Macnee, Melvyn Douglas,*
*Gloria Carlin, Allan Kolman, Jan Lapp, Norwich*
*Duff, James B. Douglas, Philip Spensley, Louis*
*Bakhache, Terrence La Brosse*
A painter makes a good living forging the works of
great masters in partnership with a businessman.
However, their cosy life is disturbed when an art
dealer discovers their activities.
DRA                                  92 min
B,V                                   POLY

## HOT WATER **                          18
Jim Hanley           CANADA           1984
*Suzanne De Laurentis, Linda Singer, Ken Roberts,*
*Jeremy Ratchford, Michael McKeever, Cotton Maher,*
*Alanne Heuff, Daisy Franklin, Brian Morgan, Tricia*
*Turner, Ken Heuff, Peter Mahoney, Howie Kirby, Tom*

*Lane, Tim Latchem*
Two prostitutes attempt to go straight after their
release from prison, by running a marina. They face
opposition from the resentful locals, who mount a
campaign to drive them out, but their troubles really
start when they find themselves menaced by a mad
killer. A low-grade and exploitative thriller.
Aka: JUNIOR
THR               77 min (ort 90 min) Cut (9 min 15 sec)
B,V                       VFLY L/A; STABL; PALAN

## HOT, FAST AND LOOSE *                 18
Dwayne Avery          USA             1973
*Carl Manson, Angela Carson, Maybe Smith*
Thriller about an ex-Marine bomber who hates hip-
pies, that masquerades as a sex film, but consists of
nothing more than the usual run of "mad killer" type
cliches.
Aka: BOOBY TRAP (LYNX)
THR                                  89 min
B,V                             LYNX L/A; PRI; PHE

## HOTEL COLONIAL *                      15
Cinzia T.H. Torrini  ITALY/USA        1987
*John Savage, Robert Duvall, Rachel Ward, Massimo*
*Troisi*
Having learned of his brother's suicide in Bogota,
Columbia, a man goes there and becomes involved in a
sinister plot. A pointless trifle that wears out its
welcome very quickly.
A/AD            102 min (ort 104 min) Cut (41 sec)
B, V/s                            CHV; BRAVE

## HOTEL DU LAC ***                      PG
Giles Foster          UK              1986
*Anna Massey, Denholm Elliott, Julia McKenzie,*
*Googie Withers, Patricia Hodge, Barry Foster, Irene*
*Handl*
After narrowly avoiding an unsuitable marriage, a
woman novelist retreats to an elegant Swiss hotel in
the off-season, where she ponders her life whilst
carefully observing her fellow guests. A nicely paced
and detailed adaptation of a Booker Prize-winning
novel, filmed amidst the lakes and mountains of
Switzerland.
Boa: novel by Anita Brookner.
DRA                               75 min mTV
V/h                                   BBC

## HOTEL NEW HAMPSHIRE, THE **          18
Tony Richardson       USA             1984
*Jodie Foster, Beau Bridges, Rob Lowe, Nastassja*
*Kinski, Wilford Brimley, Paul McCrane, Jennie*
*Dundas, Dorsey Wright, Matthew Modine, Amanda*
*Plummer, Wallace Shawn, Anita Morris*
An American moves to Bavaria to manage a hotel,
and becomes involved in a series of bizarre adven-
tures. A long and disorganised adaptation of Irving's
semi-comic work, that makes a few interesting
observations on life, and boasts a number of good
performances. Unfortunately it all wears rather thin
about halfway through.
Boa: novel by John Irving.
DRA                     110 min; 104 min (WHV)
B, V/sh               TEVP; WHV (VHS only)

## HOTLINE **                            15
Jerry Jameson         USA             1982
*Lynda Carter, Steve Forrest, Granville Van Dusen,*
*Monte Markham, James Reynolds, Joy Garrett, Harry*
*Waters Jr, James Booth, Arthur Malet, Nick Angotti,*
*Julian Fellowes, James Ingersoll, Blane Savage, Scott*
*Durnavich*
A woman takes a job at a centre for people in crisis,
and finds herself the victim of a psychotic caller, in
this standard thriller of few surprises.
Aka: REACHOUT
Boa: story by David E. Peckinpah and Stancil E.D.
Johnson.

THR 96 min mTV
B,V VFP L/A; HER

## HOTTEST SHOW IN TOWN, THE * 18
Phyllis Eberhard Kronhausen
SWITZERLAND 1974
*Brad Branden, Samantha J. Timms, Karen Zelat*
A circus is saved from financial ruin by introducing
live sex performances. The simple plot is no more than
a framework for a series of sexy and titillating turns,
in this dated European effort.
A 59 min (ort 100 min) Cut (8 sec)
B,V TOW L/A; GLOB

## HOTWIRE **
Frank Q. Dobbs USA 1980
*George Kennedy, Stropher Martin, John Terry, Jean
Sanders*
The tough story of a crooked car repossession racket.
Average.
A/AD 92 min
B,V MARKET/GOV

## HOUND OF THE BASKERVILLES, THE * 15
Paul Morrissey UK 1977
*Peter Cook, Dudley Moore, Denholm Elliott, Joan
Greenwood, Terry-Thomas, Max Wall, Irene Handl,
Kenneth Williams, Hugh Griffith, Dana Gillespie, Roy
Kinnear, Prunella Scales, Penelope Keith, Spike
Milligan, Lucy Griffiths*
Spoof version of the much filmed story of a mysterious
supernatural dog, that threatens the latest inheritor
of a Dartmoor mansion. A host of comic talent is
assembled to but little avail in this pitifully thin and
painfully unfunny effort. The script is by Peter Cook.
Boa: novella by Arthur Conan Doyle.
COM 80 min (ort 85 min)
B,V,V2 VCL/CBS

## HOUND OF THE BASKERVILLES, THE ** 15
Douglas Hickox UK 1983
*Ian Richardson, Martin Shaw, Denholm Elliott, Brian
Blessed, Connie Booth, Donald Churchill, Nicholas
Clay*
Film version of the Sherlock Holmes tale, in which the
famous detective has to solve an ancient family curse.
Competent rather than memorable.
Boa: novella by Arthur Conan Doyle.
DRA 96 min
B,V,V2 EHE; CH5 (VHS only)

## HOUND OF THE BASKERVILLES, THE *** PG
Terence Fisher UK 1959
*Peter Cushing, Christopher Lee, Andre Morell, Maria
Landi, Miles Malleson, David Oxley, Francis De Wolff,
Ewen Solon, John Le Mesurier, Sam Kydd, Helen Goss*
Hammer-style remake of the 1939 film version of the
Sherlock Holmes tale, telling of a supernatural dog
said to bring death to an aristocratic family. A fairly
decent remake of this much-filmed classic, spoilt by
the usual clumsy touches that generally find their
way into Hammer films. Despite this, Cushing is well
cast and the film doesn't lack for atmosphere.
Boa: novella by Arthur Conan Doyle.
HOR 86 min
B,V WHV

## HOUNDS OF WAR **
Terry Bourke AUSTRALIA 1982
*Chard Hayward, Ivar Kants, Margaret Lawrence,
Jennifer Cluff, Alyson Best, Les Foxcroft, Joan Bruce,
James Elliot, Moira Walker, Ricky May*
Two brothers both witness the massacre of a village in
Indonesia in 1975 and both try in their own way to
come to terms with what they have seen.
Aka: BROTHERS (POLY)
Boa: story Reflex by Roger Ward.
WAR 106 min
B,V POLY L/A; CIN

## HOUR OF THE ASSASSIN ** 15
Luis Llosa USA 1986
*Erik Estrada, Robert Vaughn, Alfredo Alvarez
Calderon, Lourdes Berninzon*
Set in a fictional South American country, with
Estrada a hit-man who has been called back in order
to assassinate the newly-elected president. Vaughn
has a good part as the CIA agent determined to stop
him. Filmed in Peru.
A/AD 92 min
B,V MGM

## HOUSE * 15
Steve Miner USA 1986
*William Katt, Kay Lenz, George Wendt, Richard Moll,
Susan French, Mary Stavin, Erik Silver, Michael
Ensign, Mark Silver*
A horror film with comic touches. After his divorce a
writer moves to the house where his aunt killed
herself and finds himself plagued by nightmarish
fantasies. A messy and disjointed film that works as
neither comedy nor horror. Followed by the inevitable
sequels.
HOR 93 min
V EIV

## HOUSE 2: THE SECOND STORY ** 15
Ethan Wiley USA 1987
*Arye Gross, Lar Park Lincoln, Jonathan Stark, Royal
Dano, John Ratzenburger, Devin Devasquez, Jayne
Modean, Ronn Carroll, Dean Cleverdon, Doug
McHugh*
As much a comedy as a horror film, this bizarre sequel
has a man moving into the house where his parents
were murdered years ago. He digs up the coffin of his
mischievous 170-year-old great-grandfather, and
together they embark on a series of rather strange
adventures. Followed by another film in the HOUSE
series.
HOR 84 min (ort 94 min)
B,V EIV

## HOUSE 3: THE HORROR SHOW ** 18
Jim Isaac USA 1989
*Lance Henriksen, Rita Taggart, Brion James, DeeDee
Pfeiffer, Aron Eisenberg*
Another weird in-name-only sequel to HOUSE, with a
mass murderer finally being sent to the electric chair
after being hunted down by an intrepid detective.
However, his death catapults him into an unearthly
plane of existence where he still has scope for more
evil. Occasionally chilling but generally just rather
gruesome.
HOR 90 min
V BRAVE

## HOUSE BY THE CEMETERY, THE ** 18
Lucio Fulci ITALY 1981
*Katherine McColl, Paolo Malco, Giovanni Frezza,
Giovanni De Nava, Dagmar Lassander, Anja Pierani,
Silvie Collatina, Daniele Doria, Carlo De Mejo*
A family moves into a house once owned by a certain
Dr Freudstein, and finds that he is alive and well and
living in their cellar, even though he is by now about
150 years old. Buckets of blood and other horrors
abound in this incredibly over-the-top Italian offering.
Cut before video submission by 34 seconds. Unlikely
to be available in an uncut form in the UK.
Aka: HOUSE OUTSIDE THE CEMETERY, THE;
QUELLA VILLA ACCANTO AL CIMITERO
HOR 85 min; 76 min (ELE) Cut (4 min 11 sec in
addition to film cuts)
B,V,V2 VDM/GHV; ELE (VHS only)

## HOUSE CALLS * PG
Howard Zieff USA 1978
*Glenda Jackson, Walter Matthau, Art Carney, Richard
Benjamin, Candice Azzara, Dick O'Neill, Thayer
David*

A doctor recently widowed after thirty-one years, goes after a bored divorcee. A mediocre comedy which not even Matthau can enliven. Jackson is seriously miscast in a comic role. Written by Max Shulman, Julius J. Epstein and Alan Mandel. Followed by a TV series.

| COM | 93 min (ort 98 min) |
| V/h | CIC |

### HOUSE OF DARK SHADOWS, THE **    18
Dan Curtis          USA          1970
*Jonathan Frid, Grayson Hall, Kathryn Leigh Scott, Roger Davis, Joan Bennett, John Karlen, Thayer David, Louis Edmonds, Nancy Barrett*
A routine vampire story based onthea TV series "Dark Shadows" from ABC, in which a female vampire searches for a cure in order to marry. Agreeable and suitably chilling in places but this one offers no new slant. Followed by "Night Of Dark Shadows".

| HOR | 93 min (ort 95 min) |
| B,V | MGM |

### HOUSE OF EVIL *    18
Mark Rosman          USA          1983
*Kathryn McNeil, Eileen Davidson, Lois Kelso Hunt, Christopher Lawrence, Robin Meloy, Janis Zido, Jodi Draigie, Harley Kozak, Ellen Dorsher*
A prank at an all-girls school misfires, and leads to the deaths of seven girl students, in this unimpressive psychotic slasher tale. The script is by Mark Rosman.
Aka: HOUSE ON SORORITY ROW, THE; SEVEN SISTERS

| HOR | 90 min; 88 min (APX) Cut (3 sec) |
| B,V | VCL L/A; APX |

### HOUSE OF GAMES ****    15
David Mamet          USA          1987
*Lindsay Crouse, Joe Mantegna, Lilia Skala, Steve Goldstein, Mike Nussbaum, J.T. Walsh, Willo Hauseman, Karen Kolhaas, Jack Wallace, Ricky Jay, G. Roy Levin, Bob Lumbra, Andy Potok, Allen Soule, Ben Blakeman, Scott Zigler*
Playwright David Mamet makes his directorial debut in this tale of a successful psychiatrist who acquires a confidence trickster as a patient and finds herself so fascinated by his world of deception, that she gets drawn into it rather more deeply than was her intention. An elegant and absorbing study, with Mantegna giving one of his best performances as the slick and convincing trickster.

| THR | 98 min |
| V/s | RCA |

### HOUSE OF SHADOWS **
Richard Wulicher   ARGENTINA          1977
*John Gavin, Yvonne De Carlo, Leonor Manso, Mecha Ortiz*
A woman witnesses a murder which took place 23 years earlier, in this strange Argentinian tale.

| HOR | 90 min (ort 103 min) |
| B,V,V2 | MED; VPD |

### HOUSE OF TERROR **    18
Sergei Goncharoff          USA          1972
*Jennifer Bishop, Arell Blanton, Mitchell Gregg, Jacquelyn Hyde*
A nurse to the invalid wife of a millionaire, plots with her boyfriend to get their hands on his fortune, in this cliche-ridden but atmospheric offering.

| THR | 90 min |
| B,V | TEM L/A; VIP |

### HOUSE OF THE LIVING DEAD **
Ray Austin          SOUTH AFRICA          1973
*Mark Burns, Shirley Anne Field, David Oxley*
A family on a South African estate are threatened by insanity and the living dead.
Aka: DOCTOR MANIAC

| HOR | 85 min |
| B,V,V2 | INT/CBS |

### HOUSE OF THE LONG SHADOWS, THE *    15
Peter Walker          UK          1983
*Vincent Price, Christopher Lee, Peter Cushing, John Carradine, Desi Arnaz Jr, Sheila Keith, Julie Peasgood, Richard Todd, Louise English, Richard Hunter, Norman Rossington*
An author goes to an isolated house to write a manuscript after making a bet, but finds strange things start to happen as soon as he gets there. A dismal and flawed spoof that is of slight interest in the casting of several horror film veterans in the one movie.
Boa: novel Seven Keys To Baldpate by Earl Derr Biggers.

| HOR | 90 min; 97 min (VCC) (ort 101 min) |
| B,V,V2,LV | GHV; VCC (VHS only) |

### HOUSE OF THE RISING SUN **    18
Chuck Vincent          USA          1985
*Tish Ambrose, Rachel Ashley, Paul Thomas, Taija Rae, Jerry Butler, Scott Baker*
The story of a brothel that undergoes a renovation by a profit-oriented businessman. A mediocre sex tale.

| A | 80 min |
| B,V | TCX; PARK |

### HOUSE OF USHER, THE **    18
Alan Birkinshaw          1989
*Oliver Reed, Donald Pleasence, Rufus Swart, Romy Windsor*
An updated version of Poe's classic tale that's set in England in modern times, where Ryan Usher and his fiancee have been invited to stay at the family home by an uncle. However, the uncle has designs on the girl, for as the last of his line he badly wants to produce an heir. A low-budget film, well photographed but devoid of the atmosphere so necessary to give substance to the work of Poe.
Boa: short story The Fall Of The House Of Usher by Edgar Allan Poe.

| HOR | 87 min |
| V | CASPIC |

### HOUSE OF WAX **    PG
Andre De Toth          USA          1953
*Vincent Price, Frank Lovejoy, Phyllis Kirk, Carolyn Jones, Paul Cavanagh, Charles Buchinski (Bronson), Paul Picerni*
A sculptor disfigured in a fire at his wax museum takes a grisly revenge on those around him, rebuilding his damaged showplace with the bodies of his victims. A remake of "The Mystery Of The Wax Museum", that's packed with sudden shocks (mainly because it was an early 3-D film) but is hampered by poor narrative development.

| HOR | 85 min (ort 88 min) |
| B,V | WHV |

### HOUSE OF WHIPCORD **    18
Pete Walker          UK          1974
*Barbara Markham, Patrick Barr, Ray Brooks, Penny Irving, Anne Michelle, Sheila Keith, Dorothy Gordon, Robert Tayman, Ivor Salter, Judy Robinson, Karen David, Jane Howard, Celia Quicke, David McGillivray, Tony Sympson*
A senile and vicious old judge is so appalled by the decline in moral standards that he sets up a private house of correction for young girls. The tale follows the ordeal of one such girl who is imprisoned after accepting an invitation on the part of her boyfriend to meet his parents. A polished sexploitation film that dissipates its power with gratuitous titillation and an implausible climax.

| HOR | 100 min |
| B,V,V2 | DFS |

## HOUSE ON CARROLL STREET ** PG
Peter Yates USA 1987
*Kelly McGillis, Jeff Daniels, Mandy Patinkin, Jessica Tandy, Christopher Rhode, Jonathan Hogan, Remak Ramsey, Ken Walsh*
A woman editor on Life magazine, sacked when she refuses to take part in the anti-Communist witch-hunt of the 1950s, inadvertently stumbles across a sinister government-inspired conspiracy to smuggle ex-Nazis into the USA. A detailed film whose improbabilities of plot weigh heavily against it.
A/AD 97 min
V VIR

## HOUSE ON GARIBALDI STREET, THE **
Peter Collinson USA 1979
*Topol (Chaim Topol), Martin Balsam, Janet Suzman, Nick Mancuso, Leo McKern, Charles H. Gray, Derren Nesbitt, Alfred Burke, John Bennett, John Carter, Fernando Hilbeck, Edward Judd, Alberto Berco, Alberto DeMendoza*
Account of the capture of Adolf Eichmann in Argentina, by Israeli agents in 1960, that is carefully made but falls into the trap of being too preachy. Filmed in Spain.
Aka: EICHMANN
Boa: book by Isser Harel.
DRA 98 min (ort 100 min) mTV
B,V VFP L/A; HER

## HOUSE ON THE EDGE OF THE PARK, THE *
Roger Franklin (Ruggero Deodato)
ITALY 1980
*David A. Hess, Annie Belle, John Morghen, Lorraine De Selle, Christian Borromeno, Marie Claude Joseph*
Two men prove to be vicious sadists when a girl at a party first leads them on and then rejects them. Unpleasant and rather vacuous exploiter. Unlikely to be available in an uncut form in the UK.
Aka: LA CASA AI CONFINI DEL PARCO; LA CASA NEL PARCO; LA CASA SPERDUTA DEL PARCO
HOR 91 min
B,V VFM

## HOUSE PARTY *** 15
Reginald Hudlin USA 1990
*Christopher Reid, Robin Harris, Tisha Campbell, Martin Lawrence, A.J. Johnson, Christopher Martin, Paul Anthony*
A zestful comedy-musical built around a party held in a house in a black neighbourhood. Will be enjoyed by fans of rap music and for its keen sense of fun. Music is by Marcus Miller and Lenny White and features: Full Force, Kid 'n' Play (Christopher Reid and Christopher Martin), L.L. Cool J, Flavor Full and others. Writer-director Hudlin's directorial debut.
COM 101 min
V RCA

## HOUSE THAT CRIED MURDER, THE *** 18
Jean-Marie Pelissie USA 1974
*Robin Strasser, John Beal, Arthur Roberts, Iva Jean Saraceni*
A couple plan to spend their honeymoon in a new house in the Connecticut countryside, but the husband has a few unpleasant surprises in store, when he is unfaithful to his wife on their wedding day in this tense thriller.
Aka: BRIDE, THE; HERE COMES THE BRIDE; NO WAY OUT (VIDAGE or GLOB)
THR 83 min; 73 min (VIDAGE or GLOB) (ort 90 min)
B,V VTC L/A; VIZ L/A; VIDAGE; GLOB

## HOUSE THAT DRIPPED BLOOD, THE **
Peter John Duffell UK 1970
*Christopher Lee, Peter Cushing, Nyree Dawn Porter, John Bennett, Denholm Elliott, Tom Adams, Jon Pertwee, John Bryans, Joanna Dunham, Ingrid Pitt, Chloe Franks, Joss Ackland, Geoffrey Bayldon*
A quartet of stories involving a detective investigating a disappearance, in a sinister mansion that has a strange history. The best stories are the first and last ones.
Boa: short stories: Method For Murder, Waxworks, Sweets To The Sweet and The Cloak by Robert Bloch.
HOR 97 min (ort 102 min)
B,V BWV/VSP

## HOUSE THAT WOULD NOT DIE, THE *
John Llewellyn Moxey USA 1970
*Barbara Stanwyck, Richard Egan, Michael Anderson Jr, Doreen Lang, Katherine Winn, Mabel Albertson*
A standard haunted house horror story, telling of witchcraft and ghosts in an inherited house, and set in Amish country. The film offers little new, except Stanwyck in her TV movie debut.
Boa: novel Ammie, Come Home by Barbara Michaels (Barbara G. Mertz).
HOR 90 min mTV
B,V GHV

## HOUSE WHERE DEATH LIVED, THE **
Alan Beattie USA 1980
*Joseph Cotten, Patricia Pearcy, David Hayward, John Dukakis*
A young woman takes up a post as nurse to an elderly invalid, but becomes emotionally involved with his 16-year-old grandson, and shortly after her arrival a series of murders begins.
Aka: DELUSION
THR 82 min (ort 93 min)
B,V VIPCO

## HOUSE WHERE EVIL DWELLS, THE * 18
Kevin Connor USA 1982
*Susan George, Edward Albert, Doug McClure, Amy Barrett, Mako Hattori, Toshiyuki Sasaki, Toshiya Maruyama*
An American family in Japan moves into a haunted house in Kyoto, despite warnings. A violent and unappealing ghost yarn, with little new to relieve the tired plot.
HOR 84 min (ort 88 min) Cut (34 sec)
V/h WHV

## HOUSE WHERE HELL FROZE OVER, THE ** 18
S.F. Brownrigg USA 1975
*Camilla Carr, Gene Ross, Stephen Tobolowsky, Ann Stafford, Sharon Bunn, Chelsea Ross, Annabelle Weenick, Bill Thurman, Jessie Lee Fulton, Lucille Baldwin, Desmond Dhooge, Skipper Richardson, Cebe Reed*
Unpleasant horror story of a mad woman who carries out a series of murders on unsuspecting victims.
Aka: KEEP MY GRAVE OPEN (CHM/PPL)
HOR 80 min
B,V CHM/PPL L/A; CLOK

## HOUSEHOLDER, THE **
James Ivory INDIA 1963
*Shashi Kapoor, Leela Naidu*
A schoolteacher and his wife try to come to terms with their arranged marriage. An absorbing and fairly perceptive character study.
Aka: GHARBAR
DRA 101 min B/W
B,V PVG

## HOUSEKEEPING *** PG
Bill Forsyth USA 1987
*Christine Lahti, Sara Walker, Andrea Burchill, Anne Pitoniak, Barbara Reese, Margot Pinvidic, Bill Smillie, Wayne Robson*
Two orphan girls go to live with their aunt, who proves to be an eccentric woman whose unconventional ways do not go down too well in the small town where they all live. An oddly charming film which follows the careers of the girls, one growing up to be a

normal and conventional young lady, the other finding herself drawn to her guardian's strange ways. Lahti gives one of her best performances to date.
Boa: novel by Marilynne Robinson.
COM 111 min (ort 117 min)
B,V RCA

## HOVERBUG **
Jan Darley-Smith UK 1971
*Jill Riddick, John Trayhorn, Francis Attard, Gary Cann, Arthur Howard, Michael Balfour, Peter Myers, Cardew Robinson*
A brother and sister enter a race for home-made hoverbugs and are helped by an inventor with a history of unreliable inventions. A pleasant little kid's film.
JUV 57 min
B,V RNK

## HOW DO I LOVE THEE? * PG
Michael Gordon USA 1970
*Jackie Gleason, Maureen O'Hara, Shelley Winters, Rosemary Forsyth, Rick Lenz, Clinton Robinson*
A philosophy professor has problems relating to his atheist father, in this overly sentimental comedy.
COM 87 min (ort 110 min)
B,V RNK; VGM

## HOW I GOT INTO COLLEGE ** 15
Savage Steve Holland USA 1989
*Anthony Edwards, Corey Parker, Christopher Rydell, Lara Flynn Boyle, Finn Carter, Charles Rocket, Brian Doyle-Murray*
This juvenile comedy starts off with a promising premise: a look at the antics ambitious kids use to get into top colleges and the tricks the colleges employ in turn to get the students they want. The flimsy plot follows the exploits of a student who applies to one such college, but only because a girl he is after is doing so. A few fantasy sequences pep up an otherwise rather dull effort.
COM 83 min (ort 89 min)
V CBS

## HOW SLEEP THE BRAVE ** 18
Lyndon James Swift USA 1981
*Lawrence Day, Luis Manuel, Thomas Pollard, Daniel Foley, Gerrany Quatro, George Gabriel, Christophe Muncke*
Whilst out on a search-and-destroy mission, a small inexperienced platoon finds itself trapped by the Viet Cong. Their only way out is by helicopter, but as their rescuers approach, the Viet Cong close in and the fighting becomes a battle to the death.
Aka: COMBAT ZONE (IVS); ONCE UPON A TIME IN VIETNAM
WAR 90 min
B,V VNET L/A; VDF L/A; IVS

## HOW THE WEST WAS WON *** PG
John Ford/Henry Hathaway/George Marshall
USA 1962
*Henry Fonda, Gregory Peck, James Stewart, George Peppard, Debbie Reynolds, John Wayne, Carroll Baker, Lee J. Cobb, Spencer Tracy, Karl Malden, Eli Wallach, Carolyn Jones, Richard Widmark, Walter Brennan, Raymond Massey*
An epic story that follows a family as it moves West, encountering many dangers along the way. The film loses much of its impact on TV (it was shown in Cinerama) but still retains considerable force, even if there are tedious moments in between the spectacular set-pieces. The fine score is by Alfred Newman. AA: Story/Screen (James R. Webb), Sound (Franklin E. Milton), Edit (Harold F. Kress).
WES 157 min (ort 165 min) Cut (2 sec)
B,V MGM

## HOW TO BEAT THE HIGH CO$T OF LIVING ** 15
Robert Scheerer USA 1980
*Susan St James, Jane Curtin, Jessica Lange, Richard Benjamin, Garrett Morris, Eddie Albert, Cathryn Damon, Ronnie Schell, Fred Willard, Dabney Coleman, Art Metrano, Sybil Danning (Sybelle Danninger)*
Three housewives plan a robbery at their local shopping centre as a way of making their housekeeping money go further. Worth a look, but the slight storyline could have been compressed into about half the running time.
COM 106 min (ort 110 min)
B,V,V2 RNK

## HOW TO GET AHEAD IN ADVERTISING ** 15
Bruce Robinson UK 1988
*Richard E. Grant, Rachel Ward, Richard Wilson, Jacqueline Tong, John Shrapnel, Susan Wooldridge. Mick Ford*
A bizarre parody on advertising, this sees a young advertising executive beset with doubts regarding his profession during a campaign for a new pimple cream. To add to his troubles a boil erupts on his neck, and develops into a talking head that spews forth a constant stream of abrasive advertising slogans. Written by Robinson, this ponderous satire on marketing has its funny moments, but is generally as tasteless as it is disagreeable.
COM 90 min
V CBS

## HOW TO KILL 400 DUPONTS *
Stefano Steno ITALY 1967
*Terry-Thomas, Johnny Dorelli, Margaret Lee, Didi Perego, Alfred Adam, Rosella Como, Jean Pierre Zola*
A master criminal eludes the police when he tries to kill 400 people.
Aka: ARRIVA DORELLIK; DORELLIK
COM 98 min
B,V,V2 VPD

## HOW TO MARRY A MILLIONAIRE ** U
Jean Negulesco USA 1953
*Marilyn Monroe, Betty Grable, Lauren Bacall, William Powell, Rory Calhoun, David Wayne, Alex D'Arcy, Fred Clark, Cameron Mitchell*
Three girls rent an expensive apartment in New York and go hunting for millionaires to marry. Monroe does her best in a dullish film that has a few bright moments, but not enough of them. A remake of a 1932 film "The Greeks Had A Word For Them".
COM 92 min (ort 95 min)
V CBS

## HOW TO MURDER YOUR WIFE *** PG
Richard Quine USA 1964
*Jack Lemmon, Virna Lisi, Terry-Thomas, Eddie Mayehoff, Claire Trevor, Sidney Blackmer, Max Showalter, Jack Albertson, Mary Wickes*
A cartoonist gets drunk and wakes up next morning to find himself married to a beautiful Italian girl. As he's a confirmed bachelor he feels honour bound to get rid of her. A delightfully wacky comedy that generally holds up pretty well, though towards the end it runs out of steam. A highlight is the courtroom scene.
COM 114 min (ort 118 min)
B,V WHV

## HOW TO PICK UP GIRLS! ** PG
Bill Persky USA 1978
*Desi Arnaz Jr, Bess Armstrong, Fred McCarren, Polly Bergen, Richard Dawson, Alan King, Abe Vigoda, Deborah Raffin, Rudolph Willrich, Forbesy Russell, Hollis Winick, Shelley Wyant, Kevin Conroy, Chrysis, Colette Blonigan*
A naive young country boy goes to New York and indulges in his fondness for the title subject. Silly, harmless, watchable and forgettable in that order.

Boa: book by Eric Weber.
COM 96 min (ort 100 min) mTV
B,V IMPACT/ODY

## HOW TO SCORE WITH GIRLS *
Ogden Lowell USA 1980
*Ron Osborne, Larry Jacobs, Richard Young, Sandra*
*McKnight, Arlana Blue, Janice Fuller*
A softcore sex comedy that masquerades as advice to
the loveless.
A 77 min
B,V MOVTIM

## HOW TO STEAL A MILLION *** U
William Wyler USA 1966
*Audrey Hepburn, Peter O'Toole, Charles Boyer, Eli*
*Wallach, Hugh Griffith*
A sophisticated comedy about a million dollar art
theft at a Paris museum, with Hepburn and O'Toole
working well together and generally overcoming the
sluggishness of the script.
COM 116 min (ort 127 min)
B,V CBS

## HOW TO STUFF A WILD BIKINI * U
William Asher USA 1965
*Annette Funicello, Dwayne Hickman, Brian Donlevy,*
*Buster Keaton, Mickey Rooney, Harvey Lembeck,*
*Beverly Adams, Jody McCrea, John Ashley, Frankie*
*Avalon*
Another one of those dreary "Beach Party" comedies,
with an advertising man out to find a typical "girl next
door". Followed by THE GHOST IN THE INVISIBLE
BIKINI.
COM 97 min
V RCA

## HOW TO SUCCEED IN BUSINESS WITHOUT U
## REALLY TRYING ***
David Swift USA 1967
*Robert Morse, Rudy Vallee, Michele Lee, Anthony*
*Teague, Maureen Arthur, Sammy Smith*
A window cleaner advances to the top of a New York
company with the aid of a helpful handbook. An
enjoyable and brash musical that moves along at a
good pace and has several well-staged musical num-
bers. Songs (by Frank Loesser) include: "I Believe In
You" and "Brotherhood Of Man".
Boa: novel by Stephen Mead/musical Abe Burrows.
MUS 121 min
B,V WHV

## HOW TO SUCCEED WITH SEX *
Bert I. Gordon USA 1969
*Zack Taylor, Mary Jane Carpenter, Keith London*
An addle-brained sex comedy of mimimal plot.
A 75 min
B,V INT/CBS

## HOWARD: A NEW BREED OF HERO * PG
William Huyck USA 1986
*Lea Thompson, Tim Robbins, Jeffrey Jones, Paul*
*Guilfoyle, Liz Sagal, Holly Robinson, Dominique*
*Davalos, Tommy Swerdlow, Richard Edson, Miles*
*Chaplin*
A duck from another planet mysteriously arrives on
Earth but is far from impressed by what he sees. A
misguided and mistaken attempt to take a Marvel
comic-strip creation and bring it to the screen.
Aka: HOWARD THE DUCK
COM 105 min (ort 111 min) (Cut at film release)
B,V CIC

## HOWARDS OF VIRGINIA, THE *** U
Frank Lloyd USA 1940
*Cary Grant, Martha Scott, Cedric Hardwicke, Alan*
*Marshal, Richard Carlson, Paul Kelly, Irving Bacon,*
*Elizabeth Risdon, Anne Revere, Tom Drake, Phil*
*Taylor, Rita Quigley, Libby Taylor, Richard Gaines,*

*George Houston*
A backwoods man is catapulted into Virginia society
when he marries a young aristocratic lady. The couple
set up home in the wilderness, but the American
Revolution shatters their happiness and they find
themselves supporting opposite sides in the conflict.
An overlong but patriotic and often rousing melodra-
ma, slightly spoilt by poor casting (though Houston is
worth a look for his portrayal of George Washington).
Aka: TREE OF LIBERTY, THE
Boa: novel Tree Of Liberty by E. Page.
DRA 111 min (ort 117 min) B/W
V RCA

## HOWLING, THE *** 18
Joe Dante USA 1980
*Dee Wallace, Patrick Macnee, Dennis Dugan,*
*Christopher Stone, Belinda Balaski, Kevin McCarthy,*
*John Carradine, Slim Pickens, Elisabeth Brooks, Dick*
*Miller*
A strange Californian encounter group community is
in reality a den of werewolves, in this spoof full of
film-buff jokes. The superb special effects are by Rob
Bottin. Followed by several "sequels" that are, in
reality, unrelated to this film.
HOR 90 min
B,V,LV EHE; CH5 (VHS only)

## HOWLING 2, THE * 18
Phillipe Mora USA 1984
*Christopher Lee, Reb Brown, Annie McEnroe, Marsha*
*A. Hunt, Ferdy Mayne, Sybil Danning (Sybelle*
*Danninger), Judd Omen, Jimmy Nail*
More werewolf nonsense in darkest Transylvania, as
an expert leads an expedition to destroy a werewolf
queen. Unrelated to the 1981 film, this clumsy
attempt at parody is one big dud.
Aka: HOWLING 2, THE: YOUR SISTER IS A
WEREWOLF
HOR 87 min (ort 90 min)
B,V GHV; VCC (VHS only)

## HOWLING 3 ** 18
Phillippe Mora AUSTRALIA 1987
*Barry Otto, Imogen Annersley, Leigh Biolos, Max*
*Fairchild, Dasha Blahova, Frank Thring, Michael*
*Pate, Ralph Cotterill, Barry Humphries*
Learning that werewolves are to be found in the
outback, a professor goes off to find them and discovers
a marsupial variety. He later casts his lot in with
them in the face of government plans for their
eradication. A gentle but uneven spoof on this horror
genre, with a few amusing touches such as Thring as a
Hitchcock-like director and Annersley's pretty female
werewolf who carries her child in a pouch on her belly.
Third film in the series.
Aka: HOWLING 3: THE MARSUPIALS
HOR 94 min
B,V PRES

## HOWLING 4: THE ORIGINAL NIGHTMARE *** 18
John Hough UK 1988
*Romy Windsor, Michael T. Weiss, Suzanne Severeid,*
*Anthony Hamilton*
A female writer is plagued by a series of disturbing
visions and decides to take a much-needed holiday in
the countryside, staying at a remote cottage her
husband has rented. However, her visions worsen and
she is soon drawn into a sinister and frightening
mystery. Despite being slow to develop, this effective
chiller is well worth a look.
HOR 89 min
V PRES

## HOWLING 5: THE RE-BIRTH * 15
Cedric Sundstrom USA 1989
*Philip Davis, Victoria Catlin, Ben Cole, Elizabeth She,*
*Mary Stavin*
Only the title bears any relation to the earlier films,

with this in-name-only sequel following the adventures of a group of European travellers who take refuge at a spooky castle that has been shut up for 500 years. The werewolf doesn't appear until near the end, by which time one no longer cares.
HOR                                                    99 min
V                                                        VES

**HOWZER ***                                             15
                           USA                          1972
*Royal Dano, Olive Deering, Virgil Frye*
A father's vengeance destroys childhood aspirations in this competent and well made melodrama.
DRA                                                    79 min
B,V                                                     POLY

**HUCKLEBERRY FINN ****
Robert Totten          USA                              1975
*Ron Howard, Donny Most, Antonio Fargas, Jack Elam, Royal Dano, Rance Howard, Merle Haggard, Clint Howard, Jean Howard, George "Shug" Fisher, Sarah Selby, Bill Erwin, Frederic Downs, James Almanzar, Patty Weaver, Woodrow Chambliss*
Film version of the famous classic that endures a folksy treatment and the loss of some of the novel's more interesting and critical aspects. OK as a pleasant family movie but of no great depth.
Boa: novel The Adventures Of Huckleberry Finn by Mark Twain.
A/AD                                               72 min mTV
B,V                                                     RNK

**HUE AND CRY ***
Charles Crichton       UK                               1946
*Harry Fowler, Alastair Sim, Jack Warner, Joan Dowling, Jack Lambert, Valerie White, Frederick Piper, Vida Hope, Gerald Fox, Grace Arnold, Douglas Barr, Stanley Escane, Ian Dawson, Gerald Fox, Paul Demel, Joey Carr, Robin Hughes*
Crooks use a boys' comic-paper to pass information for robberies, but fail to reckon with the resourcefulness of the youngsters. An excellent film with a period charm of its own. A highlight is the appearance by Sim, as the slightly dotty writer whose stories are used by the crooks. The script is by T.E.B. Clarke.
DRA                                   78 min (ort 82 min) B/W
B,V                                                    TEVP

**HUGO AND JOSEPHINE ***
Kjell Grade            SWEDEN                            1967
*Frederick Beckten, Marie Ohman, Inga Landgre, Helena Brodin, Beppe Wolgers*
A lonely eight-year-old girl finds a friend of her own age in this charming Swedish story.
Aka: HUGO OCH JOSEPHINE
JUV                                                    90 min
V                                                        INT

**HUGO THE HIPPO ***                                       U
William Feigenbaum     USA                              1976
*Voices of: Paul Lynde, Burl Ives, Robert Morley, Marie Osmond, Jimmy Osmond*
A story of a struggle between hippos and sharks on the island of Zanzibar, and of a little hippo who escapes from Zanzibar and befriends an African boy. A pleasant kiddies' musical animation.
CAR                                                    91 min
B,V,V2                             IFS L/A; HOLLY (VHS only)

**HULLABALOO OVER GEORGE AND BONNIE'S PICTURES ****
James Ivory            INDIA                             1978
*Peggy Ashcroft, Larry Pine, Aparna Sen*
An impoverished maharajah and his sister decide to sell some pictures, and various people vie with each other for the right to buy them.
DRA                                                    82 min
B,V                                            MVM; PVG/VIR

**HUMAN DUPLICATORS, THE ****
Hugo Grimaldi          USA                              1965
*George Nader, Dolores Faith, Barbara Nichols, George Macready, Hugh Beaumont, Richard Arlen, Richard Kiel*
Aliens decide to take over Earth by using android duplicates of human beings. A low-budget production, whose few good ideas never get a chance to develop.
FAN                                   80 min (ort 82 min)
B,V,V2                                                  HOK

**HUMAN ERROR ***                                          PG
Clyde Ware             USA                              1989
*Susanne Wouk, Vincent Cobb, Rob Garrison, Joe Estevez*
A revenge movie with an intriguing and original premise. A man designs a nuclear-proof shelter and agrees to test it with his family, but is unaware that they are all the subjects of an experiment involving controlled exposure to radiation. This eventually kills his wife and children, and our designer sets out to have his revenge.
HOR                                                   103 min
V                                                        VPD

**HUMAN FACTOR, THE ***                                    18
Edward Dmytryck        ITALY/UK                         1975
*George Kennedy, John Mills, Raf Vallone, Arthur Franz, Rita Tushingham, Frank Avianca, Haydee Politoff, Tom Hunter, Barry Sullivan, Flamma Verges, Danny Houston, Hillary Leaf, Robert Lowell, Shane Rimmer, Anne Ferguson*
A computer expert in Italy, tracks down the killers of his family, in this violent and bloody revenger.
DRA                                   91 min (ort 96 min)
B,V                                                     GHV

**HUMAN FACTOR, THE ****                                   15
Otto Preminger         UK                               1979
*Nicol Williamson, Richard Attenborough, Joop Doderer, John Gielgud, Derek Jacobi, Robert Morley, Ann Todd, Richard Vernon, Iman, Keith Marsh, Anthony Woodruff, Gary Forbes, Angela Forbes, Tony Haygarth, Paul Curran*
An innocent man is suspected of being a mole in the Foreign Office and is forced to defect to Russia. Despite the fine cast and an intelligent script by Tom Stoppard, the results are disappointing.
Boa: novel by Graham Greene.
DRA                               115 min; 110 min (VCC)
B,V                               RNK; VCC (VHS only)

**HUMAN JUNGLE, THE ***                                    PG
Joseph M. Newman       USA                              1954
*Gary Merril, Jan Sterling, Paula Raymond, Emile Meyer, Regis Toomey, Chuck Connors*
One day in the life of a busy American police station done in a low-key documentary fashion. Not a great film, but solid and very well done. The script is by William Sackheim and Daniel Fuchs.
DRA                                                    82 min
V                                           VMA; STABL

**HUMANOID DEFENDER ****                                   PG
Ron Satlof             USA                              1985
*Terence Knox, Gary Kaspar, William Lucking, Aimee Eccles*
A human male is genetically cloned and grows to maturity at a greatly accelerated pace. He develops some special powers and not surprisingly, the military soon have a sinister interest in him. Average.
FAN                                  89 min Cut (4 sec)
B,V                                                     CIC

**HUMANOID WOMAN ****                                      PG
Richard Victor         USSR                             1982
*Yelena Metelkina, Nadezhda Sementsova, Vatsalv Dvorzhetsky, Alexander Lazarev, Ivan Ledogora*
The beautiful title creature, survives the destruction

of her space probe and comes to Earth, in this little-known Russian science fiction tale.
Aka: CHEREZ TERNII K ZVEZDAM; PER ASPERA AD ASTRA; THORNY WAY TO THE STARS, THE; TO THE STARS
FAN                                              91 min
V                                                XTASY

## HUMANOID, THE **                          PG
George B. Lewis        ITALY                 1979
*Richard Kiel, Corinne Clery, Arthur Kennedy, Barbara Bach*
A laughable low-grade Italian fantasy, with an evil warlord converting Kiel into a powerful automaton, as part of his plan to gain control of a benignly ruled Galactic Empire. Mixed up with this tale is some downright peculiar mysticism, as a strange little boy from an unknown place (Tibet is implied) helps Kiel regain his volition and defeat this threat. The film does have some good moments, but is sorely in need of a better script.
FAN                              96 min Cut (25 sec)
B,V                                              RCA

## HUMONGOUS *                                18
Paul Lynch             CANADA                1981
*Janet Julian, David Wallace, Layne Coleman, Janit Baldwin, John Wildman*
A human beast rapes and kills a group of youngsters, whose boat is wrecked on a small island. Since most of the action takes place in the dark, we never get a good look at the monster; no great loss judging from the low standard in all other departments.
HOR              89 min (ort 93 min) Cut (1 min 3 sec)
B,V,V2                                           EHE

## HUNCHBACK HAIRBALL OF L.A., THE *         15
Jeremy Kagan           USA                   1990
*Allan Katz, Corey Parker, Cindy Williams, Melora Hardin*
Campus-comedy about a strange Quasimodo-like character who lives in a clock tower. After attempting the rescue of a pretty girl student he is eventually entrusted to the care of a none-too-bright student who teachers him to speak. A juvenile and tasteless affair that takes its single idea and drives it into the ground.
COM                                          105 min
V                                                VES

## HUNCHBACK OF NOTRE DAME, THE ***          PG
Michael Tuchner        USA                   1982
*Anthony Hopkins, Derek Jacobi, Lesley-Anne Down, Robert Powell, John Gielgud, David Suchet, Gerry Sundquist, Tim Piggott-Smith, Alan Webb, Roland Culver, Nigel Hawthorne, Rosalie Crutchley, Joseph Blatchley, Dave Hill*
A spirited version of the Hugo classic that remains faithful to the novel, and boasts Hopkins' excellent characterisation as Quasimodo, and John Stoll's detailed replica of Notre Dame Cathedral, built at Pinewood Studios, England. The adaptation of the novel is by John Gay.
Boa: novel by Victor Hugo.
DRA                     102 min (ort 150 min) mTV
B,V                                              RCA

## HUNCHBACK OF NOTRE DAME, THE ***
Wallace Worsley        USA                   1923
*Lon Chaney, Patsy Ruth Miller, Norman Kerry, Ernest Torrance, Tully Marshall, Gladys Brockwell, Kate Lester, Brandon Hurst*
An early version of this classic story, of the deformed bellringer of Notre Dame Cathedral and his unrequited love for a gypsy girl he rescues from death. Though silent, the lavish sets and incredible make-up of Chaney, ensure that this film stands the test of time.
Boa: novel by Victor Hugo.

DRA                                 93 min B/W silent
B,V                                          SPEC/POLY

## HUNCHBACK OF NOTRE DAME, THE ****        PG
William Dieterle       USA                   1939
*Charles Laughton, Cedric Hardwicke, Maureen O'Hara, Thomas Mitchell, Edmond O'Brien, Walter Hampden, George Zucco*
Laughton gives a most moving performance in this first sound version of the classic tale, as the lame and deformed bellringer of the Cathedral who is obliged to do his master's bidding when the latter (Hardwicke) falls in love with a gypsy girl. A lavish recreation of Paris of the Middle Ages that spares no expense – the assault on the Cathedral is a high-spot.
Boa: novel by Victor Hugo.
DRA                                       112 min B/W
B,V                     TEVP L/A; HER L/A; CH5

## HUNDRA **                                  18
Matt Cimber (Matteo Ottaviano)
                       SPAIN/USA             1983
*Laurence Landon, John Ghaffari, Marisa Casal*
A female warrior avenges the killing of her fellow tribeswomen in this trashy but enjoyable sword-and-sorcery epic.
FAN                           95 min (ort 104 min)
B,V                                              TEVP

## HUNGER, THE **                             18
Tony Scott             USA                   1983
*Catherine Deneuve, Susan Sarandon, David Bowie, Cliff De Young, Beth Ehlers, Dan Hedaya, Ann Magnuson, Willem Dafoe*
Two vampires live together in New York. One of them suddenly starts to age and the other is forced to try and find some way of helping him. The ageing scene is the film's highlight in an otherwise fairly bland effort.
Boa: novel by Whitley Strieber.
HOR                            92 min (ort 97 min)
V                                                MGM

## HUNK **                                    PG
Lawrence Bassoff       USA                   1986
*John Allen Nelson, Steve Levitt, Deborah Shelton, Rebeccah Bush, James Coco, Robert Morse, Avery Schreiber*
A computer wizard without any social graces, sells his soul to the Devil to become an irresistible lady's man. After the transformation, he schemes to find a way out of the contract. A foolish and muddled piece of nonsense, carried off by a good cast. Coco plays the Devil in an inspired piece of casting.
COM                            98 min (ort 102 min)
B,V                                              VES

## HUNT FOR RED OCTOBER, THE ****           PG
John McTiernan         USA                   1990
*Sean Connery, Alec Baldwin, Sam Neill, Tim Curry, Peter Firth, James Earl Jones, Scott Glenn, Joss Ackland, Richard Jordan, Courtney B. Vance, Jeffrey Jones*
Connery plays the captain of a Soviet nuclear sub who may be planning to use the vessel to defect to the West during its maiden voyage, or may be about to launch an attack. Meanwhile, Western intelligence agencies attempt to predict his every move. A long, complex and very tense Cold War thriller, with a superb cast and great direction.
Boa: novel by Tom Clancy.
THR                           130 min (ort 135 min)
V                                                CIC

## HUNTED, THE *                              15
Joseph Losey           UK                    1969
*Robert Shaw, Malcolm McDowell, Henry Woolf, Christopher Malcolm, Andrew Bradford, Roger Lloyd Pack, Pamela Brown*
Two men on the run in an unspecified country are

hunted by helicopter. Relentlessly boring, this film may be symbolic or allegorical, but good cinema it ain't.
Aka: FIGURES IN A LANDSCAPE
Boa: novel Figures In A Landscape by Barry Englund.
A/AD                                            110 min
B,V                                               CBS

## HUNTER OF THE UNKNOWN **                    18
Simon Sterling (Sergio Sollima)
              ITALY/FRANCE/SPAIN          1966
*Giorgio Ardisson, Frank Wolff, Evi Marandi*
A number of agents are sent to an island to investigate reports of a strange new weapon, in this tedious and overlong European spy thriller.
Aka: AGENTE 353, MASSACRO AL SOLE; AGENTE 353 ENVIADO SPECIAL; 353 AGENTE ESPECIAL
THR                                            124 min
B,V                                               PRV

## HUNTER, THE **                              15
Buzz Kulik              USA              1980
*Steve McQueen, Eli Wallach, LeVar Burton, Ben Johnson, Kathryn Harrold, Tracey Walter*
The true story of a modern-day bounty hunter who goes after people who have skipped bail. McQueen's last film and not a particularly well made or inspiring one, though it does have a few humorous moments. Based on the life of bounty hunter Ralph (Pappy) Thorson, this slack and unrewarding affair is a poor tribute to the late actor.
Boa: book by Christopher Keane.
A/AD                          98 min (ort 117 min)
V/h                                               CIC

## HUNTER'S BLOOD **                           18
Robert Hughes          USA              1986
*Clu Gulager, Sam Bottoms, Ken Swafford, Joey Travolta, Kim Delaney, Mayf Nutter*
An extremely violent tale of a group of deer hunters on holiday in Arkansas, who are attacked by a gang of deer poachers. Strongly echoes DELIVERANCE, but with none of that film's lightness of touch.
A/AD                          97 min (ort 102 min)
B,V                                          PAL; PVG

## HUNTER'S CROSSING **                        18
Teddy Page              USA              1985
*Richard Harrison, Bruce Baron, Philip Gamboa*
Routine Vietnam saga about American POWs left behind after the fall of Saigon.
WAR                                             90 min
B,V                                               ARF

## HUNTERS OF THE GOLDEN COBRA *
Anthony M. Dawson (Antonio Margheriti)
              ITALY                       1982
*David Warbeck, John Steiner, Almanta Suska, Alan Collins*
Two American soldiers pursue a Japanese general in order to steal a priceless treasure he owns.
Aka: I PREDATORI DEL COBRA D'ORO; RAIDERS OF THE GOLDEN COBRA
A/AD                                            97 min
B,V,V2                                            EIV

## HUNTING PARTY, THE *                        18
Don Medford            USA              1971
*Oliver Reed, Candice Bergen, Gene Hackman, Simon Oakland, L.Q. Jones, Ronald Howard, Mitchell Ryan, G.D. Spradlin, Bernard Kay, William Watson, Rayford Barnes, Ralph Brown, Marian Collier, Max Slaten, Carlos Bravo, Deal Selmier*
A man raises a posse, to track down and kill the members of a gang who kidnapped and raped his wife. A fine cast is wasted in this unpleasant revenger that

has a lot in common with CHATO'S LAND.
WES      104 min (ort 132 min) Cut (1 min 43 sec)
B,V                                               WHV

## HURRICANE *                                 15
Jan Troell              USA              1979
*Jason Robards, Mia Farrow, Max Von Sydow, Trevor Howard, Dayton Ka'ne, Timothy Bottoms, James Keach*
A useless remake of a 1937 film about the simple life on a South Seas island plagued by a nasty governor and a hurricane. $22,000,000 was blown away on this dud.
Aka: FORBIDDEN PARADISE
Boa: novel by Charles Nordhof and James Norman Hall.
A/AD                                           119 min
B,V,V2                                            GHV

## HURRICANE EXPRESS **
Armand Schaefer/J.P. McGowan
              USA                         1932
*John Wayne, Shirley Grey, Tully Marshall, Conway Tearle, Joseph Girard, J. Farrell McDonald*
Feature version of a longer 12-part serial, about a young transport pilot who tries to catch a saboteur responsible for the train crash in which his father died. Average.
DRA                     77 min (ort 223 min) B/W
B,V,V2                              VCL/CBS; WDV

## HURRICANE, THE ****                         PG
John Ford              USA              1937
*Dorothy Lamour, John Hall, C. Aubrey Smith, Mary Astor, Raymond Massey, Thomas Mitchell, John Carradine, Jerome Cowan*
The peaceful life of a tropical island comes to an abrupt halt with the arrival of a new and evil-minded governor. Contains some classic hurricane scenes. Remade in 1979 at vast cost by the Swedish director Jan Troell. The fine score is by Alfred Newman. AA: Sound (Thomas T. Moulton).
Boa: novel by Charles Nordhof and James Norman Hall.
DRA                     99 min (ort 110 min) B/W
V                                                 VGM

## HURRY UP OR I'LL BE THIRTY **               15
Joseph Jacoby          USA              1973
*John Lefkowitz, Linda De Coff, Ronald Anton, Maureen Byrnes, Danny DeVito, Steve Inwood, Francis Gallagher, David Kirk, Selma Rogoff*
An amoral slob tries to steal his friend's woman, in this offbeat and quirky tale of a man trying to get his life into some order before he reaches thirty. Occasionally funny but a misfire most of the time.
Aka: FRIEND, THE (SOV)
COM                                             88 min
B,V                                 MMA; SOV; BVP

## HUSH LITTLE BABY DON'T YOU CRY ***          15
Don Hawks              USA              1984
*Emery L. Kedocia, Garry Giem, Tony Grant, Burt Douglas, Sharon Grady*
An intense child abuse story, in which a boy subjected to his uncle's perverse cruelties, grows up to become a loving father and husband. However, his childhood experiences have left him emotionally scarred and subject to rages of murderous intensity.
DRA                                            109 min
B,V                                 STARB L/A; PALAN

## HUSH, HUSH SWEET CHARLOTTE ***              15
Robert Aldrich          USA              1964
*Bette Davis, Olivia De Havilland, Joseph Cotten, Cecil Kellaway, Agnes Moorehead, Victor Buono, William Marshall, Mary Astor, Bruce Dern*
The story of a southern belle who lives for thirty-seven years in her lonely mansion tormented by her belief

that she killed her fiance. However, some strange events begin to convince her otherwise. A moody and generally absorbing tale, supported in large measure by the star cast.

DRA 133 min B/W
V CBS

## HUSSY *
Matthew Chapman   UK   1979
*Helen Mirren, John Shea, Daniel Chasin, Jenny Runacre, Paul Angelis, Murray Salem, Patti Boulaye, Marika Rivera, Hal Gallili, Sandy Ratcliff, Jill Melford, Andy Pantelidou, Linda Polan, Janet Amsden, Vanessa Furse*
A prostitute gets involved with gangsters and illicit drugs, but eventually makes a new life for herself and her child. A sleazy and exploitative dud.

DRA 85 min (ort 95 min)
B,V,V2 VIPCO

## HUSTLE *
Robert Aldrich   USA   1975
*Burt Reynolds, Catherine Deneuve, Ben Johnson, Paul Winfield, Eddie Albert, Eileen Brennan, Ernest Borgnine, Jack Carter, Catherine Bach*
An L.A. cop has a prostitute girlfriend who wants to get away from her sordid life. At the same time he is investigating a young girl's suicide which turns out to be the start of something far more serious. A repulsive and depressing story that climbs into the gutter and stays there.

DRA 120 min
B,V CIC

## HUSTLER SQUAD *
Cesar Gallardo
PHILIPPINES/USA   1976
*John Ericson, Karen Ericson, Nory Wright, Lynda Sinclaire, Ramon Revilia*
A group of prostitutes are used behind Japanese lines in the Philippines to seduce and kill the enemy.
Aka: DIRTY HALF DOZEN

WAR 98 min
B,V MOG; CBS

## HUSTLER, THE ****   15
Robert Rossen   USA   1961
*Paul Newman, Jackie Gleason, George C. Scott, Piper Laurie, Myron McCormick, Murray Hamilton, Michael Constantine*
A poolroom hustler hits rock bottom after a severe beating, but regains his self-respect when he wins a match against a legendary champ. The seedy and unpleasant world of poolroom hustlers and drifters is realistically brought to life in this stylish and memorable film. Followed 25 years later by an excellent sequel – THE COLOR OF MONEY. AA: Cin (Eugen Shuftan), Art/Set (Harry Horner/Gene Callahan).
Boa: novel by W. Tevis.

DRA 130 min B/W
B,V,V2 CBS

## HYSTERIA **   15
Freddie Francis   UK   1964
*Robert Webber, Lelia Goldoni, Anthony Newlands, Jennifer Jayne, Maurice Denham, Peter Woodthorpe, Sandra Boize, Sue Lloyd*
An American in London suffers from amnesia due to a car accident, and becomes entangled in a murder plot, in this convoluted and fairly unsatisfying thriller.

THR 82 min (ort 85 min) B/W
B,V MGM

## HYSTERICAL *   15
Chris Bearde   USA   1983
*William Hudson, Mark Hudson, Brett Hudson, Richard Kiel, Bud Cort, Julie Newmar, Cindy Pickett, Robert Donner, Murray Hamilton, Clint Walker, Keenan Wynn, Franklin Ajaye, Charlie Callas, Gary Owens*
A spoof on horror movies such as THE EXORCIST, THE AMITYVILLE HORROR etc. A small seaside town is invaded by ghouls, zombies, ghosts and other assorted undesirables. A dismal dud that could damage any actor's career.

COM 82 min (ort 86 min)
B,V EIV

# I

## I.F.O. *   PG
Ulli Lommel   USA   1985
*Carey Shearer, Kim Kincaid, Paul Rugg, Mark Drotman, Tony Lovett*
A teenage computer freak stumbles across a top-secret device belonging to the Air Force, which possesses a dangerous intelligence of its own. He activates it unaware that it is not really under his control. A foolish effort that is not even redeemed by good special effects.

FAN 81 min
B,V VIR

## I AM A CAMERA **
Henry Cornelius   UK   1955
*Julie Harris, Laurence Harvey, Shelley Winters, Ron Randell, Lea Seidl, Anton Diffring, Jean Gargoet, Frederick Valk, Tutte Lemkow, Patrick McGoohan, Stanley Maxted, Julia Arnall, Zoe Newton, Stan Bernard Trio*
A young writer observes Berlin life in the 1930s and develops a platonic relationship with a rather reckless English girl. A stolid adaptation of the work of Isherwood and Van Druten that is enlivened by a good performance from Harris. Remade with a lot more style (if with less verisimilitude) as CABARET.
Boa: short stories by Christopher Isherwood/play by John Van Druten.

DRA 95 min (ort 98 min) B/W
B,V CBS

## I CONFESS ***   PG
Alfred Hitchcock   USA   1953
*Montgomery Clift, Anne Baxter, Karl Malden, Brian Aherne, Dolly Haas, O.E. Hasse*
A priest hears a confession and refuses to reveal what he has heard to the police, even though he is suspected himself. Despite the limitations of the plot, Hitchcock manages to imbue this one with a fair degree of tension, even if the outcome is never in doubt. Set in Quebec, with good use made of this location.
Boa: play by Paul Anthelme.

DRA 90 min (ort 93 min) B/W
V WHV

## I DRINK YOUR BLOOD *
David Durston   USA
1970 (released 1971 after re-editing)
*Bhaskar, Jadine Wong, Ronda Fultz, George Patterson, Riley Mills, Richard Bowler, Tyde Kierney, John Damon, Elizabeth Marner-Brooks, Lynn Lowry, Iris Brooks, Alex Mann, Mike Gentry*
A bunch of hippies who are also into Satanism give LSD to an old man and in revenge his son injects the blood of a rabid dog into meat pies and gives them to the hippies, who turn into foaming, blood-crazed lunatics and go on a rampage. Controversy over this film led to it being extensively re-cut and re-edited and what might have been a powerful shocker is now no more than a repulsive and muddled mess.

HOR 82 min
B,V,V2 MED; VPD

## I HEARD THE OWL CALL MY NAME ***   U
Daryl Duke   CANADA/USA   1973
*Tom Courtenay, Dean Jagger, Paul Stanley, Marianne Jones, George Clutesi, Keith Pepper, Margaret Atleo*

A young priest is sent to work in a remote Indian village in British Columbia, in this lyrical and beautifully made film.
Boa: book by Margaret Craven.
DRA                                    74 min mTV
B,V                                         ODY

## I KNOW MY FIRST NAME IS STEVEN **
Larry Elikann        USA              1989
Cindy Pickett, John Ashton, Corin Nemec, Arliss Howard, Luke Edwards
Based on a true story, this tells of a 7-year-old boy who vanished in 1972 while on his way to school. Seven years later he turns up, but can remember little of his past life. A competent drama.
DRA                                    182 min
V/h                                         ODY

## I LIVE WITH ME DAD ***                 15
Paul Moloney     AUSTRALIA            1987
Peter Hehir, Haydon Samuels, Rebecca Gibney, Tony Hawkins, Gus Mercurio, Dennis Miller, Robyn Gibbes, Esben Storm
Sentimental tearjerker based on a real story, with a young boy living with his down-and-out loafer of a father, much against the wishes of the child welfare authorities. They present the boy's father with an ultimatum; get a job or lose the kid and the pair are split up despite the father's attempts to curtail his drinking. All ends happily however, but not before there have been a series of incidents in this competent but often harsh drama.
Boa: short story by Derry Moran.
DRA                                    91 min
B,V                                         CBS

## I MARRIED A CENTREFOLD *                PG
Peter Werner         USA              1984
Teri Copley, Timothy Daly, Diane Ladd, Todd Susman, Robert Hanley, Anson Williams, Roger Aaron Brown, Richard Jamison, Suzanne LaRusch, Jack Fletcher, Rick Podell, Sharon Wyatt, Steve Yochem, Tom Kindle, Robbi Morgan
An engineer becomes obsessed with a centrefold girl he sees on TV. He wins $500 by getting a date with her and they fall in love. But this is only the beginning of their problems. An adequate stop-gap, but no more than that.
COM                       92 min (ort 100 min) mTV
B,V                             PRV L/A; CH5

## I MISS YOU HUGS AND KISSES **           18
Murray Markowitz     USA              1978
Elke Sommer, Donald Pilon, Chuck Shamata, Cindy Girling, George Touliatos, Cec Linder, George Chuvalo, Richard Davidson, Miguel Fernandes, Michele Fansett, Corinna Carlson, Linda Sorenson, Susan Hogan, Larry Solway
Based on the murder trial of Peter Denter, this story begins at the time of the Hungarian uprising, and continues twenty years later with a series of mysterious murders.
Aka: DROP DEAD DEAREST; LEFT FOR DEAD
THR            82 min (ort 96 min) Cut (1 min 6 sec)
B,V                        PPL L/A; VFP L/A; HER

## I NEVER PROMISED YOU A ROSE GARDEN **  18
Anthony Page         USA              1977
Bibi Andersson, Kathleen Quinlan, Sylvia Sidney, Reni Santoni, Signe Hasso, Diane Varsi, Susan Tyrrell, Dennis Quaid
The story of a teenage girl undergoing treatment for schizophrenia which concentrates on the relationship between her and her psychiatrist. A ponderous account that benefits from its graphic approach, but never sufficiently to make it much better than average. See also STRANGE VOICES.
Boa: novel by Hannah Green.

DRA                            88 min (ort 96 min)
B,V                                         WHV

## I OUGHT TO BE IN PICTURES **            15
Herbert Ross         USA              1982
Walter Matthau, Ann-Margret, Dinah Manoff, Lance Guest, Lewis Smith
A young girl goes to Los Angeles to meet her divorced father, in the hope that he will help her get into movies as he works as a screenwriter. A tepid comedy that is redeemed by good performances. Scripted by Neil Simon from his play.
Boa: play by Neil Simon.
COM                                    104 min
B,V,V2,LV                                   CBS

## I REMEMBER MAMA **                       U
George Stevens       USA              1948
Barbara Bel Geddes, Irene Dunne, Oscar Homolka, Philip Dorn, Cedric Hardwicke, Edger Bergen, Rudy Vallee, Barbara O'Neil, Florence Bates, Ellen Corby
A saga of a Norwegian family in San Francisco and the mother's struggle to keep them together. All the vices and virtues of Hollywood films of this period, well written and acted but a trifle over-sentimental. Later formed the basis for a TV series in the USA.
Boa: play by John Van Druten/book Mama's Account by Kathryn Forbes.
DRA                       129 min (ort 134 min) B/W
V                                           VCC

## I SAW WHAT YOU DID ***                  18
Fred Walton          USA              1987
Tammy Lauren, Shawnee Smith, Robert Carradine, David Carradine, Candace Cameron
Remake of the 1965 film, with two teenage girls playing a silly phone prank on a man who has just committed a murder, and thus making themselves prime candidates for his next crime.
Boa: novel by Ursula Walter.
THR                                    90 min
B/sh, V/sh                                  CIC

## I WAKE UP SCREAMING ***                 PG
Bruce Humberstone    USA              1941
Betty Grable, Carole Landis, Victor Mature, Laird Cregar, William Gargan, Alan Mowbray, Allyn Joslyn, Elisha Cook Jr
An absorbing mystery tale in which the sister of a murdered model teams up with the chief suspect (Mature) in order to catch the real culprit, whilst all the while being pursued by a determined cop. Sharp, concise and highly atmospheric; the twist ending is as effective as it is unexpected. Remade as "Vicki".
Aka: HOT SPOT
Boa: novel by Steve Fisher.
DRA                        79 min (ort 82 min) B/W
V                                           CBS

## I WALK THE LINE **                      15
John Frankenheimer   USA              1970
Gregory Peck, Tuesday Weld, Estelle Parsons, Ralph Meeker, Lonny Chapman
A sheriff turns a blind eye to the criminal activities of a family of moonshiners, because he is obsessed with their daughter, but disaster strikes when a local government investigator arrives. An adequate formula melodrama, with a few plot twists to sustain attention.
Boa: novel An Exile by Madison Jones.
DRA                                    95 min
B,V                                         RCA

## I WALKED WITH A ZOMBIE ***
Jacques Tourneur     USA              1943
Frances Dee, Tom Conway, James Ellison, Edith Barrett, Christine Gordon, Theresa Harris, James Bell
A nurse takes a job on a voodoo-ridden Caribbean

island in this classic zombie tale, and finds that the legends have a basis in reality. Richly atmospheric, but somewhat hampered by the thin plot.
Osca: CRACKUP

| HOR | 66 min (ort 69 min) B/W |
| B,V | KVD |

## I WANT HIM DEAD **
Paolo Bianchini       ITALY
*Craig Hill, Dea Massari, Jose Manuel Martin*
Routine bang-bang Western revenger.
Aka: LO VOGLIO MORTO

| WES | 93 min |
| B,V | VPD |

## I WAS MONTY'S DOUBLE ***
John Guillermin       UK       1958
*John Mills, Cecil Parker, Michael Hordern, Leslie Phillips, Bryan Forbes, Marius Goring, Patrick Allen, M.E. Clifton-James, James Hayter, Sidney James, Vera Day, Victor Maddern, Marne Maitland, Alfie Bass, Duncan Lamont*
A well-made tale of an actor being used to confuse the Germans, by impersonating Montgomery in the North African campaign during WW2.
Aka: HELL, HEAVEN AND HOBOKEN
Boa: book by M.E. Clifton-James.

| WAR | 97 min (ort 100 min) B/W |
| V | WHV |

## I WILL FIGHT NO MORE FOREVER ***
Richard T. Heffron       USA       1975
*James Whitmore, Sam Elliott, Ned Romero, Nick Ramus, Emilio Delgado, John Kauffman, Linda Redfearn, Frank Sotonoma Salsedo, W. Vincent St Cyr, Deloy White, Charles Ynfante*
Story of Chief Joseph of the Nez Perce Indians, who tried to lead his people from the reservation to sanctuary in Canada and his conflict with the US Army. A moving and memorable dramatisation. The script is by Jeb Rosebrook and Theodore Strauss.
Boa: novel Where the Sun Now Stands by Will Henry.

| DRA | 105 min mTV |
| B,V | GHV |

## I WILL IF YOU WILL ***                    18
Nello Rossati       ITALY       1975
*Ursula Andress, Luciana Paluzzi, Jack Palance, Lino Toffolo, Duilio Del Prete, Mario Pisu, Carla Romanelli*
A wine merchant's relatives engage a sexy nurse, in the hope of finishing the old man off, but this plan backfires when she seduces every other male in the house to satisfy her appetite. Fair Italian sex film with comic overtones.
Aka: L'INFERMIERA; NURSE, THE; SECRETS OF A SENSUOUS NURSE (BEV); SENSUOUS NURSE, THE

| A | 73 min (ort 85 min) |
| B,V | VUL L/A; 18PLAT/TOW; PHE (VHS only); BEV; KRP |

## I WILL, I WILL . . . FOR NOW **              15
Norman Panama       USA       1975
*Diane Keaton, Elliott Gould, Paul Sorvino, Victoria Principal, Robert Alda, Candy Clark*
A divorced couple come together again, but their unsatisfactory sex-life makes them seek help at a clinic, in this tasteless satire of sex-therapists and their patients.

| COM | 103 min (ort 109 min) |
| B,V | CINE |

## I WONDER WHO'S KILLING HER NOW? **
Steven Hilliard Stern       USA       1976
*Bob Dishy, Joanna Barnes, Bill Dana, Vito Scotti*
Satire on the many aspects of modern life, revolving around a husband who takes out a contract on his wife's life, but gets cold feet at the last moment. A spotty and mildly diverting farce, written by Mickey

Rose (who was Woody Allen's one-time collaborator).

| COM | 95 min |
| B,V | HVM |

## I-MAN **                                    U
Corey Allen       USA       1986
*Scott Bakula, Ellen Bry, Joey Cramer, John Bloom, Herschel Bernardi, John Anderson, Dale Wilson, Cindy Higgins, Charles E. Siegel, Joseph Golland, Jan Tracey, George Josef, Campbell Lane, Terry Moore, Lillian Carlson*
A cab driver gains super-powers, when a canister containing a sample of a gas from outer space is accidentally released. A bland Disney pilot for a prospective series.

| FAN | 91 min (ort 100 min) mTV |
| B,V | RNK L/A; WDV |

## I, MONSTER ***
Stephen Weeks       UK       1971
*Christopher Lee, Peter Cushing, Mike Raven, Richard Hurndall, Kenneth J. Warren, George Merritt, Susan Jameson, Marjie Lawrence, Aimee Delamain*
Extremely competent reworking of the Jekyll and Hyde theme, with Lee quite convincing as the doctor whose thirst for knowledge forces him to experiment on himself. Despite a slow start and some awkward melodramatic flourishes, the film builds up to a satisfactory climax.
Boa: novella The Strange Case Of Dr Jekyll And Mr Hyde by Robert Louis Stevenson.

| HOR | 74 min |
| B,V | TEVP |

## I, THE JURY **                              18
Richard T. Heffron       USA       1982
*Armand Assante, Barbara Carrera, Alan King, Laurene Landon, Geoffrey Lewis, Paul Sorvino, Judson Scott*
Updated version of the 1953 film based on Spillane's private eye Mike Hammer who is out for revenge on those who killed his friend. A harsh and brutal thriller that is sorely in need of a more consistent script. Written by Larry Cohen.
Boa: novel by Mickey Spillane.

| DRA | 102 min (ort 111 min) Cut (4 min) |
| V | WHV |

## ICE CASTLES **                             PG
Donald Wyre       USA       1978
*Robby Benson, Lynn-Holly Johnson, Colleen Dewhurst, Tom Skerritt, Jennifer Warren, David Huffman*
Boy meets girl and love blossoms at an ice-rink. He goes into hockey and she becomes a champion ice-skater, but an accident blinds her. A slick and manipulative tearjerker that's undeniably effective, but leaves no permanent impression.

| DRA | 105 min (ort 109 min) |
| V | RCA |

## ICE COLD IN ALEX ***                       PG
J. Lee Thompson       UK       1960
*John Mills, Sylvia Sims, Anthony Quayle, Harry Andrews, Liam Redmond, Peter Arne, Diane Clare, Richard Leech, Allan Cuthbertson, David Lodge*
A British ambulance driver in Libya in 1942, successfully charts his vehicle through German minefields and other dangers. An overlong but extremely engaging war film, that benefits from good direction and solid performances.
Aka: DESERT ATTACK
Boa: novel by Christopher Landon.

| WAR | 125 min (ort 132 min) B/W |
| B,V | TEVP; WHV (VHS only) |

## ICE PIRATES, THE **                         15
Stuart Raffill       USA       1984

Robert Urich, Mary Crosby, Michael D. Roberts, John
Matuszak, Anjelica Huston, Ron Perlman, John
Carradine, Robert Symonds
A spoof space opera about a future in which water is
the most important commodity. A gang of space
pirates sets out to destroy an evil empire that controls
the water supply of a distant empire. With a talky
script that is too clever by half, this one never gets a
chance to get going.
FAN                                           91 min
B,V                                            MGM

### ICE STATION ZEBRA **                        U
John Sturges            USA              1968
Rock Hudson, Ernest Borgnine, Patrick McGoohan,
Jim Brown, Tony Bill, Lloyd Nolan, Gerald S.
O'Loughlin, Alf Kjellin
Cold War tale of murder and espionage at a remote
Arctic station, with Hudson as the commander of a
submarine sailing to the North Pole, where he must
obtain the hidden film from an American spy satellite
before it falls into Russian hands. A mixture of
tension and tedium, as the various MacLean plot
convolutions unravel. Written by Douglas Heyes and
Harry Julian Fink.
Boa: novel by Alistair MacLean.
A/AD                           139 min (ort 148 min)
V                                              MGM

### ICEMAN ***                                   PG
Fred Schepisi          CANADA             1984
Timothy Hutton, Lindsay Crouse, John Lone, Josef
Sommer, David Straithairn, Danny Glover
A Neanderthal man is found frozen in a block of ice
and is thawed out. Most of the scientists regard him as
a mere specimen, only one person looks on him as a
human being. A surprisingly effective fantasy that
owes much to a great performance from Lone as the
title character. The score is by Bruce Smeaton.
FAN                                           99 min
B,V                                            CIC

### IDAHO TRANSFER **                           15
Peter Fonda             USA              1973
Kelly Bohanan, Keith Carradine, Kevin Hearst,
Caroline Hildebrand
On the eve of WW3, a scientist is preparing to transfer
a small group of people into the future.
Aka: DERANGED (SATPRO)
FAN                             82 min (ort 90 min)
B,V,V2              FOU L/A; BRNX L/A; SATPRO

### IDEAL HUSBAND, AN **                         U
Alexandra Korda         UK               1947
Paulette Goddard, Michael Wilding, Diana Wynyard,
C. Aubrey Smith, Glynis Johns, Hugh Williams,
Constance Collier, Christine Norden, Harriette Johns,
Michael Medwin, Michael Anthony, Fred Groves
A diplomat's career is threatened when an old flame
turns up, in this stuffy and stilted adaptation of
Wilde's comedy of manners.
Boa: play by Oscar Wilde.
DRA                        92 min (ort 96 min) B/W
B,V                                  POLY; CENVID

### IDOLMAKER, THE **                           15
Taylor Hackford          USA             1980
Ray Sharkey, Tovah Feldshuh, Paul Land, Peter
Gallagher, Joe Pantoliano, Maureen McCormick,
Olympia Dukakis
Fictionalised story of 1950s rock producer Bob Mar-
cucci, who guided performers such as Frankie Avalon
and Fabian to stardom. Good material is never
developed, in a cumbersome film that makes a couple
of salient points and then falters. The rock score is by
Jeff Barry.
DRA                            114 min (ort 119 min)
B/sh, V/sh                                     WHV

### IF . . . **                                  15
Lindsay Anderson        UK               1968
Malcolm McDowell, David Wood, Richard Warwick,
Robert Swann, Peter Jeffrey, Christine Noonan,
Arthur Lowe, Mona Washbourne, Graham Crowden,
Anthony Nicholls, Geoffrey Chater, Hugh Thomas,
Rupert Webster, Mary McLeod
A strange, allegorical, somewhat empty film, set in a
boys' public school and full of rather meaningless
images that you can take any way you like. Is it an
anti-establishment satire? You tell me.
DRA              107 min (ort 111 min) (B/W in parts)
B,V                                            CIC

### IF DON JUAN WERE A WOMAN **                 18
Roger Vadim            FRANCE             1973
Brigitte Bardot, Jane Birkin, Maurice Ronet, Michelle
Sand, Robert Hossein, Robert Walker Jr
A torrid tale of love, passion and murder with Bardot
cast as a female Don Juan who delights in conquering
men and then ruining them. A good vehicle for
Bardot, but not really memorable on any other count.
Aka: DON JUAN 73; DON JUAN 73 OR IF DON
JUAN WERE A WOMAN; DON JUAN 73 OU SI
DON JUAN ETAIT UNE FEMME; MS. DON JUAN;
SI DON JUAN ETAIT UNE FEMME
DRA                             87 min (ort 95 min)
V                                           CASPIC

### IF EVER I SEE YOU AGAIN *                    PG
Joe Brooks              USA              1978
Joe Brooks, Shelley Hack, Jerry Keller, Jimmy
Breslin, George Plimpton, Danielle Brisebois
A couple find that the pressures of their jobs and
family commitments threaten to put paid to their love
affair. A dreary and soppy follow-up to YOU LIGHT
UP MY LIFE, this gave Hack her starring debut but
failed to make use of her talents. Written and directed
by Brooks.
DRA                            100 min (ort 105 min)
B,V                                            POLY

### IF IT'S TUESDAY, IT STILL MUST              PG
### BE BELGIUM **
Bob Sweeney             USA              1987
Claude Akins, Lou Liberatore, Courtney Cox, Faith
Ford, Stephen Furst, Peter Graves, Bruce Weitz, Anna
Maria Horsford, Kiel Martin, Kene Holiday, David
Leisure, Tracy Nelson, Richard Moll, Doris Roberts
Planned as a showcase for various NBC stars of the
time, this weak, partial remake of the 1969 film, has
our busload of American tourists now spending most
of their time searching for the driver's missing
daughter.
COM                                        96 min mTV
B,V                                            MGM

### IF LOOKS COULD KILL *                        18
Chuck Vincent           USA              1987
Kim Lambert, Tim Gail, Alan Fisler
A man hired to spy on some individuals, finds himself
getting drawn into the obligatory web of mystery and
intrigue in this formula tale.
THR                         84 min Cut (1 min 22 sec)
B,V                                            NOVA

### IF TOMORROW COMES ***                       15
Jerry London            USA              1986
Madolyn Smith, Tom Berenger, David Keith, Richard
Kiley, Jack Weston, Liam Neeson, Joe Cortese, George
DiCenzo, Susan Hess, Jeffrey Jones, John Laughlin,
Susan Tyrell, Harold Sylvester, Lane Smith, C.C.H.
Pounder
The slick story of a pair of romantically involved jewel
thieves, and their attempts to keep one step ahead of a
persistent insurance investigator. Entertaining non-
sense helped along by colourful international loca-
tions that include Cannes, Nice, New Orleans and
Amsterdam. First shown in three parts.

Boa: novel by Sidney Sheldon.
DRA            298 min (2 cassettes – ort 420 min) mTV
B,V                                                    CBS

### IF YOU DON'T STOP IT YOU'LL GO BLIND **   18
Bob Levy/Keefe Brasselle
                    USA                    1974
*George Spencer, Pat Wright, Jane Kellem, Garth*
*Pilsbury, Russ Marin, Pat McCormick*
A feeble collection of sketches forming a mild sex
comedy. Followed in 1980 by CAN I DO IT TILL I
NEED GLASSES?
Aka: YOU MUST BE JOKING
COM                                        80 min
B,V,V2             VPD; CHV (Betamax and VHS only)

### IKE ***                                      PG
Boris Sagal/Melville Shavelson
                    USA                    1979
*Robert Duvall, Lee Remick, Dana Andrews, J.D.*
*Cannon, Darren McGavin, Paul Gleason, Laurence*
*Luckinbill, Wensley Pithey, Ian Richardson, William*
*Schallert, Stephen Roberts, Wolfgang Preiss, Bonnie*
*Bartlett*
An enjoyable biopic on the WW2 US general, that
concentrates on his affair with his female driver. Cut
down from a six-hour TV mini-series and well above-
average, mainly thanks to a fine performance from
Remick as Kay Summersby, on whose memoirs this
film is largely based.
Aka: IKE: THE WAR YEARS
Boa: book Past Forgetting by Kay Summersby
Morgan.
DRA                    180 min (ort 291 min) mTV
B,V                                            HER

### I'LL BE SEEING YOU ***
William Dieterle       USA                 1944
*Ginger Rogers, Joseph Cotten, Shirley Temple, Spring*
*Byington, Tom Tully, Chill Wills, John Derek*
A female convict on leave, meets and falls for a
shell-shocked soldier. A standard Hollywood celebra-
tion of sentiment, but done with considerable
panache.
Boa: novel by Charles Martin.
DRA                                      85 min B/W
B,V                                            GHV

### I'LL GET YOU FOR THIS **
Joseph M. Newman       UK                  1950
*George Raft, Colleen Gray, Greta Gynt, Enzo Staiola,*
*Charles Goldner, Walter Rilla, Martin Benson, Peter*
*Illing, Hugh French, Peter Bull, Donald Stewart,*
*Elwyn Brook-Jones, Jack La Roc and his Orchestra*
Gangster drama set in London, in which an American
gambler sets out to catch the forgers who framed him
for killing a US Treasury agent. An unmemorable
melodrama, scripted by George Callahan and William
Rose.
Aka: LUCKY NICK CAIN
Boa: novel High Stakes by James Hadley Chase.
DRA                    81 min (ort 83 min) B/W
B,V                                            CBS

### I'LL SEE YOU IN MY DREAMS **
Michael Curtiz         USA                 1951
*Doris Day, Danny Thomas, Frank Lovejoy, Patrice*
*Wymore, James Gleason*
Romantic and very slight handling of the career of
songwriter Gus Kahn, with Thomas giving a good
performance in an otherwise pretty forgettable film.
MUS                                      107 min B/W
V                                              WHV

### I'LL TAKE MANHATTAN: PARTS 1 AND 2 **   15
Douglas Hickox/Richard Michaels
                    USA                 1986/1987
*Valerie Bertinelli, Perry King, Francesca Annis, Barry*
*Bostwick, Staci Love, Jane Kaczmarek, Jack Scalia,*

*Paul Hecht, Timothy Daly*
Following the mysterious death of her father, a spoilt
young girl takes over his publishing empire and has to
deal with the underhand schemes of a wicked uncle. A
competent adaptation of Krantz's soap opera tale of
love, deceit and intrigue, all wrapped up in a glossy
and colourful package.
Boa: novel by Judith Krantz.
DRA            375 min (2 cassettes – ort 480 min) mTV
B,V                            IVS; BRAVE (VHS only)

### ILLEGALLY YOURS *                            PG
Peter Bogdanovich      USA                 1988
*Rob Lowe, Colleen Camp, Harry Carey Jr, Kenneth*
*Mars, Kim Myers, Marshall Colt*
A jilted lover returns home, and is called for jury duty
in the trial of a woman he has secretly adored for
many years. Naturally, he is convinced of her innocence, and tries to find evidence that will prove him
right, but finds himself getting out of his depth in the
complications that follow. Dull-witted and almost
embarrassing to watch.
COM                                      102 min
B, V/sh                                 CBS; PRES

### ILLUSTRATED MAN, THE **                      15
Jack Smight            USA                 1969
*Rod Steiger, Claire Bloom, Robert Drivas, Don*
*Dubbins, Jason Evers, Tom Weldon*
A brave but failed attempt to bring to the screen
Bradbury's collection of fantasy tales, linked by the
device of a tattooed man, each of whose pictures tells a
story. Atmospheric in parts, but generally too dis-
jointed and opaque to be effective.
Boa: book by Ray Bradbury.
FAN                        94 min (ort 103 min)
V                                              WHV

### I'M ALRIGHT JACK ***                         U
John Boulting/Roy Boulting
                    UK                     1959
*Ian Carmichael, Terry-Thomas, Peter Sellers, Richard*
*Attenborough, Dennis Price, Irene Handl, Margaret*
*Rutherford, Miles Malleson, Victor Maddern, Liz*
*Fraser, John Le Mesurier, Marne Maitland, Kenneth*
*Griffith, Terry Scott*
An idealistic graduate takes a job at his uncle's
factory, starting at the bottom. However, his well-
meaning and conscientious ways eventually provoke a
strike. Sellers is memorable as a gruff and bloody-
minded union leader. Initially a brilliant satire on
labour relations in 1950s Britain, the film progres-
sively degenerates into a contrived web of intrigue,
culminating in an ending that pulls all of its punches.
Boa: novel Private Life by Alan Hackney.
COM               104 min; 101 min (WHV) B/W
B,V                        TEVP; WHV (VHS only)

### I'M DANCING AS FAST AS I CAN **              15
Jack Hofsiss           USA                 1982
*Jill Clayburgh, Nicol Williamson, Dianne West, Joe*
*Pesci, Geraldine Page, Daniel Stern, James Sutorius,*
*Cordis Heard, Richard Masur, Ellen Greene, John*
*Lithgow*
A woman film producer becomes addicted to Valium
and is eventually rehabilitated. Despite fine perform-
ances and the potential of the subject matter, this one
is very disappointingly done. The script is by David
Rabe, Clayburgh's husband.
Boa: book by Barbara Gordon.
DRA                        101 min (ort 107 min)
B,V                                            CIC

### I'M FOR THE HIPPOPOTAMUS *                   PG
Italo Zingarelli       ITALY               1979
*Terence Hill (Mario Girotti), Bud Spencer (Carlo*
*Pedersoli), Joe Bugner*
Comic duo Spencer and Hill team up again, as
big-game hunters in Africa.

COM                              104 min (ort 106 min)
B,V                                               MED

## I'M GOING TO BE FAMOUS *
Paul Leder          USA                          1983
*Dick Sargent, Meredith MacRae, Paul Coufos*
A New York playwright holds auditions for his new
play, in a film that throws up every showbusiness
cliche in the book (and invents a few more of its own).
DRA                                           101 min
B,V,V2                                       INT/CBS

## I'M GONNA GIT YOU, SUCKA! ***                   15
Keenen Ivory Wayans     USA                      1988
*Keenen Ivory Wayans, Bernie Casey, Antonio Fargas,
Isaac Hayes, Jim Brown, Steve James, Janet DuBois,
Dawnn Lewis, John Vernon*
Written by Wayans, this is a sharp parody of 1970s
blaxploitation films that sees one Jack Spade out to
avenge the death of his brother and clean up the
ghetto at the same time. Disjointed and episodic it
may be, but the gags fly thick and fast, and most of
them hit their targets.
COM                              84 min (ort 87 min)
V/sh                                              WHV

## I'M NOT FEELING MYSELF TONIGHT *               18
Joseph McGrath        UK                         1975
*Barry Andrews, Sally Faulkner, James Booth, Billy
Harmon, Bea Aris, Mike Brady, Katya Wyeth, Brian
Murphy, Chic Murray, Graham Stark, Geraldine Hart,
Andrea Lawrence, Ronnie Brady, Juliette King, Bob
Godfrey, Rita Webb*
An unsuccessful odd-job man who works at a sex
institute, invents an electronic aphrodisiac that
changes his love life dramatically. A dreary and tame
exercise in smut and double entendres.
A                                             84 min
B,V                              WOV; ORANGE/STABL

## IMAGE OF BRUCE LEE *
Yeung Kuen       HONG KONG                        1978
*Bruce Li (Ho Tsung-Tao), Chang Wu Lang, Chang Lei*
Our martial arts hero fights to expose a ring of
international forgers in this totally forgettable tale.
MAR                                           80 min
B,V                                               VPD

## IMAGE, THE **                                  15
Peter Werner          USA                        1990
*Albert Finney, Kathy Baker, John Mahoney, Marsha
Mason, Swoosie Kurtz, Spalding Gray*
A ratings-hungry TV news anchorman begins to
believe his own reviews, and his ruthless thirst for
good audience figures creates conflict and ultimate
disillusionment. A variant on a theme explored in
NETWORK, this provocative look at telejournalism is
certainly well acted, but ultimately says nothing of
importance.
DRA                          89 min (ort 110 min) mCab
V/sh                                              WHV

## IMAGEMAKER, THE **                             15
Hal Weiner            USA                         1986
*Michael Nouri, Anne Twomey, Jerry Orbach, Jessica
Harper, Farley Granger, Maury Povich*
A presidential aide becomes involved in a nuclear
conspiracy to manipulate the media for political ends.
A spotty and undisciplined mess, though the
Washington talk show sequence is fairly entertaining.
DRA                              90 min (ort 93 min)
B,V                                               MED

## IMAGES ***
Robert Altman        EIRE                         1972
*Susannah York, Rene Auberjonais, Marcel Bozzuffi,
Hugh Millais, Cathryn Harrison, John Morley*
A disturbed woman is haunted by images of her
former lovers, in this complex tale that is difficult to
follow but rewards patience.
DRA                              98 min (ort 101 min)
B,V,V2                                            VCL

## IMMEDIATE FAMILY **                            15
Jonathan Kaplan       USA                         1989
*Glenn Close, James Woods, Mary Stuart Masterson,
Kevin Dillon, Linda Darlow, Jane Greer, Jessica
James, Mimi Kennedy*
A wealthy couple who are unable to have a child of
their own meet a pregnant and underprivileged girl
via an adoption agency, but their meeting with both
her and her boyfriend causes a good deal of soul
searching. A touching and sometimes funny character
study whose impact is weakened by its strident tone.
The somewhat uneven script is by Barbara Benedek.
DRA                                        96 min subH
V                                               20VIS

## IMMORAL MR TEAS, THE **                        18
Russ Meyer            USA                         1958
*Bill Teas, Ann Peters, Marilyn Wesley, Dawn Denelle,
Michele Roberts*
The first of many films produced by a director obsessed
with big-breasted women. This one tells the story of a
sexually frustrated bachelor, who satisfies his desires
by ogling women and imagining them naked. As time
goes on he gets better at this and the viewer is treated
to much nudity, if not action (poor Mr Teas never does
meet anyone). An innocuous and innocent film that
now looks very dated, but despite this, retains a
certain naive charm.
A                                             63 min
B,V                                               VSP

## IMMORAL TALES **
Walerian Borowczyk   FRANCE                       1974
*Lisa Danvers, Fabrice Luchini, Charlotte Alexandra,
Paloma Picasso, Pascal Christophe, Florence Bellamy,
Jacopo Berinizi*
A collection of four mediocre erotic tales that are
supposedly an essay on life, love and women, with
each episode set in a different time and place. In "The
Tide" a young man teaches his cousin the joys of sex,
"Therese, The Philosopher" tells of a girl who finds a
book of erotic drawings and learns to masturbate, in
"Erzsebet Bathory" a countess rounds up the local
virgins and in "Lucrezia Borgia" a female Borgia
makes love to Pope Alexander VI.
A                                             98 min
B,V                                              TEVP

## IMP, THE **                                    18
David De Cocteau      USA                         1987
*Linnea Quigley, Michelle Bauer, Andras Jones, Robin
Rochelle, Brinke Stevens, Kathi Orbrecht, Buck Flower*
A crazy and overblown fantasy horror tale in which a
nasty little imp is released from a bowling trophy, and
wreaks havoc among the college kids who unwittingly
released him.
Aka: SORORITY BABES IN THE SLIME BOWL-A-
RAMA
HOR               75 min (ort 85 min) Cut (1 min 9 sec)
B,V                                               CFD

## IMPACT ***                                     15
Arthur Lubin          USA                         1949
*Brian Donlevy, Ella Raines, Charles Coburn, Anna
May Wong, Helen Walker, Robert Warwick, Mae
Marsh*
A woman and her lover plan to murder her millionaire
industrialist husband, but their plans misfire and the
husband survives, taking a new identity. A convo-
luted melodrama, with enough twists in the plot to
keep one guessing right up to the end.
THR                          94 min (ort 111 min) B/W
B,V                                               KVD

## IMPORTANCE OF BEING EARNEST, THE **** U
Anthony Asquith        UK              1952
*Michael Redgrave, Michael Denison, Edith Evans,*
*Richard Wattis, Margaret Rutherford, Joan*
*Greenwood, Dorothy Tutin, Miles Malleson, Walter*
*Hudd, Ivor Barnard, Aubrey Mather*
Wilde's famous comedy of manners, about two bache-
lors and their troubled love lives. Set in Victorian
England and boasting an impeccable cast who play
their parts to perfection.
Boa: play by Oscar Wilde.
COM                             91 min (ort 95 min)
V                                           RNK

## IMPOSSIBLE SPY, THE ***                       15
Jim Goddard           UK              1987
*John Shea, Eli Wallach, Michal Bat-Adam, Sasson*
*Gabay, Rami Danon, Chaim Girafi*
True story of an Israeli civilian who was recruited into
Israel's secret service and became their most success-
ful spy, working in Damascus where he infiltrated the
Syrian political establishment and helped the Israelis
defeat them during the Six Day War. Based on the
story of Elie Cohen.
THR                                 96 min mCab
B,V                                         MGM

## IMPOSTER, THE *                               PG
Michael Pressman      USA             1984
*Anthony Geary, Lorna Patterson, Jordan Charney,*
*Penny Johnson, Ken Olandt, Billy Dee Williams, Peter*
*Syvertsen, Sara Jane Donley, Gerry Becker, Todd*
*Cerveris, Pat Rowie, Jack McLaughlin Grey, Nathan*
*Davis, Ron Parady*
A released prisoner uses his wits to become the
principal of an American high school and embarks on
a campaign to eradicate the school's drugs problem.
An implausible and not terribly interesting effort.
DRA                      120 min; 90 min (ARF) mTV
B,V                                         ARF

## IMPROPER CHANNELS *
Eric Till             CANADA          1979
*Alan Arkin, Mariette Hartley, Monica Parker, Sarah*
*Stevens, Harry Ditson*
An architect father is wrongly suspected of child
abuse, when he takes his injured daughter to hospital.
A comedy misfire that might have worked better as a
straight drama, especially with regard to the nature of
the subject matter.
COM                                      93 min
B,V                                         RNK

## IMPULSE *                                     18
William Grefe         USA             1974
*William Shatner, Harold Sakata, Ruth Roman, Kim*
*Nicholas, Jennifer Bishop, James Dobson, Marcie*
*Knight*
A low-budget account of a nasty child molester, played
by Shatner. Tedious and barely watchable.
Aka: WANT A RIDE, LITTLE GIRL?
HOR                             87 min (ort 91 min)
B,V                                         APX

## IMPULSE **                                    18
Graham Baker          USA             1984
*Meg Tilly, Tim Matheson, Hume Cronyn, John*
*Karlen, Bill Paxton, Claude Earl Jones, Amy Stryker*
The inhabitants of a small town suddenly and inex-
plicably begin to behave in a violent and irrational
way. A woman goes home to investigate her mother's
attempted suicide and gets caught up in this mystery.
A modest little fantasy-thriller that offers no explana-
tion and has no real resolution.
FAN                                      88 min
B,V                                         ODY

## IMPULSE **                                    18
                      USA             1990
*Theresa Russell, Jeff Fahey, George Dzundza*

A female undercover cop finds herself caught up in an
agonising choice between love and money, when her
one-night stand is murdered and she conceals all trace
of her involvement, but hangs onto a key to a locker
containing $1,000,000 in drugs money. An interesting
drama with a strong female lead, only its implausible
and contrived elements spoil it.
DRA                                     101 min
V                                           WHV

## IMPULSION **
                      USA             1972
*Alejandro Rey, Katherine Justice*
A crime of passion set in the world of international
jet-setters, forms the basis for this routine melodrama.
DRA                                      85 min
B,V,V2                                   VCL/CBS

## IMPURE THOUGHTS ***                           15
Michael A. Simpson    USA             1985
*Brad Dourif, Lane Davies, Terry Beaver, John Putch,*
*Mary Nell Santacroce, Mary McDonough, Benji*
*Wilhoite, Judith Anderson (narration)*
After death, four men meet up in Purgatory, and pass
the time looking back at the early part of their lives,
when they were students together at the same Catho-
lic school. An erratic comedy that has a few good
moments and a dose of tiresome symbolism.
COM                             83 min (ort 87 min)
B,V                                         FUTUR

## IN A COLT'S SHADOW *                          PG
Gianni Brimaldi    ITALY/SPAIN        1966
*Stephen Forsyth, Conrado Sanmartin, Anne Sherman,*
*Helga Line, Frank Ressel, Graham Sooty, Pepe Calvo,*
*Andrew Scott, Frankie Liston*
After quarrelling with his fellow gunfighter, one man
is left to defend a Mexican village against bandits. An
unashamed and undistinguished attempt to copy THE
MAGNIFICENT SEVEN, without any of that film's
virtues.
Aka: ALL'OMBRA DI UNA COLT; IN THE
SHADOW OF A COLT
WES                           77 min Cut (20 sec) dubbed
B,V                                         VPD

## IN A LONELY PLACE ***                         PG
Nicholas Ray          USA             1950
*Humphrey Bogart, Gloria Grahame, Frank Lovejoy,*
*Robert Warwick, Carl Benton Reid, Art Smith, Jeff*
*Donnell, Martha Stewart*
A sour and arrogant screenwriter who suffers from
self-destructive urges and a violent temper, becomes
the chief suspect when a woman he briefly met is
found murdered. Though innocent, the charge poisons
and eventually destroys the only relationship that
might have given him lasting happiness. An unusual
and harsh melodrama of little warmth.
Boa: novel by Dorothy B. Hughes.
DRA                          90 min (ort 93 min) B/W
V                                           RCA

## IN A SHALLOW GRAVE **                         15
Kenneth Bowser        USA             1987
*Michael Biehn, Michael Beach, Maureen Meuller,*
*Patrick Dempsey, Thomas Boyd Mason*
A WW2 veteran badly disfigured at Guadalcanal
returns to his desolate Virginia home and empty life,
and wallows in self pity. The arrival of a drifter gives
him a chance to communicate with his ex-fiancee, and
the young man is used as a go-between. A peculiar
love triangle is the result in this bizarre romantic
drama, whose sluggish pace and gloomy outlook are
serious flaws.
DRA                             90 min (ort 92 min)
V                                           VIR

## IN BROAD DAYLIGHT ***
Robert Day            USA             1971

*Richard Boone, Suzanne Pleshette, Stella Stevens,*
*Fred Beir, John Marley, Whit Bissell, Paul Smith,*
*Daniel Spelling, Barbara Dodd, Ken Sansom, Sam*
*Edwards, Buddy Lewis, Frank Bellu, Al C. Ward*
A recently blinded husband plans to kill his wife and
her lover, in this often tense but rather implausible
tale. The script is by Larry Cohen.
DRA                            73 min mTV
B,V                                GHV

### IN COUNTRY **                              15
Norman Jewison          USA               1989
*Bruce Willis, Emily Lloyd, Joan Allen, Kevin*
*Anderson, John Terry, Peggy Rea, Judith Ivey,*
*Richard Hamilton, Patricia Richardson, Jim Beaver*
A shell-shocked Vietnam veteran and a young girl
who lost her father in the conflict, each try to come to
terms with the war in their own way. Willis is
excellent as the girl's uncle, but the flawed script is as
uneven as it is well-intentioned, though a final
sequence set at the Veterans' Memorial in Washing-
ton D.C. is surprisingly moving.
Boa: novel by Bobbie Anne Mason.
DRA                    110 min (ort 120 min)
V/sh                               WHV

### IN DANGEROUS COMPANY **                    18
Ruben D. Preuss          USA              1988
*Tracy Scoggins, Cliff De Young*
The mistress of the leader of a gang who deal in art
forgeries, hatches a plot to steal some of them and
contacts a former lover to assist her. A watchable
thriller.
THR                                92 min
V                                   RCA

### INDIO *                                    15
                         USA              1989
*Francesco Quinn, Brian Dennehy, Marvin Hagler*
An American Indian and former marine returns to his
tribal homelands only to find that his jungle-dwelling
people are threatened by the activities of a construction company. Having seen that the company is
prepared to use murder to prevent opposition, and
having had his own father killed, he wages a lone
battle against the company and its ruthless boss. A
foolish action film of poor acting and ludicrous plotting.
A/AD                               89 min
V                             PRES; CHV

### IN GOD WE TRU$T *                          15
Marty Feldman            USA              1980
*Marty Feldman, Peter Boyle, Louise Lasser, Richard*
*Pryor, Andy Kaufman, Wilfred Hyde-White, Severn*
*Darden*
A monk goes out into the world to raise money to save
his monastery, in this pathetically unfunny attempt
to produce a religious satire. Co-written by Feldman,
whose gifts were better employed in front of the
camera than behind it.
COM                    93 min (ort 97 min)
B,V                                 CIC

### IN HOT PURSUIT **
                         USA              1982
*Don Watson, Bob Watson, Debbie Washington*
Action story with two brothers planning to make their
fortune delivering an illegal shipment of drugs.
Unknown to them the police have been tipped off. A
film of noise, action, car chases and little else.
A/AD                               90 min
B,V                                MMA

### IN LOVE WITH AN OLDER WOMAN ***           PG
Jack Bender              USA              1982
*John Ritter, Karen Carlson, Jamie Ross, Robert*
*Mandan, Jeff Altman, George Murdock, Robin Curtis,*
*Wendall Wright, Deborah Tilton, Blaine Novak,*

*Robert Townsend, Jo Anne Astrow, Mary-Alan*
*Hockanson, Michael Cummings, Sandy Ward*
A younger man and an older woman face scorn and
prejudice because of their relationship. A generally
agreeable comedy-drama that is better than one
might have expected, mainly thanks to good work
from Ritter and Carlson. The script is by Michael
Norell.
Boa: novel Six Months With An Older Woman by
David Kaufelt.
DRA                           100 min mTV
B,V                        IPC/VSP; CBS

### IN 'N' OUT *                               15
Ricardo Franco           USA              1984
*Samuel Bottoms, Pat Hingle*
A ne'er-do-well on the verge of suicide goes to Mexico
for his father's funeral, despite the fact that he has
always been told his d died some 30 years before. Once
there, he gets embroiled in a complex series of
misadventures. A flat and paltry effort whose labyrinthine plot slowly collapses beneath the weight of its
wealth of poorly realised ideas.
COM                                98 min
V                                  NWV

### IN POSSESSION *
Val Guest                UK               1984
*Christopher Cazenove, Carol Lynley, Bernard Kay,*
*Judy Loe*
A woman discovers a body in her flat just before she is
about to move.
Osca: CZECH MATE
HOR                                85 min
B,V                                BWV

### IN PRAISE OF OLDER WOMEN *                 18
George Kaczender     CANADA               1978
*Tom Berenger, Karen Black, Susan Strasberg, Helen*
*Shaver, Alexandra Stewart, Marilyn Lightstone*
The story of a Hungarian emigre and his numerous
sexual encounters, seen as a series of tiresome
flashback sequences, in which semi-clothed women
are paraded across the screen for our edification. But
for all that the film remains a boring dud.
Boa: novel by Stephen Vizinczey.
DRA                   105 min (ort 108 min)
               Cut (Cut at film release by 8 sec)
B,V                                WHV

### IN SEARCH OF A GOLDEN SKY **
Jefferson Richard        USA              1984
*Charles Napier, George Flower, Cliff Osmond*
After the death of their mother and the disappearance
of their father, two children are sent to stay with their
uncle, who lives in a remote cabin in the wilderness.
At first they are apprehensive about their new home,
but eventually come to love their new life. An
enjoyable and undemanding tale.
JUV                                94 min
B,V                                AVP

### IN SEARCH OF THE CASTAWAYS ***             U
Robert Stevenson     UK/USA               1961
*Hayley Mills, Maurice Chevalier, Wilfrid Hyde-White,*
*George Sanders, Wilfrid Brambell, Michael Anderson*
*Jr, Antonio Cifariello, Keith Hamshere, Jack Gwillim,*
*Ronald Fraser, Inia Te Waita, Norman Bird, Michael*
*Wayne*
Three children and a professor go to South America in
search of a missing sea captain, encountering various
disasters and hazards along the way. A colourful
Disney adventure tale, that suffers rather badly from
an uneven script, but is generally good clean fun.
Boa: novel Captain Grant's Children by Jules Verne.
A/AD                   94 min (ort 100 min)
B,V                                WDV

## IN THE AFTERMATH: ANGELS NEVER SLEEP **    PG
Carl Colpaert    JAPAN/USA    1987
*Tony Markes, Rainbow Dolan, Kenneth McCabe,*
*Kurtiss J. Tews, Edward Holm, Brian Ellenburg,*
*Mike Hickam*
Another post-WW3 story with the Earth reduced to a burnt out cinder. A soldier has strange dreams and discovers a girl who may hold the key to the future in this unmemorable yarn.
Aka: ANGELS NEVER SLEEP
FAN    69 min
B,V    NWV

## IN THE CUSTODY OF STRANGERS ***    15
Robert Greenwald    USA    1982
*Martin Sheen, Jane Alexander, Emilio Esterez,*
*Kenneth McMillan, Ed Lauter, Matt Clark, John*
*Hancock, Virginia Kiser, Jon Van Ness, Judyann*
*Elder, Deberah Foreman, Susan Peretz, Peter Jurasik,*
*Pat McNamara, Ramon Estevez*
Explores the troubled relationship between a father and his wild son, when the latter is put in jail on charges of drunkenness and assault, and the parents are unable to get him out. A thought-provoking melodrama with a good script by Jennifer Miller.
DRA    95 min; 91 min (NGV) (ort 100 min) mTV
B,V    VFP; NGV

## IN THE HEAT OF THE NIGHT ****    15
Norman Jewison    USA    1967
*Sidney Poitier, Rod Steiger, Warren Oates, Lee Grant,*
*Scott Wilson, Larry Gates, Quentin Dean, James*
*Patterson, Anthony James, William Schallert*
A superb drama about a black Philadelphia homicide cop who is reluctantly roped into helping a Southern sheriff in a murder case, thus exposing himself to local bigotry and hatred. Poitier and Steiger complement each other brilliantly and the music of Ray Charles is used to great effect. The inferior "They Call Me Mr Tibbs" followed. AA: Pic, Actor (Steiger), Edit (Hal Ashby), Screen (Adapt) (Stirling Silliphant), Sound (Goldwyn Studios).
Boa: novel by J. Ball.
DRA    109 min
B,V    WHV

## IN THE LINE OF DUTY **    18
Yuen Woo Ping    HONG KONG    1989
*Cynthia Khan, Michael Woods, Donnie Yen*
A police story with a strong martial arts flavour that has a tough female cop being assigned to a witness who holds vital information on a drug-smuggling ring that is being jointly operated by the CIA and a criminal gang. The requisite supply of action and fisticuffs helps enliven a film that has very few surprises in the plot department.
A/AD    90 min
V    VPD

## IN THE SHADOW OF KILIMANJARO *    18
Raju Patel    KENYA/UK/USA    1986
*John Rhys-Davis, Timothy Bottoms, Michele Carey,*
*Irene Miracle, Calvin Jung, Don Blakely, Patty Foley*
Ridiculous tale of 90,000 baboons poised to attack humans, because a drought in Africa has robbed them of their normal food. Allegedly based on a number of real events. (Baboons have been known to attack humans, but 90,000?) Filmed on location in Kenya.
A/AD    92 min
B,V    GHV

## IN THE SHADOW OF THE WIND **    15
Yves Simoneau    FRANCE
*Steve Banner, Charlotte Valendrey*
A man returns to his small conservative hometown, after leaving five years ago following an argument with his father. His arrival serves as the catalyst for some unpleasant conflicts in this repressed Protestant community.
DRA    107 min (2 cassettes) B/W
V/s    HEND

## IN WHICH WE SERVE ****    U
Noel Coward/David Lean   UK    1942
*Noel Coward, Bernard Miles, John Mills, Celia*
*Johnson, Kay Walsh, Michael Wilding, Joyce Carey,*
*Penelope Dudley Ward, Philip Friend, Frederick Piper,*
*Derek Elphinstone, Geoffrey Hibbert, Richard*
*Attenborough*
WW2 morale-booster written by Coward, that describes the life of a destroyer and those who serve on her. Told in flashbacks as the survivors of the torpedoed ship recall their lives at war and on leave. A low-key affair, but quite excellent. AA: Spec Award (Noel Coward for outstanding production achievement).
WAR    96 min (ort 114 min) B/W
V    RNK

## IN-LAWS, THE *    PG
Arthur Miller    USA    1979
*Alan Arkin, Peter Falk, Richard Libertini, Nancy*
*Dussault, Penny Peyser, Arlene Golonka, Michael*
*Lembeck, Ed Begley Jr*
Terribly strained comedy in which a dentist, played by Arkin, finds that by the marriage of one of his children, he has become involved with the CIA and their intrigues in a Latin American dictatorship. No light touch here. The music is by John Morris.
COM    99 min (ort 103 min)
B,V    WHV

## INCA *    PG
J. Lee Thompson    USA    1963
*Yul Brynner, George Chakaris, Shirley Ann Field,*
*Barry Morse, Richard Basehart, Brad Dexter*
A Mayan leader takes the remnants of his tribe to North America but has to face hostile Indians. Filmed in Mexico, this movie is deservedly obscure.
Aka: KINGS OF THE SUN
A/AD    87 min (ort 108 min)
B,V    SCAN

## INCIDENT, THE ***    PG
Josrgent    USA    1989
*Walter Matthau, Susan Blakely, Peter Firth, Robert*
*Carradine, Barnard Hughes, William Schallert, Harry*
*Morgan*
Matthau makes his TV debut as a small-town lawyer who takes on the job of defending a German POW during WW2, and becomes a social outcast in the process. An absorbing and solidly acted drama, scripted by Michael and James Norell.
DRA    95 min (ort 100 min) mTV
V    BRAVE

## INCIDENT AT CRESTRIDGE **    PG
Jud Taylor    USA    1981
*Eileen Brennan, Pernell Roberts, Bruce Davison,*
*Sandy McPeak, Walt Field, Cliff Osmond, Maria*
*Richwine, Barbara Dirickson, Max Robinson, Craig*
*Lewis, Julie Boyd, Russ McGinn, Michael Ruud, John*
*Perryman, Tip Boxell*
A woman decides to run for sheriff in a small town in Wyoming where respect for the law is somewhat lacking. Failed attempt to update the Western with a nod towards the feminist movement.
Aka: INCIDENT IN CRESTRIDGE; LADY WITH A BADGE
WES    91 min (ort 100 min) mTV
B,V    MGM

## INCOMING FRESHMAN ** 
Glenn Morgan/Eric Lewald
   USA    1979
*Leslie Blalock, Debralee Scott, Jim Overbey, Richard*

*Harriman, Cheryl Gordon*
Four young girls start college, but their minds are more on men than books in this slight comedy.
COM                          81 min (ort 84 min)
B,V,V2                                       RNK

## INCREDIBLE HULK, THE *                    PG
Kenneth Johnson        USA            1977
*Bill Bixby, Susan Sullivan, Jack Colvin, Lou Ferrigno, Susan Batson, Charles Siebert, Mario Gallo, Eric Server, Eric Deon, Jake Mitchell, Lara Parker, William Larsen, Olivia Barash, George Brenlin, June Whitley Taylor*
Pilot for a TV series based on a character created by the Marvel Comic group. Doctor David Banner is investigating strange cases of superhuman strength, and subjects himself to an experiment which results in him becoming an irritable green giant when angered. A pretty laughable affair, very much made for the small screen. An interminable TV series followed.
FAN          94 min (ort 100 min) mTV
B,V                                         CIC

## INCREDIBLE HULK RETURNS, THE ***         PG
Nicholas Corea         USA            1988
*Bill Bixby, Lou Ferrigno, Jack Calvin, Tim Thomerson, Lee Purcell, Eric Kramer*
The most recent in a series of feature spin-offs from the popular TV series based on a Marvel comics character. In this tale Dr David Banner develops a device he hopes will rid himself of his dangerous alter-ego, but the forces of evil put an end to his scheme, and as the Hulk he is forced to team up with Thor the Thunder God to fight them. Enjoyable hokum.
Aka: RETURN OF THE INCREDIBLE HULK
A/AD         93 min (ort 100 min) mTV
V/h                                         NWV

## INCREDIBLE JOURNEY, THE ***              Uc
Fletcher Markle        CANADA         1963
*Emile Genest, John Drainie, Tommy Tweed, Sandra Scott, Syme Jago*
Two dogs and a Siamese cat travel 250 miles across Canada to rejoin their owners. Wholesome Disney fare with our trio encountering various hazards in the form of unfriendly animals but arriving safe and sound in the end. A good film for the family.
Boa: book by Sheila Burnford.
JUV                                      80 min
B,V                                         WDV

## INCREDIBLE KUNG FU MISSION, THE **
Chan Hsin-Yi      HONG KONG           1982
*John Liu, Shang Kuan Lung, Chen Lung, Hso Chung-Hsu, Ting Hwa-Choong*
Five expert fighters embark on a perilous mission, to rescue a rebel agent held captive in a fortress. Average.
Aka: KUNG FU COMMANDOS
MAR                                      91 min
B,V                                         AVP

## INCREDIBLE MELTING MAN, THE *            18
William Sachs          USA            1977
*Alex Rebar, Burr DeBenning, Myron Healey, Michael Aldredge, Ann Sweeney, Cheryl Rainbeaux Smith, Lisle Wilson*
The survivor of a space mission develops a taste for human flesh as his own body begins to melt and fall apart, in this repulsive low-budget nonsense. The remarkable work of make-up expert Rick Baker partially redeems it.
FAN                                      90 min
B,V                                         RCA

## INCREDIBLE ROCKY MOUNTAIN RACE, THE **
James L. Conway        USA            1977
*Christopher Connelly, Forrest Tucker, Larry Storch, Whit Bissell, Bill Zuckert, Mike Mazurki, Jack*

*Kruschen, Parley Beer, Don Haggerty, Allen Wood, John Hansen, Sandy Gibbon, William Kazele, Robert Easton, David O'Malley*
Western about a grudge race from Missouri to California between two rivals, Mark Twain and Mike Fink. A broad and undisciplined comedy.
WES                                100 min mTV
B,V                                         RNK

## INCREDIBLE VOYAGE OF STINGRAY, THE ***   U
Alan Patillo/David Elliott/John Kelly
                   UK      1965 (re-edited 1980)
*Voices of: Don Mason, Robert Easton, Lois Maxwell, Ray Barrett*
Four episodes from this children's puppet series are compiled into a single feature-length adventure. The crew of underwater vessel "Stingray" are menaced by the denizens of the deep as they fight an evil underwater emperor who plots to take over the world. Fair kid's adventure.
CAR                                 95 min mTV
B,V                      PRV; CH5 (VHS only)

## INCUBUS, THE *                           18
John Hough            CANADA          1981
*John Cassavetes, John Ireland, Helen Hughes, Kerrie Keane, Erin Flannery, Duncan McIntosh, Harvey Atkin, Harry Ditson, Mitch Martin, Matt Birman, Wes Lee, Beverly Cooper, Brian Young, Barbara Franklin, Neil Dainard, Helene Udy*
A supernatural entity is behind a series of rapes and sex murders in a small Wisconsin town, in this unpleasant low-budget shocker.
Boa: novel by Ray Russell.
HOR                    92 min; 88 min (MAST)
B,V         VTC L/A; XTACY/KRP; MAST (VHS only)

## INDECENT EXPOSURE **
Robert McCallum        USA            1981
*Veronica Hart, Jesie St James, Richard Bolla, Eric Edwards, Georgina Spelvin, Arcadia Lake, Nicole Noir, Chelsea*
This story follows a bored fashion photographer who wants to sleep with all his models. Together with a friend and their respective girlfriends, they go off on several assignments and the men spend much of the time lovemaking with the models. On the last assignment a wealthy woman seduces our photographer, but the film ends with a reconciliation and all four drive off happily into the night. A watchable but hardly engrossing effort.
A                                        85 min
B,V                                         HAR

## INDECENT OBSESSION, AN **                18
Lex Marinos         AUSTRALIA         1985
*Wendy Hughes, Gary Sweet, Bill Hunter, Bruno Lawrence*
A WW2 story set in a military hospital in the South Pacific, that examines the relationship of a group of mentally ill men with each other, and the ward sister who cares for them.
Boa: novel by Colleen McCullough.
DRA                                     100 min
B,V                                        TEVP

## INDIANA JONES AND THE LAST
## CRUSADE ***                              PG
Steven Spielberg       USA            1988
*Harrison Ford, Sean Connery, Alison Doody, John Rhys-Davies, Denhol Elliott, Julian Glover, River Phoenix, Michael Byrne, Alex Hyde-White*
This big-budget sequel to INDIANA JONES AND THE TEMPLE OF DOOM sees Indy joining his father on a quest for the Holy Grail, when the latter vanishes whilst on that mission. Father and son are soon battling ed Nazis in a story that is almost a clone of RAIDERS OF THE LOST ARK, but lacks that film's panache. Nevertheless, this stylish sequel has many

virtues, and the two leads are great together. AA: Effects (aud) (Ben Burtt/Richard Hymns).

A/AD  121 min (ort 127 min)
V/sh  CIC

### INDIANA JONES AND THE TEMPLE OF DOOM **  PG

Steven Spielberg  USA  1984
*Harrison Ford, Kate Capshaw, Ke Huy Quan, Amrish Puri, Roshan Seth, Philip Stone, Dan Aykroyd*
A sequel to the highly enjoyable RAIDERS OF THE LOST ARK, but somewhat less successful in terms of story and entertainment, with the film whizzing along at breathtaking speed. In this tale Ford has to regain a sacred jewel whose loss has plunged a village into despair. A noisy, headache-inducing affair. Followed by INDIANA JONES AND THE LAST CRUSADE. AA: Effects (Vis) (Dennis Muren/Michael McAlister/Lorne Peterson/George Gibbs).

A/AD  112 min (ort 118 min) (Cut at film release)
V/sh  CIC

### INDISCREET *  PG

Richard Michaels  USA  1988
*Robert Wagner, Lesley-Anne Down, Maggie Henderson, Robert McBain, Jeni Barnett*
A dull remake of the 1958 Grant and Bergman film that adds nothing of interest to the thin plot, and lacks the screen presence of the two stars to make it watchable.

DRA  95 min (ort 100 min) mTV
V  VGM

### INDISCREET ***  PG

Stanley Donen  UK  1958
*Cary Grant, Ingrid Bergman, Phyllis Calvert, Cecil Parker, David Kossoff, Megs Jenkins*
A NATO officer meets a beautiful actress and falls in love with her, but protects himself by saying his is married. Despite the thin plot, both stars are in top form and carry off this charming comedy of manners. Boa: play Kind Sir by Norman Krasna.

COM  96 min (ort 100 min)
B,V,V2  BBC; VCC (VHS only)

### INDISCRETION OF AN AMERICAN WIFE *

Vittorio De Sica  ITALY/USA  1954
*Jennifer Jones, Montgomery Clift, Gino Cervi, Richard Beymer*
An American wife bids farewell to her lover in Rome's railway station, in this painfully contrived attempt to make an Italian BRIEF ENCOUNTER that barely rises above the level of a turgid melodrama. The original 87 minute running was restored in 1983. Aka: INDISCRETION; TERMINAL STATION; TERMINUS STATION

DRA  72 min (ort 87 min) B/W
B,V  GHV; VCC

### INFERNO **  18

Dario Argento  ITALY  1978
*Leigh McCloskey, Irene Miracle, Sacha Pitoeff, Eleanora Giorgi, Alida Valli, Daria Nicolodi, Feodor Chaliapin, Veronica Lazar, Gabriele Lavia*
An American returns from his studies in Rome in order to investigate the brutal murder of his sister, and discovers that it was committed by a group of Satanists. A disjointed and largely unsuccessful shocker with a few moments of surreal power. Aka: INFERNO '80

HOR  102 min (ort 107 min) Cut (28 sec)
B,V,V2,LV  CBS

### INFERNO IN PARADISE *

Edward Forsyth  USA  1974
*Jim Davis, Richard Young, Betty Ann Carr*
An arsonist threatens the island of Honolulu in this obscure little thriller.

THR  90 min
B,V,V2  VPD

### INFERNO IN SAFEHAVEN *  18

Brian Thomas Jones/James McCalmont
USA  1990
*Rick Gianasi, John Wittenbauer, Roy MacArthur*
In a brutalised post-WW3 future, a family are allocated living-quarters in "Safehaven"; they discover that this allegedly safe refuge is dominated by ruthless thugs and they are forced to fight to survive. Another poorly mounted apocalyptic vision whose paltry ideas are drowned in a welter of bad acting and cheap effects. Aka: ESCAPE FROM SAFEHAVEN

FAN  82 min
V  MED

### INFERNO THUNDERBOLT **  18

Godfrey Ho  HONG KONG  1986
*Richard Harrison, Fonda Lynn, Wang Tao, Pierre Trembley, Claire Angela, Rose Kuei, Jacky Lim*
A standard kung fu punch-and-kicker of no great plot complexity.

MAR  90 min
B,V  GAL; SID

### INGLORIOUS BASTARDS, THE **  1978

Enzo G. Castellari  ITALY
*Ian Bannen, Bo Svenson, Fred Williamson, Peter Hooten, Michael Pergolani*
Five soldiers about to be tried by a court-martial during WW2 in France, escape and make for Switzerland, in this implausible Italian effort that barely holds up but for a few good action sequences. Aka: COUNTERFEIT COMMANDOS

WAR  87 min (ort 100 min)
B,V  HOK

### INHERIT THE WIND **  PG

David Greene  USA  1988
*Kirk Douglas, Jason Robards, Darren McGavin, Jean Simmons, Megan Follows, Kyle Secor, John Harkins*
A remake of the 1960 Spencer Tracy film, with our proponent of the theory of evolution and his opponent, battling it out in a courtroom. A feeble version indeed, that makes bad use of the stars and weakens the story, by removing several important supporting characters. Written by John Gay. Boa: play by Jerome Lawrence and Robert E. Lee.

DRA  96 min (ort 100 min) mTV
V  MGM

### INHERIT THE WIND ****  U

Stanley Kramer  USA  1960
*Spencer Tracy, Gene Kelly, Fredric March, Dick York, Donna Anderson, Claude Akins, Florence Eldridge*
The famous Scopes "monkey trial" of 1925 provided the subject for this classic account of a schoolteacher brought to trial for teaching Darwin's theory of evolution in a small Southern town. Although its stage origins are always in evidence, this long but compelling courtroom film has splendid performances and a lively, articulate script. Remade for TV in 1988. Boa: play by Jerome Lawrence and Robert E. Lee.

DRA  124 min (ort 127 min) B/W
V  WHV

### INHERITANCE, THE ***  18

Mauro Bolognini  ITALY  1976
*Anthony Quinn, Dominique Sanda, Fabio Testi, Adriana Asti, Luigi Proietti, Paolo Bonalelli*
A scheming woman uses her sexual charms to extract money from her dying father-in-law. Plenty of erotic scenes in this steamy melodrama. Aka: INHERITORS, THE; L'EREDITA FERRAMONTI

DRA  105 min (ort 121 min)
B,V  HAR

## INHUMANOIDS: THE EVIL THAT LIES WITHIN ***    PG

USA    1986
The planet is threatened by the spread of the "Inhumanoid" terror and the brave Earth Corps travels to the centre of the Earth to do battle with them and the "Mutores". A lively kiddie's adventure based on some Hasbro toy characters.
CAR    85 min
V    MSD

## INITIANTS, THE **    18
1989
Two attractive female hitch-hikers encounter a strange world of the supernatural, when they stop for the night at a remote farmhouse and are used as pawns in an erotic black magic ceremony. This thinnest of plots serves as a vehicle for the standard set of sex romps. Average.
A    52 min
B,V    PHV L/A; SFI

## INITIATION ***    15
Michael Pearce    AUSTRALIA    1987
*Rodney Harvey, Bruno Lawrence, Arna Maria Winchester, Miranda Otto, Bobby Smith, Tony Barry*
A young American boy leaves the urban jungle after his mother dies and embarks on a search for his father. This takes him to a small Australian town where he eventually faces the greatest challenge of his life.
A/AD    90 min
B,V    AVA

## INITIATION, THE *    18
Larry Stewart    USA    1983
*Vera Miles, Clu Gulager, James Read, Daphne Zuniga*
A family is plagued by a dangerous maniac who has a special interest in the daughter, with whom he seems to have a strange connection. A fairly unappealing slasher tale, in which our psycho embarks on a series of murders at the girl's college. Cut before video submission by 59 sec.
THR    92 min (ort 97 min)
B,V    CBS

## INN OF THE DAMNED **    15
Terry Bourke    AUSTRALIA    1974
*Alex Cord, Michael Craig, Tony Bonner, Judith Anderson, Joseph Furst, John Meillon, Robert Quilter, Carla Hoogeveen, Linda Brown*
Travellers at an inn run by strange folk disappear, and a bounty hunter investigates in this unmemorable shocker.
HOR    111 min (ort 125 min)
B,V,V2    MED

## INN OF THE SIXTH HAPPINESS, THE ***    PG
Mark Robson    USA    1958
*Ingrid Bergman, Curt Jurgens, Robert Donat, Ronald Squire, Athene Seyler, Richard Wattis, Moultrie Kelsall*
The story of Gladys Aylward, who became a missionary in China and endured great hardship, leading 100 children to safety (singing "Knick, Knack, Paddywack") following the Japanese invasion of WW2. Overlong, but fine performances from Bergman and Donat as a Chinese mandarin (his last role) work to its advantage. The score is by Malcolm Arnold.
Boa: novel The Small Woman by Alan Burgess.
DRA    152 min (ort 158 min)
V/h    CBS

## INNERSPACE ***    PG
Joe Dante    USA    1987
*Dennis Quaid, Martin Short, Meg Ryan, Kevin McCarthy, Fiona Lewis, Vernon Wells, Robert Picard, Wendy Schaal, Harold Sylvester, William Schallert,*
*Ken Tobey, Henry Gibson, Orson Bean, Kevin Hooks, Kathleen Freeman, Dick Miller*
Comedy tale in which a Navy test pilot, miniaturised as part of a secret experiment, is accidentally injected into a hypochondriac supermarket clerk instead of a laboratory rabbit as was intended. A boisterous comedy with some good effects, and a nice performance from Short as the unhappy, comical hero. AA: Effects (Vis) (Dennis Muren/William George/Harley Jessup/Kenneth Smith).
COM    116 min (ort 120 min)
V/sh    WHV

## INNOCENT BYSTANDERS **    18
Peter Collinson    UK    1972
*Stanley Baker, Geraldine Chaplin, Donald Pleasence, Dana Andrews, Sue Lloyd, Vladek Sheybal, Derren Nesbitt, Warren Mitchell, Ferdy Mayne, John Collin, Frank Maher*
An agent is sent to bring back a defecting Russian scientist from Turkey, as his last assignment in this messy and often violent thriller that fails to make the most of an excellent cast.
Boa: novel by James Munro.
THR    110 min
B,V    HVM L/A; VUL L/A; MIA (VHS only)

## INNOCENT PREY **    18
Colin Eggleston    1984
*P.J. Soles, Martin Balsam, Kit Taylor, Susan Stenmark*
Having discovered that her husband is a multiple murderer of prostitutes, a woman flees to Sydney, where she attempts to start a new life. However, her husband sets out to find her and her troubles are compounded by the discovery that her landlord is a psychopath. A melodramatic and overblown tale.
HOR    92 min
V    TGP

## INNOCENT VICTIM ***    
Michael Winner    USA    1976
*Yvette Mimieux, Tommy Lee Jones, Robert Carradine, Frederic Cook, Severn Darden, Howard Hesseman, Mary Woronov*
A woman jailed for a minor offence is raped by one of the guards, but breaks out of jail with another inmate. A fast-paced chase story with a minor cult following. Later remade for TV as "Outside Chance".
Aka: JACKSON COUNTY JAIL
DRA    84 min
B,V    PRIME/CBS

## INSANITY **    
*Terence Stamp, Fernando Rey, Corinne Clery*
A film-maker comes under pressure to produce a sequel to his latest hit, but falls obsessively in love with a beautiful woman, in this obscure and fairly routine horror story.
HOR    90 min
B,V    GOV

## INSATIABLE **    18
Godfrey Daniels    USA    1980
*Marilyn Chambers, John C. Holmes, Jesie St James, John Leslie, Serena, Joan Turner, Mike Ranger, David Morris, Richard Pacheco*
A beautiful model loses her parents, in a tragic accident at the height of her career. She is left with an enormous fortune but is sexually unfulfilled, and searches for happiness in New York and London. A largely plotless film, that follows poor, insatiable, masochistic, aptly-named Sandra Chase, as she goes from one unsatisfying encounter to another.
A    70 min (PHE); 35 min (SHEP); (ort 85 min)
(Abridged at film release)
B,V    TCX L/A; NET L/A; PHE; SHEP

**INSATIABLE 2 \***                                R18
Godfrey Daniels II        USA                      1984
*Marilyn Chambers, Juliet Anderson, Jamie Gillis,*
*Paul Thomas, Valerie La Veaux, Craig Roberts,*
*Shanna McCullough, Billy Dee*
The continuing story of an insatiable woman whose
need for sex is coupled with masochistic tendencies.
This one doesn't even try to work the episodes around
a plot.
A            62 min (ort 79 min) Cut (6 min 18 sec)
V                                                  VPD

**INSATIABLE ALICIA AND THE MARQUIS \*\***    18
Al Bagram          SPAIN                           1982
*Concha Valero, Jorge Batalla, Paule James, James*
*Garci, Mivna Bel, Andrea Albani, Joaquin Gomez*
In Spain, the gold-digging Alicia visits her uncle (a
valet in a castle) and goes to great lengths to seduce
the Count, even though he fancies another guest, a
photographic model there on a calendar assignment.
A wildly implausible sexual melodrama shot at the
same time as SEXUAL DESIRES, using the same set
and a similar cast.
Aka: EL MARQUES, LA MENOR Y EL TRAVESTI
A      61 min (ort 71 min) Cut (6 min 32 sec in addition
to film cuts) dubbed
B,V                                                ELE

**INSEMINOID \***                                  18
Norman J. Warren      UK                           1980
*Robin Clarke, Jennifer Ashley, Stephanie Beacham,*
*Steven Grives, Judy Geeson, Barry Houghton,*
*Rosalind Lloyd, Victoria Tennant, Trevor Thomas,*
*Heather Wright, David Baxt, Dominic Jephcott, John*
*Segal, Kevin O'Shea*
An alien creature takes over the body of a female
member of a team of space archaeologists, and she
gives birth to twin monsters. A repulsive ALIEN clone
with none of the sheer style of that earlier film.
Aka: HORROR PLANET
FAN                   93 min; 89 min (INTMED)
B,V                        BWV/VSP; INTMED

**INSERTS \***                                     18
John Byrum            UK                            1975
*Richard Dreyfuss, Jessica Harper, Veronica*
*Cartwright, Bob Hoskins, Stephen Davies*
A once-famous director in Hollywood of the 1930s, is
reduced to making sexo films for a living. A boring
and pretentious affair, in which the five characters
stumble through the interminable script in search of a
few good lines.
DRA                        114 min (ort 117 min)
B,V                                                WHV

**INSIDE DESIREE COUSTEAU \***
Leon Gucci            USA                           1979
*Desiree Cousteau, Serena, Susan Nero, John C.*
*Holmes*
Plotless sex film following the exploits of the title
character as she enjoys numerous encounters.
A                                                  90 min
V                                                  RIP

**INSIDE MAN, THE \*\***                           15
Tom Clegg          SWEDEN/UK                        1985
*Dennis Hopper, Gosta Ekman, Hardy Kruger, David*
*Wilson, Cory Molder*
Routine spy thriller with Stockholm locations, and the
novel plot of a laser invention for hunting submarines,
but the usual collection of spies who are after it.
THR                                                89 min
B,V                                                CBS

**INSIDE MOVES \*\***
Richard Donner        USA                          1980
*John Savage, David Morse, Diana Scarwid, Amy*
*Wright, Tony Burton, Harold Russell, Bill Henderson,*

*Bert Remsen, Steve Kahan, Jack O'Leary*
A young would-be-suicide meets a group of handicapped people in a bar, and learns a thing or two about
self-respect. Undeniably sincere, this curious and
uncertain drama has a few tragi-comic observations,
but not enough of them to sustain the flimsy plot.
Boa: novel by Todd Walton.
DRA                                                113 min
B,V,V2                                             INT/CBS

**INSIDE OUT \*\***                                PG
Peter Duffell    UK/WEST GERMANY                   1975
*Telly Savalas, James Mason, Robert Culp, Aldo Ray,*
*Gunter Meisner, Adrian Hoven, Wolfgang Lukschy,*
*Charles Korvin, Constantin De Goguel, Richard*
*Warner, Don Fellows, Lorna Dallas, Sigrid Hanack,*
*Peter Schlesinger*
Americans break a Nazi war criminal out of prison in
East Germany in order to recover buried Nazi loot. An
implausible action story that sails along pretty well so
long as the plot is not followed too closely.
Aka: GOLDEN HEIST, THE; HITLER'S GOLD
A/AD                       93 min (ort 97 min)
B,V                            MEGA L/A; WHV

**INSIDE SEKA \*\***
Seka (Yontz)/Ken Yontz
                      USA                           1980
*Seka (Yontz/Dorothy Hundley Patton), Ken Yontz,*
*Christie Ford, Merle Michaels*
Pseudo-documentary on the career of the title porno
star, with numerous encounters that are based,
according to a concluding statement from her, on real
experiences. A peculiar film of limited range, but
much activity that may please her devotees. See also
CONFESSIONS OF SEKA.
A                                                  96 min
B,V                                                XTASY

**INSIDE STORY, THE \*\***                         U
Allan Dwan            USA                           1948
*William Lundigan, Marsha Hunt, Charles Winninger,*
*Gail Patrick*
A look at the Depression years, when a large amount
of money suddenly starts to circulate during a bank
holiday in 1933. An obscure and only slightly divert-
ing tale.
DRA                                            87 min B/W
V                                           VMA; STABL

**INSIDE THE THIRD REICH \*\*\***                  15
Marvin J. Chomsky     USA                          1982
*Viveca Lindfors, Rutger Hauer, Derek Jacobi, John*
*Gielgud, Maria Schell, Trevor Howard, Ian Holm,*
*Robert Vaughn, Stephen Collins, Randy Quaid, Elke*
*Sommer, Renee Soutendijk, Mort Sahl, Blythe Danner,*
*Zoe Wanamaker*
A well-made insider's view of life in the Third Reich,
as seen from the privileged vantage point Speer's
position gave him. Hauer's American TV debut, but
it's Jacobi's portrayal of Hitler that really stands out.
Written and produced by E. Jack Neuman and
originally shown in two parts.
Boa: book by Albert Speer.
DRA                        250 min (ort 412 min) mTV
B,V,V2                                             CIC

**INSIGNIFICANCE \*\*\*\***                        15
Nicholas Roeg         UK                            1984
*Tony Curtis, Theresa Russell, Gary Busey, Michael*
*Emil, Will Sampson, Lou Hirsch, Ray Charleson,*
*Patrick Kilpatrick, Jan O'Connell, George Holmes,*
*Richard Davidson, Mitchell Greenberg, Raynor*
*Scheine, Jude Ciceolella*
Story of a fictitious meeting at a hotel between
Einstein, McCarthy, Joe DiMaggio and Marilyn Mon-
roe. A careful and highly perceptive examination of
fame and its implications, coupled with a look at the

perils of atomic warfare, set in New York during 1953 with the four characters "unnamed" but readily identifiable. This is a film both biting and funny, and superbly acted by all concerned.
Boa: play Relatively Speaking by Terry Johnson.
DRA                                    105 min (ort 110 min)
B,V                                                      PVG

## INSOLENT, THE **
Jean Claude Roy       FRANCE              1972
Henry Silva, Sabine Glaser, Andre Pousee
Routine crime thriller involving the planning of a bullion robbery.
Aka: L'INSOLENT
DRA                                             87 min
B,V                                 HOT L/A; VIDVIC

## INSPECTOR CALLS, AN ***
Guy Hamilton          UK                  1954
Alastair Sim, Arthur Young, Brian Worth, Eileen
Moore, Bryan Forbes, Jane Wenham, Olga Lindo,
George Woodbridge, Barbara Everest, John Welsh,
Norman Bird, Pat Neal, George Cole, Jenny Jones,
Amy Green, Catherine Wilmer
A mysterious policeman calls on a wealthy family in Yorkshire in 1912, after a young girl has taken her own life with poison. As he questions them, a series of flashbacks show how each member of the family bears some of the blame for her death. A nice adaptation of Priestley's play, with a neat twist by way of a finale.
Boa: play by John Boynton Priestley.
DRA                                    77 min (ort 79 min) B/W
V                                                        WHV

## INSPECTOR CLOUSEAU *                              U
Bud Yorkin            UK                  1968
Alan Arkin, Frank Finlay, Patrick Cargill, Beryl Reid,
Barry Foster, Delia Boccardo, Clive Francis, Richard
Pearson, Michael Ripper, Tutte Lemkow, Anthony
Ainley, Wallas Eaton, Eric Pohlmann
Inspector Clouseau is called in by Scotland Yard, to deal with the threat of a series of serious robberies. A lame attempt to cash in on the success of THE PINK PANTHER films, that very quickly runs out of steam.
COM                                    92 min (ort 105 min)
V                                                        WHV

## INSPECTOR GENERAL, THE ***
Henry Koster          USA                 1949
Danny Kaye, Walter Slezak, Barbara Bates, Elsa
Lanchester, Gene Lockhart, Alan Hale, Walter Catlett
Musical version of a play about a traveller who is mistaken for a government official, with Kaye hamming it up with wild abandon and generally making up for the sluggishness of the plot.
Aka: HAPPY TIMES
Boa: play by Nikolai Vasilevich Gogol.
MUS                                    96 min (ort 102 min)
B,V                                                      MOV

## INSPECTOR MORSE: THE DEAD OF
JERICHO ***                                        15
Alistair Reid         UK                  1989
John Thaw, Kevin Whately, Gemma Jones, Patrick
Troughton, Norman Jones, Richard Durden, James
Laurenson, Peter Woodthorpe
The very first episode from a popular TV police detective series that gave Thaw one of his best-ever roles as a world-weary and highly unorthodox police officer who saw his cases as intellectual challenges as much as crimes. The body of an attractive woman who apparently committed suicide is discovered, but Morse has good reason to believe she was murdered.
DRA                                          104 min mTV
V                                 PICK; SCREL; CENTV

## INSPECTOR MORSE 2: THE SILENT WORLD OF
NICHOLAS QUINN ***                                 15
Brian Parker          UK                  1987

John Thaw, Kevin Whately, Michael Gough, Frederick
Treves, Elspet Gray, Roger Lloyd Pack, Clive Swift,
Amanda Hillwood
The second tale from this excellently-scripted crime series, in which Detective Inspector Morse could always be relied upon to use his highly intellectual and unconventional approach to solve his cases. In this episode a deaf man working for Oxford University's examinations board appears to have come into possession of a piece of information that cost him his life.
DRA                                          101 min mTV
V                                                      CENTV

## INSPIRATIONS **                                   18
Joe Sherman           USA                 1982
Lisa De Leeuw, Mai Lin, Serena
A sex-mad doctor in need of cash, videotapes his patients' erotic fantasies and sells them, in this considerably shortened UK version of a hardcore American original.
Osca: CAPTAIN LUST/TEENAGE BRIDE (ROXY)
A                            43 min (ort 89 min) Cut (12 sec)
B,V                               TCX; TOW; ROXY

## INTERFACE *                                        15
Andy Anderson         USA                 1984
John Davies, Laura Lane, Matthew Sacks, Arne
Strand, Michael Hendrix, Janet Six, Laurie Allison,
Kellie Lawson, John Williamson, Dan Foster, David
Blood, Betty Bunkhart, Lou Diamond Phillips, Chris
Jenkins, Roggie Cale
Students who dress up as crimefighters, gradually become obsessed with their role-playing, in this cliche-ridden drama.
DRA                                             88 min
B,V                                                      VES

## INTERIORS ***                                      15
Woody Allen           USA                 1978
E.G. Marshall, Geraldine Page, Diane Keaton,
Maureen Stapleton, Kristin Griffith, Mary Beth Hurt,
Richard Jordan, Sam Waterston
Woody Allen attempts a kind of Bergmanesque study of well-off but unhappy people, marking a change in direction from his earlier work that so often parodied films such as these. A film that is too lightweight to be really tragic and too anguished to be funny, but is undeniably well put together.
DRA                                    91 min (ort 93 min)
B,V                                                      WHV

## INTERLUDE **                                       PG
Kevin Billington      UK                  1968
Oskar Werner, Barbara Ferris, Virginia Maskell,
Donald Sutherland, Alan Webb, Geraldine Sherman,
Robert Lang, Nora Swinburne, Bernard Kay, John
Cleese, Humphrey Burton
A female newspaper reporter falls in love with a famous conductor, but the wife of the latter refuses to accept the situation, in this remake of the 1957 film. A manipulative tearjerker, that's all charm and no substance.
Aka: WHEN TOMORROW COMES
DRA                                    109 min (ort 113 min)
V                                                        RCA

## INTERMEZZO ***                                     PG
Gregory Ratoff        USA                 1939
Ingrid Bergman, Leslie Howard, John Halliday, Edna
Best, Cecil Kellaway
A world-famous violinist has an affair with his musical protege, but she finds the courage to leave him, thus freeing him to return to his wife and children. An overly sentimental remake of the Swedish original of 1936, which is the better film of the two. Its touching moments, and there are some, are diluted by an intrusive instrumental backing that is rarely

silenced. This was Bergman's first English-speaking film.
Aka: ESCAPE TO HAPPINESS
Osca: GARDEN OF ALLAH, THE (VCC)
DRA         70 min; 156 min (VCC – 2 film cassette) B/W
B,V                                    GHV; VCC (VHS only)

## INTERNAL AFFAIRS **                                    18
Mike Figgis              USA                    1990
*Richard Gere, Andy Garcia, Nancy Travis, Laurie Metcalf, William Baldwin, Michael Beach*
A young cop joins the Internal Affairs department of the L.A. police and becomes obsessed with busting a corrupt cop, so much so that his remorseless pursuit of justice becomes a personal vendetta. Gere gives a fine performance as the dishonest cop, in a film that for all its promise fails to develop its ideas.
DRA                          110 min (ort 117 min)
V                                                CIC

## INTERNATIONAL VELVET **                              PG
Bryan Forbes             UK                     1978
*Tatum O'Neal, Christopher Plummer, Anthony Hopkins, Nanette Newman, Peter Barkworth, Dinsdale Landen, Sarah Bullen, Jeffrey Byron, Richard Warwick, Daniel Albineri, Jason White, Martin Neil, Douglas Reith, Norman Wooland*
An attempt to produce a sequel to the 1944 hit film "National Velvet", that told of a champion horse. This story is one of an orphan girl who develops into an Olympic horsewoman, coached by her Aunt Velvet (the grown-up main character from the first film). An agreeable and undemanding tale, quite undeserving of the opprobrium heaped on it by the critics, despite the insipid dialogue.
DRA                          89 min (ort 132 min)
B,V                                              MGM

## INTERZONE **                                         18
Deran Sarafian                                  1987
*Bruce Abbott, Tegan Clive*
Another post-nuclear holocaust tale, in which the Earth is a dead wasteland except for one region, which is protected from incursions by a powerful force field. However, two rival groups find a way of gaining access.
FAN                                          88 min
V                                                EIV

## INTIMATE BETRAYAL ***                                PG
Robert M. Lewis          USA                    1987
*James Brolin, Melody Anderson, Morgan Stevens, Pamela Bellwood, Joe Spano*
A man hides a secret from his wife, and when his picture appears in a magazine a chain of events is set in motion that leads to him faking his own death. With the apparent loss of her husband, his wife begins to piece together details of his secret life. A complex and effective thriller.
THR                                          96 min
B,V                                              VIR

## INTIMATE CONFESSIONS OF STELLA **                    18
Zacarias Urbiola      FRANCE/SPAIN             1978
*Azvcena Hernandez, Teresa Gimpera, Fernando Martin, Riccardo Merino*
A schoolgirl goes home for Christmas, and sets about seducing all and sundry, regardless of sex.
Aka: UNE INGENUE LIBERTINE
A                                            87 min
B,V                                             GLOB

## INTIMATE GAMES *
Tudor Gates              UK                     1976
*Suzy Mandell, Peter Blake, Anna Bergman, George Baker, Ian Hendry, Joyce Blair, Hugh Lloyd, Queenie Watts, Mary Millington, Dudley Stevens, Barbara Eatwell, Norman Lean, Steve Amber, Norman Chappell, John Vyvyan, John Benson*

Sex comedy about university students of psychology, who have to write about their sexual fantasies. Dull serving of titillation, as smutty as a seaside postcard but not quite as funny.
A                                            90 min
B,V                                    VDM L/A; MED

## INTIMATE RELATIONS ***                               18
Luigi Russo              ITALY                  1975
*Philippe Leroy, Simonetta Steffanelli, Florence Ramon*
Newlywed couple Laura and Sandro set up home in a cottage in the grounds of his parents' estate. But the unwelcome and incessant visits of Mum and Dad seem to have doomed their marriage to failure, and in addition Sandro is making love to Laura's sister. An amusing tale of marital discord.
Aka: LA NUORA GIOVANE
A                          77 min (ort 84 min) Cut (49 sec)
B,V,V2                                        VPD; TCX

## INTIMATE STRANGERS **                                15
Robert Ellis Miller      USA                    1986
*Stacy Keach, Teri Garr, Cathy Lee Crosby, Priscilla Lopez, Justin Deas, Max Gail, Justin Deas, Max Barabas, Tresa Hughes, Bob E. Hannah, Robert Goodman, Ray Forchion, Manny Bronz, Ernest Aruba, Carol Gun, Christine Page*
A married couple worked as doctor and nurse during the Vietnam War and became separated after the fall of Saigon. After ten years in captivity the wife returns home, but is still haunted and scarred by her experiences. Meanwhile, her husband has taken up with another woman and is now forced to choose between them. An average soap opera-style melodrama.
DRA                        90 min (ort 100 min) mTV
V                                                GHV

## INTIMIDATOR, THE **                                  15
Noel Black               USA                    1988
*Bruce Boxleitner, David Graf, Pat Hingle*
A brutal thug returns to his home town after a couple of years in jail and proceeds to terrorise the inhabitants, who eventually conspire to murder him. However, the young public prosecutor is outraged by this and sets about gathering sufficient evidence to prosecute those responsible. A muddled "film with a message" that is too ambiguous to be effective.
DRA                                          97 min
B,V                                              ODY

## INTO THE HOMELAND **                                 15
Lesli Linka Glatter      USA                    1987
*Powers Boothe, Paul Le Mat, C. Thomas Howell, Cindy Pickett, David Caruso, Shelby Leverington, Emily Longstreth*
A dissipated former policeman goes after his missing daughter, and gets embroiled in a violent clash with a nasty bunch of white supremacists. A formula action yarn of no great consequence. Scripted by Anna Hamilton Phelan, this was the feature debut for Glatter.
A/AD                       90 min (ort 115 min) mCab
V/sh                                             GHV

## INTO THE LABYRINTH *                                  U
                         UK                     1983
*Ron Moody, Pamela Salem, Lisa Turner, Simon Henderson, Simon Beal, Tim Bannerman, John Abineri, Philip Manikum, Paul Lavers, Edwina Ford, Peewee Hunt*
A sorcerer sends three children off to regain the source of his power, stolen from him by an evil witch. An episode from a TV series entitled "The Third Eye".
JUV                                     75 min mTV
V                                                VGM

## INTO THE LABYRINTH 2 **                              PG
                         UK                     1989
*Simon Beal, Lisa Turner, Simon Henderson, Ron*

*Moody, Pamela Salem*
A further set of adventures for our intrepid time-travellers who encounter an evil witch in their search for the Nidus.
JUV                               97 min mTV
V                                        VGM

## INTO THE NIGHT **                    15
John Landis            USA             1985
*Jeff Goldblum, Michelle Pfeiffer, Richard Farnsworth, Irene Papas, Kathryn Harrold, Paul Mazursky, Roger Vadim, Dan Aykroyd, David Bowie, Bruce McGill, Vera Miles, Clu Gulager*
Comedy thriller about a man who becomes involved with a beautiful girl on the run from Iranian assassins. A film made for film buffs, with a number of funny cameos by directors (Don Siegel, Jonathan Demme and David Cronenberg among them) that is far too self-centred and contrived, to work as a movie for the general public.
COM                      109 min (ort 115 min)
B,V                                     CIC

## INTO THIN AIR ***                    15
Roger Young            USA             1985
*Ellen Burstyn, Robert Prosky, Sam Robards, John Dennis Johnston, Patricia Smith, Tate Donovan, Caroline McWilliams, J.P. Bumstead, Bill Calvert, Britt Leach, Ebbe Roe Smith, Elizabeth Barclay, Dale Wilson, Babs Chula*
A 19-year-old boy goes missing from home and as usual the authorities show little interest in finding him. A gripping little drama with excellent performances from the leads. Inspired by "Just Another Missing Kid", a report broadcast by the Canadian Broadcasting Company. The script is by George Rubio.
Aka: BRIAN WALKER, PLEASE CALL HOME
DRA                    93 min (ort 100 min) mTV
B,V                                 IVS; CAST

## INTOLERANCE ****
D.W. Griffith          USA             1916
*Lillian Gish, Mae Marsh, Constance Talmadge, Robert Harron, Elmo Lincoln, Eugene Pallette, Bessie Love, Elmer Clifton, Seena Owen, Alfred Paget*
A classic of the early cinema, with four parallel stories linked and intercut to demonstrate man's inhumanity to man. Despite the quaint little title cards and the over-ripe performances, this powerful work is an all-time great, with many spectacular scenes of undeniable power. Some prints have a running time of 208 minutes.
DRA              113 min (ort 123 min) B/W silent
B,V                                SPEC/POLY

## INTRIGUE *
Edwin L. Marin         USA             1947
*George Raft, Tom Tully, June Havoc, Helena Carter, Marvin Miller, Elmo Lincoln, Dan Seymour, Philip Ahn*
A man is dishonourably discharged from the army because of two women's plotting. He plans to expose the black market in Shanghai to square things with the army. A prosaic and uninventive time-filler.
DRA                             90 min B/W
B,V                         ITL L/A; BBC; VMA

## INTRIGUE **                          PG
David Drury            USA             1988
*Scott Glenn, Robert Loggia, William Atherton, Martin Shaw, Cherie Lunghi, Eleanor Bron*
A US government agent is given the job of smuggling an old buddy out of the Soviet Union to which he defected a few years earlier. He then discovers that his instructions include an order to murder. A competent if undemanding little thriller.
THR                    94 min (ort 100 min) mTV
B,V                                     EIV

## INTRUDER WITHIN, THE **              15
Peter Carter           USA             1981
*Chad Everett, Joseph Bottoms, Jennifer Warren, Rockne Tarkington, Lynda Mason Green, Paul Larson, James Hayden, Mary Ann McDonald, Matt Craven, Michael Hogan, Ed LaPlante, Mickey Gilbert, Joe Finnegan*
An oil rig crew is menaced by a nasty alien creature from the depths of the ocean, in this modest but fairly tense and effective shocker.
HOR                91 min (ort 100 min) mTV
V                                       VPD

## INTRUDER, THE ***                    15
Roger Corman           USA             1961
*William Shatner, Frank Maxwell, Beverly Lunsford, Robert Emhardt, Jeanne Cooper, Leo Gordon, Charles Beaumont*
A racist travels from one Southern town to the next, doing his best to incite the townsfolk against enforced racial integration in the local schools. One of Corman's better films which, though cheaply made, neither made any money nor was a quickie exercise in exploitation. The literate script is by Beaumont.
Aka: I HATE YOUR GUTS!; SHAME; STRANGER, THE
Boa: novel by Charles Beaumont.
DRA                                  84 min
V                                    CONNO

## INTRUDER, THE *                      18
David F. Eustace     CANADA            1981
*Pita Oliver, James B. Douglas, Gerard Jordan*
A stranger with supernatural powers comes to a small town and begins to terrorise the inhabitants.
HOR                                  90 min
B,V                                     CBS

## INTRUDER, THE **                     18
Scott Spiegel          USA             1988
*Elizabeth Cox, Danny Hicks, David Byrnes, Renee Estevez, Sam Raimi, Alvy Moore, Tom Lester, Emil Sitka*
A supermarket is the setting for a series of gruesome slasher murders, in this well made but utterly conventional formula offering.
Aka: LAST CHECKOUT, THE: NIGHT CREW
HOR          82 min (ort 90 min) Cut (1 min 53 sec)
B,V                                     CFD

## INVADERS FROM MARS **                PG
Tobe Hooper            USA             1986
*Karen Black, Timothy Bottoms, Hunter Carson, Laraine Newman, James Karen, Louise Fletcher, Bud Cort, Jimmy Hunt*
A flashy but inferior remake of the atmospheric 1953 film, about a small boy who witnesses the landing of a spacecraft near his small town and sees its inhabitants taken over one by one. There are some good moments and it's all done with great panache, but the film slowly and surely unwinds as it develops.
FAN          94 min (ort 100 min) (Cut at film release)
B,V                                     RNK

## INVADERS FROM MARS ***
William Cameron Menzies
                       USA             1953
*Helena Carter, Arthur Franz, Jimmy Hunt, Leif Erickson, Hillary Brooke, Bert Freed*
A well-made tale of a young boy, who witnesses an alien ship landing and the gradual takeover of the town's inhabitants, his own parents included. The first half of the film is by far the best. Once the aliens are exposed (all too easily, it seemed), the film develops (via the standard stock footage of tanks rolling) into a "we can shoot 'em and beat 'em" story. Originally shot in 3-D and remade in 1986.
FAN                        71 min (ort 82 min)
B,V                                 INT/CBS

## INVADERS OF THE LOST GOLD *
Alan Birkinshaw       ITALY       1981
*Stuart Whitman, Glynis Barber, Edmund Purdom,*
*Harold Sakata, Woody Strode, Britt Ekland, Laura*
*Gemser*
Thirty-six years after the end of WW2, the hunt is on
for ten missing cases containing Japanese gold.
Aka: SAFARI SENZA RITORNO
A/AD                                         86 min
B,V,V2                           AVI L/A; VIPCO

## INVASION OF CAROL ENDERS, THE **
Burt Brinckerhoff       USA       1982
*Meredith Baxter, Christopher Connelly, Sally Kemp,*
*Charles Aidman*
Two women are being treated in intensive care. One
dies of her injuries, the other recovers to find that she
has acquired the dead woman's personality and
memories. An intriguing but not entirely successful
chiller.
HOR                                          67 min
B,V                                       IVS; CBS

## INVASION OF THE BLOOD FARMERS **
Ed Adlum       USA       1972
*Norman Kelly, Cynthia Fleming, Tanna Hunter,*
*Bruce Detrick, Jack Neubeck, Paul Craig Jennings,*
*Warren D'Oyly-Rhind*
A farming community in upstate New York is
threatened by an evil sect of Druids, who seek a rare
blood type so that they can revive their queen. A
deliberately sleazy effort (made for about $40,000),
that is now well regarded, if only as an early example
of camp horror.
Aka: BLOOD FARMERS
HOR                               73 min (ort 86 min)
B,V                               VSP L/A; MOV

## INVASION OF THE BODY SNATCHERS, THE ** 15
Philip Kaufman       USA       1978
*Donald Sutherland, Brooke Adams, Leonard Nimoy,*
*Veronica Cartwright, Jeff Goldblum, Kevin McCarthy,*
*Don Siegel, Robert Duvall*
A remake of the 1956 classic now updated to the 1970s
and transplanted to San Francisco. Some superb
effects and genuinely tense moments fail to offer much
improvement on the original. Watch out for Kevin
McCarthy and director Don Siegel, both of whom have
cameo roles. The score is by Denny Zeitlin.
FAN                                         115 min
B,V                                          WHV

## INVASION OF THE BODY SNATCHERS *** PG
Don Siegel       USA       1956 (re-issued 1979)
*Kevin McCarthy, Dana Wynter, Larry Gates, King*
*Donovan, Carolyn Jones, Jean Willes, Ralph Dumke,*
*Virginia Christine, Tom Fadden, Sam Peckinpah*
Tense and atmospheric tale of alien duplicates, who
gradually hatch from pods and take over the inhabi-
tants of a small town. (Towards the end the storyline
falters, as the hero's girlfriend is taken over even
though no pod is present.) An effective demonstration
of what is possible with a limited budget. The script is
by Daniel Mainwaring. The clumsy prologue and
epilogue tacked onto the film by the studio were
removed on re-issue. Remade in 1978.
Boa: Collier's Magazine serial The Body Snatchers by
Jack Finney.
FAN                              77 min (ort 80 min) B/W
V                                            VCC

## INVASION OF THE BODYSUCKERS * 18
William Fruet       USA       1987
*Steve Railsback, Susan Anspach, Gwynyth Walsh,*
*John Vernon, Joe Flaherty, Robin Duke*
An ALIEN rip-off, in which the creature this time is a
mysterious plant whose human victim gives "birth" to
a hideous worm-like monster. Most of the film takes
place in darkness – no great handicap as it's not worth

watching under any circumstances.
Aka: BLUE MONKEY; INSECT
HOR                              90 min (ort 98 min)
B,V                                         SONY

## INVASION, USA * 18
Joseph Zito       USA       1985
*Chuck Norris, Richard Lynch, Melissa Prophet, Alex*
*Colon, Alexander Zale*
A former CIA operative takes on the combined might
of a Cuban/Soviet invasion force and single-handedly
routs them, emerging unscathed from this encounter.
Violent, bloody and sterile.
A/AD                       96 min (ort 107 min) Cut (14 sec)
B,V                                          MGM

## INVESTIGATION OF A CITIZEN ABOVE 18
## SUSPICION ***
Elio Petri       ITALY       1970
*Gian Maria Volonte, Florinda Bolkan, Salvo Randone,*
*Gianni Santuccio*
Taut drama about a police chief who murders his
mistress, and then proceeds to investigate the crime,
having implicated another of her lovers. The score is
by Ennio Morricone. AA: Foreign.
Aka: INDAGINE SU UN CITTADINO AL DI SOPRA
DI OGNI SOSPETTO; INVESTIGATION INTO A
CITIZEN ABOVE SUSPICION; INVESTIGATION
OF A PRIVATE CITIZEN; STORY OF A CITIZEN
ABOVE ALL SUSPICION
DRA                                         115 min
B,V                                          RCA

## INVINCIBLE ARMOUR, THE ** 18
                          HONG KONG
*Huang Cheng Li, Lee Lau Fer, Lar Kin Tee*
A general is framed for the murder of his superior and
has to find the real culprit in this standard martial
arts film.
MAR                             100 min Cut (10 sec)
B,V                                          VPD

## INVINCIBLE BARBARIAN, THE **
Frank Shannon (Franco Prosperi)
                          ITALY       1981
*Sabrina Siani, Peter McCoy (P. Torrisi), David*
*Jenkins, Diana Roy*
Two brothers avenge the slaughter of their tribe in
this forgettable actioner.
Aka: GUNAN, KING OF THE BARBARIANS;
GUNANA RE BARBARO
A/AD                             83 min (ort 92 min)
B,V,V2                           VSP L/A; FTV

## INVINCIBLE IRON PALM **
Chu Mu       HONG KONG       1971
*Charlie Chin (Chin Hsiang-Lin), Alan Teng (Teng*
*Kuang-Jung)*
Formula martial arts tale of honour and revenge.
Aka: WU-TI T'IEH SHA CHANG
MAR                                          85 min
V                                          VIPCO

## INVINCIBLE OBSESSED FIGHTER ** 18
John King       HONG KONG       198-
*Eton Chong, Mike Wong*
Two powerful warriors fight to possess a stolen
treasure.
MAR                             84 min Cut (26 sec)
B,V                                          VPD

## INVINCIBLE POLE FIGHTER, THE ** 18
Liu Chia Liang       HONG KONG       198-
*Chang Chan Peng, Hsaio Ho, Liu Chia Yung, Yung*
*Wang Tu, Mai Te Lo, Fu Sheng, Lou Ka Sheng,*
*Gordon Liu*
A martial arts tale set in the Sung Dynasty, and
introducing the technique of stick fighting, making
use of staffs and spears. Two brothers survive a

massacre and one enters a monastery in order to gain the skills he needs to have his revenge on the killers.
Aka: EIGHT DIAGRAM POLE FIGHTER, THE; INVINCIBLE POLE FIGHTERS, THE
MAR      95 min (ort 110 min) Cut (56 sec)
B,V      CLOK; SHOG; WHV

## INVINCIBLE SHAOLIN KUNG FU **      15
Ko Shih Hao      HONG KONG
*Hsiah Po Le, Li Yi Min, Ho Chun, Chen Wai Lan, Yue Chung Chiu, Sen Wing Je, Ying Kwok Chung*
Three men avenge the murder of a great kung fu fighter in this routine tale.
Aka: SECRET SHAOLIN KUNG FU, THE
MAR      86 min (XTASY); 91 min (DRUM) Cut (15 sec)
B,V      VPD L/A; XTASY; DRUM

## INVINCIBLE SUPER CHAN ** 
Sun Yang      HONG KONG
*Han Sinan Chin, Chin Chi*
In the Ming Dynasty all of China feared one man, an invincible fighter whose presence always spelt death. Another martial arts tale where various warriors battle over honour – if not a better script.
MAR      90 min
B,V      VPD

## INVISIBLE DEAD, THE *      18
Peter Chevalier      FRANCE/SPAIN      1970
*Howard Vernon, Brigitte Carva, Fred Sanders (Fernand Snacho), Francis Valladares, Isabel Del Rio, Evane Hanska, Arlette Balkis, May Chartrette, Christian Forges, Eugene Berthier*
A scientist creates an invisible monster that escapes and terrorises the countryside.
Aka: ORLOFF AND THE INVISIBLE MAN: ORLOFF Y El HOMBRE INVISIBLE
HOR      90 min
B,V      CAREY; GLOB

## INVISIBLE KID, THE *      15
Avery Crounse      USA      1988
*Jay Underwood, Karen Black, Chynna Phillips, Wally Ward, Brother Theodore, Mike Genovese, Jan King*
A shy teenager discovers the secret of invisibility and puts it to good comic use (e.g. spying on girls in various states of undress). A banal, low-grade comedy outing, that's not even redeemed by good performances.
COM      90 min (ort 95 min)
B,V      CHV; BRAVE

## INVITATION TO HELL *      15
Wes Craven      USA      1984
*Robert Urich, Joanna Cassidy, Susan Lucci, Kevin McCarthy, Joe Regalbuto, Patricia McCormack, Bill Erwin, Soleil Moon Frye, Barret Oliver, Nicholas Worth, Virginia Vincent, Greg Monaghan, Lois Hamilton, Cal Bartlett*
A couple move to the country and are invited to join the local club, which may be a front for more sinister activities. Despite a few nods in the direction of the Faustus legend, this horror yarn never rises above the banality of its script.
HOR      91 min (ort 100 min) mTV
B,V      PRV; CH5

## INVITATION TO HELL **      18
Michael J. Murphy      USA      1982
*Becky Simpson, Joseph Sheahan, Colin Efford, Steven Longhurst*
A young girl accepts an invitation to a friend's party unaware that she is to be a human sacrifice to satanic forces. Heavily re-edited to obtain a certification (the Videomedia release ran to 94 minutes) and despite that, still cut by a few seconds. The film would have been effective but is now barely coherent.
HOR      47 min (ort 94 min) Cut (39 sec)
B,V      VDM L/A; SENAT/PHE

## INVITATION TO THE WEDDING * 
Joseph Brooks      UK      1983
*Ralph Richardson, John Gielgud, Paul Nicholas, Elizabeth Sheperd, John Standing, Edward Duke, Susan Brooks, Ronald Lacey, Janet Burnell, Jeremy Clyde, Allan Cuthbertson, Aimee Delamain, Leslie French, Kate Harper*
During a wedding rehearsal everything that can possibly go wrong does, with an American who is standing in for the groom finding himself married to the daughter of an impoverished earl. Bad casting and a flabby script ruin an idea that might have worked well enough as a 30-minute short.
COM      85 min (ort 90 min)
B,V      AVA/CBS

## IPCRESS FILE, THE **      PG
Sidney J. Furie      UK      1965
*Michael Caine, Nigel Green, Guy Doleman, Sue Lloyd, Gordon Jackson, Frank Gatliff, Aubrey Richards, Freda Bamford, Thomas Baptiste, Peter Ashmore, Oliver MacGreevy*
Introduces Harry Palmer, the cockney secret agent. In this film he has to trace a missing scientist and discovers that his superior is a spy. A convoluted and twisty tale, that is never less than impossible to follow but has a nice understated performance from Caine. Unfortunately it all now looks rather dated. The score is by John Barry. Followed by FUNERAL IN BERLIN and BILLION DOLLAR BRAIN.
Boa: novel by Len Deighton.
THR      108 min; 103 min (RNK)
B,V,LV      BWV/VSP; RNK (VHS only)

## IRENE **      U
Herbert Wilcox      USA      1940
*Anna Neagle, Ray Milland, Roland Young, Alan Marshal, May Robson, Billie Burke, Arthur Treacher*
Milland as a wealthy playboy, romances working girl Neagle. A remake of a musical (done as a silent with Colleen More) minus most of the songs. The cast do their best with a slow and limply directed film, that charms at a few places.
Boa: play by James H. Montgomery.
DRA      82 min B/W (plus a colour sequence)
V      VCC

## IRISHMAN, THE *** 
Donald Crombie      AUSTRALIA      1978
*Michael Craig, Simon Burke, Robin Nevin, Lou Brown, Andrew Maguire, Byron Brown*
Story of a lorry-driver and his family, facing problems and progress in the 1920s. A highly rewarding drama that succeeds through great performances and intelligent handling of the subject matter.
DRA      90 min (ort 108 min)
B,V      HVH; VSP

## IRON ANGELS **      18
     JAPAN      1988
*Hideki Saiju*
After the police destroy some opium plantations in Thailand, the villains set out to have their revenge and begin to kill off the officers who took part in the operation. Eventually a group of tough crimebusters are sent for, in order to destroy the female mastermind behind these attacks. More mindless nonsense, but quite well handled.
MAR      93 min dubbed
B,V      RCA

## IRON DRAGON STRIKES BACK, THE **      18
Siu Kwai      HONG KONG
*Bruce Li (Ho Tsung-Tao), Philip Ko, Hau Kwok Choi*
Martial arts adventure involving gold smuggling, deep sea diving and a quest for revenge.
MAR      88 min
B,V      VPD

**IRON EAGLE *** 15
Sidney J. Furie          USA          1986
*Louis Gossett Jr, Jason Gedrick, David Suchet, Tim Thomerson, Larry G. Scott, Caroline Lagerfelt, Jerry Levine, Michael Bowen*
And you'll need an iron posterior to sit through this adolescent and turgid nonsense. A teenage boy steals an F-16 fighter plane to rescue his father, who is being held prisoner somewhere in the Middle East. A sequel of similar merits followed in 1988.
A/AD          112 min (ort 119 min)
V/sh          RCA

**IRON EAGLE 2 *** PG
Sidney J. Furie     CANADA/ISRAEL          1988
*Louis Gossett Jr, Stuart Margolin, Mark Humphrey, Sharon H. Brandon, Alan Scarfe, Maury Chaykin*
A foolish sequel to the first film that sees Gossett back again as Charles "Chappy" Sinclair, whose new mission is to assemble a group of Soviet and American pilots for a raid on a secret nuclear missile site somewhere in the Middle East.
A/AD          95 min (ort 105 min)
V/sh          GHV

**IRON FIST ADVENTURE, THE **** 18
Sean Lee          HONG KONG          1986
*Jimmy Wang Yu, Maria Lee, Joe Tn, Stell Ng, John Lau*
A high-action kung fu tale with the hero out for revenge against gun-toting baddies. Not a bad effort in its way, but hardly enthralling.
MAR          86 min
B,V          SENAT/PHE

**IRON FIST BOXER **** 15
Chang-Tse-Tsou     HONG KONG          1989
Two young boys become apprentices to a master of "Back Kung Fu" in order to have revenge for a savage beating they suffered at the hands of a brothel guard. An undistinguished effort – average in all departments.
MAR          85 min Cut (2 min 48 sec)
B,V

**IRON MASK, THE **** 
Allan Dwan          USA          1929
*Douglas Fairbanks Sr, Belle Bennett, Marguerite De La Motte, Dorothy Revier, Vera Lewis, William Bakewell, Nigel de Brulier, Ullrich Haupt*
Silent version of the famous Dumas novel, about a plot to place a pretender on the throne of France, one of two twin princes whose existence has been kept secret. A lavish and exciting adventure that originally had some talkie sequences. Re-issued in 1940 with narration by Fairbanks Jr. Later filmed as "The Man In The Iron Mask".
Boa: novel The Man In The Iron Mask by Alexandre Dumas.
A/AD          87 min B/W silent
V          HVS

**IRON MASTER, THE *** 15
Umberto Lenzi     FRANCE/ITALY          1982
*Sam Pasco, George Eastman (Luigi Montefiore), Elvire Audrey, Pamela Field*
Story of a Stone Age man who discovers iron and uses it to make weapons. A European costume effort without the costumes.
Aka: IL DOMINATORE DEL FERRO; IL PADRONE DEL FERRO; IRONMASTER, THE; LA GUERRA DEL FERRO; LA GUERRE DU FER
FAN          84 min (ort 90 min) Cut (24 sec)
B,V,V2          MED

**IRON NECK LI **** 18
Chang Jen Chieh     HONG KONG
*Chi Kuan Chun, Hang Han, Hang Jui, Ku Man Ching, Ng Hsiao Chan, Ching Chen, Choi Mung, So*

*Jin Ping, Chen Hoi, Kong Yang, Lung Se, Se Ho Tao, Tsai Hung*
Lightweight tale of three heroes who travel the countryside, righting wrongs kung fu-style.
Aka: IRON NECK
MAR          89 min
B,V          WOV L/A; VTEL; GLOB

**IRON OX: THE TIGER KILLER *** 18
Tse Tsung Lung     HONG KONG          1973
*Wang Kang Hsiung, Tzu Lan, Huang Fei Lung, Chin Hsiu, Kao Chin Ti, Kao Chen Peng*
A young warrior is determined to clear his home province of criminals, once and for all.
Aka: IRON OX, THE TIGER'S KILLER; T'IEH NIU FU HU
MAR          92 min (ort 96 min) (Cut at film release)
B,V          AVR L/A; SHEP

**IRON TRIANGLE, THE **** 18
Eric Weston          USA          1988
*Beau Bridges, Haing S. Ngor, Johnny Hallyday, Liem Whatley, James Ishida*
Portrait of the lives of two combatants on opposite sides during the Vietnam War, one being a US captain and the other a young guerilla fighter in the Vietcong. A diverting view of the war as seen from the other side, but hampered by a disjointed script.
WAR          90 min (ort 94 min)
V          MED

**IRON WARRIOR *** 15
Al Bradley (Alfonso Brescia)
          ITALY          1985
*Miles O'Keeffe, Savina Gersak, Tim Lane, Frank Daddi, Elizabeth Kaza, Iris Peynado*
A foolish sword-and-sorcery offering, with a muscle-bound hero out to rescue a fair damsel, from a witch who has the usual plans for world domination. A kind of slack follow-up to ATOR, THE FIGHTING EAGLE and ATOR THE INVINCIBLE, both of which starred O'Keeffe.
FAN          84 min
B,V          RNK

**IRONWEED **** 15
Hector Babenco          USA          1987
*Jack Nicholson, Meryl Streep, Carroll Baker, Michael O'Keefe, Tom Waits, Fred Gwynne, Carroll Baker, Diane Venora, Margaret Whitton, Jake Dengel, Joe Grifasi, Nathan Lane, James Gammon*
Depression-era tale set in Albany, New York, where a vagrant seeks a way back into the life he left behind a year before. Streep plays his companion in misery who, like him, is a confirmed alcoholic. Both stars give fine performances in an atmospheric but almost unbearably depressing work, Babenco's first in America. Scripted by Kennedy from his Pulitzer Prize-winning novel.
Boa: novel by William Kennedy.
DRA          134 min (ort 143 min)
B,V          RCA

**IRRECONCILABLE DIFFERENCES **** 15
Charles Shyer          USA          1984
*Drew Barrymore, Shelley Long, Ryan O'Neal, Sam Wanamaker, Allen Garfield, Sharon Stone*
A nine-year-old interferes in the planned divorce of her parents, in an effort to get them to see sense. A sharp and often perceptive comedy, with an intelligent script by Shyer (in his directorial debut) and Nancy Meyers.
COM          113 min; 108 min (VCC) (ort 117 min)
B,V          GHV; VCC (VHS only)

**IRRESISTIBLE **** 18
Edwin Brown          USA          1983
*Misha Garr, Richard Pacheco, Samantha Fox, Nicole*

*Black, Gina Gianetti, Gayle Sterling, Starr Wood,
Dorothy Le May*
A henpecked husband is unhappy with his wife and spends most of his time daydreaming about women. By a stroke of good fortune he meets a man who offers him the use of an invention that will enable him to travel back in time. He enjoys encounters with woman such as Cleopatra, Shakespeare's Juliet (the machine ignores reality) and Mata Hari, but finally tires of the novelty and returns to his wife, in this silly and contrived sex-comedy.

| | |
|---|---|
| A | 100 min; 74 min (VEXCEL) |
| B,V | SPEC/POLY L/A; VEXCEL; PLAVID; GLOB |

## IS THERE SEX AFTER DEATH? ***
Jeanne Abel/Alan Abel   USA                1971
*Buck Henry, Alan Abel, Holly Woodlawn, Marshall
Efron, Earle Doud*
A crude but rather funny satire on the world's sex films, with Abel amusing as a travelling sexologist. Look out for Efron who appears as a porno-film director.

| | |
|---|---|
| A | 97 min (ort 120 min) |
| B,V | INT |

## ISHTAR *                                    PG
Elaine May            USA                1987
*Warren Beatty, Dustin Hoffman, Isabelle Adjani,
Charles Grodin, Jack Weston, Tess Harper, Carol
Kane, Aharon Ipale*
Two untalented songwriters are advised by their agent to go as far away from him as possible, and so they head for Morocco where they become involved in a budding revolution, and wind up on opposite sides. An expensive flop that tries awfully hard to be funny without ever finding a direction to go in. The deliberately bad songs are by Paul Williams and the film is scripted by May.

| | |
|---|---|
| COM | 103 min (ort 107 min) (Cut at film release by 8 |
| sec) | |
| B,V | RCA |

## ISLAND AT THE TOP OF THE WORLD, THE **   U
Robert Stevenson      USA                1974
*David Hartman, Donald Sinden, Jacques Marin,
Mako, David Gwillim, Agneta Eckemyr*
An Arctic expedition discovers a Viking colony at the top of a remote mountain range, in this fairly mundane adventure yarn that is partially rescued by some fine specia! effects if not by the ill-advised Viking dialogue (all of which is rather tediously translated).
Boa: novel The Lost Ones by Ian Cameron.

| | |
|---|---|
| A/AD | 93 min |
| B,V | WDV |

## ISLAND OF ADVENTURE, THE **              U
Anthony Squire        UK                 1981
*Norman Bowler, Wilfrid Brambell, Catherine Schell,
Eleonor Summerfield, Leon Lissek, Patrick Field,
Chloe Franks, Perry Benson, John Rhys-Davies, Daryl
Black, Paul Williamson, Julie Neesam, John Forbes-
Robertson, Frank Williams*
Story of the adventures that befall four children on holiday in Cornwall, when they stumble across a ruthless gang of international criminals who plan to destroy the world's currency balance. Fortunately, they find help in the shape of a mysterious stranger. An example of an interesting idea spoilt by poor acting and slow plot development, most of the action occurring in the last 30 minutes.
Boa: novel by Enid Blyton.

| | |
|---|---|
| JUV | 80 min (ort 82 min) |
| B,V,V2 | GHV |

## ISLAND OF DEATH **
Narcisco Ibanez Serrador
                      SPAIN              1975

*Lewis Fiander, Prunella Ransome, Maria Durille,
Lourdes de la Camara, Roberto Nauta, Javier de la
Camara, Luis Mateos, Jose Luis Romero*
A couple go on holiday to a Spanish island where all the adults seem to be absent and the children are hostile.
Aka: DEATH IS CHILD'S PLAY; ISLAND OF THE DAMNED; QUIEN PUEDO MATAR A UN NINO?; WHO CAN KILL A CHILD?; WOULD YOU KILL A CHILD?
Boa: novel The Game by Juan Jose Plans.

| | |
|---|---|
| HOR | 90 min (ort 112 min) |
| B,V,V2 | HOK |

## ISLAND OF DOCTOR MOREAU, THE *           15
Don Taylor            USA                1977
*Burt Lancaster, Michael York, Nigel Davenport,
Barbara Carrera, Richard Basehart, Nick Cravat*
Flat, useless attempt to film the classic story of a man on a lonely Pacific island, who spends his time conducting experiments on animals, in order to give them human form. A remake of "Island Of Lost Souls". York is especially memorable for the woodenness of his acting, the others are little better.
Boa: novel by H.G. Wells.

| | |
|---|---|
| DRA | 98 min (ort 104 min) |
| B,V,V2 | GHV |

## ISLAND OF LOST WOMEN, THE **
Frank Tuttle          USA                1959
*Jeff Richards, Venetia Stevenson, John Smith, Alan
Napier, Diane Jergens, June Blair*
An atomic scientist has retired to an island with his daughters, to protect them from the world. Their isolation is broken when a plane is forced to make an emergency landing there. A middling drama with an intriguing title, to make the film appear to be more exciting than it really is.
Osca: COTTER

| | |
|---|---|
| DRA | 64 min (ort 71 min) B/W |
| B,V | KVD |

## ISLAND OF LOVE *                          18
                      USA
*Diane Hunter, Raysheena, Steve Vette, Tom Byron,
Lisa Aroo, Don Shina*
Two young couples enjoy erotic frolics in this fairly plotless sex film.

| | |
|---|---|
| A | 80 min |
| B,V | CAL |

## ISLAND OF LOVE XANAVA **                  18
Zygmunt Sulistrowski   USA
*Bettina Scheirrer, Valerie Belpy, Morgan Bittencourt*
A girl inherits a tropical island but her paradise is threatened by voodoo practices.

| | |
|---|---|
| A | 100 min |
| B,V | BLUMO/GOLD |

## ISLAND OF MUTATIONS **
Sergio Martino/Dan T. Miller
                      ITALY/USA          1979
*Barbara Bach, Richard Johnson, Joseph Cotten, Mel
Ferrer, Cameron Mitchell, Claudio Cassinelli, Beryl
Cunningham, Eunice Bolt*
A group of people are shipwrecked on an island inhabited by strange creatures in this obscure horror tale.
Aka: FISH MEN, THE: ISLAND OF MUTANTS; ISLAND OF THE FISHERMEN, THE; L'ISOLA DEGLI UOMINI PESCE; SCREAMERS; SOMETHING WAITS IN THE DARK

| | |
|---|---|
| HOR | 85 min |
| B,V | VIPCO |

## ISLAND OF SISTER TERESA, THE *
Joseph Pevney         USA                1979
*Steven Keats, Peter Lawford, Clint Walker, Jamie Lyn*

Bauer, Jayne Kennedy, Kathryn Davis, Rosalind
Chao, Deborah Shelton, Susie Coelho, Guich Koock,
Sandy McPeak, Michael McGreevey
Adventure set on a desert island peopled by beautiful
but deadly women, where an all-male oil crew is
forced to make an emergency landing. This is a
tedious little thriller that might have worked better
as a comedy.
Aka: MYSTERIOUS ISLAND OF BEAUTIFUL
WOMEN, THE
THR                          93 min (ort 100 min) mTV
V                                                VPD

## ISLAND OF TERROR *
Terence Fischer         UK                      1966
Peter Cushing, Edward Judd, Carole Gray, Eddie
Byrne, Sam Kydd, Niall MacGinnis, James Caffrey,
Liam Gaffney, Roger Heathcote, Peter Forbes
Robertson, Shay Gorman
Strange bone-eating monsters are loose on an Irish
island, having been created by a scientist as part of his
investigation into the causes of cancer. An unambi-
tious little yarn that never amounts to much.
HOR                                            89 min
B,V,V2                                            RNK

## ISLAND OF THE LOST **                          U
Richard Carlson/John Florea
                        USA                      1968
Richard Greene, Luke Halpin, Mark Hulswit, Jose De
Vega, Robin Mattson, Irene Tsu
An anthropologist and his family go in search of an
uncharted island and become shipwrecked there. A
wholesome and mildly diverting story somewhat
devoid of ideas or development. Written by Richard
Carlson and Ivan Tors, with the underwater sequ-
ences directed by Ricou Browning.
A/AD                          87 min (ort 91 min)
B,V                                              GHV

## ISLAND SONS *                                  PG
Alan J. Levi            USA                      1987
Timothy Bottoms, Joseph Bottoms, Samuel Bottoms,
Benjamin Bottoms, Clare Kirkconnell, David Wohl,
Richard Narita
A pilot for an action series set on Hawaii, that
revolves around four feuding brothers who are hard
put to hold onto the family business when their father
disappears. The gimmick of using the real-life Bot-
toms siblings is of more interest than anything the
film has to offer.
A/AD                          94 min (ort 100 min) mTV
V                                                CIC

## ISLAND, THE *                                  18
Michael Ritchie         USA                      1980
Michael Caine, David Warner, Angela Punch
McGregor, Frank Middlemass, Don Henderson,
Jeffrey Frank, Christopher F. Bean, Zakes Mokee
A reporter investigating strange happening in the
Caribbean, is captured by a colony of throwbacks from
an 18th century pirate community. A ludicrous and
sometimes unintentionally funny effort, scripted by
Benchley from his novel.
Boa: novel by Peter Benchley.
A/AD                          108 min (ort 114 min)
B,V,LV                                            CIC

## ISLE OF THE DEAD **                            15
Mark Robson             USA                      1945
Boris Karloff, Ellen Drew, Helen Thiming, Marc
Cramer, Alan Napier, Jason Robards Sr, Katherine
Emery
A group of people take refuge on a Greek island in
1912, to escape the plague and discover that one of
their number is a vampire. A sombre but atmospheric
tale.
Osca: BERLIN EXPRESS (KVD)

HOR                          69 min; 72 min (VCC) B/W
B,V                          KVD; VCC (VHS only)

## ISTANBUL *                                     15
Mats Arehn     SWEDEN/TURKEY                     1989
Timothy Bottoms, Twiggy (Lesley Hornby), Emma
Kilberg, Robert Morley, Lena Endre, Sverre Anker
Ousdal
An American journalist travels to Istanbul with his
daughter when he receives a mysterious videotape
sent by the father of his stepson, but when his
daughter is kidnapped he is drawn into a murky and
complex intrigue. A dully opaque thriller, as unin-
teresting as it is inpenetrable.
THR                                            87 min
V                                                ODY

## IT CAME FROM OUTER SPACE **                    PG
Jack Arnold             USA                      1953
Richard Carlson, Barbara Rush, Charles Drake,
Kathleen Hughes, Russell Johnson, Joe Sawyer
An alien ship crashes in the desert, and its occupants
assume the identities of some of the local townsfolk
while they undertake repairs. Originally shown in
3-D on a wide screen, this fairly competent yarn (one
of the first to use the theme of impersonation) will lose
a good deal of its impact on TV.
Boa: short story by Ray Bradbury.
FAN                          77 min (ort 81 min) B/W
B,V                                              CIC

## IT HAPPENED ONE NIGHT ****                     U
Frank Capra             USA                      1934
Clark Gable, Claudette Colbert, Walter Connolly,
Roscoe Karns, Alan Hale, Ward Bond
A film that established Columbia's reputation and
marked their change from a studio making quickies.
This tells of a runaway heiress who falls in love with a
reporter on a bus trip. A delightful comedy, the first
film to win all five top Oscars. Not until ONE FLEW
OVER CUCKOO'S THE NEST 41 years later, was
this done again. AA: Pic, Dir, Actor (Gable), Actress
(Colbert), Story (Adapt) (Robert Riskin).
Boa: story Night Bus by S.H. Adams.
COM                          101 min (ort 105 min) B/W
V                                                RCA

## IT RAINED ALL NIGHT THE DAY I LEFT **
Nicolas Gessner
                CANADA/FRANCE/ISRAEL             1979
Tony Curtis, Sally Kellerman, Louis Gossett Jr, John
Vernon, Lisa Langlois, Guy Hoffman, William
Clarkson, Bertrand A. Henry, Gabi Amrani, Peter
Bray, Dudik Somandar, Judy Arkin, Rolf Brin,
Richard Solano, Jean-Claude Houbart
Two gun-runners become involved in a private war
over water rights in a desert.
Aka: DEUX AFFREUX SUR LE SABLE; DEUX
REQUINS SUR LE SABLE
A/AD                                            100 min
B,V                                      VFP L/A; HER

## IT SEEMED LIKE A GOOD IDEA AT THE TIME **
John Trent              CANADA                   1974
Anthony Newley, Stefanie Powers, Isaac Hayes, Lloyd
Bochner, Yvonne De Carlo, Henry Ramer, Lawrence
Dane, John Candy, Moya Fenwick, Ann-Marie Sten,
Robert Silverman, Roy Wordsworth
A woman leaves her husband although she still loves
him, her reasons for doing so being mainly financial.
Average.
COM                                            110 min
V                                      CIN L/A; CYC

## IT SHOULDN'T HAPPEN TO A VET ***               U
Eric Till               UK                       1976
John Alderton, Colin Blakely, Lisa Harrow, Bill
Maynard, Richard Pearson, Paul Shelley, John
Barrett, Rosemary Martin, Philip Stone, Raymond

*Francis, May Warden, Liz Smith, Christine Hargreaves, Clifford Kershaw, Gwen Nelson*
More adventures from the country vet largely based on Herriot's experiences. A wholesome sequel to "All Creatures Great And Small", a 1974 TV film.
Aka: ALL THINGS BRIGHT AND BEAUTIFUL
Boa: books Let Sleeping Vets Lie/Vet In Harness (jointly known as All Things Bright And Beautiful) by James Herriot.

| DRA | 89 min (ort 93 min) |
| B,V | TEVP; WHV |

### IT TAKES ALL KINDS, TO CATCH A THIEF *
Eddie Davis          AUSTRALIA/USA          1969
*Robert Lansing, Vera Miles, Barry Sullivan, Sid Melton, Penny Sugg*
A woman blackmails a seaman into committing a robbery, after a sailor is killed in a brawl.

| THR | 90 min |
| B,V | MEV |

### IT TAKES TWO *
David Beaird          USA          1988
*George Newbern, Leslie Hope, Kimberley Foster, Barry Corbin, Anthony Geary, Frances Lee McCain*
A man about to be married is struck by second thoughts and decides to buy his dream car, which brings him into contact with a beautiful saleswoman.
Aka: MY NEW CAR

| COM | 76 min |
| V/sh | WHV |

### ITALIAN JOB, THE ***                                   PG
Peter Collinson          UK          1969
*Michael Caine, Noel Coward, Benny Hill, Maggie Blye, Tony Beckley, Raf Vallone, Rossano Brazzi, Irene Handl, John Le Mesurier, Fred Emney, Graham Payn, Robert Rietty, Simon Dee, Henry McGee, Robert Powell*
The rather neat story of a criminal mastermind (played by Coward) who plans a brilliant bullion robbery from inside prison, by causing the biggest traffic jam in the history of Turin. An enjoyable and ingenious film sadly let down by poor characterisation and dialogue, though Coward's cameo is a joy.

| COM | 96 min (ort 100 min) |
| B,V | CIC |

### ITALIAN STALLION, THE **
Morton Lewis          USA          1970
*Sylvester Stallone, Henrietta Holm, Jodi Van Prang, Frank Micelli, Nicholas Warren, Barbara Strom*
Said to be his first screen role, for which he is reputed to have been paid $200, Stallone stars as Stud, a loving guy frustrated by his intense sex drive. Even though his girlfriend makes love to him whenever she can, he still cannot keep his thoughts off other women. A film of minimal plot that ends with a general orgy and one that displays a naive innocence common to early sex films.
Aka: PARTY AT KITTY AND STUDS

| A | 72 min |
| B,V | DFS; GOST |

### IT'S A MAD, MAD, MAD, MAD WORLD *                      U
Stanley Kramer          USA          1963
*Spencer Tracy, Phil Silvers, Terry-Thomas, Ethel Merman, Mickey Rooney, Dick Shawn, Jimmy Durante, Milton Bearle, Jonathan Winters, Buddy Hackett, Sid Caesar, Edie Adams, Dorothy Provine, Buster Keaton, Jack Benny, Jerry Lewis*
And it's one long, long, long, long and very unfunny film, as a group of ill-assorted fortune-seekers attempt to recover the loot hidden by a dying gangster who reveals its approximate whereabouts. Endless frantic chases do not a comedy make. See also MONEY MANIA. AA: Effects (Aud) (Walter G. Elliott).

| COM | 162 min (ort 192 min) |
| B,V | WHV |

### IT'S A WONDERFUL LIFE ****                             U
Frank Capra          USA          1946
*James Stewart, Donna Reed, Lionel Barrymore, Henry Travers, Thomas Mitchell, Ward Bond, Gloria Grahame, Frank Faylen, Beulah Bondi, H.B. Warner, Frank Albertson, Todd Karns, Samuel S. Hinds, Mary Treen, Sheldon Leonard*
An angel shows a despairing man that his life has not been a failure despite what he thinks, by allowing him to see how those around him would have fared had he not been born. Wonderfully charming classic that shows film-making at its best. Remade for TV as "It Happened One Christmas".
DRA    125 min (ort 129 min) B/W (colourised version available)

| V | VCC |

### IT'S ALIVE! ***                                        18
Larry Cohen          USA          1974
*John Ryan, Sharon Farrell, Andrew Duggan, Guy Stockwell, James Dixon, Michael Ansara*
A woman's newborn babe turns out to be a terrifying monster. An unusual and chilling shocker that wore out its welcome with two further instalments. The score is by Bernard Herrmann.

| HOR | 87 min (ort 91 min) |
| V | WHV |

### IT'S ALIVE 2 *                                          15
Larry Cohen          USA          1978
*Frederic Forrest, Kathleen Lloyd, Andrew Duggan, John P. Ryan, John Marley, Eddie Constantine, James Dixon*
Sequel to IT'S ALIVE with our mutant baby and two others, escaping from a research centre and going on the obligatory rampage. Followed by a third outing for our murderous babes.
Aka: IT LIVES AGAIN

| HOR | 91 min |
| V/sh | WHV |

### IT'S ALIVE 3: ISLAND OF THE ALIVE **                   18
Larry Cohen          USA          1986
*Michael Moriarty, Karen Black, Laurene Landon, Gerrit Graham, Neal Israel, James Dixon, Art Lund, Ann Dane, Macdonald Carey, William Watson, Patch MacKenzie, C.L. Sussex, Rick Garia, Carlos Palomino*
The third instalment in this series has the father sending his "monster" son to a remote island to be with others of its kind. Years later, these creatures return to threaten civilization as we know it. A wildly overblown sequel with some touches of black humour, but still not all that good.
Aka: ISLAND OF THE ALIVE

| HOR | 90 min |
| B,V | WHV |

### IT'S ALL HAPPENING **                                  U
Don Sharp          UK          1963
*Tommy Steele, Michael Medwin, Angela Douglas, Jean Harvey, Danny Williams, Bernard Bresslaw, Walter Hudd, Richard Goolden, Dick Kallman, John Barry*
A record company talent scout stages a show for an orphanage, saving it from closure and making himself into a star in the process. A bland but fairly endearing musical comedy.
Aka: DREAM MAKER, THE

| MUS | 97 min (ort 101 min) |
| V | WHV |

### IT'S CALLED MURDER BABY **                             18
Sam Weston          USA          1982
*John Leslie, Cameron Mitchell, Lisa Trego, Lisa De Leeuw, Seka*
An ex-cop private eye is hired to stop a blackmail scheme and finds that he has bitten off more than he can chew, in this cut-down version of a hardcore film originally entitled "Dixie Ray: Hollywood Star".

Aka: DIXIE RAY: HOLLYWOOD STAR
A                           89 min (ort 129 min)
B,V                         VTC L/A; MEN/AVR

## IT'S GOOD TO BE ALIVE ***
Michael Landon          USA             1974
*Paul Winfield, Louis Gossett Jr, Ruby Dee, Ramon
Bieri, Joe DeSantis, Ty Henderson, Lloyd Gough, Eric
Woods, Ketty Lester, Julian Burton, Len Lesser,
Stymie Beard, Paul Savior, Stanley Clay, Joe E. Tata,
Nina Roman*
A baseball star rebuilds his life after a near fatal
accident, in this restrained and touching account of
the life of Roy Campanella, a former catcher for the
Brooklyn Dodgers who had to adapt to life in a
wheelchair following an auto crash in 1959.
Boa: book by Roy Campanella.
DRA                         100 min mTV
B,V,V2                      IFS

## IT'S MY LIFE TO LIVE **
Igor Auzins        AUSTRALIA          1980
*Robin Nevin, David Cameron, Judy Davis*
An ambitious chorus girl finds her life changes
dramatically when she adopts a young boy. This is the
second part of a TV series called WATER UNDER
THE BRIDGE. Fair.
DRA                         80 min mTV
B,V                         CAREY/PVG

## IT'S MY TURN ***                          15
Claudia Weill           USA             1980
*Jill Clayburgh, Michael Douglas, Charles Grodin,
Beverly Garland, Steven Hill, Teresa Baxter, Joan
Copeland, John Gabriel, Jennifer Salt, Daniel Stern,
Dianne Wiest*
A female professor falls for the son of her father's new
wife and tries to reconcile the conflicting emotional
and career aspects of her life. A diverting comedy-
drama that is packed with engaging performances and
a considerably less engaging feminist slant. Written
by Eleanor Bergstein.
DRA                         90 min
B,V                         RCA

## IVAN THE TERRIBLE *****                   PG
Sergei Eisenstein    USSR       1944 and 1946
*Nikolai Cherkassov, Serafima Birman, Ludmila
Tselikovskaya, Eric Pyriev, Mikhail Nazvanov, Pavel
Kodochnikov, Andrei Abrikosov*
A magnificent and utterly enthralling account of the
life and times of one of Russia's greatest (and most
ruthless) rulers, tracing his life from early childhood
up to cynical and embittered middle-age. A difficult,
stylised and rewarding masterpiece. Unfortunately
only a fragment of Part 3 exists as Stalin banned the
film; he took offence to the director's depiction of the
Tsar's secret police. The score is by Prokofiev.
Aka: IVAN THE TERRIBLE: PART 1 (asa);
BOYAR'S PLOT, THE: IVAN THE TERRIBLE –
PART 2 (asa)
DRA          185 min (2 cassettes) B/W (plus one colour
sequence)
V                           HEND

## IVANHOE ***                               U
Richard Thorpe          USA             1952
*Robert Taylor, Elizabeth Taylor, John Fontaine,
George Sanders, Emlyn Williams, Finlay Currie,
Robert Douglas, Felix Aylmer, Sebastian Cabot,
Frances De Wolff, Guy Rolfe, Norman Wooland, Basil
Sydney*
A spectacular tale of this famous knight that suffers
somewhat from being shallow and overlong, but is
always beautiful to look at. Filmed in England.
Boa: novel by Sir Walter Scott.
A/AD                        103 min (ort 106 min)
B,V                         MGM

## I'VE COME ABOUT THE SUICIDE **            15
Sophia Turkiewicz
                    AUSTRALIA          1987
*Barry Otto, Ralph Cotterill, Gosia Dobrowolska,
Duncan Wass, Gary Down, Gwen Plumb, Patrick
Ward*
A successful novelist who bases his writing on real
experiences, has to look further afield for new inspira-
tion.
COM                         90 min
V/sh                        GHV

## I'VE HEARD THE MERMAIDS SINGING ***       15
Patricia Rozema      CANADA            1987
*Sheila McCarthy, Paule Baillargeon, Ann-Marie
MacDonald, John Evans, Brenda Kamino, Richard
Monette*
A young and rather naive woman takes a job in an art
gallery run by another woman, but finds both her and
the art world strange and intimidating. A quirky,
low-budget comedy of manners, winner of the "Prix De
La Jeunesse" at the 1987 Cannes Film Festival.
Aka: LE CHANT DES SIRENES
COM                         85 min
V/s                         HEND

## IZZY AND MOE, THE BOOTLEG BUSTERS **      U
Jackie Cooper           USA             1985
*Art Carney, Jackie Gleason, Cynthia Harris, Zohra
Lempert, Dick Latessa, Thelma Lee, Drew Snyder,
Jesse Doran, Tom Wiggin, Rick Washburn, Sully
Boyar, Roy Brocksmith, William Hickey, Tracy
Sallows, Mary Tanner*
Two Federal agents fight against bootleggers in the
1920s. A lively but uneven and only slightly amusing
yarn, despite the good pairing of comedy veterans
Carney and Gleason (the latter also wrote the music).
Aka: IZZY AND MOE
COM                  92 min (ort 104 min) mTV
B,V                         IVS; CAST

# J

## J.D.'s REVENGE **                         18
Arthur Marks            USA             1976
*Glynn Turman, Joan Pringle, Louis Gossett Jr, James
Louis Watkins, Carl Crudup, Alice Jubert, Stephanie
Faulkner, Fred Pinkard, Jo Anne Meredith, Fuddle
Bagley, David McKnight*
After being hypnotised at a nightclub, a young
student is taken over by the spirit of a petty criminal,
dead for over 40 years but still thirsty for revenge on
his killers. A well-made, low-budget horror film.
HOR                  92 min (ort 95 min)
V                           RCA

## J.J. STARBUCK **                          PG
Corey Allan             USA             1988
*Dale Robertson, Bill Bixby, David Huddleston, Patty
Duke*
An eccentric Texas billionaire who spouts a constant
stream of homespun wisdom, devotes himself to
playing the private eye and helping those let down by
the legal system. A pilot for a TV series that depended
heavily on the character of its hero.
DRA                         91 min
B,V                         EIV

## JABBERWOCKY **                            PG
Terry Gilliam           UK              1977
*Michael Palin, Max Wall, Deborah Fallender, Neil
Innes, Dave Prowse, Harry H. Corbett, John Le
Mesurier, Annette Badland, Warren Mitchell, Rodney
Bewes, Bernard Bresslaw, Derek Francis, Alexandra
Dane, Frank Williams*
Medieval satire from the "Monty Python" team, in
which a cooper's apprentice finds himself having to

slay a dragon after having been mistaken for a prince, but it is rewarded by the hand of a princess. Patchy and largely unfunny, with the emphasis firmly on the more unpleasant aspects of life in that period. Written by Charles Alverson and Terry Gilliam.

COM                                      104 min
V                                          RCA

## JACK AND MIKE **                          15
Jack Bender          USA               1986
Shelley Hack, Tom Mason, Holly Fulger, Jacqueline Brookes, Kevin Dunn, Vincent Baggetta, Noelle Bou-Sliman
A woman journalist assigned to a rape case, becomes convinced that the man is innocent even after his conviction, and starts to campaign for his release making some enemies in the process. A pilot for a TV series that lasted just nine months.

DRA                                  67 min mTV
B,V                                        MGM

## JACK AND THE BEANSTALK **                  Uc
Lamont Johnson       USA               1982
Dennis Christopher, Elliott Gould, Jean Stapleton, Katherine Helmond, Mark Blankfield
A live-action version of this famous fairytale, of the naive youngster who swaps a cow for five magic beans and has something of a surprise when he plants them.
Boa: short story by Jakob Ludwig Karl Grimm and Wilhelm Karl Grimm.

JUV                            48 min (ort 60 min)
V                                          MGM

## JACK AND THE BEANSTALK **
Peter J. Solmo       USA               1976
A pleasant and undemanding animated version of this fairytale.
Boa: short story by Jakob Ludwig Karl Grimm and Wilhelm Karl Grimm.

CAR                                       96 min
B,V,V2                           INT/CBS; VMA

## JACK AND THE BEANSTALK ***                  U
Gene Kelly           USA               1966
Gene Kelly
A mixture of animation and live action in this musical version of the fairytale, produced by Hanna-Barbera.
Boa: short story by Jakob Ludwig Karl Grimm and Wilhelm Karl Grimm.

JUV                                       60 min
V                         VFP L/A; HER L/A; VCC

## JACK AND THE BEANSTALK **                  Uc
                                           1989
A pleasant but generally undistinguished entry in the Pickwick "Animated Classics" series.
Boa: short story by Jakob Karl Grimm and Wilhelm Karl Grimm.

CAR                                       40 min
V                                         PICK

## JACK 'N' JILL **                          R18
Mark Ubell           USA               1979
Samantha Fox, Jack Wrangler, Vanessa Del Rio, Eric Edwards
Adult sex-film with a partner-swapping theme, as two couples get acquainted whilst playing a game of strip poker. Cut before video submission by 29 min 20 sec.
Osca: FASCINATION
A             39 min (ort 70 min); 85 min (2 film cassette)
B,V,V2                       PHV L/A; TCX; SHEP

## JACK 'N' JILL 2 **                        R18
Chuck Vincent    SWEDEN/USA            1981
Samantha Fox, Jack Wrangler, Carol Cross, Jerry Butler, Crysta Cox, Taija Rae
Sequel to the first film with more swapping of more partners as Fox and Wrangler play a swinging couple out to get the most out of life. Eventually they find a

couple to their liking and swap, even to the extent of starting divorce proceedings. However, they each find their new partners not quite as agreeable as they first thought, in a glossy sex film that strains hard for laughs but hardly ever delivers them.
Aka: DESIRES OF A NAUGHTY NYMPHO
A                             79 min (ort 84 min)
B,V                                 TCX; SHEP

## JACK THE RIPPER ***                        15
David Wickes         UK                1988
Michael Caine, Lewis Collins, Jane Seymour, Susan George, Lysette Anthony, Armand Assante, Ray McAnally, Ken Bones, Jonathan Moore, Kelly Cryer, Michael Gorhard
The latest retelling of this gory tale is a lavish, well-made and well-acted film, that retraces the events in the Ripper's career in considerable detail, but adds some fictional elements, with Caine ultimately unmasking the murderer. First shown in two parts.

DRA                         183 min (ort 200 min) mTV
V                                          VCC

## JACKALS **                                 18
Gary Grillo          USA               1985
Jack Lucarelli, A. Wilford Brimley, Gerald McRaney, Jameson Parker, Jeannie Wilson
The title refers to the local police who prey on illegal Mexican immigrants, robbing and murdering them as they try to cross the border. An uncorrupted ex-city cop mounts a bloody campaign to reveal the truth, but the virtue of this interesting idea is marred by excessive gore.
Aka: AMERICAN JUSTICE
A/AD                                      92 min
B,V                                        CBS

## JACKNIFE ***                               15
David Jones          USA               1989
Robert De Niro, Ed Harris, Kathy Baker, Charles Dutton, Loudon Wainwright III
A Vietnam veteran visits an old army pal in the hope of getting him to face up to his unhappy memories of the conflict and the loss of a mutual friend, and his arrival brings a little romance into the life of the man's shy sister. A very fine drama, superbly acted and intelligently scripted by Metcalf from his stage play.
Boa: play Strange Snow by Stephen Metcalf.

DRA                          98 min (ort 102 min)
V                                          VES

## JACK'S BACK **                             18
Rowdy Herrington     USA               1987
James Spader, Cynthia Gibb, Rod Loomis, Jim Haynie, Wendell Wright, Robert Picardo, Chris Mulkey, Danitza Kingsley
The story of Jack the Ripper is updated and transplanted to modern-day L.A., where a series of grisly murders of prostitutes takes place 100 years after the crimes of the legendary Victorian figure. When the chief suspect is murdered, the police are content to close their files, but his twin brother arrives to clear his name. A sluggish tale of preposterous plot twists, but a few thrills near the end offer a partial compensation.

THR                           90 min (ort 97 min)
V                                          CBS

## JACQUELINE BOUVIER KENNEDY *
Steven Gethers       USA               1981
Jaclyn Smith, Rod Taylor, Stephen Elliott, James Franciscus, Claudette Nevins, Donald Moffat, Joseph Chapman, Heather Hobbs, Dolph Sweet, James F. Kelly, Maurice Marsac, Eve Roberts, Robert Easton, Lauree Berger, Ned Wilson
Dull biopic about Jackie Kennedy's rise to fame from

age five onwards, that proves as interesting as its subject matter.

DRA · 122 min (ort 150 min) mTV
B,V · VFP L/A; HER

## JAGGED EDGE ** 18
Richard Marquand · USA · 1985
*Jeff Bridges, Glenn Close, Peter Coyote, Robert Loggia, John Dehner, Leigh Taylor-Young, Karin Austin, Lance Henricksen, James Karen*
A woman lawyer defends a publisher on a charge of murder and falls in love with him. However, he may not be as innocent as she thinks. The title refers to the murder weapon; a hunting knife. Implausible nonsense, but quite well done.
THR · 105 min (ort 108 min)
V · RCA

## JAGUAR LIVES! ** 15
Ernest Pintoff · USA · 1979
*Christopher Lee, Barbara Bach, John Huston, Joe Lewis, Donald Pleasence, Woody Strode, Capucine, Joseph Wiseman*
A martial arts master sets out to avenge the death of a special agent, as he fights drugs smugglers in a variety of capital cities. A predictable low-budget affair.
MAR · 82 min (ort 98 min) (Cut at film release by 22 sec)
B,V,LV · RNK L/A; MIA (VHS only)

## JAIL BIRD ** 18
Liliana Cavani · ITALY · 1982
*Tom Berenger, Eleonora Giorgi, Marcello Mastroianni*
Study of the complex relationship between a girl, her father, an American engineer and a convicted murderer. Fair but far from memorable.
Aka: BEHIND THE DOOR; BEYOND OBSESSION; BEYOND THE DOOR (SUN/CAREY)
DRA · 106 min; 116 min (SUN/CAREY)
B,V · SUN/CAREY; MPV

## JAILBAIT BABYSITTER * 
John Hayes · USA · 1973
*Theresa Pare, Rosco Born, Lydia Wagner Wade Nichols, Tina Lynn*
A sexually precocious 16-year-old in the habit of servicing her classmates, takes a job babysitting, and uses the opportunity to throw a wild party whilst a couple are away from home.
A · 80 min
B,V · ATA L/A; APX

## JAKARTA ** 18
Charles Kaufman · USA · 1988
*Christopher North, Sue Francis Pai, Ronald Hunter, Franz Tumbuan*
Three years after he was sent to Jakarta to guard a beautiful and mysterious oriental woman, a New York-based CIA agent is kidnapped and taken back there. A competent action thriller with colourful locations.
A/AD · 90 min
V · MED

## JAKE SPEED * 15
Andrew Lane · USA · 1986
*Wayne Crawford, Dennis Christopher, Karel Kopins, John Hurt, Leon Ames, Roy Lindon, Donna Pescow, Barry Primus, Monte Markham, Rebecca Ashley, Alan Shearman, Millie Perkins, Karl Johnson, Sal Viscuso, Ken Lerner, Ken Gampu*
A pulp fiction hero comes to life to help a woman whose sister has been captured by white slavers. Mediocre and unfunny. The script was co-written and co-produced by Crawford.
A/AD · 100 min (ort 104 min)
B,V · NWV

## JAMAICA INN ** U
Lawrence Gordon Clark
· USA · 1982
*Patrick McGoohan, Jane Seymour, Trevor Eve, John McEnery, Billie Whitelaw, Vivien Pickles, Peter Vaughan, Michael Goldie, John Abineri, Norman Bowler, Christopher Douglas, Hubert Tucher, Nick Brimble, Howard Goorney, Tim Hooper*
A failed attempt to bring to the small screen, the sweep and grandeur of the original tale of 18th century wreckers and smugglers on the Cornish coast. Lavishly made, but murky and difficult to follow. Filmed once before by Hitchcock in 1939. The adaptation was by Derek Marlowe.
Boa: novel by Daphne du Maurier.
A/AD · 156 min (ort 200 min) mTV
V · VGM

## JAMES JOYCE'S WOMEN ** 18
Michael Pearce · USA · 1985
*Fionnula Flanagan, Timothy E. O'Grady, Chris O'Neill, Tony Lyons, Gerald Fitzmahoney, Paddy Dawson, Martin Dempsey, Joseph Taylor*
Dramatised account of James Joyce and his female characters, derived from a much-praised solo stage show by Flanagan that blended episodes from the author's life, with scenes from his books. Fair.
DRA · 85 min (ort 91 min)
B,V · CIC

## JANE AND THE LOST CITY ** PG
Terence Marcel · UK · 1987
*Kirsten Hughes, Maud Adams, Sam Jones, Jasper Carrott, Robin Bailey, Graham Stark, Ian Roberts, Elsa O'Toole, John Rapley, Charles Comyn, Ian Steadman*
Film based on a British cartoon heroine who first saw the light of day in 1932 and was a hit with the troops in WW2. A wild adventure yarn involving giant gems, a lost city and Nazi villains. A poor latecomer to the ranks of the RAIDERS OF THE LOST ARK clones.
A/AD · 89 min (ort 93 min)
V/sh · RCA

## JANE AUSTEN IN MANHATTAN * 
James Ivory · USA · 1980
*Anne Baxter, Robert Powell, Michael Wager, Tim Choate, John Guerrasio, Katrina Hodiak, Kurt Johnson, Sean Young, Nancy New, Chuck McCaughan*
Two acting teachers clash over the production of a newly discovered play by Jane Austen. An incoherent and lacklustre mess, of curiosity value only.
DRA · 108 min
B,V · HVM

## JANE DOE *** 
Ivan Nagy · USA · 1983
*Karen Valentine, William Devane, Eva Marie Saint, David Huffman, Stephen E. Miller, Jackson Davies, Anthony Holland, Jason Michas, Ann Petrie, Terry David Mulligan, Wayne Cox, Fred Latremouille, Julie Brown, Tom Heaton*
A woman victim of a multiple killer survives, but loses her memory and faces further danger, when the killer learns she is still alive and decides to silence her for good. Well above average.
THR · 96 min (ort 100 min) mTV
B,V,V2 · PRV

## JANE EYRE *** PG
Robert Stevenson · USA · 1943
*Joan Fontaine, Orson Welles, Margaret O'Brien, John Sutton, Henry Daniell, Agnes Moorehead, Elizabeth Taylor, Peggy Ann Garner, Sara Allgood, Aubrey Mather, Hillary Brooke, Edith Barrett, Ethel Griffies, Barbara Everest*
A languid but careful adaptation of Bronte's classic tale, in which a poor orphan girl obtains the post of

governess at a mansion, but finds that her master has a sullen disposition and a mysterious past. An atmospheric and often effective offering; Welles is at his menacing best as a brooding Rochester. Scripted by Stevenson, Aldous Huxley and John Houseman. The music is by Bernard Herrmann and photography by George Barnes.
Boa: novel by Charlotte Bronte.

| DRA | 96 min |
|---|---|
| V/h | CBS |

## JANE EYRE: PARTS 1 AND 2 **    U
Julian Amyes          UK          1983
*Timothy Dalton, Zelah Clarke, Judy Cornwell*
A lively, well-made TV version of this famous classic, telling of the stormy relationship that develops between a governess and her brooding and melancholy employer.
Boa: novel by Charlotte Bronte.

| DRA | 238 min (2 cassettes) mTV |
|---|---|
| B,V | BBC |

## JANITOR, THE **    15
Peter Yates          USA          1981
*William Hurt, Sigourney Weaver, Christopher Plummer, James Woods, Irene Steven Hill, Kenneth McMillan, Pamela Reed, Albert Paulsen, Sharon Goldman, Morgan Freeman, Alice Drummond, Chao-Li Chi, Keone Young, Dennis Sakamoto*
A janitor in a New York office building is infatuated with a woman TV news reporter. When a Vietnamese businessman is murdered there, he pretends to know something about the crime in order to get to know her. The characters are well delineated except for Weaver, who fails to convince as a New York Jewess. In addition, the plot device (a scheme to get Jews out of the USSR) seems strained and contrived. A flawed work. Written by Steve Tesich.
Aka: EYEWITNESS

| DRA | 108 min |
|---|---|
| B,V,LV | CBS |

## JANUARY MAN, THE *    15
Pat O'Connor          USA          1988
*Kevin Kline, Susan Sarandon, Mary Elizabeth Mastrantonio, Danny Aiello, Harvey Keitel, Rod Steiger, Alan Rickman, Faye Grant, Tandy Cronyn*
A serial killer who murders one victim a month has the New York police baffled, and the mayor is forced to call in a former ace sleuth. A muddled and unworkable mixture of action, drama and comedy, that does nothing but run on the spot. The script is by John Patrick Shanley.

| A/AD | 98 min |
|---|---|
| V | MGM |

## JASON AND THE ARGONAUTS ***    U
Don Chaffey          UK          1963
*Todd Armstrong, Niall MacGinnis, Gary Raymond, Nancy Kovack, Honor Blackman, Laurence Naismith, Nigel Green, Michael Gwynn, Douglas Wilmer, Jack Gwillim, Andrew Faulds, Patrick Troughton, John Cairney, Gernando Poggi*
Jason's voyage in search of the Golden Fleece, and his adventures, as he and his men face many hardships and dangers, are brought to life in a film with fine special effects by Ray Harryhausen. The score is by Bernard Herrmann.

| A/AD | 104 min |
|---|---|
| B,V | RCA |

## JAVA BURN *    18
Robert Chappell          USA          1988
*William Bell Sullivan, Ayu Azhari, David Thornton, Peter Fox, Ava Lazar*
A young American criminal living in Indonesia becomes romantically entangled with a beautiful woman, and she enlists his help in her efforts to locate a missing cache of diamonds. The Indonesian locations

and torrid love scenes provide some slight relief in a mediocre thriller that stands in sore need of an injection of energy and direction.
Aka: DIAMOND RUN

| THR | 86 min |
|---|---|
| V | MED |

## JAWS ****    PG
Steven Spielberg          USA          1975
*Roy Scheider, Robert Shaw, Richard Dreyfuss, Lorraine Gary, Jeffrey Kramer, Murray Hamilton*
A brilliant look at what happens when a monstrous shark attacks a small coastal island. The film really examines the relationship that develops between the three men who set out to hunt it. The script is by Benchley who has a cameo as a TV reporter. A superb film that has been followed by a series of dreadful sequels. AA: Sound (Robert L. Hoyt/Roger Herman/Earl Madery/John Carter), Score (Orig) (John Williams), Edit (Verna Fields).
Boa: novel by Peter Benchley.

| DRA | 118 min (ort 124 min) |
|---|---|
| V | CIC |

## JAWS 2 *    PG
Jeannot Szwarc          USA          1978
*Roy Scheider, Lorraine Gary, Murray Hamilton, Joseph Mascolo, Collin Wilcox, Jeffrey Kramer, Ann Dusenberry, Mark Gruner, Barry Coe, Susan French, Gary Springer, Donna Wilkes, Gary Dubin, John Dukakis, G. Thomas Dunlop*
A feeble formula spin-off attempting to cash in on the success of its predecessor. Waterlogged dialogue is coupled with an interminable final sequence in which the shark attacks a bunch of kids and is finished off by Scheider. Pity the director didn't meet up with it prior to filming.

| DRA | 111 min (ort 116 min) |
|---|---|
| B,V | CIC |

## JAWS 3 *    15
Joe Alves          USA          1983
*Dennis Quaid, Bess Armstrong, Simon MacCorkindale, Louis Gossett Jr, John Putch, Lea Thompson, P.H. Moriarty, Dan Blasko, Liz Morris, Lisa Maurer, Harry Grant, Andy Hansen, P.T. Horn, John Edson Jr, Kaye Stevens*
This time the shark is on the prowl in Florida's Sea World, where the two grown-up sons of the police chief from the first two films are now living. When a baby Great White shark is captured, its mother charges to the rescue, flattening everything in its path. A dull, silly second sequel, with the useless gimmick of 3-D. Followed by JAWS: THE REVENGE.
Aka: JAWS 3-D

| A/AD | 94 min (ort 97 min) |
|---|---|
| V/sh | CIC |

## JAWS 4 *    15
Joseph Sargent          USA          1987
*Lance Guest, Lorraine Gary, Mario Van Peebles, Karen Young, Michael Caine, Judith Barsi, Lynn Whitfield, Mitchell Anderson, Jay Mello, Cedric Scott, Charles Bowleg, Melvin Van Peebles, Mary Smith, Edna Billotto, Lee Fierro*
The widow of the sheriff from the first two films, re-lives past horrors in a nightmare that starts when her son is killed by a shark, and she goes to the Bahamas to visit her other son. There, she comes to the startling conclusion that members of her family are being deliberately attacked by a Great White shark, in a personal vendetta for the deaths of its relatives. A truly ludicrous premise, not helped by shoddy handling and an inept ending.
Aka: JAWS: THE REVENGE

| A/AD | 86 min (ort 100 min) |
|---|---|
| V/sh | CIC |

**JAWS OF THE DRAGON ***                18
Jack C. Harris      HONG KONG         1976
*James Nam, James Taylor, Jenny Kam*
In this one the bad guys wear high-heeled boots and
there's much mayhem and violence in the form of
rapes, car chases and sudden death. The violent action
sequences serve as nothing more than an acknow-
ledgement of just how empty the plot is.
Osca: EIGHT MASTER, THE (TURBO)
MAR                                  94 min
B,V                          MOV L/A; TURBO

**JAYNE MANSFIELD STORY, THE ***       PG
Dick Lowry          USA               1980
*Loni Anderson, Arnold Schwarzenegger, Raymond
Buktenica, Kathleen Lloyd, G.D. Spradlin, Dave
Shelley, Laura Jacoby, Whitney Rydbeck, John
Medici, Lewis Arquette, James Jeter, Janice Kent,
Lynne Seibel, Gwen Van Dam*
Biopic on this platinum blonde sex symbol of the
1950s, who met an untimely end in a car crash. A film
that is neither interesting nor accurate.
Aka: JAYNE MANSFIELD: A SYMBOL OF THE 50s
DRA                   100 min; 92 min (ODY) mTV
B, V/h, V2                   GHV; ODY (VHS only)

**JAZZ SINGER, THE ***                 PG
Richard Fleischer   USA               1980
*Neil Diamond, Laurence Olivier, Lucie Arnaz, Catlin
Adams, Paul Nicholas, Franklyn Ajaye, Sully Boyar,
Mike Kellin*
An updated remake of the earlier classic, in which
Diamond plays a rock singer at odds with his Ortho-
dox Jewish father (played by Olivier with appropriate
hammy cliches of "I hef no son!"). Tepid, dull and
mawkish, despite a good performance from Diamond.
Boa: novel by Samson Raphaelson.
MUS                      111 min (ort 115 min)
V/sh                           TEVP; WHV

**JAZZ SINGER, THE ****                U
Alan Crosland       USA               1927
*Al Jolson, May McAvoy, Warner Oland, Eugenie
Besserer, Otto Lederer, William Demarest, Roscoe
Karns*
Despite its corny story of how the son of a Jewish
cantor defied his father and made the big time in show
business, this film is pure cinema history. Known as
the first talkie, although it is actually a silent whose
added sound sequences caused a sensation at the time.
Now notable primarily on this account, but Jolson's
fine performance spelt certain commercial success.
Remade in 1953 and 1980. AA: Spec Award (Warner
Brothers).
Boa: play by Samson Raphaelson.
MUS          85 min (ort 90 min) silent (with sound
                               sequences) B/W
B/W
V/h                                   WHV

**JEAN DE FLORETTE ****                PG
Claude Berri        FRANCE            1986
*Gerard Depardieu, Yves Montand, Daniel Auteuil,
Elisabeth Depardieu, Marcel Champel, Ernestine
Mazurowa, Marc Betton, Bertino Benedetto, Armand
Meffre, Margarita Lozano, Pierre Jean Rippert, Andre
Dupon, Pierre Nougaro*
Lavish first part of Pagnol's tale of a simple man who
leaves the city to live on an inherited piece of land, but
is ruined when he fails to find water, the location of an
underground spring having been kept secret by two
scheming villagers. The conclusion to this story comes
in the final part, MANON DES SOURCES.
Boa: novel L'eau des Collines by Marcel Pagnol.
DRA                                  122 min
V/h                                   PAL

**JEKYLL AND HYDE: TOGETHER AGAIN ***  18
Jerry Belson        USA               1982

*Mark Blankfield, Bess Armstrong, Tim Thomerson,
Krista Errickson, George Chakiris, Michael Chakiris*
Updated spoof of this old favourite about a scientist
whose dabblings turn him into a regular nasty. A
disappointing directorial debut for Belson with but a
few scattered laughs in the whole sorry mess.
COM                        83 min (ort 87 min)
B,V                                   CIC

**JEKYLL EXPERIMENT, THE ***
James Wood          USA               1982
*James Mathers, Tom Nicholson, John Kearney, Dawn
Carver Kelly, Nadine Kalmes*
Dr Jekyll stages experiments on criminals with a
mind control serum, in this low-budget chiller.
Aka: DOCTOR JEKYLL'S DUNGEON OF
DARKNESS; DOCTOR JEKYLL'S DUNGEON OF
DEATH
HOR                                  88 min
B,V                  AVA/CBS; AVI L/A; VIPCO

**JENNIFER ****                        15
Brice Mack          USA               1978
*Lisa Pelikan, Bert Convy, Nina Foch, Amy Johnston,
John Gavin, Jeff Corey, Wesley Eure, Louise Hoven,
Ray Underwood, Florida Friebus, Georganne La Piere*
Rip-off of CARRIE, with the psychic powers of our
ostracised high school girl even extending to the
unleashing of deadly snakes against her spiteful
persecutors.
Aka: JENNIFER, THE SNAKE GODDESS
HOR            86 min; 88 min (PHE) (ort 90 min)
B,V,V2                   PYR/21ST; PHE (VHS only)

**JENNIFER: A WOMAN'S STORY ****       15
Guy Green           USA               1979
*Elizabeth Montgomery, Bradford Dillman, Scott
Hylands, James Booth, John Beal, Robin Gammell,
Doris Roberts, Kate Mulgrew, Michael Goodwin,
Arthur Franz, Basil Hoffman, Dennis Dimster, Tracey
Gold, Ted Gehring, Hope Clarke*
The widow of a wealthy shipping magnate has to fight
in the boardroom to keep control of her husband's
business. Pilot for a prospective series that was
probably inspired by the British TV series "The
Foundation". Average.
DRA                        86 min (ort 94 min) mTV
B,V                               PRV; PYR

**JENNY ***
George Bloomfield   USA               1970
*Marlo Thomas, Alan Alda, Marian Hailey, Elizabeth
Wilson, Vincent Gardenia, Stephen Strimpell*
A film-maker marries a pregnant girl to avoid the
draft, in this contrived, over-sentimental and point-
less yarn.
DRA                                  90 min
B,V                                   RNK

**JENNY'S WAR: PARTS 1 AND 2 ****      U
Steven Gethers      USA               1985
*Dyan Cannon, Robert Hardy, Nigel Hawthorne, Elke
Sommer, Patrick Ryecart, Richard Todd, Harmut
Becker, Christopher Cazenove, Sion Tudor-Owen,
John Moulder-Brown, Denis Lill, Garfield Morgan,
Michael Elphick, Hugh Grant*
An American woman goes behind German lines in
occupied Europe, disguised as a man in order to find
her POW son, an RAF pilot shot down over Germany.
Undistinguished treatment of the real-life story of
Jenny Baines.
Boa: novel by Jack Stoneley.
DRA                204 min (2 cassettes) mTV
V                                     VGM

**JEREMIAH JOHNSON ****                PG
Sydney Pollack      USA               1972
*Robert Redford, Will Geer, Allyn Ann McLerie, Stefan
Gierasch, Charles Tyner, Josh Albee, Paul Benedict,
Matt Clark, Joaquin Martinez*

Nice low-key story of an ex-soldier in the 1850s who becomes a mountain trapper to get away from civilisation but finds himself inadvertently involved in conflict with the local Indians. Overlong, but good fun. The script is by John Milius and Edward Anhalt.
Boa: book Mountain Man by Vardis Fisher.
WES                              107 min
B,V                              WHV

## JERICHO MILE, THE ***
Michael Mann          USA              1979
*Peter Strauss, Roger E. Mosley, Brian Dennehy, Billy Green Bush, Ed Lauter, Beverly Todd, Richard Lawson, William Prince, Miguel Pinero, Geoffrey Lewis, Richard Moll, Edmund Penney, Burton Gilliam, Ji-Tu Cumbuka, Wilmore Thomas*
A prisoner sentenced to life, is given a chance to run in the Olympics. An unusual tale with a thought-provoking script by Mann and Nolan.
Boa: story by Patrick J. Nolan.
DRA              97 min (ort 100 min) mTV
B,V                        VFP L/A; HER

## JERK, THE **                              15
Carl Reiner           USA              1979
*Steve Martin, Bernadette Peters, Catlin Adams, Mabel King, Richard Ward, Dick Anthony Williams, Bill Macy, Jackie Mason, M. Emmet Walsh, Dick O'Neill*
The white adopted son of black sharecroppers makes a fortune, only to lose it again. Stand-up comic Martin's first starring film role, and later remade as a TV film which he produced. Some very funny clowning moments cannot hide the sheer lack of substance.
COM              91 min (ort 94 min)
B,V                        CIC

## JERK TOO, THE **
Michael Schultz       USA              1983
*Mark Blankfield, Ray Walston, Stacey Nelkin, Thalmus Rasulala, Barrie Ingham, Mabel King, Pat McCormick, Gwen Verdon, Jimmie Walker, Martin Mull, Lainie Kazan, Robert Sampson, Patricia Barry, John LeClerc, Bill Saluga*
Not so much a TV sequel to THE JERK as a remake, this reprises the story of a white youngster brought up by black sharecroppers, who goes in search of his true love. Some bright comic moments enliven an otherwise dull film, that was intended as a TV pilot for a prospective series.
COM              88 min (ort 100 min) mTV
V                          CIC

## JERUSALEM FILE, THE **              PG
John Flynn        ISRAEL/USA          1971
*Bruce Davidson, Donald Pleasence, Nicol Williamson, Ian Hendry*
An over-complex Middle East thriller in which an archaeological expedition gets caught up in the Arab-Israeli conflict.
THR              92 min (ort 96 min)
B,V                        MGM

## JESSE **                              PG
Glenn Jordan          USA              1988
*Lee Remick, Scott Wilson, Richard Marcus, Priscilla Lopez, Leon Rippy, Albert Salmi, Kevin Conway*
A nurse in a remote desert community is charged with being an unlicensed medical practitioner and put on trial. A dull dramatisation of a true incident, scripted by James Lee Barrett.
DRA              93 min (ort 100 min) mTV
B,V                        VIR

## JESSE JAMES MEETS FRANKENSTEIN'S    PG
## DAUGHTER **
William Beaudine      USA              1966
*John Lupton, Estelita, Cal Bolder, Steven Geray, Jim Davis, Narda Onyx, Felipe Turich, Rosa Turich, Raymond Barnes, William Fawcett, Nestor Paiva, Dan*

*White, Page Slattery, Roger Creed, Fred Stromsoe, Mark Norton*
Mixture of Western and horror genres, with Jessie James battling to save the world from Frankenstein's grand-daughter, who has turned a member of his gang into a killer monster called Igor. Ludicrous, low-budget shenanigans.
HOR              63 min (ort 95 min)
B,V,V2                    EHE

## JESSE OWENS STORY, THE ***          U
Richard Irving        USA              1984
*Dorian Harewood, Debbi Morgan, Barry Corbin, Georg Stanford Brown, Kai Wulff, Lynn Hamilton, Tom Bosley, LeVar Burton, Ronny Cox, Norman Fell, Greg Morris, James B. Sikking, Vic Tayback, Ben Vereen, George Kennedy*
Story of the gifted black American runner, whose winning performance at the infamous 1936 Berlin Olympics, upset Hitler so much that he left the stadium in a fit of pique, at this rebuttal of the myth of Aryan racial superiority. The film also deals with the subsequent events in his life, including his tax battles with the government. A powerful and engrossing drama, scripted by Harold Gast. The score is by Michel Legrand. First shown in two parts.
DRA              158 min (ort 200 min) mTV
B,V                        CIC

## JESSIE AND LESTER: TWO BROTHERS IN A    15
## PLACE CALLED TRINITY **
James London (Renzo Genta)
                      ITALY            1972
*Richard Harrison, Donald O'Brien, Anna Zimmermann*
Two brothers inherit a piece of land, but fail to agree on how it should be used. One of the brothers is a gunslinger and wants to build a brothel, and the other is a priest and wants to build a church. A mediocre comedy.
Aka: JESSE AND LESTER; JESSE E LESTER, DUE FRATELLI IN UN POSTO CHIAMATO TRINITA
WES              97 min
B,V,V2              VDM; PHE (VHS only)

## JESSI'S GIRLS *                       18
Al Adamson            USA              1975
*Sondra Currie, Geoffrey Land, Ben Frank, Rod Cameron, Gavin Murrell, Regina Carroll, Rigg Kennedy, Jennifer Bishop, William Hammer, Ellen Stern, Hugh Warden, Joe Cortese, Joe Arrowsmith, Jon Shank, John Durren, Biff Yeager*
A Mormon woman survives to avenge her rape and the murder of her preacher husband, by a gang of outlaws as they were attacked on the way to Tucson. A grim saga of rape, revenge and killing, from a notorious Grade-Z Hollywood director. Written by Budd Donnelly.
Aka: WANTED WOMEN (PRI, PHE or SHEP)
WES          79 min; 81 min (SHEP) (ort 86 min)
                      Cut (1 min 27 sec)
B,V          INT/CBS L/A; PRI; PHE; XTASY; SHEP

## JESUS CHRIST, SUPERSTAR ***          PG
Norman Jewison        USA              1973
*Ted Neely, Carl Anderson, Yvonne Elliman, Barry Dennen, Joshua Mostel, Bob Bingham*
Film version of the rock opera on the life of Christ, that combines fine music with a somewhat stagebound approach. Highly unusual but definitely showing its age.
Boa: rock opera by Andrew Lloyd Webber and Tim Rice.
MUS              102 min (ort 108 min)
B,V                        CIC

## JESUS OF MONTREAL ****               18
Denys Arcand     CANADA/FRANCE         1989
*Lothaire Bluteau, Catherine Wilkening, Johanne-*

Marie Tremblay, Remy Girard, Robert Lepage, Gilles
Pelletier, Marie-Christine Barrault, Yves Jacques
Written by Arcand, this unusual film offers the
premise that a group of actors who have assembled to
mount an unconventional production of the Passion
Play may in fact be in the presence of Jesus. Bluteau
gives a superb performance in the title role, and this
insightful work loses no opportunity to examine
religious bigotry and various other issues.
DRA                                        120 min subtitles
V                                                       PAL

**JESUS OF NAZARETH** **                              PG
Franco Zeffirelli      ITALY/UK                        1977
Robert Powell, Anne Bancroft, Laurence Olivier,
Ralph Richardson, James Mason, Anthony Quinn,
Peter Ustinov, Rod Steiger, Christopher Plummer,
Ernest Borgnine, Claudia Cardinale, Valentina
Cortese, James Farentino
A long and detailed account of the life of Christ, filmed
in Morocco and Tunisia, that's best described as
sincere but rather dull.
DRA                                    383 min (4 cassettes) mTV
B,V                                    PRV L/A; CH5 (VHS only)

**JET PILOT** **                                        U
Josef Von Sternberg    USA                             1950
                                              (released 1957)
John Wayne, Janet Leigh, Jay C. Flippen, Paul Fix,
Richard Rober, Roland Winters, Hans Conried
Wayne stars as a US Air Force colonel who falls in
love with, and marries a Russian spy, who pretends to
defect to the USA. Romantic drama that sat on the
shelf for seven years before being released. Implausi-
ble nonsense carried along by a nice cast and some
rather good stunt flying sequences.
DRA                                    108 min (ort 112 min)
V/h                                                     CIC

**JEWEL IN THE CROWN, THE** ***                         15
Jim O'Brien/Christopher Morahan
                       UK                               1984
Peggy Ashcroft, Charles Dance, Saeed Jaffrey,
Geraldine James, Rachel Kempson, Rosemary Leach,
Art Malik, Tim Pigott-Smith, Zia Mohyeddin, Wendy
Morgan, Judy Parfitt, Eric Porter, Susan Wooldridge,
Anna Cropper
An account of the closing years of the British Raj.
Massive in scope but unfortunately overladen with all
the stock British "pukka" characters, and Indians who
rarely rise above the level of cardboard characters.
Boa: the Raj Quartet novels of Paul Scott.
DRA                                    752 min (5 cassettes) mTV
V                                      GRN; VES; PREST

**JEWEL OF THE NILE, THE** **                           PG
Lewis Teague          USA                              1985
Michael Douglas, Kathleen Turner, Danny DeVito,
Spiros Focas, Paul David Magid, Avner Eisenberg,
Howard Jay Patterson, Randall Edwin Nelson, The
Flying Karamazov Brothers
A sequel to ROMANCING THE STONE, with our
madcap duo getting involved in a hunt for a myste-
rious gem in the deserts of North Africa, and a race to
outwit an arch-villain. The same mixture of violent
action, romance and languors as before.
A/AD                                   101 min (ort 104 min)
V/sh                                                    CBS

**JEZEBEL** ***                                         U
William Wyler         USA                              1938
Bette Davis, Henry Fonda, George Brent, Margaret
Lindsay, Donald Crisp, Fay Bainter, Spring Byington,
Richard Cromwell, Henry O'Neill, John Litel, Eddie
Anderson, Gordon Oliver, Irving Pichel
A temperamental and self-centred Southern beauty
outrages all and sundry by her behaviour, but finally
gets a chance to redeem herself when yellow fever
strikes, and she volunteers to act as nurse to her sick

fiance and accompany him into quarantine. AA:
Actress (Davis), S. Actress (Bainter).
Boa: play by Owen Davis Sr.
DRA                                    100 min (ort 103 min) B/W
V                                                       WHV

**JIGSAW MAN, THE** **                                  15
Terence Young         UK                               1983
Michael Caine, Laurence Olivier, Susan George,
Robert Powell, Charles Gray, Michael Medwin, Vladek
Sheybal
A defector undergoes plastic surgery and is then sent
back to the UK to recover secret documents. A verbose
and muddled thriller.
Boa: novel by D. Bennett.
THR                                    95 min; 91 min (WHV)
B, V/h                                 TEVP; WHV (VHS only)

**JIGSAW MURDERS, THE** ***                             18
Jag Mundhra          USA                               1988
Chad Everett, Yaphet Kotto, Michelle Johnson,
Michael Sabatino
Two detectives are assigned to a case involving a
gruesome murder of a young girl, whose leg was found
in a factory skip. Later one of the detectives is given a
jigsaw puzzle at his stag party, featuring a photograph
of the same model's leg, which he recognises due to a
tattoo. This leads him back to the original photographer and the discovery of a vicious serial killer. A
taut and gripping thriller.
THR                                                97 min
V                                                       MGM

**JIMMY REARDON** **                                    15
William Richert      USA                               1988
River Phoenix, Ann Magnuson, Meredith Salenger,
Ione Skye, Louanne, Matthew L. Perry
A coming-of-age comedy set in 1962 and narrated by
the central character, who looks back on the turning
point in his young life which marked his transition to
manhood. Quite appealing, but patchy and unsatis-
fying.
Aka: NIGHT IN THE LIFE OF JIMMY REARDON,
THE
Boa: novel Aren't You Ever Gonna Kiss Me Goodbye?
by William Richert.
COM                                    89 min (ort 105 min)
B,V                                                    SONY

**JIMMY THE KID** *                                     PG
Gary Nelson          USA                               1983
Gary Coleman, Paul Le Mat, Walter Olkewicz, Dee
Wallace, Ruth Gordon, Don Adams, Cleavon Little,
Avery Schreiber
The son of wealthy singers is kidnapped but is in no
hurry to be returned home by his inept captors
because at last he now has a chance to enjoy his
childhood. A lame and fairly unfunny comedy.
Boa: novel by Donald Westlake.
COM                                                85 min
B,V                                                     GHV

**JINXED!** **                                          15
Don Siegel           USA                               1982
Bette Midler, Rip Torn, Ken Wahl, Jack Elam, Val
Avery, Benson Fong, Jacqueline Scott
Comedy dealing with a bunch of mixed-up characters
in Las Vegas and focusing on a small-time gambler,
his singer girlfriend and a blackjack dealer. A tedious
comedy of few laughs, scripted by Frank D. Gilroy
(who used the pseudonym of Brian Blessed).
COM                                                103 min
B,V                                                     WHV

**JO JO DANCER: YOUR LIFE IS CALLING** *               18
Richard Pryor        USA                               1986
Richard Pryor, Debbie Allen, Art Evans, Fay Hauser,
Barbara Williams, Carmen McRae, Paula Kelly,
Diahnne Abbott, Scoey Mitchill, Billy Eckstine, Wings

*Hauser, E'lon Cox, Virginia Capers, Dennis Farina*
A behind-the-scenes look at a comedian, forced to reconsider his life and ways after a serious accident at the height of his career. Largely based on Pryor's own life, this was his directorial debut, and what a jumbled and incoherent mess it is.
COM                           96 min Cut (1 min 1 sec)
V/sh                                                RCA

### JOAN OF ARC **                                        PG
Victor Fleming            USA                        1948
*Ingrid Bergman, Jose Ferrer, George Coulouris,*
*Francis L. Sullivan, J. Carroll Naish, Gene Lockhart,*
*Ward Bond, John Ireland, Leif Erickson, William*
*Conrad, John Ireland, Hurd Hatfield, George Zucco*
Bergman stars as Joan of Arc, the young French peasant girl who led the French army against the English. Betrayed to the enemy, she was forced to confess to heresy and was burnt at the stake as a witch. A competent rather than exciting adaptation of the original play, let down by a distinct lack of spectacle. AA: Cin (Joseph Valentine/William V. Skall/Winton C. Hoch), Cost (Dorothy Jeakins/ Karinska), Spec Award (Walter Wanger).
Boa: play by Maxwell Anderson.
DRA   96 min (ort 145 min) (Abridged by distributor)
B,V                           MEV L/A; VGM (VHS only)

### JOCKS **                                              15
Steve Carver           USA        1984 (released 1987)
*Scott Strader, Perry Lang, Mariska Hargitay, Richard*
*Roundtree, Christopher Lee, R.G. Armstrong, Stoney*
*Jackson, Adam Mills, Katherine Kelly Lang, Don*
*Gibb, Trinidad Silva*
A college tennis team face a tough time during a tournament, and also have to deal with the negative attitude of the college athletics director towards their sport, which he considers an unmanly game. A simple-minded teen comedy.
Aka: ROAD TRIP
COM                                              91 min
B,V                                                 WHV

### JODY **
Glenn Tucker             USA
*Joey Keeper, Ron McPherson*
When a young boy is stranded in the American wilderness in the 1880s, he faces a desperate struggle to survive.
DRA                                              83 min
B,V                                          ALLAM/MOG

### JOE **                                                15
John G. Avildsen         USA                        1970
*Dennis Patrick, Peter Boyle, Audrey Caire, K. Callan,*
*Susan Sarandon, Patrick McDermott*
A man murders his daughter's hippy boyfriend, and makes friends in a bar with a like-minded bigot, but the latter learns of his crime and decides to blackmail him. A contrived film sustained by the strong cast. This was Sarandon's film debut.
DRA                           93 min (ort 107 min)
B,V,V2                      INT/CBS; PICPAL; STABL

### JOE DANCER VOL. 1 **
Reza Badiyi              USA                        1981
*Robert Blake, JoBeth Williams, Neva Patterson, James*
*Gammon, Carol Wayne, Veronica Cartwright, Edward*
*Winter, Phillip R. Allen, Sondra Blake, Eileen*
*Heckart, A. Wilford Brimley, Kevyn Major Howard,*
*Kenneth Tigar, Bubba Smith*
A tough private eye is wrongly accused of a murder, and follows a trail of killing and corruption that leads to a wealthy family with political ambitions. The first of three TV films in a series. Fair.
Aka: BIG BLACK PILL, THE
THR                                        100 min mTV
B,V                                                 CBS

### JOE KIDD **                                           15
John Sturges             USA                        1972
*Clint Eastwood, Robert Duvall, John Saxon, Don*
*Stroud, Stella Garcia, James Wainwright, Paul Keslo,*
*John Carter, Gregory Walcott, Pepe Horn, Chuck*
*Hayward, Dick Van Patten, Buddy Van Horn, Lynne*
*Marta*
A gunfighter is hired by a landowner to hunt down some Mexican squatters. Another one of those features that helped nudge Eastwood towards stardom, but this one is little better than mediocre.
WES                           83 min (ort 88 min)
V/h                                                 CIC

### JOE PANTHER ***
Paul Krasny              USA                        1976
*Ricardo Montalban, Brian Keith, Ray Tracey, Alan*
*Feinstein, Cliff Osmond, A. Martinez, Ray Tracey, Lois*
*Red Elk*
Story of a modern-day Seminole Indian boy, his initiation into manhood and his attempts to adjust to white civilisation. A solid, entertaining tale.
WES                                             110 min
B,V,V2                                        INT/CBS

### JOE VERSUS THE VOLCANO ***                             PG
John Patrick Shanley   USA                          1990
*Tom Hanks, Meg Ryan, Lloyd Bridges, Robert Stack,*
*Abe Vigoda, Dan Hedaya, Barry McGovern, Ossie*
*Davis*
A bullied wage-slave is diagnosed as suffering from a mysterious terminal disease, but is offered a fabulous remaining six months by a millionaire if he accepts a challenge to throw himself into a live volcano on a Polynesian island, for the natives require a hero to appease their gods and the millionaire has worked out a method of getting control of the island's mineral deposits. A chaotic and disorganised screwball romantic-comedy.
COM                           98 min (ort 102 min) subH
V/sh                                                WHV

### JOHN AND YOKO: THE COMPLETE STORY **
Sandor Stern             USA                        1985
*Mark McGann, Kim Miyori, Kenneth Price, Peter*
*Capaldi, Philip Walsh, Richard Morant, Rachel*
*Laurence, Joe Randall Cutler, Samuel Wetmore, Paul*
*Lockwood, Catherine Wrigley, Larissa Anastacio,*
*Vincent Marzello, David Baxt*
A shallow account of the relationship between Yoko Ono and John Lennon, that presents them both as less than lovable human beings rather than perfect icons of popular idol worship. Apart from the Beatles' songs however, there is little entertainment to be had here. Written by Stern and first shown in two parts.
Aka: JOHN AND YOKO: A LOVE STORY
Boa: story by Sandor Stern and Edward Hume.
DRA                     132 min (ort 180 min) mTV SONY

### JOHNNY AND THE WICKED GIANT **
Jean Image             FRANCE                        1951
Animated comic fairytale in which the Queen Bee and her army help Johnny kill an evil giant. Fair.
Aka: JEANNOT L'INTREPIDE; JOHNNY THE GIANT KILLER
CAR                                              76 min
B,V                                                 VDM

### JOHNNY BE GOOD *                                      15
Bud Smith                USA                        1987
*Anthony Michael Hall, Robert Downey Jr, Paul*
*Gleason, Uma Thurman, Steve James, Seymour*
*Cassel, Michael Greene, Robert Downey Sr, Jim*
*McMahon, Howard Cosell, Jennifer Tilly, Marshall*
*Bell, Deborah May, Michael Alldredge*
A dull comedy about the illegal recruitment of high school athletes by US colleges, concentrating on one athlete who has promised his girlfriend they would

attend the local university together. Full of nudity and crude jokes, to make up for the lack of plot and competent acting.

COM  87 min (ort 98 min)
V/sh  VIR

## JOHNNY COME LATELY ** PG
William K. Howard  USA  1943
*James Cagney, Grace George, Marjorie Lord, Marjorie Main, Hattie McDaniel, Edward McNamara, Bill Henry, Robert Barrat, George Cleveland, Margaret Hamilton, Lucien Littlefield, Irving Bacon*
A wandering journalist stops at a small town where he helps an elderly editor expose the corruptness of the local politicians. Made by Cagney as an independent production, this mildly amusing piece of turn-of-the-century whimsy has a few enjoyable moments scattered here and there.
Boa: novel McLeod's Folly by Louis Bromfield.
DRA  97 min B/W
V  VIR

## JOHNNY DANGEROUSLY * 15
Amy Heckerling  USA  1984
*Michael Keaton, Joe Piscopo, Marilu Henner, Peter Boyle, Maureen Stapleton, Griffin Dunne, Richard Dimitri, Glynnis O'Connor, Byron Thames, Danny DeVito, Dom DeLuise, Ray Walston, Sudie Bond*
A wild spoof on American gangster films, that takes a look at the career of the title character. A scattering of feeble jokes serve merely to highlight the atrociousness of the whole effort.
COM  86 min (ort 90 min)
B,V  CBS

## JOHNNY GUITAR *** PG
Nicholas Ray  USA  1953
*Sterling Hayden, Joan Crawford, Scott Brady, Mercedes McCambridge, Ward Bond, Ernest Borgnine, Ben Cooper, Royal Dano, John Carradine, Paul Fix, Frank Ferguson, Rhys Williams, Ian MacDonald, Will Wright, John Maxwell*
An old flame comes to work at a saloon run by a woman whose relationship with the local townsfolk is none too friendly. Hayden as the reluctant gunslinger, and Crawford as the saloonkeeper with a penchant for outlaws, strike sparks off each other in this one. McCambridge was never more sinister. The script is by Philip Yordan.
Boa: novel by R. Chanslor.
WES  110 min
B,V  BBC; VCC

## JOHNNY HANDSOME *** 15
Walter Hill  USA  1989
*Mickey Rourke, Ellen Barkin, Charles Roven, Elizabeth McGovern, Forest Whitaker, Scott Wilson, Lance Henriksen, Morgan Feman*
A badly disfigured criminal is ditched by his comrades during a robbery, captured and sent to prison. However, once there he's given the chance to have cosmetic surgery as part of a rehabilitation programme, and on being eventually released sets out to have his revenge on his former colleagues. A moody, violent and offbeat yarn, not without its virtues despite the lack of a strong plot. Music is by Ry Cooder.
Boa: novel The Three Worlds Of Johnny Handsome by John Godey.
DRA  90 min (ort 94 min)
V  GHV

## JOHNNY SHILOH ** U
James Neilson  USA  1963
*Kevin Corcoran, Brian Keith, Daryl Hickman, Eddie Hodges, Skip Homeier*
The story of an 11-year-old drummer boy, serving with the Union forces in the American Civil War after his family is killed. A good cast do well in this undemanding family yarn. The film was originally shown in two parts on a Disney TV show.
WES  86 min (ort 90 min)
B,V  WDV

## JOINT VENTURE * USA 1978
*Gerard Damiano, Vanessa Del Rio, Bobby Astyr, Sharon Mitchell*
Sex film written around the exploits of four women who take part in a series of contests highlighting different methods of stimulation.
A  90 min
V  RIP

## JOKER, THE * 18
Peter Patzak  WEST GERMANY  1987
*Peter Maffay, Massimo Ghini, Tahnee Welch, Armin Muller-Stahl, Michael York, Elliott Gould, Bernhard Freyd, Elke Krings, Joachim D. Mues, Marquard Bohm, Andras Goczol, Werner Pochath, Monika Bleibtreu, Uwe Hacker*
A tough cop sets out on an errand of revenge when an explosion cripples one of his colleagues and kills another. A violent thriller full of murder and mayhem, but hampered by its weak plot and downbeat ending.
Aka: LETHAL OBSESSION
THR  93 min
V  RCA

## JOLSON SINGS AGAIN ** U
Henry Levin  USA  1949
*Larry Parks, Barbara Hale, William Demarest, Ludwig Donath, Bill Goodwin, Tamara Shayne, Myron McCormick*
A flaccid attempt to build on the success of THE JOLSON STORY, which takes us through the singer's second marriage and later career, in which he gained a new lease of life as an entertainer of the troops during WW2. As before, Parks mimes and Jolson sings, but apart from the songs (which include "Baby Face", "Sonny Boy" and "Back In Your Own Yard") this is a singularly uninspiring affair.
MUS  92 min (ort 96 min)
V  RCA

## JOLSON STORY, THE *** U
Alfred E. Green  USA  1946
*Larry Parks, Evelyn Keyes, William Demarest, Bill Goodwin, Ludwig Donath, Tamara Shayne, Scotty Beckett, John Alexander*
An excellent biopic on the famous singer, with Jolson dubbing his own songs, that is done very much in the traditional Hollywood style but eminently enjoyable nonetheless. Followed in 1949 by the sequel JOLSON SINGS AGAIN. Songs include: "April Showers", "Avalon", "You Made Me Love You" and "My Mammy". AA: Score (Morris Stoloff), Sound (John Livardy).
MUS  124 min (ort 129 min)
V  RCA; PREST

## JONATHAN LIVINGSTON SEAGULL ** 
Hal Bartlett  USA  1973
*Voices of: James Franciscus, Juliet Mills, Hal Holbrook, Philip Ahn, David Ladd, Dorothy McGuire, Richard Crenna*
An account of a seagull who wants to fly higher and faster than any other in the world, that offers excellent photography, jarring music and a silly voice-over, all elements that fail in their attempt to convey the mysticism of the original novel. The intrusive score is by Neil Diamond.
Boa: novel by Richard Bach.
DRA  95 min (ort 120 min)
V/sh  CIC

## JONI ** PG
James F. Collier  USA  1980
*Joni Eareckson, Bert Remsen, Katherine De Hetre,*

*Cooper Huckabee, John Milford, Michael Mancini, Richard Lineback*
A woman rebuilds her life and finds religion, after breaking her spine in a diving accident. An earnest but dull devotional film, financed by Billy Graham's organisation.
Boa: book by Joni Eareckson.

| | |
|---|---|
| DRA | 108 min |
| B,V | RVD; BAG |

**JORY ** ** PG
Jorge Fons USA 1972
*John Marley, B.J. Thomas, Brad Dexter, Robby Benson, Claudio Brook, Ben Baker, Patricia Aspillaga, Todd Martin, Linda Purl, Anne Lockhart, Betty Sheridan, Ted Markland*
A 15-year-old boy sets out to have his revenge when his father and a group of friends are murdered. Shot in Mexico and only released on an experimental basis initially, but the film is actually better than one would have expected. Benson's screen debut.
Boa: novel by Milton R. Bass.

| | |
|---|---|
| WES | 93 min (ort 97 min) Cut (5 sec) |
| B,V | EHE |

**JOSEPH AND HIS BROTHERS ** **
Jack B. Hively USA 1979
*Sam Bottoms, Walter Brooke, Harvey Jason, Bernie Koppell, Barry Nelson, Carol Rossen*
The story of Joseph being sold into slavery by his brothers. Part of the "Greatest Heroes Of The Bible" series. Fair.

| | |
|---|---|
| DRA | 55 min |
| B,V | VCL/CBS |

**JOUR DE FETE *** ** U
Jacques Tati FRANCE 1948
*Jacques Tati, Guy Decomble, Paul Fankeur, Santa Relli, Maine Vallee, Roger Rafal, Beauvais*
A village postman tries to improve the service with hilarious results, after seeing a documentary about the wondrous efficiency of the US Mail. Tati's full-length directorial debut, and expanded from an earlier work by him, a short film entitled "L'Ecole Des Facteurs". Though the film was shot in colour (using a new process) it was found to be unsatisfactory and released in B/W. However, a partially hand-coloured print has been made.

| | |
|---|---|
| COM | 80 min (ort 87 min) B/W |
| B,V,V2 | VDM L/A; VMA; STABL |

**JOURNALIST, THE ** ** 15
Michael Thornhill AUSTRALIA 1979
*Sam Neill, Jack Thompson, Liz Alexander*
A journalist leaves his job and has a mental break-down, his problems being compounded when his mistress walks out on him and his wife starts planning for a divorce. Better times are in store however.

| | |
|---|---|
| DRA | 89 min |
| B,V | PRV |

**JOURNEY ***
Paul Almond CANADA 1972
*Genevieve Bujold, John Vernon, Gale Garnett, George Sperdakos, Elton Hayes, Beata Hartig, Meg Hogarth, Mary Bellows, Judith Gault, Gary McKeehan, Ratch Wallace, Greg Adams, Luke Gibson*
A young woman believes that she is the bearer of bad luck after being saved from drowning by the head of a remote rural community. A silly drama that tries to be more important than it is.

| | |
|---|---|
| DRA | 88 min |
| B,V,V2 | VCL/CBS |

**JOURNEY AMONG WOMEN ** ** 18
Tom Cowan AUSTRALIA 1977
*Lillian Crombie, Jeune Pritchard, Martin Phelan, Nell Campbell*

A group of ill-treated woman convicts plan to escape from their suffering, and plot their revenge in this drama set in days when Australia was still a British penal colony.

| | |
|---|---|
| DRA | 93 min Cut |
| B,V | MED |

**JOURNEY INTO FEAR ** ** PG
Daniel Mann CANADA 1975
*Sam Waterston, Zero Mostel, Yvette Mimieux, Scott Marlowe, Ian McShane, Joseph Wiseman, Shelley Winters, Stanley Holloway, Donald Pleasence, Vincent Price, Meira Shore, Dimitri Papaioannou, Jackie Cooper, Christos Natsios*
A geologist in Turkey becomes involved in an international spy ring and undertakes a mission to save the government from overthrow. A remake of a 1942 film with Orson Welles, but far less exciting and a good deal more muddled.
Boa: novel by Eric Ambler.

| | |
|---|---|
| A/AD | 100 min; 95 min (MIA) |
| B,V,V2 | INT/CBS; MIA (VHS only) |

**JOURNEY OF NATTY GANN, THE ** ** PG
Jeremy Paul Kagan USA 1985
*Meredith Salenger, Ray Wise, John Cusack, Lainie Kazan, Scatman Crothers, Barry Miller, Verna Bloom, Bruce M. Fischer*
In the Depression years a young girl sets out across the USA to re-join her father, and gains an unlikely travelling companion in the shape of a wolf. A well-photographed if somewhat slow-paced and sentimental tale.
Aka: NATTY GANN

| | |
|---|---|
| JUV | 97 min (ort 105 min) |
| B,V | RNK; WDV |

**JOURNEY TO THE CENTER OF THE EARTH *** ** U
Henry Levin USA 1959
*James Mason, Pat Boone, Arlene Dahl, Diane Baker, Thayer David, Peter Ronson, Alan Napier, Alan Caillou, Ben Wright, Alex Finlayson, Frederick Halliday, Mary Brady, Robert Adler*
A superlative evocation of Verne's classic tale, of a scientific expedition that descends into the bowels of the earth, where various incredible sights await. Rather poorly remade in 1978 as "Where Time Began".
Boa: novel by Jules Verne.

| | |
|---|---|
| FAN | 129 min (ort 132 min) |
| V/h | CBS |

**JOURNEY TO THE CENTER OF TIME ** **
David L. Hewitt USA 1967
*Scott Brady, Gigi Perreau, Anthony Eisley, Abraham Sofaer, Poupee Gamin, Lyle Waggoner, Austin Green, Tracy Olsen, Andy David, Larry Evans, Jody Milhouse*
Time travellers move backwards and forwards in time, from a prehistoric jungle to a dictatorship of the year 5000. Unmemorable nonsense that wastes a few good ideas.

| | |
|---|---|
| FAN | 82 min |
| B,V | DFS |

**JOURNEY TO THE CENTRE OF THE EARTH ** ** Uc
Richard Slapczynski
AUSTRALIA 1976
Lively animated version of this classic tale of adventure and exploration in the bowels of the Earth.
Boa: novel by Jules Verne.

| | |
|---|---|
| CAR | 49 min |
| B,V,V2 | VCL/CBS; CHILD L/A; STYL (VHS only) |

**JOURNEY TO THE CENTRE OF THE EARTH ** ** PG
Rusty Lemorande USA 1988
*Nicola Cowper, Paul Carafotes, Ilan Mitchell-Smith, Geoffrey Kirkland*
Made by Cannon, this is the latest attempt to bring Verne's classic tale to the screen. Watchable, but no

more than that.
Boa: novel by Jules Verne.
A/AD 77 min (ort 86 min) Cut (37 sec)
B,V RNK

## JOURNEY TO THE SEVENTH PLANET * U
Sidney Pink DENMARK 1958
*Greta Thyssen, Ann Smyrner, Mimi Heinrich, Carl Ottosen*
A derivative Danish opus all about an Earth mission to Uranus in 2001 that encounters a strange alien civilisation. A low-budget effort hampered by both a lack of money and imagination.
FAN 74 min (ort 83 min)
V RCA

## JOY **
Serge Bergon CANADA/FRANCE 1984
*Agnes Torrent, Claudia Udy, Gerard Antoine Huart, Elisabeth Mortensen, Claire Nadeau, Septmu Sever, John Stocker, Jerome Tiberghien, Danielle Godet, Michel Caron, Jeffrey Kime, Remy Azzolini, Manuel Gelin*
The sexual adventures of a woman.
Boa: novel by J. Laurey.
A 95 min (ort 101 min)
B,V AVA/CBS

## JOY OF FOOLING AROUND, THE ***
Pierre Du Bois FRANCE 1979
*Monique Du Prez, Kevin Raymond, Valerie Ashley, Sal Pontini, Erica Swanson*
Sex film set on the Greek island of Mykonos which begins with a wealthy shipowner discovering his wife in bed with her lover. He takes off in his yacht, but causes an explosion and is thrown into the water. Washed ashore on an island and suffering from amnesia, he is rescued by a fisherman's daughter and sheltered in her shack. Complications follow with the discovery of a recent murder, but all ends happily in a well-made and intriguing tale.
A 90 min
B,V,V2 CAL

## JOY OF LETTING GO, THE **
John Gregory USA 1976
*Dominique St Pierre, Leslie Hughes, Susie Sun Lee, James Kral, Frank Dudley, Pamela Strass*
A bored rich woman is married to a man 20 years older, who is so moralistic that when he goes on trips abroad she's left in the care of a bodyguard. She becomes so sexually frustrated she has two women seduce and "imprison" her minder, and with her new-found freedom she goes to work as a prostitute. An unbelievable story, but one that benefits from good performances and some nice cinematography.
A 88 min; 58 min (ELEC)
B,V EVI L/A; ELEC

## JOY OF SEX, THE * 15
Martha Coolidge USA 1984
*Michelle Meyrink, Cameron Dye, Lisa Langlois, Charles Van Eman, Christopher Lloyd, Colleen Camp, Ernie Hudson*
A girl believes that she has only weeks to live, and decides to lose her virginity before it's too late, since dying a virgin is almost as bad as death itself. So tasteless and unfunny that it insults Dr Alex Comfort's famous sex manual, whose title (and only that) it shares.
COM 89 min (ort 93 min)
V/h CIC

## JOYRIDE **
Joseph Ruben USA 1977
*Desi Arnaz Jr, Robert Carradine, Melanie Griffith, Anne Lockhart, Tom Ligon, Cliff Lenz*
Two young couples go looking for adventure, but turn

to crime after the men get a raw deal from a union official. A confused and haphazard tale that staggers along in general aimlessness.
DRA 92 min
B,V,V2 VCL/CBS

## JOYRIDE TO NOWHERE * 15
Mel Welles USA 1978
*Leslie Ackermann, Sandy Serrano, Len Lesser, Gary Gabelich, Linda Gray, Dino Nova, Mel Welles, Ron Ross, Speed Stearns*
Two young girls on the road enjoy a variety of edifying experiences, plus sundry car chases in this aptly-named piece of pointlessness.
A/AD 80 min; 90 min (SKP)
B,V INT L/A; XTASY; SKP

## JOYRIDERS ** 15
Aisling Walsh EIRE 1988
*Patricia Kerrigan, Andrew Connolly, Billie Whitelaw, John Kavanagh*
A woman flees from her brutal husband and is forced to leave behind her two young daughters, but embarks on an affair with a young joyrider she meets on her travels.
DRA 96 min
V PATHE

## JOYSTICKS * 18
Greydon Clark USA 1983
*Joe Don Baker, Leif Green, Jim Greenleaf, Scott McGinnis, Logan Ramsey*
A video arcade is threatened by a nasty man who wants to shut it down, but the teens unite to defeat this menace to their wholesome pastime. A film as noisy and empty as the cause it champions.
Aka: JOY STICKS; VIDEO MADNESS
COM 83 min (ort 88 min)
B,V EIV

## JUAREZ *** U
William Dieterle USA 1939
*Paul Muni, Bette Davis, John Garfield, Brian Aherne, Claude Rains, Donald Crisp, Gale Sondergaard, Gilbert Roland, Louis Calhern, Pedro De Cordoba, Joseph Calleia, Henry O'Neill, Montagu Love, Harry Davenport, Grant Mitchell*
Muni gives a fine performance as this famous Mexican leader, in a colourful film full of splendid sets and locations, that describes the fight to oust the Emperor Maximillian from the Mexican throne, on which he had been placed by the troops of France's ruler Napoleon III. A film that for all its lavish sets and fine acting remains somewhat aloof and clinical.
Boa: book Phantom Crown by B. Harding.
DRA 106 min (ort 132 min) B/W
V WHV

## JUBILEE *
Derek Jarman UK 1978
*Toyah Wilcox, Jordan, Little Nell, Jenny Runacre, Hermione Demoriane, Ian Charleson, Karl Johnson, Linda Spurrier, Neil Kennedy, Orlando, Wayne County, Richard O'Brien, David Haughton, Adam Ant, Claire Davenport*
Punk-rock film with Queen Elizabeth I being transported to the present day by her astrologer, and witnessing the virtual collapse of civilisation. A typical Jarman extravaganza of shock effects and pointless nastiness. The film has something valid to say, but it never has a chance to say it.
DRA 103 min
B,V VCL/CBS

## JUDGEMENT AT NUREMBERG *** PG
Stanley Kramer USA 1961
*Spencer Tracy, Burt Lancaster, Richard Widmark, Marlene Dietrich, Judy Garland, Maximilian Schell, Montgomery Clift, William Shatner, Kenneth*

*MacKenna, Edward Binns, Werner Klemperer, Torben Meyer, Alan Baxter*
An overlong film version of what started life as an entry in a 1950s TV series, "Playhouse 90" in the USA. Here the fictional story of a Nazi judge on trial for war crimes, serves as a means of examining the atrocities committed or sanctioned by the officials of that hideous regime. AA: Actor (Schell), Screen (Adapt) (Abby Mann).
Boa: TV play by Abby Mann.
DRA                              178 min (ort 190 min) B/W
V                                                    WHV

### JUDGEMENT DAY ***
Jon Cutaia          USA                       1978
*Angel Face, Moira Benson, John Leslie, Morning Star, P.J. Whigham, Turk Lyon, Josie Farmer, John Seeman*
This sex comedy opens with a suicide, but moves on to a scene where several couples describe their sex lives to St Peter in order to enter Heaven. As most of the men died from some foolishness or other, they are sent to Hell, but St Peter relents in several cases. Finally, he reverses the suicide of the first couple who only did this because the man couldn't get a divorce. He sends them back to Earth and solves this problem for them as well.
A                                                   72 min
B,V                                                   CAL

### JUDGEMENT IN STONE, A **                     15
Ousama Rawi        CANADA                     1986
*Rita Tushingham, Tom Kneebone, Ross Petty, Shelley Peterson, Jessica Stern, Jonathan Crombie, Jackie Burroughs*
A woman housekeeper who is dyslexic, is driven mad by the pressure of trying to conceal her disability from her employers and eventually kills them. A chilling little tale that takes a long time to develop.
Aka: HOUSEKEEPER, THE
Boa: novel by Ruth Rendell.
HOR                                   94 min (ort 102 min)
B,V                                                   VIR

### JUDGEMENT, THE **                           15
Harvey Hart        CANADA/USA                 1985
*Tess Harper, Leslie Nielson, Ronny Cox, Kate Lynch, Henry Ramer, Sean McCann, Frank Adamson, Lily Franks, Tony DeSantis, Gary Reineke, Tony Lower, Barry Platman, Mark Humphrey, Patricia Idlette, Garfield Andrews*
A doctor slandered by an investigative TV reporter, fights back and engages a woman lawyer of limited experience to refute the allegations that he had used his clinic merely as a means of pushing pills. A dull fictionalised account, based on a similar case in Los Angeles in 1983, against the CBS network and its show "60 Minutes".
Aka: RECKLESS DISREGARD
DRA                                   92 min (ort 95 min) mCab
B,V                                                   ARF

### JUGGERNAUT ***                              PG
Richard Lester     UK                         1974
*Richard Harris, David Hemmings, Omar Sharif, Anthony Hopkins, Ian Holm, Shirley Knight, Roy Kinnear, Cyril Cusack, Freddie Jones, Roshan Seth, Mark Burns, Kristine Howarth, Clifton James, Jack Watson, Bob Sessions*
A luxury liner cruising at sea, becomes the object of an extortion attempt when a number of bombs are revealed to be aboard. Tension mounts right to the end, as a demolition crew races against the clock to defuse them, a task made much harder by the fact that the devices are complex and treacherous in design. An excellent, tautly directed thriller.
THR                                                 110 min
B,V                                                   WHV

### JULIA *                                     18
Sigi Rothemund    WEST GERMANY                1976
*Sylvia Kristel, Terry Torday, Ekkehardt Belle*
A young sophisticated woman comes of age in this forgettable softcore offering.
Aka: DER LIEBERSCHULER; ES WAR NICHT DIE NACHTIGALL
A                         83 min (ort 92 min) Cut (42 sec)
B,V                      WOV L/A; FANVID L/A; STABL

### JULIA ***                                   PG
Fred Zinnemann     USA                        1977
*Jane Fonda, Vanessa Redgrave, Jason Robards, Maximilian Schell, Rosemary Murphy, Hal Holbrook, Meryl Streep, John Glover, Lisa Pelikan, Cathleen Nesbitt, Maurice Denham, Susan Jones*
The story of two women and their friendship, told against the background of the resistance to the Nazis prior to WW2. Wooden direction and acting, combine in a beautifully photographed but sterile film, that is lacking in solid and credible characterisations. This was Meryl Streep's film debut. AA: S. Actor (Robards), S. Actress (Redgrave), Screen (Adapt) (Alvin Sargent).
Boa: book Pentimento by Lillian Hellman.
DRA                                  113 min (ort 118 min)
B,V,V2,LV                                             CBS

### JULIA AND JULIA *                           18
Peter Del Monte    ITALY                      1987
*Kathleen Turner, Sting (Gordon Sumner), Gabriel Byrne, Gabriele Ferzetti, Angela Goodwin, Lidia Broccolino, Alexander Van Wyk, Renato Scarpa, Norman Mozzato, Yorgo Voyagis, Mirella Falco, Francesca Muio, John Steiner*
A woman whose husband died on their wedding day, comes home one day and finds that he is still alive, they have a six-year-old son, and she has a lover. A weird, pseudo-SF tale, ineptly handled and with an irritatingly inconclusive ending. Notable only because it is the first feature to be shot on high definition video (with 1125 instead of 625 lines) and then transferred to 35 mm film.
THR                                                 98 min
V/sh                                                  CBS

### JULIUS CAESAR **
Stuart Burge       UK                         1969
*John Gielgud, Charlton Heston, Jason Robards, Richard Johnson, Diana Rigg, Robert Vaughn, Richard Chamberlain, Jill Bennett, Christopher Lee, Andrew Crawford, Alan Browning, Norman Bowler, David Dodimead, Michael Gough*
Third film version of Shakespeare's play offers a hardly exciting view of this drama. Adequate but far from inspiring, with Robards' dismal portrayal of Brutus a serious handicap.
Boa: play by William Shakespeare.
DRA                                                 117 min
B,V                                                   VFP

### JULIUS CAESAR **                            U
Herbert Wise       UK                         1979
*Richard Pasco, Charles Gray, Keith Michell, David Collings, Virginia McKenna, Elizabeth Spriggs, Sam Dastor, John Laurimore, John Sterland, Brian Coburn, Garrick Hagon, Leonard Preston, Alex Davion, Darien Angadi*
An efficient TV production of this famous play. One of a series of BBC Shakespeare adaptations which were characterised by the faithfulness of their interpretation and a pleasing lack of gimmickry, if not always by their inspiration.
Boa: play by William Shakespeare.
DRA                                          162 min mTV
V/h                                                   BBC

### JUMPIN' JACK FLASH *                        15
Penny Marshall     USA                        1986
*Whoopi Goldberg, Stephen Collins, Carol Kane,*

*Lawrence Gordon, John Wood, Joel Silver, Annie Potts, Roscoe Lee Browne, Sara Botsford, Jeroen Krabbe, Peter Michael Goetz, Jonathan Pryce, Tracy Reiner, Jim Belushi, Tony Hendra*
A computer operator is drawn into the complex world of international espionage when a British agent sends a message for help to her terminal. A confused and disjointed comedy-thriller, not improved by the fact that the original director, Howard Zieff, was replaced during shooting. The talents of Goldberg are wasted.
COM 101 min
V/sh CBS

### JUNGLE BOOK, THE *** U
Zoltan Korda USA 1942
*Sabu, Joseph Calleia, John Qualen, Frank Puglia, Rosemary De Camp*
A wonderful and lively fantasy of a boy brought up by wolves, who is at home in the jungle and at one with all (or nearly all) the animals. He dreams of killing Shere-Khan the tiger. A film of considerable visual impact with some remarkably beautiful sets. As ever, Sabu is memorable (even if the fight to the death with a stiff-jointed model tiger is less so). The score is by Miklos Rozsa. Remade by Disney as a cartoon animation in 1967.
Aka: RUDYARD KIPLING'S JUNGLE BOOK
Boa: novel by Rudyard Kipling.
JUV 109 min; 105 min (CH5)
B,V EHE; CH5 (VHS only)

### JUNGLE BOOK, THE ** Uc
1989
A further film in the Pickwick "Animated Classics" collection, telling of the adventures of young Mowgli and his jungle friends. Not a bad entry in the series, though animation is not especially memorable.
Boa: novel by Rudyard Kipling.
CAR 40 min
V PICK

### JUNGLE BURGER ** 18
Jean-Paul Walvarens (Picha and Boris Szulzinger)
BELGIUM/FRANCE 1975
*Voices of: Johnny Weissmuller Jr, John Belushi, Bob Perry, Andrew Duncan, Brian Doyle-Murray, Pat Bright, Emily Prager, Bill Murray, Guy Sorel, Deya Kent, Judy Graubart, Adolph Caesar, Christopher Guest, M. Vernon*
Mildly amusing animated adult jungle spoof, with Tarzan a weedy and sexually inadequate wimp whilst Jane becomes his strident and insatiable wife.
Aka: LA HONTE DE LA JUNGLE; TARZOON LA HONTE DE LA JUNGLE; TARZOON THE SHAME OF THE JUNGLE
A 72 min; 70 min (EIV)
B,V HOK L/A; EIV

### JUNGLE WARRIORS * 18
Ernst R. Von Theumer
MEXICO/WEST GERMANY 1984
*Nina Van Pallandt, Paul L. Smith, John Vernon, Alex Cord, Woody Strode, Sybil Danning (Sybelle Danninger), Louisa Moritz, Kai Wulff, Dana Elcar, Marjoe Gortner*
Fashion models are taken prisoner and subjected to various indignities, by a South American drugs dealer and his half-sister, when their plane crashes in the Amazon jungle. A good cast looks suitably embarrassed in this nonsense.
Aka: EUR WEG FUHRT DURCH DIE HOLLE; JUNGLE FEVER
A/AD 95 min; 88 min (INTMED) Cut (1 min 18 sec)
B,V HER; INTMED

### JUNGLE WOLF ** 18
Charlie Ordonez USA 1986
*J. Antonio Carreon, Ron Marchini, Laura Abyeta, Joe Meyor, Romy Diaz*

A US ambassador is being held hostage in the jungles of Central America, and the "lone wolf" agent sent to rescue him, has only 72 hours to complete his assignment before the US gets drawn into a new war.
Aka: WOLF
A/AD 84 min (ort 90 min) Cut (16 sec)
B,V IVS; VIP

### JUNIOR BONNER ***
Sam Peckinpah USA 1972
*Steve McQueen, Ida Lupino, Robert Preston, Ben Johnson, Joe Don Baker, Barbara Leigh, Mary Murphy*
An over-the-hill rodeo rider returns to the bosom of his family but finds his troubles are by no means over in this pleasant rodeo comedy-drama, that is sustained by fine acting and a good feel for the subject. One of the few Peckinpah films in which the characters don't end up full of bullet holes.
DRA 99 min (ort 105 min)
B,V RNK

### JUST A GIGOLO * 15
David Hemmings WEST GERMANY 1978
*David Bowie, Sydne Rome, Kim Novak, David Hemmings, Maria Schell, Curt Jurgens, Marlene Dietrich, Erika Pluhar*
A Prussian war veteran tries to make a living in Berlin of the 1920s and finds his niche before the inevitable tragic ending. A severely edited melodrama that makes little sense. Don't watch it to see Dietrich – her part is tiny.
Aka: SCHONER GIGOLO, ARMER GIGOLO
DRA 89 min (ort 147 min)
B,V,V2 VCL/CBS; VIR

### JUST ASK FOR DIAMOND *** U
Stephen Bayly UK 1988
*Peter Eyre, Susannah York, Rene Ruiz, Nickolas Grace, Patricia Hodge, Saeed Jaffrey, Dursley McLinden, Colin Dale, Michael Medwin, Roy Kinnear, Jimmy Nail, Bill Patterson, Michael Robbins*
A sharp 13-year-old boy and his incompetent elder brother are paid £200 to look after a box of confectionery. Soon, they find they are threatened by nasty characters who will stop at nothing to get the box. A witty and neat re-working of the private eye genre, set in contemporary London. The script is by Horowitz from his novel.
Aka: FALCON'S MALTESER, THE
Boa: novel The Falcon's Malteser by Anthony Horowitz.
JUV 89 min (ort 94 min)
B,V CBS

### JUST BEFORE DAWN * 18
Jeff Lieberman USA 1980
*George Kennedy, Chris Lemmon, Mike Kellin, Deborah Benson, Gregg Henry, Ralph Seymour, Kati Powell, Charles Bartlett, Jamie Rose, John Hunsaker, Hap Oslund, Barbara Spencer*
Teenagers hiking in the mountains are attacked by a hatchet-wielding maniacal killer, one of a pair of degenerate mutant twins (both played by Hunsaker). Nothing new or original here, apart from the idea of twin slashers, of course.
HOR 86 min (ort 91 min) Cut (7 sec)
B,V,LV RNK L/A; MIA

### JUST BETWEEN FRIENDS *** 15
Allan Burns USA 1986
*Mary Tyler Moore, Ted Danson, Christine Lahti, Sam Waterston, Susan Rinell, Salome Jens, Jane Greer, James MacKrell, Timothy Gibbs, Mark Blum*
Two women meet and develop a firm friendship, yet they remain unaware that they are both involved with the same man, as wife and lover respectively. The directing debut for Burns, and though the film suffers

badly from the contrived plot, fine performances
redeem it.

| DRA | 106 min (ort 120 min) |
| B,V | RCA |

## JUST DENNIS: THE MOVIE **

| | U |
| USA | 1988 |

*Victor Di Mattia, William Windom*
An adaptation of a long-running comic strip by Hank
Ketchum, this tale follows the exploits of our angelic-
looking title character, after he discovers a dinosaur
bone in his back garden. A cute little kid's film, made
very much in the same style as all those Disney
adventures.

| JUV | 97 min |
| V/h | ODY |

## JUST ONE OF THE GUYS ***

| | 15 |
| Lisa Gottlieb   USA | 1985 |

*Joyce Hyser, Billy Jacoby, Clayton Rohner, Toni
Hudson, Sherilyn Fenn, William Zabka, Leigh
McCloskey*
A teenage girl disguises herself as a boy and changes
her school in order to win a journalism contest. The
usual transsexual complications a la TOOTSIE arise,
in a film that is a lot funnier than one might have
expected. See also HER LIFE AS A MAN.

| COM | 96 min (ort 100 min) |
| V | RCA |

## JUST THE WAY YOU ARE ***

| | PG |
| Edouard Molinaro   USA | 1984 |

*Kristy McNichol, Michael Ontkean, Kaki Hunter,
Andre Dussolier, Catherine Saviat, Robert Carradine,
Lance Guest, Alexandra Paul, Timothy Daly, Patrick
Cassidy*
A girl with a crippled foot, hides her disability with a
plaster cast and goes on holiday where she falls in
love, only to be terrified that her boyfriend won't love
her when he learns of her handicap. A patchy but
pleasing and gentle little drama. The script is by
Allan Burns.
Aka: I WON'T DANCE

| DRA | 91 min (ort 95 min) |
| B,V | MGM |

## JUSTIN CASE *

| | U |
| Blake Edwards   USA | 1988 |

*George Carlin, Molly Hagan, Douglas Sill, Gordon
Jump, Timothy Stack, Paul Sand*
This pilot for a prospective series recycles the TOP-
PER theme, in its story of the earthbound spirit of a
murdered private eye, who involves a young actress in
the hunt for his murderer. Derivative and dull. The
script is by Edwards.

| COM | 78 min mTV |
| V | WDV |

## JUSTINE **

| | 18 |
| Jesse Franco  ITALY/WEST GERMANY | 1969 |

*Jack Palance, Akim Tamiroff, Maria Rohm*
A story running the whole gamut of perversions,
that's loosely based on De Sade's famous novel. See
also THE VIOLATION OF JUSTINE.
Aka: JUSTINE: LE DISAVVENTURE DELLA
VIRTU; MARQUIS DE SADE: JUSTINE
Boa: novel Justine, Ou Les Malheurs De La Vertu by
The Marquis de Sade.

| A | 104 min |
| B,V,V2 | VUL L/A; SID |

## JUSTINE ***

| | 15 |
| George Cukor   USA | 1969 |

*Anouk Aimee, Dirk Bogarde, Robert Forster, Anna
Karina, Michael York, Philippe Noiret, Jack
Albertson, Cliff Gorman, John Vernon, George Baker,
Michael Dunn, Barry Morse, Severn Darden*
A banker's wife in Alexandria in the 1930s, exerts a
powerful influence on the lives of those she meets, and

eventually becomes involved in politics. The com-
pression of four novels into a single film, loses all their
atmosphere and much of the storyline, leaving nothing but an exotic oriental melodrama. Not to be
confused with a film of the same title and year of
release, that has nothing to do with Durrell's novels.
Boa: Alexandria Quartet novels by Lawrence Durrell.

| DRA | 116 min |
| B,V | CBS |

# K

## K-9 *

| | 15 |
| Rod Daniel   USA | 1989 |

*James Belushi, Mel Harris, Kevin Tighe, Ed O'Neill,
Jerry Lee, James Handy, Cotter Smith*
Belushi gives a great performance that's all but
wasted in this tale of an unconventional cop, whose
obsessive desire to nail a bunch of drug dealers makes
him so difficult to work with that he's given a dog as a
partner. However, the mutt proves to be more than a
match for him, though the film itself is a big
disappointment.

| JUV | 97 min (ort 102 min) |
| V/h | CIC |

## K9000 *

| | 15 |
| Kim Manners   USA | 1989 |

*Catherine Oxenberg, Chris Mulkey*
Hard on the heels of K-9, comes this blatant rip-off. A
dog that has had a miniature computer implanted in
its brain is stolen by a ruthless maniac. A cop tracks
them to an abandoned warehouse, but in the ensuing
rescue is accidentally implanted with a receiver that
allows him to communicate with the dog telepathically, thereby making him a valuable ally in the fight
against crime. A poorly-realised, woodenly-acted, idiotic film.

| A/AD | 90 min |
| V | PRISM L/A |

## KADAICHA **

| | 18 |
| James Bogie   AUSTRALIA | 1988 |

*Zoe Carides, Tom Jennings, Eric Oldfield*
After experiencing a horrible nightmare, a young girl
wakes up with a strange stone in her hand, which her
teacher informs her is an Aboriginal "death stone".
After she is found cut to shreds, the stone moves on to
other kids who also meet violent deaths, in this
Australian clone of FRIDAY THE 13TH.
Aka: KADAICHA THE DEATH STONE

| HOR | 86 min |
| B,V | MED |

## KAGEMUSHA ***

| | PG |
| Akira Kurosawa   JAPAN | 1980 |

*Tatsuya Nakadai, Tsutomo Yamazaki, Kenichi
Hagiwara, Jinpachi Nezu, Hideji Otaki, Kota Yui,
Hideo Murata*
"Kagemusha" means "The Double", and refers to the
practice of Japanese warlords of employing others to
impersonate themselves during battles. In this film, a
thief about to be executed is reprieved and given the
task of impersonating a one such man. When the
latter dies the impersonation continues until he is
unmasked, whereupon the story moves on to explore
the end of a warrior clan. An impressive, lavish, but
strangely lifeless work.
Aka: KAGEMUSHA THE SHADOW WARRIOR

| WAR | 153 min (ort 181 min) |
| B, V/h, LV | CBS |

## KAMPUCHEA EXPRESS **

| | 18 |
| Lek Kitiparaporn   USA | 1982 |

*Robert Walker, Christopher George, Nancy Kwan,
Woody Strode*
An American journalist tries to get his lover out of

Kampuchea before the Khmer Rouge invade.
WAR                                          90 min
B,V                                             INT

## KANAL ****
Andrzej Wajda        POLAND            1956
*Teresa Izewska, Tadeusz Janczar, Vladek*
*(Wladyslaw) Sheybal, Wienczylaw Glinski, Emil*
*Kariewicz*
The second film in Wajda's excellent WW2 trilogy.
This one looks at a group of partisans who take part in
the 1944 Warsaw uprising and fight their way
through the sewers. Preceded by A GENERATION
and followed by ASHES AND DIAMONDS.
Aka: THEY LOVED LIFE
Boa: novel Kloakerne by Jerzy Stawinski.
WAR                        93 min (ort 96 min) B/W
B,V                                            TEVP

## KANDYLAND **                              18
Robert Schnitzer      USA              1987
*Sandahl Bergman, Kim Evenson, Charles Laulette,*
*Irwin Keyes, Bruce Baum, Cole Stevens, Alan Toy,*
*Steve Kravitz, Catlyn Day, Ja-Net Hintzen, Chrissy*
*Ratay, Brenda Winston, Israel Jurabe, Beth Peters,*
*Ken Olfson, Richard Neil*
A young girl takes a job at a sleazy nightclub as a
stripper, learning the ropes from former stripper
Bergman. She is soon drawn into a sordid world of vice
and drugs, in this inconsequential sex-thriller that
inevitably has a few similarities to STRIPPED TO
KILL, but generally manages to sustain its story right
up to the tragic ending, despite the excessive footage
devoted to actual stripping.
THR                              79 min (ort 94 min)
V/h                                             NWV

## KANE AND ABEL **                          15
Buzz Kulik            USA              1985
*Sam Neill, Peter Strauss, Veronica Hamel, David*
*Dukes, Fred Gwynne, Tom Roberts Byrd, Alberta*
*Watson, Reed Birney, Vyto Ruginus, Jill Eikenberry,*
*Richard Anderson, Kate McNeil, Lisa Banes,*
*Christopher Cazenove, Jan Rubes*
Two men, born on the same day and destined to
become powerful tycoons, become implacable enemies
and bitter rivals largely by chance, rather than due to
any personal animosity. Strauss imparts real life to
the figure of Abel Rosnovski, the Polish immigrant of
a hotel chain, but Neill gives his usual flat performance. A watchable if not excessively entertaining
adaptation of a readable if not excessively entertaining book.
Boa: novel by Jeffrey Archer.
DRA                        320 min (3 cassettes) mTV
B,V                                       EHE; NELS

## KANGAROO **                               15
Tim Burstall          USA              1986
*Judy Davis, Colin Friels, John Walton, Julie Nihill,*
*Hugh Keays-Byrne*
Film version of a famous novel dealing with a writer's
experiences in Australia of 1922, that doesn't quite
succeed in giving equal weight to all its themes,
especially the writer's tortured relationship with his
wife, and his inability to deal with the world at large.
Boa: story by D.H. Lawrence.
DRA                           100 min (ort 105 min)
B,V                                             VES

## KANSAS *                                  15
David Stevens         USA              1988
*Matt Dillon, Andrew McCarthy, Kyra Sedgwick, Leslie*
*Hope, Arlen Dean Snyder, Brent Jennings*
A young man becomes innocently embroiled in a bank
robbery, after his car and possessions are destroyed on
the road. A fast journey nowhere.
A/AD                                         110 min
B,V                                             EIV

## KANSAS CITY BOMBER *                      15
Jerrold Freedman      USA              1972
*Raquel Welch, Kevin McCarthy, Norman Alden,*
*Helena Kallianiotes, Jeanne Cooper, Dick Lane, Jodie*
*Foster*
The boring story of a rising roller-skating star, with
Welch encountering jealousy from the women and lust
from the men. Despite a good performance from the
star, this unintentionally funny piece says all it's
going to in the first ten minutes, so there's no need to
watch it right through.
DRA                            90 min (ort 99 min)
B,V,V2                                          MGM

## KANSAS CITY MASSACRE, THE ***
Dan Curtis            USA              1975
*Dale Robertson, Robert Walden, Bo Hopkins, Mills*
*Watson, Scott Brady, Matt Clark, John Karlen, Lyn*
*Loring, Elliott Street, Harris Yulin, Philip Bruns,*
*Sally Kirkland, William Jordan, Morgan Paull,*
*James Storm, Lester Maddox*
A sequel to MELVIN PURVIS G-MAN, and a descrip-
tion of the real-life events leading up to a famous
shoot-out between government agents and a gangster
organisation formed by Pretty Boy Floyd, John Dillin-
ger, Baby Face Nelson and others. Sharp direction and
good performances compensate for the mundane
script.
DRA                           97 min (ort 100 min) mTV
B,V                                    VFP L/A; HER

## KARATE GHOSTBUSTER **                     18
Lo Wei                HONG KONG        198-
*Jackie Chan*
Another Jackie Chan blend of comedy and mayhem,
but this time with a supernatural flavour as he finds
himself battling ghostly warriors.
MAR                                          90 min
V                                               TGP

## KARATE KID, THE ***                       15
John G. Avildsen      USA              1984
*Ralph Macchio, Noriyuki (Pat) Morita, Martin Kove,*
*Elisabeth Shue, Randee Heller, William Zabka, Chad*
*McQueen, Tony O'Dell, Larry Drake*
A sugar-sweet confection all about a teenager who is
taught karate by the local janitor of the apartment
block where he lives, so that he can face up to bullies.
Excellent performances from Macchio and Morita are
coupled with a solid script. Followed by two inferior
sequels.
DRA                                         126 min
V/h                                             RCA

## KARATE KID 2, THE *                       PG
John G. Avildsen      USA              1986
*Ralph Macchio, Noriyuki (Pat) Morita, Nobu*
*McCarthy, Danny Kamekona, Yuji Okumoto, Tamlyn*
*Tomita, Martin Kove*
Pupil and mentor from THE KARATE KID now
travel to Japan where they must face the latter's great
rival and enemy in a series of adventures. Strictly
kiddie-fare and inferior to the first film. A sequel
followed.
DRA                                         120 min
V/sh                                            RCA

## KARATE KID 3, THE *                       PG
John G. Avildsen      USA              1989
*Ralph Macchio, Noriyuki (Pat) Morita, Sean Kanan,*
*Robyn Elaine Lively, Thomas Ian Griffith, Martin*
*Kove, Jonathan Avildsen*
Young Daniel (an unfortunate hormonal imbalance
prevents 27-year-old Macchio from looking his age)
now has to fight to retain a karate championship title,
but finds that his old mentor is unwilling to train him.
Eventually he finds a new trainer who proves to be
secretly in league with an old enemy of the Kid. An

over-sentimental dud, of cliched homilies and a predictable outcome.
Aka: KARATE KID PART 3, THE
A/AD                          108 min (ort 111 min)
V                                          RCA

## KARATE WARRIOR **                          15
Larry Ludman (Fabrizio de Angelis)
                    ITALY                   1988
Jared Martin, Janet Agren, Kim Stuart, Ken
Watanabe
A martial arts master trains a boy who was brutally
attacked by a former pupil, and who has now turned to
crime, in this fairly standard action tale.
Aka: FIST OF POWER
A/AD                           85 min Cut (25 sec)
B,V                                        VPD

## KASHMIRI RUN *                               15
John Peyser              SPAIN              1969
Pernell Roberts, Alexandra Bastedo, Julian Mateos,
Gloria Gamata
Two men and a girl try to escape from Communist-
occupied Tibet, into Kashmir in India in this dreary
yarn.
A/AD                         96 min; 103 min (MIA)
B,V                             VUL L/A; HVM; MIA

## KATY **                                      U
Jose Luis/Santiago Moro
              MEXICO/SPAIN                 1983
Delightful animated tale of a caterpillar, and her
adventures as she searches for her identity. A lively
and colourful tale, suitable for kids of about five and
under.
Aka: KATY CATERPILLAR
CAR                             78 min (ort 85 min)
B,V                                        CBS

## KEATON'S COP ***                            18
Robert Burge             USA               1990
Lee Majors, Abe Vigoda, Don Rickles
A cop and his partner are assigned to protect a
gangster newly released from prison, whose life is in
danger from his former colleagues. Several deaths
occur and one of the cops decides that the only way to
avoid being killed is to go after the mobsters himself,
but his task is complicated by his lack of knowledge as
to the reason why the crooks are determined to silence
their erstwhile comrade. Fair.
A/AD                                     91 min
V/sh                                       PATHE

## KEEP IT UP JACK! *
Derek Ford               UK                1973
Mark Jones, Sue Longhurst, Maggi Burton, Paul
Whitsun-Jones, Frank Thornton, Queenie Watts, Steve
Viedor, Jack Le White, Linda Regan, Jenny
Westbrook, Veronica Peters, Yvette Vanson, Juliet
Groves, Marian Brown, Jan Foster
A young female impersonator inherits a brothel on the
death of his aunt. He decides to impersonate her and
run the brothel, but falls for one of the girls. A tired
attempt to squeeze a few laughs out of a one-joke
situation.
A                               85 min (ort 87 min)
B,V                                        VPD

## KEEP, THE *                                  18
Michael Mann             USA               1983
Scott Glenn, Ian McKellen, Alberta Watson, Jurgen
Prochnow, Robert Prosky, Gabriel Byrne, Morgan
Sheppard, Royston Tickner, Michael Carter, Phillip
Joseph, John Vine, Jona Jons, Wolf Kahler, Rosalie
Crutchley, Bruce Payne
The German forces in WW2 occupy a fortress in
Romania, and ignore warnings from the locals about a
strange presence it conceals. Muddled, messy and
incoherent.

Boa: novel by F. Paul Wilson.
HOR                                     96 min
B,V                                        CIC

## KEEPER, THE **                               15
Tom Y. Drake             CANADA            1976
Christopher Lee, Tell Schreiber, Sally Gray, Ross
Vezerian, Ian Tracey
The wealthy relatives at a strange mental home seem
to die like flies. Perhaps their deaths are linked to the
strange and menacing keeper of the asylum. Average.
HOR                             84 min (ort 96 min)
B,V                                        VPD

## KEEPING TRACK **                             15
Robin Spry               CANADA            1985
Margot Kidder, Michael Sarrazin, Alan Scarfe, Ken
Pogue, Vlasta Vkana, John Boylan, Daniel Pilon,
James D. Morris, Shawn Lawrence, Pierre Zimmer,
Louis Negin, Terry Haig, Patricia Phillips, Renee
Girard, Leo Ilial
A female bank executive and a work-obsessed TV
journalist witness a strange robbery and find them-
selves involved in a deadly game. Yet another one of
those tiring espionage comedies, where innocent bys-
tanders find themselves up to their necks in diverse
and complex conspiracies.
THR                                     100 min mTV
B,V                          .              MED

## KELLY'S HEROES **                           PG
Brian G. Hutton
              USA/YUGOSLAVIA              1970
Clint Eastwood, Donald Sutherland, Telly Savalas,
Don Rickles, Carroll O'Connor, Gavin MacLeod,
Stuart Margolin, (Harry) Dean Stanton
Overlong and unbelievable story of a plan to steal a
hoard of Nazi gold, from a bank behind the German
lines in the middle of a bloody battle of WW2. The
strong cast do their best and there are one or two
bright spots, but this one was sorely in need of a more
intelligent script.
WAR                            143 min (ort 145 min)
B, V/sh, LV                                MGM

## KENNONITE **                                PG
Bill Duke/Larry Gross    USA               1989
Louis Gossett Jr
Another "Gideon Oliver" tale, that follows the fortunes of a reserved and old-fashioned Amish-like sect,
who live in peace and tranquility with the other
inhabitants of a small rural region in the southern
USA, until the day a farming family are found
murdered in their home. With suspicion falling on the
son of a preacher belonging to the sect and the local
sheriff having lost his authority, a lynching seems the
likeliest outcome. Average.
DRA                                     91 min mTV
V                                          CIC

## KENT STATE ***
James Goldstone          USA               1981
Jane Fleis, Charley Lang, Talia Balsam, Keith
Gordon, Michael Higgins, John Getz, David Marshall
Grant, Roxanne Hart, Jeff McCracken, Ann Gillespie,
Shepperd Strudwick, George Coe
A dramatic account of the four days of student protests
against the Vietnam War, staged at Kent State
University in Ohio in 1970, which led to a clash with
the National Guard, leaving four students dead and
nine wounded. The powerful script is by Gerald Green
and Richard Kramer, with the director winning an
Emmy.
DRA                                     150 min mTV
B,V                                     APX; TEM

## KENTUCKIAN, THE **                          PG
Burt Lancaster           USA               1955
Burt Lancaster, Diana Lynn, Walter Matthau, Dianne

*Foster, John McIntire, Una Merkel, John Carradine*
A rugged frontiersman and his son travel to Texas in search of a place where they can start a new life. Matthau makes his film debut in this minor piece that has a few good moments, but nothing of great impact.
Boa: novel Gabriel Horn by F. Holt.
WES                                      99 min (ort 104 min)
V                                                          WHV

### KENTUCKY FRIED MOVIE, THE **                    18
John Landis            USA                        1977
*Evan Kim, Bill Bixby, George Lazenby, Henry Gibson, Donald Sutherland, Tony Dow, Richard A. Baker, Master Bong Soo Han, Boni Enten*
A series of skits and sketches satirising many themes from American TV and film; several spin-offs followed. The idea originated with a theatre troupe known as the "Kentucky Fried Theatre" which numbered Jim Abrahams, David Zucker and Jerry Zucker among its members, these three going on to make AIRPLANE! and AMAZON WOMEN ON THE MOON. Often vulgar and only occasionally funny.
COM                                        80 min Cut (9 sec)
B,V                                    VPD; EIV (VHS only)

### KES **                                              PG
Ken Loach            UK                          1969
*David Bradley, Lynne Perrie, Colin Welland, Freddie Fletcher, Brian Glover, Bob Bowes, Robert Naylor, Trevor Hesketh, Geoffrey Banks, Eric Bolderson, Joey Kaye*
A boy's harsh life in a Northern town is temporarily enlivened when he acquires a pet kestrel. A film of almost unbearable grimness where the beauty of a creature of the wild clashes harshly with the brutalised nature of the human inhabitants.
Boa: novel A Kestrel For A Knave by Barry Hines.
DRA                                    106 min (ort 113 min)
V                                                          WHV

### KEY LARGO ****                                       PG
John Huston            USA                        1948
*Humphrey Bogart, Edward G. Robinson, Lauren Bacall, Lionel Barrymore, Claire Trevor, Thomas Gomez, Marc Lawrence, Jay Silverheels, Monte Blue*
Excellent thriller about a tough hoodlum holed up in a run-down hotel during a storm, and holding its occupants captive until he can make his getaway, with the unwilling help of boat-owner Bogart. Scripted by Huston and Richard Brooks. The final shoot-out onboard Bogart's boat, and a great performance from Trevor as Robinson's alcoholic moll, are highlights. AA: S. Actress (Trevor).
Boa: play by Maxwell Anderson.
THR                                    97 min (ort 101 min) B/W
B,V                                                        WHV

### KEY, THE **                                         18
Tinto Brass            ITALY                      1984
*Frank Finlay, Stefania Sandrelli*
Story of the erotic relationship between an elderly English hotelier living in Venice in 1940 and his much younger wife, with whom he enjoys sexual fantasy games. A beautifully photographed but empty film.
Boa: novel by Junichiro Tanizaki.
A                                    105 min (Cut at film release)
B,V                                    EHE; CH5 (VHS only)

### KGB: THE SECRET WAR **                              15
Dwight Little            USA                      1984
*Michael Billington, Denise DuBarry, Michael Ansara, Walter Gotell, Sally Kellerman*
A Russian agent steals a NASA Columbia Space Shuttle code and then tries to bargain with the West over his attempted defection. Average.
A/AD                                              86 min
B,V                            VTC; XTACY/KRP; MAST (VHS only)

### KHARTOUM **                                         PG
Basil Dearden            UK                        1966
*Charlton Heston, Laurence Olivier, Ralph Richardson, Richard Johnson, Nigel Green, Michael Hordern, Alexander Knox, Johnny Sekka, Zia Mohyeddin, Marne Maitland, Hugh Williams, Ralph Michael, Douglas Wilmer, Edward Underdown*
An overlong, boring and historically inaccurate account of the conflict in Sudan of the 1880s, between the British and the charismatic leader of the Dervish; the Mahdi. Khartoum falls after a 10-month siege when British forces fail to relieve it. Olivier is excellent as the Mahdi, but no meeting between him and Gordon ever took place (though it made good cinema). Well acted throughout, but the film drags until the final attack on the city.
Boa: book by A. Caillou.
DRA                        122 min (ort 134 min) Cut (26 sec)
V                                                          WHV

### KICK BOXER **                                       18
David Worth            USA                        1989
*Jean-Claude Van Damme, Dennis Alexio, Eric Sloane, Haskell V. Anderson*
When a man's brother is deliberately paralysed in a martial arts contest, the former vows to have his revenge and undertakes a period of training in order to equip him for this task. A formula revenger with much mindless mayhem but little plotting.
MAR                                              97 min
V                                                          EIV

### KICKS **                                            15
William Wiard            USA                      1985
*Anthony Geary, Shelley Hack, Tom Mason, Ian Abercrombie, James Avery, Susan Ruttan, Larry Cedar*
A wealthy eccentric and a lady professor become lovers and indulge in a series of dangerous games, to enhance their desire to live on a knife-edge. A quirky little thriller of very limited appeal.
THR                    97 min; 94 min (CBS) (ort 100 min) mTV
B,V                                      ABCVID/RNK; CBS

### KID BLUE *                                           
James Frawley            USA                      1973
*Dennis Hopper, Warren Oates, Peter Boyle, Ben Johnson, Janice Rule, Lee Purcell, Ralph Waite, Clifton James, Jose Torvay, Mary Jackson, Howard Hesseman, Jay Varela, Emmett Walsh*
Spoof Western about an outlaw, and the problems he encounters when he tries to go straight. Set in Texas of 1902 but filmed in Mexico, this dud largely wastes a good cast on little in the way of humour or excitement.
COM                                              100 min Cut
B,V                                                        CBS

### KID DYNAMITE *                                       
Wallace Fox            USA                        1943
*Leo Gorley, Huntz Hall, Bobby Jordan, Gabriel Dell, Pamela Blake, Bennie Bartlett, Sammy Morrison*
Juvenile comedy about a boy's gang that was made as part of the "Dead End Kids" series. In this tale one of our kids suspects that another had him kidnapped so that he could take his place in a boxing contest. If this comedy is dynamite, then someone has forgotten to light the fuse.
COM                                    59 min (ort 73 min) B/W
B,V                                                        WOV

### KID FROM BROOKLYN, THE ***                          U
Norman McLeod            USA                      1946
*Danny Kaye, Virginia Mayo, Eve Arden, Vera-Ellen, Steve Cochran, Walter Abel, Lionel Stander, Fay Bainter, Clarence Kolb, Victor Cutler, Charles Cane, Jerome Cowan, Don Wilson, Knox Manning, Kay Thompson, Johnny Downs*
A Brooklyn milkman who is hardly the bravest of men, inadvertently takes up a boxing career in this

remake of the Harold Lloyd comedy "The Milky Way".
A contrived and often overblown effort, but Kaye's
considerable comic gifts carry it off.
Boa: play The Milky Way by Lynn Root and Harry
Clark.
COM                           109 min (ort 114 min)
V                                             VGM

### KID FROM LEFT FIELD, THE ***
Adell Aldrich           USA              1979
*Gary Coleman, Robert Guillaume, Tab Hunter, Tricia
O'Neil, Gary Collins, Ed McMahon, Rick Podell,
Alberto Velasquez, Peggy Browne, Don Draper, Owen
Sullivan, Stu Nahan*
A remake of the 1953 film about a bat-boy who guides
a baseball team to victory thanks to some advice from
his father, a former baseball star now reduced to
selling hot dogs for a living. A competent and
entertaining remake.
DRA                                    100 min mTV
B,V                                           VTC

### KID FROM NOT-SO-BIG, THE **
Bill Crain              USA              1978
*Jennifer McAllister, Veronica Cartwright, Paul
Tulley, Robert Viharo, Don Keefer*
A 12-year-old girl inherits the editorship of her
grandfather's frontier town newspaper. A lively and
likeable yarn.
WES                                        88 min
B,V                                           GHV

### KID GALAHAD ***                            PG
Michael Curtiz          USA              1937
*Edward G. Robinson, Bette Davis, Humphrey Bogart,
Wayne Morris, Jane Bryan, Harry Carey, Veda Ann
Borg*
A sharp boxing promoter takes a naive bellhop and
makes him into a boxing star, but jealousy blights his
relationship with the latter and he loses his girlfriend
to him for good measure. An enjoyable and fast-paced
boxing melodrama. Remade as "The Wagons Roll At
Night" and after a fashion as a Presley musical.
Aka: BATTLING BELLHOP
Boa: novel by Francis Wallace.
DRA                          98 min (ort 101 min) B/W
V                                             WHV

### KID VENGEANCE *                            15
Joe Manduke            USA              1977
*Lee Van Cleef, Jim Brown, John Marley, Leif Garrett,
Glynnis O'Connor, Matt Clark, Timothy Scott*
A youth goes looking for the bandits who murdered
his parents and abducted his sister, in this brutal,
bloody and unpleasant tale. Filmed in Israel.
WES                             90 min (ort 94 min)
B,V                                           RNK

### KID WHO LOVED CHRISTMAS, THE **           U
Arthur Allan Seidelman USA               1990
*Trent Cameron, Michael Warren, Cicely Tyson,
Sammy Davis Jr, Ray Parker Jr, Della Reese, Esther
Rolle, Vanessa Williams*
A couple are about to adopt a youngster when the wife
is killed and the adoption procedure halted. But after
the child runs away from a foster home the man finds
himself given a fresh chance to adopt. Average weepie
drama, but quite well handled.
DRA                                        93 min
V                                             CIC

### KID WITH THE 200 IQ, THE **               U
Leslie Martinson        USA              1983
*Gary Coleman, Robert Guillaume, Dean Butler, Kari
Michaelsen, Mel Stewart, Harriet Nelson, Darian
Mathias, Charles Bloom, Clayton Rohner, Harrison
Page, Starletta DuPois, Christina Murrill, Jason Max
Adams, Karen Anders*
A 13-year-old genius is sent to university, and has to

make some rapid adjustments in order to cope with
life on the campus. The expected complications arise.
Boa: story by Phil Margo.
COM                                    96 min mTV
B,V                                    VFP L/A; HER

### KID WITH THE BROKEN HALO, THE **          U
Leslie Martinson        USA              1981
*Gary Coleman, Robert Guillaume, June Allyson,
Mason Adams, Ray Walston, John Pleshette, Lani
O'Grady, Telma Hopkins, Kim Fields, Georg Stanford
Brown, Tammy Lauren, Keith Mitchell, Rance
Howard, Corey Feldman, Randy Kirby*
A young angel has to win promotion to full status by
helping to improve the fortunes of three families, in
this unashamedly whimsical comedy, a pilot for a
prospective series.
COM                          96 min (ort 100 min) mTV
B,V                              VIPCO; MIA (VHS only)

### KIDCO **
Ronald F. Maxwell       USA      1982 (released 1984)
*Scott Schwartz, Clifton James, Cinnamon Idles,
Tristine Skyler, Elizabeth Gorcey, Maggie Blye,
Charles Hallahan*
Said to be based on the true story of a bunch of kids
who went into business, this film starts off as an
enjoyable comedy that largely praises the spirit of
enterprise, but all too soon becomes a cliched effort, as
the government steps in to spoil the efforts of our
young entrepreneurs.
COM                             100 min (ort 105 min)
B,V                                       CBS/FOX

### KIDNAPPED *                                18
Howard Avedis           USA              1986
*Barbara Crampton, David Naughton, Charles Napier,
Lance LeGault, Michelle Rossi, Kim Evinson, Chick
Vennera, Jimmie Walker*
A young girl who dreams of a career in films, is offered
a part by an apparently respectable film-maker who
has a secret sideline making porno films. The girl is
kidnapped whilst on holiday with her sister, but the
latter teams up with an undercover cop in order to
mount a rescue. A cliched and unimaginative effort.
DRA                  94 min (ort 98 min) Cut (2 min 8 sec)
B,V                                           VIR

### KIDNAPPED **                               U
Robert Stevenson        UK               1959
*Peter Finch, James MacArthur, Bernard Lee, Niall
McGinnis, John Laurie, Finlay Currie, Miles
Malleson, Duncan Macrae, Peter O'Toole, Andrew
Cruickshank, Alex Mackenzie, Oliver Johnston,
Norman MacOwan, Eileen Way*
A faithful adaptation of this adventure yarn telling of
a young boy's adventures in Scotland at the time of
the Jacobite Rebellion. A strong cast and colourful
locations compensate for the dullness of the script.
Boa: novel by Robert Louis Stevenson.
A/AD                            91 min (ort 97 min)
B,V                                           WDV

### KIDNAPPED **                               U
Delbert Mann            UK               1971
*Michael Caine, Trevor Howard, Jack Hawkins,
Donald Pleasence, Gordon Jackson, Vivien Heilbron,
Lawrence Douglas, Freddie Jones, Jack Watson,
Andrew McCulloch, Eric Woodburn, Roger Booth,
Russell Waters, John Hughes*
A young boy is kidnapped and sent to sea during the
time of the Jacobite rebellion due to the machinations
of a wicked uncle, but is eventually restored to his
rightful position in this third bash at the classic yarn.
A rather stilted rendition, but Caine's performance as
Alan Breck is pleasing.
Boa: novels Kidnapped and Catriona by Robert Louis
Stevenson.

DRA                     103 min (ort 107 min)
B,V            -        RNK; VCC (VHS only)

**KIDNAPPED \*\*\***                          Uc
L. Grant        AUSTRALIA              1972
A stylish, animated version of this famous tale, done
in a rather sober style and as ever, following the
adventures that befall a young boy after he falls into
the clutches of his wicked uncle. One in a series of
cartoon animations, all of which were based on famous
classics.
Boa: novel by Robert Louis Stevenson.
CAR                            48 min mTV
B,V,V2     VCL/CBS; CHILD L/A; STYL (VHS only)

**KIDNAPPING OF BABY JOHN, THE \*\***        15
Peter Gerretson     USA               1987
*Jayne Greenwood, Geoffrey Bowes, Janet Laine-Green,*
*George Millenbach, Helen Hughes, James Loxley,*
*Chuck Shamata*
Based on a true story, this tells of a family who
struggle with a moral dilemma when the mother gives
birth to a severely retarded child. A sincere but
somewhat exploitative effort.
Aka: BABY JOHN DOE; KIDNAPPING OF BABY
JOHN DOE, THE
DRA                        86 min (ort 90 min) mTV
B,V                                CINE

**KIDNAPPING OF THE PRESIDENT, THE \*\***
George Mendeluk
                CANADA/USA            1980
*William Shatner, Hal Holbrook, Ava Gardner, Van*
*Johnson, Miguel Fernandes, Cindy Girling*
Third world terrorists kidnap the American president
on a state visit to Canada. Shatner plays the Secret
Service agent who comes to his rescue in this formula
action tale.
Boa: novel by Charles Templeton.
A/AD                           113 min
B,V                            GHV

**KIDS DON'T TELL \*\*\***                      15
Sam O'Steen        USA                1985
*Michael Ontkean, JoBeth Williams, Leo Rossi, John*
*Sanderford, Ari Meyers, Jordan Charney, Robin*
*Gammell, Shelley Morrison, Jean Bruce Scott,*
*Matthew Faison, David S. Aron, Roger Askin, Judith*
*Barsi, Gary Bayer, Earl Billings*
A documentary film-maker working on a study of
child abuse, discovers that this is the cause of his
wife's frigidity. An intelligent examination of this
issue, with a literate and thoughtful script by Peter
Silverman and Maurice Hurley.
DRA                            104 min mTV
B,V                            ODY/POLY

**KIDS LIKE THESE \*\*\***                      15
Georg Stanford Brown
                USA                   1987
*Tyne Daly, Richard Crenna, Martin Balsam, David*
*Kaufman*
A mother whose son has Down's Syndrome campaigns
for greater help and public understanding for children
with this handicap, while she faces the challenge of
bringing him up. The strong script is by Emily Perl
Kingsley, and was based on her own experiences as
the mother of a Down's Syndrome child.
DRA                            100 min mTV
V                              TGP

**KIDS WHO KNEW TOO MUCH, THE \*\*\***          U
Robert Clouse       USA               1980
*Sharon Gless, Larry Cedar, Lloyd Haynes, Jared*
*Martin, David S. Steiner, Don Knight, Rad Daly, Dana*
*Hill, Christopher Holloway, Kevin King Cooper*
This tale has a group of kids finding themselves
involved in a dangerous web of intrigue after stumb-

ling upon an espionage plot. However, they find that
no-one will believe them except an inquisitive journalist. An engaging story with better characterisations
than are usually provided in Disney kid's films.
Boa: novel Whisper In The Gloom by Nicholas Blake.
JUV                            86 min
B,V                            WDV

**KILL \***
Romain Gary                           1971
    FRANCE/ITALY/SPAIN/WEST GERMANY
*James Mason, Jean Seberg, Curt Jurgens, Stephen*
*Boyd, Daniel Emilfork*
A series of murders of key figures threatens the
international drugs trade in this violent and implausi-
ble thriller, which has Mason playing an Interpol
agent on the trail of Italian drug dealers, whilst Boyd
is his fellow agent who prefers to operate outside the
law.
Aka: KILL, KILL, KILL
THR                            107 min
B,V                            TEVP

**KILL AND KILL AGAIN \*\***                    15
Ivan Hall          USA                1981
*James Ryan, Anneline Kriel, Ken Gampu, Norman*
*Robinson, Michael Meyer, Bill Flynn, Marloe Scott-*
*Wilson, Stan Schmidt, John Ramsbottom, Eddie*
*Dorie, Mervyn Johns*
A martial arts champion rescues a scientist who has
won the Nobel Prize, from a mad scientist who wants
to take over the world. A fairly lively martial arts
outing that followed KILL OR BE KILLED. Filmed in
South Africa.
MAR           95 min (ort 100 min) Cut (1 min 13 sec)
B,V,V2                         GHV

**KILL CRAZY \***                               18
David Heavener      USA               1988
*David Heavener, Danielle Brisebois, Burt Ward, Bruce*
*Glover, Rachelle Carson, Lawrence Hilton-Jacobs,*
*Gary Owens*
A Vietnam veteran goes on a camping trip with some
friends as a way of slowly forgetting the horrors of
war, but the group are attacked by a bunch of
fanatical white supremacists. A typical Heavener
survival tale, written and directed by him.
A/AD                           90 min
V                              VPD

**KILL OR BE KILLED \*\***                      18
Ivan Hall          USA                1980
*James Ryan, Norman Combes, Charlotte Michelle,*
*Danie DuPlessis, Stan Schmidt, Norman Robinson*
A martial arts master is lured into a trap disguised in
the form of a martial arts tournament, and all to slake
the thirst for revenge of a former Nazi coach who was
beaten by his Japanese counterpart in a WW2 contest.
Not bad for this type of film, with a better-than-
average script. Followed by KILL AND KILL AGAIN.
Aka: KARATE KILL (TGP)
MAR                            90 min
B,V                            CEN L/A; TGP

**KILL SLADE \*\***                             PG
Bruce McFarlane                       1989
*Patrick Dollaghan, Lisa Brady, Anthony Frid John,*
*Danny Keogh*
The illegal diversion of food aid provides the basis for
this comedy-adventure that's set in Africa and fea-
tures mercenaries, kidnapping and all the other
requisite elements. A mildly amusing little trifle.
COM                            85 min
V                              RCA

**KILL-OFF, THE \*\*\***                         18
Maggie Greenwald    USA               1989
*Loretta Gross, Jackson Sims, Steve Monroe, Cathy*
*Haase, Andrew Lee Barrett*

A group of losers are united only by their hatred of a malicious and elderly invalid who takes a delight in spreading gossip, and one of them finally attempts to silence her for good. Not really a thriller so much as an atmospheric study of human evil, set in a resort on the US East coast during the bleak months of winter. The excellent photography is the work of Declan Quinn.

THR                        92 min
V/sh                        PAL

## KILL THE GOLDEN GOOSE **
Elliott Hang     HONG KONG       1979
*Ed Parker, Bong Soo Han, Brad Von Beltz*
A hired killer has to eliminate one remaining key witness on behalf of a multinational company in this standard actioner.
MAR                       91 min
B,V,V2                    IFS

## KILL ZONE *                                18
David A. Prior     USA            1985
*Ted Prior, David James Campbell, Fritz Matthews, David Kong, Richard Massery, William Joseph Zipp*
A Vietnam veteran still serving in the Marines runs amok, and has to be captured after killing four guards. Just one more film in an interminable series, exploiting the cliched and depressing "Vietnam veteran on the rampage" theme.
THR                        95 min
B,V                   IVS; GLOB

## KILLER CONTRACTED *                        15
James Ormerod     UK            1984
*Edward Woodward, Kate Harper, Wanda Ventham*
A businessman's daughter is kidnapped and her life is threatened, in an attempt to stop him starting production of a new fantasy. The last one in a set of three 52-minute plays filmed for Yorkshire TV. The other two were entitled KILLER IN WAITING and KILLER EXPOSED – all three were rather turgid little murder mysteries.
THR            60 min (ort 52 min) mTV
B,V                   TOW

## KILLER COP **                              15
Luciano Ercol     ITALY         1975
*Claudio Cassinelli, Arthur Kennedy, Franco Fabrizi, Sara Speruti, Bruno Zaniz*
A young detective in Milan has to defuse a bomb in a crowded hotel and then takes on some drug pushers, in this Italian DIRTY HARRY clone. Kennedy gives a nice overblown performance as a ruthless gang boss.
Aka: POLICE CAN'T MOVE, THE
THR                      93 min
B,V    ITM L/A; MARKET/GOV L/A; CINV; DIAM

## KILLER ELITE, THE *                        18
Sam Peckinpah     USA            1975
*James Caan, Robert Duvall, Arthur Hill, Bo Hopkins, Mako, Burt Young, Gig Young*
A veritable feast of gore with Caan out for revenge against Duvall, who double-crossed him whilst they were working as mercenaries. A standard offering from Peckinpah, with a trashy plot that drags in the CIA. Some good action sequences make it slightly more bearable.
Boa: novel by Robert Rostand.
DRA                      122 min
B,V                   WHV

## KILLER EXPOSED *
James Ormerod     UK            1983
*Anthony Valentine, Dearbha Molloy, Molly Radlove*
Filmed play from Yorkshire TV about a dentist who is attracted to a female patient because of a remarkable resemblance. Number 2 in a set of three forgettable little murder mysteries; numbers 1 and 3 were entitled KILLER IN WAITING and KILLER CON-

TRACTED respectively.
THR            60 min (ort 52 min) mTV
B,V                   TOW

## KILLER IN WAITING *                        18
Michael Ferguson     UK          1982
*John Thaw, Diane Keen, Stafford Gordon*
A man is threatened in his isolated home by a hired killer, in this play made for Yorkshire TV. A tepid little thriller that was the first in a set of three, the other two plays being KILLER EXPOSED and KILLER CONTRACTED.
THR                  52 min mTV
B,V                   TOW

## KILLER INSIDE ME, THE **                   18
Burt Kennedy     USA            1976
*Stacy Keach, Susan Tyrell, Keenan Wynn, Tisha Sterling, Don Stroud, Charles McGraw, John Dehner, John Carradine*
The sheriff of a small town undergoes a personality change and becomes a brutal and psychotic killer. A weird film that relies heavily on flashback sequences to show how our sheriff has got into his present state; Keach's powerful performance redeems an otherwise forgettable tale.
DRA           95 min (ort 99 min)
B,V               POLY; VFO

## KILLER INSTINCT **                         15
Cirio H. Santiago
         PHILIPPINES/USA     1987
*Robert Patrick, William Steis, Lydie Denier, Barbara Hooper, Robert Dryer, Morgan Douglas*
Vietnam war drama set in 1975. While searching for some soldiers who had gone missing, a squad leader and his men are captured by Soviet advisors to the North Vietnamese. The leader escapes and returns to his base, only to find it overrun by the enemy. Having discovered that the USA is about to pull out her troops, he decides to fight on and mount a rescue mission.
Aka: SEARCH AND DESTROY
A/AD                    90 min
B,V                   VES

## KILLER KLOWNS FROM OUTER SPACE *           15
Stephen Chiodo     USA          1987
*Grant Cramer, Suzanne Snyder, John Allen Nelson, Royal Dano, John Vernon, Michael Siegel, Peter Licassi*
Another variation on the CRITTERS theme, our aliens with a taste for human flesh this time taking the form of sadistic circus clowns who stalk their prey with a formidable arsenal of bizarre weapons, after landing their circus-tent/spaceship at a small secluded town. A gruesome comedy that leans rather too heavily on its repulsive ideas (e.g. our "klowns" like to coat their victims in candyfloss before drinking their blood).
HOR          83 min (ort 88 min)
B,V                   EIV

## KILLER LIKES CANDY, THE **
Richard Owens (Federico Chentrens)
   FRANCE/ITALY/WEST GERMANY    1968
*Kerwin Mathews, Marilu Tolu, Bruno Cremer*
Two CIA agents are assigned to protect the life of a Middle East ruler on a visit to Rome.
Aka: LE TUEUR AIME LES BONBONS; UN KILLER PER SUA MAESTA; ZUCKER FUR DEN MORDER
A/AD                    88 min
B,V                   HEL

## KILLER METEORS, THE *                      15
Lo Wei     HONG KONG         1984
*Jackie Chan, Jimmy Wang Yu*

Two masters of different fighting styles battle it out.
Aka: JACKIE CHAN VERSUS JIMMY WANG YU
MAR                                    91 min
V                                      TGP

## KILLER ON BOARD *                    PG
Philip Leacock          USA           1977
Patty Duke Astin, Claude Akins, Len Birman, Frank
Converse, William Daniels, George Hamilton, Murray
Hamilton, Susan Howard, Jeff Lynas, Jane Seymour,
Beatrice Straight, Michael Lerner, Thalmus Rasulala,
John Roper, Fred Lerner
Passengers on board a luxury cruise liner fall victim
to a dangerous virus. One of those maritime disaster
movies in which the ship stays afloat but the plot
sinks. A kind of high seas version of THE CASSAN-
DRA CROSSING.
DRA                   97 min (ort 100 min) mTV
B,V                                   POLY

## KILLER PANTHER, THE **               15
Jurgen Roland
          ITALY/WEST GERMANY          196-
Brad Harris, Marianne Koch, Horst Frank, Heinz
Drache, Dorothee Parker
A murder mystery centring on the theft of a sapphire
from a Buddhist temple in Thailand. Average.
Aka: DER SCHWARZE PANTHER VON RATANA
A/AD                                   91 min
B,V          STR L/A; MARKET/GOV L/A; VTEL

## KILLER PARTY *                        18
William Fruet           USA           1986
Martin Hewitt, Ralph Seymour, Elaine Wilkes, Paul
Bartel, Alicia Fleer, Sherry Willis-Burch, Woody
Brown, Joanna Johnson, Terri Hawkes, Deborah
Hancock, Laura Sherman, Jeff Pustil, Pam Hyatt,
Howard Busgang, Jason Warren
A variation of the slasher in the dorm movies – the
spirit of a murdered student possesses a young girl in
order to gain its revenge. An ineffective mixture of
chills and puerile high school humour.
Aka: FOOL'S NIGHT
HOR                       88 min (ort 92 min)
B,V                                    MGM

## KILLER VOLCANO **
Ernest Pintoff          USA           1981
Art Carney, David Huffman, Cassie Yates, Albert
Salmi, Ron O'Neal
An account of the Mount St Helens eruption of 1980
woven around the story of a man who refuses to leave
his home.
Aka: SAINT HELENS; SAINT HELENS: KILLER
VOLCANO
DRA                                    97 min
B,V                                    HER

## KILLER WHO WOULDN'T DIE, THE **
William Hale            USA           1976
Mike Connors, Samantha Eggar, Gregoire Aslan, Clu
Gulager, Mariette Hartley, Robert Colbert, James
Shigeta, Robert Hooks, Patrick O'Neal, Lucille Benson,
Philip Ahn, Christopher Gardner, Tony Becker, Kwan
Hi Lin
A ex-cop whose wife was killed by a bomb meant for
him, investigates the murder of a killer and uncovers
a complex conspiracy. Undistinguished pilot for an
unsold series.
Aka: OHANIAN
THR                    93 min (ort 100 min) mTV
V                                      CIC

## KILLER, THE **                        18
Chu Yuen            HONG KONG         1971
Ching Miao, Yuang Chi Ching, Chiang Nan, Cheng
Lei, Chi Lien-Kuei, Hsia Hui, Wang Kuang Yu, Ku
Feng
A naive martial arts fighter is fooled into taking the

wrong side in a dispute between the law and a local
racketeer.
MAR                       90 min Cut (57 sec)
V                                      WHV

## KILLER, THE ***                       18
John Woo            HONG KONG         1989
Chow Yun-fatt, Sally Yeh, Danny Lee
A contract killer accidentally blinds a singer and is
forced into doing one more job to pay for an operation
to restore her sight. This thin plot nonetheless holds
up well in a fast-paced tale of considerable length and
complexity. A highlight is the final decisive gunfight,
a sequence that marks this violent action tale as one
of the best films of its type.
A/AD                    110 min (ort 135 min)
V/h                                    PAL

## KILLERFISH *                          15
Anthony M. Dawson (Antonio Margheriti)
          BRAZIL/ITALY               1978
Lee Majors, Karen Black, James Franciscus, Margaux
Hemingway, Marisa Berenson, Gary Collins, Dan
Pastorini, Roy Brocksmith, Charlie Guardino, Frank
Pesce, Anthony Steffen, Fabio Sabag, Chico Arago,
Sonia Citicica
A gang of emerald thieves stash their loot in a
reservoir stocked with piranha fish. Attempts by
various parties to recover the loot form the basis for
this tired outing – the fish are deadly, and so is this
story. Filmed in Brazil. See also PIRANHA.
Aka: DEADLY TREASURE OF THE PIRANHA;
KILLER FISH
THR                     97 min (ort 101 min)
B,V                               PRV; CH5

## KILLER'S MOON
Alan Birkinshaw         UK            1978
Anthony Forrest, Nigel Gregory, Tom Marshall,
Georgina Kean, David Jackson, Paul Rattee, Peter
Spraggan, Jane Hayden, Alison Elliott, Jo-Anne
Good, Jane Lester, Lisa Vanderpump, Debbie Martyn,
Christina Jones, Lynne Morgan
A coachload of schoolgirls in a derelict house is
terrorised by four escaped lunatics. A dreary and
incompetently-made piece of exploitation, with a
half-forgotten plot that serves as no more than a
vehicle for scenes of gratuitous unpleasantness.
HOR                                    89 min
B,V,V2                                 VPD

## KILLERS OF KILIMANJARO, THE **        PG
Richard Thorpe          UK            1959
Robert Taylor, Anthony Newley, Anne Aubrey,
Gregoire Aslan, John Dimech, Martin Boddey, Alan
Cuthbertson, Martin Benson, Orlando Martins,
Donald Pleasence, Earl Cameron, Harry Baird,
Anthony Jacobs
A railway engineer undertaking a survey in East
Africa in 1900, has to contend with the attacks of a
slave trader while helping a young woman locate her
missing father and fiance. A standard stiff-upper-lip
adventure that keeps the flag flying right to the end.
Aka: ADAMSON OF AFRICA
Boa: stories African Bush Adventures by John A.
Hunter and Dan P. Mannix.
A/AD                    88 min (ort 91 min)
V                                      RCA

## KILLERS, THE ***                      18
Don Siegel              USA           1964
Lee Marvin, John Cassavetes, Angie Dickinson, Clu
Gulager, Ronald Reagan, Claude Akins, Norman Fell
Two hoodlums kill the man they were hired to
murder, but are so intrigued by the way in which he
accepted his death, that they decide to piece together
his past. An absorbing if loose adaptation of Hemingway's story, filmed originally for TV but rejected as

being too violent, and released to cinemas instead. This was Reagan's last film role.
Boa: short story by Ernest Hemingway.
DRA                               90 min (ort 95 min) mTV
B,V                                               ARENA/CIC

## KILLING AT HELL'S GATE, THE **           PG
Jerry Jameson            USA               1981
*Robert Urich, Deborah Raffin, Lee Purcell, Joel Higgins, George DiCenzo, Paul Burke, Mitch Carter, Brion James, John Randolph, Maya Braddock, Vicci Cooke, William D. Cottrell, Bob Griggs, Curtis Hanson, Kenny Kinsner*
Similar in plot to DELIVERANCE, this tells of how a canoe trip becomes a nightmare when the group is attacked by snipers. The inclusion of two women in the group does little to improve the cliched plot. Average. The initial title of the film was "Hell And High Water".
HOR                                         100 min mTV
B,V                                                   CBS

## KILLING CARS **                          15
Michael Verhoeven
                     WEST GERMANY          1985
*Jurgen Prochnow, Senta Berger, Agnes Soral, Daniel Gelin, William Conrad, Bernhard Wicki, Stefan Meinke, Peter Matic, Osman Ragheb, Axel Scholtz, Marina Larsen, Klaus Mikoleit, Wolf Gaudlitz, Oliver Rohrbeck, Uwe Hacker*
A brilliant engineer invents a car that does not run on petrol, and immediately finds that the oil producers and motor manufacturers are determined to destroy his invention at any cost, in a ruthless campaign of terror and intimidation.
THR                               96 min (ort 115 min)
B,V                                                   MGM

## KILLING DAD **                           15
Michael Austin           UK                1989
*Julie Walters, Richard E. Grant, Denholm Elliott*
A black comedy in which a man sets out to get to know his father, a cad who walked out on the family when he was a child. In order to do this he changes his name so he can get to know the man incognito. However, his father turns out to be a man so disgusting that he decides to murder him. A good cast do their best in a film that tries very hard to be zany, and merely ends up being chaotic.
COM                                           93 min
V/h                                                   PAL

## KILLING EDGE, THE *                      15
Lindsay Craig Shonteff  USA               1986
*Bill French, Mary Spencer*
In the ruins of a post-WW3 world a survivor searches for his family.
A/AD                                          85 min
B,V                                                   IVS

## KILLING 'EM SOFTLY *                     15
Max Fischer            CANADA             1985
*George Segal, Irene Cara, Joyce Gordon, Clark Johnson, Nicholas Campbell, Andrew Martin Thompson, Barbara Cook, Gail Dahms, Emidio Michetti, George Zeeman, Arleigh Peterson, Sheena Larkin, Jeffrey Cohen, Irene Kessler*
A loner has his dog killed by a teenage gang and steals their money in revenge, accidentally killing one of them in the process. When the police arrest somebody else for this crime, it looks like easy days ahead. That is, until the man's singer girlfriend starts her own investigation. A shoddy little drama.
Aka: MAN IN 5A, THE; NEIGHBOUR, THE
DRA                         90 min; 86 min (PALAN)
B,V                                   IVS L/A; PALAN

## KILLING FIELDS, THE ***                  15
Roland Joffe            UK                 1984

*Sam Waterston, Haing S. Ngor, John Malkovich, Julian Sands, Athol Fugard, Craig T. Nelson, Bill Paterson, Spalding Gray, Graham Kennedy, Katherine Kragum Chey, Oliver Pierpaoli, Edward Entero Chey, Tom Bird, Ira Wheeler*
A harrowing account of the reign of terror imposed by the Khmer Rouge, and of an American journalist who tries to get his Cambodian guide and interpreter out of the country. The depiction of a country being torn apart by war and savagery cannot be faulted. This was documentary-maker Joffe's first feature. AA: S. Actor (Ngor – who lived through the turmoil), Cin (Chris Menges), Edit (Jim Clark).
Boa: memoirs of New York Times reporter Sidney Schanberg.
DRA                               136 min (ort 142 min)
B, V/sh                             TEVP; WHV (VHS only)

## KILLING GAME, THE **                     18
Joseph Merhi             USA               1987
*Robert Zdar, Chard Hayward, Cynthia Killion, Geoffrey Sadwith, Bette Rae, Julie Noble, Monique Monet, Brigitte Burdine, Janet Jimmi Parker, Ron Gilchrist, Leia Luahiwa*
Made-for-video thriller set on the Californian "Gold Coast" where a hit-man becomes a blackmail victim after carrying out a contract killing, and the prime suspect appears to be a Las Vegas drugs baron.
A/AD                          85 min (ort 90 min) Cut (7 sec) mVid
B,V                                                   TGP

## KILLING HOUR, THE **                     18
Armand Mastroianni      USA               1982
*Kenneth McMillan, Elizabeth Kemp, Perry King, Norman Parker, Jon Polito, Joe Morton, Barbara Quinn, Antone Pagan, Thomas De Carlo, Lou Bedford, David Ramsey, Tom Stechschulte, Louise Flannigan, Olivia Negron, Steve Beauchamp*
New York is gripped by fear because of a series of macabre killings, and a talk-show host decides to use them to boost his ratings, by getting a psychic artist to draw the premonitions she gets when a murder is about to be committed. A bizarre slasher movie with a psychic twist.
Aka: CLAIRVOYANT, THE
HOR                          91 min (ort 95 min) Cut (1 min 19 sec)
B,V                                                   ARF

## KILLING MACHINE **                       18
Anthony J. Loma (J. Antonio de la Loma)
                     MEXICO/SPAIN          1983
*George (Jorge) Rivero, Margaux Hemingway, Lee Van Cleef, Willie Aames, Hugo Stiglitz, Ana Obregon, Richard Jaeckel*
An ex-terrorist turned trucker is ambushed by the Mafia, when he is caught up in European labour wars on one last trip to Germany. The multi-national casting is a drawback, but Rivero as our tough trucker out for revenge, holds the film together.
DRA                          92 min (ort 95 min) Cut (1 min 31 sec)
B,V                                                   EHE

## KILLING OF ANGEL STREET, THE **          
Donald Crombie          AUSTRALIA         1981
*Liz Alexander, John Hargreaves, Reg Lye, Alexander Archdale, Gordon McDougall*
Some property developers will stop at nothing to get their way and the authorities refuse to act. Two people take up the fight when the father of one of them dies in mysterious circumstances. An enjoyable melodrama, said to be based on real events.
DRA                                           100 min
B,V                                              VDB; KRP

## KILLING OF SISTER GEORGE, THE ***        18
Robert Aldrich           USA               1969
*Beryl Reid, Susannah York, Coral Browne, Ronald Fraser, Patricia Medina, Hugh Paddick, Cyril Delevanti*

An engrossing tragi-comedy with Reid in one of her finest roles, as an ageing lesbian who loses both her job and her lover, when she is axed from a long-running TV farmyard soap opera. Not quite retaining the light touch of the play but undeniably effective. Scripted by Lukas Heller and filmed in England.
Boa: play by Frank Marcus.
DRA                    134 min (ort 138 min)
B,V                            VGM; RNK

**KILLING TIME, THE \*\***                    15
Rick King               USA                1987
*Kiefer Sutherland, Beau Bridges, Wayne Rogers, Joe Don Baker, Camelia Kath, Janet Carroll*
An unfaithful wife and her sheriff boyfriend, hatch a plot to kill the husband of the former and pin the murder on Sutherland, but things do not turn out as expected, in this muddled thriller.
THR                      89 min (ort 94 min)
B/h, V/h                         NWV

**KILLING TOUCH, THE \***                    18
Michael Elliott         USA                1982
*Sally Kirkland, Lynn Banashek, Sean Masterson, Michael O'Leary, Teal Roberts, Melissa Prophet*
A new generation of Olympic athletes in training at a college, are menaced by a killer in this formula variant on the mad-slasher-on-the-loose theme.
Aka: FATAL GAMES
THR                   83 min; 90 min (ACAD)
B,V                        MERL/VCL/CBS; ACAD

**KILLJOY \*\*\***                            PG
John Llewellyn Moxey  USA              1981
*Kim Basinger, Robert Culp, Stephen Macht, Nancy Marchand, John Rubinstein, Ann Dusenberry, Ann Wedgeworth, Helene Winston, Francine Verrett, Terry Burns, Arthur Roberts, Kelly Jean Peters*
Murder mystery revolving round a young woman's untimely death, and the chief pathologist and other parties involved at a city hospital. Complex, witty and absorbing; the convoluted script is by Sam H. Rolfe.
THR                     96 min (ort 100 min) mTV
B,V                            POLY

**KILLPOINT \***                              18
Frank Harris            USA                1984
*Leo Fong, Richard Roundtree, Cameron Mitchell, Stack Pierce, Hope Holiday*
A cop and a secret agent team up to hunt gunrunners. Plenty of violent action is about all there is on offer, in this simple-minded and uninventive action tale. Very poor.
Aka: KILL POINT
A/AD       84 min (ort 92 min) Cut (1 min 28 sec)
B,V                        VFP L/A; HER

**KIM \*\*\***                                PG
John Davies             USA                1984
*Peter O'Toole, Bryan Brown, John Rhys-Davies, Ravi Sheth, Julian Glover, Lee Montague, Alfred Burke, Mick Ford, Bill Leadbitter, Sneh Gupta, Roger Booth, Peter Childs, Noel Coleman, Nadira, Lavlin, Jalal Agha, Sean Scanlon*
A colourful remake of the 1950 tale of colonial India, telling of a resourceful British boy who is brought up by an Indian mystic and becomes a spy for the British Secret Service. Sheth makes his debut as the title character, with O'Toole giving a splendidly over-the-top performance as a Buddhist monk. The script is by James Brabazon.
Boa: novel by Rudyard Kipling.
A/AD     121 min; 136 min (CH5) (ort 150 min) mTV
B,V,V2                     EHE; CH5 (VHS only)

**KIMBERLEY JIM \*\***                         U
Emil Nofal       SOUTH AFRICA           1965
*Jim Reeves, Madeleine Usher, Clive Parnell, Arthur Swemmer, Mike Holt*

Two gamblers take part in a rigged game of poker, from which they emerge as the proud new owners of a diamond mine. An undistinguished and undemanding musical that's worth seeing if only to catch Country singer Reeves in a rare screen appearance.
MUS                      78 min (ort 82 min)
B,V                    SPEC/POLY; CH5 (VHS only)

**KIND HEARTS AND CORONETS \*\*\*\***          U
Robert Hamer            UK                 1949
*Dennis Price, Alec Guinness, Joan Greenwood, Valerie Hobson, Miles Malleson, Hugh Griffith, Jeremy Spenser, Arthur Lowe, Audrey Fildes, Clive Morton, Lyn Evans, Cecil Ramage, John Penrose, John Salew, Eric Messiter, Anne Valery*
Superb black comedy about a man who ruthlessly eliminates eight of his relatives (all played by Guinness) in order to inherit a title and stately home; part of his motivation being as an act of revenge in memory of his disowned mother, and part just plain greed. Price is perfect in his portrayal of the villain of the piece, in this beautifully crafted comedy.
Boa: novel Israel Rank (Noblesse Oblige) by Roy Horniman.
COM                    101 min (ort 106 min) B/W
B,V                      TEVP; WHV (VHS only)

**KIND OF LOVING, A \*\*\*\***                 15
John Schlesinger        UK                 1962
*Alan Bates, June Ritchie, Thora Hird, Bert Palmer, Gwen Nelson, Malcolm Patton, Pat Keen, James Bolam, Jack Smethurst, John Ronane, David Mahlowe, Patsy Rowlands, Michael Deacon, Jerry Desmonde, Leonard Rossiter*
A young draughtsman in a Northern industrial town, is forced into an early marriage when he gets a girl at work pregnant. A fine realistic drama that examines his relationship with those around him, not least a hostile mother-in-law. All the cast are excellent but Bates as the young man and Hird as his mother-in-law are outstanding.
Boa: novel by Stan Barstow.
DRA                    107 min (ort 112 min) B/W
B,V                      TEVP; WHV (VHS only)

**KINDRED, THE \***                           18
Jeffrey Obrow/Stephen Carpenter
                        USA                 1986
*Rod Steiger, Kim Hunter, David Allen Brooks, Amanda Pays, Talia Balsam, Timothy Gibbs, Peter Frechette, Julia Montgomery, Bunki Z, Charles Grueber, Bennet Guillory, Edgar Small, James Boeke, Randy Harrington, Ben Perry*
A woman scientist creates a man-eating tentacled monster, by combining skin tissue from her son with that of a marine organism. Plenty of revolting special effects fail to enliven a dull film.
HOR                      89 min (ort 97 min)
B,V                            EIV

**KING \*\*\***                               PG
Abby Mann               USA                 1978
*Paul Winfield, Cicely Tyson, Roscoe Lee Brown, Ossie Davis, Lonny Chapman, Ossie Davis, Cliff De Young, Al Freeman Jr, Clu Gulager, Steven Hill, William Jordan, Warren Kemmerling, Lincoln Kilpatrick, Kenneth McMillan*
A biopic on the career of Martin Luther King Jr, the famous civil rights leader, that follows him from his early days as a Southern Baptist minister, up to his assassination in 1968. An absorbing and detailed account. The score, by Billy Goldenberg, was awarded an Emmy.
DRA        277 min (3 cassettes – ort 360 min) mTV
B,V                            PARA

**KING AND I, THE \*\*\*\***
Walter Lang             USA                 1956
*Deborah Kerr, Yul Brynner, Rita Moreno, Martin*

*Benson, Terry Saunders, Alan Mowbray, Rex Thompson, Geoffrey Toone*
Musical version of "Anna And The King Of Siam" telling the story of the British governess who went to Siam in 1862 and spent six years teaching the King's many children at the Royal Palace of Bangkok. A lively and appealing film tailor-made for Brynner.
AA: Actor (Brynner), Art/Set (Lyle R. Wheeler and John DeCuir/Walter M. Scott and Paul S. Fox), Sound (Carl Faulkner), Score (Alfred Newman/Ken Darby), Cost (Irene Sharaff).
Boa: musical Anna And The King Of Siam/book The English Governess At The Siamese Court by Anna Leonowens.
MUS                                        128 min (ort 133 min)
B,V,LV                                                      CBS

**KING BOXER **                                              18
Liu Chia Liang     HONG KONG                              1973
*Liu Chia-Hui, Hui Ya-Mung, Wang Lung-Wei*
A young martial arts devotee comes up against rivals, and has his hands broken as a warning. However, he makes a remarkable recovery and learns a secret "iron-fist" technique with which he has his revenge. An early martial arts offering with several good sequences, but some ludicrous dubbing and a pointless romantic sub-plot.
Aka: FIVE FINGERS OF DEATH; INVINCIBLE BOXER
MAR                        101 min Cut (7 sec) dubbed
B,V                                                        WHV

**KING BOXER 2 **                                            18
Joseph Kong       HONG KONG
*Bruce Le (Huang Kin Lung), Chang Lee, Lita Vasquez*
A follow-up to the first film, with a formula tale of honour and revenge.
MAR                                                   78 min
V                                             TRANS; ATLAS

**KING DAVID **                                              PG
Bruce Beresford     USA                                   1985
*Richard Gere, Edward Woodward, Denis Quilley, Alice Krige, Niall Buggy, Jack Klaff, Cherie Lunghi, Hurd Hatfield, John Castle*
A Hollywood biblical epic that fails, largely due to poor casting of Gere in the title role. However, despite a panning from the critics there are some good things in it, such as a fine performance from Woodward as Saul and the excellent photography of Donald McAlpine. The script is less memorable and gradually unravels as the story progresses. The score is by Carl Davis.
Aka: STORY OF DAVID, THE
DRA                                      109 min (ort 114 min)
V/sh                                                       CIC

**KING DICK **                                               18
Giorgio Terzi (Gioacchino Libratti)
                  ITALY                                   1978
Sex cartoon involving a dwarf and a witch.
Aka: IL NANO E LA STREGA; LITTLE DICK THE MIGHTY MIDGET
CAR                67 min; 63 min (AVR) (Cut at film release)
B,V                                           INT/CBS L/A; AVR

**KING KONG ***                                              PG
Merian C. Cooper/Ernest B. Schoedsack
                  USA                                     1933
*Fay Wray, Bruce Cabot, Robert Armstrong, Frank Reicher, Noble Johnson, James Flavin, Sam Hardy, Victor Wong, Steve Clemento, Ethan Laidlaw, Charlie Sullivan, Vera Lewis, Leroy Mason, Dick Curtis, Lynton Brent, Frank Mills*
A rather wooden tale of the capture of a giant ape, and its exhibition when brought back to civilisation, where it escapes and runs amok. Though terribly dated now, the film must be seen in the context of the technical limitations of the 1930s, and for that reason

can be regarded as something of a milestone in cinema. It was remade in 1976. See also MIGHTY JOE YOUNG.
Boa: novel by Edgar Wallace and Merian C. Cooper.
A/AD                       86 min; 100 min (CH5) B/W
B,V                                    HER; CH5 (VHS only)

**KING KONG ***                                              PG
John Guillermin     USA                                   1976
*Jeff Bridges, Jessica Lange, John Randolph, Charles Grodin, Julius Harris, Rene Auberjonois, Ed Lauter, Jack O'Halloran, Mario Gallo, Jorge Moreno, Sid Conrad, John Agar, John Lone, Gary Walberg, George Whitman*
Excellent remake of the rather cardboard 1933 film that handles both human and animal characters with considerable intelligence. After it captures the girl, both human and ape develop a touching and rather ambivalent relationship that is well shown. The special effects in this one are superb. AA: Spec Award (Carlo Rambaldi/Glen Robinson/Frank Van Der Meer for visual effects).
Boa: novel by Edgar Wallace and Merian C. Cooper.
A/AD                                     128 min (ort 135 min)
B,V                                                       TEVP

**KING KONG LIVES ***                                        PG
John Guillermin     USA                                   1986
*Brian Kerwin, Linda Hamilton, John Ashton, Peter Michael Goetz, Frank Maraden, Peter Elliott, George Yiasomi, Alan Sader, Lou Criscuolo, Marc Clement, Richard Rhodes, Larry Souder, Ted Prichard, Jayne Lindsay-Gray*
A sequel to the 1976 remake of the original, in which Kong is brought out of the coma caused by his fall, and restored to full health and vigour by a heart transplant. To make his happiness complete, he even gets a mate. A film that's as daft as it is unconvincing.
A/AD                                     101 min (ort 105 min)
V                                                        PRES

**KING KONG VERSUS GODZILLA **                               PG
Inoshiro Honda/Thomas Montgomery
                  JAPAN/USA                               1963
*Michael Keith, James Yagi, Tadao Takashima, Mie Hama, Kenji Sahara, Akihiko Hirata, Ichiro Arishima, Tatsuo Matsumura, Yu Fujiki, Harry Holcombe, Eiko Wakabayashi, Senkichi Omura*
Apart from an exciting finale, set atop Mount Fuji where the two title creatures clash, this is a rather slow monster film, short on action and long on talk. The good special effects raise it above the level of the usual run of these films, but cannot compensate for those long boring periods.
Aka: KINGU KONGU TAI GOJIRA
FAN                                      87 min (ort 90 min)
B,V                                                        CIC

**KING LEAR ***                                              15
Michael Elliott     UK                                    1983
*Laurence Olivier, Colin Blakely, Anna Calder-Marshall, John Hurt, Jeremy Kemp, Robert Lang, Robert Lindsay, Leo McKern, Diana Rigg, David Threlfall, Dorothy Tutin*
This well-staged adaptation represented one of Olivier's last demanding roles, and though it fails to rival the power of earlier works (such as the 1971 Peter Brook production), it is certainly made with enough care to merit attention.
Boa: play by William Shakespeare.
DRA                                      157 min (ort 180 min) mTV
V                                                         VES

**KING LEAR ***                                              PG
Peter Brook         DENMARK/UK                            1970
*Paul Scofield, Irene Worth, Alan Webb, Cyril Cusack, Tom Fleming, Jack MacGowran, Susan Engel, Patrick Magee, Robert Lloyd, Soeren Elung-Jensen, Anne-Lise Gabold*

An effective version of Shakespeare's play (filmed in Jutland and Denmark) that benefits from a strong cast and a wonderful feel for the material. This restrained version is a little hard to follow but rewards patience.
Boa: play by William Shakespeare.
DRA 132 min (ort 137 min) B/W
B,V RCA

**KING LEAR ****** PG
Jonathan Miller UK 1982
Michael Hordern, Frank Middlemass, John Shrapnel, Norman Rodway, Michael Kitchen, Gillian Barge, Brenda Blethyn, Penelope Wilton, John Bird, Julian Curry, David Weston, Harry Waters, Anton Lesser, John Grillo, Iain Armstrong
An outstanding television production, easily one of the best in this large and ambitious series of the complete set of Shakespeare's plays. Acting and direction are absolutely first rate.
Boa: play by William Shakespeare.
DRA 186 min mTV
V/h BBC

**KING OF COMEDY, THE *** PG
Martin Scorsese USA 1981 (released 1982)
Robert De Niro, Jerry Lewis, Ed Herlihy, Diahnne Abbott, Sandra Bernhard, Tony Randall, Shelley Hack, Fred de Cordova
De Niro gives a bravura performance as an obsessive would-be-comic, who kidnaps a comedian with his own TV show in order to be given the chance of making a guest appearance. Lewis is suitably insincere as the successful comic, De Niro is wonderfully obnoxious as the aspiring one. A patchy but fairly amusing comedy, scripted by Paul D. Zimmerman.
DRA 105 min (ort 109 min)
B,V TEVP

**KING OF FRIDAY NIGHT, THE ** 15
John Gray CANADA 1985
Frank Mackay, Eric Peterson, Geoffrey Bowes, Alec Willows, Andrew Rhodes, Sheree Jeacocke
A lively musical about a 1960s rock group told in a series of flashbacks.
MUS 88 min
B,V CAN; TEVP

**KING OF KONG ISLAND**
Robert Morris SPAIN 1978
Brad Harris, Esmeralda Barros, Marc Lawrence, Adriana Alben, Mark Farran
A mercenary fights a group of scientists trying to use robot-like apes to dominate the world after tinkering with their brains. Utterly ludicrous low-grade trash. The question is, who tinkered with the director's brain?
Aka: EVE OF THE WILD WOMAN; KONG ISLAND
HOR 90 min (ort 92 min)
B,V INT/CBS

**KING OF KUNG FU *** 18
Chiang I. Hsing HONG KONG 1973
Bobby Baker, Nam Chun Pan, Lam Chun Chi, Alex Lung, Christine Hui, Yukio Someno
Another production-line martial arts adventure.
Aka: HE WALKS LIKE A TIGER
MAR 90 min
B,V VIDRNG L/A; PRV L/A; NET

**KING OF LOVE, THE *** 15
Anthony Wilkinson USA 1987
Nick Mancuso, Rip Torn, Sela Ward, Michael Lerner, Alan Rosenberg, Katy Boyer, Robin Gammell
Fanciful story of the eventful rise to power of a tycoon, who seems to have been inspired by the man who founded Playboy magazine. A mishmash of a film that has everything in it, from McCarthyism to the Black Panther movement; the result is everything one

would have expected. Scripted by Donald Freed.
DRA 90 min (ort 96 min) mTV
B,V MGM

**KING OF THE GRIZZLIES *** U
Ron Kelly USA 1970
John Yesno, Chris Wiggins, Hugh Webster, Jack Van Evera, Winston Hibler (narration)
Standard Disney animal yarn, with an Indian boy coming across a full grown grizzly that he raised as a cub, and trying to tame it. A pleasant little outing, filmed in the Canadian Rockies.
Boa: novel The Biography Of A Grizzly by E.T. Seton.
JUV 89 min (ort 93 min)
B,V WDV

**KING OF THE KICKBOXERS *** 18
Lucas Lowe 1989
Loren Avedon, Keith Cooke, Billy Blanks
The murder of a man's brother by a martial arts champ leaves him filled with bitterness, but when the culprit sets about recruiting people to star in his new kickboxing movie the opportunity arises to have revenge.
MAR 93 min
V EIV

**KING OF THE MOUNTAIN *** 
Noel Nosseck USA 1981
Joseph Bottoms, Harry Hamlin, Dennis Hopper, Deborah Van Valkenburgh, Ashley Cox, Richard Cox, Dan Haggerty, Seymour Cassel, Joe Sloan, Steve Jones, Lillian Muller, Cassandra Peterson, Buddy Joe Hooker, Ron Trice, Kurt Ayers
Racing enthusiasts who pit themselves and their cars against each other as they race down L.A.'s Mulholland Drive, form the basis for this pointless effort. Unfortunately the script gets caught in a cul-de-sac, and both development and climax are predictable. Inspired by a magazine article written by Dave Barry for "New West" magazine.
DRA 86 min (ort 90 min)
B,V POLY

**KING OF THE OLYMPICS: PARTS 1 AND 2 *** PG
Lee Philips USA 1988
David Selby, Renee Soutendijk, Pat Starr, Sybil Maas, Shelagh McLeod
Overlong biopic about a man who dominated the running of the Olympic Games for so many decades that one almost expected him to go on for ever, which is exactly what this film does. Originally shown in two parts.
Aka: KING OF THE OLYMPICS: THE LIVES AND LOVES OF AVERY BRUNDAGE
DRA 177 min (ort 200 min) mTV
B,V CHV

**KING OF THE STREETS *** 18
Edmund Hunt CANADA 1985
Brett Clark, Regie DeMorton, Pamela Saunders, Nelson D. Anderson, Norman Budd, Elodie McKee, Bill Woods Jr, Rameon Witt, Tony Williams, Connie Lee Wiggins, Arturo Bonilla, Linda Lutz, Lydia Finzi, Anthony Alexander
An alien being is sent to Earth to combat evil in the form of rapists and other nasties. An incredibly stupid attempt to exploit the story of Christ that is full of phoney mysticism.
Aka: ALIEN WARRIOR
DRA 91 min Cut (3 min 16 sec)
B,V IMPACT/ODY

**KING OF THE WIND *** U
Peter Duffell UK 1989
Frank Finlay, Jenny Agutter, Nigel Hawthorne, Navin Chowdry, Glenda Jackson, Richard Harris
A mute Arab boy accompanies a stallion on a perilous

journey from North Africa to France and then Britain. They suffer many hardships and misfortunes and have a number of adventures before the inevitable happy ending. An enjoyable children's film that, despite its stereotyped characterisation and over-burdened plot, is sustained by fine photography and performances.
Boa: novel by Marguerite Henry.
DRA                                    102 min mTV
V                                            VES

### KING SOLOMON'S MINES *
J. Lee Thompson        USA            PG
                                             1985
Richard Chamberlain, Sharon Stone, John Rhys-Davies, Herbert Lom, Ken Gampu, June Buthelezi, Sam Williams, Shai K. Ophir, Fidelis Chea, Mick Lesley, Bob Greer, Vincent Van Der Byl, Oliver Tengende, Neville Thomas, Isiah Murert
A rather bad version of this classic adventure tale, somewhat influenced by RAIDERS OF THE LOST ARK etc. Cardboard characters combine with wooden acting to produce a film lacking in credibility. Never fear, there is a sequel; ALLAN QUARTERMAIN AND THE LOST CITY OF GOLD.
Boa: novel by H. Rider Haggard.
A/AD                          96 min (ort 100 min)
B,V                                          RNK

### KING SOLOMON'S MINES ***
Robert Stevenson        UK              U
                                             1937
Cedric Hardwicke, Paul Robeson, Roland Young, John Loder, Anne Lee, Sydney Fairbrother, Robert Adams, Makubalo Hlubi, Ecce Homo Toto, Frederick Leister, Alf Goddard, Arthur Sinclair, Arthur Goullet
A group of daring explorers search the African continent for the lost diamond mines of Solomon. Robeson stars as Umbopa, in the role that brought him fame. A fine adventure film, remade twice since, in lamentably inferior versions.
Boa: novel by H. Rider Haggard.
A/AD                        77 min (ort 80 min) B/W
V                                            VCC

### KING SOLOMON'S TREASURE *
Alvin Rakoff        CANADA/UK           PG
                                             1976
David McCallum, Patrick Macnee, Britt Ekland, John Colicos, Yvon Dufour, Ken Gampu, Wilfrid Hyde-White, John Quentin, Veronique Beliveau, Sam Williams, Hugh Rowse, Fiona Fraser, Camilla Hutton
A low-budget version of this famous tale of a diamond hunt in the jungle, dinosaurs and a Phoenician queen. Exotic settings cannot rescue this dud.
Boa: novel Allan Quatermain by H. Rider Haggard.
A/AD                          84 min (ort 89 min)
B,V      INT/CBS; MIA (VHS only); PARK (VHS only)

### KINGDOM IN THE CLOUDS **
Elisabeth Bostan        ROMANIA        1973
Anna Szeles, Mircea Breazu, Ion Tergeanu
A shepherd's son sets out to find the land of eternal youth in this live-action fairy-tale.
Aka: TINERETTE FARA BATRINETE
JUV                                      72 min
V                                            INT

### KINGDOM OF THE SPIDERS **
John (Bud) Cardos        USA            PG
                                             1977
William Shatner, Tiffany Bolling, Woody Strode, Lieux Dressler, David MacLean, Joy Ross, Hoke Howell, Marcy Rafferty, Roy Engel, Adele Malis, Natasha Ryan, Altovise Davis
Tarantulas in Arizona go on the march by the thousands, in this standard, surprise-free but moderately competent horror yarn.
Aka: KINGDOM OF SPIDERS
HOR                          91 min (ort 95 min)
B,V                                     IFS; APX

### KINGS AND DESPERATE MEN **
Alexis Kanner        CANADA            15
                                             1983
Patrick McGoohan, Alexis Kanner, Andrea Marcovicci, Margaret Trudeau, Budd Knapp, Dave Patrick, Robin Spry, Jean-Pierre Brown, Frank Moore, August Schellenberg, Neil Vipond, Kevin Fenlon, Peter MacNeill, Kate Nash
A broadcaster is held at gunpoint by a gang of terrorists who want to review the case of a prisoner on the air. A promising start is thrown away by clumsy development and bad direction, allowing McGoohan to over act to the point of irritation.
Aka: KINGS AND DESPERATE MEN: A HOSTAGE INCIDENT
DRA                                     118 min
B,V                                          EHE

### KINGS OF THE ROAD ***
Wim Wenders        WEST GERMANY        18
                                             1975
Rudiger Vogler, Hanns Zischler, Lisa Kreuzer, Rudolf Schundler, Marquard Bohm
A New Wave German film that provides a slow, insightful and absorbing examination of a host of issues, all wrapped up in the form of a road movie. A travelling projectionist/repairman teams up with a depressed hitch-hiker to explore a dreary, forgotten border region between East and West Germany. A film about fast cars, rock 'n' roll and industrial decline, that's well complemented by its fine rock score.
Aka: IM LAUF DER ZEIT
DRA                                176 min B/W
V                                          CONNO

### KINJITE: FORBIDDEN SUBJECTS **
J. Lee Thompson        USA             18
                                             1989
Charles Bronson, Juan Fernandez, James Pax, Kumiko Hayakawa, Perry Lopez, Peggy Lipton, Amy Hathaway, Bill McKinney, Sy Richardson, Alex Hyde-White, Richard Egan Jr
A long-serving vice cop sets out to smash a child prostitution ring, run by a ruthless pimp who has kidnapped the daughter of a Japanese businessman recently arrived in Los Angeles. Standard hard-boiled Bronson thriller dressed up with a few new angles.
Aka: KINJITE
A/AD                          94 min (ort 97 min)
V/sh                                       PATHE

### KINKY COACHES AND THE POM-POM PUSSYCATS, THE **
Mark Warren        CANADA/USA         1980
John Vernon, Norman Fell, Robert Forster, Thom Haverstock, Terry Swiednicki, Keith Brown, Christine Cattell, Lisa Schwartz, Paul Bakewich, Kimberly McKeever, Jim Murchison, Anthony Sherwood, Matt Birman-Feldmann, Jean Walker
Female supporters of an American football team try every trick in the book to ensure that their team wins the championship, in an endearingly silly comedy that refuses to take itself or anything else seriously.
Aka: CRUNCH
COM                                     100 min
B,V,V2                          NUT L/A; MARKET

### KISMET ***
Vincente Minnelli        USA            U
                                             1955
Howard Keel, Ann Blyth, Dolores Gray, Monty Woolley, Sebastian Cabot, Vic Damone, Jay C. Flippen, Mike Mazurki, Jack Elam
An entertaining Arabian Nights fantasy, with some great songs (and some dreadful ones too) about a beggar and his daughter and their adventures in Bagdad. The best songs, "Stranger In Paradise" and "Baubles, Bangles and Beads", are based on music by Borodin.
Boa: musical by Edward Knoblock.
MUS                        108 min (ort 113 min)
V/sh                                        MGM

## KISS ME GOODBYE **
Robert Mulligan          USA          1982
*James Caan, Sally Field, Jeff Bridges, Paul Dooley,*
*Claire Trevor, Mildred Natwick, Dorothy Fielding,*
*William Prince, Maryedith Burrell, Alan Haufrect,*
*Stephen Elliott, Michael Ensign, Lee Weaver, Edith*
*Fields, Gene Castle*
A young woman about to re-marry, is visited by her
late husband's ghost, in this clear remake of DONA
FLOR AND HER TWO HUSBANDS but minus that
film's charm.
COM                                  101 min
B,V                                     CBS

## KISS ME KATE ***                       U
George Sidney          USA          1953
*Howard Keel, Kathryn Grayson, Ann Miller, Bobby*
*Van, Keenan Wynn, James Whitmore, Bob Fosse,*
*Tommy Rall, Kurt Kaszner, Ron Randell*
The lead couple in a musical version of Shakespeare's
"The Taming Of The Shrew" have a married life that
in many respects resembles their on-stage roles. Many
fine tunes grace this highly enjoyable adaptation of
the smash hit Broadway musical and include numbers
such as: "So In Love", "Always True To You In My
Fashion", "Brush Up Your Shakespeare" and "From
This Moment On".
Boa: play by Samuel and Bella Spewack/musical by
Cole Porter.
MUS                          105 min (ort 111 min)
B,V                                     MGM

## KISS ME . . . KILL ME **               PG
Michael O'Herlihy          USA          1976
*Stella Stevens, Michael Anderson Jr, Dabney*
*Coleman, Claude Akins, Bruce Boxleitner, Pat*
*O'Brien, Robert Vaughn, Tisha Sterling*
When a schoolteacher is murdered, a female investi-
gator bravely agrees to act as a human decoy in a bid
to capture the killer. Some standard thrills but little
else is to be had in this generally unmemorable work.
A/AD                          69 min (ort 126 min)
V                                       RCA

## KISS ME, STUPID *                      PG
Billy Wilder          USA          1964
*Dean Martin, Ray Walston, Kim Novak, Felicia Farr,*
*Cliff Osmond, Barbara Pepper, Doro Merande, Henry*
*Gibson, John Fiedler, Mel Blanc*
A lewd comedy vehicle for Martin, in which he plays a
womanising singer who feigns interest in the work of
an unsuccessful songwriter as a ploy to bed the latter's
wife. Despite good casting of Martin and a scattering
of amusing gags, the passage of time has not been
kind to this sluggish and inept affair, as tasteless as it
is tiresome. Following a heart attack, Peter Sellers
dropped out of the role taken over by Walston.
Boa: play L'Oro Della Fantasia by Anna Bonacci.
COM                          121 min (ort 124 min)
V                                       WHV

## KISS ME WITH LUST **                   18
                         FRANCE
*Rozana Khan, Jean-Marie Pallardy, Karin Schubert*
A look at the fast jet-setting lifestyle of the super-rich.
Aka: READY AND WILLING (SHEP); VERY
SPECIAL WOMAN, A
A                66 min (ort 72 min) Cut (2 min 46 sec)
V                                 ACV L/A; PHV

## KISS OF THE SPIDER WOMAN ***          15
Hector Babenco          BRAZIL/USA          1985
*William Hurt, Raul Julia, Milton Goncalves, Sonia*
*Braga, Jose Lewgoy, Nuno Leal Maia, Antonio Petrim,*
*Denise Dummont, Miriam Pires, Fernando Torres,*
*Patricio Bisso, Herson Captri, Nildo Parente, Antonio*
*Petrin, Wilson Grey*
A much-acclaimed film about two prisoners who share
a cell in a Latin American prison. One is a revolution-

ary, the other a homosexual and a strange multi-
faceted relationship develops between them, as the
latter entertains the former with his memories of
trashy Hollywood movies. The script is by Leonard
Schrader. AA: Actor (Hurt).
Boa: novel by Manuel Puig.
DRA          120 min; 115 min (PAL) Colour and B/W
B,V                          PVG; PAL (VHS only)

## KISS OF THE TARANTULA *
Chris Munger          USA          1972
*Suzanne Ling, Eric Mason, Herman Wallner, Patricia*
*Landon, Beverly Eddins, Jay Scott Neal, Rebecca*
*Eddins, Rita French, W. James Eddins, Jared Davis*
A young teenage girl has a strange power over spiders
and uses tarantulas to kill those who incur her wrath,
such as her adulterous mother. A dull little effort
whose plot has too many twists for the meagre budget
to sustain.
Aka: SHUDDERS
HOR                                     84 min
B,V,V2                                   HOK

## KISS, THE **                           18
Pen Densham          USA          1988
*Meredith Salenger, Joanna Pacula, Mimi Kuzyk,*
*Nicholas Kilbertus, Jan Rubes*
An African voodoo priestess is subject to a curse that
is handed down from one generation to the next by
means of a woman-to-woman kiss. In a search for an
heiress she enters the lives of the family of her dead
sister, where the young girl she has chosen begins to
have doubts about the wholesomeness of her newly-
arrived aunt. A cumbersome yarn with one or two
scary moments and a general failure to explore the
premise's intriguing sexual element.
HOR                           94 min (ort 101 min)
V                                       RCA

## KISS THE NIGHT *                       18
James Ricketson          AUSTRALIA          1987
*Patsy Stevens, Warwick Moss, Garry Aron Cook*
Sex thriller set in a brothel, where one of the most
reliable girls makes the fatal mistake of falling for a
client with a number of dark secrets, and embarking
on an affair that ends in tragedy. A film that
presumably sets out to generate tension, but is
hampered by its sleazy and murky atmosphere.
Aka: CANDY REGENTAG
THR                                    102 min
B,V                          SHEER; BRAVE

## KISSING PLACE, THE **                  15
Tony Wharmby          USA          1989
*Meredith Baxter-Birney, David Ogden Stiers,*
*Nathaniel Moreau, Victoria Snow*
A young 10-year-old boy discovers his parents' dark
secret and the reason why the family is never able to
stay in one place for long. An interesting if flawed
drama whose restrained direction is singularly at odds
with Baxter-Birney's overwrought performance.
DRA                           84 min (ort 96 min)
V                                       CIC

## KITCHEN TOTO, THE ***                  15
Harry Hook          UK          1987
*Bob Peck, Phyllis Logan, Edwin Mahinda, Robert*
*Urquhart, Kirsten Hughes, Edward Judd, Nicholas*
*Charles, Nathan Dambuza Mdledle, Ann Wanjugu,*
*Job Seda*
The powerful story of a young Kikuyu boy sent to
work for the British police chief, in the White
Highlands of Kenya in 1950, the year when the
support for the Mau-Mau rebels was rapidly growing
among the Kikuyu tribe. Scripted by Hook in his
directorial debut. The film was a prizewinner at the
Tokyo Film Festival.
DRA                           92 min (ort 95 min)
B,V                                     WHV

## KLANSMAN, THE *
Terence Young          USA              1974
*Richard Burton, Lee Marvin, Cameron Mitchell, Lola
Falana, Luciana Paluzzi, Linda Evans, O.J. Simpson,
David Heddleston*
Racial tensions flare when a white girl is raped and
the local sheriff has to confront the Ku Klux Klan. A
brutal and badly acted melodrama. The film was
initially directed by Samuel Fuller but Young took
over.
Aka: BURNING CROSS, THE
Boa: novel by William Bradford Huie.
DRA                    90 min (ort 112 min)
B,V,V2                            VCL/CBS

## KLEINHOFF HOTEL *
Carlo Lizzani          ITALY            1977
*Corinne Clery, Bruce Robinson, Katya Rupe*
A married woman becomes emotionally involved with
a tourist, in this fairly insipid drama.
Aka: PASSIONATE STRANGERS, THE
DRA                              92 min
B,V,V2                              VPD

## KLONDIKE FEVER **                              PG
Peter Carter           USA              1980
*Jeff East, Rod Steiger, Angie Dickinson, Lorne Greene,
Barry Morse, Lisa Langlois, Robin Gammell, Michael
Hogan, Gordon Pinsent, Sherry Lewis, D.D. Winters*
An adventure yarn set during the Klondike Gold Rush
with Jack East cast as the great writer and adventur-
er Jack London. Despite the potential of the material,
this tale is little more than an adequate effort.
Aka: JACK LONDON'S KLONDIKE FEVER
Boa: story by Jack London.
A/AD                   102 min; 105 min (MIA or PARK)
B,V,V2  INT/CBS; MIA (VHS only); PARK (VHS only)

## KLUTE ***                                       18
Alan J. Pakula         USA              1971
*Donald Sutherland, Jane Fonda, Roy Scheider,
Charles Cioffi, Dorothy Tristan, Rita Gam, Jean
Stapleton, Vivian Nathan, Nathan George, Morris
Strassberg, Barry Snider, Anthony Holland, Richard
Shull, Betty Murray*
An ex-cop investigating a disappearance, becomes
involved with a call-girl in this excellent drama,
which offers plenty of suspense despite its downbeat
and low-key approach. AA: Actress (Fonda).
Boa: novel by William Johnston.
THR                    109 min (ort 114 min)
B,V                                 WHV

## KNIFE IN THE WATER ***
Roman Polanski         POLAND           1962
*Leon Niemczyk, Jolanta Umelka, Zygmunt
Malanowicz*
A tense and gripping tale of a young couple who pick
up a hitch-hiker and invite him onto their yacht,
where a strange game begins. The director's only
feature made in his native country, demonstrates a
sure hand in a sparse and direct style. Malanowicz's
voice was dubbed over with Polanski's.
Aka: NOZ W WODZIE
DRA                    90 min (ort 94 min) B/W
B,V                                TEVP

## KNIGHT RIDER: THE ORIGINAL TV MOVIE **  PG
Daniel Haller          USA              1982
*David Hasselhoff, Edward Mulhare, Phyllis Davis,
Richard Anderson, Vince Edwards*
A cop injured in a shoot-out is rebuilt with the aid of
plastic surgery, and becomes a one-man police force by
being given a radio link with his partner, an indes-
tructible computer-controlled car. Pilot for a TV
series. In this episode he hunts down a group of
industrial saboteurs.
A/AD                            91 min mTV
V/h                                 CIC

## KNIGHT RIDER 2: NIGHT OF THE
JUGGERNAUT **                                   PG
Georg Fenady           USA              1985
*David Hasselhoff*
Pilot for the second Knightrider TV series that started
in 1985 (the first series ran from 1982). As before,
episodes are built around the exploits of a cop who has
been equipped with an "intelligent" patrol car that has
its own built-in computer. Average.
A/AD                            91 min mTV
B,V                                 CIC

## KNIGHT WITHOUT ARMOUR ***                       U
Jacques Feyder         UK               1937
*Robert Donat, Marlene Dietrich, Irene Vanbrugh,
John Clements, Austin Trevor, Herbert Lomas, Miles
Malleson, Basil Gill, David Tree, Lawrence Hanray,
Hay Petrie, Lyn Harding, Frederick Culley, Lisa
D'Esterre*
A British agent is sent to Russia where he is captured
and sent to Siberia, but after the 1917 revolution he is
set free and appointed as commissar for a small town.
Ordered to escort a beautiful countess to Petrograd for
trial, he chooses to flee with her to the West. A fine
adventure film with just the right blend of romance
and action. The score is by Miklos Rozsa.
Boa: novel Without Armour by James Hilton.
DRA        96 min; 102 min (PICK) (ort 108 min) B/W
B,V                SPEC/POLY; PICK (VHS only)

## KNIGHTRIDERS ***                                15
George A. Romero       USA              1981
*Ed Harris, Gary Lahti, Tom Savini, Amy Ingersoll,
Patricia Tallman, Warner Shook, Christine Forrest,
Brother Blue*
A leisurely-paced tale of an itinerant group who
re-stage medieval jousting tournaments but use
motorcycles instead of horses. A highly unusual
change of subject for horror director Romero, who also
wrote the screenplay.
A/AD                   141 min (ort 145 min)
B,V                                 WHV

## KNIGHTS AND EMERALDS **                         PG
Ian Emes               UK               1986
*Christopher Wild, Warren Mitchell, Rachel Davies,
Tony Milner, Tracie Bennett, Beverly Hills, Bill
Leadbitter, Nadim Sawalha, Patrick Field, Maurice
Dee, David Keys, Andrew Goodman*
A talented drummer in a Birmingham marching band
has to contend with both a racist and a cash shortage,
that forces a merger with an all-female band. After
their defeat in the first round of a contest, he joins an
all-black group, an action that sparks off a major
family crisis. An earnest but clumsy attempt to say
something of social significance within the context of a
comedy.
COM                    87 min (ort 94 min)
V/sh                                WHV

## KNIGHTS OF THE CITY *                           18
Dominic Orlando        USA              1986
*Leon Isaac Kennedy, Nicholas Campbell, Stoney
Jackson, John Mengati, Jeff Moldovan, The Fat Boys,
Smokey Robinson, Janine Turner, Michael Ansara,
Jeff Kutash, Wendy Barry, Karin Smith, Deney Terrio,
Kurtis Blow*
Two street gangs clash to music just like in STREETS
OF FIRE. An unpleasant glamorisation of violent
thuggery without redeeming features.
A/AD                   88 min Cut (7 sec)
B,V                                 NWV

## KNOWLEDGE, THE *                                PG
Bob Brooks             UK               1979
*Nigel Hawthorne, Michael Elphick, Maureen Lipman,
Mick Ford*
Stupid and tiresome attempt to compress the ordeal

London cabbies have to go through in order to gain their badge, into a lightweight and empty film.

COM                  89 min (ort 100 min) mTV
B,V                         THAMES; VCC

## KOJAK: THE BELARUS FILE **      PG
Robert Markowitz     USA          1985
*Telly Savalas, Suzanne Pleshette, Max Von Sydow, Herbert Berghof, Betsy Aidem, Alan Rosenberg, Charles Brown, George Savalas, David Leary, Harry Davis, Rita Karin, Mark B. Russell, Vince Conti, Margaret Thomson*
A fair pilot for a new TV series about a canny bald-headed cop. Russians who survived the concentration camps are being murdered forty years on, as our detective faces one of his most baffling cases.
Aka: BELARUS FILE, THE
Boa: novel The Belarus Secret by John Loftus.
DRA                 93 min (ort 100 min) mTV
B,V                            CIC

## KOJAK: THE PRICE OF JUSTICE **     15
Alan Metzger       USA          1987
*Telly Savalas, Kate Nelligan, Jack Thompson, Pat Hingle, Brian Murray, Tony di Benedetto, John Bedford-Lloyd, Jeffrey DeMunn*
Kojak is assigned to a case involving the murder of two small boys who were found dumped in the Harlem river. Their mother is accused of the murder, but a sudden break in this tortuous case seems to point in the direction of her magnate lover. A further episode in this new series of tales that were based (somewhat unwisely) on original stories rather than specially written screenplays. Average.
Boa: novel The Investigation by Dorothy Uhnak.
THR                92 min (ort 100 min) mTV
B,V                            CIC

## KONGA *                         PG
John Lemont        UK           1961
*Michael Gough, Margo Johns, Jess Conrad, Claire Gordon*
This British rip-off of KING KONG sees London being menaced by a monster ape, the handiwork of the stock mad scientist. A silly SF film with few endearing qualities.
FAN                      86 min (ort 90 min)
V                              WHV

## KRAMER VERSUS KRAMER ***     PG
Robert Benton      USA          1979
*Dustin Hoffman, Meryl Streep, Justin Henry, Jane Alexander, Howard Duff, George Coe, JoBeth Williams*
An adman's wife gets a divorce and walks out leaving her ex-husband to take care of their son. Glossy and skilfully made production that's quite moving in parts, though a red-eyed Streep doing her best to cry her eyes out is an irritation. AA: Pic, Dir, Actor (Hoffman), S. Actress (Streep), Screen (Adapt) (Robert Benton).
Boa: novel by Avery Corman.
DRA                        105 min
B,V                           RCA

## KRAYS, THE ***                18
Peter Medak        UK           1989
*Gary Kemp, Martin Kemp, Billie Whitelaw, Susan Fleetwood, Charlotte Cornwell, Alfred Lynch, Steven Berkoff, Tom Bell*
A stylised portrayal of two of Britain's most notorious and vicious gangsters, that neglects many aspects of their early life and subsequent career in favour of a one-sided concentration on their relationships with women, most notably their mother. The Kemp brothers (of pop group Spandau Ballet) are excellent, but the script fails to probe. The allegation that the film rights cost £255,000 caused an understandable furore at the time.

DRA                        115 min
V                            RCA

## KREMLIN LETTER, THE *      18
John Huston       USA          1970
*Richard Boone, Orson Welles, Bibi Andersson, Max Von Sydow, Patrick O. Neal, Barbara Parkins, Dean Jagger, George Sanders, Raf Vallone, Ronald Radd, Nigel Green, Lila Kedrova, Michael MacLiammoir, Sandor Eles, Niall MacGinnis*
A bogus peace treaty binding the US to the USSR in an agreement to destroy Red China, has to be recovered at all costs, in this dull Cold War thriller that wastes its good international cast.
Boa: novel by Noel Behn.
THR                    113 min (ort 122 min)
B,V,LV                       CBS

## KRULL **                        PG
Peter Yates        UK           1983
*Ken Marshall, Lysette Anthony, Francesca Annis, Freddie Jones, Liam Neeson, Alun Armstrong, David Battley, Bernard Bresslaw, John Welsh, Graham McGrath, Tony Church, Bernard Archard, Belinda Mayne, Dicken Ashworth, Todd Carty*
Sword-and-sorcery SF epic with the usual theme of good versus evil, as seen in a perilous quest to rescue a beautiful maiden from captivity, at the hands of an evil creature. An abundance of special effects and elaborate settings are somewhat hampered by the slow development of the story.
FAN             121 min; 116 min (PREST)
B, V/sh            RCA; PREST (VHS only)

## KRUSH GROOVE **           15
Michael Schultz     USA          1985
*Blair Underwood, Kurtis Blow, Sheila E, Fat Boys, Run DMC, New Edition, Mark Morales, Damon Wimbley, Darren "Buffy" Robinson, Jason Mizell, Richard E. Gant, Lisa Gay Hamilton, Joseph Simmons, Daryl McDaniels*
This dull rap musical pads outs its non-existent plot, with a constant stream of numbers that will thrill fans but leave everyone else unmoved.
MUS                      91 min (ort 97 min)
V/sh                           WHV

## KUBLAI KHAN **
Denys de la Patelliere/Noel Howard
      AFGHANISTAN/FRANCE/EGYPT/ITALY/
          SWITZERLAND/YUGOSLAVIA    1964
*Anthony Quinn, Horst Buchholz, Akim Tamiroff*
A truly international attempt to provide an account of the life and travels of the explorer Marco Polo. Without doubt a brave if not altogether successful attempt.
Aka: FABULOUS ADVENTURES OF MARCO POLO, THE; LA FABULEUSE AVENTURE DE MARCO POLO; LE MERAVIGLIOSE AVVENTURE DI MARCO POLO; MARCO POLO; MARCO POLO EL AZIME
DRA                       111 min
B,V                        VCL/CBS

## KUNG FU EMPEROR **         18
Pao Shiue-Li     HONG KONG
*Din Lung, Shy Sy, Taur Ming-Ming, Tang Too-Liang, Chen Shing, Muh Sy-Cheung*
The unchallenged terror of the War Lord represents a bloody reign of evil, until a new master emerges to oppose him.
MAR                       91 min
B,V                       AVR; MKR

## KUNG FU GANGBUSTERS *
John Sur (Sun Chia-Wei)
          HONG KONG          197-
*Jason Pai Piau, Tommy Lu Chun, Ingrid Hu*
Kung fu fighters smash a criminal gang.

Aka: NAN-TZU HAN; SMUGGLERS
MAR                                    90 min
B,V                                    VPD

## KUNG FU GIRL *
Lo Wei          HONG KONG             1974
*Cheng Pei Pei, Ou Wei, James Tien*
A girl sets out to avenge the death of a student
activist. More of the same fisticuffs, but with a heroine
this time round.
Aka: NONE BUT THE BRAVE
MAR                                    77 min
B,V                                    RNK

## KUNG FU HERO *                                   15
Wan Hung Lo     HONG KONG             198-
*Cheung Lik, Christine Hui Shan, Shan Kwai*
Standard kung fu actioner with the plot little more
than a vehicle for the fighting sequences.
MAR                                   105 min
V                                      TRAX

## KUNG FU MASTER *
                HONG KONG             1979
*Chang Wu Lang, Yuen Siu Ting, Kao King*
A man tricked into smuggling diamonds has to fight to
the finish.
Aka: KUNG FU MASTER NAMED DRUNK CAT
MAR                                    84 min
B,V                                    VPD

## KUNG FU WARRIOR **                               18
                HONG KONG
*Chang Lei, Kuan Hai Shan*
A young kung fu student encounters unforeseen
setbacks, when he moves to Hong Kong to find work
and perfect his martial skills.
MAR                         82 min (ort 91 min)
B,V                                    VPD

## KURONEKO ***
Kaneto Shindo   JAPAN                 1968
*Kichiemon Nakamura, Nobuko Otowa, Kiwako
Taichi, Kei Sato, Hideo Kanze, Rokko Toura, Taiji
Tonoyama*
Two women raped and murdered by a samurai, return
to terrorise the area in this fantasy set in medieval
Japan. A celebrated warrior is dispatched to deal with
their ravages, and discovers to his horror that they are
the avenging spirits of his wife and mother. Scenes of
imaginative power alternate with ones of clumsy
horror, in a remarkable film that in many ways gives
the impression of having been made by two directors.
Aka: YABU NO NAKA KURONEKO
HOR                              99 min B/W
B,V                                    PVG

## KWAIDAN ****
Masaki Kobayashi  JAPAN               1964
*Rentaro Mikuni, Ganemon Nakamura, Katso
Nakamura, Michiyo Aratama, Keiko Kishi, Tatsuya
Nakadai, Takashi Shimura*
Four tales of the supernatural involving samurai,
monks, spirits etc. that are all put together with great
skill but are best enjoyed in two sittings. The superb
use of a wide-screen format will be lost on TV, but
fortunately the imaginative use of colour and setting
can still be enjoyed.
Aka: GHOST STORIES; WEIRD TALES
Boa: short stories by Lafcadio Hearn.
FAN                                   164 min
B,V                                    PVG

# L

## L-SHAPED ROOM, THE **                            15
Bryan Forbes    UK                    1962

Leslie Caron, Brock Peters, Tom Bell, Patricia
Phoenix, Cicely Courtnidge, Emlyn Williams, Avis
Bunnage, Nanette Newman, Harry Locke
A London suburban lodging house is inhabited by a
variety of characters including an author and a
pregnant French girl with whom he falls in love. A
mild little drama with watchable performances but
nothing of substance.
Boa: novel by Lynne Reid Banks.
DRA                     120 min (ort 142 min) B/W
V                                      WHV

## L.A. BOUNTY *                                    18
Worth Keeter    USA                   1988
*Sybil Danning (Sybelle Danning), Wings Hauser,
Robert Hanley, Lenore Kasdorf, Henry Darrow, Van
Quattro*
A woman bounty hunter and ex-cop, finds that the
psycho who killed her partner several years ago, has
now taken the city's mayor hostage, and she seizes the
chance to have her revenge. A low-grade, violent
actioner that was scripted and co-produced by Dan-
ning.
A/AD                        81 min (ort 85 min)
B,V                                    GHV

## L.A. CONNECTION ***                              18
Philip Ko       HONG KONG             1989
*Brent Gilbert, Mike Abbott*
A special agent is ordered to stop a pair of drug
runners operating a route from Hong Kong to L.A..
However, this involves the agent in taking on the
drugs producer, a vicious killer known as the "Black
Dragon". A tough, fast-paced martial arts police
adventure.
A/AD                                   85 min
V                                      VPD

## L.A. CRIMEWAVE *                                 15
Michael Mann    USA                   1989
*Scott Plank, Alex McArthur, Ely Pouget, Vincent
Custaferro, Richard Chaves, Victor Rivero, Alex
McArthur*
A disappointingly conventional crime drama built
around the three-way relationship of a dedicated cop
who heads L.A.'s robbery and murder unit, the
criminal mastermind behind a series of murders and
burglaries and the girlfriend of the former. The film
fails to blossom, mostly due to poor scripting and
acting. Devised by Mann, who has enjoyed considerably more success with an earlier creation: the TV
series "Starsky And Hutch".
Aka: MADE IN L.A.
A/AD                                   92 min
V                                      PRISM L/A

## L.A. HEAT **                                     18
Joseph Merhi    USA                   1988
*Lawrence-Hilton Jacobs, Jim Brown*
A tough detective whose partner was killed by a drugs
dealer is obsessed with bringing him to justice, and
discovers that his quarry is being protected by mobs-
ters.
A/AD                                   90 min
V                                      CINE

## L.A. LAW **                                      15
Gregory Holbit  USA                   1986
*Richard Dysart, Harry Hamlin, Corbin Bernsen, Jill
Eikenberry, Jimmy Smits, Michael Tucker, Alan
Rachins, Juanin Clay, Rob Knepper, Michele Greene,
Shannon Wilcox, Susan Dey, Susan Ruttan*
Pilot for the popular TV series about a busy L.A. legal
firm. Slick and well acted with good characterisation
but lacking in real bite as the storyline is painfully
thin and contrived.
DRA                     90 min (ort 104 min) mTV
V                                      CBS

## L.A. STREETFIGHTERS *
18
Richard Park          USA          1986
*Jun Chong, James Lew, Philip Rhee, Rosanna King*
Martial arts tale in an American setting, as two rival
drug-dealing gangs battle it out for control of the city.
Aka: NINJA TURF
MAR                    78 min (ort 90 min)
V                                    GHV

## L.B.J. – THE EARLY YEARS: PARTS 1    PG
AND 2 ***
Peter Werner          USA          1986
*Randy Quaid, Patti LuPone, Morgan Brittany, Pat
Hingle, Kevin McCarthy, Barry Corbin, Charles
Frank, James F. Kelly*
An episodic study of the political career of LBJ from
1934 to 1963, that's distinguished by excellent per-
formances from the two leads, especially with regard
to LuPone as Lady Bird and Hingle as Sam Rayburn.
DRA                            183 min mTV
B,V                                  VIR

## LA BALANCE ***
18
Bob Swain             FRANCE        1982
*Nathalie Baye, Philippe Leotard, Richard Berry,
Maurice Ronet, Christophe Maavoy, Jean-Paul
Connart*
A one-time Parisian criminal is forced by an unscru-
pulous cop, to inveigle a former associate into a
robbery in order to betray him to the police, who are
desperate to catch him. A tough and compelling
thriller that won several awards in its homeland.
THR                                104 min
B,V                                  CBS

## LA BAMBA ***
15
Luis Valdez           USA          1986
*Lou Diamond Phillips, Esai Morales, Rosana De Soto,
Elizabeth Pena, Joe Pantoliano, Danielle Von Zerneck,
Rick Dees, Marshall Crenshaw, Brian Setzer*
Biopic on the all too brief career of Ritchie Valens who
achieved almost overnight fame. The excellence of the
lead performance and the music, help make up for the
occasional cliched treatment. The music is performed
on the soundtrack by Los Lobos (who appear as the
Tijuana Band) and the score was written by Santana
and Miles Goodman.
DRA                                104 min
V/sh                                 RCA

## LA BELLE ET LA BETE *****
Jean Cocteau          FRANCE        1946
*Jean Marais, Josette Day, Mila Parely, Michel Auclair,
Marcel Andre, Nane Germon*
Cocteau's version of the classic fairy tale Beauty and
the Beast represents cinema at its best. One of the
greatest films ever made and a work of timeless and
magical beauty. The music is by Georges Auric.
Aka: BEAUTY AND THE BEAST, THE
FAN                               86 min B/W
B,V                                 TEVP

## LA CAGE AUX FOLLES ***
15
Edouardo Molinaro
                      FRANCE/ITALY   1978
*Ugo Tognazzi, Michel Serrault, Michel Galabru,
Claire Maurier, Remy Laurent, Benny Luke*
Two ageing homosexual lovers, one a nightclub owner
and the other his star "lady", pretend to be a normal
married couple for the sake of the son of the former,
who wishes to marry a respectable girl. An amusing
adaptation of a French stage farce that soon runs out
of steam, being at its best during the opening
nightclub sequences. Two sequels and a hit Broadway
musical followed.
Aka: BIRDS OF A FEATHER
Boa: play by Jean Poiret.
DRA                                91 min
B,V                                  WHV

## LA CAGE AUX FOLLES 3 **
15
Georges Lautner       FRANCE/ITALY   1985
*Michel Serrault, Ugo Tognazzi, Michel Galabru,
Benny Luke, Stephane Audran, Antonella Interlenghi*
The third attempt to extract some laughs from the
rather tired theme of a homosexual couple, one of
whom is a transvestite performer at the nightclub
owned by the other. Here, the "female" half is in line
for a vast inheritance if he marries and has a child
within 18 months. An unfunny second sequel.
Aka: LA CAGE AUX FOLLES 3: ELLES SE
MARIENT; LA CAGE AUX FOLLES 3: THE
WEDDING
COM                                87 min
B,V                                  RCA

## LA DOLCE VITA ***
18
Federico Fellini      ITALY         1961
*Marcello Mastroianni, Anouk Aimee, Claudia
Cardinale, Anita Ekberg, Alain Cuny, Yvonne
Furneaux, Magali Noel, Nadia Gray, Lex Barker*
Rambling, overlong and episodic look at the decadent
lifestyle of Roman high society, seen through the eyes
of a gossip columnist who aspires to straight journalism, but is unable to break away from his debauched
life. Some powerful scenes inevitably stick in the
memory, but the self-indulgent world shown here
inhibits any sympathy one might feel for the characters. AA: Cost (Piero Gherardi).
Aka: SWEET LIFE, THE
DRA                            174 min B/W
V                                    PAL

## LA REGLE DU JEU ****
Jean Renoir           FRANCE        1939
*Marcel Dalio, Nora Gregor, Jean Renoir, Mila Parely,
Gaston Modot, Julien Carette, Roland Toutain,
Paulette Dubost*
A weekend shooting party at a country house with
attendant sexual intrigues provides a sharply
observed picture of this type of society. Sad, funny and
wonderfully inventive; certainly one of the director's
best works.
Aka: RULES OF THE GAME
DRA                  110 min (ort 113 min) B/W
B,V                                  LNG

## LA RONDE ****
Max Ophuls            FRANCE        1950
*Anton Walbrook, Simone Signoret, Serge Reggiani,
Simone Simon, Daniel Gelin, Danielle Darieux,
Fernand Gravet, Jean Louis Barrault, Odette Joyeux,
Isa Miranda, Gerard Philipe*
Assorted amoral goings-on in Vienna of 1900. A film
of great charm and style which was considered very
daring at the time, linked together by a rather caustic
Walbrook, in a story of various Parisians having
affairs with each other that come full circle. Remade
in 1964. The music is by Oscar Straus. See also
DANCE OF LOVE.
Aka: MERRY-GO-ROUND, THE
Boa: play Merry Go Round by Arthur Schnitzler.
DRA                   93 min (ort 100 min) B/W
B,V                                  LNG

## LA VIE DU CHATEAU ***
PG
Jean-Paul Rappeneau FRANCE          1965
*Catherine Deneuve, Philippe Noiret, Pierre Brasseur,
Mary Marquet, Henri Garcin, Carlos Thompson*
Rappeneau's directorial debut is an easygoing and
often charming tale of a bored housewife living in
Normandy in WW2. A mysterious stranger discovered
at her chateau declares his love for her, but only to
protect his true identity as a Free French agent on a
secret mission. Various other complications follow in
this contrived but enjoyable blend of drama and farce.
Aka: GOOD LIFE, THE; MATTER OF RESISTANCE
DRA                                95 min B/W
V                                   CASPIC

## LABYRINTH ***
Jim Henson                USA                1986
*David Bowie, Jennifer Connelly, Toby Freud, Shelley Thompson, Christopher Malcolm, Natalie Finland, Shari Weiser, Brian Henson, Ron Mueck, Rob Mills, Dave Goetz, David Barclay, David Shaughnessy, Karen Prell, Timothy Bateson*
Elaborate fantasy tale of adventure as a young girl tries to rescue her baby stepbrother, who has been kidnapped by the king of the goblins. Enjoyable most of the time, though there are one or two sluggish moments. Written by Terry Jones.
FAN                        98 min (ort 101 min)
V/sh                              NELS L/A; CH5

## LACE *                                    15
Billy Hale                USA                1984
*Brooke Adams, Bess Armstrong, Phoebe Cates, Angela Lansbury, Anthony Higgins, Herbert Lom, Anthony Quayle, Honor Blackman, Arielle Dombrasle, Nickolas Grace, Leigh Lawson, Simon Chandler, Trevor Eve, Francois Guetary*
An international sex symbol is determined to trace her mother, having decided to ruin her life because she abandoned her as a baby. A glossy but extremely boring and empty Hollywood production soap. A sequel followed all too soon.
Boa: novel by Shirley Conran.
DRA                    240 min (2 cassettes) mTV
B,V                            VFP L/A; HER; CH5

## LACE 2 *                                   15
Billy Hale                USA                1985
*Brooke Adams, Deborah Raffin, Arielle Dombrasle, Phoebe Cates, Anthony Higgins, Christopher Cazenove, James Read, Patrick Ryecart, Michael Gough, Francois Guetary, Michael Fitzpatrick, Walter Gotell, Paul Shelley*
More of the same with Lili having to find the identity of her father in order to raise a ransom of $11,000,000 for her mother. A sequel to the earlier dross, not based on any novel this time. Very much another celebration of empty glitz, and if possible, slightly worse than its predecessor.
Boa: novel by Shirley Conran.
DRA                              180 min mTV
B,V                                VFP L/A; HER

## LACEMAKER, THE ****
Claude Goretta                              1977
FRANCE/SWITZERLAND/WEST GERMANY
*Isabelle Huppert, Yves Beneyton, Florence Giorgetti, Anne Marie Duringer, Renata Schroefer, Jean Obe*
The relationship between a young Parisian girl and a student she meets while on a holiday, fails because of differences of class and education. A rather beautiful little film, made with enormous care and attention to detail. The script is by Laine and Claude Goretta.
Aka: LA DENTELLIERE
Boa: novel La Dentelliere by Pascal Laine.
DRA                        100 min (ort 107 min)
B,V                                   VCL/CBS

## LADDER OF SWORDS **                       15
Norman Hull               UK                 1988
*Martin Shaw, Juliet Stevenson, Eleanor David, Bob Peck*
A second-rate circus act is stranded in a remote lay-by, awaiting a phone call that may result in an offer of work. When the bored wife of the troupe leader exposes herself to a passing motorist a bizarre chain of events unfolds. A very strange mixture of drama, intrigue and death, made more so by a few touches of black humour.
DRA                                   94 min
V/sh                                     ODY

## L'ADDITION **                             18
Denis Amar                FRANCE             1984
*Richard Berry, Richard Bohringer, Victoria Abril, Fadrid Chopel, David Sarky*
Murky prison melodrama in which a guard crippled in a prison break seeks revenge on those involved, including a romantic womaniser in prison on a minor charge.
Aka: ADDITION; CAGED HEART, THE
DRA                        82 min (ort 93 min) dubbed
B,V                                      RNK

## LADIES' DOCTOR **                          18
Joe D'Amato (Aristide Massaccassi)
                          ITALY              1977
*Mario Carotemuto, Massimo Serato, Paola Senatore*
A successful gynaecologist arranges to disappear whilst on holiday in the Caribbean, thus solving a number of his problems, such as paying off his gambling debts. In the meantime his fumbling assistant has become extremely popular, and helped by a nurse, has turned the clinic into a goldmine. A softcore sex farce.
Aka: IL GINECOLOGO DELLA MUTUA
A                                 81 min dubbed
B,V,V2                      VPD; ABC; NET; TCX

## LADIES' NIGHT **                          R18
Harry Lewis               USA                1980
*Annette Haven, Paul Thomas, Lisa de Leeuw, Chelsea McClane, Nicole Noie, Richard Bern, Herschel Savage, Billy Doe*
Since the football season has started and their menfolk are otherwise occupied, a group of women decide to go out in search of their own fun and games. Meeeting up at a male strip joint they enjoy a variety of sexual encounters.
Aka: PASSIONS NOCTURNES
Osca: EROTIC ADVENTURES OF CANDY, THE (asa – HAR)
A              41 min; 64 min (SHEP) (ort 74 min) Cut
B,V                       TCX; HAR; PRI; SHEP

## LADIES OF THE 80s *                       R18
Mark Richards             USA                1985
*Jacqueline Lorians, Tamara Longley, Lana Burner, Steve Drake, Dan T. Mann, Sheri St Clair, Jessie Adams, Claire Wright*
Five women come to a retreat where a female doctor offers group therapy. There is much dialogue from the doctor as the women discover the joys of loving each other, culminating in a banquet and orgy. A strange and rather pretentious offering promoting the view that women do not need men.
A                                     48 min
V                                       SHEP

## LADIES OF THE LOTUS **                     18
Lloyd A. Simanal/Douglas C. Nicolle
                          CANADA             1986
*Richard Dale, Angela Read, Patrick Bermel, Darcia Carnie, Martin Evans, Nathan Andrews*
Top models are kidnapped by a white-slavery ring in this action thriller.
A/AD                88 min (ort 120 min) Cut (37 sec)
B,V                                      VIP

## LADY AND THE HIGHWAYMAN, THE ***         PG
John Hough                UK                 1988
*Emma Samms, Oliver Reed, Claire Bloom, Christopher Cazenove, Lysette Antony, Hugh Grant, Michael York, Gordon Jackson, Gareth Hunt, John Mills, Robert Morley, Bernard Miles*
Standard British swashbuckler, set in the Civil War period and with all the stock characters. Despite being fairly predictable an excellent cast and good production values sustain it.
Boa: novel Cupid Rides Pillion by Barbara Cartland.
A/AD                       90 min (ort 100 min) mTV
V                                        PARK

## LADY AND THE TRAMP, THE ****   U
Hamilton Luske/Clyde Geronimi/Wilfred Jackson
USA                                    1955
*Voices of: Peggy Lee, Barbara Luddy, Bill Thompson,*
*Bill Baucon, Stan Freberg, Verna Felton, Alan Reed,*
*George Givot, Dallas McKennon, Lee Millar*
One of Disney's most delightful cartoons, in which a
pedigree dog runs away from home after the arrival of
a baby makes her feel unwanted, and meets up with a
stray who lives by his wits. The two dogs survive
various hazards and win through in the end, when
they prove their worth by rescuing the baby. The first
Disney film in Cinemascope, and a skilful (if anthropomorphic) blend of comedy, drama and pathos. Songs
are by Peggy Lee and Sonny Burke.
CAR                                  77 min
V/sh                                     WDV

## LADY AVENGER *                         18
David De Cocteau          USA           1987
*Peggie Sanders, Tony Josephs, Jacolyn Leeman,*
*Daniel Hirsch, Bill Butler*
Standard vigilante tale in which a woman goes back
to L.A. for her brother's funeral, and tries to find out
how he died. The gang responsible nearly beat her to
death and so she decides to takes them on herself. An
implausible exploiter with the obligatory lashings of
violence.
A/AD         77 min (ort 92 min) Cut (2 min 26 sec)
B,V                                      PAL

## LADY BEWARE ***                        18
Karen Arthur              USA           1987
*Diane Lane, Michael Woods, Cotter Smith, Viveca*
*Lindfors, Peter Nevargic, Edward Penn, Tyra Ferrell*
A psychopath becomes obsessed with a woman win-
dow dresser because he interprets the displays she
arranges as sexual signals. The usual campaign of
terror ensues. Predictable it may be, but the perform-
ances compel attention.
THR                        103 min (ort 108 min)
B,V                                      MED

## LADY BLUE **                           15
Gary Nelson               USA           1985
*Jamie Rose, Danny Aiello, Katy Jurado, Kate*
*Mahoney, Babi Besch, Jim Brown, Tony LoBianco,*
*Marco Rodriguez, Ajay Naidu, Ron Dean, Zaid Farid,*
*Henry Godinez, Ricardo Guiterrez, John Mahoney,*
*Steven Memel, Kathryn Jodsten*
A hardboiled female cop uses unconventional methods
to trap a murderer who wiped out an entire family.
Pilot for a violent and short-lived TV series. A kind of
feminist answer to DIRTY HARRY, with all the
appropriate trimmings.
DRA                    91 min (ort 104 min) mTV
B,V                                      MGM

## LADY CAROLINE LAMB *
Robert Bolt             ITALY/UK         1972
*Sarah Miles, Jon Finch, Richard Chamberlain,*
*Laurence Olivier, John Mills, Margaret Leighton,*
*Ralph Richardson, Pamela Brown, Silvia Monti, Peter*
*Bull, Charles Carson, Sonia Dresdel, Nicholas Field,*
*Robert Harris*
The tempestuous affair between a young married
aristocratic lady and the famous poet Lord Byron,
makes for a remarkably dull film that follows in
laborious detail the tortuous sequence of passion and
humiliation that outraged contemporary society. The
ridiculous script is by Bolt who also directed (if that is
not too strong a word).
DRA                        118 min (ort 123 min)
B,V                                      TEVP

## LADY CHATTERLEY'S LOVER *               18
Just Jaeckin          FRANCE/UK          1981
*Sylvia Kristel, Nicholas Clay, Shane Briant, Ann*
*Mitchell, Elizabeth Spriggs, Pascale Ridault, Anthony*

*Head, Frank Morey, Peter Bennett, Bessie Love, John*
*Tyanan, Michael Huston, Mark Colleano*
Soft-focus porno film with literary pretensions that
takes a vastly over-rated novel and turns it into a
mediocre romp, in which the wife of an impotent
mine-owner embarks on a wild affair with a
gamekeeper. Of little value except perhaps as a
chance to admire Kristel's beauty if not her acting
ability.
Aka: L'AMANT DE LADY CHATTERLEY
Boa: novel by D.H. Lawrence.
DRA                        99 min (ort 105 min)
V                                        RCA

## LADY FROM YESTERDAY, THE **            PG
Robert Day                USA           1984
*Wayne Rogers, Tina Chen, Bryan Price, Bonnie*
*Bedelia, Pat Hingle, Barrie Youngfellow, Blue Deckert,*
*Nicole Benton, Ruth Kibart, Paul Menzel, KaRan Neff*
*Reed, Beulah Quo, James Crittenden, H.F. Stone,*
*Maggie Egan*
A Vietnam veteran finds that his life is completely
upset by the arrival of his former Vietnamese girl-
friend and their son. Something like the opposite of
GREEN EYES (in which our veteran was doing the
searching) but quite competently handled.
DRA                                  92 min mTV
B,V                                      ODY

## LADY GODIVA RIDES AGAIN **             18
A.C. Stephen              USA           1969
*Liz Rene, Sherri Jackson, Vincent Barbi, Johnny Ellis,*
*Marsha Jordan, Forman Share*
Period sex comedy based on the director's own novel.
Aka: LADY GODIVA MEETS TOM JONES; LADY
GODIVA RIDES
Boa: novel Lady Godiva And Tom Jones by A.C.
Stephen.
A                                    83 min
B,V          18PLAT/TOW; PHE (VHS only)

## LADY GREY *
Worth Keeter              USA           1980
*Ginger Alden, David Allen Coe, Paul Ott, Herman*
*Bloodsworth, Ed Grady, Paula Baldwin*
The story of an aspiring female country singer and
how her career fails due to a tragic event. A rather
humdrum affair that is not even enlivened by particu-
larly good music. Filmed in North Carolina.
DRA                                 100 min
B,V                                  INT/CBS

## LADY HAMILTON ***                      PG
Alexandra Korda           USA           1941
*Laurence Olivier, Vivien Leigh, Gladys Cooper, Alan*
*Mowbray, Sara Allgood, Henry Wilcoxon, Heather*
*Angel, Halliwell Hobbes*
An excellent film about Nelson's lifelong relationship
with Emma Hamilton that is somewhat glamorised
and stiff but generally extremely effective. The music
is by Miklos Rozsa.
Aka: THAT HAMILTON WOMAN
DRA       100 min; 119 min (PICK) (ort 128 min) B/W
B,V,V2                     GOV; PICK (VHS only)

## LADY ICE *
Tom Gries                 USA           1973
*Donald Sutherland, Jennifer O'Neil, Robert Duvall,*
*Patrick Magee, Eric Braeden, Jon Cypher*
An insurance investigator teams up with the daugh-
ter of a criminal in order to steal a diamond in this
coldly unappealing thriller, that fails to exploit the
talents of a fine cast. The script is by Alan Trustman
and Harold Clemens.
Boa: story by Alan Trustman.
THR                                  92 min
B,V,V2                                   VIPCO

## LADY IN A CORNER **
Peter Levin                    USA                    PG
                                                      1989
*Lindsay Frost, Brian Keith, Loretta Young*
The editor of a fashion magazine returns from her
vacation to find that the publisher of a pornographic
magazine has launched a take-over bid. Facing the
prospect of the destruction of her career she sets out to
find an alternative investor.
DRA                                             90 min
V                                          PRISM L/A

## LADY IN RED, THE **
Lewis Teague                   USA                    18
                                                      1979
*Pamela Sue Martin, Robert Conrad, Louise Fletcher,
Robert Hogan, Laurie Heineman, Glenn Withrow,
Christopher Lloyd, Dick Miller*
A farmgirl goes to Chicago in the 1930s and finds it
impossible to make an honest living. Circumstances
force her into prostitution and into a liason with the
gangster John Dillinger. A Roger Corman production
that suffers from the low budget but works quite well.
The script is by John Sayles.
Aka: GUNS, SIN AND BATHTUB GIN
THR                                             93 min
B,V                                          EAG; GLOB

## LADY IN WHITE ***
Frank LaLoggia                 USA                    15
                                                      1988
*Lukas Haas, Katherine Helmond, Len Cariou, Alex
Rocco, Jason Presson, Jared Rushton, Renata Vanni,
Angelo Bertolini*
A youngster becomes intrigued by stories of the
mysterious title character said to haunt a nearby
house, and finds himself involved in an unsolved
murder case. Set in the 1960s, this effective chiller
doesn't lack for atmosphere, even if the final outcome
is rather easy to guess.
HOR                                  109 min (ort 112 min)
V                                               VIR

## LADY IS A WHORE, THE *
Osmiros Efstratiades  GREECE                          18
                                                      1972
*Anna Fonsou, Christos Nomikos, Andrea Barkoulis,
Marc Elliot, Helen Roda, Nina Sgouridou, E.
Georgitsis, Elias Kapetanidis, Costas Davas, G.
Matheou, M. Assariotou, V. Konstantinidou, G.
Kokalos*
A businessman's wife turns prostitute in order to
satisfy her voracious sexual appetite, and indulges in
a series of orgies but eventually commits suicide.
Edifying it is not.
Aka: NAUGHTY NIGHTS (PACEV); TWO FACES
OF LOVE, THE
A              79 min; 102 min (PACEV) (ort 125 min)
B,V                                  INT; PACEV (VHS only)

## LADY JANE **
Trevor Nunn                    UK                     PG
                                                      1985
*Jane Lapotaire, John Wood, Patrick Stewart, Sara
Kestelman, Helena Bonham Carter, Cary Elwes,
Michael Hordern, Jill Bennett, Joss Ackland, Warren
Saire, Roger Vernon, Ian Hogg, Richard Johnson*
Historical drama about Lady Jane Grey, who was
Queen of England for a mere seven days in 1553. A
solid account that is rather too slow to really hold the
attention. This story was filmed once before as "Tudor
Rose" (1936).
DRA                                  136 min (ort 142 min)
V/sh                                            CIC

## LADY OF THE HOUSE ***
Ralph Nelson/Vincent Sherman                         15
                               USA                    1978
*Dyan Cannon, Armand Assante, Zohra Lampert,
Susan Tyrrell, Colleen Camp, Christopher Norris,
Jesse Dizon, Maggie Cooper, Anthony Charnota, Sam
Freed, Kim Hamilton, Melvin Belli, Charlie Murphy,
Tom Rosqui, Chris Nelson*
A San Francisco madam gradually rises in the world

and finally attains power and respectability in this
1930s tale largely based on the career of Sally
Stanford, a celebrated San Francisco madam of the
time. (She eventually became mayor of Sausalito in
California in 1976.) The intelligent script is by Ron
Koslow.
Boa: book Sally Stanford.
DRA                                  88 min (ort 100 min) mTV
B,V                                       IFS L/A; AVR

## LADY TAKES A CHANCE, A ***
William A. Seiter              USA                    1943
*John Wayne, Jean Arthur, Phil Silvers, Charles
Winninger, Mary Field, Don Costello*
A naive girl from the big-city on holiday in Oregon
falls for a rodeo rider, in this gently appealing if
somewhat thin romantic comedy.
Aka: COWBOY AND THE GIRL, THE
Osca: FIRST TRAVELING SALESLADY, THE (asa)
COM                                  80 min (ort 86 min) B/W
B,V                                             KVD

## LADY TRUCKERS ***
Robert Greenwald               USA                    PG
                                                      1979
*Annie Potts, Kim Darby, Harry Dean Stanton, Arthur
Godfrey, Rory Calhoun, Fred Willard, Avery
Schreiber, Billy Carter, Rance Howard, Julie Mannix,
Don Pike, Robert Herron, Lorna Thayer, Ann Ryerson,
Joseph Sheer, Lawrence Bame*
Two lady truckers work very hard to keep their truck
on the road and out of the hands of the repossessors as
well as a gang out to hijack it. An enjoyable and lively
piece of nonsense. The pilot film for a TV series.
Aka: FLATBED ANNIE AND SWEETIEPIE;
FLATBED ANNIE AND SWEETIEPIE: LADY
TRUCKERS
A/AD                                 95 min (ort 100 min) mTV
B,V                                     VFP; IVS; CHV

## LADY VANISHES, THE *
Anthony Page                   UK                     PG
                                                      1979
*Elliott Gould, Cybill Shepherd, Angela Lansbury,
Herbert Lom, Arthur Lowe, Ian Carmichael, Jenny
Runacre, Gerald Harper, Jean Anderson, Vladek
Sheybal, Medlena Nedeva, Wolf Kahler, Madge Ryan,
Rosalind Knight, Jonathan Hackett*
A dismally flawed remake of the 1938 original which,
although fairly faithful to the story (lady vanishes en
route back to England from Switzerland) is fatally
ruined by incompetent casting. The script is by George
Axelrod.
Boa: novel The Wheel Spins by Ethel Lina White.
DRA                                  99 min; 96 min (VCC)
B,V,LV                                RNK; VCC (VHS only)

## LADY VANISHES, THE ****
Alfred Hitchcock               UK                     U
                                                      1938
*Margaret Lockwood, Michael Redgrave, Paul Lukas,
Dame May Whitty, Cecil Parker, Linden Travers, Mary
Clare, Naunton Wayne, Basil Radford, Emile Boreo,
Googie Withers, Philip Leaver, Catherine Lacey,
Charles Oliver*
Enjoyable film in which two people investigate the
disappearance of an old woman from a train, and
discover a plot to pretend she was never on the train in
the first place. A lively comedy-drama that, though
somewhat over-rated, has many good things in it, not
least being the witty script (by Frank Launder and
Sidney Gilliat) and some splendid performances.
Remade in 1979.
Boa: novel The Wheel Spins by Ethel Lina White.
DRA                                  93 min (ort 95 min) B/W
B,V,LV                                          RNK

## LADY WHIRLWIND *
                               HONG KONG              1971
*Angela Mao, Chang Yi*
Male and female fighters join forces in this unmemor-
able kung fu adventure.

MAR                                    85 min
B,V                                       RNK

## LADY WITH A LAMP, THE ***                U
Herbert Wilcox          UK              1951
*Anna Neagle, Michael Wilding, Gladys Young, Felix
Aylmer, Julia D'Albie, Arthur Young, Helena Pickard,
Peter Graves, Sybil Thorndike, Monckton Hoffe,
Charles Carson, Edwin Styles, Barbara Couper, Helen
Shingler, Nigel Stock*
A workmanlike account of Florence Nightingale's
pioneering efforts in the field of nursing, well acted if
somewhat less than accurate in terms of historical
detail. Neagle is particularly well cast.
Boa: play by Reginald Berkeley.
DRA                                  110 min B/W
V                                        WHV

## LADY, STAY DEAD *
Terry Bourke       AUSTRALIA          1982
*Chard Hayward, Louise Hewitt, Deborah Coulls,
Roger Ward, Lex Foxcroft, James Elliott*
A psychotic gardener preys on his female employers,
murdering them in a variety of grisly ways. A gory
tale set in an Australian beach resort.
HOR                                     91 min
B,V,V2                                 INT/CBS

## LADYHAWKE ***                            PG
Richard Donner          USA             1985
*Rutger Hauer, Michelle Pfeiffer, Leo McKern, Matthew
Broderick, John Wood, Richard Donner, Lauren
Schuler, Ken Hutchison, Alfred Molina, Giancarlo
Prete, Loris Loddi, Alessandro Serra, Charles
Borromel, Massimo Sarchielli*
Medieval fantasy in which two young lovers change at
night into a wolf and a hawk because of a spell cast by
an evil bishop. Overlong but generally quite well
sustained, despite bad casting of Broderick and the
intrusive score by Andrew Powell.
FAN                         118 min (ort 124 min)
V/sh                                      CBS

## LADYKILLERS *                            15
Robert Lewis            USA             1988
*Lesley-Anne Down, Susan Blakely, Marilu Henner,
William Lucking*
A role-reversal thriller in which a female cop investi-
gates a series of killings at a disco, the victims this
time being male strippers. Doleful nonsense.
THR                         95 min (ort 100 min) mTV
B, V/sh                                COL; MSD

## LADYKILLERS, THE ****                     U
Alexandra Mackendrick UK                1955
*Alec Guinness, Katie Johnson, Peter Sellers, Cecil
Parker, Herbert Lom, Danny Green, Frankie Howerd,
Jack Warner, Philip Stainton, Fred Griffiths, Kenneth
Connor, Edie Martin, Jack Melford, Ewan Roberts,
Harold Goodwin*
Amusing black comedy about a little old lady who lets
a room to a man who is regularly visited by his
friends. They pretend to be musicians but are really
planning a robbery. A minor classic with a wonderful
performance from Guinness. The script is by William
Rose.
COM                           86 min (ort 97 min)
B,V                           TEVP; WHV (VHS only)

## LAGUNA HEAT **                           18
Simon Langton           USA             1987
*Harry Hamlin, Jason Robards, Rip Torn, Catherine
Hicks, Anne Francis, James Gammon*
An L.A. cop goes back to his home town but finds its
former tranquility shattered by a series of murders
that seem to be linked in some way to people
associated with his father. Generally atmospheric but
a little stolid in pacing.
Boa: novel by T. Jefferson Parker.

THR                        105 min (ort 110 min) mCab
B,V                                       GHV

## LAIR OF THE WHITE WORM, THE ***           18
Ken Russell             UK              1988
*Amanda Donohue, Hugh Grant, Catherine Oxenberg,
Peter Capaldi, Sammi Davis, Stratford Johns*
The screenplay is by Russell in this overblown (as
ever) and over-ripe adaptation of Stoker's novel,
telling of an archaeologist's investigations into an
estate where a huge wormlike skull was discovered,
and his discovery that some of these bizarre creatures
are alive and well. Generally far too self-indulgent to
work as a horror yarn, but as a farce it is effective.
Boa: novel by Bram Stoker.
HOR                                     90 min
V                                         VES

## LAMA AVENGER, THE **
                       HONG KONG
*Bruce Li (Ho Tsung-Tao)*
A kung fu hero fights school bullies in this standard
effort.
MAR                                     87 min
B,V,V2                                    VPD

## LAMBADA *                                15
Joel Silberg            USA             1990
*J. Eddie Peck, Melora Hardin, Keene Curtis, Shabba-
Doo, Ricky Paull Goldin, Basil Hoffman, Dennis
Burkley*
A maths teacher at a posh Beverly Hills school has a
secret identity, for as "Blade" he dances the night
away at a seedy club in East L.A., where he tries to
stimulate an interest in education on the part of the
underprivileged kids he encounters there. A crude
attempt to exploit a sensuous Brazilian dance style
that's all surface and no depth; a few good dance
sequences (choreographed by Shabba-Doo) are the
best things in it.
Aka: LAMBADA: SET THE NIGHT ON FIRE
MUS                                    104 min
V/sh                                     PATHE

## LAMBADA: THE FORBIDDEN DANCE *            15
Greydon Clark           USA             1989
*Laura Herring, Jeff James, Sid Haig, Richard Lynch*
A rainforest princess goes to the USA to protest about
the destruction of her habitat and teaches her native
dance to a rich man with whom she falls in love. They
enter and win a dance contest, giving her a chance to
appear on TV and appeal for help in stopping a
powerful logging corporation who are cutting down
the trees. The dancing is the best thing in this
cynically exploitative film, whose ecological sub-plot
is entirely out of place.
MUS                                     97 min
V                                        PATHE

## LAMP, THE ***                            18
Tom Daly                USA             1986
*Deborah Winters, James Huston, Scott Bankston,
Andra St Ivanyi, Danny Daniels, Mark Mitchell,
Andre Chimene, Damon Merrill, Barry Coffing, Tracye
Walker, Raan Lewis, Hank Amigo, Brian Floores,
Michelle Watkins, Coy Sevier*
A girl discovers a lamp at her father's museum, and
unwittingly releases a nasty demon when she rubs it
(the lamp that is). Under the spell of said demon, she
invites some of her chums back to the museum to
spend Halloween there, and our demon arranges a
series of gruesome surprises. Quite a predictable film,
but not without a good number of chilling effects.
Aka: OUTING, THE
HOR                         85 min (Cut at film release)
B,V                                  IVS; BRAVE

## LAND BEFORE TIME, THE ***                 U
Don Bluth               USA             1988

*Voices of: Pat Hingle, Gabriel Damon, Helen Shaver, Candice Houston, Judith Barsi, Will Ryan, Burke Barnes*
When a young dinosaur is orphaned, he sets off with several of his fellows to find a secret valley where they can find safety from a plague that is ravaging the world. On the way they experience danger but also have several amusing encounters. Excellent animation work helps sustain this sluggish yarn, which could so easily have been a great deal better (and certainly more colourful).
CAR                                        69 min
V                                           CIC

## LAND OF DOOM *                          18
Peter Maris            USA               1984
*Deborah Rannard, Garrick Dowhen, Daniel Radell, Frank Garrett, Richard Allen*
In a post-atomic world peopled by mutant survivors, a man and a woman battle for survival.
FAN            83 min (ort 96 min) Cut (14 sec)
B,V                                    PEGA/MED

## LAND OF NO RETURN, THE *                 U
Kent Bateman         USA   1975 (released 1978)
*Mel Torme, William Shatner, Donald Moffat*
Typical survival epic about an animal trainer who survives a plane crash in Utah, that is of little interest except for the scenery.
Aka: CHALLENGE TO SURVIVE; SNOWMAN; SURVIVAL ELEMENT (WARAD)
DRA                    85 min; 80 min (KRP)
B,V,V2            VDB L/A; WARAD L/A; KRP

## LAND THAT TIME FORGOT, THE ***           PG
Kevin Connor           UK                1974
*Doug McClure, John McEnery, Susan Penhaligon, Keith Barron, Anthony Ainley, Declan Mulholland, Godfrey James, Bobby Farr, Ben Howard, Colin Farrell, Roy Holder, Andrew McCulloch, Grahame Mallard, Brian Hall, Peter Sproule*
Germans and Americans on board a submarine discover an island of prehistoric monsters and savages in this engaging fantasy yarn that is let down by rather poor special effects. Followed by THE PEOPLE THAT TIME FORGOT.
Boa: novel by Edgar Rice Burroughs.
A/AD                        87 min (ort 91 min)
B,V                      TEVP; WHV (VHS only)

## LANGUAGE OF LOVE 2 *                      18
Torgny Wickman      SWEDEN            1983
*Inge Hegeler, Sten Hegeler, Maj-Brith Bergstrom-Walen*
Tiresome documentary masquerading as a sex film.
Aka: KARLEKENS SPRAK 2
A       85 min (ort 92 min) (Cut cinema release version)
V                                          SHEP

## LAS VEGAS GIRLS **
Troy Benny             USA               1981
*Karen Hall, Liz Renay, Brian Jensen, Cynthia Morrow, Drea, Raymond Andres, Brad Ashley, Jesse Ronald, William Margold*
Sex film with a gambling background. A wealthy Texan hires a private eye in order to find his missing daughter, who he suspects has run off to Las Vegas and is working as a hooker (she has done this before). The detective and his female assistant visit just about every dive in town, before discovering that she has flown off to Mexico to marry a wealthy rancher. So they go to bed instead.
A                                        76 min
B,V,V2                                     ELV

## LAS VEGAS WEEKEND **                      15
Dale Trevillion        USA               1986
*Barry Hickey, Jace Damon, Macka Foley, Vickie Benson, Kimberlee Kaiser, Dyanne Di Rosario*

A compulsive gambler loses his university scholarship and goes to Las Vegas to test out a system he has evolved, in a final desperate attempt to recoup his losses.
COM                                       83 min
B,V                                  IVS; GLOB

## LASERBLAST **
Michael Raye          USA               1978
*Kim Milford, Cheryl Smith, Roddy McDowall, Ron Masak, Keenan Wynn, Dennis Burkley, Gianni Russo, Barry Cutler, Mike Bobenko, Eddie Deezen*
A teenager finds an alien weapon that gives him great power to destroy his enemies until the aliens intervene and take away his toy. A poorly conceived and low-budget yarn. The special effects are by David Allen.
FAN                                       87 min
B,V                                   INT/CBS

## LASSIE **                                 U
William Beaudine Sr    USA              1962
*Lassie, Jon Provost, Hugh Reilly, June Lockhart, Richard Simmons, Richard Kiel, Walter Stocker*
Lassie and her master are carried off in a runaway balloon and are stranded in the Canadian wilderness. An undemanding effort that now looks very dated indeed. Compiled from four segments of the TV series.
Aka: LASSIE'S GREAT ADVENTURE
JUV    90 min; 99 min (VCC) (ort 103 min) B/W mTV
B,V,V2                    VCL; VCC (VHS only)

## LASSITER **                               18
Roger Young            USA               1984
*Tom Selleck, Lauren Hutton, Jane Seymour, Bob Hoskins, Joe Regalbuto, Warren Clarke, Ed Lauter, Edward Peel, Paul Antrim, Christopher Malcolm, Barrie Houghton, Peter Skellern, Harry Towb, Belinda Mayne, Morgan Sheppard*
An ace jewel thief in London in 1936 uses his skills to steal documents from the German embassy, having been blackmailed by Scotland Yard into accepting this dangerous assignment. Quite carefully made, but the pedestrian pacing spoils it.
DRA                        96 min (ort 100 min)
B,V                                        RNK

## LAST AMERICAN HERO, THE ***              PG
Lamont Johnson        USA               1973
*Jeff Bridges, Valerie Perrine, Geraldine Fitzgerald, Art Lund, Gary Busey, Ed Lauter, Ned Beatty*
A backwoods moonshiner and racing fanatic pits his wits against the established authorities. Extremely convincing characterisations are the mainstay of this witty and offbeat hillbilly comedy-drama (based to some extent on the early career of racing driver Junior Johnson).
Aka: HARD DRIVER
DRA                         91 min (ort 95 min)
B,V                                        CBS

## LAST AMERICAN VIRGIN, THE **             18
Boaz Davidson          USA               1982
*Lawrence Monoson, Diane Franklin, Steve Autin, Louisa Moritz*
From the same team that brought us LEMON POPSICLE. Three randy kids try to get their girlfriends to co-operate. A standard comedy slightly redeemed by the attractive cast if not by the script.
COM                      92 min; 88 min (GHV)
B,V,V2                               MSD; GHV

## LAST CHANCE *                             15
Alastair Brown                           1987
*Jane Seaborn, Robin Dene, Simon Wolfe, Richard Woods*
A retired Mafia hit-man lives quietly in Australia, until the collapse of a drugs ring results in him being forced to fight some ruthless crooks sent to kill him.

A/AD                                90 min
B,V                                 PACEV

**LAST CHILD, THE ***
John Llewellyn Moxey    USA          1973
*Michael Cole, Van Heflin, Edward Asner, Harry
Guardino, Janet Margolin, Kent Smith, Michael
Larrain, Phillip Bourneuf, Barbara Babcock, Victor
Izay, James A. Watson Jr, Sondra Blake, Roy Engle,
Phyllis Avery, Ivor Francis*
Echoes the same theme as ZERO POPULATION
GROWTH; in 1994 the US Government decrees one
child per family. A couple have to flee to Canada and
are helped by a senator. Quite a compelling little
piece, despite the lack of a close examination of the
kind of society that would accept such a decree.
DRA                                 71 min mTV
B,V                                 RNK

**LAST CONFLICT, THE ***                    15
John O'Conner          USA           198-
*David Janssen, Christopher Stone*
An American Intelligence agent tries to avert a
nuclear conflict after a B52 bomber is launched by
mistake. Average.
A/AD                                90 min
V                                   ARF

**LAST DAY, THE ***                         PG
Vincent McEveety       USA           1975
*Richard Widmark, Christopher Connelly, Loretta
Swit, Robert Conrad, Gene Evans, Richard Jaeckel,
Tim Matheson, Barbara Rush, Tom Skerritt, Morgan
Woodward, Kathleen Cody, Jon Locke, Bryan O'Byrne,
William Brawley*
A retired gunman is forced to defend his town against
the Dalton gang in this simple and fairly adequate
tale, done in a restrained almost documentary style
(complete with narration – courtesy of Harry
Morgan).
Boa: story by Steve Fisher and A.C. Lyles.
WES                                 93 min (ort 100 min) mTV
B,V                                 ARENA/CIC

**LAST DAYS OF FRANK AND JESSE
JAMES, THE ***                              15
William A. Graham      USA           1986
*Johnny Cash, Kris Kristofferson, Willie Nelson, Ed
Bruce, June Carter Cash, David Allan Lee, David Allan
Coe, Andrew Stahl, June Carter Cash, Marcia Cross,
Darell Wilks, Margaret Gibson, James Sinclair, Cherie
Elledge Grapes*
Another attempt to squeeze some mileage out of the
exploits of these notorious bandits. Colourful perform-
ances (especially Nelson's as a Confederate general)
are hampered by unimaginative direction.
WES                                 96 min mTV
B,V                                 VES

**LAST DAYS OF PATTON, THE ***              PG
Delbert Mann           USA           1985
*George C. Scott, Eva Marie Saint, Richard Dysart, Lee
Patterson, Ed Lauter, Murray, Hamilton, Kathryn
Leigh Scott, Horst Janson, Daniel Benzali, Ron
Berglas, Don Fellows, Errol John, Alan
MacNaughtan, Paul Maxwell*
Scott reprises the role he created in PATTON in this
account of the last six months in the life of this
colourful WW2 general. No more than adequate with
a ludicrous and tiresome deathbed scene that just goes
on and on. The script is by William Luce.
Boa: book by Ladislas Farago.
DRA                                 140 min (ort 180 min) mTV
V/h                                 CBS

**LAST DAYS OF POMPEII, THE ***
Mario Bonnard          ITALY         1960
*Steve Reeves, Christine Kaufman, Barbara Carroll,
Anne Marie Baumann, Mimmo Palmara, Fernando*

*Rey, Guillerma Marin, Angel Aranda*
Routine version with the usual trappings of historical
costumers made in Italy during this period. Very short
on spectacle.
Boa: novel by Lord Edward Bulwer-Lytton.
DRA                                 98 min (Ort 105 min)
B,V                                 VFO

**LAST DAYS OF POMPEII, THE ***
Ernest B. Schoedsack   USA           1935
*Preston Foster, Basil Rathbone, Dorothy Wilson, Alan
Hale, David Holt, John Wood, Louis Calhern*
A gladiator fights his way to the top, and several other
dramas are played out against the background of this
doomed city. The spectacular destruction scenes are
really what make this movie, and when they arrive
they do not disappoint. Remade for TV in 1984.
Boa: novel by Lord Edward Bulwer-Lytton.
Osca: MYSTERIOUS DESPERADO, THE
DRA                                 92 min (ort 96 min) B/W
B,V                                 KVD

**LAST DETAIL, THE ***                      18
Hal Ashby              USA           1973
*Jack Nicholson, Otis Young, Randy Quaid, Clifton
James, Carol Kane, Michael Moriarty, Nancy Allen*
Two sailors escorting a prisoner, to serve a long
sentence in a naval prison for a trivial theft, try to
give him a good time before he goes inside. A complex
movie that has strong characterisations, with a
downbeat but rather appropriate ending. Written by
Robert Towne.
Boa: novel by Darryl Ponicsan.
DRA                                 100 min (ort 105 min)
V                                   RCA

**LAST DRAGON, THE ***                      15
Michael Schultz        USA           1985
*Taimak, Julius J. Carey III, Chris Murray, Leo
O'Brien, Thomas Ikeda, Faith Prince, Vanity, Mike
Starr, Jim Moody, Glen Eaton, Ernie Reyes Jr, Roger
Campbell, Esther Marrow, Keshia Knight Pullam,
Jamal Mason*
Story of a kung fu quest by a disciple of the martial
arts. On his way, he has to rescue a young damsel and
fight the self-styled Shogun of Harlem. Ponderous
overblown nonsense, very clumsy and disorganised.
Aka: BERRY GORDON'S THE LAST DRAGON;
LAST DRAGONS, THE
MAR                                 107 min Cut (1 min 59 sec)
B,V                                 CBS

**LAST ELECTRIC KNIGHT, THE ***            U
James Fargo            USA           1986
*Gil Gerard, Ernie Reyes Jr, Keye Luke, Nancy
Stafford, Jason Hervey*
The grandson of an oriental mystic acquires a cop
foster-father on the death of his own grandfather, and
he uses his strange powers to aid him in his fight
against drug dealers. A dull pilot for a TV series called
"Sidekicks".
Aka: SIDEKICKS
Osca: TWO AND A HALF DADS
JUV                                 44 min (ort 60 min) mTV
B,V                                 WDV

**LAST EMBRACE, THE ***                     18
Jonathan Demme         USA           1979
*Roy Scheider, Janet Margolin, John Glover, Sam
Levene, Christopher Walken, Charles Napier*
An agent's wife is killed in an attack meant for him
and he is forced to go underground. A tight and
punchy thriller that builds up to an exciting climax at
Niagara Falls. The score is by Miklos Rozsa.
Boa: novel The 13th Man by Murray Teigh Bloom.
THR                                 98 min (ort 101 min)
B,V                                 WHV

**LAST EMPEROR, THE ****                    15
Bernardo Bertolucci

CHINA/ITALY/UK          1987
*John Lone, Joan Chen, Peter O'Toole, Ying Ruocheng,
Victor Wong, Dennis Dun, Ryuichi Sakamoto, Maggie
Han, Ric Young, Wu Vuu, Tijger Tsou, Wu Tao, Fan
Guang*
Vast, sprawling epic account of China's last emperor
that spares no expense in following the career of Pu
Yi, from his cloistered upbringing to his enforced exile
after being deposed. A cold but lavish odyssey. AA:
Pic, Dir, Screen (Adapt) (M. Peploe/B. Bertolucci), Cin
(V. Storaro), Art/Set (F. Scarfiotti/B. Cesari and O.
Desideri), Cost (J. Acheson), Sound (B. Rowe/I. Shar-
rock), Edit (G. Cristiani), Score (Orig) (R. Sakamoto/
D. Byrne/C. Su).
Boa: book by Pu Yi.
DRA                          156 min (ort 164 min)
V/sh                                          RCA

## LAST EXIT TO BROOKLYN ***          18
Uli Edel          WEST GERMANY          1989
*Stephen Lang, Jennifer Jason Leigh, Burt Young,
Peter Dobson, Jerry Orbach, Stephen Baldwin, Ricki
Lake, John Costelloe*
Written by Desmond Nakano, this is a harsh and
gloomy adaptation of Selby's cult novel, which paints
a brutal and uncompromising picture of life around a
1950s Brooklyn waterfront, where poverty, crime and
labour unrest are the most influential features of life.
Despite being memorable for its detail and strong
characterisation, the film suffers from a lack of focus
and a shortage of sympathetic characters.
Boa: novel by Hubert Selby Jr.
DRA                          99 min (ort 102 min)
V                                             GHV

## LAST FEELINGS *          PG
Ruggero Deodato          ITALY          1978
*Maurizio Rossi, Vittoria Galeazzi, Carlo Lupo*
A boy from the streets makes the big-time as a
swimmer, before succumbing to a fatal illness in this
dreary and manipulative mess.
Aka: L'ULTIMO SAPORE DELL'ARIA
DRA   93 min (ort 98 min) Cut (4 sec in addition to film
cuts)
B,V                          ARCADE/VSP L/A; VGM

## LAST FIGHT, THE *
Fred Williamson          USA          1983
*Joe Spinell, Ruben Blades, Willie Colon, Darlanne
Fluegel, Nereida Mercado, Don King, Jose "Chegui"
Torres*
A man seeks revenge on the Mob for murdering his
father, in this dull and cliched tale of a singer-turned-
boxer who aims for the world championship.
DRA                          86 min (ort 88 min)
B,V,V2                                     VCL/CBS

## LAST FLIGHT OF NOAH'S ARK, THE *          U
Charles Jarrott          USA          1980
*Elliott Gould, Genevieve Bujold, Ricky Schroder,
Tammy Lauren, John Fujioka, Yuki Shimoda,
Vincent Gardenia, Dana Elcar*
An assorted planeload of humans and animals are
forced down on a Pacific island, and get help from an
unexpected source in their attempts to return to
civilisation. A messy and cumbersome affair, saddled
with limp direction.
Boa: story The Gremlin's Castle by Ernest K. Gann.
DRA                          97 min
B,V                                           WDV

## LAST FLIGHT OUT **          PG
USA          1989
*Richard Crenna, James Earl Jones, Haing S. Ngor*
A dullish TV drama that attempts to recreate the
chaos of those few last days in Saigon during 1975,
just before the fall of the South Vietnamese regime,
when Pan-Am was the last commercial airline operating from there. We follow the fortunes of a number of

its employees as they desperately struggle to bring
family and friends to safety.
DRA                          94 min mTV
V                                             ODY

## LAST FLING, THE **          15
Corey Allen          USA          1986
*John Ritter, Connie Selleca, Randee Heller, Paul
Sand, Scott Bakula, John Bennett Perry, Shannon
Tweed*
On the eve of her marriage to a somewhat dull
boyfriend, a woman decides to indulge in one last wild
affair. Adequately diverting if not exactly hilarious.
COM                          93 min (ort 100 min) mTV
B,V                                          SONY

## LAST FRONTIER, THE: PARTS 1 AND 2 **          15
Simon Wincer          USA          1986
*Linda Evans, Jack Thompson, Jason Robards Jr*
The story of an independent-spirited American widow
and her struggles on a farm in Australia, where when
not battling with her greedy neighbours she has to
contend with the hostile climate, financial problems
and the attraction she feels for a handsome renegade.
A flat and unconvincing performance from Evans
severely hampers this soap opera-style melodrama.
Average.
DRA                          240 min (2 cassettes) mTV
V                                             CASPIC

## LAST GIRAFFE, THE **          U
Jack Couffer          USA          1979
*Susan Anspach, Simon Ward, Gordon Jackson, Don
Warrington, Saeed Jaffrey, John Hallam, Rudoph
Walker*
Details a young conservationist couple's efforts to save
an endangered species of giraffe in Kenya, with our
couple ending up adopting an orphaned animal. A
mild safari adventure with some good outdoor work.
Boa: book Raising Daisy Rothchild by Jock and Betty
Leslie-Melville.
A/AD                          104 min mTV
B,V                                       SPEC/POLY

## LAST GLORY OF TROY, THE **
Giorgio Rivalta          ITALY          1962
*Steve Reeves, Carla Malier, Liana Orfei*
The story of the voyage from Troy to the future site of
the city of Rome, forms the basis for this routine
costumer.
Aka: AVENGER, THE; WAR OF THE TROJANS; LA
LEGGENDA DI ENEA
DRA                          100 min
B,V                                           VPD

## LAST GUN, THE **
Serge Bergen (Sergio Berganzelli)
ITALY/SPAIN          1964
*Cameron Mitchell, Carl Mohner, Celina Cely, Kitty
Carver*
A sheriff has to fight outlaws who have taken over his
town, and gets help from a mysterious former gunfigh-
ter who puts on his guns for one last shoot-out. A
standard European B-movie.
Aka: JIM IL PRIMO; KILLER'S CANYON
WES                          90 min
B,V,V2                                        VPD

## LAST HORROR FILM, THE *
David Winters          USA          1984
*Caroline Munro, Joe Spinell, Judd Hamilton, Robin
Leach, Devin Goldenberg, David Winters, Susanne
Benton, Mary Spinell, Glenn Jacobson, J'len Winters,
Sharon Hughes, Sean Casey, Don Talley, June
Chadwick, John Kelly*
A horror film star is followed to Cannes by an ardent
fan who starts killing those around her. An inadequ-
ate and messy yarn that goes nowhere.
Aka: FANATIC, THE

HOR 87 min
B,V,V2 ALPHA/INT/CBS

## LAST HOUSE ON THE LEFT PART 2, THE **
Mario Bava ITALY 1971
*Claudine Auger, Chris Avram, Luigi Pistilli, Claudio
Volonte, Anna Maria Rosati, Laura Betti, Brigitte
Skay, Isa Miranda, Leopoldo Triste, Paola Rubens*
Teenagers in an apparently deserted resort find
themselves at the mercy of a silent killer, as a series of
murders occur, all appearing to be linked in some way
to an attempt to possess a valuable piece of real estate.
A fair chiller that bears no relation to the similarly
titled "The Last House On The Left".
Aka: ANTEFFATO; BAY OF BLOOD; BEFORE THE
FACT; BLOODBATH BAY OF DEATH; CARNAGE;
ECOLOGIA DEL DELITTO; ECOLOGY OF A
CRIME, THE; REAZIONE A CATENA; TWITCH OF
THE DEATH NERVE
HOR 87 min
V MED

## LAST HUNTER, THE ** 18
Anthony M. Dawson (Antonio Margheriti)
ITALY 1980
*David Warbeck, Tisa Farrow, Tony King*
A female war correspondent and a US soldier are
caught up in the Vietnam War and find themselves
trapped behind enemy lines. Average.
Aka: IL CACCIATORE 2
WAR 92 min (ort 94 min) Cut (8 sec)
B,V INT/CBS; ILV L/A; ELE

## LAST INNOCENT MAN, THE *** 18
Roger Spottiswoode USA 1986
*Ed Harris, Roxanne Hart, David Suchet, Darrell
Larson, Bruce McGill, Rose Gregorio, Clarence
Williams III*
A disenchanted lawyer decides to leave his profession
but changes his mind after beginning a passionate
affair with a woman, who persuades him to defend her
husband against a charge of murder. An unusual
drama with arresting performances and a literate
script by Dan Bronson.
Boa: novel by Phillip M. Margolin.
DRA 109 min mCab
B,V GHV

## LAST MERCENARY, THE ** 18
Marlon Sirko 1984
*Tony Marsina, Ketty Nichols, Malcolm Duff, Louis
Walser*
A tough mercenary tries to save himself and a lady
friend from the perils of a war in the African bush.
Average.
Aka: ROLF
WAR 89 min Cut (38 sec)
B,V ECF L/A; IVS L/A; NET

## LAST MOMENTS ** PG
Mario Gariazzo ITALY 1974
*Lee J. Cobb, Renato Cestie, James Whitmore*
A small boy has to make his own way in the world of
showbiz, when his father is deserted by his wife and
partner. A real tearjerker.
DRA 100 min
B,V ARCADE/VSP; VGM

## LAST OF THE BADMEN ** 15
Nando Cicero ITALY 1977
*George Hilton, Frank Wolff, Pamela Tudor*
A ranch-hand turns outlaw and gets into trouble,
when his partner starts killing for fun in this
high-action spaghetti Western.
WES 91 min
B,V,V2 VDM L/A; STABL; PHE

## LAST OF THE MOHICANS ***
James L. Conway USA 1977

*Steve Forrest, Ned Romero, Don Shanks, Andrew
Prine, Robert Tessier, Jane Actman, Michele Marsh,
Robert Easton, Whit Bissell, Beverly Rowland, Dehl
Berti, John G. Bishop, Coleman Creel, Rosalyn Mike,
Reid Sorenson*
A "Classics Illustrated" version of this much-filmed
Western yarn about a white hunter and his Indian
blood brothers, who together help a British officer
escort two women through Indian country, at the time
of the French and Indian War. Colourful and spirited.
Boa: novel by James Fenimore Cooper.
WES 94 min (ort 100 min) mTV
B,V RNK

## LAST OF THE MOHICANS, THE *
Cano Mathew
*Jack Taylor, Barbara Loy, Paul Muller, Sara Lezana,
Luis Induni, Dan Martin*
Film version of a classic frontier story about a white
hunter and his Indian blood brother who accompany a
British officer escorting two women through Indian
country. An obscure, low-budget European produc-
tion.
Boa: novel by James Fenimore Cooper.
WES 104 min
B,V,V2 VPD

## LAST OF THE SUMMER WINE: GETTING SAM
HOME *** PG
Alan J.W. Bell UK 1983
*Brian Wilde, Bill Owen, Peter Sallis, Lynda Baron,
John Comer, Jane Freeman, Joe Gladwin, Peter
Russell, Kathy Staff*
Full-length feature based on the popular BBC comedy
series about three ageing ne'er-do-wells. In this
adventure the trio sneak a dying friend out of his
house, for one last night of passion with his mistress.
Aka: GETTING SAM HOME
COM 89 min mTV
B,V BBC

## LAST OF THE SUMMER WINE: UNCLE OF THE
BRIDE **
Alan J.W. Bell UK 1985
*Bill Owen, Peter Sallis, Michael Aldridge, Thora Hird,
Jane Freeman, Joe Gladwin, Kathy Staff*
Spin-off of a popular British TV series dealing with
the escapades of a trio of eccentric senior citizens in a
small Northern town. Various strange individuals
meet at a wedding in this feature.
Aka: UNCLE OF THE BRIDE
COM 85 min mTV
B,V BBC

## LAST OF THE VIKINGS **
Giacomo Gentilomo
FRANCE/ITALY 1960
*Cameron Mitchell, Edmund Purdom, Isabelle Corey,
Helene Remy*
An elaborate epic about the conflict between local
inhabitants and Viking raiding parties, that is made
with considerable verve but is rather handicapped by
poor casting and acting.
A/AD 100 min
B,V VPD

## LAST PLANE FROM CORAMAYA, THE ** PG
Randy Roberts USA 1989
*Louis Gossett Jr*
Another Gideon Oliver adventure, with our intrepid
professor travelling to a remote country that's in the
throes of a civil war. Once there, he attempts to find
an old colleague, despite having been told by the
military junta that the man in question committed
suicide whilst investigating an ancient religious artefact. The professor soon finds himself in much danger.
Fair. See also TONGS, SLEEP WELL, PROFESSOR
OLIVER and GIDEON'S WAR.

A/AD                                   91 min mTV
V                                            CIC

**LAST PLANE OUT** **
David Nelson           USA            1982
*Jan-Michael Vincent, Mary Crosby, Julie Carmen,*
*David Huffman, William Windom, Lloyd Battista,*
*Tonyo Melendez, Ronnie Gonzalez, Orlando Varona,*
*Anthony Feijoo, Yeg Wilson, William Fuller, Mary*
*Teahan, Juan Pedro Samoza*
An American journalist finds himself on a death-list
in Somoza's Nicaragua, and is mistrusted by both
sides. Produced by Jack Cox and largely drawn from
his experiences as a journalist, working in Nicaragua
in the final days of the Somoza regime. Average.
DRA                              90 min (ort 98 min)
B,V                                           VCL

**LAST PLATOON** *                              18
Paul D. Robinson        USA           1988
*Richard Hatch, Max Laurel, Anthony Sawyer, Vassili*
*Karis, Maricar, Donald Pleasence*
A bunch of raw recruits and their tough sergeant are
sent on a mission into the jungles of Vienam, but find
themselves trapped and at the mercy of the enemy. A
standard offering.
WAR                                        95 min
V                                            VPD

**LAST REBEL, THE** *
Denys McCoy             ITALY          1971
*Joe Namath, Jack Elam, Woody Strode, Ty Hardin,*
*Victoria George, Renato Romano, Marina Coffa,*
*Anmaria Chio, Mike Forrest, Bruce Ewelle, Jessica*
*Dublin, Larry Lawrence, Herb Andress*
Two Confederate soldiers escape rather than surren-
der and experience various adventures in this dismal
Italian effort.
WES                             85 min (ort 89 min)
B,V,V2                                        FFV

**LAST REMAKE OF BEAU GESTE, THE** *        PG
Marty Feldman           USA           1977
*Marty Feldman, Michael York, Ann-Margret, Peter*
*Ustinov, James Earl Jones, Trevor Howard, Henry*
*Gibson, Terry-Thomas, Avery Schreiber, Spike*
*Milligan, Roy Kinnear, Hugh Griffith, Irene Handl*
A spoof on those Foreign Legion films that fails to
weld a scattered collection of gags into a coherent
whole. Co-written by Feldman in his directorial debut.
COM                             80 min (ort 85 min)
B,V                                           CIC

**LAST RESORT, THE** **                        15
Zane Buzby              USA           1986
*Charles Grodin, Robin Pearson Rose, Megan Mullally,*
*John Ashton, Brenda Bakke, Gerrit Graham, Phil*
*Hartman*
A man takes his family to Club Sand, a Caribbean
resort where they find that the camp is a hangout for
sex-mad singles, with the occasional visit from the
local armed guerrillas. A scattershot comedy with a
few gems in amongst the dross. Written by Steve
Zacharias and Jeff Buhai. Buzby's directorial debut.
COM                                        76 min
B,V                                MMA L/A; VES

**LAST RITES** *                               18
Donald P. Bellisario    USA           1988
*Tom Berenger, Daphne Zuniga, Chick Vennera, Anne*
*Twomey, Dane Clark, Paul Dooley, Vassili Lambrinos*
A priest undertakes to protect a girl who is on a Mafia
hit-list and rather unsurprisingly falls in love with
her. Lifeless dross without one good idea but a host of
implausible ones (e.g. our priest is himself the son of a
Mafia boss).
DRA                                       120 min
V                                            MGM

**LAST ROMAN, THE** **
Robert Siodmak
              ROMANIA/WEST GERMANY         1968
*Orson Welles, Laurence Harvey, Sylva Koscina, Honor*
*Blackman, Michael Dunn, Harriet Andersson, Lang*
*Jeffries, Robert Hoffman*
Epic account of Roman history with the city under
attack from barbarian tribes. Spectacular this may be,
but none of the cast look as though they are enjoying
the experience. Edited down from a two-part film.
Boa: novel Kamf Und Rom by Felix Dann.
DRA                                       100 min
B,V,V2                                        VCL

**LAST RUN, THE** *                            18
Richard Fleischer       USA           1971
*George C. Scott, Tony Musante, Trish Van Devere,*
*Colleen Dewhurst*
A getaway driver retired and living in Portugal
cannot resist one last job just so as to prove he's still
up to scratch. Too bad the film isn't, though Sven
Nkvist's photography cannot be faulted. John Huston
started directing this one but Fleischer took over.
DRA                             92 min (ort 99 min)
B,V                                           MGM

**LAST SONG, THE** **
Alan J. Levi            USA           1980
*Lynda Carter, Ronny Cox, Charles Aidman, Paul*
*Rudd, Nicholas Pryor, Jenny O'Hara, Dale Robinette,*
*Bill Lucking, Don Porter, Louanne, Kene Holliday,*
*Ben Piazza, Charles Aidman, Ed Bernard, Robert*
*Phalen, Anthony Charnota*
An electronics expert on a surveillance assignment is
killed after recording a plot to cover up an industrial
waste scandal. His wife and daughter are forced to flee
for their lives whilst at the same time trying to avert a
disaster. Good ideas are ruined by unclear plotting
and stock situations, with no attempt being made to
explain why he was on the assignment in the first
place.
Aka: LADY IN DANGER
THR                                    100 min mTV
B,V                                VFP L/A; HER

**LAST STARFIGHTER, THE** **                   PG
Nick Castle             USA           1983
*Lance Guest, Dan O'Herlihy, Robert Preston,*
*Catherine Mary Stewart, Barbara Bosson, Norman*
*Snow, Chris Hebert, Kay E. Kuter, Dan Mason, John*
*O'Leary, Charlene Nelson, Bruce Abbott, George*
*McDaniel, John Maio, Robert Starr*
Space fantasy about a kid whose talents at the space
invaders game, lead to his being enlisted for combat in
a distant galaxy. An engaging fantasy that delivers
some nice effects but has no real force.
FAN                  101 min; 96 min (CH5 or POLY)
B,V       VFP L/A; HER; CH5 (VHS only); POLY (VHS
only)

**LAST TANGO IN PARIS** ***                    18
Bernardo Bertolucci
              FRANCE/ITALY/USA           1972
*Marlon Brando, Maria Schneider, Jean-Pierre Leaud,*
*Darling Legitimus, Catherine Sola, Mauro Marchetti*
A middle-aged American meets a young French girl
when they both go to view the same apartment, and
initiates a strange sexual relationship with her.
Massively over-rated when released, this is a rather
pretentious and meaningless film, though Brando
gives a wonderful performance.
Aka: ULTIMO TANGO A PARIGI
DRA                          129 min; 124 min (WHV)
B,V                                     INT; WHV

**LAST TEMPTATION OF CHRIST, THE** ***
Martin Scorsese         USA           1988
*Willem Dafoe, Harvey Keitel, Barbara Hershey, Harry*

*Dean Stanton, David Bowie, Andre Gregor*
Despite the wave of accusations of blasphemy unjustifiably heaped upon this film, this portrayal of Christ in terms of his human feelings is neither shocking nor sensational, but merely unexciting and unworthy of the novel on which it is based. There are some genuinely moving moments; if only the film had been directed in a less self-indulgent way. The score is by Peter Gabriel.
Boa: novel by Nikos Kazantzakis.
DRA                                              157 min (ort 163 min)
V/sh                                                                    CIC

## LAST TOUCH OF LOVE, THE ** PG
Philip Ottini          USA                    1978
*Christopher George, Gay Hamilton, Laura Trotter*
A boy with no resistance to germs who must live in a sterile room learns that his parents plan a divorce and makes a frantic effort to effect a reconciliation. Fair.
DRA                                                          100 min
B,V                                                        VGM; WDV

## LAST TRAIN FROM GUN HILL, THE *** 15
John Sturges          USA                    1959
*Kirk Douglas, Anthony Quinn, Carolyn Jones, Earl Holliman, Brad Dexter, Brian Hutton, Ziva Rodann, Val Avery, Walter Sande, Lars Henderson, John P. Anderson, Lee Hendry, William Newell, Sid Tomack, Charles Stevens*
A marshal's efforts to bring the killer of his wife to justice, are complicated by the fact that the latter is the son of an old friend. A taut and well-paced Western that poses the moral question as to whether turning a blind eye is the best way to resist evil.
WES                      94 min; 90 min (CH5) (ort 98 min)
B,V                                    CBS; HER; CH5 (VHS only)

## LAST TRAIN TO BERLIN **
Casey Diamond (Caslav Damjanovic)
                        YUGOSLAVIA                    1976
*Ty Hardin, Stathis Giallelis, Georgia Moll*
An American soldier joins forces with the Resistance to prevent the Nazis shipping back a load of plundered gold.
Aka: LAST RAMPAGE, THE; REKVIJEM
WAR                                                          86 min
B,V                                                                DFS

## LAST TRAIN, THE **
Pierre Granier-Deferre
                        FRANCE/ITALY                  1973
*Romy Schneider, Jean-Louis Trintignant, Serge Marquand*
A man searching for his pregnant wife in the midst of the confusion and chaos caused by the German invasion of France in 1940, has a passionate but short-lived affair.
Aka: LE TRAIN
DRA                                                          120 min
B,V                                                          VCL/CBS

## LAST TYCOON, THE *** 15
Elia Kazan          USA                    1976
*Robert De Niro, Tony Curtis, Robert Mitchum, Jeanne Moreau, Jack Nicholson, Donald Pleasence, Ray Milland, Ingrid Boulting, Dana Andrews, Peter Strauss, John Carradine, Theresa Russell, Jeff Corey, Angelica Huston*
Film adaptation of an unfinished novel about Hollywood and the film moguls of the late 1920s and 1930s. A restrained adaptation by Harold Pinter with a powerful performance from De Niro that is certainly one of his best.
Boa: novel by F. Scott Fitzgerald.
DRA                                124 min; 118 min (CH5)
B,V                              VFP L/A; HER; CH5 (VHS only)

## LAST UNICORN, THE * U
Jules Bass/Arthur Rankin Jr

                        USA                    1982
*Voices of: Alan Arkin, Jeff Bridges, Tammy Grimes, Angela Lansbury, Mia Farrow, Robert Klein, Christopher Lee, Keenan Wynn*
Animated story of a unicorn who goes in search of others of her kind and, after various adventures, frees all the other unicorns from captivity. A slack and disappointing affair.
Boa: novel by P.S. Beagle.
CAR                                    95 min; 84 min (CH5)
B,V,V2                          PRV L/A; CH5 (VHS only)

## LAST VALLEY, THE * 15
James Clavell          UK                    1970
*Michael Caine, Omar Sharif, Nigel Davenport, Florinda Bolkan, Per Oscarsson, Arthur O'Connell, Madeline Hinde, Yorgo Voyagis, Miguel Alejandro, Christian Roberts, Ian Hogg, Brian Blessed, Irene Prador, Edward Underdown*
A long boring film that goes nowhere and has nothing to say. It's supposedly about a scholar who tries to protect a hidden valley that has somehow escaped the devastation of the Thirty Years War.
Boa: novel by J.B. Pick.
DRA                      122 min; 119 min (PARK) (ort 125 min)
B,V                              INT/CBS; PARK (VHS only)

## LAST VICTIM, THE *
Jim Sotos          USA                    1975 (released
                                              1984 after re-editing)
*Tanya Roberts, Ron Max, Nancy Allen, Robin Leslie, Brian Freilino, Vasco Vallardares, Billy Longo, Michael Tucci, Beth Carlton, David Kerman, Frank Verroca, Michael Miles, Glenn Scarpelli, Ammy Levitan*
Sick saga of a psychotic killer who has an obsessive hatred of prostitutes, whom he beats, rapes and murders.
Aka: FORCED ENTRY
HOR                                                          86 min
B,V,V2                                                      INT/CBS

## LAST VIDEO AND TESTAMENT **
Peter Sasdy          UK                    1984
*Deborah Raffin, David Langton, Oliver Tobias, David Langton, Christopher Scoular, Clifford Rose, Shane Rimmer, Barbara Keogh, Geraldine Gardner, Shevaun Bryers, Hugh Dickson, Michael Fleming, Robert Rietty*
A high-tech will tempts somebody into trying to anticipate the course of events, in this standard offering in the Hammer House Of Mystery and Suspense.
Osca: CORVINI INHERITANCE, THE
HOR                                                    72 min mTV
B,V                                                                BWV

## LAST WAR, THE ***
Shue Matsubayashi    JAPAN                    1961
*Yuriko Hoshi, Frankie Sakai, Akira Takarada, Nabuko Otawa, Yumi Shirakawa*
During a period of high international tension, a misunderstanding between the superpowers leads to a nuclear exchange and Earth is destroyed. A depressing but effective film that concentrates on the harrowing experiences of the victims and for the most part eschews sensationalism. See also THE DAY AFTER and TESTAMENT.
Aka: FINAL WAR, THE; SEKAI DAISENSO
FAN                                          76 min (ort 79 min)
B,V,V2                                                            IFS

## LAST WINTER, THE ** 15
Riki Shelach Missimoff
                        ISRAEL/USA                    1983
*Kathleen Quinlan, Yona Elian, Stephen Macht, Zippora Peled, Brian Aron, Michael Schneider*
Two Israeli women form a close relationship as they

seek to discover the fate of their respective husbands, both missing after the Yom Kippur War. A kind of soap opera in an unusual setting, slightly redeemed by good performances.
Aka: HAKHOREF HAACHARON
DRA                           86 min (ort 92 min)
V                                              RCA

## LAST WITNESS **                                      18
E. Bruce Weiss            USA              1985
*Jeff Anderson, Vicki Long, Mike Schuster, Roxanne Caudy, Jeanne Finnery, Don Holbrook, Basia Lubitsch, Ken Strunk*
After a man escapes from a US Federal Institution he goes on the run, but government agents are sent after him, with orders to kill him on sight as he knows too much to be allowed to live.
A/AD                                        90 min
B,V                                            AVR

## LAST WORD, THE **
Roy Boulting             USA               1979
*Richard Harris, Karen Black, Martin Landau, Biff McGuire, Dennis Christopher*
An inventor tries to protect himself and his friends from unscrupulous property dealers, making use of clever schemes for this purpose. An unusual comedy-drama that never really gets into its stride. The script is by Michael Varhol, Greg Smith and Kit Carson.
DRA                          103 min (ort 105 min)
B,V                                            EHE

## LATE NANCY IRVING, THE **
Peter Sasdy               UK                1984
*Marius Goring, Christine Raines, Simon Willis, Mick Ford, Derek Benfield, Lewis Fiander, Tony Anholt, Zenia Merton, Tom Chadbon, Michael Elwyn, Ben Robertson, Christopher Banks, Tony Millin, David Rose*
Another offering from the Hammer House of Mystery and Suspense, about a dead woman who refuses to lie down. Average.
Osca: PAINT ME A MURDER
HOR                                      72 min mTV
B,V                                            BWV

## LATE SHOW, THE ***                                  15
Robert Benton            USA               1977
*Art Carney, Lily Tomlin, Bill Macy, Eugene Roche, Joanna Cassidy, John Considine, Howard Duff*
An ex-private eye comes out of retirement when his old partner is killed and investigates the case. Carney and Tomlin work well together, with the latter giving a convincing performance as an aimless young woman who decides to assist him. Complex, amiable and quite funny. Later gave rise to a brief TV series.
COM                                         94 min
B,V                                            WHV

## LATINO ***                                          15
Haskell Wexler           USA               1985
*Robert Beltran, Annette Cardona, Tony Plana, Ricardo Lopez, Gavin McFadden, Martu Tenorio, Michael Goodwin*
Set in Nicaragua, this purports to be an examination of the undercover wars of the US. Secretly sent into combat minus identification, a Green Beret finds himself fighting a war that is not his, and one that includes innocent civilians. An irritating film with a pronounced left-wing bias, but remarkably well directed and acted. Filmed in Nicaragua.
A/AD                                       105 min
B,V                                            CBS

## LAUGHTERHOUSE *                                      PG
Richard Eyre             UK                1984
*Ian Holm, Bill Owen, Rosemary Martin, Penelope Wilton, Richard Hope, Stephen Moore, Patrick Drury,*

*Aran Bell, Stephanie Tague, C.J. Allen, Norman Fisher, Kenneth MacDonald, Barbara Burgess, Ben Wright, Tim Seely, Stephen Phillips*
A Norfolk farmer beset by union problems decides to walk his geese to market in London; unfortunately the comic aspects of this film take a walk too. Written by Brian Glover.
Aka: SINGLETON'S PLUCK
COM                            93 min; 89 min (PAL)
B,V                                       PVG; PAL

## LAURA **
Luigi Scattine           ITALY             1974
*Carroll Baker, Leonard Mann, Zeudy, Enrico Maria Salerno*
A beautiful woman with everything in life she could wish for, falls in love with her stepson with devastating results.
Aka: BODY, THE; IL CORPO; LOVE SLAVE OF THE ISLANDS; TAKE THIS MY BODY
DRA                           91 min (ort 93 min)
B,V,V2                                         VPD

## LAURA ****                                           U
Otto Preminger           USA               1944
*Gene Tierney, Dana Andrews, Clifton Webb, Vincent Price, Judith Anderson, Dorothy Adams, Grant Mitchell, Clyde Fillmore, Ralph Dunn, Kathleen Howard, James Flavin*
A detective investigating the alleged murder of a beautiful woman finds himself falling madly in love with her. A classic example of film noir with a perfect cast and a witty script by Jay Dratler, Samuel Hoffenstein and Betty Reinhardt. The theme song is by David Raskin. Rouben Mamoulian started directing this one but Preminger took over. The 88 minute running time was reduced owing to a dispute over music rights. AA: Cin (Joseph LaShell).
Boa: novel by Vera Caspary.
THR                           84 min (ort 88 min) B/W
V/h                                            CBS

## LAURA: SHADOWS OF A SUMMER **
David Hamilton           FRANCE            1979
*Maud Adams, Dawn Dunlap, James Mitchell*
Story of the sexual awakening of a young girl, this time while posing as a model for a sculptor.
Aka: LAURA
A                               86 min (ort 95 min)
B,V                               TEVP; CHM; VPD

## LAUREL AND HARDY: A CHUMP AT
## OXFORD **                                            U
Alfred Goulding          USA               1939
*Stan Laurel, Oliver Hardy, Forrester Harvey, Wilfrid Lucas, Forbes Murray, James Finlayson, Anita Garvin, Peter Cushing*
Our two stars play a couple of street-cleaners whose efforts in foiling a bank robbery win them a college education as a reward. A highly uneven and only occasionally amusing romp, whose effectiveness is seriously diluted by unrelated comic episodes. However, with their arrival at Oxford (patience is needed) matters improve somewhat. Laurel's transmutation into Lord Paddington is a highlight.
Aka: CHUMP AT OXFORD, A
COM                           60 min (ort 63 min) B/W
V                                              VIR

## LAUREL AND HARDY: A-HAUNTING WE WILL
## GO *                                                 U
Alfred Werker            USA               1942
*Stan Laurel, Oliver Hardy, Elisha Cook Jr, Sheila Ryan, Don Costello, Dante the Magician*
A disappointing feature that finds Stan and Ollie engaged by crooks to escort a coffin, that gets accidentally switched with one used by a stage magician.
Aka: A-HAUNTING WE WILL GO

COM                      61 min (ort 68 min) B/W
V/h                                          CBS

## LAUREL AND HARDY: AIR RAID WARDENS *   U
Edward Sedgwick       USA                   1943
*Stan Laurel, Oliver Hardy, Edgar Kennedy,*
*Jacqueline White, Horace (Stephen) McNally, Nella*
*Walker, Donald Meek*
Having been rejected as unfit for military service, two
idiotic air raid wardens capture a bunch of Nazi spies
entirely by accident. A weak and flawed comedy that
had an appeal on release that has now largely faded.
Very disappointing.
Aka AIR RAID WARDENS
Osca: LAUREL AND HARDY: NOTHING BUT
TROUBLE/LAUREL AND HARDY: HEROES OF
THE REGIMENT
COM              67 min; 214 min (boxed set) B/W
V                                            MGM

## LAUREL AND HARDY: BABES IN TOYLAND ****
Gus Meins/Charles R. Rogers
                    USA                      1934
*Stan Laurel, Oliver Hardy, Charlotte Henry, Henry*
*Brandon, Felix Knight, Jean Darling, Florence*
*Roberts, Johnny Downs, Marie Wilson*
Film version of a Victor Herbert operetta which
incorporates many fairy tale figures. A wonderful
comedy-fantasy with our two comedians giving one of
their best performances, easily making the most of the
thin script.
Aka: BABES IN TOYLAND; LAUREL AND HARDY
IN TOYLAND; MARCH OF THE WOODEN
SOLDIERS; WOODEN SOLDIERS
Boa: story by Glen MacDonough/operetta by Victor
Herbert.
MUS                   75 min (ort 79 min) B/W
B,V                            JVC L/A; ART L/A

## LAUREL AND HARDY: BLOCKHEADS ***   U
John G. Blystone      USA                   1938
*Stan Laurel, Oliver Hardy, Billy Gilbert, Patricia*
*Ellis, James Finlayson, Minna Gombell*
Stan becomes a hero having guarded a trench for
twenty years since WW1. But he finds it a little
difficult to adjust to civilian life when he is taken
home by Ollie. A fresh and lively outing that is
inclined to be disjointed but has a number of classic
gags.
Aka: BLOCKHEADS
COM                   55 min (ort 60 min) B/W
B,V                                          VIR

## LAUREL AND HARDY: BOGUS BANDITS ***
Hal Roach/Charles R. Rogers
                    USA                      1933
*Oliver Hardy, Stan Laurel, Dennis King, James*
*Finlayson, Thelma Todd, Henry Armetta*
Laurel and Hardy travel to the Italian Alps by mule,
getting involved in some hilarious situations. Based
on a romantic operetta.
Aka: BOGUS BANDITS; DEVIL'S BROTHER, THE;
FRA DIAVOLO
COM                   74 min (ort 88 min) B/W
B,V,V2                                   EVC L/A

## LAUREL AND HARDY: GREAT GUNS **   U
Montague Banks        USA                   1941
*Stan Laurel, Oliver Hardy, Sheila Ryan, Dick Nelson,*
*Edmund MacDonald, Allan Webb, Charles*
*Trowbridge, Ludwig Stossel, Mae Marsh*
In this feeble comedy, Stan and Ollie join the Texas
Cavalry to be with their millionaire employer, to
whom they are entirely devoted. Quite watchable but
far off the standard set by their best work. Watch out
for Alan Ladd who puts in a brief appearance.
Aka: GREAT GUNS
COM                   70 min (ort 74 min) B/W
V/h                                          CBS

## LAUREL AND HARDY: HEROES OF THE
REGIMENT ***                                   U
James Horne           USA                   1935
*Stan Laurel, Oliver Hardy, Jimmy Finlayson, June*
*Lang, William Janney, Anne Grey, Vernon Steele*
Laurel and Hardy go to Scotland to collect an
inheritance but end up in India, having inadvertently
joined a Scottish regiment. The plotting could be
better but this is vintage stuff.
Aka: BONNIE SCOTLAND; HEROES OF THE
REGIMENT. Osca: LAUREL AND HARDY:
NOTHING BUT TROUBLE. LAUREL AND HARDY:
AIR RAID WARDENS
COM   76 min (ort 80 min); 214 min (MGM boxed set)
B/W
B, V, V2                          MGM (VHS only)

## LAUREL AND HARDY: NOTHING BUT
TROUBLE *                                      U
Sam Taylor            USA                   1944
*Stan Laurel, Oliver Hardy, Mary Boland, Philip*
*Merivale, David Leland, Henry O'Neill*
A minor Laurel and Hardy vehicle, in which they are
hired to work as servants in a household where they
inadvertently foil an attempt to poison a young king.
A weak and shallow effort, the last comedy the pair
made for MGM.
Aka: NOTHING BUT TROUBLE
Osca: LAUREL AND HARDY: AIR RAID
WARDENS/LAUREL AND HARDY: HEROES OF
THE REGIMENT
COM              69 min; 214 min (boxed set) B/W
V                                            MGM

## LAUREL AND HARDY: OUR RELATIONS ***   U
Harry Lachman         USA                   1936
*Stan Laurel, Oliver Hardy, Sidney Toler, Alan Hale,*
*James Finlayson, Daphne Pollard, Iris Adrian, Noel*
*Madison, Ralf Harolde, Arthur Housman*
Our comic duo gets into all kinds of trouble on account
of their long-lost twin brothers. A stylish work that
exhibits none of that unfortunate tendency to ramble
so often present in their films.
Aka: OUR RELATIONS
Boa: short story The Money Box by W.W. Jacobs
COM                            70 min B/W
B,V                                          VIR

## LAUREL AND HARDY: PACK UP YOUR    U
TROUBLES **
George Marshall/Raymond McCarey
                    USA                      1931
*Stan Laurel, Oliver Hardy, Charles Middleton, George*
*Marshall, James Finlayson, Donald Dillaway, Mary*
*Carr, Dick Cramer, Tom Kennedy, Billy Gilbert*
When her father dies, a young girl is entrusted to the
care of his two pals, a couple of former WW1
combatants. Good fun but disjointed and generally
aimless.
Aka: PACK UP YOUR TROUBLES
COM                   60 min (ort 68 min) B/W
B,V                                          VIR

## LAUREL AND HARDY: PARDON US **   U
James Parrott         USA                   1931
*Stan Laurel, Oliver Hardy, Wilfred Lucas, Walter*
*Long, James Finlayson, June Marlowe*
First feature from our comic duo is a rather dated
prison spoof that has some humorous moments, most
of which revolve around some difficulties Ollie has
with a loose tooth. Patchy and muddled but quite
likeable. A highlight is the unusual song-and-dance
routine about halfway through.
Aka: JAILBIRDS; PARDON US
COM                   53 min (ort 55 min) B/W
B,V                                          VIR

## LAUREL AND HARDY: SAPS AT SEA ***    U
Gordon Douglas    USA      1940
*Stan Laurel, Oliver Hardy, James Finlayson, Richard Cramer, Ben Turpin, Harry Bernard*
Laurel and Hardy's last film for Hal Roach has Ollie recuperating after suffering a breakdown brought on by his job as a horn factor. But his fishing vacation with Stan soon has them both at sea. A solid work that's a little short on gags.
Aka: SAPS AT SEA
COM        56 min (ort 60 min) B/W
V            VIR

## LAUREL AND HARDY: SONS OF THE
## DESERT ****    U
William A. Seiter    USA      1933
*Stan Laurel, Oliver Hardy, Charley Chase, Dorothy Christy, Lucien Littlefield, Mae Busch*
Having given their oath to attend a fraternal convention, Stan and Ollie discover that their wives have other ideas and are forced to employ a complex ruse that involves Ollie contracting a disease requiring a long sea voyage. One of the very best of their comedies; complex, vigorous and hilarious.
Aka: FRATERNALLY YOURS; SONS OF THE DESERT
COM        62 min (ort 69 min) B/W
V            VIR

## LAUREL AND HARDY: SWISS MISS **    U
John G. Blystone    USA      1938
*Stan Laurel, Oliver Hardy, Della Lind, Walter Woolf King, Eric Blore, Adia Kuznetzof, Charles Judels*
Two mousetrap salesmen in Switzerland become involved with an actress, who is scheming to arouse her husband's jealousy. The romantic setting doesn't give our comic duo much chance to shine, although there is a nice moment when Ollie gets to serenade his beloved.
Aka: SWISS MISS
COM        70 min (ort 73 min) B/W
V            VIR

## LAUREL AND HARDY: THE BOHEMIAN GIRL ** U
James Horne/Charles R. Rogers
      USA      1936
*Stan Laurel, Oliver Hardy, Mae Busch, Darla Hood, Jacqueline Wells (Julie Bishop), Antonio Moreno, James Finlayson, Thelma Todd*
Laurel and Hardy in their last comic opera as the guardians of a young girl who is a kidnapped princess, although nobody seems to realise this. The singing unfortunately tends to get in the way of the gags in this one, which all too often misfire.
Aka: BOHEMIAN GIRL, THE
COM        67 min (ort 74 min) B/W
V            VIR

## LAUREL AND HARDY: THE BULLFIGHTERS **    U
Mal St Clair    USA      1945
*Stan Laurel, Oliver Hardy, Margo Woode, Richard Lane, Carol Andrews, Diosa Costello*
Laurel and Hardy play two detectives, who pursue a female criminal over the border into Mexico, where Laurel is mistaken for a famous matador, and winds up having his moment of glory in the bullring. This last American feature shows a few flashes of humour but is largely a poor vehicle for their talents.
Aka: BULLFIGHTERS, THE
COM        61 min B/W
V/h          CBS

## LAUREL AND HARDY: THE DANCING    U
## MASTERS **
Mal St Clair    USA      1943
*Stan Laurel, Oliver Hardy, Trudy Marshall, Bob Bailey, Margaret Dumont, Matt Briggs, Robert Mitchum*

Laurel and Hardy are cast here as the owners of a ballet school who find themselves involved with gangsters. Our duo work well together but lack material, and the clumsily back-projected runaway bus sequence fails to amuse.
Aka: DANCING MASTERS, THE
COM        64 min B/W
V/h          CBS

## LAUREL AND HARDY: THE FLYING    Uc
## DEUCES ***
A. Edward Sutherland    USA      1939
*Stan Laurel, Oliver Hardy, Jean Parker, James Finlayson, Reginald Gardiner, Charles Middleton*
Stan and Ollie join the Foreign Legion so that Stanley can forget an unhappy romance – the usual mixture of mayhem and complications follow. A fast-paced comedy that has the charming musical number – "Shine On, Harvest Moon" and sees Ollie reincarnated as a mule.
Aka: FLYING ACES; FLYING DEUCES, THE
COM        61 min B/W
B,V        MOV; DIAM; VCC

## LAUREL AND HARDY: UTOPIA *
Leo Joannon    FRANCE      1950
*Stan Laurel, Oliver Hardy, Suzy Delair, Max Elloy*
An island paradise is threatened by the discovery of uranium. Our comic duo's last film, and not one of their best.
Aka: ATOLL K; ROBINSON CRUSOELAND; UTOPIA
COM        80 min B/W
B,V        EVC L/A

## LAUREL AND HARDY: WAY OUT WEST ****    U
James W. Horne    USA      1937
*Stan Laurel, Oliver Hardy, Sharon Lynn, James Finlayson, Rosina Lawrence, Stanley Fields, Jim Mason, James C. Morton, Frank Mills, Dave Pepper, Vivien Oakland, Harry Bernard, Mary Gordon, May Wallace, The Avalon Boys, Jack Hill*
Well-paced and funny Laurel and Hardy comedy, with our inept pair being tricked into handing over the deeds to a mine, to a girl who is impersonating the rightful heiress. Easily one of their best films with great routines and some charming musical interludes.
Aka: WAY OUT WEST
COM        60 min (ort 66 min) B/W
B,V          VIR

## LAVENDER HILL MOB, THE ****    U
Charles Crichton    UK      1951
*Alec Guinness, Stanley Holloway, Sidney James, Alfie Bass, John Gregson, Marjorie Fielding, Clive Morton, Ronald Adams, Sydney Tafler, Jacquis Brunius, Meredith Edwards, Edie Martin, Patrick Barr, Marie Burke*
Sparkling Ealing comedy about an underpaid bank clerk who plans and executes a brilliant gold robbery, but his colleague's botched attempt to hide the loot leads to some bizarre complications. Look out for Audrey Hepburn, who appears very briefly. AA: Story/Screen (T.E.B. Clarke).
COM        78 min
B,V        TEVP; WHV (VHS only)

## LAW AND DISORDER ***    U
Charles Crichton    UK      1958
*Michael Redgrave, Robert Morley, Joan Hickson, Lionel Jeffries, Ronald Squire, Elizabeth Sellars*
A smuggler is forced to lead a double life in which he poses as a cleric in order to hide the truth from his staid and law-abiding son. When he faces arrest for his activities his colleagues come to the rescue. An amusing and well-paced criminal caper.
Boa: novel Smuggler's Circuit by Denys Roberts.
COM        83 min (ort 76 min) B/W
V            WHV

## LAW AND DISORDER *** 18
Ivan Passer            USA            1974
*Ernest Borgnine, Carroll O'Connor, Karen Black, Ann
Wedgeworth, Anita Dangler, Leslie Ackerman*
Two well-off New Yorkers form a vigilante group to
combat crime. At first they treat their role as something of a joke but soon get drawn into more sinister
conflicts. An uneven comedy-drama that starts off in a
light vein and gradually becomes quite sombre,
though there are some good observations along the
way.
DRA                        97 min (ort 102 min)
B,V                                          POLY

## LAW OF THE UNDERWORLD **
Lew Landers            USA            1938
*Eduardo Cianelli, Anne Shirley, Chester Morris,
Richard Bond, Walter Abel, Lee Patrick, Paul
Guilfoyle, Frank M. Thomas, Eddie Acuff, Jack
Arnold, Jack Carson*
Two lovers are robbed of their life savings and become
involved in a desperate plot to regain their money. A
remake of "The Pay-Off Time" from 1930.
Boa: story/play by John B. Hymer and Samuel
Shipman. Osca: OUTLAW, THE
DRA                              59 min B/W
B,V                                           KVD

## LAW OF VIOLENCE, THE * 15
ITALY
*George Greenwood, Conrad Steve, Angel Aranda,
Manuel Bronchud*
A man wrongly convicted of a crime gets his revenge
and kills the sheriff of a small town, but finds that his
successor is much tougher. An obscure and forgettable
effort.
WES                               81 min
B,V                                           VPD

## LAWLESS LAND, THE * 18
Jon Hess               USA            1988
*Nick Corri, Amanda Peterson, Leon Xander Berkeley*
Another tale set in the ruins of a post-holocaust world,
with two lovers fleeing the girl's land baron father in
order to get married, and finding themselves pursued
by a posse of gunslingers. Mindless high-action with a
sharp strand of viciousness.
FAN                               77 min
V                                            MGM

## LAWRENCE OF ARABIA *** PG
David Lean             UK             1962
*Peter O'Toole, Omar Sharif, Arthur Kennedy, Anthony
Quinn, Jack Hawkins, Claude Rains, Anthony Quayle,
Jose Ferrer, Alec Guinness, Michel Ray, Zia
Mohyeddin, Donald Wolfit, I.S. Johar, Howard
Marion Crawford, Hugh Miller*
An exciting but highly romanticised look at the life of
T.E. Lawrence, which established O'Toole as a star
but unfortunately provides little insight into the inner
drives of the title character. A film of great beauty
whose 70 mm wide-screen camerawork will be largely
lost on TV. AA: Pic, Dir, Cin (Fred A. Young), Art/Set
(John Box and John Stoll/Dario Simoni), Score (Orig)
(Maurice Jarre), Sound (John Cox), Edit (Ann Coates).
Boa: book Seven Pillars Of Wisdom by T.E. Lawrence.
DRA                221 min; 191 min (PREST)
B,V                       RCA; PREST (VHS only)

## LAZARUS SYNDROME, THE ***
Jerry Thorpe           USA            1979
*Louis Gossett Jr, Ronald Hunter, E.G. Marshall*
A doctor joins forces with a patient and former
journalist to expose the negligence of a hospital, and
has to confront the surgeon-administrator responsi-
ble. A good pilot for a prospective TV series.
DRA                        70 min (ort 90 min) mTV
B,V                                          VIPCO

## LE BAL ** PG
Ettore Scola
ALGERIA/FRANCE/ITALY            1982
*Christophe Allwright, Marc Berman, Regis Bouquet,
Chantal Capron, Nani Noel, Danielle Rochard, Jean-
Claude Penchenat, Etienne Guichard, Jean-Francois
Perrier, Liliane Delval, Monica Scattini*
Set in a Parisian ballroom, this is a survey of life and
love between 1936 and 1983, all told in musical form
without dialogue. Highly original and certainly styl-
ish, but it all becomes something of a strain after a
while. Those who like films without dialogue will like
this one a lot. Written by Scola, Ruggero Maccari,
Furio Scarpelli and Jean-Claude Penchenat, and
based on a stage production by the Theatre du
Campagnol.
MUS                               112 min
B,V                                           WHV

## LE CHANT DU MONDE *** PG
Marcel Camus           FRANCE         1965
*Catherine Deneuve, Hardy Kruger, Charles Vanel*
A Romeo and Juliet-style tale of the passionate love
affair between two members of rival clans that are
forever locked in conflict. An enjoyable drama, set in
the French department of Haute-Provence.
Aka: WORLD SONG, THE
DRA                               95 min
V                                            CASPIC

## LE DERNIER MILLIADAIRE **
Rene Clair             FRANCE         1934
*Max Dearly, Renee Saint-Cyr, Marthe Mellot,
Raymond Cordy*
A small principality invites a financial wizard to
restore its fortunes, but things fail to go as planned.
An uneven and sluggishly-handled tale with a few
good sequences. One of the director's poorer efforts.
Aka: LAST MILLIONAIRE, THE
COM                88 min (ort 100 min) B/W
B,V                                           TEVP

## LE JOUR SE LEVE ****
Marcel Carne           FRANCE         1939
*Jean Gabin, Jules Berry, Arletty, Jacqueline Laurent,
Rene Genin, Mady Berry, Bernard Blier, Marcel Peres,
Jacques Baumer, Rene Bergeron, Gabrielle Fontan,
Arthur Devere, George Douking, Germaine Lix*
A murderer trapped in an attic by a police siege
recalls the events that led to his present predicament.
A marvellously poetic example of classic French film
noir. Later remade as "The Long Night".
Aka: DAYBREAK
DRA                93 min (ort 95 min) B/W
B,V                                           PVG

## LE SILENCE EST D'OR ***
Rene Clair             FRANCE         1947
*Maurice Chevalier, Marcelle Derrien, Francois Perier*
A middle-aged film-maker falls in love with his ward,
but she prefers his young assistant. Good perform-
ances and period charm (circa 1906) help pad out this
thin story.
Aka: MAN ABOUT TOWN; SILENCE IS GOLDEN
DRA                87 min (ort 99 min) B/W
B,V                                           TEVP

## LEADER OF THE BAND *** 15
Nessa Hyams            USA            1987
*Steve Landesberg, Mercedes Ruehl*
The story of a musician who dreams of leading a
marching band and gets his opportunity when a local
band comes off worst in an argument with a bus. An
amusing little tale that makes the most of its
material.
COM                               87 min
B,V                                           CBS

## LEAGUE OF GENTLEMEN, THE ***
Basil Dearden          UK                    1960
*Jack Hawkins, Nigel Patrick, Richard Attenborough,
Roger Livesey, Bryan Forbes, Kieron Moore, Terence
Alexander, Norman Bird, Robert Coote, Melissa
Stibling, Nanette Newman, Gerald Harper, Patrick
Wymark, David Lodge*
Nice stylish film about a military man who assembles
a bunch of ex-officers who left the service for a variety
of reasons, and trains them to carry out a bank
robbery with military precision. The manner in which
they get caught is painfully contrived, as one feels
almost inclined to believe they should have got way
with it.
Boa: novel by John Boland.
DRA                    112 min (ort 115 min) B/W
B,V                                          RNK

## LEAP OF FAITH **                          PG
Stephen Gyllenhaal     USA                   1988
*Anne Archer, Sam Neill, Frances Lee McCain, Louis
Giambalvo, James Tolkan, Elizabeth Ruscio, C.C.H.
Pounder, Michael Constantine*
A woman learns that she has terminal cancer but
refuses to accept the verdict of her doctors and turns
instead to alternative medicine in her search for a
cure. A sincere story, told with conviction; its obvious
TV origins tend to dilute its impact.
DRA                    94 min (ort 100 min) mTV
V                                          BRAVE

## LEATHER BOYS, THE **                      15
Sidney J. Furie        UK                    1963
                           (released in USA 1966)
*Rita Tushingham, Colin Campbell, Dudley Sutton,
Gladys Henson, Avice Landone, Lockwood West, Betty
Marsden, Martin Matthews, Johnny Briggs, James
Chase, Geoffrey Dunn, Sandra Caron*
A sleazy study of a teenage marriage and its gradual
break-up. Well-observed but profoundly gloomy, and
with a few daring (for the time) observations on
homosexuality.
Boa: novel by Eliott George (Gillian Freeman).
DRA                    90 min (ort 108 min) B/W
V                                            MIA

## LEATHERNECKS **                           18
Paul D. Robinson       USA                   1988
*Richard Hatch, James Mitchum*
Standard war heroics tale that's set in Vietnam,
where a US Marines sergeant is ordered to bring in
two deserters and learns that one of them is his
much-decorated close friend. The latter is subsequently captured by the Vietcong and the sergeant and his
unit find themselves fighting a desperate battle
against a numerically superior force. A predictable
low-budget affair with ample action but little else.
WAR                                       91 min
V                                            VPD

## LEAVE 'EM LAUGHING ****
Jackie Cooper          USA                   1981
*Mickey Rooney, Anne Jackson, Allen Goorwitz, Elisha
Cook Jr, William Windom, Red Buttons, Carol Ann
Susi, Bruce French, DeVoreaux White, Adrienne
Kingman, Jan Stratton, Candy Mobly, Gray Miller,
Joseph Pon, Dick Paxton*
An inspiring and moving account of a real-life clown
and his wife who took into their home no less than 37
homeless children over the years. Faced with terminal
cancer, he worries about what will happen to them
after he dies. Superb acting by the entire cast allows
the film to neatly side-step the pitfall of sentimental-
ity, and achieve genuine feeling. Rarely has Rooney
been better.
Boa: story by Peggy Chantler-Dick.
COM                                      104 min mTV
B,V                                   VFP L/A; HER

## LEAVE YESTERDAY BEHIND **                  PG
Richard Michaels       USA                   1978
*John Ritter, Carrie Fisher, Buddy Ebsen, Ed Nelson,
Robert Urich, Carmen Zapata, Barbara Stuart, Walter
Maslow, Lucia Straiser, Carol Ann Williams, Josh
Hall, Dan Harrison*
A young student is crippled in a polo match but still
finds love; in fact, a girl ditches her boyfriend to be
with him. Insipid and mawkish, this film has all the
ingredients of a good tale, but does little with them.
DRA                                       97 min mTV
B,V                                          HER

## LEFT HAND OF THE LAW, THE *
Giuseppe Rosati        ITALY                 1975
*Leonard Mann, Janet Agren, Stephen Boyd*
A dedicated policeman is prepared to do everything he
can to fight crime.
Aka: LA POLIZIA INTERVIENE: ORDINE DI
UCCIDERE!
DRA                                          97 min
B,V,V2                                       VPD

## LEFT-HANDED GUN, THE ***                   PG
Arthur Penn            USA                   1958
*Paul Newman, John Dehner, Lita Milan, Hurd
Hatfield, James Congdon, James Best, Colin Keith-
Johnston, John Dierkes, Bob Anderson, Wally Brown,
Ainslie Pryor, Martin Garralaga, Denver Pyle, Nestor
Paiva, Robert Foulk, Paul Smith*
Penn's debut is a psychological study of Billy the Kid
and his quest for revenge on the four men who
murdered his friend. Harsh and realistic, but not
always successful in its aspirations to explain the
workings of a pathological mind. See also BILLY THE
KID.
Boa: TV play by Gore Vidal.
WES                                       102 min B/W
V                                            WHV

## LEFTOVERS, THE *                            U
Paul Schneider         USA                   1986
*John Denver, Cindy Williams, Jason Presson, George
Wyner, Pamela Segall, Andrea Barber, Matthew
Brooks, Douglas Emerson, Jaleel White, Matthew
Laurance, Henry Jones, Anne Seymour, Bernadette
Birkett, Lucy Butler*
Tale in which Denver stars as an employee of an
orphanage, under threat of closure to make way for a
factory. The orphans devise a wild plan of action to
save their home. Unfortunately they can't do much to
save this cloying Disney romp. Denver's TV movie
debut.
Boa: story by Steven Slavkin and Gen LeRoy.
COM                    90 min (ort 100 min) mTV
B,V                                          WDV

## LEG FIGHTERS, THE ***                      18
Li Tso-Nan             HONG KONG             1980
*Tan Tao-Liang, Hsia Kuan-Li, Chin Lung, Peng
Kang, Sun Yung-Chi, Wang Hsieh, Tsai Hung, Wang
Yiu, Cheng Pao*
A couple of stubborn students have to learn leg
fighting techniques in order to defeat a villain. A
simple-minded film with some excellent action sequ-
ences.
Aka: INVINCIBLE KUNG FU LEGS, THE
MAR                                          90 min
B,V                                         VTEL

## LEGACY OF BLOOD *                          18
Carl Monson            USA                   1971
*John Carradine, Faith Domergue, Jeff Morrow, John
Russell, Merry Anders, Richard Davalos, Rudolfo
Acosta, Norman Bartold, Ivy Bethune, John Smith,
Buck Kartalian, Brooke Mills, Mr. Chin*
A wealthy American businessman requires four heirs
to his fortune, to remain in his house for seven days
after his death, in order to inherit. They do so but find

themselves at the mercy of a killer. A good cast are hard put to breathe life into this old chestnut.
Aka: BLOOD LEGACY; WILL TO DIE
HOR                                           90 min
B,V                          CIN L/A; PRV; VIDRNG

### LEGACY OF HORROR **                         18
Andy Milligan            USA                1978
*Elaine Boies, Chris Broderick, Marilee Troncone,*
*Jennifer Cusick, Julia Curry, Peter Barcia, Stanley*
*Schwartz, Louise Galandra, Dale Hansen*
Three sisters must live in harmony in the family mansion for 72 hours to inherit their father's estate. Evil lurks however, ready to cause death and mayhem. Average.
Aka: LEGACY OF BLOOD (SID)
HOR                      77 min; 79 min (SID)
B,V,V2                               VPD; SID

### LEGACY, THE *
Richard Marquand         UK                 1978
*Katherine Ross, Sam Elliott, Ian Hogg, John*
*Standing, Margaret Tyzack, Charles Gray, Lee*
*Montague, Roger Daltrey, Hildegard Neil, Marianne*
*Broome, William Abney, Patsy Smart, Reg Harding,*
*Mathias Kilroy*
All of the guests at a country house have been inveigled there, in order to determine which one is to inherit a satanic legacy. The selection proceeds with the progressive murder of each guest who is deemed not to qualify. A streak of viciousness mars this tale, and the expected revelation has all the horror of a bad joke.
Aka: LEGACY OF MAGGIE WALSH, THE
HOR                         95 min (ort 102 min)
B,V,V2                                  VIPCO

### LEGAL EAGLES **                            PG
Ivan Reitman             USA                1986
*Robert Redford, Debra Winger, Daryl Hannah, Brian*
*Dennehy, Terence Stamp, Steven Hill, John McMartin,*
*Jennie Dundas, Roscoe Lee Browne*
An assistant D.A. becomes involved with a woman defence attorney when they are brought together in a fraud case. A frantic attempt to recreate the witty partnership of Tracy and Hepburn in their best comedies, but this one fails to come anywhere near. The music is by Elmer Bernstein.
COM                                          115 min
B,V                                          CIC

### LEGEND **                                  PG
Ridley Scott             USA                1985
*Tim Curry, Tom Cruise, Mia Sara, David Bennent,*
*Alice Playton, Billy Barty*
Fairytale about a princess who inadvertently causes the death of a unicorn, thus unleashing the powers of darkness against her forest domain. Tim Curry is excellent as the demon who desires her as his bride, in an otherwise lavishly produced but shallow offering.
FAN                                           90 min
V/sh                            CAN L/A; WHV

### LEGEND OF ALFRED PACKER, THE **
Jim Robertson Dray       USA                1980
*Patrick Day, Ron Haines, Bob Damon, Jim Dratfield,*
*Dave Ellingson, Ron Holiday*
A harsh tale of survival and cannibalism in Colorado in 1877.
DRA                                           90 min
B,V,V2                                INT/CBS

### LEGEND OF BILLY JEAN, THE *                15
Matthew Robbins          USA                1985
*Helen Slater, Christian Slater, Peter Coyote, Keith*
*Gordon, Martha Gehman, Richard Bradford, Dean*
*Stockwell, Barny Tubb, Yeardley Smith, Mona Fultz,*
*John M. Jackson, Rodney Rincon, Caroline Williams,*
*Rudy Young*

A girl becomes a national figure when she resorts to rough methods to get justice after she, her brother and two friends are involved in a shooting incident. A standard "shoot 'em up" actioner with a message as thin as the characterisations.
Aka: LEGEND OF BILLIE JEAN, THE
A/AD                        91 min (ort 96 min)
V/sh                                     RCA

### LEGEND OF BLACK THUNDER
### MOUNTAIN, THE **                           U
Tom Breemer              USA                1979
*Holly Beeman, Steve Beeman, F.A. Milovich, Ron*
*Brown, Keith Sexson, John Sexson, Vance Cleveland,*
*Dick Albertson, Glen Porter, Tim Stabb*
Two children lost in the mountains are adopted by a grizzly bear in this lighthearted kid's adventure.
JUV                                           90 min
B,V                                   IVS; VPM

### LEGEND OF BLOOD CASTLE, THE ***
Jorge Grau          ITALY/SPAIN            1972
*Ewa Aulin, Lucia Bose, Espartaco Santoni, Ana*
*Farra, Franca Grey, Silvano Tranquili, Lola Gaos,*
*Angel Memendes, Enrico Vico*
On the same theme as COUNTESS DRACULA, this is an effective and moody tale loosely based on the notorious 17th century Countess Elizabeth Bathory whose penchant it was to bathe in the blood of female virgins as a means of preserving her beauty if not her popularity. Here, her husband the Count is a vampire, and keeps her well supplied with blood.
Aka: BLOODY COUNTESS; CEREMONIA
SANGRIENTA; COUNTESS DRACULA; FEMALE
BUTCHER, THE; LADY DRACULA; LE VERGINI
CAVALCANO LA MORTE
HOR                        87 min (ort 102 min)
B,V,V2                                   VPD

### LEGEND OF BOGGY CREEK, THE **
Charles B. Pierce        USA                1972
*Willie E. Smith, John P. Nixon, John W. Gates, Jeff*
*Crabtree, Buddy Crabtree, Herb Jones*
A horrifying swamp monster is sighted in a remote Arkansas community in this soggy docu-drama that blends alleged sightings of the creature with re-enacted footage. See also RETURN TO BOGGY CREEK.
DRA                        76 min (ort 87 min)
B,V,V2                                   IFS

### LEGEND OF FRANK WOODS, THE **
Hagen Smith/Richard Robinson
                         USA                1977
*Brad Stewart, Troy Donahue, Kitty Vallacher, Michael*
*Christian*
A gunman disguises himself as a priest in order to avoid an ambush. Average.
WES                                          107 min
V                                 CIN L/A; CYC

### LEGEND OF FRENCHIE KING, THE *
Christian-Jacque/Guy Casaril
                  FRANCE/ITALY/SPAIN/UK     1971
*Brigitte Bardot, Claudia Cardinale, Michael J.*
*Pollard, Patty Shepard, Micheline Presle, Emma*
*Cohen*
A sort of poor man's "Viva Maria" with five sisters turning outlaws and disguising themselves as men, at a French settlement in New Mexico in the 1880s. A messy attempt at a Western romp that gets very tiresome very quickly.
Aka: LES PETROLEUSES; PETROLEUM GIRLS
WES                     90 min (ort 97 min) dubbed
B,V,V2                               VCL/CBS

### LEGEND OF HELL HOUSE, THE **               PG
John Hough               UK                 1973

*Pamela Franklin, Roddy McDowall, Clive Revill,*
*Gayle Hunnicutt, Roland Culver, Peter Bowles,*
*Michael Gough*
A scientist, his wife and a medium are hired by a
millionaire who is obsessed with knowing whether
there is life beyond the grave, and sent to investigate
a haunted house, where previous hauntings have
often led to the death of the psychics who attempted to
probe its secret. There are certainly chilling moments
but the expected revelation is hardly the stuff of which
nightmares are made. Scripted by Matheson.
Boa: novel Hell House by Richard Matheson.
HOR                                          94 min
V                                         CBS L/A

## LEGEND OF KING ARTHUR, THE **          U
Rodney Bennett   AUSTRALIA/UK            1985
*Andrew Burt, David Robb, Felicity Dean*
Condensation of a TV series about Camelot and the
Knights of the Round Table. Fair.
DRA                                    110 min mTV
B,V                                           BBC

## LEGEND OF LIZZIE BORDEN, THE ***        15
Paul Wendkos      USA                    1975
*Elizabeth Montgomery, Ed Flanders, Fionnuala*
*Flanagan, Katherine Helmond, Fritz Weaver, Don*
*Porter, Bonnie Bartlett, John Beal, Helen Craig, Alan*
*Hewitt, Gail Kobe, Robert Symonds, Hayden Rorke,*
*Iggie Wolfington*
The story of the New England spinster who was
accused of the axe murders of her father and step-
mother in 19th century Massachusetts, thereby giving
rise to the famous nursery rhyme. Quite an interest-
ing account with a literate script and intense but not
overblown performances. Written by William Best.
DRA                           92 min (ort 100 min) mTV
B,V                                     ARENA/CIC

## LEGEND OF LOBO, THE ***                 U
James Algar       USA                    1962
*Rex Allen (narration), Sons of the Pioneers (songs)*
The life of a forest wolf forms the basis for this
anthropomorphic tale in which the wolf is followed
from his cub days to adulthood, when he succeeds in
saving his mate from bounty hunters. A bright and
cheerful outdoors adventure of the sort Disney studios
excelled at.
Boa: book Lobo And Other Stories by Ernest
Thompson-Seton.
JUV                      64 min (ort 67 min) Cut (44 sec)
B,V                                           WDV

## LEGEND OF ROBIN HOOD, THE **            U
                  AUSTRALIA               1972
Pleasant animated version of this famous tale.
CAR                            46 min (ort 60 min)
V                                 CHILD L/A; STYL

## LEGEND OF SLEEPY HOLLOW, THE **
Henning Schellerup   USA                 1980
*Jeff Goldblum, Dick Butkus, Paul Sand, Meg Foster,*
*James Griffith, Laura Campbell, John Sylvester*
*White, Michael Ruud, Karin Isaacson, H.E.D.*
*Redford, Tiger Thompson, Michael Witt*
A "Classics Illustrated" tale of a ghostly headless rider
and the bumbling schoolteacher who has an encounter
with him in the little town of Sleepy Hollow. A fairly
bland family adventure that was done with a good
deal more verve as a cartoon in 1949.
Aka: ADVENTURES OF ICHABOD AND MR TOAD
Boa: story by Washington Irving.
FAN                                    98 min mTV
B,V                                        VIPCO

## LEGEND OF THE GOLDEN PEARL, THE ***    PG
Teddy Robin Kwan HONG KONG               1987
*Ti Lung, Bruce Baron, Teddy Robin Kwan, Wong Joe*
*Yin, Heidi Makinen, Lo Ta Yu, Peter Pau*

An explorer well versed in the martial arts, is asked
by a man to find the title object, which is reputed to
have been left behind by a flying dragon and to possess
great power. He refuses to be drawn into the quest
until a boyhood friend takes him to a monastery in
Katmandu, where he finds the pearl and learns a little
more about its properties. A lively action adventure
with a strong mystical flavour.
A/AD                           77 min (ort 80 min)
B,V                                           EIV

## LEGEND OF THE HOLY ROSE **             PG
Henry Winkler      USA                   1989
*Dana Elcar, Lise Cutter, Richard Dean Anderson*
A free-spirited adventurer joins forces with an old
girlfriend when the latter, an archaeologist, calls on
his help in her search for a priceless 12th century
artifact. Together, they experience many dangers
before reaching their goal.
A/AD                                      95 min
V                                             CIC

## LEGEND OF THE LONE RANGER, THE **      PG
William A. Fraker    USA                 1981
*Klinton Spilsbury, Jason Robards, Matt Clark,*
*Christopher Lloyd, Michael Horse, Juanin Clay, John*
*Bennett Perry, David Hayward, John Hart, Richard*
*Farnsworth, Lincoln Tate, Ted Flicker, Marc Gilpin,*
*Patrick Montoya*
An attempt to tell the story of the origins of our
masked avenger and his first contact with Tonto, his
Indian friend and subsequent sidekick. Episodes of
humour alternate with ones in a more serious vein
and the film starts off with promise, unfortunately bad
casting (plus the clumsy dubbing of Spilsbury) and the
awkward narrative style eventually pull the film
down.
WES            94 min; 92 min (CH5) (ort 98 min)
B,V,V2                   PRV L/A; CH5 (VHS only)

## LEGEND OF THE SEA WOLF, THE *
Joseph Green (Giuseppi Vari)
                  ITALY                  1975
*Chuck Connors, Barbara Bach, Giuseppi Pambieri*
The exploits of a sadistic sea captain form the basis for
his uninspired Italian adaptation of the tale by Jack
London, done once before as "Wolf Larsen" in 1958.
Aka: WOLF LARSEN; WOLF OF THE SEVEN SEAS
Boa: novel The Sea Wolf by Jack London.
DRA                                      92 min
B,V                                           MOV

## LEGEND OF THE SEVEN GOLDEN             18
## VAMPIRES, THE **
Roy Ward Baker  HONG KONG/UK             1973
*Peter Cushing, Julie Ege, John Forbes-Robertson,*
*David Chiang, Robin Stewart, Shih Szu, Chan Shen,*
*Robert Hanna, James Ma, Liu Chia Yung, Feng Ko*
*An, Wong Han Chan*
In 1904 Professor Van Helsing finds Dracula behind a
cult of Chinese vampires. An uneasy mix of horror and
martial arts genres that does nothing for either.
Aka: DRACULA AND THE SEVEN GOLDEN
VAMPIRES; SEVEN BROTHERS MEET DRACULA,
THE
HOR                      85 min (ort 89 min) Cut (12 sec)
B,V                                           WHV

## LEGEND OF THE WEREWOLF, THE *          18
Freddie Francis     UK                   1974
*David Rintoul, Peter Cushing, Ron Moody, Hugh*
*Griffith, Roy Castle, Lynn Dalby, Stefan Gryff, Renee*
*Houston, Marjorie Yates, Norman Mitchell, Patrick*
*Holt, John Harvey, Mark Weavers, David Bailie,*
*Michael Ripper, Pamela Green*
Poorly realised account of a werewolf who grows up
with a travelling circus but finds his true vocation
after a few false starts. Cushing investigates.

HOR                                     88 min (ort 90 min)
B,V                                                    RNK

## LEGEND OF THE WHITE HORSE, THE ***        PG
Jerzy Domaradsk                                        1986
*Christopher Lloyd, Dee Wallace Stone, Soon-Teck Oh,*
*Christopher Stone, Luke Askew*
Enjoyable action tale in which an environmentalist
and his young son travel to a distant country, where
the father is carrying out a study of a mining
operation. Together, father and son have some strange
encounters and a series of exciting adventures.
A/AD                                                 87 min
V                                                      CBS

## LEGEND OF VALENTINO, THE **               15
Melville Shavelson         USA                         1975
*Franco Nero, Suzanne Pleshette, Judd Hirsch, Lesley*
*Ann Warren, Milton Berle, Yvette Mimieux, Harold J.*
*Stone, Alicia Bond, Michael Thoma, Brenda Venus,*
*Constance Forslund, Ruben Moreno, Penny Stanton,*
*Jane Alice Brandon*
A so-so biopic on the romantic heart-throb of the 1920s
that is about as incisive as a magazine interview and
just as glossy. Nero is adequate as this silent-screen
star, but certainly displays nothing one could label
charisma. The 1977 film VALENTINO is somewhat
better.
DRA                          92 min (ort 120 min) mTV
B,V,V2                                                  GHV

## LEGEND OF WOLF LODGE, THE ***             15
Graeme Campbell       CANADA                           1987
*Susan Anspach, Lee Montgomery, Art Hindle, Olivia*
*D'Abo*
A drifter takes a job at the title establishment and
becomes involved in a murder intrigue in this solid
little thriller, falling a victim to the charms of
Anspach, the seductive wife of the loutish owner. A
film that starts off slowly but really becomes quite
gripping as the plot unfolds.
Aka: INTO THE FIRE
THR                                     86 min (ort 93 min)
B,V                                                    VES

## LEGEND OF YOUNG DICK TURPIN, THE **        U
James Neilson       UK                                 1964
*George Cole, William Franklyn, David Weston,*
*Bernard Lee, Maurice Denham, Leonard Whiting,*
*Roger Booth, William Mervyn, Colin Blakely, Richard*
*Pearson, Harry Locke, Gladys Henson*
A romanticised account of the life of Dick Turpin,
following his exploits when, after prosecution by a
gambling nobleman for poaching, he becomes a legen-
dary highwayman. Fair.
JUV                                                  89 min
B,V                                                    WDV

## LEGENDARY WEAPONS OF KUNG FU **           15
Liu Chia-Liang     HONG KONG                           1982
*Liu Chia-Liang, Liu Chia Jung, Hui Ying Hing, Hsiao*
*Hou*
A martial arts expert runs off to Canton to avoid
having to obey the orders of the Dowager Empress,
but before long finds himself having to make use of his
fighting skills.
MAR                     99 (ort 105 min) Cut (5 min 16 sec)
V                                                      WHV

## LEGION OF IRON *                           18
Yakov Bentsvi                                          1989
*Kevin T. Walsh, Erica Nann, Reggie De Morton,*
*Camille Carrigan*
A young couple are mysteriously abducted to a
strange desert region, where they find themselves
fighting to stay alive and under threat from an evil
warlord.
FAN                                                  87 min
V                                                      EIV

## LEMON POPSICLE **                          18
Boaz Davison       ISRAEL                              1977
*Yiftach Katzur, Anat Atzmon, Jonathan Segal*
A comic look at three 17-year-olds growing up in
Israel. A carbon-copy of all those American youth
movies, only with a more exotic location. Followed by
GOING STEADY, the first in a line of innumerable
sequels, each of which was slightly more inane than
the one before.
Aka: ESKIMO LIMON
COM                                                  95 min
B,V,V2                                         HOK; TAKE2

## LEMORA *
Richard Blackburn        USA                           1973
*Cheryl Smith, Lesley Gilb, William Whitton, Richard*
*Blackburn, Steve Johnson, Maxine Ballantyne, Monte*
*Pyke, Parker West, John Drury, Jack Fisher, Charla*
*Hall, Alice Baird Johnson, Buck Buchanan*
A lesbian female vampire hunts for fresh blood in this
awkward low-budget offering in which a flabby plot is
complemented by unconvincing acting.
Aka: LADY DRACULA; LADY VAMPIRE;
LEGENDARY CURSE OF LEMORA; LEMORA,
THE LADY DRACULA
HOR                                                  95 min
B,V                                                    CIN

## LENA: MY HUNDRED CHILDREN ***             U
Ed Sherin       USA                                    1988
*Linda Lavin, Torquil Campbel, Lenore Harris, George*
*Touliatos, Cynthia Wilde, Suzannah Hoffman, John*
*Evans, Sam Mackin, Victoria Wauchophe, Megan*
*Fahlenbock*
A Jewess who survived WW2 by pretending to be
Aryan, tries to purge the guilt she feels as a survivor,
by taking care of a large group of Jewish orphans in
Poland. An above-average and well-handled drama,
based on the life of Lena Kuchler-Silberman, who died
in 1987.
Aka: LENA: MY 100 CHILDREN
Boa: book by Lena Kuchler-Silberman.
DRA                          95 min (ort 100 min) mTV
B,V                                                   SONY

## LENNY ***                                 18
Bob Fosse       USA                                    1974
*Dustin Hoffman, Valerie Perrine, Jan Miner, Stanley*
*Beck, Gary Morton*
Film biography of stand-up comic Lenny Bruce and
his controversial brand of humour, which made him
both admired and derided in the 1950s. Hoffman is
well cast, but the film owes much to the fine camer-
awork of Bruce Surtees. Scripted by Julian Barry.
Boa: play by Julian Barry.
DRA                                            111 min B/W
B,V,V2                                              INT/CBS

## LEONARD PART 6 *                           PG
Paul Weiland       USA                                 1987
*Bill Cosby, Tom Courtenay, Joe Don Baker, Gloria*
*Foster, Pat Colbert, Anna Levine, Victoria Powell,*
*David Maier, William Hall, Grace Zabriskie, George*
*Maguire, John Hostetter, Hal Bokar*
A fanatical vegetarian unleashes trained animals on
an unsuspecting world in a bid for power, but is
combated by a retired restaurateur. A leaden dud that
proves that Cosby's charm and talents are best
employed within the confines of the small screen, and
makes one glad he skipped over parts 1 to 5. Look out
for a brief appearance by Jane Fonda.
COM                                     82 min (ort 85 min)
V/sh                                                   RCA

## LEONOR *
Juan Bunuel
                 FRANCE/ITALY/SPAIN                    1975
*Liv Ullmann, Michal Piccoli, Ornella Muti, Antonio*

*Ferrandis, Jorge Rigaud, Jose Maria Caffared, Angel
Del Pozo*
An aristocratic lady rises from the dead ten years
after being sealed up in her tomb by her husband. A
film of mind-numbing boredom that makes one wish
she had stayed in her tomb.

| HOR | 90 min (ort 100 min) |
| B,V | VDM |

## LEONORA ** 18
Derek Strahan    AUSTRALIA    1986
*Mandi Miller, Leon Marrell, David Egans, Angela
Menzies-Wills, Ron Beck*
The story of an open marriage where the husband gets
cold feet when the wife starts to take him at his word.

| A | 84 min Cut (50 sec) |
| B,V | VIP; TAME (VHS only) |

## LEOPARD FIST NINJA, THE *** 18
Godfrey Ho    HONG KONG
*Jack Lam, Willie Freeman, James Exshaw, Dick Hunt,
Chung Wok, Peter Sho, Chuck Horry*
Story of a loner who has travelled across the country,
honing his martial arts skills to perfection with the
sole aim of avenging the death of his parents.
However, his adversary awaits his arrival with the
support of a band of Ninja warriors in this enjoyable
adventure.

| MAR | 83 min |
| B,V | VPD |

## LEOPARD IN THE SNOW ** 
Gerry O'Hara    CANADA/UK    1977
*Keir Dullea, Susan Penhaligon, Kenneth More, Billie
Whitelaw, Jeremy Kemp, Yvonne Manners, Gordon
Thompson, Peter Burton, Tessa Dahl, Terence Durrant*
A girl caught in a blizzard in the Lake District is
offered shelter by a mysterious recluse with a pet
leopard. An adequate melodrama with the expected
thick layer of sentiment; it was, after all, the first film
produced by the publishers of Harlequin romantic
novels.
Boa: novel by Anne Mather.

| DRA | 94 min |
| B,V | DFS |

## LEPKE ** 18
Menahem Golan    USA    1974
*Tony Curtis, Anjanette Comer, Michael Callan,
Warren Berlinger, Milton Berle, Vic Tayback, Gianni
Russo*
Story of the rise of the man who became the head of
what was known as "Murder Inc." in the gangster-
ridden USA of the 1930s. A violent and fairly
unpleasant drama, faithful to the facts but generally
unappealing.

| DRA | 105 min (ort 110 min) |
| V | WHV |

## LES BIJOUTIERS DU CLAIR DE LUNE ** 18
Roger Vadim    FRANCE    1957
*Brigitte Bardot, Alida Valli, Stephen Boyd*
A young convent girl elopes to Spain with her lover,
who murdered her uncle and seduced her aunt. Their
passion intensifies as time runs out and they are
eventually cornered in the mountains. Well-made
nonsense that serves as a good showcase for Bardot,
but is certainly one of her least memorable films.
Aka: HEAVEN FELL THAT NIGHT; NIGHT
HEAVEN FELL, THE

| DRA | 95 min |
| V | CASPIC |

## LES ENFANTS DU PARADIS *****
Marcel Carne    FRANCE    1945
*Arletty, Jean-Louis Barrault, Pierre Brasseur, Marcel
Herrand, Maria Casares, Louis Salou, Pierre Renoir,
Gastin Modot, Jane Marken*

An exploration of the lives and loves of a group of
characters, whose fates are all linked by their involvement with a seductive courtesan (Arletty), in the
theatre world of 1840s Paris. This magnificent tapestry of a bygone age is too detailed and rich for any
description to do it justice, but is without doubt one of
the most enthralling and evocative films ever made.
Aka: CHILDREN OF PARADISE

| DRA | 180 min (ort 195 min) B/W |
| B,V | TEVP |

## LES GIRLS *** U
George Cukor    USA    1957
*Gene Kelly, Kay Kendall, Mitzi Gaynor, Taina Elg,
Jacques Bergerac, Leslie Phillups, Henry Daniell,
Patrick Macnee*
Three dancers fall out when one of the girls publishes
her memoirs in a film that, though hampered by a
narrative that makes much use of flashbacks, remains
a lively affair, if a little short on wit. The use of Cole
Porter's music is a major asset. AA: Cost (Orry-Kelly).
Boa: novel by Vera Caspary.

| MUS | 113 min |
| V | MGM |

## LES GRANDES MANOEUVRES *** PG
Rene Clair    FRANCE    1955
*Brigitte Bardot, Michele Morgan, Gerard Philipe, Yves
Robert*
Clair's first colour film is a witty and ironic romantic-
comedy set in a pre-WW1 garrison town. A dragoon
with a reputation as a ladies' man accepts a bet that
he can seduce an icy divorcee. He sets to this challenge
with gusto only to fall in love with her, but his hopes
are dashed by the notoriety his many affairs have
achieved. A film of both charm and insight.
Aka: GRAND MANEUVER, THE; SUMMER
MANOEUVRES

| DRA | 106 min |
| V | CASPIC |

## LES LIAISONS DANGEREUSES *** 18
Roger Vadim    FRANCE    1959
*Gerard Philipe, Jeanne Moreau, Annette Vadim,
Jeanne Valerie, Jean-Louis Trintignant*
An updating of the 18th century novel that has
Valmont (Philipe) and his wife Juliette (Moreau)
encouraging each other in their sexual conquests, for
they delight in nothing so much as comparing notes.
When they plan the seduction of an innocent and
sweet-natured young girl, they fall into a trap created
by their actions and reap a fitting reward for their
callousness. An absorbing little moral fable. See also
DANGEROUS LIAISONS.
Boa: novel by Choderlos de Laclos.

| DRA | 105 min B/W |
| V | CASPIC |

## LES MISERABLES *** PG
Glenn Jordan    USA    1978
*Richard Jordan, Anthony Perkins, Cyril Cusack,
Claude Dauphin, John Gielgud, Flora Robson, Celia
Johnson, Joyce Redman, Christopher Guard, Ian
Holm, Caroline Langrishe, Angela Pleasence, John
Moreno, Roy Evans, David Swift*
The story of a man sentenced to serve in the galleys in
France of 1796, his escape and ultimate redemption. A
lavish and effective remake that, though lacking the
sheer power of the 1935 Charles Laughton classic,
nevertheless remains a respectable effort. This was
Dauphin's last film.
Boa: novel by Victor Hugo.

| DRA | 131 min (ort 180 min) mTV |
| B,V | PRV; CH5 (VHS only) |

## LES PATTERSON SAVES THE WORLD ** 15
George Miller    AUSTRALIA    1987
*Barry Humphries, Pamela Stephenson, Thaao
Penghlis, Andrew Clarke, Henri Szeps*

A wild, over-the-top spoof with Humphries' two famous creations, Dame Edna Everage and Sir Les Patterson, blundering about in a Gulf state and discovering a sinister plan to use a biological weapon to blackmail the world. The appeal of this one is likely to be restricted to fans of Humphries.

COM 85 min
B,V CBS

## LES PORTES DE LA NUIT ***
Marcel Carne       FRANCE       1946
*Pierre Brasseur, Yves Montand, Nathalie Nattier,*
*Serge Reggiani, Jean Vilar, Saturnin Fabre, Raymond*
*Bussieres, Julien Carette, Mady Berry, Dany Robin*
Story of the interwoven destinies of a group of people in Paris after the end of the German occupation of WW2 – with the figure of "Destiny" appearing from time to time in the guise of a tramp. A stylish exercise in post-war angst, to some extent inspired by a ballet – "La Rendevous", by Prevert.
Aka: GATES OF NIGHT
DRA 106 min B/W
B,V TEVP

## LESS THAN ZERO *
                                  18
Marek Kanievska       USA       1987
*Andrew McCarthy, Robert Downey Jr, James Spader,*
*Nicholas Pryor, Donna Mitchell, Jami Gertz, Tony*
*Bill, Michael Bowen*
An attempt to examine the superficial lifestyle of the Beverly Hills crowd that results in a film that's generally as unappealing as the characters in it.
Boa: novel by Bret Easton Ellis.
DRA 94 min (ort 98 min)
V/sh CBS

## LET GEORGE DO IT ***
Marcel Varnel       UK       1940
*George Formby, Phyllis Calvert, Garry Marsh,*
*Romney Brent, Bernard Lee, Coral Browne, Torin*
*Thatcher, Hal Gordon, Donald Calthrop, Diana*
*Beaumont, Johnnie Schofield, Ian Fleming, Jack*
*Hobbs, Ronald Shiner, Albert Lieven*
Our ukelele-strumming friend goes to Bergen in Norway instead of Blackpool and is mistaken for a spy. One in a series of films made as vehicles for this entertainer, and generally acknowledged as one of his best efforts. Written by John Dighton, Austin Melford, Angus MacPhail and Basil Dearden.
COM 81 min B/W
B,V TEVP

## LETHAL GAMES **
                                  18
John Bowen       USA       1989
*Frank Stallone, Brenda Vaccaro*
A ruthless millionaire calls in a brutal thug to help him gain conrtrol of a piece of land by evicting all its tenants. However, when the thug murders a local nightclub owner and kidnaps the man's girlfriend, her sister calls in a tough former GI to help her get revenge.
A/AD 85 min
V HIFLI

## LETHAL PURSUIT **
                                  18
Don Jones       USA       1987
*Mitzi Kapture, John Stuart Wildman, Blake Baker*
A rock star and her boyfriend visit her home town, but what they intended to be no more than a relaxing break, becomes a nightmare when the girl's former high school sweetheart decides to kill them.
A/AD 89 min Cut (19 sec)
B,V MED

## LETHAL WEAPON **
                                  18
Richard Donner       USA       1987
*Mel Gibson, Danny Glover, Gary Busey, Gustav*
*Vintas, Mitchell Ryan, Tom Atkins, Darlene Love,*
*Traci Wolfe, Jackie Swanson, Damon Hines, Ebonie*

*Smith*
Two cops team up to tackle a drugs ring – one carries a gun but the other doesn't, as he is a lethal weapon in his own right. A fast-moving saga of loud bangs and nasty villains, who all too soon get what's coming to them. A sequel followed in 1989.
A/AD 105 min (ort 110 min)
V/sh WHV

## LETHAL WEAPON 2 ***
                                  18
Richard Donner       USA       1989
*Mel Gibson, Danny Glover, Joe Pesci, Joss Ackland,*
*Derrick O'Connor, Patsy Kensit, Darlene Love, Traci*
*Wolfe, Steve Kahan*
This flashy and violent sequel sees the return of our maverick police duo, this time out to bust a drug smuggler who does not scruple to hide behind diplomatic immunity. The mixture of humour and non-stop action is as before, in a stylised cartoon-like film that will certainly appeal to fans of the first one.
A/AD 109 min (ort 113 min)
V/sh WHV

## LET'S DO IT *
                                  18
Bert I. Gordon       USA       1982
*Greg Bradford, Britt Helfer, Amanda Cleveland*
A young student at UCLA is asked by his girlfriend to give her a special birthday present – one she can celebrate in bed. But our hero has a problem making love to girls he likes, so his friends suggest some practice in this trite and superficial comedy.
COM 82 min
B,V ARF

## LET'S GET HARRY **
                                  18
Stuart Rosenburg
                   USA       1986
*Robert Duvall, Gary Busey, Mark Harmon, Glen Frey,*
*Ben Johnson, Michael Schoeffling, Tom Wilson, Rick*
*Rossovich, Matt Clark, Gregory Sierra, Elpidia*
*Carrillo*
The somewhat misleading title refers to five ordinary guys who decide to mimic "Rambo", when a sixth member of their little bunch is kidnapped by South American revolutionaries. Enjoyable in a mindless way, though it tends to suffer from the disjointed plotting. The director Stuart Rosenberg was involved with this film but disliked it so much that he had his name taken off the credits.
A/AD 99 min (ort 107 min)
B,V RCA

## LET'S GET LAID *
                                  18
James Kenelm Clarke       UK       1977
*Fiona Richmond, Robin Askwith, Graham Stark,*
*Anthony Steel, Linda Hayden, Roland Curram, Tony*
*Haygarth, Patrick Holt, Fanny Carby, Shaun Curry,*
*Charles Pemberton, Richard Manuel, David Sterne,*
*James Marcus, Anna Chen*
Set in the 1940s, this tells of how a film star inadvertently becomes involved in international espionage, when she acquires a cigarette lighter that has a secret device hidden inside. A dull dud.
Aka: FIONA
COM 92 min (ort 96 min)
B,V INT L/A; NEWDIR/AVR

## LET'S GET MARRIED *
Peter Graham Scott       UK       1959
*Anthony Newley, Anne Aubrey, Bernie Winters,*
*Hermione Baddeley, James Booth, Lionel Jeffries,*
*Diane Clare, John Le Mesurier, Victor Maddern, Joyce*
*Carey, Sydney Tafler, Betty Marsden, Cardew*
*Robinson, Meier Tzelniker*
A medical student finds that love and marriage are far from simple, when he weds a pregnant model and finds himself delivering her baby. A tired attempt to squeeze a few laughs out of that old stock-in-trade of British comedy, the medical farce.

Boa: novel Confessions Of A Kept Woman by Gina Klausen.
COM                           88 min (ort 91 min) B/W
B,V                                                   CBS

## LET'S MAKE A DIRTY MOVIE *                      18
Gerrard Pires          FRANCE             1976
*Claude Brasseur, Robert Castel, Nathalie Coural*
The director of a low-budget film has problems getting things together, so he decides to make a porno film.
Aka: ATTENTION: LES YEUX!; WATCH FOR THE EYES
A                    75 min (ort 85 min) Cut (2 min 37 sec)
B,V            DFS L/A; PRI; PHE (VHS only); SHEP

## LET'S MAKE LOVE ***                              U
George Cukor            USA               1960
*Marilyn Monroe, Yves Montand, Tony Randall,*
*Wilfrid Hyde-White, Frankie Vaughan, David Burns,*
*Bing Crosby, Gene Kelly, Milton Berle*
A millionaire learns that he is to be lampooned in an off-Broadway show and tries to have it stopped, but changes his mind after meeting Monroe, falls for the female lead and is eventually hired to play himself. A lightweight musical, inspired by "On The Avenue", that's redeemed by excellent interaction between the two leads.
MUS                            115 min (ort 118 min)
V                                                     CBS

## LETTER FROM AN UNKNOWN WOMAN, A ***
Max Ophuls             USA               1948
*Joan Fontaine, Louis Jourdan, Marcel Journet, Mady*
*Christians, Art Smith*
A woman has a lifelong infatuation with a musician although she finally marries another man in this opulent and atmospheric melodrama, in which the predictability of the script is forgotten in the face of fine direction and performances.
Boa: novel by Stefan Zweig.
DRA                                         90 min B/W
B,V,V2                                          INT/CBS

## LETTER TO BREZHNEV **                           15
Chris Bernard          UK                 1985
*Margi Clarke, Peter Firth, Alfred Molina, Alexandra*
*Pigg, Neil Cunningham, Ken Campbell, Angela*
*Clarke, Tracy Lea, Susan Dempsey, Ted Wood, Carl*
*Chase, Sharon Power, Robbie Dee, Eddie Ross, Syn*
*Newman, Gerry White, Pat Riley*
Two bored unemployed Liverpool lasses out for an evening's fun, meet up with a couple of Russians visiting Britain as part of a public relations exercise. Love blossoms between the young couples who have only 24 hours to spend together before parting, perhaps for ever. A charming idea ruined by the stereotyped portrayal of the working class as lewd, crude and vulgar, and of the critics of the Soviet Union as ignorant bigots.
DRA                            91 min (ort 95 min)
V                                                 PVG/PAL

## LETTER TO THREE WIVES, A ***                    U
Joseph L. Mankiewicz   USA               1949
*Jeanne Crain, Linda Darnell, Ann Sothern, Kirk*
*Douglas, Paul Douglas, Jeffrey Lynn, Thelma Ritter,*
*Barbara Lawrence, Connie Gilchrist, Florence Bates,*
*Hobart Cavanaugh, Patti Brady, Ruth Vivian, Celeste*
*Holm (voice only)*
Details the story of three wives who each receive a letter from the same woman, claiming that she has run off with their husbands. An absorbing comedy-drama that is full of sharp dialogue but little development. Holm narrates in the role of the writer of the letters. Remade for TV in 1985. AA: Dir, Screen (Mankiewicz).
Boa: novel by John Klempner.
DRA                         98 min (ort 103 min) B/W
B,V                                                   CBS

## LETTER, THE ****                                PG
William Wyler          USA               1940
*Bette Davis, Herbert Marshall, James Stephenson, Sen*
*Yung, Frieda Inecort, Gale Sondergaard, Bruce Lester,*
*Tetsu Komai*
A plantation owner's wife in the former British colony of Malaya claims to have killed a man in self-defence, but a letter that proves it was a crime of passion is used to blackmail her. A remake of the 1929 film (which also starred Marshall), with Davis excellent in a difficult and unsympathetic role. Remade several times since.
Boa: play/story by William Somerset Maugham.
DRA                            91 min (ort 95 min) B/W
V                                                     WHV

## LETTING GO ***                                  PG
Jack Bender            USA               1985
*Sharon Gless, John Ritter, Joe Cortese, Max Gail, Kit*
*McDonough, Peter Dvorsky, Michael Fantini, Barbara*
*Gordon, Debra Turnbull, Rhonda D'Amour, Richard*
*Hardacre, Elena Kudaba, Gordon Clapp, Laura*
*Owens, Sandra Scott*
A widower meets a woman jilted by her lover but the second time around proves difficult for both of them. An engaging comedy-drama given more appeal than it really merits thanks to fine performances from the leads. The script is by Charlotte Brown.
Boa: book by Zev Wanderer and Tracy Cabot.
DRA                           91 min (ort 100 min) mTV
B,V                                                   PRV

## LEVIATHAN **                                    18
George P. Cosmatos     USA               1989
*Peter Weller, Richard Crenna, Amanda Pays, Daniel*
*Stern, Ernie Hudson, Michael Carmine, Lisa*
*Eilbacher, Hector Elizondo*
An underwater clone of ALIEN, in which the crew of an undersea mining platform discover a sunken Soviet ship that was deliberately scuttled to prevent an aborted and potentially disastrous genetic experiment from endangering the world. An unoriginal and derivative film with little to sustain interest except the expected gruesome effects. Music is by Jerry Goldsmith.
THR                           93 min (ort 98 min) subH
V                                                     CBS

## LIANNA ***
John Sayles            USA               1983
*Linda Griffiths, Jane Hallaren, Jon De Vries, Jo*
*Henderson, Jessica Wight MacDonald, Jessie*
*Solomon, Maggie Renzi*
A young married woman has a hard time accepting the fact that she is a lesbian, when she discovers that she is sexually attracted to another woman. An overlong saga that makes up in sincerity and perceptiveness for what it lacks in development. Written by Sayles.
DRA                                          112 min
B,V                                               EHE

## LIAR'S MOON **                                  15
David Fisher           USA               1981
*Matt Dillon, Cindy Fisher, Christopher Connelly, Hoyt*
*Axton, Maggie Blye, Susan Tyrrell, Yvonne De Carlo,*
*Broderick Crawford*
A poor man and a rich woman fall in love and embark on a secret relationship despite their different backgrounds. A trite little yarn, made with two different endings. The script is by Fisher.
DRA                                          105 min
B,V                                           ODY/CBS

## LIBERACE: THE UNTOLD STORY ***                  PG
David Greene           USA               1987
*Victor Garber, Saul Rubinek, Michael Dolan, Maureen*
*Stapleton, Shawn Levy*
A portrait of this pianist and showman that attempts

to strip away the myths and examine the man behind the public personna, resulting in a far more interesting film than the "approved" Billy Hale version. Garber attempts to give his character some substance rather than merely attempting mimicry, and Stapleton is quite memorable as the performer's dominating mother.
Aka: LIBERACE: BEHIND THE MUSIC
DRA                            90 min (ort 100 min) mTV
B,V                                                    MOG

## LIBERATORS, THE **                                    U
Kenneth Johnson          USA                    1987
Robert Carradine, Larry B. Scott, Cynthia Dale, Renee Jones, Bumper Robinson, Caryn Ward, James B. Douglas
A plantation owner and an escaped slave who become friends, get involved in an organisation known as the Underground Railroad, that helped slaves escape to the North in the 1850s. Based on the life of John Fairchild, a real plantation owner of the time. Fair.
A/AD                          90 min (ort 100 min) mTV
B,V                                                    WDV

## LICENSE TO DRIVE **                                  PG
Greg Beeman              USA                     1988
Corey Haim, Corey Feldman, Carol Kane, Richard Masur, Heather Graham, Harvey Miller, Michael Manasseri, Grant Goodeve, Parley Baer
A 16-year-old boy fails his driving test, but this doesn't stop him from borrowing his grandfather's car for a date, that turns into an endless catalogue of mishaps. A likeable comedy whose lack of a coherent narrative dilutes strong performances from Haim and Masur.
COM                          86 min (ort 88 min) Cut (7 sec)
V/sh                                                   CBS

## LICENSE TO KILL ***                                  15
John Glen                UK                      1989
Timothy Dalton, Carey Lowell, Robert Davi, Talisa Soto, Anthony Zerbe, Frank MacRae, Wayne Newton, Everett McGill, Benecio Del Toro, Desmond Llewelyn, David Hedison, Priscilla Barnes
The second Bond outing for Dalton (following his debut in THE LIVING DAYLIGHTS) in which he goes after a drugs mobster in order to avenge the maiming of his best friend and murder of the man's bride. Despite the lack of Connery's suave sophistication, Dalton brings a toughness and intensity to his role that makes this violent adventure entertaining, if occasionally a little disagreeable. Some spectacular stunts are an additional attraction.
A/AD                         127 min (ort 133 min)
V/sh                                                   WHV

## LICENSED TO KILL **
Lindsay Shonteff         UK                      1965
Tom Adams, Karel Stepanek, Peter Bull, Veronica Hurst, John Arnatt, Francis De Wolff, Felix Felton, George Pastell, Judy Huxtable, Billy Milton, Stuart Saunders, Tony Wall
James Bond spoof about a Russian attempt to steal an anti-gravity invention. Followed in 1978 by a similar parody (though it was not a sequel) – NUMBER ONE OF THE SECRET SERVICE. Not all that badly done, though the comic elements have begun to look creaky with the passing years.
Aka: SECOND BEST SECRET AGENT IN THE WHOLE WIDE WORLD, THE
COM                          95 min (ort 97 min)
B,V                                                    DFS

## LICENSED TO LOVE AND KILL *
Lindsay Shonteff         UK                      1979
Gareth Hunt, Nick Tate, Fiona Curzon, Gary Hope, Geoffrey Keen, Don Fellows, Jay Benedict, John Arnatt, Toby Robins, Noel Johnson, John Junkin, Me Me Lai, Eiji Kusuhara, Imogen Hassall, Douglas

Robinson, Deep Roy
A further sub-Bond parody, with Charles Bind of the British Secret Service on a mission to foil a mad scientist's scheme to replace the US President with a duplicate. See also NUMBER ONE OF THE SECRET SERVICE, the film that preceded this dreary effort.
Aka: NO. 1 LICENSED TO LOVE AND KILL
COM                          92 min (ort 94 min)
B,V,V2                                                 INT

## LIES **                                              18
Ken Wheat/Jim Wheat      USA                     1983
Ann Dusenberry, Bruce Davison, Gail Strickland, Clu Gulager, Terence Knox, Bert Remsen, Dick Miller
A young actress is hired to portray a wealthy heiress who committed suicide, but finds that this is a cover for an elaborate and devious plot, engineered as a means of getting her inheritance through a skilful deception. A neat but somewhat contrived little thriller.
DRA                          100 min; 98 min (MPV or XTASY)
B,V               ALPHA/INT/CBS L/A; MPV; XTASY

## LIFE AND DEATH (A STRUGGLE) **
Leong Po-Chih            HONG KONG               1985
John Sam, Tse Ching Yuen, Ronald Wong
A family living on a deserted island come into conflict with six students on a camping holiday. Average.
Aka: ISLAND, THE
MAR                                             80 min
B,V                                                    MMA

## LIFE AND DEATH OF COLONEL BLIMP, THE ***  U
Michael Powell/Emeric Pressburger
                         UK                      1943
Roger Livesey, Anton Walbrook, Deborah Kerr, John Laurie, James McKechnie, Albert Lieven, Roland Culver, Arthur Wontner, David Hutcheson, Ursula Jeans, Harry Welchman, Reginald Tate, Carl Jaffe, Valentine Dyall, Patrick Macnee
The title character bears no relation to the famous character created by cartoonist David Low. This is a story of a British soldier's career through three wars and, but for a final descent into clumsy farce, would have been a remarkable film.
Aka: COLONEL BLIMP
COM                                             163 min
B,V                                                    RNK; VCC

## LIFE AND TIMES OF JUDGE ROY BEAN ***   15
John Huston              USA                     1972
Paul Newman, Ava Gardner, Stacy Keach, Victoria Principal, John Huston, Anthony Perkins, Ned Beatty, Jim Burk, Tab Hunter, Roddy McDowall, Anthony Zerbe, Jacqueline Bisset, Richard Farnsworth, Roy Jenson, LeRoy Johnson
A self-appointed judge rules over a vast territory, and dispenses rough justice to all and sundry, in a colourful and slightly tongue-in-cheek tale, whose appeal largely resides in a series of engaging vignettes. Scripted by John Milius.
WES                                             124 min
B,V                                                    WHV

## LIFE IS BEAUTIFUL **                                 18
Grigori Chukhrail   ITALY/USSR                   1979
Giancarlo Giannini, Ornella Muti, Nikolai Dupak, Regimantas Adomitis, Stefano Maria, Yevgeni Lebediev
A military pilot becomes a Lisbon taxi-driver and inadvertently gets involved in the anti-Salazar resistance of the 1960s.
Aka: BETRAYED (TURBO); FREEDOM TO LOVE; LA VITA E BELLA; LIFE IS WONDERFUL; THEY MADE HIM A CRIMINAL; ZHIZN PREKRASNA
DRA                          102 min; 90 min (TURBO)
B,V                                                    ABA L/A; TURBO

**LIFE OF NINJA, A \*\*** 18
HONG KONG
The police are powerless in the face of a Ninja mob who appear able to carry out their assassinations with impunity. However, a man steeped in their traditions and skills is inadvertently drawn into a conflict with them and challenges their dominance. A set of well staged fight sequences are on offer in this utterly predictable martial arts movie.
Aka: LIFE OF A NINJA, A
MAR 84 min Cut (23 sec)
B,V VPD

**LIFEBOAT \*\*\*\*** PG
Alfred Hitchcock USA 1944
William Bendix, Tallulah Bankhead, Walter Slezak, Mary Anderson, John Hodiak, Henry Hull, Heather Angel, Hume Cronyn, Canada Lee
The survivors of a torpedoed liner are adrift in a lifeboat. Having picked up the U-boat commander responsible for their plight, they are forced to rely on him to steer the vessel. A gripping propaganda film, with unusual casting and a literate script (by Jo Swerling). The director uses the constraints imposed by the cramped set to his advantage. Bankhead, playing a spoilt rich girl in her one major role, was never better.
Boa: story by John Steinbeck.
DRA 96 min B/W
V CBS

**LIFEFORCE \*\*** 18
Tobe Hooper USA 1985
Frank Finlay, Steve Railsback, Mathilda May, Peter Firth, Patrick Stewart, Nicholas Ball, Michael Gothard, Aubrey Morris, Nancy Paul, John Hallam, John Keegan, Paul Cooper, Christopher Jagger, Bill Malin, Jerome Willis
An alien spacecraft is brought back to Earth where its occupants escape and wreak havoc, by draining people they contact of their life-force, after which the victims become short-lived sex-crazed zombies. A blend of intriguing SF and ridiculous supernatural elements, with the latter eventually gaining precedence.
Boa: story The Space Vampires by Colin Wilson.
FAN 97 min (ort 100 min)
B,V GHV; VCC (VHS only)

**LIFEGUARD \*\*** 15
Daniel Petrie USA 1976
Sam Elliott, Anne Archer, Kathleen Quinlan, Stephen Young, Parker Stevenson, Steve Burns, Sharon Weber
A middle-aged Californian lifeguard begins to have doubts about his future career prospects after attending a high school reunion. Well made but of passing interest only.
DRA 93 min (ort 96 min)
B,V CIC

**LIFESPAN \*\*** 18
Alexander (Sandy) Whitelaw
NETHERLANDS/USA 1975
Klaus Kinski, Hiram Keller, Tina Aumont, Fons Rademakers, Eric Schneirer, Franz Mulder, Lyde Polak, Joan Remmelts, Andre Van Den Heuvel, Onno Molenkamp, Dick Schefer, Albert Van Doorn, Adrian Brine, Helen Van Meurs
A wealthy industrialist fights a young scientist for control of a drug that promises to be an elixir of life, conferring immortality on its recipients.
FAN 77 min (ort 85 min) Cut (1 min 14 sec)
B,V VES

**LIFETAKER, THE \*\*** 18
Michael Papas UK 1975
Terence Morgan, Peter Duncan, Lea Dregorn, Dimitris Andreas, Leon Silver, Paul Beech, Anna Mottram
A husband plays a cat-and-mouse game with his faithless wife, and eventually kills her, pinning the blame on her young lover.
THR 103 min
B,V,V2 INT/CBS; MPV

**LIFT, THE \*\*\*** 15
Dick Maas NETHERLANDS 1983
Huub Stapel, Willeke Van Ammelrooij, Josine Van Dalsun, Hans Verman, Hans Dagelet, Ab Abspoel, Frederick DeGroot, Onno Molenkamp, Henri Serge Valcke, Liz Snijdijink, Wiske Sterringa, Huib Broos, Pieter Lutz, Dick Scheffer
A lift seems to have the ability to cause a series of nasty killings in a new apartment block, in this flashy and taut chiller that unfortunately ends without any clear resolution or explanation.
Aka: DE LIFT; GOING UP
HOR 94 min (ort 99 min) dubbed
B,V WHV

**LIGHT AT THE EDGE OF THE WORLD, THE \*\*** 
Kevin Billington
LIECHTENSTEIN/SPAIN/USA 1971
Kirk Douglas, Yul Brynner, Samantha Eggar, Jean-Claude Druout, Fernando Rey, Renato Salvatori, Aldo Sambrell, Massimo Ranieri, Tito Garcia, Tony Skios, Victor Israel, Luis Barbo, Raul Castro, Alejandro De Enciso, John Clark
A lighthouse keeper near Cape Cod has to battle a gang of pirates and shipwreckers who are out to take control of the island. A simple tale that generates a modicum of excitement, but also a generous dose of tedium.
Boa: novel by Jules Verne.
A/AD 95 min (ort 120 min)
B,V TEVP

**LIGHT IN THE FOREST, THE \*\*** U
Herschel Daugherty USA 1958
James MacArthur, Carol Lynley, Fess Parker, Wendell Corey, Joanne Dru, Jessica Tandy, Joseph Calleia, John McIntire, Rafael Campos, Frank Ferguson, Norman Frederic, Marian Seldes, Stephen Bekassy, Sam Buffington
A young man, kidnapped and raised by Indians, is forcibly returned to his parents when a peace treaty is concluded in 1764, but finds it hard to adjust to white civilisation. A dose of typical Disney sentimentality hampers this adaptatation of a classic American novel.
Boa: novel by Conrad Richter.
A/AD 89 min (ort 92 min)
B,V WDV

**LIGHT OF DAY \*\*** PG
Paul Schrader USA 1987
Michael J. Fox, Joan Jett, Gena Rowlands, Jason Miller, Michael McKean, Thomas G. Waites, Cherry Jones, Michael Dolan
A working-class teenage brother and sister in Cleveland find a refuge from the pressures of growing-up and their family, in a local rock band that seems poised to make a breakthrough. A disjointed tearjerker of clumsy scripting and strong performances.
DRA 103 min (ort 107 min) Cut (8 sec)
B,V RCA L/A; BRAVE; VCC (VHS only)

**LIGHT PRINCESS, THE \*\*** U
Andrew Gosling UK 1985
Irene Handl, Stacy Dorning, John Fortune
Mixed animation and live-action fairytale based on a Victorian children's story, telling of a handsome prince who frees a princess from a spell placed on her by a witch.
Boa: short story by George MacDonald.
JUV 56 min mTV
B,V BBC

**LIGHTBLAST \*\*** 18
Enzo G. Castellari ITALY 1985

*Erik Estrada, Thomas Moore, Mike Pritchard, Ennio Girolami, Peggy Rowe, Bob Taylor, Massimo Vanni, Francesca Giordani, Louis Geneva, Robert Feldner, Thaddeus Golas, Robert Paul Weiss, Sheldon Feldner, John X. Heart*
A mad scientist with a powerful laser weapon, holds San Francisco to ransom but is opposed by a tough police inspector.
Aka: COLPI DI LUCE; RAY OF LIGHT
THR                                             85 min (ort 89 min)
B,V                                                           MED

## LIGHTHORSEMAN, THE **        PG
Simon Wincer            AUSTRALIA              1987
*Jon Blake, Peter Phelps, Anthony Andrews, Tony Bonner, Sigrid Thornton, Bill Kerr, John Walton, Tim McKenzie*
A simple-minded WW1 actioner, dealing with the exploits of a small cavalry contingent in Palestine. Beautifully filmed, but spoilt by one-dimensional characterisations and excessive length.
WAR                   110 min (ort 128 min) Cut (6 sec)
B,V                                                           MED

## LIGHTNING RAIDERS **
Sam Newfield            USA                    1946
*Buster Crabbe, Al St John, Mady Lawrence, Henry Hall, Steve Darrell, Karl Hackett, I. Stanford Jolley, Roy Brent, Marin Sais, Al Ferguson, John Cason*
A crooked banker heads a gang that steals mail, thus enabling him to obtain land by foreclosure when debts fail to be paid. An average "Billy Carson" Western in which his sidekick provides a little comic relief when he eats some Mexican jumping beans.
Osca: THEY MADE ME A CRIMINAL (WOOD)
WES                                             61 min B/W
V                                                    ELPIC; WOOD

## LIGHTNING, THE WHITE STALLION *     U
William A. Levey        USA                    1986
*Mickey Rooney, Susan George, Isabel Lorca, Billy Wesley*
A wealthy gambler's racehorse is stolen by a criminal and he is helped in his efforts to recover it by two young friends. An undistinguished family film that largely wastes Rooney's considerable talents and the viewer's time.
A/AD                                            88 min (ort 93 min)
B,V                                                           RNK

## LIGHTSHIP, THE **                15
Jerzy Skolimowski       USA                    1985
*Robert Duvall, Klaus Maria Brandauer, Tom Bower, Robert Costanzo, Badja Djola, William Forsythe, Arliss Howard, Michael Lyndon*
Three criminals are rescued by the crew of a lightship whom they harass and terrorise. A stylish film full of rather opaque symbolism – some critics saw the lightship as representing the Weimar Republic.
Boa: novel Das Feuerschiff by Siegfried Lenz.
DRA                                             84 min (ort 89 min)
B,V                                                           CBS

## LIKE FATHER AND SON **        15
Eric Weston             USA                    1983
*John Cassavetes, Gibran Brown, Billy Dee Williams, Fay Hauser, Denise Nicholas-Hill*
A boy on his own strikes up a strange friendship with an alcoholic drifter after the former tried to commit suicide, in this watchable but hardly enthralling melodrama.
Aka: LIKE FATHER LIKE SON; MARVIN AND TIGE
DRA                                             100 min
B,V                                                          POLY

## LIKE FATHER, LIKE SON *        15
Rod Daniel              USA                    1987
*Kirk Cameron, Dudley Moore, Sean Astin, Margaret*

*Colin, Catherine Hicks, Patrick O'Neal*
A father and son accidentally change bodies with predictable complications all round. A limp and unfunny comedy built around this "Vice Versa" idea, followed by several films that handled this perennial favourite with a good deal more style. See also EIGHTEEN AGAIN!
COM                                             96 min (ort 98 min)
B,V                                                           RCA

## LIKELY LADS, THE *          PG
Michael Tuchner         UK                     1976
*Rodney Bewes, James Bolam, Brigit Forsyth, Mary Tamm, Sheila Fearn, Zena Walker, Anulka Dubinska, Judy Brixton, Alun Armstrong, Vicki Michelle, Penny Irving, Michelle Newell, Susan Tracy, Gordon Griffin, Edward Wilson*
Two Geordie friends and their girlfriends go on a caravan holiday together. Spin-off from a long-running TV series but with none of the latter's sharply observed social comment. Written by Dick Clement and Ian La Frenais.
COM                               86 min (ort 90 min) B/W
V                                                    TEVP L/A; WHV

## LILAC DREAM **             15
Marc Voizard            CANADA                 1987
*Dack Rambo, Susan Almgren, Walter Massey, Arthur Grosser*
A woman jilted by a lover, nurses an amnesiac back to health and gradually falls in love with him. Another entry in the "Shades of Love" series of adaptations of works of romantic fiction.
Boa: story by Serita Deborah Stevens.
DRA                                             74 min (ort 83 min)
B,V                                                           VCC

## LILACS IN THE SPRING *** 
Herbert Wilcox          UK                     1954
*Anna Neagle, Errol Flynn, David Farrar, Kathleen Harrison, Peter Graves, Helen Haye, Scott Sanders, Jennifer Mitchell, Alan Gifford, George Margo, Alma Taylor, Hetty King, Gillian Harrison, Sean Connery*
A young actress in the Blitz is knocked unconscious and has various fantasies before waking up, among others dreaming of herself as Nell Gwyn and Queen Victoria. Happy and insubstantial nonsense, with no clear narrative but a spirited performance from Neagle.
Aka: LET'S MAKE UP
Boa: play The Glorious Days by Harold Purcell.
DRA                                             95 min
B,V                                                           VDM

## LILI MARLEEN **           15
Rainer Werner Fassbinder
                        WEST GERMANY           1981
*Hanna Schygulla, Giancarlo Giannini, Mel Ferrer, Christine Kaufman, Karl Heinz, Udo Kier, Hark Bohm, Karin Baal*
The story of a female singer who is catapulted to fame by singing an old song during WW2 in Nazi Germany. A strange film that never seems able to make up its mind whether to become a satire or a straight drama, and ultimately does justice to neither genre.
Boa: novel The Sky Has Many Colours By Lale Anderson.
DRA                                             116 min (ort 120 min)
B,V                                       INT/CBS; MIA (VHS only)

## LIMBO LINE, THE ** 
Samuel Gallu            UK                     1967
*Craig Stevens, Kate O'Mara, Norman Bird, Vladek Sheybal, Eugene Deckers, Moira Redmond, Yolande Turner, Jean Marsh, Rosemary Rogers, Robert Urquhart, Ferdy Mayne, Joan Benham*
A secret agent uses a Russian ballerina as bait to find out how defectors are being kidnapped and taken back to the USSR.

Boa: novel by Victor Canning.
THR                                              99 min
B,V,V2                                       INT/CBS

## LIMIT UP **                                    PG
Richard Martini         USA                     1989
Nancy Allen, Dean Stockwell, Brad Hall, Danitra
Vance, Ray Charles, Rance Howard, Luana Anders,
Sally Kellerman
A modernised version of the Faust legend, in which a
female would-be commodities broker does a deal with
the Devil, who acquires her soul in return for allowing
her to gain control of the world's trade in soybeans.
Not quite the success it might have been, as the
fantasy elements do not blend well with the comedy,
but casting Ray Charles as God is a nice touch. Look
out for Kellerman, who has a cameo as a nightclub
singer.
COM                              85 min (ort 88 min)
V                                                MED

## LINCOLN **                                     PG
Lamont Johnson         USA                      1987
Sam Waterston, Mary Tyler Moore, John Houseman,
Richard Mulligan, John McMartin, Ruby Dee,
Cleavon Little, Jeffrey DeMunn, James Gammon,
Deborah Adair, Robin Gammell
A ponderous biopic, adapted from Vidal's equally
heavy-going bestseller, tracing the events that occur-
red during Lincoln's time in office. Good performances
are dissipated by the slow pace. The careful adapta-
tion is by Ernest Kinoy and the score is by Ernest
Gold. Johnson won an Emmy for his direction.
Aka: GORE VIDAL'S LINCOLN
Boa: novel by Gore Vidal.
DRA                                      188 min mTV
B,V                                            SHEER

## LINCOLN CONSPIRACY, THE *
James L. Conway         USA                     1977
Bradford Dillman, John Dehner, John Anderson,
Robert Middleton, Whit Bissell
Purports to throw new light on an alleged Senate
conspiracy that lay behind Lincoln's assassination,
but this shoddy effort is both dull and inaccurate.
DRA                              87 min (ort 104 min)
B,V                                              QUA

## LINDA LOVELACE FOR PRESIDENT **
Claudio Guzman         USA                      1975
Linda Lovelace, Mickey Dolenz, Joey Forman
What purports to be a spoof on the American political
system using the actress from "Inside Linda Lovelace"
turns out to be just another sex film.
Aka: HOT NEON
A                                                93 min
B,V,V2                                VUL L/A; WOV

## LINE OF DUTY **                                PG
Christian I. Nyby II    USA                     1987
Charles C. Hill, Justin Deas, William Hootkins, Bob
Tzudiker
Story of two US marshals and their battles to break a
gun and munitions smuggling gang. Average.
A/AD                                             90 min
B,V                                              RNK

## LINE UP AND LAY DOWN **                        18
                        FRANCE/ITALY            1973
Philippe Gaste, Malissa Longo, Anne Libert, Monique
Vitta, Gely Genca, Karine Geantet, Pierre Dany, Jean
Roche, Christiane Duroc, Antoine Marin, Lita Rescio,
Phillippe Dumet, Fred Pasquali
A used car salesman rapidly becomes exhausted
keeping three affairs going at the same time in this
trite sex farce.
Aka: PRENEZ LA QUEUE COMME TOUT LE
MONDE

A                       87 min (ort 91 min) Cut (1 min 2 sec)
V                                               DRUM

## LINE, THE *
Robert J. Siegel        USA                     1980
Russ Thacker, Brad Sullivan, David Doyle, Lewis J.
Stadlen, Jacqueline Brooks, Kathleen Tolan, Erik
Estrada, Gil Rogers
An anti-military drama set in an American military
"stockade" where 27 prisoners stage a sit-down strike.
A poorly made and tiresome affair that makes much
use of footage from an earlier film by the director –
"Parades".
DRA                                              95 min
B,V                                              QUA

## LINK *                                          15
Richard Franklin        UK                      1986
Terence Stamp, Elizabeth Shue, Steven Pinner,
Richard Garnett, David O'Hara, Kevin Lloyd, Joe
Belcher
A female zoology student in charge of research
animals at a lonely house, finds that the tables are
turned and that she is their prisoner. A flabby thriller
that generates few surprises and no suspense.
THR                             99 min (ort 116 min)
B,V                                              CAN

## LINK, THE ***                                   18
Alberto De Martino      ITALY                   1982
Michael Moriarty, Penelope Milford, Cameron Mitchell
A psychic link develops between twins separated at
birth, one a respected psychiatrist, the other a
murderer.
HOR                              94 min Cut (22 sec)
B,V                                              MED

## LION IN WINTER, THE ***                         15
Anthony Harvey          UK                      1968
Peter O'Toole, Katharine Hepburn, Jane Merrow,
Timothy Dalton, Anthony Hopkins, Nigel Terry, Nigel
Stock, O.Z. Whitehead, Kenneth Griffith
King Henry II and his Queen meet at Christmas to
consider the question of a successor to the throne. An
overlong talk-show that meanders interminably be-
tween farce and high drama, but has a few moments of
brilliance among the dross. Hepburn tied with Barbra
Streisand (in FUNNY GIRL) at the Academy Awards.
AA: Actress (Hepburn), Score (Orig) (John Barry),
Screen (Adapt) (John Goldman).
Boa: play by James Goldman.
DRA                     134 min; 128 min (CH5)
B,V                          CBS; CH5 (VHS only)

## LION OF AFRICA, THE **                          PG
Kevin Connor            USA                      1987
Brooke Adams, Brian Dennehy, Josef Shiloa, Don
Warrington, Carl Andrews, Katherine Schofield
A woman missionary tricks a safari guide into helping
her obtain medicine for the sick villagers in her
charge, and together they face the perils of a long trek
through the jungle. Fair.
A/AD                            105 min (ort 115 min) mCab
B,V                                              GHV

## LION OF THE DESERT **                           15
Moustapha Akkad
                        LIBYA/UK/USA           1979
                                    (released 1980)
Anthony Quinn, Oliver Reed, Irene Papas, Rod
Steiger, John Gielgud, Raf Vallone, Gastone Moschin,
Andrew Keir, Takis Emmanuel, Stefano Patrizi, Sky
Dumont, Robert Brown, Eleonora Stathopoulou,
Adolfo Lastretti
Quinn plays Omar Mukhtar, a Libyan guerilla leader
who fought Italy's occupation of the country from 1911
to 1931. A glamorised account of some spectacle but
little verisimilitude. Steiger gives a good performance
as Mussolini.

Aka: OMAR MUKHTAR
DRA                          156 min (ort 163 min)
B,V                              ASV L/A; MALEK

## LION OF THEBES, THE **
Richard McNamara (Giorgio Ferroni)
                 ITALY/FRANCE              1964
*Mark Forest, Yvonne Furneaux*
Routine sword-and-sandal view of ancient history.
Helen of Troy escapes to Thebes where she faces even
greater dangers.
Aka: IL LEONE DI TEBE; HELENE, REINE DE
TROIE
DRA                                         89 min
B,V                                     AVI; IOVID

## LION, THE WITCH AND THE WARDROBE *     Uc
Bill Melendez            UK/USA             1978
*Voices of: Rachel Warren, Susan Sokol, Reg Williams,
Simon Adams, Victor Spinetti, Dick Vosburgh, Don
Parker, Liz Proud, Stephen Thorne, Beth Porter*
Fantasy animation about a country kept in eternal
winter by the power of an evil witch and telling of the
three children who journey there. A rather insipid
adaptation that has none of the poetry or magic of
Lewis' novel, though somewhat surprisingly, it did
win an Emmy in the category reserved for children's
features. Written by Melendez and David Connell.
Boa: novel by C.S. Lewis.
CAR                          90 min (ort 96 min) mTV
B,V                              VES/PVG; PREST

## LIONMAN **
Natuch Baitan          TURKEY               1980
*Steve Arkin, Barbara Luke, Allison Soames, Charles
Garrett*
A colourful story set against the background of the
Christian and Moslem conflicts of the Crusades,
telling of a man who was orphaned and brought up by
lions.
A/AD                                       109 min
V                                    REX L/A; APX

## LIONMAN AND THE WITCHQUEEN **     PG
Michael Arslan                             1984
*Frank Morgan, Dee Taylor, Erich Akman, Henrietta
Voight*
Standard sword-and-sorcery fare that tells of a boy
raised by lions who grows up to become a mighty
warrior king, and engages in a deadly conflict with a
sworn enemy and his witchqueen ally. An average
offering somewhat constrained by its low budget.
Aka: LIONMAN; LIONMAN: WRATH OF THE
WITCH QUEEN; LIONMAN 2 VERSUS THE
WRATH OF THE WITCH QUEEN
A/AD                                        90 min
B,V                                     IVS; GLOB

## LIONS FOR BREAKFAST **
William Davidson     CANADA                 1974
*Jan Rubes, Jim Henshaw, Danny Forbes, Susan
Petrie, Paul Bradley, Pixie Bigelow, Stu Daly, Peg
Secord, Les Rubie, Jim Barron, Ernie Severn, John C.
Rutter, Anne-Marie Sten, William Osler, Dwayne
McLean, Frank Moore*
A young boy and his older brother go in search of a
better life in the country, in this undemanding family
film.
COM                          86 min (ort 97 min)
B,V,V2                               VCL/CBS

## LIP SERVICE **
W.H. Macy              USA                  1985
*Sharon Mitchell, Mai Lin, Lee Carol*
The adventures of a porno film-maker, formerly a
director of straight movies who has fallen on hard
times.

A                                           80 min
B,V                                            ELV

## LIPPS AND McCAINE ***     18
Bob C. Chinn            USA                 1978
*Paul Thomas, Amber Hunt, Rick Lutz*
Two men refuse to give up their cowboy fantasies and
enjoy various erotic adventures in this light-hearted
and cheerful sex film. Cut before video submission by
5 min.
Aka: HOT COWGIRLS (HAR); SEXY
ADVENTURES OF LIPPS AND McCAINE, THE
A               57 min (ort 95 min) Cut (2 min 44 sec)
B,V                          HVS L/A; HAR (VHS only)

## LIPSTICK *     18
Lamont Johnson          USA                 1976
*Margaux Hemingway, Anne Bancroft, Robin
Gammell, Chris Sarandon, Perry King, Mariel
Hemingway*
A raped model takes revenge when the courts fail her
in this nasty little exploiter that treads the same
well-worn path as DEATHWISH. This was Mariel
Hemingway's film debut. See also THE SISTER-
HOOD.
DRA             83 min (ort 90 min) Cut (2 min 54 sec)
B,V                                            CIC

## LIQUID SKY **
Slava Tsukerman         USA                 1983
*Anne Carlisle, Paula E. Sheppard, Susan Doukas,
Otto Von Wernherr, Bob Brady, Elaine Grove, Stanley
Knap, Jack Adalist, Lloyd Ziff, Roy MacArthur, Harry
Lum, Sara Carlisle, Nina V. Kerova, Alan Preston,
Christine Hatfull*
A lesbian punk in Manhattan becomes involved with
a UFO and other strange happenings, in this utterly
bizarre low-budget effort that has some good moments
but not much of a plot.
DRA                                        112 min
B,V                                            VTC

## LIQUIDATOR, THE *     PG
Jack Cardiff            UK                  1965
*Rod Taylor, Trevor Howard, Jill St John, Wilfrid
Hyde-White, Eric Sykes, David Tomlinson, Derek
Nimmo, Akim Tamiroff, Gabriella Licudi, John Le
Mesurier, Jeremy Lloyd, Jennifer Jayne, Betty
McDowell, Richard Wattis*
A limp and overlong spoof on a phoney reluctant war
hero who is pressed into service with British Intelli-
gence.
Boa: novel by John Gardner.
COM                          100 min (ort 105 min)
B,V                                            MGM

## LISA AND THE DEVIL *     18
Mickey Lion (Mario Bava)
                     ITALY                 1975
*Telly Savalas, Elke Sommer, Sylva Koscina, Robert
Alda, Alida Valli, Gabriele Tinti, Alessio Orano,
Eduardo Fajardo, Carmen Silva, Franz Von Treuberg,
Espartaco Santoni*
A tourist in Rome sees a church fresco of the Devil and
becomes drawn into a strange world of Satanism. An
incoherent and mudddled film that exists in two
versions, this original and another called (among
other titles) "The House Of Exorcism", that incorpo-
rates new footage featuring Robert Alda as a priest.
Both however, do not spare us the graphical effects of
possession.
Aka: DEVIL AND THE DEAD, THE; DEVIL IN THE
HOUSE OF EXORCISM; EL DIABOLO SE LLEVA A
LOS MUERTOS; HOUSE OF EXORCISM, THE; IL
DIAVOLO E I MORTI; IL DIAVOLO E IL MORTO;
LA CASA DELL'EXORCISMO; LISA E IL DIAVOLO
HOR                          92 min (ort 100 min)
B,V                                    VTC L/A; GHV

**LISBON \*\***                                PG
Ray Milland            USA            1956
*Ray Milland, Maureen O'Hara, Claude Rains, Yvonne*
*Furneaux, Francis Lederer, Percy Marmont, Edward*
*Chapman*
An account of an attempt to free a millionaire tycoon
imprisoned behind the Iron Curtain, with an interna-
tional thief hiring a skipper to help him. However, the
man's wife has other ideas. A flashy little thriller that
goes nowhere in particular.
THR                                     90 min
B,V                       BBC; VMA; STABL

**LISTEN TO ME \***                           15
Douglas Day Stewart     USA           1990
*Kirk Cameron, Jami Getz, Roy Scheider, Amanda*
*Peterson*
Thoroughly pretentious film built around the exploits
of several students at a prestigious college, who are all
intent on making their mark in life, and hone their
talents at the college debating society. With all
concerned nursing their share of secret ambitions or
pains, this soap opera-style drama has very little to
say, but uses about a million words to prove it.
Aka: TALKING BACK
DRA                       105 min (ort 117 min)
V                                        RCA

**LISZTOMANIA \***                            18
Ken Russell            UK             1975
*Roger Daltrey, Sara Kestelmann, Paul Nicholas, Fiona*
*Lewis, Ringo Starr, John Justin, Veronica Quilligan,*
*Nell Campbell, Andrew Reilly, Anulka Dziubinska,*
*Imogen Claire, Rick Wakeman, Rikki Howard, Felicity*
*Devonshire*
Ken Russell's usual uncontrolled excercise in self-
indulgence is this time applied to the life of Liszt, seen
in terms of pop performers. A visual and aural
inundation.
MUS                       99 min (ort 105 min)
B,V                                     WHV

**LITTLE ARK, THE \*\***                      PG
James B. Clark          USA           1971
*Theodore Bikel, Philip Frame, Genevieve Ambas, Max*
*Croiset, Johan De Slaa*
Two war orphans and their pets find safety from floods
in a houseboat in this slightly allegorical but general-
ly unsatisfactory effort.
Boa: story by Jan de Hartog.
A/AD                                    96 min
B,V                                      CBS

**LITTLE BIG MAN \*\*\***                     15
Arthur Penn            USA            1970
*Dustin Hoffman, Faye Dunaway, Chief Dan George,*
*Martin Balsam, Richard Mulligan, Jeff Corey, Amy*
*Eccles, Jean Peters, Carole Androsky, Cal Bellini,*
*Robert Little Star, Thayer David, James Anderson,*
*Jesse Vint, Jack Bannon*
Long, rambling and episodic account of the Old West
seen through the eyes of a 121-year-old man, who was
brought up by the Indians and was present at the
Battle of the Little Big Horn. The best incidents are
quite excellent, but there are not enough of them. The
script is by Calder Willingham.
Boa: novel by Thomas Berger.
WES                       133 min (ort 150 min)
V                                        CBS

**LITTLE BOY LOST, A \*\***                   PG
Terry Bourke         AUSTRALIA        1978
*Tony Barry, Lorna Lesley, John Hargreaves, John*
*Jarrat, James Elliott, Nathan Dawes*
A recreation of some true events of the 1960s, when a
massive search took place to discover the whereabouts
of a small boy. Quite well handled but otherwise
unmemorable.
DRA                                     92 min
B,V                                      ABC

**LITTLE CAESAR \*\*\*\***                    1930
Mervyn Le Roy           USA
*Edward G. Robinson, Douglas Fairbanks Jr, Glenda*
*Farrell, Stanley Fields, Sidney Blackmer, George E.*
*Stone*
Robinson is excellent as the central character in this
tale of the rise and fall of a small-time crook, based on
the career of Al Capone. The script is by Francis
Faragoh and Robert E. Lee.
Boa: novel by W.R. Burnett.
THR                       80 min B/W
B,V                                      WHV

**LITTLE CONVICT, THE \*\***                  U
Yoram Gross          AUSTRALIA        1979
*Narrated by Rolf Harris*
Story of an Australian convict in New South Wales
who has many adventures before he wins his freedom.
A mixture of animation and live-action.
JUV                                     80 min
B,V,V2                    INT/CBS; CINV

**LITTLE DARLINGS \***                        15
Ronald F. Maxwell       USA           1980
*Tatum O'Neal, Kristy McNichol, Armand Assante,*
*Matt Dillon, Maggie Blye, Nicolas Coster, Krista*
*Erickson, Alexa Kenin, Cynthia Nixon*
Tacky and contrived story of a group of girls sent on a
summer camp, where two compete to see who will be
the first to lose her virginity.
COM                       90 min (ort 95 min)
B,V                                      CIC

**LITTLE DARLINGS \*\***                      18
Jim Clark              USA            1981
*Richard Bolla, Jake Teague, Lysa Thatcher, Jerry*
*Butler, Juliet Jay, Suzannah Ash, Lorelei Palmer*
The story of a camping trip arranged for a group of
young "Eager Beavers" by their leader. En route to the
campsite their van breaks down and the girls fortu-
nately find a hotel down the road where they can stay.
Here the manager enjoys their charms and the girls
have a most pleasant stay.
A                                       80 min
V                         BLUES; TURBO

**LITTLE DRUMMER GIRL, THE \*\*\***           15
George Roy Hill         USA           1984
*Diane Keaton, Klaus Kinski, Sami Frey, Yorgo*
*Voyagis, Anna Massey, Thorley Walters, Michael*
*Cristofer, David Suchet, Eli Danker, Kerstin De Ahna,*
*Dana Wheeler-Nicholson, Robert Pereno, Moti Shirin*
A young American actress gets herself involved in the
Arab-Israeli conflict and is forced to take sides. A
ponderous and pompous thriller that remains worth
seeing for an electric performance from Keaton.
Boa: novel by John Le Carre.
DRA                       125 min (ort 130 min)
B/h, V/h                                 WHV

**LITTLE FAUSS AND BIG HALSY \*\***           15
Sidney J. Furie        USA            1970
*Michael J. Pollard, Robert Redford, Lauren Hutton,*
*Noah Beery, Linda Gaye Scott, Lucille Benson*
A mediocre offbeat film that examines the lives of a
couple of motorcycle racers, whose opposing tempera-
ments are part of their complex relationship. One of
those 1970s "buddy-films" popular during the period.
The song score is by Johnny Cash.
DRA                                     97 min
B,V                                      CIC

**LITTLE FOXES, THE \*\*\*\***                PG
William Wyler           USA           1941
*Bette Davis, Herbert Marshall, Teresa Wright, Dan*
*Duryea, Richard Carlson, Patricia Collinge, Charles*
*Dingle, Carl Benton Reid, Jessie Grayson*
Film version of a play about a mean and scheming
family in the post-Civil War period, with Davis quite

outstanding and the other stars almost as good. The film debuts for Collinge, Duryea, Reid and Wright, with the first three actors recreating the roles they had in the Broadway version of the play.
Boa: play by Lillian Hellman.
DRA                                          116 min B/W
V                                                   VGM

## LITTLE GIRL LOST **                              15
Sharron Miller            USA               1988
Tess Harper, Frederic Forrest, Patricia Kalember, Lawrence Pressman, Christopher McDonald, Marie Martin
The story of a couple and their struggle to keep their foster child, in the knowledge that she has been abused by her real father. A competent but rather depressing drama.
DRA                           96 min (ort 100 min) mTV
V                                                  PRISM

## LITTLE GIRL, BIG TEASE **                        18
Roberto Mitrotti          USA               1975
Jody Ray, Rebecca Brooke, Robert Furey, Phil Bendene, Garry Casten, Joe Adinaro
A young girl is kidnapped and becomes sexually involved with her captors.
A                             80 min (ort 88 min) Cut
B,V,V2                      INT/CBS; SKP; XTACY/KRP

## LITTLE GIRLS LOST ***
Ted Roter                 USA               1983
Veronica Hart, John Leslie, Eric Edwards, Tigr (Chelsea Manchester), Gena Lee, John Hollyfield, Jennifer West, Ron Jeremy, William Margold
The story of three aspiring actresses who meet at acting school and take rooms together. The film examines their contrasting attitudes towards the practice of sleeping with directors and producers in order to get parts. One of the girls refuses to compromise her principles and still gets offered a part in a top Hollywood production. Well acted and with a more interesting story than is usual for these films.
A                                          80 min
B,V                                    ROXY L/A; WOV

## LITTLE GODFATHER FROM HONG KONG **
                          HONG KONG
Bruce Liang, Gordon Mitchell
Formula kung fu thriller set in Hong Kong and Rome.
MAR                                        93 min
B,V,V2                                       VPD

## LITTLE HERO OF THE SHAOLIN TEMPLE, THE * 18
                          HONG KONG            198-
Cheng-Taid Syh
The heir to the throne of China is forced to hide in a Shaolin temple, after the Emperor orders his assassination by a band of Ninja killers.
Aka: LITTLE HEROES OF SHAOLIN TEMPLE
MAR            82 min (ort 90 min) Cut (1 min 1 sec)
V                                             VPD

## LITTLE LORD FAUNTLEROY ***                       U
Jack Gold                 USA               1980
Alec Guinness, Eric Porter, Colin Blakely, Ricky Schroder, Connie Booth, Rachel Kempson, Gerry Cowper, Barry Jackson, Antonia Pemberton, Tony Melody, John Southworth, Carmel McSharry, Edward Wylie, Rolf Saxon, John Carter
A fair remake of the classic 1936 film about a Brooklyn street urchin, who goes from rags to riches when his aristocratic heritage comes to light, and finds that he has inherited an English stately home and estate. An Emmy Award went to Arthur Ibbetson for his photography. The script is by Blanche Hanalis.
Boa: novel by Frances Hodgson Burnett.
DRA                          90 min (ort 100 min) mTV
B,V                                           TEVP

## LITTLE MATCH GIRL, THE **                        U
Michael Lindsay-Hogg   USA                  1987
William Daniels, John Rhys-Davies, Keshia Knight Pulliam, Rue McClanahan, Jim Metzler, William Youmans, Hallie Foote, Maryedith Burrell
A version of this famous tale set in the 1920s and altered somewhat to have our poor waif taken in by a wealthy family. Quite good to look at, but lacking sufficient material to develop into a full-length feature. The script is by Maryedith Burrell.
Boa: short story by Hans Christian Andersen
JUV                          90 min (ort 100 min) mTV
V                                              MIA

## LITTLE MATCH GIRL, THE **                        U
Michael Constance      UK                   198-
Twiggy (Lesley Hornby), Roger Daltrey, Natalie Morse
A film version of the famous fairytale.
Boa: short story by Hans Christian Andersen.
JUV                               81 min (ort 90 min)
V                                             VGM

## LITTLE MERMAID, THE **
Tomoharu Katsumata  JAPAN                   197-
An adequate animated version of the famous fairytale.
Aka: NINGYO HIME
Boa: story by Hans Christian Andersen.
CAR                          66 min (ort 75 min)
B,V,V2                             INT/CBS; POLY

## LITTLE MERMAID, THE *                            U
                                            1989
Fairly unmemorable adaptation of Andersen's fairytale of a mermaid who falls in love with a prince she saves from drowning, and chooses to become human in order to have a chance of winning him.
Boa: short story by Hans Christian Andersen.
CAR                                        71 min
V                                            BRAVE

## LITTLE MISS MARKER *                             U
Walter Bernstein          USA               1980
Walter Matthau, Julie Andrews, Tony Curtis, Bob Newhart, Lee Grant, Sara Stimson, Brian Dennehy, Kenneth McMillan
A little girl is left with a bookmaker as an I.O.U. and reforms the entire gambling fraternity. A flat and uninspired remake of the charming Shirley Temple film of 1934, and one that marked the directorial debut for screenwriter Bernstein.
Boa: short story by Damon Runyon.
COM                          99 min (ort 103 min)
B,V                                           CIC

## LITTLE MONSTERS **                               PG
Richard Alan Greenberg USA                  1989
Howie Mandel, Fred Savage, Daniel Stern, Margaret Whitton, Ben Savage, Frank Whaley, Rick Ducommun, Amber Barretto
A fantasy comedy with a strong BEETLEJUICE flavour, in which a youngster finds a mischievous gremlin under his bed, and their resultant friendship and adventures create havoc for all concerned. The fascinating premise is let down by a lack of inventiveness, bad editing and a decidedly spiteful outlook.
COM                          97 min (ort 100 min)
V                                             VES

## LITTLE NEZHA FIGHTS GREAT                        U
## DRAGON KINGS *
Louis Elman (English version)
                          CHINA               198-
Animated story of a dragon fighting child.
CAR                                        59 min
B, V/h, V2                                    BBC

## LITTLE NIGHT MUSIC, A **
Harold Prince

AUSTRIA/WEST GERMANY    1978
*Elizabeth Taylor, Diana Rigg, Lesley-Anne Down, Len Cariou, Hermione Gingold, Lawrence Guittard, Christopher Guard*
Film version of a Stephen Sondheim stage musical which is in turn based on an Ingmar Bergman film, about a weekend party at a country estate – "Smiles Of A Summer Night", and tells of a middle-aged lawyer who rekindles an affair with an old flame in Vienna at the turn of the century. Pleasant enough but hardly the stuff of greatness, and suffering badly from a stilted script. Filmed in Austria. AA: Score (Adapt) (Jonathan Tunick).
Boa: musical by Stephen Sondheim and Hugh Wheeler.
MUS                                    102 min (ort 125 min)
B,V,V2                                                   GHV

## LITTLE NIKITA **                                    15
Richard Benjamin        USA            1988
*Sidney Poitier, River Phoenix, Richard Bradford, Richard Lynch, Caroline Kava, Loretta Devine, Lucy Deakins*
A teenager's parents are revealed as Soviet sleeper agents when their teenage son applies to the Air Force Academy, and he is caught in an agonising conflict of loyalties, when they are eventually instructed to undertake an espionage mission. This fascinating idea makes for a rather disappointing film that does little with its central idea, though Poitier is good as an FBI agent.
DRA                                     93 min (ort 98 min)
B,V                                                      RCA

## LITTLE PRINCE, THE: FOR THE LOVE
## OF ANIMALS **                                       Uc
                                                        1983
The Little Prince visits other planets and makes friends with various animals, in this pleasant adaptation of Saint Exupery's fable.
Boa: short story by Antoine de Saint Exupery.
CAR                                     50 min (ort 60 min)
V                                                        VES

## LITTLE PRINCESS, THE ***                             U
Walter Lang             USA            1939
*Shirley Temple, Richard Greene, Anita Louise, Ian Hunter, Cesar Romero, Arthur Treacher, Marcia Mae Jones, Mary Nash, Sybil Jason, Miles Mander*
A delightful piece of Hollywood nonsense with our diminutive star cast as a Victorian kid who goes from rags to riches. And not a dry eye in the house.
Boa: novel Little Lord Fauntleroy by Frances Hodgson Burnett.
COM                                     91 min (ort 93 min)
B,V                                          VIDCLB; DIAM; GLOB

## LITTLE ROMANCE, A ***                                PG
George Roy Hill      FRANCE/USA        1979
*Laurence Olivier, Dane Lane, Thelonius Bernard, Arthur Hill, Sally Kellerman, Broderick Crawford*
A pair of 13-year-old lovers run away to Venice where an ageing Frenchman (played by Olivier) acts as their guide and mentor. A film loaded with sentiment that nevertheless remains rather appealing, mainly due to winning performances from the leads. AA: Score (Orig) (Georges Delerue).
COM                                                  108 min
B,V                                                      WHV

## LITTLE SEX, A **                                     15
Bruce Daltrow           USA            1982
*Tim Matheson, Kate Capshaw, John Glover, Edward Herrmann, Joan Copeland, Susanna Dalton, Wallace Shawn, Wendie Malic, Melinda Culea*
A man marries a long-term girlfriend in a vain hope of becoming a reformed character, but finds that mar-

riage is no cure for his compulsive womanising. A one-joke film that relies too heavily on its good performances and picturesque New York locations. This was Capshaw's film debut.
COM                                     90 min (ort 94 min)
V                                                        GHV

## LITTLE SHOP OF HORRORS ***                           PG
Frank Oz                USA            1986
*Rick Moranis, Ellen Greene, Steve Martin, Vincent Gardenia, John Candy, Bill Murray, Jim Belushi, Christopher Guest, Tichinia Arnold, Tisha Campbell, Michelle Weeks, Levi Stubbs (voice of Audrey II)*
Film version of the off-Broadway musical that was itself based on the 1960 Roger Corman film, about a young man and his attachment to a man-eating plant. A wonderfully tacky black comedy with our hero thinking the plant will make him his fortune, only things don't quite turn out as expected. Unfortunately, the film has a vicious streak which tends to spoil the fun.
Boa: musical by Howard Ashman and Alan Menken.
MUS                                                   91 min
V/sh                                                     WHV

## LITTLE SHOP OF HORRORS, THE ***                      15
Roger Corman       USA    1960 (re-released 1987)
*Dick Miller, Jonathan Haze, Jackie Joseph, Mel Welles, Jack Nicholson, Myrtle Vail, Charles B. Griffith (voice of Audrey)*
A high camp horror comedy all about Seymour, a shy errand boy for a run-down flower shop, who creates a hybrid plant that develops a taste for blood. As the plant grows it begins to develop a voracious appetite which becomes ever harder to satisfy. Originally a B/W offering with Nicholson in his first film performance, which was later colourised and re-released. Written by Charles B. Griffith. Later made as a musical both on the stage and on film.
COM                                     71 min (colourised)
B,V                                         SEE; VES; PREST

## LITTLE SPIES **                                      U
Greg Beeman             USA            1986
*Mickey Rooney, Robert Constanzo, Peter Smith, Candace Camero, Adam Carl, Sean Hall, James Tolkan, Jamie Abbott, Jason Harvey, Sarah Jo Martin, Scot Neames, Kevin King Cooper, J.J. Hardy, Laura Jacoby, Eric Walker*
A group of kids prove to be highly resourceful when their dog is stolen by kidnappers. Standard Disney romp with all the usual ingredients.
Boa: story by John Greg Pain, Stephen Bonds and Stephen Greenfield.
JUV                                    89 min (ort 100 min) mTV
B,V                                                      WDV

## LITTLE SWEETHEART **                                 15
Anthony Simmons      UK/USA           1988
*John Hurt, Karen Young, Cassie Barasch, Guy Boyd, John McMartin, Barbara Bosson*
A 9-year-old girl appears to be a sweet young child but has a more sinister side, resorting to burglary and blackmail to get her own way.
Boa: novel The Naughty Girls by Arthur Wise.
DRA                                                  104 min
B,V                                                     NELS

## LITTLE TREASURE **                                   15
Alan Sharp              USA            1985
*Margot Kidder, Ted Danson, Burt Lancaster, Joseph Hacker, Malena Doria, John Pearce*
A stripper goes to see her father in Mexico but their reunion is cut short by his death, whereupon she teams up with a fellow American, in order to find the loot from a bank robbery hidden in an old ghost town by her father. An offbeat tale which doesn't do much with its unusual plot elements. Sharp's directing debut.

DRA 94 min
B,V RCA

**LITTLE WOMEN ** **  Uc
JAPAN 1983
Adequate animated version of a classic story.
Boa: novel by Louisa May Alcott.
CAR 68 min
B,V PRV; CH5 (VHS only)

**LITTLE WOMEN ** ** **  U
George Cukor  USA  1933
*Katharine Hepburn, Paul Lukas, Joan Bennett,*
*Frances Dee, Jean Parker, Spring Byington, Edna May*
*Oliver, Henry Stephenson, Douglass Montgomery,*
*John Davis Lodge, Samuel Hinds, Mabel Colcord,*
*Marion Ballou, Nydia Westman*
A faithful adaptation of the book telling of the
growing up of four sisters in America during the
period just before and after the Civil War. A fine cast
perform well in a film of considerable visual beauty.
Remade several times since. AA: Story (Adapt) (Sarah
Y. Mason/Victor Heerman).
Boa: novel by Louisa May Alcott.
DRA 111 min (ort 115 min) B/W
V MGM

**LITTLEST OUTLAW, THE ** * **  U
Robert Gavaldon  USA  1955
*Andres Velasquez, Pedro Armendariz, Joseph Calleia,*
*Rodolfo Acosta, Pepe Ortiz, Laila Maley, Gilberto*
*Gonzales, Jose Torvay, Ferrusquilla, Enriqueta*
*Zazueta, Margarito Luna*
A Mexican boy steals a horse to stop it being killed in
this diverting and highly enjoyable little Disney
romp, filmed on location.
JUV 70 min (ort 75 min) Cut (17 sec)
B,V WDV

**LITTLEST REBEL, THE ** ** **  PG
David Butler  USA  1935
*Shirley Temple, John Boles, Jack Holt, Karen Morley,*
*Bill "Bojangles" Robinson, Guinn Williams, Willie*
*Best, Frank McGlynn Sr*
A small Southern girl visits President Lincoln to
persuade him to release her Confederate father from
imprisonment in the North. A classic Temple vehicle,
done with enormous style and wit.
MUS 75 min B/W
V CBS

**LITTLEST WARRIOR, THE ** **  U
SPAIN 1975
Animated feature about a boy who lives in the forest
with the animals after having been separated from his
family. They were on their way to the Emperor's
palace to help their father, wrongly imprisoned on
false charges of starting a forest fire.
CAR 70 min dubbed
B,V HVM L/A; XTASY

**LIVE A LITTLE, STEAL A LOT ** **  15
Marvin Chomsky  USA  1974
*Robert Conrad, Don Stroud, Donna Mills, Robyn*
*Millan, Luther Adler, Burt Young, Paul Stewart*
Two Florida beach bums pull off an "impossible"
diamond robbery in this diverting tale based on a
real-life robbery, the item in question being the
564-carat Star of India.
Aka: MURPH THE SURF; YOU CAN'T STEAL
LOVE
DRA 101 min
B,V RNK

**LIVE AND LET DIE ** **  PG
Guy Hamilton  UK  1973
*Roger Moore, Jane Seymour, Yaphet Kotto, Clifton*
*James, Bernard Lee, Lois Maxwell, David Hedison,*
*Julius W. Harris, Geoffrey Holder, Gloria Hendry,*

*Tommy Lane, Earl Jolly Brown, Roy Syewart, Lon*
*Satton, Arnold Williams*
James Bond adventure about a drug smuggling racket
in the Caribbean run by a black mastermind who isn't
averse to using voodoo to control and terrify the locals.
A plethora of stunts and high-speed action masks a
very thin plot. Number eight in the series with THE
MAN WITH THE GOLDEN GUN following.
Boa: novel by Ian Fleming.
A/AD 116 min (ort 121 min)
V WHV

**LIVE TODAY, DIE TOMORROW ** **
Kaneto Shindo  JAPAN  1970
*Daijiro Harada, Nobuko Otowa, Keiko Torii*
A young man from the country goes to the city but
meets only failure and disappointment in this satis-
factory drama.
Aka: HADAKA NO JUKYUSAI
DRA 95 min B/W
B,V PVG

**LIVING DAYLIGHTS, THE ** * **  PG
John Glen  UK  1987
*Timothy Dalton, Maryam D'Abo, Jeroen Krabbe, Joe*
*Don Baker, Art Malik, John Rhys-Davies, Geoffrey*
*Keen, Desmond Llewelyn, Andreas Wiesniewski,*
*Robert Brown, Thomas Wheatley, Caroline Bliss,*
*Walter Gotell*
Dalton gives a good demonstration of his acting
ability in his debut as James Bond, making him a
credible figure at last. Still as action-packed as ever
and not without some tongue-in-cheek humour, but a
welcome relief from the increasingly irritating paro-
dies that Roger Moore starred in. Bliss has her debut
as Miss Moneypenny.
A/AD 126 min (ort 130 min)
V/sh WHV

**LIVING DEAD AT THE MANCHESTER  18
MORGUE, THE ** * **
Jorge Grau  ITALY/SPAIN  1974
*Ray Lovelock, Christine Galbo, Arthur Kennedy, Aldo*
*Massasso, Giorgio Trestini, Roberto Posse, Jeanine*
*Mestre, Jose Ruiz Lifante, Fernando Hilbeck, Isabel*
*Mestre*
An ultrasonic pest control device brings the dead back
to life in a small village. They rapidly increase in
number by annointing the eyes of other corpses with
their blood and the hero sets out to destroy them, but
is shot by a dumb cop and returns as a zombie himself.
A chilling and generally effective film rendered
slightly less so by some black humour and uneven
direction. Cut before video submission by 1 min 27 sec.
Aka: BREAKFAST AT THE MANCHESTER
MORGUE; DON'T OPEN THE WINDOW; FIN DE
SEMANA PARA LOS MUERTOS; LIVING DEAD,
THE; NO PROFANAR EL SUENO DE LOS
MUERTOS; NON SI DEVE PROFANARE IL SONO
DEI MORTI
HOR 88 min (ort 93 min) Cut (26 sec)
B,V ECF L/A; NET

**LIVING DOLL ** **  18
Peter Litton/George Dugdale
USA 1989
*Mark Jax, Katie Orgill, Gary Martin, Eartha Kitt*
A man is so besotted with his lover that he cannot
accept the reality of her death, and removes her from
the cemetery in order to make her his "wife". A dark
and dreary horror yarn.
HOR 94 min
V MGM

**LIVING FREE ** **  U
Jack Couffer  UK  1972
*Susan Hampshire, Nigel Davenport, Geoffrey Keen,*
*Edward Judd, Peter Lukoye, Shane De Louvre, Robert*
*Beaumont, Nobby Noble, Charles Hayes, John Hayes*

Sequel to BORN FREE taking up the story of Elsa and her three cubs. A film that ambles along very pleasantly, but can be enjoyed just as much with eyes half closed.
Boa: book by Joy Adamson.

| DRA | | 87 min (ort 92 min) |
| B,V | | RCA |

## LIVING LEGEND *
| Worth Keeter | USA | 1980 |

*Earl Owensby, Ginger Alden, William T. Hicks, Jerry Rushing, Greg Carswell, Toby Wallace*
Story of a Presley-type entertainer whose private life suffers because of the pressures caused by his success. Aldem (Presley's last girlfriend) plays his girlfriend; she later graduated to portraying a singer in LADY GREY from the same independent North Carolina studios owned by Owensby. A brash and annoying display of emptiness.

| DRA | 100 min |
| B,V | ITL |

## LIVING NIGHTMARE **
| | 15 |
| Arthur Allan Seidelman USA | 1983 |

*Richard Alfieri, Nathalie Nell, Ruth Roman, Mercedes McCambridge, Gale Sondergaard, Mike Kellin, John Spencer, Paul Joynt, Leonard Crofoot, Barbara Monte-Britton, Duncan Quinn, Julie Burger, Sheila Coonan, Robin Karfo*
A man finds his life being complicated by dreams and encounters with psychic phenomena, with visions of his twin brother who died just before birth attempting to kill him. The good start to this film is deflated by the disappointing ending.
Aka: ECHOES (AST)

| DRA | 90 min; 87 min (AST) |
| B,V | AST L/A (VHS only); ARF |

## LIVING PROOF ***
| | | PG |
| Dick Lowry | USA | 1983 |

*Richard Thomas, Lenora May, Liane Langland, Ann Gillespie, Merle Kilgore, Clu Gulager, Allyn Ann McLerie, Barton Heyman, Noble Winningham, Christian Slater, Jay O. Sanders, Jonathan Hogan, Randy Patrick, Mickey Jones*
A well-acted account of the problems faced by a young Country singer in trying to establish himself in his own right, whilst coping with the legend surrounding his famous father. Scripted by Stephen Kandel and I.C. Rapoport.
Aka: LIVING PROOF: THE HANK WILLIAMS JR STORY
Boa: book by Hank Williams Jr and Michael Bane.

| DRA | 92 min (ort 100 min) mTV |
| B,V | MGM |

## LIZARD IN A WOMAN'S SKIN, A **
| Lucio Fulci | ITALY | 1973 |

*Florinda Balkan, Jean Sorel, Stanley Baker*
Whodunnit involving a mysterious murder and a woman who has strange dreams.

| DRA | 99 min |
| B,V | VIP; HER L/A; GVC L/A; APX |

## LIZARDS **
| Lina Wertmuller | ITALY | 1963 |

*Tony Petruzzi, Stefano Sattaflores, Sergio Farrannino*
A study of a small town in Southern Italy and its slothful inhabitants.

| DRA | 85 min B/W |
| B,V | PVG |

## LOADED GUNS *
| Fernando di Leo | ITALY | 1974 |

*Ursula Andress, Woody Strode, Marc Porel*
A female undercover agent who poses as a stewardess is instructed to destroy a drug-smuggling ring.
Aka: COLPO IN CANNA; STICK 'EM UP, DARLINGS

| DRA | 90 min |
| B,V,V2 | VPD |

## LOBSTER MAN FROM MARS **
| | | PG |
| Stanley Sheff | USA | 1989 |

*Tony Curtis, Deborah Foreman, Patrick Macnee, Billy Barty, Anthony Hickox, Tommy Sledge*
Silly but enjoyable film-within-a-film spoof that borrows its central idea from THE PRODUCERS. A movie mogul desperately in need of a tax loss meets a young man who has penned the title epic, and we then get to see the film being made in all its atrocious glory. A few laughs are on offer but like most parodies, once the central idea has been uncovered, it's slowly downhill from that point on.

| COM | 78 min |
| V | EIV |

## LOCAL HERO ***
| | | PG |
| Bill Forsyth | UK | 1983 |

*Burt Lancaster, Peter Riegart, Denis Lawson, Fulton MacKay, Peter Capaldi, Jenny Seagrove, Christopher Rozycki, Jennifer Black, Christopher Asante, Rikki Fulton, Alex Norton, Norman Chancer, David Anderson, Sandra Voe*
An oil company representative tries to buy up a Scottish village for use as a refinery site, but encounters unexpected difficulties. A quirky little comedy that is amusing rather than hilarious.

| COM | 107 min (ort 111 min) |
| B, V/h | TEVP; WHV (VHS only) |

## LOCH NESS HORROR, THE *
| Larry Buchanan | USA | 1981 |

*Sandy Kenyon, Miki McKenzie, Barry Buchanan, Preston Hansen, Eric Scott, Karey-Louis Scott*
Nessie comes after a scuba diver who has stolen her one and only egg in this low-budget and laughable piece of nonsense.

| HOR | 93 min |
| B,V | VFP L/A; HER |

## LOCK UP **
| | | 18 |
| John Flynn | USA | 1990 |

*Sylvester Stallone, Donald Sutherland, John Amos, Darlanne Fluegel, Frank McRae, Sonny Landham*
A model prisoner with only 6 months left to serve is transferred to a prison hellhole at the behest of its sadistic governor, who aims to exact a cruel revenge for a past humiliation, and hopes to provoke Stallone into a breach of the rules. Much brutality now follows, but our prisoner escapes to have his revenge and this simple-minded tale delivers the expected happy resolution. Music is by Bill Conti.

| A/AD | 104 min |
| V/sh | GHV |

## LOCK UP YOUR DAUGHTERS! *
| | | 15 |
| Peter Coe | UK | 1969 |

*Christopher Plummer, Jim Dale, Susannah York, Glynis Johns, Ian Bannen, Kathleen Harrison, Roy Kinnear, Richard Wordsworth, Roy Dotrice, Vanessa Howard, Fenella Fielding, Peter Bayliss, Georgia Brown, Fred Emney*
A dull farce set in 18th century London, and following the exploits of an aristocrat and three sailors, all of whom set off in search of female companionship and suffer the consequences of mistaken identity. A brash and vulgar effort, that tries hard to achieve some of the verve of TOM JONES, but is held back by its crudity and lack of wit.
Boa: plays by Bernard Miles, Laurie Johnson and Lionel Bart/Rape Upon Rape by Henry Fielding/The Relapse by John Vanbrugh.

| COM | 96 min (ort 103 min) |
| V | RCA |

## LOG OF THE BLACK PEARL, THE **
| | | U |
| Andrew V. McLaglen | USA | 1974 |

*Ralph Bellamy, Kiel Martin, Jack Kruschen, Anne Archer, Henry Wilcoxon, Glenn Corbett, John Alderson, Edward Faulkner, Pedro Armendariz Jr, Jose Angel Espinosoa, Dale Johnson*
A young man embarks on a modern-day treasure hunt after receiving a strange message from his grandfather. A pretty fair yarn.
Boa: story by Eric Bercovici and Jerry Ludwig.
A/AD                                     86 min (ort 100 min) mTV
V                                                                CIC

**LOGAN ***                                                      PG
Gerald Potterton        CANADA                         1973
*Donald Pleasence, Kate Reid, Don Calfa, Leonard George, Stanley James, Greg George, Paul Lam, David Thomas, Bernard Edwards, Yvonne Weisner, Isaac Paul, Frederick Earl*
Three drifters find gold only to lose it again in this unmemorable yarn.
Aka: RAINBOW BOYS, THE; RAINBOW GANG, THE
A/AD                                                      90 min
B,V                                                           MOG

**LOGAN'S RUN ***                                                PG
Michael Anderson        USA                            1976
*Michael York, Jenny Agutter, Richard Jordan, Peter Ustinov, Farrah Fawcett, Roscoe Lee Browne, Michael Anderson Jr, Randolph Roberts, Lara Lindsay, Gary Morgan, Michelle Stacy, Denny Arnold, Bob Neill*
In a city of the future no-one is permitted to live beyond thirty. A member of the elite death squad responsible for enforcing this rule escapes from the city and discovers the truth about his society. A hammy and irksome display of bad acting and worse direction with a flashy first half and a dreary second.
AA: Spec Award (L.B. Abbott/Glen Robinson/Matthew Yuricich for visual effects).
Boa: novel by William F. Nolan and George Clayton Johnson.
FAN                                     114 min (ort 120 min)
V/sh                                                          MGM

**LOLA'S SECRET ****                                             18
                            ITALY
*Donatella Damiani*
Remake of PRIVATE LESSONS with Damiani as the new housekeeper whose arrival heralds some lessons in love for the inexperienced 17-year-old son. But her seduction of the son Albert has a motive.
A                                                        87 min
V                                                           ELE

**LONDON CONNECTION, THE ****                                    U
Robert Clouse           UK                             1979
*Jeffrey Byron, Larry Cedar, Roy Kinnear, Lee Montague, Mona Washbourne, David Kossoff, Frank Windsor, Walter Gotell, Nigel Davenport, Dudley Sutton, David Battley, Julian Orchard, Kathleen Harrison, Percy Herbert, Don Fellows*
A young American in London becomes involved with an espionage ring after witnessing the abduction of a scientist. Average.
Aka: OMEGA CONNECTION, THE
THR 83 min (ort 84 min) Cut (Cut at film release by 26 sec)
B,V                                                          WHV

**LONDON'S BURNING: THE MOVIE ****                               15
Les Blair               UK                             1986
*Mark Arden, Rupert Baker, Sean Blowers, James Hazeldine, Gerard Horan, Katherine Rogers, Richard Walsh*
The feature-length pilot that launched a popular TV series dealing with the exploits of the London Fire Brigade. Blue Watch B25 are joined by a female recruit who has to prove herself in their almost exclusively male environment. Meanwhile, there are fires to be put out. Not exactly brilliant drama, but

nicely handled and quite watchable.
DRA                                     102 min mTV
V                                                VCC

**LONE RANGER, THE ****                                          U
Stuart Heisler          USA                            1956
*Clayton Moore, Jay Silverheels, Lyle Bettger, Bonita Granville, Perry Lopez, Robert J. Wilke, John Pickard, Beverly Washburn, Michael Ansara, Frank DeKova, Charles Meredith, Mickey Simpson, Zon Murray, Lane Chandler*
Tonto and his masked friend investigate Indian unrest and unearth a plan to block the territory's achievement of statehood. A pleasant feature version of a highly popular TV series of the same name.
WES                                     85 min (ort 87 min)
B,V                                                          MGM

**LONE RUNNER ***                                                15
Roger Deodato           ITALY                          1988
*Miles O'Keeffe, Ronald Lacey, Savina Gersak, John Steiner*
O'Keeffe sets out to rescue a kidnapped princess in this banal and lacklustre effort.
A/AD                                                     84 min
V                                                           EIV

**LONE WOLF ***                                                  18
John Callas             USA                            1988
*Dyann Brown, Kevin Hart, Jamie Newcomb*
A pair of high school students investigate a series of murders and find that the evidence points to a werewolf. A fairly amateurish effort that offers no shortage of gory effects but is seriously deficient in the plot department.
HOR                                                     88 min
B,V                                            COL; WATER

**LONE WOLF McQUADE ****                                         18
Steve Carver            USA                            1983
*Chuck Norris, David Carradine, Barbara Carrera, Leon Isaac Kennedy, Robert Ryan, L.Q. Jones*
A martial arts Texas Ranger takes on a gun-running operation in this fast and eventful tale that gives Norris a good chance to show off his skill in the fisticuffs department. Shallow but entertaining.
A/AD                                     105 min (ort 107 min)
B,V                                                          RNK

**LONELIEST RUNNER, THE ****
Michael Landon          USA                            1976
*Lance Kerwin, Michael Landon, Brian Keith, DeAnn Mears, Melissa Sue Anderson, Walter Edminson, Rafer Johnson, Dermott Downs, Herb Vigran, Cliff Bellow, Neil Russell, Robert Hackman, Barbara Collentine, Hank Stohl*
A sensitive teenager overcomes his feelings of inadequacy and lack of self-confidence due to his chronic bed-wetting and goes on to become an Olympic star. A perceptive story, thankfully free of mawkishness. The script is by Landon.
DRA                                     74 min (ort 90 min) mTV
B,V                                                 STARX/SEL

**LONELINESS OF THE LONG DISTANCE RUNNER, THE ****                15
Tony Richardson         UK                             1962
*Tom Courtenay, Michael Redgrave, James Bolam, John Thaw, Alec McCowen, Avis Bunnage, Peter Madden, James Fox, Julia Foster, Joe Robinson*
An engrossing character study examining the life of a rebellious and dishonest youngster, who is sent to reform school following a robbery. There his prowess as a runner leads to his selection in an inter-school competition, and as he runs he thinks back over his pointless and empty life. Screenplay is by Sillitoe.
Boa: short story by Alan Sillitoe.
DRA                                     99 min (ort 104 min) B/W
V                                                         CASPIC

## LONELY GUY, THE ** 15
Arthur Hiller          USA          1983
*Steve Martin, Charles Grodin, Judith Ivey, Robyn Douglass, Steve Lawrence, Merv Griffin, Joyce Brothers*
A man is thrown out by his girlfriend and discovers an entire society of lonely guys in New York, being introduced to said society by Grodin, who is quite wonderful in this otherwise low-key and sombre comedy. Adapted from Friedman's book by Neil Simon and scripted by Ed Weinberger and Stan Daniels.
Boa: novel by Bruce Jay Friedman.
COM          87 min (ort 90 min)
V/h          CIC

## LONELY HEARTS ***
Paul Cox          AUSTRALIA          1981
*Norman Kaye, Wendy Hughes, John Finlayson, Julia Blake, Jonathan Hardy*
Story of an unlikely romance between a middle-aged piano tuner and a shy office worker who come together courtesy of a dating agency. An uneven and offbeat tale, done with considerable warmth. Screenplay is by Cox.
DRA          95 min
B,V          FTV/VSP

## LONELY KNIGHTS ** 15
Henry Less          198-
*Dack Rambo, Jennifer Dale*
A generous businessman sets up a charity for the homeless but finds his wish to remain anonymous compromised by the efforts of a female reporter.
DRA          96 min
B,V          BRAVE

## LONELY LADY, THE * 18
Peter Sasdy          USA          1982
*Pia Zadora, Lloyd Bochner, Bibi Besch, Joseph Cali, Anthony Holland, Jared Martin*
A female screenwriter is used, abused and much else as she climbs to the top in Hollywood in this trashy adaptation of a trashy novel. Filmed for the most part in Italy.
Boa: novel by Harold Robbins.
DRA          87 min (ort 92 min) Cut (3 sec)
B,V          TEVP; CAN

## LONELY PASSION OF JUDITH HEARNE, THE *** 15
Jack Clayton          UK          1988
*Maggie Smith, Bob Hoskins, Wendy Hiller, Marie Kean, Ian McNeice, Prunella Scales, Alan Devlin, Rudi Davies*
An Irish spinster finds love at long last, but discovers that her young lover is only interested in her money. Sparkling performances save this flawed adaptation that tends to wallow in melodrama at the expense of its characters.
Boa: novel by Briane Moore.
DRA          112 min (ort 120 min)
B,V          PATHE

## LONERS, THE **
Sutton Roley          USA          1972
*Dean Stockwell, Scott Brady, Gloria Grahame, Todd Susman, Pat Stitch, Alex Dreier, Tim Rooney*
An Indian accidentally kills a cop and joins up with two drop-outs on bikes as they flee from the law. We've seen it all before and there are no surprises in this one.
DRA          98 min
B,V,V2          VPD

## LONESOME COWBOYS **  18
Andy Warhol          USA          1968
*Viva, Taylor Mead, Tom Hompertz, Louis Waldon, Joe Dallesandro, Eric Emerson, Julian Burroughs,*

*Francis Francine*
A look at Warhol's world of misfits built around a kind of sex Western, in which affection between the cowboys depicted forms the central theme for the work. Not terribly well acted and with no discernible plot, this high camp exercise is by turns comic, bizarre, poignant and boring.
DRA          90 min (ort 110 min)
B,V          PVG

## LONESOME DOVE: PARTS 1, 2 AND 3 ***  15
Simon Wincer          USA          1988
*Robert Duvall, Anjelica Huston, Tommy Lee Jones, Danny Glover, Robert Urich, Ricky Schroder, Diane Lane, Frederic Forrest, D.B. Sweeney, Barry Corbin*
The story of two ageing Texas Rangers and their cattle drive from a town in Texas to Montana. An enjoyable old-fashioned Western and an absorbing character study.
Boa: novel by Larry McMurtry.
WES          360 min (3 cassettes) mTV
B,V          PARK

## LONG AND THE SHORT AND THE TALL, THE ***
Leslie Norman          UK          1960
*Richard Todd, Laurence Harvey, Richard Harris, David McCallum, Ronald Fraser, John Meillon, John Rees, Kenji Takaki*
WW2 drama set in Malaysia. A British patrol capture a Japanese scout and agonise over whether to shoot him or not. A powerful character study that has not aged too well but still retains impact.
Aka: JUNGLE FIGHTERS
Boa: play by Willis Hall.
WAR          101 min (ort 110 min) B/W
V          WHV

## LONG ARM OF THE GODFATHER, THE *
Nardo Bonomi          ITALY
*Adolfo Celi, Erika Blanc, Kim Dimon*
A Mafia boss seeks revenge after being double-crossed by a young thug in this cliched melodrama.
DRA          90 min
B,V          INT/CBS

## LONG DAY'S JOURNEY INTO NIGHT ***
Sidney Lumet          USA          1961
*Ralph Richardson, Katharine Hepburn, Dean Stockwell, Jason Robards Jr, Jean Barr*
The anguish of an American family as it tears itself apart. Set in 1910, this acutely-observed melodrama pulls out all the stops in an effort to tug at our hearts, with the wife a drug addict, one son an alcoholic, and the other dying of TB. Overblown (it largely exhibits the faults of the play) but powerful. The script is by O'Neill.
Boa: play by Eugene O'Neill.
DRA          135 min (ort 174 min) B/W
B,V          SPEC/POLY

## LONG DUEL, THE *
Ken Annakin          UK          1967
*Yul Brynner, Trevor Howard, Andrew Keir, Harry Andrews, Charlotte Rampling, Maurice Denham, Imogen Hassall, Zorah Segal, Paul Hardwick, Norman Florence, Antonio Ruiz, Kent Christian, Terence Alexander*
Another dull Indian adventure film, set in the 1920s among the British forces guarding the North-West frontier from unruly tribesmen, with Brynner leading a revolt of the peasants.
A/AD          115 min
B,V          RNK

## LONG GOOD FRIDAY, THE ***  18
John Mackenzie          UK          1980
*Bob Hoskins, Helen Mirren, Eddie Constantine, Dave*

King, Brian Hall, Bryan Marshall, Derek Thompson, Stephen Davis, George Coulouris, P.H. Moriarty, Paul Freeman, Charles Cork, Paul Barber, Patti Love, Ruby Head, Loe Dolan
Rival gangsters in London battle it out in an East End setting unaware that a far more powerful criminal organisation has become involved. A brutish and unpleasant saga, redeemed by a strong performance from Hoskins and a number of sharp observations.
THR                                        109 min (ort 114 min)
B,V                          TEVP L/A; CBS (VHS only)

## LONG GOODBYE, THE **                           18
Robert Altman           USA                      1973
Elliott Gould, Nina Van Pallandt, Mark Rydell, Sterling Hayden, Henry Gibson, Jim Bouton, David Arkin, Warren Berlinger
Private detective Philip Marlowe gets involved south of the border helping out a friend suspected of murdering his wife. A less than completely serious treatment, that adds comedy at the expense of suspense and the feeling of paranoia that this genre demands. The score is by John Williams. Arnold Schwarzenegger pops up briefly, but I leave you to guess his role.
Boa: novel by Raymond Chandler.
DRA                                              111 min
B,V                                              WHV

## LONG GRAY LINE, THE **                          U
John Ford               USA                      1954
Tyrone Power, Maureen O'Hara, Robert Francis, Donald Crisp, Ward Bond, Betsy Palmer, Philip Carey, Harry Carey Jr, Patrick Wayne, Sean McClory
A look at the life of an Irish immigrant who becomes an athletic trainer at West Point and enjoys many happy years there. An overlong and sentimental journey.
Boa: book Bring Up The Brass by Merty Maher.
DRA                                     132 min (ort 138 min)
V                                                RCA

## LONG HOT SUMMER, THE ***
Martin Ritt             USA                      1958
Paul Newman, Joanne Woodward, Anthony Franciosa, Orson Welles, Lee Remick, Angela Lansbury
A tyrannical rancher tries to play God with the lives of his family but comes into conflict with a drifter, who decides to stay and marry his daughter. An atmospheric and full-blooded adaptation with a flawed narrative but great performances. The score is by Alex North, with screenplay by Irving Ravetch and Harriet Frank Jr. Remade for TV in 1985.
Boa: short stories/novel The Hamlet by William Faulkner.
DRA                                     116 min (ort 118 min)
B,V                                              CBS

## LONG HOT SUMMER, THE: PARTS 1          PG
AND 2 ***
Stuart Cooper           USA                      1985
Don Johnson, Jason Robards, Cybill Shepherd, Judith Ivey, Ava Gardner, Wings Hauser, William Russ, Alexandra Johnson, Stephen Davies, Charlotte Stanton, Albert Hall, William Forsythe, James Gammon, Rance Howard, Bill Thurman
An excellent remake of the 1958 film that tells of a tyrannical Southerner and his conflict with a tenant farmer in a small Mississippi town. The screenplay is by Dennis Turner and makes use of the one for the earlier film. Originally shown in two parts.
Boa: short stories/novel The Hamlet by William Faulkner.
DRA                                      185 min mTV
V                                                CBS

## LONG JOURNEY HOME *                            15
Rod Holcomb             USA                      1987

David Birney, Ray Baker, Meredith Baxter Birney, Mike Preston, James Sutorius, Daphne Maxwell (Reid), Kevin McCarthy
When her husband suddenly appears after having gone missing in Vietnam, a woman finds herself becoming gradually implicated in a complex espionage plot. A disjointed and implausible chase thriller of no great impact.
THR                                      88 min (ort 100 min) mTV
B,V                                              GHV

## LONG RIDE HOME, A **                           15
Phil Karlson            USA                      1967
Glenn Ford, George Hamilton, Inger Stevens, Paul Peterson, Max Baer, Timothy Carey, Kenneth Tobey, Dick Miller, (Harry) Dean Stanton
Towards the end of the Civil War, some Confederates escape from their Union captors and kidnap the fiancee of a Union captain, who has no option but to go after them. A minor Civil War tale, no better or worse than a hundred others.
Aka: TIME FOR KILLING, A
WES                                      80 min (ort 88 min)
V                                                RCA

## LONG RIDE, THE **                              15
Pal Gabor               USA                      1983
John Savage, Kelly Reno, Ildiko Bansagi
An American pilot attempts to flee from occupied Hungary and is helped by a boy and his horse.
DRA                                              90 min
B,V,V2                                           TEVP

## LONG RIDERS, THE **                            18
Walter Hill             USA                      1980
Stacy Keach, James Keach, Pamela Reed, David Carradine, Keith Carradine, Robert Carradine, Dennis Quaid, Randy Quaid, Kevin Brophy, Harry Carey Jr, Christopher Guest, Nicholas Guest, Shelby Leverington, Felice Orlandi
The story of various outlaw gangs in the Old West told in violent detail with little else in the way of fresh ideas, except perhaps the novelty of using a bunch of brothers to play almost all the leading parts. The score is by Ry Cooder.
WES                          95 min (ort 99 min) Cut (1 min 35 sec)
V                                                WHV

## LONG SHIPS, THE **                             PG
Jack Cardiff         UK/YUGOSLAVIA               1963
Richard Widmark, Sidney Poitier, Russ Tamblyn, Rosanna Schiaffino, Oscar Homolka, Edward Judd, Lionel Jeffries, Beba Loncar, Clifford Evans, Gordon Jackson, Paul Stassino, Colin Blakeley, Jeanne Moody, David Lodge
A colourful costumed romp that follows the adventures of some Vikings who come into conflict with a Moorish prince over a golden bell. The stilted and rather shallow script is a major handicap, as is the shortage of action.
Boa: novel by Frank G. Bengtsson.
A/AD        120 min (ort 126 min) Cut (13 sec in addition
                                              to film cuts)
V                                                RCA

## LONG WAY FROM HOME, A: DADAH IS         15
DEATH **
Jerry London            USA                      1988
Julie Christie, Hugo Weaving, John Polson, Kerry Armstrong, Sarah Jessica Parker, Victor Banerjee, Robin Ramsay
Two Western tourists in Malaysia face the death penalty after having been found guilty of possessing drugs. Based on an actual case that took place in 1983.
Aka: DADAH IS DEATH
DRA                          180 min (available as 2 cassette version)
B,V                                              CHV

## LONG WAY HOME, A ***
Robert Markowitz          USA                1981
*Timothy Hutton, Brenda Vaccaro, Rosanna Arquette,*
*George Dzundza, Paul Regina, John Lehne, Bonnie*
*Bartlett, Wil Wheaton, Seven Anne McDonald, Floyd*
*Levine, Brendan Klinger, Neta Lee Noy, Lauren*
*Peterson, Paul Haber*
A young man searches relentlessly to find his brother
and sister from whom he was separated at an early
age, when all three children were sent to different
foster homes. A sad and engrossing drama of fine
performances and skilful direction.
DRA                       94 min (ort 120 min) mTV
B,V,V2                                         GHV

## LONGARM **                                PG
Virgil Vogel              USA                1988
*John T. Terlesky, Whitney Kershaw, Deborah Dawn*
*Slaboda, Daphne Ashbrook, Lee De Broux, John*
*Dennis Johnston, John Quade, Shannon Tweed, John*
*Laughlin, Rene Auberjonois*
A pilot for a comedy Western series telling of a tough
marshal who has an eye for the ladies. Based on a
character of that name created in a series of "Long-
garm" books by Tabor Evans. Mildly amusing, but
only in places. The script is by David J. Chisholm.
WES                       68 min (ort 96 min) mTV
V                                              CIC

## LONGEST BRIDGE, THE **                    15
Ting Shan Si       HONG KONG                 1977
*Kuo Chuan-Hsiung, Lin Chin-Hsia, Hsu Feng*
War film set in China in 1937. During the siege of
Shanghai a small Chinese detachment have to hold off
a far more numerous invading Japanese force.
Aka: BA-PAI CHUANG-SHIN
WAR                                       108 min
B,V                              FILINT L/A; 21ST

## LONGEST DAY, THE ***                      PG
Ken Annakin/Andrew Martin/Bernard Wicki
                          USA                1962
*John Wayne, Rod Steiger, Robert Ryan, Robert*
*Mitchum, Henry Fonda, Robert Wagner, Mel Ferrer,*
*Paul Anka, Fabian, Tommy Sands, Richard Beymer,*
*Jeffrey Hunter, Sal Mineo, Roddy McDowall, Stuart*
*Whitman, Richard Burton*
Vast sprawling epic of a film that attempts to recreate
the Allied landing on Normandy during WW2. Bril-
liant handling of spectacle is hampered by lack of
focus, making it rather difficult to follow and a little
tiring to watch. AA: Cin (Jean Borgoin/Walter Wot-
titz), Effects (Robert MacDonald/Jacques Maumont).
Boa: novel by Cornelius Ryan.
WAR                      169 min (ort 180 min) B/W
V                                              CBS

## LONGEST NIGHT, THE **                     15
Jack Smight               USA                1972
*David Janssen, James Farentino, Phyllis Thaxter,*
*Mike Farrell, Syke Aubrey, Sallie Shockley, Joel*
*Fabiani, Charles McGraw, Richard Anderson, John*
*Kerr, Robert Cornthwaite, Ross Elliott*
The daughter of wealthy parents is kidnapped and
imprisoned in an underground chamber while her
parents and the police mount a frantic search. A
fact-based tale, generally tense but rather unsatisfac-
tory as a thriller.
THR                       71 min (ort 74 min) mTV
V                                              CIC

## LONGSHOT *                                15
E.W. Swackhammar          USA                1981
*Leif Garrett, Linda Manz, Ralph Seymour*
Teenagers enter the World Table Football Cham-
pionships, but disaster strikes when one of the players
breaks his wrists. A film of somewhat limited appeal.
Aka: LONG SHOT

DRA                       89 min (ort 100 min)
B,V                                            CBS

## LONGSHOT, THE *                           PG
Paul Bartel               USA                1986
*Tim Conway, Harvey Korman, Jack Weston, Ted*
*Wass, Jonathan Winters, Stella Stevens, Anne Meara,*
*George DiCenzo, Jorge Cervera, Joseph Ruskin,*
*Jonathan Winters*
Four unfortunate gamblers borrow $5,000 from a Mob
loanshark to back a certainty, but blow it all on the
wrong horse. A feeble, low-brow comedy.
COM                       86 min (ort 110 min)
B,V                                            RCA

## LOOK BACK IN ANGER **
Tony Richardson           UK                 1959
*Richard Burton, Claire Bloom, Edith Evans, Mary*
*Ure, Gary Raymond, Donald Pleasence, Glen Byam-*
*Shaw, Phyllis Neilson-Terry, Stanley Van Beers, John*
*Dearth, Jordan Lawrence, Michael Balfour, George*
*Devine, Anne Dickins*
A film adaptation of one of the first of the influential
British dramas dealing with anti-establishment senti-
ments. Burton is rather striking as our irascible
young man who has decided to rebel against life and
family, but the play on which this film was based is
now looking very dated. Scripted by Nigel Kneale.
Boa: play by John Osborne.
DRA                       95 min (ort 101 min) B/W
B,V                                           TEVP

## LOOK WHAT'S HAPPENED TO ROSEMARY'S
BABY *                                        15
Sam O'Steen               USA                1976
*Stephen McHattie, Patty Duke Astin, Broderick*
*Crawford, Ruth Gordon, Lloyd Haynes, David*
*Huffman, Tina Louise, George Maharis, Ray Milland,*
*Donna Miles, Philip Boyer, Brian Richards, Beverly*
*Sanders, Buck Young*
Uninspired sequel to ROSEMARY'S BABY in which
our demon baby has grown up. Sometimes one won-
ders who dreams up these pathetic titles for unneces-
sary and unloved films, that merely trade on the
success of the original and offer little entertainment
in their own right.
Aka: ROSEMARY'S BABY 2
HOR                       92 min (ort 95 min) mTV
B,V,V2                                         CIC

## LOOK WHO'S TALKING ***                    15
Amy Heckerling            USA                1989
*John Travolta, Kirtsie Alley, Olympia Dukakis,*
*George Segal, Abe Vigoda, Bruce Willis (voice only)*
An unmarried mother is ditched by her boyfriend and
sets out to find a perfect surrogate father for the child.
Travolta becomes the baby's somewhat unconvention-
al sitter and most of the humour is derived from the
baby's sharp observations, which from conception to
the age of one are relayed courtesy of the Bruce Willis
voiceover.
Aka: DADDY WANTED
COM                       92 min (ort 96 min) subH
V                                            20VIS

## LOOKER *                                  15
Michael Crichton          USA                1981
*James Coburn, Albert Finney, Susan Dey, Leigh*
*Taylor-Young, Dorian Harewood, Tim Rossovich,*
*Darryl Hickman, Kathryn Witt, Terri Welles, Ashley*
*Cox, Donna Benz, Michael Gainsborough, Catherine*
*Parks, Terry Kiser, Georgann Johnson*
A plastic surgeon becomes intrigued by a series of
murders where the victims are famous models on
whom he has operated, and discovers a sinister plot on
the part of a powerful conglomerate chief. A confused
and ineffective modification of a theme handled in
THE STEPFORD WIVES, done with neither flair nor
imagination.

THR                          89 min (ort 94 min)
B/sh, V/sh                                    WHV

## LOOKIN' TO GET OUT *                           15
Hal Ashby            USA                        1980
*Jon Voight, Burt Young, Ann-Margret, Bert Remsen,*
*Jude Farese, Allen Keller, Richard Bradford*
Two losers have a plan to win a lot of money in Las
Vegas to pay their gambling debts to New York
criminals. Remsen is rather engaging as a card shark,
but the comedy suffers from banality and simple-
mindedness.
Aka: LOOKING TO GET OUT
COM                         100 min (ort 105 min)
B,V,V2                                         GHV

## LOOKING FOR MR GOODBAR *                        18
Richard Brooks       USA                        1977
*Diane Keaton, Tuesday Weld, Richard Kiley, Richard*
*Gere, William Atherton, Tom Berenger, LeVar Burton*
A woman teacher of deaf children haunts singles bars
by night for one-night stands. A film that starts off in
an engrossing manner and then degenerates into a
tiresome and pretentious display of sordidness. Later
gave rise to the TV movie "Trackdown: Finding The
Goodbar Killer".
Boa: novel by Judith Rossner.
DRA                         130 min (ort 136 min)
B,V                                            CIC

## LOOKING GLASS WAR, THE *                        15
Frank R. Pierson     UK                         1969
*Christopher Jones, Pia Degermark, Ralph Richardson,*
*Anthony Hopkins, Paul Rogers, Susan George, Anna*
*Massey, Ray McAnally, Maxine Audley, Cyril Shaps,*
*Robert Urquhart, Frederick Jaegar, Paul Maxwell,*
*Vivien Pickles*
Story of a spy mission to photograph a missile site in
East Germany. A dull and incoherent spy thriller that
fails to do justice to the original novel. Jones just does
not convince as the young Pole sent over to do British
Intelligence's dirty work for them. Written by Pierson.
Boa: novel by John Le Carre.
DRA                         103 min (ort 108 min)
V                                              RCA

## LOOPHOLE **                                     PG
John Quested         UK                         1980
*Albert Finney, Martin Sheen, Susannah York, Colin*
*Blakely, Jonathan Pryce, Alfred Lynch, Robert Morley,*
*Tony Doyle, Christopher Guard, Gwyneth Powell,*
*Jerry Harte, James Grout, Terence Hardiman, Bridget*
*Brice, Ian Howarth*
The story of the various people who plan to rob the
vaults of a reputedly impregnable bank. A glib little
thriller of no great merit. The music is by Lalo
Schifrin.
THR                          105 min; 94 min (VGM)
B,V                              BWV; VGM (VHS only)

## LOOSE CANNONS *                                 15
Bob Clark            USA                         1990
*Gene Hackman, Dan Aykroyd, Dom DeLuise, Ronny*
*Cox, Nancy Travis*
A pair of mismatched police detectives solve a serial
murder case that involves an incriminating video tape
of Hitler and his henchmen that could ruin the career
of a German politician. A clumsy farce that throws in
just about every ingredient on offer, but the whole is
very definitely less than the sum of the parts.
COM                                        90 min
V                                              RCA

## LOOSE CONNECTIONS **
Richard Eyre         UK                         1983
*Lindsay Duncan, Stephen Rea, Carole Harrison,*
*Frances Low, Andre De La Tour, David Purcell, Keith*
*Allen, Robbie Coltrane, Ruth Bruck, Gary Olsen, Jan*
*Niklas, Henny Reinheimer, Eberhard Meltzer*

Story of the adventures of an old mis-matched couple
on the road in Europe, consisting of a radical feminist
on her way to a convention in Munich and a macho
male football supporter. A pleasant way to kill ninety
minutes, but no more than that.
COM                          96 min (ort 100 min)
B,V                                            PVG

## LOOSE SHOES **
Ira Miller           USA                         1980
*Bill Murray, Howard Hesseman, David Landsburg,*
*Ed Lauter, Susan Tyrell, Avery Schreiber, Jaye P.*
*Morgan, Buddy Hackett, Misty Rowe, Murphy Dunne,*
*Theodore Wilson, David Downing, Lewis Arquette,*
*Danny Dayton, Ira Miller*
Mixed bag of short spoofs on film trailers with a few
hilarious sequences (especially "Darktown After
Dark") and a mass of mediocre ones. This was
Murray's first film. The score and songs were com-
posed by Dunne.
Aka: COMING ATTRACTIONS
COM                          70 min (ort 84 min)
B,V                                            HOK

## LOOT ***                                        15
Silvio Narizzano     UK                         1970
*Hywel Bennett, Richard Attenborough, Lee Remick,*
*Milo O'Shea, Dick Emery, Joe Lynch, Roy Holder,*
*John Cater, Aubrey Woods, Robert Raglan, Jean*
*Marlow*
A funny but uneven black comedy about bank robbers
who make frantic efforts to retrieve the proceeds of a
robbery, having hidden it in the coffin of the mother of
one of them. However, they do not bargain for
Attenborough's Inspector Truscott who fancies him-
self as something of a sleuth. Bad casting of Remick is
a handicap.
Aka: LOOT . . . GIVE ME MONEY, HONEY!
Boa: play by Joe Orton.
COM                          96 min (ort 101 min)
B,V                          TEVP; WHV (VHS only)

## LORCA AND THE OUTLAWS *                         PG
Roger Christian      UK                         1985
*John Tarrant, Deep Roy, Cassandra Webb, Donogh*
*Rees, Ralph Cotterill, Hugh Keays-Byrne, Joy*
*Smithers, Tyler Coppin, James Steele, Peter Morris,*
*Arthur Sherman, Steve Jodder III, Arky Michael*
A group of miners rebel and plot their escape from the
planet they're kept on, when they learn of plans to
replace them with robots. Unsophisticated SF yarn. A
lacklustre quickie inspired by STAR WARS, but
hampered by poor characterisation and a shortage of
action.
Aka: 2084; STARSHIP
FAN                          90 min (ort 100 min)
B,V                                            POLY

## LORD JIM **                                     PG
Richard Brooks       UK                         1964
*Peter O'Toole, James Mason, Eli Wallach, Curt*
*Jurgens, Jack Hawkins, Paul Lukas, Akim Tamiroff,*
*Daliah Lavi, Ichizo Itami, Christian Marquand,*
*Andrew Keir, Jack MacGowran, Noel Purcell, Walter*
*Gotell*
A poor and shallow adaptation of Conrad's novel
telling of a young sailor who commits an act of
cowardice, and then spends the rest of his life
struggling to find some way to atone and regain his
self-respect. An outstanding cast do their best.
Scripted by Brooks.
Boa: novel Joseph Conrad.
A/AD                         148 min (ort 154 min)
V                                              RCA

## LORD OF THE FLIES **                            15
Harry Hook           USA                         1990
*Paul Balthazar Getty, Chris Furrh, Danuel Pipoly,*
*Michael Greene, Badgett Dale, Edward Taft, Andrew*

*Taft*
A lush updating of Golding's classic apocalyptic fable that turns our British schoolboys into American kids, adding a certain contemporary feel to the story, but at the expense of the novel's sub-Freudian insights. The excellent score is by Phillipe Sarde, and a fine cast (largely of unknowns) play their parts well, but the depth and compelling (if sporadic) force of the earlier Peter Brook film is entirely absent.
Boa: novel by William Golding.
DRA                                          95 min
V/h                                          PAL

**LORD OF THE FLIES ***                      PG
Peter Brook            UK                    1963
*James Aubrey, Tom Chapin, Roger Elwin, Hugh Edwards, Tom Gaman, Surtees Twins*
Having been stranded on a remote tropical island by a plane crash, a group of English schoolboys slowly descend into savagery and tribalism. A flawed attempt to adapt Golding's book, it has some powerful moments but is generally weighed down by the novel's symbolism rather than assisted by it. A semi-professional production that is sometimes a little too ambitious for its own good. Screenplay is by Brook.
Boa: novel by William Golding.
DRA                      87 min (ort 91 min) B/W
V                                            WHV

**LORD OF THE RINGS, THE ***                 15
Ralph Bakshi           USA                   1978
*Voices of: Christopher Guard, William Squire, John Hurt, Michael Sholes, Dominic Guard*
Animated version of this fantasy saga dealing with the battle between good and evil in the realm of "Middle Earth", and a struggle for possession of a magical ring which can confer great power on its owner. An ambitious but flawed adaptation of the Tolkien saga that ends rather abruptly, having only got halfway through the trilogy. One interesting aspect is the way in which the cartoon was made, using film of live actors as a basis.
Boa: trilogy The Lord Of The Rings by J.R. Tolkien.
CAR                      60 min (ort 133 min) Cut (2 sec)
B,V                                    TEVP L/A; VES

**LORDS OF DISCIPLINE, THE ***               15
Franc Roddam           USA                   1982
*David Keith, Mark Breland, Robert Prosky, G.D. Spradlin, Rick Rossovitch, Mitchell Lichtenstein, Barbara Babcock, Michael Biehn, Judge Reinhold, Bill Paxton*
An ugly story of racism at a military academy in South Carolina in 1964, where the first black student is being systematically assaulted by a secret society. Good performances hold up the murky and unappealing script. Filmed in England.
Boa: novel by Pat Conroy.
DRA                      98 min (ort 103 min)
B,V,V2                                       CIC

**LORDS OF FLATBUSH, THE ***                 15
Stephen F. Verona/Martin Davidson
                       USA                   1974
*Sylvester Stallone, Henry Winkler, Perry King, Paul Mace, Susan Blakely, Dolph Sweet, Maria Smith, Paul Jabara*
Excellent story of a New York gang in 1957 with fine performances all round and good period detail. Some of the dialogue was written by Stallone.
DRA                      80 min (ort 88 min)
V                                            RCA

**LORDS OF MAGICK, THE ***                   18
David Marsh                                  1989
*Brendan Dillon Jr, Mark Gauthier, Jarrett Parker, David Snow*
When an evil wizard abducts a young girl in a bid for

world domination, two young sorcerers set out to rescue her. Standard blend of sword and sorcery.
FAN                                          99 min
V                                            NEON

**LORDS OF THE DEEP ***                      PG
Mary Ann Fisher        USA                   1988
*Bradford Dillman, Priscilla Barnes, Daryl Haney*
The crew of an underwater research station become trapped by an earthquake but discover an alien colony beneath the seabed. Like "The Abyss" and DEEPSTAR SIX, this film explores a late 1980s interest in underwater fantasies.
FAN                                          75 min
V                                            MGM

**LORELEI'S GRASP, THE ***                   18
Armando de Ossorio    SPAIN                  1972
*Tony Kendall (Luciano Stella), Helga Line, Silvia Tortosa, Loretta Tovar, Luis Induin, Jose Theman, Angel Menendez, Luis Barboo, Josefina Jartin*
A low-budget quickie, very loosely based on the German legend of a siren who ate the hearts of young people to keep her beauty. This tale combines elements of the "Nibelungen" myth and has our creature living in a cave, from where she ventures forth as a monster to attack young women and tear out their hearts. A warrior is hired to destroy her and eventually does so, with a blade forged from the sword of Siegfried.
Aka: LAS GARRAS DE LORELEI; LORELEY'S GRASP, THE; WHEN THE SCREAMING STOPS
HOR                   81 min (ort 102 min) Cut (37 sec)
B,V                                          VPD

**LOS ANGELES CONNECTION, THE ***
                       USA                   198-
*John Ireland, Dorothy Malone*
A journalist investigates a friend's mysterious death and finds his own life in danger.
DRA                                          90 min
B,V,V2                                       VPD

**LOSERS, THE ***                            18
Jack Starrett          USA                   1970
*Bernie Hamilton, William Smith, Adam Roarke, Daniel Kemp, Houston Savage, Gene Cornelius, Paul Koslo, John Garwood, Ana Koita, Lilliam Margarejo, Paralumen Paul Nuckles*
Five Hell's Angels are recruited for active service on armoured cycles in Cambodia, where they frighten the Viet Cong and rescue an American advisor from the Chinese. Formula mindless mayhem. See also NAM ANGELS.
Aka: MEAN COMBAT (WARAD); MISERS, THE
WAR                                          95 min
B,V                                    VUL L/A; WARAD

**LOSIN' IT ***                              18
Curtis Hanson          USA                   1983
*Tom Cruise, Jackie Earle Haley, John Stockwell, Shelley Long, John P. Nevin Jr, Henry Darrow*
Three teenagers go to Tijuana for a wild time and hope to become sexually experienced. An empty-headed comedy made slightly more diverting by the strong cast.
COM                      96 min (ort 104 min)
B,V                              NET; GLOB; INT/CBS

**LOST AND FOUND ***                         15
Melvin Frank          USA                    1979
*George Segal, Glenda Jackson, Maureen Stapleton, John Cunningham, Hollis McLaren, Paul Sorvino, John Candy, Martin Short*
An attempt to remake A TOUCH OF CLASS with a British divorcee meeting and marrying a widowed American college professor, and the couple rather quickly discovering just how incompatible they are. A

flawed comedy that strains hard for a few laughs. Written by Frank and Jack Rose.

COM 104 min (ort 112 min)
V RCA

## LOST BOYS, THE ** 15
Joel Schumacher USA 1987
Corey Feldman, Jami Gertz, Corey Haim, Jason Patric, Kiefer Sutherland, Edward Herrmann, Barnard Hughes, Dianne Wiest, Jamison Newlander, Brooke McCarter, Billy Wirth, Alexander Winter
Two brothers move to a new town and discover that the local biker gang members are really undead. The younger one has his work cut out when his older brother falls for the lone female in this bunch of motorised vampires. A flashy but predictable chiller with some humorous touches. The climax is the best thing in the film.

HOR 94 min (ort 98 min)
V/sh WHV

## LOST COMMAND ** 15
Mark Robson USA 1966
Anthony Quinn, Alain Delon, Claudia Cardinale, George Segal, Michele Morgan, Maurice Ronet, Gregoire Aslan, Jean Servais
The story of a French paratroop regiment and its anti-guerilla operations during the Algerian struggle for independence. A competent action film with Quinn excellent as a peasant leader but the script is merely adequate.
Boa: novel The Centurions by Jean Larteguy.

WAR 125 min (ort 129 min)
V/sh RCA

## LOST EMPIRE, THE **
Jim Wynorski USA 1983
Melanie Vincz, Raven De La Croix, Angus Scrimm, Angela Aames, Paul Coufos, Bob Tessier, Blackie Dammett, Linda Shayne, Angelique Pettyjohn, Kenneth Tobey, Garry Goodrow, Art Hern, Annie Gaybis, Jason Stuart, Gary Don Cox
An action fantasy about a woman out to avenge the death of her policeman brother, who stumbles across a secret society that is planning to dominate the world.

A/AD 80 min (ort 86 min)
B,V AVA/CBS

## LOST HORIZON **** U
Frank Capra USA 1937
Ronald Colman, Jane Wyatt, John Howard, Thomas Mitchell, Edward Everett Horton, Sam Jaffe, H.B. Warner, Isabel Jewell, Margo
A brilliant evocation of our longing for a land beyond time and human imperfection finds expression in this exquisite tale of five travellers who are abducted and brought to the remote Himalayan community of Shangri La, the intention being to select a new leader. Originally 130 min but released at 118 min. Unfortunately portions of the original uncut film are now lost. AA: Art (Stephen Goosen), Edit (Gene Havlick/Gene Milford). Remade in 1972.
Boa: novel by James Hilton.

A/AD 112 min (ort 118 min) B/W
V RCA

## LOST IDOL, THE ** 15
P. Chalong USA 1988
Erik Estrada, James Phillips, Myra Chason, Christoph Kluppel, Pierre Delande
A former US Army officer discovered a priceless golden statue in Kampuchea during the Vietnam War, then massacred his unit, hid the statue, and hoped to retrieve it after the war. He returns with a bunch of mercenaries with this intention, but discovers that one of his men survived and now lives in the country. A fair action yarn.

A/AD 105 min
V COL

## LOST IN AMERICA *** 15
Albert Brooks USA 1985
Julie Hagerty, Albert Brooks, Michael Greene, Gary Marshall, Art Frankel, Tom Tarpey, Ernie Brown
Peeved at not being promoted, an executive and his wife drop out and buy a camper, intending to rediscover the promise of life on the road as shown in EASY RIDER. A restrained but often highly amusing satire. The script is by Brooks and Monica Johnson.

COM 88 min (ort 91 min)
V/h WHV

## LOST IN LONDON * U
Robert Lewis USA 1986
Emmanuel Lewis, Ben Vereen, Lynne Moody, Freddie Jones, Basil Hoskins, Courtney Roper Knight, Bobby Collins, Horace Oliver, Amber Jane Raab, Wayne Michelle Welch, Wayne Goddard, Peter Hughes, Deidre Costello, Linda Regan
A young boy alone in London after his parents' divorce gets lost and falls in with a modern-day Fagin. A dreary little yarn that tries for whimsy but merely achieves mediocrity.

JUV 93 min mTV
B,V HER

## LOST MOMENT, THE ***
Martin Gabel USA 1947
Robert Cummings, Susan Hayward, Agnes Moorehead, Joan Lorring, Eduardo Ciannelli
A publisher goes to Italy in search of a famous poet's love letters, written to a lady who is now 105, and discovers her living with a young female companion who suffers from a split personality. A contrived melodrama, strong on atmosphere and period detail but a little short on plausibility.
Boa: novel The Aspern Papers by Henry James.

DRA 89 min B/W
B,V INT/CBS

## LOST TRIBE, THE ** 18
John Laing NEW ZEALAND 1983
John Bach, Darien Takle, Emma Takle, Don Selwyn, Terry Connolly, Martyn Sanderson, Ian Watkin, Adele Chapman
Some terrifying events on a deserted island result in death, as a missing archaeologist is sought by his wife and twin brother.

THR 95 min
B,V CBS

## LOST! ** 15
Peter Rowe CANADA 1986
Helen Shaver, Kenneth Walsh, Michael Hogan, Linda Goranson, Charles Joliffe
Two brothers and a woman have to share a life-raft for 70 days, as they await rescue in the Pacific.
Aka: LOST! – A TRUE STORY
Boa: book by Thomas Thompson.

DRA 95 min
B,V AVA

## LOTS OF LUCK ** U
Peter Baldwin USA 1985
Martin Mull, Annette Funicello, Fred Willard, Polly Holliday, Mia Dillon, Tracey Gold, Jeremy Licht, Christina Nigra, Hamilton Camp, Dick O'Neill, Jack Riley, Vincent Schiavelli, Frederick Long, Joseph Chapman
A couple win a big prize in a lottery but find that money does not bring happiness. Average.

COM 88 min mCab
B,V WDV

## LOTTERY * U
Lee Philips USA 1983
Marshall Colt, Ben Murphy, Allan Goorwitz, Reni Santoni, Christopher McDonald, Renee Taylor
A lottery company hires two people to help it find

those who have won cash prizes. A witless TV movie that spawned a series of 22 one-hour episodes.
COM                                    74 min mTV
B,V                                        STABL

## LOUIS ARMSTRONG – CHICAGO STYLE *        15
Dee Philips              USA              1976
*Ben Vereen, Red Buttons, Margaret Avery, Janet MacLachlan, Ketty Lester, Albert Paulsen*
In the 1930s Armstrong received a death threat from the Chicago underworld when he refused to play at a club they controlled, but the threat backfired and brought him international prominence. This film attempts to examine that incident, but the flat script (by James Lee) fails to imbue it with any dramatic significance.
DRA                    74 min (ort 78 min) mTV
V                                          CASPIC

## LOUISIANA **                             15
Philippe de Broca
            CANADA/FRANCE/ITALY          1984
*Ian Charleson, Margot Kidder, Victor Lanoux, Len Cariou, Lloyd Bochner, Andrea Ferreol, Hilly Hicks, Ken Pogue, Akosua Busia, Raymond Pellegrin, Corinne Marchand, Jim Bearden, Larry Lewis, Wayne Best, Ron Lewis*
A 19th century epic about a ruined heiress fighting to regain her lost home and fortune. A glitzy piece of enjoyable hokum, first shown in two parts.
Aka: LOUISANE
Boa: novels Louisiana and Fausse-Riviere by Maurice Denuziere.
DRA                               285 min mCab
B,V                                      ODY/POLY

## LOVE AMONG THE RUINS ****
George Cukor            USA              1975
*Laurence Olivier, Katharine Hepburn, Joan Sims, Colin Blakely, Richard Pearson, Leigh Lanson, Gwen Nelson, Robert H. Harris, Peter Reeves, John Dunbar, Arthur Hewlett, John Blythe, Lain Sinclair, Mervyn Pascoe*
When faced with the prospect of a breach of promise suit brought by her young lover, an ageing actress turns for help to an old flame who is a brilliant barrister. A witty and romantic comedy that won Emmy Awards for Hepburn, Olivier and Cukor as well as for the teleplay by James Costigan, art and set decoration and costumes.
COM                               100 min mTV
B,V                                        GHV

## LOVE AMONG THIEVES **                    PG
Roger Young             USA              1987
*Audrey Hepburn, Robert Wagner, Jerry Orbach, Patrick Bauchau, Brion James, Samantha Eggar, Christopher Neame*
A synthetic blend of romantic comedy and action adventure set in Mexico, where a female jewel thief goes to ransom her kidnapped fiancee with the booty from her latest robbery. Hepburn's TV movie debut.
COM                    98 min (ort 100 min) mTV
B,V                                        GHV

## LOVE AND BULLETS **                       15
Stuart Rosenberg        UK              1978
*Charles Bronson, Jill Ireland, Rod Steiger, Henry Silva, Strother Martin, Bradford Dillman*
A policeman falls in love with the girlfriend of a powerful gangleader. Bronson's wife, Jill Ireland get to plays the girlfriend. Average.
A/AD         97 min (ort 103 min) Cut (1 min 24 sec)
B,V,V2  PRV L/A; CH5 (VHS only); POLY (VHS only)

## LOVE AND DEATH **                         PG
Woody Allen             USA              1975
*Woody Allen, Diane Keaton, Harold Gould, Alfred Lutter, Olga Georges-Picot, Jessica Harper, Zvee*

*Scooler, Despo, Frank Adu, James Tolkan, Henry Czarniak*
A very uneven Woody Allen look at Russian literature and its obsession with the meaning of life, made in the form of a spoof on foreign films. The one-line jokes are the best things in it.
COM                      81 min (ort 85 min)
V                                          WHV

## LOVE AND HATE ***                         15
Francis Mankiewicz  CANADA              1989
*Kate Nelligan, Kenneth Welsh, John Colicos, R.H. Thomson, Duncan Ollerenshaw*
Courtroom drama based on the true case of the murder of Jo-Ann Thatcher, whose body was discovered in a small Canadian town in 1983. As the ex-wife of Colin Thatcher, the millionaire cabinet minister and son of the Premier, the case received massive publicity, especially when the woman's former husband was arrested, tried and convicted of her murder (a charge he denies to this day). An overlong but compelling tale.
DRA                                184 min mTV
V/h                                         ODY

## LOVE AND LARCENY **                       PG
Ron Iscove              CANADA          1985
*Jennifer Dale, Douglas Rain, Brent Carver*
A poor farm girl achieves fame and fortune by becoming a lady confidence trickster. Average.
DRA                     140 min (ort 148 min)
B,V                           CAREY/PVG; PARK

## LOVE AND MONEY *
James Toback
            USA/WEST GERMANY            1980
*Ray Sharkey, Klaus Kinski, Ornella Muti, King Vidor, Armand Assante, Susan Heldfond, William Prince*
A millionaire businessman plans a complex scheme in which a young man becomes entangled through his infatuation with the former's wife. Despite having the sex scenes between Sharkey and Muti toned down somewhat after completion, this generally incoherent effort was barely released; deservedly so.
DRA                                     95 min
B,V,V2                                     GHV

## LOVE AND WAR ***                          15
Paul Aaron              USA              1987
*Jane Alexander, James S. Woods, Haing S. Ngor, Concetta Tomei, Jon Cedar, Richard McKenzie, James Pax*
Another film with a Vietnam background, dealing with a couple, and telling of how their love survived the husband's captivity at the hands of the Viet Cong. Despite enduring years of torture by his captors, the husband did not crack and was even able to secrete coded messages in his letters home to his wife, alerting her as to the conditions he was enduring. A harrowing and well-made tale.
Boa: book by Jim and Sybil Stockdale.
DRA                                     92 min
B,V                                       SONY

## LOVE AT FIRST BITE ***
Stan Dragoti            USA              1979
*George Hamilton, Susan St James, Richard Benjamin, Dick Shawn, Arte Johnson, Sherman Hemsley, Isabel Sandford, Eric Laneuville, Barry Gordon, Michael Pataki, Robert Ellenstein, Rolfe Sedan, Bab Bassim, Hazel Shermet*
Count Dracula is evicted from his home in Transylvania and comes to New York where he falls in love with a model. Hamilton is quite outstanding in a spirited and entertaining comedy. The script is by Robert Kaufman.
COM                                     96 min
B,V,V2                                     GHV

**N THE AFTERNOON** ***
hmer          FRANCE          1972
, Bernard Verley, Francoise Verley, Daniel
di, Malvina Penne, Babette Ferrier, Frederique
r, Claude-Jean Philippe, Sylvaine Charlet,
e Malat, Suze Randall, Tina Michelino, Jean
Livi, Pierre Nunzi
rried man becomes innocently involved with the
r mistress of a friend in this absorbing drama.
CHLOE IN THE AFTERNOON; L'AMOUR
RES-MIDI
                                    98 min
                                    INT

**E IS A MANY-SPLENDORED THING, A** **
ry King          USA          1955
iam Holden, Jennifer Jones, Isobel Elsom, Jorja
twright, Virginia Gregg, Torin Thatcher, Richard
, Murray Matheson
Eurasian woman doctor falls in love with an
erican war correspondent at the time of the
rean War. Mediocre plot beautifully realised in a
m that is only memorable for its tragic ending and
scar-winning theme song. AA: Score (Alfred New-
an), Song ("Love Is A Many Splendoured Thing" –
ammy Fain – music/Paul Francis Webster – lyrics),
ost (Charles LeMaire).
ka: MANY-SPLENDORED THING, A
3oa: novel A Many Splendoured Thing by Han Suyin.
DRA                                 102 min
V                                   CBS L/A

**LOVE IS A SPLENDID ILLUSION** **          18
Tom Clegg          UK          1969
Simon Brent, Andree Flamand, Lisa Collings, Peter
Hughes, Mark Kingston, Fiona Curzon, Maxine
Casson, Anna Matisse, Carl Ferber, Nancy Nevinson
A young philandering husband and father brings
tragedy on himself and his family.
Aka: SWEDISH DREAM (SHEP)
DRA                       87 min; 84 min (SHEP)
B,V,V2                              INT/CBS

**LOVE IS NEVER SILENT** ****          PG
Joseph Sargent          USA          1985
Mare Winningham, Phyllis Frelich, Ed Waterstreet,
Fredric Lehne, Cloris Leachman, Sid Caesar, Susan
Ann Curtis, Mark Hildreth, Lou Fant, Julianna Fjeld,
Jeremy Christall, Stephen E. Miller, Alex Diakun,
Gregory Hayes
A girl with normal hearing has to function as the ears
of her deaf parents and is torn between this role and a
desire for a life of her own. The sensitive script is by
Darlene Craviotto. A splendid drama with fine per-
formances. The film won Emmy Awards for Outstand-
ing Director and Outstanding Drama Special.
Aka: SHATTERED SILENCE
Boa: novel In The Sign by Joanne Greenberg.
DRA                     97 min (ort 100 min) mTV
V                                   VCC

**LOVE LEADS THE WAY** *          U
Delbert Mann          USA          1984
Timothy Bottoms, Eva Marie Saint, Arthur Hill,
Glynnis O'Connor, Susan Dey, Patricia Neal, Ernest
Borgnine, Ralph Bellamy, Gerald Hiken, George
Wallace, Michael Anderson Jr, Stephen Young,
Richard Roat, Richard Speight Jr
The story of the people who pioneered the use of guide
dogs for the blind in the USA. Rather badly made and
loaded with sentiment, a little too sweet to digest in
one sitting. Scripted by Henry Denker.
Boa: book First Lady Of The Seeing Eye by Morris
Frank and Blake Clark.
DRA                     95 min (ort 110 min) mCab
B,V                                 WDV

**LOVE LETTERS** ***          18
Amy Jones          USA          1983

Jamie Lee Curtis, James Keach, Amy Madigan, Bud
Cort, Matt Clark, Bonnie Bartlett, Brian Wood, Phil
Coccioletti, Larry Cedar, Michael Villella, Betsy Toll,
Lyman Ward, Shelby Leverington, Emma Chapman,
Scott Henderson
Story of an obsessive affair between an older married
man and a young girl, in which her dead mother's love
letters play a key but tragic role. An engrossing
low-budget melodrama that is effective and quite
touching.
Aka: MY LOVE LETTERS
DRA                     84 min (ort 102 min)
B,V                                 VES

**LOVE MACHINE, THE** *          18
Jack Haley Jr          USA          1971
John Philip Law, Dyan Cannon, Robert Ryan, Jackie
Cooper, David Hemmings, Shecky Green, Maureen
Arthur, William Roerick
The rise and fall of a cold and callous TV executive
who ruthlessly exploits all who come into his path for
the sake of advancement. As melodramatic as the
book on which it is based and no more entertaining.
Scripted by Samuel Taylor.
Boa: novel by Jacqueline Susann.
DRA                     104 min (ort 110 min)
V                                   RCA

**LOVE ON THE RUN** **          15
Gus Trikonis          USA          1985
Stephanie Zimbalist, Alec Baldwin, Ernie Hudson,
Constance McCashin, Howard Duff, Madison Mason,
Francine Lembi, Kit LeFever, Matthew Cowles, Arnold
Turner, David Hayward, Ken Lerner, Savannah
Smith Boucher, Burke Byrnes
A female lawyer falls for a client and helps to spring
him from prison. Based on a real-life case but no more
than adequate.
DRA                     96 min (ort 102 min) mTV
B,V                                 RCA

**LOVE PILL, THE** *          18
Kenneth Turner          UK          1971
Toni Sinclair, David Pugh, Henry Woolf, Melinda
Churcher, Kenneth Waller, John Stratton, Flanagan,
Jacqueline Andrews, Tilly Tremaine
A village shopkeeper invents a combined contracep-
tive and aphrodisiac with dire results. Another exam-
ple of the genre of British sex comedies and barely
worth the effort.
COM                     79 min (ort 82 min)
B,V                                 APX; INTMED

**LOVE PLAY** *          18
John Thomas          FRANCE          1977
                                    (released 1984)
Emmanuelle Parezee, Martine Grimaud, Isabel,
Charles Schneider, Nicole Avril, Evon Evier, Alain
Saury, Pierre Danny
A wealthy man is unhappy with his wife's abilities in
bed so he takes to buying ladies' underwear, which he
gets a woman in a boutique to model for him. Not
surprisingly, he ultimately ends up with both women
in this extravagant piece of nonsense.
A                                   82 min
B,V,V2                              ELV

**LOVE STORY** **          PG
Arthur Hiller          USA          1970
Ryan O'Neal, Ali MacGraw, Ray Milland, John
Marley, Katherine Balfour, Russell Nype, Tom
(Tommy) Lee Jones
Synthetic weepie that was a huge box-office success in
which boy meets girl, boy and girl fall in love, girl dies
suddenly of something quite painless that is never
mentioned by name. High-grade romantic slush that
was followed by a sequel, OLIVER'S STORY in 1978.
Scripted by Segal. AA: Score (Orig) (Francis Lai).
Boa: novelette by Erich Segal.

## LOVE AT STAKE **

John Moffitt          USA               1987
Kelly Preston, Patrick Cassidy, Bud Cort, David Graf,
Stuart Pankin, Barbara Carrera, Dave Thomas, Anne
Ramsey, Georgia Brown, Annie Golden
An attempt to spoof the Salem witch trials in the style
of a Mel Brooks film, that scatters a variety of gags in
every direction (nothing is spared, the trials are even
linked to some property deals) with only some hitting
home. Carrera makes an alluring witch and the
strong cast do their best to breathe life into this wacky
but overwrought parody.
COM                                    85 min
V                                      20VIS

## LOVE BOX, THE **          18

Billy White/Teddy White
                      UK               1972
Chris Williams, Flanagan, Paul Aston, Maggie
Wright, John Mattocks, Lizbeth Lindeborg, Jane
Cardew, Basil Clarke, Ann Henning, Raymond
Young, Peter Burton, Charlie Miller, Dick Hayden,
Joan Alcorn, Simon Legree, Laurie Goode
A set of comedy shorts revolving around a "love box"
put in the lonely hearts column of a sex magazine, to
enable people to fulfil their fantasies. Episodes are:
"Peter The Boy Virgin", "The Sex Kittens", "The
Young Wives' Club", "Massage Wanted", "The Trade
Descriptions Act", "The Refined Couple", "The Wife
Swappers", "Orgy In Kilburn", "The Bored House-
wife", "Trying New Colours" and "The Love Park".
Mildly amusing, but far, far too episodic.
Aka: LOVE CAMP; SEX BOX, THE (PHV or SHEP)
A                            85 min (ort 89 min)
B,V                           NOV L/A; PHV; SHEP

## LOVE BUG, THE ***          U

Robert Stevenson      USA               1968
Dean Jones, Michele Lee, Buddy Hackett, David
Tomlinson, Joe Flynn, Benson Fong, Iris Adrian, Joe
E. Ross, Robert Reed, Bert Convy, Hope Lange, Barry
Kelley, Andy Granatelli, Dale Van Sickel, Regina
Paton, Bob Drake
A Volkswagen has a mind of its own and gets up to all
sorts of mischief in this fast and furious celebration of
slapstick and mayhem. Followed by three rather less
inventive "Herbie" sequels, the first one being HER-
BIE RIDES AGAIN.
COM                       107 min (ort 110 min)
B,V                                    WDV

## LOVE BUTCHER, THE **

Mike Angel/Don Jones
                      USA      1975 (released 1982)
Erik Stern, Kay Neer, Robin Sherwood, Jeremiah
Beecher, Edward Roehm, Don Jones, Eve Mac, Robert
Walter, Louis Ojena, John Stoglin, Marilyn Jones,
Joan Vigman, Marcus Flower, Darlene Chaffee, Neal
Byers, Peter Netzband
The police are completely baffled by a series of strange
murders, which are in fact the work of a crippled
gardener who hates his lady employers and returns to
murder them whenever he is insulted or dismissed. A
low-budget, tongue-in-cheek effort that pre-dated the
craze for slasher films by several years.
DRA                                    90 min
B,V,V2                                 INT/CBS

## LOVE BY APPOINTMENT *          18

Armando Nannuzzi     ITALY              1976
Ernest Borgnine, Francoise Fabian, Corinne Clery,
Armand Nanuzzi, Silvia Dionisio, Fabrizio Jovine,
Jole Fierro, Maurizio Bonuglia, Mimmo Palmara
Two unscrupulous businessmen spend most of their
free time at a luxury brothel.
Aka: CHRISTMAS AT THE BROTHEL;
CHRISTMAS TIME IN A BROTHEL; NATALE IN
CASA D'APPUNTAMENTO

DRA
B,V                   VTC

## LOVE CAMP **

Christian Anders WEST GERM
Laura Gemser, Christian Ander
The leader of a free-love cu
millionaire's daughter for financ
Aka: DIE TODESGOTTIN DES
A
B,V

## LOVE CHILD *

Larry Peerce          USA
Amy Madigan, Beau Bridges, Albert
Philips, Joanna Merlin, Rhea Perlma
A woman prisoner becomes pregna
warder and fights to keep her child.
on a true story, but a tedious and mi
that.
DRA                   93 n
B,V

## LOVE CIRCLES **

Gerard Kikoine       UK
John Sibbit, Marie Frances, Michel Siu, J
Jacqueline Jones, Pierre Burton
A young man travels the world in search
sexual experience.
A                     94 min (
B,V

## LOVE FOR SALE **

David Miller          USA
Lisa Eilbacher, Annette O'Toole, Rhonda Flem
Darren McGavin, Eugene Roche, David Selby,
Catherine Hicks, Bert Remsen, Robin Strand,
Woods, Severn Darden
Two sisters go to Los Angeles, but end up
priced call-girls in this glossy, formula time-fill
Aka: LOVE FOR RENT (VFP)
Boa: Playboy Magazine story by Donn Pearce.
DRA                   96 min; 90 min (AVR or ARAMA
B,V                           VFP; AVR; A

## LOVE GAMES OF YOUNG GIRLS *

F.J. Gottlieb         WEST GERMANY
Karin Gotz, Mattis Bottcher, Peter Kranz
Sex film disguised as a survey of young girl's att
and pretty dull stuff it is too.
Aka: HUNGRY FOR SEX; LIEBESSPIELE JUN
MADCHEN; LOVE GAMES FOR YOUNG GIRI
A                                      6
B,V                   FANVID L/A; TAKE2

## LOVE IN A WOMEN'S PRISON **

Rino Di Silvestro     ITALY
Anita Strindberg, Eva Czemerys, Olga Bisera, Jen
Tamburi, Paolo Senatore, Roger Browne, Valeria
Fabrizi, Cristina Gaioni, Jane Avril, Gabriella
Giorgelli, Bedy Moratti, Massimo Serato, Valeria
Mongardini, Umberto Raho
Typical women's prison melodrama with a m
sub-plot and a series of the usual exploitative scene
Aka: DIARIO SEGRETO DI UN CARCERE
FEMMINILE; WOMEN IN CELL BLOCK 7
A                     60 min (ort 100 min)
V                                      K

## LOVE IN FOUR EASY LESSONS **

Sergio Martino       ITALY              19
Ursula Andress, Barbara Bouchet, Johnny Dorelli
A quartet of stories about love, lust and jealousy.
Aka: SPOGGLIAMOCI COSI' SENZA PUDOR
A                                      80 mi
B,V                                    INT/CBS

DRA 96 min (ort 100 min)
B,V CIC

## LOVE STREAMS **
John Cassavetes USA 15
 1984
*John Cassavetes, Gena Rowlands, Seymour Castel,*
*Diahnne Abbott, Risa Martha Blewitt, Margaret*
*Abbott, Jakob Shaw*
A typically Cassavetes-style talky drama about the
trials and tribulations of a couple's relationship at a
difficult period in their lives. Not everyone's idea of a
fun film but it has won many European film awards.
The script was by Cassavetes and Ted Allan.
Boa: play by Ted Allan.
DRA 135 min (ort 141 min)
V GHV

## LOVE THEATRE ***
Beate Ushe WEST GERMANY 1985
*Mona, Edith Argentina, Robert Zellis, Sherri Breyer,*
*Sharon Wolfen, Larry Kiebasa*
The Love Troupe are a group of actors and actresses
who arrive at the castle of a count to perform a
scenario he has written. However, when the women
discover that he wants them to perform an orgy they
leave in disgust. But their bus breaks down, and after
having it repaired they are obliged to return and
perform for the count after all. An amusing romp.
A 80 min
B,V HAR

## LOVE TO ETERNITY *
Ferreri FRANCE/ITALY 1976
*Catherine Deneuve, Marcello Mastroianni, Pascal*
*Lapperrousaz, Corinne Marchand, Michel Piccoli*
A woman comes to an isolated island inhabited by a
male recluse and takes the place of his dog, even to the
extent of wearing a collar and lead. A tiresome "art"
film that takes a long time to say absolutely nothing.
Aka: LIZA
Boa: novel by Ennio Flaiano.
DRA 100 min
B,V VCL/CBS L/A

## LOVE WAR, THE *
George McCowan USA 1970
*Lloyd Bridges, Angie Dickinson, Harry Basch, Dan*
*Travanty (Daniel J. Travanti), Byron Foulger, Judy*
*Jordan, Bill McLean, Allen Jaffe, Bob Nash, Pepper*
*Martin, Art Lewis*
Two planets' representatives fight a duel in a small
town for control of Earth. This incredibly stupid tale is
worth seeing if only as an example of how not to make
a film.
FAN 90 min mTV
B,V GHV

## LOVE WITH A PERFECT STRANGER **  PG
Desmond Davis (uncredited)
 UK/USA 1986
*Marilu Henner, Daniel Massey, Sky Dumont, Stephen*
*Greif, Delia Paton, Tim Stern, Shirin Taylor, Robert*
*Rietty, Phillip O'Brien, Gay Barnes, Tim Price, Rita*
*Lester, Ray Marioni, Bruce Lidington, Anthony*
*Wingate*
A beautiful, successful and wealthy American
businesswoman travelling by train to Italy, finds love
in the shape of a dashing Irishman. First in a series of
TV films from Harlequin – purveyors of romantic
novels.
Boa: novel by Pamela Wallace.
DRA 90 min (ort 98 min) mCab
V CIC

## LOVE YOU ***  R18/18
John Derek USA 1980
*Annette Haven, Wade Nichols, Leslie Bovee, Rob*
*Everett*
Two happily married couples embark on an erotic

adventure designed to allow them to indulge their
fantasies, when they hire a helicopter to take them to
an inaccessible island off the Californian coast for the
weekend. Initially the swapping of partners leads to
some jealousy but the film ends with this resolved by
way of a group discussion. This may sound trite, but
this work is both warm and perceptive, unusual for
films of this genre.
A 72 min Cut (6 min 18 sec – 18); 76 min Cut (1 min 15
 sec – R18)
B,V EVI L/A; PHV L/A; SHEP

## LOVE YOU TO DEATH *  18
Robert Bergman USA 1989
*Nadia Capone, Yaphet Kotto, Silvio Oliviero,*
*Lawrence Bane, Denise Ryan*
A struggling actress takes a job with a phone sex
company and in order to make her bizarre work more
bearable, creates different "characters" with her voice.
A psycho who works as a sound recordist at a strip
club becomes infatuated with her voice and embarks
on a series of murders, repeatedly calling her for more
"inspiration". An unpleasant and sleazy film, with a
contrived and predictable climax. Avoid it if
possible.
THR 96 min
V CINE

## LOVE-IN ARRANGEMENT, THE ***
Charles Larkin USA 1980
*Merle Michaels, Arcadia Lake, Carol Cat, Rick*
*Iversen, Eric Edwards, Vanessa Del Rio, Ron Jeremy,*
*Dave Ruby, Kandi Barbour, Bobby Astyr*
A couple's sex life is seen in flashbacks during a court
hearing in which the woman is bringing a palimony
action for half her partner's wealth. The contrived film
structure allows both parties to voice their grievances
and leads to some amusing sequences and an eventual
reconciliation.
Osca: EAGER FINGERS, EAGER LIPS/SLIP UP
(asa)
A 71 min
B,V HAR

## LOVE, HATE, LOVE **
George McCowan USA 1970
*Ryan O'Neal, Peter Haskell, Lesley Ann Warren,*
*Henry Jones, Jeff Donnell, Jack Mullaney, Stanley*
*Adams, Shannon Farnon, Ryan MacDonald, Fred*
*Holliday, Mark Tapscott, Charlene Polite*
A fashion model's romance turns into a nightmare
when the object of her attentions turns out to have a
hidden side, which surfaces when she takes up instead
with an engineer. Suggested by the novel "Color Of
Green" by Lenard Kaufman and scripted by Eric
Ambler. Average.
DRA 70 min (ort 73 min) mTV
B,V RNK

## LOVE, HONOR AND OBEY **  15
Robert Mandel USA 1983
*David Keith, Kathleen Quinlan, Cliff De Young,*
*Frances Sternhagen, Dianne Wiest, Josef Sommer,*
*Bert Remsen, Richard Farnsworth, Brooke Alderson,*
*Noble Winningham, Susan Rutman*
The story of an independent-minded woman itching to
leave her small town behind her is coupled to the story
of a battered housewife, in what appears to be two
quite separate films rather clumsily joined together.
Aka: FOLLOW YOUR DREAMS; INDEPENDENCE
DAY
DRA 106 min (ort 110 min)
B/h, V/h WHV

## LOVE, LUST AND ECSTASY **
Ilia Milonako GREECE 1983
*Ajita Wilson, Mireille Damien, Danilo Micheli,*
*Missimo Saudurmy, Starto Zasimis, George Minter*

A young woman married to a shipowner has an affair with tragic consequences in this fairly well acted melodrama.

DRA                                    79 min
B,V,V2                                 VPD

## LOVELESS, THE *                     18
Kathryn Bigelow/Monty Montgomery
                    USA                1982
Willem Dafoe, J. Don Ferguson, Marin Kantner, Robert Gordon, Tina L'Hotsky, Liz Gans
A motorcycle gang stop in a small Southern town to repair a bike and a tragic love affair begins between the gang leader and a local 16-year-old girl. Well photographed but generally plotless and uninteresting. A kind of update to THE WILD ONE hampered by the anaemic script.
Aka: BREAKDOWN
DRA          82 min; 79 min (PAL) (ort 85 min)
B, V/h                                 PVG; PAL

## LOVELINES *                         15
Rod Amateau            USA             1985
Greg Bradford, Mary Beth Evans, Michael Winslow, Tammy Taylor, Joanna Lee, Stacey Toten
Rival groups of teenagers behave as only they can in this witless comedy that follows the exploits of rival bands.
COM                                    93 min
B,V                                    CBS

## LOVELY BUT DEADLY *                 18
David Sheldon          USA             1983
Lucinda Dooling, John Randolph, Richard Herd, Mel Novak, Susan Meschner
A girl high school student wages a ruthless war against drug-pushers after her brother dies from an overdose. An overblown melodrama.
Aka: DEADLY AVENGER
DRA                                    90 min
B,V                                    MPV; NICK/CBS

## LOVER, THE *                        18
                    ISRAEL             1985
Michel Bat-Adam, Roberto Pollack, Yehoram Gaon, Abigail Arieli, Fanny Lubitsch, Awas Khatib
A somewhat mawkish drama that follows the amorous exploits of the title character. A derivative and cliched time-filler.
Aka: HAME'AHEV
Boa: novel by A.B. Yehoshua.
DRA                    87 min Cut (54 sec)
B,V                                    RNK

## LOVERBOY *                          15
Joan Micklin Silver    USA             1989
Patrick Dempsey, Kate Jackson, Robert Ginty, Nancy Valen, Charles Hunter Walsh, Barbara Carrera, Bernie Coulson, Ray Girardin, Robert Camilletti, Vic Tayback, Kim Miyori, Kirstie Alley, Carrie Fisher
A pizza delivery boy uses his job as a front for his real enterprise, satisfying sexually frustrated older women. The expected complications and gags do nothing to enliven this disappointing sex farce.
COM                                    98 min
V                                      RCA

## LOVERS AND OTHER STRANGERS ****     15
Cy Howard              USA             1969
Gig Young, Bonnie Bedelia, Anne Jackson, Harry Guardino, Michael Brandon, Beatrice Arthur, Richard Castellano, Cloris Leachman, Robert Dishy, Diane Keaton, Anne Meara, Marian Hailey
After having lived together, a young couple get married only to discover that there are still many problems to be faced. A witty, charming and splendidly directed farce, full of memorable moments and great performances. This was Diane Keaton's film

debut. AA: Song ("For All We Know" – Fred Karlin – music/Robb Royer and James Griffin – lyrics).
Boa: play by Renee Taylor and Joseph Bologna.
COM                    91 min (ort 106 min)
B,V                                    RNK; VGM

## LOVES OF HERCULES, THE *            PG
Carlo Ludonico Bragaglia
                FRANCE/ITALY           1960
Jayne Mansfield, Micky Hargity, Massimo Serato, Rosella Como
Sword-and-sandal epic with a love theme replacing the usual adventure. A wonderful celebration of bad acting and worse dubbing, but undeniably funny, although I don't think that was the intention of the director.
Aka: GLI AMORI DI ERCOLE; LES AMOURS D'HERCULE
DRA                    100 min dubbed
B,V                                    MOV L/A; VDN

## LOVE'S SAVAGE FURY *
Joseph Hardy           USA             1979
Jennifer O'Neill, Perry King, Raymond Burr, Connie Stevens, Robert Reed, Ed Lauter, Howard McGilin, Vernee Watson, Deborah Morgan, Jeffrey Byron, Robert Cornthwaite, Edward Power, Slim Gaillard, Aarika Wells, Mark Hager
A bare-faced copy of GONE WITH THE WIND in which a Southern belle fights to hold onto the family estate during the Civil War and its aftermath. Well below average, with most of the action set in a ghastly Yankee prison camp, where the makers of this nonsense should have been sent.
DRA                    100 min mTV
B,V                                    IPC/PVG

## LOVESICK *                          15
Marshall Brickman      USA             1983
Dudley Moore, Alec Guinness, Elizabeth McGovern, Wallace Shawn, John Huston, Ron Silver, Alan King, Gene Saks, Selma Diamond
A New York psychiatrist falls in love with a new patient and lands in all kinds of crazy predicaments. A flawed and flabby effort that needs a couch of its own.
COM                    93 min (ort 95 min)
B,V                                    WHV

## LOW BLOW **                         18
Frank Harris           USA             1986
Leo Fong, Akosua Busia, Cameron Mitchell, Troy Donahue
A rich father hires an ex-cop to get his daughter out of the clutches of a powerful and sinister sect. Average.
Aka: SAVAGE SUNDAY
A/AD                                   85 min
B,V                                    RCA

## LT. ROBIN CRUSOE U.S.N. *           U
Byron Paul             USA             1966
Dick Van Dyke, Nancy Kwan, Akim Tamiroff, Arthur Malet, Tyler McVey
A modern day Robinson Crusoe is lucky enough to find not one, but several native girls in this creaky Disney comedy. Written by Bill Walsh and Don da Gradi.
Aka: LIEUTENANT ROBIN CRUSOE U.S.N.
COM                    110 min (ort 114 min)
B,V                                    RNK; WDV

## LUCAN **                            15
David Greene           USA             1977
Kevin Brophy, Stockard Channing, Ned Beatty, William Jordan, John Randolph, Lou Frizzell, Ben Davison, George Wyner, Hedley Mattingly, John Finnegan, Richard C. Adams, Todd Olsen, George Reynolds, Virginia Hawkins
Pilot for a series about a young man who was raised by wolves in Northern Minnesota and spent the first ten years of his life living wild. Not a bad yarn in its way,

that handles a theme first explored by Truffaut's "The Wild Child" (1970).

A/AD 73 min (ort 79 min) mTV
B,V MGM

## LUCAS ***
David Seltzer USA 1986 · 15
Corey Haim, Kerri Green, Charlie Sheen, Courtney Thorne-Smith, Winona Ryder, Thomas E. Hodges, Guy Bond
A tale of teenage love between a 14-year-old boy and an older girl of 16 and how their affair affects those around them. A delightful little drama that has engaging performances and sharply delineated but believable characters. The directorial debut for Seltzer.
DRA 96 min (ort 100 min)
B,V CBS

## LUCIFER **
John Eyres UK 1987 · 18
Emma Sutton, Frank Rozelaar Green, Jared Morgan, Jane Price
The child survivor of a playground massacre by a psychotic murderer faces further terror as he tries to eliminate her as the only person who can identify him.
Aka: GOODNIGHT, GOD BLESS
HOR 90 min
B,V MOG

## LUCIFER COMPLEX, THE *
Kenneth Hartford USA 1978
Robert Vaughn, Aldo Ray, Merrie Lynn, Keenan Wynn, William Lanning, Victoria Carroll, Glen Ranson, Lynn Cartwright, Ross Durfee, Kieu Chinh, Colin Eliot Brown, Gustof Unger, Carol Terry, Corinne Cole, Bertil Unger
A mad scientist on a remote island plots to take over the world using clones of world leaders, said scientist being none other than Adolf Hitler! A wonderfully tacky effort with not a dry eye in the house – but mostly from laughing at the ineptness of it all.
FAN 91 min
B,V,V2 HER

## LUCKY JIM **
John Boulting UK 1957
Ian Carmichael, Hugh Griffith, Terry-Thomas, Sharon Acker, Jean Anderson, Clive Morton, Maureen Connell, Kenneth Griffith, John Welsh, Jeremy Hawk, Reginald Beckwith, Harry Fowler, John Cairney, Charles Lamb, Ian Wilson
A junior history lecturer at a provincial university staggers from one mishap to another in this mildly enjoyable farce that (unlike the novel) relies on broad humour rather than subtlety.
Boa: novel by Kingsley Amis.
COM 91 min (ort 95 min) B/W
B,V TEVP

## LUCKY LUCIANO **
Francesco Rosi · 18
FRANCE/ITALY/USA 1974
Rod Steiger, Edmond O'Brien, Gian-Maria Volonte, Vincent Gardenia, Charles Cioffi
The story of an infamous gangster and the fight to bring him to justice, well told and generally convincing. Look out for Charles Siragusa, the real-life federal agent who helped put Luciano away.
DRA 106 min (ort 112 min)
B,V HEL; PARK (VHS only); HOLLY (VHS only);
MIA

## LUCKY LUKE **
Rene Goscinny
BELGIUM/FRANCE 1971
Animated story of a cowboy's fight to free a peaceful town from the grip of the Dalton gang. Followed by LUCKY LUKE AND THE DALTON GANG.

Aka: LUCKY LUKE: DAISY TOWN
CAR 85 min
B,V SEL

## LUCKY LUKE AND THE DALTON GANG **
Rene Goscinny/Rene Morris
BELGIUM/FRANCE 1978
Second in the series of animated features about our hero's running battle with the Dalton Gang. Fair.
Aka: LE BALLADE DES DALTON; LUCKY LUKE: THE BALLAD OF THE DALTONS
CAR 82 min
B,V SEL

## LUCKY STAR, THE **
Max Fischer CANADA 1980
Rod Steiger, Louise Fletcher, Lou Jacobi, Brett Marx, Helen Hughes, Yvon Dufour, Isabelle Mejias, Guy L'Ecuyer, Kalman Steinberg, Pierre Gobeil, Rijck De Gooyer, Joop Admiraal, Derek De Unt, Aubert Pallascio, Lex Goudsmit
During the Nazi occupation of Holland, a young Jewish boy acts out Western fantasies, believing that he is a sheriff because of his yellow star. When his parents are taken away by the Nazis he decides to take on the local German officer. Well made, but the ending disappoints and the trivialisation of the subject matter strikes a sour note.
DRA 110 min
B,V GHV

## LUCKY TEXAN **
Robert North Bradbury · U
USA 1934
John Wayne, Barbara Sheldon, Yakima Canutt, George "Gabby" Hayes, Lloyd Whitlock, Gordon D. (Demain) Woods, Eddie Parker, Earl Dwire, Jack Rockwell, Artie Ortego, Tex Palmer, Tex Phelps, George Morrell
A young man comes West to work his late father's share of a gold claim with the latter's partner but has to contend with claim jumpers. A fairly undemanding but enjoyable effort, one in a series of John Wayne "Lone Star" Westerns, produced by Paul Malvern.
WES 54 min (ort 61 min) B/W
V CH5

## LUGGAGE OF THE GODS! **
David Kendall USA 1983 · PG
Mark Stolzenberg, Gabriel Barre, Gwen Ellison, Martin Haber, Rochelle Robins, Lou Leccese, Dog Thomas, John Tarrant, Corad Bergschneider
The life of a tribe is dramatically altered when a jet plane drops its cargo on them in this offbeat and only slightly amusing tale. Bears no relation to THE GODS MUST BE CRAZY.
COM 72 min (ort 87 min)
B,V CBS

## LULLABY OF BROADWAY **
David Butler USA 1951
Doris Day, Gene Nelson, Billy De Wolfe, Gladys George, Florence Bates, S.Z. Sakall, Anne Triola
A woman achieves stardom in a musical comedy but is unaware of the fact that her mother is in urgent need of a helping hand. A competent but uninspired musical, lively but hardly memorable. A few good songs keep it going.
MUS 89 min (ort 92 min)
V WHV

## LUNATIC ***
Laslo Benedek USA 1970
Max Von Sydow, Liv Ullmann, Trevor Howard, Per Oscarsson, Rupert Davies, Andrew Keir, Gretchen Franklin, Arthur Hewlett, Jim Kennedy, Hanne Bork, Lottie Freddie, Bjorn Watt Boolsen
An inmate of an asylum for the criminally insane plans to escape for one night to exact his revenge on

the people he holds responsible for his predicament. A carefully made but sluggish film, though one that maintains a good deal of tension. Filmed in Denmark and Sweden.
Aka: NIGHT VISITOR, THE
HOR                                         106 min
B,V                              VFP L/A; HER

## LUNCH WAGON ***
Ernest Pintoff          USA              1980
*Rick Podell, Pamela Jean Bryant, Rosanne Katon, Candy Moore, Chuck McCann, Vic Dunlop, Jimmy Van Patten, Rose Marie, Michael Mislove, Dick Van Patten, Anthony Charnota, Gary Levy, Peggy Mannix, Steve Tannen*
Three girls with a lunch wagon become innocently embroiled with rival gangs, a hit-man and the cops. Strong direction and acting turn a banal story into something of value.
Aka: COME AND GET IT; LUNCH WAGON GIRLS
COM                         84 min (ort 88 min)
B,V,V2                                     VPD

## LURKERS *                                18
Roberta Findlay          USA              1987
*Christine Moore, Gary Warner, Marina Taylor, Carisa Channing, Tom Billett*
Poorly realised, confused horror tale whose central figure is a young woman plagued by recurrent nightmares, and burdened by a demented mother and a Satanist boyfriend.
HOR                         89 min (ort 95 min)
B,V                                        MOG

## LUST ***                                 18
Joe D'Amato              ITALY            1985
*Laura Gemser, Martin Philips, Lilli Carati, Al Cliver (Pier Luigi Conti), Annie Bell, Noemie Chelkoff, Ursula Foti*
A white hunter returns from Africa with a native girl who he promptly installs in his home. His wife and servants are none too pleased at first, but soon find that the girl is very free with her favours – our hunter now finding that he has to get to the back of the queue. Not a bad effort from D'Amato.
Aka: LUSSURIA
A          88 min Cut (1 min 6 sec in addition to film cuts)
B,V                                        ELE

## LUST FOR A VAMPIRE **
Jimmy Sangster           UK              1970
*Ralph Bates, Suzanna Leigh, Michael Johnson, Barbara Jefford, Yutte Stensgaard, Mike Raven, Helen Christie, Pippa Steel, David Healy, Michael Brennan, Jack Melford, Erik Chitty*
A pupil at a European finishing school for girls is a vampire and wreaks havoc on the pupils. A typical period Hammer film (circa 1830) with the appropriate wooden performances.
Aka: TO LOVE A VAMPIRE
Boa: novel Carmilla by J. Sheridan Le Fanu.
HOR                         85 min (ort 95 min)
B,V                                       TEVP

## LUST FOR FREEDOM *                       18
Eric Louzil              USA             1988
*Melanie Coll, William J. Kulzer, Judi Trevor*
A rubbishy women-in-prison yarn, with bad dialogue (clumsily dubbed) and similar acting. And through it all, the low production values shine out, like a warning to film-makers everywhere.
A/AD       84 min (ort 91 min) Cut (5 min 34 sec) dubbed
B,V                                 HER; BRAVE

## LUST FOR REVENGE *
Andreas Kalia            GREECE          1975
*Larry Daniels, George Christianson, Yvonne Rion*
The father of a victim of a horrible crime sets out to kill those responsible in this cliche-ridden revenge tale.

DRA                                      85 min
B,V,V2                                  INT/CBS

## LUST IN SPACE **                        R18
Miles Kidder             USA
*Ron Jeremy, Harry Reems, Lana Burner, Gina Carrera, Ali Moore*
Sex film with a space opera flavour.
Aka: LUST IN SPACE: CONTACT IS MADE
A                                        56 min
V                                         SHEP

## LUST IN THE DUST **                      15
Paul Bartel              USA             1984
*Tab Hunter, Divine (Glenn Milstead), Lianie Kazan, Geoffrey Lewis, Henry Silva, Cesar Romero, Woody Strode, Gina Gallegro, Pedro Gonzales-Gonzales, Nedra Volz, Courtney Gains, Daniel Fishman, Al Cantu, Ernie Shinagawa*
Spoof Western about hidden gold and sundry fortune seekers, with Divine trying to locate the treasure in order to achieve "her" ambition of becoming a saloon singer. A high-camp celebration of bad taste and general nonsense, but enjoyable in small doses.
COM                         81 min (ort 87 min)
V/h                                        RCA

## LUST ON THE ORIENT XPRESS ***           18
Tim McDonald             USA             1986
*Gina Carrera, John Leslie, Tracy Adams, Eric Edwards, Jamie Gillis, Paul Thomas, Pat Manning, Kelly Fitzpatrick*
A husband and wife team write sexy mystery novels and are being harassed by a publisher for their next book. They take a trip on the Orient Express to recharge their batteries, but in the course of the journey a murder is committed and a priceless diamond goes missing. They set out to probe each suspect in a well made sex film with more than a few twists in the plot.
A          60 min; 77 min (ELV) Cut (3 min 51 sec)
B,V                              ELHOL L/A; ELV

## LUSTFUL VICAR *                          18
Torgny Wickman           SWEDEN          1970
*Jarl Borssen, Margit Carlquist, Magali Noel*
A vicar has problems of a sexual nature due to a curse.
Aka: KYRKOHERDEN; VICAR, THE
A          71 min (ort 82 min) (Cut at film release)
B,V                              INT L/A; SHEP

## LUSTY MEN, THE **
Nicholas Ray             USA             1952
*Robert Mitchum, Susan Haywood, Arthur Kennedy, Arthur Hunnicutt, Burt Musin, Frank Faylen, Walter Coy, Carol Nugent, Maria Hart, Lorna Thayer, Karen King, Jimmie Dodd, Eleanor Todd, Riley Hill, Robert Bray, Sheb Wooley*
Semi-documentary in style, this is an account of the tough world of rodeo riders and the strains which this way of life imposes on friends and family. A sound and atmospheric tale, with a rather disappointing ending.
DRA                         90 min (ort 113 min) B/W
B,V                                    VCL/CBS

## LYDIA ***                                U
Julien Duvivier          USA             1941
*Merle Oberon, Joseph Cotten, Alan Marshal, Edna May Oliver, Hans Yaray, George Reeves, John Halliday, Sara Allgood*
An ageing lady meets her former lover and looks back at an earlier time of happiness in this sentimental but quite moving remake of "Carnet De Bal". Written by Ben Hecht and Samuel Hoffenstein and with music by Miklos Rozsa.
Boa: story by Julien Duvivier and Laszlo Bus-Fekete.
DRA                        94 min (ort 104 min) B/W
V                                         PICK

# M

## M*A*S*H **                                                  15
Robert Altman          USA                          1970
*Donald Sutherland, Elliott Gould, Sally Kellerman,*
*Tom Skerritt, Robert Duvall, Gary Burghoff, Jo Ann*
*Pflug, Rene Auberjonois, Roger Bowen, John Schuck,*
*G. Wood, Fred Williamson, Bud Cort, Danny*
*Goldman, Dawne Damon*
Wildly episodic black comedy about the antics of a
couple of crazy surgeons posted to a field hospital
during the Korean War. A disappointing effort with
the emphasis firmly on the crazy antics and sexual
exploits of all concerned, with little or no attention
paid to the absurd horror of patching up combat
personnel so as to send them back into action. Gave
rise to a superior TV series that just ran and ran.
Screen (Adapt) (Ring Lardner Jr).
Boa: novel by Richard Hooker.
COM                           111 min (116 min)
V/sh                                              CBS

## M*A*S*H – GOODBYE, FAREWELL          PG
## AND AMEN *
Alan Alda              USA                          1983
*Alan Alda, Loretta Swit, Mike Farrell, Harry Morgan,*
*Jamie Farr, William Christopher, David Ogden Stiers*
Final full-length episode from a long-running TV
series that should have been put out of its misery
years earlier. The medics who patch up US soldiers
fighting in the Korean War have to pack up and go
home when peace finally breaks out. A feature-length
wake for a show that outstayed its welcome, lasting no
less than eight years more than the duration of the
Korean War. Sloppy, silly and sentimental.
WAR                      115 min (ort 120 min) mTV
B,V                                               CBS

## MAC AND ME **                                          U
Stewart Raffill        USA                          1988
*Christine Ebersole, Jonathan Ward, Katrina Caspary,*
*Lauren Stanley, Jade Calegory*
A family of fairly grotesque but quite harmless aliens
are accidentally brought to Earth by a returning space
probe, and rapidly make themselves at home in this
deliberate clone of E.T. THE EXTRA-TERRESTRIAL.
See also ALF.
JUV                            95 min (ort 99 min)
V/sh                                              GHV

## MACABRE **                                              18
Lamberto Bava          ITALY                        1980
*Bernice Stegers, Stanko Molnar, Veronica Zinny,*
*Roberto Posse, Ferdinand Orlandi, Fernando*
*Pannullo, Elisa Kadiga Bove*
A woman who has lost both her small son and her
lover, keeps the severed head of the latter, which she
takes to bed with her at night. A nosy neighbour hears
strange noises coming from her apartment and de-
cides to investigate.
Aka: FROZEN TERROR; MACABRO
HOR                            86 min (ort 91 min)
B,V                                   GOV L/A; MOG

## MACAO **                                               PG
Josef Von Sternberg    USA                          1952
*Robert Mitchum, Jane Russell, William Bendix,*
*Gloria Grahame, Thomas Gomez, Philip Ahn*
A singer has a tempestuous affair with a wandering
adventurer, against a background of Oriental intrigue
and suspense set in the port of Macao, and together
they set out to capture a gangster wanted in the USA.
A disappointing yarn, with stylish direction but an
unimaginative script.
DRA                         78 min (ort 81 min) B/W
B,V                                        KVD; VCC

## MACARONI **                                            PG
Ettore Scola           ITALY                        1985

*Jack Lemmon, Marcello Mastroianni, Daria Nicolodi,*
*Isa Daieli, Maria Luisa Saniella, Patrizzie Sacchi,*
*Bruno Esposito, Marc Berman, Jean-Francois*
*Perriere, Fabio Tenore*
An American businessman revisits Naples after forty
years, and meets a former friend and romantic rival.
Various complications ensue but even excellent acting
cannot redeem an overly light and fluffy story.
Aka: MACCHERONI
COM                           101 min (ort 104 min)
B,V                                               PAL

## MacARTHUR **                                           PG
Joseph Sargent         USA                          1977
*Gregory Peck, Ed Flanders, Dan O'Herlihy, Sandy*
*Kenyon, Dick O'Neil, Marj Dusay, Ivar Bonar, Ward*
*Costello, Art Fleming*
Biopic tracing the career of this famous general
during both WW2 and the Korean War. Sincere and
well crafted but lacking in dramatic impact.
Aka: MacARTHUR THE REBEL GENERAL
DRA                           124 min (ort 144 min)
V/h                                               CIC

## MACBETH **                                             PG
Jack Gold              UK                           1983
*Nicol Williamson, Jane Lapotaire, Tony Doyle, Ian*
*Hogg, Brenda Bruce, Eileen Way, Anne Dyson, Mark*
*Dignam, James Hazeldine, Christopher Ellison, John*
*Rowe, Gawn Grainger, David Lyon, Gordon Kane*
A fairly efficient TV adaptation, a little spoilt by a
bland performance from Williamson in the title role,
that lacks both vigour and conviction. One of a
number of BBC adaptations of Shakespeare's many
plays.
Boa: play by William Shakespeare.
DRA                      119 min (ort 149 min) mTV
V                                        BBC; THAMES

## MACBETH ***
Orson Welles           USA                          1948
*Orson Welles, Jeanette Nolan, Dan O'Herlihy, Edgar*
*Barrier, Roddy McDowall, Robert Coote, Erskine*
*Sanford, Alan Napier, John Dierkes, Peggy Webber*
Welles' version of the famous play is sorely hampered
by lack of money, but is well worth seeing for its sheer
inventiveness and exuberance, as well as its excellent
use of interiors to create a heightened mood, entirely
in keeping with the sombre spirit of the play. The
cheap-looking sets and an ill-advised attempt to
present an authentic Scottish accent are unfortunately, major flaws.
Boa: play by William Shakespeare.
DRA                       107 min (ort 111 min) B/W
B,V                                          INT/CBS

## MACBETH ****                                           15
Roman Polanski         UK                           1971
*Jon Finch, Francesca Annis, Martin Shaw, Nicholas*
*Selby, John Stride, Stephan Chase, Paul Shelley,*
*Terence Bayler, Andrew Laurence, Frank Wylie,*
*Bernard Arcgard, Brian Purchase, Keith Chegwin,*
*Noel Davis, Elsie Taylor*
Ranks almost equally with Kurosawa's "Throne Of
Blood", as one of the most powerful adaptations of
Shakespeare's famous tragedy, telling of lust for
power, murder, treachery and a final reckoning.
Brilliantly acted, this full-blooded rendition has some
graphic scenes of violence that may disturb those used
to a more restrained presentation.
Boa: play by William Shakespeare.
DRA                           134 min (ort 140 min)
B,V                                               RCA

## MACHINE GUN McCAIN *                                   15
Giuliano Montaldo      ITALY                        1970
*John Cassavetes, Peter Falk, Britt Ekland, Gabriele*
*Ferzetti, Salvo Randone, Gena Rowlands*
A gangster just out of jail plans to rob a Mafia-owned

casino, in this unmemorable caper.
THR                    94 min; 91 min (XTASY)
B,V                             VTC L/A; XTASY

## MACHINE-GUNNER *
                                            PG
                    UK                      1976
*Leonard Rossiter, Kate O'Mara, Colin Welland*
A private detective who works as a debt-collector bites
off more than he can chew when he takes on a difficult
case.
DRA                                      72 min
V                                          VGM

## MACHO CALLAHAN **
                                            15
Bernard Kowalski        USA                 1970
*David Janssen, Lee J. Cobb, David Carradine, Jean
Seberg, Pedro Armendariz Jr, James Booth, Anne
Revere, Richard Anderson, Matt Clark, Richard
Evans, Bo Hopkins, Diane Ladd, Robert Morgan*
A Civil War prisoner escapes to get his revenge on the
man who arrested him, wreaking havoc and generally
making himself disliked. A moody and violent tale,
with bad dialogue and some gratuitous brutality.
WES                         94 min (ort 100 min)
B,V,V2                       EHE; CH5 (VHS only)

## MACK AND HIS PACK, THE *
                                            18
Michael Campus         USA                  1973
*Max Julien, Don Gordon, Richard Pryor, Carol Speed,
Roger E. Mosley, William C. Watson*
A violent excursion among the world of pimps, drug
pushers and prostitutes in Oakland, where a black
member of that fraternity sets about those who
wronged him. A dismal and unrewarding experience.
Aka: MACK, THE (STABL)
DRA                         87 min (ort 110 min)
B,V,V2               VTC L/A; VMA L/A; STABL

## MacKENNA'S GOLD **
                                            15
J. Lee Thompson        USA                  1969
*Gregory Peck, Omar Sharif, Telly Savalas, Camilla
Sparv, Keenan Wynn, Lee J. Cobb, Julie Newmar,
Raymond Massey, Eli Wallach, Edward G. Robinson,
Anthony Quayle, Burgess Meredith, Eduardo
Ciannelli, Rudy Diaz, Ted Cassidy*
The story of a long and difficult hunt for a lost
treasure of gold, confuses both the audience and the
searchers, in this dull epic that was not improved by
pre-release cutting. Written by Carl Foreman with
narration by Victor Jory. The score is by Quincy
Jones.
Boa: novel by Will Henry.
WES                        123 min (ort 135 min)
B,V                                         RCA

## MACKINTOSH AND T.J. **
Marvin J. Chomsky      USA                  1975
*Roy Rogers, Clay O'Brien, Billy Green Bush, Andrew
Robinson, Joan Hackett, James Hampton, Walter
Barnes, Dean Smith, Larry Mahan*
An ageing cowpuncher takes on the difficult task of
straightening out a tough young boy. Rogers' first
starring role in 22 years. The music is by Waylon
Jennings. Fair.
WES                          93 min (ort 96 min)
B,V                                         RNK

## MACKINTOSH MAN, THE **
                                            15
John Huston            UK                   1973
*Paul Newman, James Mason, Harry Andrews,
Dominique Sanda, Ian Bannen, Nigel Patrick, Michael
Hordern, Peter Vaughan, Roland Culver, Percy
Herbert, Leo Genn, Robert Lang, Jenny Runacre, John
Bindon, Hugh Manning, Wolfe Morris*
A complex spy thriller about a government agent
deliberately framed and sent to prison, so that he can
eventually expose a criminal gang led by a powerful
politician. A strictly run-of-the-mill affair that wastes
both time and talent. The script is by Walter Hill.

Boa: novel The Freedom Trap by Desmond Bagley.
DRA                         95 min (ort 100 min)
B,V                                         WHV

## MACON COUNTY LINE **
                                            18
Richard Compton        USA                  1973
*Alan Vint, Cheryl Waters, Max Baer Jr, Jesse Vint,
Joan Blackman, Geoffrey Lewis, James Gammon, Leif
Garret, Doodles Weaver*
Three strangers are chased by the local sheriff in the
mistaken belief that they murdered his wife. Alleged-
ly based on a true incident that took place in Georgia
in 1954, but really just another re-run for that tired
old theme of corrupt power-crazy Southern lawmen
doing their own thing. Followed by RETURN TO
MACON COUNTY. The script is by Max Baer Jr.
Aka: KILLING TIME (POR)
DRA                          90 min; 84 min (POR)
B,V                            VFO; MKR; POR

## MAD BOMBER, THE *
Bert I. Gordon         USA                  1972
*Chuck Connors, Vince Edwards, Neville Brand, Hank
Brandt, Cristina Hart*
A tough cop tracks down a psychotic bomber, who
punishes those he believes to have wronged him by
blowing them up. A violent police actioner of the
strictly routine kind, from a director of many ultra
low-budget films.
DRA                                      100 min
B,V                                         DFS

## MAD BULL **
Walter Doniger/Len Steckler
                       USA                  1977
*Alex Karras, Susan Anspach, Elisha Cook Jr,
Nicholas Colasanto, Steve Sandor, Mike Mazurki,
Christopher De Rose, Danny Dayton, Richard Karron,
Titos Vandis, Tracey Walter, Bill Baldwin, Dennis
Burkley, Walker Edmiston*
Drama about a professional wrestler who sets out to
avenge the death of his kid brother. In the midst of his
quest he falls in love with a gentle and sensitive
woman who brings out the better aspects of his
character. Fair.
Aka: AGGRESSOR, THE
Boa: story by Wayne Wellons and Stanley Mann.
DRA                                   96 min mTV
B,V                                    HER; IVS

## MAD DOG **
Philippe Mora          AUSTRALIA            1976
*Dennis Hopper, Jack Thompson, David Gulpilil,
Frank Thring, Michael Pate*
Story of a youth in the 1853 Gold Rush, who is
sentenced to 12 years for a petty crime and eventually
becomes a legendary Australian outlaw. Replete with
typically Aussie touches, showing sympathy for the
underdog and a good dose of violence, but unremark-
able in all other respects.
Aka: MAD DOG MORGAN
A/AD                        95 min (ort 102 min)
B,V                                         PRV

## MAD FOXES, THE *
Paul Gray              USA
*Robert O'Neal, Laura Prenika, Laly Espinet*
Hell's Angels take a brutal revenge on a driver who
accidentally kills one of them, in this cliched and
forgettable offering.
DRA                                       73 min
B,V                                         VCL

## MAD MAX ***
                                            18
George Miller          AUSTRALIA            1979
*Mel Gibson, Joanne Samuel, Steve Bisley, Hugh
Keays-Byrne, Tim Burns, Roger Ward, Geoff Parry,
Paul Johnstone, John Ley, Jonathan Hardy, Vince Gil,
Sheila Florence, Reg Evans, Stephen Clark, Howard*

*Eynon, John Farndale*
The weird story of a desolate post-WW3 world, in which the police have their hands full combating roving motorcycle gangs, and one cop seeks revenge for the slaughter of his family. A visually impressive cult favourite that has spawned several sequels and a clutch of imitations.
FAN                              88 min (ort 100 min) Cut (48 sec)
B,V                                                                 WHV

### MAD MAX 2 ***                                            18
George Miller          AUSTRALIA              1981
*Mel Gibson, Bruce Spence, Emil Minty, Vernon Wells,
Mike Preston, Virginia Hay, Kjell Nilsson, Syd
Heylen, Moira Claux, David Slingsby, Max Phipps,
Steve J. Spears, Arkie Whitely, William Zappa, Jimmy
Brown*
Sequel to MAD MAX, with our hero helping a small oil-producing community defend itself against gangs desperate for fuel, in this post-WW3 world. Plenty of incredible car stunts make this a must, even if the script has a good deal less imagination. Followed by MAD MAX: BEYOND THE THUNDERDOME.
Aka: ROAD WARRIOR, THE
FAN                                    91 min (ort 96 min)
B,V                                                                 WHV

### MAD MAX: BEYOND THE THUNDERDOME *** 15
George Miller/George Ogilvie
                        AUSTRALIA              1985
*Mel Gibson, Tina Turner, Angelo Rossitto, Helen
Buday, Rod Zuanic, Frank Thring, Angry Anderson,
Bruce Spence, Robert Grubb, George Spartels, Adam
Cockburn, Paul Larsson, Mark Spain, Mark Kounnas,
Tom Jennings, Adam Willits*
Third in the MAD MAX series, and as ever set in a post WW3 world, where civilisation has broken down, and scattered enclaves struggle for survival. Here the action takes place in Bartertown, where Max arrives in search of some stolen property and has to fight a duel in the Thunderdome arena. With the same formula as the two earlier films, but showing a definite lack of freshness or energy.
FAN                                                      103 min
V/sh                                                                WHV

### MAD MISS MANTON, THE **                      15
Leigh Jason             USA                        1938
*Barbara Stanwyck, Henry Fonda, Sam Levene,
Frances Mercer, Stanley Ridges, Vicki Lester, Hattie
McDaniel, Whitney Bourne, Ann Evers, Catherine
O'Quinn, Linda Terry, Eleanor Hansen, James Burke,
Paul Guilfoyle, Penny Singleton*
Comedy murder mystery in which a female socialite, stumbling over a body that disappears by the time the police arrives, sets out to solve the crime herself, with a little assistance from her friends. A fairly effective mixture of two genres, superficial but good fun. Written by Philip G. Epstein.
COM                                    76 min (ort 80 min) B/W
B,V                                                                 KVD

### MAD MISSION 2 **                                    PG
Eric Tsang (Tsang Chi Wai)
                        HONG KONG             1982
*Carl Mak, Sam Hui, Sylvia Chang, Dean Shak*
Story of gang warfare revolving around a hoard of diamonds and the rivalry between a female police inspector and a detective. A kind of Hong Kong answer to THE CANNONBALL RUN, with some good car stunts but little else. Two more sequels soon followed.
Aka: ACES GO PLACES; MAD MISSION 2: ACES GO PLACES; MAD MISSION PART 2: ACES GO PLACES (VTC)
A/AD                                    79 min (ort 101 min)
B,V,V2                          VTC L/A; INT/CBS L/A; MIA

### MAD MISSION 3: OUR MAN IN BOND          PG
STREET *
Tsui Mark              HONG KONG             1984
*Carl Mak, Sam Hui, Peter Graves, Richard Kiel,
Sylvia Chang, Tsunehara Sugiyama*
Second sequel in this spoof series, with a gang of international crooks being pursued from Paris to Hong Kong. A further film in the series followed.
Aka: ACES GO PLACES 3; OUR MAN FROM BOND STREET
A/AD                                    81 min (ort 87 min)
B,V                                                                 TEVP

### MAD MISSION 4 *                                      18
Ringo Lam              HONG KONG             1986
*Ronald Lacey, Sally Yeh, Karl Marka, Sam Hui,
Sylvia Chang, Peter McCaully, Onno Boulee, Sandi
Dexter, Gayle-Anne Jones*
Another in this series of non-stop action spoofs, with a professor inventing a crystal prism that can turn ordinary people into supermen, by stimulating their brains. As one might expect, this device is eagerly sought by some whose motives are less than pure. Unfortunately, the film fails to stimulate the viewer's brain.
A/AD                                                      86 min
B,V                                                                 HER

### MAD MONSTER PARTY? *                          U
Jules Bass              USA                        1967
*Voices of: Boris Karloff, Phyllis Diller, Ethel Ennis,
Gale Garnett*
Animated feature about a monster's convention to which Dr Frankenstein summons the monsters, because he wants to retire and appoint a successor. A good idea founders on the twin rocks of banality and tiresomeness.
CAR                                                      94 min
B,V,V2                                EHE; CH5 (VHS only)

### MADAME CLAUDE *                                    18
Just Jaeckin            FRANCE                 1977
*Francoise Fabian, Klaus Kinski, Robert Webber, Dayle
Haddon, Murray Head, Jean Craven, Viveke Knudsen,
Andre Falcon, Francois Perrot, Marc Michel*
A tale of blackmail, sex and murder, involving French government ministers and their visits to a house of ill-repute, in this softcore saga from the director of EMMANUELLE. A sequel followed.
Aka: FRENCH WOMAN, THE
Boa: novel Allo Oui Les Memoirs De Madame Claude by Jacques Quoirez.
DRA                                    105 min (ort 110 min)
V                                                                   RCA

### MADAME CLAUDE 2 **
Francois Mimet          FRANCE                 1981
*Alexandra Stewart, Bernard Fresson, Kim Harlow,
Dirke Altevogt*
A French newspaper plans to expose an international organisation of prostitutes who cater for diplomats and their perversions.
Aka: INTIMATE MOMENTS (TEVP)
A                                                        86 min
B,V                                                                TEVP

### MADAME SIN ***                                      PG
David Greene            USA                        1971
*Bette Davis, Robert Wagner, Roy Kinnear, Paul
Maxwell, Denholm Elliott, Gordon Jackson, Dudley
Stratton, Pik-Sen Lim, David Healy, Alan Dobie, Al
Mancini, Charles Lloyd Pack, Arnold Diamond, Frank
Middlemass, Burt Kwouk*
An evil female oriental genius plots to take over the world, using an ex-CIA agent in order to gain control of a Polaris submarine. An entertaining pilot for a

proposed series, well worth seeing for Davis' performance.

THR                                            86 min mTV
B,V,V2                          PRV; CH5 (VHS only)

## MADAME SOUSATZKA ***                          15
John Schlesinger        UK                      1988
*Shirley MacLaine, Peggy Ashcroft, Navin Chowdray,*
*Leigh Lawson, Twiggy (Lesley Hornby), Shabana*
*Azmi, Geoffrey Bayldon, Lee Montague*
The story of an eccentric, ageing Russian piano
teacher, who takes on a
15-year-old Indian boy as a pupil, and is drawn into an
obsessive desire to both teach him music and instruct
him in life. Extremely well made, but MacLaine's role,
calling for her to wear a ludicrous amount of make-up
and jewellery, has an air of absurdity about it.
DRA                              116 min (ort 121 min)
V                                              VIR

## MADAME ZENOBIA **
Eduardo Cemano          USA                     1973
*Christina Russel, Elizabeth Donovan, Rick Livermore*
A widow has problems with her sex life after her
husband's death.
Aka: ZENOBIA
A                                             64 min
B,V                                        MOV; APX

## MADE *                                         15
John Mackenzie          UK                      1972
*Carol White, John Castle, Roy Harper, Margery*
*Mason, Doremy Vernon*
An unhappy telephonist cares for her invalid mother
and illegitimate son, but has no-one to care for her.
She seeks an escape from her dreary life and finds
possible salvation in an encounter with a priest and a
folk singer. A typically British celebration of blighted
lives and empty souls that revels in misery and for all
its apparent stab at social realism, says nothing of any
relevance whatsoever.
Boa: play No One Was Saved by Howard Barker.
DRA                                          107 min
V                                              WHV

## MADE FOR EACH OTHER ***                        PG
John Cromwell           USA                     1938
*James Stewart, Carole Lombard, Lucile Watson,*
*Charles Coburn, Alma Kruger, Ward Bond, Harry*
*Davenport, Eddie Quillan, Esther Dale, Louise Beavers*
A touching and skilful romantic examination of the
married life of a young couple, and the pitfalls that lie
ahead as they struggle with babies, poverty and
interfering in-laws. Written by Jo Swerling.
DRA                          87 min (ort 95 min) B/W
B,V                                     APV L/A; DIAM

## MADE IN HEAVEN **                              PG
Alan Rudolph            USA                     1987
*Timothy Hutton, Kelly McGillis, Maureen Stapleton,*
*Don Murray, Anne Wedgeworth, Mare Winningham,*
*Amanda Plummer, Ellen Barkin, Debra Winger, Maej*
*Dusay, Ray Gideon, Timothy Daly, Neil Young, Tom*
*Petty, Ric Ocasek*
After a man has accidentally cut short his life, he and
a woman "newly created" fall madly in love. When she
is sent to Earth to live her first life, the man follows,
but has just thirty years in which to find her. A sugary
romantic comedy spoilt by two many gags and a
reliance on funny cameos instead of a funny script.
COM                              98 min (ort 103 min)
B,V                                            GHV

## MADE IN USA **                                 18
Ken Friedman            USA                     1988
*Christopher Penn, Adrian Pasdar, Lori Singer*
Two coalminers' sons leave their former lives behind
them when they set out for California in pursuit of the
Great American Dream. Along the way they pick up a

young girl and the three youngsters enjoy plenty of
excitement as they try to keep one jump ahead of the
law.
A/AD                                          85 min
B,V                                            CHV

## MADHOUSE **                                    18
James Clark             UK                      1974
*Vincent Price, Peter Cushing, Adrienne Corri, Robert*
*Quarry, Linda Hayden, Natasha Pyne, Michael*
*Parkinson, Barry Dennen, Ellis Dayle, Catherine*
*Wilmer, John Garrie, Ian Thompson, Jenny Lee*
*Wright, Julie Crosthwaite*
A mad horror film star comes out of retirement to take
revenge for the murder of his girlfriend, and is soon
implicated in a series of grisly murders, in this
entertaining but uneven yarn. A few touches of grim
humour help it along somewhat.
Aka: REVENGE OF DOCTOR DEATH, THE
Boa: novel Devilday by Angus Hall.
HOR                              88 min (ort 92 min)
V                                              RCA

## MADIGAN'S MILLION *
Stanley Prager       ITALY/SPAIN               1967
*Dustin Hoffman, Elsa Martinelli, Cesar Romero*
A US Treasury official is sent to Italy to recover
money stolen by a mobster, who died there after being
deported from the USA. A hollow and amateurish
effort.
DRA                                           89 min
B,V,V2                                         VPD

## MADMAN *                                       18
Joe Giannone            USA                     1980
*Alexis Dubin, Tony Fish, Harriet Bass, Seth Jones,*
*Jan Claire, Alex Murphy, Jimmy Steele, Paul Ehlers,*
*Carl Fredericks, Michael Sullivan, Gaylen Ross*
Several years ago a demented farmer went on a bloody
rampage, killing his family and escaping into the
woods. When a summer camp that was closed by this
event, is reopened as a training camp for counsellors,
our bloodthirsty farmer puts in an appearance. A dull
and derivative effort that adds nothing new to this
genre. Good photography and special effects cannot
redeem it.
Aka: MADMAN MARZ
HOR                                           88 min
B,V                                   VDF L/A; VFO

## MADRON **
Jerry Hopper            USA                     1970
*Richard Boone, Leslie Caron, Paul Smith, Gabi*
*Amrani, Chaim Banai, Avraham Telya, Sam Red,*
*Willy Gafni*
An Indian hunter falls in love with a nun, the sole
survivor of an Apache massacre, as they trek across
the desert. A rarity in that it was shot in Israel's
Negev desert. Average.
WES                              77 min (ort 97 min)
B,V,V2                                     VCL/CBS

## MAE WEST *
Lee Philips             USA                     1982
*James Brolin, Roddy McDowall, Ann Jillian, Piper*
*Laurie, Chuck McCann, Louis Giambalvo, Lee*
*DeBroux, Donald Hotton, Ian Wolfe, Bill Morey, Rita*
*Taagart, Michael Currie, Jay Garner, Burke Byrnes,*
*Bridgette Anderson, Debbie Lytton*
A less-than-accurate biopic on the life and times of
this famous entertainer with little of interest and
even less titillation. Scripted by E. Arthur Kean.
DRA                          90 min (ort 97 min) mTV
B,V                                            PCV

## MAFIA PRINCESS **                              15
Robert Collins          USA                     1986
*Susan Lucci, Tony Curtis, Tony De Santis, Jonathan*

Welsh, David McWraith Kathleen Widdoes, Chuck Shamata, Louie Di Blanco, David McIlwraith, Marsha Moreau, Albert Schultz, Norma Edwards, Ken Pogue, Tom Harvey, Bill Lake
The story of the family life of the head of a Mafia clan who rules their lives with a rod of iron. THE GODFATHER it may not be, but the performances largely redeem the dismal script.
Boa: book by Antoinette Giancana and Thomas C. Renner.
DRA                          90 min (ort 100 min) mTV
B,V                                      IVS; VCC (VHS only)

**MAFIA VERSUS NINJA \***                            18
                         HONG KONG              1985
Alexander Lou, Charles Wong, Alan Lan, Silvio Azzolini, Wang Hsia, Pad Yku La
Mafia efforts to take over a town are resisted by a black-clad Ninja, in this rather clumsy attempt to blend two genres.
MAR                          85 min Cut (1 min 40 sec)
B,V                                              NINJ/VPD

**MAFIA WARFARE \***
Jose Giovanni      FRANCE/ITALY            1972
Jean-Paul Belmondo, Claudia Cardinale, Michel Constantin
Two gangsters cheated by the Mafia plan to get their revenge in this tediously predictable effort.
Aka: HIT MAN; KILLER MAN; LA SCOUMOUNE; SCOUNDREL
DRA                                                97 min
B,V                                                  VCL

**MAFU CAGE, THE \*\***
Karen Arthur        USA                       1978
Lee Grant, Carol Kane, Will Geer, James Olson
An astronomer takes care of her deranged sister in this bizarre battle of wills, with each sister assuming the aspect of their caged pet orang-utan, "Mafu" – hence the title. Weird and muddled but certainly unusual.
Aka: CAGE, THE; DEVIATION; MY SISTER, MY LOVE
Boa: play by Eric Wespha.
DRA                                               101 min
B,V                                       MVM L/A; HVH

**MAGEE \*\***
Gene Levitt       AUSTRALIA/USA            1978
Tony LoBianco, Sally Kellerman, Ann Semler, Rod Mullinnar, Kevin Leslie
A man fights off a takeover bid for his freighter, by kidnapping the spoilt daughter of a businessman so as to force a meeting. Their mutual hostility slowly turns to affection as they fight off various perils together. A standard romantic adventure, with contrived dialogue and a predictable resolution. Now turn to THE AFRICAN QUEEN to see how it really should have been done.
Aka: MAGEE AND THE LADY; SHE'LL BE SWEET
A/AD                                       92 min mTV
B,V                                     MOG; CBS; PMA

**MAGGIE, THE \*\***
Alexander Mackendrick  UK                 1953
Paul Douglas, Alex Mackenzie, James Copeland, Abe Barker, Hubert Gregg, Geoffrey Keen, Tommy Kearins, Dorothy Alison, Andrew Keir, Fiona Glyne, Meg Buchanan, Jameson Clark, Mark Dignam, Moultrie Kelsall, Sheila Shand Gibbs
The captain of a rusty old bucket of a cargo ship in the Western Isles of Scotland, tricks the agent for an American businessman, into letting him carry a valuable cargo. Quite competent but inclined to slackness in pacing.
Aka: HIGH AND DRY

Boa: novel by J.D. White.
COM                          90 min (ort 92 min) B/W
B,V                                                TEVP

**MAGIC \*\*\***                                     15
Richard Attenborough   USA                 1978
Anthony Hopkins, Ann-Margret, Burgess Meredith, Ed Lauter, Jerry Houser, E.J. Andre, David Ogden Stiers
Excellent and gripping tale of a ventriloquist whose attachment to his dummy becomes an unhealthy dependence, to the point where he is driven "by the dummy" to murder. Hopkins gives a remarkable performance, for which he had to learn the skills of a ventriloquist. Screenplay is by William Goldman.
Boa: novel by William Goldman.
DRA                                               106 min
B,V,V2                                             VGM

**MAGIC ADVENTURE \*\***
Cruz Delgado          SPAIN                  1973
A lively animated fantasy inspired by some of the tales of Hans Christian Andersen, with two children being taken to a magical land and enjoying a series of adventures.
Aka: MAGICA AVENTURA
CAR                                                65 min
B,V,V2                                  VUL L/A; KRP

**MAGIC BOX, THE \*\*\***                            U
John Boulting         UK                     1951
Robert Donat, Maria Schell, Margaret Johnston, John Howard Davies, Renee Asherson, Richard Attenborough, Robert Beatty, Michael Denison, Leo Genn, Joyce Grenfell, Marius Goring, Robertson Hare, Kathleen Harrison
Made for the Festival of Britain, and with a host of guest stars, this is devoted to the life and career of William Friese-Greene, a British portrait photographer who helped pioneer the development of the cine camera. A careful and expensive biopic, in which sincerity replaces inventiveness and a series of vignettes replace the narrative.
Boa: book Friese-Greene by Ray Allister.
DRA                          107 min (ort 118 min)
V                                                  WHV

**MAGIC CHRISTIAN, THE \***                          15
Joseph McGrath        UK                     1970
Peter Sellers, Ringo Starr, Richard Attenborough, Raquel Welch, Yul Brynner, Laurence Harvey, Christopher Lee, Wilfrid Hyde-White, Spike Milligan, Dennis Price, Leonard Frey, Isabel Jeans, Caroline Blakiston, Roland Culver
Dreadful garbage this one. An eccentric millionaire sets out to prove that people will do anything for money. Hopelessly unfunny, it sank into well-deserved oblivion. Scripted by McGrath and Terry Southern with help from Cleese, Sellers and Chapman, and like so many British faltering attempts at comedy, it contains an array of star cameos adding nothing to the paper-thin plot. The catchy music is by Badfinger.
Boa: novel by Terry Southern.
COM       88 min (ort 95 min) (Cut at film release)
B,V                                   VFP; MIA (VHS only)

**MAGIC ROUNDABOUT, THE: DOUGAL AND THE BLUE CAT \*\***                             U
                         UK
Voice of Eric Thompson
A feature-length spin-off of a popular puppet animation series (originally created by Serge Danot for French TV and then adapted by Thompson) that concerned the adventures of a variety of creatures in the Beautiful Wood, and the ubiquitous Mr Zebedee who was always on hand to tell them when it was bed-time. In this tale Dougal the dog finds himself up

against the mysterious "Blue Cat", who is intent on turning everything in sight blue.
Aka: DOUGAL AND THE BLUE CAT
CAR                                         85 min
V                                           CH5

## MAGIC STICKS *                           PG
Peter Keglevic        USA                   1987
*George Kranz, Kelly Curtis, John Gallagher, Jack McGee, Chico Hamilton*
An unemployed jazz drummer acquires a pair of magic sticks that ensure that people will always dance to his beat. A contrived and fairly pointless effort. Jazz drummer Hamilton puts in an appearance.
COM                                         87 min
V                                           VES

## MAGIC SWORD, THE ***                     U
Bert I. Gordon        USA                   1962
*Basil Rathbone, Estelle Winwood, Gary Lockwood, Anne Helm, Liam Sullivan, Jacques Gallo, John Mauldin, Leory Johnson, Angus Duncan, David Cross, Taldo Kenyon, Jack Kosslyn, Maila Nurmi, Danille De Metz, Merritt Stone*
A young knight has to rescue a damsel in distress, held captive by an evil sorcerer and a dragon. A fantasy adventure far above the usual level for the work of this director, but still somewhat unfocused and messy.
Aka: SORCERER'S CURSE, THE (BUDPAC)
FAN                     76 min (ort 85 min)
B,V,V2              EVC L/A; SVC L/A; BUDPAC

## MAGIC TOYSHOP, THE **                    15
David Wheatley        UK                    1986
*Tom Bell, Caroline Milmoe, Kilian McKenna, Patricia Kerrigan, Lorcan Cranitch, Gareth Bushill, Marlene Sidaway, Georgina Hulme, Marguerite Porter, Lloyd Newson*
After their mother's death, three children go to live with their sadistic uncle at his old toyshop, where they experience a series of bewildering events.
Boa: story by Angela Carter.
THR                                        103 min
B,V                                         PAL

## MAGICIAN OF LUBLIN, THE *                15
Menahem Golan
        ISRAEL/WEST GERMANY                 1979
*Alan Arkin, Louise Fletcher, Lou Jacobi, Valerie Perrine, Shelley Winters, Warren Berlinger*
Film version of a story about a magician with a strange power over women, that he uses to reach the top of Warsaw society at the turn of the century. A slack and ponderous rendition of Singer's novel, with a few clever moments but a general air of apathy.
Boa: novel by Isaac Bashevis Singer.
DRA                     101 min (ort 114 min)
B,V                                         RNK

## MAGNIFICENT AMBERSONS, THE ****          U
Orson Welles          USA                   1942
*Tim Holt, Joseph Cotten, Dolores Costello, Anne Baxter, Agnes Moorehead, Ray Collins, Richard Bennett, Erskine Sanford*
This film might have been Welles' masterpiece but was cut to pieces by the studio. It tells of a family unable to come to terms with a changing world, and of a mother and son conflict over her lover. Many of the Welles touches are still there but re-cutting and re-shooting by the studio all but ruined it.
Boa: novel by Booth Tarkington.
DRA                                         88 min
V                                           VCC

## MAGNIFICENT BODYGUARDS *                 15
Lo Wei        HONG KONG                     1984
*Jackie Chan*
Another mass-produced Chan adventure, with our

hero hired to act as bodyguard to a woman who is taking her seriously ill brother to the only doctor who can cure him.
MAR                         97 min Cut (38 sec)
V                                  TGP; SQUARE

## MAGNIFICENT MATADOR, THE **              
Budd Boetticher       USA                   1955
*Anthony Quinn, Maureen O'Hara, Manual Rojas, Thomas Gomez, Richard Denning, Lola Albright, William Brooks Ching, Eduardo Noriega, Lorraine Chanel, Anthony Caruso, Joaquin Rodriguez*
Another venture into the world of bullfighting for this director, in this tale of a matador and his illegitimate son, who seems destined to follow in his father's footsteps. Fair.
Aka: BRAVE AND THE BEAUTIFUL, THE
DRA                                         94 min
B,V,V2                                  INT/CBS

## MAGNIFICENT NATURAL FIST *               18
Godfrey Ho        HONG KONG                 198-
*Elton Chong, Mike Wong, Beau Wan, Lewis Ko, Natassa Chan, Leung Yuen, Kelly Lon*
Standard kung fu mayhem.
MAR                                         85 min
B,V                                         VPD

## MAGNIFICENT SEVEN DEADLY SINS, THE *
Graham Stark        UK                      1971
*Bruce Forsyth, Joan Sims, Roy Hudd, Harry Secombe, June Whitfield, Julie Ege, Leslie Phillips, Harry H. Corbett, Cheryl Kennedy, Ian Carmichael, Alfie Bass, Spike Milligan, Ronald Fraser, Arthur Howard, Stephen Lewis*
A compilation of comedy sketches of variable quality, not one of which is memorable, but all of which attempt to highlight a legendary human failing. The sins examined are avarice, envy, gluttony, lust, pride, sloth and wrath.
COM                                        107 min
B,V                                         GHV

## MAGNIFICENT SEVEN, THE ***               PG
John Sturges          USA                   1960
*Yul Brynner, Steve McQueen, James Coburn, Eli Wallach, Horst Buchholtz, Charles Bronson, Robert Vaughn, Brad Dexter, Vladimir Sokoloff, Rosenda Monteros, Jorge Martinez de Hoyos, Whit Bissell, Val Avery, Bing Russell*
Seven gunfighters come together, when their services are required by a poor Mexican village subject to periodic raids by bandits. A direct steal from Kurosawa's brilliant film "The Seven Samurai", yet quite enjoyable for all that, and with a memorable score by Elmer Bernstein. Followed by a spate of sequels, beginnning with "Return Of The Seven".
WES                     123 min (ort 138 min)
V                                           WHV

## MAGNIFICENT SHOWMAN, THE **             U
Henry Hathaway        USA                   1964
*John Wayne, Rita Haywoth, Claudia Cardinale, John Smith, Richard Conte, Lloyd Nolan, Wanda Rotha, Kay Walsh*
An American circus tours Europe, while the owner seeks to find a performer he once loved, in this standard romance set against the world of circus artistes. The inevitable big fire comes as a blessed relief from the tedium of it all. Filmed in Spain.
Aka: CIRCUS WORLD (IFS/CBS or VCC)
DRA                     132 min (ort 135 min)
B,V              IFS/CBS; VCC (VHS only)

## MAGNUM FORCE **                          18
Ted Post        USA                         1973
*Clint Eastwood, David Soul, Mitchell Ryan, Hal Holbrook, Felton Perry, Tim Matherson, Robert Urich*
A police inspector in San Francisco has to find out who

is responsible for a wave of gangster killings. Second in the DIRTY HARRY series with Eastwood as mean and tough as ever but the script showing a distinct lack of imagination. Written by John Milius and Michael Cimino. Followed by THE ENFORCER.

DRA 116 min (ort 124 min)
V WHV

## MAHLER **
Ken Russell UK 1974
Robert Powell, Georgina Hale, Richard Morant, Lee Montague, Rosalie Crutchley, Antonia Ellis, Benny Lee, David Collings, Ronald Pickup, Ken Colley, Arnold Yarrow, Dana Gillespie, Elaine Delmar, Michael Southgate

Here we go, it's Ken Russell time and we're in for another wild, overblown extravaganza in which the music of a great composer once more serves as a vehicle for Russell's fantasies. Looks pretty dated now (it looked pretty dated at the time).

DRA 115 min
B, V/sh, V2 GHV

## MAID IN SWEDEN **
Floch Johnson USA 1971
Kristina Lindberg, Monika Ekman, Krister Ekman
A country girl visiting Stockholm for the first time, has some strange encounters with men.

A 72 min
B,V INT

## MAID TO ORDER ***
Amy Jones USA 1987
Ally Sheedy, Beverly D'Angelo, Michael Ontkean, Valerie Perrine, Dick Shawn, Tom Skerritt, Merry Clayton, Begona Plaza, Rainbow Phoenix
A spoilt rich girl is transformed into a penniless brat, when her father wishes that he did not have a daughter. What's worse, she forced to work as a maid for a couple just as rich and insufferable as she used to be. A cute fairytale, with lively performances and a couple of nice songs too.

COM 89 min (ort 96 min) mTV
B,V PRES

## MAIGRET **
Paul Lynch UK 1988
Richard Harris, Patrick O'Neal, Victoria Tennant, Barbara Shelley, Don Henderson, Ian Ogilvy, Eric Deacon, Caroline Munro, Andrew McCulloch
A Parisian policeman searches for the killer of his best friend, who worked as a private eye. This pilot for a prospective series based on Georges Simenon's famous creation fails to convince (despite its locations) largely on account of the inability of the cast to breathe life into the characters they portray or give them realistic accents.

DRA 95 min (ort 100 min) mTV
V VGM

## MAIN EVENT, THE *
Howard Zieff USA 1979
Barbra Streisand, Ryan O'Neal, Paul Sand, Whitman Mayo, James Gregory, Richard Lawson
A businesswoman finds gerself almost totally bankrupt, with no assets but a broken-down boxer about to retire. To save her perfume business, she becomes his manager and tries to force him to make a comeback. Poorly scripted and indifferently acted, this comedy is an unworthy vehicle for the talents of all concerned.

COM 105 min (ort 112 min)
B,V WHV

## MAJESTIC THUNDERBOLT **
Godfrey Ho HONG KONG 1985
Richard Harrison, Philip Lo, Roc Tien, John Ladedski
A formula thriller involving diamond smuggling and criminal double-dealing.

THR 83 min Cut (4 min 57 sec)
B,V BRNX L/A; SAT

## MAJOR DUNDEE *** PG
Sam Peckinpah USA 1965
Charlton Heston, Richard Harris, Jim Hutton, James Coburn, Michael Anderson Jr, Senta Berger, Slim Pickens, Mario Adorf, Brock Peters, Warren Oates, Ben Johnson, R.G. Armstrong, L.Q. Jones, Karl Swenson, Michael Pate
An assorted bunch of Confederate soldiers fight Apaches and antagonise the French in Mexico. Peckinpah disowned the film which was re-cut by others, but it's certainly better than one might have expected, and the excellent cast and spectacular battles more than compensate for the lack of warmth or coherence. Written by Harry Julian Fink, Oscar Saul and Peckinpah.

WES 117 min (ort 134 min)
B,V RCA

## MAJOR LEAGUE ** 15
David S. Ward USA 1989
Tom Berenger, Charlie Sheen, Corbin Bernsen, Margaret Whitton, James Gammon, Rene Russo, Bob Uecker
A low-brow comedy about a no-hope baseball team of misfits and oddball characters, that's groomed for stardom by their new lady boss, who has inherited the team. Strident and rather crude, but the attractive cast make the most of their material.

COM 102 min
V BRAVE

## MAKING A CASE FOR MURDER: THE HOWARD BEACH STORY ** 15
Dick Lowry USA 1989
Daniel J. Travanti, William Daniels, Joe Morton, Cliff Gorman, Bruce Young, Dan Lauria
A state prosecutor faces an uphill struggle when he tries to solve the murder of a black man in a white working-class district. A straightforward account of the notorious murder that took place at Queens, New York City in 1986. Fair.
Aka: HOWARD BEACH: MAKING A CASE FOR MURDER

DRA 94 min (ort 100 min) mTV
V PRISM L/A

## MAKING CONTACT ** 15
Roland Emmerich/Klaus Dittrich
WEST GERMANY 1985
Joshua Morrell, Tammy Shields, Eva Kryll, Jan Zierold, Barbara Klein
A young boy with psychic powers enabling him to contact his dead father, comes across a ventriloquist's dummy that is possessed by evil forces. The dummy lures him and some friends to a deserted house, where they are attacked by a series of savage creatures unleashed by it.
Aka: JOEY

HOR 80 min (ort 83 min)
B,V MGM

## MAKING LOVE ** 18
Arthur Hiller USA 1982
Kate Jackson, Harry Hamlin, Michael Ontkean, Wendy Hiller, Arthur Hill, Nancy Olson, John Dukakis, Terry Kiser, Dennis Howard, Asher Brauner
A couple's marriage is jeopardised, when the husband comes out of the closet and admits his homosexuality to his wife. A serious topic is given an undeservedly dull treatment.
Boa: story by A. Scott Berg.

DRA 112 min
B,V CBS

**MAKING MR RIGHT** ** 15
Susan Seidelman            USA            1987
*John Malkovich, Ann Magnuson, Glenne Headly, Ben*
*Masters, Laurie Metcalf, Polly Bergen, Harsh Nayyar,*
*Hart Bochner, Susan Anton*
A woman public relations expert is hired to promote a
scientist's android creation. An interesting comic
premise fails to develop its full potential. Filmed in
Miami Beach, and set there too.
COM                                    95 min
V/sh                                       RCA

**MAKING THE GRADE** ** 15
Dorian Walker              USA            1984
*Judd Nelson, Jonna Lee, Carey Scott, Dana Olsen,*
*Gordon Jump, Ronald Lacey*
A rich kid attending prep school, faces losing his
supply of family money unless he gets good grades, so
he hires a streetwise Jersey kid to impersonate him,
unaware that he is on the run from the Mob. A dullish
comedy aimed at the teen end of the market.
Aka: LAST AMERICAN PREPPY, THE; PREPPIES
(AVA/CBS)
COM                      105 min; 100 min (MSD)
B,V                          AVA/CBS; MSD; GHV

**MAKO: THE JAWS OF DEATH** ** PG
William Grefe              USA            1976
*Richard Jaeckel, Jennifer Bishop, Harold Sakata,*
*John Chandler, Buffy Dee*
A low-budget film, a kind of poor man's JAWS in
reverse, with Jaeckel protecting the sharks from the
hunters of the deep.
Aka: JAWS OF DEATH, THE
DRA                                    90 min
B,V                                        PRV

**MALACHI'S COVE** ** U
Henry Herbert              UK             1973
*Donald Pleasence, Dai Bradley, Arthur English, David*
*Howe, Veronica Quilligan, Peter Vaughan, Lillian*
*Walker, Kennaley Hoyle, John Barrett, Alan Hockney,*
*George Malpas, Meg Wynn Owen*
A young girl is forced to live by selling seaweed when
her father is drowned, but comes into conflict with
another family whose son does his best to make her
life unpleasant. Despite this, she saves him from
suffering the same fate as her father. A dull tale of life
among the coastal folk of Cornwall in the 1880s.
Aka: SEAWEED CHILDREN, THE
Boa: short story The Seaweed Children by Anthony
Trollope.
DRA                        75 min; 85 min (MAST)
B,V,V2                 INT/CBS; VMA; MAST (VHS only)

**MALCOLM** *** 15
Nadia Tass             AUSTRALIA          1986
*Colin Friels, John Hargreaves, Lindy Davies, Chris*
*Haywood, Charles Tingwell, Beverly Phillips, Judith*
*Stratford*
When an eccentric inventor loses his job at the tram
depot where he works, he turns his talents to committing a series of unusual crimes. A charming and
inventive comedy that marked the directorial debut
for Tass, with a script by David Parker (her husband),
who based the title character on his brother. The film
won eight Australian Film Institute awards in 1986,
including one for Best Picture.
COM                        83 min (ort 88 min) B/W
B,V                                    VIR; PVG

**MALEDICTION** * 18
Bert I. Gordon             USA            1989
*Robert Forster, Lydie Denier, Caren Kaye*
A former cop-turned-private-eye is hired to find a
missing girl and gets involved with the female owner
of a modelling agency. He sees a strange medieval
protrait that hangs in her office, but its significance is
not revealed until later, in a mediocre and gory film,

that's as devoid of logic as it is of conviction on the
part of its actors.
Aka: SATAN'S PRINCESS
HOR                            87 min Cut (57 sec)
V                                          CIC

**MALIBU EXPRESS** * 18
Andy Sidaris              USA             1984
*Darby Hinton, Sybil Danning (Sybelle Danninger),*
*Art Metrano, Niki Dantine, Lynda Wiesmeier, Shelly*
*Taylor, Lori Sutton, Barbara Edwards, Kimberly*
*McArthur*
A private eye becomes involved in a plot to steal
high-tech secrets and give them to the Russians, but
this corny story takes second place in a film that
serves merely as a vehicle to display the talents of a
number of Playboy models. A very loose remake of
STACEY, an earlier film by this director. Followed by
a similar film (though not a sequel) entitled PICASSO
TRIGGER.
THR                            97 min (ort 101 min)
B,V                                        CIC

**MALIBU HIGH** * 18
Irv Berwick               USA             1979
*Jill Lansing, Stuart Taylor, Katie Johnson, Tammy*
*Taylor, Garth Howard, Phyllis Benson, Al Mannino*
A pretty schoolgirl gets involved in a life of crime and
ends up as a Mafia assassin. Unpleasant and exploita-
tive nonsense.
DRA                                    92 min
B,V,V2                         INT/CBS; XTASY

**MALIBU HOT SUMMER** * 18
Richard Brander        USA     1974 (released 1986)
*Terry Congie, Leslie Brander, Roselyn Royce, Robert*
*Acey, Kevin Costner, Larry DeCraw, James Pascucci,*
*Justin Scott*
Three young women go to Los Angeles to fulfil their
ambitions in various fields. Low-grade nonsense. This
poor offering gave Costner his first screen role.
Aka: SIZZLE BEACH; SIZZLE BEACH, USA
DRA                            82 min (ort 93 min)
B,V                                   DFS; XTASY

**MALLEN CURSE, THE** ** PG
Mary McMurray/Brian Mills
                           UK             1980
*Juliet Stevenson, Gerry Sundquist, Caroline Blakiston*
The second series of tales based on Cookson's "The
Mallens" tells of Barbara who, rejected by her cousin,
enters a loveless marriage with the son of the
Benshams, who now own the High Banks Hall since
the bankruptcy of her late father. Meanwhile, the
widowed Mr Bensham has propposed to Anna Brig-
more, who has ambitions of her own regarding the
former home of the Mallens. A glossy soap opera-style
yarn, but somewhat better than the first series.
Boa: The Mallen trilogy by Catherine Cookson.
DRA                                   147 min mTV
V                                        CHEREN

**MALLEN GIRLS, THE** ** PG
Richard Martin/Ronald Wilson/Brian Mills
                           UK             1978
*John Duttine*
The second part of the first TV series of "The Mallens".
The once wealthy squire has squandered his money
and is forced to vacate High Banks Hall and move to a
small cottage with his two wards. His two bastard
sons become regular visitors there and one night
Barbara is savagely raped.
Boa: The Mallen trilogy by Catherine Cookson.
DRA                                   178 min mTV
V                                        CHEREN

**MALLEN SECRET, THE** ** PG
Mary McMurray/Roy Roberts
                           UK             1980

*Juliet Stevenson, Gerry Sundquist, Caroline Blakiston*
Based on the second series of tales in "The Mallens",
this follows the career of Barbara, one of the late
Squire's many illegitimate children, who has been
kept from the truth of her origins by her governess.
However, matters become complicated when she falls
in love with her cousin Michael, who has also had the
truth of his illegitimacy kept from him. A fair drama
of no great weight, but absorbing enough in its way.
Boa: The Mallen trilogy by Catherine Cookson.

DRA                           140 min mTV
V                                CHEREN

## MALLEN STREAK, THE **          PG
Richard Martin/Ronald Wilson/Brian Mills
UK                                 1978
*John Duttine*
The story of a wealthy squire who squanders his
money and fathers a number of illegitimate children,
each of whom is recognisably his child, thanks to a
streak of white hair. Compiled from "The Mallens",
this rather tedious drama wended its weary way, but
improved somewhat by the time the second series
began dealing with the fortunes of the squire's many
offspring.
Boa: The Mallen trilogy by Catherine Cookson.

DRA                           171 min mTV
V                                CHEREN

## MALLENS, THE *             PG
Roy Roberts       UK               1978/80
*John Duttine, John Hallam, Caroline Blakiston*
Put together from a historical series made for TV, this
tale is full of wild squires and bastard children in the
best tradition of romantic fiction. An expensive but
not terribly convincing effort. A second series followed
that was somewhat better.
Boa: novel by Catherine Cookson.

DRA               345 min (3 cassettes) mTV
B,V                          GRN; VES

## MALOMBRA ***               18
Bruno Gaburrp      ITALY            1983
*Paola Senatore, Maurice Poli, Gloria Brini, Gino Milli,*
*Stefano Alesandrini, Scilla Jacu*
An unusual erotic mystery story, in which a young
man's fantasies become reality.
Aka: MALOMBRA, LE PERVERSIONI SESSUALI
DI UNA ADOLESCENTE; MALOMBRA, THE
SEXUAL PERVERSIONS OF AN ADOLESCENT
Boa: novel by Antonio Foguzzano

A                                 91 min
B,V                             BLUMO

## MALONE **               18
Harley Cokliss      USA             1987
*Burt Reynolds, Cliff Robertson, Scott Wilson, Kenneth*
*McMillan, Lauren Hutton, Cynthia Gibb*
An ex-CIA agent, disillusioned with the workings of
the intelligence agencies, is poised to leave his job,
when he suddenly unearths a strange conspiracy in a
small town, that poses a major threat to national
security. Amiable high-action dross that is best
enjoyed with the mind disengaged.
Boa: novel Shotgun by William Wingate.

THR           88 min (ort 92 min) Cut (1 sec)
B,V                      RNK L/A; VIR

## MALPERTUIS ***            18
Harry Kumel
BELGIUM/FRANCE/WEST GERMANY   1972
*Orson Welles, Susan Hampshire, Michel Bouquet,*
*Mathieu Carriere, Walter Rilla, Daniel Pilon, Jean-*
*Pierre Cassel, Dora Van Der Groen, Sylvia Vartan*
An old sailor discovers the gods of ancient Greece, who
are exhausted by years of neglect. He captures them
and sews them into human skins with the aid of a
taxidermist, and they are brought to a house where
they live fairly drab lives, but occasionally reveal

their true natures. When a young sailor strays into
their abode he is turned into a statue by Medusa. An
opulent and surreal tale, quite unlike any other
horror film.
Aka: MALPERTUIS: HISTOIRE D'UNE MAISON
MAUDITE; MAUDITE: THE LEGEND OF DOOM
HOUSE
Boa: novel by Jean Ray.

HOR                                89 min
B,V,V2             INT L/A: MPV; GLOB

## MALTA STORY, THE ***        U
Brian Desmond Hurst    UK           1953
*Alec Guinness, Jack Hawkins, Anthony Steel, Flora*
*Robson, Muriel Pavlow, Renee Asherson, High*
*Burden, Nigel Stock, Reginald Tate, Ralph Truman,*
*Rosalie Crutchley, Michael Medwin, Ronald Adam,*
*Stuart Burge, Jerry Desmonde*
Thrilling account of the RAF action during WW2, in a
battle to prevent the island fortress of Malta from
falling into German hands. Low-key it may be, but
this only serves to highlight the merits of this
well-crafted flag-waver.

WAR           99 min (ort 103 min) B/W
V                                  VCC

## MALTESE FALCON, THE ***     PG
John Huston       USA            1941
*Humphrey Bogart, Sydney Greenstreet, Peter Lorre,*
*Mary Astor, Gladys George, Ward Bond, Elisha Cook*
*Jr, Jerome Cowan, Lee Patrick, Barton MacLane,*
*Walter Huston*
Vastly over-rated mystery about the hunt for a
statuette, so valuable that murders are committed to
gain it. Doors fly open, doors fly shut, bodies turn up
here, there, everywhere. In the end the effect is as
deadening as wading through sawdust. A fine cast and
some splendid dialogue rescue it from disaster. This
was Huston's directorial debut and Greenstreet's first
screen role.
Boa: novel by Dashiell Hammett.

DRA                         101 min B/W
B,V                              WHV

## MAMA'S DIRTY GIRLS **      18
John Hayes        USA            1974
*Gloria Grahame, Candice Rialson, Sondra Currie,*
*Paul Lambert, Mary Stoddard*
A woman murders her first husband but discovers
that he was penniless, so she goes off in search of
another suitable candidate.

THR          80 min; 76 min (XTASY)
B,V                VTC L/A; XTASY

## MAME *                
Gene Saks         USA            1974
*Lucille Ball, Robert Preston, Beatrice Arthur, Jane*
*Connell, Bruce Davison, Kirby Furlong, Joyce Van*
*Patten, John McGiver*
After his father dies, a nine-year-old boy goes off to
live with his aunt and discovers that she is a strange
and flamboyant person. This film version of the
musical is much inferior to the straight 1958 "Auntie
Mame" in which Rosalind Russell gave an outstand-
ing performance in the title role.
Boa: novel by Patrick Dennis/play by Jerome
Lawrence and Robert E. Lee.

MUS                   127 min (ort 131 min)
V                                WHV

## MAMMA DRACULA *          18
Boris Szulzinger
BELGIUM/FRANCE        1988
*Louise Fletcher, Maria Schneider, Marc-Henri*
*Wajnberg, Alexander Wajnberg, Jess Hahn*
A female vampire who enjoys bathing in the blood of
virgins, is forced by the increasing rarity of this
commodity to employ a scientist who makes artificial

blood. However, the mass disappearances have focused attention on her, and her birthday party to which she has invited a bevy of girls, is joined by an undercover female cop. A slack-witted and disappointing horror spoof.

COM          80 min
V          EIV

## MAN ABOUT THE HOUSE *    PG
John Robins    UK    1974
*Paula Wilcox, Sally Thomsett, Richard O'Sullivan, Yootha Joyce, Brian Murphy, Peter Cellier, Patrick Newell, Spike Milligan, Arthur Lowe, Doug Fisher, Aimi MacDonald, Jack Smethurst, Melvyn Hayes, Michael Ward*
Another dreadful TV spin-off from an even worse TV series, in which a man and the two girls he shares the flat with, join forces with their disreputable landlord to fight off redevelopment of the area. The script could have used some redevelopment.

COM      86 min (ort 90 min)
B.V      TEVP

## MAN ALONE, A ***    U
Ray Milland    USA    1955
*Ray Milland, Mary Murphy, Raymond Burr, Ward Bond, Lee Van Cleef, Arthur Space, Alan Hale, Douglas Spencer, Thomas Browne Henry, Grandon Rhodes, Martin Garralaga, Kim Spalding, Howard Negley, Julian Rivero, Lee Roberts*
Western revolving around a fugitive from a lynching party, who exposes the outlaw-leader responsible for the massacre of stagecoach passengers. An absorbing and well-crafted effort that marked Milland's directorial debut.

WES    92 min (ort 96 min)
V    VMA L/A; HOLLY; STABL; PARK

## MAN AND A WOMAN, A: TWENTY YEARS  15
## LATER *
Claude Lelouch    FRANCE    1986
*Anouk Aimee, Jean-Louis Tritignant, Richard Berry, Evelyne Bouix, Charles Gerard, Marie-Sophie Pochat, Antoine Sire, Andre Engel, Patrick Poivre D'Arvor*
Twenty years may have gone by, but they've made very little difference in terms of either plot or conception to this delayed remake, with a film producer seeking out his old love in order to immortalise their romance on celluloid. Music is by Francis Lai.
Aka: UN HOMME ET UNE FEMME: VINGT ANS DEJA

DRA    108 min (ort 120 min)
B/sh, V/sh    WHV

## MAN AT THE TOP **
Mike Vardy    UK    1973
*Kenneth Haigh, Nanette Newman, Harry Andrews, John Quentin, Mary Maude, Danny Sewell, Paul Williamson, Margaret Heald, Angela Bruce, Charlie Williams, Anne Cunningham, William Lucas, John Collin, Norma West*
An attempt to cash in on the success of a popular TV series of the same name, that was inspired by John Braine's novel "Room At The Top", and followed the adventures of Joe Lampton, a character who first saw the light of day in the 1958 film ROOM AT THE TOP (followed by the 1965 sequel "Life At The Top"). In this predictable spin-off, Lampton is now a successful executive, and faces a nasty dilemma over the use of a new, untested drug.

DRA    95 min
B,V    TEVP

## MAN CALLED BLADE, A *    18
Sergio Martino    ITALY    1977
*John Steiner, Sonja Jeannie, Donald O'Brien, Maurizio Merli, Phillip Leroy, Marine Brochard*
A routine revenge Western about an axe-wielding hero and his various conflicts.

Aka: MANNAJA
WES    91 min (ort 96 min) Cut (7 sec)
B,V    VTC L/A; CBS L/A; XTASY

## MAN CALLED HORSE, A ***    15
Elliot Silverstein    USA    1970
*Richard Harris, Judith Anderson, Jean Gascon, Manu Tupou, Corinna Tsopei, Dub Taylor, William Jordan, James Gammon, Eddie Little Sky, Manuel Padilla, Iron Eyes Cody, Lina Marin*
In 1825 an English aristocrat is captured by the Sioux, but eventually proves his worth as a warrior by undergoing torture, and becoming their leader in the process. An intense and often bloody film, with a fine Leonard Rosenman score. Followed by RETURN OF A MAN CALLED HORSE and TRIUMPHS OF A MAN CALLED HORSE.
Boa: short story by Dorothy M. Johnson.

WES    110 min
B,V    CBS

## MAN CALLED INTREPID, A *
Peter Carter    CANADA/UK/USA    1979
*David Niven, Michael York, Barbara Hershey, Paul Harding, Peter Gilmore, Gayle Hunnicutt, Renee Asherson, Ferdy Mayne, Nigel Stock, Ken James, Robin Gammell, Joseph Golland, Chris Wiggins, Larry Reynolds, Colin Fox*
This purports to be the inside story of British Intelligence in WW2, but is a flat and lifeless piece of fiction, despite the potential inherent in the subject matter. Originally shown as three 96-minute episodes. The script is by William Blinn.
Boa: book by William Stevenson.

WAR    130 min (ort 288 min) mTV
B,V    VFP L/A; HER

## MAN CALLED SARGE, A *    15
Stuart Gillard    1989
*Gary Kroeger, Gretchen German, Marc Singer, Jennifer Runyon, Bobby Di Cicco*
An AIRPLANE!-style comedy that attempts to spoof war movies, and is set in the North African desert where a group of deserters from the Foreign Legion set out to help the Allies win WW2. However, their plans to blow up a German fuel dump are somewhat over-ambitious in the face of their total lack of fighting ability. Very dull.

COM    85 min
V/sh    PATHE

## MAN CALLED SLEDGE, A *    15
Vic Morrow    ITALY    1970
*James Garner, Dennis Weaver, Claude Akins, John Marley, Laura Antonelli, Paola Barbara, Mario Valgoi, Lorenzo Piani, Wade Preston, Laura Betti, Tony Young, Ken Clark, Franco Giornelli*
A gang tries to steal gold stored in a prison but then fight among themselves, in this violent and all-too-predictable Western. Garner plays a villain, an unusual role for this amiable actor.

WES    88 min (ort 96 min)
V    RCA

## MAN FOR ALL SEASONS, A **    U
Fred Zinnemann    UK    1966
*Paul Scofield, Wendy Hiller, Susannah York, Leo McKern, Robert Shaw, Orson Welles, John Hurt, Nigel Davenport, Corin Redgrave, Colin Blakely, Vanessa Redgrave, Cyril Luckham, Jack Gwyllim*
Mechanical version of a play about how Sir Thomas More's opposition to Henry VIII's divorce inevitably led to his execution. Despite its excellent photography and costumes, this stiff piece is weighed down by leaden prose and wooden acting; though this did not prevent it winning several Oscars. Remade for cable in 1988. AA: Pic, Dir, Actor (Scofield), Cin (Ted Moore). Cost (Elizabeth Haffenden/Joan Bridge), Screen (Adapt) (Robert Bolt).

Boa: play by Robert Bolt.
DRA                          116 min (ort 120 min)
V                                          RCA

## MAN FOR ALL SEASONS, A ***              PG
Charlton Heston           USA             1988
*Charlton Heston, Vanessa Redgrave, John Gielgud,*
*Richard Johnson, Roy Kinnear, Martin Chamberlain*
A full-blooded and vigorous adaptation of Bolt's fine
play, telling of the conflict between Thomas More and
Henry VIII, that arose when the latter broke with the
Vatican. Heston plays More, the role he had in the
stage version of the work.
Boa: play by Robert Bolt.
DRA                                   150 min mCab
V                                      TURNER

## MAN FRIDAY *                             PG
Jack Gold                 UK              1975
*Peter O'Toole, Richard Roundtree, Peter Cellier,*
*Christopher Cabot, Joel Fluellen, Sam Seabrook,*
*Stanley Clay*
Preachy film about the evils of colonialism, which
merely uses the story of Robinson Crusoe as a vehicle
and nothing more. Oh yes, Man Friday is shown to be
cleverer than Crusoe in this one. Originally produced
as a TV play in 1972.
Boa: play by Adrian Mitchell.
DRA        104 min; 110 min (CH5) (ort 115 min) mTV
B,V                         PRV; CH5 (VHS only)

## MAN FROM ATLANTIS, THE *
Lee H. Katzin             USA             1977
*Patrick Duffy, Belinda J. Montgomery, Victor Buono,*
*Art Lund, Dean Santoro, Lawrence Pressman, Mark*
*Jenkins, Allen Case, Joshua Bryant, Steve Franken,*
*Virginia Gregg, Curt Lowens, Charles Davis, Lilyan*
*Chauvin, Alex Rodine*
Pilot for a mercifully short-lived TV series, about a
strange man whose ability to breathe underwater plus
other aquatic skills, make him a valuable recruit to
the US Navy, after he is unable to find his way back to
his underwater homeland. Written by Mayo Smith.
Aka: MAN FROM ATLANTIS: THE DEATH
SCOUTS
FAN                                   105 min mTV
B,V                                        VFP

## MAN FROM BUTTON WILLOW, THE *            U
David Detiege             USA             1975
*Voices of: Dale Robertson, Edgar Buchanan, Howard*
*Keel, Herschel Bernardi, Barbara Jean Wong, Ross*
*Martin, Verna Felton, Shep Menken*
Animated feature about a rancher who leads a double
life as a secret agent. He suddenly finds himself the
guardian of a four-year-old girl and also prevents
crooks from stealing land from settlers. Mild kiddie
fare, set in 1869.
CAR          79 min; 77 min (MAST) (ort 81 min)
B,V,V2              INT/CBS; VMA; STABL; MAST

## MAN FROM GLOVER GROVE, THE **
William Hillman           USA             1974
*Ron Masak, Cheryl Miller, Jed Allan, Rose Marie,*
*Paul Winchell, Stu Gilliam*
A small town sheriff has his hands full, coping with a
nutty toy inventor and the crooks who are trying to
steal his inventions.
COM                                      96 min
B,V                                 VPD L/A; MED

## MAN FROM HONG KONG, THE **
Brian Trenchard Smith
          HONG KONG/AUSTRALIA           1975
*George Lazenby, Jimmy Wang Yu, Ros Spiers, Hugh*
*Keays-Byrne, Rebecca Gilling*
A Hong Kong police inspector is asked to go to Sydney

to trap a drugs ring. Plenty of action and stunts for
undemanding viewers.
Aka: DRAGON FLIES, THE
A/AD                         99 min (ort 103 min)
B,V                                        RNK

## MAN FROM SNOWY RIVER, THE ***           PG
George Miller           AUSTRALIA         1982
*Kirk Douglas, Tom Burlinson, Sigrid Thornton, Jack*
*Thompson, Loraine Bayly, Bruce Kerr, Chris*
*Haywood, Terrence Donovan, June Jago, Tony*
*Bonner, John Nash, Gus Mercutio, David Bradshaw,*
*Tommy Dysart*
Based on an epic Australian poem, this tells the story
of a young man who falls in love with the daughter of
his employer, a power-hungry rancher. A splendid
old-fashioned saga, with wonderful scenery and good
performances. Written by John Dixon and Fred
Cullen. Followed by THE UNTAMED in 1988.
Boa: poem by A.B. Paterson.
A/AD                         104 min (ort 115 min)
B,V,V2                                     CBS

## MAN FROM THE HIGH COUNTRY, THE *        PG
                        AUSTRALIA
*John Waters, Terry Serio, Tom Oliver*
A man returns to the mountain ranch that killed his
wife and broke up his family, and finds that ranchers
are trying to steal his land. Poor.
DRA                                      80 min
B,V                                        ARF

## MAN FROM UTAH, THE **                    U
Robert North Bradbury USA                 1934
*John Wayne, Polly Ann Young, George "Gabby"*
*Hayes, Yakima Canutt, Ed Piel Sr, Anita Campillo,*
*Lafe McKee, George Cleveland, Earl Dwire, Artie*
*Ortego*
A cowboy sets out to bring to justice a gang of crooks
who are killing rodeo riders in this fair actioner. The
rather clumsy use of stock rodeo footage is an
annoyance in an otherwise well-made tale.
WES                          52 min (ort 55 min)
V                                          CH5

## MAN IN LOVE, A *                         18
Diane Kurys     FRANCE/ITALY/USA          1987
*Peter Coyote, Jamie Lee Curtis, Greta Scacchi, Peter*
*Riegert, John Barry, Claudia Cardinale, John Barry,*
*Vincent Lindon, Jean Pigozzi, Elia Katz, Constantin*
*Alexandrov, Jean Claude de Goros, Michele Melega,*
*Iole Silvani*
An actor playing an important role embarks on a
torrid romance with a fellow player. Impressive sex
scenes but little else, make for a very slight drama.
Written by Kurys and Israel Horovitz.
Aka: UN HOMME AMOUREUX
DRA                          106 min (ort 110 min)
B,V                                        VIR

## MAN IN THE BROWN SUIT, THE ***          PG
Alan Grint                USA             1988
*Stephanie Zimbalist, Rue McClanahan, Edward*
*Woodward, Tony Randall, Ken Howard, Nickolas*
*Grace, Simon Dutton*
A resourceful young woman witnesses a man's death
in front of an underground train at London's Hyde
Park Corner station, and becomes intrigued by the
circumstances of his death. A few clues lead her to a
sinister organisation headed by someone known as
The Colonel, with whom she engages in a deadly
cat-and-mouse game aboard a luxury liner off the
African coast.
Boa: novel by Agatha Christie.
THR                                      91 min
V                                          WHV

## MAN IN THE IRON MASK, THE ***           PG
Mike Newell               USA             1977

*Richard Chamberlain, Patrick McGoohan, Jenny
Agutter, Ian Holm, Louis Jourdan, Ralph Richardson,
Vivien Merchant, Brenda Bruce, Esmond Knight,
Godfrey Quigley, Emrys James, Denis Lawson, Anne
Zelda, Stacy Davis*
Film version of a classic novel about the strange fate
of a prisoner forced to wear an iron mask so as to hide
his identity. This lively remake of the
1939 film has Chamberlain well cast and ably sup-
ported by a fine cast. The adaptation is by William
Bast.
Boa: novel by Alexandre Dumas.

| DRA | 101 min mTV |
| B,V | PRV |

## MAN IN THE SANTA CLAUS SUIT, THE **    U
Corey Allen          USA                    1978
*Fred Astaire, Gary Burghoff, John Byner, Bert Convy,
Nanette Fabray, Tara Buckman, Brooke Bundy, Eddie
Barth, Ron Feinberg, Harold Gould, Ray Vitte, Debbie
Lytton, Patrick Peterson, Danny Wells, André Gower*
Yuletide fantasy about a costume shop where three
people who rent Santa Claus outfits get a little help
with their lives from no less than eight different
individuals (all played by Astaire). A pleasant little
diversion.
Boa: story by Leonard Gershe.

| FAN | 93 min (ort 100 min) mTV |
| V | CH5 |

## MAN IN THE STEEL MASK, THE **
Jack Gold            UK                      1974
*Elliott Gould, Trevor Howard, Joseph Bova, Ed
Grover, James Noble, John Lehne, Kay Tornborg,
Lyndon Brook, Joy Garrett, Michael Lombard, Ivan
Desny, John Stewart, Alexander Allerson, Bruce Boa,
Dan Sazarino*
An American physicist is so horribly mutilated in a
car accident in East Germany, that he can only be
saved with mechanical aids plus a steel mask that
covers his face, but the American government is
suspicious about allowing him to return home. A
clumsy mixture of drama and SF elements, shown
only on TV in 1976 and never released to the cinema.
Aka: MAN WITHOUT A FACE; WHO?
Boa: novel Who? by Algis Budrys.

| DRA | 87 min (ort 93 min) |
| B,V | MVM; HVH |

## MAN IN THE WHITE SUIT, THE ***    U
Alexander McKendrick  UK                    1951
*Alec Guinness, Joan Greenwood, Cecil Parker,
Michael Gough, Ernest Thesiger, Miles Malleson, Vida
Hope, Howard Marion Crawford, John Rudling,
Patric Doonan, Duncan Lamont, Harold Goodwin,
Colin Gordon, Joan Harben*
A mere laboratory assistant invents a cloth that is
virtually indestructible and so causes a panic in the
textile industry, which sees his invention as a deadly
threat. Unions and management unite in a bid to stop
the march of progress in a witty farce that unfortu-
nately, pulls its punches at the end, neatly restoring
the status quo by having the fabric ultimately prove to
be a little flawed. Written by Macdougall, John
Dighton and McKendrick.
Boa: play by Roger Macdougall.

| COM | 81 min (ort 84 min) B/W |
| B,V | TEVP; WHV |

## MAN IN THE WILDERNESS **    PG
Richard C. Sarafian   USA                    1971
*Richard Harris, John Huston, John Bindon, Ben
Carruthers, Prunella Ransome, Henry Wilcoxon,
James Doohan, Bruce M. Fisher, Percy Herbert, Bryan
Marshall, Norman Rossington, Robert Russell, Dennis
Waterman, Paul Castro*
A trapper abandoned in the wilderness fights to
survive and get his revenge in this harsh and brutal
tale set in the Canadian Northwest of the 1820s.

| WES | 103 min (ort 105 min) |
| B,V | WHV |

## MAN OF FLOWERS *    18
Paul Cox             AUSTRALIA               1984
*Norman Kaye, Alyson Best, Chris Haywood, Sarah
Walker, Julia Blake, Bob Ellis, Barry Dickins*
Pretentious story of a mother-fixated rich man unable
to have a relationship with a woman, who hires a
young girl to strip for him and conceives a suitable
artistic revenge on her brute of a boyfriend. An empty,
depressing and sterile work, predictably raved over by
the critics, telling us more about their taste than it
does about the film.

| DRA | 91 min; 87 min (PAL) |
| B,V | PVG; PAL |

## MAN OF LA MANCHA *    PG
Arthur Miller        USA                      1972
*Peter O'Toole, Sophia Loren, James Coco, Harry
Andrews, John Castle, Brian Blessed*
Ponderous attempt to make a film of the Broadway
musical which has Cervantes telling the story of Don
Quixote to his fellow inmates, after having been cast
into prison by the Inquisition. A flashy but hollow
work.
Boa: play by Dale Wasserman/musical by Mitch Leigh
and Joe Darion.

| MUS | 124 min (ort 132 min) |
| V | WHV |

## MAN OF THE EAST **    PG
E.B. Clucher (Enzo Barboni)
                     ITALY                    1972
*Terence Hill (Mario Girotti), Gregory Walcott, Harry
Carey Jr, Yanti Somer, Dominic Barton*
Western spoof in which an eccentric Englishman is
taught how to be a great gunfighter when he comes to
the USA to take over his dad's ranch. Overlong but
quite good fun.
Aka: E POI LO CHIAMORONI IL MAGNIFICO

| WES | 112 min (ort 122 min) |
| B,V | WHV |

## MAN OF VIOLENCE *
Peter Walker         UK                       1970
*Michael Latimer, Luan Peters, Derek Aylward,
Maurice Kaufmann, Derek Francis, Kenneth Hendel,
George Balbin, Erika Raffael, Virginia Wetherell,
Andreas Malandrinos*
A loan operator investigating some property deals,
finds himself involved in a struggle between rival
gangs for possession of a stolen gold shipment.
Aka: SEX RACKETEERS, THE

| THR | 107 min |
| B,V | EVI L/A; KRP |

## MAN ON A STRING **    PG
Joseph Sargent       USA                      1972
*Christopher George, William Schallert, Joel Grey,
Keith Carradine, Paul Hampton, Kitty Winn, Jack
Warden, Michael Baseleon*
An undercover agent infiltrates the underworld, and
brings about a conflict between two rival Mafia
families, but is almost killed when his identity is
discovered. A pilot for a prospective series based on
"Tightrope", an American series than ran from 1959 to
1960. Average.

| A/AD | 71 min (ort 73 min) mTV |
| V | RCA |

## MAN ON FIRE *    18
Elie Chouraqui   FRANCE/ITALY                 1987
*Brooke Adams, Scott Glenn, Danny Aiello, Joe Pesci,
Paul Shenar, Jonathan Pryce, Jade Malle, Laura
Morante, Giancarlo Prati, Inigo Lezzi, Alessandro
Haber, Franco Trevis, Lou Castel, Lorenzo Piani*
A disillusioned former CIA agent goes on a rampage

when the 12-year-old girl he was hired to protect is kidnapped. A disagreeable mixture of violence and implausibility, wasting a good cast.
A/AD                         89 min (ort 92 min) Cut (31 sec)
B,V                                                              VES

## MAN OUTSIDE, THE **
Samuel Gallu            UK                    1968
*Van Heflin, Heidelinde Weis, Pinkas Braun, Peter Vaughan, Charles Gray, Paul Maxwell, Ronnie Barker, Linda Marlowe, Gary Cockrell, Bill Nagy, Larry Cross, Willoughby Gray, Carole Ann Ford*
A CIA agent fired from his job gets involved in an international plot over a Soviet defector. A standard mediocre espionager.
Boa: novel Double Agent by Gene Stackleborg.
THR                                                       97 min
B,V                                                          INT

## MAN WHO FELL TO EARTH, THE **        PG
Robert J. Roth          USA                   1986
*Lewis Smith, Beverly D'Angelo, James Laurenson, Wil Wheaton, Bruce McGill, Robert Picardo, Annie Potts, Henry Sanders, Bobbi Jo Lathan, Carmen Argenziano, Chris De Rose, Ritch Shydner, Rob Neilson, Steve Natole*
An alien from a dying world lands on Earth, where he tries to find a means of saving his home planet. Although this represents a somewhat unnecessary remake when one considers the 1976 British production starring David Bowie, it does at least attempt a more straightforward version of the original story. The script is by Richard Kletter. Pilot for a prospective series.
Boa: novel by Walter Tevis.
FAN                         93 min (ort 100 min) mTV
B,V                                                          MGM

## MAN WHO FELL TO EARTH, THE ***        18
Nicolas Roeg            UK                    1976
*David Bowie, Rip Torn, Candy Clark, Buck Henry, Bernie Casey, Jackson D. Kane, Tony Mascia, Rick Ricardo, Linda Hutton, Adrienne Larussa, Hillary Holland, Peter Prouse, Richard Breeding, Lilybell Crawford, James Lovell*
Confusing story of an alien who comes to Earth to save his arid planet from dying, but is prevented from leaving when he is in a position to complete his mission. Excellent camerawork and inspired casting of Bowie as the alien fail to rescue an incoherent plot, and Roeg shows his limitations as a director. Written by Paul Mayersburg and remade for TV in 1987.
Boa: novel by Walter Tevis.
FAN                         134 min (ort 138 min)
B,V                                                        TEVP

## MAN WHO HAD POWER OVER WOMEN, THE *  15
John Krish               UK                    1970
*Rod Taylor, Carol White, James Booth, Penelope Horner, Charles Korvin, Clive Francis, Alexandra Stewart, Keith Barron, Marie-France Boyer, Magali Noel, Jimmy Jewel*
Black comedy about a public relations man and the ethical problems he faces after he comes to hate his job. An overblown exercise in breast-beating with few endearing aspects, despite the fine work of the cast. Written by Andrew Meredith.
Boa: novel by Gordon Williams.
COM                                                       89 min
B,V                                                          CBS

## MAN WHO HAUNTED HIMSELF, THE **
Basil Dearden            UK                    1970
*Roger Moore, Hildegard Neil, Hugh MacKenzie, Alastair MacKenzie, Anton Rodgers, Freddie Jones, Olga Georges-Picot, Thorley Walters, John Carson, John Welsh, Gerald Sim, Edward Chapman, Laurence Hardy, Charles Lloyd Pack*
After recovering from a serious road accident, a businessman discovers that he has an evil double who has taken over his life. An intriguing idea is not allowed to develop sufficiently to provide enough material for a full-length tale.
Boa: short story The Case Of Mr Pelham by Anthony Armstrong.
DRA                                              91 min (ort 94 min)
B,V                                                        TEVP

## MAN WHO KNEW TOO MUCH, THE **        PG
Alfred Hitchcock        USA                   1956
*James Stewart, Doris Day, Bernard Miles, Brenda De Banzie, Ralph Truman, Alan Mowbray, Daniel Gelin, Christopher Olsen, Mogens Wieth, Alan Mowbray, Hilary Brooke, Reggie Nalder, Richard Wattis, Noel Willman, Alix Talton*
Hitchcock's remake of his own 1934 film about an American couple who become involved in an international conspiracy to assassinate an important figure. A thoroughly disappointing film that shows none of the lightness of touch the director exhibited in the earlier film. AA: Song ("Whatever Will Be, Will Be" (Que Sera, Sera) – Jay Livingston/Ray Evans).
THR                         115 min (ort 120 min)
V/h                                                          CIC

## MAN WHO LOVED CAT DANCING, THE **    18
Richard C. Sarafian     USA                   1973
*Burt Reynolds, Sarah Miles, Lee J. Cobb, George Hamilton, Jack Warden, Bo Hopkins, Robert Donner, Sandy Kevin, Nancy Malone, Jay Silverheels, Jay Varela, Owen Bush, Larry Littlebird*
An unhappily married woman is taken hostage in the course of a robbery and finally falls for one of the outlaws. Fairly slow-moving but moderately diverting, and somewhat inspired by "No Orchids For Miss Blandish". The script is by Eleanor Perry.
Boa: novel by Marilyn Durham.
WES                                                      118 min
V                                                            MGM

## MAN WHO LOVED WOMEN, THE *          15
Blake Edwards           USA                   1983
*Burt Reynolds, Julie Andrews, Kim Basinger, Marilu Henner, Barry Corbin, Cynthia Sikes, Jennifer Edwards, Tracy Vaccaro*
An American remake of a 1977 Truffaut film, about a bachelor obsessed with women to the point of eventually seeking help from a female psychologist. A ponderous and wordy affair that lacks the verve of the earlier film, despite a winning performance from Reynolds. Written by Milton Wexler, Geoffrey Edwards and Blake Edwards, who gives a good demonstration of his inadequacies as a director.
COM                         106 min (ort 110 min)
V                                                            RCA

## MAN WHO WASN'T THERE, THE *         15
Bruce Malmuth           USA                   1983
*Steve Guttenberg, Lisa Langlois, Art Hindle, Jeffrey Tambor, Morgan Hart, Bill Forsythe, Vincent Baggetta*
Originally made for 3-D, this dull espionage comedy centres around a liquid that when swallowed confers invisibility. Naturally, it becomes the avid object of attention for agents from several countries.
COM                         107 min (ort 111 min)
B,V                                                          CIC

## MAN WHO WOULD BE KING, THE ***       PG
John Huston             USA                   1975
*Sean Connery, Michael Caine, Saeed Jaffrey, Christopher Plummer, Jack May, Doghmi Larbi, Karroom Ben Bouih, Mohammad Shamsi, Albert Moses, Paul Antrim, Graham Acres, Shakira Caine*
Caine and Connery star as two engaging soldiers of fortune who ply their less-than-respectable trade in 19th century India. They contrive and carry out a daring plan to become rulers in the small isolated land

of Kafiristan. A splendid, full-blooded adventure yarn
of the old-fashioned kind; highly entertaining and
well-made, but lacking the genuine Indian locations
that would have added more to the atmosphere.
Boa: short story by Rudyard Kipling.
A/AD                        123 min (ort 129 min)
V                                              RCA

## MAN WITH BOGART'S FACE, THE **
Robert Day              USA              1980
*Olivia Hussey, Robert Sacchi, Franco Nero, Michelle
Phillips, Victor Buono, Herbert Lom, Sybil Danning
(Sybelle Danninger), George Raft, Yvonne De Carlo,
Jay Robinson, Mike Mazurki, Henry Wilcoxon, Victor
Sen Yung*
A detective has cosmetic surgery to resemble his hero
Bogart, and immediately becomes involved in a case
that seems to be a re-run of THE MALTESE FAL-
CON, but where the object of everyone's greed is a set
of gems known as the "Eyes of Alexander". A silly
spoof, but played straight. Adapted by Fenady from
his novel. This was the last film for Raft.
Aka: SAM MARLOWE, PRIVATE EYE
Boa: novel by Andrew J. Fenady.
COM                          95 min (ort 106 min)
B,V                                          CBS

## MAN WITH ONE RED SHOE, THE *          PG
Stan Dragoti            USA              1985
*Tom Hanks, Jim Belushi, Lori Singer, Dabney
Coleman, Carrie Fisher, Charles Durning, Edward
Herrmann, Irving Metzman, Tom Noonan, David L.
Lander, Ritch Brinkley, Gerrit Graham, Frank
Hamilton, Dortha Duckworth, Art La Fleur*
A CIA boss uses a young man as a decoy in a plot to
outwit his rivals within the organisation. Loosely
based on a French film of 1972, and no more entertain-
ing than that over-rated dud.
Aka: MISCHIEF; TALL BLOND MAN WITH ONE
BLACK SHOE, THE
COM            92 min (ort 93 min) Cut (5 sec)
B,V                                          CBS

## MAN WITH THE DEADLY LENS, THE **       15
Richard Brooks          USA              1982
*Sean Connery, George Grizzard, Katherine Ross,
Robert Conrad, Henry Silva, Leslie Nielsen, John
Saxon, G.D. Spradlin, Robert Webber, Dean Stockwell,
Rosalind Cash, Hardy Kruger, Ron Moody, Jennifer
Jason Leigh*
An ace reporter discovers a US government plot to
assassinate an Islamic leader, in this unusual satire
that cracks along at a fair pace but tends to miss most
of its targets. The script is by Brooks.
Aka: WRONG IS RIGHT
Boa: novel The Better Angels by C. McCarry.
A/AD          113 min (ort 117 min) Cut (2 sec)
B,V                                          RCA

## MAN WITH THE GOLDEN ARM, THE ***       15
Otto Preminger          USA              1955
*Frank Sinatra, Kim Novak, Darren McGavin, Eleanor
Parker, Arnold Stang, Doro Merande, Robert Strauss,
John Conte, George E. Stone*
A gambler tries to kick his addiction to drugs and
eventually succeeds in this harrowing drama that's
enlivened by a fine performance from Sinatra and a
memorable jazz score by Elmer Bernstein. The mud-
dled narrative and some bad casting are minor faults.
Boa: novel by Nelson Algren.
DRA                              119 min B/W
B,V                                    INT; CBS

## MAN WITH THE GOLDEN GUN, THE **       PG
Guy Hamilton            UK               1974
*Roger Moore, Christopher Lee, Britt Ekland, Maud
Adams, Marc Lawrence, Bernard Lee, Herve
Villechaize, Clifton James, Lois Maxwell, Desmond
Llewellyn, Richard Loo, Soon-Teck Oh, James*

*Cossins, Chan Yiu Lam*
Another espionage adventure with James Bond get-
ting involved in a plan to liquidate a professional
assassin in the East. Good car stunts and exotic
locations are all this sluggish film has to offer.
Number nine in the series and followed by THE SPY
WHO LOVED ME.
Boa: novel by Ian Fleming.
A/AD                        119 min (ort 125 min)
V                                              WHV

## MAN WITH THE SYNTHETIC BRAIN, THE *
Al Adamson              USA              1972
*John Carradine, Kent Taylor, Tommy Kirk, Regina
Carrol, Roy Morton, Rich Smedley, Arne Warde, Tacey
Robbins, Kirk Duncan, Tanya Maree, John Armond,
Lyle Felice, Barney Gelfen, John Talbert, Joey Benson*
Should have been re-titled The Director With The
Synthetic Brain. The title says it all in this lumbering
tale of a demented doctor whose experiments in
transplanting brains lead to murder, mayhem and one
singularly inept movie.
Aka: BLOOD OF GHASTLY HORROR; FIEND
WITH THE ATOMIC BRAIN, THE; FIEND WITH
THE ELECTRONIC BRAIN, THE; LOVE MANIAC,
THE; PSYCHO A GO-GO!
HOR                          79 min (ort 87 min)
B,V                                          VIV

## MAN WITH TWO BRAINS, THE **           15
Carl Rainer             USA              1983
*Steve Martin, David Warner, Kathleen Turner, Paul
Benedict, James Cromwell, Richard Brestoff, James
Cromwell, George Furth, Randi Brooks, Peter Hobbs,
Earl Boen, Bernie Hern, Frank McCarthy, William
Taylor, Bernard Behrens*
A surgeon falls in love with a woman's brain and
starts looking for a body to put it in. A wild spoof that
unfortunately loses all the jokes and ideas in a
rambling and disorganised script.
COM                          86 min (ort 93 min)
V                                              WHV

## MAN WITH X-RAY EYES, THE **            PG
Roger Corman            USA              1963
*Ray Milland, Diana Van Der Vlis, Harold J. Stone,
John Hoyt, Don Rickles, John Dierkes, Kathryn Hart,
Lorie Summers, Vicki Lee, Carol Irey, Dick Miller,
Barboura Morris*
A surgeon discovers a means of giving himself X-ray
vision and is at first intoxicated by his discovery, but
eventually becomes an outcast and finally succumbs
to madness. A moody and compelling little story that
starts off with promise but eventually gets bogged
down in cheap effects and a muddled script. The
unpleasant climax ends the film abruptly without
resolving anything.
Aka: X: THE MAN WITH X-RAY EYES
HOR                          76 min (ort 79 min)
B,V                                          RNK

## MAN, A WOMAN, A BANK, A **            15
Noel Black              CANADA           1979
*Donald Sutherland, Brooke Adams, Paul Mazursky,
Allen Magicovsky, Leigh Hamilton*
Two men plan to rob a bank but a romantic attach-
ment complicates their plans in this charming and
lighthearted heist film.
Aka: VERY BIG WITHDRAWAL, A
COM              101 min; 97 min (CH5)
B,V,V2,LV               EHE; CH5 (VHS only)

## MAN, PRIDE AND VENGEANCE **           15
Luigi Bazzoni ITALY/WEST GERMANY        1967
*Franco Nero, Klaus Kinski, Tina Aumont*
Routine spaghetti Western, with a young officer
hunted by the law for murder and desertion, seeking
revenge on the lieutenant who made fun of his love for
a gypsy girl.

Aka: L'UMO, L'ORGOGLIO, LA VENDETTA; MIT
DJANGO KOM DER TOD
WES                                         99 min
B,V,V2                        VDM; PHE (VHS only)

## MAN, WOMAN AND CHILD ***          PG
Dick Richards          USA            1982
*Martin Sheen, Blythe Danner, Sebastian Dungan,*
*Craig T. Nelson, David Hemmings, Nathalie Nell,*
*Arlene McIntyre*
A happily married man learns that a brief affair ten
years before produced a son who has just become an
orphan. Scripted by Erich Segal and David Selag and
despite the expected lashings of sentimentality, sur-
prisingly effective.
Boa: novel by Erich Segal.
DRA                      96 min (ort 100 min)
V                                          RCA

## MANAOS **                              18
Alberto Vazques Figueroa
             ITALY/MEXICO/SPAIN          1980
*Agostina Belli, Fabio Testi, Alberto de Mendoza, Jorge*
*Rivero*
Steamy story of love and cruelty on a rubber planta-
tion.
DRA            90 min; 93 min (MPV) Cut (23 sec)
B,V                                  DFS; MPV

## MANDELA ***                            PG
Philip Saville         USA            1987
*Danny Glover, Alfre Woodard, John Matshikiza,*
*Warren Clarke, Allan Corduner, Julian Glover*
An absorbing examination of the life of Nelson and
Winnie Mandela and the former's struggle against the
South African apartheid regime. Despite a tendency
to glamorise the subject and an unwillingness to
examine the more questionable activities of the ANC,
the film certainly has many effective moments. The
script is by Ronald Harwood. Filmed on location in
Zimbabwe.
DRA                              144 min mCab
V                                       CASVIS

## MANDINGO *                             18
Richard Fleischer      USA            1975
*James Mason, Perry King, Susan George, Richard*
*Ward, Ken Norton, Brenda Sykes, Lillian Hayman,*
*Paul Benedict, Ji-Tu Cumbuka, Ben Masters*
Passions run high on a slave-breeding plantation in
the steamy South, with Mason playing a bigoted
plantation owner to perfection, one of the few good
things in this trashy and overblown melodrama.
Followed by the sequel DRUM.
Boa: novel by Kyle Onstott/play by Jack Kirkland.
DRA            120 min (ort 127 min) Cut (47 sec)
V/h                                        CIC

## MANHANDLERS, THE *                     18
Lee Madden             USA            1973
*Cara Burgess, Judy Brown, Rosalind Miles, Vince*
*Cannon, Henry Brandon*
A woman inherits a massage parlour from her uncle,
blissfully unaware that he was murdered by the Mob
who use the business as a front for prostitution. A
low-grade sexploiter.
A                        83 min (ort 87 min)
B,V                        VTC L/A; XTACY/KRP

## MANHATTAN ****                         15
Woody Allen            USA            1979
*Woody Allen, Diane Keaton, Mariel Hemingway,*
*Michael Murphy, Anne Byrne, Meryl Streep*
A wry film about the life and loves of a New York
writer and his friends, built around his love affair/
obsession with New York and everything about it. A
rich, funny, sharp and poignant comedy, and one that
sums up this director's idiosyncratic view of life better
than any of his earlier works. The music of Gershwin
is used to great effect and the wonderful photography
is by Gordon Willis.
COM                    92 min (ort 96 min) B/W
V                                          WHV

## MANHUNT *
Fernando Di Leo
             ITALY/WEST GERMANY          1972
*Sylva Koscina, Woody Strode, Henry Silva, Adolfo*
*Celi, Mario Adorf, Cyril Cusack*
A pimp on the run from the Mafia has to find those
responsible for framing him, after drugs worth mil-
lions of dollars disappear, in this totally forgettable
European gangster thriller.
Aka: DER MAFIA BOSS: SIE TOTEN WIE
SCHAKALE; LA MALA ORDINA; MAN ON THE
RUN (AVI or IOVID)
THR                                       95 min
B,V,V2                    AVI L/A; IOVID; VPD

## MANHUNT: SEARCH FOR THE NIGHT
## STALKER ***                            15
Bruce Seth Green       USA            1989
*Richard Jordan, Lisa Eibacher, Julie Carmen*
Very much a straightforward account of two cops and
their investigation of a serial killer, that follows the
mounting pressures on them both at work and at
home as the murders continue unabated. Despite the
lack of action a strong sense of tension is maintained
throughout.
THR                               89 min mTV
V                                        BRAVE

## MANHUNT, THE **                        15
Larry Ludman (Fabrizio De Angelis)
             ITALY      1984 (released 1986)
*John Ethan Wayne, Rayumnd Harmstorf, Henry*
*Silva, Bo Svenson, Ernest Borgnine*
A young man wrongly branded as a horse thief,
escapes and is chased across the country by a huge
police posse. A routine tale made watchable by the
work of the cast. Filmed in the USA.
DRA                       83 min (ort 89 min)
B,V                                        EIV

## MANHUNTER ***                          18
Michael Mann           USA            1986
*William L. Petersen, Joan Allen, Stephen Lang, Brian*
*Cox, Tom Noonan, Dennis Farina, Kim Griest, David*
*Seaman, Benjamin Hendrickson*
An FBI agent who has received special psychological
training and possesses the ability to read the minds of
killers and understand their thinking, is recalled from
retirement to deal with a very difficult case; a serial
killer who chooses his victims with great care.
Boa: novel Red Dragon by Thomas Hope.
A/AD                                     115 min
V/sh                                       CBS

## MANIAC *
William Lustig         USA            1980
*Joe Spinell, Caroline Munro, Gail Lawrence (Abigail*
*Clayton), Kelly Piper, Rita Montone, Tom Savini, Hyla*
*Marrow*
A deranged murderer kills and scalps his female
victims – and all because he loves his dear old mum
too much. A sickening wallow in gory effects that
makes no attempt to explore the workings of a
diseased mind.
HOR                                       83 min
B,V                                        INT

## MANIAC COP *                           18
William Lustig         USA            1988
*Tom Atkins, Bruce Campbell, Laurene Landon,*
*Richard Roundtree, Sheree North, William Smith,*
*Robert Z'Dar*
A series of brutal murders in New York prove to be
the handiwork of a deranged cop, causing a situation

that culminates in clashes between the police and menmbers of the public. Some clumsy attempts at black humour and flat direction kill this one before it even gets started.

THR 81 min (ort 92 min) Cut (5 sec)
B,V MED

## MANIFESTO *** 18
Dusan Makavejev
USA/YUGOSLAVIA 1988
*Camilla Soeberg, Alfred Molina, Simon Callow, Lindsay Duncan, Eric Stoltz, Rade Serbedzija, Svetozar Svetlovic, Chris Haywood, Patrick Godfrey, Linda Marlowe, Ronald Lacey*
Very loosely inspired by a story by Emile Zola, this 1920s tale is set in a small Balkan community that's alive with murderous intrigues and repression. A cheerfully bold and lively comedy, somewhat hampered by a lack of discipline imposed on the varied strands of the narrative.

COM 93 min (ort 96 min)
B,V CAN

## MANIPULATOR, THE ***
Ken Hughes    UK/WEST GERMANY 1974
*James Coburn, Lee Grant, Harry Andrews, Ian Hendry, Michael Jayston, Keenan Wynn, Christine Kruger, Terence Alexander, Philip Anthony, David Swift, Ray Callaghan, Julian Glover, Kevin Scott, Richard Marner, Ewan Roberts*
An international tycoon controls an industrial espionage organisation which is threatened by the activities of a Washington journalist and attempts to arrange the elimination of several spies that could harm his political ambitions. A flashy and well-paced thriller with no lack of style but a definite lack of warmth.
Aka: INTERNECINE PROJECT, THE
Boa: novel The Internecine Project by Mort W. Elkind.

THR 95 min
B,V HVM L/A; HVH

## MANITOU, THE * 18
William Girdler    USA 1978
*Tony Curtis, Susan Strasberg, Michael Ansara, Ann Sothern, Burgess Meredith, Stella Stevens, Jon Cedar, Paul Muntee, Jeanette Nolan, Lurene Tuttle, Joe Glieb, Ann Mantee, Hugh Corcoran, Tenaya, Jan Heininger, Carole Hemingway*
An Indian medicine man is resurrected in a growth on a girl's neck and bursts upon the world in a welter of gory special effects. A graphic foray in territory explored by "The Exorcist" with a silly plot but rather good special effects.
Boa: novel by Graham Masterton.

HOR 105 min
B,V,V2 EHE

## MANKILLERS * 18
David A. Prior    USA 1987
*Edd Byrnes, Gail Fischer, Edy Williams, Linda Aldon, Marilyn Stafford, Suzanne Tegman*
A tough female squad take on a vicious drugs dealer in a race against time. A fairly mundane tale given a title that promises more excitement than the film can deliver.

A/AD 87 min (ort 90 min) Cut (1 min 45 sec) mVid
B,V AVA

## MANNEQUIN * PG
Michael Gottlieb    USA 1987
*Andrew McCarthy, Kim Cattrall, Estelle Getty, G.W. Bailey, James Spader, Meshach Taylor, Carole Davis*
A window dresser in a large store, falls in love with a mannequin who comes to life, in this forlorn attempt to recapture the sparkling life-affirming Hollywood comedies of yesteryear. See also ONE TOUCH OF VENUS.

COM 87 min (ort 90 min)
V/sh WHV

## MANON DES SOURCES *** PG
Claude Berni    FRANCE 1987
*Yves Montand, Daniel Auteiul, Emmanuelle Beart, Hippolyte Girardot, Andre Dupon, Margarite Lozano, Elisabeth Depardieu, Gabriel Bacquier, Armand Meffre, Pierre Nougaro, Jean Maurel, Roger Souza, Didier Pain*
Second and concluding part of the story that began with JEAN DE FLORETTE, that deals with the revenge inflicted by Jean's daughter on those responsible for his death. An absorbing tale that makes its leisurely way to an unexpected climax.
Aka: MANON OF THE SPRING
Boa: novel by Marcel Pagnol.

DRA 114 min (ort 120 min)
V/h PAL

## MANSFIELD PARK: PARTS 1 AND 2 ** U
David Giles    UK 1986
*Anna Massey, Bernard Hepton, Angela Pleasance*
Television adaptation of a story about a poor girl of good family snubbed by her arrogant rich relatives. Fair.
Boa: novel by Jane Austen.

DRA 260 min (2 cassettes) mTV
V/h BBC

## MANTIS UNDER FALCON CLAWS * 18
Mitch Wong    HONG KONG
*Alan Ko, Sonny Man, Gary Cho, Bob Yuen, Bob Ng, Mike Cheun, George Tai*
A silk merchant has to learn to fight in order to recover his stolen property.
Aka: MANTIS VERSUS FALCON CLAWS

MAR 82 min
B,V VTEL; DIAM

## MANY HAPPY RETURNS ** PG
Steven Hilliard Stern    USA 1987
*George Segal, Ron Leibman, Helen Shaver, Walter Olkewicz, Linda Sorenson, Sean McCann, Paul Brown, Michael Donaghue, Alfie Scoop, Lawrence Dane, Michael Riley, Jason Blicker, Ben Lennick, Sylvia Lennick, James Kidnie*
A tax audit makes life hell for an average middle-class American until he finds a way to hit back. Despite good work from Segal and Leibman this comedy remains no more than adequate.

COM 90 min (ort 100 min) mTV
B,V EIV

## MARATHON ** PG
Jackie Cooper    USA 1980
*Bob Newhart, Herb Edelman, Dick Gautier, Leigh Taylor-Young, Anita Gillette, John Hillerman, Rene Enriquez, Valerie Landsburg, Richard Roat, Don Keefer, Bill Smillie, Kathy Beaudine, Jerry Colker, John Dukakis, Greg Friedkin*
A middle-aged businessman takes up running and is tempted into an adulterous relationship by a young girl runner. Average.

COM 92 min (ort 100 min) mTV
B,V,V2 GHV

## MARATHON MAN *** 18
John Schlesinger    USA 1976
*Dustin Hoffman, Laurence Olivier, Roy Scheider, William Devane, Marthe Keller, Fritz Weaver, Marc Lawrence, Richard Bright, Allen Joseph, Ben Dova, Tito Goya, Lou Gilbert, Jacques Marin, James Wing Woo, Nicole Deslauriers*
A marathon runner gets drawn into an intricate web of intrigue and finds himself the quarry of a Nazi war criminal, who has returned from Uruguay to the USA in order to obtain some diamonds that were being kept for him by his now dead brother. An over-complex film that appears to be about to make some valid observations, when it changes direction and becomes a vicious thriller. It is however, very well done. Written by

Goldman.
Boa: novel by William Goldman.
THR                           119 min (ort 126 min)
B,V                                          CIC

## MARCH OR DIE *                          PG
Dick Richards          USA               1977
Gene Hackman, Terence Hill (Mario Girotti),
Catherine Deneuve, Max Von Sydow, Ian Holm, Rufus,
Jack O'Halloran, Marcel Bozzuffi, Andre Penvern,
Paul Sherman, Vernon Dobtcheff, Marne Maitland,
Gigi Bonos, Walter Gotell
A more recent film written around the French Foreign
Legion with this being the story of how a detail from
the Legion is sent off to protect an archaeological
expedition threatened by the local Arab tribesmen. A
good cast is wasted on this tedious film and can do
little with it. Should be re-titled "Plod Or Die".
DRA            99 min; 102 min (CH5) (ort 107 min)
B,V                                  PRV L/A; CH5

## MARCIANO *
Bernard L. Kowalski    USA               1979
Tony LoBianco, Vincent Gardenia, Richard Head,
Belinda J. Montgomery, Dolph Sweet, Michael Pataki,
Simmy Bow, Vanna Salviati, Melo Alexandria, Susan
Plumb, Booth Colman, Don Dunphy, Peter Marciano,
Natasha Ryan, Paul Picerni
Biopic on the life of the famous heavyweight boxer
with the focus being on his somewhat sordid private
life. A flabby and messy drama.
DRA                             112 min mTV
B,V                               VFP L/A; HER

## MARCO POLO *                            PG
Giuliano Montaldo   ITALY/USA            1984
Ken Marshall, Denholm Elliott, Tony Vogel, John
Gielgud, Burt Lancaster, Anne Bancroft, Tony
LoBianco, Sada Thompson, David Warner, Ying
Ruocheng, James Hong, Junichi Ishida, Ian McShane,
Leonard Nimoy, Kathryn Dowling
Spectacle about the famous explorer who opened up
the trade routes to China. This film took four years to
make and sometimes seems just as long to watch.
Despite its sumptuousness, the pedestrian pacing of
the story and the dubbed dialogue make it an effort of
will to sit through.
DRA            500 min (3 cassettes) dubbed mTV
B,V                                          RCA

## MARDI GRAS MASSACRE *
Jack Weis              USA               1982
Curt Dawson, Gwen Arment, Laura Misch, Bill Metzo,
Cathryn Lacey, Nancy Daneer, Ayne Mack, Butch
Benit, Ronald Tanet
Murders of prostitutes during the festival of Mardi
Gras seem to have a ritual significance. Unlikely to be
available in an uncut form in the UK.
Aka: CRYPT OF DARK SECRETS
DRA                                      92 min
B,V,V2                                       DFS

## MARGARET BOURKE-WHITE: THE TRUE     PG
## STORY **
Lawrence Schiller      USA               1989
Farrah Fawcett, Frederic Forrest, David Huddleston,
Jay Patterson, Ken Marshall, Mitchell Ryan
The story of a woman who realised her ambition to
make a career for herself in photography and was one
of the most highly regarded photographers to work on
Life magazine in the 1930s and 1940s. An average
drama with Fawcett well and truly miscast.
Boa: book by Vicki Goldberg.
DRA                      93 min (ort 105 min) mCab
V                                          FUTUR

## MARGIN FOR MURDER **               15
Daniel Haller          USA               1981
Kevin Dobson, Charles Hallahan, Cindy Pickett,

Donna Dixon, Asher Brauner, Floyd Levine, Aarika
Wells, John Considine, Renata Vanni, Charles
Picerni, Nicholas Hormann, David Downing,
Elizabeth Wickenshaw, Ivan Saric
Pilot for a series which didn't sell, based on a Spillane
character Mike Hammer, who works as a private eye.
In this story he has to track down a friend's killer.
Average.
Aka: MICKEY SPILLANE'S MARGIN FOR
MURDER
THR                      90 min (ort 100 min) mTV
B,V,V2                     GHV; MSD (VHS only)

## MARIAH **                            15
Victor Lobel           USA               1990
John Getz, Wanda De Jesus, Tovah Feldshuh, Philip
Baker Hall, William Allan Young
Tough prison yarn set inside Mariah State Penitentiary, an overcrowded and understaffed prison that's
ruled by a ruthless and old-fashioned warden who is
largely blind to the tensions being generated. The
arrival of a deputy superintendent with some new
ideas sparks off the expected conflict. Meanwhile
others face more personal problems. A kind of soap-
opera behind bars, not all that endearing, but quite
well-handled.
A/AD                                     93 min
V                                            NWV

## MARIA'S LOVERS ***                   15
Andrei Konchalovsky    USA               1984
Nastassia Kinski, John Savage, Robert Mitchum,
Keith Carradine, Anita Morris, Bud Cort, Tracy
Nelson, Vincent Spano
An American GI returns home from a Japanese POW
camp to marry his childhood sweetheart, but is unable
to consummate their marriage because of harrowing
wartime experiences. A detailed and absorbing tale
that would have been far better if the general air of
gloom had been less somewhat less pronounced. The
opening sequence makes rather good use of footage
from a John Huston documentary – "Let There Be
Light".
DRA                      104 min (ort 110 min)
B,V                                          GHV

## MARIE: A TRUE STORY ***             15
Roger Donaldson        USA               1985
Sissy Spacek, Jeff Daniels, Keith Szarabajka, Lisa
Banes, Morgan Freeman, Don Hood, Fred Thompson,
Lisa Barnes, Trey Wilson, John Cullum, Graham
Beckel, Macon McCalman, Colin Wilcox Paxton,
Robert Green Benson III
A single-parent mother gets a job with a state parole
board and then proceeds to buck the entire corrupt
system, finding herself in some difficulties. An absorb-
ing and salutary tale.
Aka: MARIE
Boa: book by Peter Maas.
DRA                      107 min (ort 112 min)
B,V                                   CAN; TEVP

## MARIHUANA: THE DEVIL'S WEED
Dwain Esper            USA               1936
Harley Wood, Hugh McArthur, Pat Carlyle, Paul Ellis,
Dorothy Dehn, Richard Erskine
A 1930s tale that cautions on the dangers of smoking
dope. Wonderfully inept and overblown, and a fine
companion to REEFER MADNESS and ASSASSIN
OF YOUTH.
Aka: MARIHUANA; MARIHUANA: DEVIL'S WEED
WITH ROOTS IN HELL
DRA                      54 min (ort 56 min) B/W
B,V                                      VCL/CBS

## MARILYN, MY LOVE **                  18
Michel Lemoine (Michel Leblanc)
                       SWITZERLAND       1985
Olinka (Olinka Hardimann), Laura Clair, Cathy

*Miller, Andre Kay, Gabriel Pontello, Maria Granada, Elaine, Klaus Bini, Nicky Rocha, Gerard Gregory*
Unsavoury attempt to exploit a Monroe lookalike in a story of the rise of a porno queen, who walks out on her cheating boyfriend and gets involved in steamy antics at a lakeside retreat.
Aka: MARILYN, MON ARMOUR

| | |
|---|---|
| A | 80 min Cut |
| B,V | CASS/IVS; GLOB |

## MARILYN: THE UNTOLD STORY ***
Jack Arnold/John Flynn/Lawrence Schiller
USA                1980
*Catherine Hicks, Viveca Lindfors, Richard Basehart, Frank Converse, John Ireland, Jason Miller, Sheree North, Kevin Geer, Tracey Gold, Priscilla Morrill, John Christy Ewing, Bill Vint, Larry Pennel, Heath Jobes*
Excellent attempt to get at the person behind the legend of Monroe with a script by Dalene Young based on work by Mailer. Well above average and with fine work from Hicks in the title role.
Boa: book Marilyn by Norman Mailer.

| | |
|---|---|
| DRA | 120 min (ort 156 min) mTV |
| B,V | VTC |

## MARINE ISSUE **                18
Christopher Bentley (Denis Amar)
GIBRALTAR            1986
*Michael Pare, Tawny Kitaen, Peter Crook, Charles Napier*
When his sister is brutally murdered by drug smugglers, a young marine soldier feels compelled to resign in order to track down and punish the culprits. Good action sequences partially redeem a hackneyed plot.
Aka: INSTANT JUSTICE

| | |
|---|---|
| A/AD | 97 min (ort 101 min) |
| V/sh | WHV |

## MARK OF THE DEVIL *
Val Guest        UK            1984
*Dirk Benedict, Jenny Seagrove, Burt Kwok, George Sewell, John Paul, Tom Adams*
A man about to marry and in desperate need of money to repay a gambling debt, murders a Chinese (!) voodoo priest in the course of robbing him. He suffers a frightening revenge in the form of a tattoo, which tells of his crime and slowly speads until his body is completely covered. An intriguing idea is hampered by poor acting and plot development.
Osca: SWEET SCENT OF DEATH

| | |
|---|---|
| HOR | 72 min |
| B,V | BWV |

## MARK OF THE DEVIL **
Michael Armstrong
UK/WEST GERMANY        1969
*Herbert Lom, Olivera Vuco, Udo Kier, Reginald Nalder, Herbert Fuchs, Michael Maien, Ingeborg Schoener, Gaby Fuchs, Dorothea Carrera, Adrian Hoven*
Story of a cult of devil worshippers who bring death and destruction to the countryside during the 18th century. Followed by a sequel in 1972. Average.
Aka: AUSTRIA 1700; BRENN HEXE BRENN; HEXEN BIS AUFS BLUT GEQUAELT; MARK OF THE WITCH; SATAN

| | |
|---|---|
| HOR | 84 min; 90 min (INT/CBS) |
| B,V | INT/CBS; SLA; LON |

## MARK OF ZORRO, THE ***
Fred Niblo        USA            1920
*Douglas Fairbanks Sr, Marguerite De La Motte, Noah Beery, Robert McKim, Charles Mailes*
Classic silent movie about a masked avenger who defends the rights of oppressed Mexican peasants, harassing the Spanish tyrants and carving his initials wherever his search for injustice takes him. Though inevitably dated, the film remains highly enjoyable,

not least for some good stunt-work from the star. Remade several times since.
Boa: novel The Curse Of Capistrano by Johnston McCulley.

| | |
|---|---|
| A/AD | 82 min (ort 90 min) B/W silent |
| B,V | SPEC/POLY |

## MARK, I LOVE YOU **
Gunnar Hellstrom    USA        1979
*Kevin Dobson, James Whitmore, Cassie Yates, Dana Elcar, Peggy McCay, Molly Cheek, Lane Smith, Justin Dana, Jay W. MacIntosh, Raleigh Bond, Pat Corley, Michael Currie, Jack Murdock, Lloyd Nelson, Maurice Hill, Susan Niven*
A widower engages in a legal battle with his in-laws over the custody of his small son, in this standard tearjerker. The adaptation is by Sue Grafton.
Boa: book by Hal W. Painter.

| | |
|---|---|
| DRA | 104 min mTV |
| B,V | VFP L/A; HER |

## MARKED FOR MURDER *                15
Rick Sloane        USA            1989
*Wings Hauser, Renee Estevez, James Mitchum, Ken Abraham, Ross Hagen*
A good cast is wasted in this run-of-the-mill mystery tale, which concerns a videotape that implicates the corrupt director of a TV station. He sends two innocent employees to retrieve it, but they don't know that federal agents are after the tape as well. A dreary thriller of little merit, the brief appearance of Martin Sheen in a small cameo is one of its few points of interest.

| | |
|---|---|
| THR | 87 min (ort 93 min) |
| V | NWV |

## MARLOWE: PRIVATE EYE **                15
David Wickes/Sidney Haysers/Peter Hunt/ Bryan Forbes    UK        1984
*Powers Boothe, Kathryn Leigh-Scott, William Kearns*
Five episodes from a TV series that fairly successfully re-created the atmosphere of the original stories. Easygoing and quite good fun, without ever becoming too demanding. Originally shown as a set of six 60 min episodes, followed in 1986 by a further six.
Aka: CHANDLERTOWN; PHILIP MARLOWE: PRIVATE EYE
Boa: stories by Raymond Chandler.

| | |
|---|---|
| THR | 350 min mTV |
| B,V | PAL |

## MAROC 7 *
Gerry O'Hara        UK            1967
*Gene Barry, Elsa Martinelli, Cyd Charisse, Leslie Phillips, Denholm Elliott, Alexandra Stewart, Eric Parker, Angela Douglas, Tracey Reed, Maggie London, Lionel Blair, Paul Danquah*
A lady fashion editor who lives a double life as a jewel thief, finds herself involved in an international espionage plot. An over-complex tale with so many twists to the plot that it all becomes rather tiresome to watch.

| | |
|---|---|
| THR | 90 min |
| B,V | RNK |

## MAROONED **                U
John Sturges        USA            1969
*Gregory Peck, Richard Crenna, David Janssen, James Franciscus, Gene Hackman, Lee Grant, Nancy Kovak, Mariette Hartley, Scott Brady, George Gaynes, Walter Brooke, Mauritz Hugo, Craig Huebling, John Carter, Frank Marth*
A rescue mission is mounted to bring back three astronauts stranded in space when their retro-rockets fail to ignite and they are left with only a 42-hour supply of oxygen. Despite the flashy effects and sets, the film moves along at such a pedestrian pace that no tension is ever developed. Written by Mayo Simon.
AA: Effects (Vis) (Robbie Robertson).

Boa: novel by Martin Caidin.
FAN 124 min (ort 134 min)
V RCA

## MARRIAGE ITALIAN STYLE ** 15
Vittorio De Sica FRANCE/ITALY 1964
*Sophia Loren, Marcello Mastroianni, Aldo Puglisi, Pia Lindstrom, Vito Moriconi, Giovani Ridolfi, Generoso Cortini*
A prostitute has to use all her wits to get a client of long-standing to take the plunge and marry her when he announces his forthcoming marriage to a young girl. A likeable comedy that makes a few sharp points about Italy's cumbersome divorce laws.
Aka: MATRIMONIO ALL'ITALIANA
Boa: play Filomena by Eduardo de Filippo.
COM 96 min (ort 102 min) dubbed
V CH5

## MARRIAGE OF MARIA BRAUN, THE *** 18
Rainer Werner Fassbinder
WEST GERMANY 1978
*Hanna Schygulla, Klaus Lowitsch, Ivan Desny, Gottfried John, Gisela Uhlen, Gunter Lamprecht, Mark Bohm, George Byrd*
A bride in the post-war period builds an industrial empire after her husband is imprisoned for murdering her black GI boyfriend. A heavy mixture of irony and drama, but never less than fully absorbing. The first of three post-WW2 accounts by the director, with "Lola" and then VERONIKA VOSS following.
DRA 116 min (ort 119 min)
B,V VCL/CBS L/A; APX; INTMED

## MARRIED TO THE MOB *** 15
Jonathan Demme USA 1989
*Michelle Pfeiffer, Matthew Modine, Dean Stockwell, Mercedes Ruehl, Alec Baldwin, Joan Cusack, Trey Wilson, Charles Napier, Tracey Walter, Al Lewis*
When a woman's gangster husband is killed she goes on the run, intending to make a new life for herself. However, she is pursued by both an FBI agent, who wants information, and the Mafia boss who had her husband killed, who is besotted with her. A screwball comedy that has several engaging cameos and some witty dialogue, but is a little too chaotic for its own good. The score is by David Byrne.
COM 99 min (ort 103 min)
V VIR

## MARSEILLE CONTRACT, THE ** 15
Robert Parrish FRANCE/UK 1974
*Michael Caine, Anthony Quinn, James Mason, Maurice Ronet, Maureen Kerwin, Catherine Rouvel, Alexandra Stewart, Marcel Bozzufi, Patrick Floersheim, Andre Oumansky, Vernon Dobtcheff, Barbara Sommers, Danik Zurakowska*
A tough US drugs agent based in Paris goes after the head of a drugs ring and puts his own life at risk. Caine gives a good performance as an amiable assassin but the colourless script and slightly less-than-serious direction are handicaps.
Aka: DESTRUCTORS, THE; THAT'S WHAT FRIENDS ARE FOR; WHAT ARE FRIENDS FOR?
THR 87 min (ort 89 min)
B,V WHV

## MARSEILLES CONNECTION, THE ** 18
Enzo G. Castelli ITALY 1983
*Franco Nero, James Whitmore*
Drugs thriller with a dedicated police commissioner using unorthodox means to deal with a syndicate who have abandoned Marseilles and transferred their base of operations to Genoa.
A/AD 97 min
B,V PHV L/A; MIDAS

## MARTIAL HERO, THE * 15
Le Cho Kwan HONG KONG

*Cheung Lung, Kin Fang*
Standard fisticuffs with the title character engaging in the usual round of pugilistic engagements.
MAR 90 min
V NINCOL; MART

## MARTIAL MONKS OF SHAOLIN ** 18
Godfrey Ho HONG KONG 1983
*Dragon Lee, Wong Chen Li, Petty Suh, Jose Wong*
All-action martial arts tale as a villain tries to seize control of a monastery. As ever, the plot is no more than a vehicle for some exciting sequences that display a variety of fighting styles.
Aka: MARTIAL MONKS OF SHAOLIN TEMPLE
MAR 85 min (ort 90 min) Cut (56 sec)
B,V VPD

## MARTIAN CHRONICLES, THE * 
Michael Anderson UK/USA 1980
*Rock Hudson, Gayle Hunnicutt, Darren McGavin, Roddy McDowall, Maria Schell, Bernadette Peters, Fritz Weaver, Bernie Casey, Christopher Connelly, Joyce Van Patten, Nicholas Hammond, Linda Lou Allen, Michael Anderson Jr*
A film version of a group of stories telling of the early colonisation of Mars by settlers from Earth. Rather flat with none of the poetic strength of the original work and seriously hampered by the writer's dated vision of the future (the stories were written about thirty years ago). Originally shown in three 75-minute episodes.
Aka: MARTIAN CHRONICLES PART 1, THE: THE EXPEDITIONS; MARTIAN CHRONICLES PART 2, THE: THE SETTLERS; MARTIAN CHRONICLES PART 3, THE: THE MARTIANS; EXPEDITIONS, THE; SETTLERS, THE; MARTIANS, THE
Boa: book The Silver Locusts by Ray Bradbury (several stories only).
FAN 300 min (3 cassettes) mTV
B,V VFP

## MARTIN *** 
George A. Romero USA 1977
*John Amplas, Lincoln Maazel, Sarah Venable, Christine Forrest, Elayne Nadeau, Tom Savini, Fran Middleton, George A. Romero, Al Levitsky*
A 17-year-old boy thinks he is a vampire and carries out a number of attacks using razor blades in place of the fangs he lacks. Eventually his notoriety comes to the attention of a local radio station and he becomes a celebrity, phoning in to discuss his problem. A chilling little piece of work, bleak and disturbing but undeniably well done.
Boa: story by George A. Romero.
HOR 95 min
B,V HEL

## MARTIN'S DAY ** 15
Alan Gibson CANADA/UK 1985
*Richard Harris, James Coburn, Justin Henry, Lindsay Wagner, Karen Black, John Ireland*
A lifer denied parole escapes from prison taking a small boy hostage, and a strange rapport soon develops between them. Unfortunately this rapport fails to extend to the viewer and the film remains flat and uninteresting.
DRA 95 min (ort 98 min)
B/h, V/h WHV

## MARTY **** U
Delbert Mann USA 1955
*Ernest Borgnine, Betsy Blair, Joe Mantell, Joe De Santis, Esther Minciotti, Jerry Paris, Karen Steele*
A touching, warm and wholesome tale of a lonely Bronx butcher who lives with his mother and dreams rather forlornly of finding love, and rather unexpectedly (for him at least) does. A charming film, as fresh and vibrant as when it was made. AA: Pic, Dir,

Actor (Borgnine), Screen (Chayevsky).
Boa: play by Paddy Chayevsky.
DRA                          86 min (ort 91 min) B/W
V                                             WHV

## MARVELLOUS KUNG FU *                    15
Chin Sheng-En      HONG KONG
*Ling Yun, Wang Kuan-Hsing, Hsia Ling-Ling, Ling Fei, Chang Kuan-Lung*
This rather misleading title hides a very ordinary film about violence, revenge and sudden death, with our hero a brash young man who learns kung fu in order to take on some bullies.
Aka: MARVELLOUS STUNTS OF KUNG FU
MAR                                         92 min
B,V                       ICL L/A; VTEL; GLOB

## MARX BROTHERS: A DAY AT THE RACES ***  U
Sam Wood             USA              1937
*Groucho Marx, Chico Marx, Harpo Marx, Allan Jones, Maureen O'Sullivan, Sig Rumann, Margaret Dumont, Douglass Dumbrille, Esther Muir*
The Marx Brothers team up with a girl who owns both a sanatorium and a racehorse, but they create havoc at the sanatorium when they pay it a visit. Contains several of their funniest sequences, but is let down by a feeble storyline that holds back their zany humour, and some truly forgettable songs. Often cited as the first film to show signs of their decline, but the comic elements (especially the racecourse climax) remain potent.
Aka: DAY AT THE RACES, A
Osca: MARX BROTHERS: GO WEST/MARX BROTHERS: THE BIG STORE
COM            111 min; 273 min (boxed set) B/W
V                                              MGM

## MARX BROTHERS: A NIGHT          U
## AT THE OPERA ****
Sam Wood             USA–              1935
*Groucho Marx, Harpo Marx, Chico Marx, Kitty Carlisle, Allan Jones, Margaret Dumont, Sig Ruman, Walter Woolf King*
One of the greatest of the Marx Brothers' zany comedies with a fast-paced plot that almost defies description. Some nice songs sung by Carlisle and Jones blend well with Marx Brothers lunacy, as Groucho and company become involved in the production of a Sig Ruman opera, but ultimately destroy it. The script is by George S. Kaufman and Morrie Ryskind. From this film onwards, Zeppo no longer appeared.
Aka: NIGHT AT THE OPERA, A
COM                          87 min (ort 96 min) B/W
V                                              MGM

## MARX BROTHERS: ANIMAL CRACKERS ****  U
Victor Heerman        USA             1930
*Groucho, Harpo, Chico and Zeppo Marx, Margaret Dumont, Lilian Roth, Louis Sorin, Hal Thompson, Robert Greig*
Though this, their second film, suffers from a stage-bound approach and is somewhat patchy, the comic exchanges are still extremely funny after all these years. Adapted from a successful Broadway run, the story, such as it is, deals with a stolen painting that turns up at an elegant party.
Aka: ANIMAL CRACKERS
COM                          93 min (ort 98 min) B/W
B,V                                           CIC

## MARX BROTHERS: DUCK SOUP ***      U
Leo McCarey          USA             1933
*Groucho Marx, Harpo Marx, Chico Marx, Zeppo Marx, Margaret Dumont, Louis Calhern, Raquel Torres, Edgar Kennedy, Edmund Breese*
Crazy but very uneven Marx Brothers' comedy set in a fictitious country that declares war on one of its

neighbours. The jokes and comic sequences (especially the mirror one) are quite wonderful; if only the plot had been sharper and the ending less abrupt. But still worth seeing for all that. This was the last film in which Zeppo appeared.
Aka: DUCK SOUP
COM                          70 min (ort 72 min) B/W
B,V                                            CIC

## MARX BROTHERS: GO WEST **           U
Edward Buzzell        USA             1940
*Groucho Marx, Chico Marx, Harpo Marx, John Carroll, Diana Lewis, Walter Woolf King, Robert Barrat*
This humdrum story of three zany characters and their adventures out west has a funny opening sequence at a ticket office and a wonderful finale in which they dismantle a moving train. Unfortunately, what comes between these two highlights is some of their weakest material.
Aka: GO WEST; MARX BROTHERS GO WEST, THE
Osca: MARX BROTHERS: A DAY AT THE RACES/MARX BROTHERS: THE BIG STORE
COM              81 min; 273 min (boxed set)
V                                             MGM

## MARX BROTHERS: LOVE HAPPY ***      U
David Miller          USA             1949
*Groucho Marx, Harpo Marx, Chico Marx, Ilona Massey, Vera-Ellen, Marion Hutton, Raymond Burr, Eric Blore, Marilyn Monroe*
Not the funniest of the Marx Brothers' films but still quite watchable, this story is built around the exploits of a bunch of impoverished actors who come into possession of the Romanov diamonds. It all looks a trifle strained now and the comic gags have given way to doses of mawkishness. Look out for Marilyn Monroe who appears very briefly.
Aka: LOVE HAPPY
COM                          81 min (ort 91 min) B/W
V                                             VCC

## MARX BROTHERS: ROOM SERVICE ****  U
William A. Seiter     USA             1938
*Groucho Marx, Harpo Marx, Chico Marx, Lucille Ball, Ann Miller, Frank Albertson, Donald MacBride*
The Marx Brothers play penniless playwrights who have to find a way to avoid eviction from their hotel room, while waiting for a Broadway backer to turn up. Adapted in the inimitable Marx style from a Broadway farce and written by Morris Ryskind. Later remade as the musical STEP LIVELY.
Aka: ROOM SERVICE
Boa: play by John Murray and Alan Boretz.
COM                          75 min (ort 78 min) B/W
B,V                           CH5 (VHS only)

## MARX BROTHERS: THE BIG STORE ***  U
Charles Riesner       USA             1941
*Groucho Marx, Chico Marx, Harpo Marx, Tony Martin, Virginia Grey, Margaret Dumont, Douglass Dumbrille, Henry Armetta*
Groucho plays an unconventional detective who's hired to investigate the running of a department store. When not creating the usual mayhem with his brothers, he manages to save it from crooks. One of the most conventionally plotted of their comedies, this one has some excellent comic moments separated by dull interludes. Often cited as the weakest comedy they made for MGM, this was their last feature for that studio.
Aka: BIG STORE, THE
Osca: MARX BROTHERS: A DAY AT THE RACES/MARX BROTHERS: GO WEST
COM              80 min; 273 min (boxed set)
V                                             MGM

## MARY AND JOSEPH *
Eric Till             USA             1979

*Blanche Baker, Jeff East, Colleen Dewhurst, Stephen McHattie, Lloyd Bochner, Paul Hecht, Shay Duffin, Marilyn Lightstone, Murray Matheson, Tuvia Tavi, Dina Dovon, Gabi Amrani, Joseph Bee, Jacob Ben Shira, Yossi Yadin*
Story of Christ's parents made on location in the Holy Land, depicting them as a struggling young couple in the early years of their marriage. Despite the biblical setting this is the stuff of soap operas, not epics. Very poor.
Aka: MARY AND JOSEPH: A STORY OF FAITH
DRA                    115 min (ort 147 min) mTV
B,V                                              POLY

## MARY POPPINS ***
Robert Stevenson          USA                      U
                                                 1964
*Julie Andrews, Dick Van Dyke, Glynis Johns, David Tomlinson, Ed Wynn, Hermione Baddeley, Karen Dotrice, Matthew Garber, Arthur Treacher, Reginald Owen*
The story of a magical nanny whose arrival at the home of a staid and stuffy bank employee heralds some magical adventures for his two children. Some good song and dance routines plus lively animated sequences make this a charming film. Andrews' screen debut. AA: Actress (Andrews), Score (Orig) (Richard M. Sherman/Robert B. Sherman), Edit (Cotton Warburton), Song ("Chim Chim Cheree" – Sherman/Sherman), Effects (Vis) (Ellenshaw et al.).
Boa: novel by P.L. Travers.
MUS                                          133 min
V                                              WDV

## MARY! MARY! ***
Bernard Morris            USA                    R18
                                                 1977
*Constance Money, John Leslie, Sharon Thorpe, Jeremy Smith*
Study of a couple whose sex problems are remedied with a little help from the Devil. The man trades his soul for sexual prowess. Despite some rather silly dialogue, this one is made with a good deal of care, especially in the cinematography department. And, oh yes, the Devil does come to collect.
Osca: CHORUS CALL/FEMALE FANTASIES (asa)
A                                             80 min
B,V                                 HVS L/A; HAR

## MASCARA ***
Patrick Conrad         BELGIUM                    18
                                                 1987
*Charlotte Rampling, Derek De Lint, Michael Sarrazin, Romy Haag, Jappe Claes, Herbert Flack, Harry Cleven, Serge-Henri Valcke, Eva Robbins, John Van Dreelen, Norma Christine Deummer, Pascale Jean-Louis Berghe*
A police inspector leads a secret life as a transvestite, and murders a number of transsexuals and the boyfriend of his sister, for whom he harbours an incestuous desire.
DRA                      95 min (ort 99 min)
B,V                                             WHV

## MASH'D *
Emton Smith             USA                      1976
*Annie Spinkles, Andrea True, Mike Jefferson, J.J. Jones, George Arthur*
A porno version of the hit film M*A*S*H with our wartime nurses and doctors making love at every opportunity. Contrived and coarse with not a plot in sight.
A                                             71 min
B,V                              VCO; BUVID; RIP

## MASK ****
Peter Bogdanovich        USA                      15
                                                 1985
*Eric Stoltz, Cher, Sam Elliott, Estelle Getty, Richard Dysart, Harry Carey Jr, Laura Dern, Nicole Mercurie, Harry Carey Jr, Dennis Burhley, Laurence Monoson, Ben Piazza, Alexandra Powers, L. Craig King, Todd Allen, Joe Unger*

Based on a true life account, this is the study of a teenager suffering from a disorder that causes his cranial bones to continue growing, giving him a grotesque masklike appearance and leading to his eventual death. His relationship with his mother and others is sympathetically dealt with in a film that carefully eschews sentimentality. Stolz and Cher give fine performances. AA: Make (Michael Westmore/Zoltan Elek).
DRA                    115 min (ort 120 min)
V/h                                              CIC

## MASK OF MURDER **
Arne Mattson           SWEDEN                     18
                                                 1986
*Christopher Lee, Rod Taylor, Valerie Perrine, Sam Cook*
After the police trap and shoot a nasty masked killer, a series of similar killings occur, and in all cases the culprit wears a similar mask and uses the same techniques. The evidence begins to point to the killer being a deranged police officer.
THR                     83 min Cut (2 min 4 sec)
B,V                                   SHEER; BRAVE

## MASQUE OF THE RED DEATH *
Alan Birkinshaw          USA                      18
                                                 1989
*Herbert Lom, Frank Stallone, Brenda Vaccaro*
This version of Poe's classic has a contemporaray setting in Germany, where a young woman attends a ball at the home of a reclusive industrialist, held in a castle built in the 19th century by Ludwig, the mad king of Bavaria. As the evening progresses, the guests are murdered one at a time by a strange masked figure. A rather dismal film that attempts (and fails) to generate some atmosphere, but is really just one more slasher movie.
Boa: short story by Edgar Allan Poe.
HOR                                           89 min
V                                               CBS

## MASQUE OF THE RED DEATH, THE ***
Roger Corman             USA                      15
                                                 1964
*Vincent Price, Jane Asher, Hazel Court, David Weston, Patrick Magee, Skip Martin, John Westbrook, Nigel Green*
Probably the most successful of Corman's attempts to adapt an Edgar Allan Poe story to the screen, thanks largely to the photography of Nicholas Roeg. While plague devastates an Italian province in the 12th century, its ruler, a sadist and Satanist, holds a masked ball to which Death comes as an uninvited guest. The tale "Hopfrog" is presented by way of a sub-plot.
Boa: short stories The Masque Of The Red Death/Hopfrog by Edgar Allan Poe.
HOR          85 min (ort 89 min) (Cut at film release)
V/sh                                            WHV

## MASQUE OF THE RED DEATH, THE **
Larry Brand              USA                      18
                                                 1989
*Adrian Paul, Patrick Macnee, Tracy Reiner, Claire Hoak, Jeff Osterhage*
Produced by Roger Corman, this is effectively a remake of one of his better works, that adds a smattering of sex and violence to Poe's tale of paranoia and death. The debauched character of Prince Prospero is carefully delineated, and the pleasing sets and costumes help sustain a film whose lack of momentum and limited budget are serious handicaps.
Boa: short story by Edgar Allan Poe.
HOR                      80 min (ort 83 min)
V                                               MGM

## MASQUERADE **
Bob Swaim                USA                      18
                                                 1988
*Rob Lowe, Meg Tilly, Kim Cattrall, Doug Savant, John Glover, Dana Delaney, Erik Holland*
A wealthy woman whose mother has recently died

falls in love with a charming man, unaware that there is a sinister plan to kill her for her money A loose remake of of the Hitchcock classic SUSPICION (1941) that might have been very good indeed without Lowe, who is too bland to be the least bit sinister.

| THR | 88 min (ort 91 min) |
|---|---|
| B,V | MGM |

## MASS APPEAL *** 15
Glenn Jordan          USA          1984
*Jack Lemmon, Zeljko Ivanek, Charles Durning, Louise Latham, Lois De Banzie, James Ray, Talia Balsam, Gloria Stuart*
Two Catholic priests clash over the different ways in which they preach the Gospel to their congregation. An amusing screen version of David's two-character play, expanded somewhat but definitely a winner.
Boa: play by Bill C. David.

| COM | 95 min (ort 100 min) |
|---|---|
| B,V | CIC |

## MASSACRE AT CENTRAL HIGH ** 18
Renee Daalder          USA          1976
*Andrew Stevens, Robert Carradine, Derrel Maury, Kimberly Beck, Steve Bond, Roy Underwood, Steve Sikes, Lani O'Grady, Damon Douglas, Rainbeaux Smith*
Nine students are brutally murdered at a Californian high school when a newcomer decides on a novel way to combat bullying and eliminates an entire gang. A brutal and offbeat tale that gives a new twist to an old formula.
Aka: BLACKBOARD MASSACRE

| HOR | 84 min |
|---|---|
| B,V,V2 | VCL; APX |

## MASSACRE AT FORT HOLMAN ** 15
Tonino Valerii          1974
          FRANCE/ITALY/SPAIN/WEST GERMANY
*James Coburn, Telly Savalas, Bud Spencer (Carlo Pedersoli), Robert Burton, Georges Geret, Ralph Goodwin, Joseph Mitchell*
Story of a suicide mission to capture a Confederate fort in the Civil War, undertaken by seven condemned prisoners. Somewhat reminiscent of THE DIRTY DOZEN but considerably less exciting.
Aka: REASON TO LIVE, A REASON TO DIE, A (IFS or GHV)

| WES | 84 min; 87 min (IFS) (ort 91 min) |
|---|---|
| B,V,V2 | GHV; IFS |

## MASSACRE IN ROME *** 15
George Pan Cosmatos
          FRANCE/ITALY          1973
*Richard Burton, Leo McKern, Peter Vaughan, John Steiner, Anthony Steel, Marcello Mastroianni, Delia Boccardo*
Burton plays a German colonel who must execute 330 Roman hostages as a reprisal for the death of 33 German soldiers. Mastroianni plays the priest who opposes him in a desperate attempt to save them. Based on a true WW2 incident and on the whole effectively handled.
Boa: novel Death In Rome by R. Katz.

| WAR | 97 min (ort 104 min) |
|---|---|
| B,V | IFS; VGM (VHS only) |

## MASSAGE GIRLS IN BANGKOK ** 18
J.A. Morn          HONG KONG          197-
*Varee Pornsavan, Supree Ya Vichit, Mariam Boonkonk*
Two men become involved in murder after visiting a massage parlour in this dreary and exploitative look at Bangkok's red-light district.
Aka: MASSAGE GIRLS (ABC or ELV)
A     68 min (ort 72 min) Cut (18 sec in addition to film cuts)

| B,V | HOK L/A; ABC; ELV; TCX; NET |
|---|---|

## MASSAGE PARLOUR WIFE ** 18
Barry Spinello          USA
*Jen Gillian, Steve Rodgers, Brandy Saunders, Susan Snow*
Routine sex film of little plot.

| A | 84 min |
|---|---|
| B,V | TCX; 18PLAT/TOW |

## MASSIVE RETALIATION * PG
Thomas A. Cohen          USA          1984
*Peter Donat, Karlene Crockett, Jason Gedrick, Michael Pritchard, Tom Bower, Marilyn Hasset, Susan O'Connell, Jason Gedrick, Mimi Farina*
Survivalist epic set on the eve of WW3. A family attempt to reach their fortified ranch when hostilities break out, but the car their children are travelling in separately, breaks down as people evacuate the city. As unconvincing as it is uninteresting.

| THR | 89 min |
|---|---|
| B/s, V/s | VES |

## MASTER NINJA, THE * PG
          USA          1984
*Lee Van Cleef, Claude Akins, Clu Gulager, Sho Kosugi, Timothy Van Patten, David McCallum, Terri Treas, Art Hindle, George Maharis, Tara Buckman*
An ageing and embarrassingly miscast Cleef plays a Ninja warrior in search of a long lost daughter in this feature consisting of two TV episodes – "The Good, The Bad and The Priceless", and "High Rollers". "Return Of The Ninja Master" followed, the pilot for a dreadful TV series, some episodes of which were cobbled up into yet more features.
Aka: NINJA MASTER

| MAR | 90 min Cut mTV |
|---|---|
| B,V | VPD |

## MASTER NINJA 2, THE * PG
          USA          1984
*Lee Van Cleef, Timothy Van Patten, David McCallum, George Lazenby, Sho Kosugi*
A follow-up to the previous film, consisting of two episodes from the US TV series "Ninja Master" made up into a feature. These episodes were "State of the Union" and "Hostages". As ever, our geriatric Master and the faithful Max are stalked by the deadly Ninja Osaka. A waste of both time and film.
Aka: NINJA MASTER 2

| MAR | 90 min Cut mTV |
|---|---|
| B,V | VPD |

## MASTER OF BALLANTRAE, THE *** U
Douglas Hickox          USA          1984
*Richard Thomas, Michael York, John Gielgud, Timothy Dalton, Ian Richardson, Nickolas Grace, Finola Hughes, Brian Blessed, Kim Hicks, Donald Eccles, Pavel Douglas, James Cosmo, Brian Pettifer, Robert James, James Coyle*
A remake of the 1953 film telling of a plot to make Bonnie Prince Charlie King of England in the rebellion of 1745. A lavish and well-made yarn made more enjoyable by good casting.
Boa: novel by Robert Louis Stevenson.

| A/AD | 156 min mTV |
|---|---|
| V | VGM |

## MASTER OF DRAGONARD HILL ** 18
Gerard Kikoine          1987
*Oliver Reed, Eartha Kitt, Herbert Lom, Patrick Warburton, Annabel Schofield*
A West Indian slave plantation in colonial times is the setting for this steamy drama, in which Reed plays the brutal governor and Kitt the local madame. An enjoyable slice of hokum.
Aka: DRAGONARD

| A/AD | 86 min Cut (1 min 19 sec) |
|---|---|
| B,V | CAN |

## MASTER OF THE FLYING GUILLOTINE *
Jimmy Wang Yu    HONG KONG    1975
*Jimmy Wang Yu, Kam Kong, Lung Kun Yee*
Another fast-paced but forgettable kung fu adventure, with our hero making use of the title technique.
Aka: ONE-ARMED BOXER VERSUS THE FLYING GUILLOTINE
MAR                                      80 min
B,V                                         ARI

## MASTER OF THE GAME: PARTS 1 AND 2 ***    15
Kevin Connor/Harvey Hart
USA                            1984
*Dyan Cannon, Leslie Caron, Harry Hamlyn, Ian Charleson, Fernando Allende, Cliff De Young, Liane Langland, Donald Pleasence, Cherie Lunghi, Jean Marsh, Barry Morse, Johnny Sekka, Angharad Rees, Maryam D'Abo, David Suchet*
The colourful saga of a mining family who found a dynasty forms the basis for this tale, which opens with Charleson as a young Scot going to South Africa to seek his fortune. A kind of lively mining soap opera, with Cannon playing the woman who eventually becomes head of the business empire, and portraying her from age 17 to age 90. Filmed on location in Kenya, England, France and New York, and first shown in three parts.
Aka: MASTER OF THE GAME 1: JAMES MCGREGOR; MASTER OF THE GAME 2: KATE BLACKWELL; MASTER OF THE GAME 3: EVE AND ALEXANDRA
Boa: novel by Sidney Sheldon.
DRA          410 min; 419 min (BRAVE) (3 cassettes
                              – ort 540 min) mTV
B,V                       VTC L/A; BRAVE (VHS only)

## MASTER OF THE WORLD **
William Witney    USA    1961
*Vincent Price, Charles Bronson, Mary Webster, Henry Hull, Richard Harrison, David Frankham, Mary Webster, Richard Harrison, Vito Scotti, Ken Terrell, Wally Campo, Steve Masino, Peter Besbas*
A man in possession of a strange flying machine attempts to become the ruler of the world, proclaiming his opposition to war even as he is prepared to use force to achieve his ends. A sort of aerial equivalent to Captain Nemo and the Nautilus from TWENTY-THOUSAND LEAGUES UNDER THE SEA, well-handled and robust, but relying rather too heavily on stock footage and cheap-looking sets.
Boa: novel by Jules Verne.
A/AD                        98 min (ort 104 min)
B,V,V2                                      GHV

## MASTER WITH CRACKED FINGERS, THE *    15
HONG KONG    198-
*Jackie Chan*
Kung fu revenger, with Chan demonstrating his skills as he avenges his father's death.
MAR                                      78 min
V                                           VPD

## MASTERBLASTER **    18
Glen R. Wilder    USA    1986
*Jeff Moldovan, Donna Rosae, Joe Hess, Peter Lundblad, Robert Goodman, Richard St George, George Gill, Earleen Carey, Jim Reynolds, Julian Byrd, Ron Burgs, Tracy Hutchinson, Bill Whorman, Ray Forchion, Lou Ann Carroll*
Participants in a military conflict game find that the rules have been changed and that what started as a game has become a real life-and-death struggle. Average.
A/AD            80 min (ort 90 min) Cut (31 sec)
B,V                                         MED

## MASTERMIND ***
Alex March    USA    1969 (released 1976)
*Zero Mostel, Keiko Kishi, Bradford Dillman, Gawn Grainger, Herbert Berghof, Jules Munshin, Sorrell Brooke*
A spoof on all those "Charlie Chan" films with a crazy plot that has a Japanese police inspector protecting a midget robot. A happy and mindless celebration of slapstick and car chases.
COM                        92 min (ort 131 min)
B,V                                         RNK

## MASTERS OF MENACE *    15
Daniel Raskov    USA    1990
*David Rasche, Catherine Bach, Lance Kinsey, David L. Lander, James Belushi, Dan Aykroyd*
Outrageous and excessive spoof on biker movies, that is built around the efforts made by a gang to give one of their members the funeral he deserves; in Las Vegas no less. To do this, however, they have to violate the terms of their probation, which brings their old adversary the local D.A. after them. A tedious chase yarn whose crude attempts at humour are more embarrassing than amusing.
COM                                      97 min
V                                           VES

## MASTERS OF THE UNIVERSE: THE    PG
MOTION PICTURE **
Gary Goddard    USA    1987
*Dolph Lundgren, Frank Langella, Courtney Cox, Cristina Pickles, Billy Barty, James Tolkan, Meg Foster, Jon Cypher, Chelsea Field, Tony Carroll, Pons Mar, Anthony DeLongis, Robert Towers, Barry Livingston*
A live-action feature based on the incredibly popular but banal children's animated series, in which the heroic He-Man battles the evil Skeletor on the war-devastated planet Eternia, in his bid to defeat the forces of darkness.
Aka: MASTERS OF THE UNIVERSE
FAN                        101 min (ort 106 min)
V/sh                                        WHV

## MATA HARI *    18
Curtis Harrington    UK    1985
*Sylvia Kristel, Oliver Tobias, Christopher Cazenove, Gaye Brown, Gottfried John, William Fox, Michael Anthony, Vernon Dobtcheff, Anthony Newlands, Brian Badcoe, Tutte Lemkow, Taylor Ryan, Tobias Rolt, Victor Langley*
Film version of the life and death of the famous female spy whose activities on behalf of the Germans during WW1 attracted more attention on account of fact that she was exotic, than as any reflection of the use she was to the Germans. A plodding effort in which plotting is abandoned in favour of glimpses of an unclothed Kristel.
DRA                        103 min (ort 108 min)
B,V                       GHV; VCC (VHS only)

## MATANGO: FUNGUS OF TERROR *    15
Inoshiro Honda    JAPAN    1963
*Akiro Kubo, Yoshiro Tsuchiya, Horishi Koizumi, Hiroshi Tachikawa*
Shipwrecked expedition members turn into mushrooms after eating a strange fungus. Low-grade nonsense – watch this and you'll do the same.
Aka: ATTACK OF THE MUSHROOM PEOPLE; MATANGO
HOR                                      73 min
B,V                       JVI L/A; SHEP

## MATCH OF DRAGON AND TIGER **
Yu Kuan Jen    HONG KONG    1973
*Yu Tien Lung, Teng Mei Fang, Lei Ming*
A kung fu fighter avenges his parents' death but hesitates when he falls in love with the daughter of one of the criminals responsible.
MAR                                      87 min
B,V,V2                                    IOVID

**MATEWAN** **** 15
John Sayles        USA        1987
*Chris Cooper, Will Oldham, Mary McDonnell, Bob
Gunton, Ken Jenkins, James Earl Jones, Kevin Tighe,
Gordon Clapp, David Straithairn, Josh Motel, Joe
Grifasi, Maggie Renzi*
A realistic account of the coal-miners' struggles for
trade union rights in the 1920s, and their fight
against the gangster methods employed by the mine-
owners. A splendid period piece without a single
discordant note. The script is by Sayles (who even
wrote some labour songs) and the fine photography is
by Haskell Wexler.
Boa: novel Union Dues by John Sayles.
DRA                126 min (ort 130 min)
B,V                MGM

**MATILDA** * U
Daniel Mann        USA        1978
*Elliott Gould, Robert Mitchum, Harry Guardino, Roy
Clark, Clive Revill, Lionel Stander, Karen Carlson,
Art Metrano, Larry Pennell, Gary Morgan (the
kangaroo)*
A world boxing champion is tricked into a match
against a kangaroo in this fine example of that old
adage about never appearing on-screen with children
or animals (or for that matter, a man in a kangaroo
suit).
Boa: novel by Paul Gallico.
COM                89 min (ort 105 min)
B,V                RNK; MIA (VHS only)

**MATINEE IDOL** *** 18
Henri Pachard      USA        1986
*John Leslie, Jesie St James, Angel, Kay Parker,
Herschel Savage, David Friedman, Colleen Brennan,
Elmer Fox*
Adult film-maker Dave Friedman appears as Bernie
Kuntz, who is out to make a sex film, but has
difficulties arising from the dislike his two leads have
for each other. He decides to replace them both and
conducts a series of interviews. Some peculiar com-
plications then take place, in this fairly amusing and
light-hearted sex romp.
A                  60 min (ort 82 min)
B,V                SCRN

**MATING SEASON, THE** ** 
John Llewellyn Moxey USA       1980
*Lucie Arnaz, Laurence Luckinbill, Swoosie Kurtz,
Diane Stilwell, Joe Brooks, Bob Herman, Anne Haney,
Megan Follows, Marian Hailey, Truman Gaige,
Imogene Bliss, Timothy Farmer, Georgine Hall*
A lady lawyer falls in love with a small businessman
at a bird sanctuary in this music-drenched stab at a
romantic comedy. Average.
COM                100 min mTV
B,V                VIPCO

**MATTER OF TIME, A** * PG
Vincente Minelli   ITALY/USA  1976
*Ingrid Bergman, Liza Minnelli, Charles Boyer, Spiros
Andros, Tina Aumont, Anna Proclemer, Gabriele
Ferzetti, Fernando Rey, Isabella Rossellini*
A crazy countess teaches her chambermaid how to
take a positive view of life and so acquire the
self-confidence vital to success. Set in pre-WW1
Europe, with Rossellini (Bergman's daughter) making
her debut in a film that was the last one for both the
director and Boyer. An inept and flaccid effort.
Boa: novel The Film Of Memory by Maurice Druon.
DRA                99 min (ort 165 min)
B,V                EIV

**MATTIG THE GOOSEBOY** ** PG
Attila Dargay      HUNGARY    1978
Animated version of a traditional family story of a
village boy who vows to get even with a wicked baron.
Aka: LUDAS MATYI; MATT THE GOOSEBOY;

**MATTIE THE GOOSEBOY**
CAR                77 min
B,V                GHV

**MAURICE** *** 15
James Ivory        UK         1987
*James Wilby, Hugh Grant, Rupert Graves, Denholm
Elliot, Simon Callow, Billie Whitelaw, Barry Foster,
Judy Parfitt, Phoebe Nicholls, Ben Kingsley, Patrick
Godfrey, Helena Bonham-Carter*
Story of a boy's growing awareness of his own
sexuality, that's set in pre-WW1 England, where two
young men studying at Cambridge meet and fall in
love, but find their relationship fraught with dangers
and difficulties owing to the repressive attitudes
prevalent at the time. Overlong but quite effective.
Co-scripted by Ivory and Kit Hesketh-Harvey.
Boa: story by E.M. Forster.
DRA                134 min (ort 140 min)
B,V                NELS

**MAUSOLEUM** ** 18
Michael Dugan      USA        1983
*Marjoe Gortner, Bobbie Bresee, Norman Burton, La
Wanda Page, Maurice Sherbanee, Laura Hippe, Sheri
Mann, Julie Christy Murray*
A woman who becomes possessed by evil forces,
commits a series of violent murders, in this kind of
melding of PSYCHO and THE EXORCIST, and her
husband is forced to fight the forces of evil in an
attempt to free her from a terrible curse. Good special
effects and a gory climax are the highlights of this
undistinguished effort.
HOR                92 min (ort 96 min)
B,V,V2 FTV/VSP; GHV L/A; APX (Betamax and VHS
only)

**MAVERICK QUEEN, THE** ** U
Joseph Kane        USA        1955
*Barbara Stanwyck, Barry Sullivan, Scott Brady, Mary
Murphy, Wallace Ford, Jim Davis, Howard Petrie,
Emile Meyer, Walter Sande, George Keymas, John
Doucette, Taylor Holmes, Pierre Watkin*
An undercover Pinkerton detective attempts to break
up a gang of rustlers by becoming friendly with a
woman hotel-keeper who is working with them. A dull
story is enlivened by good acting and direction.
Boa: novel by Zane Grey.
WES                92 min; 86 min (HOLLY)
V                  VMA; HOLLY; STABL; PARK

**MAX** **
Claude Sautet      FRANCE     1970
*Romy Schneider, Bernard Fresson, Michel Picoli*
A police inspector takes the law into his own hands
when some criminals go free.
Aka: MAX ET LES FERRAILLEURS
DRA                112 min
B,V,V2             VCL/CBS

**MAX DUGAN RETURNS** *** PG
Herbert Ross       USA        1983
*Marsha Mason, Jason Robards, Donald Sutherland,
Matthew Broderick, Dody Goodman, Sal Viscuso,
David Morse, Kiefer Sutherland, Panchito Gomez,
Charlie Lau*
Film version of a stage comedy about a long-lost
father trying to make amends for his long absence,
through exaggerated generosity to his single-parent
daughter, who is struggling to raise her teenage son
and hang on to their small house. A film of consider-
able vigour and charm, splendidly acted and marking
the film debut of Broderick.
Boa: play by Neil Simon.
COM                98 min
B,V                CBS

**MAX HEADROOM FILM, THE** *** PG
Annabel Jankel/Rocky Morton

UK                                    1985
*Matt Frewer, Nickolas Grace, Amanda Pays*
A fascinating and highly original look at the near
future, with a story of an investigative journalist's
search for the truth behind "blipverts" i.e. compressed
adverts, used by powerful TV corporations as they
fight ratings battles. Actually a pilot for a pop music
show compered by the title character, a computer-
simulated talking head. Several "Max Headroom"
episodes followed, in an attempt to cash in on the
success of this one.
Aka: MAX HEADROOM: THE ORIGINAL STORY;
MAX HEADROOM STORY, THE
FAN                                60 min mTV
B/h, V/h                    VIR/POLY; VIR/PVG

## MAXIE **                                PG
Paul Aaron            USA               1985
*Glenn Close, Mandy Patinkin, Ruth Gordon, Barnard
Hughes, Michael Ensign, Michael Laskin, Valerie
Curtin, Googy Gess, Harry Hamlin*
A "flapper" from the 1920s is reincarnated in the body
of the private secretary to the Bishop of San Francisco
in this light comedy very much in the vein of ALL OF
ME. Gordon's last film.
Aka: FREE SPIRIT; I'LL MEET YOU IN HEAVEN
Boa: novel Marion's Wall by Jack Finney.
COM                        94 min (ort 98 min)
B,V                                      RNK

## MAXIMUM OVERDRIVE *                      18
Stephen King           USA              1986
*Emilio Estevez, Pat Hingle, Laura Harrington,
Christopher Murvey, John Short, Yeardley Smith,
Ellen McElduff, J.C. Quinn, Holter Graham, Frankie
Faison, Pat Miller, Jack Canon, Barry Bell, John
Brasington, J. Don Ferguson*
King's directorial debut tells of a rogue comet that
passes close to Earth causing mechanical devices to
initially malfunction and then take on a life of their
own. At first the problem is one of only minor
inconveniences but the situation eventually deterio-
rates when trucks come to life and start attacking the
population. A poor affair.
HOR                                    97 min
B,V                                      CBS

## MAXIMUM SECURITY **                      18
Bill Duke             USA               1987
*Robert Desiderio, Jean Smart, Geoffrey Lewis*
A juvenile serving a long sentence at a new maximum
security prison for a minor offence, is recommended
for parole but has it refused. He takes some hostages
in a bid to escape, in this tough prison drama that
tries to avoid the usual cliches and stereotyped
characterisations.
DRA                                   112 min
B,V                                      NWV

## MAYBE BABY **                            15
John G. Avildsen      USA               1988
*Molly Ringwald, Randall Batinkoff, Kenneth Mars,
Miriam Flynn, Conchata Ferrell, Sean Frye, Allison
Roth, Trevor Edmond, Hailey Ellen Agnew, Jaclyn
Bernstein, Michelle Downey, Janet MacLachlan, Steve
Eckholdt, Robin Morse*
Two high school students in love find their world
turned upside down by an unexpected pregnancy and
are forced to make some tough decisions at a tender
age. A well acted and assembled teenage bubblegum
comedy.
Aka: FOR KEEPS
COM                        94 min (ort 98 min)
B,V                                      RCA

## MAYBE BABY ... AGAIN? **                 PG
Tom Moore             USA               1988
*Dabney Coleman, Jane Curtin, Julia Duffy, Florence
Stanley, David Doyle, Peter Michael Goetz*

A happily-married businesswoman of 39, sets her
heart on having a baby before it's too late, but just
about everyone else including her husband try to
dissuade her. A mild little blend of comedy and pathos
that's not quite one thing or the other. Fair.
Aka: MAYBE BABY
Osca: SECOND CHANCE (asa)
COM                       90 min (ort 100 min) mTV
V                                       CASPIC

## MAYBE THIS TIME *                        18
AUSTRALIA                  1981
*Judy Morris, Bill Hunter, Mike Preston*
A woman is torn between two lovers, one of whom is a
married man who keeps on avoiding the question of a
divorce in this fairly uninteresting melodrama.
DRA                                    92 min
B,V                                      PRV

## MAYERLING *
Terence Young         FRANCE/UK          1968
*Omar Sharif, James Mason, Catherine Deneuve, Ava
Gardner, James Robertson Justice, Genevieve Page,
Andreas Parisy, Ivan Desny, Charles Millot, Maurice
Teynac, Fabienne Dali, Moustache*
Remake of the 1936 film about the events that led up
to the suicide pact between the heir to the Hapsburg
empire and his mistress. Overlong, tedious and uncon-
vincing, with Sharif miscast for the umpteenth time.
Boa: novel by Claude Anet.
DRA                        135 min (ort 141 min)
B,V                                      TEVP

## MAYFLOWER MADAM *                        18
Lou Antonio           USA               1987
*Candice Bergen, Chris Sarandon, Chita Rivera,
Caitlin Clarke, Jim Antonio, Sydney Biddle Barrows*
The story of Sidney Biddle Barrows, a young socialite
descended from a Mayflower family founder, who ran
a highly lucrative call-girl operation until the law
caught up with her in 1984. Despite the potential
inherent in her story, this is very much a standard
soap opera treatment, and a poor one at that.
DRA                        93 min (ort 100 min) mTV
B,V                                      FUTUR

## MAYHEM *                                 18
Joseph Merhi          USA               1986
*Raymond Martino, Pamela Dixon, Wendy McDonald,
Robert Grillo, Jean Levine, Sonia Kara*
Two strangers embark on a search for their missing
women in this violent and predictable effort.
A/AD              79 min (ort 90 min) Cut (1 min 4 sec)
B,V                                   IVS; CAST

## McCONNELL STORY, THE **                   U
Gordon Douglas        USA               1955
*Alan Ladd, June Allyson, James Whitmore, Frank
Faylen, Willis Bouchey*
A test pilot finds that his job imposes a strain on his
marriage. Romantic version of a true story done in
suitably melodramatic style.
Aka: TIGER IN THE SKY
DRA                                   107 min
B,V                                      WHV

## McMASTERS, THE **
Alf Kjellin           USA               1969
*Brock Peters, David Carradine, Burl Ives, Nancy
Kwan, Jack Palance, Dane Clark, John Carradine,
L.Q. Jones, R.G. Armstrong*
A rancher in the South sells half his ranch to his black
adopted son at which point a feud breaks out between
various groups. Made and released with two endings;
the good guys win or the bad guys win. A bleak look at
bigotry and greed, overlaid with a strong coating of
violence.
DRA                                    90 min
B,V,V2                                 VCL/CBS

## McQ *
John Sturges            USA            1974
*John Wayne, Eddie Albert, Diana Muldaur, Colleen*
*Dewhurst, Clu Gulager, David Huddleston, Julie*
*Adams, Al Lettieri*
A cop leaves the force and stops at nothing to get the
crooks who killed a couple of his buddies. A number of
good action sequences are about all there is to find in
this embarrassing effort, in which an ageing Wayne
stumbles through a muddled and rambling mess.
A/AD                          107 min (ort 116 min)
B,V                                          WHV

## McVICAR **
Tom Clegg              UK             1980
*Roger Daltrey, Adam Faith, Cheryl Campbell, Bill*
*Murray, Georgina Hale, Steven Berkoff, Brian Hall,*
*Peter Jonfield, Matthew Scurfield, Leonard Gregory,*
*Joe Turner, Jeremy Blake, Anthony Trent, Terence*
*Stuart*
Film based on the true story of a violent criminal, his
escape from Durham Prison, his capture, reform and
eventual rehabilitation. Exploitative and dreary,
though Daltrey is certainly convincing. Scripted by
McVicar from his book.
Boa: book McVicar By Himself by John McVicar.
DRA                    112 min; 107 min (SPEC/POLY)
V                                    SPEC/POLY; CH5

## ME AND THE COLONEL **                          U
Peter Glenville         USA            1958
*Danny Kaye, Curt Jurgens, Nicole Maurey, Francoise*
*Rosay, Akim Tamiroff, Martita Hunt, Alexander*
*Scourby, Liliane Montevecchi, Ludwig Stossel*
In 1940 an anti-Semitic Polish officer flees France in
the company of a Jewish refugee, in this uneven and
rather contrived satire. Despite a promising start, the
film never develops into anything substantial. Filmed
in France.
Boa: play Jacobowsky And The Colonel by Franz
Werfel.
COM                    105 min (ort 110 min) B/W
V                                             RCA

## ME AND THE GIRLS **                           PG
Jack Gold               UK             1985
*Tom Courtenay, Nichola McAuliffe, Robert Glenister*
The story of a homosexual actor who refuses to
compromise his principles and deny his true inclina-
tions. Quite a competent little character study, but
dealing with a subject that has now become rather
mundane. See also MRS CAPPER'S BIRTHDAY,
MISTER AND MRS EDGEHILL and WHAT MAD
PURSUIT?
Boa: story by Noel Coward.
DRA                                        54 min
V                                           PICK

## MEAN BUSINESS *                               15
Bobby Suarez           HONG KONG
*Cynthia Rodrigo, Marrie Lee, Johnny Wilson, Dick*
*Adair*
Routine drugs mayhem in Hong Kong.
Aka: DEVIL'S THREE
DRA                                        90 min
B,V                                          FOX

## MEAN DOG BLUES **                             18
Mel Stuart             USA            1978
*George Kennedy, Gregg Henry, Kay Lenz, Scatman*
*Crothers, Tina Louise, Felton Perry, Gregory Sierra,*
*James Wainwright, William Windom, Gregory Sierra*
Story of a man railroaded onto a prison farm run by a
warden who imposes order with a team of ferocious
dogs. Made with good deal of care but a little short of
surprises. The script is by George Lefferts.
DRA                    108 min; 104 min (VES)
B,V                               VES/PVG; VES

## MEAN JOHNNY BURROWS **                        18
Fred Williamson         USA            1976
*Roddy McDowall, Elliott Gould, Jenny Sherman, Fred*
*Williamson, Luther Adler, Mike Henry, Stuart*
*Whitman, R.G. Armstrong, Anthony Caruso*
A Vietnam hero dishonourably discharged from the
Army is shunned by his town and is unable to find
honest work. Drawn into the Mafia, he meets a woman
who, unknown to him, is a spy for a rival family. A
ponderous and unconvincing drama that marked
Williamson's directing debut.
Aka: HIT MAN, THE; STREET WARRIOR (NET)
DRA      81 min; 76 min Cut (NET: 12 sec) (ort 90 min)
B,V                          INT; GOV; MPV; NET

## MEAN MACHINE, THE **                          15
Robert Aldrich          USA            1974
*Burt Reynolds, Eddie Albert, Ed Lauter, Barbara*
*Bouchet, Arthur Kennedy, Michael Conrad,*
*Bernadette Peters, Jim Hampton, Charles Tyner, Mike*
*Henry, Harry Caesar, Richard Kiel, Robert Tessier,*
*Malcolm Atterbury*
A football star imprisoned for drunken driving, is
blackmailed into forming a team to play a match
against the prison guards. A brutal and disjointed
comedy that fires off lots of gags in every direction
without the benefit a clear narrative drive would have
supplied. Scripted by Tracy Keenan Wynn.
Aka: LONGEST YARD, THE
COM                          116 min (ort 121 min)
B,V                                          CIC

## MEAN SEASON, THE **                           15
Phillip Borsos          USA            1985
*Kurt Russell, Mariel Hemingway, Richard Jordon,*
*Richard Masur, Andu Garcia, Joe Pantoliano,*
*Richard Bradford, Rose Portrillo, William Smith,*
*John Palmer, Lee Sandman, Dan Fitzgerald, Cynthia*
*Caquelin, Fred Ornstein*
A crime reporter finds himself the unwilling confidant
of a crazy killer who supplies him with exclusive
details of each murder he commits, until the reporter's
growing celebrity status causes the murderer to
kidnap the reporter's girlfriend in a fit of jealousy. The
intriguing basic premise that underpins the film is
wasted in the second half. The music is by Lalo
Schifrin.
Boa: novel In The Heat Of The Summer by John
Katzenbach.
THR                          99 min (ort 106 min)
B,V                                          RNK

## MEAN STREETS **
Martin Scorsese         USA            1973
*Robert De Niro, Harvey Keitel, David Proval, Amy*
*Robinson, Richard Romanus, Cesare Danova, George*
*Memmoli, Robert Carradine, David Carradine*
Realistic account of the lives of four young Italian-
American men and their involvement in the world of
the Mafia and small-time criminals. The film provides
a harsh and violent look at their world but ultimately
has nothing to say worth hearing.
DRA                          105 min (ort 110 min)
B,V                                          HOK

## MEAN STREETS OF KUNG FU *                     18
Yang Teo               HONG KONG       1983
*Barry Chan*
A kung fu master comes into conflict with a local
businessman, who has a girl killed in order to frame
him for the murder. Our hero gathers his students
together for a bloody battle.
MAR      78 min (ort 84 min) Cut (5 min 12 sec) dubbed
B,V                              TURBO; XTASY

## MEASURE FOR MEASURE ***                       PG
Desmond Davis           UK             1979
*Tim Pigott-Smith, Kenneth Colley, Kate Nelligan,*
*Christopher Strauli, John McEnery, Jacqueline*

Pearce, Frank Middlemass, Alun Armstrong,
Adrienne Corri, Ellis Jones, John Clegg, William
Sleigh, Neil McCarthy
A competent TV production of the Shakespeare play.
Casting is strong and as ever in this ambitious BBC
series, the text of the play is rendered in full.
Boa: play by William Shakespeare.

| | |
|---|---|
| DRA | 147 min mTV |
| V/h | BBC |

### MEATBALL **
Gerard Damiano          USA            1974
Harry Reems, Singe Low, Linda Sanderson
A crazy doctor sprinkles a new chemical compound on
a hamburger he's cooking in his lab, and it grows so
big it pops out of the pan. When he eats said
hambuger, the same thing happens to him. Rapidly
wearing himself out, he is obliged to come up with a
solution to his problems before he drops dead. He now
reverses his preparation and it turns him gay. Amusing in parts, this silly sex comedy is best enjoyed after
a few beers.

| | |
|---|---|
| A | 90 min |
| V | RIP |

### MEATBALLS *                                    15
Ivan Reitman           CANADA         1979
Bill Murray, Harvey Atkin, Kate Lynch, Russ
Banham, Kristine DeBell, Sarah Torgov, Chris
Makepeace, Jake Blum, Keith Knight, Cindy Girling,
Todd Hoffman, Margot Pinvidic, Matt Craven, Norma
Dell'Agnese, Michael Kirby
A low-brow look at a summer camp and the strange
characters who inhabit it. Followed by two equally
unfunny sequels.

| | |
|---|---|
| COM | 89 min (ort 92 min) |
| V/h | CIC |

### MEATBALLS 2 *                                  15
Ken Wiederhorn         USA            1984
Richard Mulligan, John Mengatti, Hamilton Camp,
Kim Richards, Tammy Taylor, John Laroquette,
Archie Hahn, Misty Rowe, Pee-Wee Herman (Paul
Reubens), Vic Dunlop, Felix Silla, Elayne Boosler
Not really a sequel, more a desperate attempt to wring
some laughs out of a number of disparate elements
such as a juvenile alien with amazing powers, sex-
mad camp counsellors, a manic coach driver etc. As
before the action is set at a summer camp. Pretty
feeble stuff.
Aka: MEATBALLS: PART 2

| | |
|---|---|
| COM | 84 min (ort 90 min) |
| B,V | EIV |

### MEATBALLS 3 *                                  18
George Mendeluk        USA            1987
Sally Kellerman, Patrick Dempsey, Al Waxman,
Isabelle Mejias, Shannon Tweed, Ian Taylor, George
Buza
A dead porno queen has to help a young lad lose his
virginity before she can enter heaven. Thankfully this
ended a series that began badly and never got any
better.
Aka: MEATBALLS 3: SUMMER JOB

| | |
|---|---|
| COM | 90 min (ort 95 min) |
| B,V | IVS |

### MECHANIC, THE ***                             15
Michael Winner         USA            1972
Charles Bronson, Keenan Wynn, Jan-Michael Vincent,
Jill Ireland, Linda Ridgeway, Frank De Kova
A professional hit-man takes on an apprentice but
finds that he has made a serious error of judgement.
Harsh and brutal, but definitely engrossing, with a
neat twist at the end. Scripted by Lewis John Carlino.
Aka: KILLER OF KILLERS

| | |
|---|---|
| DRA | 96 min (ort 100 min) Cut (7 sec) |
| B,V | WHV |

### MEDEA *                                        PG
Pier Paolo Pasolini
            ITALY/WEST GERMANY        1969
Maria Callas, Guiseppe Gentile, Massimo Girotti,
Laurent Terzieff
Following his successful quest, Jason returns to
Corinth with the Golden Fleece and Medea, the High
Priestess who helped him. Having lived together for
several years with their children, he grows tired of her
and she is driven to seek vengeance. Despite the
unusual casting of Callas in the title role, this
sluggish and uninspiring adaptation is hampered by
poor direction and does little with the fiery (and
dubbed) star.
Boa: play by Euripides.

| | |
|---|---|
| DRA | 104 min (ort 118 min) |
| V | CONNO |

### MEDUSA TOUCH, THE *                           15
Jack Gold              FRANCE/UK      1978
Richard Burton, Lino Ventura, Lee Remick, Harry
Andrews, Alan Badel, Jeremy Brett, Derek Jacobi,
Michael Hordern, Gordon Jackson, Michael Byrne,
Robert Lang, Avril Edgar, John Normington, Robert
Flemyng, Philip Stone
A novelist able to use his telekinetic powers to kill and
cause disasters seeks help from a psychiatrist in
controlling his unconscious destructive impulses.
Where tight scripting might have produced a film of
considerable tension, this one opts for general havoc;
the result is a disaster for all concerned.
Boa: novel by Peter Van Greenway.

| | |
|---|---|
| A/AD | 104 min (ort 109 min) |
| B,V | PRV; CH5 (VHS only) |

### MEET ME IN ST LOUIS ****                       U
Vincente Minnelli      USA            1944
Judy Garland, Tom Drake, Mary Astor, Margaret
O'Brien, Leon Ames, Marjorie Main, Lucille Bremer,
June Lockhart, Harry Davenport, John Carroll, Hugh
Marlowe, Robert Sully, Chill Wills
Musical about the life and times of a family in St
Louis during the 1903 World Fair. Judy sings several
numbers that became classics including: "The Boy
Next Door", "Have Yourself A Merry Little Christ-
mas" and "The Trolley Song". An uneven but captivat-
ing tale. Songs are by Ralph Blane and Hugh Martin
and the script is by Irving Brecher and Fred F.
Finkelhoffe. AA: Spec Award (Margaret O'Brien as
outstanding child actress).
Boa: novel by Sally Benson.

| | |
|---|---|
| MUS | 110 min (ort 113 min) |
| B,V | MGM |

### MEETING, THE *                                18
                       USA
Gary Martin, Sonja Robertson
A pop singer rescues a damsel in distress and they
embark on a passionate affair in this dreary softcore
romance.

| | |
|---|---|
| A | 80 min |
| V | PUFF |

### MEGAFORCE *                                    PG
Hal Needham            USA            1982
Barry Bostwick, Persis Khambatta, Henry Silva,
Michael Beck, Edward Mulhare, George Furth,
Michael Kulsar, Ralph Wilcox, Anthony Penya, J.
Victor Lopez, Michael Carven, Bobby Bass, Samir
Kamoun, Ray Hill
Story of an ultra-modern fighting force which is
recruited for a dangerous mission. An over-the-top
fantasy adventure that never really hits its stride.

| | |
|---|---|
| A/AD | 94 min; 95 min (VCC) (ort 99 min) |
| B,V | GHV; VCC (VHS only) |

### MEGAFORCE 7.9 **
Kenjiro Ohmori         JAPAN          1980

*Hiroshi Katsuno, Toshiyuki Nugashima, Yumi Takigawa*
A young scientist predicts that an earthquake will devastate Tokyo but nobody will believe him. Competent effects slightly redeem this effort.
Aka: EARTHQUAKE 7.9; JISHIN RETTO

A/AD                                    90 min
B,V                                     GOV

## MEGAVILLE *                          15
Peter Lehner          USA              1989
*Daniel J. Travanti, Billy Zane, Grace Zabriskie, J.C. Quinn, Kirsten Cloke*
Stylish but failed futuristic thriller hampered by its confusing plot. In the corrupt title city of the future, a law enforcement employee is persuaded to impersonate a vanished racketeer, but is unaware that a monitoring device has been implanted in his skull and is responsible for his paralysing headaches. A disjointed film that never realises more than a fraction of its potential.

FAN                                     90 min
V                                       BRAVE

## MELANIE **                           15
Rex Bromfield        CANADA            1982
*Glynnis O'Connor, Don Johnson, Jamie Dick, Burton Cummings, Trudy Young, Paul Sorvino, Donann Cavin, Jodie Drake, Lisa Dal Bello, Yvonne Murray, Martha Gibson, Rocco Bellusci, David Wills, Jim Martin*
A father abducts his son, and his mother is forced to search for him in the strange world of pop music and its musicians. Good acting partially redeems a worthless script.

DRA                          103 min (ort 109 min)
B,V,V2                       VSP L/A; IPC L/A; CBS

## MELBA **                             PG
Rodney Fisher        AUSTRALIA         1987
*Linda Cropper, Hugo Weaving, Michael Lerner, Peter Carroll, Joan Greenwood, Googie Withers, Maria Aitken, Jean Pierre Aumont, June Bronhill, Margo Lee, John Serge, Daphne Grey, Nell Schofield, Julie Haseler, Judi Farr*
An account of the life of Nellie Melba that follows her from her obscure beginnings to her later triumphs and fame. Very much a run-of-the-mill TV biopic. Originally shown in eight 50-minute episodes.

DRA                          146 min (ort 400 min) mTV
V                                       SCRN

## MELODY *                             PG
Waris Hussein         UK               1971
*Jack Wild, Mark Lester, Tracy Hyde, Sheila Steafel, Kate Williams, Roy Kinnear, Ken Jones, Hilda Barry, James Cossins, June Jago, June Ellis, Tim Wylton, John Gorman*
Two adolescent boys undergo the usual phase of rebellion against adult society – and all to the music of the Bee Gees too. A trite little comedy-drama.
Aka: S.W.A.L.K.

DRA                          103 min (ort 106 min)
V                                       MIA

## MELODY IN LOVE *                     18
George Morton (Hubert Frank)
                     WEST GERMANY       1978
*Britta Glatzeder, Sascha Hehn, Claudine Bird, Melody O'Brien*
A woman visits her female cousin in Mauritius and discovers that she and her husband have various lovers. She subsequently has a number of relationships with various men and women. A first-class yawn-inducer.

A                      92 min (ort 94 min) Cut (11 sec)
B,V                                     VPD

## MEMED MY HAWK *                      15
Peter Ustinov      UK/YUGOSLAVIA       1984
*Peter Ustinov, Herbert Lom, Dennis Quilley, Michael Elphick, Simon Dutton, Leonie Mellinger, Reija Basic, Edward Burnham, Ernest Clark, Rosalie Crutchley, Barry Denen, Walter Gotell, Michael Gough, Marne Maitland*
Drama set in Turkey of the 1920s where a young rebel fights a tyrant who controls the mountain villages. Ustinov's laughable accent is the best thing in this clumsy mixture of comedy and drama.
Boa: book by Yashar Kemal.

DRA                          101 min (ort 110 min)
B,V                          VTC L/A; XTASY

## MEMOIRS OF A SURVIVOR **
David Gladwell        UK               1981
*Julie Christie, Leonie Mellinger, Christopher Guard, Nigel Hawthorne, Debbie Hutchings, Pat Keen, Georgina Griffiths, Christopher Tsangarides, Mark Dignam, Alison Dowling, John Franklyn-Robbins, Rowena Cooper, Adrienne Byrne*
In the near future civilisation is collapsing, and a housewife finds that she is able to escape from the unpleasantness of reality by retreating into a strange dreamworld. A flat and uninspired attempt to deal with a fascinating idea.
Boa: novel by Doris Lessing.

DRA                          111 min (ort 115 min)
B,V                                     TEVP

## MEMORIES OF ME **                    15
Henry Winkler         USA              1988
*Billy Crystal, Alan King, JoBeth Williams, Janet Carroll, David Ackroyd, Phil Fondacaro, Robert Pastorelli, Sidney Miller*
A New York surgeon recovering from a mild heart attack visits Los Angeles to effect a reconciliation with his estranged father whom he finds terminally ill. A messy and contrived affair that is too superficial to be anything more than mediocre.

COM                          99 min (ort 105 min)
V                                       MGM

## MEMORIES WITHIN MISS AGGIE ****
Gerard Damiano        USA              1974
*Deborah Ashira, Kim Pope, Eric Edwards, Harry Reems, Darby Loyd Raines*
A woman who lives on an isolated farmhouse tells a strange man (whose face we do not see until the end) all about her early sexual experiences. But the memories of Miss Aggie are really just her daydreams, in which she sees herself as a sultry temptress rather than a homely spinster. Ultimately, the horrific reason for the man being in her life is revealed. A classic sex film quite unlike any other and without a doubt one of Damiano's best.

A                            58 min (ort 73 min) Cut
B,V                                     WOV

## MEMORY OF US ***
H. Kaye Dyal          USA              1974
*Ellen Geer, Jon Cypher, Barbara Colby, Peter Brown, Robert Hogan, Will Geer, Rose Marie*
A housewife begins to tire of being a wife and mother and looks around for a new identity in this unambitious but diverting account. The script is by Geer.

DRA                          87 min (ort 93 min)
B,V,V2                                  INT

## MEN FROM THE MONASTERY **            18
Chang Cheh        HONG KONG            1973
*Fu Sheng, Chi Kuan-Chun, Lu Ti, Chiang Tao, Tang Yen-Tsan, Li Cheng-Pao, Chen Kuan-Tai*
Four tales from the Shaolin temple putting the martial arts into a mythical and historic context.
Aka: DRAGON'S TEETH, THE

MAR          92 min; 85 min (KMV or WOV) Cut (39 sec)
B,V,V2              KMV L/A; WOV; WHV (VHS only)

## MEN, THE ****
Fred Zinnermann    USA
PG    1950
*Marlon Brando, Teresa Wright, Jack Webb, Everett
Sloane, Howard St John*
An ex-GI tries to readjust to civilian life, in this story
of paraplegics who face more difficulties than other
veterans. A restrained but powerful drama that was
shocking at the time for its honest examination of the
sexual frustrations such people suffered. The script is
by Carl Foreman. This was Brando's film debut.
Aka: BATTLE STRIPE
DRA    85 min B/W
V    VCC

## MENACE OF THE MOUNTAIN **
Vincent McEveety    USA
U    1970
*Patricia Crowley, Albert Salmi, Mitch Vogel, Charles
Aidman*
In the final days of the American Civil War, a young
boy and his father are obliged to battle to save their
mountain-top home, which has been taken over by a
murderous gang of army deserters. A competent but
unmemorable action tale.
Aka: MENACE ON THE MOUNTAIN
A/AD    86 min
B,V    WDV

## MEN'S CLUB, THE *
Peter Medak    USA
18    1986
*Roy Scheider, David Dukes, Richard Jordan, Harvey
Keitel, Frank Langella, Craig Wasson, Treat Williams,
Stockard Channing, Gina Gallegos, Cindy Pickett,
Gwen Welles, Jennifer Jason Leigh, Ann Wedgeworth,
Ann Dusenberry*
Seven men meet and talk mainly about woman and
their relationships with them. Later on five of them
visit a brothel. Despite its curious theme, this was a
major hit in the cinemas.
Boa: novel by Leonard Michaels.
DRA    101 min
B,V    EIV

## MEPHISTO ***
Istran Szabo    HUNGARY
15    1981
*Klaus Maria Brandauer, Krystyna Janda, Rolf Hoppe,
Ildiko Bansagi, Karin Boyd, Christine Harbot, Rolf
Hoppe, Gyorgy Cserhalmi, Martin Hellberg,
Christiane Graskoff, Peter Andorai, Ildiko Kishonti,
Tamas Major*
An actor remains in Germany after 1933 and becomes
the willing tool of the Nazis in order to further his
career. A confusing but powerful examination of how
ideals are betrayed by the desire for fame. The first
film in a trilogy by the director that was followed by
COLONEL REDL and "Hanussen". AA: Foreign.
Boa: novel by Klaus Mann.
DRA    144 min; 138 min (PAL)
B,V    PVG; PAL

## MEPHISTO WALTZ, THE ***
Paul Wendkos    USA
1971
*Alan Alda, Jacqueline Bisset, Barbara Parkins, Curt
Jurgens, William Windom, Bradford Dillman,
Kathleen Widdoes, Pamelyn Ferdin, Khigh Dheigh,
Barry Kroeger, Lylyan Chauvin, Gregory Morton, Curt
Lowens, Alberto Morin*
A young journalist becomes possessed by the soul of a
Satanic concert pianist and is drawn into a web of
occult events. A chilling film with some sequences of
genuine power but hampered by an over-complex
script. Adapted from the novel by Ben Maddow.
Boa: novel by Fred Mustard Stewart.
HOR    105 min (ort 109 min)
B,V    CBS

## MERCHANTS OF WAR *
Peter M. Mackenzie    USA
18    1988
*Asher Brauner, Jessie Vint, Bonnie Beck*
A fast and furious revenge tale, in which a group of

CIA-backed mercenaries embark on a mission in
Angola and are ambushed by terrorists. One is able to
escape and mounts a rescue mission to save his
buddies. There is no lack of action in this tale, but the
simple-mindedness of it all is a major handicap, as is
Brauner's woodenness.
A/AD    90 min
B,V    FUTUR

## MERCY OR MURDER? **
Steven Gethers    USA
PG    1987
*Robert Young, Frances Reid, Eddie Albert, Michael
Learned, Marshall Colt, Shawn Allister*
Like a confusingly similiarly titled film "Murder Or
Mercy", this is also an exploration of the rights and
wrongs of mercy-killing. Here a man is sent to prison
for killing his wife who was suffering from Alzheim-
er's disease. Based on the real-life case of Roswell
Gilbert, who took the life of his wife under similar
tragic circumstances. Unfortunately the film is mere-
ly adequate.
DRA    92 min (ort 97 min) mTV
B,V    MGM

## MERLIN AND THE SWORD *
Clive Donner    UK/USA
PG    1985
*Malcolm MacDowell, Candice Bergen, Edward
Woodward, Dyan Cannon, Lucy Gutteridge, Rupert
Everett, Joseph Blatchley, Liam Nelson, Rosalyn
Landor, Patrick Ryecart, Philip Sayer, Dennis Lill,
John Quarmby*
A 20th century sorceress goes back in time to Camelot
to give Merlin a hand. A bizarre but generally flawed
and disappointing yarn.
Aka: ARTHUR THE KING
JUV    90 min (ort 150 min) mTV
B,V,V2    GHV; VCC (VHS only)

## MERRILL'S MARAUDERS ***
Samuel Fuller    USA
U    1962
*Jeff Chandler, Ty Hardin, Peter Brown, Andrew
Duggan, Will Hutchins, Claude Akins*
War film set in Burma and describing the actions of a
real-life American guerrilla force. A tough and brutal
film of much bloodshed and combat.
WAR    94 min (ort 98 min)
B,V    WHV

## MERRY WIVES OF WINDSOR, THE **
David Jones    UK
U    1983
*Richard Griffiths, Prunella Scales, Alan Bennett, Ben
Kingsley, Elizabeth Spriggs, Bryan Marshall, Judy
Davis, Richard O'Callaghan, Tenniel Evans, Gordon
Gostelow, Nigel Terry, Michael Robbins*
One in a series of BBC adaptations of Shakespeare's
plays, most of which are competent rather than
inspired. This one is no exception.
Boa: play by William Shakespeare.
DRA    169 min mTV
V    BBC

## MESMERIZED *
Michael Laughlin
15
AUSTRALIA/NEW ZEALAND/UK    1984
*Jodie Foster, John Lithgow, Michael Murphy, Harry
Andrews, Dan Shor, Philip Holder, Reg Evans, Beryl
Te Wiata, Jonathan Hardy, Don Selwyn, Derek
Hardwick*
A young orphan girl marries a man many years older
only to find that she's landed up with a violent and
sadistic husband. Revenge begins to dominate her
thoughts and one day she sees her chance to get even.
Far-fetched and unsatisfactory, with a script by
Laughlin (from an earlier Jerzy Skolimowski one).
Aka: MESMERISED
DRA    94 min (ort 97 min)
B,V    CAN

## MESSAGE TO MY DAUGHTER ***
Robert Michael Lewis    USA                1973
*Martin Sheen, Bonnie Bedelia, Kitty Winn, Neva
Patterson, Mark Slade, King Moody, Bob Goldstein,
Lucille Benson, John Crawford, John Lasell, Richard
McMurray, Jan Shutan, Peg Shirley, Della Thomas,
Dick Balduzzi, Jerry Ayres*
A confused teenager derives strength and guidance
from tapes which her dead mother recorded many
years earlier. A run-of-the-mill tearjerker redeemed
by some excellent performances.
DRA                        72 min (ort 78 min) mTV
B,V                                         IFS

## MESSAGE, THE **                         PG
Moustapha Akkad
          LEBANON/LIBYA/SAUDI ARABIA    1976
*Anthony Quinn, Irene Papas, Michael Ansara, Johnny
Sekka, Michael Forrest, Neville Jason, Andre Morell,
Martin Benson*
The story of the career and life of Mohammed, with
the Prophet never appearing in the film so as to avoid
offending Moslem sensibilities. The film was made in
both an English and an Arabic version. Visually
impressive it may be, but this tedious film is made
more so by over-reverential direction, and is fatally
flawed by the decision never to show Mohammed.
Aka: MOHAMMED, MESSENGER OF GOD
DRA                                      182 min
B,V                                         ASV

## MESSENGER OF DEATH **                    18
J. Lee Thompson    USA                     1988
*Charles Bronson, Trish Van Devere, Laurence
Luckinbill, John Ireland, Daniel Benzali, Marilyn
Hassett*
Bronson plays a reporter who has the task of trying to
unravel a murder case that involved two hostile
Mormon sects. A production-line affair.
Boa: novel The Avenging Angel by Rex Burns.
THR                        87 min (ort 91 min)
B,V                                         CAN

## MESSENGER OF DEATH **                    18
Fred Williamson    USA                     1987
*Fred Williamson, Christopher Connelly, Joe Spinelli,
Cameron Mitchell, Val Avery, Jasmine Maimone,
Sandy Cummings*
A man just released from prison seeks revenge for the
murder of his wife, and begins to pick off his targets
from a hit-list of underworld figures. He soon finds
himself in danger from her killers in this tough
B-movie actioner, a fairly typical Williamson product.
Aka: MESSENGER, THE
THR                   93 min (ort 95 min) Cut (26 sec)
B,V                                         VPD

## MESSIAH OF EVIL **
William Huyck    USA                       1972
*Michael Greer, Marianna Hill, Joy Bang, Anitra Ford,
Royal Dano, Elisha Cook Jr*
A group of blood-drinking zombies kidnap people to
slake their thirst, and a woman who visits a small
California town in search of her father comes into
contact with them. A fairly restrained horror yarn,
executed with a little more style than most films on
this theme.
Aka: DEAD PEOPLE; RETURN OF THE LIVING
DEAD; REVENGE OF THE SCREAMING DEAD;
SECOND COMING, THE
HOR                                       90 min
B,V,V2                                      VPD

## MESSING AROUND *                         18
Mickey Nivelli                             1988
*Kentworth Jackson, Michael Walker*
Two youngsters enjoy a lively round of parties and a
promiscuous lifestyle until they begin to realise the
perils. An irritating sermon posing as a film.

COM                                       81 min
V                                       INTMED

## METAL FORCE **                           18
Joseph L. Scanlan    USA                   1987
*Bruce Fairbairn, Robert Vaughn, John Vernon, Isaac
Hayes, Leslie Nielsen, Kerrie Keane*
A standard cops and robbers actioner, with a tough
cop taking on gangsters in Manhattan, whose latest
ploy is to blow up the warehouses of their enemies.
There's almost non-stop shooting in this tale, which
despite the simple nature of the plot, is quite a
well-made effort for its kind.
Aka: CALHOUN; METALFORCE; NIGHTSTICK
A/AD                                      95 min
B,V                                        SONY

## METAL MESSIAH *
Tibor Takacs    CANADA                     1978
*David Jensen, Richard Allen, John Paul Young,
Linda Hogan, Neil Lees, Paul Gilmore, Philip Cairns,
Diane Neill, Charlotte Freelander, James Wilson,
James Reynolds, Gavin Rhodes, Anna Pinchak, Anita
Ludera, Tony Morone*
Dated rock opera about a messiah who saves society
by means of his guitar.
MUS                                       73 min
B,V                                     VCL/CBS

## METALSTORM *                             PG
Charles Band    USA                        1983
*Jeffrey Byron, Kelly Preston, Mike Preston, Tim
Thomerson, Richard Moll, Larry Pennell, D. David
Smith, Mickey Fox, Marty Zagon, Winston Jones, J.
Bill Jones, Mike Jones, Mike Walter, Rick Militi*
A peace-keeping ranger finds two megalomaniacs who
want to take over a desert planet in this dull MAD
MAX rip-off, that adds elements from the genre of
Westerns.
Aka: METALSTORM: THE DESTRUCTION OF
JARED-SYN
FAN                        80 min (ort 84 min)
B,V                                         EIV

## METAMORPHOSIS *                          18
Kenneth J. Hall    USA                     1988
*Bobbie Bresee, Pamela Gilbert, Drew Godderis, John
Terence, Donna Shock (Dawn Wildsmith), Jerry Fox,
John Carradine, Mark Anthony, Leslie Eve, Chris
Kobin, Sue Mashaw, Gary J. Levinson, Michael S.
Deak, Roger McCoin*
A fading movie star is given injections that help
restore her youth, but this experimental treatment
has strange and fateful side effects, as she is trans-
formed occasionally into a repulsive insect-like crea-
ture. Low-grade nonsense.
Aka: ALIVE BY NIGHT; DEADLY STING; EVIL
SPAWN
HOR                                       80 min
B,V                                        MOG

## METEOR *                                 PG
Ronald Neame    USA                        1979
*Sean Connery, Natalie Wood, Karl Malden, Brian
Keith, Henry Fonda, Trevor Howard, Martin Landau,
Joseph Campanella, Richard Dysart, Bo Brundin,
Katherine DeHetre, Trevor Howard, Joseph
Campanella, James Richardson*
Disaster movie in which an enormous meteor
threatens the Earth and all the parties involved in
averting this danger immediately fall out and start
bickering. See A FIRE IN THE SKY for a far better
treatment of this theme.
FAN                        103 min (ort 107 min)
B,V                                         WHV

## METHOD, THE **                           15
Joseph Destein    USA                      1987
*Melanie Dreisbach, Richard Arnold, Deborah*

Swisher, Anthony Cistaro, Taylor Gilbert, Richard
Arnold, Rob Reece, Robert Elvoss, Jean Shelton
A look at a method-acting school and the experiences
of a group of students who will submit to any degree of
self-discipline in their search for verisimilitude.
DRA                                        90 min
B,V                                        AVA

## METROPOLIS ****                         U
Fritz Lang          GERMANY           1926
Brigitte Helm, Alfred Abel, Gustav Frohlich, Rudolf
Klein-Rogge, Fritz Rasp, Theodor Loos, Erwin
Biswanger, Heinrich George, Olaf Storm, Hanns Leo
Reich, Georg John, Margaretta Lanner, Heinrich
Gotho, Max Dietze, Walter Kohle
Classic early SF story of a dehumanised future society
in which the workers toil below ground for the benefit
of an elite who live above. Fascinating if dated
sequences are woven into the sentimental story of the
romance between the son of the city's ruler and a
saintly girl from below ground. (The VES/PVG tape is
the re-edited and tinted version, which has some
restored scenes and a rather badly-chosen modern-
music soundtrack.)
Boa: novel by Thea Von Harbou.
FAN                 86 min (ort 120 min) B/W silent
B, V/sh                              TEVP; VES/PVG

## MEXICAN SPITFIRE AT SEA **
Leslie Goodwins      USA              1941
Donald Woods, Lupe Velez, Leon Errol
One of a series of second feature comedies about a
businessman and his Mexican wife. Here she goes
after an advertising contract for her husband. A mild
comedy of hectic situations and little plot.
Osca: MISTER BLANDINGS BUILDS HIS DREAM
HOUSE
COM                 70 min (ort 73 min) B/W
B,V                                    KVD

## MEXICO IN FLAMES **                     15
Sergei Bondarchuk
                ITALY/MEXICO/USSR     1982
Franco Nero, Ursula Andress, Eraclio Sapedo, Blanka
Gerra
The first part of a two-part film following the career of
US journalist John Reed. This one deals with the
period of the Mexican Revolution.
Aka: CAMPANOS ROJAS; INSURGENT MEXICO;
KRASNYE KOLOKOLA; LIFE OF JOHN REED,
THE; RED BELLS
A/AD                121 min (ort 131 min) Cut (38 sec)
V                                      GHV

## MIAMI SUPERCOPS *                       15
Bruno Corbucci       ITALY             1985
Mario Girotti (Terence Hill), Jackie Castellano, Bud
Spencer (Carlo Pedersoli), C.V. Wood Jr
Our comic duo indulge in the usual brawling and
mayhem that passes for both plot and acting in their
films.
COM                                    93 min
V                                      RCA

## MIAMI VICE ***                          15
Thomas Carter        USA              1984
Don Johnson, Philip Michael Thomas, Michael Talbot,
Saundra Santiago, John Diehl, Gregory Sierra, Bill
Smitrovich, Jimmy Smits, Belinda Montgomery,
Michael Santoro, Martin Ferrero, Jossie DeGuzman,
Harold Bergman
Pilot episode for a popular TV series showing the
sleazy side of Miami. A cop seeks revenge on a drug
dealer who murdered another cop, his brother. Quite a
stylish opener for a series that got progressively more
disagreeable as it developed.
A/AD                90 min (ort 99 min) mTV
V/h                                    CIC

## MIAMI VICE: DOWN FOR THE COUNT **       15
Richard Compton      USA              1987
Don Johnson, Philip Michael Thomas, Saundra
Santiago, Michael Talbot, Pepe Serna, Olivia Brown,
Edward James Olmos, Dan King, Mark Breland
Based on the popular police series, this has detectives
Crockett and Tubbs on the trail of a major narcotics
importer. The crook has a passion for boxing and
gambling, and the two detectives pose as cable TV
promoters looking for a deal, in order to trap him. A
glossy and shallow tale that's redeemed by the
colourful locations and cheerfully mindless action.
A/AD                88 min (ort 93 min) mTV
V/h                                    CIC

## MIAMI VICE: GOLDEN TRIANGLE *           15
Georg Stanford Brown/David Aspaugh
                    USA              1985
Don Johnson, Philip Michael Thomas, Edward James
Olmos, Keye Luke, Joan Chen
Feature spin-off from a popular TV series cop series.
Our two detectives are sent to work under cover in
Thailand in order to crack a drug-smuggling ring, but
there's little in terms of plot or action, and the same
minimalist style of acting, plus musical montages for
the boring bits, very much in the style of a pop video.
A/AD                92 min Cut (5 sec) mTV
B,V                                    CIC

## MIAMI VICE: THE PRODIGAL SON *          15
Paul Michael Glaser  USA              1985
Don Johnson, Philip Michael Thomas, Saundra
Santiago, Edward James Olson, Michael Talbot, Penn
Jilette, John Diehl, Olivia Brown, Pam Grier
Pilot for the second series of TV cop films, with our two
heroes tracking down a drugs ring, and discovering a
link between a trafficker and a New York bank in the
jungles of Latin America.
A/AD                94 min mTV
V/sh                                   CIC

## MICHEL'S MIXED UP MUSICAL BIRD **       U
Michel Legrand       USA              1978
Live action combine with cartoon animation in this
story of a Parisian music student who rescues a baby
bird that has fallen out of its nest. Fair.
JUV                                    44 min
B,V,V2                  VDM L/A; VMA; STABL

## MICKI AND MAUDE ***                     PG
Blake Edwards        USA              1984
Dudley Moore, Anne Reinking, Amy Irving, Richard
Mulligan, George Gaynes, Wallace Shawn, Lu
Leonard, Priscilla Pointer, Andre the Giant, John
Pleshette
A man's career-minded wife refuses to have children
so he finds another woman who will. When she
becomes pregnant, he decides to divorce his wife and
marry her, but before he can do this she triumphantly
announces that she is pregnant too. Bigamy soon
seems to be a small price to pay in order to keep both
women happy. A lighthearted farce that runs out of
ideas and steam after a while, but in the main
remains extremely effective.
COM                 113 min (ort 118 min)
V                                      RCA

## MIDAS RUN, THE **
Alf Kjellin          USA              1969
Fred Astaire, Richard Crenna, Anne Heywood, Ralph
Richardson, Roddy McDowall, Adolfo Celi, Maurice
Denham, Cesar Romero
A British secret agent passed over for an honour plots
to steal a gold shipment as an act of revenge. Unusual
(and inspired) casting of Astaire makes an otherwise
unremarkable and muddled film worth watching.
THR                 102 min (ort 104 min)
B,V                                    BWV; IFS

## MIDNIGHT **
John Russo                  USA                    1981
*Lawrence Tierney, Melanie Verlin, John Amplas,*
*John Hall, Charles Jackson, Doris Hackney*
A young woman leaves home and hitch-hikes to see a
friend but gets caught up with a group of Satanists. A
pretty fair low-budget offering, adapted from the
novel by Russo.
Aka: BACKWOODS MASSACRE
Boa: novel by John Russo.
HOR                                  89 min (ort 94 min)
B,V,V2                                              INT

## MIDNIGHT BLUE *
                            ITALY
*Michael Coby, Monica Camo, Vincenzo Cio*
Tiresome tale of violent passions in a hot climate.
A                                                90 min
B,V,V2                                              VPD

## MIDNIGHT COP **                                      15
Farhad Mann                 USA                    1989
*Rick Springfield, Michael Nader, Laura Johnson*
A young cop is assigned to a bizarre case in which a
series of people have been found drained of blood. He
attempts to use some rather unusual skills to solve the
mystery, while at the same time hiding the fact that
he is himself a vampire. An interesting idea is only
partially explored.
THR                                              87 min
V                                                  NWV

## MIDNIGHT COP ***                                     18
Peter Patzak                USA                    1988
*Armin Mueller-Stahl, Michael York, Morgan*
*Fairchild, Frank Stallone, Julia Kent, Monica*
*Bleibtreu, Allegra Curtis, Harry Friedman*
A West Berlin detective investigating a dancer's
death comes into contact with a drug dealer and a
hooker. Murky and sordid in equal amounts, but after
an uncertain start the film becomes engrossing.
THR                                 93 min (ort 100 min)
V                                                  RCA

## MIDNIGHT COWBOY ****                                 18
John Schlesinger            USA                    1969
*Dustin Hoffman, Jon Voight, Sylvia Miles, John*
*McGiver, Brenda Vaccaro, Barnard Hughes, Bob*
*Balaban, Viva, Taylor Mead, Paul Morrissey, Jennifer*
*Salt, Ruth White*
Sharp and offbeat story of a simple-minded "cowboy"
who arrives in New York determined to make his
fortune as a stud to rich ladies. Hoffman is superb as
the crippled loser he teams up with on the strength of
a promise to find him work in this line. The fine score
is by Harry Nillson. AA: Pic, Dir, Screen (Adapt)
(Waldo Salt).
Boa: novel by James Leo Herlihy.
DRA                                110 min (ort 113 min)
B,V                                                WHV

## MIDNIGHT CROSSING *                                  18
Roger Holzberg              USA                    1988
*Faye Dunaway, Daniel J. Travanti, Kim Cattrall,*
*John Laughlin, Ned Beatty*
A businessman arranges a trip to the Caribbean on
board a luxury yacht as a present for his blind wife.
But, unknown to her, his real reason for the trip is to
recover a hoard of stolen money from a tiny island.
The trip soon turns into a nightmare of deceit,
violence and treachery. A better title for this boring
mess would have been "Mayhem At Midnight".
THR                                 92 min (ort 104 min)
B,V                                                VES

## MIDNIGHT EXPRESS ***                                 18
Alan Parker                 UK/USA                 1978
*Brad Davis, Irene Miracle, Bo Hopkins, Randy Quaid,*
*John Hurt, Mike Kellin, Paul Smith, Paolo Bonacelli,*
*Norbert Weisser, Mike Kellin, Franco Diogene,*
*Michael Ensign, Gigi Ballista, Kevork Malikyan, Peter*
*Jeffrey*
Traces a young American's descent into the hell of a
Turkish prison after being convicted of drug-
smuggling and facing the ghastly prospect of years of
imprisonment. A powerful drama that strays rather
too often from the real-life events on which it was
based. AA: Screen (Adapt) (Oliver Stone), Score (Orig)
(Giorgio Moroder).
Boa: book by Billy Hayes and William Hoffer.
DRA                                116 min (ort 120 min)
B,V                                                RCA

## MIDNIGHT HEAT **                                     18
Richard Mahler              USA                    1983
*Jamie Gillis, Howard Feline, Cheri Champagne,*
*Sharon Mitchell, Susan Nero, Joey Carson, Tish*
*Ambrose, Lucretia Love, Michelle Perelo*
A contract killer hiding out from a gangster recalls his
career, in this blend of sex and gangster genres.
A                                   75 min (ort 78 min)
B,V                                                ELV

## MIDNIGHT MADNESS *                                   PG
David Wechter/Michael Nankin
                            USA                    1980
*David Naughton, Debra Clinger, Eddie Deezen, Brad*
*Wilkin, Maggie Roswell, Stephen Furst, Michael J.*
*Fox*
A bunch of students devise an all-night scavenger
hunt where Los Angeles itself is the game-board and
clues have to be found at various locations. A stupid
and incoherent tale that gave Michael J. Fox his film
debut.
COM                                             110 min
B,V                                                WDV

## MIDNIGHT OFFERINGS *                                 15
Rod Holcomb                 USA                    1981
*Melissa Sue Anderson, Mary Beth McDonough,*
*Patrick Cassidy, Marion Ross, Ray Girardin, Gordon*
*Jump, Cathryn Damon, Peter McLean, Dana Kimmell,*
*Jack Garner, Jeff Mackay, Michael Morgan, Wendy*
*Rastatter, Dino Shorte, Dean Wein*
A young couple encounter and battle a sinister witch
with frightening powers in this inept dud.
HOR                                91 min (ort 100 min) mTV
B,V                                                CIC

## MIDNIGHT RUN ***                                     15
Martin Brest                USA                    1988
*Robert De Niro, Charles Grodin, John Ashton, Dennis*
*Farina, Yaphet Kotto, Joe Pantoliano, Wendy Phillips,*
*Richard Foronjy*
An ex-cop bounty hunter goes after a bail-jumper
wanted by both the FBI (for his testimony) and the
Mafia. A well-focused and witty script is nicely
complemented by good work from the leads. Written
by George Gallo and with a score by Danny Elfman.
COM                                             121 min
V/sh                                               CIC

## MIDNIGHT WARRIOR **                                  18
Joseph Merhi                USA                    1989
*Kevin Bernhardt, Lilly Melgar, Bernie Angel, Michelle*
*Beger*
A popular reporter finds himself getting too involved
in a story he is covering.
A/AD                                             90 min
V                                                 CINE

## MIDNITE SPARES *                                     15
Quentin Masters     AUSTRALIA                      1982
*James Laurie, Max Cullen, Bruce Spence, Gia Carides*
A group of criminals strip cars for their parts and are
involved in a kidnapping. When the man's son returns
home after a long absence, he embarks on a chaotic

rescue mission with the help of a few friends.
COM                                      85 min Cut
B,V                                      MED


## MIDSUMMER NIGHT'S DREAM, A ***          U
Max Reinhardt/William Dieterle
                    USA                  1935
*James Cagney, Olivia De Havilland, Mickey Rooney,*
*Dick Powell, Joe E. Brown, Jean Muir, Ross*
*Alexander, Hugh Herbert, Arthur Treacher, Frank*
*McHugh, Otis Harlan, Dewey Robinson, Victor Jory,*
*Verree Teasdale, Anita Louise*
A star-packed, visually impressive version of this
famous fantasy telling of two lovers who sort out their
problems in a magical wood in Athens with a little
help from the fairies. Imaginative casting gave Cag-
ney the role of Bottom, a part he makes the most of,
whereas Rooney as Puck becomes somewhat tiresome.
The music of Mendelssohn is used to good effect. This
was the film debut of De Havilland. AA: Cin (Hal
Mohr), Edit (Ralph Dawson).
Boa: play by William Shakespeare.
MUS                     112 min (ort 133 min) B/W
V                                        WHV


## MIDSUMMER NIGHT'S DREAM, A **           U
Elijah Moshinsky        UK               1981
*Helen Mirren, Peter McEnery, Nigel Davenport, Estelle*
*Kohler, Hugh Quarshie, Geoffrey Lumsden, Pippa*
*Guard, Nicky Henson, Robert Lindsay, Cherith Mellor,*
*Geoffrey Palmer, Brian Glover, John Fowler*
Another BBC television adaptation, generally well
cast and agreeable despite the constraints of the
studio setting.
Boa: play by William Shakespeare.
COM                                      113 min mTV
V/h                                      BBC


## MIDSUMMER NIGHT'S SEX COMEDY, A **    15
Woody Allen             USA              1982
*Woody Allen, Mia Farrow, Jose Ferrer, Mary*
*Steenburgen, Tony Roberts, Julie Hagerty, Mary*
*Steenburgen, Tony Farentino*
Allen's version of Bergman's 1955 film "Smiles Of A
Summer Night" about the sexual relations among
three couples spending a summer weekend on a
country estate around 1900. Mildly diverting but
rather slack, though the photography of Gordon Willis
is an asset.
COM                                      84 min (ort 88 min)
V                                        WHV


## MIGHTY JACK *                           PG
Kazuho Mitsoti          JAPAN
*Hideaki Nitani, Naoko Kobo, Hiroshi Ninanzi*
Another standard low-budget space-epic from Japan.
FAN                                      95 min
V                                        XTASY


## MIGHTY JOE YOUNG ***
Ernest B. Schoedsack    USA              1949
*Terry Moore, Ben Johnson, Robert Armstrong, Frank*
*McHugh, Douglas Fowley, Regis Toomey, Dennis*
*Green, Paul Guilfoyle, Nestor Paiva, Dale Van Sickel,*
*Primo Carnera, Wee Willie Davis, Henry Kulky,*
*Sammy Stein, Karl David*
An updated version of KING KONG with the giant
ape being captured to form the main attraction at a
night club, running amok when taunted, but later
redeeming himself when he saves some kids from a
fire. A tongue-in-cheek effort that is surprisingly well
crafted. The splendid effects are by Willis O'Brien and
Ray Harryhausen. AA: Effects (Cooper/R.K.O. Radio).
Osca: LITTLE ORVIE
DRA                     90 min (ort 94 min) B/W
B,V                                      KVD


## MIGHTY JUNGLE, THE **
David Dalie/Ismael Rodriguez/Arnold Belgard
                    MEXICO/USA           1964
*Marshall Thompson, Dave Dalie*
A jungle adventure with primitive tribes, human
sacrifice etc. Quite enjoyable in its way but hardly
memorable.
A/AD                                     88 min
B,V                                      MMA


## MIGHTLY MOUSE: THE GREAT
## SPACE CHASE **                          U
E. Friedman/L. Kachivas/M. Lamore/G. Wetzler/
K. Wright/L. Zukor      USA              1983
*Voices of: Allen Oppenheimer, Diane Pershy*
An animated feature assembled from no less than
sixteen episodes, that tells of the title character and
his battle to save Queen Pearl Parakeet from the
wicked Harry the Heartless. Repetitive and overlong,
but quite good fun for four-year-olds.
Aka: MIGHTY MOUSE IN THE GREAT SPACE
CHASE
CAR                                      83 min
B,V                                      VGM


## MIGHTY QUINN, THE **                     15
Carl Schenker           USA              1989
*Denzel Washington, Robert Townsend, James Fox,*
*Mimi Rogers, M. Emmet Walsh, Sheryl Lee Ralph, Art*
*Evans, Esther Rolle, Norman Beaton, Keye Luke*
A police chief on an island in the Caribbean is
determined to solve a murder mystery but comes into
conflict with a childhood friend, who has now become a
crook. A routine tale placed in an exotic setting. The
lively reggae soundtrack features some hits by UB40.
Boa: novel Finding Maubee by A.H.Z. Carr.
A/AD                                     95 min (ort 98 min)
V                                        MGM


## MIKE'S MURDER *                          18
James Bridges           USA     1982 (released 1984)
*Debra Winger, Mark Keyloun, Darrell Larson, Paul*
*Winfield, Brooke Alderson, William Ostrander, Dan*
*Shor, Robert Crosson, Gregory Hormel, John Michael*
*Stewart, Victor Perez, Mark High, Ken Y. Nmaba,*
*Ruth Winger, April Ferry*
A woman bank-teller's sometime boyfriend is killed in
a drugs deal and she decides to go looking for clues to
his murder, aided by the man's addict friend who is
next on the hit-list. After less than ecstatic reviews,
the film was withdrawn for extensive re-cutting and
received very limited release in 1984. An interminable film that fails in all departments.
DRA                                      97 min (ort 105 min)
B,V                                      WHV


## MIKEY AND NICKY *                        15
Elaine May              USA              1976
*Peter Falk, John Cassavetes, Ned Beatty, Sandford*
*Meisner, Rose Arrick, Joyce Van Patten, William*
*Hickey, M. Emmet Walsh, Carol Grace*
Story of two small-time hoods who were childhood
friends. One of them is wanted by the Mob and the
other may be setting him up to be hit by them. An
opaque and over-sentimental mess that is made
barely watchable by excellent performances from the
leads.
DRA                                      101 min (ort 119 min)
B,V                                      POLY


## MILAGRO BEANFIELD WAR, THE ***          15
Robert Redford          USA              1987
*Sonia Braga, Chick Vennera, Ruben Blades,*
*Christopher Walken, Daniel Stern, John Heard,*
*Melanie Griffith, Carlos Riquelme, Freddy Fender,*
*Tony Genaro, Jerry Hardin, Ronald G. Joseph, Mario*
*Arrambide, Alberto Morin, Julie Carmen*
A poor bean farmer in New Mexico illegally diverts
water in a desperate attempt to save his parched
fields. His action rouses and unites his poor, downtrod-

den community, but at the same time sets it on a collision course with local big business interests. A vivid and entertaining tale, scripted by Nichols and David Ward. AA: Score (Orig) (Dave Grusin).
Boa: novel by John Nichols.
COM                                    113 min (ort 117 min)
B,V                                                      CIC

## MILES FROM HOME ***                              15
Gary Sinise              USA                        1988
Richard Gere, Kevin Anderson, Penelope Ann Miller,
Laurie Metcalf, John Malkovich, Brian Dennehy,
Judith Ivey, Helen Hunt, Terry Kinney, Francis
Guinan, Randy Arney
An Iowa farm goes from success in the 1950s to bankruptcy in the 1980s, so Gere burns it down rather see have a bank take it over. He then takes off with his brother on a crime spree, the pair becoming folk heroes in the process. A kind of distant cousin to BONNIE AND CLYDE but a good deal more perceptive, despite miscasting of Gere.
A/AD                                     104 min (ort 114 min)
V/sh                                                   BRAVE

## MILES TO GO **                                    15
David Greene              USA                        1986
Jill Clayburgh, Tom Skeritt, Mimi Kuzyk, Rosemary
Dunsmore, Cyndy Preston, Andrew Bednarski, Peter
Dvorsky, Caroline Arnold, Sheena Larkin, Catherine
Golvey, Lorena Gale, Linda Smith, Danette Mackay,
Donna Faron, Ian Finlay
A close-knit loving family have to come to terms with the fact that their mother is dying of cancer. A real weepie in the manner of LOVE STORY that is sustained by a dignified performance from Clayburgh.
Aka: LEAVING HOME
Boa: story by Beverly Levitt.
DRA                                      94 min (ort 100 min) mTV
B,V                                                       ODY

## MILLENNIUM *                                      PG
Michael Anderson          USA                        1989
Kris Kristofferson, Cheryl Ladd, Robert Joy, Daniel J.
Travanti, Brent Carver, Maury Chaykin, David
McIlwraith, Al Waxman, Lloyd Bochner
A mysterious woman from another time takes people off aircraft just as they are about to crash, her intention being to repopulate a disease-ridden world of the future. Kristofferson is the suspicious crash investigator who becomes involved with time-travelling Ladd, who is their agent from the future. The fascinating opening premise is not done justice by the script, which decays into cliched tedium. The script is by Varley.
Boa: short story Air Raid by John Varley.
FAN                                      102 min (ort 108 min)
V/sh                                                     WHV

## MILLION DOLLAR COLLAR, THE **                    PG
Vincent McEveety          USA                        1963
Guy Stockwell, Craig Hill, Eric Potilmann
A dog gets separated from its owner and is used by criminals to smuggle diamonds, but as is usual with Disney, everything is resolved happily.
COM                                               61 min
B,V                                                      WDV

## MILLION DOLLAR DIXIE DELIVERANCE,                PG
THE **
Russ Mayberry             USA                        1978
Brock Peters, Christian Courtland, Chip Courtland,
Alicia Fleer, Joe Dorsey, Christian Berrigan, Kyle
Richards, Kip Niven
A wounded Union soldier helps rescue five schoolchildren kidnapped by the Confederate forces and held for ransom in this enjoyable family film. This was the first Disney feature made specifically for network TV.
JUV                                      91 min (ort 100 min) mTV
B,V                                                      WDV

## MILLION DOLLAR DUCK **                            U
Vincent McEveety          USA                        1971
Dean Jones, Sandy Dennis, Joe Flynn, Tony Roberts
After accidental exposure to radiation a duck starts to lay golden eggs. Both gangsters and government are interested in getting hold of the bird. A mild Disney comedy inspired by "Mister Drake's Duck".
Aka: $1,000,000 DUCK
COM                                               92 min
B,V                                                      WDV

## MILLION DOLLAR MADNESS **                         15
Yankul Goldwasser         ISRAEL                      1985
Seffi Rivlin
A neurotic and overworked bank manager swaps places with a forger he meets in a taxi, and the next thing he knows, he has been taken off to a sanatorium where he discovers a bunch of forgers at work making banknotes. However, he decides to stay and have a rest, in this simple-minded but good-natured effort.
COM                                               85 min
B,V                                      CAN L/A; RNK

## MILLION POUND NOTE, THE **                        U
Ronald Neame              UK                          1954
Gregory Peck, Jane Griffith, Joyce Grenfell, Ronald
Squire, A.E. Matthews, Wilfrid Hyde-White, Maurice
Denham, Reginald Beckwith, Brian Oulton, John
Slater, Hartley Power, George Devine, Bryan Forbes,
Ann Gudrun, Ronald Adam
A man is given a million pound note and will be given any job that can be found for him if he can return it unspent after a month. Though this amiable comedy is hard to fault in terms of production values, it wears out its one joke very quickly.
Aka: MAN WITH A MILLION
Boa: short story by Mark Twain.
COM                                 91 min; 85 min (VCC)
B,V                                           RNK; VCC

## MIND KILLER ***                                   18
Michael Krueger           USA                        1987
Joe McDonald, Christopher Wade, Shirley Ross, Kevin
Hart, Tom Henry, Diana Calhoun, George Flynn,
Crystal Niedel, Edd Nichols, Dawn Jacobs, Sharlene
Wanger, Rebecca Toma, Kelly Holsopple, Lisa Prawel,
Sard H. Lies
A socially inept librarian is very susceptible to self-help manuals. While reading one he discovers that by expanding his mind he can control his environment and the actions of others. However, he loses control and his overtaxed brain turns into a monster which bursts from his skull. Despite the ludicrous nature of the plot, the unusual and repulsive special effects make this one worth seeing, but not on a full stomach.
Aka: BRAIN CREATURE; MINDKILLER
HOR                                               90 min
B,V                                                     CINE

## MIND OVER MURDER *                                13
Ivan Nagy                 USA                         1979
Deborah Raffin, David Ackroyd, Andrew Prine, Bruce
Davidson, Robert Englund, Christopher Cary,
Penelope Willis, Wayne Heffley, Carl Anderson, Paul
Reid Roman, Jan Burrell, Paul Lukather, Larry
Duncan, Rex Riley, Jack Griffin
A young model with psychic powers senses that she is being pursued by a mass murderer in this remarkably untense thriller.
Aka: ARE YOU ALONE TONIGHT?
THR                                      92 min (ort 100 min) mTV
B,V                                                      CIC

## MINDER ON THE ORIENT EXPRESS **                   PG
Francis Megahy            UK                          1985
Dennis Waterman, George Cole, Patrick Malahide,
Glynn Edwards, Honor Blackman, Adam Faith,
Ronald Lacey, Robert Beatty, Maurice Denham, Ralph

*Bates, Linda Hayden, Amanda Pays, Peter Childs*
Based on the TV series "Minder", here our seedy
heroes our involved in an adventure on the world's
most famous train. Other countries make films, the
UK makes TV spin-offs. What plot there is involves
the daughter of a dead crook, the hidden number of his
Swiss bank account, and a collection of greedy characters all out to get the money. This one does at least
have good dialogue and characterisation.

| | |
|---|---|
| COM | 106 min mTV |
| V | VCC |

## MINDER: AN OFFICER AND A CAR SALESMAN **   PG

Roy Ward Baker    UK     1988
*George Cole, Dennis Waterman, Richard Briers, Diana
Quick, Simon Williams*
A full-length episode from this popular TV series in
which Cole and Waterman find themselves involved
in a deal with a war games enthusiast, who has
something of a Napoleon complex.

| | |
|---|---|
| COM | 73 min (ort 90 min) mTV |
| V | VCC |

## MINDFIELD *   15

Jean-Claude Lord    CANADA    1989
*Michael Ironside, Lisa Langlois, Christopher
Plummer, Sean McCann, Stefan Wodoslawsky*
Poorly plotted, acted and directed nonsense about a
Montreal cop who gets implicated in a top secret
government project that involves research in mind
control. Control your own mind and skip this dud.

| | |
|---|---|
| THR | 87 min (ort 117 min) |
| V | BRAVE/MGM |

## MINES OF KILIMANJARO, THE ***   18

Mino Guerrini    ITALY    1986
*Christopher Connelly, Gordon Mitchell, Elena Pompei,
Tobias Hoesl, Francesca Ferre, Peter Berling, Matteo
Corsini, Josette Martial, Franco Diogene, Tino
Castaldi, Al Cliver (Pier Luigi Conti), Kit Dickinson,
Luca Giordana*
In 1934 the Third Reich is re-arming, and when an
exiled German professor is murdered, his student sets
off for Africa in search of his killers, stumbling on the
mines of Kilimanjaro and a secret Nazi undertaking.
A lively but derivative clone of RAIDERS OF THE
LOST ARK, complete with hat-wearing hero.

| | |
|---|---|
| A/AD | 93 min |
| B,V | VPD |

## MINI-SKIRT MOB, THE *   15

Maury Dexter    USA    1968
*Jeremy Slate, Diane McBain, Sherri Jackson, Ross
Hagen, Patty McCormack*
A fairly ludicrous effort revolving around the exploits
of a bunch of female bikers.

| | |
|---|---|
| A | 80 min (ort 85 min) Cut (1 min 12 sec) |
| V | RNK |

## MINT CONDITION ***   U

Robert Michael Lewis    USA    1973
*E.G. Marshall, Mildred Natwick, Alejandro Rey,
Cleavon Little, David Doyle, Charles McGraw, Ronald
Feinberg, Lou Frizzell, Robert Karnes, Lew Brown,
Paul Sorenson, Mel Allen, Peggy Walton, Morris
Buchanan*
A prisoner profits from his time behind bars to forge a
million dollars in counterfeit bills and masterminds a
complex scheme to exchange them for the real thing.
A clever little comedy that's mildly amusing rather
than hilarious.
Aka MONEY TO BURN

| | |
|---|---|
| COM | 70 min (ort 73 min) mTV |
| B,V | EAG |

## MINX, THE *

Raymond Jacobs    USA    1969
*Jan Sterling, Robert Rodan, Shirley Parker*

A man uses sexual blackmail for business purposes in
this highly forgettable effort.

| | |
|---|---|
| DRA | 90 min |
| B,V | VCL/CBS |

## MIRACLE LANDING ***   PG

Dick Lowry    USA    1989
*Connie Selleca, Wayne Rogers, Michelle Honda, Mimi
Thompkins, Robert Schornsteimer*
Competent drama that follows the fate of Flight 243,
which took off from Hawaii in 1988 on a routine flight
and miraculously escaped disaster when a section of
the roof gave way at 24,000 feet.

| | |
|---|---|
| DRA | 84 min |
| V/h | CBS |

## MIRACLE MAN, THE *

Burt Topper    USA    1976
*Fabian Forte, Larry Bishop, Tony Russel, Hal Bonner,
Casey Kasem*
A miracle worker gets himself on the wrong side of the
law.
Aka: DAY THE LORD GOT BUSTED, THE

| | |
|---|---|
| DRA | 81 min |
| B,V | GOV |

## MIRACLE OF LOVE ***   PG

Glenn Jordan    USA    1984
*James Farentino, Katheryn Harrold, Stephen Elliott,
Henry Olek, Michael Adams, Kerry Sherman, Casey
Adams, Missy Francis, Shelby Balik, Erica Yohn, Don
Chastain, Richard Doyle, Rachel Bard, Barbara
Carney, Amentha Dymally*
A couple are shocked to discover that their third child
is autistic, but decide to devote all their energies to
finding a way to treat him themselves. Based on a true
story and enlivened by remarkable performances from
Michael Adams and Casey Adams, the two youngsters
who shared the role of the child.
Aka: SON RISE: A MIRACLE OF LOVE
Boa: book Son-Rise by Barry Neil Kaufman.

| | |
|---|---|
| DRA | 96 min; 93 min (INTMED) mTV |
| B,V | HER; INTMED |

## MIRACLE OF THE BELLS, THE *

Irving Pichel    USA    1948
*Fred MacMurray, Frank Sinatra, Alida Valli, Lee J.
Cobb, Charles Meredith*
A miracle occurs in a small town when a glamorous
film star dies, but this film isn't part of it. A tepid little
oddity. The script is by Ben Hecht and Quentin
Reynolds.
Boa: novel by Russell Janney.

| | |
|---|---|
| DRA | 120 min B/W |
| B,V,V2 | INT |

## MIRACLE OF THE WHITE STALLIONS, THE *   U

Arthur Hiller    USA    1962
*Robert Taylor, Lilli Palmer, Curt Jurgens, Eddie
Albert, James Franciscus, John Larch*
The director of the Spanish Riding School in Vienna
during WW2 decides to smuggle the famous Lippizan-
er horses to safety in the countryside. An interminable and verbose drama that does end eventually,
although it seems as if it never will.
Aka: FLIGHT OF THE WHITE STALLIONS, THE

| | |
|---|---|
| DRA | 89 min (ort 118 min) |
| B,V | WDV |

## MIRACLE ON 34TH STREET ****   U

George Seaton    USA    1947
*Edmund Gwenn, Maureen O'Hara, John Payne, Gene
Lockhart, Natalie Wood, James Seay, Porter Hall,
Philip Tonge, Harry Antrim, Mary Field, William
Frawley, Thelma Ritter, Percy Helton, Jerome Cowan*
A man who works as a Santa Claus in a department
store has to convince a sceptical child that he is the
real McCoy. Despite some ill-advised romantic in-

terest, this fresh and energetic fantasy is now rightly regarded as a classic. This was Ritter's screen debut. Remade for TV in 1973. AA: S. Actor (Gwenn), Story (Orig) (Valentine Davies), Screen (George Seaton).
Aka: BIG HEART, THE
Boa: story by Valentine Davies.
COM                          92 min (ort 96 min) B/W
V/h                                                CBS

## MIRACLE ON ICE **
Steve Hilliard Stern    USA              1981
Karl Malden, Andrew Stevens, Steven Guttenberg,
Jerry Houser, Jessica Walter, Robert F. Lyons, Robert
Peirce, Michael Cabanaugh, Lucinda Doolling,
Eugene Roche, Thomas Babson, Jack Blessing,
Michael Cummings, Richard Dano
An account of the triumphs of the US hockey team in the 1980 Winter Olympics who were in fact a group of amateurs welded into a winning unit by a controversial coach. Malden is totally convincing as Coach Herb Brooks and there is nothing wrong with the skating, but away from the ice this film sags badly. Written by Lionel Chetwynd.
DRA                                  152 min mTV
B,V                                   VFP L/A; HER

## MIRACLES **
Jim Kouf              USA                  PG
                                          1985
Tom Conti, Teri Garr, Paul Rodriguez, Harry McGray,
Christopher Lloyd, Adalberto Martinez, Jorge Russek
A well-off New York couple become involved in a series of totally improbable situations, including being taken prisoner by a Mexican bank robber. A fast and brainless chase-caper that tries to make much of little. Written by Kouf whose directorial debut this was.
COM                          83 min (ort 87 min)
B,V                                          RNK

## MIRACLES STILL HAPPEN *
Guiseppe Scotese    ITALY/USA               PG
                                            1974
Susan Penhaligon, Paul Muller, Graziella Galvani,
Clyde Peters
A teenage girl survives a plane crash in the Amazon and finally makes it back to civilisation. Based on a true story but hardly enthralling.
A/AD                         87 min (ort 93 min)
B,V                                          CINE

## MIRACLES: THE CANTON GODFATHER ***    15
Jackie Chan      HONG KONG              1989
Jackie Chan, Anita Mui, Richard Ng
A GODFATHER-inspired martial-arts thriller that's set in Hong Kong in the 1930s, where a penniless country boy rescues a mortally-wounded gang boss and inadvertently becomes his successor. As his power grows, he inevitably heads for the final conflict with the rival gangster who murdered his predecessor. A well-made Jackie Chan vehicle, fast, furious and enlivened with the the occasional flash of humour.
MAR                                      101 min
V                                           VPD

## MIRAGE *
                                           18
                 USA                       1990
Jennifer McAllister, Todd Schafer, Kenneth Johnson,
Kevin McParland, Nicola Anton
A couple on a camping trip await two other friends as they set up camp in the desert. The arrival of the other couple was delayed by a strange jeep that forced them off the road, and later that night its mysterious driver turns murderous and sets out to kill them all, until the remaining survivor is forced into a battle for survival. No new ideas are on offer here, in this stale and derivative distant cousin to DUEL.
HOR                                      85 min
V                                           NWV

## MIRROR CRACK'D, THE **
Guy Hamilton         UK                    PG
                                           1980
Angela Lansbury, Geraldine Chaplin, Elizabeth
Taylor, Rock Hudson, Tony Curtis, Edward Fox, Kim
Novak, Marella Oppenheim, Charles Gray, Maureen
Bennett, Carolyn Pickles, Eric Dodson, Charles Lloyd
Pack, Richard Pearson
Agatha Christie's female detective, Miss Marple, investigates a series of murders being committed in an English village, where a film is being made with a star-studded cast. All the stereotyped English characters are here, as in so much of the British cinema. Flat, lifeless and extremely boring.
Boa: novel The Mirror Crack'd From Side To Side by Agatha Christie.
DRA                          101 min (ort 105 min)
B,V,V2                      TEVP; WHV (VHS only)

## MIRROR, MIRROR *
Joanna Lee           USA                   1979
Robert Vaughn, Loretta Swit, Janet Leigh, Lee
Meriwether, Peter Bonerz, Christopher Lemmon,
Robin Mattson, Walter Brooke, McKee Anderson,
Elizabeth Robinson, Shelley Smith, Michael Hughes,
Angus Duncan, Ken Medlock
The story of three women who undergo cosmetic surgery for a variety of reasons, including their respective men. A well-intentioned film that is never less than painfully earnest and never more than tediously dull.
Boa: story by Leah Appet.
DRA                                  100 min mTV
B,V                                          VTC

## MIRRORS *
Noel Black           USA                   1974
Kitty Winn, Peter Donat, William Swetland, Mary-
Robin Redd, William Burns, Lou Wagner, Don Keefer,
Vanessa Hutchinson, Barbara Coleman, Becki Davis,
Tom Alden, Charles Keel, Carol Sutton, Warren
Kenner, Kuumba Williams
A tale of the supernatural set in New Orleans, with a couple on honeymoon staying at a very strange hotel.
Aka: MARIANNE
HOR                          86 min (ort 89 min)
B,V,V2                               VCL L/A; TCV

## MIRRORS **
Harry Winer          USA                   15
                                           1985
Timothy Daly, Shanna Reed, Antony Hamilton,
Nicholas Gunn, Ron Field, Signe Hasso, Keenan
Wynn, Marguerite Hickey, Patricia Morison, Laurence
Haddon, Milton Selzer, Don Johanson, Cheryl
Anderson, Mitchell Kreindel, Haru Aki
A young teenage dancer leaves her home in the Midwest and heads for New York to take what she hopes will be her first steps on the road to fame. A slight little variant of A CHORUS LINE with all the expected cliches.
Boa: novel by James Lipton.
DRA                          90 min (ort 100 min) mTV
B,V                                  IVS L/A CAST

## MISADVENTURES OF MERLIN JONES, THE *    U
Robert Stevenson    USA                   1964
Tommy Kirk, Annette Funicello, Leon Ames, Stuart
Erwin, Alan Hewitt, Connie Gilchrist, Michael Fox,
Bert Mustin, Norman Grabowski, Dal McKennon
A brainy college student comes a cropper when he dabbles in hypnotism and mind-reading. A limp Disney comedy, followed by THE MONKEY'S UNCLE.
JUV                          88 min (ort 91 min)
B,V                                          WDV

## MISBEHAVIN' **
Chuck Vincent       USA                   18
                                           1978
Gloria Leonard, Arkadia, Leslie Bovee, Jack Wrangler,
Kurt Mann, Molly Malone, Dick Gallan, Eric Edwards

Erotic take-off of the story of Job, with an angel and devil betting that, given the choice of love or money, one or the other must win. They decide to settle this by visiting a rich, four-times married socialite, who's lining up her next rich husband. Meanwhile a former spouse threatens suicide if she doesn't return to him. The outcome is never made clear in a silly film replete with one-liners. Cut before video submission by 17 min 36 sec.

A                                   62 min (ort 84 min)
B,V                                     TCX L/A; SHEP

## MISBEHAVING HUSBANDS **
William Beaudine        USA               1940
*Harry Langdon, Betty Blythe, Ralph Byrd*
A couple who have stayed married for 20 years are nearly split up by a barrage of gossip.
Osca: SECOND CHORUS
DRA                                       65 min B/W
B,V                                           WOOD

## MISCHIEF **                                    15
Mel Damski             USA                1984
*Doug McKeon, Catherine Mary Stewart, Kelly Preston, Chris Nash, D.W. Brown, Jami Gertz, Graham Jarvis*
Predictable teenage sex comedy about a boy anxious to lose his virginity and his more suave and self-assured friend. Set in the 1950s and strong on period flavour. If only the script gave the appealing cast more to work with.
Aka: HEART AND SOUL
COM                                       93 min
B,V                                           CBS

## MISFITS **                                     15
Kevin Inch             USA                1988
*Lewis Collins, Daphne Ashnrook, Cyril O'Reilly*
A female clerk employed by the US Justice Department becomes involved in a scheme to help the Indians on a reservation, "hiring" a bunch of peculiar characters to help her.
COM                                       80 min
B,V                                           TGP

## MISFITS OF SCIENCE *                           PG
James D. Parriott      USA                1985
*Dean-Paul Martin, Kevin Peter Hall, Mark Thomas Miller, Courtney Cox, Mickey Jones, Jennifer Holmes, Eric Christmas, Edward Winter, Larry Linville, Kenneth Mars*
An assorted band of strange characters join forces to prevent a research project from destroying the world. A feeble pilot for a failed TV series.
COM                                       90 min mTV
V/h                                           CIC

## MISFITS, THE **                                PG
John Huston            USA                1961
*Clark Gable, Marilyn Monroe, Montgomery Clift, Eli Wallach, Thelma Ritter, Estelle Winwood, James Barbon, Kevin McCarthy*
The story of a group of drifters in Arizona who are brought together by chance and rope some wild mustangs. An ill-fated melodrama in which the stars do their best but with little success. Scripted by Arthur Miller. This was the last film for both Gable (who did his own stunts) and Monroe.
DRA                                       124 min B/W
B,V                                           WHV

## MISHIMA: A LIFE IN FOUR CHAPTERS ***          15
Paul Schrader       JAPAN/USA            1985
*Ken Ogata, Kenji Sawada, Yasosuke Bando, Mashayuki Shionya, Junkichi Orimoto, Go Riju, Naoko Otani, Masato Aizawa, Yuki Nagahara, Hisako Manda, Kyuzo Kobayashi, Yasosuke Bando, Sachiko Hidari, Toshiyuki Nagashima*
A stylised four-part account of the life and ritual suicide of a famous Japanese writer. In Japanese with

sub-titles, and an English narration read by Roy Scheider. An exotic, difficult, powerful and generally self-indulgent work, that will be hard to follow for any except those who are familiar with the writings and/or the life of the character. The script is by Paul and Leonard Schrader.
Boa: novels Runaway Horses/Temple Of The Golden Pavilion by Yukio Mishima.
DRA               116 min (ort 120 min) B/W and Colour
B/sh, V/sh                                    WHV

## MISS ANNIE ROONEY *                            U
Edwin L. Marin         USA                1942
*Shirley Temple, William Gargan, Peggy Ryan, Guy Kibbee, Dickie Moore, Gloria Holden, Jonathan Hale, Selmer Jackson, Mary Field, June Lockhart, Virginia Sale*
An attempt to give Miss Temple a more adult role, this is the trite tale of a girl from a poor family who falls for a boy from a rich one. Not quite the success its makers hoped for, this vehicle for the former child star is as routine as it is forgettable.
DRA                                       87 min
V                                             RCA

## MISS ARIZONA **                                15
Pal Sandor                                1988
*Marcello Mastroianni, Hanna Schygulla*
Set in the years just before the Nazi invasion of Europe, this tells of a Hungarian cabaret performer who rescues a fellow performer from the police, and goes on tour with her and her young son to Italy, where they perform as a trio. However, their lampooning of Italy's Fascist regime forces them to flee once more, and they arrive in Budapest and set up a nightclub. A colourful but confused saga.
DRA                                       109 min
B,V                                           MED

## MISS FIRECRACKER ***                           PG
Thomas Schlamme        USA                1988
*Holly Hunter, Tim Robbins, Mary Steenburgen, Alfre Woodard, Scott Glenn, Ann Wedgeworth, Trey Wilson, Amy Wright, Bert Remsen*
A young Mississippi woman's desire for self-respect propels her into her hometown beauty queen competition – the Yagoo City Miss Firecracker Contest. Hunter is wonderful as the foolish and vulnerable girl, recreating the role she had in Henley's play, which is well transferred to the screen. A warm, zany and colourful comedy; of the excellent cast Steenburgen is particularly memorable as a former beauty queen. Schlamme's feature debut.
Boa: play The Miss Firecracker Contest by Beth Henley.
COM                             90 min (ort 102 min)
V                                             MGM

## MISS MARPLE: A MURDER IS
## ANNOUNCED ****                                 PG
David Gilies           UK                 1985
*Joan Hickson, Ursula Howells, Renee Asherson, John Castle, Kevin Whately, Sylvia Syms, Joan Sims, Simon Shepherd, Samantha Bond, Mary Kerridge, Ralph Michael, Paola Dionosotti*
Excellent adaptation to the small screen of the Christie mystery. Fine acting and a carefully recreated period atmosphere make this well worth watching
Aka: MURDER IS ANNOUNCED, A
Boa: novel by Agatha Christie.
DRA                                       154 min mTV
V                                             BBC

## MISS MARPLE: A POCKETFUL OF RYE ***            PG
Guy Slater             UK                 1985
*Joan Hickson, Peter Davison, Clive Merrison, Annette Badland, Selina Cadell, Fabia Drake, Timothy West,*

*Tom Wilkinson, Stacey Dorning, Susan Gilmore,*
*Louis Mahoney, Jon Glover*
The murder of a London financier by poison sets in
motion a macabre train of events in this excellent TV
adaptation, one in a series. The script is by T.R.
Bowen.
Boa: story by Agatha Christie.
DRA                        100 min mTV
V/h                            BBC

## MISS MARPLE: THE BODY IN THE   PG
LIBRARY ***
Silvio Narizzano          UK           1985
*Joan Hickson, Gwen Watford, Trudie Styler, Andrew*
*Cruickshank, Anthony Smee, Moray Watson,*
*Valentine Dyall, Frederick Jaeger, David Horovitch*
The discovery of the body of a retired colonel in a
library marks the start of a complex tale of murder.
One in an excellent series of adaptations of Agatha
Christie mysteries with Hickson playing Marple as if
made for the part.
Boa: novel by Agatha Christie.
DRA                        154 min mTV
V/h                            BBC

## MISS MARPLE: MURDER AHOY *        U
George Pollock            UK           1964
*Margaret Rutherford, Lionel Jeffries, Charles*
*Tingwell, William Mervyn, Joan Benham, Stringer*
*Davis, Nicholas Parsons, Miles Malleson, Henry*
*Oscar, Derek Nimmo, Francis Matthews, Gerald Cross*
Miss Rutherford once again plays our lady detective in
her own inimitable way, this time out to solve the
deaths of trustees of a cadet training ship, set up to
give wayward youngsters a dose of naval discipline.
Despite Rutherford's considerable screen presence,
this weak yarn (the last in the series) rapidly gets
bogged down with excessive dialogue.
Aka: MURDER AHOY
DRA                    89 min (ort 93 min) B/W
V                             MGM

## MISS MARPLE: MURDER AT THE GALLOP ***   U
George Pollock            UK           1963
*Margaret Rutherford, Robert Morley, Flora Robson,*
*Charles Tingwell, Duncan Lamont, Stringer Davis,*
*James Villiers, Robert Urquhart, Katya Douglas*
The second film in a series of four, this one has our
elderly detective investigating the death of a wealthy
cat-hating recluse and his sister, the man having been
apparently frightened to death by a cat. Spirited
performances and a good script make this the best of
the Rutherford-Miss Marple whodunnits.
Aka: MURDER AT THE GALLOP
Boa: novel After The Funeral by Agatha Christie.
DRA                    87 min (ort 81 min) B/W
V                             MGM

## MISS MARPLE: MURDER MOST FOUL **   U
George Pollock            UK           1964
*Margaret Rutherford, Ron Moody, Charles Tingwell,*
*James Bolam, Francesca Anniss, Terry Scott, Andrew*
*Cruickshank, Stringer Davis, Dennis Price, Megs*
*Jenkins, Ralph Michael*
Despite what appears to be conclusive evidence con-
cerning the murder of an actress, Rutherford refuses
to return a guilty verdict whilst serving as a juror and
mounts her own investigation. This takes her to a
second-rate repertory company which she joins in
order to unmask the real culprit. A fairly good murder
mystery held back by a lack of vigour.
Aka: MURDER MOST FOUL
Boa: novel Mrs McGinty's Dead by Agatha Christie.
DRA                        91 min B/W
V                             MGM

## MISS MARPLE: MURDER SHE SAID *     PG
George Pollock            UK           1961

*Margaret Rutherford, Charles Tingwell, Muriel*
*Pavlow, Arthur Kennedy, James Robertson Justice,*
*Thorley Walters, Gerald Cross, Conrad Phillips*
An elderly and inquisitive spinster spots a girl
apparently being strangled when she happens to
glance across to a passing train. Her attempt to solve
this mystery takes her to a strange country mansion
where she poses as the new housekeeper. The first of
four Miss Marple murder mysteries, inspired casting
gave Rutherford the chance to demonstrate her considerable screen presence, apart from which this
tedious affair has little to offer.
Aka: MURDER SHE SAID
Boa: novel 4.50 From Paddington by Agatha Christie.
DRA                        87 min B/W
V                             MGM

## MISS MARY **                      15
Maria Luisa Bemberg
                ARGENTINA             1986
*Julie Christie, Donald McIntire, Eduardo Pavlovsky,*
*Nacha Guevara, Tato Pavlovsky, Sofia Viruboff,*
*Barbara Bunge, Luisina Brando, Iris Marga, Gerard*
*Romano*
A British governess in Argentina in 1938 becomes
deeply involved with the son of the family she is
employed by. A steamy tale of repressed passions and
desires, all done with great style but no more memor-
able on that account.
DRA                    95 min (ort 100 min)
B,V                           NWV

## MISS-ADVENTURES AT MEGA BOOB      18
MANOR ***
                          UK           198-
*Pat D.D. Wynn, Janie Hamilton*
A group of businessmen are delighted when they find
they have won a civic award; a week at the famed
"Megaboob Manor", where their every wish is to be
pandered to by some buxom ladies. Whilst they are
having fun and frolics in the jacuzzi, their wives start
getting lonely. Made with some care and sure to be
enjoyed by connoisseurs of the outsize female form,
but don't expect too much by way of a plot.
A                             88 min
B,V                           SFI

## MISSILE-X **
Leslie Martinson
        IRAN/SPAIN/USA/WEST GERMANY  1978
*Michael Dante, Peter Graves, Curt Jurgens, John*
*Carradine*
A top-secret missile is stolen by an international
crime syndicate who use it to hold the world to
ransom.
Aka: CRUISE MISSILE; MISSILE-X:
GEHEIMAUFTRAG NEUTRONENBOMBE;
MISSILE-X: THE NEUTRON BOMB INCIDENT
THR                    90 min (ort 100 min)
B,V,V2                        VCL/CBS

## MISSILES OF OCTOBER, THE ***      U
Anthony Page              USA          1974
*William Devane, Martin Sheen, Ralph Bellamy,*
*Howard da Silva, John Dehner, Andrew Duggan*
A tense and detailed recreation of the Cuban missile
crisis of the 1960s when the USA and the USSR
nearly came into conflict over the Soviet missile bases
in Cuba. Devane particularly well chosen to play John
F. Kennedy.
DRA                    149 min (ort 155 min) mTV
B,V                           RNK

## MISSING ***                       15
Constantine Costa-Gavras
                          USA          1982
*Jack Lemmon, Sissy Spacek, Melanie Mayron, John*
*Shea, Charles Cioffi, David Clennon, Janice Rule,*

*Richard Venture, Richard Bradford, Ward Costello, Jerry Hardin, John Doolittle, Felix Gonzalez, Robert Hitt*
A father goes to a troubled Latin American country in search of his son who has disappeared, and finds that the American authorities are not telling him the truth. Based on the real-life experiences of Ed Horman, this gripping and well-made account never falters, and Lemmon's wonderful performance as the dogged father is a gem. AA: Screen (Adapt) (Costas-Gavras/Donald Stewart).
Boa: novel The Execution Of Charles Horman by Thomas Hauser.

| | |
|---|---|
| DRA | 116 min (ort 122 min) |
| B,V | CIC |

## MISSING IN ACTION ** 15
Joseph Zito            USA            1984
*Chuck Norris, M. Emmet Walsh, James Hong, David Tress, Lenore Kasdorf*
A routine rescue-our-brave-boys film, with Norris as a walking arsenal rescuing American POWs held in Vietnam after the war there. A standard "Rambo-style effort, unalloyed with anything as superficial as a plot. And of course the obligatory sequels followed. Written (if that is the right word) by James Bruner.

| | |
|---|---|
| A/AD | 96 min (ort 101 min) |
| B,V | GHV |

## MISSING IN ACTION 2: THE BEGINNING * 18
Lance Hool            USA            1985
*Chuck Norris, Soon-Teck Oh, Cosie Costa, Steven Williams, Bennett Ohta, Joe Michael Terry*
A prequel to MISSING IN ACTION detailing the treatment of American POWs at the hands of the Vietnamese with the expected one-sidedness of portrayal. Flat and predictable, and followed by one that's (by way of a variation) predictable and flat.
Aka: BATTLE RAGE

| | |
|---|---|
| WAR | 95 min; 91 min (VCC) |
| B,V | GHV; VCC (VHS only) |

## MISSING IN ACTION 3 * 18
Aaron Norris            USA            1988
*Chuck Norris, Aki Aleong, Yehuda Efroni, Roland Harrah III, Miki King, Ron Barker*
This time round our hero returns to Vietnam to rescue the wife he thought was dead, as well as his child. Norris co-scripted and his brother directed. A flat and one-dimensional affair.
Aka: BRADDOCK: MISSING IN ACTION 3 (WHV)

| | |
|---|---|
| A/AD | 98 min |
| V/sh | WHV |

## MISSING LINK *** PG
David Hughes/Carol Hughes
USA            1988
*Peter Elliott*
From the makers of BATMAN and RAIN MAN comes this documentary-style tale, set in Africa more than a million years ago, that follows the imagined last days in the life of the mythical creature thought to provide the evolutionary link between man and ape. Make-up is by Rick Baker of AN AMERICAN WEREWOLF IN LONDON fame.

| | |
|---|---|
| FAN | 88 min |
| V/sh | CIC |

## MISSING ONE, THE * 18
Arturo Martinez            SPAIN            1989
*Valentin Trujillo, Luis Aguilar, Veronica Castro, Patricia Aspillaga*
A loner returns to his hometown, the scene of much bullying he suffered as a youngster, but once there finds himself caught up in a violent confrontation. Standard one-man-against-the-mob Western boasting all the expected ingredients.

| | |
|---|---|
| WES | 93 min |
| V | VPD |

## MISSION BLOODY MARY * 
Terence Hathaway (Sergio Grieco)
FRANCE/ITALY/SPAIN            1965
*Ken Clark, Helga Line, Phillipe Hersent, Umberto Raho, Susan Terry, Antonio Gradoli, Andrea Scotti, Brand Lyonell, Peter Blades, Franca Polesello, Pulloa Coy, Mirko Ellis, Dario Michaelis, Erik Bianchi, Alfredo Mayo*
Mediocre Euro-adventure involving murder, mayhem and espionage. One in a set. See also FURY IN ISTANBUL and SPECIAL MISSION LADY CHAPLIN.
Aka: 077: MISSION BLOODY MARY; AGENTE: MISSIONE BLOODY MARY; LA MUERTE ESPERA EN ATHENAS

| | |
|---|---|
| A/AD | 99 min |
| V | IOVID; VPD |

## MISSION FOR THE DRAGON * 18
Godfrey Ho            HONG KONG
*Dragon Lee, Martin Chiu, Sheila Kim, Roger Wong, Burt Lim*
The fight sequences are the only thing of interest in this highly confusing martial arts film that has an evil man causing much grief and bloodshed by his desire to possess a priceless antique.

| | |
|---|---|
| MAR | 83 min Cut (2 min 27 sec) |
| B,V | VPD |

## MISSION GALACTICA: THE CYCLON ATTACK * U
Vince Edwards/Christian I. Nyby II
USA            1980
*Richard Hatch, Lorne Greene, Lloyd Bridges, Dirk Benedict, Herbert Jefferson Jr*
A sequel to BATTLESTAR GALACTICA with Lorne Greene leading a few struggling survivors in a desperate battle against the human-hating Cyclons. This feeble effort, cobbled together from episodes of the "Battlestar Galactica" TV series, has our heroic band of humans embarking on a plan to destroy the Cyclons. Their efforts very nearly prove fatal, just as this film does.

| | |
|---|---|
| FAN | 102 min (ort 107 min) mTV |
| V | CIC |

## MISSION HILL *** 15
Robert Jones            USA            1982
*Alice Barrett, Brian Burke, Barbara Orson, Robert Kerman, Daniel Silver, Nan Mallenaux, John Mahoney*
A brother and sister grow up in a tough neighbourhood where crime is a way of life, but try to overcome their disadvantaged background, while their aspiring singer mother struggles to bring the teenage son back onto the straight and narrow, after he has committed a series of petty crimes. A harsh and perceptive study, filmed in Boston.
Aka: NEIGHBOURHOOD, THE; NEIGHBOURHOOD, THE: MISSION HILL (PHE)

| | |
|---|---|
| DRA | 85 min; 80 min (PHE or PYR) |
| B,V | PHE; PYR; VFP |

## MISSION IMPOSSIBLE: THE GOLDEN SERPENT * PG
Don Chaffey            AUSTRALIA            1989
*Peter Graves, Jane Badler, Phil Morris, Patrick Bishop, Rod Mullinar*
Pilot for the revived TV series that has Graves as the only familiar face and was produced on the cheap in Australia. The "Serpent" of the title refers to a heroin producer who Jim Phelps and the "Mission Impossible" team are ordered to neutralise. The technology is more advanced than in the original series, but the stunts and plotting are as improbable as ever, and do nothing to enliven this dull undercover adventure.

| | |
|---|---|
| A/AD | 101 min |
| V | CIC |

**MISSION KILL *** 18
David Winters          USA          1984
*Robert Ginty, Merete Van Kemp, Cameron Mitchell,*
*Olivia D'Abo*
A man seeks revenge for the death of his friend during
a gun-running mission in the jungle. A low-grade
actioner.
A/AD                                    92 min
B,V                                      AVA

**MISSION MANILA *** 18
Peter M. MacKenzie          1987
*Larry Wilcox, James Wainwright, Robin Eisenman,*
*Tetchie Agabyani, Sam Hennings, Al Mancini, Neil*
*French, Maria Isabel Lopez*
A man goes to Manila to locate his missing brother
who has vanished with $1,000,000 worth of heroin
belonging to a drugs syndicate, who have sent their
hit-men after him to recover the drugs and kill him as
a warning to others. Eventually they meet up and get
to take on the villains together in the final reel of this
poorly-made action thriller, that resembles nothing so
much as a formula TV movie.
Aka: WEB
A/AD                                    97 min
V                                       PRES

**MISSION, THE *** PG
Roland Jaffe          USA          1986
*Robert De Niro, Jeremy Irons, Ray McAnally, Aidann*
*Quinn, Ronald Pickup, Liam Neeson, Cherie Lunghi,*
*Chuck Low, Daniel Berrigan*
Colourful historical drama set in South America in
the 18th century, when the jurisdiction of a region is
to be transferred from Spain to Portugal. A Jesuit
missionary joins forces with a reformed slave trader,
to stop the Portuguese from enslaving the Guarani
Indians. Well-intentioned but terribly patronising in
its attitudes to the natives. Winner of the Best Picture
Award at the Cannes Film Festival. Scripted by Bolt.
AA: Cin (Chris Menges).
Boa: novel by Robert Bolt.
DRA                          120 min (ort 125 min)
B, V/sh                       PAL; WHV (VHS only)

**MISSION, THE *** PG
Parviz Sayad
          USA/WEST GERMANY          1983
*Parviz Sayad, Mary Apick, Hedyeh Apick, Houshang*
*Touzie, Mohammed B. Gaffari, Hatem Anvar, Kamran*
*Nozad*
An Iranian assassin sent to kill an ex-secret police
colonel now living in New York, gets inextricably
involved in a personal relationship with his quarry
and the latter's family. A perceptive and well-acted
study of the complexities and double-dealing of poli-
tics.
Aka: FERESTADEH
DRA                          104 min (ort 110 min)
B,V                                      PAL

**MISSION: TERMINATE *** 18
Anthony Maharaj  HONG KONG          1986
*Richard Norton, Dick Wei, Franco Guerrero, Rex*
*Cutter, Lu Shao Lung*
The members of a former platoon stationed in Viet-
nam, are being killed off in revenge for the massacre
of a village, even though the conflict is now over. Our
usual killing machine is sent to deal with this problem
in a nasty, mindless and exploitative effort. Scripted
by Joe Avallon.
WAR                          84 min Cut (14 sec)
B,V                                      VPD

**MISSIONARY, THE *** 15
Richard Loncraine          UK          1983
*Michael Palin, Maggie Smith, Trevor Howard, Phoebe*
*Nichols, Denholm Elliott, Michael Hordern, Graham*
*Crowden, Roland Culver, David Suchet, Tricia*

*George, Valerie Whittington, Rosamund Greenwood,*
*Timothy Small*
Dreadfully stilted and unfunny story of a missionary
who, newly returned from Africa, is given the job of
running a refuge for fallen women ("What, women
who have fallen over?" – illustrates the level of
humour). A pathetic example of British comedy at its
worst, with all the usual class-system cliches. Screenplay is by Palin.
COM                          82 min (ort 86 min)
B,V                                      TEVP

**MISSISSIPPI BURNING *** 18
Alan Parker          USA          1988
*Gene Hackman, Willem Dafoe, Brad Dourif, Frances*
*McDormand, R. Lee Ermey, Gailand Sartain, Stephen*
*Tobolowsky, Michael Rooker, Pruitt Taylor Vince,*
*Park Overall*
A potent, vivid drama telling of two FBI agents, who
are sent to investigate the mysterious disappearance
of three civil rights workers, in Mississippi in the
1960s. The script (inspired by real-life events) occa-
sionally falters, but there is nothing wrong with the
period-detail or performances, especially Hackman's,
as a small-town sheriff who finally solves the case.
AA: Cin (Peter Biziou).
DRA                          121 min (ort 127 min)
V                                       VIR

**MISSOURI BREAKS, THE *** 15
Arthur Penn          USA          1976
*Marlon Brando, Jack Nicholson, Kathleen Lloyd,*
*Randy Quaid, Frederic Forrest, Harry Dean Stanton,*
*John McLiam, John Ryan, Sam Gilman, Steve*
*Franken, Richard Bradford, James Greene, Luana*
*Anders, R.L. Armstrong*
Ranchers clash with rustlers and hire a gunman to
help them out. Supposedly a spoof of sorts, but it's
hard to see where the jokes are in this disorganised
and interminable mess.
WES                                     126 min
B,V                                      WHV

**MISTER AND MRS EDGEHILL *** PG
Gavin Miller          UK          1985
*Judi Dench, Ian Holm, Rachel Gurney*
The story of an English couple and their unconven-
tional lifestyle on the South Pacific island of Cowrie.
See also ME AND THE GIRLS, MRS CAPPER'S
BIRTHDAY and WHAT MAD PURSUIT?
Boa: play by Noel Coward.
DRA                                     82 min
V                                 PICK; START

**MISTER BILLION *** PG
Jonathan Kaplan          USA          1977
*Terence Hill (Mario Girotti), Valerie Perrine, Slim*
*Pickens, Jackie Gleason, Chill Wills, Dick Miller, R.G.*
*Armstrong, Dave Cass, Sam Lewis, Johnny Ray*
*McGhee, William Redfield*
A humble Italian mechanic embarks on a cross-
country chase in a mad search for a billion dollar
legacy, while varied bad guys attempt to beat him to
it. A standard chase movie devoid of new ideas or wit.
Hill's US debut.
COM                          90 min (ort 93 min)
B,V                                      CBS

**MISTER BIRD TO THE RESCUE *** U
Paul Grimault          FRANCE          1980
Loosely inspired by Andersen's tale and scripted by
Jacques Prevert, the famous poet and screenwriter,
this complex and imaginative story follows the chang-
ing fortunes of the King of Tachacardia, who one day
loses his power. An elegant and skilfully executed
animation that is certain to have wide appeal.
Aka: KING AND MISTER BIRD, THE; KING AND
THE BIRD, THE; KING AND THE MOCKINGBIRD,
THE; LE ROI ET L'OISEAU; MY BIRD TO THE

RESCUE
Boa: short story The Shepherdess And The
Chimneysweep by Hans Christian Andersen.
CAR                                    80 min (ort 87 min)
B,V                                              EIV

## MISTER BLANDINGS BUILDS HIS DREAM    U
## HOUSE ***
H.C. Potter              USA                    1948
*Cary Grant, Myrna Loy, Melvyn Douglas, Reginald
Denny, Nestor Paiva, Jason Robards, Louise Beavers,
Ian Wolfe, Harry Shannon, Sharyn Moffett, Connie
Marshall, Lurene Tuttle, Lex Barker, Emory Parnell*
A couple from the city attempt to build a house in the
countryside, but find this no easy task. Though the
film is nowhere near as subtle as the novel, this bright
and cheerful comedy has the two stars in top form. The
script is by Norman Panama and Melvin Frank. See
also THE MONEY PIT.
Boa: novel by Eric Hodgkin. Osca: MEXICAN
SPITFIRE AT SEA
COM                            84 min; 90 min (VCC) B/W
B,V                                           KVD; VCC

## MISTER CHRISTMAS DINNER **    15
Anthony Perkins          USA                    1988
*Joe Alaskey, Donna Dixon, Jeff Kober, Morgan
Sheppard, Barbara Howard, Charles Frank, Fran
Ryan, Leigh McCloskey, Bill Quinn*
A cannibalism comedy, with a fat guy falling under
the spell of a seductive siren who has decided that he
will make a fitting Christmas dinner for her degener-
ate family. A slow start gives way to a rather better
second half, but this uneven black comedy never
really gets into its stride.
Aka: LUCKY STIFF
COM                                80 min (ort 82 min)
V                                                RCA

## MISTER DEATHMAN *
Michael Moore            USA
*David Broodnax, Stella Stevens, Arthur Brauss, Lena
Nicols, Brian O'Shaugnessy*
An agent undertaking one last job for the CIA before
retiring, experiences the usual hazards.
THR                                           90 min
B,V                            VIDKNG/TEM L/A; APX

## MISTER DEEDS GOES TO TOWN ****    U
Frank Capra              USA                    1936
*Gary Cooper, Jean Arthur, Raymond Walburn, Lionel
Stander, Walter Catlett, George Bancroft, Douglass
Dumbrille, H.B. Warner, Ruth Donnelly, Margaret
Seddon, Margaret McWade*
A man must defend his sanity in a courtroom battle
when he inherits a vast fortune, and proclaims his
intention of using the money to help ordinary people
suffering the effects of the Depression to make a fresh
start. Vintage Capra, that's neither dated nor stilted,
but simply a joy to watch. The script is by Robert
Riskin. Later a brief TV series. AA: Dir.
Boa: story Opera Hat by Clarence Budington Kelland.
COM                         111 min (ort 118 min) B/W
V                                                RCA

## MISTER HALPERN AND MISTER JOHNSON *    U
Alvin Rakoff             USA                    1983
*Lawrence Olivier, Jackie Gleason*
Two men meet during the funeral of the wife of one of
them, and find they both had a relationship with her.
Remarkably uninspiring.
DRA                               52 min (ort 104 min) mCab
V                                                VGM

## MISTER HORN **    PG
Jack Starett             USA                    1979
*David Carradine, Richard Widmark, Karen Black,
Richard Masur, Clay Tanner, Pat McCormick, Jack*

Starrett, John Durren, Jeremy Slate, Enrique Lucero,
Stafford Morgan, Don Collier, James Oliver, George
Reynolds, Ian McLean
Long, episodic Western about a legendary frontier
figure, who captured the Apache chief Geronimo.
Average. See also TOM HORN.
WES                            134 min (ort 200 min) mTV
B,V                                             POLY

## MISTER INSIDE, MISTER OUTSIDE **    PG
William A. Graham        USA                    1974
*Hal Linden, Tony Lo Bianco, Phil Bruns, Paul
Benjamin, Marcia Jean Kurtz, Stefan Schnabel,
Arnold Soboloff, Melody Santangelo, Ed Van Nuys,
Robert Risel, Sam Coppola, Joe Cirillo, Robert Levine,
Matt Russo, Larry Sherman*
Pilot for a prospective series with two cops, one of
whom works undercover, trying to bust a drug
smuggling operation involving a foreign embassy
official. Good action sequences slightly redeem the
mediocre script. Inspired by an idea by Sonny Grosso.
DRA                                           74 min mTV
B,V                                              VPD

## MISTER JERICO ***
Sidney Hayers            USA                    1970
*Patrick Macnee, Marty Allen, Connie Stevens, Herbert
Lom, Leonardo Pieroni, Bruce Boa, Joanne Dainton,
Paul Darrow, Jasmina Hilton, Peter Yapp, Anne
Godfrey, June Cooper, Nancy Egerton*
Story of a diamond robbery set in Malta, with several
crooks after the same gem, and con-man Macnee out
to beat them all to it. Good locations and dialogue are
somewhat hampered by the convoluted and cumber-
some script. Inspired by an idea by David T. Chantler.
DRA                              81 min (ort 85 min) mTV
B,V                                              PRV

## MISTER KINGSTREET'S WAR ***
Percival Rubens          USA                    1973
*John Saxon, Tippi Hedren, Rossano Brazzi, Brian
O'Shaughnessy*
A game warden and his wife try to protect a wildlife
reserve from opposing sides in WW2, in this colourful
and unusual tale.
Osca: GHOST SHIP
DRA                               89 min (ort 92 min)
B,V                                              KVD

## MISTER KLEIN ***
Joseph Losey        FRANCE/ITALY               1976
*Alain Delon, Jeanne Moreau, Michel Lonsdale, Juliet
Berto, Suzanne Flon, Louise Seigner*
In 1942 a Parisian antiques dealer profits from the
plight of Jews who are forced to sell him their
priceless items for a trifle. However, by a series of
strange coincidences, he is mistaken for a shadowy
Jewish figure called Klein and begins to assume his
identity, ultimately sharing the fate of Jews being
sent to their deaths. A ponderous and unsatisfying
drama, whose surreal undertones are never fully
developed.
Aka: MR KLEIN
DRA                                          122 min
V                                                INT

## MISTER LOVE **    15
Roy Battersby            UK                     1986
*Barry Jackson, Marcia Warren, Julia Deakin, Maurice
Denham, Margaret Tyzack, Linda Marlowe, Christina
Collier, Helen Cotterill, Donal McCann, Janine
Roberts, Tony Melody, Patsy Byrne, Robert Bridges,
Jacki Piper, Alan Starkey*
A gentle comedy about a man in charge of Southport's
municipal gardens who in his own quiet way becomes
something of a Don Juan. The treatment is strangely
old-fashioned and the theme never amounts to much.
Made as one in a series for TV called "First Love".
Aka: FIRST LOVE . . . MISTER LOVE

COM                                88 min (ort 91 min)
B/h, V/h                                        WHV

**MISTER MAGOO: 1001 ARABIAN NIGHTS \***    U
Jack Kinney            USA                    1959
*Voices of: Jim Backus, Kathryn Grant (Crosby),*
*Dwayne Hickman, Hans Conried, Herschel Bernardi,*
*Alan Reed*
An animated reworking of a few classic tales, given
the standard one-joke treatment as our shortsighted
hero stumbles from one disaster to the next. Fans of
Magoo will adore it, others may find it interminable.
Aka: 1001 ARABIAN NIGHTS
CAR                                73 min (ort 75 min)
V                                               RCA

**MISTER MAGOO IN SHERWOOD FOREST \***    U
Abe Levitow            USA                    1964
*Voice of Jim Backus*
This boring and unfunny cartoon character now gets
to grips with the legend of Robin Hood.
CAR                                       83 min mTV
B,V,V2                              VTC L/A; VMA

**MISTER MAGOO IN THE KING'S SERVICE \***    U
Abe Levitow            USA                    1964
*Voice of Jim Backus*
Two cartoons starring our shortsighted hero. They are
"The Three Musketeers" and "King Arthur". Tiresome
and poorly animated dross.
CAR                                       81 min mTV
B,V                                VTC L/A; VMA

**MISTER MAGOO: MAN OF MYSTERY \***    U
Abe Levitow            USA                    1964
*Voice of Jim Backus*
Magoo plays the Count of Monte Christo, Dr Watson,
Dr Frankenstein and Dick Tracy in this crudely-
drawn and interminable animation.
CAR                                       96 min mTV
B,V                                             VPD

**MISTER MAGOO'S CHRISTMAS CAROL \*\***    U
Abe Levitow            USA                    1962
*Voices of: Jim Backus, Jack Cassidy, Morey*
*Amsterdam, Royal Dano, Paul Frees*
Mr Magoo, the shortsighted one, bumps into the
famous Dickens tale, in this cartoon from a mediocre
series of "Mister Magoo" adventures. This one is
somewhat better than average and the lively score is
by Jules Styne and Bob Merrill.
Boa: story A Christmas Carol by Charles Dickens.
CAR                                       52 min mTV
B,V                                VTC L/A; VMA

**MISTER MAGOO'S STORY BOOK \***    U
Abe Levitow            USA                    1964
*Voice of Jim Backus*
Cartoon versions of the stories of "Snow White", "Don
Quixote and "A Midsummer Night's Dream", form the
basis for this utterly uninteresting and shoddy effort.
CAR                                      113 min mTV
B,V                                VTC L/A; VMA

**MISTER MAJESTYK \*\***    18
Richard Fleischer      USA                    1974
*Charles Bronson, Al Lettieri, Linda Cristal, Lee*
*Purcell, Paul Koslo, Alejandro Rey*
The great stoneface plays a Colorado melon farmer,
who runs into trouble with gangsters when he refuses
to pay protection money. A well-paced, violent film in
which the melons act beautifully. (Bronson comes a
close second). The script is by Elmore Leonard.
DRA                                100 min (ort 103 min)
B,V                                             WHV

**MISTER MEAN \*\***    18
Fred Williamson    ITALY/USA                  1977
*Fred Williamson, Charles Wolf, Tracey Reed, Virginia*

*Grege, Stack Pierce, Dan Cornelis, Mike Henry, Gene le*
*Bell, Kitty Carl, Dean Franklin, Aroy Allen, Debby*
*Wood*
A Vietnam veteran scratches a living as a kind of
modern-day bounty hunter, tracking down criminals
and bail jumpers. Filmed in Rome.
Aka: TRACER, THE (STAT)
DRA                                           80 min
B,V                                PMA L/A; STAT

**MISTER MUM \*\***    PG
Stan Dragoti           USA                    1983
*Michael Keaton, Teri Garr, Martin Mull, Ann Jillian,*
*Christopher Lloyd, Frederick Koehler, Graham Jarvis,*
*Taliesin Jaffe, Courtney White, Brittany White, Tom*
*Leopold, Carolyn Seymour, Michael Alaimo, Jeffrey*
*Tambor*
A couple switch domestic roles when the husband gets
fired and the wife finds a job. As is usual, the fun
revolves around Hollywood's obsession with men
being useless at housework.
Aka: MISTER MOM
COM                                           91 min
B,V                                             TEVP

**MISTER NORTH \*\***    PG
Danny Huston           USA                    1988
*Anthony Edwards, Robert Mitchum, Anjelica Huston,*
*Lauren Bacall, Harry Dean Stanton, Virginia Madsen,*
*Mary Stuart Masterson, David Warner, Hunter*
*Carson, Christopher Durang, Mark Metcalf, Katherine*
*Houghton*
In the 1920s, a young man takes Newport society by
storm thanks to his charm and charisma. A likeable if
somewhat patchily realised fantasy, with fine loca-
tions and a good cast. The feature debut for the
director, who wrote the script with his father, John
Huston.
Boa: novel Teophilus North by Thornton Wilder.
COM                                90 min (ort 92 min)
B,V                                             RCA

**MISTER RICCO \*\***    15
Paul Bogart            USA                    1975
*Dean Martin, Eugene Roche, Thalmus Rasulala,*
*Geraldine Brooks, Denise Nicholas, Cindy Williams,*
*Frank Puglia*
A criminal lawyer is involved with a weird selection of
nasty crimes and even nastier criminals, when he
risks his life to defend a black client. A convoluted and
murky thriller, with a tired-looking star trying to
work up some energy, and generally not succeeding.
THR                                95 min (ort 98 min)
B,V                                             MGM

**MISTER ROBERTS \*\*\*\***    U
John Ford/Mervyn Le Roy
                       USA                    1955
*Henry Fonda, James Cagney, William Powell, Jack*
*Lemmon, Betsy Palmer, Ward Bond, Nick Adams,*
*Phlip Carey, Harry Carey Jr, Ken Curtis*
Story of a cargo ship in WW2, and an officer who is
itching for transfer to where the fighting is. The film
hovers between comedy and pathos, and has some
enjoyable, if not really believable moments. Cagney as
the martinet captain, provides a fine counterweight to
Fonda, as the officer determined to obtain a transfer.
This was Powell's last film. The vastly inferior sequel
"Ensign Pulver" followed. AA: S. Actor (Lemmon).
Boa: play by Thomas Heggen and J. Logan.
COM                                      115 min B/W
B,V                                WHV; MGM

**MISTER ROBINSON CRUSOE \*\*\***
Edward Sutherland      USA                    1932
*Douglas Fairbanks Sr, William Farnum, Earle*
*Browne, Maria Alba*
A man accepts a bet that he can live on a desert island
just like Robinson Crusoe did, and sets out to prove it.

An unusual little comedy with an ageing, but still fit Fairbanks, the chief asset in a work of some charm. The score is by Alfred Newman. The film was also released in a silent version.

COM 67 min (ort 76 min) B/W
B,V VCL/CBS

## MISTER ROSSI LOOKS FOR HAPPINESS * U
Bruno Bozzetto ITALY 197-
A man travels everywhere thanks to a golden whistle, and has adventures in various countries and periods.
CAR 80 min
V VDM L/A; VMA

## MISTER SYCAMORE * PG
Pancho Kohner USA 1974
Jason Robards, Sandy Dennis, Jean Simmons, Robert Easton, Mark Miller
A mild-mannered postman with a nagging wife decides to opt out of the rat race by turning into a tree in this limp comedy fantasy.
COM 85 min (ort 88 min)
B,V,V2 INT; VMA

## MISTER TEN PER CENT *
Peter Graham Scott UK 1966
Charlie Drake, George Baker, Annette Andre, John Le Mesurier
A builder who writes plays as a hobby has one of them accepted by a top London impresario and finds his drama being staged as a successful comedy. A film of little humour that fails to fully exploit the talents of its diminutive star.
COM 85 min
V WHV

## MISTRAL'S DAUGHTER: PARTS 1, 2 AND 3 ** PG
David Hickox
FRANCE/LUXEMBOURG/USA 1984
Stefanie Powers, Lee Remick, Stacy Keach, Timothy Dalton, Robert Urich, Stephane Audran, Ian Richardson, Stephanie Dunnam, Cotter Smith, Alan Adair, Pierre Malet, Philippine Leroy Beaulieu, Alexandra Stewart, Joanna Lumley
Overlong, dull as ditchwater saga, of a painter over a period from the 1920s to the 1950s, and mainly examining his relationship with the first model and the daughter she bears him. Not one scene carries dramatic conviction as the one-dimensional characters progress through their parts in a variety of unconvincing ways. Originally shown in three parts.
Boa: novel by Judith Krantz.
DRA 540 min (3 cassettes) mTV
B,V,V2 VFP L/A; CH5 (VHS only)

## MISTRESS OF PARADISE **
Peter Medak USA 1981
Genevieve Bujold, Chad Everett, Anthony Andrews, Olivia Cole, John McLiam, Lelia Goldoni, Carolyn Seymour, Myron Natwick, Fred D. Scott, Bill Wiley, Tonea Stuart, Valarian Smith
A Northern beauty marries a plantation owner from the Deep South, and becomes involved in voodoo. The talents of Bujold (in her TV movie debut) are largely wasted in this murky and insipid nonsense.
DRA 95 min (ort 100 min) mTV
B,V POLY

## MISTRESS OF THE APES *
Larry Buchanan USA 1979
Barbara Leigh, Jenny Neumann, Stuart Lancaster, Garth Pilsbury, Walt Robin
A woman goes to Africa in search of her missing anthropologist husband.
THR 84 min
B,V INT

## MISTRESS, THE * 15
Michael Tuchner USA 1988
Victoria Principal, Alan Rachins, Kerri Keane, Joanna Kerns, Don Murray
A mistress enjoys a perfect relationship, until her lover suddenly dies of a heart attack whilst on vacation. Her grief is compounded by the fact that after a nine-year relationship, she is left with nothing and must now start supporting herself. An empty and rather tiresome little tale.
DRA 93 min (ort 96 min) mTV
B,V VIR

## MISTRESS, THE ** 18
Mario Lanfranchi ITALY 1976
Senta Berger, Maurizio Arena, Bruno Zanin, Erika Blanc
A man buys the estate of the late Count Origoni, and finds that he has acquired the Count's pretty wife and lustful daughters as well.
Aka: DIE HERRENREITERIN; LA PADRONA E SERVITA
A 78 min (ort 105 min)
B,V,V2 VPD

## MISTRESS, THE *** 18
Jack Remy USA 1982
Kelly Nichols, Eric Edwards, Randy West, Susan Key, Richard Pacheco, Brooke West, Juliette Anderson, Anne Turner
An office girl works for a powerful New York company and enjoys weekends with her married boss. She is also involved with another married man. Both are prize egotists who simply make use of her, her boss in particular gets her to give sexual favours in order to win contracts for his company. The film brings out her attitude to men, and shows how her lack of commitment to just one man allows all and sundry to take advantage of her.
A 80 min
B,V CAL; NET

## MISTY BEETHOVEN ***
Henry Paris (Radley Metzger)
USA 1976
Jamie Gillis, Gloria Leonard, Constance Money, Terri Hall, Ras King, Mary Stuart, Jacqueline Beudant
This erotic version of Pygmalion looks at one Seymour Love, who runs the House Of Love in New York, and has written many books on human sexuality. In Paris he discovers Misty, an American woman working in a brothel and plainly just in it for the money. He convinces her that he can turn her into a high-class hooker and sets about his task, instructing her by earphone as she services a top model in Rome. An amusing and well made sex film.
Aka: OPENING OF MISTY BEETHOVEN, THE
Osca: HALF THE ACTION (asa)
A 88 min
B,V HUS L/A; HAR

## MISUNDERSTOOD ** PG
Jerry Schatzberg USA 1982
Gene Hackman, Henry Thomas, Huckleberry Fox, Rip Torn, Maureen Kerwin, Susan Anspach
A man is devastated by the death of his wife, and neglects his two young children, causing serious consequences. A well-acted, but somehow rather unappealing tale, filmed in Tunisia, and remade in Italy in 1988.
DRA 97 min
B,V ARCADE/VSP L/A; ODY

## MIXED BLOOD * 18
Paul Morrissey FRANCE 1984
Marilia Pera, Richard Ulacia, Geraldine Smith, Linda Kerridge, Angel David, Ulrich Berr, Rodney Harvey, Pedro Sanchez, Alvaro Rodriguez, William Rodriguez,

*Eduardo Gonzalez, Steven Garcia, Edwin Ebron, Andres Castillo*
Two gangs struggle for control of the drugs trade on the streets of New York's Lower East Side. A violent and exploitative film, unrelieved by some feeble attempts at comic relief.
Aka: AVENUE O; COCAINE; DOWN TOWN; NEW YORK, AVENUE O
THR                    94 min (ort 97 min) Cut (34 sec)
B,V                                         EHE; NELS

## MOB WAR **                                         18
Bobby Davis            USA                  1978
*Larry Hauck, Charlotte Sigmund, Andre Laborde, R.J. Cox*
This epic purports to tell the story of the struggle for control of New Orleans between rival gangs. Set in the 1930s.
DRA                              88 min (ort 100 min)
B,V                                      ALLAM/MOG

## MOBILE-HOME GIRLS **                              18
Michel Lemoine (Michel Leblanc)
                       FRANCE               1985
*Olinka (Olinka Hardiman), Patricia Violet, Andre Kay, Anthony Ray, John Oury, Gabriel Pontello, Francoise-Pierre Martinelli, Laura Clair, Marianne Aubert, Eric Saville*
Four prostitutes go on holiday in a mobile home which doubles as a brothel, when they decide to raise some pocket money. Mind-numbing and tedious, with but a few moments of titillation.
Aka: JOUISSANCES A DOMICILE; JOUISSANCES ROULANTES
A                                83 min (ort 117 min) Cut
B,V                                      CASS; LATE/IVS

## MOBY DICK **
                                            1977
A competent animated version of this classic tale with an introduction by Jon Pertwee.
Boa: novel by Herman Melville.
CAR                              49 min; 50 min (STYL)
B,V                              VCL/CBS; STYL (VHS only)

## MOBY DICK ***
John Huston            USA                  1956
*Gregory Peck, Richard Basehart, Leo Genn, Friedrich Ledebur, Orson Welles, James Robertson Justice, Harry Andrews, Bernard Miles, Noel Purcell, Edric Connor, Joseph Tomelty, Mervyn Johns*
A whaling skipper swears vengeance on the great white whale that cost him a leg in an earlier encounter. This slow-moving remake of the 1930 film, has some remarkable photography and scenes, but Peck makes a disappointing Ahab and the intrusive music is a severe distraction. Nevertheless, an enjoyable film, with screenplay by Huston and Ray Bradbury. A highlight is the sermon given by Father Mapple, which Welles did in a single take.
Boa: novel by Herman Melville.
A/AD                             110 min (ort 116 min)
B,V                                             TEVP

## MODEL BEHAVIOUR **                                18
Bud Gardner            USA                  1984
*Richard Bekins, Bruce Lyons, Anne Howard*
A couple of college graduates pretend to be film-makers so as to get into the world of modelling, and find themselves caught up in a web of lies and pretence.
COM                                          85 min
B,V                                         EHE; NELS

## MODERN GIRLS *                                    15
Jerry Kramer           USA                  1986
*Daphne Zuniga, Virginia Madsen, Cynthia Gibb, Clayton Rohner, Chris Nash, Steve Shellen, Rich Overton, Pamela Springsteen*
Three beautiful girls have a wild night out in this tedious, low-brow exercise in murky unpleasantness and coarse humour.
COM                              81 min (ort 84 min)
B,V                                             EIV

## MODERN PROBLEMS *
Ken Shapiro            USA                  1981
*Chevy Chase, Patti D'Arbanville, Mary Kay Place, Neil Carter, Dabney Coleman, Brian Doyle-Murray, Mitch Kreindel, Arthur Sellers, Sandy Helberg, Neil Thompson, Carl Irwin, Ron House, Buzzy Linhart, Henry Corden*
An air traffic controller aquires telekinetic powers in a freak accident, and uses them to further his career and love life. A hollow little effort with a shortage of gags.
COM                                          93 min
B,V                                             CBS

## MODERN ROMANCE ***                               15
Albert Brooks          USA                  1981
*Albert Brooks, Kathryn Harrold, Bruno Kirby, Jane Hallaren, James L. Brooks, George Kennedy, Bob Eisenstein, Tyann Means, Karen Chandler, Dennis Kort, Virginia Feingold, Thelma Leeds, Candy Castillo, Ed Weinberger*
A neurotic man is obsessed with his girlfriend, but is unable to maintain a normal relationship with her. A perceptive and generally witty exercise with some nice cameos, and a few in-jokes aimed at movie buffs. Written by Brooks and Monica Johnson.
COM                              90 min (ort 93 min)
V                                               RCA

## MODERNS, THE ***
Alan Rudolph           USA                  1988
*Keith Carradine, Linda Fiorentino, Genevieve Bujold, Geraldine Chaplin, Wallace Shawn, Kevin J. O'Connor, John Stone*
The story of a group of Americans living in Paris in 1926 provides the basis for this lavish and complex tale. Carradine (badly miscast) plays an art forger who meets a former lover who is now married to a ruthless businessman. They rekindle their romance, which takes place against the background of the cafes and salons that were the haunt of the intellectuals of the period. Ponderous and uneven, but visually engrossing.
DRA                              121 min (ort 126 min)
V                                               VES

## MODESTY BLAISE **                                 PG
Joseph Losey           UK                   1966
*Monica Vitti, Terence Stamp, Dirk Bogarde, Harry Andrews, Michael Craig, Clive Revill, Scilla Gabel, Tina Marquand, Rosella Falk, Joe Melia, Lex Schoorel, Alexander Knox*
A film version of a comic strip female super-heroine hired to protect a diamond shipment, with Bogarde extremely well cast as the villain out to get it. A high-camp spoof in the 1960s tradition, that loses its direction rather too often. The comic strip was by Peter O'Donnell.
COM                                          120 min
B,V                                             CBS

## MOHAWK **
Kurt Neumann           USA                  1956
*Scott Brady, Rita Gam, Lori Nelson, Neville Brand, Allison Hayes, John Hoyt, Vera Vague, Rhys Williams, Ted de Corsia, Mae Clarke, John Hudson, Tommy Cook, Michael Granger, James Lilburn, Chabon Jadi*
The story of frontier conflict between Indians and settlers, with the local landowners out to prevent Indians settling in the Mohawk Valley, by inciting them to war. Fortunately an Easterner and his Indian girlfriend thwart their plans. A deft little tale, that

borrows footage from "Drums Along The Mohawk".
WES                                    80 min
B,V,V2                                    INT

## MOLLY AND LAWLESS JOHN **
Gary Nelson          USA              1972
Vera Miles, Clu Gulager, Sam Elliott, John Anderson,
Cynthia Mayers, Charles A. Pinney, Robert
Westmoreland, Melinda Chavaria, George LeBow,
Grady Hill
An outlaw in jail persuades the sheriff's wife to help
him escape and they run away together, but as their
journey proceeds, his interest in her starts to wane. A
competent little time-filler.
WES                                    98 min
B,V                                      MOV

## MOLLY MAGUIRES, THE ***           PG
Martin Ritt          USA              1970
Sean Connery, Richard Harris, Samantha Eggar,
Frank Finlay, Art Lund, Bethel Leslie, Anthony Zerbe,
Anthony Costello
This tells the true story of a secret Irish terrorist
group which conspired amongst Irish miners in Penn-
sylvania in 1876, and of the informer who infiltrated
the group in order to betray them to the authorities. A
sombre and detailed film, that lacks depth to the
characters and an effective climax. Arthur Conan
Doyle also made use of these events in his tale "The
Valley Of Fear".
Boa: book Lament For Molly Maguires by A.H. Lewis.
DRA                      119 min (ort 123 min)
B,V                                      CIC

## MOM **                              18
Patrick Rand          USA              1989
Mark Thomas Miller, Jeanne Bates, Brion James,
Mary McDonough, Stella Stevens
A young reporter is assigned his first big story, which
involves investigating a series of gruesome murders of
women, in which the remains of each victim was found
to have been partially eaten. Finding a lead that takes
him to his mother's blind lodger, he discovers that the
man is really a demon from Hell and has turned his
mother into a similar creature.
HOR                                    92 min
V                                        EIV

## MOMENT OF TRUTH **                  18
Larry Gross          USA              1984
Adam Baldwin, Deborah Foreman, Ed Lauter, Rene
Auberjonois, Danny De La Paz, Scott McGinnis, John
Scott Clough, Mario Van Peebles
A gang member becomes a reformed character, falling
out with the gang leader and refusing to help him beat
a drugs charge. One of those standard teen-gang
movies in which the story unfolds in an entirely
predictable manner.
Aka: 3.15; 3.15: MOMENT OF TRUTH
DRA              81 min (ort 95 min) Cut (54 sec)
B,V                                      VIR

## MOMENT TO KILL, THE **             15
Anthony Ascott (Giuliano Carmineo)
                     ITALY
George Hilton, Walter Barnes, Loni von Friedel
A judge hires two gunmen, to find a large fortune in
gold belonging to the Confederacy that has been
hidden in the area. Okay for the action sequences, but
the ludicrous dubbing prevents any tension de-
veloping.
WES                              89 min dubbed
B,V,V2          VDM; MOVLAND L/A; PHE (VHS only)

## MOMENTS OF LOVE **                 18
B. Hershey          USA              1975
John C. Holmes, Nicole Black, Ron Jeremy, Rhonda
Jo Petty, Lisa De Leeuw, Herschel Savage, Danielle,
Jesse Adams

An inept doctor mistakenly tells a woman she only
has a year to live. She has always wanted to be a
writer, and so she decides to embark on a series of
sexual escapades in order to have something to write
about. When our doctor realises his error he telephones her with the good news, but by that time her
lurid tales have made her a celebrity.
A                                      39 min
B,V                              TCX; TOW

## MOMMIE DEAREST **                  15
Frank Perry          USA              1981
Faye Dunaway, Diana Scarwid, Steve Forrest, Howard
Da Silva, Mara Hobel, Rutanya Alda, Harry Goz,
Michael Edwards, Jocelyn Brando, Priscilla Pointer,
Joe Abdullah, Garry Allen, Selma Archered, Adrian
Aron, Xander Berkeley
Film version of a book by Crawford's adopted daugh-
ter describing her loveless upbringing at the hands of
this star. The book caused a stir when published, as it
upset many of Crawford's fans, this film may do the
same. Despite being undeniably well put together and
acted, it's hard to see what audience the film is aimed
at, as its appeal is so limited.
Aka: MOMMY DEAREST
Boa: book by Christine Crawford.
DRA                      124 min (ort 129 min)
B,V                                      CIC

## MON ONCLE ***                       U
Jacques Tati          FRANCE          1956
Jacques Tati, Jean Pierre Zola, Adrienne Servantie,
Yvonne Arnaud, Alain Becourt
An accident-prone uncle visits his nephew at his
ultra-modern gadget-ridden home, and causes havoc.
This second Tati excursion suffers badly from its lack
of dialogue and depends rather too heavily on a nearly
continuous succession of sight gags. For all that, it is
still well worth a look. Followed by PLAYTIME. AA:
Foreign.
Aka: MY UNCLE; MY UNCLE MISTER HULOT
COM                      105 min (ort 116 min)
B,V,V2          VDM L/A; VMA L/A; STABL

## MONA LISA ***                       18
Neil Jordan          UK              1986
Bob Hoskins, Cathy Tyson, Michael Caine, Robbie
Coltrane, Clarke Peters, Kate Hardie, Zoe Nathenson
A small-time crook fresh out of prison, is given the job
of acting as chauffeur to a high-class prostitute, and
becomes deeply involved with her, while not being
aware of just how sordid her life is. Excellent perform-
ances are combined with a sound if squalid story.
Written by Jordan and David Leland.
DRA                      104 min; 99 min (WHV)
B, V/h              CAN; WHV (VHS only)

## MONDO TRASHO
John Waters          USA              1969
Divine (Glenn Milstead), Mary Vivian Pearce, Mink
Stole, David Lochary
Another bad taste cult film, best described (in the
director's own words) as a "gutter film". In this
mishmash of sleaze, Divine runs over Pearce in her
Cadillac, and decides to take the body of her victim
along for the ride. This is all done to the accompani-
ment of 1960s pop tunes. This was Waters' first
feature-length effort, and lacks the sharp dialogue
that made his later films a good deal more enjoyable.
Osca: SEX MADNESS
COM                      94 min (ort 130 min)
B,V                                      PVG

## MONEY MANIA ***                      U
Richard Fleischer          USA          1987
Tom Bosley, Eddie Deezen, Rich Hall, Wendy
Sherman, Rick Overton, Mona Lyden, Douglas
Emerson, Royce D. Applegate, Pam Matteson, Daniel
McDonald, Penny Baker, Tawny Fere, LaGena Hart,

*Mack Dryden*
Comedy thriller about a mad hunt for a missing four
million dollars, the clues to its whereabouts contained
in the last words of a dying government agent. Highly
reminiscent in its concept of ITS A MAD, MAD, MAD,
MAD WORLD but a good deal more spirited.
Aka: MILLION DOLLAR MYSTERY
COM                                          90 min
B,V                                          CBS

### MONEY MOVERS ***
Bruce Beresford      AUSTRALIA              1978
*Charles Tingwell, Terence Donovan, Ed Devereaux,*
*Tony Bonner, Lucky Grills, Allan Cassel, Frank*
*Wilson, Candy Richmond*
An armoured payroll van is attacked and robbed, but
this is merely an overture to a much larger multi-
dollar theft by the members of a security company. An
adroit thriller, based on a real incident.
THR                                          95 min
B,V,V2                                       GHV

### MONEY ON THE SIDE **                      15
Robert Collins       USA                    1982
*Jamie Lee Curtis, Karen Valentine, Christopher Lloyd,*
*Linda Purl, Richard Masur, Gary Graham, Edward*
*Edwards, John Bennett Perry, Joe Lambie, Susan*
*Flannery, Arthur Rosenberg, Lee DeBroux, Terry*
*Burns, John H. Fields*
Two housewives turn to prostitution to make some
extra money, but find themselves ensnared by a vice
syndicate. Average.
Boa: story by Mort Fine.
DRA                        91 min (ort 100 min) mTV
V                                            RCA

### MONEY PIT, THE *                           15
Richard Benjamin     USA                    1986
*Tom Hanks, Shelley Long, Alexander Godunov,*
*Maureen Stapleton, Joe Mantegna, Philip Bosco, Josh*
*Mostel, Yakov Smirnoff, Carmine Caridi, Brian*
*Backer, Mia Dillon, Billy Lombardo, John Van*
*Dreelan, Douglass Watson, Lucille Dobrin*
Essentially an updating of MISTER BLANDINGS
BUILD HIS DREAM HOUSE but without the latter's
wit and charm. A young couple buy a fine house in the
country at an unbelievably low price, and find them-
selves stuck with a worthless property that just
swallows money. This strains their patience. (And
mine.)
COM                        88 min (ort 91 min)
V/sh                                         CIC

### MONEY, POWER, MURDER **                    15
Lee Philips          USA                    1989
*Kevin Dobson, Blythe Danner, Josef Sommer, John*
*Cullum*
A reporter for a cable news station investigates the
disappearance of a network anchor-woman and in-
advertently uncovers a nasty conspiracy involving a
network chief and a TV preacher.
THR                                          91 min
V                                            CBS

### MONEY TO BURN **
Virginia Lively Stone    USA                1976
*Jack Kruschen, David Wallace, Meegan King, Phillip*
*Pine*
Three senior citizens plan to rob a Federal Reserve
Bank of 50 million dollars. A pleasant but unmemor-
able comedy.
COM                        80 min (ort 104 min)
B,V                                          PRV

### MONGREL *                                  15
Robert Burns         USA                    1983
*Aldo Ray, Terry Evans, Mitch Peleggi, Catherine*
*Molloy, Jonathan M. Ingraffia, Andy Tiemann, Rachel*
*Winfree, Daniel Medina, John Dodson, Saint Blaze,*

*Dennis Hall, Janis Dickerson, Bryan Spires, Allen*
*Eaves, David Minter*
A man living in a rundown boarding house in Texas,
believes himself to be a dog and goes around attacking
people.
HOR                        84 min (ort 90 min)
B,V                                INT L/A; XTASY

### MONKEY BUSINESS **                          U
Howard Hawks         USA                    1952
*Cary Grant, Ginger Rogers, Charles Coburn, Marilyn*
*Monroe, Hugh Marlow, Henri Leondal, Robert*
*Cornthwaite, Larry Keating, Douglas Spencer, Esther*
*Dale, George Winslow, Emmett Lynn, Jerry Sheldon*
A research chemist invents a rejuvenation drug,
which a laboratory chimpanzee accidentally pours into
the water cooler, so that he, his wife and his boss all
suffer from its effects. A laboured comedy, with plenty
of star talent, but disappointingly few laughs. Written
by Ben Hecht, Charles Lederer and I.A.L. Diamond.
Aka: DARLING I AM GROWING YOUNGER
COM                        91 min (ort 97 min) B/W
V                                            CBS

### MONKEY GRIP *
Ken Cameron          AUSTRALIA              1982
*Noni Hazelhurst, Colin Friels, Harold Hopkins, Alice*
*Garner, Candy Raymond*
A single mother faces a whole lot of problems in her
life, including a boyfriend who is a drug addict. A
dreary and pointless yarn.
Boa: novel by H. Garner.
DRA                        101 min (ort 117 min)
B,V                                          FTV

### MONKEY SHINES: AN EXPERIMENT IN
### FEAR **                                     18
George A. Romero     USA                    1988
*Jason Beghe, John Pankow, Melanie Parker, Kate*
*McNeil, Joyce Van Patten, Christine Forrest, Stephen*
*Root*
Written by Romero, this horror-thriller concerns a
young man who is confined to a wheelchair as a
quadraplegic, following a serious accident. A super-
intelligent monkey (it has been injected with human
brain cells) is brought in as a companion, and begins
to anticipate his every wish, but this includes a desire
for revenge against those he blames for his predica-
ment. A strange blend of horror and black humour.
Music is by David Shire.
Boa: novel by Michael Stewart.
HOR                        108 min (ort 115 min)
V                                            VIR

### MONKEY'S UNCLE, THE **                      U
Robert Stevenson     USA                    1964
*Tommy Kirk, Leon Arnes, Annette Funicello, Frank*
*Faylen, Arthur O'Connell, Norman Grabowski*
A college student experiments with both sleep-
learning and flying machines. A sequel to THE
MISADVENTURES OF MERLIN JONES, that's
short on laughs and long on banality. The flying
sequences are a highlight.
COM                                          87 min
B,V                                          WDV

### MONKEYS, GO HOME! *                         U
Andrew V. McLaglen   USA                    1966
*Dean Jones, Maurice Chevalier, Yvette Mimieux,*
*Bernard Woringer, Clement Harari, Yvonne Constant,*
*Marcel Hillaire*
A man inherits an olive grove in France, and trains
monkeys to pick the crop. An insubstantial comedy
with precious few jokes, and an almost invisible plot.
This was Chevalier's last film appearance.
Aka: MONKEYS GO HOME
Boa: novel The Monkeys by G.R. Wilkinson.
JUV                        86 min (ort 101 min)
B,V                                          WDV

## MONSIEUR HIRE *** 15
Patrice Leconte    FRANCE    1989
*Michel Blanc, Sandrine Bonnaire, Andre Wilms, Luc Thuiller*
A restrained and wisely underplayed adaptation of the original novel, whose central figure is a voyeuristic middle-aged tailor who becomes the chief suspect following the murder of a young girl. He spends much of his time spying through his window at a young girl who lives opposite, and a strange and touching relationship develops, and the two disparate strands of this story are eventually brought together in this absorbing and unusual drama.
Boa: novel Les Fiancailles De M. Hire by Georges Simenon.
DRA                                    80 min
V                                       PAL

## MONSIEUR HULOT'S HOLIDAY *** U
Jacques Tati    FRANCE    1953
*Jacques Tati, Nathalie Pascaud, Michelle Rolla, Valentine Camax, Louis Perrault*
An accident-prone bachelor reduces a seaside resort to chaos in the first Tati comedy (rather charmingly done in the style of a silent) to introduce this character. Beautifully timed routines make this a memorable work. Followed by: MON ONCLE, PLAYTIME and TRAFFIC, in that order.
Aka: LES VACANCES DE MONSIEUR HULOT; MISTER HULOT'S HOLIDAY
COM                     91 min (ort 114 min) B/W
B,V                              VDM L/A; VMA

## MONSIEUR VINCENT *****
Mauriche Cloche    FRANCE    1947
*Pierre Fresnay, Aime Clairiond, Gabrielle Dorziat, Lise Delamare, Jean Debucourt, Michel Bouquet*
A marvellous and deeply moving biographical film on the work of Saint Vincent de Paul, who devoted his life to the service of the poor, and founded an order of nuns in the 17th century. Made with financial assistance from the Catholic Church, but an inspiring work that delivers no sermons. AA: Spec Award (most outstanding foreign language film released in the USA in 1948 – at this time there was no separate Best Foreign Film category).
DRA                                  118 min B/W
B,V                                      PVG

## MONSIGNOR * 15
Frank Perry    USA    1982
*Christopher Reeve, Genevieve Bujold, Fernando Rey, Jason Miller, Joe Cortese, Adolfo Celi, Leonardo Cimino, Tomas Milian, Robert J. Prosky*
Long, boring tale of an American Army chaplain, who rises to a position of great power within the Vatican by apparently breaking every moral rule in the book, including having an affair with a nun. An affront to both Catholics and film-lovers in equal measure.
Boa: novel by Jack Alain Leger
DRA                     116 min (ort 121 min)
B,V                                      CBS

## MONSTER * 18
Barbara Peeters    USA    1980
*Doug McClure, Vic Morrow, Ann Turkel, Cindy Weintraub, Anthony Penya, Denise Galik*
Underwater vegetable monsters go on the rampage in a small coastal resort, raping all the women in sight, and generally making a thorough nuisance of themselves in this garish low-grade yarn. Another ludicrously bad offering from the Roger Corman studios, but be warned, the ending is not for the squeamish.
Aka: HUMANOIDS FROM THE DEEP; HUMANOIDS OF THE DEEP
HOR                     77 min (ort 80 min)
B,V                                      WHV

## MONSTER CLUB, THE * 15
Roy Ward Baker    UK    1980
*Vincent Price, John Carradine, Barbara Kellerman, Simon Ward, Donald Pleasence, Richard Johnson, Britt Ekland, Stuart Whitman, Lesley Dunlop, Patrick Magee, Roger Sloman, James Laurenson, Geoffrey Bayldon, Warren Saire*
A vampire takes his victim to a club, at which assorted monsters tell their stories. A tongue-in-cheek horror yarn, with no chills and fewer laughs.
Boa: short stories by R. Chetwynd-Hayes.
HOR            93 min; 94 min (CH5) (ort 97 min)
B,V                     PRV L/A; CH5 (VHS only)

## MONSTER DOG * 18
Clyde Anderson (Claudio Fragusso)
                        USA    1986
*Alice Cooper, Eduard Sarli, Victoria Vera, Carlos Samurio, Pepita Sames, Emilio Linder, Jose Sarsa, B. Barita Bari, Ricardo Palacios, Luis Mallenda, Charly Bravo, Fernando Conde, Fernando Baeza, Nino Bastida*
A musician is accused of being a werewolf by the local villagers after a series of strange murders occur. A silly monster film of little merit.
HOR                                    81 min
B,V                                 VPD; TWE

## MONSTER HIGH * 18
Rudiger Poe    USA    1988
*Diana Frank, Dean Landoli, David Mariott, Robert M. Lind*
A witless spoof on the theme of extra-terrestrial invaders. A bunch of dumb aliens from the planet Polyester attempt to destroy Earth but are thwarted by an even dumber bunch of high school kids.
COM                                    96 min
V                                       RCA

## MONSTER IN THE CLOSET, THE * 15
Bob Dahlin    USA    1983 (released 1986)
*Donald Grant, Denise DuBarry, Claude Akins, Howard Duff, Donald Moffat, Paul Dooley, John Carradine, Stella Stevens, Henry Gibson, Frank Ashmore, Paul Walker, Jesse White*
A fine cast can do little with this silly 1950s horror spoof, in which an indestructible monster lurking in a closet, causes a national emergency as it goes on the rampage. Written by Dahlin.
HOR                     86 min (ort 100 min)
B,V                                      VPD

## MONSTER SQUAD, THE ** 15
Fred Dekker    USA    1987
*Andre Gower, Duncan Regehr, Stan Shaw, Stephen Macht, Tom Noonan, Robby Kiger, Brent Chalem, Ryan Lambert, Ashley Bank*
Some kids get the thrill of their lives when their favourite monsters make an unexpected visit to their home town, and all to find a magic amulet, desperately required by Dracula. A likeable homage to this genre, that remains rather too insipid to really get going, although the ending is suitably climactic (courtesy of Richard Edlund's special effects).
COM                     79 min (ort 82 min)
B,V                                 RCA; VCC

## MONSTROID * 
Kenneth Hartford    USA    1978
*John Carradine, Jim Mitchum, Phil Carey, Tony Eisley, Keenan Wynn, Cesar Romero, Diane McBain, Roger Clark, Stella Calle, John Lamont, Kelly Sill, Fernando Corredor, Jade Stuart, Glenn Ransom*
A village in the jungles of Columbia is attacked by a flesh-eating monster from the depths of a lake, in this predictable effort.
Aka: IT CAME FROM THE LAKE; MONSTER
HOR                     80 min (ort 93 min)
B,V,V2                                   INT

## MONTANA BELLE *
Allan Dwan                    USA                    1952
*Jane Russell, George Brent, Scott Brady, Andy Devine,*
*Forrest Tucker, Jack Lambert, Ray Teal, Rory*
*Mallinson, Roy Barcroft, John Litel, Ned Davenport,*
*Dick Elliott, Eugene (Gene) Roth, Stanley Andrews,*
*Holly Bane*
Belle Starr is involved with the Dalton Gang, but is
persuaded to go straight and help the law. A very dull
Western that even the considerable charms of Russell
cannot save.
Osca: BUNDLE OF JOY
WES                          79 min (ort 82 min) B/W
B,V                                                KVD

## MONTANA TRAP *
Peter Schamoni
            SPAIN/WEST GERMANY                1976
*Hardy Kruger, Peter Schamoni, Stephen Boyd*
A tale of robbery, treachery etc. in the Old West.
Aka: MASSACRE ON CONDOR PASS; POTATO-
FRITZ
WES                                          96 min
B,V                                        VCL/CBS

## MONTE CARLO OR BUST! *                      PG
Ken Annakin          UK/USA                    1969
*Tony Curtis, Terry-Thomas, Peter Cook, Dudley*
*Moore, Eric Sykes, Susan Hampshire, Gert Frobe, Jack*
*Hawkins, Bourvil (Andre Raimbourg), Lando*
*Buzzanca, Walter Chiari, Mireille Darc, Marie Dubois,*
*Nicoletta Machiavelli*
Limply directed and wildly unfunny account of a car
journey through Europe to Monte Carlo. Set in the
1920s and misfiring on all cylinders.
Aka: THOSE DARING YOUNG MEN IN THEIR
JAUNTY JALOPIES
COM                                         132 min
B,V                                            CIC

## MONTE CARLO: PARTS 1 AND 2 **              PG
Anthony Page            USA                    1986
*Joan Collins, George Hamilton, Lauren Hutton,*
*Malcolm McDowell, Robert Carradine, Leslie Phillips,*
*Lisa Eilbacher, Philip Madoc, Peter Vaughn, Henri*
*Garcin, Clement Harari, Rainer Harold, Steve Kalfa,*
*David Quilter*
Set in Monaco in 1940, this tells of a glamorous band
of refugees, for whom the principality is a haven from
the harsh realities of WW2. A beautiful international
cabaret singer arrives, who leads a secret life as a
double agent working for the Allies. Soon involved in
a love affair with a writer, she is arrested by the
Gestapo when they learn of her exploits. A kind of big,
glossy and superficial follow-on to SINS.
Boa: novel by Stephen Sheppard.
DRA          180 min (2 cassettes – ort 240 min) mTV
B,V                                            NWV

## MONTENEGRO **                               18
Dusan Makavejev   SWEDEN/UK                    1981
*Susan Anspach, Erland Josephson, Per Oscarsson,*
*John Zacharias, Svetozar Cvetkovic, Patricia Gelin,*
*Bora Todorovic*
A bored American housewife living in Sweden, takes
up with Yugoslavian workers at a noisy bar which
they frequent, eventually finding herself a lover, but
ultimately murdering him. A reasonably entertaining
drama, that tries to be a good deal more meaningful
than its script allows.
Aka: MONTENEGRO: OR PIGS AND PEARLS
DRA                                          96 min
B,V,V2                                  GHV; VGM

## MONTH IN THE COUNTRY, A **                  PG
Quentin Lawrence        USA                    1985
*Susannah York, Ian McShane, Linda Thorson*
Film version of a play about a passionate affair
between a young tutor and a young woman. Compe-

tent but unmemorable.
Boa: play by Ivan Turgenev.
DRA                                          90 min
B,V                                            PRV

## MONTH IN THE COUNTRY, A ***                 PG
Pat O'Connor            UK                      1987
*Colin Firth, Kenneth Branagh, Natasha Richardson,*
*Patrick Malahide, Tony Haygarth, Jim Carter,*
*Richard Vernon, Tom Baker, Vicki Arundale, Martin*
*O'Neil, Ellen O'Brien, Elizabeth Anson, Barbara*
*Marten, Kenneth Kitson*
Two young men, both worn out veterans of the WW1
trenches, meet when they come to a church in a little
Yorkshire village. One slowly uncovers a medieval
fresco inside, whilst the other proceeds to excavate
Saxon relics in the churchyard. An engrossing study,
charting the slow recovery of two men from the
rigours of war, and their developing friendships with
the local people.
Boa: novel by J.R. Carr.
DRA                              93 min (ort 96 min)
B/sh, V/sh                                     WHV

## MONTH OF SUNDAYS, A ***                     PG
Allan Kroeker           USA                    1989
*Hume Cronyn, Vincent Gardenia, Michelle Scarabelli,*
*Tandy Cronyn*
A poignant look at the problems of old age as seen in
the lives of two friends who are spending their final
days in a retirement home. The story is simple and
lacking in action, but the refreshing lack of sen-
timentality makes for an absorbing drama whose tone
is lightened by a few comic touches.
DRA                                          98 min
V                                            FUTUR

## MONTY PYTHON AND THE HOLY GRAIL ***    15
Terry Gilliam/Terry Jones
            UK                                 1975
*Graham Chapman, John Cleese, Terry Gilliam, Eric*
*Idle, Terry Jones, Michael Palin, Carole Cleveland,*
*Connie Booth, Neil Innes, John Young, Bee Duffell,*
*Rita Davies, Sally Kinghorn*
First feature from the team who produced the TV
series "Monty Python's Flying Circus". This is a
surreal look at the legend of the Knights of the Round
Table and their quest for the Holy Grail. No more
than a linked series of sketches of uneven quality, but
held together by a good feel for the period. Followed by
MONTY PYTHON'S LIFE OF BRIAN.
COM                           90 min; 88 min (CBS)
B,V                          BWV; CBS (VHS only)

## MONTY PYTHON'S LIFE OF BRIAN ***          15
Terry Jones             UK                      1979
*John Cleese, Graham Chapman, Eric Idle, Terry*
*Gilliam, Terry Jones, Michael Palin, Carol Clevland,*
*Neil Innes, Spike Milligan, Ken Colley, Gwen Taylor,*
*Terrence Bayler, Charles McKeown, Sue Jones,*
*Bernard McKenna, Chris Langham*
Intermittently amusing satire on a failure whose life
runs parallel to that of Christ, to the extent of even
having a following (of sorts) of his own. When
released, it caused considerable offence among some
religious groups, and was even banned in Norway.
Certainly not one for the devout. Written by John
Cleese and the other members of the "Monty Python"
team, and their most sustained effort to date. Fol-
lowed by MONTY PYTHON'S MEANING OF LIFE.
Aka: LIFE OF BRIAN, THE
COM                           93 min; 90 min (CBS)
B,V,V2                       TEVP; CBS (VHS only)

## MONTY PYTHON'S MEANING OF LIFE ***        15
Terry Jones             UK                      1983
*Graham Chapman, John Cleese, Terry Gilliam, Eric*
*Idle, Terry Jones, Michael Palin, Carol Cleveland,*
*Simon Jones, Patricia Quinn, Judy Loe, Andrew*

*MacLachlan, Valerie Whittington, Jennifer Franks, Angela Mann*
The third film spin-off from the surrealistic TV comedy series "Monty Python's Flying Circus", that began with MONTY PYTHON AND THE HOLY GRAIL (if we exclude AND NOW FOR SOMETHING COMPLETELY DIFFERENT). This cheerfully chaotic look at life and death takes shots at a whole range of subjects, and has some remarkable (if nauseating) sequences. Best enjoyed on an empty stomach.
Aka: MEANING OF LIFE, THE

| COM | 86 min (ort 107 min) |
| V/h | CIC |

## MOON 44 **  15
Roland Emmerich                          1989
*Michael Pare, Malcolm McDowell, Lisa Eichhorn, Brian Thompson, Leon Rippy, Stephen Geoffreys, Roscoe Lee Browne, Dean Devlin*
High-budget, low-brow SF thriller set in a future that's controlled by interplanetary mining corporations who provide the chemicals that are now the only source of fuel on Earth. An undercover cop posing as a helicopter pilot is sent to stop ore freighters being hijacked, but the impressive special effects of Volker Engel fail to maintain interest in this elaborate Europroduction that's filmed in Germany.

| FAN | 95 min |
| V | MED |

## MOON CHILD *
Alan Gadney                USA                1972
*Victor Buono, John Carradine, Janet Landgard, Mike Travis, Pat Renella, Frank Corsentino, William Challee, Marie Denn*
An unearthly child reincarnates every 25 years, and is caught up in a world of ghosts and demons.
Aka: MOONCHILD

| HOR | 90 min |
| B,V,V2 | GOV |

## MOON IN SCORPIO **  18
Gary Graver                USA                1987
*Britt Ekland, John Philip Law, William Smith, Lewis Van Bergen, April Wayne, Jillian Kesner, Bruno Marcotulli, Ken Smolka, Thomas Bloom, James Booth, Donna Kei Benz, Don Scribner*
A woman goes on a honeymoon cruise with her Vietnam veteran husband but discovers that two of the passengers are former comrades, and that all three are haunted by memories of wartime atrocities they committed. After several gruesome murders are committed, the passengers become gripped with fear, in this competent thriller.

| THR | 83 min (ort 90 min) |
| B,V | MGM |

## MOON IN THE GUTTER, THE **  18
Jean-Jacques Beineix FRANCE              1983
*Nastassia Kinski, Gerard Depardieu, Victoria Abril, Vittorio Mezzogiorno, Dominique Pinon, Bertice Reading, Milena Vukotic, Bernard Farcy, Anne-Marie Coffient, Katia Berger, Jacques Herlin, Rudo Alberti*
A man seeks out the rapist responsible for his sister's suicide, and becomes involved with a mysterious femme fatale. A highly stylised film, whose flashy camerawork and visual effects totally swamp the plot. Made by the director of DIVA, a film of similar qualities.
Aka: LA LUNE DANS LE CANIVEAU

| DRA | 120 min; 126 min (PAL) |
| B,V | PVG; PAL |

## MOON IS BLUE, THE *  PG
Otto Preminger              USA                1953
*David Niven, William Holden, Maggie McNamara, Tom Tully, Dawn Addams*
A man has a romance with a woman he meets at the top of the Empire State Building, and the usual complications ensue. At the time it caused quite a stir, by using words such as "virgin" and "mistress"; apart from such great excitement it ranks as a flat and boring comedy. Adapted by Herbert.
Boa: play by F. Hugh Herbert.

| COM | 97 min (ort 99 min) B/W |
| B,V | CBS |

## MOON OVER MIAMI ***  U
Walter Lang                USA                1941
*Don Ameche, Betty Grable, Carole Landis, Jack Haley, Charlotte Greenwood, Robert Cummings, Cobina Wright Jr, Robert Greig*
Two sisters leave Texas and head for Florida in the hope of landing rich husbands, in this enjoyable musical remake of "Three Blind Mice". Not a great musical, but tuneful and nicely put together. Songs include "You Started Something", probably the most memorable number. Remade as "Three Little Girls In Blue" and HOW TO MARRY A MILLIONAIRE.
Boa: play Three Blind Mice by Stephen Powys.

| MUS | 88 min (ort 91 min) |
| V | CBS |

## MOON OVER PARADOR **
Paul Mazursky              USA                1988
*Richard Dreyfuss, Raul Julia, Sonia Braga, Jonathan Winters, Michael Greene, Polly Holliday, Charo, Marianne Sagebrecht, Sammy Davis Jr, Dick Cavett, Edward Asner, Ike Pappas*
An American actor is unwillingly persuaded to impersonate a recently-deceased Latin American dictator, and soon finds himself enjoying his role (and the late dictator's sexy mistress). Extremely likeable but hardly the stuff of classic comedy, with a few too many gags that misfire. Co-written by Mazursky (who has a cameo in drag).

| COM | 105 min |
| V | CIC |

## MOON PILOT *  U
James Neilson              USA                1961
*Tom Tryon, Brian Keith, Edmond O'Brien, Dany Saval, Tommy Kirk, Kent Smith, Bob Sweeney, Nancy Culp, Muriel Landers, Simon Scott, Sarah Selby, Bert Rensen, Dick Whittinghill, Robert Brubaker, William Hudson*
An astronaut encounters a strange female alien who seems to know all about him, just prior to his own scheduled trip to the moon. The US Army and the FBI frantically try to keep them apart, in this feeble Disney comedy.

| JUV | 98 min |
| B,V | WDV |

## MOON SPINNERS, THE **  U
James Neilson              UK/USA              1964
*Hayley Mills, Eli Wallach, Joan Greenwood, Pola Negri, Peter McEnery, John Le Mesurier, Irene Papas, Sheila Hancock, Michael Davis, Paul Stassino, Andre Morell, George Pastell, Tutte Lemkow, Steve Plytas, Harry Tardios*
A young girl on holiday in Crete with her aunt, gets involved in helping a young man track down a gang of jewel thieves. A colourful but muddled children's thriller, that goes on rather too long.
Boa: novel by Mary Stewart.

| JUV | 114 min (ort 118 min) |
| B,V | WDV |

## MOON STALLION, THE **  U
Dorothea Brooking
                UK/WEST GERMANY              1978
*James Greene, Sarah Sutton, David Pullan*
A blind girl discovers that she possesses psychic powers as her father, an archaeologist, prepares to undertake an excavation.

| JUV | 95 min |
| B,V | BBC |

## MOONCUSSERS, THE ** U
James Neilson          USA          1962
*Oscar Homolka, Kevin Corcoran, Rian Garrick*
Set in the 1840s, this tells of the plunderers who were
in the habit of causing ships to founder in order to
plunder the wreckage. A worried ship-owner sends his
son to infiltrate a gang of these plunderers and
together with another young companion and his
sister, they enjoy a series of adventures. A wholesome
and fairly undemanding family film.
Boa: novel Flying Ebony by I. Vinton.
JUV                                    82 min
B,V                                    WDV

## MOONLIGHT ** 15
Alan Smithee (Rod Holcomb/Jackie Cooper)
                       USA          1982
*Robert Desiderio, Michelle Phillips, William Porzini,
Carmine Mitore, Penny Santon, Benson Fong, Sandra
Kearns, Christa Linder, Christopher Pennock,
Alexander Zale, Rosalind Chao, Martin Rudy, Hank
Brandt*
A prospective pilot about a fast-food delivery man who
is recruited by a secret intelligence organisation to
help combat international terrorists. The pseudony-
mous name Smithee was credited as director after
Cooper and Holcomb (who took over direction) both
had their names removed. Average.
Aka: MOONLIGHT: MURDER TO GO
THR          72 min Cut (24 sec) (ort 90 min) mTV
V/h                                    CIC

## MOONLIGHTING ***
Jerzy Skolimowski      UK           1982
*Jeremy Irons, Eugene Lipinski, Jiri Stanislaw,
Eugeniusz Haczkyewicz, Dorothy Zienciowska,
Edward Arthur, Denis Holmes, Renu Setna, David
Calder, Judy Gridley, Claire Toeman, Catherine
Harding, David Squire, Mike Sarne*
Four Polish workers come to England to renovate a
house for a rich ex-compatriot. Only their foreman
speaks English, and he keeps them from learning
about the declaration of martial law during the
military takeover in their homeland. A film that is
perceptive, wry and utterly cynical. The script is by
Jerzy Haczkiewicz.
DRA                                    97 min mTV
B,V,V2                                 3MVID

## MOONLIGHTING: THE ORIGINAL TV PG
## MOVIE **
Robert Butler          USA           1985
*Cybill Shepherd, Bruce Willis, Allyce Beasley, Robert
Ellenstein, Jim Mackrell, James Karen, Rebecca
Stanley, Dennis Lipscomb, John Medici, Dennis
Stewart*
A disjointed, overlong pilot for a popular American TV
detective series. A former model is swindled by her
business manager, and is reluctantly forced into a
partnership with the head of the tax-loss agency she
finds her manager has foisted on her. Their first case
involves a confused hunt for Nazi loot, in the form of a
cache of diamonds. A continual emphasis on the
interaction between the two characters takes the
place of a decent plot.
Aka: MOONLIGHTING
A/AD                   93 min (ort 97 min) mTV
V                                      VCC; FUTUR

## MOONRAKER ** PG
Lewis Gilbert          UK           1979
*Roger Moore, Lois Chiles, Richard Kiel, Michael
Lonsdale, Corinne Clery, Bernard Lee, Desmond
Llewelyn, Lois Maxwell, Geoffrey Keen, Emily Bolton,
Toshiro Suga, Blanche Ravalec, Jean-Pierre Castaldi,
Leila Shenna*
Another "James Bond" adventure, with 007 investi-
gating cases of disappearing space shuttles, and
discovering yet another baddy out to control the world

and replace its population with his own genetically
engineered race. Despite a much enlarged budget and
the usual gadgetry, this feels like a tired and mechanical rehash of the previous films. Number eleven in a
series that was beginning to look its age. Followed by
FOR YOUR EYES ONLY.
Boa: novel by Ian Fleming.
A/AD                  121 min (ort 126 min)
V/sh                                   WHV

## MOONRAKER, THE ***
David MacDonald        UK           1957
*George Baker, Sylvia Syms, Peter Arne, Marius
Goring, Richard Leech, Clive Morton, Paul Whitsun-
Jones, Gary Raymond, John Le Mesurier, Patrick
Troughton, Michael Anderson Jr*
This well mounted swashbuckler tells of how, during
the English Civil War, supporters of Charles Stuart
succeed in carrying the King's son off to the safety of
France. An enjoyable blend of action and suspense.
Boa: play by Arthur Watkyn.
A/AD                   79 min (ort 82 min)
V                                      WHV

## MOONRISE ** PG
Frank Borzage          USA           1948
*Ethel Barrymore, Dane Clark, Gail Russell, Allyn
Joslyn, Harry Morgan, Lloyd Bridges, Henry Morgan,
Rex Ingram*
The son of a convicted murderer kills one of his
tormentors and is forced to go on the run, accompanied
by his girlfriend. A good cast make the most of this
carefully detailed but undistinguished melodrama.
DRA                                    90 min B/W
V                                      VMA; STABL

## MOONSHINE COUNTY EXPRESS **
Gus Trikonis           USA           1977
*John Saxon, Susan Howard, William Conrad, Morgan
Woodward, Claudia Jennings, Jeff Corey, Maureen
McCormick, Dub Taylor*
Three daughters decide to carry on their dead father's
moonshining business, after he is murdered by the
local villain. Routine stuff, sustained by a good cast, if
not by the dialogue and plotting.
A/AD                                   90 min
B,V                                    PICMED; VFO

## MOONSTRUCK **** PG
Norman Jewison         USA           1987
*Cher, Nicholas Cage, Olympia Dukakis, Vincent
Gardenia, Danny Aiello, Julie Bovasso, John
Mahoney, Louis Guss, Feodor Chaliapin, Anita
Gillette, Nadia Despotovich, Joe Grifasi, Gina
DeAngelis, Robin Bartlett, Helen Hanft*
Set in Brooklyn, this tells of an Italian-American
woman who falls madly in love with the brother of the
man she is engaged to marry. A refreshing and
sharply observed Fellini-style look at life, transported
to the New World. AA: Actress (Cher), S. Actress
(Dukakis), Screen (Orig) (John Patrick Shanley).
COM                   98 min (ort 103 min)
V                                      MGM

## MOONTRAP ** PG
Robert Dyke            USA           1988
*Walter Koenig, Bruce Campbell, Leigh Lombardi*
On a routine space flight, two astronauts discover an
abandoned alien ship and retrieve a strange metal
sphere from it. A mission to the Moon follows where
remnants of an ancient civilisation are discovered
together with a woman held in suspended animation.
A film that bears some similarity to LIFEFORCE and
is in many ways as foolish, although the special effects
are excellent.
FAN                                    86 min
B,V                                    PARK

**MOONTREK \*** U
Jean Image      FRANCE      1984
Animated story of an expedition from 18th century France to the moon, in order to discover the secret of eternal life; the expedition being commissioned by an astronomer aptly named Sirius. Some good ideas are let down by indifferent animation and a thin plot.
Aka: LE SECRET DES SELENITES; MOON MADNESS
CAR      80 min
B,V      GHV; PHE (VHS only)

**MOONWALKER \*\*** PG
Jerry Kramer/Colin Chilvers
     USA      1988
*Michael Jackson, Sean Lennon, Joe Pesci, Brandon Adams, Kellie Parker*
A musical fantasy vehicle for Jackson, that rather clumsily intercuts some of his best numbers with a series of bizarre images, that purport to show a struggle between good and evil. Really nothing more than a crudely exploitative pop video/fairytale that's worth hearing but not worth seeing.
MUS      89 min
V/sh      GHV

**MORE DESIRES WITHIN YOUNG GIRLS \*\*** 18
     WEST GERMANY      198-
*Marianne Albert, Kitty Hilaire, Laurence Eymazel*
Six Swedish girls on holiday in Ibiza have a thoroughly good time.
Aka: SECHS SCHWEDINNEN AUF IBIZA
A      73 min (Cut at film release)
B,V      18PLAT/TOW L/A; PRI L/A; SHEP

**MORE THAN SISTERS \***
Russ Carlson      USA      1979
*Jamie Gillis, Leslie Murray, Eric Edwards, Coleen Anderson, Russ Carlson, Marlene Willoughby*
The story is about Siamese twins who have been separated at birth, and have no knowledge of each other's existence (or body scars for that matter). One is happily, married whilst the other is being held in an insane asylum, where she suffers sexual abuse at the hands of the doctors. Finding that they can communicate telepathically, the incarcerated woman relays the trauma of her experiences to her twin, in this nasty and disturbing film.
A      90 min
V      RIP

**MORE THINGS CHANGE, THE \*\*** PG
Robyn Nevin      USA
*Barry Otto, Judy Morris, Victoria Longley*
A couple decide to give up living in the city and move to a farm, where the husband takes over the job of looking after their young son whilst his wife continues her city job. To relieve the tension arising from their change of roles they hire a childminder, but this only complicates matters.
DRA      91 min
V      RCA

**MORECOMBE AND WISE: NIGHT TRAIN TO MURDER \*** PG
Joe McGrath      UK      1984
*Eric Morecombe, Ernie Wise, Lysette Anthony, Fulton MacKay, Kenneth Haigh*
Comic-duo Morecombe and Wise star in this parody of some of the writings of great thriller writers such as Edgar Wallace, Raymond Chandler and Agatha Christie, and get involved in a 1940s murder mystery when they decide to take care of Eric's niece.
Aka: NIGHT TRAIN TO MURDER
COM      70 min mTV
V      VCC

**MORECOMBE AND WISE: THAT RIVIERA TOUCH \*** PG
Cliff Owen      UK      1966
*Eric Morecombe, Ernie Wise, Suzanne Lloyd, Paul Stassino, Armand Mestral, George Eugeniou, George Pastell, Peter Jeffrey, Gerald Lawson, Michael Forest, Paul Danquah, Francis Matthews, George Moon*
Dreadful, utterly dreadful. Our comedy duo of TV fame are now tourists on the Riviera, and become involved with jewel thieves. British comedy at its absolute rock bottom worst.
Aka: THAT RIVIERA TOUCH
COM      98 min; 94 min (VCC)
B,V      RNK; VCC

**MORECOMBE AND WISE: THE INTELLIGENCE MEN \*** U
Robert Asher      UK      1965
*Eric Morecombe, Ernie Wise, William Franklyn, April Olrich, Richard Vernon, Gloria Paul, David Lodge, Jacqueline Jones, Terence Alexander, Francis Matthews, Warren Mitchell, Brian Oulton, Peter Bull, Joe Melia, Tutte Lemkow*
Comedy duo Morecombe and Wise are here cast as two incompetent spies who go from mishap to mishap, eventually saving a Russian ballerina from assassination, with the help of a waitress. One of those ghastly British attempts at comedy that almost makes one squirm with embarrassment.
Aka: INTELLIGENCE MEN, THE; SPYLARKS
COM      104 min; 99 min (VCC)
B,V      RNK; VCC (VHS only)

**MORECOMBE AND WISE: THE MAGNIFICENT TWO \*** PG
Cliff Owen      UK      1967
*Eric Morecombe, Ernie Wise, Margit Saad, Cecil Parker, Isobel Black, Martin Benson, Virgilio Teixeira, Michael Godfrey, Sue Sylvaine, Andreas Malandrinos, Victor Maddern*
Third, and thankfully last, film in the 1960s series employing the talents of the popular TV comedy duo. This time round, one of a pair of fairly useless travelling salesmen is mistaken for the leader of a coup in a Latin American country. Grade zero on the laugh scale.
Aka: MAGNIFICENT TWO, THE
COM      96 min; 91 min (VCC) (ort 100 min)
B,V      RNK; VCC

**MORGAN: A SUITABLE CASE FOR TREATMENT \***
Karel Reisz      UK      1966
*Vanessa Redgrave, David Warner, Irene Handl, Robert Stephens, Newton Blick, Nan Munro, Bernard Bresslaw, Arthur Mullard, Graham Crowden, John Rae, Peter Collingwood*
An artist refuses to accept that his wife is divorcing him, and does everything he can to win her back. Good ideas swim about aimlessly in what is neither a comedy nor a satire. Screenplay is by David Mercer from his own play.
Aka: MORGAN!
Boa: TV play by David Mercer.
COM      93 min (ort 97 min) B/W
B,V      TEVP

**MORITURI \*\*** 15
Bernard Wicki      USA      1965
*Marlon Brando, Yul Brynner, Janet Margolin, Trevor Howard, Wally Cox, William Redfield, Carl Esmond*
A convoluted WW2 adventure telling of how an anti-Nazi pacifist onboard a German freighter and apparently out to help the British, is in reality a German spy. A few moments of suspense give way to general tedium, though the photography of Conrad Hall is a distinct asset.
Aka: MORITURI: THE SABOTEUR; SABOTEUR, THE: CODE NAME MORITURI

Boa: novel by Werner Jeorg Kosa

WAR 123 min B/W
V/h CBS

## MORITZ * 18
Mark Bohm    WEST GERMANY    1978
*Michael Kebschull, Kershin Wehlmann, Uwe
Enkelmann, Grete Mosheim*
A troubled teenage boy retreats into a world of
fantasy, but eventually re-emerges via his involve-
ment with a rock band.
Aka: MORITZ, DEAR MORITZ; MORITZ, LIEBER
MORITZ

DRA 92 min (ort 97 min)
B,V JVI L/A; WISE

## MORNING AFTER, THE * 15
Sidney Lumet    USA    1986
*Jane Fonda, Jeff Bridges, Raul Julia, Diane Salinger,
Richard Foronjy, James Haake, Geoffrey Scott,
Kathleen Wilhoite, Don Hood, Fran Bennett, Michael
Flanagan, Bruce Vilanch, Michael Prince, Frances
Bergen, Bob Minor*
A fading actress with a drink problem wakes up to
find a corpse on her bed, and is unable to understand
how it got there. A star cast are saddled with a heavy
and opaque script, that never develops beyond a few
meaningless exchanges.

THR 102 min (ort 104 min)
V/sh GHV

## MORNING MAN, THE ** 18
Daniele J. Suissa    USA    1986
*Bruno Doyon, Kerrie Keane, Alan Fawcett, Marc
Strange, Linda Smith, Marc Blutman, Walter Massey,
Rob Roy*
A man sentenced to twenty years jail for a spate of
armed robberies, decides to prove he can live honestly
and escapes, getting a job as a radio announcer at a
local station. However, his past soon begins to catch
up with him.

THR 99 min
B,V TGP

## MORONS FROM OUTER SPACE * PG
Mike Hodges    UK    1984
*Mel Smith, Griff Rhys Jones, Dinsdale Landen, James
B. Sikking, Paul Brown, Joanne Pearce, Jimmy Nail,
Tristram Jellinek, George Innes, John Joyce, Mark
Jones, Leonard Fenton, Andrew Maranne, Joanna
Dickens, R.J. Bell*
Some not very intelligent aliens land on Earth in
what must have looked like a very funny idea, that
might have worked as a 10-minute sketch, but just
does not develop sufficiently to sustain a full-length
feature. A few good sight gags simply do not suffice.

COM 86 min (ort 97 min)
B,V TEVP

## MORTUARY ** 18
Howard Avedis    USA    1981
*Christopher George, Lynda Day George, Bill Paxton,
Mary McDonough, David Wallace, Curt Ayers, Beth
Schaffel*
A young woman has nightmares which have a habit of
coming true. She and a friend discover that the local
mortician is the head of a witches' coven, and find
themselves in deadly peril. A low-budget chiller with
a few good moments.
Aka: EMBALMED (MIG)

HOR 87 min (ort 91 min) Cut (2 min 13 sec)
B,V HOK L/A; MIG

## MORTUARY ACADEMY * 18
Michael Schroeder    USA    1988
*Paul Bartel, Mary Woronov, Perry Lang, Christopher
Atkins, Cesar Romero*
Two brothers stand to inherit a fortune from their late
uncle, but only if they graduate from the title

establishment. The usual foolish capers and juvenile
humour ensues. A film that is best described as
slapstick with corpses; which in the utterly over-the-
top climax come to life – more than can be said for the
script.

COM 82 min (ort 91 min)
B,V FUTUR

## MOSCOW ON THE HUDSON *** 15
Paul Mazursky    USA    1984
*Robin Williams, Maria Conchita Alonso, Cleavant
Derricks, Alejandro Rey, Savely Kramarov, Elya
Baskin, Yakov Smirnoff, Oleg Rudnik, Alexander
Beniaminov, Ludmilla Kramarevsky, Ivo Vrzal,
Natalie Iwanov, Tiger Haynes*
A Russian defector in New York tries to adjust to the
problems of living in a new and strange country. A
nicely observed tale, that's not without the inevitable
dose of sentimentality, but is redeemed by a stand-out
performance from Williams (who worked hard on his
pronunciation), ably assisted by an excellent supporting cast. Written by Mazursky and Leon Capetanos.

COM 112 min (ort 117 min)
V/sh RCA

## MOSES ** 15
Charles Davis    USA    1980
*Julie Adams, Robert Alda, Anne Francis, John
Marley, Joseph Campanella, Frank Gorshin*
Part of those "Greatest Heroes of the Bible" series.
Competent but hardly inspired.

DRA 50 min (ort 58 min)
B,V VCL/CBS

## MOSES THE LAWGIVER * 15
Gianfranco DeBosio    ITALY/UK    1976
*Burt Lancaster, Ingrid Thulin, Anthony Quayle, Irene
Papas, William Lancaster, Mariangela Melato,
Laurent Terzieff, Simonetta Stefanelli, Aharon Ipale,
Melba Englander, Mario Ferrari, Antonio Piovanelli,
Marina Berti*
A lethargic and ponderous account of the life of this
biblical hero, made for TV, and filmed in Israel.
Screenplay is by Anthony Burgess and Vittorio
Bonicelli.
Aka: MOSES (CH5)

DRA 135 min (ort 300 min) Cut (1 sec) mTV
B,V,LV PRV L/A; CH5

## MOSQUITO COAST, THE ** PG
Peter Weir    USA    1986
*Harrison Ford, River Phoenix, Helen Mirren, Jadrien
Steele, Andre Gragory, Conrad Roberts, Martha
Plimpton, Dick O'Neill, Hilary Gordon, Rebecca
Gorden, Butterfly McQueen, Jason Alexandre, Dick
O'Neill, Alice Sneed*
An idealistic inventor turns his back on modern
America with all its problems, and takes his family to
live in a remote part of Central America, where he
attempts to create an idyllic lifestyle. Ford is quite
wonderful as a narrow-minded idealist who eventual-
ly destroys himself, but the subtleties of the novel do
not translate well to the screen.
Boa: novel by Paul Theroux.

DRA 113 min (ort 119 min)
B,V CBS

## MOST WANTED ** 18
Walter Grauman    USA    1976
*Robert Stack, Shelly Novack, Leslie Charleson, Tom
Selleck, Kitty Winn, Sheree North, Stephen McNally*
A police story taken from a 1976 to 1977 TV series,
which had Stack in charge of a special police unit set
up to catch dangerous and often psychopathic killers.
In this tale he has the task of catching a killer of
Catholic nuns. Average.

A/AD 78 min mTV
V CASPIC

## MOTEL *
Michael J. MacFarland USA 1982
*Slim Pickens, Phyllis Diller, Terri Borland, Brad Cowgill, Cathryn Hart, Tony Long*
The story of a no-tell motel and the couples who use it. Sluggish and dull, with lousy dialogue and plotting.
Aka: PINK MOTEL
COM 84 min (ort 90 min)
B,V ODY

## MOTEL HELL *
Kevin Connor USA 1980
*Nancy Parsons, Rory Calhoun, Paul Linke, Nina Axelrod, Wolfman Jack, Elaine Joyce, Dick Curtis, Monique St Pierre, Rosanne Katon, E. Hampton Beagle*
A sort of "Sweeney Todd" tale set in a motel where you wonder just what goes into the sausages the owner and his sister sell there. A grisly black comedy in which shudders replace the laughs the film was presumably expected to provoke.
HOR 97 min (ort 106 min) Cut (2 sec)
B,V WHV

## MOTHER ****
Vsevolod I. Pudovkin USSR 1926
*Vera Baranovskaya, Nikolai Batalov, A.P. Khristialov, Ivan Koval-Samborski, Anna Zemtsova, Vsevolod Pudovkin*
A mother inadvertently turns her son in to the authorities, after he leads an illegal strike, but eventually she comes to see the error of her ways and embraces Communism. A potent tale of a family caught up in the abortive 1905 revolution, and at the same time a brilliant piece of social-realist propaganda.
Aka: MAT
Boa: novel by Maxim Gorky.
DRA 81 min (ort 84 min) B/W silent
V HEND

## MOTHER LODE **
Charlton Heston USA 1982
*Charlton Heston, Nick Mancuso, Kim Basinger, John Marley, Dale Wilson, Ricky Zantolas, Marie George*
A bush pilot and a young woman venture into the mountains of British Columbia, in search of the man's gold-seeking friend, but find a Scottish miner who is determined to protect his claim. An enjoyable tale with good photography, but a rather predictable script. Written and produced by Fraser Clarke Heston. Filmed in the Cassair Mountains of British Columbia.
Aka: LAST GREAT TREASURE, THE; SEARCH FOR THE MOTHER LODE
A/AD 98 min (ort 106 min)
B,V GHV L/A; VGM; PARK

## MOTHER, JUGS AND SPEED ***
Peter Yates USA 1976
*Bill Cosby, Raquel Welch, Harvey Keitel, Allen Garfield, Larry Hagman, Bruce Davidson, Dick Butkus, L.Q. Jones, Toni Basil*
An account of the incidents in the lives of private ambulance drivers at an L.A. based service that has seen better days, and is now forced to cut corners all round, in order to stay in business. A chaotic but generally highly amusing black comedy.
COM 99 min
B,V CBS

## MOTHER'S DAY *
Charles Kaufman USA 1980
*Tiana Pierce, Nancy Hendrickson, Deborah Luce, Rose Ross, Holden McGuire, Billy Ray McQuade*
Three college girls clash with a hillbilly family in a bloody conflict, when the former are caught and tortured, and two survive, returning to have their revenge. An unpleasant horror yarn, that's devoid of

originality but well supplied with gore.
HOR 98 min
B,V VTC

## MOTOWN'S MUSTANG **
Mark Robinson USA 1985
*Clyde James, Christi Shay, Louis Carr Jr*
Merely an excuse to play some classic Tamla Motown hits of the 1960s, thinly disguised as the story of a red mustang and the various owners it has.
MUS 43 min
B,V CIC

## MOULIN ROUGE ****
John Huston USA 1952
*Jose Ferrer, Suzanne Flon, Zsa Zsa Gabor, Eric Pohlmann, Colette Marchand, Katherine Kath, Christopher Lee, Michael Balfour, Peter Cushing*
A lovingly-made portrayal of the life and work of French impressionist painter Toulouse Lautrec, that has a remarkable performance by Ferrer (he also plays the painter's father). An accomplished and moving work, with the excitement and glamour of the Moulin Rouge splendidly captured. The theme song is by Georges Auric. AA: Art/Set (Paul Sheriff/Marcel Vertes), Cost (Marcel Vertes).
Boa: novel by Pierre La Mure.
DRA 123 min
B,V CBS; VCC

## MOUNTAIN CHARLIE **
George Stapleford USA 1982
*Denise Neilson, Dick Robinson, Rick Guinn, Lynne Seus*
A young girl goes to live with her father who works as a miner in the Rockies.
A/AD 96 min
B,V VPD

## MOUNTAIN FAMILY ROBINSON **
John Cotter USA 1979
*Robert F. Logan, Susan Damante Shaw, William Bryant, Heather Rattray, Ham Larsen, George "Buck" Flower, Calvin Bartlett*
A family in the city go off to live in the mountains and have to fight to keep their land. Last in a trilogy of films that began with THE ADVENTURES OF THE WILDERNESS FAMILY, and continued with THE FURTHER ADVENTURES OF THE WILDERNESS FAMILY. Quite well done, but the plot is as unchanging as those mountains.
A/AD 102 min
B,V,V2 VPD; IVS (Betamax and VHS only)

## MOUNTAIN MAN ***
David O'Malley USA 1977
*Denver Pyle, John Dehner, Ken Berry, Cheryl Miller, Don Shanks, Cliff Osmond, Jack Kruschen, Ford Rainey, Norman Fell, Prentiss Rowe, Brett Palmer, Melissa Jones*
A miner with lung disease has to live in the wilderness, if he is to have a chance of recovering. He and his family move to a valley where they come into conflict with logging interests. Enjoyable 1860s family tale, based on the true story of Galen Clarke, whose efforts led to the Yosemite Valley becoming a national park.
Aka: GUARDIAN OF THE WILDERNESS
A/AD 93 min (ort 104 min)
B,V RNK

## MOUNTAIN MEN, THE *
Richard Lang USA 1980
*Charlton Heston, Brian Keith, Victoria Racimo, Stephen Macht, John Glover, Victor Jory, Seymour Cassell, David Ackroyd, John Glover, Carl Bellini, Bill Lucking, Ken Ruta, Danny Zapien, Tim Haldeman, Bob Terhume, Chuck Roberson*
Two fur trappers have to fight off attacks by Indians, in a film that is dull and boring, but rather bloody in

parts. Poor direction and dialogue are helped slightly by some good photography. Screenplay is by Chuck's son, Fraser Clarke Heston.

WES       96 min (ort 102 min) (Cut at film release)
V                    RCA

## MOUNTAINS OF THE MOON ****    15
Bob Rafelson      USA       1989
*Patrick Bergin, Iain Glen, Richard E. Grant, Fiona Shaw, John Savident, James Villiers, Adrian Rawlins, Delroy Lindo, Paul Onsongo, Bernard Hill, Roshan Seth, Anna Massey, Leslie Phillips*
A colourful and enthralling account of Richard Burton's search for the source of the Nile in 1857. Beautifully photographed by Roger Deakins, and directed in a way that highlights both the Victorian sense of adventure and its foibles. Bergin as Burton and Glen as his companion John Hanning Speke both give outstanding performances. Scripted by Rafelson and Harrison and based on the latter's biographical novel and the journals of the period.
Boa: novel Burton and Speke by William Harrison.
A/AD           130 min (ort 135 min)
V/sh                GHV

## MOUNTAINTOP MOTEL MASSACRE *    18
Jim McCullough Sr    USA      1984
*Bill Thurman, Anna Chappell, Will Mitchell, Jill King, Virginia Loridans, Major Brock, James Bradford, Amy Hill, Marian Jones, Greg Brazzel, Rhonda Atwood, Foster Litton, Linda Blankenship, Angela Christine*
The only good thing about this one is the alliterative title. A woman motel owner slaughters her Satanist daughter, and in a state of deranged grief sets about doing the same for the guests, in assorted gory ways. All blood and guts, but no substance; in short, a typical Corman New World Company offering.
Aka: MOUNTAINTOP MOTEL
HOR          85 min (ort 95 min)
B,V               NWV

## MOUNTBATTEN: THE LAST VICEROY ***    15
Tom Clegg      UK       1985
*Nicol Williamson, Ian Richardson, Janet Suzman, Nigel Davenport, Wendy Hiller, Sam Dastor, Vladek Sheybal, Malcolm Terris*
Epic account of the last years of the British Raj in India, when Mountbatten was made Viceroy, and given the task of overseeing the country's change to independence. Originally shown in six 50-minute episodes, this well-mounted, but rather unmoving drama, spends more time focusing on Gandhi, Jinnah and Nehru than on the title character.
DRA      292 min; 110 min (VGM) mTV
B,V      BWV; VGM (VHS only)

## MOUSE AND HIS CHILD, THE *    U
Fred Wolf/Chuck Swenson
            USA       1977
*Voices of: Peter Ustinov, Alan Barzman, Andy Devine, Sally Kellerman, Marcy Swenson, Cloris Leachman*
Animated fantasy about two toy mice, who have various adventures in their search for a means by which to become self-winding. A verbose and stolid effort, that needed winding up itself.
CAR         81 min (ort 83 min)
B,V,V2    VSP L/A; SAT; VCC (VHS only)

## MOUSE AND THE WOMAN, THE ** 
Karol Francis      UK       1981
*Dafydd Hywell, Karen Archer, Patrick Napier, Alan Devlin, Peter Sproule, Howard Lewis, Ionette Lloyd Davies, Beti Jones, Basil Painting, John Pierce Jones, John Lehman, Robert Blythe, Simon Coady, Ozi and Glesne*
Story of the steamy affair between a muscular poet and a mine-owner's wife, in the Welsh valleys during WW1. Fair.

Aka: IN THE AFTERNOON OF WAR
Boa: story by Dylan Thomas.
DRA            105 min
B,V,V2           GOV/HER

## MOUSE THAT ROARED, THE ***    U
Jack Arnold      UK       1959
*Peter Sellers, Jean Seberg, David Kossoff, William Hartnell, Leo McKern, Harold Kasket, Monty Landis, Colin Gordon, George Margo, Macdonald Parke, Robin Gatehouse, Jacques Cey, Stuart Saunders, Ken Stanley, Bill Nagy*
The near-bankrupt Duchy of Grand Fenwick plans to declare war on the USA, be defeated and thus be eligible for Marshall Aid to rebuild its economy. One of those films in which Sellers engagingly plays three parts, effectively carrying the entire film. Written by Roger Macdougall and Stanley Mann. Followed by "The Mouse On The Moon".
Boa: novel The Wrath Of The Grapes by Leonard Wibberley.
COM         80 min (ort 85 min)
B,V              RCA

## MOVE *
Stuart Rosenberg      USA       1970
*Elliott Gould, Paula Prentiss, Genevieve Waite, John Larch, Joe Silver, Ron O'Neal*
A playwright tries to make some money by writing pornography, and moves to a larger apartment. Unfortunately, he is unable to move to a better script, and this dull dud sank soon after release. Written by Lieber and Stanley Hart.
Boa: novel by Joel Lieber.
COM         86 min (ort 88 min)
B,V              CBS

## MOVE OVER, DARLING **    PG
Michael Gordon      USA       1963
*Doris Day, Polly Bergen, James Garner, Chuck Connors, Thelma Ritter, Fred Clark, Don Knotts, Elliott Reid, John Astin, Pat Harrington Jr*
Following a plane crash and 5 years spent on a desert island, Day returns home to find that her husband is about to remarry. A sporadically entertaining remake of MY FAVOURITE WIFE that has little going for it except the professionalism of the cast. It originally started production as "Something's Got To Give" and was to have starred Marilyn Monroe.
COM       99 min (ort 103 min)
V/h              CBS

## MOVERS AND SHAKERS *    15
William Asher      USA       1985
*Steve Martin, Walter Matthau, Charles Grodin, Vincent Gardenia, Tyne Daly, Bill Macy, Gilder Radner, Penny Marshall, Nita Talbot, Luana Anders*
A wild but unfunny spoof on Hollywood in the 1980s, as a studio head fighting to avoid bankruptcy, decides to make a film version of a best-selling sex manual. A plotless mess of gags and anecdotes, thrown together without care or thought. The script is by Grodin.
COM       76 min (ort 100 min)
B,V             WHV

## MOVIE, MOVIE **    PG
Stanley Donen      USA       1978
*George C. Scott, Trish Van Devere, Eli Wallach, Red Buttons, Barbara Harris, Harry Hamlin, Barry Bostwick, Art Carney, Ann Reinking, Kathleen Beller, Rebecca York, Michael Kidel, George Burns*
A fair parody of a 1930s double bill, complete with a "coming attractions" trailer, introduced by George Burns. The two parodies are "Dynamite Hands", a boxing tale, and "Baxter's Beauties of 1933", a spoof on all those Busby Berkeley musicals. Generally quite agreeable to watch, but don't expect to be any more than mildly amused.

COM                102 min (ort 106 min) B/W and Colour
B,V                PRV L/A; CH5 (VHS only)

## MOVING **                                           15
Alan Metter            USA                         1988
*Richard Pryor, Randy Quaid, Dana Carvey, Dave
Thomas, Beverly Todd, Rodney Dangerfield, Stacey
Dash*
A transit engineer has to move from New Jersey to a
new job in Idaho, and encounters a string of problems.
A by-the-numbers comedy, made in the style of
Disney, with a few laughs buried beneath the dross.
COM                        86 min (ort 89 min)
V/sh                                           WHV

## MOVING IN **                                        15
Michael Apted          USA                         1984
*Teri Garr, Peter Weller, Christopher Collett, Corey
Haim, Sarah Jessica Parker*
A divorced woman and her two children find them-
selves having to cope with the fact that her lover is a
drug-dealing psychotic, after he moves into their
apartment and takes over. Convincing performances
are drowned in a welter of unpleasantness, and an
utterly over-the-top ending.
Aka: FIRSTBORN
DRA                        96 min (ort 103 min)
B,V                                            CIC

## MOVING TARGET **                                    15
Chris Thompson         USA                         1988
*Jason Bateman, John Glover, Jack Wagner, Chynna
Phillips, Richard Dysart, Tom Skerritt*
A youngster returns home from summer camp to find
his family gone, his house cleaned out, and some
killers after him. A good start is thrown away by poor
acting and little development. Pity, it could have been
really gripping.
THR                        96 min (ort 100 min) mTV
B,V                                            MGM

## MOVING VIOLATION **                                 15
Charles S. Dubin       USA                         1976
*Stephen McHattie, Kay Lenz, Eddie Albert, Lonny
Chapman, Will Geer, Jack Murdock, John S. Ragin,
Dennis Redfield, Michael Ross Verona*
A corrupt redneck sheriff initiates a massive hunt for
a young couple who witnessed him committing a
murder. A hackneyed plot is given a few new thrills
and dished up again.
A/AD                       88 min (ort 91 min)
B,V                                            CBS

## MOVING VIOLATIONS **                                15
Neal Israel            USA                         1985
*Sally Kellerman, Jennifer Tilly, James Keach, Lisa
Hart Carroll, Ned Eisenberg, Ben Mittleman, Victor
Campos, John Murray, Brian Backer, Wendie Jo
Sperber, Fred Willard, Clara Peller, Nedra Volz*
Traffic offenders are sent to school to mend their ways,
and fall victim to a plot to defraud them of their cars.
From the same team who produced POLICE
ACADEMY, so don't expect anything too cerebral.
COM                        86 min (ort 90 min)
B,V                                            CBS

## MRS CAPPER'S BIRTHDAY **                            PG
Mike Ockrent           UK                          1985
*Patricia Hayes, Max Wall, Paula Wilcox, Nicholas
Gecks, John Bird*
The story of a woman's 50th birthday and the
celebrations that take place. A modest little work that
serves as one of Coward's character studies. See also
ME AND THE GIRLS, MISTER AND MRS EDGE-
HILL and WHAT MAD PURSUIT?
Boa: story by Noel Coward.
DRA                                            59 min
V                                             PICK

## MRS R'S DAUGHTER **
Dan Curtis             USA                         1979
*Cloris Leachman, Season Hubley, Donald Moffat,
John McIntire, Ron Rifkin, Stephen Elliott, John
Fitzpatrick, Craig Wasson, Kerry Sherman, Don
Megowan, Deborah Benson, Barbara Tarbuck, Charles
Gray, Nan Martin, Peggy McCay*
A mother fights to bring her daughter's rapist to
justice, and then embarks on her own plan to mete out
vengeance, when the courts fail her. A so-so version of
a real story.
DRA                        93 min (ort 100 min) mTV
B,V                                            SEL

## MRS SOFFEL **                                       PG
Gillian Armstrong      USA                         1984
*Mel Gibson, Diane Keaton, Matthew Modine, Edward
Hermann, Trini Alvarado, Jennie Dundas, Danny
Corkill, Harley Cross, Terry O'Quinn, William
Youmans, Maury Chaykin, John W. Carroll, Wayne
Robson*
A couple of brothers go to prison, where the warden's
wife falls for one of them, eventually joining them on
the run. Set in Pittsburgh of 1901, this is a detailed
but sombre version of a real-life incident. Remarkably
unappealing, despite the care that went into produc-
tion.
DRA                        107 min (ort 113 min)
V                                             MGM

## MRS VERSUS MISTRESS **                              15
Naftaly Alter          ISRAEL                      1986
*Hanan Goldblatt, Leora Grossman, Irit Alter*
A bored housewife becomes friendly with a single lady
lawyer who has a liberated lifestyle, and the two
women agree to change places for a while. A formula
comedy that draws its inspiration from a remarkably
hackneyed idea. See also ONE MONTH LATER.
COM                                            89 min
B,V                                            RNK

## MS MAGNIFICENT **
Joe Sherman            USA                         1979
*Desiree Cousteau, Jesie St James, John Seeman, Holly
McCall, Robert McCallum*
Sex film with a science-fiction theme, in which
"Superwoman" (the original film title until the owners
of SUPERMAN forced them to withdraw it), is a tough
chick, who rescues various females from assorted
unpleasant characters. Poor stuff indeed.
Aka: MISS MAGNIFICENT
A                                              84 min
B,V                            ROXY L/A; SEL

## MUGSY'S GIRLS *                                     18
Kevin Brodie           USA                         1985
*Ruth Gordon, Laura Branigan, Steve Brodie, Eddie
Deezen, Estrelita, Rebecca Forstadt, Candace
Pandolfo, Kristi Somers, James Marcel, Ken Norton,
Rex Meredith, Ben Kronen, Steve Brodie*
Six college girls take up mud-wrestling when they
find they can't pay the rent, in this simple-minded
comedy that's as messy and unappealing as the mud
they slither about in.
Aka: DELTA PI
COM                84 min (ort 90 min) Cut (17 sec)
B,V                         PEGA/MED; MED

## MULTIPLE MANIACS **
John Waters            USA                         1970
*Divine (Glenn Milstead), Mary Vivian Pearce, Edith
Massey, Mink Stole, Paul Swift, David Lochary,
Cookie Mueller, Susan Lowe, Rick Morrow, Howard
Gruber, Vince Peranio, Jim Thompson, Dee Vitolo, Ed
Peranio, Bob Skidmore*
The notorious overweight female impersonator
(Divine playing him/herself) and her boyfriend, run a
travelling sideshow at which the audience is robbed
and sometimes murdered. Somewhat less disjointed

than Waters' films usually are, this one has some genuinely funny moments. Unfortunately the sleaze of it all dilutes the comedy.
Osca: COCAINE FIENDS
COM                                    90 min B/W
B,V                                        PVG

## MUMMY, THE **         15
Karl Freund          USA            1932
*Boris Karloff, Zita Johann, David Manners, Arthur Byron, Edward Van Sloan, Bramwell Fletcher, Noble Johnson, Leonard Mudie, Eddie Kane, Henry Victor, Kathryn Byron, James Crane, Arnold Grey, Tony Marlow*
A mummy is accidentally revived, and goes off in search of its ancient soul-mate. Some atmospheric sequences are present, but on the whole the film is let down by stilted acting and ludicrous dialogue. Followed by a large number of films that made use of this theme.
Osca: MUMMY'S HAND, THE
HOR      72 min; 137 min (2 film cassette) B/W
V/h                                        CIC

## MUMMY'S GHOST, THE *      PG
Reginald LeBorg      USA            1944
*Lon Chaney Jr, John Carradine, Ramsay Ames, Robert Lowery, Barton MacLane, George Zucco*
A sequel to THE MUMMY'S TOMB that has our bandaged one on the trail of a women he believes is a reincarnation of his beloved princess. A flat and hollow affair, directed without energy or conviction. Followed by "The Mummy's Curse" (1944), which ended this "Kharis" series.
Osca: MUMMY'S TOMB, THE
HOR      60 min; 117 min (2 film cassette) B/W
V/h                                        CIC

## MUMMY'S HAND, THE ***      15
Christy Cabanne      USA            1940
*Dick Foran, Wallace Ford, Peggy Moran, Cecil Kellaway, George Zucco, Tom Tyler, Eduardo Ciannelli, Charles Trowbridge*
A mummy is revived thanks to an infusion of tanna leaves, and seeks out the reincarnation of his former princess, wreaking havoc on those who desecrated her tomb. A kind of partial sequel to THE MUMMY that makes use of some footage from that earlier film, and starts off weakly but builds up to an excellent and chilling climax. This was the first of the "Kharis" mummy films. Several sequels followed, starting with THE MUMMY'S TOMB (1942).
Osca: MUMMY, THE
HOR      67 min; 137 min (2 film cassette) B/W
V/h                                        CIC

## MUMMY'S TOMB, THE **      PG
Harold Young         USA            1942
*Lon Chaney Jr, Elyse Knox, John Hubbard, Turhan Bey, Dick Foran, Wallace Ford, George Zucco, Mary Gordon*
A dreary re-run of THE MUMMY'S HAND, not improved by its borrowed footage from that earlier film, THE MUMMY (1932) and FRANKENSTEIN (1931). This was the first sequel in a series of "Kharis" films, in which our revived mummy dispensed rough justice to those who violated his tomb and spent the rest of the time searching from the reincarnation of his ancient beloved. Followed by THE MUMMY'S GHOST.
Osca: MUMMY'S GHOST, THE
HOR      61 min; 117 min (2 film cassette) B/W
V/h                                        CIC

## MUNCHIES *         PG
Bettina Hirsch       USA            1987
*Harvey Korman, Charles Stratton, Alex Elias, Nadine Van Der Velde, Charles Philips, John Stafford, Hardy Rawls, Robert Picardo, Wendy Schaal, Scott Sherk, Lori Birdsong, Traci Huber-Sheridan, Paul Bartel,*

*Ellen Albertini*
A horror spoof, telling of junk food junkies from outer space, who menace the residents of a small American town in a variety of crazy ways. A lo-budget rip-off of GREMLINS.
COM                                78 min (ort 88 min)
B,V                                        MGM

## MUPPET MOVIE, THE **      U
James Frawley        UK/USA         1979
*The Muppets, Frank Oz, Jerry Nelson, Richard Hunt, Dave Goelz, Bob Hope, Charles Durning, Austin Pendleton, Scott Walker, Edgar Bergen, Milton Berle, Mel Brooks, Madeleine Kahn, Steve Martin, Dom DeLuise, Elliott Gould*
A tale using puppets from a TV series, with this being the story of the rise to fame of Kermit from a swamp to Hollywood. Though the characters are cleverly transferred to the screen, the material is very weak, and the film just drags on and on. Followed by several more "Muppet" movies.
JUV                          94 min; 98 min (VIR)
B, V/h, V2                      PRV L/A; VIR

## MUPPETS TAKE MANHATTAN, THE ***   U
Franz Oz             USA            1984
*The Muppets, Joan Rivers, Liza Minelli, Linda Lavin, Louis Zorich, Lonny Price, Juliana Donald, Art Carney, James Coco, Dabney Coleman, John Landis, Gregory Hines, Elliott Gould, Brooke Shields, Edward I. Koch*
Third in the series of "Muppet" adventures with these puppets from a popular TV series trying to make the big time in New York. Packed with a host of guest stars, and for the most part a lively and entertaining affair.
JUV                                        94 min
V                                          CBS

## MUPPETS: HEY CINDERELLA ** 
Jim Henson           USA            1970
The muppet characters of Jim Henson are employed in this humorous retelling of the Cinderella tale.
Aka: HEY CINDERELLA
JUV                                        58 min
B,V                                        RCA

## MURDER! ***         PG
Alfred Hitchcock     UK             1930
*Herbert Marshall, Norah Baring, Phyllis Konstam, Edward Chapman, Esme Percy, Miles Mander, Donald Calthrop, Amy Brandon Thomas, Marie Wright, Hannah Jones, Una O'Connor, R.E. Jeffrey, Violet Farebrother, Kenneth Kove*
One of the jurors who convicted a woman of murder at her trial, turns amateur sleuth to prove her innocence in this interesting example of an early Hitchcock work.
Boa: play Enter Sir John by Clemence Dane and Helen Simpson. Osca: NUMBER SEVENTEEN
DRA      92 min; 100 min (SCRN) (ort 108 min) B/W
B,V                              TEVP L/A; SCRN

## MURDER AT MIDNIGHT ** 
Eric C. Kenton       USA            1931
*Wallace Ford, Gavin Gordon, Sarah Pudden, Alice White, Leslie Fenton, Eileen Pringle, Hale Hamilton*
An elderly woman takes her revenge on her relatives, who tried to have her declared insane in an attempt to get their hands on her money, and in a party game of charades, real bullets are substituted for blanks with the expected results.
DRA                          63 min (ort 69 min) B/W
B,V                                        VCL/CBS

## MURDER AT THE WORLD SERIES *   PG
Andrew V. McLaglen   USA            1977
*Lynda Day George, Karen Valentine, Murray Hamilton, Gerald S. O'Loughlin, Michael Parks, Janet Leigh, Hugh O'Brian, Nancy Kelly, Johnny Seven,*

*Tamara Dobson, Joseph Wiseman, Bruce Boxleitner,*
*Larry Mahan, Cooper Huckabee*
A strange kidnapping takes place during the World
Series in Houston. A cast packed with stars cannot
save this one, which never develops any tension owing
to the predictability of the script.
THR                                    100 min mTV
B,V                              VFP L/A; HER

## MURDER BY DEATH ***                          PG
Robert Moore              USA                   1976
*Peter Falk, Peter Sellers, David Niven, Maggie Smith,*
*Alec Guinness, Eileen Brennan, Truman Capote,*
*James Coco, Elsa Lanchester, Nancy Walker, Estelle*
*Winwood*
Beautifully made detective parody, in which the
world's greatest detectives are invited to the home of a
rich eccentric, who involves them in solving a murder.
Scripted by Neil Simon and hosting a variety of
spoofed characters, including Charlie Chan, Miss
Marple and Sam Spade. The sets are by Stephen
Grimes.
COM                         91 min (ort 94 min)
V                                              RCA

## MURDER BY DECREE ***                         15
Bob Clark              CANADA/UK                1978
*Christopher Plummer, James Mason, Donald*
*Sutherland, Genevieve Bujold, Susan Clark, David*
*Hemmings, Anthony Quayle, John Gielgud, Frank*
*Finlay, Chris Wiggins, Teddi Moore, Catherine*
*Kessler, Terry Duggan, Peter Jonfield*
Sherlock Holmes and Watson investigate the Jack the
Ripper killings, and come close to discovering the
truth behind these crimes. An ambitious idea, with
good casting of Plummer and Mason as Holmes and
Watson respectively. Only the fumbling development
of the narrative, and a few grisly touches spoil it.
DRA                     112 min; 121 min (CH5)
B,V                CBS; POLY; CH5 (VHS only)

## MURDER BY NIGHT **                           15
Paul Lynch              USA                     1989
*Robert Urich, Kay Lenz, Michael Ironside, Jim*
*Metzler, Michael Williams*
A man found unconscious at the scene of a murder and
suffering from amnesia, seems to hold the key to the
murderer's identity, but as his treatment at the hands
of a police therapist progresses, a suspicious cop
becomes increasingly convinced that he is the killer.
However, the real killer soon learns of the danger the
man poses, and sets out to silence him. A thin, grim,
assembly-line thriller lacking a much-needed injection of tension.
THR                     89 min (ort 100 min) mCab
V                                              CIC

## MURDER BY TELEVISION *
Clifford Sandforth        USA                   1935
*Bela Lugosi, June Collyer, Huntley Gordon, George*
*Meeker, Claire McDowell, Henry Mowbray, Hattie*
*McDaniel*
While demonstrating his new television process, an
electronics genius is murdered in front of the cameras.
A real camp curio, in which Lugosi plays two brothers.
The static dialogue and lack of development make it a
struggle to watch.
THR                                    70 min B/W
V                                              HVS

## MURDER BY THE BOOK **                         PG
Mel Damski              USA                     1986
*Robert Hays, Catherine Mary Stewart, Fred Gwynne,*
*Celeste Holm, Christopher Murney*
Another variation on the much used theme of a
mystery writer investigating and solving a real crime.
Here the creator of fictional detective "Biff Deegan"
witnesses the kidnapping of a beautiful woman, and
being a perfect gentleman, sets out to rescue her.

Average.
Aka: ALTER EGO
Boa: novel Alter Ego by Mel Arrighi.
THR                     90 min (ort 104 min) mTV
B,V                              CAPIT/STABL

## MURDER IN COWETA COUNTY ***                  15
Gary Nelson             USA                     1983
*Johnny Cash, Andy Griffith, Earl Hindman, June*
*Carter Cash, Cindi Knight, Ed Van Nuys, Robert*
*Schenkkan, Jo Henderson, Daniel Keyes, Brent*
*Jennings, Norman Matlock, Danny Nelson, James*
*Neale, Earl Poole Ball, Dan Biggers*
A sheriff spares no effort to prove that a local
dignitary committed a murder. An entertaining,
low-key affair, with above average performances that
embrace a realistic, rather than sensationalist
approach to the subject matter. Adapted by Dennis
Nemac from Barnes' book, which in turn was based on
a real-life incident that took place in Georgia in 1984.
Aka: LAST BLOOD (FOX)
Boa: book by Margaret Anne Barnes.
DRA                     97 min (ort 100 min) mTV
B,V                CAP/CBS L/A; FOX; 21ST

## MURDER IN TEXAS ***                          15
Billy Hale              USA                     1981
*Farrah Fawcett, Sam Elliot, Katherine Ross, Andy*
*Griffith, Craig T. Nelson, Dimitra Arliss, G.W. Bailey,*
*Barry Corbin, Pamela Myers, Royce Wallace, Jude*
*Farese, Philip Sterling, Vernon Weddle, Lesley Woods,*
*Parley Baer*
Based on a real-life incident, this is the account of a
prominent plastic surgeon accused of killing his first
wife. An intriguing tale, made with care and style.
The script is by John McGreevey and is based on the
book by the second wife of Dr John Hill, the man in
question.
Boa: book Prescription Murder by Ann Kurth.
DRA                     102 min (ort 200 min) mTV
B,V                                            POLY

## MURDER, MY SWEET ****                         PG
Edward Dmytryk          USA                     1944
*Dick Powell, Claire Trevor, Ann Shirley, Otto Kruger,*
*Mike Mazurki, Miles Mander, Douglas Watson, Ralf*
*Harolde, Don Douglas, Esther Howard, Jack Carr,*
*John Indrisano, Shimen Ruskin, Ernie Adams, Dewey*
*Robinson, Larry Wheat*
Powell as the hard-boiled detective Philip Marlowe,
has a new image in this version of Chandler's novel,
with our 'tec getting mixed up in murder and black-
mail. Well-acted and with a good supporting cast, this
is a splendid example of its genre – moody, imagina-
tive and totally absorbing. Remade in 1975 as
FAREWELL, MY LOVELY.
Aka: FAREWELL, MY LOVELY
Boa: novel Farewell, My Lovely by Raymond
Chandler.
THR                                    95 min B/W
V                                              VCC

## MURDER OF MARY PHAGAN, THE ****              15
Billy Hale              USA                     1988
*Jack Lemmon, Richard Jordan, Robert Prosky, Peter*
*Gallagher, Paul Dooley, Rebecca Miller, Kathryn*
*Walker, Charles Dutton, Kevin Spacey, Wendy J.*
*Cooke*
Based on a real incident in Atlanta, Georgia in 1913,
this tells of John Slaton, the governor of Georgia, who
had to make a decision whether or not to allow the
execution of Leo Frank, who was convicted of Pha-
gan's murder. An excellent reconstruction of events,
with fine performances and a literate script by George
Stevens Jr and Jeffrey Lane. The acting debut of
Miller, the daughter of playwright Arthur Miller.
First shown in two parts.
Boa: story by Larry McMurtry.

DRA 112 min (ort 250 min) (available as 223 min 2 cassette version) mTV
B,V VIR

## MURDER ON FLIGHT 502 ** PG
George McCowan    USA    1975
*Theodore Bikel, Polly Bergen, Ralph Bellamy, Sonny Bono, Dane Clark, Walter Pidgeon, Fernando Lamas, Larraine Day, George Maharis, Hugh O'Brien, Farrah Fawcett, Molly Picon, Robert Stack, Brooke Adams, Danny Bonaduce*
A 747 jumbo jet is threatened by the presence on board of a psychotic killer. A hackneyed theme, badly utilised in a film that lacks both tension and drive.
A/AD 92 min (ort 100 min) mTV
B,V,V2 GHV

## MURDER ON THE ORIENT EXPRESS * PG
Sidney Lumet    UK    1974
*Albert Finney, Lauren Bacall, Martin Balsam, Ingrid Bergman, Jacqueline Bisset, Sean Connery, Richard Widmark, Vanessa Redgrave, John Gielgud, Wendy Hiller, Jean-Pierre Cassel, Anthony Perkins, Rachel Roberts, Michael York*
A pretty awful adaptation of an Agatha Christie whodunnit, involving a murder that takes place on the Orient Express, eventually solved by her famous detective Monsieur Hercule Poirot (miscasting of Finney here). Slow moving and uninspired. As ever, a cast full of stars can do nothing to save it. AA: S. Actress (Bergman).
Boa: novel by Agatha Christie.
DRA 122 min (ort 131 min)
B,V TEVP L/A; WHV

## MURDER ONCE REMOVED **
Charles Dubin    USA    1971
*Richard Kiley, Barbara Bain, Wendell Burton, John Forsythe, Reta Shaw, Joseph Campanella, Laurence Haddon*
A respectable doctor plots to commit a perfect crime when he falls in love with the wife of a wealthy patient. Despite good work from the cast, the hackneyed plot leaves little scope for surprise.
THR 73 min (ort 78 min) mTV
B,V IFS

## MURDER ONE, MURDER TWO * 15
Paul Leder    USA    1990
*Sam Behrens, Shari Belafonte, Ronee Blakeley, Stanley Kamel, Jayne Meadows, Dick Sargent, Cleavon Little, Debra Sandlund*
A former lawyer working as a private eye is hired by his ex-wife to locate her missing brother and gets himself embroiled in a murder mystery. Written by Leder, this low-budget quickie combines poor camerawork with worse acting. Not an edifying experience – the use of AIDS as the red herring gives it a dated and contrived look.
Aka: MURDER BY NUMBERS
THR 90 min
V FUTUR

## MURDER ORDAINED: A TRUE STORY *** 15
Mike Robe    USA    1987
*Keith Carradine, JoBeth Williams, Terry Kinney, M. Emmet Walsh, Terence Knox, Guy Boyd, Darrell Larson*
An absorbing tale inspired by real-life events telling of two murders that took place in Kansas and involved a priest, his married lover and their respective spouses. The literate script is by Robe and James Sadwith and is based on the newspaper reports of the time. First shown in two parts.
Aka: MURDER ORDAINED PART 1: A DARK CONSPIRACY; MURDER ORDAINED PART 2: THE PRICE OF JUSTICE; MURDER ORDAINED: PARTS 1 AND 2
THR 186 min (2 cassettes) mTV
B,V SHEER; VCC (VHS only)

## MURDER RAP ** 18
Kliff Kuehl    USA    1987
*John Hawkes, Seita Kathleen Feigny, David Frizzell, Conquina Dunn*
An audio expert finds himself taking the rap for a couple of murders after he agrees to help a young woman by operating some recording equipment.
THR 107 min
B,V CHV L/A; BRAVE

## MURDER RUN * 18
George F. Hood    USA    1989
*Russell Fast, Marcie Severson*
Unappetising story based on the shortlived but violent career of a couple of losers who murdered seven innocent people along a stretch of highway in 1958.
DRA 93 min
V HIFLI

## MURDER STORY *** 15
Arno Innocenti    USA    1989
*Christopher Reeve, Bruce Boa*
A thriller writer helps out an apprentice, but the story he picks up from the press-cuttings he has collected for his current work may prove to be his undoing. Fair.
THR 90 min
V REEVE

## MURDER: ULTIMATE GROUNDS FOR DIVORCE ** 15
Morris Barry    UK    1984
*Roger Daltrey, Toyah Wilcox, Lesley Ash, Terry Raven*
Two married couples go on a camping holiday together, and the cracks in their marriages start to show.
DRA 90 min
B,V CAREY; MSD (VHS only)

## MURDERER'S ROW * PG
Henry Levin    USA    1966
*Dean Martin, Ann-Margret, Karl Malden, Camilla Sparv, James Gregory, Beverly Adams, Robert Eastman, Marcel Hilliaire, Duke Howard, Tom Reese, Ted Hartley, Robert Terry, Corinne Cole, Mary Jane Mangler, Dale Brown*
The second "Matt Helm" secret agent adventure in which he has to tackle a villain who threatens to melt Washington with his secret weapon. One of those pseudo-Bond espionage capers that were typical of the 1960s, that now looks unbelievably dated and dull. The script is by Herbert Baker.
Boa: novel by Donald Hamilton.
COM 101 min (ort 108 min)
V RCA

## MURDERLUST * 18
Donal Jones    USA    1987
*Eli Rich, Rochelle Taylor, Dennis Gannon, Bonnie Schneider*
A seemingly kind security guard is really a serial killer of prostitutes, in this low-budget shocker.
Aka: MASS MURDERER
HOR 87 min (ort 90 min) Cut (2 min 33 sec)
V CAST

## MURDERS IN THE RUE MORGUE ** 15
Gordon Hessler    USA    1971
*Jason Robards, Herbert Lom Jr, Christine Kaufman, Lilli Palmer, Adolfo Celi, Maria Perschy, Michael Dunn*
This film has little to do with Poe's short story of the same name, except the title. A series of murders are committed in a theatre in the Rue Morgue, and a detective investigates. A remake of the 1932 film, set in Paris but filmed in Spain. A good film to watch late at night if one has nothing better to do.
HOR 86 min
B,V RNK; PARK

## MURDERS IN THE RUE MORGUE **

Robert Florey     USA     15   1932
*Bela Lugosi, Sidney Fox, Leon Ames, Bert Roach,*
*Brandon Hurst, Arlene Francis*
An Expressionist reworking of Poe's short story, with
Lugosi a demented doctor, who uses his trained ape to
commit a series of nasty murders. Apart from some
atmospheric touches, there's little here to frighten, or
even sustain interest. Remade as "Phantom Of The
Rue Morgue".
Boa: short story by Edgar Allan Poe.
HOR     62 min (ort 75 min) B/W
V     ORION/PVG

## MURDERS IN THE RUE MORGUE, THE **

Jeannot Szwarc     USA     15   1986
*George C. Scott, Rebecca DeMornay, Ian McShane,*
*Neil Dickson, Val Kilmer, Maud Rayer, Maxence*
*Mailfort, Fernand Guiot, Patrick Floersheim, Roger*
*Lumont, Erick Desmarestz, Yvette Peti, Serge Ridoux,*
*Mak Wilson*
The stylish Paris locations and Scott's performance as
a retired police inspector, are the best things in this
fourth version of Poe's classic murder mystery. The
script is by David Epstein and the photography by
Bruno De Keyzer.
Boa: short story by Edgar Allan Poe.
THR     89 min (ort 100 min) mTV
B,V     HOLLY; CHROME

## MURPHY'S LAW **

J. Lee Thompson     USA     18   1986
*Charles Bronson, Kathleen Wilhoite, Carrie*
*Snodgress, Richard Romanus, Angel Thompkins,*
*Robert F. Lyons, Bill Henderson, James Luisi, Janet*
*MacLachlan, Lawrence Tierney*
Formula Bronson vehicle, in which he plays a tough
cop (surprise, surprise), framed for the murder of his
ex-wife by a psychotic woman. Plenty of action and
violence, and of course the usual Bronson stoneface
acting.
A/AD     96 min (ort 101 min)
B,V     MGM

## MURPHY'S ROMANCE **

Martin Ritt     USA     15   1985
*Sally Field, James Garner, Brian Kerwin, Corey*
*Haim, Dennis Burkley, Charles Lane, Georgeann*
*Johnson, Charles Lane, Dortha Duckworth, Michael*
*Prokopuk, Billy Ray Sharkey, Michael Crabtree, Anna*
*Levine, Bruce French, Henry Slate*
A woman and her 12-year-old son make a new start in
a small Arizona town, where she falls in love with an
unconventional drugstore owner. A relaxed perform-
ance from Garner and a pleasant story make this an
amiable, if undemanding comedy. The script is by
Irving Ravetch and Harriet Frank Jr.
Boa: novella by Max Schott.
COM     103 min (ort 107 min)
B,V     RCA

## MURPHY'S WAR **

Peter Yates     UK     1970
*Peter O'Toole, Sian Phillips, Phillipe Noiret, Horst*
*Janson, John Hallam, Ingo Morgendorf, Lawrence*
*Tierney*
A British sailor survives a torpedo attack on his ship
by a German U-boat, and swears revenge on it and its
murderous crew. Similar in theme to THE AFRICAN
QUEEN and SHOUT AT THE DEVIL, and though
gripping in parts, generally let down by long periods
of sluggishness. Scripted by Stirling Silliphant.
Boa: novel by Max Catto.
DRA     100 min (ort 108 min)
B,V     VCL/CBS

## MUSIC LOVERS, THE *

Ken Russell     UK     18   1970
*Glenda Jackson, Christopher Gable, Richard*

*Chamberlain, Max Adrian, Kenneth Colley, Maureen*
*Pryor, Isabella Telezynska, Sabina Maydelle, Andrew*
*Faulds, James Russell, Victoria Russell, Alexander*
*Russell, Georgina Parkinson*
A wildly overblown account of Tchaikovsky's life and
career, with all the self-indulgent excesses one expects
from the director. This looks mostly at the composer's
homosexuality and his wife's alleged nymphomania.
The few visually memorable moments sink in the
morass.
Boa: book Beloved Friend by Catherine Drinker
Bowen and Barbara Von Meck.
DRA     123 min
B,V     WHV

## MUSIC MACHINE, THE *

Ian Sharp     UK     PG   1979
*Gerry Sundquist, Patty Boulaye, David Easter,*
*Michael Feast, Ferdy Mayne, Clarke Peters, Richard*
*Parmentier, Billy McColl, Chrissy Wickham, Frances*
*Lowe, Johnny Wade, Many Perryment, Thomas*
*Baptiste, Esther Rantzen*
An unemployed youth enters a disco dancing competi-
tion, unaware that the owner of the disco has already
fixed the result with a crooked promoter. A feeble
British attempt to copy the infinitely superior Amer-
ican disco movies with London locations. All the
characters are one-dimensional, including the hero's
partner – a black diplomat's daughter.
MUS     87 min (ort 93 min) (Cut at film release)
B,V     INT; PHE (VHS only); AVR

## MUSIC MAN, THE ****

Morton Da Costa     USA     U   1962
*Robert Preston, Shirley Jones, Buddy Hackett,*
*Hermione Gingold, Paul Ford, Pert Kelton, Ron*
*Howard*
A con-man comes to a small town, and persuades its
inhabitants to start a marching band with himself as
its leader. An exuberant and highly successful trans-
fer to the screen makes this one of the few screen
musicals that really works. Numbers include: "76
Trombones", "Till There Was You" and "Trouble". AA:
Score (Adapt) (Ray Heindorf).
Boa: musical by Meredith Wilson.
MUS     146 min (ort 151 min)
V/sh     WHV

## MUSSOLINI **

Carlo Lizzani     ITALY/USA     1974
*Rod Steiger, Henry Fonda, Franco Nero*
A competent biopic dealing with the last days of
Mussolini's reign in April 1945.
Aka: LAST FOUR DAYS, THE; MUSSOLINI, THE
LAST ACT; MUSSOLINI ULTIMO ATTO
DRA     132 min
B,V     VFP L/A; HER

## MUSSOLINI AND I **

Alberto Negrin     PG
    FRANCE/ITALY/SPAIN/USA     1985
*Bob Hoskins, Anthony Hopkins, Susan Sarandon,*
*Annie Girardot, Barbara De Rossi, Fabio Testi,*
*Dietlinde Turban, Vittorio Mezzogiorno, Pier Paolo*
*Capponi, Francesca Rinaldi, Kurt Raab, Oliver*
*Dominick, Hans Dieter Asner*
This production concentrates on the struggle for
power between Mussolini and his son-in-law, with
Hoskins playing the former in a lavish production
that recreates the events which accompanied the
dictator's downfall after ruling Italy for more than
twenty years. Unfortunately, the film fails to organise
its material in a coherent way. First shown in two
parts.
Aka: MUSSOLINI: THE DECLINE AND FALL OF IL
DUCE

Boa: story by Nicola Badalucco.
DRA        144 min; 130 min (CH5) (ort 200 min) mCab
B,V                                 EHE; CH5 (VHS only)

## MUTANT *                                          18
John (Bud) Cardos        USA                       1984
*Wings Hauser, Bo Hopkins, Lee Montgomery, Jennifer
Warren, Jody Melford, Cary Guffey, Marc Clement,
Danny Nelson, Mary Nell Santacroce, Stuart
Culpepper, Ralph Redpath, Johnny Popwell Sr, Ralph
Pace, Lit Cannah*
Two hitch-hikers arrive in a small town, where toxic
waste is turning the locals into nasty monsters who
crave human flesh. A run-of-the-mill zombie movie.
Aka: NIGHT SHADOWS
HOR                                 95 min (ort 100 min)
B,V                                                  EIV

## MUTANT 2 *                                        18
Deran Sarafian        SPAIN                         1984
*Martin Hewitt, Dennis Christopher, Lynn Holly-
Johnson, Luis Prendes, J.O. Bosso*
Rip-off of THE MUTATIONS with three friends
discovering that alien microbes are taking over
human beings, turning their unwitting hosts into
hideous lizard-like creatures. They join forces with a
scientist to combat this menace. A lacklustre effort
with dismal effects.
Aka: ALIEN PREDATOR; ALIEN PREDATORS;
FALLING, THE
HOR                                 85 min (ort 92 min)
B,V                                                  EIV

## MUTANT HUNT **                                    18
Tim Kincaid        USA                             1987
*Rick Gianasi, Mary Fahey, Ron Reynaldi, Taunie
Vernon, Bill Peterson, Marc Umile, Stormy Spell,
Doug De Vos, Warren Ulaner, Mark Legan, Asle Kid,
Leanne Baker, Nancy Arons, Adriane Lee, Ed Malia,
Eliza Little, Owen Flynn*
Originally designed for hazardous occupations, huma-
noid cyborgs have been turned into violent mutants,
with a drug secretly administered by the head of a
powerful corporation. He plans to sell them to the
highest bidder, but meanwhile they are terrorising
the city, and the inventor of the cyborgs calls in a
private operative to destroy them. A BLADE RUN-
NER clone set in New York of the 21st century.
Aka: MATT RYKER: MUTANT HUNT
FAN                                 76 min (ort 90 min) mVid
B,V                                                  EIV

## MUTANT KID, THE *                                 18
William Szarka        USA                          1986
*David Pike, Mary Beth Pelshaw, Danny Guerra*
A doctor's evil experiments with plutonium lead to a
woman's death, which he conceals in this dreary dud.
Aka: PLUTONIUM BABY
DRA                                                 81 min
V                                   SHEER; PVG; SCRN

## MUTANT ON THE BOUNTY **                           18
Robert Torrance        USA                         1989
*John Roarke, Deborah Benson, John Furey, Victoria
Catlin, John Fleck, Kylie T. Heffner*
Life on a spaceship is rather dull, until the arrival of a
crazy musician, who has been beamed aboard in a
somewhat altered state. When two more strangers
follow, chaos ensues. A silly blend of SF and comedy.
COM                                                 90 min
V                                                  FUTUR

## MUTATIONS, THE *                                  18
Jack Cardiff        UK                             1974
*Donald Pleasence, Tom Baker, Brad Harris, Julie Ege,
Michael Dunn, Jill Haworth, Scott Antony, Lisa
Collings, Richard Davies, John Wreford, Eithne
Dunne, Tony Mayne, Kathy Kitchen, Fran
Fullenwider, Molly Tweedie, Fay Bura*

A scientist experiments in cross-breeding people with
plants, in this Grade-Z horror film. A badly-made and
rather repulsive film, with little style or imagination.
HOR                                 89 min (ort 92 min)
B,V                                                  RCA

## MUTINY AT FORT SHARP *
Fernado Cerchio        SPAIN                        1966
*Broderick Crawford, Elisa Montes, Mario Valdemain,
Umberto Ceriani, Hugo Arden, Julio Pena, Carlos
Mendi, Tomas Pico, Nando Angelini*
Set in 1864, this tells of a group of French troops who
cross by accident into Confederate territory, and then
find themselves forced to join the rebels in defending a
fort under attack from Indians. A poorly made and
badly dubbed effort.
WES                                 91 min dubbed
B,V                                                  VCL

## MUTINY IN THE SOUTH SEAS **                       15
Wolfgang Becker
           FRANCE/ITALY/WEST GERMANY               1965
*Joachim Hansen, Frank Fielding, Gisella Arden,
Alfredo Varelli, Jacques Bezard, Horst Frank, Horst
Niendorf*
At the end of WW2, German refugees in the Pacific
turn to piracy.
Aka: DIE LETZEN DREI DER ALBATROS
A/AD                                                87 min
B,V                                 DAV L/A; VTEL

## MUTINY ON THE BOUNTY ***                          15
Lewis Milestone        USA                         1962
*Marlon Brando, Trevor Howard, Richard Harris,
Hugh Griffith, Richard Haydn, Gordon Jackson, Tim
Seely, Percy Herbert, Tarita, Duncan Lamont, Chips
Rafferty, Noel Purcell*
Remake of the 1935 film which tells of the famous
mutiny against Captain Bligh during a voyage to the
South Seas. This one is a little fairer to Bligh (a good
performance by Trevor Howard), but otherwise weak-
er and less interesting as a piece of drama. Brando is
miscast as Fletcher Christian, but, if nothing else, the
film is a visual treat. Another remake followed in
1984 with THE BOUNTY.
Boa: book by Charles Nordhoff and James Hall.
DRA                                 177 min (ort 185 min)
V/sh                                                 MGM

## MUTINY ON THE BUSES *
Harry Booth        UK                              1973
*Reg Varney, Stephen Lewis, Bob Grant, Anna Karen,
Michael Robbins, Doris Hare, Pat Ashton, Janet
Mahoney, Caroline Dowdeswell, Kevin Brennan, Bob
Todd, David Lodge, Tex Fuller, Jan Rennison,
Damaris Hayman, Juliet Duncan*
Another dreary spin-off for your collection, based on a
popular British TV series "On The Buses" all about
the lives of a bus company crew and their families. In
this one Varney teaches his brother-in-law to drive
and they enjoy a day out at Windsor Safari Park.
Preceded by ON THE BUSES and followed by HOLI-
DAY ON THE BUSES.
COM                                 84 min (ort 88 min)
V                                   TEVP L/A; WHV

## MY AMERICAN COUSIN ***                            PG
Sandy Wilson        CANADA                         1986
*Margaret Langrick, John Wildman, Richard Donat,
Jane Mortifee, J.T. Scott, Camille Henderson, Darcy
Bailey, Allison Hail, Samantha Jocelyn, Babs Chula,
Terry Moore, Brent Severson, Carter Dunham, Julie
Nevlon, Alexis Peat*
A 1950s drama about a 17-year-old girl, who finds the
isolated life at "Paradise Ranch" less than idyllic.
Come the summer of '59 and she is looking towards
another season of cherry picking, until the arrival of
her cousin from California, who draws up one night in
a red Cadillac. A charming and nostalgic coming-of-

age tale, that won six "Genies" or Canadian Film
Academy awards.
DRA                              85 min (ort 94 min)
B,V                                              VES

## MY APPRENTICESHIP ***                        PG
Mark Donskoi            USSR                    1939
Part 2 of Donskoi's Maxim Gorky trilogy that began
with THE CHILDHOOD OF MAXIM GORKY and
continues with MY UNIVERISITIES.
Aka: OUT IN THE WORLD
DRA                        95 min (ort 98 min) B/W
V                                              HEND

## MY BEAUTIFUL LAUNDRETTE **                    15
Stephen Frears          UK                     1985
Saeed Jaffrey, Daniel Day Lewis, Shirley Anne Field,
Roshan Seth, Gordon Warnecke, Derreck Branche,
Rita Wolf, Souad Faress, Richard Graham, Winston
Graham, Dudley Thomas, Gary Cooper, Charu Bala
Choksi, Neil Cunningham
A contemporary and offbeat look at the Asian com-
munity in Britain, with a young Asian boy running a
luxurious laundrette with the help of a former class-
mate, who has become his homosexual lover. Amusing
in parts, violent in others, with a message buried in
there somewhere.
DRA                      97 min; 93 min (VIR) mTV
B,V                           PVG; VIR (VHS only)

## MY BEST FRIEND IS A VAMPIRE *                 15
Jimmy Huston            USA                     1987
Robert Sean Leonard, Cheryl Pollak, Rene
Auberionois, David Warner, Evan Mirand, Fannie
Flagg, Paul Wilson. Kenneth Kimmins, Cecilia Peck
A high school student is bitten and becomes a
vampire, in this reworking of the TEEN WOLF
theme. A one-joke film that really has nowhere to go,
but the cast struggle along gamely.
COM                          85 min (ort 89 min)
B,V                                             CINE

## MY BLOODY VALENTINE *                         18
George Mihalka          CANADA                  1981
Paul Kelman, Lori Hallier, Neil Affleck, Keith Knight,
Alf Humphreys, Don Franks, Cynthia Dale, Terry
Waterland, Jack Van Evera, Peter Cowper, Helene
Udy, Rob Stein, Toma Kovacs, Carl Marotte, Jim
Murchison, Gina Dick
A maniac axes various victims of both sexes to death
in a small town on Valentine's Day. An unedifying
and not especially memorable HALLOWEEN clone.
HOR                                          91 min
B,V                                              CIC

## MY BODYGUARD **                               PG
Tony Bill               USA                     1980
Adan Baldwin, Ruth Gordon, Matt Dillon, Chris
Makepeace, Martin Mull, John Houseman, Craig
Richard Nelson, Paul Quandt, Joan Cusack
A 15-year-old hires a classmate to protect him from
the school bullies in this enjoyable but hardly memor-
able tale, filmed in and around Chicago. This was
Bill's directorial debut.
COM                          92 min (ort 97 min)
B,V                                              CBS

## MY BOYS ARE GOOD BOYS **
Bethel Buckalew         USA                     1978
Ralph Meeker, Ida Lupino, Lloyd Nolan, David F.
Doyle, Sean T. Roche
Three juvenile delinquents in detention, carry out a
successful robbery of an armoured car, in an unusual
little film whose second half deals with the aftermath
of their robbery.
DRA                          85 min (ort 90 min)
B,V,V2                                           INT

## MY BRILLIANT CAREER ***
Gillian Armstrong   AUSTRALIA                   1979
Judy Davis, Sam Neill, Wendy Hughes, Robert Grubb,
Max Cullen, Pat Kennedy
A bush farmer's daughter dreams of life in the big city
and takes steps to make her dreams come true, in this
engaging drama set in turn-of-the-century Australia.
Based on a true story.
Boa: novel by Miles Franklin.
DRA                                         101 min
B,V,V2                                           GHV

## MY CHAUFFEUR **                               15
David Beaird            USA                     1985
Deborah Foreman, Sam Jones, E.G. Marshall, Sean
McLory, Howard Hesseman, Penn and Teller
Zany comedy about a girl who becomes the first female
employee of a posh L.A. limosine service. She has to
cope with both the distrust and jealousy of her male
colleagues and the crazy antics of her wealthy passengers. Good fun, but hampered but an uneasy mixture
of madcap 1930s style comedy and somewhat less
appealing 1980s humour.
COM                          94 min (ort 97 min)
B,V                                             VES

## MY DARLING SLAVE **                           15
Giorgio Capitani        ITALY                   1973
Lando Bazzanca, Catherine Spaak, Adrienne Asti,
Veronica Meril
A henpecked husband has various adventures in this
stupid and dated sex comedy.
Aka: LA SCHIAVA IO CE LINO E TU NO
A                                            96 min
B,V                                   VFP L/A; HER

## MY DEMON LOVER ***                            15
Charlie Loventhal       USA                     1987
Scott Valentine, Michelle Little, Arnold Johnson,
Robert Trebor, Alan Fudge, Gina Gallego, Calvert De
Forest, Eva Charney, David Cass, Rasia Valenza, Dan
Patrick Brady, Donovan Baker, Teresa Bowman,
Frank Colangelo
A boy has a little problem when it comes to girls;
every time he gets aroused, he literally turns into a
fur-covered demon. An inventive horror spoof that's a
lot better than one might have expected.
COM                          84 min (ort 90 min)
B,V                                              RCA

## MY DOG, THE THIEF **                          U
Robert Stevenson        USA                     1969
Dwayne Hickman, Mary Ann Mobley, Joe Flynn, Elsa
Lanchester, Roger C. Carmel, Mickey Shaughnessy,
John Van Dreelan
Undemanding Disney tale of a canine kleptomaniac
and his rehabilitation.
JUV                          85 min (ort 88 min)
B,V                                             WDV

## MY FAIR LADY ***                              U
George Cukor            USA                     1964
Rex Harrison, Audrey Hepburn, Stanley Holloway,
Wilfrid Hyde-White, Gladys Cooper, Jeremy Brett,
Theodore Bikel, Isobel Elsom, Mona Washbourne,
Walter Burke
A sumptuous but clinical version of PYGMALION,
with some fine Lerner and Loewe songs (and some
poor ones too). A linguist teaches a cockney girl to talk
posh and passes her off as a lady. Good as light
entertainment, but a trifle stilted. AA: Pic, Dir, Actor
(Harrison), Cost (Cecil Beaton), Cin (Harry Stradl-
ing), Art/Set (Gene Allen and Cecil Beaton/George
James Hopkins), Score (Adapt) (Andre Previn), Sound
(George R. Groves).
Boa: play Pygmalion by George Bernard Shaw/
musical by Frederick Loewe and Allan J. Lerner.
MUS                         163 min (ort 175 min)
V                                                CBS

## MY FATHER, MY SON ***
Jeff Bleckner      USA          15 / 1988
*Karl Malden, Keith Carradine, Margaret Klenk,*
*Michael Horton, Dirk Blocker, Jenny Lewis, Billy*
*Sullivan, Grace Zabriskie*
Admiral Zumwalt was Secretary of the Navy at the
time of the Vietnam War, and authorised the use of
the defoliant Agent Orange, which caused his son
(who was fighting in Vietnam at the time), and others
to develop cancer. This poignant but remarkably
restrained account focuses on their relationship and
the guilt Zumwalt Sr felt. Zumwalt Jr died a short
while after the film was released.
Boa: book by Admiral Elmo Zumwalt and Elmo III
Zumwalt.
DRA            96 min (ort 100 min) mTV
B,V                       MGM

## MY FAVOURITE BRUNETTE ***
PG
Elliott Nugent     USA         1947
*Bob Hope, Dorothy Lamour, Peter Lorre, Lon Chaney*
*Jr, John Hoyt, Reginald Denny, Charles Dingle*
A photographer gets involved with gangsters when he
chivalrously offers to help a lady in trouble. A good
vehicle for Hope, with Lorre and Chaney adding some
substance to an otherwise rather insubstantial piece
of nonsense. The script is by Edmund Beloin.
COM                  90 min B/W
B,V                 DFS L/A; GLOB

## MY FAVOURITE WIFE ***
U
Garson Kanin     USA        1940
*Cary Grant, Irene Dunne, Gail Patrick, Randolph*
*Scott, Anne Shoemaker, Scotty Beckett, Donald*
*MacBride*
Witty comedy about a man whose first wife was
presumed dead but returns home to find him remar-
ried. Our hapless hubby now has to choose between
them. Written by Sam and Bella Spewack and Leo
McCarey. Remade as "Move Over, Darling".
Osca: BRINGING UP BABY
COM    87 min; 183 min (2 film cassette) B/W
V                       VCC

## MY FAVOURITE YEAR ***
PG
Richard Benjamin   USA      1982
*Peter O'Toole, Mark Linn-Baker, Jessica Harper,*
*Joseph Bologna, Bill Macy, Lainie Kazan, Anne De*
*Salvo, Lou Jacobi, Adolph Green, George Wyner,*
*Selma Diamond, Cameron Mitchell, Gloria Stuart*
An aspiring young TV writer has to take care of an
ageing but carousing screen swashbuckler, who is
appearing in a 1950s TV show as that week's guest
star. A cheerfully lighthearted romp, with O'Toole
perfectly cast, and a mass of well researched period
detail adding substance to the thin plot.
COM           88 min (ort 92 min)
B,V,LV                   MGM

## MY FOOLISH HEART ***
U
Mark Robson     USA        1949
*Dana Andrews, Susan Hayward, Kent Smith, Lois*
*Wheeler, Jessie Royce Landis, Robert Keith, Gigi*
*Perreau*
The story of a WW2 romance between a soldier and a
young girl that is adroitly handled and has winning
performances that easily overcome the rather cont-
rived plot elements. The memorable theme song is by
Victor Young.
Boa: story Uncle Wiggly In Connecticut by J.D.
Salinger
DRA                  98 min B/W
V                       VGM

## MY FRIENDS NEED KILLING *
Paul Leder       USA        1976
*Greg Mullarey, Meredith MacRae, Clayton Wilcox,*
*Carolyn Ames, Elaine Partnow, Roger Cruz, Laurie*
*Burton, Bill Michael, Savannah Bently, Eric Morris*

A Vietnam veteran takes revenge on former colleagues and their wives, whom he tortures before
killing.
HOR                    85 min
B,V               VIV L/A; INT

## MY LEARNED FRIEND ***
Basil Dearden/Will Hay  UK      1943
*Will Hay, Claude Hulbert, Mervyn Johns, Ernest*
*Thesiger, Charles Victor, Derna Hazell, Eddie*
*Phillips, Maudie Edwards, G.H. Mulcaster, Lloyd*
*Pearson, Gibb Mclaughlin, Aubrey Mallalieu, Ernest*
*Butcher, Lawrence Hanray*
A mad ex-convict has a list of murder candidates,
composed of all those responsible for his imprison-
ment, and a crooked lawyer discovers that his name is
last on the list. A crazy black comedy that was Hay's
last film vehicle and contains some of his best gags.
COM        71 min (ort 76 min) B/W
B,V                    TEVP

## MY LEFT FOOT ***
15
Jim Sheridan     UK         1989
*Daniel Day Lewis, Ray McAnally, Brenda Fricker*
A film based on the true story of Christy Brown, who
was born with cerebral palsy into a large, working
class Irish family, and endured years of humiliating
helplessness. Eventually however, he learns to use his
foot to both paint and write, and secures recognition
and independence. A moving and inspiring tale. See
also GABY: A TRUE STORY.
DRA                    98 min
V/h                      PAL

## MY LIFE AS A DOG ***
15
Lasse Hallstrom   SWEDEN   1985
*Anton Glanzelius, Anki Liden, Tomas Von Brumssen,*
*Melinda Kinnaman, Kicki Rundgren, Ing-Marie*
*Carlsson, Manfred Serner, Lennart Hjulstrom, Leif*
*Ericsson, Christina Carlwind, Ralph Carlsson*
A 12-year-old boy is sent to stay with relatives in the
countryside while his sick mother recuperates. A
lighthearted and touching look at childhood in
Sweden of the 1950s, with the boy (who compares
himself to the Russian dog shot into space) finding
unexpected friendship and adventure among the
town's warmhearted eccentrics. Jonsson's novel is
largely autobiographical.
Aka: MITT LIV SOM HUND
Boa: novel by Reidar Jonsson.
DRA    101 min (2 versions available: dubbed or
sub-titled)
V/s                      HEND

## MY LITTLE PONY: THE MOVIE *
U
Michael Joens    USA       1986
*Voices of: Danny DeVito, Cloris Leachman, Tony*
*Raindall, Rhea Pearlman, Jon Bauman, Alice Playten*
Animated feature based on a popular series of soft
toys. The ponies have to prevent the evil "Smooze"
from over-running everything in sight after it has
been created by a wicked witch. A poor animation
with worse music. A TV series followed.
CAR              87 min (ort 100 min)
V                       VES

## MY LUCKY STARS ***
15
Samo Hung    HONG KONG   1985
*Jackie Chan, Samo Hung, Richard Ng*
Another Jackie Chan blend of comedy and martial
arts action. This one is a police thriller in which he
plays an undercover cop assigned to capture a noto-
rious criminal.
A/AD      84 min (ort 99 min) Cut (2 sec)
V                       VPD

## MY MAN ADAM **
15
Roger L. Simon    USA      1985
*Raphael Sbarge, Page Hannah, Veronica Cartwright,*

*Dave Thomas, Charlie Barnett, Austin Pendleton*
A teenager working as a pizza delivery boy has an active fantasy life, especially when it comes to the girl he's yearning to meet. However, he becomes involved in a real crime in this bland comedy.

| COM | 84 min |
| V/sh | CBS |

## MY MOTHER, THE GENERAL **

| Zoel Gilberg | ISRAEL | 1979 |

*Gila Almagor, Zachi Noy*
A Jewish mother visits her son in the Sinai, in a tank loaded with all sorts of good things, and meets an Egyptian mother on a similar mission.
Aka: IMI, HAGENERALIT

| COM | 76 min |
| B,V | RNK |

## MY NAME IS NOBODY **                    15

Tonino Valerii
FRANCE/ITALY/WEST GERMANY    1974
*Henry Fonda, Terence Hill (Mario Girotti), Leo Gordon, Geoffrey Lewis, R.G. Armstrong, Jean Martin, Piero Lulli, Neil Summers, Steve Kanaly*
An overlong Western spoof, about a young gunman who hero-worships an elderly gunslinger who is about to retire. Filmed in the USA and Spain and produced by Sergio Leone of A FISTFUL OF DOLLARS fame.

| COM | 115 min Cut |
| B,V | MED |

## MY NIGHTS WITH SUSAN, OLGA, ALBERT, JULIE, PIET AND SANDRA **

| Pin de la Parra | NETHERLANDS | 1975 |

*Nelly Frijda, Jerry Broujer, Hans van der Gragt, Willeke Van Ammelrooij*
An account of a strange sex community and its bizarre rituals.
Aka: MIJN NACHTEN MET SUSAN, OLGA, ALBERT, JULIE, PIET AND SANDRA; MY NIGHTS WITH SUSAN, SANDRA, OLGA AND JULIE; SECRETS OF NAUGHTY SUSAN (BEV)

| DRA | 81 min |
| B,V | ABA L/A; BEV |

## MY OLD MAN **

| John Erman | USA | 1979 |

*Kristy McNichol, Warren Oates, Eileen Brennan, Mark Arnold, David Margulies, Howard E. Rollins, Joseph Mather, Joseph Leon, Jess Osuna, Michael Jeter, Peter Maloney, Kenneth Kimmins, Carol Teitel*
A girl has a tough time taking care of her seedy horse-training father in this engaging little yarn that was filmed once before as "Under My Skin".
Boa: short story by Ernest Hemingway.

| DRA | 102 min mTV |
| B,V | IPC; CIC |

## MY PLEASURE IS MY BUSINESS *

| Al Waxman | CANADA | 1974 |

*Xaviera Hollander, Henry Ramer, Colin Fox, Kenneth Lynch, Jayne Eastwood, Don Cullen, George Sperdakos, Marvin Goldhar, Michael Kirby, Renata Plestina, Monica Parker, Nick Nichols, Sydney Brown, Richard Davidson*
An attempt at an autobiographical account of a high class prostitute Xaviera Hollander, who wrote an autobiography called "The Happy Hooker". A bland and uninteresting comedy that has Hollander totally miscast as Hollander. Almost any other actress could have done it better. See also THE HAPPY HOOKER.
Boa: book by Xaviera Hollander.

| COM | 96 min |
| B,V,V2 | VCL |

## MY SCIENCE PROJECT *                    15

| Jonathan Betnel | USA | 1985 |

*Dennis Hopper, John Stockwell, Fisher Stevens, Danielle Von Zerneck, Barry Corbin, Richard Masur, Raphael Sbarge, Ann Wedgeworth, Candace Silvers, Beau Dremann, Pat Simmons, John Vidor, Vincent Barbour, Jaime Alba*
Two high school kids devise a science project that brings them unexpected problems, when come across an alien device that's able to distort time. As they tinker with it, the place fills up with assorted creatures, but unfortunately, despite its undoubted virtues, the device is unable to fill the film with humour.

| COM | 91 min (ort 94 min) |
| B,V | TOUCH/WDV |

## MY SISTER'S KEEPER **                    15

| David Saperstein | USA | 1985 |

*Peter Weller, Kathy Baker, John Glover, Bill Smitrovich, Rhetta Hughes*
A woman finds her husband has been brutally murdered on their isolated island home and their boat is missing. There follows a terrifying life and death struggle with the murderer.

| THR | 96 min |
| B,V | AVA |

## MY SON THE VAMPIRE *

| John Gilling | UK | 1952 |

*Arthur Lucan, Bela Lugosi, Kitty McShane, Dora Bryan, Richard Wattis, Judith Furse, Philip Leaver, Maria Mercedes, Roderick Lovell, David Hurst, Hattie Jacques, Graham Moffat, Dandy Nichols, Arthur Brander, Ian Wilson*
Last in a series of dated British comedies in which our heroine helps trap an evil foreign scientist known as The Vampire, who has invented a robot to help him in his dastardly plans.
Aka: KING ROBOT; MOTHER RILEY MEETS THE VAMPIRE; OLD MOTHER RILEY MEETS THE VAMPIRE; VAMPIRE AND THE ROBOT, THE; VAMPIRE OVER LONDON

| COM | 74 min B/W |
| B,V | MOV L/A; PORVI |

## MY STEPMOTHER IS AN ALIEN *                    15

| Richard Benjamin | USA | 1988 |

*Dan Aykroyd, Kim Basinger, Jon Lovitz, Alyson Hannigan, Joseph Maher, Seth Green, Wesley Mann. Voices of: Ann Prentiss, Harry Shearer*
A widowed scientist inadvertently transports a beautiful alien to Earth and marries her, but she only wants to save her planet from imminent destruction. An unsatisfactory blend of comedy and SF that does nothing for either.

| COM | 104 min (ort 108 min) |
| V | RCA |

## MY THERAPIST ***                    18

| Al Rossi (Gary Legon) | USA | 1983 |

*Marilyn Chambers, David Winn, Judith Jordan, Kate Ward, Buck Flower, Robbie Lee*
Kelly Carson is a big-hearted Californian woman who works in a sex clinic helping men with their problems. She often becomes involved emotionally with the difficulties her clients face, but has a boyfriend who has fallen in love with her. He cannot accept that she does this kind of work, and the film ends with a sorrowful parting on a beach. Well made and acted, with a pretty good story too.

| A | 77 min (ort 81 min) (Cut at film release) |
| B,V | CIC; APX |

## MY TUTOR *                    18

| George Bowers | USA | 1982 |

*Martin Lattanzi, Caren Kaye, Kevin McCarthy, Arlene Golonka, Clark Brandon, Bruce Bauer, Crispin Glover*
A boy's parents get him a beautiful tutor to help him pass his French exams, but she gives him lessons in sex as well. A dire comedy that might well have been

better as a straight drama.
COM 97 min
B,V,V2 VDM; STABL

**MY UNIVERSITIES *** PG
Mark Donskoi USSR 1940
The final part of Donskoi's 3-part work on the life of
Gorky that began with THE CHILDHOOD OF MAX-
IM GORKY and then MY APPRENTICESHIP.
DRA 95 min (ort 104 min) B/W
V HEND

**MY WAY ** PG
Emil Nofal/Roy Sargent
SOUTH AFRICA 1972
Ken Leach, Madeleine Usher, Richard Loring, Diane
Ridler, John Higgins, Joe Stewardson, Tony Jay,
Marie Du Toit
An Olympic athlete ruthlessly demands the same
qualities and dedication that he possesses from his
three sons.
Aka: WINNERS
DRA 90 min (ort 107 min)
B,V TURBO

**MY YOUNG MAN ** PG
Mario Garriazzo ITALY 1974
Renato Cestie, Lee J. Cobb, James Whitmore, Marina
Malfatti, Adolfo Celi, Cyril Cusack
A small boy has to make his own way in the world of
showbiz, when his father is deserted by his wife and
partner. A real tearjerker.
Aka: BALLOON VENDOR, THE; LAST MOMENTS
(ARCADE/VSP; VGM); LAST CIRCUS SHOW, THE;
VENDITORE DI PALLANCINI
DRA 100 min (ARCADE/VSP or VGM); 105 min
B,V ARCADE/VSP; VGM; VPD

**MYRA BRECKENRIDGE ** 18
Michael Sarne USA 1970
Raquel Welch, John Huston, Mae West, Rex Reed,
Farrah Fawcett, Roger C. Carmel, George Furth,
Calvin Lockhart, Jim Backus, John Carradine, Andy
Devine, Grady Sutton, Tom Selleck
A film critic has a sex-change operation, and goes to
Hollywood to get her own back on both men and
mankind. A highly disjointed attempt to bring Vidal's
novel to the screen, making use both of old movie clips
and stars such as West. The film's greatest failing is
not its vulgarity, but simply its sheer lack of coher-
ence. Despite this, it hardly deserves the degree of
critical abuse that has been heaped on it.
Boa: novel by Gore Vidal.
COM 93 min (ort 100 min)
V/h CBS

**MYRIAM ** 18
Lester C. Williams
WEST GERMANY 1982
Bea Fielder, Eleanore Melzer, Susi Herman, Mario
Pollak, Herbert Stiny, Wolfgang Sammer, Robert
Dengl
The story of an open marriage in which both partners
indulge in a series of extra-marital affairs.
A 61 min (ort 89 min) Cut
B,V ELV

**MYSTERIANS, THE ** 
Inoshiro Honda JAPAN 1959
Kenji Sahara, Yumi Shirakawa, Momoko Koshi,
Akihiko Hirata, Takashi Shimura, Susumu Fujita,
Fuyki Murakami, Yoshio Kosugi, Hisaya Ito,
Minosuke Yamada, Harold S. Conway
Highly intelligent aliens invade Earth when their
own planet is destroyed, and seek to mate with Earth
women in an effort to create a new species. Not a bad
effort, with good sets and considerable inventiveness.
Aka: CHIKYU BOIGUN; EARTH DEFENSE
FORCES

Osca: SONS OF THE MUSKETEERS
FAN 82 min (ort 85 min) dubbed
B,V KVD

**MYSTERIOUS DESPERADO, THE ** 
Leslie Selander USA 1949
Tim Holt, Richard Martin, Movita, Robert Livingston,
Edward Norris, Frank Wilcox, William Tannen,
Robert B. Williams, Kenneth MacDonald, Frank
Lackteen
A standard second feature Western, in which the hero
helps a young heir recover his inheritance, stolen from
him by land-grabbing crooks.
Osca: LAST DAYS OF POMPEII, THE
WES 61 min B/W
B,V KVD

**MYSTERIOUS ISLAND *** U
Cy Endfield UK 1961
Michael Craig, Herbert Lom, Joan Greenwood,
Michael Callan, Gary Merrill, Beth Rogan, Percy
Herbert, Dan Jackson, Nigel Green
Two Confederate officers escape from their Union
captors by balloon and land on a strange island
inhabited by prehistoric monsters (special effects are
by Ray Harryhausen). An uneven but highly enjoy-
able adventure with excellent monsters. The score is
by Bernard Herrmann. Filmed once before in 1929
and as a cinema serial in 1951.
Boa: novel by Jules Verne.
JUV 101 min
B,V VCL/CBS; STYL

**MYSTERIOUS MISTER WONG, THE ** 
William Nigh USA 1935
Bela Lugosi, Arline Judge, Wallace Ford, Fred
Warren, Lotus Long, Robert Emmett O'Connor,
Edward Peil Sr, Luke Chan, Lee Shumway, Etta Lee,
Ernest F. Young, Theodor Lorch, James B. Leong,
Chester Gan
A ruthless mandarin strikes terror into the heart of
San Francisco's Chinatown in his search for the
twelve coins of Confucius, which legend says will
bring their owner great power. However, he has not
reckoned on having to deal with the formidable Mr
Wong. One in a series of "Mr Wong" films that offers
mild diversion and a few thrills. The script is by Nina
Howatt.
Boa: novel The Twelve Coins Of Confucius by Harry
Stephen Keeler.
THR 70 min B/W
V HVS

**MYSTERIOUS TWO ** 
Gary Sherman USA 1982
John Forsythe, Priscilla Pointer, Karen Werner, James
Stephens, Noah Beery, Vic Tayback, Robert Pine,
Robert Englund, Renny Roker, Candy Mobley, James
Parker, Constance Pfeiffer, Bill Quinn, Bill Smillie, Ed
Call, Georgie Paul
A couple of extra-terrestrials promise society's out-
casts a better future when they arrive on a recruiting
drive for their home planet. A pilot for a failed TV
series. Average.
Aka: FOLLOW ME IF YOU DARE
FAN 97 min (ort 100 min) mTV
B,V,V2 GHV

**MYSTERY MANSION, THE ** PG
David E. Jackson USA 1983
Dallas McKennon, Greg Wynne, Jane Ferguson, Randi
Brown, Lindsay Bishop, David Wagner
The descendants of a pioneer family who were killed
by bank robbers after being taken hostage, go on a
dangerous hunt for the money from the original
robbery. Fair.
A/AD 95 min
B,V IVS

## MYSTERY SUBMARINE **
C.M. Pennington-Richards
                          UK                1962
*Edward Judd, James Robertson Justice, Laurence*
*Payne, Albert Lieven, Joachim Fuchsberger, Arthur*
*O'Sullivan, Robert Flemyng, Richard Carpenter,*
*Richard Thorp, Jeremy Hawk, Robert Brown,*
*Frederick Jaeger, Leslie Randall*
A German submarine is captured and then put to sea
again with a British crew, who use it to find out the
movements of a German wolfpack. Standard WW2
heroics, scripted by Jon Manchip White, Hugh Wood-
house and Bertram Ostrer.
Aka: DECOY; MYSTERY SUBMARINES
Boa: play by Jon Manchip White.
WAR                                    91 min B/W
B,V                                         IFS; INT

## MYSTERY TRAIN ***                          15
Jim Jarmusch          USA                1989
*Screamin' Jay Hawkins, Masatoshi Nagase, Joe*
*Strummer, Youki Kudoh, Cinque Lee, Nicoletta*
*Braschi, Elizabeth Bracco, Rick Aviles, Steve Buscemi,*
*Tom Noonan, Rockets Redglare, Rufus Thomas, Tom*
*Waits (voice only)*
Three interwoven tales from the director of DOWN
BY LAW and STRANGER THAN PARADISE, and
likewise marked by a quirky set of observations and
feel for the bizarre. The stories are all set at a seedy
Memphis hotel, and revolve around the foreign guests
who check in. A weird, minimalist comedy that's often
surprisingly droll. Music is by John Lurie.
COM                            110 min (ort 113 min)
V/h                                          PAL

## MYSTIC PIZZA **                             15
Donald Petrie         USA                1988
*Annabeth Gish, Julia Roberts, Lili Taylor, Vincent*
*Phillip D'Onofrio, William R. Moses, Adam Storke,*
*Conchata Ferrell, Joanna Merlin*
Three pizza-house waitresses in the Connecticut re-
sort of Mystic, discover that life offers more than they
could have hoped for in this superficial but often quite
touching coming-of-age comedy. The fine New Eng-
land locations and an excellent cast help mask the
basic shallowness of the script.
COM                                        104 min
V                                            VIR

## N

## NADIA *                                      U
Alan Cooke
          FRANCE/USA/YUGOSLAVIA         1984
*Talia Balsam, Jonathan Banks, Joe Bennett, Simone*
*Blue, Johann Carlo, Carrie Snodgress, Conchata*
*Ferrell, Carl Strano, Karrie Ullman, Leslie Weiner,*
*Geza Posca, Sonja Kereskenji, Marcia Frederick,*
*Karin Aderente, Par Starr*
The superb athletic performance by the Rumanian
gymnast Nadia Comaneci at the 1976 Olympics
contrasts markedly with this attempt to tell the story
of how her career started, with all the joys, sorrows
and hard work that her training demanded. A totally
flat and lifeless work, with the only redeeming feature
worthy of mention being the performance sequences.
Boa: book by Nadia Comaneci/story by James T.
McGinn.
DRA                                     99 min mTV
B,V                        ODY; PARK (VHS only)

## NADINE **                                   PG
Robert Benton         USA                1987
*Jeff Bridges, Kim Basinger, Rip Torn, Gwen Vernon,*
*Glenne Headly, Jerry Stiller, Jay Petterson, William*
*Youmans, Gary Grubbs, Mickey Jones*
A hairdresser about to get a divorce from her husband,
accidentally witnesses a murder, and is forced to call
on his assistance to get her out of trouble. Pleasant
but bland comedy set in Austin, Texas, in 1954.
COM                            80 min (ort 83 min)
V/h                                          CBS

## NAIROBI *                                   PG
Marvin J. Chomsky     USA                1984
*Charlton Heston, Maud Adams, John Rhys-Davies,*
*John Savage, Connie Booth, Shane Rimmer, Thomas*
*Baptiste, Bill Wright, Elizabeth McConnell*
An ex-US Green Beret turned Kenyan game warden
combats poachers while his estranged father, a former
hunter, is reduced to running tourist safaris. Badly
scripted, indifferently acted and best forgotten.
Filmed entirely on location in Kenya.
Aka: NAIROBI AFFAIR, THE
A/AD                           90 min (ort 100 min) mTV
B,V                           EHE; CH5 (VHS only)

## NAKED AFTERNOON, THE **
Alan Colberg          USA                1976
*Abigail Clayton, Joey Civera, Sarah Mills, Turk Lyon,*
*Mark McIntyre, John Leslie, Annette Have, Clair Dia*
Whilst in bed with his girlfriend, a boring computer
programmer tells his girl that he wants to marry her.
But Thomasina, who is working in a massage parlour,
aspires to be an actress. She makes a porno film but
then finds herself out of work when the police close
down the parlour. However, when a film producer sees
the movie he decides to give her a screen-test, and she
becomes a legitimate actress. An interesting but
contrived story.
A                                           80 min
V                                            CAL

## NAKED AND THE DEAD, THE **                  PG
Raoul Walsh           USA                1958
*Cliff Robertson, Aldo Ray, Raymond Massey, William*
*Campbell, Richard Jaeckel, James Best, Joey Bishop,*
*L.Q. Jones, Robert Gist, Lili St Cyr, Barbara Nichols,*
*Jerry Paris, Casey Adams*
A platoon is assigned to undertake a dangerous
mission behind Japanese lines on a Pacific island
during WW2. A diluted adaptation of the original
novel with its intensity lost in the cliches and
conventions of a standard war film.
Boa: novel by Norman Mailer.
Osca: TARGET (KVD)
WAR                    123 min; 130 min (ODY)
B,V                        KVD; ODY (VHS only)

## NAKED ARE THE CHEATERS **
Derek Ashburne        USA                1971
*Angela Carmen, Robert Warner, Vickie Corbe*
Totally forgettable sex drama.
A                                           63 min
B,V                                          MED

## NAKED CAGE, THE *                           18
Paul Nicholas         USA                1985
*Shari Shattuck, Angel Tompkins, Lucinda Crosby,*
*Christina Whitaker, Carole Ita White, Faith Minton*
A female bank employee is falsely implicated when
her bank is robbed by her ex-husband and his new
girlfriend. The woman's lying testimony is instrumental in sending her to a brutal women's prison,
where she encounters the usual range of humiliations
at the hands of all and sundry. Another tawdry
exploitation piece with zero entertainment value, and
a prime example of this genre.
DRA               89 min (ort 91 min) (Cut at film release by 3
                                             min 29 sec)
B,V                                          RNK

## NAKED CAME THE STRANGER ***               R18/18
Henry Paris (Radley Metzger)
                      USA                1975

*Mary Stuart, Alan Marlow, Christina Hutton, Darby Lloyd Raines, Levi Richards, Helen Madigan*
A married couple run a radio chat show together. The husband has started to play around, so his wife starts seeking encounters as a way of getting her revenge. None too successful at first, she turns her attentions to her husband's lover, seducing the girl so expertly that she wants to leave him for her. One of Metzger's best films, made with some care. The 18 version was cut before video submission by 23 min 12 sec.
Osca: FANTASY WORLD (TCX)
A                49 min (18 version); 67 min (R18 version)
                                                (ort 91 min)
B,V                        PICVID L/A TCX L/A; SHEP

**NAKED CELL, THE ***                                    18
John Crome              USA                    1987
*Vicky Jeffrey, Richard Fallon, Jacquetta May*
A rather sordid thriller in which a businesswoman is obsessed with sex and is drawn into a succession of shallow relationships. After one of her boyfriends is found murdered at her apartment she is charged and held in prison, where she is subjected to endless interrogations. Crome's first feature film is a ponderous mess that has little tension or interest. The script is by Berkeley Burdock.
THR                                              90 min
B,V                                              CHV

**NAKED CIVIL SERVANT, THE ****                          15
Jack Gold              UK                      1975
*John Hurt*
A fine TV play based on the life and times of Quentin Crisp, an effeminate homosexual who recounts his experiences with style and wit. Both touching and amusing; a work of considerable charm.
Boa: book by Quentin Crisp.
DRA                      80 min; 78 min (VCC) mTV
B,V                                      THAMES; VCC

**NAKED COUNTRY, THE ****                               18
Tim Burstall          AUSTRALIA              1984
*John Stanton, Ivar Kants, Rebecca Gilling, Tommy Lewis, John Jarratt, Simon Chilvers, Neela Day*
An Australian adventure story telling of a rancher who is forced to venture far into the outback to bring back his wife, who has run away.
Boa: novel by Morris West.
A/AD                    88 min (ort 91 min) Cut (36 sec)
B,V                                      PACEV; PAN

**NAKED FACE, THE ****                                  18
Bryan Forbes          USA                    1984
*Roger Moore, Rod Steiger, Elliott Gould, Anne Archer, David Heidson, Art Carney, David Hedison, Deanna Dunagan, Ron Parady*
A psychiatrist's patients are being murdered and the cops investigate, coming to the startling conclusion that he is the prime suspect, which forces him to try and solve the mystery through his own efforts, and thus clear his name. A confused and ramshackle thriller that gets lost in its own absurdities.
Boa: novel by Sidney Sheldon.
THR                      100 min (ort 135 min)
B,V                                              GHV

**NAKED GUN, THE: FROM THE                               15
FILES OF POLICE SQUAD ****
David Zucker          USA                    1988
*Leslie Nielsen, Priscilla Presley, O.J. Simpson, George Kennedy, Ricardo Montalban, Nancy Marchand, John Houseman, Reggie Jackson, Jeanette Charles, Curt Gowdy, Al Yankovic, Joyce Brothers, Ken Minyard, Bob Arthur*
An over-rated slapstick comedy based on a short-lived TV show, that fires off gags in all directions, few of which hit the viewer's funny-bone. A combined creative effort from the writing team responsible for AIRPLANE!, that amply demonstrates how hard it is

to take a 30-minute TV format and turn it into a sustained feature-length comedy. The script is by Jim and Jerry Zucker, Jim Abrahams and Pat Profit.
Aka: NAKED GUN, THE
COM                              81 min (ort 85 min)
V/h                                              CIC

**NAKED KISS, THE ****                                  
Samuel Fuller          USA                    1964
*Anthony Eisley, Constance Towers, Michael Dante, Virginia Grey, Betty Bronson, Patsy Kelly*
A prostitute turns over a new leaf and takes a job caring for handicapped children, but her past is revealed when she is arrested for murder. A grim melodrama competently filmed by a director not afraid to put his own stamp on all the work he did.
DRA                                        95 min B/W
B,V                                          VUL L/A

**NAKED LIE ****                                         15
Richard A. Colla      USA                    1989
*Victoria Principal, James Farentino, Glenn Withrow, William Lucking, Dakin Matthews*
A woman D.A.'s private and professional lives collide when she and her judge lover find themselves both dealing with a case of blackmail and murder that has dangerous political overtones. Average.
DRA                      90 min (ort 100 min) mTV
V                                                CHV

**NAKED PREY, THE ****                                  PG
Cornel Wilde    SOUTH AFRICA/USA             1966
*Cornel Wilde, Ken Gampu, Gert Van Den Bergh, Patrick Mynhardt, Bella Randels*
A group of whites on a hunting safari are captured by an African tribe, and all of them are brutally murdered except one, who is given a sporting chance by being allowed to escape prior to natives being sent after him. A film made with enormous skill, that blends African music with superb locations, to produce a work of considerable atmosphere and suspense.
A/AD                            92 min (ort 94 min)
B,V                                              CIC

**NAKED RUNNER, THE ****                                PG
Sidney J. Furie        UK                    1967
*Frank Sinatra, Michael Newport, Peter Vaughan, Derren Nesbitt, Nadia Gray, Tony Robins, Inger Stratto, Cyril Luckham, Edward Fox, Michael Newport*
An American businessman becomes ensnared in a plot by British intelligence to have him kill an agent behind the Iron Curtain. A tedious and insipid espionage thriller, whose fancy camerawork fails to conceal its poor plot and indifferent acting. The script is by Stanley Mann.
Boa: novel by Francis Clifford.
THR                      100 min (ort 104 min)
B,V                                              WHV

**NAKED TRUTH, THE ****                                 U
Mario Zampi            UK                    1957
*Peter Sellers, Terry-Thomas, Peggy Mount, Dennis Price, Shirley Eaton, Georgina Cookson, Joan Sims, Miles Malleson, Kenneth Griffith, Moultrie Kelsall, Wilfrid Lawson, Wally Patch, John Stuart, George Benson*
Outraged celebrities join forces to silence the blackmailing publisher of a scandal magazine who has dared to expose their private lives to the public gaze. An amusing and well-made black comedy.
Aka: YOUR PAST IS SHOWING
COM                      92 min; 88 min (VCC) B/W
B,V                                      RNK; VCC

**NAKED VENGEANCE ***                                   18
Cirio H. Santiago      USA                    1985
*Deborah Tranelli, Kaz Garaz, Bill McLaughlin*
Another dreary outing on the justice equals revenge

theme. This time our avenging angel is a woman who suffers both a brutal rape and the murder of her husband at the hands of a gang of local thugs. Tiresome beyond belief.

A/AD                          74 min (ort 97 min) Cut (33 sec)
B,V                                                        VES

## NAKED WEREWOLF WOMAN **                    18
Rick Miller            ITALY            1982/1983
*Tina Carraro, Andrea Scall, Frederick Staltini*
Obscure and uninteresting sex film with some horror elements.
Aka: WEREWOLF WOMAN
A                          73 min; 89 min (SHEP) Cut (42 sec)
B,V                          18PLAT/TOW; GLOB; SHEP

## NAM ANGELS *                                18
Cirio H. Santiago        ITALY            1988
*Brad Johnson, Vernon Wells, Kevin Duffis*
Hell's Angels are sent to Vietnam to rescue some missing soldiers. A film that repeats the theme of THE LOSERS from 1970 and has nothing to offer apart from ample action sequences.
A/AD                                              90 min
V                                                        RCA

## NAME FOR EVIL, A *
Bernard Girard          USA              1973
*Samantha Eggar, Robert Culp, Clarence Miller, Sheila Sullivan, Mike Lane, Reed Sherman, Sue Hathaway*
After quitting his job, a man decides to restore an ancient house by a lake that has been in his family for many years, and during the restoration work he and his wife uncover a secret room.
HOR                                              90 min
B,V                                                      VCD

## NAME OF THE ROSE, THE ***                    18
Jean-Jacques Annaud
        FRANCE/ITALY/WEST GERMANY        1986
*Sean Connery, F. Murray Abraham, Christian Slater, Elya Baskin, Feodor Chaliapin Jr, William Hickey, Michael Lonsdale, Ron Perlman, Helmut Qualtinger, Volker Prechtel, Michael Habeck, Urs Althaus, Valentina Vargas*
A senior monk and his novice investigate a spate of deaths at a monastery, and reveal the seamier side of abbey life in the 14th century. Lovingly recreated exteriors, and a wonderful set of grotesque figures provide a great feeling of authenticity, but their sheer visual impact detracts from the more intellectual ramifications of the novel.
Boa: novel by Umberto Eco.
DRA                          124 min (ort 130 min)
V/sh                          NELS L/A; CH5

## NANA **                                      18
Dan Wolman              ITALY            1980
*Katya Berger, Mandy Rice-Davies, Jean-Pierre Aumont, Paul Mueller*
A young girl who sells her body, has a tragic affair that leads to her downfall in this dull, softcore rendition of Zola's classic novel.
Boa: novel by Emile Zola.
DRA                          88 min (ort 92 min)
V                                              GHV; MSD

## NANNY, THE ***                              15
Seth Holt              UK                1965
*Bette Davis, Wendy Craig, Jill Bennett, James Villiers, William Dix, Pamela Franklin, Maurice Denham, Jack Watling, Alfred Burke, Nora Gordon, Harry Fowler*
A young boy discovers his nanny's guilty secret, and has to devise a means of thwarting her efforts to silence him. A taut psychodrama made with a degree of insight and subtlety not usually associated with Hammer productions. The script is by Jimmy Sangster.

Boa: novel by Evelyn Piper.
DRA                          89 min (ort 93 min) B/W
V/h                                                      WHV

## NAPOLEON AND JOSEPHINE:                      PG
## A LOVE STORY – PARTS 1, 2 AND 3 ***
Richard T. Heffron      USA              1987
*Armand Assante, Jacqueline Bisset, Jean-Pierre Stewart, Anthony Perkins, Anthony Higgins, Stephanie Beacham, Jane Lapotaire, William Lucking, Nickolas Grace, Patrick Cassidy, Leigh Taylor-Young*
A lavish and glossy mini-saga, that follows the career of Napoleon from his rise to power to his defeat and exile on St Helena. Much of the tale was filmed at the original locations of the events portrayed, and this adds to the period atmosphere. However, the slow unfolding of the plot is a drawback and the film is marred by the gory execution sequence at the beginning.
DRA                          264 min (3 cassettes) mTV
V/sh                                                    WHV

## NAPOLEON AND SAMANTHA **
Bernard McEveety        USA              1972
*Jodie Foster, Michael Douglas, Will Geer, Johnny Whitaker, Arch Johnson, Henry Jones*
Two kids run away and take their pet lion with them, as they trek through the wilds of Oregon. A rather dull example of family entertainment.
JUV                                              92 min
B,V                                                      WDV

## NARCO DOLLAR *
J.M. Avellana          USA              1989
*Leo Damien, Marcia Kerr, Morgan Hunter*
A tough Miami-based detective mounts his own violent campaign against drug dealers and finds himself caught up in a conflict between Cubans and Colombians, with the latter kidnapping his son and holding him to ransom. He later learns that the entire conflict has been engineered by a former CIA chief anxious to take over the local drugs trade. A dismal actioner of poor production values and feeble dialogue. Barely watchable.
A/AD                                              90 min
V                                                        VES

## NASTY BOYS **                                15
Rick Rosenthal          USA              1989
*Benjamin Bratt, Don Franklin, Craig Burley, Jeff Kaahe, James Pax, William Russ, Melissa Leo, Sandy McPeak, Nia Peeples, Thomas Mikal Ford, Soon-Teck Oh, Whip Hubley*
A crack squad of narcotics officers based in Las Vegas, don masks and the other trappings of Ninja warriors, going undercover to combat local drug barons. The title and plot basis is inspired by the "Nasty Boys" of North Las Vegas, a real-life elite drugs unit; but for all that, this is yet one more production-line cops adventure. The pilot for a series.
A/AD                          88 min (ort 100 min) mTV
V                                                        CIC

## NASTY BOYS 2: KILL OR BE KILLED **          15
Leo Penn                USA              1990
*James Pax, Jeff Kaake, Craig Hurley, Don Franklin, Benjamin Bratt*
A formula sequel to the first film, in which an undercover cop sets out to nail a vigilante who has set himself up as judge and executioner, and now threatens the life of a local drug baron.
A/AD                                              86 min
V                                                        CIC

## NASTY HABITS **                              PG
Michael Lindsay-Hogg USA                1976
*Glenda Jackson, Melina Mercouri, Geraldine Page, Sandy Dennis, Anne Jackson, Susan Penhaligon,*

*Edith Evans, Anna Meara, Rip Torn, Eli Wallach, Jerry Stiller*
Scandalous goings-on at an American convent where the death of the abbess unleashes a veritable power struggle. An over-obvious attempt to satirise Watergate that is just a bit too far-fetched to be really effective.
Boa: novel The Abbess Of Crewe by Muriel Spark.
COM                    92 min; 88 min (HOLLY or VGM)
B,V          CBS; HOLLY (VHS only); VGM (VHS only)

### NATAS: THE REFLECTION *                     18
Jack Dunlap              USA                    1983
*Randy Mulkey, Pat Bolt, Craig Hensley, Fred Perry, Nino Cochise, Tom Martinelli, Bob Cota, Richard Aufmuth, Jerry Crutsinger, Leslie Donnelly, Gloria Goodman, Ted Karadenes, Rea Orcutt, Roy Gunzberg, Leo Hohler*
Routine account of Satanic terrors with a reporter investigating an ancient Indian legend about a figure that guards the gateway to Hell.
Aka: NATAS
HOR                          87 min Cut (5 sec)
B,V                                    ALPHA/INT

### NATHALIE **
Ilia Milonako           GREECE
*Roger Beach, Mario Cutini, Grazia di Giorgi, Marcella Petri,*
Sex film set on a beautiful Greek island, where a young girl is seduced by a film-maker who makes her the leading lady in his latest movie.
Aka: NATHALIE COMES OF AGE
A                              84 min (ort 93 min)
B,V                                    HVM; HVH

### NATIONAL HEALTH, THE ***                   PG
Jack Gold                UK                      1973
*Lynn Redgrave, Colin Blakely, Eleanor Bron, Jim Dale, Donald Sinden, Clive Swift, Sheila Scott-Wilkinson, Neville Aurelius, Mervyn Johns, David Hutcheson, Bob Hoskins, John Hamill, Robert Gillespie, Patience Pryor*
A fairly amusing black comedy set in the men's ward of a large and seedy hospital, that uses a mixture of pathos, comedy and fantasy to make a number of sharp observations on the nature of life in 1970s Britain. Written by Nichols, this stilted work is too hampered by its obvious stage origins to be really effective.
Boa: play by Peter Nichols.
COM                          93 min (ort 97 min)
V                                          RCA

### NATIONAL LAMPOON'S ANIMAL HOUSE **   15
John Landis              USA                    1978
*John Belushi, Tim Matheson, John Vernon, Stephen Furst, Verna Bloom, Thomas Hulce, Peter Riegert, Donald Sutherland, Mary Louise Weller*
Unfunny spoof on American college life during the 1960s, with a mass of crazy pranks and coarse jokes to cover up a threadbare plot about the conflict between rival fraternities. Gave rise to a number of follow-ups and the TV series "Delta House". Written by Harold Ramis.
Aka: ANIMAL HOUSE (CIC)
COM                       104 min (ort 109 min)
V/h                                         CIC

### NATIONAL LAMPOON'S CHRISTMAS
### VACATION **                                PG
Jeremiah S. Chechik   USA                      1989
*Chevy Chase, Beverly D'Angelo, Randy Quaid, Diane Ladd, E.G. Marshall, Doris Roberts, John Randolph, Julia Louis-Dreyfuss, Mae Questel, William Hickey, Brian Doyle-Murray, Juliette Lewis, Johnny Galecki, Nicholas Guest*
When the Griswold family decide to stay at home for the holidays, they little suspect that their peace and tranquility will be destroyed by an invasion of bickering relatives and a catalogue of disasters. A strained and often quite tasteless farce, with a few comic moments, a predictable outcome and a memorable performance from Quaid as an obnoxious cousin.
COM                    93 min (ort 97 min) subH
V/sh                                        WHV

### NATIONAL LAMPOON'S CLASS REUNION *    18
Michael Miller          USA                    1982
*Gerrit Graham, Michael Lerner, Fred McCarren, Miriam Flynn, Stephen Furst, Marya Small, Shelley Smith, Zane Buzby, Anne Ramsey, Jacklyn Zeman, Blackie Dammett, Barry Diamond, Art Evans, Maria Pennington, Randolph Powers*
Unfunny and unpleasant spoof on all those high school reunion films where the ex-classmates are terrorised by a maniacal killer. The level of humour can be gauged from the fact that the school is the Lizzie Borden High. The feeble script is by John Hughes.
Aka: CLASS REUNION (RNK)
COM                          84 min; 82 min (VCC)
B,V,V2                         RNK; VCC (VHS only)

### NATIONAL LAMPOON'S
### EUROPEAN VACATION *                         15
Amy Heckerling          USA                    1985
*Chevy Chase, Beverly D'Angelo, Eric Idle, Dana Hill, Victor Lanoux, John Astin, Jason Lively*
Feeble sequel to NATIONAL LAMPOON'S VACATION in which a strange and wimpish family of Americans decide to take a motoring holiday in Europe. Needless to say, everything goes disastrously wrong in a work reminiscent of the worst of the British "Carry On" films. Written by John Hughes and Robert Klane.
COM                          90 min (ort 94 min)
V/h                                         WHV

### NATIONAL LAMPOON'S MOVIE MADNESS *   15
Henry Jaglom            USA                    1981
*Bob Giraldi, Peter Riegert, Diane Lane, Candy Clark, Teresa Ganzel, Robert Culp, Ann Dusenberry, Bobby DiCenzo, Fred Willard, Joe Spinell, Mary Woronov, Dick Miller, Robby Benson, Richard Widmark, Christopher Lloyd*
A collection of three parodies or spoofs on various movie genres, that deal with personal growth, soap operas and cop movies. Thankfully, a fourth parody on disaster movies was removed, leaving only these three unbelievably lame efforts.
Aka: NATIONAL LAMPOON GOES TO THE MOVIES
COM                                     89 min
B,V                                         WHV

### NATIONAL LAMPOON'S VACATION *              15
Harold Ramis            USA                    1983
*Chevy Chase, Beverly D'Angelo, Anthony Michael Hall, Imogene Coca, Randy Quaid, Christie Brinkley, Dana Barron, John Candy*
A typical American family make a cross-country trip by car, and, needless to say, everything goes wrong in true Disney style. But, on the other hand, perhaps Disney could have made a funnier and more interesting film than this episodic collection of predictable situations. Written by John Hughes.
Aka: VACATION
COM                          95 min (ort 98 min)
B,V                                         WHV

### NATIVE SON **                              15
Jerrold Freedman        USA                    1986
*Carroll Baker, Akosua Busia, Matt Dillon, Victor Love, Art Evans, John Karlen, Elizabeth McGovern, John McMartin, Geraldine Page, Oprah Winfrey, David Rasche, William E. Pugh*
A poor black chauffeur in Chicago of the 1930s

accidentally kills a white woman and hides the body in a bid to escape detection. A fair adaptation of a powerful novel from 1940, made once before in Argentina in 1950, when the author played the title role, but with the inevitable compromises that blunt the force of the original.
Boa: novel/play by Richard Wright.

| DRA | 100 min (ort 112 min) |
| B,V | VES |

## NATURAL, THE **

| | PG |
| Barry Levinson    USA | 1984 |

*Robert Redford, Robert Duvall, Glenn Close, Kim Basinger, Wilford Brimley, Richard Farnsworth, Barbara Hershey, Joe Don Baker, Robert Prosky, Darren McGavin, Kim Basinger, Wilford Brimley*
A man with a strange, almost supernatural talent for baseball, reaches the top, from where only one direction is left for him to go in this curiously oblique and bare adaption of Malamud's strange updating of the King Arthur legend. Written by Roger Towne and Phil Dusenberry. Photography is by Caleb Deschanel.
Boa: novel by Bernard Malamud.

| DRA | 118 min (ort 137 min) |
| V | CBS |

## NAUGHTY BLUE KNICKERS **

| | 18 |
| Andre Genoues    FRANCE | 1984 |

*Marsha Grant, Andre Genoues, Caroline Aguilar, Charlotte Walini, Yves Massaret, Martine Mercadier*
Sex film about the adventures of the various wearers of the title garment.
Aka: LES FOLIES D'ELODIE; SECRETS OF THE SATIN BLUES (BEV or KRP)

| A | 89 min; 86 min (TOW) 85 min (KRP) |
| | Cut (1 min 6 sec) |
| B,V | TOW; BEV; GLOB; KRP |

## NAUGHTY DREAMS OF MISS OWEN, THE *

| | 18 |
| UK | 1988 |

A big-busted woman is left in charge of her aunt's house. The arrival of another well-endowed lady livens things up as they jump into the swimming pool, causing it to overflow somewhat. Unashamed and unadorned sexploiter.

| A | 53 min |
| B,V | PHV L/A; SFI |

## NAUGHTY GIRLS *

| | 18 |
| Peter Shillingford    UK | 1975 |

*Brenda Holder, Angela Unwin*
Not even mildly titillating, this is a film of unrelieved dullness. A feeble comedy in phoney documentary style, describing the experiences of four career girls who travel the world working in enticing exotic locations. Boring, but beautifully photographed.

| A | 59 min (ort 62 min) Cut (1 min 32 sec) |
| V | SFI |

## NAUGHTY NETWORK **

| | R18 |
| Linus Gator    USA | 1981 |

*Delia Cosner, Tina Jordan, Mike Ranger, Ray Cooper, Lauren Hart, Chris Parker, Sandy Browne, Nicole Noir, Stephanie Taylor*
WHAC-TV is the number one x-rated network in the States, having produced such gems as "The Little Whorehouse On The Prairie" and "The Mating Game". The president of the network is determined to knock out all the rivals and previews a series of shows to mark the start of their new season. Funny in parts but pretty low-brow stuff.

| A | 68 min (ort 78 min) Cut (1 min 44 sec) |
| B,V | TCX L/A; SHEP |

## NAUGHTY STEWARDESSES **

| | 18 |
| Al Adamson    USA | 1973 |

*Robert Livingstone, Connie Hoffman, Donna Desmond*
A tale of four flat-sharing stewardesses and their sexual escapades.

| A | 95 min Cut (1 min 43 sec) |
| B,V | VPD |

## NEAPOLITAN CAROUSEL **

| Ettore Gianni    ITALY | 1953 |

*Sophia Loren, Nadia Gray*
So-so musical entertainment about the history of Naples.
Aka: CAROSELLO NAPOLETANO

| MUS | 126 min |
| B,V,V2 | FFV |

## NEAR DARK ***

| | 18 |
| Kathryn Bigelow    USA | 1987 |

*Adrian Pasdar, Jenny Wright, Lance Hendriksen, Bill Paxton, Jenette Goldstein, Tim Thomerson, Marcie Leeds, Joshua Miller, Kenny Call, Ed Corbett, Troy Evans, Bill Cross, Roger Aaron Brown, Thomas Wagner*
A young farmhand gets passionately involved with a young girl who proves to be a member of a band of small-town vampires. In no time, he finds himself a member of a strange band of wandering vampires, whose leader gives him one week in which to make his first kill and thus become truly one of them. A well-crafted and unusual horror film that skifully blends elements of various genres.

| HOR | 90 min (ort 95 min) Cut (14 sec) |
| B,V | EIV |

## NECESSITY *

| | PG |
| Michael Miller    USA | 1988 |

*Loni Anderson, John Heard, James Naughton, Harris Laskawy*
A fashion model runs away from her husband when she learns than he is a top Mafia drugs dealer, and is forced to leave her baby behind. Undaunted however by the prospect of having to find a way into their heavily guarded home, she enlists a pilot to help her mount a rescue. As unimaginative as it is unconvincing.
Boa: novel by Brian Garfield.

| DRA | 92 min (ort 100 min) mTV |
| V/h | MED |

## NECROMANCER *

| | 18 |
| Dusty Nelson    USA | 1989 |

*Elizabeth Kaitan, Russ Tamblyn, John Tyler, Rhonda Durton, Stan Hurwitz*
A supernatural revenge tale in which a woman who is raped by a couple of thugs resorts to witchcraft in order to have her revenge. A tiresome affair that has a contrived and flimsy script and a definite lack of fresh ideas.
Aka: NECROMANCER: SATAN'S SERVANT

| HOR | 84 min (ort 90 min) Cut (35 sec) |
| V | CBS |

## NECROPOLIS *

| | 18 |
| Bruce Hickey    USA | 1986 |

*Michael Conte, Leeanne Baker, Jacquie Fitz, William K. Reed, George Anthony-Bayza, Jett Julian, Nadine Hartsein, Anthony Gioia, Jennifer Stahl, Guy Mirano, Paul Reuben, Andrew Bausili, Letnam Vexim, Jacqueline Pearson*
A witch burnt at the stake in 1685 reincarnates 300 years later to take over where she left off, but her evil-doing is opposed by other figures from her past life. A hackneyed Hammer-style theme resurrected for the 1980s, but just as lacking in skill as ever.

| HOR | 75 min |
| B,V | EIV |

## NED KELLY *

| | 15 |
| Tony Richardson    UK | 1970 |

*Mick Jagger, Allen Bickford, Geoff Gilmour, Mark McManus, Serge Lazareff, Peter Sumner, Ken Shorter,*

*James Elliott, Clarissa Kaye, Frank Thring, Diana
Craig, Susan Lloyd, Alexei Long, Bruce Barry, Janne
Wesley*
Dullish and overlong story of the life and times of this
19th century Australian outlaw and sometime folk-
hero. The script is by Richardson.
Aka: NED KELLY, OUTLAW
DRA                       100 min (ort 103 min)
B,V                                          WHV

## NEGATIVE CONTACT **                    PG
Junga Sato          JAPAN              1975
*Ken Takakura, Shinchi Chiba, Kenji Amao, Etsuko
Shiomi, Fumio Watanabe, Takashi Shimura, Ken
Utsui, Tetsuro Tanba, Eiji Goh, Masayo Utsunomiya,
Tomoo Nagai, Raita Ryu, Yumi Takigawa, Mizuho
Suzuki*
Terrorists plant a bomb on one of the famous "bullet"
trains in order to extort money from the Japanese
government.
Aka: BULLET TRAIN, THE; SHINKANSEN
DAIBABUHA
THR                       85 min (ort 155 min)
V                               FILV; INTCON

## NEGATIVES **
Peter Medak         UK                1968
*Peter McEnery, Diane Cilento, Glenda Jackson,
Maurice Denham, Steven Lewis, Norman Rossington,
Billy Russell*
The strange story of an unmarried couple who run an
antiques shop together and dress up to play a variety
of roles as a way of improving their love-life, being
joined in their strange hobby by an equally kinky
photographer. A well made but somewhat detached
curiosity.
Boa: novel by Peter Everett.
DRA                        90 min (ort 98 min)
V                                            INT

## NEIGHBOURS *                            15
John G. Avildsen    USA               1981
*John Belushi, Dan Aykroyd, Kathryn Walker, Cathy
Moriarty, Lauren-Marie Taylor, Tim Kazurinsky,
Igors Gavon, Dru-Ann Chukron, Tino Insana, P.L.
Brown, Henry Judd Baker, Lauren-Marie Taylor, Dale
Two Eagle, Sherman Lloyd*
A stuffy man is irritated when new, swinging neigh-
bours move in, but worse is to follow when their
strange antics drive him to the edge of insanity.
Watch this one and it will do the same to you. Scripted
by Larry Gelbart. This was Belushi's last film.
Boa: novel by Thomas Berger.
COM                        91 min (ort 94 min)
V                                            RCA

## NEITHER THE SEA NOR THE SAND **
Fred Burnley        UK                1972
*Susan Hampshire, Michael Petrovich, Frank Finlay,
Michael Craze, Jack Lambert, David Garth, Betty
Duncan, Anthony Booth*
A woman on holiday in Jersey falls deeply in love, but
finds that the object of her affections has an un-
pleasant surprise in store when he appears to suffer a
fatal heart attack but returns from the dead. A film
that attempts to a create a heightened mood of
romantic mysticism, but is let down badly by its
pedestrian approach and travelogue camerawork.
Boa: novel by Gordon Honeycombe.
HOR                                  94 min
B,V                                          GHV

## NEON MANIACS **                         18
Joseph Mangine      USA               1985
*Alan Hayes, Donna Locke, Leilani Sarelle, Victor
Elliot Brandt, James Atcheson, Marta Kober, David
Muir, Gene Bickell, Katherine Heard, Jessie Lawrence
Ferguson, Amber Austin, Bo Sabato, John LaFeyette,
Clarke Coleman*

A young girl is pursued by a variety of creatures, best
described as supernatural punks. Her companions are
all killed but she escapes to tell the police, who are
less than willing to believe her. High-grade nonsense
on a low-grade budget.
HOR                        85 min (ort 91 min)
B,V                                      NDH/MED

## NEON NIGHTS ***                         18
Cecil Howard        USA               1982
*Lysa Thatcher, Kandi Barbour, Veronica Hart,
Arcadia Lake, Jody Maxwell, Linda Vale, Jamie Gillis*
After being caught with her mother's boyfriend, a girl
leaves home and has some strange encounters. She is
picked up by a magician who hypnotises her into
levitating. Later, in New York she finds her mother's
boyfriend waiting to cast her in his new show. And
then, lo and behold, she is back in bed and we are led
to believe her encounters to have been merely her
fantasies. A bizarre and absorbing film. Cut before
video submission by 19 min 29 sec.
A         58 min (ort 90 min) Cut (1 min 25 sec)
B,V                                  TCX L/A; SHEP

## NEPTUNE DISASTER, THE *
Daniel Petrie       CANADA            1972
*Ben Gazzara, Yvette Mimieux, Walter Pidgeon, Ernest
Borgnine, Chris Wiggins, Donnelly Rhodes, Ed
McGibbon, Michael J. Reynolds, David Yorston,
Stuart Gillard, Mark Walker, Kenneth Pogue, Frank
Perry, Dan MacDonald, Les Carlson*
A diving submersible has to rescue three oceanolog-
ists trapped in an underwater laboratory but its
mission of mercy fails to provide enough interest to
save this film from its all-pervading dullness.
Aka: NEPTUNE FACTOR, THE; UNDERWATER
ODYSSEY, AN
THR                        94 min (ort 98 min)
B,V                                          CBS

## NEST, THE **                            18
Terence H. Winkless  USA              1987
*Robert Lansing, Lisa Langlois, Franc Luz, Terri
Treas, Stephen Davies, Diana Bellamy, Nancy
Morgan, Jack Collins, Jeff Wrinkless, Steve Tannen,
Heidi Helmer, Karen Smyth, Noel Steven Geray*
A small quaint island becomes a centre for strange
experiments undertaken by a powerful and myste-
rious company, which creates mutant super roaches
that are meat-eating and assume the form of their
victims. Predictably, there is only one person who can
save mankind and destroy these blood-curdling bugs.
A low-budget effort that has a loony charm all of its
own.
HOR                        85 min (ort 89 min)
V                                            MGM

## NESTING, THE **                         18
Armand Weston       USA               1980
*Gloria Grahame, John Carradine, Robin Groves,
Christopher Loomis, Michael David Lally, Bill Rowley,
David Tabor, Patrick Farelley, Bobo Lewis, June
Berry, Cecile Lieman, Ann Varley, Ron Levine, Bruce
Kronenberg, Jim Nixon*
A woman writer of Gothic novels attempts to cure her
agoraphobia by moving to a remote country house
that was once a brothel, and proves to be haunted by
the spirits of the prostitutes who worked there. Truth,
however, soon turns out to be stranger than fiction,
when she learns that they were brutally murdered
there, and want to use her as a means of realising
their revenge. A good start leads to a disappointing
climax.
Aka: PHOBIA
HOR                       99 min (ort 104 min)
B, V/h                                VIPCO; WHV

## NETWORK ****                            15
Sidney Lumet        USA               1976

Peter Finch, Faye Dunaway, William Holden, Robert
Duvall, Ned Beatty, Beatrice Straight, Wesley Addy,
William Prince, Marlene Warfield, Arthur Burghardt,
Kathy Cronkite, John Carpenter, Bill Burrows, Jordan
Charney
With a biting script by Paddy Chayevsky and a superb
performance from Finch in one of his last roles, this is
a sharp and powerful satire on the world of broadcast-
ing. A news commentator for a TV network becomes
an overnight media prophet when he has a breakdown
on the air. Finch's last film which earned him a
posthumous Oscar. AA: Actor (Finch), Actress (Dunaway), S. Actress (Straight), Screen (Orig) (Paddy
Chayefsky).
DRA                      121 min; 117 min (WHV)
B,V,V2                    INT; WHV (VHS only)

## NEVER A DULL MOMENT **                  15
Henry Hathaway          USA               1966
Steve McQueen, Karl Malden, Brian Keith, Arthur
Kennedy, Raf Vallone, Janet Margolin, Howard Da
Silva, Pat Hingle, Martin Landau, Suzanne Pleshette,
Paul Fix, Gene Evans, Josephine Hutchinson, John
Doucette, Val Avery
Western loosely based on the "early life" of a
character in Robbins' novel, and dealing with his
violent quest for revenge on the three outlaws who
murdered his parents, a plot that also served as the
basis for the 1975 TV movie of the same name.
Scripted by John Michael Hayes.
Boa: novel The Carpetbaggers by Harold Robbins.
WES                     125 min (ort 135 min)
V/h                                       CIC

## NEVER A DULL MOMENT *                     U
Jerry Paris             USA               1967
Dick Van Dyke, Edward G. Robinson, Henry Silva,
Dorothy Provine, Joanna Moore, Tony Bill, Slim
Pickens, Jack Elam, Ned Glass, Mickey Shaughnessy
A struggling actor is mistaken for a gangster and is
forced by circumstances to continue playing this role.
Unfortunately, the title is not an accurate description
of this tired comedy.
Boa: novel by John Godey.
COM                     87 min (ort 100 min)
B.V                                       WDV

## NEVER CRY DEVIL **                        18
Rupert Hitzig           USA               1989
Elliott Gould, Richard Roundtree, Michael J. Pollard,
Derek Rydall, Allen Garfield
A college student with an over-active imagination
discovers that one of his teachers is a Satanist who has
ritually murdered a prostitute who was his next-door
neighbour. Predictably, both his friends and the cop
leading the murder investigation dismiss his claims in
a reasonably entertaining thriller that borrows some
of its plot elements from FRIGHT NIGHT.
THR                                       88 min
V                                         MED

## NEVER CRY WOLF ***                        PG
Carroll Ballard         USA               1983
Charles Martin Smith, Brian Dennehy, Samson Jorah,
Zachary Ittimangnaq, Samson Jorah, Hugh Webster,
Martha Ittimangnaq, Tom Dahlgren, Walker Stuart,
C.M. Smith, Eugene Corr, Christina Luescher
(narration)
A Canadian author braves the perils of the Arctic to
study wolves and their behaviour, and comes to a
better understanding of both himself and them.
Inevitably, however, the human performances are
muted by the animals and the sheer majesty and
beauty of their habitat. Written by Curtis Hanson,
Sam Hamm and Richard Ketter.
Boa: book by Farley Mowat.
A/AD                                      105 min
B,V                                       WDV

## NEVER ENDING STORY, THE ***              U
Wolfgang Petersen
           UK/WEST GERMANY                1984
Noah Hathaway, Barrett Oliver, Patricia Hayes, Tami
Stronach, Moses Gunn, Sydney Bromley, Gerald
McRaney, Alan Oppenheimer (voice only)
A young boy who doesn't much care for reading, is
given a magical book that takes him of a journey to a
fantasy kingdom which he alone can save from
extinction. Good effects and visuals make this an
enjoyable fantasy although the lack of humour and an
over-simplistic message are major irritants. This was
Petersen's first English language film.
Boa: novel by Michael Ende.
JUV                                       90 min
V/sh                                      WHV

## NEVER GIVE AN INCH **                     15
Paul Newman             USA               1971
Paul Newman, Henry Fonda, Lee Remick, Michael
Sarrazin, Richard Jaeckel, Linda Lawson
Massive drama about a family of modern-day Oregon
loggers whose members all have egos every bit as big
as the trees they fell while the title (their family
motto) sums up their attitude to life. Excellent
performances and some good sequences enliven a dull
film.
Aka: SOMETIMES A GREAT NOTION
Boa: novel by Ken Kesey.
DRA                     110 min (ort 114 min)
B,V                                       CIC

## NEVER LOVE A HOOKER **                    18
Christian Gion          FRANCE            1978
Nicole Calfan, Francis Huster, Jacques Francois,
Nicole Seguin, Sophie Deschamp, Catherine Alvic,
Henri Guylet, Claire Duval
A young girl is forced to work in a Paris brothel
during the 1930s and becomes the object of an
infatuation on the part of one of her clients.
Aka: CENT VINGT-DEUX RUE DE PROVENCE;
ONE TWO TWO (INT); ONE TWO TWO RUE DE
PROVENCE
DRA                                       84 min
B,V            ABA L/A; INT; AMBAS; KRP

## NEVER LOVE A STRANGER **                  PG
Robert Stevens          USA               1958
John Drew Barrymore, Robert Bray, Lita Milan, Peg
Murray, Steve McQueen, R.G. Armstrong
Gangster melodrama with two boys growing up in
Manhattan. One becomes a gangster and the other
and assistant district attorney. The gangster helps the
assistant D.A. trap a vicious hoodlum. A predictable
adaptation of a mediocre novel.
Boa: novel by Harold Robbins.
DRA                                       88 min B/W
V                                         VCC

## NEVER ON FRIDAY *
Ken Dixon               USA               1976
Lawrence Casey, Eva Carson, Malisa Long
A man shipwrecked on an island populated solely by
female castaways uses sex to save his life.
A                                         78 min
B,V                                       INT

## NEVER ON TUESDAY *                        15
Adam Rifkin             USA               1988
Charlie Sheen, Judd Nelson, Claudia Christian,
Andrew Lauer
Two naive but brash youngsters, get a lesson in
maturity and manner from a self-possessed young
woman, when they wreck her car whilst driving across
the desert on the way to California. A puerile
coming-of-age comedy.
COM                                       87 min
B,V                                       CBS

## NEVER SAY NEVER AGAIN ***　PG
Irvin Kershner　　　UK　　　　　1983
*Sean Connery, Edward Fox, Max Von Sydow, Klaus*
*Maria Brandauer, Barbara Carrera, Alex McCowen,*
*Kim Basinger, Bernie Casey, Rowan Atkinson, Milow*
*Kirek, Valerie Leon, Anthony Sharp, Gavan O'Herlihy,*
*Pat Roach, Prunella Gee*
Routine Bond adventure which is a virtual remake of
THUNDERBALL; well, they had to run out of Ian
Fleming novels eventually. Happily, it also marked a
much-needed return to an earlier style, where soph-
isticated gadgets played a less important role. All in
all an enjoyable action film. The music is by Michel
Legand. Followed by A VIEW TO A KILL.
Boa: novel Thunderball by Ian Fleming.
A/AD　　　128 min (ort 134 min) (Cut at film release)
V/sh　　　　　　　　　　　　　　　　WHV

## NEVER TOO YOUNG TO DIE *　18
Gil Bettman　　　USA　　　　　1986
*John Stamos, George Lazenby, Peter Kwong, Ed*
*Brock, Vanity, John Anderson, Robert Englund, Gene*
*Simmons*
An agent's son becomes involved with his late father's
fellow spies in an attempt to find and punish his
murderers. Routine and mediocre, the only original
touch being the hermaphrodite villain.
A/AD　　　　　　　　　92 min Cut (16 sec)
B,V　　　　　　　　　　　　　　NELS; EHE

## NEW ADVENTURES OF HEIDI, THE **
Ralph Senensky　　USA　　　　　1978
*Katy Kurtzman, Burl Ives, John Gavin, Marlyn*
*Mason, Sean Marshall, Marylyn Mason, Sherrie Wills,*
*Alex Henteloff, Charles Aidman, Walter Brooke, Amzie*
*Strickland, Molly Dodd, Adrienne Marden, Arlen*
*Stuart, Barry Cahill*
Heidi trades the mountain peaks of her beloved
Switzerland for the charmless concrete canyons of
New York, where she becomes the companion to the
spoilt daughter of a wealthy businessman. A musical
background and modern setting are poor substitutes
for the charm of the original classic story.
Boa: novel Heidi by Joanna Spyri.
JUV　　　　　　　　　　　　100 min mTV
B,V　　　　　　　　　　　　　　VCL/CBS

## NEW ADVENTURES OF PIPPI
LONGSTOCKING, THE **　U
Ken Annakin　　USA　　　　　1988
*Tami Erin, David Seaman Jr, Cory Crow, Eileen*
*Brennan, Dick Van Patten, Dennis Dugan, Dianne*
*Hull, George Di Cenzo, John Schuck, J.D. Dickinson,*
*Chub Bailey, Branscombe Richmond, Evan Adam,*
*Fay Masterson, Romy Mehlman,*
The most colourful creation of the Swedish children's
author Astrid Lindgren gets the full Hollywood
treatment in this dull dud. Much spectacular action
but not an ounce of the playful charm that endeared
the earlier Pippi Longstocking films to adults and
children alike, far beyond the author's native country.
Boa: novels by Astrid Lindgren.
JUV　　　　　　　　　97 min (ort 100 min)
V/sh　　　　　　　　　　　　　　　RCA

## NEW AVENGERS, THE: TARGET!/FACES **　PG
Ray Austin/James Hill　UK　　　　　1976
*Patrick Macnee, Gareth Hunt, Joanna Lumley, Robert*
*Beatty, Roy Byrd, Deep Roy, John Paul, Suzanna*
*MacMillan, Robert Tayman, Frederick Jaeger, David*
*De Keyser, Edward Petherbridge, Neil Hallett,*
*Annabel Leventon, David Webb*
Two further episodes from a popular, slightly tongue-
in-cheek series, in which a trio of undercover agents
fight espionage. In "Target!" some unpleasant encoun-
ters with poison-tipped darts take place, and in
"Faces", doubles of our team members create some
rather awkward problems.

A/AD　　　　　　　　　　100 min mTV
V　　　　　　　　　　　　　　　CH5

## NEW AVENGERS, THE: THE EAGLE'S NEST/THE
GLADIATORS **　PG
Desmond Davis/George Fournier
　　　　　　UK　　　　　1976
*Joanna Lumley, Patrick Macnee, Gareth Hunt, Peter*
*Cushing, Derek Farr, Frank Gatliff, Louis Zorich, Neil*
*Vipond, Bill Starr*
Two episodes from the popular TV action series. In the
first story Steed, Purdey and Gambit investigate a
murder, and are drawn to a barren island where they
encounter an order of monks, who in reality are
neo-Nazis who have hatched a bizarre plan to resur-
rect Hitler. In the second adventure the ambitious
plans of a group of supermen are foiled by our
crime-busting trio. Average.
A/AD　　　　　　　　　　105 min mTV
V　　　　　　　　　　　　　　　CH5

## NEW AVENGERS, THE: THE LAST OF THE　PG
CYBERNAUTS?/SLEEPER **
Sidney Hayers/Graeme Gordon
　　　　　　UK　　　　　1976
*Patrick Macnee, Gareth Hunt, Joanna Lumley, Robert*
*Lang, Oscar Quitak, Basil Hoskins, S. Newton*
*Anderson, David Horovitch, Eric Carte, Keith Buckley,*
*Sara Kestelman, Prentis Hancock, Mark Jones, Leo*
*Dolan, Gavin Campbell*
Two episodes from a popular semi-serious action
series, that attempted to recapture some of the verve
of the original 1960s series "The Avengers". In the
first tale our heroes meet up with an old enemy, in the
shape of unstoppable killing machines controlled by a
ruthless megalomaniac, and in the second tale the
team are givem the job of testing out a new anti-
terrorist weapon.
A/AD　　　　　　　　　　100 min mTV
V　　　　　　　　　　　　　　　CH5

## NEW BARBARIANS, THE *
Enzo G. Castellari　ITALY　　　　　1983
*Timothy Brent (Giancarlo Prete), Fred Williamson,*
*George Eastman (Luigi Montefiore), Anna Kanakis,*
*Venantino Venantini, Enzo G. Castellari, Zora Kerova,*
*Massimo Vanni, Andrea Coppola, Patsy May*
*McLachlan, Giovanni Frezza*
Another post-nuclear holocaust saga of a world where
great motorised metal monsters terrorise the survi-
vors. And films like this terrorise the audience.
Aka: I NUOVI BARBARI; WARRIORS OF THE
WASTELAND
FAN　　　　　　　　　　　　91 min
B,V　　　　　　　　　　　　　　EIV

## NEW CENTURIANS, THE ***　15
Richard Fleischer　USA　　　　　1972
*George C. Scott, Stacy Keach, Jane Alexander,*
*Rosalind Cash, Scott Wilson, Erik Estrada, Clifton*
*James, Isabel Sanford, James B. Sikking, Ed Lauter,*
*William Atherton, Roger E. Mosley*
A look at L.A. rookies being shown the ropes by an old
cop who knows how to survive in a violent and
dangerous city. An excellent adaptation of the au-
thor's novel (largely based on his own experiences)
which has inspired many a TV police series, from
"Police Woman" and "Police Story" to "Hill Street
Blues". Inevitably episodic in structure but still worth
a look. The script is by Stirling Silliphant.
Aka: PRECINCT 45: LOS ANGELES POLICE
Boa: novel by Joseph Wambaugh.
DRA　　　　　　　　　99 min (ort 103 min)
B,V　　　　　　　　　　　　　　RCA

## NEW FIST OF FURY **　18
Lo Wei　　　HONG KONG　　　　　1976
*Jackie Chan, Nora Miao, Chang King, Chan Sing, Lo*
*Wei*

A pickpocket becomes a hero during the Japanese WW2 occupation of China, when his girlfriend's martial arts school is destroyed and its master murdered.
MAR   90 min; 106 min (TGP or SQUARE) Cut (1 min
                                1 sec of abridged version)
B,V                 AVR; SQUARE; TGP (VHS only)

**NEW GIRL \***                                      PG
Charles Ison            USA                         1985
*David Andrews, Beth Abernathy*
A guy gets up to all sorts of strange pranks, not least dressing as a girl and joining a women's basketball team.
COM                                        108 min
B,V                                          APOL

**NEW GODFATHERS, THE \***                          15
Alfonso Brescia         ITALY
*Edmund Purdom, Jeff Blynn, Antonio Sabato, Mario Merola, Lorraine De Selle,*
Cliched formula Mafia saga.
THR                                         90 min
B,V                          ITM L/A; DIAM; GLOB

**NEW LIFE, A \*\***                                 15
Alan Alda               USA                        1988
*Alan Alda, Ann-Margret, Hal Linden, Veronica Hamel, Mary Kay Place, Beatrice Alda, John Shea, David Eisner, Victoria Snow, Paul Hecht, Celia Weston, Bill Irwin, John Kozak, Alan Jordam*
A reluctantly divorced man has a tough time starting over in his search for a new partner, but eventually finds his ideal in a lady doctor. A glib and shallow look at man-woman relationships and their pitfalls. Written by Alda.
DRA                          100 min (ort 104 min)
B,V                                           CIC

**NEW MAFIA BOSS, THE \***                          15
                        ITALY                      1974
*Telly Savalas, Antonio Sabato*
A routine tale of intrigue and murder in the Sicilian Mafia.
DRA                           90 min (ort 96 min)
B,V                                          MED

**NEW ONE-ARMED SWORDSMAN, THE \***                 18
Chang Cheh          HONG KONG                      1972
*David Chiang, Li Chang, Ti Lung*
A swordsman swears revenge on the warlord responsible for him losing an arm.
MAR                                         98 min
B, V/h                              TEVP L/A; WHV

**NEW YEAR'S EVIL \***                              
Emmett Alston           USA                        1980
*Roz Kelly, Kip Niven, Chris Wallace, Louisa Moritz, Grant Cramer, Jed Mills, Taafe O'Connell, Jon Greene, Teri Copley, Anita Crane, Alice Dhanifu, John London, Barry Gibberman, Jennie Anderson, Wendy-Sue Rosloff, John Alderman*
A crazed psycho calls the hostess of a coast-to-coast TV New Year's party, and tells her of his exploits as he kills one person per hour. But to round off his performance, he gate-crashes the party and tries to kill her. Another by-numbers slasher film, that is as sick as its poor demented killer.
THR                           86 min (ort 90 min)
B,V                                          RNK

**NEW YORK AFTER MIDNIGHT \*\***                     18
Jacques Scandelari
                     FRANCE/USA                    1983
*John Ferris, Florence Giorgetti, Barry Woloski, Todd Isaacson, Ragner Wallwork, Pierre Zimmer, Lisa Raggio, Rolyn Peterson*
A woman marries after a successful career, but is troubled by recurrent nightmares that drive her to the brink of madness, and cause her to react violently to her husband's infidelity.
Aka: AFTER MIDNIGHT; FLASHING LIGHTS; MONIQUE; NEW YORK AFTER DARK
HOR                                         89 min
B,V,V2          DFS L/A; SKP L/A; REV L/A; XTASY

**NEW YORK NIGHTS \*\***                             18
Simon Nuchtern         USA                         1984
*Corinne Alphen, George Ayer, Brent Walker, Cynthia Lee, Bobbi Burns, Peter Matthey, Missy O'Shea, Nicholas Cortland, Marcia McBroom, William Dysart*
Story of nine interlinked love affairs in the best New York nightspots. Written by Romano Vanderbes. Average.
A                         105 min (Cut at film release)
B,V                                 BWV; INTMED

**NEW YORK, NEW YORK \*\*\***                        PG
Martin Scorsese         USA                        1977
*Robert De Niro, Liza Minnelli, Lionel Stander, George Auld, Barry Primus, Dick Miller, Mary Kay Place, George Memmoli, Diahnne Abbott*
Excellent musical drama about a saxophonist and a vocalist and their troubled relationship, that was unfairly panned by the critics (always keen to echo each other's opinions), despite its fine music and excellent acting. Very loosely based on "The Man I Love", and scripted by Earl Mac Rauch and Mardik Martin. Musical direction was by Ralph Burns.
MUS                          156 min (ort 163 min)
B,V                                          WHV

**NEW YORK STORIES \*\*\***                          15
Martin Scorsese/Francis Coppola/Woody Allen
                        USA                        1989
*Nick Nolte, Rosanna Arquette, Steve Buscemi, Peter Gabriel, Deborah Harry, Heather McComb, Talia Shire, Giancarlo Giannini, Don Novello, Chris Elliott, Carole Bouquet, Woody Allen, Mia Farrow, Mae Questel, Julie Kavner*
A trio of three separate tales. Scorsese's ponderous "Life Lessons" explores the obsessive love a famous painter develops for his protegee/lover. Coppola's "Life Without Zoe" is a charming but superficial fantasy that tells of a rich girl and the adventures she has in New York City whilst her wealthy parents globetrot. Finally Allen's hilarious "Oedipus Wrecks" gives us the tale of a lawyer who cannot escape the influence of his mother.
COM                          119 min (ort 123 min)
V                                          TOUCH

**NEW YORK'S FINEST \***                             18
Chuck Vincent           USA                        1987
*Ruth Collins, Jennifer Delora, Heide Paine, Scott Baker, Jane Hamilton, Alan Naggar, John Altamura, Alan Fisler, Josey Duval, Daniel Chapman, T. Boomer Tibbs, Harvey Siegel, Russ Batt, Loretta Palma, Rick Savage*
Tired of constant harassment by the vice squad, three hookers transform themselves into classy ladies and start to hunt for millionaire husbands. Their efforts, however, soon run into trouble when a former madame threatens to blackmail them into resuming their former station. Tasteless and dull with few (if any) redeeming moments.
COM                                         86 min
B,V                                         SCRN

**NEWMAN SHAME, THE \*\***                          
                     AUSTRALIA                     1978
*George Lazenby, Joan Bruce, Diane Craig, Alwyn Kurts, Judy Nunn*
An ex-Hong Kong police inspector investigates a suicide and discovers a blackmailing sex ring in this TV film.

THR 95 min mTV
B,V ALPHA/INT

## NEWSFRONT ***
Philip Noyce          AUSTRALIA          1978
*Bill Hunter, Gerard Kennedy, Wendy Hughes, Angela*
*Punch McGregor, Chris Hayward, John Ewart, Bryan*
*Brown*
An excellent look at the world of newsreel camera-
men, focussing on the lives of two rival brothers in a
film that skilfully incorporates real newsreel footage
of the 1940s and 1950s. Written by Noyce.
DRA                                    110 min
B,V                          ENT/HOMEX; HVH

## NEXT MAN, THE ***                          PG
Richard C. Sarafian    USA              1976
*Sean Connery, Cornelia Sharpe, Albert Paulsen,*
*Adolfo Celi, Charles Cioffi*
A female assassin is assigned to murder the Saudi
Arabian ambassador because of his efforts to bring
peace to the Middle East, but complicates matters
when she falls in love with her target. Quite effective
despite the implausibility of the plot.
Aka: DOUBLE HIT
DRA                          104 min (ort 108 min)
B,V                                       RNK

## NEXT OF KIN *                              15
John Irvin             USA              1989
*Patrick Swayze, Adam Baldwin, Helen Hunt, Liam*
*Neeson, Andreas Katsulas, Bill Paxton, Ben Stiller,*
*Michael J. Pollard*
When his younger brother is killed by a local mobster,
Chicago cop Swayze sets out to have his revenge and
goes after the culprits. A formula action film of little
originality, spoilt (as much as such a film can be) by a
foolish ending. Music is by Jack Nitzsche.
A/AD                         104 min (ort 108 min)
V                                         GHV

## NEXT ONE, THE **
Nico Mastorakis        USA              1981
*Keir Dullea, Adrienne Barbeau, Peter Hobbs, Jeremy*
*Licht, Peter Hobbs, Phaedon Georgitis, Betty Arvanitis*
A childlike stranger is washed up on a Greek island,
and his arrival arouses jealousy and hatred in some
quarters in this unclear fantasy.
DRA                          100 min (ort 105 min)
B,V                              VSP L/A; FTV

## NIAGARA ***                               PG
Henry Hathaway         USA              1952
*Joseph Cotten, Jean Peters, Marilyn Monroe, Don*
*Wilson, Casey Adams, Don Wilson, Richard Allan*
A couple spend their honeymoon at Niagara Falls, but
the young wife is already devising ways in which to
murder her husband. Monroe's first major role in a
competently-made and suspenseful thriller. Written
by Charles Brackett, Walter Reisch and Richard
Breen.
THR                           84 min (ort 89 min)
V                                         CBS

## NICE GIRL LIKE ME, A *
Desmond Davis          UK               1969
*Barbara Ferris, Harry Andrews, Gladys Cooper, Bill*
*Hinnant, James Villiers, Joyce Carey, Christopher*
*Guinee, Fabia Drake, Irene Prador, Erik Chitty, Totti*
*Truman Taylor, Ann Lancaster, Douglas Wilmer*
A young girl who had a sheltered upbringing gets
pregnant, not once but twice, in this silly romance,
and is looked after by a kind caretaker whom she
really loves. The attractive cast do what they can with
this dross.
Boa: story Marry At Leisure by Anne Piper.
COM                           87 min (ort 91 min)
B,V                                       CBS

## NICE GIRLS DON'T EXPLODE *                 PG
Chuck Martinez         USA              1987
*Barbara Harris, Michelle Meyrink, Wallace Shawn,*
*William O'Leary, James Nardini, Margot Gray, Jonas*
*Baugham, William Kuhlke*
A girl suffers from a rare handicap in her dealings
with the opposite sex: whenever she becomes aroused,
fires break out spontaneously. Unfortunately, this
film smoulders on dismally, to its feeble ending, but is
probably destined to become a cult favourite on
account of its daft title.
COM                           79 min (ort 92 min)
B,V                                       NWV

## NICHOLAS AND ALEXANDRA **                  PG
Franklin J. Schaffner  UK               1971
*Michael Jayston, Janet Suzman, Tom Baker, Harry*
*Andrews, Jack Hawkins, Fiona Fullerton, Laurence*
*Olivier, Roderic Noble, Ania Marson, Ian Holm,*
*Michael Bryant, Lynne Frederick, Maurice Denham,*
*Curt Jurgens, Eric Porter*
Flat and wooden account of the last 14 years of Czarist
Russia. The sets and photography are very good, but
never has such an exciting and colourful period of
history been treated in such a lifeless and uninspired
way. By some oversight, Omar Sharif does not have a
part in this film. The script is by James Goldman. AA:
Art/Set (John Box, Ernest Archer, Jack Maxted and
Gil Parrondo/Vernon Dixon), Cost (Yvonne Blake/
Antonio Castillo).
Boa: book by Robert K. Massie.
DRA                          165 min (ort 189 min)
V                                         RCA

## NICHOLAS NICKLEBY ***
Alberto Cavalcanti     UK               1947
*Derek Bond, Cedric Hardwicke, Alfred Drayton,*
*Bernard Miles, Sally Ann Howes, Mary Merrall, Sybil*
*Thorndike, Cathleen Nesbitt, Aubrey Woods, Jill*
*Balcon, Stanley Holloway, Cyril Fletcher, Vera Pearce,*
*Athene Seyler*
In 1831 a young schoolmaster struggles to gain his
rightful fortune, and protect his family from a schem-
ing uncle in this solid, workmanlike adaptation of
Dickens' novel. Written by John Dighton.
Boa: novel by Charles Dickens. DRA    107 min B/W
B,V                                       TEVP

## NICKELODEON **                             U
Peter Bogdanovich      USA              1976
*Ryan O'Neal, Burt Reynolds, Tatum O'Neal, Brian*
*Keith, Stella Stevens, John Ritter, Jane Hitchcock,*
*Harry Carey Jr*
An attempt to recreate the early days of Hollywood
silent film-making that is entertaining in parts but
ultimately fails to get across any true feeling of the
period. Scripted by Bogdanovich and W.D. Richter.
DRA                          117 min (ort 122 min)
B,V                                       TEVP

## NICKY AND GINO ***                         15
Robert M. Young        USA              1987
*Tom Hulce, Ray Liotta, Jamie Lee Curtis, Robert*
*Levine, Todd Graff, Bill Cobbs, Mimi Cecchini, David*
*Strahairn*
A sentimental but quite touching account of the
relationship between a bright medical student and his
more simple-minded twin brother. Hulce is memor-
able as the retarded brother.
Aka: DOMINICK AND EUGENE
DRA                          104 min (ort 111 min)
V                                         VIR

## NICO ***                                   18
Andrew Davis           USA              1988
*Steven Seagal, Pam Grier, Sharon Stone, Daniel*
*Faraldo, Henry Silva, Ron Dean, Nicholas Kusenko,*
*Joe V. Greco, Chelcie Ross, Thalmus Rasulala, Jack*

*Wallace, Jospeh Kosala, John Drummond, Ronnie Barron*
Real-life aikido master Seagal, uncovers a CIA plot in this non-stop violent action film that provides a fine showcase for his martial arts skills, and was a big hit at the USA box office.
Aka: ABOVE THE LAW; NICO: ABOVE THE LAW
A/AD                                95 min Cut (15 sec)
V/sh                                                        WHV

### NIGHT AND DAY **                          U
Michael Curtiz            USA            1946
*Cary Grant, Alexis Smith, Monty Woolley, Jane Wyman, Mary Martin, Ginny Simms, Eve Arden, Victor Francen, Alan Hale, Dorothy Malone*
Poor biography of Cole Porter with Grant well and truly miscast in the role of the great composer; rarely have we seen him give such an uncomfortable and stiff performance, although the musical numbers offer some compensation. Musical direction is by Max Steiner and Ray Heindorf.
MUS                                  123 min (ort 132 min)
V                                                          WHV

### NIGHT ANGELS *                            18
Luis San Andres           USA            1979
*Angel Lindberg, Henderson Forsythe, Gabriel Walsh, Jose Perez, Sabra Jones*
Two Vietnam veterans try to re-adjust to civilian life but sadly go astray, and go on the all too predictable psychotic rampage.
Aka: NIGHT FLOWERS (HOK)
DRA                           84 min; 92 min (HOK)
B,V                                          HOK L/A; KES

### NIGHT AT THE MAGIC CASTLE, A **          U
Icek Tenenbaum            USA            1988
*Arte Johnson, Matt Shakeman, Blackie Dammett, John Franklin, Max Thayer*
On his tenth birthday a small boy gets caught up in an exciting adventure.
JUV                                               88 min
B,V                                                        CHV

### NIGHT BEFORE, THE **                      15
Thom Eberhardt            USA            1988
*Keanu Reeves, Lori Loughlin, Theresa Saldana, Trinidad Silva, Suzanne Snyder, Morgan Lofting, Gwil Greene*
A daft high school kid tries to recall what he got up to the night before when he attended a concert. A feeble little comedy with a few funny moments.
COM                                               86 min
V/sh                                                       WHV

### NIGHT CALLER, THE ***
Henri Verneuil        FRANCE/ITALY        1975
*Jean-Paul Belmondo, Charles Denner, Adalberto-Maria Meril, Lea Massari, Rosy Varte*
A tough French detective has to deal with both a bank robbery and a mad killer in this well-made example of French police films, a genre in which both Belmondo and Alain Delon have specialised.
Aka: PEUR SUR LA VILLE
Osca: HIJACKERS, THE and ECHOES
A/AD                                              91 min
V                                                          DFS

### NIGHT CREATURE *                          15
Lee Madden                USA            1978
*Donald Pleasence, Nancy Kwan, Ross Hagen, Lesly Fine, Jennifer Rhodes*
A writer living on an island retreat in near Thailand becomes obsessed with a man-eating leopard in this flaccid thriller of few ideas and much lethargy.
Aka: OUT OF THE DARKNESS
THR                           83 min; 90 min (MPV)
B,V                                          INT; MPV

### NIGHT CROSSING **                         PG
Delbert Mann              USA            1982
*John Hurt, Beau Bridges, Jane Alexander, Glynnis O'Connor, Doug McKeon, Ian Bannen*
The true story of how two East German families escaped to the West in a home-made hot air balloon forms the basis for a matter-of-fact and rather pedestrian piece of family entertainment.
DRA                                  104 min (ort 106 min)
B,V                                                        WDV

### NIGHT GAME *                              18
Peter Masterson          USA            1988
*Roy Scheider, Karen Young, Richard Bradford, Paul Gleason, Carlin Glynn, Lane Smith*
A homicide detective assigned to a case involving a series of mutilation killings of young women, discovers that a murder takes place every time a star player wins a game for his favourite baseball team. When he finds that his girlfriend is likely to be the next victim, matters are brought to a head in this slow and unexciting thriller.
THR                                               92 min
V                                                          EIV

### NIGHT GAMES *                             18
Roger Vadim               USA            1980
*Cindy Pickett, Joanna Cassidy, Barry Primus, Paul Jenkins, Gene Davis*
A frigid housewife is terrified of sexual contact with men and is only able to make love to a man who shows up at night dressed in a bird suit (having flown over from the other side of town no doubt). Another obscure, tedious and utterly self-indulgent Vadim offering.
A                                                102 min
B,V                                    RNK; VCC (VHS only)

### NIGHT GOD SCREAMED, THE *
Lee Madden                USA            1973
*Jeanne Crain, Alex Nicol, Daniel Spelling, Michael Sugich, Barbara Hancock, James B. Sikking, Dawn Cleary, Gary Morgan*
A fanatical group of Jesus freaks who crucified a preacher, are sentenced to death on evidence supplied by the man's widow. The woman is tricked by some bored teenagers into believing that a revenge attack is being planned, and suffers a night of frightening pranks before having her revenge. A sluggish and feeble tale.
Aka: SCREAM
HOR                                               85 min
B,V                                                        GHV

### NIGHT IN HEAVEN, A **                     18
John G. Avildsen          USA            1983
*Lesley Anne Warren, Christopher Atkins, Robert Logan, Carrie Snodgress, Deborah Rush, Sandra Beall, Denny Terrio, Alix Elias*
A married woman teacher becomes obsessed with a boy pupil who is an exotic dancer in a nightclub. A disappointing study of an unusual romance.
DRA                                               80 min
B,V                                                        CBS

### 'NIGHT MOTHER ***                         15
Tom Moore                 USA            1986
*Sissy Spacek, Anne Bancroft, Ed Berke, Carol Robbins, Jennifer Roosendahl*
Film adaptation of a Pulitzer Prize-winning play about an unhappy woman who one evening suddenly tells her mother of her intention to end her life. An absorbing character study that remains faithful to the stage original, rather too faithful in fact, to make it really work as a film.
Boa: play by Marsha Norman.
DRA                                  93 min (ort 96 min)
V/h                                                        CIC

## NIGHT MOVES *** 18
Arthur Penn            USA            1975
*Gene Hackman, Jennifer Warren, Susan Clerk,*
*Edward Binns, Harris Yulin, Melanie Griffith, James*
*Woods, Janet Ward, Anthony Costello, John Crawford,*
*Ben Archibek, Maxwell Gail Jr, Victor Paul, Louis*
*Elias, Carey Loftin*
A Los Angeles private eye tracks a missing teenage
girl to Florida and returns her to her actress mother,
only to learn of her death during a movie stunt. After
watching footage of the accident, he comes to the
conclusion that she was murdered and decides to
investigate. An intricate, downbeat thriller, scripted
by Alan Sharp.
DRA                    96 min (ort 99 min)
B,V                                     WHV

## NIGHT OF COURAGE, A ** 15
Elliott Silverstein    USA            1987
*Barnard Hughes, Daniel Hugh Kelly, Geraldine*
*Fitzgerald, Tom Hodges, David Hernandez*
A young Hispanic boy meets his death on a couple's
doorstep when they refuse to allow him in to hide from
his white pursuers. Prompted by the media attention,
his teacher tries to unearth the truth about what
really happened. Fair, but nothing like as powerful as
it could have been.
Boa: play In This Fallen City by Brian Williams.
DRA                    93 min (ort 100 min) mTV
B,V                                     TGP

## NIGHT OF RETRIBUTION ** 18
Robert Bergman         USA            1987
*Robert Bideman, Nadia Capone, Robbie Fox, Paul*
*Sanders*
A policeman who has vowed not to bear firearms after
an accidental killing, has to rescue his family when
they are held hostage by escaped convicts.
Aka: SKULL: A NIGHT OF TERROR
THR                    80 min
V                                     CASVIS

## NIGHT OF TERROR ** 15
Jeannot Szwarc         USA            1972
*Martin Balsam, Catherine Burns, Chuck Connors,*
*Agnes Moorehead, Donna Mills, Agnes Moorehead,*
*Viv Vallardo, John Karlen, Peter Hooten, David*
*Spielberg, William Gray Espy, Mary Grace Canfield,*
*Bart LaRue, Johnny Martino*
A young woman teacher becomes the prey of a
dangerous syndicate killer but is at a total loss to
understand his motive for pursuing her. She's not the
only one. Average.
THR                    71 min (ort 73 min) mTV
V                                     CIC

## NIGHT OF THE ALIEN * 18
Ronald W. Moore        USA            1985
*Edwin Neal, Marilyn Burns, Gabriel Folse, Wade*
*Reese, Baron Faulks, Rob Rowley, Craig Kannet,*
*Jeffrey Scott*
Fraternity house members get caught on the wrong
side of time where they encounter anti-nuclear punks,
one of whom has been exposed to radiation. A
futuristic SF thriller that is wildly over-derivative
and fails to deliver anything of real interest.
Aka: FUTURE KILL; SPLATTER
FAN                    78 min (ort 90 min)
B,V                                     EIV

## NIGHT OF THE BIG HEAT * 
Terence Fisher         UK             1967
*Christopher Lee, Peter Cushing, Patrick Allen, Sarah*
*Lawson, Jane Merrow, William Lucas, Kenneth Cope,*
*Jack Bligh, Thomas Heathcote, Sidney Bromley, Percy*
*Herbert*
Creatures from outer space cause a heatwave on an
isolated Scottish island in order to survive, but are
eventually destroyed when it begins to rain. Little of

interest happens in a dull and dreary film evidently
made on a restricted budget.
Aka: ISLAND OF THE BURNING DAMNED;
ISLAND OF THE BURNING DOOMED
Boa: novel by John Lymington.
FAN                    94 min
B,V,V2                                 RNK

## NIGHT OF THE COMET ** 15
Thom Eberhardt         USA            1985
*Robert Beltran, Sharon Farrell, Kelli Maroney,*
*Geoffrey Lewis, Catherine Mary Stewart, Mary*
*Woronov, John Achorn, Michael Bowen, Ivan Roth,*
*Devon Ericson, Peter Fox, Lissa Leyng, Janice Kawaye,*
*Chance Boyer, Andrew Boyer*
Rays from a returning comet reduce most of the
world's population to dust apart from a few survivors,
a clutch of nasty zombies and the inevitable mad
scientists. Believe it or not, this is in fact a satire, and
not a bad one at that.
FAN                    95 min
B,V                                     CBS

## NIGHT OF THE CREEPS ** 18
Fred Dekker            USA            1986
*Jason Lively, Steve Marshall, Jill Whitlow, Tom*
*Atkins, Wally Taylor, Bruce Salomon, Vic Polizos,*
*Allan J. Kayser, Ken Heron, Alice Cadogan, June*
*Harris, David Paymer, David Oliver, Evelyne Smith,*
*Ivan E. Roth, Dick Miller*
Alien parasites turn their human victims into zombies
at a college dance, but the care lavished on special
effects would have been put to better use if it had been
applied to the script of this lacklustre horror-comedy.
HOR                    85 min (ort 89 min)
B,V                                     CBS

## NIGHT OF THE CYCLONE ** 18
David Irving           USA            1989
*Kris Kristofferson, Jeff Meek, Marisa Berenson, Alla*
*Korot*
A tough cop who has difficulty communicating with
his daughter sets out to find her when she takes up a
modelling job that involves a journey to a remote
island in the Indian Ocean.
DRA                    86 min
V                                     EIV

## NIGHT OF THE DEMONS ** 18
Kevin G. Tenney        USA            1987
*Linnea Quigley, Alvin Alexis, Lance Fenton, William*
*Gallo, Hal Havins, Mimi Kinkade, Cathy Podewell,*
*Phillip Tanzani, Jill Terashita, Allison Barron,*
*Donnie Jeffcoat*
A routine shocker in which a bunch of dumb teens
decide to hold a Halloween party in an abandoned
funeral parlour and are picked off one at a time by a
bunch of unpleasant and vicious demons. The special
effects cannot be faulted, but the tired old storyline is
no more than a vehicle for them.
HOR                    86 min Cut (4 sec)
V/h                                    PAL

## NIGHT OF THE EAGLE *** 15
Sidney Hayers          UK             1962
*Margaret Johnston, Peter Wyngarde, Janet Blair,*
*Anthony Nicholls, Reginald Beckwith, Kathleen Byron*
A medical professor and his wife fall prey to evil forces
when a jealous crippled woman uses the black arts to
animate a stone eagle. Filmed once before as "Weird
Woman", this genuinely creepy supernatural thriller
is sustained by good direction, if somewhat less so by
the leading players. Later spoofed in the remake
"Witches' Brew". The script is by Charles Beaumont
and Richard Matheson.
Aka: BURN, WITCH, BURN!
Boa: novel Conjure Wife by Fritz Leiber Jr.
HOR                    83 min (ort 87 min) B/W
V                                     WHV

## NIGHT OF THE EXORCIST **                    15
Delbert Mann          USA              1971
*Patty Duke, David McCallum, Lew Ayres, Dorothy*
*McGuire, Beulah Bondi, James Callahan, Nelson*
*Olmsted*
A young bride becomes possessed by the vengeful
spirit of her husband's first wife who was murdered in
this unoriginal tale of the supernatural.
Aka: SHE WAITS
HOR                   71 min (ort 91 min) mTV
B,V                         COU L/A; DRUM

## NIGHT OF THE GENERALS *                     15
Anatole Litvak     FRANCE/UK           1967
*Omar Sharif, Tom Courtenay, Peter O'Toole, Donald*
*Pleasence, Joanna Pettet, Christopher Plummer, Coral*
*Browne, Harry Andrews, John Gregson, Nigel Stock,*
*Juliette Greco, Charles Gray, Yves Brainville, Gerald*
*Buhr, Gordon Jackson*
A Nazi intelligence officer tries to discover the
identity of a disturbed general who has made a career
out of murdering prostitutes. It's hard to believe that
the Nazis cared tuppence about his behaviour, and by
the end of this interminably boring film such consid-
erations matter little. A clear waste of a good cast and
large budget.
Boa: novel by Hans Helmut Kirst.
DRA                   138 min (ort 148 min)
V                                        RCA

## NIGHT OF THE JUGGLER **                     18
Robert Butler         USA              1980
*James Brolin, Richard Castellano, Cliff Gorman,*
*Abby Bluestone, Linda G. Miller, Robert Butler, Julie*
*Carmen, Barton Heyman, Mandy Patinkin, Dan*
*Hedaya*
A mentally disturbed man mistakenly kidnaps an
ex-cop's daughter, and the father begins to comb the
city in a hunt for her. An average action thriller with
no shortage of car chases.
THR                   96 min (ort 101 min)
B,V                                   VCL/CBS

## NIGHT OF THE LIVING DEAD ***                18
George A. Romero      USA              1968
*Judith O'Dea, Duane Jones, Karl Hardman, Russell*
*Streiner, Marilyn Eastman, Keith Wayne, Judith*
*Ridley, Kyra Schon, Bill Hinzman, Charles Craig,*
*Frank Doak, George Kosana, Bill Cardille, Vince*
*Survinski, John A. Russo*
Flesh-eating zombies are activated by rays from a
space rocket and ravage the countryside, trapping a
small group of survivors in a deserted farm house.
Followed by two sequels, ZOMBIES: DAWN OF THE
DEAD (1979) and DAY OF THE DEAD (1985). A
harsh and uncompromising chiller, done in a low-key,
almost documentary style.
Aka: NIGHT OF ANUBIS; NIGHT OF THE FLESH
EATERS
HOR            93 min; 96 min (PAL) (ort 98 min) B/W
                              (available colourised)
B,V,V2          INT; PAL (Betamax and VHS only)

## NIGHT OF THE SEAGULLS *
Amando de Ossorio   SPAIN             1975
*Victor Petit, Maria Kosti, Sandra Mazarosky, Julie*
*James, Julia Saly, Jose Antonio Calvo*
A doctor and his wife move to a seaside village with a
sinister and deadly secret, and eventually learn of
nightly sacrifices of virgins. One of a series of Spanish
horror films, featuring the eyeless zombie figures of
the Knights Templar. The powerful and moody open-
ing is let down by a lack of plot development and the
film tends to drag badly until the climax. See also
THE RETURN OF THE EVIL DEAD and TOMBS OF
THE BLIND DEAD.
Aka: BLOOD FEAST OF THE BLIND DEAD; LA
NOCHE DE LOS GAVIOTAS; NIGHT OF THE
DEATH CULT

HOR                   85 min (ort 90 min)
B,V                            MOV L/A

## NIGHT OF THE SHARKS *                        15
Anthony Richmond (Antonio Riccamonza)
                      ITALY            1987
*Treat Williams, Antonio Fargas, Janet Agren, John*
*Steiner*
A cheap JAWS rip-off, in which a lazy beach bum who
spends his days in idleness, is galvanised into action
by the murder of his brother by gangsters, and has his
revenge. However, the shark gets to play an important part in this one, and incidentally has the best
lines. Cut before video submission by 4 min and 16
sec.
A/AD                  87 min
V/h                            MED

## NIGHT OF THE TERROR, THE *                   15
Roger Corman          USA              1963
*Boris Karloff, Jack Nicholson, Sandra Knight, Dick*
*Miller, Dorothy Neumann, Jonathan Haze*
A young officer in Napoleon's army in the 1800s, is
trapped on the Baltic coast in the castle of a depraved
baron. A shoddy horror spoof made over one weekend
on the same set as THE RAVEN and with some of the
same actors. The other claim to fame is its inclusion in
the film "Targets".
Aka: TERROR, THE (MOVLAND or CAB2)
HOR                   71 min (ort 86 min)
B,V                 APV L/A; MOVLAND; CAB2

## NIGHT OF THE ZOMBIES, THE *                  15
Joel M. Reed          USA              1980
*Jamie Gillis, Ryan Hilliard, Ron Armstrong,*
*Shoshana Ascher, Dick Carballo, Richard DeFaut,*
*Alphonse DeNoble, Samantha Grey, Juni Kulis, Lorin*
*E. Price, Noel M. Reed, Renate Schlessinger, Kuno*
*Sponholtz, John Barilla*
Low-budget shocker about a CIA agent on the trail of
cannibalistic Nazi soldiers who became zombies after
they were exposed to an experimental nerve gas.
Aka: CHILLING, THE (SATPRO); GAMMA 693;
NIGHT OF THE WEHRMACHT ZOMBIES
HOR      85 min; 75 min (SATPRO) (ort 101 min)
B,V                       APV L/A; SATPRO

## NIGHT PARTNERS **
Noel Nosseck          USA              1983
*Yvette Mimieux, Diana Canova, Arlen Dean Snyder,*
*M. Emmet Walsh, Patricia McCormack, Patricia*
*Davis, Michael Cavanaugh, Peter Brocco, Larry*
*Linville, Dick Anthony Williams, Nellie Bellflower,*
*Dee Dee Bridgewater, Eb Lottimer*
Two housewives find themselves menaced by a crimin-
al, when they volunteer to help crime victims in a
small Californian town. Pilot for a TV series that was
never made.
DRA                   98 min (ort 100 min) mTV
B,V                            PRV

## NIGHT PATROL *                               18
Jackie Kong           USA              1984
*Linda Blair, Pat Laulsen, Billy Barty, Jaye P. Morgan,*
*Jack Riley, Murray Langston*
A policeman who has a comedy act in which he wears
a paper bag over his head, comes under suspicion
when boys begin to be robbed by a criminal similarly
attired. A shabby rip-off of POLICE ACADEMY with
gags of similar feebleness.
COM                   82 min
B,V                            CBS

## NIGHT PORTER, THE *                          18
Liliana Cavani     ITALY/USA          1973
*Dirk Bogarde, Charlotte Rampling, Philippe Leroy,*
*Gabriele Ferzetti, Isa Miranda, Giuseppe Addobbati,*
*Isa Miranda, Nino Bignamini, Marino Mase, Amedeo*
*Amodio, Piero Vida*

A woman resumes her sado-masochistic affair with a former SS guard at a concentration camp, when she finds that he is now employed as the night porter at a hotel. A dismal and exploitative tale, set in the 1950s.
Aka: IL PORTIERE DI NOTTE
DRA                          117 min; 113 min (VCC)
B,V                          INT; VCC (VHS only)

### NIGHT RIDER **                                    U
Hy Averback            USA                    1979
David Selby, Percy Rodriguez, Pernell Roberts, George Grizzard
This TV film has a plot that recalls those of countless B-movies of earlier years. A man returns to Virginia City to take revenge on the outlaws who killed his parents and sister in a bid to seize the family silver mine. During the day our hero masquerades as a slow-witted individual while at night he performs heroic deeds. Another unremarkable time-filler representing a belated attempt to revive interest in the Western.
WES                          83 min mTV
V                            CIC

### NIGHT SCREAMS *                                  18
Allen Plone            USA                    1986
Joe Manno, Ron Thomas, Megan Wyss, Randy Lunsford, Janette Allyson Caldwell, John Hines, Diana Martin, Jerry Goehring, Susan Lyles, Barbara Schoenhofer, Dan Schramm, Mike Roark, Tony Brown, Dennis Arno
Party guests are terrorised by both a couple of escaped convicts and an unseen killer, in this uninspired variation on the "mad slasher" theme.
HOR          74 min (ort 85 min) Cut (1 min 27 sec)
B,V                          IVS L/A; BRAVE

### NIGHT SHADOW **                                  18
Randolph Cohlan        USA                    1990
Brenda Vance, Dane Chan, Tom Boylan
A series of brutal murders which appear to be the work of a large and powerful animal, coincide with the arrival of a mysterious stranger who takes a room at a local hotel. Three young guys become suspicious and their investigations reveal the murders as the handiwork of a werewolf. Competent acting and direction help maintain a sense of tension in this tale.
HOR                          90 min
V                            BOX

### NIGHT STALKER, THE ***
John Llewellyn Moxey   USA                    1971
Darren McGavin, Carol Lynley, Simon Oakland, Ralph Meeker, Claude Akins, Kent Smith, Larry Linville, Jordan Roberts, Barry Atwater, Stanley Adams, Elisha Cook
A reporter investigates a series of strange murders in Las Vegas and uncovers an incredible answer to this riddle. An extremely well-made film that maintains a fine sense of suspense throughout. Followed by THE NIGHT STRANGLER and a rather disappointing TV series. Written by Richard Matheson who skilfully blends tension and touches of humour in a memorable script.
Boa: story by Jeff Rice.
THR                          73 min mTV
B,V                          GHV

### NIGHT STALKER, THE **                            18
Max Cleven             USA                    1985
Charles Napier, Michelle Reese, Katherine Kelly Lang, Robert Viharo, Robert Z'dar, John Goff, Joey Gian, Leila Carlin, Gary Crosby, James Louis Watkins, Ola Ray, Tally Chanel, Joan Chen
A Vietnam veteran obsessed with the martial arts and mysticism sets off on a murder spree, his main target being prostitutes, and a seedy and alcoholic detective is assigned to the case. A standard B-movie, not

especially well acted but quite tense and well worth a look.
HOR                          90 min
V                            VES

### NIGHT THE LIGHTS WENT OUT IN               15
### GEORGIA, THE **
Ronald F. Maxwell      USA                    1981
Kristy McNichol, Dennis Quaid, Don Stroud, Mark Hamill, Barry Corbin, Lulu McNichol, Royce Clark, Marilyn Hickey, Jerry Rushing, Jerry Campbell, Bill Bribble, Maxwell Morrow, Lonnie Smith
Film inspired by title hit song that tries to paint a cohesive picture of a a brother and sister Country music team struggling to make the big time in Nashville. The trite and uneven script hampers appealing performances.
DRA                          115 min (ort 120 min)
B,V,V2,LV                    EHE

### NIGHT THEY SAVED CHRISTMAS, THE ***        U
Jackie Cooper          USA                    1985
Art Carney, Jaclyn Smith, Paul Le Mat, Mason Adams, June Lockhart, Paul Williams, Scott Grimes, Laura Jacoby, R.J. Williams, James Staley, Albert Hall, Anne Haney, Buddy Douglas, Billy Curtis, Michael Keys Hall
A mother and her three kids help save Santa's home from an oil company's prospecting operations. Scripted by James C. Moloney and David Niven Jr, this film provides Christmas entertainment for kids of all ages.
Boa: story by James C. Moloney, David Niven Jr and Rudy Dochterman.
COM                89 min (ort 100 min) mTV
B,V                          EHE; CH5 (VHS only)

### NIGHT TO REMEMBER, A ***                    PG
Richard Wallace        USA                    1942
Loretta Young, Brian Aherne, Jeff Donnell, William Wright, Sidney Toler, Gale Sondergaard, Donald MacBride, Lee Patrick, Blanche Yurka
A woman married to a mystery writer tries to get him to write a romantic novel, and even finds them a quiet apartment where he can work. However, these good intentions go out the window when a body turns up and they turn to amateur sleuthing instead. A lively comedy-mystery with appealing madcap touches. Written by Richard Flournoy and Jack Henley.
COM                          91 min B/W
V                            RCA

### NIGHT TO REMEMBER, A ***                    PG
Roy Baker              UK                     1958
Kenneth More, Honor Blackman, Michael Goodliffe, David McCallum, George Rose, Anthony Bushell, Ronald Allen, Robert Ayres, John Cairney, Jane Downs, Kenneth Griffith, Frank Lawton, Michael Bryant, Jill Dixon
A straight and unadorned account of the sinking of the Titanic in 1912, with many star cameos in a film that makes highly effective use of its plain semi-documentary style. Puts the later films on this subject in the shade. Adapted from the book by Eric Ambler. See also S.O.S. TITANIC.
Boa: book by Walter Lord.
DRA                          118 min (ort 123 min) B/W
V                            RNK

### NIGHT TRAIN TO KATHMANDU, THE **           U
Robert Wiemer          USA                    1988
Milla Jovovitch, Pernell Roberts, Eddie Castrodad, Kavi Raz, Tim Eyster, Robert Stoeckle
A young girl accompanies her family on a research trip to Nepal and meets a mysterious stranger on a train. Mediocre teenage adventure movie that takes us to exotic locations.
A/AD                         99 min (ort 105 min) mCab
B,V                          CIC

## NIGHT TRAIN TO TERROR * 18
J. Schlosberg-Cohen/J. Carr/P. Marshak/T. McGowan/
G. Tallas USA 1984
*John Philip Law, Charles Moll, Cameron Mitchell,*
*Mark Lawrence, Robert Bristol, Faith Cliff*
Horror film on the theme of God and the Devil
contending for the souls of the individuals featured in
three tales, cobbled together from footage drawn from
three films, two of which were unreleased. The tales
are: "The Case of Harry Billings", "The Case of Gretta
Connors" and "The Case of Claire Hanson", the last
tale comprising footage from the released film
CATACLYSM. A muddled and disjointed mess.
HOR 89 min Cut (4 min 17 sec)
B,V PVG; PALAN

## NIGHT VISION * 18
Michael Krueger USA 1987
*Stacey Carson, Shirley Ross, Tony Carpenter, Ellie*
*Martins, Stacy Shane, Tom Henry, Glen Reed*
A writer from Kansas comes to Denver, where he is
forced to take a job in a video store to make ends meet.
Unfortunately, he comes into contact with a stolen
VCR containing a tape of horrifying rituals made by a
Satanic cult, and soon becomes possessed by evil
spirits that transform him into a demented murderer.
A dreary horror film that recycles familiar ideas in a
new guise (i.e. a video tape instead of a book).
HOR 102 min mVid
V VIR

## NIGHT VISITORS * 15
David Fulk USA 1988
*Daniel Hirsch, David Schroeder, Rochelle Savitt, Joe*
*Whyte*
As a family enjoy their Christmas, four carol singers
turn up and gain entrance, taking over the celebrations and forcing the family to take part in a series of
bizarre and humiliating games. As each member of
the family are degraded, they begin to see themselves
in a new light. A sick little tale, written and directed
by Fulk.
DRA 91 min
V VPD

## NIGHT WARS ** 18
David A. Prior USA 1987
*Dan Haggerty, Brian O'Connor, Steve Horton,*
*Cameron Smith, Chet Hood, Jill Foor, Mike Hickam,*
*David Ott, Kimberley Casey*
Two former POWs are haunted by recurrent night-
mares of their captivity in Vietnam and subsequent
escape. Upon waking, their bodies bear the wounds
suffered in their dreams and so they decide to purge
their guilt for good, by going back in their dreams to
rescue the comrade-in-arms they were forced to leave
behind. A low-budget entry that combines MIA films
with the theme of A NIGHTMARE ON ELM
STREET. Intriguing but poorly realised.
Aka: NIGHTWARS
A/AD 90 min
B,V SCRN

## NIGHT WATCH ** 15
Brian G. Hutton UK 1973
*Elizabeth Taylor, Laurence Harvey, Billie Whitelaw,*
*Robert Lang, Tony Britton, Bill Dean, Michael*
*Danvers-Walker, Rosario Serrano, Pauline Serrano,*
*Pauline Jameson, Linda Hayden, Kevin Colson, Laon*
*Maybanke*
An cultured lady reports a murder but her sanity is
called into question when the police are unable to find
the body. A flat mystery thriller that fails to create
any feeling of suspense.
Boa: play by Lucille Fletcher.
THR 98 min (ort 100 min)
B,V CINE

## NIGHT ZOO ** 18
Jeane-Claude Lauzon CANADA 1987
*Gilles Maheu, Roger Le Bel, Lyne Adams, Lorne Brass,*
*Germain Houde*
An offbeat melodrama that blends two stories: one
being an urban thriller of drug dealers and corrupt
cops in Montreal and the other the poignant tale of
renewed love between a grown son and his dying
father. The film moves from the harshness of its
Montreal crime element to a weird climax that takes
place on a nocturnal visit to the local zoo (hence the
title). An over-rated and quirky film that is both
impressive and self-indulgent.
DRA 115 min subH
V HEND

## NIGHT WITH MESSALINA, A *** 18
Jacob Most SPAIN 1982
*Ajita Wilson, Carla Day, Racquel Evans, King Gomes,*
*Pipper, Tony Marono, Mirna Vec, Red Mills, Julia*
*Caballero, Concha Valero, Eva Wagner, Olga*
*Rodriguez, Carlos Perez, Anjo Solon*
A fairly well made costumer set at the time of
Imperial Rome.
Aka: BACANALES ROMANAS; MY NIGHTS WITH
MESSALINA (CAN)
A 73 min (ort 77 min) (Cut at film release)
B,V CAN; BLUMO/GOLD

## NIGHTBREAKER *** 15
Peter Markle USA 1989
*Martin Sheen, Emilio Estevez, Lea Thompson,*
*Melinda Dillon, Joe Pantoliano, Nicholas Pryor*
Flashback style story of a neurologist whose success-
ful career conceals his involvement with nuclear
testing in which soldiers were used as unwitting
guinea pigs. Somewhat overwrought but generally
effective. The script is by T.S. Cook.
Aka: ADVANCE TO GROUND ZERO
Boa: novel Atomic Soldiers by Howard Rosenberg.
DRA 94 min (ort 100 min) mCab
V PRES

## NIGHTCOMERS, THE * 18
Michael Winner UK 1971
*Marlon Brando, Stephanie Beacham, Harry Andrews,*
*Thora Hird, Verna Harvey, Christopher Ellis, Anna*
*Palk*
An attempt to describe what happened to the children
featured in the Henry James novel "The Turn Of The
Screw" and how they became evil prior to the period at
which the original story starts. An unappealing story
is combined with bad direction to produce a work that
is more wearisome than chilling. See also THE TURN
OF THE SCREW.
Boa: novel by Michael Hastings.
HOR 96 min; 92 min (CH5)
B,V EHE; CH5 (VHS only)

## NIGHTFALL * 18
Paul Mayersberg USA 1988
*David Birney, Alexis Kanner, Sarah Douglas, Andra*
*Millian, Charles Hayward, Susie Lindeman, Starr*
*Andreff*
A far-off planet in a solar system with three suns
awaits its extinction with the coming of night, a
phenomenon previously totally unknown on this world.
Fears of the unknown and apprehension at the
possible end of their civilisation, cause dissension
among the inhabitants, who divide into two hostile
groups. A little-seen, low-budget adaptation that is
highly confused and very incoherent.
Boa: short story by Isaac Asimov.
FAN 80 min (ort 82 min)
V MGM

## NIGHTFLYERS * 18
T.C. Blake (Robert Collector)
USA 1987

*Michael Praed, John Standing, Michael Des Barres,*
*James Avery, Catherine Mary Stewart, Lisa Blount,*
*Glenn Withrow, Helene Udy, Annabel Brooks*
The members of an expedition into deep space are
confronted by an evil presence aboard an ancient
space freighter, and a series of mysterious accidents
begin to claim the lives of the crew. A pointless and
derivative dud that the director virtually disowned by
having his name removed from the credits.
Boa: novel by George R. Martin
FAN                                      85 min (ort 89 min)
B,V                                                    CBS

**NIGHTFORCE** **                                          18
Lawrence D. Foldes       USA                    1987
*Linda Blair, James Van Patten, Claudia Udy,*
*Cameron Mitchell, Chad McQueen, Richard Lynch,*
*James Wilder, Dean R. Miller, Bruce Fisher, James*
*Marcel*
A group of young people organise a rescue mission
when a US senator's daughter is kidnapped by
terrorists in Central America. Undistinguished
actioner with a well-worn theme.
Aka: NIGHT FIGHTERS
A/AD                       78 min (ort 82 min) Cut (21 sec)
B,V                                                    VES

**NIGHTFRIGHT** *                                          PG
James A. Sullivan        USA                    1968
*John Agar, Carol Gilley, Roger Ready, Bill Thurman,*
*Ralph Baker Jr, Dorothy Davis, Gary McLain, Bill*
*Holly, Byron Lord, Janiz Menshaw, Russ Marker,*
*Tony Pearce, Darlene Drew, Frank Jolly, Christi*
*Simmons*
A meteor crash leads to a spate of murders in a small
town. A sheriff and his deputy investigate, and
discover that the meteor was in fact the remains of a
spaceship launched from Earth, with hundreds of
animals aboard that were turned into mutants by
radioactivity. An unimaginative and poorly-made
monster-from-beyond entry.
Aka: E.T: THE EXTRA-TERRESTRIAL NASTIE;
EXTRA-TERRESTRIAL NASTIE (WOV); NIGHT
FRIGHT
HOR                                                 91 min
V                                              FIFTH; WOV

**NIGHTHAWKS** ***                                         18
Bruce Malmuth            USA                    1981
*Sylvester Stallone, Billy Dee Williams, Rutger Hauer,*
*Nigel Davenport, Persis Khambatta, Lindsay Wagner*
Two New York cops are assigned to a special unit on
the trail of an international terrorist, in this tense and
exciting yarn.
THR                                                 99 min
B,V,V2                                                 CIC

**NIGHTINGALE SANG IN BERKELEY           PG
SQUARE, A** **
Ralph Thomas             USA                    1979
*David Niven, Richard Jordan, Oliver Tobias, Elke*
*Sommer, Gloria Grahame, Hugh Griffith, Richard*
*Johnson*
An American released from prison is blackmailed into
taking part in a bank robbery. A rather humdrum tale
is brought to life by a splendid cast.
THR                                      90 min (ort 102 min)
B,V                                                   POLY

**NIGHTKILL** **                                           15
Ted Post                 USA                    1980
*Robert Mitchum, Jaclyn Smith, Mike Connors, James*
*Franciscus, Fritz Weaver, Sybil Danning (Sybelle*
*Danninger)*
Muddled mystery drama where a wealthy woman and
a mysterious figure play out strange and deadly
games after the former becomes involved in securing a
"quickie" divorce. Filmed in Arizona.

DRA                                      95 min (ort 97 min)
B,V,V2                                               VIPCO

**NIGHTLIFE** *                                            18
Louis Lewis              USA                    1983
*Bridgette Monet, Loni Sanders, Don Hart, Herschel*
*Savage, Dorothy Le May, Joey Civera, Ginger, Michael*
*Morrison, David Smith, Gayle Sterling, Annette Haven*
A daft sexploiter that opens with a couple in bed
discussing why they can't get married. Although he is
a millionaire, she is a hooker and enjoys her work so
much that she can't bear the thought of giving it up.
We next meet an assortment of weirdos who like to
make love in various bizarre ways. The film concludes
with her agreeing to be as nice to him as she is to
everyone else. Great stuff Louie. Cut before video
submission by 35 min 51 sec.
Osca: BRIEF AFFAIR (INTMED)
A                      34 min; 73 min (2 film cassette)
V                                          HAR; INTMED

**NIGHTLIFE** *                                            15
Daniel Taplitz           USA                    1989
*Ben Cross, Maryam D'Abo, Keith Szarabajka, Jessie*
*Cortie, Camille Saviola, Oliver Clark, Glenn Shadix*
A comedy-horror yarn in which a modern-day female
vampire living in Mexico City starts a romance with a
doctor running the local blood clinic. Matters are
complicated when a former lover comes back into her
life. An example of a one-idea film that starts off fairly
well but goes rapidly downhill.
HOR                                      89 min (ort 100 min) mCab
V                                                      CIC

**NIGHTMARE AT BITTER CREEK** **                           15
Tim Burstall             USA                    1988
*Lindsay Wagner, Tom Skerritt, Constance McCashin,*
*Joanna Cassidy, Janne Mortil*
Four woman undertake a wilderness expedition under
the leadership of an alcoholic guide and encounter a
gang of gun-crazed right-wing extremists. A dreary
re-run of DELIVERANCE that marked the US TV
debut for Australian director Burstall.
THR                                      88 min (ort 96 min) mTV
V                                                     SONY

**NIGHTMARE AT NOON** **                                   18
Nico Mastorakis          USA                    1988
*George Kennedy, Wings Hauser, Bo Hopkins, Brion*
*James, Kimberley Beck*
Three tourists stop at a small-town diner and find
themselves trapped by its crazed inhabitants, who
have been poisoned by a deadly toxin.
HOR                                                 92 min
V/sh                                                   MED

**NIGHTMARE CITY** *                                       18
Umberto Lenzi     ITALY/SPAIN                   1980
*Mel Ferrer, Hugo Stiglitz, Laura Trotter, Francisco*
*Rabal, Maria Rosaria Omaggio, Sonia Viviani,*
*Eduardo Fajardo, Manolo Zarzo, Alejandro De Enciso,*
*Ugo Bologna, Stefania D'Amario, Sara Franchetti,*
*Toni Felleghi*
A plane lands at an airport with a cargo of zombies
onboard, who proceed to terrorise the living, multi-
plying faster than they can be destroyed by the
military. A low-budget exercise in chilling tedium.
Aka: ATAQUE DE LOS ZOMBIES ATOMICOS;
CITY OF THE WALKING DEAD; INCUBO SULLA
CITTA CONTAMINATA; INVASION BY THE
ATOMIC ZOMBIES; INVASION OF THE ATOMIC
ZOMBIES; LA INVASION DE LOS ZOMBIES
ATOMICOS; ZOMBIES ATOMICOS
Osca: ALIEN TERROR
HOR                       84 min (ort 92 min) Cut (3 min 5 sec)
B,V                                          VTC L/A; STABL

**NIGHTMARE CITY** **                                      18
David Mitchell           USA                    1987

*John P. Ryan, Paul Coufos, Paul Harding, Tony Rosato*
A tough cop goes after a vicious serial killer in the title city, which is aptly named as no effort was spared in depicting it in all its disgusting sordidness. An atmospheric film let down by the muddled storyline.
Aka: CITY OF NIGHT; CITY OF SHADOWS
A/AD                                    93 min Cut (31 sec)
B,V                                                    MED

### NIGHTMARE COUNTY *                          15
Sean McGregor        USA                      1977
*Beau Gibson, Sean McGregor, Gayle Hemingway*
A band of hippies face a serious confrontation with the locals, and violence erupts.
A/AD                                              86 min
B,V                                     DFS L/A; SKP

### NIGHTMARE IN BLOOD **
John Stanley         USA                      1976
*Jerry Walter, Dan Caldwell, Barrie Youngfellow, Kathleen Quinlan, Kerwin Mathews, John P. Cochran, Ray K. Gorman, Hy Pyke, Drew Eshelman, Irving Israel, Morgan Upton, Justin Bishop, Charles Murphy, Mike Hitchcock*
An actor in horror films attends a meeting of his fan club at which his ghastly secret is revealed, i.e. the world learns at last that he is a real vampire. Anti-climactic spoof aimed at film buffs, with many in-jokes.
HOR                                              89 min
B,V                                           ATA; APX

### NIGHTMARE IN WAX **
Bud Townsend         USA                      1969
*Cameron Mitchell, Anne Helm, Scott Brady, Barry Kroeger, Victoria Carol, Johnny Cardos, Hollis Morrison, James Forrest, Philip Baird, James Forrest, Virgil Frye, Mercedes Alberti, Barry Donahue, Ingrid Dittman, Reni Martin*
A former film make-up man keeps a grisly wax museum, stocked with actors he has abducted and put into suspended animation. He does this in revenge for his disfigurement, at the hands of a studio boss he used to work for, when a fight with the man left him scarred for life. He plans to add the studio boss to his collection, but his "exhibits" eventually come back to life and kill him. A tired and amateurish re-run of other horror films on this theme.
Aka: CRIMES IN THE WAX MUSEUM
HOR                                              91 min
B,V                                           AVA/CBS

### NIGHTMARE ON ELM STREET, A ***            15
Wes Craven           USA                      1984
*Robert Englund, John Saxon, Heather Langenkamp, Ronee Blakely, Amanda Wyss, Nick Corri, Johnny Depp, Charles Fleischer, Joseph Whipp, Joe Unger, Lin Shaye, Mimi Meyer-Craven, Jack Shea, Ed Call, Sandy Lipton, David Andrews*
A dead child-killer returns to murder the children of those responsible for burning him alive, and first appears to them in terrifying and identical nightmares. The horrifying special effects and the deliberate blurring of the line between reality and illusion made this a tremendous hit for the makers, and for Englund, who plays the delightful Freddy Kreuger. Several sequels and a spin-off "Freddy" TV series followed. The script is by Craven.
HOR                                  88 min (ort 91 min)
V                                                     CBS

### NIGHTMARE ON ELM STREET, A: PART 2 –   18
### FREDDY'S REVENGE **
Jack Sholder         USA                      1985
*Mark Patton, Kim Myers, Robert Ruster, Clu Gulager, Hope Lange, Robert Englund, Marshall Bell, Melinda O. Fee, Thom McFadden, Sydney Walsh, Edward*

*Blackoff, Christie Clark, Lyman Ward, Donna Bruce, Hart Sprager*
Sequel to A NIGHTMARE ON ELM STREET that continues the story five years on. A teenage boy is tormented by nightmares after his family move into their new house, dreaming of a rotting corpse-like creature who has returned from the dead. The latter does indeed return, taking over the young man's body and forcing him to commit grisly crimes. Another slasher tale, not quite as effective but a lot bloodier than the earlier one. Written by David Chaskin.
Aka: FREDDY'S REVENGE
HOR                                  82 min (ort 87 min)
V                                                    WHV

### NIGHTMARE ON ELM STREET, A: PART 3 –   18
### DREAM WARRIORS **
Chuck Russell        USA                      1987
*Robert Englund, John Saxon, Heather Langenkamp, Craig Wasson, Patricia Arquette, Larry Fishburne, Priscilla Pointer, Brooke Bundy, Rodney Eastman, Dick Cavett, Zsa Zsa Gabor*
Second sequel in what promised to be a long-running study in terror akin to FRIDAY THE 13TH, with the same excellent if repulsive effects but little else. A small town is plagued by a series of suicides among teenagers, and a young psychiatrist finds a group of teenagers who are all suffering nightmares featuring the same horrific figure.
HOR                                  93 min (ort 96 min)
V/sh                                                 WHV

### NIGHTMARE ON ELM STREET, A: PART 4 –   18
### THE DREAM MASTER ***
Renny Harlin         USA                      1988
*Robert Englund, Rodney Eastman, Ken Sagoes, Tuesday Knight, Hope Marie Carlton, Brooke Theiss, Danny Hassel, Andras Jones, Toy Newkirk, Lisa Wilcox, Brooke Bundy, Jeffrey Levine, Nicolas Mele*
Third sequel marks the arrival of a more playful and humorous attitude to the central figure of Freddy who, having finished off all the surviving children of his killers, now turns attention to their young friends. Good special effects and camerawork abound, but don't look for any logic in the plot. A TV series followed. See FREDDY'S NIGHTMARES: A NIGHTMARE ON ELM STREET.
HOR                                              94 min
V                                                     CBS

### NIGHTMARE ON ELM STREET, A: PART 5 – THE
### DREAM CHILD **                              18
Stephen Hopkins      USA                      1989
*Robert Englund, Lisa Wilcox, Kelly Jo Minter, Beatrice Boepple, Erika Anderson, Whitby Hertford, Danny Hassel*
The novel idea of an unborn child communicating its dreams to the mother, is the one fresh element in this by now tired and repetitive series. Despite his defeat in previous films, Freddy returns to Main to terrorise again, preying on the heroine (Wilcox) and her lover. As ever, the special effects are memorable, but that's all that is.
HOR                                  86 min (ort 89 min)
V                                                     CBS

### NIGHTMARE VACATION *                        18
Robert Hiltzak       USA                      1984
*Mike Kellin, Felissa Rose, Jonathan Tierston, Karen Fields, Paul De Angelo, Christopher Collins, Robert Earl Jones, Katherine Kamhi, Tom Van Dell, Loris Sallahian, John Dunn, Willy Kuskin, Desiree Gould, Owen Hughes, Susan Glaze*
Boys and girls attending a summer camp become the prey of an unseen killer who murders them in various grisly ways. A clumsy, untalented slasher tale that was followed by the inevitable sequel.

Aka: SLEEPAWAY CAMP
HOR                 80 min (ort 88 min) Cut (57 sec)
B,V                                                CBS

## NIGHTMARE VACATION **                         18
John Llewellyn Moxey    USA                      1976
*Deborah Raffin, Lynne Moody, Ralph Bellamy, Chuck
Connors, Tina Louise, Fionnuala Flanagan, Robert
Reed, Della Reese, Lana Wood, Kim Wilson, Leslie
Albers, Simpson Hemphill, Annette Henley, Tom
Keith, John Malloy*
Two attractive girls are thrown into prison after
rejecting the advances of a small-town sheriff.
Another cliched exploration of rural corruption with
all the stock figures of this genre.
Aka: NIGHTMARE; NIGHTMARE IN BADHAM
COUNTY
THR            81 min; 98 min (PYR/CBS) (ort 100 min)
                          Cut (2 min 45 sec) mTV
B,V          VFP L/A; PYR/CBS; PHE (VHS only)

## NIGHTMARE VACATION 2 *                         18
Michael A. Simpson    USA                        1987
*Pamela Springsteen, Walter Gotell, Renee Estevez,
Brian P. Clarke, Susan Marie Snyder, Heather Binion,
Tony Higgins, Terry Hobbs, Kendall Bean, Valerie
Hartman, Julie Murphy, Carol Chambers, Amy Fields*
Lame sequel to the first film in which ill-behaved
pupils at a summer camp promptly vanish and are
later found to have been murdered. Plenty of gore and
nudity but nothing to hold the interest.
Aka: SLEEPAWAY CAMP 2; SLEEPAWAY CAMP
2: UNHAPPY CAMPERS
HOR            77 min (ort 91 min) Cut (2 min 16 sec)
B,V                                         CBS; FUTUR

## NIGHTMARE VACATION 3 *                         18
Michael A. Simpson    USA                        1989
*Pamela Springsteen, Tracy Griffith, Michael J.
Pollard*
The third film in the series and the most feeble one
yet. The summer camp that was the scene for the
previous murders is re-opened and naturally, it isn't
long before our mad lady killer is doing her stuff once
more. A dull and depressing production-line horror
yarn.
HOR                                            75 min
V                                               FUTUR

## NIGHTMARE VOYAGE *                             18
Frank Mitchell         USA                       1976
*Jonathan Lippe, Peter Kellett, Midori, Mora Modair,
John Hart, Laurie Rose, Gene Tyburn*
The passengers on a voyage are murdered one by one
in this predictable and unappealing yarn.
Aka: BLOOD VOYAGE
HOR            68 min (ort 80 min) Cut (4 min 30 sec)
V                    TRANS L/A; POLY L/A; ATLAS

## NIGHTMARE WEEKEND *                            18
Henry Sala       FRANCE/UK/USA                   1986
*Debbie Laster, Debra Hunter, Lori Lewis, Dale
Midkiff, Preston Maybank, Wellington Meffert, Nick
James, Kimberley Stahl, Kim Dossin, Karen Mayo,
Andrea Thompson, Bruce Morton, Robert Burke, Dean
Gates, Marc Gottlieb*
A device invented by a brilliant scientist is used by his
evil female assistant to turn people into computer-
controlled zombies that will do her will, but this
process turns them into mad mutants. Somewhat
reminiscent of those pulp SF films of the 1950s but
with the dubious benefit of ample nudity.
FAN                                            88 min
B,V                                               AVA

## NIGHTMARES **                                  15
Joseph Sargent        USA                        1983
*Cristina Raines, Timothy James, William Sanderson,*

*Emelio Estevez, Moon Zappa, Lance Henriksen, Robin
Gammell, Richard Masur, Rose Marie Campos,
Bridgette Andersen, Veronica Cartwright, Albert
Hague, Howard F. Flynn*
Quartet of strange stories of the same type as were
shown on the TV series "The Twilight Zone" and
entitled: "The Bendiction", "Bishop Of Battle", "Night
Of The Rat" and "Terror In Topanga". A mixture of the
macabre and the supernatural, but neither particular-
ly imaginative nor gripping.
FAN                 95 min (ort 99 min) mTV
B,V                                     VIV L/A; CIC

## NIGHTMARES IN A DAMAGED BRAIN *
Romano Scavolini      USA                        1981
*Baird Stafford, Sharon Smith, Mik Cribben, C.J.
Cooke, Kathleen Ferguson, Danny Ronen, John
Watkins, William Milling, Scot Praetorius, William S.
Kirksey, Christina Keefe*
An allegedly cured schizophrenic begins to kill upon
his release from a mental home. A crude and deriva-
tive work that offers little apart from the usual gore.
Unlikely to be available in an uncut form in the UK.
Aka: NIGHTMARE
HOR                      89 min (ort 97 min) Cut
B,V                                               WOV

## NIGHTS AND LOVES OF DON JUAN, THE *
Luigi Mondello        ITALY
*Barbara Bouchet, Ira Furstenburg, Robert Hoffman*
Mediocre softcore account of this famous lover's
adventures.
A                                              91 min
B,V,V2                                        INT; VPD

## NIGHTS IN WHITE SATIN **                       15
Michael Barnard       USA                        1987
*Kenneth David Gilman, Kim Waltrip, Priscilla Harris,
Michael Laskin*
A photographer hires a young street girl as his
assistant and soon becomes romantically involved
with her.
DRA                                            90 min
B,V                                              CINE

## NIGHTS OF CABIRIA ****                         15
Federico Fellini
                    FRANCE/ITALY                 1957
*Francois Perier, Amedeo Nazzari, Giulietta Masina,
Franca Marzi, Dorian Gray, Aldo Silvani, Franca
Marzi, Mario Passante, Pina Gualandri, Polidor,
Ennio Girolami, Christian Tassou, Jean Molier,
Ricardo Fellini*
A Rome prostitute fantasises about love and a normal
life, but is betrayed when she puts her trust in others.
A powerfully moving film that formed the basis for the
Broadway musical "Sweet Charity", which was itself
filmed. AA: Foreign.
Aka: CABIRIA; LE NOTTI DI CABIRIA
DRA                106 min (ort 110 min) B/W
B,V                                        TEVP; CAN

## NIGHTS OF TERROR, THE *                        18
Andrea Bianchi        ITALY                      1980
*Karin Well, Peter Bark, Maria Angela Giordan,
Roberto Caporali, Simone Mattioli, Antonella
Antinori, Gian Luigi Chrizzi*
Zombie horror film where the undead gate-crash a
weekend party, and a gory carnage ensues. Despite
being edited down for the UK market, the film was
still cut before video submission by a further 10 min 6
sec.
Aka: LE NOTTI DEL TERRORE; ZOMBIE 3;
ZOMBIE HORROR
HOR      59 min; 66 min (APX) Cut (3 min 11 sec - ort 92
min)
B,V                                        3APX; APX

**NIGHTSHIFT \*\*\***                                                    15
Ron Howard              USA                  1982
*Henry Winkler, Michael Keaton, Shelley Long, Gina
Hecht, Pat Corley, Nita Talbot, Bobby DiCicco, Kevin
Costner*
A man takes a night job at a morgue but gets lured
into starting a call-girl operation by his smart,
fast-talking assistant. Despite the unpromising na-
ture of the setting, this is a likeable, imaginative and
amusing tale, scripted by Lowell Ganz and Babaloo
Mandel.
Aka: NIGHT SHIFT
COM                          102 min (ort 108 min)
V/sh                                        WHV

**NIGHTSIDE \*\***                                                      15
Bernard Kowalski        USA                  1980
*Doug McClure, Michael Cornelison, John DeLancie,
Roy Jenson, Jason Kincaid, Melinda Naud, Michael
D. Roberts, Danny Wells, Michael Winslow, Joe
Spinell, Wayne Heffley, Vincent Schiavelli, Timothy
Agoglia Carey, Sondra Blake*
Pilot for a prospective cop series about an experienced
Los Angeles cop and his more naive partner, who work
the dusk-to-dawn shift. Fair.
COM                          70 min (ort 78 min) mTV
B,V                                          CIC

**NIGHTWALK \***                                                       15
Jerrold Freedman        USA                  1989
*Robert Urich, Lesley-Anne Down, Mark Joy, Ryan
Urich, Bert Remsen*
A woman sees a murder take place on a lonely beach
but fails to convince the police of this when the body
disappears. However, the murderer decides to silence
her for good by bringing in a contract killer. A weak
thriller with an overly familiar plot.
THR                          90 min (ort 100 min) mTV
V/sh                                         CBS

**NIGHTWING \***                                                       15
Arthur Hiller      NETHERLANDS               1979
*David Warner, Kathryn Harrold, Steven Macht,
Strother Martin, Nick Mancuso, Ben Piazza, George
Clutesi, Donald Hotton, Charles Hallahan, Judith
Novgrod, Alice Hirson, Pat Corley, Charlie Bird,
Danny Zapien, Peter Prouse*
Vampire bats in Arizona prove to be behind a series of
mysterious deaths in an obviously derivative and
poorly plotted film, that generates little interest or
suspense.
Boa: novel by Martin Cruz Smith.
HOR                                         105 min
B,V                                          RCA

**NIGHTWISH \*\***                                                     18
Bruce R. Cook           USA                  1989
*Clayton Rohner, Jack Starrett, Robert Tessier, Brian
Thompson*
Parapsychology students take part in a strange
experiment at a remote house in the desert, where an
unconventional professor is convinced that he can
unlock the mind's psychic powers by making his
subjects confront their innermost fears. However, the
outcome is somewhat different. Good special effects
and acting help push this competent chiller along,
though the convoluted plot is an irritation.
HOR                                          86 min
V                                            MED

**NIJINSKY \*\***
Herbert Ross           UK/USA                1980
*Alan Bates, George De La Pena, Leslie Browne, Alan
Badel, Colin Blakely, Carla Fracci, Ronald Pickup,
Ronald Lacey, Jeremy Irons, Janet Suzman, Sian
Phillips, Anton Dolin*
The turbulent life of this famous dancer who married
despite being homosexual, provides the subject matter

for a less than enthralling biopic, that concentrates on
his lovers to the exclusion of his professional career. A
glossy but sterile work.
Boa: book by Romolo Nijinsky.
DRA                          120 min (ort 125 min)
B,V                                      MOV; CIC

**NIKKI, WILD DOG OF THE NORTH \*\*\***                                 U
Don Haldane/Jack Couffer
                        USA                  1961
*Jean Coutu, Emile Genest, Uriel Luft, Robert Rivard.
Narrated by: Jacques Fauteux, Dwight Hauser*
A young puppy becomes separated from its fur-trapper
owner and has various adventures together with a
bear cub. A lively Disney film and a perfect piece of
family entertainment.
Boa: novel Nomads Of The North by James Oliver
Curwood.
JUV                          70 min (ort 74 min) Cut (24 sec)
B,V                                          WDV

**NINE AGES OF NAKEDNESS \***
George Harrison Marks   UK                   1972
*Harrison Marks, Max Wall, Cardew Robinson, Max
Bacon, Julian Orchard, Big Bruno Elrington, June
Planer, Oliver McGreavey, Rita Webb*
A historical pageant with the theme of female nudity
through the ages, as recounted by a photographer. A
dull and innocent romp from an age where female
nudity on screen was the height of wickedness.
DRA                          89 min (ort 95 min)
B,V                                          DFS

**NINE AND A HALF WEEKS \***                                           18
Adrian Lyne             USA                  1986
*Kim Basinger, Mickey Rourke, Margaret Whitton,
David Margulies, Christine Baranski, Dwight Weist,
Roderick Cook, Karen Young, William De Acutis,
Victor Truro, Justine Johnson, Cintia Cruz, Kim
Chan, Lee Lai Sing*
The title refers to the duration of a steamy sex-
obsessed relationship between a man and a woman,
that seems to imply sado-masochistic aspects in a
softcore film. Despite the great media mega-hype
surrounding it on release, the film has nothing
interesting to say in its threadbare plot.
Aka: 9 1/2 WEEKS
Boa: novel 9 1/2 Weeks by Elizabeth McNeill.
DRA                                         112 min
V                                            CBS

**NINE DEATHS OF THE NINJA \*\***                                      18
Emmett Alston           USA                  1985
*Sho Kosugi, Brent Huff, Emilia Lesniak, Blackie
Dammett, Regina Richardson*
A martial arts anti-terrorist squad is sent to rescue a
group of kidnapped tourists in Manila in the standard
adventure yarn.
Aka: 9 DEATHS OF THE NINJA; DEADLY
WARRIORS
MAR                          90 min Cut (4 min 5 sec)
B,V                                          RCA

**NINE LIVES OF FRITZ THE CAT \***                                     18
Ralph Bakshi            USA                  1974
*Voices of: Skip Hinnant, Reva Rose, Bob Holt, Fred
Smoot, Pat Harrington Jr*
Animated sequel to FRITZ THE CAT with more
adventures of our cool feline hero. Where the earlier
film had some relevant and witty things to say about
the 1960s, this one just sets out to shock with its
crudity. A tiresome and banal effort. See also HEAVY
TRAFFIC, WIZARDS, FIRE AND ICE and THE
LORD OF THE RINGS - four more films by this
director.
CAR                                          72 min
B,V,V2                      POLY; CH5 (VHS only)

**NINE SEVEN SIX: EVIL \*\***                                          18
Robert Englund          USA                  1988

*Stephen Geoffreys, Sandy Dennis, Jim Metzler, Maria Rubell, Patrick O'Bryan, Lezlie Deane, J.J. Cohen, Darren Burrows*
A young boy calls a phone number that connects him to an evil force, which soon comes to dominate his life. A splendid idea fails to get the treatment it deserves, though the film does have its moments.
Aka: 976: EVIL
HOR          95 min (ort 105 min) Cut (8 sec including
                                        film cuts)
B,V                                                MED

## NINE TO FIVE ***                                        15
Colin Higgins            USA                      1980
*Jane Fonda, Lily Tomlin, Dolly Parton, Dabney Coleman, Sterling Hayden, Elizabeth Wilson, Henry Jones, Lawrence Pressman, Marian Mercer*
Three girls in an office work for a sexist boss who constantly makes lewd advances. They eventually find a way of teaching him a lesson. A surprisingly fresh and inventive comedy that never sags, despite its length. Tomlin gives a superb performance and Coleman is in peak form too. Later gave rise to a so-so TV series.
Aka: 9 TO 5
COM                          105 min (ort 110 min)
B,V,V2,LV                                          CBS

## 1984 ****                                              15
Michael Bradford         UK                       1984
*John Hurt, Suzanna Hamilton, Richard Burton Cyril Cusack, Gregor Fisher, James Walker, Andrew Wilde, David Trevena, David Cann, Anthony Benson, Peter Frye, Phyllis Logan, Pam Gems, Joscik Barbarossa, John Boswell, Bob Flag*
A later version of Orwell's brilliantly prophetic satire on totalitarianism, examining the life of Winston Smith, a man living in the dictatorship of Oceana. Unlike the earlier film, it stays remarkably faithful to the book. Originally written in 1948, his nightmarish vision is accurately captured by sets that portray the future from the standpoint of the 1940s. Burton's last film in which he gives a superb portrayal of chief inquisitor O'Brien.
Boa: novel by George Orwell.
DRA                                           110 min
B,V                                                PVG

## 1941 **                                                PG
Steven Spielberg         USA                      1979
*John Belushi, Tim Matheson, Nancy Allen, Dan Aykroyd, Ned Beatty, Toshiro Mifune, Christopher Lee, Robert Stack, Treat Williams, Warren Oates, Murray Hamilton, Dianne Kay, Slim Pickens, Bobby DiCicco, Lorraine Gary, John Candy*
Los Angeles is thrown into panic during a power cut, when a Japanese submarine is supposed to have been sighted off the coast following the Pearl Harbor attack. A vastly expensive and overblown slapstick comedy, where the time and effort yield a disappointing dividend of laughs.
COM                          112 min (ort 118 min)
V/h                                                CIC

## 1969 **                                                15
Ernest Thompson          USA                      1988
*Robert Downey Jr, Kiefer Sutherland, Bruce Dern, Winona Ryder, Joanna Cassidy, Mariette Hartley, Christopher Wynne, Keller Kuhn, Steve Foster*
A failed attempt to focus on the generation gap and social conflict, that shook the USA during the title year, when opposition to the Vietnam War was beginning to grow, as seen in the lives of a group of teenagers. Features the music of The Pretenders, Jimi Hendrix, Cream, The Animals, Canned Heat, The Moody Blues and many others. A directorial debut by writer Thompson, who is better known for having scripted ON GOLDEN POND. Intelligent scripting is

hampered by haphazard direction.
DRA                                            96 min
V                                                  EIV

## NINETY-TWO IN THE SHADE ***
Thomas McGuane           USA                      1975
*Peter Fonda, Warren Oates, Margot Kidder, Burgess Meredith, Harry Dean Stanton, Sylvia Miles, Elizabeth Ashley, William Hickey, Louise Latham*
Film adaptation of a novel about hard-working, tough fishermen in Florida, and the conflict between two rival skippers. A patchy comedy-drama with many effective moments.
Aka: 92 IN THE SHADE
Boa: novel by Thomas McGuane.
DRA                                            96 min
B,V                                                PRV

## NINJA 2: THE REVENGE OF THE NINJA **          18
Sam Firstenberg          USA                      1983
*Sho Kosugi, Keith Vitali, Virgil Frye, Arthur Roberts, Mario Gallo*
Kung fu high kicks once more, as evil Ninjas and drug smugglers get what they deserve. This one followed ENTER THE NINJA and gave rise in turn to NINJA 3: THE DOMINATION.
Aka: REVENGE OF THE NINJA, THE
MAR          80 min (ort 88 min) Cut (57 sec)
B,V,V2,LV              GHV L/A; VCC (VHS only)

## NINJA 3: THE DOMINATION **                    18
Sam Firstenberg          USA                      1984
*Lucinda Dickey, Jordan Bennett, Sho Kosugi, David Chung, T.J. Castronova, Dale Ishimodo, James Hong, Bob Craig, Pamela Ness, Roy Padilla, Moe Mosley, John LaMotta, Ron Foster, Alan Amiel, Steve Lambert, Earl Smith, Karen Petty*
In this sequel to NINJA 2: THE REVENGE OF THE NINJA, the spirit of a Ninja killed by the police takes over the body of a young girl, and proceeds to wreak havoc. Lots of action compensates for the mindlessness of it all.
MAR                                            95 min
B,V                                                GHV

## NINJA ACADEMY *                                18
Nico Mastorakis                                   1988
*Will Egan, Kelly Randall, Gerald Okomura*
A martial arts answer to POLICE ACADEMY, with a parade of the usual screwballs lining up for lessons in fisticuffs. One or two of the spoofs are funny, but this is basically a one-joke film.
COM                                            89 min
V                                                  GHV

## NINJA AMERICAN WARRIOR **                      18
Tommy Cheng      HONG KONG                        198-
*Joff Houston, John Wilford, Peter Davis, Glen Carson, Julie Luk, Laura Ma, Patrick To, Joan Leung*
The evil head of a crime empire resists the combined forces of the USA drug enforcement agency and the police, in an action-packed martial arts tale set in Asia and America.
MAR                          85 min Cut (50 sec)
B,V                          PACEV L/A; DRUM

## NINJA AND THE WARRIORS OF FIRE *              18
Bruce Lambert                                     1973
*Peter Davis, Jeff Houston, Glen Carson, Christine Warren*
The leader of a Ninja band rapes and then murders the fiancee of a man who refused to give them secret information. The woman's sister takes revenge.
A/AD              86 min Cut (1 min 24 sec)
V                               MIA L/A; FALCON

## NINJA APOCALYPSE *                             18
Tommy Lee        HONG KONG                        1985
*Don Wong, Linda Young, Yusuaki Kura To*

Standard martial arts adventure.

MAR                84 min (ort 89 min) Cut (2 min 37 sec)
B,V                                                    MOG

## NINJA CHAMPION *                                        18
Joseph Lai        HONG KONG                             1986
Bruce Baron, Pierre Tremblay, Nancy Chan, Richard
Harrison, Jack Lam, Philip Ching, Dragon Lee
An Interpol agent's girlfriend is raped by a criminal
gang, which gives our agent an excuse for a no-holds-
barred high-kicking showdown with them.
MAR                                               87 min
B,V                                             NINJ/VPD

## NINJA COMMANDMENTS *                                    15
Joseph Lai        HONG KONG                             1987
Richard Harrison, Dave Wheeler
In this tale, some Ninja are expelled from the society
for breaking some of its secret laws.
MAR                                     88 min Cut (6 sec)
B,V                                             NINJ/VPD

## NINJA DESTROYER **                                      18
Godfrey Ho        HONG KONG                             1986
Stuart Smith, Bruce Baron, Sorapong Chatri, Na Yen
Ha, Richard Berman, Timothy Nugent
Assorted Ninja fighters battle for control of an emer-
ald mine, in this tale set on the Thai-Cambodian
border.
MAR                84 min (ort 92 min) Cut (41 sec)
B,V                                             NINJ/VPD

## NINJA DRAGON **                                         18
Godfrey Ho        HONG KONG                             1986
Richard Harrison, Bruce Stallion, Melvin Pitcher,
Konrad Chang, Lily Lan, Freya Patrick
Kung fu actioner set in modern times and telling of
the conflict between two rival criminal gangs, and
their battle for control of the streets of Greater
Shanghai.
MAR                                    87 min Cut (23 sec)
B,V                                           IVS; BRAVE

## NINJA FIST OF FIRE *                                    18
                  HONG KONG
Chor Yim Yung, Cheung Ching Ching
Kung fu costume drama.
MAR                                               87 min
V                                                  ATLAS

## NINJA HOLOCAUST *                                       18
                  HONG KONG                             1985
Bruce Chen, Jim Brooks, Martin Lee, Jon Resnick,
Michael Swift
Formula martial arts tale, set in the twilight world of
South-East Asian gangsters.
MAR                                               92 min
B,V                                                   MOG

## NINJA HUNT **                                           18
Joseph Lai        HONG KONG                             1986
Richard Harrison, Stewart Smith
A CIA agent has to recover a secret formula stolen
from the US government in this agreeable martial
arts thriller.
MAR                85 min (ort 91 min) Cut (1 min 6 sec)
B,V                                          CAN L/A; ARC

## NINJA IN THE KILLING FIELDS *                           18
York Lam          HONG KONG                             198-
Stuart Sheen, Louis Roth, Patricia Greenfield, Jane
Kingsley
An American secret agent heads to Thailand to
destroy a drugs trafficking operation and comes up
against a ruthless Ninja band, which embarks on a
series of terrorist attacks.
Aka: NINJA CONNECTION
A/AD                                   85 min Cut (37 sec)
B,V                                       ARF; MIA (VHS only)

## NINJA KIDS: KISS OF DEATH **                            18
Joseph Kuo        HONG KONG
Lo Yiu, Luk Yee Fung, Luk Fung, Kwong Sang, Loong
Koon Mo
More high-kicking action but with a supernatural
slant.
Aka: NINJA KISS OF DEATH KIDS (MKR)
MAR                87 min Cut (ATL version: 5 sec; POR
                                     version: 19 sec)
B,V            AVR L/A; MKR L/A; ATLAS; POR

## NINJA KILL *                                            15
Joseph Lai        HONG KONG
Mark White, Clayton Rice, Richard Harrison, Stuart
Smith
A ruthless Ninja gang plots to assassinate a senator
and replace him with a double who is under their
control. Only two men can stop these devilish plans,
but they must first take on an evil woman and her
female gang. Another strictly routine blend of im-
plausibility and fisticuffs.
MAR                                   86 min Cut (1 min 25 sec)
V                                                     VPD

## NINJA KILLER *                                          18
Lawrence Chan     HONG KONG
Kau Ka Wen, Joey Louis, Carter Wong
A smuggler absconds to Istanbul with an associate's
loot, but is followed b police agent who finds himself
embroiled in a battle between rival gangs.
MAR                                    87 min Cut (3 sec)
B,V                                                   VPD

## NINJA MISSION, THE *                                    18
Mats Helge Olsson  SWEDEN/UK                            1984
Christopher Kohlberg, Hans Rosteau, Hana Pola, Curt
Brober, Bo F. Munthe
A scientist has to be rescued from captivity in the
USSR, and a specially trained force is sent to get him.
Bad dubbing and lousy direction make this a film of
memorable badness. However, this did not prevent it
becoming a commercial success.
A/AD               97 min Cut (1 min 1 sec) dubbed
B,V            VTC L/A; ACAD; APX; XTACY/KRP

## NINJA OPERATION: KNIGHT AND WARRIOR *  15
Joseph Lai        HONG KONG                             1987
Richard Harrison, Alphonse Beni, Stuart Smith,
Grant Temple
An Interpol agent is sent on a drugs busting operation
and comes up against four assassins who murder his
wife. He seeks help from an old friend. Formula
mayhem followed by a sequel.
Aka: KNIGHT AND WARRIOR
A/AD                                   85 min Cut (1 min 7 sec)
B,V                                                   VPD

## NINJA OPERATION 2: WAY OF CHALLENGE *   15
Joseph Lai        HONG KONG                             1988
Richard Harrison, Geoffrey Zeibart
Another formula offering from the Ninja factory, this
time telling of the efforts made to retrieve a sword of
remarkable properties.
Aka: WAY OF CHALLENGE
A/AD                                    86 min Cut (20 sec)
V                                                     VPD

## NINJA OPERATION 3: LICENSED TO           18
TERMINATE *
Joseph Lai        HONG KONG                             1987
Richard Harrison, Grant Temple, Paul Marshall, Jack
McPeat, Louis Ruth, Bob Corridge, Alvin Blacksmith,
Sandra Lee
Good Ninja warriors take on bad ones as the Golden
Ninja and the Prince of Justice confront the Black
Ninja Empire. More mindless mayhem, made slightly
ludicrous by the pretentions of the script.
Aka: LICENSED TO TERMINATE (VPD)

MAR    87 min (ort 89 min) Cut (29 sec)
V    VPD

## NINJA OPERATION 4: THUNDERBOLT
## ANGELS *    18
Joseph Lai    HONG KONG    1988
*Richard Harrison, George Ajex*
Two childhood friends become involved in a gang war
and are jailed. On their release a new conflict develops
and they soon find themselves on opposite sides when
one is recruited by a cop to destroy a criminal gang.
More martial arts mayhem, barely sustained by the
usual thin plot.
Aka: THUNDERBOLT ANGELS
MAR    86 min Cut (51 sec)
V    VPD

## NINJA OPERATION 5: GODFATHER THE
## MASTER *    18
Joseph Lai    HONG KONG    1988
*Richard Harrison, Grant Temple*
The head of a criminal clan is preparing to hand over
the family business to his son when he is murdered by
rival gang leaders. The son now embarks on a course
of training to become a Ninja fighter, and relentlessly
pursues the culprits. A tired formula offering.
Aka: GODFATHER THE MASTER
MAR    85 min
V    VPD

## NINJA OPERATION 7: ROYAL WARRIORS **    18
    HONG KONG    1989
*Richard Harrison, Mike Abbott*
Martial arts adventure set near the Burmese border
where the head of an evil Ninja gang seeks a fortune
in gold, having murdered two explorers for their
treasure map. When he brings in an old partner, who
runs a sex-slave operation, he fails to realise that this
may cause his downfall. Average entry in this long-
running series.
Aka: ROYAL WARRIORS
MAR    73 min
V    VPD

## NINJA OPERATION 8: CHAMPION ON FIRE **    18
Joseph Lai    HONG KONG    1988
*Richard Harrison, Stuart Smith*
Yet another story in this interminable series, this
time telling of a peaceful priest who, after using a
cross to great effect when caught in a train robbery,
makes an enemy of an evil Ninja criminal. Later our
priest befriends a martial arts expert, little realising
that this friendship will save his life. Average production-line violence and mayhem tale.
Aka: CHAMPION ON FIRE
A/AD    79 min
V    VPD

## NINJA SHOWDOWN, THE *    18
Joseph Lai    HONG KONG    198-
*Richard Harrison, Donald Linke, Peter Hibbard,*
*Kenneth Lundh*
A good Ninja has to defend his honour and his village
from a warlord and his gang of hired killers.
MAR    83 min Cut (3 min 30 sec) (ort 90 min)
V    ECF; VIDLNE

## NINJA SQUAD **    15
Wo Kuo-Jen    HONG KONG    1986
*Alexander Lou, Y.T. Thomas, Yang Sang*
When a New York cop arrives in Hong Kong seeking
information as to the identity of the killer of his
girlfriend's father, he soon finds that he has become a
target for assassination.
MAR    86 min Cut (1 min 17 sec)
B,V    VPD

## NINJA STRIKES BACK, THE *    18
    HONG KONG    1983

*Bruce Le (Huang Kin Lung), Harold Sakata, Wang*
*Jang Lee, Chuck Norris, Bolo Yeung*
Two martial arts masters slug it out.
MAR    78 min (ort 90 min) Cut (2 min 59 sec)
B,V    XTASY L/A; SPECTA L/A; STABL

## NINJA TERMINATOR **    18
Godfrey Ho    HONG KONG    1985
*Richard Harrison, Jonathan Wattis, Maria Francesca,*
*Wong Cheng Li, Philip Ko, Jack Lam*
Routine Ninja shenanigans with the usual complex
web of intrigue involving drugs, the underworld, a
missing statuette etc.
MAR    85 min Cut (2 min 7 sec)
B,V    IVS L/A; VCC

## NINJA THE PROTECTOR *    18
    HONG KONG    1985
*Richard Harrison, Warren Chan, Morna Lee, David*
*Butler*
A special unit headed by a Ninja is formed to smash a
nationwide forgery ring that has flooded the country
with counterfeit money.
MAR    84 min (ort 90 min) Cut (1 min 12 sec)
B,V    ECF L/A; VCC (VHS only)

## NINJA THUNDERBOLT *    18
Godfrey Ho
    HONG KONG/PHILIPPINES/TAIWAN    1985
*Richard Harrison, Anna Lewis, Wang Tao, Jackie*
*Chan, Randy To, Kulada Yusuaki, Barbara Yuen*
A corrupt businessman plans an insurance fraud but
is foiled by our nimble Ninja warriors in this standard
kung fu yarn.
MAR    88 min (ort 90 min) Cut (34 sec)
B,V    VPD

## NINJA USA *    18
Wu Kuo-Jen    HONG KONG
*Alexander Lou, George Nicholas Albergo, You Jin*
*Thomas, Yip Yong, Yong Song*
A Ninja in the pay of a Vietnam veteran turned
drug-runner kills one of the latter's friends, thus
setting the stage for another tale of bloody revenge.
MAR    85 min (ort 90 min) Cut (3 min 15 sec)
B,V    PACEV L/A; DRUM

## NINJA WARRIORS *    18
John Lloyd    USA    1985
*Ron Marchini, Paul Vance, Ken Watanabe, Romano*
*Kristoff, Mike Cohen, Charlotte Cain*
Routine story of revenge and in-fighting among a
Ninja band, when a secret document is stolen from a
research establishment.
MAR    83 min (ort 90 min) Cut (33 sec)
B,V    3APX; MEDPER

## NINOTCHKA ***    U
Ernst Lubitsch    USA    1939
*Greta Garbo, Melvyn Douglas, Ina Claire, Bela Lugosi,*
*Sig Rumann, Felix Bressart, Alexander Granach,*
*Richard Carle*
In her first "laughing" role, Garbo plays a severe
Russian emissary, sent to Paris to sell off some Tsarist
jewels. Douglas is the American playboy who woos
her, teaching her something about life and love in the
process. A fairly engaging comedy of manners, albeit a
trifle dated and mawkish. The film later formed the
basis for the Broadway musical and film SILK
STOCKINGS.
Boa: short story by Melchior Lengyel.
COM    108 min (ort 110 min) B/W
V    MGM

## NINJA WARS *    18
Kosei Saito    JAPAN    1982
*Duke Sanada, Sonny (Shinichi) Chiba*
A Ninja takes on five assassins who have kidnapped
his girlfriend.

MAR                                    96 min
B,V                            VTC L/A; VMA

## NINTH CONFIGURATION, THE **
William Peter Blatty     USA          1980
*Stacy Keach, Scott Wilson, Jason Miller, Ed Flanders,*
*Neville Brand, Moses Gunn, George DiCenzo, Robert*
*Loggia, Tom Atkins, Alejandro Rey, Joe Spinell, Steve*
*Sandor, Richard Lynch*
An unconventional psychiatrist is called in to find out
why some of the US's top military men are having
nervous breakdowns, in this confused and often
incomprehensible film, which exists in several diffe-
rent versions, all with varying running times. Some
hilarious moments offer a little compensation.
Aka: TWINKLE, TWINKLE, KILLER KANE
Boa: novel Twinkle, Twinkle, Killer Kane by William
Peter Blatty.
THR                      108 min (ort 140 min)
B,V                                     GHV

## NO BIG DEAL **
Robert Charlton                          PG
Robert Charlton          USA          1983
*Kevin Dillon, Christopher Gartin, Mary Joan Negro,*
*Jane Krakowski, Tammy Grimes, Sylvia Miles*
The story of an unhappy, alienated teenager who is
unable to fit in forms the basis for this appealing but
rather contrived tale.
DRA                                   90 min
V                                      CINE

## NO BLADE OF GRASS **
Cornel Wilde                             15
Cornel Wilde             UK           1970
*Nigel Davenport, Jean Wallace, John Hamil, Patrick*
*Holt, Lynn Frederick, Anthony May, Wendy*
*Richmond, Anthony Sharp, George Coulouris, M.J.*
*Mathews, Tex Fuller, Michael Percival, Ruth*
*Kettlewell, Simon Merrick, Max Hartnell*
A deadly virus destroys grass and other vegetation,
forcing a British family to flee to the Lake District,
where they have to contend with motorcycle thugs and
other symptoms of a total breakdown of society.
Unfortunately, the ecological impact of the original
novel, is lessened by excessive dwelling on the absence
of law and order.
Boa: novel The Death Of Grass by John Christopher.
FAN          92 min (ort 97 min) Cut (1 min 20 sec)
B,V                                     MGM

## NO DEAD HEROES *
J.C. Miller                              18
J.C. Miller              USA          1987
*Max Thayer, John Dresden, Toni Nero, David*
*Anderson, Nick Nicholson*
A Green Beret captain trapped in the jungles of North
Vietnam, becomes the victim of a KGB plot when he is
turned by them into a killing machine whose intended
victims include the Pope and the US President. Very
poor.
A/AD        81 min (ort 90 min) Cut (1 min 45 sec)
B,V                                     VES

## NO DEPOSIT, NO RETURN **
Norman Tokar                             U
Norman Tokar             USA          1976
*David Niven, Darren McGavin, Don Knotts, Herschel*
*Bernardi, Barbara Feldon, Brad Savage, Kim*
*Richards, Vic Tayback, John Williams*
Two neglected rich kids stage a fake kidnapping to
create a stir and get themselves shipped off to their
mother in Hong Kong. A likeable Disney comedy of no
great depth.
COM                                  112 min
B,V                                     WDV

## NO HOLDS BARRED **
Thomas J. Wright                         15
Thomas J. Wright         USA          1989
*Hulk Hogan, Kurt Fuller, Joan Severance, Tiny Lister,*
*Mark Pelligrino, Jesse (The Body) Ventura, Bill*
*Henderson*
A vehicle for wrestling star Hogan, in which he

appears as a TV wrestling star who comes up against
a ruthless businessman, who is prepared to do anything necessary to get him to switch TV networks. A
rather crude and predictable ROCKY 3-style film,
that attempts to cash in on the growing popularity of
TV wrestling.
A/AD                                  93 min
V                                       VPD

## NO KIDDING **
Gerald Thomas                            PG
Gerald Thomas            UK           1960
*Leslie Phillips, Julia Lockwood, Geraldine McEwan,*
*Noel Purcell, Irene Handl, Joan Hickson, Cyril*
*Raymond*
A couple inherit an old house and promptly turn it
into a holiday home for children of the rich. Pleasant
enough in its way, this anaemic comedy squeezes out
one or two laughs.
Aka: BEWARE OF CHILDREN
Boa: novel Beware Of Children by Verity Anderson.
COM                  83 min (ort 86 min) B/W
V                                       WHV

## NO MAN'S LAND **
Peter Werner                             15
Peter Werner             USA          1987
*Charlie Sheen, D.B. Sweeney, Randy Quaid, Lara*
*Harris, Bill Duke, Arlen Dean Snyder, R.D. Call, M.*
*Emmett Walsh*
A rookie cop working underground to solve a murder
gets drawn into a glamorous lifestyle and eventually
faces an agonising choice between love and profession-
al honour. Sluggish and uninspired treatment of a
promising idea.
A/AD      101 min (ort 107 min) (Cut at film release by
                                     1 min 5 sec)
V                                       VIR

## NO MERCY *
Richard Pearce                           18
Richard Pearce           USA          1986
*Richard Gere, Kim Basinger, Jeroen Krabbe, George*
*Dzundza, William Atherton, Bruce McGill, Ray*
*Sharkey, Terry Kinney, Gary Basaraba*
A cop lusting for revenge for the murder of his partner
meets up with a femme fatale, a Southern belle who's
the personal slave of the master criminal behind it all.
Slick and unappealing, with a lack of logic all of its
own.
DRA                      102 min (ort 105 min)
B,V                                     CBS

## NO MERCY MAN, THE *
Daniel J. Vance                          
Daniel J. Vance          USA          1973
*Rockne Tarkington, Stephen Sander, Heidi Vaughn,*
*Richard X. Slattery, Michael Lane*
A Vietnam veteran returns to his home town only to
find that his fighting days are not yet over as he
clashes with a local gang. Unoriginal and vicious,
low-budget nonsense.
Aka: TRAINED TO KILL
HOR                                   91 min
B,V                                     INT

## NO PLACE TO HIDE **
Robert Allen Schnitzer                   15
Robert Allen Schnitzer   USA          1973
*Sylvester Stallone, Antony Page, Rebecca Grimes*
A radical student is torn between his political loyal-
ties and his emotional commitments in this competent
but unmemorable melodrama.
Aka: REBEL (VGM or HVH)
DRA                  86 min; 89 min (HVH)
B,V          HOK L/A; AST L/A; VGM; HVH

## NO RETREAT, NO SURRENDER *
Corey Yuen                               15
Corey Yuen               USA          1985
*Kurt McKinney, Jean-Claude Van Damme, Kathie*
*Sileno, J.W. Fails, Kim Tai Chong, kent Lipham, Ron*
*Pohnel, Dale Jacoby, Pete Cunningham, Tim Baker,*
*Gloria Marziano, Joe Vance*
A student learns karate in order to beat a bully, and

ends up taking on a tough Russian boxer in this derivative nonsense that blends ROCKY with THE KARATE KID. The inevitable sequel followed.

| | |
|---|---|
| MAR | 79 min (ort 90 min) Cut (35 sec) |
| V | EIV |

## NO RETREAT, NO SURRENDER 2: RAGING THUNDER **  18

Corey Yuen            USA              1989
*Cynthia Rothrock, Loren Avedon, Max Thayer*
When a man's fiancee is kidnapped and disappears in the dense jungles of South-East Asia, he enlists the aid of two martial arts experts in his efforts to locate and rescue her.

| | |
|---|---|
| MAR | 85 min (ort 92 min) |
| B,V | EIV |

## NO RETREAT, NO SURRENDER 3: BLOOD BROTHERS *  18

Lucas Lo          HONG KONG            1989
*Loren Avedon, Keith Vitali*
Two martial artists set out to catch an international terrorist responsible for the death of their father. The usual collection of flying fists and bullets is on display.

| | |
|---|---|
| MAR | 92 min |
| V | EIV |

## NO SAFE HAVEN **  18

Ronnie Rondell         USA              1987
*Wings Hauser, Robert Tessier, Robert Ahola, Marina Rice, Branscombe Richmond*
A footballer involved with a drugs gangster antagonises the latter by failing to lose a game, and his family is almost entirely wiped out as a reprisal. However, the surviving member is an FBI agent who decides to go after said gangster and exact his own revenge, in this cliched and gory actioner.

| | |
|---|---|
| A/AD | 88 min (ort 92 min) |
| B,V | MED |

## NO SEX PLEASE, WE'RE BRITISH *  PG

Cliff Owen            UK               1973
*Ronnie Corbett, Beryl Reid, Arthur Lowe, Ian Ogilvy, Susan Penhaligon, David Swift, Cheryl Hall, Michael Bates, Valerie Leon, Margaret Nolan, Gerald Sim, Robin Askwith, John Bindon, Stephen Greif, Michael Ripper, Michael Robbins*
Film adaptation of a strained and unfunny typically British farce that enjoyed a long stage run. It deals with the complications that arise when a parcel of pornographic material is delivered in error to a bank employee. Dated isn't the word - geriatric comes closer. Written by Marriott, Johnnie Mortimer and Brian Cooke.
Boa: play by Anthony Marriott and Alistair Foot.

| | |
|---|---|
| COM | 91 min |
| V | RCA |

## NO SMALL AFFAIR **  15

Jerry Schatzberg       USA              1984
*Jon Cryer, Demi Moore, George Wendt, Peter Frechette, Elizabeth Daily, Ann Wedgeworth, Jeffrey Tambor, Jennifer Tilly, Tim Robbins, Rick Ducommun*
A 16-year-old boy falls for a rock singer seven years older and is prepared to do anything to gain her attention. In due course, his patience is rewarded. Watchable, but lacking in warmth and good characterisation.

| | |
|---|---|
| COM | 98 min (ort 102 min) |
| V/sh | RCA |

## NO SURRENDER ***  15

Peter Smith            UK               1985
*Michael Angelis, Bernard Hill, Joanne Whalley, Ray McAnally, Avis Bunnage, James Ellis, Mark Mulholland, Michael Ripper, Elvis Costello, Tom Georgeson, J.G. Devlin, Vince Earl, Ken Jones, Marjorie Sudell, Joan Turner, Ina Clough*

Comedy set in a run-down Liverpool nightclub owned by criminals, that is taken over by an ex-singer. To add to his problems, he finds that it has been inadvertently double-booked by both a Protestant and a Catholic group. A wry comment on community relations and religious bigotry.

| | |
|---|---|
| COM | 100 min (ort 104 min) |
| V | PAL |

## NO TIME FOR ROMANCE *  PG

Cory Cook             USA
*Ernice Wilson, William Walker, Joe Fluellin, Sherley Haren, De Forest Covan, Austin McCoy*
A group of aspiring stars find that there are obstacles a-plenty on the road to fame.

| | |
|---|---|
| DRA | 70 min |
| V | FIFTH; GLOB |

## NO TIME FOR SERGEANTS **  U

Mervyn Le Roy         USA              1958
*Andy Griffith, William Fawcett, Murray Hamilton, Nick Adams, Don Knotts, Jamie Farr, Myron McCormick, Bartlett Robinson*
The army adventures of a dumb Georgia farm boy conscript, who gives his sergeant a hard time by his inability to carry out the simplest tasks without making a mess of them. An agreeable if contrived slapstick affair, that was adapted from a successful stage show and still retains much of its theatrical stiffness. Gave rise to a TV series some years later. The script is by John Lee Mahin.
Boa: novel by Mac Hyman and Ira Levin.

| | |
|---|---|
| COM | 114 min B/W |
| V | WHV |

## NO TIME TO DIE *  15

Helmut Ashley
                   INDONESIA/WEST GERMANY    1985
*John Philip Law, Horst Janson, Barry Prima, Grazyana Dylong, Christopher Mitchum, Francis Glutton, Win Gatty*
A woman journalist becomes unwittingly involved in a deadly intrigue as she single-mindedly pursues a hot story on the development of a top-secret laser weapon that's part of the "Star Wars" project. A brainless thriller of foolish plotting and unbelievable dialogue.
Aka: HIJACKED TO HELL

| | |
|---|---|
| THR | 82 min |
| B,V | EHE |

## NO WAY BACK **  18

Michael Borden        USA              1988
*Campbell Scott, Bernie White, Virginia Lantry, Len Lesser*
A hunting trip for a pair of friends becomes a nightmare when they run into a bunch of degenerate mountain folk, in this DELIVERANCE-style survival saga.

| | |
|---|---|
| A/AD | 88 min |
| B,V | CHV |

## NO WAY OUT ***  15

Roger Donaldson       USA              1987
*Kevin Costner, Gene Hackman, Sean Young, Will Patton, Howard Duff, Iman, George Dzundza, Jason Bernard, Fred Dalton Thompson, Leon Russom, Dennis Burkley, Marshall Bell, Chris D., Michael Shillo, Nicholas Worth, Leo Geter*
A heavily disguised remake of "The Big Clock", which substitutes the setting of a crime magazine for a tale of high-level conspiracy and corruption in the Pentagon, where a naval officer investigates a murder committed by his boss. A competent thriller let down by a foolish ending. Scripted by Robert Garland and with music by Maurice Jarre.
Boa: novel The Big Clock by Kenneth Fearing.

| | |
|---|---|
| THR | 110 min (ort 114 min) |
| V/sh | RCA |

## NOAH'S ARK PRINCIPLE, THE ** 15
Roland Emmerich
WEST GERMANY 1984
*Richy Fuller, Matthias Fuchs, Franz Buchrieser, Avival Joel*
SF film set in the year 1997 onboard a European-American space-station that is being used to study and influence Earth's weather patterns. With the arrival of some unexpected orders, a decision has to be taken that could have catastrophic consequences for the planet.
Aka: DAS ARCHE NOAH PRINZIP
FAN 95 min
V TGP

## NOBODY RUNS FOREVER ** PG
Ralph Thomas UK 1968
*Christopher Plummer, Rod Taylor, Lilli Palmer, Camilla Sparv, Daliah Lavi, Clive Revill, Franchot Tone, Leo McKern, Lee Montague, Calvin Lockhart, Derren Nesbitt, Edric Connor, Russell Napier, Charles Tingwell*
An Australian detective is sent to arrest the country's high commissioner in London for murdering his first wife at just the time when the latter is involved in delicate East-West negotiations. Intermittently absorbing but hampered by poor dialogue and plotting. Written by Wilfred Greatorex.
Aka: HIGH COMMISSIONER, THE
Boa: novel The High Commissioner by Jon Cleary.
DRA 97 min (ort 101 min)
B,V RNK; RCA

## NOBODY'S BOY **
Yugo Serikawa/Jim Flocker JAPAN 1970
*Jim Backus (narration)*
Full-length animation telling of an orphan boy sold to a circus and of his faithful dog.
Aka: CHIBIKO REMI TO MEIKEN KAPI
Boa: story by Hector Henri Malot.
CAR 82 min
B, V MOV

## NOBODY'S FOOL ** 15
Evelyn Purcell USA 1986
*Rosanna Arquette, Eric Roberts, Mare Winninham, Louise Fletcher, Jim Youngs, Gwen Welles, Stephen Tobolowsky, Charlie Barnett, Lewis Arquette, Ann Hearn, Belita Moreno*
A downtrodden waitress, shunned by the locals because she is an unwed mother, finds acting and love when a visiting troupe comes to town. A modern Cinderella tale that is neither very credible nor entertaining, despite a nice performance from Arquette. Written by Beth Henley.
COM 103 min (ort 107 min)
B,V SONY

## NOBODY'S PERFEKT * U
Peter Bonerz USA 1981
*Gabe Kaplan, Alex Karras, Robert Klein, Susan Clark, Paul Stewart, Alex Rocco, Peter Bonerz*
Three misfits decide to take on City Hall when their car is wrecked by a pothole in the road, and because of a legal technicality they are unable to sue. A bone-headed comedy whose script should have been buried in a pothole. The directing debut for Bonerz. Written by Tony Kenrick.
COM 95 min
B,V RCA

## NOBODY'S THE GREATEST ** PG
Damiano Damiani ITALY 1977
*Terence Hill (Mario Girotti), Patrick McGoohan, Klaus Kinski*
A routine spaghetti Western sequel to "My Name Is Nobody", with the usual contrived and slightly tongue-in-cheek plot of betrayal and revenge.
Aka: GENIO, DUE COMPARI, UN POLLO;

GENIUS, THE; UN GENIE, DEUX ASSCIES, UNE CLOCHE
WES 120 min
B,V MED

## NOMAD RIDERS * 18
Frank Roach USA 1981
*Wayne Chema, Rick Cluck, Ron Gregg*
A man seeks revenge on the gang of bikers who killed his family in this dreary and exploitative effort.
A/AD 80 min (ort 82 min) Cut (1 min 36 sec)
B,V,V2 MED

## NOMADS ** 18
John McTiernan USA 1985
*Pierce Brosnan, Lesley-Anne Down, Adam Ant, Anna Maria Monticelli, Hector Mercado, Mary Woronov, Josie Cotton, Frank Doubleday, Frances Bay, Tim Walker, Alan Autry, Jeannie Elias, Nina Foch, J.J. Saunders, Paul Anselmo*
A doctor gives emergency treatment to an apparently insane derelict and later learns that he is a French anthropologist, who has come to L.A. to study a strange gang of street people, who seem to be more than human. A supernatural thriller that fails to develop its initial premise to any degree.
HOR 89 min (ort 100 min)
B,V CBS

## NONNI: PARTS 1, 2 AND 3 *** PG
Agust Gudmundsson 1988
*Lisa Harrow, Luc Merenda, Stuart Wilson*
An unusual tale set in Iceland, and telling of the career of two brothers who find themselves in danger when they attempt to clear an innocent friend of a a charge of murder.
Boa: novel by Jon Svensson.
A/AD 600 min (3 cassettes) mTV
V ODY

## NORMA RAE *** PG
Martin Ritt USA 1979
*Sally Field, Ron Leibman, Beau Bridges, Pat Hingle, Barbara Baxley, Gail Strickland, Lonny Chapman*
The story of how a female textile worker became militant and helped the union gain a foothold in the factory where she worked. Very well made and enjoyable, but the triumph of unionisation is made to appear far too easy and the victory too complete. AA: Actress (Field), Song ("It Goes Like It Goes" – David Shire – music/Norman Gimbel – lyrics).
DRA 110 min (ort 114 min)
B,V CBS

## NORMAN IS THAT YOU? * 15
George Schlatter USA 1976
*Redd Foxx, Pearl Bailey, Dennis Dugan, Michael Warren, Tamara Dobson, Vernee Watson*
An angry father decides the time has come to straighten out his homosexual son. A one-joke film and a not very funny one at that. Shot on videotape and transferred to film.
Boa: play by by Ron Clark and Sam Bobrick.
COM 87 min (ort 91 min)
B,V MGM

## NORMAN LOVES ROSE **
Henri Safran AUSTRALIA 1982
*Carol Kane, Tony Owen, David Downer, Warren Mitchell, Myra De Groot*
A mildly amusing case of confused paternity, as a teenager falls in love with his sister-in-law who then becomes pregnant.
COM 98 min
B,V MMA; EIV

## NORSEMAN, THE ** PG
Charles B. Pierce USA 1978
*Lee Majors, Mel Ferrer, Cornel Wilde, Jack Elam,*

*Chris Connelly, Kathleen Freeman, Charles B. Pierce Jr, Susan Coelho (Bono), Denny Miller*
Majors has his first starring role as a Viking prince of the 11th century, who voyages to North America to find his father who has been abducted by Indians. A limp adventure film that is much less exciting than the period in which it is set.
A/AD                              86 min (ort 90 min)
B,V                                               RNK

### NORTH BY NORTHWEST ****                        PG
Alfred Hitchcock        USA               1959
*Cary Grant, Eva Marie Saint, James Mason, Leo G. Carroll, Martin Landau, Jessie Royce Landis, Philip Ober, Adam Williams, Josephine Hutchinson, Edward Platt, Robert Ellenstein, Les Tremayne, Philip Coolidge, Ken Lynch*
An innocent man becomes inextricably entangled in a complex espionage plot, in an exciting thriller full of non-stop action that drives the story forwards at a furious pace, culminating in a memorable and justly famous fight sequence atop the Mount Rushmore Memorial. Scripted by Ernest Lehman and with a fine score by Bernard Herrmann.
THR                             131 min (ort 136 min)
V                                                MGM

### NORTH DALLAS FORTY ***                          18
Ted Kotcheff           USA                1979
*Bo Svenson, Nick Nolte, Steve Forrest, Mac Davis, Charles Durning, Dayle Haddon, Dabney Coleman, John Matuszak, G.D. Spradlin, Savannah Smith, Marshall Colt, Guich Koock, Deborah Benson, James F. Boeke, John Bottoms*
A close look at the tough world of professional American football, with all its cynicism, manipulation and brutality, both on and off the field. One of the best films of its kind, with an articulate and perceptive script by Kotcheff, Gent and Frank Yablans (who produced it).
Boa: novel by Peter Gent.
DRA                             113 min (ort 119 min)
B,V                                               CIC

### NORTH SEA HIJACK **                             15
Andrew V. McLaglen     UK                 1979
*Roger Moore, James Mason, Anthony Perkins, Michael Parks, David Hedison, Jack Watson, George Baker, Jeremy Clyde, David Wood, Faith Brook, Anthony Pullen Shaw, Lea Brodie, Philip O'Brien, John Westbrook, Jennifer Hillary*
An eccentric counter-insurgency expert is called in by the British government when a North Sea oil rig and the 700 men aboard it are captured and held to ransom by terrorists. A rather anaemic adventure tale with a script by Jack Davies.
Aka: ASSAULT FORCE; FFOLKES; FFOULKES
Boa: novel Esther, Ruth And Jennifer by Jack Davies.
A/AD                             95 min (ort 100 min)
V                                                 CIC

### NORTH SHORE *                                   PG
William Phelps         USA                1987
*Matt Adler, Nia Peeples, John Philbin, Gerry Lopez, Gregory Harrison, Laird Hamilton, Robert Page, Mark Occhilupo, John Parragon, Cristina Raines, Lord James Blears*
A surfing champion from Arizona goes to Hawaii to realise his dream of riding the waves of its perilous north shore. Filmed on location and of truly limited appeal.
A/AD                              92 min (ort 96 min)
V/sh                                              CIC

### NORTH TO ALASKA ***                             U
Henry Hathaway         USA                1960
*John Wayne, Stewart Granger, Ernie Kovacs, Fabian,*

*Capucine, Mickey Shaughnessy, Karl Swenson, Joe Sawyer, John Qualen*
Two gold prospectors strike it rich and one sends his partner south to bring back his fiancee. When the partner finds that the girl has since married, he sets out to find a substitute. Set in the 1900s, this vigorous and lighthearted adventure yarn has a lot going for it, excessive length is its only flaw.
Boa: play Birthday Gift by Ladislas Fodor.
WES                             117 min (ort 122 min)
V                                                 CBS

### NORTHANGER ABBEY **                             PG
Giles Foster           UK                 1987
*Peter Firth, Googie Withers, Robert Hardy*
Careful adaptation of Austen's novel of mystery and suspense, with a woman arriving at the Abbey and discovering much intrigue hidden beneath the bland exterior.
Boa: novel by Jane Austen.
DRA                                        90 min mTV
V/h                                               BBC

### NORTH-EAST OF SEOUL *
David Lowell Rich       USA               1972
*Anita Ekberg, John Ireland, Victor Buono, Irvan Stansby*
Various individuals become involved in the theft of an ancient jewelled sword in this rather tired adventure tale.
THR                              91 min (ort 98 min)
B,V,V2                                            DFS

### NORTHVILLE CEMETERY MASSACRE, THE *
William Dear/Thomas L. Dyke
                        USA               1979
*David Hyry, J. Craig Collicott, Jan Silk, Herb Sharples*
A motorcycle gang clash with the local residents and police, with predictably violent results.
DRA                                           86 min
B,V,V2                                        INT; APX

### NORTHWEST FRONTIER ***
J. Lee Thompson        UK                 1959
*Kenneth More, Lauren Bacall, Herbert Lom, Ursula Jeans, Wilfrid Hyde-White, I.S. Johar, Eugene Deckers, Ian Hunter, Govind Raja Ross, Jack Gwillim, Basil Hoskins, Moultrie Kelsall, Lionel Murton, S.M. Asgarelli, Homi Bode*
A British officer has to get a young Indian prince to safety during a tribal rebellion and embarks, on hazardous train journey. Set in 1905, this enjoyable "Boy's Own"-style film offers just the right blend of action and suspense. The script is by Robin Estridge.
Aka: FLAME OVER INDIA
A/AD                             87 min (ort 129 min)
B,V                                               RNK

### NORTHWEST STAMPEDE **
Albert S. Rogell       USA                1948
*Jack Oakie, Joan Leslie, James Craig, Chill Wills, Victor Kilian, Stanley Andrews, Lane Chandler, Ray Bennett, Harry Shannon, Kermit Maynard*
Routine tale of the clash between a lady ranch foreman and a cowboy who wants to corral a wild stallion. A good cast make the most of their mundane lines.
WES                                        76 min B/W
B,V,V2                                            INT

### NOSFERATU ****
F.W. Murnau            GERMANY            1921
*Max Schreck, Gustav Von Wangenheim, Greta Schroeder, Alexander Granach, G.H. Schnell, Ruth Landshoff, John Gottow, Max Nemetz*
The original classic film on the Dracula theme. Written by Henrik Galeen and remade in 1979 as

NOSFERATU THE VAMPYRE. Interestingly, it was later films that moved the vampire teeth to the sides of the mouth, a true vampire bat has them in the centre. An atmospheric and eerie film that has a number of imaginative touches absent in later works.
Aka: DRACULA; EINE SYMPHONIE DES GRAUENS; NOSFERATU, A SYMPHONY OF TERROR; NOSFERATUR, EINE SYMPHONIE DES GRAUENS; NOSFERATU, THE VAMPIRE
HOR                        63 min (ort 72 min) B/W silent
B,V                                                TEVP

## NOSFERATU THE VAMPYRE ***                      15
Werner Herzog   WEST GERMANY                      1979
*Klaus Kinski, Isabelle Adjani, Bruno Ganz, Roland Topor, Walter Ladengast, Jacques Dufilho, Dan Van Husen, Jan Groth, Carsten Bodinus, Martje Grohmann, Ryk De Gooyer, Tim Beekman, Clemens Scheitz, Lo Van Hartingsveld*
This virtually scene-for-scene remake of the silent 1921 classic is beautifully crafted but unfolds at such a slow pace that the film seems more like a succession of static scenes that a living story. Written and directed by Herzog.
Aka: NOSFERATU: PHANTOM DER NACHT
Boa: novel Dracula by Bram Stoker.
HOR                               96 min (ort 107 min)
V/h                                                 CBS

## NOT FOR PUBLICATION **                         15
Paul Bartel          UK/USA                       1984
*David Naughton, Nancy Allen, Laurence Luckinbill, Alice Ghostley, Richard Paul, Barry Dennen, Paul Bartel, Cork Hubbert*
A woman reporter discovers a nasty secret about a politician campaigning for office on an anti-vice ticket and decides to investigate by joining his campaign workers. A failed attempt to recreate some of the verve of an old-fashioned madcap comedy, that's hampered by the unappealing nature of the subject matter.
COM                                83 min (ort 88 min)
B,V                                                TEVP

## NOT JUST ANOTHER AFFAIR **                      PG
Steven Hilliard Stern   USA                       1982
*Victoria Principal, Gil Gerard, Robert Webber, Barbara Barrie, Richard Kline, Markie Post, Judy Stranglis, Ed Begley Jr, Steve Franken, Jill Jacobson, Carmen Zapata, William Dozier, Luis Avalos, Sharon Stone*
A womanising lawyer falls for a marine biologist who won't go to bed with him unless they're married. A pleasant little romantic comedy.
Aka: SMUG FIT (KSV or GLOB)
COM                         116 min (IFS); 91 min mTV
V                             IFS L/A; KSV; GLOB; VCC

## NOT MY KID ***                                  15
Michael Tuchner        USA                        1984
*George Segal, Stockard Channing, Andrew Robinson, Gary Bayer, Nancy Cartwright, Christa Denton, Tate Donovan, Laura Harrington, John Philbin, Kathleen Wilhoite, Kathleen York, Viveka Davis, Dionne Parens, Jack Axelrod*
A couple have to come to terms with the fact that one of their daughters is a drug addict, in an above-average drama that takes a mature and sensible look at a major social problem. Scripted by Christopher Knopf.
Boa: book by Beth Polson and Dr Miller Newton.
DRA                             91 min (ort 97 min) mTV
B,V                                           PRV; CH5

## NOT NOW DARLING *
Ray Cooney/David Croft UK                         1972
*Leslie Phillips, Joan Sims, Julie Ege, Moira Lister, Ray Cooney, Barbara Windsor, Derren Nesbitt, Jack*

*Hulbert, Cicely Courtneidge, Bill Fraser, Jackie Pallo, Trudi Van Doorn*
A furrier complicates his life when he tries to save money on a fur coat for his girlfriend. A dull version of a none-too-brilliant stage farce, shot in Multivista for good measure (an early forerunner to videotape that was not known for its clarity).
Boa: play by Ray Cooney.
COM                               93 min (ort 97 min)
B,V                                                 GHV

## NOT OF THIS EARTH *                             18
Jim Wynorski          USA                         1988
*Traci Lords, Arthur Roberts, Lenny Juliano, Ace Mask, Rebecca Pearle, Roger Lodge, Michael Delano, Cynthia Thompson, Becky LeBeau*
Remake of the Corman film from 1957 about an alien who lands to Earth and sets about collecting blood which is badly needed by the inhabitants of his home planet. Not a jot better or more inventive than the original.
FAN                       77 min (ort 82 min) Cut (23 sec)
V                                                   MGM

## NOT QUITE HUMAN *                               U
Steve Hilliard Stern    USA                       1987
*Alan Thicke, Robyn Lively, Robert Harper, Joseph Bologna, Jay Underwood*
A human android is given great intelligence and strength by its creator as well as the power of total recall, and is programmed to tell the truth under all circumstances, which leads to some awkward situations for all concerned. A juvenile comedy reminiscent of many a lame Disney effort.
JUV                             87 min (ort 97 min) mCab
B,V                                                 WDV

## NOT QUITE HUMAN 2 **                            U
Eric Luke              USA                         1989
*Robyn Lively, Jay Underwood, Alan Thicke, Greg Mullavey, Katie Barberi, Mark Arnott*
The further adventures of our lovable male android as he attends college, provides the story for this predictable sequel to the 1987 film. Agreeable as family entertainment but no more than that.
COM                            92 min (ort 105 min) mCab
V                                                   WDV

## NOT QUITE JERUSALEM **                          15
Lewis Gilbert         UK                          1985
*Joanna Pacula, Sam Robards, Todd Graff, Ewan Stewart, Libby Morris, Selina Cadell, Kevin McNally, Bernard Strother, Sawally Srinonton, Kate Ingram, Gary Cady, Zafir Kochanovsky, Poli Reshef, Yaacov Ben Sira, Shlomo Tarshish*
Story of a group of volunteers on a kibbutz in Israel and their various reasons for being there. Not quite a hit that had to be given an alternative title in some countries to avoid hurting Arab/Moslem sensibilities. The rather unappealing and one-dimensional script is by Kember.
Aka: NOT QUITE PARADISE
Boa: play by Paul Kember.
COM                               110 min (ort 114 min)
B,V                                                 RNK

## NOTHING BUT THE NIGHT *
Peter Sasdy           UK                          1972
*Christopher Lee, Peter Cushing, Diana Dors, Georgia Brown, Keith Barron, Fulton Mackay, Gwyneth Strong, John Robinson, Morris Perry, Michael Gambon, Shelagh Fraser, Duncan Lamont, Kathleen Byron, Geoffrey Frederick*
Murder mystery set in an orphanage where the children seem to be possessed by demonic forces after being injected with the life essences of dead trustees. A hopelessly confused attempt to adapt the original novel to the screen results in yet another British horror dud.

Aka: DEVIL'S UNDEAD, THE; RESURRECTION
SYNDICATE, THE
Boa: novel Children Of The Night by John Blackburn.
HOR                                88 min (ort 90 min)
B,V                                              RNK

## NOTHING IN COMMON **                    15
Gary Marshall           USA              1986
*Tom Hanks, Jackie Gleason, Eva Marie Saint, Hector
Elizondo, Barry Corbin, Bess Armstrong, Sela Ward,
John Kapelos*
An immature advertising executive is forced to take
care of his diabetic father after his aged parents
divorce after 36 years together. An overlong and
patchy comedy-drama, with touching moments set
like little gems in the dross of a muddled script. Later
a TV series.
COM                          114 min (ort 118 min)
B,V                                              RCA

## NOTHING PERSONAL *                      15
George Bloomfield CANADA/USA             1980
*Donald Sutherland, Suzanne Somers, Lawrence Dane,
Roscoe Lee Browne, Dabney Coleman, John Dehner,
Saul Rubinek, Catherine O'Hara, Kate Lynch, Eugene
Levy, Joe Flaherty, Joe Rosato, Craig Russell*
An unlikely couple, a female lawyer and a professor,
join forces to oppose seal hunting, a serious topic that
serves as a poor basis for this unfunny romantic
comedy. Written by Robert Kaufmann.
COM                                          97 min
B,V                                              RNK

## NOTHING TO HIDE ***                     18
Anthony Spinelli         USA             1981
*John Leslie, Richard Pacheco, Elizabeth Randolph,
Chelsea Manchester, Erica Boyer, Misty Hagen, Holly
McCall, Raven Turner*
A guy who is hopeless with women can only look on in
wonder at his friend Jack's easy conquests. Lenny is
not unlike his retarded namesake from Steinbeck's
story. He tags along with his buddy and Jack tries to
fix him up with a woman. When he eventually meets
his soul-mate and tells Jack he wants to get married,
the latter, who regards him as his "son", becomes quite
jealous. A well-scripted and often quite touching sex
film.
A          60 min; 81 min (SHEP) (ort 101 min) Cut
                                    (1 min 4 sec)
B,V                            TCX; PHV; SHEP

## NOTHING UNDERNEATH ***                  18
Carlo Vanzina           ITALY            1985
*Donald Pleasence, Tom Schanley, Renee Simonson,
Nicola Perring, Paola Tomei*
A thriller with a telepathy theme in which a number
of models are murdered and a young man experiences
the death of his model sister, a twin with whom he
shared a unique closeness. The police are unable to
catch the killer and he resolves to seek him out
himself. A film that's slow to start but generates
considerable tension and has a neat twist.
Aka: SOTTO IL VESTITO NIENTE
Boa: novel by Mario Parma
THR                                          90 min
B,V                                              AVA

## NOTORIOUS ****                           U
Alfred Hitchcock        USA              1946
*Cary Grant, Ingrid Bergman, Claude Rains, Louis
Calhern, Leopoldine Konstantin, Rienhold Schunzel,
Moroni Olsen, Ivan Triesault, Alex Minotis, Wally
Brown, Gavin Gordon, Charles Mendl, Ricardo Costa,
Fay Baker*
A classic period thriller about the daughter of a
convicted Nazi spy who is persuaded to marry a
suspected Nazi sympathiser to help US intelligence
discover his plans. She agrees, but falls in love with
the agent sent to contact her, which proves a danger-
ous complication in this highly exciting and enjoyable
film. The superb script is by Ben Hecht.
Osca: SPELLBOUND (VCC)
THR        97 min (GHV or VCC) (ort 101 min); 203 min
                            (VCC: 2 film cassette) B/W
B,V                            GHV; VCC (VHS only)

## NOTORIOUS CLEOPATRA, THE **             18
A.P. Stootsberry        USA              1970
*Sonora, John Rocco, Jay Edwards*
Sex film on the life and loves of the Queen of Egypt.
A                                            84 min
B,V                          ECF; TCX; 18PLAT/TOW

## NOW AND FOREVER **                      PG
Adrian Carr             AUSTRALIA        1983
*Cheryl Ladd, Robert Coleby, Christine Amor, Carmen
Duncan, Aileen Brittan*
A woman's unfaithful husband is unjustly accused of
rape and thrown into prison, thus putting a consider-
able strain on their marriage. A serious theme is
given a glossy and insubstantial treatment, as befits a
work based on one of Harlequin's many romantic
novels.
Boa: novel by Danielle Steel.
DRA                          93 min; 88 min (VGM)
B,V                          VSP L/A; VGM (VHS only)

## NOW YOU SEE HIM, NOW YOU DON'T **        U
Robert Butler           USA              1972
*Kurt Russell, Joe Flynn, Jim Backus, Cesar Romero,
William Windom, Michael McGreevy, Joyce Menges,
Richard Bakalyan, Alan Hewitt, Kelly Thordsen, Neil
Russell, George O'Hanlon, John Myhers, Pat Delany,
Robert Rothwell*
Sequel to THE COMPUTER WORE TENNIS SHOES
with a nearly bankrupt college saved when one of its
students invents an invisibility spray. This wonderful
scientific advance soon attracts a gang of crooks who
want to use it to rob the local bank. The special effects
compensate for the banality of the script.
COM                                          88 min
B,V                                              WDV

## NOW, VOYAGER ***                        PG
Irving Rapper           USA              1942
*Bette Davis, Claude Rains, Paul Henreid, Gladys
Cooper, Bonita Granville, Janis Wilson, Ilka Chase,
John Loder, Lee Patrick, Charles Drake, Franklin
Pangborn*
A lonely, frustrated spinster is transformed by her
psychiatrist and becomes involved in an ill-fated love
affair. Classy, romantic melodrama that wins through
on the strength of the performances of its stars and the
beauty of its music. Scripted by Casey Robinson. AA:
Score (Max Steiner).
Boa: novel by Olive Higgins Prouty.
DRA                          113 min (ort 117 min) B/W
V                                                WHV

## NOWHERE TO HIDE **                      1977
Jack Starrett          USA               1977
*Lee Van Cleef, Tony Musante, Charles Robinson, Lelia
Goldoni, Edward Anhalt, Noel Fournier, Russell
Johnson*
A former hit-man turns state's evidence and has to be
kept alive in order to testify, although his former
Mafia boss has sworn to kill him before he can come to
court. Average thrills only in a below-par suspenser.
The script is by Edward Anhalt.
DRA                          74 min (ort 78 min) mTV
B,V                          VFP L/A; HER

## NOWHERE TO HIDE **                      15
Mario Azzopardi         CANADA           1987
*Amy Madigan, Michael Ironside, John Colicos, Chuck
Shamata, Daniel Hugh Kelly, Robin MacEachern*

A woman finds herself caught up in a violent life-and-death struggle, when her husband is murdered after investigating a series of baffling crashes of Marine Corps helicopters. A violent, production-line, conspiracy yarn.

THR 90 min
V/sh GHV

## NOWHERE TO RUN *
USA 1989
*David Carradine*
The corrupt sheriff of a small Texas town is up for re-election and faces tough opposition. His opponents are out to make political capital out of his freeing of a man serving a long prison sentence, and a violent confrontation develops. At the same time a number of high school students about to graduate find themselves in a position of influence regarding the election outcome. Allegedly based on a true story, but an utterly mundane affair.

A/AD 87 min
V MGM

## NOWHERE TO RUN **
Carl Franklin USA 1989
*David Carradine, Jason Priestley, Kieran Mulroney, Jillian McWhirter*
Based on a true story, this thriller examines the events surrounding a series of nasty murders that took place in a small Texas town in 1960.

THR 87 min
V MGM

## NUCLEAR CONSPIRACY, THE *
Rainer Erler
AUSTRALIA/UK/WEST GERMANY 1986
*Birgit Doll, Albert Fortrell, Mark Lee, Kitty Myers, Lucia Bensasson, Frank Wilson*
A journalist investigating a shipment of nuclear waste disappears, and the usual paranoid conspiracy unfolds in this poorly made film.
Aka: NEUESBERICHT UBER EINE REISE IN EINE STRAHLENDE ZUKUNFT

THR 114 min dubbed
B,V TURBO; VCC

## NUCLEAR COUNTDOWN **
Robert Aldrich
USA/WEST GERMANY 1977
*Burt Lancaster, Richard Widmark, Joseph Cotten, Charles Durning, Melvyn Douglas, Paul Winfield, Roscoe Lee Brown, Burt Young, Vera Miles, Richard Jaeckel, William Marshall, Charles Aidman, Charles McGraw, Leif Erickson*
An ex-general captures a missile base, and blackmails the White House into revealing some political truths about its policies during the Vietnam War. A mildly gripping little yarn, but seriously diluted by excessive length. The music is by Jerry Goldsmith.
Aka: TWILIGHT'S LAST GLEAMING; VIPER THREE (KRP)
Boa: novel Viper Three by Walter Wager.

THR 116 min (ort 146 min)
B,V VCL/CBS; KRP/XTACY; KRP

## NUDE BOMB, THE *
Clive Donner USA 1980
*Don Adams, Pamela Hensley, Sylvia Kristel, Vittorio Gassman, Rhonda Fleming, Dana Elcar, Andrea Howard, Norman LLoyd*
The secret agent 86 from the "Get Smart" spoof spy TV series of the 1960s is brought out of retirement to stop a maniac who has a bomb that can destroy all the clothing in the world. An unsatisfying time-filler that fails to breathe new life into an old idea. Followed by GET SMART, AGAIN!
Aka: RETURN OF MAXWELL SMART, THE

COM 89 min (ort 94 min)
B,V CIC

## NUDITY REQUIRED *
John Bowen USA 1989
*Troy Donahue, Julie Newmar, Brad Zutaut*
Two teenagers are given the job of looking after a Beverly Hills mansion and decide to pose as Hollywood film producers, getting aspiring actresses to pose in the nude for them at the mansion. Various complications ensue with the arrival of a real film producer, several gangsters and other assorted characters. A low-grade, slapstick romp.

COM 90 min
B,V CFD

## NUMBER ONE **
Les Blair UK 1984
*Bob Geldof, Mel Smith, Alison Steadman, P.H. Moriarty, Phil Daniels, Alfred Molina, James Marcus, David Howey, Ian Dury, David Squire, Ron Cook, Alun Armstrong, Tony Scott, Kate Hardie, Ray Winstone, Albie Woodington*
The story of a world snooker champion and his rise to fame, including his sleazy compromises and corrupt deals. A sordid and disagreeable melodrama.

DRA 98 min (ort 106 min)
B,V HER; CH5

## NUMBER ONE OF THE SECRET SERVICE *
Lindsay Shonteff UK 1978
*Nicky Henson, Richard Todd, Aimi MacDonald, Geoffrey Keen, Dudley Sutton, Sue Lloyd, Jon Pertwee, Milton Reid, Baker Twins, Fiona Curzon, Jenny Till, Katya Wyeth, Roberta Gibbs, Oliver MacGreevy*
An unfunny parody on those James Bond films, with a secret agent battling a villainous millionaire who is having prominent financiers murdered. A film that treads the same ground as LICENSED TO KILL (1965), an earlier film by Shonteff. Followed by LICENSED TO LOVE AND KILL in 1979.
Aka: MAN FROM S.E.X., THE; NO. 1 OF THE SECRET SERVICE; ORCHID FOR NO. 1, AN; UNDERCOVER LOVER

COM 89 min (ort 93 min)
B,V INT L/A; MPV

## NUMBER ONE WITH A BULLET **
Jack Smight USA 1986
*Billy Dee Williams, Robert Carradine, Peter Graves, Doris Roberts, Valerie Bertinelli*
Two San Francisco narcotics cops refuse to accept demotion to desk jobs and decide to continue their investigation into a major drugs syndicate. A standard "odd couple" detective yarn. Average.

A/AD 97 min (ort 103 min)
B,V RNK

## NUMBER SEVENTEEN ***
Alfred Hitchcock UK 1932
*Leon M. Lion, Anne Grey, John Stuart, Donald Calthrop, Barry Jones, Garry Marsh, Donald Calthrop, Ann Casson, Henry Caine, Herbert Langley*
A reformed female jewel thief helps the police catch the gang she once belonged to. A remake of a 1928 British silent, that is technically competent and moderately exciting, despite some obviously crude effects. Written by Hitchcock, Alma Reville and Rodney Ackland.
Boa: play by J. Jefferson Farjeon.
Osca: MURDER DRA 64 min; 61 min (SCRN) B/W
B,V TEV ; SCRN

## NUNS ON THE RUN ***
Jonathan Lynn UK 1990
*Eric Idle, Robbie Coltrane, Camille Coduri, Janet Suzman, Doris Hare, Lila Kaye, Robert Patterson*
Written by Lynn, this wacky comedy tells of two career crooks who, tired of working for their nasty boss, decide to pull off a job and keep the loot for themselves. But the robbery is bungled and they have

to flee, and hide out in a convent disguised as nuns. A bit patchy and slow at times, but Idle and Coltrane are great together and the film is generally very funny.
COM                    88 min (ort 90 min) subH
V                                          CBS

## NURSE ON WHEELS **                      U
Gerald Thomas          UK              1963
Juliet Mills, Ronald Lewis, Noel Purcell, Joan Sims, Raymond Huntley, Athene Seyler, Jim Dale
The new district nurse arrives at a rural community where she falls for a local farmer and enjoys various other encounters. A likeable if soppy comedy that attempts to give district nurses the "Carry On" treatment.
Boa: novel Nurse Is A Neighbour by Joanna Jones.
COM              82 min (ort 86 min) B/W
V                                          WHV

## NURSES OF THE 407TH *                   R18
Tony Kendrick          USA             1982
Jesie St James, Paul Thomas, John Martin, Joey Silvera
A dreary sex spoof inspired by M*A*S*H.
A                           68 min (ort 90 min)
V                                          VPD

## NUTCASE **                              U
Roger Donaldson  NEW ZEALAND          1979
Melissa Donaldson, Peter Shand, Aaron Donaldson, Nevan Rowe, Ian Watkin, Ian Mune, Michael Wilson
Kids stop criminals from pulling off a crime which involves holding Auckland to ransom.
COM                                  50 min
B,V                                      POLY

## NUTCRACKER *                            18
Anwar Kawadri          UK              1982
Joan Collins, Carol White, Paul Nicholas, Finola Hughes, William Franklyn, Murray Melvin, Vernon Dobtcheff, Geraldine Gardner, Cherry Gillespie, Jane Wellman, John Vye, Gess Whitfield, Fran Fullenwider, Trevor Baxter, Jo Warne
A defecting Russian ballerina discovers that she has been manipulated as a mere pawn in the Cold War. A drama that never rises above the level of a banal soap opera.
Aka: NUTCRACKER SUITE
DRA                                 101 min
B,V                                      RNK

## NUTCRACKER FANTASY **                   U
Takeo Nakamura    JAPAN/USA           1979
Voices of: Melissa Gilbert, Roddy McDowall
A lively animated puppet film based on a classic story about a prince who rescues a princess from evil mice.
Aka: NUTCRACKER; NUTCRACKER FANTASIES
Boa: story The Nutcracker And The Mouseking by E.T.A. Hoffman.
JUV                                  81 min
B,V                         VSP L/A; SAT; MYTV

## NUTCRACKER: THE MOTION PICTURE **       U
Carroll Ballard        USA             1986
Hugh Bigney, Vanessa Sharp, Kent Stowell, Francia Russell, Wade Walthall, Russell Burnett, Julie Harris (voice only)
A performance of the Tchaikovsky suite, by the Pacific Northwest Ballet, in the form of a feature-length dance film with production and sets by Maurice Sendak, the famous illustrator and author of children's books. The music and sets cannot be faulted, but clumsy camerawork and cutting are a serious irritation.
Aka: NUTCRACKER, THE
Boa: ballet by Peter Illych Tchaikovsky.
MUS                      81 min (ort 85 min)
V                                          EIV

## NUTS ***                                18
Martin Ritt            USA             1987
Barbra Streisand, Richard Dreyfuss, Karl Malden, Maureen Stapleton, Eli Wallach, Robert Webber, James Whitmore, Karl Malden, Leslie Nielsen, William Prince, Dakin Matthews, Haley Taylor Block, Peter Eilbling, Shera Danese
A prostitute who killed one of her clients, goes to court to prove herself sane and fit to stand trial, rather than be certified insane and placed in an institution, which would suit her family, who are anxious to hide their guilty shame. An absorbing piece that is almost believable until the end, when a dreary monologue from Streisand spoils it all. Scripted by Topor, Darryl Ponicsan and Alvin Sargent.
Boa: play by Tom Topor.
DRA                     111 min (ort 116 min)
V/sh                                       WHV

## NUTS IN MAY ***                         PG
Mike Leigh             UK              1976
Roger Sloman, Alison Steadman, Anthony O'Donnell
An amusing TV play about an ill-matched pair on a camping holiday, that consists of a series of mishaps brought about by the man's obsessive need to do everything "by the book". A sharp character study, one of several tales, all of which were written by Leigh.
COM                              81 min mTV
V                                          BBC

## NUTTY PROFESSOR, THE **                 PG
Jerry Lewis            USA             1963
Jerry Lewis, Stella Stevens, Del Moore, Kathleen Freeman, Med Flory, Howard Morris, Elvia Allman, Henry Gibson
A college professor undergoes a Jekyll and Hyde transformation, in this very unfunny Lewis comedy, which like so many of his other efforts demonstrates clearly the limits of his talent. One of Lewis' best vehicles – but that's not saying much. Scripted by Lewis and Bill Richmond.
COM                     103 min (ort 107 min)
B,V                                        CIC

## NYMPHO GIRLS **                         18
Walter Boos-Buch  WEST GERMANY        1980
Tanya Scholl, Giggi Ludwig, Uta Koepke, Frank Lang, Paul Edwin Roth, Nick Werup
Three young girls, including one who's pretending to be having an affair with her tutor, go off for a weekend of sexual adventure in Hamburg. They meet three boys from their school but give them the elbow, and wind up at a club where they are mistaken for hookers. Meanwhile the boys are having a hard time losing their virginity, in a confused tale that for good measure adds a sex-mad US senator, a classy hooker and assorted heavies.
Aka: DREI SCHWEDINNEN AUF DER REEPERBAHN; THREE SWEDISH GIRLS IN HAMBURG (VPD); THREE SWEDISH GIRLS ON THE REEPERBAHN
A                                    82 min
B,V                       ILV L/A; PRI; BLUES; VPD

# O

## O LUCKY MAN! **                         15
Lindsay Anderson       UK              1973
Malcolm McDowell, Arthur Lowe, Ralph Richardson, Rachel Roberts, Alan Price, Lindsay Anderson, Helen Mirren, Mona Washbourne, Dandy Nichols, Graham Crowden, Peter Jeffrey, Philip Stone, Mary MacLeod, Wallas Eaton
An Anderson feast of disjointed and strange images, as a trainee salesman journeys erratically through life on his way to the top before settling down to do good

deeds. Several actors have multiple roles and Anderson makes a brief appearance as himself. A film that's really got nothing to say once one digs below the surface. The music is by Alan Price. A "sequel" of sorts to IF . . .
Aka: OH LUCKY MAN
COM                    167 min (ort 174 min)
B,V                    WHV

## O.C. AND STIGGS *                    15
Robert Altman          USA             1985
Daniel H. Jenkins, Dennis Hopper, Tina Louise, Neill Barry, Paul Dooley, Jane Curtin, Jon Cryer, Ray Walston, Louis Nye, Martin Mull, King Sunny Ade and his African Beats
This strange title refers to a pair of kids who spend their summer vacation indulging their warped and weird sense of humour by pestering the life out of people they despise. An erratic and dull comedy that must rank as one of the low spots in the director's career.
Aka: UGLY, MONSTROUS, MIND-ROASTING SUMMER OF O.C. AND STIGGS
COM                    105 min (ort 109 min)
B,V                    MGM

## OASIS, THE **                    18
Sparky Greene          USA             1984
Chris Makepeace, Scott Hylands, Richard Cox, Dori Brenner, Rick Podell, Mark Metcalf, Ben Slack, Anne Lockhart, Suzanne Snyder
After their plane crashes in the Mexican desert, the surviving passengers face a gruelling test of endurance as they struggle to find their way back to civilization. Quite gripping, but the unrelieved gloom of it all is a bit hard to take.
DRA                    90 min
B,V                    IVS L/A; VCC

## OBJECT OF DESIRE *
Ji Boung Jiune         USA             1983
Juliet Anderson, June Buthelezi, Ron Jeremy
Story of a brothel madam and her girls.
Osca: NYMPHO SECRETS/SISSY'S HOT SUMMER (asa)
A                      69 min
B,V                    HAR

## OBJECTIVE BURMA! ***                    PG
Raoul Walsh            USA             1944
Errol Flynn, James Brown, William Prince, George Tobias, Henry Hull, Warner Anderson, John Alvin, Stephen Richards, Tony Caruso, Joel Allen, Dick Erdman
Withdrawn for seven years in Britain following a public outcry over the fact it makes no mention of the British role in Burma, this one spawned the joke that Flynn won the war single-handed. A group of American paratroopers are dropped behind Japanese lines with orders to destroy a radio station. They eventually achieve their aim, but only at great cost in human lives, which effectively atones for any lack of historical verisimilitude.
WAR                    136 min (ort 142 min) B/W
V                      WHV

## OBLONG BOX, THE **                    15
Gordon Hessler         UK/USA          1969
Vincent Price, Christopher Lee, Rupert Davies, Sally Geeson, Uta Levka, Peter Arne, Alastair Williamson, Hilary Dwyer, Maxwell Shaw, Carl Rigg, Michael Balfour, Harry Baird
A man is horribly disfigured by an African witch doctor in revenge for his brother's killing of a native child. Upon their return to England, he is imprisoned in a tower room of the family mansion, from which he eventually escapes by faking his death. The inevitable revenge rampage then ensues. A gory horror offering that sails under false colours, by borrowing its title

from an Edgar Allan Poe story to which it bears no resemblance.
HOR                    95 min (Cut at film release)
B,V                    GHV

## OBSESSED *                    15
Robin Spry             CANADA          1987
Kerrie Keane, Daniel Pilon, Saul Rubinek, Colleen Dewhurst, Alan Thicke
Shocked at the death of her son in a hit-and-run accident, and the impotence and indifference of the legal authorities, who make the usual token and lukewarm efforts to deal with the driver, a young mother decides that justice can only be served if she takes the law into her own hands. A formula revenger that adds nothing new to this genre.
Aka: HITTING HOME
Boa: novel Hit And Run by Tom Alderman.
THR                    100 min
B,V                    FUTUR

## OBSESSION *                    R18
Jonathan Ross          USA             1985
Harry Reems, Sheri St Claire, Jessica Wylde, Joey Silvera, Jon Martin, Mike Horner, Lili Marlene
A millionaire invites six of his married high school friends to his mansion for the weekend. None of the group know who their host is and while they enjoy themselves with each other he watches through hidden TV cameras. Before they leave the ladies discover our millionaire and give him a thorough going over. But as to why they were invited in the first place; well, perhaps the director forgot to tell us.
A                      36 min
V                      VEXCEL

## OBSESSION ***                    15
Brian De Palma         USA             1976
Cliff Robertson, Genevieve Bujold, John Lithgow, Sylvia Kuumba Williams, Wanda Blackman, Patrick McNamara, Stanley J. Reyes, Nick Kreiger, Stocker Fontelieu, Don Hood, Andrea Esterhazy
A wealthy businessman's wife and child disappear after he follows police instructions and substitutes blank paper for the ransom money. Some years later he and his partner are on a visit to Florence when he meets a woman who is his wife's double and becomes obsessed with discovering her true identity. A derivative thriller with a little violence and much suspense, although its best feature is the superb score by Bernard Herrmann.
THR                    94 min (ort 98 min)
V                      RCA

## OBSESSIVE LOVE **                    PG
Steven Hilliard Stern  USA             1984
Simon MacCorkindale, Yvette Mimieux, Jill Jacobson, Constance McCashin, Kim Shriner, Allan Miller, Louise Latham, Jonathan Goldsmith, Lainie Kazan, Jerry Supiran, Greg Monaghan, Robert DoQui, Tony Miller, Barry Michlin
A typist addicted to TV soap operas indulges her passion for the leading man in her favourite show, by pursuing him to Los Angeles where she uses every trick in the book to arouse his interest. Average. Mimieux co-wrote this one.
Boa: story by Petru S. Popescu.
DRA                    96 min (ort 100 min) mTV
B,V                    PRV

## OCCUPATIONAL KILLER *                    18
Gilberto de Andas                      1989
A drugs ring kidnaps a child to use as a carrier for drugs, but in an airport shootout with the police the child is inadvertently killed and the gang destroys itself in a series of vicious internal conflicts. A confused and violent action-thriller of little worth.
A/AD                   88 min Cut (29 sec)
B,V                    VPD

## OCEAN'S ELEVEN **                                    PG
Lewis Milestone          USA              1960
*Frank Sinatra, Dean Martin, Sammy Davis Jr, Peter*
*Lawford, Angie Dickinson, Richard Conte, Cesar*
*Romero, Patrice Wymore, Joey Bishop, Akim Tamiroff,*
*Henry Silva, Ilka Chase*
A criminal gang plans to rob five Las Vegas casinos in
a single daring heist, but any suspense that such an
ambitious operation could be expected to develop is
dissipated by a silly, jokey attitude on the part of all
concerned. The unexpected ending is the best thing in
it.
COM                                      127 min
B,V                                      WHV

## OCEANS OF FIRE **                                  PG
Steven Carver            USA              1986
*Gregory Harrison, Billy Dee Williams, David*
*Carradine, Cynthia Sykes, Ken Norton, Ray "Boom*
*Boom" Mancini, Lyle Alzado, Tony Burton, Ramon*
*Bieri, Alan Fudge, David Wohl, Jeff Cooper, Jorge*
*Rusek, Roger Cudney, Sergio Calderon*
In a plot reminiscent of THE DIRTY DOZEN, high-
security prisoners serving long sentences are re-
cruited for an offshore oil project, where lives are
readily sacrificed so that a short completion deadline
can be met. Fair.
A/AD                     93 min (ort 100 min) mTV
B,V                                      IVS

## OCTAGON, THE **                                    18
Eric Karson             USA               1980
*Chuck Norris, Karen Carlson, Lee Van Cleef, Art*
*Hindle, Jack Carter, Carol Bagdasarian*
A secret terrorist training camp sets the scene for a
battle royal between our hero and sundry villains, all
of them versed in the martial arts. There's plenty of
violent action to satisfy Norris fans but little else.
MAR              99 min (ort 103 min) Cut (32 sec)
B,V    VTC L/A; VMA L/A; MAST (VHS only); STABL;
VCC

## OCTAVIA **                                         18
David Beaird            USA               1982
*Susan Curtis, Neil Kinsella, Jake Foley, G.B. File,*
*Tom Wayne*
A blind backwoods girl living in a shack with her
sadistic father, suffers the unwelcome attentions of a
nasty biker gang. One day, however, her saviour
arrives in the unlikely guise of a convict on the run.
DRA                                      85 min
B,V                                      EIV

## OCTOBER ***                                        PG
Sergei Eisenstein       USSR              1927
*Grigori Alexandrov, Boris Livanov, Nikandrov,*
*Vladimir Popov*
One of the films commissioned by the Soviet govern-
ment to celebrate the tenth anniversary of the Revolu-
tion, this is a lavish recreation of the actual events
and deservedly ranks as a masterly piece of propagan-
da. The use of montage is quite remarkable. Interes-
tingly, Trotsky had figured prominently in the film,
but with his fall from grace all sequences that
included him were removed.
Aka: OKTYABR; TEN DAYS THAT SHOOK THE
WORLD
DRA                     101 min (ort 164) B/W silent
V                                        HEND

## OCTOBER MAN, THE ***                               PG
Roy (Ward) Baker        UK                1947
*John Mills, Joan Greenwood, Edward Chapman, Kay*
*Walsh, Joyce Carey, Felix Aylmer, Catherine Lacey,*
*Patrick Holt, Frederick Piper, Adrianne Allen, Jack*
*Melford, George Benson, John Salew, John Boxer,*
*Esme Beringer, Ann Wilton*
A man suffers head injuries in an accident that killed

a young child and begins to develop suicidal tendencies. After a young model, a fellow guest at his hotel,
is murdered, he finds himself cast in the role of prime
suspect and begins to collapse under the strain. A
murder mystery with a psychological emphasis that
benefits greatly from the script, adapted from the
novel by Ambler, the thriller writer.
Boa: novel by Eric Ambler.
DRA            98 min; 91 min (VCC) B/W (ort 110 min)
B,V                                      RNK; VCC

## OCTOPUSSY ***                                      PG
John Glen               UK                1983
*Roger Moore, Maud Adams, Louis Jourdan, Kristina*
*Wayborn, Kabir Bedi, Steven Berkoff, Desmond*
*Llewellyn, Vijay Amritraj, David Meyer, Anthony*
*Meyer, Lois Maxwell, Robert Brown, Walter Gotell,*
*Geoffrey Keen, Cherry Gillespie*
An excellent and entertaining Bond adventure with a
complex Cold War plot, involving efforts by a Soviet
general to create chaos by exploding a nuclear device
at a NATO base in West Germany. High production
values and the breathtaking Indian locations make
this entry a winner. The script is by George McDonald
Fraser, with music by John Barry. Number thirteen
in this series, followed by NEVER SAY NEVER
AGAIN.
Boa: short stories Octopussy/The Property Of A Lady
by Ian Fleming.
A/AD                     126 min (ort 131 min)
V/sh                                     WHV

## ODD ANGRY SHOT, THE ***
Tom Jeffrey             AUSTRALIA         1979
*John Hargreaves, Graham Kennedy, Bryan Brown,*
*John Jarratt, Graeme Blundell*
A group of professional Australian soldiers on service
in Vietnam find that the reality of jungle warfare is
far different from what they expected, and begin to
question the reasons for their involvement. An un-
usually mature work that concentrates on personal
relationships rather than combat.
WAR                                      92 min
B,V                                      GHV

## ODD JOB, THE **                                    15
Peter Medak             UK                1978
*David Jason, Graham Chapman, Michael Elphick,*
*Simon Williams, Diana Quick, Edward Hardwicke*
When an insurance executive loses his wife to a
friend, he hires a hit-man to murder him, but
following a change of heart has to persuade the killer
to call the job off. The slight "Monty Python" flavour to
the script is the work of Chapman, who co-scripted
this sporadically amusing but generally strained
effort.
Boa: TV play by Bernard McKenna.
COM                     90 min (ort 87 min)
V                                        MIA

## ODD MAN OUT ****                                   PG
Carol Reed              UK                1946
*James Mason, Robert Newton, Kathleen Ryan, Elwyn*
*Brook-Jones, Robert Beatty, F.J. McCormick, William*
*Hartnell, Fay Compton, Beryl Measor, Cyril Cusack,*
*Dan O'Herlihy, Roy Irving, Maureen Delany, Kitty*
*Kirwan, Min Milligan*
An IRA man escapes from prison in Belfast and tries
to make his way to the docks but is shot in a police
raid on a mill. Hampered by his injuries, he encoun-
ters various individuals before meeting his inevitable
and tragic end. A memorable work that is enormously
effective despite a lack of warmth. Scripted by R.C.
Sheriff and F.L. Green from the latter's novel. Remade
in 1969 as "The Lost Man".
Aka: GANG WAR
Boa: novel by F.L. Green.
DRA            113 min; 111 min (VCC) (ort 115 min) B/W
B,V                                      RNK; VCC

## ODD SQUAD, THE *                               15
E.B. Clucher (Enzo Barboni)
                    ITALY                        1985
*Jackie Basehart, Vincent Gardenia, Carmen Russo,*
*Gil Gemma, Johnny Dorelli*
"Make love, not war", is the happy maxim of a group of
crazy soldiers in Sicily in WW2. Both they and the
enemy find a local brothel, whose employees are more
than happy to help them put this philosophy to the
test. A low-budget, broad farce.
COM                                          93 min
B,V                                       IVS; GLOB

## ODDS AND EVENS *                              PG
Sergio Corbucci      ITALY                      1978
*Terence Hill (Mario Girotti), Bud Spencer (Carlo*
*Pedersoli)*
Our comic duo become involved with the Mafia in
Miami, and enjoy various slapstick encounters that
amply demonstrate their lack of fresh ideas, in this
mediocre comedy.
COM                                         112 min
V                                             RCA

## ODE TO BILLY JOE **                           15
Max Baer             USA                        1976
*Robby Benson, Glynnis O'Connor, Joan Hotchkis,*
*Sandy McPeak, James Best, Terence Goodman*
A hit song from 1967 by Bobbie Gentry is far too thin a
prop for this empty story of a Southern teenage
romance, although we do learn why Billy Joe jumped
off the bridge.
DRA                              101 min (ort 108 min)
B,V                                           WHV

## ODESSA FILE, THE **                           PG
Ronald Neame         UK                         1974
*Jon Voight, Maximilian Schell, Maria Schell, Mary*
*Tamm, Derek Jacobi, Peter Jeffrey, Klaus Lowitsch,*
*Kurt Meisel, Hans Messemer, Garfield Morgan,*
*Shmuel Rodensky, Ernst Schroeder, Gunter Strack,*
*Noel William, Martin Brandt*
A reporter infiltrates a secret Nazi organisation in
West Germany in his search for some former members
of the SS, after reading the diary of a camp survivor. A
confused and slow-paced thriller that does little with
material that should have guaranteed a high level of
suspense. Written by Kenneth Ross and George
Markstein.
Boa: novel by Frederick Forsyth.
THR                              123 min (ort 129 min)
V                                   HOLLY L/A; RCA

## OEDIPUS REX **
Pier Paolo Pasolini   ITALY                     1967
*Franco Citti, Silvana Mangano, Julian Beck, Carmelo*
*Bene, Alida Valli*
A visually satisfying but sluggish and flat adaptation
of two Sophocles tragedies, telling of the unfortunate
Oedipus who murdered his father and married his
mother in fulfilment of a prophecy.
Aka: EDIPO RE
Boa: plays Oedipus Rex/Oedipus At Colonus by
Sophocles.
DRA                              106 min (ort 110 min)
V                                           CONNO

## OF MICE AND MEN ***
Reza Badiyi          USA                        1981
*Robert Blake, Randy Quaid, Mitchell Ryan, Lew*
*Ayres, Pat Hingle, Cassie Yates, Ted Neeley, Whitman*
*Mayo, Dennis Fimple, Pat Corley, Sondra Blake*
Modern film version of this story of two ranch hands;
one small and clever, the other massively strong and
mentally retarded, who travel around together look-
ing for work. Competent rather than inspired.
Boa: novella by John Steinbeck.
DRA                              116 min (ort 125 min) mTV
B,V,V2                                         IFS

## OF PURE BLOOD **                              15
Joseph Sargent       USA                        1986
*Lee Remick, Patrick McGoohan, Robert Bowman,*
*Gottfried John, Richard Munch, Katharina Bohm,*
*Edith Schneider, Carolyn Nelson, Catherine*
*McGoohan, Jem Wall, Hans Jurgen Schatz, Pascal*
*Breuer, Beate Finckh, Thomas Kylau*
The Nazi Lebensborn selective breeding programme,
intended to eventually result in a master race,
provides the factual background to this mediocre
thriller set some forty years after the demise of the
Third Reich, when a mother travels to West Germany
to investigate the circumstances surrounding her
son's violent death. See also THE BOYS FROM
BRAZIL.
Boa: story by Del Coleman and Michael Zagor/book by
Marc Hillel and Clarissa Henry.
DRA                              89 min (ort 100 min) mTV
B/h, V/h                                       WHV

## OF UNKNOWN ORIGIN **                          15
George Pan Cosmatos  CANADA                     1983
*Peter Weller, Jennifer Dale, Lawrence Dane, Kenneth*
*Welsh, Louis Del Grande, Shannon Tweed, Keith*
*Knight, Maury Chaykin, Leif Anderson, Jimmy Tapp,*
*Gayle Garfinkle, Earl Pennington, Jacklin Webb,*
*Bronwen Mantel, Monik Nantel*
A businessman tries to rid his Manhattan apartment
of a rat that seems to possess a curiously high degree
of intelligence, but the constant failure of his efforts
creates an unhealthy obsession that threatens both
his sanity and professsional life.
Boa: short story The Visitor by Chauncey G. Parker
III.
THR                              85 min (ort 90 min)
V/h                                            WHV

## OFF BEAT **                                   PG
Michael Dinner       USA                        1986
*Judge Reinhold, Meg Tilly, Cleavant Derricks, Joe*
*Mantegna, Jacques D'Amboise, James Tolkan, Amy*
*Wright, John Turturro, Anthony Zerbe, Julie Bovasso,*
*Fred Gwynne, Harvey Keitel, Austin Pendleton, Penn*
*Jilette*
A shy librarian finds himself pretending to be a cop,
after meeting a pretty policewoman at a benefit show
where he was standing in for a friend. A modest litte
comedy, where all concerned work hard for laughs, of
which there are too few. Written by Mark Medoff.
COM                              89 min (ort 95 min)
B,V                                            RNK

## OFF THE WALL *                                15
Rick Friedberg       USA                        1982
*Paul Sorvino, Rosanna Arquette, Patrick Cassidy,*
*Billy Hufsey, Monte Markham, Mickey Gilley, Garry*
*Goodrow, Lewis Arquette*
The antics of the crazy prisoners in an even crazier
prison forms the basis for this frantic screwball
comedy where the cast seem desperate in their
attempts to raise a laugh.
Aka: SNAKE CANYON PRISON
COM                              86 min Cut (10 sec)
B,V                              VSP L/A; MKR; POR

## OFFENCE, THE ***                              18
Sidney Lumet         UK                         1972
*Sean Connery, Ian Brennen, Vivien Merchant, Trevor*
*Howard, Derek Newark, John Hallam, Peter Bowles,*
*Ronald Radd, Anthony Sagar, Howard Goorney,*
*Richard Moore, Maxine Gordon*
A tired and disillusioned police inspector goes over the
top when confronted with a suspected child murderer.
Connery gives a fine portrayal of a man at the end of
his tether, in a fine psychological drama that was too
serious and grim to be a hit. Scripted by John Hopkins
from his play.
Boa: play This Story Of Yours by John Hopkins.

DRA                        108 min (ort 113 min)
B,V                                          WHV

## OFFENSIVE SHAOLIN LONGFIST *          18
Philip Chan          HONG KONG          1989
*Natassa Tang, Lewis Ko, Chan Fung, Bruce Cheung*
Two martial artists, one an expert and the other a
student, meet in a bloody and violent confrontation.
The set-piece battles are well-handled, but the lack of
a strong plot allows one's attention to wane.
MAR                                        85 min
V                                            VPD

## OFFERINGS *                             18
Christopher Reynolds   USA             1989
*Loretta Leigh Brown, Jerry Brewer, Elizabeth Greene,
G. Michael Smith*
A man is released after spending ten years in the
mental ayslum to which he was committed, after a
prank by the local kids caused him to lose his mind.
Another re-run of the avenging maniac theme.
HOR                                        90 min
V                                          PRISM

## OFFICER AND A GENTLEMAN, AN ***        15
Taylor Hackford        USA             1981
*Richard Gere, Debra Winger, David Keith, Louis
Gossett Jr, Robert Loggia, Lisa Blount, Lisa Eilbacher,
Tony Plana, Harold Sylvester, David Caruso, Victor
French, Grace Zabriskie, Tommy Petersen, Mara Scott
Wood*
The story of a misfit becoming a US Naval Officer
candidate and meeting a girl doing a dead-end job in a
factory. The contrived plot, though violent and dis-
jointed in parts, has touching moments as he is seen
gaining maturity at the hands of his drill instructor (a
superb performance from Gossett) and learning to
care for others. AA: S. Actor (Gossett), Song ("Up
Where We Belong" – Jack Nitzche/Buffy Sainte-Marie
– music/Will Jennings – lyrics).
Boa: novel by Stephen P. Smith.
DRA                        119 min (ort 126 min)
V/h                                          CIC

## OFFICIAL VERSION, THE **               15
Luis Puenzo          ARGENTINA          1985
*Norma Aleandro, Guillermo Battaglia, Patrizio
Contreras, Hector Alterio, Analia Castro, Chunchuna
Villafane*
A woman discovers to her horror that her adopted
child was taken from political prisoners, killed by the
military junta who ruled Argentina up to 1984. A
terribly disappointing film that demonstrates how
good intentions alone cannot compensate for poor
acting and an incoherent plot. Moreover, it fails to do
justice to those whose loved ones perished at the hands
of this brutal and benighted dictatorship.
AA: Foreign.
Aka: LA HISTORIA OFICIAL; OFFICIAL STORY,
THE
DRA                                       109 min
B,V                                          PVG

## OH GOD! ***                             PG
Carl Reiner          USA               1977
*George Burns, John Denver, Teri Garr, Ralph
Bellamy, William Daniels, Paul Sorvino, George
Furth, Barnard Hughes, Barry Sullivan, Dinah Shore,
Jeff Corey, Donald Pleasence, David Ogden Stiers*
God appears to the manager of a supermarket in the
guise of an old man, and persuades him to deliver a
message of hope and love. After a while, the joke of
seeing God wearing a baseball cap wears a bit thin. A
better story and dialogue would have helped, though
Burns carries off the role of the Almighty with
considerable panache. Two sequels followed. The
script is by Larry Gelbart.
Boa: novel by Avery Corman.

COM                         99 min (ort 104 min)
B,V                                          WHV

## OH GOD: BOOK 2 *                        PG
Gilbert Cates         USA              1980
*George Burns, Suzanne Pleshette, David Birney,
Louanne, Howard Duff, Hans Conried, Wilfrid Hyde-
White, John Louie, Conrad Janis, Anthony Holland,
Joyce Brothers, Bebe Drake Massey, Hugh Downs,
Marian Mercer, Mari Gorman*
Second of the OH GOD! films with God using a child to
tell the world he is still there. A poor sequel with few
ideas or laughs to offer.
COM                                        94 min
B,V                                          WHV

## OH GOD, YOU DEVIL! **                   15
Paul Bogart          USA               1984
*George Burns, Ted Wass, Ron Silver, Roxanne Hart,
Eugene Roche, Robert Desiderio, John Doolittle, Julie
Lloyd, Ian Giatti, Janet Brandt, Betita Moreno, Danny
Ponce, Jason Wingreen, Danny Mora, Jane Dulo,
Susan Peretz*
Third in the OH GOD! series uses the plot device of a
young singer who sells his soul to the Devil in return
for success, but changes his mind after the initial
euphoria. God and Satan (both played by Burns)
eventually face each other over a Las Vegas poker
table. The blandness of it all is a serious handicap
which not even Burns can overcome. Scripted by
Andrew Bergman.
COM                         92 min (ort 96 min)
B,V                                          WHV

## OH HEAVENLY DOG! *                      PG
Joe Camp             USA               1980
*Jane Seymour, Chevy Chase, Omar Sharif, Donnelly
Rhodes, Robert Morley, Alan Sues, Stuart Germain,
John Stride, Barbara Leigh-Hunt, Frank Williams,
Margaret Courtney, Albin Pahernik, Susan
Kellerman, Benji (the dog)*
A private eye is killed and returns to solve his own
murder – in the form of a dog. Reverse of "You Never
Can Tell" from 1951 where a dog returned as a man.
An idea that was used in THE SHAGGY D.A. with
our mutt going through his paces well enough, but
there's little for him to chew on in this limp comedy.
Joe Camp went on to make BENJI THE HUNTED.
COM                         99 min (ort 103 min)
V/s, LV/s                                    CBS

## OH! CALCUTTA! *
Jacques Levy         USA               1972
*Bill Macy, Raina Barrett, Mark Dempsey, Samantha
Harper, Mitchell McGuire, Margo Sappington, Nancy
Tribush, George Welbes*
A videotaped performance of the original Broadway
sex show with an added outdoor scene. Its ten sketches
deal with sex and nudity in a painfully contrived and
unfunny way. Of value only as a dated curio.
Boa: play by Kenneth Tynan.
A                           95 min (ort 105 min)
V                                            HOK

## OH! MR PORTER ***                        U
Marcel Varnel        UK                1937
*Will Hay, Moore Marriott, Graham Moffatt, Dave
O'Toole, Dennis Wyndham, Sebastian Smith, Agnes
Laughlan, Percy Walsh, Frederick Piper*
An inept Irish railwayman lands a position as station-
master thanks to the influence of his powerful
brother-in-law, and finds himself in charge of an
isolated halt on the border between Northern Ireland
and the Irish Free State. He and his two assistants
find themselves troubled by supernatural happenings,
but the ghosts eventually prove to be a group of
gunrunners whom they eventually unmask and
arrest. See also THE GHOST TRAIN.
Boa: story The Ghost Train by Frank Launder.

COM                           82 min (ort 84 min)
B,V                                          RNK

## OH! WHAT A LOVELY WAR ***  PG
Richard Attenborough    UK              1969
*Laurence Olivier, John Gielgud, Kenneth More, Ralph
Richardson, Jack Hawkins, Michael Redgrave, John
Mills, Dirk Bogarde, Susannah York, Maggie Smith,
Vanessa Redgrave, Vincent Ball, Pia Colombo, Paul
Daneman*
An excellent and imaginative adaptation of a stage
show that brings home the futility of WW1, with songs
of the period imaginatively woven into both semi-
comical dance routines and scenes of carnage, that are
equally moving. Attenborough shows a fine flair for
the cinematic in his directorial debut, though the
excessive length is a handicap. Scripted by Len
Deighton.
Boa: play The Long, Long Trail by Charles Tilton/
musical by Joan Littlewood.
MUS                          137 min (ort 144 min)
B,V                                          CIC

## O'HARA'S WIFE **
William S. Bartman      USA             1982
*Edward Asner, Jodie Foster, Perry Lang, Mariette
Hartley, Tom Bosley, Ray Walston, Allen Williams,
Richard Schaal, Nehemiah Persoff*
A man's wife dies but returns as a ghost only he can
see, to continue to help and advise him from beyond
the grave. A limp reworking of "Topper" minus the
humour.
COM                                   87 min mTV
B,V                                         POLY

## OIL *
Mircea Dragan          ITALY            1977
*Stuart Whitman, Ray Milland, Woody Strode, George
Dinica, William Berger, Tony Kendall*
Sabotage leads to an oil field blaze where the flames
act beautifully but fail to inspire the cast to follow
their lead.
Aka: OIL: THE BILLION DOLLAR FIRE
A/AD                                       95 min
B,V,V2                                        INT

## OKLAHOMA KID, THE ***  PG
Lloyd Bacon            USA              1939
*James Cagney, Humphrey Bogart, Donald Crisp,
Rosemary Lane, Harvey Stephens, Ward Bond, Hugh
Sothern, Charles Middleton, Edward Pawley, Lew
Harvey, John Miljan, Trevor Bardette, Arthur
Aylesworth, Irving Bacon, Joe Devlin*
Action-packed Western comedy in which Cagney
plays a Robin Hood figure who seeks revenge for his
father's murder. Bogart plays the bad guy with his
customary aplomb.
WES                        77 min (ort 82 min) B/W
V                                            WHV

## OKLAHOMA! ****  U
Fred Zinnemann         USA              1955
*Gordon MacRae, Shirley Jones, Rod Steiger, Charlotte
Greenwood, Gloria Grahame, Eddie Albert, Gene
Nelson, James Whitmore, Barbara Lawrence, J.C.
Flippen, Roy Barcroft, James Mitchell, Bambi Linn,
Jennie Workman*
A much-loved and vibrant version of the classic
Broadway musical, written by Sonya Levien and
William Ludwig, with songs by Rodgers and Hammer-
stein, from their 1943 Broadway hit. The slight story
has a cowboy almost lose his girl to a hired hand
before eventually winning her back. Songs include
"The Surrey With The Fringe On Top" and "Oh, What
A Beautiful Morning". AA: Score (Robert Russell
Bennett/Jay Blackton/Adolph Deutsch), Sound (Fred
Hynes).
Boa: musical by Richard Rodgers and Oscar
Hammerstein.

MUS                          134 min (ort 143 min)
B,V                                          CBS

## OLD DARK HOUSE, THE ****  PG
James Whale            USA              1932
*Melvyn Douglas, Charles Laughton, Raymond Massey,
Boris Karloff, Ernest Thesiger, Eva Moore, Gloria
Stuart, Lilian Bond, Brember Wills, John Dudgeon
(Elspeth Dudgeon)*
A group of travellers seek shelter in title building
which contains a household composed of very strange
individuals. A classic horror-comedy replete with
witty lines and wonderful vignettes.
Boa: novel Benighted by J.B. Priestley.
HOR                        69 min (ort 71 min) B/W
V                                            VIR

## OLD GRINGO ***  15
Luis Puenzo            USA              1989
*Gregory Peck, Jimmy Smits, Jane Fonda, Patricio
Contreras, Jenny Gago, Jim Metzler, Gabriela Rosi,
Anne Pitoniak, Pedro Armendariz Jr*
A complex epic adventure that sees an American
schoolteacher with a thirst for adventure and the
ageing writer Ambrose Bierce, crossing paths with
each other and a young Mexican general when they
find themselves caught up in the 1913 revolution of
Pancho Villa. This ambitious and often spectacular
tale was plagued with production difficulties and has
many flaws, but remains quite memorable. Scripted
by Puenzo and Aida Bortnik.
Boa: novel by Carlos Fuentes.
A/AD                        116 min (ort 119 min)
V                                            RCA

## OLD MAN RHYTHM ***
Edward Ludwig          USA              1935
*Charles "Buddy" Rogers, George Barbier, Barbara
Kent, Grace Bradley, Betty Grable, Eric Blore*
A businessman returns to college to keep tabs on his
playboy son. Songwriter Johnny Mercer puts in an
appearance as one of the students in this pleasant and
typical production, where the flimsy plot is merely a
backdrop for the musical numbers.
Osca: DAMSEL IN DISTRESS
MUS                        71 min (ort 75 min) B/W
B,V                                          KVD

## OLD MAN WHO CRIED WOLF, THE **
Walter Grauman         USA              1970
*Edward G. Robinson, Martin Balsam, Diane Baker,
Percy Rodrigues, Ruth Roman, Edward Asner, Martin
E. Brooks, Paul Picerni, Sam Jaffe, Robert Yuro, Bill
Elliott, James A. Watson Jr, Naomi Stevens, Virginia
Christine, Pepe Brown*
A man sees a friend beaten to death but fails to
convince the police or his family that this really
happened. A flawed and limp drama that wasted a
good cast.
DRA                                   74 min mTV
B,V                                          GHV

## OLD TESTAMENT, THE *  PG
                       ITALY            1963
*Brad Harris, Susan Paget, John Heston, Margaret
Taylor*
The five sons of a prophet called Matatia throw the
Syrians out of the temple in this dull Italian biblical
epic.
DRA                          85 min (ort 94 min)
B,V                                  PRV L/A; CH5

## OLD YELLER ***  U
Robert Stevenson       USA              1957
*Dorothy McGuire, Fess Parker, Tommy Kirk, Kevin
Corcoran, Jeff York, Chuck Connors, Beverly
Washburn, Spike (the dog)*
A mongrel mutt taken in by a Texas farming family
proves his worth in Disney's very first boy-and-his-dog

tale. Set in 1869, this has a father leaving his 15-year-old son in charge, when he takes part in a 3-month cattle drive. Gave rise to a sequel, SAVAGE SAM, in 1963.
Boa: novel by Fred Gipson.

| A/AD | | 80 min (ort 82 min) Cut (16 sec) |
| B,V | | RNK; WDV |

## OLIVER TWIST **
Clive Donner          USA
PG
1982
*George C. Scott, Tim Curry, Michael Hordern, Timothy West, Eileen Atkins, Cherie Lunghi, Oliver Cotton, Martin Tempest, Matthew Drew, Eleanor David, Philip Locke, Spencer Rheult, Ann Tirard, Ann Beach, Brenda Cowling*
Yet another version of this famous story which offers little except a fine performance from Scott as Fagin. The script is by James Goldman.
Boa: novel by Charles Dickens.

| DRA | 98 min (ort 100 min) mTV |
| B,V | ODY |

## OLIVER TWIST ****
David Lean          UK
U
1948
*Alec Guinness, Robert Newton, Francis L. Sullivan, John Howard Davies, Kay Walsh, Anthony Newley, Henry Stephenson, Mary Clare, Ralph Truman, Josephine Stuart, Kathleen Harrison, Gibb McLaughlin, Amy Veness, Diana Dors, W.G. Fay*
Lean's version of this classic is the best one ever; a brilliant tale of a workhouse boy running away and getting drawn into a life of crime but making good in the end. Several remakes have followed (including OLIVER! – a 1968 musical), but none approach it in terms of power. Guinness and Newley make a fine team as Fagin and the Artful Dodger respectively. Written by Lean and Stanley Haynes.
Boa: novel by Charles Dickens.

| DRA | 111 min (ort 116 min) B/W |
| V | RNK; CH5 |

## OLIVER! ****
Carol Reed          UK
U
1968
*Ron Moody, Shani Wallis, Oliver Reed, Harry Secombe, Hugh Griffith, Jack Wild, Clive Moss, Mark Lester, Peggy Mount, Leonard Rossiter, Hylda Baker, Joseph O'Conor, Sheila White, Kenneth Cranham, Megs Jenkins, James Hayter*
A splendid musical version of this classic tale with fine settings and songs by Lionel Bart, many of which are now classics. Photography is by Oswald Morris and a special prize was awarded for choreography. Uneven but great fun. AA: Pic, Dir, Art/Set (John Box and Terence Marsh/Vernon Dixon and Ken Muggleston), Score (Adapt) (John Green), Sound (Shepperton Studio Sound Dept.), Hon Award (Onna White for choreography).
Boa: novel by Charles Dickens/musical by Lionel Bart.

| MUS | 146 min; 140 min (PREST) |
| B, V/h | RCA; PREST (VHS only) |

## OMEGA COP **
Paul Kyriazi          USA
18
1989
*Ron Marchini, Adam West, Meg Thayer, Stuart Whitman, Troy Donahue*
In the year 1999 only one cop remains alive, and assisted by his robot officers, battles hordes of murderous mutants out to destroy the few remnants of humanity. A standard post-holocaust work with all the trimmings.

| A/AD | 89 min |
| V | BIGPIC |

## OMEGA SYNDROME **
Joseph Manduke          USA
18
1986
*Ken Wahl, George DiCenzo, Nicole Eggert, Doug McClure, Xander Berkley, Ron Kuhlman*
A down-at-heel journalist teams up with a Vietnam

veteran friend turned black-market arms dealer, when his daughter is kidnapped by an army of right-wing terrorists, and together they embark on a mission to rescue her. Average action, below average plot.

| A/AD | 88 min |
| V/h | NWV |

## OMEN OF EVIL **
Peter Sharp          NEW ZEALAND
18
1984
*Patrick McGoohan, Emma Piper, Andy Anderson, Terence Cooper, Frank Whitten, Sean Duffy*
A beautiful and vulnerable young girl wants to break away from her puritanical father, but her need for freedom and his need for her love and respect creates an emotional tightrope that leads to tragedy.
Aka: TRESPASSES

| DRA | 99 min |
| B,V | PVG |

## OMEN, THE **
Richard Donner          USA
18
1976
*Gregory Peck, Lee Remick, Billie Whitelaw, David Warner, Patrick Troughton, Leo McKern, Harvey Stephens, Martin Benson, Robert Rietty, Holly Palance, Anthony Nicholls, Sheila Raynor, Robert MacLeod, John Stride, Tommy Duggan*
A ridiculously overblown and unbelievable story of the coming of the anti-Christ that spawned two sequels: DAMIEN: OMEN 2 and THE FINAL CONFLICT. Peck inherited the main role from Charlton Heston who wisely turned it down. The script is by David Seltzer. AA: Score (Orig) (Jerry Goldsmith).
Boa: novel by David Seltzer.

| HOR | 106 min (ort 111 min) |
| B, V/sh, V2, LV | CBS |

## ON DANGEROUS GROUND ***
Chuck Bail          USA
PG
1986
*Stephen Collins, Bo Svenson, Janet Julien, Lance Henriksen, Victoria Racimo, Nicholas Pryor*
A scientist conducting experiments to harness sound energy which involve Halley's Comet, uncovers a conspiracy to dump industrial waste illegally and decides to fight back against those responsible. An unusual SF thriller with some memorable aerial sequences.
Aka: CHOKE CANYON

| THR | 91 min (ort 94 min) |
| V/sh | WHV |

## ON GOLDEN POND ***
Mark Rydell          USA
PG
1981
*Henry Fonda, Katharine Hepburn, Jane Fonda, Doug McKeon, Dabney Coleman, William Lanteau*
Fonda's last film is a fine tribute in his portrayal of an 80-year-old professor who has to cope with a crisis in his life and marriage. Plenty of sentimentality, a good script and the presence of three stars made this a sure hit and a firm contender for the Oscars. Simplistic it may be, but touching it is too. AA: Actor (Henry Fonda), Actress (Hepburn), Screen (Adapt) (Ernest Thompson).
Boa: play by Ernest Thompson.

| DRA | 104 min (ort 109 min) |
| B,V | PRV; CH5 (VHS only); POLY (VHS only) |

## ON HER MAJESTY'S SECRET SERVICE **
Peter Hunt          UK
PG
1969
*George Lazenby, Diana Rigg, Telly Savalas, Ilse Steppat, Yuri Borienko, Bernard Lee, Lois Maxwell, Gabriele Ferzetti, Bernard Horsfall, George Baker, Desmond Llewelyn, Angela Scoular, Catherina Von Schell, John Gay*
Lazenby had a great chance when Connery took a break from these Bond films, but muffed it as the most wooden secret agent one could imagine. Savalas plays a master criminal out, as they usually are, to take over the world and as such gives a much meatier

performance. This film, the sixth in the series, was followed by DIAMONDS ARE FOREVER.
Boa: novel by Ian Fleming.

A/AD 127 min (ort 142 min)
V WHV

## ON THE AIR LIVE WITH CAPTAIN MIDNIGHT **  PG
Beverly C. Sebastian/D. Ferd Sebastian
USA 1979
*Tracy Sebastian, John Ireland, Dena Dietrich, Ted Gehring, Mia Kovacs*
A boy plays truant from school and decides that his role in life is to be a disc jockey, on his own illegal radio station that broadcasts from the back of his van. A mild little comedy.
Aka: CAPTAIN MIDNIGHT
COM 80 min (ort 93 min)
B,V CIC

## ON THE BEACH ***
Stanley Kramer USA 1959
*Gregory Peck, Anthony Perkins, Donna Anderson, Ava Gardner, Fred Astaire, John Tate, Lola Brooks, Guy Doleman, John Meillon, Harp McGuire, Richard Meikle, Ken Wayne, Joe McCormick, Lou Vernon, Basil Buller-Murphy*
A downbeat version of the end of the world as a consequence of a nuclear exchange between East and West. The action is set in Australia, where most of the population await the arrival of drifting radioactive clouds, which have already killed off the rest of mankind. Good performances are hampered by the lethargic script, written by John Paxton. This was the first dramatic role for Astaire, whose performance is a highlight.
Boa: novel by Nevil Shute.
DRA 133 min B/W
V CBS

## ON THE BEAT ***
Robert Asher UK 1962
*Norman Wisdom, Jennifer Jayne, Raymond Huntley, David Lodge, Esma Cannon, Eric Baker, Eleanor Summerfield, Ronnie Stevens, Terence Alexander, Maurice Kaufman, Dilys Laye*
A car-park attendant at Scotland Yard dreams of becoming a policeman just like his dear old dad, but unfortunately is too short to be accepted. He is however, elevated to the ranks when it's discovered that he bears an uncanny resemblance to an Italian jewel thief, whom the police are anxious to catch. A lively Wisdom comedy with good routines making up for the deficiencies in the story.
Aka: NORMAN WISDOM: ON THE BEAT
Osca: TROUBLE IN STORE COM 105 min B/W
B,V RNK

## ON THE BUSES *  PG
Harry Booth UK 1971
*Reg Varney, Doris Hare, Anna Karen, Michael Robbins, Stephen Lewis, Bob Grant, Andrew Lawrence, Pat Ashton, Brian Oulton, Pamela Cundell, Pat Coombs, Wendy Richard, Peter Madden, David Lodge, Maggie McGrath*
First spin-off from a popular TV comedy series about the lives and loves of the crews of a Northern bus depot. In this story female bus drivers cause problems. Hardly a celebration of life, more like a dreary and depressing night out in the rain. MUTINY ON THE BUSES and HOLIDAY ON THE BUSES soon followed and were equally forgettable.
COM 88 min; 84 min (WHV)
B,V TEVP; WHV (VHS only)

## ON THE EDGE **  15
Rob Nilsson USA 1985

*Bruce Dern, Bill Bailey, Jim Haynie, John Marley, Pam Grier*
A 44-year-old runner risks everything to win a gruelling race, which has become such an obsession that he is prepared to sacrifice his career, health and self-respect in the pursuit of a fleeting moment of glory as the winner. A strong beginning soon gives way to a less energetic performance.
DRA 82 min (ort 92 min)
B,V VES

## ON THE GAME *  18
Stanley Long UK 1974
*Pamela Manson, Charles Hodgson, Suzy Bowen, Nicola Austine, Allen Morton, Peter Duncan, Louise Pajo, Allan McClelland, Eva, Val Penny, Francis Batson, Fiona Victory, David Brierley, Mandy Murfitt, Natalie Shaw, June Palmer*
A potted history of prostitution through the ages with a number of sketches on this theme. A poorly scripted and dated sex film.
A 83 min (ort 87 min) Cut (2 min 6 sec)
B,V MOV L/A; PICVID (VHS only); SHEP

## ON THE LINE *  15
Jose Luis Borau SPAIN 1982
*David Carradine, Scott-Wilson, Victoria Abril, Jeff Delger, Paul Richardson, Jesse Vint, Sam Jaffe*
Action-drama set against the Texan-Mexican border and the traffic in illegal immigrants. A reworking of familiar ground covered many times before.
Aka: RIO ABAJO
A/AD 95 min
B,V MED

## ON THE NICKEL **
Ralph Waite USA 1979
*Donald Moffatt, Penelope Allen, James Gammon, Ralph Waite, Hal Williams, Jack Kehoe*
A deft, sentimental view of life among the down-and-out inhabitants of Los Angeles skid row that is both slow-paced and unsensational. The script is by Waite, who also produced the film.
DRA 90 min (ort 96 min)
B,V IFS

## ON THE RIGHT TRACK **  PG
Lee Philips USA 1981
*Gary Coleman, Maureen Stapleton, Michael Lembeck, Lisa Eilbacher, Norman Fell, Bill Russell*
A 10-year-old boy who lives in a railway station locker has an uncanny ability to pick winners, and soon endears himself to a variety of people who try to help him. A slight and sentimental comedy that over-stretches its material. Coleman's first starring role.
COM 94 min (ort 98 min)
B,V VES/PVG; VES

## ON THE RUN **
Pat Jackson UK 1969
*Dennis Conoley, Robert Kennedy, Tracey Collins, Gordon Jackson, John Hollis, Bari Johnson, Olwen Brooks, Dan Jackson, Harry Locke*
Adventure film about the son of a deposed African chief who is rescued from his kidnappers by a group of cockney kids.
Boa: novel by Nina Bawden.
JUV 57 min
B,V RNK

## ON THE TOWN ****  U
Gene Kelly/Stanley Donen
USA 1949
*Gene Kelly, Frank Sinatra, Jules Munshin, Vera-Ellen, Betty Garrett, Ann Miller, Tom Dugan, Florence Bates, Alice Pearce*
A marvellously enjoyable and vibrant musical built around the adventures of three sailors on a day's leave in New York. Gene Kelly choreographed the dance

routines and Leonard Bernstein wrote the ballet "Fancy Free". Shot on location in New York City with "New York, New York" and the other songs by Roger Edens and Lennie Hayton. This memorable offering was Kelly's directorial debut. AA: Score (Roger Edens/Lennie Hayton).

MUS　　　　　　　　　　　　94 min (ort 98 min)
V　　　　　　　　　　　　　　　　　　MGM

## ON THE WATERFRONT *** 　　　　　PG
Elia Kazan　　　　USA　　　　　1954
*Marlon Brando, Lee J. Cobb, Eve Marie Saint, Karl Malden, Pat Henning, Leif Erickson, Rod Steiger, James Westerfield, John Hamilton, Fred Gwynne*
A dramatic account of dockland corruption that's not without its sentimental moments, but has powerful performances and excellent direction. The music by Leonard Bernstein and the script by Budd Schulberg are two of its memorable features. Interestingly, the novel's ending was altered to allow Brando to survive. AA: Pic, Dir, Actor (Brando), S. Actress (Saint), Art/Set (Richard Day), Cin (Boris Kaufman), Edit (Gene Milford), Story/Screen (Schulberg).
Boa: novel by Budd Schulberg.
DRA　　　　　　　103 min (ort 108 min) B/W
B,V　　　　　　　　　　　　　　　　RCA

## ON THE YARD ** 　　　　　　　15
Raphael D. Silver　　USA　　　　1979
*John Heard, Thomas D. Waites, Mike Kellin, Richard Bright, Joe Grifasi, Lane Smith*
A routine prison drama that is well and truly based on all the expected stereotyped figures and stock situations, with Heard coming into conflict with the prison kingpin who runs all the rackets.
Boa: novel by Malcolm Braly.
DRA　　　　　　　　97 min (ort 102 min)
B,V　　　VFP L/A; HER L/A; INTMED (VHS only)

## ON VALENTINE'S DAY ** 　　　　PG
Ken Harrison　　　USA　　　　　1989
*William Converse Roberts, Michael Higgins, Hallie Foote, Steven Hill, Rochelle Oliver, Richard Jenkins, Carol Goodheart, Horton Foote Jr, Matthew Broderick*
A simple love story set in a small town in Texas, where in 1917 a young couple find themselves coming up in the world, which is just as well for the girl's wealthy parents disowned her after the couple's elopement. A pleasant drama with nice characterisations but not much of a plot. Scripted by Horton Foote, this formed part of a nine-play semi-autobiographical cycle.
Aka: STORY OF A MARRIAGE
DRA　　　　　　　　　　　　280 min
V　　　　　　　　　　　　　PRISM L/A

## ON WINGS OF EAGLES ** 　　　　PG
Andrew V. McLaglen　USA　　　1986
*Burt Lancaster, Richard Crenna, Paul Le Mat, Louis Giambalvo, Jim Metzler, Lawrence Pressman, Robert Wightman, Cyril O'Reilly, Esai Morales, Martin Doyle, Bob Delegall, Bill Bumiller, James Sutorius, Richard Crenna Jr*
A millionaire mounts a private military expedition, to rescue two of his executives from prison in Iran after the downfall of the Shah. Apart from its well-excecuted action scenes, a typically undistinguished TV product. Originally shown in two parts.
Boa: novel by Ken Follet.
A/AD　　　　　　235 min (ort 250 min) mTV
V　　　　　　　　　　　　　　　　HER

## ONCE A HERO ** 　　　　　　　PG
Claudia Weill/Kevin Inch
　　　　　　　　　　USA　　　　　1987
*Jeff Lester, Robert Forster, Caitlin Clarke, Milo O'Shea*
A comic book hero really does exist in another

dimension, and is forced to enter the real world and confront his creator when he discovers that a lack of new ideas is causing him to fade away. Once there, he becomes involved in the problems of the real world and has to rescue his foremost fan, when the latter and his mother are kidnapped by criminals. A highly unusual and witty but not entirely successful effort.
FAN　　　　　　　　　　　　　74 min
B,V　　　　　　　　　　　　　　　NWV

## ONCE AGAIN ** 　　　　　　　15
Amin Q. Chaudhri　USA　　　　1986
*Richard Cox, Jessica Harper, Martin Balsam, Frances Sternhagen, Harley Cross*
A couple whose marriage has been virtually dead for a long time, are unpleasantly surpised when they hear that their respective parents are planning to get hitched. A disappointing mishmash that never finds a clear direction or theme.
DRA　　　　　103 min (ort 105 min) Cut (8 sec)
B,V　　　　　　　　　　　　　　　GHV

## ONCE BITTEN * 　　　　　　　15
Howard Storm　　　USA　　　　1985
*Lauren Hutton, Jim Carrey, Cleavon Little, Karen Kopins, Thomas Ballatore, Skip Lacey, Jeb Adams, Joseph Brutsman, Stuart Charno, Robin Klein, Glen Mauro, Gary Mauro, Carey Moore, Peter Ebling, Richard Schaal, Peggy Pope*
A beautiful lady vampire stays young thanks to a supply of young male virgins provided by her faithful butler. A dull vampire spoof badly in need of a transfusion of wit.
COM　　　　　　　　89 min (ort 94 min)
B,V　　　　　　　　　　　　　　　VES

## ONCE IN PARIS *** 　　　　　
Frank D. Gilroy　　USA　　　　1978
*Wayne Rogers, Gayle Hunnicutt, Jean Lenoir, Clement Harrari, Tanya Lopert, Doris Roberts, Philippe March*
Three people meet in Paris and embark on various relationships, among them a Hollywood writer who has been engaged to re-write a script. Once there, he learns about life Parisian-style from his worldly wise chauffeur. Despite the lack of plot this is a charming little work.
DRA　　　　　　　　　　　　100 min
B,V　　　　　　　　　　　　ATA; APX

## ONCE UPON A BROTHERS GRIMM ** 　
Norman Campbell　USA　　　　1977
*Dean Jones, Paul Sand, Chita Riviera*
Musical fantasy in which the Brothers Grimm meet some of their best known characters.
MUS　　　　　　　　　　　　102 min
B,V　　　　　　　　　　　　VCL/CBS

## ONCE UPON A SCOUNDREL ** 　　U
George Schaefer　　USA　　　　1973
*Zero Mostel, Katy Jurado, Tito Vandis, Priscilla Garcia, A. Martinez*
Mexican villagers trick their tyrannical mayor into thinking he has died, so that he can see the error of his ways and make suitable amends. An uneven and cluttered comedy with a few hilarious moments. This was Mostel's last film and was not released for several years, as it became the subject of litigation.
COM　　　　　　　　　　　　90 min
B,V　　　　　　　　　　　　　　　PRV

## ONCE UPON A SPY *** 　　　　　PG
Ivan Nagy　　　　USA　　　　　1980
*Ted Danson, Marie Louise Weller, Eleanor Park, Christopher Lee, Leonard Stone, Terry Lester*
In this James Bond-style yarn, a secret agent obtains the reluctant services of a computer expert, and the two attempt to foil the crazy schemes of a power-mad megalomaniac, who has just stolen NASA's latest super-computer. Entertaining nonsense, made with

some style and wit. The script is by Jimmy Sangster.
A/AD                          91 min (ort 100 min) mTV
V                                                   RCA

## ONCE UPON A STARRY NIGHT **
Jack B. Hively            USA                    1978
Denver Pyle, Dan Haggerty, Jack Kruschen, Ken
Curtis
A story in the "Grizzly Adams" TV series about a
couple of kids and their uncle forced to shelter in his
cabin from the winter, while he searches for their
parents. A corny little kid's adventure yarn.
JUV                           71 min (ort 78 min) mTV
B,V                                                 EVI

## ONCE UPON A TEXAS TRAIN **                      U
Burt Kennedy             USA                     1987
Willie Nelson, Richard Widmark, Stuart Whitman,
Angie Dickinson, Shaun Cassidy, Jack Elam, Dub
Taylor, Ken Curtis, Willie Nelson, Royal Dano, Kevin
McCarthy, Gene Evans, Harry Carey Jr
An ageing criminal and his gang plan to rob a train
but face tough opposition from a sheriff and his posse,
who are equally long in the tooth. A pleasant comedy
whose plot has less life in it than the ageing cast.
Written by Kennedy.
WES                          87 min (ort 100 min) mTV
V/h                                                MED

## ONCE UPON A TIME *
                                                    198-
The story of a beautiful princess and a stubborn prince
who become enemies when they are involved in a
dispute over water rights.
CAR                                           93 min
V                                                  MAST

## ONCE UPON A TIME IN AMERICA ****              18
Sergio Leone             USA                     1984
Robert De Niro, James Woods, Elizabeth McGovern,
Tuesday Weld, Larry Rapp, William Forsythe, Treat
Williams, Burt Young, Danny Aiello
A strange disjointed film full of powerful images
tracing the career of four Jewish gangsters, from their
beginnings as New York street punks up to a final
reckoning when one of them is being sought for
betraying the others. Difficult to follow as it jumps
back and forth in time, but it rewards close attention.
Music by Ennio Moricone. The US release was cut to
88 minutes, thus becoming quite incomprehensible.
Boa: novel by L. Hays.
DRA                    218 min (ort 228 min) Cut (10 sec)
B, V/sh, V2                     TEVP; WHV (VHS only)

## ONCE UPON A TIME IN THE WEST ****            15
Sergio Leone             ITALY/USA              1969
Charles Bronson, Henry Fonda, Claudia Cardinale,
Jason Robards, Jack Elam, Woody Strode, Frank
Wolff, Gabriele Ferzetti, Keenan Wynn, Paolo Stoppa,
Marco Zuanelli, Lionel Stander, John Frederick, Dino
Mele
Long, violent and highly atmospheric Western with a
woman landowner being the target for a hired gun. An
inspired piece of casting gave Fonda the chance to
show his worth as one of the meanest, most sinister
villains ever to hit the screen. The music is by Ennio
Moricone and the film has the longest credits roll ever
– 12 minutes in all. Scripted by Leone, Bernardo
Bertolucci and Dario Argento.
Aka: C'ERA UNA VOLTA IL WEST
WES                          159 min (ort 165 min)
B,V                                                 CIC

## ONE AND ONLY, GENUINE, ORIGINAL,             U
FAMILY BAND, THE ***
Michael O'Herlihy        USA                     1967
Walter Brennan, Buddy Ebsen, Lesley Ann Warren,
John Davidson, Janet Blair, Kurt Russell, Wally Cox,
Richard Deacon, John Davidson, Goldie Hawn
The rousing tale of a musical family who settle in the
American Northwest in the 1880s, becoming
embroiled in a political battle between two over-
zealous presidential candidates. The music is com-
posed by the Sherman Brothers (of MARY POPPINS
fame) and is no more than adequate. This was Hawn's
screen debut – she has a miniscule part as a dancer.
MUS                          105 min (ort 110 min)
B,V                                                 WDV

## ONE BLOW TOO MANY ***                         PG
Joseph Sargent           USA                     1984
James Cagney, Art Carney, Ellen Barkin, Peter
Gallagher, Joseph Sirola, Edward I. Koch, Floyd
Patterson, Harris Laskaway, Lawrence Tierney, Terry
Ellis, Peter Deanello, Susan Lowden, Anna Berger,
Andrew MacMillan
A retired prizefighter has a visit from his granddaugh-
ter who needs to find some money, to pay off a debt her
good-for-nothing boyfriend owes the Mafia. Whilst
staying at his home she begins to write his life story
and they start to develop a touching relationship.
Cagney's last film and his only TV movie shows that
he could still pack a punch as an actor. Art Carney is
good too.
Aka: TERRIBLE JOE MORAN
DRA                                          96 min mTV
B,V,V2                                             CBS

## ONE BRIEF SUMMER *
John Mackenzie           UK                      1969
Clifford Evans, Jennifer Hilary, Peter Egan, Felicity
Gibson, Jan Holden, Richard Vernon, Brian Wilde,
Fanny Carby, Helen Lindsay, Basil Moss
A divorced financier grows tired of his girlfriend and
becomes attracted to, and eventually marries a young
girl who is a friend of his daughter. A dull melodrama
that is hardly improved by the slight hint of incest
present in the script. Written by Wendy Marshall.
Boa: play Valkyrie's Armour by Harry Tierney.
DRA                                          87 min
B,V                                                 PRV

## ONE BY ONE *                                  18
Bill Hinzman             USA                     1986
Kevin Kindlin, Terrie Godfrey, Colin Martin, Dana
Maiello, Bill Hinzman, John Russo, Mark Jevicky,
Sueanne Seamens, Russ Streiner
When a demented killer stalks and murders some
majorettes at a local high school, a town is gripped
with terror. An average, predictable shocker.
Aka: MAJORETTES, THE
THR                   87 min (ort 90 min) Cut (1 min 31 sec)
B,V                                         IVS; BRAVE

## ONE COOKS, THE OTHER DOESN'T **               PG
Richard Michaels         USA                     1983
Joseph Bologna, Rosanna Arquette, Suzanne
Pleshette, Oliver Clark. Evan Richards, Carl Franklin,
Robin Strand, Allyce Beasley, Gregg Berger, Tony
Craig, Jim Weston, Don Bovingloh, Paddi Edwards,
Shelby Leverington
A divorced real-estate agent finds himself unable to
meet his alimony payments to his ex-wife, and
eventually hits on the ingenious solution of allowing
her and his teenage son to come and live with him and
his young bride, to the eventual embarrassment of all
concerned. A slight one-joke comedy that soon ex-
hausts its potential.
COM                          92 min (ort 100 min) mTV
B,V                                                POLY

## ONE CRAZY SUMMER **                           PG
Savage Steve Holland     USA                     1986
John Cusack, Demi Moore, Curtis Armstrong, Joel
Murray, Tom Villard, Bobcat Goldthwait, William
Hickey, Joe Flaherty, Bruce Wagner, Kimberly Foster,
John Matuszak

A maladjusted teenager spends a summer in New England and gets involved in defending the land of a local family from greedy developers. A disappointing and episodic comedy that offers no more than a few sporadic laughs.

| | |
|---|---|
| COM | 90 min (ort 93 min) |
| V/h | WHV |

## ONE DARK NIGHT ** 18
Tom McLoughlin   USA   1983
*Meg Tilly, Robin Evans, Leslie Speights, Elizabeth Daily, Adam West, David Mason Daniels, Melissa Newman*
A dead man with psychic powers returns from the grave when two young college girls are forced by their sorority, to spend the night in the mausoleum where he is interred. He soon takes over their bodies, draining them of their bio-energy and bringing all the other corpses there back to shambling life. An unoriginal, derivative horror film.
Aka: ENTITY FORCE, THE (FILV); NIGHT OF DARKNESS (ARAMA, AVR or PAUSE)

| | |
|---|---|
| HOR | 87 min (PAUSE); 83 min (FILV); 90 min (AVR) (ort 94 min) |
| B,V | AVP L/A; AVR; FILV; ARAMA; PAUSE |

## ONE DEADLY SUMMER *** 18
Jean Becker   FRANCE   1983
*Isabelle Adjani, Alain Souchon, Francois Cluzet, Manuel Gelin, Jenny Cleve, Suzanne Flon, Michel Gaalbru, Maria Machado*
A sexy young woman comes to a village in France to exact a secret revenge, on the men who raped and assaulted her mother. Written by Sebastian Jarrisot from his novel, with the story seen (as in "Rashomon") through the eyes of several characters. Overlong but totally absorbing, and with Adjani giving one of her best performances.
Aka: L'ETE MEURTRIER
Boa: novel by Sebastian Jarrisot.

| | |
|---|---|
| DRA | 126 min (ort 133 min) Cut (5 sec) |
| B,V | GHV; MSD |

## ONE DOLLAR TOO MANY * PG
ITALY   1988
*John Saxon, Antonio Sabato, Frank Wolff*
Routine continental Western in which the three members of a gang persist in double-crossing each other in their search for $3000,000, the proceeds of a robbery. Eventually, they find themselves confronted by a common enemy.

| | |
|---|---|
| WES | 96 min |
| B,V | VPD |

## ONE DOWN, TWO TO GO **
Fred Williamson   USA   1982
*Fred Williamson, Jim Kelly, Jim Brown, Richard Roundtree*
A professional karate fight promoter takes on the Mob who are rigging fights, but the story merely serves to provide an excuse for the action. A typical Williamson product.

| | |
|---|---|
| MAR | 87 min |
| B,V | POLY |

## ONE FLEW OVER THE CUCKOO'S NEST **** 18
Milos Forman   USA   1975
*Jack Nicholson, Louise Fletcher, William Redfield, Brad Dourif, Michael Berryman, Danny DeVito, Scatman Crothers, Will Sampson, Peter Brocco*
A brilliant film version of a powerful book describing the claustrophobic world of an insane asylum, its inmates and staff. The first film since IT HAPPENED ONE NIGHT to win all five top Oscars and without doubt it deserved them. AA: Pic, Dir, Actor (Nicholson), S. Actress (Fletcher), Screen (Adapt) (Bo Goldman/Lawrence Hauben).
Boa: novel by Ken Kesey.

| | |
|---|---|
| DRA | 129 min (ort 134 min) |
| B,V | TEVP |

## ONE FROM THE HEART ** 15
Francis Ford Coppola   USA   1982
*Frederic Forrest, Teri Garr, Raul Julia, Nastassia Kinski, Lainie Kazan, Harry Dean Stanton, Luana Anders*
A married couple quarrel, seek out new partners and make-up again in this highly stylised but empty-headed romantic comedy, made at great expense with Las Vegas virtually re-created in the studio. Written by Coppola and Armyan Bernstein.

| | |
|---|---|
| COM | 103 min |
| B,V | CBS |

## ONE HUNDRED AND ONE DALMATIANS ****
Wolfgang Reitherman/Hamilton S. Luske/Clyde Geromini   USA   1961
*Voices of: Rod Taylor, Lisa Davis, Cate Bauer, Ben Wright, Fred Warlock, Tom Conway, J. Pat O'Malley, Betty Lou Gerson, Martha Wentworth, Barbara Beaird, Micky Maga, Queenie Leonard, Marjorie Bennett, Tudor Owen, Mimi Gibson*
A pair of Dalmatians produce a litter of no less than 101 puppies that the owners refuse to sell to an insistent woman, who is secretly planning to make a coat from their skins. She has them stolen and when human efforts to locate them fail, the dogs of London work against the clock to mount a rescue operation. One of Disney's best animated features that took three years and the work of three hundred artists to produce.
Boa: story The Hundred And One Dalmatians by Dodie Smith.

| | |
|---|---|
| CAR | 80 min |
| V | WDV |

## ONE IS A LONELY NUMBER ** 15
Mel Stuart   USA   1972
*Trish Van Devere, Monte Markham, Janet Leigh, Melvyn Douglas, Jane Elliott, Jonathan Lippe*
After splitting up with her husband, a young woman finds comfort in the arms of other men in this typically glib view of the problems of divorced people. An appealing performance from Van Devere sustains this thin little tale.
Boa: novel by Rebecca Morris.

| | |
|---|---|
| DRA | 93 min (ort 97 min) |
| B,V | MGM |

## ONE LITTLE INDIAN ** U
Bernard McEveety   USA   1973
*James Garner, Vera Miles, Clay O'Brien, Pat Hingle, Andrew Prine, Jodie Foster, Morgan Woodward, Jim Davis, John Doucette, Robert Pine, Rudy Diaz, Bruce Glover, Ken Swafford, Jay Silverheels, Walter Brooke, John Flynn*
An army deserter escapes through the desert together with two unlikely companions: an Indian boy and a camel. A rather thin Disney tale that fails to generate much interest or mirth. Written by Harry Spalding.

| | |
|---|---|
| COM | 91 min |
| B,V | WDV |

## ONE MAGIC CHRISTMAS ** U
Phillip Borsos   CANADA   1985
*Mary Steenburgen, Gary Basaraba, Harry Dean Stanton, Arthur Hill, Robbie Magwood, Élisabeth Harnois, Michelle Meyrink, Elias Koteas, Wayne Robson, Jan Rubes*
Seasonally sentimental tale with Santa restoring the flagging spirits of a long-suffering wife and mother, in a film showing Disney at its cutest and in chronic need of new ideas and a fresh approach to family entertainment.

| | |
|---|---|
| JUV | 88 min |
| B,V | WDV |

## ONE MILLION YEARS B.C. ** PG
Don Chaffey          UK          1966
*Raquel Welch, John Richardson, Percy Herbert,*
*Robert Brown, Martine Beswick, Jean Waldon, Lisa*
*Thomas, Malaya Nappi, William Lyon Brown*
Remake of a 1940 film with prehistoric tribes clashing
in a landscape filled with fantastic monsters. A little
laughable in parts with Richardson fleeing from his
tribe and meeting up with a bikini-clad Welch before
returning. Short on dialogue, grunts suffice. Ray
Harryhausen handles the monsters and the unusual
percussion score is by Mario Nascimbene.
A/AD                   96 min (ort 100 min)
B,V               TEVP; WHV (VHS only)

## ONE MONTH LATER ** 18
Nouchka Van Brake
          NETHERLANDS          1988
*Renee Soutendijk, Edwin De Vries, Monique Van De*
*Ven*
Two women decide to exchange places for a month.
One is the bored wife of a psychiatrist and the other a
journalist doing an article on marriage. A mildly
amusing effort.
COM                              95 min
V/sh                             WHV

## ONE NIGHT ONLY * 18
Timothy Bond          USA          1983
*Lenore Zann, Helene Udy, Tarorah Johnson, Jeff*
*Braunstein, Grant Alidnak*
A girl is offered $50,000 by a hockey team if she can
fulfil their coach's most secret sexual fantasy.
A                                86 min
B,V                              CBS

## ONE NIGHT STAND ** 15
Simon Wincer          AUSTRALIA          1984
*Cassandra Delaney, Saskia Post, Jay Hackett, Tyler*
*Coppin*
On the eve of WW3, a group of people amuse
themselves in a variety of ways in a deserted Sydney
Opera House. An uncomfortable mixture of comedy
and drama that attempts to make a few political
statements, but generally just succeeds in being
pretentious.
DRA                   90 min (ort 94 min)
B,V                              VES

## ONE OF OUR AIRCRAFT IS MISSING *** U
Michael Powell/Emeric Pressburger
          UK          1941
*Godfrey Tearle, Eric Portman, Hugh Williams, Hugh*
*Burden, Bernard Miles, Emrys Jones, Googie Withers,*
*Pamela Brown, Peter Ustinov, Joyce Redman, Hay*
*Petrie, Robert Helpmann, Alec Clunes, Roland Culver,*
*Stewart Rome*
A WW2 bomber crew is forced to bail out over Holland
and is helped back to Britain by the Resistance. A
competent and workmanlike propaganda effort that is
quite entertaining despite some slow-moving sequ-
ences. Written by Powell and Pressburger.
Boa: story by Emeric Pressburger.
WAR                   98 min (ort 106 min) B/W
B,V                          BBC; VCC

## ONE OF OUR DINOSAURS IS MISSING *
Robert Stevenson          UK/USA          1976
*Peter Ustinov, Derek Nimmo, Joan Sims, Helen Hayes,*
*Clive Revill, Bernard Bresslaw, Natasha Payne, Roy*
*Kinnear, Joss Ackland, Derek Guyler, Andrew Dove,*
*Max Harris, Richard Pearson, Jon Pertwee, Amanda*
*Barrie, John Laurie*
A roll of microfilm hidden inside a dinosaur skeleton
in the Natural History Museum provides the excuse
for this feeble family comedy, filmed in the UK and
written by Bill Walsh.
Boa: novel The Great Dinosaur Robbery by David
Forrest.

COM                   90 min (ort 101 min)
B,V                              WDV

## ONE ON ONE *** 15
Lamont Johnson          USA          1977
*Robby Benson, Annette O'Toole, G.D. Spradlin, Gail*
*Strickland, Melanie Griffith*
A new basketball player fresh from high school has to
re-adjust to the harsh, competitive atmosphere of
university sports. Director Johnson puts in an appear-
ance as Benson's big brother as well as co-writing the
script.
DRA                   94 min (ort 98 min)
B,V                              WHV

## ONE ON TOP OF THE OTHER **
Lucio Fulci          ITALY          1970
*Elsa Martinelli, Marisa Mell, Jean Sorel*
Two friends help a man wrongly convicted of murder-
ing his wife.
Aka: UNA HISTORIA PERVERSA; UNA
SULL'ALTRA
DRA                              99 min
B,V,V2                           VPD

## ONE POLICE PLAZA ** 15
Jerry Jameson          USA          1986
*Robert Conrad, George Dzundza, Jamey Sheridan,*
*Larry Riley, James Olsen, Anthony Zerbe, Lisa Banes,*
*Joe Grifasi, Earl Hindman, Janet-Laine Green, Peter*
*McNeil, Barton Heyman, Nicholas Hormann, David*
*Cryer, Alar Aedma*
A simple case of murder proves to be linked to a major
scandal involving the top echelons of the police force.
A police lieutenant is determined to investigate, even
at the cost of defying the orders and authority of his
superiors. Sound but hardly memorable, and filmed
mainly in Montreal despite the New York location.
Followed by THE RED SPIDER.
Boa: novel by William J. Caunitz.
THR          90 min (ort 100 min) Cut (10 sec) mTV
B,V                              CBS

## ONE SHOE MAKES IT MURDER **
William Hale          USA          1982
*Robert Mitchum, Mel Ferrer, Angie Dickinson, Jose*
*Perez, John Harkins, Howard Hesseman, Asher*
*Brauner, Bill Henderson, Cathee Shirriff, Bill*
*Schilling, Sandy Martin, Grainger Hines, Peter*
*Renaday*
A private eye investigates the disappearance of a
casino owner's wife and unearths the title clue in his
search for the truth. Mitchum makes his TV acting
debut in a far from memorable film. Written by Felix
Culver.
Boa: novel So Little Cause For Caroline by Eric
Bercovici.
DRA                   90 min (ort 100 min) mTV
B,V,LV                           POLY

## ONE SILVER DOLLAR **
Calvin Jackson Paget (Giorgio Ferroni)
          FRANCE/ITALY          1965
*Montgomery Wood (Guiliano Gemma), Evelyn Stewart*
*(Ida Galli), Peter Cross, John MacDouglas (Giuseppe*
*Aldobbati), Frank Farrel, Tor Altmayer, Max Dean,*
*Peter Surtess, Nicholas St John, Benny Farber, Frank*
*Liston, Andrew Scott*
After the defeat of the South in the Civil War two men
head West together. They are forced into a gunfight
and one kills the other, the survivor's life being saved
by a silver dollar which stops the bullet meant for
him. He now sets out to avenge himself on the gang
responsible in this violent, routine Western.
Aka: BLOOD FOR A SILVER DOLLAR; UN
DOLLAR TROUE; UN DOLLARO BUCATO
WES                   90 min (ort 95 min)
B,V,V2                           VPD

## ONE SUMMER LOVE **                    15
Gilbert Cates          USA          1976
*Beau Bridges, Susan Sarandon, Mildred Dunnock,*
*Ann Wedgeworth, Michael B. Miller, Linda Miller*
After being released from a mental home after many
years, a man goes in search of his estranged family
and enjoys a romantic entanglement with a woman
working at a cinema. A diverting little tale, written
by N. Richard Nash.
Aka: DRAGONFLY
DRA                          94 min (ort 97 min)
B,V                              RNK; ORION

## ONE THAT GOT AWAY, THE ***
Roy Baker              UK            1957
*Hardy Kruger, Colin Gordon, Michael Goodliffe,*
*Terence Alexander, Jack Gwillim, Andrew Faulds,*
*Julian Somers, Alec McCowen, John Van Eyssen,*
*Harry Lockhart, Robert Crewdson, George Mikell,*
*George Roubicek*
Well-produced true-life account of WW2 flier Franz
Von Werra, who was the only German POW ever to
escape from all the camps in which he was confined.
An entertaining and gripping film with a script by
Howard Clewes.
Boa: novel by Kendal Burt and James Leasor.
DRA                            111 min B/W
B,V                                RNK

## ONE TOUCH OF VENUS ***
William A. Seiter       USA           1948
*Robert Walker, Ava Gardner, Dick Haymes, Eve*
*Arden, Olga San Juan, Tom Conway*
A young man working as a store window-dresser falls
in love with a statue of Venus which comes to life.
Music is by Kurt Weill in an amusing romantic
comedy that still retains a considerable charm. See
also MANNEQUIN.
Boa: play by S.J. Perelman and Ogden Nash.
COM                             82 min B/W
B,V,V2                              INT

## ONE WAY OUT *                        18
Paul Kyriazi           USA           1980
*Ivan Rogers, Sandy Brook, Rick Sutherlin, Doug Irk,*
*Mike Rizk, Norman Matthews*
A black cop seeks revenge on the drugs ring that
killed his wife, and becomes involved with a special
police task force that unearths a web of corruption and
vengeance.
A/AD                          83 min Cut (27 sec)
B,V                              PACEV; VIP

## ONE WOMAN'S LOVER *                  18
Sergio Buzzani        ITALY
*Joe Dallesandro, Andrea Ferreol*
A student is distracted from his studies by some
willing women.
A                                  73 min
V                          18PLAT/TOW; TOW; PRI

## ONE-ARMED BOXER **
Wang Yu          HONG KONG           1972
*Wang Yu, Tang Shin, Tien Yeh*
A student loses an arm in a fight, and learns a style of
one-armed combat in order to exact his revenge.
Followed by a sequel.
Aka: DOP BEY KUAN WAN
MAR                                76 min
B,V                                RNK

## ONE-EYED SOLDIERS, THE *
Jean Christophe
              UK/USA/YUGOSLAVIA      1966
*Dale Robertson, Luciana Paluzzi, Andrew Faulds, Guy*
*Deghy, Mila Auramovic*
A dying man's last words give a clue to the location of
a large sum of money that soon attracts a horde of
fortune-seekers. One of those international co-

productions that never achieves even a mediocre level
of entertainment and is best forgotten.
THR                                80 min
B,V                                DFS

## ONE-HUNDRED RIFLES ***              15
Tom Gries              USA           1969
*Jim Brown, Burt Reynolds, Raquel Welch, Fernando*
*Lamas, Dan O'Herlihy, Michael Forest, Soledad*
*Miranda, Alberto Dalbes, Jose Manuel Martin, Hans*
*Gudegast, Aldo Sambrell, Carlos Bravo*
A deputy chases a consignment of stolen rifles into
Mexico, where he falls in love with a woman revolu-
tionary desperate to prevent an Indian massacre. A
tough action film with plenty of blood-letting.
Aka: 100 RIFLES
Boa: novel The Californio by Robert MacLeod.
WES                          110 min Cut (4 sec)
B,V                                CBS

## ONE-MAN JURY *
Charles Martin         USA           1978
*Jack Palance, Christopher Mitchum, Angel Tompkins,*
*Pamela Shoop, Joe Spinell, Cara Williams*
A cop takes the law into his own hands by dispensing
brutal justice to criminals. Very much inspired by
DIRTY HARRY and other films of that ilk.
THR                                104 min
B,V                                INT

## ONE, TWO, THREE ****                 U
Billy Wilder           USA           1961
*James Cagney, Arlene Francis, Horst Buchholz,*
*Pamela Tiffin, Lilo Pulver, Howard St John, Leon*
*Askin, Red Buttons*
This deliciously wicked Cold War satire never stops
for breath, as it tells the story of a Coca-Cola executive
posted to West Berlin, who is more than a little
outraged at his daughter's involvement with a Com-
munist. The gags come fast and furious and Cagney's
performance is a joy to watch. This was his last screen
role until RAGTIME in 1981. Written by Wilder and
I.A.L. Diamond and very, very loosely based on
Molnar's one-act play.
Boa: play by Ferenc Molnar.
COM                             115 min B/W
V                                  WHV

## ONIBABA ***
Kaneto Shindo         JAPAN          1964
*Nobuko Otowa, Jitsuko Yoshimura, Kei Sato*
In medieval Japan a woman and her daughter-in-law
live by killing samurai and selling their armour.
However, the girl eventually takes one as a lover and
her mother-in-law becomes jealous. This slow and
brooding folk-tale has moments of eerie horror and
good locations, but is hampered by excessive sen-
timentality. The script is by Shindo.
Aka: HOLE, THE
DRA                            105 min B/W
B,V                             PVG; INT;

## ONION FIELD, THE ***               18
Harold Becker          USA           1979
*James Woods, Franklyn Seales, John Savage, Ted*
*Danson, Ronny Cox, Dianne Hull, David Huffman,*
*Christopher Lloyd*
Factually based account of two cops held hostage by
two thugs. One is murdered but his killers escape
justice, through legal technicalities and clever manipulation of the judicial system. The surviving policeman has to face accusations of cowardice that result in
a breakdown and his resignation from the force. A film
with a fine script by Joseph Wambaugh that asks
some uncomfortable questions about the nature of
justice.
Boa: novel by Joseph Wambaugh.
DRA                          121 min (ort 126 min)
B,V          EHE; CH5 (VHS only); POLY (VHS only)

## ONLY ONE WINNER **

Robert Dai          USA          1983
*Richard Chamberlain, Rod Steiger, Michael Gross,
Diane Venora, Samm-Art Williams, Louis Negin,
Mark Welker, Barry Blake, Bronwen Mantel, Tara
O'Donnel, Daniel Nalbach, Philip Spensley, Antony
Parr, Don Robinson*
A rather slow-paced account of the race to reach the
North Pole, between the two famous explorers Cook
and Peary, that suggests this work would have been
more effective as a documentary.
Aka: COOK AND PEARY: THE RACE TO THE
POLE; RACE TO THE POLE, THE
DRA                              100 min mTV
B,V                              CBS

## ONLY THE VALIANT **                          PG

Gordon Douglas          USA          1950
*Gregory Peck, Barbara Payton, Ward Bond, Gig
Young, Lon Chaney, Warner Anderson, Jeff Corey,
Steve Brodie, Neville Brand, Terry Kilburn, Herbert
Heyes, Art Baker, Hugh Sanders, Michael Ansara,
Nana Bryant, Harvey Udell*
Following a disastrous skirmish with Indians, a
disciplinarian cavalry officer finds that he has lost the
respect of his men. When he leads a detachment
through hostile territory, he has to work hard to
regain their respect, eventually proving his courage
by holding off rampaging Apaches. A competent
action Western, technically well made but not all that
interesting.
WES                              105 min (ort 107 min) B/W
V                                VIR

## ONLY TWO CAN PLAY **                          PG

Sidney Gilliat          UK          1962
*Peter Sellers, Mai Zetterling, Virginia Maskell,
Richard Attenborough, Raymond Huntley, Kenneth
Griffith, John Le Mesurier, Maudie Edwards, John
Arnatt, David Davies, Meredith Edwards, Frederick
Piper, E. Eynon Evans*
A married Welsh librarian attempts to have a pas-
sionate affair with the Norwegian-born wife of a local
councillor, but is prevented at every turn from
consummating their relationship. A dated and bitter-
sweet comedy that is only occasionally funny. Music is
by Richard Rodney Bennett and the script by Bryan
Forbes.
Boa: novel That Uncertain Feeling by Kingsley Amis.
COM                              101 min (ort 106 min) B/W
B,V                              TEVP; WHV

## ONLY WAY, THE *

Bengt Christensen
          DENMARK/PANAMA/USA          1970
*Jane Seymour, Martin Potter, Ebbe Rude, Ove Sprogoe*
A Jewish ballerina escapes with her family from
Denmark in order to avoid deportation by the SS, in
this dull account of how the Danes courageously saved
nearly all the country's Jews in 1943.
Aka: OKTOBER-DAGE
DRA                              86 min
B,V                              VUL L/A; VDB

## ONLY WAY TO SPY, THE *                          18

Michael Ullman
*Mike Paris, Pamela Palm, Rusty Blitz, Andrea Adler,
Barrett Cooper, Jinaki Milele, Richard M. Fisher*
A missile nose-cone goes astray and is avidly sought
by the customary bunch of international spies usually
found in espionage spoofs of this kind.
COM                              108 min, 85 min (AVR)
B,V,V2                           VPD L/A; AVR; MKR

## ONLY WHEN I LAUGH **                          15

Glenn Jordan          USA          1981
*Marsha Mason, Kristy McNichol, James Coco, Joan
Hackett, David Dukes, John Bennett Perry*
This film version of a failed Neil Simon play (he also
wrote the script) focuses on an alcoholic actress, who is
trying to break the habit and get her life back in
shape, and mend her troubled relationship with her
teenage daughter. Moderately entertaining, but the
manipulative script is a serious handicap.
Aka: IT ONLY HURTS WHEN I LAUGH
Boa: play The Gingerbread Lady by Neil Simon.
COM                              120 min
B,V                              RCA

## OOH, YOU ARE AWFUL **                          PG

Cliff Owen          UK          1972
*Dick Emery, Derren Nesbitt, Ronald Fraser, Pat
Coombs, William Franklyn, Cheryl Kennedy, Norman
Bird, Roland Curram, Liza Goddard, Ambrosine
Philpotts, Brian Oulton, Steve Plytas, Louis Negin,
Neil Wilson*
Comedy vehicle for the popular TV comedian Emery.
Here he gets a chance to try out many disguises in the
role of a con-man, searching for a Swiss bank account
number tattoed on the backsides of four girls. Fortu-
nately, his hilarious impersonations save a film that is
woefully inadequate in the plot department.
Aka: GET CHARLIE TULLY; OOH . . . YOU ARE
AWFUL
COM          93 min (ort 97 min) (Cut at film release)
B,V                              TEVP; WHV

## OPEN ALL HOURS **                          PG

Sydney Lotterby          UK          1984
*Ronnie Barker, David Jannsen, Lynda Baron*
Spin-off from a successful TV series about a randy
Northern grocer and his attempts to bed the local
district nurse. Strictly so-so despite the considerable
comic talents of Barker and Jannsen.
COM                              90 min mTV
V/h                              BBC

## OPEN HOUSE **                          18

Jag Mundhra          USA          1987
*Joseph Bottoms, Rudy Ramos, Adrienne Barbeau,
Mary Stavin, Scott Thompson Baker*
A psychologist working on a radio talk show, studies a
baffling series of murders where the victims are all
real estate agents and their clients.
HOR                              91 min Cut (1 min 18 sec)
B,V                              HER L/A; BRAVE

## OPERATION AMSTERDAM ***                          PG

Michael McCarthy          UK          1958
*Peter Finch, Tony Brittan, Eva Bartok, Alexander
Knox, Malcolm Keen, Tim Turner, Christopher
Rhodes, John Horsley, Keith Pyott, Melvyn Hayes,
Oscar Quitak, John Bailey, John Richardson*
Semi-documentary account of a mission to smuggle
out a consignment of industrial diamonds from Am-
sterdam in 1940. Well acted with good locations and
nice taut direction.
Boa: novel Adventure In Diamonds by David Walker.
WAR                              98 min (ort 104 min) B/W
B,V                              RNK; STRAND

## OPERATION BIG TEN *                          18

John Sun          HONG KONG
*Shirley Lee, Patrick Chase, Irene Bail, Jean East,
Ramon Kobe, Dennis Ho, Susan Leigh*
A mission is mounted to rescue girls being held in
captivity in Asian camps.
A/AD                              80 min
B,V                              DIAM

## OPERATION BRAINDRAIN **                          PG

Philip Leacock          USA          1971
*Doug McClure, Chuck Connors, Richard Basehart,
Rene Auberjonois, Max Baer Jr, Don Knight, Tom
Skerrit, Greg Mullavey, Barry Brown, Paul Koslo,
Genadii Biegouloff, Rolf Niehus, Peter Hellman, Karl
Swenson, Karl Bruck*
A group of Allied POWs plot their escape from

imprisonment in a fortress perched on a steep mountain peak, by building a glider and flying to nearby Switzerland. With them they plan to bring a Norwegian scientist whose knowledge is invaluable to the war effort. A standard WW2 adventure.
Aka: BIRDMEN, THE; ESCAPE OF THE BIRDMEN
WAR                                    90 min mTV
B,V                                         SCAN

**OPERATION COUNTERSPY ***                 15
Nick Nostro   FRANCE/ITALY/SPAIN          1965
*George Ardisson, Leontine May, Joaquin Diaz*
A routine Bond rip-off, in which the hero has to find six pictures in the possession of the Russians and decipher the code they contain.
Aka: AS DE PIL (OPERACION CONTRAESPIONAJE); ASSO DI PICCHE OPERAZIONE CONTROSPIONAGGIO
THR                                       100 min
B,V                                          PRV

**OPERATION CROSS EAGLES ****
Richard Conte   USA/YUGOSLAVIA            1969
*Richard Conte, Rory Calhoun, Aili King, Phil Brown*
A secret mission is planned to secure the release of a captured American officer, in Yugoslavia during WW2, by mounting a commando raid to snatch a suitable German hostage for whom he can be exchanged. Fair but unmemorable.
WAR                                        90 min
B,V                                          MMA

**OPERATION CROSSBOW *****                  PG
Michael Anderson   UK                     1965
*George Peppard, John Mills, Sophia Loren, Trevor Howard, Tom Courtenay, Anthony Quayle, Lilli Palmer, Richard Johnson, Jeremy Kemp, Paul Henreid, Helmut Dantine, Richard Todd, Sylvia Syms, John Fraser, Barbara Rueting*
Trained scientists parachute behind the lines during WW2 to destroy a secret Nazi missile base, and their mission ends successfully with its total destruction. A routine war epic with music by Ron Goodwin and a script by Robert Imrie (Emeric Pressburger), Derry Quinn and Ray Rigby.
Aka: GREAT SPY MISSION, THE
WAR                        112 min (ort 116 min)
B,V                                          MGM

**OPERATION DAYBREAK ****                    15
Lewis Gilbert   USA                       1975
*Timothy Bottoms, Martin Shaw, Joss Ackland, Nicola Pagett, Anthony Andrews, Anton Diffring*
A re-enactment of how Czech patriots killed the hated Reinhard "Hangman" Heidrich, the Nazi "Protector" of Czechoslovakia, and were then hunted down and murdered by the Nazis, who also razed the village of Lidice to the ground as a further reprisal, and deported or killed all its inhabitants. Competently made but somewhat lacking in impact.
Aka: PRICE OF FREEDOM
Boa: novel Seven Men At Daybreak by Alan Burgess.
WAR                                       119 min
B,V                                          WHV

**OPERATION GANYMED ****
Rainer Erler   WEST GERMANY               1977
*Horst Frank, Dieter Laser, Uwe Friedrichsen, Juergen Prochnoww (Jurgen Prochnow), Claus Theo Gaestner, Vicky Roskilly, Wolf Mittler*
A UN-sponsored mission to Ganymede is lost, but against all the odds a single spaceship returns and lands in the Mexican desert. The five surviving crew members are ill-equipped for the rigours of the desert and, driven mad with thirst, murder each other, with but a single survivor remaining. A tense and unusual film.
Aka: OPERATION GANYMEDE

FAN                                       120 min
B,V                                          AVP

**OPERATION INCHON ***
Terence Young   KOREA/USA                 1981
*Laurence Olivier, Jacqueline Bisset, Ben Gazarra, Toshiro Mifune, Richard Roundtree, David Janssen, Gabriele Ferzetti, Rex Reed*
The landing of United Nations forces at Inchon during the Korean War is here restaged at vast cost, and was allegedly bankrolled courtesy of the Moonies sect. It cost a total of $48,000,000 to make and has to date grossed only $650,000. A badly scripted and badly cast mess.
Aka: INCHON
WAR                        90 min (ort 140 min)
B,V                             SVC L/A; MARKET

**OPERATION PACIFIC ****                     PG
Keith Larson   USA                        1969
*Dennis Weaver, Vera Miles, Keith Larson, Helen Thompson, Vic Diaz*
A pilot who only wants to make his fortune out of WW2 by evacuating people for money, gets caught up in an Allied operation to keep a hoard of gold out of the hands of the Japanese and inadvertently becomes a hero. Average.
Aka: MISSION BATANGAS
WAR                   100 min; 96 min (TURBO)
B,V                                  IVS; TURBO

**OPERATION PARATROOPER ***                  18
Frank De Palma   USA                      1988
*Martin Hewitt, Joe Dallesandro, Kimberly Beck, Reggie Johnston, George Shannon, B.J. Turner*
An experienced training sergeant is still haunted by memories of an incident in Vietnam, when he escaped from the Vietcong but left his buddy behind to die. He finally loses his sanity and his dangerous training methods (including the use of live ammunition) degenerate into a brutal conflict and a final clash with the son of the man whose death he caused. A corny amalgam of just about every Vietnam-veteran-on-the-loose cliche going.
A/AD                                       90 min
V                                            MED

**OPERATION PETTICOAT *****                   U
Blake Edwards   USA                       1959
*Cary Grant, Tony Curtis, Joan O'Brien, Dina Merrill, Gene Evans, Arthur O'Connell, Virginia Gregg, Gavin McLeod, Marion Ross*
A crippled submarine has a captain who is determined to make his craft seaworthy again by fair means or foul. Grant and Curtis work together well in an enjoyable, lighthearted comedy. Remade as a TV movie in 1977 that served in its turn as a pilot for a brief TV series.
COM                       115 min (ort 124 min)
V                                            VCC

**OPERATION THUNDERBOLT *****
Menahem Golan   ISRAEL                     1977
*Klaus Kinski, Assaf Dayan, Yehoram Gaon, Shai K. Ophir, Ori Levy, Sybil Danning (Sybelle Danninger), Mark Heath*
An account of the Entebbe raid when a group of hostages were rescued from Uganda by Israeli commandos, after being abducted by terrorists operating with the connivance of Idi Amin. Generally acknowledged to be the most realistic and authoritative of the three films dealing with this operation, as the other two, RAID ON ENTEBBE and VICTORY AT ENTEBBE, were rushed out quickly by US TV.
Aka: ENTEBBE: OPERATION THUNDERBOLT
THR                        119 min (ort 125 min)
B,V                                          RNK

## OPERATION: WAR ZONE *
David A. Prior    USA        18
1988
*Joe Spinell*
A low-budget Vietnam tale telling of a group of GIs who find themselves caught behind enemy lines and break out, rescuing some captured soldiers in the process. A formula effort that is without doubt one of the most inept and clumsy films of this genre.
A/AD      82 min
B,V      BRAVE

## OPPONENT, THE **
Sergio Martino    ITALY    18
1987
*Daniel Greene, Guiliano Gemma, Mary Stavin, Ernest Borgnine*
A young amateur boxer dreams of a chance at turning professional, but is unable to find a backer until by chance he saves a woman from three attackers and finds that her boyfriend is a top promoter. He becomes a successful fighter but finds there is a heavy price to pay, as various conflicts mar his relationship with both his promoter and his father. A competent ROCKY clone.
Aka: BLOODFIGHT
DRA    85 min (ort 90 min) Cut (2 sec)
B,V    VES

## OPTIMISTS OF NINE ELMS, THE **
Anthony Simmons    UK    PG
1973
*Peter Sellers, Donna Mullane, John Chaffey, David Daker, Marjorie Yates, Patricia Brake, Don Crown, Michael Graham Cox, Bruce Purchase, Tommy Wright, Jane Brandl*
London slum kids strike up a friendship with a busker down on his luck. A quiet and sentimental piece that offers passable entertainment. Written by Simmons and Tudor Gates.
Aka: OPTIMISTS, THE
Boa: novel by Anthony Simmons.
COM    110 min
B,V,V2    HVM; PARK (VHS only)

## OPTIONS **
Camilo Vila    USA    PG
1988
*Matt Salinger, Joanna Pacula, John Kani, Susan Anton, James Keach, Eric Roberts*
A Hollywood agent goes to Africa, and fights his way through the jungle to contact a princess and buy her life story, only to be turned down flat when she rejects any idea of a deal. A second chance, however, seems to be on the cards when she is kidnapped, and he proves to be the only one who can rescue her.
COM    89 min (ort 105 min)
V    VES

## ORACLE, THE **
Roberta Findlay    USA    18
1984
*Victoria Dryden, Caroline Capers Powers, Roger Neil, Pam Latesta, Stefanie Powers, Chris Maria DeKoron, Dan Lutzky, Stacey Graves, G. Gordon Cronce, Ethel Mark, Alexandria Blade, John Leonard, Irma Saint Paule*
A girl plays with a ouija board and becomes possessed by the spirit of a man who was murdered by his wife.
HOR    93 min Cut (1 min 13 sec)
B,V    IVS; CDC (VHS only); BRAVE

## ORCA: KILLER WHALE **
Michael Anderson    USA    PG
1977
*Richard Harris, Charlotte Rampling, Bo Derek, Will Sampson, Keenan Wynn, Robert Carradine, Peter Hooten, Don Barry, Scott Walker, Wayne Heffley, Vincent Gentile*
A whale takes revenge for the accidental killing of its mate by a deep-sea fisherman off Newfoundland. Not a film for the squeamish (Derek in her screen debut has her leg bitten off) but enlivened by music composed by Ennio Morricone. Unfortunately, the poor script is a major drawback.
Aka: ORCA; ORCA, THE KILLER WHALE
Boa: novel by Arthur Herzog.
A/AD    88 min (ort 92 min)
B,V,V2    TEVP

## ORDEAL BY INNOCENCE *
Desmond Davis    UK    15
1985
*Donald Sutherland, Christopher Plummer, Faye Dunaway, Sarah Miles, Ian McShane, Diana Quick, Annette Crosbie, Michael Elphick, Phoebe Nicholls, George Innes, Valerie Whittington, Michael Maloney, Cassie Stuart*
A paleontologist investigates the case of an innocent man hung for murder in this rather routine detective yarn, that is markedly lacking in excitement or logic. The score is by Dave Brubeck.
Aka: AGATHA CHRISTIE'S ORDEAL BY INNOCENCE
Boa: novel by Agatha Christie.
THR    86 min (ort 90 min)
B,V    MGM

## ORDEAL OF BILL CARNEY, THE **
Jerry London    USA    1981
*Ray Sharkey, Richard Crenna, Betty Buckley, Ana Alicia, Jeremy Licht, Martin Milner, Vincent Baggetta, C.J. Hicks, David Faustino, Lynnette Mettey, Tony Dow, Douglas Dirkson, Allan Rich, Robert Prosky, Lara Staley, Noam Pitlik*
A disabled man fights in the courts for the custody of his two small sons, in this tale of a celebrated case that proved to be a legal landmark. Fair.
DRA    90 min (ort 104 min) mTV
B,V    VUL L/A; KRP

## ORDEAL OF DOCTOR MUDD, THE ***
Paul Wendkos    USA    1980
*Dennis Weaver, Susan Sullivan, Nigel Davenport, Richard Dysart, Michael McGuire, Arthur Hill, Mary Nell Santacroce, Larry Larson, Teddy Milford, Angela Tully, Ryan Grady, Panos Eli Karatassos, Ben Gribble, Luke Halpin*
A well-acted account of the true story of Dr Mudd sentenced unjustly to a term of life imprisonment, for unwittingly treating James Wilkes Booth just after Lincoln's assassination, mainly since the authorities believed (without any real evidence) that he was somehow involved in planning this deed. The same material has been filmed twice before as "Prisoner Of Shark Island" and "Hellgate".
DRA    136 min (ort 143 min) mTV
B,V    PRV

## ORDEAL OF PATTY HEARST, THE **
Paul Wendkos    USA    1979
*Dennis Weaver, Lisa Eilbacher, Stephen Elliott, David Haskell, Dolores Sutton, Felton Perry, Tisa Farrow, Jonathan Banks, Anne DeSalvo, Kathryn Butterfield, Karen Landry, Nancy Wolfe, Brendan Burns, Roy Poole*
Patty Hearst's kidnapping by the Symbionese Liberation Front is related here by one of the FBI agents assigned to the case. Not a terribly impressive dramatisation of material that was later to form the basis of the 1988 film PATTY HEARST: HER OWN STORY.
DRA    138 min (ort 156 min) mTV
B,V    VFP

## ORDEAL, THE **
Julian Pringle    USA    1981
*George Lazenby, Diane Craig, Joan Bruie*
An ex-cop decides to get the head of an extortion ring after his friend commits suicide.
A/AD    90 min
B,V    INT

## ORDER OF DEATH ***
Roberto Faenza    ITALY    18
1983
*Harvey Keitel, Nicole Garcia, Leonard Mann, John Lydon, Sylvia Sidney*

A policeman in New York is drawn into the hunt for a cop killer and becomes involved with a strange man who begins to victimise him. An absorbing, psychological thriller with a complex, unusual plot. Lydon was formerly in the punk rock group The Sex Pistols where he was known as Johnny Rotten.
Aka: COP KILLERS; CORRUPT
THR                    100 min; 97 min (VIR) (ort 113 min)
B,V                                    PVG; VIR

## ORDER OF THE BLACK EAGLE *                    18
Worth Keeter          USA          1987
*Ian Hunter, Charles K. Bibby, William T. Hicks, Jill Donnellan, Anna Rappagna, Flo Hyman, Stephan Krayn*
When a brilliant scientist is kidnapped by a bunch of neo-Nazis who want him to perfect a proton beam weapon, a secret agent and his assistant are sent on a rescue mission to South America. There they discover a sinister plot to use the body of Hitler (being kept in suspended animation) to usher in a new Nazi era. A film as ludicrous as it is incoherent.
A/AD                    89 min (ort 93 min) Cut (13 sec)
B,V                                    CBS

## ORDER OF THE EAGLE *                    15
Tom Baldwin          USA          1988
*Frank Stallone*
Tedious little actioner with a corrupt corporation involved in some nasty deals in order to win a major defence contract. When a scientist disappears with some vital computer discs Stallone and his chums go after the man, whose crashed plane has been found by a boy scout. All ends in bloodshed and mayhem with our scout fortunately rescued in the nick of time from some rather disagreeable heavies.
A/AD                    91 min
B,V                                    BRAVE

## ORDERS ARE ORDERS **                    U
David Paltenghi          UK          1954
*Peter Sellers, Tony Hancock, Sid James, Brian Reece, Margot Grahame, Raymond Huntley, Maureen Johnson, June Thorburn, Bill Fraser, Donald Pleasence, Peter Martyn, Edward Lexy, Eric Sykes, Barry Mackay, Clive Morton*
An American film unit totally disrupts life at an army barracks when they are given permission to film there. Remake of an earlier film from 1933 and of little interest except to film historians.
Boa: play by Ian Hay and Anthony Armstrong.
COM                    78 min B/W
B,V                                    VMA; STABL; DER

## ORDINARY HEROES **                    15
Peter H. Cooper          USA          1985
*Valerie Bertinelli, Richard Dean Anderson, Doris Roberts, Jesse D. Goins, Matthew Laurence, Richard Baxter, Liz Torres*
A Vietnam conscript, blinded towards the end of his tour of duty when he rescues a friend, encounters the normal re-adjustment problems upon his return to civilian life. A familiar drama on a familiar theme.
Aka: ORDINARY GUY, AN
Boa: novel Pride Of The Marines by Albert Maltz.
DRA                    87 min (ort 105 min)
B,V                                    VES

## ORDINARY PEOPLE ****                    15
Robert Redford          USA          1980
*Donald Sutherland, Mary Tyler Moore, Judd Hirsch, Timothy Hutton, M. Emmet Walsh, Elizabeth McGovern, James B. Sikking*
Redford's directorial debut (for which he won an Oscar) is an impressive drama about the hidden tensions and failings behind the facade of an ordinary "happy" family. Music is by Marvin Hamlisch. AA: Pic, Dir, S. Actor (Hutton), Screen (Adapt) (Alvin Sargent).

Boa: novel by Judith Guest.
DRA                    119 min (ort 124 min)
B,V                                    CIC

## ORIENTAL BLUE **
Philip T. Drexler          USA          1975
*Peonie Jung, Jamie Gillis, Bree Anthony, C.J. Laing, Bobby Astyr, Allan Mario, Kim Pope, Steven Lark*
Madame Blue works in New York's Chinatown, arranging to have girls of all nationalities kidnapped and sent to work in brothels around the world. She holds them prisoner until she has overcome their inhibitions by forcing them to drink a potent aphrodisiac. When her procurer refuses to hand over a new girl, Madame has her kidnapped. The film ends with both Madame and procurer killing each other. A competent sex film with rather good cinematography.
A                    61 min (ort 84 min) Cut
B,V                                    PRV

## ORIGINAL SIN **                    15
Ron Satlof          USA          1988
*Ann Jillian, Robert Desiderio, Charlton Heston, Louis Guss, Lou Liberatore*
When his 4-year-old son is kidnapped, a man suspects that this may be the work of his estranged father, a Mafia chieftain, a fact he has kept secret from his wife. Average.
THR                    94 min (ort 100 min) mTV
V/h                                    NWV

## ORION'S BELT ***                    15
Ola Solum          NORWAY          1985
*Helge Jordal, Hans Ola Sorlie, Sverre Anker Ousdal, Kjersti Holmen, Vidar Sandem, Nils Johnson, Jon Eikemo, Johan Sverre, Jan Harstad, Holger Vistisen, Erik Oksnes, Bjorg Telsted, John Ousland, Jarl E. Goli, Tor Stokke*
A gripping thriller about three men who stumble across secret Soviet listening station, and flee in panic after an exchange of fire in which one of them is wounded. The sole survivor of this encounter finally manages to return home, where the authorities are less than enthusiastic about his story, and both sides prove ultimately to be equally cynical and ruthless, in the defence of what they see as vital national security interests.
Aka: ORION'S BELTE
Boa: novel by Jon Michelet.
THR                    93 min (ort 103 min)
B,V                                    EHE

## ORPHANS ***                    15
Alan J. Pakula          USA          1987
*Albert Finney, Matthew Modine, Kevin Anderson, John Kellog, Anthony Heald, Novella Nelson, Elizabeth Parrish, B. Constance, Frank Ferrara, Clifford Fearl*
A gangster is "kidnapped" by two streetwise orphans and ends up a reformed character as he soon assumes the role of a surrogate father. The performances in this one make the most of the thin plot. Scripted by Kessler.
Boa: play by Lyle Kessler.
DRA                    111 min (ort 120 min)
B,V                                    GHV

## ORPHEE ****                    PG
Jean Cocteau          FRANCE          1949
*Jean Marais, Maria Casares, Francois Perier, Marie Dea, Edouard Dermithe, Juliette Greco, Roger Blin*
An updating of the famous legend with Orpheus a poet who meets and becomes obsessed with the Princess of Death. Encouraged by this, she carries off his wife, but Orpheus retrieves her and the unhappy princess sacrifices herself so as not to blight their mortal happiness. A display of cinematic tricks makes the film's evocation of the underworld as memorable as it

is unique. The haunting score is by Georges Auric.
Remade by Jacques Demy as "Parking".
Aka: ORPHEUS
Boa: play by Jean Cocteau.
FAN                      90 min (ort 112 min) B/W
V                                            CONNO

**OSS \***                                        PG
Walter Grauman        USA              1970
*Stuart Whitman, Joan Collins, Pikas Braun, Martin*
*Jarvis, Gunther Neutze, Margit Saad, Johnny Briggs,*
*Patrick Jordan, David Taylor, Richard Abbot*
An OSS operative is given the dangerous job of
smuggling a German scientist out of Germany to-
wards the end of WW2 ahead of the advancing
Russians. A dull and predictable war film.
Aka: LAST ESCAPE, THE
WAR                                        90 min
B,V                                          SCAN

**OSSESSIONE \*\*\***                             PG
Luchino Visconti      ITALY            1942
*Clara Calamai, Massimo Girotti, Juan de Landa, Elio*
*Marcuzzo*
A handsome drifter falls for the unhappy wife of an
elderly innkeeper and the two conspire to murder him,
after which their relationship proceeds to its inevitable conclusion. This unofficial adaptation of Cain's
novel (later to be filmed in Hollywood in 1945 and
1981) marked the start of the Italian neo-realist
period, but difficulties over the rights to the novel kept
the film out of the USA until 1975. Visconti's debut is
clinical but effective.
Boa: novel The Postman Always Rings Twice by
James M. Cain.
DRA                  140 min (ort 135 min) B/W
V                                            CONNO

**OSTERMAN WEEKEND, THE \*\***              18
Sam Peckinpah         USA              1983
*Rutger Hauer, John Hurt, Burt Lancaster, Craig T.*
*Nelson, Dennis Hopper, Chris Sarandon, Meg Foster,*
*Helen Shaver, Cassie Yates, Sandy McPeak, Cheryl*
*Carter, Christopher Starr, John Bryson, Anne Haney*
The host of a TV show is persuaded by the CIA to help
expose some of his friends who somehow just happen
to be Soviet agents. The director's last film is one of
those confused espionage thrillers where nobody
seems to have a clue as to what is happening most of
the time. Scripted by Alan Sharp and Ian Masters.
Boa: novel by Robert Ludlum.
THR                   102 min; 98 min (WHV)
B,V,V2                      TEVP; WHV (VHS only)

**OTHELLO \*\***                                   U
Trevor Nunn           UK               1989
*Willard White, Ian McKellen, Imogen Stubbs, Zoe*
*Wanamaker, Sean Baker, Michael Grandage, Clive*
*Swift, Marsha Hunt, Phillip Sully, John Burgess*
The Royal Shakespeare Company bring their talents
to bear in this unusual adaptation that's set at the
time of the American Civil War.
Boa: play by William Shakespeare.
DRA                                       204 min
V                                            PICK

**OTHELLO: PARTS 1 AND 2 \*\*\***               U
Jonathan Miller       UK               1981
*Anthony Hopkins, Bob Hoskins, Penelope Wilton,*
*Rosemary Leach, Anthony Pedley, Geoffrey Chater,*
*Alexander Davion, David Yelland, Joseph O'Conor,*
*Peter Walmsley, John Barron, Seymour Green,*
*Howard Goorney*
An excellent television adaptation, marked by good
casting and sets, and without doubt one of the better
Shakespeare renditions in this somewhat uneven
series.
Boa: play by William Shakespeare.

DRA                     207 min (2 cassettes) mTV
V/h                                          BBC

**OTHER CINDERELLA, THE \***
Stanley Long/Michael Pataki
                      USA               1977
*Cheryl Smith, Kirk Scott, Brett Smiley, Yana Nirvana,*
*Marilyn Corwin, Sy Richardson*
A softcore musical version of this tale with our
heroine being endowed by her fairy godmother with
superb abilities in the lovemaking department. The
prince has never climaxed and in this story he spends
most of the ball blindfolded in bed, searching among
numerous commoners for the woman who can cure
him. A film of very few ideas.
Aka: CINDERELLA
A                                          83 min
B,V                                          INT

**OTHER LOVE, THE \*\***
Andre De Toth         USA              1947
*Barbara Stanwyck, David Niven, Richard Conte,*
*Maria Palmer, Joan Lorring, Gilbert Roland, Richard*
*Hale, Lenore Aubert*
A woman suffering from a terminal illness decides to
enliven her last days by indulging in a fling with a
gambler, much to the chagrin of the doctor who is
madly in love with her. Hardly the stuff of realism but
quite diverting.
Boa: novel by Erich Maria Remarque.
DRA                                     96 min B/W
V                                            INT

**OTHER SIDE OF JULIE, THE \*\*\***
Anthony Riverton      USA              1978
*John Leslie, Suzannah French, Gloria Roberts,*
*Richard Logan, Joey Maseia, Jackie O'Neil, Paula*
*Donnelly*
A man runs a brothel that supplies women to half the
male population of San Francisco. Worn out from his
daily sexual encounters, he is unable to make love to
his unsuspecting wife. She eventually does discover
how he makes his living and takes over the organisation herself. Quite an entertaining film, this opens
with a spectacular car crash in which the man's two
partners are killed, thus leaving him to run the
organisation single-handed.
A                                          89 min
B,V                                          CAL

**OTHER SIDE OF MIDNIGHT, THE \***          18
Charles Jarrott       USA              1977
*Marie-France Pisier, John Beck, Susan Sarandon, Raf*
*Vallone, Clu Gulager, Christian Marquand, Sorrel*
*Brooke*
A young Frenchwoman makes her way in the world
from 1939 to 1947, during which period she exploits
her charms in order to become a film star, and dallies
with an American flier until her husband takes a
cruel revenge. A faithful adaptation of a dull original
novel with a script by Herman Raucher and music by
Michel Le Grand.
Boa: novel by Sidney Sheldon.
DRA                      159 min (ort 166 min)
B,V                                          CBS

**OTHER WOMAN, THE \*\*\***                       PG
Melville Shavelson    USA              1983
*Hal Linden, Anne Meara, Jerry Stiller, Janis Paige,*
*Steven Bisley, Madolyn Smith, Warren Berlinger, Joe*
*Regalbuto, Alley Miles, P.J. Soles, Selma Jane Dulo,*
*Gregory Itzin, Fran Myers, Stephen Nathan, Robert*
*Picardo*
A widower marries a woman half his age but soon
discovers that they have little in common and throws
her over in favour of a middle-aged grandmother. An
entertaining and original tale.
DRA                      93 min (ort 100 min) mTV
B,V                              INT L/A; XTASY

**OTLEY ** **  PG
Dick Clement          UK          1968
*Tom Courtenay, Romy Schneider, Alan Badel, James
Villiers, Leonard Rossiter, James Bolam, Fiona Lewis,
Freddie Jones, Jamew Cossins, James Maxwell,
Ronald Lacey, Barry Fantoni, Pete Murray, Jimmy
Young, The Herd*
Spoof on spy films written by successful TV script-
writing team Ian La Frenais and Dick Clement, and
telling of a petty thief who becomes involved with
criminals and espionage. Appealing performances
help enliven this disjointed and dated comedy.
Boa: novel by Martin Waddell.
COM                   87 min (ort 91 min)
V                                     RCA

**OUR MAN FLINT ** **  PG
Daniel Mann           USA          1965
*James Coburn, Lee J. Cobb, Gila Golan, Edward
Mulhare, Benson Fong, Gianna Serra, Rhys Williams,
Peter Brocco, Russ Conway, Steven Geray, Alberto
Morin, William Walker, Sigrid Valdis, Shelby Grant,
Helen Funai, Ena Hartman*
A Bond spoof that is short of laughs as super-hero
Coburn fights an organisation out to dominate the
world by controlling the weather. A sequel, "In Like
Flint", followed. Music is by Jerry Goldsmith.
COM            102 min (ort 108 min) Cut (26 sec)
B,V,V2                                CBS

**OUR MISS FRED ** *  PG
Bob Kellett           UK          1972
*Danny La Rue, Alfred Marks, Lance Percival, Lally
Bowers, Frances De La Tour, Walter Gotell*
When a troupe of actors is captured by the Nazis in
wartime France, one of them escapes by disguising
himself as a woman. An ill-conceived vehicle for a
popular female impersonator whose talents are best
enjoyed in a theatrical setting.
COM                   92 min (ort 96 min)
V                                     WHV

**OUT OF AFRICA ** ***  PG
Sydney Pollack        UK/USA        1985
*Meryl Streep, Robert Redford, Klaus Maria
Brandauer, Michael Kitchen, Joseph Thiaka, Mallick
Bowens, Stephen Kinyanjui, Michael Gough, Suzanna
Hamilton, Rachel Kempson, Graham Crowden, Leslie
Phillips, Shane Rimmer*
A long, heavily romanticised account of the life of
Karen Blixen who wrote under the name of Isak
Dinesen. Redford as an Englishman was an error but
worse still was the use of Africa and Africans as an
exotic backdrop to a mundane love story. AA: Pic, Dir,
Cin (David Watkin), Screen (Adapt) (Kurt Luedtke),
Art/Set (Stephen Grimes/Josie MacAvin), Sound
(Chris Jenkins/Gary Alexander/Larry Stensvold/
Peter Handford), Score (Orig) (John Barry).
Boa: novel Silence Will Speak by Errol Trzebinski/
novel Isak Dinesen by Judith Thurman/letters of
Karen Blixen.
DRA                   155 min (ort 161 min)
B,V                                   CIC

**OUT OF BOUNDS ** **  15
Richard Tuggle        USA          1986
*Anthony Michael Hall, Jeff Korber, Jenny Wright,
Glynn Turman, Raymond J. Barry, Pepe Serna, Meat
Loaf, Michelle Little, Jerry Levine, Ji-Tu Cumbuka,
Kevin McCorkle, Linda Shayne, Maggie Gwinn, Ted
Gehring, Allan Graf*
A young man accidentally collects the wrong luggage
and finds himself with a million dollars worth of
heroin that belongs to the Mafia. To add to his
troubles, the police are also after him for a murder he
did not commit. A contrived and overblown thriller.
THR                   93 min
V/h                                   RCA

**OUT OF CONTENTION ** **  15
Herschel Daugherty    USA          1972
*Elizabeth Montgomery, George Maharis, Eileen
Heckart, Sue Anne Langdon, Jess Walton, Ross Elliott,
Richard Derr, George Jue, John Furlong, Michael
Keller*
A woman gets a call for help from her sister and
responds, only to find that her own life is now in
jeopardy after she arrives at her house, and is trapped
there by a tremendous storm that has brought down
both power and telephone lines. Good performances
are wasted in a film that is deficient in suspense.
Aka: VICTIM, THE
Boa: story by McKnight Malmar.
THR                   71 min (ort 90 min) mTV
B,V                              EAG L/A; KRP

**OUT OF CONTROL ** *  18
Allan Holzman         USA          1985
*Martin Hewitt, Andrew J. Lederer, Claudia Udy, Betsy
Russell, Cindi Dietrich, Richard Kantor, Martin Mull,
Jim Youngs, Sherilyn Fenn*
A group of teenagers get involved with drug smug-
glers when their private plane crash-lands on a small
island. A muddled adventure yarn that tries to do too
many things at once.
Aka: CROSSWINDS
A/AD           75 min (ort 78 min) Cut (19 sec)
B,V                                   MED

**OUT OF ORDER ** ***  15
Carl Schenkel    WEST GERMANY       1984
*Gotz George, Renee Sontendijk, Wolfgang Kieling,
Hannes Jaenicke, Klaus Wennemann, Ralph Richter,
Kurt Raab, Jan Groth, Ekmekyemez Firdevs, Hans
Schwofker*
A straightforward thriller that follows the changing
relationship between four people trapped in an eleva-
tor over a weekend. As the occupants begin to suffer
from fatigue and claustrophobia their behaviour be-
comes ever more desperate and uncontrolled. Though
the tension is well handled, the use of dubbed
American accents is something of a distraction.
Aka: ABWARTS; ABWARTS: DAS DUELL UBER
DER TIEFE; DER AUFZUG
Boa: novel by Wilhelm Heyne.
THR            90 min; 83 min (VIR) dubbed
B,V                              PVG; VIR

**OUT OF SEASON ** **  18
Alan Bridges          UK          1975
*Vanessa Redgrave, Susan George, Cliff Robertson,
Edward Evans, Frank Jarvis*
Overblown melodrama about a man returning to an
English seaside boarding house to resume a rela-
tionship after a lapse of 20 years, and finding that his
former lover now has a teenage daughter.
Aka: WINTER RATES
DRA                   87 min (ort 90 min)
B,V                                   TEVP

**OUT OF THE ASHES ** ***  15
Peter Werner                        1990
*Max Von Sydow, Judd Nelson, Noriyuki "Pat" Morita,
Ben Wright, Tamlyn Tomita, Kim Miyori*
Absorbing drama built around the lives of some of the
people who lived through the dropping of the atomic
bomb on Hiroshima in 1945.
DRA                   94 min
V                                ODY/CBSDIS

**OUT OF THE BLUE ** ***
Dennis Hopper         USA          1980
*Dennis Hopper, Linda Manz, Sharon Farrell,
Raymond Burr, Don Gordon*
An account of an incestuous relationship between a
father and daughter, with the latter trying to cope
with the problem of having a drug-addict mother and
an ex-biker father. A taut and low-key drama.

DRA                                    94 min
B,V                                      CBS

**OUT OF THE BODY **                    18
Brian Trenchard-Smith
                   AUSTRALIA            1988
*Tessa Humphries, Mark Hembrow*
A young university researcher experimenting with
the paranormal sees visions of inexplicable murders
as they are committed, but on telling the police of his
visions he becomes their main suspect. A further
series of experiments only results in his body being
taken over by the being responsible. Fair.
HOR                          87 min (ort 91 min)
B,V                                      MED

**OUT OF THE DARK ***                   18
Michael Schroeder        USA           1988
*Cameron Dye, Karen Black, Bud Cort, Lainie Kazan,
Tab Hunter, Paul Bartel, Karen Witter, Divine (Glenn
Milstead), Tracey Walter, Geoffrey Lewis*
The girls who work for a telephone sex service are
murdered one by one, by a mysterious killer clown
who is known only as Bobo. An unappealing shocker
in which Divine makes his last screen appearance.
THR        84 min (ort 89 min) (Cut at film release by
                                    1 min 34 sec)
V/sh                                     MED

**OUT OF THE PAST ****                   PG
Jacques Tourneur        USA            1947
*Kirk Douglas, Robert Mitchum, Jane Greer, Richard
Webb, Rhonda Fleming, Dickie Moore, Steve Brodie,
Virginia Huston, Paul Valentine, Ken Niles, Lee
Elson, Frank Wilcox, Mary Fields, Jess Escobar,
James Bush, Hubert Brill*
A private eye, hired to find a hoodlum's girlfriend,
ends up falling in love with her. Film noir with plenty
of intrigue and double dealing. The script is by
Geoffrey Homes (Daniel Mainwaring). Later remade
as AGAINST ALL ODDS.
Aka: BUILD MY GALLOWS HIGH (VCC)
Boa: novel Build My Gallows High by Geoffrey
Homes.
Osca: HELL'S HIGHWAY
THR               92 min (ort 97 min) B/W
B,V                      KVD L/A; VCC (VHS only)

**OUT OF TIME **                         PG
Robert Butler            USA           1988
*Bruce Abbott, Bill Maher, Leo Rossi, Rebecca
Schaeffer, Adam Ant, Kristian Alfonso, Ray Girardini*
A detective from the 21st century travels back in time
to the present day, to enlist the help of his great-
grandfather in capturing a master criminal. A
pleasant comedy-drama of no great substance that
formed the pilot for a prospective series.
DRA                      92 min (ort 96 min) mTV
B,V                                      EIV

**OUT ON BAIL **                         18
Gordon Hessler          USA            1990
*Robert Ginty, Kathy Shower, Tom Badal*
A loner arrives at a small Southern town and gets
entangled in the usual morass of stock situations,
including the ubiquitous corrupt sheriff, murder
frame-up and attractive young widow etc. Badal is
good as the sadistic sheriff and a set of well-executed
stunts adds a little zip to this unoriginal low-budget
actioner.
A/AD                                    98 min
V                                        EIV

**OUTBACK ***
Ted Kotcheff      AUSTRALIA/USA        1970
*Gary Bond, Donald Pleasence, Sylvia Kay, Chips
Rafferty, Jack Thompson*
A sensitive schoolteacher finds life in a remote
outback town too much to take in all its brutality and

narrow-mindedness. Paints the same stark and un-
flattering picture of Australian behaviour and hospi-
tality, especially towards strangers, reflected in so
many films from down under. Scripted by Evan Jones.
Aka: WAKE IN FRIGHT
Boa: novel Wake In Fright by Kenneth Cook.
DRA                      95 min (ort 114 min)
B,V                                   INT/CBS

**OUTBACK BOUND **                      15
John Llewelyn Moxey      USA           1988
*Donna Mills, John Schneider, John Meillon, Andrew
Clarke, Colette Mann, Nina Foch, Robert Harper*
A Beverly Hills woman cheated out of all she owns
inherits a disused opal mine in Australia, and decides
to move there to sell it and start a new life. Fair.
A/AD                     90 min (ort 96 min) mTV
V                                        CBS

**OUTBACK VAMPIRES **                   15
Colin Eggleston      AUSTRALIA         1986
*John Doyle, Brett Climo, Richard Morgan, Angela
Kennedy, Maggie Blinco, David Gibson, Antonia
Murphy*
A horror-spoof in which some travellers find them-
selves stranded in the middle of nowhere and become
the unwilling guests of a family of vampires. The story
leaves a lot to be desired, but the gags and visual jokes
help sustain it.
COM                                     88 min
V/sh                                     GHV

**OUTCAST **                            18
Roman Buchnok                          1990
*Peter Tench*
A young loser sells his soul to the Devil in return for
the power to take revenge on all those who used to
bully or humiliate him. However, by fathering a child
he finds that he has committed an act of disobedience
to his master, for which he can only atone by
murdering the child. A fairly unusual and tense
horror tale.
HOR                                     94 min
V                                        NWV

**OUTCAST OF THE ISLANDS, AN ***         PG
Carol Reed               UK            1951
*Trevor Howard, Kerima, Robert Morley, Ralph
Richardson, Wendy Hiller, George Coulouris,
Frederick Valk, Wilfrid Hyde White, Betty Ann Davies*
At a Far Eastern trading post a selfish and misguided
reprobate reveals a secret sea route in order to curry
favour with an island princess, but his plan misfires
and he is left with nothing. A full-blooded adaptation
of Conrad's complex character study; Howard is
compelling in the title role.
Boa: novel by Joseph Conrad.
A/AD                     96 min (ort 102 min) B/W
V                                        WHV

**OUTER LIMITS, THE: VOL. 1 **           PG
Byron Haskin/Laslo Benedek
                         USA           1963
*Robert Culp, Geraldine Brooks, Leonard Stone, Martin
Wolfson, Donald Pleasence, Priscilla Morrill, Edward
C. Platt, Fred Beir*
Two episodes from a popular and often very well made
SF series. "The Architects Of Fear" sees a group of
scientists creating a mock alien to shock mankind into
less-aggressive behaviour, while "The Man With The
Power" sees a timid professor finding himself with
awesome powers after a brain operation.
FAN                        104 min mTV B/W
V                                        MGM

**OUTER LIMITS, THE: VOL. 2 ***          PG
Leslie Stevens/Byron Haskin
                         USA           1963
*Cliff Robertson, Lee Philips, Jacqueline Scott, William*

*O. Douglas, Mavis Neal, Allyson Ames, Sidney Blackmer, Phil Pine, Mark Roberts, Nancy Rennick, Joan Camden, Clarence Lung, Richard Loo*
The very first and second episodes from a popular and well-mounted SF series. "The Galaxy Being" tells of a radio-station engineer whose experiments bring a benign creature of fearful appearance to Earth from a distant galaxy. In "The Hundred Days Of The Dragon" the new American president is replaced by an Oriental despot who has the ability to alter his appearance and cellular structure.

| | |
|---|---|
| FAN | 104 min mTV B/W |
| V | MGM |

### OUTER LIMITS, THE: VOL. 3 **    PG
James Goldstone/Leonard Horn
USA                1963
*David McCallum, Edward Mulhare, Jill Haworth, Constance Cavendish, Nora Marlowe, Robert Doyle, Martin Landau, Shirley Knight, John Considine, Karl Held, Maxine Stuart*
"The Sixth Finger" follows the experiments a scientist conducts in the acceleration of evolution, and the changes he brings about in an illiterate miner. In "The Man Who Was Never Born" a spaceman passes through a time barrier and finds Earth of the 21st century a barren, blighted wasteland, but returns home with one of its inhabitants in an effort to change the future.

| | |
|---|---|
| FAN | 104 min mTV B/W |
| V | MGM |

### OUTFIT, THE **    15
John Flynn        USA        1973
*Karen Black, Robert Duvall, Joe Don Baker, Robert Ryan, Timothy Carey, Richard Jaeckel, Sheree North, Marie Windsor, Jane Greer, Elisha Cook Jr*
An ex-con takes on the mobsters who murdered his brother. A shallow tale that can be enjoyed for its strong characterisations if not for its generous dose of gratuitous violence. Scripted by Flynn.
Boa: novel by Richard Stark (Doanld E. Westlake)

| | |
|---|---|
| DRA | 99 min (ort 103 min) |
| B,V | MGM |

### OUTLAND **    15
Peter Hyams        USA        1981
*Sean Connery, Peter Boyle, Frances Sternhagen, James B. Sikking, Kika Markham, Clarke Peters, Steven Berkoff, John Ratzenberger, Nicholas Barnes, Manning Redwood, Pat Starr, Hal Galili, Angus MacInnes, Stuart Milligan*
This SF version of HIGH NOON (complete with digital clock) has a tough investigator being sent out to a mining colony on one of Jupiter's moons, to solve a rash of apparent suicides. He becomes the target of a murder squad and awaits their arrival. A flashy but unsatisfying film with a script by the director.

| | |
|---|---|
| FAN | 105 min |
| V | WHV |

### OUTLAW BLUES **    15
Richard T. Heffron        USA        1977
*Peter Fonda, Susan Saint James, John Crawford, James Callahan, Michael Lerner*
Ex-con Fonda becomes a Country and Western star thanks to the efforts of his back-up singer (Saint James in her first film role) and has to take on an established star who has stolen his song. An enjoyable if none too convincing look at this branch of showbusiness. Written by B.W.L. Norton.

| | |
|---|---|
| DRA | 97 min (ort 101 min) |
| B,V | WHV |

### OUTLAW FORCE *    18
David Heavener        USA        1987
*Paul Smith, Frank Stallone, David Heavener, Warren Berlinger, Robert Bjorklund, Devin Dunsworth, Stephanie Cicero*
When his wife is killed and his daughter kidnapped by gangsters, a sideshow cowboy gives chase in order to rescue her and exact his revenge. A dismal effort that serves as no more than a vehicle to parade the appropriate sequences of unpleasantness, with the hero almost as disagreeable a person as the villains he is chasing. Written by Heavener.

| | |
|---|---|
| A/AD | 91 min Cut (54 sec) |
| B,V | NOVA; CAST |

### OUTLAW JOSEY WALES, THE ***    18
Clint Eastwood        USA        1976
*Clint Eastwood, Chief Dan George, Sondra Locke, John Vernon, Bill McKinney, Sam Bottoms, Paula Trueman, Geraldine Keams, Woodrow Parfrey, Joyce Jameson, Sheb Wooley, Royal Dano, Matt Clark, John Verros, Will Sampson, John Quade*
A man becomes an outlaw when Union soldiers murder his family in a tale that is long and violent but extremely well made. Followed by THE RETURN OF JOSEY WALES without Eastwood. The screenplay was by Philip Kaufman and Sonia Chernus, with the former directing until Eastwood took over.
Boa: novel Gone To Texas by Forrest Carter.

| | |
|---|---|
| WES | 130 min (ort 135 min) |
| B,V | WHV |

### OUTLAW OF GOR *    18
John (Bud) Cardos        ITALY        1987
*Urbano Barberini, Jack Palance, Donna Denton, Rebecca Ferrati, Nigel Chipps, Russel Savadier, Alex Heyns, Tulio Monetta, Larry Taylor, Michelle Clarke*
A sequel to GOR with our professor making a return trip to this primitive world for some further adventures. A dreary excursion into the world of sword-and-sorcery, only in this one the sorcery is in short supply.
Boa: novel by John Norman.

| | |
|---|---|
| FAN | 85 min (ort 89 min) |
| B,V | WHV |

### OUTLAW RIDER, THE **    15
Willy S. Regan        USA
*Sean Todd, Ken Wood, Isabella Savona, Rick Garett*
A man kills a poker cheat and finds that a bounty of $50,000 has been put on his head, forcing him to run for cover.

| | |
|---|---|
| WES | 93 min Cut (2 sec) |
| B,V | VPD |

### OUTLAW RIDERS *
Tony Houston        USA        1972
*Darlene Duralia, Bryan Sonny West, Rafael Campos, Bambi Allen, Bill Bonner*
Routine biker film of noise, dust and general unpleasantness.

| | |
|---|---|
| A/AD | 76 min |
| B,V | INT |

### OUTLAW, THE ***    U
Howard Hughes        USA        1943
*Jane Russell, Walter Huston, Jack Buetel, Thomas Mitchell, Mimi Aguglia, Joe Sawyer, Gene Rizzi, Frank Darien, Pat West, Carl Stockdale, Nena Quartaro, Martin Garralaga, Julian Rivero, Dickie Jones, Ethan Laidlaw, Ed Brady*
A pretentious but unusual version of the Billy the Kid legend, with our outlaw enjoying a little romance when he meets up with Doc Holliday and Pat Garrett, at a half-way station where they quarrel over a half-breed girl. This famous "sex" Western marked Russell's screen debut, and excessive interest in her bosom is certainly evident. The music is by Victor Young. Filmed in 1941 and directed mostly by Howard Hawks.
Osca: LAW OF THE UNDERWORLD

| | |
|---|---|
| WES | 114 min (ort 126 min) B/W |
| B,V | KVD L/A; VCC (VHS only) |

## OUTLAWS **
Peter Werner                    USA                     PG
                                                        1986
*Rod Taylor, William Lucking, Richard Roundtree,*
*Charles Napier, Patrick Houser, Christine Belford,*
*Lewis Van Bergen, Wendy Girard*
A group of Texas cowboys are catapulted forward in
time to the 20th century and have to cope with the
bewildering complexities of our technological age.
Pilot for a series that lasted a mere six months.
COM                             92 min (ort 104 min) mTV
B,V                                                     CIC

## OUTRAGE **
Richard T. Heffron      USA                     1973
*Robert Culp, Marlyn Mason, Beah Richards,*
*Jacqueline Scott, Ramon Bieri, Thomas Leopold, Mark*
*Lenard, Nicholas Hammond, Don Dubbins, Ivor*
*Francis, Sid Grossfeld, James B. Sikking, Paul*
*Jenkins, Christopher Gardner*
A doctor becomes a vigilante in order to combat
teenage gangs who are terrorising his wealthy neigh-
bourhood. There are no surprises here.
DRA                                     77 min mTV
B,V                                                     GHV

## OUTRAGEOUS FORTUNE ***
Arthur Hiller           USA                     15
                                                1987
*Shelley Long, Bette Midler, Peter Coyote, George*
*Carlin, John Schuck, Anthony Heald, Robert Prosky,*
*Ji-Tu Cumbuka*
Two struggling actresses who detest each other on
sight become bosom buddies, especially when they
find themselves involved with the same worthless
man. A screen celebration of female friendship with a
calculated feminist slant. The script is by Leslie
Dixon.
COM                             95 min (ort 100 min)
B,V                                                     RNK

## OUTRAGEOUS PARTY *
Jacki McKimmie    AUSTRALIA                     18
                                                1989
*Graeme Blundel, John Jarrall, Noni Hazelhurst*
Neighbours take turns organising monthly parties.
One such man invites his boss to his bash to curry
favour, but the party gets wildly out of hand.
COM                                     84 min
V                                                       EQUIN

## OUTSIDERS, THE ***
Francis Ford Coppola    USA                     PG
                                                1983
*C. Thomas Howell, Matt Dillon, Ralph Macchio, Diane*
*Lane, Patrick Swayze, Rob Lowe, Tom Cruise, Leif*
*Garrett, Emilio Estevez, Tom Waits*
A study of teenagers growing up in Oklahoma in the
1960s as seen through the eyes of one boy. An
ambitious if not exactly successful attempt to trans-
pose Hinton's likeable novel. The score is by Carmine
Coppola. Followed by RUMBLE FISH, another film
based on the work of Hinton.
Boa: novel by S.E. Hinton.
DRA                                     87 min (ort 95 min)
V/sh                                                    WHV

## OUTSIDERS, THE *
Sharron Miller/Alan Shapiro                     15
                        USA                     1990
*Jay R. Ferguson, Rodney Harvey, Boyd Kestner*
Three young orphaned brothers have a tough time
surviving, and their difficulties are soon compounded
by the release from jail of the leader of a rival
street-gang. Average urban melodramatics.
DRA                                     83 min
V                                                       CIC

## OVER THE BROOKLYN BRIDGE *
Menahem Golan           USA                     15
                                                1983
*Elliott Gould, Margaux Hemingway, Sid Caesar,*

*Shelley Winters, Carol Kane, Burt Young*
A Jewish restaurant owner wants to borrow money
from his uncle, but he and his family refuse to help
him unless he breaks with his non-Jewish girlfriend.
A comedy whose stupidity makes one cringe, with a
script by Arnold Somkin.
COM                             102 min (ort 106 min)
B,V                                                     GHV

## OVER THE EDGE ***
Jonathan Kaplan        USA                     18
                                                1979
*Michael Kramer, Matt Dillon, Vincent Spano, Pamela*
*Ludwig, Tom Fergus, Andy Romano, Ellen Geer,*
*Harry Northup*
Dillon's film debut is a powerful study of disturbed
and alienated youths living in the suburbs. A fine
score by Sol Kaplan complements it well. The percep-
tive script is by Charlie Haas and Tim Hunter.
DRA                                     90 min (ort 95 min)
B,V                                                     CBS

## OVER THE MOON **
Thornton Freeland      UK                       U
                                                1937
                                (released in UK 1940)
*Merle Oberon, Rex Harrison, Ursula Jeans, Robert*
*Douglas, Louis Borell, Zena Dare, Peter Haddon,*
*David Tree, Mackenzie Ward, Carl Jaffe, Elizabeth*
*Welch, Herbert Lomas, Wilfred Shine, Bruce Winston,*
*Frank Atkinson, Evelyn Ankers*
A young girl inherits a vast fortune which she
squanders on a lavish tour of Europe, but her romance
with a young doctor fails to progress until the loss on
her wealth puts them on an even footing again. A
slight, romantic comedy.
COM                                     76 min (ort 78 min)
V                                               SCREL; CENVID

## OVER THE TOP *
Menahem Golan          USA                      PG
                                                1986
*Sylvester Stallone, Robert Loggia, Susan Blakely, Rick*
*Zumwalt, David Mendenhall, Chris McCarty, Terry*
*Funk*
The title is an apt description for this story of a strong
but determined truck driver who fights to gain
custody of his young son, against his wealthy and
influential father-in-law. Stallone tries a softer image
but winds up being merely inaudible.
A/AD                                    100 min
B,V                                                     RNK

## OVERBOARD **
Gary Marshall          USA                      PG
                                                1987
*Goldie Hawn, Kurt Russell, Edward Herrmann,*
*Katherine Helmond, Michael Hagerty, Roddy*
*McDowall, Jared Rushton, Jeffrey Wiseman, Brian*
*Price, Jamie Wild, Frank Campanella, Harvey Alan*
*Miller, Frank Buxton, Carol Willard*
An insufferably overbearing and arrogant rich woman
falls off her yacht, losing her memory in the process,
and ends up living the life of an ordinary mortal as a
housewife and mother to a carpenter's three kids. A
pleasant comedy vehicle of appealing performances
and banal scripting.
COM                             107 min (ort 112 min)
B,V                                                     MGM

## OVERKILL *
Ulli Lommel             USA                     18
                                                1987
*Steve Rally, John Nishio, Laura Burkett, Allen Wisch,*
*Roy Summersett, Antonio Caprio*
Los Angeles-based action tale of a tough undercover
cop and his vow of vengeance on a ruthless Japanese
crime syndicate, who killed his partner while he was
investigating their terrifying protection racket aimed
at Japanese living in the USA. The title is an apt
description of the direction.
A/AD                                    78 min (ort 81 min)
B,V                                                     RCA

## OVERLORD ***
Stuart Cooper     UK     1975
*Brian Stirner, Davyd Harries, Nicholas Ball, Julie Neesam, Sam Sewell, John Franklyn-Robbins, Stella Tanner, Harry Shacklock, David Scheur, Lorna Lewis, Elsa Minelli*
A semi-documentary tracing the life of an 18-year-old boy from the day he is called up until his death in the Normandy landings. A sensitive and touching character study with a minimal plot. Written by Stuart Cooper and Christopher Hudson.
DRA     83 min B/W
B,V     TEVP

## OWL AND THE PUSSYCAT, THE ***    15
Herbert Ross     USA     1970
*Barbra Streisand, George Segal, Robert Klein, Allen Garfield, Roz Kelly*
Beautifully acted zany comedy about an unlikely pair; a semi-illiterate prostitute and a bookseller who are thrown together by circumstance and fall in love. The script by Buck Henry is adapted from a hit Broadway comedy.
Boa: play by Bill Manhoff.
COM     96 min
V/sh     RCA

## OXFORD BLUES *    15
Robert Boris     USA     1984
*Rob Lowe, Ally Sheedy, Julian Sands, Amanda Pays, Michael Gough, Aubrey Morris, Gail Strickland, Alan Howard, Julian Forth*
A poor remake of the 1938 film "A Yank At Oxford" with a young rough diamond pursuing a blue-blooded beauty, and trying to win her heart by volunteering for the rowing team. A curiously lifeless film that tries hard to please with a few comic episodes, but Lowe and the snobs he comes into conflict with are so obnoxious that this stilted work is all too easy to dislike.
COM     93 min (ort 97 min)
B,V     GHV/PARK

# P

## P.O.W. **    18
Quentin Lawrence     UK     1965
*Jack Hedley, Charles Tingwell, Patrick Wymark, Barbara Shelley, Bill Owen, Peter Welch, Lee Montague, Edwin Richfield, Michael Ripper, Philip Latham, Glyn Houston*
A Hammer film telling of the exploits of a WW2 woman agent, who parachutes into a Malayan prison that's behind enemy lines, where she is sheltered by POWs who help her elude the Japanese. Fair.
Aka: P.O.W. – PRISONERS OF WAR; SECRET OF BLOOD ISLAND, THE
WAR     90 min
B,V     KES; GLOB

## P.O.W. – THE ESCAPE *    15
Gideon Amir     USA     1986
*David Carradine, Charles Floyd, Steve James, Phil Brock, Mako*
A small group of crack US soldiers are sent into North Vietnam, to rescue American prisoners being held in jungle camps, and they make their way to freedom as Saigon falls to the Communists. An energetic feast of action and mindlessness, plotted like clockwork and acted in much the same way.
Aka: BEHIND ENEMY LINES
A/AD     85 min (ort 90 min) Cut (19 sec)
B,V     MGM

## PABLO AND THE DANCING CHIHUAHUA **    U
Walter Perkins     USA     1972

*Armando Islas, Francesca Jarvis, Walter Tilley, Manual Rivera*
Typical Disney story of a young Mexican boy's trip through the desert with his dog, to join his uncle in Tucson.
JUV     87 min
B,V     WDV

## PACIFIC BANANA **
John Lamond     AUSTRALIA     1981
*Alyson Best, Robin Stewart, Deborah Gray, Graeme Blundell*
An airline pilot who has a problem with girls gets some unexpected help in this bawdy comedy.
COM     84 min
B,V     ITM L/A; APX

## PACIFIC CONNECTION **
Luis Nepomuceno     PHILIPPINES
*Dean Stockwell, Roland Dantes, Nancy Kwan, Alejandro Rey, Guy Madison, John Drew Barrymore*
Historical action-adventure set in the Philippines during the period of Spanish rule. The ruthless governor has his son trained in the martial arts but an expert stickfighter arises to defend his people from the governor's oppressive rule. Mildly entertaining, but no more than that.
Aka: STICKFIGHTER
A/AD     90 min
B,V     VIPCO

## PACIFIC INFERNO **    15
Rolf Bayer     PHILIPPINES/USA     1978
*Jim Brown, Wilma Reading, Richard Jaeckel, Tad Horino, Vic Diaz*
A fortune in silver pesos is to be recovered from Manila Bay where it was dumped just prior to WW2. The Japanese occupation forces use American POWs as divers.
Aka: DO THEY EVER CRY IN AMERICA?
A/AD     90 min; 86 min (MED)
B, V/h     VDM; MED

## PACK OF LIES **    PG
Anthony Page     USA     1987
*Ellen Burstyn, Teri Garr, Alan Bates, Ronald Hines, Clive Swift, Sammi Davis, Daniel Benzali*
In the 1960s a London couple allow their home to be used by British Intelligence to spy on their Canadian neighbours, who unknown to them, are KGB agents. The film (very loosely inspired by real events) focuses on the strains the couple endure in having to keep up the pretence of normality under these difficult circumstances. Whitemore's clumsy play is improved by Ralph Gallup's adaptation, and the fine performances help slightly. Average.
Boa: play by Hugh Whitemore.
DRA     103 min mTV
B,V     FUTUR

## PACK, THE **    15
Robert Clouse     USA     1977
*Joe Don Baker, Hope Alexander Willis, Richard B. Shull, R.G. Armstrong, Ned Wertimer, Bibi Besch, Delos V. Smith Jr, Richard O'Brien, Sherry Miles, Paul Wilson, Eric Knight, Steve Lytle, Rob Narke, Peggy Price, Steve Butts*
The inhabitants of an island resort are terrorised by a pack of abandoned dogs, in this competent but predictable thriller. Written by Clouse.
Aka: LONG DARK NIGHT, THE; WE'VE GOT A BONE TO PICK WITH YOU
Boa: novel by Dave Fisher.
THR     98 min
B,V     WHV

## PACKAGE, THE **    15
Andrew Davis     USA     1989

Gene Hackman, Joanna Cassidy, Tommy Lee Jones, John Heard, Dennis Franz, Pam Grier, Reni Santoni, Kevin Crowley, Ike Pappas, Thalmus Rasulala
Political thriller that casts Hackman as an army sergeant who is reprimanded after a security breach at a disarmament conference and given the menial job of escorting a court-martialled soldier back to the States. Following the escape of his prisoner, he begins to discover that he has been used as a dupe by Soviet and American military dissidents. A film that initially develops tension, only to lose it in the face of progressive implausibility.
THR                              103 min (ort 108 min)
V                                             VIR/RCA

## PACKAGE TOUR **                           PG
Lasse Aberg          SWEDEN                  1980
Lasse Aberg, Jon Skolmen, Kim Anderzon, Lottie Ejebrant, Ted Astrom, Roland Jansson, Magnus Harenstam, Weibron Holmberg, Sven Melander, Margarita Calahorra, Maria Esperanza Santos, German Perez, Svante Grunberg, Eva Orn
A broad Swedish farce about the misadventures of a group of holiday-makers. One of the highest grossing domestic successes for Sweden of all time.
COM                                       102 min
B,V,V2                                        GHV

## PAID IN BLOOD *
USA
Jeff Cameron, Donald O'Brian, Christa Neil
A man seeks revenge for the murder of his brother in this little-known and forgettable Western.
WES                                         88 min
B,V,V2                                         FFV

## PAINT IT BLACK **                          18
Tim Hunter           USA                     1989
Rick Rossovich, Julie Carmen, Doug Savant, Jason Bernard, Martin Landau, Sally Kirkland, Peter Frechette
A rather flashy mystery thriller in which Rossovich plays a talented young sculptor whose affair with an unscrupulous gallery owner seems to bring him no success. He decides to end their relationship, but before he can do so he has an accidental encounter with a weirdo that results in her murder. Not unnaturally, he becomes the prime suspect. Clever and competent this film may be, but the implausible plot takes some swallowing.
THR                                         97 min
V                                              VES

## PAINT ME A MURDER *
Alan Cooke           UK                      1984
Michelle Phillips, James Laurensen, David Robb, Alan Lake, Tony Steedman, Morgan Sheppard
Story of an artist who forms one of the partners in a love triangle that ends in tragedy.
Osca: LATE NANCY IRVING, THE
HOR                                         72 min
B,V                                            BWV

## PAINT YOUR WAGON ***                       PG
Joshua Logan         USA                     1969
Lee Marvin, Clint Eastwood, Jean Seberg, Harve Presnell, Ray Walston, Tom Ligon, Alan Baxter, William O'Connell, Paula Trueman, Robert Eastman, Geoffrey Morgan, H.B. Haggerty, Terry Jenkins, Karl Bruck
A glossy and expensive musical about the California Gold Rush, with some fine Lerner and Loewe songs and plenty of action. Marvin and Eastwood share Seberg – the wife they bought at an auction. Marred in parts by poor singing, but Presnell's "They Call the Wind Maria" and Marvin's rendition of "Wanderin' Star" are highlights. The witty script is by Paddy Chayevsky.

Boa: musical by Alan Jay Lerner and Frederick Loewe.
MUS                                        167 min
V/s                                           CIC

## PAIR OF ACES **                            15
Aaron Lipstadt       USA                     1989
Willie Nelson, Kris Kristofferson, Rip Torn, Helen Shaver, Jane Cameron, Michael Marich, Emily Warfield
A low-key re-working of 48 HOURS that's given a Western flavour but has a modern setting. This time our mismatched couple are a Texas Ranger and a safecracker who's awaiting trial, and they form a reluctant partnership in pursuit of a serial killer. Quite entertaining, but most of the interest in this formula story resides in the pairing of the two stars.
WES                          94 min (ort 100 min) mTV
V/sh                                           WHV

## PAJAMA GAME, THE ****                       U
Stanley Donen        USA                     1957
Doris Day, John Raitt, Eddie Foy Jr, Reta Shaw, Carol Haney, Barbara Nichols
Workers at a pajama factory go on strike for higher wages, but complications ensue when their female negotiator falls in love. A fine version of a Broadway musical that, despite the unlikely subject, works boths as an entertaining musical and a fluid and effective piece of cinema. Songs (by Richard Adler and Jerry Ross) include: "There Once Was A Man", "Hey, There" and "Hernando's Hideaway". Choreography is by Bob Fosse.
Boa: musical/book Seven And A Half Cents by Richard Bissel.
MUS                               97 min (ort 101 min)
V                                              WHV

## PAL JOEY ***                               PG
George Sidney        USA                     1957
Rita Hayworth, Frank Sinatra, Kim Novak, Bobby Sherwood, Hank Henry, Elizabeth Patterson, Barbara Nichols
A brash cabaret entertainer lands in San Francisco determined to make it big, but scores his biggest hits with a wealthy socialite and a chorus line cutie. The classic Rodgers and Hart score includes: "The Lady Is A Tramp", "There's A Small Hotel", "I Could Write A Book" and "My Funny Valentine".
Boa: play/short stories by John O'Hara/musical by Richard Rodgers and Lorenz Hart.
MUS                         105 min (ort 111 min) B/W
V                                             PREST

## PALAIS ROYALE **                           15
Martin Lavut         CANADA                  1988
Kim Catrall, Matt Craven, Kim Coates, Brian George, Michael Hogan, Jan Rubes, Dean Stockwell
Period melodrama circa 1959, with a Toronto advertising executive getting drawn into fronting for local crooks, when he meets the girl of his dreams, a gangster's moll whose face has appeared on cigarette advertising hoardings. Once enrolled, his money-making talents blossom as he develops the legitimate front his colleagues need so badly. An interesting film that's flawed by a disappointing climax.
DRA                               88 min (ort 100 min)
V                                              EIV

## PALE RIDER **                              15
Clint Eastwood       USA                     1985
Clint Eastwood, Michael Moriarty, Christopher Penn, Carrie Snodgrass, John Russell, Sydney Penny, Richard Dysart, Richard Kiel, Doug McGrath
Eastwood's first Western since THE OUTLAW JOSEY WALES is essentially a re-run of HIGH PLAINS DRIFTER. A violent and mysterious stranger comes to the aid of a mining community

threatened by the local baddies who are in the pay of a large mining corporation. Well made it may be, but the clumsy attempts at symbolism and shameless cloning of SHANE give the whole work an air of heavy-handed pretentiousness.
Boa: novel by A.D. Foster.

| WES | 116 min |
| V/sh | WHV |

## PALS *** PG
Lou Antonio      USA      1987
*George C. Scott, Don Ameche, Sylvia Sidney, Susan Rinell, James Greene, Jean Hale, Lenka Peterson, Richard Hamilton, Kenneth French, Marc Gowan, Georgia Allen, Bruce Taylor, Randy Martin, Jane Berman, Rick Maley, Tim Maley*
A real gem of a comedy that rises far above its mTV format. Two pensioner pals stumble across a fortune in drug cash hidden in the boot of a car, and decide to keep the money. Needless to say, this changes them and their way of life somewhat. Witty and engaging, with fine performances all round.

| COM | 87 min (ort 100 min) mTV |
| B,V | FUTUR |

## PANCHO VILLA **
Eugenio Martin      SPAIN      1972
*Clint Walker, Telly Savalas, Chuck Connors, Anne Francis, Angel Del Pozo, Luis Davila, Jose Maria Prada, Monica Randall, Antonio Casas, Berta Barri, Eduardo Calvo, Dan Van Husen, Norman Bailey, Tony Ross*
Biopic on the famous Mexican revolutionary leader, that's nothing like as good as the 1934 film "Viva Villa" with Wallace Beery. The remarkable climax has two trains colliding, and on that account is worth sitting through; but only just.

| DRA | 92 min |
| B,V | VCL/CBS |

## PANDA AND THE MAGIC SERPENT ** U
     JAPAN      1961
*Narrated by Marvin Miller*
Animated feature about young lovers separated by the intervention of a cruel wizard, and telling how the two are finally united after many perils. Based on a Chinese fairytale.

| CAR | 78 min |
| B,V | HVH; XTASY |

## PANDEMONIUM * 15
Alfred Sole      USA      1982
*Carol Kane, Miles Chapin, Candy Azzara, Tom Smothers, Debralee Scott, Marc McClure, Judge Reinhold, Paul Reubens, Tab Hunter, Madeline Kahn, Eve Arden, Eileen Brennan, Donald O'Connor*
A sluggish spoof on all those killer-at-the-college films, with a few funny ideas but a general air of desperation.
Aka: THURSDAY THE 12TH

| COM | 78 min (ort 82 min) |
| B,V | WHV |

## PANIC * 18
Anthony Richmond (Antonio Riccamonza)
     ITALY/SPAIN/UK      1980
*Janet Agren, David Warbeck, Franco Ressel, Jose R. Lifante, Fabian Conde, Roberto Ricci, Miguel Herrera, Ovidio Taito, Eugenio Benito, Jose Maria Labernie, Ilaria Maria Bianchi, Vittorio Calo*
An accident during secret experiments with bacteriological weapons, leads to a disappearance and several brutal murders. A detective is given 12 hours in which to solve the mystery, before the town is destroyed by the military in order to cover up the incident. Implausible nonsense.
Aka: PANICO

| HOR | 90 min |
| B,V | BRO L/A; VHS L/A |

## PANIC CITY *
William Girdler      USA      1974
*Austin Stoker, James Pickett, Hugh Smith, Charles Kissinger*
An unconscious witness to a murder is one of the reasons for a cunning killer being able to elude a police dragnet.
Aka: ZEBRA KILLER, THE

| DRA | 92 min |
| B,V,V2 | INT |

## PANIC IN NEEDLE PARK, THE *** 18
Jerry Schatzberg      USA      1971
*Al Pacino, Kitty Winn, Richard Bright, Kiel Martin, Michael McClanathan, Warren Finnerty, Alan Vint, Marcia Jean Kurtz, Raul Julia, Larry Marshall, Gil Rogers, Paul Sorvino*
A young girl meets a small-time crook, who becomes hooked on heroin and drags her down with him. A sobering examination of the nether world of the junkie, scripted by Joan Didion and John Gregory Dunne. Pacino and Winn both give performances of remarkable conviction.
Boa: novel by James Mills.

| DRA | 104 min (ort 110 min) Cut (57 sec) |
| B,V | CBS |

## PANIC IN THE CITY **
Eddie Davis      USA      1967
*Linda Cristal, Howard Duff, Stephen McNally, Nehemiah Persoff*
Terrorists try to detonate an A-bomb in Los Angeles in an attempt to provoke a nuclear exchange between the USA and the USSR. A slow-moving thriller of little power.

| THR | 96 min |
| B,V | VFP L/A; HER |

## PANIC ON THE 5:22 ** 15
Harvey Hart      USA      1974
*Bernie Casey, Linda Chiles, Ina Balin, James Sloyan, Andrew Duggan, Dana Elcar, Eduard Franz, Lynda Day George, Laurence Luckinbill, Reni Santoni, James Sloyan, Robert Walden, Dennis Patrick, Robert Mandan, Charles Lampkin*
Passengers on a commuter train are held up and terrorised by three armed thugs. Average.

| THR | 75 min (ort 78 min) mTV |
| B,V | TURBO; BRAVE |

## PAPER CHASE, THE *** PG
James Bridges      USA      1973
*Timothy Bottoms, Lindsay Wagner, John Houseman, Graham Beckel, Edward Herrmann, Craig Richard Nelson, James Naughton, Bob Lydiard*
The story of a Harvard law school as seen through the eyes of its first-year students. Bridges wrote the screenplay as well as directing. This film gave Houseman his first taste of stardom in the role of Professor Kingsfield, that he continued in a mediocre TV series. A blend of comedy and drama, with student Bottoms discovering that his girlfriend is Kingsfield's daughter. Photography is by Gordon Willis. AA: S. Actor (Houseman).
Boa: novel by John Jay Osborn Jr.

| DRA | 107 min (ort 111 min) |
| B,V | CBS |

## PAPER TIGER ** PG
Ken Annakin      UK      1975
*David Niven, Toshiro Mifune, Hardy Kruger, Ando, Ivan Desny, Irene Tsu, Miiko Taka, Jeff Corey, Ronald Fraser, Patrick Donahue, Kunt Christian, Jeanine Siniscal, Gatz Shariff*
The tutor to the son of a Japanese ambassador, has to act out his heroic fantasies in reality when his young pupil is kidnapped. A messy blend of action and saccharine cuteness that is hardly riveting. The script is by Jack Davies.

A/AD                              96 min (ort 99 min)
B,V,V2       RNK; MIA (VHS only); PARK (VHS only)

## PAPERHOUSE ***                           15
Bernard Rose             UK                     1988
*Charlotte Burke, Glenne Headly, Gemma Jones, Ben Cross, Elliot Spiers, Sarah Newbold*
In this intriguing tale, a young girl on the verge of puberty experiences a series of fainting fits, later drawing a sketch of a house she has seen in her dreams. As she alters the drawing the dream house alters too, but eventually the visions of it begin to dominate her life. A tense and chilling psychological fantasy, the feature debut of music-video director Rose.
Boa: novel Marianne Dreams by Catherine Storr.
THR                           89 min (ort 94 min)
V                                      VES

## PAPILLON ****                             18
Franklin J. Schaffner     USA            1973
*Steve McQueen, Dustin Hoffman, Victor Jory, Don Gordon, Anthony Zerbe, George Coulouris, Woodrow Parfrey, Bill Mumy, Gregory Sierra, William Smithers*
An expensive and lovingly produced account of Henri Charriere, known as "Papillon", who made repeated attempts to escape from his incarceration on Devil's Island, the French Caribbean penal colony off the coast of French Guyana, where he was sent after being convicted of murder. The colourful locations and attention to detail make this a most rewarding film. Written by Dalton Trumbo and Lorenzo Semple Jr, with music by Jerry Goldsmith.
Boa: novel by Henri Charriere.
DRA                     144 min (ort 150 min)
B,V                                 RCA

## PARADE, THE ***                         PG
Peter H. Hunt           USA            1984
*Michael Learned, Frederic Forrest, Rosanna Arquette, Maxwell Caulfield, James Olson, Geraldine Page, Tom Wees, Angela Wallace, Karla Burns, Adam Mueller, Steve Frazier, Troy Mays, Andy Musick, James Erickson, Tim McGill*
After seven years in prison, a man returns to his home town for revenge, bringing chaos to the lives of three women. A spare little piece, of considerable power. Scripted by Nash.
Boa: short story by N. Richard Nash.
DRA                     92 min (ort 100 min) mTV
B,V                                 ODY

## PARADINE CASE, THE **
Alfred Hitchcock      USA           1947
*Gregory Peck, Charles Laughton, Louis Jourdan, Ann Todd, Charles Coburn, Ethel Barrymore, Alida Valli, Leo G. Carroll*
A barrister falls in love with the woman he is defending on a charge of murder. Despite the stilted and excessively verbose nature of the script, Hitchcock's treatment largely redeems it, though this is far from one of his best works. Produced and written by David O. Selznick.
Boa: novel by Robert Hichens.
DRA              115 min (ort 132 min) B/W
B,V                           GHV; VCC

## PARADISE *                                 15
Stuart Gillard         USA            1982
*Willie Aames, Phoebe Cates, Tuvia Tavi, Richard Curnock, Neil Vipond, Aviva Marks*
Two teenagers stranded at a lush desert oasis, imitate Adam and Eve when they discover sex, in this 1820s tale. A re-run of THE BLUE LAGOON and just as forgettable.
DRA                                 102 min
B,V,V2                              EHE

## PARADISE ALLEY **                      15
Sylvester Stallone     USA            1978
*Sylvester Stallone, Lee Canalito, Armand Assante, Frank McRae, Anne Archer, Kevin Conway, Joy Ingalls*
Stallone's directing debut (he also wrote the script) tells of three brothers from the slums of New York hoping for the big time when one of them becomes a professional wrestler. A kind of fashionable update of CITY FOR CONQUEST with a shallower treatment.
DRA           102 min (ort 109 min) (Cut at film
                                   release by 42 sec)
B,V                                 CIC

## PARADISE MOTEL *                        18
Cary Medoway         USA            1984
*Gary Hershberger, Robert Krantz, Bob Basso, Jonna Leigh Stack, Rick Gibbs, Jeffrey Jay Hea*
The son of a motel owner is obliged to let his snobby classmates use a spare room at his father's motel for their sexual fumblings, as a way of gaining acceptance. Though slightly reminiscent of THE APARTMENT, this rather witless teen comedy is light years away in terms of plot.
Aka: NEW KID IN TOWN
COM                                    87 min
B,V                             POLY; CH5

## PARALLAX VIEW, THE ****                15
Alan J. Pakula         USA            1974
*Warren Beatty, Paula Prentiss, William Daniels, Walter McGinn, Hume Cronyn, Kenneth Mars, Kelly Thordsen, Earl Hindman, Chuck Waters, Bill Joyce, Bettie Johnson, Bill McKinney, Joanne Harris, Ted Gehring, Lee Purlford, Doria Cook*
Taut thriller about a conspiracy to eliminate all the witnesses to a political killing. Script is by David Giler and Lorenzo Semple Jr. The same director-photographer-design team went on to make ALL THE PRESIDENT'S MEN, but that film is not nearly as exciting as this entertaining work.
Boa: novel by Loren Singer.
THR                                 101 min
B,V,V2                              CIC

## PARAMEDICS *                            15
Stuart Margolin        USA            1987
*George Newbern, Ray Walston, Lawrence-Hilton Jacobs, John P. Ryan, Sally Kellerman, Christopher McDonald*
Now paramedics get the POLICE ACADEMY treatment, as they are transferred from a rich uptown district to a poorer and rougher neighbourhood.
COM           87 min (ort 90 min) Cut (15 sec)
B,V                                 VES

## PARANOIA *
Umberto Lenzi     ITALY/FRANCE       1969
*Carroll Baker, Lou Castel, Collette Descombes, Tino Carraro*
A widow becomes involved in betrayal and blackmail by those she once trusted, or so it would seem. A grim dud with a vicious streak.
Aka: ORGASMO; UNE FOLLE ENVIE D'AIMER
DRA                                  94 min
B,V                          VFP L/A; HER

## PARAPSYCHICS **                       18
Nico Mastorakis      GREECE         1974
*Jessica Dublin, Maria Alfieri, Peter Winter, Chris Nomikos, Peter Winter*
A cool blonde possesses strange and terrifying paranormal powers which she uses to gain her own ends.
Aka: BLUE EYES OF DEATH; DEATH HAS BLUE EYES (NET)
HOR      77 min (ort 90 min) (Abridged at film release)
B,V                              KSV; NET

## PARASITE *
Charles Band        USA        1982
*Robert Glaudini, Demi Moore, Luca Bercovici, James Davidson, Al Fann, Cherie Currie, Vivian Blaine, Tom Villard*
Nasty creatures prey on victim after victim, and not only thrive inside their hosts but leap out to attack others. An amateurish ALIEN clone that was filmed in 3-D, to make this experience a little more sickening (though this will be lost on the TV screen – a small blessing perhaps).
HOR        80 min (ort 85 min)
V        EIV

## PARENT TRAP, THE **        U
David Swift        USA        1961
*Hayley Mills, Maureen O'Hara, Brian Keith, Charlie Ruggles, Una Merkel, Leo G. Carroll, Joanna Barnes, Cathleen Nesbitt, Ruth McDevitt, Nancy Kulp*
Twin sisters meet for the first time at a summer camp, and eventually hatch a plot to re-unite their divorced parents. A cute Disney comedy of the dated and sentimental kind, with Mills playing both parts. Written by Swift and followed by two TV sequels in 1986 and 1989. Filmed once before as "Twice Upon A Time".
Boa: novel Das Doppelte Lottchen (Lottie And Lisa) by Erich Kastner.
COM        122 min (ort 124 min)
B,V        WDV

## PARENT TRAP 2 **        U
Ronald F. Maxwell        USA        1986
*Hayley Mills, Tom Skerritt, Bridgette Anderson, Carrie Kei Heim, Alex Harvey, Gloria Cromwell, Judith Tannen, Janice Tesh, Duchess Tomasello, Daniel Brun, Antonio Fabrizio, Ted Science, Margaret Woodall*
Sequel to THE PARENT TRAP, with Mills playing the dual role of twin sisters, now both grown up, divorced and moving from Florida to New York. She finds that her daughter and her best friend are both just as conniving as she and her sister were as children. Glossy, romantic nonsense that was followed by a further sequel in 1989. Filmed on location in Tampa, Florida.
DRA        81 min (ort 95 min) mCab
B,V        WDV

## PARENT TRAP 3 **        U
Mollie Miller        USA        1989
*Hayley Mills, Barry Bostwick, Ray Baker, Patricia Richardson, Joy Creel, Leanna Creel, Monica Creel*
Third time round, this second sequel to the 1961 film has moved quite far from the original idea, with our grown-up twins falling out when they both decide to marry the same man, a widowed father of triplets. A light and frothy comedy, followed by "Parent Trap Hawaiian Honeymoon".
COM        85 min (ort 100 min) mTV
V        WDV

## PARENTHOOD ****        15
Ron Howard        USA        1989
*Steve Martin, Mary Steenburgen, Dianne Wiest, Jason Robards, Rick Moranis, Tom Hulce, Martha Plimpton, Keanu Reeves, Harley Kozak, Dennis Dugan, Leaf Phoenix, Paul Linke*
A warm and insightful character study that focuses on the problems of parenthood, as seen through the eyes of several parents who belong to the same large family. While Martin and Steenburgen cope with careers and kids, and Moranis' 3-year-old copes with Kafka, Wiest finds herself the mother of problem teenagers and Robards learns that parenthood doesn't end when the kids grow up. The music is by Randy Newman. A TV series followed.
Boa: story by Lowell Ganz, Babaloo Mandel and Ron Howard.

COM        118 min (ort 124 min)
V        CIC

## PARENTS **        18
Bob Balaban        USA        1989
*Randy Quaid, Mary Beth Hurt, Sandy Dennis, Bryan Madorsky, Juno Mills-Cockell, Kathryn Grody, Deborah Rush, Graham Jarvis*
A comedy-horror yarn set in the 1950s, and telling of an inquisitive 10-year-old boy who begins to wonder where the tasty leftovers come from that father brings home every night, and just what goes on in their cellar. Fairly well handled and there are one or two laughs, but the lack of a good story sinks this one. The directorial debut of actor Balaban.
HOR        94 min
V        VES

## PARIS BY NIGHT **        15
David Hare        UK        1988
*Charlotte Rampling, Jane Asher, Michael Gambon, Iain Glen, Robert Hardy, Andrew Ray, Niamh Cusack, Robert Flemyng*
A tough and self-possessed female politician finds that an old associate, who was ruined by her husband, is out to destroy her career. She decides that murder is her only option. An untidy and banal muddle that largely wastes the talents of its cast.
THR        99 min
V        VIR

## PARIS, TEXAS ***        15
Wim Wenders
        FRANCE/WEST GERMANY        1984
*Harry Dean Stanton, Dean Stockwell, Nastassia Kinski, Aurore Clement, Hunter Carson, Bernard Wicki*
The strange story of a man returning after a long absence, and looking for his wife in an effort to rebuild his life. He eventually finds her working in a brothel (of sorts). Richly atmospheric and beautifully photographed (by Robby Muller) and acted, but excruciatingly slow and murky. A hit with the critics, who probably read their own meanings into the enigmatic Sam Shepard script. The excellent score is by Ry Cooder. Filmed in English.
DRA        148 min; 139 min (PAL) (ort 150 min)
B,V,V2        PVG; PAL

## PARK IS MINE, THE **        15
Steven Hilliard Stern
        CANADA        1985
*Yaphet Kotto, Tommy Lee Jones, Helen Shaver, Peter Dvorsky, Eric Peterson, Lawrence Dane, Dennis Simpson, Reg Dreger, Louis DiBianco, Gale Garnett, Carl Marotte, Dennis O'Connor, Tom Harvey, R.D. Reid, George Bloomfield*
A frustrated Vietnam veteran takes over Central Park in New York by force, in order to give vent to his emotions, resulting in a violent conflict taking place. Despite its powerful emotional content, whatever point the film is trying to make never becomes clear. Filmed in Toronto, despite the setting of the tale.
Boa: novel by Stephen Peters.
A/AD        102 min (ort 105 min) mCab
B,V        CBS

## PARKER **        15
Jim Goddard        UK        1984
*Bryan Brown, Cheri Lunghi, Kurt Raab, Hannelore Eisner, Simon Rouse, Dana Gillespie, Bob Peck, Beate Finkh, Gwyneth Strong, Uwe Ochsenknecht, Ingrid Pitt, Phil Smeeton, Tom Wilkinson, Alexander Duda*
A businessman is held captive for 11 days, and then released without a ransom being demanded. No-one believes him and he becomes obsessed with the need to know the reasons for his ordeal. A suspense tale that

is largely made ineffective by a lack of direction. Written by Trevor Preston.
Aka: BONES
THR 96 min; 93 min (VIR) (ort 100 min)
B,V PVG; VIR

**PARTIZAN \*\***
Stole Jankovic
USA/LIECHTENSTEIN/YUGOSLAVIA 1974
Rod Taylor, Adam West, Xenia Gratsos, Olivera Katarina, Brako Plesa
The heroic but ultimately unsuccessful attempts, by a band of Yugoslav partisans to resist the onslaught of the Nazi war machine during 1941, form the basis for this routine WW2 action tale.
Aka: PARTIZANI
WAR 91 min
B,V POR L/A; MMA

**PARTNERS \***                                   15
James Burrows USA 1982
Ryan O'Neal, John Hurt, Kenneth McMillan, Robyn Douglass, Jay Robinson, Denise Galik, Rick Jason
A straight policeman has to pretend to be homosexual in order to investigate a gay murder. A clone of CRUISING that wastes the assembled talents of the cast. Written by Francis Veber (of LA CAGE AUX FOLLES fame), this puerile comedy-thriller was the feature debut for Burrows, who prior to this directed TV comedy shows.
THR 88 min (ort 98 min)
B,V CIC

**PARTY ANIMAL, THE \***                          18
David Beaird USA 1984
Matthew Causey, Timothy Carhart, Robin Harlan, Jerry Jones, Suzanne Ashley
A freak experiment turns a totally unattractive youth into a super-stud, in this dreary exercise in silliness.
COM 73 min (ort 77 min)
B,V EIV

**PARTY CAMP \*\***                               15
Gary Graves USA 1987
April Wayne, Billy Jacoby, Kirk Cribb, Kerry Brennan, Peter Jason, Andrew Ross, Jewel Shepard
A summer camp with the usual complement of crazy counsellors and mad campers is the subject for this broad comedy.
COM 92 min (ort 96 min) Cut (11 sec)
B,V VES

**PARTY LINE \***                                 18
William Webb USA 1988
Richard Hatch, Leif Garrett, Richard Roundtree, Greta Blackburn, Shawn Weatherly, James O'Sullivan, Terrence McGovern
A series of murders in Los Angeles is linked to a telephone party-line which youngsters use to make dates. A slack effort that attempts to exploit a popular telephone service, but brings neither talent nor care to the story.
HOR 91 min
B,V SONY

**PARTY STOOGE \***                               PG
Chuck Workman USA 1985
Josh Mostel, Melanie Chartoff, Josh Miner, Sid Caesar, Thom Sharp
A young boy who hero-worships the Three Stooges, grows to manhood but cannot shake off his obsession with the comic trio and seeks medical help. A weak comedy that flogs its central idea to death in a desperate search for laughs. Not surprisingly, much use is made of actual footage from Three Stooges films.
Aka: STOOGEMANIA
COM 80 min (ort 95 min)
B,V EIV

**PARTY, PARTY \***                               15
Terry Windsor UK 1983
Daniel Peacock, Karl Howmon, Perry Fenwick, Sean Chapman, Phoebe Nichols, Caroline Quentin, Gary Olsen, Clive Mantle, Ken Thomson, Kate Williams, Kenneth Farrington, Phillip Martin Brown, Annabel Mednick, Sallyanne Law
A boy holds a New Year's party while his parents are not at home and it rapidly gets out of hand. Tiresome dross with not a single gag worth remembering.
COM 98 min
B,V VSP L/A; A&M

**PARTY, THE \*\***                               18
R.T. Megginson USA
"Bud" Whancey, Mary Mitchell, Cindy Tree, Bobby Astyr, Billy Padgett, The Amazing Dorin
A young musician sets out for New York to seek his fortune and gets more than he bargained for, in this look at what happens at a party when the guests really let their hair down.
A 81 min
B,V PANA; PHE; DIAM

**PARTY, THE \*\***                               PG
Blake Edwards USA 1968
Peter Sellers, Claudine Longet, Marge Champion, Denny Miller, Gavin MacLeod, Fay McKenzie, Steve Franken, Buddy Lester
A clumsy Indian actor is invited to a party at the home of a Hollywood studio boss in error, and proceeds to wreck his house in a series of accidents. The script is by Edwards, and Tom and Frank Waldham and the film is every bit as loose and episodic as one might expect. There are however, several very funny sight gags.
COM 95 min (ort 99 min)
B,V WHV

**PASCALI'S ISLAND \*\***                         15
James Dearden UK 1988
Ben Kingsley, Charles Dance, Helen Mirren, George Murcell, Sheila Allen, Nadim Sawalha
A love and espionage triangle set on an Aegean island, in the last dying days of the Turkish Empire just prior to WW1, with a bogus English archaeologist plotting with a disaffected Turkish spy to smuggle out an archaeological treasure. A well-acted drama (written by the director) whose modest budget severely hampers it.
DRA 99 min (ort 106 min)
B,V VIR

**PASSAGE TO INDIA, A \*\*\***                     PG
David Lean UK 1984
Judy Davis, James Fox, Peggy Ashcroft, Victor Banerjee, Alec Guinness, Art Malik, Saeed Jaffrey, Richard Wilson, Michael Culver, Antonia Pemberton, Clive Swift, Ann Firbank, Roshah Seth, Sandra Holz, Ishaq Bux
An examination of the clash of cultures between the British and Indians in the 1920s, when a young and foolish woman goes to India accompanied by the mother of her fiance. Finding her honour compromised by a trip to the hills in the company of a native Indian, she accuses him of attempted rape. This overlong and stilted film is partially redeemed by its images of great beauty. AA: S. Actress (Ashcroft), Score (Orig) (Maurice Jarre).
Boa: novel by E.M. Forster.
DRA 157 min (ort 163 min)
B,V TEVP

**PASSAGE TO MARSEILLES \*\***                    PG
Michael Curtiz USA 1944
Humphrey Bogart, Michele Morgan, Claude Rains, Sidney Greenstreet, Philip Dorn, Peter Lorre, Helmut Dantine, George Tobias, John Loder, Victor Francen, Eduardo Ciannelli

Five convicts escape from Devil's Island in order to join up with the Free French forces. The film's complex structure (and use of flashbacks within flashbacks) belies its rather simplistic story, and despite the presence of many of the same actors and production crew, totally fails to recapture the the feeling of CASABLANCA.

A/AD 105 min (ort 110 min) B/W
V WHV

## PASSAGE, THE *
J. Lee Thompson UK 1978
*James Mason, Anthony Quinn, Malcolm McDowell, Patricia Neal, Kay Lenz, Christopher Lee, Paul Clemens, Robert Rhys, Michael Lonsdale, Marcel Bozzuffi, Peter Arne, Neville Jason, Robert Brown, Rosa Alba*
A chemist and his family escaping over the Pyrenees into Spain, are pursued by a fanatical Nazi. Quinn plays the Basque guide who helps them escape. A simplistic chase thriller with a vicious streak, and an over-the-top performance from McDowell that carries little conviction. Scripted by Nicolaysen.
Boa: novel The Perilous Passage by Bruce Nicolaysen.
THR 98 min
B,V VCL/CBS

## PASSAGE, THE ** PG
Harry Thompson USA 1987
*Brian Keith, Alexandra Paul, Dee Law, Ned Beatty, Barbara Barrie*
The daughter of a wealthy family marries her boyfriend after becoming pregnant and is duly ostracised by her father who's outraged at her refusal to fall in with the plans he had for her. After enduring several years of estrangement, the young couple finally learn that something has happened to make him relent.
DRA 102 min
V RCA

## PASSENGER, THE ** PG
Michelangelo Antonioni
FRANCE/ITALY/SPAIN 1975
*Jack Nicholson, Maria Schneider, Jenny Runacre, Ian Hendry, Steven Berkoff, Ambrose Bia*
A disenchanted TV reporter in Africa, decides to take over the identity of an Englishman who died suddenly in a hotel room, and discovers that he is now a gunrunner being slowly drawn into a web of intrigue, that can only result in his death. An enigmatic and ponderous thriller whose opaque plotting makes it difficult to follow, but as an exercise in sinister mood creation it works perfectly.
Aka: PROFESSION: REPORTER; PROFESSIONE: REPORTER
THR 113 min (ort 119 min)
B,V MGM

## PASSION AND THE GLORY, THE ** 15
Chris Thomson USA 1989
*Frank Gallacher, Tony Richards, Greta Scacchi, Jack Thompson, Mark Little, Jay Mannering*
A long and detailed melodrama set during the Depression Years, when a union chief falls for the leader of a group of Italian immigrants brought in by the bosses to work as cheap labour. Fair.
DRA 120 min
V TGP L/A

## PASSION HOTEL ** 18
Ilja Neutrof WEST GERMANY 197-
*Peter Hamm, Margaret-Rose Keil, Eva Gross, Rose Gardner, Al Price*
A young man works in a luxury hotel, and finds this has compensations, not least being the beautiful women who go there to get away from their boring husbands. A trite and dated little sex romp.
Aka: HAPPY GIGOLO, THE

A 64 min (ort 75 min) Cut (3 min 28 sec)
B,V BLUMO/GOLD; CAN

## PASSION ISLAND ** 18
Jacques Regis FRANCE/SPAIN 1983
*Stacey King, Kim Moon, Scris Murphy, Vera Floux, Dirke Altenvogt, Beatrice Philip*
Two models and a photographer on an assignment in Sri Lanka find it hard to keep their minds on their work when they get involved with a sinister sect.
Aka: ISLAND OF PASSION; L'ILE DES PASSIONS; SAMANKA
THR 71 min (ort 80 min)
B,V ABA L/A; PINK; CASS/IVS

## PASSION OF LOVE ** 15
Ettore Scola FRANCE/ITALY 1981
*Laura Antonelli, Bernard Giroudeau, Valerie D'Obici, Jean-Louis Trintignant, Bernard Blier, Massimo Girotti*
In 1862 an army captain arrives at a small frontier post, where a woman of hideous appearance conceives a hopeless passion for him. When he leaves to visit his mistress, she falls dangerously ill, and a feeling of pity and moral obligation draws him into a relationship with her. A flawed and generally ineffective variant on the story of Beauty and the Beast.
Aka: PASSIONE D'AMORE
DRA 118 min
B,V PVG; VES

## PASSION SEKA ** R18/18
Richard Pacheco USA
*Seka (Dorothy Hundley Patton), Mike Horner, Kay Parker, Shanna McCullough, Misha Garr, Toni Brooks*
A happily married housewife lives a double life, changing by night into an X-rated superstar called Molly Flame.
A 56 min (18 version) Cut (5 min 16 sec); 69 min (R18 version)
B,V ELV

## PASSPORT TO PIMLICO *** U
Henry Cornelius UK 1949
*Stanley Holloway, Basil Radford, Hermione Baddeley, Paul Dupuis, John Slater, Barbara Murray, Margaret Rutherford, Naunton Wayne, Raymond Huntley, Sidney Tafler, Betty Warren, Jane Hylton, Charles Hawtrey, James Hayter*
An unexploded bomb from WW2 is detonated in the London district of Pimlico, exposing a hidden cache of treasure and an ancient document that reveals the area to be part of the old French kingdom of Burgundy. The inhabitants exploit this loophole to secede from the UK and various complications arise. A charmingly whimsical comedy, dated but well executed. Screenplay was by Cornelius and T.E.B. Clarke.
COM 80 min (ort 84 min) B/W
V WHV

## PASSPORT TO TERROR *** PG
Lou Antonio USA 1989
*Lee Remick, Norma Aleandro*
Whilst on holiday in Turkey, an American woman is jailed on a charge of attempting to smuggle historical relics. Released on bail but fully expecting a long prison sentence she plans an escape, helped by the head of the American Consul. A tense thriller, largely based on a true story.
THR 90 min
V VIR

## PAT GARRETT AND BILLY THE KID ** 
Sam Peckinpah USA 1973
*James Coburn, Kris Kristofferson, Richard Jaeckel, Katy Jurado, Chill Wills, Jason Robards, Bob Dylan,*

R.G. Armstrong, Luke Askew, John Beck, Richard Bright, Matt Clark, Rita Coolidge, Jack Dodson, Jack Elam, Emilio Fernandez

A sombre retelling of this Western myth that has been filmed a number of times before. This version has too many character actors walking on for minor parts, and too little in the story to make it a success, though the full-length version (which only turned up in 1989) is somewhat better, if a good deal more bloody. Music is by Bob Dylan.

WES                          102 min (ort 122 min)
B,V,V2                                        MGM

## PATERNITY *                                15
David Steinberg          USA              1981
Burt Reynolds, Beverly D'Angelo, Norman Fell, Paul Dooley, Elizabeth Ashley, Lauren Hutton, Peter Billingsley, Jacqueline Brooks, Linda Gillin, Mike Kellin, Victoria Young, Elsa Raven, Carol Locatell, Kay Armen, Juanita Moore

A man who yearns to be a father, hires a waitress to act as a surrogate mother, in this predictable comedy of few laughs and much tedium. This was Steinberg's directing debut.

COM                          89 min (ort 94 min)
B,V                                            CIC

## PATHFINDER ***                             15
Nils Gaup              NORWAY            1987
Mikkel Gaup, Helgi Skulason, Nils Utsi, Sara Marit Gaup, Svein Scharfenberg, Knut Walle, John Sigurd Kristensen, Ann-Marja Blind, Sverre Porsanger, Ailu Gaup, Sven Birger Olsen, Nils-Aslek Valkeapaa, Marius Muller

This first film in the Lapp language, is the brutal tale of how a young boy achieves revenge on the invading nomads who slaughtered his parents and younger sister, when he offers to become their pathfinder. A memorable tale, made more so by the stark landscape in which it takes place. Only the dubbing is an annoyance, sub-titles would have been far better.

A/AD                             83 min dubbed
B,V                                            GHV

## PATHS OF GLORY ****
Stanley Kubrick          USA              1957
Kirk Douglas, Adolphe Menjou, George Macready, Wayne Morris, Ralph Meeker, Richard Anderson, Timothy Carey, Suzanne Christian, Bert Freed

Three French soldiers in 1916 face a court-martial on the charge of cowardice, which carries the death penalty, but are in fact innocent of these charges, and have been selected as scapegoats to save the reputation of a general. A harrowing, anti-war film, intelligently written by Calder Willingham, Jim Thompson and Kubrick, and based on Cobb's book which in turn was based on a true incident.
Boa: novel by Humphrey Cobb.

DRA                          80 min (ort 86 min) B/W
V                                             WHV

## PATRICK ***
Richard Franklin
                     AUSTRALIA           1978
Susan Penhaligon, Robert Helpman, Rod Mullinar, Robert Thompson, Bruce Barry, Julia Blake, Maria Mercedes, Helen Hemmingway, Everett de Roche, Walter Pym

A psychotic killer with telekinetic powers lies in a coma after killing his mother, but strange things begin to happen around him. A fair chiller with rather good effects but little development.

HOR                          104 min (ort 115 min)
B,V                                        VCL/CBS

## PATRIOT, THE **                            15
Frank Harris             USA              1986
Jeff Conaway, Michael J. Pollard, Leslie Nielson, Gregg Henry, Simone Griffeth, Stack Pierce

An ex-navy commando fights to save the world from a gang of terrorists, who plan to steal nuclear warheads on their way to a government base. A low-key and rather clumsy actioner that has a few good underwater sequences and a generous dose of violence.

A/AD                         98 min Cut (9 sec)
B,V                                            RCA

## PATSY, THE **                               U
Jerry Lewis              USA              1964
Jerry Lewis, Everett Sloane, Ed Wynne, Phil Harris, Keenan Wynn, Peter Lorre, John Carradine, Hans Conreid, Phil Foster, Richard Deacon, Scatman Crothers, Nancy Culp, Ed Wynn, Ed Sullivan, Mel Torme, Hedda Hopper

A bellboy is groomed for stardom after a popular entertainer dies in a plane crash. Sad to relate, this unfunny turkey was Lorre's last film.

COM                                       101 min
V                                             COL

## PATTON ****                                PG
Franklin Schaffner       USA              1970
George C. Scott, Karl Malden, Stephen Young, Michael Strong, Frank Latimore, James Edwards, Lawrence Dobkin, Michael Bates, Tim Considine, Karl Michael Vogler, Cary Loftin, Albert Dumortier, Morgan Paull, Bill Hickman

A brilliant performance by Scott, as one of America's most famous generals, plus a fine supporting cast, make this a most enjoyable film and a classic in screen biographies. Scott won an Oscar but didn't accept it. The score is by Jerry Goldsmith. AA: Pic, Dir, Actor (Scott), Story/Screen (Francis Ford Coppola/Edmund H. North), Art/Set (U. McCleary and G. Parrondo/P. Thevenet and A. Mateos), Edit (H. Fowler), Sound (Williams/Bassman).
Aka: PATTON: LUST FOR GLORY
Boa: book by L. Farago.

DRA                          169 min (ort 171 min)
B, V/h, V2                                      CBS

## PATTY HEARST: HER OWN STORY *             18
Paul Schrader            USA              1988
Natasha Richardson, William Forsythe, Ving Rhamer, Dana Delany, Frances Fisher, Jodi Long, Olivia Barash, Scott Kraft, Ermal Washington, Gerald Gordon

Dramatisation of the kidnap and subsequent brainwashing of Patty Hearst, by the Symbionese Liberation Army in the 1970s. An ill-advised attempt early on to portray her brainwashing from the victim's point of view, kills any dramatic impact the narrative (such as it is) might have achieved. Scripted by Nicholas Kazan. See also THE ORDEAL OF PATTY HEARST.
Aka: PATTY HEARST
Boa: book Every Secret Thing by Patty Hearst.

DRA                          105 min (ort 108 min)
B,V                                            EIV

## PAWNBROKER, THE ****
Sidney Lumet             USA          ,   1965
Rod Steiger, Geraldine Fitzgerald, Brock Peters, Jaimie Sanchez, Thelma Oliver, Juano Hernandez, Marketa Kimbrell, Raymond St Jacques

A survivor of the Auschwitz death-camp, scratches a living from his pawnbroker's shop situated in Harlem, but is haunted by his memories. A beautiful and moving film for which Steiger received an Oscar nomination. The script is by David Friedkin and Morton Fine and the score by Quincy Jones. Note the excellent intercutting of harrowing deathcamp sequences; the editing was done by Ralph Rosenblum.
Boa: novel by Edward Lewis Wallant.

DRA                          109 min (ort 114 min) B/W
B,V                                            POLY

## PAYBACK *                                  15
Russell Solberg          USA              1990

Corey Michael Eubanks, Bert Remsen, Michael
Ironside, Teresa Blake, Don Swayze, Vincent Van
Patten
Following a prison-yard brawl, a young man is put
into a hard-labour gang, but eventually escapes and
sets out to avenge the death of his brother at the
hands of an evil drugs baron. Fast, furious and
forgettable.
A/AD                                    90 min
V                                        VES

## PAYDAY ***
Daryl Duke            USA               1972
Rip Torn, Ahna Capri, Elayne Heilveil, Cliff Emmich,
Michael C. Gwynne
A detailed account of the depressing life of a touring
Country and Western singer who, despite his limited
talent, is determined to make it to the top by
exploiting everybody he can. A downbeat but thor-
oughly absorbing study, scripted by Don Carpenter.
DRA                          98 min (ort 103 min)
B,V                                     TEVP

## PEACEKILLERS, THE *                     18
Douglas Schwartz      USA               1971
Michael Ontkean, Clint Richie, Paul Krokop, Jessie
Walton, Darlene Duralia, Lavelle Roby
A young girl is raped and an all-out war erupts
between biker gangs. A cynical piece of sick exploita-
tion.
DRA    82 min; 79 min (VCC) Cut (3 min 26 sec) (ort 86
min)
B,V            FRON/GHV L/A; VCC (VHS only)

## PEACEMAKER **                           18
Kevin S. Tenney      USA                1990
Robert Davi, Robert Forster, Hilary Shepard, Lance
Edwards
An alien mass murderer escapes to Earth, but is
pursued by the title figure, a sort of galactic cop, who
enlists the help of an Earth girl. However, she
encounters their quarry and becomes somewhat confused when he claims to be the "Peacemaker". A fairly
well-structured cat-and-mouse story, with adequate
special effects, though the film might well have been
better.
FAN                                     87 min
V                                        MED

## PEACHES AND CREAM ***                   R18
Robert McCallum      USA                1982
Annette Haven, Abigail Reed, Chelsea McLane, Jerry
Health, Paul Thomas, Dale Meadar, Aaron Stuart
A naive young girl has been brought up on a farm by
her drunken, lecherous stepfather. She is next seen as
super-sophisticated and we realise that she has been
working for a pimp for the last four years. Returning
home to visit an old boyfriend, she finds that he is now
married and that her stepfather is dead. She returns
to the city but finally walks out on her pimp. Haven
brings a lot of conviction to her role in this superior
adult movie.
A                                       71 min
B,V                         EVI L/A; PRI; SHEP

## PEANUT BUTTER SOLUTION, THE ***          PG
Michael Rubbo        CANADA             1985
Mathew Mackay, Michael Hogan, Alison Podbrey,
Edgar Fruitier, Siluck Sayanasy, Michel Maillot,
Helen Hughes, Griffith Brewster, Harry Hill, Patricia
Thompson, Terrence La Brosse, Doug Smith, Nick
Manekos, Vicki Lee
A young boy loses his hair after an encounter in a
haunted house, but fortunately is supplied with the
title substance by one of his teachers, a strange figure
who likes to collect children and sell their hair. Told to
use only the smallest amount of the solution, he uses
too much and quickly turns into a walking hair
factory. A witty and lively children's fantasy.

Aka: MICHAEL'S FRIGHT
JUV                          90 min (ort 98 min)
B,V                                     NWV

## PEE-WEE'S BIG ADVENTURE **               U
Tim Burton           USA                1985
Pee-Wee Herman (Paul Reubens), Elizabeth Daily,
Mark Holton, Diana Salinger, Judd Owen, James
Brolin, Morgan Fairchild
Feature-length vehicle for Herman, a famous Amer-
ican comic, whose humour involves a grown-up man
acting and thinking like a child. Pee-Wee searches for
his stolen bicycle and has other adventures, but
despite a wonderfully overblown performance from
Herman, the film has little of substance. The score is
by Danny Elfman.
COM                          88 min (ort 92 min)
V/sh                                    WHV

## PEEPER **                                PG
Peter Hyams          USA                1975
Michael Caine, Natalie Wood, Kitty Winn, Thayer
David, Liam Dunn, Dorothy Adams
A private eye is hired to find a criminal's daughters
who have taken their father's loot and run away. A
sort of weak spoof of those detective films of the 1940s.
Aka: FAT CHANCE
Boa: novel Deadfall by Keith Laumer.
COM                          83 min (ort 87 min)
B,V                                     CBS

## PEEPING TOM ***                          R18
Michael Powell       UK                 1959
Carl Boehm, Moira Shearer, Anna Massey, Maxine
Audley, Brenda Bruce, Martin Miller, Esmond Knight,
Bartlett Mullins, Michael Goodliffe, Jack Watson,
Shirley Ann Field, Pamela Green, Michael Powell
A demented photographer is fascinated by the idea of
murdering women and taking pictures of the fear on
their faces, so he sets out with a camera and tripod
(with concealed spike) to do this. Additionally he
documents the police investigation that follows and
finally his own suicide. A remarkable film in many
ways, this sick saga of insanity created a storm of
controversy on release. It's still strong stuff.
THR            65 min (ort 109 min) Cut (1 min 6 sec)
V                                    VEXCEL

## PEG LEG, MUSKET AND SABRE *              PG
Kirk Douglas        ITALY/USA          1973
Kirk Douglas, Mark Lester, Neville Brand, George
Eastman (Luigi Montefiore), Don Stroud, Lesley-Anne
Down, Danny DeVito, Mel Blanc, Phil Brown, Davor
Antolic, Stole Arandjelovic, Fabijan Sovagovic, Shaft
Douglas
A turgid pirate adventure aimed at a juvenile audi-
ence, that follows the exploits of a peg-legged pirate
who leads his gang on a treasure hunt in California. A
lousy film, made worse by the addition of some truly
forgettable songs. Filmed in Yugoslavia.
Aka: SCALAWAG
A/AD                                    93 min
V                            WARAD; GLOB

## PEGGY SUE GOT MARRIED ***               15
Francis Ford Coppola  USA              1986
Kathleen Turner, Nicholas Cage, Barry Miller,
Catherine Hicks, Barbara Harris, Joan Allen, Kevin J.
O'Connor, Don Murray, Maureen O'Sullivan, Leon
Ames, Helen Hunt, John Carradine
A woman about to divorce her husband, gets taken
back in time to her last year at high school, and finds
that she has a second chance to make some important
decisions. A pleasant and nostalgic little fantasy that
leaves too much unresolved, but is put together with
considerable flair.
COM                          98 min (ort 104 min)
B,V                                     CBS

**PEKING BLONDE ***
Nicolas Gessner        FRANCE             1967
*Mireille Darc, Claude Brook, Pascale Roberts, Edward
G. Robinson, Francoise Brion*
The intelligence services of the USA, the USSR and
China race to get hold of some secret information
about missiles. A little-known thriller whose lack of
renown is well deserved. Robinson looks bored acting
in this one (he has a small part), so will you after
watching it.
Aka: BLONDE FROM PEKING, THE
THR                          78 min (ort 80 min)
B,V                                          VCL/CBS

**PELLE THE CONQUEROR ****                      15
Billie August   DENMARK/SWEDEN            1987
*Pelle Hvenegaard, Max Von Sydow, Erik Paaske,
Kristina Tornqvist, Morten Jorgensen, Axel Strobye,
Astrid Villaume, Bjorn Granath, Lena Pia
Bernhardsson, Troels Asmussen, John Wittig, Nis
Bank-Mikkelsen*
A poor Swedish widower takes his young son Pelle to
Denmark, where he hopes they can find a better life.
Once there they are forced to face even greater
hardships, but this serves to strengthen the bond
between father and son. Set in the 19th century, this
poignant period drama is as moving as it is memor-
able. It deservedly won the Palme d'Or at the 1988
Cannes Film Festival. AA: Foreign.
Boa: novel by Martin Anderson Nexo.
DRA                                      150 min
V                                          BRAVE

**PENALTY PHASE ***                            PG
Tony Richardson        USA                1986
*Peter Strauss, Jonelle Allen, Karen Austin, Jane
Badler, John Harkins, Millie Perkins, Mitchell Ryan,
Richard Bright, Richard Chaves, Ross Harris, Art
LaFleur, Melissa Gilbert, Mark Allen, Ron Campbell,
Stuart Duckworth*
A judge discovers a technical flaw in the handling of a
murder case and agonises over his decision. He must
either risk public anger and a possible end to his
career by allowing a convicted murderer to go free, or
act against the dictates of his conscience. A well-
focused and literate drama, the script is by Gale
Patrick Hickman.
DRA                     89 min (ort 94 min) mTV
B,V                                          NWV

**PENDULUM ***                                 15
George Schaefer        USA                1969
*George Peppard, Jean Seberg, Richard Kiley, Charles
McGraw, Robert F. Lyons, Madeline Sherwood, Frank
Marth, Paul McGrath, Stewart Moss, Isabell Sanford,
Dana Elcar, Harry Lewis, Mildred Trares, Robin
Raymond*
A police captain is accused of murder when his wife
and her lover are killed, and finds it difficult to get at
the truth. A flashy and efficient melodrama, well put
together but hardly enthralling. The score is by
Walter Scharf.
DRA                     97 min (ort 106 min)
B,V                                          RCA

**PENITENT, THE ***
Cliff Osmond           USA                1986
*Raul Julia, Armand Assante, Rona Freed, Julie
Carmen, Lucy Reina*
This unusual little fable is set in a remote village
where each year and extreme religious sect re-enact
the Crucifixion, by leaving a cult member nailed to a
cross for a whole day in the desert. An examination of
this largely falls victim to a further sub-plot that sees
Julia having his young wife seduced by an old friend.
Osmond's directing debut is a flawed blend of interest-
ing ideas and muddled plotting.
DRA                                      94 min
V                                          CBS

**PENITENTIARY ***                             18
Jamaa Fanaka           USA                1979
*Leon Isaac Kennedy, Thommy Pollard, Hazel Speers,
Badja Djola, Gloria Delaney, Chuck Mitchell*
A young black man who has been wrongly imprisoned,
uses his skill as a boxer to improve his lot. Fanaka
produced, directed and wrote this one which, despite
being predictable in development, is carried along by
its acute observation and unflinching portrayal of
prison brutality. Several less commendable sequels
followed.
DRA                                      99 min
B,V,V2                           VDM L/A; STABL

**PENITENTIARY 2 ***
Jamaa Fanaka           USA                1984
*Leon Isaac Kennedy, Ernie Hudson, Mr T, Glynn
Turman, Peggy Blow, Malik Carter, Cephaus Jaxon,
Marvin Jones*
A sequel to the first film, with very much the same
theme of a young black prisoner using his boxing
skills to make his life in prison a little more bearable.
Unfortunately, this one lacks the care that was
lavished on the earlier work, and represents little
more than a cynical exercise in exploitation.
DRA                103 min (ort 108 min) Cut (29 sec)
B,V                                    VDM; STABL

**PENITENTIARY 3 ***                           18
Jamaa Fanaka           USA                1987
*Leon Isaac Kennedy, Anthony Geary, Steve Antin,
Kessler Raymond, Ric Mancini, Jim Bailey*
A further outing for this boxer-in-prison theme, with
Kennedy back in jail where he finds that both the
warder, and the local Mr Big who runs life inside,
want him to fight on their boxing teams. Slightly
better than the preceding film but still puerile.
DRA                           87 min Cut (25 sec)
B,V                                          WHV

**PENNIES FROM HEAVEN ***                      15
Herbert Ross           USA                1982
*Steve Martin, Bernadette Peters, Christopher Walken,
Jessica Harper, Vernel Bagneris, John McMartin, Jay
Garner, Tommy Rall, Eliska Krupka, Toni Kaye,
Frank McCarthy, Raleigh Bond, Gloria LeRoy, Nancy
Parsons, Shirley Kirkes*
The story of a sheet-music salesman and his bleak life,
is compared to the carefree world of the songs of the
1930s. Superb photography (by Gordon Willis) and
sets (by Ken Adam) are intelligently combined with
the music of the period. Only the transposition of the
story (originally a BBC TV production with Bob
Hoskins) to the USA lets it down. Musical direction
was by Marvin Hamlisch.
Boa: TV play by Dennis Potter.
MUS                     103 min (ort 108 min)
V/h                                          MGM

**PENNY GOLD ***
Jack Cardiff           UK                 1973
*James Booth, Una Stubbs, Sue Lloyd, Micky Henson,
Francesca Annis, Joseph O'Connors, Richard Heffer,
Joss Ackland, George Murcell, Marianne Stone*
When a young woman is murdered, the detective
investigating the case finds that her twin is party to
an elaborate deception involving a rare stamp.
DRA                                      90 min
V                                          HVS

**PENNY SERENADE ***                           U
George Stevens         USA                1941
*Cary Grant, Irene Dunne, Beulah Bondi, Edgar
Buchanan, Ann Doran, Eva Lee Kuney, Leonard
Willey*
Weepy drama about a couple who adopt a baby when
their own child dies. A film that pulls out all the
emotional stops and yet still retains the power to
retain interest and stimulate belief. The script is by
Morrie Ryskind.

DRA          115 min (ort 125 min) B/W
V          VCC

## PENTHOUSE PARADISE **        PG
George Schaefer    USA       1988
*Karen Austin, Joel Higgins, Lee Richardson,*
*Katharine Hepburn*
A best-selling authoress writes a book that flops, and
is persuaded to spend a week with a normal family as
a way of gaining inspiration.
COM               95 min
B,V          EMP; BRAVE

## PEOPLE **                18
Gerard Damiano    USA       1978
*Serena, Samantha Fox, Jamie Gillis, Richard Bolla,*
*John Thomas, Paula Pretense, Kasey Rodgers, Eric*
*Edwards, Bobby Asyr, Sue Swan, Kelly Green*
Six completely unrelated erotic tales, that were
probably intended to make some statement regarding
human sexuality, but end up only titillating. "The
Game" looks at a husband and wife, "Goodbye" has a
man leaving to go on a long journey, "Once Upon A
Time" is a costumed ball, "The Exhibition" observes a
dominatrix at work, an untitled story examines
incest, and lastly "The Hooker" explores an encounter
with a prostitute.
A      63 min (ort 80 min) Cut (9 min 9 sec)
B,V          XTACY/KRP; MOIRA

## PEOPLE ACROSS THE LAKE, THE **    18
Arthur Allen Seidelman
         USA       1988
*Valerie Harper, Gerald McRaney, Barry Corbin,*
*Dorothy Lyman, Daryl Anderson, Tammy Lauren, Jeff*
*Kizer*
A couple from the city move to a quiet lakeside
community, and find themselves embroiled in a
murder mystery when bodies start appearing in their
basement. A slow and illogical thriller that has
nothing of novelty, except perhaps the setting.
THR      96 min (ort 100 min) mTV
V          RCA

## PEOPLE THAT TIME FORGOT, THE **    U
Kevin Connor     UK       1977
*Patrick Wayne, Sarah Douglas, Doug McClure, Dana*
*Gillespie, Thorley Walters, Shane Rimmer, Tony*
*Britton, John Hallan, Dave Prowse, Milton Reid,*
*Kiran Shah, Richard Parmentier*
A sequel to THE LAND THAT TIME FORGOT, with
a man leading an expedition to a mysterious island to
rescue a friend who disappeared there three years
before. Set in 1919, the film has a few effective
moments but is generally a pedestrian exercise. Even
the monsters don't come up to scratch.
Boa: novel by Edgar Rice Burroughs.
A/AD         87 min (ort 90 min)
B,V          RNK

## PERCY * 
Ralph Thomas     UK       1970
*Hywel Bennett, Elke Sommer, Britt Ekland, Denholm*
*Elliott, Cyd Hayman, Janet Key, Tracey Crisp,*
*Antonia Ellis, Tracy Reed, Patrick Mower, Adrienne*
*Posta, Julia Foster, Arthur English, Margaretta Scott*
Tasteless story of the world's first penis transplant,
with the recipient setting out to discover the identity
of the owner. Written by Hugh Leonard and followed
by PERCY'S PROGRESS.
Boa: novel by Raymond Hitchcock.
COM        96 min (ort 103 min)
B,V          TEVP

## PERCY'S PROGRESS 
Ralph Thomas     UK       1974
*Elke Sommer, Denholm Elliott, Leigh Lawson, Judy*
*Geeson, Harry H. Corbett, Vincent Price, Adrienne*
*Posta, Julie Ege, Barry Humphries, James Booth, Milo*

*O'Shea, Ronald Fraser, Anthony Andrews, Bernard*
*Lee, Madeline Smith*
Sequel to PERCY, with all the men in the world
becoming impotent except the owner of the world's
first transplanted organ. Unalloyed dross of a very
high order.
Aka: IT'S NOT SIZE THAT COUNTS; IT'S NOT THE
SIZE THAT COUNTS
COM        97 min (ort 101 min)
B,V          TEVP

## PERFECT *                15
James Bridges    USA       1985
*John Travolta, Jamie Lee Curtis, Marilu Henner,*
*Jann Wenner, Anne De Salvo, Stefan Gierasch,*
*Laraine Newman*
A reporter for a music magazine, researching for an
article on health clubs, finds his objectivity in danger
when he falls for an aerobics instructress working in a
club he was intending to write a bad piece on. A
superficial, vain and pompous little film that never
found an audience, and no wonder. Scripted by
Bridges and Aaron Latham.
DRA        115 min (ort 120 min)
V/sh         RCA

## PERFECT CRIME, THE * 
Aaron Leviathon (Giuseppe Rosati)
         ITALY     1978
*Gloria Guida, Anthony Steel, Leonard Mann, Alida*
*Valli, Janet Agren, Joseph Cotten*
A series of murders decimates the top management of
a worldwide company. Scotland Yard investigates.
Aka: INDAGINE SU UN DELITTO PERFETTO
THR             105 min
B,V,V2        VPD

## PERFECT FRIDAY ** 
Peter Hall       UK       1970
*Ursula Andress, Stanley Baker, David Warner,*
*Patience Collier, T.P. McKenna, David Waller, Joan*
*Benham, Julian Orchard, Trisha Mortimer, Ann*
*Tirard, Carleton Hobbs*
A bank manager becomes infatuated with the wife of
an impoverished aristocratic couple, and decides to
break free from his staid life, robbing his own bank of
£30,000 with their help. A mildly amusing caper with
a few good twists. The music is by Johnny Dankworth.
COM        92 min (ort 95 min)
B,V          VCL/CBS

## PERFECT GENTLEMAN ***       PG
Jackie Cooper    USA       1978
*Lauren Bacall, Ruth Gordon, Sandy Dennis, Lisa*
*Pelikan, Robert Alda, Stephen Pearlman, Stevie Allie*
*Collura, Dick O'Neill, Rick Garcia, Robert Kay-Hill,*
*Ken Olfson, Ralph Manza*
An old lady and three prisoners' wives plan a daring
bank robbery in this diverting yarn. Scripted by Nora
Ephron. This was Bacall's TV movie debut.
COM        93 min (ort 100 min) mTV
B,V          CIC

## PERFECT MATCH **           PG
Mark Deimel     USA       1987
*Marc McClure, Jennifer Edwards, Diane Stilwell, Rob*
*Paulsen*
A couple meet through a newspaper personal column
and attempt to conceal their real circumstances,
which turns their relationship into a tangle of decep-
tion and subterfuge. Fair.
COM        90 min (ort 93 min)
B,V          RCA

## PERFECT PEOPLE ***         PG
Bruce Seth Green   USA       1988
*Lauren Hutton, Perry King, Priscilla Barnes, Karen*
*Valentine, June Lockhart, David Leisure*
A couple decide to go in for a massive bout of

self-improvement but find that diet and exercise is not enough, so they eventually resort to the drastic measure of plastic surgery in their search for perfection. A likeable effort, whose success is largely derived from the appealing performances of the leads. Scripted by Greg Goodell.

COM                         93 min (ort 96 min) mTV
B,V                                              SONY

## PERFECT TIMING *                                18
Rene Bonniere          USA                      1984
*Stephen Markle, Michelle Scarabelli, Paul Boretski,*
*Nancy Cser*
A photographer trying to make some money, turns a humdrum session into an orgy in a bid to raise the cash he needs to avoid eviction.
Aka: SOFT FOCUS; SOHO BLUES; SWEETHEARTS
COM                                           83 min
B,V                                              VES

## PERFORMANCE ***                                18
Nicolas Roeg/Donald Cammell
UK                                              1970
*James Fox, Mick Jagger, Anita Pallenberg, Michele*
*Breton, Johnny Shannon, Ann Sidney, John Bindon,*
*Allan Cuthbertson, Stanley Meadows, Antony Morton,*
*Anthony Valentine*
Fox is remarkable as a vicious gangster, on the run from his boss who has decided to eliminate him. Arriving at the house of a former rock star, he is slowly drawn into a world of drugs and fantasy. A highly innovative film, full of powerful if somewhat pretentious images. Written by Donald Cammell and with musical direction by Randy Newman. Ry Cooder contributes several excellent musical numbers.
DRA                       101 min (ort 105 min)
B,V                                              WHV

## PERILS OF MANDY, THE **
Ken Rowles             USA                      1982
*Gloria Brittain, Elizabeth Kosek, Amanda Clasper,*
*Louise Cohen, Derrick Slater*
A teenage schoolgirl faces grave danger, when she applies for a part in a sex film in this spoofy sex comedy.
A                                             60 min
B,V                                          VIV; STV

## PERILS OF PAULINE, THE ***                      U
George Marshall        USA                      1947
*Betty Hutton, John Lund, Constance Collier, Billy De*
*Wolfe, Frank Faylen, William Demarest, William*
*Farnum, Paul Panzer, Chester Conklin, Hank Mann,*
*Snub Pollard, Creighton Hale, James Finlayson, Bert*
*Roach, Francis McDonald*
Musical entertainment feature that's supposed to be a film biography of the heroine of the silents – Pearl White, but is really just an enjoyable spoof in which Hutton, as the daughter of a famous scientist, attempts to find a secret deadly gas formula in the Far East. Enjoyable and high-spirited nonsense. The songs are by Frank Loesser.
MUS                                       96 min B/W
B,V                                         MMA; GLOB

## PERMANENT RECORD ***                            15
Marisa Silver          USA                      1988
*Alan Boyce, Keanu Reeves, Richard Bradford,*
*Jennifer Rubin, Michelle Meyrink, Pamela Gidley,*
*Michael Elgart, Barry Corbin, Kathy Baker*
A teenage boy's suicide, and the pressures that drove a seemingly happy high school kid and grade A student to end his life, form the basis for this powerful and unusual drama.
DRA                       88 min (ort 92 min)
V                                                CIC

## PERMISSION TO KILL ***                          15
Cyril Frankel          UK                       1975

*Ava Gardner, Dirk Bogarde, Bekim Fehmiu, Nicole*
*Calfan, Frederic Forrest, Timothy Dalton, Alf Joint,*
*Peggy Sinclair, Anthony Dutton, Klaus Wildbolz, John*
*Levene, Dennis Blanch, Vladimir Popric, Peter Garell*
An exiled politician is prevented from returning to his dictator-ruled homeland by the machinations of the West. A good spy drama written by Robin Estridge from his novel. The music is by Richard Rodney Bennett.
Boa: novel by Robin Estridge.
THR                        93 min (ort 97 min)
B,V                                              WHV

## PERMISSIVE *
Lindsay Shonteff       UK                       1970
*Maggie Stride, Gay Singleton, Gilbert Wynne, Alan*
*Gorrie, Robert Daubigny, Forever More*
Story of rock music groupies, with an examination of the life of a teenage girl who likes to live with pop groups. Wearisome drivel.
DRA                                           75 min
B,V                                              VDM

## PERRI ***                                        U
Ralph Wright/N. Paul Kenworthy Jr
USA                                             1957
*Narrated by Winston Hibler*
The first of Disney's True Life Fantasies, this combination of live-action footage and cartoon backgrounds follows the life of a squirrel through several seasons in its wood. A charming if heavily romanticised nature tale.
Boa: novel by Felix Salten.
JUV                                           74 min
B,V                                         RNK; WDV

## PERRY MASON RETURNS **                          PG
Ron Satlof             USA                      1985
*Raymond Burr, Barbara Hale, William Katt, Patrick*
*O'Neal, Holland Taylor, James Kidne, Kerrie Keane,*
*Roberta Weiss, Richard Anderson, Cassie Yates,*
*David McIlwraith, Al Freeman Jr, Paul Hubbard,*
*Lindsay Merrithew*
Feature based on a popular 1960s series about a defence lawyer, who in this tale is now a judge. He makes a comeback appearance to defend his former female assistant on a charge of murdering her boss. A run-of-the-mill effort that was followed by PERRY MASON: THE CASE OF THE NOTORIOUS NUN. Based on the character created by Erle Stanley Gardner. The script is by Dean Hargrove. A prime example of an idea that had passed its sell by date.
DRA                        89 min (ort 100 min) mTV
B,V                                              VPD

## PERRY MASON: THE CASE OF THE ALL STAR
ASSASSIN *                                         PG
Christian I. Nyby II   USA                      1989
*Raymond Burr, Barbara Hale, Alexandra Paul,*
*William R. Moses, Shari Belafonte, Deidre Hall,*
*Pernell Roberts, Bruce Greenwood, Jason Beghe*
A hockey star is accused of killing the team's owner, but is resolutely defended by Mason in another entry in this series, based on the earlier (and far more popular) television show. Like most of them, this overlong and painfully pedestrian drama has few bright moments to relieve the tedium.
DRA                        95 min (ort 100 min) mTV
V                                              BRAVE

## PERRY MASON: THE CASE OF THE AVENGING
ANGEL **
Christian I. Nyby II   USA                      1988
*Raymond Burr, Barbara Hale, William Katt, Patty*
*Duke, Erin Gray, Larry Wilcox, Charles Siebert, James*
*Sutorius, James McEachin, Richard Sanders, David*
*Ogden Stiers*
Mason gets a chance to help an innocent man he once

sentenced to prison in his capacity as a judge. When a new witness steps forward, he gamely undertakes the man's defence at a second trial. Average.
DRA                                        100 min mTV
V                                              BRAVE

## PERRY MASON: THE CASE OF THE LADY IN THE LAKE *
Ron Satlof            USA                      1988
*Raymond Burr, Barbara Hale, William Katt, David Hasselhoff, David Ogden Stiers, John Beck, Doran Clark, John Ireland, Liane Langland, Audra Lindley*
An undistinguished mystery-style entry in the series, that revolves around a kidnap and murder plot, involving a young heiress to a vast fortune and her lakeside disappearance.
DRA                                        100 min mTV
V                                              BRAVE

## PERRY MASON: THE CASE OF THE LETHAL LESSON **
                                               PG
Christian I. Nyby II      USA                  1989
*Raymond Burr, Barbara Hale, Alexandra Paul, William R. Moses, Brian Keith, Leslie Ackerman, Richard Allen, Karen Kopins*
In this tale, Mason defends a young law student accused of murder, but his brief is complicated by the fact that the father of the victim is an old friend of many years' standing. Average.
DRA                                        100 min mTV
V                                              BRAVE

## PERRY MASON: THE CASE OF THE LOST LOVE **
Ron Satlof            USA                      1987
*Raymond Burr, Barbara Hale, William Katt, Jean Simmons, Gene Barry, Robert Walden, Stephen Elliott, Robert Mandan, David Ogden Stiers*
Perry Mason is re-united with an old flame he once knew 30 years before, when she finds herself accused of murder, and he gallantly comes to the rescue. A dull and overlong drama, watchable but soon fades from the memory.
DRA                                        100 min mTV
V                                              BRAVE

## PERRY MASON: THE CASE OF THE MURDERED MADAM *
Ron Satlof            USA                      1987
*Raymond Burr, Barbara Hale, William Katt, David Ogden Stiers, Ann Jillian, Anthony Geary, Daphne Ashbrook, John Rhys-Davies, Bill Macy, Vincent Baggetta*
A scheming former brothel-keeper gets herself murdered and Mason, of course, is on hand to defend his innocent client who is accused of her murder. This involves a long investigation as he ferrets out the truth, but by the time this tedious tale reaches its predictable outcome, one no longer cares.
DRA                                        100 min mTV
V                                              BRAVE

## PERRY MASON: THE CASE OF THE MUSICAL MURDER **
                                               PG
Christian I. Nyby II      USA                  1989
*Raymond Burr, Barbara Hale, Alexandra Paul, William R. Moses, Debbie Reynolds, Jerry Orbach, Dwight Schultz, Mary Cadorette, Raymond Singer*
A Broadway background adds a dash of much-needed colour to this story of a murdered director whose domineering and underhand methods earned him no shortage of enemies. For all that, this entry is no more than an average effort, with much talk but little else.
DRA                                        100 min mTV
V                                              BRAVE

## PERRY MASON: THE CASE OF THE NOTORIOUS NUN **
                                               PG
Ron Satlof            USA                      1986
*Raymond Burr, Barbara Hale, William Katt, Timothy Bottoms, Jon Cypher, Michele Greene, James McEachin, Gerald S. O'Loughlin, William Prince, Edward Winter, Barbara Parkins, David Ogden Stiers, Tom Bosley, Arthur Hill*
An ageing lawyer helps a nun accused of killing a priest, who was alleged to have been her lover. The lead character is based on the popular American TV series of the 1960s – "Perry Mason". Second in the series that started with PERRY MASON RETURNS. Followed by "Perry Mason: The Case Of The Shooting Star". Average.
Aka: CASE OF THE NOTORIOUS NUN, THE
DRA                          96 min (ort 100 min) mTV
B,V                                        CONQ/VPR

## PERRY MASON: THE CASE OF THE SCANDALOUS SCOUNDREL **
                                               PG
Christian I. Nyby II      USA                  1988
*Raymond Burr, Barbara Hale, William Katt, David Ogden Stiers, Robert Guillaume, Morgan Brittany, Rene Enriquez, George Grizzard, Wings Hauser, Yaphet Kotto*
The publisher of a muck-raking scandal sheet is silenced for ever, and a female reporter on his paper is charged with the murder. Another long and tiresome murder mystery whose outcome is never in doubt.
DRA                          95 min (ort 100 min) mTV
V                                              BRAVE

## PERRY MASON: THE CASE OF THE SHOOTING STAR **
                                               PG
Ron Satlof            USA                      1987
*Raymond Burr, Barbara Hale, William Katt, Joe Penny, Ron Glass, Alan Thicke, Ivan Dixon, Wendy Crewson, David Ogden Stiers, Jennifer O'Neill, Ross Petty, Mary Kane, Lisa Howard, J. Kenneth Campbell, Lee Wilkof, Bryan Genesse*
The host of a popular chat-show is murdered on prime-time TV, and a famous film star is made to carry the can until Mason and his associates inevitably triumph, in yet another assembly-line production.
DRA                          95 min (ort 100 min) mTV
V                                              BRAVE

## PERRY MASON: THE CASE OF THE SINISTER SPIRIT *
                                               PG
Richard Lang          USA                      1987
*Raymond Burr, Barbara Hale, William Katt, Robert Stack, David Ogden Stiers*
A novelist is thrown to his death from the top of a resort hotel and a publisher is accused of his murder. This yarn attempts to compensate for the lack of plot development by way of tired "haunted house" cliches, that add absolutely nothing to the story and are never resolved.
DRA                          95 min (ort 104 min) mTV
V                                              BRAVE

## PERSECUTION **
Don Chaffey           UK                       1974
*Lana Turner, Trevor Howard, Ralph Bates, Olga Georges-Picot, Suzan Farmer, Ronald Howard, Patrick Allen, Mark Weavers, Shelagh Fraser*
A rich, crippled American woman living in England dominates her son who hates and fears her. A stilted and overblown melodrama that's all atmosphere and no direction.
Aka: TERROR OF SHEBA, THE
DRA                  93 min; 90 min (TELS) (ort 96 min)
B,V                            RNK; TELS (VHS only)

## PERSONAL BEST ***
                                               18
Robert Towne          USA                      1982

*Mariel Hemingway, Scott Glenn, Patrice Donnelly, Kenny Moore, Jim Moody, Larry Pennell*
Two female athletes in training for the 1980 Olympics, fall in love in a rare and quite sensitive portrayal of a lesbian relationship. Some clumsy camerawork is an annoyance, but the work as a whole remains engrossing and perceptive. Towne's directorial debut.
DRA                                    122 min (ort 124 min)
B,V                                                        WHV

## PERSONAL EXEMPTIONS **                              15
Peter Rowe              USA                            1988
*Nanette Fabray*
A look at a single-minded tax inspector and her domestic life, which gradually begins to collapse in the face of her obsessive interest in her work.
COM                                                  90 min
V                                                        CFD

## PERSONAL FOUL **                                     PG
Ted Lichtenfeld        USA                            1987
*David Morse, Adam Arkin, Susan Wheeler Duff, F. William Parker*
Two bosom buddies fall out over the same girl in this celebration of male pair-bonding. Quite an entertaining little yarn, though the pace is on the slow side at times.
COM                                                  96 min
V                                                        GHV

## PERSONAL SERVICES **                                 18
Terry Jones            UK                             1986
*Julie Walters, Alec McGowan, Shirley Stelfox, Terry Jones, Danny Schiller, Victoria Hardcastle, Tim Woodward, Dave Atkins, Leon Lissek*
Fictionalised account of the career of brothel keeper Cynthia Payne, who came to public notice by way of a prominent police prosecution. This film follows her life from humble beginnings, to the exalted position as purveyor of kinky sexual services to the rich and famous. An on-and-off comedy that handles the rather unfunny scenes of kinky sex in a remarkably stilted way. See also WISH YOU WERE HERE.
COM                                                 109 min
B,V                                                      VIR

## PERSONAL VENDETTA **                                 18
John Llewellyn Moxey   USA                           1987
*Susan Lucci, Michael Nader, Roscoe Born, Joseph Wiseman*
After the parents of a girl are murdered, she is brought up by a gangster and later goes off to study law, returning to help him move from crime to a legitimate hotel operation. However, rival gangsters start a war and she finds herself drawn into it when her husband, the gangster's son, is murdered. A well-made but implausible gangster yarn.
DRA                                                  91 min
V                                                       SONY

## PERSUADERS, THE: LONDON CONSPIRACY ** U
James Hill/David Greene UK                            1976
*Roger Moore, Tony Curtis, Laurence Naismith, Arthur Brough*
Spin-off from the TV series "The Persuaders". Here a family mansion is being used for some sinister purpose. Average.
Aka: LONDON CONSPIRACY
A/AD                                            98 min mTV
B,V                                    PRV; CH5 (VHS only)

## PERSUADERS, THE:
## MISSION MONTE CARLO **                               PG
Roy Ward Baker/Basil Dearden
                       UK                             1975
*Tony Curtis, Roger Moore, Laurence Naismith*
Feature-length episode from the TV series "The Persuaders", with our duo in the French Riviera for a

holiday but soon finding themselves called upon to solve a murder.
Aka: MISSION MONTE CARLO
A/AD                       96 min; 92 min (CH5) mTV
B,V                                    PRV; CH5 (VHS only)

## PERSUADERS, THE: SPORTING CHANCE **    PG
Leslie Norman/Peter Medak
                       UK                             1972
*Tony Curtis, Roger Moore, Laurence Naismith*
Another compilation from the British TV series "The Persuaders", about two ill-matched crime-busting gentlemen of leisure.
Aka: SPORTING CHANCE
A/AD                                            98 min mTV
B,V                                        PRV L/A; CH5

## PERSUADERS, THE: THE SWITCH **
Roy Ward Baker/Val Guest
                       UK                             1972
*Tony Curtis, Roger Moore, Laurence Naismith*
A compilation episode from the British TV series "The Persuaders", that followed the exploits of two wealthy playboys who fought crime for the sheer fun of it. This story is set at the Cannes Film Festival, where our intrepid duo have to protect one of the guests, a union boss due to give testimony on corruption at a Congressional hearing.
Aka: SWITCH, THE
A/AD                                            60 min mTV
B,V                                               PRV L/A

## PERVERSION STORY *
Julio Buchs            ITALY/SPAIN                    1969
*Brett Halsey, Romina Power, Marilu Tolo, Fabrizio Maroni, Gerard Tichy*
A man investigates his sister's suicide and discovers corruption, drugs and sexual perversions.
Aka: I CALDI AMORI DI UNA MINOR ENNE
DRA                                                  91 min
B,V,V2                                                   VPD

## PET SEMATARY ***                                     18
Mary Lambert           USA                            1989
*Fred Gwynne, Dale Midkiff, Denise Crosby, Brad Greenquist, Michael Lombard, Blaze Berdahl, Miko Hughes*
A family is unwise enough to move to a home in the Maine woods that's sited near an ancient Indian burial ground, now used as a pet's cemetary. The death of the family cat and apparent accidental death of their son heralds the start of a chronicle of horror, and when the distraught parents wish for their son's return, the forces of evil work a horrible fulfilment. Scripted by King, this is one of his darkest and most effective fantasies.
Boa: novel by Stephen King.
HOR                                     98 min (ort 103 min)
V                                                        CIC

## PETE TOWNSHEND: WHITE CITY,                           15
## THE MUSIC MOVIE *
Richard Lowenstein     UK                             1985
*Pete Townshend, Andrew Wilde, Francis Barber*
Disjointed, overlong attempt at a musical exploration of the London district where Townshend grew up.
Aka: PETE TOWNSHEND: WHITE CITY; WHITE CITY: PETE TOWNSHEND; WHITE CITY (VES)
MUS                                                  57 min
V                                                        VES

## PETER GUNN **                                         15
Blake Edwards          USA                            1988
*Peter Strauss, Barbara Williams, Peter Jurasik, David Rappaport, Pearl Bailey, Jennifer Edwards*
A TV detective series that Edwards directed from 1958 to 1961, formed the inspiration for this re-run which has most of the original characters, but an

entirely new cast. In this tale a detective finds himself
caught in an intrigue involving gangsters and corrupt
cops. The Henry Mancini score is the best thing in it.
A/AD                            95 min (ort 100 min) mTV
V                                                 NWV

## PETER THE GREAT *                                15
Marvin K. Chomsky/Lawrence Schiller
                            USA                   1985
*Maximilian Schell, Ursula Andress, Omar Sharif,*
*Vanessa Redgrave, Trevor Howard, Laurence Olivier,*
*Helmut Griem, Jan Niklas, Renee Soutendijk, Mel*
*Ferrer, Hanna Schygulla, Mike Gwilym, Gunter-*
*Maria Halmer, Jan Malmsjo*
Enormously long and rather over-rated attempt to tell
the story of the Czar who attempted to modernise
Russia single-handedly, at vast expense in terms of
human lives. Full of stars but still as dull as
ditchwater, and what's worse, at the end of this
overlong saga we emerge none the wiser as to Peter's
personality or his achievements.
Boa: book by Robert K. Massie.
DRA                360 min (3 cassettes – ort 366 min)
B,V                                      IVS L/A; BRAVE

## PETER-NO-TAIL **                                 U
Jan Gissberg/Stig Lasseby/Michael Bakewell (English
version)                    SWEDEN                 1983
Animated feature about a tail-less cat and his friends.
Average.
Aka: PELLE SVANSLOS
CAR                                             81 min
B,V,V2                                  VDM L/A; VCC

## PETE'S DRAGON **                                 U
Don Chaffey                 USA                   1977
*Helen Reddy, Jim Dale, Shelley Winters, Mickey*
*Rooney, Red Buttons, Jim Backus, Jeff Conaway, Sean*
*Marshall, Jean Kean, Joe E. Ross, Ben Wrigley,*
*Charlie Callas (voice only)*
Live action mixes with animation in this story of a
lonely orphan boy befriended by a dragon named
Elliott. A Disney production that's marred by by poor
animations and clumsy and plodding development.
MARY POPPINS it ain't.
Boa: story by Seton I. Miller and S.S. Field.
MUS                            102 min (ort 134 min)
B,V                              RNK; WDV (VHS only)

## PETS **
Raphael Nussbaum            USA                   1973
*Candy Railson, Ed Bishop, Joan Blackman, Teri*
*Guzman, Bret Parker, Matt Greene*
Story of a young runaway who gets mixed up with
underworld figures.
Aka: SUBMISSION
A                                               89 min
B,V                                                INT

## PETTICOAT AFFAIR **                              U
John Astin/Norman Abbott/William Asher
                            USA                   1977
*Jamie Lee Curtis, John Astin, Richard Gilliland,*
*Yvonne Wilder, Jackie Cooper, Richard Brestoff,*
*Christopher Brown, Kraig Cassity, Wayne Long,*
*Richard Marion, Michael Mazes, Jack Murdock, Peter*
*Schuck, Raymond Singer*
A pilot for a subsequent series that is essentially a
remake of the 1959 film OPERATION PETTICOAT,
which tells of a WW2 submarine and what happens to
the crew when they rescue five nurses. Average.
Aka: LIFE IN THE PINK; OPERATION PETTICOAT
Boa: story by Paul King and Joe Stone.
COM                                    89 min mTV
B,V                                             CIC

## PETTICOAT PIRATES **                             U
David MacDonald             UK                     1961
*Charlie Drake, Anne Heywood, Cecil Parker, John*

*Turner, Maxine Audley, Thorley Walters*
With the seizure of a frigate by a bunch of WRNS, the
nervous captive stoker decides it's safer to pose as one
of them. Popular comedian Drake does what he can
with this contrived comedy vehicle.
COM                             83 min (ort 87 min)
V                                               WHV

## PHANTASM ***                                     18
Don Coscarelli              USA                   1977
*Michael Baldwin, Bill Thornburg, Reggie Bannister,*
*Kathy Lester, Angus Scrimm*
A young boy is constantly drawn to a morgue that's
patrolled by a strange sinister figure. Plucking up the
courage to enter the building, he finds that it appears
to be used for some horrific purpose. A rather flawed
film that is hampered by a low budget but has some
powerful and highly imaginative sequences. A sequel
followed in 1987.
HOR                             85 min (ort 87 min)
B,V                 VCL/CBS L/A; BRAVE; VCC (VHS only)

## PHANTASM 2 **                                    18
Don Coscarelli              USA                   1987
*James Le Gros, Reggie Bannister, Angus Scrimm,*
*Paula Irvine, Samantha Phillips, Kenneth Tigar*
This sequel to the 1977 film covers pretty much the
same ground, but with the dubious benefits of bigger
money and more explicit effects. The "Tall Man" and
his deadly spheres return to raise another army of the
dead for construction work on his home planet.
HOR                                             93 min
V/sh                                            GHV

## PHANTOM EMPIRE **                                15
Fred Olen Ray               USA                   1987
*Sybil Danning (Sybelle Danninger), Ross Hagen,*
*Jeffrey Combs, Robert Quarry, Susan Stokey, Michelle*
*Bauer, Dawn Wildsmith, Russ Tamblyn*
Whilst searching for a lost city, a group of scientists
encounter a variety of dangers, including cannibals
and an Amazon queen, in this slightly tongue-in-
cheek adventure yarn.
A/AD                           80 min (ort 85 min) Cut (7 sec)
V                                               VES

## PHANTOM OF DEATH **                              18
Ruggero Deodato             ITALY                 1987
*Michael York, Edwige Fenech, Donald Pleasence*
A gifted pianist contracts a rare disease that acceler-
ates the ageing process, and his sufferings so unhinge
his mind that he goes on a murderous rampage.
Another predictable, assembly-line horror offering.
Aka: OFF BALANCE (AVA)
HOR                            88 min; 95 min (TGP)
B,V                                      AVA; TGP

## PHANTOM OF THE MALL: ERIC'S REVENGE ** 18
Richard Friedman            USA                   1989
*Derek Rydall, Morgan Fairchild, Kari Whitman,*
*Jonathan Goldsmith*
A girl takes a job in a shopping centre built on the site
of her late boyfriend's house, which was burnt down
with him inside. A spate of strange murders soon
occurs as the dead man unleashes his supernatural
revenge for the act of arson which took his life. What
might so easily have been an effective horror film
degenerates into a confused welter of special effects.
HOR                                             90 min
V                                          PRISM L/A

## PHANTOM OF THE OPERA, THE **                     PG
                                                  1987
*Voices of: Aiden Grennell, Daniel Reardon, Collette*
*Porter, Jim Reid, Joseph Taylor*
A fair animated adventure based on this classic tale,
and following the exploits of our phantom after he
kidnaps a young soprano, with the intention of
making her into a star.

CAR               60 min
V               STYL

## PHANTOM OF THE OPERA, THE **   18
Dwight H. Little    USA      1989
*Robert Englund, Jill Schoelen, Alex Hyde-White, Bill Nighy, Terence Harvey, Stephanie Lawrence*
Despite some attempt to keep faithful to the original novel, this muddled remake is a gory, slow-moving film that is closer to the spirit of a slasher movie than anything else. Englund is alternately hammy and compelling, as a Phantom who has made a pact with the Devil and instead of a mask, uses the skin of those he murders to cover his ruined face. Schoelen makes an appealing heroine. Filmed in Budapest but curiously sited in London.
Boa: novel by Gaston Leroux.
HOR             91 min
V              CASPIC

## PHANTOM OF THE OPERA, THE ***   PG
Rupert Julian    USA      1925
*Lon Chaney, Norman Kerry, Mary Philbin, Gibson Gowland, Snitz Edwards, Arthur Edmond Carewe*
An early version of this much-filmed story, of the disfigured composer who haunts the Paris Opera and lives in the catacombs. Chaney gives one of his most memorable performances, as the tormented creature who kidnaps a young girl to train as his protegee. A flawed classic that still retains considerable power.
Boa: novel by Gaston Leroux.
HOR  74 min (ort 101 min) B/W or tinted (CH5) silent
B,V        POLY; CH5 (VHS only)

## PHANTOM OF THE OPERA, THE **   PG
Terence Fisher    UK      1962
*Herbert Lom, Heather Sears, Thorley Walters, Edward De Souza, Michael Gough, Ian Wilson, Martin Miller, John Harvey, Miriam Karlin, Miles Malleson*
The third version of this classic tale, in which a hideously disfigured composer takes refuge in the sewers below the Paris Opera House, eventually abducting a girl to sing in his opera. A stolid remake that delivers a few shocks but conveys a general air of lifelessness.
Boa: novel by Gaston Leroux.
HOR      81 min (ort 84 min)
V              CIC

## PHANTOM OF THE OPERA, THE ***
Robert Markowitz    USA    1983
*Jane Seymour, Maximilian Schell, Michael York, Jeremy Kemp, Diana Quick, Philip Stone, Paul Brooke, Andras Miko, Gellert Rakasanyi, Laszlo Nemeth, Jeno Kis, Laszlo Sos, Denes Ujlaky, Terez Bod, Agnes David, Sandor Halmagyi*
This version of the story is set in Budapest but remains essentially the same, telling of a disfigured composer who kidnaps a young girl to train as a singer. Schell is well cast and the excellent make-up of Stan Winston adds the appropriate chill. Adapted by Sherman Yellen.
Boa: novel by Gaston Leroux.
HOR      104 min mTV
B,V            VFP

## PHANTOM OF THE OPERA, THE ***   15
Tony Richardson    UK/USA    1990
*Charles Dance, Burt Lancaster, Teri Polo, Ian Richardson, Andrea Ferreol, Adam Storke, Jean-Pierre Cassel*
A lush, sentimental and melodramatic re-telling of this much-filmed classic, that benefits from its French locations but teeters dangerously on the edge of parody. Dance makes an effective if somewhat romantic Phantom, though the poor dubbing of the opera sequences is an annoyance. Originally shown in two parts. Adapted by Kopit from his stage play.
Boa: novel by Gaston Leroux/play by Arthur Kopit.

DRA        210 min mTV
V             STYL

## PHANTOM OF THE PARK, THE **   15
Gordon Hessler    USA    1978
*Kiss (Paul Stanley, Gene Simmons, Ace Frehley, Peter Criss), Anthony Zerbe, Carmine Caridi, Deborah Ryan, Terry Lester, John Dennis Johnston, John Lisbon, Lisa Jane Persky, John Chappell, Don Steele, Richard Hein*
An elaborate promo for this hard rock group, set amidst the opening of a high-tech amusement park owned and run by an evil engineer, who has made four robot Kiss replicas and turned them loose in his amusement park.
Aka: ATTACK OF THE PHANTOMS; KISS: THE PHANTOM OF THE PARK; KISS MEETS THE PHANTOM OF THE PARK
MUS    94 min (ort 100 min) mTV
B, V/sh        IVS; HEND

## PHANTOM TOLLBOOTH, THE **   U
Chuck Jones/Abe Levitow/David Monahan
        USA    1969
*Butch Patrick, voices of: Hans Conreid, Mel Blanc, Candy Candido, Shep Menken, Les Tremayne, Larry Thor, Daws Butler, June Foray*
Live-action changes to animation as a boy is catapulted into the strange world of the Kingdom of Wisdom, inhabited by numbers and letters that are now at war. A rather intellectual cartoon whose best aspects are derived from the novel. The slow start and poor songs are drawbacks. The animation sequences were directed by Levitow. Scripted by Jones and Sam Rosen.
Boa: novel by Norton Juster.
JUV      85 min (ort 90 min)
B,V           MGM

## PHANTOMS **   18
Charles Band    USA    1990
*Sherilyn Fenn*
An American woman inherits an ancestral castle in Italy and goes there to take up residence. This sets the scene for a rather traditional horror tale (remarkably gore-free) that involves ghosts, werewolves, a family curse, a haunted house and elements of Beauty and the Beast. And all of this has its place in a series of supernatural events that unfold when she invites a troupe of travelling players to dine at the castle. Fair.
HOR         90 min
V             EIV

## PHAR LAP **   PG
Simon Wincer    AUSTRALIA    1983
*Tom Burlinson, Ron Leibman, Judy Morris, Martin Vaughan, Celia De Burgh, Vincent Ball, Richard Morgan, Robert Grubb, Georgie Carr, James Steele, Peter Whitford, John Stanton, Roger Newcombe, Len Wasserman*
A battered racehorse is nursed back to health by his trainer, when everyone else has given up on it. However, after winning many races, it dies under mysterious circumstances. A fact-based drama that largely follows the career of this horse, which died in 1932. Average.
Aka: PHAR LAP: HEART OF A NATION
DRA     103 min (ort 118 min)
B,V           CBS

## PHASE 4 ***   PG
Saul Bass    USA    1973
*Nigel Davenport, Lynne Frederick, Michael Murphy, Alan Gifford, Helen Horton, Robert Henderson*
An unusual tale in which ants of normal size become super-intelligent, and attack a research station in the desert. Attempts to communicate with them fail and eventually a researcher enters the nest to kill the queen, but is "changed" by the insects instead. A film

of striking images (documentary footage is cleverly used), opaque symbolism and stilted acting, in roughly that order. This was Bass' feature directing debut.
Aka: PHASE IV
FAN 80 min (ort 86 min)
B,V CIC

**PHILADELPHIA EXPERIMENT, THE \*\*** PG
Stewart Raffill USA 1984
*Michael Pare, Nancy Allen, Eric Christmas, Bobby Di Cicco, Kene Holliday, Louise Latham, Michael Currie, James Edgcomb, Joe Dorsey, Gary Brockette, Stephen Tobolowsky, Debra Troyer, Miles McNamara, Ralph Manza, Ed Bakey*
An experiment designed to make a battleship invisible goes wrong, and a sailor is drawn forward in time from 1943 to 1984. Reasonably diverting, but a little thin to pad out into a full-length feature. Scripted by William Gray and Michael Janover.
Boa: novel by William J. Moore and Charles Berlitz.
FAN 102 min
B,V TEVP

**PHILBY, BURGESS AND MACLEAN \*\*\*** PG
Gordon Flemyng UK 1977
*Derek Jacobi, Anthony Bates, Michael Culver, Elizabeth Seal, Arthur Lowe*
A dramatised reconstruction of the entire sordid tale of three Oxford graduates who worked for British Intelligence and betrayed the country to the USSR, and of the bumbling and incompetent failure on the part of the security services to catch them. An absorbing and complex character study, written by Ian Curteis.
Aka: BURGESS, PHILBY AND MACLEAN: SPY SCANDAL OF THE CENTURY
DRA 78 min (ort 83 min) mTV
B,V GRN

**PHOBIA \*** 15
John Huston CANADA 1980
*Paul Michael Glaser, John Colicos, Susan Hogan, David Bolt, David Eisner, Patricia Collins, Lisa Langlois, Robert O'Ree, Alexandra Stewart, Marian Waldman, Neil Vipond, Kenneth Walsh, Gwen Thomas, Paddy Campanaro*
Five phobics who are all convicted murderers and the patients of the same psychiatrist, are murdered one by one after being released from prison. A muddled mixture of horror and mystery that falls far below the level one would have expected from a director of this calibre.
THR 85 min (ort 91 min)
B,V TEVP

**PHOENIX THE NINJA \*** 15
Fong Ho HONG KONG 1986
*Pearl Cheung, Chung Wah, Rose Kuei, Wang Shan, James Tyan*
Kung fu revenger about an orphan girl and an evil monk, with our heroine doing battle with the murderers of her family.
MAR 87 min
B,V VPD

**PHOENIX THE WARRIOR \*\*** 18
Robert Hayes USA 1988
*Persis Khambatta, Kathleen Kinmont, Sheila Howard*
Another saga of post-WW3 devastation. Here, savage female warriors contend for the last man on the planet, in a desperate bid to save the human race from extinction.
FAN 85 min (ort 110 min)
B,V 2020

**PHOENIX, THE \*** U
Douglas Hickox USA 1981
*Judson Scott, E.G. Marshall, Fernando Allende, Shelley Smith, Daryl Anderson, Hersha Parady,*

*Jimmy Mair, Lyman Ward, Carmen Argenziano, Stanley Kamel, Angus Duncan, Wayne Storm, Terry Jastrow, Bret Williams, Paul Marin*
A being with supernatural powers is brought back to life and must come to terms with modern civilisation, in this banal pilot for a short-lived TV series.
HOR 78 min; 71 min (VPD) mTV
B,V TWE L/A; VPD (VHS only)

**PHOTOGRAPHER, THE \*** 18
William B. Hillman USA 1975
*Michael Callan, Spencer Milligan, Harold J. Stone, Isabel Sanford*
A photographer who hates his mother takes a gruesome revenge on his models in this dreary piece of dross.
DRA 93 min
B,V,V2 EHE

**PHYSICAL \*\*** R18
USA 198-
*Juliet Anderson, Hershel Steed, Linda Shaw, Mike Ranger, Dorothy LeMay*
The publishers of a pornographic magazine decide to hold an erotic Olympics with a grand prize of $50,000. However, not having any money themselves, they are obliged to take part in their own competition.
A 84 min
V EVI L/A; SHEP

**PHYSICAL EVIDENCE \*** 18
Michael Crichton USA 1989
*Burt Reynolds, Theresa Russell, Ned Beatty, Kay Lenz, Kenneth Welsh, Tom O'Brien, Ted McGinley, Ray Baker, Ken James*
Having already been suspended from the force, a violent and unorthodox cop is accused of murder, following the death of a notorious gangster. An ambitious female lawyer sets out to defend him. A flabby and unconvincing drama with precious little suspense and a poor performance from Russell, hampering a somewhat better one from Reynolds.
DRA 95 min (ort 99 min)
V/sh WHV

**PIAF: THE EARLY YEARS \*\*** 
Guy Casaril FRANCE/USA 1974 (released in USA 1982)
*Brigitte Ariel, Pascale Christophe, Guy Trejan, Pierre Vernier, Jacques Duby, Anouk Ferjac*
Biopic on the early career and life of this world famous French singer, based on the bestseller by her half-sister (who is played by Christophe). Good songs and fine performances are of little use when they are hampered by such a messy and disjointed script. A great pity, the film could have been magical.
Boa: book by Simone Berteaut.
DRA 105 min
B,V VSP

**PICASSO TRIGGER \*\*** 15
Andy Sidaris USA 1987
*Steve Bond, Hope Marie Carlton, Roberta Vasquez, John Aprea, Bruce Penhall, Harold Diamond, Guich Kook*
A lethal hit-man is preparing to kill a number of federal employees, and is tracked by an agent in an attempt to thwart him – not an easy task as he is fond of using ingenious methods to kill his victims. A kind of follow-up to MALIBU EXPRESS with the same blend of action and pretty girls (who in this tale are employed as bait to trap the killer). Mildly entertaining, low-budget nonsense.
A/AD 96 min (ort 99 min)
V RCA

**PICK-UP ARTIST, THE \*** 15
James Toback USA 1987
*Robert Downey, Molly Ringwald, Dennis Hopper,*

Harvey Keitel, Danny Aiello, Mildred Dunnock, Brian
Hamil, Vanessa Williams, Victoria Jackson
A young man whose romantic philosophy is of the love
'em and leave 'em kind, gets more than he bargained
for when he takes up with the daughter of a gambler
who owes money to the Mafia. A dull waste of time
and talent.
COM                                   78 min (ort 81 min)
B, V/sh                                              CBS

**PICK-UP GIRLS, THE \*\***                              18
Jesse Franco            SPAIN
Rosa Valenty, Lina Romay, Robert Foster
Young men and women get up to the usual in this
Spanish effort.
A                                 85 min Cut (2 min 44 sec)
B,V                                                 ATLAS

**PICKWICK PAPERS, THE \*\*\***                           U
Noel Langley            UK                          1952
James Hayter, Nigel Patrick, James Donald, Kathleen
Harrison, Hermione Baddeley, Joyce Grenfell,
Hermione Gingold, Donald Wolfit, Harry Fowler, Sam
Costa, George Robey, Mary Merrall, Athene Seyler,
Alexander Gauge
A loosely-structured and episodic comedy built around
the incidents that befall the members of the Pickwick
Club in the 1830s. Humorous and well acted, but a
little too insubstantial to work as anything more than
a series of pleasing sketches.
Noa: novel by Charles Dickens.
COM                          107 min (ort 115 min) B/W
V                                                  BRAVE

**PICKWICK PAPERS, THE:**                              U
**PARTS 1 AND 2 \*\***
Brian Lighthill         UK                          1985
Nigel Stock
A colourful BBC adaptation of Dickens' tale of the
amusing adventures of the Pickwick Club. Narrated
by Ray Brooks.
Boa: book by Charles Dickens.
DRA                       148 min (2 cassettes) mTV
V/h                                                  BBC

**PICNIC \*\*\*\***                                         U
Joshua Logan            USA                         1955
William Holden, Rosalind Russell, Kim Novak, Betty
Field, Cliff Robertson, Arthur O'Connell, Verna
Felton, Susan Strasberg, Nick Adams, Phyllis
Newman, Reta Shaw
In a small Kansas town, a drifter looks up an old
friend but winds up stealing the man's girl. Scripted
by Daniel Taradash, this fine adaptation of Inge's play
marked the start of a more realistic style of Hollywood
melodrama. The tendency towards over-acting from
the leads is more than made up for by the strong
supporting cast. AA: Art/Set (William Flannery and
Jo Mielziner/Robert Priestley), Edit (Charles Nelson/
William A. Lyon).
Boa: play by William Inge.
DRA                          109 min (ort 115 min)
V                                                    RCA

**PICNIC AT HANGING ROCK \*\*\***
Peter Weir              AUSTRALIA                   1975
Rachel Roberts, Dominic Guard, Helen Morse, Jacki
Weaver, Vivean Gray, Margaret Nelson, Kirsty Child
A beautifully-filmed but empty mystery about the
disappearance of a party of Australian schoolgirls that
took place in 1900. Scripted by Cliff Green and
certainly not lacking in atmosphere. The music is by
Bruce Smeaton.
Boa: novel by Joan Lindsay.
DRA                                              115 min
B,V                                                  VSP

**PICTURE SHOW MAN, THE \*\*\***
John Power              AUSTRALIA                   1977

Rod Taylor, John Meillon, John Ewart, Harold
Hopkins, Judy Morris, Patrick Cargill
Entertaining account of the adventures of a travelling
cinema in Australia of the 1920s. A rewarding tale,
lacking in dramatic impact but certain to appeal to
anyone with an interest in the early days of cinema.
Aka: TRAVELLING PICTURE SHOW MAN, THE
Boa: book by Lyle Penn.
COM                                              99 min
B,V                                                  GHV

**PIECE OF THE ACTION, A \*\***                          15
Sidney Poitier          USA                         1977
Bill Cosby, Sidney Poitier, James Earl Jones, Denise
Nicholas, Hope Clark, Tracy Reed, Janet DuBois
Two black conmen blackmail local crooks as they help
a social worker keep kids on the straight and narrow.
An overlong and sanctimonious effort, quite well
made but of little appeal. Written by Charles Black-
well and followed by a sequel, "Let's Do It Again".
Boa: story by Timothy March.
COM                      129 min (ort 135 min) Cut (10 sec)
B,V                                                  WHV

**PIED PIPER \*\***                                       PG
Norman Stone                                        1989
Peter O'Toole, Mare Winningham
A solicitor on holiday in France sets out to leave on
the eve of the German invasion, and is asked by a
woman staying at his hotel to take her two children to
the safety of England. A competent adventure.
A/AD                                            110 min
V                                                CASPIC

**PIED PIPER OF HAMELIN, THE \*\***                      Uc
Nicholas Meyer          USA                         1984
Eric Idle
A newer version of this famous legend telling of the
mysterious stranger who leads away the children of
Hamelin when he is not paid for clearing the town of
vermin.
Aka: PIED PIPER, THE
JUV                                  49 min (ort 60 min)
B,V                                                  MGM

**PIED PIPER, THE \***                                    PG
Jacques Demy            UK                          1971
Donovan, Donald Pleasence, Jack Wild, Michael
Hordern, John Hurt, Cathryn Harrison, Roy Kinnear,
Peter Vaughan, Diana Dors, Keith Buckley, Peter Eyre,
Arthur Hewlett, Hamilton Dyce, Andre Van
Gyseghem, John Falconer, John Welsh
A musical fantasy based on the famous legend that is
given a hard edge by the director, and succeeds in
painting a convincing but disagreeable picture of the
period (the tale is set in 1349). Hard to know to whom
this would appeal, adults would be bored and children
might find it too horrific. The music is by Donovan.
JUV                                              90 min
B,V     HVM; VUL L/A; VGM (VHS only); PARK (VHS
only)

**PILOT, THE \***                                         PG
Cliff Robertson         USA                         1979
Cliff Robertson, Frank Converse, Diana Baker, Dana
Andrews, Milo O'Shea, Gordon MacRae, Ed Binns
An airline pilot has a drink problem which threatens
to end in disaster for both him and his passengers. A
run-of-the-mill melodrama that is both predictable
and depressing. The photography by Walter Lassally
and the score by John Addison seem almost too good
for this dud.
Aka: DANGER IN THE SKIES
DRA                                              91 min
B,V                         DFS L/A; VMA; STABL

**PIMPERNEL SMITH \*\*\***                                U
Leslie Howard           UK                          1941
Leslie Howard, Mary Morris, Francis L. Sullivan,

*Hugh McDermott, Raymond Huntley, David Tomlinson, Manning Whiley, Peter Gawthorne, Allan Jeayes, Dennis Arundell, Joan Kemp-Welch, Phillip Friend, Lawrence Kitchen*
An updating of the Scarlet Pimpernel legend, set during WW2, with an archaeology professor smuggling prisoners out of Germany under the noses of the Gestapo. After a slow start, some good scenes (Howard disguised as a scarecrow) are worked into what is essentially a wartime propaganda film which shows the Nazis as being remarkably stupid. The script is by Anatole De Grunwald, Roland Pertwee and Ian Dalrymple.
Aka: FIGHTING PIMPERNEL, THE; MISTER V
DRA                        116 min (ort 121 min) B/W
B,V                                         BBC; VCC

**PIN ***                                          18**
Sandor Stern          CANADA              1988
*David Hewlett, Cyndy Preston, John Ferguson, Terry O'Quinn, Bronwen Mantel, Jacob Tirney, Michelle Anderson, Steven Bernarski, Katie Shengler*
A psychological thriller telling of a young man's obsession with an anatomical dummy, that was the only means his cold and withdrawn father used to communicate with him and his sister. After the untimely death of their parents, the boy brings the dummy home and begins to plan a life of solitude for him and his sister, in which the dummy is to be their only companion.
Boa: novel by Andrew Neiderman.
HOR                                         99 min
B,V                                          NWV

**PIN-UP GIRL **                                    U**
Bruce Humberstone     USA               1944
*Betty Grable, John Harvey, Martha Raye, Joe E. Brown, Eugene Pallette, Dave Willcock, Mantan Moreland, Charlie Spivak Orchestra*
One of Grable's less memorable vehicles in which she plays a Washington secretary who meets a navy hero and is catapulted to national fame. A poor attempt to exploit the star's musical and comic talents, this flimsy affair has moments of verve and some good sets, but for the most part remains curiously lifeless.
MUS                                         82 min
V                                            CBS

**PINBALL SUMMER ***                               15**
George Mihalka        CANADA              1981
*Michael Zelniker, Carl Marotte, Helen Udy, Karen Stephen, Tom Kovacs, Joey McNamara, Joy Boushel, J. Robert Maze, Matthew Stevens, Sue Ronne, Robert King, Rob Stein, Rob Ferguson, Roland Nincheri, Lyn Jackson, Riva Spier*
A bunch of awful kids go on holiday and indulge in the expected pastimes: pinball machines, beauty contests etc. A bland affair.
Aka: PICK-UP SUMMER; PINBALL PICK-UP
COM                                         95 min
B,V,V2                                       MED

**PINK CHAMPAGNE ***                               **
Steve Conrad          USA               1980
*Jon Steele, Lisa De Leeuw, Rick Fonte, Jeff Parker, Ron Jeremy, Loreli Winston, Aimee Leigh, Lauri Pearl, Tiffany Clark*
This sex-spoof on 1930s Hollywood has all the actresses performing sex in order to get ahead. And none more so than April, who lives in a Beverly Hills mansion with top producer Zagfield. April believes that a star depends on those that help make her one and she sets out to thank all the boys in publicity, whilst Zagfield enjoys an audition of girls for his next musical. All ends in a big party in which our producer meets the woman of his dreams.
A                                           70 min
B,V                                          CAL

**PINK CHIQUITAS, THE **                            15**
Anthony Currie        CANADA              1986
*Frank Stallone, Claudia Udy, Bruce Pirrie, Elizabeth Edwards, Cindy Valentine, John Hemphill, Don Lake*
A meteorite crashes near a small town, and turns the local women into nymphomaniacs in this cheerfully vulgar SF spoof. Not bad, but ten minutes is all that's required to get the gist of it. Written by Currie.
COM                          80 min (ort 86 min)
B,V                                          RCA

**PINK FLAMINGOS ***                                **
John Waters           USA               1973
*Divine (Glenn Milstead), Mink Stole, Edith Massey, David Lochary, Mary Vivian Pearce, Danny Mills, Cookie Mueller, Channing Wilroy, Paul Swift, Susan Walsh*
Two groups vie for the honour of being "the filthiest people in the world" in this Waters offering of low-budget nausea. There are one or two funny moments, but on the whole the show put on by Divine and friends is a trivial affair, celebrating high-camp dialogue and low-grade activities (coprophagia being but one of them).
COM                                         95 min
B,V                                          PVG

**PINK FLOYD: THE WALL ***                         15**
Alan Parker           UK                1982
*Bob Geldof, Christine Hargreaves, James Laurenson, Eleanor David, Bob Hoskins, Kevin McKeon, David Bingham, Jenny Wright, Alex McAvoy, Ellis Dale, James Hazeldine, Marjorie Mason, Marie Passarelli, Winston Rose, Eddie Tagoe*
An account of a pop star who has come to the end of the road, with some brilliant animated sequences. This combination of live-action, animation and concert footage was inspired by a Pink Floyd record album of the same name. Despite the potency of the images, the unrelenting tone of self-pity is a serious flaw. Animations were designed by political cartoonist Gerald Scarfe.
Aka: WALL, THE
MUS                          92 min (ort 95 min)
B, V/sh                            TEVP L/A; CAN

**PINK NIGHTS **                                   PG**
Phillip Koch          USA               1985
*Shaun Allen, Kevin Anderson, Peri Kaczmarek, Larry King, Jonathan Michaels, Jessica Vitkus*
Teenage sex comedy, with a young high school boy dreaming of finding a girlfriend and suddenly being landed with three girls all at once. Light, frothy and insubstantial.
COM                          80 min (ort 87 min)
B,V                                          SONY

**PINK PANTHER, THE ***                            PG**
Blake Edwards         USA               1963
*Peter Sellers, David Niven, Capucine, Claudia Cardinale, Robert Wagner, John Le Mesurier, Fran Jeffries, Colin Gordon, Brenda de Banzie, Colin Gordon, Fran Jeffries*
An unfunny comedy about a bumbling French police inspector who creates chaos all around him. The title character in turn spawned a whole series of pointless TV cartoons. Scripted by Maurice Richlen and Blake Edwards with animation by De Patie-Freleng. The music is by Henry Mancini. Followed by A SHOT IN THE DARK.
COM                         110 min (ort 113 min)
V                                            WHV

**PINK PANTHER STRIKES AGAIN, THE ***              PG**
Blake Edwards         UK                1976
*Peter Sellers, Herbert Lom, Colin Blakely, Leonard Rossiter, Lesley-Anne Down, Burt Kwouk, Andre Maranne, Richard Vernon, Michael Robbins, Briony McRoberts, Dick Crockett, Byron Kane, Paul Maxwell,*

*Jerry Stovin, Phil Brown*
I wish the actors would strike, then we would be rid of these endless idiotic sequels. Our bumbling Inspector Clouseau comes up against an organisation created by Chief Inspector Dreyfus that is designed to rid the world of Clouseau. This was the fourth of five sequels. Written by Frank Waldman and Blake Edwards with music by Henry Mancini. Followed by THE RE-VENGE OF THE PINK PANTHER.
COM                              98 min (ort 103 min)
V                                                      WHV

**PINOCCHIO \*\***                                     U
Cenci Brothers         ITALY              1967
Animated rendition of this famous tale of a wooden puppet boy who becomes a real little boy after a series of adventures. This version is based on the original illustrations for the 1867 story. Different from Disney, but still worth watching.
Aka: ADVENTURES OF PINOCCHIO, THE (MAST); LE AVVENTURE DI PINOCCHIO
Boa: novel by Carlo Collodi (Carlo Lorenzini).
CAR                                                  98 min
B,V,V2                      MAST (VHS only); FFV

**PINOCCHIO \*\***                                    Uc
Barry Letts            UK                  1985
*Derek Smith, Rhoda Lewis, Roy McCready, Neil Fitzwilliam*
Mixed puppet and live-action version of this famous story compiled from four 30-minute episodes. Fair.
Boa: novel by Carlo Collodi (Carlo Lorenzini).
JUV                                          108 min mTV
B,V                                                     BBC

**PINOCCHIO \*\***
Sid Smith/Ron Field    USA                1976
*Danny Kaye, Sandy Duncan, Flip Wilson, Clive Revill, Liz Torres, Gary Morgan, Don Correa, Roy Smith*
Feature-length musical version of this famous tale, of a puppet that has many adventures before being granted his dearest wish; to become a real boy.
Boa: novel by Carlo Collodi (Carlo Lorenzini).
MUS                                                  76 min
B,V                                                VCL/CBS

**PINOCCHIO \*\***                                    Uc
Peter Medak            USA                1984
*James Coburn, Carl Reiner, Paul Reubens, Lainie Kazan, Pee-Wee Herman (Paul Reubens), Jim Belushi, Don Novello (narration)*
Another version of this famous classic tale in the "Faerie Tale Theatre" series.
Boa: novel by Carlo Collodi (Carlo Lorenzini).
JUV                                                  50 min
V                                                      MGM

**PINOCCHIO \*\*\*\***                                 U
Ben Sharpstein/Hamilton Luske
                       USA                1940
*Voices of: Dickie Jones, Cliff Edwards, Evelyn Venerable, Charles Judels, Don Brodie*
The original classic Walt Disney animation of the tale of a carpenter whose dream of a son comes true, in the form of a wooden puppet. A film that combines technical brilliance with an imaginative and atmospheric script. AA: Score (Orig) (Paul J. Smith/Ned Washington), Song ("When You Wish Upon A Star" – Leigh Harline – music/Ned Washington – lyrics).
Boa: novel by Carlo Collodi (Carlo Lorenzini).
CAR                                84 min (ort 88 min)
B,V                                                    WDV

**PINOCCHIO AND THE**                                 U
**EMPEROR OF THE NIGHT \***
Hal Sutherland         USA                1987
*Voices of: Edward Asner, Tom Bosley, Lana Beeson, Linda Gary, Jonathan Harris, James Earl Jones,*

*Ricky G. Paull, Ted Richert, Leslie Graves, Carole*
This full-length cartoon is a flawed attempt to produce a sequel to the 1940 Disney classic, with Pinocchio celebrating his first birthday as a real boy. However, he is led into temptation by a mysterious carnival owner and experiences many adventures and perils. A flat and anaemic effort, of poor animation and banal dialogue.
CAR                                83 min (ort 95 min)
V                                                      VCC

**PINOCCHIO IN OUTER SPACE \***                       U
Ray Goosens            FRANCE/USA         1964
*Voices of: Arnold Stang, Jess Cain, Minerva Pious, Peter Lazer, Conrad Jameson, Cliff Owens, Mavis Mims, Kever Kennedy*
Pinocchio battles a flying whale that is attacking space vessels. A mediocre cartoon with forgettable songs and shoddy animation.
Aka: PINOCCHIO DANS L'ESPACE
CAR                                62 min (ort 71 min)
B,V                                                    GHV

**PIONEER BUILDERS \*\***
William A. Wellman     USA                1932
*Richard Dix, Ann Harding, Donald Cook, Edna May Oliver, Guy Kibbee, Julie Haydon, Harry Holman, Skeets Gallagher, Walter Walker, Wally Albright Jr, Marilyn Knowlden, Jason Robards, Jed Prouty, E.H. Calvert, J. Carrol Naish*
A newlywed man moves West with his wife, and builds a banking empire in this enjoyable if cliched tale (inspired by "Cimarron"), that covers a 50-year period from the 1870s to the 1930s.
Aka: CONQUERORS, THE
Osca: BIG LAND, THE
DRA                                81 min (ort 88 min) B/W
B,V                                                    KVD

**PIPE DREAMS \*\*\***
Stephen Verona         USA                1976
*Gladys Knight, Barry Hankerson, Bruce French, Sherry Buin, Wayne Tippit, Sally Kirkland, Altovise Davis*
A woman moves to Alaska to work on the pipeline, but her real reason for going was to find her ex-husband. Singing star Knight makes her acting debut, and teams up with her backing group The Pips, for the soundtrack. A warm and appealing tale, in an unusual setting.
DRA                                                  89 min
B,V                                                    PRV

**PIPPIN \*\***
Kathryn Doby           USA                1981
*Ben Vereen, William Katt, Chita Rivera, Martha Raye*
A video production of the original Broadway stage show about a young man's search for the meaning of life.
Boa: musical by Roger O. Hirsch (book) and Stephen Schwartz (music and lyrics).
MUS                                                 120 min
B,V                                             HVM; HVH

**PIRANHA \*\*\***                                    18
Joe Dante              USA                1978
*Bradford Dillman, Heather Menzies, Kevin McCarthy, Keenan Wynn, Dick Miller, Belinda Balaski, Barbara Steele*
A stock of man-eating fish are accidentally released into local rivers in this fast-paced spoof on JAWS that attempts to parody SF films of the 1950s. The script is by John Sayles. Followed by a sequel in name only.
Boa: novel by John Sayles.
COM                                90 min (ort 94 min)
B,V                                                    WHV

**PIRANHA 2: FLYING KILLERS \***                      18
James Cameron          ITALY/USA          1981

*Tricia O'Neal, Steve Marachuk, Lance Henriksen, Ricky G. Paul, Ted Richert, Leslie Graves, Carole Davis, Arnie Ross, Connie Lynn Hadden, Tracy Berg, Anne Pollack, Albert Sanders*
Bears no relation to the original title film and tells of nasty killer fish that go on a rampage in the Caribbean. This was Cameron's debut as a director (he went on to make THE TERMINATOR) and is little more than a gratuitously gory mess.
Aka: PIRANHA 2: THE SPAWNING
HOR                              92 min (ort 95 min)
B,V                                             RCA

## PIRANHA WOMEN *                              15
J.D. Athens            USA                    1988
*Adrienne Barbeau, Shannon Tweed, Barry Primus, Bill Maher, Karen Mistal*
A famous anthropologist heads an expedition to find the long-lost Dr Kurtz and they discover a tribe ruled over by a demented feminist. A low-budget jungle movie spoof, written and directed by Athens.
Aka: CANNIBAL WOMEN IN THE AVOCADO JUNGLE OF DEATH
COM             85 min (ort 87 min) Cut (16 sec)
B,V                                             CFD

## PIRATE MOVIE, THE *                           PG
Ken Annakin         AUSTRALIA               1982
*Kristy McNichol, Christopher Atkins, Ted Hamilton, Bill Kerr, Maggie Kirkpatrick, Garry McDonald*
An updated teenage version of The Pirates of Penzance, with a girl dreaming that she is in the musical, but changing some of the details. Not really very successful as it attempts to be both a silly bubblegum comedy and a parody of other films. Sequences of slapstick and swordplay are thrown together in the hope that this unlikely combination is sufficiently funny to not require a script.
Boa: musical The Pirates Of Penzance by Gilbert and Sullivan.
COM                            94 min (ort 105 min)
B, V/s, V2                                      CBS

## PIRATE, THE ***                                U
Vincente Minnelli      USA                   1948
*Judy Garland, Gene Kelly, Walter Slezak, Gladys Cooper, Reginald Owen, George Zucco, The Nicholas Brothers*
A girl living in a West Indian port takes a circus clown for a pirate, and he happily strings her along to win her attention. Though studio-bound in conception, the film is saved by the songs and Kelly's dancing, in which he shows his usual exhilaration and zest. Music and lyrics are by Cole Porter and Lennie Hayton, with the script by Albert Hackett and Frances Goodrich.
Boa: play by S.N. Behrman.
MUS                            97 min (ort 102 min)
V                                               MGM

## PIRATES **                                     PG
Roman Polanski
              FRANCE/TUNISIA               1986
*Walter Matthau, Damien Thomas, Richard Pearson, Cris Campion, Charlotte Lewis, Michael Elphick, Bill Fraser, Roy Kinnear, Ferdy Mayne, Cardew Robinson, Olu Jacobs*
Polanski's homage to pirate adventure films but taken to extremes (the replica galleon cost $8,000,000 to build) and lacking the care he usually gives to the plot. Despite excellent performances, this expensive dud is no more than a lavish, robust, empty mess. The score is by Philippe Sarde. Cut before video submission by 1 min 30 sec.
A/AD                          106 min (ort 124 min)
B,V                                        CAN; WHV

## PIRATES OF SPRING COVE, THE ***                U
Richard Thorpe        UK                     1965
*John Mills, Hayley Mills, James MacArthur, Lionel*

*Jeffries, Harry Andrews, Niall MacGinnis, David Tomlinson, Lionel Murton*
A young girl meets a millionaire's son who helps her to save her father's treasure map from falling into the hands of pirates. A rousing and enjoyable film for kids.
Aka: TRUTH ABOUT SPRING, THE
Boa: novel Satan by Henry de Vere Stacpoole.
JUV                            96 min (ort 102 min)
B,V                                        EAG; GLOB

## PIRATES OF THE MISSISSIPPI **                  15
Jurgen Roland    WEST GERMANY               1963
*Brad Harris, Dorothee Parker, Horst Frank, Sabine Singen, Hans Jorg Felmy, Werner Peters*
A sheriff goes after an outlaw but is captured by river pirates.
Aka: DIE FLUSSPIRATEN DES MISSISSIPPI
A/AD                                         101 min
B,V            STR L/A; MARKET/GOV L/A; VTEL

## PIT AND THE PENDULUM, THE **                   15
Roger Corman          USA                    1961
*Vincent Price, John Kerr, Barbara Steele, Luana Anders, Antony Carbone, Patrick Westwood, Lynne Bernay, Mary Menzies, Charles Victor, Larry Turner*
Corman mutilates a fine Poe story, in this tale of a man who locks his sister and her lover in a torture chamber, after going mad and thinking he is his late father (who used to work for the Inquisition). A slow and lacklustre film that's partially redeemed by good sets, especially the pendulum sequence. This was Corman's second foray into Poe territory. The script is by Richard Matheson.
Boa: short story by Edgar Allan Poe.
HOR                        85 min; 77 min (VGM)
B,V,V2                                    GHV; VGM

## PIXOTE ****                                     18
Hector Babenco        BRAZIL                 1981
*Fernando Ramos da Silva, Marilia Pera, Jorge Juliao, Gilberto Moura, Jose Nilson dos Santos, Edilson Lino, Zenildo Oliveira Santos, Claudio Bernardo, Tony Tornado, Jardel Filho, Rubens de Falco*
A 10-year-old boy is abandoned and slowly drifts into crime, eventually becoming a murderous criminal, in this shocking indictment of the social conditions in the slums of Brazil. Not for the squeamish.
Aka: PIXOTE: LA LEY DEL MAS DEBIL
DRA       119 min (ort 125 min) (Cut at film release)
V                                               PVG

## PLACE IN HELL, A **
Joseph Warren (Giuseppe Vari)
                       ITALY                 1968
*Guy Madison, Monty Greenwood, Fabio Testi, Helene Chanel, Lee Burton*
An American correspondent in Manila during WW2 and a prostitute, escape to a small island, joining US troops trapped there by the Japanese, and become involved in a mission to blow up a radar station.
Aka: COMMANDO ATTACK; UN POSTO ALL'INFERNO
WAR                                          105 min
B,V,V2                                   AVI L/A; VPD

## PLACE OF WEEPING ***                            PG
Darrell Roodt      SOUTH AFRICA             1986
*James Whyle, Charles Comyn, Geina Mhlophe, Norman Coombes, Michelle du Toit, Ramolao Makhene, Patrick Shai*
A clumsy but sincere appeal for change in South Africa, following the story of a black woman who fights for justice after a brutal white farmer beats one of his workers to death. This was South Africa's first home-grown indictment of apartheid.
DRA                            85 min (ort 88 min)
B/h, V/h                                        NWV

## PLACES IN THE HEART ***
Robert Benton      USA

PG
1984

*Sally Field, Lindsay Crouse, Ed Harris, Amy Madigan, John Malkovich, Danny Glover*
A widow struggles to keep her farm and family together during the Depression years, enduring many hardships in this over-sentimental but generally effective tale. AA: Actress (Field), Screen (Orig) (Benton).
Aka: WAITING FOR MORNING
DRA      111 min
B,V      CBS

## PLAGUE *
Ed Hunt      CANADA

15
1978

*Daniel Pilon, Kate Reid, Celine Lomez, Michael J. Reynolds, Brenda Donohue, Barbara Gordon, Johna Rayston, Jack Van Evera, Trevor Rose, Renata Bosacki, Michael Donaghue, Joseph Golland, Allan Habberfield, Lynda Kemp, John Kerr*
A deadly strain of bacteria is on the loose – with dire results, one of which was this movie.
Aka: INDUCED SYDROME (KRP); M3: THE GEMINI STRAIN
FAN 88 min; 84 min (MANHAT or KRP) (ort 110 min)
B,V      AVP; MANHAT; KRP

## PLAGUE DOGS, THE ***
Martin Rosen      UK/USA

PG
1982

*Voices of: John Hurt, James Bolam, Christopher Benjamin, Judy Geeson, Barbara Leigh-Hunt*
Animation telling of two dogs that are infected with a deadly virus at a research laboratory and escape, threatening to infect the entire countryside with an epidemic. Somewhat heavy-going to start with, but held together by fine animation and the sincere script, which is as much a plea to respect the rights of animals as it is an adventure tale.
Boa: novel by Richard Adams.
CAR      99 min (ort 103 min)
B,V      TEVP; WHV

## PLAGUE OF THE ZOMBIES, THE ***
John Gilling      UK

15
1965

*Andre Morell, Diane Clare, Jacqueline Pearce, John Carson, Brook Williams, Michael Ripper, Alex Davion, Marcus Hammond, Roy Royston, Dennis Chinnery*
An epidemic in a Cornish village is traced to the local squire, who uses voodoo to create zombies who are then made to work in his tin mine. Quite an effective little chiller, made by Hammer Films and well above their usual quality.
Aka: ZOMBIE, THE; ZOMBIES, THE
HOR      87 min (ort 91 min)
B,V      WHV

## PLAIN CLOTHES **
Martha Coolidge      USA

PG
1988

*Arliss Howard, George Wendt, Seymour Cassel, Diane Ladd, Suzy Amis, Robert Stack*
A local teacher is murdered, and a cop goes undercover in his high school in a bid to find the killer, experiencing once more all the things he had to contend with when he was a student. A messy mystery-comedy sustained by the fine cast.
COM      94 min (ort 98 min)
V      CIC

## PLAN 9 FROM OUTER SPACE
Edward D. Wood Jr      USA      1959
*Gregory Walcott, Tom Keene, Duke Moore, Mona McKinnon, Dudley Manlove, Lyle Talbot, Bela Lugosi, Tor Johnson, Vampira (Maila Nurmi), Criswell*
Here it is. One of the very worst films ever made. So bad that it achieves a kind of greatness. Lugosi died after only four days of shooting, but don't let that put you off; it's OK, a double took over. The tale is one of aliens re-animating corpses to use in an invasion of Earth, this is the dreaded "Plan 9". This masterpiece

was followed by NIGHT OF THE GHOULS.
Aka: GRAVE ROBBERS FROM OUTER SPACE
FAN      79 min B/W
B,V      PVG

## PLANES, TRAINS AND AUTOMOBILES ***
John Hughes      USA

15
1987

*Steve Martin, John Candy, Laila Robbins, Michael McKern, Kevin Bacon, Dylan Baker, Carol Bruce, Olivia Burnette, Diana Douglas, Martin Ferrero, Larry Hankin, Richard Herd, Susan Kellerman, Matthew Lawrence, Edie McClurg*
A businessman hurrying home to celebrate Thanksgiving with his family, gets inextricably involved with his boorish travelling companion, and together they experience an incredible succession of mishaps on their cross-country odyssey. Good characterisation and a certain measure of warmth sustain the rather thin plot.
COM      88 min (ort 93 min)
V/sh      CIC

## PLANET EARTH **
Marc Daniels      USA

PG
1974

*John Saxon, Janet Margolin, Ted Cassidy, Diana Muldaur, Johana De Winter, Christopher Gary, Majel Barrett, Jim Antonio, Sally Kemp, Claire Brennan, Corinne Camacho, Sarah Chattin, John Quade, Patricia Smith, Raymond Sutton*
An American scientist wakes from suspended animation in the year 2133 to find that future society is a matriarchy where men are mere slaves. A kind of reworking of a slightly earlier film, "Genesis 2" (1973). Fair.
Boa: story by Gene Roddenberry.
FAN      71 min mTV
B,V      WHV

## PLANET OF THE APES ***
Franklin J. Schaffner      USA

PG
1968

*Charlton Heston, Roddy McDowall, Kim Hunter, Maurice Evans, James Whitmore, James Daly, Linda Harrison, Robert Gunner, Lou Wagner, Woodrow Parfrey, Jeff Burton, Buck Kartalian, Norman Burton, Wright King*
Astronauts crash-land on a planet where apes rule and man is dumb and enslaved. An interesting and stimulating film with a surprise ending. Rod Serling and Michael Wilson scripted the film, which spawned several sequels, a TV series and a cartoon. Folowed by BENEATH THE PLANET OF THE APES, ESCAPE FROM THE PLANET OF THE APES, CONQUEST OF THE PLANET OF THE APES and BATTLE FOR THE PLANET OF THE APES. AA: Hon Award (John Chambers for make-up).
Boa: novel La Planete Des Singes (Monkey Planet) by Pierre Boulle.
FAN      112 min (ort 119 min)
V      CBS

## PLANET OF THE VAMPIRES ***
Mario Bava      ITALY

15
1965

*Barry Sullivan, Norma Bengell, Angel Aranda, Evi Marandi, Fernando Villena, Stelio Candelli, Mario Morales, Massimo Righi, Franco Andrei, Ivan Rassimov, Alberto Cevenini, Rico Boido*
A mission to a strange mist-covered planet comes under attack from its invisible inhabitants who take over the minds of the crew members. A low-budget chiller with considerable atmosphere.
Aka: DEMON PLANET, THE; HAUNTED PLANET; OUTLAW PLANET; PLANET OF TERROR; TERROR FROM SPACE; TERRORE NELLO SPAZIO
Boa: short story One Night Of 21 Hours by Renato Pestriniero.
HOR      86 min
B,V      RCA

## PLANK, THE ** U
Eric Sykes UK 1967
*Eric Sykes, Tommy Cooper, Graham Stark, Stratford Johns, Jim Dale, Hattie Jacques, Jimmy Tarbuck*
One of those endearingly idiotic comedies that is done without a word of dialogue and inevitably features several workmen making a mess of the simplest of tasks. This tale follows the havoc caused by two such men and their plank of wood.
COM 46 min
V PICK

## PLATOON *** 15
Oliver Stone USA 1986
*Tom Berenger, Willem Dafoe, Charlie Sheen, Forest Whitaker, Francesco Quinn, John C. McGinley, Richard Edson, Kevin Dillon, Reggie Johnson, Keith David, Johnny Depp, David Neidorf*
A realistic look at the experiences of a front-line American soldier in Vietnam that says what has been said many times before: war is hell, and meaningless to boot. What we're still waiting for is a film that puts this conflict in its historical context as THE BATTLE OF ALGIERS did for the Algerian liberation struggle. AA: Pic, Dir, Sound (John K. Wilkinson/Richard Rogers/Charles "Bud" Grenzbach/Simon Kaye), Edit (Claire Simpson).
WAR 115 min (ort 120 min)
V/sh RCA

## PLATOON LEADER ** 18
Aaron Norris USA 1988
*Michael Dudikoff, Robert F. Lyons, William Smith, Rick Fitts, Brian Libby, Michael De Lorenzo*
An inexperienced commander whose military knowledge is purely academic, receives a baptism of fire in the trenches, when his unit comes into conflict with Communist forces in South-East Asia. Mindless high-action nonsense.
A/AD 92 min (ort 97 min)
B, V/sh CAN; PATHE

## PLATOON WARRIORS * 18
Philip Ko USA 1987
*James Miller, Alex Sylvian, Don Richard, David Coley, Mark Watson, Mike Abbott*
Two drug gangs fight it out in this underworld actioner.
Aka: PLATOON THE WARRIORS
MAR 83 min (ort 90 min) Cut (3 min 47 sec)
B,V CINE

## PLATYPUS COVE ** 
Peter Maxwell AUSTRALIA 1983
*Tony Barry, Carmen Duncan, Bill Kerr, Allen Bickford, Aileen Briccon, Paul Smith, Simone Buchanan, Martin Lewis, Henri Szeps, Mark Hembrow, Dennis Miller, Brian Anderson, Robin Bowering, Robert Carnamolis*
A widowed tugboat captain and his two children, clash with the local crooked businessman who is out to ruin them. Predictable but enjoyable entertainment for kids.
JUV 72 min
B,V AVP L/A

## PLAY DEAD * 18
Peter Wittman USA 1982
*Yvonne De Carlo, Stephanie Dunham, David Cullinane, Glenn Kezer, Ron Jackson, David Elizey, Carolyn Greenwood*
A rich woman decides to murder her relatives one by one, and presents each in turn with the gift of a dog, one that has been duly imbued with Satanic evil. An incoherent and unmemorable yarn.
Aka: SATAN'S DOG (VIDVIS)
HOR 90 min; 86 min (VIDVIS)
B,V VFO L/A; VIDVIS

## PLAY IT AGAIN, SAM *** 15
Herbert Ross USA 1972
*Woody Allen, Diane Keaton, Susan Anspach, Tony Roberts, Jerry Lacy, Jennifer Salt, Joy Bang, Viva*
An entertaining and charming Woody Allen comedy, with a film critic being helped in his love life by the figure of Humphrey Bogart, and finding that his life begins to follow Bogart's in CASABLANCA. A good deal less disjointed than most of Allen's work, this one actually has a coherent script.
Boa: play by Woody Allen.
COM 82 min (ort 86 min)
B,V CIC

## PLAY MISTY FOR ME *** 18
Clint Eastwood USA 1971
*Clint Eastwood, Donna Mills, Jessica Walter, John Larch, Irene Hervey, Jack Ging, Johnny Otis, James McEachin, Clarice Taylor, Donald Siegel, Duke Everts, George Fargo, Mervin W. Frates, Tim Frawley, Otis Kadani*
Eastwood's directorial debut is a highly-skilled piece of work with a good sense of suspense. He plays a late-night radio D.J. who is pursued by a deranged woman who has developed an obsessive interest in him. Don Siegel puts in an appearance as a bartender. Scripted by Jo Heims and Dean Reisner.
THR 98 min (ort 102 min)
V CIC

## PLAYBIRDS, THE * 18
Willy Roe UK 1978
*Mary Millington, Glynn Edwards, Gavin Campbell, Alan Lake, Windsor Davies, Derren Nesbitt, Suzy Mandel, Ballard Berkely, Sandra Dorne, Alec Mango, Penny Spencer, Michael Gradwell, Tony Kenyon, Dudley Sutton, John East*
A policeman goes under cover to investigate a series of murders of nude porno magazine models. Another tired, unsexy attempt to bilk the public.
Aka: SECRETS OF A PLAYGIRL (BEV or KRP)
A 90 min (ort 94 min) (Cut at film release)
B,V HOK L/A; BEV; KRP; MIG

## PLAYBOY OF THE WESTERN WORLD, THE ***
Brian Desmond Hurst EIRE 1962
*Siobhan McKenna, Gary Raymond, Elspeth March, Michael O'Brian, Liam Redmond, Niall MacGinnis*
Film version of a famous play, telling of a boastful young man who arrives at a sleepy County Mayo village with a tale of how he killed his father, and other stories that generally charm and intrigue the inhabitants. A colourful romp that clearly shows its stage origins but is no less enjoyable for that.
Boa: play by John Millington Synge.
COM 96 min (ort 100 min)
B,V TEVP

## PLAYERS * PG
Anthony Harvey USA 1979
*Ali MacGraw, Maximilian Schell, Pancho Gonzalez, Dean-Paul Martin, Steve Guttenberg, Melissa Prophet*
A tennis player falls in love with another man's mistress and finds his feelings are having an adverse effect on his game. A curiously empty film built around a match at Wimbledon, but with the script probably left behind in the changing rooms.
DRA 115 min (ort 120 min)
B,V CIC

## PLAYGIRL, THE ***
Roberta Findlay USA 1982
*Veronica Hart, Samantha Fox, Tiffany Clark, Sharon Cain, Merle Michaels, Candida Royalle, Ashley Moore, R. Bolla, Bobby Astyr*
The wife of a wealthy publisher patronises artists and writers, offering them something more than mere moral support; and all with her husband's approval. Once her men achieve success, she tires of them and

looks for new companions. Love finally catches up with her in the shape of a frustrated novelist who works for her husband. Made with something of a feminist slant, this is a lighthearted fun film.

| | |
|---|---|
| A | 90 min |
| B,V,V2 | ELV |

## PLAYING FOR KEEPS ** 15
Harvey Weinstein/Bob Weinstein
USA                 1986
*Daniel Jordano, Matthew Penn, Leon W. Grant,*
*Harold Gould, Jimmy Baio, Marisa Tomei, Mary B.*
*Ward, Kim Hauser*
Three boys in New York City are anxious for adventure after their graduation, and spend their time playing a childhood game they invented. However, when one of the boys finds that his family has inherited an old hotel he decides to turn it into a resort for teenagers. Amiable nonsense.

| | |
|---|---|
| COM | 102 min (ort 105 min) |
| V/sh | GHV |

## PLAYING FOR TIME ***
Daniel Mann          USA          1980
*Vanessa Redgrave, Jane Alexander, Maud Adams,*
*Viveca Lindfors, Shirley Knight, Marisa Berenson,*
*Verna Bloom, Donna Haley, Lenore Harris, Max*
*Wright, Mady Kaplan, Will Lee, Anna Levine, Melanie*
*Mayron*
The story of Fania Fenelon, a Jewish woman who survived the horrors of Auschwitz by playing in the camp orchestra. Screenplay is by Arthur Miller, with effective (if somewhat insensitive) casting of Redgrave as Fenelon. The film won four Emmy awards: Outstanding Actress (Redgrave), Outstanding Drama Special, Outstanding Lead Actress in a Limited Special (Alexander), Outstanding Writing in a Limited Special (Arthur Miller).
Boa: book by Fania Fenelon.

| | |
|---|---|
| DRA | 150 min mTV |
| B,V | POLY L/A; VCL |

## PLAYING WITH FIRE * 18
Howard (Hikmet) Avedis
USA          1984
*Eric Brown, Sybil Danning (Sybelle Danning),*
*Andrew Prine, Paul Clemens, K.T. Stevens, Gene*
*Bickell*
A pupil falls in love with his teacher, but murder complicates the path of true love somewhat. He soon discovers that his lover wants his help in order to kill her mother and gain an inheritance. A nasty little drama that starts off like PRIVATE LESSONS but rapidly becomes a good deal more sordid.
Aka: THEY'RE PLAYING WITH FIRE

| | |
|---|---|
| DRA | 92 min (ort 96 min) |
| B,V | CBS |

## PLAYTIME **** U
Jacques Tati          FRANCE          1968
*Jacques Tati, Barbara Dennek, Henri Piccoli,*
*Jacqueline Lecomte, Valerie Camille, France Romilly,*
*Leon Doyen, Jack Gautier*
Tati's famous bumbling, fumbling character, Monsieur Hulot, wanders through a Paris he does not recognise, as he attempts to keep an appointment in this very Gallic assault on the confusing complexities of modern civilisation. Tati's understanding of the possibilities inherent in a 70 mm screen (largely lost on TV) is remarkable. Followed by TRAFFIC.

| | |
|---|---|
| COM | 115 min (ort 155 min) |
| B,V,V2 | VDM L/A; VMA; STABL |

## PLAZA SUITE *** PG
Arthur Hiller          USA          1971
*Walter Matthau, Maureen Stapleton, Barbara Harris,*
*Lee Grant, Louise Sorel, Jennie Sullivan, Tom Carey*
Three stories set in the same hotel suite with Matthau playing all three parts: a successful businessman who

has taken his wife out to celebrate an anniversary (poignant rather than funny), a sex-starved film director (acid-sharp but only slightly funny), and a pompous father whose daughter is about to get married but has locked herself in the bathroom (extremely funny). Written by Neil Simon.
Boa: play by Neil Simon.

| | |
|---|---|
| COM | 109 min (ort 114 min) |
| B,V | CIC |

## PLEASE SIR! * PG
Mark Stuart          UK          1971
*John Alderton, Deryck Guyler, Joan Sanderson, Noel*
*Howlett, Eric Chitty, Richard Davies, Patsy Rowlands,*
*Peter Cleall, Carol Hawkins, Liz Gebhardt, David*
*Barry, Peter Denyer, Malcolm McFee, Aziz Resham,*
*Brinsley Forde*
Spin-off from a British TV series about a teacher and his unruly class at a run-down school. Here, he takes the kids off to a summer camp; laughs are few and far between. The script is by John Esmonde.

| | |
|---|---|
| COM | 97 min (ort 101 min) |
| B,V | RNK; VCC (VHS only) |

## PLEASURE DOME ** 18
Paul Aubin          FRANCE
*Alban, Nadia, Danielle Troyer*
A female aristocrat has to find her daughter in order to inherit a fortune, and is aided in her search by a powerful aphrodisiac potion.

| | |
|---|---|
| A | 60 min; 87 min (TAR) |
| B,V | ELV L/A; TAR |

## PLEASURE ISLAND ** 18
FRANCE
*Nadine Roussail*
Emmanuelle's sex adventure on a tropical isle. Average.

| | |
|---|---|
| A | 67 min (ort 71 min) |
| B,V | VPD; NET; TCX |

## PLEASURE PALACE **
Walter Grauman          USA          1980
*Omar Shariff, Victoria Principal, Hope Lange, Jose*
*Ferrer, J.D. Cannon, Gerald S. O'Loughlin, Teddi*
*Siddall, John Fujioka, Alexander Zale, Joseph*
*Bernard, Chuck Hicks, Dave Burton, Eddie Sherman,*
*George LaForge*
A high-rolling gambler risks his reputation by helping a lady casino owner in this routine caper, scripted by Blanche Hanalis.

| | |
|---|---|
| DRA | 92 min (ort 100 min) mTV |
| B,V | PRV |

## PLEASURE PALACE ***
Edward Hunt          CANADA          1973
(re-released 1980)
*Serena, Eric Edwards, R. Bolla, Jamie Gillis, Joey*
*Silvera, Roger Caine, Bobby Astyr, Janice Duval,*
*Nicki Flynn, Tomi Celli, Art Roberts*
A vice squad cop who has been fired for being too lenient on a pimp, goes into partnership to buy up a bordello in Connecticut. The whorehouse is very profitable and they discover that the reason the owner is keen to sell is that a local gangster has decided to take it over. Meanwhile, the ex-cop has fallen for the brothel Madame. Complications ensue in this well made but occasionally violent adult film.

| | |
|---|---|
| A | 70 min |
| B,V | CAL L/A |

## PLEASURE SO DEEP ** R18
Miller Dirksen          ITALY          1983
*Lauren St Jermain, Brigitte De Palma, Stephen*
*Sheldon, Richard Hammer, Kathleen Kinski, Paul*
*Myerson, Nolan Velours, Elsa McDonald, Ursula*
*Fontaine*
A Mafia godfather runs a funeral business as a front for a counterfeiting operation. He sends Mario, his

second-in-command, to bring back his daughter who is working in a massage parlour. Mario falls for the girl, despite the fact that he is already having an affair with his boss's new wife. The girl initially rejects him, but after various mishaps they end up together in this contrived but mildly diverting tale.

A 77 min dubbed
V SHEP

## PLEASURE, THE ** 18
Joe D'Amato (Aristide Massaccesi)
ITALY 1985
*Isabelle Andrea Guzon, Steve Wyler, Marco Mattioli, Lilli Carati, Laura Gemser, Dagmar Lassander*
A widower is eventually seduced by his step-daughter, in a story set against the background of the carnival in pre-WW2 Venice.
Aka: IL PIACERE
A 87 min (ort 90 min) Cut (3 sec in addition
to film cuts)
B,V ELE

## PLENTY ** 15
Fred Schepisi UK 1985
*Meryl Streep, Sam Neill, Charles Dance, John Gielgud, Tracy Ullman, Sting (Gordon Sumner), Ian McKellen, Andre Maranne, Tristram Jellinek, Peter Forbes-Robertson, Hugo De Vernier, James Taylor, Ian Wallace, Burt Kwouk*
A former female intelligence agent is unable to adapt to civilian life, in post-WW2 Britain which she finds depressingly dull and meaningless. Remarkably convincing performances and a few sharp observations are hampered by the tedious nature of the story. The film's use of a wide-screen frame will be lost on TV. Scripted by Hare from his play.
Boa: play by David Hare.
DRA 119 min (ort 124 min)
B,V TEVP

## PLOT TO KILL HITLER, THE ** PG
Lawrence Schiller USA 1990
*Brad Davis, Madolyn Smith, Ian Richardson, Mike Gwilyn, Helmut Griehm, Jonathan Hyde, Kenneth Colley*
Drama based on the events of the summer of 1944, when Germany was facing certain defeat and Hitler's underlings were convinced that the country would fare better with a conditional surrender to the Allies rather than wait until they were comprehensively beaten. An interesting but patchy affair, that attempts to show some humanity within the German camp, but never develops tension and miscasts Davis as the ringleader of the plotters.
DRA 87 min (ort 100 min) mTV
V WHV

## PLOUGHMAN'S LUNCH, THE *** 
Richard Eyre UK 1983
*Jonathan Pryce, Tim Curry, Rosemary Harris, Frank Finlay, Charlie Dore, David De Keyser, Nat Jackley, Bill Paterson, David Lyon, Pearl Hackney, Simon Stokes, Orlando Wells, Witold Schejbal, Libba Davies, Sandra Voe*
Sharply observed study of contemporary Britain during the Falklands War, with Pryce excellent as an obnoxious and self-centred radio reporter. A minor piece that is confined within the narrow boundaries of its outlook, but pungent and thought-provoking.
DRA 100 min (ort 107 min)
B,V PVG

## PLUCKING THE DAISY * 15
Marc Allegret FRANCE 1956
*Brigitte Bardot, Daniel Gelin, Robert Hirsch*
An early Bardot vehicle, with her cast as the authoress of a scandalous bestseller who is forced to flee from her disapproving father to Paris, where she finds herself destitute. To earn some money she enters a

striptease competition, and finds her supposedly strait laced father among the judges. A dated and tame comedy of limited interest.
Aka: EN EFFLUEILLANT LA MARGUERITE
COM 101 min
V CASPIC

## PLUNGE INTO DARKNESS ** 15
Peter Maxwell AUSTRALIA 1977
*Olivia Hammett, Bruce Barry, Peter Maxwell, Ashley Grenville, Tom Richards, John Jarratt, Wallace Eaton*
An ex-Olympic runner and his wife are on holiday, and find a boy in the bush who is the only survivor of an entire family murdered by gangsters. Naturally, they decide to seek help, but when their car breaks down the husband has to put his former skills to the test.
THR 74 min (ort 77 min)
B,V XTASY; INT/CBS; VEXCEL

## POCKET MONEY ** PG
Stuart Rosenberg USA 1972
*Paul Newman, Lee Marvin, Strother Martin, Christine Belford, Kelly Jean Peters, Wayne Rogers, Fred Graham, Hector Elizondo, Mickey Gilbert*
A none-too-bright debt-ridden cowboy and his drunk pal become involved in cattle rustling, in this flabby comedy that's slightly redeemed by Marvin's deliberate hamming. The fine photography is by Laszlo Kovacs and the script is by Terry Malick.
Boa: novel by Jim Kane.
COM 102 min
B,V GHV; VMA; STABL

## POINT, THE *** U
Fred Wolf USA 1970
*Ringo Starr (narration only)*
A charming, animated parable about a young boy who is unique in having a rounded head, not a pointed one like everyone else in the Land of Point. This "crime" earns him banishment from the kingdom and he has a series of entertaining adventures on his travels. Inspired by a record album produced by rock musician Harry Nilsson, and featuring some of his bright tunes. The occasional dollops of moralising and the expected puns are minor failings.
CAR 74 min mTV
V VES

## POINT BLANK ***
John Boorman USA 1967
*Lee Marvin, Angie Dickinson, Keenan Wynn, Carroll O'Connor, Lloyd Bochner, John Vernon, Michael Strong, Sharon Acker*
A man is shot and left for dead by his wife and her lover, but survives the shooting to get his revenge two years later. This harsh, brutal and opaque thriller was a failure at the time, but is now regarded as a near classic. Written by Alexander Jacobs, David Newhouse and Rafe Newhouse.
Boa: novel The Hunter by Richard Stark (Donald E. Westlake).
THR 88 min (ort 92 min)
B,V MGM

## POIROT: PERIL AT END HOUSE *** PG
Renny Rye UK
*David Suchet, Hugh Fraser, Philip Jackson, Pauline Moran*
Suchet is excellent as Hercule Poirot, one of Christie's most popular sleuths, in this tale of mystery and murder set on the Cornish Riviera, to which our detective and his friend Captain Hastings have travelled for a holiday.
Boa: story by Agatha Christie.
DRA 100 min mTV
V VCC

## POIROT: VOLUME 1 ** PG
UK 1988

*David Suchet, Hugh Fraser, Philip Jackson, Pauline Moran*
Two episodes from the TV series that followed the exploits of Christie's famous sleuth. The tales are entitled "The Adventure Of The Clapham Cook" and "Murder In The Mews". In the first, the strange disappearance of a cook leads to Poirot uncovering a complex intrigue, and in the second he discovers that an apparent suicide is not quite all it appears to be. Fair.
Boa: stories by Agatha Christie.
DRA                          100 min mTV
B,V                          CASVIS

### POIROT: VOLUME 2 **                     PG
Edward Bennet          UK              1989
*David Suchet, Hugh Fraser, Philip Jackson, Pauline Moran*
Two more tales from this generally well made adaptation of stories featuring Christie's famous sleuth. These episodes are entitled "The Third Floor Flat" and "The Incredible Theft".
Boa: stories by Agatha Christie.
DRA                          100 min mTV
V                            CASVIS

### POIROT: VOLUME 3 **                     PG
Renny Rye              UK              1989
*David Suchet, Hugh Fraser, Philip Jackson, Pauline Moran*
Two episodes entitled "The Adventure Of Johnnie Waverly" and "Four And Twenty Blackbirds", and as before based on the character created in the stories of Agatha Christie.
Boa: stories by Agatha Christie.
DRA                          100 min mTV
V                            CASVIS

### POIROT: KING OF CLUBS/THE DREAM ***   PG
Renny Rye/Edward Bennett
                       UK              1989
*David Suchet, Hugh Fraser, Philip Jackson, Pauline Moran, Joely Richardson, Alan Howard, Niamh Cusack*
Two stories from a well-made and popular series of adaptations of Agatha Christie tales – "King Of Clubs" and "The Dream", in which Poirot is consulted by an industrialist who has been experiencing disturbing nightmares.
Boa: stories by Agatha Christie.
DRA                          100 min mTV
V                            CASVIS

### POISON IVY **                          PG
Larry Elikann          USA             1984
*Michael J. Fox, Nancy McKeon, Robert Klein, Caren Kaye, Adam Baldwin, Joe Wright, Tommy Nowell, Matthew Shugallo, Derek Googe, Gary Guffey, Hoke Reece, Cameron Arnett, Ryan Langhorn, Brett Rice, Lou Walker, Jarett Beal*
Teen comedy set in a boy's summer camp, where the camp director has problems of his own with his crazy wife. Fairly run-of-the-mill for this genre with few surprises.
COM                          92 min (ort 100 min) mTV
B,V                          RCA

### POKER ALICE **                         PG
Arthur Seidelman       USA             1987
*Elizabeth Taylor, Tom Skerrit, George Hamilton, Richard Mulligan, David Wayne, Susan Tyrell, Pat Corley*
A female gambler wins a brothel in a high-stakes game and finds her life will never be the same again. The script is by James Lee Barrett, who has done better work. Average.
WES                          91 min (ort 109 min) mTV
B,V                          NWV

### POLICE ACADEMY **                      15
Hugh Wilson            USA             1984
*Steve Guttenberg, Kim Cattrall, G.W. Bailey, George Gaynes, Bubba Smith, Michael Winslow, David Graf, Donovan Scott, Andrew Rubin, Bruce Mahler, Georgina Spelvin, Leslie Easterbrook*
A police commissioner lowers the recruiting standards of the police academy with the result that assorted misfits and weirdos enrol. Several sequels have followed, each one spinning out to gossamer thinness, a comic idea that was never more than moderately amusing to begin with.
COM                          92 min (ort 96 min)
V/sh                         WHV

### POLICE ACADEMY 2 *                     15
Jerry Paris            USA             1985
*Steve Guttenberg, Bubba Smith, George Gaynes, David Graf, Michael Winslow, Bruce Mahler, Marion Ramsey, Colleen Camp, Howard Hesseman, Art Metrano, Ed Merlihy*
The continuing story of the world's most unlikely police graduates; funny if you like that sort of thing.
Aka: POLICE ACADEMY 2: THEIR FIRST ASSIGNMENT
COM                          84 min (ort 87 min)
B,V                          WHV

### POLICE ACADEMY 3 **                    PG
Jerry Paris            USA             1986
*Steve Guttenberg, Bubba Smith, David Graf, Michael Winslow, Marion Ramsey, Leslie Easterbrook, Art Metrano, Tim Kazurinsky, George Gaynes, Bobcat Goldthwait*
Yet aonther attempt to squeeze a few more laughs (and some cash) out of a tired plot, revolving round a zany police training academy. In this one, the academy is faced with budget cuts that may close it; our rookie cops find a way to save it.
Aka: POLICE ACADEMY 3: BACK IN TRAINING
COM                          80 min (ort 82 min)
B,V                          WHV

### POLICE ACADEMY 4 *                     PG
Jim Drake              USA             1987
*Steve Guttenberg, G.W. Bailey, Bobcat Goldthwait, George Gaynes, Bubba Smith, Michael Winslow, David Graf, Tim Kazurinsky, Marion Ramsey, Sharon Stone, Leslie Esterbrook, Lance Kinsey, Billie Bird*
Another tired sequel, this time featuring police attempts to involve the local citizens in crime prevention.
Aka: POLICE ACADEMY 4: CITIZEN'S PATROL
COM                          83 min (ort 87 min) Cut (8 sec)
V                            WHV

### POLICE ACADEMY 5 *                     PG
Alan Myerson           USA             1987
*Bubba Smith, Michael Winslow, George Gaynes, David Graf, Janet Jones, Matt McCoy, Leslie Easterbrook, Marion Ramsey, G.W. Bailey, Rene Auberjonois, George Gaynes, Lance Kinsey*
Bottom-of-the-barrel time, with this fourth sequel in which an accidental switch of luggage at an airport deprives some crooks of their stolen diamonds, which thus come into the possession of Chief Lassed, who's in Miami to address a police convention.
Aka: POLICE ACADEMY 5: ASSIGNMENT MIAMI BEACH
COM                          87 min (ort 90 min)
V                            WHV

### POLICE ACADEMY 6 *                     PG
Peter Bonerz           USA             1989
*Kenneth Mars, G.W. Bailey, George Gaynes, Bubba Smith, Michael Winslow, David Graf, Leslie Easterbrook, Lance Kinsey, Marion Ramsey, Matt McCoy, Bruce Mahler, Gerrit Graham*
Yet another tale in this increasingly dismal and

strained series, this time following the exploits of our cops as they try to solve a crime wave.
Aka: POLICE ACADEMY 6: CITY UNDER SIEGE
COM                                         82 min
V/sh                                          WHV

## POLICE ASSASSINS **                        18
David Chung        HONG KONG            1986
*Michelle Khan, Henry Sanada, Harry Khan, Michael Wong*
A team of anti-terrorists foil an attempt to hijack a jet, killing two of the would-be hijackers in the process. However, they now find themselves targeted by an international group of terrorists, who have sworn revenge. A fast-paced and violent action tale, followed by a sequel.
A/AD                                        92 min
B,V                                    PVG; SCRN

## POLICE ASSASSINS 2 *                       18
                   HONG KONG            1987
*Michelle Khan, Cynthia Rothrock*
A tough Scotland Yard woman detective is sent to Hong Kong to take part in a hazardous investigation, in this formula blend of crimebusting and martial arts mayhem.
A/AD                         85 min (ort 90 min)
B,V                                         SCRN

## POLICE GIRLS ACADEMY *                     18
Richard Hieronymous   USA              1987
*Kirsten Baker, Perry Lang*
A low-budget effort that attempts to cash in on the success of the POLICE ACADEMY series, by virtue of its title if not its plot, which is bland to the point of tedium. The script has two college girls helping the local police during their vacations and causing the expected mishaps.
COM                    84 min Cut (1 min 59 sec)
B,V                                     VPD; POR

## POLICE IN ACTION 1: THE BROKEN BADGE **  15
Lee H. Katzin        USA               1978
*Claude Akins, Dennis Dugan, Michael Bell, Warren Stevens, Barbara Luna*
The first tale in a series of cop thrillers, this tells of a dedicated cop whose involvement with a prostitute inadvertently leads to him being convicted of murder and sent to San Quentin.
Aka: BROKEN BADGE, THE
THR                                    94 min mTV
V                                            RCA

## POLICE IN ACTION 2: MAN ON A STRING **   PG
Joseph Sargent       USA               1971
*Christopher George, William Schallert, Michael Baseleon, Keith Carradine, Joel Grey, Kitty Winn, Paul Hampton, Jack Warden, J. Duke Russo, Jack Bernardi, Lincoln Demyan, Bob Golden, Jerome Guardino, Byron Morrow*
An undercover agent for the government infiltrates the Mob, and lands in the middle of a violent struggle between various gangs. One of several full-length features in a series.
Aka: MAN ON A STRING
THR                                    71 min mTV
V                                            RCA

## POLICE IN ACTION 3: STIGMA **            15
                   USA                 1977
*Mike Connors, Cameron Mitchell, James Darren*
Another tale in a series that attempts to present a less stereotyped image of police officers, showing something of their feelings and frailties. On a day out with their families, two cops become involved in a nasty shoot-out and one is taken hostage and then shot. His partner now finds himself unable to overcome feelings of guilt. Competent.

Aka: STIGMA
THR                                    92 min mTV
B,V                                          RCA

## POLICE IN ACTION 4: KISS ME ... KILL ME ** PG
Michael O'Herlihy    USA               1976
*Stella Stevens, Robert Vaughn, Claude Akins, Michael Anderson Jr, Dabney Coleman, Bruce Boxleitner, Alan Fudge, Bruce Glover, Morgan Paull, Tisha Sterling, Charles Weldon, Pat O'Brian, Arnold Soboloff, Helena Carroll*
Prospective pilot about a woman assistant investigator for the D.A., who takes on a murder case where the victim was a respectable young teacher. Competent but certainly not memorable.
Aka: KISS ME ... KILL ME
THR                                    69 min mTV
V                                            RCA

## POLICE IN ACTION 5: A CRY FOR JUSTICE **  15
Robert Kelljan       USA               1978
*Dennis Weaver, Diane Muldaur, Sharon Acker, Biff McGuire, Michael Conrad, Jerry Douglas, Don Mitchell, Nehemiah Persoff, Warren Kennedy, Bruce Glover, Al Ruscio, Janet Wood, Larry Hagman, Robert Culp*
Another story in this fairly entertaining series. In this one a police officer is disabled following a brutal attack, and much bitterness is created within the force, leading to a ruthless search for those responsible.
Aka: CRY FOR JUSTICE, A
A/AD                                   94 min mTV
V                                            RCA

## POLICE IN ACTION 6: DAY OF TERROR, NIGHT OF FEAR *                                   PG
E. Arthur Kean       USA               1977
*Chad Everett, Sandy Dennis, Bruce Davison, Tom Simcox, Michael Baseleon, Malcolm Atterbury, Ward Costello, Andy Romano, Sheila Larkin, Warren Oates*
This further entry in the series, created by writer Joseph Wambaugh, is the stereotyped tale of a pair of armed robbers who take five people hostage on the 12th floor of an office block after their heist fails. A smart cop is given the job of persuading them to surrender. Despite the realistic view of police procedure, the conventional and somewhat sentimental script fails to engage the interest.
Aka: DAY OF TERROR, NIGHT OF FEAR; POLICE STORY: DAY OF TERROR, NIGHT OF FEAR
DRA                                    94 min mTV
V                                            RCA

## POLICE STORY ***                          15
Jackie Chan          HONG KONG         1986
*Jackie Chan, Briget Lin, Maggie Cheung, Cho Yuen, Bill Tung, Kenneth Tong, Lam Kok Hung*
A tough Hong Kong cop is given the assignment of protecting a key witness in a drugs trial, in this simple-minded but enjoyable mixture of martial arts, comedy and action genres. Chan does his own stunts, most of which are incredible. Switch the brain off and enjoy this one.
Aka: JACKIE CHAN'S POLICE STORY; JINGCHA GUSHI; POLICE FORCE
A/AD                         84 min (ort 89 min)
B,V                                          PAL

## POLICE STORY 2 ***                         15
Jackie Chan          HONG KONG         1989
*Jackie Chan, Maggie Cheung, Bill Tung, Lam Kwok Hung, Charles Chao*
Following his one-man battle with drug dealers, Chan has been demoted from a detective to a traffic cop. When Hong Kong is hit by a wave of bomb threats, he finds himself caught up in a private investigation that results in the kidnapping of his girlfriend by those

responsible. An entertaining and often spectacular follow-up to his earlier film.

A/AD 92 min
V VPD

## POLICE STORY: THE FREEWAY KILLINGS ** 15
William (Billy) Graham USA 1987
*Richard Crenna, Angie Dickinson, Ben Gazzara, James B. Sikking, Gloria Loring, Tony Lo Bianco, Don Meredith*
A prospective pilot for a new series of "Police Story" episodes and following the exploits of a cop who is out to catch a vicious serial killer, who stalks his victims on the freeways. Fair.

THR 139 min (ort 156 min) mTV
B,V MGM

## POLICEWOMAN * 18
Lee Frost USA 1974
*Sondra Currie, Tony Young, Phil Hoover, Elizabeth Stuart, Jeanie Bell*
When a group of female prisoners succeed in a bold jail escape, a special officer is recruited and trained in the martial arts. She then leads the hunt for these naughty girls, in a film full of sex and violence.

A/AD 94 min (ort 99 min) Cut (6 sec in addition to film cuts)
V VPD L/A; SHEP

## POLICEWOMAN CENTREFOLD * 15
Reza Badiyi USA 1983
*Melody Anderson, Ed Marinaro, Donna Pescow, Bert Remsen, David Spielberg, Michael LeClair, Greg Monaghan, David Haskell, Jerry Supiran, Corinne Carroll, Vince Ferragamo, Jill Jacobson, John Milford, Andrea Howard*
Based on the true story of a female police officer of Springfield Ohio who appeared in Playboy Magazine, this tells of a policewoman who finds that her life is not the same after she poses nude for a magazine. A very dull and uninteresting film.

DRA 100 min mTV
B,V PRV

## POLLY *** U
Debbie Allen USA 1989
*Phylicia Rashad, Keshia Knight Pulliam, Celeste Holm, Brock Peters, Dorian Harewood, Butterfly McQueen, Larry Riley, Ken Page*
This bright and breezy Disney offering recasts their 1960 film POLLYANNA as a musical, with the action transferred to a small town in Alabama where virtually all the inhabitants are black. Choreographed by the director, and with a score by Joel McNeely.

MUS 90 min (ort 100 min) mTV
V WDV

## POLLYANNA ** U
David Swift USA 1960
*Hayley Mills, Jane Wyman, Richard Egan, Karl Malden, Adolphe Menjou, Nancy Olson, Donald Crisp, Agnes Moorehead, Kevin Corcoran, Reta Shaw*
A young girl goes to stay with her aunt and brightens up the lives of the inhabitants of a small New England town. Swift also wrote the script as well as directing this pleasant but rather humourless adaptation of Porter's tale. AA: Hon Award (Mills – for the most outstanding juvenile performance).
Boa: novel by Eleanor Porter.

JUV 129 min (ort 134 min)
B,V WDV

## POLTERGEIST ** 15
Tobe Hooper USA 1982
*JoBeth Williams, Beatrice Straight, Dominique Dunne, Craig T. Nelson, Zelda Rubinstein, Heather O'Rourke, Oliver Robins, James Karen*
A family's home is invaded by hostile supernatural entities who kidnap the family's 5-year-old daughter. It starts well but soon goes downhill as the special effects take over from the plot. Written by Steven Spielberg, Michael Grais and Mark Victor. As is so often the case, dazzling special effects cannot hide the lack of substance. The inevitable sequels followed.

HOR 110 min
V/sh MGM

## POLTERGEIST 2 ** 15
Brian Gibson USA 1986
*JoBeth Williams, Craig T. Nelson, Heather O'Rourke, Oliver Robins, Zelda Rubinstein, Will Sampson, Julian Beck, Geraldine Fitzgerald*
This sequel is set four years on and finds the family facing a return encounter with these strange creatures from another world. As with the first film the special effects cannot be faulted, only the story lacks substance.
Aka: POLTERGEIST 2: THE OTHER SIDE

HOR 87 min (ort 90 min)
B,V MGM

## POLTERGEIST 3 * 15
Gary Sherman USA 1988
*Tom Skerritt, Nancy Allen, Heather O'Rourke, Zelda Rubinstein, Lara Flynn Boyle, Kip Wentz, Richard Fire*
Third time round, there's little that's new or fresh left to extract from the story of a family pursued by hideous ghosts. Here, they are summoned up by the daughter, when her therapist refuses to acknowledge the reality of the supernatural.

HOR 94 min (ort 97 min)
B,V MGM

## POLYESTER ** 
John Waters USA 1981
*Divine (Glenn Milstead), Tab Hunter, Edith Massey, Mary Garlington, Ken King, David Samson, Mink Stole, Stiv Bators, Joni Ruth White, Hans Kramm, George Stover, Steve Yeagers*
Middle-class satire on a housewife's inability to cope with her life. For fans of Waters/Divine only. Originally released in "Odorama" with audience members being given smelly cards to scratch and sniff. This was Waters' first mainstream effort and the bad taste of his earlier films is but partially replaced by wit. There are however, some funny moments.

COM 86 min
B,V ARCADE/VSP L/A

## POM-POM GIRLS, THE ** 
Joseph Ruben USA 1976
*Jennifer Ashley, Robert Carradine, Lisa Reeves, Michael Mullins, Bill Adler*
Teenage comedy with girls at a college enjoying the usual pursuits as they celebrate their final year with a plethora of mindless mayhem.

COM 90 min
B,V,V2 INT/CBS

## POOR ALBERT AND LITTLE ANNIE * 
Paul Leder USA 1972 (re-released 1983)
*Zooey Hall, Geri Reischl, Joanne Moore, Greg Mullaway, Marlene Tracy, Frank Whiteman, Elaine Partnow, Rosella Olson, Robert Christopher*
A deranged psychopath escapes from the asylum where he was held, in order to have his revenge on his rich mother who sent him there and cut him off. However, he also feels the need to avenge himself against women in general, and embarks on an orgy of murder of attractive women until he falls for the nine-year-old child of his mother's housekeeper. A low-budget shocker offering a morbid and depressing view of insanity.
Aka: I DISMEMBER MAMA

HOR 82 min
B,V INT/CBS

**POOR COW \*\***     15
Ken Loach     UK     1967
*Carol White, Terence Stamp, John Bindon, Kate*
*Williams, Queenie Watts, Geraldine Sherman, Ellis*
*Dale, Gerald Young, Gladys Dawson*
While a thief is away in prison, his wife moves in with
his best friend. A typical 1960s kitchen-sink drama
full of squalor and despair but little else.
Boa: novel by Nell Dunn.
DRA     98 min (ort 101 min)
V     WHV

**POOR LITTLE RICH GIRL:**
**PARTS 1 AND 2 \*\***     15
Charles Jarrott     USA     1987
*Kevin McCarthy, Nicholas Clay, Bruce Davison,*
*Sascha Hehn, Stephane Audran, Burl Ives, Farrah*
*Fawcett, James Read, Anne Francis, David Ackroyd,*
*Tony Peck, Zoe Wanamaker*
A two-part soap telling the story of Woolworth heiress
Barbara Hutton and her turbulent life. She inherited
a vast fortune but frittered it away and died in 1979
almost penniless. Rather superficial but quite enter-
taining.
Aka: POOR LITTLE RICH GIRL: THE BARBARA
HUTTON STORY
Boa: book by C. David Heymann.
DRA     232 min; 180 min (BRAVE)
    (2 cassettes – ort 280 min) mTV
B,V     CINE; BRAVE (VHS only)

**POOR WHITE TRASH \***    
S.F. Brownrigg     USA     1983
*Gene Ross, Ann Stafford, Norma Moore*
A mad axe murderer disturbs the peace and tranquil-
ity of a couple's summer holiday in this sick offering.
Aka: POOR WHITE TRASH 2; SCUM OF THE
EARTH
HOR     90 min
B,V,V2     INT/CBS

**POPE JOAN \***    
Michael Anderson     UK     1972
*Liv Ullmann, Olivia De Havilland, Lesley-Anne*
*Down, Trevor Howard, Jeremy Kemp, Patrick Magee,*
*Franco Nero, Maximilian Schell, Natasa Nicolescu,*
*Sharon Winter, Richard Bebb, Peter Arne, George*
*Innes, Susan Macready*
A woman disguises herself as a man and eventually
becomes Pope. Possibly inspired by the legend of a 9th
century German prostitute who found a vocation to
preach and eventually became Pope. A feeble attempt
to combine spectacle with sensationalism that would
have been better as a comedy (or even a musical).
Written by John Briley.
Aka: DEVIL'S IMPOSTER, THE
DRA     111 min (ort 132 min)
B,V     GHV

**POPE JOHN PAUL II \*\*\***    
Herbert Wise     USA     1984
*Albert Finney, Michael Crompton, Hans Frank, Robert*
*Austin, Caroline Bliss, Antony Brown, Alfred Burke,*
*Brian Cox, Sam Dastor, Victoria Fairbrother, John*
*Forgeham, Derek Francis, Nigel Hawthorne, Marne*
*Maitland*
Biopic covering the life of this Pope from his youth up
to 1978, that benefits hugely from a wonderful
performance by Finney (in his US TV debut). The
script is by Christopher Knopf. See also FROM A FAR
COUNTRY: POPE JOHN PAUL II.
DRA     147 min (ort 150 min) mTV
B,V     CBS

**POPE OF GREENWICH VILLAGE, THE \*\*\***     15
Stuart Rosenberg     USA     1984
*Mickey Rourke, Eric Roberts, Daryl Hannah,*
*Geraldine Page, Kenneth McMillan, Tony Musante,*
*Burt Young, M. Emmet Walsh, Jack Kehoe, Philip*

*Bosco, Val Avery, Joe Grifasi*
Two small-time crooks plan a robbery and find that
they've stolen from the Mafia, but the story takes
second place to a funny series of observations and
character studies. The script is by Patrick from his
novel.
Boa: novel by Vincent Patrick.
COM     116 min (ort 120 min)
V/h     WHV

**POPEYE \*\***     U
Robert Altman     USA     1980
*Robin Williams, Shelley Duvall, Ray Walston, Paul*
*Smith, Paul Dooley, Richard Libertini, Wesley Ivan*
*Hurt, Linda Hunt*
An ambitious attempt to bring this famous comic-strip
character (based on the work of E.C. Segar) to the
screen. The script is by Jules Feiffer, and has the
character returning to Sweethaven in search of the
father who abandoned him. Unfortunately the film is
nothing like as inventive as those old Max Fleischer
shorts and very little action takes place until near the
end.
COM     92 min (ort 114 min)
B,V     WDV

**POPPIES ARE ALSO FLOWERS \***    
Terence Young     USA     1966
*Yul Brynner, Omar Sharif, Trevor Howard, Senta*
*Berger, Stephen Boyd, Angie Dickinson, Rita*
*Hayworth, Trini Lopez, E.G. Marshall, Gilbert*
*Roland, Anthony Quayle, Eli Wallach, Jack Hawkins,*
*Marcello Mastroianni*
Many stars have cameo roles in this story of drug
smuggling, made by the United Nations as part of an
initiative to combat the heroin trade. A well-
intentioned sluggish mess, poorly acted and badly
scripted.
Aka: DANGER GROWS WILD; POPPY IS ALSO A
FLOWER, THE
Boa: story by Ian Fleming.
A/AD     85 min (ort 105 min)
B,V,V2     EHE

**PORK CHOP HILL \*\*\***    
Lewis Milestone     USA     1959
*Gregory Peck, Harry Guardino, Rip Torn, George*
*Peppard, James Edwards, Bob Steele, Woody Strode,*
*Robert Blake, George Shibata, Barry Atwater*
Realistic account of the Korean War, set in the closing
stages. An American commander has to take and hold
a hill, that will be of vital significance in fixing the
final truce line.
WAR     94 min (ort 98 min) B/W
V     WHV

**PORKY'S \*\*\***     18
Bob Clark     CANADA     1981
*Dan Monahan, Mark Herrier, Wyatt Knight, Roger*
*Wilson, Kim Cattrall, Chuck Mitchell, Scott Colomby,*
*Kaki Hunter, Nancy Parsons, Alex Karras, Susan*
*Clarke, Tony Ganios, Cyril O'Reilly, Boyd Gaines,*
*Dough McGrath, Art Hindle*
Set in South Florida circa 1954, where some high
school kids try to patronise the local brothel as an
attempt to discover sex. A number of sequels followed
this film, that's essentially a recycling of the "Amer-
ican Graffiti" theme of adolescent pimply youth. A
happy low-brow film that made a fortune and spawned
several sequels. Written by Clark.
COM     94 min (ort 98 min)
B,V     WHV; CBS (VHS only)

**PORKY'S 2 \***     18
Bob Clark     CANADA     1983
*Dan Monahan, Wyatt Knight, Mark Herrier, Roger*
*Wilson, Kaki Hunter, Scott Colomby, Nancy Parsons,*
*Edward Winter, Tony Ganios, Cyril O'Reilly, Joseph*
*Running Fox, Eric Christmas, Cisse Cameron, Else*

*Earl*
The first sequel to the original bears little resemblance to it, and is set in a Florida high school where the inevitable high-jinks and low-brow comedy abound.
Aka: PORKY'S 2: THE NEXT DAY
COM                                     94 min
B,V                                     CBS

## PORKY'S REVENGE *                    18
James Komack          USA               1985
*Dan Monahan, Wyatt Knight, Tony Ganios, Kaki Hunter, Mark Herrier, Scott Colomby, Nancy Parsons, Chuck Mitchell, Kimberly Everson*
Third in this rather tedious PORKY'S series of teenage comedies. This time the school's basketball coach has gambling debts to the brothel owner.
COM                          88 min (ort 92 min)
V/h                                     CBS

## PORRIDGE **                          PG
Dick Clement          UK                1979
*Ronnie Barker, Richard Beckinsale, Fulton Mackay, Brian Wilde, Peter Vaughan, Geoffrey Bayldon, Julian Holloway, Christopher Godwin, Barrie Rutter, Daniel Peacock, Sam Kelly, Ken Jones, Philip Locke, Gordon Kaye*
A spin-off from a witty and observant British TV series, about the life of the prisoners at H.M. Slade Prison. Not as funny as the TV series, with a plot revolving around the attempt of old lags to arrange an escape for a first offender. The TV show came to the States as "On The Rocks". Scripted by Dick Clement and Ian La Frenais.
Aka: DOING TIME
COM                          96 min; 90 min (POLY)
B, V/h   PRV L/A; CH5 (VHS only); POLY (VHS only)

## PORTNOY'S COMPLAINT *               18
Ernest Lehman         USA               1972
*Karen Black, Lee Grant, Richard Benjamin, Jack Somack, Jill Clayburgh, Jeannie Berlin*
The story of a neurotic Jewish boy's innumerable hangups and his downright peculiar relationship with his mother. The directorial debut for Lehman is a flawed film, with barely a trace of the humour that made the novel so successful. The music is by Michel Le Grand. Lehman also scripted this.
Boa: novel by Philip Roth.
COM                                     101 min
B,V                                     WHV

## PORTRAIT OF A HIT MAN **            PG
Alan A. Buckhantz     USA               1977
*Jack Palance, Rod Steiger, Bo Svenson, Richard Roundtree, Ann Turkel, Philip Ahn*
The story of a Mafia killer who finds he has divided loyalties when he is hired to kill a friend who once saved his life. A messy film with too many unresolved elements. The script is by Harold Yablonsky.
Aka: JIM BUCK
THR                          82 min (ort 86 min)
B,V                                     VIP

## PORTRAIT OF A STRIPPER *
John A. Alonzo        USA               1979
*Lesley Ann Warren, Edward Herrimann, Vic Tayback, Sheree North, Allan Miller, K.C. Martel, Thomas Hill, Michael Cavanaugh, Udana Power, Louise Foley, Lucy Lee Flippin, Jeff Donnell, Julie Mannix, Lilyan Chauvin*
A young widow earns her keep as a stripper, while fighting her in-laws over the custody of her young son, as they have decided that she is an unfit mother. Exploitative dross with a few good nightclub sequences. The choreography (dance sequence) was by Steven Merritt.
DRA                         97 min (ort 100 min) mTV
B,V                                  VFP L/A; HER

## PORTRAIT OF JENNIE ****             U
William Dieterle      USA               1948
*Jennifer Jones, Joseph Cotten, Ethel Barrymore, Lilian Gish, David Wayne, Henry Hull*
A struggling artist meets a strange girl in a park and falls in love with her, despite the fact that she is a ghost. A film rich in visual imagery, with remarkable photography and a fine score by Dmitri Tiomkin (after Debussy). Written by Peter Berneis, Paul Osborn and Leonard Bernovici, and produced by David O. Selznick. AA: Effects (Paul Eagler/J. McMillan/Russell Sherman/Clarence Sliffer – vis; Charles Freeman/James G. Stewart – aud).
Aka: JEANNIE; TIDAL WAVE
Boa: novella by Robert Nathan.
DRA                                  86 min B/W
B,V                                  GHV; VCC

## PORTRAIT OF SEDUCTION, A ***
Anthony Spinelli      USA               1976
*Vicky Lyon, Robert Cole, Jeffrey Stern (Jon Martin), Monique Cardin, Rita Stone*
A young woman marries an older man who has a teenage son by a previous marriage. The son is a randy art student and has already decided that he is going to seduce his stepmother even though he has a girlfriend. When the husband discovers his wife's infidelity he refuses to forgive her, and she leaves to set up with the son as part of a threesome. A dramatic if somewhat contrived story, sustained by some excellent acting.
A                                       60 min
B,V                                     EVI

## PORTRAITS OF PLEASURE *
Bo Koup               USA               1974
*Jon Black, Susan McBain, Sharon Mitchell, Juan Pedos, Four Huck, Candy Split, Bud Wipp*
A look at Candy Split; the obnoxious wife of a man unable to satisfy her voracious needs. Not very likeable himself, the husband is seen arranging a date of his own with a former lesbian. This girl tells her roommate who suggests that both they and Candy (who is a friend of theirs) go out and pick up guys. And no-one is more surprised than Candy when one of the girls brings back her husband. A dull and sleazy sex film.
A                                       60 min
V                                       RIP

## POSEIDON ADVENTURE, THE ***         PG
Ronald Neame          USA               1972
*Gene Hackman, Ernest Borgnine, Shelley Winters, Roddy McDowall, Red Buttons, Carol Lynley, Jack Albertson, Stella Stevens, Leslie Nielsen, Pamela Sue Martin, Arthur O'Connell, Eric Shea*
An exciting drama of a band of survivors, trying to escape from a liner that has turned over completely, after a tidal wave has overwhelmed it. Harrowing in parts but generally quite gripping. Written by Stirling Silliphant and Wendell Mayes. The excellent score is by John Williams. AA: Song ("The Morning After" – Al Kasha/Joel Hirschhorn), Spec Award (L.B. Abbott/A.D. Flowers for visual effects).
Boa: novel by Paul Gallico.
DRA                         112 min (ort 117 min)
V                                       CBS

## POSITIVE I.D. ***                   18
Andy Anderson         USA               1987
*Stephanie Rascoe, John Davies, Steve Fromholz, Laura Lane, Gail Cronauer, Matthew Sacks*
A young and attractive housewife is viciously assaulted and raped, and finds herself unable to continue her life as before. She leaves her family and adopts a new identity, drawing up a plan of revenge. A well-made thriller, scripted by Anderson.
THR                          91 min (ort 96 min)
B/h, V/h                                CIC

**POSSESSED, THE \*** 18
Lucio Fulci ITALY 1982
*Christopher Connelly, Martha Taylor, Brigitta Boccoli,*
*Giovanni Frezza, Cinzia De Ponti, Andrea Bosic, Carlo*
*DeMejo, Antonio Pulci, Lucio Fulci, Vincenzo*
*Bellanich, Mario Moretti*
An American Egyptologist is struck by blindness
whilst exploring a strange tomb, and after much
hardship, returns to New York with a strange medal-
lion in the shape of an eye. This proves to be a
mistake, for when his daughter takes to wearing it she
becomes an instrument of evil. The usual violent
bloodshed results in a film chiefly remembered for the
presence of De Ponti, who was Miss Italy of 1979.
Aka: EYE OF THE EVIL DEAD, THE; L'OCCHIO
DEL MALE; MANHATTAN BABY
HOR 87 min; 84 min (EIV) (ort 91 min)
B,V EIV; CBS

**POSSESSED, THE \*\*** 15
Jeremy Thorpe USA 1977
*James Farentino, Joan Hackett, Claudette Nevins,*
*Eugene Roche, Harrison Ford, Ann Dusenberry, Diana*
*Scarwid, Dinah Manoff, Carol Jones, P.J. Soles,*
*Ethelinn Block, Susan Walden, Lawrence Bame,*
*James Parkes, Catherine Cunneff*
A defrocked minister takes on strange forces responsi-
ble for a spate of fires at a girls' school, when he is
called in to perform an exorcism. Average.
HOR 71 min (ort 78 min) mTV
V WHV

**POSSESSION \*\***
Andrzej Zulawski
FRANCE/WEST GERMANY 1981
*Isabelle Adjani, Sam Neill, Heinz Bennett, Margit*
*Carstensen, Michael Hogben, Johanna Hofer, Shaun*
*Lawtor*
A love triangle drama that reaches a weird climax
when the wife "creates" a hideous monster, confusing
both her husband and us. Rather stylishly directed
but somewhat incomprehensible. Filmed in English.
HOR 87 min (ort 127 min)
B,V VTC

**POSSESSION OF JOEL DELANEY, THE \*\***
Waris Hussein USA 1971
*Shirley MacLaine, Perry King, Lisa Kohane, David*
*Ellacott, Lovelady Powell, Miriam Colon, Michael*
*Hordern, Barbara Trentham*
A woman's brother is taken over by the spirit of a dead
Puerto Rican murderer, in this uneven but potent tale
that struggles to make some kind of social comment.
Written by Matt Robinson and Grimes Grice.
Boa: novel by Ramona Stewart.
HOR 105 min (ort 108 min)
B,V PRV

**POSTMAN ALWAYS RINGS TWICE, THE \*\*** 18
Bob Rafelson USA 1981
*Jack Nicholson, Jessica Lange, John Colicos, Michael*
*Lerner, John P. Ryan, Anjelica Huston, William*
*Taylor, Tom Hill, Jon Van Ness, Brian Farrell,*
*Raleigh Bond, William Newman, Albert Henderson,*
*Ken Magee, Eugene Peterson*
A remake of the 1946 film, with a drifter taking up
with the young wife of a middle-aged cafe owner and
plotting with her to kill her husband. Far more
faithful to the novel than the earlier film, but far less
stylish too. Some vicious touches mark its 1980s
origins. Written by David Mamet and with photogra-
phy by Sven Nkvist.
Boa: novel by James M. Cain.
DRA 122 min; 116 min (VCC)
B,V,V2,LV GHV; VCC (VHS only)

**POUND PUPPIES:**
**THE LEGEND OF BIG PAW \*** U
Pierre DeCelles USA 1987

*Voices of: George Rose, B.J. Ward, Ruth Buzzi,*
*Brennan Howard*
A rather mundane cartoon feature based on toys of the
same name, with the title characters trying to regain
a magical bone. Very dull and unlikely to have much
appeal for kids.
Aka: POUND PUPPIES AND THE LEGEND OF BIG
PAW
CAR 74 min (ort 76 min)
V/sh GHV

**POWER \*\*** 15
Sydney Lumet USA 1985
*Richard Gere, Julie Christie, Gene Hackman, Kate*
*Capshaw, Denzel Washington, E.G. Marshall, Beatrice*
*Straight, Fritz Weaver, Michael Learned, J.T. Walsh,*
*E. Katherine Kerr, Polly Rowles, Matt Salinger*
The story of a political media man who markets his
politicians like just another commodity, and prides
himself on his shrewdness but discovers that others
are smarter. A flashy and insincere tale of implausi-
bility and pompousness that makes a few sharp
points, but even these are no longer fresh or original.
DRA 107 min (ort 111 min)
B,V CBS

**POWER GAME \*\*** 15
Faustu Canel SPAIN/USA 1982
*Jon Finch, Cattriona MacColl, Isabel Garcia Lorca,*
*May Heatherly, Jose Lifante, Fernando Hilbeck,*
*Simon Andreu*
The head of a nuclear plant under construction in
Spain, refuses to start operations until all safety
measures have been taken. He is consequently terro-
rised by those in the pay of the multinational company
that is financing the project.
Aka: 72 HOURS OR DIE (SOV); LA AMENALA;
SEVENTY-TWO HOURS OR DIE; SEVENTY-TWO
HOURS TO DIE; THREAT, THE
THR 102 min; 95 min (SOV)
B,V BBHV L/A; MED; PORVI; SOV

**POWER PLAY \*** 18
Martyn Burke CANADA/UK 1978
*Peter O'Toole, Barry Morse, Donald Pleasence, David*
*Hemmings, Jon Granik, Marcella Saint-Amant,*
*George Touliatos, Gary Reineke, Chuck Shamata, Eli*
*Rill, Harvey Atkin, August Schellenberg, Dick Cavett,*
*David Calderisi*
The anatomy of a military coup in a corrupt but
unnamed country. It looks as though it could be in
Europe but it's rather hard to care. A plodding and
verbose affair, written by Burke. (Some second unit
shooting was done in
1974.)
Aka: STATE OF SHOCK
Boa: book Coup D'Etat by Edward N. Luttwak.
DRA 102 min (ort 109 min)
B,V RNK

**POWER, THE \*\*** 18
Steven Carpenter/Jeffrey Obrow
USA 1983
*Susan Stokey, Warren Lincoln, Lisa Erikson, Chad*
*Christian, Ben Gilbert, J. Dinan Myrtetus, Chris*
*Morrill, Rod Mays, Jay Fisher, Costy Basile, Juan Del*
*Valle, Alice Champlin, Gabe Cohen, Milton Robinson,*
*Steve Nagle*
An American steals an Aztec idol and is overcome by
evil forces, in this competent but generally uninspired
tale.
HOR 81 min (ort 95 min)
B,V EIV

**POWERS OF EVIL \*\*\*** 15
Roger Vadim/Frederico Fellini/Louis Malle
FRANCE/ITALY 1968
*Jane Fonda, Terence Stamp, Peter Fonda, Brigitte*
*Bardot, Alain Delon, James Robertson Justice*

Three horror tales involving Satanism (and loosely based on stories by Edgar Allan Poe), form the basis for this colourful and engaging work. The tale directed by Fellini is easily the best one, but all three are well worth watching.

Aka: HISTOIRES EXTRAORDINAIRE; SPIRITS OF THE DEAD; TALES OF MYSTERY

HOR                              78 min (ort 120 min)
B,V                              INT L/A; XTASY

## POWWOW HIGHWAY ***                          15
Jonathan Wacks           USA                   1988
*Gary Farmer, A. Martinez, Amanda Wyss, Joanelle Romero, Sam Vlahos, Wayne Waterman, Margo Kane*
This humorous look at Indian mistreatment and the clash of cultures, follows a Cheyenne and an Indian activist friend as they take a trip to New Mexico. Despite the stereotyping of the racists they encounter along the way, this immensely likeable film is both mature and insightful.

COM                              87 min (ort 90 min)
V                                             PATHE

## PRANCER ***                                  U
John Hancock             USA                   1989
*Sam Elliott, Cloris Leachman, Rebecca Harrell, Abe Vigoda, Rutanya Alda, Michael Constantine, Ariana Richards*
A family film revolving around a troubled young girl whose widowed father is in danger of losing their farm. When the girl finds an injured reindeer just before Christmas, she becomes convinced that it belongs to Santa Claus and sets out to nurse it back to health. Slow-moving, but a film that repays patience.

A/AD                             98 min (ort 103 min)
V                                               MED

## PRANKS *
Jeffrey Obrow/Stephen Carpenter
                         USA                   1982
*David Snow, Laurie Lapinski, Stephen Sachs, Pamela Holland, Dennis Ely, Woody Roll, Jake Jones, Daphne Zuniga, Robert Frederick, Chris Morill, Chandre, Billy Criswell, Richard Cowgill, Kay Beth, Jimmy Betz*
A group of students clearing a derelict building of its furniture is threatened by a psychotic killer.

Aka: DEATH DORM; DORM THAT DRIPPED BLOOD, THE

HOR                                          83 min
B,V,V2                                     VPD L/A

## PRAY FOR DEATH *                             18
Gordon Hessler           USA                   1985
*Sho Kosugi, James Booth, Donna Kai Benz, Michael Constantine, James Booth, Shane Kosugi, Kane Kosugi, Robert Ito*
A master Ninja has his family wiped out just as he is about to retire, and swears vengeance on the killers. A messy, noisy and unbelievably hackneyed effort that substitutes fisticuffs for dialogue and sudden death for a plot.

MAR         89 min (ort 93 min) (Cut at film release)
V                                               VPD

## PRAY TV **                                   U
Robert Markowitz         USA                   1982
*John Ritter, Ned Beatty, Richard Kiley, Madolyn Smith, Louise Latham, Jonathan Prince, Michael Currie, Kenneth Tigar, Lois Areno, Jason Bernard, Frank Birney, James Keane, Richard Kennedy, Mel Torme, Ronald Craig*
As with the earlier film, this is also the tale of a TV station that is faced with the prospect of closure unless it can improve its ratings. In this slack comedy, a newly-ordained priest falls into the clutches of a TV evangelist. Written by Lane Slate who presumably had something interesting to say – unfortunately it

isn't in this film.

COM                      96 min (ort 100 min) mTV
V                                               HER

## PRAY TV **                                   15
Rick Friedberg           USA                   1980
*Dabney Coleman, Jamie Lyn Bauer, Sidney Miller, Joyce Jameson, Ruth Silveira, Lewis Arquette, Archie Hahn*
An impoverished TV station turns to religion to improve its ratings, and becomes a textbook example of religious broadcasting, complete with quiz shows, soap operas etc. all with a faith slant. A satire on religious programming, that's easily confused with the identically titled film in the same theme from 1982.

Aka: KGOD

COM                              84 min (ort 92 min) mTV
B,V                                             RCA

## PRAYER FOR THE DYING, A *                    15
Mike Hodges              UK/USA                1987
*Mickey Rourke, Bob Hoskins, Alan Bates, Sammi Davis, Christopher Fulford, Liam Neeson, Alison Doody*
An IRA hit-man is forced to fulfil one more contract before retiring. A stolid and hardly successful adaptation of the original novel.

Boa: novel by Jack Higgins.

A/AD                             103 min (ort 108 min)
V/sh                                            VES

## PRAYING MANTIS **                            15
Jack Gold       UK/WEST GERMANY                1982
*Jonathan Pryce, Cherie Lunghi, Carmen de Sautoy, Pinkas Braun, Anna Cropper*
A professor's young wife plots with her lover, his assistant, to kill her husband, but their plans go awry in this complex tale of a weak young man caught in a web of deception.

Boa: novel Les Mantes Religieuses by Hubert de Monteilhet.

THR                              119 min (ort 145 min)
B,V                              CAN; CAREY; SCRN

## PREACHERMAN **
Albert T. Viola          USA                   1971
*Amos Huxley, Ilene Kristen, Esty F. Davis, Adam Hesse, Marian Brown*
A man of God proves to have a weakness for women and money.

Aka: PREACHERMAN MEETS WIDDERWOMAN

DRA                                          90 min
B,V,V2                   ATA L/A; VUL L/A; KRP; APX

## PREDATOR ***                                 18
John McTiernan           USA                   1987
*Arnold Schwarzenegger, Carl Weathers, Elpidia Carrillo, Bill Duke, Jesse Ventura, R.G. Armstrong, Kevin Peter Hall, Sonny Landham, Richard Chaves, Shane Black, Gregory Barnett, Bobby Bass, Gene Baxley, Steve Boyum*
A crack team of agents are sent by the US Government to the jungles of South America on a rescue mission, but find themselves up against an elusive alien that is able to change its appearance and pick them off one at a time. An implausible feast of gore and special effects, but certainly not without considerable tension.

THR                              102 min (ort 107 min)
V/sh                                            CBS

## PREMATURE BURIAL, THE **
Roger Corman             USA                   1961
*Ray Milland, Hazel Court, Richard Ney, Heather Angel, Alan Napier, John Dierkes, Dick Miller, Brendan Court*
Another Corman misadaptation of Poe, with Milland

playing a man so terrified of being buried alive that he employs an elaborate series of precautions to prevent this. Lavish sets and an effective dream sequence cannot mask the director's lack of empathy with his material.
Boa: short story by Edgar Allan Poe.
HOR                                         81 min
B,V,V2                                        GHV

## PREMONITION, THE *                          15
Robert Allen Schnitzer   USA               1975
*Sharon Farrell, Richard Lynch, Ellen Barber, Edward Bell, Jeff Corey, Chitra Neogy, Danielle Brisebois, Rosemary McNamara, Roy White*
A young girl disappears, and her parents seek parapsychological help in an attempt to discover her whereabouts. A heavy-going affair that combines a difficult subject with a muddled script.
HOR                          88 min (ort 91 min)
B,V                                           EHE

## PRESIDIO, THE **                            18
Peter Hyams        USA                     1988
*Sean Connery, Mark Harmon, Meg Ryan, Jack Warden, Dana Gladstone, Mark Blum, Jenette Goldstein, Don Calfa*
A cop clashes with the provost marshal at a military base in San Francisco, when he has to investigate a murder there. The latter used to be his commanding officer, and the fact that he is now dating the marshal's daughter, adds yet more fuel to their old enmity. A formula plot that ill-serves an actor of Connery's stature.
A/AD                         95 min (ort 97 min)
V/sh                                          CIC

## PRESS FOR TIME **
Robert Asher        UK                     1966
*Norman Wisdom, Derek Bond, Angela Browne, Tracey Crisp, Allan Cuthbertson, Noel Dyson, Derek Francis, Peter Jones, David Lodge, Stanley Unwin, Frances White, Michael Balfour, Tony Selby*
The story of an accident-prone newspaper seller, who is sent by his prime minister grandfather to work as a cub reporter on a provincial newspaper, in an attempt to keep him out of trouble. A feeble comedy that makes poor use of Wisdom's comic gifts. However, there are some good things here, not least Wisdom playing three roles, and a nice score by Mike Vickers. This was the last of Wisdom's old-style comedy films.
Aka: NORMAN WISDOM: PRESS FOR TIME
Boa: novel Yea, Yea, Yea by Angus McGill.
COM                         94 min (ort 102 min)
B,V                                           RNK

## PRESSURE **
Horace Ove          UK                     1975
*Herbert Norville, Oscar James, Frank Sanguineau, Lucita Lijertwood, Sheila Scott-Wilkinson, Ed Deveraux, T-Bone Wilson, Ramjohn Holder, Norman Beaton, John Landry, Archie Pool, Whitty Vialva Forde, Marlene Davis, Dave Konoshi*
A documentary-style film about the West Indian community in North Kensington, with an unemployed youth from Trinidad drifting into crime and drugs. A sincere attempt to portray the life of blacks in Britain, but ultimately too strident for its own good. The script is by Ove and Samuel Selvon.
DRA                         101 min (ort 110 min)
V                                             INT

## PRETTY BABY **                              15
Louis Malle         USA                    1978
*Brooke Shields, Keith Carradine, Susan Sarandon, Frances Faye, Antonio Fargas, Matthew Anton, Gerrit Graham, Mae Mercer, Diana Scarwid, Barbara Steele*
A photographer in New Orleans becomes obsessed by a 12-year-old prostitute and eventually marries her. Carradine is badly cast in this lacklustre WW1 tale,

but Shields is rather appealing. This was Malle's first US work and was written by him and Polly Platt. The photography was by Sven Nykvist, but even that can do little for this film.
DRA                         106 min (ort 109 min)
B,V                                           CIC

## PRETTY IN PINK **                           15
Howard Deutch       USA                    1986
*Molly Ringwald, Andrew McCarthy, Harry Dean Stanton, Jon Cryer, Annie Potts, James Spader*
A poor but pretty girl falls in love with a handsome boy from a wealthy family, but their budding romance is not helped along by their differing social backgrounds. A pleasant tale of growing pains and teenage insecurities, but nothing memorable. Written by John Hughes.
COM                          93 min (ort 96 min)
V/sh                                          CIC

## PRETTY PEACHES **
Alex De Renzy       USA                    1978
*Desiree Cousteau, John Leslie, Joey Civera, Carol Connors*
A happy-go-lucky girl is out for a drive in her jeep, when it flips over and she is knocked out. Now suffering from amnesia, she embarks on a series of sexual encounters in order to regain her past. A mildly amusing and fairly well made sex romp.
A                                           82 min
B,V,V2                                        TCX

## PRETTY POISON ***                           15
Noel Black          USA                    1968
*Anthony Perkins, Tuesday Weld, Beverly Garland, John Randolph, Dick O'Neill, Clarice Blackburn*
A psychotic arsonist teams up with a high school student, to carry out sabotage at a chemicals factory, but soon discovers that she's weirder than he is. A bizarre mixture of drama and black comedy, but quite effectively done. Written by Lorenzo Semple Jr.
Boa: novel She Let Him Continue by Stephen Geller.
DRA                          85 min (ort 89 min)
B,V                                           CBS

## PRETTY SMART *                              18
Dimitri Logothetis  USA                    1986
*Tricia Leigh Fisher, Patricia Arquette, Paris Vaughn, Lisa Loricht, Lisa Vice, Dennis Cole, Tricia Leigh Fraser*
A maladjusted girl who foils a bank robbery by stripping, gets sent by her parents to a girls' school on an isolated Mediterranean island where they hope she'll learn some decorum. Once there, she sets out to get expelled as soon as possible, but the headmaster seems to be impervious to her ploys. After joining the school gang, she learns that drugs are being sold to the students and decides to take some action. A boring, self-satisfied dud.
Aka: BENTLEY ACADEMY, THE
COM                          80 min (ort 90 min)
B,V                                           NWV

## PRETTY WOMAN ***                            15
Garry Marshall      USA                    1990
*Richard Gere, Julia Roberts, Ralph Bellamy, Jason Alexander, Laura San Giacomo, Hector Elizondo, Alex Hyde-White, Elinor Donahue, Larry Miller*
A runaway now working as a hooker is hired by a cold-blooded businessman, and the latter spruces her up so that she can act as his escort for a week while he wheels and deals. However, an unlikely love affair blossoms. Roberts is delightful in a frothy and derivative variant on the PYGMALION theme. Despite managing to include just about every romantic cliche to be had, this appealing comedy retains great charm.
COM                   115 min (ort 117 min) subH
V                                           TOUCH

## PRETTYKILL *                                    18
George Kaczender          USA          1986
*Susannah York, Season Hubley, Suzanne Snyder,*
*David Birney, Yaphet Kotto, Germaine Houde*
As a favour to a friend, a high-class call-girl agrees to
take in another girl, unaware that she has a dangerous personality disorder. After her new room-mate
nearly kills the Swedish Ambassador, following a
meeting she set up, she decides to give up her life of
prostitution and evict her. However, her room-mate
has other ideas. An unpleasant and exploitative effort
that tries to do for prostitution what PSYCHO did for
motels.
Aka: TOMORROW'S A KILLER
THR                          97 min (ort 105 min)
V/sh                                        GHV

## PREY *                                          18
Norman J. Warren          UK           1977
*Barry Stokes, Sally Faulkner, Glory Annen, Sandy*
*Chimney, Eddie Stacey, Jerry Crampton*
A strange young man has dinner with two lesbians,
but unfortunately for them, he is in fact a replica of a
man murdered by aliens who are searching for
supplies of protein. Although the film does develop
some atmosphere, its gratuitous dwelling on cannibalism and dismemberment makes it very hard to relate
to. A kind of gruesome low-budget black comedy
without the laughs.
Aka: ALIEN PREY
HOR                  74 min (ort 85 min) Cut (10 sec)
B,V,V2                          VDM L/A; STABL

## PREY, THE *                                     18
Edwin Scott Brown         USA          1980
*Steve Bond, Debbie Thureson, Lori Lethin, Robert*
*Wald, Gayle Gannes, Philip Wenckus, Jackson*
*Bostwick, Jackie Coogan, Connie Hunter, Ted Hayden,*
*Garry Goodrow, Carel Struycken*
Six teenagers hiking in the forests of the Colorado
Rockies, are stalked by something connected with a
terrifying tragedy that happened 30 years before.
Routine kids-in-peril movie of the cheaper kind.
HOR                                        92 min
B,V                                       TWE/VPD

## PRICE OF DEATH, THE *
Vincent Thomas (Enzo Gicca)
                          ITALY          1971
*Klaus Kinski, Gianni Garko, Gely Gerka, Luciano*
*Lorcas, Franco Abbina, Laura Giandi*
A hired killer becomes involved in violent happenings
in a Texan town. Poor.
Aka: IL VENDITORE DI MORTE
WES                                       102 min
B,V,V2                                        VPD

## PRICE OF PASSION, THE **                        15
Leonard Nimoy             USA          1988
*Diane Keaton, Liam Neeson, Jason Robards, Ralph*
*Bellamy, Teresa Wright, James Naughton, Asia*
*Vieira, Joe Morton, Katey Sagal, Tracy Griffith,*
*Charles Kimbrough*
For the first time in her life a divorced mother finds
romance and sexual fulfillment, but her unconven-
tional and open method of child rearing, leads to a
nightmare when her ex-husband sues for custody of
their daughter, after having become convinced that
her boyfriend is sexually abusing the child. A dreary
and disagreeable adaptation of Miller's novel, flatly
directed and lacking dramatic impact.
Aka: GOOD MOTHER, THE
Boa: novel by Sue Miller.
DRA                          100 min (ort 103 min)
V                                          TOUCH

## PRICE OF POWER, THE **                          15
Tonino Valerii   ITALY/SPAIN           1969
*Van Johnson, Giuliano Gemma, Warren Vanders,*

*Fernando Rey, Jose Suarez, Benito Stefanelli, Maria*
*Cuadra, Ray Saunders, Maria Luisa Sala*
A man sets out to clear his dead friend's name, as the
latter was accused of being involved in the assassina-
tion of a US President in Dallas in 1880.
Aka: IL PREZZO DEL POTERRE; LA MUERTE DE
UN PRESIDENTE
WES                 118 min; 107 min (PHE) (ort 122 min)
B,V,V2              VDM L/A; SCV; PHE (VHS only)

## PRICELESS BEAUTY *                              15
Charles Finch             ITALY         1987
*Christopher Lambert, Diane Lane*
A standard tale of love and passion etc.
DRA                                        88 min
V                                            VPD

## PRICK UP YOUR EARS ***                          18
Stephen Frears            UK           1987
*Gary Oldman, Alfred Molina, Vanessa Redgrave,*
*Julie Walters, Wallace Shawn, James Grant, Frances*
*Barber, Lindsay Duncan, Janet Dale, Margaret*
*Tyzack, Dave Atkins*
The story of Joe Orton and his stormy relationship
with his lover Kenneth Halliwell, who eventually
murdered him when he found himself being left in the
shadows as Orton's fame grew. A convincing and
absorbing piece, with Oldman and Molina giving
remarkable performances as Orton and Halliwell
respectively. The script is by Alan Bennett.
Boa: book by J. Lahr.
DRA                                       111 min
B,V                                           VIR

## PRIDE AND PREJUDICE ***                          U
Cyril Coke            AUSTRALIA/UK      1980
*Elizabeth Garvie, David Rintoul*
A faithful adaptation of Austen's classic, with good
period detail and an excellent cast.
Boa: novel by Jane Austen.
DRA                  225 min (2 cassettes) mTV
V/h                                           BBC

## PRIDE AND PREJUDICE ****                         U
Robert Z. Leonard         USA          1940
*Laurence Olivier, Greer Garson, Edmund Gwenn,*
*Mary Boland, Melville Cooper, Edna May Oliver,*
*Maureen O'Sullivan, Ann Rutherford, Frieda Inescort,*
*Bruce Lester, Karen Morley, E.E. Clive, Heather Angel,*
*Marsha Hunt*
Story of five sisters hunting for husbands in Victorian
England. Fine period flavour is retained in this
elegant comedy of manners, and an excellent cast adds
to the enjoyment. Written by Aldous Huxley and Jane
Murfin. AA: Art (Cedric Gibbons/Paul Groesse).
Boa: novel by Jane Austin/play by Helen Jerome.
DRA                  113 min (ort 116 min) B/W
V                                            MGM

## PRIDE OF JESSIE HALLAM, THE **
Gary Nelson               USA          1981
*Johnny Cash, Eli Wallach, Guy Boyd, Brenda*
*Vaccaro, Ben Marley, Chrystal Smith, Earl Poole Ball,*
*Linda Bennett, Viola Borden, Michael Burnham, Tara*
*Cash, Malinda Comer, Ray Comier, William*
*Dickenson, Dale Doerman, Brad Zinn*
A man is forced to face the unpleasant fact that he is
illiterate, when he brings his daughter to a hospital in
the city. A fair little drama, written by Suzanne
Clauser. The music is by Cash, and he sings it with his
wife, June Carter Cash.
DRA                  100 min (ort 105 min) mTV
B,V                                           HVH

## PRIEST OF LOVE, THE **                          15
Christopher Miles         UK           1981
*Janet Suzmann, Ian McKellen, Ava Gardner, Penelope*
*Keith, John Gielgud, Helen Mirren, Sarah Miles,*
*James Faulkner, Jorge Rivero, Maruizio Merli, Mike*

*Gwilym, Massimo Ranieri, Marjorie Yates, Jane Booker, Wendy Alnutt,*
Dull biopic about the life of the writer D.H. Lawrence, written by Alan Plater and largely following his last years and the publication of "Lady Chatterly's Lover". A ponderous affair that fails to provide us with any insight into the character. The director also worked on Lawrence's THE VIRGIN AND THE GYPSY some years before.
Boa: book by Harry T. Moore.

| | DRA 120 min (ort 125 min) |
|---|---|
| B,V | HVH; CH5 (VHS only) |

## PRIMAL RAGE ** 18
Vittorio Rambaldi  USA  1989
*Patrick Lowe, Bo Svenson, Cheryl Arutt, Mitch Watson, Sarah Buxton, Doug Sloan*
When a student is bitten by a monkey that was being used in animal experiments, he goes on an insane rampage and is killed, but not before he has infected others. A competent chiller with special effects by Carlo Rambaldi.

| HOR | 90 min |
|---|---|
| V | CHV |

## PRIMARY TARGET ** 15
Clark Henderson  USA  1989
*John Calvin, John Ericson, Miki Kim, Chip Lucia, Colleen Casey*
A group of Vietnam veterans hire themselves out as mercenaries in the Golden Triangle. When they agree to rescue a woman who has been kidnapped by a former comrade they see this as just another routine mission, but are soon disabused of this idea. A standard action film that offers no surprises.

| A/AD | 92 min |
|---|---|
| V | RCA |

## PRIME CUT * 18
Michael Ritchie  USA  1972
*Lee Marvin, Gene Hackman, Angel Tompkins, Gregory Walcott, Sissy Spacek, Janit Baldwin, Eddie Egan*
A Kansas mobster is sentenced to death by his Chicago superiors, in this sleazy chase thriller that has a few grimly humorous touches. This was Spacek's first film. The music is by Lalo Schifrin.

| THR | 82 min (ort 91 min) |
|---|---|
| B,V | CBS |

## PRIME EVIL * 18
Roberta Findlay  USA  1989
*William Beckwith, Christine Moore, Mavis Harris, Max Jacobs, George Krause, Tim Gail, Gary Warner, Amy Bretano*
A group of Satanists is obliged to make a human sacrifice every 13 years, in order to maintain the immortality granted them by the Devil. A brave nun infiltrates their group in an attempt to foil their plans. A badly acted and thinly plotted film of little interest, whose highlight is a few good special effects near the climax.

| HOR | 90 min |
|---|---|
| B,V | SCRN |

## PRIME OF MISS JEAN BRODIE, THE ***
Ronald Neame  UK  1969
*Maggie Smith, Gordon Jackson, Celia Johnson, Robert Stephens, Jane Carr, Pamela Franklin, Diane Grayson, Shirley Steedman, Margo Cunningham, Isla Cameron, Rona Anderson, Molly Weir*
A character study of a romantic Edinburgh lady schoolteacher who has a hypnotic effect on her pupils. Written by Jay Presson Allen, with music and lyrics by Rod McKuen. Filmed on location. The story later formed the basis for a TV mini-series. AA: Actress (Smith).
Boa: novel by Muriel Spark.

| DRA | 99 min (ort 116 min) |
|---|---|
| B,V | GHV; VCC |

## PRIME RISK ** PG
Michael Farkas  USA  1985
*Lee Montgomery, Toni Hudson, Keenan Wynn, Sam Bottoms, Clu Gulager, John Lukes, Roy Stuart, Lois Hall, Rick Rakowski, John Lykes, James O'Connell, Randy Pearlman, Timothy Rice, Helen Duffy, Christopher Murphy*
Two teenage computer hackers enter a bank's system, but become aware of a terrorist plan, to create economic chaos by destroying the US monetary system through its computers. An intermittently engaging thriller which fails to make the most of its promising start.

| THR | 94 min (ort 98 min) |
|---|---|
| B,V | MED |

## PRIME SUSPECT ** PG
Noel Black  USA  1982
*Mike Farrell, Teri Garr, Lane Smith, Veronica Cartwright, Barry Corbin, James Sloyan, Charles Aidman, Matthew Faison, Ron Joseph, Nan Martin, Peter Hobbs, Terry Kiser, Ray Girardin, Martina Deignan, Penelope Windust*
The actions of a zealous TV reporter lead to a law-abiding citizen becoming the prime suspect in a murder case, in this uninspired ABSENCE OF MALICE clone.
Aka: CRY OF INNOCENCE
Boa: story by Jeffrey Bloom and Steven Nalevansky.

| DRA | 96 min (ort 100 min) mTV |
|---|---|
| B,V | VFP L/A; HER |

## PRIME SUSPECT ** PG
Jeffrey Hayden  USA  1974
*Jessica Walter, William Shatner, Peter Haskell, Mills Watson*
One of three TV films about a woman police chief. Here she faces a case of industrial espionage and murder that seems to implicate an old family friend. Fair.
Aka: AMY PRENTISS: BAPTISM OF FIRE

| DRA | 93 min mTV |
|---|---|
| B,V | EAG |

## PRIME TARGET ** PG
Robert Collins  USA  1989
*Angie Dickinson, Joseph Bologna, David Soul, Yaphet Kotto, Joe Regalbuto, Dennis Lipscomb, Mills Watson, Charles Durning*
Mystery surrounds the murder of a number of female police officers as the fact that the first two victims were vigorous defenders of equal treatment for women seems to point to their killer being a local cop. When a female cop investigates, she uncovers a deep-seated (but unbelievable) conspiracy. Dickinson gives a re-run of the type of role she made so familiar in the "Police Woman" TV series. Average.

| THR | 91 min (ort 100 min) mTV |
|---|---|
| V | MGM |

## PRINCE AND THE PAUPER, THE **
Don Chaffey  USA  1962
*Guy Williams, Laurence Naismith, Donald Houston, Jane Asher, Walter Hudd*
A pleasant Disney style retelling of the classic Twain novel.
Boa: novel by Mark Twain.

| A/AD | 93 min |
|---|---|
| V | WDV |

## PRINCE AND THE PAUPER, THE ***
William Keighley  USA  1937
*Errol Flynn, Billy Mauch, Bobby Mauch, Claude Rains, Alan Hale, Barton MacLane, Henry Stephenson, Eric Portman, Montagu Love, Lionel Pape, Halliwell Hobbes, Fritz Leiber*
Prince Edward VI (the son of Henry VII) finds a boy beggar who is his exact double and benefits from this strange coincidence to change places with him. A

lavish and spirited rendition of Twain's tale, with a fine score by Erich Wolfgang Korngold. Remade in 1962 and 1977.
Boa: novel by Mark Twain.

| A/AD | 114 min (ort 118 min) B/W |
| V | WHV |

### PRINCE AND THE PAUPER, THE ** Uc
AUSTRALIA 1971
Animated version of Twain's classic tale of the young prince who changes places with his double. Fair.
Boa: story by Mark Twain.

| CAR | 46 min (ort 60 min) |
| V | CHILD L/A; STYL |

### PRINCE AND THE SHOWGIRL, THE ** PG
Laurence Olivier UK 1957
Marilyn Monroe, Laurence Olivier, Richard Wattis, Sybil Thorndike, Jeremy Spencer, Jean Kent, Esmond Knight, David Horne, Charles Victor, Daphne Anderson, Vera Day, Gillian Owen, Maxine Audley, Gladys Henson
Set in London, this tells of an American showgirl who becomes the object of a foreign Prince's attentions during the coronation of George V in 1911. A ponderous comedy with much lavishness but little mirth. The script is by Terence Rattigan, with music by Richard Addinsell and photography by Jack Cardiff. Part of a series called "A Night At The Movies", the tape includes a cartoon, a newsreel and a trailer.
Boa: play The Sleeping Prince by Terence Rattigan.

| COM | 117 min |
| B,V | WHV |

### PRINCE JACK *
Bert Lovitt USA 1984
Robert Hogan, James F. Kelly, Kenneth Mars, Lloyd Nolan, Cameron Mitchell, Theodore Bikel, Robert Guillaume, Jim Backus, Dana Andrews
A supposedly realistic biopic on the Kennedy clan that concentrates on the personalities of its male members. Very dull, very shallow. See also YOUNG JOE: THE FORGOTTEN KENNEDY.

| DRA | 100 min |
| B,V | VCL/CBS |

### PRINCE OF BEL-AIR * 15
Charles Braverman USA 1986
Mark Harmon, Kirstie Alley, Robert Vaughn, Patty Labyorteaux, Bartley Braverman, Deborah Harmon, Katherine Moffat, Scott Geltin, Michael Horton, Jonathan Stark, Sherry Hursey, Lisanne Falk, Dean Cameron, Don Swayze
A swimming-pool service-man who has his own business, finds his love-life taking a turn for the worse when he is asked to look after a friend's 18-year-old son for the summer. Glossy and empty, this serves as no more than an effort to exploit the popularity of the star.

| COM | 90 min (ort 95 min) mTV |
| B,V | ARF |

### PRINCE OF DARKNESS ** 18
John Carpenter USA 1987
Donald Pleasence, Lisa Blount, James Parker, Victor Wong, Dennis Dun, Susan Blanchard, Anne Howard, Alice Cooper, Ann Yen, Peter Jason, Dirk Blocker
All hell literally breaks loose, when a cannister containing a foul liquid is broken in an abandoned church, and an up-to-then imprisoned demonic creature is let loose. Written by the director (under the pseudonym of Martin Quatermass) and containing a number of chilling moments but little of substance.

| HOR | 101 min (ort 110 min) |
| | GHV |

### PRINCE OF PENNSYLVANIA, THE ** 15
Ron Nyswaner USA 1988
Fred Ward, Keanu Reeves, Bonnie Bedelia, Amy Madigan, Jeff Hayenga, Tracey Ellis
A bizarre character study with a weird young man slowly finding himself, not really being helped in this by his equally unconventional dad. Despite many comic moments the film is too disorganised to work as anything more than a set of funny vignettes. Nyswaner's directorial debut.

| COM | 91 min |
| V | RCA |

### PRINCE OF THE CITY, THE *** 15
Sidney Lumet USA 1981
Treat Williams, Jerry Orbach, Richard Foronjy, Don Billett, Carmine Caridi, Kenny Marino, Paul Roebling, Lindsay Crouse, Michael Beckett, Norman Parker, Bob Balaban, James Tolkan, Steve Inwood, Matthew Laurance, Tony Turco
An undercover cop reveals police corruption in the department, but is frozen out when his colleagues close ranks against him. A powerful and provocative tale that is far longer than it need have been, but makes a number of points that are all the more disturbing for being based on a real-life incident. Written by Jay Presson Allen and Lumet. See also SERPICO, which is just as effective but a good deal shorter.
Boa: novel by Robert Daley

| DRA | 160 min (ort 167 min) |
| V | WHV |

### PRINCESS AND THE PEA, THE ** Uc
Tony Bill USA 1983
Liza Minnelli, Tom Conti, Nancy Allen, Pat McCormack, Beatrice Straight
Film version of a classic fairytale and part of the "Faerie Tale Theatre" series. The story tells of a young princess and the sleepless night she endures when a pea is placed beneath her twenty mattresses.
Boa: short story by Hans Christian Andersen.

| JUV | 60 min |
| B,V | MGM |

### PRINCESS AND THE PIRATE, THE *** U
David Butler USA 1944
Bob Hope, Virginia Mayo, Walter Brennan, Walter Slezak, Victor McLaglen, Marc Lawrence, Maude Eburne, Hugo Haas
Our hero is on the run from a mean pirate, and gets into sundry scrapes in this lighthearted and crazy Hope vehicle. Brennan is well cast as a pirate, but many of the jokes will, unfortunately, seem a little dated now. The music is by David Rose.

| COM | 94 min |
| B,V | VGM |

### PRINCESS BRIDE, THE *** PG
Rob Reiner USA 1987
Cary Elwes, Peter Falk, Mandy Patinkin, Carol Kane, Billy Crystal, Chris Sarandon, Robin Wright, Fred Savage, Andre the Giant, Christopher Guest, Mel Smith, Wallace Shawn, Peter Cook, Willoughby Gray, Malcolm Story
A tongue-in-cheek fairytale aimed at adults and children alike, and telling of a man who must rescue his own true love from an evil villain. This uneven mixture of sparkling action and lacklustre comedy, is loosely bound together by the muddled William Goldman script. There are however, some memorable moments.
Boa: novel by William Goldman.

| A/AD | 94 min (ort 98 min) |
| V | VES |

### PRINCESS DAISY *
Warris Hussein USA 1983
Merete Van Kemp, Lindsay Wagner, Paul Michael Glaser, Robert Urich, Claudia Cardinale, Rupert Everett, Ringo Starr, Barbara Bach, Stacy Keach, Alexa Kenin, Nicolas Coster, Sal Viscuso, Lysette

*Anthony, David Haskell*
Glossy, trashy story of a poor little rich girl who is the daughter of a Russian prince and one of a pair of twins. This overblown melodrama has our heroine overcoming many obstacles as she rises to a position of great wealth, but discovering that it counts for little without true love. As contrived as it sounds and a good deal more boring. Originally shown in two parts.
Boa: novel by Judith Krantz.
DRA                                    200 min mTV
B,V                                    VFP L/A; HER

### PRINCESS WARRIOR *                          18
Lindsay Norgard                                1989
*Sharon Lee Jones, Dana Fredsti, Tony Riccardi*
Space opera set in a future off-world society, where women are the aggressors and men serve as concubines. Two sisters enter a contest to determine the ruler of the planet Venus.
FAN                                    90 min
V                                      BCB

### PRINCIPAL, THE **                           18
Christopher Cain          USA                  1987
*James Belushi, Louis Gossett Jr, Rae Dawn Chong, Michael Wright, J.J. Cohen, Esai Morales, Troy Winbush, Jacob Vargas, Thomas Ryan, Reggie Johnson, Kelly Mintner*
An idealistic teacher is appointed principal of the worst high school in the district – a hotbed of juvenile crime and violence – and faces the seemingly impossible task of imposing some kind of order and discipline. An awkward mixture of comedy and tension that is partially redeemed by the final showdown between the title character and the school's toughest thug.
DRA                            106 min (ort 109 min)
B,V                                    RCA

### PRISON **                                   18
Renny Harlin              USA                  1988
*Lane Smith, Viggo Mortensen, Chelsea Field, Lincoln Kilpatrick, Andre De Shields, Ivan Kane, Steven Little, Tom Lister Jr, Michael Yablans, Larry Flash Jenkins, Arlen Dean Snyder, Hal Landon Jr*
A prisoner executed in 1964, returns from the dead to take his revenge on the warden. Good special effects and atmosphere (the film was shot in a Wyoming prison) help bolster the thin plot. See also THE CHAIR for a dose of something similar.
HOR                            99 min (ort 102 min)
B,V                                    EIV

### PRISON SHIP STAR SLAMMER **                  18
Fred Olen Ray             USA                  1986
*John Carradine, Sandy Brooke, Aldo Ray, Susan Stokey, Ross Hagen, Bobbie Bresee, Dawn Wildsmith, Marya Grant, Michael D. Sonye, Richard Alan Hench, Lindy Skyles, Johnny Legend, Jade Barrett, Danita Aljuwani, Liat Mathias*
An innocent young woman is sent to a women's space penitentiary, controlled by sadistic humanoids and stocked with depraved inmates, and soon finds herself being persecuted by the chief executioner. She begins to plot her escape. Average.
Aka: ADVENTURES OF TAURA PART 1, THE; PRISON SHIP; STAR SLAMMER; STAR SLAMMER: THE ESCAPE
FAN                                    83 min
B,V                                    SHEER

### PRISONER OF RIO *                           15
Lech Majewski             UK                   1987
*Steven Berkoff, Paul Freeman, Peter Firth, Florinda Bolkan, Jose Wilker, Zeze Motta, Breno Morani*
Very loosely based on a Scotland Yard plan, to bring former Great Train Robber Biggs back to the UK, this follows the exploits of a police officer who goes there posing as a journalist and attempts to entice Biggs onboard a Royal Navy vessel as part of a publicity

stunt. A meaningless and exploitative effort with little value as entertainment.
DRA                                    90 min
B,V                                    PAL

### PRISONER OF SECOND AVENUE, THE ***          PG
Melvin Frank              USA                  1975
*Jack Lemmon, Gene Saks, Anne Bancroft, Elizabeth Wilson, Florence Stanley, M. Emmet Walsh*
An executive faces a nervous breakdown when he suddenly becomes unemployed, in this unusual comedy that treads a thin line between comedy and pathos. Bancroft is cast as his understanding wife. Look out for an appearance by Sylvester Stallone as an alleged pickpocket. Written by Neil Simon and with music by Marvin Hamlisch.
Boa: play by Neil Simon.
COM                            93 min (ort 101 min)
B,V                                    WHV

### PRISONER OF THE CANNIBAL GOD *
Sergio Martino            ITALY                1978
*Ursula Andress, Stacy Keach, Claudio Cassinelli, Franco Fantasia, Antonio Marsina, Lamfranco Spinola, Carlo Longhi, Dudley Wanagura, Luisina Rocchi, Akushlaa Sellajaah, T.M. Munna, M. Suki*
A woman and her brother go searching for her missing husband in the jungles of New Guinea, and are captured by the natives.
Aka: LA MONTAGNA DEL DIO CANNIBALE; SLAVES OF THE CANNIBAL GOD
A/AD                                   96 min
B,V,V2                                 HOK

### PRISONER OF ZENDA, THE **                   U
Richard Thorpe            USA                  1952
*Stewart Granger, Louis Calhern, Deborah Kerr, Robert Coote, Robert Douglas, James Mason, Jane Greer, Lewis Stone*
A remake of the 1937 original, that lacks any feeling for this story of intrigue at the court of Ruritania, when a double has to stand in at the coronation of the country's new king. Granger plays both king and his English double – in both roles he is without presence or feeling.
Boa: novel by Anthony Hope.
A/AD                           97 min (ort 100 min)
V                                      MGM

### PRISONER OF ZENDA, THE *                    PG
Richard Quine             USA                  1979
*Peter Sellers, Lynne Frederick, Lionel Jeffries, Elke Sommer, Gregory Sierra, Stuart Wilson, Jeremy Kemp, Catherine Schell, Simon Williams, Norman Rossington, John Laurie*
A dreadful remake of the famous Anthony Hope adventure that was played strictly for laughs but provided precious little amusement. Among his roles Sellers plays a London cabbie who is asked to impersonate the King of Ruritania when the latter dies in a hot-air balloon. This painfully vacuous film came filled with its own supply of hot air, and did nothing to advance the careers of any of its passengers.
COM                            104 min (ort 108 min)
V                                      CIC/CBSDIS

### PRISONER WITHOUT A NAME, CELL WITHOUT A NUMBER *
Linda Yellen              USA                  1983
*Sam Robards, Liv Ullman, David Cryer, Roy Scheider, Michael Pearlman, Zach Galligan*
Dramatisation of the experiences of Jacob Timerman, an Argentinian Jewish newspaper editor who was imprisoned and tortured for two and a half years, by the military junta that was then in power. As the editor of La Opinion, the country's leading liberal newspaper, he was a leading opponent of the repressive government of that time. Co-scripted by Budd

Schulberg (who had his name replaced by a pseudonym in the credits). Flat and uninspired.
Aka: JACOBO TIMMERMAN: PRISONER WITHOUT A NAME, CELL WITHOUT A NUMBER
Boa: book by Jacobo Timerman/story by Oliver P. Drexell Jr and Stan Silverman.

DRA                    90 min (ort 100 min) mTV
V                                              FTV

## PRISONER, THE ***          PG
Pat Jackson/Don Chaffey/Peter Graham Scott and
others                    UK                1967
*Patrick McGoohan, Leo McKern, Angelo Muscat, Colin Gordon, Peter Wyngarde, Mary Morris, Guy Doleman, Alexis Kanner. Guest stars: Finlay Currie, Paul Eddington, Eric Portman, Anton Rodgers, John Castle, Donald Sinden*
This cult TV series tells of a British Intelligence agent who, after resigning is kidnapped and taken to a strange village from which he cannot escape. There he is subjected to attempts to brainwash him and discover the reasons behind his resignation. A highly imaginative series that began with great promise but eventually became repetitive. Some episodes were better than others, but the final one was inconclusive. Filmed at Portmeirion.
FAN                819 min (17 cassettes) mTV
V                                              CH5

## PRISONERS OF THE LOST UNIVERSE **    PG
Terry Marcel              UK                1983
*Kay Lenz, John Saxon, Richard Hatch, Dawn Abraham, Peter O'Farrell, Ray Charleson, Kenneth Hendel, Philip Van Der Byl, Larry Taylor, Ron Smerczak, Charles Comyn, Ian Steadman, Bikll Flynn, Danie Vogles, Myles Robertson*
A warrior chief on a distant planet, captures two people who accidentally enter another dimension and find themselves on his planet. Average.
FAN                    87 min (ort 90 min) mCab
B,V                        POLY; NICK; MPV

## PRIVATE BENJAMIN **          15
Howard Zieff              USA                1980
*Goldie Hawn, Armand Assante, Eileen Brennan, Robert Webber, Sam Wanamaker, Barbara Barrie, Mary Kay Place, Hal Williams, Harry Dean Stanton, Albert Brooks, P.J. Soles, Sally Kirkland*
A Goldie Hawn vehicle, with Hawn playing a spoilt rich girl who enlists in the US Army and discovers to her surprise that it's not a bed of roses. After an initial shock she finds that life in the army does have certain advantages. Hawn gurgles and squeals her way through this one very pleasantly, but somehow it just isn't enough. A TV series followed.
COM                    106 min (ort 110 min)
B,V                                            WHV

## PRIVATE EYE **          15
Mark Tinker               USA                1987
*Michael Woods, Josh Brolin, Stanley Kamel, Frederick Coffin, Lisa Jane Persky, Jamey Sheridan, Susan Blakely, Ed Marinaro, Bill Sadler, Faye Grant, J.O. Sanders, Anthony Charnota*
Pilot film for a TV series in which a former cop, kicked out of the police force because of alcoholism and corruption, sobers up quickly and sets out to have his revenge, when his brother, a private eye, is killed by gangsters. Set in the 1950s, the best thing about this uninspired effort is the authentic period atmosphere.
A/AD                            93 min mTV
B,V                                            CIC

## PRIVATE EYE: WAR BUDDY/      15
## NICKY THE ROSE **
Donald Petrie/Rob Cohen
                          USA                1987
*Michael Woods, Josh Brolin, Bill Sadler, Lisa Jane*

*Persky, Ed Marinaro, Susan Blakely*
Two stories following the exploits of a couple of private detectives. In the first they help an old friend whose life is in danger and in the second are hired by a woman to keep tabs on her boyfriend.
A/AD                            92 min mTV
B,V                                            CIC

## PRIVATE FUNCTION, A **        15
Malcolm Mowbray          UK                1984
*Maggie Smith, Michael Palin, Denholm Elliott, Richard Griffiths, Tony Haygarth, John Normington, Bill Paterson, Liz Smith, Alison Steadman, Jim Carter, Peter Postlethwaite, Eileen O'Brien, Rachel Davies, Reece Dinsdale*
The story of the fate of a black-market pig, being secretly raised for the Royal Wedding celebrations in post-WW2 Britain. The humour, such as it is, focuses on the fact that rationing is still in force, making our grunter the centre of attention. Some nice character studies add a modicum of mirth. The script is by Alan Bennett.
COM                    92 min (ort 94 min)
B,V                        TEVP L/A; WHV

## PRIVATE INVESTIGATIONS **      18
Nigel Dick               USA                1987
*Clayton Rohner, Ray Sharkey, Martin Balsam, Talia Balsam, Paul Le Mat, Vernon Wells, Anthony Zerbe, Phil Morris, Roberto Ito, Anthony Geary, Justin Lord, Richard Cummings Jr, Desiree Boschetti, Andy Romano, Sydney Walsh*
A complex Los Angeles thriller that's set in the present day, but is full of references to past works in this genre, and follows the exploits of an architect who, after discovering a corpse in his bathroom, finds himself the prey of a demented hit-man who also happens to be a cop. A stylish and slightly tongue-in-cheek tale, but somewhat deficient in terms of plotting and characterisation. This was Dick's feature film debut.
Aka: P.I. – PRIVATE INVESTIGATIONS
THR                    87 min (ort 100 min)
B,V                        AVR; GLOB; POLY

## PRIVATE LESSONS **          18
Alan Myerson             USA                1981
*Sylvia Kristel, Howard Hesseman, Eric Brown, Pamela Bryant, Ed Begley Jr*
A young boy in a rich family is given a hand with his sexual initiation by the maid, unaware that she has more ambitious plans in this inconsequential little piece. The script is by Dan Greenburg.
COM 80 min (ort 87 min) (Cut at film release by 3 min 20 sec)
B,V                                            CIC

## PRIVATE LIFE OF HENRY VIII, THE ****    U
Alexander Korda          UK                1933
*Charles Laughton, Elsa Lanchester, Robert Donat, Merle Oberon, Wendy Barrie, Binnie Barnes, Everley Gregg, Lady Tree, Franklin Dyall, John Loder, Miles Mander, Claud Allister, William Austin, Gibb McLaughlin, Sam Livesey*
A wonderfully lively and sparkling portrayal of the much-married British monarch, that is not always strictly true to historical fact but more than makes up for this, through its excellent cast and fine production values. Laughton is quite magnificent in the title role.
AA: Actor (Laughton).
DRA                97 min; 90 min (PICK) B/W
V                        CENVID; PICK

## PRIVATE LIFE OF SHERLOCK HOLMES,    PG
## THE ***
Billy Wilder            UK/USA              1970
*Robert Stephens, Colin Blakely, Genevieve Page, Irene Handl, Eric Francis, Stanley Holloway, Christopher*

Lee, Clive Revill, Tamara Toumanova, George Benson,
Catherine Lacey, Mollie Maureen, Peter Madden,
Robert Cawdron
The discovery of a secret Watson manuscript, reveals
that the famous detective did have relationships with
women, in this uneven but affectionate and occasionally humorous film, constructed around two stories. The abrupt ending is the only sour note in a work
of great charm. Written by Wilder and I.A.L. Diamond, with music by Miklos Rozsa.
DRA                          120 min (ort 125 min)
B,V                                           WHV

## PRIVATE LIVES OF ELIZABETH AND          U
## ESSEX, THE ***
Michael Curtiz          USA                 1939
Errol Flynn, Bette Davis, Donald Crisp, Vincent Price,
Olivia De Havilland, Alan Hale, Nanette Fabray,
Henry Stephenson, Henry Daniell, Leo G. Carroll,
Robert Warwick, John Sutton
Solid account of the stormy relationship between
Elisabeth I and the Earl of Essex, which led to his
rebellion and subsequent execution as a traitor.
British history gets the grand Hollywood treatment,
but the inspired pairing of Davis and Flynn makes for
excellent drama. Written by Norman Reilly Raine and
with music by Erich Wolfgang Korngold.
Boa: play Elizabeth The Queen by Maxwell Anderson.
DRA                          102 min (ort 106 min)
V                                             WHV

## PRIVATE MANOEUVRES *                      18
Ziv Shissel          ISRAEL                 1983
Zachi Noy, Joseph Shiloah, Sybil Rauch, Moshe
Ishkasit, Dvorah Bekon
A sequel to BABY LOVE, with our heroes re-enlisting
and being sent on a military exercise. Number six in
the LEMON POPSICLE series. Followed by UP
YOUR ANCHOR.
COM                      81 min; 78 min (VCC)
B,V                          GHV; VCC (VHS only)

## PRIVATE PARTS **
Paul Bartel          USA                    1972
Ann Ruymen, Lucille Benson, Laurie Main, John
Ventantonio
A runaway teenage girl stays at her aunt's hotel,
where strange things are afoot and the hotel guests
are somewhat unusual. Several murders take place,
but they are hardly central to this bizarre comedy-
drama that spends more time examining the sexual
eccentricities of the guests. Bartel's directorial debut.
DRA                          83 min (ort 86 min)
B,V                                           MGM

## PRIVATE PLEASURES *                       18
Alex C. Englund          USA                198-
Elona Glen
A woman with a voracious sexual appetite, is torn
between love of her husband and self-gratification.
A                                           80 min
B,V                                            VPD

## PRIVATE POPSICLE *                        18
Boaz Davidson
                 ISRAEL/WEST GERMANY        1983
Yftach Katzur, Zachi Noy, Jonathan Segall, Sonja
Martin
Third sequel to LEMON POPSICLE, with the three
boys from the original yarn now doing their 3-year
stint of military service. Followed by BABY LOVE.
Aka: LEMON POPSICLE 4; SAPICHES
COM                  96 min (ort 111 min) dubbed
B,V                          GHV; VCC (VHS only)

## PRIVATE PROPERTY *                        R18
Leslie Stevens          USA                 1959
Corey Allen, Kate Manx, Warren Oates, Robert Wark,
Jerome Cowan

Two young men try hard to seduce a married woman,
in this boring sex comedy which was (before cutting)
explicit if nothing else.
A              33 min (ort 60 min) Cut (3 min 26 sec)
B,V                                   DAP L/A; SHEP

## PRIVATE RESORT *                          18
George Bowers          USA                  1985
Rob Morrow, Johnny Depp, Karyn O'Bryan, Emily
Longstreth, Tony Azib, Hector Elizondo, Dody
Goodman, Leslie Easterbrook
Two teenage boys enjoy a riotous time at a Miami
resort, in an empty-headed and energetic exercise in
the inconsequential.
COM                          78 min (ort 85 min)
B,V                                            RCA

## PRIVATE RIGHT, THE **
Michael Papas          GREECE/UK            1966
Dimitris Andreus, George Kafkaris, Tamara Hinchco,
Cristos Demetriou, Charlotte Selwyn, Seraphim
Nicola, John Brogan
After Cyprus becomes independent, a former guerilla
leader goes to London to get his revenge on the man
who betrayed him.
DRA                          81 min (ort 86 min)
B,V,V2                                    INT/CBS

## PRIVATE ROAD *                            18
Ralph Nussbaum          USA                 1987
George Kennedy, Greg Evigan, Mitzi Kapture, Patty
McCormack, Brian Patrick Clarke, E.J. Peaker, James
Van Patten
A young stock car racer is knocked off his motorcycle
by a drunken heiress and his brought back to her
family home to recuperate. The girl's father is attemp-
ting to win a government contract to produce an
all-terrain attack vehicle, and is persuaded to give the
man a job in order to avoid a scandal. Complications
now follow in a film that is both hard to classify and
boring to watch.
Aka: PRIVATE ROAD: NO TRESPASSING
DRA                                         97 min
V                                             MGM

## PRIVATE SCHOOL *                          18
Noel Black          USA                     1983
Phoebe Cates, Betsy Russell, Matthew Modine, Michael
Zorek, Fran Ryan, Ray Walston, Sylvia Kristel
Plenty of teenage high-spirits are in evidence at a
girls' school, in yet another dumb youth movie. This
one was made to what the producers thought was a
certain recipe for success (i.e. boys from nearby school
break into girl's school for sexual frolics). It flopped on
release; deservedly so.
Aka: PRIVATE SCHOOL FOR GIRLS
COM                          85 min (ort 97 min)
V/h                                            CIC

## PRIVATE SESSIONS **                       15
Michael Pressman          USA               1984
Maureen Stapleton, Mike Farrell, Denise Miller,
Kathryn Walker, Mary Tanner, David Labiosa, Tom
Bosley, Robert Vaughn, Kelly McGillis, Greg Evigan,
Hope Lange, Kim Hunter, Victor Garber, John
Cunningham, Wendie Malick
A pilot for a prospective series about a psychologist
who unwisely becomes involved in the lives of his
patients; the patient in this tale being a woman who
seeks a cure for her nymphomania, the result of a
trauma in early life. Music is by Lalo Schifrin. This
was McGillis' TV movie debut. A fair low-key drama
that's hampered by a contrived plot.
DRA                      89 min (ort 95 min) mTV
B,V                                           TEVP

## PRIVATE VICES AND PUBLIC VIRTUES **
Miklos Jancso  ITALY/YUGOSLAVIA             1977
Lajos Balazsovitz, Franco Branciaroli, Pamela

*Villoresi, Therese-Ann Savoy, Laura Betli, Ivica Pajer*
The young heir to a central European kingdom
neglects his wife and indulges in womanising, drinking etc.
Aka: VIZI PRIVATI, PUBBLICHE VIRTU

| A | 104 min |
| B,V | INT |

## PRIVATES ON PARADE **                          15
Michael Blakemore          UK               1982
*John Cleese, Denis Quilley, Michael Elphick, Nicola*
*Pagett, Joe Melia, Bruce Payne, Patrick Pearson,*
*David Bamber, Simon Jones, Phil Tan, Vincent Wong,*
*Neil Pearson, John Standing, John Quayle, Brigitte*
*Kahn, Tim Barlow*
The story of an army entertainment troupe in Singa-
pore in 1948, that's a clumsy mixture of drama, satire
and farce. Quilley is excellent as the homosexual
director of the troupe, but the film as a whole lacks
substance. Written by Nichols.
Boa: play by Peter Nichols.

| COM | 107 min (ort 113 min) |
| B,V | TEVP |

## PRIVATE'S PROGRESS ***                          U
John Boulting          UK               1956
*Ian Carmichael, Terry-Thomas, Richard*
*Attenborough, Dennis Price, John Le Mesurier, Peter*
*Jones, Thorley Walters, William Hartnell, Ian Bannen,*
*Jill Adams, Victor Maddern, Kenneth Griffith, George*
*Coulouris, Miles Malleson*
An undergraduate with no visible talents joins the
army in WW2, and soon learns the best ways of
avoiding work, before getting involved in a scheme to
steal German art treasures for his uncle. A light-
hearted and splendid farce on army life, though it's
not quite the satire it was intended to be. Look out for
Christopher Lee in an early part – he plays a German.
Boa: novel by Alan Hackney.

| COM | 96 min (ort 102 min) B/W |
| V | WHV |

## PRIZE FIGHTER, THE *                          
Michael Preece          USA               1979
*Tim Conway, Don Knotts, David Wayne, Robin Clarke,*
*Cissie Cameron, Mary Ellen O'Neil*
Depression-era story of a none-too-smart boxer and
his manager, with broad comedy but little wit. See
THE PRIVATE EYES, a later and far better pairing
of Conway and Knotts.

| COM | 99 min |
| B,V,V2 | MED; VPD |

## PRIZE OF PERIL, THE **                          18
Yves Boisset   FRANCE/YUGOSLAVIA          1984
*Gerrard Lanvin, Marie France Pisier, Michel Picolli*
In an ultimate TV quiz of the near future, contestants
stand to win a prize of $1,000,000 if they can elude
capture by gangs of paid murderers. See THE RUN-
NING MAN for another film on this game-show
theme.
Aka: LE PRIX DU DANGER
Boa: short story by Robert Sheckley.

| DRA | 85 min (ort 95 min) |
| B,V | BWV |

## PRIZZI'S HONOR ***                          15
John Huston          USA               1985
*Jack Nicholson, Kathleen Turner, Anjelica Huston,*
*Robert Loggia, William Hickey, Lawrence Tierney,*
*John Randolph, Lee Richardson, Michael Lombard,*
*Joseph Ruskin*
Skilfully directed account of the complex life of the
Mafia. A hit-man falls in love with the widow of his
latest victim and discovers that she's in the same
business. Many bizarre twists transpire in a most
enjoyable film in which John Huston made his last
screen appearance. Written by Condon and Janet
Roach and with music by Alex North. The photogra-

phy is by Andrzej Bartkowiak. AA: S. Actress
(Huston).
Boa: novel by Richard Condon.

| COM | 129 min; 124 min (CH5) |
| B,V | EHE; CH5 (VHS only) |

## PROBABILITY ZERO **                          15
Maurizio Lucidi/Dario Argento
                       ITALY               1968
*Henry Silva, Luigi Casellato, Riccardo Salvino*
A British aeroplane with a new type of radar crashes
after being attacked by German fighters. A commando
mission is then mounted to destroy the equipment
before it is captured.
Aka: PROBABILITA ZERO

| WAR | 95 min |
| B,V | VPD; KRP/XTASY |

## PRODIGAL BOXER *
Au Yang Chun   HONG KONG               1980
*Meng Fei, Tan Tao Liang, Shoji Karata, Lu Ping,*
*Lung Chun Er, Wei Ping Ao, Suma Wah Lung*
A man is blamed for the death of a friend of some local
thugs, so in revenge they kill his father and injure his
mother. After rigorous training, our hero sets out to
have his own revenge, and enters a martial arts
contest with this in mind. No surprises here.

| MAR | 101 min |
| B,V | VIDRNG; VIR |

## PRODUCERS, THE ***                          PG
Mel Brooks          USA               1967
*Zero Mostel, Gene Wilder, Kenneth Mars, Dick Shawn,*
*Lee Meredith, Estelle Winwood, Renee Taylor,*
*Christopher Hewett, Andreas Voustinas, Bill Hickey*
A funny black comedy that is marred by a terribly
lame ending. A Broadway producer comes up with a
surefire scheme for making money, on a musical
production that he is absolutely certain must be a flop,
as it's a hymn of praise to the Nazis. For sheer bad
taste this one is hard to beat, a highlight being the
"Springtime for Hitler" number, but from this point on
it's downhill all the way. AA: Story/Screen (Brooks).

| COM | 84 min (ort 88 min) |
| B,V | CBS; EHE; CH5 (VHS only); POLY (VHS only) |

## PROFESSIONALS, THE ***                          PG
Richard Brooks          USA               1966
*Burt Lancaster, Lee Marvin, Jack Palance, Robert*
*Ryan, Claudia Cardinale, Ralph Bellamy, Woody*
*Strode, Joe De Santis, Rafael Bertrand, Jorge*
*Martinez De Hoyos, Maria Gomez, Jose Chavez, Carlos*
*Romero, Robert Conteras*
A wealthy rancher hires four gunslingers to rescue his
wife from kidnappers. A well-paced film, with good
action sequences, that may be a little implausible, but
is still highly enjoyable. The fine photography is by
Conrad Hall. Written by Brooks.
Boa: novel A Mule For The Marquesa by Frank
O'Rourke.

| WES | 112 min (ort 123 min) |
| B,V | RCA |

## PROFESSIONALS, THE:
## A MAN CALLED QUINN/NO STONE **                          15
Horace Ove/Chris Burt   UK               1978
*Gordon Jackson, Martin Shaw, Lewis Collins, Steven*
*Berkoff, Bernard Archard, Del Henney, Sarah Neville,*
*John Wheatley, Philip York*
Two TV episodes following the exploits of a secret
intelligence unit, set up to solve crimes the police are
not equipped to deal with. In the first one a former
intelligence agent threatens the lives of his one-time
colleagues and in the second (the last episode in the
series) a terrorist group that has carried out a number
of attacks is foiled.

| A/AD | 102 min mTV |
| V | VCC |

## PROFESSIONALS, THE: HUNTER, HUNTED/ PRIVATE MADNESS, PUBLIC DANGER ** 15

Anthony Simmons/Douglas Camfield
UK 1978
*Gordon Jackson, Lewis Collins, Martin Shaw, Bryan Marshall, Cheryl Kennedy, Tom Caunter, Keith Barron, Di Trevis, Angus Mackay*
Two episodes from a popular British TV series detailing the exploits of a secret undercover crime-busting unit. In the first tale a secret gun with laser sights is stolen and must be recovered, and in the second, the mysterious deaths of an industrialist and his secretary are investigated.
A/AD                         102 min mTV
V                                    VCC

## PROFESSIONALS, THE: KLANSMAN/STAKE-OUT ** 15

Pat Jackson/Benjamin Wickers
UK 1978
*Gordon Jackson, Martin Shaw, Lewis Collins, Jules Walter, Trevor Thomas, Anthony Booth, Frank Collings, Barry Jackson, Pamela Stephenson*
Two episodes from a popular series that followed the exploits of an undercover criminal intelligence unit. In the first episode a black community is being threatened by men wearing Ku Klux Klan robes, and in the second, terrorists attempt to blackmail the government by theatening to explode a nuclear device.
Boa: story by Simon Masters ("Klansman" episode only).
A/AD                         103 min mTV
V                                    VCC

## PROFESSOR, THE *** 18

Giuseppe Tornatore    ITALY    1986
*Ben Gazzara, Laura Del Sol, Franco Interlenghi, Luciano Bartoli, Leo Gullotta, Nicola Di Pinto*
A Mafia leader is sentenced to prison for murder, but continues to control all the criminal rackets of Naples from inside jail. An overlong and somewhat overcomplex but absorbing saga.
Aka: CAMORRA MAN, THE; CAMORRA MEMBER, THE; IL CAMORRISTA
Boa: novel by Giuseppe Marrazzo.
THR          145 min (ort 147 min) Cut (26 sec)
B,V                                  AVA

## PROJECT A *** PG

Jackie Chan    HONG KONG    1985
*Jackie Chan, Samo Hung, Yuen Biao Mars, Dick Wei, Isabella Wong*
A high-action tale set at the turn of the century, and telling of a unit of marines who are sent to eradicate a gang of cutthroats who infest the China Seas. A sequel followed.
MAR                              100 min
V                                    VPD

## PROJECT A: PART 2 *** 15

Jackie Chan    HONG KONG    1987
*Jackie Chan, Maggie Cheung, David Lam, Rosalind Kwan*
This sequel to the first film is another actioner set in Hong Kong at the turn of the century, when an intrepid police inspector fights crooks and a corrupt policeman. A lively and mindless blend of martial arts mayhem and comedy, with Chan as ever, choreographing and performing his own stunts.
MAR                           94 min dubbed
B,V                                  VPD

## PROJECT X ** PG

Jonathan Kaplan    USA    1987
*Matthew Broderick, Helen Hunt, Bill Sadler, Johnny Ray McGhee, Jonathan Stark, Robin Gammell, Stephen Lang, Jean Smart, Dick Miller, Chuck*

*Bennett, Daniel Roebuck, Mark Harden, Marvin J. McIntyre, Swede Johnson*
The story of a young airman who is assigned to a secret research base, where chimps are taught to operate aircraft simulators. He befriends one highly intelligent chimp that is able to communicate with sign language, and eventually rebels when he learns more of the true nature of the project. A tense and absorbing tale let down by a predictable plot and an implausible ending.
THR                      103 min (ort 108 min)
V/sh                                 CBS

## PROJECT: KILL ** 

William Girdler    USA    1977
*Leslie Nielsen, Gary Lockwood, Nancy Kwan, Vic Silayan, Vic Diaz, Galen Thompson, Pamela Parsons, Maurice Down, Carlos Salazar*
A government agent finds himself being pursued by his ex-partner. Average.
THR                        90 min (ort 104 min)
B,V                                  VFO

## PROJECTED MAN, THE ** 

Ian Curteis    UK    1966
*Mary Peach, Bryant Halliday, Norman Wooland, Ronald Allen, Derek Farr, Tracey Crisp, Derrick De Marney, Gerard Heinz, Sam Kydd*
A scientist conducting experiments in which laser energy is used to transport matter, tries the experiment out on himself, but an accident occurs and he emerges from the chamber with a warped mind, a deadly touch and a disfigured face. A watchable variant on THE FLY.
Osca: GUNS DON'T ARGUE
FAN                        86 min (ort 90 min)
B,V                                  KVD

## PROM NIGHT ** 18

Paul Lynch    CANADA    1980
*Leslie Nielsen, Jamie Lee Curtis, Casey Stevens, Robert Silverman, Antoinette Bower, Eddie Benton, Michael Tough, David Mucci, Pita Oliver, Marybeth Rubens, Joy Thompson*
A deranged killer threatens college students, who were responsible for the death of a little girl six years before. A standard slasher tale that's quite well handled, but adds nothing original to this genre.
DRA                        88 min (ort 91 min)
B,V                                  EHE

## PROM NIGHT 2: HELLO MARY LOU ** 18

Bruce Pitman    CANADA    1987
*Michael Ironside, Wendy Lyon, Justin Louis, Lisa Schrage, Richard Monette*
Not really a sequel to the earlier PROM NIGHT, this tale has students being menaced by a murdered prom queen, who has returned from the grave after thirty years to have her revenge. Fair.
Aka: HELLO MARY LOU: PROM NIGHT 2
HOR          95 min; 92 min (VCC) (ort 97 min)
B,V              VPM L/A; SHEER; VCC (VHS only)

## PROM NIGHT 3: THE LAST KISS * 18

Ron Oliver/Peter Simpson
CANADA 1990
*Tim Conlon, Cyndy Preston, Courtney Taylor, David Stratton*
Mediocre horror films tend to beget even worse series, and this one is no exception, with our murdered prom queen returning from the grave to seduce a high school boy and embark on the expected bout of supernatural murder and mayhem.
HOR                              95 min
V/sh                                 CBS

## PROMISE AT DAWN ** 15

Jules Dassin    FRANCE/USA    1970

*Melina Mercouri, Assaf Dayan, Francois Raffoul,*
*Despo, Fernand Gravey, Perlo Vita (Jules Dassin)*
A biopic on the life and career of writer Romain Gary
and his mother, that follows them as they journey
across Europe during the last years of her life. Well
acted but patchy and unsatisfying. The script is by
Dassin.
Boa: play First Love by Samuel Taylor.
DRA                          101 min; 98 min (CH5)
B,V                          EHE; CH5 (VHS only)

## PROMISE MADE, A ** U
Beau Bridges          USA          1986
*Beau Bridges, Millie Perkins, Jordan Bridges, Lloyd*
*Bridges*
A boy makes a pet of a stray gosling, that was found
and brought to his family for rearing, on the under-
standing that it was to be fattened up for a Thanksgiv-
ing dinner. A typical happy little Disney film, with
our boy saving his pet, but not until they have enjoyed
various adventures together.
JUV                          90 min Cut (2 sec)
B,V                          WDV

## PROMISE OF LOVE, THE *
Don Taylor          USA          1980
*Valerie Bertinelli, Jameson Parker, Andy Romano,*
*Joanna Miles, David James Carroll, Lauri Hendler,*
*Virginia Kiser, Craig T. Nelson, Karlene Crockett, Dey*
*Young, Shelley Long, Don Caldwell, Anne Gee Byrd,*
*Heath Kaye*
A young widow has a tough time rebuilding her life,
after her US Marines husband is killed in Vietnam.
Sincere and well meaning but terribly dull.
DRA                          96 min mTV
B,V                          POLY

## PROMISED A MIRACLE *** 15
Steven Gyllenhaal          USA          1988
*Rosanna Arquette, Judge Reinhold, Tom Bower,*
*Vonni Ribisi, Gary Bayer, Maria O'Brien*
The true story of a deeply religious couple, who
believed that they could cure their diabetic son
through the power of prayer, and refused to allow him
to be treated by doctors. When he died they were
charged with manslaughter. Arquette and Reinhold
give performances of great sincerity in this moving
tale. The excellent script is by David Hill.
Boa: book We Let Our Son Die by Larry Parker.
DRA                          95 min (ort 100 min) mTV
B,V                          VIR

## PROMISED LAND ** 15
Michael Hoffman          USA          1987
*Kiefer Sutherland, Meg Ryan, Jason Gedrick, Tracy*
*Pollan, Googy Gess, Deborah Richter, Oscar Rowland,*
*Sondra Seacat*
Four friends in small-town America, leave school with
high hopes for their future. Their paths cross two
years later, when there are surprises in store for them.
An atmospheric but patchy melodrama redeemed by
articulate performances.
DRA                          110 min
B,V                          VES

## PRONTO * 18
Franco Prosperi
          ITALY/WEST GERMANY          1976
*Ray Lovelock, Martin Balsam, Elke Sommer, Ettore*
*Manni*
A routine thriller in which a hardbitten cop seeks
revenge when his mother is killed by the bullet that
was meant for him. A typical Italian effort, of jerky
dubbing and muddled plotting.
Aka: PIZAZ; PIZZAZ (MOVLAND); PRONTO AD
UCCIDERE; RISKING (VIP)
THR                          90 min dubbed
B,V     REN L/A; VIP L/A; GLOB; MOVLAND (VHS
only)

## PROPHECIES, THE ** 18
Tom McLoughlin          USA          1989
*John D. Le May, Chris Wiggins*
Grieving over the death of his brother, a young man
travels to France to join his friend at a holy shrine
where people seek cures for body and soul. Unfortu-
nately, a disciple of the Devil has taken up residence
there and is intent on fulfilling six prophecies from a
Satanic book.
HOR                          93 min
V                          CIC

## PROPHECY * 15
John Frankenheimer          USA          1979
*Talia Shire, Robert Foxworth, Armand Assante,*
*Richard Dysart, Victoria Racimo*
A doctor and his musician wife investigate an out-
break of mutant animals in the forests of Maine, and
discover the cause to be mercury poisoning. A point-
less chiller with an ecological slant, that's neither
shocking nor especially interesting, but does deliver a
few unintentional moments of mirth.
HOR                          98 min (ort 102 min) Cut
                           (Cut at film release by 8 sec)
B,V                          CIC

## PROSTITUTE, THE * 18
Tony Garnett          UK          1980
*Eleanor Forsythe, Kate Crutchley, Kim Lockett, Nancy*
*Samuels, Richard Mangan, Phyllis Hickson, Joseph*
*Senior, Ann Whitaker, Paul Arlington, Carol Palmer,*
*Pat Manning, Brigid Phillipa Williams, Colin*
*Hindley, John Evans*
A documentary-style drama on a Birmingham prosti-
tute and her attempts to become a London call-girl. A
dull drama done in the seedy style reserved by British
film-makers for this kind of material.
DRA                          90 min (ort 98 min) Cut (8 sec)
B,V                          VSP L/A; SHEP

## PROSTITUTION RACKET, THE ***
Carlo Lizzani          ITALY          1975
*Cinzia Mambretti, Christina Moranzoni, Lia Di*
*Corato, Danila Grassini, Anna Curti, Anna Rita*
*Grapputi*
Story of six prostitutes and how they take up their
profession, forced into it by the violence and poverty of
their environment.
Aka: PROSTITUTE, THE (PRI); STORIE DI VITA E
MALAVITA
A                          91 min
B,V                          KRP L/A; KMV L/A; PRI

## PROTECTOR, THE ** 18
James Glickenhaus
          HONG KONG/USA          1985
*Jackie Chan, Danny Aiello, Sandy Alexander, Roy*
*Chiao, Bill Wallace*
A tough Chinese cop is sent to Hong Kong to combat
drug dealers. Plenty of martial arts and other action
in a violent and undemanding film. Switch your brain
off and enjoy this fast-paced nonsense.
MAR                          91 min
V/sh                          WHV

## PROTOCOL * PG
Herbert Ross          USA          1984
*Goldie Hawn, Chris Sarandon, Richard Romanus,*
*Andre Gregory, Ed Begley Jr, Gail Strickland, Cliff De*
*Young, Kenneth Mars, Kenneth McMillan*
A cocktail waitress accidentally saves the life of an
Arab sheikh by being shot in the bottom. From such
an unpromising beginning she is given an important-
sounding diplomatic appointment, that is in reality a
sinecure, and finds herself being used as a pawn in
political shenanigans. The film even tries to make a
point, but this gets lost in the silliness of it all.
COM                          91 min (ort 96 min)
V/sh                          WHV

## PROTOTYPE ***
David Greene USA 1983 U

*Christopher Plummer, David Morse, Frances
Sternhagen, James Sutorius, Arthur Hill, Stephen
Elliott, Alley Mills, Ed Call, Jonathan Estrin, Richard
Kuss, Pat McNamara, Vahan Moosekian*

An updated version of the Frankenstein story, with a
Nobel Prize-winner creating a humanoid that arouses
the interests of the military authorities. An unusual
and intriguing basic premise is given an intelligent
treatment, by scriptwriters Richard Levinson and
William Link.

FAN 96 min (ort 100 min) mTV
B,V VFP L/A; HER

## PROUD AND THE DAMNED, THE **
Ferde Grofe Jr USA 1973

*Chuck Connors, Cesar Romero, Jose Greco, Aron
Kincaid, Anita Quinn, Henry Capps, Peter Ford,
Smoky Roberds, Maria Grimm, Dana Lorca, Conrad
Packman, Alvaro Ruiz*

Four Civil War veterans hire out their services as
mercenaries in Latin America, in this routine tale
that doesn't even have particularly interesting performances to enliven it.

WES 93 min (ort 95 min)
B,V,V2 VCL/CBS

## PROUD MEN *
William A. Graham USA 1987 15

*Charlton Heston, Peter Strauss, Belinda Belaski, Alan
Autry, Nan Martin, Maria Mayenzet*

A rancher and his son have a hard time getting along,
and are hardly helped by the inadequacies of the
script in this dreary offering. Heston as the dying,
tough old rancher grinds his jaw a lot, but even this
doesn't suffice.

DRA 99 min mTV
B,V GHV

## PROUD REBEL ***
Michael Curtiz USA 1958 U

*Alan Ladd, David Ladd, Olivia De Havilland, Dean
Jagger, Cecil Kellaway, John Carradine, Henry Hull,
James Westerfield*

At the end of the Civil War, a Southern veteran
wanders the country in search of a doctor who can cure
his mute son (played by Ladd's real-life son David)
and falls for the farm woman he goes to work for. A
predictable piece of family entertainment, but wholesome and quite endearing in a simple-minded way.

WES 99 min (ort 103 min)
V CASPIC

## PRUDENCE AND THE PILL *
Fielder Cook UK 1968 15

*David Niven, Deborah Kerr, Edith Evans, Keith
Michell, Judy Geeson, Joyce Redman, Robert Coote,
Irina Demick, David Dundas, Vickery Turner, Hugh
Armstrong, Peter Butterworth, Moyra Fraser*

A girl borrows her mother's birth pills, replacing them
with aspirins. Naturally, both end up in a state of
pregnancy, in this trite and feeble comedy. The script
is by Mills.
Boa: play by Hugh Mills.

COM 92 min (ort 98 min)
B,V CBS

## PSYCH-OUT **
Richard Rush USA 1968 18

*Susan Strasberg, Dean Stockwell, Jack Nicholson,
Adam Roarke, Max Julien, Bruce Dern, Henry
Jaglom, The Strawberry Alarm Clock, The Seeds*

An attractive deaf runaway, meets up with rock
musicians and assorted weirdos in San Francisco,
when she sets off in search of her missing brother. A
nostalgia trip to the 1960s that serves up an extravaganza of psychedelic effects and some over-heated

acting and dialogue. Not so much a film as a gloriously
dated parody of how it all was.

DRA 85 min
V RCA

## PSYCHO ***
Alfred Hitchcock USA 1960 15

*Anthony Perkins, Vera Miles, Janet Leigh, John
Gavin, Martin Balsam, John McIntire, Patricia
Hitchcock, Simon Oakland, Frank Albertson*

A legendary shocker that may seem tame by today's
standards, but reflects a skill in direction that cannot
be denied. Though slow to develop, it retains moments
of great power. Perkins is superb as the deranged
owner of a motel to which a girl flees after she has
defrauded her employer. Written by Joseph Stefano
with music by Bernard Herrmann. Several sequels
have followed.
Boa: novel by Robert Bloch.

HOR 108 min B/W
B,V CIC

## PSYCHO 2 ***
Richard Franklin USA 1983 18

*Anthony Perkins, Vera Miles, Meg Tilly, Robert
Loggia, Dennis Franz, Hugh Gillin*

An competent sequel to the 1960 film, with Norman
Bates now released from his mental hospital after 22
years, and returning to his motel where he tries to
carry on running his business. Unfortunately, the
murders soon start afresh and poor Norman begins to
doubt his sanity. Suspense is nicely maintained right
up to the surprise ending. Followed by PSYCHO 3.

HOR 109 min (ort 113 min)
V/sh CIC

## PSYCHO 3 *
Anthony Perkins USA 1986 18

*Diana Scarwid, Jeff Fahey, Anthony Perkins, Roberta
Maxwell, Maureen Coyle, Hugh Gillin, Lee Garlington,
Robert Alan Browne, Gary Bayer, Juliette Cummins,
Patience Cleveland, Steve Guevara, Kay Heberle,
Donovan Scott*

Perkins' directing debut marks yet another return to
the Bates Motel, where poor Norman Bates finds that
one of his guests is intent on creating her own
personal bloodbath. He begins to fall in love with her,
but the disapproval of his "mother", and several other
events soon drive him over the edge into his bloodiest
massacre to date. A feast of gore and unpleasantness
that's devoid of tension or style.

HOR 89 min (ort 96 min)
V/sh CIC

## PSYCHO FROM TEXAS *
Jim Faezell USA 1974 18

*John Henry III, Candy Dee, Janel King, Joanne
Bruno, Tommy Lamey, Reed Johnson, Jack Collins,
Herschell Mays*

A violent story of kidnapping and murder in a quiet
Southern town, with a battered child growing up into
a murderer and rapist.
Aka: BUTCHER, THE (SATRO); EVIL + HATE =
KILLER (MARKET); HURTING, THE; MAMMA'S
BOY, THE; WHEELER

HOR 78 min (ort 85 min) Cut (5 min 20 sec)
B,V SATPRO L/A; MARKET

## PSYCHO GIRLS *
Gerald Ciccoritti CANADA 1984 18

*John Haslett Cuff, Agi Gallus, Darlene Mignacco, Pier
Giorgio DiCicco, Silvio Oliviero, Rose Graham*

An innocent married couple are captured and terrorised by a pair of deranged sisters. Unpleasant,
exploitative dross. See also DEATH GAME, for something similar.

HOR 92 min (ort 96 min)
V CIC

## PSYCHOCOP *                                  18
Wallace Potts              USA              1989
*Bobby Ray Shafer, Jeff Qualle*
Confused attempt by the same producers to exploit the
appeal of MANIAC COP, that combines the concept of
a murderous police enforcer with elements of horror
and slasher films. The title figure pursues a group of
college students and their girlfriends, who are on their
way to a weekend in the country, and the expected
series of sinister events unfolds.
HOR                                        84 min
V                                            RCA

## PSYCHOMANIA **
Don Sharp                  UK               1972
*Beryl Reid, George Sanders, Nicky Henson, Mary*
*Larkin, Patrick Holt, Robert Hardy, Ann Michelle, Roy*
*Holder, Denis Gilmore, Miles Greenwood, Rocky*
*Taylor, Peter Whiting, June Brown, Jacki Webb,*
*David Millett, Linda Gray*
A nasty gang of motorcyclists make a deal with the
Devil and become virtually indestructible, as they
proceed to ravage and destroy the surrounding coun-
tryside. Bizarre, violent and occasionally uninten-
tionally amusing. Written by Arnaud D'Usseau.
Aka: DEATH WHEELERS, THE; FROG, THE;
LIVING DEAD, THE; PSYCHO MANIA
HOR                                        95 min
B,V                                       VCL/CBS

## PSYCHOPATH, THE **                           18
Curtis Harrington          USA               1973
*John Savage, Cindy Williams, Ann Sothern, Ruth*
*Roman, Luana Anders, Sue Bernard, Helene Winston,*
*Marjorie Eaton, Peter Brocco*
A St Louis investigator is called in to help a small
town plagued by a series of brutal murders, and learns
of a young man who is out to exact revenge on those
who had him framed on a rape charge.
Aka: KILLING KIND, THE (INT/CBS)
DRA          90 min; 88 min (INT/CBS) Cut (9 sec)
B,V                     INT/CBS; MPV; GLOB; IFS; DFS

## P'TANG, YANG, KIPPERBANG *                   PG
Michael Apted              UK               1982
*John Albasiny, Alison Steadman, Garry Cooper,*
*Abigail Cruttenden, Maurice Dee, Mark Brailsford,*
*Chris Karallis, Frances Ruffelle, Robert Urquhart,*
*Garry Cooper, Maurice O'Connell, Tim Seeley,*
*Richenda Carey, Peter Dean*
The story of young teenage love in Britain of 1948.
Another trip down nostalgia lane; an all too frequent
destination for British film-makers. Written by Jack
Rosenthal.
Aka: KIPPERBANG
COM                          77 min (ort 80 min) mTV
B,V                                         TEVP

## PUBERTY BLUES **                             15
Bruce Beresford     AUSTRALIA              1981
*Neil Schofield, Jad Capelja, Geoff Rhoe, Tony Hughes,*
*Sandy Paul*
The growing pains of two teenage girls who are
Australian surfing groupies, are examined in this
hackneyed effort that does at least have the unusual
aspect of telling it all from the girls' point of view. The
script is by Margaret Kelly.
Boa: novel by Kathy Lette and Gabrielle Carey.
COM                          81 min (ort 86 min)
B,V,V2                                      TEVP

## PUBLIC ENEMY, THE ***                        PG
William Wellman            USA               1931
*James Cagney, Edward Woods, Jean Harlow, Joan*
*Blondell, Donald Cook, Mae Clarke, Beryl Mercer,*
*Leslie Fenton*
This powerful and entertaining film put Cagney on
the road to stardom. It tells of two slum kids who grow
up into gangsters and eventually get their just

deserts. Contains the fondly remembered scene in
which Cagney pushes a grapefruit into Mae Clarke's
face. Written by Harvey Thew, Kubec Glasmon and
John Bright.
Aka: ENEMIES OF THE PUBLIC
DRA                       80 min (ort 96 min) B/W
V                                            WHV

## PULSE ***                                    18
Paul Golding               USA               1988
*Cliff De Young, Roxanne Hart, Joey Lawrence*
A family is terrorised by domestic appliances that
become deadly, when a massive electrical surge
becomes imbued with a malevolent intelligence. An
unusual tale told with skill and directness.
HOR                           87 min (ort 90 min)
B,V                                          RCA

## PUMPING IRON ***                             PG
George Butler/Robert Fiore
                           USA               1976
*Arnold Schwarzenegger, Lou Ferrigno, Matty*
*Ferrigno, Victoria Ferrigno, Mike Katz*
This excellent documentary on male bodybuilding
follows Schwarzenegger and Ferrigno as they compete
for the Mr Universe title. A fascinating behind-the-
scenes look at a very specialised sport, that benefits
considerably from a strong sense of respect for the
competitors and Schwarzenegger's engaging personality. Followed by "Pumping Iron 2: The Women", an
altogether inferior film.
Boa: book by C. Gaines/George Butler.
DOC                           82 min (ort 85 min)
V                                            HEND

## PUNCH AND JODY **
Barry Shear                USA               1974
*Glenn Ford, Pam Griffin, Ruth Roman, Kathleen*
*Widdoes, Susan Brown, Parley Baer, Donald Barry,*
*Billy Barty, Mel Stewart, Cynthia Hayward, Patty*
*Maloney, Pat Morita, Peter Ford, Read Morgan,*
*Barbara Rhoades*
A circus manager suddenly finds himself left with the
custody of a teenage daughter he never knew he had,
when his wife dies. A pleasant little melodrama of no
great consequence.
DRA                                       78 min mTV
B,V                                          IFS

## PUNCH THE CLOCK **                           18
Eric L. Schlagman          USA               1988
*Mike Rogen, Chris Moore*
A female criminal and a prison administrator fall in
love and are drawn into a murderous intrigue.
A/AD                                       90 min
V                                            BOX

## PUNCHLINE ***                                15
David Seltzer              USA               1988
*Tom Hanks, Sally Fields, John Goodman, Mark*
*Rydell, Kim Griest, Pam Matteson, Taylor Negron,*
*Barry Neikrug, Mae Robbins, Max Alexander, Paul*
*Kozlowski, Barry Sobel*
An odd couple help each other make their way in the
world of New York stand-up comedians. Fields is a
housewife and aspiring comedienne and Hanks her
mentor and would-be lover; both are excellent in this
surprisingly effective if overlong look at two obsessed
individuals. The perceptive and witty script is by
Seltzer.
COM                           122 min (ort 128 min)
V                                            RCA

## PUNISHER, THE *                              18
Mark Goldblatt             USA               1990
*Dolph Lundgren, Louis Gossett Jr, Jeroen Krabbe,*
*Nancy Everhard, Kim Miyori, Barry Otto*
Inspired by the Marvel Comics character, this sees a
cop going underground to take his revenge when his

family is wiped out by gangsters. He appears to be all set for retirement until a Yakuza kidnaps the children of a Mafia leader in a bid for dominance, and he embarks on a rescue mission. A humourless film of relentless violence and action.

A/AD 86 min
V 20VIS

## PUPPET MASTER ***
David Schmoeller    USA    18    1989
*Paul LeMat, Jimmie F. Scaggs, Irene Miracle, Robin Frates, Matt Roe, William Hickey, Barbara Crampton*
A master puppet-maker has used an ancient Egyptian power to imbue his creations with life, and following his suicide a group of psychics gather at a creepy hotel to locate them. However, the demonic creations have other ideas in this implausible but rather scary film. The special effects and animation work of David Allen are excellent. A sequel followed.

HOR 86 min (ort 90 min)
V EIV

## PUPPET MASTER 2 **
David Allen    USA    18    1989
*Elizabeth MacLellan, Collin Bernsen, Greg Webb, Nita Talbot*
Sequel to the first film that sees our murderous puppets back for another bout of murder, this time the victims are a team of scientific researchers. Average.

HOR 87 min
V EIV

## PUPPET ON A CHAIN **
Geoffrey Reeve    UK    1970
*Sven-Bertil Taube, Alexander Knox, Patrick Allen, Barbara Parkins, Vladek Sheybal, Peter Hutchins, Ania Mason, Penny Casdagli, Henri Orri, Stewart Lane*
A rather wooden adaptation of a story about an American narcotics agent hunting drug smugglers in Amsterdam. Remembered chiefly for an excellent chase sequence that makes use of Amsterdam's waterways and is, in fact, the highlight of the film.
Boa: novel by Alistair MacLean.

THR 98 min
B,V,V2 GHV

## PURE HELL OF ST TRINIANS, THE *
Frank Launder    UK    U    1957
*Cecil Parker, Joyce Grenfell, George Cole, Eric Baker, Thorley Walters, Irene Handl, Dennis Price, Sidney James, Julie Alexander, Lloyd Lamble, Raymond Huntley, Nicholas Phipps, Liz Fraser, John Le Mesurier, Lisa Lee*
Yes, and it's pure hell watching this garbage, with our wayward schoolgirls back in their second sequel. In this one a rich Arab sheikh visits the school, looking for fresh recruits for his harem. Like so much British comedy – tame, tedious and trite. Followed by THE GREAT ST TRINIANS TRAIN ROBBERY.

COM 90 min (ort 94 min)
(Cut at film release) B/W
V WHV

## PURELY PHYSICAL ***
Billy Thornberg    USA    R18    1982
*Jade Wong, Juliet Anderson, Joey Civera, Laura Lazore, Kitty Shane, Lysa Thatcher, Michael Morrison, Sidney Fellows, Tiger (Chelsea Manchester), Dana Moore*
A female student studying writing at a local university, takes a job in a motel and decides to keep a journal of her experiences. The film then moves on to explore a variety of liaisons between couples and singles that check into the motel. Some scenes are funny, some sad, and most are convincing. Eventually, our writer falls for a travelling salesman and they decide to get married.

A 80 min
B,V EVI

## PURPLE HEARTS **
Sidney J. Furie    USA    15    1984
*Cheryl Ladd, Ken Wahl, Stephen Lee, David Harris, Lane Smith, James Whitmore Jr, Lee Ermey, Annie McEnroe, Paul McCrane*
A navy surgeon in the Vietnam War falls in love with a nurse, and volunteers for a dangerous mission in order to qualify for leave. An overlong and underplotted saga, one in a series of Harlequin romances.

DRA 110 min (ort 115 min)
B,V WHV

## PURPLE PEOPLE EATER, THE **
Linda Shayne    USA    U    1988
*Ned Beatty, Shelley Winters, Neil Patrick Harris, Peggy Lipton, Chubby Checker, Little Richard, James Houghton, Thora Birch, Molly Cheek*
Inspired by a 1959 pop song, this silly kid's tale has a friendly alien arriving on Earth, just in time to help out some senior citizens faced with the prospect of eviction, and some local teens who want to form a rock band. Corny fun for six-year-olds and under.

JUV 85 min (ort 91 min)
B,V CIC

## PURPLE PLAIN, THE ***
Robert Parrish    UK    1954
*Gregory Peck, Maurice Denham, Win Min Than, Bernard Lee, Lyndon Brook, Ram Gopal, Brenda De Banzie, Anthony Bushell, Josephine Griffin, Peter Arne, Jack McNaughton, Dorothy Alison, Mya Mya Spencer, Soo Ah Song*
A WW2 pilot is slowly cracking up under the strain of flying, whilst trying to forget the death of his wife in an air-raid. When he meets and falls in love with a beautiful Burmese girl, he realises that he does have a reason to go on living after all. After crashing in the jungle with two comrades, he decides to spare no effort to get back to his base, despite the fact that his navigator cannot walk. The intelligent script is by Eric Ambler.
Boa: novel by H.E. Bates.

WAR 96 min (ort 100 min)
B,V RNK

## PURPLE RAIN **
Albert Magnoli    USA    15    1984
*Prince, Appollonia Kotero, Morris Day, Olga Karlatos, Jerome Benton, Billy Sparks, Clarence Williams III*
Really just a vehicle for singer Prince, this is the story of a performer struggling to gain acceptance in his fight to reach the top. Without the score, this dull effort would have little merit in its own right. Prince's film debut. AA: Score (Prince/John L. Nelson/The Revolution).

MUS 107 min (ort 113 min)
V/s WHV

## PURPLE ROSE OF CAIRO, THE ***
Woody Allen    USA    PG    1984
*Mia Farrow, Danny Aiello, Jeff Daniels, Dianne Wiest, Van Johnson, Milo O'Shea, Zoe Caldwell, Edward Herrmann, Stephanie Farrow, Karen Akers, John Wood, Deborah Rush, Michael Tucker*
The downtrodden housewife in a small American town in the 1930s, finds escape from reality by repeatedly visiting the cinema to see the title film. Things take an unexpected turn when the film's leading man falls in love with her and steps down from the screen. A clinically effective comedy, that would be cold indeed without the warmth Farrow and Aiello bring it.

COM 78 min (ort 82 min)
B,V RNK; VIR (VHS only)

## PURSUED **
Raoul Walsh    USA    PG    1947
*Teresa Wright, Robert Mitchum, Judith Anderson, Dean Jagger, Alan Hale, John Rodney, Harry Carey Jr, Clifton Young, Ernest Severn, Charles Bates, Peggy*

*Miller, Norman Jolley, Lane Chandler, Elmer Ellingwood, Jack Montgomery*
Having been brought up by a couple who have never shown him any affection, an orphan eventually goes off to fight in the Spanish-American War. He returns determined to find out who killed his father years ago, but causes a tragedy for his adoptive parents, before ultimately learning the truth. A grim and offbeat Western, well acted but rather unappealing.

WES                                        101 min B/W
V                                                    VIR

## PURSUIT **                                    15
Roger Spottiswode          USA            1981
*Treat Williams, Robert Duvall, Kathryn Harrold, Ed Flanders, Paul Gleason, R.G. Armstrong, Nicolas Coster, Cooper Huckabee, Christopher Curry, Dorothy Fielding, Howard K. Smith, Ramon Chavez, Stacy Newton, Pat Ast, Jack Dunlap*
The true story of a former Green Beret who stole $200,000, parachuted from a Boeing 707 and was never heard of again. Written by Jeffrey Alan Fiskin. A flawed adventure yarn with comic overtones and a lack of substance and competence.
Aka: IN PURSUIT OF D.B. COOPER; PURSUIT OF D.B. COOPER, THE
Boa: novel Free Fall by J.D. Reed.

A/AD                                       100 min
B,V                                          POLY

## PURSUIT ***                                   15
Thomas Quillen             USA            1975
*Ray Danton, DeWitt Lee, Troy Nabors, Diane Taylor, Eva Kovacs, Jason Clark*
After being wounded in an encounter with a bear, an army scout finds that he has become prey to a more dangerous enemy – an Indian brave, out to kill him in revenge for the massacre of an Apache camp by the Cavalry. A taut and unusual Western thriller. The screenplay is by DeWitt Lee and Jack Lee.

WES                                         92 min
B,V                   PMA L/A; VIV L/A; POLY

## PUSHING UP DAISIES **
Ivan Nagy                  USA            1972
*Ross Hagen, Kelly Thordsen, Christopher George, Hoke Howell, Eric Lidberg, Dal Jenkins, Jack Sowards, Tony Lorea, Lu Dorn, Arne Warda, Lenny Geer, Kenny MacKenzie, Bob Padilla, Vince Garcia, Leslie McRay, Gay Hearsum*
After a daring bank raid, a sheriff pursues four members of the gang across the border into Mexico.
Aka: THEIR BREAKFAST MEANT LEAD

WES                        85 min; 96 min (INT)
B,V                                 MEV L/A; INT

## PUSS IN BOOTS **                               U
Eugene Marner              USA            1987
*Jason Connery, Christopher Walken, Yossi Graber*
Film version of this famous fairytale, of the cat that helped young Dick Whittington become Lord Mayor of London.
Boa: short story by Charles Perrault.

JUV                           93 min (ort 96 min)
V/sh                              VCC L/A; WHV

## PUSS 'N BOOTS *                              R18
Chuck Vincent              USA            1983
*Kelly Nichols, Jade East, Sharon Kane, J.T. Ambrose, Cheri Champagne, Ron Hudd, David James, George Payne, Michael Knight*
Sex film trading on the success of PRIVATE BEN-JAMIN, with a female soldier scheming to get pregnant so that she can gain her discharge. A unappealing and rather brutal film, whose deficiencies of plot are largely balanced by an excess of coarseness.

A                      62 min Cut (4 min 36 sec)
B,V                                 EVI; SHEP

## PUSSY TALK **
Danille Bellus/Claude Mulot (Frederic Lanzac)
                         FRANCE            1975
*Francis Le Roy, Nils Hortz, Penelope Lamour, Ellen Earl-Cauprey, Sylvia Bourdon*
A bizarre sex comedy in which a woman is unable to control her talkative sexual organ, which insists on telling her husband about her sex life both before and during marriage as well as contradicting her expressions of marital devotion. A most peculiar film whose basic idea (not really quite as funny as it sounds) hampers its development.
Aka: PUSSY TALK: LE SEXE QUI PARLE

A                            91 min dubbed
B,V                                          WOV

## PUSSYCAT SYNDROME **                           18
Irvin Miles          WEST GERMANY         1983
*Ajita Wilson, Jacqueline Marcan, Tina Eklund, Herbert Hofer, Cristus Nicoeul, Tony Woolf, Don Caverman, Nastassja Nataly, George Filipou, Carmella Bassi, Nina Georgiou, Marcella Banezi, Bobies Provatas*
Two models in Greece enjoy a variety of adventures and end up staying on a millionaire's yacht.

A                            73 min (ort 85 min)
                            (Abridged at film release)
B,V                                          ELV

## PYGMALION ****                                 U
Anthony Asquith/Leslie Howard
                         UK               1938
*Wendy Hiller, Leslie Howard, Wilfrid Lawson, Marie Lohr, Scott Sunderland, Jean Cadell, David Tree, Everley Gregg, Leueen McGrath, Esme Percy, Violet Vanbrugh, Iris Hoey, Viola Tree, Irene Browne, Wally Patch, H.F. Maltby*
An excellent straight version of Shaw's play, with sparkling, witty performances, following the exploits of a professor who, having boasted to a friend that he could teach a flower girl to talk like a duchess, is presented with the opportunity to do so. Remade as the musical MY FAIR LADY. Shaw's screenplay and its adaptation both won Oscars. AA: Screen (George Bernard Shaw and Ian Dalrymple/Cecil Lewis/W.P. Lipscomb for adaptation).
Boa: play by George Bernard Shaw.

COM                                        95 min B/W
V                                               CH5

## PYX, THE ***
Harvey Hart              CANADA           1973
*Karen Black, Christopher Plummer, Donald Pilon, Lee Broker, Jacques Grodin, Yvette Brind'Amour, Jean-Louis Roux, Terry Haig, Robin Gammell, Louise Rinfret, Julie Wildman, Francine Morand, Jean-Louis Paris*
A detective investigating the death of a prostitute stumbles across a strange black magic cult, in this unusual blend of detective, horror and SF genres.

THR                                        111 min
B,V                                          BWV

# Q

## Q PLANES *                                     U
Tim Whelan               UK               1939
*Laurence Olivier, Ralph Richardson, Valerie Hobson, George Merritt, George Curzon, Gus McNaughton, David Tree, Sandra Storme, Hay Petrie, Frank Fox, Gordon McLeod, John Longden, Reginald Purdell, George Butler, John Laurie*
A test pilot and a Scotland Yard detective join forces to investigate the disappearance of a number of aircraft on test flights, and discover an espionage conspiracy. The first half of the film is exciting but it descends rapidly into a disappointingly cliched chase

movie, with a few comic touches.
Aka: CLOUDS OVER EUROPE
THR                                          82 min B/W
V                                            PICK

## Q: THE WINGED SERPENT *
Larry Cohen          USA                     1982
*David Carradine, Michael Moriarty, Richard*
*Roundtree, Candy Clark, John Capodice, James*
*Dixon, Malachy McCourt, Fred J. Scollay, Peter Hock,.*
*Ron Cey, Mary Louise Weller*
An Aztec deity finds its way to New York, where it
carries out a number of grisly murders from its safe
perch atop the Chrysler building. A small-time crook
discovers its nest and holds the city to ransom,
demanding a huge payment to reveal the location, in
this cheerfully trashy nonsense.
Aka: Q; WINGED SERPENT, THE
HOR                                          92 min
B,V                                          HOK

## QUACKSER FORTUNE HAS A COUSIN
## IN THE BRONX **
Warris Hussein       EIRE                    1970
*Gene Wilder, Margot Kidder, Eileen Colgen, Seamus*
*Ford, May Ollis, Liz Davis, Caroline Tully, Paul*
*Murphy, David Kelly*
A young Dubliner who makes his living by collecting
horse manure, falls for an American exchange stu-
dent, but is bitterly disappointed when he realises that
the social gap between them is too wide to bridge. At
the same time, plans to pension off the remaining
horse-drawn vehicles force him to re-assess his life. A
none-too-convincing fairytale that doesn't really
work.
Aka: FUN LOVING
COM                                          90 min
B,V                                          VFP; VCC

## QUADROPHENIA ***                          18
Franc Roddam         UK                      1979
*Phil Daniels, Mark Wingett, Philip Davis, Sting*
*(Gordon Sumner), The Who, Kate Williams, Michael*
*Elphick, John Bindon, Garry Cooper, Leslie Ash,*
*Toyah Wilcox, Trevor Laird, Raymond Winstone, Gary*
*Shail, Kim Neve, John Phillips*
Highly enjoyable rock-musical combining the music of
The Who with a nice feel for the mood of the 1960s,
when Mods and Rockers battled it out on the beaches
of Britain's seaside resorts. Written by Dave Hum-
phries, Martin Stellman and Franc Roddam. Sting's
acting debut. Inspired by a record album of the same
name.
DRA                              113 min (ort 120 min)
B,V                              POLY; CH5 (VHS only)

## QUARANTINE *                              18
Charles Wilkinson    USA                     1989
*Beatrice Boepple, Garwin Sanford, Jerry Wasserman*
Confused SF thriller set in a bleak future, where those
suspected of being contaminated with a deadly virus
are forcibly quarantined in vast prison camps. When a
power-mad senator begins to abuse this system for his
own ends, he is opposed by a brave woman who enlists
the help of a brilliant scientist, and together they
mount a campaign to stop him. A set of good ideas
never come to fruition in this poorly made affair.
FAN                                          89 min
V                                            BOX

## QUARE FELLOW, THE ***                     15
Arthur Dreifuss      EIRE                    1962
*Patrick McGoohan, Sylvia Syms, Walter Macken,*
*Dermot Kelly, Jack Cunningham, Hilton Edwards*
At a Dublin prison a new warder learns the reasons
behind a condemned man's murder of his brother and
comes to doubt the usefulness of capital punishment.
A competent adaptation of the successful stage play,

this engaging tragi-comedy retains some of the
humour but most of the melancholy of the original.
McGoohan is well cast as the uncertain young warder
and the articulate script is by Dreifuss.
Boa: play by Brendan Behan.
DRA                              80 min (ort 90 min) B/W
V                                            CONNO

## QUARTET ***
Ralph Smart/Harold French/Arthur Crabtree/Ken
Annakin              UK                       1948
*Basil Radford, Naunton Wayne, Mai Zetterling,*
*Angela Baddeley, Dirk Bogarde, Francoise Rosay,*
*Honor Blackman, Irene Browne, Hermione Baddeley,*
*Mervyn Johns, Susan Shaw, George Cole, Cecil*
*Parker, Linden Travers, Nora Swinburne*
Four short stories each with a different cast and
director, each tale being introduced by Maugham. The
episodes are of variable quality but the whole effort
works extremely well. Stories are entitled: "The Facts
Of Life", "The Alien Corn", "The Kite", and "The
Colonel's Lady". The success of this film prompted the
sequel "Trio".
Aka: SOMERSET MAUGHAM'S QUARTET
Boa: short stories by William Somerset Maugham.
DRA                             118 min (ort 120 min) B/W
B,V                                          RNK

## QUARTET ***                               18
James Ivory          FRANCE/UK               1981
*Isabelle Adjani, Alan Bates, Maggie Smith, Anthony*
*Higgins, Pierre Clementi, Daniel Mesguich, Virginie*
*Thevenet, Suzanne Flon, Sheila Gish, Daniel Chatto,*
*Paulita Sedgewick, Bernice Stegers, Isabelle Canto da*
*Maya*
Traces the lives of four expatriates in Paris in the late
1920s, with Adjani being taken in by Bates when her
husband is imprisoned. A drama of decadence and
decay, written by Ruth Prawer Jhabvala.
Boa: novel by Jean Rhys.
DRA                             96 min (ort 101 min)
B,V                                          CBS

## QUATERMASS AND THE PIT **                 PG
Rudolph Cartier      UK        1957 (shown 1958/59)
*Andre Morell, Cec Linder, Christine Finn, Anthony*
*Bushell, John Stration*
Compilation of the six 30-minute episodes, of the third
series of a popular set of SF stories, that ran
intermittently from 1953 until 1979. This tale deals
with the discovery of an alien spacecraft at a new
excavation for a London underground station. Closer
examination reveals that the vessel is imbued by its
makers with a hostile form of energy that has the
potential to enslave mankind. Written by Nigel
Kneale and remade in 1967. Fair.
FAN                              178 min B/W mTV
V/h                                          BBC

## QUATERMASS CONCLUSION, THE **            15
Piers Haggard        UK                      1980
*John Mills, Barbara Kellerman, Simon*
*MacCorkindale, Margaret Tyzack, Brewster Mason*
A late addition to those "Quatermass" films of the
1950s, in which our intrepid professor had to battle it
out with alien menaces. Here Professor Quatermass
finds that aliens are trying to take over the Earth by
affecting the minds of young people, and causing
society to break down. Fairly imaginative but seriously hampered by the low budget.
FAN                        107 min; 102 min (VCC) mTV
B,V                             TEVP; VCC (VHS only)

## QUEEN CHRISTINA ****                       U
Rouben Mamoulian     USA                      1933
*Greta Garbo, John Gilbert, Lewis Stone, Ian Keith,*
*Elizabeth Young, C. Aubrey Smith, Gustav von*
*Seyffertitz, Reginald Owen*

Unable to face the prospect of an arranged marriage, the queen of 17th century Sweden dons man's clothes and goes off in search of adventure, only to fall in love with the newly-arrived Spanish ambassador. Stilted, over-sentimental and historically inaccurate it may be, but this charming romance shows the star to her best advantage, the tragic ending is quite moving. Garbo never looked more radiant.

DRA 100 min B/W
V MGM

## QUEEN FOR CAESAR, A **
Victor Tourjansky  FRANCE  1962
*Pascale Petit, Gordon Scott, Akim Tamiroff*
The story of the struggle for power between Cleopatra and her brother.

DRA 95 min
B,V,V2 VPD

## QUEEN OF EVIL **
18
Oliver Stone  CANADA  1974
*Herve Villechaize, Jonathan Frid, Martine Beswicke, Christina Pickles, Henry Baker, Mary Woronov, Joe Sirola, Troy Donahue, Roger De Koven, Anne Meacham, Timothy Ousey, Richard Cox, Lucy Bingham, Emil Meola, Timothy Rowse*
A horror writer's weekend party, is interrupted by three sinister guests who seem to be figments of his imagination and who force him and his family to play strange games. Flashy but disjointed and ultimately unsatisfying. This was Stone's directorial debut.
Aka: SEIZURE! (WHV)

HOR 94 min
V GOV L/A; AST L/A; MARKET; WHV; RCA

## QUEEN OF HEARTS **
PG
Jon Amiel 1989
*Vittorio Duse, Joseph Long, Anita Zagaria, Eileen Way*
An account of the life of an Italian immigrant couple, from the days when they fled an arranged marriage in Italy to their arrival and eventual prosperity in England. Some years later, a threat to their happiness appears in the shape of a figure from the past. A standard melodrama.

DRA 112 min
V MGM

## QUEEN OF SPADES, THE ***
Thorold Dickinson  UK  1948
*Anton Walbrook, Edith Evans, Ronald Howard, Yvonne Mitchell, Mary Jerrold, Anthony Dawson, Miles Malleson, Athene Seyler, Michael Medwin, Pauline Tennant, Ivor Barnard, Valentine Dyall, Yusef Ramart, Gibb McLaughlin*
An impoverished Russian army officer tries to extract the secret of winning at cards from an aged countess. A rather slow story with some macabre moments. Written by Rodney Ackland and Arthur Boys, with music by Georges Auric. Set in 1806.
Boa: novel by Alexander S. Pushkin.

DRA 92 min (ort 96 min) B/W
B,V TEVP

## QUEEN OF THE BLUES *
18
Willie Roe  UK  1979
*John M. West, Allen Warren, Lynn Dean, Ballard Berkeley, Robert Russell, Felix Browness, Milton Reid, Geraldine Hooper, Mary Millington, Cindy Truman, Nicola Austin, Lydia Lloyd, Rosalind Watts, Rosemary England*
A stuffy gentleman's club is turned into a strip joint using an uncle's money, but the club is threatened by racketeers. A feeble sex comedy that goes nowhere.

A 62 min
B,V,V2 HOK L/A; MIG

## QUEENIE: PARTS 1 AND 2 **
PG
Larry Peerce  USA  1987
*Kirk Douglas, Mia Sara, Joel Grey, Topol (Chaim*

*Topol), Claire Bloom, Sarah Miles, Leigh Lawson, Martin Balsam, Joss Ackland, Rosalie Crutchley*
A young woman from the slums of Calcutta becomes a Hollywood star, but finds that fame and fortune inevitably arouse resentment among the less fortunate. A lush but undistinguished adaptation of Korda's bestseller, said to be based to some extent on the life of Merle Oberon.
Boa: novel by Michael Korda.

DRA 245 min (2 cassettes) mTV
B/h, V/h NWV

## QUEEN'S RANSOM, A **
Ting Shan-Si  HONG KONG  1976
*George Lazenby, Judith Brown, Jimmy Wang Yu, Ko Chun-Hsuing, Angela Mao Ying, Tien Ni, Hsing Hwa-Chiang*
A squad of terrorists plans to immobilise Hong Kong in a daring gold robbery.

THR 87 min
B,V RNK L/A

## QUERELLE **
18
Rainer Werner Fassbinder
FRANCE/WEST GERMANY 198
*Brad Davis, Jeanne Moreau, Franco Nero, Gunther Kaufmann, Hanno Poschl, Laurent Malet*
Fassbinder's final film tells of a French sailor who, after murdering a fellow seaman, goes to a notorious brothel in Brest and discovers his homosexuality. Here he comes to terms with his true nature, and the other habitues of the place fall victim to his charms. Shot in a garish series of studio sets, replete with macho icons, this film attempts to say something of interest but is ultimately overwhelmed by layers of tedium.
Aka: QUERELLE DE BREST
Boa: novel by Jean Genet.

DRA 106 min; 103 min (PAL) (ort 120 min)
B,V PVG; PAL (VHS only)

## QUEST FOR EDEN **
15
William Olsen  USA  1988
*Sam Bottoms, Page Hannah, Renee Coleman, Edward Binns, James Farkas, Robert Lansing, Dick Cavett*
A young student becomes hopelessly smitten with her attractive professor, and they embark on a passionate affair.
Aka: AFTER SCHOOL

DRA 90 min
B,V CINE

## QUEST FOR FIRE ***
15
Jean-Jacques Annaud
CANADA/FRANCE 1981
*Everett McGill, Rae Dawn Chong, Ron Perlman, Nameer El Kadi, Gary Schwartz, Frank Olivier Bonnet, Kurt Schiegl, Brian Gill, Terry Fitt, Bibi Caspari, Peter Elliott, Michelle Leduc, Robert Lavoie, Matt Birman, Christian Benard*
Saga of a Stone Age tribe which loses its fire and has to discover how it is made, so three members of the tribe go off in search of some. Despite some unintentionally funny moments, the film works well enough. The special sign language used was devised by Anthony Burgess, and Desmond Morris advised with regard to body language. The film was shot in Kenya, Canada, Scotland and Iceland. AA: Make (Sarah Monzani/Michele Burke).
Aka: LA GUERRE DU FEU
Boa: novel Le Felin Geant (Quest Of The Dawn Man) by J.H. Rosny Sr.

FAN 96 min (ort 100 min) Cut
(Cut at film release by 8 sec)
B,V CBS

## QUEST FOR KING SOLOMON'S
U
## MINES, THE **
Kurt Neumann  USA  1959

*George Montgomery, Taina Elg, David Farrar, Rex Ingram, Dan Seymour*
A dull sequel to KING SOLOMON'S MINES, made on the cheap by using footage from the 1950 version of that film. Not quite as bad as one might have expected, but not all that good either.
Aka: WATUSI

| A/AD | | 80 min (ort 85 min) |
| V | | CROS; GLOB; KRP |

### QUEST FOR LOVE *** PG
Ralph Thomas          UK          1971
*Tom Bell, Joan Collins, Denholm Elliott, Laurence Naismith, Lyn Ashley, Neil McCallum, Simon Ward, Juliet Harmer, Trudy Van Doorn, Jeremy Child, Ray McAnally, John Hallam, Geraldine Moffatt, David Weston, Drewe Henley*
A scientist is projected into a parallel universe, where he finds that he's a writer married to a woman who is soon to die. An engaging SF yarn with a good basic premise and a rather neat plot.
Boa: short story Random Quest by John Wyndham.

| FAN | | 87 min (ort 90 min) (Cut at film release) |
| B,V | | RNK; VCC |

### QUEST FOR LOVE ** 15
Helena Noguiera                    1989
*Sandra Prinsloo, Jana Cilliers, Wayne Bowman*
Alex (Cilliers) is a bigoted journalist and political activist who sets out to find herself but instead gets caught up in a web of violence, lust and intrigue. Average melodramatics.

| DRA | | 91 min |
| V | | NWV |

### QUEST, THE * U
Rod Holcomb          USA          1982
*Perry King, Noah Beery, Ray Vitte, Karen Austin, John Rhys Davies, Michael Billington, William Lucking, Ralph Michael, James Sloyan*
A mythical kingdom is bound by a treaty that could cause it to revert to France, should rule of the kingdom fail to pass to a direct descendant of the throne. The present ruler discovers the existence of four youngsters who are eligible, and presents them with a set of tasks in order to select one to rule. A pilot for a failed series, this banal little affair is not even enlivened by interesting action sequences.

| A/AD | | 90 min mTV |
| B,V | | CIC |

### QUESTION OF GUILT, A ** 15
Robert Butler          USA          1978
*Tuesday Weld, Ron Leibman, Viveca Lindfors, Lana Wood, Peter Masterson, Alex Rocco, Stephen Pearlman, Ron Rifkin, David Wilson, Jim Antonio, M. Emmet Walsh, Kelly Jean Peters, Mari Gorman, Katherine Bard, Nicky Blair*
A loose-living woman is accused of murdering her two children, and has to contend with both a prejudiced policeman and a power-hungry D.A. who is anxious for re-election. Fairly run-of-the-mill melodrama inspired by the real-life case of New Yorker Alice Crimmins.

| DRA | | 91 min (ort 96 min) mTV |
| B,V | | POLY |

### QUESTION OF LIFE, A *** PG
Lou Antonio          USA          1977
*Geraldine Page, Gerald S. O'Loughlin, Marc Singer, Jeff Lynas, Linda Kelsey, Steve Guttenberg, Paul Picerni, Linda Kelsey, Brian Farrell, Katherine Beller, Stephen Parr, David Hooks, June Dayton, James Karen, David Garfield*
A football star has to cope with the fact that his younger brother is terminally ill with leukaemia. A dramatisation of the real-life relationship between football star John Cappelletti and his brother, that holds its sentiment well in check and is all the better

for it.
Aka: SOMETHING FOR JOEY

| DRA | | 89 min (ort 100 min) mTV |
| V | | CROS |

### QUESTION OF LOVE, A *** 
Jerry Thorpe          USA          1978
*Gena Rowlands, Jane Alexander, Ned Beatty, Clu Gulager, Bonnie Bedelia, James Sutorius, Jocelyn Brando, Keith Mitchell, Josh Albee, Gwen Arner, John Harkins, Nancy McKeon, S. John Launer, Phillip Sterling, Donald Hotton*
A lesbian mother fights her ex-husband for custody of their young son, in this touching and articulate study. A fine cast gives the whole film considerable depth. Written by William Blinn.
Aka: PURELY A LEGAL MATTER

| DRA | | 104 min mTV |
| B,V | | HVM L/A; HVH |

### QUESTOR TAPES, THE ** U
Richard A. Colla          USA          1974
*Mike Farrell, Robert Foxworth, Dana Wynter, Lew Ayres, John Vernon, James Shigeta, Ellen Weston, Majel Barrett, Reuben Singer, Walter Koenig, Fred Sadoff, Gerald Saunderson Peters, Eyde Girard, Alan Caillou, Lal Baum*
An android undertakes a search for the scientist who created him and has now gone missing. A pilot for a series that was never made, and no wonder, for despite the interesting premise, this effort is little better than mediocre.
Boa: story by Gene Roddenberry.

| FAN | | 92 min (ort 100 min) mTV |
| V | | CIC |

### QUICK AND THE DEAD, THE ** PG
Robert Day          USA          1987
*Sam Elliott, Tom Conti, Kate Capshaw, Matt Clark, Patrick Kilpatrick, Kenny Morrison, Jerry Porter, Billy Streater, Del Shores, Kurt D. Lott*
A family struggle to build in the lawless frontier lands of 1860s and find a mysterious stranger coming to their aid when they are attacked by a criminal gang. A variant on SHANE, with good atmosphere but poor characterisations. The husband's Civil War experiences have made him unwilling to fight, but this is merely used to illustrate just how ill-prepared the couple are for the rigours of frontier life. Scripted by James Lee Barrett.
Boa: novel by Louis L'Amour.

| WES | | 87 min (ort 93 min) mCab |
| B,V | | GHV |

### QUICKSILVER * 15
Tom Donnelly          USA          1986
*Kevin Bacon, Jami Gertz, Paul Rodriguez, Rudy Ramos, Andrew Smith, Gerald S. O'Loughlin, Larry Fishburne, Louis Anderson, Whitney Kershaw*
A young New York stockholder gives up the rat race after a series of financial disasters and becomes a bicycle messenger. However, the usual nutty psychopath lurks in the background. Only recommended for music-mad cycling enthusiasts.

| A/AD | | 102 min (ort 106 min) |
| B,V | | RCA |

### QUIET COOL ** 18
Clay Borris          USA          1986
*James Remar, Jared Martin, Nick Cassavetes, Adam Coleman Howard, Daphne Ashbrook, Fran Ryan*
A New York cop travels to a small town in California, on behalf of a former girlfriend who is worried by the sudden disappearance of her brother and his wife. Once there, he discovers that they have in fact been murdered by growers of cannabis. A fast-paced action tale, with some memorable stunts but a merely

adequate script.
A/AD                              78 min (ort 100 min)
V                                             RCA


## QUIET EARTH, THE ***                          15
Geoff Murphy      NEW ZEALAND              1985
*Bruno Lawrence, Alison Routledge, Peter Smith,*
*Norman Fletcher, Tom Hyde*
A haunting film in which a scientist wakes up to find
that the Earth has been virtually depopulated as a
result of an experiment that went wrong.
Boa: novel by Craig Harrison.
FAN                               95 min (ort 100 min)
B,V                                           CBS


## QUIET MAN, THE ****                            U
John Ford             USA                  1952
*John Wayne, Maureen O'Hara, Barry Fitzgerald,*
*Victor McLaglen, Mildred Natwick, Francis Ford,*
*Arthur Shields, Ward Bond, Eileen Crowe, Sean*
*McClory, Jack McGowran*
An Irish-American boxer goes to live in Ireland where
he falls in love with a local girl. Though he has sworn
never to fight again (a superb flashback sequence tells
why), he is forced to in order to win her hand. A kind
of Irish "Taming of the Shrew" of considerable charm
and wit. Written by Frank Nugent and with a score by
Victor Young. AA: Dir, Cin (Winton C. Hoch/Archie
Stout).
Boa: novel by Maurice Walsh.
DRA                              124 min (ort 129 min)
V                                             VCC


## QUIET THUNDER **                               15
David Rice            USA                  1988
*Wayne Crawford, June Chadwick, Victor Steinbach,*
*Romalou Makhene, Karla Johnson*
A senator's wife and a bush pilot become targets, after
witnessing an assassination in the African jungle. A
RAIDERS OF THE LOST ARK-style adventure, with
some imaginative action sequences but little energy
expended on the tired formula script.
A/AD                                        94 min
B,V                                           VES


## QUIET VICTORY ***                             PG
Roy Campanella II     USA                  1987
*Michael Nouri, Pam Dawber, Bess Meyer, Peter Berg,*
*James Handy, Dan Lauria, Gracie Harrison*
The story of a former football star who developed Lou
Gehrig's disease in the 1970s but refused to succumb
to despair, going on to become a highly-regarded high
school football coach. By the 1980s he was still
teaching, despite being confined to a wheelchair. An
inspiring and remarkably restrained account, with a
literate script (by Barry Morrow) that, like the
character portrayed, has no time for self-pity.
Aka: QUIET VICTORY: THE CHARLIE
WEDEMEYER STORY
DRA                         90 min (ort 100 min) mTV
V/sh                                          ODY


## QUILLER MEMORANDUM, THE ***                   15
Michael Anderson      UK/USA               1966
*George Segal, Max Von Sydow, Alec Guinness, Senta*
*Berger, George Sanders, Robert Helpmann, Robert*
*Flemyng, Peter Carsten, Edith Schneider, Gunter*
*Meisner, Robert Stass, Ernst Walder, Philip Madoc,*
*John Rees*
A British agent is given the task of investigating
neo-Nazis in modern-day Berlin. Nothing sensational,
but adroit and well handled. The script is by Harold
Pinter with music by John Barry.
Boa: novel The Berlin Memorandum by Adam Hall
(Elleston Trevor).
DRA              99 min; 103 min (VCC) (ort 105 min)
B,V                            RNK; VCC (VHS only)


## QUINCY'S QUEST **
Robert Reed           UK                   1979
*Tommy Steele, Mel Martin, Charles Morgan, Lila*
*Kaye, Frederick Schiller, Tony Aitken, Lance Percival,*
*Aubrey Woods*
Quincy tries to save the toys in a department store
from being destroyed, in this musical special, that's
little more than a vehicle for Steele. Mildly diverting
but undistinguished kid's entertainment.
JUV                                      77 min mTV
B,V                                           TEVP


## QUINNS, THE **
Daniel Petrie         USA                  1977
*Barry Bostwick, Blair Brown, Susan Browning,*
*Geraldine Fitzgerald, Peter Masterson, Penny Peyser,*
*William Swetland, Pat Corley, Virginia Vestoff*
Three generations of New York Irish firemen come
under the microscope, in a drama that for once, deals
with the lives of ordinary citizens. A detailed and
mildly diverting tale, based on an idea by Phyllis
Minoff and Fran Sears.
DRA                          74 min (ort 78 min) mTV
B,V                                           QUA


## QUINTET *                                      15
Robert Altman         USA                  1979
*Paul Newman, Bibi Andersson, Fernando Rey,*
*Vittorio Gassman, Nina Van Pallandt, Brigitte Fossey,*
*David Langton, Tom Hill, Craig Richard Nelson,*
*Marcuska Stankova, Monique Mercure, Anne Gerety,*
*Francoise Berd, Max Fleck*
One of the most boring films that has ever been made.
A slow and utterly pointless look at the uneventful
lives of a community living in a frozen world of the
future. They while away their futile existence by
playing "Quintet" – a meaningless game that often
ends in death. At the end of this film you'll feel like
joining them.
FAN                             113 min (ort 118 min)
B,V                                           CBS


## QUITE BY CHANCE *                              18
Francesco Massaro     USA                  1989
*Kate Capshaw, Michele Placido, David Naughton,*
*Luca Barbareschi*
A look at the world of fashion and TV entertainment,
where behind each bland exterior are hidden depths of
passion, torment and intrigue. Standard soap opera
melodramatics.
DRA                                         90 min
V                                             BOX


## QUO VADIS? ***                                PG
Mervyn Le Roy         USA                  1951
*Robert Taylor, Deborah Kerr, Peter Ustinov, Leo Genn,*
*Patricia Laffin, Finlay Currie, Abraham Sofaer,*
*Marina Berti, Buddy Baer, Felix Aylmer, Nora*
*Swinburne, Ralph Truman, Norman Wooland*
Describes Rome at the time of Nero, focusing on a
Roman commander who falls in love with a Christian
girl and becomes a convert himself. A spectacular film
with many fine sequences but marred by a tendency to
be tedious in some places, brutal in others. The film is
at its most effective where it examines the lives of the
early Christians. The Miklos Rozsa score was based on
music of the time. Remade for Italian TV in 1985.
Boa: novel by Henryk Sienkiewicz.
DRA                             168 min (ort 171 min)
B,V                                           MGM


# R

## R.O.T.O.R. **                                 15
Cullen Blaine         USA                  1988
*Richard Gesswein, Margaret Trigg, James Cole, Clark*
*Moore, James Cole, Caroll Brandon Baker*

A special team is given the task of developing a robot police officer, in order to combat the soaring crime rate. However, the robot rapidly goes out of control and becomes a threat to everyone. See also ROBOCOP.

| A/AD | 88 min (ort 90 min) |
| B,V | RCA |

## R.S.V.P. **
John Amero/Lem Amero
USA                         1984
*Adam Mills, Lynda Weismeier, Veronica Hart, Harry Reems, Ray Colbert, Kat Shea, Carey Hayes, Lola Mason, Steve Nave, Robert Pinkerton, Allene Simmons, Arlene Steiger, Dustin Stevens*
A film-maker auditions a host of girls in his Beverly Hills mansion, with the intention of choosing one to cast in his new movie. Financed by the Playboy TV channel, this movie has the auditions taking place during a huge party with far too many characters and far too little plot. More or less an excuse to parade a succession of beauties, this has neither the wit nor sensuality of the far superior Australian film – DON'S PARTY.

| A | 83 min mTV |
| B,V | AVA/CBS |

## RABBIT TEST *                         15
Joan Rivers                USA          1978
*Billy Crystal, Alex Rocco, Joan Prather, Doris Roberts, George Gobel, Jimmie Walker, Imogene Coca, Alice Ghostley, Paul Lynde, Rosey Grier, Joan Rivers*
Comedienne Joan Rivers presents her first film, telling of the world's first pregnant man. An unutterably silly affair, with a few zany ideas and a host of star cameos, neither of which can redeem it. See also THE SLIGHTLY PREGNANT MAN.

| COM | 84 min (ort 86 min) |
| B,V | EHE |

## RABID ***
David Cronenberg   CANADA           1977
*Marilyn Chambers, Frank Moore, Joe Silver, Patricia Gage, Susan Roman, Howard Ryspan, J. Roger Periard, Lynne Deragon, Victor Deay, Gary McKeehan, Terry Schonblum, Julie Anna, Terrence G. Ross, Robert O'Ree, Greg Von Riel*
Following an accident, a woman motorcyclist receives an experimental skin graft of "morphologically neutral" skin. However, this develops into a repulsive growth that drains the blood from her lovers and a rabies-like epidemic develops. Quite a forceful little chiller.

| HOR | 90 min |
| B,V | INT; EMP |

## RABID GRANNIES *                         18
Emmanuel Kervyn                         1988
*Catherine Aymerie, Danielle Daven, Ann Marie Fox*
Immensely bad movie, courtesy of Troma Productions (of TOXIC AVENGER fame), in which a birthday party for the elderly relatives of a large family turns a little sour, when they are sent a present by a devil-worshipping relative that turns them all into murderous demons. Needless to say, the bodies soon start to pile up, in a badly dubbed and edited offering that verges on the unwatchable.

| HOR | 88 min |
| V | VIR |

## RACCOONS AND THE LOST STAR, THE ***   Uc
Kevin Gilles               USA          1983
*Rich Little (narration)*
Heavily inspired by STAR WARS, this animation tells of two raccoons who, together with their dog, fight the evil Cyril Sneer, who threatens to take over the Earth with an army of pigs. An inventive and enjoyable episode in a series of adventures for these creatures.

| CAR | 45 min (ort 49 min) |
| D,V,V2 | EHE; CH5 (VHS only) |

## RACCOONS' BIG SURPRISE, THE **          U
Kevin Gilles               USA          1985
Musical animated adventure featuring the title creatures. Average.

| CAR | 50 min |
| V | NELS/CBS; CH5 |

## RACE AGAINST THE HARVEST **            PG
Dick Lowry                 USA          1986
*Wayne Rogers, Mariclare Costello, Fredric Lehne, Jill Carroll, Earl Holliman*
A farmer races against the clock to bring in his harvest before the arrival of an approaching storm. Average.

| DRA | 93 min mTV |
| B,V | CHV |

## RACE FOR THE YANKEE ZEPHYR **          PG
David Hemmings
AUSTRALIA/NEW ZEALAND           1981
*Ken Wahl, Lesley Anne Warren, Donald Pleasence, George Peppard, Bruno Lawrence, Grant Tilly, Robert Bruce*
Several men learn of a wrecked DC-3 plane that crashed in 1944 carrying $50,000,000 in gold. As they make plans to retrieve the loot, one man prepares to get it all for himself. The nice locations are the chief point of interest in this clumsy adventure.
Aka: RACE TO THE YANKEE ZEPHYR; TREASURE OF THE YANKEE ZEPHYR

| A/AD | 108 min |
| V | TEVP |

## RACE TO DANGER **                         15
Joseph Louis Agraz         USA          1987
*Asher Brauner, Don Calfa, Linnea Quigley, Jo Ann Ayers*
A woman singer travels to the jungles of Central America to entertain, but is kidnapped by pirates because of her uncanny resemblance to a Moon goddess worshipped by a tribe of Indians. Fair adventure yarn.
Aka: TREASURE OF THE MOON GODDESS

| A/AD | 91 min (ort 96 min) |
| B,V | TGP |

## RACE WITH THE DEVIL **                  15
Jack Starrett              USA          1975
*Peter Fonda, Warren Oates, Loretta Swit, Lara Parker, R.G. Armstrong, Wes Bishop, Clay Tanner, Carol Blodgett, Ricci Ware, Paul A. Partain, Arkey Blue, James Harrell, Karen Miller, Jack Starrett, Phil Hoover*
Two pairs of holiday-makers stumble upon a group of Satanists about to sacrifice a human being and are forced to run for their lives. A smoothly directed film with a good sense of tension, but the poor ending lets it down badly. Written by Lee Frost and Wes Bishop.

| THR | 84 min (ort 88 min) |
| B,V | CBS |

## RACHEL PAPERS, THE ***                  18
Damien Harris                         1989
*Dexter Fletcher, Ione Skye, Jonathan Pryce, James Spader, Bill Paterson, Michael Gambon, Shirley Anne Field*
A computer buff has programmed his machine with every chat-up line under the sun, and has become a master of seduction. However, when his best efforts are stymied by an aloof girl he seeks advice from his coarse brother-in-law (a great performance from Pryce). Eventually he wins her over and she movies in with him, but once the chase is ended he finds himself bored. A coy updating the Amis novel, sustained by a few amusing cameos.
Boa: novel by Martin Amis.

COM                                         91 min
V                                            VIR

## RACHEL'S MAN **
Moshe Mizrachi        ISRAEL            1974
*Mickey Rooney, Rita Tushingham, Michael Bat-*
*Adam, Leonard Whiting*
The story of the love of Rachel and Jacob as told in the
Old Testament. Filmed on location in Israel. Average.
Aka: ISH RACHAEL
DRA                          87 min (ort 115 min)
B,V                                      VCL/CBS

## RACING WITH THE MOON **            15
Richard Benjamin      USA              1984
*Sean Penn, Elizabeth McGovern, Nicolas Cage, John*
*Karlen, Rutanya Alda, Carol Kane, Max Showalter,*
*Crispin Glover*
Teenagers have a love affair in a small Californian
town in the 1940s, but their relationship is oversha-
dowed by the spectre of WW2. Much attention was
lavished on attempts to create a genuine period
atmosphere, but this alone fails to rescue the film from
its stiflingly leisurely pace. Written by Steven Kloves.
DRA                          103 min (ort 108 min)
B,V                                          CIC

## RACQUET *
David Winters         USA              1979
*Bert Convy, Edie Adams, Lynda Day George, Phil*
*Silvers, Bobby Riggs, Susan Tyrell, Bjorn Borg*
A former tennis star embarks on a scheme to raise the
money for his own tennis club, by exploiting his charm
and ability to fascinate the opposite sex. An addle-
brained and inane dud.
COM                                         89 min
B,V,V2                                       GHV

## RADIO DAYS ***                      PG
Woody Allen           USA              1986
*Dianne Wiest, Julie Kavner, Michael Tucker, Mia*
*Farrow, Danny Aiello, Tony Roberts, Diane Keaton,*
*Josh Mostel, Seth Green, Jeff Daniels, Wallace Shawn,*
*Tito Puente, Gina DeAngelis, Kitty Carlisle Hart, Julie*
*Kurnitz*
A nostalgic homage to the joys of a 1940s childhood
and the mass medium of that era. Not much in the
way of a plot, more a succession of episodes that
largely focus on a young boy's upbringing, with a mass
of period detail and host of affectionate vignettes. The
photography is by Carlo Di Palma and the excellent
sets are by Santo Loquasto.
COM                                         85 min
B,V                                          RCA

## RADIOACTIVE DREAMS *               18
Albert F. Pyun        USA              1986
*John Stockwell, Lisa Blount, George Kennedy, Michael*
*Dudikoff, Don Murray, Michele Little, Norbert*
*Weisser, Paul Keller Galan, Demian Slade, Chris*
*Andrew*
A post-WW3 epic, with two young men emerging from
their fallout shelter after 15 years, and setting off in
exploration of their surroundings, armed only with a
knowledge of the world derived from reading pulp
detective fiction. A bizarre post-apocalypse teen com-
edy, as unfunny as it is tasteless.
FAN                                         94 min
B,V                          GHV L/A; NDH; MED

## RAFFERTY AND THE GOLD DUST TWINS ** 15
Dick Richards         USA              1975
*Alan Arkin, Sally Kellerman, Mackenzie Phillips, Alex*
*Rocco, Charlie Martin Smith, Harry Dean Stanton,*
*Louis Prima, John McLiam*
Two women force a driving instructor to drive them
from Los Angeles to New Orleans and embroil him in
a series of adventures. A likeable but rather aimless
road movie that has neither direction nor purpose.

Aka: RAFFERTY AND THE HIGHWAY HUSTLERS
COM                                         92 min
B,V                                          WHV

## RAFFLES ***                          U
Sam Wood              USA              1940
*David Niven, Olivia De Havilland, Dudley Digges,*
*Dame May Whitty, Douglas Walton, Lionel Pape, E.E.*
*Clive, Peter Godfrey*
A remake of the 1930 film telling of a wily gentleman
thief who always stays one step ahead of the law. Will
appeal to those old enough to recall Hollywood films of
this period, but Niven is a poor substitute for Col-
man's original gentleman burglar. Written by John
Van Druten and Sydney Howard with music by Victor
Young.
Boa: novel Raffles The Amatuer Cracksman by E.W.
Hornung.
DRA                          69 min (ort 72 min) B/W
B,V                                  VGM; PARK

## RAFFLES: MR JUSTICE RAFFLES **     PG
Christopher Hodson    UK               1977
*Anthony Valentine, Charles Dance, Christopher*
*Strauli, Lynette Davies, John Savident*
An episode from the TV series based on the exploits of
a gentleman jewel-thief and cracksman who is not
averse to taking the law into his own hands when his
friends are in need of his help. In this story he dishes
out his own form of justice when a disreputable
money-lender bullies a friend for non-payment of a
loan.
A/AD                                    55 min mTV
V                                           HEND

## RAFFLES: THE GIFT OF THE EMPEROR ** PG
James Goddard         UK               1977
*Anthony Valentine, Christopher Strauli, John*
*Hallam, John Carson, Victor Carin*
Raffles becomes involved in an international incident
when he comes up against a dishonest politician who
tries to con him.
A/AD                                    55 min mTV
V                                           HEND

## RAGE **                             15
George C. Scott       USA              1972
*George C. Scott, Richard Basehart, Martin Sheen,*
*Barnard Hughes, Nicolas Beauvy, Paul Stevens, Ed*
*Lauter, Dabbs Greer, Ken Tobey, Lou Frizzell, John*
*Dierkes, Stephen Young, William Jordan*
The US Army's tests of a new chemical agent, result
in the accidental death of a young boy. The boy's
father finds his grief turning to anger as he discovers
that a vast cover-up has taken place. This was Scott's
debut as a director, in a film that starts off well but
goes gradually downhill in a welter of violent action,
that eclipses whatever message it might have been
intended to convey.
DRA                          95 min (ort 104 min)
B,V                                          WHV

## RAGE ***                            15
William A. Graham     USA              1980
*David Soul, James Whitmore, Yaphet Kotto, Caroline*
*McWilliams, Vic Tayback, Sharon Farrell, Craig T.*
*Nelson, Tom Noonan, Randy Brooks, Darleen Carr,*
*Garry Walberg, John Durren, James Gammon, Robert*
*Davi, Jonathan Banks*
A man convicted of rape undergoes intensive aversion
therapy in prison and is eventually able to locate the
inner source of his rage against women. Well acted
and often quite harrowing, with a literate script by
George Rubino.
DRA                                     99 min mTV
B,V                          VFP L/A; HER L/A; RCA

## RAGE OF ANGELS 1 **                 15
Buzz Kulik            USA              1983

*Jaclyn Smith, Ken Howard, Armand Assante, Ron Hunter, Kevin Conway, George Coe, Joseph Wiseman, Deborah May, Joseph Warren, Wesley Addy, Bill Cobbs, James Greene, Pauline Flanagan, Lois Smith, Art Vasil, Edward J. Lynch*
A woman lawyer fights her way to the top, enjoying various love affairs as a diversion from the pressures of her profession. A glossy and unmemorable celebration of pulp fiction, followed by a sequel of similar merits. First shown in two parts.
Boa: novel by Sidney Sheldon.
DRA                              200 min (2 cassettes) mTV
B,V                                            SEL; HER; STRAND

### RAGE OF ANGELS 2: PARTS 1 AND 2 **    15
Paul Wendkos          USA                           1983
*Jaclyn Smith, Ken Howard, Michael Nouri, Susan Sullivan, Mason Adams, Linda Dano, Brad Dourif, Paul Roebling, Michael Woods, Ronald Hunter, Paul Shenar, Angela Lansbury, Philip Bosco, Danny Gerard, Michael O'Hare, Jay O. Sanders*
The continuing story of Jennifer Parker, a high-powered Manhattan lawyer who has fought her way to the top, enjoying various love affairs and a rather complex past. A former lover has just been elected US Vice President and is anxious to rekindle their relationship, much against his wife's wishes. The brother of yet another lover, now dead, turns up to blackmail her. Even her mother, who abandoned her as a child, re-appears. A busy day.
Aka: RAGE OF ANGELS: THE STORY CONTINUES
DRA              176 min (2 cassettes – ort 240 min) mTV
B,V                                                      SHEER

### RAGE OF HONOR **    18
Gordon Hessler        USA                           1987
*Sho Kosugi, Lewis Van Bergen, Robin Evans, Chip Lucia, Gerry Gibson, Richard Wiley, Carlos Estrada, Alan Amiel*
A narcotics agent who is an martial arts expert, mounts his own one-man vendetta after his partner is murdered. Kosugi gives his all in a film that's short on plot but long on action. Poor dialogue is another drawback.
Aka: RAGE OF HONOUR
MAR              87 min (ort 91 min) Cut (25 sec)
B,V                                                       VPD

### RAGE TO KILL *
David Winters         USA                           1987
*James Ryan, Oliver Reed, Cameron Mitchell, Henry Cele, John Phillip Law*
A secret missile base is established on a Caribbean island, with a revolutionary regime that is promoting terrorism, and a group of American students find themselves trapped there. Fortunately, help arrives in the form of the tough, racing driver brother of one of the kids, and in no time at all he has formed his own guerilla force to deal with the villains. Brutal, uninspiring drivel.
A/AD                                                  91 min
V                                                        BRAVE

### RAGEWAR *    15
Rosemarie Turko et al.   USA                        1983
*Jeffrey Byron, Leslie Wing, Richard Moll, Blackie Lawless, Danny Dick, Gina Calebrese, Daniel Dion, Bill Bestolarides, Scott Campbell, Ed Dorini, R.J. Miller, Don Moss, Alanna Roth, Kim Connell, Janet Welsh, Carol Soloman*
A girl is held hostage by an alien, and a computer expert is given seven challenges to overcome in order to free her. Seven directors worked on this dismal effort. (For the curious, the other six were: John Buechler, Charles Band, David Allen, Steve Ford, Peter Manoogian and Ted Nicolau.)
Aka: DIGITAL KNIGHTS; DUNGEONMASTER, THE

FAN                                                  73 min
B,V                                                      EIV

### RAGGEDY ANN AND ANDY:    U
### A MUSICAL ADVENTURE *
Richard Williams      USA                           1977
*Voices of: Didi Conn, Mark Baker, Fred Stuthman, Joe Silver, Nikki Flacks, Arnold Stang, George S. Irving, Alan Sues, Lynne Stuart, Sheldon Harnick, Ardyth Kaiser, Allen Swift, Hetty Gordon, Paul Dooley, Mason Adams*
A full-length animated musical, based on the famous rag-doll characters who set off in search of adventure and rescue a French doll from pirates. A lethargic and unfocused experience, with adequate animation but an interminable stream of tuneless songs by Joe Paposo.
Boa: stories by Johnny Gruelle.
CAR                              76 min (ort 87 min)
V                                                        VGM

### RAGGEDY MAN **    15
Jack Fisk             USA                           1981
*Sissy Spacek, Eric Roberts, William Sanderson, Tracey Walter, Sam Shepard, Henry Thomas, R.G. Armstrong, Carey Hollis Jr*
Art director Fisk makes his directorial debut, in a story of a divorced woman raising her two sons in a small town in Texas during WW2. A detailed and engrossing study of 1940s America, that's spoilt by a melodramatic climax and a certain lack of warmth.
DRA                              89 min (ort 94 min)
B,V                                                      CIC

### RAGGEDY RAWNEY, THE ***    15
Bob Hoskins           UK                            1988
*Dexter Fletcher, Zoe Nathenson, Bob Hoskins, Zoe Wanamaker, Ian Dury*
An anti-war satire, telling of a young shell-shocked soldier who deserts his post in war-torn Europe and, disguised as a woman, joins a band of gypsies who care nothing for the conflict. A potent blend of humour and savage comment, co-written by Hoskins in his directorial debut.
DRA                                                 103 min
V                                                       PATHE

### RAGING BULL ****    18
Martin Scorsese       USA                           1980
*Robert De Niro, Cathy Moriarty, Joe Pesci, Frank Vincent, Nicholas Colasanto, Theresa Saldana*
Biopic on the prizefighter Jake La Motta, who went from obscurity to fame and then back again. A powerful film with violent fight scenes that may disturb. The central character is remarkably unappealing but De Niro's superb performance and the care lavished on period detail, combine to produce a most engrossing work. Written by Paul Schrader and Mardik Martin. AA: Actor (De Niro) Edit (Thelma Schoonmaker).
Boa: book by Jake La Motta.
DRA                                                 124 min
V/sh                                                     WHV

### RAGING FURY *    18
Douglas Grossman      USA                           1986
*Christopher Stryker, Maureen Mooney, Jason Brill, Millie Prezioso, Christopher Cousins*
In return for being humiliated in class, a boy and his friends terrorise their teacher, to such an extent that she turns into a murderous psychopath and takes a gory revenge. Not so much a horror film as a celebration of viciousness.
HOR              78 min (ort 85 min) Cut (1 min 36 sec)
B,V                                                      POLY

### RAGING MOON, THE **    PG
Bryan Forbes          UK                            1970

*Malcolm McDowell, Nanette Newman, Bernard Lee,*
*Georgia Brown, Gerald Sim, Michael Flanders,*
*Margery Mason, Barry Jackson, Geoffrey Whitehead,*
*Constance Chapman, Jack Woolgar, Norman Bird,*
*Brook Williams*
Two physically handicapped youngsters in a home,
fall in love, but their happiness is short-lived in this
sincere but dull film, scripted by Forbes.
Aka: LONG AGO TOMORROW
Boa: novel by Peter Marshall.
DRA                            111 min; 107 min (WHV)
B, V/s                         TEVP; WHV (VHS only)

## RAGMAN'S DAUGHTER, THE ***                        15
Harold Becker            UK                        1972
*Simon Rouse, Victoria Tennant, Leslie Sands, Patrick*
*O'Connell, Rita Howard, Brenda Peters, Brian*
*Murphy, Jane Wood*
A Nottingham working-class petty criminal and
layabout, recalls his tragic love for a good-looking
middle-class girl, whose parents were implacably
opposed to what they considered to be an unsuitable
match. A thin but quite touching drama that was
scripted by Sillitoe. Becker's feature debut.
Aka: TEA-LEAF, THE (GLOB or KRP)
Boa: short story by Alan Sillitoe.
DRA                            94 min; 90 min (KRP)
B,V                            CBS; FILV; GLOB

## RAGS TO RICHES ***                                 U
Bruce Seth Green         USA                       1986
*Joseph Bologna, Tisha Campbell, Kimiko Gelman,*
*Douglas Seale, Bianca DeGarr, Bridget Michele*
A self-made millionaire moves to Beverly Hills, and
decides to improve his public image in order to
successfully negotiate a merger for his company. To do
this he gives five orphan girls a temporary home, but
finds that he has taken on more than he bargained for.
Set in the 1960s, this likeable pilot for a TV series
makes good use of the music of the period.
COM                            96 min mTV
B,V                            NWV

## RAGTIME ***                                         15
Milos Forman             USA                       1981
*Elizabeth McGovern, Howard E. Rollins Jr, James*
*Olson, Mary Steenburgen, James Cagney, Pat O'Brien,*
*Norman Mailer, Brad Dourif, Moses Gunn, Donald*
*O'Connor, Ken McMillan, Mandy Patinkin*
Film version of a novel that attempted to present a
picture of American life in 1906. Fine performances
are let down by early concentration on a single strand
of the novel to the exclusion of all else – the obsessive
search for justice undertaken by a black man, after
humiliation at the hands of some racists. This was
Cagney's last cinema role, after a 20-year absence.
The score is by Randy Newman.
Boa: novel by E.L. Doctorow.
DRA                            149 min (ort 155 min)
B,V                            TEVP

## RAID ON CAESARS *                                   15
Noel Nosseck             USA                       1976
*Stella Stevens, Stuart Whitman, George DiCenzo,*
*Lynne Moody, Linda Scruggs, Joseph Della Sorte,*
*Jesse White*
A security guard falls in love with a woman and
becomes involved in a robbery. A flaccid heist movie
with poor acting and an unbelievable script.
Aka: LAS VEGAS LADY
THR            83 min; 87 min (21ST) (ort 90 min)
B,V                            FILINT L/A; 21ST; FILV

## RAID ON ENTEBBE **                                  PG
Irvin Kershner           USA                       1977
*Peter Finch, Charles Bronson, Horst Buchholz, Martin*
*Balsam, John Saxon, Jack Warden, Sylvia Sidney,*
*Yaphet Kotto, Tige Andrews, Eddie Constantine,*
*Warren Kemmerling, Robert Loggia, David Opatoshu,*

*Allan Arbus, James Woods*
Another version of the Entebbe hijack drama and
subsequent rescue of the hostages, by a crack unit of
Israeli commandos on July 4th 1976 (no thanks to
Uganda's dictator Idi Amin). Finch's last film, for
which he received only an Emmy nomination, though
Bill Butler received an Emmy award for his cinema-
tography. See also VICTORY AT ENTEBBE and
OPERATION THUNDERBOLT.
THR                            113 min; 120 min (VCC) mTV
B,V                            TEVP; VCC (VHS only)

## RAID ON ROMMEL *                                    15
Henry Hathaway           USA                       1971
*Richard Burton, John Colicos, Clinton Greyn,*
*Wolfgang Preiss, Danielle Demetz*
A British officer posing as a Nazi, gathers together a
group of POWs for an attack on Rommel's fuel dump,
intended to be a prelude to a raid on the guns at
Tobruk before the Allied invasion of North Africa. A
dull dud, filmed in Mexico and with its battle footage
borrowed from TOBRUK.
WAR                            93 min (ort 99 min)
V/h                            CIC

## RAIDERS IN ACTION *                                 PG
Benni Schvily                                      198-
*Paul Smith, Pierre Henry*
A formula WW2 offering, with a group of commandos
parachuting into occupied Europe in order to learn the
nature of a new German secret weapon.
WAR                            89 min
V/sh                           WHV

## RAIDERS OF THE LIVING DEAD **                       15
Samuel M. Sherman        USA                       1986
*Scott Schwarz, Robert Deveau, Donna Asali, Bob*
*Sacchetti, Zita Johann, Bob Allen*
Once more the Earth resounds to the tread of the living
dead and their insatiable appetite for human flesh,
when a reporter, who was originally covering a
terrorist story, stumbles across a sinister farm where
the dead are brought back to life.
HOR                            85 min
B,V                            IVS L/A; BRAVE

## RAIDERS OF THE LOST ARK ****                        PG
Steven Spielberg         USA                       1981
*Harrison Ford, Karen Allen, Wolf Kahler, Paul*
*Freeman, Ronald Lacey, John Rhys-Davies, Denholm*
*Elliott, Anthony Higgins, Alfred Molina, Vic Tablian,*
*William Hootkins, Don Fellows, Fred Sorenson, Bill*
*Reimbold, Patrick Durkin*
A lavish blockbuster, with Ford as a freelance hunter
of lost treasures, sent to find the lost Ark of the
Hebrews before the Nazis do. Conceived by George
Lucas, Philip Kaufman and Spielberg, with music
John Williams and the script by Lawrence Kasdan.
Followed by INDIANA JONES AND THE TEMPLE
OF DOOM. AA: Art/Set (Reynolds and Dilley/Ford),
Edit (Kahn), Sound (Varney et al.), Effects (Vis)
(Edlund et al.), Spec Award (Burtt et al for sound
effects).
A/AD                           112 min (ort 115 min)
B,V                            CIC

## RAILWAY CHILDREN, THE ***                           U
Lionel Jeffries          UK                        1970
*Dinah Sheridan, William Mervyn, Jenny Agutter,*
*Bernard Cribbens, Iain Cuthbertson, Gary Warren,*
*Sally Thomsett, Peter Bromilow, Ann Lancaster,*
*Gordon Whiting, David Lodge*
Three children who live by a railway line, have
various adventures whilst waiting for their father to
be found innocent of the charge of spying. An aimless
work redeemed by nice locations and a charming feel
for the period. The script is by Jeffries.
Boa: novel by E. Nesbit.

JUV                                    104 min (ort 108 min)
B,V                            TEVP L/A; WHV (VHS only)

## RAIN MAN ***                                        15
Barry Levinson            USA                        1988
Dustin Hoffman, Tom Cruise, Valeria Golino, Jerry
Molden, Jack Murdock, Michael D. Roberts
A brash young layabout goes home for his father's
funeral and discovers that he has an autistic older
brother, who quite unexpectedly has been made the
sole beneficiary of his father's estate. He kidnaps his
brother, intending to have him declared incompetent
and get control of the inheritance, but in time a bond
of affection grows between them. A contrived but
likeable film. AA: Pic, Dir, Actor (Hoffman), Screen
(Orig) (Ronald Bass/Barry Morrow).
DRA                                     128 min (ort 140 min)
V/sh                                                   WHV

## RAINBOW **                                           U
Jackie Cooper             USA                        1978
Andrea McArdle, Don Murray, Piper Laurie, Martin
Balsam, Michael Parks, Jack Carter, Rue
McClanahan, Nicholas Pryor, Donna Pescow, Erin
Donovan, Moosie Drier, Johnny Doran, Philip
Sterling, Ben Frank, Peggy Walton, Carol Leigh
This follows Judy Garland's career, from her early
days as one of three singing sisters up to her role in
The Wizard of Oz. Fairly accurate, but McArdle is
woefully miscast and has not one tinge of the Garland
charisma. An Emmy went to the cinematographer,
Howard R. Schwartz.
Boa: book by Christopher Finch.
DRA                          73 min (ort 100 min) mTV
B,V                          ATA L/A; APX L/A; VCC

## RAINBOW, THE ***                                     15
Ken Russell               UK                         1989
Sammi Davis, Paul McGann, Amanda Donohoe,
Christopher Gable, David Hemmings, Glenda
Jackson, Ken Colley
A remarkable restrained film from Russell that serves
as a prequel to WOMEN IN LOVE, and follows the
career of a naive and sheltered young girl who learns
of love and life at the hands of both her teacher and a
soldier. This mature study of adolescence and growth
is visually pleasing if a little disjointed. Jackson has a
part as the mother of the character she played in the
earlier work. Screenplay is by Ken and Vivian
Russell.
Boa: novel by D.H. Lawrence.
DRA                                              104 min
B,V                                                   VES

## RAINBOW BRITE AND THE                                U
## STAR STEALER *
Bernard Degries/Kimio Yabuki
                          USA                        1985
Voices of: Bettina, Patrick Fraley, Peter Cullen, Robbie
Lee, Andre Stojka, David Mendenhall, Rhonda
Aldrich, Les Tremayne, Mona Marshall, Jonathan
Harris, Marissa Mendenhall, Scott Menville, Charles
Adler, David Workman
Animated feature that looks (and sounds) as if it was
made on an assembly-line, all about a little girl who
must stop the forces of evil from extinguishing the last
star.
CAR                                      81 min (ort 85 min)
V/sh                                                   WHV

## RAINBOW BRITE: THE MIGHTY                            Uc
## MONSTROMURK MENACE **
Herb Sevush               USA                        1983
Rainbow Land is menaced by a colour-draining mons-
ter in this energetic and fairly competent cartoon
animation.
CAR                               60 min; 42 min (PREST)
B,V                                            VES; PREST

## RAINBOW JACKET, THE **                               PG
Basil Dearden             UK                         1954
Kay Walsh, Bill Owen, Edward Underdown, Fella
Edmonds, Robert Morley, Wilfrid Hyde White, Charles
Victor, Ronald Ward, Howard Marion Crawford,
Honor Blackman, Sidney James, Michael Trubshawe,
Frederick Piper
A veteran jockey, barred from racing owing to dishon-
esty, takes on a young novice and teaches him all he
knows. However, the boy is blackmailed by crooks
who want him to lose the St Leger. A colourful
racetrack melodrama with good racing sequences but
an entirely predictable outcome.
DRA                                      96 min (ort 99 min)
V                                                      WHV

## RAINY DAY FRIENDS *                                  15
Gary Kent                 USA                        1985
Esai Morales, Carrie Snodgress, Janice Rule, Lelia
Goldoni, John Philip Law
The story of a teenager and his fight against cancer.
An over-sentimental and uninspiring tale, done in the
style of a mawkish soap opera.
DRA                                     99 min (ort 101 min)
B,V                                                   APOL

## RAISE THE TITANIC! *                                 PG
Jerry Jameson             USA/UK                     1980
Jason Robards, Richard Jordan, David Selby, Anne
Archer, Alec Guinness, J.D. Cannon, Paul Carr,
Michael C. Gwynne, Dirk Blocker, Norman Barfold,
Bo Brundin, Charles Macauley, Elya Baskin, Harvey
Lewis, M. Emmet Walsh
Lew Grade who produced this film, later said that it
would have been cheaper to lower the Atlantic. One
must agree, this dismal flop tells of the largest salvage
operation ever; the ridiculous plot involving the
presence on board the title vessel of a rare ingredient
used in nuclear weapons. Written by Adam Kennedy
and Eric Hughes and cut down from 121 minutes just
prior to release but still a good 100 minutes too long.
Boa: novel by Clive Cussler.
A/AD                                    109 min (ort 114 min)
B,V                               PRV; CH5 (VHS only)

## RAISING ARIZONA ***                                  15
Joel Coen                 USA                        1987
Nicolas Cage, Holly Hunter, Trey Wilson, John
Goodman, William Forsythe, Sam McMurray, Frances
McDormand, Randall "Tex" Cobb
A rather odd couple decide to kidnap one child from a
set of quintuplets as they are unable to have a child of
their own. A crazy blend of unfocused energy and wild
slapstick sequences, but highly enjoyable in its way.
The script is by Ethan and Joel Cohen with the score
by Carter Burwell and cinematography by Barry
Sonnenfeld.
COM                                      90 min (ort 94 min)
B,V                                                    CBS

## RALLY ROUND THE FLAG BOYS! *                         PG
Leo McCarey               USA                        1958
Paul Newman, Joanne Woodward, Joan Collins, Jack
Carson, Dwayne Hickman, Tuesday Weld, Gale
Gordon, Murvyn Vye
A small community mounts a vigorous protest in
order to prevent a missile base being sited nearby. A
brash and witless waste of energy which, for all its
efforts, produces barely a ripple of mirth.
Boa: novel by Max Shulman.
COM                                     102 min (ort 106 min)
V/h                                                    CBS

## RAISING THE WIND **                                  U
Gerald Thomas             UK                         1961
James Robertson Justice, Leslie Phillips, Paul Massie,
Kenneth Williams, Sidney James, Liz Fraser, Eric
Barker, Jennifer Jayne, Jimmy Thompson, Esma
Cannon, Geoffrey Keen, Jill Ireland, David Lodge,

*Lance Percival, Jim Dale*
A "Carry On" style look at the lives of students at a music academy, with one of them facing the loss of a scholarship for writing a pop song. Mildly entertaining but generally inconsequential.

| COM | 87 min (ort 91 min) |
| V | WHV |

### RAMB-OOH: THE FORCE IS IN YOU *   R18
Von Rogel   USA
*Careena Collins, Candie Evans, Peter North, Krista Lane, Tom Byron, Ray Hardin, Francois Papillon, Pauline Pepper, Barbie Blake*
Story of a soldier of fortune and the women who lust after him – a kind of tedious sex spoof on those "Rambo"-type films.

| A | 79 min (ort 82 min) Cut (4 sec) |
| V | SHEP |

### RAMB-OOH: THE SEX PLATOON *   R18
Wolfgang Gower   USA   1988
*Tracey Adams, Alicia Monet, Peter North, Tiffany Storm, Meegan Leigh, Jerry Butler, Mike Horner, Bill Dee*
Silly sex movie set in a secret military camp somewhere in the USA, where a new meaning is given to the phrase "training exercises".

| A | 69 min (ort 82 min) |
| V | SHEP |

### RAMBO 3 *   18
Peter McDonald   USA   1988
*Sylvester Stallone, Richard Crenna, Marc De Jonge, Kurtwood Smith, Spiros Focas, Sasson Gabai, Doudi Shoua, Randy Raney*
This time the cartoon action is set in Russian-occupied Afghanistan, where our walking one-man arsenal has to rescue a former superior from captivity in an impregnable fortress. An almost non-stop series of loud bangs is a poor substitute for a plot.

| A/AD | 94 min (ort 101 min) Cut (3 min 3 sec) |
| V/sh | GHV |

### RAMBO: FIRST BLOOD, PART 2 *   15
George Pan Cosmatos   USA   1985
*Sylvester Stallone, Richard Crenna, Steven Berkoff, Charles Napier, Julia Nickson, Martin Kove, Andy Wood, George Kee Cheung, William Ghent, Steve Williams, Don Collins, Chris Grant, John Sterlini, Alain Hocquenghem*
Unbelievable and incredibly violent fantasy about one-man arsenal Stallone, a Vietnam veteran out to rescue POWs held by the Viet Cong. One of many gung-ho fantasies produced since the Vietnam War – Chuck Norris and Arnold Schwarzenegger being other valued contributors to this genre. A callous film that totally fails to address the very real problem of those GIs still being held.

| A/AD | 92 min |
| B, V/sh | TEVP; GHV/PARK (VHS only) |

### RAMBO: THE RESCUE **   U
USA   1986
A cartoon animation using the character from the "Rambo" movies, who is now the leader of an undercover team known as The Force Of Freedom. In this tale Rambo leads his team to a small Latin American country to help ward off an invasion attempt. Quite a likeable effort that has a lot of shooting but shows no one being killed, a welcome relief from the films that provided its inspiration.

| CAR | 99 min |
| B,V | SHEER |

### RAMPAGE *   18
William Friedkin   USA   1987
*Michael Biehn, Alex McArthur, Deborah Van Valkenburgh, Nicholas Campbell, Billy Greenbush, John Harkins, Art LaFleur, Royce D. Applegate, Grace*

*Zabriskie, Roy London, Donald Hotton, Andy Roman*
A psychotic forces his way into a house, murders and eviscerates a family of three and a short while later mounts another attack. When he even murders the cops who tried to arrest him, a liberal-minded assistant D.A. finds his opposition to the death penalty beginning to waver. A film with a fairly simple message, driven home with a sledgehammer.
Boa: novel by William P. Wood.

| DRA | 97 min |
| B,V | CBS |

### RAN ****   15
Akira Kurosawa   FRANCE/JAPAN   1985
*Tatsuya Nakadai, Akira Terao, Jinpachi Nezu, Daisuke Ryu, Mieko Harada, Hisashi Igawa, Peter (Shinnosuke Ikehata), Hitoshi Veki, Jun Tazaki, Norio Matsui, Hisachi Igawa, Kenji Kodama, Toshiya Ito, Takeshi Kato, Mayayuki Yui*
Brutal, bloody and brilliant. Kurosawa's epic version of King Lear is perfectly adapted to Japanese customs and history, and tells of a warlord who turns his kingdom over to his eldest son, a rash action that sows dissension and splits his family. AA: Cost (Emi Wada).
Boa: play King Lear by William Shakespeare.

| DRA | 155 min (ort 162 min) |
| V | CBS |

### RANCH OF THE NYMPHOMANIAC GIRLS *   18
Erwin C. Dietrich
SWITZERLAND   1974
*Helga Blaost, Laurel Lonic, Peter Capra, Nadine De Rangot*
Abysmal sex farce, one more in a series of dreary Swiss efforts.
Aka: DIE BUMSFIDELEN MADCHEN VON BIRKENHOF; RANCH OF THE NYMPHO-MANIACS

| A | 70 min; 81 min (SHEP) Cut (23 sec in addition to film cuts) |
| B,V | 18PLAT/TOW; GLOB; SHEP |

### RANCH, THE **   15
Stella Stevens   USA   1988
*Andrew Stevens, Gary Fjellgaard*
A New York executive learns that he's bankrupt and then loses both his home and his girlfriend. However, when he learns that he has inherited a run-down ranch he decides to see if he can do something to improve his luck. A mildly diverting but contrived comedy.

| COM | 97 min |
| V | BOX |

### RANCHO DELUXE ***   15
Frank Perry   USA   1974
*Jeff Bridges, Sam Waterston, Elizabeth Ashley, Charlene Dallas, Clifton James, Slim Pickens, Harry Dean Stanton, Richard Bright, Patti D'Arbanville*
Two modern-day cowboys make a living rustling cattle from a local rancher, until he hires a detective to deal with them. A relaxed and disorganised comedy, but unusual enough to be worth seeing. Written by Thomas McGuane and with music by Jimmy Buffett. Now something of a cult film.

| COM | 90 min (ort 95 min) |
| B,V | WHV |

### RANCHO NOTORIOUS ***   PG
Fritz Lang   USA   1952
*Marlene Dietrich, Mel Ferrer, Arthur Kennedy, Lloyd Gough, Gloria Henry, William Frawley, Jack Elam, George Reeves, Lisa Ferraday, John Raven, Frank Ferguson, Francis McDonald, Dan Seymour, John Kellogg, Redd Redwing*
A cowboy in search of the murderer of his girlfriend, arrives at an outlaw's hideout run by Dietrich, and proceeds to upset her life. An unusual if rather slow

Western, with a good script by Daniel Taradash

| WES | 89 min |
| B,V | VCC |

## RANDY, THE ELECTRIC LADY **
Phillip Schumann     USA     1980
*Desiree Cousteau, Juliet Anderson, Roger Frazer,*
*Cyrus Jones, Lisa Rush, Monica Sands*
A woman is experiencing orgasmic problems, but
finally climaxes in an experiment and her body begins
to produce a powerful aphrodisiac, that is able to turn
women into nymphomaniacs and men into tireless
lovers. A slight and predictable erotic comedy. The
screenplay is by Terry Southern.

| A | 84 min |
| B,V | TCX |

## RANDY RIDES ALONE **                          U
Harry Fraser     USA     1934
*John Wayne, Alberta Vaughn, George "Gabby" Hayes,*
*Yakima Canutt, Earl Dwire, Tex Phelps, Artie Ortego,*
*Herman Hack, Mack V. Wright*
A drifter finds himself being blamed for robbery and a
series of murders, and helped by a young girl, he sets
out to clear his name and catch those rsponsible. A
fairly standard offering from Monogram that is considerably enlivened by some nice work from Hayes as
the killer.

| WES | 54 min B/W |
| V | CASPIC |

## RANSOM *                                      PG
Caspar Wrede     UK     1975
*Sean Connery, Ian McShane, Norman Bristow, John*
*Cording, Isabel Dean, William Fox, Robert Harris,*
*Richard Harrison, Harry Landis, Preston Lockwood,*
*James Maxwell, John Quentin, Jeffrey Wickham, Knut*
*Hansson*
The British ambassador to a Scandinavian country is
kidnapped by terrorists and has to be rescued. An
unenthralling adventure thriller offering little excite-
ment, though the splendid photography (by Sven
Nykvist, a long-time associate of Ingmar Bergman) is
a slight compensation. Filmed in Norway.
Aka: TERRORISTS, THE

| THR | 89 min (ort 98 min) |
| B, V/h | TEVP; WHV (VHS only) |

## RANSOM **
Richard Compton     USA     1977
*Oliver Reed, Stuart Whitman, John Ireland, Deborah*
*Raffin, Jim Mitchum, Paul Koslo*
A town is haunted by a mysterious killer who is
demanding four million dollars to stop the slaughter.
A competent time-filler.
Aka: ASSAULT ON PARADISE; MANIAC

| DRA | 84 min |
| B,V,V2 | GHV |

## RAPE OF RICHARD BECK, THE ***
Karen Arthur     USA     1985
*Richard Crenna, Meredith Baxter Birney, Pat Hingle,*
*Frances Lee McCain, Cotter Smith, George Dzundza,*
*Joanna Kerns, Mark Dickison, Jason Bernard,*
*Nicholas Worth, M.C. Gainey, Stanley Kamel, James*
*Goodwin Rice, Troy Evans*
A tough cop re-assesses his view of sex offenders, after
suffering a brutal sexual assault by a pair of cop-
haters. Crenna won an Emmy for his outstanding
performance. The powerful script is by James G.
Hirsch.

| DRA | 90 min (ort 100 min) mTV |
| B,V | IVS |

## RAPPIN' *                                     PG
Joel Silberg     USA     1985
*Mario Van Peebles, Charles Flohe, Tasia Valenza,*
*Eriq La Salle, Leo O'Brien, Richie Abanes, Ruth*
*Jaroslow, Kadeem Hardison, Harry Goz*

The story of Pittsburgh street gangs, their lives and
internecine rivalries, all done to a rap music background. To paraphrase Abe Lincoln – people who like
this sort of film will find this the sort of film they like.

| DRA | 89 min (ort 92 min) |
| B,V | MGM |

## RASCAL **                                     U
Norman Tokar     USA     1969
*Steve Forrest, Bill Mumy, Elsa Lanchester, Pamela*
*Toll, Bettye Ackerman, Henry Jones*
The story of a lonely young boy's childhood, and of his
pet raccoon that causes plenty of mischief in a small
Wisconsin town. A competent Disney mixture of
charm and tears, based on North's largely autobiog-
raphical novel.
Boa: novel by Sterling North.

| JUV | 84 min |
| B,V | WDV |

## RASCALS AND ROBBERS **                        U
Dick Lowry     USA     1982
*Patrick Creadon, Anthony Michael Hall, Anthony*
*James, Allyn Anne McLerie, Ed Begley Jr, Cynthia*
*Nixon, John Harkins, Hansford Rowe, Anthony Zerbe,*
*J.D. Hall, William LaMassena, Gretchen West,*
*Eugenia Wright, Ed Bakey, John Quern*
Some of Mark Twain's famous characters are given a
series of completely new adventures, with Tom and
Huck joining a circus and enjoying various pranks and
exploits. A pleasant if undemanding kid's film.
Aka: RASCALS AND ROBBERS: THE SECRET AD-
VENTURES OF TOM SAWYER AND HUCK FINN

| JUV | 95 min (ort 100 min) mTV |
| B,V | CBS |

## RASPUTIN ***                                  PG
Elem Klimov     USSR     1975
*Alexie Petrenko, Velta Linei, Alisa Freindlikh, Anatoly*
*Romashin*
A sumptuous account of the last two years before the
Russian Revolution, and dealing mainly with the
sinister influence of Rasputin.
Aka: AGONY; AGONIJA; AGONY: DEATH
THROES

| DRA | 142 min (ort 148 min) |
| B,V | TEVP |

## RAT PFINK A BOO-BOO *                         15
Ray Dennis Steckler     USA     1966
*Vin Saxon, Carolyn Brandt, Titus Moede, George*
*Caldwell, James Bowie, Mike Cannon, Keith Webster,*
*Romeo Barrymore, Bob Burns, Dean Danger*
*(narration)*
An abysmally inept film, that starts out as a thriller
but turns into pure corny slapstick, as the two title
superheroes attempt to rescue the kidnapped girl-
friend of a singing idol. Despite the sometime cult
status of the director, most will find this offering
tedious in the extreme.
Aka: RAT FINK AND BOBO; RAT FINK AND
BOO-BOO

| COM | 72 min (ort 90 min) B/W |
| B,V | PAL |

## RATBOY **                                     PG
Sondra Locke     USA     1986
*Sondra Locke, Sharon Baird, Robert Townsend,*
*Sydney Lassick, Christopher Hewitt, Gerrit Graham,*
*Larry Hankin, Louie Anderson, S.L. Baird, Billie*
*Bird, Gordon Anderson*
A gentle, rodent-like alien is discovered by a depart-
ment store window-dresser, who attempts to turn him
into a media celebrity and exploit his notoriety by
becoming his manager. Locke's directorial debut is a
curious blend of comedy and pathos, that has no clear
message but a powerful charge of earnestness. Writ-

ten by Rob Thompson.
DRA                      100 min (ort 104 min) Cut (3 sec)
B,V                                              WHV

## RATS, THE **                                        18
Robert Clouse          USA                     1982
*Sam Groom, Sara Botsford, Scatman Crothers, Lisa
Langolis, Cec Linder, James B. Douglas, Lesleh
Donaldson, Lee-Max Walton, Joseph Kelly, Kevin
Foxx, Jon Wise, Wendy Bushell, Charles Joliffe, Dora
Dainton, Michael Fawkes*
Giant rats go on the rampage, but are combated by a
teacher and a health inspector who prove more than a
match for them, if not for the hackneyed script.
Aka: DEADLY EYES
Boa: novel by James Herbert.
HOR                                            83 min
B,V,V2                                      GHV; VCC

## RATS: NIGHT OF TERROR **                            18
Vincent Dawn (Bruno Mattei)/Clyde Anderson
                       FRANCE/ITALY            1984
*Richard Raymond, Richard Cross, Cindy Leadbetter*
Post-nuclear holocaust time again folks – now the
survivors find that an uncontaminated city has been
over-run by rats. A shlock-horror film from a famed
director of many.
Aka: RATS
HOR                                            85 min
B,V                                             MED

## RATTLE OF A SIMPLE MAN **
Muriel Box             UK                       1964
*Harry H. Corbett, Diane Cilento, Thora Hird, Michael
Medwin, Charles Dyer, Hugh Futcher, Carole Gray,
Brian Wilde, Barbara Wilde, Barbara Archer, David
Saire, Alexander Davion, Marie Burke*
A Northern football fan comes to London for a Cup
Final match and spends the night with a woman of
easy virtue. A mildly pleasing farce that outstays its
welcome. Written by Dyer and with music by Stanley
Black.
Boa: play by Charles Dyer.
COM                       91 min (ort 95 min) B/W
B,V                                            TEVP

## RATTLERS **                                         15
John McCauley          USA                     1976
*Sam Chew, Elizabeth Chauvet, Dan Priest, Ron Gold,
Richard Lockmiller, Tony Ballen, Jo Jordan, Al
Dunlap, Ancel Cook, Gary Van Ormand, Darwin
Jostin, Travis Gold, Alan Decker*
A series of unprovoked attacks by a snake are traced
to secret military experiments with nerve gas.
THR                                            80 min
B,V                                            POLY

## RAVAGERS, THE *                                     15
Richard Compton        USA                     1979
*Richard Harris, Ann Turkel, Ernest Borgnine, Art
Carney, Anthony James, Woody Strode, Alana
Hamilton*
In 1991 after a nuclear war, the few normal survivors
are terrorised by degenerate humans that have re-
verted to animal behaviour. After his wife is mur-
dered by a gang of bikers, Harris joins forces with
Carney in the hope of having his revenge. A messy
blend of DEATHWISH and MAD MAX, with neither
skill shown in direction nor scripting (by Donald
Sanford).
FAN                                            87 min
B,V                                             RCA

## RAVEN, THE ***
Roger Corman           USA                     1963
*Boris Karloff, Vincent Price, Peter Lorre, Hazel Court,
Jack Nicholson, Olive Sturgess, Connie Wallace,
William Baskin, Aaron Saxon*
Horror spoof about a contest that takes place between

two powerful wizards. Set in the 15th century, this is
one of the few Corman films that actually succeeds in
telling a credible tale; one that's inspired by an Edgar
Allan Poe poem. Richard Matheson wrote the screenplay.
HOR                                            86 min
B,V                                             RNK

## RAVINE, THE *                                       PG
Paolo Cavara   ITALY/YUGOSLAVIA                1969
*David McCallum, John Crawford, Lars Loch,
Nicoletta Machiavelli, Demeter Bietnc*
During WW2 a German soldier falls in love with a
Yugoslav girl sniper he has been sent to kill. A weak
war melodrama that has a message buried in there
somewhere.
WAR                                93 min (ort 97 min)
B,V,V2                                          INT

## RAW DEAL *                                          18
John Irvin             USA                     1986
*Arnold Schwarzenegger, Kathryn Harrold, Darren
McGavin, Sam Wanamaker, Steven Hill, Paul Shenar,
Joe Regalbuto, Robert Davi, Blanche Baker*
Schwarzenegger plays a retired agent, blackmailed by
the FBI into going after a Chicago Mob family. Plenty
of gore as Arnie wipes 'em out, but the film suffers
badly from its comic-book approach. A few flashes of
humour are a poor compensation.
A/AD                              101 min (ort 106 min)
V                                               CBS

## RAW DEAL ***
Anthony Mann           USA                     1948
*Dennis O'Keefe, Claire Trevor, Raymond Burr,
Marsha Hunt, John Ireland*
A man escapes from prison with the help of his
girlfriend, and sets out to catch up with the crook who
framed him, whilst a police posse follows in hot
pursuit. A brutal and forceful tale, with Burr making
a memorable villain.
DRA                                       78 min B/W
V/sh                                            GHV

## RAW FORCE *
Edward Murphy HONG KONG/USA                    1981
*Cameron Mitchell, Geoff Binney, Jillian Kessner, John
Dresden, Jennifer Holmes, Ralph Lombardi, Hope
Holiday, Rey King, Vic Diaz*
A strange blend of martial arts action and zombie
shenanigans. Monks on an island eat human flesh, in
order to raise martial arts warriors from the dead. A
grisly and rather inept affair.
HOR                                            86 min
B,V                            EVI; WEC L/A; KRP

## RAW TALENT ***                                     R18
Larry Revene           USA                     1984
*Lisa De Leeuw, Cassandra Leigh, Jerry Butler,
Danielle, Trish Ambrose, Chelsea Blake, Rhonda Jo
Petty, Joey Silvera, Jose Duvall, Ron Jeremy*
A big handsome guy comes to Hollywood and gets
involved in the world of porno movies, but merely to
earn some money whilst trying to make it as a serious
actor. He's exploited by an unscrupulous female porno
director and makes some movies for her. Later he
achieves nationwide TV fame as a legitimate actor,
but she ruins his career by releasing his earlier films.
A complex and absorbing story with an interesting
role-reversal slant.
A                  75 min (ort 90 min) Cut (1 min 50 sec)
B,V                                             ELV

## RAWHEAD REX **                                      18
George Pavlou          EIRE/UK                 1986
*David Dukes, Kelly Piper, Niall Toibin, Niall O'Brian,
Ronan Wilmot, Hugh O'Connor, Heinrich Von
Schellendorf, Cora Lunny, Donal McCann, Gladys
Sheehan, Madely Erskine, Gerry Walsh, Noel*

*O'Donovan, John Olohan*
An old-fashioned horror film, in which a farmer ploughing his field accidentally releases a huge demon who was pent up below ground for centuries. Having gained his freedom, our monster embarks on a rampage until a very nice American arrives to deal with him. The screenplay is by Clive Barker, in this moderately enjoyable effort that would have benefited from a better climax and a more convincing monster.
Aka: RAWHEAD
Boa: novel by Clive Barker.
HOR                                      85 min (ort 103 min)
B,V                                                          VES

## RAY BRADBURY'S NIGHTMARES
## VOLUME 1 ***                                              15
Bruce Pittman/William Fruet
              USA                                          1985
*Drew Barrymore, Janet Laine-Greene, Roger Dunn, Allan Scarfe, Ian Heath, Ken James, Jacqueline McLeod, Michael Copeman, Mary Anne Coles, William Shatner Keith Dutson, Kate Trotter, Miko Malish, Steven Andrade, Barry Flatman*
Two supernatural tales adapted from Bradbury stories. In "The Screaming Woman", an inquisitive kid discovers the existence of a murdered woman, who has been secretly buried in a wood, and in "The Playground", a meek insurance salesman tries to prevent his kid from going near a sinister playground. Two chilling and well-handled tales.
Boa: short stories by Ray Bradbury.
FAN                              57 min (ort 70 min) mCab
B,V                                                          VES

## RAY BRADBURY'S NIGHTMARES
## VOLUME 2 **                                               15
Douglas Jackson/Ralph Thomas
              USA                                          1985
*Charlie Martin Smith, Peter O'Toole, Jennifer Dale, Michael Copeman, Redmond Gleeson, Wendy Wilcox, Nick Mancuso, R.H. Thompson, David Hughes, Victor Eartmantis*
Two supernatural tales based on the writings of Bradbury. In "Banshee", a man visiting a film director is challenged to locate the source of a strange howling, whilst in "The Crowd", a man who nearly dies in an accident, discovers a nightmarish secret behind the speed with which people gather following an accident. A fair offering, with the second tale by far the better of the two.
Boa: short stories by Ray Bradbury.
FAN                              57 min (ort 70 min) mCab
B,V                                                          VES

## RAZORBACK **                                              18
Russell Mulcahy   AUSTRALIA                              1984
*Gregory Harrison, Bill Kerr, Judy Morris, Arkie Whiteley, Chris Haywood, David Argue*
Music video director Russell Mulcahy's directing debut is a story of a female animal rights campaigner who vanishes in the outback. Her husband sets out to find her, coming up against a monstrous wild boar that's terrorising the countryside. A hammy version of JAWS.
Boa: novel by Paul Brennan.
A/AD                                     90 min (ort 95 min)
B, V/sh                         TEVP L/A; WHV (VHS only)

## RAZOR'S EDGE, THE **                                      15
John Byrum        USA                                   1984
*Bill Murray, Theresa Russell, Catherine Hicks, Denholm Elliott, James Keach, Peter Vaughan, Brian Doyle-Murray, Saeed Jaffrey, Faith Brook*
A remake of a 1946 film telling of a young man's search for peace of mind after experiencing the horrors of WW1. A well-meaning but anachronistic attempt, severely hampered by Murray's lack of emotion. Written by Byrum and Murray.

Boa: novel by William Somerset Maugham.
DRA                                     124 min (ort 128 min)
B,V                                                          RCA

## RE-ANIMATOR **                                            18
Stuart Gordon      USA                                  1985
*Jeffrey Combs, Bruce Abbott, Barbara Crampton, Robert Sampson, David Gale, Gerry Black, Carolyn Purdy-Gordon, Peter Kent, Barbara Picters*
A grisly black comedy not without its moments of humour, as a young man experiments with a fluid that is able to reanimate the dead. Undeniably gross and overblown in terms of its effects, this film could never be accused of showing lightness of touch. Gordon's directing debut. Written by Gordon, Dennis Paoli and William J. Norris.
Boa: short stories in series Herbert West – The Reanimator by H.P. Lovecraft.
COM              81 min (ort 86 min) Cut (1 min 42 sec)
B,V                            WHV L/A; EIV (VHS only)

## RE-ANIMATOR 2 **                                          18
Brian Yuzna        USA                                  1990
*Jeffrey Combs, Bruce Abbott, David Gale, Kathleen Kinmont*
Sequel to the first horror film with our mad inventor moving on to greater things and creating living beings from dismembered limbs in the expected haphazard way. Inevitably his creations turn on him, but the flow of ideas has by now dried up and a few desperate attempts at black humour are all that's left to sustain the film.
HOR                                                  93 min
V                                                          MED

## REACH FOR THE SKY **                                       U
Lewis Gilbert      UK                                   1956
*Kenneth More, Muriel Pavlow, Lyndon Brook, Alexander Knox, Sydney Tafler, Lee Patterson, Dorothy Alison, Howard Marion Crawford, Jack Watling, Michael Warre, Nigel Green, Anne Leon, Walter Hudd, Eddie Byrne, Charles Carson*
The story of Douglas Bader, a WW2 flying ace, who put up a heroic struggle to prove himself capable of returning to active service, after he lost both his legs in a crash in 1931. He eventually succeeded but was shot down and imprisoned by the Germans, remaining in captivity for the duration of the war, despite making numerous attempts to escape. A sincere but stilted affair that is more boring than inspiring.
Boa: book by Paul Brickhill.
DRA                                            136 min B/W
V                                                          RNK

## REACHING FOR THE MOON **
Edmund Goulding    USA                                  1931
*Douglas Fairbanks Sr, Bebe Daniels, Bing Crosby, Edward Everett Horton, Claud Allister, Jack Mulhall, Helen Jerome Eddy*
The story of an on-off romance between a Wall Street financier and a young girl on a transatlantic liner, with a new cocktail having having a strange effect on the former. A lightweight comedy set in the Depression era. Crosby sings one Irving Berlin number.
COM                          64 min (ort 91 min) B/W
B,V               CHM L/A; KRP L/A; PPL L/A; VCL/CBS

## REACTOR **                                                PG
Al Bradley (Alfonso Brescia)
              ITALY                                        1985
*Yanti Somer, Melissa Long, James R. Stuart, Robert Barnes, Nick Jordan, Patricia Gore*
Aliens leave Earth an unwelcome gift in the form of a nuclear reactor that seems to be impossible to de-activate. Adequate.
FAN                                                  90 min
B,V                                                          MOG

## READY WHEN YOU ARE, MISTER McGILL! *  PG
Mike Newell                    UK          1976
*Joe Black, Diana Davies, Joe Belcher*
A comic behind-the-scenes look at the disasters that
befall a film crew working on their latest project.
COM                                       55 min
V                                           GRN

## REAL BRUCE LEE, THE *                    18
Jim Markovic         HONG KONG             1979
*Bruce Lee, Dragon Lee, Bruce Li (Ho Tsung-Tao)*
Undistinguished kung fu feature cobbling together
clips from Bruce Lee's early non-martial arts films.
MAR          115 min (ort 120 min) Cut (3 min 28 sec)
B,V,V2             INT L/A; RAP969 L/A; RVD

## REAL BULLETS *                           18
Lance Lindsay         USA                  1988
*Martin Landau, John Gazarian, Merritt Yohnka,*
*Darlene Landau*
When two female members of a stunt team stumble
onto a drug baron's desert fortress and are captured,
the remaining team members have to mount a rescue.
A/AD                                      90 min
B,V                                        APOL

## REAL GENIUS **                           15
Martha Coolidge       USA                  1985
*Val Kilmer, Gabe Jarret, Jonathan Gries, Michelle*
*Meyrink, William Atherton, Patti D'Arbanville, Robert*
*Prescott, Louis Gaiambalvo, Jonathan Gries*
The story of a kid genius exploiting his college chums,
by conning them into joining his team of high-flyers,
where their talents are put to good use. An interesting
idea that never gets past the teen comedy stage.
COM                          102 min (ort 108 min)
V/sh                                        RCA

## REAL GLORY, THE ***                      PG
Henry Hathaway        USA                  1939
*Gary Cooper, David Niven, Broderick Crawford,*
*Andrea Leeds, Reginald Owen, Kay Johnson,*
*Vladimir Sokoloff, Russell Hicks, Henry Kolker*
An excellent actioner set in the Philippines during
and just after the Spanish-American War. Cooper
plays a medic solving both medical and military
problems with a little help from others.
A/AD                      92 min (ort 95 min) B/W
B,V                                         VGM

## REAL LIFE *                              PG
Francis Megahy        UK                   1983
*Rupert Everett, Cristina Raines, Norman Beaton,*
*Warren Clarke, Isla Blair, James Faulkner, Catherine*
*Rabett, Gillian Adams, Michael Fenton, Una*
*Brandon-Jones, Carolyn Colquhoun, Julia Josephs,*
*Royce Mills, Ann Castle*
The idle and boastful assistant of an estate agent
indulges in wild daydreams, until he meets an
American girl and becomes involved with stolen
Rembrandts. A tedious and feeble comedy. Written by
Megahy.
COM                          89 min (ort 96 min)
B,V                                         EIV

## REAL MEN *                               15
Dennis Feldman        USA                  1988
*James Belushi, John Ritter, Barbara Barrie, Bill*
*Morey, Isa Anderson, Mark Herrier, Gail Barl*
An unfunny spy spoof, with a secret agent on a
mission to save the world from a deadly toxin,
eventually obtaining the antidote from some friendly
aliens.
COM                          82 min (ort 86 min)
B,V                                         WHV

## REAR WINDOW ***                          PG
Alfred Hitchcock      USA                  1954
*James Stewart, Grace Kelly, Wendell Corey, Thelma*
*Ritter, Raymond Burr, Judith Evelyn, Ross*
*Bagdasarian, Georgine Darcy, Sara Berner, Frank*
*Cady, Jesslyn Fax, Irene Winston, Harris Davenport,*
*Marla English, Alan Lee*
A news photographer confined to bed with a broken
leg, spends his time looking through his window over
to the window of a room on the other side of the
building, but this harmless pursuit changes when he
witnesses a murder. An interesting idea severely
hampered by the restriction of action and location.
Written by John Michael Hayes, with music by Franz
Waxman.
Boa: novel by Cornell Woolrich.
THR                          107 min (ort 112 min)
B,V                                         CIC

## REASON TO DIE **                         18
Tim Spring            USA                  1989
*Wings Hauser, Anneline Kriel, Arnold Vosloo*
A nasty bail-jumper goes on the run after a killing
spree and complete with a new identity, settles in
Africa where he once worked with the CIA. However,
he is pursued by a bounty hunter who is not averse to
using similar methods to achieve his ends. A fair
blend of action and tension.
A/AD                                      87 min
V                                           NWV

## REBECCA ****                             PG
Alfred Hitchcock      USA                  1940
*Laurence Olivier, Joan Fontaine, George Sanders,*
*Judith Anderson, Nigel Bruce, Reginald Denny, C.*
*Aubrey Smith, Gladys Cooper, Philip Winter, Edward*
*Fielding, Florence Bates, Melville Cooper, Leo G.*
*Carroll*
A country house holds some strange secrets that
torment the life of the young second wife of a Cornish
landowner. Hitchcock's first American film has a fine
cast and splendid photography. Screenplay is by
Robert E. Sherwood and Joan Harrison, with music by
Franz Waxman. AA: Pic, Cin (George Barnes).
Boa: novel by Daphne du Maurier.
DRA                       130 min; 127 min (VCC) B/W
B,V                            GHV; VCC (VHS only)

## REBECCA OF SUNNYBROOK FARM **            U
Allan Dwan            USA                  1938
*Shirley Temple, Randolph Scott, Gloria Stuart, Jack*
*Haley, Phyllis Brooks, Helen Westley, Slim*
*Summerville, Bill Robinson*
A radio presenter finds a child star only to lose her
again, but they are re-united once more. Not to be
compared to the 1921 silent, with Mary Pickford or
the 1932 remake, this version does not follow the Kate
Douglas Wiggin novel at all. Screenplay is by Karl
Tunberg and Don Ettinger.
COM                          77 min (ort 80 min) B/W
V                                           CBS

## REBEL *                                  15
Robert Allen Schnitzer  USA               1973
*Sylvester Stallone, Antony Page, Rebecca Grimes, Roy*
*White*
A former terrorist has a change of heart and sets out
on a lone crusade against those who manufacture
weapons, but his good intentions are marred by his
destructive methods.
A/AD                                      78 min
V                                  CASPIC/TERRY

## REBEL **                                 15
Michael Jenkins       AUSTRALIA           1986
*Matt Dillon, Debbie Byrne, Bryan Brown, Bill Hunter,*
*Ray Barrett, Julie Nihill, John O'May, Kim Deacon,*
*Sheree Do Costa*
Dillon is badly cast as an American soldier who goes
AWOL in Sydney, meeting up with Byrne, as a
cabaret performer. This flashy but shallow yarn
recalls part of the plot of FROM HERE TO ETERNI-

TY, but is hampered by an intrusive musical soundtrack, that seriously diminishes its dramatic impact.
DRA                                                    98 min
B,V                                                       VES

**REBEL LIEUTENANT, THE **                          15
Calvin Jackson Paget (Giorgio Ferroni)
                      FRANCE/ITALY
*Montgomery Wood (Guiliano Gemma), Dan Vadis,*
*Sophie Daumier, Jacques Sernas, Jose Calvo*
An American Civil War story, with Southern prisoners fighting alongside their captors to beat off an attack by a criminal gang.
WES                                                    95 min
B,V                                                       VPD

**REBEL ROUSERS, THE **                             18
Martin B. Cohen          USA               1967
*Cameron Mitchell, Jack Nicholson, Bruce Dern, Diane*
*Ladd, Harry Dean Stanton*
A road-movie that captures the spirit of the motorcycle gangs of the 1960s, with Dern holding a drag race with Mitchell to see who gets to have the girlfriend of the former. A mildly engaging and slightly amusing offering.
DRA                                     64 min; 80 min (MIA)
B,V                                MOV L/A; MIA (VHS only)

**REBEL WITH A CAUSE ***                               1969
Paolo Heusch            ITALY               1969
*Francisco Rabal, John Ireland, Susan Martinkova,*
*Howard Ross, Giacomo Rossi, Stuart Andrea Checchi,*
*Vittorio Sanipoli*
The life and death of Che Guevara forms the basis for this dull and turgid biopic.
Aka: BLOODY CHE CONTRA; EL CHE GUEVARA;
LA MUERTE DEL CHE GUEVARA
Boa: book by Adriano Bolzoni.
WAR                                                    89 min
B,V                                          ATA L/A; APX

**REBEL WITHOUT A CAUSE ****                          PG
Nicholas Ray            USA                 1955
*James Dean, Natalie Wood, Sal Mineo, Jim Backus,*
*Ann Doran, Corey Allen, Edward Platt, Dennis*
*Hopper, William Hopper, Rochelle Hudson, Nick*
*Adams*
The film that propelled Dean to stardom. He plays an unhappy, insecure youth alienated from his parents. He hangs around with the local youths and causes the death of one in a car stunt. A classic story of youthful alienation that was a well-deserved hit, Dean's wonderful portrayal is supported by a fine cast. Written by Stewart Stern.
Boa: novel Children Of The Dark by I. Schulman.
DRA                                    106 min (ort 111 min)
V                                                        WHV

**REBELS, THE **                                     15
Russ Mayberry           USA                 1979
*Andrew Stevens, Don Johnson, Doug McClure,*
*Richard Basehart, Joan Blondell, Jim Backus, Tom*
*Bosley, Rory Calhoun, Macdonald Carey, Kim*
*Cattrall, John Chappell, William Daniels, Anne*
*Francis, Peter Graves, Pamela Hensley*
A sequel to THE BASTARD, with our hero deeply involved in the American Revolution and its leading lights, and helping to foil a plot to assassinate George Washington. See also THE SEEKERS. Average.
Boa: novel by John Jakes.
A/AD                              188 min (ort 200 min) mTV
B,V                                                       CIC

**REBORN **
Bigas Luna           ITALY/SPAIN/USA          1981
*Dennis Hopper, Michael Moriarty, Antonella Margia,*
*Francisco Rabal, Xavier Elorriaga*
A faith healer uses the services of a talent scout, to find actors able to fake various ailments. Average.

Aka: BLOODY MARY (FFV); RENACER;
RENACIDA
DRA                                                    91 min
B,V                                VTC L/A; FFV (VHS only)

**RECKLESS ***                                        18
James Foley             USA                 1984
*Aidan Quinn, Daryl Hannah, Kenneth McMillan, Cliff*
*De Young, Lois Smith, Adam Baldwin, Dan Hedaya*
A rebellious teenage boy starts a relationship with a rich girl from a really conventional family, who finds in the relationship some of the excitement she craves. All very ponderous and earnest, and done to the beat of an intrusive rock score.
DRA                                                    90 min
B,V                                                       MGM

**RECOMMENDATION FOR MERCY **
Murray Markowitz      CANADA                1974
*Andrew Skidd, Karen Martin, Robb Judd, Mike*
*Upmalis, Michele Fansett, Barry Belchamber, Tom*
*Brennan, Henry Cohen, George Cunninghamfee,*
*Michael Lambert, Michael Lewis, David Murray, Ruth*
*Peckham, Tom Storey, David Wideman*
An 11-year-old boy is accused of the murder of a 13-year-old girl. Based on a real case that took place in 1959.
DRA                                                    81 min
B,V,V2                                                    VPD

**RECON GAME ***                                      18
Peter Collinson         SPAIN               1974
*Peter Fonda, John Philip Law, Cornelia Snarpe,*
*William Holden, Richard Lynch, Albert Mendola*
Three Vietnam veterans (there must be a factory somewhere) continue to kill after the war comes to an end, having become sadistic killers by virtue of their training. An unconvincing and cliched plot unrelieved by any freshness of approach. One day someone will make a film showing what these veterans really had to put up with on their return home.
Aka: OPEN SEASON; RECON HUNT
A/AD                                   99 min (ort 103 min)
B,V                                              KES; KRP

**RECRUITS ***                                        15
Rafal Zelinski          USA                 1986
*Alan Deveau, Annie McCauley, Thor (John Michael),*
*Lolita David, Steve Osmond, Doug Annear, Tracey*
*Tanner, John Terrell, Tony Travis, Mike McDonald,*
*Colleen Karney, Caroline Tweedle, Mark Blutman*
A hopeless bunch of assorted misfits are recruited by the local police chief, in this unashamed encroachment on POLICE ACADEMY territory. Ring down for the Grade-Z awards, here's another one on the way.
COM                                                    87 min
B,V                                                       MED

**RED ALERT ***                                       PG
Billy Hale              USA                 1977
*William Devane, Michael Brandon, Adrienne*
*Barbeau, Ralph Waite, David Hayward, M. Emmett*
*Walsh, Malcolm Wittman, Don Wiseman, Howard*
*Finch, Charles Krohn, Dixie Taylor, Jim Siedow, Lois*
*Fleck, Don Rausch, Jim Danko*
An accident at a nuclear power station causes the computer to seal the building, thereby trapping a group of technicians. A taut and well handled thriller.
Boa: novel Paradigm Red by Harold King.
THR                                                91 min mTV
B,V                                                       CIC

**RED BADGE OF COURAGE, THE ***                        U
John Huston             USA                 1951
*Audie Murphy, Bill Mauldin, Douglas Dick, Royal*
*Dano, John Dierkes, Andy Devine, Arthur Hunnicutt*
An excellent drama dealing with the American Civil War, as seen through the eyes of a young and uncertain hero. Good performances and realistic bat-

tle scenes make this a powerful yet un-cliched attack on the suffering caused by war. The troubled production of this film is told in Lillian Ross' book, "Picture". Vastly under-rated at the time, distributors were unwilling to handle it (it shows American soldiers running away). Remade for TV in 1974.
Boa: novel by Stephen Crane.
WES                              67 min (ort 69 min) B/W
V                                                    MGM

### RED BALLOON, THE *****                          U
Albert Lamorisse    FRANCE                         1955
*Pascal Lamorisse*
Whilst on his way to school, a lonely little boy finds a balloon which seems to have a life of its own. It becomes his faithful companion and when its life is tragically brought to an end, the child receives unexpected comfort. First shown at Cannes (where it received a standing ovation) this exquisite fantasy is one of the great film shorts. Written by Lamorisse and photographed by Edmond Sechan. AA: Screen (Orig) (Albert Lamorisse).
Aka: LE BALLON ROUGE
JUV                              35 min (ort 36 min)
V                                                  BRAVE

### RED BERETS, THE **                              18
Mario Siciliano     ITALY                          1982
*Ivan Rassimov, Priscilla Drake, Kirk Morris*
Mercenaries are sent into a rebel held area of the Congo to recover important documents now in the hands of nationalist guerilars. A formula war film.
Aka: REBELLION
WAR              91 min (ort 100 min) Cut (2 min 52 sec)
B,V                       VDM L/A; GHV L/A; STABL

### RED DAWN *                                      15
John Milius         USA                            1984
*Charlie Sheen, Patrick Swayze, C. Thomas Howell, Lea Thompson, Powers Boothe, Ben Johnson, Harry Dean Stanton, William Smith, Vladek Sheybal, Ron O'Neal, Darren Dalton, Jennifer Grey*
Ridiculous film with a real bubble-gum plot – Soviet forces invade the USA only to be eventually defeated by teenage guerillas. A violent and poorly thought out effort.
A/AD                             109 min (ort 114 min)
V/sh                                                WHV

### RED FLAG: THE ULTIMATE GAME ***
Don Taylor          USA                            1981
*Barry Bostwick, William Devane, Joan Van Ark, Fred McCarren, Debra Feuer, Fred McCarren, Linden Chiles, Arlen Dean Snyder, Jay Kerr, Alan Campbell, Eve McVeagh, Vic Villaro, Joan O'Connell, Tom Daniels, Dick Padgett*
Tragedy strikes during pilot training exercises conducted by the US Air Force, as the direct result of old rivalries between two pilots. A lot of care went into this one, and the simulated battle conditions under which the fighter pilots train, provide a realistic touch. The articulate script is by T.S. Cook.
Aka: RED FLAG
DRA                              92 min mTV
B,V                                                 PRV

### RED HEAT *                                      18
Robert Collector
                    USA/WEST GERMANY               1985
*Linda Blair, Sylvia Kristel, William Ostrander, Sue Kiel, Albert Farrell, Elisabeth Volkmann, Herb Andress, Barbara Spitz*
A woman is imprisoned in East Germany, and her boyfriend decides to get her out to save her from sexual abuse. An absurd plot coupled with poor acting, ensure that this remains a non-starter.
Aka: ROTE HITZE
THR              101 min (ort 104 min) Cut (31 sec)
B/sh, V/sh                                         POLY

### RED HEAT *                                      18
Walter Hill         USA                            1988
*Arnold Schwarzenegger, James Belushi, Peter Boyle, Ed O'Ross, Gina Gershon, Larry Fishburne, Richard Bright, Oleg Vidov*
A Chicago cop is teamed up with a Russian detective, in order to capture a Russian drugs dealer. Standard guns-and-oaths action film, whose only claim on posterity is that it represents the first time the Soviet authorities allowed an American film team to film in Red Square.
A/AD                             100 min (ort 106 min)
V/sh                                                RCA

### RED KING, WHITE KNIGHT *                        15
Geoff Murphy                                       1988
*Max Von Sydow, Helen Mirren, Tom Skerritt, Tom Bell*
Confused thriller set in the era of glasnost, with the CIA helping to foil a plot by the KGB to assassinate Gorbachev by sending a former agent to the USSR to work with an old Soviet girlfriend, who (as one might expect) is played by Mirren. A film whose single interesting idea rapidly gets bogged down in a morass of sub-plots and distractions.
THR                              100 min
V                                                 FUTUR

### RED NIGHTS *                                    18
Izhak Hanooka       USA                            1987
*Christopher Parker, Jack Carter, Brian Matthews*
A man moves to Hollywood to realise his dream of becoming an actor, but finds himself falling into every pitfall on offer, in this remarkably tedious and violent tale.
A/AD                             85 min (ort 92 min)
B,V                                                 EIV

### RED PONY, THE ***                               PG
Lewis Milestone     USA                            1949
*Myrna Loy, Robert Mitchum, Louis Calhern, Peter Miles, Shepperd Strudwick, Margaret Hamilton, Beau Bridges*
The story of a young boy and his life on a farm, his love of his pony and how he loses faith in his father when it dies. Attractive, slow-moving and atmospheric, but somewhat thinly plotted – the story being rather too short to stretch into a full-length feature. The fine score is by Aaron Copeland. Scripted by Robert Totten and Ron Bishop and remade for TV in 1973.
Boa: short story by John Steinbeck.
DRA                              89 min
B,V                        BBC L/A; VMA; STABL

### RED RIDING HOOD ***                             PG
Adam Brooks         USA                            1987
*Isabella Rossellini, Craig T. Nelson, Amelia Shankley*
A colourful live-action version of this fairytale, telling of wicked Sir Godfrey, who wants to marry the wife of his brother, but is opposed by his young niece. He hatches a fiendish plan to get rid of her.
Aka: CANNON MOVIE TALES: RED RIDING HOOD
Boa: short story by Jakob Ludwig Karl Grimm and Wilhelm Karl Grimm.
JUV                              78 min (ort 84 min)
V/sh                                                WHV

### RED RIVER **                                    PG
Richard Michaels    USA                            1988
*James Arness, Gregory Harrison, Bruce Boxleitner, Ray Walston, Laura Johnson, Stan Shaw, Ty Hardin, Robert Horton, John Lupton, Guy Madison*
Based on the 1948 version starring John Wayne and Montgomery Clift, the story follows a cattle ranch owner who sets out with his adopted son and a bunch of tough cowboys to drive a herd across 1,000 dangerous miles of Texas landscape. A textbook illustration

of how unnecessary remakes generally are. Richard Fielder adapted the Borden Chase and Charles Schnee screenplay from the original.
Boa: novel by Borden Chase.
WES                                        91 min (ort 96 min) mTV
B,V                                                            MGM

## RED RIVER ****                                           U
Howard Hawks            USA                    1948
*John Wayne, Montgomery Clift, Joanne Dru, Walter Brennan, Coleen Gray, John Ireland, Noah Beery Jr, Harry Carey Sr, Harry Carey Jr, Paul Fix, Mickey Kuhn, Chief Yowlachie, Ivan Perry, Hank Worden, Hal Taliaferro, Paul Fiero*
A vast, open-spaced and sprawling epic Western, set mainly on a cattle drive along the Chisholm trail, undertaken by a rancher and his rebellious son. Wayne gives one of his best performances as the tyrannical guardian, and Clift is excellent in his first film role. The score is by Dimitri Tiomkin and the photography by Russell Harlan. Written by Borden Chase and Charles Schnee and remade for TV in 1988.
Boa: novel by Borden Chase.
WES                                        122 min (ort 133 min)
V                                                              WHV

## RED SCORPION *                                           U
Joseph Zito             USA                    1989
*Dolph Lundgren, M. Emmet Walsh, Al White, T.P. McKenna, Carmen Argenziano, Alex Colon, Brion James*
Lundgren plays a Russian Spetznaz agent, sent to Africa to murder a rebel African leader in this overlong and flat action tale. A couple of good action sequences cannot save it.
A/AD                                                     102 min
V                                                              VES

## RED SHOES, THE ****
Michael Powell/Emeric Pressburger
UK                    1948
*Anton Walbrook, Moira Shearer, Marius Goring, Robert Helpmann, Leonide Massine, Ludmilla Tcherina, Frederick Ashton, Albert Basserman, Esmond Knight, Irene Browne, Austin Trevor, Marcel Poncon, Jerry Verno, Jean Short*
A great ballet dancer is torn between love for her art and her love of two men, finally being driven to a tragic end. A beautiful film that gives an intimate backstage view of the world of ballet. This was Shearer's screen debut. The photography is by Jack Cardiff and the script by Powell and Pressburger. AA: Score (Brian Easdale), Art/Set (Hein Heckroth/Arthur Lawson).
DRA                                        132 min (ort 136 min)
B,V                                                            RNK

## RED SONJA *                                           PG/15
Richard Fleischer       USA                    1985
*Arnold Schwarzenegger, Brigitte Nielsen, Sandahl Bergman, Paul Smith, Ernie Reyes Jr, Ronald Lacey, Pat Roach, Terry Richards, Janet Agren, Donna Ostabuhr, Lara Naszinsky, Hans Meyer, Tutte Lemkow, Tad Horino*
Sword-and-sorcery adventure with all the standard ingredients, telling how Sonja avenges her sister's death and deposes a wicked queen. A pulp adventure, based on the writings of Robert E. Howard of "Conan" fame. In this one the actors are as unconvincing as the monsters.
A/AD    85 min (ort 89 min) (Cut at film release for PG version)
B,V                                                            TEVP

## RED SPIDER **                                           18
Jerry Jameson           USA                    1988
*James Farentino, Amy Steel, Jennifer O'Neill, Philip Casnoff, Soon-Teck Oh, Stephen Joyce, Ed Hindman*
As sequel to ONE POLICE PLAZA with a different cast stepping into the same roles. A dogged New York police lieutenant investigates a series of bizarre Chinatown murders, in which the victims are all marked with a spider emblem, and a Vietnam link is discovered. A production-line thriller.
THR                                        89 min (ort 96 min) mTV
B,V                                                            CBS

## RED SUN *                                           15
Terence Young
FRANCE/ITALY/SPAIN              1971
*Charles Bronson, Toshiro Mifune, Ursula Andress, Alain Delon, Capucine, Satoshi Nakamoura, Bart Barry, Lee Burton, Anthony Dawson, John Hamilton, George W. Lycan, Jose Nieto, Julio Pena, Monica Randall, Luc Merenda*
In 1870s Arizona a samurai teams up with an outlaw to recover a ceremonial sword, a present from the Emperor of Japan to the President of the USA. A thorough let-down, with a good idea spoilt by excessive emphasis on violence. The conflict of cultural values remains an unexplored theme.
Aka: SOLEIL ROUGE
WES                                  103 min; 109 min (CH5)
B,V                           POLY; CH5 (VHS only)

## RED-HEADED STRANGER, THE *                        15
Bill Wittliff           USA        1984 (released 1986)
*Willie Nelson, Katherine Ross, Morgan Fairchild, R.G. Armstrong, Royal Dano, Sonny Carl Davis*
A Montana preacher and his beautiful wife arrive in a Western town to preach the word of God, and discover that the town is in the grip of a gang of thugs. Since the weak sheriff is unable to impose law and order, the preacher decides to do so for him. A flat and unappealing yarn, inspired by a Willie Nelson album of 1975. Wittliff's directorial debut.
WES                                                     105 min
B,V                                                            NELS

## RED-LIGHT STING, THE **                           15
Rod Holcomb             USA                    1984
*Farrah Fawcett, Beau Bridges, Harold Gould, Paul Burke, Conrad Janis, Lawrence Pressman, Katherine Cannon, Alex Henteloff, Sunny Johnson, James Luisi, Philip Charles MacKenzie, Macon McCalman, Eddie Barth, Stanley Kamel*
A high-class prostitute is engaged to work in a brothel, which is really an elaborate front being used to trap a gang leader. A relaxed and mildly diverting tale.
Boa: book The Whorehouse Sting by Henry Post.
DRA                                        92 min mTV
B,V                                                            CIC

## REDEEMER, THE *
Constantine S. Gochis   USA                    1976
*Damien Knight, Jeanette Arnette, T.G. Finkbinder, Michael Hollingsworth, Gyr Patterson, Nikki Barthen, Christopher Flint, Eric Kjoenes, Larry Mooney, Nick Carter*
Six people arrive at their old school for a class reunion, only to find themselves alone and at the mercy of a sinister killer. Another standard killer-on-the-prowl offering.
Aka: REDEEMER . . . SON OF SATAN, THE
THR                                                     83 min
B,V                                                            DFS

## REDNECK *
Silvio Narizzano        ITALY/UK               1972
*Franco Nero, Telly Savalas, Mark Lester, Ely Galleani, Dulio Del Prete, Maria Michi, Beatrice Clary, Bruno Boschetti, Aldo De Carellis, Tommy Duggan, Wanda Pellini, Michael Barnes*
Two jewel thieves on a job accidentally "kidnap" a young boy, and use him as a hostage as they shoot their way out of a succession of tight corners. A disagreeable and implausible dud with a streak of

nastiness.
DRA 84 min (ort 92 min)
B,V POLY

**REDS ✶✶** 15
Warren Beatty USA 1981
*Warren Beatty, Diane Keaton, Jack Nicholson,*
*Edward Herrmann, Paul Sorvino, Jerzy Kosinski,*
*Maureen Stapleton, Gene Hackman, Nicolas Coster, M.*
*Emmet Walsh, Ian Wolfe, Bessie Love, MacIntyre*
*Dixon, Pat Starr, George Plimpton*
Vast sprawling biopic on the life and loves of idealistic
journalist John Reed; an eyewitness to the Russian
Revolution. Heavily weighed down with its political
content and dealing with Reed's affair with Louise
Bryant in a superficial way, this represents a film
ruined by over-ambition. Despite this it won three
Oscars. AA: Dir, S. Actress (Stapleton), Cin (Vittorio
Storaro).
DRA 187 min (ort 200 min) (Cut at film
release by 3 sec)
B,V CIC

**REEFER MADNESS**
Louis Gasnier USA 1936
*Dave O'Brien, Dorothy Short, Warren McCollum,*
*Lillian Miles, Carleton Young, Thelma White,*
*Kenneth Craig*
Unbelievable, campy anti-marihuana warning, that is
as ill-informed as it is exploitative and counter-
productive, claiming as it does, that smoking dope
turns kids into drug-crazed murderers and perverts.
As might be expected, this laughable and moronic tale
now enjoys cult status. See also ASSASSIN OF
YOUTH and MARIHUANA: THE DEVIL'S WEED.
Aka: BURNING QUESTION, THE; DOPE ADDICT;
DOPED YOUTH; LOVE MADNESS; TELL YOUR
CHILDREN
DRA 70 min B/W
V HVS

**REFLECTION OF FEAR, A ✶✶** 18
William A. Fraker USA 1971
*Robert Shaw, Sally Kellerman, Mary Ure, Sondra*
*Locke, Signe Hasso, Mitchell Ryan, Gordon De Vol,*
*Liam Dunn, Victoria Risk, Michael St Clair, Michele*
*Marvin, Gordon Anderson, Leonard John Crofoot*
An adolescent girl has been kept secluded from the
outside world by her mother and grandmother. The
return of her father after a 10-year absence, leads to
the murder of the mother and grandmother, and the
attempted murder of the man's girlfriend. All the
signs point to the attacker being male and this turns
out to be so, with our "girl" revealed to be a boy who
has been brought up as a girl by his man-hating
mother. A murky and ponderous tale.
Aka: AUTUMN CHILD; LABYRINTH
Boa: novel Go To Thy Deathbed by Stanton Forbes.
HOR 86 min (ort 90 min)
B,V RCA

**REFORM SCHOOL GIRLS ✶** 18
Tom De Simone USA 1986
*Linda Carrol, Wendy O. Williams, Pat Ast, Sybil*
*Danning (Sybelle Danninger), Charlotte McGinnis,*
*Sherri Stoner, Denise Gordy, Tiffany Schwartz*
A ridiculous over-the-top spoof on women-in-prison
movies, this time concentrating on a reform school for
girls where the staff and inmates are equally rotten,
evil and sadistic. Hard to believe that a film in which
one of the characters commits suicide could be looked
on as a form of comic entertainment.
COM 90 min (ort 98 min) Cut (8 sec)
B,V NWV

**REFUGE OF FEAR ✶** 15
Jose Manuel Ulloa SPAIN 1973
*Craig Hill, Patty Shepard, Teresa Gimpera, Fernando*
*Millet, Pedro Maria Sanchez, Fernando Hilbeck*

Routine post-WW3 account of a devastated world.
Aka: EL REFUGIO DEL MIEDO; SURVIVORS OF
THE LAST RACE (NET)
HOR 92 min
B,V VPD; NET

**REGAN ✶✶** 15
Tom Clegg UK 1974
*John Thaw, Dennis Waterman, Lee Montague,*
*Garfield Morgan, David Daker. Janet Key, Maureen*
*Lipman*
Tough cop thriller with Thaw and Waterman from the
popular TV police series "The Sweeney" searching for
the murderer of a colleague.
THR 80 min mTV
V THAMES/VCC

**REGENERATOR ✶✶** 18
G.L. Eastman USA 1988
*Gene LeBrock, Stephen Brown, Catherine Baranov,*
*Harry Cason*
A brilliant scientist unlocks the secret of genetic
replication and tries to convince his colleagues that he
has found the key to eternal life. Their scepticism is
such that he decides to experiment on himself, but
soon finds himself changing into a monster. A low-
budget film of good effects and an effective climax.
FAN 90 min
B,V CFD

**REILLY: ACE OF SPIES ✶✶** 15
Jim Goddard UK 1983
*Sam Neill, Leo McKern, Norman Rodway, Peter Egan,*
*Sebastian Shaw*
First episode of a multi-part serial about a famous spy.
Sub-titled "An Affair with a Married Woman". The
background is recreated with loving care but the story
proceeds so slowly that no suspense is generated.
Here, Reilly is inside Russia gathering information on
its oil industry when the train he is on is stopped and
he and his fellow passengers are detained by the
authorities.
Aka: REILLY: THE ACE OF SPIES
Boa: book by R.B. Lockhart.
DRA 80 min mTV
B,V THAMES/TEVP

**REJUVENATOR ✶✶** 18
Brian Thomas Jones USA 1988
*Vivian Lanko, John MacKay, James Hogue, Jessica*
*Dublin*
A woman develops homicidal tendencies as a side-
effect of a rejuvenation treatment that is based on the
use of dead brain tissue. Not the freshest of plots, but
done with a certain amount of flair and quite enter-
taining.
Aka: REJUVENATRIX; REJUVENATRIX: A
CLASSIC TALE OF TERROR
HOR 84 min (ort 90 min)
B,V CHV

**RELATIVE SECRETS ✶✶** PG
Don Cato USA 1987
*Karen Black, Art Hindle, Hoyt Axton, Tina Louise,*
*Ruth Nissen, Nina Foch, Moses Gunn, Chris Rydell,*
*Pamela Springsteen, John Vernon*
The story of a wild family reunion that takes place in
a small American town at the end of WW2.
Aka: DIXIE LANES
COM 83 min (ort 90 min)
B,V CHV

**RELATIVES ✶✶** PG
Anthony Bowman AUSTRALIA 1985
*Bill Kerr, Rowena Wallace, Ray Barrett, Norman*
*Kaye, Carol Raye, Brett Climo*
A family gathers to celebrate their grandfather's 80th
birhday, and all the hidden tensions and conflicts
begin to emerge. Average.

COM                                    85 min
B,V                                       ODY

## RELENTLESS **                           18
William Lustig          USA              1989
*Judd Nelson, Robert Loggia, Leo Rossi, Meg Foster,*
*Patrick O'Bryan, Ken Lerner, Mindy Seeger, Angel*
*Tompkins*
A neat little police thriller that casts Rossi as a New
York cop now working in L.A., where he sets out to
solve a series of killings with his new partner. Nelson
is memorable as the psychotic killer who, having been
abused as a child, has taken to random killings by
selecting his victims from phone books. Despite its
share of cliches, this well-acted tale benefits from its
strong script, the work of Phil Alden Robinson.
THR                           88 min (ort 93 min)
V/sh                                      WHV

## RELUCTANT HEROES, THE **                PG
Robert Day             USA              1971
*Ken Berry, Jim Hutton, Trini Lopez, Cameron*
*Mitchell, Warren Oates, Ralph Meeker, Don Marshall,*
*Richard Young, Michael St George, Soon-Teck Oh*
An assorted group of soldiers have to capture a
keypoint, Hill 656 during the Korean War, but are led
by an inexperienced officer who was formerly an army
historian. Excellent performances and good action
sequences make up for the poor dialogue and im-
plausible plotting.
Aka: EGGHEAD ON HILL 656, THE
Osca: HELL IN THE PACIFIC (VCC)
WAR         71 min; 168 min (2 film cassette) mTV
B,V                          GHV; VCC (VHS only)

## REMBRANDT ****                            U
Alexander Korda         UK               1936
*Charles Laughton, Gertrude Lawrence, Elsa*
*Lanchester, Edward Chapman, Walter Hudd, Roger*
*Livesey, John Bryning, Sam Livesey, Herbert Lomas,*
*Allan Jeayes, John Clements, Raymond Huntley,*
*Abraham Sofaer, Lawrence Hanray, Basil Gill*
A lavish examination of the life of this 17th century
Dutch painter, made as a set of vignettes exploring
episodes in his life. A handsome, austere and gently
tragi-comic work, loosely held together by a memor-
able performance from Laughton. Photography is by
Georges Perinal and Richard Angst.
DRA                           80 min (ort 84 min) B/W
V                                        PICK

## REMEMBRANCE OF LOVE ***
Jack Smight            USA              1982
*Kirk Douglas, Pam Dawber, Chana Eden, Robert*
*Clary, Yoram Gall, Michael Goodwin, Eric Douglas,*
*Irit Frank, Gladys Gewirtz, Yossi Yadin, Gideon*
*Singer, Reuben Singer, Irv Kaplan, Warren Feign,*
*Dina Doronne, Yehuda Efroni*
A widowed Holocaust survivor meets the woman he
loved when they were both teenagers in the Warsaw
Ghetto. A melodramatic love story played out against
the background of painful historical events whose
consequences are still with us. Filmed entirely on
location in Israel and written by Harold Jack Bloom.
Boa: magazine article by Rena Dictor LeBlanc.
DRA                                  96 min mTV
B,V                            VFP L/A; HER

## REMO: UNARMED AND DANGEROUS **          15
Guy Hamilton           USA              1985
*Fred Ward, Joel Grey, Wilford Brimley, J.A. Preston,*
*George Coe, Charles Cioffi, Kate Mulgrew, Michael*
*Pataki, William Hickey, Patrick Kilpatrick, Davenia*
*McFadden, Cosie Costa, J.P. Romano, Joel J. Kramer,*
*Frank Ferrara*
A tough New York cop is drafted into a top-secret
intelligence agency and assigned to the care of a
Korean martial arts instructor for training. What
promises to be an enjoyable adaptation, true to the

spirit of the pulp "Destroyer" novels of Richard Sapir
and Warren Murphy, rapidly goes downhill and is
hardly helped by some remarkably cheap effects. Only
Grey's engaging performance as the Korean martial
arts master makes this worth watching.
Aka: REMO WILLIAMS: THE ADVENTURE
BEGINS; REMO WILLIAMS: THE ADVENTURE
CONTINUES
A/AD       111 min (ort 121 min) (Cut at film release)
B,V            ORION/PVG; RNK; VIR (VHS only)

## REMOTE CONTROL **                        15
Jeff Lieberman          USA              1987
*Kevin Dillon, Jennifer Tilly, Deborah Goodrich,*
*Christopher Wynne, Frank Beddor, Bert Remsen,*
*Jaimie McEnnan, Jerold Pearson, Jennifer Buchman,*
*Will Nye, Deborah Downey, Marilyn Adams, Richard*
*Warlock, Ann Walker, Ty Kelley*
A spoof horror yarn, the title of which refers to a
videotape that is supposedly a 1950s film looking
forward to the 1980s, but is in reality a tape created by
aliens in order to destroy mankind. Those who watch
the tape are driven to violence, and with more and
more people clamouring for it, a young man working
in a video store realises that all copies must be
destroyed.
HOR                           85 min (ort 88 min)
B,V                                       CBS

## RENEGADE **                              15
E.B. Clucher (Enzo Barboni)
                       ITALY             1987
*Terence Hill (Mario Girotti), Robert Vaughn, Ross*
*Hill, Norman Bowler*
A drifter travels across the States living by selling his
horse which, no sooner sold, returns to its owner. A
jailed friend asks him to look after his young son and
take over the running of a ranch, but as he heads
there he finds that his friend has enemies who are out
to stop him. A relaxed and quite enjoyable tale that
makes a nice change from all those abysmal Hill-
Spencer comedy actioners.
A/AD                          100 min Cut (34 sec)
B,V                                       VES

## RENEGADES **                             18
Jack Sholder           USA              1989
*Kiefer Sutherland, Lou Diamond Phillips, Rob*
*Knepper, Bill Smitrovich, Jami Gertz, Floyd*
*Westerman*
A pilot for a short-lived series that has a Philadelphia
cop and a Lakota Indian teaming up to bust a
gun-running operation and settle a few old scores at
the same time. Written by David Rich, it combines a
paper-thin plot with a series of well-handled action
scenes.
A/AD                      102 min (ort 106 min) subH
V                                        20VIS

## RENEGADES, THE **                        15
John Patterson          USA              1988
*John Bennett Perry, Anthony Zerbe, Amanda Wyss,*
*Sandy McPeak*
A brave sheriff who lost his family to a vicious outlaw
gang, builds a new life for himself in a frontier town.
When the same gang turns up to threaten his new
family, he sets out to have his revenge.
WES                                     101 min
V                                         TGP

## RENT-A-COP *                             15
Jerry London           USA              1987
*Burt Reynolds, Liza Minnelli, James Remar, Richard*
*Masur, Bernie Casey, John Stanton, John P. Ryan,*
*Dionne Warwick, Robby Benson*
After a drugs bust goes tragically wrong, a suspended
cop teams up with a prostitute to get a crazy killer
who is their common enemy. A careless and meander-
ing tale, made even less enjoyable by Minnelli's

constant stream of wisecracks.

A/AD 92 min (ort 97 min)
V VES

**RENTADICK *** PG
Jim Clark/Richard Loncraine
UK 1972
*James Booth, Richard Briers, Julie Ege, Ronald
Fraser, Donald Sinden, Tsai Chin, Kenneth Cope,
John Wells, Richard Beckinsale, Michael Bentine,
Derek Griffiths, Leon Sinden, Kristopher Kum,
Veronica Clifford, Cheryl Hall*
A shapeless detective spoof from a couple of members
of the "Monty Python" TV team, with a private
detective hired to recover an experimental nerve gas
that paralyses from the waist down. Unfortunately,
this flabby comedy paralyses from the neck up.
Written by John Cleese, Graham Chapman, John
Wells and John Fortune.
COM 94 min; 89 min (VCC)
B,V RNK; VCC

**REPO MAN *** 18
Alex Cox USA 1984
*Emilio Esterez, Harry Dean Stanton, Vonetta McGee,
Olivia Barash, Sy Richardson, Susan Barnes, Tracey
Walter, Fox Harris, The Circle Jerks*
A young punk gets a job repossessing cars but finds
himself involved in a strange series of events. A
curious blend of film noir and macabre fantasy that is
intermittently engaging but is best enjoyed in small
doses. Written by Cox.
A/AD 88 min (ort 92 min)
V/h CIC

**REPORT TO THE COMMISSIONER *** 15
Milton Katselas USA 1974
*Michael Moriarty, Yaphet Kotto, Susan Blakely,
Hector Elizondo, Tony King, Michael McGuire, Dana
Elcar, Robert Balaban, William Devane, Stephen
Elliott, Richard Gere, Vic Tayback, Sonny Grosso*
The police department mount a cover-up when a
rookie cop accidentally kills an experienced undercov-
er one. A harsh melodrama that veers wildly from
realism to melodrama and back again. Gripping but
implausible. Written by Abby Mann and Ernest
Tidyman with music by Elmer Bernstein. This was
Gere's film debut.
Aka: OPERATION UNDERCOVER
Boa: novel by James Mills.
DRA 108 min (ort 112 min)
B,V WHV

**REPULSION **** 18
Roman Polanski UK 1965
*Catherine Deneuve, Ian Hendry, John Fraser, Patrick
Wymark, Yvonne Furneaux, Renee Houston, James
Villiers, Valerie Taylor, Hugh Futcher, Helen Fraser,
Monica Merlin, Mike Pratt, Imogen Graham, Wally
Bosco, Roman Polanski*
Polanski's first English language film is a brilliant
but harrowing tour de force, charting the slow descent
of a withdrawn young girl into madness, when left
alone in a flat for a few days while her sister goes on
holiday. An abundance of powerful images serve to
underline her growing insanity, culminating in a
nightmarish climax. Written by Polanski and Gerald
Brach.
HOR 104 min; 100 min (ODY) B/W
B,V VDM; VMA; STABL; ODY (VHS only)

**RESCUE ME *** PG
Jubel Harshaw USA 1988
*Teri Austin, Ted Shackleford*
A divorced woman embarks on an affair with an
architect and then finds herself locked in a dangerous
love triangle when her jealous former husband returns.

DRA 96 min
B,V BRAVE

**RESCUE OF JESSICA McCLURE, THE *** PG
Mel Damski USA 1989
*Beau Bridges, Patty Duke, Pat Hingle, Roxana Zal*
Dramatisation of the true story of an 18-month-old
girl who fell into a well-shaft and was trapped there
for 56 hours until her rescue. This apparently simple
task was revealed to be fraught with unforeseen perils
and the rescue attracted worldwide attention. An
adequate TV film that generally maintains a good
sense of momentum, despite the fact that the outcome
is never in question.
Aka: EVERYBODY'S BABY: THE RESCUE OF
JESSICA McCLURE
DRA 91 min mTV
V/h ODY

**RESCUE, THE *** PG
Ferdinand Fairfax USA 1988
*Marc Price, Kevin Dillon, Charles Haid, Edward
Albert, Christina Harnos, Ned Vaughan, Ian Giatti,
Timothy Carhart*
A group of kids invade North Korea to rescue their
fathers, all members of US armed forces, from Com-
munist captivity. A mindless and puerile action tale,
produced by Touchstone Pictures, who clearly display
their Disney origins.
A/AD 93 min (ort 98 min)
B,V BUENA; TOUCH

**RESISTANCE *** PG
Arthur H. Nader UK 1970
*Robert Goulet, Danielle Gaubert, Laurence Dobkin,
Carl Duering, Joachim Hansen, Roger Delgado,
Alexander Prag, George Pravda, Leon Lissek,
Sebastian Breaks, Nicole Croisell, Derry Power*
A German general is kidnapped from occupied France,
by an American major working together with the
French resistance, in this run-of-the-mill war film.
Aka: UNDERGROUND
WAR 89 min (ort 100 min)
V FILV; GLOB

**REST IN PIECES *** 18
Joseph Braunstein USA 1987
*Scott Thompson Baker, Lorin Jean, Dorothy Malone,
Jack Taylor, Patty Shepherd, Jeffrey Segal, Fernando
Bilbao, Carol James, Robert Case, Daniel Katz, Tony
Isbert, Antonio Ross*
A woman inherits an eerie Spanish estate that proves
to be the focus for a Satanist cult.
HOR 85 min (ort 90 min)
B,V CINE

**RESTING PLACE *** PG
John Korty USA 1986
*John Lithgow, Richard Bradford, Morgan Freeman,
C.C.H. Pounder, M. Emmet Walsh, Frances
Sternhagen, G.D. Spradlin, John Philbin, Brian
Tarantina, Tegan West, Buck Herron, Bob Hannah,
Mert Hatfield, Hugh Jarrett*
A Vietnam veteran brings the body of a black fellow
soldier home for burial in the whites only cemetery in
his home town, and encounters a good deal of opposi-
tion to this, as well as learning of a conspiracy to
conceal the manner in which the soldier really died.
Slightly reminiscent of "Bad Day At Black Rock", but
lacking power, despite the "we're all rascists" message
heavily worked into the script.
Aka: HALLMARK HALL OF FAME
DRA 98 min (ort 100 min) mTV
B,V CAN

**RESTLESS BREED, THE *** 
Allan Dwan USA 1957
*Scott Brady, Anne Bancroft, Jim Davis, Scott
Marlowe, Evelyn Rudie, Jay C. Flippen, Leo Gordon,*

*Rhys Williams, Myron Healy, Scott Marlowe, Eddy Waller, Harry V. Cheshire, Gerald Milton, Dennis King Jr, James Flavin*

A Western lawyer is out to get the killer of his secret service father, and arrives at a frontier town to do just that. Very much a standard revenge Western, well made but hardly memorable.

| WES | 81 min |
| B,V,V2 | INT |

## RESTLESS NATIVES *                    PG
Michael Hoffman            UK          1985
*Vincent Friell, Joe Mullaney, Teri Lally, Bernard Hill, Mel Smith, Robert Urquhart, Ned Beatty, Bryan Forbes, Nanette Newman, Anne Scott-James, Rachel Boyd, Iain McColl, Dave Anderson, Eiji Kusuhara, Ed Bishop, Laura Smith*

Two youths become bored with their jobs and make themselves unemployed, but decide to improve their dull and impecunious lifestyle by dubbing themselves the "Clown" and the "Wolfman" and robbing tourist coaches in Scotland. Soon these latter-day highwaymen find themselves becoming media celebrities. A flat and unsatisfactory comedy that fails to make the most of its one idea.

| COM | 89 min |
| B,V | TEVP; WHV |

## RESURRECTED **                        18
Paul Greengrass           UK          1989
*Tom Bell, Rita Tushingham, David Thewlis, Rudi Davis*

An attempt to provide an account of Kevin Deakin, a British soldier who went missing during the Falklands War and was presumed dead, but turned up 49 days later, apparently suffering from amnesia. Despite statements to the contrary from his superiors, he was seen as an embarrassment and was eventually obliged to resign. A competent blend of fact and fiction, but of limited appeal.

| DRA | 92 min |
| V | CBS |

## RESURRECTION OF EVE, THE ***
Jim Mitchell/Artie Mitchell
                          USA          1973
*Marilyn Chambers, Mimi Morgan, Matthew Armon, Johnny Keyes, Kani Jones*

This film follows the changes in Eve's life, from age 13 to adulthood, and her relationship with a jealous disc jockey. A serious road accident leaves her badly scarred but she has cosmetic surgery, emerging as Chambers. She then marries her D.J. and embarks on a swinging lifestyle. A competent and well-acted tale, and one that cleverly interweaves earlier sequences of her life into the main narrative.

| A | 82 min |
| B,V | TCX |

## RETALIATOR *                           18
Allan Holzman            USA          1987
*Robert Ginty, Sandahl Bergman, Louise Claire Clark, James Booth*

A former CIA agent is brought out of retirement to mount a rescue mission, when two American kids are snatched during a terrorist outrage in Greece. The mission is successful and the terrorists are killed, but the body of a female terrorist is used in a gruesome experiment in which she is resurrected as a vengeance-seeking cyborg. Gory, derivative and mind-numbing nonsense.
Aka: PROGRAMMED TO KILL

| A/AD | 87 min |
| B,V | VPD |

## RETRIBUTION *                          18
Guy Magar                USA          1986
*Hoyt Axton, Suzanne Snyder, Leslie Wing, Dennis Lipscomb, Jeff Pomerantz, George Murdock, Pamela Dunlap, Susan Peretz, Clare Peck, Chris Caputo, Ralph Manza*

An artist whose suicide attempt failed, is possessed by the spirit of a man seeking revenge on his killers, thus beginning another orgy of special effects and gory deaths. A dull and derivative film that rapidly becomes quite tiresome to watch.

| HOR | 103 min (ort 107 min) Cut (1 min 24 sec) |
| V/sh | MED |

## RETURN FROM THE RIVER KWAI ***        15
Andrew V. McLaglen       USA          1988
*Christopher Penn, Edward Fox, Denholm Elliott, Tatsuya Nakadai, George Takei, Nick Tate*

US Air Force planes destroy a set of bridges over the River Kwai in Japanese occupied Thailand during WW2, and a pilot parachutes to safety after his plane is hit by anti-aircraft fire. After joining a unit of Thai guerrillas, led by an English major, he takes part in an attempt to free POWs being held at a local camp, is himself captured but eventually escapes. A vigorous and well handled if somewhat stereotyped war film.

| WAR | 98 min |
| V | BRAVE |

## RETURN FROM WITCH MOUNTAIN **          U
John Hough               USA          1978
*Bette Davis, Christopher Lee, Ike Eisenmann, Kim Richards, Denver Pyle, Jack Soo, Anthony James, Ward Costello, Dick Bakalyan, Brad Savage, Christian Juttner, Jeffrey Jacquet*

A sequel to ESCAPE TO WITCH MOUNTAIN, in which a group of criminals try to exploit the supernatural powers of the two alien children. Quite inventive in terms of its special effects, but coy and lacking in strong characterisation with regard to the two kids. An undemanding Disney outing.

| FAN | 89 min (ort 95 min) |
| B,V | RNK |

## RETURN OF A MAN CALLED HORSE, THE ***  15
Irvin Kershner           USA          1976
*Richard Harris, Gale Sondergaard, Bill Lucking, Geoffrey Lewis, Jorge Luke, Enrique Lucero, Ana DeSade, Claudio Brook, Jorge Russek, Pedro Damien*

Sequel to A MAN CALLED HORSE, with Harris returning to the Yellow Hand Sioux to help them resist the onslaught of the white man. A harsh and brutal adventure, written by Jack De Witt. The memorable score is by Laurence Rosenthal. Followed by TRIUMPHS OF A MAN CALLED HORSE.
Boa: novel by Dorothy M. Johnson.

| WES | 119 min (ort 125 min) Cut (1 min 46 sec) |
| B,V | WHV |

## RETURN OF BRUCE *
Joseph Velasco
                    HONG KONG/PHILIPPINES
*Bruce Le (Huang Kin Lung), Lo Lieh, Kong Tau, James Num, Gina Velasco, Pak Chi Sang, Leopoldo Salcedo, Richard Merchant*

Bruce kills a gangster and then flees to Manila where he deals with a white slavery ring. Another below-average spin-off using a Bruce Lee lookalike to capitalise on the popularity of the late star.

| MAR | 85 min |
| V | ICL |

## RETURN OF CAPTAIN INVINCIBLE, THE **   PG
Philippe Mora   AUSTRALIA/USA          1982
*Alan Arkin, Christopher Lee, Kate Fitzpatrick, Michael Pate, Bill Hunter, John Bluthal*

An ageing and alcoholic superhero comes out of retirement to save the world. A curious attempt to produce a campy comedy that occasionally works but is generally ineffective. One of those films that looked better on paper. Written by Steven E. De Souza and Andrew Gaty.

Aka: LEGEND IN LEOTARDS
COM                              90 min
B,V                                 EIV

**RETURN OF FRANK CANNON, THE \*\***      PG
Corey Allen          USA          1980
*William Conrad, Arthur Hill, Allison Argo, Burr
DeBenning, Taylor Lacher, Diana Muldaur, Ed
Nelson, Joanna Pettet, William Smithers, Rafael
Campos*
Private detective Frank Cannon comes out of retire-
ment (if not back into a new TV series) and leaves his
comfortable life as a restaurateur, to solve a myste-
rious suicide when he learns that the victim, a former
Army Intelligence agent, was an old friend of his. A
re-tread of all the standard detective cliches follows,
in this uninspired attempt to revive a popular TV
character.
DRA                              96 min mTV
V                                CASPIC

**RETURN OF JOSEY WALES, THE \***         15
Michael Parks        USA          1986
*Michael Parks, Raphael Campos, Bob Magruder, Paco
Vela, Everett Sifuentes, Charlie McCoy*
A follow-on to the original THE OUTLAW JOSEY
WALES minus Clint Eastwood, and telling of the
exploits of our title character as he takes on an
incompetent but stubborn lawman. A limp and hollow
dud that would have worked better as a comedy.
WES                              90 min mTV
B,V                                 ABC

**RETURN OF KID BARKER, THE \***          15
Robert J. Emery      USA
*Big John Hamilton, Glenn Corbett, Ivy Jones, Morgan
Woodward*
Vietnam veteran goes to hostile town. Vietnam
veteran finds that his girlfriend is now married.
Vietnam veteran accidentally kills a man in a fight.
The words may have changed, but the song remains
the same.
DRA                              86 min
B,V                                 KSV

**RETURN OF MARTIN GUERRE, THE \*\***     15
Daniel Vigne         FRANCE       1982
*Gerard Depardieu, Nathalie Baye, Roger Planchon,
Maurice Jacquemont, Bernard Pierre Donnadieu,
Sylvie Meda, Maurice Barrier, Stephane Peau*
A 16th century peasant boy disappears from his
village and returns seven years later as a man, but
there are suspicions that he may be an imposter.
Mildly entertaining and always good to look at, but
hampered by a lack of narrative drive. Written by
Jean-Claude Carriere and Daniel Vigne.
Aka: LE RETOUR DE MARTIN GUERRE
DRA               110 min; 105 min (PAL) (ort 123 min)
B,V                             PVG; PAL

**RETURN OF SAM McCLOUD, THE \***         PG
Alan J. Levi         USA          1989
*Dennis Weaver, J.D. Cannon, Terry Carter, Diana
Muldaur, Patrick Macnee, Kerrie Keane, Roger Rees,
Simon Williams, Melissa Anderson, David McCallum*
Corny attempt to breathe new life into the title
character, the cowboy cop from the popular TV series.
Here, he is now a US senator fighting powerful
chemical corporations over their pollution of the
environment. When he arrives in London for the
funeral of his niece, his enemies attempt his assas-
sination. A stereotyped view of England, with chirpy
cockneys and steam trains adds nothing to this dud.
See BRANNIGAN for something similar.
DRA                              96 min
V                                   CIC

**RETURN OF SHERLOCK HOLMES, THE \*\***   PG
Kevin O'Connor       USA          1987

*Margaret Colin, Connie Booth, Michael Pennington,
Lila Kaye, Barry Morse, Nicholas Guest*
An American descendant of Dr Watson inherits a
property in Britain and finds the frozen body of the
famous sleuth in the cellar. She revives him and
together they go back to the USA, where our detective
has more than a little difficulty coming to terms with
the 20th century. A good premise is spoilt by flippant
treatment and poor development.
Boa: short story by Arthur Conan Doyle.
COM                   90 min (ort 104 min) mTV
B,V                                 CBS

**RETURN OF SHERLOCK HOLMES, THE:**       PG
**SILVER BLAZE \*\*\***
Brian Mills          UK           1986
*Jeremy Brett, Edward Hardwicke*
In this tale Holmes embarks on an attempt to discover
exactly why a valuable race-horse vanished on the eve
of a major race. Another enjoyable adaptation.
Boa: short story by Arthur Conan Doyle. Osca:
RETURN OF SHERLOCK HOLMES, THE: THE
DEVIL'S FOOT
DRA               105 min (2 film cassette) mTV
B,V                                HEND

**RETURN OF SHERLOCK HOLMES, THE:**
**THE ABBEY GRANGE \*\*\***
Peter Hammond        UK           1986
*Jeremy Brett, Edward Hardwicke, Paul Williamson,
Conrad Phillips, Anne Louise Lambert*
Holmes is called in to investigate the murder of a
certain Sir Eustace Brackenstall and soon finds that
what appears to be a simple case has deeper implica-
tions. Another episode in this detailed and entertain-
ing series of adaptations. The script is by Trevor
Bowen.
Boa: short story by Arthur Conan Doyle. Osca:
RETURN OF SHERLOCK HOLMES, THE: THE
EMPTY HOUSE
DRA               103 min (2 film cassette) mTV
B,V                                HEND

**RETURN OF SHERLOCK HOLMES, THE:**
**THE BRUCE PARTINGTON PLANS \*\*\***
John Gorrie         UK            1986
*Jeremy Brett, Edward Hardwicke*
In this intriguing mystery, Holmes attempts to solve a
baffling case that revolves around the discovey of the
body of a young man on a railway line. His pockets
were found to contain secret plans for construction of a
submarine and Holmes sets out to determine whether
or not he was a traitor.
Boa: short story by Arthur Conan Doyle. Osca:
RETURN OF SHERLOCK HOLMES, THE:
WISTERIA LODGE
DRA               105 min (2 film cassette) mTV
B,V                                HEND

**RETURN OF SHERLOCK HOLMES, THE:**      PG
**THE DEVIL'S FOOT \*\***
Ken Hannam          UK            1986
*Jeremy Brett, Edward Hardwicke, Peter Barkworth,
Norman Bowler, Dennis Quilley, Damien Thomas*
Holmes sets out for Cornwall and a much-needed
holiday, but spends his time solving a mysterious
murder in which the victim, a young woman, has no
visible wounds.
Boa: short story by Arthur Conan Doyle. Osca:
RETURN OF SHERLOCK HOLMES, THE: SILVER
BLAZE
DRA               105 min (2 film cassette) mTV
V                                  HEND

**RETURN OF SHERLOCK HOLMES, THE:**      PG
**THE EMPTY HOUSE \*\*\***
Howard Baker        UK            1986

*Jeremy Brett, Edward Hardwicke, Patrick Allen, Colin Jeavons*
After the success of the first set of Holmes tales this new series began, starting where the last episode (see THE ADVENTURES OF SHERLOCK HOLMES: THE FINAL PROBLEM) concluded. Three years have passed since the apparent death of his colleague at the Reichenbach Falls, and Watson attempts to solve a puzzling murder case. A mysterious stranger appears to offer him some help. Written by John Hawkesworth.
Boa: short story by Arthur Conan Doyle.
Osca: RETURN OF SHERLOCK HOLMES, THE: THE ABBEY GRANGE
DRA                    103 min (2 film cassette) mTV
V                                              HEND

## RETURN OF SHERLOCK HOLMES, THE:   PG
## THE MAN WITH THE TWISTED LIP ***
Patrick Lau            UK                    1986
*Jeremy Brett, Edward Hardwicke, Clive Francis, Eleanor David, Terence Longdon*
In this story Holmes is called in by the distraught wife of a missing businessman and finds that the clues lead him to a mysterious, unwashed beggar, who has been arrested as a possible suspect. Written by Alan Plater.
Boa: short story by Arthur Conan Doyle.
Osca: RETURN OF SHERLOCK HOLMES, THE: THE PRIORY SCHOOL
DRA                    105 min (2 film cassette) mTV
V                                              HEND

## RETURN OF SHERLOCK HOLMES, THE:
## THE MUSGRAVE RITUAL ***
David Carson           UK                    1986
*Jeremy Brett, Edward Hardwicke, Michael Culver, James Hazeldine, Johanna Kirby*
An aristocrat calls in our sleuth to assist him in solving the mysterious death of his butler, but Holmes uncovers a deeper mystery, and one that involves the long-lost crown of Charles I. Written by Jeremy Paul.
Boa; short story by Arthur Conan Doyle.
Osca: RETURN OF SHERLOCK HOLMES, THE: THE SECOND STAIN
DRA                    104 min (2 film cassette) mTV
B,V                                            HEND

## RETURN OF SHERLOCK HOLMES, THE:
## THE PRIORY SCHOOL ***
John Madden            UK                    1986
*Jeremy Brett, Edward Hardwicke, Christopher Benjamin, Alan Howard*
When the son of a duke is kidnapped Holmes finds himself working on one of his most puzzling cases ever. Another excellent episode in this series of adaptations. The script is by T.R. Bowen.
Boa: short story by Arthur Conan Doyle.
Osca: RETURN OF SHERLOCK HOLMES, THE: THE MAN WITH THE TWISTED LIP
DRA                    105 min (2 film cassette) mTV
B,V                                            HEND

## RETURN OF SHERLOCK HOLMES, THE:   PG
## THE SECOND STAIN ***
John Bruce             UK                    1986
*Jeremy Brett, Edward Hardwicke, Patricia Hodge, Harry Andrews, Colin Jeavons*
A call from the Prime Minister involves our detective in the hunt for a stolen letter whose contents could, were it made public, lead to a state of war. Written by John Hawkesworth.
Boa: short story by Arthur Conan Doyle.
Osca: RETURN OF SHERLOCK HOLMES, THE: THE MUSGRAVE RITUAL
DRA                    104 min (2 film cassette) mTV
V                                              HEND

## RETURN OF SHERLOCK HOLMES, THE:   PG
## THE SIX NAPOLEONS ***
David Carson           UK                    1986
*Jeremy Brett, Edward Hardwicke, Colin Jeavons, Eric Sykes*
A burglar steals six busts of Napoleon from a statuette shop and smashes them to bits. Further similar incidents occur at the homes of people who had bought such busts. Eventually Holmes discovers that the culprit is searching for something he secreted in the plaster used to make the busts. The script is by John Kane.
Boa: short story by Arthur Conan Doyle.
DRA                                  52 min mTV
V                                              HEND

## RETURN OF SHERLOCK HOLMES, THE:   PG
## WISTERIA LODGE ***
Peter Hammond          UK                    1986
*Jeremy Brett, Edward Hardwicke, Freddie Jones, Charles Gray*
In "Wisteria Lodge" Holmes sets out to solve a murder, and finds himself embroiled in an intrigue that involved a foreign ruler.
Boa: short story by Arthur Conan Doyle.
Osca: RETURN OF SHERLOCK HOLMES, THE: THE BRUCE PARTINGTON PLANS
DRA                    105 min (2 film cassette) mTV
V                                              HEND

## RETURN OF THE BADMEN **
Ray Enright            USA                   1948
*Randolph Scott, Robert Ryan, Anne Jeffreys, Jacqueline White, Steve Brodie, George (Gabby) Hayes, Richard Powers (Tom Keane), Robert Bray, Lex Barker, Walter Reed, Michael Harvey, Dean White, Robert Armstrong, Tom Tyler*
An Oklahoma sheriff has his hands full dealing with several notorious outlaws such as Billy the Kid, the Dalton Gang, the Younger Brothers and the Sundance Kid. In between all this, he still finds time for a little romance with a female desperado. A competent Western that served as a semi-sequel to "Badman's Territory". Followed by BEST OF THE BADMEN.
Osca: GIRL IN EVERY PORT, A
WES                    86 min (ort 90 min) B/W
B,V                                            KVD

## RETURN OF THE DEMONS                        18
Donald G. Jackson/Jerry Younkins
                       USA
*Christmas Robbins, Val Mayerik, Gunnar Hansen, Tom Hutton, Sonny Bell, Linda Conrad, Phil Foreman, Carol Lasowski, Ron Hively, Susan Bullen, David Howard, Jan Porter, Michael McGivern, Kathy Stewart, Kyra Nash*
A group of hippies dabble in black magic under the guidance of an experienced devotee of the occult. However, when they refuse to take part in a Satanic ritual, he conjures up a demon that murders several of them. A bottom-of-the-barrel effort, as inept as it is unwatchable.
HOR                                      80 min
B,V                                            CLOK

## RETURN OF THE EVIL DEAD, THE **             18
Amando de Ossorio
                       PORTUGAL/SPAIN        1973
*Tony Kendall (Luciano Stella), Esther Ray (Esperanza Roy), Fernando Sancho, Lone Fleming, Frank Blake (Frank Brana), Loretta Tovar, Jose Canalejas*
An evil medieval sect is resurrected and wreaks havoc on a small Portuguese town. Second in this series of films about our dear old eyeless Knights Templar, who were executed in the Middle Ages but now have returned as vengeance-seeking zombies. A competent, low-budget sequel to TOMBS OF THE BLIND DEAD. See also NIGHT OF THE SEAGULLS.

Aka: EL ATAQUE DE LOS MUERTOS SIN OJOS;
RETURN OF THE BLIND DEAD
HOR                                83 min (ort 91 min)
B,V                                    PRV L/A; INT L/A

## RETURN OF THE FAMILY MAN *                18
John Murlowski          USA              1989
*Ron Smerczak, Liam Cundill, Terence Reis*
A mass murderer whose speciality is to wipe out
entire families escapes from a prison bus and travels
to his hometown where he begins to pick off the
holidaymakers who have rented his childhood house.
Eventually, the survivors fight back, making use of a
set of ingenious home-made weapons. A low-grade and
moronic offering of little discernible merit.
HOR                                           88 min
V                                              MGM

## RETURN OF THE FLY *                         15
Edward L. Bernds       USA               1959
*Vincent Price, Brett Halsey, David Frankham, John
Sutton, Danielle De Metz, Dan Seymour, Michael
Mark, Janine Grandel, Pat O'Hara, Jack Daly, Barry
Bernard, Richard Flato, Joan Cotton, Florence Strom,
Gregg Martell*
A rubbishy sequel to THE FLY, with the son of the
ill-fated scientist reconstructing his dad's matter
transporter and suffering a similar fate. Followed six
years later by "The Curse Of The Fly".
HOR                         75 min (ort 78 min) B/W
V/h                                            CBS

## RETURN OF THE GUNFIGHTER **                 U
James Neilson          USA               1966
*Robert Taylor, Chad Everett, Ana Martin, Mort Mills,
Lyle Bettger, John David Chandler, Michael Pate,
Barry Atwater, John Crawford, Willis Bouchey,
Rodolfo Hoyos, Read Morgan, Henry Wills, Robert
Shelton, Loretta Miller*
A retired gunfighter arrives in town, having been
summoned there by a friend in trouble. He arrives too
late to prevent his friend being murdered, but stays to
see justice done. A formula revenge 'n' justice West-
ern, but quite nicely done.
Aka: AS I RODE DOWN TO LAREDO
Boa: story by Robert Buckner and Burt Kennedy.
WES                         92 min (ort 98 min) mTV
B,V                                            MGM

## RETURN OF THE JEDI ****                     U
Richard Marquand       USA               1983
*Mark Hamil, Harrison Ford, Billy Dee Williams,
Carrie Fisher, Anthony Daniels, Dave Prowse, Alec
Guinness, Peter Mayhew, Sebastian Shaw, Ian
McDiarmid, Kenny Baker, Frank Oz, James Earl
Jones (voice of Darth Vader)*
Third in the STAR WARS trilogy, with the plot a
continuation of the battle between the heroic rebels
and the decadent Galactic Empire. A highly inventive
and sparkling fantasy, but largely aimed at kids.
Written by Lawrence Kasdan and George Lucas with
music by John Williams. AA: Spec Award (Richard
Edlund/Dennis Muren/Ken Ralston/Phil Tippett for
visual effects).
FAN                         126 min (ort 132 min)
V                                              CBS

## RETURN OF THE KILLER TOMATOES! *           15
John DeBello           USA               1989
*Anthony Starke, George Clooney, Karen Mistal, Steve
Lundquist, John Astin, Charlie Jones*
Sequel to ATTACK OF THE KILLER TOMATOES
that promises more of the same, with one joke being
over-extended ad nauseum. A mad scientist turns
tomatoes into people and people into tomatoes, and
our hero falls in love with a former tomato. Unfortunately, unless you're heavily into tomatoes, this just
isn't very funny.

COM                                           99 min
B,V                                            NWV

## RETURN OF THE LIVING DEAD **               18
Dan O'Bannon           USA               1985
*Clu Gulager, James Karen, Don Calfa, Thom
Mathews, Beverly Randolph, John Philbin, Linnea
Quigley, Miguel Nunez, Brian Peck, Jewel Shepard*
A sequel to NIGHT OF THE LIVING DEAD, in which
the zombie plague is once more unleashed on human-
ity and the cinema-going public. Much comic mayhem
mixes with gory effects, but what starts out as a spoof
turns nasty about halfway through. This was the
directorial debut for SF screenwriter O'Bannon. Fol-
lowed by a sequel.
Aka: NIGHT OF THE LIVING DEAD
HOR                         87 min (ort 96 min)
V/s                                            VES

## RETURN OF THE LIVING DEAD: PART 2 *        18
Ken Wiederhorn         USA               1987
*James Karen, Thom Mathews, Michael Kenworthy,
Dana Ashbrook, Philip Bruns, Marsha Dietlein,
Suzanne Snyder*
A sequel to the 1985 film that has a group of
irresponsible kids causing the dead to rise up again,
when they open strange barrels that have fallen off an
army truck. Good effects are combined with a ponder-
ous and uninventive script.
HOR                                           89 min
B,V                                            GHV

## RETURN OF THE MAN FROM                      PG
U.N.C.L.E., THE **
Ray Austin             USA               1983
*Robert Vaughn, David McCallum, Patrick Macnee,
Tom Mason, Gayle Hunnicutt, Anthony Zerbe, Keenan
Wynn, George Lazenby, Geoffrey Lewis, Simon
Williams, John Harkins, Jan Triska, Susan Woollen,
Carolyn Seymour, Judith Chapman*
An attempt to cash in on a popular TV series of the
1960s, with Napoleon Solo and Illya Kuryakin, our
two anti-espionage agents, returning after a fifteen-
year absence (in fact this pilot tale was subtitled "The
Fifteen Years Later Affair"). A pleasant resurrection
with an above-average script.
A/AD                        100 min; 92 min (CH5) mTV
B,V                         CINE L/A; HER; CH5 (VHS only)

## RETURN OF THE MUSKETEERS, THE **           PG
Richard Lester         UK                1988
*Michael York, Oliver Reed, Frank Finlay, C. Thomas
Howell, Kim Cattrall, Geraldine Chaplin, Roy
Kinnear, Christopher Lee, Richard Chamberlain,
Philippe Noiret*
A lavish but dispirited follow-up to Lester's THE
THREE MUSKETEERS, that has many of the same
stars in the same roles as the earlier film. The complex
story is almost impossible to follow, largely consisting
of kidnapping and murder plots plus a good dose of
swashbuckling. It moves along rapidly, but has too
many shortcomings to be all that effective. Kinnear
died during shooting after falling from a horse – this
film is dedicated to him.
Boa: novel Twenty Years After by Alexandre Dumas.
A/AD                                          97 min
V                                              EIV

## RETURN OF THE PINK PANTHER, THE *          PG
Blake Edwards          UK                1974
*Peter Sellers, Christopher Plummer, Herbert Lom,
Catherine Schell, Peter Arne, Peter Jeffrey, Burt
Kwouk, Gregoire Aslan, Andre Maranne, Victor
Spinetti, David Lodge, Graham Stark, Eric Pohlmann,
John Bluthal*
Another unfunny PINK PANTHER film, with Sellers
once more playing our bumbling Inspector Clouseau,
this time investigating the theft of the Pink Panther
diamond. Music is by Henry Mancini. The opening

titles, animated by Richard Williams and Ken Harris, are the best part of the film. (Benny Green wrote in Punch that this was the first movie to be upstaged by its own credits.) Followed by THE PINK PANTHER STRIKES AGAIN.

COM                          108 min (ort 113 min)
B,V                                        PRV; CH5

### RETURN OF THE SHAGGY DOG, THE *        U
Stuart Gillard            USA              1987
Cindy Morgan, Todd Waring, Gary Kroegar, Michelle Little, Jane Carr, Gavin Reed, K. Callan
A feeble attempt to exploit the success of the 1959 Disney film, "The Shaggy Dog", with a young boy finding that he is able to change into a dog thanks to a magic ring. An uninspired and wearisome effort. See also THE SHAGGY D.A.

COM              85 min (ort 100 min) mTV
B,V                                        WDV

### RETURN OF THE SIX MILLION DOLLAR      PG
### MAN AND THE BIONIC WOMAN **
Ray Austin                USA              1987
Lindsay Wagner, Lee Majors, Lee Majors II, Tom Schanley, Richard Brooks, Martin Landau, Gary Lockwood, Martin E. Brooks, Tom Schonley
The title characters plus their bionic son are reunited in this pilot for a relaunched series that was never made. Here, as ever, they take on the bad guys and emerge triumphant thanks to their super-human powers. Average. See also THE SIX MILLION DOLLAR MAN.

A/AD             95 min (ort 100 min) mTV
B,V                                        CIC

### RETURN OF THE SOLDIER, THE **         PG
Alan Bridges              UK               1982
Alan Bates, Julie Christie, Glenda Jackson, Ann-Margret, Ian Holm, Frank Finlay, Jeremy Kemp, Edward De Souza, Jack May, Emily Irvin, William Booker, Elizabeth Edmonds, Hilary Mason, John Sharp, Valerie Aitken, Amanda Grinling
A soldier returns home in a state of shell-shock, with no memory of the past twenty years and his marriage to a haughty woman. Nor does he realise that two other women are in love with him. A delicate and touching love story by West, becomes a bleak and ponderous tale that, despite good performances, never develops into anything of substance. Scripted by Hugh Whitemore.
Boa: novel by Rebecca West.
DRA                          98 min (ort 102 min)
B,V                                  GHV L/A; VGM

### RETURN OF THE STREETFIGHTER **
Shigehiro Osawa       JAPAN              1976
Sonny (Shinichi) Chiba, Yoko Ichiji, Masafumi Suzuki, Donald Nakajima
This violent sequel to "The Streetfighter" has the hardly original plot of a lone fighter battling an evil criminal. Certain to be heavily cut or edited if available. See also ENTER THE STREETFIGHTER and THE STREETFIGHTER'S LAST REVENGE.
MAR                                       75 min
B,V                                     VTC L/A

### RETURN OF THE SWAMP THING, THE **     12
Jim Wynorski            USA               1989
Louis Jordan, Heather Locklear, Sarah Douglas, Dick Durock, Joey Segal
Based on the D.C. Comics series, this sequel to THE SWAMP THING is a spoof horror tale, in which a girl searching for the reasons behind her mother's death gains an unlikely ally in the shape of a man-vegetable creature, who helps her escape the clutches of her mad scientist stepfather and thwarts his fiendish plans. A thoroughly silly effort that tries too hard to parody early B-movie horror films and ends up merely parodying itself.

HOR                                       87 min
V                                          MED

### RETURN OF THE TIGER *
Jimmy Shaw (James Fung Shaw)
             HONG KONG/TAIWAN            1973
Bruce Li (Ho Tsung-Tao), Paul Smith, Angela Mao Ying, Chang I, Lung Fei, Hsieh Hsing
An undercover agent combats narcotics smugglers in Bangkok, being assisted n his efforts by a female cop. Another cynical attempt to exploit the popularity of the late star by using a Bruce Lee clone.
Aka: SILENT KILLER FROM ETERNITY
MAR                                       95 min
B,V                                         VPD

### RETURN TO BOGGY CREEK **
Tom Moore                 USA              1977
Dawn Wells, Dana Plato, Louis Belaire, John Hofeus
A sequel to THE LEGEND OF BOGGY CREEK, with another monster sighted near a small isolated fishing village. Two youngsters find themselves involved with our creature, who ends up saving them during a violent storm in this mildly exciting kid's adventure. Followed by "Boggy Creek 2", a confusingly titled third "Boggy Creek" outing, to which this film bears little relation.
JUV                          80 min (ort 87 min)
B,V                                         CBS

### RETURN TO HORROR HIGH **              18
Bill Froehlich            USA              1987
Alex Rocco, Vince Edwards, Brendan Hughes, Philip McKeon, Scott Jacoby, Lori Lethin, Andy Romano, Richard Brestoff, Al Fann, Pepper Martin, Maureen McCormick, Panchito Gomez, Michael Eric Kramer
A film crew go to a deserted high school to make a low-budget movie about a series of gruesome murders that took place there five years earlier. Soon, the murders start once more, in this fairly effective slasher tale that is hampered by poor direction and a muddled script.
HOR                          90 min (ort 95 min)
V/h                                         NWV

### RETURN TO MACON COUNTY *              15
Richard Compton           USA              1975
Don Johnson, Nick Nolte, Robin Mattson, Robert Viharo, Eugene Daniels, Matt Greene, Devon Ericson
A follow-up to MACON COUNTY LINE, in which our 1950s teenagers get involved in drag racing and murder and run into trouble from a brutal cop. A forgettable effort that has a few unintentionally funny moments, but nothing else of interest. Nolte's first film.
Aka: RETURN TO MACON COUNTY LINE
DRA                                       90 min
B,V                                         RNK

### RETURN TO OZ **                        U
Arthur Rankin             USA              1964
A musical, animated sequel to THE WIZARD OF OZ. Fair.
Boa: novels The Land Of Oz/Ozma Of Oz by Lyman Frank Baum.
CAR                     60 min; 52 min (CH5)
B,V                          ODY; CH5 (VHS only)

### RETURN TO OZ **                        PG
Walter Murch              USA              1985
Fairuza Balk, Nicol Williamson, Jean Marsh, Piper Laurie, Matt Clark, Tim Rose, Michael Sundin, Stewart Larange, Justin Case, John Alexander, Deep Roy. Voices of: Sean Barrett, Denise Bryer, Brian Henson, Lyle Conway
This unattractive directing debut for sound technician Murch, is a partial sequel to THE WIZARD OF OZ. Oz now lies in ruins and Dorothy ventures there to save her old friends from petrification. Though loosely

based on Baum's classic tales, this film is dark in tone and no more than coldly efficient. A highlight is the sequence in which rock faces come to life – courtesy of Will Vinton's Claymation technique. Written by Murch and Gill Dennis.
Boa: novels The Land Of Oz/Ozma Of Oz by Lyman Frank Baum.
JUV                                108 min (ort 110 min)
B,V                                                    WDV

### RETURN TO SALEM'S LOT, A ***                  18
Larry Cohen             USA                       1987
*Michael Moriarty, Samuel Fuller, Andrew Duggan, June Havoc, Evelyn Keyes, Richard Addison Reed, Ronee Blakely, Jill Gatsby, James Dixon, Tara Reid, David Holbrook, Natja Crosby, Brad Rijn, Robert Burr, Jacqueline Britton*
A sequel to SALEM'S LOT with an anthropologist and his son going to the New England town where he has inherited a cottage from his aunt, and discovering that the area is the home of vampires who have kept their existence there secret for over 300 years. He eventually teams up with an ex-Nazi hunter in an effort to lift the curse from the town. A highly effective film that balances the chills with some nice touches of humour.
HOR                                            97 min
B,V                                               WHV

### RETURN TO THE 36TH CHAMBER **                 PG
Liu Chia-Liang     HONG KONG                      1980
*Lo Lieh, Liu Chia-Hui, Huiu Ya Hung, Wang Lung Wei*
A young mill worker learns the martial arts to avenge the death of a workmate killed by a gang. A sequel to THE THIRTY-SIXTH CHAMBER OF SHAOLIN.
MAR                                            100 min
B,V                                               WHV

### RETURN TO WATERLOO ***                        PG
Ray Davies             UK                         1984
*Ken Colley, Valerie Holliman, Dominique Barnes*
The mid-life crisis of a middle-aged commuter, told mainly in music and visual imagery with little dialogue. The directing debut for Ray Davies of the rock group The Kinks, this unusual little film has many memorable images but no clear structure.
Aka: RAY DAVIES' RETURN TO WATERLOO
MUS                                57 min (ort 60 min)
B,V                                                    RCA

### RETURNING, THE *
Joel Bender             USA                       1983
*Gabriel Walsh, Susan Strasberg, Brian Foleman, Victor Arnold, Ruth Warrick*
A Utah family on a visit to the Mojave desert pick up a rock as a souvenir, which later appears to have strange powers and a sinister influence. Very dull.
HOR                                            88 min
B,V                                               APX

### REUBEN, REUBEN ***                            15
Robert Ellis Miller     USA                       1983
*Tom Conti, Kelly McGillis, Roberts Blossom, Cynthia Harris, E. Katherine Kerr, Joel Fabiani, Kara Wilson, Lois Smith*
A drunken, burnt-out Scottish poet lives off his female admirers in a small university town in New England, but then falls in love with a beautiful young student (McGillis in her screen debut). A curious and offbeat comedy in which mirth often gives way to a feeling of irritation. Written by Julius J. Epstein.
Boa: novel by Peter De Vries/play Spofford by Herman Shumlin.
COM                       101 min; 95 min (CH5 or POLY)
B,V            EHE; CH5 (VHS only); POLY (VHS only)

### REVENGE **
Jud Taylor             USA                        1971

*Shelley Winters, Stuart Whitman, Bradford Dillman, Carol Rossen, Roger Perry, Gary Clarke, Johnny Scott Lee, Leslie Charleson*
A woman plots to imprison the man she suspects of having raped her daughter, having provided a cage in her basement for this purpose. Winters' overblown performance gives a slightly hammy feeling to this drama, but the photography of John A. Alonzo is a compensation. Screenplay is by Joseph Stefano.
Boa: novel by Elizabeth Davis.
DRA                                          78 min mTV
B,V                                               GHV

### REVENGE **                                    18
Alberto De Martino     ITALY                      1979
*Franco Nero, Barbara Bach, Reno Palmer*
A couple of survivors of a brutal robbery decide to form their own crime fighting duo when they realise that the local police force is corrupt.
Aka: STREET LAW; VIGILANTE 2 (IVS)
A/AD                         90 min; 105 min (IVS)
B,V                TURBO L/A; IVS; SATPRO

### REVENGE **                                    18
Tony Scott             USA                        1989
*Kevin Costner, Madeleine Stowe, Anthony Quinn, Sally Kirkland, Tomas Milian, Joaquin Martinez, James Gammon, Miguel Ferrer, Joe Santos*
Navy pilot Costner pays a visit to a Mexican gangster whose life he once saved, but unwisely embarks on an affair with the man's beautiful wife. For this act of betrayal, a brutal revenge follows (hence the title), and this sordid tale quickly descends into nastiness. A competently made film that blends good camerawork with unpleasant violence, and hides nothing beneath its flashy exterior.
DRA                                119 min (ort 124 min)
V                                                  20VIS

### REVENGE IS MY DESTINY **
Joseph Adler           USA                        1971
*Sidney Bluckmer, Chris Robinson, Elisa Ingram, Joe E. Ross*
A Vietnam veteran comes back home only to find that his wife has mysteriously disappeared, and eventually unravels a sordid intrigue when he learns of her death. An awkwardly scripted tale, that never develops any tension. Mediocre.
Osca: TENSION AT TABLE ROCK
DRA                                86 min (ort 95 min)
B,V                                               KVD

### REVENGE OF AL CAPONE, THE ***                 18
Michael Pressman     USA                          1988
*Keith Carradine, Ray Sharkey, Debrah Farentino, Charles Haid, Scott Paulin, Jayne Atkinson, Charles Hallahan*
Sharkey plays Capone and Carradine the FBI agent who put him behind bars, in this overblow but enjoyable account, told in flashback form by Capone from the cell in which he lives out his last days. The vigorous and fast-paced script is by Tracy Keenan Wynn.
DRA                                90 min (ort 100 min) mTV
B,V                                             BRAVE

### REVENGE OF FRANKENSTEIN, THE **               15
Terence Fisher         UK                         1958
*Peter Cushing, Francis Matthews, Eunice Grayson, Michael Gwynn, Lionel Jeffries, Oscar Quitak, John Welsh, Richard Wordsworth, Charles Lloyd Pack, John Stuart, Arnold Diamond, Margery Cresley*
After the death of his monster, the good doctor resumes his experiments in another town, under an assumed name after escaping the guillotine. A slow-moving horror yarn enlivened by a few touches of ghoulish humour. This was the second "Frankenstein" film from Hammer, being preceded by THE CURSE

OF FRANKENSTEIN. Followed by "The Evil Of Frankenstein".

HOR                                87 min (ort 89 min)
V                                              RCA

**REVENGE OF THE BARBARIANS** **
Giuseppi Vari        ITALY                 1960
*Robert Alda, Anthony Steel, Daniela Rocca*
One of those typical Italian costumers of the 1960s telling of the Roman Empire under threat from advancing barbarian armies.
Aka: LA VENDETTA DEI BARBARI
A/AD                                          99 min
B,V                                              VPD

**REVENGE OF THE CHEERLEADERS** *        18
Richard Lerner       USA                   1976
*Jerii Woods, Rainbeaux Smith, Helen Lang, Patrice Rohmer, Susie Elene, Eddra Gale, David Hasselhoff, Carl Ballantine*
Witless sex comedy about the title characters, full of the usual silly jokes and knowing innuendos.
Aka: HOTS 3 (MANHAT or KRP)
COM                                          87 min
B,V            UNIV L/A; SLA L/A; MANHAT; KRP

**REVENGE OF THE DRAGONS** **        18
Robert Tai            HONG KONG
*Alexander Lou, Liu Hau Yi, Lou Chun, Tien Lung, Yang Hsiung, Chien Hsun, Wang Hau, Tsing Kuo Chung*
A group of children survive a massacre and study the martial arts in order to mount the obligatory vengeance crusade.
Aka: REVENGE OF THE DRAGON
MAR                                          90 min
B,V                                            CLOK

**REVENGE OF THE DRUNKEN MASTER** **        18
Godfrey Ho            HONG KONG           198-
*Johnny Chan, Eagle Han, Wang Sao, Si-Fu*
A young man masters the technique of Drunk Fist and use his newly acquired skills to fight an evil Ninja gang, who are forced to unite in an effort to destroy him.
MAR                                          81 min
B,V                                              VPD

**REVENGE OF THE NERDS** **        18
Jeff Kanew           USA                   1984
*Robert Carradine, Anthony Edwards, Julie Montgomery, Curtis Armstrong, Ted McGinley, Bernie Casey, Tim Busfield, Andrew Cassese, Larry B. Scott, Brian Tochi*
Brainy college students get tired of being humiliated by sporty types and form their own fraternity, leading to a humorous conflict on the campus. A simple-minded teen comedy of appealing performances and obvious gags. The script is by Tim Metcalfe, Miguel Tejada-Flores, Steve Zacharias and Jeff Buhai. A sequel followed.
COM                                87 min (ort 90 min)
B,V                                              CBS

**REVENGE OF THE NERDS 2** *        15
Joe Roth             USA                   1987
*Robert Carradine, Curtis Armstrong, Larry B. Scott, Timothy Busfield, Andrew Cassesse, Barry Sobel, Courtney Thorne-Smith, Michelle Meyrink, Anthony Edwards, Ed Lauter, Donald Gibb, Bradley Whitford*
Once again the nerds prove themselves worthy of our respect, as they triumph over their traditional enemies at a fraternity convention held at Fort Lauderdale. A production-line comedy that is even less inspired than the original.
Aka: REVENGE OF THE NERDS 2: NERDS IN PARADISE
COM                                85 min (ort 95 min)
B,V                                              CBS

**REVENGE OF THE PINK PANTHER** *        PG
Blake Edwards        USA                   1978
*Peter Sellers, Herbert Lom, Robert Webber, Dyan Cannon, Burt Kwouk, Robert Loggia, Paul Stewart, Graham Stark, Andre Maranne, Sue Lloyd, Tony Beckley, Valerie Leon, Alfie Bass, Danny Schiller, Douglas Wilmer, Ferdy Mayne*
Sellers' final portrayal (whilst alive that is) of the bumbling and totally unfunny Inspector Clouseau. In this painfully tedious yawn-inducer, our detective is supposedly murdered and attempts to find his "killer". A nice performance from Cannon is thrown away on this dud. As ever, Henry Mancini provides the music. THE TRAIL OF THE PINK PANTHER followed, Sellers' death notwithstanding.
COM                               99 min; 94 min (WHV)
B,V                            INT; WHV (VHS only)

**REVENGE OF THE RADIOACTIVE REPORTER** *  18
Craig Pryce          USA                   1988
*David Scammell, Kathryn Boese, Richard Sali, Randy Pearlstein*
An investigative reporter examining alleged irregularities at a nuclear plant is deliberately plunged into a barrel of radioactive waste as a way of getting rid of him. However, just as in TOXIC AVENGER, far from causing his demise, he emerges all the better equipped to fight evil. A low-budget spoof of flat jokes and questionable taste.
FAN                                          80 min mTV
V                                                CIC

**REVENGE OF THE TEENAGE VIXENS**        15
**FROM OUTER SPACE, THE** **
Jeff Farrell         USA                   1985
*Lisa Schwedop, Howard Scott, Amy Crumpacker, Sterling Ramberg, Julian Schembri*
A 16-year-old boy discovers that his mother was an alien, when she returns to Earth in the company of four others who are looking for a good time. A chaotic and ludicrous SF spoof, but quite good fun in its way.
FAN                                          83 min
V                                                TAR

**REVOLUTION** *        PG
Hugh Hudson          NORWAY/UK             1985
*Al Pacino, Nastassja Kinski, Donald Sutherland, Joan Plowright, Dave King, Steven Berkoff, John Wells, Annie Lennox, Dexter Fletcher, Sid Owen, Richard O'Brien, Paul Brooke, Eric Milota, Felicity Dean, Jo Anna Lee, Cheryl Miller*
A lavish but badly cast and clumsy account of the American War of Independence. An unmitigated disaster from start to finish, with a constant reliance on hand-held cameras giving the film a nice "shaky" feel that makes it painful to watch. Severely panned by the critics, and deservedly so, this film was one of the biggest flops in recent cinema history, and at £18,000,000 an expensive dud for British cinema.
DRA                               121 min (ort 125 min)
V/sh                                            WHV

**REWARD** **        PG
E.W. Swackhamer      USA                   1980
*Michael Parks, Richard Jaeckel, Louis Giambalvo, Malachy McCourt, Annie McEnroe, Andrew Robinson, Calvin Jung, Bridget Hanley, Lane LeGault, David Clennon, James A. Watson Jr, Martin Cassidy, Byron Webster, Biff Warren*
After 15 years, a San Francisco cop leaves his job to solve the murder of his best friend. A pilot for a series that was never made, scripted by Jason Miller. Average.
A/AD                              72 min (ort 105 min) mTV
B,V                                            POLY

**RHINESTONE** *        PG
Bob Clark            USA                   1984
*Sylvester Stallone, Dolly Parton, Richard Farnsworth,*

*Ron Leibman, Tim Thomerson, Steven Apostle Pec, Penny Santon, Russell Buchanan, Ritch Brinkley, Perry Potter, Jesse Welles, Phil Rubinstein, Thomas Ikeda*
A New York cabbie becomes a singer to raise money to replace his crashed cab, helped by Parton who bets that she can turn anyone into a Country and Western singer. Stallone's singing debut (and almost certainly his finale too). A clumsy and foolish concoction that's best left in obscurity.
COM                                   106 min (ort 111 min)
B,V                                                        CBS

**RICCO **                                                    18
Tulio Demichelli
                          ITALY/SPAIN                    1973
*Christopher Mitchum, Arthur Kennedy, Barbara Bouchet, Malisa Longo*
The son of a murdered Mafia chief is slowly drawn into the world of forgery and drugs in order to avenge his father's murder. A standard gangster drama.
Aka: DIRTY MOB, THE; RICO; UN TIPO CON UNA FACCIA STRANA TI CERCA PER UCCIDERTI
DRA                                                     90 min
B,V                                                   DFS L/A

**RICH AND FAMOUS ***                                         18
George Cukor            USA                             1981
*Jacqueline Bisset, Candice Bergen, David Selby, Hart Bochner, Steven Hill, Meg Ryan, Matt Lattanzi, Michael Brandon*
Cukor's last film (he was eighty-two when it was shot) is a remake of "Old Acquaintance" and deals with two women who maintain their friendship over twenty years, despite being rivals in both love and career. A painfully contrived and muddled effort, made worse by excessive dialogue and an ill-advised attempt to spice up a straightforward story with some 1980s sex.
Boa: play Old Acquaintance by John Van Druten.
DRA                                  112 min (ort 117 min)
B,V                                                        MGM

**RICH BITCH ***                                              18
                          ITALY
*Maria Cantudo, Claudia Gravi, Anita Wilson, Ali Moore, April Maye, Susan Hart, Paul Thomas, Alan Royce, Marc Wallace*
Sexual adventures of a pleasure-seeking woman. Another mediocre Italian softcore offering.
A                                                      110 min
B,V                                                        AVR

**RICHARD III ***                                              U
Laurence Olivier        UK                             1955
*Laurence Olivier, John Gielgud, Ralph Richardson, Claire Bloom, Alex Clunes, Cedric Hardwicke, Stanley Baker, Pamela Brown, Michael Gough, John Laurie, Norman Wooland, Laurence Naismith, Mary Kerridge, Helen Heye, Clive Morton*
This famous play is brought to the screen by a host of Shakespearian actors. Now considered to be a classic, this is a remarkably theatrical production, that refuses to rely on the marvellous language of the play, and resorts instead to an over-reliance on visual effects. Nor are the battle scenes all that impressive. A rather disappointing and faded epic.
Boa: play by William Shakespeare.
DRA                                  150 min (ort 161 min)
V                                                          VCC

**RICHEST CAT IN THE WORLD, THE ***                           U
Gregg Beeman            USA                             1986
*Ramon Bieri, Steven Kampmann, Caroline McWilliams, George Wyner, Kellie Martin, Stephen Vinovich, Jesse Welles, Brandon Call, J.A. Preston, Christina Cocek, Thomas Hill, Richard Cuss, Thomas Oglesby, Palmer the Cat*
A talking moggy inherits its millionaire owner's fortune, and enlists human help to keep his greedy

relatives at bay (the millionaire's that is). One of those cute and syrupy Disney offerings that are seen once and promptly forgotten.
Boa: story by Les Alexander and Steve Ditlea.
COM                                    90 min (ort 100 min) mTV
B,V                                                        WDV

**RICHIE ***                                                  15
Paul Wendkos           USA                             1983
*Ben Gazzara, Eileen Brennan, Robbie Benson, Lance Kerwin, Charles Fleischer, Clint Howard, Harry Gold, Cindy Eilbacher, Rose Gregorio, Sean Thomas Roach, Anne Newman Mantee, Shirley O'Hara, Jennifer Rhodes, John Zaremba*
A family is torn apart by the son's drug addiction and his inability to kick the habit, provoking the father into taking drastic steps that have tragic consequences. An often harrowing film that carries a mite too much sentimentality at times. Scripted by John McGreevey.
Aka: DEATH OF RICHIE, THE
Boa: book Richie by Thomas Thompson.
DRA                                    93 min (ort 100 min) mTV
B,V                                                        ODY

**RICKY 1 ***                                                 15
Bill Naud               USA                             1986
*Michael Michaud, Maggie Hughes, Peter Zellars, Lane Montano, Jon Chaney, Steve Welles, James Herbert, Lisa Traficante*
When his girlfriend walks out on him, leaving a note saying that she does not wish to stand in the way of his career, a boxer decides to hang up his gloves and gets a job as an executive trainee at a fish market. Slipping into debt, he is eventually forced to fight in a rigged fight and surprises everyone by winning, but this is only the start of his problems. A fresh and light-hearted comedy.
Aka: HEART TO WIN
COM                                                    84 min
B,V                                                        EIV

**RIDDLE OF THE SANDS, THE ***                                18
Tony Maylam            UK 1978 (released USA 1984)
*Simon MacCorkindale, Michael York, Jenny Agutter, Alan Badel, Jurgen Anderson, Olga Lowe, Michael Sheard, Hans Meyer, Wolf Kahler, Ronald Markham*
A British yachtsman on holiday in the North Sea in 1901, accidentally discovers German plans to invade Britain. A slow-moving and stilted thriller that fails to make the most of a good premise. Written by Maylam and John Bailey.
Boa: novel by Erskine Childers.
THR                                   102 min; 98 min (PARK)
B,V          RNK; MIA (VHS only); PARK (VHS only)

**RIDE A NORTHBOUND HORSE ***                                 U
Robert Totten          USA                             1969
*Carroll O'Connor, Michael Shea, Ben Johnson, Jack Elam, Andy Devine, Edith Atwater, Dub Taylor, Harry Carey Jr*
Disney adventure tale set in Texas, and telling of a young man who wins a horse and then has it stolen. When he sets out to regain it, he is branded a horse thief and thrown into jail. Quite enjoyable in an undemanding way.
Boa: novel by Richard Wormser.
WES                                                    89 min
B,V                                                        WDV

**RIDE A WILD PONY ***                                        U
Don Chaffey            AUSTRALIA                        1976
*Michael Craig, John Meillon, Robert Bettles, Eva Griffith, Graham Rouse*
The son of a poor farmer and a crippled rich girl, compete for a pony in this sentimental but rather appealing kid's film, set in the Edwardian era.
Boa: story A Sporting Proposition by James Aldridge.
JUV                                    86 min (ort 91 min)
B,V                                                        WDV

**RIDE IN A PINK CAR ***
Robert J. Emery          USA               1978
*Glenn Corbett, Morgan Woodward, Ivy Jones*
A Vietnam veteran accidentally shoots a man and is
pursued by a lynching party, in this contrived and
predictable offering.
A/AD                                       80 min
B,V                                            ARI

**RIDEOUT CASE, THE ***                        15
Peter Levin              USA               1980
*Mickey Rourke, Linda Hamilton, Rip Torn, Eugene
Roche, Conchata Ferrell, Gail Strickland, Bonnie
Bartlett, Richard Venture, Gerald McRaney, Alley
Mills, Paul Koslo, Mo Malone, Camilla Ashlend, Brad
Blaisdell, Rob Colbin*
Based on an actual case that came to the courts in
Oregon in 1978, this courtroom drama recreates the
trial of a husband who was involved in a case that
made legal history, when he was accused by his wife of
raping her. Fair.
Aka: RAPE AND MARRIAGE: THE RIDEOUT
CASE
DRA                      96 min; 92 min (CH5) mTV
B,V                           POLY; CH5 (VHS only)

**RIDER ON THE RAIN ***                        18
Rene Clement        FRANCE/ITALY           1970
*Charles Bronson, Marlene Jobert, Annie Cordy, Jill
Ireland*
An investigator on the trail of an escaped prisoner,
involves a woman as his unwilling accomplice in this
coldly effective thriller. Implausible, but convoluted
enough to keep one watching through to the end.
Aka: LE PASSAGER DE LA PLUIE
THR                        113 min (ort 119 min)
B,V                                            EHE

**RIDERS OF DESTINY ***                         U
Robert North Bradbury USA                  1933
*John Wayne, Cecilia Parker, George "Gabby" Hayes,
Forrest Taylor, Al St John, Heinie Conklin, Earl
Dwire, Yakima Canutt, Lafe McKee, Fern Emmett, Hal
Price, Si Jenks, Horace B. Carpenter*
A government agent poses as an outlaw, to aid settlers
whose water rights have been usurpeed by a corrupt
businessman. The only "Singin' Sandy" film made,
with competentt action sequenncess annddd dubbed
sinnging on the part of the star.
WES                      449 min (ort 59 min) B/W
V                                            CCH5

**RIDING HIGH ***
Ross Cramer              UK                1980
*Eddie Kidd, Irene Handl, Murry Salem, Zoot Money,
Marella Oppenheim, Bill Mitchell, Paul Humpoletz,
Lynda Bellingham, Daniel Peacock, Owen Whittaker,
Claire Toeman, Ken Kitson, Vivienne McKone, Peter
Whitman, Patricia Hodge*
A motorcycle enthusiast is given a chance to challenge
the World Stunt Champion and win a gold-plated
motorcycle. Real-life stunt-rider Kidd plays the chal-
lenger. Of limited appeal, but possibly worth seeing
for some good stunt riding if not for the script.
Aka: HEAVY METAL; VERY HEAVY METAL
DRA                        92 min (ort 96 min)
B,V                                       VCL/CBS

**RIGHT OF THE PEOPLE, THE ***                  15
Jeffrey Bloom            USA               1985
*John Randolph, Michael Ontkean, Billy Dee Williams,
Jane Kaczmarek, M. Emmet Walsh, Jamie Smith
Jackson, Janet Carroll, Joanne Linville, Chuck
Shamata, Jeffrey Josephson, Scott Michael Wilson,
Sandra Lynn Currie, Ken Pogue*
A man campaigns for the right to carry weapons, after
his family dies in a restaurant shoot-out. A strictly
formula offering that provides no insight into this
problem, nor an explanation of how arming everyone

will deal with armed maniacs. Written by Bloom.
DRA                                        91 min mTV
B,V                                            CBS

**RIGHT OF WAY ***
George Schaefer          USA               1983
*Bette Davis, James Stewart, Melinda Dillon, Priscilla
Morrill, John Harkins, Louis Schaefer, Jacque Lynn
Colton, Charles Walker, Philip Littell, Edith Fields,
East Carlo, Jodi Hicks, Erin Karpf, Bobby Jacoby,
Michael Murphy*
An elderly couple decide to commit suicide, when the
wife learns that she has terminal cancer and the
husband decides that he does not want to be left alone.
However, when their married daughter learns of their
plan she does all she can to prevent them. The ending
was changed and some characters removed shortly
before the film was released, due to the controversial
nature of the subject matter. A depressing drama of
little merit.
Boa: play by Richard Lee.
DRA                                       110 min mCab
B,V                                         VCL/CBS

**RIGHT STUFF, THE ***                          15
Philip Kaufman           USA               1983
*Sam Shepard, Scott Glenn, Ed Harris, Dennis Quaid,
Fred Ward, Charles Frank, Barbara Hershey, Kim
Stanley, Veronica Cartwright, Scott Paulin, Pamela
Reed, Donald Moffat, Levon Helm, Scott Wilson, Jeff
Goldblum, Harry Shearer*
A behind-the-scenes look at the development of the
US space programme. Seen as a certain boost to
Senator John Glenn's presidential ambitions, it failed
to get off the ground; perhaps due to writer-director
Kaufman making all the characters one-dimensional
except the pilots. A disappointment. AA: Sound (Ber-
ger/Scott/Thom/MacMillan), Edit (Farr/Rolf/Frucht-
man/Rotter/Stewart), Score (Orig) (Bill Conti), Effects
(Aud) (Jay Boekelheide).
Boa: book by Tom Wolfe.
DRA                       185 min (ort 193 min)
V/sh                                           WHV

**RIGHT TO DIE ***                              15
Paul Wendkos            USA               1987
*Raquel Welch, Michael Gross, Bonnie Bartlett, Peter
Michael Goetz, Joanna Miles, Ed O'Neil*
A woman suffering from an incurable disease, fights
for the right to end her suffering through suicide.
Unusual casting of Welch makes this over-
sentimental drama more interesting than it might
otherwise have been.
DRA                      93 min; 100 min (SHEER) mTV
B,V                           SHEER; VCC (VHS only)

**RIGHT TO KILL? ***                            15
John Erman              USA               1985
*Frederic Forrest, Chris Collet, Karmin Murcelo,
Justine Bateman, Ann Wedgeworth, Terrance
O'Quinn, Lisa Blake Richards, J.T. Walsh, Alison
Bartlett, John M. Jackson, Randy Moore, Norman
Bennett, Jerry Haynes*
A young boy shoots his father dead to save his sister
from a beating, and ends up being charged with
murder. Based on a true case. Written by Joyce
Eliason and well above average.
DRA                       90 min (ort 100 min) mTV
B,V                           CBS/FOXVID; CBS

**RING OF BRIGHT WATER ***                       U
Jack Couffer             UK                1969
*Bill Travers, Virginia McKenna, Peter Jeffrey,
Jameson Clark, Helena Gloag, Roddy McMillan,
Willie Joss, Jean Taylor-Smith, Archie Duncan, Kevin
Collins*
A man buys an otter and takes it to live with him in
the Scottish Highlands, where the pair enjoy various
escapades. A wholesome and likeable tale, carefully

made and well photographed. The script is by Jack
Couffer and Bill Travers.
Boa: book by Gavin Maxwell.
DRA                                    109 min; 102 min (VCC)
B,V,V2,LV                              GHV; VCC (VHS only)

### RING OF DESIRE ***                                  R18
Pierre Balakoff            USA                          1981
*Georgina Spelvin, Gena Lee, Hillary Summers,*
*Jennifer West, Monique Faberge, Ron Jeremy, Paul*
*Thomas, Chris Parker, William Margold*
A lawyer buys a magical ring that instantly makes
whoever wears it sexually irresistible. From him it
passes to his secretary, who loses it to a magazine
photographer. The film follows the ring as it passes
from hand to hand, leaving a trail of affairs in its
wake. Eventually it returns to our lawyer and arrives
on his night table, placed there by his wife's masseur.
A funny tale with good dialogue and a fair story.
A                           77 min (ort 84 min) Cut (1 sec in
                                    addition to film cuts)
B,V,V2                                                  ELV

### RIO BRAVO ***                                        PG
Howard Hawks               USA                          1959
*John Wayne, Dean Martin, Ricky Nelson, Angie*
*Dickinson, Walter Brennan, Ward Bond, Claude*
*Akins, John Russell, Pedro Gonzalez, Estelita*
*Rodriguez, Harry Carey Jr, Malcolm Atterbury, Bob*
*Steele, Bing Russell, Myron Healey*
A classic Western, with a brave sheriff trying to
prevent a killer being sprung from jail. More or less
remade in 1966 as "El Dorado", and in 1970 as RIO
LOBO. Despite a fine cast who give credible perform-
ances, little suspense is generated, and the film's
inordinate length makes this failing even more notice-
able. Written by Jules Furthman and Leigh Brackett.
WES                                    136 min (ort 141 min)
V                                                       WHV

### RIO GRANDE ****                                       U
John Ford                  USA                          1950
*John Wayne, Maureen O'Hara, Ben Johnson, Harry*
*Carey Jr, Victor McLaglen, Claude Jarman Jr, Chill*
*Wills, J. Carol Naish, Grant Withers, Peter Ortiz, Steve*
*Pendleton, Karolyn Grimes, Alberto Morin, Stan*
*Jones, Jack Pennick*
An excellent account of the US Cavalry and their
struggle with the Apache in the post-Civil War period.
The last of a Ford trilogy that dealt with the same
subject matter, the other two being FORT APACHE
and SHE WORE A YELLOW RIBBON. Written by
James Kevin McGuinness, with music by Victor
Young and songs by the Sons of the Pioneers. The
splendid photography is by Bert Glennon and Archie
Stout.
Boa: story by James Warner Bellah.
Osca: FLAME OF THE BARBARY COAST
WES    102 min (ort 105 min); 189 min (2 film cassette)
B/W
V                                                       VCC

### RIO LOBO ***                                         PG
Howard Hawks               USA                          1970
*John Wayne, Jorge Rivero, Jennifer O'Neill, Jack*
*Elam, Victor French, Chris Mitchum, Jim Davis,*
*Susana Dosamantes, Mike Henry, David Huddleston,*
*Bill Williams, Edward Faulkner, Sherry Lansing,*
*Dean Smith, Robert Donner*
At the end of the Civil War, a Union colonel sets out to
expose a traitor and recover a gold shipment. A long
and rambling tale, but highly enjoyable for its good
dialogue and action sequences. Written by Leigh
Brackett and Burton Wohl. This was Hawks' final
film.
WES                                    103 min (ort 114 min)
B,V                                                     MGM

### RIOT IN CELL BLOCK 11 ***                            15
Don Siegel                 USA                          1954
*Neville Brand, Emile Meyer, Leo Gordon, Frank*
*Faylen, Robert Osterloh, Paul Frees, Don Keefer*
A powerful and realistic prison movie, telling of three
convicts who seize their guards and barricade them-
selves in their cell-block, intending to use the result-
ing press coverage to expose their brutal treatment.
The script is by Richard Collins and the photography
by Russell Harlan.
DRA                           77 min (ort 80 min) B/W
V                                                       VCC

### RIOT ON SUNSET STRIP *                               18
Arthur Dreifuss            USA                          1967
*Aldo Ray, Mimsy Farmer, Michael Evans, Tim*
*Rooney, Laurie Mock, Bill Baldwin*
The real-life riots of the mid-1960s, provide the
backdrop to this exploitative tale of a cop's daughter,
whose involvement with drugs and hippies sparks off
a violent reaction from her father, which in turn helps
usher in the notorious riots. A dreary melodrama that
blends nostalgia and nonsense.
DRA                                    82 min (ort 85 min)
V                                                       RCA

### RIP OFF *
James Polakof              USA                          1977
*Linda Cristal, Colleen Camp, Michael Parks, Scott*
*Jacoby, John Ireland, Rory Calhoun, Rod Cameron*
A group of farmworkers decide that there are easier
ways of making money, such as opening a brothel
where the local rich set can be taken for all they're
worth. They then become involved in an attempt to
combat some crooked politicians, aided by the leader
of a gang dealing in stolen car parts. A ponderous
action comedy with the gags signalled well in advance.
Aka: LOVE AND THE MIDNIGHT AUTO SUPPLY;
MIDNIGHT AUTO SUPPLY
COM                                                    94 min
B,V                                                    CBS

### RIP VAN WINKLE **
Francis Ford Coppola     USA                           1985
*Talia Shire, Hunter Carson, Harry Dean Stanton, Ed*
*Begley Jr, Tim Conway, Mark Blankfield*
A feature-length version of a classic story, and one in
the "Faerie Tale Theatre" series.
JUV                                                    60 min
B,V,V2                                                 INT/CBS

### RIP-OFF, THE **
Anthony M. Dawson (Antonio Margheriti)
                           ITALY                        1978
*Lee Van Cleef, Karen Black, Edward Albert, Robert*
*Alda, Lionel Stander*
An ex-safe cracker comes back for one last job and
proves that he can outsmart his companions.
Aka: CONTRORAPINA; HO TENTATO DI VIVERE
A/AD                                                   98 min
B,V                                                    INT

### RISE AND FALL OF IDI AMIN, THE **
Sharad Patel              KENYA                         1981
*Joseph Olita, Geoffrey Keen, Denis Hills, Leonard*
*Trolley, Diane Mercier, Andre Maranne, Tony*
*Sibbald, Thomas Baptiste, Louis Mahoney, Ka*
*Vundla, Marlene Dogherty*
A film account of the horrors that were inflicted on the
people of Uganda, during the reign of "President for
Life" Idi Amin. Olita gives a chillingly realistic
portrayal of this hideous and degenerate dictator, who
ruled the country from 1971 to 1978, but the script
veers far too often towards gratuitous gore, rarely
attempting to examine the personality of the title
character.

Aka: AMIN: THE RISE AND FALL.
DRA                                      101 min (ort 105 min)
B,V                                                  VIPCO L/A

**RISE AND FALL OF LEGS DIAMOND, THE *** PG**
Budd Boetticher          USA                    1960
*Ray Danton, Karen Steele, Elaine Stewart, Jessie
White, Simon Oakland, Robert Lowery, Warren Oates,
Judson Pratt*
An excellent account of the rise of a notorious
gangster of the 1920s, with Danton well cast as an
aspiring criminal, who takes shooting lessons from his
old sergeant in a bid for the top. Part of a not
altogether successful effort on the part of Warner, to
resurrect the gangster genre. Written by Joseph
Landon and with photography by Lucien Ballard.
DRA                                        101 min B/W
B,V                                                     WHV

**RISE OF CATHERINE THE GREAT, THE **        U**
Paul Czinner             UK                      1934
*Douglas Fairbanks Jr, Elisabeth Bergner, Flora
Robson, Joan Gardner, Gerald Du Maurier, Irene
Vanbrugh, Griffith Jones, Lawrence Hanray, Gibb
McLaughlin, Clifford Heatherley, Allan Jeayes*
Creaky, melodramatic account of how an unsophisti-
cated German princess became absolute ruler of
Russia, through both marriage and military power,
after forcing her husband to abdicate in her favour.
Written by Biro, Arthur Wimperis and Marjorie
Deans.
Aka: CATHERINE THE GREAT
Boa: play The Czarina by Lajos Biro and Melchior
Lengyel.
DRA                             84 min (ort 96 min) B/W
V                                  CENVID; PICK; SCREL

**RISING DAMP ***                               PG
Joe McGrath              UK                      1980
*Leonard Rossiter, Frances De La Tour, Don
Warrington, Denholm Elliott, Christopher Strauli,
Carrie Jones, Glyn Edwards, John Cater, Derek
Griffiths, Ronnie Brody, Alan Clare, Jonathan Cecil*
A feature-length spin-off from a mediocre British TV
comedy, telling of the lodgers who live in a run-down
boarding house owned by a seedy and disreputable
landlord. Made without Richard Beckinsale, who
appeared in the TV series but died prematurely. The
thin and dreary little plot tells of a female tenant who
develops an interest in one of the new arrivals, much
to the chagrin of the landlord. Written by Eric
Chappell.
COM                                     94 min (ort 98 min)
B,V,V2   GHV L/A; PRV L/A; CH5 (VHS only); POLY
                                                    (VHS only)

**RISING STORM ***                               18
Francis Schaeffer        USA                    1989
*Wayne Crawford, Jane Chadwick, John Rhys-Davies,
Zach Galligan*
Bleak vision of a future authoritarian America, set in
Los Angeles circa 2099. A man is released from jail
and joins his brother in the search for a fortune and a
videotape that may enable them to overthrow the
regime. A low-budget SF thriller that fails to realise
any of its potential.
FAN                                              95 min
V                                                     RCA

**RISKY BUSINESS ***                             18
Paul Brickman            USA                     1983
*Tom Cruise, Rebecca De Mornay, Curtis Armstrong,
Bronson Pinchot, Raphael Sbarge, Nicholas Pryor, Joe
Pantoliano, Richard Masur*
A boy's parents go out of town on a visit and leave him
to look after the house. He begins to enjoy himself, but
decides things have gone a little too far when a couple
of hookers start using the house as a brothel. An
utterly banal comedy, combining a stilted and witless

script with wooden acting; the whole set off by a loud
and monotonous dirge (courtesy of Tangerine Dream)
that often drowns the dialogue out entirely.
COM                                     96 min (ort 99 min)
V/sh                                                    WHV

**RITA, SUE AND BOB TOO ***                      18
Alan Clarke              UK                      1987
*George Costigan, Siobhan Finneran, Michelle Holmes,
Lesley Sharp, Willie Ross, Patti Nichols, Kulvinder
Ghir, Danny O'Dea, David Britton, Maureen Long,
Mark Crompton, Stuart Goodwin, Max Jackman,
Simon Waring, Andrew Krauz*
A married man with a frigid wife indulges in a
threesome with his two young babysitters until his
wife finds out. An unappealing sex comedy with a few
hilarious sequences. Written by Dunbar from his play.
Boa: play by Andrea Dunbar
COM                                     89 min (ort 95 min)
B,V                                                     VIR

**RITUALS ***
Peter Carter             CANADA                 1976
*Hal Holbrook, Lawrence Dane, Robin Gammell, Ken
James, Gary Reineke, Murray Westgate, Jack Creley,
Michael Zenon*
Five doctors on holiday are terrorised by an evil
presence, and have to fight to survive in this rip-off of
DELIVERANCE. Quite suspenseful, but hardly ori-
ginal in conception or development.
Aka: CREEPER, THE
HOR                                     96 min (ort 100 min)
B,V,V2                                                 VPD

**RITZ, THE ***                                  15
Richard Lester           USA                     1976
*Jack Weston, Rita Moreno, Jerry Stiller, Kaye Ballard,
F. Murray Abraham, Treat Williams, Paul B. Price,
John Everson, Christopher J. Brown, Dave King,
Bessie Love, Tony De Santis, Ben Aris, George
Coulouris, Hugh Fraser*
A man on the run from his murderous brother-in-law,
hides out in one of New York's gay Turkish baths.
Moreno is memorable in a reprise of her Tony-winning
role as the untalented entertainer Googie Gomez, but
the whole affair has a very stagebound look about it.
Filmed in the UK.
Boa: play by Terrence McNally.
COM                                     88 min (ort 90 min)
B,V                                                     WHV

**RIVERBEND ***                                  18
Sam Firstenberg          USA                     1990
*Steve James, Margaret Avery, Tony Frank*
Wildly over-the-top tale of the racist South, that's set
in mid-1960s Georgia, where a small town is ruled by
a sadistic and murderous sheriff who oppesses the
local blacks. When some black marines on the run
from a court martial (they refused to massacre
Vietnamese villagers) meet the widow of a murdered
black civil rights activist, they decide to stay and
teach the folk to fight back. An improbable and
clumsily exploitative tale.
A/AD                                            106 min
V                                                     PRISM

**RIVER OF DEATH ***                             15
Steve Carver             USA                     1988
*Michael Dudikoff, Donald Pleasence, Robert Vaughn,
Herbert Lom, L.Q. Jones, Cynthia Erland*
At the end of WW2, a Nazi doctor escapes to South
America and hides out in the Amazon jungle, where
he continues his work trying to perfect a virus that
will only kill non-Aryans. Twenty years later, a
plague is found to be killing off Amazonian Indians
living near a lost city, and a party of explorers become
embroiled in a conflict with him. A loose adaptation of
MacLean's novel, that is as flat as a cartoon but not as
entertaining.

Boa: novel by Alistair MacLean.

A/AD 98 min
V PATHE

**RIVER OF NO RETURN \*\*** PG
Otto Preminger USA 1954
*Robert Mitchum, Marilyn Monroe, Tommy Rettig,*
*Rory Calhoun, Murvyn Vye, Wil Wright, Douglas*
*Spencer, Ed Hinton, Don Beddoe, Claire Andre, Jack*
*Mather, Edmund Cobb, Jarma Lewis, Hal Baylor,*
*Barbara Nichols, Fay Morley*
Set at the time of the California Gold Rush, this tells
of a widower and his young son, who meet a saloon
singer whose husband has deserted her. She hires the
man to take her downriver in pursuit of her husband,
and all three experience various hazards along the
way. The plot is insubstantial but the film moves
along briskly and the lovely locations are an asset. An
early Cinemascope film, whose impact will be dimi-
nished on TV.
WES 87 min (ort 91 min)
V CBS

**RIVER RAT, THE \*\*** 15
Tom Rickman USA 1984
*Tommy Lee Jones, Nancy Lea Owen, Brian Dennehy,*
*Martha Plimpton, Shawn Smith, Norman Bennett,*
*Tony Frank, Angie Bolling*
This directorial debut for screenwriter Rickman (he
went on to script COAL MINER'S DAUGHTER) tells
of a man wrongly imprisoned for murder for 13 years,
who arrives home to find his troubles are just
beginning. An uneven and only intermittently effec-
tive drama.
DRA 89 min (ort 93 min)
B,V CIC

**RIVER, THE \*\*\*** 15
Mark Rydell USA 1984
*Mel Gibson, Sissy Spacek, Shane Bailey, Becky Jo*
*Lynch, Scott Glenn, Don Hood, Billy Green Bush,*
*James Tolkan, Bob W. Douglas*
A film about the trials and tribulations of American
farmers, with a close-knit family struggling to make a
living, but constantly threatened by the river that
flows nearby. An old-fashioned family drama, written
by Robert Dillon and Julian Barry. The excellent
photography is by Vilmos Zsigmond. AA: Spec Award
(Kay Rose for sound effects editing).
DRA 119 min (ort 122 min)
B,V CIC

**RIVER'S EDGE, THE \*\*\*** 18
Tim Hunter USA 1987
*Crispin Glover, Dennis Hopper, Daniel Roebuck,*
*Keanu Reeves, Ione Skye Leitch, Roxanna Zal, Joshua*
*Miller, Josh Richman, Phil Brock, Tom Bower,*
*Constance Forslund, Leo Rossi, Jim Metzler, Tammy*
*Smith*
A study in teenage alienation and callousness, telling
of a teenage boy who strangles his girlfriend and
leaves her body on the river bank. An unpleasant and
disturbing film, based on a real incident.
THR 95 min (ort 99 min)
B,V PAL

**RIVKIN: THE BOUNTY HUNTER \*\***
Harry Harris USA 1981
*Rob Leibman, Harry Morgan, Harold Gary, Verna*
*Bloom, George DiCenzo, Glenn Scarpelli, John Getz,*
*Harry Bellaver, Jim Moody, Bo Rucker, Manuel*
*Martinez, Carl Don, Barry Ford, Jamie Aff, Mort*
*Freeman, Tony Turco, Richelle Williams*
The story of a small-time modern-day bounty hunter
in the state of New York. A pilot for a TV series.
Average.
DRA 114 min mTV
B,V HVM

**ROAD GAMES \*\*** 15
Richard Franklin AUSTRALIA 1981
*Stacy Keach, Jamie Lee Curtis, Marion Edward, Grant*
*Page, Bill Stacey*
A truck driver on the trail of a murderer picks up a
young hitch-hiker. A competent thriller hampered by
slow development. The director went on to make
PSYCHO 2, an altogether more effective film. Written
by Everett De Roche.
THR 88 min (ort 110 min)
B,V,V2,LV EHE

**ROAD RAIDERS \*\*** PG
Richard Lang USA 1989
*Bruce Boxleitner*
A former US Army officer with a talent for insub-
ordination, now runs a bar in the Philippines. With
the Japanese advancing, he attempts to escape the
war by taking over the identity of a dead officer and
assuming command of a plane that's taking a bunch of
misfits back to the States. When the plane crashes in
Japanese occupied territory, the group have to use
their wits to survive. A fast-paced but messy blend of
comedy, romance and action.
COM 91 min
V CIC

**ROAD TO BALI \*\*** 
Hal Walker USA 1952
*Bob Hope, Dorothy Lamour, Bing Crosby, Murvyn Vye,*
*Ralph Moody, Jerry Lewis, Jane Russell, Dean*
*Martin, Carolyn Jones, Bernie Gozier, Harry Cording,*
*Herman Cantor, Michael Ansara, Jack Claus, Allan*
*Nixon*
A routine comedy in the "Road To" series (the only
colour one), with Hope and Crosby rescuing Lamour
from various perils in the jungle. The film debut for
Jones. Number six in a series of seven films.
COM 90 min
B,V CHM/PPL

**ROAD TO MOROCCO \*\*\*** U
David Butler USA 1943
*Bing Crosby, Bob Hope, Dorothy Lamour, Anthony*
*Quinn, Vladimir Sokoloff, Monte Blue, Yvonne De*
*Carlo, Andrew Tombes, Leon Belasco, Dan Seymour,*
*Mikhail Rasumny, George Givot, Dona Drake, Jamiel*
*Hasson,*
Another entry in the series, with both heroes becom-
ing involved with a beautiful Arab princess. A frothy
and well paced excursion, with attractive locations
and some good gags. This was the third "Road To" film.
COM 78 min (ort 83 min) B/W
V CIC

**ROAD TO SINGAPORE \*\*** U
Victor Schertzinger USA 1940
*Bob Hope, Bing Crosby, Dorothy Lamour, Charles*
*Coburn, Anthony Quinn, Judith Barrett, Jerry*
*Colonna*
Two men hide out in Singapore, and forswear women
until they meet one who makes them change their
minds. The first in what proved to be a long series of
light and frothy comedies starring Hope, Crosby and
Lamour, all invariably being entitled "Road To . . .".
Boa: story by Harry Hervey.
COM 81 min (ort 84 min) B/W
V CIC

**ROAD TO UTOPIA \*\*** PG
Hal Walker USA 1945
*Bob Hope, Bing Crosby, Dorothy Lamour, Hillary*
*Brooke, Douglass Dumbrille, Jack La Rue, Robert*
*Barrat, Nestor Paiva, Will Wright, Billy Benedict,*
*Alan Bridge, Robert Benchley, Stanley Andrews,*
*Edgar Dearing, Arthur Loft*
The fourth "Road To" movie set in the Klondike with
talking animals, songs and the usual gags, plus
Robert Benchley's witty commentary. The plot is

flimsy but a few good gags are to be found.
COM                          86 min (ort 90 min) B/W
B,V                                              CIC

## ROAD TO ZANZIBAR **                          PG
Victor Schertzinger    USA                      1941
*Bob Hope, Bing Crosby, Dorothy Lamour, Una Merkel,
Eric Blore, Luis Alberni, Douglass Dumbrille, Charles
Coburn, Anthony Quinn*
This entry is set in Africa, where two circus artists go
on a jungle safari in search of a diamond mine. The
second film in this long-running series.
COM                          88 min (ort 92 min) B/W
V                                               CIC

## ROADBLOCK ***
Harold Daniels         USA                      1951
*Charles McGraw, Joan Dixon, Lowell Gilmore, Louis
Jean Heydt, Milburn Stone*
Under the influence of a greedy woman, an insurance
investigator is drawn into crime and begins to sell
information to criminals. A solid and highly atmos-
pheric little tale.
Osca: BACK TO BATAAN
DRA                          70 min (ort 73 min) B/W
B,V                                             KVD

## ROADHOUSE *                                   18
Rowdy Herrington       USA                      1989
*Patrick Swayze, Kelly Lynch, Sam Elliott, Ben
Gazzara, Marshall Tighe, Kathleen Wilhoite, The Jeff
Healey Band*
A philosophy student is taken on as a bouncer at an
ultra-tough Midwest bar and proceeds to break heads
at speed, which ultimately leads to an encounter with
the local crime boss. A feat of mindless violence that
tires the eye and exhausts the mind.
A/AD                         109 min (ort 114 min)
V/sh                                            WHV

## ROADHOUSE 66 *                                18
John Mark Robinson     USA                      1984
*Willem Dafoe, Judge Reinhold, Kaaren Lee, Kate
Vernon, Stephen Elliott, Alan Autry*
Two men on the road discover that the locals are none
too friendly, as they travel across the US in a 1955
Thunderbird on route 66. Sounds reminiscent of the
TV series "Route 66". A film with little going for it, not
least being the uninteresting plot.
A/AD                          90 min (ort 96 min)
B,V                                             EIV

## ROAR *                                        PG
Noel Marshall          USA                      1981
*Tippi Hedren, Noel Marshall, Jerry Marshall, John
Marshall, Melanie Griffith, Kyalo Mativo*
A research biologist in the bush is visited by his wife
and kids, in a dull pro-wildlife tract that has a
sub-plot involving evil game hunters. This poor effort
cost $17,000,000 to make and took eleven years to
complete. Some roar.
A/AD                         96 min (ort 102 min)
B,V                                   INT; VGM; MIA

## ROARING FIRE **                               18
Norry Suzuki          JAPAN                      1981
*Sonny (Shinichi) Chiba, Duke (Hiroyuki) Sanada, Sue
Shiomi, Miki Yamasita, Emily Yokoyama, Abdullah
The Butcher, Mickey Narita*
A man kidnapped and raised in Texas, returns to
Japan where he finds that his wicked uncle intends to
use a family heirloom to buy heroin. Standard martial
arts action with the usual flimsy plot.
MAR                  90 min (ort 95 min) Cut (7 sec)
B,V                                   VTC L/A; XTASY

## ROARING TWENTIES, THE ***                     PG
Raoul Walsh            USA                      1939
*James Cagney, Priscilla Lane, Humphrey Bogart,*

*Gladys George, Jeffrey Lynn, Frank McHugh, Paul
Kelly, Elizabeth Risdon, Joe Sawyer*
A classic gangster movie, that shows how a WW1
veteran returns to New York and builds a bootlegging
empire. Fast-paced, with fine acting and excellent
direction. The script is as predictable as they come,
but the whole effort is done with great style. This was
one of the last in a series of gangster movies from
Warner, and is generally regarded as one of the best.
Boa: story by Mark Hellinger.
A/AD                         102 min (ort 106 min) B/W
V                                               WHV

## ROB ROY *                                     U
Harold French          UK                       1953
*Richard Todd, Glynis Johns, James Robertson
Justice, Michael Gough, Finlay Currie, Geoffrey Keen,
Jean Taylor Smith, Archie Duncan, Michael Goodliffe,
Marjorie Fielding, Russell Waters, Eric Pohlmann,
Malcolm Keen*
After the defeat of the Scottish highland clans in 1715,
their leader evades capture by the English, and has
quite a few adventures before he obtains a royal
pardon. A sluggish and unconvincing yarn.
Aka: ROB ROY, THE HIGHLAND ROGUE
A/AD                                            88 min
B,V                                             WDV

## ROBBERS OF THE SACRED MOUNTAIN **             15
Bob Schulz            CANADA                     1982
*Simon MacCorkindale, John Marley, Louise Vallance,
George Touliatos, Blanca Guerra, Jorge Reynaldo,
Roger Cudney, Martin LaSalle, Enrique Lucero, Jorge
Santoyo, Jose Chavez Trowe, Pedro Montero, Salvador
Codinez, Harry Kopolan*
A remote monastery in Mexico in 1931 houses fabu-
lous treasures, which attract the attention of fortune-
hunters. This was announced as the first movie made
for US pay TV. (Well I thought you'd better know
that.) A RAIDERS OF THE LOST ARK clone, spirited
but hardly memorable. The music is by Lalo Schifrin.
Aka: FALCON'S GOLD
Boa: novel Challenger's Gold by Arthur Conan Doyle.
A/AD                                        90 min mTV
B,V,V2                                          GHV

## ROBBERY **                                    15
Michael Thornhill    AUSTRALIA                   1985
*John Sheerin, Tony Rickards, Tim Hughes, Regina
Gaigalas, Duncan Wass, Rhys McConnochie*
Sydney bookmakers are robbed of millions by six men
operating from an exclusive gentleman's club.
Average.
THR                          91 min (ort 94 min)
B,V                                             MPV

## ROBBERY **                                    PG
Peter Yates            UK                        1967
*Stanley Baker, James Booth, Frank Finlay, Joanna
Pettet, Barry Foster, William Marlowe, George Sewell,
Clinton Greyn, Michael McStay, Patrick Jordan*
Written by Edward Boyd, Peter Yates and George
Markstein, this is a fictional account of the Britain's
1963 Great Train Robbery. A deft account that is
fairly predictable but has several good chase sequ-
ences.
A/AD                         109 min (ort 113 min)
B,V                                 EHE; CH5 (VHS only)

## ROBBERY UNDER ARMS **                         PG
Ken Hannam/Donald Crombie
                      AUSTRALIA                  1985
*Sam Neill, Ed Devereux, Andy Anderson, Christopher
Cummins, Stephen Vidler, Liz Newman*
The story of Captain Starlight, an Australian folk
hero of the 19th century. A remake of a classic 1920
Australian film, (a 1957 British version also exists)
that tells of a likeable "Raffles"-type rogue who has a
taste for the finer things in life, and a talent for

robbery under arms, especially of other men's cattle. A competent cut-down version of a TV series, that had a longer running time of about 180 minutes.
Boa: novel by Rolf Boldrewood.
A/AD                    105 min (ort 141 min) Cut (6 sec)
B,V                                        IVS L/A; PRV

### ROBE, THE **                                        U
Henry Koster            USA                        1953
Richard Burton, Jean Simmons, Michael Rennie,
Victor Mature, Jay Robinson, Torin Thatcher,
Richard Boone, Dean Jagger, Betta St John, Richard
Morrow, Ernest Thesiger, Dawn Addams
First film in Cinemascope, but simultaneously shot flat (that's what's seen on TV), with the robe worn by Jesus at his crucifixion, attracting attention from both Romans and Christians. First cast with Tyrone Power in Burton's role and Burt Lancaster in Mature's. Written by Philip Dunne with music by Alfred Newman. DEMETRIUS AND THE GLADIATORS followed. AA: Art/Set (Lyle Wheeler and G.W. Davis/ W. Scott and P. Fox), Cost (C. LeMaire/E. Santiago).
Boa: novel by Lloyd C. Douglas.
DRA                             129 min (135 min)
V/h                                                CBS

### ROBIN AND MARION *                            PG
Richard Lester          USA                        1976
Sean Connery, Audrey Hepburn, Robert Shaw,
Richard Harris, Nicol Williamson, Denholm Elliott,
Kenneth Haigh, Ian Holm, Ronnie Barker, Bill
Maynard, Esmond Knight, Peter Butterworth
A kind of downbeat version of the legend of Robin of Sherwood, with our hero returning after an absence of many years, and finding the conditions in England somewhat depressing. However, he rekindles his romance with Maid Marion and even kills his old enemy the Sheriff of Nottingham, but dies in the attempt. A cold and unappealing tale, with not one trace of magic or sparkle. Written by James Goldman.
DRA                             102 min (ort 107 min)
V                                                  RCA

### ROBIN AND THE SEVEN HOODS ***                U
Gordon Douglas          USA                        1964
Frank Sinatra, Dean Martin, Sammy Davis Jr, Peter
Falk, Barbara Rush, Bing Crosby, Victor Buono, Sig
Rumann, Allen Jenkins, Hans Conried, Jack La Rue,
Edward G. Robinson, Barry Kelley
The Robin Hood legend is updated to 1920s Chicago, where a gangster and his cronies become local heroes by stealing from the rich and giving to the poor. A set of sharp routines and some good jokes keep this rather shallow spoof on the move. Music is by Nelson Riddle for which he received an AAN, as did songwriter-lyricist team James Van Heasen and Sammy Cahn for "My Kind Of Town". The unnecessary use of Panavision will be lost on TV.
COM                             118 min (ort 123 min)
                                                   WHV

### ROBIN HOOD *                                    U
Wolfgang Reitherman     USA                        1973
Voices of: Brian Bedford, Peter Ustinov, Terry-
Thomas, Phil Harris, Andy Devine, Pat Buttram,
Roger Miller, George Lindsey, Carole Shelley
An unusual animated version of this famous legend, with a fresh approach in that all the parts are played by animals. However, despite good dialogue, the songs and animation leave a lot to be desired.
CAR                              80 min (ort 83 min)
V                                                  WDV

### ROBIN HOOD ***                                 PG
Allan Dwan              USA                        1922
Douglas Fairbanks, Wallace Beery, Alan Hale Sr,
Enid Bennett
The story of this legendary hero and his battles with the villainous Sheriff of Nottingham. An excellent

(albeit silent) version of this tale, with ambitious sets and some exciting stunts and swordplay.
A/AD                117 min (ort 127 min) B/W silent
V                                                  VIR

### ROBIN OF SHERWOOD **                            U
Ian Sharp               UK                         1983
Michael Praed, Anthony Valentine, Nickolas Grace,
Clive Mantle, Judi Trott, Peter Llewellyn-Williams,
Phil Rose, Phillip Jackson, John Abineri, Ray
Winstone, Robert Addie, Mark Audley, Paul Duggan,
Mark Ryan, Toby Lee
Pilot for a TV series, that added elents of magic and mysticism to a familiar story. Well made and acted, but not aimed at too young an audience, with Robin now cast as the semi-mortal offspring of a pagan god. A strange and not altogether successful variant.
Aka: ROBIN HOOD AND THE SORCERER; ROBIN HOOD, THE LEGEND
A/AD                            100 min (ort 115 min) mTV
V                                                  VGM

### ROBIN OF SHERWOOD 2 **                         PG
Ian Sharp               UK                         1984
Michael Praed, Judi Trott, Jason Connery, Clive
Mantle, Ray Winstone, Peter Llewellyn, Phil Rose,
Mark Ryan, Nickolas Grace, Robert Addie, John
Abineri
Episodes 3 and 4 from the first series. In "Seven Poor Knights From Acre" a group of fanatical Knights Templars attack Robin and his men, whom they blame for the theft of a sacred emblem. "Alan a'Dale" has Robin called upon to assist Alan, whose beloved Mildred is about to be forced into an arranged marriage with the Sheriff of Nottingham.
Osca: ROBIN OF SHERWOOD (asa)/ROBIN OF SHERWOOD 3 (asa)
A/AD                100 min; 300 min (boxed set) mTV
V                                                  VGM

### ROBIN OF SHERWOOD 4 **                         PG
Robert Young/James Allen/Alex Kirby
                        UK                         1985
Michael Praed, Judi Trott, Jason Connery, Clive
Mantle, Ray Winstone, Peter Llewellyn, Phil Rose,
Mark Ryan, Nickolas Grace, Robert Adie, John
Abineri, John Nettles, Philip Davies, George Baker,
David de Keyser, Amy Rosenthal
The first two episodes from the second series. In "The Prophecy" Robin hears the death of King Richard foretold and learns of a hooded prisoner being kept in the dungeons of Nottingham Castle by Prince John. "The Children Of Israel" sees the Sheriff of Nottingham using the massacre of the Jews of York as a precedent to stir up a riot and avoid paying his debts to a moneylender.
A/AD                                        100 min mTV
V                                                  VGM

### ROBINSON CRUSOE **                              U
Gibba                   AUSTRALIA                  1972
Voices of: Alan Thornton, Frank Driver, Anthony
Victor
An engaging animated version of this classic tale, with an introduction by Jon Pertwee.
CAR                              47 min (ort 86 min)
B,V                 VCL L/A; CHILD L/A; STYL (VHS only)

### ROBINSON CRUSOE AND THE TIGER ***             PG
Rene Cardona Jr         MEXICO                     1969
Hugo Stiglitz, Ahui
Written by Mario Marzac and Rene Cardona Jr, this has the addition of a tiger that Crusoe takes with him to the island. A well made and attractive version of the famous tale.
Aka: ROBINSON CRUSOE
Boa: novel by Daniel Defoe.
JUV                 105 min (ort 110 min) Cut (1 min 11 sec)
B,V                                 EHE; CH5 (VHS only)

## ROBINSON CRUSOE ON MARS ***
Byron Haskin          USA                    1964
*Paul Mantee, Vic Lundin, Adam West*
Having crashlanded on Mars, an astronaut faces a
harsh struggle to survive, but he receives unexpected
help when he offers sanctuary to a slave-worker newly
escaped from his alien masters. A surprisingly good
adaptation of Defoe's classic, the use of Death Valley
locations and the photography of Winton C. Hoch are
its greatest strengths, although the juvenile plotting
and resolution are drawbacks.
FAN                              105 min (ort 109 min)
V                                               CIC

## ROBO NINJA **                                    18
Keita Amamiya                                     1988
A futuristic action tale that blends martial arts and
SF genres into an account of an armed conflict
between two warrior clans. When the leader of one is
captured the title character, a kind of Ninja answer to
THE TERMINATOR, is called in to mount a rescue
and prevent a possible world catastrophe. Competent
enough, but neither particularly original nor memor-
able.
FAN                                            90 min
V                                                 BOX

## ROBOCOP ***                                      18
Paul Verhoeven          USA                       1987
*Peter Weller, Nancy Allen, Dan O'Herlihy, Ronny Cox,
Kurtwood Smith, Miguel Ferrer, Robert DoQui, Ray
Wise, Felton Perry, Paul McCrane, Jesse Goins, Del
Zamora, Calvin Jung, Rick Leiberman, Lee DeBroux,
Mark Carlton*
In the not-too-distant future, policing has become the
responsibility of a private corporation who, in their
search for greater efficiency, resurrect a murdered
police officer and turn him into a bionic law enforce-
ment officer. However, he still seeks revenge for his
murder, in this brutal and effective fantasy. See also
R.O.T.O.R. AA: Spec Award (Stephen Flick/John
Pospisil for sound effects editing).
FAN                               98 min (ort 103 min)
B,V                                              VIR

## ROBOT JOX ***                                    15
Stuart Gordon          USA                        1989
*Gary Graham, Anne-Marie Johnson, Paul Koslo,
Robert Sampson, Danny Kamekona, Hilary Mason,
Michael Alldredge*
In the post-WW3 future, war has been outlawed and
all armed conflicts are decided by single combat
between trained fighters in vast robot machines. The
American champ, upset by the death of 300 spectators
caused when his machine fell on them, refuses to fight
the Soviet champ over the sovereignty of Alaska, but a
femme fatale is sent to persuade him otherwise. A
competent effort, inspired by the Peter Watkins story
"The Gladiators".
FAN                                            81 min
V                                                 EIV

## ROBOT MONSTER
Phil Tucker          USA                          1953
*George Nader, Gregory Moffett, Claudia Barrett,
Selena Royle, John Mylong, George Barrows, Pamela
Paulson*
A legendary Grade-Z movie that achieves a greatness
eluding lesser films. A young boy has a fall and loses
consciousness, dreaming that Earth has been invaded
by a powerful robot. (Yes, I know the robot looks like a
gorilla wearing a diving helmet, but this is LOW
budget stuff.) Shot in 3-D originally (except for some
stock dinosaur footage), and with an utterly incomprehensible finale.
FAN                                       63 min B/W
B,V                                               BWV

## ROBOTECH: THE MOVIE ***                          PG
Carl Macek/Ishiguro Noburo
                      USA                         1986
*Voices of: Ryan O'Flannigan, Brittany Harlowe,
Muriel Fargo, Greg Sbow, Jeffrey Platt, Guy Garrett,
Abe Lasser, Merle Pearson, Penny Sweet, Wendee
Swan, Wayne Anthony, Spike Niblick, Bruce Nielson,
Ike Medlick, Tom Warner*
A full-length animation, set in the year 2027, and
telling of an alien space fleet assembled to invade
Earth, but requiring information held on a master
computer to be certain of success. When the man in
charge of the planet's defences is captured, he is
replaced by a duplicate, and a young mechanic who
has learnt of this, tries to foil the duplicate's plans. A
lively adventure helped along by its well thought-out
script.
CAR                                            82 min
B,V                                               RNK

## ROCK AND RULE **                                 PG
Clive A. Smith          CANADA                    1983
*Voices of: Don Francks, Paul Le Mat, Susan Roman,
Sam Langevin, Catherine O'Hara, Dan Hennessey,
Greg Daffell, Chris Wiggins, Brent Titcomb, Donny
Burns, Martin Lavut, Catherine Gallant, Keith
Hampshire, Melleny Brown*
A futuristic cartoon, about a wicked plot to release a
monster from another dimension into a civilisation
based on rock and roll music. Unfortunately, the
excellent animation is hampered by the flimsy story.
The enjoyable rock score includes music by: Lou Reed,
Debbie Harry, Cheap Trick, Earth, Wind and Fire and
Iggy Pop.
Aka: ROCK 'N' RULE
CAR                            85 min; 74 min (CH5)
B,V                          EHE; CH5 (VHS only)

## ROCK 'N' ROLL COWBOYS *                          15
Rob Stewart          AUSTRALIA                    1987
*David Franklin, Nikki Coghill, Peter Phelps*
A bunch of conservatives are out to ban rock music,
and take samples of the brainwaves of musicians in an
effort to understand what they oppose. However, the
music turns them into mindless zombies, in this
foolish satire.
MUS                                            83 min
B,V                                               GHV

## ROCK 'N' ROLL HIGH SCHOOL ***                    15
Allan Arkush          USA                         1979
*P.J. Soles, Vincent Van Patten, Clint Howard, Dey
Young, The Ramones, Mary Woronov, Paul Bartel,
Dick Miller, Alix Elias, Don Steele, Loren Lester,
Daniel Davies, Lynn Farrell, Grady Sutton, Herbie
Braha, Barbara Ann Walters*
The new headmistress at a school tries to ban rock and
roll, while her pupils do all they can to defy her. A
boisterous musical of minimal plotting but much
energy, and worth a look for some hilarious sequences.
Music is supplied by the Ramones.
MUS              88 min (ort 91 min) Cut (1 min 39 sec)
B,V                                               WHV

## ROCK 'N' ROLL MUM **                             U
Michael Schultz          USA                      1988
*Dyan Cannon, Heather Locklear, Michael Brandon,
Joe Pantoliano, Telma Hopkins, Nancy Lenehan, Josh
Blake, Fran Drescher, Alex Rocco*
A woman rock singer tries to reconcile the conflicting
demands of being a musician and a mother, in this
undemanding Disney effort.
COM                             92 min (ort 100 min) mTV
B,V                                               WDV

## ROCK, ROCK, ROCK **                              U
Will Price          USA                           1956
*Tuesday Weld, Jacqueline Kerr, Ivy Schulman, Alan
Freed, The Moonglows, Teddy Randazzo, Chuck*

Berry, Fats Domino, Lavern Baker, The Johnny
Burnette Trio, The Flamingos, Frankie Lymon and the
Teenagers, Cirino and the Bowties
Classic 1950s corn, filmed in the Bronx. A teenage girl
has to find the money she needs to buy a strapless
evening gown to wear to the school dance. Fortunately
she does so to the sound of some fine rock 'n' roll
numbers. Weld's singing voice was dubbed by Connie
Francis and the effect is unintentionally hilarious.
The screen debut for Weld.

| MUS | 84 min B/W |
| B,V | DFS; STABL |

### ROCKERS **
Theodoros Bafaloukos  JAMAICA                    1978
Leroy Wallace, Richard Hall, Monica Craig, Marjorie
Norman, Jacob Miller
An impoverished Rasta musician tries to break into
the music establishment, and comes into contact with
some of its less honest elements. A loud reggae score
features Peter Tosh, Bunny Wailer, Burning Spear,
Third World and Gregory Isaacs. A contrived but
quite entertaining effort.

| MUS | 100 min |
| B,V | ISLPIC/PVG |

### ROCKET GIBRALTAR ***                          PG
Daniel Petrie       USA                          1988
Burt Lancaster, Suzy Amis, Patricia Clarkson,
Frances Conroy, Sinead Cisack, John Glover, Bill
Pullman, Kevin Spacey, Macauley Culkin
Relatives gather to celebrate the 77th birthday of the
family patriarch, in this difficult but ultimately
rewarding study of family loyalties and conflicts. The
script is by Amos Poe. Filmed on Long Island.

| DRA | 95 min (ort 100 min) |
| V | RCA |

### ROCKETTES **                                  PG
Jerrold Freedman       USA                       1983
Gwen Verdon, John Heard, Sheree North, David
Marshall Grant, Ron Karabatsos, Shanna Reed,
Maureen Teefy, Deborah Geffner, Eileen Collins,
Barson Heyman, Vera Lockwood, Carol Harbich,
Ethyl Will, Mace Barrett, Marilyn Cooper
A behind-the-scenes look at a famous New York dance
troupe working at Radio City Hall, and a look at the
competition that's run to recruit them. A kind of less
glamorous version of A CHORUS LINE. Verdon's TV
movie debut.
Aka: LEGS (VFP)

| DRA | 91 min; 100 min (VFP) (ort 120 min) mTV |
| B,V | VFP; AMBAS; GLOB |

### ROCKING HORSE WINNER, THE ***                PG
Anthony Pelissier       UK                       1949
Valerie Hobson, John Mills, John Howard Davies,
Ronald Squire, Cyril Smith, Hugh Sinclair, Charles
Goldner, Susan Richards, Antony Holles, Melanie
McKenzie, Caroline Steer, Michael Ripper
A young boy develops a strange ability to pick
winning horses after being inspired by the thrilling
stories of a groom. At first everything goes well, but
events begin to take an unexpected turn. A competent
little drama, put together with wit and care, but
hampered by the thin plot. Remade as a 33-minute
short in 1983
Boa: short story by D.H. Lawrence.

| DRA | 88 min (ort 90 min) B/W |
| V | VCC |

### ROCKING WITH SEKA *
Ziggy Zigowitz Jr       USA                      1980
Seka (Dorothy Hundley Patton), Serena, John C.
Holmes, Jamie Gillis, Judy Carr, Patricia Lee
A stewardess tells her girlfriends about her sexual
experiences on the Los Angeles to San Francisco, run
in this plotless, tiresome epic of sex and more sex.

Aka: ROCKIN' WITH SEKA (VCO); SEKA'S
CRUISE

| A | 78 min |
| B,V | VCO L/A; BUVID |

### ROCKULA **                                    PG
Luca Bercovici       USA                          1989
Dean Cameron, Tawny Fere, Susan Tyrrell, Bo
Diddly, Thomas Dolby, Toni Basil
In this utterly silly vampire musical a vampire falls in
love every 22 years, but cannot lose his virginity due
to a centuries-old curse. A film that plays very much
like a pop video, but a few good songs and some funny
lines provide a modicum of entertainment if not wit.

| COM | 87 min |
| V/sh | PATHE |

### ROCKY ****                                    PG
John G. Avildsen       USA                        1976
Sylvester Stallone, Talia Shire, Burt Young, Carl
Weathers, Thayer David, Burgess Meredith
Stallone finally broke into the big time with this
excellent story (written by him) of a fading small-time
boxer who gets a chance to regain his self respect by
taking a crack at the heavyweight championship.
Music by Bill Conti. Four sequels have followed so far,
each slightly more hollow than the one before. AA:
Pic, Dir, Edit (Richard Halsey/Scott Conrad).

| DRA | 119 min; 114 min (WHV) |
| B,V | INT; WHV (VHS only) |

### ROCKY 2 **                                    PG
Sylvester Stallone       USA                      1979
Sylvester Stallone, Talia Shire, Burt Young, Carl
Weathers, Burgess Meredith
Sequel to ROCKY with our boxer marrying his girl
and working towards another bout. There's nothing
new in this one, although the film remains watchable.
Written once more by Stallone with music by Bill
Conti.

| DRA | 114 min (ort 119 min) |
| B, V/sh, LV | WHV |

### ROCKY 3 **                                    PG
Sylvester Stallone       USA                      1982
Sylvester Stallone, Talia Shire, Burt Young, Burgess
Meredith, Carl Weathers, Tony Burton, Mr. T, Hulk
Hogan
The second sequel to ROCKY, with the champ beaten
at his first match against a tough opponent. He trains
under Weathers to get his revenge. More of the same
with a script by Stallone.

| DRA | 95 min (ort 99 min) |
| V/sh | WHV |

### ROCKY 4 **                                    PG
Sylvester Stallone       USA                      1985
Sylvester Stallone, Dolph Lundgren, Carl Weathers,
Talia Shire, Burt Young, Brigitte Nielsen, Michael
Pataki, James Brown, R.J. Adams, Al Dandiero,
Dominic Barto, Daniel Brown, Rose Mary Campos,
Jack Carpenter, Marty Denkin
The fourth in the "Rocky" series pits the champ
against a mighty Soviet fighting-machine (played
admirably by Lundgren – who's Swedish). When his
buddy dies at the hands of this monster, our perennial
pugilist swears revenge. Did I hear you ask about a
new plot?

| DRA | 88 min (ort 91 min) |
| V/sh | WHV |

### ROCKY HORROR PICTURE SHOW, THE ***          15
Jim Sharman       UK                              1975
Tim Curry, Susan Sarandon, Barry Bostwick, Richard
O'Brien, Jonathan Adams, Meatloaf, Charles Gray,
Little Nell (Neil Campbell), Patricia Quinn, Peter
Hinwood, Hilary Labow, Jeremy Newson, Koo Stark,
Christopher Biggins
A camp spoof on horror movies, with a straight couple

taking refuge in a house full of weirdos. An outrageous blend of sex, transvetism and rock, with music and lyrics by O'Brien. Now something of a cult film, it was followed by SHOCK TREATMENT.
COM                 95 min (ort 101 min)
B,V                                     CBS

**RODEO GIRL ** **
Jackie Cooper          USA           1980
*Katherine Ross, Bo Hopkins, Candy Clark, Jacqueline Brookes, Wilford Brimley, Parley Baer, Elise Caitlin, Savannah Bentley, Nancy Priddy, Bucklind Perry, Dee Croxton, Arlene Banas, June Evett, Pamela Earnhardt*
An adaptation by Kathryn Micaelian Powers of the true story of Sue Pirtle, a world champion rodeo star who in this tale is shown as a bored rodeo wife who joins an all-girl rodeo outfit. Average.
DRA                 92 min (ort 100 min) mTV
B,V                                     PRV

**ROLLER BLADE ***                         18
Donald G. Jackson      USA           1985
*Katina Garner, Suzanne Solari, Jeff Hutchinson, Robby Taylor, Sam Mann, Shaunn Michelle, Chris Douglas-Olen Ray, Michelle Bauer, Lisa Marie, Barbara Peckinpaugh*
A post-WW3 survival epic, with mutant baddies and the other stock characters that crop up in this genre. This one's set in a devastated L.A. but has nothing new on offer except the appearance of roller-skating heroines.
FAN                                  88 min
B,V                                     NWV

**ROLLER BOOGIE ***                         
Mark L. Lester         USA           1979
*Linda Blair, Jim Bray, Beverly Garland, Roger Perry, Mark Goddard, Sean McClory, Jimmy Van Patten, Kimberly Beck*
A musical prodigy studying in Venice, heads the fight to prevent a local roller skating rink from being closed. Made purely and simply to cash in on a brief roller-disco craze, but certainly not worth watching in its own right.
DRA                                 103 min
B,V                                     VPD

**ROLLERBABIES ***
Carter Stevens         USA           1979
*Robert Random, Yolanda Salvas, David Williams, Susan McBain, Terri Hall*
In the 21st century sex has been outlawed because of the population explosion and people take sex-suppressant pills. An insane and disjointed mess featuring a sexy bald-headed woman who appears on a TV show, a female android who gets pregnant and a bunch of guys and girls who make love on roller-skates.
A                                    90 min
V                                       RIP

**ROLLERBALL ***                          15
Norman Jewison         USA           1975
*James Caan, John Houseman, Ralph Richardson, Maud Adams, John Beck, Moses Gunn, Pamela Hensley. Shane Rimmer, Bert Kwouk, Barbara Trentham, Alfred Thomas, Burnell Tucker, Angus MacInnes, Nancy Blair, Rick Le Permentier*
A bleak, pointless and hollow look at a futuristic society, where aggression is channelled into the following of a violent spectator sport – a kind of hockey on roller-skates and motorcycles. A hero of the sport has achieved such a following that the state sees him as a threat, and he is ordered in no uncertain terms to retire. One of the most empty and sterile films ever made. Written by William Harrison.
Boa: short story Rollerball Murder by William Harrison.

FAN                 119 min (ort 129 min)
B,V,V2                           INT; WHV

**ROLLING MAN ** **
Peter Hyams           USA           1972
*Dennis Weaver, Don Stroud, Donna Mills, Jimmy Dean, Sheree North, Slim Pickens, Agnes Moorehead, Linda Scott, Devra Korwin, Donald Larkin, Jack Haley, Joe Nixon, Marion Hall, Joanie Hall, Gary Marsh, Carol Swenson*
A man just out of prison, for the attempted murder of a driver who ran over and killed his wife, goes in search of his missing children. An atmospheric but muddled and overblown drama. Written by Stephen and Elinor Knarpf.
DRA                 73 min (ort 90 min) mTV
B,V                                     RNK

**ROLLING THUNDER ***                      18
John Flynn            USA           1977
*William Devane, Tommy Lee Jones, Linda Haynes, James Best, Dabney Coleman, Lisa Richards, Luke Askew*
A Vietnam POW sees his family murdered and sets out to get his revenge in a standard revenger that might have been better (though not much) without its graphic violence. Written by Paul Schrader.
DRA                                  99 min
B,V,V2                                  RNK

**ROLLING VENGEANCE ***                    18
Steven Hilliard Stern  USA           1987
*Don Michael Paul, Lawrence Dane, Ned Beatty, Lisa Howard*
A trucker takes revenge for the rape of his girlfriend and the murder of his family, fitting out his truck with a range of weapons and explosive devices. A low-grade and repulsive offering.
A/AD                 87 min Cut (21 sec)
V/h                                     MED

**ROLLOVER ** **                          15
Alan J. Pakula         USA           1981
*Jane Fonda, Kris Kristofferson, Hume Cronyn, Josef Sommer, Bob Gunton, Macon McCalman, Ron Frazier, Jodi Long, Crocker Nevin, Martin Chatinover, Ira B. Wheeler, Paul Hecht, Norman Snow, Nelly Hoyos, Lansdale Chatfield*
The murder of a financial tycoon leads to the discovery of a major conspiracy, with far-reaching implications for the economy of the West. The title refers to the use made of funds by large institutions, when they are used to finance further loans. A complex and barely intelligible tale that tries to be more important than it is. Written by David Shaber.
DRA                 112 min (ort 115 min)
B,V                                     WHV

**ROMAN HOLIDAY ***                        U
Noel Nosseck          USA           1987
*Tom Conti, Catherine Oxenberg, Ed Begley Jr, Eileen Atkins*
A dull remake of the William Wyler classic with neither charm nor skill, and sorely missing the presence of Audrey Hepburn and Gregory Peck, who made the thin little tale of a runaway princess and her affair with a reporter so enjoyable in the original.
DRA                 96 min (ort 100 min) mTV
B,V                                     CIC

**ROMAN SCANDALS *** ***                   PG
Frank Tuttle          USA           1933
*Eddie Cantor, Ruth Etting, Gloria Stuart, David Manners, Edward Arnold, Verree Teasdale, Alan Mowbray*
Hilarious musical, with Cantor dreaming that he's back in ancient Rome, where he gets caught up in some crazy intrigues. Great songs and Busby Berkeley numbers ("Keep Young and Beautiful" features

Lucille Ball) combine with brilliant comic routines to produce a memorable film. The story is by George S. Kaufman and Robert E. Sherwood, with photography by Gregg Toland.

MUS           88 min (ort 93 min) B/W
V           VGM

## ROMANCE WITH A DOUBLE BASS *    PG
Robert Young      USA      1974
*John Cleese, Connie Booth, Graham Crowden, Desmond Jones, Freddie Jones, Jonathan Lynn, Andrew Sachs, Denis Ramsden*
A bass player and a princess both have their clothes stolen, and have to get back into the palace in this silly comedy, set in 19th century Russia.
Boa: short story by Anton Chekhov.
COM         40 min
B,V         CIC

## ROMANCING THE STONE ***    PG
Robert Zemeckis      USA      1984
*Michael Douglas, Kathleen Turner, Danny DeVito, Zack Norman, Alfonso Arau, Mary Ellen Trainor, Manuel Ojeda, Holland Taylor, Eve Smith, Joe Nesnow, Jose Chavez, Camillo Garcia, Rodrigo Puebla, Paco Morayta, Jorge Zamora*
A writer of romantic fiction gets into trouble in South America and is helped out by an American fortune-hunter. The action proceeds at a breakneck pace and both Turner and Douglas turn in credible performances, but this isn't enough to gloss over the lack of a solid plot. The unnecessarily violent ending also strikes a sour note. Written by Diane Thomas and produced by Michael Douglas. THE JEWEL OF THE NILE followed.
Boa: novel by J. Wilder.
A/AD      101 min (ort 106 min) Cut (23 sec)
V/sh      CBS

## ROMANTIC COMEDY *    15
Arthur Hiller      USA      1983
*Dudley Moore, Mary Steenburgen, Frances Sternhagen, Janet Eilber, Robyn Douglass, Ron Leibman*
A playwright tries to suppress his feelings for his female partner, in this unsuccessful attempt to transfer a hit Broadway play to the screen. Written by Slade.
Boa: play by Bernard Slade.
COM      98 min (ort 103 min)
B,V      WHV

## ROMANTIC ENGLISHWOMAN, THE **    15
Joseph Losey      FRANCE/UK      1975
*Michael Caine, Glenda Jackson, Helmut Berger, Marcus Richardson, Kate Nelligan, Rene Kolldehof, Michel Lonsdale, Beatrice Romand, Anna Steele, Nathalie Delon, Bill Wallis, Julie Peasgood, David De Keyser, Phil Brown*
The wife of a novelist goes on holiday, falling in love with another man and so initiating a strange, three-cornered relationship. An uncertain blend of drama and fantasy, that attempts to make a few portentous statements on the meaning of life, but ultimately becomes merely tiresome. Written by Tom Stoppard and Thomas Wiseman.
Boa: novel by Thomas Wiseman.
DRA      115 min
B, V/h      VCL/CBS; ODY

## ROME 2033: THE FIGHTER CENTURIONS **    18
Lucio Fulci      ITALY      1983
*Jared Martin, Fred Williamson, Howard Ross, Eleonor Gold, Claudio Cassinelli*
A complex plot revolving around televised gladiatorial games held in Rome's New Colosseum and a sports hero who's framed for murder.
Aka: NEW GLADIATORS, THE; ROME 2033

FAN      90 min Cut
B,V      MED

## ROME AGAINST ROME ** 
Giuseppi Vari      ITALY      1963
*John Drew Barrymore Jr, Susy Anderson, Ettore Mani, Ida Galli, Mino Doro, Philippe Hersent*
A Roman centurian is sent to Asia Minor to investigate the threat of an uprising and discovers that a magician has created an army of zombie warriors. A run-of-the-mill Italian effort buoyed up by slightly better than average production values.
Aka: NIGHT STAR: GODDESS OF ELECTRA; ROMA CONTRA ROMA; WAR OF THE ZOMBIES
A/AD      83 min (ort 105 min)
B,V      VPD

## ROME EXPRESS ***    U
Walter Forde      UK      1932
*Conrad Veidt, Esther Ralston, Joan Barry, Gordon Harker, Cedric Hardwicke, Harold Huth, Donald Calthrop, Hugh Williams, Finlay Currie, Frank Vosper, Muriel Aked, Eliot Makeham*
A prototype for those train thrillers such as THE LADY VANISHES and MURDER ON THE ORIENT EXPRESS, with thieves and blackmail victims among the passengers on the Paris-Rome express. An entertaining but verbose thriller. Written by Clifford Grey, Sidney Gilliat, Frank Vosper and Ralph Stock.
THR      91 min (ort 94 min) B/W
B,V      RNK; VCC

## ROMEO AND JULIET **    PG
Alvin Rakoff      UK      1979
*Patrick Ryecart, Rebecca Saire, Celia Johnson, Michael Hordern, John Gielgud, Joseph O'Conor, Laurence Naismith, Anthony Andrews, Alan Rickman, Jacqueline Hill, Christopher Strauli, Christopher Northey, Paul Henry*
A standard BBC adaptation, competent but unmemorable.
Boa: play by William Shakespeare.
DRA      169 min mTV
V      BBC

## ROMEO AND JULIET ***    PG
Franco Zeffirelli      ITALY/UK      1968
*Leonard Whiting, Olivia Hussey, Milo O'Shea, Michael York, John McEnery, Pat Heywood, Robert Stephens, Bruce Robinson, Paul Hardwick, Natasha Parry, Antonio Piefederici, Esmeralda Ruspoli, Roberto Bisacco, Keith Skinner*
Whiting and Hussey were only 17 and 15 respectively when this was made, and are ideal as lovers in a glossy screen version of this famous play, telling of the doomed love affair between the children of feuding families. A brave attempt, but Shakespeare's verse suffers badly from the brisk pace. The beautiful score is by Nino Rota and the prologue is read by Laurence Olivier. AA: Cin (Pasqualino De Santis), Cost (Danilo Donati).
Boa: play by William Shakespeare.
DRA      133 min (ort 152 min)
B,V      CIC

## ROMERO ***    15
John Duigan      USA      1989
*Raul Julia, Richard Jordan, Ana Alicia, Eddie Velez, Tony Plana, Alejandro Bracho, Lucy Reina, Harold Gould, Al Ruscio, Robert Viharo*
An absorbing movie with a message that attempts to chart the career of Oscar Romero, the Archbishop of El Salvador, who changed from obedient cleric to opponent of the state, and was assassinated by right-wing thugs in 1980. Ponderous and vague with regard to US support for the repressive government, but Julia's fine performance compensates. Scripted by John Sacret Young, this was the first feature financed by the US Roman Catholic Church.

DRA                          101 min (ort 102 min)
V/sh                                           WHV

## ROOFTOPS **                                   15
Robert Wise               USA               1989
*Jason Gedrick, Troy Beyer, Eddie Velez, Tisha*
*Campbell, Alexis Cruz, Allen Payne*
The director of WEST SIDE STORY returns with
another urban musical, dealing with the tough New
York kids who dance, fight and survive on the streets.
This time round, the starcrossed lovers are a white
boy and his Hispanic girlfriend, and the unusual but
rather awkwardly inserted "combat" dancing sequ-
ences blend kung fu movements with DIRTY DANC-
ING sexuality. If only the dreary plot were not there
to dissipate the energy of it all.
MUS                             91 min (ort 95 min)
V                                               CBS

## ROOM AT THE TOP ****                           15
Jack Clayton               UK               1958
*Laurence Harvey, Simone Signoret, Heather Sears,*
*Hermione Baddeley, Donald Wolfit, Donald Houston,*
*Allan Cuthbertson, John Westbrook, Raymond*
*Huntley, Ambrosine Phillpots, Richard Pasco, Beatrice*
*Varley, Delena Kidd, Mary Peach*
An ambitious young man decides to take a short cut in
the struggle to reach the top by marrying his boss'
daughter, ultimately ditching an older woman he had
a loving relationship with. A memorable drama,
excellently acted, and perfectly capturing the atmos-
phere of the grimy Northern town where the story is
set. Followed by the inferior LIFE AT THE TOP, a TV
series and then MAN AT THE TOP. AA: Actress
(Signoret), Screen (Adapt) (Neil Paterson).
Boa: novel by John Braine.
DRA                          113 min (ort 117 min) B/W
B,V                                        CBS; VCC

## ROOM UPSTAIRS, THE ***                         PG
Stuart Margolin           USA               1987
*Stockard Channing, Sam Waterston, Linda Hunt,*
*Sarah Jessica Parker, James Handy, Clancy Brown,*
*Joan Allen*
A touching comedy-drama telling of a lonely female
teacher, who is brought out of her shell by a gentle
musician who takes a room in her boarding house. The
script is by Steve Lawson.
Boa: novel by Norma Levinson.
DRA                                 101 min mTV
B,V                                           FUTUR

## ROOM WITH A VIEW, A ***                        PG
James Ivory                UK               1985
*Maggie Smith, Helena Bonham Carter, Judi Dench,*
*Julian Sands, Daniel Day Lewis, Denholm Elliott,*
*Simon Callow, Rosemary Leach, Joan Henley, Maria*
*Britneva, Amanda Walker, Rupert Graves, Fabia*
*Drake*
Upper-class mores are put under the microscope, in
one of those typically British class-conscious studies.
The story is of a young couple who indulge in a
passionate affair while on holiday in Florence. A
detailed period tale. AA: Art/Set (Gianni Quaranta
and Brian Ackland-Snow/Brian Savegar and Elio
Altramura), Screen (Adapt) (Ruth Prawer Jhabvala),
Cost (Jenny Beavan/John Bright).
Boa: novel by E.M. Forster.
DRA                          113 min (ort 115 min)
B,V                             EHE; CH5 (VHS only)

## ROOM, THE **                                   PG
Robert Altman             USA               1987
*Linda Hunt, Annie Lennox, Julian Sands, Donald*
*Pleasence*
A woman and her husband living in one cramped but
cosy room, are faced with eviction by their sinister
landlord.

DRA                                         49 min
V                                               IVA

## ROOMMATE, THE ***                              PG
Neil Cox                  USA               1984
*Lance Guest, Barry Miller, Tony Mockus, Deanna*
*Dunagan, Melissa Ford, Elaine Wilkes, David*
*Bachman*
A quiet college student finds his beatnik roommate
hard to take, and is eventually led into bad ways in
this witty and engaging comedy, set in a 1950s
university.
Aka: AMERICAN PLAYHOUSE: ROOMMATES
Boa: novel Christian Roommates by John Updike.
COM                          92 min (ort 96 min) mTV
B,V                                             CBS

## ROOMMATES ***                                  
Chuck Vincent             USA               1982
*Samantha Fox, Veronica Hart, Jamie Gillis, Jerry*
*Butler, Kelly Nichols, Bobby Astyr, Jack Wrangler*
The story of a former high-class hooker who is trying
to get out of the business and start a new life.
Although she now works making TV commercials, she
is in debt to her former pimp, and is forced to take on
two female roommates to help share the costs of her
apartment. A sophisticated and strongly plotted tale,
following the experiences of all three women as they
make their way in the world.
A                                           89 min
B,V                                             EVI

## ROOSTER *                                      15
Brice Mack                USA               1983
*Vincent Van Patten, Ty Hardin, Ruta Lee, Jeff Corey,*
*Kristine DeBell*
An unpleasant and tasteless story built around the
illegal sport of cock-fighting.
Aka: ROOSTER: SPURS OF DEATH
A/AD            85 min (ort 90 min) Cut (3 min 29 sec)
V                         MAST L/A; SKP L/A; XTASY

## ROOSTER COGBURN **                             U
Stuart Miller             USA               1975
*John Wayne, Katharine Hepburn, Richard Jordan,*
*Anthony Zerbe, John McIntire, Paul Koslo, Tommy*
*Lee, Strother Martin, Jack Colvin, Jon Lormer,*
*Richard Romancito, Lane Smith, Warren Vanders,*
*Jerry Gatlin, Mickey Gilbert*
A woman missionary teams up with a hard-fighting,
hard-drinking marshal, to bring in the outlaws who
killed her father. A kind of misguided sequel to TRUE
GRIT by way of THE AFRICAN QUEEN, with
neither the freshness nor verve of either.
Aka: ROOSTER COGBURN AND THE LADY
WES                          103 min (ort 108 min)
V/h                                             CIC

## ROOTS **                                       PG
Marvin Chomsky/John Erman/David Greene/Gilbert
Moses                     USA               1977
*Edward Asner, Chuck Connors, Cicely Tyson, Lloyd*
*Bridges, Doug McClure, Vic Morrow, George*
*Hamilton, Lorne Greene, Louis Gossett Jr, Richard*
*Roundtree, Maya Angelou, Moses Gunn, Thalmus*
*Rasulala, Harry Rhodes, William Watson*
A long, loose and rambling film version of a bestseller,
that looks at black history from the capture of an
African slave and his transportation to the States up
to the time of the Civil War. Well made and acted, but
terribly idealistic in terms of the view of life portrayed
in Africa. The impact is severely diluted by the
sluggish script. See also ROOTS: KUNTE KINTE'S
GIFT.
Boa: novel by Alex Hailey.
DRA              538 min (6 cassettes) Cut (16 sec) mTV
B,V                                             WHV

## ROOTS OF EVIL *
Christian Anders
WEST GERMANY 1979
*Christian Anders, Deep Roy, Fred Harris, Dunja Rayter*
An evil midget masterminds a drug-running racket and comes into conflict with a karate champion. Ludicrous nonsense.
Aka: DIE BRUT DES BOSEN
MAR 90 min
B,V TEM L/A; APX

## ROOTS: KUNTA KINTE'S GIFT **
Kevin Hooks USA PG 1988
*LeVar Burton, Louis Gossett Jr, Avery Brooks, Shaun Cassidy, John McMartin, Jerry Hardin, Kate Mulgrew, Michael Learned, Fran Bennett, Annabella Price, Tim Russ*
Another dose of glamorised history, that began with ROOTS and the tale of a young black boy who is taken into slavery. Three years have passed since an unsuccessful escape attempt, and Kunte Kinte now becomes involved in an ambitious scheme to lead his fellow slaves to freedom. Average.
Aka: KUNTA KINTE'S GIFT; ROOTS: THE GIFT
DRA 89 min (ort 100 min) mTV
V WHV

## ROPE **
Alfred Hitchcock USA PG 1948
*James Stewart, John Dall, Farley Granger, Cedric Hardwicke, Constance Collier, Joan Chandler, Edith Evanson, Douglas Dick*
Two homosexuals murder a friend for kicks and hide his body in a trunk. They then proceed to throw a party, using the trunk as a cocktail bar. The entire action takes place in one room, and was inspired by the real case of Leopold Loeb. A really stagebound work, with irritatingly long takes, and performances that just don't convince. Written by Arthur Laurents, this over-rated experiment was Hitchcock's first colour film.
Boa: play by Patrick Hamilton.
DRA 77 min (ort 81 min)
B,V CIC

## ROSALIE GOES SHOPPING ***
Percy Adlon WEST GERMANY 15 1989
*Marianne Sagebrecht, Brad Davis, Judge Reinhold, William Harlander, Alex Winter, Erika Blumberger, Patricia Zehentmayr*
Bavarian-born Sagebrecht and her weird family settle in Little Rock, Arkansas, where she becomes obsessed with the Great American Dream. Having taken this to mean an endless spending spree and a house full of possessions, she devises a crazy way to beat her creditors. A wonderfully screwy satire on American consumerism, that fires off gags in almost every direction and is as uneven as it is hilarious. The script is by Percy Adlon.
COM 93 min
V PAL

## ROSARY MURDERS, THE **
Fred Walton USA 18 1987
*Donald Sutherland, Charles Durning, Belinda Bauer, Josef Sommer, James Murtaugh, John Danelle, Addison Powell, Kathleen Tolan, Tom Mardirosian, Anita Barone*
A priest knows the identity of the man who has been murdering nuns and priests in Detroit, but cannot reveal this information to the police as he gained this knowledge in the confessional. A film that starts off well but cannot sustain itself, and degenerates into an exercise in tedium. Filmed on location in Detroit and scripted by Elmore Leonard.
Boa: novel by William X. Kienzle.
THR 100 min (ort 105 min)
B,V VIR

## ROSE CAFE, THE *
Daniele J. Suisa CANADA PG 1987
*Parker Stevenson, Linda Smith, Damir Andrei*
A woman neglects her love life to make a go of a restaurant venture. More romantic nonsense from the purveyors of Harlequin novels.
THE
DRA 75 min
V VCC

## ROSE GARDEN, THE ***
Fons Rademakers 15
USA/WEST GERMANY 1989
*Liv Ullmann, Maximilian Schell, Peter Fonda, Jan Niklas, Kurt Hubner*
A man accused of assualt claims in his defence that he recognised his elderly victim as the commander of the death camp in which his family perished. Fine performances and a dollop of sincerity are not enough to round out this superficial and excessively oblique attempt to deal with the issues raised by the Holocaust.
DRA 109 min (ort 111 min)
V PATHE

## ROSE MARIE ***
Mervyn Le Roy USA U 1954
*Howard Keel, Ann Blyth, Fernando Lamas, Bert Lahr, Marjorie Main, Joan Taylor, Ray Collins, Chief Yowlachie, James Logan, Turl Ravenscroft, Abel Fernandez, Billy Dix, Al Ferguson, Frank Magney, Marshall Reed, Sheb Wooley*
A remake of the 1936 musical in which a mountie falls for a tomboy girl of the woods, eventually "taming" her and winning her love. Not as good as the earlier film but closer to the original operatta. A highlight is Lahr singing "I'm The Mountie Who Never Got His Man". The choreography is by Busby Berkeley.
Boa: play by Rudolf Friml, Otto Harbach and Oscar Hammerstein II
MUS 97 min (ort 115 min)
B,V MGM

## ROSE, THE **
Mark Rydell USA 15 1979
*Bette Midler, Alan Bates, Frederic Forrest, Harry Dean Stanton, Barry Primus, David Keith*
A spin-off from the rather sad life of singer Janis Joplin, this has Midler starring in a powerful but overlong story, of a self-destructive singer who engineers her own downfall and death. The photography is by Vilmos Zsigmond, and is one of the best features of this depressing work.
DRA 129 min (ort 134 min)
B,V CBS

## ROSEBUD BEACH HOTEL, THE *
Harry Hurwitz USA 15 1984
*Peter Scolari, Colleen Camp, Christopher Lee, Fran Drescher, Eddie Deezen, Monique Gabrielle, Chuck McCann*
A seaside hotel is the setting for another low-brow comedy romp, with a ragbag collection of unfunny antics, and a hotel operator who hires a bunch of hookers to act as porters.
Aka: BIG LOBBY, THE
COM 80 min; 82 min (VES) (ort 87 min)
B,V VES/CBS; VES

## ROSELAND ***
James Ivory USA 1977
*Teresa Wright, Lou Jacobi, Geraldine Chaplin, Helen Gallagher, Christopher Walken, Joan Copeland, Lilia Skala, Don De Natale, Louise Kirkland, Conrad Janis, David Thomas, Edward Kogan, Madeline Lee, Stan Rubin*
Three stories set against the background of a famous New York ballroom. The first is weak but the other two are much better, with good attention paid to the

habitues of the dancehall and their bittersweet lives.
Written by Ruth Prawer Jhabvala.

DRA                                          103 min
B,V                                          PVG

## ROSELYNE AND THE LIONS *                  15
Jean-Joacques Beineix
                    FRANCE                   1989
*Isabelle Pasco, Gerard Sandoz*
Another slice of flashy, over-stylised emptiness from
the director of DIVA. A young man falls in love with a
beautiful girl and together they form a lion-taming
act with a travelling circus. A sub-plot involving a
schoolmaster keen to turn their exploits into fiction
adds nothing of substance to this lightweight effort.

DRA                                          125 min
V                                            PAL

## ROSEMARY'S BABY ***                       18
Roman Polanski          USA                  1968
*Mia Farrow, John Cassavetes, Ruth Gordon, Sidney
Blackmer, Maurice Evans, Ralph Bellamy, Patsy
Kelly, Angela Dorian, Elisha Cook Jr, Charles Grodin*
The frightening tale of a woman, the wife of an actor,
who is befriended by Satanists and unwittingly
becomes pregnant by the Devil. Written by Polanski.
It sounds foolish but is actually very well done.
Followed some years later by the ludicrous TV sequel,
LOOK WHAT'S HAPPENED TO ROSEMARY'S
BABY. AA: S. Actress (Gordon).
Boa: novel by Ira Levin.

HOR                                131 min (ort 137 min)
B,V                                          CIC

## ROSEMARY'S KILLER *
Joseph Zito             USA                  1981
*Farley Granger, Vicky Dawson, Christopher Goutman,
Lawrence Tierney, Cindy Weintraub, Lisa Dunsheath,
David Sederholm, Bill Nunnery, Thom Bray, Diane
Rode, John Seitz*
A mad GI kills his former girlfriend and her new lover
with a pitchfork, and then waits 35 years, after which
time he begins another round of savagery, this time
killing high school students. A mindless and absurd
shocker with rather unpleasant effects (courtesy of
Tom Savini).
Aka: GRADUATION, THE; PROWLER, THE

HOR                                          87 min
B,V                                          EIV

## ROSES ARE FOR THE RICH: PARTS 1           PG
AND 2 **
Michael Miller          USA                  1987
*Lisa Hartman, Bruce Dern, Joe Penny, Richard
Masur, Howard Duff, Morgan Stevens, Jim Youngs,
Betty Buckley, Kate Mulgrew*
A two-part soap opera, telling of a determined Appa-
lachian woman who sets out to have her revenge on
the coal magnate whom she blames for the death of
her husband. Hartman is unconvincing in her role,
but this enjoyable piece of escapist nonsense has
enough in it to sustain interest if not credibility.

DRA                                177 min (ort 200 min) mTV
B,V                                          GHV

## ROSIE DIXON: NIGHT NURSE *                18
Justin Cartwright       UK                   1977
*Debbie Ash, Caroline Argyle, Beryl Reid, John Le
Mesurier, Arthur Askey, Liz Fraser, Lance Percival,
John Junkin, Bob Todd, David Timson, Leslie Ash,
Jeremy Sinden, Peter Mantle, Ian Sharp, Christopher
Ellison, Patricia Hodge*
A young nurse encounters various over-sexed indi-
viduals in her work, in this ghastly attempt at a sex
comedy.
Boa: novel Confessions Of A Night Nurse by Rosie
Dixon.

COM                                84 min (ort 88 min)
V                                            RCA

## ROSIE: THE ROSEMARY CLOONEY
STORY ***                                    PG
Jackie Cooper           USA                  1982
*Sondra Locke, Tony Orlando, Penelope Milford,
Katherine Helmond, Kevin McCarthy, John Karlen,
Cheryl Anderson, Robert Ridgely, Joey Travolta*
A simple account of the career of singer Clooney, that
charts her rise from an act on Cincinnati radio,
through to stardom, a mental breakdown and a
courageous struggle back into the limelight. This
predictable rise-and-fall story benefits from Locke's
fine performance (she lip-synchs to Clooney's singing
voice) and an above-average script that's largely
based on Clooney's autobiography. Poor casting of
Orlando as Jose Ferrer is a minor failing.
Boa: autobiography This For Remembrance by
Rosemary Clooney.

DRA                                93 min (ort 100 min) mTV
V                                            CASPIC

## ROTTWEILER: THE DOGS OF HELL *            18
Worth Keeter            USA                  1982
*Earl Owensby, Herman Bloodsworth, Jerry Rushing*
Ten dogs trained for use in warfare escape, and spread
terror and death in a small town. An unappealing
version of JAWS on four legs.

HOR                                          89 min
B,V,V2                                       TEVP

## ROUGH CUT **                              PG
Donald Siegel           USA                  1980
*Burt Reynolds, Lesley-Anne Down, David Niven,
Timothy West, Patrick Magee, Joss Ackland, Al
Matthews*
A gentleman jewel thief, living in London and in-
volved in a multi-million dollar diamond heist, becom-
es the prey of a Scotland Yard detective about to
retire, who decides to trap his quarry with a pretty
woman. An adequate romantic comedy that was
plagued by production difficulties, and had four
directors and a clumsily re-filmed ending. Written by
Larry Gelbart (who used the pseudonym Francis
Burns).
Boa: novel Touch the Lion's Paw by Derek Lambert.

COM                                106 min (ort 112 min)
V/h                                          CIC

## ROUGHNECKS **                             15
Bernard McEveety        USA                  1980
*Steve Forrest, Sam Melville, Ana Alicia, Cathy Lee
Crosby, Stephen McHattie, Vera Miles, Harry Morgan,
Wilford Brimley, Kevin Geer, A. Martinez, Andrew
Rubin, Sara Rush, Timothy Scott, Rockne Tarkington,
Louise Heath*
Originally shown in two parts, this is the story of a
bunch of wildcatters or unofficial oil prospectors, who
follow after big-shot oil prospectors, drilling holes
where the chances of success are limited. Average.
Boa: story by Michael Michaelian and Charles Pieper.

A/AD                               178 min (ort 180 min) mTV
B,V                                          GHV

## ROUND MIDNIGHT ***                        15
Betrand Tavernier
                    FRANCE/USA               1986
*Dexter Gordon, Francois Cluzet, Lonette McKee,
Gabrielle Haker, Martin Scorsese, Herbie Hancock,
Sandra Reaves-Phillips, Christine Pascal, Bobby
Hutcherson, Wayne Shorter, John Berry, Philippe
Noiret, Liliana Rovere*
The enjoyable story of an expatriate black jazz
musician, and his struggle to create the be-bop sound
in 1959 Paris. A kind of homage to the world of jazz
and its musicians, and to some extent inspired by the
lives of Bud Powell and Lester Young. Real-life tenor
sax Gordon gives a great performance as an ageing
sax player in his film debut, for which he received a
nomination but unfortunately no Oscar. AA: Score
(Orig) (Herbie Hancock).

MUS 126 min (ort 133 min)
V/sh WHV

## ROVER, THE *
Terence Young ITALY 1967
*Anthony Quinn, Rita Hayworth, Richard Johnson,*
*Rosanna Schiaffino, Ivo Garrani, Mino Doro*
An 18th century French pirate comes under suspicion
of being an English spy but escapes from custody and
forms a friendship with a simple girl. A lacklustre and
slow-moving tale.
Boa: story by Joseph Conrad.
A/AD 107 min
B,V VPD

## ROXANNE **
PG
Fred Schepisi USA 1987
*Steve Martin, Daryl Hannah, Rick Rossovich, Shelley*
*Duvall, John Kapelos, Fred Willard, Max Alexander,*
*Michael J. Pollard*
An updating of Rostand's famous play "Cyrano de
Bergerac", with our romantic Captain of the Guard in
17th century France transformed into a modern-day
fire-chief, played with considerable panache by Mar-
tin. Hannah is the object of his affections in this
amiable but slack comedy.
COM 103 min (ort 107 min)
V/sh RCA

## ROYAL FLASH *
15
Richard Lester UK 1975
*Malcolm McDowell, Florinda Bolkan, Alan Bates,*
*Oliver Reed, Britt Ekland, Lionel Jeffries, Alastair*
*Sim, Michael Hordern, Tom Bell, Christopher*
*Cazenove, Joss Ackland, Leon Greene, Richard*
*Hurdall, Roy Kinnear*
A man is forced to impersonate a Prussian nobleman
and marry a beautiful woman, in this long-winded
and unfunny adventure, very much inspired by the
original novel. McDowell does his best as Flashman, a
Victorian bully and accomplished cad, but the film
just goes nowhere. Written by Fraser and very loosely
based on his novel.
Boa: novel by George MacDonald Fraser.
A/AD 97 min (ort 118 min)
B,V CBS

## ROYAL WEDDING **
U
Stanley Donen USA 1951
*Fred Astaire, Jan Powell, Sarah Churchill, Peter*
*Lawford, Keenan Wynn, Albert Sharpe, Viola Roche,*
*James Finlayson*
A musical revolving around a group of journalists and
performers in London for the Royal Wedding. Some
good scenes are interspersed throughout a film that's
rather tedious. Highlights are Astaire dancing on the
ceiling and Powell singing "Too Late". Music is by
Alan Jay Lerner (who also wrote the script) and
Burton Lane.
Aka: WEDDING BELLS
MUS 89 min (ort 93 min)
V MGM

## RUBY **
Curtis Harrington USA 1977
*Stuart Whitman, Piper Laurie, Janit Baldwin, Roger*
*Davis, Crystin Sinclaire, Paul Kent, Len Lesser, Jack*
*Perkins, Sal Vecchio, Edward Donno, Fred Kohler*
A deaf-mute girl becomes possessed by the spirit of a
dead gangster and causes much violence and mayhem,
leaving a trail of death behind her at a drive-in
cinema. A kind of supernatural thriller of muddled
direction and occasional chills.
HOR 80 min (ort 85 min)
B,V BWV

## RUBY AND OSWALD **
U
Mel Stuart USA 1978
*Michael Lerner, Frederic Forrest, Doris Roberts, Lou*

*Frizzell, Lanna Saunders, Brian Dennehy, Bruce*
*French, Sandy McPeak, Sandy Ward, James E.*
*Brodhead, Gwynne Gilford Jump, Erick Kilpatrick,*
*Walter Mathews*
A reconstruction of the four days prior to and follow-
ing the assassination of President John Kennedy, in
Dallas in November 1963, drawn from authenticated
events and eyewitness accounts. A sincere effort but
never rises above the level of a competent but
unmemorable drama.
Aka: FOUR DAYS IN DALLAS
DRA 102 min (ort 156 min) mTV
B, V/h GHV; ODY (VHS only)

## RUBY GENTRY **
King Vidor USA 1952
*Jennifer Jones, Charlton Heston, Karl Malden,*
*Josephine Hutchinson*
Brought up as a tomboy on the wrong side of the North
Carolina swamps, a young girl associates with a local
aristocrat, but eventually settles for marriage to a
wealthy businessman in order to spite those who
looked down on her. A ponderous, overblown and
remarkably unrealistic melodrama.
DRA 82 min B/W
B,V GHV; VCC

## RUCKUS **
15
Max Kleven USA 1982
*Dirk Benedict, Linda Blair, Ben Johnson, Matt Clark,*
*Richard Farnsworth*
A Vietnam veteran defends himself against his tor-
mentors in a small town and is pursued by massive
forces. Much the same plot as the later and better-
known Sylvester Stallone film – FIRST BLOOD.
DRA 91 min
B,V PRV

## RUDE AWAKENING **
15
Peter Sasdy UK 1984
*Denholm Elliott, Pat Heywood, James Laurenson,*
*Lucy Gutteridge, Eleanor Summerfield, Gareth*
*Armstrong, Patricia Mort*
An estate agent, married to a woman he does not love,
gets involved in a strange series of events when he
goes to view an old house. A predictable Hammer
House of Horror offering that runs out of steam very
early on.
Osca: TWO FACES OF EVIL, THE (CH5)
HOR 54 min; 101 min (2 film cassette) mTV
B,V PRV; CH5 (VHS only)

## RUDE BOY **
18
Jack Hazan/David Mingay
UK 1980
*Ray Gange, Joe Strummer, Mick Jones, Paul*
*Simonon, Nicky Headon, Johnny Green, Barry Baker,*
*Terry McQuade, Carole Coon, Elizabeth Young, Sarah*
*Hall, Colin Bucksey, Lizard Brown, Hicky Etienne,*
*Inch Gordon, Lee Parker*
An angry young man gets a job helping a punk rock
group on tour. Fans of punk rock may enjoy this one,
but others will find the lack of a story too much of an
irritation.
MUS 127 min (ort 133 min) (Cut at film release)
B,V VSP/PVG L/A; HEND

## RULERS OF THE CITY **
Fernando Di Leo
ITALY/WEST GERMANY 1977
*Jack Palance, Gisela Hahn, Edmund Purdom, Harry*
*Baer, Al Cliver (Pier Luigi Conti), Vittorio Caprioli*
A gambling boss has a hard time punishing those who
cheated him out of large sums of money. Standard
gangster melodramatics.
Aka: I PADRONI DELLA CITTA DI MISTER
SCARFACE; ZWEI SUPERTYPEN RAUMEN AUF
DRA 96 min
B,V,V2 VPD

**RUMBLE FISH \*\*** 18
Francis Ford Coppola    USA    1983
*Matt Dillon, Mickey Rourke, Diane Lane, Dennis
Hopper, Vincent Spano, Diana Scarwid, William
Smith, Nicolas Cage, Tom Waits*
An account of two adolescent brothers who get
involved in gang warfare. The title refers to one of the
brothers, who works in a petshop and identifies with
the bad-tempered and ferocious rumble fish. A power-
ful but unfocused effort. This was Dillon's third
Hinton film and Coppola's second (following THE
OUTSIDERS). Written by Coppola and with music by
Stewart Copeland.
Boa: novel by S.E. Hinton.
DRA    91 min (ort 94 min) B/W and Colour sequences
B,V    CIC

**RUMOR OF WAR, A \*\*\*** 15
Richard T. Heffron    USA    1980
*Brad Davis, Keith Carradine, Stacy Keach, Brian
Dennehy, Michael O'Keefe, Christopher Mitchum,
Steve Forrest, Richard Bradford, John Friedrich,
Perry Lang, Dan Shor, Lane Smith, Nicholas
Woodeson, Gail Youngs, Phillip R. Allen*
A college student is gradually transformed from a
young idealist into a battle-hardened and bitter
veteran, in this excellent adaptation of Caputo's book,
one of the first TV films to tackle the subject of the
Vietnam War. The script is by John Sacret Young.
Boa: book by Philip Caputo.
DRA    194 min (available as 2 cassette version)
    (ort 200 min) mTV
V    HER

**RUMPELSTILTSKIN \*\*** U
David Irving    USA    1986
*Amy Irving, Clive Revill, Billy Barty, Priscilla Pointer,
Robert Symonds, John Moulder-Brown*
A young woman is imprisoned in the King's castle and
given the task of spinning a bale of straw into gold.
When she begins to despair at her seemingly impossi-
ble task, a magic dwarf appears, and offers to help her
if she will promise him her first-born son. A feeble
musical adaptation, filmed in Israel.
Aka: RUMPLESTILTSKIN
Boa: short story by Jakob Ludwig Karl Grimm and
Wilhelm Karl Grimm.
JUV    81 min (ort 85 min)
V/sh    WHV

**RUN FOR THE ROSES \*\*** PG
Henry Levin    USA    1978
*Vera Miles, Stuart Whitman, Panchito Gomez, Sam
Groom, Theodore Wilson, Lisa Eilbacher*
A Puerto Rican boy raises a lame foal, and nurses it
back to health so that it can run in the Kentucky
Derby. Everything that one would expect from this
type of film is present, where the human actors are
obliged to play second fiddle to their more talented
equine colleagues.
Aka: THOROUGHBRED
JUV    93 min
B,V    VTC L/A; VMA; STABL

**RUN FOR YOUR LIFE \*\*** 15
William Webb    USA    1984
*Tom Eplin, Danny Williams, John Mayall*
A photographer in L.A. gets entangled in attempts by
organised crime, to gain control of a rock club on
Sunset Strip.
DRA    87 min
B,V    IMPACT/ODY

**RUN IF YOU CAN \*\*** 18
Virginia Lively Stone    USA    1987
*Martin Landau, Yvette Nidar, Jerry Van Dyke*
The people of L.A. are terrified by a series of baffling
murders. A tough, disillusioned cop is assigned to the
case and in the course of his investigations meets a
young girl who claims to have witnessed several of the
killings. Although the cop initially refuses to believe
her, he soon becomes convinced she is telling the truth
and realises that he must stop her from becoming the
next victim.
HOR    89 min (ort 93 min) Cut (2 min 22 sec)
B,V    AVA

**RUN LIKE A THIEF \*\*** PG
Harry Spalding    SPAIN/USA
*Kieron Moore, Ina Balin, Keenan Wynn, Fernando Rey*
A diamond thief conspires with the mistress of a gang
leader over a cache of stolen diamonds. Average.
THR    92 min Cut (17 sec)
B,V    VDF L/A; APX; SID

**RUN OF THE ARROW \*\*\***
Samuel Fuller    USA    1956
*Rod Steiger, Charles Bronson, Brian Keith, Sarita
Montiel, Ralph Meeker, Jay C. Flippen, Tim McCoy,
Olive Carey, H.M. Wynant, Neyle Morrow, Frank De
Kova, Stuart Randall, Frank Warner, Billy Miller,
Chuck Hayward, Don Orlando*
A Confederate soldier is given the chance to become a
Sioux warrior, by surviving their initiation ceremony,
an endurance test known as the "Run of the Arrow".
He does so, proving his bravery and worth as a
warrior. Steiger is excellent, in a violent and bloody
film that's still worth watching. The script is by
Fuller, and Angie Dickinson is reputed to have
dubbed Montiel. See also A MAN CALLED HORSE,
for something very similar.
Osca: CRY DANGER
WES    86 min
B,V    KVD

**RUN SILENT, RUN DEEP \*\*\*** U
Robert Wise    USA    1958
*Clark Gable, Burt Lancaster, Jack Warden, Brad
Dexter, Don Rickles, Nick Cravat, Mary LaRoche,
Eddie Foy III, Joe Maross, H.M. Wynant*
A submarine captain pursues a single-minded cam-
paign of revenge against the Japanese destroyer that
sank the previous sub he commanded. A tense por-
trayal of men facing the stresses of combat. The script
is by John Gay.
Boa: novel by Commander Edward L. Beach.
WAR    89 min (ort 93 min) B/W
V    WHV

**RUN WILD, RUN FREE \*\*** U
Richard C. Sarafian    UK    1969
*John Mills, Sylvia Syms, Mark Lester, Bernard Miles,
Gordon Jackson, Fiona Fullerton*
A 10-year-old mute and withdrawn boy, gains self
confidence through his love of animals, when he
encounters a wild colt on the moors. A pleasant
enough family film with nothing of great consequence.
Nicely photographed by Wilkie Cooper and written by
Rook from his novel.
Boa: novel The White Colt by David Rook.
JUV    97 min
B,V    RCA

**RUN, CHRISSIE, RUN \*\***
Chris Langman    AUSTRALIA    1984
*Carmen Duncan, Michael Aitkins, Shane Briant,
Nicholas Eadie, Annie Jones*
A 15-year-old girl finds herself being chased by an
assortment of unsavoury thugs; and all because of
some stolen money her mother has been given. Fair.
DRA    95 min
B,V    EIPT/CBS; KRP

**RUN, COUGAR, RUN \*\*** U
Jerome Courtland    USA    1972
*Stuart Whitman, Frank Aletter, Lonny Chapman,
Douglas V. Fowley, Harry Carey Jr, Alfonso Arau,
Seeta (the cougar)*

The story of a female cougar and her three cubs, who are befriended by a shepherd in the remote mountains of Utah. However, their happy idyll is soon to be threatened by the activities of an obsessive hunter.
Boa: novel The Mountain Lion by Robert Murphy.
JUV                                              85 min
V                                                WDV

**RUN, MAN, RUN ***
Sergio Sollima          ITALY          1968
Thomas Milian, John Ireland, Donald O'Brien, Linda Beras, Edward Ross, Gianni Rizzo, Chelo Alonso
A Mexican revolutionary group in desperate need of funds, joins in a treasure hunt for $3,000,000.
Aka: CORRI, UOMO, CORRI
WES                                              90 min
B,V,V2                                           VPD

**RUNAWAY ****                                    15
Michael Crichton        USA            1984
Tom Selleck, Cynthia Rhodes, Gene L. Simmons, Kirstie Alley, Stan Shaw, Joey Cramer, G.W. Bailey, Chris Mulkey, Anne-Marie Martin, Michael Paul Chan, Elizabeth Norment, Carol Teesdale, Paul Batten, Babs Chulls
The head of a police squad that deals with runaway robots, discovers a sinister plot masterminded by an electronics genius, but his superiors refuse to believe him, forcing him to fight on alone. A well-paced and imaginative fantasy, scripted by Crichton and with a score by Jerry Goldsmith.
FAN                                96 min (ort 100 min)
V/sh                                             RCA

**RUNAWAY TRAIN ****                              18
Andrei Konchalovsky     USA            1985
Jon Voight, Eric Roberts, Rebecca DeMornay, Kyle T. Heffner, John P. Ryan, T.K. Carter, Kenneth McMillan, Stacey Pickren, Walter Wyatt, Edward Bunker, Reid Cruikshanks, Michael Lee Gogin, John Bloom, Norton E. Warden
Two escaped convicts stow away on a speeding freight train, out of control after the driver suffers a fatal heart attack, but find the chief warden hot on their trail. A solid exciting thriller, based on a script by master director Akira Kurosawa and adapted by Djordje Milicevic, Paul Zindel and Edward Bunker.
THR                              109 min (ort 111 min)
B,V                                         MGM; CAN

**RUNNER STUMBLES, THE ***
Stanley Kramer          USA            1979
Dick Van Dyke, Kathleen Quinlan, Maureen Stapleton, Ray Bolger, Tammy Grimes, Beau Bridges
A nun and a Catholic priest fall in love, but their relationship comes to an abrupt end with him being accused of her murder. Written by Stiff from his Broadway play, which in turn was based on a true story. A cold and stilted work.
Boa: play by Milan Stiff.
DRA                              88 min (ort 110 min)
B,V                                             GHV

**RUNNERS ***                                     15
Charles Sturridge       UK             1983
James Fox, Jane Asher, Kate Hardie, Eileen O'Brien, Ruti Simon, Max Hafler, Peter Turner, Bridget Turner, Robert Lang, Shay Gorman, Paul Angelis, Tim Faulkner, Sarah London, Holli Hoffman, Bernard Hill, Chris Tummings
Distraught parents search the underworld to find out what has happened to their missing children. A realistic but somewhat ponderous and unmoving drama. Written by Stephen Poliakoff.
DRA                                             110 min
B,V                                        VCL; PVG/VIR

**RUNNING ***
Steven Hilliard Stern

CANADA          1979
Michael Douglas, Susan Anspach, Lawrence Dane, Eugene Levy, Chuck Shamata, Philip Akin, Trudy Young, Murray Westgate, Jennifer McKinney, Lesleh Donaldson, Jim McKay, Deborah Burgess, Gordon Clapp
A man who has been a lifelong failure, decides to compete in the Olympic marathon, in a last attempt to regain his self respect. A forgettable little melodrama.
DRA                              98 min (ort 103 min)
B,V,V2                                           IFS

**RUNNING BEAR ***                               PG
Abraham Polonsky
            USA/YUGOSLAVIA          1971
Elsa Martinelli, Jane Birkin, Serge Gainsbourg, Yul Brynner, Eli Wallach, Oliver Tobias, Lainie Kazan, David Opatoshu
Historical drama set in Russian-occupied Poland at the turn of the century, when a young man has several love affairs and many adventures. An ambitious adventure tale that lacks a really strong narrative.
Aka: ROMANCE OF A HORSE THIEF
A/AD                             93 min (ort 100 min)
B,V                                             VDEL

**RUNNING BRAVE ***                              PG
D.S. Everett (Donald Shebib)
            CANADA          1983
Robby Benson, Pat Hingle, Claudia Cron, Jeff McCracken, August Schellenberg, Denis Lacroix, Graham Greene, Michael J. Reynolds, Kendall Smith, Margo Kane, George Clutesi, Maurice Wolfe, Carmen Wolfe, Fred Keating
A Sioux Indian leaves his reservation to pursue a career as a runner, and wins a gold medal in the 1964 Tokyo Olympics. Based on the story of Billy Mills, a real-life champion. A corny exercise in good intentions and melodrama. The POLY tape has a 12 minute feature on the ill-fated South African runner Zola Budd.
Osca: STORY OF ZOLA BUDD, THE (POLY)
DRA                     105 min; 97 min (POLY or CH5)
B,V              K-TEL/PRV; POLY; CH5 (VHS only)

**RUNNING FROM THE GUNS ***                      15
John Dixon              USA            1987
Jon Blake, Mark Hembrow, Nikki Coghill, Terence Donovan, Bill Kerr, Peter Whitford, Warwick Sims
Yet another one of those stories of Mob money that goes missing, this time being found by a couple of friends who go on the run when they realise they are in danger. A fairly good time-filler, but hardly unusual.
A/AD                       83 min (ort 87 min) Cut (13 sec)
B,V                                             RCA

**RUNNING MAN, THE ***                           18
Paul Michael Glaser     USA            1987
Arnold Schwarzenegger, Richard Dawson, Maria Conchita Alonso, Yaphet Kotto, Jim Brown, Jesse Ventura, Mike Fleetwood, Dweezil Zappa, Erland Van Lidth, Marvin J. McIntyre, Gus Rethwisch, Toru Tanaka, Karen Leigh Hopkins
In a totalitarian USA of 2019, a framed murderer gets a chance at freedom when he competes on a TV show, in which convicted felons race for their lives through a ruined L.A. A violent and predictable tale, but done on a big budget. See also THE PRIZE OF PERIL.
Boa: novel by Richard Bachman (Stephen King).
A/AD                       101 min; 97 min (RCA)
V                                        BRAVE; RCA; VCC

**RUNNING ON EMPTY ****                          15
Sidney Lumet            USA            1987
Christine Lahti, River Phoenix, Judd Hirsch, Martha Plimpton, Jonas Arby, Ed Crowley, L.M. Kit Carson, Steven Hill, Augusta Dabney
Two former 1960s student radicals have been on the

run from the FBI for 17 years, but now have two children in tow. Unable to stay anywhere for long, they live out of suitcases, but are faced with a dilemma when their talented teenage son is accepted at a music college. A well-made and convincing tale that unfortunately takes a wrong turning and concentrates on the plight of the son. Scripted by Naomi Foner, the film's co-executive producer.
DRA                           110 min (ort 116 min)
V                                                    GHV

## RUNNING OUT OF LUCK *                    18
Julien Temple        · USA                    1986
*Mick Jagger, Jerry Hall, Rae Dawn Chong, Dennis Hopper*
Mick Jagger plays himself (no-one does it better) lost in the jungle surrounding Rio and desperate to get back to Britain. He has adventures a-plenty in this musical extravaganza (from the creator of ABSO-LUTE BEGINNERS) which is nothing more than a promo for Jagger's L.P. "She's The Boss".
Aka: SHE'S THE BOSS
MUS                                           86 min
V                                                    CBS

## RUNNING SCARED **                        15
Peter Hyams            · USA                   1986
*Gregory Hines, Billy Crystal, Steven Bauer, Darlanne Fluegel, Dan Hedaya, Joe Pantoliano, Jimmy Smits, Jonathan Gries, Tracy Reed, John DiSanti, Larry Hankin, Don Calfa, Robert Lesser, Betty Carvalho*
Two unorthodox Chicago cops decide that it's time to retire to Key West, and decide to nab a notorious drug runner as their last case. A routine mixture of comedy and thrills, with a good car chase and a nice performance from Crystal, but nothing else of note.
COM                          102 min (ort 106 min)
V                                                   MGM

## RUNNING SCARED **
Paul Glicker            USA                    1973
*John Saxon, Bradford Dillman, Ken Wahl, Judge Reinhold, Lonny Chapman, Pat Hingle, Annie McEnroe*
Two men returning from military service in the Panama Canal Zone are inadvertently taken for spies. Average.
Boa: novel by G. McDonald.
DRA                                           98 min
V/sh                                  VFP L/A; HER

## RUNNING WILD ***                          U
Robert McCahon         USA                    1973
*Lloyd Bridges, Pat Hingle, Dina Merril, Morgan Woodward, Gilbert Roland, Lonny Chapman, R.G. Armstrong*
A news photographer on assignment in Colorado, is shocked by the treatment of wild horses and makes a protest. An enjoyable family film of nice locations and good intentions.
DRA                           95 min (ort 103 min)
B,V                                  MOV/PRV; VIZ

## RUSH WEEK **                              18
Bob Bralver            USA                     1989
*Dean Hamilton, Pamela Ludwig, Courtney Gebhart, Ray Thinnes, Dean Grail*
The title refers to the period that begins the new college year in the USA, when fraternities and sororities recruit new members. A mad axe killer whose victims are invariably women takes advantage of the general excitement to seek out new victims, but these disappearances attract the attention of a journalist on the college paper. A conventional slasher movie that's partially redeemed by an effective ending.
THR                                           92 min
V                                                    GHV

## RUSSIAN ROULETTE *                        15
Lou Lombardo           USA                     1975
*George Segal, Gordon Jackson, Denholm Elliott, Cristina Raines, Richard Romanus, Bo Brundin, Louise Fletcher, Nigel Stock, Peter Donat, Val Avery*
The Soviet premier Kosygin is the target of an assassination plot during a visit to Vancouver, and a secret agent is assigned to capture those responsible. A messy and unsatisfying thriller that consists of little more than a series of tiresome chases. Filmed in Canada and written by Tom Ardies, Stanley Mann and Arnold Margolin.
Boa: novel Kosygin Is Coming by Tom Ardies.
THR                   ·86 min (ort 93 min) Cut (4 sec)
B,V                           PRV L/A; CH5 (VHS only)

## RUSSICUM *                                15
                       ITALY                   1989
*Treat Williams, F. Murray Abraham, Danny Aiello*
An over-plotted, labyrinthine thriller involving the Vatican, CIA and KGB, all of whom are apparently involved in the same plan to relocate the Holy See in the USSR. Poorly dubbed dialogue and lousy camerawork makes this film harder to follow than the average Italian production.
THR                                   108 min dubbed
V                                                    RCA

## RUSSKIES **                               PG
Rick Rosenthal         USA                     1987
*Whip Hubley, Leaf Phoenix, Peter Billingsley, Stefan DeSalle, Susan Walters, Patrick Kilpatrick, Vic Polizios, Charles Frank, Susan Blanchard, Carole King, Summer Phoenix*
Three humanitarian teenagers aid a Russian sailor, who was washed ashore in Florida after his secret mission was aborted. A sincere attempt to promote a message of goodwill and fellowship, but hardly memorable. The music is by James Newton Howard and the photography by Reed Smoot.
A/AD                          98 min (ort 100 min)
V/s                                                  GHV

## RUSTLER'S RHAPSODY *                      PG
Hugh Wilson            USA                     1985
*Tom Berenger, G.W. Bailey, Marilu Henner, Andy Griffith, Fernando Rey, Sela Ward, Patrick Wayne, Brant Van Hoffman, Christopher Malcolm, Jim Carter, Billy J. Mitchell*
An unfunny Western spoof on singing B-movie Westerns of former years, that has little to offer in the way of humour or entertainment, and deservedly died at the box office.
COM                           85 min (ort 88 min)
B,V                                                  CIC

## RUTANGA TAPES, THE **                     15
David Lister           USA                     1989
*David Dukes, Susan Anspach*
When a US Government Agent investigating the illegal shipment of chemical weapons attempts to discover the reasons for the disappearance of an African village, he is approached by an East German scientist working at the local fertiliser factory who promises him information in return for political asylum.
THR                                           85 min
V                                                    EIV

## RUTHERFORD COUNTY LINE, THE ***           18
Thom McIntyre          USA                     1985
*Earl Owensby, Terry McLoughlin, Marilyn Carter, Dean Whitworth, Gene Kusterer, Rodney Orton*
A story based on the true exploits of Damon Huskey, an unconventional sheriff in North Carolina. Done in semi-documentary style, the film follows some of Huskey's more memorable encounters, culminating in the capture of a crazed gunman who surrenders, and who in fact became the first man to be executed in the

state for 23 years. Written by McIntyre.
DRA                94 min (ort 112 min) Cut (50 sec)
B,V                                                    CIC

## RUTHLESS ***
Edgar G. Ulmer          USA                1947
*Zachary Scott, Sydney Greenstreet, Diana Lynn, Louis*
*Hayward, Martha Vickers, Lucille Bremer, Raymond*
*Burr*
A Southern tycoon lets absolutely nothing stand in his
way, as he climbs to the top in this powerful and
absorbing tale. Written by S.K. Lauren and Gordon
Kahn.
Boa: novel Prelude To Night by Dayton Stoddert.
DRA                              104 min B/W
B,V                                                    INT

## RUTHLESS PEOPLE **                                18
Jim Abrahams/David Zucker/Jerry Zucker
                        USA                1986
*Danny DeVito, Bette Midler, Judge Reinhold, Helen*
*Slater, Anita Morris, Bill Pullman, William G.*
*Schilling, Art Evans, Clarence Felder, Gary Riley, J.E.*
*Freeman, Phyllis Applegate, Jeannine Bisignano*
A clothing manufacturer refuses to pay his wife's
ransom because he's very happy since she's been
kidnapped. In fact, he was planning to have her
bumped off anyway. An enjoyable farce with a neat
twist but a somewhat over-extended gag. Written by
Dane Launer.
COM                          91 min (ort 93 min)
B, V/s                                      TOUCH; RNK

## RYAN WHITE STORY, THE **                          15
John Herzfeld            USA                1988
*Judith Light, Lukas Haas, George C. Scott, George*
*Dzundza, Valerie Landsburg, Sarah Jessica Parker,*
*Mitchell Ryan, Nikki Cox, Peter Scolari, Grace*
*Zabriskie*
Based on a true story, this tells of a teenage
haemophiliac who is diagnosed as having AIDS, and
whose mother is forced to campaign for him to be
allowed to attend school.
DRA                        90 min (ort 100 min) mTV
V/h                                                    ODY

## RYAN'S DAUGHTER ***                               15
David Lean              UK                 1970
*Robert Mitchum, Sarah Miles, Christopher Jones,*
*John Mills, Trevor Howard, Leo McKern, Barry*
*Foster, Archie O'Sullivan, Marie Kean, Barry Jackson*
A flawed attempt to produce a romantic masterpiece,
set in 1916 against the the background of the Irish
troubles, when a teacher's wife has an affair with a
British soldier. Well-acted and visually impressive,
but overlong and remarkably unmoving. Mills' per-
formance as the village idiot is the chief highlight.
The music is by Maurice Jarre and the script by
Robert Bolt. AA: S. Actor (Mills), Cin (Freddie
Young).
DRA                          186 min (ort 206 min)
B/s, V/s                                               MGM

# S

## S*H*E **                                          18
Robert Lewis            USA                1980
*Omar Sharif, Cornelia Sharpe, Anita Ekberg, Robert*
*Lansing, Fabio Testi, Isabella Rye, William Traylor,*
*Thom Christopher, Mario Colli, Claudio Ruffini,*
*Geoffrey Copplestone, Fortunato Arena, Emilio*
*Messina*
Story of international espionage as a female super-spy
crosses swords with the suave playboy who is the
mastermind of an international crime syndicate. Not
to be confused with the Rider Haggard tale – the
cryptic title stands for "Security Hazards Expert". A

tepid little adventure, scripted by Richard Maibaum.
A/AD                              100 min mTV
B,V                                         IFS L/A; CBS

## S*P*Y*S *
Irvin Kershner          USA                1974
*Donald Sutherland, Elliott Gould, Joss Ackland,*
*Zouzou, Vladek Sheybal, Kenneth Griffith, Kenneth J.*
*Warren, Yuri Borisenko, Michael Petrovitch, Pierre*
*Oudry, Jacques Marin, Shane Rimmer, George Pravda*
Spy spoof about a defecting Russian dancer and a list
of KGB agents in China. A lame-brained and ludic-
rous attempt to do for espionage what M*A*S*H did
for war.
COM                          87 min (ort 100 min)
B,V                                                    TEVP

## S.O.B. *
Blake Edwards           USA                1981
*Julie Andrews, William Holden, Richard Mulligan,*
*Robert Preston, Robert Vaughn, Loretta Swit, Larry*
*Hagman, Shelley Winters, Marisa Berenson*
A film producer decides to liven up a hopeless film
with a little nudity provided by his wife, the title
being an acronym for "Standard Operation Bullshit".
Art mirrors life, for in reality Andrews is the direc-
tor's wife and this supposed satire on Hollywood is
truly a hopeless film consisting of a mishmash of
nudity, slapstick and black humour.
COM                                      120 min
B,V                                                    GHV

## S.O.S. PACIFIC **
Guy Green               UK                 1959
*Richard Attenborough, Pier Angeli, John Gregson,*
*Eddie Constantine, Eva Bartok, Jean Anderson,*
*Clifford Evans, Cec Linder, Gunnar Moller, Harold*
*Kasket*
Survivors of a plane crash in the Pacific are washed up
on an island that is soon to be used for testing an
H-bomb. A competent and fairly taut little tale. The
music is by Georges Auric.
A/AD                              91 min B/W
B,V,V2                                                 INT

## S.O.S. TITANIC **                                 PG
William Hale            UK/USA             1979
*David Janssen, Cloris Leachman, Susan St James,*
*David Warner, Ian Holm, Helen Mirren, Harry*
*Andrews, Beverly Ross, David Battley, Ed Bishop,*
*Tony Caunter, Nicholas Davies, Matthew Guinness,*
*Jerry Houser, Victor Langley*
Documentary-style drama about the famous sea disas-
ter of 1912, which mirrors fictional elements of the
1958 film A NIGHT TO REMEMBER and the 1953
one "Titanic" but still remains dull and unconvincing,
even in its shortened version. Scripted by James
Costigan.
DRA                          98 min (ort 140 min) mTV
B,V                                                    TEVP

## S.S. GIRLS *
                        ITALY              1976
*Gabriele Carrara, Marina Davnia, Thomas Rudy*
After the attempt on Hitler's life in 1944, a special
group of prostitutes is recruited to test the loyalties of
the Wehrmacht generals. Low-grade nonsense.
DRA                                       82 min
B,V                                                    VPD

## S.T.A.B. **                                       PG
Chalong Pakdivijt    THAILAND              1976
*Greg Morris, Tham Thuy Hang, Sombat Metanee,*
*Krung Srivilai, Anoma Pulalak, Krisana Amnveyporn*
Thriller involving the hunt for a fortune in gold, used
as payment for drugs in South-East Asia during the
Vietnam War, which has now attracted the attentions
of various adventurers.
Aka: SPOILERS, THE; THONG

A/AD                                          96 min
B,V                                            RNK

## SABOTAGE ***                                PG
Alfred Hitchcock        UK                    1936
*Sylvia Sidney, Oscar Homolka, John Loder, Desmond
Tester, Joyce Barbour, Matthew Boulton, S.J.
Warmington, William Dewhurst, Austin Trevor, Torin
Thatcher, Aubrey Maher, Peter Bull, Charles Hawtrey,
Pamela Bevan*
A woman begins to suspect that her husband is a spy
working for a foreign power, and it soon transpires
that he is a dangerous terrorist whose contempt for
humanity extends to using his wife's little brother as
the unwitting messenger boy who delivers his bombs.
A tense and well-realised adaptation of Conrad's
novel. Musical direction is by Louis Levy. Written by
Charles Bennett, Ian Hay and Helen Simpson.
Aka: WOMAN ALONE, A (WOOD); WOMAN
ALONE, THE
Boa: novel The Secret Agent by Joseph Conrad.
Osca: BULLDOG DRUMMOND'S REVENGE
(WOOD)
THR                          74 min (ort 76 min) B/W
B,V                               WOOD L/A; RNK

## SADIE **                                     18
Bob C. Chinn           USA                   1980
*Chris Cassidy, Jerome Deeds, Gary Dana, Deborah
Sullivan, Joseph Daling, John Hires, Diahana Holt,
Larry Price*
An amateurish attempt to spice up Maugham's origin-
al story, which is now updated to the time of the
Vietnam War, and replaces the original righteous
minister with a right-wing moralistic senator. The
story follows the exploits of Sadie Johnson, a prosti-
tute who leaves Danang and comes to Borneo. On the
way she has various sexual encounters and meets the
senator who tries to get her to repent of her sinful
ways. Pleasant but unmemorable.
Boa: story Rain by William Somerset Maugham.
A                       73 min (ort 88 min) Cut (2 min)
B,V                          CIN L/A; CYC; PACEV

## SADIST, THE *
William Allan Castleman
                        USA                   1973
*Kipp Whitman, Dennis Burkley, Carol Speed, David
Amkrum, Connie Strickland, David Buchanan*
A wild party attended by a rock group and complete
with go-go dancers, ends in a violent tragedy because
of what the bass player does to two groupies. A dismal
and unpleasant effort.
Aka: BUMMER
DRA                                           98 min
B,V          GOV L/A; HIK L/A; ABV L/A; PORVI L/A;
MARKET

## SAFARI RALLY **
Albert Thomas (Adalberto Albertini)
                        ITALY/KENYA           1977
*Joe Dallesandro, Marcel Bozzuffi, Olga Bisera*
A rally in Africa is the background for this tale of two
pilots and their rivalry.
Aka: SEIMILLE CHILOMETRI DI PAURA
DRA                                           90 min
B,V,V2                                        VPD

## SAGEBRUSH TRAIL ***                          U
Armand L. Schaefer      USA                   1933
*John Wayne, Nancy Shubert, Lane Chandler, Yakima
Canutt, Henry Hall, Wally Wales, Art Mix, Bob Burns,
Bill Dwyer, Earl Dwire, Hank Bell, Slim Whitaker,
Hal Price*
A man is falsely accused of murder and thrown into
jail, but escapes and joins an outlaw gang in a bid to
find the real culprit. A brisk and enjoyable film, the

second offering in producer Paul Malvern's "Lone
Star" series.
Aka: RANDY RIDES ALONE
WES                        53 min (ort 55 min) B/W
V                                             CH5

## SAHARA ****                                  PG
Zoltan Korda           USA                   1943
*Humphrey Bogart, Bruce Bennett, J. Carrol Naish,
Lloyd Bridges, Rex Ingram, Richard Nugent, Dan
Duryea, Kurt Kreuger*
A mixed nationality tank crew, trapped in the desert
during the WW2 retreat from Tobruk, outwit their
Nazi opponents and cause considerable damage. Taut
and well handled, the simpleminded plot takes very
much second place to the strong characterisations and
excellent action sequences. Later remade as the
Western "Last Of The Comanches".
A/AD                       93 min (ort 97 min) B/W
V                                             RCA

## SAHARA *                                     PG
Andrew V. McLaglen      USA                   1984
*Brooke Shields, Lambert Wilson, Ronald Lacey, Horst
Buchholz, John Mills, John Rhys-Davies, Steve
Forrest, Cliff Potts*
A woman participating in a car race across North
Africa in the 1920s, is kidnapped by an Arab sheikh.
A trashy and contrived effort.
A/AD                    106 min (ort 111 min) Cut (11 sec)
B,V,V2                                    GHV; MSD

## SAHARA CROSS *
Tonino Valerii          ITALY                 1977
*Franco Nero, Michael Coby, Michael Constantin*
A petrol research station is attacked by violent
saboteurs in this cheap-looking and thoroughly
mediocre effort.
A/AD                                          96 min
B,V,V2                                        VPD

## SAIGON *                                     18
Christopher Crowe       USA                   1987
*Willem Dafoe, Gregory Hines, Fred Ward, Scott Glenn,
Amanda Pays, Kay Tong Lim, David Alan Grier,
Keith David, Raymond O'Connor, Richard Brooks*
Tough cop story set in Saigon in 1968, where two cops
seek the killers of six prostitutes with American
babies. A careless and sleazy tale in which the
identity of the murderer is rather too easy to guess.
Aka: OFF LIMITS
A/AD                    97 min (ort 102 min) Cut (22 sec)
B,V                                           CBS

## SAIGON COMMANDOS *                          18
Clark Henderson         USA                   1987
*Richard Young, P.J. Soles, John Allen Nelson, Jimi B.
Jr*
A police actioner set in the chaotic city of Saigon in
the 1970s, where the US Military Police are investigating a connection between drug dealers and a
high-ranking Vietnamese politician. When the ex-
commando police officer leading the investigation is
framed on a murder charge, he forms a private strike
force from former buddies to take on those responsible.
A kind of Far East answer to DIRTY HARRY, with
little new in the plot department.
A/AD                         84 min (ort 88 min)
B,V                                           MED

## SAIGON: THE YEAR OF THE CAT **              PG
Stephen Frears          UK                   1983
*Judi Dench, Frederic Forrest, E.G. Marshall*
Story of a romance between a British bank employee
and a CIA agent, and set in Saigon in 1974 with the
impending fall of South Vietnam an ever-present
threat in the background.
DRA                                          105 min
B,V              THAMES/TEVP; VCC (VHS only)

## SAILOR WHO FELL FROM GRACE WITH THE SEA, THE ** 18

Lewis John Carlino       UK       1976
*Sarah Miles, Kris Kristofferson, Jonathan Kahn, Margo Cunningham, Earl Rhodes, Paul Tropea, Gary Lock, Stephen Black, Peter Clapham, Jennifer Tolman*
In an English coastal town, a sailor courts a sexually repressed widow while her unhappy son looks on. The torrid love scenes climax in a repulsive ending when the woman's son castrates his mother's lover. A bizarre mixture of sexuality, torture and symbolism. Photography is by Douglas Slocombe and the locations are on the Dartmouth coast. Written and directed by Carlino.
Boa: novel Gogo No Eiko by Yukio Mishima.
DRA                         104 min; 100 min (CH5)
B,V                         EHE; CH5 (VHS only)

## SAINT AND THE BRAVE GOOSE, THE ** PG

Cyril Frankel           UK       1978
*Ian Ogilvy, Gayle Hunnicutt, Stratford Johns, Derren Nesbitt, Joe Lynch*
The Saint, a character based on the novels of Leslie Charteris, helps a mysterious widow involved in a treasure hunt. A full-length episode from the TV series "The Return of the Saint". In the original TV series, "The Saint", Roger Moore had the lead and was far better than Ogilvy.
A/AD                        94 min mTV
B,V                         PRV L/A; CH5 (VHS only)

## SAINT ELMO'S FIRE ** 15

Joel Schumacher         USA      1985
*Rob Lowe, Emilio Estevez, Andrew McCarthy, Demi Moore, Judd Nelson, Ally Sheedy, Mare Winningham, Martin Balsam, Andie MacDowell, Joyce Van Patten*
Seven college graduates stick together as a group once they leave, out of fear of losing the cosiness of college life. An uninspiring and unimpressive attempt to dramatise the conflict between immature aspirations and the harsh realities of life. Written by Schumacher and Carl Kurlander.
DRA                         104 min (ort 108 min)
V/sh                        RCA

## SAINT IN LONDON, THE ** PG

John Paddy Carstairs    UK       1939
*George Sanders, Sally Gray, David Burns, Henry Oscar, Ralph Truman, Nora Howard, Gordon McLeod, Carl Jaffe, Ballard Berkeley, Charles Carson, Athene Seyler, Ben Williams, Hugh McDermott, John Abbott, Charles Paton*
The third "Saint" film in a series of eight, that started with THE SAINT IN NEW YORK (1938) and ended with "The Saint Meets The Tiger" (1943). In this tale, he becomes involved in dealing with a gang who are planning to pass off a fortune in forged notes. Fair.
Boa: novel The Million Pound Day by Leslie Charteris.
A/AD                        72 min (ort 77 min) B/W
V                           STABL

## SAINT IN NEW YORK, THE ** PG

Ben Holmes              USA      1938
*Louis Hayward, Kay Sutton, Jack Carson, Jonathan Hale, Sig Ruman, Frederick Burton, Paul Guilfoyle, Ben Weldon, Charles Halton, Cliff Bragdon, Frank M. Thomas, George Irving, Paul Fix, Lee Phelps*
A refined crimefighter is asked by anxious citizens, to deal with a gangster group who have been terrorising the city. First in a series of eight films built around a character created in the novels of Leslie Charteris. A competent adventure built around a somewhat dated idea.
Boa: novel by Leslie Charteris.
A/AD                        72 min B/W
V                           STABL

## SAINT IVES * 15

J. Lee Thompson         USA      1976
*Charles Bronson, John Houseman, Jacqueline Bisset, Harry Guardino, Elisha Cook Jr, Maximilian Schell, Harry Yulin, Dana Elcar, Michael Lerner, Dick O'Neill, Val Bisoglio, Burr De Benning, Daniel J. Travanti, Joe Roman*
A crime reporter and aspiring novelist is asked to recover stolen records that could trigger a violent gang war, and after reluctantly accepting this assignment finds himself faced with a labyrinthine conspiracy that baffles both him and the audience. Less violent, and somewhat better acted than is usual for Bronson's films, but the unnecessarily convoluted plot is a recipe for tedium. Written by Barry Beckerman.
Boa: novel The Procane Chronicle by Oliver Bleeck.
DRA                         90 min (ort 98 min)
B,V                         VML L/A; WHV

## SAINT TROPEZ VICE ** 18

Nicole Boisserie        FRANCE   1986
*Yves Jourtroy, Henri Poivier, Vanda Mendres, Laure Sabardin, Michel Duperret, Peter Ulrich*
An innocent-seeming love affair between a young girl and a playboy degenerates into a sordid business when he entices her to pose nude, and she soon finds herself being drawn into the seedy world of prostitution. Average adult movie with some exotic locations.
Aka: POLICE DES MOEURS: LES FILLES DE SAINT TROPEZ
Boa: novel Les Filles De Barbe Bleu by Pierre Lucas.
A                           74 min (ort 90 min) (Cut at film release)
B,V                         ELV L/A; ATLAN

## SAINT VALENTINE'S DAY MASSACRE, THE **

Roger Corman            USA      1967
*Jason Robards Jr, George Segal, Ralph Meeker, Jean Hale, Joseph Campanella, Bruce Dern, Clint Ritchie, Richard Bakalayan, David Canary, Harold J. Stone, Kurt Krueger, Paul Richards, John Agar, Alex D'Arcy*
Recreation of one of the bloody events that took place during the gangland wars of Chicago in the 1920s, done in the usual Corman style but on a bigger budget. The guns act beautifully, but human talent is sadly wasted on this disappointing epic.
DRA                         97 min (ort 99 min)
B,V                         CBS

## SAKHAROV ** PG

Jack Gold               USA      1984
*Jason Robards, Glenda Jackson, Frank Finlay, Michael Bryant, Anna Massey, Paul Freeman, Joe Melia, Lee Montague, Jim Norton, Valentine Pelka, Catherine Hall, John McAndrew, Debbie Farrington*
Uninspired and flat story of the career of the Nobel Prize-winning physicist Andrei Sakharov, and his growing commitment to the struggle for human rights in the Soviet Union. A thoroughly unconvincing affair, this film never attempts to examine the process by which the creator of the Soviet hydrogen bomb came to question his absolute loyalty to party and state. The script is by David W. Rintels.
DRA                         117 min; 120 min (VES) mCab
B,V                         PVG; VES

## SAKURA KILLERS ** 18

Richard Ward            USA      1986
*Chuck Connors, George Nichols, Mike Kelly, John Ladalski, Manji Otsuki, Brian Wong, Thomas Lung*
Standard Ninja capers involving the theft of a secret video tape, and the efforts of two top agents to recover it.
MAR                         87 min Cut (40 sec)
B,V                         EIV

## SALAMANDER, THE ** 15

Peter Zinner            ITALY/UK/USA   1981
*Franco Nero, Anthony Quinn, Martin Balsam,*

*Christopher Lee, Sybil Danning (Sybelle Danninger),*
*Eli Wallach, Cleavon Little, Paul Smith, Claudia*
*Cardinale*
A strange series of events alerts an Italian army
colonel to the existence of a Fascist plot to stage a coup
d'etat, but this exciting premise is not sustained in a
film that rapidly dissipates all tension and ends up
resembling all those ten-a-penny Italian Mafia melo-
dramas.
Boa: novel by Morris West.
DRA                                      101 min
B,V                                         PRV

**SALEM'S LOT ***                           18
Tobe Hooper          USA            1979
*David Soul, James Mason, Lance Kerwin, Bonnie*
*Bedelia, Lew Ayres, Reggie Nalder, Ed Flanders,*
*Elisha Cook, Marie Windsor, Fred Willard, Clarissa*
*Kaye, James Gallery, Kenneth McMillan, George*
*Dzundza*
Vampires run riot in a small New England town,
where an old hilltop house forms the focus for the
all-pervasive deadly evil. Soul plays a writer return-
ing home to these strange events. Well-made and
quite chilling, but Soul is somewhat uninspiring,
though Mason is a good deal better as a malevolent
antique dealer. Followed by A RETURN TO SALEM'S
LOT.
Aka: SALEM'S LOT: THE MOVIE
Boa: novel by Stephen King.
HOR                    106 min (ort 200 min) mTV
V                                           WHV

**SALESMAN COMES, THE ***                   18
*Jackie Hunter*
Fairly mindless adult film with two women meeting
for their weekly coffee morning. The arrival of a
salesman selling fantasy tea, heralds the start of an
erotic encounter for them all.
A                          59 min Cut (32 sec)
B,V                                    SFI; PHV

**SALLY OF THE SAWDUST ***                   U
D.W. Griffith          USA            1925
*W.C. Fields, Carol Dempster, Alfred Lunt, Erville*
*Alderson, Effie Shannon*
The owner of a sideshow tries to effect a reconciliation,
between his ward and her grandparents, who dis-
approve of performing artistes. An enjoyable tale that
was remade in 1936 as "Poppy". Written by Forrest
Halsey.
Boa: play by Dorothy Donnelly.
DRA                          86 min B/W silent
B,V                                  POLY; CH5

**SALOME ***                                 18
Claude D'Anna          ITALY          1986
*Tomas Millan, Pamela Salem, Joe Ciampa, Tim*
*Woodward*
This mangled and updated version of the Wilde play,
tells of the erotic young dancer who obtains the
promise from her stepfather, the King of Judea, that
she will be rewarded with whatever she desires in
return for performing the Dance Of The Seven Veils.
A baffling and incoherent hotchpotch made worse by
low-key lighting and lousy acting. Definitely an
experience to miss.
Boa: play by Oscar Wilde.
A                          91 min (ort 100 min)
B,V                                         RNK

**SALOME ***                                 18
William Dieterle        USA            1953
*Rita Hayworth, Charles Laughton, Stewart Granger,*
*Judith Anderson, Cedric Hardwicke, Alan Badel,*
*Maurice Schwartz, Basil Sydney, Rex Reason, Arnold*
*Moss*
A film version of the biblical story that undergoes
some distortion, with Salome falling in love with a

Christian, and leaving home when her dancing fails to
save John the Baptist. A good cast struggles bravely
with this nonsense. Scripted by Harry Kleiner and
Jesse L. Lasky Jr.
DRA                          84 min (ort 103 min)
B,V                                    MOV L/A

**SALOME'S LAST DANCE ***                   18
Ken Russell          UK            1988
*Imogen Millais-Scott, Glenda Jackson, Stratford*
*Johns, Nickolas Grace, Linzi Drew, Douglas Hodge*
Set in a Victorian London brothel, this adaptation of
Wilde's play is a stiff studio-bound production, which
finds the author (a miscast Grace) lounging about, as
the brothel proprietor stages a production of the title
work. A fairly typical flight of Russellian self-
indulgence, though slightly less oppressive than some
of his other recent works.
Boa: play Salome by Oscar Wilde.        86 min
A
B,V                                         VES

**SALSA ***                                 PG
Boaz Davidson          USA            1988
*Robby Rosa, Rodney Harvey, Magali Alvarado,*
*Miranda Garrison, Moon Orona, Angela Alvarado,*
*Celia Cruz, Tito Puente*
This attempt to cash in on the success of DIRTY
DANCING, has resulted in a Latin variant with little
plot or substance, as a young man sees success in a
dance competition as his ticket to a better life.
MUS          94 min; 93 min (PATHE) (ort 97 min)
                        (Cut at film release)
B,V                  CAN L/A; WHV; PATHE

**SALUTE OF THE JUGGER, THE ***             18
David Webb Peoples
              AUSTRALIA/USA          1988
*Rutger Hauer, Joan Chen, Vincent D'Onofrio, Anna*
*Katerina, Delroy Linda*
Echoes of MAD MAX and ROLLERBALL abound in
this futuristic post-WW3 world where gladiatorial
games are played by teams using a dog's skull instead
of a ball and a few meagre scraps from the previous
era serve as prizes. A flashy and heavily derivative
film that soon exhausts its stock of ideas but retains
considerable visual impact.
A/AD                                    99 min
V                                           VIR

**SALVADOR ***                              18
Oliver Stone          USA            1986
*James Woods, James Belushi, John Savage, Michael*
*Murphy, Elpedia Carrillo, Tony Plana, Colby Chester,*
*Cindy (Cynthia) Gibb, John Doe*
Seduced by the lure of cheap drink, drugs and sex, an
experienced photo-journalist goes with his friend to El
Salvador in the early 1980s. Once there, they see the
turmoil and brutality of the country as it is being
destroyed by the conflict, and learn of American
involvement. A patchy but effective piece of propagan-
da, largely based on the experiences of Richard Boyle,
a journalist there in the 1980s.
WAR                          117 min (ort 123 min)
B,V                                        PREST

**SALVATION! ***                            18
Beth B.          USA            1986
*Stephen McHattie, Dominique Davalos, Viggo*
*Mortensen, Rockets Redglare, Billy Bastani, Exene*
*Cervenka*
The Rev. Edward Randall is a TV evangelist with a
powerful following. Rhonda is a rock 'n' roller turned
"born-again" housewife, who wants to help him bring
the Lord's message to the youth of America, via a
heavy metal band. However, when her slob of a
husband Jerome loses his job, he conspires with her
sister Lenore, to blackmail the Reverend after Lenore
has seduced him. A wildly overblown comedy, badly in

need of more disciplined direction.
Aka: SALVATION! HAVE YOU SAID YOUR
PRAYERS TODAY?
COM                                80 min (ort 85 min)
V                                  RECREL L/A; COL

## SALVATORE GIULIANO ***
Francesco Rosi          ITALY                1961
*Frank Wolff, Salvo Randone, Federico Zardi, Pietro
Cammarata, Fernando Cicero*
Seen in the form of flashbacks detailing his rise to
power, this film opens with the discovery of the
bullet-riddled body of Salvatore Giuliano, one of
Italy's most famous gangsters, being found in a
courtyard in 1950. A complex, vivid and rather
difficult work, but certainly an absorbing one. This
film prompted the Palermo government to launch an
inquiry into the activities of the Mafia. Remade by
Michael Cimino as THE SICILIAN.
Aka: DREADED MAFIA, THE; SALVATORE
GIULIANO: THE DREADED MAFIA
DRA                    123 min (ort 125 min) B/W
B,V                                        PVG

## SALZBURG CONNECTION, THE *            PG
Lee H. Katzin           USA                  1972
*Barry Newman, Anna Karina, Klaus-Maria
Brandauer, Karen Jensen, Joe Maross, Wolfgang
Preiss*
An American lawyer on holiday in Salzburg gets
mixed up with spies, when a chest of incriminating
Nazi war documents is discovered in an Austrian lake.
Soon a host of foreign agents are out to obtain it. A
gimmicky and dated yarn, made worse by its
annoying reliance on slow motion and freeze-frame
photography.
Boa: novel by Helen MacInnes.
THR                                89 min (ort 93 min)
V                                          CBS

## SAMAR **
George Montgomery
                 PHILIPINES/USA            1962
*George Montgomery, Gilbert Roland, Ziva Rodann,
Joan O'Brien, Nico Minardos, Mario Barri*
In order to put an end to their inhumane treatment at
the hands of their Japanese captors, a group of
American prisoners held on an island in the Philip-
pines plan an escape. Average.
THR                                        89 min
B,V                                  ATA L/A; APX

## SAME TIME NEXT YEAR **                  15
Robert Mulligan         USA                  1978
*Ellen Burstyn, Alan Alda, Ivan Bonar, Bernie Kuby,
Cosmo Sardo, David Northcutt, William Cantrell*
A couple have an affair lasting 26 years, but only meet
once a year for a weekend together. Through their
meetings we see a cavalcade of recent American social
history and changing ideas and attitudes. An enter-
taining trifle enlivened by an excellent performance
from Burstyn. Scripted by Slade from his successful
Broadway play.
Boa: play by Bernard Slade.
COM                                113 min (ort 119 min)
V/h                                        CIC

## SAMMY AND ROSIE GET LAID **            18
Stephen Frears          UK                   1987
*Shashi Kapoor, Claire Bloom, Frances Barber, Ayub
Khan Din, Roland Gift, Wendy Gazelle, Badi
Uzzmann, Suzetta Llewellyn, Meera Syal, Tessa
Wojtczak, Emer Gillespie, Lesley Manville, Mark
Sproston, Cynthia Powell, Dennis Colon*
The story of a couple whose open relationship is upset
by the arrival of the man's old-fashioned father. A
pointless attempt at social commentary built around
the lives of Indians living in Britain. Written by Hanif
Kureishi.

DRA                                97 min (ort 100 min)
B,V                                     NELS; PAL

## SAMMY THE WAY-OUT SEAL **              U
Norman Tokar            USA                  1962
*Robert Culp, Jack Carson, Billy Mumy, Patricia
Barry, Elizabeth Fraser, Ann Jillian, Michael
McGreevey*
Two brothers smuggle a seal into their home and try
to keep its existence a secret from their parents. A
wholesome kid's comedy, first shown on American TV
as a two-part feature from Disney.
JUV                                86 min (ort 90 min)
B,V                                        WDV

## SAMSON **                              PG
Gianfranco Parolini     ITALY                1961
*Brad Harris, Brigitte Corey, Alan Steel, Mara Berni,
Walter Reeves, Carlo Tamberlani, Irene Prosen*
Samson battles an evil minister who is plotting
against the rightful queen, but as usual the plot
hardly matters, in this typical Italian historical (or
more accurately, ahistorical) epic.
Aka: SANSONE
A/AD                                    94 min dubbed
B,V                                        PRV

## SAMSON AND DELILAH **                  PG
Lee Philips             USA                  1984
*Max Von Sydow, Belinda Bauer, Antony Hamilton,
Stephen Macht, Maria Schell, Jose Ferrer, Victor
Mature, Daniel Stern, Clive Revill, Jennifer Holmes,
David S. Eisner, David Byrd, Angelica Aragon, Rene
Ruiz, Brandon Scott*
Another film version of the famous biblical story
that's a lavish remake of the 1949 film. As Mature was
too old to play the hero again, he settled for the role of
Samson's father in his TV debut. Fair.
Boa: novel Husband Of Delilah by Eric Linkletter.
DRA                                91 min (ort 95 min) mTV
B,V                                        CBS

## SAMSON AND DELILAH ***                 U
Cecil B. De Mille       USA                  1949
*Victor Mature, Hedy Lamarr, Angela Lansbury,
George Sanders, Henry Wilcoxon, Olive Deering, Fay
Holden, Russ Tamblyn*
An entertaining film version of the biblical story, with
good costumes and sets. Mature as Samson is good,
even if the lion fight is as phoney as Lansbury's
Philistine accent. However, the final scene in which
the temple is destroyed is splendid. Written by Jesse
L. Lasky Jr with music by Victor Young. AA: Art/Set
(Hans Dreier and Walter Tyler/Sam Comer and Ray
Moyer), Cost (Edith Head/Dorothy Jeakins/Elois Jens-
sen/Gile Steele/Gwen Wakeling).
DRA                                122 min (ort 128 min)
V/h                                        CBS

## SAMSON AND SALLY **                    U
Jannik Hastrup
                 DENMARK/SWEDEN            1984
Two young whales set off in search of the legendary
Moby Dick in the belief that only he can help them
with pollution and other threats to themselves and
their environment.
Aka: SAMSON AND SALLY: THE SONG OF THE
WHALES
Boa: book Song Of The Whales by Bent Haller.
CAR                                60 min (ort 70 min)
V                                          PARK

## SAMURAI *                              U
Lee H. Katzin           USA                  1979
*Joe Penny, Dana Elcar, Beulah Quo, James Shigeta,
Charles Cioffi, Geoffrey Lewis, Norman Alden,
Morgan Brittany, Ralph Manza, Shane Sinutko,
Michael Pataki, James McEachin, Philip Baker Hall,*

*Randolph Roberts, Diana Webster*
A young San Francisco district attorney takes on the identity of a crusading samurai warrior, to stop a property developer armed with a machine that can cause earthquakes. This silly and poorly-acted nonsense, was the pilot for a TV series that thankfully was never made.
A/AD                    70 min (ort 90 min) mTV
B,V                                               CIC

**SAMURAI \***
Sergio Corbucci    ITALY/USA         1979
*Eli Wallach, Giuliano Gemma, Tomas Milian*
A samurai warrior joins forces with a sheriff and a bandit in order to recover a holy Japanese pony that has been stolen by the Indians. A clumsy melding of disparate genres.
COM                                     107 min
B,V                                          IFS

**SAMURAI REINCARNATION \*\***          18
Kinji Fukasaku    JAPAN              1981
*Sonny (Shinichi) Chiba, Ken (Kenji) Sawada, Duke (Hiroyuki) Sanada, Akiko Kana*
An executed samurai is reincarnated to lead a revolt against the rule of the Tokagawa shoguns, forming an army composed of the ghosts of other rebellious warriors. A few sequences of genuine power partially sustain this overlong offering.
Aka: MAKAI TENSHO
HOR         107 min; 117 min (XTASY) Cut (5 sec)
                                  (ort 122 min)
B,V                          VTC L/A; XTASY

**SAN ANTONIO \*\***
David Butler       USA               1945
*Errol Flynn, Alexis Smith, S.Z. Sakall, John Litel, Victor Francen, Paul Kelly, Florence Bates, Robert Shayne, Monte Blue, John Alvin, Robert Barrat, Pedro De Cordoba, Tom Tyler, Chris-Pin Martin, Charles Stevens, Dan White*
Having returned to San Antonio from Mexico, a cattleman sets out to prove that the owner of a saloon is the ringleader of a gang of cattle rustlers. A thinly plotted but well-paced tale.
WES                   100 min (ort 109 min)
V                                           WHV

**SAND PEBBLES, THE \*\***               15
Robert Wise        USA               1966
*Steve McQueen, Richard Crenna, Richard Attenborough, Candice Bergen, Mako, Simon Oakland, Larry Gates, Marayat Andriane, Gavin MacLeod, Ford Rainey, Charles Robinson, Joe Turkel*
Follows the crew of a US gunboat on patrol in the Yangtze River in China in 1926, and their involvement with Chinese warlords. McQueen gives a fine performance in this film as a cynical sailor, but the mixture of action and romance is a recipe for confusion. Written by Robert Anderson, and well photographed by Joseph MacDonald.
Boa: novel by Richard McKenna.
DRA                   179 min (ort 195 min)
B,V                                         CBS

**SANDERS OF THE RIVER \*\***             U
Zoltan Korda       UK                1935
*Leslie Banks, Paul Robeson, Nina Mae McKinney, Robert Cochran, Martin Walker, Richard Grey, Marquis De Portago, Eric Maturin, Allan Jeayes, Charles Carson, Orlando Martins*
An adventure tale set in Nigeria in colonial times, and following the exploits of a river patrol officer and his black servant. A curious and dated tale, with Robeson giving a dignified performance that lends weight to an otherwise unmemorable effort.
Aka: BOSAMBO
Boa: novel by Edgar Wallace.
A/AD    84 min (ort 98 min) (Abridged by distributor)

B/W
V                                   CENVID; PICK

**SANDINISTA: WAR IS HELL \*\***          18
Michael Kennedy    USA               1989
*Stephen McHattie, Deborah Van Valkenburgh, Aharon Ipale*
A Vietnam veteran who now works for a military dictator in Central America decides to quit, but finds that he is not allowed to and is blackmailed into a drug smuggling operation which requires the murder of a female reporter. When he refuses to carry out his mission, they are both obliged to go on the run. Fair.
A/AD                                    90 min
V                                CBS; CASPIC

**SANDOKAN STRIKES BACK \***             PG
Luigi Capuano      ITALY             1964
*Ray Danton, Guy Madison, Franca Bettoja, Mino Doro*
Sandokan, also named the invincible Tiger of Malaysia, is the hero in this action movie set against the background of the Malaysian jungle. One of a series of adventure films featuring the title character. Mediocre.
Aka: SANDOKAN FIGHTS BACK
A/AD            86 min (ort 96 min) Cut (35 sec)
B,V                                         ELE

**SANDPIPER, THE \*\***                  15
Vincente Minnelli  USA               1965
*Elizabeth Taylor, Richard Burton, Eva Marie Saint, Charles Bronson, Robert Webber, Torin Thatcher, Morgan Mason, Tom Drake*
Story of a love triangle involving a female beatnik and a respected pillar of the community, whose passionate love affair comes close to breaking up his marriage and ruining his career. Written by Dalton Trumbo and Michael Wilson. Glossy but shallow. AA: Song ("The Shadow Of Your Smile" – Johnny Mandel – music/Paul Francis Webster – lyrics).
DRA                   112 min (ort 116 min)
V                                           MGM

**SANDS OF IWO JIMA \*\*\***             PG
Allan Dwan         USA               1949
*John Wayne, John Agar, Adele Mara, Forrest Tucker, Arthur Franz, Julie Bishop, Richard Jaeckel, Wally Cassell, James Brown, Martin Milner*
A young Marine gradually accepts the need for military discipline, in a film with excellent and realistic battle scenes. Wayne's role as a tough sergeant brought him his first nomination for an Oscar, although he was not to win one until TRUE GRIT.
Osca: FLYING TIGERS (asa)
WAR        108 min; 199 min (2 film cassette) B/W
V                                           VCC

**SANDS OF THE DESERT \***                U
John Paddy Carstairs  UK             1960
*Charlie Drake, Peter Arne, Sarah Branch, Raymond Huntley, Rebecca Dignam, Peter Illing, Harold Kasket*
A clumsy and disorganised vehicle for Drake in which he plays a travel agent who investigates sabotage at a desert holiday camp and saves a girl from an Arab sheikh at the same time. The script is by Carstairs.
COM                    88 min (ort 92 min)
V                                           WHV

**SANDWICH MAN, THE \***                 PG
Robert Hartford-Davies  UK           1966
*Michael Bentine, Suzy Kendall, Norman Wisdom, Dora Bryan, Bernard Cribbins, Harry H. Corbett, Stanley Holloway, Alfie Bass, Ian Hendry, Warren Mitchell, John Le Mesurier, John Junkin, Ron Moody, Diana Dors, Wilfrid Hyde-White*
One of those daft British comedy-mimes, in which there's no dialogue, just a series of oh-so-funny

encounters. This one is about the daily life of a sandwich-board man, and looks at the eccentrics he encounters.
COM  93 min (ort 95 min)
B,V  VCC

## SANJURO ***
Akira Kurosawa  JAPAN  1962
*Toshiro Mifune, Tatsuya Nakadai, Takashi Shimura, Yuzo Kayama, Reiko Dan, Masao Shimizu, Yunosuke Ito, Takako Irie*
Spoof samurai film, in which a shabby warrior helps young clan members root out corruption among the elders of their clan. A kind of sequel to YOJIMBO, with excellent fighting sequences and effective moments of humour.
Aka: TSUBAKI SANJURO
COM  96 min
B,V  PVG

## SANTA AND THE THREE BEARS *
Tony Benedict  USA  1970
Animated Christmas story of three bears who discover what the Yuletide season is all about.
CAR  63 min
B,V,V2  INT

## SANTA CLAUS **  U
Jeannot Szwarc  UK  1984
*David Huddleston, Dudley Moore, John Lithgow, Burgess Meredith, Jeffrey Kramer, Judy Cornwell, Christian Fitzpatrick, Carrie Kei Heim, John Barrard, Anthony O'Donnell, Peter O'Farrell, Tim Stern, Christopher Ryan, Don Estelle*
The Santa Claus legend is here milked for all it's worth, as Santa sets off for New York to rescue an unhappy elf from the grip of a toymaker. A poorly executed film with an abysmally low level of humour. Only the eye-catching opening, telling of the origin of Santa, has any memorable sequences.
Aka: SANTA CLAUS: THE MOVIE (WHV)
COM  100 min; 103 min (WHV) (ort 112 min)
V/sh  CAN; WHV (VHS only)

## SANTA CLAUS CONQUERS THE MARTIANS *  Uc
Nicholas Webster  USA  1964
*John Call, Leonard Hicks, Vincent Beck, Donna Conforti, Pia Zadora, Victor Stiles, James Cahill, Carl Donn, Jim Bishop, Leila Martin, Charles G. Renn, Christopher Month, Bill McCutcheon, Josip Eric, Lin Thurmond*
Santa and two Earth kids are kidnapped by Martians but eventually succeed in winning over their captors. Silly fantasy that is on the way to becoming a cult film. Watch out for Pia Zadora who pops up in an early role as one of the Martian kids. The score is by Milton Delugg.
FAN  78 min
B,V  CH5 (VHS only); EHE

## SANTA FE TRAIL **  U
Michael Curtiz  USA  1940
*Errol Flynn, Olivia De Havilland, Raymond Massey, Ronald Reagan, Alan Hale, Guinn "Big Boy" Williams, Van Heflin, William Lundigan, Gene Reynolds, Henry O'Neill, Alan Baxter, John Litel, Moroni Olsen, David Bruce, Joseph Sawyer*
Long rambling Western. Massey as John Brown is tracked down by J.E.B. Stuart (Flynn) and George Armstrong Custer (Reagan), both of whom were classmates at West Point and are rivals for De Havilland. The music is by Max Steiner.
WES  107 min (ort 110 min) B/W
B,V  MOV L/A; GLOB

## SANTA SANGRE ****  18
Alejandro Jodorowsky  ITALY  1989

*Axel Jodorowsky, Blanca Guerre, Guy Stockwell, Thelma Tixou*
After 17 years, the director "El Topo" returns with this profoundly disturbing and surrealistic tale of madness and eventual liberation. A series of dreamlike images recount the career of a child circus-magician who was driven insane by his father's violent attack on his mother, but escapes his asylum to rejoin his mother in a bizarre stage act. A film of violent extremes and limited appeal, that is as memorable as it is shocking.
HOR  123 min
V/h  PAL

## SANTEE ***  15
Gary Nelson  USA  1972
*Glenn Ford, Michael Burns, Dana Wynter, Charles Courtney, Jay Silverheels, Harry Townes, John Larch, Robert J. Wilke, Robert Donner, Taylor Lacher, Lindsay Crosby, Chuck Courtney, X. Brands, John Hart, Boyd "Red" Morgan*
The son of an outlaw goes West to find his father, and befriends the bounty hunter who, unknown to him, killed him. A competent if violent tale, with good performances and a strong script.
Aka: TURN OF THE BADGE (KRP)
WES  87 min (ort 93 min) Cut (4 sec)
B,V,V2  PHE; CBS; INT; KSV; KRP; PYR

## SAPPHIRE ***  PG
Basil Dearden  UK  1959
*Nigel Patrick, Yvonne Mitchell, Michael Craig, Paul Massie, Bernard Miles, Rupert Davies, Olga Lindo, Earl Cameron, Gordon Heath, Jocelyn Britton, Harry Baird, Orlando Martins, Robert Adams, Yvonne Buckingham*
A black music student is murdered, and the investigators discover that her ability to pass for white had some bearing on the case, as did the fact that she was pregnant. A mixture of social comment and melodrama, but quite effective.
Boa: novel by E.G. Cousins.
THR  92 min
B,V  RNK; STRAND

## SARA DANE **
Rod Hardy/Gary Conway
AUSTRALIA  1981
*Juliet Jordan, Harold Hopkins, Brenton Whittle, Sean Scully, Barry Quinn*
A woman is falsely accused of theft and transported to an Australian penal colony, but ultimately achieves great wealth in her new life. Good period detail and competent acting help sustain the thin story. Written by Alan Seymour. Originally shown in eight 50-minute episodes.
Boa: novel by Catherine Gaskin.
DRA  255 min (2 cassettes) (ort 400 min) mTV
B,V  IPC/PVG

## SARTANA, ANGEL OF DEATH **
Anthony Ascott (Giuliano Carmineo)
ITALY  1969
*Gianni Garko, Klaus Kinski, Frank Wolff*
A landowner who is also the local sheriff in a lawless province, is unjustly accused of having masterminded a bank robbery.
Aka: I AM SARTANA: YOUR ANGEL OF DEATH; SONO SARTANA IL VOSTRO BECCHINO
WES  93 min
B,V  VTC

## SARTANA, PRAY FOR YOUR DEATH **  15
Frank Kramer (Gianfranco Parolini)
ITALY/WEST GERMANY  1968
*Gianni Garko, Sidney Chaplin, Klaus Kinski*
Various outlaws fight over a bullion chest stolen from a coach. One in a series of so-so "Sartana" adventures.
Aka: IF YOU MEET SARTANA PRAY FOR YOUR DEATH; SARTANA; SARTANA BETE UM DEINEN

TOD; SE INCONTRI SARTANA PREGA PER LA
TUA MORTE
WES                                       91 min
B,V                                         PRV

## SATANIC RITES OF DRACULA, THE *        18
Alan Gibson          UK                    1973
*Peter Cushing, Christopher Lee, Michael Coles,*
*William Franklyn, Freddie Jones, Joanna Lumley,*
*Richard Vernon, Patrick Barr, Barbara Yu Ling,*
*Richard Mathews, Lockwood East, Maurice O'Connell,*
*Valerie Van Ost, Peter Adair*
An outbreak of vampirism is traced to the presence in
London of Dracula, who is masquerading as a property
developer and plans to unleash a deadly plague on the
world. The modern setting for this ancient myth adds
absolutely nothing to a tired and dispirited produc-
tion.
Aka: COUNT DRACULA AND HIS VAMPIRE
BRIDE; DRACULA IS DEAD AND WELL AND
LIVING IN LONDON
HOR              84 min (ort 88 min) Cut (1 sec in
                              addition to film cuts)
V                                            WHV

## SATAN'S BLADE *                         18
Scott Castillo Jr       USA                1984
*Tom Bongiorno, Stephanie Leigh Steel, Thomas Cue,*
*Elisa R. Malinovitz, Janeen Lowe, Ski Mark Ford,*
*Ramona Andrada, Diane Taylor, Marti Neal, Susan*
*Bennet, Fred Armond, Meg Greene, Mary Seaman,*
*Richard Taecker, Paul Batson*
Innocent teenagers fall victim to a series of sadistic
killings, in this totally derivative and unimaginative
offering.
HOR              76 min (ort 87 min) Cut (3 min 35 sec)
B,V                            GOV L/A; MOG

## SATAN'S BREW **
Rainer Werner Fassbinder
              WEST GERMANY                 1976
*Kurt Raab, Margit Carstensen, Helen Vita, Volker*
*Spengler, Ingrid Craven, Y Sa Lo*
An unproductive poet has trouble getting money out
of his publishers, so he murders his mistress then
takes over the identity of another poet, even adopting
his homosexual predilections. A bizarre mixture of
German Expressionism and zany escapism, with the
director at pains to express his own sexuality. Not a
very effective film, but certainly an unusual one.
COM                                      100 min
B,V                                         PVG

## SATISFACTION *                          15
Joan Freeman          USA                  1988
*Justine Bateman, Liam Neeson, Trini Alvarado, Britta*
*Phillips, Scott Coffey, Julia Roberts*
Story of a rock band consisting of four girls and just
one guy, who get a chance to break into the big time
when they land an engagement at a summer resort. A
cliched little tale that was designed for the teen
market but aimed too low.
DRA                              89 min (ort 93 min)
B,V                                         CBS

## SATISFACTION *                          18
Alex De Renzy         USA                  1989
*Annette Haven, John Leslie, Eva Nicole*
The standard tale of a ruthless woman and her pursuit
of happiness and sexual freedom.
A                              54 min Cut (54 sec)
V                                           ELV

## SATISFIERS OF ALPHA BLUE, THE **       R18
Gerard Damiano        USA                  1981
*Lysa Thatcher, Richard Bolla, Herschel Savage,*
*George Payne, Sharon Mitchell, Annie Sprinkles*
In a future society of the twenty-first century, sex is
one of the few human activities left. The satisfiers are

male and female individuals whose job is to spread
suitable cheer around, for this purpose they are each
coded according to their speciality. This tale examines
the frustrations of Algon, a man who believes in love
and would like to return to the past, but cannot find
anyone to reciprocate his feelings. An unusual idea,
poorly developed.
A                74 min (ort 82 min) Cut (2 min 45 sec)
B,V                              TCX L/A; SHEP

## SATURDAY NIGHT AND SUNDAY
## MORNING ****                            PG
Karel Reisz           UK                   1960
*Albert Finney, Shirley Ann Field, Hylda Baker,*
*Rachel Roberts, Bryan Pringle, Norman Rossington*
The life of a coarse, fun-loving factory hand in
Nottingham, who has an affair with the wife of a
workmate, gets beaten up for his trouble but eventual-
ly finds a girl of his own. One of the first of a batch of
fresh, raw working-class dramas, this faithful adapta-
tion broke new ground both in its frank attitude
towards sexuality and its unashamed anti-authority
stance. Finney's zestful performance deservedly shot
him to stardom.
Boa: novel by Alan Sillitoe.
DRA                     86 min (ort 89 min) B/W
V                                         CASPIC

## SATURDAY NIGHT AT THE BATHS **
David Buckley         USA                  1974
*Ellen Sheppard, Robert Aberdeen, Don Scotti, Steve*
*Ostrow*
At New York's Continental Baths, a straight piano
player finds himself falling for one of the homosexuals
who frequent this meeting place.
DRA                                       81 min
B,V,V2                                      INT

## SATURDAY NIGHT FEVER ***               PG
John Badham           USA                  1978
*John Travolta, Karen Lynn Gorney, Joseph Cali,*
*Barry Miller, Paul Pape, Bruce Ornstein, Donna*
*Pescow, Julie Bovasso*
A young man doing a dead-end job only comes to life at
the local disco on Saturday nights, when he becomes
the local dancing sensation. A flashy and vigorous
musical that skilfully blends exciting dancing with
foul-mouthed language. The PG rated version dropped
some scenes and dialogue. Written by Norman Wex-
ler, with songs written and performed by the Bee
Gees. This was Travolta's first starring film. Followed
by STAYING ALIVE.
Boa: story by Nik Cohn.
MUS   104 min (ort 119 min) (Abridged at film release)
V/h                                         CIC

## SATURDAY THE 14TH *                     15
Howard R. Cohen       USA                  1981
*Richard Benjamin, Paula Prentiss, Severn Darden,*
*Jeffrey Tambor, Rosemary De Camp, Kari Michaelson,*
*Kevin Brando, Nancy Lee Andrews, Roberta Collins,*
*Craig Coulter, Thomas Newman, Carol Androvsky,*
*Annie O'Donnell, Irwin Russo*
A dreadful horror spoof with the usual strange house
and weird characters, as Transylvania comes to
downtown Pennsylvania, and a family find them-
selves having to resort to DIY exorcism. As crude as it
is unfunny. Followed by SATURDAY THE 14TH
STRIKES BACK - an unnecessary sequel if ever
there was one.
COM                              73 min (ort 75 min)
B,V,V2                          EHE; CH5 (VHS only)

## SATURDAY THE 14TH STRIKES BACK *       PG
Howard R. Cohen       USA                  1988
*Ray Walston, Avery Schreiber, Patty MacCormack,*
*Jason Presson, Julianne McNamara, Rhonda Aldrich,*
*Leo V. Gordon*

A sequel to the first horror spoof that remains firmly stuck at the same level as its predecessor. In this one Presson finds that a sour note enters his birthday celebrations as a variety of monsters set out to get him.

COM                                          76 min (ort 79 min)
B,V                                                              MGM

### SATURN 3 **                                              15
Stanley Donen            UK                              1980
Kirk Douglas, Farrah Fawcett, Harvey Keitel, Douglas Lambert, Ed Bishop, Christopher Muncke
Two research scientists enjoy an idyllic existence on a deserted space station until the arrival of an unbalanced scientist, whose sinister robot takes on some of the less desirable aspects of his personality. A glossy and menacing exercise in emptiness. Written by Martin Amis and scored by Elmer Bernstein.
Boa: short story by John Barry.
FAN                              88 min; 84 min (CH5)
B,V,V2                        PRV L/A; CH5 (VHS only)

### SAVAGE BEES, THE **
Bruce Geller             USA                            1976
Ben Johnson, Michael Parks, Horst Buchholz, Gretchen Corbett, Paul Hecht, Bruce French, James Best, David L. Gray, Richard Charles Boyle, Elliot Keener, Boardman O'Connor, Danny Barker, Don Hood, Bill Holliday
New Orleans at carnival time is menaced by a vast swarm of African killer bees in this fairly well handled thriller. Written by Guerdon Trueblood and followed by TERROR OUT OF THE SKY.
THR                                              94 min mTV
B,V                                                            TEVP

### SAVAGE BRIDGE *                                     PG
Herold Crawford          USA                          1976
Walter Stevenson, Saul Peters
Tiresome war epic in which a small group have to hold a bridge against an onslaught mounted by Nazi troops.
WAR                                                        92 min
B,V                                              CENCOM/BUDGE

### SAVAGE DAWN *                                         18
Simon Nuchtern          USA                            1984
George Kennedy, Karen Black, Richard Lynch, Claudia Udy, Bill Forsythe, Lance Henrikson
An ex-soldier has to stop a bike gang that is terrorising a small town, as all good bikers are wont to do. Offers nothing new in a throwback to a virtually extinct genre.
THR                                    98 min (ort 102 min) Cut (6 sec)
B,V                                                          POLY

### SAVAGE ENCOUNTER *
Bernard Buys        SOUTH AFRICA
John Parsonson, Lieb Bester, Tessa Marie Ziegler
A man avenges the rape of his wife in this obscure and highly forgettable revenger.
DRA                                                       80 min
B,V                                                            DFS

### SAVAGE HARBOUR *                                     18
Carl Monson             USA                            1988
Frank Stallone, Chris Mitchum, Karen Mayo-Chandler, Anthony Caruso, Nicholas Worth, Lisa Loring, Greta Blackburn, Gary Wood
A sullen merchant seaman and his buddy, come ashore at a tough port where the former falls for a girl who, unknown to him, is on the run from her gangster boyfriend. When she is callously murdered on the orders of the gangster, the sailor teams up with his friend for the usual revenge spree. A mediocre effort, done with neither conviction nor subtlety.
Aka: RAGGEDY ANNE

A/AD                                                      80 min
V                                                            BRAVE

### SAVAGE HARVEST **                                   15
Robert Collins           USA                            1981
Tom Skerritt, Michelle Phillips, Melinda Dillon, Tana Helfer, Shawn Stevens, Anne-Marie Martin, Derek Patridge
During a prolonged drought in the African bush, a lonely family plantation comes under attack, from wild predators that have developed a taste for human flesh, triggering a tense and bloody struggle for survival. Quite gripping but rather implausibly plotted.
A/AD                                                      85 min
V                                                              WHV

### SAVAGE INNOCENTS, THE **
Nicholas Ray     FRANCE/ITALY/UK              1960
Anthony Quinn, Yoko Tani, Peter O'Toole, Marie Yang, Anna May Wong, Carlo Justini, Lee Montague, Ed Devereaux
The conflict between Western values and Eskimo civilisation, forms the background to this story of an Eskimo who accidentally kills a missionary and is forced to flee. A film of splendidly photographed locations (by Aldo Tonti and Peter Hennessy) and rather unconvincing dialogue, with the actors speaking in a kind of broken English. Written and directed by Ray. O'Toole's voice was dubbed over.
Boa: novel Top Of The World by Hans Ruesch.
DRA                                        105 min (ort 107 min)
B,V                                                            RNK

### SAVAGE IS LOOSE, THE *
George C. Scott          USA                            1974
George C. Scott, Trish Van Devere, John David Carson, Lee H. Montgomery
Traces the strains that occur in the relationship between a mother, father and son, who have been stranded on a desert island for 20 years, culminating in an eventual incestuous relationship between mother and son. Not an inspiring work.
DRA                                                      114 min
B,V                                            HVM L/A; HVH

### SAVAGE ISLAND *                                        18
Nicholas Beardsley/Edward Muller
                          ITALY/SPAIN/USA            1985
Nicholas Beardsley, Ajita Wilson, Christina Lai, Anthony Steffen, Leon Askin, Linda Blair
A group of women are kept captive in the jungle and forced to mine emeralds. One of them escapes to take the usual bloody revenge in this depressing exploitation film. This mess was cobbled up from the original European film entitled "Escape From Hell" and some American film footage featuring Blair was added.
Aka: ESCAPE FROM HELL
A/AD                              73 min (ort 96 min) Cut (22 sec)
B,V                                                            EIV

### SAVAGE ISLANDS **                                    PG
Ferdinand Fairfax
                          NEW ZEALAND                1983
Tommy Lee Jones, Jenny Seagrove, Michael O'Keefe
This attempt to recreate one of those Errol Flynn pirate movies transfers the action to the South Pacific. Average action, almost non-existent plot.
A/AD                                                      96 min
B,V                                                              CIC

### SAVAGE JUSTICE *                                      18
Joey Romero             USA                            1988
Steven Memel, Julia Montgomery
The daughter of a US ambassador sees her parents murdered in a revolution, and is raped by the leader. She eventually escapes and teams up with a former Green Beret for the obligatory revenge mission.

A/AD 83 min
B,V BRAVE

## SAVAGE SAM ** PG
Norman Tokar USA 1962
*Brian Keith, Tommy Kirk, Kevin Corcoran, Dewey
Martin, Jeff York, Royal Dano, Marta Kristen, Rafael
Campos, Slim Pickens, Rodolfo Acosta, Pat Hogan,
Dean Fredericks, Brad Weston*
A sequel to OLD YELLER, with another mongrel
mutt proving his worth in order to gain acceptance, by
tracking down Apaches who have kidnapped some
children. A fairly routine outing, but pleasant enough.
Boa: novel by F. Gipson.
DRA 103 min
B,V WDV

## SAVAGE SISTERS * 18
Eddie Romero USA 1974
*Gloria Hendry, Cheri Caffaro, Tosanna Ortiz, John
Ashley, Sid Haig, Eddie Garcia*
Two revolutionaries who are sisters, are betrayed and
captured while planning to attack an army convoy. A
mediocre action yarn of much foolishness.
A/AD 80 min (ort 89 min) Cut (2 min 21 sec)
B,V ORION/RNK; RNK

## SAVAGE SOLDIER * 18
Stu Phillip USA
*Claudia Jennings, Joseph Kaufman, Alix Wyeth,
Robert Derman*
A Vietnam veteran suffers the by now familiar
adjustment problems.
DRA 84 min
B,V CBS L/A; KRP

## SAVAGE STREETS * 18
Danny Steinmann USA 1983
*Linda Blair, John Vernon, Robert Dryer, Johnny
Venocur, Sal Landi, Scott Meyer*
A tough high school girl turns vigilante, against a
street gang of rapists and murderers known as "The
Scars". A gratuitously violent and fairly repulsive
updating of DEATH WISH. Cut before video submis-
sion by 11 min 28 sec.
A/AD 80 min (ort 93 min) Cut (1 min 4 sec)
B,V MED

## SAVAGE WATER * 15
Paul W. Kener USA 1982
*Ron Berger, Gil Van Wagoner, Bridget Agnew, Mike
Wactor, Clayton King, Pat Comer, Jo Mickelson, Dawn
Deanne, Rashad Javeri, Valerie Kittel, Gene Eubanks*
Boating enthusiasts on the Colorado River are
menaced by unseen killers, in this low-grade
DELIVERANCE-style saga of survival.
HOR 95 min (ort 105 min)
V FIFTH; GLOB

## SAVAGES * PG
James Ivory USA 1972
*Susan Blakely, Sam Waterston, Louis J. Stadlen,
Anne Francine, Thayer David, Salome Jens, Neil
Fitzgerald*
A primitive tribe comes across a deserted mansion and
becomes influenced by its civilising effect. An obscure
parable whose meaning (if there was one) is lost on
everyone, its makers included.
DRA 108 min
B,V HVH L/A; PVG

## SAVAGES *** PG
Lee H. Katzin USA 1974
*Andy Griffith, Sam Bottoms, Noah Beery, James Best,
Randy Boone, Jim Antonio, James Chandler*
A young man is hired to guide a hunting party, but
discovers that he is to be the quarry, as a sadistic
killer pursues him in the desert. Quite a predictable
and derivative effort, but taut and fairly gripping.

Boa: novel Death Watch by Rob White.
THR 69 min (ort 71 min) mTV
B,V,V2 GHV

## SAVANNAH SMILES ** PG
Pierre De Moro USA 1982
*Mark Miller, Donovan Scott, Peter Graves, Bridgette
Andersen, Chris Robinson, Michael Parks*
A rich little girl who has run away from home meets
two crooks and eventually gets them to reform. A
sweet and harmless tale, no doubt conceived by
someone with a fondness for Shirley Temple films.
Written by Miller.
COM 99 min (ort 105 min)
B,V CBS

## SAVING GRACE ** PG
Robert M. Young USA 1985
*Tom Conti, Giancarlo Giannini, Donald Hewlitt,
Fernando Rey, Angelo Evans, Erland Josephson,
Patricia Manceri, Edward James Olmos*
A newly-elected Pope is overcome by a feeling of
distaste for the meaningless routine, that forms an
important part of his job, and sneaks out of the
Vatican in disguise. He winds up in an Italian village
and enjoys various encounters along the way. An
amusing idea, but fatally hampered by slow develop-
ment.
Boa: novel by Celia Gittelson.
COM 107 min (ort 111 min)
B,V EHE

## SAVIOR OF THE EARTH * PG
Roy Thomas HONG KONG 1989
A further fantasy-adventure from the producer of
FALCON 7 and CAPTAIN COSMOS, in which three
heroes are given the task of stopping a mad scientist
from wrecking Earth's computer network in his bid for
world domination. A contrived futuristic tale that
runs along predictable lines.
CAR 65 min
V VPD

## SAY ANYTHING *** 15
Cameron Crowe USA 1989
*John Cusack, Ione Skye, John Mahoney, Lili Taylor,
Amy Brooks, Pamela Segall, Jason Gould, Joan
Cusack, Eric Stoltz, Lois Chiles*
Comedy-drama that takes a look at first love with an
unexceptional high school kid falling for a clever and
seemingly unattainable girl, and finding that she is
not quite so unapproachable after all. Despite the use
of a well-worn theme, this refreshing film has both
charm and wit. Lois Chiles has an unbilled cameo as
the girl's mother. Scripted by Crowe in his directing
debut.
DRA 96 min (ort 100 min)
V/sh CBS

## SAY HELLO TO YESTERDAY *
Alvin Rakoff UK 1970
*Jean Simmons, Evelyn Laye, Leonard Whiting, John
Lee, Jack Woolgar, Derek Francis, Constance
Chapman, Geoffrey Bayldon, Frank Middlemass,
Gwen Nelson, Laraine Humphreys, Nora Nicholson*
A middle-aged woman on a shopping trip in London,
has a romance with a young man half her age. An
uninspired yawn, best suited to chronic insomniacs,
for whom it was probably designed. Written by Rakoff
and Peter King.
DRA 92 min
B,V BWV

## SAY YES ** PG
Larry Yust USA 1982 (released 1986)
*Jonathan Winters, Art Hindle, Lissa Layng, Logan
Ramsey, Maryedith Burrel, Jensen Collier, Jacque
Lynn Colton, Devon Ericson, Art La Fleur, John
Milford*

An eccentric tycoon leaves a will, stipulating that his grandson will only inherit his fortune, if he is able to wed within 24 hours of the death of the former. A predictable comedy that delivers the expected sequences of frantic endeavour, but little else.

COM                    86 min (CBS); 90 min
B,V                                  CBS; MED

**SAYONARA** ***
Joshua Logan          USA              1957
*Marlon Brando, Miiko Taka, Ricardo Montalban, Miyoshi Umeki, Red Buttons, Martha Scott, James Garner, Patricia Owens, Kent Smith*
American servicemen in Japan become deeply involved with Japanese women, and learn that neither side is prepared to accept such relationships, as pilot Brando discovers when he falls for Japanese entertainer Taka. Written by Paul Osborn, with an Irving Berlin theme song and music by Franz Waxman. AA: S. Actor (Buttons), S. Actress (Umeki), Art/Set (Ted Hawarth/Robert Priestley), Sound (George Groves).
Boa: novel by James A. Michener.

DRA                    141 min (ort 147 min)
B,V                                        CBS

**SCALPEL** **
John Grissmer         USA                15
*Robert Lansing, Judith Chapman, Arlen Dean Snyder, David Scarroll, Sandy Martin*              1976
A plastic surgeon transforms a girl into a copy of his missing daughter so that she can collect an inheritance of 5 million dollars. A violent and generally unpleasant tale, partially redeemed by a neat twist ending.
Aka: FALSE FACE

THR                    89 min (ort 95 min)
V                                          RCA

**SCALPHUNTERS, THE** **
Sydney Pollack        USA                PG
*Burt Lancaster, Shelley Winters, Telly Savalas, Ossie Davis, Dan Vadis, Armando Silvestre, Dabney Coleman, Paul Picerni, Nick Cravat, John Epper, Jack Williams, Chuck Roberson, Tony Epper, Agapito Roldan, Gregorio Acosta*                     1968
A fur trapper and his highly-educated slave, track down a gang who specialise in killing Indians for their scalps. A strange subject for a comedy, that that meanders aimlessly despite one or two good moments.

WES                    99 min (ort 102 min)
V                                          WHV

**SCALPS** *
Fred Olen Ray         USA                18
*Kirk Alyn, Roger Maycock, Richard Hench, Jo Anne Robinson, Frank McDonald, Carroll Borland, Barbara Magnusson, Forrest J. Ackerman, Carol Flockhart*   1983
When a group of students foolishly desecrate an Indian burial site, some demons emerge from the earth to take revenge in this unconvincing horror yarn.

HOR                                      90 min
B,V                                        ARF

**SCANDAL** **
Michael Caton-Jones   UK                 18
*John Hurt, Joanne Whalley-Kilmer, Ian McKellen, Bridget Fonda, Britt Ekland, Daniel Massey, Roland Gift, Jeroen Krabbe*                            1988
A recreation of a sex scandal of the early 1960s, when government minister John Profumo became involved with call-girl Christine Keeler, whom he had been introduced to by Stephen Ward, a curious social-climbing figure of the time. The fact that Keeler (and her colleague Mandy Rice-Davies) had been involved with a Soviet diplomat, was felt to compromise Profumo's integrity and he was forced to resign. A competent directing debut for Caton-Jones.

DRA                                      110 min
V/sh                                        PAL

**SCANDAL IN A SMALL TOWN** *
Anthony Page          USA                15
*Raquel Welch, Christa Denton, Frances Lee McCain, Peter Van Norden, Robin Gammell, Ronny Cox*       1988
The story of one woman's lone fight with the establishment, when she learns that her daughter's teacher is promoting anti-Semitism. An unconvincing and exploitative effort, that covers much the same ground as EVIL IN CLEAR RIVER.

DRA                    96 min (ort 100 min) mTV
B,V                                        EMP

**SCANDAL IN THE FAMILY** **
Marcello Andrei       ITALY              18
*Gloria Guida, Gianluigi Ghirizzi, Lucretia Love, Giuseppe Anatrelli, Loredana Martinez, Luciana Turina*                                           1975
Mildly amusing Italian sex comedy.
Aka: SCANDALO IN FAMIGLIA (GRAZIE ZIO)

A                                        77 min
B,V                                        HER

**SCANDAL SHEET** **
David Lowell Rich     USA                PG
*Burt Lancaster, Robert Urich, Lauren Hutton, Pamela Reed, Bobby DiCicco, Peter Jurasik, Trey Wilson, Susan Peretz, Lois DeBanzie, Max Wright, Penelope Windust, Doug Rose, Belita Moreno, Jim B. Baker, Frances McDormand*                           1985
An editor is determined to dig out the truth about an alcoholic Hollywood star, and is unconcerned about how many lives he ruins in the process, just so long as he increases circulation of his glossy magazine. Average.

DRA                    95 min (ort 100 min) mTV
B,V                                        CBS

**SCANDALOUS JOHN** *
Robert Butler         USA                U
*Brian Keith, Michele Carey, Alfonso Arau, Rick Lenz, Harry Morgan, Simon Oakland, Bill Williams, Christopher Dark, Fran Ryan, Richard Hale, James Lydon, John Ritter, Iris Adrian, Larry D. Mann, Jack Raine, Booth Coleman*                       1971
An old rancher, deep in debt and unable to adapt to modern times, makes a last stand to save his ranch from property developers. An overlong, tedious and unattractive effort.
Boa: novel by Richard Gardner.

WES                                      117 min
B,V                                        WDV

**SCANDALOUS!** *
Rob Cohen             USA                15
*Robert Hays, Pamela Stephenson, John Gielgud, Jim Dale, M. Emmet Walsh, Nancy Wood, Ed Dolan, Paul Reeve, Alita Kennedy, Kevin Elyot, Peter Dennis, Duncan Preston, Maureen Bennett, Preston Lockwood, Bow Wow Wow*                              1984
A TV reporter gets involved in murder and industrial espionage when he runs foul of con artists and has to extricate himself from a murder charge. An addle-brained and fairly disagreeable farce, that strains for laughs but never gets going. Written by Cohen.

COM                    88 min (ort 92 min)
V                                          GHV

**SCANNERS** ***
David Cronenberg      CANADA             18
*Stephen Lack, Jennifer O'Neill, Patrick McGoohan, Lawrence Dane, Charles Shamata, Michael Ironside, Robert Silverman, Lee Broker, Mavor Moore, Adam Ludwig, Lee Murray, Fred Doederlein, Geza Kovacs, Sony Forbes*                               1981
A tranquiliser test-marketed on pregnant women in the 1940s, led to the creation of "scanners" – powerful

telepaths, some of whom have telekinetic powers. The corporation responsible for their creation tracks down one with the intention of sending him to infiltrate a dangerous group of subversive scanners. Gory effects are coupled to a sound if rather convoluted story. Written by Cronenberg.

HOR                                        103 min
B,V,V2,LV        GHV; VIR (Betamax and VHS only)

## SCARAB *                                    18
Steven-Charles Jaffe
                 SPAIN/USA              1982
*Robert Ginty, Rip Torn, Cristina Hachael, Jose-Luis De Villalonga, Dan Pickering*
An American reporter investigates the mysterious death of a number of heads of state, and discovers a maniac with supernatural powers.

THR                                         91 min
B,V                                VTC L/A; XTASY

## SCARECROW *                                 18
Jerry Schatzberg     USA               1973
*Gene Hackman, Al Pacino, Eileen Brennan, Dorothy Tristan, Ann Wedgeworth, Richard Lynch*
Two drifters on the road, meet and become friends. One of them believes against all the odds in his own carwash business, while the other has just walked out on his wife. A downbeat and depressing little film. Written by Garry Michael White. The photography of Vilmos Zsigmond and the good use of locations are a slight compensation.

DRA                        108 min (ort 115 min)
B,V                                          WHV

## SCARECROWS ***                              18
William Wesley       USA               1988
*Ted Vernon*
Five army deserters hijack a plane carrying a large amount of money, but one of them decides to keep it all for himself. After throwing the loot out he parachutes down after it. However, he lands in a field of murderous, living scarecrows, and these creatures soon kill him and prepare a welcome for the others. A gripping and quite scary film, that attempts no rational explanation, but merely delivers a set of gruesome shocks.

HOR                                         79 min
V                                            MED

## SCARED STIFF **                             18
Richard Friedman     USA               1986
*Andrew Stevens, Mary Page Keller, Josh Segal, David Ramsey*
The tale of a female singer who moves into a new house with her boyfriend and young son. She finds a strange talisman in the attic that soon begins to exert a sinister influence on their lives.

HOR                         81 min (ort 85 min)
B,V                                          CBS

## SCARED STRAIGHT: ANOTHER STORY ***          15
Richard Michaels     USA               1980
*Cliff De Young, Stan Shaw, Terri Nunn, Randy Brooks, Tony Burton, Linden Chiles, Don Fullilove, Eric Laneuville, William Sanderson, Nathan Cook, John Hammond, Michael Fairman, S. John Launer, Bebe-Drake-Massey, Al White*
Hardened criminals are used to shock juvenile delinquents out of their nasty ways, in this powerful but fictional follow-up to an award-winning TV documentary. A harsh and uncompromising look at life behind bars and the men who endure it, built around a set of encounter groups where the convicts warn their young visitors about the realities of life inside.
Aka: SCARED STRAIGHT

DRA                        96 min (ort 100 min) mTV
B,V                                         POLY

## SCARED TO DEATH **
Christy Cabanne      USA               1947
*Bela Lugosi, Douglas Fowley, Joyce Compton, George Zucco, Nat Pendleton, Angelo Rossitto, Molly Lamont, Roland Varno, Gladys Blake, Lee Bennett, Stanley Andrews, Stanley Price*
A murderess is confronted with the evidence of her crimes and goes insane. This low-budget thriller was Lugosi's only colour film and is far from one of his best, though the film's structure, in which the facts of the case are slowly revealed by the central character, is quite unusual.

THR                                         65 min
B,V                            NEON L/A; VCL/CBS

## SCARED TO DEATH **                          18
Bill Malone          USA               1980
*John Stinson, Diana Davidson, Jonathan David Moses, Pamela Brown, Toni Jannotta, Kermit Eller, Walker Edminston, Mike Muscat, Pam Bowman*
A man-made monster on the prowl in the city's sewers, surfaces from time to time to attack humans and suck out their bone marrow. A low-budget film that's mildly scary, but suffers from an over-reliance on that good old horror standby – the man in the rubber suit.

HOR                         87 min (ort 94 min)
B,V          GOV L/A; PPL L/A; VTC L/A; AVA

## SCAREMAKER, THE *                           18
Robert Deubel        USA               1982
*Rutanya Alda, Suzanne Barnes, Hal Holbrook, David Holbrook, Lauren-Marie Taylor, James Carroll*
A scavenger hunt turns into a nightmare as college students are murdered one by one. Sounds familiar?
Aka: GIRL'S NITE OUT; GIRL'S NIGHT OUT

HOR                 92 min (ort 98 min) Cut (22 sec)
B,V                                 VTC L/A; AVR

## SCARFACE *                                  18
Brian De Palma       USA               1983
*Al Pacino, Steven Bauer, Michelle Pfeiffer, Mary Elizabeth Mastrantonio, Robert Loggia, Paul Shenar, Harris Yulin, F. Murray Abraham, Miriam Colon*
An updated version of the 1932 film, with the central figure now a Cuban refugee who becomes a powerful drugs dealer, and the setting changed from Chicago to Miami. An abundance of of graphic brutality, coarse language and drug-taking, gives it an authentic 1980s flavour but we are offered no new insights. Not so much a film, as a static and disagreeable wallow in the gutter. Written by Oliver Stone.

A/AD              162 min (ort 170 min) (Cut at film
                                  release by 25 sec)
V                                            CIC

## SCARFACE ***                               15
Howard Hawks      USA     1931 (released 1932)
*Paul Muni, Ann Dvorak, George Raft, Boris Karloff, Karen Morley, Vince Barnett, Osgood Perkins, C. Henry Gordon, Henry Armetta, Edwin Maxwell*
A detailed chronicle of the life and death of Chicago gangster Al Capone, with Dvorak as an incestuous sister thrown in for good measure. This brutal and graphic film was made in 1931, but its release was delayed by the censors. Written by Ben Hecht, Seton I. Miller, John Lee Mahin, Fred Pasley and W.R. Burnett. Remade in 1983 with Al Pacino in the title role.
Aka: SCARFACE: THE SHAME OF THE NATION; SHAME OF A NATION, THE
Boa: novel by Armitage Traill.

DRA                    86 min (ort 99 min) B/W
B,V                                          CIC

## SCARFACE MOB, THE ***                       PG
Phil Karlson         USA               1962
*Robert Stack, Neville Brand, Barbara Nichols, Keenan*

Wynn, Pat Crowley, Bruce Gordon, Walter Winchell (narration)
The original pilot episode for the TV series "The Untouchables", the story of FBI agent Elliot Ness, who heads a team of handpicked men to break Al Capone's grip during the Prohibition years in America. Originally shown in 1959, but still retaining considerable force.
Boa: book The Untouchables by Elliot Ness and O. Fraley.

| | |
|---|---|
| A/AD | 91 min B/W mTV |
| V/h | CIC |

## SCARLET AND THE BLACK, THE ***     PG
Jerry London     ITALY/USA     1981
Gregory Peck, Christopher Plummer, Raf Vallone, John Gielgud, Barbara Bouchet, Edmund Purdom, Kenneth Colley, Walter Gotell, Julian Holloway, Angelo Infanti, Olga Karlatos, Michael Byrne, T.P. McKenna, Vernon Dobtcheff
In 1943, when Italy has capitulated and been taken over by the Nazis, an Irish priest founds an organisation to help Allied prisoners escape, and fights a cat-and-mouse game with a Nazi officer who is out to catch him. Peck's first dramatic starring role for TV, with Pope Pius XII played by Gielgud. A competent thriller, adapted by David Butler.
Boa: book The Scarlet Pimpernel Of The Vatican by J.P. Gallagher.

| | |
|---|---|
| THR | 138 min (ort 155 min) mTV |
| B,V,V2 | PRV L/A; CH5 (VHS only) |

## SCARLET PIMPERNEL, THE ****     U
Harold Young     UK     1934
Leslie Howard, Merle Oberon, Raymond Massey, Nigel Bruce, Anthony Bushell, Bramwell Fletcher, Joan Gardner, Walter Rilla, Mabel Terry-Lewis, O.B. Clarence, Ernest Milton, Edmund Breon, Melville Cooper, Gibb McLaughlin
Classic story of the English aristocrat who rescued French compatriots from the guillotine, with Howard first class as a dashing Englishman playing a dangerous game with consummate skill. Written by Robert E. Sherwood, Sam Berman, Arthur Wimperis and Lajos Biro. The music is by Arthur Benjamin. Remade as "The Elusive Pimpernel" in 1950 and also as a 1982 TV series.
Boa: novel by Baroness Orczy.

| | |
|---|---|
| A/AD | 93 min (ort 98 min) B/W |
| B,V | SCREL; POLY; PICK |

## SCARLET STREET ***
Fritz Lang     USA     1945
Edward G. Robinson, Joan Bennett, Dan Daryea, Margaret Lindsay, Rosalind Ivan, Jess Barker, Samuel S. Hinds, Arthur Loft
A weak man becomes tragically involved with a prostitute and her pimp, in this fairly effective but ponderous tale. Interestingly, this was the first Hollywood film to show a crime going unpunished, for when the prostitute is murdered her pimp is wrongfully executed for the crime. Written by Dudley Nichols. The play on which this is based was filmed once before by Jean Renoir in 1932.
Boa: play La Chienne by George De La Fouchardiere.

| | |
|---|---|
| DRA | 90 min (ort 103 min) B/W |
| B,V | NOVA L/A |

## SCARLET WOMAN, THE **
Jean Valere     FRANCE/ITALY     1968
Monica Vitti, Maurice Ronet, Robert Hossein, Claudio Brook, Francisco Rabal
A rich woman decides to get her revenge on her lover by murdering him, but her plans take an unexpected turn.
Aka: LA FEMME ECARLATE

| | |
|---|---|
| COM | 83 min |
| B,V,V2 | FFV L/A |

## SCARRED **
Rose-Marie Turko     USA     1983
Jennifer Mayo, Jackie Berryman, David Dean, Randolph Pitts, Shandra Beri, Neva Miner
Young girls in Los Angeles are forced to become prostitutes in order to survive. A harsh but not especially convicing drama.
Aka: STREET LOVE

| | |
|---|---|
| DRA | 81 min (ort 85 min) |
| B,V | VFP L/A; HER |

## SCARS OF DRACULA, THE **
Roy Ward Baker     UK     1970
Christopher Lee, Dennis Waterman, Wendy Hamilton, Jenny Hanley, Christopher Matthews, Anoushka Hempel, Patrick Troughton, Michael Gwynn, Delia Lindsay, Michael Ripper, Bob Todd
A young couple looking for the husband's missing brother, stumble across Count Dracula. Yet another reworking of this old legend, with our lovable vampire being resurrected by bat's blood and commencing his anti-social activities all over again. Plenty of irrelevant sex and sadism are thrown in, but there is nothing of lasting value in a film that was one more nail in the coffin of a series approaching its end. DRACULA A.D. 1972 followed.

| | |
|---|---|
| HOR | 96 min; 92 min (WHV) |
| B,V | TEVP; WHV (VHS only) |

## SCAVENGER HUNT *
Michael Schultz     USA     1979
Richard Benjamin, Cloris Leachman, Ruth Gordon, James Coco, Scatman Crothers, Roddy McDowall, Richard Mulligan, Vincent Price, Robert Morley, Tony Randall, Dirk Benedict, Willie Aames, Richard Masur, Avery Schreiber
A man dies and his relatives and servants are obliged by the terms of his will, to assemble a collection of strange objects within a set time, in order to be eligible for a share of his inheritance. An original plot idea never develops beyond a scatter-brained chase, much in the same mould as IT'S A MAD, MAD, MAD, MAD WORLD.

| | |
|---|---|
| COM | 116 min mTV |
| B,V | GHV |

## SCAVENGERS *     15
Duncan McLachlan     USA     1987
Kenneth David Gilman, Brenda Bakke, Crispen De Nys, Ken Gampu, Norman Anstey
A coded message in a bible, leads a researcher and his girlfriend on a dangerous chase all the way to Africa, in this very poor spy thriller.

| | |
|---|---|
| A/AD | 90 min (ort 94 min) |
| B,V | BRAVE |

## SCAVENGERS, THE **
R.L. Frost     USA     1969
Jonathan Bliss, Maria Lease, Michael Dikova
A group of Confederate soldiers are tricked into believing that the war is still on, and commit various bloody and brutal crimes, having been instilled with hatred by their captain, who exploits them for his own ends.

| | |
|---|---|
| WES | 85 min |
| B,V | DFS |

## SCENES FROM A MARRIAGE ***     15
Ingmar Bergman     SWEDEN     1973
Liv Ullman, Erland Josephson, Bibi Andersson, Jan Malmsjo, Anita Wall, Gunnel Lindblom
Gloomy and depressing look at an unhappy marriage and its disintegration. An intimate and perceptive examination of human misery, with superb performances rom Ullman and Josephson as a couple, who divorce and find new partners. The upbeat ending does, however, see them eventually come together as lovers once more, if not as husband and wife. Original-

ly shown on TV in 6 episodes, but edited into a feature by the director.
Aka: SCENER UR ETT AKTENSKAP
DRA                    168 min (ort 300 min) mTV
B,V                                          VCC

## SCENES FROM THE CLASS STRUGGLE IN
BEVERLY HILLS ***                             18
Paul Bartel            USA                  1988
*Jacqueline Bisset, Ray Sharkey, Mary Woronov,*
*Robert Beltran, Ed Begley Jr, Wallace Shawn, Arnetia*
*Walker, Paul Bartel, Paul Mazursky, Rebecca*
*Schaeffer*
A bizarre sex farce set in Beverly Hills where two gardeners each bet that they can be first to bed the other's employer. This scattershot comedy of musical beds among the rich and not-so-rich, tries hard to be a satire but remains just one more wacky sex romp. A highlight is Bisset as an ex-sitcom star whose dead husband keeps re-appearing to pledge his undying love. The screenplay is by Bruce Wagner.
Boa: story by Paul Bartel and Bruce Wagner.
COM                    99 min (ort 102 min)
V                                            MGM

## SCENT OF HEATHER, A **                     18
Phillip Drexler        USA                  1981
*Tracy Adams, Christine Ford, Veronica Hart, Vanessa*
*Del Rio, Paul Thomas, Jessica Teal, Lisa Be, Richard*
*Bell, R. Bolla, Neil Peters, Felix Krull*
A silly Gothic romance set in an English castle, with a naive young woman getting married and then discovering that her husband is really her brother. The story now has both parties remaining married but making alternative arrangements to obtain sexual satisfaction. Finally, the husband decides that they should have one night together and then commit suicide, but just before this happens they discover they are not brother and sister after all.
A                      69 min (ort 99 min) Cut (1 min 38 sec
                                in addition to film cuts)
B,V                                     ELV; HAR

## SCHEHERAZADE **                            18
Stephen Lucas          USA                  1982
*Annette Haven, John Leslie, Lisa De Leeuw, Mai Lin*
Porno version of the famous collection of stories from the "Tales of the
1001 Nights", suitably cut in those small places for UK consumption. The plot revolves around a sultan who finds it necessary to be kept aroused at all times, using of exotic stories and dancers for that purpose.
Aka: SCHEHERAZADE ONE THOUSAND AND ONE NIGHTS
A          54 min (ort 80 min) (Abridged by distributor)
B,V,V2 NET L/A; TCX L/A; 18PLAT/TOW L/A; SHEP

## SCHIZO *                                   18
Pete Walker            UK                    1976
*Lynne Frederick, John Leyton, Stephanie Beacham,*
*John Fraser, Jack Watson, Queenie Watts, Trisha*
*Mortimer, John McEnery, Paul Alexander, Colin*
*Jeavons, Victoria Allum, Wendy Gilmore, Diana King,*
*Pearl Hackney, David McGillivray*
A famous ice-skater is terrorised by a maniac after her impending marriage is announced, but things are not quite as they appear to be. A predictable and pointless exercise in the third-rate.
Aka: AMOK
HOR                    103 min (ort 109 min) Cut (1 min 3 sec
                                including film cuts)
B,V                                          WHV

## SCHIZOID *                                 18
David Paulsen          USA                  1980
*Klaus Kinski, Mariana Hill, Craig Wasson, Donna*
*Wilkes, Christopher Lloyd, Richard Herd, Joe*
*Regalbuto, Kiva Lawrence, Cindy Dolan, Claude*

*Duvernoy, Flo Gerrish, Jon Greene, Richard Balin*
Patients attending a group therapy centre, are being murdered one by one, in this incoherent psychological shocker.
HOR                                      91 min
B,V                                          RNK

## SCHOOL DAZE **                             18
Spike Lee              USA                  1988
*Larry Fishburne, Giancarlo Esposito, Tisha Campbell,*
*Kyme, Joe Seneca, Art Evans, Julian Eaves, Ellen*
*Holly, Ossie Davis, Spike Lee, Branford Marsalis*
A comedy set at a black college in the South, where a serious-minded student fights against both the college establishment and the juvenile antics of his fellow students. An unusual comedy, written by Lee, that unfortunately fails to make the most of its opening premise.
COM                                     121 min
V/sh                                         RCA

## SCHOOL FOR SCOUNDRELS **                    U
Robert Hamer           UK                    1960
*Ian Carmichael, Alastair Sim, Terry-Thomas, Janette*
*Scott, Dennis Price, Edward Chapman, Kynaston*
*Reeves, Irene Handl, John Le Mesurier, Hugh*
*Paddick, Peter Jones, Gerald Campion, Hattie*
*Jacques, Anita Sharp Bolster*
The story of a failure in life who enrols at the College of One-Upmanship, in the hope that he will learn the secret of coming out on top in any situation. Not really a film, but a series of amusing sketches that are drawn from the books of Potter. Written by Patricia Mayes and Hal E. Chester. Mildly entertaining, but no more than that.
Boa: books: Gamesmanship/Oneupmanship/Lifemanship by Stephen Potter.
COM                    91 min (ort 94 min) B/W
V                                            WHV

## SCHOOL SPIRIT **                           15
Allan Holeb            USA                  1985
*Tom Nolan, Elizabeth Foxx, Roberta Collins, John*
*Finnegan, Larry Linville, Daniele Arnaud, Marta*
*Kober, Tom Hudson*
A boy comes back from the dead in ghostly form to conclude unfinished business with his girlfriend. A juvenile blend of slapstick and fantasy that remains ineffective for most of the film.
COM                    87 min (ort 90 min)
B,V                                          MED

## SCI-BOTS 1: CONFLICT *                      U
Jim Terry              JAPAN
Evil mutants destroy a distant planet and the survivors flee to Earth, in this typical production-line Japanese animation. Followed by SCI-BOTS 2.
CAR                    56 min (KRP); 45 min
B,V                                    KRP; GLOB

## SCI-BOTS 2: STRIKE BACK *                   U
Jim Terry              JAPAN
Survivors from the mutant attack in the first film, launch a counter-attack in an attempt to destroy their aggressors.
CAR                                      45 min
B,V                                    KRP; GLOB

## SCOOBY-DOO AND THE GHOUL SCHOOL *           U
Charles B. Nicholas    USA                  1988
*Voices of: Remy Auberjonois, Susan Blu, Hamilton*
*Camp, Jeff B. Cohen, Glynis Johns, Casey Kasem, Zale*
*Kessler, Ruta Lee, Aaron Lohr, Patty Maloney, Scott*
*Menville, Don Messick, Pat Musick, Bumper Robinson,*
*Donnie Schell*
Another feature-length adaptation based on the cowardly canine hero of a long-running TV series. Poor.
CAR                                      90 min
V                                            VCC

## SCOOBY-DOO AND THE RELUCTANT WEREWOLF *

U

Ray Patterson          USA          1988
*Voices of: Don Messick, Casey Kasem, Hamilton Camp, Jim Cummings, Joanie Gerber, Ed Gilbert, Brian Mitchell, Pat Musick, Alan Oppenheimer, Rob Paulsen, Mimi Seton, B.J. Ward, Frank Welker*
When his former werewolf escapes to Florida, and is thus prevented from competing in the annual monster rally, Count Dracula turns Shaggy into his replacement and has him and his friends kidnapped and forced to compete in the race. An overlong and extremely poorly produced feature that is weak in both plot and animation.
CAR          94 min
V          VCC

## SCOOBY-DOO IN GHASTLY GHOST TOWN *          U
Joseph Barbera/William Hanna
USA          1972
*Voices of: Don Messick, Frank Welker, Heather North, Casey Kasem, Pat Stevens, Marla Frumkin*
Mystery Inc. plus their canine mascot come to a desert ghost town where they meet up with The Three Stooges and get embroiled in a series of sinister events. Another dreary animation in this interminable series.
CAR          41 min
V          VCC

## SCOOP **          PG
Gavin Millar          UK          1986
*Denholm Elliott, Michael Hordern, Michael Maloney, Herbert Lom, Jack Shepherd, Nicola Pagett, Donald Pleasence, Renee Soutendijk*
In 1938 a young writer is mistaken for a successful novelist of the same name and takes a post as special correspondent to cover the war that's breaking out in the African country of Ishmaelia. A series of events are set in motion by a meeting with an old friend and he eventually emerges with a valuable scoop.
DRA          120 min
V          VCC

## SCORCHY **
Hikmet Avedis          USA          1976
*Connie Stevens, Cesare Danova, William Smith, Marlene Schmidt, Norman Burton, Joyce Jameson*
A Seattle undercover policeman works to trap a high-level drugs syndicate in this lurid and fairly meaningless tale. Some good action sequences offer a slight compensation.
DRA          99 min
B,V          MHO L/A; HVH

## SCORPIO **          15
Michael Winner          USA          1972
*Burt Lancaster, Alain Delon, Gayle Hunnicutt, Paul Scofield, John Colicos, J.D. Cannon, Joanne Linville*
The complex tale of some CIA agents who try to double-cross each other and a hit-man who wants to retire. A convoluted and disorganised jumble, with a few well-handled action sequences and the obligatory dose of brutality.
THR          114 min
B,V          WHV

## SCORPION **          15
William Riead          USA          1986
*Tonny Tulleners, Don Murray, Robert Logan, Allen Williams, Kathryn Daley, Ross Elliott, John Anderson, Bart Braverman, Thom McFadden, Bill Hayes, Adam Pearson*
A tough karate-chopping secret agent foils a terrorist plane hijacking, and is then given the job of guarding a terrorist-turned-informer. When the man is killed and our agent's cover is blown, he is forced to embark on a revenge mission. A straightforward action film with few frills, but the story moves along fast enough

to hold one's interest. Tulleners' film debut.
Aka: THE SUMMONS
A/AD          100 min
B,V          WHV

## SCORPION THUNDERBOLT **          18
Godrey Ho          HONG KONG
*Bernard Tsui, Juliet Chan, Nancy Lim, Richard Harrison*
A serpentine monster is attacking and killing people in Hong Kong. A police inspector investigates in this strange mixture of martial arts and horror.
HOR          84 min Cut (2 min 8 sec)
B,V          BRNX; SAT

## SCORPION, THE **          18
Ben Vebong          NETHERLANDS          1983
*Peter Tuinman, Monique van de Van, Rima Melati, Senne Rouffaer, Walter Kous, Adrian Brine, Huub Stapel, Henk Van Ulsen, Edwin De Vries, Teddy Schaank, Marike Veugelers, Hans Holtkamp, Hans Kerckhoffs, Albert Abspoel*
A truck driver discovers a closely-guarded secret, and has to run from the man who will stop at nothing to keep the truth from getting out.
Aka: DE SCHORPIOEN; NEVER KILL A SCORPION
THR          97 min
B,V          SCRN; TEVP

## SCOTT OF THE ANTARCTIC ***          U
Charles Frend          UK          1948
*John Mills, Derek Bond, Harold Warrender, James Robertson Justice, Kenneth More, Reginald Beckwith, James McKechnie, John Gregson, Norman Williams, Barry Letts, Clive Morton, Anne Firth, Diana Churchill, Christopher Lee*
An account of the ill-prepared and ill-fated British expedition to the South Pole in 1912, which perished largely because of a lack of professionalism as compared to the Norwegians. Ignore the "stiff-upper-lip" syndrome so typical of British films of this genre, and this becomes quite a decent film. Written by Mary Hayley Bell (Mills' wife), Ivor Montagu and Walter Meade, and with music by Ralph Vaughan Williams.
DRA          105 min (ort 111 min)
B,V          TEVP; WHV (VHS only)

## SCOUT'S HONOR **
Henry Levin          USA          1980
*Gary Coleman, Katherine Helmond, Wilfrid Hyde-White, Harry Morgan, Meeno Peluce, Pat O'Brien, Angela Cartwright, Lauren Chapin, Jay North, Marcello Krakoff, Paul Petersen, John Louie, Joanna Moore, Peter Hobbs, Al Fann*
An orphan dreams of becoming a cub scout in this cute and quite appealing little comedy yarn. This was the final film of Levin, who died on the last day of production.
COM          96 min mTV
B,V          VTC

## SCRATCH HARRY *
Alex Matter          USA          1969
*Harry Walker Staff, Victoria Wilde, Christine Kelly*
A man's instincts get him into trouble in this run-of-the-mill adult movie.
Aka: EROTIC THREE, THE
A          94 min
B,V,V2          INT

## SCREAM AND DIE! *
Joseph Larraz          UK          1973
*Andrea Allan, Karl Lanchbury, Joseph Larraz, Maggie Walker, Judy Matheson, Peter Forbes-Robertson, Annabella Wood, Alex Leppard, Lawrence Keane, Daphne Lea, Raymond Young, Richard Aylen, Barbara Meale, Joshua Leppard*
A model witnesses a sadistic murder after breaking

into a house with her boyfriend, and finds herself being pursued by the killer. A dreary and unconvincing dud that is as absurd in its use of red herrings and tawdry sexploitation footage, as it is in the predictability of the final outcome.
Aka: DON'T GO IN THE BEDROOM; HOUSE THAT VANISHED, THE; PSYCHO SEX FIEND; SCREAM OR DIE!

| | |
|---|---|
| HOR | 85 min (ort 99 min) |
| B,V,V2 | REP/VPD |

## SCREAM AND SCREAM AGAIN ** 18
Gordon Hessler    UK    1969
*Vincent Price, Christopher Lee, Peter Cushing, Judy Huxtable, Alfred Marks, Peter Sallis, Anthony Newlands, David Lodge, Uta Levka, Christopher Matthews, Judy Bloom, Clifford Earl, Kenneth Benda, Yutte Stensgaard*
Confused and disjointed film about a mad scientist's attempts to create a race of super-beings, by using the limbs and organs taken from kidnapped people. Lurid and quite unpleasant, but there are occasional flashes of power. Written by Christopher Wicking.
Aka: SCREAMER
Boa: novel The Disorientated Man by Peter Saxon.

| | |
|---|---|
| HOR | 91 min (ort 94 min) |
| B,V | RCA |

## SCREAM BLOODY MURDER ** 
Marc B. Ray/Robert J. Emery
    USA    1972
*Fred Holbert, Leigh Mitchell, Robert Knox, Paul Vincent, A. Maana Tanelah, Paul Ecenta*
A maniac killer with a steel claw, is released from a mental home only to kill again, in this disagreeable horror yarn.

| | |
|---|---|
| HOR | 83 min (ort 90 min) |
| B,V | VCL/CBS |

## SCREAM FOR HELP * 18
Michael Winner    UK/USA    1984
*Rachel Kelly, David Brooks, Marie Masters, Rocco Sisto, Lolita Lorre, Corey Parker, Tony Sibbald, Sandra Clark, Stacey Hughes, David Baxt, Leslie Lowe, Morgan Deare, Sarah Brackett, Clare Burt, Matthew Peters, Diane Ricardo*
A young girl discovers that her stepfather is plotting the murder of her mother, but is not believed when she tries to get help. A trite and tiresome thriller full of bad dialogue and worse acting.

| | |
|---|---|
| THR | 86 min (ort 90 min) |
| B,V | VFP L/A; HER |

## SCREAM IN THE STREETS, A ** 18
Carl Monson    USA    1972
*John Kirkpatric, Frank Barton, Rosee Stone, Brandy Lyman, Con Covert, Linda York, Tony Scaponi*
Two cops have to track down a sadistic rapist and murderer, who specialises in killing attractive women in this grimly unpleasant tale.
Aka: GIRLS IN THE STREETS (EROT/ATLAS)

| | |
|---|---|
| THR | 65 min (ort 90 min) Cut (14 min 53 sec) |
| B,V | LVC L/A; EROT/ATLAS |

## SCREAMTIME * 18
Al Beresford    UK    1983
*Vincent Russo, Michael Gordon, Robin Bailey, Ian Saynor, Yvonne Nicholson, David Van Day, Marie Scinto, Kevin Smith, Jonathon Morris, Boscoe Hogan, John Styles, Lully Bowers, Veronica Doran, Brenda Kempner, Dora Bryan*
A fairly dreary horror spoof in the form of three sketches, the opening device being the theft of three videotapes from a shop in Times Square. In "Killer Punch" a Punch and Judy puppeteer takes out his anger on his wife and stepson, with the aid of Mr Punch, in "Scream House" a young couple move into a house that's haunted by the ghost of a knife-wielding maniac, and in "Garden Of Blood" a gardener's new

employers own a sinister garden.
Aka: SCREAM TIME

| | |
|---|---|
| COM | 91 min mTV |
| B,V | MED |

## SCREEN TEST * 
Sam Auster    USA    1985
*Michael Allen Bloom, Monique Gabrielle, Robert Bundy, Paul Leuken, David Simpatico, Mari Laskarin*
Adolescents set up a phoney porno video company to ogle girls arriving for "auditions", but they get more than they bargained for. A smutty display of puerile humour.

| | |
|---|---|
| COM | 81 min (ort 84 min) Cut (6 sec) |
| B,V | RCA |

## SCREWBALL ACADEMY * 15
Reuben Rose    USA    1985
*Colleen Camp, Ken Welsh, Christine Cattell, Charles Dennis, Angus MacInnes*
A crazy comedy set in a chaotic educational establishment. A mixture of the usual madcap antics and comic capers. Very dull.

| | |
|---|---|
| COM | 88 min |
| B,V | BRAVE/IVS |

## SCREWBALL HOTEL * 18
Rafal Zielinski    USA    1988
*Michael Bendetti, Andrew Zeller, Jeff Greenman, Kelly Monteith*
The manager of a seedy Miami hotel has a month to find $2,500,000 before gangsters take it over. His one faint hope is to stage a "Miss Purity" pageant, but unfortunately he finds "pure" girls to be in short supply. When three military school rejects take jobs there, they set up an illegal casino and then use an inhibition-releasing drug to stage a wild party. A brash, vulgar comedy, the third film in the "Screwball" series.

| | |
|---|---|
| COM | 97 min |
| B,V | BRAVE |

## SCREWBALLS * 18
Rafal Zielinski    USA    1983
*Peter Keleghan, Linda Speciale, Alan Daveau, Linda Shayne, Kent Deuters*
Routine comedy about sex-mad adolescents who are determined to get a topless view of a particular young girl. Made with neither wit nor care and followed by two sequels.

| | |
|---|---|
| COM | 80 min |
| B,V,V2 | AVA/CBS |

## SCREWBALLS 2: LOOSE SCREWS * 18
Rafal Zielinski    CANADA    1985
*Bryan Genesse, Lance Van Der Kolk, Annie McAutey, Alan Deveau, Jason Warren, Cyd Belliveau, Mike MacDonald, Karen Wood, Annie McAuley, Liz Green, Beth Gondek, Deborah Lobdan, Stephanie Sulik, Terrea Oster, Wayne Fleming*
A production-line sequel with our four heroes going to a summer school and getting up to the usual pranks. Followed by SCREWBALL HOTEL.
Aka: LOOSE SCREWS; SUMMER SCHOOL

| | |
|---|---|
| COM | 85 min |
| B,V | AVA |

## SCROOGE *** 
Ronald Neame    UK    1970
*Albert Finney, Alec Guinness, Edith Evans, Kenneth More, Michael Medwin, Laurence Naismith, David Collings, Richard Beaumont, Kay Walsh, Anton Rodgers, Suzanne Neve, Frances Cuka, Derek Francis, Roy Kinnear, Mary Peach*
An enjoyable, exuberant musical version of this seasonal story, with Finney giving a lovely overblown performance as dear old Mr Scrooge, who learns the meaning of Christmas from a trio of ghosts. Guinness makes an excellent Marley. Only the poor songs of

Leslie Bricusse let it down. The sets were designed by Terry Marsh, and Ronald Searle did the title design. Richard Harris and Rex Harrison were both sought for the role before Finney.
Boa: novel A Christmas Carol by Charles Dickens.
MUS                                    115 min (ort 118 min)
B,V                                                          CBS

### SCROOGE ***                                               U
Brian Desmond-Hurst    UK                              1951
Alastair Sim, Mervyn Johns, Kathleen Harrison, Jack Warner, Hermione Baddeley, Clifford Millison, Michael Hordern, George Cole, Rona Anderson, John Charlesworth, Glyn Dearman, Francis De Wolff, Carol Marsh, Brian Worth
A lively, vivid and highly enjoyable version of this classic tale, with fine performances and intelligent direction and casting. Dickens' tale has been adapted many times, but this work is without doubt one of the most memorable.
Boa: novella A Christmas Carol by Charles Dickens.
DRA                                              94 min B/W
V                                                        BRAVE

### SCROOGED ***                                             PG
Richard Donner          USA                            1988
Bill Murray, Karen Allen, John Forsythe, David Johanson, Carol Kane, John Glover, Bobcat Goldthwait, Robert Mitchum, Michael J. Pollard, Nicholas Phillips, Alfre Woodard, Mabel King, John Murray, Jamie Farr, Robert Goulet
An amusing update of Dicken's tale "A Christmas Carol", with Murray playing a mean and unpleasant network TV executive out to spread gloom and misery amongst his employees and the public at large. Following a visit from his dead former boss, he makes a half-hearted effort to mend his ways, but is only really convinced of the need to change with the arrival of the ghosts of past, present (Kane as a fairy with a mean left hook) and future.
COM                                      97 min (ort 101 min)
V                                                          CIC

### SCRUBBERS *                                               15
Mai Zetterling          UK                             1982
Chrissie Cotterill, Amanda York, Kate Ingram, Elizabeth Edmonds, Eva Motley, Kathy Burke, Amanda Symonds, Debbie Bishop, Imogen Bain, Honey Bane, Camille Davis, Rachael Weaver, Dawn Archibald, Faith Tingle, Anna McKeown
An unrelenting look at the enclosed world of a girls' borstal, with all its squalor and hopelessness. A film that provides neither entertainment nor education. Written by Mai Zetterling, Roy Minton and Jeremy Watt. See SCUM, which covers similar ground.
DRA                                        89 min (ort 93 min)
B,V                                                  TEVP; CAN

### SCRUFFY *                                                 U
                        USA                            1980
Voices of: Alan Young, June Foray, Hans Conreid, Nancy McKeon
A puppy loses his parents and is involved in many perilous situations before finding his true love.
CAR                                        60 min (ort 72 min)
V                                                          VCC

### SCUM **
Alan Clarke             UK                             1979
Ray Winstone, Mick Ford, John Blundell, Julian Firth, Phil Daniels, John Fowler, Ray Burdis, Patrick Murray, Herbert Norville, George Winter, Alrick Riley, Peter Francis, Philip Da Costa, Perry Benson, Alan Igbon, Andrew Paul
A graphic account of the horrors of a boys' borstal that was originally made as a TV play and then banned by the BBC. Not for the squeamish. See also SCRUBBERS for a look at a female institution.
Boa: TV play by Roy Minton.

DRA                          98 min; 96 min (ODY)
B, V/sh, V2               VCL/CBS; ODY (VHS only)

### SCUMBUSTERS *                                            18
Gorman Bechard          USA                            1987
Debi Thiebeault, Karen Nielson, Lisa Schmidt, Ruth Collins, Simone, Griffin O'Neal, Christina Whitaker, Elizabeth Kaitan, Nick Cassavetes, Jamie Bozian, Tammara Souza
A group of cheerleaders take the law into their own hands when one of their number is raped. They enjoy the experience so much they decide to form a female vigilante group to rid the streets of undesirables, using hatchets and chainsaws for this purpose. A clumsy mixture of bloodshed and slapstick, this noisome film was intended to be a horror spoof, but winds up being merely repellent.
Aka: ASSAULT OF THE KILLER BIMBOS (EIV); HACK 'EM HIGH
HOR                     80 min; 70 min (CFD) (ort 85 min)
B,V                                                  EIV; CFD

### SEA DEVILS **
Raoul Walsh             UK                             1953
Yvonne De Carlo, Rock Hudson, Maxwell Reed, Denis O'Dea, Michael Goodliffe, Bryan Forbes, Jacques Brunius, Ivor Barnard, Arthur Wontner, Gerard Oury, Keith Pyott
In Napoleonic France, a fisherman-turned-smuggler saves the life of a beautiful English spy, who is out to foil plans for the invasion of England. Standard costumed high spirits, hearty and instantly forgettable.
Boa: novel Toilers Of The Deep by Victor Hugo.
A/AD                                       87 min (ort 90 min)
V                                                          WHV

### SEA HAWK, THE ****                                        U
Michael Curtiz          USA                            1940
Errol Flynn, Flora Robson, Brenda Marshall, Henry Daniell, Claude Rains, Donald Crisp, Alan Hale, Una O'Connor, James Stephenson, William Landigan, Gilbert Roland, Julien Mitchell, Montague Love, J.M. Kerrigan, Fritz Leiber
A splendid swashbuckling classic, with Flynn in fine form in this tale of intrigue at the court of Elizabeth I. Written by Seton I. Miller with a fine score by Erich Wolfgang Korngold. Unfortunately the film is currently only available on the nearly obsolete CED recording system.
Boa: novel by Rafael Sabatini. A/AD    122 min B/W
CED                                                  MGM; WHV

### SEA OF LOVE ***                                          18
Harold Becker           USA                            1989
Al Pacino, Ellen Barkin, John Goodman, Michael Rooker, William Hickey, Richard Jenkins, Christine Estabrook, Barbara Baxley, Patricia Barry, Jacqueline Brookes
When a smart New York detective in the throes of a mid-life crisis, begins investigating a series of killings apparently linked to lonely hearts small ads, he finds himself falling for the chief suspect. A tough and sexy urban thriller, held together by a knockout performance from Pacino. The script is by Richard Price.
THR                                      108 min (ort 112 min)
V                                                          CIC

### SEA QUEST **
Carl Schultz            AUSTRALIA                      1978
Hardy Kruger, Greg Rowe, Elspeth Ballantyne, Liddy Clark, John Jaratt
A father and son not on the best of terms, find themselves having to pull together when things go wrong on a tuna fishing expedition. A pleasant family adventure.
Aka: BLUE FIN
A/AD                                                   90 min
B,V                                                  VCL/CBS

**SEA WIFE ‡‡** PG
Bob McNaught UK 1957
*Joan Collins, Richard Burton, Basil Sydney, Ronald*
*Squire, Cy Grant, Harold Goodwin, Roddy Hughes,*
*Gibb McLaughlin, Lloyd Lamble, Nicholas Hannen,*
*Ronald Adam, Beatrice Varley*
Three men and a girl survive in a dinghy when their
ship is torpedoed off Singapore during WW2, but are
unware that the lady in question is a nun. Done in
awkward flashback style, this uneven and fairly
ineffectual film is a poor adaptation of a rather minor
novel.
Boa: novel Seawyf And Biscuit by J.D. Scott.
DRA 82 min
V/h CBS

**SEA WOLF, THE ‡‡‡** PG
Michael Curtiz USA 1941
*Edward G. Robinson, John Garfield, Ida Lupino,*
*Alexander Knox, Gene Lockhart, Barry Fitzgerald,*
*Stanley Ridges, David Bruce, Howard Da Silva*
The tyrannical and unbalanced captain of a freighter
picks up three survivors from a ferry crash but holds
them captive. Robinson gives an intense and utterly
believable performance in London's brutal tale, but
the action takes second place to the dialogue rather
too often. Remade several times since, most notably as
"Wolf Larsen".
Boa: novel by Jack London.
DRA 84 min (ort 100 min) B/W
V WHV

**SEA WOLVES, THE ‡‡** PG
Andrew V. McLaglen
SWITZERLAND/UK/USA 1980
*Gregory Peck, Roger Moore, David Niven, Trevor*
*Howard, Barbara Kellerman, Patrick Macnee, Patrick*
*Allen, Bernard Archard, Martin Benson, Faith Brook,*
*Allan Cuthbertson, Kenneth Griffith, Donald Houston,*
*Glyn Houston*
A retired British cavalry unit in India undertakes a
hazardous sabotage operation against a German ship,
in the neutral Portuguese enclave of Goa in 1943.
More of a stiff-jointed romp than a war film, with a
curiously old-fashioned look to it, but mildly enter-
taining in its way. Written by Reginald Rose and
based to some extent on a true story.
Boa: novel Boarding Party by James Leasor.
WAR 115 min (ort 122 min)
B,V RNK L/A; VCC (VHS only)

**SEALED CARGO ‡‡‡** 
Alfred L. Werker USA 1951
*Dana Andrews, Claude Rains, Carla Balenda, Philip*
*Dorn*
A tense tale of German submarine activity off the
Newfoundland coast during WW2, with a fishing
vessel rescuing the captain of a Danish ship, who in
reality is in command of a group of German subs. Good
performances and tight direction make this a gripping
account.
Osca: BEST OF THE BADMEN
THR 85 min B/W
B,V KVD

**SEALED TRAIN, THE ‡‡** PG
Damiano Damiani 1987
*Ben Kingsley, Jason Connery, Timothy West*
A sluggish and none too interesting docu-drama about
Lenin's return to Russia in 1917, when the German
government sent him back in a sealed train in the
hope that he would successfully lead an uprising that
would take Russia out of the war. Though this was
indeed an event that shaped history, little effort has
been made to imbue the subject matter with the
dramatic impact it requires.
Aka: LENIN, THE SEALED TRAIN
DRA 120 min mTV
V FUTUR

**SEARCH AND DESTROY ‡** 15
William Fruet CANADA/USA 1978
(released in 1981)
*Perry King, Tisa Farrow, Park Jong Soo, Don Stroud,*
*George Kennedy, Tony Sheer, Phil Aiken, Rummy*
*Bishop, Daniel Buccos, Rob Garrison, John Kerr, Geza*
*Kovacs, Bill Starr, Kirk McColl*
A South Vietnamese official comes to the USA on a
mission of revenge against former GIs, in this
mediocre effort.
DRA 89 min (ort 93 min)
B,V RNK

**SEARCH AND DESTROY ‡‡** 18
J. Christian Ingvordsen USA 1988
*Stuart Garrison Day, John Christian, Kosmo Vinyl*
Terrorists attempt to take over a biochemical research
station in a small town, and in the ensuing fighting, a
virus is released that has a strange effect on the local
inhabitants. Average.
A/AD 94 min
V/h MED

**SEARCHERS OF THE VOODOO MOUNTAIN ‡** 18
Bobby A. Suarez USA 1984
*Michael James, Debrah Moore, Ken Metcalfe, Mike*
*Cohen*
Post-WW3 saga with all the usual ingredients: punks,
mutants, strange civilisations etc.
FAN 90 min
B,V GHV

**SEARCHERS, THE ‡‡‡‡** U
John Ford USA 1956
*John Wayne, Jeffrey Hunter, Natalie Wood, Vera*
*Miles, Ward Bond, John Qualen, Henry Brandon,*
*Harry Carey Jr, Olive Carey, Ken Curtis, Antonio*
*Worden, Lana Wood, Walter Coy, Dorothy Jordan,*
*Pippa Scott, Patrick Wayne*
A classic film describing the years a man spends
searching for his niece who has been kidnapped by
Indians. A dramatic and rather solemn film, written
by Frank S. Nugent and with music by Max Steiner.
Boa: novel by Alan Le May.
WES 114 min (ort 119 min)
B,V WHV

**SEASON FOR ASSASSINS ‡** 
Marcello Andrei ITALY 1976
*Martin Balsam, Rossano Brazzi, Joe Dallesandro,*
*Magali Noel, Guido Leontini*
A teenage gang terrorises the helpless citizens of
Rome.
Aka: IL TEMPO DEGLI ASSASSINI
DRA 104 min
B,V VPD

**SEASON OF DREAMS ‡‡** PG
Martin Rosen USA 1988
*Frederic Forrest, Christine Lahti, Peter Coyote, Megan*
*Fellows, Ray Baker, Jason Gedrick, James Gammon,*
*Kaiulani Lee, Jacqueline Brookes, Irene Daily*
The story of a young teenager growing up in the
countryside, forms the basis for this slack and unin-
teresting tale, somewhat redeemed by a handful of
excellent performances.
Aka: STACKING
DRA 91 min (ort 109 min)
B,V RCA

**SEBASTIANE ‡** 18
Derek Jarman/Paul Humfress
UK 1976
*Leonardo Treviglio, Barney James, Neil Kennedy,*
*Richard Warwick, Donald Dunham, Ken Hicks,*
*Junusz Romanov, Steffano Massari, David Finbar,*
*Gerald Incandela, Robert Medley, Graham Cracker,*
*Lindsay Kemp and Troupe*
An account of the martyrdom of St Sebastiane with

the emphasis on the homosexual aspects of Roman life. If for nothing else, memorable for being the only film made in Latin (it carries English subtitles).
DRA                              86 min (Latin dialogue)
B,V                                                      PVG

**SECOND CHANCE \*\***
Rudolph Mate            USA                  1953
*Robert Mitchum, Jack Palance, Linda Darnell,*
*Reginald Sheffield, Roy Roberts*
A boxer and a gambler's girlfriend on the run in Mexico, fall in love but are threatened by a hired killer. A competent melodrama with a gripping climax set on a cable car. Written by Oscar Millard and Sidney Boehm. Made in 3-D.
Boa: story by D.M. Marshman Jr.
Osca: GREAT DAY IN THE MORNING
DRA                              80 min (ort 82 min)
B,V                                                      KVD

**SECOND CHANCE \*\***                        PG
Gilbert Cates           USA                  1988
*Beatrice Arthur, Richard Kiley, Joan Van Ark*
A bored and unfulfilled woman meets up with an old flame who is now a successful doctor, and the latter sweeps her off her feet once more. However, his jealous former girlfriend begins to hatch a series of schemes with the intention of breaking them up forever. A mildly entertaining comedy.
Osca: MAYBE BABY . . . AGAIN? (asa)
COM                                               90 min
V                                                   CASPIC

**SECOND CHORUS \*\***                          U
H.C. Potter             USA                  1940
*Fred Astaire, Paulette Goddard, Burgess Meredith,*
*Charles Butterworth, Artie Shaw and Orchestra,*
*Frank Melton, Jimmy Conlon*
Two members of a band fall in love with the same girl in this pleasant and undemanding tale. Music is by Artie Shaw with lyrics by Johnny Mercer.
MUS                             80 min (ort 84 min) B/W
B,V                    VCL/CBS L/A; VIDCLB; DIAM; GLOB

**SECOND COMING OF EVA, THE \*\*\***
Mac Ahlberg            SWEDEN               1975
*Bridget Maier, Teresa Svenson, Peter Berg, Jack*
*Frank, Jim Styf, Kim Frank, Agda Daal, Suzy*
*Anderson*
Rather lighthearted sex film, looking at a live-in school for young ladies set up by a count, when he inherited his wealthy uncle's manor estate. Unknown to the parents, the count has hired a team of young men to give the girls a sexual education, one to which virginal Eva quickly adapts on her arrival. A lawyer now makes his appearance, having been sent to inspect the "school", but he meets a similar fate too.
A                                                 80 min
B,V,V2                            MOV L/A; TCX; CAL

**SECOND DEGREE, THE \***                      15
Ralph Colelli           USA                  1981
*Michael Speero, Dennis Romer, Jenny Herron*
A man and his girlfriend keep getting mixed up with criminals in this unsatisfactory thriller.
THR                                               96 min
B,V                                                   POLY

**SECOND SERVE \*\***                           15
Anthony Page            USA                  1986
*Vanessa Redgrave, Martin Balsam, William Russ,*
*Alice Krige, Kerrie Keane, Reni Santoni, Richard*
*Venture, Louise Fletcher, Jeff Corey, Alan Feinstein,*
*Nina Van Pallandt, Michael Cavanaugh, Kenneth*
*Tigar, Alison LaPlaca*
A 40-year-long wallow in the private hell of one man, Richard Radley, who finally changed sex to become Renee Richards, ending up as a controversial female

tennis player and coach. Redgrave plays the lead both before and after.
Aka: RENEE RICHARDS STORY, THE
Boa: book The Renee Richards Story: Second Serve by Renee Richards and John Ames.
DRA                                               91 min mTV
B,V                                                   GHV

**SECOND SIGHT \***                             PG
Joel Zwick              USA                  1989
*John Larroquette, Bronson Pinchot, Bess Armstrong,*
*Stuart Pankin, John Schuck, James Tolkan, William*
*Prince, Christine Estabrook, Cornelia Guest*
Larroquette is the boss of a detective agency that solves its cases with the help of psychic Pinchot. A love interest sub-plot involving a nun is thrown in as an afterthought. A fairly mindless film of amusing bits and pieces that deservedly died at the box office. As a TV sitcom it might well have done better.
COM                             81 min (ort 84 min)
V/sh                                                  WHV

**SECOND SIGHT: A LOVE STORY \*\*\***           PG
John Korty              USA                  1984
*Elizabeth Montgomery, Barry Newman, Nicholas*
*Pryor, Michael Horton, Ben Marley, Richard*
*Romanus, Susan Ruttan, Mitzi Hoag, Frances Bey, Liz*
*Sheridan, Marta Kober, Christian Jacobs, Sanford*
*Jensen, Lance Gordonear*
A blind woman has her sight restored after being urged to take a chance on an operation by her boyfriend, but after 15 years of blindness, finds it hard to part with her guide dog. Quite a touching little tale, scripted by Dennis Turner.
Boa: book Emma And I by Sheila Hocken (adapted by Susan Miller).
DRA                             93 min (ort 100 min) mTV
B,V                                                   ODY

**SECOND SPRING, A \*\***                       18
Ulli Lommel      WEST GERMANY              1975
*Curt Jurgens, Irmgard Schonberg, Eddie Constantine,*
*Anna Orso, Umberto Raho, Philippe Heysent*
An ageing Italian gossip columnist settles in New York and marries a young nurse, only to revert to his former ways and associates.
Aka: DER ZWEITE FRUHLING
DRA                                               75 min
B,V                       VTC L/A; QLV L/A; XTASY

**SECOND THOUGHTS \***                          15
Lawrence Turman         USA                  1982
*Lucie Arnaz, Craig Wasson, Ken Howard, Anne*
*Schedeen, Arthur Rosenberg, Peggy McCay*
A female lawyer divorces her banker husband and plunges into a new relationship with a middle-aged hippie, which is complicated by the fact that his ideas and attitudes are still firmly rooted in the 1960s. One of those ideas that looked good on paper, and should have been left there.
COM                             93 min (ort 98 min)
B,V                                         TEVP; CANN

**SECOND TIME LUCKY \***                        15
Michael Anderson        USA                  1984
*Roger Wilson, Diane Franklin, Robert Morley,*
*Jonathan Gadsby, Bill Ewens, John-Michael Honson,*
*Robert Helpmann*
The Devil and God decide on a return match in a new Garden of Eden, in this painfully unfunny offering.
COM                             87 min (ort 98 min)
B,V                                                   VGM

**SECOND VICTORY, THE \*\***                    15
Gerald Thomas      AUSTRALIA               1986
*Anthony Andrews, Helmut Griem, Mario Adorf, Renee*
*Soutendijk, Birgit Doll, Max Von Sydow*
Story set in Austria just after WW2, when the death of a British sergeant at the hands of a sniper, leads to a

manhunt on the part of an officer. A blend of intrigue and action that is fairly well done, but offers little that's memorable. Written by West.
Boa: novel by Morris West.

| WAR | 98 min (ort 112 min) |
| B,V | CHV |

## SECOND WIND **
Don Shebib          CANADA          1976
*James Naughton, Lindsay Wagner, Ken Pogue, Tedde Moore, Tom Harvey, Louis Del Grande, Gerard Parkes, Jonathan Welsh, Cec Linder, Allan Levson, Vivian Reis, Robert Goodier, Mike Hurley, Robyn Jaffe, Robert Slee*
A young couple discover the pleasure of making an effort to get the things they want. Average.

| DRA | 92 min |
| B,V | PRV |

## SECOND-HAND HEARTS *
Hal Ashby          USA          1979
(released in 1981)
*Barbara Harris, Robert Blake, Collin Boone, Amber Rose Gold, Bert Remsen, Shirley Stoler*
A middle-aged slob goes to a party, gets drunk and wakes up to find that he has just got married. A stupid and tiresome comedy that is as incoherent and muddled as it is unfunny and contrived.
Aka: HAMSTER OF HAPPINESS, THE

| COM | 97 min (ort 102 min) |
| B,V | TEVP; GHV |

## SECRET ADMIRER *          15
David Greenwalt          USA          1986
*C. Thomas Howell, Lori Loughlin, Kelly Preston, Fred Ward, Dee Wallace Stone, Cliff De Young, Leigh Taylor-Young, Casey Siemaszko, Scott McGinnis, Geoffrey Blake*
An anonymous love letter complicates the lives of a group of teenagers and their parents, in this totally forgettable comedy. Attractive performances and a catchy score by Jan Hammer do little to rescue it.

| COM | 94 min (ort 98 min) |
| B,V | RNK |

## SECRET AGENT, THE **          U
Alfred Hitchcock          UK          1936
*Peter Lorre, Robert Young, Madeleine Carroll, John Gielgud, Percy Marmont, Lilli Palmer, Florence Kahn, Charles Carson, Michel Saint-Dennis, Andrea Malandrinos, Tom Helmore, Michael Redgrave, Howard Marion Crawford*
A pair of secret agents, posing as husband and wife, are sent to Switzerland on a mission of murder, in this blend of comedy and thriller genres. A curious film for Hitchcock, and one that doesn't work all that well, although there are some funny moments. Written by Charles Bennett and with musical direction by Louis Levy. The photography is by Bernard Knowles.
Boa: play by Campbell Dixon/short stories The Hairless Mexican and Triton from "Ashenden" by William Somerset Maugham.

| THR | 82 min (ort 86 min) B/W |
| B,V | RNK; VCC |

## SECRET BEYOND THE DOOR, THE **
Fritz Lang          USA          1948
*Michael Redgrave, Joan Bennett, Anne Revere, Barbara O'Neill, Natalie Schafer, Paul Cavanagh, Anabel Shaw, Rosa Rey, James Seay, Mark Dennis, Virginia Brissac, Houseley Stevenson, Marie Harmon, Kay Morley, Paul Fierro*
An heiress on vacation in Mexico meets a man she marries after a brief whirlwind courtship. However, as soon as the honeymoon is over she begins to suspect that her husband may have murdered his first wife and be planning to murder her too. Somewhat reminiscent of Hitchcock's SUSPICION, but too verbose and sluggish to build up any tension. Written by

Sylvia Richards and with music by Miklos Rozsa.
Boa: short story Museum Piece No. 13 by Rufus King.

| DRA | 79 min (ort 98 min) B/W |
| B,V | INT |

## SECRET DIARY OF ADRIAN MOLE AGED 13¾, PG THE *
Peter Sasdy          UK          1985
*Julie Walters, Stephen Moore, Gian Sammarco, Beryl Reid, Lindsay Stagg, Bill Fraser, Freddie Jones, Paul Greenwood, Doris Hare*
TV dramatisation of a laboured comedy that revolves around the obsessive self-interest of a young boy and his observations on life. Twee and almost unbearably unfunny, the series that inspired this dismal film was a real low water mark in the tradition of profoundly depressing and life-denying British comedies, their humour derived from an attitude of mind that portrays existence as something to be stoically endured.
Boa: novel by Sue Townsend.

| COM | 150 min (2 cassettes – ort 171 min) mTV |
| B,V | THAMES; VCC |

## SECRET EXECUTIONERS **          18
HONG KONG          198-
*Wong Chen-Li, Jim Norris, Peggy Min*
A martial arts expert forms a little band of fighters in an effort to free the city from the grip of a criminal gang. The gang responds by hiring some American assassins to remove this threat to their operations.

| MAR | 86 min (ort 90 min) |
| B,V | VPD |

## SECRET GARDEN, THE ***          U
Fred McLeod Wilcox          USA          1949
*Margaret O'Brien, Dean Stockwell, Herbert Marshall, Gladys Cooper, Elsa Lanchester, Brian Roper*
In Victorian times, a young orphan girl goes to live with her morose and secretive uncle. Her friendship with a strange boy and their adventures in a walled garden whose gate is always kept locked, has unexpected consequences but a happy outcome. A charming moral fable; slow, careful and atmospheric. Remade for TV in 1987.
Boa: novel by Frances Hodgson Burnett.

| JUV   89 min (ort 92 min) B/W (with colour sequences) |
| V | MGM |

## SECRET GARDEN, THE ***          U
Dorothea Brooking          UK          1975
*Sarah Hollis Andrews, David Patterson*
The story of a young girl who lives with her uncle in Yorkshire, and learns of a secret garden where she makes some new friends. A pleasant adaptation of Burnett's famous classic.
Boa: novel by Francis Hodgeson Burnett.

| JUV | 106 min (ort 210 min) mTV |
| V | BBC |

## SECRET HONOR **          15
Robert Altman          USA          1984
*Philip Baker Hall*
A mythical portrayal of US President Richard Nixon's attempts to cope with the death of his own political career after the huge Watergate scandal. The film is really a one-man show, with Hall as Nixon pacing his study and raging against all his real and imagined enemies. A weird experience that is a little hard to take in a single dose.

| COM | 86 min (ort 90 min) |
| V/s | HEND |

## SECRET INVASION, THE ***
Roger Corman          USA          1964
*Stewart Granger, Raf Vallone, Mickey Rooney, Edd Byrnes, Henry Silva, Mia Massini, William Campbell, Peter Coe*
A WW2 story, telling of five convicts who are given the chance to do their bit by working behind enemy

lines in Yugoslavia. An exciting and well-handled tale, exploring a theme that was to be used a little later in THE DIRTY DOZEN.
WAR                              94 min (ort 98 min)
V                                              WHV

## SECRET KILLING **                          PG
Charles Dubin          USA              1971
*Barbara Bain, John Forsythe, Richard Kiley, Joseph Campanella, Wendell Burton, Reta Shaw, Laurence Haddon*
A doctor attempts to commit a perfect murder but is finally brought to book. Undistinguished, despite good work from the cast.
Aka: MURDER ONCE REMOVED
DRA                    73 min; 71 min (KRP) mTV
B,V                                 VDEL L/A; KRP

## SECRET LIFE OF WALTER MITTY, THE ***        U
Norman Z. McLeod       USA              1947
*Danny Kaye, Virginia Mayo, Boris Karloff, Fay Bainter, Ann Rutherford, Florence Bates, Thurston Hall, Gordon Jones, Reginald Denny, Fritz Feld*
Danny Kaye is splendid as an incorrigible daydreamer in this very, very loose adaptation of a James Thurber short story. He spends his days dreaming of heroic deeds but is a little taken aback when he finds himself involved in a real-life spy plot. The early fantasy sequences are the highlight of the film, and the later complexities are far less amusing.
Boa: short story by James Thurber.
COM                             106 min (ort 110 min)
V                                              VGM

## SECRET LIVES OF THE BRITISH
## PRIME MINISTERS, THE: ASQUITH **
David Cunliffe         UK               1983
*David Langton, Dorothy Tutin, Michelle Sachs, Rupert Frazer, Tony Steedman, Alan Rowe, Neville Barber*
A potted biography of Sir Henry Asquith during his time as P.M. that concentrates on his controversial social reforms such as old-age pensions and unemployment insurance.
Aka: ASQUITHS, THE; ASQUITH: THE TAX SCANDAL; SIR HENRY ASQUITH
DRA                             55 min (ort 60 min) mTV
B,V                                         CAREY

## SECRET LIVES OF THE BRITISH
## PRIME MINISTERS, THE: DISRAELI **
Alvin Rakoff           UK               1981
*Richard Pasco, Nicholas Jones, James Grant, Zena Walker, Elizabeth Sellars, Evelyn Laye, Geoffrey Toone*
A biography of the life of Disraeli, one of Britain's most flamboyant and colourful prime ministers.
Aka: BENJAMIN DISRAELI; DISRAELI; DIZZY; NUMBER                              DIZZY
DRA                             55 min (ort 60 min) mTV
B,V                                         CAREY

## SECRET LIVES OF THE BRITISH
## PRIME MINISTERS, THE: GLADSTONE **
Herbert Wise           UK               1981
*Dennis Quilley, Celia Johnson, Frank Middlemass*
Yet another biography of a British P.M. which this time concentrates on Gladstone and his efforts at helping fallen women, which were easily and somewhat deliberately misconstrued.
Aka: GLADSTONE: THE PROSTITUTE SCANDAL; OLD GLAD EYES
DRA                             55 min (ort 60 min) mTV
B,V                                         CAREY

## SECRET LIVES OF THE BRITISH
## PRIME MINISTERS, THE: LLOYD GEORGE **
Herbert Wise           UK               1983
*John Stride, Rhoda Lewis, Barbara Kellerman*

A potted biography of the career of Lloyd George, with the emphasis firmly placed on the more lurid aspects of his private life.
Aka: DAVID LLOYD GEORGE; LLOYD GEORGE: THE MENAGE A TROIS SCANDAL; WOMAN OF STYLE, A
DRA                             55 min (ort 60 min) mTV
B,V                                         CAREY

## SECRET LIVES OF THE BRITISH
## PRIME MINISTERS, THE: MACDONALD **
David Reynolds         UK               1983
*Ian Richardson, Emma Piper, Antonia Pemberton, Emrys James, Marian Owen Smith, Robert Urquhart, Norman Jones*
A dramatised account of the private life of one of Britain's first Labour Party prime ministers.
Aka: JAMES RAMSAY MACDONALD; MACDONALD; UNDERDOG
DRA                             55 min (ort 60 min) mTV
B,V                                         CAREY

## SECRET LIVES OF THE BRITISH
## PRIME MINISTERS, THE: PITT **
David Reynolds         UK               1983
*Jeremy Brett, Albert Burke, Keith Barron, Patrick Newell, William Simons, Jeffrey Wickham*
Fictionalised biography of both the elder and the younger Pitt.
Aka: BLOODLINE; PITT: THE YOUNGER GIRL SCANDAL
DRA                                     55 min mTV
B,V                                         CAREY

## SECRET LIVES OF THE BRITISH
## PRIME MINISTERS, THE: THE IRON DUKE **
John Glenister         UK               1983
*Bernard Archer, Gabrielle Drake, Philip Latham, Derek Royle, Michael Barrington*
A fictionalised biography, that concentrates on the private life of the Duke of Wellington when he was prime minister, and explains how he managed to go from national wartime hero to a political embarrassment and the most despised man in the country (his house was stoned by a furious mob) in a mere 18 months.
Aka: DUKE OF WELLINGTON, THE; IRON DUKE, THE; SECRET LIVES OF THE BRITISH PRIME MINISTERS, THE: THE DUKE OF WELLINGTON; WELLINGTON: THE DUEL SCANDAL
DRA                             55 min (ort 60 min) mTV
B,V                                         CAREY

## SECRET NINJA, ROARING TIGER **          18
Godfrey Ho             HONG KONG         198-
*Dragon Lee, Wong Cheng Li, Jack Lam*
When the daughter of a millionaire is kidnapped by a Ninja sect, a martial arts master undertakes a perilous mission to rescue her.
MAR                        80 min Cut (1 min 37 sec)
B,V                                           VPD

## SECRET OF MY SUCCESS, THE **             PG
Herbert Ross           USA               1987
*Michael J. Fox, Helen Slater, Margaret Whitton, Richard Jordan, John Pankow, Christopher Murney, Gerry Bamman, Fred Gwynne, Carol-Ann Susi*
An ambitious and clever country boy comes to the big city where he works his way up in the world, encountering various complications along the way. A bright and cheerful comedy that is sustained by an attractive performance from Fox, but eventually runs out of ideas.
COM                             106 min (ort 110 min)
V/sh                                           CIC

## SECRET OF NIMH, THE ***                   U
Don Bluth              USA               1982

*Voices of: Derek Jacobi, Dom DeLuise, John Carradine, Peter Strauss, Aldo Ray, Elizabeth Hartman, Hermione Baddeley, Edie McClurg*
Quality animated feature produced by a group of defectors from the Disney studios, all about a widowed mouse who fights to save her family homestead from imps and seeks help from super-intelligent rats. Written by Bluth (in his directorial debut), John Pomeroy, Gary Foldman and Will Finn. The music is by Jerry Goldsmith.
Boa: novel Mrs Frisby And The Rats Of Nimh by Robert C. O'Brien.
CAR                          79 min (ort 82 min)
V                                          WHV

**SECRET OF SEAGULL ISLAND, THE ****
Nestore Ungaro       ITALY            1981
*Jeremy Brett, Nicky Henson, Prunella Ransom*
An attractive blind girl disappears and the search points to a mysterious bleak island. Compiled from a 300-minute TV mini-series and based on a story by the director.
Aka: SEAGULL ISLAND
DRA                                 103 min mTV
B,V                                        PRV

**SECRET OF THE BLACK DRAGON, THE ****   PG
Sigi Rothemund                          1985
        NETHERLANDS/USA/WEST GERMANY/
                YUGOSLAVIA
*Julian Glover, Tommi Ohrner, Charles Braure, Ritza Brown, Oleg Vidov, Sarah Lam, Ronald Beer, Kunihiro Ohta, Heinz Wanitschek, Relja Basic, Andy Ho, Ake Lindman, Zdenko Jelcic, Drago Mitrovic*
Historical tale set in 1648 amidst the chaos of the Thirty Year War, when a German baron sends an expedition to find a new land route to China and conclude a trade treaty with that country. Along the way, they have many a close shave and find themselves embroiled in the search for a fabulous gold treasure. A watchable if undistinguished adventure romp.
A/AD                              228 min dubbed
V                                         PALAN

**SECRET OF THE ICE CAVE, THE ****       PG
Radu Gabrea                             1989
*Sally Kellerman, Michael Moriarty, David Mendenhall*
A youngster decides to visit his scientist mom whom he hasn't seen for years, but as she is now working in a remote part of Chile he is obliged to stowaway onboard a private plane in order to complete his journey. He survives a plane crash and when the dying pilot gives him a map to hidden treasure he sets out to find it. A fast-moving, juvenile romp that is always diverting but never memorable.
A/AD                                     102 min
V                                         PATHE

**SECRET OF THE SAHARA ****              15
Alberto Negrin       ITALY            1988
*Michael York, Ben Kingsley, James Farentino, Andie McDowell, David Soul, Mathilda May, Delia Boccardo*
An archaeologist sets out to find the legendary "Talking Mountain" and has to fight off attacks from Foreign Legion deserters and others hazards. A watchable action yarn.
A/AD                       110 min; 123 min (BRAVE)
B,V                    IVS L/A; BRAVE (VHS only)

**SECRET OF THE SHAOLIN POLES, THE ****
                HONG KONG              197-
*Meng Fei, Delon Tam, Shoji Karada, Chang Yi*
This martial arts film features the art of pole fighting.
MAR                                       90 min
B,V                                       OCEAN

**SECRET PLACES ****                      15
Zelda Barron         UK               1984
*Marie-Therese Relin, Tara MacGowran, Claudine Auger, Jenny Agutter, Cassie Stuart, Ann-Marie Gwatkin, Pippa Hinchley, Klaus Barner, Sylvia Coleridge, Rosemary Martin, Amanda Grinling, Veronica Clifford, Adam Richardson*
The enclosed world of a girls' boarding school in England during WW2, forms the backdrop to a story of friendship between two girls. Despite the appeal of the leads this story lacks substance, although there are a few touching moments.
Boa: novel by Janice Elliott.
DRA                          94 min (ort 98 min)
B,V                                        RNK

**SECRET SEX LIVES OF ROMEO
AND JULIET, THE ****                     18
A.P. Stootsberry     USA              1969
*Dicora Carse, Forman Chane, Mickey Jines*
An attempt to turn Shakespeare's tragedy into a sex film, and only really remarkable for having been banned in the USA at one time.
Aka: SECRET LOVE LIVES OF ROMEO AND JULIET, THE; SECRET SEX LIFE OF ROMEO AND JULIET, THE
A                            88 min (ort 96 min)
B,V                          TCX; 18PLAT/TOW

**SECRETS ***                             15
Philip Saville       USA              1971
*Jacqueline Bisset, Per Oscarsson, Shirley Knight Hopkins, Robert Powell, Takra Kings, Martin C. Thurley*
Three members of one family, husband, wife and daughter, all have sex during the same day and must keep this a secret from the others. This one will pin you to your armchair – asleep. Remade for TV in 1978.
DRA                          75 min (ort 86 min)
B,V,V2                       MMA; INT; GHV

**SECRETS OF A DOOR-TO-DOOR SALESMAN ***  18
Wolf Rilla           UK               1973
*Brendan Price, Graham Stark, Chic Murray, Bernard Spear, Sue Longhurst, Felicity Devonshire, Jean Harrington, Johnny Briggs, Elizabeth Romilly, Jacqueline Logan, Victoria Burgoyne, Noelle Finch, Geraldine Hart*
A lobster fisherman sells up and moves to London, but his attempts to make a living as a door-to-door salesman are ruined by all the oversexed housewives he keeps meeting. Feeble.
COM                  54 min; 79 min (STABL)
B,V                         WOV L/A; STABL

**SECRETS OF A FRENCH MAID ****           18
Michael Thomas (Erwin C. Dietrich)
                SWITZERLAND
*Brigitte Lahaie, Celina Mood, Nadine Pascal, Erwin C. Dietrich*
A young maid provides a wide variety of services to all members of her household, in this unmemorable sex romp.
A                            80 min (ort 90 min)
B,V                              BEV L/A; KRP

**SECRETS OF A MARRIED MAN ***            18
William A. Graham
                ITALY/UK/USA           1984
*William Shatner, Michelle Phillips, Cybill Shepherd, Glynn Turman, Jackson Davies, Kevin George, Wally Marsh, Tiffany Michas, Dameon Clark, Dale Wilson, Blu Mankuma, J.C. Roberts, Shirley Barekay, Don MacKay, Moira Walley*
A married man finds himself having an affair with a prostitute, which puts his marriage in jeopardy. A silly melodrama with very little going for it.
DRA                     92 min (ort 100 min) mTV
B,V                            PRV L/A; CH5

## SECRETS OF A STUDENT NURSE **
Stephanie Rothman        USA               1970
*Karen Carlson, Elaine Giftos, Brioni Farrell, Barbara
Leigh, Keri Stanton, Reni Santoni, Richard Rust*
The first film produced by Roger Corman's New World
Pictures studio was also the first of five films purport-
ing to deal with the lives and antics of a group of
nurses. None are as titillating as their titles suggest,
though this one has a good script (co-written by the
director) that includes a thoughtful sub-plot dealing
with a nurse's guilt feelings at having caused an
accidental death. See also THE YOUNG NURSES
and CANDY STRIPE NURSES.
Aka: STUDENT NURSES, THE
COM                          81 min (ort 89 min)
B,V                          ATA L/A; CYC; APX

## SECRETS OF A SUPERSTUD *
Morton M. Lewis        UK                 1975
*Anthony Kenyan, Mark Jones, Jenny Westbrook, Janet
Adler, Bobby Sparrow, Alan Hendrick, Paula Martin,
Joanna Richards, Juliette Groves, Margaret Burton,
Raymond Young, David Pugh, Alan Selwyn, Candida
Hershman*
In order to inherit a fortune, a man must marry and
produce an heir within a year. A relative and her son
do all they can to frustrate his plans in this dismal
British sex farce.
A                                      103 min
B,V                                    MOV; APX

## SECRETS OF LADY TRUCKERS *              18
Stu Segall        USA                     198-
*Valdesta, Jack Barnes, Elke Van, Janice Jordan,
Catherine Barkley*
Hookers use a trucking business as a front for their
more horizontal activities.
A                            72 min (ort 90 min)
B,V                          BEV L/A; KRP

## SECRETS OF THE PHANTOM CAVERNS **        15
Don Sharp        USA        1983 (released 1984)
*Robert Powell, Lisa Blount, Timothy Bottoms, Anne
Heywood, Richard Johnson, A.C. Weary, Jackson
Bostwick, Richard Beauchamp, William Gribble, Carl
Spurlock, Jason Laskay, Liam Sullivan, Carlos
Cervantes, Tim Powell*
A race of cave dwellers turn nasty, when they are
disturbed by a group of soldiers, who are part of an
expedition to install a sonar device in an underground
cavern. A strong cast can do little with this flabby
yarn.
Aka: WHAT WAITS BELOW
HOR                                    88 min
B,V                                    RNK

## SECRETS OF THE PIRATE'S INN **           U
Gary Nelson        USA                    1969
*Ed Begley, Charles Aidman, Jimmy Bracken, Annie
McEverty, Patrick Creamer*
Compiled from a TV serial, this adventure follows the
exploits of a retired sea captain and three kids, who
embark on a search for treasure in a deserted
mansion.
A/AD                                   89 min mTV
B,V                                    WDV

## SECRETS OF YOUNG NURSES *
Clinton Kimbro        USA                 1973
*Jean Manson, Ashley Porter, Angela Gibbs, Zack
Taylor, Jack La Rue Jr, William Joyce*
A nurse tracks down the drug dealer responsible for
her friend's death. A wild mixture of second-rate
simulated sex, not helped by a plot that is every bit as
limp.
Aka: GAMES THAT NURSES PLAY; YOUNG
NURSE, THE
A                                      72 min
B,V                          ATA L/A; APX

## SEDUCED **                                15
Jerrold Freedman        USA               1985
*Gregory Harrison, Cybill Shepherd, Jose Ferrer, Mel
Ferrer, Adrienne Barbeau, Michael C. Gwynne, Paul
Stewart, Ray Wise, Karmin Murcelo, Jordan
Christopher, Felton Perry, Wally Taylor, Michele
Greene, Barbara Pilavin*
A mediocre tale of power politics among the beautiful
and rich, as a politician tracks down the murderer of
his mistress, the wife of a rich businessman.
DRA                          91 min (ort 100 min) mTV
B,V                                    CBS

## SEDUCTION OF JOE TYNAN, THE ***          15
Jerry Schatzberg        USA               1979
*Alan Alda, Meryl Steep, Rip Torn, Barbara Harris,
Charles Kimbrough, Melvyn Douglas, Blanche Baker,
Adam Ross, Carrie Nye, Chris Arnold*
An examination of the corroding effect of political
power on integrity and family relationships, with the
central figure a liberal senator who has to contend
with a variety of pitfalls in his climb to the top. Not
quite in the same league as "All The King's Men" but
not bad either, though the climax is a big let down.
Written by Alda.
DRA                          102 min (ort 107 min)
V/h                                    CIC

## SEDUCTION OF LYNN CARTER, THE ***
Wes Browne        USA                     1974
*Jamie Gillis, Sharon Thorpe, Andrew True, Tony
Rousso, Peter Gibbs*
On their last night together before he goes off on a
business trip, a man and his wife discuss extramarital
affairs. The very next day she finds herself drawn into
an adulterous relationship, and by the time her
husband returns, she is well and truly hooked and
unable to break free. An absorbing and quite believable tale that ends with her confessing her infidelity
to her husband, but makes no attempt to resolve their
marital crisis.
A                                      84 min
B,V                                    VCO L/A

## SEE CHINA AND DIE **                     PG
Larry Cohen        USA                    1981
*Yaphet Kotto, Andrew Duggan, Esther Rolle, Joyce
Van Patten, Kene Holliday, Frank Converse, Paul
Dooley, Claude Brooks, William Walker III, Jean
Marsh, Laurene Luckinbill, Fritz Weaver, Jack Straw,
Jane Hickox*
A black hotel cleaner teams up with her cop son, to
solve the mystery of a guest she found murdered in his
room. Fair pilot for a series that was never made.
Aka: HEARSAY (TRUE); MOMMA THE
DETECTIVE
DRA                                    87 min mTV
B,V                          SKP; TRUE; REV; XTASY

## SEE HOW SHE RUNS ***
Richard T. Heffron        USA             1978
*Joanne Woodward, John Considine, Lissy Newman,
Mary Beth Manning, Barnard Hughes, Barbara Meek,
James Houghton, Linda Peterson, Chris Anastasio,
Harvey Reed, Tom Kemp, Nancy Tates, Annette Miller,
Frank Dolan*
A divorced woman teacher over 40 takes up running
and jogging as a means of coming to terms with her
life, and eventually enters the Boston marathon. One
of her daughters is played by real-life daughter
Newman in her acting debut. A likeable and rather
touching drama. An Emmy Award went to Woodward.
DRA                                    104 min mTV
B,V                                    CAP; CBS

## SEE NO EVIL, HEAR NO EVIL **             15
Arthur Hiller        USA                  1989
*Richard Pryor, Gene Wilder, Joan Severance, Kevin
Spacey, Kirsten Childs, Alan North, Anthony Zerbe*

Wilder and Pryor are two handicapped buddies who are respectively deaf and blind. Having witnessed a murder and become suspects, each tries to hide his disability and they go on the run from both killer and cops. The two stars work well together and although the comic sequences are never cruel, the utterly contrived and disagreeably foul-mouthed script gives them little chance to shine.
COM 98 min (ort 103 min) subH
V 20VIS

### SEE YOU IN THE MORNING ** 15
Alan J. Pakula USA 1988
*Jeff Bridges, Alice Krige, Farrah Fawcett, Linda Lavin, Drew Barrymore, Lukas Haas, David Dukes, Frances Sternhagen, Theodore Bikel*
A New York psychiatrist struggles to get over the trauma of his failed marriage, and balance the obligations he still has to his former wife and kids, against his role as stepfather to his new wife's children. A touching character study that blends comedy and drama fairly agreeably, but is spoilt by contrived scripting and a disappointing ending. The screenplay is by Pakula.
COM 114 min (ort 119 min)
V/sh GHV

### SEED OF INNOCENCE ** 
Boaz Davidson USA 1980
*Tim Wead, Mary Cannon, T.K. Carter, Vincent Schiavelli, Azizi Johari, Shirley Stoler*
Two teenagers fall in love and run away to New York after the girl becomes pregnant. An overblown and somewhat contrived melodrama.
DRA 86 min (ort 91 min)
B,V RNK

### SEEKERS, THE ** 15
Sidney Hayers USA 1979
*Randolph Mantooth, Edie Adams, Neville Brand, John Carradine, Delta Burke, George DeLoy, Julie Gregg, Rosey Grier, George Hamilton, Alex Hyde-White, Harriet Karr, Brian Keith, Donald Mantooth, Ross Martin, Gary Merrill*
Third instalment in the saga consisting of THE BASTARD and THE REBELS, with Philip Kent and his two sons off on an expedition exploring the Northwest. A colourful but rather slow-moving and predictable tale, adapted from the American Revolution novels of John Jakes.
Boa: novel by John Jakes.
DRA 182 min (ort 200 min) mTV
B,V CIC

### SEEMS LIKE OLD TIMES *** PG
Jay Sandrich USA 1980
*Goldie Hawn, Chevy Chase, Charles Grodin, Robert Guillaume, Harold Gould, George Grizzard, Yvonne Wilder, T.K. Carter, Judd Omen, Marc Alaimo*
Film version of a play about a woman living in the 1930s, whose life with her new husband is jeopardised by the crazy antics of her old one. A lightweight farce that ambles along most enjoyably with but the occasional lapse. Written by Simon. This was the feature debut of TV director Sandrich.
Boa: play by Neil Simon.
COM 98 min (ort 121 min)
V RCA

### SEIZE THE DAY *** PG
Fielder Cook USA 1986
*Robin Williams, Joseph Wiseman, Jerry Stiller, Glenne Headly, Tony Roberts, Richard Shull, John Fielder, Jo Van Fleet, William Hickey, Eileen Heckart*
The story of a middle-aged failure who has lost his job, and the manner in which he attempts to come to terms with his life. An absorbing but depressing tale of naive trust and broken promises. Despite the unappealing nature of the material, a fine performance

from Williams gives it substance. Written by Ronald Ribman.
Boa: novel by Saul Bellow.
DRA 94 min
V VES

### SELL-OUT, THE ** 15
Peter Collinson ISRAEL/ITALY/USA 1976
*Richard Widmark, Oliver Reed, Gayle Hunnicutt, Sam Wanamaker, Ori Levy, Vladek Sheybel, Assaf Dayan, Shmuel Rodensky, Peter Frye*
A double agent is lured to Jerusalem where both sides try to kill him. An over-complex spy thriller, with a veneer of violence that does little to mask the shallowness of the plot.
Aka: LA SPIA SENZA DOMANI; MELIMOT BEYERUSHALAIM
THR 97 min (ort 102 min)
B,V WHV

### SEMI-TOUGH ** 15
Michael Ritchie USA 1977
*Burt Reynolds, Kris Kristofferson, Jill Clayburgh, Robert Preston, Bert Convy, Lotte Lenya, Roger E. Mosley, Richard Masur, Carl Weathers, Brian Dennehy, Mary Jo Catlett*
A comic look at two football stars and their girlfriends, that is meandering and unstructured, though not without one or two mildly amusing moments. Adapted from the novel by Ring Lardner Jr (who took his name off the credits) and Walter Bernstein. Later a brief TV series.
Boa: novel by Dan Jenkins.
COM 105 min (ort 107 min)
B,V WHV

### SENATOR'S DAUGHTER, THE *** 
Don Flowers USA 1979
*John C. Holmes, Leslie Bovee, Linda West, Peter Whigam, Gloria Throate, Bert Hupley*
Amusingly silly spoof on the TV series "The Six Million Dollar Man", telling the story of women being kidnapped by Russian agents and brainwashed into working as "seduction units". In order to rescue them, the government creates a well-endowed bionic man, using as a subject a man badly injured in a car crash. Needless to say, he rescues all the women, but not before he has thoroughly sampled their charms.
A 70 min
B,V CAL

### SENDER, THE *** 18
Roger Christian UK 1982
*Zeljko Ivanek, Kathryn Harrold, Shirley Knight, Paul Freeman, Sean Hewitt, Harry Ditson, Olivier Pierre, Tracy Harper, Al Matthews, Marsha Hunt, Angus MacInnes, Jana Sheldon, Monica Buferd, Manning Redwood, John Stephen Hill*
A telepathic individual is unable to control his nightmares, and causes havoc in a hospital to which he has been confined with amnesia, after making a suicide attempt. An intriguing and quite gripping tale.
THR 87 min (ort 91 min)
B,V CIC

### SENSATIONS ** 18
Chuck Vincent USA 1987
*Rebecca Lynn, Blake Bahner, Jennifer Delora, Rick Savage, Loretta Palma, Frank Stewart*
A prostitute and a hustler find they each have half of a winning lottery ticket and will have to get married in order to collect. Unfortunately, they cannot stand each other.
COM 88 min (ort 91 min)
B,V FUTUR

## SENSE AND SENSIBILITY ** U
Rodney Bennett UK 1980
*Irene Richard, Tracey Childs, Diana Fairfax*
A compilation of a TV serial adaptation of the famous novel, telling of the hapless Dashwoods who suffer indignity and the loss of their family home at the hands of their snobbish relatives. A lavish and detailed saga that draws on the strengths of Austen's work, but is somewhat sluggish in development.
Boa: novel by Jane Austen.
DRA 173 min mTV
V/h BBC

## SENSE OF FREEDOM, A ** 18
John McKenzie UK 1979
*David Hayman, Alex Norton, Fulton MacKay, Jake D'Arcy, Sean Scanlon*
Partially based on the true story of Jimmy Boyle, this tells of the imprisonment and eventual rehabilitation of a convicted murderer. An abundance of unpleasant detail cannot mask the superficial treatment his story is given. Average. Written by Peter MacDougall.
Boa: book by Jimmy Boyle.
DRA 85 min (ort 104 min) mTV
B,V TEVP

## SENSITIVE PASSIONATE MAN, A * 15
John Newland USA 1977
*David Janssen, Angie Dickinson, Richard Venture, Mariclare Costello, Todd Lookinland, Justin Randi, Rhodes Reason, Richard Bull, Terry Hinz, Marged Wakely, Laura Campbell, Beverly Carter, Frederick Hoffman, Craig Littler*
An aerospace engineer who has lost his job is, as if by magic, immediately transformed into a self-destructive and alcoholic nutter, in this overwrought and quite tedious dud.
Boa: book by Barbara Mahoney.
DRA 100 min; 96 min (PARA) mTV
B,V VFP: PARA

## SENSUAL FIRE * R18
Troy Benny USA 1979
*Serena, Dorothy LeMay, Jesie St James, Lucy Tellerman, Jamie Gillis*
A man remarries and finds that he has developed an obsession for his new wife's pretty teenage daughter. As his obsession grows, he tries to find ways of controlling it, even to the extent of searching for a lookalike of the girl. But even that doesn't help and so he eventually takes the opportunity of a costumed ball to make love to her, in this slight and vacuous tale.
A 83 min Cut (1 min 48 sec)
B,V,V2 ELV

## SENSUALIST, THE *** 18
Paul Verhoeven NETHERLANDS 1973
*Monique Van de Ven, Rutger Hauer, Tonny Huurdeman, Wim Van Den Brink, Hans Bokamp*
A hippie sculptor marries a girl from a well-to-do family, but they eventually split up and he tries to find solace by sleeping with as many women as possible. Some time later they meet, but under sad circumstances. A vigorous, uncompromising and quite disturbing tale, hampered slightly by ponderous direction and a few clumsy attempts at satire.
Aka: TURKISH DELIGHT; TURKS FRUIT
Boa: novel by Jan Wolkers.
DRA 101 min (ort 106 min) Cut (39 sec)
B,V RCA

## SENSUOUS DETECTIVE, THE ** 18
M.M. Dimitri USA
*John Leslie, Serena, Laurien Dominique, Jesie St James*
Sex film using the familiar plot of a private eye being hired to find the missing heirs to a fortune. Average.
Osca: ONE WAY AT A TIME/SEX HUNTERS, THE (asa)
A 53 min (ort 67 min) Cut
B,V HAR

## SENTINEL, THE ** 18
Michael Winner USA 1976
*Cristina Raines, Ava Gardner, Chris Sarandon, Burgess Meredith, Sylvia Miles, Jose Ferrer, John Carradine, Arthur Kennedy, Deborah Raffin, Eli Wallach, Christopher Walken, Jerry Orbach, Beverly D'Angelo, Tom Berenger*
A fashion model discovers that the apartment block she has rented in Brooklyn Heights is inhabited by demons, and that she is destined to be the next sentinel guarding the gateway to Hell, over which the block has (rather unwisely it would seem) been built. A flashy but rather shallow yarn. See also THE BEYOND for something on a similar theme.
Boa: novel by Jeffrey Konvitz.
HOR 88 min (ort 92 min)
B,V CIC

## SEPARATE TABLES ** PG
John Schlesinger UK 1983
*Alan Bates, Julie Christie, Claire Bloom, Irene Worth, Liz Smith, Bernard Archard, Brian Deacon, Kathy Staff*
A TV version of the well-known one-act play, exploring the hopes and lives of a group of boarders staying at a small guest house. Quite well made, but almost unbearably stagebound.
Boa: play by Terence Rattigan
DRA 113 min mTV
B,V MGM

## SEPARATE VACATIONS ** 18
Michael Anderson USA 1986
*David Naughton, Jennifer Dale, Mark Keyloun, Lally Cadeau, Blanca Cuerra, Susan Almgren, Laurie Holdeu, Tony Rosato*
A husband with a seven-year-itch, goes on holiday by himself to Mexico in search of a quick fling, but makes a complete mess of it while his wife enjoys success without even trying. A hackneyed old formula comedy.
Boa: novel by Eric Webber.
COM 90 min (ort 94 min)
B,V MED

## SEPTEMBER ** PG
Woody Allen USA 1987
*Mia Farrow, Denholm Elliott, Sam Waterston, Dianne Wiest, Jack Warden, Elaine Strich, Ira Wheeler, Jane Cecil, Rosemary Murphy*
Back to the serious side of life as seen through Allen's distorting mirror, as six characters on summer vacation in Vermont indulge their assorted anxieties and obsessions. Despite good performances and an intelligent script, this one becomes very tiresome very quickly.
DRA 79 min (ort 82 min)
B,V VIR

## SERGEANT DEADHEAD ** U
Norman Taurog USA 1965
*Frankie Avalon, Deborah Walley, Eve Arden, Cesar Romero, Fred Clark, Buster Keaton, Gale Gordon, Harvey Lembeck, John Ashley*
An accident prone US sergeant is shot into space together with a chimp, and undergoes a personality change in this dated and silly comedy. Written by Louis M. Heyward.
Aka: SERGEANT DEADHEAD, THE ASTRONAUT
COM 86 min (ort 89 min) B/W
B,V RCA

## SERGEANT KLEMS ** 
Sergio Grieco ITALY 1972
*Peter Strauss, Howard Ross, Tina Aumont, Pier Paolo Capponi*

A sergeant decides to desert from the Foreign Legion.
Average.
Aka: IL SERGENTE KLEMS
DRA                                         96 min
B,V,V2                                       VPD

## SERGEANT PEPPER'S LONELY          PG
## HEARTS CLUB BAND *
Michael Schultz          USA               1978
*Peter Frampton, The Bee Gees, George Burns, Donald*
*Pleasence, Frankie Howerd, Sandy Farina, Dianne*
*Steinberg, Paul Nicholas, Earth, Wind and Fire, Billy*
*Preston, Steve Martin*
A failed and sorry attempt to add a set of visual
sequences and a storyline to the songs from the
Beatles' album of the same name. Give this one a miss
and get the album instead.
MUS                                        108 min
B,V                                         CIC

## SERGEANT YORK ****                 U
Howard Hawks             USA               1941
*Gary Cooper, Walter Brennan, Joan Leslie, George*
*Tobias, Noah Beery Jr, June Lockhart, David Bruce,*
*Stanley Ridges, Margaret Wycherly, Dickie Moore,*
*Ward Bond, George Tobias*
The true story of a one-time hillbilly and pacifist
Sergeant Alvin York, who became a hero in WW1 by
singlehandedly capturing 132 German soldiers. An
excellent tale that never becomes maudlin yet still
manages to make its points with considerable force.
Written by Abem Finkel, Harry Chandler, Howard
Koch and John Huston. AA: Actor (Cooper).
Boa: book Sergeant York And His People by S.K.
Cowan.
WAR                       129 min (ort 134 min) B/W
V                                           WHV

## SERIAL ***                          18
Bill Persky              USA               1980
*Martin Mull, Tuesday Weld, Sally Kellerman, Bill*
*Macy, Christopher Lee, Tom Smothers, Pamela*
*Bellwood, Jennifer McAlister, Sam Chew Jr, Nita*
*Talbot, Anthony Battaglia, Barbara Rhoades, Peter*
*Bonerz*
An amusing and satirical look at assorted Californian
trendies and their various obsessions and fads. Mull's
first starring role. Written by Rich Eustis and Michael
Elias.
Boa: novel by Cyra McFadden.
COM                         87 min (ort 91 min)
B,V                                         CIC

## SERIOUS CHARGE **                  PG
Terence Young            UK                1959
*Anthony Quayle, Andrew Ray, Sarah Churchill, Irene*
*Browne, Percy Herbert, Cliff Richard, Liliane Brousse,*
*Noel Howlett, Wensley Pithey, Leigh Madison, Wilfred*
*Pickles, Jean Cadell, Oliver Sloane*
After a local layabout is accused by a priest of being
instrumental in causing the death of a girl, the former
has his revenge by accusing the priest of making
homosexual advances towards him. One of those films
that was formerly daring and therefore absorbing, but
now looks merely dated.
Boa: play by Philip King.
DRA                         90 min (ort 99 min) B/W
V                                           ODY

## SERPENT AND THE RAINBOW, THE ***   18
Wes Craven               USA               1987
*Bill Pullman, Cathy Tyson, Zakes Mokae, Paul*
*Winfield, Brent Jennings, Theresa Merritt, Michael*
*Gough*
Supposedly based on the experiences of Wade Davis,
this tells of an anthropologist who is sent to investi-
gate the phenomenon of zombies, who have been
created by the use of drugs and voodoo rituals. Despite
support from a local psychiatrist, he soon finds that

the tribal leaders are determined to protect their
secrets, in this predictable but highly effective shock-
er. Filmed on location in Haiti.
Boa: book by Wade Davis.
HOR                    94 min (ort 98 min) Cut (5 sec)
B,V                                         CIC

## SERPENT, THE **
Henri Verneuil      FRANCE/ITALY           1974
*Yul Brynner, Henry Fonda, Dirk Bogarde, Philippe*
*Noiret, Virna Lisi, Farley Granger, Robert Alda*
Brynner as a top Soviet official defects to the West and
various problems arise, not least being the manner in
which the international cast gets bogged down in the
muddled and over-complex plot. Written by Henri
Verneuil and Giles Perrault. Photography is by
Claude Renoir.
Aka: NIGHT FLIGHT FROM MOSCOW
Boa: novel Le 13e Suicide by Pierre Nord.
THR                         117 min (ort 124 min)
B,V                                         VPD

## SERPENT'S EGG, THE **             18
Ingmar Bergman
                     USA/WEST GERMANY      1977
*Liv Ullmann, David Carradine, Gert Frobe, Heinz*
*Bennett, Glynn Turman, James Whitmore*
An American Jewish trapeze artist in Berlin at the
time of Hitler's rise to power is surrounded by
depravity and corruption. A cluttered mess of splendid
photography (by Sven Nykvist), interesting art direc-
tion and general nastiness. A big misfire for the
director, who also wrote the script.
DRA                                        120 min
V                                           CASPIC

## SERPICO ****                       18
Sidney Lumet             USA               1973
*Al Pacino, John Randolph, Jack Kehoe, Biff McGuire,*
*Barbara Eda-Young, Cornelia Sharpe, Tony Roberts,*
*James Tolkan, Lewis J. Stradlen, M. Emmet Walsh, F.*
*Murray Abraham, Kenneth McMillan*
Based on a true story, this tells of a New York cop who
is so shocked at the widespread corruption inside the
force that he stages a one-man crusade. A harsh and
uncompromising film, with powerful performances
and a good script. Written by Waldo Salt and Norman
Wexler, with music by Mikis Theodorakis. Followed
in 1976 by the pilot for a TV series – "Serpico: The
Deadly Game". See also THE PRINCE OF THE CITY.
Boa: book by Peter Maas.
DRA                         125 min (ort 130 min)
B,V                                         CIC

## SERVANT, THE ***                   15
Joseph Losey             UK                1963
*Dirk Bogarde, James Fox, Sarah Miles, Wendy Craig,*
*Catherine Lacy, Patrick Magee, Richard Vernon,*
*Brian Phelan, Dorothy Bromiley, Hazel Terry, Alison*
*Seebohm, Philippa Hare, Alun Owne, Harold Pinter*
A crafty servant eventually comes to dominate his
weak-willed master, in this fine drama with Fox well
cast as the ineffectual employer, gradually debased by
servant Bogarde and his sister. Written by Harold
Pinter with music by Johnny Dankworth.
Boa: novel by Robin Maugham.
DRA        112 min; 111 min (WHV) (ort 116 min) B/W
B,V                        TEVP; WHV (VHS only)

## SESSIONS **                        18
Richard Pearce           USA               1983
*Veronica Hamel, Jeffrey DeMunn, Jill Eikenberry,*
*David Marshall Grant, Deborah Hedwall, George Coe,*
*Doris Belack, Henderson Forsythe, Jo Henderson, Ann*
*Lange, Tracy Pollan, Heather Denna, Carrie Kei Hein,*
*Lenny Von Dohlen*
A high-class call girl begins to have doubts about her
way of life in this fairly unmemorable effort. This
gave Hamel her first starring role after her prominent

part in the TV police series "Hill Street Blues".
DRA                          92 min (ort 100 min) mTV
B,V                          VCL L/A; VIR

## SEVEN **                                              18
Andy Sidaris           USA                       1979
*William Smith, Guich Koock, Barbara Leigh, Art*
*Metrano, Martin Kove, Richard Le Pore, Susan Kiger*
A muscleman is hired by US Intelligence, and sent to
Hawaii to stop seven crime families from negotiating
a merger of their empires into a super-syndicate. A
violent drama with a few redeeming touches of
humour.
DRA                          97 min (ort 102 min) Cut (23 sec)
B,V                          RNK

## SEVEN ALONE **
Earl Bellamy           USA                       1975
*Dewey Martin, Aldo Ray, Anne Collins, Dean Smith,*
*Stewart Peterson, James Griffith, Dehl Berti, Bea*
*Morris*
Whilst on the way to Oregon in 1843, the parents of
seven children are killed, and the oldest boy leads
them on a 2,000 mile journey west to reach their
destination. Solid family film based on a true story.
Boa: novel On To Oregon by Honore Morrow.
A/AD                         90 min (ort 97 min)
B,V                          VCL/CBS

## SEVEN BEAUTIES ****                                  18
Lina Wertmuller        ITALY                     1975
*Giancarlo Giannini, Fernando Rey, Shirley Stoler,*
*Elena Fiore, Enzo Vitale, Piero Di Iorio*
A small-town Don Juan has to learn to survive in a
concentration camp during WW2, with all the atten-
dant horrors. Written and directed by Wertmuller,
this is an unforgettable and quite harrowing film, and
one that mixes satire and unpleasantness with con-
siderable skill.
Aka: PASQUALINO SETTEBELLEZZE
DRA                          115 min
B,V                          WHV

## SEVEN BRIDES FOR SEVEN BROTHERS ****   U
Stanley Donen          USA                       1954
*Howard Keel, Jane Powell, Jeff Richards, Russ*
*Tamblyn, Tommy Rall, Virginia Gibson, Julie*
*Newmeyer (Newmar), Ruta Kilmonis (Lee), Matt*
*Mattox, Nancy Kilgas, Betty Carr, Jacques d'Amboise,*
*Norma Doggett, Ian Wolfe, Earl Burton*
Classic musical about seven brothers who decide on a
radical method of settling down and getting married,
and kidnap seven local girls. Written by Frances
Goodrich, Albert Hackett and Dorothy Kingsley, with
the lively songs by Johnny Mercer and Gene DePaul.
The brilliant choreography is by Michael Kidd. AA:
Score (Adolph Deutsch/Saul Chaplin).
Boa: short story Sobbin' Women by Stephen Vincent
Benet.
MUS                          104 min
V/sh                         MGM

## SEVEN DIALS MYSTERY, THE *                    PG
Tony Wharmby           UK                        1980
*John Gielgud, Harry Andrews, Cheryl Campbell,*
*James Warwick, Terrence Alexander, Rula Lenska,*
*Lucy Gutteridge, Lesley Sands, Christopher Scoular,*
*Brian Wilde, Joyce Redmond*
The theft of a secret formula by a foreign power, and
the murder of two Foreign Office officials, leads an
amateur female sleuth to a secret society in Soho. An
overlong and tiresome adaptation of one of Christie's
minor novels, and featuring one of her less memorable
characters, a certain Lady Brent.
Aka: novel by Agatha Christie.
DRA                          120 min mTV
V                            MSD

## SEVEN DOLLARS TO KILL **                     15
Albert Cardiff (Alberto Cardone)
                       ITALY                     1974
*Anthony Steffen, Gerry Wilson, Frank Farrel, Carol*
*Brown, Fernando Sancho*
A father and his long-lost son are drawn into fighting
a duel, when they are thrown together by circumst-
ances, and neither one recognises the other. A violent
and moody Western.
WES                          95 min Cut (5 sec)
B,V                          VPD

## SEVEN GOLDEN MEN **
Marco Vicario                          1965 (released
          FRANCE/ITALY/SPAIN  in USA 1969)
*Philippe Leroy, Rossana Podesta, Gastone Moschin,*
*Gabriele Tinti, Jose Suarez*
Routine thriller about a gang who plan to steal
several tons of gold from a Swiss bank. A flashy but
empty heist film, written by Vicario and followed by
SEVEN GOLDEN MEN STRIKE AGAIN.
THR                          87 min (ort 91 min) dubbed
B,V                          IOVID; VPD

## SEVEN GOLDEN MEN STRIKE AGAIN **
Marco Vicario          ITALY                     1966
*Philippe Leroy, Rossana Podesta, Gastone Moschin,*
*Giampiero Albertini, Gabriele Tinti, Maurice Poli*
Sequel to SEVEN GOLDEN MEN. This time round an
espionage agent plans another gold robbery, while
under pressure from US agents to spy on a Latin
American general. An over-complex mixture of heist
and espionage genres.
THR                          102 min
B,V                          VPD

## SEVEN HOURS TO JUDGEMENT **                  15
Beau Bridges           USA                       1988
*Beau Bridges, Ron Leibman, Julianne Phillips, Reggie*
*Johnson, Tiny Ron Taylor, Al Freeman Jr*
In a desperate bid to ensure the conviction of the men
who murdered his wife, a grief-stricken husband
kidnaps the wife of the judge trying the case, giving
him just seven hours in which to find evidence that
will ensure a guilty verdict. A gripping but utterly
inplausible tale.
DRA                          89 min
B,V                          EIV

## SEVEN MAGNIFICENT FIGHTS **
Lo Wei                 HONG KONG                 1972
*Jimmy Wang Yu, Maria Yi, James Tien, Uruma*
*Toshiko, Tien Feng Li Kun*
Kung fu thriller set on location in Japan. Average.
Aka: HAI-YUAN CH'I-HAO; SEAMAN NUMBER
SEVEN; WANG YU'S 7 MAGNIFICENT FIGHTS
MAR                          91 min (ort 140 min)
B,V                          RNK

## SEVEN MAGNIFICENT                             PG
## GLADIATORS, THE **
Vincent Dawn (Bruno Mattei)
                       USA                       1983
*Lou Ferrigno, Sybil Danning (Sybelle Danninger),*
*Brad Harris, Dan Vodis, Mandy Rice-Davies, Carla*
*Ferrigno, Barbara Pesante, Yehuda Efroni, Claudia*
*Bridges, Robert Maura, Ivan Beshears, Jody Wanger,*
*Kristin Kline, Mary Rader*
An attempt to exploit the theme of "The Seven
Samurai" with a marked sword-and-sorcery flavour,
as villagers, anxious to save their village from annual
bandit attacks, seek a warrior pure enough to wield
their magic sword without burning his hands.
A/AD                         83 min (ort 86 min)
B,V                          GHV

## SEVEN MINUTES IN HEAVEN **                    15
Linda Feferman        USA                        1986

*Jennifer Connelly, Bryon Thames, Alan Boyce, Maddie Corman, Billy Wirth, Polly Draper, Marshall Bell*
A light comedy-drama in which a runaway teenager is invited by a female friend to move in whilst her father is away, but the latter finds that their platonic relationship leads to complications with her friends. This contrived formula tale has production-line teen appeal but little to offer an older audience.

| COM | 85 min |
| V/h | WHV |

## SEVEN NIGHTS IN JAPAN *

| Lewis Gilbert | FRANCE/UK | PG |
| | | 1976 |

*Michael York, Hidemi Aoki, James Villiers, Peter Jones, Charles Gray, Anne Lonnberg, Eleonore Hirt, Lionel Murton, Yolande Donlon*
Limp story of seven nights of passion, when the Crown Prince to the throne in the UK falls for a geisha he meets on a visit to Japan. A flat and unappealing tale of insipid dialogue and wooden performances.

| DRA | 100 min (ort 104 min) |
| B,V | TEVP L/A; WHV |

## SEVEN PERCENT SOLUTION, THE ***

| Herbert Ross | USA | 15 |
| | | 1976 |

*Nicol Williamson, Alan Arkin, Robert Duvall, Vanessa Redgrave, Laurence Olivier, Joel Grey, Samantha Eggar, Jeremy Kemp, Charles Gray, Georgia Brown, Regine, Anna Quayle, Jill Townsend, John Bird, Alison Leggatt*
Watson lures Holmes to Vienna so that Freud can cure him of his addiction to morphine (the title refers to the concentration he uses). An excellent idea is just thrown away by the slapstick antics of the last third of the film. Written by Nicholas Meyer from his novel.
Boa: novel by Nicholas Meyer.

| DRA | 110 min (ort 114 min) |
| B,V | CIC |

## SEVEN TIMES DEATH **

| Paul Harrison | USA | 1973 |

*John Ireland, Faith Domergue, John Carradine, Carol Wells, Jerry Strickler, Charles McCauley, Larry Record, Ron Foreman, Marty Hornstein, Charles Bail, Jeff Alexander, Jo Anne Mower, Lucy Doheny, Ron Garcia, Wells Bond*
A film crew making a film about a horrific incident of black magic, find that history is repeating itself when they set up their equipment at a deserted Victorian house. A film clearly hampered by a lack of money, but fairly atmospheric.
Aka: HOUSE OF SEVEN CORPSES, THE; HOUSE OF THE SEVEN CORPSES, THE

| HOR | 90 min |
| B,V | NUT L/A; MARKET; DFS |

## SEVEN UP *

| John D. Lamond | AUSTRALIA | PG |
| | | 1982 |

*Robin Nedwell, Juliet Jordan, John Ewart*
A happy-go-lucky bachelor with an active love life accidentally undergoes a vasectomy, but is then confronted by seven girls who all claim to be pregnant by him. An empty-headed sex farce.
Aka: SLICE OF LIFE, A

| COM | 90 min |
| B,V | IVS |

## SEVEN WINCHESTERS FOR A MASSACRE **

| E.G. Rowland (Enzo G. Castellari) | | 15 |
| | ITALY | 1969 |

*Edd Byrnes, Louise Barrett, Enio Girolami, Guy Madison*
Routine Western about a bloody conflict on the Texas-Mexico border, telling of defeated Confederate forces who refuse to accept that the war is over, and turn to banditry as a way of continuing the struggle.

Aka: FINAL DEFEAT, THE (KSV); SETTE WINCHESTER PER UN MASSACRO

| WES | 86 min; 90 min (KSV) |
| B,V | FFV L/A; KSV |

## SEVEN YEAR ITCH, THE ***

| Billy Wilder | USA | PG |
| | | 1955 |

*Marilyn Monroe, Tom Ewell, Evelyn Keyes, Sonny Tufts, Oscar Homolka, Victor Moore, Robert Strauss, Marguerite Chapman, Carolyn Jones, Doro Merande*
Enjoyable classic comedy about a man alone in his New York apartment while his wife and kids are on holiday in the country. Monroe gives a marvellous performance as the girl in another apartment in the block that he almost has a wild fling with, but beneath the witty lines there is little of substance. Written by Wilder and George Axelrod and with music by Alfred Newman.
Boa: play by George Axelrod.

| COM | 105 min |
| V | CBS |

## SEVEN-UPS, THE ***

| Philip D'Antoni | USA | 15 |
| | | 1973 |

*Roy Scheider, Tony Lo Bianco, Bill Hickman, Richard Lynch, Victor Arnold, Jerry Leon, Larry Haines, Ken Kercheval, Ed Jordan, David Wilson, Robert Burr, Rex Everhart, Matt Russo*
A secret unit is formed within the New York police, to combat drug peddlars, with Scheider playing a tough cop. Shot in New York City, this thriller boasts one of the best car chase sequences on film. Directed by the producer of THE FRENCH CONNECTION, in what is an unofficial sequel to that film.

| THR | 99 min (ort 103 min) |
| B,V | CBS |

## SEVENTEEN **

| Annelise Meineche | DENMARK | 1965 |

*Ole Soltoft, Ghita Norbig, Haas Christensen, Ole Monty, Jorgen Kiil, Bodil Steen, Susanne Heinrich, Lily Broberg, Ingolf David, Lise Rosendahl, Hugo Herrestrup, Annie Birgit Garde, Arthur Jensen, Jutte Abildstrom*
In the summer of 1913, a young boy is perplexed by the onset of sexual maturity. On a trip away from home he enjoys a variety of encounters and is thoroughly experienced by the time he returns. An innocent and fairly innocuous sex film of no great merit, that now looks very dated indeed.
Aka: SYTTEN

| A | 88 min |
| V | INT |

## SEVENTH SIGN, THE *

| Carl Schultz | USA | 18 |
| | | 1988 |

*Demi Moore, Michael Biehn, Jurgen Prochnow, Peter Friedman, Manny Jacobs, John Taylor, Lee Garlington, Akosua Busia*
A flabby and unconvincing supernatural yarn, in which a pregnant woman becomes convinced that the end of the world is approaching, whilst a mysterious boarder she has taken in would appear to have some sinister plan for her unborn child.

| HOR | 93 min (ort 98 min) |
| B,V | RCA |

## SEVENTH VEIL, THE ***

| Compton Bennett | UK | 1945 |

*James Mason, Ann Todd, Herbert Lom, Albert Lieven, Hugh McDermott, Yvonne Owen, David Horne, Manning Whiley, Grace Allardyce, Ernest Davies, Beatrice Varley, John Slater, Margaret Withers, Arnold Goldsborough*
A well-acted melodrama in which a psychiatrist uses hypnosis, to probe the mind of a young woman who tried to drown herself in the Thames, gradually unearthing the secrets of her unhappy life and

enabling her to be restored to the man she loves. The music is by Benjamin Frankel. AA: Screen (Orig) (Muriel Box/Sydney Box).

| | |
|---|---|
| DRA | 94 min B/W |
| B,V | PRV |

## SEVENTY-TWO DESPERATE REBELS, THE ** 15
Lin Bin          HONG KONG          197-
*Pai Ying, Shao Gn, Wei Hai-Bing, Shieh Han, Ma Tien, Tsai Hung, Chen Shing, Wei Ts-Yon, Lung Fei*
Martial arts adventure set at the beginning of the Ming Dynasty, when a group of men rebel against the emperor.
Aka: 72 DESPERATE REBELS, THE

| | |
|---|---|
| MAR | 90 min |
| B,V | VIDPLY/GOLD; DIAM |

## SEVERANCE **                                        18
David Steinberg          USA          1989
*Lou Liotta, Lisa Wolpe*
A former US Air Force hero is haunted by the tragic accident that killed his wife and shattered his family, and has become a down-and-out. His estranged daughter works as a stripper in a sleazy nightclub. In an effort to rekindle their relationship he gets a job as a truck driver, intending to use the money to buy her a birthday present. However, when he discovers that he is working for mobsters the inevitable conflict ensues. Average.

| | |
|---|---|
| A/AD | 90 min |
| V | CFD |

## SEWERS OF PARADISE, THE **
Jose Giovanni          FRANCE          1979
*Lila Kedrova, Jean-Francois Balmer, Francis Huster, Andre Pousse, Anouk Ferjac*
Based on a true incident, this is a re-creation of a famous bank robbery in Nice in which the gang tunnelled through the city's sewers.
Aka: LES EGOUTS DU PARADIS

| | |
|---|---|
| THR | 107 min |
| B,V | VCL/CBS |

## SEX ACADEMY **                                     18
SPAIN
*Tamara Longley, Kristara Barrington, Marie Harper, Helga Line, Jessica Wilde, Jorge Gonce*
Madrid stands in for London, in this laughable and dated tale of a seductive madame who owns a luxurious bordello in London, patronised by the rich and famous. The brothel also doubles as a spy school, and when one of her clients falls in love, the establishment's future is put at risk.
Aka: MADAME OLGA'S PUPIL'S

| | |
|---|---|
| A | 78 min (ort 82 min) Cut (1 min 10 sec) |
| V | ABC L/A; TCX; NET |

## SEX AIRLINES **                                    R18
USA
*Georgina Spelvin, Bridgette Grahame, Pauline Atkins*
Routine sex film set on an airline flight.

| | |
|---|---|
| A | 62 min |
| V | VPD |

## SEX AND THE OTHER WOMAN *                           18
Stanley Long          UK          1972
*Richard Wattis, Bartlett Mullins, Peggy Ann Clifford, Maggie Wright, Anthony Bailey, Margaret Burton, Gordon Gale, Jane Cardew, Peter Dunn, Gillian Brown, Anthony Howard, Stacy Davies, Raymond Young, Felicity Devonshire*
Four sketches dealing with the dangers represented by the "other woman". A tepid and dated sex farce, with Wattis presenting each episode.

| | |
|---|---|
| A | 83 min (ort 88 min) Cut (9 min 30 sec) |
| B,V | MOV L/A; SHEP |

## SEX APPEAL *                                        18
Chuck Vincent          USA          1986

*Louie Bonanno, Tally Britanny, Marcia Kerr, Jerome Brenner, Marie Sawyer, Jeff Eagle, Molly Morgan, Veronica Hart*
Witless comedy about a man so starved of sex, that he alters his entire lifestyle in a vain attempt to become a great seducer, only to find his efforts landing him in a variety of ludicrous situations.

| | |
|---|---|
| COM | 81 min |
| B,V | VES |

## SEX AT 7,000 FEET **                                18
F.J. Gottlieb (Erich Tomek)
WEST GERMANY          1977
*Ajita Wilson, Olivia Pascal, Betty Verges, Frits Hassoldt, Corinne Cartier, Gianni Garko*
A girl overcomes her fear of flying and sex at the same time, thanks to the autopilot and inspiration she gains from reading Erica Jong's "Fear of Flying".
Aka: FREUDE AM FLIEGEN; JOY OF FLYING

| | |
|---|---|
| A | 83 min |
| B,V | WOV L/A; STABL |

## SEX BOAT *
David I. Frazer/Svetlana
USA          1980
*Kelly Nichols, Dana Dennis, Kandi Bartour, Randy West, Silver Miser, Roxanne Potts, Linda Revves, Jeanette James, Pene La Paz*
Erotic version of TV's "The Love Boat". Two men dress up as women and sneak onto a ship that caters only for young married women, whose husbands want to get rid of them for a few weeks by sending them on a cruise. An excuse for a non-stop series of sexual encounters not complicated by anything as extraneous as a plot, though by way of a diversion there is a pirate attack in the last reel.

| | |
|---|---|
| A | 63 min (ort 90 min) |
| B,V | ELV |

## SEX CLINIC **
Don Chaffey          UK          1972
*Georgina Ward, Alex Davion, Polly Adams, Mike Lewin, Carmen Silvera, Vincent Ball, Basil Moss, Tony Wright, Geoffrey Morris, Maria Coyne, April Olrich, Windsor Davies, John Joyce, Peter Halliday, Donald Bissett*
The story of the woman owner of a health clinic, who uses her position to blackmail her clients, and how justice catches up with her.
Aka: CLINIC XCLUSIVE; WITH THESE HANDS

| | |
|---|---|
| A | 90 min |
| B,V | INT L/A; WEV |

## SEX CONNECTION, THE **                              18
Charles Ferrer          WEST GERMANY          1969
*Joanna Jung, Alfred Bettner, Rose Ningy, Christophe Alberola, Yves Jofa, Elisabeth Felchner*
Three girls and two boys tour Europe in an old bus, and have various adventures in this innocent little early sex romp.

| | |
|---|---|
| A | 82 min |
| B,V | DFS L/A; XTACY/KRP; VPD |

## SEX DENS OF BANGKOK **                              18
SWITZERLAND
*Angela May Wong, Patty Patpun, Angela Yu Chen, Mailing Chen*
Routine sex film set in a more exotic location.

| | |
|---|---|
| A | 66 min Cut (45 sec) |
| B,V | KTC |

## SEX DIARY ***                                       18
Bruno Gaburro          ITALY          1975
*Rossana Podesta, Renzo Montagnani, John Ireland, Sherry Buchanan, Giuseppe Anatrelli, Franco Bracardi*
The respectable citizens of a small village find the affairs of a womaniser a source of annoyance, but one day this man's life becomes complicated when he

saves the unhappy, disfigured daughter of a business-
man from suicide.
Aka: IL LETTO IN PIAZZA
Boa: novel by Nantas Salvalaggio.

A                                            75 min
B,V                        HOK L/A; ABC; NET; VPD; TCX

**SEX FARM \***
Arnold L. Miller         UK                  1973
*Hilary Lebow, Amber Kammer, Kim Alexander,*
*Tristan Rogers, Gordon Whiting, Claire Gordon, Max*
*Mason, Ray Edwards, Tommy Wright, Barry Rhode,*
*Steve Patterson, Sui Lin, Sue Glanville, Pamela*
*Sholto, Elsie Winsor*
Witless softcore sex comedy set at a health farm, with
some unsatisfied wives spending a weekend there.

A                                            90 min
B,V                                          INT

**SEX HUNGRY GIRLS \*\***                      18
*Marika Pica, Jackie Lombard, Alain Saury*
A prisoner on the run finds himself taking refuge in
the home of two insatiable females, and soon wishes
he were safely back in prison in this routine farce.
Aka: DEADLY WHEN AROUSED; LOVE HUNGRY
GIRLS

A                          79 min Cut (2 min 38 sec)
V                                  NET; TCX; SHEP

**SEX IN THE HEAD \***                         18
Sergio Ammirata          ITALY
*Corra Scot, Tina Andreas, Pilar Velasquez*
An attractive university student chooses to study the
reactions of men in large cities to prostitution, as part
of her thesis. In order to do this she decides to live as a
prostitute, an approach that brings the expected
rewards, in this rather cliched adult tale.
Aka: SEX ON THE BRAIN

A                                            76 min
B,V                            18PLAT/TOW; PHE

**SEX KITTENS GO TO COLLEGE**                  15
Albert Zugsmith          USA                 1960
*Mamie Von Doren, Tuesday Weld, Mickey*
*Shaughnessy, Mijanou Bardot, Louis Nye, Martin*
*Milner, Pamela Mason (Norman), "Woo Woo"*
*Grabowski, Jackie Coogan, John Carradine*
The title is the best thing in this dreary and unfunny
effort, that has the new head of a college department
turning out to be a former stripper. A trashy dud that
should be re-titled so that it can be left in obscurity.
Aka: BEAUTY AND THE ROBOT, THE

COM                                      94 min B/W
V/h                                          CBS

**SEX, LIES AND VIDEOTAPE \*\*\***              18
Steven Soderbergh        USA                 1989
*James Spader, Andie MacDowell, Peter Gallagher,*
*Laura San Giacomo*
This bizarre morality tale has a selfish lawyer married to a frigid woman, but having an affair with her
sister. An old college chum visits their home, and his
strange project of videotaping women as they discuss
their sexuality serves to put the lives of all concerned
onto a new footing. Writer-director Soderburgh's first
feature is a disturbing blend of honesty and preten-
sion. Winner of the 1989 International Critic's Prize
and Palme d'Or at Cannes.

DRA                        96 min (ort 100 min)
V                                            VIR

**SEX O'CLOCK NEWS, THE \***                   18
Romano Vanderbes         USA                 1983
*Romando Vanderbes, Lydia Mahan, Wayne Knight,*
*Don Pardo, Doug Ballard, Jerry Winsett, Judith*
*Drake, Philip McKinley, Rob Bartlett, Kate Weiman*
A satire on contempary sexual mores, which attempts
to cash in on such spoofs as "The Groove Tube",
KENTUCKY FRIED MOVIE etc. Merely a gross and

unfunny exercise in low-brow smut.
Aka: GUIDE TO AMERICA

A                                            83 min
B,V                                          VIP/IVS

**SEX ON THE ROCKS \*\***                      18
Siggi Gotz               WEST GERMANY
*Tanya Spiess, Regis Porte, Beate Granitz, Heide Stroh,*
*Michael Gsandl, Regis Pork, Cesa Thoma, Tanja*
*Speiss*
Bright and cheerful sun, surf and sand sex film.
Aka: BEAUTIFUL AND WILD ON IBIZA; DIE
SCHONEN WILDEN VON IBIZA

A                                            80 min
B,V                              ILV L/A; BLUES

**SEX SLAVES \***                              18
Hubert Frank             WEST GERMANY        1977
*Olivia Pascal, Philippe Garnier, Marine Merril, Bea*
*Fiedler, Lili Murati, Elisa Servier, William Levine,*
*Scarlett Cunden*
Tiresomely witless sex film set in a harem, with some
well-endowed young men (no eunuchs here) both
guarding the girls and sampling them.
Aka: DIE INSEL DER 1000 FREUDEN; SEX FEVER
(STABL or XTASY); SEX FEVER ON AN ISLAND
OF 1,000 DELIGHTS

A                          70 min Cut (15 min 13 sec)
B,V                WOV L/A; SHAD L/A; XTASY; STABL

**SEX SLEUTH \*\***                            18
                         FRANCE
*Marilyn Jess, Patricia Violet, Dominique St Claire*
A sex-mad private eye has various adventures in the
course of his work.

A                          80 min (AVR); 50 min
B,V                               AVR; CASS/AVR

**SEX SYMBOL, THE \*\***                       15
David Lowell Rich        USA       1973 (released 1974)
*Connie Stevens, Shelley Winters, Jack Carter, William*
*Castle, Don Murray, Nehemiah Persoff, James Olson,*
*Madlyn Rhue, Milton Selzer, Tony Young, William*
*Smith, Rand Brooks, Malachi Throne, Frank Loverde,*
*Bing Russell*
The story of a movie queen of the 1940s and 1950s,
following her climb to super-stardom and her fall. A
fictitious account, but inspired by the story of Monroe.
The film was threatened by a libel suit just prior to its
March 1974 premiere and was severely edited for USA
release, with Throne's voice being redubbed by
Eduard Franz. Average.
Boa: novel The Symbol by Alvah Bessie.

DRA                                     106 min mTV
B,V                                          RCA

**SEX TAPES SCANDAL, THE \*\***                18
Noel Nosseck             USA                 1989
*Anthony Dennison, Sarah Dutton, Vanessa Williams*
An investigation into the murder of a high-class
hooker takes a more sinister turn when it is discovered that a videotape, used to record the more bizarre
activities of her clients, has been stolen.

DRA                                          92 min
V                                            CHV

**SEX THIEF, THE \***
Martin Campbell          UK                  1973
*David Warbeck, Diane Keen, Terence Edmond,*
*Deirdre Costello, Christopher Neil, Michael*
*Armstrong, Harvey Hall, Jenny Westbrook, Gerald*
*Taylor, Gloria Walker, Eric Deacon, Christopher*
*Mitchell, Christopher Biggins, Val Penny*
A jewel thief makes love to his women victims, who
then give the police deliberately misleading informa-
tion. Tired and dated.

COM                                          89 min
B,V                                          MED

## SEX TO THE END *

Vilgot Sjoman    SWEDEN    18
                          1971
*Solveig Ternstrom, Borje Ahlstedt, Margaretha
Bystrom, Frej Lindqvist, Sven Bjorling, Jan-Olof
Strandberg, Gosta Bredefeldt, Akke Carlsson, Nina
Gaines, Vilgot Sjoman, Barbro Ericsson, Ingegard
Kall, Rolf Bjorling*
A young couple infatuated with each other, cannot
make love because of their strange hang-ups; he has a
granny fetish and she prefers other women. Initially
they try partner-swapping but this doesn't help.
Finally the only thing that saves their relationship is
when the wife decides to try prostitution. Another one
of those silly Scandinavian sex comedies, neither
especially lascivious nor particularly funny.
Aka: TILL SEX US DO PART; TROLLS

A                                   91 min
V                              PHV; SHEP

## SEX WITH THE STARS *

Anwar Kawadri    UK    18
                       1980
*Martin Burrows, Thick Wilson, Janie Love, Carrie
Allen, Susie Sylvie, Terri Mitchell, Simon St Laurent,
Nicola Austine, Poula Griffith Jada, Faith Daykin,
Clair Bastin, Lorreta Smith, Caroline Grenville,
Suzannah Willis*
A sedate women's magazine undergoes a startling
transformation, when the astrology journalist is
ordered to pep up his column, in this tired and
tiresome sex comedy.
Aka: CONFESSIONS OF THE NAUGHTY
NYMPHOS; SECRETS OF A GIRL FRIDAY

COM                          88 min (ort 92 min)
B,V,V2              HOK L/A; PINK L/A; KRP

## SEX WORLD **

Anthony Spinelli    USA    R18
                          1978
*Leslie Bovee, John Leslie, Sharon Thorpe, Annette
Haven, Amber Hunt*
The story of a fantasy resort/sexual health centre,
designed to cater for an individual's deepest fantasy
desires. A glossy and well made series of vignettes.

A                                   90 min
B,V                                  EVI

## SEX-A-VISION ***

Ned Morehead    USA    18
                       1985
*Joey Silvera, Gina Carrerra, Herschel Savage, Tamara
Longly, Sheri St Clair, Melissa Melendez, Colleen
Brennan*
Daryl is a weedy nerd who has no friends except his
dog, and spends most of his time watching sex videos.
Whilst watching one such film he expresses a desire to
change places with Dick, the porno star. And this does
actually happen, with Dick helping Daryl climb in
through the TV screen whilst Dick climbs out and
goes in search of a lady who deserted the film. A silly,
amusing sexy spoof, almost certainly inspired by THE
PURPLE ROSE OF CAIRO.

A                                   44 min
V                                 DREAM

## SEXORCIST, THE ***

Mario Gariazzo    ITALY    18
                          1974
*Chris Avram, Lucretia Love, Stella Carnacina, Luigi
Pistilli, Gianrico Tondinelli, Umberto Raho, Ivan
Rassimov, Gabriele Tinti*
Sex film combining "The Exorcist" effects with sexual
activities. An art student becomes possessed by an evil
spirit that dwells within a crucifix taken from a
desecrated church that his mother is restoring. This
interesting combination of genres helps lift this one a
cut or two above the usual run of such films.
Aka: DEVIL OBSESSION, THE; EERIE MIDNIGHT
HORROR SHOW, THE; ENTER THE DEVIL
(SCAN); L'OSSESSA; OBSESSED, THE (SKP);
OBSESSION, THE; SEXORCISTS, THE;
TORMENTED, THE; TORMENTORS, THE

A                    83 min (ort 92 min) Cut (XTASY: 40 sec);
                        81 min Cut (PHE: 45 sec)
B,V    PYR/CBS L/A; SKP; SCAN; COBRA/HOMCO;
                                    PHE; XTASY

## SEXPIONAGE *

Don Taylor    USA    15
                    1984
*Sally Kellerman, Linda Hamilton, Hunt Block, Viveca
Lindfors, Geena Davis, Barrie Ingham, Christopher
Atkins, James Franciscus, Donald Pilon, John
Cassatio, Linda Clune, Vlastra Vrana, Catherine
Lafonde, Fernanda Tavares*
An attempt to describe how the KGB allegedly recruit
and train beautiful girls for work as spies in the USA.
An exploitative and muddled effort that is neither
interesting nor titillating.
Aka: SECRET WEAPONS; SECRETS OF THE RED
BEDROOM
Boa: book Sexpionage: The Exploitation Of Sex By
Soviet Intelligence by David Lewis.

DRA                          92 min (ort 131 min) mTV
B,V                              PRV L/A; CH5

## SEXPLORER, THE *

Derek Ford    UK    18
                    1975
*Monika Ringwald, Andrew Grant, Tanya Ferova,
Albin Pahernik, Tony Kenyon, Maria Ski, Michael
Cronin, Dave Carter, Catriona Nurse, Prudence Drage,
Ros Strang*
Sex comedy about a blonde Venusian who lands in
London's Soho, and is so fascinated by the sexual
practices she finds there, that she decides not to return
home. Another dreary dud from the British film
industry.
Aka: DIARY OF A SPACE VIRGIN; GIRL FROM
STARSHIP VENUS

A                            83 min (ort 85 min)
B,V                      MED; ROXY L/A; TOW

## SEXTETTE *

Ken Hughes/Irving Rapper    PG
                    USA    1978
*Mae West, Tony Curtis, Ringo Starr, Dom DeLuise,
Timothy Dalton, Walter Pidgeon, George Raft, George
Harrison, Alice Cooper, Keith Moon, George Hamilton,
Rona Barrett, Van McCoy*
An ageing sex queen is disturbed on her latest
honeymoon, by the presence of well-wishers and
ex-husbands. An embarrassing attempt (the last) by
this 86-year-old ex-star to portray herself. Of curiosity
value only. Written by Herbert Baker from West's
play.
Boa: play by Mae West.

COM                          84 min (ort 91 min)
B,V                              VPD L/A; CH5

## SEXUAL DESIRES ***

Al Bagram    SPAIN    18
                     1982
*Concha Valero, Paula Mejei, Andrea Albani, Jorge
Batalla*
The erotic story of a young girl's desire to possess her
large family fortune. First she seduces her uncle and
then her aunt and, helped by her friend, the pair use
their charms to turn the entire household upside
down. Enjoyable piece of softcore nonsense, made at
the same time as INSATIABLE ALICIA AND THE
MARQUIS and using the same set and a similar cast
and plot.
Aka: COLEGIALAS LESBIANAS Y EL PLACER DE
PERVERTIR

A                    64 min (ort 75 min) Cut (9 min 39 sec
                                    in addition to film cuts)
B,V APX L/A; NET (VHS only) L/A; TCX L/A; TURBO

## SEXUAL DEVIANTS **

*Amanda Stone, Tom Celli, Brenda Cole*    18
Two young men go on a sordid week-long escapade,
indulging in every form of vice, and even risking their
lives on the toss of a coin.

A                    68 min (ort 90 min) Cut (6 min 2 sec)
B,V                                                  CLOK

## SEXUAL EXPLOITS OF NAUGHTY PENNY, THE ***
Mark Ubell          USA                             1978
*Samantha Fox, Molly Malone, Don Peterson, Kurt*
*Mann, Richard Bolla, Anna St James*
Interesting hardcore tale of a young girl who must
solve a riddle in order to inherit a fortune, whilst
avoiding succumbing to the schemes of the person
next in line who is plotting to kill her.
A                              63 min (ort 74 min)
B,V                                               HAR

## SEXUAL EXTASY **                                 18
Claus Tiedemans WEST GERMANY                        1979
*Margit Man, Sascha Hehn, Marlette Soy, Claus*
*Obalski*
A couple go to Greece on separate holidays but
unwittingly end up at the same resort, where they
both fall for a beautiful blonde lady courier. One more
in a long line of formula German sex films, but the
exotic locations compensate.
Aka: HIGH SEASON; NACKT UND HEISS AUF
MYKONOS
A                                              88 min
B,V                                      POLY; PLAVID

## SEXUAL FREEDOM *                                 18
Conrad Brueghel     ITALY                           1984
*Lilli Carati, Zara Keen, Filip Degara*
Four girl terrorists escape from prison and take a
coachload of tennis players hostage. Having forced a
judge to shelter them in his home and whilst holding
the police at bay, they relieve their sexual frustrations
with the hostages, in this dreary and feeble dud.
A                              91 min; 80 min (PHE)
B,V              PHE (VHS only); PRI; 18PLAT/TOW

## SEXY DOZEN, THE **                               18
Norbert Terry       SWITZERLAND                     1969
*Barbro Hedstrom, Vincent Gauthier, Renee St Cyr,*
*Noel Roquevert, Lovis Navarre, Julie Jordan, Bruno*
*Kaspar*
After being caught making love to her boyfriend on
the carpet, a young girl is sent to a finishing school in
the Swiss Alps. However, she gets her boyfriend to
dress up as a girl and successfully smuggles him into
the school in this dated and tepid farce.
Aka: CHARLEY'S TANTE NACKT
A                              94 min (ort 104 min)
B,V                            GOV L/A; DFS; VPD

## SEXY SECRETS OF THE KISSOGRAM GIRLS, THE *       18
*Donna, Georgina, Jackie, Karen, Sue, Zoe*
Allegedly a look at the kissogram business and a
kissogram training course, but little more than a
chance to look at some well-endowed girls. Pleasant
enough in its way, but hardly enthralling.
Aka: KISSOGRAM GIRLS (PRI)
A                                              90 min
B,V                                         SFI; PRI

## SEXY SECRETS OF THE SEX THERAPISTS, THE *        18
                    UK                              1986
*Debee Ashby, Nicola Clair, Terry St John, Jackie*
*Hunt, Chris Moor, Phillip Kaleb, Mark Yule*
An expose of the strange fetishes of clients attending a
London sex clinic. Ashby's film debut, in which she
seduces the doctor at the clinic, and causes havoc at a
local radio station. A banal and poorly acted dud.
Aka: SEXY SECRETS OF A SEX THERAPIST, THE
A                                             100 min
B,V                                               SFI

## SEXY SISTERS **
Arnold Baxter       DENMARK                         1974
*Greta Young (Gertie Jung), Paul Glargaard, Emmett*
*Hennessy, Preben Mahrt, Paul Kirby, Susan Bowen,*
*Jeanne Darville*
Sex drama about a model whose fortunes have begun
to decline.
Aka: OVERKLASSENS HEMLIGE SEXGLAEDER
A                                              75 min
B,V                                               VIV

## SHADEY **                                        15
Philip Saville      UK                              1985
*Antony Sher, Patrick Macnee, Bernard Hepton, Billie*
*Whitelaw, Katherine Helmond, Leslie Ash, Larry*
*Lamb, Jesse Birdsall, Olivier Pierre, Stephen Persaud,*
*Jon Cartwright, Basil Henson, Peter Kelly, Madhav*
*Sharma*
Convoluted, surrealistic black comedy, about an un-
assuming businessman who raises the cash for his
sex-change operation, by selling his ability to capture
his mental images on film, to the intelligence service.
The plot has so many twists and turns that one soon
loses interest in the outcome.
COM                           103 min (ort 106 min)
B,V                                               VIR

## SHADOW BOX, THE ***                              15
Paul Newman         USA                             1980
*Christopher Plummer, Joanne Woodward, Valerie*
*Harper, James Broderick, Sylvia Sidney, Melinda*
*Dillon, Ben Masters, Curtiss Marlowe, John Considine*
Follows three terminally ill patients at a country
home, who are visited by their families during the
course of one day. A potent and moving drama,
adapted by Cristofer from his Pulitzer Prize and Tony
Award-winning play.
Boa: play by Michael Cristofer.
DRA                                   103 min mTV
B,V                                               HER

## SHADOW DANCING **                               15
Lewis Furey         USA                             1988
*Nadine Van Der Velde, Christopher Plummer*
A talented dancer gains a part in a new show when a
mysterious accident befalls a member of the troupe.
She begins to undergo a strange personality change
that threatens the entire troupe, when the spirit of a
dead dancer who died on stage 50 years ago, begins to
take her over.
HOR                                           100 min
V                                                 COL

## SHADOW DREAM **                                 15
Rimas Poskaitis                                     1987
*Jeong Sook Lee, Al Myles, Kirk Bruner, Bob Roberts,*
*James Edwards, Bert Wood, Amber Jade*
A young man returns to Los Angeles only to find that
his family's business has burnt down, and his rela-
tives have perished. After rescuing a warehouse
worker, the two become firm friends, and together
they set out to investigate the disaster.
DRA                            89 min Cut (6 sec)
B,V                                              NELS

## SHADOW MAKERS **                                PG
Roland Joffe        USA                             1989
*Paul Newman, Dwight Schultz, Bonnie Bedelia, John*
*Cusack, Laura Dern, John C. McGinley, Ron Frazier,*
*Natasha Richardson*
The story of the creation of the world's first two atom
bombs (nicknamed "Fat Man" and "Little Boy") that
details their creation at the Manhattan Project and
the subsequent destruction of Hiroshima and Nagasaki. An episodic and verbose drama of sporadic impact,
that is weakened by its lack of authenticity and a
failure to examine the Project's political background
as a response to Japanese aggression. Music is by
Ennio Morricone.

Aka: FAT MAN AND LITTLE BOY
DRA 110 min (ort 126 min)
V CIC

## SHADOW OF CHIKARA, THE ***
Earl A. Smith USA 1978
*Slim Pickens, Joe Don Baker, Sondra Locke, Ted Neeley, Dennis Fimple, John Chandler, Joy Houck Jr, Linda Dano*
An ex-Confederate army captain leads an expedition in search of buried treasure, but this ends in unforeseen hazards after they rescue a woman who appears to have survived a massacre. An intriguing blend of supernatural and Western genres, with a disturbing twist ending.
Aka: WISHBONE CUTTER
WES 94 min (ort 114 min)
B,V HOK

## SHADOW OF DEATH ** 18
Robert Kirk USA 1988
*Deborah Foreman, Lyle Alzado, Clayton Rohner, Anthony Perkins*
A standard slasher tale following the exploits of a murderous lunatic who stalks the corridors of an abandoned prison. The film opens with this maniac about to be electrocuted, but being saved by a convenient power cut. Having escaped, he returns 20 years later to have his revenge, murdering a film crew who have come to the prison to make a low-budget film. An unpleasant but quite well-handled shocker.
HOR 94 min
B,V SONY

## SHADOW OF THE COBRA ** 15
Mark Joffe USA 1987
*Rachel Ward, Michael Woods, Art Malik*
Based on a true story, this tale is set in 1977, when two journalists are commissioned to write on the life of Charles Sobhraj, a dangerous criminal of great charm and murderous ruthlessness.
THR 104 min
V FUTUR

## SHADOW OF THE TIGER ** 15
Yeung Kuen HONG KONG 198-
*Cliff Look, Ka Sa Fa, Lam Man Wei*
A group of top fighters join forces, in this standard kung fu action tale.
Aka: DUEL OF THE SEVEN TIGERS
MAR 92 min Cut (8 sec)
V VPD

## SHADOW PLAY ** 15
Susan Shadburne USA 1986
*Dee Wallace Stone, Cloris Leachman, Ron Kuhlman, Barry Laws, Delia Slavi, Al Strobel, Susan Dixon, Glen Baggerly, Juleen Murray, Michele Mariana, Bob Griggs, Marjorie Card Hughes, Richard Wilshire, George Stokes*
A woman obsessed by the death of her lover, who fell from a lighthouse, experiences much terror before she finally learns the truth about how he died. A trifle of few chills and much tedium.
THR 101 min
B,V NWV

## SHADOWLANDS *** PG
Norman Stone
NETHERLANDS/UK/USA 1985
*Joss Ackland, Claire Bloom, Philip Stone, Tim Preece, David Waller, Max Harvey, Rupert Baderman, Rhys Hopkins, Alan MacNaughton, Norman Rutherford, John Ringham, Henry Moxon, Michael Cunningham, Jim Kirby, Dilys Price*
Beautifully acted, sensitive and restrained account, of how love came to the writer and theologian C.S. Lewis late in life, when he was sought out by an unhappily married American lady who was soon to die of cancer.

Though the subject of his literary work is only touched on, and the film has a tendency to have Lewis mouthing pompous platitudes, the story is never less than wholly absorbing. Scripted by William Nicholson.
Boa: book by P. Straub.
DRA 89 min mTV
V/h BBC

## SHADOWMAN *** 15
Piotr Andreyev 1989
*Tom Hulce, Jeroen Krabbe, Manouk Van Der Meulen*
WW2 drama set in Amsterdam where a penniless Jewish refugee comes to a man prepared to help him for a price. When his would-be rescuer abandons him, he is persuaded to relent by his wife, and the refugee is drawn into a passionate affair with her. However, he is soon obliged to choose between carrying on the relationship or escaping with his life. A competent and fairly absorbing tale.
DRA 93 min
V NWV

## SHADOWZONE *** 18
USA 1989
*David Beecroft, James Hong, Shawn Weatherly, Louise Fletcher*
Scientists researching into sleep patterns accidentally bring back a being from another dimension. As in THE THING, the creature is a shape-changer that rapidly depletes the members of the research team, until a way is found to repatriate it. An intelligent, low-budget horror-thriller of minimal gore.
HOR 82 min
V EIV

## SHADOWS IN THE STORM * 18
Terrell Tannen USA 1989
*Ned Beatty, Mia Sara*
A married man who loses his job, tells his wife that he's taking a fishing trip and goes off into the mountains, where he rents a cabin. He falls for a woman who, with her violent husband, is staying in the cabin next door. A secret tryst with the woman leads to murder, when the husband confronts them and is shot by the wife. They dump the body and take off, but soon discover that they were seen. An unconvincing and predictable thriller.
THR 90 min
B,V CHV

## SHADOWS ON THE WALL *** 15
Patrick C. Poole USA 1987
*A. Wilford Brimley, Gary Swanson, Lou Michaels*
An investigative journalist goes to a small Texas town to research a bizarre 50-year-old murder case, where a returning cowboy's visit home ended in murder and suicide. He finds the town to be largely deserted, apart from a few frightened and suspicious locals. When a new series of deaths occur he is obliged to solve the past mystery in order to understand the present one. An ingenious but implausible story.
THR 86 min
B,V RCA

## SHADOWS RUN BLACK * 18
Howard Heard USA 1981 (released 1983)
*William J. Kulzer, Elizabeth Trosper, Shea Porter, Dianne Hinkler, George J. Engelson, Terry Congie, Kevin Costner*
A failed attempt to vary the slasher movie theme, that takes the position that killer's crimes are meant to be seen as the justifiable actions of a vigilante, since his victims are all members of a group of high school students operating drugs and prostitution rackets.
THR 89 min
V VES

**SHAFT \*\*\*** 15
Gordon Parks          USA          1971
*Richard Roundtree, Moses Gunn, Charles Cioffi,*
*Christopher St John, Drew Bundini Brown, Gwenn*
*Mitchell, Lawrence Pressman, Antonio Fargas*
A black detective is hired to find a Harlem gangster's
kidnapped daughter, and gets caught up in the usual
rackets. Violent, flashy and competent. Written by
Ernest Tidyman and John D.F. Black, and followed by
SHAFT IN AFRICA and SHAFT'S BIG SCORE! plus
a rather unmemorable TV series. AA: Song ("Theme
From Shaft" – Isaac Hayes).
Boa: novel by Ernest Tidyman.
A/AD                              96 min (ort 100 min)
B,V                                            MGM

**SHAFT IN AFRICA \*** 18
John Guillermin          USA          1973
*Richard Roundtree, Frank Finlay, Vonetta McGee,*
*Neda Arneric, Cy Grant, Jacques Marin*
A rubbishy further sequel to SHAFT, with an African
nation calling on our black detective to put an end to
the local slave trade. A violent and brutal piece of
dross. Written by Sterling Silliphant.
A/AD                                          112 min
B,V                                            MGM

**SHAFT'S BIG SCORE! \*\*** 15
Gordon Parks          USA          1972
*Richard Roundtree, Moses Gunn, Drew Bundini*
*Brown, Joseph Mascolo, Kathy Imrie, Wally Taylor,*
*Joe Santos*
First sequel to SHAFT with our private eye getting
into trouble when he sets out to investigate the
murder of a friend. A fast and flashy film, quite
enjoyable in its way, and containing an excellent
chase sequence. Written by Ernest Tidyman and with
music by Gordon Parks. SHAFT IN AFRICA followed.
A/AD                              101 min (ort 104 min)
B,V                                            MGM

**SHAG \*\*\*** 15
Zelda Barron          USA          1988
*Phoebe Cates, Bridget Fonda, Page Hannah, Annabeth*
*Gish, Scott Coffey, Robert Rusler, Tyrone Power Jr,*
*Jeff Yagher, Carrie Hamilton, Shirley Anne Field*
A Southern high school graduate is about to get
married, so her three friends decide to take her out for
one last wild weekend. A bright and breezy comedy set
in the 1960s.
COM                              96 min (ort 98 min)
V/h                                            PAL

**SHAGGY D.A., THE \*\*** U
Robert Stevenson          USA          1976
*Dean Jones, Suzanne Pleshette, Tim Conway, Keenan*
*Wynn, Jo Anne Worley, Dick Van Patten, Vic Tayback*
Sequel to "The Shaggy Dog" with a contender for the
job of D.A. having to cope with the fact that he
changes into a dog from time to time, whilst at the
same time trying to expose corruption in high places.
A mildly entertaining slapstick romp, very much a
Disney film in both conception and development. See
also OH HEAVENLY DOG!
COM                                            91 min
B,V                                            WDV

**SHAKA ZULU: PARTS 1, 2 AND 3 \*\*** 15
William C. Faure
                    SOUTH AFRICA/USA          1986
*Henry Cele, Dudu Mkhize, Edward Fox, Robert*
*Powell, Fiona Fullerton, Christopher Lee, Trevor*
*Howard, Roy Dotrice, Kenneth Griffith*
A lavish mini-epic set in South Africa of the early
18th century, and telling of the rise to power of Shaka,
who welded disparate tribes into the powerful Zulu
nation that was later to battle the British. An
expensive, earnest tale that's somewhat hampered by

a ponderous script. Filmed on location where it all
happened, in the rolling hills of Zululand. Originally
shown in ten 50-minute episodes.
A/AD          448 min (3 cassettes – ort 500 min) mTV
B,V                                            MGM

**SHAKEDOWN ON THE SUNSET STRIP \*\*** 15
Walter Grauman          USA          1987
*Perry King, Season Hubley, Joan Van Ark, Vincent*
*Baggetta, Michael McGuire, David Graf, Charles*
*Siebert*
A patchy blend of comedy and thriller genres, with an
ambitious L.A. vice squad detective out to nab a
notorious madam and finding himself coming up
against some unexpected obstacles when he discovers
that she has powerful friends in high places.
THR                              90 min (ort 96 min) mTV
B,V                                            CBS

**SHAKER RUN \*\*** 15
Bruce Morrison   NEW ZEALAND          1985
*Cliff Robertson, Leif Garrett, Lisa Harrow, Shane*
*Briant, Peter Hayden, Peter Rowell, Bruce Phillips,*
*Ian Mune, Fiona Samuels, Deirdre O'Connor, Mat*
*Lees, Daniel Gillion, Geoffrey Heath, Dave Smith, Igo*
*Kantor, Barry Dorking*
Following a chance meeting with a beautiful scientist,
a stunt driver and his young mechanic get themselves
hopelessly entangled in the delivery of a deadly
biological virus to the CIA, while being pursued by
enemy agents and military forces alike. A standard
car chase tale with fine scenery and a good performance from Robertson, slightly compensating for the
shortcomings of the script.
A/AD                              86 min (ort 91 min)
B,V                                            MGM

**SHAKESPEARE WALLAH \*\*** 15
James Ivory          INDIA          1965
*Felicity Kendal, Shashi Kapoor, Madhur Jaffrey,*
*Geoffrey Kendal, Laura Liddell, Utpal Dutt*
An English troupe of Shakespearean actors tour
post-Raj India trying to eke out a living, and Kendal
finds herself being courted by a wealthy playboy. A
languid and atmospheric tale, quite unusual but not
terribly interesting. Written by Ruth Prawer Jhab-
vala.
DRA                              115 min (ort 125 min) B/W
B,V                              HVH L/A; PVG; VIR

**SHALAKO \*\***
Edward Dmytryck          UK          1968
*Sean Connery, Brigitte Bardot, Stephen Boyd, Jack*
*Hawkins, Peter Van Eyck, Honor Blackman, Woody*
*Strode, Eric Sykes, Alexander Knox, Valerie French,*
*Julian Mateos, Donald (Don "Red") Barry, Rodd*
*Redwing, Chief Tug Smith*
A party of European aristocrats, on a hunting expedi-
tion in New Mexico in the 1880s, come into conflict
with the Apache, but despite this encounter the film
remains a slow-moving and ponderous Western. Writ-
ten by J.J. Griffith, Hal Hopper and Scot Finch, and
with music by Robert Farnon.
Boa: novel by Louis L'Amour.
WES                              116 min (ort 118 min)
B,V                              JVC L/A; TEVP

**SHALL WE DANCE? \*\*\*** U
Mark Sandrich          USA          1937
*Fred Astaire, Ginger Rogers, Edward Everett Horton,*
*Eric Blore, Jerome Cowan, Ketti Gallian, Ann*
*Shoemaker*
A dancing duo pretend to be married to simplify their
lives but eventually decide to do so. A flimsy little plot
that has no bearing on this highly enjoyable musical.
Songs are by George and Ira Gershwin and include
"Let's Call The Whole Thing Off", "They All Laughed"
and "They Can't Take That Away From Me".

MUS                                    116 min B/W
B,V                        TEVP; CH5 (VHS only)

## SHALLOW GRAVE ***                             18
Richard Styles          USA                    1987
*Tony March, Lisa Stahl, Thomas Law, Carol Cadby,*
*Donna Blatron, Just Kelly*
Four convent girls on vacation are driving through
redneck country when a flat tyre forces them to stop,
and they inadvertently see a local sheriff commit
murder. The sheriff embarks on a chase in order to
silence them in this predictable but taut and well
handled thriller.
THR                                       85 min
B,V                                          EHE

## SHAMAN, THE **                               18
Michael Yakub           USA                    1987
*Michael Conforti, Sean Ashby, Ilene Kristen, James
Farkas, Lynn Weaver, Elvind Harum*
As an evil wizard searches for one to whom he can
pass on his powers, a young boy is forced to oppose his
friend, who has been chosen as successor.
HOR                            86 min (ort 88 min)
B,V                                         CINE

## SHAME **                                     15
Steve Jodrell        AUSTRALIA                 1989
*Deborra-Lee Furness, Tony Barry, Simone Buchanan,
Gillian Jones, Peter Aanensen, Margaret Ford*
A female attorney on vacation is stranded in a small
outback town when her bike breaks down. She
discovers that local women are being subjected to a
reign of sexual violence and uncovers a nasty conspiracy of silence over the rape of a young girl. Despite
the danger she faces, she persuades her victim to
bring charges against her assailants. An uneven
blend of various genres and not a terribly successful
effort.
DRA                                       90 min
V/sh                                 CBS; OASIS

## SHAMPOO *                                    18
Hal Ashby               USA                    1975
*Warren Beatty, Julie Christie, Goldie Hawn, Jack
Warden, Lee Grant, Carrie Fisher, Tony Bill, Jay
Robinson*
A Beverly Hills hairdresser tries to borrow money
from an investment counsellor, with whom he has a
few things in common as the former is having an
affair with the man's wife, mistress and daughter. A
dismal comedy-drama that is sluggish when it should
be funny, and feeble when it should be dramatic. AA:
S. Actress (Grant).
DRA                           106 min (ort 110 min)
V                                           PREST

## SHAMUS **                                    18
Buzz Kulik              USA                    1972
*Burt Reynolds, Dyan Cannon, Giorgio Tozzi, John
Ryan, Joe Santos, Kevin Conway, Ron Weyland, Barry
Beckerman, Kay Frye*
A private eye has to solve a strange case, and suffers
the usual indignities at the hands of assorted villains.
A 1940s film done 1970s style, with the obligatory
violence and a few jokes for film buffs. Written by
Barry Beckerman.
THR                            94 min (ort 106 min)
V                                             RCA

## SHAMWARI **
Clive Harding     SOUTH AFRICA                 1980
*Ian Yule, Ken Gampu, Tamara Franke*
Two convicts in Rhodesia, one white the other black,
escape. Though they hate each other they must
co-operate to survive. This theme was originally
tackled in "The Defiant Ones", which did it with far
more style.

WAR                                       99 min
B,V                                      VCL/CBS

## SHANE ****                                   PG
George Stevens          USA                    1953
*Alan Ladd, Jean Arthur, Van Heflin, Jack Palance,
Brandon De Wilde, Ben Johnson, Edgar Buchanan,
Emile Meyer, Elisha Cook Jr, Douglas Spencer, John
Dierkes, Ellen Corby, Paul McVey, John Miller, Edith
Evanson, Leonard Strong*
A beautiful classic Western, with Ladd as the quiet
lone gunfighter who only wants to hang up his guns
and retire, but is finally forced to aid the homestead-
ers he is living with and whose son idolises him.
Palance gives a remarkably sinister performance as a
gunfighter who is far from retired. Written by A.B.
Guthrie Jr. AA: Cin (Loyal Griggs).
Boa: novel by Jack W. Schaefer.
WES                           113 min (ort 117 min)
V                                             CIC

## SHANGHAI SURPRISE *                          15
Jim Goddard             UK                     1986
*Sean Penn, Madonna (Madonna Ciccone), Paul
Freeman, Richard Griffiths, Philip Sayer, Clyde
Kusatsu, Kay Tong Lim, Sonserai Lee, Victor Wong,
Toru Tanaka, Michael Aldridge, Sarah Lam, George
She*
Romantic adventure, set in 1930s China, following the
exploits of a fortune hunter who is looking for a
chance to earn his fare out of the country, and who
meets up with a woman missionary looking for a
missing cache of opium, needed for her clinic. A most
uncharismatic pairing of erstwhile husband-and-wife
team Penn and Madonna, each totally miscast and
showing not a trace of the panache and acting ability
so vital to films of this kind.
Boa: novel Faraday's Flowers by Tony Kenrick.
A/AD                            93 min (ort 97 min)
V/sh                                          WHV

## SHAOLIN CHALLENGES NINJA **                  15
Liu Chia-Liang     HONG KONG                   1979
*Liu Chia-Hui, Kurata Yasubki, Yuka Mizuno*
When a Chinese martial arts teacher goes to Japan to
persuade his wife to return to him, he finds that he is
obliged to battle a Ninja fighter in order to win her
back.
MAR                        97 min Cut (5 min 40 sec)
V                                             WHV

## SHAOLIN CHAMBER OF DEATH **                  15
Chen Chi Hua       HONG KONG                   1984
*Jackie Chan*
A warrior undergoes a deadly test at the hands of his
Shaolin teachers, in order to discover whether or not
he has the skill needed to avenge the death of his
father.
Aka: SHAOLIN WOODEN MEN
MAR                                      103 min
V                                  TGP; SQUARE

## SHAOLIN DEATH SQUAD **                       18
Joseph Kuo         HONG KONG                   1977
*Polly Shian Kuan, Tin Peng, Carter Wong, Cheung
Yeh, Chin Kang*
The daughter of a murdered statesman, gets aid in her
revenge quest from the title warriors. Standard
mayhem, but quite nicely done.
Aka: SHAOLIN KIDS, THE
MAR                                       90 min
B,V                                          CBS

## SHAOLIN DEVIL AND SHAOLIN ANGEL **           15
                   HONG KONG                   198-
*Chen Sing*
When a series of inexplicable events leads the Emper-
or to conclude that one of his Shaolin warriors is a

traitor, he sends a young fighter to discover his identity.
Aka: SHAOLIN DEVIL, SHAOLIN ANGEL
MAR                                          83 min
B,V                                          VPD

## SHAOLIN DRUNKEN FIGHTER **                        15
Tao Man Po        HONG KONG                 1986
*Wong Tien Lung, Ting Lan*
A man who survived an attack on himself and his family, hides in a Shaolin monastery where he is instructed by the priests, and acquires the skill needed to have his revenge.
Aka: SHAOLIN DRUNK FIGHTER
MAR          85 min (ort 95 min) Cut (1 min 42 sec)
B,V                                          VPD

## SHAOLIN DRUNKEN MONK, THE **                      18
Au Yeung Chun      HONG KONG               197-
*Lau Ka-Fai, Chin Yuen-San, Wong Yat-Tso*
Revenge tale with a little comic relief, told in a flashback to the hero's childhood, but mainly built around his search for the killers of his father.
MAR            77 min (ort 90 min) Cut (2 min 15 sec)
B,V                                          ATLAS

## SHAOLIN INVINCIBLE STICKS **                      18
Lee Tso-Nam
*Don Wong Tao, Chang Yi, Hsia Kuang-Li, Kam Kang, King Kong, Lo Ei Lon*
The heir to the leadership of a stick fighting clan, is pitted against an evil warrior in the formula tale. Superb fighting sequences redeem it.
MAR                                          90 min
B,V                                          NORM

## SHAOLIN IRON CLAWS **                             18
Ko Shih Hao       HONG KONG
*Wang Tao, Lee I Min, Chang Yh, Cheng Shing, Hwa Ling, Chu Li*
A Shaolin assassin is hired to threaten members of the Ching Dynasty into signing a letter, calling for the restoration of the monarchy. When a police chief investigates this plot and his friend is murdered as a warning, it becomes clear that the treacherous assassin must be captured in order to save the Dynasty.
MAR                                          85 min
B,V                        CHAM L/A; NORM L/A; VPD

## SHAOLIN NINJA **                                  18
Wong Tai Loy       HONG KONG              1985
*David Chang, Hsu Shao Chiang, Yasuaki Kurata, Wang Ching Lee, Doris King, Lo Lieh, Pamela Yang, Bruce Liang, Yang Chak Lam, Flora Cheung, Isamu Nakamura*
A master Ninja fights a prolonged battle against a martial arts expert bearing the name of "The Deadly Blade". A dull film with a well-staged set of fight sequences.
Boa: story Return Of One Deadly Blade by Ko Lung.
MAR                                          81 min
B,V                                          IVS

## SHAOLIN RED MASTER *                              18
Sung Ting Mei      HONG KONG
An orphan expelled from the mighty Hang Saih Shaolin Temple, goes in search of the man who murdered his family. The usual revenge-based developments occur.
MAR                       84 min (ort 90 min)
B,V                                          CLOK

## SHAOLIN TEMPLE **                                 18
Chang Hsin Yen     HONG KONG              1976
*Chang Cheh, Wang Chung, Shan Mao, Lung Wei, Ti Lung, Shee Fong, Lin Kuang-Tseng, Li Lin Jei, Yue Chen Wei, Yue Hai, Din Nam*
A secret that is of vital importance to the Emperor, is guarded by kung fu masters prepared to protect it

with their lives. When two pupils, who learnt kung fu in order to avenge their fathers' deaths, return to their Shaolin temple, they find it under siege and unite with the other pupils to fight off the attackers.
MAR          113 min Cut (3 min 22 sec); 95 min
                          Cut (8 sec) (ort 117 min)
B,V                          WHV L/A; VIDPAC

## SHAOLIN TEMPLE 2 **                               18
Joseph Kuo        HONG KONG
*Chen Chien Chang, Sun Kuo Ming*
Kung fu adventure set in the last days of the Ming Dynasty, and telling of how the last Ming princess seeks refuge in a Shaolin mountain temple, where the priests prepare to defend her from her attackers.
Aka: SHAOLIN TEMPLE STRIKES BACK
MAR                                          86 min
B,V                                          VPD

## SHAOLIN WARRIOR *                                 15
Li Chao           HONG KONG
*Chen Sing, Kam Fong, Chen Wai Man, Chan Fei, Jia Ren*
A Tartar warlord obsessed with the desire to possess a sword, causes a massacre in which the single survivor takes an oath of revenge against him.
MAR            82 min (ort 88 min) Cut (58 sec)
V                                            DRUM

## SHAOLIN: THE BLOOD MISSION ***                    18
Leung Wing Chan   HONG KONG              1984
*Sun Kok Ming, Poou Cheung, Huang Tang Ming (Huang Cheng-Li), Lo Wah Sing, Wong Yin Fong*
An evil general is sent to discover the names of any people who oppose the rule of the Manchu Dynasty, and becomes convinced that the peaceful monks of a Shaolin temple are hiding rebels. He has the temple burned to the ground, but this is only the prelude to a fast-paced martial arts adventure.
MAR                                          85 min
B,V                                          VPD

## SHAPE OF THINGS TO COME, THE *                    PG
George McCowan     CANADA                1979
*Jack Palance, Carol Lynley, Barry Morse, John Ireland, Nicholas Campbell, Eddie Benton*
Nothing to do with the classic 1936 film based on an H.G. Wells script, this one is about a megalomaniac who tries to take over a colony on the moon, that contains the remnants of those who escaped Earth's nuclear destruction. A low-budget SF dud.
FAN                                          94 min
B,V                          INT L/A; XTASY

## SHAPE UP *                                        18
Marice Tobias      USA                   1985
*Daniel Greene, Alice Moore, Lee Taylor Allen, Bob Small, Alex Intriage, Carol James, Earleen Carey*
A rather mindless film, set at a health club where the patrons go through their workouts to a throbbing, pulsating soundtrack.
COM                                          89 min
B,V                                          RCA

## SHARK! **                                         15
Samuel Fuller      MEXICO/USA            1968
*Burt Reynolds, Barry Sullivan, Arthur Kennedy, Silvia Pinal, Enrique Lucero, Charles Berriochoa*
A treasure hunt in shark-infested water gets a gunrunner in the Sudan involved with unscrupulous divers searching for wrecks, in this tepid effort. A stunt diver was killed by a shark during filming, earning the film a bad advance revue. Written by Fuller (who disowned this production) and John Kingsbridge. The film was badly re-edited after Fuller lost control of it.
Aka: MANEATER
Boa: novel His Bones Are Coral by Victor Canning.

A/AD                                89 min (ort 92 min)
B,V,V2        IFS L/A; VGM; MIA; PARK (VHS only)

**SHARK'S CAVE, THE ***
Anthony Richmond (Antonio Riccamonza)
                ITALY/SPAIN                    1978
*Arthur Kennedy, Andres Garcia, Janet Agren, Pino
Colizzi, Maximo Valverde, Sergio Doria*
A skin-diver with amnesia, turns up six months after
his ship and its crew disappeared in the Bermuda
triangle.
Aka: BERMUDAS: LA CUEVA DE LOS
TIBURONES; BERMUDE: LA FOSSA
MALEDETTA; CAVE OF THE SHARKS
DRA                                              83 min
B,V,V2                                           HOK

**SHARK'S PARADISE ***                              PG
Michael Jenkins    AUSTRALIA                      1986
*David Reyne, Sally Taylor, Ralph Cotterill, Ron Becks,
Lynda Stoner, John Paramor, Dennis Miller*
A team of detectives in Australia join forces, in an
attempt to catch a vicious blackmailer who claims
that he is able to lure killer sharks to the beaches of a
popular surfing resort. His threats to kill the local
tourist trade are taken seriously by the mayor, who
puts together an unconventional unit in order to track
the culprit down. Very much a TV movie, this is
glossy, shallow and totally forgettable.
THR                       94 min (ort 120 min) mTV
B,V                                              VES

**SHARK'S TREASURE ***                              PG
Cornel Wilde        USA                          1974
*Cornel Wilde, Yaphet Kotto, John Neilson, Cliff
Osmond, David Canary, David Gilliam*
A fortune in gold in a sunken Spanish treasure fleet,
lures four men into a dangerous Caribbean adventure.
A likeable piece of nonsense with the usual heroics
from the star, and a couple of enjoyable sequences.
A/AD            91 min (ort 95 min) (Cut at film release)
B,V                                              WHV

**SHARKY'S MACHINE ***                              18
Burt Reynolds        USA                         1981
*Burt Reynolds, Rachel Ward, Brian Keith, Vittorio
Gassman, Charles Durning, Bernie Casey, Henry
Silva, Earl Holliman, Richard Libertini, John Fiedler,
Darryl Hickman, Joseph Mascolo, Carol Locatell, Hari
Rhodes, James O'Connell*
Extremely bloody and violent film about a vice cop
and his crusade against the underworld, falling for a
beautiful prostitute in the process. Written by Gerald
Di Pego.
Boa: novel by William Diehl.
THR                       117 min (ort 120 min) Cut
                        (Cut at film release by 9 sec)
B,V                                              WHV

**SHATTERED ***                                     15
Lamont Johnson      USA                          1989
*Shelley Long, Tom Conti, John Rubinstein, Alan
Fudge, Jamie Rose, Christine Healy, Frank Converse*
A woman suffering from multiple personalities undergoes therapy and learns that this condition results
from abuse she suffered as a child, when both she and
her sister were sexually abused by her brutal stepfather. Having discovered that he is still alive, she
leaves – apprently on a mission of vengeance.
Allegedly based on a true story, but Long's lack of
range and the script implausibilites do not work to the
film's advantage.
DRA                                             120 min
V                                               NWV

**SHATTERED INNOCENCE ***                           15
Sandor Stern        USA                          1987
*Jonna Lee, John Pleshette, Melinda Dillon, Kris
Kamm, Ben Frank, Dennis Howard, Richard Cox*
A naive young cheerleader from a small town dreams
of Hollywood stardom, but becomes a porno actress
instead. A fictionalised account of the tragic life of
real-life porno star Shauna Grant, who committed
suicide. Her story was told once before in the TV
documentary "Death Of A Porn Queen". Fair.
DRA                       90 min (ort 100 min) mTV
V                                               GHV

**SHATTERED SPIRITS ***                             PG
Robert Greenwald    USA                          1986
*Martin Sheen, Melinda Dillon, Matthew Laborteaux,
Roxana Zal, Lukas Haas, Jill Schoelen, Jenny Gago,
Gabrielle Mandelik, Lenny Hicks, Dyana Ortelli, John
Herzfeld, John Miranda, Ed Call, Francine Lembi,
Freddie Dawson*
An alcoholic who has previously been protected by his
wife, suddenly finds his life crumbling around him
when he loses his job, and the whole family is put on
the poverty line, forcing him to try to tackle the
situation himself. An absorbing drama with convinc-
ing performances from all concerned.
DRA                        89 min (ort 100 min) mTV
B,V                                             IVS

**SHATTERED VOWS ***
Jack Bender         USA                          1984
*David Morse, Valerie Bertinelli, Caroline McWilliams,
Tom Parsekian, Millie Perkins, Leslie Ackerman, Lisa
Jane Persky, Elayne Heilveil, Ben Powers, Patricia
Neal, Matt Adler, Joseph Battaglia, Susan Blackstone*
A young nun and priest fall in love and have to make a
difficult decision. Based on the story of Dr Mary
Gilligan Wong who gave up her calling to become a
clinical psychologist. Average.
Boa: book Nun: A Memoir by Mary Gilligan Wong.
DRA                        90 min (ort 100 min) mTV
B,V                                        IPC/VSP L/A

**SHE ***                                           18
Avi Nesher         ITALY    1982 (released 1985)
*Sandahl Bergman, Harrison Muller, David Goss,
Quinn Kessler, Elena Wiedermann, Gordon Mitchell,
Laurie Sherman, Andrew McLeay, Cyrus Elias, David
Brandon, Susan Adler, Gregory Snegoff, Mary
D'Antin, Mario Pedone*
Very loose adaptation of the classic story of a female
warrior who leads her tribe against its enemies. A
vacuous and feeble yarn.
Boa: novel by H. Rider Haggard.
A/AD                                            104 min
B,V                                             AVA

**SHE-DEVIL ***                                     15
Susan Seidelman    USA                           1989
*Meryl Streep, Roseanne Barr, Ed Begley Jr, Sylvia
Miles, Linda Hunt, Bryan Larkin, Elizabeth Peters, A.
Martinez*
A mutilated version of Weldon's comic novel, that
follows the revenge plotted by dowdy Barr, as she sets
out to destroy the life of her unfaithful husband after
he goes off to live with a romantic novelist. This crude
and somewhat grotesque comedy is hampered by
sluggish plotting and Barr's lack of range, but Streep
is wonderful as the glamorous writer, and does all she
can with her part. Very disappointing.
Boa: The Life And Loves Of A She-Devil by Fay
Weldon.
COM                                      95 min (ort 99 min)
V                                               VIR

**SHE KNEW NO OTHER WAY ***                         18
Osmiros Efstratiadis  GREECE                      1977
*Maria Vassililou, Chris Nomikos, Dino Theodorelos,
John Petro-Poulos, Dimis Bouloukos, Andreas
Barkoulis*
Young people stranded on Rhodes, try various ways of
making ends meet in this routine sex farce.

A      73 min Cut (4 min 10 sec in addition to film cuts)
B,V                                         PRI L/A; SHEP

## SHE KNOWS TOO MUCH **                                PG
Paul Lynch            USA                         1988
*Meredith Baxter Birney, Robert Urich, Erik Estrada*
A prominent congressman is accompanied on his
campaign trail by a former criminal, who is now his
spokesman on minority affairs. Wherever the politician goes a series of crimes occur, but when a special
agent begins an investigation, he finds that things are
far from simple. A workmanlike blend of comedy and
mystery, with an unlikely plot and a shortage of good
gags.
COM                                          89 min
B,V                                             MGM

## SHE'S OUT OF CONTROL *                                15
Stan Dragoti          USA                         1989
*Tony Danza, Catherine Hicks, Wallace Shawn, Dick
O'Neill, Ami Dolenz, Laura Mooney, Derek McGrath,
Dana Ashbrook*
Danza plays a widower whose precocious and rapidly
maturing daughter gives him a few headaches when
she is transformed into a raving beauty via some
beauty tips, courtesy of his girlfriend. A one-idea
comedy that takes an idea more suited to a 30-minute
TV sketch and stretches it just about as far as it will
go.
COM                              90 min (ort 95 min) subH
V                                             20VIS

## SHE WAS FAIR GAME ***                                18
Mario Andreacchio AUSTRALIA                       1985
*Garry Uho, Cassandra Delaney, Peter Ford, David
Sandford*
An attractive female game warden runs into a trio of
boozy kangaroo hunters, and a series of tit-for-tat
incidents quickly develops into a full-scale conflict,
with their hunting activities being transferred to her.
A taut and surprisingly gripping tale.
THR                                          90 min
B,V                                             EHE

## SHE WORE A YELLOW RIBBON ****                          U
John Ford             USA                         1949
*John Wayne, Joanne Dru, John Agar, Victor
McLaglen, Ben Johnson, Harry Carey Jr, Mildred
Natwick, George O'Brien, Arthur Shields, Francis
Ford, Harry Woods, Chief Big Tree, Cliff Lyons, Noble
Johnson, Michael Dugan*
The second in Ford's cavalry trilogy, with Wayne as
the dutiful officer reluctant to retire in the face of an
imminent Indian uprising. Excellent. Followed by
RIO GRANDE. Filmed in Technicolor and written by
Frank Nugent and Lawrence Stallings. AA: Cin
(Winton C. Hoch).
Boa: short story by James Warner Bellah.
Osca: FIRST REBEL, THE
WES      98 min (ort 103 min); 169 min (2 film cassette)
B/W
V                                               VCC

## SHEENA *                                             15
John Guillermin       USA                         1984
*Tanya Roberts, Ted Wass, Donovan Scott, Elizabeth of
Toro, France Zobda, Trevor Thomas*
The dull adventure story of a female Tarzan in Kenya
and her struggle with game poachers. Possibly in-
tended as a spoof, but neither funny nor especially
well made. Written by David Newman and Lorenzo
Semple Jr.
Aka: SHEENA: QUEEN OF THE JUNGLE
A/AD                111 min (ort 117 min) Cut (1 sec)
B,V                                             RCA

## SHE'LL BE WEARING PINK PYJAMAS **                     15
John Goldschmidt      UK                          1984
*Julie Walters, Jane Evers, Janet Henfrey, Anthony*

*Higgins, Paula Jacobs, Penelope Nice, Maureen
O'Brien, Alyson Spiro, Jane Wood, Pauline Yates, Bill
Lund, Paul Butterworth, Nicky Puttnam, Paul
Atkinson, Gail Herring*
Eight mostly ill-prepared women, tackle a week-end
survival course in the Lake District, baring their souls
to each other in the process, and spending a good deal
of their time moaning about men. An intermittently
engaging tale, with good ensemble performances but a
contrived script.
COM                              86 min (ort 90 min)
B,V                                             PVG

## SHE'LL FOLLOW YOU ANYWHERE *
David C. Rea          UK                          1971
*Keith Barron, Kenneth Cope, Hilary Pritchard,
Philippa Gail, Richard Vernon, Penny Brahms,
Sandra Bryant, Anna Matisse, Andrea Allan,
Josephine Baxter, Mary Collinson, Madeleine
Collinson, Linda Cunningham, Valerie Stanton*
Two perfume-makers create a scent that women find
irresistible, in this lightweight and dated sex comedy.
COM                                          98 min
B,V,V2                                       INT L/A

## SHENANDOAH ***                                       PG
Andrew V. McLaglen    USA                         1965
*James Stewart, Doug McClure, Glenn Corbett,
Rosemary Forsyth, Katherine Ross, Patrick Wayne,
Phillip Alford, Charles Robinson, Denver Pyle, George
Kennedy, Paul Fix, Tim McIntire, James McMullan,
James Best, Warren Oates*
Saga of the American Civil War and how it affects a
Virginia family. Stewart as a widower is indifferent to
the struggle between the states, until his family is
reluctantly drawn into it. A moving and intelligent
tale that formed the basis for a later Broadway
musical. This was Ross' film debut. Written by James
Lee Barrett.
WES                             100 min (ort 105 min)
B,V                                             CIC

## SHERIFF AND THE SATELLITE KID, THE **               PG
Michele Lupo          ITALY                       1979
*Bud Spencer (Carlo Pedersoli), Joe Bugner, Raymond
Harmstorf, Pupa De Luca, Carlo Reali, Gigi Bonos,
Harold E. Finch, Dino Emmanuelli, Giancarlo
Bastinianoni, Giavanni Cianfriglia, Ottaviano
Dell'Acqua, Vincenzo Maggio*
A comedy Western in which a young boy claims to be a
visitor from outer space, but the local sheriff has his
doubts. An aimless, lightweight comedy, followed by
WHY DID YOU PICK ON ME? in 1981.
Aka: CHISSA PERSCHE . . . CAPITANO TUTTO A
ME; LO SCERIFFO E L'EXTRATERRESTRE; UNO
SCERIFFO EXTRATERRESTRE . . . POCO EXTRA
E MOLTO TERRESTRE
COM                              89 min Cut (5 sec)
B,V                                             MED

## SHERLOCK HOLMES ***
Alfred L. Werker      USA                         1939
*Basil Rathbone, Nigel Bruce, George Zucco, Ida
Lupino, Alan Marshal, Terry Kilburn, E.E. Clive,
Mary Gordon, Henry Stephenson*
Released together with THE HOUND OF THE BAS-
KERVILLES, both these films marked the start of a
series based on Conan Doyle's famous sleuth. In this
engaging yarn, Holmes is sent on a false trail by his
old enemy Moriarty, as the latter is planning to steal
the Crown Jewels. Look out for the sequence where
Rathbone sings a charming little ditty in disguise.
Written by Edwin Blum and followed by SHERLOCK
HOLMES AND THE VOICE OF TERROR.
Aka: ADVENTURES OF SHERLOCK HOLMES,
THE
DRA                                          83 min B/W
B,V                                          CBS L/A

## SHERLOCK HOLMES AND THE SECRET WEAPON **
Roy William Neill          USA          1942
*Basil Rathbone, Nigel Bruce, Lionel Atwill, Kaaren Verne, William Post Jr, Dennis Hoey, Mary Gordon, Harry Woods, George Burr MacAnnan, Paul Fix, Henry Victor, Holmes Herbert, Harold De Becker, Harry Cording, Paul Bryar*
The fourth film in a long series, this is set rather unexpectedly in London of the 1940s, with our sleuth now involved in foiling a Nazi attempt to steal an experimental bomb-sight. This one contains a few elements from the Arthur Conan Doyle story "The Dancing Men". SHERLOCK HOLMES IN WASHINGTON followed. Average.
DRA                                    68 min B/W
B,V                                        MOV

## SHERLOCK HOLMES AND THE VOICE OF TERROR **
John Rawlins              USA          1942
*Basil Rathbone, Nigel Bruce, Hillary Brooke, Evelyn Ankers, Reginald Denny, Montagu Love, Mary Gordon, Thomas Gomez, Henry Daniell, Olaf Hytten, Harry Stubbs, Edgar Barrier, Robert O. Davies, Lon Chaney Jr*
An outbreak of sabotage leads Holmes to a traitor in the Cabinet Office of His Majesty's Government. Number 3 in a long-running series, and followed by SHERLOCK HOLMES AND THE SECRET WEAPON. Fair. The script is by Lynn Riggs.
Boa: short story His Last Bow by Arthur Conan Doyle.
Osca: ADVENTURES OF SHERLOCK HOLMES, THE
THR                                    65 min B/W
B,V                                        MGM

## SHERLOCK HOLMES AND THE WOMAN IN GREEN **
Roy William Neill          USA          1945
*Basil Rathbone, Nigel Bruce, Hillary Brooke, Henry Daniell, Paul Cavanagh, Matthew Boulton, Eve Amber, Frederic Worlock, Tom Bryson, Sally Shepherd, Mary Gordon, Percival Vivian, Olaf Hytten, Harold de Becker, Tommy Hughes*
A number of strange murders baffle the police (don't they always?) and our sleuth is called in, discovering the existence of a blackmail outfit that makes use of a lady hypnotist. A fairly enjoyable adventure (the eleventh) in a long-running series.
Aka: WOMAN IN GREEN, THE
THR                                    66 min B/W
B,V                    MOV L/A; PORVI; VCL/CBS

## SHERLOCK HOLMES AND THE SPIDERWOMAN ***                              U
Roy William Neill          USA          1943
*Basil Rathbone, Nigel Bruce, Gale Sondergaard, Dennis Hoey, Mary Gordon, Arthur Hohl, Alec Craig*
Holmes comes up against Sondergaard, in the guise of a femme fatale who is responsible for a series of unexplained "suicides", the victims all being found to have large insurance policies. One of the best in the series, this adventure has an alluring villainess and a gripping climax set in a shooting gallery.
Aka: SPIDER WOMAN
DRA                          60 min (ort 62 min) B/W
V/h                                        CBS

## SHERLOCK HOLMES: DRESSED TO KILL **
Roy William Neil           USA          1946
*Basil Rathbone, Nigel Bruce, Tom Dillon, Edmond Breon, Patricia Morison, Frederic Worlock, Carl Harbord, Patricia Cameron, Tom P. Dillon, Topsy Glyn, Harry Cording, Mary Gordon, Ian Wolfe, Lillian Bronson, Cyril Delevanti*
A Sherlock Holmes adventure in a long-running

series made in the 1940s. In this tale Holmes and Watson are on the trail of three wooden boxes. The last in a series of 14 films, that made use of Rathbone and Bruce as Holmes and Watson respectively, and started with THE HOUND OF THE BASKERVILLES and SHERLOCK HOLMES. Fair but by no means one of their best.
Aka: DRESSED TO KILL; SHERLOCK HOLMES AND THE SECRET CODE
DRA                                    68 min B/W
B,V                                        MOV

## SHERLOCK HOLMES FACES DEATH ***       U
Roy William Neill          USA          1943
*Basil Rathbone, Nigel Bruce, Hillary Brooke, Milburn Stone, Halliwell Hobbes, Arthur Margetson, Dennis Hoey, Gavin Muir, Frederic Worlock, Olaf Hytten, Gerald Hamer, Mary Gordon, Vernon Downing*
Watson asks Holmes to solve a series of bizarre deaths at a convalescent home for retired officers. A good film in the series that sticks fairly closely to the basics of the story. A highlight is Holmes' demonstration of his deductive powers, when he gathers all the suspects together and moves them about like so many chess pieces.
Boa: short story The Musgrave Ritual by Arthur Conan Doyle.
DRA                          66 min (ort 68 min) B/W
V/h                                        CBS

## SHERLOCK HOLMES IN WASHINGTON ***    U
Roy William Neill          USA          1942
*Basil Rathbone, Nigel Bruce, Marjorie Lord, Henry Daniell, George Zucco, John Archer, Gavin Muir*
Another updated but enjoyable entry in this variable series, with Holmes now in Washington where he breaks a Nazi spy ring and prevents an important microfilmed document from falling into the wrong hands. A strong beginning gives way to a sluggish middle portion, but the film is redeemed by the gripping climax.
DRA                          68 min (ort 71 min) B/W
V/h                                        CBS

## SHERLOCK HOLMES: TERROR BY NIGHT **
Roy William Neil           USA          1946
*Basil Rathbone, Nigel Bruce, Alan Mowbray, Dennis Hoey, Renee Godfrey, Mary Forbes, Billy Bevan, Frederic Worlock, Leyland Hodgson, Geoffrey Steele, Boyd Davis, Janet Murdoch, Skelton Knaggs, Gerald Hamer, Harry Cording*
Routine Sherlock Holmes adventure, in which a stolen jewel is recovered and murders are solved on a speeding train, complete with interposed shots of the supposed scenery to be seen between London and Edinburgh. Number 13 in a long-running series.
Aka: TERROR BY NIGHT
DRA                                    60 min B/W
B,V                                    PORVI; MOV

## SHERLOCK HOLMES: THE BASKERVILLE       U
CURSE **
Alex Nicholas              UK            1983
*Voice of Peter O'Toole*
Animated version intended for kids. Average.
Aka: BASKERVILLE CURSE, THE; SHERLOCK HOLMES AND THE BASKERVILLE CURSE
Boa: novel The Hound Of The Baskervilles by Arthur Conan Doyle.
CAR                                      67 min
B,V                    RPTA/PVG; MSD (VHS only)

## SHERLOCK HOLMES: THE HOUND OF THE BASKERVILLES ***                      PG
Sidney Lanfield            USA          1939
*Basil Rathbone, Nigel Bruce, Richard Greene, Wendy Barrie, Lionel Atwill, John Carradine, Beryl Mercer, Mary Gordon, E.E. Clive, Morton Lowry, Ralph*

*Forbes, Barlowe Borland, Eily Malyon, Ivan Simpson*
Having inherited a Dartmoor estate from his uncle, who met a tragic end, a young man calls in Holmes in order to avoid a similar fate. Rathbone's first appearance as the sleuth gives ample demonstration of his suitability, and this careful though studio-bound adaptation is atmospheric if a little languid. A highlight is Rathbone's appearance as a tramp (Holmes was after all a master of disguise).
Aka: HOUND OF THE BASKERVILLES, THE
Boa: story by Arthur Conan Doyle.
DRA                                           80 min B/W
V                                                  CBS

## SHERLOCK HOLMES: THE MASKS OF      PG
## DEATH **
UK                          1984
*Peter Cushing, John Mills, Anne Baxter, Ray Milland, Gordon Jackson*
Set in 1913, this tale has Holmes coming out of retirement to solve a case that threatens the security of Britain, and whose trail of murder leads him to an old and dangerous enemy.
DRA                                           80 min mTV
V                                                  TELS

## SHERLOCK HOLMES: THE SCARLET
## CLAW ***                                       PG
Roy William Neill          USA              1944
*Basil Rathbone, Nigel Bruce, Gerard Hamer, Arthur Hohl, Miles Mander, Ian Wolfe, Paul Cavanaugh, Kay Harding*
A series of nasty murders takes place at a remote Canadian village, but fortunately Holmes is on hand to nab the culprit. One of the best in this updated Holmes series, the mood is unashamedly patriotic and the settings realistic. Only the plot (loosely based on "The Hound Of The Baskervilles") is decidedly weak.
Aka: SCARLET CLAW, THE
DRA                                70 min (ort 74 min) B/W
V                                                  CBS

## SHERLOCK HOLMES: THE VALLEY OF FEAR ** U
UK                          1983
*Voice of Peter O'Toole*
A competent animated version of this tale.
Aka: VALLEY OF FEAR, THE; SHERLOCK HOLMES AND THE VALLEY OF FEAR
Boa: short story The Valley Of Fear by Arthur Conan Doyle.
CAR                                           48 min
V                                                  MSD

## SHE'S BACK *                                   18
Tim Kincaid                USA              1988
*Carrie Fisher, Robert Joy*
A tasteless comedy in which a man's wife is murdered by a gang of thugs, just after they move into their new home. Her ghost returns to nag her husband until he satisfies her desire for revenge.
COM                                           88 min
B,V                                                VES

## SHE'S GOTTA HAVE IT ***                        18
Spike Lee                  USA              1986
*Tracy Camila Johns, Tommy Redmond Hicks, John Canada Terrell, Spike Lee, Raye Dowell, Bill Lee*
The story of a sexy young woman, her complicated love life and the three men who compete for her affections. A vigorous if uneven little film, quite charming in its way. The director's father, Bill Lee, provides the catchy jazz score.
COM                                85 min B/W and Colour
B,V                                                PAL

## SHE'S HAVING A BABY **                         15
John Hughes                USA              1988
*Kevin Bacon, Elizabeth McGovern, Alec Baldwin, Isabel Lorca, William Windom, Cathryn Damon,*

*Holland Taylor, James Ray, Dennis Dugan, John Ashton, Edie McClurg, Paul Gleason*
A lighthearted look at the problems facing a newly-married couple, all told from the point of view of the husband who is beginning to feel trapped by it all. Not quite the fresh and witty comedy it was intended to be, but despite the rather tedious plot, the stars perform well enough to make it watchable.
COM                                102 min (ort 106 min)
V/sh                                               CIC

## SHE'S IN THE ARMY NOW **                       PG
Hy Averback                USA              1981
*Kathleen Quinlan, Jamie Lee Curtis, Susan Blanchard, Julie Carmen, Melanie Griffith, Janet MacLachlan, Dale Robinette, Robert Peirce, Lynn Barbara Block, Rocky Bauer, Douglas Dirkson, Damita Jo Freeman, Susan Barnes*
A PRIVATE BENJAMIN clone that formed the pilot for a TV series, and tells of the comic mishaps and romantic entanglements of five young women who join the army. A film as unfunny as it is unoriginal.
COM                                96 min Cut (7 sec) mTV
B,V                                           CBS; IVS

## SHINBONE ALLEY **
John D. Wilson/David Detiege
USA                          1970
*Voices of: Eddie Bracken, Carol Channing, John Carradine, Alan Reed Sr*
Animated musical about a cockroach and an alley cat, who form a song-writing team. A lively if hardly memorable adaptation of a Joe Darion musical, based on the characters created by Don Marquis.
CAR                                76 min (ort 86 min)
B,V                                           VCL/CBS

## SHINING, THE **                                18
Stanley Kubrick            UK               1980
*Jack Nicholson, Shelley Duvall, Danny Lloyd, Scatman Crothers, Barry Nelson, Joe Turkel, Philip Stone, Lia Beldam, Billie Gibson, Barry Dennan, David Baxt, Lisa Burns, Alison Coleridge, Kate Phelps, Anne Jackson, Tony Burton*
A man takes on the job of caretaker to a deserted hotel, in its closed season. As he begins to fall victim to evil supernatural forces, he undergoes an unpleasant personality change that threatens his wife and son. A moody but cumbersome tale, that has Nicholson over-acting so wildly that it all becomes rather ludicrous. Nevertheless, there are some genuinely powerful moments.
Boa: novel by Stephen King.
HOR                                114 min (ort 146 min)
B,V                                                WHV

## SHINOBI NINJA **                               18
Lik Chuen/Syuji Gotho
JAPAN                        1984
*Tadashi Yamashita, Eric Lee, Karen Lee Shepard*
A karate expert is called in to deal with a threat to Japan's security from evil Ninja warriors.
MAR                        98 min (ort 103 min) Cut (2 min 12 sec)
V                                          RAP969 L/A; RVD

## SHIPWRECK! ***                                 U
Stewart Raffill            USA              1978
*Robert Logan, Mikki Jamison-Olson, Heather Rattray, Cjon Damitri Patterson, Shannon Saylor*
A family sets off on a journey around the world but is shipwrecked on an island off the Alaskan coast. A rousing family adventure, made even more enjoyable by the colourful locations.
Aka: SEA GYPSIES, THE; SHIPWRECKED
A/AD                                           100 min
B,V                                                WHV

## SHIRLEY VALENTINE ***                          15
Lewis Gilbert              UK/USA           1989

*Pauline Collins, Tom Conti, Alison Steadman, Julia McKenzie, Joanna Lumley, Bernard Hill, Sylvia Syms*
Collins repeats her stage role in this quirky little comedy about a bored middle-aged housewife, who leaves her dull life behind when she heads for the Greek isles and a spot of extra-marital romance. Written by Russell, who also gave us EDUCATING RITA, this wry little film is sustained by its witty observations on life, delivered by Collins in a splendid Tony Award-winning performance. Not exactly a masterpiece, but quite charming.
Boa: play by Willy Russell.
COM                                104 min (ort 108 min)
V                                                     CIC

**SHIVERS **
David Cronenberg    CANADA             1975
*Paul Hampton, Joe Silver, Lyn Lowry, Alan Migicovsky, Barbara Steele, Susan Petrie, Ronald Mlodzik, Barrie Baldaro, Camille Ducharme, Al Rochman, Hanna Poznanska, Wally Martin, Vlastra Vrana, Charles Perley, Julie Wildman*
The tenants of an apartment block fall victim to nasty parasites that cause violent sexual excesses. The first big film from the director, with an abundance of gruesome effects that have now become his trademark. A TV version was made, but was cut to 77 minutes.
Aka: PARASITE MURDERS, THE; THEY CAME FROM WITHIN
HOR                                                   86 min
B,V,V2                                                INT

**SHOCK ***
Mario Bava          ITALY                         18
                                                   1977
*John Steiner, Daria Nicolodi, David Colin Jr, Ivan Rassimov, Nicola Salerno*
Bava's last feature tells of a woman's son who is possessed by the spirit of his late father, and used as a tool to drive his mother insane, as a way for the dead man to avenge his brutal murder at her hands. A highly atmospheric film, but one in which much gratuitous gore tends to detract from the narrative. A loose remake called UNTIL DEATH, was made by Bava's son in 1987.
Aka: ALL 33 DI VIA OROLOGIO FA SEMPRE FREDDO; BEYOND THE DOOR 2; SHOCK (TRANSFER SUSPENSE HYPNOS); SUSPENSE
HOR                                                   87 min
B,V                                         VDM L/A; STABL

**SHOCK CORRIDOR ***
Samuel Fuller       USA                         1963
*Peter Breck, Constance Towers, Gene Evans, James Best, Hari Rhodes, Philip Ahn, Paul Dubov, Frank Gerstle, William Zuckert, John Matthews, John Craig, Larry Tucker, Chuck Roberson, Neyle Morrow, Linda Randolph, Rachel Roman*
A reporter pretends to be mad in order to solve the mystery surrounding the death of an inmate of an asylum, but soon finds himself overwhelmed by the experience. A taut and gripping drama that still retains considerable power. Scripted by Fuller and photographed by Stanley Cortez.
DRA              95 min (ort 101 min) B/W and Colour
B,V,V2                                           VUL L/A

**SHOCK TREATMENT **                              PG
Jim Sharman         USA                         1981
*Jessica Harper, Cliff De Young, Richard O'Brien, Patricia Quinn, Charles Gray, Ruby Wax, Nell Campbell, Barry Humphries, Rik Mayall, Manning Redwood, Darlene Johnson, Wendy Raebeck, Jeremy Newson, Betsy Brantley, Chris Malcolm*
Satire of American life, in which an entire town has become a non-stop TV show. A failed spin-off from the musical THE ROCKY HORROR PICTURE SHOW, with the same director and many of the original cast.

Unfortunately this unusual basic premise is never allowed to develop.
COM                                 91 min (ort 95 min)
V/sh                                                   CBS

**SHOCK TREATMENT **                              18
Julian Doyle        USA                         1987
*Nancy Paul, John Rowe, Robert Ashby, Norman Chancer*
An American father places his heroin addict daughter in an English clinic, that is known for its controversial methods of treatment. Once there, she finds herself a prisoner, and learns that the clinic engages in far more sinister activities. A fair thriller, scripted by Dolyle and Mark Ezra.
THR                                                   86 min
V                                                     VES

**SHOCK TROOP ***                                 18
J. Christian Ingvordsen
                    USA                         1988
*John Christian, Oliver Daniels*
This out-dated idea has a tough American GI being captured by the Soviets, and sent to a harsh forced labour camp. He soon escapes and makes his way to Afghanistan, where he joins the Mujahedeen freedom fighters. A mindless and barely watchable film, with a few competent action sequences that do little to redeem it.
A/AD                                                 113 min
V                                                     RCA

**SHOCK WAVES ***
Ken Weiderhorn      USA                         1977
*Peter Cushing, Brooke Adams, John Carradine, Fred Buch, Jack Davidson, Luke Halpin, D.J. Sidney, Don Stout, Tony Moskal, Gary Levinson, Bob Miller, Bob White, Jay Meader, Talmadge Scott*
Tourists land on a Caribbean island, and discover that a former SS officer has been conducting strange experiments in the creation of Nazi androids. A low-budget effort that has been somewhat ignored, but is well worth seeing for the imaginative handling of its ideas.
Aka: ALMOST HUMAN; DEATH CORPS; DEATH WAVES
HOR                                                   86 min
B,V,V2                                                GHV

**SHOCKER ***                                     18
Wes Craven          USA                         1989
*Michael Murphy, Peter Berg, Mitch Pileggi, Cami Cooper, Theodore Raimi*
A demented TV repairman with a penchant for hacking families to death in the evenings, is finally caught and executed, but continues to live on within TV sets, and terrorises the family of his last victim. Craven's new creation is a larger-than-life monster of massive personality, well placed to take over from Freddy of the NIGHTMARE ON ELM STREET films. Written by Craven, this gruesome shocker employs some remarkable state-of-the-art visual effects.
HOR                                 105 min (ort 110 min)
V/sh                                                  GHV

**SHOESTRING **                                   15
Douglas Camfield    UK                     1979/1980
*Trevor Eve, Michael Medwin, Doran Godwin, Liz Crowther*
A local radio phone-in DJ works as a kind of citizens private eye, in this compilation from a TV series that was well made, but a little short on plot development and suspense. The original series consisted of twenty-six 50-minute episodes.
THR                                              105 min mTV
B,V                                                   BBC

**SHOGUN ***                                      15
Jerry London        JAPAN/USA               1981

*Richard Chamberlain, Toshiro Mifune, Yoko Shimada, Frankie Sakai, Yuki Meguro, John Rhys-Davies, Michael Hordern, Alan Badel, Damien Thomas, Leon Lissek, Nobuo Kaneko, Vladek Sheybal, Hideo Takamatsu, Hiromi Senno*
A cut down version of the 12-hour TV saga, loosely based on the true story of the rise of Toranaga, first of the Japanese Shoguns, and his relationship with Blackthorne, one of a group of English sailors shipwrecked off the coast of Japan. A colourful and detailed account that suffers somewhat from the degree of editing required to compress it. This was Badel's last film. Orson Welles narrates.
Boa: novel by James Clavell.
DRA                 119 min (ort 720 min) Cut (10 sec) mTV
V                                                         CIC

## SHOOT *
Harvey Hart          CANADA                 1976
*Cliff Robertson, Ernest Borgnine, James Blendick, Henry Silva, Les Carlson, Larry Reynolds, Kat Reid, Helen Shaver, Gloria Carlin Chetwynd, Allan McRae, Ed McNamara, Peter Langley, Helena Hart, James Ince, George Markos*
A misunderstanding between two groups of hunters, that arose from the accidental shooting of one hunter, escalates into a full-scale conflict in this brutal and unattractive variant on DELIVERANCE.
A/AD                              90 min (ort 98 min)
B,V                                              HVM; HVH

## SHOOT THE MOON **                              15
Allan Parker         USA                     1981
*Albert Finney, Diane Keaton, Karen Allen, Peter Weller, Dana Hill, Viveka Davis, Leora Dana, Tracey Gold, Tina Yothers*
A study of marital breakdown set in Marin County, California, that largely explores the effect this has on the children, and the new relationships the partners embark on. A competent but depressing piece offering no memorable insights or fresh ideas. Written by Bo Goldman.
DRA                              118 min (ort 123 min)
B,V                                                 MGM

## SHOOTDOWN **                                  PG
Michael Pressman     USA                     1989
*Angela Lansbury, George Coe, Molly Hagan, Kyle Secor, Jennifer Savidge, John Cullum*
The relatives of passengers on a civilian airliner that strayed over Soviet territory and was shot down, press the American government for a full investigation into the circumstances surrounding the flight. The first of two TV films that attempted to examine this tragic event, when a South Korean aeroplane was shot down by Soviet fighter planes in 1983. Average.
DRA                              93 min (ort 100 min) mTV
B,V                                                SONY

## SHOOTER *                                     PG
Gary Nelson          USA                     1988
*Jeffrey Nordling, Alan Ruck, Helen Hunt, Noble Willingham, Carol Huston, Rosalind Chao, Kario Salem, Jeffrey Alan Chandler, Cu-Ba Nguyen, Nick Cassavetes, Grace Zabriskie*
A pilot for a failed series that explores the work of combat photographers in Vietnam. A verbose and dreary bore, with cardboard characters and dialogue to match.
A/AD                                    105 min mTV
B,V                                               CIC

## SHOOTING PARTY, THE ***                       15
Alan Bridges         UK                      1984
*James Mason, Edward Fox, Dorothy Tutin, John Gielgud, Gordon Jackson, Cheryl Campbell, Robert Hardy, Aharon Ipale, Rupert Frazer, Judi Bowker, Joris Stuyck, Rebecca Saire, Sarah Badel, John Carney, Ann Castle, Daniel Chatto*

A weekend party in 1913 recreates the vanished world of the British aristocracy, that is mistakenly thought to have ended with WW1. An absorbing but ultimately rather meaningless character study, made enjoyable by some appealing performances. The screenplay is by Julian Bond.
Boa: novel by Isabel Colegate.
DRA                              93 min (ort 108 min)
B,V                       TEVP; WHV (VHS only)

## SHORT CIRCUIT ***                             PG
John Badham          USA                     1986
*Steve Guttenberg, Ally Sheedy, Fisher Stevens, Austin Pendleton, Brian McNamara, G.W. Bailey, Martin McIntyre, John Garaber, Penny Santon, Vernon Weddle, Barbara Tarbuck, Tom Lawrence, Fred Slyter, Tim Blaney (voice only)*
A brilliant but totally reclusive inventor has constructed robots which possess the capacity to destroy entire cities. At a military demonstration, the fifth one in the series is struck by lightning and becomes aware. Eager to escape from those who wish to terminate it, it takes refuge with animal-lover Sheedy, who protects it from the commandos sent to track it down. An amusingly quirky tale, followed by the inevitable sequel.
FAN                              95 min (ort 99 min)
B,V                                               CBS

## SHORT CIRCUIT 2 **                            PG
Kenneth Johnson      USA                     1988
*Fisher Stevens, Cynthia Gibb, Michael McKean, Jack Weston, David Hemblen, Dee McCaffrey, Tim Blaney (voice only)*
Sequel to the first film with Stevens and Number 5 now having further adventures as they meet up with several strange characters. An overlong bore that has little of the verve of the first film, but is watchable if one has nothing better to do.
FAN                              106 min (ort 110 min)
V/sh                                               RCA

## SHORT EYES ***
Robert M. Young      USA                     1977
*Bruce Davison, Jose Perez, Nathan George, Don Blakely, Shawn Elliott, Miguel Pinero, Tito Goya, Joe Carberry, Kenny Steward, Bob Maroff, Keith Davis, Curtis Mayfield, Willie Hernandez, Bob O'Connell, Tony De Benedetto*
A grim and realistic view of prison life – the title is a prison slang term for a child molester. This brutal and compelling film was shot in New York's now closed house of detention, known as The Tombs. Written by Pinero.
Aka: SLAMMER
Boa: play by Miguel Pinero.
DRA                                        104 min
B,V                                               WOV

## SHOT IN THE DARK, A **                        PG
Blake Edwards        USA                     1964
*Peter Sellers, Elke Sommer, George Sanders, Herbert Lom, Tracy Reed, Graham Stark, Moira Redmond, Vanda Godsell, Maurice Kaufmann, Ann Lynn, David Lodge, Andre Maranne, Martin Benson, Reginald Beckwith, Bryan Forbes*
Sellers plays bumbling detective Clouseau, who attempts to clear Sommer of a murder charge in this so-so sequel to THE PINK PANTHER, the first in a line of progressively feebler comedies. Followed by THE RETURN OF THE PINK PANTHER. The script is by Edwards and William Peter Blatty and as ever, the score is by Henri Mancini. See also INSPECTOR CLOUSEAU.
Boa: plays by Harry Kurnitz and Marcel Archard.
COM                              98 min (ort 101 min)
V                                                 WHV

## SHOT, THE **
Dean Hargrove     USA     15     1975
*Tony Curtis, Brenda Vaccaro, Roscoe Lee Browne,*
*Larry Hagman, Allan Royal, John Dehner, Morgan*
*Woodward*
A crook designs an ingenious scheme to swindle
kidnappers out of their ransom money, in this compe-
tent thriller that inevitably reminds one of THE
STING.
Aka: BIG RIP-OFF, THE
THR     85 min
B,V     KES

## SHOUT AT THE DEVIL **
Peter R. Hunt     UK     15     1976
*Lee Marvin, Roger Moore, Barbara Parkins, Ian Holm,*
*Rene Koldehoff, Gernot Endemann, Karl Michael*
*Vogler, Horst Janson, Gerard Pasquis, Maurice*
*Denham, Jean Kent, Heather Wright, George*
*Coulouris, Murray Melvin, Bernard Horsfall*
In Zanzibar, a poacher, his daughter and an English
adventurer, set out to blow up a German cruiser at the
beginning of WW1. A ponderous and overlong tale,
that has a few good action sequences but a clutch of
characters too disagreeable for one to identify with.
Written by Wilbur Smith, Stanley Price and Alastair
Reid, and with music by Maurice Jarre.
Boa: novel by Wilbur Smith.
WAR     115 min (ort 147 min)
B, V/h     VDM L/A; MED

## SHOUT, THE ***
Jerzy Skolimowski     UK     15     1979
*Alan Bates, Tim Curry, John Hurt, Susannah York,*
*Robert Stephens, Julian Hough, Carol Drinkwater,*
*Nick Stringer, John Rees, Susan Woolridge*
A man visiting an asylum is told a strange tale by one
of the inmates, of how after learning secret powers
from the Aborigines, he came to dominate and ultimately destroy the lives of a married couple he stayed
with. Bates gives a hypnotic performance as the
inmate with these strange powers, that include the
ability to kill by shouting (the film's best sequence). A
pointless but powerful film. Written by Skolimowski
and Michael Austin.
Boa: short story by Robert Graves.
DRA     83 min (ort 86 min)
B, V/h     RNK L/A; ODY

## SHOUT: PARTS 1 AND 2 **
Ted Robinson     AUSTRALIA     15     1985
*Terry Serio, John McTernan, Marcelle Schmitz, Tony*
*Barry, Melissa Jaffer, John Paramor, Michelle Giddy,*
*Russell Newman, Steve Shaw, Greg Stone, Jared Kerr,*
*John Polson, Simon Eddy, Bryan Nicholls, Nicholas*
*Comroy*
The story of Johnny O'Keefe, Australia's most famous
rock performer, is told here in a direct and tedious way
that robs the story of much of its drama. Only the
music remains to hold the interest, and we emerge
none the wiser as to the forces that took O'Keefe to the
top in the late 1950s, and impelled him on to
self-destruction by the age of 39.
Aka: SHOUT!; SHOUT: THE STORY OF JOHNNY
O'KEEFE
DRA     197 min
B,V     MOG

## SHOW OF FORCE, A *
Bruno Barreto     USA     15     1990
*Amy Irving, Andy Garcia, Robert Duvall, Lou*
*Diamond Phillips, Kevin Spacey, Joe Campanella,*
*Erik Estrada, Priscilla Pointer, Hattie Winston*
Brazilian director Barreto's first US movie is very
loosely based on a true 1978 incident, when two
Puerto Rican radicals were apparently shot dead as
terrorists with the connivance of the FBI. Irving plays
a TV news reporter who sets out to get at the truth
and in so doing puts her own life in danger. What

might well have worked as an examination of US
covert action serves as little more than a dreary
political thriller of no great force.
THR     89 min (ort 93 min)
V     CIC

## SHOWBOAT **
George Sidney     USA     U     1951
*Ava Gardner, Howard Keel, Kathryn Grayson, Joe E.*
*Brown, Marge Champion, Gower Champion, Robert*
*Sterling William Warfield, Agnes Moorehead*
A reasonable remake of the film version of a famous
musical about riverboat life along the Mississippi
which, though no more than a pale imitation of the
1936 classic, is enjoyable for its songs. Written by
John Lee Mahin.
Boa: novel by Edna Ferber.
MUS     104 min (ort 108 min)
V     MGM

## SHOWDOWN **
George Seaton     USA     PG     1972
*Rock Hudson, Dean Martin, Susan Clark, Donald*
*Moffat, John McLiam, Ben Zeller, John Richard Gill,*
*Charles Baca, Jackson Kane, Phillip L. Mead, Rita*
*Rogers, Vic Mohica, Raleigh Gardenhire, Ed Begley*
*Jr, Dan Boydston*
Two men who were in love with the same woman, find
themselves on opposite sides of the law when they
meet again. A routine Western, but quite competently
done. This was Seaton's last film.
WES     95 min (ort 99 min)
B,V     CIC

## SHOWGIRLS **
Robert McCallum     USA     R18     1986
*Joanna Storm, Stacey Donovan, Eric Edwards, Joey*
*Silvera, Nina Hartley, Jessica Wylde, Misty Regan,*
*Sandy Summer, Liz Randall, Jack Baker, Mike*
*Horner, Tiffany Dupont, Jon Martin*
A Las Vegas nightclub is hovering on the verge of
bankruptcy and the owner wants to close it. The girls
persuade him to give them time to put on a new show,
and with some help from the choreographer, they save
the nightclub. A simple and quite deft story, swamped
by the numerous sexual encounters that make up the
bulk of the film.
A     52 min
V     VEXCEL

## SHY PEOPLE **
Andrei Konchalovsky     USA     15     1987
*Jill Clayburgh, Barbara Hershey, Martha Plimpton,*
*Merritt Butrick, John Philbin, Pruitt Taylor Vince,*
*Don Swayze, Michael Audley, Brad Leland, Paul*
*Landry, Mare Winningham, Tony Epper, Warren*
*Battiste, Edward Bunker*
A New York woman journalist, with her protesting
daughter in tow, travels to the Louisiana backwoods
to write an article on a distant branch of the family
and discovers some dark secrets. A muddled, uncon-
vincing and uninteresting melodrama, though the
photography of Chris Menges offers a slight com-
pensation.
DRA     114 min (ort 118 min)
B/sh, V/sh     WHV

## SICILIAN CLAN, THE ***
Henri Verneuil     FRANCE     15     1969
*Jean Gabin, Alain Delon, Lino Ventura, Irina Demick,*
*Amadeo Nazzari, Sydney Chaplin*
A crime family plans a complex jewel theft, that
involves stealing a cache of diamonds from a plane en
route to New York, and Delon is sprung from jail to
help them. A far-fetched but engrossing heist movie,
made with considerable style and wit.
Aka: ATTACO ALLA PIOVRA; LE CLAN DES
SICILIENS
THR     121 min
V/h     CBS

## SICILIAN CONNECTION, THE **
ITALY                                    1974
*Ben Gazzara, Silvia Monti, Fausto Tozzi*
One man battles the whole Mafia heroin operation in
Sicily in this little-known but quite competent
thriller.
THR                                   97 min
B,V                                      HER

## SICILIAN CONNECTION, THE **                      18
Damiano Damiani     ITALY              1985
*Michele Placido, Mark Chase, Simona Cavallari, Ida
di Benedetto, Massimo di Francour*
The owner of a pizza parlour in Brooklyn, is sent to
Palermo by the Mafia to carry out a contract killing,
and enlists the aid of his brother. Bears no relation to
a similar title from 1974. Average.
Aka: ATTACO ALLA PIOURA; AMORE A
PALERMO; PIZZA CONNECTION
DRA                                  116 min
B,V                                      MGM

## SICILIAN CROSS *                                 18
Maurizio Lucidi/William Garroni
ITALY                                    1976
*Roger Moore, Stacy Keach, Ivo Garrani, Fausto Tozzi,
Ettore Manni*
A San Francisco Mafia boss imports a jewel-encrusted
cross as a present for his church, but a rival gangster
uses it for smuggling heroin. He sends Moore (laugh-
ably cast as a Sicilian) and Keach to discover the
culprit, in this flabby effort in which tedium alter-
nates with car chases.
Aka: EXECUTORS, THE (VPD); GLI ESECUTORI;
LA CROCE SICILIANA; STREET PEOPLE
DRA                                   99 min
B,V,V2                             EVC L/A; VPD

## SICILIAN, THE *                                  18
Michael Cimino     USA                 1987
*Christopher Lambert, Joss Ackland, Terence Stamp,
John Turturro, Richard Bauer, Barbara Sukowa,
Barry Miller, Aldo Ray*
The story of Salvatore Giuliano and his struggle to
achieve Sicily's secession from Italy in the 1940s. This
dull dud fails to make anything of its material and
unimaginably bad casting of Lambert ensures its
failure. A haphazard blend of drama and pathos, with
neither humour nor pace, this film is also available in
a special "director's cut" version of 146 minutes, which
is slightly better. The 1961 film SALVATORE
GIULIANO is far better.
Boa: novel by Mario Puzo.
A/AD                        111 min (ort 115 min)
B,V                                      CBS

## SID AND NANCY *                                  18
Alex Cox           UK                  1986
*Gary Oldman, Chloe Webb, David Hayman, Drew
Schofield, Debby Bishop, Tony London, Perry Benson,
Gloria LeRoy*
An account of the bizarre relationship between Sid
Vicious (of the British punk rock group The Sex
Pistols) and his American groupie girlfriend Nancy
Spungen. A kind of overblown docu-drama, in which
the two utterly repellent characters battle it out on
the way to self-destruction, culminating in the murder
of Spungen and the suicide of Vicious. Two powerful
performances cannot redeem this. See also THE
GREAT ROCK 'N' ROLL SWINDLE.
DRA                         109 min (ort 111 min)
V                                        CH5

## SIDE BY SIDE ***
Jack Bender         USA                1988
*Danny Thomas, Milton Berle, Sid Caesar, Morey
Amsterdam, Marjorie Lord, Georgann Johnson,
Michael Lembeck*
The story of three senior citizens who launch a

clothing company to cater for people of their age.
Corny it may be, but this warm-hearted tale has much
to commend it.
COM                                 102 min mTV
V                                       SONY

## SIEGE **                                         18
Paul Donovan/Maura O'Connell
CANADA                                   1976
*Tom Nardini, Brenda Baizinet, Darel Haeny, Doug
Lennox, Terry-David Despres, Jack Blum, Jeff Pustil,
Keith Knight, Fred Wadden, Gary Dempster, Dennis
O'Connor, Richard Collins, Alison Outhit, Tricia Fish,
Vicky Price*
A self-appointed group of so-called vigilantes, mas-
sacres the clientele of a gay bar. Based on the true
story of the events that took place after a police strike
in Canada.
DRA                       77 min (Cut at film release)
B,V                                  TEVP; CAN

## SIEGE OF FIREBASE GLORIA, THE **                 18
Brian Trenchard-Smith
AUSTRALIA                                1988
*Wings Hauser, R. Lee Ermey, Robert Abivalo, Gary
Hershberger*
An account of a true incident that took place during
the Tet offensive in the course of the Vietnam War.
During a 36-hour truce in 1968, some US Marines
carry out a patrol and learn of an imminent attack
against a US Army base, but the sergeant is unable to
get the base commander to believe him. Standard war
heroics, with the usual plotting, characterisation, and
dialogue.
WAR                                   99 min
V                                       SONY

## SIESTA *                                         18
Mary Lambert        UK/USA             1987
*Ellen Barkin, Gabriel Byrne, Julian Sands, Martin
Sheen, Jodie Foster, Grace Jones, Isabella Rossellini,
Alexei Sayle*
A professional stuntwoman awakens on a Spanish
runway, semi-nude and covered in blood. A deliberate-
ly arty and pretentious effort, in which our heroine
slowly discovers the reasons for her predicament, by
way of a series of flashbacks and weird encounters.
Not so much a film as a failed experiment. The jazz
score by Miles Davis, is one bright spot in this mess.
Boa: novel by Patrice Chaplin.
THR                         93 min (ort 96 min)
B/h, V/h                                 PAL

## SIGN OF FOUR, THE ***                            PG
Desmond Davies      UK                 1983
*Ian Richardson, David Healy, Thorley Walters, Cherie
Lunghi, Joe Melia, Terence Rigby*
A remake of the 1932 Sherlock Holmes mystery in
which our sleuth finds himself working on a mystery
that involves a secret pact, hidden treasure and a
murderous pygmy. Richardson gives a most enjoyable
performance that recalls much of the attraction of
those Basil Rathbone B-movies of the 1940s.
Aka: SHERLOCK HOLMES' THE SIGN OF THE
FOUR
Boa: short story by Arthur Conan Doyle.
A/AD                   100 min; 90 min (CH5)
B,V                       EHE; CH5 (VHS only)

## SIGHT UNSEEN ***                                 18
Greydon Clark       USA                1989
*Susan Blakely, Eddie Albert, Kurt Williams, Wings
Hauser, Lynn-Holly Johnson, Richard Masur*
A wealthy woman suffers trauma caused by the
murder of her boyfriend and young daughter, and
almost cracks up under the relentless questioning of a
cop, who is investigating a series of similar attacks,
and the constant interference of her ex-husband. A
neat, cleverly conceived and executed thriller, whose

over-fondness for flashbacks and dream sequences is a drawback.
Aka: OUT OF SIGHT, OUT OF MIND

| | |
|---|---|
| THR | 90 min |
| V | BOX |

**SILAS MARNER** ***

| | | PG |
|---|---|---|
| Giles Foster | UK | 1985 |

*Ben Kingsley, Jenny Agutter, Patrick Ryecart,*
*Jonathan Coy, Patsy Kensit, Freddie Jones, Rosemary*
*Martin, Frederick Treves, Angela Pleasence*
Adaptation of Eliot's classic story of an old, miserly linen weaver, who is consumed with bitterness and anger until he adopts an abandoned child, who brings much joy into his life. A bright and appealing work, beautifully acted and produced.
Boa: novel by George Eliot.

| | |
|---|---|
| DRA | 91 min mTV |
| V/h | BBC |

**SILENCE** ***

| | | |
|---|---|---|
| John Korty | USA | 1974 |

*Will Geer, Ellen Geer, Richard Kelton, Ian Geer*
*Flanders, Craig Kelly*
A young autistic boy on a camping trip gets lost, and has to face a variety of dangers, both from the harsh environment and an unbalanced recluse who takes him captive. An offbeat and quite engrossing tale.
Aka: CRAZY JACK AND THE BOY

| | |
|---|---|
| A/AD | 88 min |
| B,V | GOV |

**SILENCE IN THE NORTH** **

| | | PG |
|---|---|---|
| Allan Winton King | CANADA | 1981 |

*Tom Skerritt, Ellen Burstyn, Gordon Pinsent, Jennifer*
*McKinney, Colin Fox, Donna Dobrijevic, Chapelle*
*Jaffe, Thomas Hauff, David Fox, Richard Farrell,*
*Larry Reynolds, Frank C. Turner, Ute Blunck, Tom*
*Harvey, Ken Babb*
An account of a young woman's struggle to survive against the elements and the Canadian wilderness. Based on a true story, this enjoyable tale has good performances and beautiful locations – only the predictability of the script lets it down.
Aka: SILENCE OF THE NORTH
Boa: book by Ben East and Olive Reamer Frederickson

| | |
|---|---|
| DRA | 90 min (ort 94 min) |
| B,V | CIC |

**SILENCE OF THE HEART** ***

| | | PG |
|---|---|---|
| Richard Michaels | USA | 1984 |

*Mariette Hartley, Howard Hesseman, Dana Hill, Chad*
*Lowe, Silvana Gallardo, Elizabeth Berridge,*
*Alexandra Powers, Charlie Sheen, Lynnette Mettey,*
*Rick Fitts, Ray Giradin, Jaleel White, Rad Daly,*
*Melissa Hayden, Jim Boyle*
A poignant study of how one family is affected by a teenage suicide, with the parents unable to come to terms with the death of their son, whilst his sister tries to discover the reasons behind it. The perceptive and moving script is by Phil Penningroth.

| | |
|---|---|
| DRA | 91 min (ort 100 min) mTV |
| B,V | CBS |

**SILENCE THE WITNESS** **

| | | |
|---|---|---|
| Giuseppe Rosati | ITALY | 1974 |

*Bekim Fehimu, Rosanna Schaffino, Aldo Guiffre,*
*Guido Alberti*
A doctor returns with the police, to the scene of a fatal car accident but finds that all traces of the incident have vanished.
Aka: IL TESTIMONE DEVE TACERE

| | |
|---|---|
| THR | 100 min |
| B,V,V2 | VPD |

**SILENCERS, THE** ***

| | | PG |
|---|---|---|
| Phil Karlson | USA | 1966 |

*Dean Martin, Daliah Lavi, Stella Stevens, Cyd*
*Charisse, Victor Buono*
The first of the "Matt Helm" movies, this likeable spy spoof stars Martin as a secret agent, sent to outsmart a Chinese mastermind who intends using one of America's own missiles to destroy a weapons base in New Mexico. A flashy and fairly enjoyable effort, but followed by three inferior sequels. See also THE AMBUSHERS and THE WRECKING CREW.

| | |
|---|---|
| A/AD | 97 min |
| V | RCA |

**SILENT ACTION** **

| | | |
|---|---|---|
| Sergio Martino | ITALY | 1975 |

*Mel Ferrer, Luc Merendu, Delia Boccardo, Paola*
*Tedesco, Michele Gammino, Tomas Milian*
Police have to cope with a gang of urban terrorists who are systematically assassinating key government figures.
Aka: IL SERVIZIO SEGRETO UCCIDE; LA POLIZIA ACCUSA

| | |
|---|---|
| A/AD | 80 min |
| V | GOV |

**SILENT ASSASSINS** *

| | 18 |
|---|---|
| Lee Doo Yong/Scott Thomas | |
| USA | 1987 |

*Linda Blair, Mako, Sam J. Jones, Jun Chong, Phillip*
*Rhee, Bill Erwin, Gustav Vintas, Rebecca Ferratti,*
*Stuart Damon*
A cop tries to stop a former CIA agent now involved with international terrorism, from stealing germ warfare secrets. Another standard, by-the-book low-budget actioner, with a couple of good fight sequences.

| | | |
|---|---|---|
| A/AD | 87 min (ort 90 min) Cut (1 min 18 sec) | |
| B,V | | MED |

**SILENT FLUTE, THE** *

| | | 18 |
|---|---|---|
| Richard Moore | USA | 1978 |

*Jeff Cooper, Eli Wallach, David Carradine, Roddy*
*McDowall, Christopher Lee, Erica Creer*
A silly, utterly pretentious film about a quest for a strange book, which is reputed to contain great knowledge. A man who wishes to go on the quest is obliged to compete in a martial arts tournament in order to prove his worth. The film is full of supposedly allegorical tableaux, which are presented without any real significance or reason. Carradine plays four parts. Filmed in Israel.
Aka: CIRCLE OF IRON

| | | |
|---|---|---|
| MAR | 92 min (ort 95 min) Cut (51 sec including film cuts) | |
| B,V | | RNK; MIA |

**SILENT HEROES** **

| | | 15 |
|---|---|---|
| Richard Driscoll | UK | 1987 |

*Robert Wilford, Martin Arlott*
Set during the Falklands War, this tale follows the exploits of a group of SAS soldiers, who are given the task of infiltrating islands prior to the British landings. Average.

| | |
|---|---|
| WAR | 92 min |
| B,V | ABC |

**SILENT KILL** **

| | | 15 |
|---|---|---|
| John Florea | USA | 1983 |

*Robert Foxworth, Stefanie Powers, Elke Sommer, Sue*
*Lyon*
A silent maniac murders blondes, leaving no clues behind that might reveal his identity, and a cop is given the seemingly impossible task of catching him.

| | |
|---|---|
| THR | 83 min (ort 85 min) |
| B,V | POLY |

**SILENT MADNESS** *

| | | 18 |
|---|---|---|
| Simon Nuchtern | USA | 1984 |

*Belinda Montgomery, Viveca Lindfors, Sydney*
*Zassick, David Greenan, Solly Max, Roderick Cook, Ed*
*Van Nuys, Stanja Lowe, Dennis Helfend, Philip Levy,*
*Toni Hartman, Katherine Kamhi, Katie Bull, Rick*

*Aiello, Jeffrey Bingham*
A computer error leads to the release of a homicidal mental patient instead of one who is fully recovered, and the doctor in charge goes to the town where this man committed a series of murders in an attempt to catch him. However, two hospital orderlies follow with instructions to kill the doctor and cover up the mistake. As laughable as it is ludicrous. Originally shot in 3-D.
Aka: NIGHT KILLER; OMEGA FACTOR
HOR                87 min (ort 90 min) Cut (1 min 34 sec)
B,V                                                    AVA

## SILENT MOVIE **                                       PG
Mel Brooks              USA                    1976
*Mel Brooks, Marty Feldman, Dom DeLuise, Bernadette Peters, Sid Caesar, Liza Minnelli, James Caan, Madeline Kahn, Harold Gould, Fritz Feld, Paul Newman, Burt Reynolds, Anne Bancroft, Marcel Marceau, Carol Arthur, Chuck McCann*
An attempt to revive silent film comedy, revolving around the efforts of a producer to get back into the big time. An interesting experiment that never really succeeds. Look out for Marcel Marceau who utters the only word in the the movie – "non". Written by Brooks, Ron Clark, Rudy De Luca and Barry Levinson.
COM                            83 min (ort 88 min)
B,V                                                    CBS

## SILENT NIGHT, BLOODY NIGHT **
Theodore Gershuny       USA                    1973
*Patrick O'Neal, James Patterson, John Carradine, Mary Woronov, Astrid Heeren, Candy Darling, Walter Abel, Walter Klavun, Fran Stevens, Jay Garner, Philip Burns, Lisa Richard, Alex Stevens, Debbie Parness, Donelda Dunne*
A moody maniac-on-the-loose film, set as always in some small American town in New England. A lawyer arrives to sell a house, a former asylum, for his client. He spends the night there with his girlfriend and both are killed. Later other murders occur. The use of flashbacks explains all, in this fairly effective tale.
Aka: DEATH HOUSE; NIGHT OF THE DARK FULL MOON; ZORA
HOR                            84 min (ort 90 min)
B,V,V2                                                 INT

## SILENT PARTNER, THE ***                               18
Daryl Duke              CANADA                  1978
*Elliot Gould, Christopher Plummer, Celine Lomez, Susannah York, Michael Kirby, Kenneth Pogue, John Candy, Gail Dahms, Michael Donaghue, Jack Duffy, Sean Sullivan, Nancy Simmonds, Nuala Fitzgerald*
Slick and rather violent tale of a bank teller who, discovering that there is to be a robbery, secretes a large amount of money in order to pretend that more has been stolen than was actually the case. A battle of wits now ensues, with Plummer excellent as the vicious and sadistic robber, bent on revenge. Written by Curtis Hanson with music by Oscar Peterson.
Aka: DOUBLE DEADLY (MKR)
Boa: novel Think Of A Number by Anders Bodelson.
THR                                         105 min
B,V                            QUA; MKR; VIDVIS

## SILENT RAGE **                                        18
Michael Miller          USA                    1982
*Chuck Norris, Ron Silver, Steven Keats, Stephen Furst, Toni Kalem, William Finley, Brian Libby, Stephanie Dunnam*
Norris stars as the tough street-fighting sheriff of a small town, which is being terrorised by a psychotic killer. An average blend of mayhem and gore, with little new on offer in the plot department except Norris' opponent – a super-human zombie. Written by Joseph Fraley.
THR                96 min (ort 105 min) Cut (41 sec)
V                                                     RCA

## SILENT RUNNING ****                                    U
Douglas Trumbull        USA                    1971
*Bruce Dern, Cliff Potts, Ron Rifkin, Jesse Vint, Mark Persons, Steven Brown, Larry Whisenhunt, Cheryl Sparks, Roy Engel*
In the future all that remains of Earth's plant-life is preserved on huge spaceship-domes. When it is decided that these can be destroyed, a "keeper" resorts to murder in order to save one. An excellent film, with a beautiful opening and memorable effects. Scripted by Michael Cimino, Steve Bochco and Deric Washburn. The directorial debut for special effects man Trumbull. The unusual score is by Peter Schickele, with Joan Baez singing.
FAN                            85 min (ort 90 min)
V                                                     CIC

## SILENT SCREAM **
Denny Harris            USA                    1980
*Rebecca Balding, Cameron Mitchell, Avery Schreiber, Barbara Steele, Yvonne De Carlo, Brian Cox, Steve Doubet, Julie Andelman, Brad Reardon, Tina Taylor, John Widelock, Jack Stryker, Jason Zahler, Thelma Pelish, Joan Lemmo*
A pretty American college girl is trapped in an old house with dark secrets, where the various tenants have fallen victim to a knife-wielding maniac. Quite stylish, but the hackneyed plot is a major drawback.
HOR                                          87 min
B,V                                                   INT

## SILENT SCREAM, THE **                                 15
Alan Gibson             UK                     1981
*Peter Cushing, Elaine Donnelly, Anthony Carrick, Robin Browne, Terry Kinsella, Brian Cox*
A released convict finds himself trapped again, when he unwisely breaks into a pet shop and is imprisoned by the weird owner. A Hammer House of Horror tale. Fair.
Aka: HAMMER HOUSE OF HORROR: SILENT SCREAM
Osca: WITCHING TIME (CH5)
HOR        54 min (ort 60 min); 108 min (2 film cassette)
mTV
B,V                            PRV; CH5 (VHS only)

## SILENT VOICE **                                       PG
Mike Newell             USA                    1987
*Jamie Lee Curtis, Alex English, Gregory Peck, William L. Peterson, Joshua Zuehlke, Dennis Lipscomb, Lee Richardson*
A cute little story of a 12-year-old boy, who decides to stop playing baseball until the leaders of the world's countries agree to total nuclear disarmament. As other athletes around the world begin to follow suit, the pressure to disarm becomes intense. A cloyingly sweet piece of hokum, dripping with sentiment and good intentions.
Aka: AMAZING GRACE AND CHUCK
JUV                            111 min (ort 115 min)
V/sh                                                  RCA

## SILENT WITNESS **                                     18
Michael Miller          USA                    1985
*John Savage, Valerie Bertinelli, Chris Nash, Melissa Leo, Jacqueline Brookes, Katie McCombs, Tom Badal, Billy Elmer, Alex McArthur, Steven Williams, Pat Corley, Dennis Harrington, Bruce Kirkpatrick, Tom Signorelli*
A female witness to a brutal rape, keeps silent because of the involvement of her brother-in-law, but when the victim commits suicide after a gruelling courtroom battering, she is placed in a moral predicament, and decides to act and live with the consequences. An exploitative effort that makes use of a real-life rape trial that took place in Massachusetts. Average.
DRA            92 min (ort 97 min) Cut (48 sec) mTV
B,V                                         IVS L/A; CAST

**SILK \***                                        18
Cirio H. Santiago       ITALY               1986
*Cec Verrell, Fred Bailey, Bill McLaughlin*
Story of a tough lady cop who is bent on getting even
with the usual nasty felons. A B-movie from a director
of many.
A/AD                            79 min Cut (5 sec)
B,V                                          MED

**SILK STOCKINGS \*\*\***                     U
Rouben Mamoulian       USA               1957
*Fred Astaire, Cyd Charisse, Janis Paige, Peter Lorre,*
*George Tobias, Jules Munshin, Joseph Buloff, Barrie*
*Chase*
A musical remake of NINOTCHKA, with Charisse a
female commissar on a mission to Paris, where she is
to persuade a Russian composer to return home. A
lively but overlong effort. Songs include "All Of You"
and "Stereophonic Sound". Lyrics are by Andre Previn
with a Cole Porter score. Written by Leonard Spiegel-
gass and Leonard Gershe. This was the director's last
film.
Boa: musical by George S. Kaufman, Leueen McGrath
and Abe Burrows/play by Melchior Lengyel.
MUS                          114 min (ort 116 min)
V                                            MGM

**SILKEN PUSSYCAT, THE \***                  18
Bob C. Chinn           USA               1977
*John C. Holmes, Steve Ballint, Georgina Spelvin,*
*Linda Wong*
Another film in which Holmes plays Johnny Wadd, a
tough private eye who has been hired to find a missing
jade statuette of a cat, stolen from a museum in Tokyo.
A fairly mindless hardcore spoof that was followed by
a further instalment – THE CHINA CAT. Cut by
distributor by 35 min 16 sec before submission.
Aka: JADE PUSSYCAT, THE
A                      45 min (ort 80 min) Cut (23 sec)
V                                            HAR

**SILKWOOD \*\*\***                           15
Mike Nichols           USA               1983
*Meryl Streep, Kurt Russell, Cher, Craig T. Nelson,*
*Diana Scarwid, Fred Wurd, Ron Silver, Charles*
*Hallahan, Josef Summer, Sudi Bond, Henderson*
*Forsythe, E. Katherine Kerr, Bruce McGill*
Recreates the story of Karen Silkwood, who died in
mysterious circumstances when she set out to expose
the total disregard for statutory safety procedures at a
nuclear facility she worked at. Fine performances and
care in production, sustain this film further than the
thin little script would carry it. Written by Nora
Ephron and Alice Arlen. See also THE PLUTONIUM
INCIDENT.
DRA                          128 min (ort 131 min)
B,V                                          RNK

**SILVER BEARS \*\*\***                       PG
Ivan Passer            UK                1977
*Michael Caine, Cybill Shepherd, Louis Jourdan,*
*Martin Balsam, David Warner, Stephane Audran,*
*Charles Gray, Tom Smothers, Jay Leno, Tony Mascia,*
*Jeremy Clyde, Joss Ackland, Moustache, Mike Falco,*
*Philip Mascellino, Steve Plytas*
Complex but highly entertaining story, of a Mafia
plan to launder money by buying a bank in Switzer-
land, and telling of their subsequent involvement in a
plan to manipulate the world silver market. Written
by Peter Stone and filmed in Switzerland and
Morocco.
Boa: novel by Paul Erdman.
COM                          108 min (ort 114 min)
B,V                                  TEVP; WHV

**SILVER BULLET \*\***                        18
Daniel Attias         USA                1985
*Corey Haim, Gary Busey, Megan Follows, Everett*
*McGill, Kent Bradhurst, Terry O'Quinn, Robin*

*Groves, Leon Russom, Bill Smitrovich, James*
*Gammon, Heather Simmons, Joe Wright, James A.*
*Baffico, Rebecca Fleming, Lawrence Tierney*
A small town is terrorised by a series of brutal
murders that seem to be the work of a werewolf. A
crippled boy, his sister and their uncle become in-
volved in the hunt for the killer. A limp horror movie
that could have done with a stronger storyline.
Aka: STEPHEN KING'S SILVER BULLET
Boa: novelette Cycle Of The Werewolf by Stephen
King.
HOR                           90 min (ort 95 min)
B,V                                          CAN

**SILVER CITY \*\*\***                        15
Sophia Turkiewicz
                       AUSTRALIA          1985
*Gosia Dobrowolska, Ivar Kants, Anna Jemison, Steve*
*Bisley, Debra Lawrance, Ewa Brok, Tim McKenzie,*
*Dennis Miller, Joel Cohen, Annie Byron, Adam*
*Bowen, Halina Abramowicz, Cheryl Walton, Ron*
*Blanchard, Noel Hodda, Robert Newman*
A poignant evocation of a love-triangle among Polish
immigrants recently arrived in the title transit camp,
in the early 1950s. The warmth and passion in their
lives contrasts pointedly with the hostile unfriendli-
ness they receive from the native-born Australians.
Sensitive, well-acted and convincing; one of the best of
recent Australian films.
DRA                           97 min (ort 110 min)
B,V                                      IPC/PVG

**SILVER DRAGON NINJA \*\***                  18
Don Kong           HONG KONG             198-
*Harry Caine, Sam Yosida, Jim Gross, Guy Samson,*
*Eddy Chan, Conrad Chow, Anne McDonald*
A young female cop goes undercover, in an attempt to
learn the secrets of a sinister Ninja sect, and foil its
plans for domination of the free world.
MAR                           85 min Cut (55 sec)
B,V                                    NINJ; VPD

**SILVER DREAM RACER \*\***                   15
David Wickes           UK                1980
*David Essex, Christina Raines, Beau Bridges, Clarke*
*Peters, Diane Keen, Harry H. Corbett, Lee Montague,*
*Sheila White, Peter Ryecart, David Baxt, Ed Bishop,*
*T.P. McKenna, Barrie Rutter, Malya Woolf, Stephen*
*Hoye, Nick Brimble*
Story of a garage mechanic who becomes a successful
racing motorcyclist and eventually achieves his ambi-
tion of winning a big race. A very minor piece of
limited appeal. The musical score is written and
performed by Essex.
A/AD               109 min; 106 min (PARK) (ort 111 min)
B,V,LV                 RNK; VGM; PARK (VHS only)

**SILVER STREAK \*\*\***                      PG
Arthur Hiller          USA               1976
*Gene Wilder, Jill Clayburgh, Richard Pryor, Patrick*
*McGoohan, Ned Beatty, Clifton James, Richard Kiel,*
*Ray Walston, Valerie Curtin, Stefan Gierasch,*
*Scatman Crothers, Fred Willard, Len Birman*
A publisher on a train becomes involved in a murder,
and finds himself menaced by the crooks, in this
high-spirited and madcap mixture of comedy and
mayhem. A rather patchy effort, with the humour
distinctly strained in a few places, but generally a
highly effective film – something of a spoof on
Hitchcock-style thrillers. The script is by Colin Hig-
gins.
COM                          109 min (ort 113 min)
B,V                                          CBS

**SILVER TWILIGHT, THE \*\***                 PG
Roy Thomas         HONG KONG             1989
Another Joseph Lai/Betty Chan production, made
very much in the same style as FALCON 7 or THE
COSMOS CONQUEROR, and as ever, featuring a set

of nasty rebel aliens out to conquer Earth. When the ruler of the home planet sends his son to help us, he thoughtfully provides him with a magical staff, but when this is stolen things begin to look very bleak indeed. Average.

CAR 60 min
V VPD

**SILVERADO ** PG**
Lawrence Kasdan        USA            1985
*Kevin Kline, Scott Glenn, Brian Dennehy, John Cleese, Linda Hunt, Kevin Costner, Rosanna Arquette, Danny Glover, Jeff Goldblum, Marvin J. MacIntyre, Brad Williams, Todd Allen, Kenny Call Hartline, Rusty Meyers*
As the result of a strange meeting, four strangers are drawn together in a violent conflict at a crooked Western town, in this attempt to revive the old-style Western. A lumbering affair that has nothing noteworthy on offer, yet moves along fast enough to mask its shortcomings.

WES 127 min (ort 132 min)
V RCA

**SIMBA ****
Brian Desmond Hurst        UK            1955
*Dirk Bogarde, Donald Sinden, Virginia McKenna, Basil Sydney, Marie Ney, Joseph Tomelty, Earl Cameron, Orlando Martins, Frank Sanguineau*
Melodrama about the Mau-Mau emergency in Kenya, and its impact on a family of white farmers. A brutal but quite competent tale.
Boa: novel by Anthony Perry.

DRA 99 min
B,V RNK

**SIMON ** PG**
Marshall Brickman        USA            1980
*Alan Arkin, Madeline Kahn, Austin Pendleton, Judy Graubart, William Finley, Fred Gwynne, Wallace Shawn, Max Wright, Adolph Green, Ann Risley, Keith Szarabajka, Pierre Epstein, Roy Cooper, Rex Robbins, David Warrilow*
A psychology professor is brainwashed into thinking that he is an alien, in a well-made film that tries to make a few points but is little more than a solemn and only slightly funny farce. Written by Brickman in his directorial debut.

COM 100 min
B,V WHV

**SIMON BOLIVAR ****
Alessandro Blasetti
                ITALY/SPAIN            1969
*Maximilian Schell, Rosanna Schiaffino, Francisco Rabal*
Biopic on the life and struggle of Simon Bolivar to free Latin America from Spain's control.

DRA 90 min (ort 110 min)
B,V VUL; GHV

**SIMPLE JUSTICE ** 18**
Deborah Del Prete        USA            1988
*Cesar Romero, Doris Roberts, John Spencer, Priscilla Lopez, Kevin Geer, Candy McClain, Matthew Galle*
A happy couple are looking forward to the birth of their first child when, in the course of a bank raid, the wife is murdered. After the trial collapses due to the disappearance of a key witness, the culprits are set free, but soon begin to fall victim to a mysterious assailant. Simple-minded revenge tale with a twist ending.

A/AD 97 min
V VPD

**SIN * 15**
George Pan Cosmatos
                GREECE            1971
*Raquel Welch, Richard Johnson, Flora Robson*

Story of passion and forbidden love on a Mediterranean island, with an ending just like a Greek tragedy. The pretty scenery is a compensation.

DRA 93 min
B,V,V2 MIA; INT

**SINAI COMMANDOS ** PG**
Raphael Nussbaum
                ISRAEL/ITALY/WEST GERMANY      1968
*Robert Fuller, Aviva Marr, Esther Ullman, Avraham Mor, Avraham Hafner, Ruffi Natan, John Hudson*
An Israeli patrol is ordered to blow up the radar installation at Sharm-el-Sheikh during the Six Day War. Apart from a few good action sequences, this film has very little else to offer. Poor dubbing is a distraction.
Aka: HAMMATRA TIRAN; KOMMANO SINAI; MISSIAN TIRAN

WAR 99 min; 95 min (STABL) dubbed
B,V VTC L/A; STABL (VHS only); VMA

**SINBAD AND THE EYE OF THE TIGER ** U**
Sam Wanamaker        UK            1977
*Patrick Wayne, Taryn Power, Jane Seymour, Margaret Whiting, Patrick Troughton, Kurt Christian, Nadim Sawalha, Damien Thomas, Bruno Barnabe, Bernard Kay, Samali Coker, David Sterne*
Some further adventures of Sinbad, in this rather limp sequel to THE GOLDEN VOYAGE OF SINBAD, with our hero freeing a city from the grip of an evil spell. An overlong film that really drags after a while – even Ray Harryhausen's monsters begin to look tired.

FAN 113 min; 108 min (PREST) (ort 117 min)
B,V RCA; PREST (VHS only)

**SINBAD OF THE SEVEN SEAS ** PG**
E. Castellari            1988
*Lou Ferrigno, John Steiner*
Updated version of the kind of costume adventure films made by the hundreds in Italy in the 1950s and 1960s. Ferrigno plays the title role largely on account of his splendid physique, but is far from impressive in the acting department. The simple plot has Sinbad and his men embarking on a perilous mission to recover sacred gems stolen from his home city by an evil wizard.

A/AD 89 min
V PATHE

**SINBAD THE SAILOR *** U**
Richard Wallace        USA            1947
*Douglas Fairbanks Jr, Maureen O'Hara, Anthony Quinn, Walter Slezak, Jane Greer, George Tobias, Mike Mazurki, Sheldon Leonard*
A lavish swashbuckling version of a much told story. A classic Hollywood film with Fairbanks well cast as Sinbad, who goes off on his eighth voyage in search of the lost treasure of Alexander. Only the occasional lack of pace lets it down.
Osca: three short films

A/AD 112 min (ort 117 min)
B,V KVD; VCC (VHS only)

**SINBAD THE SAILOR * U**
Taiji Yabushita        JAPAN
Animated adventure of Sinbad and his friend Ali who hear of the existence of a South Seas island which hides many precious jewels.

CAR 81 min
V MAST; MYTV

**SINCE YOU WENT AWAY *****
John Cromwell        USA            1944
*Claudette Colbert, Jennifer Jones, Joseph Cotten, Shirley Temple, Monty Wooley, Agnes Moorehead, Lionel Barrymore, Guy Madison, Hattie McDaniel, Robert Walker, Craig Stevens, Keenan Wynn, Albert Basserman, Nazimova*

Story of a family on the home front in the USA, and their sufferings during WW2. A memorable flagwaver that has inevitably dated, but still demonstrates the power Hollywood could bring to bear on a subject when need be. Written by David O. Selznick and well photographed by Lee Garmes and Stanley Cortez. This was the film debut for Guy Madison and John Derek, with the latter having a tiny part as an extra. AA: Score (Max Steiner).
Boa: book by Margaret Buell Wilder.
DRA                                    172 min B/W
B,V                                          GHV

### SINCERELY VIOLET *                              PG
Mort Ransen          CANADA              1987
*Simon MacCorkindale, Patricia Phillips*
A woman academic encounters a problem, when a man refuses to give up a document in his possession, that would prove her theory that a woman was among the signatories to the Declaration of Independence. Undaunted by this, she becomes a cat burglar in an effort to steal it, but is caught by him whilst burgling his apartment, and the two promptly fall in love. A glossy, superficial and cloying romance, one in the "Shades Of Love" series.
DRA                            78 min (ort 86 min)
B,V                                   VCC; FUTVI

### SING *                                          15
Richard Baskin        USA               1989
*Peter Dobson, Lorraine Bracco, Jessica Steen, Patti La Belle*
A hot-tempered but talented street punk is chosen to take part in a high school song-and-dance contest, and has to overcome his self-destructive urges. Scripted by Dean Pritchford (who worked on FAME: THE MOVIE and FOOTLOOSE), this mediocre musical has a host of stereotyped characters ambling through a tired and predictable script. Not really a movie, merely an excuse for a seemingly endless series of forgettable musical numbers.
DRA                            95 min (ort 98 min)
V                                            RCA

### SINGER NOT THE SONG, THE **
Roy Ward Baker        UK                1961
*Dirk Bogarde, John Mills, Mylene Demongeot, Eric Pohlmann, John Bentley, Laurence Naismith, Leslie French, Nyall Florenz, Roger Delgado, Laurence Payne, Lee Montague*
A Catholic priest in a remote Mexican town comes into conflict with a local bandit who is trying to gain control. With time, a strange ambivalent relationship based on a degree of mutual respect, develops between them. A brooding and sluggish tale, written by Nigel Balchin.
Boa: novel by Audrey Erskine Lindop.
DRA                                    132 min
B,V                                          RNK

### SINGIN' IN THE RAIN ****                         U
Gene Kelly/Stanley Donen
                      USA               1952
*Gene Kelly, Donald O'Connor, Debbie Reynolds, Jean Hagen, Cyd Charisse, Rita Moreno, Millard Mitchell, Douglas Fowley, Madge Blake*
Two friends go to Hollywood in the transitional period, as silent film is giving way to talkies. Their rise to fame is shown to good effect in this classic Hollywood musical, which contains one of the most famous dance sequences ever filmed, notably Gene Kelly (who did the choreography) singing the title song. Written by Adolph Green and Betty Comden. Music is by Nacio Herb Brown with lyrics by Arthur Freed.
MUS                            98 min (ort 102 min)
V                                            MGM

### SINGLE BARS, SINGLE WOMEN **                    15
Harry Winer           USA               1984
*Paul Michael Glaser, Tony Danza, Keith Gordon, Shelley Hack, Christine Lahti, Frances Lee McCain, Kathleen Wilhoite, Mare Winningham, Christopher Allport, Rick Rossovich, Richard Hamilton, Ivan Bonar, Brett Cullen*
A song by Dolly Parton provided the inspiration for this fairly uninteresting comedy-drama, telling of the bright young things who enjoy life at a swinging nightspot.
DRA                   95 min (ort 100 min) mTV
B,V                              IMPACT/PVG; ODY

### SINGLE ROOM FURNISHED *
Matt Cimber (Matteo Ottaviano)
                      USA               1968
*Jayne Mansfield, Dorothy Keller, Fabian Dean, Billy M. Greene, Terri Messina, Martin Horsey, Walter Gregg*
After many humiliations and hardships, a woman is forced to become a prostitute. A sorry mess that has nowhere to go but down. This was the star's last film and was released after her untimely death. It opens with a tribute from Walter Winchell.
DRA                                     93 min
B,V                                     VCL/CBS

### SINGLE WOMEN, MARRIED MEN **                    15
Nick Havinga          USA               1989
*Michele Lee, Lee Horsley, Margaret Avery, Carrie Hamilton, Julie Harris*
A woman deserted by her husband trains as a psychotherapist as a way of coming to terms with her life, but finds herself becoming involved with a married man.
DRA                                     91 min
V                                            CBS

### SINNER'S BLOOD *                                18
Neil Douglas          USA               1969
*Stephen Jacques, Nanci Sheldon, John Tait, Cristy Beal, Parker Herriot, Julie Connors, Drucilla Hoy*
Two girls on a visit to their aunt in a small town in North Carolina, are corrupted by the members of a biker gang, who introduce them to the pleasures of sex, drugs and rock 'n' roll.
DRA             77 min (ort 80 min) Cut (2 min 21 sec)
B,V                              VTC L/A; XTASY

### SINS OF DORIAN GRAY, THE **                     PG
Tony Maylam           USA               1983
*Anthony Perkins, Joseph Bottoms, Belinda Bauer, Olga Karlatos, Michael Ironside, Caroline Yeager, Patsy Rahn, Roxanne Moffitt, Jeff Braunstein, Roy Wordsworth, Peter Hanlon, Carol Robinson, Mark Duffy, Bob Collins*
A modernised version of Wilde's famous novel, but this time Dorian Gray is cast as a female photographer's model, and it's her screen test that ages. Average.
Boa: novel The Picture Of Dorian Gray by Oscar Wilde.
DRA                            100 min mTV
B,V                                          POLY

### SINS OF THE FATHER **                           15
Peter Werner          USA               1985
*James Coburn, Ted Wass, Glynnis O'Connor, Marion Ross, John Prather, Channing Mitchell, Kathleen Lloyd, John O'Leary, Pepper Davis, Nico Stevens, Liz Sheridan, Donald V. Allen, Janell Baca, Victoria Cardosa, Al Checco*
An unusual love triangle, in which a woman employee at a law firm falls for both the boss and his son. A fair little soap opera.
Boa: story by Elizabeth Gill.
DRA                   92 min (ort 100 min) mTV
B,V                                          CBS

## SINS WITHIN THE FAMILY *
Bruno Gambuno          ITALY                    1974
*Michele Placido, Juliette Magniel, Renzo Montagnani,*
*Simonetta Stefanelli*
A young man ruins a middle-class family by catering
to their sexual appetites in this dull trashy film.
Aka: PECCATI IN FAMIGLIA; SINS IN THE
FAMILY
A                                             77 min
B,V                                           WOV

## SINS: PARTS 1, 2 AND 3 **                    15
Douglas Hickox          USA                    1986
*Joan Collins, Marisa Berenson, Jean-Pierre Aumont,*
*Joseph Bologna, Steven Berkoff, Elizabeth Bourgine,*
*Judi Bowker, Capucine, Timothy Dalton, Arielle*
*Dombasle, James Farentino, Paul Freeman, Allen*
*Garfield, Giancarlo Giannini*
A soapy mini-series about the terrible secret of a
beautiful female millionairess and head of a business
empire. Can she leave the past behind her and find
true happiness? Sit through this for five hours or so
and you may find out.
Boa: novel by Judith Gould.
DRA          315 min (3 cassettes – ort 420 min) mTV
B,V                                            NWV

## SIR HENRY AT RAWLINSON'S END *             15
Steve Roberts          UK                      1980
*Trevor Howard, Patrick Magee, Denise Coffey, J.G.*
*Devlin, Sheila Reed, Harry Fowler, Vivian Stanshall,*
*Jeremy Child, Susan Porrett, Liz Smith, Ben Aris,*
*David Geroll, Suzanne Danielle, Gary Waldhorn,*
*Simon Jones, Michael Crane*
An aristocrat tries to rid his estate of a family ghost.
The idea for this film came from the work of the pop
group the Bonzo Dog Doodah Band, who once released
an album with a track entitled "Rawlinson's End".
This film bears no other relation to it and is best
described as a sterile, laboured comedy. Written by
Vivien Stanshall and Steve Roberts.
Boa: radio play by Vivien Stanshall.
COM                      72 min; 75 min (IVA)
B,V                      CHM L/A; IVA; POLY

## SIROCCO **                                   PG
Curtis Bernhardt        USA                    1951
*Humphrey Bogart, Marta Toren, Lee J. Cobb, Everett*
*Sloane, Gerald Mohr, Zero Mostel, Onslow Stevens*
Set in 1920s Damascus, this sluggish yarn has an
American gunrunner helping the rebels and finding
time for a little romance on the side.
Boa: novel Coup De Grace by Joseph Kessel.
A/AD                     95 min (ort 98 min) B/W
V                                              RCA

## SISSY'S HOT SUMMER *
                        USA                    1981
*Candida Royalle, Jennifer Walker, Jeremy Harden,*
*Michelle Moore, Laurien Dominique, John C. Holmes,*
*Tony Bond*
Royalle appears as hostess of a TV show on station
WYSEX, which is running the title movie. This tells
of two girls and a guy who are forced to sell their
bodies, in order avoid being evicted from their apart-
ment for failing to pay their rent. In between clips of
the movie Royalle, demonstrates a few sex aids, in this
clumsily contrived and disjointed story.
Osca: NYMPHO SECRETS/OBJECT OF DESIRE
(asa)
A                                             55 min
B,V                                           HAR

## SISTER STREETFIGHTER *                       18
Kazuhiko Yamaguchi  JAPAN                      1976
*Sue (Etsuko) Shiomi, Sonny (Shinichi) Chiba*
A female martial arts student searches for her
brother's murderer. Yet another formula tale of
honour and revenge.

Aka: SISTER STREET FIGHTERS
MAR          73 min (ort 82 min) Cut (3 min 41 sec)
B,V                      VTC L/A; VMA L/A; STABL

## SISTER-IN-LAW, THE ***
Joseph Ruben            USA                    1974
*John Savage, W.G. McMillan, Anne Saxon, Meredith*
*Baer, Joe Oppenheim, Tom Mahoney*
A man becomes involved in drug smuggling because of
his sister-in-law's machinations. An absorbing drama
with a downbeat ending. The score is by Savage who
also sings several folk ballads.
DRA                                           85 min
B,V                                        VCL/CBS

## SISTER, SISTER *                             18
Bill Condon            USA                      1987
*Eric Stoltz, Jennifer Jason Leigh, Judith Ivey, Dennis*
*Lipscomb, Anne Pitoniak, Benjamin Mouton, Natalia*
*Nogulich, Richard Minchenberg, Bobby Pickett, Jason*
*Saucier, Jerry Leggio, Fay Cohn, Ashley McMurray,*
*Ben Book*
A man goes away for a quiet weekend, but unwisely
chooses a hotel in New Orleans that's run by two
sisters, and has many a dark secret. A flawed and
ineffective tale.
HOR                      86 min (ort 91 min)
B,V                                            NWV

## SISTERHOOD, THE *                            18
A.K. Allen             USA                      1984
*Diana Scarwid, Karen Austin, Christine Belford,*
*Bruce Davidson, Shera Danese, Beverly Todd, Marilyn*
*Kagan, Kit McDonough, Arliss Howard, Randee*
*Heller, Paul Carafotes, Nicholas Worth, Scott Lincoln*
A nasty and exploitative piece telling of a group of
rape victims, who band together in order to castrate
rapists whom the law has not punished. A version of
DEATHWISH by way of women's lib, which totally
fails to offer any real insight into the true nature of
rape and rapists. Something like ACT OF
VENGEANCE, only more vicious.
Aka: LADIES' CLUB, THE
Boa: novel by Betty Black and Casey Bishop.
DRA                      79 min (ort 90 min)
B,V                                            MED

## SISTERHOOD, THE *                            18
Cirio H. Santiago  ITALY                        1988
*Rebecca Holden, Lynn-Holly Johnson, Barbara*
*Hooper, Chuck Wagner*
In a world of the future, women are held as mere
chattels in a male-dominated society, except for a
gang of women known as "The Sisterhood". Another
silly blend of fantasy and exploitative violence.
FAN                                           82 min
V                                            PRISM

## SISTERS **                                   15
Michael Hoffman        USA                      1987
*Patrick Dempsey, Jennifer Connelly, Lila Kedrova,*
*Florinda Bolkan*
A young teenage boy goes to stay with his girlfriend's
family in Quebec but finds himself ill at ease with the
family; which comprises two other predatory sisters, a
devoutly Catholic mother, an atheist father (who is
writing a biography of Pascal in the nude) and the
dying granny, who has escaped from her hospital bed.
A sporadically amusing comedy, littered with occa-
sional bouts of irritating symbolism.
Aka: SOME GIRLS
COM                                           89 min
V                                             MGM

## SISTERS ***                                  18
Brian De Palma         USA                      1972
*Margot Kidder, Jennifer Salt, Charles Durning,*
*Barnard Hughes, William Finley, Mary Davenport,*
*Dolph Sweet, Lisle Wilson*

Siamese twins are separated at birth, one becomes a psychopath, the other a normal person. Various complications follow in the wake of a series of murders. Salt plays a reporter who thinks she has witnessed one of the killings. A tense blend of mystery and horror, with an excellent score by Bernard Herrmann.
Aka: BLOOD SISTERS
HOR                                    90 min (ort 93 min)
B,V,LV                              POLY; CH5 (VHS only)

## SISTERS OF DEATH *
Joseph A. Mazzuca        USA              1977
Arthur Franz, Claudia Jennings, Cherie Howell, Paul Carr, Sherry Boucher, Joe Tata, Sherry Alberoni, Roxanne Albee, Elizabeth Bergen, Paul Fierro, Vern Mathison
A reunion of five members of a college sorority is haunted by a crazed killer. It's that same old song again, only the actors change.
HOR                                              87 min
B,V,V2                                              INT

## SITTING TARGET ***                          18
Douglas Hickox          UK               1972
Oliver Reed, Jill St John, Ian McShane, Edward Woodward, Frank Finlay, Jill Townsend, Freddie Jones, Robert Beatty, Tony Beckley, Mike Pratt, Robert Russell, Joe Cahill, Robert Ramsey, Susan Shaw
An extremely well made but very brutal film, with Reed playing a psychopathic killer to perfection. He escapes from prison with the intention of punishing his unfaithful wife. Some neat twists in the plot lead to a violent if not unexpected climax. Written by Alexander Jacobs.
Boa: novel by Lawrence Henderson.
THR                                    89 min (ort 92 min)
B,V                                                MGM

## SITTING TARGET **                           18
Philip J. Roth          USA              1989
David Sinclair, Albert Marsh
A cop who has embarked on his own one-man war against drug dealers finds himself at considerable risk when his luck runs out.
A/AD                                             90 min
V                                                  BOX

## SIX AGAINST THE ROCK ***                    15
Paul Wendkos           USA               1987
David Carradine, Charles Haid, Jan-Michael Vincent, Richard Dysart, Dennis Farina, David Morse, Howard Hesseman, Paul Sanchez
A harsh prison tale that following the exploits of a group of prisoners who attempted to escape from Alcatraz in 1946, and were embroiled in a siege that lasted 41 hours, finally being brought to an end by a detachment of US Marines. The script is by John Gay.
A/AD                                96 min (ort 100 min) mTV
B,V                                                VES

## SIX DIRECTIONS OF BOXING, THE ***
Tyrone Hsu            HONG KONG            1979
David Chaing, Simon Yuen, Yo Hua
A policeman is given the task of catching the brother of a warlord, and finding out his arms-smuggling plans, using every means possible to do so. An expensive and well-choreographed production, with much better production values than are usually found in films of this genre.
MAR                                              90 min
B,V                                               POLY

## SIX GUN GOLD **
David Howard          USA               1941
Tim Holt, Ray Whitley, Jan Clayton, Lee "Lasses" White, Lane Chandler, LeRoy Mason, Eddy Waller, Davidson Clark, Harry Harvey Sr, Slim Whitaker, Jim Corey, Fern Emmett

A phoney sheriff heads a gang after a gold shipment, but a young pioneer eventually routs the outlaws. A typical Western of the period.
Osca: TYCOON
WES                                    55 min (ort 57 min)
B,V                                                KVD

## SIX MILLION DOLLAR MAN, THE **             U
Richard Irving          USA              1973
Lee Majors, Darren McGavin, Martin Balsam, Barbara Anderson, Charles Knox Robinson, Dorothy Green, Ivor Barry, Anne Whitfield, George Wallace, Robert Cornthwaite, Olan Soule, Norma Storch, Maurice Sherbanee, John Mark Robinson
A test-pilot is so badly injured in a crash that only advanced technology can save him, albeit in a rebuilt form with several artificial limbs, plus superhuman strength and senses. The US government then persuades him to undertake a secret mission. The pilot for a long-running TV series that in turn gave rise to several more feature spin-offs (see also RETURN OF THE SIX MILLION DOLLAR MAN AND THE BIONIC WOMAN). Adequate.
Boa: novel Cyborg by Martin Caidin.
A/AD                                    72 min (ort 90 min) mTV
B,V                                                CIC

## SIX PACK **
Daniel Petrie          USA              1982
Kenny Rogers, Diane Lane, Erin Gray, Barry Corbin, Terry Kiser, Bob Hannah, Tommy Abernathy, Ronny Still, Anthony Michael Hall, Benji Wilhoite, Robbie Fleming
A stock car racer making a comeback adopts six orphans as his pit crew, whose idea of fun is to strip down cars. An old-fashioned family film of somewhat limited appeal. This was Rogers' theatrical debut.
COM                                  108 min (ort 110 min)
B,V,V2                                             CBS

## SIX WIVES OF HENRY VIII, THE ***          PG
John Glenister/Naomi Capon
                        UK               1970
Keith Michell, Annette Crosbie, Dorothy Tutin, Patrick Troughton, Anne Stallybrass, Sheila Burrell, Elvi Hale, Angela Pleasence, Rosalie Crutchley, John Ronane
A stylish and painstakingly-produced set of TV plays, that explored the character of Henry VIII and his relationship with his wives, with one play being devoted to each wife. Originally shown in six parts and later used as a basis for the film HENRY VIII AND HIS SIX WIVES.
DRA                                  541 min (6 cassettes) mTV
V/h                                                BBC

## 633 SQUADRON **                            PG
Walter Grauman         UK               1964
George Chakiris, Maria Perschy, Cliff Robertson, Harry Andrews, Michael Goodliffe, Donald Houston, Angus Lennie, John Meillon, Scot Finch, John Bonney, Suzan Farmer, Barbara Archer
WW2 story in which Mosquito aircraft are sent to destroy a munitions factory in occupied Norway, by attempting to cause the cliff that overhangs it to collapse. A standard stiff-upper-lip war film with plenty of heroics and action, but not much else. The script is by James Clavell and Howard Koch.
Boa: novel by Frederick E. Smith.
WAR                                    92 min (ort 94 min)
V                                                  WHV

## SIXTEEN CANDLES **                          U
John Hughes          USA               1984
Molly Ringwald, Anthony Michael Hall, Michael Schoeffling, Justin Henry, Paul Dooley, Carlin Glynn, Blanche Baker, Gedde Watanabe, Edward Andrews, Billie Bird, Carole Cook, Max Showalter, John Cusack, Joan Cusack,

A girl becomes sixteen and wants to find her "Mister Right", but unknown to her he is already making plans of his own. Quite a perceptive little comedy, but flawed by muddled direction and some sequences of dubious appeal. A lovely performance from Ringwald carries the film. Written by Hughes.

COM 93 min
V/h CIC

## SIXTY-EIGHT ** 18
Steven Kovacs  USA  1988
*Eric Larson, Robert Locke, Sandor Tecsi, Neil Young, Anna Dukasz, Mirlan Kwun, Terra Vandergaw, Shony Alex Braun, Donna Pecora*
The story of a Hungarian immigrant, who tries to start up a cafe in San Francisco in the late 1960s, as the city becomes involved in a wave of protest movements. One of his sons becomes politically active but the other turns out to be gay – dad is pleased with neither. A nostalgia movie that just isn't very appealing or particularly well made.
Aka: 68
DRA 95 min (ort 97 min)
B,V NWV

## SIXTY-SEVEN DAYS ** 15
Zika Mitrovic  YUGOSLAVIA  1978
*Boris Buzancic, Bozidarka Frajt, Ivan Jugodic, Neda Arneric*
Describes the aftermath of the German invasion of Yugoslavia in 1941. Fair.
Aka: 67 DAYS; VZICKA REPUBLIKA
WAR 114 min
B,V VCL/CBS; APX; INTMED

## SIZZLE ** 18
Mark Ubell  USA  1981
*Samantha Fox, Merle Michaels, Veri Knotty, Roger Caine, George Payne*
Uneven and only slightly amusing sex comedy featuring five unrelated tales. First there is gangster-style story of a moll and her obedient gang of hoods, a kidnap tale follows, the third story is built around a conventional bedroom scene, this is followed by a spoof on a family soap opera and finally there is a tale in which Fox drowns herself but then returns to continue her affairs.
Aka: SIZZLE PANTS
Osca: BANG BANG/SLIPPERY WHEN WET (asa)
A 49 min (ort 79 min) Cut (3 min 45 sec)
B,V HAR

## SKAG *** 
Frank Perry  USA  1980
*Karl Malden, Piper Laurie, Craig Wasson, Peter Gallagher, Leslie Ackerman, Kathryn Holcomb, George Voskovec, Powers Boothe, M. Emmet Walsh, Tom Atkins, Charles Hallahan, Juanin Clay, Gwen Humble, Bert Freed, Tony Burton*
A hardworking steelworker is struck down by a stroke and finds that time hangs heavy on his hands. This was later adapted for a TV series. A simple drama carried along by Malden's vigorous performance. Written by Abby Mann.
DRA 120 min (ort 150 min) mTV
B,V POLY

## SKEEZER *** 
Peter H. Hunt  USA  1982
*Karen Valentine, Leighton Greer, Tom Atkins, Dee Wallace, Justin Lord, Mariclare Costello, Jeremy Licht, Jack DeMave, Christine Hutter, Max Hunt, Flonisha Powell, Kyle Oliver, Bunny Summers, Sandi Cornell*
A woman uses a dog as a form of therapy in her work with emotionally disturbed children. A touching little drama that is neither contrived nor mawkish. Adapted from the book by Robert Hamilton.
Boa: book Skeezer, Dog With A Mission by Elizabeth Yates.
DRA 91 min (ort 96 min) mTV
B,V PRV

## SKELETON COAST ** 15
John Cardos  USA  1987
*Ernest Borgnine, Daniel Greene, Oliver Reed, Herbert Lom, Robert Vaughn, Leon Isaac Kennedy, Nancy Mulford, Peter Kwong, Robin Townsend*
A bunch of renegade mercenaries mount a dangerous mission to Angola, in order to rescue a CIA agent who has been captured by Cuban guerrillas.
A/AD 93 min (ort 98 min) Cut (34 sec)
B,V SHEER; VCC (VHS only)

## SKI BUM, THE * 
Bruce Clark  USA  1971
*Charlotte Rampling, Zalman King, Joseph Mell, Dimitra Arliss, Anna Karen, Tedd King*
Film about the involvement of the title character in a shady business deal, that he undertakes in order to further his social-climbing career. Very dull.
Boa: novel by Romain Gary.
DRA 94 min (ort 136 min)
B,V EHE

## SKI PATROL * PG
Richard Correll  USA  1990
*Roger Rose, T.K. Carter, Paul Feig, Ray Walston, Yvette Nipar, Martin Mull, Tess, Corby Timbrook*
Poorly made, screwball comedy from the producer of POLICE ACADEMY that attempts to do the same for a ski resort, where the staff are struggling to fend off a development tycoon with plans of his own for their establishment. As dreadful as it sounds.
COM 88 min (ort 91 min)
V EIV

## SKIN DEEP ** 18
Marcello Aliprandi  ITALY/SPAIN
*Lilli Carati, Miki Youk, Maurizio Interlandi, Ilona Stauer*
A young man has his first sexual experience on holiday on an island near Sicily when, in the company of several friends, he looks after his mother's holiday home for a fortnight and holds a series of pool-side parties that soon degenerate into orgies.
Aka: SENZA BUCCIA
A 90 min
B,V PHE L/A; DAV L/A; 18PLAT/TOW; TCX; SHEP

## SKIN DEEP ** 18
Blake Edwards  USA  1988
*John Ritter, Vincent Gardenia, Alyson Reed, Julianne Phillips, Joel Brooks, Chelsea Field, Nina Foch, Denise Crosby, Michael Kidd, Bryan Genesse, Sgerl Lee Ralph*
A slob still loves his ex-wife but is unwilling to reform in order to get her back. A patchy comedy, written by Edwards, that's very much a hit-and-miss affair.
COM 96 min (ort 102 min)
V BRAVE

## SKIN ON SKIN ** 
Anthony Spinelli  USA  1981
*John Leslie, Eva Houseman, Richard Pacheco, Pat Manning, Jon Martin, Aaron Stuart, Mai Lin, Juliet Anderson, Erica Boyer*
No story to this one, just a set of about six unrelated tales that follow the exploits of several individuals, as they enjoy sexual encounters both real and imaginary.
A 80 min
B,V CAL

## SKINHEADS * 18
Greydon Clark  USA  1989
*Chuck Connors, Barbara Bain, Jason Culp, Elizabeth Sagal, Brian Brophy*

A appallingly unattractive piece of dross, that deals with the activities of a group of L.A. neo-Nazis who flee to North California when one of them shoots a black man. It's not long before they start a vicious feud with a bunch of college kids, two of whom survive to mete out the expected vengeance.

A/AD 90 min
V PRISM L/A

## SKINTIGHT *
Ed de Priest USA 1981
*Annette Haven, Lisa De Leeuw, Paul Thomas, Randy West, Aaron Stuart, Mai Lin, Lee Carroll, Maria Tortuga*
The story of a pretty sex clinic therapist and her patients. The film follows her as she deals with a number of cases, but has a real problem of her own in the form of obscene phone calls. These are eventually traced to the doctor who runs the clinic, who arrives to try out some of his sadistic fantasies on her. But Haven has left and no longer works there, so he rapes her room-mate instead, in an unpleasant and violent conclusion.

A 90 min
B,V TCX

## SKOKIE ***
Herbert Wise USA 1981 PG
*Danny Kaye, John Rubinstein, Carl Reiner, Kim Hunter, Eli Wallach, Lee Strasberg, Brian Dennehy, George Dzundza, Ed Flanders, Charles Levin, Stephen D. Newman, James Sutorius, Marin Kanter, Michele Shay*
A dramatisation of true events, when a group of neo-Nazis tried to hold a meeting in a suburb inhabited by many survivors of the Nazi deathcamps. An engrossing tale, with a powerful performance from Kaye in his TV debut. Written by Ernest Kinoy.

DRA 125 min mTV
B,V VFM; HER

## SKULDUGGERY **
Gordon Douglas USA 1969
*Burt Reynolds, Susan Clark, Roger C. Carmel, Chips Rafferty, Edward Fox, Wilfrid Hyde-White, Paul Christian, Alexander Knox, Pat Suzuki, William Marshall, Mort Marshall, Booker Bradshaw, Michael St Claire, Rhys Williams*
Story of the search for the missing link by a scientific expedition to New Guinea, who discover a tribe of ape-like beings. In order to prevent their slaughter, a court case is mounted to prove their humanity. An unusual tale that is both unconvincing and contrived. Written by Nelson Gidding, who had his name removed from the credits.

DRA 105 min
B,V CBS

## SKY BIKE, THE **
Charles Frend UK 1968 U
*Spencer Shires, Liam Redmond, Ian Ellis, William Lucas, Ellen McIntosh, Della Rands, John Howard, Bill Shine, David Lodge, Harry Locke*
Children enter a competition for man-powered flying machines, and an inventor's flying bike wins the contest. Fair.

JUV 62 min
B,V RNK

## SKY HIGH **
Nico Mastorakis USA 1984 15
*Daniel Hirsch, Clayton Norcross, Frank Schultz, John Lawrence, Lauren Taylor, Janet Taylor, Karen Verlaine, Gary Wayton, Jeff McGrail, Michelle McDaniel, Alan White*
When three kids on holiday in Greece stumble across a KGB secret, they soon find themselves embroiled in a complex intrigue.

COM 105 min
B,V POLY

## SKY IS FALLING, THE **
Silvio Narizzano CANADA 1976
*Dennis Hopper, Carroll Baker, Richard Todd, Faith Brook, Win Wells*
Violence, shocks and eroticism, and all set in a secluded Spanish coastal village which is home to a strange sect. Average.
Aka: BLOODBATH

HOR 91 min
B,V DFS; AMBAS

## SKY PIRATES **
Colin Eggleston AUSTRALIA 1986 PG
*John Hargreaves, Max Phipps, Meredith Phillips, Bill Hunter, Simon Chilvers, David Parker, Adrian Wright, Peter Cummins, Tommy Dysart, Wayne Cull, Alex Menglett, Nigel Bradshaw, Chris Gregory, John Murphy, Bill Fozz*
Survivors of a plane crash in the Pacific find themselves thrown back in time, in this confused, pale imitation of an "Indiana Jones"-style adventure.

A/AD 83 min (ort 89 min) Cut (51 sec)
V/s VES

## SKY PIRATES, THE **
Pennington Richards UK 1977
*Bill Maynard, Reginald Marsh, Ewan Solon, Adam Richens, Michael McVey, Sylvia O'Donnell, Jamie Forman, Kenneth Watson, John Lee*
Two boys wage war against diamond thieves, who steal the radio-controlled plane belonging to one of them, to use as a means of smuggling their loot.

JUV 60 min
B,V RNK

## SKY RIDERS **
Douglas Hickox USA 1976 PG
*James Coburn, Susannah York, Robert Culp, Charles Aznavour, Werner Pochath, Kenneth Griffith, Harry Andrews, John Beck*
Hang-glider daredevils help to rescue hostages held by terrorists in Greece. A routine adventure tale redeemed by some splendid aerial sequences.

A/AD 87 min (ort 91 min)
B,V CBS

## SKY TRAP, THE **
Jerome Courtland USA 1978 PG
*Jim Hutton, Marc McClure, Kitty Ruth*
A glider pilot becomes reluctantly drawn into a conspiracy to smuggle drugs, in this amiable Disney adventure.

A/AD 96 min mTV
B,V WDV

## SKY WEST AND CROOKED **
John Mills UK 1966 PG
*Hayley Mills, Ian McShane, Laurence Naismith, Geoffrey Bayldon, Annette Crosbie, Norman Bird, Hamilton Dyce, Pauline Jameson, Rachel Thomas, Judith Furse*
Mills as a beautiful mentally-retarded girl who runs off with a gypsy to find her first romance, in this atmospheric but muddled tale. Written by Mary Hayley Bell and John Prebble. The score is by Malcolm Arnold.
Aka: GYPSY GIRL

DRA 101 min
B,V RNK; STRAND

## SKYJACKED **
John Guillermin USA 1972 PG
*Charlton Heston, Yvette Mimieux, James Brolin, Claude Akins, Jeanne Crain, Susan Dey, Roosevelt*

Grier, Walter Pidgeon, Leslie Uggams, Mariette
Hartley
A commercial flight is hijacked to Russia, as a mad
bomber diverts a Boeing 707 on a flight from L.A. to
Minneapolis and forces it to fly to Moscow. A fairly
straightforward tale that starts off with great promise
but slowly runs out of steam. Written by Stanley R.
Greenbers.
Aka: SKY TERROR
Boa: novel Hijacked by David Harper.
DRA                                            100 min
B,V                                             MGM

### SKY'S THE LIMIT, THE **                     U
Edward H. Griffith       USA                   1943
Fred Astaire, Robert Ryan, Joan Leslie, Robert
Benchley, Marjorie Gateson, Elizabeth Patterson,
Clarence Kolb, Richard Davis, Peter Lawford, Eric
Blore
A flier on leave meets a lady photographer and they
make sweet music together. Worthwhile episodes are
Benchley's dinner speech and Astaire's "One For My
Baby" and "My Shining Hour". Written by Frank
Fenton and Lynn Root.
Osca: STEP LIVELY
MUS                       87 min (ort 89 min) B/W
B,V                            KVD; VCC (VHS only)

### SKY'S THE LIMIT, THE **                     U
Tom Leetch               USA                   1975
Pat O'Brien, Lloyd Nolan, Jeanette Nolan
A boy is sent to live with his grandfather on his farm
and discovers an old biplane which they decide to
restore. A likeable little film.
JUV                                             89 min
B,V                                             WDV

### SKYWARD ***
Ron Howard               USA                   1980
Bette Davis, Howard Hesseman, Marion Ross, Ben
Marley, Clu Gulager, Lisa Whelchel, Suzy Gilstrap,
Jana Hall, Mark Wheeler, Jessie Lee Fulton, Rance
Howard, Bill Thurman, Bill Blackwood, Rhonda
Minton, Gene Pietragallo
A handicapped teenager in a wheelchair learns how to
fly a plane, with a little help from a former stunt pilot
and an airport watchman. An engaging tale, scripted
by Nancy Sackett. The TV acting debut of real-life
paraplegic Gilstrap.
Boa: story by Anson Williams.
DRA                      90 min (ort 100 min) mTV
B,V                              VDB L/A; KRP

### SLAMDANCE *                                 15
Wayne Wang               UK/USA                1987
Tom Hulce, Harry Dean Stanton, Mary Elizabeth
Mastrantonio, Virginia Madsen, Adam Ant, Millie
Perkins, Judith Barsi, Rosalind Chao, Sasha Delgado,
Joshua Caceras, Don Opper, John Doe, Marty Levy,
John C. Slade, Julian Deyer
An underground cartoonist is framed by a bunch of
corrupt cops, for the murder of a girl he formerly had a
relationship with. A flat and unconvincing attempt at
film noir that is just rather empty and tiresome.
THR                      93 min (ort 99 min)
B/h, V/h                                        PAL

### SLAMMER GIRLS *                             18
Chuck Vincent            USA                   1987
Jeff Eagle, Tally Brittany, Devon Jenkin, Ron
Sullivan, Jane Hamilton
A spoof on all those women-in-prison films that tells of
a male reporter who dons drag and gets himself put in
a woman's penitentiary in order to find evidence to
prove a woman's innocence. Once inside, he encounters a host of bizarre characters, including an ex-
hooker, a nymphomaniac and a young innocent
woman who hatches a plan for a mass breakout. A
low-brow and smutty affair.

Aka: BIG SLAMMER, THE
COM                      77 min (ort 82 min)
B,V                                             VES

### SLAMS, THE *                                18
Jonathan Kaplan         USA                   1973
Jim Brown, Judy Pace, Ted Cassidy, Rowland "Bob"
Harris, Frank De Kova, Paul E. Harris, Ted Cassidy,
Frenchia Guizon, Quinn Redeker, Joe Emel, Jan
Merlin
A run-of-the-mill tale with a man being sent to prison
after having hidden a cache of heroin and $1.500,000.
The film brightens up about halfway, but still remains
barely watchable.
A/AD                     86 min (ort 97 min)
B,V                                             MGM

### SLAPSTICK OF ANOTHER KIND *
Steven Paul              USA                   1982
Jerry Lewis, Madeline Kahn, Marty Feldman, Jim
Backus, John Abbott, Pat Morita, Samuel Fuller, Merv
Griffin, Virginia Graham, Ben Frank, Robert
Hackman, Eugene Choy, Ken Johnson, Peter Kwong,
Orson Welles (voice only)
A man's wife gives birth to enormous twins, that are
in reality aliens on a mission to solve the problems of
the world, but they can only do this if they are kept
together. Almost nothing of Vonnegut's novel remains
in this plodding and unfunny movie, despite it having
been scripted by the writer.
Aka: SLAPSTICK
Boa: novel by Kurt Vonnegut.
COM                      82 min (ort 87 min)
B,V                                             PVG

### SLASH *                                     18
John Gale                USA                    198-
Ron Kristoff, Nick Nichols, Paul Van, Michael Monty,
Gwen Hung, Patrick Lee, Ronnie Patterson
Standard heroics with a former Vietnam veteran
being sent into enemy territory to rescue political
prisoners, being equipped for this task with an
impressive amount of weaponry. When he discovers
that he has been betrayed he sets out to have his
revenge.
A/AD                     80 min (ort 84 min)
B,V                                             TGP

### SLATE, WYN AND ME *                         18
Don McLennan            AUSTRALIA             1987
Simon Burke, Sigrid Thornton, Martin Sacks,
Michelle Torres, Tommy Lewis, Lesley Baker
Having robbed a bank and killed a cop, two brothers
kidnap Thornton, who witnessed it all. A lacklustre
yarn that starts off well enough but never develops.
Aka: SLATE, WYN AND MACBRIDE
THR                                             91 min
B,V                                             PAL

### SLAUGHTER *                                 18
Jack Starrett            USA                   1972
Jim Brown, Rip Torn, Stella Stevens, Don Gordon,
Cameron Mitchell, Marlene Clark
A black Vietnam veteran and ex-Green Beret, goes
after the crime syndicate that had his parents killed,
in this mind-numbing and sterile nonsense. Followed
by "Slaughter's Big Rip-Off".
A/AD              88 min (ort 90 min) Cut (14 sec)
B,V                                             GHV

### SLAUGHTER HIGH *                            18
George Dugdale/Mark Ezra/Peter Litten
                         USA                   1985
Caroline Munro, Simon Scuddamore, Sally Cross,
Donna Yeager, Dick Randall, Kelly Baker
An April Fool's Day prank that went wrong, left a
student deformed and insane, and he was confined to a
local asylum. Years later, a bunch of former students
are invited to a school reunion and our lunatic escapes

to have his revenge. There's nothing new in this formula shocker.
Aka: APRIL FOOL'S DAY
HOR                         86 min (ort 89 min) Cut (32 sec)
B,V                                                    VES

## SLAUGHTER IN SAN FRANCISCO *
William Lowe          HONG KONG               1973
*Don Wong, Chuck Norris, Sylvia Channing, Robert Jones, Dan Ivan, Bob Talbot, James Economides, Chuck Boyde*
A former cop seeks revenge for the murder of his partner. Not released in the USA until 1981, when it added in some measure to the growing popularity of Norris, who here plays a baddie. A poor effort that is flawed in almost every department.
MAR                                      84 min (ort 87 min)
B,V                                                    RNK

## SLAUGHTERHOUSE *                                    18
Rick Roessler          USA                     1987
*Don Barrett, Sherry Bendorf, Joe Barton, William Houck*
A clumsy, low-budget tale in which the retarded son of a man who owns a pig-slaughtering plant murders a bunch of teenagers and hangs their corpses up in the plant. Soon his father realises that he can use the same method to rid himself of the property developers who are trying to put him out of business. A film that tries to be a spoof of THE TEXAS CHAINSAW MASSACRE, but produces neither mirth nor shocks.
HOR                                                80 min
B,V                                                    IVS

## SLAUGHTERHOUSE FIVE ***                             15
George Roy Hill          USA                    1972
*Michael Sacks, Ron Leibman, Eugene Roche, Sharon Gans, Valerie Perrine, Sorrel Booke, John Dehner, Perry King, Roberts Blossom, Friedrich Ledebur, Holly Near, Lucille Benson, Kevin Conway, Nick Belle, Stan Gottlieb*
Entertaining and polished rendition of a novel about an American optometrist who has become displaced in time. He finds himself constantly flitting back and forth between various important passages in his life, such as his time as a POW in Germany or the period he spent living on another planet. The music of J.S Bach and Vivaldi is used to good effect. Written by Stephen Geller.
Boa: novel Slaughter House Five; Or, The Children's Crusade by Kurt Vonnegut.
FAN                                     99 min (ort 104 min)
V/h                                                    CIC

## SLAVE GIRLS FROM BEYOND INFINITY **                 18
Ken Dixon          USA                          1987
*Elizabeth Clayton, Cindy Beal, Brinke Stevens, Don Scribner, Carl Horner, Kirk Grave, Randolph Roebling, Bud Graves, Jeffrey Blanchard, Mike Cooper, Greg Cooper, Sheila White, Fred Tate, Jacques Scardo*
A low-budget SF sex fantasy done in the style of a 1950s Roger Corman film, with some amusing tongue-in-cheek touches and a plot similar to that of "The Most Dangerous Game". The story tells of a couple of slave girls who escape their cruel master and are forced to fight for survival on a planet full of androids, monsters and various other hazards.
FAN                                                87 min
B,V                                                    CFD

## SLAVE WARRIOR **                                    PG
Richard McNamara     ITALY                      1965
*Rossana Podesta, Guy Madison, Jack Stuart (Giancorno Rossi-Stuarti)*
A centurian falls in love with a slave girl in this routine sword-and-sandal offering.
A/AD                                               89 min
B,V                                                    VPD

## SLAVERS *                                           18
Jurgen Goslar     WEST GERMANY                  1978
*Trevor Howard, Britt Ekland, Ray Milland, Ron Ely, Jurgen Goslar, Ken Gampu, Cameron Mitchell, Don Jack Rousseau*
A low-grade account of slave trading in 19th century Africa, with a star cast struggling bravely with their ludicrous lines, but finding they are unequal to the task.
DRA                                94 min (ort 102 min) Cut (2 sec)
B,V                                             INT L/A; MPV

## SLAVES OF NEW YORK **                               15
James Ivory          USA                        1989
*Bernadette Peters, Adam Coleman Howard, Chris Sarandon, Mary Beth Hurt, Nick Corri, Madeleine Potter, Mercedes Ruehl, Betty Comden, Steve Buscemi, Jonas Abry, Michael Schoeffling, Tammy Grimes, Stephen Bastone, Charles McCaughan*
Janowitz's set of tales about the arty inhabitants of downtown New York are cobbled together into an episodic adaptation, with the central character an intelligent woman who is constantly humiliated by her inability to fit in with her boyfriend's cliquey friends. Written by Janowitz, this long and cluttered film is all gloss and no substance.
Boa: book by Tama Janowitz.
COM                                    120 min (ort 125 min)
V                                                      RCA

## SLAYGROUND *                                        18
Terry Bedford          UK                       1983
*Peter Coyote, Mel Smith, Billie Whitelaw, Philip Sayer, Bill Luhrs, Marie Masters, Clarence Felder, Ned Eisenberg, David Hayward, Michael Ryan, Barret Mulligan, Kelli Maroney, Margareta Arvidssen, Rosemary Martin, Jon Morrison*
A robber who caused the death of a child, goes on the run from a killer hired by the dead child's father, taking refuge in a deserted amusement park owned by Whitelaw. A slick and sterile film in which the bad guy wins.
Boa: novel by Richard Stark (Donald E. Westlake)
THR                                     85 min (ort 89 min)
B,V                                              TEVP; WHV

## SLEEP MY LOVE ***                                   PG
Douglas Sirk          USA                       1948
*Claudette Colbert, Robert Cummings, Don Ameche, Rita Johnson, George Coulouris, Raymond Burr, Hazel Brooks, Keye Luke*
A husband tries to drive his wife mad in order to be rid of her, but his schemes are foiled. A hackneyed plot is given new life by an excellent cast. Written by St Clair McKelway. The memorable photography is by Joseph Valentine.
Boa: novel by Leo Rosten.
THR                                                97 min B/W
V                                              VMA; STABL

## SLEEP OF DEATH, THE **                              15
Calvin Floyd          EIRE/SWEDEN               1981
*Curt Jurgens, Patrick Magee, Per Oscarsson, Marilu Tolo, Brendan Price, Kay MacLaren, Niall Toibin, Barry Cassins, Christopher Casson, John Malloy, Ray McAnally, Archie O'Sullivan, Bill Foley, Jacintha Martin, Olwen Fouere*
Slow-moving account of a young English aristocrat's encounter with a strange man and his beautiful, mysterious wife.
Aka: DEVIL SLEEP; INN OF THE FLYING DRAGON, THE; ONDSKANS VARDSHUS
DRA                                    90 min; 86 min (SID)
B,V                                        VDB L/A; KRP; SID

## SLEEP WELL, PROFESSOR OLIVER **                     15
John Patterson          USA                     1989
*Louis Gossett Jr, Shari Headley, Michael Roker, Cynthia Nixon*

When his close friend is killed in what appears to be a street robbery, and the cop investigating the crime is also attacked, a professor leaves the tranquility of his sheltered academic life and embarks on a search for the killer. A pilot for a TV series. See also TONGS and GIDEON'S WAR.

A/AD                                    91 min mTV
V                                            CIC

## SLEEPER ***                                PG
Woody Allen          USA              1973
*Woody Allen, Diane Keaton, John Beck, Mary Gregory, Don Keefer, John McLiam*
One of Allen's more consistent comedies, in which he plays a health store owner who was deep frozen after a minor operation went wrong and wakes up 200 years later into a totalitarian society. A succession of splendid sight gags and some memorable lines keep this one moving along, despite one or two pauses and a rather feeble ending. The jazz score is by the Preservation Hall Jazz Band. As ever, Allen writes and directs.
COM                         84 min (ort 88 min)
V                                            WHV

## SLEEPING BEAUTY **                          U
David Irving          USA              1986
*Morgan Fairchild, Tahnee Welch, Nicholas Clay, Sylvia Miles, Kenny Baker, David Holliday*
A competent but unmemorable version of this classic fairytale.
Aka: CANNON MOVIE TALES: SLEEPING BEAUTY
JUV                                       89 min
V                                            WHV

## SLEEPING BEAUTY ***                         U
Clyde Geronimi          USA           1958
*Voices of: Mary Costa, Bill Shirley, Eleanor Audley, Verna Felton, Barbara Jo Allen (Vera Vague), Barbara Luddy, Bill Thompson, Taylor Holmes, Candy Candido*
One of Disney's most expensive and successful animations, this tells simply and without unnecessary embellishment, the story of the beautiful princess who pricks her finger on a spinning wheel and is cast into a deep sleep. A splendid example of a classic Disney animation. The music is adapted from Tchaikovsky. Filmed in wide-screen, an aspect that will be lost on TV.
CAR                         72 min (ort 85 min)
B,V          FFV L/A; RNK L/A; WDV (VHS only)

## SLEEPING BEAUTY ***                        Uc
Jeremy Kagan          USA             1983
*Beverly D'Angelo, Christopher Reeve, Bernadette Peters, Ron Rifkind, George Dzunda, Sally Kellerman, Carol Kane, Rene Auberjonois*
A more polished version of this fairytale, one in the "Faerie Tale Theatre" series, with a handsome prince who longs to be wed, hearing of a beautiful woman doomed to sleep for a hundred years by an evil fairy. An enjoyable blend of live-action and animation.
JUV                                       58 min
V                                            MGM

## SLEEPING CAR, THE **                        18
Douglas Curtis          USA           1989
*David Naughton, Jeff Conaway, Judie Aronson, Kevin McCarthy*
When a man leaves his wife to further his ambitions in journalism he starts a course at college and rents part of an old train to live in. However, the former and now deceased occupant was very particular about it being kept tidy, and takes a gruesome revenge when a jealous student vandalises it.
HOR                                       84 min
V                                           CASPIC

## SLEEPING DOGS **
Roger Donaldson
                  NEW ZEALAND           1977
*Sam Neill, Ian Mune, Warren Oates, Nevan Rowe, Donna Akersten, Clyde Scott, Bill Juliffe, Ian Watkin, Bill Johnson, Dorothy McKegg, Tom Groser, Bernard Kearns, Don Selwyn, Raf Irving, Melissa Donaldson*
An apolitical loner finds himself becoming gradually involved in the events surrounding a strike, in this murky political tale that suffers badly from uncertain direction. The first New Zealand film to open in the US.
DRA                        100 min (ort 107 min)
B,V                                          QUA

## SLEEPING FIST **
Yeh Yang-Ju          HONG KONG
*Yan Hsiao-Tien, Shepherd Wong*
A young man must learn the martial arts in order to rescue his kidnapped girlfriend. Average.
MAR                                       85 min
B,V                                          VPD

## SLEUTH ***                                  15
Joseph L. Mankiewicz   USA            1972
*Laurence Olivier, Michael Caine, Alec Cawthorne, Margo Channing, John Matthews, Teddy Martin*
Based on a successful play, this tells of how a writer of detective stories decides to give his wife's lover the fright of his life, by playing a series of nasty tricks on him after he has been inveigled down to his country home. Both actors are excellent as players in this game of wits, though a contrived ending disappoints. Written by Shaffer with sets by Ken Adam.
Boa: play by Anthony Shaffer.
DRA                        132 min (ort 139 min)
B,V                                          CBS

## SLIGHTLY PREGNANT MAN, THE *
Jacques Demy          FRANCE/ITALY    1973
*Marcello Mastroianni, Catherine Deneuve, Mirelle Mathieu, Marisa Pavan, Micheline Presle*
Unfunny comedy about a pregnant man and what happens when the news breaks. See also RABBIT TEST.
Aka: L'EVENEMENT LE PLUS IMPORTANT DEPUIS QUE L'HOMME A MARCHE SUR LA LUNE; MOST IMPORTANT EVENT SINCE MAN EVER SET FOOT ON THE MOON, THE
COM                                       92 min
B,V                                          VCL

## SLIP UP *
Robert Walters/Manny Manchcunt
                       USA              1974
*Jamie Gillis, Darby Lloyd Raines, Candida, Mark Stevens, Eric Edwards, Amy Weller*
One of those inane and tiresomely unfunny slapstick efforts from the 1970s. At the Tighttwat Institute for Sexual Research, an inventor has produced a device that could, under the right conditions, permanently arouse every male in the USA. His plan is to take over the government in the resulting confusion. Fortunately our dastardly inventor is stopped, but not before much foolishness has come to pass.
Osca: LOVE-IN ARRANGEMENT, THE/EAGER FINGERS, EAGER LIPS (asa)
A                                         77 min
B,V                                          HAR

## SLIPPER AND THE ROSE, THE *                  U
Bryan Forbes          UK              1976
*Richard Chamberlain, Kenneth More, Gemma Craven, Michael Hordern, Edith Evans, Margaret Lockwood, Annette Crosbie, Christopher Gable, Lally Bowers, Julian Orchard, John Turner, Sherrie Hewson, Rosalind Ayres, Keith Skinner*
An overlong and quite dreadful musical version of

Cinderella. The actors are wooden, the dialogue stilted and the songs terrible. A film that is almost painful to watch. The end when it does come is a blessed relief. Written and directed by Forbes with Richard Sherman. Songs (such as they are) appear courtesy of Robert and Richard Sherman.
Boa: short story Cinderella by Perrault.
MUS                                    136 min (ort 146 min)
B,V                                         IFS L/A; VGM

## SLIPPERY WHEN WET **
Karl Anderson          USA                    1976
*Ursula Austin, Annie Sprinkles, C.J. Laing, Hope Stockton*
Story of a beautiful Soho artist whose abilities in erotic art lead to her enormous popularity among the local college lads.
Osca: BANG BANG/SIZZLE (asa)
A                                             91 min
B,V                                              HAR

## SLIPSTREAM *
David Acomba          CANADA          U    1972
*Luke Askew, Patti Oatman, Eli Rill, Scott Hylands, Danny Freedman, Debbie Peck, Debbie Rotenberg, Allan G. Anderson, Joseph Golland, Linda Houston, Michael Hollingsworth, Karen Peterson, Elizabeth Murphy, Ed Potts*
A popular DJ becomes the object of a national manhunt in this mediocre little tale.
DRA                                    57 min (ort 93 min)
V                                               CHRY

## SLIPSTREAM **
Steven M. Lisberger     USA            PG    1988
*Mark Hamill, Bob Peck, Bill Paxton, Kitty Aldridge, Ben Kingsley, Eleanor David, Robbie Coltrane, F. Murray Abraham*
Fantasy set in a world where the laws of nature are in disarray, and the main mode of transport is in craft carried along by the powerful winds. A man being taken to prison escapes from his captors, and is kidnapped by a young adventurer who intends claiming a reward. Despite imaginative ideas, this story soon degenerates into a standard chase movie. The music is by Elmer Bernstein.
FAN                                           101 min
V                                                 EIV

## SLITHER ***
Howard Zieff           USA             15    1972
*James Caan, Peter Boyle, Sally Kellerman, Louise Lasser, Allen Garfield, Richard B. Shull*
An assorted bunch of criminals chase across California in search of a cache of loot. A wild mixture of slapstick and thrills that develops erratically but is fast-paced enough to be effective. Written by W.D. Richter.
COM                                           96 min
B,V                                              MGM

## SLITHIS *
Stephen Traxler        USA                    1979
*Alan Blanchard, Judy Motulsky, Mello Alexandria, Dennis Lee Falt, Hy Pyke, Win Condict, Don Cummins, Rocky Fumarelli, John Hatfield, Daphnae Cohan, Steven J. Hoag, Wendy Rastattar, Dan Coles, David Riddenauer*
Nuclear waste leads to the creation of an unstoppable monster which menaces the citizens of a Californian town. Low-grade and poorly handled dross.
Aka: SPAWN OF THE SLITHIS
HOR                                           86 min
B,V                                        MED; VPD

## SLOANE *
Daniel Rosenthal                       18
                        PHILIPPINES            1984
*Robert Resnik, Debra Blee, Paul Aragon, Ann*

*Milhench, Carissa Carlos, Arthur Cervantes, Charles Black*
A tough ex-cop and martial arts expert, goes to Manila to rescue his ex-girlfriend from her kidnappers. Very dull, very predictable.
A/AD                                   88 min Cut (58 sec)
B,V                                              MED

## SLOW BURN **
Matthew Chapman        USA             15    1986
*Eric Roberts, Beverly D'Angelo, Raymond J. Barry, Dan Hedaya, Henry Gibson, Dennis Lipscomb, Emily Longstreth, Johnny Depp, Ann Schedeen, Frank Schuller, Edward Bunker, Ruth Richards, Pat Ast, Linda Rae Barre*
An ex-reporter turns private eye in Palm Springs, but soon finds himself in too deep when an apparently simple case embroils him in drugs, murder and blackmail. A slow-moving thriller that is fairly lacking in tension.
Boa: novel Castles Burning by Arthur Lyons.
THR                                    91 min mCab
B,V                                              CIC

## SLUGGER'S WIFE, THE *
Hal Ashby               USA            15    1985
*Michael O'Keefe, Rebecca DeMornay, Martin Ritt, Randy Quaid, Cleavant Derricks, Lisa Langlois, Loudon Wainwright III*
A baseball player marries a pop star but finds that married life is far from easy. A disjointed and fairly unattractive dud, written by Neil Simon.
COM                                    100 min (ort 105 min)
B,V                                              RCA

## SLUGS *
J.P. Simon              USA            18    1989
*Michael Garfield, Kim Terry, Philip McHale*
This first film version of one of Hutson's books, opens with several people meeting nasty accidents arising from their contact with deadly, mutated slugs. Despite a lack of belief on the part of the police, who put the deaths down to a series of accidents, a health inspector who has learnt the truth sets out to destroy them. A repulsive and far-fetched story, of poor dialogue and little imagination.
Boa: novel by Shaun Hutson.
HOR                                           89 min
V                                                NWV

## SLUMBER PARTY '57 *
William A. Levey        USA                   1977
*Debra Winger, Noelle North, Bridget Hollman, Mary Anne Appleseth, Rainbeaux Smith, Janet Wood, Rafael Campos, Will Hutchins*
Six girls recall how they lost their virginity, at a slumber party held when their basketball team was away that weekend. A shoddy and vulgar comedy, built around a series of flashbacks. This was Winger's first film.
Aka: TEENAGE SLUMBER PARTY
COM                                    83 min (ort 89 min)
B,V                                              INT

## SLUMBER PARTY MURDERS *
Amy Jones               USA            18    1982
*Michele Michaels, Robin Stille, Michael Villela, Andre Honore, Debra DeLiso, Gina Mari, David Millbern, Joe Johnson, Pamela Roylance, Brinke Stevens, Rigg Kennedy, Howard Furgason, Anna Patton, Jim Boyce, Jennifer Meyers*
A crazed killer stalks a girl's overnight party, in what is allegedly a parody of such films, with a sequel following in 1987. An unrewarding and barely watchable effort. Screenplay is by Rita Mae Brown.
Aka: SLUMBER PARTY MASSACRE
HOR                                    72 min (ort 78 min) Cut (30 sec)
B,V                                              TEVP

**SMALL KILLING, A ** **                                              15**
Steven Hilliard Stern    USA
*Edward Asner, Jean Simmons, Andrew Prine, J. Pat*
*O'Malley, Mary Jackson, Sylvia Sidney, John*
*Steadman, Kent Williams, Matthew Faison, Anne*
*Ramsey, Barbara Edelman, Nicholas Guest, Enrique*
*Castillo, Doug Johnson, Noel Conlon*
An undercover cop gets some unexpected help from a
female college professor, in tracking down hired
killers working for a drug syndicate, when he per-
suades her to pose as a bag lady. Fair.
Boa: novel The Rag Bag Clan by Richard Barth.
THR                         96 min (ort 100 min) mTV
B,V                                                    HER

**SMALL SACRIFICES ** * **                                         15**
David Greene        USA                              1988
*Farrah Fawcett, Ryan O'Neal, John Shea, Gordon*
*Clapp, Emily Perkins*
Fawcett gives a convincing performance in her role as
Diane Downs, an Oregon mother who was accused of
shooting her three children. An intense and powerful
melodrama that is often quite disturbing to watch.
Originally shown in two parts.
DRA                        180 min (ort 200 min) mTV
V                                                   PRISM L/A

**SMALL TOWN GIRLS ** **                                            **
Tom Janovich       USA                               1979
*John Seeman, Blair Harris, Serena, Valerie Darlyn,*
*Harry Freeman, Dave Morris, Aaron Stuart, Dorothy*
*Le May, Jesse Adams, Michael Morrison*
A sex magazine stages a $50,000 competition, to find
the best article a woman can write about her sexual
fantasies. Each of the four finalists is given $5,000 to
live out their fantasy, and unknown to them, the
magazine has hired four men to help them do this.
Fantasies range from voyeurism to sado-masochism,
and by the time the women are done, each is declared
a winner.
Aka: ECSTASY GIRLS
A                            53 min (ort 84 min)
B,V                                                    KTC

**SMALL TOWN IN TEXAS, A ** **                                      15**
Jack Starrett        USA                             1976
*Timothy Bottoms, Susan George, Bo Hopkins, Art*
*Hindle, Morgan Woodward, John Karlen*
A man plots revenge against the sheriff, who framed
him on a drugs charge and then proceeded to steal his
girlfriend. He gets his chance to put his plans into
operation on release from prison, in this violent tale.
Quite well made, but there are no surprises on offer.
THR                         92 min (ort 96 min)
B,V                                                    RNK

**SMALL TOWN MASSACRE ***                                          18**
Michael Laughlin
                   AUSTRALIA/NEW ZEALAND           1981
*Michael Murphy, Louise Fletcher, Arthur Dignam,*
*Dan Shor, Fiona Lewis, Marc McClure, Scotty Brady,*
*Dey Young, Charles Lane, Jim Boelsen, Beryl Te*
*Wiata, B. Courtenay Leigh, William Hayward,*
*Elizabeth Cheshire, Billy Al Bengston*
A small town is terrorised by a brutal and crazed
killer who leaves the usual trail of corpses in this
low-budget shocker. Supposed to be set in the Midwest
but actually filmed in New Zealand.
Aka: DEAD KIDS; STRANGE BEHAVIOUR
HOR                                                  97 min
B,V,V2  VIDGOL/CBS; SCO (Betamax and VHS only)

**SMALLEST SHOW ON EARTH, THE ** **                                U**
Basil Dearden       UK                               1957
*Virginia McKenna, Bill Travers, Peter Sellers,*
*Margaret Rutherford, Bernard Miles, Leslie Phillips*
Very British, slightly unreal comedy with a young
couple inheriting a flea-pit cinema, complete with

drunken projectionist and other eccentric characters.
Against all the odds they manage to make it pay and
the humour derives from the various underhand ploys
they use. An uncomfortable blend of sentiment and
farce that carries little force in either area.
Aka: BIG TIME OPERATORS
COM                                               81 min B/W
V                                                  CASPIC

**SMASH PALACE ** **                                               18**
Roger Donaldson
                   NEW ZEALAND                       1981
*Bruno Lawrence, Anna Jemison, Greer Robson, Keith*
*Aberdein, Desmond Kelly*
A junkyard owner is so engrossed in smashing up cars
that he fails to notice the crisis affecting his family. A
murky and muddled melodrama slightly redeemed by
good performances.
DRA                        103 min (ort 108 min)
B,V                                                    CBS

**SMASH-UP ON INTERSTATE FIVE ** **                                15**
John Llewellyn Moxey   USA                           1976
*Robert Conrad, Sian-Barbara Allen, Buddy Ebsen,*
*David Groh, Scott Jacoby, Herb Edelman, Joe Knapp,*
*Sue Lyon, Vera Miles, Donna Mills, Harriet Nelson,*
*George O'Hanlon Jr, Terry Moore, David Nelson,*
*Bonnie Ebsen, Joel Parks*
Traces the story of those who become part of a crash,
involving 39 cars on a Californian motorway. A
multi-character movie with a series of flashbacks,
showing events in the lives of the characters prior to
the accident, which happens at the start, the story
unfolding from that point. Average.
Boa: novel Expressway by Elleston Trevor.
DRA                        100 min mTV
B,V                                                    HER

**SMITH! ** * **                                                   U**
Michael O'Herlihy     USA                            1969
*Glenn Ford, Nancy Olson, Dean Jagger, Keenan*
*Wynn, Warren Oates, Chief Dan George, Frank*
*Ramirez, Jay Silverheels*
The story of a liberal-minded farmer who comes to the
defence of an Indian accused of murder. Quite an
unusual drama from Disney, and done in a nice
restrained way.
WES                         97 min (ort 112 min)
B,V                                                    WDV

**SMITHEREENS ** * **                                              15**
Susan Seidelman     USA                              1982
*Susan Berman, Brad Rinn, Richard Hill, Roger Jett,*
*Nada Despotovitch, Kitty Summerall*
A selfish young punk girl comes to New York and
hopes to fulfil her dream of becoming a rock star, but
soon finds herself in desperate straits. A realistic and
absorbing character study.
DRA                        93 min; 89 min (ACAD)
B,V                         ACAD; MERL/VCL; APX

**SMOKE ** * **                                                    U**
Vincent McEveety     USA                             1970
*Earl Holliman, Ron Howard, Jacqueline Scott*
Pleasant story of a teenage boy who finds a weak and
wounded dog, and nurses it back to health. However,
his step-father is concerned that it will worry his
sheep and when the pet's real owner turns up both boy
and dog go into hiding.
Boa: novel by W. Corbin.
DRA                         89 min (ort 98 min) mTV
B,V                                                    WDV

**SMOKEY AND THE BANDIT ** * **                                    PG**
Hal Needham        USA                               1977
*Burt Reynolds, Jackie Gleason, Sally Field, Jerry*
*Reed, Mike Henry, Paul Williams, Pat McCormick*
A bootlegging truck driver and his sidekick, outwit a
redneck sheriff in hot pursuit across several states.

The cars act beautifully but the overall effect is one of motion without progress. Followed by the inevitable trail of sequels.

COM                                      92 min (ort 97 min)
V/h                                                       CIC

### SMOKEY AND THE BANDIT 2 *                          PG
Hal Needham              USA                           1980
*Burt Reynolds, Jackie Gleason, Sally Field, Jerry Reed, Dom DeLuise, Paul Williams, Pat McCormick, Mike Henry, Brenda Lee, Mel Tillis*
This time around our heroes agree to take a pregnant elephant to Texas. Unlike the first film, this one is short on action, with few gags to enliven the boring bits.
Aka: SMOKEY AND THE BANDIT RIDE AGAIN
COM                                      97 min (ort 101 min)
V/h                                                       CIC

### SMOKEY AND THE BANDIT: PART 3 *                    18
Dick Lowry               USA                           1983
*Jackie Gleason, Paul Williams, Jerry Reed, Pat McCormick, Mike Henry, Colleen Camp, Burt Reynolds*
Third film in the series, with the redneck sheriff accepting a bet that he can drive from Miami to Texas in 24 hours. A vapid yawn-inducer. Originally filmed with Gleason playing two roles and then re-shot with Reed.
Aka: SMOKEY IS THE BANDIT
COM                                      84 min (ort 88 min)
B,V                                                       CIC

### SMOKEY AND THE HOTWIRE GANG *
Anthony Cardoza          USA                           1979
*James Keach, Tony Lorea, Alvy Moore, Stanley Livingston, Carla Ziegfield, Skip Young, George Barris*
Another one of those mindless car chase movies.
A/AD                                                  85 min
B,V                                                       MOV

### SMOKEY BITES THE DUST *                            15
Charles B. Griffiths     USA                           1981
*Jimmy McNichol, Janet Julian, Walter Barnes, Patrick Campbell, Kari Lizer, John Blythe Barrymore, William Forsythe*
A hot-rod enthusiast kidnaps the local sheriff's daughter. This serves as an excuse for the usual car chase sequences. Somewhat reminiscent of EAT MY DUST! but a good deal more mindless.
COM                                                   85 min
B,V                                                  BWV; VGM

### SMOOTH TALK **                                     15
Joyce Chopra             USA                           1985
*Treat Williams, Laura Dern, Mary Kay Place, Levon Helm, Elizabeth Berridge, Sarah Inglis, Margaret Welch*
A young girl's adolescence is complicated when she meets an older man who is very glib and persuasive. A disappointing drama that marked the debut of documentary director Chopra. The script is by Tom Cole.
Boa: short story by Joyce Carol Oates.
DRA                                      90 min (ort 92 min)
B,V                                                       ODY

### SMORGASBORD *                                      PG
Jerry Lewis              USA                           1983
*Jerry Lewis, Herb Edelman, Zane Buzby. Guest stars: Dick Butkus, Milton Berle, Sammy Davis Jr, Foster Brooks, Buddy Lester*
A sketch-type film in which Lewis tries extremely hard to amuse, this time as a near suicidal patient who is being treated by a psychiatrist. Shelved (understandably) for some time after production.
Aka: CRACKING UP
COM                                                   85 min
B,V                                                       CBS

### SMUGGLER, THE *                                    18
Lucio Fulci              ITALY
*Fabio Testi, Ivana Marti, Guido Alberti*
Standard Mafia drama with all the usual ingredients, put together in an entirely predictable way.
A/AD                                     88 min Cut (2 min 52 sec)
V                                                ELE L/A; VIZ

### SMURFS AND THE MAGIC FLUTE, THE *                  U
Jose Dutillieu
                         BELGIUM/FRANCE                1984
Animated feature set in the Middle Ages at the royal court, and following the exploits of a family of little elfin creatures. The discovery of a magic flute leads to much chaos, as it turns out that it has the power to make all who hear it dance uncontrollably. A sluggish and uninspired tale.
Aka: LA FLUTE A SIX SCHTROUMPFS; SIX-SMURF FLUTE, THE
CAR                                                   73 min
B,V                                                  INT; VCC

### SNAKE **                                           15
Bernard L. Kowalski      USA                           1973
*Strother Martin, Robert Gilgorov, Dirk Benedict, Heather Menzies, Richard B. Shull, Jack Ging, Tim O'Connor, Reb Brown, Kathleen King, Ted Grossman, Felix Silla, Charles Seel, Ray Ballard, Brendan Burns, Rick Beckner*
A ludicrous horror yarn, telling of a demented scientist whose experiments result in his creation of a cobra-man. Quite nicely put together (the make-up was by John Chambers) but the silly plot is a major handicap.
Aka: SSSSNAKE; SSSSSSS
HOR                                      94 min Cut (27 sec)
B,V                                                       CIC

### SNAKE AND CRANE: ARTS OF SHAOLIN ***              18
Chen Chi Hua             HONG KONG                     1984
*Jackie Chan*
A warrior is unjustly accused of the murder of a number of Shaolin masters and is pursued by warriors, but has to survive long enough to prove his innocence. Another fast-paced and enjoyable Jackie Chan adventure.
MAR                                                   96 min
V                                                   AVR; TGP

### SNAKE EATER, THE *                                 18
George Erschbamer        CANADA                        1989
*Lorenzo Lamas, Josie Bell, Ronnie Hawkins, Robert Scott, Cheryl Jeans, Larry Csonka, Ron Palilo*
When his sister is kidnapped and the other members of his family murdered by a psychotic, an ex-Marine takes off in pursuit. He ultimately tracks his quarry to a swamp where his military skills give him the edge he needs to survive and achieve his ends. A violent and disagreeable actioner of no great merit.
A/AD                                                  89 min
V                                                      20VIS

### SNAKE IN THE EAGLE'S SHADOW ***                   18
Yuen Woo Ping            HONG KONG                     1978
*Jackie Chan, Juan Jon Lee, Simon Yuen, Shi Tien, Chiu Chi-Ling, Chen Hsia, Wang Chang, Louis Feng*
The last remaining master of the snake style of kung fu, decides to take on a student to ensure the survival of this style of combat. A vigorous blend of kung fu and comedy, the first film of this type starring Jackie Chan.
Aka: EAGLE'S SHADOW, THE; SNAKES IN EAGLE SHADOW; SNAKE IN EAGLE'S SHADOW
MAR                                      92 min (ort 97 min) Cut (34 sec)
B,V                                                       RNK

### SNAKE IN THE EAGLE'S SHADOW: PART 2 **            15
                         HONG KONG                     1989
*Long Fei*

Four different kung fu styles are on display here in this competent sequel to the first film, that as expected, uses the formula honour-must-be-avenged plot as a vehicle for some fancy footwork.

MAR 89 min
B,V VPD

## SNAKE IN THE MONKEY'S SHADOW **
Chang Shen    HONG KONG    1979
*John Chong (Chang Wu Lang), Wilson Tang (Tang Wei-Cheng), Hou Chao-Sheng, Charlie Chan, Domson Shi*
Two rival fighting styles are put to the test in a series of bloody clashes.
Aka: HOU HSING K'OU SHOU

MAR 85 min
B,V VPD

## SNAKE STRIKES BACK, THE **    18
HONG KONG    198-
*Eagle Han, Elton Chung, Kim Miou*
A ruthless fighter plots to achieve control of a kung fu school, and thus gain possession of a secret book of invincible fighting techniques. Only the favourite pupil of the current master is able to oppose his wicked plans.

MAR 83 min Cut (4 sec)
B,V VPD

## SNAP *    PG
Chuck Vincent    USA    1981
*Chris Lemmon, Marlyn Joi, Olivia Pascal*
A one-man advertising agency is given the task of persuading famous women to use a certain brand of bra. Very silly.
Aka: C.O.D.

COM 90 min
B,V AVA/CBS

## SNAPSHOT *
Allan Eastman    CANADA    1975
*Jim Henshaw, Susan Petrie, Susan Hogan, Peter Jobin, Allan Migicovsky, David Bolt, Linda Houston, Deni Allaire, Nick Mancuso, Lise Granik, George Kee, Terry Lynch, David Main, Richard Davidson, Doug Fetherling, Dale Wilson*
An accident-prone sports photographer finds himself getting involved in some very strange situations.
Aka: SWEETER SONG, A

COM 82 min
B,V VCL/CBS

## SNAPSHOT: AUSTRALIAN STYLE *
Simon Wincer    AUSTRALIA    1978
*Chantal Contouri, Robert Brunning, Sigrid Thornton*
A young girl becomes a model and is disowned by her family for posing in the nude.
Aka: DAY AFTER HALLOWEEN; SNAPSHOT

DRA 90 min
B,V VCL/CBS

## SNEAKERS *    15
Daryl Duke    USA    1981
*Carl Marotte, Lisa Langlois, Charlaine Woodward*
A fairly routine look at teenage life in the 1960s.

DRA 105 min
B,V POLY

## SNOOPY, COME HOME! ***    U
Bill Melendez    USA    1972
*Voices of: Bill Melendez, Stephen Shea, David Carey, Chad Webber, Robin Kahn, Johanna Baer, Hilary Momberger, Chris De Faria, Linda Ercoli, Linda Mendelson*
Animation based on a famous comic strip cartoon by Schulz – "Peanuts" – with Snoopy, the beagle, getting so annoyed at the number of "No Dog" signs, that he decides to run away with Woodstock, his feathered friend. A distraught Charlie Brown searches every-

where for him. An enjoyable second outing for the "Peanuts" gang. See also CHARLIE BROWN: A BOY NAMED CHARLIE BROWN.

CAR 77 min
B,V CBS

## SNOW BUNNIES: NERDS ON VACATION **    15
Robert Gibson    AUSTRALIA    1982
*David Argue, Lance Curtis*
Two men win a car and decide to take a vacation to a ski resort, where they indulge in the usual buffoonery.
Aka: SNOW: THE MOVIE

COM 90 min
B,V TGP

## SNOW QUEEN, THE **    U
Andrew Gosling    UK    1976
*Linda Slater, Joshua le Touzel, Hilda Barry, Mercedes Burleigh*
Live-action and animated version of the famous children's tale.
Boa: short story by Hans Christian Andersen.

CAR 56 min
B,V BBC

## SNOW SPIDER, THE **    U
Pennant Roberts    198-
*Sian Phillips, Osian Roberts*
A kid's fantasy tale in which a 9-year-old who receives five unusual gifts on his birthday, sets out on a strange quest to a mythical land. Fair.

JUV 90 min
V VGM

## SNOW TREASURE **
Irving Jacoby    USA    1968
*James Franciscus, Ilona Rodgers, Paul Anstad, Raoul Oyen, Randi Borch*
The Norwegian Resistance plan to smuggle out the country's gold reserves under the noses of the German occupying forces, with the help of some teenage patriots. A satisfactory but hardly engrossing story, written by Jacoby and Peter Hansen
Boa: novel by Marie McSwigan.

WAR 95 min
B,V HVM L/A; VUL L/A; HVH

## SNOW WHITE AND THE SEVEN DWARFS **    U
Michael Berz    USA    1987
*Diana Rigg, Sara Patterson, Doug Sheldon, Nicola Stapleton, Billy Barty, Mike Edmunds, Ricardo Gil, Malcolm Dixon, Gary Friedkin, Tony Cooper, Douglas Sheldon, Dorit Adi, Ian James, Amnon Meskin, Julien Joy Chagrin*
A live-action version of this famous fairytale, telling of how the daughter of a king was forced by the jealousy of her stepmother to flee to the forest for safety, where she was adopted by a family of dwarfs. A competent work.
Aka: CANNON MOVIE TALES: SNOW WHITE
Boa: short story by Jakob Ludwig Karl Grimm and Wilhelm Karl Grimm.

JUV 82 min (ort 85 min)
V/sh WHV

## SNOW WHITE AND THE SEVEN DWARFS ***    Uc
Peter Medak    USA    1983
*Elizabeth McGovern, Vanessa Redgrave, Rex Smith, Vincent Price*
An adaptation of the classic tale from the "Fairie Tale Theatre" series, with an evil queen plotting to kill the beautiful Snow White with a poisoned apple, when she learns that the latter is more beautiful than her. Price makes a fine talking mirror in this effective rendition.
Boa: short story by Jakob Ludwig Karl Grimm and Wilhelm Karl Grimm.

JUV 53 min
V MGM

## SNOW WHITE CHRISTMAS, A ** U
Kay Wright USA 1979
Cartoon adventure in which Snow White makes friends with seven giants and they fight the evil Queen, who has hatched a plan to spoil the spirit of Christmas.
CAR 46 min (ort 60 min)
V VGM

## SNOWBALL EXPRESS **
Norman Tokar USA 1972
*Dean Jones, Nancy Olson, Harry Morgan, Keenan Wynn, Johnny Whittaker, Mary Wickes, Michael McGreevey, David White, Dick Van Patten, George Lindsey*
An accountant inherits a rundown hotel and tries to turn it into luxury accommodation for skiers. A standard Disney comedy, with a madcap ski chase the highlight of the film.
Boa: novel Chateau Bon Vivant by Frankie and John O'Rear.
JUV 99 min; 93 min (WDV)
B,V RNK; WDV

## SNOWBALLING * 15
Charles E. Sellier USA 1984
*Alan Segus, Mary McDonough, Jim Carroll, P.R. Paul, Bob Hastings*
Formula teen comedy with American college students at a ski resort in search of sex and adventure.
COM 94 min
B,V CBS

## SNOWS OF KILIMANJARO, THE ** PG
Henry King USA 1952
*Gregory Peck, Susan Hayward, Ava Gardner, Hildegarde Neff, Leo G. Carroll, Torin Thatcher, Marcel Dalio*
In Africa, a wounded hunter has ample time to review his past life as he awaits rescue. Despite the star-studded cast, Hemingway's tale of a man trying to find a meaning to life falls victim to that common Hollywood failing, in short, a lack of conciseness. A muddled mess of unconvincing performances, spectacular locations and rambling dialogue.
Boa: story by Ernest Hemingway.
DRA 109 min (ort 117 min)
V/h CBS

## SO DEAR TO MY HEART ** U
Harold Schuster USA 1948
*Burl Ives, Beulah Bondi, Harry Carey, Bobby Driscoll, Luana Patten*
A small boy is determined to tame his pet black sheep and enter it in a country fair in a country farm in 1903 that may appeal to some. Contains several animated sequences. Music is by Eliot Daniels with lyrics by Larry Morey. Written by John Tucker Battle.
Boa: novel Midnight And Jeremiah by Sterling North.
JUV 84 min
B,V WDV

## SO FINE ** 15
Andrew Bergman USA 1981
*Ryan O'Neal, Jack Warden, Richard Kiel, Mariangela Melato, Fred Gwynne, Mike Kellin, David Rounds*
Comedy set in the New York garment industry, where a professor of literature tries to save his garment manufacturer dad from gangsters, and gets caught up in some strange adventures. The directing debut for Bergman, who wrote the script. Music is by Ennio Morricone. Fair, but somewhat chaotic.
COM 87 min (ort 91 min)
B,V WHV

## SO LONG AT THE FAIR **
Terence Fisher/Anthony Darnborough
UK 1950
*Jean Simmons, Dirk Bogarde, David Tomlinson, Honor Blackman, Cathleen Nesbitt, Marcel Poncin, Betty Warren, Felix Aylmer, Andre Morell, Zena Marshall, Austin Trevor, Eugene Deckers, Natasha Sokolova*
A brother and sister visit the 1889 Paris Exposition, and the day after their arrival he disappears from the hotel and everybody denies ever having seen him. A modest little mystery, somewhat lacking in force.
Boa: novel by Anthony Thorne.
DRA 86 min (ort 90 min) B/W
B,V RNK

## SO PROUDLY WE HAIL * 15
Lionel Chetwynd USA 1989
*David Soul, Edward Herrmann, Chad Lowe, David Lowe, Gloria Carlin, Raphael Sbarge, Kevin Conroy, Peter Dobson, Harley Jane Kozak*
Dull examination of resurgent neo-Nazism that focuses on a gullible university professor, whose propagation of a theory to explain cultural differences makes him a useful tool for a white supremacist group. A poor drama that trivialises and exploits a disturbing issue. The script is by Chetwynd.
DRA 91 min (ort 100 min) mTV
V CBS

## SO SWEET, SO DEAD **
Roberto Montero ITALY 1972
*Farley Granger, Sylva Koscina, Susan Scott, Silvano Tranquilli, Annabella Incontreux*
A series of murders of women baffle the police since they appear to have no underlying motive.
Aka: RIVELAZIONI DI UN MANIACO SESSUALE AL CAPO DELLA SQUADRA MOBILE
THR 95 min
B,V,V2 VPD

## SOCIETY *** 18
Brian Yuzna USA 1989
*Billy Warlock, Devin Devasquez, Evan Richards, Ben Meyerson*
A surreal horror-comedy that's based on the bizarre premise that the rich folk of Beverly Hills are a separate race who literally feed on the poor. A alienated youngster learns the frightful truth about his family when his sister's jilted boyfriend gives him a videotape showing the things the family get up to with other like-minded individuals. Weird, horrific and unforgettable; the nauseating special effects are by Screaming Mad George.
HOR 94 min
V MED

## SOCIETY AFFAIR **
Robert McCallum USA 1982
*Veronica Hart, Harry Reems, Richard Bolla, Kelly Nichols, Tiffany Clark, Jack Newtown, Tara Aire, Frank Holowell, Lauri Smith*
Rick is a small-time crook who's contacted by his former partner when she discovers that the bridegroom in a rich society wedding is Rick's double. Having hatched a plot for Rick to marry into the family instead, they dope the bridegroom and put their plan into action. Rick never does get married though, for when he learns of a plot to defraud the bridegroom he denounces the whole thing and absconds with his old partner and the wedding gifts.
A 80 min
B,V EVI

## SODOM AND GOMORRAH ** PG
Robert Aldrich
FRANCE/ITALY/USA 1963
*Stewart Granger, Pier Angeli, Stanley Baker, Rossana Podesta, Anouk Aimee, Rik Battaglia, Giacomo Rossi Stuart*
Long account of the fate of two sinful cities. Said to be based on the Bible account, but frankly I have my

doubts. A mixture of spectacle and tedium, with music by Miklos Rozsa.
DRA     112 min (ort 154 min) (Abridged by disributor)
V                                                    VPD

## SOFT BEDS, HARD BATTLES *                    15
Roy Boulting            UK              1973
*Peter Sellers, Lila Kedrova, Curt Jurgens, Gabriella Licudi, Jenny Hanley, Beatrice Romand, Francoise Pascal, Rula Lenska, Daphne Lawson, Carolle Rousseau, Hylette Adophe, Douglas Sheldon, Timothy West, Patricia Burke*
The occupants of a Paris brothel in WW2 make their contribution to the Allied victory. Sellers plays six roles including Hitler, in this awkward mishmash of jokes and tired routines. Written by Leo Marks and Roy Boulting.
Aka: SOFT BEDS AND HARD BATTLES; UNDERCOVER HERO; UNDERCOVERS HERO
Boa: novel by P. Evans.
COM                      95 min (ort 107 min)
B,V                               RNK; STRAND

## SOFT PLACES *
Wray Hamilton           USA              1978
*Annette Haven, Phil Tobias, Paul Thomas*
A husband dies and leaves a will that is his revenge for an unsatisfactory sex life with his wife. According to its conditions she has to engage in several sexual activities in order to inherit, the last one being that she finds a man to love totally. She begins to carry out the terms of the will but ultimately winds up in bed with her husband's lawyer, in this utterly foolish and far-fetched tale.
A                                        70 min
B,V                                        WOV

## SOGGY BOTTOM, USA **
Ted Flicker             USA              1981
*Ben Johnson, Ann Wedgeworth, Lois Nettleton, Jack Elam, P.J. Soles, Lane Smith, Don Johnson, Anthony Zerbe, Dub Taylor*
A town in the USA seems unaffected by the Depression and business continues as normal, its business being moonshine.
COM                                      97 min
B,V,V2                                    GHV

## SOLAR ADVENTURE *                          PG
Roy Thomas          HONG KONG            1989
Yet another Joseph Lai/Betty Chan production (see FALCON 7 or CAPTAIN COSMOS) that blends rather nondescript animation techniques with an ambitious fantasy plot. Once again Earth is under threat from evil aliens, and this time our would-be conqueror has captured the only weapon that can stop him – the "Canon Robot". Fortunately, a friendly alien is on hand, and finds a group of children able to control the robot with their minds.
CAR                                      63 min
V                                        VPD

## SOLARWARRIORS *                            15
Alan Johnson            USA              1986
*Richard Jordan, Jami Gertz, Jason Patric, Lukas Haas, James Le Gros, Claude Brooks, Peter DeLuise, Peter Kowanko, Adrian Pasdar, Sarah Douglas, Charles Durning, Frank Converse, Terrence Mann, Alexei Sayle, Bruce Payne*
A lame fantasy about a group of teenage skateboarders, held prisoner by an evil megalomaniac ruler on a desert planet, and their attempts to rebel and save a mystical alien from destruction.
Aka: SOLARBABIES
FAN                      91 min (ort 95 min)
B,V                                        MGM

## SOLDIER BLUE *                             18
Ralph Nelson            USA              1970

*Candice Bergen, Peter Strauss, Donald Pleasence, John Anderson, Dana Elcar, Jorge Rivero, Martin West, Jorge Russek, Marco Antonio Arzate, Ron Fletcher, Barbara Turner, Aurora Clavell*
The love affair between the two survivors of an Indian attack, one a naive cavalry officer, the other a determined resourceful girl, serves as background to an account of the inhuman treatment meted out to the Indians courtesy of the US Cavalry. A meandering and cliched affair that culminates in a rather sickening massacre of an Indian village. Written by John Gay.
Boa: novel Arrow In The Sun by Theodore V. Olsen.
WES             109 min (ort 114 min) Cut (36 sec)
B,V,V2,LV                 EHE; CH5 (VHS only)

## SOLDIER OF FORTUNE **                       PG
Pasquale Festa Campi ITALY
*Bud Spencer (Carlo Pedersoli), Andrea Ferreol*
Very loosely based on the tale of the Challenge of Barletta that took place in 1503, this tells of a French soldier who inadvertently insults a group of Italian horsemen. The latter propose a contest between French and Italian horseriding champions as a way of fighting a duel of honour.
COM                                      91 min
B,V                                        VPD

## SOLDIER'S REVENGE, A *                       15
David Worth       ARGENTINA/USA
                               1984 (released 1986)
*John Savage, Maria Socas, Edgardo Moreira, Frank Cane, Paul Lambert, Sebastian Larrie, George Wellurtz, Jack Arndt, Albert Uris, Brian McKlunn, Fiona Keyne*
When a 6-year-old Vietnamese girl dies in his arms, a US soldier refuses to fight any longer and is sent to prison. After his release he resolves to help small nations preserve their independence, but these ideals lead to his involvement with a revolution in Latin America, which proves to be a dangerous experience. A foolish and implausible combination of pacifist sentiments and explosive action.
Boa: story by Eduard Sarlui.
DRA                                      90 min
B,V                                        EIV

## SOLDIER'S STORY, A ***                       15
Norman Jewison          USA              1984
*Howard E. Rollins Jr, Adolph Caesar, Art Evans, Dennis Lipscombe, Denzel Washington, Larry Riley, Wings Hauser, Patti LaBelle, David Alan Grier, David Harris*
A university-trained black US army investigator, is assigned to tackle the case of a young black sergeant murdered at a training camp in Louisiana. Based on Fuller's Pulitzer Prize-winning play, which was in turn inspired by Melville's "Billy Budd", the film features most of the black cast from the original stage production. A somewhat stilted but absorbing drama.
Boa: play by Charles Fuller.
DRA                      97 min (ort 101 min)
V/sh                                       RCA

## SOLE SURVIVOR **
Thom Eberhardt          USA              1982
*Anita Skinner, Kurt Johnson, Caren Larkey, Andrew Drake, Daniel Cartmell, William Snare, Toni Lawrence, Rudy Challenger, Laurie Wendorf, Susan Malter, Gino Gaudio, Al Valletta, Eldon Randall, Barbara Renee*
A girl survives a plane crash and finds that she has become the victim of terrifying occult forces. Fair.
THR                                      102 min
B,V,V2                                     INT

## SOLITAIRE *                                 R18
Mike Freeman
*Inga Radstrom, Bob Wildman*

Fairly plotless film revolving around the title character, who as a writer of erotic novels, is paid a visit by a
pushy male journalist.

A                                            80 min
V                                            PUFF

**SOME CALL IT LOVING *** 18
James B. Harris          USA          1973
*Zalman King, Carole White, Richard Pryor, Tisa
Farrow, Logan Ramsey, Brandy Herrod, Veronica
Anderson*
A young jazz musician lives in a mansion in California
with two women, in an erotic fantasy world of their
own. On a visit to a carnival he becomes obsessed with
a strange "sleeping beauty" in a sideshow – a girl who
has been in a drug-induced sleep for a year. He buys
up the sideshow and waits for her to awaken, not
having realised that life does not generally resemble
fairy tales. A pretentious and contrived little fantasy.
Aka: DREAM CASTLE; DREAM CASTLES
Boa: short story Sleeping Beauty by John Collier.
DRA                                 90 min (ort 103 min)
B,V                                    CBS L/A; MPV

**SOME GIRLS DO ***
Ralph Thomas             UK           1969
*Richard Johnson, Daliah Lavi, Bebi Loncar, Sydne
Rome, James Villiers, Vanessa Howard, Robert
Morley, Maurice Denham, Florence Desmond, Ronnie
Stevens, Adrienne Posta, Nicholas Phipps, Yutte
Stensgaard, Virginia North*
Bulldog Drummond investigates sabotage of Britain's
supersonic aircraft programme, in this updated story
of the adventures of a famous detective from the radio.
He finds that the sabotage is linked to a gang of
murderous female assassins. Quite fast-paced, but
nothing more than a dated parody of the character
created by Sapper. A sequel to "Deadlier Than The
Male".
THR                                 91 min (ort 93 min)
B,V                                           RNK

**SOME KIND OF HERO *** 15
Michael Pressman         USA          1981
*Richard Pryor, Margot Kidder, Ray Sharkey, Ronny
Cox, Lynne Moody, Olivia Cole, Paul Benjamin, David
Adams, Martin Azarow, Shelly Batt, Susan Berlin*
A Vietnam veteran returns home after 6 years as a
POW, only to find that things are not as he expected to
find them. A patchy and irritating blend of comedy
and drama, that is unappealing in both departments.
Boa: novel by James Kirkwood.
DRA                                 93 min (ort 97 min)
V/h                                           CIC

**SOME KIND OF MIRACLE *****
Jerrold Freedman         USAS         1979
*David Dukes, Andrea Marcovicci, Michael C. Gwynne,
Art Hindle, Dick Anthony Williams, John Herzeld,
Bruno Kirby, Nancy Marchand, Stephen Elliott,
Marilyn Chris, Katherine Pass, Art Evans, Michael
LaGuardia, Lee Kessler*
A man injures his spine in a surfing accident and his
entire life is drastically changed, although the film
tends to focus on the sexual frustrations suffered by
him and his fiancee. A solid and unpretentious tale.
Boa: book But There Are Always Miracles by Mary
Pleshette Willis.
DRA                                 100 min mTV
B,V                                           HER

**SOME KIND OF WONDERFUL *** 15
Howard Deutch            USA          1987
*Eric Stoltz, Lea Thompson, Mary Stuart Masterson,
Craig Sheffer, John Ashton, Elias Koteas, Molly
Hagan, Maddie Corman, Jane Elliot, Candice
Cameron*
A young man struggles to find his own identity,
despite the pressure to conform on the part of both

family and friends. Eventually, he finds true love in
the company of the tomboy girl he ignored in favour of
a flashy but empty-headed girl. A film exploring a
similar theme to that of PRETTY IN PINK, but with a
gender change.
DRA                                 91 min (ort 93 min)
V/sh                                           CIC

**SOME LIKE IT HOT ******** U
Billy Wilder             USA          1959
*Tony Curtis, Jack Lemmon, Marilyn Monroe, Joe E.
Brown, George Raft, Pat O'Brien, Nehemiah Persoff,
Joan Shawlee, Mike Mazurki, George E. Stone*
Having inadvertently witnessed the St Valentine's
Day Massacre, two unemployed musicians evade
capture by posing as women and joining an all-girl
dance band that's on its way to Miami. A romance
between one of them and the pretty singer and the
other and a playboy millionaire, leads to incredible,
hilarious complications. Wilder's best comedy is a
trifle uneven but has sharp performances and great
dialogue. AA: Cost (Orry-Kelly).
Boa: novel by Billy Wilder/I.A.L. Diamond.
COM                          117 min (ort 119 min) B/W
V                                             WHV

**SOME MAY LIVE *****
Vernon Sewell            USA          1967
*Joseph Cotten, Martha Hyer, Peter Cushing, John
Ronane*
Set in Saigon, this has Cotten trying to trap the
traitor in his intelligence department. A sluggish
little thriller.
Aka: IN SAIGON, SOME MAY LIVE
THR                                87 min (ort 105 min) mTV
V                                             INT

**SOME WILL, SOME WON'T *** PG
Duncan Wood              UK           1969
*Ronnie Corbett, Thora Hird, Michael Hordern,
Barbara Murray, Leslie Phillips, James Robertson
Justice, Dennis Price, Wilfrid Brambell, Eleanor
Summerfield, Arthur Lowe, Stephen Lewis*
The four heirs to a fortune find that the will stipulates
they are each obliged to perform uncharacteristic
tasks in order to inherit. A flaccid remake of "Laugh-
ter In Paradise" that's as unfunny as it is unmemor-
able.
COM                                 87 min (ort 90 min)
V                                             WHV

**SOMEBODY KILLED HER HUSBAND ***
Lamont Johnson          USA          1978
*Farrah Fawcett-Majors (Fawcett), Jeff Bridges, John
Wood, Tammy Grimes, John Glover, Patricia Elliott*
A woman's lover becomes the prime suspect when her
husband is killed in mysterious circumstances. A
feeble little comedy-mystery that has very little going
for it except the title. Written by Reginald Rose and
filmed in Manhattan. This was the first starring role
for Fawcett after her spell in the TV series "Charlie's
Angels".
COM                                          96 min
B,V,V2                                        GHV

**SOMEBODY'S STOLEN OUR RUSSIAN SPY ***
James Ward          SWITZERLAND/UK      1967
*Tom Adams, Tim Barrett, Diana Lorgs, Mari Paz
Pondal, Barta Barry, Maria Silvia*
A typical spy spoof in which a British agent has to
rescue a Russian colonel kidnapped by the Chinese
(ably assisted by the Albanians). A weak and dated
offering.
COM                                          77 min
B,V                                          WOV

**SOMEONE BEHIND THE DOOR ***** 15
Nicolas Gessner          FRANCE       1971
*Charles Bronson, Anthony Perkins, Jill Ireland, Henry*

*Garcin, Andre Penvern, Adriano Magestretti, Agathe
Natanson, Viviane Everly*
An amnesiac patient who may have caused a murder,
becomes a pawn in the hands of the psychiatrist
treating him, since the latter sees him as a means of
inflicting the ultimate revenge on his faithless wife.
An implausible and suspense-free tale.
Aka: BRAINKILL (DRUM or COU); QUELQU'UN
DERRIERE LA PORTE; TWO MINDS FOR
MURDER
THR                       91 min; 97 min (COU) Cut (36 sec)
B,V                                VCL/CBS; DRUM; COU

## SOMEONE IS BLEEDING **
Georgos Lautner       FRANCE                1974
*Alain Delon, Mireille Darc, Claude Brasseur, Nicoletta
Machiavelli*
A man and a woman have a strange relationship in an
isolated house run by a disturbed caretaker.
Aka: LES SEINS DE GLACE
Boa: novel by Richard Matheson.
DRA                                          120 min
B,V                                          VCL/CBS

## SOMEONE TO LOVE *
Henry Jaglom          USA                   1988
*Henry Jaglom, Michael Emil, Andrea Marcovicci,
Orson Welles, Sally Kellerman, Monte Hellman, Oja
Kodar, Stephen Bishop, Dave Frishberg, Ronee
Blakely, Kathryn Harrold, Jeremy Kagan, Miles
Kreuger*
A film-maker looking for love, invites all his friends to
a St Valentine's party, and films their replies to his
questions about love and life. A boring experiment
with neither insight nor wit. Of curiosity value as the
last film of Welles, who in this sorry effort does no
more than mouth a few philosophical platitudes.
COM                               103 min (ort 110 min)
V                                              CIC

## SOMEONE TO WATCH OVER ME ***          15
Ridley Scott          USA                   1987
*Tom Berenger, Jerry Orbach, Mimi Rogers, Lorraine
Bracco, John Rubinstein, Andreas Katsulas, Tony
DiBenedetto, James Moriarty, Mark Moses, Daniel
Hugh Kelly, Harley Cross*
A New York cop is assigned to protect a wealthy
woman who has received death threats, and gradually
becomes infatuated with her. A gripping romantic
thriller made with a good deal of flair.
THR                               103 min (ort 106 min)
V/s                                            RCA

## SOMETHING ABOUT LOVE ***             15
Tom Berry             CANADA               1988
*Jan Rubes, Stefan Wodoslawsky, Jennifer Dale,
Lenore Zann*
A touching drama in which a man returns to his
family home in Canada after spending years living in
L.A., and finds that his father has grown old and
forgetful. The simple plot is sustained and made
worthwhile by the fine performances.
DRA                                89 min (ort 93 min)
B,V                                            VES

## SOMETHING IN COMMON ***             15
Glenn Jordan          USA                   1986
*Ellen Burstyn, Tuesday Weld, Patrick Cassidy, Don
Murray, Eli Wallach, Marc Poppel, Amanda Wyss,
Kenneth Kimmins, Terri Treas, Gertrude Flynn,
George O. Petrie, Elizabeth Kerr, Anita Dangler,
Douglas Emerson, Shannon Farnon*
A 40-year-old woman book editor is forced to re-
examine her life when her 22-year-old son, who still
lives at home, becomes romantically involved with a
woman almost twice his age. An appealing romantic
comedy. The perceptive script is by Susan Rice.
COM                               94 min (ort 100 min) mTV
V                                              NWV

## SOMETHING IS OUT THERE **            18
Richard A. Colla      USA                   1988
*Joe Cortese, Maryam D'Abo, Gregory Sierra, John
Putch, Kim Delaney, George Dzundza, Robert Webber*
A police officer is baffled by a series of brutal,
motiveless murders, where there are neither clues nor
witnesses. Eventually he learns that the murderer is
the last member of a dangerous alien species. Fortunately, help arrives in the form of an attractive alien
woman. Worth seeing for the special effects of John
Dykstra, and Rick Baker's monster, but rather poorly
plotted. A pilot for a brief TV series, and first shown in
two parts.
HOR                               178 min (ort 192 min) mTV
B,V                                            EIV

## SOMETHING SHORT OF PARADISE **       15
David Helpern Jr      USA                   1979
*Susan Sarandon, Marilyn Sokol, Jean-Pierre Aumont,
David Steinberg, Joe Grifasi, Robert Hitt*
The story of an on-and-off runaway romance and
something of an ANNIE HALL rip-off. A film with
little appeal except for movie buffs, who may find the
title sequence of old movie trailers of interest.
DRA                                87 min (ort 91 min)
B,V                                            RNK

## SOMETHING SO RIGHT ***               PG
Lou Antonio           USA                   1982
*Ricky Schroder, Patty Duke Austin, James Farentino,
Fred Dryer, Annie Potts, Carole Cook, Dick Anthony
Williams, Neva Patterson, Newell Alexander, Ed Call,
Henry G. Sanders, Stuart Boyd, Gregory Cassel,
Marilyn Coleman*
A divorced woman looks for an older brother for her
young son who is always getting into trouble, and gets
a little bit more than she expected. An amiable and
relaxed tale. Written by Shelley List and Jonathan
Estrin.
DRA                                          100 min mTV
B,V                                            HER

## SOMETHING TO SING ABOUT **            U
Victor Schertzinger    USA                  1937
*James Cagney, Evelyn Daw, William Frawley, Mona
Barie, Gene Lockhart*
A New York bandleader starts a new career in
Hollywood where he becomes involved with a schem-
ing producer, in this lightweight musical made by
Cagney as an independent, during his rift with
Warner Studios. The unmemorable songs are by
Schertzinger with musical direction by Constantin
Bakaleinikoff.
Aka: BATTLING HOOFER
MUS   88 min (ort 90 min) B/W (available colourised –
VCC)
B,V                    VCL/CBS; VCC (VHS only); GLOB

## SOMETHING WICKED THIS WAY COMES ***  PG
Jack Clayton          USA                   1983
*Shawn Carson, Vidal Peterson, Jason Robards,
Jonathan Pryce, Royal Dano, Pam Grier, Diane Ladd,
Mary Grace Canfield, James Stacy, Jake Dengel, Bruce
M. Fischer, Richard Davalos, Brendan Klinger,
Arthur Hill (narration)*
A mysterious carnival visits a small American town
in Illinois and fulfils some of the inhabitants' dreams,
but at a heavy price. The intelligent and often poetic
script is by Bradbury, with Pryce giving a remarkably
intense performance as the demonic carnival owner
who tries to ensnare two small boys who have
discovered his true identity. An unusually mature
Disney treatment of a fantasy tale.
Boa: novel Ray Bradbury.
DRA                                91 min (ort 94 min)
B,V                                            WDV

## SOMETHING WILD **                     18
Jonathan Demme        USA                   1986

*Jeff Daniels, Melanie Griffith, Ray Liotta, Margaret Colin, Tracey Walter, Dana Preu, Jack Gilpin, Su Tissue, Kristin Olsen, John Sayles, John Waters*
Comedy thriller about a yuppie tax consultant, who gets embroiled in a series of adventures with an unconventional girl, eventually the pair findng themselves on the run from the police. A careless blend of comedy and melodrama, with a few funny sequences and a contrived ending.

| COM | 109 min (ort 116 min) |
|---|---|
| V/sh | RCA |

## SOMETIMES AUNT MARTHA DOES DREADFUL THINGS ** 18
Thomas Casey USA 1971
*Abe Zwick, Scott Lawrence, Don Craig, Robin Hughes, Yanka Mann, Marty Cordova, Maggie Wood, Mike Mingoia, Robert DeMeo, Sandra Lurie, Brad Ginter, Charlie Guanci, Francelia Waterbury, Victor Anchipolovsky, Joseph Bracci*
A thief with a split personality becomes a homicidal maniac.
Aka: SOMETIMES AUNT MARTHA DOES TERRIBLE THINGS

| HOR | 95 min |
|---|---|
| V | GLOB |

## SOMEWHERE IN TIME ** PG
Jeanot Szwarc USA 1980
*Christopher Reeve, Jane Seymour, Christopher Plummer, Teresa Wright, Bill Erwin, George Voskovec, Susan French, John Alvin, Eddra Gale, Sean Hayden, Audrey Bennett, W.H. Macy, Laurence Coren*
A young playwright becomes fascinated by a locket containing a portrait of an actress from 70 years ago. By an effort of will, he travels back to Chicago 1912 in order to meet her, but they are soon parted. A lightweight romantic fantasy, written by Matheson from his novel. The pretty scenery is of Mackinac Island. Music is by John Barry.
Boa: novel Bid Time Return by Richard Matheson.

| DRA | 99 min (ort 104 min) |
|---|---|
| B,V | CIC |

## SON OF BLOB * 15
Larry Hagman USA 1972 (re-issued 1982)
*Robert Walker, Gwynne Gilford, Godfrey Cambridge, Richard Webb, Shelley Berman, Carol Lynley, Burgess Meredith, Cindy Williams, Gerrit Graham, Larry Hagman, Richard Stahl, Marlene Clark, Dick Van Patten*
A comedy sequel to the 1958 film THE BLOB, that was re-issued in 1982 with the tag line "The Film That J.R. Shot". Really no more than a one-joke film that soon becomes quite tedious.
Aka: BEWARE! THE BLOB

| FAN | 88 min |
|---|---|
| B,V | VTM; BRAVE (VHS only) |

## SON OF KONG ** 15
Ernest B. Schoedsack USA 1933
*Robert Armstrong, Helen Mack, Victor Wong, John Marston, Frank Reicher, Lee Kohlmar, Ed Brady, Noble Johnson, Clarence Wilson, Katherine Ward, Gertrude Sutton, Steve Clemento, Gertrude Short, James L. Leong, Frank O'Connor*
A sequel to the classic KING KONG, with the original expedition going back to Skull Island and finding the giant ape's little son. A feeble offering rushed out in a hurry, with little attention paid to the script. The film was so ludicrous that it was promoted as a comedy, but in fact Willis O'Brien's effects are still potent. The music is by Max Steiner.
Osca: YOU'LL FIND OUT

| A/AD | 66 min (ort 69 min) B/W |
|---|---|
| B,V | KVD |

## SON OF SINBAD ** U
Ted Tetzlaff USA 1955
*Dale Robertson, Vincent Price, Sally Forrest, Lili St Cyr, Mari Blanchard, Leon Askin, Jay Novello, Raymond Greenleaf, Ian MacDonald, Larry Blake, Donald Randolph, Nejla Ates, Kalantan*
Sinbad is captured by the Caliph and forced to save Bagdad from the wicked Tamerlane in order to win his freedom. A lively and rather silly Arabian Nights yarn, with harem girls playing the forty thieves. Look out for Kim Novak who appears briefly in a full-length hooded cape. The music is by Victor Young.
Osca: CYCLONE ON HORSEBACK plus one short.

| A/AD | 88 min |
|---|---|
| B,V | KVD |

## SON OF THE SHEIK, THE *** U
George Fitzmaurice USA 1926
*Rudolph Valentino, Vilma Banky, Agnes Ayres, Karl Dane, Bull Montana*
A sequel to "The Sheik" with the star playing both father and son, in the tale of a desert leader who abducts a dancing girl he thinks has betrayed him, and then falls in love with her. One of Valentino's best films, done in slightly jocular style. A 1934 re-release had a music soundtrack by Jack Ward.

| DRA | 64 min; 58 min (CH5) (ort 74 min) B/W silent |
|---|---|
| B,V | POLY; CH5 (VHS only) |

## SONG IS BORN, A ** PG
Howard Hawks USA 1948
*Danny Kaye, Virginia Mayo, Hugh Herbert, Steve Cochran, Felix Bressart, J. Edward Bromberg, Mary Field, Ludwig Stossel, Louis Armstrong, Charlie Barnet, Benny Goodman, Lionel Hampton, Tommy Dorsey, Mel Powell*
A stuffy professor working on an encyclopedia of music with seven others, discovers jazz and life while becoming romantically entangled with a gangster's girl, in this remake of the 1941 film "Ball Of Fire" by the same director. A mild and fairly anodyne musical comedy. Look out for guest stars: Louis Armstrong, Benny Goodman, Tommy Dorsey, Lionel Hampton and Charlie Barnet.

| COM | 113 min (ort 120 min) B/W |
|---|---|
| V | VGM |

## SONG OF BERNADETTE, THE **** U
Henry King USA 1943
*Jennifer Jones, William Eythe, Charles Bickford, Vincent Price, Lee J. Cobb, Anne Revere, Gladys Cooper, Roman Bohnen, Patricia Morison, Aubrey Mather, Charles Dingle, Mary Anderson, Edith Barrett, Sig Rumann*
In the 1800s a peasant girl has a vision of the Virgin Mary (Linda Darnell in an unbilled role) at the spot that becomes the shrine of Lourdes. Despite its length and lack of historical accuracy, fine production values and a wonderfully ethereal performance from Jones ensured the film was an enormous success. AA: Actress (Jones), Cin (Arthur C. Miller), Art/Int (James Basevi and William Darling/Thomas Little), Score (Alfred Newman).
Boa: novel by Franz V. Werfel.

| DRA | 154 min (ort 156 min) B/W |
|---|---|
| V/h | CBS |

## SONG OF NORWAY * U
Andrew L. Stone USA 1970
*Florence Henderson, Toralv Maurstad, Christina Schollin, Frank Poretta, Edward G. Robinson, Harry Secombe, Robert Morley, Oscar Homolka, Elizabeth Larner, Bernard Archard, Richard Wordsworth*
A musical fantasia on the life of Grieg, in a variety of styles. Weak as a biographical work, though the Super Panavision photography helps enhance the beauty of the landscapes, but this will be lost on TV. Written by Stone.
Boa: musical by Milton Lazarus, Robert Wright and

George Forrest.
MUS                                    139 min (ort 143 min)
B,V                     RNK; VGM; PARK (VHS only)

## SONG OF TEXAS ***                                   U
Joseph Kane            USA                  1943
*Roy Rogers, Harry Shannon, Sheila Brady, Bob
Nolan, Barton Lane, Sons of the Pioneers, Arline
Judge, William Haade, Hal Taliaferro, Yakima
Canutt, Tom London, Forrest Taylor, Eve March*
Rogers helps an alcoholic former rodeo star, fake
wealth and success when his daughter comes to visit.
A reworking of "Lady For A Day" (1933) in a Western
setting, that provides Rogers with an enjoyable
vehicle.
WES                        51 min (ort 69 min) B/W
V                                        HOLVID

## SONG OF THE SOUTH ***                               Uc
Harve Foster           USA                  1946
*Ruth Warrick, Bobby Driscoll, James Baskett, Luana
Patten, Lucile Watson, Hattie McDaniel, Glenn Leedy,
George Nokes, Gene Holland, Erik Rolf, Mary Field,
Anita Brown, Voices of: Nicodemus Stewart, Johnny
Lee, James Baskett*
Live-action and animated musical fantasy, set on a
Southern plantation where an old "Uncle Remus"
recounts "Brer Rabbit" stories. The three excellent
animated sequences feature Brer Rabbit, Brer Fox
and Brer Bear. Animation is by Wilfred Jackson, with
music by Daniele Amfitheatrof and photography by
Gregg Toland. Uneven, but great fun. AA: Song
("Zip-A-Dee-Doo-Dah" – Allie Wrubel – music/Ray
Gilbert – lyrics), Spec Award (James Baskett).
Boa: short stories Tales Of Uncle Remus by Joel
Chandler Harris.
MUS                             91 min (ort 94 min)
B,V                                     RNK; WDV

## SONG TO REMEMBER, A **                              U
Charles Vidor          USA                  1944
*Cornel Wilde, Merle Oberon, Paul Muni, Stephen
Bekassy, Nina Foch, George Coulouris, Sig Arno,
Howard Freeman, George Macready*
A lavish but stilted biopic on the life of Chopin, with
Wilde woefully inadequate for the part, but Oberon
appealing as George Sand. The ludicrous script tends
to sink this one early on. Worth listening to but not
seeing.
Boa: novel Polonaise by D. Leslie.
MUS                            108 min (ort 113 min)
V                                       PREST; RCA

## SONGWRITER **                                      15
Alan Rudolph           USA                  1984
*Willie Nelson, Kris Kristofferson, Rip Torn, Melinda
Dillon, Lesley Ann Warren, Mickey Raphael, Richard
C. Sarafian*
Musical comedy about a Country-and-Western song-
writer and his lack of business sense. Rather too
loosely structured to be effective as a film, but there
are some good moments, not least an appearance by
director Richard C. Sarafian who appears as a greedy
backer. Written by Bud Shrake.
COM                             90 min (ort 94 min)
B,V                                         RCA

## SONNY BOY *                                        18
Robert Martin Carrol   USA                  1988
*David Carradine, Paul L. Smith*
A sick film telling of a baby boy brought up in a
nightmare of cruelty by a psychotic, who had his
parents murdered in order to have the opportunity to
create a monster he could unleash on his enemies.
HOR                                      99 min
V                                          EIV

## SONS OF THE MUSKETEERS **
Lewis Allen            USA                  1953

*Maureen O'Hara, Cornel Wilde, Alan Hale*
Loosely based on the Dumas stories, this re-unites the
sons of the original four musketeers in a perilous
quest to save the reputation of the French Queen.
Lively and fairly entertaining nonsense.
Osca: MYSTERIANS, THE
A/AD                                     80 min
B,V                                         KVD

## SOPHIE'S CHOICE ***                                15
Alan J. Pakula         USA                  1982
*Meryl Streep, Kevin Kline, Peter MacNicol, Rita Karin,
Stephen D. Newman, Josh Mostel, Josef Sommer
(narration)*
A Polish woman who survived the death camps, lives
in New York in the 1940s but is still tormented by her
experiences, and the memory of an agonising decision
forced on her in the camps. A ponderous and gloomy
piece about guilt and despair, with Streep giving one
of her finest performances. The music is by Marvin
Hamlisch and the photography by Nestor Nestor
Almendros. Written by Pakula. AA: Actress (Streep).
Boa: novel by William Styron.
DRA               140 min; 144 min (CH5) (ort 157 min)
B,V                       PRV L/A; CH5 (VHS only)

## SORCERERS, THE *
Michael Reeves         UK                   1967
*Boris Karloff, Catherine Lacey, Ian Ogilvy, Elizabeth
Ercy, Susan George, Victor Henry, Meier Tzelniker,
Dani Sheridan, Ivor Dean, Peter Fraser*
An evil scientist couple devise a way of exercising
control of other people's minds and hypnotise a young
man to do their bidding. An interesting idea receives
the usual low-budget treatment. Written by Reeves,
Tom Baker and John Burke.
HOR                                      86 min
B,V,V2                                      WAL

## SORORITY HOUSE MASSACRE *                          18
Carol Frank            USA                  1986
*Angela O'Neill, Wendy Martel, Pamela Ross, Nicole
Rio, John C. Russell, Marcus Vaughter, Vincent
Bilancio, Joe Nassi, Gillian Frank, Mary Anne, Axel
Roberts, Joseph Mansier, Fitzhough Houston, Marsha
Carter, Alan Eugster*
A group of girls is terrorised by a crazed knife-
wielding killer, who is drawn to their sorority house
because of mysterious past connections. More of the
same in yet another sorority-girls-in-peril offering.
HOR                                      86 min
B,V                                         MED

## SORORITY SWEETHEARTS *                             18
                       USA
*Bridgette Monet, Lisa De Leeuw, Linda Shaw,
Gretchen Sweet*
Banal story of some sorority girls who have plenty of
time for the boys at their college but never any time
for classes.
A                                        50 min
B,V                                      VEXCEL

## SORRY, WRONG NUMBER **                             15
Tony Wharmby           USA                  1989
*Loni Anderson, Carl Weintraub, Patrick Macnee, Hal
Holbrook*
A flat and unconvincing remake of the minor 1948
classic, which starred Barbara Stanwyck as an invalid
overhearing a murder plan on the telephone and then
realising that she is to be the victim. Here she is
replaced by a surprisingly healthy-looking Anderson
as the worried woman, who gradually becomes aware
of the plans others have in store for her. The insertion
of a sub-plot all about drug dealing is an unnecessary
distraction.
Boa: story by Lucille Fletcher.
THR                          85 min (ort 100 min) mCab
V                                           CIC

## SOUL MAN ** 15
Steve Miner      USA      1986
*C. Thomas Howell, Rae Dawn Chong, Leslie Nielsen, James Earl Jones, Arye Gross, Melora Hardin, James B. Sikking, Max Wright, Jonathan Leonard, Jeff Altman, Julia Louis Dreyfus, Ron Reagan*
When his father refuses to support him through college, a young boy takes an overdose of tanning pills in order to win a black scholarship to Harvard Law School. There he is subject to the usual ethnic stereotyping and finds himself falling in love with a black student who, he learns, failed to win the scholarship because of his ruse. A clumsy attempt at a social satire.
COM      100 min
B,V      NWV

## SOUND BARRIER, THE *** U
David Lean      UK      1952
*Ralph Richardson, Ann Todd, Nigel Patrick, Dinah Sheridan, John Justin, Joseph Tomelty, Denholm Elliott, Jack Allen, Ralph Michael, Leslie Phillips, Jolyon Jackley*
An aircraft engineer who is obsessed with proving that the sound barrier can be broken, and takes many risks to prove it, in this taut story of the early days of jet flight. AA: Sound (London Films).
Aka: BREAKING THE SOUND BARRIER
DRA      111 min (ort 118 min) B/W
V      WHV

## SOUND OF FURY, THE *** PG
Cyril Endfield      USA      1951
*Lloyd Bridges, Frank Lovejoy, Richard Carlson, Katherine Locke, Adele Jergens, Irene Vernon, Art Smith, Katherine Ryan*
A kidnapper kills his victim and is hunted by the police while the town is stirred to a lynching fury by a journalist. A brutal and uncompromising study of mob rule. The script is by Pagano.
Aka: TRY AND GET ME!
Boa: novel The Condemned by Jo Pagano.
DRA      85 min (ort 91 min) B/W
V      VMA; STABL

## SOUND OF MUSIC, THE *** U
Robert Wise      USA      1965
*Julie Andrews, Christopher Plummer, Eleanor Parker, Peggy Wood, Anna Lee, Richard Haydn, Marni Nixon, Heather Menzies, Charmian Carr, Duane Chase, Angela Cartwright, Nicholas Hammond, Debbie Turner, Kym Karath*
In 1938 a novice nun becomes governess to a musical family, and falls in love with their widower father, helping the family escape from the Nazis when Austria is occupied. Based on the life of the Von Trapp family, this has fine songs set in a syrupy confection. Written by Ernest Lehman. Music and lyrics are by Richard Rodgers and Oscar Hammerstein II. AA: Pic, Dir, Score (Adapt) (Irwin Kostal), Sound (F. Hynes et al), Edit (W. Reynolds).
Boa: book The Trapp Family Singers by Maria Augusta Von Trapp, Russell Crouse and Howard Lindsay.
MUS      167 min (ort 172 min)
V/s      CBS

## SOUNDER *** 
Martin Ritt      USA      1972
*Cicely Tyson, Paul Winfield, Kevin Hooks, Carmen Matthews, James Best, Taj Mahal, Janet MacLachlan, Yvonne Jarrell, Eric Hooks, Sylvia Kuumba Williams, Teddy Airhart, Thomas N. Phillips, William Thomas Bennett, Inez Durham*
A romanticised view of the experiences of a black sharecropping family in Louisiana of the 1930s. A detailed and carefully made tale, with excellent characterisation and an intelligent script. Only the lack of pace is a drawback. Music is by Taj Mahal.

Written by Lonnie Elder III and followed by a sequel.
Boa: novel by William H. Armstrong.
DRA      105 min
B,V      POLY

## SOUP FOR ONE ** 18
Jonathan Kaufer      USA      1982
*Saul Rubinek, Marcia Strassman, Teddy Pendergrass, Gerrit Graham, Richard Libertini, Andrea Martin, Lewis J. Stradlen*
A single man in New York goes searching for the woman of his dreams, in this likeable but patchy comedy. Engaging performances carry the film along.
COM      81 min (ort 87 min)
B,V      WHV

## SOUR GRAPES * PG
John De Bello      USA      1986
*Richard Gilland, Jamie Farr, Tawny Kitaen, Rich Little, Ty Henderson, Debbie Gates, Eddie Deezen*
A secret formula developed to end world hunger but proving to be irresistibly addictive, provides the excuse for this routine chase film, as all and sundry attempt to steal this latest boon to mankind. Another flabby "food" comedy from the director of ATTACK OF THE KILLER TOMATOES.
Aka: HAPPY HOUR
COM      85 min (ort 88 min)
B,V      MED

## SOURSWEET ** 15
Mike Newell      UK      1988
*Sylvia Chang, Danny Dun, Soon-Teck Oh, Jodi Lang*
A look at the struggles of a family of emigrants from Hong Kong, who come to London and struggle for success in a seedy part of London, with the husband working as a waiter to save enough money for his own business, and then losing it all at cards. A bleak, cheerless but rather touching tale.
Boa: novel by Timothy Mo.
DRA      110 min
V/h      PAL

## SOUTH BRONX HEROES ** 18
William Szarka      USA      1985
*Mario Van Peebles, Brendan Ward, Megan Van Peebles*
Two sets of teenage orphans, brother and sister, black and white, have to fend for themselves in a run-down crime-ridden neighbourhood. Average.
Aka: RUNAWAYS; REVENGE OF THE INNOCENTS
DRA      90 min
B,V      AVR

## SOUTH OF ALGIERS *** PG
Jack Lee      UK      1952
*Van Heflin, Wanda Hendrix, Eric Portman, Charles Goldner, Jacques Francois, Jacques Brunius, Alec Margo, Marne Maitland*
In the Sahara a reporter accompanies an archaeological expedition searching for a fabulous buried treasure: the Golden Mask of Moloch. Unfortunately, some rather less scrupulous hunters are also interested. A straightforward and unadorned outdoors adventure with good plotting and colourful locations.
Aka: GOLDEN MASK, THE
A/AD      86 min (ort 95 min)
V      WHV

## SOUTH OF HELL MOUNTAIN ** 
William Sachs/Louis Leahman
     USA      1971
*Sam Hall, Anna Stewart, Martin J. Kelly, Nicol Britton, Elsa Raven, David Willis, Paul Heller, Mark Mellet*
A family of gold thieves, on the run from the law, stop at the cabin of a lonely wife and her beautiful daughter and hold them captive, but complications

arise when the girl falls for one of her captors. An obscure, occasionally violent tale. The insane asylum sequences were directed by Leahman.

WES                                                92 min
B,V                                                 RNK

**SOUTH PACIFIC ***                                    U
Joshua Logan              USA              1958
*Rossano Brazzi, Mitzi Gaynor, John Kerr, Ray Walston, Juanita Hall, France Nuyen, Tom Laughlin, Giorgio Tozzi (voice only)*
Enjoyable musical, about life for US troops and natives on an island in the South Pacific during 1943, when an American Army nurse falls in love with a French planter (Brazzi). The fine songs include such gems as "Bali H'ai", "There Is Nothing Like A Dame", "Happy Talk" and others. Written by Paul Osborn, Richard Rodgers, Oscar Hammerstein II and Joshua Logan, and based on the successful stage show. AA: Sound (Fred Hynes).
Boa: short stories Tales Of The South Pacific by James A. Michener/musical by Richard Rodgers and Oscar Hammerstein II.
MUS                                143 min (ort 171 min)
B,V                                                 CBS

**SOUTHERN COMFORT ***                                 18
Walter Hill               USA              1981
*Keith Carradine, Powers Boothe, Fred Ward, Franklyn Seales, T.K. Carter, Lewis Smith, Peter Coyote*
National Guardsmen on an exercise in the Louisiana swamps come into conflict with the locals, and this initial clash escalates into full-scale hostilities. A brutal DELIVERANCE-style yarn that's quite well made but is devoid of originality.
THR                                102 min (ort 106 min)
B, V/sh                          TEVP L/A; WHV (VHS only)

**SOYLENT GREEN ***                                    15
Richard Fleischer         USA              1973
*Edward G. Robinson, Charlton Heston, Leigh Taylor-Young, Chuck Connors, Joseph Cotten, Brock Peters, Paula Kelly, Mike Henry, Leonard Stone, Lincoln Kilpatrick, Whit Bissell, Celia Lousky, Dick Van Patten, Morgan Farley*
A grim view of an Earth so overpopulated in the year 2022, that life has become an endless struggle, with the resources of the planet utterly spent. The film soon degenerates into a routine murder mystery, involving Heston as a cop and Robinson his "book" (giving a fine performance in his last film). A pretentious, ponderous and unsatisfying effort, scripted by Stanley R. Greenberg.
Boa: novel Make Room! Make Room! by Harry Harrison.
FAN                                 94 min (ort 100 min)
B,V                                                 MGM

**SPACE 1999: ALIEN ATTACK ***                         PG
Lee H. Katzin/Charles Crichton/Bill Lenny
                          UK               1977
*Barbara Bain, Martin Landau, Barry Morse, Roy Dotrice, Anthony Valentine, Nick Tate, Catherine Schell, Tony Anholt, Isla Blair, Zienia Merton, Yasuko Magazumi*
A spin-off from the TV series "Space 1999", which dealt with the adventures encountered by the personnel on Moonbase Alpha, who were sent off on a journey into deep space, when a freak nuclear accident wrenched the Moon from its orbit. In this tale they explore a rogue planet, suffer a mysterious illness and experience a nuclear explosion that affects the Moon's orbit.
Aka: ALIEN ATTACK
FAN                                        122 min mTV
B,V                             PRV L/A; CH5 (VHS only)

**SPACE 1999: COSMIC PRINCESS ***                      PG
Charles Crichton/Peter Medak

                          UK               1976
*Martin Landau, Barbara Bain, Catherine Schell, Barry Morse, Anouska Hempel, Brian Blessed, Tony Anholt, Zienia Merton, Nick Tate*
An alien creature able to change shape comes to the rescue of Moonbase Alpha, when the drifting space station begins to approach a sinister planet. This tale comprises two episodes of the TV series – "Metamorph" and "Space Warp", directed by Crichton and Medak respectively.
Aka: COSMIC PRINCESS
FAN                      95 min (PRV); 105 min mTV
B,V,V2                       PRV L/A; CH5 (VHS only)

**SPACE 1999: DESTINATION MOONBASE**            PG
**ALPHA ***
Tom Clegg                 UK               1979
*Martin Landau, Barbara Bain, Barry Morse, Nick Tate, Tony Anholt, Catherine Schell, Zienia Merton, Yasuko Magazumi*
An episode from the rather cheap-looking "Space 1999" TV SF series. In this tale visitors to Moonbase Alpha, claiming to be sent to rescue the personnel and take them back to Earth, are not quite what they appear.
Aka: DESTINATION MOONBASE ALPHA
FAN                                         96 min mTV
B,V                             PRV L/A; CH5 (VHS only)

**SPACE 1999: JOURNEY THROUGH THE**             U
**BLACK SUN ***
Ray Austin/Lee Katzin  UK                 1975
*Martin Landau, Barbara Bain, Barry Morse, Margaret Leighton, Paul Jones, Nick Tate, Tony Anholt, Catherine Schell, Zienia Merton, Yasuko Magazumi*
Feature-length film from the first "Space 1999" TV series, with the crew of Moonbase Alpha encountering a new alien civilisation. Adequate.
Aka: JOURNEY THROUGH THE BLACK SUN
FAN                            89 min (ort 96 min) mTV
B,V                                PRV; CH5 (VHS only)

**SPACE CRUISER: GUARDIAN OF THE**              U
**GALAXY ***
Yoshinobu Nishizaki   JAPAN               1977
*Voices of: Marvin Miller, Rex Krolls, Paul Shiveley, Mercy Goldman*
A cartoon feature about a space cruiser given an urgent mission to a distant planet, in order to help Earth achieve victory in an interplanetary war.
Aka: SPACE CRUISER; UCHUSENKAN YAMATO
CAR                                           85 min
B,V                            DFS L/A; VGM; MIA

**SPACE ISLAND ***                                     PG
Anthony M. Dawson (Antonio Margheriti)
                 ITALY/WEST GERMAY        1987
*Anthony Quinn, Ernest Borgnine, David Warbeck, Haco Nardulli, Philippe Leroy, Klaus Loewitsch, Ida Di Benedetto, Renato De Carmine, Giovanni Lombardo Rodice, Andy Luotto*
This lively SF version of "Treasure Island", has a 12-year-old boy and his companions, learning of a map that tells of the location of hidden treasure on a distant planet. To reach it they charter a spaceship and engage a motley collection of rough characters. An enjoyable and lighthearted parody.
Aka: TREASURE ISLAND IN OUTER SPACE
FAN                110 min; 145 min (BRAVE) Cut (16 sec)
B,V                             BRAVE/IVS; BRAVE

**SPACE RAIDERS ***                                    PG
Howard R. Cohen           USA              1983
*Vince Edwards, David Mendenhall, Patsy Pease, Thom Christopher, Drew Snyder, Luca Bercovi, Ray Stewart, George Dickerson, Dick Miller, Virginia Kiser, Don Washburn, Michael Miller, Bill Boyett, Howard Dayton, Elizabeth Charlton*

Space opera-type adventure, produced by Roger Corman and using special effects, footage and music from BATTLE BEYOND THE STARS. A watchable time filler.

| | |
|---|---|
| FAN | 82 min; 80 min (EIV) |
| B,V | VTC L/A; EIV |

## SPACE RIDERS *                                              PG

Joe Massot            UK                          1983
Barry Sheene, Gavin O'Herlihy, Toshiya Ito, Stephanie McLean, Sayo Inaba, Caroline Evans, Hiroshi Kato, Jeff Harding, Marina Sirtis, Yuriko Tagaki, Maureen Moody, Steve Parrish, Andrew Marriott
The story of a motorcycle team and their bid to win the world championships, with Sheene playing a top rider who is signed up to ride for a Japanese corporation. Very dull.

| | |
|---|---|
| DRA | 97 min (ort 99 min) |
| B,V | TEVP |

## SPACE TRANSFORMER **                                        PG

Johnny T. Howard  HONG KONG                      1989
Another film in a seemingly endless stream of Hong Kong animated space adventures (see SOLAR ADVENTURE, CAPTAIN COSMOS or FALCON 7) that inevitably feature an Earth under attack from aliens. This time round, our only saviour is a genius who has succumbed to a virulent bacteriological weapon. In an idea borrowed from FANTASTIC VOYAGE, a rescue crew is miniaturised and injected into her bloodstream to save her.

| | |
|---|---|
| CAR | 60 min |
| V | VPD |

## SPACEBALLS **                                               PG

Mel Brooks            USA                         1987
Mel Brooks, John Candy, Rick Moranis, Bill Pullman, Daphne Zuniga, Dick Van Patten, George Wyner, Michael Winslow, Lorene Yarnell, Ronny Graham, Leslie Bevis, Sal Viscuso, John Hurt. Voices of: Joan Rivers, Dom DeLuise
STAR WARS gets the Mel Brooks treatment in this soggy spoof, that has a plot loosely revolving around the rescue of a princess, but is really little more than a succession of visual and verbal gags, with most of the latter being simple parodies of names used in the earlier film. Quite amusing, but only in 10-minute doses.

| | |
|---|---|
| COM | 92 min (ort 96 min) Cut (1 sec) |
| V | MGM |

## SPACECAMP *                                                 PG

Harry Winer            USA                        1986
Kate Capshaw, Lea Thompson, Tom Skerritt, Kelly Preston, Larry B. Scott, Leaf Phoenix, Tate Donovan, Barry Primus, Terry O'Quinn, Mitchell Anderson, T. Scott Coffey, Daryl Roach, Peter Scranton, Holly Rebecca Suggs
Five teenagers are chosen to train at a NASA summer camp and by accident get launched, together with their instructor, into space. They now have to get safely back to Earth. A vacuous little effort that isn't even memorable in the special effects department.
Aka: SPACE CAMP

| | |
|---|---|
| FAN | 107 min |
| V/s | CBS |

## SPACEHUNTER *                                               15

Lamont Johnson       CANADA                       1983
Peter Strauss, Molly Ringwald, Ernie Hudson, Andrea Marcovicci, Michael Ironside, Beeson Carroll, Hrant Alianak, Deborah Pratt, Aleisa Shirley, Cali Timmins, Paul Boretski, Patrick Rowe, Reggie Bennett
A space salvage man rescues three space maidens on a dangerous planet in the "Forbidden Zone" of the 22nd century, who are being held captive by a nasty mutant who goes under the title of "Overdog". The Elmer Berstein score is the best thing in this bleak yarn. Written by Edith Ray, David Preston, Dan Goldberg

and Len Blum.
Aka: SPACEHUNTER: ADVENTURES IN THE FORBIDDEN ZONE

| | |
|---|---|
| FAN | 86 min (ort 90 min) |
| V/sh | RCA |

## SPACEMAN AND KING ARTHUR, THE **              U

Russ Mayberry          UK                         1979
Dennis Dugan, Ron Moody, Jim Dale, Kenneth More, John Le Mesurier, Rodney Bewes, Sheila White, Robert Beatty, Cyril Shaps, Kevin Brennan, Ewen Solon, Reg Lye
Two time travellers find themselves at the court of King Arthur, in this Disney reworking of Mark Twain's classic, in which Dugan and a lookalike robot are catapulted back into medieval times. A pleasant but undemanding little tale.
Aka: UNIDENTIFIED FLYING ODDBALL
Boa: novel A Connecticut Yankee In The Court Of King Arthur by Mark Twain.

| | |
|---|---|
| JUV | 93 min |
| B,V | RNK; WDV |

## SPACERAGE *                                                 18

Conrad E. Palmisano    USA                        1986
Michael Pare, Richard Farnsworth, John Laughlin, William Windom, Lewis Van Bergen, Lee Purcell, Dennis Redfield, Harold Sylvester, Hank Worden, Frank Doubleday, Wolfe Perry, Ricky Supiran, Nick Palmisano, Rick Weber
A story set on a prison planet called Botany Bay, where a bunch of thugs are causing considerable trouble until an ex-cop arrives to teach them a lesson. A silly tale that plays like a lousy Western, and has acting to match.
Aka: BREAKOUT ON PRISON PLANET; DOLLAR A DAY, A: LAST FRONTIER, THE; TRACKERS; TRACKERS: 2180

| | |
|---|---|
| FAN | 74 min (ort 77 min) |
| B,V | VES |

## SPACESHIP *                                                 PG

Bruce Kimmel           USA                        1981
Cindy Williams, Bruce Kimmel, Leslie Nielsen, Gerrit Graham, Patrick Macnee, Ron Kurowski
A spoof on the theme of an alien creature on the loose in a spaceship, with Nielsen the officer in command, Macnee a scientist and Williams the only woman on board. Disagreeable nonsense.
Aka: CREATURE WASN'T NICE, THE

| | |
|---|---|
| FAN | 77 min (ort 82 min) |
| B,V | ENT L/A; EIV |

## SPANISH GARDENER, THE ***                      U

Philip Leacock         UK                         1956
Dirk Bogarde, Michael Hordern, Cyril Cusack, Geoffrey Keen, Maureen Swanson, Lyndon Brook, Josephine Griffin, Bernard Lee, Rosalie Crutchley, Ina De La Haye, Harold Scott, Jack Stewart
The son of a diplomat develops a strong friendship with their gardener, which is resented by the father. A slow, careful and interesting character study, that is a little too languid but remains quite absorbing. Written by Lesley Storm and John Bryan.
Boa: novel by A.J. Cronin

| | |
|---|---|
| DRA | 88 min (ort 97 min) |
| V | VCC |

## SPANISH MAIN, THE **                           U

Frank Borzage          USA                        1945
Maureen O'Hara, Paul Henreid, Walter Slezak, Binnie Barnes, John Emery, J.M. Kerrigan, Barton MacLane, Nancy Gates, Fritz Leiber, Mike Mazurki, Jack La Rue, Victor Kilian
A well done if rather routine adventure set in the Caribbean, with Henreid a pirate who foils the villainous governor Slezak and wins O'Hara. Photography is by George Barnes and musical direction by Constantin Bakaleinikoff.

Osca: three shorts
A/AD                            95 min (ort 105 min) B/W
B,V                                          KVD; VCC

## SPARKLE **                                        15
Sam O'Steen              USA                        1976
*Philip Michael Thomas, Irene Cara, Lonette McKee,*
*Dwan Smith, Dorian Harewood, Tony King, Mary*
*Alice*
This film charts the rise of a three-girl group in the
1950s and their encounters within the pop world,
especially in its most sordid aspect. A film of flashy
direction and a cliched script. Musical numbers are by
Curtis Mayfield.
DRA                      93 min (ort 100 min) Cut (26 sec)
B,V                                               WHV

## SPARROWS CAN'T SING *                              PG
Joan Littlewood          UK                         1962
*James Booth, Barbara Windsor, Roy Kinnear, George*
*Sewell, Barbara Ferris, Avis Bunnage, Murray*
*Melvin, Arthur Mullard*
After a couple of years at sea, a sailor returns home to
find that his wife and baby have gone off to live with a
bus driver. He searches for them relentlessly. A
cheerful, chirpy, cockney caricature; the characters
are generally a little too disagreeable for one to
sympathise. Barbara Windsor sings the title song.
Boa: play Sparrers Can't Sing by Stephen Lewis.
COM                           88 min (ort 94 min) B/W
V                                                  WHV

## SPARTACUS ****                                     15
Stanley Kubrick          USA                        1960
*Kirk Douglas, Laurence Olivier, Jean Simmons,*
*Charles Laughton, Tony Curtis, Peter Ustinov, Herbert*
*Lom, John Gavin, Woody Strode, Nina Foch, John*
*Ireland, John Dall, Charles McGraw*
A splendid film about an actual slave rebellion that
took place in 71 B.C., led by a famous gladiator who
defeated several Roman armies sent against him.
Produced by Kirk Douglas and written by Dalton
Trumbo, with the fine score by Alex North. AA: S.
Actor (Ustinov), Cin (Russell Metty), Art/Set (Alexan-
der Golitzen and Eric Orbom/Russell A. Gausman and
Julia Heron), Cin (Russell Metty), Cost (Valles/Bill
Thomas).
Boa: novel by Howard Fast.
DRA                           180 min (ort 196 min)
V/sh                                               CIC

## SPASMO **
Umberto Lenzi            ITALY                       1974
*Robert Hoffman, Suzy Kendall, Monica Monet, Ivan*
*Rassimov, Guido Alberti*
A young playboy falls in love with a girl, but their
relationship is threatened when a man is killed in
their bathroom. An unsatisfying crime thriller.
THR                                             120 min
B,V                                                HER

## SPASMS *                                           18
William Fruet            CANADA                      1982
                                          (released 1983)
*Peter Fonda, Oliver Reed, Kerrie Keane, Al Waxman,*
*Marilyn Lightstone, Angus MacInnes, George*
*Bloomfield, Miguel Fernandes, Gerard Parkes, Sandra*
*Awalt, Laurie J. Brown, William Needles, Denis*
*Simpson, Patrick Bryner, Al Maini*
Reed plays a man who finds that he has a telepathic
link with a killer snake in this silly piece of hokum.
Aka: DEATH BITE
Boa: novel Death Bite by Brent Monahan.
HOR                                              86 min
B,V                              VTC L/A; XTACY/KRP

## SPECIAL DAY, A ***
Ettore Scola      CANADA/ITAALY                    1977

*Sophia Loren, Marcello Mastroianni, John Vernon,*
*Francoise Berd, Nicole Magny*
An attempt to produce a drama with political overtones, telling of an unhappy housewife and a frustrated homosexual who meet at the time of Hitler's
1938 visit to Rome. Despite their opposing political
views they find themselves drawn together. An
absorbing film that never quite makes the important
statements it seemed likely to.
DRA                                             105 min
V                                                  INT

## SPECIAL DELIVERY **                               15
Paul Wendkos            USA                         1976
*Bo Svenson, Cybill Shepherd, Michael C. Gwynne,*
*Tom Atkins, Sorrell Booke, Vic Tayback, Gerrit*
*Graham, Jeff Goldblum, John Quade*
Three disabled Vietnam veterans rob a bank, but only
one escapes with the loot, and he has to contend with
killers and various other complications. A moderately
entertaining blend of comedy and action.
A/AD                        99 min; 95 min (VES)
B,V                                         PVG; VES

## SPECIAL EFFECTS **                                18
Larry Cohen             USA                         1985
*Zoe Tamerlis, Brad Rijn, Eric Bogosian, Kevin*
*O'Connor, Bill Oland, Richard Greene, Heidi Bassett,*
*Steven Pudenz, John Woerhle, Kitty Summerall, Kris*
*Evans, Mike Alpert*
An insane director makes a "snuff movie", that is to
say he actually kills the actress on screen and then
tries to build a film around his deed, with the woman's
husband given a part too. A tale that attempts to
make a few sharp points about the film world, but soon
gets bogged down in its over-inventive plot.
THR                      101 min (ort 103 min) Cut (30 sec)
B,V                                         EHE; NELS

## SPECIAL MISSION LADY CHAPLIN *                    PG
Alberto De Martino
                    FRANCE/ITALY/SPAIN            1966
*Ken Clark, Helga Line, Phillipe Hersent, Evelyn*
*Stewart (Ida Galli), Danida Biani, Jacques Bergerac*
A third-rate Continental spy-thriller that offers little
suspense and even less entertainment. See also FURY
IN ISTANBUL and MISSION BLOODY MARY, two
more films in the series.
Aka: 077: SPECIAL MISSION LADY CHAPLIN;
LADY CHAPLIN STORY, THE; MISSIONE
SPECIALE LADY CHAPLIN; OPERACION LADY
CHAPLIN; OPERAZIONE LADY CHAPLIN
A/AD                            97 min Cut (3 sec)
V                                                  VPD

## SPECIAL PEOPLE ***                                PG
Marc Daniels            CANADA                      1984
*Brooke Adams, Susan Roman, Sandra Ciccone, Lesleh*
*Donaldson, Albert Gentile, Benny D'Onofrio, Ron*
*James, Joseph Kelly, Greg Kozak, Renato Marulli,*
*Isabelle Mejias, Glenn Milligan, Brenda Woods,*
*Nicholas Kilbertus, Liberace*
A drama group composed of mentally retarded young
people, finds self respect through the efforts of their
young woman teacher, who shows them how to run
their own puppet theatre. A touching drama based on
the work of Canada's Famous People Players, some of
whom appear in the film as themselves. The script is
by Corey Blechman, who also wrote BILL.
DRA                          96 min (ort 100 min) mTV
B,V                                                ODY

## SPECIAL TRAIN FOR HITLER *
James Gartner           FRANCE                      1976
*Claudine Beccarie, Erik Muller, Monica Swann, Bob*
*Askloff, Francoise Quenie, Pamela Stanford, Sandra*
*Mozarousky*
A female Nazi leaves her stage act to lead a group of
women soldiers at the front.

Aka: TRAIN SPECIAL POUR HITLER; TRAIN
SPECIAL POUR SS
DRA                                      90 min
B,V,V2                                       VPD

## SPECIALIST, THE *
                    ITALY                   1976
*Franco Gaspari, John Saxon, John Steiner*
A CIA agent infiltrates a terrorist group but finds his
life threatened after a murder attempt.
DRA                                      90 min
B,V                                          HER

## SPECTERS *                                 18
Marcello Avallone    ITALY               1987
*Donald Pleasence, John Pepper, Katrine Michelsen,
Massimo De Rossi, Riccardo De Torrebruna, Lavinia
Grizi, Riccardo Parisio Perrotti, Giovanni Bilancia,
Erna Schurer*
A group of men working on a new subway line, reveal
a hidden Roman tomb that has been undisturbed for
centuries, and when archaeologists investigate, they
disturb a demonic creature. A cumbersome and de-
rivative film that starts off well enough, but gets
rather silly when the creature is finally revealed. In
between the few second-rate effects are acres of
tedium, that dissipate any tension before it can
develop.
Aka: SPECTRES; SPETTRI
HOR                                      96 min
B,V                                          AVA

## SPEED FEVER *                              15
Mario Morra           ITALY              1978
*Michael York, Gene Hackman, James Coburn*
Docu-drama about the world of motor racing. Forgett-
able.
Aka: FORMULA UNO FEBBRE DELLA VELOCITA
DRA                                      98 min
B,V                                          MED

## SPEED KILLS **                            15
John Stewart          USA                1988
*Burri Murray, Gregory Scott Cummins*
Two FBI agents given the job of locating a fortune in
diamonds and an important witness, have to get both
safely across the state border, but find that the Mafia
are out to stop them at any price.
A/AD                                     93 min
V                                            HIFLI

## SPEEDTRAP *
Earl Bellamy          USA                1974
*Joe Don Baker, Tyne Daly, Richard Jaeckel, Robert
Loggia, Morgan Woodward, Timothy Carey*
A private eye teams up with a lady cop to catch a
slippery car thief in this formula effort. If you like
screeching tyres and a minimal plot then this one is
for you.
A/AD                                     98 min
B,V                                          VCL/CBS

## SPELLBINDER *                              18
Janet Greek           USA                1988
*Timothy Daly, Kelly Preston, Rick Rossovich, Audra
Lindley, Diana Bellamy, Cary-Hiroyuki Tagawa,
Anthony Crivello, Roderick Cook, Stefan Gierasch*
A man rescues a woman from a beating, but is
horrified to learn that she is on the run from a ruthless
cult who are prepared to use any amount of violence to
get her back, as they are intending to sacrifice her. An
unpleasant and predictable supernatural thriller.
HOR                             95 min (ort 99 min)
B,V                                          MGM

## SPELLBOUND ***                             PG
Alfred Hitchcock      USA                1945
*Ingrid Bergman, Gregory Peck, Leo G. Carroll, John
Emery, Michael Chekhov, Wallace Ford, Rhonda*

*Fleming, Jean Acker, Donald Curtis, Norman Lloyd,
Steven Geray, Paul Harvey, Erskine Sanford, Janet
Scott, Victor Kilian*
Bergman as a female psychiatrist tries to probe Peck's
mind, in this solid psychological mystery with in-
teresting dream sequences and a good cast. Written by
Ben Hecht and Angus MacPhail. AA: Score (Miklos
Rozsa).
Boa: novel The House Of Dr Edwardes by Francis
Beeding.
Osca: NOTORIOUS (VCC)
DRA          111 min; 106 min (VCC); 203 min
                        (2 film cassette) B/W
B,V                          GHV; VCC (VHS only)

## SPETTERS **                                18
Paul Verhoeven    NETHERLANDS            1980
*Renee Soutendijk, Hans van Tongeren, Toon
Agterberg, Marianne Boyer, Rutger Hauer, Maarten
Spanjer*
An unusual drama telling of motobike freaks and
their lives in Holland, with Hauer a race champ who
is idolised by all. A rather chaotic but vigorous blend
of sexuality and teenage escapades, that's quite
enjoyable in a mindless way.
DRA          103 min (ort 115 min) (Cut at film release)
B,V                                          EHE

## SPHINX **                                  15
Franklin J. Schaffner   USA             1980
*Lesley-Anne Down, Frank Langella, John Rhys-
Davies, Maurice Ronet, John Gielgud, Martin Benson,
Vic Tablian, Nadim Sawalha, Tutte Lemkow, Saeed
Jaffrey, Eileen Way, William Hootkins, James Cossins*
An Egyptologist finds her life in danger in her search
for a lost tomb. An uneasy blend of comedy and chills
that muddles along fairly aimlessly, delivering a few
good sequences along the way. Worth a look for the
Egyptian locations if not for the rather ludicrous
script and poor performances. Written by John
Byrum.
Boa: novel by Robin Cook.
THR                                      118 min
B,V                                          WHV

## SPIDER BABY **
Jack Hill             USA                1964
*Lon Chaney Jr, Carol Ohmart, Mantan Moreland, Jill
Banner, Quinn Redeker, Beverly Washburn, Sid Haig,
Karl Schanzer*
An obscure black comedy telling of a very strange and
very sick family, who suffer from a unique disease
caused by inbreeding, and are inclined to murder the
inquisitive. A nightmarish and highly unusual film,
that is packed with disturbing images but has little
plot.
Aka: CANNIBAL ORGY; LIVER EATERS, THE;
MADDEST STORY EVER TOLD, THE; SPIDER
BABY, OR THE MADDEST TALE EVER TOLD
HOR                                      80 min
B,V                                          HVS

## SPIDERMAN: THE MOVIE *                     U
E.W. Swackhamer       USA                1976
*Nicholas Hammond, Lisa Eilbacher, Thayer David,
Michael Pataki, David White, Ivor Francis, Jeff
Donnell, Hilly Hicks, Dick Balduzzi, Bob Hastings,
Barry Cutler, Norman Rice, Len Lesser, Ivan Bonar,
Carmelita Pope, George Cooper*
A spider's bite gives a weedy student superhuman
powers, which he uses to fight crime. In this pilot for a
brief series, our hero sets out to expose a multi-million
dollar extortion racket. A not terribly successful or
well-conceived adaptation, of one of the most popular
comic book characters to grace the pages of Marvel
Magazine's comics. Followed by a couple of sequels.
Aka: SPIDER-MAN
FAN                            90 min (ort 92 min) mTV
B,V                          RCA; PREST (VHS only)

## SPIDERMAN: STRIKES BACK *          U
Ron Satlof          USA          1978
*Nicholas Hammond, Joanna Cameron*
In this adventure, our masked crusader against crime
sets out to foil an attempt to destroy L.A. Another
mediocre effort, based on a character created by
Marvel Comics, but lacking both flair and imagina-
tion.
FAN                    89 min Cut (17 sec) mTV
V                                        RCA

## SPIDERMAN: THE DRAGON'S CHALLENGE *    U
Don McDougall          USA          1979
*Nicholas Hammond, Robert F. Simon, Benson Fong,
Eileen Bry, Chip Fields, Myron Healey, Rosalind Chao*
A sequel to SPIDERMAN: THE MOVIE, with our
masked crime-fighter setting out to clear the name of
a Chinese official who has been accused of being a
WW2 traitor. Very poor.
Aka: CHINESE WEB, THE; SPIDERMAN AND THE
DRAGON'S CHALLENGE
FAN                    93 min (ort 95 min) mTV
V                                        RCA

## SPIES A GO-GO *
James Landis          USA          1964
*Arch Hall Jr, Micha Terr, Melissa Morgan, John
Akana*
A weak spy spoof in which the wicked Russkies plan to
attack the US with an infected rabbit.
Aka: NASTY RABBIT, THE
COM                                    84 min
B,V                                      VIV

## SPIES LIKE US *          PG
John Landis          USA          1985
*Chevy Chase, Dan Aykroyd, Steve Forrest, Donna
Dixon, Bruce Davison, Tom Hatten, William Prince,
Bernie Casey, Michael Apted, Frank Oz, Constantin
Costa-Garvas, Terry Gilliam, Ray Harryhausen,
Martin Brest, Bob Swain*
A silly farce about a pair of incompetent bumbling
agents who are used as decoys in a complex plot. An
infantile exercise made in the style of a "Road To"
movie, but far too chaotic and muddled to deliver
much in the way of humour. Written by Dan Aykroyd,
Lowell Ganz and Babaloo Mandel.
COM                    98 min (ort 109 min)
V/h                                      WHV

## SPIES, LIES AND ALIBIS **          15
Anthony Thomas          USA          1989
*Robert Loggia, David Warner, Brian Kerwin, Diane
Ladd, Alice Krige*
A group of spies have to create a phoney world crisis in
order to spark off a fall in the futures market, on
which they have gambled large sums. The action is set
in a small Indian Ocean island known as Moressa, and
as one might expect, their plans go somewhat awry. A
well-conceived and ingenious comedy-thriller that's
let down by poor realisation and an uneven tone.
Aka: SPIES INC.; SPOOKS
COM                                    93 min
V                                        VES

## SPIES, LIES AND NAKED THIGHS **          PG
James Frawley          USA          1989
*Harry Anderson, Ed Begley Jr, Wendy Crewson, Linda
Purl, Rachel Ticotin*
A madcap comedy telling of a strange house guest,
who embroils his hosts in a crazy mystery revolving
around the activities of a rather bizarre killer. The
script is by Ed Self.
COM                    90 min (ort 100 min) mTV
V                                        PRISM

## SPIRAL STAIRCASE, THE ****          PG
Robert Siodmak          USA          1945
*Dorothy McGuire, George Brent, Ethel Barrymore,*

*Kent Smith, Rhonda Fleming, Elsa Lanchester,
Gordon Oliver, James Bell, Charles Wagenheim, Ellen
Corby, Rhys Williams, Richard Tyler, Erville
Alderson, Sara Allgood, Myrna Dell*
In 1906, a New England town is terrorised by a
psychopath who murders three handicapped girls. A
mute servant working in a strange, dark household,
has her own suspicions as to the identity of the
murderer. An atmospheric thriller that doesn't miss a
single chance to convey a feeling of tension and fear.
Written by Mel Dinelli and remade in the UK in 1975.
Boa: novel Some Must Watch by Ethel Lina White.
THR                    80 min (ort 83 min) B/W
B,V                        GHV L/A; VCC (VHS only)

## SPIRIT OF SAINT LOUIS, THE *          U
Billy Wilder          USA          1957
*James Stewart, Marc Connelly, Patricia Smith,
Murray Hamilton*
Dramatisation of Charles A. Lindbergh's epic 3,600-
mile solo flight across the Atlantic, when he took off
from Roosevelt Field, New York, and landed 33 hours
later in France. Overlong and full of numerous boring
flight sequences. Written by Billy Wilder and Wendell
Mayes. The music is by Franz Waxman.
Boa: book by Charles A. Lindbergh.
A/AD                    129 min (ort 138 min)
B,V                                      WHV

## SPIRIT, THE **          15
Joel Bender          USA          1986
*Susan Strasberg, Gabriel Walsh, Victor Arnold, Ruth
Warrick*
When a lorry driver kills a youngster in an accident
the father seeks revenge, for both he and the driver
were bitter enemies in a previous existence.
HOR                                    90 min
B,V                                      NET

## SPIRITS OF BRUCE LEE *
Shang Lung          HONG KONG
*Michael Chan, Sun Chia Ling, Poon Lok, Wong Tip
Lam, Guh Men Tong, Chan Fei Lung*
A man goes to Thailand to look for his missing brother
and finds that he was murdered by a gang of Thai
boxers. A dismal effort.
MAR                                    90 min
B,V                                      POLY

## SPITTIN' IMAGE **          U
Russell S. Kern          USA          1983
*Sunshine Parker, Trudi Cooper, Sharon Barr*
A young girl gets lost out West, and is befriended by
an old pioneer who teaches her how to spit tobacco, an
invaluable aid to her survival.
COM                                    89 min
B,V                                      VPD

## SPLASH **          PG
Ron Howard          USA          1984
*Daryl Hannah, Tom Hanks, Eugene Levy, Dody
Goodman, John Candy, Richard B. Shull, Shecky
Greene, Bobby Di Cicco, Howard Morris, Tony Di
Benedetto*
Twice in his life a man is saved from drowning, once
as a boy and then as a young man. His saviour is a
beautiful and mysterious girl who one day comes in
search of him. She is however a mermaid except when
on dry land. Some comic moments vie with some
touching ones, but a weak plot lets it all down. Looks a
bit like an update of MIRANDA. Written by Lowell
Ganz, Babaloo Mandel, Bruce Jay Friedman and
Brian Grazer. Followed by SPLASH, TOO.
COM                                    110 min
B,V                                      WDV

## SPLASH, TOO *          U
Greg Antonacci          USA          1988
*Todd Waring, Amy Yasbeck, Donovan Scott, Rita*

*Taggart, Noble Willingham, Dody Goodman, Mark Blankfield*
In this Disney-style sequel to the first film, Waring and his mermaid wife Yasbeck settle into happy domesticity, until our mermaid takes off to save a dolphin friend. Unfortunately, nothing can save this ill-conceived and poorly executed effort.
COM                                    100 min mTV
B,V                                         BUENA

**SPLIT DECISIONS **                               15
David Drury          USA                     1986
*Craig Sheffer, Jeff Fahey, Gene Hackman, Jennifer Beals, John McLiam, Eddie Velez, Carmine Caridi, James Tolkan*
A tough boxing family constantly argue, until the eldest son is murdered for refusing to fix a fight, at which point they close ranks. A violent and generally unappealing tale that covers much the same territory as ROCKY.
DRA                              91 min (ort 95 min)
V/sh                                          GHV

**SPLIT IMAGE ***                                  15
Ted Kotcheff         USA                     1982
*Michael O'Keefe, Karen Allen, Peter Fonda, James Woods, Elizabeth Ashley, Brian Dennehy, Michael Sacks, Ronnie Schribner, Pamela Ludwig*
A boy meets a girl who seduces him into joining a strange cult, where he is subsequently brainwashed before being forcibly abducted by a deprogrammer, hired by his despairing parents. A competent and quite gripping tale with Dennehy giving a fine performance as the boy's father.
THR                            107 min (ort 111 min)
B,V                                          POLY

**SPLIT SECOND ***                                 
Dick Powell          USA                     1953
*Stephen McNally, Alexis Smith, Jan Sterling, Paul Kelly, Richard Egan, Keith Andes, Arthur Hunnicutt, Robert Paige*
A convict holds a group of people at gunpoint in an Arizona ghost town that, unknown to all except him, is scheduled for use as a nuclear test site. A taut and offbeat tale, written by Irving Wallace and William Bowers. This was Powell's directing debut.
THR                                  85 min B/W
B,V                                           KVD

**SPLIT, THE **                                    
Gordon Flemyng       USA                     1968
*Jim Brown, Diahann Carroll, Julie Harris, Ernest Borgnine, Gene Hackman, Jack Klugman, Warren Oates, James Whitmore, Donald Sutherland*
A gang plan to rob a famous Los Angeles stadium during a match, in this cliche-ridden caper movie. Well paced but hardly enthralling.
Boa: novel by The Seventh Richard Stark.
DRA                                      91 min
B,V                                           CBS

**SPLITZ ***                                       15
Dominic Paris        USA                     1984
*Robin Johnson, Shirley Stoler, Patti Lee, Chuck McQuarry, Raymond Serra, Barbara M. Bingham*
A female college head threatens to close a sorority house, but the girls have a few powerful protectors who come to their aid. Standard high school nonsense.
COM                                      83 min
B,V                                           EIV

**SPONTANEOUS COMBUSTION ***                       18
Tobe Hooper          USA                     1989
*Brad Dourif, Cynthia Bain, Jon Cypher, William Prince, Melinda Dillon, Dey Young, Dick Butkus, John Landis*
Not a serious examination of an alleged "scientific" reality, but another Hooper extravaganza of special effects, in this tale of a man whose strange pyrotechnic powers seem to be due to the exposure to radiation his parents underwent in the 1950s. The use of flamethrower effects cannot hide the sheer absurdity of it all in this poorly conceived dud.
HOR                             93 min (ort 108 min)
V                                           BRAVE

**SPOOK WHO SAT BY THE DOOR, THE ***               
Ivan Dixon           USA                     1973
*Lawrence Cook, Paula Kelly, Janet League, J.A. Preston, Paul Butler, Byron Marrow, Don Blakely, David Lemieux, Joseph Mascolo, Jack Aaron, Beverly Gill, Bob Hill, Martin Golar, Jeff Hamilton, Margaret Kromgols, Kathy Berk*
A black CIA agent organises an anti-white teenage guerilla movement. A bizarre film that is insulting to black people and filmlovers in equal measure, and is rather poorly done too.
Aka: CERTAIN HEAT (ARCTIC); KEEPERS (MARKET/GOV)
A/AD                                     102 min
B,V     MARKET/GOV L/A; DIAM/MOV L/A; ARCTIC

**SPOOKIES **                                      18
Eugenie Joseph/Thomas Doran/Brendan Faulkner
                     USA                     1986
*Felix Ward, Dan Scott, Alec Nemser, Maria Pechukas, A.I. Lowenthal, Pat Wesley Bryan, Peter Din, Nick Giorta, Lisa Fried, Joan Ellen Delaney, Peter Lasillor Jr, Charlotte Seely, Kim Merrill, Anthony Valburg, Soo Paek*
A horror spoof that tells of a mysterious count, who lives in a coffin in a graveyard and needs some human sacrifices, to revitalise his dead bride. When a bunch of bored kids venture into his cemetery for fun, he decides to seize his chance. An utterly silly and overblown effort, but done with a lot of verve.
Aka: TWISTED SOULS
HOR                              85 min (ort 98 min)
B,V                                           PAL

**SPORTING CLUB, THE ***                           
Larry Peerce         USA                     1971
*Robert Fields, Nicolas Coster, Maggie Blye, Jack Warden, Richard Dysart, William Roerick, Ralph Waite, Linda Blair*
A study of the life and times of well-off citizens in Northern Michigan. Violence and promiscuity abound in a badly directed offering.
Boa: novel by Thomas McGuane.
A                                        105 min
B,V                                           EHE

**SPOT MARKS THE X ***                             U
Mark Rossman         USA                     1986
*Barret Oliver, Natalie Gregory, Richard B. Schull, Vic Dunlop, Jerry Wasserman, Geoffrey Lewis, David Huddleston, Frances Flanagan, David Wilson, Pat Armstrong, Gary Chalk, Don Davis, Duncan Fraser, Mike the Dog*
A dog is part of a gang that buried their loot before they were jailed, and only he knows where to find it. The problem is that he now wants to go straight, after being rescued from the pound by a young boy. A typical little Disney tale – cute, wholesome and forgettable.
JUV                                    90 min mTV
B,V                                           WDV

**SPRING BREAK ***                                 15
Sean S. Cunningham   USA                     1983
*David Knell, Steve Bassett, Perry Lang, Paul Land, Corinne Alphen, Richard B. Schull, Jayne Modean, Daniel Faraldo, Donald Symington, Jessica James*
A study of teenagers by the sea in all its boring emptiness. What little plot there is revolves around two boys sharing a room with a couple of cool New Yorkers, whilst on a short holiday at Fort Lauderdale.

A feeble and witless sex comedy, written by David Smilow.
Aka: SPRINGBREAK

| | |
|---|---|
| COM | 97 min (ort 101 min) |
| V | RCA |

**SPRING FEVER ***           15
Joseph L. Scanlan    CANADA      1983
*Susan Anton, Frank Converse, Carling Bassett, Jessica Walter, Stephen Young, Lisa Brady, David Main, Barbara Cook, Alan Fawcett, Derrick Jones, Lisa Foster, Brian Crabb, Martin Schechter, Stephen Shellen*
Bassett as a young girl struggles to become a champion tennis player, in this anodyne exercise in tedium.
Aka: SNEAKERS

| | |
|---|---|
| DRA | 100 min |
| B,V | ODY |

**SPRING FEVER USA ***          18
William Milling      USA        1988
*Darrel Gullbeau, Michelle Kemp, Jeff Greenman, Lara Belmonte, Janine Lindenmulden*
Two over-sexed teenagers spend their holiday in search of women, in this thinly plotted sex-comedy. Written by Milling.

| | |
|---|---|
| COM | 92 min |
| V | VPD |

**SPRINGFIELD RIFLE ***          U
Andre De Toth     USA        1952
*Gary Cooper, Phyllis Thaxter, David Brian, Paul Kelly, Philip Carey, Lon Chaney Jr, James Millican, Martin Milner, Guinn Williams, James Brown, Jack Woody, Alan Hale, Vince Barnett, Fess Parker, Richard Lightner*
Gary Cooper stars as an officer in the Union Army who gets himself cashiered, joins the Confederates as a spy, and finds out who is behind the theft of government arms. A solid Western with good production values but no real zest.

| | |
|---|---|
| WES | 89 min (ort 93 min) Cut (3 sec) |
| V | WHV |

**SPRINGTIME IN THE ROCKIES ***      U
Irving Cummings    USA      1942
*Betty Grable, John Payne, Carmen Miranda, Cesar Romero, Charlotte Greenwood, Edward Everett Horton, Jackie Gleason, Frank Orth, Harry James and his Music Makers*
At a mountain retreat a Broadway couple repeatedly bicker and make up, while others enjoy more romantic encounters. Grable is at her prettiest in this thinly plotted but colourful and very typical wartime musical. The feeble storyline is forgotten in the face of the gorgeous Technicolor photography and catchy numbers, that include: "Chattanooga Choo Choo" and "I Had The Craziest Dream". Songs are by Mack Gordon and Harry Warren.

| | |
|---|---|
| MUS | 87 min (ort 91 min) |
| V | CBS |

**SPY ***          15
Philip F. Messina    USA      1989
*Bruce Greenwood, Catherine Hicks, Jameson Parker, Michael Tucker, Ned Beatty, Tim Choate*
An intelligence yarn that faintly echoes THREE DAYS OF THE CONDOR in its premise of a "freebooter" group at work inside the CIA. When a former operative stumbles across their existence he soon finds himself paying a high price for this unwelcome knowledge. A reasonably entertaining espionage thriller.

| | |
|---|---|
| A/AD | 81 min (ort 100 min) mCab |
| V | CIC |

**SPY IN BLACK, THE ***        U
Michael Powell    UK        1938
*Conrad Veidt, Valerie Hobson, Sebastian Shaw,*

*Marius Goring, June Duprez, Athole Stewart, Agnes Lauchlan, Helen Haye, Cyril Raymond, Hay Petrie, Grant Sutherland, Robert Rendel, Mary Morris, George Summers, Margaret Moffatt*
In WW1, a German agent is pursued by the British in the Orkneys, after escaping from a trap, in which the wife of a naval officer replaced the schoolmistress he was supposed to contact. An absorbing tale of twists and complexities, with a little romance added for good measure. The script is by Emeric Pressburger and Roland Pertwee.
Aka: U-BOAT 29
Boa: novel by J. Storer Clouston.

| | |
|---|---|
| DRA | 82 min B/W |
| V | PICK |

**SPY KILLER, THE ***       
Roy Ward Baker    USA      1968
(released in USA 1970)
*Robert Horton, Sebastian Cabot, Jill St John, Eleanor Summerfield, Douglas Sheldon, Lee Montague, Robert Russell, Barbara Shelley, Donald Morley, Kenneth Warren, Philip Mardoc, Michael Segal, Timothy Bateson*
A confused spy thriller in which the machinations revolve around attempts to recover a secret list of agents. A muddled and almost incomprehensible tale, that begins to make sense by the time one has lost interest. Followed by "Foreign Exchange".
Boa: novel Private I by Jimmy Sangster.

| | |
|---|---|
| THR | 72 min (ort 74 min) mTV |
| B,V | RNK |

**SPY STORY ***       
Lindsay Shonteff    UK      1976
*Don Fellows, Michael Gwynne, Philip Latham, Michael Petrovitch, Nicholas Parsons, Tessa Wyatt, Toby Robins, Ciaran Maddan, Nigel Plaskitt, Bernard Kay, Derren Nesbitt*
An undistinguished and fairly typical 1970s spy thriller, that received scant publicity on release (despite being based on a Deighton novel). An intelligence operative employed at a war games institute, becomes involved in the planning surrounding the defection of a Soviet admiral.
Boa: novel by Len Deighton.

| | |
|---|---|
| THR | 92 min (ort 102 min) |
| B,V,V2 | INT |

**SPY WHO LOVED ME, THE ***      PG
Lewis Gilbert    UK      1977
*Roger Moore, Barbara Bach, Richard Kiel, Curt Jurgens, Caroline Munro, Lois Maxwell, Bernard Lee, Sydney Tafler, Walter Gotell, Geoffrey Keen, Olga Bisera, Shane Rimmer, Bryan Marshall, Michael Billington, Desmond Llewellyn*
Another "James Bond" film (the tenth) with East joining West, in an attempt to prevent a megalomaniac from achieving world domination, by instigating a nuclear war between the USA and the USSR. Not one of the best but still good, with Moore as suave as ever and the undersea battle a high-spot. Music is by Marvin Hamlisch with Carly Simon singing. Written by Christopher Wood and Richard Maibaum. Followed by MOONRAKER.
Boa: novel by Ian Fleming.

| | |
|---|---|
| A/AD | 123 min (ort 125 min) |
| V | WHV |

**SPYDER ***          18
J.M. Avellana        1988
*Blake Bahner, Roxanne Baird*
A cop leaves Los Angeles for Hawaii in pursuit of his investigations and gets caught up in a world of corruption, drugs and illegal immigration.

| | |
|---|---|
| A/AD | 76 min |
| V | RCA |

## SQUARE DANCE *** 15
Daniel Petrie USA 1986
*Jason Robards, Jane Alexander, Wynona Ryder, Rob*
*Lowe, Deborah Richter, Guich Koock, Elbert Lewis*
A rather charming tale of a young girl and her growth
to womanhood, with her setting off from her grand-
father's farm to be with her irresponsible mother. An
overlong film that moves along somewhat sluggishly,
but is sustained by some great performances, especial-
ly from Lowe as a retarded young man and Alexander
as the girl's mother.
Aka: HOME IS WHERE THE HEART IS
DRA 112 min
B,V SONY

## SQUARE PEG, THE *** 
John Paddy Carstairs UK 1958
*Norman Wisdom, Edward Chapman, Campbell*
*Singer, Hattie Jacques, Brian Worth, Terence*
*Alexander, Honor Blackman, John Warwick, Arnold*
*Bell, Eddie Leslie, Andre Maranne, Frank Williams,*
*Oliver Reed*
Period comedy with a star whose immense talent was
rarely done justice by his material. An army recruit
turns out to be the exact double of a German general,
so of course Norman gets to play both parts with his
usual hilarious panache. A dated but enjoyable com-
edy. Look out for the mirror sequence that even rivals
the one in DUCK SOUP. Written by Jack Davies.
Aka: NORMAN WISDOM: THE SQUARE PEG
Osca: BULLDOG BREED, THE
COM 86 min (ort 89 min)
B,V TEVP

## SQUARE RING, THE **
Michael Relph/Basil Dearden
UK 1953
*Jack Warner, Kay Kendall, Joan Collins, Robert*
*Beatty, Bill Owen, Maxwell Reed, Bernadette*
*O'Farrell, Eddie Byrne, Sidney James, Alfie Bass*
A collection of stories revolving around a single night
at a boxing stadium. A motley set of episodes, well
mounted but of variable interest.
Boa: play by Ralph Peterson.
DRA 80 min (ort 83 min) B/W
V WHV

## SQUEEZE A FLOWER **
Marc Daniels AUSTRALIA 1969
*Dave Allen, Walter Chiari, Jack Albertson*
A cunning monk takes his monastery's secret liquor
formula with him to Australia and sets up in business
for himself.
COM 105 min
B,V,V2 INT

## SQUEEZE PLAY *
Samuel Weil USA 1980
*Jim Harris, Jenni Hetrick, Rick Gitlin, Helen*
*Campitelli, Al Corley, Jim Metzler*
A vulgar comedy about a man-woman softball match,
with humour reminiscent of those saucy English
seaside postcards of Donald McGill. Jokes about
human anatomy and various bodily functions abound
in this smutty and unrewarding experience.
COM 92 min
B,V TEM L/A; APX

## SQUEEZE, THE *
Roger Young USA 1987
*Michael Keaton, Rae Dawn Chong, John Davidson,*
*Ric Abernathy, Danny Aiello, Bobby Bass, Jophrey*
*Brown, Leslie Bevis, Lou Criscoulo, Ray Gabriel,*
*George Gerdes, Ronald Guttman, Paul Herman,*
*Richard E. Huhn, John Dennis Johnston*
A man is tricked by his former wife into collecting a
package containing a magnet, that crooks intend
using to score with on a TV game show lottery. A
scatterbrained comedy with very few laughs but a
good many chases, as Keaton and Chong uncover this
fiendish plot.
COM 97 min (ort 101 min) Cut (6 sec)
B,V CBS

## SQUEEZE, THE **
Michael Apted UK 1977
*Stacy Keach, David Hemmings, Edward Fox, Stephen*
*Boyd, Carol White, Freddie Starr, Hilary Gasson, Rod*
*Beacham, Stewart Harwood, Alan Ford, Leon Greene,*
*Maureen Sweeney, Lucinda Duckett, Alison Portes,*
*Lionel Ngakane*
An ex-cop who lost his job because of his addiction to
drink, mounts a lone crusade to rescue his ex-wife and
daughter who are being held as hostages. A fast-paced
thriller that tries hard for realism but merely
achieves unpleasantness. Written by Leon Griffiths.
Boa: novel by David Craig.
THR 102 min (ort 107 min)
B,V WHV

## SQUIRM *** 18
Jeff Lieberman USA 1976
*Don Scardino, Patricia Pearcy, Jean Sullivan, R.A.*
*Dow, Peter MacLean, Fran Higgins, William Newman,*
*Barbara Quinn, Angel Sande, Carl Dagenhart, Carol*
*Jean Owens, Walter Dimmick, Kim Iocouvozzi, Julia*
*Klopp*
On one rainy night, a falling power line causes nasty
worms to turn into maneaters and attack a small town
in Georgia. Lieberman both wrote and directed this
shocker, which has several repulsive sequences and
one or two touches of gruesome black humour.
HOR 93 min
B,V RNK

## SQUIZZY TAYLOR ** 15
Kevin Dobson AUSTRALIA 1982
*David Atkins, Jacki Weaver, Alan Cassell, Michael*
*Long, Kim Lewis, Steve Bisley*
A period piece recreating 1920s Melbourne and deal-
ing with the career of the title character – its famous
gangster. An interesting but rather pointless homage
to an obscure figure.
DRA 89 min (ort 97 min)
B,V ITM L/A; DIAM; APX

## STACEY **
Andy Sidaris USA 1973
*Anne Randall, Alan Landers, James Westmoreland,*
*Cristina Raines, Anitra Ford, Marjorie Bennett*
A female detective investigates a wealthy woman's
potential heirs and discovers a complex web of black-
mail and murder. A slick and violent tale, fairly
unmemorable apart from the presence of former
Playmate Randall. Remade after a fashion as MALI-
BU EXPRESS.
Aka: STACEY AND HER GANGBUSTERS
A/AD 83 min
B,V,V2 DFS

## STAGE DOOR *** U
Gregory La Cava USA 1937
*Katharine Hepburn, Ginger Rogers, Adolphe Menjou,*
*Andrea Leeds, Ann Miller, Lucille Ball, Gail Patrick,*
*Eve Arden, Samuel S. Hinds, Franklin Pangborn,*
*Constance Collier, Jack Carson*
A rich girl tries to make it as an actress on her own
merits, while staying at a theatrical boardinghouse.
Excellent performances and a good script carry the
thin storyline, though the latter half of the movie
strikes a more sombre note, that seems strangely at
odds with the contrived comic aspects. Written by
Morrie Ryskind and Anthony Veiller.
Boa: play by Edna Ferber and George S. Kaufman.
DRA 92 min B/W
V VCC

## STAGE FRIGHT **
Michele Soavi          USA                18
                                          1986
*David Brandon, Barbara Cupisti, Robert Gilgorov,
John Morghen, Mary Sellers, Jo Anne Smith, Lori
Parrel, Martin Philips, Ulrike Schwerk, Clain Parker,
Piero Vida, James E.R. Sampson, Don Fiore, Richard
Berkley*
A gripping but quite unpleasant slasher tale, in which
a performance group are rehearsing in an obsolete
theatre, for a horror musical that's inspired by the
exploits of a mass murderer. What they don't realise is
that the demented psycho, who inspired their play,
has escaped from an asylum and is heading their way.
Aka: AQUARIUS; STAGEFRIGHT
HOR                             86 min (ort 95 min)
B,V                                        AVA

## STAGE STRUCK **
Sidney Lumet          USA                1957
*Henry Fonda, Susan Strasberg, Herbert Marshall,
Christopher Plummer, Joan Greenwood*
The story of an aspiring actress and her climb to
Broadway stardom, that is little more than a dated
remake of "Morning Glory". A film that's strong on
detail but is spoilt by poor casting, with Strasberg
rather unappealing in the central role. Written by
Ruth and Augustus Goetz.
Boa: play by Zoe Atkins.
Osca: GIRL MOST LIKELY, THE
DRA                      91 min (ort 95 min) B/W
B,V                                        KVD

## STAGECOACH **
Ted Post              USA                  U
                                          1986
*Willie Nelson, Waylon Jennings, Kris Kristofferson,
Johnny Cash, Anthony Newley, John Schneider, Mary
Crosby, Tony Franciosa, Elizabeth Ashley, Merritt
Butrick, June Carter Cash, Jesse Colter, Alex Kubik,
David Allan Coe*
The second remake of the classic 1939 Western,
telling of the assorted passengers on a long stagecoach
journey, and how they react to the strains of the
journey, not least the hazard of an Indian attack. An
unconvincing effort, made more so by packing the cast
with an assortment of Country and Western singing
stars, wives and others.
Boa: short story Stage To Lordsburg by Ernest Lee
Haycox.
WES                            94 min (ort 100 min) mTV
B,V                                        MOG

## STAGECOACH ****
John Ford             USA                1939
*John Wayne, John Carradine, Claire Trevor, Thomas
Mitchell, Andy Devine, Tim Holt, Louise Platt, George
Bancroft, Donald Meek, Berton Churchill, Francis
Ford, Tom Tyler, Chris-Pin Martin, Elvira Ross,
Yakima Canutt, Bill Cody*
Classic film about a group of travellers on a
stagecoach, their fears and conflicts as they are
attacked by Indians etc. Highly entertaining but don't
expect realism. The stuntwork is by a famous stunt-
man of the time – Yakima Canutt. Written by Dudley
Nichols and remade in 1966 and 1986. AA: S. Actor
(Mitchell), Score (Richard Hageman/Frank Harling/
John Lepold/Leo Shuken).
Boa: short story Stage To Lordsburg by Ernest Lee
Haycox.
Osca: DEADLINE AT DAWN
WES                      92 min (ort 99 min) B/W
B,V                                   KVD; MOGP

## STAKEOUT ***
John Badham           USA                15
                                          1987
*Richard Dreyfuss, Emilio Estevez, Madeleine Stowe,
Aidan Quinn, Dan Lauria, Forest Whitaker, Ian
Tracey, Earl Billings, Jackson Davies, J.J. Makaro,
Scott Anderson, Tony Pantages, Beatrice Boepple,
Kytle Woida, Jan Speck*

Two cops are sent on a routine assignment to keep
watch on a beautiful woman, but one of them falls in
love with her. This fairly improbable and rather
shallow plot is transformed into a witty and lively
comedy, by fine performances from Dreyfuss and
Estevez and some memorable dialogue. The script is
by Jim Kouf.
COM                            112 min (ort 115 min)
B,V                                      BUENA

## STALAG 17 ****
Billy Wilder          USA                PG
                                          1953
*William Holden, Don Taylor, Otto Preminger, Robert
Strauss, Harvey Lembeck, Peter Graves, Sig Ruman,
Neville Brand, Richard Erdman*
A classic wartime POW story mixing comedy and
pathos, as a group of American POWs begin to suspect
that one of their number (Holden) is a traitor, because
their escape attempts are so easily foiled. The mixture
of comedy and pathos is at times uneasy but it's a fine
film just the same. Written by Wilder and Edwin
Blum with music by Franz Waxman. The humour is
supplied by Strauss and Lembeck repeating their
Broadway roles. AA: Actor (Holden).
Boa: play by Donald Bevan and Edmund Trzinski.
WAR                     118 min (ort 120 min) B/W
V/h                                        CIC

## STAND ALONE **
Alan Beattie          USA                18
                                          1986
*James Keach, Charles Durning, Pam Grier, Bert
Remsen, Barbara Sammeth, Lu Leonard, Luis
Contreras*
A WW2 hero witnesses a gangland killing and
becomes reluctantly involved in helping the police.
This makes him a target and he is forced to use his
military skills to defend himself. Standard heroics are
coupled to an unlikely and overweight hero to make
for an unconvincing tale.
THR                                        90 min
B,V                                        NWV

## STAND AND DELIVER ***
Ramon Menendez        USA                PG
                                          1988
*Edward James Olmos, Lou Diamond Phillips, Rosana
De Soto, Andy Garcia, Will Gotay, Ingrid Oliu,
Virginia Paris, Mark Eliot*
Based on a real-life story, this tells of a determined
and dedicated teacher who instils in his unruly
students a sense of pride and self-worth, when his
teaching methods enable them to pass a difficult
examination. Olmos gives a remarkable performance
in this warmhearted and enthralling tale. The script
is by Menendez and Tom Musca.
DRA                            99 min (ort 105 min)
V/h                                        WHV

## STAND BY ME ***
Rob Reiner            USA                15
                                          1986
*River Phoenix, Corey Feldman, Wil Wheaton, Jerry
O'Connell, John Cusack, Richard Dreyfuss, Kiefer
Sutherland, Casey Siemaszko, Gary Riley, Marshall
Bell, Bradley Bregg, Jason Oliver, Frances Lee, Bruce
Kirby, William Bronder*
A trip back to a 1950s American boyhood, that follows
the friendships and adventures of four young misfit,
who take a trip into the woods to have a look at a dead
body. An overly sentimental and contrived tale, based
on King's autobiographical story, but sustained by
some appealing performances. The constant stream of
profanities seems somewhat out of place in the 1950s.
Boa: novella The Body by Stephen King.
DRA                            85 min (ort 87 min)
B,V                                        RCA

## STAND UP VIRGIN SOLDIERS *
Norman Cohen          UK                 15
                                          1977
*Robin Askwith, Nigel Davenport, George Layton,
Robin Nedwell, Warren Mitchell, Edward Woodward,*

*John Le Mesurier, Irene Handl, Fiesta Mei Lung,*
*Pamela Stephenson, Lynda Bellingham, David Auker,*
*Robert Booth*
Sequel to THE VIRGIN SOLDIERS, depicting more
sexual adventures in 1950 for British recruits in
Singapore. A vulgar farce lacking any of the authen-
ticity of the 1969 film. Written by Leslie Thomas.
Boa: novel by Leslie Thomas.
COM                                          90 min
B,V                                          WHV

## STAR! ***
Robert Wise            USA              1968
*Julie Andrews, Richard Crenna, Michael Craig,*
*Daniel Massey, Robert Reed, John Collin, Bruce*
*Forsyth, Beryl Reed, Jenny Agutter*
The story of Gertrude Lawrence and her rise from
poverty to international stardom. This incredibly
overlong saga boasts some huge musical numbers that
are worth seeing for their sheer novelty. Apart from
that the film has very little to offer. It was later cut to
120 minutes and retitled after it flopped at the box
office. The script is by William Fairchild. The title
song (which received an AAN) is by James Van
Heusen and Sammy Cahn.
Aka: THOSE WERE THE HAPPY DAYS; THOSE
WERE THE HAPPY TIMES
MUS                        175 min (ort 194 min)
B,V                                          CBS

## STAR 80 ***
Bob Fosse              USA              1983
*Mariel Hemingway, Eric Roberts, Cliff Robertson,*
*Carroll Baker, Josh Mostel, Roger Rees, David*
*Clennon, Sidney Miller, Jordan Christopher, Keenan*
*Ivory Wyans, Stuart Damon, Ernest Thompson*
Biopic about the tragic life and death of Playboy
magazine centrefold Dorothy Stratton, who was mur-
dered by her jealous small-time hustler husband, Paul
Snider. A well-handled but sordid tale that draws fine
performances from all concerned, but provides no
insights or interesting observations. This was Fosse's
last film. See also DEATH OF A CENTREFOLD, a TV
film that covers similar ground.
DRA                        99 min (ort 104 min)
B,V                                          WHV

## STAR CHAMBER, THE **
Peter Hyams            USA              1983
*Michael Douglas, Hal Holbrook, Yaphet Kotto, Sharon*
*Gless, James B. Sikking, Joe Regalbuto, Don Calfa,*
*Hohn Di Santi, DeWayne Jessie, Jack Kehoe, Larry*
*Hankin, Dick Anthony Williams, Margie Impert, Dana*
*Gladstone, Fred McCarren*
A young judge is so annoyed at having to release
criminals because of legal niceties, that he joins a
secret society that dispenses its own justice. A simplis-
tic and implausible affair, written by Hyams and
Roderick Taylor. (The title comes from the chamber,
complete with star motifs on the ceiling, used by
Henry VIII to conduct business with his ministers,
which later became a court with summary and
arbitrary powers.)
DRA                        104 min (ort 109 min)
B,V                                          CBS

## STAR CHASERS **
David Lowell Rich      USA              1984
*Sharon Gless, Dee Wallace, Anne Archer, David*
*Ackroyd, Barnard Hughes, Paul Menzel, Gary Moody,*
*Alex Harvey, Joe Rainer, Dan Ammerman, Robin*
*Mosley, Jerry Briggs, Theresa Graham, Nicole*
*Fusselman, Jo Perkins*
Three women compete to be the first one to travel
aboard the space shuttle, in this forgettable melod-
rama.
Aka: SKY'S NO LIMIT, THE
DRA                    92 min (ort 100 min) mTV
B,V                                          ARF

## STAR CRYSTAL **                          18
Lance Lindsay          USA              1985
*C. Jutson Campbell, Faye Bolt, John Smith, Taylor*
*Kingsley, Marcia Linn, Eric Moseng, Lance Brucker,*
*Thomas Williams, Don Kingsley, Robert Allen, Emily*
*Longstreth, Lisa Goulian, Charles Linza, Frank*
*Alexander*
A strange crystal found aboard a derelict spacecraft is
taken for scientific tests. However, it contains a
malevolent lifeforce that threatens the existence of
mankind.
FAN                        97 min; 88 min (CDC)
B,V                        IVS; CDC (VHS only)

## STAR FORCE *                             PG
Kiyosumi Kukazawa/Minora Kanaga
                    JAPAN
*Tatsuya Azuma, Miyuki Tanigawa, Joe Shisido, Choei*
*Takakashi*
Another low-grade and forgettable Japanese space
opera.
Aka: STAR FORCE: FUGITIVE ALIEN 2
FAN                                          103 min
V                                            XTASY

## STAR IS BORN, A **                       15
Frank Pierson          USA              1976
*Barbra Streisand, Kris Kristofferson, Paul Mazursky,*
*Gary Busey, Oliver Clark, Marta Heflin, M.G. Kelly,*
*Sally Kirkland, Vanetta Fields, Clydie King*
A remake of the 1937 original, telling of a Hollywood
love affair that ends in tragedy. This one is updated to
the 1970s and is well supplied with screaming crowds
and some high decibel numbers, plus an overblown
and insensitive performance from Streisand. Howev-
er, the movie does come to life when she sings. A
flashy but irritating and rather empty work. AA: Song
("Evergreen" – Streisand – music/Paul Williams –
lyrics).
DRA                        134 min (ort 140 min)
V                                            WHV

## STAR IS BORN, A ***                      U
George Cukor           USA              1954
*Judy Garland, James Mason, Charles Bickford, Jack*
*Carson, Tommy Noonan, Amanda Blake, Lucy*
*Marlow*
First remake of the 1937 film done as a musical, with
Garland and Mason in fine form as the ill-fated
Hollywood lovers. A lack of depth in the story is
noticeable in the second half and the film suffered
from excessive editing, that took place after its
premiere. The songs are by Harold Arlen and Ira
Gershwin, and with the exception of "The Man That
Got Away" are not all that good. A restored version
put together in 1983 is now the one generally seen.
MUS                        168 min (ort 181 min)
V/h                                          WHV

## STAR IS BORN, A ****
William Wellman        USA              1937
*Janet Gaynor, Fredric March, Adolphe Menjou, May*
*Robson, Andy Devine, Lionel Stander, May Robson,*
*Owen Moore, Franklin Pangbourn*
The story of an actress on the way up, who marries a
leading man whose career is on the way down. A
classic film with the two stars in peak form. The
sharply observant script is by Dorothy Parker, Alan
Campbell and Robert Carson and is partly based on
the 1932 film "What Price Hollywood". Remade in
1954 and 1976. AA: Story (Orig) (Robert Carson/
William A. Wellman), Spec Award (W. Howard
Greene for colour cinematography).
Boa: story by William A. Wellman.
DRA                                          110 min B/W
B,V                        GOV L/A; EVC L/A

## STAR KNIGHT **                           PG
Fernando Colombo       SPAIN            1986

*Klaus Kinski, Harvey Keitel, Fernando Rey, Maria Lamor, Miguel Bose*
A spaceship is transported back to medieval Spain where the locals take it to be a dragon. Apart from a few special effects, this one has very little to offer. Only Keitel escapes dubbing.
Aka: KNIGHT OF THE DRAGON, THE
FAN                        87 min (ort 90 min) dubbed
B,V                                                    VES

## STAR PACKER, THE ***                               U
Robert North Bradbury  USA                        1934
*John Wayne, Verna Hillie, Gabby Hayes, Yakima Canutt, Earl Dwire, Eddie Parker, George Cleveland, Tom Lingham, David Aldrich, Tex Palmer, Billy Franey*
A young cowboy becomes sheriff but goes underground to ferret out a mysterious cowboy gang, led by a man known as "The Shadow". An unusual and intriguing story.
Aka: WEST OF THE DIVIDE
WES                                           53 min B/W
V                                                    CH5

## STAR QUALITY **                                    PG
UK                                                1985
*Susannah York, Ian Richardson, David Yelland*
A young man's dream of having his first play performed in the West End comes true, but success is not quite as he imagined it would be.
Boa: story by Noel Coward.
DRA                                               78 min
V                                                   PICK

## STAR TREK ***                                      U
Robert Wise                USA                    1979
*Willian Shatner, Leonard Nimoy, DeForest Kelley, Stephen Collins, Persis Khambatta, James Doohan, George Takei, Walter Koenig, Nichelle Nichols, Mark Lenard, Majel Barrett, Grace Lee Whitney, David Gautreaux, Marcy Lafferty*
Earth is threatened by a massive energy field and the Starship Enterprise is sent to investigate, in this spin-off of the popular TV series. Wooden acting and stilted dialogue let down a good plot enlivened by some superb special effects. Screenwriters were Alan Dean Foster and Harold Livingstone with music by Jerry Goldsmith. Followed by several sequels.
Aka: STAR TREK: THE MOTION PICTURE
FAN                         124 min (ort 132 min)
V                                                    CIC

## STAR TREK 2: THE WRATH OF KHAN **                  PG
Nicholas Meyer             USA                    1982
*William Shatner, Leonard Nimoy, DeForest Kelley, Ricardo Montalban, Walter Koenig, James Doohan, George Takei, Paul Winfield, Nichelle Nichols, Bibi Besch, Merritt Butrick, Kirstie Alley, Ike Eisenmann, Judson Scott*
A further adventure of the crew of the Enterprise but this time the plot is an amplified version of a TV episode from 1967 ("Space Seed"), in which our heroes are menaced by a selectively bred superman. A laughable and wholly inferior sequel. Followed by STAR TREK 3.
Aka: WRATH OF KHAN, THE
FAN                         109 min (ort 114 min)
B,V                                                  CIC

## STAR TREK 3: THE SEARCH FOR SPOCK **               PG
Leonard Nimoy              USA                    1984
*William Shatner, DeForest Kelley, James Doohan, George Takei, Walter Koenig, Christopher Lloyd, Nichelle Nichols, Jane Wyatt, Mark Lenard, Robin Curtis, James B. Sikking, Catherine Hicks, Leonard Nimoy, Robert Ellenstein*
Third "Star Trek" adventure continuing from the previous one. Captain Kirk goes on a mission to find the body of his dead lieutenant but has to overcome various problems, not least being a hostile Klingon warship and the rapid self-destruction of a barren world, artificially seeded with life. Seriously overlong and totally uninspired. STAR TREK 4: THE VOYAGE HOME followed.
Aka: SEARCH FOR SPOCK, THE
FAN                         101 min (ort 105 min)
V/sh                                                 CIC

## STAR TREK 4: THE VOYAGE HOME ***                   PG
Leonard Nimoy              USA                    1986
*William Shatner, Leonard Nimoy, DeForest Kelley, James Doohan, Jane Wyatt, Walter Koenig, George Takei, Nichelle Nichols, Catherine Hicks, Mark Lenard, Robin Curtis, Robert Ellenstein, John Schuck, Brock Peters, Michael Snyder*
Fourth outing for the crew of the Enterprise, with a comedy flavour and a contemporary setting. The crew travel back in time on a mission that involves them with a marine biologist and the saving of one of Earth's most precious life forms. A lightweight but fairly entertaining tale.
Aka: VOYAGE HOME, THE
FAN                         117 min (ort 119 min)
V/sh                                                 CIC

## STAR TREK 5: THE FINAL FRONTIER **                 PG
William Shatner            USA                    1989
*William Shatner, Leonard Nimoy, DeForest Kelley, James Doohan, Walter Koenig, Nichelle Nichols, George Takei, David Warner, Laurence Luckinbill, Charles Cooper*
The crew of the Enterprise are recalled from a camping trip, and head for a distant planet that has been taken over by a renegade Vulcan, in search of spiritual enlightenment. Having captured their ship, he forces them to set off in search of the ultimate goal – God. Shatner's feature directing debut (which he also co-wrote) starts off slowly, gets slightly better, but ultimately disappoints. Music is by Jerry Goldsmith.
FAN                         102 min (ort 106 min)
V                                                    CIC

## STAR TREK: A PIECE OF THE ACTION/BY ANY OTHER NAME **                                       U
James Komack/Marc Daniels
USA                                              1968
*William Shatner, Leonard Nimoy, DeForest Kelley, James Doohan, George Takei, Nichelle Nichols, Anthony Caruso, Vic Tayback, Lee Delano, Steve Marlo, John Harmon, Warren Stevens, Barbara Bouchet, Stewart Moss, Julie Cobb, Carl Byrd*
The first of these stories takes Kirk to a remote planet that has evolved into a society resembling Chicago in the Prohibition-era. The second finds the captain and his crew being abducted by creatures intent on destroying humanity.
FAN                                         98 min mTV
V                                                    CIC

## STAR TREK: A PRIVATE LITTLE WAR/THE GAMESTERS OF TRISKELION **                            PG
Marc Daniels/Gene Nelson
USA                                           1967/68
*William Shatner, Leonard Nimoy, DeForest Kelley, James Doohan, George Takei, Nancy Kovak, Michael Whitney, Ned Romero, Janos Prohaska, Joseph Ruskin, Angelique Pettyjohn, Steve Sandor, Victoria George*
In the first of these episodes the Klingons arm the natives of a primitive planet and Kirk is forced to intervene, despite a Starfleet Command ruling to the contrary. The second story sees Kirk, Uhura and Chekov being abducted to a strange world whose powerful rulers enjoy using other races to stage

set-piece tournaments.

FAN 98 min mTV
V/h CIC

## STAR TREK: A TASTE OF ARMAGEDDON/ PG
## SPACE SEED **
Joseph Pevney/Marc Daniels
USA 1967
*William Shatner, Leonard Nimoy, DeForest Kelley,*
*James Doohan, George Takei, Nichelle Nichols, Walter*
*Koenig, Gene Lyons, David Opatoshu, Robert*
*Sampson, Barbara Babcock, Ricardo Montalban,*
*Madlyn Rhue, Blaisdell Makee, Mark Tobin*
In the first of these tales, Kirk visits a planet where
battles are fought with a rival world by computer, and
in the second tale the Captain has to outsmart a
ruthless race of supermen. Fair.

FAN 98 min mTV
V/h CIC

## STAR TREK: ARENA/THE ALTERNATIVE PG
## FACTOR **
Joseph Pevney/Gerd Oswald
USA 1967
*William Shatner, Leonard Nimoy, DeForest Kelley,*
*James Doohan, George Takei, Nichelle Nichols,*
*Walter Koenig, Carole Shelyne, Jerry Ayers, Tom*
*Troupe, Grant Woods, Sean Kenney, Robert Brown,*
*Janet MacLachlan, Richard Derr*
Another two episodes from the popular TV series. In
the first one Kirk has to fight an alien creature sent
against him by a strange civilisation. The second story
tells of a man who has a double in another dimension,
and must prevent him from ever entering this uni-
verse.

FAN 98 min mTV
V/h CIC

## STAR TREK: ASSIGNMENT EARTH/SPECTRE OF
## THE GUN * U
Marc Daniels/Vincent McEveety
USA 1968
*William Shatner, Leonard Nimoy, DeForest Kelley,*
*James Doohan, George Takei, Walter Koenig, Nichelle*
*Nichols, Robert Lansing, Teri Garr, Bonnie Beacher,*
*Ron Soble, Rex Holman, Sam Gilman, Bill Zuckert,*
*Abraham Sofaer*
In the first of these stories the Enterprise is sent to
investigate the old world, which according to the
records narrowly escaped destruction in 1968. In the
second Kirk decides to explore a forbidden planet, and
finds himself and his officers trapped in a reconstruc-
tion of the Gunfight at the O.K. Corral.

FAN 98 min mTV
V/h CIC

## STAR TREK: BALANCE OF TERROR/
## CHARLIE X ** U
USA 1966
*William Shatner, Leonard Nimoy, DeForest Kelley,*
*James Doohan, George Takei, Nichelle Nichols, Walter*
*Koenig, Mark Lenard, Paul Comi, Lawrence*
*Montaigne, Robert Walker Jr, Abraham Sofar,*
*Patricia McNulty, Charles J. Stewart*
In the first tale the Enterprise finds itself up against
an invisible alien ship, and in the second story, a man
with deadly powers is brought on board and threatens
the lives of the crew.

FAN 96 min mTV
V CIC

## STAR TREK: BREAD AND CIRCUSES/JOURNEY
## TO BABEL ** PG
Ralph Senensky/Joseph Pevney
USA 1967/68
*William Shatner, Leonard Nimoy, DeForest Kelley,*
*James Doohan, George Takei, William Smithers,*
*Logan Ramsey, Ian Wolfe, Lois Jewell, Rhodes*

*Reason, Mark Lenard, Janet Wyatt, William*
*O'Connell, Reggie Nalder*
"Bread and Circuses" sees Kirk locked in combat to
save the lives of his crew, when they encounter a
society similar to that of ancient Rome. The second
adventure sees Spock meeting his father, from whom
he parted bitterly many years before.

FAN 98 min mTV
V/h CIC

## STAR TREK: ELAAN OF TROYIUS/THE
## PARADISE SYNDROME * PG
Jud Taylor/John Meredyth
USA 1968
*William Shatner, Leonard Nimoy, DeForest Kelley,*
*James Doohan, George Takei, Walter Koenig, Nichelle*
*Nichols, France Nuyen, Jay Robertson, Tony Young,*
*Victor Brandt, Lee Duncan, Sabrina Scharf, Rudy*
*Solari*
The first story has Kirk dealing with an alien woman
whose tears have remarkable powers, the second has
Kirk getting married and apparently taking no
further interest in the running of the ship.

FAN 98 min mTV
V/h CIC

## STAR TREK: ERRAND OF MERCY/THE CITY ON
## THE EDGE OF FOREVER ** U
John Newland/Joseph Pevney
USA 1967
*William Shatner, Leonard Nimoy, DeForest Kelley,*
*James Doohan, George Takei, Nichelle Nichols, John*
*Abbott, John Colicos, Peter Brocco, Victor Lundin,*
*David Hillary Huge, Joan Collins, John Harmon, Hal*
*Baylor*
Another two Star Trek adventures. In the first tale
Kirk warns the rulers of a planet about an imminent
Klingon invasion, but finds them unconcerned. In the
second story, a time vortex drags McCoy back to New
York in the 1920s and Kirk and Spock follow.

FAN 98 min mTV
V/h CIC

## STAR TREK: FRIDAY'S CHILD ** PG
Joseph Pevney USA 1967
*William Shatner, Leonard Nimoy, DeForest Kelley,*
*James Doohan, Nichelle Nichols, George Takei, Julie*
*Newmar, Tige Andrews, Michael Dante, Ben Gage,*
*Cal Boulder, Kirk Raymone, Robert Bralver*
In this "Star Trek" adventure, Captain Kirk becomes
involved in a conflict with his old enemies the
Klingons.
Osca: STAR TREK: METAMORPHOSIS (asa)

FAN 51 min; 98 min (2 film cassette) mTV
V CIC

## STAR TREK: I, MUDD/THE TROUBLE WITH
## TRIBBLES ** U
Marc Daniels/Joseph Pevney
USA 1967
*William Shatner, Leonard Nimoy, DeForest Kelley,*
*James Doohan, George Takei, Roger C. Carmel,*
*Richard Tatro, Kay Elliot, Stanley Adams, William*
*Schallert, William Campbell, Whit Bissell*
"I, Mudd" tells of the abduction of Kirk and his
colleagues to a planet where a disreputable man
appears to live a life of ease with android servants. In
"The Trouble With Tribbles" the Enterprise is
threatened by a plague of cuddly little creatures that
possess the ability to multiply rapidly.

FAN 98 min mTV
V/h CIC

## STAR TREK: METAMORPHOSIS ** PG
Ralph Senensky USA 1967
*William Shatner, Leonard Nimoy, DeForest Kelley,*
*James Doohan, Nichelle Nichols, George Takei, Glenn*
*Corbett, Elinor Donahue*

Another episode from the poular TV series "Star Trek". In this story Captain Kirk, Spock and McCoy are taken prisoner when they visit a strange planet.
Osca: STAR TREK: FRIDAY'S CHILD (asa)
FAN          51 min; 98 min (2 film cassette) mTV
V                                              CIC

## STAR TREK: MIRI/THE CONSCIENCE OF THE KING **                                    PG
Vincent McEveety/Gerd Oswald
                    USA                    1966
*William Shatner, Leonard Nimoy, DeForest Kelley, James Doohan, George Takei, Nichelle Nichols, Kim Darby, Michael J. Pollard, John Megna, Steven McEveety, Ed McCready, Arnold Moss, Barbara Anderson, Bruce Hyde*
Two episodes from the TV series. In "Miri" the Enterprise crew visit a planet whose inhabitants appear to stay forever young, while in "The Conscience Of The King" suspicions are aroused when a troupe of actors visits the starship, for their leader resembles a notorious criminal.
FAN                              100 min mTV
V                                              CIC

## STAR TREK: MIRROR, MIRROR/THE DEADLY YEARS **                                      U
Marc Daniels/Joseph Pevney
                    USA
*William Shatner, Leonard Nimoy, DeForest Kelley, James Doohan, George Takei*
In the first of these Star Trek adventures the Enterprise is caught up in an ion storm during transportation, and Captain Kirk and his buddies find themselves in a parallel universe, while their doubles appear aboard the ship. The second tale deals with a strange infection caught on a visit to a new planet, that causes Kirk and his three chief officers to age rapidly.
FAN                               96 min mTV
V/h                                            CIC

## STAR TREK: MUDD'S WOMEN/THE ENEMY WITHIN **                                      U
Harvey Hart/Leo Penn
                    USA                    1966
*William Shatner, Leonard Nimoy, DeForest Kelley, James Doohan, George Takei, Nichelle Nichols, Roger C. Carmel, Karen Steele, Susan Denberg, Maggie Thrett, Gene Dynarski, Edward Maden, Garland Thompson*
Episodes 4 and 5 of the original TV series. The first one deals with a passenger and his cargo of three beautiful girls and the second sees Captain Kirk being split by a transporter malfunction into two people of distinctly opposite qualities.
FAN                               98 min mTV
V/h                                            CIC

## STAR TREK: OBSESSION/THE IMMUNITY SYNDROME **                                      U
Joseph Pevney          USA            1967/68
*William Shatner, Leonard Nimoy, DeForest Kelley, James Doohan, George Takei, Walter Koenig, Nichelle Nichols, Jeffrey Ayres, Stephen Brooks, John Winston*
In the first of these stories Kirk encounters a deadly gaseous creature that once killed two of his crew, and disregards orders in a bid to destroy it. The second story tells of a vast, shapeless creature that confronts the Enterprise and of Spock's efforts to overcome it.
FAN                               98 min mTV
V/h                                            CIC

## STAR TREK: OPERATION ANNIHILATE!/ CATSPAW **                                      U
Herschel Daugherty/Joseph Pevney

                    USA                    1967
*William Shatner, Leonard Nimoy, DeForest Kelley, James Doohan, George Takei, Nichelle Nichols, Dave Armstrong, Maurishka Taliferro, Craig Hundley, Joan Swift, Antoinette Bowers, Theo Marcuse, Michael Barrier*
The first of these stories concerns a spaceship hurtling towards the sun, and of its occupants who prefer death to insanity at the mercy of an alien parasite. The second tale deals with a landing on a sinister planet, where Kirk and his officers find themselves involuntary guests.
FAN                               98 min mTV
V/h                                            CIC

## STAR TREK: PLATO'S STEPCHILDREN/WINK OF AN EYE **                                   PG
David Alexander/Jud Taylor
                    USA                    1968
*William Shatner, Leonard Nimoy, DeForest Kelley, James Doohan, George Takei, Walter Koenig, Nichelle Nichols, Michael Dunn, Liam Sullivan, Barbara Babcock, Kathie Brown, Jason Evers, Geoffrey Binney, Eric Holland*
The first of these stories finds the crew of the Enterprise responding to a distress call and risking enslavement by a creature with telepathic powers. In the second story the ship is invaded by a creature that lives at an incomparably faster rate than human beings.
FAN                               98 min mTV
V                                    CIC/CBSDIS

## STAR TREK: RETURN TO TOMORROW/ PATTERNS OF FORCE *                               U
Ralph Senensky/Vincent McEveety
                    USA                    1968
*William Shatner, Leonard Nimoy, DeForest Kelley, James Doohan, George TAkei, Walter Koenig, Nichelle Nichols, Diana Muldaur, Skip Homeier, Richard Evans, Valora Norand, David Brian, William Wintersole, Gilbert Green*
"Return To Tomorrow" sees the Enterprise embarking on a flight to an apparently lifeless world in response to a distress call, while "Patterns Of Force" has Spock and Kirk landing on a remote world ruled by a Nazi-like regime.
FAN                               98 min mTV
V/h                                            CIC

## STAR TREK: SHORE LEAVE/THE SQUIRE OF GOTHOS **
                    USA                1966/1967
*William Shatner, Leonard Nimoy, DeForest Kelley, James Doohan, George Takei, Nichelle Nichols, Walter Koenig, Emily Banks, Oliver McGowan, Bruce Mars, Perry Lopez, William Campbell, Richard Carlyle, Michael Barrier*
In the first of these tales the crew of the Enterprise enjoy some leave on an Earth-like planet, but a surprise awaits them. The second story tells of a powerful alien who tries to take over the Enterprise.
FAN                               98 min mTV
V                                              CIC

## STAR TREK: SPOCK'S BRAIN/IS THERE IN TRUTH NO BEAUTY? **                           PG
Marc Daniels/Ralph Senensky
                    USA                    1968
*William Shatner, Leonard Nimoy, DeForest Kelley, James Doohan, George Takei, Walter Koenig, Nichelle Nichols, Marj Dusay, Diane Muldaur, David Frankham*
In the first of these tales a mysterious woman causes Spock to suffer a severe brain-drain that may cause his death, and in the second special visors are required when an ambassador representing the benign but

hideous Medusans visits the Enterprise. Average.
FAN                                98 min mTV
V/h                                         CIC

## STAR TREK: THAT WHICH SURVIVES/LET THAT
## BE YOUR LAST BATTLEFIELD **            U
Herb Wallerstein/Jud Taylor
                   USA                    1968
*William Shatner, Leonard Nimoy, DeForest Kelley,*
*James Doohan, George Takei, Walter Koenig, Nichelle*
*Nichols, Arthur Batanides, Naomi Pollack, Lee*
*Meriwether, Lou Antonio, Frank Gorshin*
"That Which Survives" has Kirk and McCoy stranded
on a hostile planet when the Enterprise is flung
light-years away and "Let That Be Your Last Bat-
tlefield" sees two warring aliens bringing their
50,000-year-old dispute onto the Enterprise.
FAN                                98 min mTV
V                                   CIC/CBSDIS

## STAR TREK: THE CAGE ***               U
Robert Butler          USA                1964
*Leonard Nimoy, John Hoyt, Peter Duryea, Jeffrey*
*Hunter, Susan Oliver, Majel Barrett, Meg Wylie*
The original pilot for the long-running TV series, in
which the USS Starship Enterprise "boldly goes where
no man has gone before". Here Captain Kirk's prede-
cessor runs into a good deal of trouble on a strange
planet. It was never televised in its original form, but
was later edited down to provide the flashback
sequences for the TV series' only two-part episode –
STAR TREK: THE MENAGERIE from 1966.
FAN                                73 min mTV
V/h                                         CIC

## STAR TREK: THE CHANGELING/THE APPLE ** U
Marc Daniels/Joseph Pevney
                   USA                    1967
*William Shatner, Leonard Nimoy, DeForest Kelley,*
*Keith Andes*
Two more adventures from this long-running TV
series. In the first tale, Captain Kirk has to battle a
computer that threatens to destroy the Earth, while in
the second story, the crew of the Enterprise inadver-
tently anger a powerful being who controls life on two
planets. Average.
FAN                                98 min mTV
V                                           CIC

## STAR TREK: THE DOOMSDAY MACHINE/WOLF
## IN THE FOLD **                        PG
Marc Daniels/Joseph Pevney
                   USA               1978/1967
*William Shatner, Leonard Nimoy, DeForest Kelley,*
*James Doohan, George Takei, Walter Koenig, Nichelle*
*NIchols, William Windom, John Copage, Elizabeth*
*Rogers, Richard Compton, John Fiedler, Charles*
*Macauley, Pilar Seurat*
Two more tales in this series. In the first an awesome-
ly powerful "doomsday machine" nearly destroys the
Enterprise, while in the second Scottie would appear
to have murdered three women, until the real culprit
is exposed.
FAN                                98 min mTV
V/h                                         CIC

## STAR TREK: THE EMPATH/THE THOLIAN WEB
## **                                    PG
John Erman/Ralph Senensky
                   USA                    1966
*William Shatner, Leonard Nimoy, DeForest Kelley,*
*James Doohan, George Takei, Walter Koenig, Nichelle*
*Nichols, Kathryn Hays, Alan Bergman, William Sage*
"The Empath" sees Kirk, Spock and McCoy being held
on a doomed planet, where powerful aliens have
devised a series of tests involving personal sacrifice, in
order to determine the viability of another species. In
"The Tholian Web" Kirk is trapped onboard a wrecked

Starship, unable to reach his own vessel which faces
destruction from an energy field.
FAN                                98 min mTV
V                                           CIC

## STAR TREK: THE ENTERPRISE INCIDENT/AND
## THE CHILDREN SHALL LEAD **            PG
John Meredyth Lucas/Marvin J. Chomsky
                   USA                    1968
*William Shatner, Leonard Nimoy, DeForest Kelley,*
*James Doohan, George Takei, Walter Koenig, Nichelle*
*Nichols, Joanne Linville, Melvin Belli, Craig Hundley,*
*James Wellman*
The first of these stories sees Kirk ordering his ship
into the Romulan neutral zone where it is captured,
the second finds the crew of the Enterprise brought by
a distress call to the planet Triacus, where an alien
creature finds a way of manipulating them through
fear.
FAN                                98 min mTV
V/h                                         CIC

## STAR TREK: THE GALILEO SEVEN/COURT
## MARTIAL **                            PG
Robert Gist/Marc Daniels
                   USA                    1967
*William Shatner, Leonard Nimoy, DeForest Kelley,*
*James Doohan, George Takei, Nichelle Nichols, Don*
*Marshall, John Crawford, Peter Marko, Phyllis*
*Douglas, Grant Woods, Percy Rodriguez, Elisha Cook*
*Jr*
Two further episodes from the popular TV series. In
"The Galileo Seven" Spock gains his first independent
command, but finds himself under attack from the
inhabitants of Taurus II. In "Court Martial" the death
of a fellow officer is blamed on Kirk, and he is put on
trial for negligence.
FAN                                98 min mTV
V                                           CIC

## STAR TREK: THE MAN TRAP/THE NAKED      PG
## TIME **
                   USA                    1966
*William Shatner, Leonard Nimoy, DeForest Kelley,*
*James Doohan, George Takei, Nichelle Nichols, Walter*
*Koenig, Jeanne Bal, Alfred Ryder, Michael Zaslow,*
*Bruce Watson, Vince Howard, Stewart Moss, John*
*Bellah, Bruce Hyde*
In the first of these episodes an alien being threatens
the lives of the crew of the Enterprise, and in the
second Spock and Kirk are obliged to confront their
innermost fears.
FAN                                98 min mTV
V                                           CIC

## STAR TREK: THE MENAGERIE ***          PG
Marc Daniels       USA                    1966
*William Shatner, Leonard Nimoy, Jeffrey Hunter,*
*Susan Oliver, Meg Wylie, Malachi Throne, Julie*
*Parrish, Majel Barrett, John Hoyt, Peter Duryea,*
*Hagen Beggs*
The only two-part episode from the original TV series,
which has Spock on trial for mutiny, after he took
control of the Enterprise and "kidnapped" Captain
Pike, the ship's former commander. This episode
makes considerable use of footage from the original
pilot episode – STAR TREK: THE CAGE, in which the
first captain of the Enterprise was imprisoned on a
strange planet, by creatures that live off the emotions
of others.
FAN                          93 min (ort 98 min) mTV
V                                           CIC

## STAR TREK: THE NEXT GENERATION 1 **    U
Corey Allen        USA                    1987
*Patrick Stewart, Jonathan Frakes, LeVar Burton,*
*Denise Crosby, Brent Spiner, Gates McFadden,*
*Marina Sirtis, John De Lancie, Michael Bell, Colm*

*Meaney, DeForest Kelley, Cary-Hirooyuki, Timothy Dang, David Erskine*
The first in a series of new "Star Trek" adventures, "Encounter At Farpoint" is set 85 years after the time of Captain Kirk, and tells of how the crew of the new Enterprise are sent on a mission, to determine whether a space station can be used as a new Starfleet base.
FAN                                            91 min mTV
V/sh                                                 CIC

## STAR TREK: THE NEXT GENERATION 2 **    PG
Russ Mayberry/Paul Lynch
             USA                               1987
*Patrick Stewart, Jonathan Frakes, LeVar Burton, Gates McFadden, Wil Wheaton, Karole Selmon, James Louis Watkins, Jessie Lawrence, Michael Rider, Brooke Bundy, David Renan, Skip Stellrecht, Kenny Koch*
Two episodes from a new series of "Star Trek" adventures – "Code Of Honor" and "The Naked Time", in which the crew of the Enterprise come across an abandoned spaceship that contains a few corpses but no survivors.
FAN                                            88 min mTV
V/sh                                                 CIC

## STAR TREK: THE NEXT GENERATION 3 **    PG
Richard Colla/Rob Bowman
             USA                               1987
*Jonathan Frakes, Patrick Stewart, Wil Wheaton, LeVar Burton, Brent Spiner, Gates McFadden, Marina Sirtis, Darryl Henriques, Armin Shimerman, Tracey Walter, Jake Dengel, Mike Domez, Stanley Kamel, Eric Menyuk, Herta Ware*
Two more adventures from the TV series. In "Last Outpost" Commander Ryker has to face an alien inquisition in order to free his crew, and in "Where No One Has Gone Before" the crew of the Enterprise find themselves taken to a distant galaxy by an alien visitor. A watchable blend of fair effects and wooden acting.
FAN                                            89 min mTV
V/sh                                                 CIC

## STAR TREK: THE NEXT GENERATION 4 **    PG
James L. Conway/Cliff Bole
             USA                      1987
*Patrick Stewart, Jonathan Frakes, LeVar Burton, Denise Crosby, Brent Spiner, Gates McFadden, Marina Sirtis, Kavi Raz, Colm Meaney, John Durbin*
Two episodes from the popular TV series: "Lonely Among Us" and "Justice". In the first story two very different alien lifeforms send representatives to attend a Federation peace conference and in the second tale, a Ferengi captain uses a thought-controlling device to have his revenge on Captain Picard, whom he blames for the death of his son.
FAN                                            89 min mTV
V/sh                                                 CIC

## STAR TREK: THE NEXT GENERATION 5 *    PG
Rob Bowman/Cliff Bole
             USA                               1987
*Patrick Stewart, Jonathan Frakes, LeVar Burton, Denise Crosby, Brent Spiner, Gates McFadden, Michael Dorn, Elaine Nalee, William A. Wallace, Majel Barrett. Rob Knepper, Nan Martin, Robert Ellenstein, Carel Struycken*
These two episodes are entitled "The Battle" and "Hide And Q". In the first the ship's captain meets up with an old enemy and in the second a strange force disables the Enterprise.
FAN                                            89 min mTV
V                                                    CIC

## STAR TREK: THE NEXT GENERATION 6 **    PG
Joseph L. Scanlon/Richard Crompton
             USA                               1987

*Patrick Stewart, Jonathan Frakes, LeVar Burton, Denise Crosby, Brent Spiner, Gates McFadden, Marina Sirtis, Wil Wheaton, Michael Dorn*
Two more stories from the new series of "Star Trek" adventures, entitled "The Big Goodbye" and "Haven", in which the Enterprise meets another vessel whose crew are suffering from a deadly disease.
FAN                                            89 min mTV
B,V                                                  CIC

## STAR TREK: THE NEXT GENERATION 7 **
Rob Bowman/Michael Rhodes
             USA                               1987
*Patrick Stewart, Jonathan Frakes, LeVar Burton, Denise Crosby, Brent Spiner, Gates McFadden, Marina Sirtis, Wil Wheaton, Michael Dorn*
These two episodes are entitled "Datalore" and "Angel One", with the latter telling of a mission to pick up survivors of a crippled vessel, that leads the Enterprise to a planet ruled by women.
FAN                                            89 min mTV
B,V                                                  CIC

## STAR TREK: THE NEXT GENERATION 8 **    U
Paul Lynch/Michael Vejar
             USA                               1987
*Patrick Stewart, Jonathan Frakes, LeVar Burton, Denise Crosby, Brent Spiner, Gates McFadden, Marina Sirtis, Wil Wheaton*
Two more adventures from this series. "11001001" tells of a race of creatures who live in symbiosis with computers, and contrive to steal the Enterprise by meddling with its computer. "Coming Of Age" tells of an investigation of Captain Picard mounted by Starfleet Command, and of how another crew member was tested for a place in the Cadet Academy. Average.
FAN                       88 min (ort 90 min) mTV
B,V                                                  CIC

## STAR TREK: THE NEXT GENERATION 9 **    PG
Rob Bowman/Kim Manners
             USA                               1987
*Patrick Stewart, Jonathan Frakes, LeVar Burton, Denise Crosby, Brent Spiner, Gates McFadden, Marina Sirtis, Wil Wheaton, Michael Dorn*
Episodes are entitled "Hearts Of Glory" and "When The Bough Breaks", which tells of a visit by the Enterprise to a seemingly peaceful planet that hides a sinister secret.
FAN                                            89 min mTV
B,V                                                  CIC

## STAR TREK: THE NEXT GENERATION 14 *    PG
Maurice Hurley/Cliff Bole
             USA                               1989
*Patrick Stewart, Jonathan Frakes*
Two episodes from the new (and vastly inferior) Star Trek series entitled "Q Who?" and "The Emissary", the latter story telling of the Enterprise's interception of a Klingon battleship whose occupants have been kept in suspended animation for 70 years.
FAN                                            89 min mTV
V                                                    CIC

## STAR TREK: THE ULTIMATE COMPUTER/THE OMEGA GLORY ***    U
John Meredyth Lucas/Vincent McEveety
             USA                               1968
*William Shatner, Leonard Nimoy, DeForest Kelley, James Doohan, George Takei, Nichelle Nichols, Sabrina Scharf, Rudy Solari, Morgan Woodward, Roy Jensen, David L. Ross, Ed McCready, Irene Kelly*
The first of these adventures deals with a super-intelligent computer that is installed in the Enterprise to replace its human crew, but goes berserk and becomes a dangerous menace. The second story sees the Enterprise crew picking up a strange warning from a deserted starship that leads Kirk to beam down

to a planet surface where one man claims to have the secret of immortality.

FAN 98 min mTV
V/h CIC

## STAR TREK: THE WORLD IS HOLLOW AND I HAVE TOUCHED THE SKY/DAY OF THE DOVE ** PG
Tony Leader/Marvin Chomsky
USA 1968
*William Shatner, Leonard Nimoy, DeForest Kelley, James Doohan, George Takei, Walter Koenig, Nichelle Nichols, Kate Woodville, Michael Ansara, Susan Howard, David L. Rose*
The first of these adventures sees McCoy, who has just learned he has a year to live, submitting to enslavement by the alien queen of a mysterious asteroid; while the second story concerns a strange presence that invades and Enterprise, and nearly causes a catastrophe with its ability to "feed" on hostility.

FAN 98 min mTV
V CIC/CBSDIS

## STAR TREK: THIS SIDE OF PARADISE/ PG THE DEVIL IN THE DARK **
Ralph Senensky/Joseph Pevney
USA 1967
*William Shatner, Leonard Nimoy, DeForest Kelley, James Doohan, George Takei, Nichelle Nichols, Walter Koenig, Jill Ireland, Frank Overton, Dick Scotter, Grant Woods, Ken Lynch, Barry Russo, Brad Weston, Biff Elliott*
In the first of these tales the Enterprise attempts an exploration of a strange planet whose appearance is deceptive, and the second story tells of a mining operation on the planet Janus VI, which is threatened by attacks from an alien creature.

FAN 98 min mTV
V/h CIC

## STAR TREK: TOMORROW IS YESTERDAY/ PG RETURN OF THE ARCHONS **
USA 1978
*William Shatner, Leonard Nimoy, DeForest Kelley, James Doohan, George Takei, Nichelle Nichols, Walter Koenig, Roger Perry, Ed Peck, Hal Lynch, Richard Merrifield, Harry Townes, Torin Thatcher, Charles Macauley, Christopher Held*
In the first of these tales the Enterprise is transported back in time to the 20th century and in the second, a planet populated by strange zombie-like people is investigated by Captain Kirk.

FAN 98 min mTV
V/h CIC

## STAR TREK: WHAT ARE LITTLE GIRLS PG MADE OF: DAGGER OF THE MIND **
James Goldstone/Vincent McEveety
USA 1966
*William Shatner, Leonard Nimoy, DeForest Kelley, James Doohan, George Takei, Nichelle Nichols, Walter Koenig, Michael Strong, Harry Basch, Ted Cassidy, Sherry Jackson, James Gregory, Marianna Hill, Morgan Woodward*
The first of these stories follows Kirk as he sets out to find a missing scientist on a distant planet, and the second has the crew of the Enterprise in grave danger when they visit the planet Tantalus, which contains a penal colony.

FAN 98 min mTV
V/h CIC

## STAR TREK: WHERE NO MAN HAS GONE BEFORE/THE CORBOMITE MANEUVER *** U
James Goldstone/Joseph Sargent
USA 1966
*William Shatner, Leonard Nimoy, DeForest Kelley,*

*James Doohan, George Takei, Nichelle Nichols, Gary Lockwood, Paul Carr, Sally Kellerman, Paul Fix, Lloyd Haynes, Anthony Call, Clint Howard, Ted Cassidy (voice only)*
In the first of these stories, the Enterprise is ordered to penetrate beyond the region of explored space, but after passing through a strange force-field a crew member begins to mutate into a being with unlimited powers. The second adventure concerns an alien space-craft that appears to pose a threat to the Enterprise.

FAN 96 min mTV
V CIC

## STAR TREK: WHO MOURNS FOR ADONAIS/ PG AMOK TIME **
Marc Daniels/Joseph Pevney
USA 1967
*William Shatner, Leonard Nimoy, DeForest Kelley, James Doohan, George Takei, Nichelle Nichols, Walter Koenig*
In the first of these "Star Trek" stories Captain Kirk has to confront Apollo, the last of the Greek gods, and in the second tale the Enterprise takes Spock back to the planet Vulcan, in order for him to participate in a strange marriage ritual.

FAN 98 min mTV
V/h CIC

## STAR VIRGIN *
Linus Gator USA 1979
*Mike Ranger, Johnny Harden, Karl Black, Tracy Walton, Jeanette Harlow*
Plotless series of sexual encounters, ranging from a high school football game to a surrealistic black and white vampire sequence.

A 90 min Colour and B/W
V RIP

## STAR WARS *** U
George Lucas USA 1977
*Mark Hamill, Harrison Ford, Carrie Fisher, Alec Guinness, Dave Prowse, Peter Cushing, Anthony Daniels, Kenny Baker, Peter Mayhew, Phil Brown, Eddie Byrne, Shelagh Fraser, James Earl Jones (voice of Darth Vader)*
SF blockbuster with heroic rebels fighting a corrupt galactic empire of long ago. Features aliens, robots, spaceships and much more. Shallow but good fun. Written by Lucas with THE EMPIRE STRIKES BACK and THE RETURN OF THE JEDI following. AA: Art/Set (Barry et al./Christian), Cost (Mollo), Edit (Hirsch/Lucas/Chew), Score (Orig) (Williams), Effects (Vis) (Stears et al.), Sound (MacDougall et al.), Spec Award (B. Burtt Jr for sound effects).

FAN 116 min (ort 121 min)
V/s CBS

## STARBIRD AND SWEET WILLIAM
Jack Hively USA 1976
*A. Martinez, Louise Fitch, Ancil Cook*
A grizzly bear cub and a raccoon help a young Indian to survive in the wild, when he is stranded there after a plane crash. A pleasant family adventure.

A/AD 90 min
B,V VCL/CBS

## STARBIRDS *
USA 1980
Animated space-age story about Earth's struggle against alien invaders.

CAR 72 min
B,V DFS

## STARCHASER: THE LEGEND OF ORIN *** PG
Steven Hahn USA 1985
*Voices of: Joe Colligan, Carmen Argenziano, Noelle North, Anthony Delongis, Les Tremayne, Tyke*

*Carvelli, Ken Sanson, John Moschitta Jr, Mickey Morton, Herb Vigran, Dennis Alwood, Mona Marshall, Tina Romanus, Ryan MacDonald*
Animated story of an evil intergalactic ruler, who tries to enslave Earth but is baulked by our hero. A solid and entaining kid's adventure. The imaginative use of 3-D will not translate well to TV.
CAR                      100 min (ort 107 min)
B,V                                        EIV

## STARCRASH *                              PG
Lewis Coates (Luigi Cozzi)
                         ITALY            1979
*Marjoe Gortner, Caroline Munro, Christopher Plummer, David Hasselhoff, Joe Spinell, Robert Tessier, Hamilton Camp (voice only)*
A very poor story in which three space adventurers are out to save the planet from domination, at the hands of a power-mad megalomaniac. Inferior even to those 1930s serials such as "Flash Gordon" and the like.
FAN                   95 min; 93 min (VGM)
B,V              VIPCO L/A; VGM (VHS only)

## STARCROSSED *                            PG
Jeffrey Bloom            USA             1984
*James Spader, Belinda Bauer, Clark Johnson, Peter Kowanko, Jacqueline Brookes, Edward Groenenberg, Chuck Shamata, James Kidnie, Fred Lee, Barbara Barnes, Andy Maton*
An extra-terrestrial falls in love with an earthling while being pursued by alien assassins. A dumb clone of STARMAN with a gender change.
FAN                    95 min (ort 100 min) mTV
B,V                                        CBS

## STARDUST ***                             15
Michael Apted            UK              1974
*David Essex, Adam Faith, Larry Hagman, Keith Moon, Dave Edmunds, Ines Des Longchamps, Rosalind Ayres, Marty Wilde, Edd Byrnes, Paul Nicholas, Karl Howman, Rick Lee Parmentier, Peter Duncan, John Normington, Dave Daker*
An excellent sequel to THAT'LL BE THE DAY charting the career and inevitable decline of a rock group's lead singer. Well made, well acted and very enjoyable. The script is by Ray Connolly and musical direction is by Dave Edmunds and David Puttnam.
DRA                    97 min (ort 111 min)
B,V                                       TEVP

## STARDUST MEMORIES ***                    15
Woody Allen              USA             1980
*Woody Allen, Charlotte Rampling, Jessica Harper, Marie-Christine Barrault, Tony Roberts, Daniel Stern, Laraine Newman, Amy Wright, Helen Hanft, Louise Lasser*
A Woody Allen look at life – a film producer attends a weekend conference and is pursued by fans, producers, lovers, relatives etc. One of Allen's most uneven and self-indulgent films, but there are some sharp and witty moments. As ever, Allen writes and directs.
DRA                    85 min (ort 88 min) B/W
V                                          WHV

## STARFLIGHT ONE **                        U
Jerry Jameson            USA             1983
*Lee Majors, Hal Linden, Lauren Hatton, Ray Milland, Gail Strickland, Robert Webber, George Di Cenzo, Tess Harper, Terry Kiser, Heather McAdam, Michael Sacks, Gary Bayer, Pat Corley, Jocelyn Brando, Diane Stilwell, Peter Jason*
A new type of aircraft accidentally goes into orbit and has to be rescued. The special effects are by John Dykstra, but they fail to compensate for the overlong and humdrum script.
Aka: STARFLIGHT: THE PLANE THAT COULDN'T LAND

Boa: story by Peter R. Brooke and Gene Warren.
DRA              155 min (ort is 180 min) mTV
B,V                                        RNK

## STARHOPS **                              15
Barbara Peeters          USA             1978
*Dorothy Buhrman, Sterling Frazier, Jillian Kesner, Peter Paul Liapis, Paul Ryan, Anthony Mannino, Dick Miller*
Three waitresses at a drive-in pool their savings to go into business for themselves. A simple little tale somewhat hampered by a clear lack of money. The script is by Stephanie Rothman.
DRA                    78 min (ort 92 min)
B,V,V2                       INT L/A VEXCEL

## STARLIGHT HOTEL ***                      PG
Sam Pillsbury    NEW ZEALAND             1987
*Peter Phelps, Greer Robson, Marshall Napier, The Wizard, Alice Fraser, Patrick Smyth*
An unhappy teenager strikes up an unlikely friendship with a disturbed veteran from WW1 in this warmhearted and unusual tale. The excellent photography is by Warrick Attewell.
DRA                                      93 min
B,V                                       COLS

## STARMAN ***                              PG
John Carpenter           USA             1984
*Jeff Bridges, Karen Allen, Richard Jaeckel, Charles Martin Smith, Robert Phalen, Tony Edwards, John Water Davis, Ted White, Dirk Blocker, Sean Faro, M.C. Gainey, George Buck Flower, Russ Benning, Ralph Cosham, Jim Deeth*
Some splendid special effects are used in this story, of an alien visitor sent to investigate the Earth as a result of the 1970's Voyager II space probe. He assumes the form of a woman's dead husband and she falls in love with him, and shelters him from inquisitive government agents. Bridges plays to perfection the part of a creature slowly learning to be human. The action is set in Wisconsin. Later a TV series.
FAN                   110 min (ort 115 min)
V/sh                                       RCA

## STARS AND BARS **                        15
Pat O'Connor             USA             1988
*Daniel Day Lewis, Martha Plimpton, Harry Dean Stanton, Maury Chaykin, Joan Cusack, Matthew Cowles, Keith David, Spalding Gray, Glenne Headly, Deidre O'Connell, Will Patton, Steven Wright, Laurie Metcalf, Rockets Redglare*
A British art collector goes to the USA to purchase a long-lost Renoir from an eccentric Southern family, and instead finds himself meeting a succession of weird characters. A mildly amusing comedy of little substance but one or two funny cameos.
COM                                      91 min
B,V                                        RCA

## STARSTRUCK *                             PG
Gillian Armstrong  AUSTRALIA            1982
*Jo Kennedy, Ross O'Donovan, Pat Evison, Margo Lee, Max Cullen, John O'May*
A teenage boy works hard to promote the career of his rock singer cousin. A tongue-in-cheek outing that's not very funny or enjoyable despite some good reviews.
COM                    95 min (ort 102 min)
B,V                                        EIV

## START THE REVOLUTION WITHOUT ME **      PG
Bud Yorkin               USA             1969
*Donald Sutherland, Gene Wilder, Hugh Griffith, Jack MacGowran, Billie Whitelaw, Victor Spinetti, Orson Welles, Ewa Aulin*
Two pairs of twins are separated at birth – one pair are raised as peasants, the others as aristocrats. Set in

the period just prior to the French Revolution. A historical spoof that sank without a trace in the 1970s but now has a minor cult following. Fair, but certainly not hilarious.

| | |
|---|---|
| COM | 90 min |
| B,V | WHV |

**STARTING OVER **              15
Alan J. Pakula          USA          1979
*Burt Reynolds, Jill Clayburgh, Candice Bergen, Charles Durning, Austin Pendleton, Frances Sternhagen, Mary Kay Place, Wallace Shawn*
A divorced man in love with a teacher is still haunted by his feelings for his ex-wife. A shallow comedy-drama with the stars making the most of the thin script. Written by James L. Brooks with music by Marvin Hamlisch.
Boa: novel by Dan Wakefield.

| | |
|---|---|
| COM | 101 min (ort 106 min) |
| V/h | CIC |

**STATE FAIR ***              U
Walter Lang          USA          1945
*Dana Andrews, Jeanne Crain, Dick Haymes, Vivian Blaine, Fay Bainter, Charles Winninger, Frank McHugh, Percy Kilbride, Donald Meek*
A charming remake of the 1933 film telling of the adventures of a family out for the day at the Iowa State Fair. A cheerful and attractive film, its fine Rodgers and Hammerstein songs (their only film score), include "A Grand Night For Singing" and "That's For Me" as well as the Oscar-winner. The film was retitled for TV. AA: Song ("It Might As Well Be Spring" – Richard Rodgers – music/Oscar Hammerstein II – lyrics).
Aka: IT HAPPENED ONE SUMMER

| | |
|---|---|
| MUS | 100 min |
| V | CBS |

**STATE OF DIVISION ***              
David Lowell Rich          USA          1973
*Lloyd Bridges, Roy Thinnes, Eric Braeden, Doug McClure, Dennis Rucker, Christopher Cary, Brendon Boone, Ivor Burry, Dennis Dugan, William Beckley, Eric Micklewood*
Set in North Africa against the background of Rommel's retreat after El Alamein, this is an uninspired war film telling of two Americans in a damaged fighter plane who have to face German tanks. The Milton Rosen score was originally written for a 1967 film – "The Young Warriors".
Aka: DEATH RACE

| | |
|---|---|
| WAR | 90 min mTV |
| B,V | EAG |

**STATE OF EMERGENCY, A ***              PG
Richard Bennett          USA          1986
*Martin Sheen, Peter Firth, Tim Pigott-Smith, Frances Tomelty, Kenneth Haigh, Dudley Sutton, Fionnula Flanagan*
A brilliant scientist learns that under the right conditions a single nuclear explosion could destroy all life on the planet. He sets out to warn the super-powers before it's too late. Average.
Aka: CHAIN REACTION

| | |
|---|---|
| THR | 100 min |
| B,V | TGP |

**STATIC ***              15
Mark Romanek          USA          1986
*Keith Gordon, Amanda Plumber, Bob Gunton, Barton Heyman, Lily Knight, Jane Hoffman, Reathel Bean, Kitty Mei-Mei, Eugene Lee, Joel K. Rehbeil, Jack Murakami, Mike Murakami, Uma Ridenhour, Janice Abbott, Tamma Allgood*
Critically acclaimed off-beat film, involving an obsessive inventor who claims to have produced a TV that tunes into Heaven, but most people only see a blank screen and hear static. An incoherent comedy-drama

that has some poignant and funny moments but for most of the time has a lot in common with that blank screen. Written by Gordon and Romanek.

| | |
|---|---|
| DRA | 90 min (ort 93 min) |
| B,V | VES |

**STAY HUNGRY ***              18
Bob Rafelson          USA          1976
*Jeff Bridges, Sally Field, Arnold Schwarzenegger, R.G. Armstrong, Roger E. Mosley, Helena Kallianiotes, Scatman Crothers, Ed Begley Jr, Gary Godorow, Joanna Cassidy, Robert Englund, Fannie Flagg, Richard Gilliland*
A wealthy heir to an Alabama estate is not interested in the family business but becomes involved with body builders, when he is sent on a crooked mission to buy up a health club. A curious and rather meaningless story, with good performances but no clear direction. Written by Rafelson and Charles Gaines.
Boa: novel by Charles Gaines.

| | |
|---|---|
| DRA | 103 min |
| B,V | WHV |

**STAY TUNED FOR MURDER ***              15
Gary W. Jones          USA          1988
*Tery Reeves-Wolf, Christopher Ginnaven, B.J. Hardin, Dominique St Croix*
A woman TV reporter makes herself a target when she presents a story on a crooked lawyer and his links with the financial establishment.

| | |
|---|---|
| THR | 86 min (ort 92 min) Cut (27 sec) |
| B,V | CINE |

**STAYING ALIVE ***              PG
Sylvester Stallone          USA          1983
*John Travolta, Cynthia Rhodes, Finola Hughes, Stevie Inwood, Julie Bovasso, Frank Stallone*
An aspiring Broadway dancer has problems with both his girlfriend and his leading lady, in this sequel to the hugely successful SATURDAY NIGHT FEVER that offers little of the vigour of the earlier film, except for the "Satan's Alley" finale. Written by Stallone and Norman Wexler.

| | |
|---|---|
| MUS | 92 min (ort 96 min) |
| B,V | CIC |

**STAYING ON ***              PG
Silvio Narizzano/Waris Hussein
UK          1980
*Trevor Howard, Celia Johnson, Saeed Jaffrey, Zia Mohyeddin, Pearl Padamsee, Ajit Saldanha*
An elderly British couple stay on in India after its independence, passing their days quietly at a small Himalayan hill-station. An engaging character study.
Boa: novel by Paul Scott.

| | |
|---|---|
| DRA | 87 min mTV |
| B,V | GRN |

**STEAGLE, THE ***              
Paul Sylbert          USA          1971
*Richard Benjamin, Chill Willis, Cloris Leachman, Sandra Giles, Susan Tyrell, Jean Allison*
During the Cuban missile crisis a college professor decides to recreate his nostalgic 1940s fantasies on a trip from Long Island to Hollywood. An offbeat and unconvincing tale.

| | |
|---|---|
| DRA | 90 min |
| B,V | EHE |

**STEAL THE SKY ***              
John Hancock          USA          1988
*Mariel Hemingway, Ben Cross, Sasson Gabai, Mark Rolston, Nicolas Surovy, Ronald Guttman, Sam Gray*
An American spy is recruited by Israeli Intelligence, in order for her to seduce an Iraqi pilot and get him to fly his MIG fighter plane to Israel. As implausible as it is contrived, but partially sustained by some good

aerial sequences.

A/AD            105 min (ort 120 min) mCab
V                                CIC

### STEALING HEAVEN ***       15
                                          1989
*Kim Thomson, Derek De Lint, Denholm Elliott*
A lavishly-shot film version of the story of the 12th century love story of Abelard and Heloise, with the former a young cleric who falls hopelessly in love with Heloise, who has been promised in marriage to the highest bidder by her rich uncle. When she becomes pregnant, a gruesome revenge is taken on her lover. Always a pleasure to watch, this film is perhaps a trifle overlong and it not quite as well acted as it might have been.
DRA                          111 min
V                               20VIS

### STEALING HOME **       15
Steven Kampmann/Will Aldis
                   USA               1988
*Mark Harmon, Jodie Foster, Blair Brown, Harold Ramis, William McNamara, John Shea*
A 1940s coming-of-age tale in which a former baseball player looks back over the years, dwelling on his experiences with the attractive babysitter who changed his life. A muddled, aimless and rather pointless film.
DRA             94 min (ort 98 min)
V/sh                            WHV

### STEAMIE, THE **         PG
                  UK               1989
*Eileen McCallum, Dorothy Paul, Katy Murphy*
Comedy set in 1953 and built around a communal wash-house and the women using it on the eve of their annual Hogmanay celebration.
Boa: play by Tony Roper.
COM                           85 min
V                                CH5

### STEAMING *            18
Joseph Losey           UK               1985
*Vanessa Redgrave, Sarah Miles, Diana Dors, Patti Love, Brenda Bruce, Sally Sagoe, Felicity Dean, Anna Tzelniker*
A dreary adaptation of a play set in a women's Turkish baths, in which a motley collection of women unite across class (always a feature of British films) and age barriers to prevent the closure of their baths. The last film for both Losey and Dors. Scripted by Patricia Losey.
Boa: play by Nell Dunn.
DRA             92 min (ort 95 min)
B,V                           RCA

### STEEL **           15
Steve Carver         USA            1980
*Lee Majors, Jennifer O'Neill, Art Carney, George Kennedy, Harris Yulin, Terry Kiser, Richard Lynch, Roger Mosley, Albert Salmi, R.G. Armstrong*
A vigorous construction yarn, telling of workers who struggle to complete a skyscraper on time and battle various hazards and dangers. A kind of macho soap opera, with an abundance of labour disputes, spectacular explosions, heroics etc. Implausible but quite entertaining.
Aka: LOOK DOWN AND DIE; MEN OF STEEL
DRA            97 min (ort 99 min)
V                               RCA

### STEEL ARENA **       PG
Mark Lester          USA           1972
*Dusty Russell, Laura Brooks, Gene Drew, Buddy Love, Dutch Schnitzer*
A look at the hazard-filled world of stunt car driving, built around the exploits of Dusty Russell, and following his career from demolition derby days, to his

later performances as star of the Circus of Death auto show.
A/AD                          99 min
B,V                           VES

### STEEL CLAW, THE ***            
George Montgomery     USA           1961
*George Montgomery, Charito Luna, Mario Barri, Paul Sorenson, Amelia de la Rama*
An American soldier in WW2 Philippines loses his hand (hence the title) but not his bravery, turning partisan leader after his discharge so that he can carry on fighting. A solid and action-filled war tale.
WAR                         96 min
B,V                 ATA L/A; APX

### STEEL DAWN **         18
Lance Hool           USA            1987
*Patrick Swayze, Lisa Niemi Swayze, Anthony Zerbe, Christopher Neame, John Fujioka, Brion James, Brett Hool, Marcel Van Heerden, Arnold Vosloo, James Whyle, Russell Savadier*
A re-run of SHANE in a futuristic setting, with Swayze protecting an attractive farmer and her son from a bunch of villainous thugs. A derivative and fairly unappealing effort, filmed in the deserts of southern Africa.
FAN        96 min (ort 102 min) Cut (21 sec)
V/sh                           VIR

### STEEL MAGNOLIAS ***      PG
Herbert Ross         USA           1989
*Sally Field, Dolly Parton, Shirley MacLaine, Daryl Hannah, Olympia Dukakis, Julia Roberts, Tom Skerritt, Dylan McDermott, Kevin J. O'Connor, Sam Shepard, Bill McCutcheon*
A comedy-drama featuring an all-star cast, and following the lives of six friends who over several years, congregate at Parton's beauty-salon in a small Louisiana town. The film is light and cheerful to begin with, but becomes progressively more poignant and culminates with an emotion-charged ending. Written by Harling from his one-set play, the film lacks some of the wit and insight of the original, but remains highly entertaining.
Boa: play by Robert Harling.
DRA           113 min (ort 118 min) subH
V                               RCA

### STEEL WREATH **         15
Marvin Chomsky     USA           1971
*Telly Savalas, Sally Field, Anne Francis, Martin Sheen, Charles Cioffi, Joe Don Baker, Johnny Haymer, Harry Basch, Howard Dayton, Ned Glass, Angelo Rossito, Gregg Palmer*
A man recently released from prison comes back to his home town, having been hired by his brother to kill a rival. A sluggish and brutal exercise in moodiness, well directed if rather unappealing.
Aka: MONGO'S BACK IN TOWN
Boa: novel by E. Richard Johnson.
DRA                       83 min mTV
B,V                           SID

### STEELE JUSTICE *         18
Robert Boris         USA           1987
*Martin Kove, Sela Ward, Ronny Cox, Bernie Casey, Joseph Campanella, Jan Gan Boyd, Soon-Teck Oh, Robert Kim, Peter Kwong, Shannon Tweed, Sarah Douglas, Astrid Plane*
Yet another one of those Vietnam veteran revenge tales, with Kove investigating the murder of a former buddy and his family, and deciding to take on an ex-Vietnam general who has become a wicked drug baron. These films are being churned out in a factory somewhere.
A/AD                         95 min
B,V                           EIV

## STEELYARD BLUES ** 15
Alan Myerson        USA        1972
*Jane Fonda, Donald Sutherland, Peter Boyle, Garry Goodrow, Howard Hesseman, John Savage*
An assorted group of misfits plan to rebuild an abandoned seaplane and fly away to a better life. Their efforts are hampered by the local D.A. who is the brother of one of them. Funny in parts but disappointing overall. The script is by David S. Ward.
Aka: FINAL CRASH, THE
COM        89 min (ort 92 min)
B,V        WHV

## STELLA DALLAS *** U
King Vidor        USA        1937
*Barbara Stanwyck, John Boles, Anne Shirley, Barbara O'Neil, Alan Hale, Tim Holt, Marjorie Main*
A remake of a 1925 silent weepie, dealing with a woman who has to make great sacrifices for the sake of her daughter's happiness. Despite the mawkish nature of the script, an excellent performance from Stanwyck turns a rather mundane soap opera into a touching film of considerable power.
Boa: novel by Olive Higgins Prouty.
DRA        101 min (ort 106 min) B/W
V        VGM

## STEP LIVELY *** U
Tim Whelan        USA        1944
*Frank Sinatra, George Murphy, Adolphe Menjou, Gloria De Haven, Eugene Pallette, Anne Jeffreys, Walter Slezak*
A musical remake of "Room Service", with a producer having to wheel and deal as never before to get his show off the ground. A fast and furious romp with witty dialogue and good performances. Songs are by Jule Styne and Sammy Cahn with musical direction by Constantin Bakaleinikoff.
Boa: play Room Service by J. Murray and A. Boret.
MUS        85 min (ort 88 min) B/W
B,V        KVD; STABL

## STEPFATHER, THE *** 18
Joseph Ruben        USA        1987
*Terry O'Quinn, Shelley Hack, Jill Schoelen, Stephen Shellen, Charles Lanyer, Stephen E. Miller, Robyn Stevan, Jeff Schultz, Lindsay Bourne, Anna Hagan, Gillian Barber, Blu Mankuma, Jackson Davies, Sandra Head, Gabrielle Rose*
An apparently mild-mannered family man is in reality a ruthless and demented killer, who marries widows with children in a constant search for a "perfect" family, erupting into a murderous rage when they disappoint him. A frightening film with O'Quinn giving a chilling performance in his lead debut. Written by Donald Westlake.
HOR        86 min (ort 89 min)
B,V        VIR

## STEPFORD CHILDREN, THE * 15
Alan J. Levi        USA        1987
*Barbara Eden, Don Murray, Tammy Lauren, Randal Batikoff, Richard Anderson, Ken Swofford, Pat Corley, Dick Butkus, Sharon Spelman, James Coco*
A sequel of sorts to THE STEPFORD WIVES, with the nice men of Stepford now turning their attention to their children as well as their wives – replacing them with perfect android copies. A film that starts off slowly, gets progressively sillier and builds up to a ludicrous climax. Enjoy it as a comedy.
HOR        96 min (ort 100 min) mTV
B,V        PACE; SCRN

## STEPFORD WIVES, THE *** 15
Bryan Forbes        USA        1974
*Katherine Ross, Paula Prentiss, Peter Masterson, Nanette Newman, Patrick O'Neal, Tina Louise, Carol Rossen, William Prince, Carole Mallory, Barbara Rucker, Tonie Reid, Judith Baldwin, George Coe, Michael Higgins*
A couple newly arrived at a small Connecticut town find many of the young wives obsessively houseproud and totally obedient to their husbands, with new arrivals changing after a time too. A good idea with some genuinely horrific moments, but one that fails to work completely. Followed by two trashy sequels – "The Revenge Of The Stepford Wives" and THE STEPFORD CHILDREN. The script is by William Goldman.
Boa: novel by Ira Levin.
FAN        115 min; 110 min (VIR)
B,V        VCL/CBS L/A; VIR

## STEPHEN KING'S NIGHT SHIFT COLLECTION ** 15
Frank Darabont/Jeff C. Schiro/James Greco
        USA        1985
*Dee Croxton, Brian Libby, Michael Reid, Bert Linder, Mindy Silverman, Bob Brunson, George Russel, Terence Brady, Jerome Bynder, Bobby Persichetti, Michael Dagostino, Nancy Linderberg, James Holmes, John MacDonald, Dave Buff*
Three student films (two of which are based on Stephen King short stories), apparently made as amateur and film-school works. Tales are entitled: "The Woman In The Room", "The Bogeyman" and "Stranglehold", the latter written by James Greco.
Aka: NIGHTSHIFT
Boa: short stories by Stephen King.
HOR        90 min
B,V        VIR

## STEPS * PG
Lenny Hirschfield        USA        1972
*Irene Papas, Umberto Orsini*
A Greek survivor of the Nazi terror is haunted by the question of whether any of her family are still alive.
DRA        91 min
B,V        PRV

## STEPTOE AND SON * PG
Cliff Owen        UK        1972
*Wilfrid Brambell, Harry H. Corbett, Carolyn Seymour, Arthur Howard, Victor Maddern, Fred Griffiths, Queenie Watts, Patsy Smart, Alec Mango, Perri St Clare, Lon Satton, Vivien Lloyd, Mike Reid, Barry Ingham, Joan Heath*
A popular and very witty TV series about a father and son junkyard business, is brought rather unsuccessfully to the screen. When the son falls for a stripper it looks as though true love is only a whisker away, but taking his father on the honeymoon is not a very good idea. Pitifully weak and unfunny. Written by Ray Galton and Alan Simpson and followed by STEPTOE AND SON RIDE AGAIN.
Aka: STEPTOE AND SON: THE FEATURE
COM        93 min (ort 98 min) (Cut at film release)
B,V        TEVP L/A; WHV (VHS only)

## STEPTOE AND SON RIDE AGAIN * PG
Peter Sykes        UK        1973
*Harry H. Corbett, Wilfrid Brambell, Milo O'Shea, Diana Dors, Neil McCarthy, Bill Maynard, George Tovey, Sam Kydd, Yootha Joyce, Olga Lowe, Henry Woolf, Geoffrey Bayldon, Frank Thornton, Peter Thornton, Grazina Frame*
A follow-on to STEPTOE AND SON with our rag-and-bone man using his father's savings to buy a greyhound. A feeble attempt to build a full-length feature out of material, that would just about sustain an episode of the original and well-loved TV series "Steptoe And Son" (1964-73).
COM        95 min (ort 99 min)
V        WHV

## STEVIE ** 
Robert Enders        UK/USA        1978
*Glenda Jackson, Mona Washbourne, Trevor Howard,*

*Alex McCowen, Emma Louise Fox*
Biopic about the recluse and poetess Stevie Smith who won the Queen's award for poetry. A claustrophobic little film with limited appeal that will be enjoyed mostly by fans of Jackson and/or the woman she plays. Written by Whitemore.
Boa: play by Hugh Whitemore.
DRA                           102 min
B,V                            HVH

## STEWARDESS SCHOOL *                15
Ken Blancato          USA          1986
*Judy Landers, Mary Cadorette, Donald Most, Brett Cullen, Sandahl Bergman, Sherman Hemsley, Vicki Frederick, Corinne Bohrer, Julia Montgomery, Wendi Jo Sperber, Vito Scotti*
Now it's the turn of a training school for stewardesses to get the POLICE ACADEMY treatment. Limp and vulgar in equal measure.
COM                            92 min
B,V                             RCA

## STICK *                             18
Burt Reynolds         USA          1985
*Burt Reynolds, Candice Bergen, George Segal, Charles Durning, Jose Perez, Richard Lawson, Dar Robinson, Tricia Leigh Fisher, Castulo Guerra, Alex Rocco*
An ex-con released from prison seeks revenge for his friend's murder in a drugs deal that went wrong. A murky melodrama of little action but much introspection. Written by Leonard.
Boa: novel by Elmore Leonard.
THR            104 min (ort 109 min) Cut (13 sec)
V/sh                            CIC

## STICK, THE ***                      15
Darrell Roodt    SOUTH AFRICA      1988
*Greg Later, Sean Taylor, Frantz Dobrowsky, James Whyle, Nicky Villiers, Gys De Villiers, Frank Opperman, Dickson Malele, Winston Ntshona*
Set in South Africa, this follows the exploits of an army squad sent across the border to deal with the threat posed by a powerful native tribe. As they venture further into the bush the tension mounts and the fragile unity of the group is lost, with a series of atrocities committed on villagers leading to the inevitable retaliation. Written by Roodt and Carole Shore, this harsh and effective film is a little too contrived for its own good.
A/AD                           90 min
V                              PARK

## STICKY FINGERS *                    15
Catlin Adams          USA          1988
*Helen Slater, Melanie Mayron, Carol Kane, Danitra Vance, Eileen Brennan, Loretta Devine, Stephen McHattie, Christopher Guest, Gwen Welles, Shirley Stoler*
A failed attempt to produce a madcap comedy, with a couple of empty-headed female musicians coming into possession of a suitcase full of drug money and going on a wild spending spree. A frantic scrabble for laughs that gets ever more grating and disagreeable. Vigorous performances from the stars do nothing to redeem it. The script is by Adams and Mayron.
COM                    84 min (ort 97 min)
B,V                            VIR

## STIGMA **                           15
Barry Shear           USA          1975
*Mike Connors, Cameron Mitchell, James Darren, Diane Baker, Eddie Egan, David Ladd, Kim Richards*
Two cops are firm friends and honest officers, but when one is taken hostage by criminals the other sticks to police procedure, and in the ensuing shootout his friend is killed. Filled with self-doubt and guilt he begins to question the value of his training.
A/AD                           92 min
V                              RCA

## STILETTO **                         18
Bernard Kowalski      USA          1969
*Alex Cord, Britt Ekland, Patrick O'Neal, Joseph Wiseman, Roy Scheider, John Dehner, Barbara McNair, Eduardo Ciannelli*
A Mafia leader rescues a young rapist from a Mob and he later becomes a contract killer, leading a rich and unconcerned life until the day he decides that he would like to retire from his chosen profession. A flashy and depressing soap opera style gangland saga.
Boa: novel by Harold Robbins.
DRA          95 min (ort 101 min) Cut (35 sec)
B,V                            EHE

## STILL LIFE *                        15
Graeme Campbell       USA          1989
*Jessica Steen, Jason Gedrick, Stephen Shellen*
A TV art critic and her kooky friend are drawn into a series of murders in Lower Manhattan that are linked to the art world, when her musician boyfriend is framed. A contrived and not terribly effective murder mystery.
THR                            83 min
V                              RCA

## STILL OF THE NIGHT **               15
Robert Benton         USA          1982
*Meryl Streep, Roy Scheider, Jessica Tandy, Joe Grifasi, Sara Botsford, Josef Sommer, Rikke Borge, Irving Metzman, Larry Joshua, Tom Norton, John Bentley, Richmond Hoxie, Hyon Cho, Danielle Cusson, George A. Tooks, Sigrunn Omark*
A psychiatrist falls for a woman who might have killed one of his patients, in this Hitchcock-style murder mystery that lacks the latter's economy of direction. Written by Benton and David Newman.
DRA                    87 min (ort 91 min)
B,V                            WHV

## STILLWATCH **                       15
Rod Holcomb           USA          1986
*Angie Dickinson, Lynda Carter, Don Murray, Stuart Whitman, Louise Latham, Bibi Osterwald, Walter Olkewicz, Jack Heller, John Wesley, John M. Jackson, Eunice Christopher, Gary Werntz, Michael Dan Wagner, Dan Peters, Lin Shaye*
A female TV reporter begins to delve into the murky past of a senator and is plunged into a bizarre mystery, when she discovers a link with her own rented home, the scene of a murder many years before. A muddled and sluggish tale.
Boa: novel by Mary Higgins Clark.
THR            94 min (ort 100 min) mTV
B,V                           SHEER

## STING 2, THE **                     PG
Jeremy Paul Kagan     USA          1983
*Jackie Gleason, Mac Davis, Karl Malden, Teri Garr, Oliver Reed, Bert Remsen*
Sequel to THE STING with our two con-artists arranging a complicated fraud, this time a rigged boxing match, in order to put one over on a bigwig. A flat and unappealing tale in which the complexities of the plot overshadow the performances. Written by David S. Ward and with music by Lalo Schifrin.
COM                    98 min (ort 102 min)
B,V                            CIC

## STING, THE ***                      PG
George Ray Hill       USA          1973
*Paul Newman, Robert Redford, Robert Shaw, Charles Durning, Eileen Brennan, Harold Gould, Ray Walston, Dana Elcar, Jack Kehoe, Dimitra Arliss, Charles Dierkop*
Clever film about two con-men who set up a completely fake scenario in order to fleece a gangleader (played by a miscast Robert Shaw), who had one of their friends killed. Scott Joplin's music is used to good effect. THE STING 2 followed. AA: Pic, Dir, Art/Set

(Henry Bumstead/James Payne), Edit (William Reynolds), Cost (Edith Head), Story/Screen (David S. Ward), Score (Marvin Hamlisch).
COM                                    129 min
B,V                                        CIC

## STINGIEST MAN IN TOWN, THE **          U
Daniel Petrie            USA              1956
*Narrated by Walter Matthau*
Lighthearted, animated musical version of Dickens' famous tale. Fair.
Boa: story A Christmas Carol by Charles Dickens.
CAR                      51 min; 47 min (CH5)
B,V                        HER; CH5 (VHS only)

## STINGRAY **
Richard Taylor           USA              1978
*Christopher Mitchum, Sherry Jackson, Bill Watson, Les Lannom, Sondra Theodore, Bert Hinchman*
The title refers to a model of fast American sports car which two men in St Louis buy, without being aware that it conceals a fortune in cash and and drugs. As usual, the crooks give chase. An unattractive blend of comedy and violence, with a couple of good action sequences.
A/AD                     95 min (ort 100 min)
B,V,V2                              IFS; NET

## STINGRAY: INVADERS FROM THE DEEP **    U
David Elliott/John Kelly/Desmond Saunders
                          UK              1964
Captain Tempest and the crew of Stingray struggle to save an underwater city from alien invaders. A compilation feature made up from episodes of a popular TV puppet series of the 1960s.
Aka: INVADERS FROM THE DEEP
CAR                                      92 min
B,V,LV                     PRV; CH5 (VHS only)

## STIR CRAZY **                          15
Sidney Poitier           USA              1980
*Gene Wilder, Richard Pryor, Georg Stanford Brown, JoBeth Williams, Craig T. Nelson, Barry Corbin, Erland van Lidth de Jeude, Lee Purcell, Miguelangel Suarez*
Two unfortunate men are sent to jail by mistake, when the woodpecker outfits they were hired to wear to promote the opening of a new bank, are stolen and used to rob the bank. Once there they suffer the usual indignities, more so when the warden discovers that they can be persuaded to ride for him in a rodeo contest. An over-extended farce whose highlights are appearances by the massive (and melodious) de Jeude. Written by Bruce Jay Friedman.
COM                      106 min (ort 111 min)
B,V                        RCA; VCC (VHS only)

## STITCHES *                             18
Alan Smithee (Rod Holcomb)
                          USA              1985
*Parker Stevenson, Geoffrey Lewis, Eddie Albert, Brian Tochi, Robin Dearden*
Three medical students are far more interested in chasing nurses than in their studies at the Brantford School of Medicine. A feeble sex comedy that was badly edited after production, prompting the director to have his name removed from the credits.
COM                      87 min (ort 90 min)
B,V                                        MED

## STOCKS AND BLONDES ***                 18
Arthur Greenstands       USA              1984
*Leigh Wood, Veronica Hart, Jamie Kantor (Jamie Gillis), Dick Biel*
The story of Wanda Brandt, the ruthless and manipulative boss of Tyler Industries, who uses her sexuality in a meteoric rise to power in this well made

softcore tale.
A                                        78 min
B,V                                        VES

## STOGIES **                             15
Marty Davidson           USA              1987
*William L. Petersen, Virginia Madsen, Larry Riley, Dermot Mulroney*
A sentimental tale following the changing fortunes of a minor league baseball team in the 1950s. A tough and hard-drinking coach takes on a new catcher and turns the team into a success. All the expected cliches are here, plus a few more besides, but the movie is put together with a good deal of care.
Boa: novel by Paul Hemphill.
DRA                      107 min (ort 112 min)
B,V                                        GHV

## STONE **                               18
Sandy Harbutt    AUSTRALIA               1974
*Ken Shorter, Deryck Barnes, Sandy Harbutt, Helen Morse, Hugh Keays-Byrne, Vincent Gil*
A motorcycle cop investigating a political assassination becomes involved with a gang of bikers.
THR                      95 min (ort 100 min)
B,V                          VTC L/A; XTASY

## STONE COLD DEAD ***                    18
George Mendeluk    CANADA               1980
*Richard Crenna, Paul Williams, Linda Sorenson, Belinda J. Montgomery, George Chuvalo, Charles Shamata, Alberta Watson, Monique Mercure, Andree Cousineau, Frank Moore, Jennifer Dale, George Touliatos, Dennis Strong*
A taut and well-made crime drama with tough cop Crenna out to nail a ruthless mobster, played with equal conviction by Williams.
Aka: POINT TWO TWO
DRA                      98 min (ort 100 min)
B,V                                    EVI; KSV

## STONE KILLER, THE **                   18
Michael Winner           USA              1973
*Charles Bronson, Martin Balsam, David Sheiner, Norman Fell, Ralph Waite, Christina Raines, Stuart Margolin, John Ritter, Frank Campanella, Kelly Miles*
A police officer unravels a complex plot involving Vietnam veterans and a gangland boss. One of the director's customary violent offerings. Written by Gerald Wilson.
Boa: novel A Complete State Of Death by John Gardner.
THR                      91 min (ort 96 min)
V                                          RCA

## STONER *
Huang Feng        HONG KONG             1976
*George Lazenby, Angela Mao, Betty Ting Pei, Whang In-Sik, Joji Takagi, Hung Chin-Po*
A man and woman team of narcotic agents fights an underworld gang, in this violent and undistinguished crime thriller, typical of the vast bulk of Hong Kong productions.
THR                                      95 min
B,V                                        RNK

## STONES FOR IBARRA ***                  PG
Jack Gold                USA              1988
*Glenn Close, Keith Carradine, Alfonso Arau, Jorge Cervera Jr, Trindad Silva, Angie Porres*
A simple and quite touching story of an American couple, who move to a small Mexican village and re-open an inherited copper mine. When the husband is found to be suffering from cancer their dream of a better life is shattered. This perceptive and thoughtful film spends much time exploring the cultural gap between the newcomers and their Mexican neighbours.

Boa: novel by Harriett Doerr.
DRA                          96 min (ort 100 min) mTV
B,V                                        CINE; PARK

## STONING, A **                          15
Larry Elikann          USA                1988
*Ken Olin, Jill Eikenberry, Ron Perlman*
Story set in the Amish community with a young
Amish boy killed, following the taunts of four boys
from outside the community. No-one will testify and
though the D.A. is keen to prosecute, he finds that his
only witness is a young Amish girl whose parents do
not believe in secular courts. A rather clinical offering
which remains aloof and unmoving, despite good work
from the cast.
DRA                                        97 min
V/h                                           ODY

## STOPOVER TOKYO **                        U
Richard L. Breen       USA                1957
*Joan Collins, Robert Wagner, Edmond O'Brien, Ken
Scott, Reiko Oyama, Larry Keating, Sarah Selby, Solly
Nakamura, H. Okhawa, K.J. Seijto, Demmei Susuki,
Yuki Kaneko, Michei Miura*
An American intelligence agent in Japan discovers a
plot to assassinate the US ambassador there, but the
intended victim refuses to take the threat seriously.
The Japanese locations are very pretty, but the flabby
script and unconvincing performances get in the way.
Written by Breen and Walter Reisch.
Boa: novel by John P. Marquand.
THR                                      100 min B/W
V/h                                           CBS

## STORM *                                 15
David Winning          CANADA             1987
*David Palfry, Stan Kane, Harry Freedman, Lawrence
Elion, Tom Schider*
Following a robbery in the 1940s, two crooks bury
their loot in a forest and return for it forty years and a
prison sentence later. However, they are seen by two
students on a camping trip and set out to silence them.
A cumbersome and largely incoherent dud.
THR                          96 min (ort 99 min)
B,V                                           WHV

## STORM BOY ***
Henri Safran           AUSTRALIA          1976
*Peter Cummings, Grag Rowe, David Gulpilil, Judy
Dick, Michael Moody, Tony Allison, Graham Dow,
Frank Foster-Brown, Eric Mack, Michael Caulfield,
Paul Smith, Hedley Cullen*
Touching story of a boy and his friendship with an
Aborigine.
Boa: novel by Colin Thiele.
JUV                                        89 min
B,V                                           GHV

## STORM OVER ASIA ***                      PG
Vsevolod Pudovkin      USSR               1928
*I. Inkizhinov, Valeri Inkizhanov, A. Dedintsev, V.
Tzoppi, Paulina Belinskaya*
The British intervene in Mongolia in 1918 and
attempt to create a puppet government, headed by a
fur trapper who claims to be heir to Genghis Khan,
but who eventually rejects his imperialist role and
leads a rebellion. An unusual film of great beauty but
made with the expected political overtones. This was
Pudovkin's last major silent work, but a sound track
was added under his direction in 1950.
Aka: HEIR TO GENGHIS KHAN, THE; POTOMOK
CHINGIS-KHANA
DRA                        87 min (ort 149 min) B/W silent
V                                             HEND

## STORM OVER THE NILE **                   U
Terence Young/Zoltan Korda
                       UK                 1955
*Laurence Harvey, Anthony Steel, Ronald Lewis, Ian*

*Carmichael, James Robertson Justice, Mary Ure,
Geoffrey Keen, Jack Lambert, Ferdy Mayne, Michael
Hordern, Christopher Lee, Sam Kydd, John Wayne,
Avis Scott*
A remake of THE FOUR FEATHERS that fails to
provide a satisfying cinematic experience, despite
some good action sequences such as the Battle of
Omdurman. The use of stock footage from the original
does little for this film. Music is by Benjamin Frankel
and the script is by R.C. Sherriff.
Boa: novel The Four Feathers by A.E.W. Mason.
A/AD                                      111 min
B,V                                           CBS

## STORMQUEST **                           15
Alex Sessa                                1987
*Brent Huff, Kai Baker, Linda Lutz, Monica Gonzaga,
Rocky Giordani, Dudizile Mkhize*
A standard fantasy adventure telling of a female
dominated kingdom ruled by a despotic warrior
queen, and of a rebellion on the part of some men, who
escape from prison and battle to achieve freedom and
equality.
FAN                                        93 min
B,V                                           PAL

## STORMRIDER **                           18
Giancarlo Santi
              FRANCE/ITALY/WEST GERMANY    1972
*Lee Van Cleef, Peter O'Brien, Marc Mazza, Klaus
Grunberg, Horst Frank, Jess Hahn, Anthony Vernon,
Sandra Sandrini*
A veteran gunfighter becomes the protector of an
innocent young man, who was wrongfully convicted of
the murder of a gang leader, and together the pair
fight to free the town from the grip of this gang.
Average.
Aka: BIG SHOWDOWN, THE (VUL); DREI
VATERUNSER FUR VIER HALUNKEN; GRAND
DUEL, THE (VUL); IL GRANDE DUELLO; LE
GRAND DUEL
WES                          89 min (ort 93 min) Cut (3 sec)
B,V                 VFP L/A; OREG L/A; VUL L/A; DRUM

## STORMY MONDAY ***                        15
Mike Figgis            UK                 1988
*Melanie Griffith, Tommy Lee Jones, Sting (Gordon
Sumner), Sean Bean, James Cosmo, Mark Long, Brian
Lewis*
An atmospheric thriller set in Newcastle where Sting
is the owner of a nightclub, and a ruthless American
businessman arrives with the intention of making a
fortune from re-development of the area. A slowly-
paced but stylish film of little substance, with all the
leads performing well. Written by Figgis (who also did
the score) and with photography by Roger Deakins.
THR                          89 min (ort 93 min)
V/sh                                          VIR

## STORY OF DAVID, THE **                   PG
Alex Segal/David Lowell Rich
                       USA                1976
*Timothy Bottoms, Keith Michell, Anthony Quayle,
Jane Seymour, Susan Hampshire, Norman Rodway,
Oded Teumi, Mark Dignam, Yehuda Efroni, Tony
Tarruella, Ahuva Yuval, Irit Benzer, Avram Ben-
Yossef, Yakar Semach*
Biblical epic on the life of the boy king and his later
lust for Bathsheba. A carefully told but rather slug-
gish account, scripted by Ernest Kinoy. First shown in
two parts.
DRA                        183 min (ort 250 min) mTV
B,V                                           RCA

## STORY OF ESTHER **
                       USA                1979
*Victoria Principal, Michael Ansara, Robert Mandan,
Eddie Mekka, Noah Beery*
Part of the "Greatest Heroes of the Bible" series.

Average.
DRA                                    45 min
B,V                                  VCL/CBS

## STORY OF JESUS, THE **
Peter Sykes/John Kirsh
                    USA              1979
Brian Deacon, Rivka Noiman, Yossef Shiloah, Niko
Nitai, Gadi Roi, David Goldberg, Alexander Scourby
(narration)
Matter-of-fact portrayal of the life of Jesus. Filmed in
Israel and earnest but hardly enthralling.
Aka: JESUS
DRA                       110 min (ort 117 min)
B,V                                    TEVP

## STORY OF JOANNA ***
Gerard Damiano          USA          1975
Jamie Gillis, Terri Hall, Zebedy Colt, Juliet Graham,
Stephen Lark
A woman meets a moody and malevolent libertine in a
restaurant on the Continent, and is taken back to his
ancestral castle. She falls in love with him, despite his
affirmation that he can never love her in return.
Scenes of torture and degradation follow, but her
affection never wavers. Finally he reveals that he is
dying of cancer and wishes to die at the hands of a
woman who loves him. A strange, intense and decadent tale.
A                                      86 min
B,V                                    INT

## STORY OF O, THE **
Just Jaeckin            USA          1975
Udo Kier, Anthony Steel, Corrine Clery, Jean Gaven,
Martine Kelly, Alain Noury, Christianne Minazzoli, Li
Seligreen, Gabriel Cattand
Film version of an erotic novel about a woman who
gives herself body and soul to a lover, whose demands
become progressively more depraved. From the direc-
tor of the first EMMANUELLE film.
Boa: novel by Pauline Reage.
A                                      93 min
B,V,V2                                 INT

## STORY OF ROBIN HOOD AND HIS
## MERRIE MEN, THE **
Ken Annakin             UK           1952
Richard Todd, Joan Rice, James Hayter, James
Robertson Justice, Peter Finch, Hubert Gregg, Marita
Hunt, Anthony Forwood, Elton Hayes, Patrick Barr,
Bill Owen, Michael Hordern, Reginald Tate, Hal
Osmond, Anthony Eustrel
Yet another version of a famous legend, in which an
excellent cast do their best to breathe some life into
this story of the outlawed Earl of Sherwood, who leads
his band against the corrupt Sheriff of Nottingham in
the 12th century. Quite colourful but rather anaemic,
the legend having received the standard Disney
treatment.
Aka: STORY OF ROBIN HOOD, THE
A/AD                                   83 min
B,V                                    WDV

## STORY OF VERNON AND IRENE CASTLE,  U
## THE ***
H.C. Potter             USA          1939
Fred Astaire, Ginger Rogers, Edna May Oliver, Walter
Brennan, Lew Fields, Etienne Girardot, Janet Beecher,
Rolfe Sedan, Leonid Kiskey, Robert Strange, Douglas
Walton, Clarence Derwent, Sonny Lamont, Frances
Mercer
The last major film starring Astaire and Rogers, in
which they appear as a husband and wife team, who
achieve fame in Paris just before the outbreak of
WW1. Somewhat cramped by slow pacing but still a
pleasure to watch. Numbers include: "Little Brown
Jug", "Too Much Mustard" and "Only When You're In

My Arms".
Boa: books by Irene Castle.
MUS                       90 min (ort 93 min) B/W
V                                      VCC

## STOWAWAY ***                        U
William A. Seiter       USA          1936
Shirley Temple, Alice Faye, Robert Young, Eugene
Pallette, Helen Westley, Arthur Treacher, J. Edward
Bromberg, Astrid Allwyn
The orphan daughter of an American missionary
smuggles herself aboard a ship and has various
adventures. Young and Faye provide the romantic
interest. A good vehicle for Temple in which she
performs some enjoyable numbers, including a song in
Chinese. Songs are by Mack Gordon and Harry Revel,
with musical direction by Louis Silvers.
MUS                                    86 min B/W
V                                      CBS

## STOWAWAY IN THE SKY ***            U
Albert Lamorisse        FRANCE       1962
Pascal Lamorisse, Andre Gille, Maurice Baquet, Jack
Lemmon (narration)
Having sneaked aboard his grandfather's latest in-
vention, a sixty foot balloon, a youngster enjoys a
scenic tour of France. A pleasantly diverting tale from
the director of THE RED BALLOON.
JUV                                    82 min
V                                      BRAVE

## STRAIGHT TIME **                    18
Ulu Grosbard            USA          1978
Dustin Hoffman, Theresa Russell, Gary Busey, Harry
Dean Stanton, M. Emmet Walsh, Rita Taggart
A man released from prison goes steadily downhill
despite his best efforts to go straight. An absorbing
but rather unattractive tale that's sustained by its
performers. Hoffman started directing this one but
Grosbard took over. Scripted by Alvin Sargent, Ed-
ward Bunker and Jeffrey Boam.
Boa: novel No Beast So Fierce by E. Bunker.
DRA                                    114 min
B,V                                    WHV

## STRAIGHT TO HELL *                  15
Alex Cox                USA          1986
Sy Richardson, Dennis Hopper, Courtney Love, Elvis
Costello, Grace Jones, Joe Strummer, Dick Rude, Jim
Jarmusch, The Pogues
A dull Western spoof that attempts to parody Sergio
Leone's spaghetti epics, but which has nothing to
sustain it except some campy dialogue, and even that
soon loses its charm. Should be retitled Straight To
Oblivion.
WES                       83 min (ort 86 min)
B,V                                    NELS

## STRANDED **                         15
Tex Fuller              USA          1987
Ione Skye, Joe Morton, Maureen O'Sullivan, Susan
Barnes, Cameron Dye, Michael Green, Brendan
Hughes, Michael Burke
Aliens escape from one planet and risk capture on
another, but are given shelter by an independent-
minded old lady and her grand-daughter. Dye is the
young man also comes to their rescue, helping them
escape the clutches of a sheriff's posse and an other-
worldly assassin. Not a story that amounts to much,
though it has better characterisation than one usually
finds in an SF film.
FAN                       78 min (ort 80 min)
V                                      20VIS

## STRANGE AFFAIR OF UNCLE HARRY, THE **  15
Robert Siodmark         USA          1945
George Sanders, Geraldine Fitzgerald, Ella Raines,
Sara Allgood, Moyna MacGill, Samuel S. Hinds,
Harry Von Zell, Ethel Grimes

A man falls in love, but cannot escape from his overbearing sisters, and plans the murder of one of them. A stilted film that develops a modicum of suspense, but is then completely spoilt by a poor resolution tacked on, to comply with the constraints of 1940s censorship. Produced by Joan Harrison, one of Hitchcock's associates and written by Stephen Longstreet and Keith Winter.
Aka: UNCLE HARRY
Boa: play by Thomas Job.
THR                           77 min (ort 82 min) B/W
V                                              VMA; STABL

## STRANGE BREW **                           PG
Dave Thomas/Rick Moranis
                    USA                        1983
Dave Thomas, Rick Moranis, Max Von Sydow, Paul Dooley, Lynne Griffin, Brian McConnachie, Tom Harvey, Douglas Campbell, David Beard, Leon Doncheff, Jill Frappier, Thick Wilson, Robert Windsor, Sid Lynas, Mel Blanc (voice only)
Saga of two beer swilling brothers and their equally addicted dog, who discover a plot by a master brewer to take over the world, by adulterating his product with a mind-controlling drug. A slack and chaotic film that fires off shots in every direction and occasionally comes up with some hilarious sequences. Written by Thomas and Moranis.
COM                            87 min (ort 90 min)
V                                                     MGM

## STRANGE CASE OF DOCTOR JEKYLL AND    18
## MISS OSBOURNE, THE **
Walerian Borowczyk  FRANCE               1981
Udo Kier, Marina Pierro, Clement Harari, Patrick Magee, Howard Vernon
A variation on the original R.L. Stevenson story. Here a girl is murdered on arriving at the home of Dr Jekyll whilst Mr Hyde is prowling around outside.
Aka: BLOODBATH OF DR JEKYLL; BLOOD OF DR JEKYLL, THE; DOCTOR JEKYLL AND MISS OSBOURNE; DOCTOR JEKYLL AND MISTER HYDE; DOCTEUR JEKYLL ET LES FEMMES; LE CAS ETRANGE DU DR JEKYLL ET DE MISS OSBOURNE
HOR                            90 min; 84 min (SID)
                   Cut (14 sec in addition to film cuts)
B,V                                        VTC L/A; SID

## STRANGE INVADERS **                        PG
Michael Laughlin         USA                 1983
Paul Le Mat, Nancy Allen, Diana Scarwid, Michael Lerner, Louise Fletcher, Fiona Lewis, Kenneth Tobey, Wallace Shawn, Charles Lane, June Lockhart, Lulu Sylbert, Joel Cohen, Dan Shor, Dey Young, Jack Kehler, Mark Goddard
A spoof on SF films with a Midwestern town being taken over by aliens, that parodies INVASION OF THE BODY SNATCHERS and other such 1950s films. Patchy and disorganised but generally agreeable. The script is by William Condon and Laughlin, and the evocative score is supplied by John Addison.
FAN                            90 min (ort 93 min)
B,V                                                 TEVP

## STRANGE NEW WORLD *                        PG
Robert Butler            USA                 1975
John Saxon, Kathleen Miller, Keene Curtis, Martine Beswick, James Olson, Reb Brown, Ford Rainey, Catherine Bach, Richard Farnsworth, Gerrit Graham, Bill McKinney, Norland Benson
After being held in suspended animation for nearly 200 years, three astronauts return to Earth and find that scientists have learnt the secret of eternal life. An attempt to produce a pilot for a series, inspired by the earlier TV films "Genesis 2" and PLANET EARTH, both of which were superior to this dud.
FAN                                        94 min mTV
B,V                                                  WHV

## STRANGE VOICES **                          PG
Arthur Allan Seidelman USA                   1988
Valerie Harper, Nancy McKeon, Stephen Macht, Tricia Leigh Fisher, Millie Perkins, Robert Krantz, Jack Blessing
McKeon plays a happy teenager who develops schizophrenia, in this dreary clone of the infinitely superior I NEVER PROMISED YOU A ROSE GARDEN.
DRA                           95 min (ort 100 min) mTV
V/h                                                  ODY

## STRANGENESS, THE *                         15
David Michael Hillman USA                    1984
Dan Lunham, Terri Berland, Rolf Theisen, Keith Hurt, Mark Sawicki, Chris Huntley, Diane Borcyckowski, Robin Sortman, Arlene Buchmann
An expedition in search of gold becomes trapped in a cave, where they are confronted by a strange creature and much dullness, in this dreary and ponderous horror yarn.
HOR                                            89 min
B,V                                        VTC L/A; AVR

## STRANGER AND THE GUNFIGHTER, THE **    18
Anthony M. Dawson (Antonio Margheriti)
             HONG KONG/ITALY/SPAIN          1976
Lee Van Cleef, Lo Lieh, Patty Shepard, Julian Ugarte, Karen Yeh, Femi Benussi, Erika Blanc, George Rigaud, Richard Palacios, Goyo (Gregorio) Peralta, Al Tung, Alfred Boreman, Bart Barry, Paul Costello
A clumsy spoof attempt to marry two diverse genres that is only partially successful, and tells of a gunfighter who joins forces with a kung fu expert in order to regain a missing fortune, the whereabouts of which is tattoed on the backsides of several girls.
Aka: BLOOD MONEY
WES                           95 min (ort 107 min)
B,V                                 IFS L/A; PACE; NET

## STRANGER FROM CANTON *                     18
Yeo Ban Yee            HONG KONG            1981
Pai Paio, Lu Chun, Kao Kang
A routine kung fu adventure that is no more than typical of this genre.
Aka: KUAI KO
MAR                             87 min Cut (35 sec)
B,V                                                  VPD

## STRANGER FROM SHAOLIN **
Loo Chun              HONG KONG
Wong Hang Sav, Thomson Kao Kun
A girl learns kung fu to get revenge for the murder of her family by the emperor's men.
MAR                                            94 min
B,V                                        AVI L/A; IOVID

## STRANGER IN SACRAMENTO, A *               15
Serge Bergon (Sergio Bergonzelli)
             ITALY/SPAIN                    1969
Mickey Hargitay, Barbara Frey, James Hill, Steve Saint-Claire, Johnny Gordon
When a man's family is ruthlessly murdered and his cattle stolen, he sets out to have his revenge. A typical tale of bloodshed and vengeance, done in the usual violent and overblown style of a spaghetti Western.
WES                                           100 min
B,V,V2                          VDM L/A; PHE (VHS only)

## STRANGER IS WATCHING, A **                 18
Sean S. Cunningham   USA                     1981
Kate Mulgrew, Rip Torn, James Naughton, Shawn Von Schreiber, Barbara Baxley, Stephen Joyce, James Russo
A deranged murderer kidnaps a young girl and a female TV reporter, holding them hostage in part of the New York subway system, below Grand Central Station. A tense but over-complex tale done with the obligatory 1980s style touches of viciousness, from the

director of FRIDAY THE 13TH. Written by Earl MacRaugh and Victor Miller.
Boa: novel by Mary Higgins Clark.

| | |
|---|---|
| THR | 88 min (ort 92 min) |
| B,V | MGM |

## STRANGER ON MY LAND **                                    15
Larry Elikann          USA          1988
*Tommy Lee Jones, Ben Johnson, Dee Wallace Stone, Pat Hingle, Richard Anderson, Terry O'Quinn, Ned Romero, Barry Corbin*
The story of a Vietnam veteran who finds that the government intends to compulsorily purchase his ranch for use as a missile base. Understandably, he decides to fight back. Similar to the TV film "Fire On The Mountain" but with the dubious benefit of added violence.

| | |
|---|---|
| A/AD | 93 min (ort 96 min) mTV |
| B,V | TGP |

## STRANGER ON THE THIRD FLOOR ****
Boris Ingster          USA          1940
*Peter Lorre, John McGuire, Margaret Tallichet, Charles Waldron, Elisha Cook Jr, Charles Halton, Ethel Griffies, Cliff Clark, Oscar O'Shea, Alec Craig, Otto Hoffman, Charles Judels, Frank Yaconelli, Paul McVey, Robert Dudley*
A reporter begins to have second thoughts about his evidence in a murder case, which has led to the conviction of Cook as a murderer. Lorre appears fleetingly as the real murderer, while the striking dream sequence is a highspot in this excellent drama. Photography is by Nicholas Musuraca.
Osca: THING FROM ANOTHER WORLD, THE

| | |
|---|---|
| DRA | 62 min (ort 64 min) B/W |
| B,V | KVD |

## STRANGER THAN PARADISE ***                               15
Jim Jarmusch USA/WEST GERMANY          1984
*John Lurie, Eszter Balint, Richard Edson, Cecilia Stark*
A gray view of America seen through the eyes of a young girl from Budapest, who meets up with her cousin and his best friend. Together they visit New York, Cleveland and Florida. An offbeat tale, divided into three segments, that's alternately funny, perceptive and dull. Written by Jarmusch and essentially an expanded version of a 30 minute short. The music is by John Lurie.

| | |
|---|---|
| DRA | 85 min (ort 90 min) B/W |
| B,V | PVG; VIR |

## STRANGER WAITS, A **                                     15
Robert Lewis          USA          1987
*Suzanne Pleshette, Tom Atkins, Paul Benjamin, Justin Deas, Ann Wedgeworth, Kenneth Walsh*
After the death of her wealthy husband, a woman retreats to her seaside resort where she becomes involved with several men, all of whom have designs on her wealth. A flat little thriller, written by Durrell Royce Crays.
Boa: story by Bruce Lansbury.

| | |
|---|---|
| THR | 90 min (ort 100 min) mTV |
| B,V | GHV |

## STRANGER WITHIN, THE ***                                 15
Lee Philips          USA          1974
*Barbara Eden, George Grizzard, Joyce Van Patten, David Doyle, Nehemiah Persoff*
Written by Richard Matheson and slightly reminiscent of ROSEMARY'S BABY, this unpleasant drama tells of a woman whose unborn child begins to control her. A chilling tale that builds up to an effective climax. Originally the film was to have been entitled "Trespass".
Boa: short story by Richard Matheson.

| | |
|---|---|
| THR | 78 min mTV |
| B,V | POLY |

## STRANGER WITHIN, THE ***                                 18
Tom Holland          USA          1990
*Kate Jackson, Chris Sarandon*
With the death of her husband in the Vietnam War being followed by the abduction of her 3-year-old son, a woman's life is shattered. However, she slowly rebuilds it, and 15 years later has buried her trauma and entered a new relationship. But the appearance of a stranger who claims to be her long-lost son threatens to unhinge her mind, especially as his behaviour becomes ever more erratic. A tense psychological thriller.

| | |
|---|---|
| THR | 93 min |
| V | NWV |

## STRANGERS IN LOVE **                                     
Chuck Vincent          USA          1983
*Samantha Fox, Tish Ambrose, Kelly Nichols, Jerry Butler, Jack Wrangler, Joanna Storm*
Two lovers who first met in 1962 have separated but cannot forget each other in this story of an obsessive love affair.
Aka: IN LOVE

| | |
|---|---|
| A | 88 min |
| B,V | KRP; CBS |

## STRANGERS KISS ***                                       
Matthew Chapman          USA          1984
*Peter Coyote, Victoria Tennant, Blaine Novak, Dan Sher, Richard Romanus, Linda Kerridge*
Encouraged by the director, the two leads in a 1955 low-budget movie fall in love, causing difficulties with the woman's gangster boyfriend who is financing the production. An unusual and quite gripping tale, written by Novak and Chapman and inspired by "Killer's Kiss".

| | |
|---|---|
| DRA | 96 min |
| B,V,V2 | EHE |

## STRANGERS ON A TRAIN ****                                PG
Alfred Hitchcock          USA          1951
*Robert Walker, Farley Granger, Ruth Roman, Leo G. Carroll, Marion Lorne, Patricia Hitchcock, Laura Elliott, Jonathan Hale, Howard St John, John Brown, Norma Varden, Robert Gist, John Doucette, Dick Wessel*
When an obsessive young man (brilliantly played by Walker) meets a stranger on a train, he discusses how they might each be rid of their respective problems, by collaborating in a murder plan. They part and the former assumes he has the latter's agreement. A marvellously taut and exciting film and one of Hitchcock's best. Written by Raymond Chandler and Czenzi Ormonde. Remade in 1970 as "Once You Kiss A Stranger".
Boa: novel by Patricia Highsmith.

| | |
|---|---|
| THR | 96 min (ort 98 min) B/W |
| V | WHV |

## STRANGERS WHEN WE MEET **                                15
Richard Quine          USA          1960
*Kirk Douglas, Kim Novak, Walter Matthau, Barbara Rush, Ernia Kovacs, Virginia Bruce, Helen Gallagher, Kent Smith*
An unhappily married architect falls in love with his neighbour, but faces a conflict between his emotional needs and his career, when he is suddenly presented with an attractive job opportunity in Hawaii. A glossy and quite superficial soap opera, with lots of misery but no real problems. The script is by Hunter.
Boa: novel by Evan Hunter.

| | |
|---|---|
| DRA | 113 min (ort 117 min) |
| V | RCA |

## STRANGLER OF VIENNA, THE **                              18
Guido Zurli   ITALY/WEST GERMANY          1971
*Victor Buono, Brad Harris, Karin Field, Franca Polcelli, Hannsi Linder, John Ireland, Sybil Martin, Arthur Mann, Carl Stearns, Michael Turner*

In Vienna in 1934 a rash of disappearances of young girls is traced to a butcher's shop, whose sausages are much in demand. Stock Euro-horror with faint touches of macabre humour.
Aka: DER WURGER KOMMT AUF LEISEN SOCKEN; IL STRANGOLATORE DI VIENNA; MAD BUTCHER, THE (VALIV); MAD BUTCHER OF VIENNA, THE; MEAT IS MEAT; VIENNA STRANGLER, THE
HOR                                        84 min
B,V          STABL; VAMP/VDM; VALV/VREL

**STRAPLESS ***                              15
David Hare          UK                     1988
*Blair Brown, Bruno Ganz, Bridget Fonda, Alan Howard, Hugh Laurie, Alexandra Pigg, Billy Roche, Camille Coduri, Michael Gough, Gary O'Brien*
Scripted by playwright Hare, this complex and rather slow-moving character study tells of an American doctor who lives and works in London and reaches a mid-life crisis on her 40th birthday, just at the time her younger sister is paying a visit. Brown and Fonda are excellent as respectively, the older and younger woman, and this unusual adult romantic-drama makes up in atmosphere what it lacks in momentum.
DRA                                        95 min
V                                        VIR/RCA

**STRAW DOGS ***                             
Sam Peckinpah       UK                     1971
*Dustin Hoffman, Susan George, Peter Vaughan, T.P. McKenna, Peter Falk, David Warner, Del Henney, Ken Hutchinson, Colin Welland, Jim Norton, Len Jones, Sally Thomsett, Donald Webster, Michael Mundell, Peter Arne, Robert Keegan*
An American academic and his wife settle in a Cornish village but find that the atmosphere is far from welcoming. An extremely unpleasant film in which the locals are portrayed as a bunch of brutish thugs and rapists. The ending is violent and bloody. Written by Peckinpah and David Zelag. Filmed in England.
Boa: novel The Siege Of Trencher's Farm by Gordon M. Williams.
THR                      113 min (ort 118 min)
B,V,V2                               GHV; VCC

**STRAWBERRY BLONDE, THE ***                 U
Raoul Walsh         USA                    1941
*James Cagney, Olivia De Havilland, Rita Hayworth, George Tobias, Alan Hale, Jack Carson, Una O'Connor, George Reeves*
Set in New York in the 1890s, this tells of a dentist who becomes infatuated with one woman but marries another, and then has doubts as to whether he made the right choice. A lively and witty remake of "One Sunday Afternoon", with Cagney's bouncy performance sustaining the thin plot. Remade in 1948 by Walsh, but using the original title once more.
Boa: play One Sunday Afternoon by James Hagan.
COM                94 min (ort 97 min) B/W
V                                          WHV

**STREAK CAR COMPANY, THE ***                15
Paul W. Kener       USA
*Roger Darbonne, Shelly Stevenson, Richard Jewkes, Ron Ivie, Becky Mechan, Zinda Mensel*
American bubblegum comedy with spoilt teens in flash cars. Supremely vacuous.
COM                                        82 min
V                                          REN

**STREAMERS ***                              18
Robert Altman       USA                    1983
*Matthew Modine, Michael Wright, Mitchell Lichtenstein, David Alan Grier, Guy Boyd, George Dzundza*
Film version of a powerful play ostensibly about four soldiers in an army barracks, waiting to be sent to

Vietnam and facing mounting tension at the training camp of the 83rd Airborne Division. Written by Rabe, this overlong and sombre tale is a little too claustrophobic for its own good, but has many striking moments.
Boa: play by David Rabe.
DRA                      113 min (ort 118 min)
B,V                             VTC L/A; MED

**STREET FLEET ***                           15
Joel Schumacher     USA                    1983
*Gary Busey, Mr. T, Adam Baldwin, Charlie Barnett, Irene Cara, Anne DeSalvo, Max Gail, Gloria Gifford, Jose Perez*
A Washington taxi company is pulled together by its staff of wacky misfits and their equally strange methods. A rambling series of funny encounters are very losely strung together into a rather likeable film.
Aka: D.C. CAB
COM                        95 min (ort 99 min)
B,V                                        CIC

**STREET GIRLS ***                           
Michael Miller      USA                    1974
*Carol Case, Art Burke, Christine Souder, Jay Derringer, Paul Pompian, Fred Garrett, John Freeman, Jimmy Smith, Michael Albert Weber*
A father searches desperately for his daughter in an unfamiliar world of drug addicts, thieves, prostitutes and pimps.
Aka: CRACKERS
DRA                                        72 min
B,V                                 PRIME; CBS

**STREET HERO ***                            15
Michael Pattison    AUSTRALIA              1984
*Vince Colosimio, Sigrid Thornton, Sandy Gore, Bill Hunter, Roy Marshall, Amanda Muggleton*
A young teenage boy has to choose between the Mafia, a career as a professional boxer and the local rock group.
DRA                                        98 min
B,V                                        MED

**STREET JUSTICE ***                         18
Richard Safarian    CANADA                 1987
*Michael Ontkean, William Windom, Catherine Bach, Joanna Kerns*
Following his escape from a Siberian prison camp after twelve years, a CIA agent returns home to a rather less than warm welcome. Deliberately set up years ago to be captured, he was long thought to be dead, and his return is a severe political embarrassment. Sent to a high-security prison, he escapes and heads for his home town in this standard revenge tale. Watchable, but no more than that.
THR                                        89 min
V/sh                                       GHV

**STREET KILLING ***                         PG
Harvey Hart         USA                    1976
*Andy Griffith, Bradford Dillman, Harry Guardino, Robert Loggia, Don Gordon, Adam Wade, Anna Berger, Deborah White, Sandy Faison, Gigi Semone, John O'Connell, Fred Sadoff, Paul Hecht, Gerrit Graham, Stan Shaw, Ben Hammer*
A New York D.A. has to prove that the Mafia were behind an apparently run-of-the-mill fatal mugging. Fair.
THR                      78 min (ort 90 min) mTV
B,V                                        HER

**STREET MUSIC ***                           15
Jenny Bowen         USA                    1981
*Elizabeth Daily, Larry Breeding, Ned Glass, Marjorie Eaton, W.F. Walker, Miriam Phillips, D'Alan Moss*
A singer and her boyfriend fight to save an old people's hotel from being demolished. A very minor tale with good performances but an inadequate script.

COM                    92 min; 88 min (VES)
B,V                              PVG; VES

## STREET OF DREAMS **      15
William A. Graham     USA              1988
*Morgan Fairchild, Ben Masters, John Hillerman,*
*Diane Salinger, Michael Cavanaugh, Alan Autry,*
*David Marciano*
A seedy private eye gets involved with a mysterious
blonde who's down on her luck, and finds himself
embroiled in a strange Hollywood killing. A glossy but
rather insubstantial thriller, scripted by Bill Stratton.
Boa: novel Good Night And Good Bye by Timothy
Harris.
THR                       90 min (ort 100 min) mTV
B,V                              CHV; WATER

## STREET OF NO RETURN *      18
Samuel Fuller  FRANCE/PORTUGAL         1989
*Keith Carradine, Valentina Vargas, Bill Duke, Andrea*
*Ferreol*
A disappointing and muddled adaptation of Goodis'
tale of a once-popular singer who has fallen on hard
times and yet is drawn back into a meeting with those
responsible for his fall from popularity. The clumsy
insertion of an upbeat ending and the sheer ineptitude
of it all will confuse those familiar with the excellent
work this director has produced in the past.
Boa: novel by David Goodis.
DRA                          89 min (ort 90 min)
V                                      RCA

## STREET OF SHADOWS **      PG
Richard Vernon        UK               1953
*Cesar Romero, Kay Kendall, Edward Underdown,*
*Victor Maddern*
Thriller set in and around some of London's less
salubrious locations, with a Soho arcade owner being
framed for the murder of his mistress. A fairly routine
underworld outing with a few good moments and an
effective air of seediness.
Aka: SHADOW MAN
Boa; novel The Creaking Chair by Lawrence Meynall.
THR                      81 min (ort 84 min) B/W
V                                      WHV

## STREET OF THE DAMNED **      18
Giles Behat           FRANCE           1983
*Bernard Giraudeau, Bernard-Pierre Donnadieu,*
*Christine Boisson, Jean-Pierre Kalfon, Michel Aumont*
A man gets into trouble with a savage street gang
when he helps a girl raped by the gang boss.
Aka: RUE BARBARE; STREET OF THE LOST
THR             95 min (ort 102 min) Cut (30 sec)
B,V                              EHE; NELS

## STREET SMART **      18
Jerry Schatzberg      USA              1987
*Christopher Reeve, Mimi Rogers, Kathy Baker, Jay*
*Patterson, Andre Gregory, Morgan Freeman*
A down-on-his-luck magazine writer tries to get back
in favour by cobbling together a fake study of New
York pimps, but finds that its success embroils him in
a murder investigation. Written by David Freeman
and based to some extent on his own experiences, but
something of a hit-and-miss affair that tries to make a
few sharp observations about journalistic corruption.
A great performance from Freeman as a ruthless pimp
is a highlight.
THR                          93 min (ort 97 min)
B,V                                    WHV

## STREET SOLDIERS *      18
Lee Harry             USA              1990
*Jeff Rector, David Homb, Jonathan Gorman,*
*Katherine Armstrong*
Formula urban action film that focuses on the violent
clash between two nasty street-gangs.

A/AD                                  92 min
V                                      BCB

## STREET TRASH *      18
Jim Muro Jr           USA              1987
*Karen Krawiec, Ellen O'Neil, Dave Weckerman, Vic*
*Noto, Nicole Potter, Bill Chepil, Mike Lackey, Mark*
*Sferrazza, Jane Arakawa, Clarenze Jarmon, Bernard*
*Perlman, Miriam Zucker, M. D'Jango Krunch, James*
*Corinz, Morty Storm*
Two brothers and a cop help street tramps get their
own back on a ruthless gang, but a strange rotgut
liquor presents new problems. An incoherent low-
grade mess of melting bodies and exploding heads,
that is difficult to follow and almost impossible to
watch. This effective shocker has little in the way of a
plot, and consists of a seemingly endless stream of
nauseating effects and violent encounters. A Grade 10
shocker.
HOR                    89 min (ort 96 min) Cut (6 sec)
B,V                                    AVA

## STREET WAR **      18
Jamaa Fanaka/John Evans
                      USA              1974
*Rod Perry, Jimmy Witherspoon, Timothy Byer,*
*Pamela Woodruff, Marie Burrell, Lee Boek, Damu*
*King, Diane Sommerfield, Don Chastain*
After his best friend dies on the run from the police, a
crook reforms completely and declares war on the
organised drugs trade, thus threatening the local
crime syndicate.
Aka: BLACK GODFATHER, THE
A/AD                                  84 min
B,V         COBRA; PYR/CBS L/A; 21ST L/A; APX

## STREETCAR NAMED DESIRE, A ***      15
John Erman            USA              1984
*Treat Williams, Ann-Margret, Beverly D'Angelo,*
*Randy Quaid, Rafael Campos, Erica Yohn, Ric*
*Mancini, Fred Sadoff, Elsa Raven, Tina Menard,*
*Raphael Sbarge*
A remake of the 1951 classic of repressed emotions
and blighted lives that, although nowhere near the
earlier film in terms of sheer power, has many good
aspects, not least a fine performance from Ann-
Margret as Blanche. The adaptation is by Oscar Saul.
Boa: play by Tennessee Williams.
DRA              124 min; 115 min (CH5) mTV
B,V                    EHE; CH5 (VHS only)

## STREETCAR NAMED DESIRE, A ****      15
Elia Kazan            USA              1951
*Marlon Brando, Vivien Leigh, Kim Hunter, Karl*
*Malden*
Powerful screen version of a famous play about
steamy Southern passions, with Brando memorable as
Stanley Kowalski and Leigh equally good as Blanche
Dubois, his sister-in-law. The fine jazz score is by Alex
North. Written by Williams from his play and photo-
graphed by Harry Stradling. Remade for TV in 1984.
AA: Actress (Leigh), S. Actor (Malden), S. Actress
(Hunter), Art/Set (Richard Day/George James Hop-
kins).
Boa: play by Tennessee Williams
DRA              122 min; 116 min (VCC) B/W
B,V                    GHV; VCC (VHS only)

## STREETFIGHTER, THE **      15
Walter Hill           USA              1975
*Charles Bronson, James Coburn, Strother Martin,*
*Maggie Blye, Michael McGuire, Jill Ireland*
Bronson plays a barefist fighter in the Depression
years in a story set in New Orleans. An interesting if
rather unsatisfying film, although Bronson is certain-
ly believable in his role. Written by Hill (his directing
debut), Bryan Gindoff and Bruce Henstell.
Aka: HARD TIMES

A/AD                    89 min (ort 97 min)
B,V                                    RCA

## STREETFIGHTER'S LAST REVENGE, THE **    18
JAPAN                                 1977
*Sonny (Shinichi) Chiba, Sue (Etsuko) Shiomi*
A pharmaceutical company develops a form of synthetic heroin that arouses the intense interest of the underworld, and a famous martial arts fighter is hired to stop their attempts to steal it. One in a series of "Streetfighter" films. See also ENTER THE STREETFIGHTER and RETURN OF THE STREETFIGHTER.
Aka: STREETFIGHTER COUNTER-ATTACKS, THE
MAR                      75 min Cut (31 sec)
B,V                              VTC L/A; VMA

## STREETHAWK **                           PG
Vigil W. Vogel          USA           1984
*Rex Smith, Joe Regalbuto, Richard Venture, Jeannie Wilson*
A motorcycle cop patrols the streets in a high-tech, laser-equipped flying bike, in this pilot for a brief TV series.
Aka: STREET HAWK
A/AD                            90 min mTV
B,V                                    CIC

## STREETS ***
Katt Shea Ruben         USA           1989
*Christina Applegate, David Mendenhall, Ed Lottimer, Patrick Richwood*
A well directed tale of L.A. street-kids that somehow manages to transcend its essentially exploitative approach and achieve a measure of rapport with the lost souls it portrays. The insertion of the standard sub-plot revolving around a psychotic killer on the prowl, provides the expected dose of violence.
A/AD                                82 min
V                                      MGM

## STREETS OF FIRE **                       15
Walter Hill             USA           1984
*Michael Pare, Diane Lane, Rick Moranis, Amy Madigan, Willem Dafoe, Elizabeth Daily, Deborah Van Valkenburgh, Lee Ving, Marine Jahan, Ed Begley Jr, The Blasters*
Damsel in distress theme of a rock singer kidnapped by a bike gang. Plenty of violence tastefully set to music with her boyfriend setting out to rescue her. A kind of superficial, comic strip style melodrama that's all sham gilt and pulsating music. The stylish photography is by Andrew Laszlo.
DRA                     90 min (ort 94 min)
V/sh                                   CIC

## STREETS OF GOLD **                       15
Joe Roth                USA           1986
*Klaus Maria Brandauer, Adrian Pasdar, Angela Molina, Wesley Snipes, Elya Baskin, Rainbow Harvest*
A ROCKY type action movie about a former Soviet boxing champion, who defects to the USA and becomes the coach of two promising young boxers. A routine outing that not even a great performance from Brandauer can enliven.
DRA                     89 min (ort 95 min)
B,V                                    VES

## STREETS OF JUSTICE **                    18
Christopher Crowe       USA           1985
*John Laughlin, Robert Loggia, Lance Henriksen, Jack Thibeau, Paul Shenar, Cristina Raines, Fred Taylor, Don Gibb, Wayne Anderson, Roger Aaron Brown, John Hancock, Richard Foronjy, Kate Charleson, Pepe Serna, Robin Gammell*
When the wife and young child of a mechanic are murdered by bikers, the husband is outraged to find the culprits released on a legal technicality and takes

his own revenge. A brutal DEATH WISH clone that was made as the pilot for a prospective series.
A/AD          90 min (ort 100 min) Cut (15 sec) mTV
B,V                                    CIC

## STREETS OF SAN FRANCISCO, THE: 1 – THRILL KILLERS **                                 PG
USA                                   1976
*Karl Malden, Michael Douglas, Richard Hatch, Patty Duke Astin*
The first episode of a popular police detective series. When two members of a family of dangerous activists are put on trial, their supporters kidnap the entire jury.
A/AD                            90 min mTV
V                                   CASVIS

## STREETS OF SAN FRANCISCO, THE: 2 – CROSSFIRE **                                 PG
USA                                   1974
*Karl Malden, Michael Douglas, Pamela Franklin, Celeste Holm*
Another episode in a popular TV detective series from the 1970s, that now shows its age but was always enjoyable. In this story Mike Stone and his partner find a connection between the shooting of a student and the murder of a professor.
A/AD                            50 min mTV
V                                   CASVIS

## STREETS OF SAN FRANCISCO, THE: 3 – BETRAYED **                                  PG
USA                                   1973
*Karl Malden, Michael Douglas, Martin Sheen, Colin Wilcox-Horne*
The third episode in the series sees a female bank clerk giving a man details of her bank, but finding her life put in danger when she recognises him in the course of a robbery.
A/AD                            50 min mTV
V                                   CASVIS

## STREETWALKER, THE **                     18
Walerian Borowczyk   FRANCE           1976
*Sylvia Kristel, Joe Dallesandro, Mireille Audibert, Denis Manuel, Andre Falcon, Louise Chevalier*
After his wife dies, a businessman becomes emotionally involved with a prostitute in the Parisian red light district.
A                                   86 min
B,V                                    PVG

## STREETWALKIN' *                          18
Joan Freeman            USA           1985
*Melissa Leo, Julie Newmar, Antonio Fargas, Leon Robinson, Dale Midkiff, Annie Golden*
The sordid story of a teenage New York prostitute and her pimp, both portrayed as stereotyped figures with neither depth nor credibility.
Aka: COOKIE
DRA                     80 min (ort 85 min)
B,V                                    VES

## STRICTLY DYNAMITE *
Elliott Nugent          USA           1934
*James Durante, Lupe Velez, Norman Foster*
An aspiring poet wins media fame on the radio but loses his wife, until a final reconciliation.
DRA                             68 min B/W
B,V                                    KVD

## STRIKE ****                              15
Sergei Eisenstein       USSR          1924
*Maxim Shtraukh, Grigori Alexandrov, Mikhail Gomarov, I. Ivanov, I. Kluvkin*
The feature debut for Eisenstein, this remarkable film tells of how a strike on the part of factory workers in 1912, is brutally suppressed by the authorities. Much

use is made of visual montage and caricature, with disturbing slaughterhouse sequences used to highlight the brutal tactics employed by the police. A brilliant, harrowing and difficult film.
Aka: STACHKA; TOWARDS THE DICTATORSHIP OF THE PROLETARIAT

DRA 80 min (ort 82 min) B/W silent
V HEND

## STRIKE BACK ** 18
Karl Schenkel WEST GERMANY 1980
*Dave Balko, Brigitte Wollner*
A man makes a violent break from prison, in order to have revenge on the gang of motorbike thieves for whom he took the rap.

THR 87 min
B,V ABA L/A: NET

## STRIKE COMMANDO * 18
Vincent Dawn (Stefan Oblowski)
ITALY 1986
*Reb Brown, Christopher Connelly, Locs Kamme, Alan Collins*
A group of highly trained soldiers in Vietnam are sent to stop an undercover Soviet platoon.

WAR 87 min (ort 90 min) Cut (48 sec)
B,V AVA

## STRIKE FORCE * PG
Barry Shear USA 1975
*Cliff Gorman, Donald Blakely, Richard Gere, Edward Grover, Joe Spinell, Marilyn Chris, Mimi Cecchini, Allan Rich, Billy Longo, Arnold Soboloff, Carl Don, Randy Jurgensen*
Set in New York, this crime story has a Federal agent, a New York cop and a state trooper joining forces to smash a drugs ring. A sluggish and uninspired effort that is just one more failed TV pilot.
Boa: story by Sonny Grosso.

A/AD 74 min (ort 90 min) mTV
B,V VPD

## STRIKE OF THE PANTHER, THE ** 18
Brian Trenchard-Smith
AUSTRALIA 1987
*Eddie Stazak, John Stanton, Paris Jefferson, Michael Carman, Jim Richards, Rowena Wallace*
This sequel to DAY OF THE PANTHER is strictly more of the same, as Jason Blade continues to enforce law and order, this time setting up a task force to assist in recapturing a criminal mastermind, who is also a martial arts expert and one of Blade's old enemies.
Aka: FISTS OF BLOOD

A/AD 83 min Cut (1 min 38 sec)
V GHV

## STRIKE OF THUNDERKICK TIGER ** 18
Henry Wong HONG KONG
*Casanova Wong, Charles Han, Billy Yuen*
A girl's father is murdered, and $1,000,000 is stolen from him and his criminal accomplices, who set out to regain it. However, only the dead man's daughter has a clear idea where to search, and so she sets out with her friends to recover the money before they do.

MAR 80 min Cut (33 sec)
B,V VPD

## STRIKER * 18
Enzo Castellari ITALY 1988
*Frank Zagarino, Paul Werner, Melanee Rogers, John Steiner, John Philip Law*
Finding himself unable to adapt to civilian life, a former Vietnam veteran is pressured into mounting a rescue mission to save a former friend, who has become a reporter and is now being held in Nicaragua. When he finds his buddy has been killed he embarks on the usual revenge-seeking mission.

A/AD 89 min (ort 93 min) Cut (1 min 51 sec)
B,V VPD

## STRIKING BACK ** 18
Sean S. Cunningham USA 1985
*Shannon Presby, Lori Loughlin, James Spader, John Philbin, Eddie Jones, Eric Stoltz, Tom Atkins*
A pair of orphans move to a small town where they fall victim to the local gang of bullies. A routine cycle of aggression, revenge, violence and murder.

DRA 85 min Cut (54 sec)
V RCA

## STRIKING CHANCE ** PG
Rick King USA 1986
*Jim Youngs, Pele, Mario Van Peebles*
A rich young kid who dreams of becoming a football star is suspended from his club because of indiscipline, and sets off for Brazil to meet his idol, a former football star named Santos. He persuades Santos to pass on his skill and returns home to success and fame. A wholesome if glib tale.

DRA 95 min Cut (6 sec)
V/sh RCA

## STRIPES ** 15
Ivan Reitman USA 1981
*Bill Murray, Harold Ramis, Warren Oates, P.J. Soles, Sean Young, John Candy, John Larroquette, John Voldstad, Lance LeGault, Roberta Leighton, Nick Toth, Judge Reinhold, Glenn-Michael Jones, Bill Lucking, Fran Ryan, Dave Thomas*
This box office success is no more than a routine army comedy, about a loser who enlists and ends up in a platoon of volunteer misfits that a sergeant is doing his best to train. Written by Len Blum, Dan Goldberg and Harold Ramis and the music is by Elmer Bernstein.

COM 102 min (ort 105 min)
B,V RCA

## STRIPPED TO KILL *** 18
Katt Shea Ruben USA 1986
*Kay Lenz, Greg Evigan, Norman Fell, Tracy Crowder, Debbie Nassar, Pia Kamakahi, Athena Worthey*
A policewoman poses as a stripper to find out who is responsible for a wave of killings of L.A. strippers. Despite a tendency to concentrate rather too much attention on the strip numbers, this fast and well paced film, from the studios of Roger Corman, has much to commend it. A sequel followed.

THR 83 min (ort 88 min)
B,V MGM

## STRIPPED TO KILL 2: LIVE GIRLS * 18
Katt Shea Ruben USA 1988
*Maria Ford, Eb Lottimer, Karen Mayo Chandler, Marjean Holden, Birke Tan, Debra Lamb*
More of the same, but this time the heroine is a woman with ESP powers, who dreams of the murders as they occur. Very poor.
Aka: LIVE GIRLS

THR 80 min
V MGM

## STROKER ACE * PG
Hal Needham USA 1983
*Burt Reynolds, Ned Beatty, Jim Nabors, Loni Anderson, Parker Stevenson, Bubba Smith, Frank O'Hill, John Byner*
A stock car racer falls into the clutches of an unscrupulous tycoon, in this corny and low-brow effort, without doubt one of Reynolds' worst films.

COM 90 min (ort 96 min)
B,V CIC

## STROMBOLI * 
Roberto Rossellini ITALY 1949
*Ingrid Bergman, Mario Vitale, Renzo Cesana, Mario*

*Sponza*
A homeless girl marries an Italian and settles down to life on a remote island, but finds herself resenting her bleak lifestyle. A sluggish and uninteresting tale that not even the erupting volcano can enhance. Written by Rossellini et al. and with music by Renzo Rossellini.
Aka: STROMBOLI, TERRA DI DIO
Osca: WHILE THE CITY SLEEPS
DRA                    79 min (ort 107 min) B/W
B,V                                        KVD

## STRONGEST MAN IN THE WORLD, THE ** U
Vincent McEveety      USA            1976
*Kurt Russell, Joe Flynn, Eve Arden, Cesar Romero, Phil Silvers, Dick Van Patten, Harold Gould, James Gregory, William Schallert, Roy Roberts, Fritz Feld, Raymond Bailey, Eddie Quillan, Burt Mustin*
A student attracts the attention of crooks when he invents a formula that gives him super-strength, in this predictable Disney romp. Written by Joseph L. McEveety and Herman Groves.
JUV                    88 min (ort 92 min)
B,V                                        WDV

## STRONGHOLD ** 18
Bobby Eehart
        BELGIUM/NETHERLANDS          1986
*Jack Monkau, Hidde Mars, Annick Christians, Josse De Pauw, Chrise Lomme, Marc Van Eeghem*
A pair of armed and ruthless robbers hold a family hostage in their own home, using the daughter's baby as the main hostage. Eventually however, the spiralling tension culminates in violence. Quite an effective if unappealing tale, but somewhat let down by awkward sets (the makers seemed to be uncertain as to where the story is set) and poor dubbing.
Aka: GAMEKEEPER; WILDSCHUT
Boa: novel by Felix Thijssen.
THR              90 min (Cut at film release) dubbed
B,V                                        RNK

## STROSZEK *** 
Werner Herzog    WEST GERMANY        1976
*Bruno S, Eva Mattes, Clemens Scheitz, Tom Paxton, Chet Atkins, Sonny Terry*
Three Berlin misfits find life in the USA is not all roses in their pursuit of The American Dream, in a film that is clearly an outsider's view of the States, largely reflecting the director's own feelings towards the country.
DRA                                    107 min
B,V                                        PVG

## STRYKER * 18
Cirio H. Santiago  PHILIPPINES/USA   1983
*Steve Sandor, Andria Savio, William Ostrander, Michael Lane, Julie Gray, Monique St Pierre, Jon Harris III, Ken Metcalfe, Joe Zucchero, Michael De Mesa, Catherine Schroeder, Tony Carreon, Pete Cooper, Corey Casey*
Survivors of the nuclear war fight desperately for the remaining supplies of uncontaminated water, in yet another variation on an all too familiar theme. Cut before video submission by 1 min 12 sec.
FAN                    81 min (ort 86 min)
B,V                                TEVP L/A; CAN

## STUCK ON YOU * 18
Michael Herz/Samuel Weil
                USA                  1982
*Irwin Corey, Virginia Penta, Mark Mikulski, Albert Pia, Norma Pratt, Daniel Silbert, Eddie Brill, June Martin, John Bigham, Robin Burroughs, Julie Newdow, Pat Tallman, Mr. Kent, Barbie Kielian, Louis Homyak, Ben Kellman*
A review of lovers and their problems through the ages, from Adam and Eve onwards.

COM                    88 min; 81 min (CH5)
B,V                    POLY; CH5 (VHS only)

## STUCKEY'S LAST STAND **
Lawrence G. Goldfarb    USA          1980
*Whit Reichart, Tom Murray, Richard Cosentino, Will Shaw, Ray Anzalone*
Teenage comedy set in a summer camp, where the title character and other counsellors have a tough time keeping their young charges in order. A trite and predictable effort, written by Goldfarb.
COM                                    92 min
B,V            ITM L/A; GOV L/A; MARKET

## STUD, THE * 18
Quentin Masters    UK               1978
*Joan Collins, Oliver Tobias, Sue Lloyd, Mark Burns, Walter Gottell, Emma Jacobs, Tony Allyn, Doug Fisher, Peter Lukas, Natalie Ogle, Constantin De Goguel, Guy Ward, Sarah Lawson, Jeremy Child, Franco de Rosa, Minah Bird*
The sexual cavortings of the super-rich and highly unpleasant are looked at in this successful soap opera, telling of a waiter who works his way up in the world by sleeping with his boss's wife, who has an insatiable sexual appetite. Pure dross this one may be, but it resurrected Collins' career. Written by Joan's sister Jackie Collins and followed by THE BITCH.
Boa: novel by Jackie Collins.
Osca: BITCH, THE (PARK)
DRA          92 min; 189 min (PARK: 2 film cassette)
B,V                      BWV; VGM; PARK

## STUDENT BODIES * 15
Mickey Rose        USA              1981
*Richard Brando, Kristen Riter, Matthew Goldsby, Joe Flood, Joe Talarowski, Mimi Weddell, Carl Jacobs, Janice E. O'Malley, Peggy Cooper, Kevin Mannis, Sara Eckhardt, Brian Batytis, Cullen G. Chambers, Joan Browning Jacobs*
Horror spoof on the slasher-in-the-college theme, with embracing couples being plagued by a heavy-breather who never appears onscreen. Its low level of humour demonstrates the difficulty of parodying a genre, that itself balances precariously on the verge of parody most of the time.
COM                    82 min (ort 86 min)
V/h                                        CIC

## STUDENT BODY, THE * 18
Gus Trikonis      USA               1976
*Warren Stevens, Jillian Hesner, Janice Heiden, June Fairchild, Peter Hooten, Alan McRae, David Akrum, Judith Roberts, Vic Jolley, Faith Barnhart, Sanford Lee, Holmes Osborne, Gary Gitchell, Joseph Kanter, Henry Effertz, Cindy Jaco*
Mindless comedy about a bunch of female juvenile delinquents, who enjoy themselves at a college campus where they've been sent to take part in voluntary medical experiments.
COM                                    89 min
V                                    GLOB; VIZ

## STUDENT CONFIDENTIAL * 15
Richard Horian    USA               1986
*Richard Horian, Eric Douglas, Susan Scott, Marlon Jackson, Elizabeth Singer, Ronee Blakely*
A boring look at four college students and the various problems they experience as they grow up. Written by Horian.
DRA                                    94 min
B,V                                        SHEER

## STUDENT EXCHANGE ** PG
Mollie Miller    USA                1988
*Viveka Davis, Todd Field, Mitchell Anderson, Heather Graham, Gavin McLeod, Maura Tierney, Moon Zappa, Lindsay Wagner, Lisa Hartman, O.J. Simpson*
A couple of high school kids pretend to be exchange

students in order to experience some popularity. The usual Disney complications occur.

| COM | 86 min (ort 100 min) mTV |
| B,V | WDV |

## STUDY IN TERROR, A ***
James Hill   UK/WEST GERMANY   1965
*John Neville, Donald Houston, John Fraser, Anthony Quayle, Robert Morley, Cecil Parker, Barbara Windsor, Georgia Brown, Barry Jones, Adrienne Corri, Frank Finlay, Judi Dench, Charles Regnier, Dudley Foster, Peter Carsten*
Sherlock Holmes tracks down Jack the Ripper but is always one step behind, in this clever and entertaining film. See also MURDER BY DECREE. Written by Donald and Derek Ford.
Aka: FOG; SHERLOCK HOLMES' GROSSTER FALL
Boa: novel by Ellery Queen.

| DRA | 94 min |
| B,V | VDM |

## STUFF, THE **   15
Larry Cohen   USA   1985
*Michael Moriarty, Paul Sorvino, Andrea Marcovicci, Garrett Morris, Scott Boom, Danny Aiello, Alexander Scourby, Russell Nype, James Dixon, Gene O'Neill, James Dukas, Peter Hock, Colette Blonigan, Frank Telfer*
A strange white substance lands on Earth and is exploited commercially as a breakfast food. It does prove, however, to have rather unpleasant side effects. A somewhat chaotic and messy blend of comedy and horror, done in the style of 1950s SF films.

| HOR | 83 min (ort 93 min) |
| B,V | CBS |

## STUNT MAN, THE ***
Richard Rush   USA   1978
*Peter O'Toole, Steve Railsback, Barbara Hershey, Chuck Bail, Allen Goorwitz, (Garfield), Adam Roarke, Alex Rocco, Sharon Farrell, Philip Bruns*
A Vietnam veteran on the run accidentally kills a stuntman, and has to take his place in return for not being handed over to the police by the director. An offbeat and rather witty comedy-drama that almost looks as if it has some deeper meaning. Written by Lawrence B. Marcus and with music by Dominic Frontiere.
Boa: novel by Paul Brodeur.

| DRA | 129 min |
| B,V | GHV |

## STUNNERS *   18
   UK   1989
*Debee Ashby, Lu Varley*
Allegedly an explicit expose of how national newspapers in the UK recruit their nude models as well as an account of their investigations of sex scandals, but in reality little more than a vehicle for some mildly titillating frolics.

| A | 60 min |
| V | SFI |

## STUNT SEVEN **
John Peyser   USA   1979
*Christopher Connelly, Christopher Lloyd, Bill Macy, Peter Haskell, Elke Sommer, Patrick Macnee, Bob Seagren, Soon-Teck Oh, Brian Brodsky, Juanin Clay, Morgan Brittany, Morgan Paul, Lynda Beattie, Santy Josol*
Pilot for a series on law and order enforcing stuntmen that was never made. Here they rescue a film star being held for a $10,000,000 dollar ransom. Average.
Aka: FANTASTIC SEVEN

| A/AD | 100 min mTV |
| B,V | WAL |

## STUNTS: THE DEADLY GAME ***
Mark L. Lester   USA   1977
*Robert Forster, Fiona Lewis, Joanna Cassidy, Darrell Fetty, Bruce Glover, James Luisi, Ray Sharkey*
When his stuntman brother is killed in what later proves to be a deliberate murder, a man decides to take his place in order to find the murderer. A well made film with many good action sequences.
Aka: DEADLY GAME, THE; STUNTS; WHO IS KILLING THE STUNTMEN?

| A/AD | 89 min |
| B,V | DER L/A; MAST L/A; RNK; VMA |

## SUBSTITUTE, THE *   15
Glenn Jordan   USA   1986
*Bruce Dern, Lee Remick, Piper Laurie, Jason Patric, Eric Schiff, Dee Dee Pfeiffer*
A young man's life could not be more promising, but he decides to experiment with drugs, with predictable results. A typically sanitised Hollywood contribution to the anti-drugs lobby.

| DRA | 91 min |
| B,V | CBS |

## SUBURBAN WIVES *
Derek Ford   UK   1972
*Eva Whishaw, Maggie Wright, Peter May, Barry Linehan, Heather Chasen, Gabrielle Drake, Richard Thorpe, Nicola Austine, Claire Gordon, Paul Antrim, James Donnelly, Denys Hawthorne, Yokki Rhodes, Jane Cardew, Robin Culver*
A woman journalist on a local paper investigates how non-working wives pass their time in this pseudo-documentary. Another silly British attempt at a sex comedy.

| COM | 82 min (ort 87 min) |
| B,V,V2 | VPD |

## SUBURBIA *   18
Penelope Spheeris   USA   1983
*Chris Pedersen, Bill Coyne, Jennifer Clay, Timothy Eric O'Brien, Don Allen, Andrew Pece, Grant Miner, Michael Bayer, Wade Walston, Dee Waldron, Maggie Ehrig, Christina Beck, Andre Boutiler, Robert Peyton*
Alienated youngsters take over an abandoned building and clash with the locals, in this trite examination of a serious social problem. The film attempts to be serious but succeeds in being merely violent and unpleasant.
Aka: WILD SIDE, THE

| DRA | 91 min (ort 94 min) Cut (28 sec) |
| B,V | VES/PVG; VES |

## SUBWAY **   15
Luc Besson   FRANCE   1985
*Christopher Lambert, Isabelle Adjani, Richard Bohringer, Jean-Hughes Anglade, Jean Bouise, Michel Galabru, Jean Reno, Jean-Pierre Bacri, Eric Serra, Pierre-Ange Le Pogam, Arthur Simms, Constantin Alexandrov*
A stylish thriller concerning the strange drop-outs who live in the Paris subway system, and the young thief who takes refuge there after robbing a wealthy couple. A well-made triumph of style over content. Written by Besson and others.

| THR | 98 min (ort 104 min) |
| V/sh | CBS |

## SUBWAY RIDERS
Amos Poe   USA   1981
*Robbie Coltrane, Charlene Kaleina, Cookie Mueller, John Lurie, Amos Poe, Susan Tyrell, Bill Rice*
Underground film about the lives of six New Yorkers, that consists of little more than a series of static images observing the non-activities of a junkie, a cop, a musician, a psychotic and various other characters. A piece of self-indulgent dross masquerading as a film.

| A/AD | 118 min |
| B,V | 3MVID/PVG |

**SUCCESS \*\***                                  PG
Steven Gethers            USA            1983
*Mary Crosby, Robert Conrad, Jennifer Warren, Lance*
*Guest, Ann Dusenberry, Bettye Ackerman, Don*
*Gordon, Walker Edmiston, Ben Hammer, John*
*O'Leary, Ann Weldon, Red West, Fred Claussen,*
*Erwin Fuller, Charles Hutchins, Lola Mason*
A man turns his back on a successful life and
abandons his wife and family when he falls in love
with a young woman. Average.
Aka: CONFESSIONS OF A MARRIED MAN
DRA                                     91 min mTV
B,V                                           ODY

**SUCCESS \*\***                                  15
William Richert          USA            1979
*Jeff Bridges, Bianca Jagger, Ned Beatty, Belinda*
*Bauer, Steven Keats, John Glover*
A dissatisfied businessman decides to drop out from
success and all its trappings, and acts out a fantasy by
becoming a streetwise tough guy. Richert twice
re-edited and re-issued this film – in 1981 as "An
American Success" and in 1983 as SUCCESS, but for
all that it remains decidedly uneven and loose, though
there are funny moments.
Aka: AMERICAN SUCCESS; AMERICAN SUCCESS
COMPANY, THE; RINGER, THE
Boa: story by Larry Cohen.
COM                               88 min; 80 min (MIA)
B,V                               HVP L/A; MIA (VHS only)

**SUCCESS IS THE BEST REVENGE \*\***
Jerzy Skolimowski FRANCE/UK             1984
*Michael York, Joanna Szczerbic, Michael Lyndon,*
*Jerry Skol (George Skolimowski), Michel Piccoli, John*
*Hurt, Anouk Aimee, Ric Young, Claude Le Sache,*
*Malcolm Sinclair, Hilary Drake, Jane Asher, Adam*
*French, Mark Sarne*
Explores the conflicts between first and second gen-
eration Polish immigrants in the UK. By inference, an
indirect comment on the state of Poland today.
Written by Jerzy Skolimowski and Michael Lyndon
and something of a surreal follow-up to MOON-
LIGHTING.
COM                                        91 min
B,V                                      GTO; VGM

**SUDDEN DEATH \*\***
Eddie Romero            USA            1975
*Robert Conrad, Felton Perry, Don Stroud, John*
*Ashley, Nancy Conrad, Jenny Green*
Two contract killers ply for hire and are given various
assignments.
A/AD                                       84 min
B,V,V2                                   VPD; MED

**SUDDEN FURY \*\***
D. Brian Damude      CANADA            1975
*Dominic Hogan, Ray Gowan, Dan Hannessey, Hollis*
*McLaren, David Yorston, Eric Clavering, Sean*
*McCann, Robin Ward, Steve Weston, Gerry Huckstep*
A man leaves his wife to bleed to death in a car crash
in order to inherit her money, and accuses an innocent
motorist who tried in vain to save her life.
DRA                                        93 min
B,V                                      IFS; CBS

**SUDDEN IMPACT \*\***                             18
Clint Eastwood          USA            1983
*Clint Eastwood, Sondra Locke, Pat Hingle, Bradford*
*Dillman, Paul Drake, Jack Thibeau, Audrie J.*
*Neenan, Michael Currie, Albert Popwell, Mark*
*Keyloun*
Our tough cop from DIRTY HARRY aids and abets a
rape victim in her crusade of vengeance, leaving a
trail of corpes behind them. The music is by Lalo
Schifrin. This was the third sequel, with THE DEAD
POOL following.

A/AD                              112 min (ort 117 min)
V                                            WHV

**SUDDEN JUSTICE \*\***                            18
                        ITALY           1989
*Maurizio Merli, John Saxon, Barry Sullivan*
A tough cop fights back against the underworld,
playing by the same vicious rules. One more mean and
moody urban thriller, with little to distinguish it from
a hundred others.
THR         90 min Cut (2 sec in addition to film cuts)
B,V                                           VPD

**SUDDENLY SINGLE \*\***
Jud Taylor              USA            1971
*Hal Holbrook, Barbara Rush, Margot Kidder, Agnes*
*Moorehead, Michael Constantine, Cloris Leachman,*
*Pamela Rodgers, David Huddleston, Fred Beir, Steve*
*Dunne, Kate Porter, Devra Korwin*
A young divorced man finds single life somewhat
traumatic as he tries to make it in the singles world.
An uneven blend of comedy and drama with a rather
poor resolution.
Boa: story by Arnold and Lois Peyser.
DRA                            71 min (ort 78 min) mTV
B,V                                           RNK

**SUDDENLY, LAST SUMMER \*\*\***                  15
Joseph L. Mankiewicz    UK            1960
*Katharine Hepburn, Elizabeth Taylor, Montgomery*
*Clift, Albert Dekker, Mercedes McCambridge, Gary*
*Raymond, Mavis Villiers, Patricia Marmont, Joan*
*Young*
An adaptation of a one-act play that tells of a young
woman, who went mad when she saw her homosexual
cousin raped and murdered by beach boys, whose
attentions he had courted. However, this is only
revealed in the climax, with the bulk of the film
consisting of a talky examination of her plight. A
flawed but engrossing tale, scripted by Gore Vidal.
Boa: play by Tennessee Williams.
DRA                          109 min (ort 114 min) B/W
V                                             RCA

**SUGAR COOKIES \*\***
Theodore Gershuny       USA            1973
*Mary Woronov, Monique Van Vooren, Lynn Lowry,*
*Maureen Byrnes, George Shannon, Daniel Sadur,*
*Ondine, Jennifer Welles*
Routine erotic story of love and death, with a sex film
director murdering an actress and asking a lady
friend to provide an alibi.
DRA                                        82 min
B,V                                      VCL/CBS

**SUGARLAND EXPRESS, THE \*\*\***                  PG
Steven Spielberg        USA            1974
*Goldie Hawn, Ben Johnson, Michael Sacks, William*
*Atherton*
Though he has only a short time left to serve in jail, a
young man is persuaded by his girlfriend to escape, so
as to prevent their baby from being forcibly adopted.
On the way they abduct a cop as hostage and with the
police in hot pursuit, attempt to rescue the child.
Based on a true story and written by Hal Barwood and
Matthew Robbins. A fair blend of drama and comedy,
with a downbeat ending. Spielberg's first theatrical
venture.
DRA                                       109 min
B,V                                           CIC

**SUICIDE CLUB, THE \***                           18
James Bruce             USA            1988
*Mariel Hemingway, Robert Joy, Lenny Henry,*
*Madeleine Potter, Michael O'Donoghue*
A bored and somewhat alienated young heiress be-
comes involved with a decadent group of wealthy
dilettantes who delight in rituals and bizarre games.
Hemingway looks very appealing, which is more than

can be said for this incomprehensible mess.
Aka: WELCOME TO THE SUICIDE CLUB
DRA                                        90 min
V                                          CFD

## SUICIDE COMMANDO **
Camillo Bazzoni      ITALY            1969
Aldo Ray, Pamela Tudor, Gaetano Cimarosa, Luis
Davila, Manuel Zarzo
Routine war film telling of a commando mission to
destroy a German air base prior to the D-Day
landings. Average.
WAR                      90 min (ort 94 min)
B,V                              HVP L/A; HVH

## SUICIDE CULT *
Jim Glickenhaus      USA             1977
Mark Buntzman, Monica Tidwell, Bob Byrd, Al
Narcisse, Alison McCarthy, Julie Ragoo
The CIA perfect astrology as a science and a scientist
delving into the Second Coming discovers an evil cult.
Obscure and laughable.
Aka: ASTROLOGER, THE
THR                                        82 min
B,V                                        MEGA

## SUICIDE MISSION *                        15
Jose Luis Merino     SPAIN           1968
Craig Hill, Alan Parker
A group of American marines are sent to Germany to
capture Rommel, but their mission does not go
according to plan.
WAR                                        79 min
B,V,V2                                     VPD

## SUICIDE'S WIFE, THE **
John Newland         USA             1979
Angie Dickinson, Gordon Pinsent, Zohra Lampert,
Todd Lookinland, Peter Donat, Lane Davies, Don
Marshall, Majel Barrett, Walt Davis, Martin Rudy,
Luana Anders, Elaine Princi, Mario Machado, Lorna
Thayer, Denis Berkfeldt
A woman has to come to terms with her husband's
suicide in this competent but rather stolid tale.
Aka: NEW LIFE, A
Boa: novel by David Madden.
DRA                                  100 min mTV
B,V                                        HER

## SUMMER AT 17 **                           PG
John Downey          USA
Kyle Brown, Bryan Cupp
Standard teen-comedy set in summery California.
COM          77 min (ort 87 min) Cut (1 min 19 sec)
V                                    FIFTH; GLOB

## SUMMER CAMP *                             18
Chuck Vincent        USA             1979
Colleen O'Neill, Ray Holland, John C. McLaughlin,
Michael Abrams, Matt Michaels, Jake Barnes, Bud
Bogart, Alexis Schreiner, Verkina Flower, Brenda
Fogarty, Barbara Gold, Dustin Pacino Jr
A low-brow and predictable sex comedy set at a
summer camp, where a 10-year re-union is in progress
and most of the sporting events are sexual.
COM                                        90 min
B,V                                     MED; IVS

## SUMMER CITY **                            15
Christopher Fraser   USA             1977
Mel Gibson, Steve Bisley, Phil Avalon, John Jarret,
James Elliott, Debbie Forman
An Australian version of AMERICAN GRAFFITI
with four young men setting out for a weekend at the
beach and the usual innocent fun and frolics. This
mindless beach film gave Gibson his first starring
role.
DRA                      82 min (ort 90 min)
B,V                                        CINE

## SUMMER DOG **
John Clayton         USA             1977
James Congdon, Elizabeth Eisenman
A family on holiday in the country adopt a playful
stray dog.
A/AD                                   85 min B/W
B,V                                        INT

## SUMMER DREAMS: THE STORY OF THE BEACH
BOYS **                                       15
Michael Switzer      USA             1989
Bruce Greenwood, Greg Kean, Bo Foxworth, Arlen
Dean Snyder, Casey Sander, Andrew Myler
An unauthorised biopic on the lives of one of Amer-
ica's most successful bands, who promoted a light-
weight and happy style of music that became inextric-
ably bound up with sun, sand and surfing in Califor-
nia. Features many of their most popular songs, but
these are not performed by them.
MUS                                        90 min
V                                          CH5

## SUMMER FANTASY *                          15
Noel Nosseck         USA             1984
Julianne Phillips, Ted Shackelford, Michael Gross,
Dorothy Lyman, Danielle Von Zerneck, Paul Keenan,
Richard Eden, Chip Lucia, Eddie Velez, Winnie
Gardner, Dennis Burkley, Brent Huff, Leonard
Lightfoot, John Howard Swain
A teenage student becomes the first female lifeguard
on the beach, in this odd little throwback to the
sun-and-sand beach films of the 1950s.
DRA                                  100 min mTV
B,V                                        PRV

## SUMMER FEVER **                           15
William Webb         USA             1987
Leif Garrett, Martin Landau, Denver Pyle, Wendy Jo
Sperber, Katherine Kelly Lange, Tom Eplin, Will
Bledsoe
The son of the owner of a boat house gives little
thought to his future and is content to enjoy life as a
water ski instructor. With the arrival of his attractive
cousin his attitudes change, and the death of his
father gives him the opportunity to turn the boat
house into a successful ski resort, with the help of a
friend. However, to do this he has to win a water
skiiing contest. A cheerful, inane and pleasantly
forgettable summer movie.
DRA                                        90 min
V/h                                        NWV

## SUMMER GIRL **                            15
Robert Michael Lewis   USA           1983
Barry Bostwick, Kim Darby, Martha Scott, Murray
Hamilton, Millie Slavin, Diane Franklin, Hunt Block,
David Faustino, Laura Jacoby, Linda Ryan, Benjamin
C. Jaus, David Kraul, Jim Lansbury, Randy Spangler,
Lee Gaber
A young girl who has been engaged as a babysitter
seems to exert a strange influence over the whole
family. A dull drama, written by A.J. Crothers.
Boa: novel by Caroline Crane.
DRA                                  120 min mTV
B,V                                        POLY

## SUMMER HEAT *                             15
Michie Gleason       USA             1987
Lori Singer, Anthony Edwards, Bruce Abbott, Kathy
Bates, Clu Gulager
A woman who is neglected by her farmer husband
falls for the hired hand in this dreary effort.
DRA                      77 min (ort 93 min)
B,V                                        EIV

## SUMMER HEAT *
Christy McCabe       USA             1980
Desiree Cousteau, Jamie Gillis, Juliet Anderson

Fantasy story focusing on a look into the mind of a young voyeur after he is hypnotised by his promiscuous aunt.
Osca: BELLA (asa – HAR)

| | |
|---|---|
| A | 81 min |
| B,V | ROXY L/A; HAR |

## SUMMER HEAT ** 15
Barbara Peeters   USA   1975
*Candice Rialson, Pat Anderson, Rhonda Leigh-Hopkins, Will Carney, Grainger Haines, Christopher Wales, Dick Miller*
Three country girls come to town and take up jobs in the local high school, teaching the boys a thing or two about life and generally causing havoc, in this episodic but lighthearted effort.
Aka: SUMMER SCHOOL TEACHERS

| | |
|---|---|
| COM | 81 min (ort 87 min) |
| V | MPV; GLOB |

## SUMMER IN SAINT TROPEZ, A **
David Hamilton   FRANCE   1981
An ethereal and dream-like film in which seven young women explore their sexuality, whilst living on an expensive country estate in St. Tropez. A film without dialogue and with none of the actors or actresses identified, yet of interest in the way it attempts to create what is in effect a series of still-life portraits. A more enjoyable effort than his 1977 film BILITIS, but at 60 minutes it's a little too sweet to take in one dose.

| | |
|---|---|
| A | 60 min |
| B,V | TEVP L/A |

## SUMMER JOB * 15
Paul Madden   USA   1988
*Sherrie Rose, James Summer, Amy Baxter, Can Mayor, Renee Shugart, Fred Bourdin, Chantal, Dave Clouse, Kirt Earhardt, George O.*
Another predictable and carefree comedy about a group of indolent and lustful teenage students who take summer jobs at a holiday resort, but set out to do as little work as possible. A puerile piece of nonsense that offers minimal entertainment.

| | |
|---|---|
| COM | 88 min |
| V | MED |

## SUMMER LOVERS * 18
Randal Kleiser   USA   1982
*Peter Gallagher, Daryl Hannah, Barbara Rush, Valerie Quennessen, Carole Cook, Hans Van Tongeren, Lydia Lenos, Vladimiros Kiriakos, Carlos Rodriguez Ramos, Henir Behar, Rika Dialina*
The story of a menage-a-trois on a Greek island that's all surface gloss and meaningless dialogue. Another boring dud from the director of THE BLUE LAGOON.

| | |
|---|---|
| DRA | 98 min |
| B,V | ORION/RNK |

## SUMMER MAGIC ** U
James Neilson   USA   1963
*Hayley Mills, Burl Ives, Dorothy McGuire, Deborah Walley, Eddie Hodges, Una Merkel, Jimmy Mathers, Michael J. Pollard, Darren McGavin, Wendy Turner, Peter Brown, James Stacy, O.Z. Whitehead, Eddie Quillan, Norman Leavitt*
A Disney remake of "Mother Carey's Chickens", with a poor widow struggling to raise her family in a big rambling house in New England. A mildly pleasing but hardly memorable tale. Songs are by the Sherman Brothers.
Boa: novel Mother Carey's Chickens by K.D. Wiggins.

| | |
|---|---|
| DRA | 109 min |
| B,V | WDV |

## SUMMER NIGHT FEVER ** 18
Siggi Gotz   WEST GERMANY   1978
*Stephanie Hillel, Olivia Pascal, Klaus Obalski, Betty Verges, Edwige Pierre, Bea Fiedler, Claudine Bird, Joseph N. Delnegor, Giani Garko, Jacques Herlin*

Three teenagers search for sexual adventures while travelling by car in Spain.

| | |
|---|---|
| A | 96 min; 87 min (DREAM) |
| B,V | PRV; DREAM |

## SUMMER OF '42 *** 15
Robert Mulligan   USA   1971
*Jennifer O'Neill, Gary Grimes, Jerry Houser, Oliver Conant, Katherine Allentuck, Christopher Norris, Lou Frizell*
Touchingly nostalgic look at a young boy's relationship with the young wife of a soldier. Skilfully put together if rather soft-focus and followed by CLASS OF '44. Written by Raucher. AA: Score (Orig) (Michel Legrand).
Boa: novel by Herman Raucher.

| | |
|---|---|
| DRA | 98 min (ort 103 min) |
| B,V | WHV |

## SUMMER OF FEAR ***
Wes Craven   USA   1978
*Linda Blair, Lee Purcell, Jeff East, Jeremy Slate, Jeff McCracken, Carol Lawrence, MacDonald Carey, James T. Jarnagin, Gwil Richards, Kerry Arquette, Beatrice Manley, Patricia Wilson, Ed Wright, Fran Drescher, Billy Beck*
A young girl spending the summer at her relative's farm, is menaced by the occult power of an evil cousin, who turns up at the house and begins to use witchcraft to dominate the family. Quite a gripping little yarn.
Aka: STRANGER IN OUR HOUSE
Boa: novel by Lois Duncan.

| | |
|---|---|
| DRA | 93 min (ort 120 min) Cut mTV |
| B,V | HOK L/A; RNK L/A; VSP L/A; BWV |

## SUMMER OF MY GERMAN SOLDIER ***
Michael Tuchner   USA   1978
*Kristy McNichol, Bruce Davidson, Esther Rolle, Michael Constantine, Barbara Barrie, James Noble, Robyn Lively, Margaret Hall, Anne Haney, Sonny Shroyer, Jane Hickey, Mary Nell Santacroce, Roy Morris, William Ovell, G.W. Bailey*
A young Jewish girl gets involved with an escaped German POW in a small Georgia town during WW2. A rather over-sentimental but quite effective romance, adapted by Jane-Howard Hammerstein. An Emmy went to Rolle for her fine performance as the family housekeeper.
Boa: novel by Bette Greene.

| | |
|---|---|
| DRA | 98 min (ort 100 min) mTV |
| B,V,V2 | IFS |

## SUMMER RENTAL ** PG
Carl Reiner   USA   1985
*John Candy, Karen Austin, Rip Torn, Richard Crenna, Kerrir Green, Pierrino Mascarino, Joey Lawrence, Aubrey Jene, Richard Herd, Lois Hamilton, Carmine Caridi, John Laroquette*
A family on holiday in Florida runs into all kinds of trouble, in this very minor comedy that fails to make much use of Candy's considerable comic gifts.

| | |
|---|---|
| COM | 83 min (ort 86 min) |
| B,V | CIC |

## SUMMER SCHOOL ** 15
Carl Reiner   USA   1987
*Mark Harmon, Kirstie Alley, Dean Cameron, Gary Riley, Shawnee Smith, Patrick Laborteaux, Ken Olandt, Courtney Thorne-Smith*
A high school teacher has his work cut out when he has to cancel his vacation, to take over a remedial class teaching assorted misfits and no-hopers. An amiable, mindless comedy, quite enjoyable if one isn't too demanding.

| | |
|---|---|
| COM | 93 min (ort 98 min) Cut (48 sec) |
| V/h | CIC |

## SUMMER STORY, A *** PG
Piers Haggard UK 1988
*James Wilby, Imogen Stubbs, Ken Colley, Sophie Ward, Susannah York, Jerome Flynn*
Set in 1902, this tells of a romance between a young London lawyer and a naive and poorly educated country girl. A beautifully made and rather bittersweet tale. The script is by Penelope Mortimer.
Boa: novella The Apple Tree by John Galsworthy.
DRA 93 min (ort 95 min)
V/sh WHV

## SUMMER TO REMEMBER, A *** U
Robert Lewis USA 1985
*James Farentino, Tess Harper, Bridgette Anderson, Sean Justin Gerlis, Burt Young, Louise Fletcher, Dennis Haysbert, Molly Cheek, Dennis Fimple, Taylor Lacher, Tom Lovinger, Corey Brunish, B. Joe Medley, C.J. the Orang-utan*
An ape trained to understand sign language, escapes and becomes the pet of a deaf and dumb boy with whom it can communicate. An engrossing and touching comedy-drama.
Boa: story by Scott Swanton and Robert Lloyd Lewis.
DRA 90 min (ort 100 min) mTV
V CIC

## SUMMER WITH MONIKA ***
Ingmar Bergman SWEDEN 1952
*Harriet Andersson, Lars Ekborg, John Harryson, Georg Skarstedt, Dagmar Ebbesen, Ake Gronberg, Ake Fridell, Naemi Briese*
A young couple's brief and defiant affair results in pregnancy and marriage, and when the girl finds married life not to her liking she leaves her husband and child. A standard Nordic gloomy look at life, made with both care and sensitivity by a master director.
Aka: MONIKA; SOMMAREN MED MONIKA
Boa: novel by Per Anders.
DRA 97 min B/W
B,V LNG

## SUNBURN **
Richard C. Sarafian UK/USA 1979
*Farrah Fawcett-Majors (Fawcett), Charles Grodin, Art Carney, Joan Collins, William Daniels, John Hillerman, Eleanor Parker, Keenan Wynn, Robin Clarke, Joan Goodfellow, Jack Kruschen, Alejandro Joanna Lehman, Alex Sharpe*
An insurance investigator teams up with a model to pursue a case of fraud and murder. A carelessly made and dated comedy, set in Acapulco. The script is by John Daly, Stephen Oliver and James Booth.
Boa: novel The Bind by Stanley Ellin.
COM 98 min
B,V VCL/CBS

## SUNDAY DRIVE * U
Mark Cullingham USA 1986
*Tony Randall, Carrie Fisher, Audra Lindley, Hillary Wolf, Raffi DiBlasio, Ted Wass, Norman Alden, Claudia Cron, Norman Alden, Charley Garrett, James Avery, Lynnette Mettey, Chip Johnson, Branscombe Richmond, William Utay*
Standard Disney shenanigans arise when two identical cars are mistaken by their respective owners. A film as short of laughs as it is of originality.
COM 90 min mTV
B,V WDV

## SUNDAY IN THE COUNTRY ** 18
John Trent CANADA/UK 1973
*Cec Linder, Ernest Borgnine, Michael J. Pollard, Louis Zorich, Al Waxman, Hollis McLaren, Tim Henry, Vladimir Valenta, Murray Westgate, Ratch Wallace, Ralph Endersby, Franz Russell, Susan Petrie, Mark Walker, Gary Reineke*
A religious farmer takes a terrible revenge on three armed killers who invade his property.

Aka: VENGEANCE IS MINE
A/AD 88 min (ort 92 min)
B,V INT L/A; SKP; XTASY

## SUNDOWN: THE VAMPIRE IN RETREAT *** 15
Anthony Hickox USA 1988
*David Carradine, Maxwell Caulfield, Bruce Campbell, Morgan Brittany, Jim Metzler*
At long last a vampire spoof with an original idea, that sees the entire population of the isolated desert town of Purgatory a community of vampires, who have devised both a synthetic blood substitute and a means of surviving in direct sunlight. When a group of traditionalists vampire demand a return to the old ways the inevitable conflict results. A well-paced film that unfortunately doesn't make the most of its amusing premise.
HOR 99 min
V VES

## SUNFLOWER ** 15
Vittorio De Sica ITALY 1970
*Sophia Loren, Marcello Mastroianni, Ludmilla Savelyeva, Anna Carena, Galina Andreyeva, Germano Longo*
A woman searches for her lost husband who failed to return from Stalingrad. After much effort she traces him to Moscow, but is dismayed to find that he has since remarried. A foolish and uninspiring melodrama.
Aka: I GIRASOLI
DRA 103 min
B,V EHE

## SUNNYBOY AND SUGARBABY * 18
1989
*Sabine Wollin, Gina Janssen, Bernie Paul*
A girl living in a remote Alpine village with her two boyfriends inherits her uncle's taxi and fast-food businesses in the Far East. Our trio immediately fly off to take control of these enterpries, but find them to be worthless and are forced to find work to pay for their passage home. A trite romantic-comedy of pleasant locations and occasional humour.
COM 86 min
V VPD

## SUNSET ** 15
Blake Edwards USA 1988
*Bruce Willis, James Garner, Malcolm McDowall, Mariel Hemingway, Jennifer Edwards, Kathleen Quinlan, Patricia Hodge, Richard Bradford, M. Emmet Walsh, Dermot Mulroney, Joe Dallesandro*
Lighthearted comedy-thriller with 1920s actor Tom Mix cast to play Wild West legend Wyatt Earp, this latter having come along as an advisor. Besides making a movie, they wind up solving a murder that shocks all of Hollywood. Often irritating, generally disjointed, this disorganised effort is largely saved by a good performance from Garner.
COM 103 min (ort 107 min)
B,V RCA

## SUNSET BOULEVARD **** PG
Billy Wilder USA 1950
*William Holden, Gloria Swanson, Eric Von Stroheim, Fred Clark, Nancy Olson, Jack Webb, Hedda Hopper, Anna Q. Nilsson*
Brilliant classic film looking at the relationship between a struggling young writer and an ageing faded movie star. Full of powerful psychological insights helped along by a great script and fine acting; Swanson was never better. Hedda Hopper, Buster Keaton and Cecil B. De Mille appear briefly. AA: Art/Set (H. Drier and J. Meehan/S. Comer and R. Moyer), Score (Franz Waxman), Story/Screen (Wilder/Charles Brackett/D.M. Marshman Jr).
DRA 106 min (ort 110 min) B/W
B,V CIC

**SUNSET GIRLS ***                                         R18
          USA
*Terri Johnson, Debbie Osborne, Christy Anna*
Dull sex film about prostitutes in downtown Holly-
wood.
Aka: MIDNIGHT PLOWBOY
A                                        61 min (ort 85 min)
B,V                                        ROXY L/A; TOW

**SUNSET LIMOUSINE ***                                       U
Terry Hughes          USA                    1983
*John Ritter, Susan Dey, Lainie Kazan, Martin Mull,*
*Paul Reiser, Audrie J. Neenan, George Kirby, Martin*
*Short, James Luisi, Louise Sorel, Michael Ensign,*
*Charles Lane, Joyce Little, Stacey Nelkin, John Snee,*
*Tom Dreesen*
A chauffeur who is trying to become a stand-up comic
unwittingly gets involved with criminals. Not without
its moments but overlong. The script is by Dick
Clement and Ian La Frenais.
COM                                   92 min (ort 100 min) mTV
B,V                                        PRV

**SUNSET STRIP ***                                          15
William Webb          USA                    1984
*Tom Eplin, John Mayall, Cheri Cameron Newell, John*
*Smith, Danny Williams*
A music club is threatened by hoodlums who want to
use it to sell guns to kids. A photographer uncovers
this plot and tries to get evidence to take to the police.
Aka: L.A. THRILLER
A/AD                                        87 min
B,V                                        IMPACT/ODY

**SUNSHINE BOYS, THE ***                                    PG
Herbert Ross          USA                    1975
*Walter Matthau, George Burns, Richard Benjamin,*
*Lee Meredith, Carol Arthur, Howard Hesseman, Ron*
*Rifkin, Fritz Feld, Jack Bernardi, F. Murray Abraham*
A witty look at what happens when two old and
cantankerous comedians, once a successful stage duo,
are brought together for a TV special. Burns stepped
in when Jack Benny fell ill and died, and this film was
largely responsible for relaunching his career. AA: S.
Actor (Burns).
Boa: play by Neil Simon.
COM                                   106 min (ort 111 min)
V                                        MGM

**SUPER COPS, THE ***                                       15
Gordon Parks          USA                    1974
*Ron Leibman, David Selby, Sheila Frazier, Pat Hingle,*
*Dan Frazer*
A cop team called Batman and Robin use unusual
methods to stop drug trafficking in a black district of
Brooklyn. A lighthearted thriller with a good many
touches of humour mixed in among the action.
Written by Lorenzo Semple Jr.
Boa: story by L.H. Whittemore.
THR                                   90 min (ort 94 min)
B,V                                        MGM

**SUPER NINJA MASTER, THE ***                               18
Charles Lee          HONG KONG                1988
*Pierre Kirby, Edowan Bersnea, Dewy Bosworth,*
*Thomas Harthan, Reuto Sala*
Yet another tale that revolves around the murder of a
man's family. This time our hero escapes and is taken
under the protection of the Zombie Ninja Master, who
teaches him the techniques he requires for revenge.
MAR                                        87 min
B,V                                        CINE

**SUPER SEAL ***
Michael Dugan          USA                    1976
*Foster Brooks, Sterling Holloway, Sarah Brown, Bob*
*Shepard, Nada Rowland*
An injured seal pup is cared for by a girl and her
grandfather. Fair.

JUV                                   80 min (ort 95 min)
B,V                                        INT

**SUPERBITCH ***                                            18
Massimo Delmano    ITALY/UK                   1973
*Stephanie Beacham, Ivan Rassimov, Patricia Hayes,*
*Cec Linder, Verna Harvey, Red Carter, Luciano*
*Catenacci, Giacomo Rossi Stuart, Leon Vitali*
A narcotics agent goes undercover and becomes
emotionally involved with a woman member of the
drugs ring. Average.
Aka: BLUE MOVIE BLACKMAIL; SERVIZIO DI
SCORTA
DRA                                   90 min (ort 97 min)
B,V                                        IVS; BOOK

**SUPERCARRIER ***                                          PG
William A. Graham      USA                    1987
*Robert Hooks, Richard Jaeckel, Paul Gleason, Alex*
*Hyde White, Ken Olandt, Wendy Malick*
Another parade of the usual macho heroics and
posturing, as a tough sergeant puts a bunch of US
Navy pilots through their paces on an aircraft carrier,
where they compete to see who is best. The pilot for a
short-lived series, this derivative dud is nothing more
than TOP GUN for TV. Followed by several sequels.
A/AD                                        90 min mTV
B,V                                        CINE

**SUPERCARRIER 2 ***                                        PG
William A. Graham      USA                    1987
*Robert Hooks, Dale Dye, Ken Olandt, Cec Verrel*
A further episode of this action-filled but rather dull
adventure series, set on a US Navy aircraft carrier
and inspired by the film TOP GUN. In this tale our
brave pilots have to deal with threats from a Soviet
submarine and a MIG fighter plane.
A/AD                                        95 min mTV
B,V                                        CINE

**SUPERCARRIER 3: THE LAST BATTLE ***                       PG
Corey Allen          USA                    1988
*Robert Hooks, Ken Olandt, Cec Verrell, Richard*
*Jaeckel*
The final part of a three-part TV saga dealing with the
exploits of the pilots aboard an American aircraft
carrier. As with the earlier episodes, the flimsy plot
serves as nothing more than a vehicle for the flying
sequences.
A/AD                                        133 min mTV
B,V                                        CINE

**SUPERCHIC ***                                            R18
Ed Forsythe          USA                    1973
*Joyce Jillson, John Caradine*
Tiresome piece of softcore all about an insatiable
airline stewardess.
Aka: SUPER CHICK (VOR or SHEP)
Osca: LOVE GAMBLER (PPL)
A          48 min (ort 94 min) Cut (4 min – VOR version;
                                1 min 34 sec – SHEP version)
B,V                       DPV L/A; PPL L/A; PRI; VOR; SHEP

**SUPERDAD ***                                              U
Vincent McEveety      USA                    1974
*Bob Crane, Kurt Russell, Barbara Rush, Joe Flynn,*
*Kathleen Cody, Dick Van Patten*
A generation gap comedy with a man competing with
his daughter's boyfriend. Another dated dud from
Disney.
COM                                        96 min
B,V                                        WDV

**SUPERDOME ***
Jerry Jameson          USA                    1978
*David Janssen, Edie Adams, Ken Howard, Van*
*Johnson, Donna Mills, Jane Wyatt, Peter Haskell,*
*Clifton Davis, Tom Selleck, Bubba Smith, Dick*

*Butkus, Susan Howard, Vonetta McGee, Ed Nelson,*
*Shelly Novack, Robin Mattson*
A killer is loose among the crowds enjoying a sports
event, in New Orlean's Super Bowl giant enclosed
stadium. An insubstantial thriller that develops
neither tension nor interest.
Boa: story by Barry Oringer.
THR                                    100 min mTV
B,V                                            CBS

**SUPERFLY ** **                                   18
Gordon Parks Jr         USA                      1972
*Ron O'Neal, Carl Lee, Sheila Frazier, Julius W.*
*Harris, Charles McGregor*
Flashy black consciousness film all about a heroin
dealer trying to retire after one last big deal. All the
white cops are wicked racists and the blacks are
portrayed very sympathetically, whether drug dealing
or not. For all that, a very slick and well acted film
with some good moments and a fine score by Curtis
Mayfield. SUPERFLY T.N.T. followed.
Boa: novel by Philip Penty.
DRA                                  90 min (ort 98 min)
B,V                                            WHV

**SUPERFLY T.N.T. ***                              18
Ron O'Neal             USA                       1973
*Ron O'Neal, Roscoe Lee Brown, Sheila Frazier,*
*Jacques Sernas, William Berger, Roy Bosier*
A sequel to SUPERFLY with our ex-pusher getting
involved in an African revolution. A messy and
generally worthless yarn.
A/AD                                 83 min (ort 87 min)
B,V                                            CIC

**SUPERGANG, THE ** **                             18
                HONG KONG                        198-
*Bruce Le (Huang Kin Lung)*
Two rival street gangs battle for control, but one gang
member is in love with the sister of the rival
gangleader. When the latter finds out about his
sister's relationship, the conflict turns into a full-scale
war.
MAR                                85 min Cut (32 sec)
B,V                                            VPD

**SUPERGIRL ***                                    PG
Jeannot Szwarc         USA                       1984
*Helen Slater, Faye Dunaway, Peter O'Toole, Mia*
*Farrow, Brenda Vaccaro, Peter Cook, Simon Ward,*
*Marc McClure, Hart Bochner, Maureen Teefy, David*
*Healy, Sandra Dickinson, Robyn Mandell, Diana*
*Ricardo, Nancy Lippold, Sonya Leite*
Superman's female cousin comes to Earth to regain a
lost power source, that has fallen into the hands of
arch-villainess Dunaway. A lethargic and disappoint-
ing follow-on to SUPERMAN: THE MOVIE that just
drags and drags.
A/AD                                111 min (ort 124 min)
B, V/sh                              TEVP L/A; WHV

**SUPERGRASS, THE ** **                            15
Peter Richardson       UK                        1985
*Adrian Edmondson, Jennifer Saunders, Peter*
*Richardson, Dawn French, Nigel Planer, Keith Allen,*
*Robbie Coltrane, Daniel Peacock, Alexei Sayle,*
*Michael Elphick, Ronald Allen, Patrick Durkin,*
*Marika Rivera, Rita Treisman*
A careless boast in a pub leads to a teenage boy being
forced to work as a police informer, a job not without
its share of dangerous complications. A funny but
fairly lightweight comedy, from the same team that
produced all those "Comic Strip Presents.." episodes
for Channel Four TV.
COM                                 105 min (ort 107 min)
V/h                                            CBS

**SUPERKNIGHTS ***
Raphael Nussbaum       USA               .       1976

*Corey John Fischer, Hy Pike*
The sexual adventures of Don Quixote and his ser-
vant, form the basis for this limp attempt to turn
Cervantes' classic work into an erotic musical comedy.
Aka: AMOROUS ADVENTURES OF DON
QUIXOTE AND SANCHO PANZA, THE;
SUPERKNIGHT
COM                                            100 min
B,V,V2                                         INT

**SUPERMAN ** ** **                                PG
Richard Donner         UK/USA                    1978
*Christopher Reeve, Margot Kidder, Marlon Brando,*
*Gene Hackman, Glenn Ford, Jackie Cooper, Ned*
*Beatty, Susannah York, Phyllis Thaxter, Trevor*
*Howard, Valerie Perrine, Marc McClure, Jeff East,*
*Terence Stamp, Maria Schell*
Updated attempt to bring the DC Comics superhero to
life, with Superman out to thwart arch-criminal Lex
Luthor's scheme to activate the San Andreas fault.
Music is by John Williams with several sequels
following. The witty script is by Mario Puzo, David
Newman, Robert Benton and Leslie Newman. The
superb effects won an Oscar. AA: Spec Award (Les
Bowie/Colin Chilvers/Denys Coop/Roy Field/Derek
Meddings/Zoran Perisic for visual effects).
Aka: SUPERMAN: THE MOVIE
FAN                                137 min (ort 142 min)
V/sh                                           WHV

**SUPERMAN 2 ** ** **                              PG
Richard Lester         USA                       1980
*Christopher Reeve, Margot Kidder, Gene Hackman,*
*Terence Stamp, Ned Beatty, Sarah Douglas, Jackie*
*Cooper, Valerie Perrine, Susannah York, E.G.*
*Marshall, Jack O'Halloran, Marc McClure, Clifton*
*James, Shane Rimmer, Michael Shannon*
Newly escaped from imprisonment in the Phantom
Zone, three super-villains (a great performance from
Stamp) arrive on Earth and battle Superman for
world domination. The story may be weaker but the
special effects are even better. Slightly more tongue-
in-cheek than before but well worth seeing.
FAN                                            127 min
B,V                                            WHV

**SUPERMAN 3 ***                                   PG
Richard Lester         USA                       1983
*Christopher Reeve, Richard Pryor, Robert Vaughn,*
*Annette O'Toole, Jackie Cooper, Marc McClure, Annie*
*Ross, Pamela Stephenson, Margot Kidder, Gavan*
*O'Herlihy, Nancy Roberts, Graham Stark, Henry*
*Woolf, Gordon Rollings*
A further "Superman" film that is such a spoof that
the good ideas in it are really spoilt. The story is inane
(an attempt to control the world's oil tankers) and the
dialogue is flat. An unworthy successor to the two
previous films that's possibly worth seeing for the
special effects, but only just.
FAN                                120 min (ort 125 min)
V/sh                                           WHV

**SUPERMAN 4: THE QUEST FOR PEACE ***             PG
Sidney J. Furie        USA                       1987
*Christopher Reeve, Gene Hackman, Jackie Cooper,*
*Marc McClure, Jon Cryer, Sam Wanamaker, Mark*
*Pillow, Mariel Hemingway, Margot Kidder, Damian*
*McLawhorn, Jim Broadbent, William Hootkins,*
*Stanley Lebor, Don Fellows, Robert Beatty*
Superman is out to rid the world of nuclear weapons,
but Lex Luthor, now a nuclear arms entrepreneur,
creates a superhero of his own, a genetic clone whose
powers are equal to those of Superman. The two do
battle and though the final outcome is never in doubt,
things look bad for our hero at times. The weakest
entry in the series, with shoddy, second-rate effects
and a plot with holes large enough to push Krypton
through. Hard to enjoy on any level.
Aka: QUEST FOR PEACE, THE

FAN                                87 min (ort 90 min)
V/sh                                              WHV

### SUPERMAN AND THE MOLE MEN *        U
Lee Sholem            USA                 1951
*George Reeves, Phyllis Coates, Jeff Corey, Walter Reed*
One of the dreary 1950s adventures featuring the Man
of Steel and the usual plethora of all-too-easily
defeated villains. This episode features a set of
creatures who inhabit the centre of the Earth and
reach the surface via an oil well.
A/AD                                      59 min B/W
V                                                 WHV

### SUPERMEN **
Bitto Albertini        ITALY              1976
*Brad Harris, Sal Borges, George Martin*
Action adventure set in Africa involving the Russians,
a uranium mine, a tribe of Amazons and much more.
A/AD                                          97 min
B,V                                   DFS; MARKET

### SUPERNATURAL **
Eugenio Martin        SPAIN               1980
*Maximo Valverde, Candida Losada, Cristina Galbo,*
*Gerardo Malla, Juan Jesus Valverde, Lola Lemos*
An unfaithful wife is haunted by the vengeful ghost of
her tyrannical husband, whose malevolent presence
pervades her home, causing several nasty accidents.
Eventually she frees herself with the aid of a priest
and a medium. Despite being very well produced, a
distinct lack of tension hampers the film's effective-
ness.
Aka: SOBRENATURAL
HOR                                          100 min
B,V                                               IDS

### SUPERNATURALS, THE *               18
Armand Mastroianni     USA               1986
*Maxwell Caulfield, Nichelle Nicholls, Levar Burton,*
*Talia Balsam, Bradcroft Bancroft, Bobby Di Cicco,*
*Margaret Shenal, Patrick Davis, James Kirkwood,*
*Scott Jacoby, Richard Pachorek, John Zarchen, Robert*
*Barron, Mark Schneider*
A National Guard unit on exercises in the swamps,
stumble across a group of zombies that were killed
during the Civil War and then revived. A boring dud
that was never released theatrically. Watch it and
you'll find out why.
Aka: GHOST SOLDIERS
HOR                                          87 min
B,V                                   EHE; NELS

### SUPERPOWER **
Lin Chan Wei       HONG KONG             1980
*Billy Chang, Chaing Tao, Hau Chiu Sing, Liu An Li,*
*William Liu Tan, Liu Hao-Nien*
A kung fu student returns home to see his dying
father, and learns that many years ago he was the
head of the Manchu Imperial guard, but was beaten in
a martial arts contest by five kung fu experts. The son
vows to regain the family honour by taking on and
beating the son of one of the experts. This thin plot
serves as a vehicle for some competent action sequences.
MAR                                          89 min
B,V,V2                                           VPD

### SUPERSNOOPER *                     PG
Sergio Corbucci      ITALY/USA           1981
*Terence Hill (Mario Girotti), Ernest Borgnine, Joanne*
*Dru, Marc Lawrence, Julie Gordon, Lee Sandman*
A Miami cop acquires superpowers after accidental
exposure to radiation and takes on mobster Lawrence.
A hammy affair of poor effects and worse acting.
Aka: SUPER FUZZ
A/AD                               92 min (ort 106 min)
B,V                                               WHV

### SUPERSONIC MAN *
Piquer Simon (Juan Piquer)
                      SPAIN               1979
*Michael Coby, Cameron Mitchell, Diana Polakow,*
*Richard Yesteran, Jose Maria Caffarel, Frank Brana,*
*Javier De Campos, Tito Garcia, Quique Camoiras,*
*Luis Barboo, Angel Ter*
A super-being is sent to Earth to discover why
deliveries of a radioactive substance are disappearing,
and ends up doing battle with an evil scientist out for
the usual bid at world domination. Instantly forgett-
able, despite a few good special effects.
FAN                                          90 min
B,V,V2                                           VPD

### SUPERSTITION **                    18
James Robertson        USA               1982
*Albert Salmi, Lynn Carlin, Larry Penwell, James*
*Houghton, Maylo McCaslin, Joshua Cadman,*
*Jacquelyne Hyde, Heidi Bohay, Billy Jacoby, Kim*
*Marie, Robert Symonds, Stacy Keach Sr, John*
*Alderman, Carole Goldman, Johnny Doran*
A witch burnt at the stake exerts a deadly power over
an old house by a lake some 200 years later, in this
gruesome and gory horror yarn.
Aka: WITCH, THE
Boa: short story by Michael Sajbel.
HOR                                          95 min
B,V                                   VTC L/A; STABL

### SUPERTRAIN **
Dan Curtis            USA                 1979
*Steve Lawrence, Keenan Wynn, Don Meredith, Don*
*Stroud, Char Fontaine, Stella Stevens, George*
*Hamilton*
Sabotage aboard an atomic-powered luxury train
travelling at 200 mph leads to panic among the
passengers. Pilot for a short-lived TV series of eight
episodes.
Aka: EXPRESS TO TERROR
THR                                       92 min mTV
B,V                                   SEL L/A; STARX/CIC

### SUPERVAN *                         15
Lamar Card            USA                 1977
*Mark Schneider, Katie Saylor, Morgan Woodward,*
*Len Lesser, Skip Riley, Tom Kindle, Bruce Kimball,*
*Ralph Seeley, Richard Sobek*
The title refers to a sophisticated super vehicle used in
the fight against crime. An abundance of car smash
sequences will appeal to some.
A/AD                              86 min; 77 min (MAST)
B,V                                VTC L/A; MAST (VHS only)

### SUPERVIXENS *
Russ Meyer            USA                 1975
*Shari Eubank, Charles Pitts, Charles Napier, Henry*
*Rowland, Jack Provan, Ushi Digard, Christy*
*Hartsburg, Haji, Ann Marie, Sharan Kelly*
First sequel to "The Vixens" has Clint working at a
gas station and living with insanely jealous Angel.
Clint beats her up so badly the cops arrive. Later,
when Clint is out one calls to see her. She teases the
cop because he is impotent and in a rage he kills her.
Clint now flees but months later meets a "reincarna-
tion" of Angel running a gas station! The cop arrives
and tries to kill them both but kills himself. A
ludicrous and violent tale.
A                                            106 min
B,V                                               BWV

### SUPPORT YOUR LOCAL GUNFIGHTER **   U
Burt Kennedy          USA                 1971
*James Garner, Suzanne Pleshette, Jack Elam, Harry*
*Morgan, John Dehner, Joan Blondell, Chuck Connors,*
*Marie Windsor, Henry Jones, Dub Taylor, Kathleen*
*Freeman, Willis Bouchey, Walter Burke, Gene Evans,*
*Dick Haymes, Ellen Corby*
A con-man passes off bumbling Elam as a notorious

gunfighter so as to benefit from a mining dispute. A sequel to SUPPORT YOUR LOCAL SHERIFF that disappoints despite a good cast.
Aka: LATIGO
COM                                    89 min (ort 92 min)
B,V                                              WHV

### SUPPORT YOUR LOCAL SHERIFF! ***          PG
Burt Kennedy              USA              1968
*James Garner, Walter Brennan, Joan Hackett, Harry Morgan, Jack Elam, Bruce Dern, Henry Jones, Walter Burke, Dick Peabody, Gene Evans, Willis Bouchey, Kathleen Freeman, Gayle Rogers, Richard Hoyt, Marilyn Jones*
Western spoof about a sheriff bringing law to a tough town by any means he can muster. Though well acted, the film is only slightly amusing rather than really funny, despite some clever parodies from countless Westerns. Brennan's role as Old Man Clanton from "My Darling Clementine" adds a nice touch. Written and produced by William Bowers and followed in 1971 by SUPPORT YOUR LOCAL GUNFIGHTER.
COM                                            93 min
B,V                                              WHV

### SUPPOSE THEY GAVE A WAR AND          15
### NOBODY CAME? ***
Hy Averback               USA              1969
*Tony Curtis, Ernest Borgnine, Brian Keith, Suzanne Pleshette, Ivan Dixon, Bradford Dillman, Tom Ewell, Arthur O'Connell, Robert Emhardt, John Fiedler, Don Ameche*
A satire on the deteriorating relationship between the army personnel at a base and the inhabitants of the nearby town. An unusual film that is a lot better than its clumsy title would lead one to believe.
Aka: WAR GAMES
COM                          113 min; 107 min (VCC)
B,V                                          GHV; VCC

### SURABAYA CONSPIRACY, THE **
Roy Davis                 USA              1975
*Richard Jaeckel, Michael Rennie, Barabara Bouchet, Mike Preston*
Adventure story set in Indonesia and the Philippines, and involving the smuggling of weapons.
A/AD                                           90 min
B,V                                          VCL/CBS

### SURE THING, THE **                         15
Rob Reiner                USA              1985
*John Cusack, Daphne Zuniga, Anthony Edwards, Viveca Lindfors, Lisa Jane Persky, Boyd Gaines, Tim Robbins, Nicollette Sheridan*
Story of an unlikely romance that develops between two college students, who are thrown together by chance on a cross-country journey. Something of an attempt to update IT HAPPENED ONE NIGHT, that's contrived and predictable, but quite watchable.
COM                                    91 min (ort 94 min)
B,V                               EHE; CH5 (VHS only)

### SURF 2 *                                   18
Randall Badat             USA              1984
*Linda Kerridge, Ruth Buzzi, Eddie Deezen, Cleavon Little, Peter Isaacksen, Eric Stoltz, Lyle Waggoner, Morgan Paull, Ruth Buzzi, Carol Wayne, Terry Kiser*
A spoof on those beach-party and teenage-slasher films. There never was a "Surf 1" which is one of the funnier jokes of the film. Ha Ha.
COM                                    89 min (ort 91 min)
B,V                                              ODY

### SURF NAZIS MUST DIE *                      18
Peter George              USA              1987
*Barry Brenner, Gail Neely, Michael Sonye, Dawn Wildsmith, Tom Shell, Dawne Ellison, Bobbie Bresee, Robert Harden, Joel Hile, Gene Mitchell, Terry Lee,*

*Brian Krutoff, Ted Prior, Andrew Bick, Berta Dahl, Willa Reynolds*
In the near future, Californian beaches are taken over by various gangs following a devastating earthquake. The most vicious gang consists of a bizarre bunch of ruthless punk neo-Nazis. When an innocent black youth is murdered by the gang his mother swears vengeance. A ludicrous and rather boring mess, that despite a much-hyped release is neither shocking nor interesting.
Aka: SURF NAZIS (PARK)
A/AD                      78 min (ort 90 min) Cut (31 sec)
B,V                               CINE L/A; TOW; PARK

### SURRENDER *                                PG
Jerry Belson              USA              1987
*Sally Field, Michael Caine, Steve Guttenberg, Peter Boyle, Jackie Cooper, Julie Kavner, Louise Lasser*
A struggling artist and a successful author embark on an affair, in this banal comedy that not even good performances can do anything for. The script is by Belson.
COM                                    91 min (ort 96 min)
V/sh                                             WHV

### SURROGATE, THE ***                         18
Don Carmody               CANADA          1983
*Art Hindle, Carole Laure, Shannon Tweed, Michael Ironside, Jackie Burroughs, Marilyn Lightstone, Barbara Law, Gary Reineke, Jean-Claude Poitras, Jonathan Welsh, Tony Scott, Dean Hagopian, Mark Burns, Jim Hanley*
A couple whose marriage is on the rocks are advised to seek a sex therapist, who seems to be linked in some way with a series of murders. A contrived but intriguing tale that suffers slightly from over-complexity.
Aka: BLIND RAGE
THR                                            95 min
B,V                                              MED

### SURVIVAL GAME *                            15
Herb Freed                USA              1987
*Mike Norris, Deborah Goodrich, Seymour Cassel, Ed Bernard, Arlene Golonka*
A combat expert employed by a war games resort, is forced to put his skills to the test when he finds himself up against a gang of ruthless criminals. Very poor.
A/AD                                    87 min (ort 91 min)
V                                                EIV

### SURVIVAL QUEST **                          15
Don Coscarelli            USA              1988
*Lance Henriksen, Mark Rolston, Ben Hammer, Dominic Hoffman, Traci Lin, Catherine Keener, Dermot Mulroney*
Standard survival saga with a group of youngsters battling the elements and other hazards in the Rockie Mountains. Average.
A/AD                                    90 min (ort 92 min)
B,V                                              CINE

### SURVIVAL RUN *                             15
Larry Spiegel             USA              1980
*Peter Graves, Ray Milland, Vincent Van Patten, Pedro Armendariz Jr, Alan Conrad, Marianne Savage*
Teenagers on an excursion into the desert stumble across drug smugglers and have to escape on foot after their vehicle is destroyed. Unfortunately, they cannot escape from this banal film.
THR                                    85 min (ort 90 min)
B,V,V2                                    HOK L/A; SID

### SURVIVAL RUN ***                           15
Paul Verhoeven   NETHERLANDS              1977
*Rutger Hauer, Jeroen Krabbe, Edward Fox, Susan Penhaligon, Peter Faber, Derek De Lint, Eddy Habbema*
Good Biopic of a Dutch resistance group, its famous

leader and the fate that befell its various members, during the long years of the German occupation in WW2. Based on the experiences of a Dutch resistance leader.
Aka: SOLDAT VAN ORANGE; SOLDIER OF ORANGE
Boa: book by Erik Hazelhoff.
WAR                          115 min (ort 144 min)
B,V                                          RNK

## SURVIVAL ZONE *                          15
Percival Reubens        USA             1984
*Gary Lockwood, Camilla Sparv, Morgan Stevens, Zoli Markey, Ian Steadman, Arthur Hall, Karl Eric Kostlin, Elizabeth Meyer, Lillian Randall, Jeanne Combrink, Mimi Kheswa*
Post-WW3 survivors are menaced by motorcycle maniacs in this painfully unoriginal yarn.
A/AD                                      90 min
B,V                          CBS; PYRAM; PHE

## SURVIVALIST, THE **                      18
Sig Shore              USA              1986
*Steve Railsback, Susan Blakely, Cliff De Young, David Wayne, Morjoe Gortner*
Another post-nuclear holocaust tale, with a man setting out on a dangerous quest across a devastated land in search of his son. Cut before video submission by 12 sec.
Aka: JACK TILLMAN: THE SURVIVALIST
A/AD                                      92 min
V                              HER L/A; BRAVE

## SURVIVE! *                               18
Rene Cardona          MEXICO           1976
*Hugo Stiglitz, Luz Maria Aguilar, Pablo Ferrel, Fernando Larranga, Norma Lazareno*
The story of how the survivors of a plane that crashed in the Andes in 1972 survived with neither food nor water for 16 days, being forced to turn to cannibalism. An exploitative film with little to be said in its favour.
Aka: SUPERVIVIENTES DE LOS ANDES
Boa: book by Charles Blair Jr.
DRA                          82 min (ort 86 min)
B,V                                         TEVP

## SURVIVING ***                            15
Waris Hussein          USA             1985
*Ellen Burstyn, Len Cariou, Zach Galligan, Marsha Mason, Molly Ringwald, Paul Sorvino, Heather O'Rourke, William Windom, Marc Gilpin, Paddi Edwards, River Phoenix, Camilla Ashlend, Jane Simoneau, Joe Berryman, Lon Coggeshall*
A powerful and quite harrowing look at the effect a suicide pact has on the two families concerned, when a teenage couple decide to take their lives. A well-acted and intelligent film that occasionally becomes overwrought but is always absorbing. The script is by Joyce Eliason.
DRA                    138 min (ort 150 min) mTV
B,V                                          VCC

## SURVIVOR *                               18
Michael Shackleton    USA              1987
*Chip Mayer, Richard Moll, Sue Kiel, Richard Haines, John Carson, Rex Garner, Sandra Duncan, Ben Dekker, Andre Roothman, Sven Forsell, Bima Stagg, Pedro Reis, Mo Maralis, Andre Roberts, Jimmy Nel, Hennie Bosman, Maria Schooman*
An astronaut who returns to Earth a year after a nuclear war, finds it a barren place peopled by savages. In his determination to survive he sets out in search of a rumoured hidden city and has various adventures along the way. A feeble MAD MAX clone with neither wit nor originality.
FAN                                       88 min
B,V                                          NDH

## SURVIVOR, THE ***                        15
David Hemmings   AUSTRALIA             1980
*Robert Powell, Jenny Agutter, Angela Punch McGregor, Peter Sumner, Joseph Cotten, Ralph Cotterill, Denzil Howsen, Lorna Lesley, Kirk Alexander, Adrian Wright*
A bizarre and unusual tale of supernatural forces. A pilot is tortured with guilt at being the only survivor of a plane crash and is haunted by an evil force from amidst the wreckage. A few ponderous moments are minor shortcomings.
Boa: novel by James Herbert.
HOR                          93 min (ort 100 min)
B,V              ARCADE/VSP L/A; VGM (VHS only)

## SURVIVORS, THE **                        15
Michael Ritchie       USA              1983
*Walter Matthau, Robin Williams, Jerry Reed, James Wainwright, Annie McEnroe, Kristen Vigard*
Two men, an executive and a gas station attendant, find their lives changed out of all recognition when they identify a robber, and are forced as a result of their civic courage to take refuge in the mountains of Vermont. A patchy black comedy, written by Michael Leeson.
COM                98 min (ort 102 min) Cut (20 sec)
V                                            RCA

## SUSPECT ***                              15
Peter Yates           USA              1987
*Dennis Quaid, Cher, Liam Neeson, John Mahoney, Joe Mantegna, Philip Bosco, E. Katherine Kerr*
A defence lawyer takes on a seemingly hopeless case when she agrees to represent a deaf tramp accused of murder. Convincing performances lift the film above its contrived plot.
DRA                          117 min (ort 121 min)
B,V                                          RCA

## SUSPICION *                              15
Andrew Greive         UK               1987
*Anthony Andrews, Jane Curtin, Jonathan Lynn, Betsy Blair, Michael Hordern, Vivian Pickles*
A naive country girl becomes suspicious of her husband when she thinks she has stumbled on a murder plot that would benefit him. An almost slavish remake of the earlier Hitchcock classic that includes all the required elements, but moves along at such a ponderous pace that no tension is ever generated. Andrews is good as the possibly villainous husband, but Curtin is badly cast and this dull dud lacks both subtlety and wit.
Boa: novel Before The Facts by Francis Iles.
DRA                                  97 min mTV
V                                            VGM

## SUSPICION ***                            PG
Alfred Hitchcock      USA              1941
*Cary Grant, Joan Fontaine, Cedric Hardwicke, Nigel Bruce, Dame Mary Whitty, Isabel Jeans, Heather Angel, Leo G. Carroll, Auriol Lee, Reginald Sheffield, Maureen Roden-Ryan, Carol Curtis-Brown, Constance Worth, Violet Shelton*
A wife believes that her husband is out to murder her, but the sense of suspense in this film is muted by the need to observe the moral restraints that film-makers had to contend with at that time. Written by Samson Raphaelson, Alma Reville and Joan Harrison and with music by Franz Waxman. Remade for TV in 1988. AA: Actress (Fontaine).
Boa: novel Before The Fact by Francis Iles.
THR                          95 min (ort 99 min) B/W
V                                            CH5

## SUSPICION OF MURDER **
Ralph Baum/Suzanne Wiesenfeld
                       FRANCE          1973
*Alain Delon, Simone Signoret, Catherine Allegret*
A murder investigation causes family tensions to erupt.

DRA 96 min
B,V VCL/CBS

## SUSPIRIA ***
Dario Argento ITALY 1976
*Jessica Harper, Stefania Casini, Udo Kier, Joan*
*Bennett, Alida Valli, Flavio Bucci, Miguel Bose,*
*Barbara Magnolfi, Susanna Javicoli, Margherita*
*Horowitz, Jacopo Mariani, Fulvio Mingozzi, Renato*
*Zamengo, Rudolf Schundler, Eva Axen*
A new pupil at a German ballet school discovers a
hotbed of Satanism and other diabolical practices. A
kind of melding of PSYCHO and "The Exorcist",
with several good moments and an effective score by
Argento and the rock group Goblin. Written by
Argento and Dario Nicolodi.
HOR 93 min (ort 97 min)
B,V TEVP

## SUZIE SUPERSTAR ***
R18/18
Robert McCallum USA 1983
*Shauna Grant, John Leslie, Gayle Sterling, Sharon*
*Mitchell, Joey Silvera, Jon Martin, Ron Jeremy, Laura*
*Lazarre, Tara Aire, Stephanie Taylor, Ross Roberts*
Story of a rock star who together with her backing
band, is locked into a contract that prevents them
playing with any other group for four years. Eventual-
ly, they break their contract with a little help from a
gangster godfather, at whose birthday they are hired
to sing by the daughter. A better-than-average story
lifts this one above the usual run of adult films.
A 68 min (R18 version – ort 90 min); 53 min Cut
(13 min 14 sec – 18 version)
B,V TCX L/A; SHEP

## SVENGALI **
Anthony Harvey USA 1983
*Peter O'Toole, Jodie Foster, Elizabeth Ashley, Larry*
*Joshua, Pamela Blair, Barbara Byrne, Ronald Wyand,*
*Robin Thomas, Brian Carney, Madeline Potter, Holly*
*Hunter, Vera Mayer, Paul O'Keefe, Stu Charno, Peter*
*Boruchowitz*
Modern updating of the story of the hypnotic and
domineering voice teacher and his female protegee,
who rises to stardom under his guidance. An offbeat
performance from O'Toole makes this film watchable,
but Foster is so lacking in charisma that it's hard to
see how anyone could turn her into a rock star with a
devoted following. Written by Frank Cucci.
Boa: story Trilby by George de Maurier/story by Sue
Grafton.
DRA 100 min mTV
B,V HER

## SWALLOWS AND AMAZONS **
Claude Whatham UK 1974
*Virginia McKenna, Ronald Fraser, Simon West,*
*Sophie Neville, Zanna Hamilton, Stephen Grendon,*
*Kit Seymour, Lesley Bennett, John Franklyn-Robbins,*
*Jack Woolgar, Mike Prat, David Blagden, Brenda*
*Bruce*
A boring film version of a famous children's book
about a group of children on holiday in the Lake
District in 1929. Much of the action takes place at
night when one cannot see a thing, but just hear the
voices of the children as they go about their adven-
tures. Written by David Wood.
Boa: novel by Arthur Ransome.
JUV 88 min (ort 92 min)
B,V TEVP

## SWAMP THING ***
15
Wes Craven USA 1981
*Louis Jourdan, Adrienne Barbeau, Ray Wise, Don*
*Knight, David Hess, Nicholas Worth, Dick Durock, Al*
*Ruban, Ben Bates, Tommy Madden*
A scientist becomes a monster after being contamin-
ated with an experimental growth inducing chemical.
However, our scientist still remains benevolent, even

though he has become a walking vegetable. A ludic-
rous but enjoyable offering. Followed by THE RE-
TURN OF THE SWAMP THING.
HOR 88 min (ort 90 min)
B,V WHV

## SWAP MEET *
Brice Mack USA 1979
*Ruth Cox, Jonathan Gries, Debi Richter, Cheryl Rixon,*
*Danny Goldman*
Teenagers use a "swap meet" as an excuse for the
usual irresponsible escapades.
COM 84 min
B,V SVC L/A; APX

## SWAP, THE *
Jordan Leondopoulos (John Shade/John C. Broderick)
USA 1969
*Robert De Niro, Jennifer Warren, Jered Mickey,*
*Martin Kelley, Viva, Terrayne Crawford, Lisa Blount,*
*Sybil Danning (Sybelle Danninger)*
A man just out of prison goes in search of his brother's
killers. Of minor interest for an early appearance by
De Niro, this film was re-shot and new characters
played by Danning and Blount were added – it was
then re-issued under the above title. It now largely
concentrates on a weekend Long Island party,
attended by a New York film editor and a highly
disruptive character. Despite these changes, it remains a dreary and pointless dud.
Aka: SAM'S SONG
DRA 90 min (ort 104 min)
B,V RNK

## SWARM, THE *
PG
Irwin Allen USA 1978
*Michael Caine, Katherine Ross, Richard Widmark,*
*Richard Chamberlain, Henry Fonda, Olivia De*
*Havilland, Lee Grant, Fred MacMurray, Patty Duke*
*Astin, Ben Johnson, Jose Ferrer, Slim Pickens,*
*Cameron Mitchell, Bradford Dillman*
Cliche-ridden effort about an unstoppable swarm of
killer bees, invading the USA from South America
and stinging all and sundry (except the director
unfortunately). A good cast is wasted on this dross.
Written by Stirling Silliphant. See also THE BEES.
Boa: novel by Arthur Herzog.
HOR 111 min (ort 116 min)
B,V WHV

## SWASHBUCKLER *
PG
James Goldstone USA 1976
*Robert Shaw, James Earl Jones, Peter Boyle,*
*Genevieve Bujold, Beau Bridges, Geoffrey Holder,*
*Avery Schreiber, Anjelica Huston*
An attempt to resurrect the pirate genre with rivals in
love helping a much-wronged lady. Made with neither
zest nor imagination, this feeble effort did nothing to
advance the careers of the stars.
Aka: SCARLET BUCCANEER, THE; SCARLETT
BUCKANEER
A/AD 97 min (ort 101 min)
V CIC

## SWEDISH CONFESSIONS *
Andrew Whyte (Andrei Feher)
SWEDEN 1977
*Barbara Scott, Jack Frank, Anne von Lindberger*
Ghastly Swedish sex film with the ostensible plot of an
international gang of art thieves, whose leader ex-
ploits his relationship with the wife of a banker.
Aka: JAG VILL LIGGA MED DIN AYSKARE
MAMMA; KARLEKSSVINGEL;
KARLEKSVIRVELN
A 90 min
B,V DFS

## SWEDISH PLAYBIRDS **
18
Michel Lemoine (Michel Leblanc)

SWITZERLAND
*Gabrielle Portello, Claudia Nabel, Olivia Flores,*
*Anthony Debray*
A new arrival at a ski resort is mistaken for a
notorious nymphomaniac and despite initial shyness,
soon loses her inhibitions in this formula story.
A                              62 min (ort 75 min) Cut (3 sec)
B,V                                          ELV; SUP

## SWEDISH SEX CLINIC ** 18
Andrew Whyte (Andrei Feher)
                    SWEDEN                    1981
*Gabriel Rivera, Christina Andersson, Marina*
*Delestrade, Barbro Pettersson, Silvia Merino, Marilyn*
*Tess, Marie Laffont, Ursula Angel, Brigitte Laton*
A sex therapist with a successful clinic and practice
finds that he has problems of his own.
Aka: ECSTASY INC.; HEAT AND LUST (ATLAN);
HEAT AND LUST: DIARY OF A SEX THERAPIST;
RASPOUTINE
A                              77 min (ort 90 min) Cut (8 sec)
B,V                       VIC L/A; ELV L/A; ATLAN

## SWEDISH SEX GAMES * 18
Torgny Wickman    SWEDEN/UK               1974
*Borje Nyberg, Chris Chitell, Stellan Skarsgard*
Blackmail with sexual overtones proves to be a
dangerous game with unforeseen consequences.
Aka: INKRAKTARNA; INTRUDER, THE;
INTRUDERS, THE (SHEP); LET US PLAY SEX
A                              81 min (ort 97 min) Cut (21 sec)
B,V                                      ACT L/A; SHEP

## SWEDISH SEX KITTEN * 18
Bert Torn (Mac Ahlberg)
                    SWEDEN                    1974
*Maria Lyn (Marie Forsa), Kim Frank, Anita*
*Anderson, Jack Frank, Gunilla Goransson, Karl*
*Goransson, Marianne Larsson, Lars Dahlgard, Gosta*
*Bergkvist, Tomas Svensson*
Out walking in Stockholm one day, a foreign embassy
official meets a mysterious woman who invites him
back to a mansion, where he is introduced to an
attractive young girl whom he eventually seduces.
The rest of the film is largely devoted to the far from
entrancing story of their relationship and her recollec-
tions of affairs past. A slack and amateurish effort,
even compared to other films of the time.
Aka: FLOSSIE
Boa: novel by John Archer.
A                      63 min (Cut at film release – ort 93 min)
V                                            PHV; SHEP

## SWEENEY! *** 18
David Wickes              UK                    1976
*John Thaw, Dennis Waterman, Barry Foster, Ian*
*Bannen, Colin Welland, Joe Melia, Michael Coles,*
*Brian Glover, Lynda Bellingham, Morris Perry, Nick*
*Brimble, Bernard Kay, Anthony Brown, Sally Osborne*
Quite good spin-off from a TV police series, telling of
an international oil cartel that uses blackmail and
murder for its own ends. Followed by an inferior
sequel. Written by Ranald Graham.
A/AD                                          93 min
B,V                                            TEVP

## SWEENEY 2 * 18
Tom Clegg                  UK                    1978
*John Thaw, Dennis Waterman, Barry Stanton,*
*Denholm Elliott, John Flanagan, David Casey,*
*Derrick O'Connor, John Aikin, James Warrior, Guy*
*Standevin, Nigel Hawthorne, Ken Hutchinson, Brian*
*Gwaspari, Frederick Treves*
The new head of the Flying Squad is over-ambitious
for results, after the failure to net a gang of bank
robbers who return to Malta after each heist. A second
feature-length spin-off from a popular British police
series, but let down by limp direction and an unin-
spired script. Written by Troy Kennedy Martin.

A/AD                          103 min (ort 108 min)
B,V                                            TEVP

## SWEENEY: JACKPOT ** 15
Tom Clegg                  UK                    1975
*Dennis Waterman, John Thaw, Garfield Morgan, Ed*
*Devereaux, Morgan Shepherd, Morris Perry*
An episode from the popular British TV police series
"The Sweeney", that tells of an investigation mounted
when £30,000 goes missing and the evidence seems to
point to police corruption. Fair. Written by Tony
Marsh.
A/AD                                          55 min mTV
V                                              VCC

## SWEET DREAMS *** 15
Karel Reisz               USA                    1985
*Ed Harris, Jessica Lange, Ann Wedgeworth, David*
*Clennon, James Staley, David Clennon, P.J. Soles,*
*Gary Gasabara*
A biopic on the life of Patsy Cline, an American singer
of the 1950s, that tends to focus on her marital
problems to the detriment of the more interesting
performing sequences. Some gutsy performances and
memorable songs redeem it. Lange mimes to Cline's
original recordings.
DRA                          114 min; 110 min (WHV)
B, V/sh               TEVP L/A; WHV (VHS only)

## SWEET GEORGIA * 18
Edward Boles              USA                    1972
*Marsha Jordan, Barbara Miles, Al Wilkins, Gene*
*Drew, Chuck Lawson, Bill King Jr*
Yet another insatiable heroine and her willing ways.
Georgia has one ambition in life, to find enough men
around the ranch to satisfy her.
A                              70 min (ort 80 min) Cut (56 sec)
B,V                                      ROXY L/A; TOW

## SWEET HOSTAGE *** 15
Lee Philips               USA                    1975
*Linda Blair, Martin Sheen, Jeanne Cooper, Bert*
*Remsen, Lee DeBroux, Dehl Berti, Al Hopson, Bill*
*Sterchi, Valentino DeLeon, Michael C. Eiland, Mary*
*Michael Carnes, Don Hann, Ross Elder, Chris*
*Williams*
A young man escapes from the asylum where he was
being held and goes off to live in the mountains in
New Mexico. Later he kidnaps a young girl and a
touching rapport develops between them. A talky
melodrama redeemed by fine performances.
Boa: novel Welcome To Xanadu by Nathaniel
Benchley.
DRA                                          93 min mTV
B,V                                            CINE

## SWEET KILL *** 
Curtis Hanson             USA                    1970
*Tab Hunter, Nadyne Turney, Roberta Collins, Isabell*
*Jewell*
A psychopath cannot deal with relations with the
opposite sex, so he murders them instead. Set in
Venice, California and despite the nature of the
subject matter, extremely gripping.
Aka: AROUSERS, THE; KISS FROM EDDIE, A
THR                                          90 min
B,V                                      PRIME; CBS

## SWEET LIBERTY ** 15
Alan Alda                 USA                    1986
*Alan Alda, Saul Rubinek, Michael Caine, Lise*
*Hilboldt, Bob Hoskins, Lillian Gish, Michelle Pfeiffer,*
*Lois Chiles, Linda Thorson, Diane Agostini, Alvin*
*Alexis, Christopher Bergman, Leo Burmester, Cynthia*
*Burr, Timothy Carhart*
A history teacher in a small town writes a book on the
American Revolution that becomes a bestseller. When
the film rights are sold to Hollywood a film crew are
sent out to make a film on location. In charge of them

is a bad-tempered and anarchic director who proceeds to turn the book into a gag-filled sex romp, clashing with the writer in the process. A few laughs cannot hide the emptiness of this one. The script is by Alda.
COM      102 min (ort 107 min)
V/h      CIC

**SWEET LIES \***      15
Nathalie Delon      USA      1987
*Treat Williams, Julianne Phillips, Joanna Pacula, Laura Manszky*
An American goes to Paris to catch an insurance swindler and at his hotel the daughter of the concierge tries to seduce him. She fails and tells her two older friends, who make a bet as to which of them will seduce him first, and the pair employ the most outrageous tactics in order to do this. A disjointed and empty-headed comedy that is both unfunny and quite pointless.
COM      93 min
B,V      SONY

**SWEET LORRAINE \*\*\***      PG
Steve Gomer      USA      1987
*Maureen Stapleton, Trini Alvarado, Lee Richardson, John Bedford Lloyd, Giancarlo Esposito, Edith Falco, Todd Graff, Evan Handler, Freddie Roman*
A remote hotel in the Catskills finally faces its last summer season as it stands in need of extensive repairs, and the owner has received a tempting offer from developers. An atmospheric slice-of-life tale with little direction but a host of interesting observations.
DRA      97 min
V      PRISM

**SWEET MURDER \*\***      18
Percival Rubens      USA      1990
*Helene Udy, Embeth Davidtz, Russell Todd*
Two girls from very different backgrounds become room-mates and friends, but when one inherits a fortune and gets herself a handsome boyfriend, the other has a brainstorm and decides to do away with her.
THR      93 min
V      NWV

**SWEET REVENGE \*** 
Jerry Schatzberg      USA      1977
*Stockard Channing, Sam Waterston, Franklin Ajaye, Richard Doughty*
A lawyer defends a female car thief and falls in love with her. Unfortunately, this dismal offering is very hard to love.
Aka: DANDY, THE ALL-AMERICAN GIRL
DRA      85 min (ort 90 min)
B,V      MGM

**SWEET REVENGE \*\***      15
Mark Sobel      USA      1986
*Ted Shackelford, Nancy Allen, Martin Landau, Sal Landi, Michele Little, Gina Gershon, Stacey Adams*
A mediocre film about a female journalist kidnapped by a white slavery ring while investigating the disappearance of women in Los Angeles.
A/AD      77 min (ort 80 min)
B,V      VES

**SWEET SCENT OF DEATH, THE \*\***
Peter Sasdy      UK      1984
*Dean Stockwell, Shirley Knight, Carmen Du Saute, Robert Lang, Allan Gifford, Michael Gothard*
An American couple come to live in London and experience problems relating to the wife's former career as a lawyer.
Osca: MARK OF THE DEVIL HOR      75 min
B,V      BWV

**SWEET SEXUAL AWAKENING \*\***      18
     GREECE

*Maria Constant, Samantha Roman, Angela Stanon*
Routine story with a theme used countless times before; that of a young woman and her growing awareness of her own sexuality.
Aka: JANE'S SEXUAL AWAKENING
A      75 min (ort 98 min) (Cut at film release)
B,V      18PLAT/TOW L/A; SHEP

**SWEET SINS OF SEXY SUSAN, THE \*\***
Franz Antel (Francois Lergand)
     AUSTRIA/ITALY/HUNGARY      1967
*Mike Marshall, Pascale Petit, Terry Corday, Rosemary Lindt, Harold Leipnitz*
Historical romp, set in the 19th century, about the resistance of the women of Westphalia to the French occupation.
Aka: DIE WIRTIN VON DER LAHN; I DOLCI VIZI DELLA CASTA SUSANNA; SUSANNE, DIE WIRTIN VON DER LAHN; SUZANNE: THE HOSTESS OF THE LAHN
COM      87 min
V      REX L/A; APX

**SWEET SIXTEEN \***      18
Jim Sotos      USA      1982
*Bo Hopkins, Susan Strasberg, Aleisa Shirley, Don Stroud, Patrick MacNee, Dana Kimmell, Steve Antin, Sharon Farrell, Don Shanks, Logan Clarke, Michael Pataki, Henry Wilcoxon, Larry Storch, Michael Cutt*
A sensuous young girl has a string of boyfriends who, one by one are found murdered, in this predictable thriller in which the identity of the murderer comes as no surprise.
Aka: SWEET 16
THR      84 min (ort 90 min)
B,V      VPD

**SWEET WILLIAM \*\***
Claude Whatham      UK      1980
*Sam Waterston, Jenny Agutter, Anna Massey, Geraldine James, Daphne Oxenford, Rachel Bell, Arthur Lowe, Peter Dean, Tim Pigot-Smith, Emma Bakhle, Victoria Fairbrother, Ivor Roberts, Joan Cooper, David Wood, Billy Milton*
A very minor tale in which a woman discovers that her American boyfriend is incapable of being faithful but refuses to accept his philandering ways.
Boa: novel by Beryl Bainbridge.
DRA      88 min (ort 92 min)
B,V,V2      HOK

**SWEET, SWEET RACHEL \***
Sutton Roley      USA      1971
*Alex Dreier, Stefanie Powers, Pat Hingle, Louise Latham, Brenda Scott, Steve Inhat, Chris Robinson, Mark Tapscott, William Bryant, Len Wayland, Rod McCary, John Alvin, John Hillerman*
An ESP expert tries to track down the source of a strange force, which has caused one man's murder and is driving his widow insane. A messy and incoherent tale that was the pilot for the TV series "The Sixth Sense".
HOR      73 min mTV
B,V      RNK

**SWEETHEART'S DANCE \*\*\***      15
Robert Greenwald      USA      1988
*Don Johnson, Susan Sarandon, Jeff Daniels, Elizabeth Perkins, Kate Reid, Justin Henry, Holly Marie Combs, Heather Coleman*
Set in a small town in Vermont, this bittersweet comedy tells of a couple whose marriage is just about ending, while their close friend is at the beginning of a serious relationship. A charming little tale, not very profound or funny, but quite endearing. Scripted by Ernest Thompson.
COM      97 min (ort 100 min)
B,V      RCA

## SWIM TEAM *
James Polakof         USA              1979
*James Daughton, Stephen Furst, Richard Young,*
*Jenny Neumann, Buster Crabbe, Kim Day*
Spurred on by a determined new coach, a swimming
team gets into shape. This is truly a film of limited
appeal.
COM                          78 min (ort 92 min)
B,V,V2                                     VPD

## SWING HIGH, SWING LOW ***
Mitchell Leisen       USA              1937
*Carole Lombard, Fred MacMurray, Dorothy Lamour,*
*Charles Butterworth, Jean Dixon, Harvey Stephens,*
*Franklin Pangborn, Anthony Quinn*
A singer helps a soldier start a career as a trumpet
player but their subsequent marriage is threatened by
his success. Corny but quite enjoyable. Also filmed as
"Dance of Life" and "When My Baby Smiles At Me".
The music is by Victor Young and the script by
Virginia Van Upp and Oscar Hammerstein II.
Boa: play Burlesque by George Manker Walters and
Arthur Hopkins.
DRA                       93 min (ort 97 min) B/W
B,V                                     VCL/CBS

## SWING SHIFT *                         PG
Jonathan Demme        USA              1984
*Goldie Hawn, Kurt Russell, Christine Lahti, Ed*
*Harris, Fred Ward, Sudi Bond, Roger Corman, Holly*
*Hunter, Patty Maloney, Belinda Carlisle*
During WW2, American housewives were recruited to
work in the factories. One such woman finds her life
complicated when she dons overalls for Uncle Sam. A
feeble romantic comedy written by several top writers
(Ron Nyswaner, Bo Goldman and Nancy Dowd) under
the pseudonym Rob Morton.
Aka: SWINGSHIFT
COM             96 min (ort 112 min) Cut (2 sec)
B,V                                        WHV

## SWING TIME ****                       U
George Stevens        USA              1936
*Fred Astaire, Ginger Rogers, Victor Moore, Helen*
*Broderick, Eric Blore, Betty Furness, George Metaxa*
The love affair between the two partners of a dance
team is complicated by his engagement to another
girl. Forget the plot and just enjoy the dance routines,
in one of the best of the Astaire-Rogers musicals. AA:
Song ("The Way You Look Tonight" – Jerome Kern –
music/Dorothy Fields – lyrics).
MUS                      103 min (ort 114 min) B/W
V                                          CH5

## SWINGIN' SUMMER, A **
Robert Sparr          USA              1965
*Raquel Welch, James Stacey, Allan Jones, William*
*Wellman Jr, Quinn O'Hara, The Righteous Brothers,*
*The Rip Chords, Garry Lewis and The Playboys*
Three boys open a dance hall in this lightweight
musical.
MUS                                    88 min
B,V                                    VCL/CBS

## SWINGING BARMAIDS, THE ***           18
Gus Trikonis          USA              1975
*Bruce Watson, Laura Hippe, Katie Saylor, William*
*Smith, Dyanne Thorne, John Alderman, Renie*
*Radich, Zitto Kazann*
A cop goes after a mad killer whose victims are all
barmaids. A well made B-thriller with a strong plot
and convincing performances. The script is by Charles
Griffith.
Aka: EAGER BEAVERS
THR                      83 min Cut (2 min 26 sec)
B,V                                 SKP; XTASY

## SWINGING CHEERLEADERS *
Jack Hill             USA              1974
*Jo Johnston, Rainbeaux Smith, Colleen Camp,*
*Rosanne Katon, Ron Hajeck, Jason Summers, Mae*
*Mercer*
Story of two cheerleaders and their adventures with
the college football team, as told by a woman journal-
ist who goes undercover for this assignment.
COM                                    88 min
B,V,V2                                  IFS L/A

## SWISS CONSPIRACY, THE *              15
Jack Arnold
            USA/WEST GERMANY           1975
*David Janssen, Senta Berger, John Ireland, John*
*Saxon, Elke Sommer, Ray Milland, Anton Diffring*
The head of a Swiss bank hires a detective to
investigate the blackmailing of five of his customers.
An over-complex and dated tale in which the nice
locations are more memorable than any aspects of the
plot.
Aka: PER SALDO MORD
THR                       85 min (ort 92 min)
B,V                                        WHV

## SWISS FAMILY ROBINSON **             U
            AUSTRALIA                  1971
An adequate animated version of Wyss's children's
classic.
Boa: novel by Johann Wyss.
CAR                                    47 min
B,V       RNK L/A; VCL/CBS L/A; CHILD; STYL

## SWISS FAMILY ROBINSON ***            U
Ken Annakin           USA              1960
*John Mills, Dorothy McGuire, James MacArthur,*
*Tommy Kirk, Kevin Corcoran, Janet Munro, Sessue*
*Hayakawa, Cecil Parker, Andy Ho, Milton Reid, Larry*
*Taylor*
A family are shipwrecked on an island and have
various adventures, including a clash with a horde of
pirates that they fight off with supreme ease. Light-
weight enjoyable nonsense. First made in 1940 and
remade for TV in 1975.
Boa: novel by Johann Wyss.
JUV                                    126 min
B,V                                    RNK; WDV

## SWITCH HITTERS **                    R18
            USA
*Stacey Donovan, Matt Forrest*
Instantly forgettable adult comedy telling of a sexy
young woman and her exploits with the members of a
baseball team.
A                                      64 min
V                                      VEXCEL

## SWITCH IN TIME, A **                 15
Paul Donovan          USA              1987
*Tom McCamus, Laurie Paton, Brian Downey*
The story of three people who are accidentally trans-
ported back in time to Switzerland of the 1st century.
Whilst two of them are content to bask in adulation
from a barbarian tribe, the third begins to introduce
them to the secrets of technology, much to the dismay
of the Romans. A lighthearted and fairly amusing
romp.
COM                                    86 min
B,V                                    CBS

## SWITCHBLADE SISTERS, THE **          18
Jack Hill             USA              1975
*Robbie Lee, Joanne Nail, Monica Gayle, Rosalie Cole,*
*Kitty Bruce, Marlene Clark, Michael Miller*
The story of a female gang and its wide range of
criminal activities. A low-budget tale, but quite
effective. Originally released as "The Jezebels", which
was the gang's name.
Aka: JEZEBELS, THE; PLAYGIRL GANG
DRA              86 min (ort 90 min) Cut (8 sec)
B,V,V2                             IFS; STAT; NET

## SWITCHING CHANNELS *** PG
Ted Kotcheff USA 1987
*Kathleen Turner, Christopher Reeve, Burt Reynolds,
Ned Beatty, Henry Gibson, George Newbern, Al
Waxman, Ken James, Barry Flatman, Ted Simonett,
Anthony Sherwood, Joe Silver, Charles Kimbrough*
Another re-run of "His Girl Friday" but updated to the
present day and set in a TV news network, where a
cunning editor will stop at nothing to keep his ace
reporter from leaving to get married. Quite enjoyable,
but somewhat bland, although the stars do their best
to overcome this.
COM 100 min (ort 108 min)
V/sh WHV

## SWORD AND THE ROSE, THE *** U
Ken Annakin USA 1952
*Richard Todd, Glynis Johns, James Robertson
Justice, Michael Gough, Jane Barrett, Peter Copley,
Rosalie Crutchley, D.A. Clarke-Smith, Ernest Jay,
John Vere, Phillip Lennard, Bryan Coleman, Jean
Mercure*
Period drama depicting the ill-fated romance between
the captain of Henry VII's palace guard and Princess
Mary Tudor, played out against the backdrop of court
intrigue. A minor historical yarn, thinly plotted but
quite colourful. Written by Laurence E. Watkin and
filmed in England.
Boa: novel When Knighthood Was In Flower by
Charles Major.
DRA 88 min (ort 93 min)
B,V WDV

## SWORD AND THE SORCERER, THE ** 18
Albert Pyun USA 1982
*Lee Horsley, Kathleen Beller, Simon MacCorkindale,
George Maharis, Richard Lynch, Richard Moll, Robert
Tessier, Nina Van Pallandt, Anna Bjorn, Jeff Corey*
Fantasy adventure about a sword-wielding hero, who
saves a kingdom from an evil wizard and his nasty
demon, rescuing a fair damsel into the bargain. A
standard fantasy with passable effects.
FAN 98 min (ort 100 min)
B,V,V2 RNK

## SWORD IN THE STONE, THE ** U
Wolfgang Reitherman USA 1963
*Voices of: Ricky Sorenson, Sebastian Cabot, Karl
Swenson, Junius Matthews, Alan Napier, Norman
Alden, Martha Wentworth, Ginny Taylor, Barbara Jo
Allen, Richard Reithermann, Robert Reithermann*
An animated version of the Arthurian legend follow-
ing the adventures of a youngster called "Wart", who
is destined to become King Arthur. One of the poorer
Disney animations, fast paced but flat, with ponderous
dialogue and unmemorable Sherman Brothers songs.
Boa: novel The Once And Future King by T.H. White.
CAR 76 min (ort 80 min)
V WDV

## SWORD OF BUSHIDO, THE ** 18
Adrian Carr 1989
*Richard Norton, Rochelle Asana, Toshishiro Obata,
Judy Green, Kovik Wattankoon*
Martial arts mayhem with an American karate expert
in Thailand to find out what happened to his grandfather, who was onboard a plane that crashed there
during WW2. When he learns that his grandpa
survived the crash but was executed by the Japanese
for stealing a sacred sword, he resolves to locate and
return it to the original owners. Abundant action
sequences (and a few softcore ones) partially bolster
the flabby and mindless script.
MAR 90 min (ort 100 min)
V FUTUR

## SWORD OF HEAVEN ** 18
Byron Meyers USA 1985
*Tadashi Yamashita, Mel Novak, Gerry Gibson, Katie
Mullin, Karen McManus, Joe Randazzo*
A martial arts expert is engaged to find a stolen sacred
sword, which possesses magical properties as it was
forged from a meteorite.
MAR 91 min (FRON/GHV); 81 min (VCC) Cut (50 sec)
B,V FRON/GHV; VCC (VHS only)

## SWORD OF HONOUR: PARTS 1 AND 2 * 15
Pino Amenta/Catherine Millar
AUSTRALIA 1986
*Andrew Clarke, Tracy Mann, Alan Fletcher, Nikki
Coghill, Andrew Sharp, Linda Newton, Wynn Roberts,
Margaret Ford, Paul Hampton, Julia Blake, Pauline
Chan, Alan Hopgood, Gus Mercurio, Stephanie
Nicholson, Tony Richards*
Dull and unimaginative drama dealing with the
effects of the Vietnam War on an Australian family.
Apart from a few token appearances of groups opposed
to Australian participation in this conflict, this film
rather firmly avoids exploring any of the larger issues
raised by Australian involvement.
DRA 267 min (3 cassettes) Cut (2 sec)
V CHV; IVS

## SWORD OF MONTE CHRISTO *
Maurice Geraghty USA 1951
*George Montgomery, Paula Corday, Berry Kroeger,
Steve Brodie, Robert Warwick, William Conrad*
A woman finds the legendary title sword with the key
to the fabulous treasure of Monte Christo inscribed on
it and sets out in search of it, joined in her quest by an
army officer. However, a corrupt minister is also
seeking the treasure. A feeble adventure yarn, made
on the cheap.
A/AD 80 min
B,V,V2 INT

## SWORD OF SHERWOOD FOREST ** U
Terence Fisher UK 1960
*Richard Greene, Peter Cushing, Niall McGinnis,
Richard Pasco, Jack Gwillim, Sarah Branch, Dennis
Lotis, Nigel Green, Vanda Godsell, Derren Nesbitt,
Oliver Reed*
Recreating the TV role that brought him fame,
Greene as Robin fights the villainous Sheriff of
Nottingham and foils a plot on the part of the Earl of
Newark, to murder the Archbishop of Canterbury. A
mildly enjoyable spin-off from the popular 1950s TV
series "The Adventures Of Robin Hood", that has little
to offer except the enthusiasm of the actors.
A/AD 77 min (ort 80 min)
V PREST

## SWORD OF THE BARBARIANS **
Michael E. Lemick (Franco Prosperi)
ITALY 1983
*Peter MacCoy, Margareta Range, Yvonne Fraschetti,
Anthony Freeman, Sabrina Siani*
A young chieftain undertakes a perilous journey in
order to attempt to restore a young girl to life.
Standard sword-and-sorcery fantasy.
Aka: GUNAN, KING OF THE BARBARIANS;
GUNAN NO. 2: THE INVINCIBLE SWORD; LA
SPADA BARBARI; LE SPADE DEI BARBARI
FAN 90 min
V VFP L/A; APX

## SWORD OF THE VALIANT ** PG
Stephen Weeks UK 1984
*Miles O'Keeffe, Cyrielle Claire, Leigh Lawson, Sean
Connery, Trevor Howard, Peter Cushing, Ronald
Lacey, Emma Sutton, Douglas Wilmer, Lila Kedrova,
John Rhys Davies, Bruce Lidington, Thomas
Heathcote, John Serrat, Brian Coburn*
A remake of "Gawain And The Green Knight" by the
same director. Based on a medieval legend, this tells
of a squire who has a year to solve a riddle and save a
maiden, after he accepts a challenge from a strange,
magical knight. A clumsy mixture of fantasy and

realism, with the all-too-brief appearances of Connery the film's highlights. Written by Weeks, Philip M. Breen, Howard C. Pen, Roger Towne, Rosemary Sutcliff and Therese Burdon.
Aka: CLASH OF SWORDS
A/AD                     97 min (ort 101 min) Cut (38 sec)
B,V                                       GHV L/A; VCC

**SWORDKILL **                                           15
Jo Larry Carroll          USA                          1984
*Janet Julian, Charles Lumpkin, Hiroshi Fujioka,*
*John Calvin, Frank Schuler*
The deep-frozen body of a samurai is discovered and he is brought back to life. He now finds himself having to survive on the streets of L.A. and deal with the criminals he comes into contact with. A predictable tale enlivened by some good special effects.
A/AD                     77 min (ort 81 min) Cut (21 sec)
B,V                                                     EIV

**SWORN TO SILENCE **                                    15
Peter Levin               USA                          1987
*Peter Coyote, Dabney Coleman, Caroline McWilliams,*
*Ed Nelson, David Spielberg, Liam Neeson*
Two defence lawyers take on the case of a psychopathic recluse charged with murder but learn that he killed two other girls in the course of their interviews, thus presenting them with the dilemma of having to choose between their moral and professional obligations. An intriguing drama that fails to really tackle the issues it raises. Written by Robert L. Joseph.
Boa: novel Priveleged Information by Tom Alibrandi and Frank M. Armani.
DRA                                      94 min (ort 100 min) mTV
B,V                                                     IVS

**SYLVESTER ***                                          PG
Tim Hunter                USA                          1985
*Melissa Gilbert, Richard Farnsworth, Michael*
*Schoeffling, Constance Towers, Pete Kowanko,*
*Yankton Hatten, Shane Serwin, Angel Salazar, Chris*
*Pederson, Arliss Howard, Shizuko Hoshi, Richard*
*Jamison, James Gammon, Ariane de Vogue*
The familiar tale of a young girl turning a broken-down nag into a champion jumper. (One day they'll try it the other way round – it'll be more interesting.) Written by Carol Sobieski.
Boa: novel by Ray Stark.
JUV                                      99 min (ort 104 min)
B,V                                                     RCA

**SYLVIA ***                                             PG
Michael Firth    NEW ZEALAND                           1985
*Nigel Terry, Eleanor David, Mary Regan, Martyn*
*Sanderson, Tom Wilkinson, Terence Cooper, David*
*Letch, Sarah Peirse, James Cross, Peter Thorpe, Roy*
*Pearse, Ian Harrop, Te Whatanui Skipwith, Norman*
*Forsey, Margaret Murray*
A drama based on the work of famed educationalist Sylvia Ashton-Warner, who made herself unpopular with the educational authorities in New Zealand in the 1940s, with her innovative methods of teaching reading to Maori children. An inspiring and sincere tale.
Boa: books Teacher and I Passed This Way by Sylvia Ashton-Warner.
DRA                                                    97 min
B,V                                                    ODY

**SYLVIA SCARLETT ***                                    U
George Cukor              USA                          1935
*Katharine Hepburn, Cary Grant, Brian Aherne,*
*Edmund Gwenn, Natalie Paley, Lennox Pawle, Dennie*
*Moore*
First time teaming of Hepburn and Grant in a screwball comedy, where she has to leave town disguised as a boy when her no-good father gets into trouble. A rambling and offbeat tale that was a failure on release, mainly due its languid pace. Written by

Gladys Unger, John Collier and Mortimer Offner.
Boa: novel by Compton Mackenzie.
COM                          86 min (ort 94 min) B/W
V                                                       VCC

**SYMPHONY OF EVIL **                                    15
Craig Lahiff      AUSTRALIA                            1987
*Penny Cook, Arna-Maria Winchester, Liddy Clark,*
*Olivia Hammett, Patrick Frost, Vivienne Graves*
Set in a music academy, this tense tale revolves around an independent female student who is haunted by a "phantom of the opera" type spectre. Average.
Aka: CODA
HOR                                                    96 min
B,V                                       CINE L/A: VIP

**SYNDICATE VICE **                                      18
Al Adamson                USA                          1980
*Timothy Brown, Russ Tamblyn, Jana Belland*
A women's hotel in Los Angeles is the scene for many intrigues.
Aka: GIRLS' HOTEL
A                            89 min (ort 97 min) Cut (11 sec)
B,V                              SVC L/A; ILV L/A; MIG

# T

**T.N.T. JACKSON **
Cirio H. Santiago         USA                          1975
*Jeanne Bell, Stan Shaw, Pat Anderson, Ken Metcalf*
Low-budget martial arts adventure with a black heroine, played by shapely former Playboy Playmate Wells starring as a karate expert who is looking for her missing brother. Filmed in the Philippines. Fair.
MAR                                                    87 min
B,V                                       CAP; ZOD/PVG

**TABLE FOR FIVE ***                                     PG
Robert Lieberman          USA                          1983
*John Voight, Richard Crenna, Millie Perkins, Marie-*
*Christine Barrault, Roxana Zal, Robby Kiger, Son*
*Hoang Bui, Maria O'Brien*
A divorced man takes his three children on a European cruise as a way of making up for his absence and has to tell them that their mother has been killed. A slow and quite competent tearjerker, written by David Seltzer.
DRA                                      116 min (ort 123 min)
B,V                                                    CBS

**TABOO ISLAND ***                                       18
Enzo D'Ambrosio     ITALY                              1976
*Laura Gemser, Arthur Kennedy, Paolo Giusti, Nicola*
*Pagrone*
A young man adrift at sea lands on a remote island and meets a beautiful girl.
Aka: LA SPIAGGIA DEL DESIDERIO
A                                                      90 min
B,V                                       PRV; VPD

**TAFFIN **                                              18
Francis Megahy          UK                             1987
*Pierce Brosnan, Alison Doody, Ray McAnally, Jeremy*
*Child, Dearbhla Molloy, Jim Bartley, Alan Stanford,*
*Gerald McSorley, Patrick Bergin, Britta Smith*
A debt collector battles ruthless property developers determined to push through a project to build a chemical plant on the local athletics field. A dull action tale partially enlivened by a couple of exciting sequences.
Aka: TAFFIN: A DIFFERENT KIND OF HERO
A/AD                                                   96 min
V                                                      VES

**TAG: THE ASSASSINATION GAME **
Nick Castle               USA                          1982
*Robert Carradine, Linda Hamilton, Bruce Abbott,*

*Kristine DeBell, Frazer Smith, Perry Lang, John Mengatti, Michael Winslow, Ivan Bonar*
Students play games with rubber-tipped dart guns, but one of them begins to take this pastime too seriously. Another predictable campus-kids-in-peril offering.
Aka: T.A.G. – THE ASSASSINATION BUREAU
THR 92 min
B,V 3MVID/PVG

## TAGGART: DOUBLE JEOPARDY *** 15
Jim McCann UK 1988
*Mark MacManus, James Macpherson, James Laurenson, Sheila Ruskin, Valerie Gogan, Rose McBain, Herbert Trattnigg, Claus Ellsman, Harriet Buchan, Alec Heggie, Barbara Rafferty, John Shedelen, Iain Anders, Robert Robertson*
A woman commits suicide in a wood but the absence of a note and other circumstances convinces Taggart that she was murdered by her common-law husband. Unable to find evidence to prove the man's guilt, he mounts a dogged campaign of surveiilance that takes him to Germany and finally back to Glasgow. A well-plotted murder mystery that moves along at a fast pace, maintaining interest right up to the end.
DRA 77 min mTV
V TELS

## TAGGART: IN COLD BLOOD *** 15
Haldane Duncan UK 1988
*Mark McManus, Diane Keen, James Macpherson, Harriet Buchan, Iain Anders, Freddie Boardley, Leonard O'Malley, Mona Bruce, Patricia Ross, Robert Robertson*
Jim Taggart finds his approaching 24th wedding anniversary having to take a back seat to a baffling case in which a woman shot a man in a parked car and then tried to take her own life. However, it soon transpires that she cannot be charged with murder as a forensic investigation reveals that her intended victim was already dead. A competent movie-length feature based on the popular TV detective series.
DRA 77 min mTV
V TELS

## TAI-PAN * 18
Daryl Duke USA 1986
*Bryan Brown, John Stanton, Joan Chen, Tom Guinee, Bill Leadbitter, Russell Wong*
An overlong and rambling film based on Clavell's book of similar merits, telling of the adventures of a 19th century trader who is based in Hong Kong. A film that looks as if it should be a major epic but isn't really about anything in particular. Written by John Briley and Stanley Mann.
Boa: novel by James Clavell.
DRA 123 min (ort 127 min)
B, V/sh CAN; PATHE

## TAINTED ** 18
Orestes Matacena USA 1985
*Shari Shattuck, Park Overall, Gene Tootle, Magilla Schaus*
An innocent rape victim is accused of murder and has to contend with many difficulties in her struggle to prove her innocence.
DRA 90 min
B,V AVA; CAN

## TAKE A GIRL LIKE YOU * 15
Jonathan Miller UK 1970
*Hayley Mills, Oliver Reed, Sheila Hancock, Noel Harrison, John Bird, Aimi MacDonald, Ronald Lacey, Geraldine Sherman, Imogen Hassall, Penelope Keith*
A sexually inexperienced Northern girl moves to the South to work as a teacher, and becomes the target of small-town womanisers. A dated little tale of very minor appeal. Written by George Melly.
Boa: novel by Kingsley Amis. DRA 94 min (ort 101 min)
V RCA

## TAKE DOWN ** PG
Keith Merrill USA 1978
*Lorenzo Lamas, Kathleen Lloyd, Edward Herrmann, Maureen McCormick, Nick Beauvy, Kevin Hooks, Stephen Furst*
A high school tries to put all its efforts into winning a wrestling contest in this engaging semi-comic account.
DRA 107 min
B,V VPD

## TAKE ME OUT TO THE BALL GAME *** U
Busby Berkely USA 1949
*Frank Sinatra, Esther Williams, Gene Kelly, Betty Garrett, Edward Arnold, Jules Munshin, Richard Lane, Tom Dugan, Murray Alper, Wilton Graf, Charles Regan, Mack Gray, Douglas Fowley, Eddie Parkes, James Burke*
Bright and cheerful musical set in the 1890s, telling of a young woman who takes over a baseball team. Full of humour and enjoyable lines, this served as something of a trial run for ON THE TOWN. Numbers include "O'Brien To Ryan To Goldberg" and "The Hat My Father Wore On St Patrick's Day". Songs are by Betty Comden, Adolph Green and Roger Edens.
Aka: EVERYBODY'S CHEERING
MUS 89 min (ort 93 min)
V MGM

## TAKE MY BODY ** 18
Michel Le Blanc FRANCE 1984
*Olinka (Olinka Hardimann), Gabrielle Pontello, Laura Clair, Kathleen Menard, Mary Monroe, John Oury, Eric Dray*
On a train heading for Paris, Natasha (Monroe) invites a guy into her compartment for a session. A complex espionage plot then unfolds, with the guy turning out to be employed by an intelligence agency that is tracking a blonde spy onboard the train. Mind-numbing nonsense.
A 78 min
B,V PRI; GLOB

## TAKE NO PRISONERS * 18
Tom Shaw USA 1987
*G.F. Russell, Edgar Reynolds*
The inventor of a revolutionary bugging device and his family are kidnapped by a secret agent in an attempt to foil a Soviet assassination attempt. A film that is so carelessly thrown together and ineptly directed that it is best enjoyed as a faintly ludicrous parody.
Aka: OPERATION: TAKE NO PRISONERS
THR 86 min
V VES

## TAKE OFF ** 18
Armand Weston USA 1978
*Wade Nichols, Leslie Bovee, Georgina Spelvin, Annette Haven, Eric Edwards*
An erotic update of the Oscar Wilde tale "The Picture of Dorian Gray", about a man who never ages. Three decades of Daren Blue's life are examined in flashback form as he tells his story to a woman invited to one of his parties. Much use of black and white film ensues, as we see Wade's life from the gangster era (when he first wished to remain young) through to the 1970s. Interesting in a rather contrived and hammily acted way.
A 76 min (ort 103 min) Cut
B,V 18PLAT/TOW; PHE (VHS only); NET; TCX;
SHEP

## TAKE THE MONEY AND RUN ** PG
Woody Allen          USA            1968
*Woody Allen, Janet Margolin, Marcel Hillaire,*
*Jacquelyn Hyde, Lonny Chapman, Louise Lasser, Jan*
*Merlin, Jackson Beck (narration)*
A look at the career of a compulsive thief, with plenty
of visual gags of variable quality. Louise Lasser
appears briefly. This was Allen's first film as writer,
director and star, and shows a few flashes of brilliance,
but is far too incoherent to be effective.
COM                          83 min (ort 85 min)
B,V                                RNK; VGM

## TAKE THIS JOB AND SHOVE IT ** PG
Gus Trikonis         USA            1981
*Robert Hays, Art Carney, David Keith, Tim*
*Thomerson, Barbara Hershey, Martin Mull, Charlie*
*Rich, Eddie Albert, Penelope Milford*
A young executive is given the job of modernising the
brewery in his home town, but being with a one-time
girlfriend and old cronies affects his attitude. The title
(taken from a 1970s hit by Johnny Paycheck) prom-
ises more than the plot can deliver, but the film is
likeable enough.
COM                          98 min (ort 100 min)
B,V                                     EHE

## TAKE TIME TO SMELL THE FLOWERS **
Chris Caras          USA            1977
*Viju Krem, David Anthony, Greta Hartog, Richard*
*Salamon, Harrington Smith, Thea Caradino, Fred L.*
*Cherrick*
Two people make love and devise plots for possible sex
films which then come to life.
Aka: COME WITH ME MY LOVE
A                                     64 min
B,V                                 INT L/A

## TAKE TWO * 18
Peter Rowe           USA            1987
*Grant Goodeve, Robin Mattson, Frank Stallone,*
*Warren Berlinger, Nita Talbot, Darwyn Swalve*
On her deathbed, a mother tells her son of his twin
brother, who was brought up by a millionaire. He sets
out to meet him, but finds him to be a ruthless tycoon.
Soon embroiled in an affair with the man's wife, the
two begin to plot a murder. A wildly uneven thriller
that veers from pathos to comedy to gore, without ever
finding a point of focus.
THR                          100 min (ort 101 min)
B,V                                    NOVA

## TAKE, THE **
Robert Hartford-Davis  USA          1974
*Vic Morrow, Billy Dee Williams, Frankie Avalon,*
*Eddie Albert, Albert Salmi*
A policeman accepts a bribe yet still tries to stop a
gangland boss in this mediocre crime story. A good
cameo from Avalon as a petty criminal, adds a little
colour.
Boa: novel Sir, You Bastard by G.F. Newman.
DRA                                   92 min
B,V                                     RNK

## TAKE, THE ** 18
Leon Ichaso          USA            1989
*Ray Sharkey, Lisa Hartman, Larry Manetti, R. Lee*
*Ermey, Joe Lala, Julia Mechoso*
Absolutely undistinguished action movie about an
ex-prisoner, a former cop, who gets mixed up with
drug dealers and lives to regret it. Resembles nothing
so much as an episode of "Miami Vice" in its predict-
able blend of violent thrills and poor scripting, but at
least the acting is well above average.
A/AD                         87 min (ort 100 min) mCab
V                                        CIC

## TAKIN' IT OFF *
Ed Hanson            USA            1984

*Kitten Navidad, Adam Hadum, Ashley St John,*
*Angelique Pettyjohn*
A stripper with a 48 inch bust has to lose three inches
in order to make it big in the filmworld. Dross of a
high order.
COM                          85 min Cut (4 min 9 sec)
B,V                                IMPACT/ODY

## TAKING OF FLIGHT 847, THE *** 15
Paul Wendkos         USA            1988
*Lindsay Wagner, Eli Danker, Sandy McPeak, Ray*
*Wise, Leslie Easterbrook, Laurie Walters, Joseph*
*Nasser*
A gripping account of the real-life drama that took
place in 1985, when a plane was hijacked and the
coolness of the flight attendant was generally reck-
oned to have been instrumental in averting a blood-
bath. Written by Norman Morrill.
Aka: TAKING OF FLIGHT 847, THE: THE ULI
DERICKSON STORY
DRA                          96 min (ort 100 min) mTV
B,V                                     EIV

## TAKING OF PELHAM 123, THE *** 15
Joseph Sargent       USA            1974
*Walter Matthau, Robert Shaw, Martin Balsam, Hector*
*Elizondo, Earl Hindman, Dick O'Neill, James*
*Broderick, Doris Roberts, Tony Roberts, Jerry Stiller,*
*Lee Wallace, Kenneth McMillan, Julius Harris, Sal*
*Viscuso*
Taut, well made thriller about the ruthless hijacking
of a New York subway train. Shaw and three accom-
plices take over a train, and demand a ransom pay-off
of one million dollars to be delivered in one hour. The
script is by Peter Stone and the music by David Shire.
Boa: novel by John Godey.
THR                          100 min (ort 104 min)
B,V                                     WHV

## TAKING OFF *** 18
Milos Forman         USA            1971
*Lynn Carlin, Buck Henry, Linnea Heacock, Audra*
*Lindley, Paul Benedict, Georgia Engel*
A wry look at suburban America, with distraught
parents seeking runaway children and gradually
becoming involved in a hippie sub-culture. This was
Forman's first American film. Written by Forman,
John Guare, Jean-Claude Carriere and John Klein.
COM                          89 min (ort 92 min)
B,V                                     CIC

## TALE OF THE BUNNY PARK, THE ** U
Jim Henson           UK             198-
*Voices of: Steve Whitmore, Richard Hunt, Camille*
*Bonara, Ron Mueck, Karen Prell, Kevin Clash, Louise*
*Gold, Martin P. Robinson, Mike Quinn, David*
*Rudman, Jim Henson*
From the creator of "The Muppets" comes this tale of
rabbits and their annual celebration – the famous
Bunny Picnic. A cheerful blend of songs and lively
animation.
Aka: BUNNY PICNIC, THE; TALE OF THE BUNNY
PICNIC, THE
JUV                                   50 min
V                                        VIR

## TALE OF THE FROG PRINCE, THE *** PG
Eric Idle            USA            1984
*Robin Williams, Teri Garr, Rene Auberjonois, Candy*
*Clark*
A good film version of a famous fairytale from the
"Faerie Tale Theatre". This one tells of a prince who is
transformed into a frog but is saved from this fate by
the kiss of a beautiful princess.
Boa: short story by Jakob Ludwig Karl Grimm and
Wilhelm Karl Grimm.
JUV                                   54 min
V                                        MGM

## TALE OF TWO CITIES, A ** PG
Jim Goddard    USA    1980
*Chris Sarandon, Kenneth More, Peter Cushing, Billie
Whitelaw, Flora Robson, Barry Morse, Alice Krige,
Norman Jones, Nigel Hawthorne, George Innes, Kevin
Stoney, Robert Urquhart, Bernard Hug, Martin
Carroll, Valerie Tilburg*
One of many versions of this famous classic tale, of a
carefree lawyer who finds his true purpose in life
when he aids victims of the Reign of Terror that
followed on the heels of the French Revolution. A film
that is certainly good to look at but has little depth
and uncharismatic leads. The script is by John Gay.
Boa: novel by Charles Dickens.
DRA    156 min mTV
B,V    PRV

## TALE OF TWO CITIES, A ** U
Ralph Thomas    UK    1958
*Dirk Bogarde, Dorothy Tutin, Stephen Murray, Athene
Seyler, Christopher Lee, Rosalie Crutchley, Ernest
Clark, Paul Guers, Cecil Parker, Donald Pleasence,
Ian Bannen, Marie Versini, Alfie Bass, Freda Jackson,
Duncan Lamont*
A faithful adaptation of the famous novel. Bogarde as
Sydney Carton does his best as the lawyer who saves a
man from the guillotine by taking his place, but the
film cannot compare to the 1935 Ronald Colman
classic. Remade for TV in 1980. Written by T.E.B.
Clarke.
Boa: novel by Charles Dickens.
DRA    112 min (ort 117 min) B/W
V    RNK

## TALE OF TWO CITIES, A *** PG
Michael E. Briant    UK
*Paul Shelley, Nigel Stock, Ralph Michael, Judy
Parfitt, Vivien Merchant*
A solid interpretation of the Dickens novel of the
French Revolution and one man's heroic sacrifice to
save the life of another.
Boa: novel by Charles Dickens.
DRA    172 min mTV
V    BBC

## TALES FROM THE CRYPT ** 18
Freddie Francis    UK    1972
*Ralph Richardson, Geoffrey Bayldon, Peter Cushing,
Joan Collins, Ian Hendry, Richard Greene, Chloe
Franks, Oliver MacGreevey, Susan Denny, Angie
Grant, Robin Phillips, David Markham, Robert
Hutton, Barbara Murray, Roy Dotrice*
Five visitors exploring catacombs are confronted by a
strange monk who predicts their futures. Episodes are
entitled: "And All Through The House", "Reflection Of
Death", "Poetic Justice", "Wish You Were Here" and
"Blind Alley" A sort of sequel, VAULT OF HORROR,
followed. Fair. Written by Milton Subotsky and based
on the comic strips of William Gaines.
Osca: VAULT OF HORROR
HOR    92 min (Cut at film release)
B,V    CBS

## TALES FROM THE CRYPT ** 18
Robert Zemeckis/Richard Donner/Walter Hill
    USA    1989
*Mary Ellen Trainor, Larry Drake, Marshall Bell,
Lindsey Whitney Barry, Bill Sadler, Gustav Vintas,
Joe Pantoliano*
Three simplistic horror tales, with each having a
rather childish introduction by a corpse. In "The Man
Who Was Death" a state executioner takes matters
into his own hands when capital punishment is
abolished, in "And All Through The House" an
adulterous wife is pursued by a maniac disguised as
Santa Claus, and finally "Dig That Cat . . .He's Real
Gone" tells of a drifter who is given nine lives by a
mad scientist.
HOR    79 min
V    CIC

## TALES OF BEATRIX POTTER ** U
Reginald Mills    UK    1971
*Carol Ainsworth, Sally Ashby, Frederick Ashton,
Avril Bergen, Michael Coleman, Lesley Collier, Jill
Cooke, Leslie Edwards, Graham Fletcher, Bridget
Goodricke, Alexander Grant, Garry Grant, Ann
Howard, Brenda Last*
Performed by members of the Royal Ballet, this
pleasant little diversion tells of the adventures of
some of the creatures created by Beatix Potter in her
charming (if somewhat bland) children's stories.
Choreography is by Frederick Ashton.
Aka: PETER RABBIT AND THE TALES OF
BEATRIX POTTER
Boa: stories by Beatrix Potter.
JUV    85 min (ort 90 min)
V/sh    TEVP; WHV

## TALES OF MYSTERY AND IMAGINATION ** 18
Roger Vadim/Louis Malle/Federico Fellini
    FRANCE    1967
*Brigitte Bardot, Jane Fonda, Terence Stamp, Alain
Delon*
Three short films loosely adapted from Poe's stories
and entitled: "Don't Bet Heads", "William Wilson's
Sketch" and "Metzengerstein". A variable set of tales,
of which the last two are the best.
Aka: HISTOIRES EXTRAORDINAIRES; TRE PASSI
NEL DELIRIO; SPIRITS OF THE DEAD
Boa: short stories by Edgar Allan Poe.
FAN    120 min
V    CASPIC

## TALES OF ORDINARY MADNESS * 18
Marco Ferreri    FRANCE/ITALY    1983
*Ben Gazzara, Ornella Muti, Tanya Lopert, Susan
Tyrrell, Roy Brocksmith, Katia Berger*
Describes the life and fantasies of a Los Angeles poet
(Gazzara) who boozes his life away and meets a
variety of women. A disorganised wallow in self-
indulgence and platitudes, mostly set on Venice
Beach, California. The script (such as it is) is by
Ferreri and others.
Boa: short stories from Erections, Ejaculations
Exhibitions And Tales Of Ordinary Madness by
Charles Bukowski.
DRA    97 min (ort 108 min)
B,V    VCL L/A; APX; INTMED

## TALES OF TERROR ***
Roger Corman    USA    1961
*Vincent Price, Peter Lorre, Basil Rathbone, Debra
Paget, Maggie Pierce, Leona Gage, Joyce Jameson*
Three Poe stories get the Corman treatment. In
"Morella" a dying woman comes home to find her
father brooding over the mummified body of his wife.
In "The Black Cat" (which contains elements of "The
Cask Of Amontillado") Lorre walls up his faithless
wife and her lover in a vault. Finally "The Facts In
The Case Of M. Valdemar" has a man being kept alive
by hypnosis, following his death. A variable display of
atmospheric effects and sluggish plotting.
Boa: short stories Morella, The Black Cat and The
Facts In The Case Of M. Valdemar by Edgar Allan
Poe.
HOR    90 min
B,V    GHV

## TALES OF TERROR 1: SHE FREAK ** 15
Byron Mabe    USA    1967
*Claire Brennan, Lee Raymond, Lynn Courtney, Bill
McKinney, Van Teen, Felix Silla, Claude Smith, Bill
Bagdad, Marsha Drake, Bobby Matthews, Ben Moore,
David Boudrot, Madame Lee*
Exploitative recycling of "Freaks", with a waitress
marrying the owner of a carnival show, being unfaith-
ful to him, and suffering a ghastly retribution at the
hands of the freaks.
Aka: SHE FREAK

HOR    87 min (3 films in this series available as a set)
B,V                                    GOV L/A; AVR

## TALES OF TERROR 2: THE IMPURE,    18
## WILD RIDERS **
Richard Kanter          USA              1971
*Alex Rocco, Sherry Bain, Elizabeth Knowles, Arell*
*Blanton, Ted Hayden, Jax Carroll, Steve Vincent, Bill*
*Collins, Ray Galvin, Linda Johanesen, Diana Jones,*
*Frank Charolla, Gail Liddle, Dirty Denney, Carl Crow,*
*Tim Ray*
A gang of Hell's Angels breaks into a house where two
young girls are alone. They proceed to ransack the
place and generally enjoy themselves until the owner
of the house, a concert cellist, arrives home. They force
him to play his instrument, not realising that it
controls Satanic forces.
Aka: HEAD; IMPURE, THE; WILD RIDERS
HOR        85 min; 90 min (TURBO) (ort 91 min)
B,V                              AVR; AST; TURBO

## TALES OF TERROR 3: DROPS OF BLOOD ***    15
Giorgio Ferroni      FRANCE/ITALY         1960
*Pierre Brice, Wolfgang Preiss, Scilla Gabel, Dany*
*Carrel, Liana Orfei, Marco Gugliemi, Herbert Boehme,*
*Olga Solbelli*
A professor kills women and injects their blood into
his dying daughter in an attempt to keep her alive. As
a final macabre touch, he turns the corpses into
statues and keeps them in the windmill where he
lives. An impressive film of nightmarish ideas and
gruesome sequences.
Aka: DROPS OF BLOOD; HORRIBLE MILL
WOMEN, THE; HORROR OF THE STONE WOMEN;
IL MULINO DELLE DONNE DI PIETRA; LE
MOULIN DES SUPPLICES; MILL OF THE STONE
MAIDENS; MILL OF THE STONE WOMEN
Boa: Flemish Tales By Peter Van Weigen.
HOR        90 min; 82 min (AVR) (ort 94 min)
B,V                    MARKET/GOV L/A; MAGNUM; AVR

## TALES THAT WITNESS MADNESS **
Freddie Francis         UK               1973
*Kim Novak, Georgia Brown, Joan Collins, Jack*
*Hawkins, Donald Houston, Peter McEnery, Suzy*
*Kendall, Donald Pleasence, Russell Lewis, Frank*
*Forsyth, Beth Morris, Michael Jayston, Michael*
*Petrovich, Mary Tamm*
A black comedy with four strange stories set in a
mental home, and recounted as case histories by
Pleasence to a sceptical Hawkins (in one of his last
roles, his voice being dubbed by Charles Gray). "Mr
Tiger" is about a boy who gets an imaginary tiger to
kill his parents. In "Penny Farthing" an antique
dealer travels back in time. In "Mel" a living tree kills
a man's wife, and in "Luau" an author uses a young
girl as a sacrifice. Unmemorable.
HOR                                      90 min
B,V                                        RNK

## TALK DIRTY TO ME **                     R18
Anthony Spinelli        USA              1980
*John Leslie, Jesie St James, Richard Pacheco, Juliet*
*Anderson*
The story of one man who claims to be able to bed any
woman whilst his friend is too shy to even ask. Little
in the way of a plot as Jack (the unshy one), makes
love to a succession of adoring women. The title refers
to Jack's sexy conversations with his lady friends, in
this lighthearted but rather silly tale.
A                    60 min (ort 80 min) Cut (27 sec)
B,V                                        EVI

## TALK NAUGHTY TO ME **                    18
Chris Warfield          USA              1981
*Lesley Bovee, John Leslie, Ken Scudder, Bonnie*
*Holliday, Kandy Barbour, Kay Parker*
A silly but amusing story of an overworked female

executive, who uses men (she hires studs to service
her) but has never had fulfilment from one. The film
follows her adventures and those of her chauffeur
(who pretended to be gay in order to be hired) as they
embark on encounters of their own, before finding true
happiness in each other's arms.
Aka: CHAMPAGNE FOR BREAKFAST
A                               75 min (ort 99 min)
B,V                                 HAR; TOPART

## TALK OF THE TOWN, THE ***                U
George Stevens          USA              1942
*Cary Grant, Ronald Coleman, Edgar Buchanan, Jean*
*Arthur, Glenda Farrell, Charles Dingle, Emma Dunn,*
*Rex Ingram, Tom Tyler, Lloyd Bridges*
A suspected murderer goes on the run and hides out at
a boarding house, where he engages in debate with an
unsuspecting law professor, while making up to the
attractive landlady. A delicious comedy-thriller with
the three leads making the most of their thin mate-
rial. The script is by Irwin Shaw and Sidney
Buchman.
THR               112 min (ort 118 min) B/W
V                                          RCA

## TALKING PARCEL, THE **                    U
Brian Cosgrove          UK               1978
*Voices of: Lisa Norris, Freddie Jones, Mollie Sugden,*
*Roy Kinnear, Windsor Davies, Michael Hordern*
A young girl finds a talking parcel on the seashore and
discovers a parrot inside, who takes her on a journey
to a magical land where the animals of myth and
legend are to be found.
Boa: story by Gerald Durell.
CAR                  45 min; 40 min (VCC)
B,V             THAMES/TEVP; VCC (VHS only)

## TALK RADIO ***                           18
Oliver Stone            USA              1988
*Eric Bogosian, Alec Baldwin, Ellen Greene, Leslie*
*Hope, John C. McGinley, John Pankow, Michael*
*Wincott*
The story of a controversial and abrasive talk-show
host, whose hectoring and controversial style leads to
a notoriety that puts his life in danger. Powerfully
acted and directed, this fascinating film is set mainly
in the confines of a radio studio, but is never
claustrophobic. A perfect vehicle for writer Bogosian,
who co-wrote the screenplay with Stone, adding
elements of the true story of Alan Berg – a DJ
assassinated by white supremacists.
Boa: play by Eric Bogosian and Tad Savinar/book
Talked To Death: The Life And Murder Of Alan Berg
by Stephen Singular.
THR                  104 min (ort 110 min)
V                                          CBS

## TALKING WALLS **                         18
Stephen Verona          USA              1986
*Stephen Shellen, Marie Laurin, Barry Primus, Sybil*
*Danning (Sybelle Danninger), Sally Kirkland*
A young sociology student writing a research thesis on
human sexuality, uses some high-tech videotaping
equipment to spy on the intimate moments of couples
staying at a seedy motel, observing them through a
hole he has drilled through the wall of his room. See
also FOREPLAY.
COM                  80 min (ort 85 min)
B,V                                        NWV

## TALL GUY, THE **                         15
Mel Smith               USA              1988
*Jeff Goldblum, Emma Thompson, Rowan Atkinson*
A talented but accident-prone American actor works
as nothing more than a stooge to an obnoxious and
self-centred comedian. When he falls for a nurse who
is treating him for hay fever, he misses a performance
and gets fired. Many fruitless interviews later, he gets
his break playing in a musical version of "The

Elephant Man". Smith's directorial debut is an original but tepid work, that fails to stretch the comic talents of all concerned.

COM                                              88 min
V/sh                                             VIR

### TALL STORY **                                U
Joshua Logan            USA              1960
*Jane Fonda, Anthony Perkins, Ray Walston, Marc Connelly, Anne Jackson, Murray Hamilton, Elizabeth Patterson*
College romance set against the background of a vital baseball match against a Russian team. This was Fonda's film debut, as a co-ed in love with college basketball star Perkins. An unmemorable comedy with badly-cast leads. The script is by Julius J. Epstein.
Boa: novel The Homecoming Game by Howard Nemoor/play by Howard Lindsay and Russel Crouse.
COM                                        91 min B/W
B,V                                              WHV

### TALL STRANGER, THE **                        PG
Thomas Carr             USA              1957
*Joel McCrea, Virginia Mayo, Michael Ansara, Barry Kelley, Whit Bissell, James Dobson, George Neise, Adam Kennedy, Michael Pate, Leo Gordon, Ray Teal, Robert Foulk, George J. Lewis, Guy Prescott*
Story of a wagon train crossing Colorado, with McCrea being rescued by the pioneers and cared for after having been shot, and coming to be accepted as their leader. A colourful but not especially memorable yarn. Written by Christopher Knopf.
Boa: novel by Louis L'Amour.
WES        81 min; 79 min (PARK) (ort 83 min) B/W
V                                    VMA; STABL; PARK

### TAMARIND SEED, THE ***                        15
Blake Edwards           USA              1974
*Julie Andrews, Omar Sharif, Anthony Quayle, Daniel O'Herlihy, Sylvia Sims, Oscar Homolka, Bryan Marshall, David Baron, Celia Bannerman, Roger Dann, Sharon Duce, George Mikell, Kate O'Mara, Constantin De Goguel*
An innocent romance between an attractive widow and a Russian military attache in Barbados, leads to complications for the intelligence community when he decides to defect. A blend of romance and espionage that's well handled and fairly modest in scope. Written by Edwards.
Boa: novel by Evelyn Anthony.
THR                           119 min (ort 125 min)
B,V,V2                          PRV; RCA; CH5 (VHS only)

### TAMING OF THE SHREW, THE ***                  U
Jonathan Miller         UK               1980
*John Cleese, Sarah Badel, Frank Thornton, Susan Penhaligon, John Bird*
A full-blooded and diverting version of this play of love and conquest, with Cleese effective as Petruchio and Badel equally good as Katharine, the woman he pursues and ultimately wins.
Boa: play by William Shakespeare.
DRA                                      128 min mTV
V/h                                              RCA

### TAMING OF THE SHREW, THE ***                  U
Franco Zeffirelli
                        ITALY/USA        1967
*Richard Burton, Elizabeth Taylor, Michael Hordern, Vernon Dobtcheff, Natasha Pyne, Michael York, Cyril Cusack, Alan Webb, Victor Spinetti, Alfred Lynch*
Excellent film version of the famous comedy with Burton and Taylor in fine form, ably supported by a good cast and splendid photography. The musical score is by Nino Rota. More of a film in the true sense than is generally the case with adaptations of this playwright's works, which so often become mere filmed plays. A colourful and bawdy romp.

Boa: play by William Shakespeare.
COM                                          126 min
B,V                                              RCA

### TAMPOPO ***                                   15
Juzo Itami              JAPAN            1987
*Tsutomu Yamazaki, Nobuko Miyamoto, Koji Yakusho, Ken Watanabe, Rikiya Yasuoka*
The story of a truck driver who helps a widow both make a success of her noodle shop and discover the secret of the perfect noodle, forms the basis for this bizarre comedy. Not so much a film as a series of comical vignettes, all of which revolve around food.
COM                                          117 min
V                                                PAL

### TANAMERA: PARTS 1, 2 AND 3 ***               15
Kevin Dobson/John Power
                        AUSTRALIA/UK     1989
*Christopher Bowen, Lewis Fiander, Kay Tong Lim, Anne-Louise Lambert, Kyhm Lam, Ed Devereaux*
A lavish mini-saga that tells of the idle rich English expatriates who lived a life of luxury in Singapore up to its fall to the Japanese in 1942. The son of a wealthy aristocratic family falls for a Chinese girl but his parents do all they can to keep them apart, and when WW2 breaks out they are soon separated. A well-acted and detailed film that delivers all the usual soap opera-style cliches.
Boa: novel by Noel Barber.
DRA                            340 min (3 cassettes)
V                                              CENTV

### TANGERINE **                                 R18
Roger McCallum          USA              1979
*Cece Malone, Holly McCall, Laurie Blue, Angela Desmond, Ken Scudder, Howie Greene, Milt Ingersoll*
Story of a man who provides three young girls to cater for men who fantasise about having teenage lovers. A cheerfully silly and brightly photographed piece of nonsense.
A                              70 min (ort 90 min)
B,V                        WEC L/A; EVI; RIP; XTASY

### TANGO AND CASH **                             15
Andre Konchalovsky/Albert Magnoli
                        USA              1989
*Sylvester Stallone, Kurt Russell, Terri Hatcher, Brion James, Geoffrey Lewis, Jack Pallance, James Hong, Marc Alaimo, Michael J. Pollard*
Stallone and Russell team up as rival L.A. detectives who are framed by a drugs mobster and have to unite in order to clear their names. Reputed to have had a $55,000,000 budget, this juvenile buddy-movie starts off well with excellent action sequences (a highlight is the prison break) but soon descends into self-parody. Mostly directed by Konchalovsky, it was completed by Magnoli after the former quit in a dispute over the film's ending.
A/AD                                          97 min
V                                                WHV

### TANK **                                       15
Marvin Chomsky          USA              1984
*James Garner, Shirley Jones, C. Thomas Howell, Jenilee Harrison, Mark Herrier, Dorian Harewood, G.D. Spradlin, James Cromwell, Eddie Murphy*
A military man uses his restored Sherman tank to free his teenage son who has been imprisoned by a nasty redneck sheriff. An absorbing look at injustice and one man's fight against it, but an example of a good idea ruined by overkill. Somewhat reminiscent of SUPPOSE THEY GAVE A WAR AND NOBODY CAME? but lacking the depth of that film.
A/AD                          108 min (ort 113 min)
B,V                                              CIC

### TANK MALLING *                                18
James Marcus            UK               1989

*Jason Connery, Amanda Donohoe, Ray Winstone,*
*Marsha Hunt, Peter Wyngarde*
Heavy-footed and inept British thriller that overplays
its hand with the tale of an investigative journalist
who takes on the Establishment when he sets out to
uncover corruption in high places. Having been
framed and imprisoned for perjury once before, his
acquisition of a stolen diary gives him the confidence
to mount a second assault. Despite Donohoe's strong
presence in the film, the lack of money and imagination are serious flaws.

THR                                           96 min
V                                              CINE

**TAP ***                                         PG
Nick Castle               USA               1989
*Gregory Hines, Suzzanne Douglas, Sammy Davis Jr,*
*Savion Glover, Joe Morton, Dick Anthony Williams,*
*Terrence McNally, Sandman Sims, Bunny Briggs,*
*Steve Condos, Jimmy Slyde, Pat Rico, Arthur Duncan,*
*Harold Nicholas, Etta James*
A trite but highly enjoyable story of an ex-con who has
shunned the use of his dancing skills for a life of crime
and easy pickings. When the pull of tap dancing
becomes too strong, he forsakes his old ways and
learns a new set of values from an old-time hoofer. A
loving tribute to tap, with little plot but some great
dance sequences and a charming performance from
Davis as "Little Mo", a tap dancing legend.

DRA                                           110 min
V/h                                            RCA

**TAPEHEADS ***                                   15
Bill Fishman              USA               1989
*Tim Robbins, John Cusack, Doug McClure, Connie*
*Stevens, Clu Gulager, Mary Crosby, Katy Boyer, Lyle*
*Alzado, Jessica Walter, Susan Tyrrell, Junior Walker,*
*Sam Moore*
A brash, energetic but puerile comedy in which
con-artist Cusack teams up with video genius Robbins
to make some music videos. As they struggle to make
it in the L.A. rock music scene they encounter a
succession of wacky characters. A disorganised and
cluttered film, with some enjoyable celebrity cameos
and a rather good soundtrack.

COM                                  88 min (ort 97 min)
V                                              RCA

**TAPS ***                                        PG
Harold Becker             USA               1981
*Timothy Hutton, George C. Scott, Ronny Cox, Sean*
*Penn, Tom Cruise, Brendan Ward*
Army cadets occupy their academy by force, in order
to prevent the building from being demolished, but
the dispute escalates into violence. A kind of modern
moral fable that climaxes too soon and then has
nowhere to go. Written by Darryl Ponicsan and Robert
Mark Kamen. This was Penn's screen debut.
Aka: T.A.P.S.
Boa: novel Father Sky by Devery Freeman.

DRA                              121 min (ort 126 min)
V/sh                                           CBS

**TARGET ***                                      15
Arthur Penn               USA               1985
*Gene Hackman, Matt Dillon, Josef Sommer, Guy Boyd,*
*Gail Strickland, Gayle Hunnicutt, Victoria Fyodorova,*
*Ilona Grubel, Herbert Berghof, Richard Munch, Ray*
*Fry, Jean-Pol Dubois, Werner Pochath, Ulrich Haupt,*
*James Selby*
A son discovers a different side to his ex-CIA father,
when the latter is galvanised into action following the
kidnapping of his wife in Europe, by a former rival
bent on revenge for an incident that took place
eighteen years ago. A stolid and cliche-ridden tale,
that is so overlong that the few good action scenes are
able to do nothing for it.

THR                             112 min (ort 117 min)
V/sh                                           CBS

**TARGET ***                                      15
David Wickes              UK                 1977
*Patrick Mower, Philip Madoc, Brendan Price, Vivien*
*Heilbronn*
One episode of a TV series about the work of a
regional crime squad. Quite gritty and well handled
but too humourless to be appealing.

THR                                         50 min mTV
B,V                                            BBC

**TARGET ***                                       
Stuart Gilmore            USA               1952
*Tim Holt, Richard Martin, Linda Douglas, Walter*
*Reed, Harry Harvey, John Hamilton, Lane Bradford,*
*Riley Hill, Mike Ragan*
A fast-paced Tim Holt vehicle (one of the last films he
made in a series for RKO) in which he joins forces with
another cowboy to take on a corrupt land agent and
his gang of outlaws.

WES                          54 min (ort 60 min) B/W
B,V                                            KVD

**TARGET EAGLE ***                                PG
Anthony Loma (Jose Antonio de la Loma)
                          MEXICO/SPAIN          1982
*George Peppard, Maud Adams, Max Von Sydow,*
*George (Jorge) Rivero, Chuck Connors, Susana*
*Dosamantes*
Free-fall parachutists run a smuggling racket in the
Mediterranean but the gang is infiltrated by Rivero, a
mercenary in the pay of the Spanish police. An
adequate action thriller.

A/AD              98 min; 94 min (MAST) (ort 100 min)
B,V,V2              DFS L/A; VMA; MAST (VHS only)

**TARGET EARTH ***                                 
Sherman Rose              USA               1952
*Richard Denning, Virginia Grey, Kathleen Crowley,*
*Richard Reeves, Robert Roark, Steve Pendleton, Whit*
*Bissell, Arthur Space, House Peters Jr, Jim Drake,*
*Mort Marshall*
People in a deserted American city are trapped when
it is attacked by robots from Venus. A typical example
of 1950s SF, that starts off well enough but suffers
badly from sluggish and uninspired development.
Pity.

FAN                                         74 min B/W
B,V                                   GAMM L/A; APX

**TARGET REMOVED ***                              15
Antonio Isasi
                    FRANCE/ITALY/SPAIN       1972
*Karl Malden, Olivia Hussey, Christopher Mitchum,*
*Raf Vallone, Claudine Auger, Gerard Tichy*
A 6-year-old boy witnesses his father's murder at the
hands of hired thugs, and waits 20 years before taking
his revenge in a series of bloody killings. There's little
logic to the plot, but no lack of action.
Aka: SUMMERTIME KILLER, THE

A/AD              88 min; 94 min (AMBAS) Cut (13 sec)
B,V                                  AMBAS; GLOB

**TARGET: HARRY ***                               18
Henry Neill (Roger Corman)
                          USA               1969
*Vic Morrow, Victor Buono, Stanley Holloway, Suzanne*
*Pleshette, Cesar Romero, Charlotte Rampling, Michael*
*Ansara*
The owner of a seaplane is given the job of taking
some stolen banknote plates to Istanbul, in this
mediocre reworking of THE MALTESE FALCON.
Originally made for TV but released theatrically.
Aka: HOW TO MAKE IT; WHAT'S IN IT FOR
HARRY?

THR                78 min (ort 83 min) Cut (49 sec) mTV
B,V                                      VGM; RNK

**TARKA THE OTTER ***                             PG
David Cobham              UK                 1978

Peter Bennett, Edward Underdown, Brenda
Cavendish, John Leeson, Reg Lye, George Waring,
Stanley Lebor, Max Faulkner, Peter Ustinov
(narration)
A tale following the life of an otter, from birth to
adulthood, and telling of the man who attempted to
keep it as a household pet. A warm and appealing film
for nature lovers, set in Devon of the 1920s. The script
is by Gerald Durrell.
Boa: novel by Henry Williamson.

| DRA | 87 min (ort 91 min) |
| V | VCC; RNK |

## TARZAN IN MANHATTAN **     PG
Michael Schultz     USA     1989
Joe Lara, Jan-Michael Vincent, Kim Crosby, Tony
Curtis, Jimmy Medina Taggert
A lighthearted action tale that was the pilot for a
prospective series, with Tarzan coming to the big city
on the trail of some nasty vivisectionists who have
disturbed his jungle abode. Mild entertainment of the
undemanding kind.

| A/AD | 95 min (ort 100 min) mTV |
| V | RCA |

## TARZAN, THE APEMAN     15
John Derek     USA     1981
Bo Derek, Richard Harris, Miles O'Keeffe, John
Phillip Law, Wilfrid Hyde-White
This unbearably dreary remake is merely a vehicle for
Bo Derek's talents. A dull and wearisome production.
See also GREYSTOKE: THE LEGEND OF TARZAN,
LORD OF THE APES.

| A/AD | 107 min (ort 112 min) |
| B,V,V2 | MGM |

## TASTE FOR FEAR, A **     18
Piccio Raffani     ITALY     1987
Virginia Hey, Gerard Darmon, Kid Creole, Eva
Grimaldi
An attractive former model now makes her living as a
photographer and hires models to engage in a series of
role-playing activities as part of an ambitious project.
When one after another of her models is found
murdered, our photographer is drawn into a murky
web of violence. A slow-moving and bizarre psychological thriller, strong on atmosphere and quite carefully plotted, but somewhat self-indulgent.
Aka: OBSESSION: A TASTE FOR FEAR

| THR | 90 min |
| B,V | AVA |

## TASTE OF EVIL, A * 
John Llewellyn Moxey    USA     1971
Barbara Parkins, Barbara Stanwyck, Roddy
McDowall, William Windom, Arthur O'Connell, Bing
Russell, Dawn French
A woman is released after seven years in a mental
home because of a rape, and returns home to find a
chilly welcome, and nearly has another breakdown
when she finds herself being terrorised. A film that
should have been gripping but isn't.

| HOR | 90 min mTV |
| B,V | GHV |

## TASTE OF HELL, A *
Neil Yarema/Basil Bradbury
    UK     1973
John Garwood, William Smith, Lisa Lorena, Vic Diaz,
Lloyd Kino, Angel Buenaventura
An American officer disfigured when fighting the
Japanese in the Philippines, wages a personal crusade
of vengeance.

| WAR | 86 min |
| B,V,V2 | VPD |

## TASTE OF HONEY, A ***     15
Tony Richardson     UK     1961
Rita Tushingham, Robert Stephens, Dora Bryan,
Murray Melvin, Paul Danquah
In Salford the wayward teenage daughter of a widow
has an affair with a black sailor and is helped through
her pregnancy by a homosexual friend. A poignant
and moving performance from Tushingham in her
film debut, is complemented by good location work
and strong characterisation.
Boa: play by Shelagh Delaney.

| DRA | 96 min (ort 100 min) B/W |
| V | CASPIC |

## TASTE OF MONEY, A **     R18
Richard Mailer     USA     1983
Constance Money, Sharon Mitchell, Gina Canetti,
Jamie Gillis, Paul Thomas, Blair Harris, Don Hart
This follow-up to Money's appearance in the 1978 film
MISTY BEETHOVEN, sees her debating whether to
make another sex film after a six year absence. Her
lover leaves to pursue his musical career, and she is
contacted by a film producer who has rounded up her
old friends to persuade her to make a comeback. She
very nearly does so too, but the sudden return of her
lover sees her forswearing the whole nasty business
forever.

| A | 87 min |
| V | SHEP |

## TASTE THE BLOOD OF DRACULA *
Peter Sasdy     UK     1969
Christopher Lee, Linda Hayden, Geoffrey Keen, Gwen
Watford, Peter Sallis, Anthony Corlan, Isla Blair,
John Carson, Michael Jarvis, Ralph Bates, Roy
Kinnear, Michael Ripper
This was the fourth Hammer stab at the Dracula
legend (preceded by DRACULA HAS RISEN FROM
THE GRAVE) and has a bunch of bored seekers of
excitement murdering a servant of the Count, when
the decadence he promised them turns out to be more
than they can stomach. Dracula sets out to have his
revenge, using a variety of people for this purpose. A
flabby yarn that gets bogged down very quickly.
Followed by THE SCARS OF DRACULA.

| HOR | 87 min (ort 95 min) |
| V | WHV |

## TATTOO *     18
Bob Brooks     USA     1981
Bruce Dern, Maud Adams, Leonard Frey, Rikke Borge,
John Getz, Peter Iachangelo
A mentally ill artist becomes obsessed with a famous
model, and kidnaps her in order to use her body as a
canvas. A sordid and offbeat tale that ends with our
girl covered in tattoos and our artist dead. Written by
Joyce Bunuel, the daughter-in-law of director Luis
Bunuel.
Boa: novel by Earl Thompson.

| DRA | 103 min |
| B,V | TEVP |

## TAXI DRIVER ***     18
Martin Scorsese     USA     1976
Robert De Niro, Cybill Shepherd, Harvey Keitel, Jodie
Foster, Peter Boyle, Leonard Harris, Albert Brooks, Joe
Spinell, Martin Scorsese
A very bloody look at life in New York City viewed
through the eyes of one man, a crazed and lonely
Vietnam veteran now working as a taxi driver.
Written by Paul Schraeder, who says that the story
was inspired (if that is the right word) by the diaries of
would-be assassin Arthur Bremer. The music is by
Bernard Herrmann.

THR     109 min (ort 116 min) (Cut at film release by 1
sec)

| B,V | RCA |

## TAXI GIRLS ** 
Jaacov Jaacovi     USA     1979
Nancy Suiter, Serena, John C. Holmes, Candida
Royalle, Nancy Hoffman, Ric Lutz, Mike Ranger

After spending yet another night in the cells, a bunch
of hookers decide to go into business using taxis as a
means of providing both transportation and premises.

| A | 80 min |
| B,V | CAL |

## TAXI TO THE TOILET **
Frank Ripploh    WEST GERMANY    1981
*Frank Ripploh, Bernd Broderup, Magdalena
Montezuma, Tabea Blumenschein, Gitte Lederer*
A sleazy look at the world of Berlin homosexuals, and
more particularly, the adventures of a teacher who is
driven by his lover's jealousy to go out in search of
fresh encounters, an action which eventually costs
him his job.
Aka: TAXI TO THE JOHN; TAXI TO THE LOO;
TAXI ZUM KLO

| DRA | 92 min |
| B,V | PVG |

## TEACHER, THE **
Hikmet Avedis    USA    1974
*Angel Tompkins, Jay North, Anthony James, Marlene
Schmidt, Sivi Aberg, Rudy Herera Jr, Med Flory,
Barry Atwater*
A beautiful high school teacher seduces her star pupil
but their affair arouses the jealousy of a psychopathic
killer just released from an asylum. A highly im-
plausible but quite well-made story.
Aka: SEDUCTRESS, THE

| A | 85 min |
| B,V | TCX |

## TEACHERS *      15
Arthur Hiller    USA    1984
*Nick Nolte, Richard Mulligan, JoBeth Williams, Judd
Hirsch, Lee Grant, Ralph Macchio, Allen Garfield,
Royal Dano, William Schallert, Crispin Glover, Zohra
Lampert, Art Metrano, Laura Dern*
A satirical look at the American high school system,
set in a school that is nothing more than a chaotic
mess. The movie is a thoroughly disappointing mess
in its own right. Filmed in Columbus, Ohio and
written by W.R. McKinney.

| COM | 102 min (ort 106 min) |
| V/sh | WHV |

## TEAM, THE **      PG
Earl Bellamy    AUSTRALIA    1975
*Ben Murphy, Wendy Hughes, Peter Graves, John
Clayton, John Derum, Peter Gwynne, Paul Bertram,
John Meillon, Patrick Ward, John Devon, Serge
Lazareff*
A behind-the-scenes look at the tensions and conflicts
in the world of sidecar racing, with Murphy a visiting
American who teams up with an Australian to win the
big race. Well-handled but very noisy.
Aka: SIDECAR RACERS

| DRA | 90 min |
| B,V | KES |

## TEDDY RUXPIN: THE ADVENTURES OF    U
## TEDDY RUXPIN ***
     USA    1985
A teddy-bear-like creature and his companions go on a
treasure-hunt, but the evil "Tweeg" switches treasure
maps, and they are sent on a wild journey that
embroils them in a series of exciting adventures.
Aka: ADVENTURES OF TEDDY RUXPIN, THE

| CAR | 43 min |
| V | VCC |

## TEEN VAMP *      18
Samuel Bradford    USA    1988
*Clu Gulager, Beau Bishop, Karen Carlsen, Angie
Brown*
A young jerk, constantly bullied at school, is bitten by
a vampire prostitute and is magically transformed
into an attractive hunk who now stands an excellent

chance with the girl of his dreams. A poorly plotted
and under-developed cousin to TEEN WOLF that
lacks Fox's engaging personality to give it sparkle.

| COM | 86 min |
| V | 20VIS |

## TEEN WITCH **      PG
Dorian Walker    USA    1989
*Robyn Lively, Dan Gauthier, Joshua Miller, Dick
Sargent, Zelda Rubinstein, Lisa Fuller, Shelley
Berman*
A virtuous little teen comedy in which a girl discovers
just before her 16th birthday that she has descended
from a long line of Salem witches. She promptly uses
her powers to attract the school's football hero. Quite a
pleasant effort but nothing substantial.

| COM | 90 min (ort 105 min) |
| V | EIV |

## TEEN WOLF **      PG
Rod Daniel    USA    1985
*Michael J. Fox, James Hampton, Susan Ursitti, Jerry
Levine, Jim MacKrell, Scott Paulin, Lorie Griffin,
Mark Arnold, Matt Adler, Mark Holton, Elizabeth
Gorcey, Jay Tarses, Melanie Manos, Doug Savant,
Charles Zucker, Clare Peck*
A teenager finds that he is a werewolf, just like his
dad, who now has some explaining to do. But this
change gives him a certain popularity with his
classmates. Fox is very appealing in his role and this
is what largely carries the aimless story along.
Followed by a sequel and an animated TV series.
Aka: TEEN WOLF 1

| COM | 92 min (Cut at film release by 13 sec) |
| B,V | EIV |

## TEEN WOLF TOO *      PG
Christopher Leitch    USA    1987
*Jason Bateman, Kim Darby, John Astin, Paul Sand,
James Hampton, Mark Holton, Estee Chandler, Robert
Neary, Stuart Fratkin, Beth Ann Miller, Rachel Sharp*
In this moronic sequel, the adventures of Teen Wolf's
cousin are explored. Not a rewarding experience.

| COM | 90 min (ort 95 min) |
| B,V | EIV |

## TEENAGE CRUISERS *
Martin Margulies/Tom Denucci
     USA    1979
*Christine Schaeffer, Lynne Marguiles, Tony Cohn,
Serena, John C. Holmes, Jerry Sokorski, William
Margold*
A disc-jockey working on a youth programme provides
a detailed guide to adolescent sexual habits. A long,
uneven series of skits and insanities, examine various
aspects of sexuality such as masochism and bestiality,
with no unifying story to hold them together. What
might have been funny in the 1970s, now looks very
dated indeed.

| A | 77 min |
| B,V | TCX |

## TEENAGE HITCH-HIKERS **
Gerri Sedley    USA    1974
*Kathie Christopher, Sandra Peabody, Nikki Lynn,
Dennis O'Neill, Victor Paul, Michael Paul*
Two girls hitch-hike across the country and have
various sexual adventures.

| A | 80 min |
| B,V | MOV L/A; MMA |

## TEENAGE INNOCENCE *      18
Chris Warfield    USA
*John Alderman, Sandra Dempsey, Judy Medford*
Two young girls decide to hitch-hike their way to
pleasure, and after being picked up by a middle-aged
man they spend two days trying to love him to death.
Aka: INNOCENT SEX; LITTLE MISS INNOCENCE

(RED); LITTLE MISS INNOCENT; TEENAGE
INNOCENTS
Osca: DEVILS IN THE CONVENT (NET)
A          72 min; 60 min (MKR) (ort 79 min) 93 min
                                (2 film cassette – NET)
B,V     TURBO; RED; NET; MKR; REX L/A; CIN L/A;
TCX

**TEENAGE PSYCHO MEETS BLOODY MARY,**   15
**THE **
Ray Dennis Steckler     USA          1963
*Cash Flagg (Ray Dennis Steckler), Brett O'Hara,*
*Carolyn Brandt, Atlas King, Sharon Walsh, Madison*
*Clarke, Erina Enyo, Jack Brady, Toni Camel, Neil*
*Stillman, Son Hooker*
Now a camp classic, this is probably the world's first
(and last?) horror musical, about a gypsy fortune-
teller who turns her customers into zombies. Badly
acted, with dreadful dialogue, but well-filmed and
surprisingly atmospheric.
Aka: INCREDIBLY STRANGE CREATURES WHO
STOPPED LIVING AND BECAME MIXED-UP
ZOMBIES
HOR                          81 min (ort 90 min)
V                                        PAL

**TELEFON **                                 PG
Don Siegel            USA          1977
*Charles Bronson, Lee Remick, Tyne Daly, Donald*
*Pleasence, Patrick Magee, Alan Badel, Sheree North,*
*Frank Marth, Helen Page Camp, Roy Jenson, Iggie*
*Wolfington, Jacqueline Scott, Ed Bakey, John*
*Mitchum, Kathleen O'Malley*
A renegade Stalinist hardliner reactivates some sleep-
er agents in the USA, who have been hypnotically
conditioned to perform acts of sabotage. To avoid a
super-power conflict, the Kremlin send their top agent
to deal with this menace. A tedious yarn devoting too
much time to the relationship between the agent
(Bronson) and his assistant (Remick). As ever, Fin-
land provides the Soviet locations. Written by Peter
Hyams and Stirling Silliphant.
Boa: novel by Walter Wager.
THR                                      103 min
B,V                                        MGM

**TELEPHONE, THE ***                           15
Rip Torn             USA          1987
*Whoopi Goldberg, Severn Darden, Elliott Gould, John*
*Heard, Amy Wright*
The story of an out-of-work actress and her many
problems, mostly psychological, and her penchant for
conducting her life over the telephone. With a talent
like Goldberg's, it's really a shame to see her working
with such poor material; she sued to prevent this
version being released, and no wonder. A dismal film
that goes nowhere. Written by Terry Southern and
Harry Nilsson. This was Torn's directorial debut.
COM                          80 min (ort 82 min)
B,V                                        NWV

**TELL THEM WILLIE BOY IS HERE ****          15
Abraham Polonsky       USA          1969
*Robert Redford, Katherine Ross, Robert Blake, Susan*
*Clark, Barry Sullivan, John Vernon, Charles*
*McGraw, Charles Aidman, Shelly Novack, Ned*
*Romero, John Day, Lee De Broux, George Tyne, Robert*
*Lipton, Steve Shermayne, Lloyd Gough*
A slow-paced re-enactment of a true incident in 1909,
when an Indian was pursued by a massive posse after
an accidental killing. Undoubtably sincere in its
desire to redress the balance in favour of the Indians,
this film is not helped by casting Ross and Blake as
Indians. Written and directed by Polonsky – his first
film since making "Force Of Evil" in 1948 and his
subsequent blacklisting.
Boa: novel Willie Boy by Harry Lawton.
DRA                          93 min (ort 98 min)
V/h                                        CIC

**TEMPEST, THE ***                           15
Paul Mazursky          USA          1982
*John Cassavetes, Gena Rowlands, Susan Sarandon,*
*Vittorio Gassman, Raul Julia, Sam Robards, Molly*
*Ringwald, Paul Stewart, Jackie Gayle, Lucianne*
*Buchanan, Jerry Hardin, Tony Holland, Vassilis*
*Glezakos, Sergio Nicolai*
An architect runs away to a Greek island in an
attempt to solve his personal problems, but events
there seem to echo the famous play by Shakespeare.
An ill-advised attempt to update Shakespeare, that
sputters with a couple of jokes early on and then just
settles down to smoulder. Written by Mazursky and
Leon Capetanos.
COM                          136 min (ort 142 min)
V                                          RCA

**TEMPEST, THE ***                           15
Derek Jarman          UK          1980
*Heathcote Williams, Karl Johnson, Toyah Wilcox,*
*Peter Bull, Richard Warwick, Elisabeth Welch, Jack*
*BIrkett, Ken Campbell, David Meyer, Neil*
*Cunningham, Christopher Biggins, Peter Turner,*
*Claire Davenport, Kate Temple*
Film version of the famous play telling of a deposed
duke who, by the use of magic, engineers the ship-
wrecking of his enemies on his island. Fair.
Boa: play by William Shakespeare.
DRA                          87 min (ort 95 min)
B,V                                     PVG; PAL

**TEMPEST, THE ***                           U
*Richard Burton, Lee Remick, Roddy McDowall,*
*Maurice Evans*
Standard TV production of the famous play.
Boa: play by William Shakespeare.
DRA                          80 min mTV
V                                       LEISUR

**TEMPEST, THE ****                          U
John Gorrie          UK          1980
*Michael Hordern, Derek Godfrey, David Waller,*
*Warren Clarke, David Dixon, Nigel Hawthorne,*
*Andrew Sachs, John Nettleton, Alan Rowe, Pippa*
*Guard, Christopher Guard, Kenneth Gilbert, Edwin*
*Brown*
A fairly well mounted and enjoyable television
adaptation, one in a series produced by the BBC in the
1970s and 1980s.
Boa: play by William Shakespeare.
DRA                          126 min mTV
V/h                                        BBC

**TEMPLE OF THE**
**DRAGON ***                                18
Chang Cheh          HONG KONG          1973
*Chen Kuan-Tai, Fu Sheng, Chu Mu, Fang Hsin, Wang*
*Chiang*
Action adventure set in China during the Ming
Dynasty.
Aka: HEROES TWO (WHV)
MAR                   97 min Cut (2 min 43 sec)
B,V          ICY L/A; NEON L/A; WHV (VHS only)

**TEMPTER, THE ***                           18
Alberto De Martino    ITALY          1974
*Carla Gravina, Mel Ferrer, Arthur Kennedy, George*
*Coulouris, Alida Valli, Umberto Orsini, Anita*
*Strandberg, Mario Scaccia*
A rip-off of "The Exorcist", with a young girl
becoming possessed by the evil spirit of a female
ancestor, burnt at the stake in the Middle Ages on
charges of witchcraft, her presence not making itself
felt until the girl is paralysed as a result of a car
accident. Tormented by horrific and obscene visions,
her despairing father finally summons a priest to
perform an exorcism.

Aka: ANTICHRIST, THE; ANTICHRISTO;
L'ANTICRISTO
HOR                    96 min (HER); 91 min (VPM)
                          (ort 111 min) Cut (13 sec)
B,V                    CBS L/A; INT L/A; VPM; HER

**TEMPTER, THE ***                              18
Damiani Damiano    ITALY/UK              1975
*Glenda Jackson, Lisa Harrow, Adolfo Celi, Arnoldo
Foa, Claudio Cassinelli, Gabriele Lavia, Rolf Tasna,
Duilio Del Prete, Francisco Rabal*
Tiresome Satanist epic set in a convent, with Jackson
the head of a religious hostel using various unsavoury
methods to control the residents. Unpalatable non-
sense. The music is by Ennio Morricone.
Aka: DEVIL IS A WOMAN, THE; IL SORRISO DEL
GRANDE TENTATORE
HOR                                        106 min
B,V                                           ARF

**TEMPTRESS, THE ****                           18
                    FRANCE
*Christine Croguennec, Jean-Louis Vattier, Patrick
Segalas*
When her husband goes on a business trip to London,
his young wife seizes the opportunity to enjoy some
extramarital affairs.
A                      64 min (ort 70 min) Cut (23 sec)
V                                        APX; MPV

**TEN ***                                       18
Blake Edwards        USA                 1979
*Dudley Moore, Julie Andrews, Bo Derek, Robert
Webber, Dee Wallace, Sam Jones, Brian Dennehy, Max
Showalter, Don Calfa, Nedra Volz, James Noble*
A successful songwriter suddenly meets his perfect
woman, and determines to woo and win her at any
cost. The title refers to his habit of scoring his
girlfriends out of ten. Another tiresomely awful
Edwards offering. See THE WOMAN IN RED for a
similar and far funnier treatment of this idea. The
music is by Henry Mancini with Ravel's Bolero a
recurrent theme.
Aka: "10"
COM                                        118 min
B,V                                           WHV

**TEN AND A HALF WEEKS ****                    R18
Robert McCallum      USA                 1986
*Barbara Dare, Jerry Butler, John Leslie, Keisha, Nikki
Knights, Dana Dylan, Siobhan Hunter, Tom Byron,
Jon Martin, Joey Silvera*
A more explicit version of the novel than NINE AND
A HALF WEEKS, with Butler the lover obsessed with
Barbara Dare. After telling Dare that he's madly in
love with her they embark on a wildly passionate
affair, exploring some of the sado-masochistic ele-
ments considerably subdued in the earlier film.
Aka: 10 1/2 WEEKS
Boa: novel 9 1/2 Weeks by E. McNeill.
A                        40 min Cut (16 sec)
V                                         VEXCEL

**TEN BROTHERS OF SHAOLIN ***
Ting Cheng           HONG KONG          1979
*Chia Ling, Chang Yi, Liang Chia-Jen, Don Wong Dao,
Wang Tao*
Ten Shaolin fighters protect a Ming ruler from the
Chings. Good period detail is largely wasted on this
plodding effort.
MAR                                         90 min
B,V                                          POLY

**TEN COMMANDMENTS, THE *****                   U
Cecil B. De Mille    USA                 1956
*Charlton Heston, Yul Brynner, Anne Baxter, Edward
G. Robinson, Yvonne De Carlo, Debra Paget, Cedric
Hardwicke, John Derick, Nina Foch, Martha Scott,
Judith Anderson, Vincent Price, John Carradine,
Eduard Franz, Olive Deering*

A stilted and flat retelling of the events described in
Exodus, but well worth seeing for the good effects and
some moments of genuine power. The story traces the
life of Moses from his birth and abandonment through
to manhood, and his leading of the Israelites out of
Egypt. A vivid but dated epic, filmed once before by De
Mille as a silent in 1923. The music is by Elmer
Bernstein AA: Effects (John Fulton).
A/AD                    217 min (ort 219 min)
V/sh                                          CIC

**TEN FINGERS OF STEEL ****
Kien Lun             HONG KONG          1968
*Wang Yu, Chang Chin Chin, Kan Kai*
A man seeks revenge on the bandit leader who raped
his sister in this standard fists 'n feet actioner.
MAR                                         95 min
B,V                                           DFS

**TEN LITTLE INDIANS ***
Peter Collinson                          1975
    FRANCE/ITALY/SPAIN/UK/WEST GERMANY
*Oliver Reed, Elke Sommer, Herbert Lom, Richard
Attenborough, Gert Frobe, Adolpho Celi, Charles
Aznavour, Stephane Audran, Teresa Gimpera, Alberto
de Mendoza, Maria Rohm, Orson Welles (voice only)*
Euro-version of the much-filmed murder mystery,
that fails to be anything but a tired and pedestrian
rendition of this tale, with assorted suspects of a series
of murders becoming victims as well. Set in Iran, this
is the third version of Christie's novel – it was first
filmed in 1945 and then in 1966.
Aka: AND THEN THERE WERE NONE (TEVP);
DEATH IN PERSEPOLIS; DIEZ NEGRITOS; TEN
LITTLE NIGGERS
Boa: novel by Agatha Christie.
THR                    100 min; 94 min (TEVP)
B,V                                          TEVP

**TEN LITTLE INDIANS ***                        15
Alan Birkinshaw      USA                 1989
*Donald Pleasence, Brenda Vaccaro, Frank Stallone,
Herbert Lom, Sarah Maur Thorp, Warren Berlinger,
Paul L. Smith, Yehuda Efroni, Moira Lister*
This is the third stab at Christie's murder mystery on
the part of producer Harry Alan, and is by far the
worst. The action is set at an African safari camp in
the 1930s, and as the sluggish plot wends its weary
way, we are treated to the expected succession of
slayings until the final denouement. A stiff and poorly
acted adaptation of minimal virtue.
Boa: novel by Agatha Christie.
DRA                    96 min (ort 98 min)
V                                   WHV; PATHE

**TEN RILLINGTON PLACE *****                    15
Richard Fleischer    UK                  1970
*Richard Attenborough, Judy Geeson, John Hurt, Pat
Heywood, Isobel Black, Phyllis MacMahon, Geoffrey
Chater, Robert Hardy, Bernard Lee, Andre Morell,
Robert Keegan, David Jackson, Edward Evans, Sam
Kydd, Gabrielle Daye*
A restrained and sombre account of the murderer
Christie, whose tenant, Timothy Evans, was hanged
for his deeds. Both Attenborough and Hurt give
remarkably fine performances, in a film that is
gruesome but of undeniable power. Scripted by Clive
Exton and with photography by Denys Coop.
Boa: book by Ludovic Kennedy.
DRA                                        111 min
B,V                                           RCA

**TEN TO MIDNIGHT ***                           18
J. Lee Thompson     USA                  1983
*Charles Bronson, Andrew Stevens, Gene Davis, Lisa
Eilbacher, Wilford Brimley, Geoffrey Lewis*
Re-run of DEATHWISH, in which an ex-cop hunts
down a psychotic woman-killer, who molested his
daughter after he planted evidence on him, an action

that got him dismissed from the force. Freed from the last restraints of any respect for the law, Bronson (giving a more than usually lifeless performance) embarks on his own hunt for the murderer.
Aka: 10 TO MIDNIGHT
A/AD                96 min (ort 102 min) Cut (1 min 42 sec)
B,V                                         GHV L/A; VCC

## TEN VIOLENT WOMEN *
Ted V. Mikels          USA              1978
Sherry Vernon, Dixie Lauren, Sally A. Gamble,
Georgia Morgan, Jane Farnsworth, Ted V. Mikels,
Anne Gaylis
A group of women become tired of working for a living and plan a massive jewel robbery.
THR                                        105 min
B,V,V2                                        VPD

## TEN WHO DARED *                             PG
William Beaudine       USA              1960
Brian Keith, John Beal, James Drury, R.G.
Armstrong, Ben Johnson, L.Q. Jones, Dan Sheridan,
David Stollery, Stan Jones, David Frankham, Pat
Hogan, Ray Walker, Jack Bighead, Roy Barcroft,
Dawn Little Sky
Account of an expedition to the Colorado River in 1869 based on the exploits of Major John Wesley Powell. A cliche-ridden and unappealing adventure, with little action and a lack of direction.
WES                                         92 min
B,V                                          WDV

## TENANT, THE ****                            18
Roman Polanski    FRANCE/USA           1976
Roman Polanski, Isabelle Adjani, Melvyn Douglas, Jo
Van Fleet, Shelley Winters, Bernard Fresson, Lila
Kedrova, Claude Dauphin, Claude Pieplu, Jacques
Monod, Patrice Alexandre, Josiane Balasko, Jean
Pierre Bagot
Polanski plays a withdrawn bank clerk who moves into a furnished apartment whose previous tenant is in hospital after a suicide attempt. Little by little, he becomes drawn into a strange and nightmarish world in which he adopts the previous tenant's identity. Stylish, well acted and very, very intense. Written by Polanski and Gerard Brach.
Aka: LE LOCATAIRE
Boa: novel by Roland Topor.
HOR                120 min (ort 125 min) Cut (6 sec)
B,V                                          CIC

## TENDER AGE, THE **                          18
Jan Egelson            USA              1984
John Savage, Tracy Pollan, Roxanne Hart, Richard
Jenkins, Jack Kehoe, Henry Tomaszewski
An idealistic probation officer is torn between his home life and the demands imposed by his latest case. A flawed and uneven drama that largely wastes some very good performances.
Aka: LITTLE SISTER, THE
DRA                      99 min (ort 103 min) mTV
B,V                                   TWE/VPD; TWE

## TENDER IS THE NIGHT **                       15
Robert Knights         UK               1985
Peter Strauss, Mary Steenbergen, Edward Asner, Sean
Young, Laurie Piper, John Heard, Jurgen Brugger,
Erwin Kohlund, Joris Stuyck, Kate Harper, Nancy
Paul, Astrid Frank, Francois Guetary, Rosario
Serrano, Richard Linford
Overlong film about a psychologist who cures and marries a wealthy female patient, only to find the tables turned. Not bad, although the 1961 version was somewhat better. Filmed in Paris, Switzerland and the South of France. The adaptation was by Dennis Potter.
Boa: novel by F. Scott Fitgerald.
DRA                311 min (2 cassettes – 360 min) mTV
B,V                                          BBC

## TENDER LOVING CARE **
Don Edmonds            USA              1973
Donna Desmond, Michael Asher, Leah Simon, Tony
Victor, Anita King, John Daniels
Three nurses get mixed up with blackmail, drugs, murder and sex, in this predictable effort.
Aka: NAUGHTY NURSES
A                       85 min (ort 102 min) Cut
B,V,V2                                        VPD

## TENDER MERCIES **                           PG
Bruce Beresford        USA              1982
Robert Duvall, Tess Harper, Allan Hubbard, Betty
Buckley, Ellen Barkin, Wilford Brimley, Lenny Von
Dohlen, Paul Gleason
An attractive widow and her young son help a Country and Western singer rebuild his life, in a sweet but insipid concoction that's easy to watch but leaves no trace on the memory. Duvall wrote his own songs for this. AA: Actor (Duvall), Screen (Orig) (Horton Foote).
DRA                      88 min (ort 93 min) mTV
B,V                               TEVP; WHV (VHS only)

## TENEBRAE ***
Dario Argento          ITALY            1982
Anthony Franciosa, John Saxon, Christian Borromeo,
Daria Nicolodi, Giuliano Gemma, Mirella D'Angelo,
John Steiner, Veronica Lario, Lara Wendel, Ania
Pieroni, Eva Robins, Mirella Banti, Isabella Amadeo,
Carola Stagnaro
A bizarre horror film, with an author going to Rome to promote his book, and getting involved in a strange series of killings. Gory but atmospheric, with good photography by Luciano Tovoli. Unlikely to be available in an uncut form in the UK.
Aka: SOTTO GLI OCCHI DELL'ASSASSINO;
UNSANE
HOR                                        101 min
B,V,V2                                        VDM

## TENNESSEE BUCK *                            18
David Keith            USA              1987
David Keith, Kathy Shower, Brent Van Hoffman,
Sydney Lassick
An intrepid hunter has to rescue his girlfriend from headhunters in the jungles of darkest Borneo. A low-budget adventure that inevitably reminds one of the kind of films being churned out by Monogram in the 1930s. The script is by Keith.
Aka: FURTHER ADVENTURES OF TENNESSEE
BUCK, THE: SACRIFICE
A/AD                    86 min (ort 90 min)
B,V                                          EIV

## TENNIS COURT, THE **
Peter Sasdy            UK               1984
Peter Graves, Hannah Gordon, Ralph Arliss, Isla St
Clair, Annis Joslin, George Little
A woman tries to flee from something evil in her past. A Hammer film made for TV as one in a series. Average.
HOR                                         72 min mTV
B,V                                          BWV

## TENSION AT TABLE ROCK **
Charles Marquis Warren
                       USA              1956
Richard Egan, Dorothy Malone, Cameron Mitchell,
Billy Chapin, Royal Dano, Edward Andrews, John
Dehner, DeForrest Kelley, Angie Dickinson, Joe
DeSantis
Routine Western about a man on the run because of a killing committed in self-defence. A competent but unmemorable tale, written by Winston Miller.
Boa: novel Bitter Sage by Frank Gruber.
Osca: REVENGE IS MY DESTINY

WES                          89 min (ort 93 min)
B,V                                        KVD

## TENSPEED AND BROWNSHOE ***          PG
E.W. Swackhamer        USA               1979
*Jeff Goldblum, Ben Vereen, Robert Webber, Jayne
Meadows, Richard Romanus, John Harkins, Simon
Griffeth, Larry Maretti, A.C. Weary, Luke Andreas,
Robyn Douglass*
Pilot for a TV series about a mismatched pair of
private investigators, one being a staid stockbroker
and the other a street-wise con artist. A slick and
extremely well-handled tale that was, unfortunately,
followed by an inferior series.
A/AD                               95 min mTV
B,V                                        CIC

## TENTH MAN, THE **                     15
Jack Gold              UK                 1988
*Anthony Hopkins, Kristin Scott Thomas, Derek
Jacobi, Cyril Cusack, Brenda Bruce, Paul Rogers*
The story of a successful French lawyer who becomes a
Nazi prisoner during WW2, and signs over all his
property to another prisoner so that the latter will
take his place in front of a firing squad. After the war
he returns to his villa, which has now become the
property of the dead man's family, and takes a job
there. A languid and rather murky fable, attractively
staged, but ultimately pointless.
Boa: novel by Graham Greene
DRA                               100 min mTV
B,V                                        MGM

## TENTH MONTH, THE **
Joan Tewkesbury        USA               1979
*Carol Burnett, Keith Michell, Dina Merrill, Melissa
Converse, Cristina Raines, Richard Venture, Yvonne
Wilder, Martine Beswick, Woodrow Parfrey, Joe
Ponazecki, Del Hinkley, Jossie DeGuzman, Rex
Robbins, Harriet Medin*
A middle-aged divorced woman becomes pregnant
after having an affair with a world-famous pianist,
and faces a dilemma about keeping the child, a fact
that has added poignancy as this is her first baby. An
overlong but touching melodrama.
Boa: novel by Laura Z. Hobson.
DRA                               123 min mTV
B,V                                     VTC L/A

## TENTH OF A SECOND *                   15
Darrell Roodt     SOUTH AFRICA          1987
*James Whyle, Janet Buckland, John Carson, Norman
Coombes, Nicky Rebelo, Greg Latter*
A white liberal South African teacher who supports
the anti-apartheid movement becomes involved in a
terrorist bombing that causes the death of an innocent
family. A murky and bleak film, with little action but
an abundance of moodiness.
THR                                   77 min
B/h, V/h                                   NWV

## TEQUILA SUNRISE **                    15
Robert Towne           USA               1988
*Mel Gibson, Michelle Pfeiffer, Kurt Russell, Raul
Julia, J.T. Walsh, Arliss Howard, Ann Magnuson,
Ayre Gross*
Two lifelong buddies go their separate ways, with one
becoming a drug dealer and the other a cop. They
come into conflict when they both start taking an
interest in the same woman. A film that starts off as if
it's really going somewhere, and then just peters out.
Written by Towne.
DRA                            111 min (ort 116 min)
V/sh                                       WHV

## TERMINAL CHOICE **                    18
Sheldon Larry         CANADA             1982
                                  (released 1985)
*Joe Spano, David McCallum, Diane Venora, Robert*

*Joy, Don Francks, Nicholas Campbell, Ellen Barkin,
Chapelle Jaffe, Clare Coulter, James Kidnie, Martha
Gibson, Chas Lawther, Les Rubie, Teri Austin, Tom
Harvey, Sandra Warren*
A doctor has to unravel a strange conspiracy in his
high-tech clinic, when he discovers that some of his
patients are dying because of deliberate interference
with the computer controlling their life-support sys-
tems. A gory thriller with little tension.
THR                             94 min (ort 98 min)
B,V                                        CBS

## TERMINAL ENTRY **                     15
John Kincade          USA                1986
*Paul Smith, Yaphet Kotto, Kabir Bedi, Edward Albert,
Yvette Nipar, Patrick Laborteaux, Rob Stone, Sam
Tempeles*
A group of young computer hackers rent a secluded
cabin, and spend a weekend breaking into restricted
databases, one of which takes the form of a strange
computer game. Having entered the game, they start
ordering a series of random "assassinations", but find
that these are actually being carried out.
A/AD                                   95 min
B,V                                        IVS

## TERMINAL EXPOSURE *                   15
Nico Mastorakis       USA                1986
*John Vernon, Steve Donmeyer, Joe Phelan, Tara
Buckman, Mark Hennessy, Scott King, Hope-Marie
Carlton, Patrick St Esprit, Ted Lange, Christina
Carda*
Two boys accidentally film a murder carried out by a
nightclub performer, but the only clue to her identity
is a rose tattoo on her behind. A silly mystery that
would have played better as a comedy.
THR                                  105 min
B,V                                       POLY

## TERMINAL ISLAND *
Stephanie Rothman     USA                1973
*Phyllis Elizabeth Davis, Don Marshall, Tom Selleck,
Barbara Leigh, Sean David Kennedy, Roger E. Mosley,
Ena Hartman, Marta Kristen, Clyde Ventura, Randy
Boone, Ford Clay, Jo Morrow, Richard Stahl, Frank
Christi, Sandy Ward*
In the future murderers are imprisoned in offshore
prisons instead of being executed, but one such prison,
formerly for men, starts taking in women. A weari-
some blend of mayhem and heavy breathing, with a
poor plot and worse dialogue. This film was re-issued a
decade later to take advantage of the popularity of
Selleck in the TV series "Magnum".
FAN                                   88 min
B,V                              WAL L/A; MMA

## TERMINAL MAN, THE **                  15
Mike Hodges           USA                1974
*George Segal, Joan Hackett, Richard Dysart, Jill
Clayburgh, Donald Moffat, Matt Clark, James B.
Sikking, Michael C. Gwynne, Ian Wolfe, Jason
Wingreen, Normann Burton, William Hansen, Robert
Ito, Matt Clark*
A computer scientist becomes a violent killer, when a
computer program is implanted in his brain after he
volunteers to undergo an experimental form of treat-
ment, in an attempt to control his violent outbursts of
rage. This adaptation of a best-selling novel starts off
with promise, but goes rapidly downhill in the second
half, in which the film concentrates heavily on the
series of murders he commits after escaping from the
hospital.
Boa: novel The Andromeda Strain by Michael
Crichton.
FAN                            100 min (ort 107 min)
B,V                                        WHV

## TERMINATE WITH EXTREME PREJUDICE **
Raoul Coutard

FRANCE/WEST GERMANY          1982
*Miles O'Keeffe, Dagmar Lassander, Catherine Jarrett,*
*Raimund Harmstorf, Anton Diffring*
A psychotic ex-CIA agent runs amok in El Salvador,
and has to be stopped before he carries out his
assignment to kill a powerful politician. A routine spy
thriller.
Aka: S.A.S. SAN SALVADOR
THR                                          95 min
B,V                                           EIV

## TERMINATOR, THE ***                        18
James Cameron          USA                   1984
*Arnold Schwarzenegger, Linda Hamilton, Paul*
*Winfield, Michael Biehn, Lance Henriksen, Rick*
*Rossovich, Earl Boen, Dick Miller, Bess Motta, Shawn*
*Shepps, Bruce M. Kerner, Franco Columbo, Bill*
*Paxton, Brian Thompson, Tom Oberhaus*
A humanoid killer cyborg is sent back in time from a
future society ruled by machines. Its task is to track
down and kill a woman whose as yet unborn son will
overthrow the rule of the robots. Schwarzenegger as
the unstoppable man-machine is frightening. A vio-
lent action film and the director's debut. Produced by
Gale Anne Hurd who co-wrote with Cameron.
FAN                                         135 min
B,V                                          RNK

## TERMINUS *                                  15
Pierre William Glenn
         FRANCE/WEST GERMANY          1986
*Johnny Hallyday, Jurgen Prochnow, Karen Allen,*
*Gabriel Damon, Julie Glenn, Louise Vincent, Dieter*
*Schidor, Janos Kulka, Dominique Valera, Jean-Luc*
*Montama, Ray Montama, Bruno Ciarrochi, David*
*Jalil, Andre Nocquet*
A MAD MAX variant that's set in the near future, and
tells of a truck race between the driver of a huge
computer-guided vehicle and his pursuers, who are
out to stop him at all costs. An incoherent mess with a
feeble script and a budget to match.
FAN                                          80 min
B,V                                          NELS

## TERMS OF ENDEARMENT ***                     15
James L. Brooks        USA                   1983
*Shirley MacLaine, Debra Winger, Jack Nicholson,*
*John Lithgow, Jeff Daniels, Danny DeVito, Lisa Hart*
*Carroll*
The relationship between a mother and her daughter
over the years has its ups and downs in this finely
-balanced mixture of comedy and drama, which tips
over into melodrama when the daughter dies of
cancer. Nicholson gives an amusing performance as a
former astronaut unable to cope with the lack of
excitement in everyday life. AA: Pic, Dir, Actress
(MacLaine), S. Actor (Nicholson), Screen (Adapt)
(Brooks).
Boa: novel by Larry McMurtry.
DRA                             126 min (ort 132 min)
V/h                                          CIC

## TERRAHAWKS: EXPECT THE UNEXPECTED     U
– PARTS 1 AND 2 **
Alan Patillo           UK                    1983
*Voices of: Windsor Davies, Denise Bryer, Jeremy*
*Hitcher, Anne Ridler, Ben Stevens*
Two episodes from a puppet animation series set in
the year 2020. They tell of how Earth was forced to
defend itself against an attack by evil aliens who,
having destroyed a base on Mars, set out to conquer
the galaxy. An elite fighting force known as the
Terrahawks is formed to defend the planet. This
two-part story tells of the investigation of a mysterious energy source and the capture of the Terrahawks' leader by the ruthless alien commander.
CAR                                      92 min mTV
V                                            CH5

## TERRIBLE QUICK SWORD OF SIEGFRIED, THE **
Adrian Hoven/David Friedman
         USA/WEST GERMANY             1971
*Lance Boyle (Raymond Harmstorf), Sybill Danning*
*(Sybelle Danninger), Heide Bohlen (Heide Ho), Peter*
*Hard*
Sex film about a warrior aptly named Siegfried, and
set at the Burgundian court.
Aka: EROTIC ADVENTURES OF SIEGFRIED, THE;
LONG SWIFT SWORD OF SIEGFRIED, THE;
MAIDEN QUEST; SIEGFRIED UND DAS
SAGENHAFTE LIEBESLEBEN DER
NIBELUNGEN
A                                            92 min
B,V                                          INT

## TERRITORY, THE **                           PG
Edgar Bold      SOUTH AFRICA
                               1985 (released 1986)
*Gordon Mulholland, Ian Roberts, Roc. E. Palmer*
*Gumib*
Another routine survival epic in which a Namib
Desert recluse and a young geologist form an uneasy
truce after a period of tension, but find that the lack of
water is their biggest threat.
Aka: ONE OF ONE
THR                                      75 min mTV
B,V                                        PACEV

## TERROR *                                    15
Franco Prosperi        ITALY                 1977
*Florinda Balkan, Ray Lovelock, Flavio Andreini,*
*Sherry Buchanan*
Three psychotic killers imprison and humiliate seven
women, but one of them plans a devastating revenge.
A disagreeable, low-grade offering.
Aka: LA SETTIMA DONNA
THR                                         102 min
B,V,V2                                        VPD

## TERROR AT RED WOLF INN **                   15
Bud Townsend           USA                   1972
*Linda Gillin, Arthur Space, John Nielson, Janet*
*Wood, Margaret Avery, Earl Parker, Michael*
*Macready*
A young college student wins a holiday at a strange
hotel run by an elderly couple and their grandson, but
discovers that they are in fact cannibals. A horror
spoof that relies on wit more than gore and for the
most part, is successful. The final credits roll in the
form of a menu – a nice touch.
Aka: FOLKS AT RED WOLF INN, THE; TERROR
HOUSE; TERROR ON THE MENU (COU or DRUM)
HOR                             79 min (ort 90 min)
B,V                    VNET L/A; COU L/A; DRUM

## TERROR EYES *                               18
Ken Hughes             USA                   1980
*Leonard Mann, Rachel Ward, Drew Snyder, Annette*
*Miller, Joseph R. Sicari, Nicholas Cairis, Karen*
*MacDonald, Bill McCann, Margo Skinner, Holly*
*Hardman, Elizabeth Barnitz, Leonard Corman, Ed*
*Higgins, Belle McDonald, John Blood*
Women attending a Boston night school are being
decapitated, and the killer may be one of the teachers.
Not a graphic film, but repulsive nonetheless. This
sorry effort was Ward's feature film debut.
Aka: NIGHT SCHOOL
HOR           84 min (ort 90 min) Cut (1 min 16 sec)
B,V,V2                                        GHV

## TERROR IN BEVERLY HILLS **                  18
John Myhers            USA                   1988
*Frank Stallone, Behrouz Vossoughi, Cameron*
*Mitchell, William Smith, Lysa Hayland*
An ex-Marine is sent to rescue the daughter of the US
President, when she is taken hostage by Middle East
terrorists who have also kidnapped his family to stop

the mission. Standard formula heroics that serves as a good vehicle for Stallone.

A/AD                                              89 min
V                                                     GHV

## TERROR IN THE JUNGLE **
Tom De Simone/Andy Janzack/Alex Graton
                    MEXICO/USA              1968
*Jimmy Angle, Robert Burns, Fawn Silver, Joan
Addis, Ivan Stephen, Henry Clayton Jr, Cee Childress*
A little boy goes missing in the Amazon jungles after a plane crash, and is hunted by Indians who want to sacrifice him.

A/AD                                              84 min
B,V                               CRO L/A; MARKET

## TERROR IN THE SWAMP *                        15
Joseph J. Catalanotto    USA              1983
*Billy Holliday, Chuck Long, Mike Thomas, Chuck
Bush, Michael Tedesco, Ray Saadie, Keith Barker,
Gerald Daigal, Mark Peterson, Claudia Wood, Albert
Dykes*
Down in the swamps of Louisiana, strange mutant creatures are on the prowl, the result of scientific experiments where rodents have been bred for their value to the fur industry.
Aka: NUTRIA MAN

HOR                                               87 min
B,V                                                   ODY

## TERROR IN THE WAX MUSEUM *
Georg Fenady            USA              1973
*Ray Milland, Broderick Crawford, Elsa Lanchester,
Maurice Evans, Shani Wallis, John Carradine, Louis
Hayward, Patric Knowles, Mark Edwards, Steven
Marlo, Nicole Shelby, Leslie Thompson, Lisa Lu, Ben
Wright, Matilda Calnan*
Low-budget murder mystery set in a Victorian exhibition of figures of famous murderers. The owner is found murdered, apparently by the figure of Jack the Ripper, before he can sell his collection to an American showman. Later this man is killed too. It finally transpires that a fortune was hidden among the figures and the murderer wanted to find it before the collection left the country. A poor effort – look closely and you'll see the exhibits moving.

HOR                                               93 min
B,V                                                   DFS

## TERROR OF DOCTOR HICHCOCK, THE **          18
Robert Hampton (Riccardo Freda)
                           ITALY              1962
*Barbara Steele, Robert Flemyng, Teresa Fitzgerald
(Maria Teresa Vianello), Montgomery Glen (Silvano
Tranquil), Harriet White, Spencer Williams*
A re-married mad doctor tries to revive his long dead first wife in this typical Gothic chiller.
Aka: HORRIBLE DR HICHCOCK, THE;
L'ORRIBILE SEGRETO DEL DOTTORE
HICHCOCK; RAPTUS

HOR                                               84 min
B,V              PHE (VHS only); STABL; VDM

## TERROR OF TINY TOWN, THE ***
Sam Newfield            USA              1938
*Billy Curtis, Yvonne Moray, Little Billy, John
Rambary, Billy Platt, Charles Becker, Joseph Herbert,
Nita Krebs, George Ministeri, Karl Casitzky, Fern
McDill, W.H. O'Dogharty*
In this one the baddie sets two families against each other in the hope that they'll all get killed off and he can get their lands. This bizarre film is in fact a musical Western with midget actors playing all the parts. Not terribly interesting or even well acted but worth a look as a curiosity. See also EVEN DWARFS STARTED SMALL.

WES                                              63 min B/W
B,V                                                   BWV

## TERROR ON HIGHWAY 91 **                      15
Jerry Jameson            USA              1988
*Ricky Schroder, George Dzundza, Matt Clark, Brad
Dourif, David Sherrell, Lara Flynn Boyle, Frederic
Lehne*
A young man joins the local police force and is dismayed to find it riddled with greed and corruption. Supposedly based on a true incident, but no more interesting for that.

DRA                     89 min (ort 100 min) mTV
V                                                     CBS

## TERROR ON TOUR *
Don Edmunds              USA              1982
*Dave Galluzzo, Richard Styles, Rich Pemberton, Jeff
Morgan, Dave Thompson, Larry Thomasof, Lisa
Rodriguez, Sylvia Wright, John Green, Lindy Leah,
John Wintergate, Kalassu, Ann Davis, Verkina
Flower, Rhonda Cacioppo, Frank James*
A rock group with a sadistic stage act become prime suspects when a number of prostitutes are murdered, since the psychopath responsible dresses as a member of the group. They are obliged to spring into action to clear their name. A gruesome and unrewarding blend of exploitation and tedium.
Aka: TERROR, THE

HOR                                               90 min
B,V                                            MED; VPD

## TERROR OUT OF THE SKY *
Lee H. Katzin            USA              1978
*Efrem Zimbalist Jr, Tovah Feldshuh, Dan Haggerty,
Lonny Chapman, Steve Franken, Ike Eisenmann,
Bruce French, Richard Herd, Joe E. Tata, Ellen Blake,
Philip Baker Hall, Charles Hallahan, Steve Tannen,
Melinda Peterson*
This sequel to THE SAVAGE BEES, has New Orleans terrorised by swarms of the usual buzzers, whose invasion is prevented by a pilot and two bee experts. Very dull.
Aka: TERROR FROM THE SKY

HOR                     81 min (ort 98 min) mTV
B,V                                            DFS; TEVP

## TERROR TRAIN **                               18
Roger Spottiswoode
                    CANADA/USA              1980
*Jamie Lee Curtis, Ben Johnson, Hart Bochner, David
Copperfield, Sandee Currie, Derek MacKinnon,
Timothy Webber, Anthony Sherwood, Howard
Busgang, Greg Swanson, D.D. Winters, Joy Boushel,
Victor Knight, Donald Lamoureux*
A masked fancy-dress party aboard a train chartered by a college fraternity, is the unusual setting for a run-of-the-mill entrant to the teen slasher stakes. The culprit turns out to be a former student, demented by a fraternity initiation prank, and out to get his revenge. One interesting twist is the killer donning the disguise of each successive victim. The photography of John Alcott slightly redeems this routine affair.

HOR                                               98 min
V                                                     MGM

## TERROR VISION *                               15
Ted Nicolaou            USA              1986
*Diane Franklin, Gerrit Graham, Mary Woronov, Chad
Allen, Jonathan Gries, Jennifer Richards, Alejandro
Rey, Bert Remsen, Randi Brooks, Sonny Clark Davis,
Ian Patrick Williams, John Leamer, William Paulson*
A family of strange characters find their satellite TV antenna attracts the unwelcome attentions of an alien creature, which comes to Earth and takes up residence in their television set. A comedy-horror yarn that sinks under the weight of its overblown special effects and clumsy humour.
Aka: TERRORVISION

COM                          81 min (ort 85 min)
B,V                                                   EIV

## TERROR WITHIN, THE **

| | | 18 |
|---|---|---|
| Tierry Notz | USA | 1988 |

*Andrew Stevens, Starr Andreeff, Terri Treas, George Kennedy, John LaFayette, Tommy Hinchley*

In a bleak world of the future, plague has killed of most of the planet's population and a horde of mutants attack an underground medical centre. A low-budget tale from Roger Corman's studios that's certainly grim enough, but has no more inspiration than is usual for such films.

HOR                                    85 min (ort 88 min)
V                                                        MGM

## TERROREYES **

| | | 18 |
|---|---|---|
| Eric Parkinson | USA | 1988 (released 1991) |

*Daniel Roebuck, Vivian Schilling*

Gruesome horror spoof about a demon sent from Hell to recruit new scriptwriters. Having murdered the husband of a writer, he takes the man's place in order to help her complete her script for the Devil's next horror film. An over-the-top effort that tries for a type of humour reminiscent of BEETLEJUICE, but largely fails.

HOR                                                   89 min
V                                                        VPD

## TERRY FOX STORY, THE ***

| | | |
|---|---|---|
| Ralph Thomas | CANADA | 1983 |

*Eric Fryer, Robert Duvall, Rosalind Chao, Chris Makepeace, Michael Zelniker, Frank Adamson, Elva Mai Hoover, Marie McCann, Clyde Rose, Austin Davis, Matt Craven, Jeremy Brown, Sheldon Rybowski, Dorothy Wyatt, Steven Hunter*

The true and moving story of a one-legged athlete, who ran across Canada raising funds for a project, before eventually dying of cancer. First-time actor Fryer, a real amputee, brings realism to the role of Fox in an example of perfect casting.

Boa: story by John and Rose Kastner.

DRA                                              97 min mCab
B,V                                                     POLY

## TESS **

| | | PG |
|---|---|---|
| Roman Polanski | FRANCE/UK | 1979 |

*Nastassia Kinski, Leigh Lawson, Peter Firth, John Collin, John Bett, Tony Church, Tom Chadbon, Rosemary Martin, Sylvia Coleridge, Richard Pearson, Fred Bryant, Carolyn Pickles, Arielle Dombasle, David Markham*

Film version of a classic novel about a peasant girl who tries to prove her aristocratic origins but comes unstuck when confronted by her betters. A solid, overlong and glossy work, quite evocative but not especially entertaining. The script is by Polanski, Gerard Brach and John Brownjohn. AA: Cin (Geoffrey Unsworth/Ghislain Cloquet), Art/Set (Pierre Guffroy and Jack Stephens), Cost (Anthony Powell).

Boa: novel Tess Of The D'Urbervilles by Thomas Hardy.

DRA                                     164 min (ort 180 min)
B,V                                                     TEVP

## TESTAMENT ***

| | | PG |
|---|---|---|
| Lynne Littman | USA | 1983 |

*Jane Alexander, William Devane, Roxana Zal, Ross Harris, Lukas Haas, Lilia Skala, Leon Ames, Philip Anglim, Lurene Tuttle, Rebecca DeMornay, Kevin Costner, Mako, Mico Olmos*

A restrained view of how a small town is affected by a nuclear attack, that focuses on the effect this catastrophe has on one family. Quite harrowing, and infinitely better than THE DAY AFTER, but not well known as it was not well publicised. Written by John Sacret Young. See also THE LAST WAR.

Boa: short story The Last Testament by Carol Amen.

DRA                                       86 min (ort 89 min)
B,V                                                      CIC

## TESTAMENT OF ORPHEUS, THE ***

| | | |
|---|---|---|
| Jean Cocteau | FRANCE | 1959 |

*Jean Cocteau, Edouard Dermithe, Maria Cesares, Francois Perier, Henri Cremieux, Yul Brynner, Jean-Pierre Leaud, Daniel Gelin, Jean Marais, Pablo Picasso, Charles Aznavour, Francoise Christophe, Nicole Courcel*

A surreal journey with the director through time and space, as a poet seeks the meaning of existence. This self-indulgent and slightly mocking exercise of Cocteau's, fails as a statement of his values, but is of interest for the melancholy array of bizarre images it presents. Written by Cocteau.

Aka: LE TESTAMENT D'ORPHEE

FAN                                               83 min B/W
B,V                                                      PVG

## TEX ***

| | | PG |
|---|---|---|
| Tim Hunter | USA | 1982 |

*Jim Metzler, Meg Tilly, Bill McKinney, Frances Lee McCain, Ben Johnson, Mat Dillon, Emilio Estevez, Phil Brock, Jack Thibeau, Tom Virtue*

A young boy is raised by his brother because one parent is dead and the other absent. A simple and unadorned account, the first of Hinton's novels about young adults to be made into a film. Look out for Hinton, who has a cameo as a teacher. The script is by Hunter and Charlie Haas.

Boa: novel by S.E. Hinton.

DRA                                                 103 min
B,V                                                     WDV

## TEXAS ACROSS THE RIVER **

| | | PG |
|---|---|---|
| Michael Gordon | USA | 1966 |

*Alain Delon, Dean Martin, Joey Bishop, Rosemary Forsyth, Peter Graves, Tina (Aumont) Marquand, Andrew Prine, Michael Ansara, Linden Chiles, Stuart Anderson, Roy Barcroft, George Wallace, Richard Farnsworth, John Harmon*

Western spoof with an assortment of characters and a complex plot, that has a Texan, an Indian and a Spanish nobleman going on the run to escape their enemies and experiencing various encounters along the way. A rambling affair to which the gags seem to have been added as an afterthought.

COM                                     96 min (ort 101 min)
B,V                                                      CIC

## TEXAS ADIOS **

| | | |
|---|---|---|
| Ferinando Baldi | ITALY/SPAIN | 1966 |

*Franco Nero, Cole Kitosch, Elisa Montes*

A Texas sheriff pursues his father's killer across the border into Mexico and finally tracks him down, only to experience a bitter disappointment when his identity is revealed.

Aka: ADIOS, TEXAS; TEXAS, ADDIO

WES                                                  85 min
B,V                                                      VPD

## TEXAS DETOUR **

| | | |
|---|---|---|
| Hikmet Avedis | USA | 1978 |

*Patrick Wayne, Mitch Vogel, Lindsay Bloom, R.G. Armstrong, Cameron Mitchell, Priscilla Barnes*

Low-budget drama about a stunt car driver and his family, who find that the theft of their van is merely the prelude to a succession of dangerous situations.

DRA                                                  92 min
B,V                                           CEN L/A; HOK

## TEXAS GLADIATORS 2020 *

Kevin Mancuso/Joe D'Amato (Aristide Massaccesi)
                                        ITALY           1982

*Al Cliver (Pier Luigi Conti), Sabrina Siani, Harrison Muller, Daniel Stephen, David Green, Al Yamanouchi, Peter Hooten, Donal O'Brien*

A cheap MAD MAX clone, with all the expected trimmings and a shortage of originality.

Aka: SUDDEN DEATH; 2020 TEXAS GLADIATORS; 2020 TEXAS FREEDOM FIGHTERS

A/AD                                          91 min
B,V                          FTV/VSP L/A; CBS

## TEXAS LADY **                              U
Tim Whelan           USA            1955
*Claudette Colbert, Barry Sullivan, Gregory Walcott,*
*Ray Collins, Horace McMahon, John Litel, James Bell,*
*Walter Sande, Douglas Fowley, Dan Haggerty, Celia*
*Lovsky*
Story of a female newspaper editor in a Western town
who decides to run an anti-corruption campaign and
faces the usual dangers and hazards. Colbert's charm
partially enlivens the routine script.
WES                                          86 min
V                                VMA; STABL

## TEXAS LIGHTNING **                         18
Gary Graver          USA            1981
*Cameron Mitchell, Peter Jason, Channing Mitchell,*
*Maureen McCormick*
A boy goes on a hunting trip with his father and soon
learns to chase more than game when he meets a
shapely waitress.
COM                                          93 min
B,V                                     VPD

## THANK GOD IT'S FRIDAY *                    15
Robert Klane         USA            1978
*Valerie Landsburg, Jeff Goldblum, Donna Summer,*
*Terri Nunn, Chick Vennera, Debra Winger, Andrea*
*Howard, Paul Jabara, Ray Vitte, The Commodores*
*(with Lionel Ritchie)*
The story of a Hollywood disc-jockey and his problems,
set against the background of the disco where he
works. A pounding, uninspiring and monotonous
experience. The script is by Barry Armyan Bernstein.
AA: Song ("Last Dance" – Paul Jabara).
MUS                                          90 min
B,V                                     RCA

## THANK YOUR LUCKY STARS ****                U
David Butler         USA            1943
*Eddie Cantor, Dinah Shore, Joan Leslie, Errol Flynn,*
*Bette Davis, Humphrey Bogart, Edward Everett*
*Horton, John Garfield, Alan Hale, Ann Sheridan,*
*Jack Carson, Dennis Morgan, Olivia De Havilland,*
*Ida Lupino, S.Z. Zakall*
Cantor and his double (also, amazingly enough,
played by Cantor) get involved in mounting a patriotic
show. Not so much a film as a parade of talented
performers. A lively, funny and most satisfying
musical. Numbers include: "They're Either Too Young
Or Too Old", "Love Isn't Born It's Made", "I'm Going
North" and "That's What You Jolly Well Get". Songs
are by Frank Loesser and Arthur Schwartz.
MUS                          122 min (ort 127 min) B/W
V/h                                     WHV

## THAT CHAMPIONSHIP SEASON **               15
Jason Miller         USA            1982
*Bruce Dern, Stacy Keach, Robert Mitchum, Martin*
*Sheen, Paul Sorvino, Arthur Franz*
Former members of a high school basketball team,
attend a reunion with their erstwhile coach after 25
years, but this meeting only serves to highlight
long-standing bitterness and enmity. A stolid adapta-
tion of a Pulitzer prize-winning play, that has none of
the intense performances that made the original stage
version such a success. Written by Miller.
Boa: play by Jason Miller.
DRA                          105 min (ort 108 min)
V                            PAL L/A; GHV; MSD

## THAT DARN CAT! **                          U
Robert Stevenson     USA            1965
*Hayley Mills, Dean Jones, Dorothy Provine, Roddy*
*McDowall, Neville Brand, Elsa Lanchester, William*
*Demarest, Frank Gorshin, Richard Eastman, Grayson*
*Hall, Ed Wynn, Tom Lowell, Richard Deacon, Iris*

*Adrian, Liam Sullivan*
A pet cat accidentally helps a hostage to get free of the
bank robbers who have kidnapped her, in this feeble
and overlong comedy. A typical 1960s Disney kiddies'
comedy – safe, tame and wrapped in a sugar-candy
coating.
Boa: novel Undercover Cat by Mildred Gordon and G.
Gordon.
COM                          112 min (ort 116 min)
B,V                                     RNK

## THAT GIRL IS A TRAMP **                    18
Jack Guy
*Bente Nielsen, Sam Maree, Laura Viala, Yves*
*Collignan*
After running away from home, a young girl meets up
with another girl and the two of them take on a job as
nude models for photographers. Soon they graduate to
more ambitious enterprises, such as fleecing the
customers of their wallets.
Aka: LADY IS A TRAMP, THE; THAT LADY IS A
TRAMP; THIS GIRL IS A TRAMP
A                            86 min Cut (10 min 53 sec)
B,V                              TCX L/A; VPD

## THAT LUCKY TOUCH *                         PG
Christopher Miles    UK             1975
*Roger Moore, Susannah York, Shelley Winters, Lee J.*
*Cobb, Jean-Pierre Cassel, Raf Vallone, Sydne Rome,*
*Donald Sinden, Michael Shannon, Alfred Hoffman,*
*Aubrey Woods, Timothy Carlton, Fabian Cevellos,*
*Vincent Hall*
An arms dealer and a lady journalist covering the
NATO exercises in Brussels, fall for each other. A
lightweight muddle of unconvincing romance and
unamusing comedy. Written by John Briley.
Boa: story by Moss Hart.
COM                          93 min; 89 min (VCC)
B,V                              VCL/CBS; VCC

## THAT MAGIC MOMENT *                        15
Daryl Duke           USA            1990
*Jace Alexander, Lindsay Frost, Cynthia Gibb, Jane*
*Krakowski, Eric La Salle*
Soap opera-style story of a group of American high
school teenagers about to graduate in a small town
during the summer of 1959, whose tight-knit camar-
aderie is shattered by the tragic deaths of two of its
members. Further events contrive to split the group
still further, with some of them going off to college
whilst others stay behind. A dreary coming-of-age
drama that never comes up with a strong and coherent
narrative.
DRA                                          96 min
V                                       NWV

## THAT MAN BOLT **                           18
Henry Levin/David Lowell Rich
                     USA            1973
*Fred Williamson, Bryon Webster, Miko Mayama,*
*Teresa Graves, Jack Ging*
An international syndicate courier versed in the
martial arts has various adventures. A mix of comedy
and kung fu, filmed in Hong Kong, Las Vegas and
L.A. A watchable actioner of nice locations and
routine plotting, written by Quentin Werty and
Charles Johnson.
MAR                          98 min (ort 103 min) Cut (1 min 6 sec)
B,V                                     CIC

## THAT SECRET SUNDAY **                      15
Richard A. Colla     USA            1986
*James Farentino, Parker Stevenson, William Lucking,*
*Daphne Ashbrook, Michael Lerner, Dan Hedaya,*
*Charles Frank, Robert Romanus, Joe Regalbuto,*
*Patrick Dollaghan, George Grizzard, Sondra Blake,*
*Wendy Van Riesen, Lesley Ewen*
Two reporters investigate an attempt to cover up the
deaths of two young women, at a party attended

mainly by police officers. A standard drama that sags rather badly, despite a strong performance from Farentino.

| DRA | 90 min (ort 92 min) mTV |
| B,V | CBS |

### THAT SINKING FEELING ** PG
Bill Forsyth UK 1979
*Tom Mannion, Eddie Burt, Richard Demarco, Alex McKenzie, Margaret Adams, Kim Masterson, Danny Benson, Robert Buchanan, Drew Burns, Billy Greenlees, John Hughes, Eric Joseph, Alan Love, Derek Millar, James Ramsey, Janette Rankin*
Very unfunny account of a gang of unemployed Glaswegian teenagers who think they've broken into the big time, when their leader unveils a scheme to boost their morale by stealing stainless steel sinks from a warehouse. Released in the US after the success of GREGORY'S GIRL and LOCAL HERO, both of which were also by Forsyth, though this film marked his directorial debut.

| COM | 90 min (ort 93 min) |
| B,V | PVG; PAL |

### THAT SUMMER OF WHITE ROSES *** 15
Rajko Grlic 1989
*Tom Conti, Susan George, Rod Steiger, Nitzan Sharron, Alun Armstrong, John Gill, John Sharp, Geoffrey Whitehead, Miljenko Brlecic, Vanja Drach, Slobodan Sembera, Stanka Gjuric*
An atmospheric drama set in Nazi-occupied Yugoslavia where a naive and kindhearted lifeguard puts his life in danger by taking in the young widow of a partisan and her son, both of whom are on the run from the Nazis. His later action in saving a drowning Nazi officer leads to him being branded as a traitor, and his innocent world is brought to a shattering end. A film of improbabilities that's redeemed by fine performances and direction.

| DRA | 99 min |
| V/sh | AVALON |

### THAT TOUCH OF MINK ** U
Delbert Mann USA 1962
*Cary Grant, Doris Day, Gig Young, Audrey Meadows, John Astin, Dick Sargent*
Typical period sex comedy. Grant as his usual wooden self plays an unmarried executive who chases his chaste secretary, the lovely Doris. Mildly amusing to start with, but as the film progresses it rapidly becomes quite tiresome. Written by Stanley Shapiro and Nate Monaster.
Osca: THE GRASS IS GREENER (VCC)

| COM | 95 min (ort 99 min) |
| B,V | BBC L/A; VCC (VHS only) |

### THAT WAS THEN, THIS IS NOW ** 15
Christopher Cain USA 1985
*Emilio Estevez, Craig Sheffer, Kim Delaney, Barbara Babcock, Larry B. Scott, Jill Schoelen, Frank Howard, Matthew Dudley, Frank McCarthy, Steven Pringle, Diane Dorsey, Roman Sheen, David Miller, Bob Swain, John O'Brien, Paul Lane*
A boy's relationship with his elder brother is threatened when a girlfriend arrives on the scene. An intense but patchy account of teenagers and their emotions, based on another of Hinton's gloomy and angst-filled accounts. The script is by Estevez.
Boa: novel by S.E. Hinton.

| DRA | 98 min (ort 102 min) |
| B,V | EHE |

### THAT'LL BE THE DAY *** 15
Claude Whatham UK 1973
*David Essex, Ringo Starr, Rosemary Leach, James Booth, Billy Fury, Keith Moon, Deborah Watling, Robert Lindsay, Brenda Bruce, Verna Harvey, Rosalind Ayres, James Ottoway, Beth Morris, Daphne Oxenford, Kim Braden, Ron Hackett*

This tells of the beginnings of a young man's involvement in the world of rock music, and how it affects his life. Essex and Starr are splendid in a piece of well crafted entertainment. Followed by STARDUST which continues his story. Written by Ray Connolly, with musical direction by Keith Moon and Neil Aspinall.

| DRA | 87 min (ort 91 min) |
| B,V | TEVP; WHV (VHS only) |

### THAT'S ADEQUATE ** 15
Harry Hurwitz USA 1987
*Tony Randall, James Coco, Bruce Willis, Robert Downey Jr, Robert Vaughn, Susan Dey*
The story of a film studio called "Adequate Pictures" that uses underhand methods and the theft of ideas from other studios to make its movies.

| DRA | 90 min |
| V | CASPIC/TERRY |

### THAT'S DANCING! *** U
Jack Haley Jr USA 1985
*Narrated by: Gene Kelly, Sammy Davis Jr, Mikhail Baryshnikov, Liza Minnelli, Ray Bolger*
A selection of dance sequences from a wide range of movie musicals, with a host of poor sequences but several memorable ones too. A fascinating compilation in which the earlier numbers such as the Astaire-Rogers routines show just how deficient 1980s musicals are in comparison. Of added interest is a Ray Bolger number cut from THE WIZARD OF OZ.

| MUS | 103 min (ort 105 min) |
| V/sh | MGM |

### THAT'S ENTERTAINMENT: PART 1 *** U
Jack Haley Jr USA 1974
*Fred Astaire, Bing Crosby, Gene Kelly, Peter Lawford, Liza Minnelli, Donald O'Connor, Debbie Reynolds, Frank Sinatra, James Stewart, Mickey Rooney, Elizabeth Taylor, Judy Garland, Esther Williams, Eleanor Powell (and others)*
A compilation movie consisting of a selection of highlights from MGM musicals released between 1929 and 1958. A celebration of nostalgia and talent, slightly spoilt by being clumsily organised and edited and sentimentally narrated. Nevertheless, there are many fine sequences. Written by Haley Jr and followed by a sequel. The selections are introduced by many of the stars that appeared in them.

| MUS | 122 min (ort 137 min) |
| V | MGM |

### THAT'S ENTERTAINMENT: PART 2 *** U
Gene Kelly USA 1976
*Jeanette MacDonald, Nelson Eddy, the Marx Brothers, Laurel and Hardy, Jack Buchanan, Judy Garland, Ann Miller, Mickey Rooney, Oscar Levant, Louis Armstrong (and others)*
Introduced by Fred Astaire and Gene Kelly, this second compilation film has highlights from another collection of MGM movies, but lacks the verve of the first film. However, much of the material is memorable, and this time includes sequences from comedies and dramas.

| MUS | 121 min (ort 133 min) |
| V | MGM |

### THAT'S LIFE! *** 15
Blake Edwards USA 1986
*Jack Lemmon, Julie Andrews, Sally Kellerman, Robert Loggia, Chris Lemmon, Emman Walton, Rob Knepper, Jennifer Edwards, Matt Lattanzi, Cynthia Sikes, Dana Sparks, Felicia Farr, Theodore Wilson, Nicky Blair, Jordan Christopher*
A sharp but sour look at the emotional problems afflicting the members of an affluent family, most especially the father, who has just turned 60, and his wife who thinks she may have cancer. Often quite touching, but hampered by the contrived script and an

unrelenting tone of bitterness. One of the director's more substantial films.

| | |
|---|---|
| DRA | 101 min |
| B,V | VES |

## THEATRE OF BLOOD *** 18
Douglas Hickox          UK          1973
*Vincent Price, Diana Rigg, Ian Hendry, Harry Andrews, Coral Browne, Jack Hawkins, Michael Hordern, Arthur Lowe, Robert Morley, Dennis Price, Milo O'Shea, Diana Dors, Robert Coote, Joan Hickson, Renee Asherson, Eric Sykes*
A mad actor in classical theatre decides to take a gruesome revenge on all the critics who have panned him over the years, by engineering a series of elaborate murder schemes, each of which recalls a scene from one of Shakespeare's plays. A black comedy of inventive plotting and repulsive effects.

| | |
|---|---|
| HOR | 100 min (ort 102 min) |
| B,V | WHV |

## THEM! * PG
Gordon Douglas          USA          1954
*Edmund Gwenn, James Arness, Joan Weldon, James Whitmore, Onslow Stevens, Don Shelton, Sean McClory, Chris Drake, Sandy Descher, Mary Ann Hokanson, Olin Howlin, William Schallert, Dub Taylor, Fess Parker, Leonard Nimoy*
Radiation from a nuclear test causes ants to grow to giant size; the plot and acting are shrunk in proportion, thus achieving a kind of balance. The climax is in the sewers of L.A. Written by Ted Sherdeman, this is an example of a perfectly good idea that's a hostage to those "this is a job for the army" cliches of the 1950s. Fess Parker has a small role, as does Leonard Nimoy. The music is by Bronislau Kaper.
Boa: short story by George Worthing Yates.

| | |
|---|---|
| FAN | 94 min B/W |
| B,V | WHV |

## THEODORA, QUEEN OF BYZANTIUM ** PG
Riccardo Freda    FRANCE/ITALY          1954
*Irene Papas, George Marchal, Gianna Maria Canale, Renato Baldini, Henri Guisol*
Historic epic about the rise to power of a slave girl to the position of Empress of Byzantium. A standard European work, slightly redeemed by nice sets and costumes.
Aka: THEODORA, SLAVE EMPRESS

| | |
|---|---|
| DRA | 87 min (ort 92 min) Cut (7 sec) |
| B,V,V2 | VDM L/A; STABL |

## THERE GOES THE BRIDE * PG
Terence Marcel          UK          1980
*Twiggy (Lesley Hornby), Tom Smothers, Martin Balsam, Sylvia Syms, Michael Whitney, Geoffrey Sumner, Graham Stark, Hermione Baddeley, Phil Silvers, Jim Backus, Broderick Crawford, Margot Moser, Toria Fuller, John Terry*
Tale of the chaotic events that befall an advertising man on the day of his daughter's wedding, when he is so overcome by events that he begins to hallucinate, and finds himself haunted by the ghost of a flapper. Generally plotless and fairly witless, with a script by Marcel and Ray Cooney.
Boa: play by Ray Cooney and John Chapman.

| | |
|---|---|
| COM | 90 min |
| B,V | HVH; MIA (VHS only) |

## THERE WAS A CROOKED MAN *** 15
Joseph L. Mankiewicz    USA          1970
*Kirk Douglas, Henry Fonda, Warren Oates, Hume Cronyn, Burgess Meredith, John Randolph, Arthur O'Connell, Martin Gabel, Michael Blodgett, Claudia McNeil, Alan Hale, Victor French, Lee Grant, C.K. Yang, Pamela Hensley, Bert Freed*
A murderer tries to escape from jail and recover his loot, but finds this rather difficult. An entertaining comedy that derives its humour from a battle of wits

between Douglas and Fonda, as inmate and warden respectively. Written by David Newman and Robert Benton.

| | |
|---|---|
| WES | 125 min |
| B,V | WHV |

## THERE'S A GIRL IN MY SOUP ** 15
Roy Boulting          UK          1970
*Peter Sellers, Goldie Hawn, Tony Britton, Nicky Henson, John Comer, Diana Dors, Judy Campbell, Gabrielle Drake, Nicola Paget, Geraldine Sherman, Thorley Walters, Christopher Cazenove, Raf de la Torre, Avril Angers*
A TV personality who is something of an ageing Don Juan, finds his life is vastly complicated when he picks up a young girl. A slightly amusing comedy that ends with all concerned back at the point they started. Sellers is miscast in this flimsy screen version of the long-running play. The script is by Frisby.
Boa: play by Terence Frisby.

| | |
|---|---|
| COM | 92 min (ort 96 min) |
| V | RCA |

## THERE'S NO BUSINESS LIKE SHOW U
## BUSINESS ***
Walter Lang          USA          1954
*Ethel Merman, Donald O'Connor, Marilyn Monroe, Dan Dailey, Johnnie Ray, Mitzi Gaynor, Hugh O'Brian, Frank McHugh*
An account of a family stage-act and their ups and downs, built around the songs of Irving Berlin. An entertaining musical that's well worth a look, despite the lack of plotting and a tendency to show off the fact that it was made in Cinemascope (a series of lavish and crowded numbers serving to fill up the screen). The music is by Lionel and Alfred Newman.

| | |
|---|---|
| MUS | 115 min (ort 117 min) |
| V | CBS |

## THEY ALL LAUGHED ** 
Peter Bogdanovich    USA          1982
*Ben Gazzara, John Ritter, Audrey Hepburn, Colleen Camp, Dorothy Stratten, Blaine Novak, Patti Hansen, George Morfogen, Sean Ferrer*
Romantic comedy following the adventures of four private detectives working in New York, who enjoy various encounters, including ones of the romantic kind. An episodic and rambling comedy, barely sustained by its excellent use of New York City locations. Written and directed by Bognanovich. Stratten was murdered prior to release of the film.

| | |
|---|---|
| COM | 115 min |
| B,V | VTC |

## THEY CALL ME HALLELUJAH **
Anthony Ascott (Giuliano Carmineo)
                      ITALY          1978
*George Hilton, Charlie Southwood, Agatha Florry*
A group of men planning to overthrow the Mexican government, embark on a search for a hidden fortune in jewels, to pay for the guns they need.

| | |
|---|---|
| WES | 96 min |
| B,V | ABA L/A |

## THEY CALL ME TRINITY *** PG
E.B. Clucher (Enzo Barboni)
                      ITALY          1971
*Terence Hill (Mario Girotti), Bud Spencer (Carlo Pedersoli), Farley Granger, Steffan Zacharias, Dan Sturkie, Gisela Hahn, Elena Pedemonte, Ezio Marano, Luciano Rossi, Michelle Spaeara, Remo Capitani, Michele Cimarosa*
A spoof on the THE MAGNIFICENT SEVEN, in which two half-brothers protect a Mormon settlement from Mexican bandits. A high-spirited succession of slapstick gags and affectionate parodies. Followed by TRINITY IS STILL MY NAME.
Aka: TRINITY IS MY NAME

WES 109 min
B,V EHE

## THEY CALL THAT AN ACCIDENT **
Nathalie Delon     FRANCE                        1982
*Nathalie Delon, Patrick Norbert, Gilles Segal*
A mother is convinced that her son's death during a
routine operation was murder, and plans revenge on
the three surgeons involved.
THR                                              90 min
B,V                                          ISLPIC/PVG

## THEY CALLED HIM AMEN *
Alfio Caitabiano     USA                         1982
*Sydne Rome, Luc Merenda*
Undistinguished spaghetti Western.
Aka: THEY CALL HIM AMEN
WES                                              89 min
B,V                                              VPD

## THEY DIED WITH THEIR BOOTS ON ***          U
Raoul Walsh          USA                         1941
*Errol Flynn, Olivia De Havilland, Gene Lockhart,
Regis Toomey, Stanley Ridges, Arthur Kennedy, John
Litel, Sydney Greenstreet, Hattie McDaniel, Anthony
Quinn, Charles Grapewin, Walter Hampden, G.P.
Huntlet Jr*
An attempt to retell the story of the events leading up
to the Battle of the Little Big Horn, with Custer cast
in a romantic and honourable light, and the blame for
this disaster firmly pinned on gunrunners. An episo-
dic account, but mounted with a good deal of style.
Photography is by Bert Glennon.
WES                        135 min (ort 140 min) B/W
V                                                WHV

## THEY GOT ME COVERED **                     U
David Butler         USA                         1943
*Bob Hope, Dorothy Lamour, Lenore Aubert, Otto
Preminger, Eduardo Ciannelli, Donald Meek, Marion
Martin, Donald MacBride, Walter Catlett, Philip Ahn,
John Abbott, Florence Bates*
Wartime comedy tale of a bungling newspaper repor-
ter who gets mixed up in a foreign spy ring. A good
mixture of laughs and thrills done in the expected
manic style. Written by Harry Kurnitz.
COM                        90 min (ort 93 min) B/W
V                                            VGM; PARK

## THEY LIVE **                               18
John Carpenter                                   1988
*Roddy Piper, Keith David, Meg Foster, George "Buck"
Flower, Peter Jason, Raymond St Jacques, Jason
Robards III, Larry Franco*
This film's unusual premise is that aliens have
succeeded in dominating society and walk undetected
among the inhabitants, who are constantly bom-
barded with subliminal messages of obedience and
consumption. A drifter who arrives in L.A. discovers
this when he acquires a special pair of glasses,
enabling him to see the true appearance of the aliens.
A good idea is thrown away, with the film becoming
just one more urban actioner.
Boa: story Eight O'Clock In The Morning by Ray
Faraday Nelson.
FAN                        90 min (ort 97 min)
V/sh                                             GHV

## THEY MADE ME A CRIMINAL ***               PG
Busby Berkeley       USA                         1939
*John Garfield, Claude Rains, Ann Sheridan, Gloria
Dickson, May Robson, Billy Halop, Leo Gorcey, Huntz
Hall, Bobby Jordan, Gabriel Dell*
Following a drunken brawl in which a man was killed,
a boxer hides at a strange ranch out West, where he
meets Robson and the "Dead End Kids". An effective
remake of the 1933 film "The Life Of Jimmy Dolan",
that is sustained by Garfield's sensitive performance

rather than by any merits to be found in the script.
Osca: LIGHTNING RAIDERS (WOOD)
DRA                        70 min (ort 92 min) B/W
B,V                          VCL/CBS; VCC; WOOD; GLOB

## THEY PAID WITH BULLETS *
Guilio Diamanti     ITALY/SPAIN                  1969
*Peter Lee Lawrence (Karl Mirenbach), William Bogart,
Ingrid Schoelly*
Gangster movie set in the 1920s in Chicago and
telling of the conflict between rival gangs. Unmemor-
able.
Aka: THEY PAID WITH BULLETS: CHICAGO 1929;
TEMPO DI CHARLESTON: CHICAGO 1929;
TIEMPOS DE CHICAGO
DRA                                              85 min
B,V,V2                                           INT

## THEY SHOOT HORSES, DON'T THEY? ***       15
Sydney Pollack       USA                         1969
*Jane Fonda, Michael Sarrazin, Susannah York, Gig
Young, Red Buttons, Bruce Dern, Bonnie Bedelia,
Allyn Ann McLerie*
A dance marathon in 1932 in California is used as a
microcosm of life in the Depression years, intertwined
with many subplots built around the lives of the
characters. Young as the unctuous promotor is espe-
cially memorable. Written by James Poe and Robert
E. Thompson. AA: S. Actor (Young).
Boa: novel by Horace McCoy.
DRA                108 min; 114 min (VGM) (ort 129 min)
B,V                                          RNK; VGM

## THEY STILL CALL ME BRUCE *               15/PG
James Orr/Johnny Yune USA                        1987
*Johnny Yune, Robert Guillaume, Pat Paulsen, David
Mendenhall, Joey Travolta, Bethany Wright, Don Gibb*
A young Korean finds he has a wonderful talent for
getting into trouble, as he travels the USA in search of
the GI who once saved his life. An aimless farce that is
a sequel in name alone to THEY CALL ME BRUCE.
COM        90 min Cut (15 version: 22 sec); 89 min Cut
                   (Abridged PG version: 51 sec)
V/h                                              MED

## THEY WENT THAT-A-WAY AND                  PG
## THAT-A-WAY *
Edward Montagne/Stuart E. McGowan
                     USA                         1978
*Tim Conway, Chuck McCann, Richard Kiel, Dub
Taylor, Reni Santoni, Lenny Montana, Timothy Blake*
Two fumbling policemen are sent to prison to discover
the location of the proceeds of a robbery. When the
prison governor, the only one who knew of the ruse,
dies of a heart attack, our inept cops are faced with a
tricky situation. A stupid comedy with tired gags and
an flabby plot. The script Tim Conway.
Aka: UNDERCOVER CAPER, THE (TURBO)
COM                 95 min; 102 min (TURBO)
B,V                                     TEM L/A; TURBO

## THEY'RE A WEIRD MOB **
Michael Parell       AUSTRALIA                   1966
*Walter Chiari, Clare Dunne, Chips Rafferty, Alida
Chelli, Ed Devereaux, John Meillon, Slim De Gray,
Charles Little, Muriel Steinbeck, Gloria Dawn*
An Italian immigrant arrives in Sydney in this wry
look at Australia and Australians, taking up the
building trade and falling in love with his cousin's
ex-girlfriend.
Boa: book by Nino Culotta.
COM                                              112 min
B,V                                              RNK

## THICKER THAN WATER **                     PG
Gray Hofmeyr        SOUTH AFRICA
                                    1985 (released 1986)

*Russel Savadier, Aletta Bezuidenhout, Wilson Dunster, Gillian Garlick*
Two families living on adjoining farms in a desert area clash over water rights, when the owner of the poorer farm finds that his supply will only last a few more days.
Aka: WATER WAR

| | |
|---|---|
| A/AD | 90 min mTV |
| B,V | CINE |

**THIEF ** **
William A. Graham     USA                    1971
*Richard Crenna, Angie Dickinson, Cameron Mitchell, Hurd Hatfield, Robert Webber, Bruce Kirby, Michael Lerner, Michael C. Gwynne, Mark Gregory, Ed Peck, Barbara Perry, Richard Stahl, Jo De Winter, Todd Martin, Rick Metzler*
An ex-prisoner must raise the cash needed to repay a debt at very short notice, and sees no other way out than to temporarily resume his career as a burglar in one last heist. Tight direction and an interesting central character enliven a formula plot. Scripted by John D.F. Black.

| | |
|---|---|
| DRA | 72 min (ort 74 min) mTV |
| B,V,V2 | AFE/IFS |

**THIEF OF BAGDAD, THE ** **                    U
Clive Donner     FRANCE/UK                    1978
*Roddy McDowall, Kabir Bedi, Frank Finlay, Marina Vlady, Peter Ustinov, Terence Stamp, Pavla Ustinov, Ian Holm, Daniel Emilfork, Ahmed El-Shenawi, Kenji Tanaki, Neil McCarthy, Vincent Wong, Leon Greene, Bruce Montague*
A fourth attempt at this Arabian Nights fantasy, that has Ustinov as the Caliph of Bagdad trying to find a suitable match for his daughter. Quite pleasant to look at, but hardly an inspired version.
Boa: novel by Achmed Abdullah.

| | |
|---|---|
| FAN | 86 min (ort 104 min) Cut (5 sec) mTV |
| V | EHE |

**THIEF OF BAGDAD, THE *** **
Raoul Walsh     USA                    1924
*Douglas Fairbanks Sr, Julanne Johnston, Anna May Wong, Snitz Edwards, Charles Belcher, Etta Lee, Brandon Hurst, Sojin*
The first version of this famous adventure story, with the title character having many adventures before rescuing Bagdad from the Mongol hordes, and winning the hand of the Caliph's daughter. A dated but vigorous and faithful rendition of the tale, written by Fairbanks and Lotta Woods. The sets are by William Cameron Menzies. Remade in 1940, 1961 and 1978.
Boa: novel by Achmed Abdullah.

| | |
|---|---|
| A/AD | 137 min B/W silent |
| B,V | POLY |

**THIEF OF BAGDAD, THE **** **                    U
L. Berger/M. Powell/T. Whelan/Z. Korda/W.C. Menzies/A. Korda     UK                    1940
*Sabu, Conrad Veidt, June Duprez, John Justin, Morton Selten, Rex Ingram, Miles Malleson, Mary Morris, Bruce Winston, Hay Petrie, Roy Emerton, Allan Jeayes, Miki Hood, David Sharpe, Adelaide Hall*
An entertaining Arabian Nights-style adventure which, though bearing little resemblance to the Achmed Abdullah novel, is a skilful blend of action and magic, as Sabu (aided by Ingram's splendid genie) outwits a wicked magician and saves a princess. Produced by Korda with music by Miklos Rozsa. AA: Cin (George Perrival), Art (Vincent Korda), Effects (Lawrence Butler – vis/Jack Whitney – aud).

| | |
|---|---|
| A/AD | 102 min (ort 109 min) |
| B,V | POLY; CENVID; PICK |

**THIEF OF HEARTS ** **                    18
Douglas Day Stewart     USA                    1984
*Steven Bauer, Barbara Williams, John Getz, David Caruso, Christine Ebersole, George Wendt*

A cat burglar steals a woman's intimate diaries and uses them to seduce her. Written by Stewart and re-edited to include some spicier footage for video release, this glossy and sexy drama has had great care lavished on it, but remains shallow and stilted. The score is by George Moroder. This was the director's debut.

| | |
|---|---|
| DRA | 96 min (ort 100 min) |
| B,V | CIC |

**THIEF WHO CAME TO DINNER, THE ** **                    15
Bud Yorkin     USA                    1973
*Ryan O'Neal, Jacqueline Bisset, Warren Oates, Jill Clayburgh, Ned Beatty, Charles Cioffi, Austin Pendleton, John Hillerman*
A Houston computer expert becomes a cat burglar, going after the jewellery of Houston's wealthy social set. A failure as a comedy caper that throws away a good cast. Scripted by Walter Hill.
Boa: novel by Terence L. Smith.

| | |
|---|---|
| COM | 100 min (ort 109 min) Cut (16 sec) |
| B,V | WHV |

**THIEVES ** **                    PG
John Berry     USA                    1976
*Marlo Thomas, Charles Grodin, Irwin Corey, Hector Elizondo, Mercedes McCambridge, John McMartin, Gary Merrill, Ann Wedgeworth*
An unconventional New York couple split up and try to rediscover their former innocence, in a city brimming over with corruption and violence. A pretentious slab of nonsense enlivened by a few witty lines and one or two pleasant cameos.
Boa: play by Herb Gardner.

| | |
|---|---|
| COM | 90 min (ort 92 min) |
| B,V | CINE |

**THIEVES AND ROBBERS * **
Bruno Corbucci     ITALY
*Carlo Pedersoli (Bud Spencer), Marc Lawrence, Tomas Milian*
A Miami police sergeant goes on the trail of a Mafia chief.

| | |
|---|---|
| COM | 96 min |
| B,V | RCA |

**THIN LINE, THE * **                    18
Andreas O. Loucka     USA                    1988
*Joseph Orlando, Jay Gonzalez, Terri Prinz, Matt Mitler, Jill Cumer, Donna Davidge, Joseph Pacifico III, Francis Reilly, Greg Zaragoza*
An ex-cop teams up with a trans-sexual hooker for revenge on his partner's murderer. Dreary and exploitative dross.

| | |
|---|---|
| A/AD | 90 min |
| V | INTMED |

**THING FROM ANOTHER WORLD, THE ** **
Christian Nyby     USA                    1951
*Kenneth Tobey, Margaret Sheridan, Robert Cornthwaite, Dewey Martin, Douglas Spencer, Paul Frees, Robert Nichols, Eduard Franz, John Dierkes, William Self, Everett Glass, Tom Steele, James Arness (the Thing)*
Scientists at a polar base discover a frozen alien and unwisely proceed to defrost it. A disappointing and rather moralistic adaptation of Campbell's story, promising great excitement early on and then simply failing to deliver. Produced by Howard Hawks (who is often credited with direction). The music is by Dmitri Tiomkin and the script by Charles Lederer. Remade as THE THING in 1982.
Aka: THING, THE
Boa: short story Who Goes There? by J.W. Campbell Jr.
Osca: STRANGER ON THE THE THIRD FLOOR

| | |
|---|---|
| FAN | 83 min (ort 87 min) B/W |
| B,V | KVD |

## THING, THE ** 18
John Carpenter    USA    1982
*Kurt Russell, A. Wilford Brimley, Richard Dysart,*
*Richard Masur, Donald Moffat, T.K. Carter, David*
*Clennon, Charles Hallahan, Peter Maloney, Keith*
*David, Joel Polis, Thomas Waites, Norbert Weisser,*
*Larry Franco, Nate Irwin*
A remake of the 1951 film THE THING FROM
ANOTHER WORLD, which tells of the discovery at a
frozen polar station of an alien creature, able to
invade and control the bodies of those it comes into
contact with. More faithful than its predecessor to the
original story, this is a dull film, only memorable for
some of the most repulsive special effects ever put on
film. Written by Bill Lancaster. Music by Ennio
Moricone.
Boa: short story Who Goes There? by John W.
Campbell.
FAN    103 min
V    CIC

## THINGS CHANGE ** PG
David Mamet    USA    1988
*Don Ameche, Joe Mantegna, Robert Prosky, J.J.*
*Johnson, Ricky Jay, Mike Nussbaum, Jack Wallace,*
*Dan Conway, J.T. Walsh*
A small-time gangster is given the job of "minding" a
simple Italian cobbler, who has agreed for a fee, to
take the rap for a Mob killing. However, instead of
merely keeping him out of trouble, the gangster takes
him out for one last wild fling. A minor comedy tale,
sustained by appealing performances. The script is by
Mamet and Shel Silverstein.
COM    97 min (ort 100 min)
V    RCA

## THINGS TO COME **** PG
William Cameron Menzies
    UK    1936
*Raymond Massey, Ralph Richardson, Cedric*
*Hardwicke, Edward Chapman, Ann Todd, Margaretta*
*Scott, Maurice Braddell, Sophie Stewart, Derrick De*
*Marney, Pearl Argyle, Kenneth Villiers, Ivan Brandt,*
*Patricia Hilliard, Patrick Barr*
The script is by H.G. Wells, in this look at the
evolution of a World State after a devastating war.
Despite a studio-bound feel, this is one of the most
ambitious films in British cinema, which had great
impact when first shown. This dated but classic work
takes the form of a sequence of verbose tableaux; the
vibrant music of Arthur Bliss and the striking
Menzies sets, are its greatest strengths. Produced by
Alexander Korda.
Boa: novel The Shape Of Things To Come by H.G.
Wells.
FAN    89 min (ort 113 min) B/W
B,V    POLY; SCREL; CENVID; PICK (VHS only)

## THINKIN' BIG * 15
S.F. Brownrigg    USA    1986
*Bruce Anderson, Nancy Buechler, Darla Ralston,*
*Kenny Sargent, Randy Jandt, Derek Hunter, Regina*
*Mikel, Claudia Church, April Burrage*
A smutty comedy about an over-endowed stud and
other sex-obsessed characters on a beach holiday.
COM    96 min
B,V    IVS L/A; CAST

## THIRD DEGREE BURN ** 
Roger Spottiswoode    USA    1989
*Treat Williams, Virginia Madsen*
A former cop becomes a private detective, and takes
on a case for a woman who wants a divorce from her
husband. When this man is found murdered, all the
evidence would appear to point to the detective's
girlfriend.
DRA    80 min
V    CIC

## THIRD MAN, THE **** PG
Carol Reed    USA    1949
*Orson Welles, Joseph Cotten, Alida Valli, Trevor*
*Howard, Bernard Lee, Ernst Deutsch, Wilfrid Hyde-*
*White, Paul Hoerbiger, Erich Ponton, Siegfried*
*Breuer, Bernard Lee, Geoffrey Keen, Hedwig Bleibtreu,*
*Annie Rosar*
An American writer of cheap Westerns arrives in
Vienna shortly after WW2, and finds that his friend
whom he was to have met, has been killed in
mysterious circumstances. His attempts to solve this
mystery are strangely hampered. A brilliant atmos-
pheric film with memorable zither music by Anton
Karas. Written by Graham Greene. The US version
has a different opening narration. AA: Cin (Robert
Krasker).
Boa: novel by Graham Greene.
DRA    99 min; 95 min (WHV) B/W
B,V    TEVP; WHV (VHS only)

## THIRST *** 
Rod Hardy    AUSTRALIA    1979
*David Hemmings, Henry Silva, Chantal Contouri,*
*Max Phipps, Shirley Cameron, Rod Mullinar, Robert*
*Thompson, Walter Pym, Rosie Sturgess, Amanda*
*Muggleton, Lulu Pinkus*
A vampire cult kidnaps a woman executive descended
from a Hungarian countess (who bathed in the blood
of virgins in order to preserve her beauty) and
brainwashes her, in an attempt to ensure that she has
the right views in order to become their leader. A
well-handled and quite unusual chiller.
HOR    90 min (ort 98 min)
B,V    VCL/CBS

## THIRSTY DEAD, THE * 15
Terry Becker    USA    1974
*John Considine, Jennifer Billingsley, Judith*
*McConnell, Tani Guthrie, Chique Da Rosa, Frederick*
*Meyers, Elena Sampson, Mary Walters, Vic Diaz, Rod*
*Navarro, Rick Rohrke*
A stupid Dracula-style horror yarn, in which a guide
kidnaps an actress and her friends, and takes them to
a jungle lair where a tribe is waiting to drink their
blood. Made in the Philippines.
Osca: DREAM NO EVIL (AVR)
HOR    82 min; 88 min (AVR) (ort 90 min)
B,V    DAV; AVR (VHS only)

## THIRTEEN AT DINNER * U
Lou Antonio    USA    1985
*Peter Ustinov, Faye Dunaway, David Suchet,*
*Jonathan Cecil, Bill Nighy, John Stride, Diane Keen,*
*Benedict Taylor, Lee Horsley, Allan Cuthbertson, Glyn*
*Baker, John Barron, Peter Clapham, Lesley Dunlop,*
*Avril Elgar, Roger Milner*
Yet another adaptation of an Agatha Christie novel,
with Hercule Poirot (the familiar mellifluous tones as
Ustinov attempts another accent) investigating a
murder among English aristocrats. Set in the 1980s, it
opens with a TV interview of Poirot. Limp, uninspir-
ing, tiresome and tedious. Adapted from the novel by
Rod Browning and filmed in England.
Aka: AGATHA CHRISTIE'S THIRTEEN AT
DINNER
Boa: novel by Agatha Christie.
DRA    91 min (ort 100 min) mTV
V    WHV

## THIRTEEN RUE MADELAINE *** U
Henry Hathaway    USA    1946
*James Cagney, Annabella, Richard Conte, Frank*
*Latimore, Melville Cooper, Walter Abel, Sam Jaffe,*
*E.G. Marshall, Blanche Yurka, Karl Malden, Red*
*Buttons*
During WW2, OSS agents attempt to locate a German
missile site in occupied France. Cagney takes over as
leader of the mission when one of his agents is killed
by the Nazis. One of several films inspired by "The

March Of Time" and done in appropriate semi-documentary style. A taut and gripping espionage tale.

| A/AD | 95 min B/W |
| V/h | MED |

## THIRTEENTH FLOOR, THE ** 18
Chris Roach          AUSTRALIA          1988
*Lisa Hemsley, Tim McKenzie, Miranda Otto*
A little girl sees her ruthless gangster father electrocute the child of an informer, and later runs away from home. However, she eventually returns to live in that same building years later, and discovers a sinister presence. Finally, her dad is lured back there and meets a fitting end, in this utterly predictable effort.
Aka: 13TH FLOOR, THE

| HOR | 86 min Cut (22 sec) |
| B,V | MED |

## THIRTY-NINE STEPS, THE ** 15
Don Sharp          UK          1978
*Robert Powell, David Warner, Eric Porter, Karen Dotrice, John Mills, George Baker, Ronald Pickup, Donald Pickering, Timothy West, Miles Anderson, Andrew Keir, Robert Flemyng, William Squire, Paul McDowell, David Collings*
A remake of the 1935 film that is more faithful to the original novel, and tells of a man pursued by crooks who think he has obtained information on their plot to instigate WW1. Not a terribly suspenseful film, and spoilt by the climax on the face of Big Ben, which no doubt was inspired by the Will Hay film MY LEARNED FRIEND. The script is by Michael Robson.
Boa: novel by John Buchan.

| THR | 102 min |
| B,V | RNK; VCC |

## THIRTY-NINE STEPS, THE ** U
Ralph Thomas          UK          1959
*Kenneth More, Taina Elg, Brenda de Banzie, Barry Jones, Reginald Beckwith, Faith Brook, Michael Goodliffe, James Hayter, Duncan Lamont, Jameson Clark, Andrew Cruikshank, Leslie Dwyer, Betty Henderson, Joan Hickson, Sidney James*
A virtually scene-for-scene remake of the original film, with the dubious added attraction of colour. The cast do their best in this curiously flat and wooden adaptation, telling of a young man who finds himself embroiled in murder and intrigue. Guaranteed suspense free.
Boa: novel by John Buchan.

| A/AD | 91 min (ort 93 min) |
| V | VCC |

## THIRTY-NINE STEPS, THE **** U
Alfred Hitchcock          UK          1935
*Robert Donat, Madeleine Carroll, Lucy Mannheim, Godfrey Tearle, John Laurie, Peggy Ashcroft, Helen Haye, Wylie Watson, Frank Cellier, Peggy Simpson, Gus McNaughton, Jerry Verno, Hilda Trevelyan, John Turnbull, Miles Malleson*
An innocent man is embroiled in murder and espionage, in this sophisticated comedy-thriller, that deviates quite considerably from the original novel. Donat and Carroll make a fine pair, and in one memorable sequence find themselves being chased across Scotland while chained together. The climax is suitably dramatic. Written by Charles Bennett and Alma Reville, and with musical direction by Louis Levy. Remade several times since.
Boa: novel by John Buchan.

| THR | 78 min (ort 87 min) B/W |
| V | RNK |

## THIRTY-SIXTH CHAMBER OF SHAOLIN, THE ** 18
Liu Chia-Liang     HONG KONG          1977

*Liu Chia-Hui, Huang Yu (Young Wang Yu), Lo Leih, Liu Chia-Yung, Hsu Shao-Chiang, Yu Yong*
A young man masters the secrets of kung fu, so as to avenge his family's death at the hands of the Manchu invaders. A competent film that spends rather too much time following the training the hero is obliged to undergo. Followed in 1980 by RETURN TO THE 36TH CHAMBER.
Aka: 36TH CHAMBER OF SHAOLIN, THE; MASTER KILLER

| MAR | 89 min (ort 109 min) |
| B,V | TEVP |

## THIS CHILD IS MINE ** PG
David Greene          USA          1985
*Lindsay Wagner, Chris Sarandon, Michael Lerner, John Philbin, Kathleen York, Frank Dent, Joan McMurtrey, Matthew Faison, Nancy McKeon, Carolyn Coates, Eve Roberts, Jennifer Parsons, Leigh French, Paul Teurpe, Susan Peretz*
The story of a teenager who gives her child up for adoption, and then has to battle the childless couple who have gained custody, when she has second thoughts. Average TV movie melodramatics.

| DRA | 93 min (ort 100 min) mTV |
| V | VCC |

## THIS GIRL FOR HIRE *** PG
Jerry Jameson          USA          1983
*Bess Armstrong, Celeste Holm, Cliff De Young, Hermione Baddeley, Scott Brady, Howard Duff, Jose Ferrer, Beverly Garland, Roddy McDowall, Percy Rodrigues, Ray Walston, Elisha Cook, William Lanteau, Fredric Lehne*
A lady detective is hired to investigate the murder of a mystery writer and find his latest manuscript. A fine cast adds depth to this enjoyable but contrived take-off of the 1940s detective genre.
Boa: story by Barbara Avedon, Barbara Corday and Barney Rosenzweig.

| COM | 96 min (ort 100 min) mTV |
| B,V | STABL |

## THIS HAPPY BREED *** 
David Lean          UK          1944
*Robert Newton, Celia Johnson, Stanley Holloway, John Mills, Kay Walsh, Amy Veness, Alison Leggatt, Eileen Erskine, Guy Verney, Merle Tottenham, Betty Fleetwood, John Blythe, Laurence Olivier (narration)*
A saga of a British working-class family with interesting detail on the period it covers, this being 1919 to 1939. A hit with the public but somewhat less so with the critics. Scripted by Lean, Ronald Neame and Anthony Havelock-Allan, and with photography by Neame.
Boa: play by Noel Coward.

| DRA | 114 min |
| B,V | RNK |

## THIS IS CALLAN ** 15
Don Sharp          UK          1974
*Edward Woodward, Eric Porter, Carl Mohner, Catherine Schell, Peter Egan, Russell Hunter, Kenneth Griffith, Veronica Lang, Michael da Costa, Dave Prowse, Don Henderson, Joe Dunlop, Nadim Sawalha*
Spin-off from a TV series about a secret agent who eliminates undesirables on behalf of the British Secret Service. In this story, our agent has to kill a German gun-runner in order to win reinstatement. Fair. See also CALLAN.
Aka: CALLAN
Boa: novel A Red File For Callan by James Mitchell.

| DRA | 90 min (ort 106 min) |
| B,V | POLY; CH5 (VHS only) |

## THIS IS ELVIS *** PG
Malcolm Lee/Andrew Solti
USA          1981
*David Scott, Paul Boensh III, Johnny Harra, Lawrence*

*Koller, Rhonda Lyn, Debbie Edge, Larry Raspberry,*
*Furry Lewis*
Both documentary footage and acted sequences are
used, in this intriguing and carefully made examination of the famous rock star, that ultimately leaves us
none the wiser as to his motivation and private
thoughts. An exploitative and flawed biopic, but quite
fascinating. See also ELVIS AND ME and ELVIS:
THE MOVIE.
DOC                                    144 min Colour and B/W
V                                                          WHV

### THIS IS SPINAL TAP **                              15
Rob Reiner                UK                          1984
*Rob Reiner, Michael McKean, Christopher Guest,*
*Harry Shearer, Tony Hendra, June Chadwick, R.J.*
*Parnell, David Kaff, Paul Benedict, Patrick Macnee,*
*Billy Crystal, Fred Willard, Ed Begley Jr, Howard*
*Hesseman, Paul Shaffer*
An uneven spoof about a heavy-metal rock band,
whose ageing members have embarked on an Amer-
ican tour. The use of documentary techniques success-
fully satirises many of the aspects of the music
business, but for the most part the end result is just
not all that funny.
MUS                                    79 min (ort 82 min)
B,V                                                        EHE

### THIS ISLAND EARTH **                              PG
Joseph M. Newman          USA                         1955
*Jeff Morrow, Rex Reason, Faith Domergue, Russell*
*Johnson, Douglas Spencer, Robert Nichols, Karl*
*Lindt, Lance Fuller, Reg Parton, Eddie Parker, Olan*
*Soule, Richard Deacon, Robert B. Williams, Mark*
*Hamilton, Guy Edwards*
In a desperate attempt to save their civilisation,
benevolent aliens plan to kidnap some Earth scien-
tists, but arrive at their embattled planet too late to
save it. A film that starts off with great promise,
showing how the scientists are tricked into agreeing
to work at a remote base, prior to their abduction.
Unfortunately, the film is spoilt by clumsy develop-
ment and cliche-ridden dramatics.
Boa: novel by Raymond F. Jones.
FAN                                    83 min (ort 86 min)
V                                                          CIC

### THIS MAN STANDS ALONE **
Jerrold Freedman          USA                         1979
*Louis Gossett Jr, Clu Gulager, Mary Alice, Barry*
*Brown, James McEachin, Barton Heyman, Lonny*
*Chapman, Philip Michael Thomas, Helen Martin,*
*John Crawford, Burton Gilliam, Clebert Ford, Nick*
*Smith, Mary Kay Place*
A black man attempts to resist the powerful white
family that dominates the town. An interesting film
let down by poor characterisations, and largely based
on the true story of a black civil rights activist, who
ran for sheriff in a Southern town.
DRA                                    78 min (ort 90 min) mTV
B,V                                                        VCL/CBS

### THIS PROPERTY IS CONDEMNED **                     15
Sydney Pollack            USA                         1966
*Natalie Wood, Robert Redford, Kate Reid, Charles*
*Bronson, Robert Blake, Mary Badham, Jon Provost,*
*John Harding, Alan Baxter*
An out of town railway official falls in love with his
landlady's daughter, and has to face both her anger
and that of the railway workers he has laid off. An
implausible story, with unconvincing dialogue and
aimless plotting, but quite stylishly done. Written by
Francis Ford Coppola, Fred Coe and Edita Sommer.
Photography is by James Wong Howe.
Boa: play by Tennessee Williams.
DRA                                    105 min (ort 110 min)
B,V                                                        CIC

### THIS SPORTING LIFE ***                            15
Lindsay Anderson          UK                          1963
*Richard Harris, Rachel Roberts, Alan Badel, William*
*Hartnell, Colin Blakely, Arthur Lowe, Vanda Godsell,*
*Anne Cunningham, Jack Watson, Harry Markham*
Powerful adaptation of a fine novel, telling of the
career of a successful rugby player and his ambiguous
relationship with his landlady. Retains much of the
feeling of Northern life that came through so well in
the book, and is helped along by splendid perform-
ances all round. A sombre but excellent piece, with
Harris perfectly cast as the sullen rugger player.
Written by Storey.
Boa: novel by David Storey.
DRA                                    128 min (ort 134 min) B/W
V                                                          RNK

### THIS TIME FOREVER **
Larry Kent                CANADA                      1980
*Claire Pimpare, Vince Van Patten, Eddie Albert,*
*Nicholas Campbell, Daniel Gadovas, Jacques Godin,*
*Cloris Leachman, Jack Wetherall, Marthe Mercure,*
*Gerard Parkes, Jonathan Barrett, Michel Blais, John*
*Boylan*
A hockey player has a love affair with an art student.
Set in Canada and of no great substance.
Aka: GABRIELLE; SCORING; VICTORY, THE;
YESTERDAY
DRA                                    98 min
B,V                                    SVC L/A; APX

### THIS, THAT AND THE OTHER *                        18
Derek Ford                UK                          1969
*Victor Spinetti, Vanessa Howard, Dennis Waterman,*
*Vanda Hudson, John Bird*
Three trite and slightly comical stories with erotic
overtones.
Aka: PROMISE OF BED, A
A                                      83 min
B,V                                    NET; GLOB

### THOMAS CROWN AFFAIR, THE ***                      PG
Norman Jewison            USA                         1968
*Steve McQueen, Faye Dunaway, Paul Burke, Jack*
*Weston, Biff McGuire, Yaphet Kotto*
An interesting and rather beautiful but empty film,
which makes good use of the split-screen technique. A
millionaire amuses himself by carrying out a bank
robbery, and then playing a cat-and-mouse game with
a female insurance investigator. Written by Alan R.
Trustman. Split-screen will suffer on TV. AA: Song
("The Windmills Of Your Mind" – Michel Legrand –
music/Alan and Marilyn Bergman – lyrics).
DRA                                    102 min
B,V                                    WHV

### THOMPSON'S LAST RUN **                            PG
Jerrold Freedman          USA                         1986
*Robert Mitchum, Wilfred Brimley, Kathleen York, Guy*
*Boyd, Royce Wallace, Susan Tyrell, Daniel McDonald,*
*Benjamin Gregory, Joe Berryman, Jerry Biggs,*
*Johnny Brink, Sa'mi Chester, Jack Gould, Joe*
*Graham, Kerry Graves*
Two boyhood friends end up on different sides of the
law, one as a safe-cracker serving a life sentence and
the other, the cop who takes him from one prison to
the next. Fair but unmemorable.
Aka: LAST RUN, THE
DRA                                    95 min (ort 104 min) mTV
B,V                                    IVS L/A; CAST

### THOR THE CONQUEROR **                             18
Anthony Richmond (Antonio Riccamonza)
                          ITALY                       1982
*Conrad Nichols, Christopher Holm, Maria Romano,*
*Malisa Lang, Raf Falcone*
A sword-and-sorcery epic with the legendary Norse
god battling his enemies.
Aka: THOL IL CONQUISTATORE

FAN                           90 min; 87 min (APX)
B,V                                    VIP L/A; APX

## THORN, THE *
Peter Alexander          USA                  1980
*Bette Midler, John Bassberger*
Satire on commercialised religion in the form of spoofy
bible stories, with Midler playing the Virgin Mary.
Forgettable.
Aka: DIVINE MR J, THE
COM                                         90 min
B,V                                    SVC L/A; APX

## THOSE CALLOWAYS ***                        PG
Norman Tokar             USA                  1964
*Brian Keith, Vera Miles, Brandon de Wilde, Walter
Brennan, Ed Wynn, Linda Evans, Philip Abbott, John
Larkin, Parley Baer, Frank De Kova, Tom Skerritt,
John Qualen, Roy Roberts, Paul Hartman, Russell
Collins, John Davis Chandler*
A New England eccentric and family fight to turn a
local lake into a bird sanctuary for migrating geese,
opposed by others who are more concerned with the
possible profits to be made from the organisation of
shooting parties. Overlong and uneven, but quite
charming. Written by Louis Pelletier with music by
Max Steiner.
Boa: novel Swift Water by Paul Annixter.
COM                           129 min (ort 131 min)
B,V                                            WDV

## THOSE DEAR DEPARTED *                       15
Ted Robinson             AUSTRALIA            1987
*Garry McDonald, Pamela Stephenson*
When an actor is murdered he finds a way of returning
to Earth with a pack of malevolent spirits and plotting
a ghostly revenge.
COM                                         88 min
B,V                                            MED

## THOSE MAGNIFICENT MEN IN THEIR           U
## FLYING MACHINES *
Ken Annakin              UK                   1965
*Terry-Thomas, James Fox, Stuart Whitman, Sarah
Miles, Robert Morley, Alberto Sordi, Gert Frobe, Eric
Sykes, Benny Hill, Sam Wanamaker, Flora Robson,
Fred Emney, Gordon Jackson, William Rushton, Tony
Hancock, John Le Mesurier*
Totally unfunny comedy about a sponsored air race
from London to Paris in the early days of flying. A film
of immense tedium that never gets off the ground. Red
Skelton has a funny cameo in an amusing prologue,
tracing the history of aviation. Written by Annakin
and Jack Davies.
Aka: HOW I FLEW FROM LONDON TO PARIS IN
25 HOURS AND 11 MINUTES
COM                                        138 min
V                                              CBS

## THOSE SHE LEFT BEHIND **                    PG
Waris Hussein            USA                  1989
*Gary Cole, Joanna Kerns, Mary Page Keller, Colleen
Dewhurst, George Coe, Maryedith Burrell*
Weepy drama about a young father whose life is
shattered by the death of his wife in childbirth and his
feelings of inadequacy in the face of the prospect of
having to bring up his baby daughter alone. Good
performances sustain a film that is hampered by
excessive sentimentality and spoilt by the contrived
ending.
DRA                           87 min (ort 100 min) mTV
V/h                                            ODY

## THRASHIN' *                                 15
David Winters            USA                  1986
*Josh Brolin, Robert Rusler, Pamela Gidley, Chuck
McCann, Brooke McCarter, Brett Marx, Josh Richman*
Rival gangs of skateboarding teenagers meet in a
violent confrontation, as a boy and girl from either

side meet and fall in love. A kind of non-musical
WEST SIDE STORY, devoid of charm and of truly
limited appeal.
A/AD                          88 min (ort 92 min)
B,V                                            CBS

## THREADS ***                                 15
Mick Jackson      AUSTRALIA/UK              1985
*Karen Meagher, Reece Dinsdale, Rita May, David
Brierly, Harry Beety, June Broughton, Sylvia Stoker,
Nicholas Lane, June Hazelgrove, Ashley Barker,
Victoria O'Keefe, Henry Moxon*
A critically acclaimed but chilling story of a nuclear
strike on Britain, that explores the aftermath of the
conflict through the eyes of two Sheffield families.
Extremely restrained in its examination of grief,
hypothermia and starvation, and certainly not ending
on a hopeful note. See also TESTAMENT and THE
DAY AFTER.
DRA                           114 min (ort 125 min) mTV
V                                              BBC

## THREE A.M. ***
Robert McCallum          USA                  1976
*Georgina Spelvin, Clair Dia, Rhonda Gellard, Charles
Hooper, Rob Rose, Sharon Thorpe, Judith Hamilton*
Extremely sensitive story of a couple who share their
home with their sister, who has lived with them for
many years, even bringing up their children.
Although his wife believes he has been faithful, the
husband has been sleeping with his sister-in-law. She
tries to get him to leave his wife and during an
argument accidentally causes his death. Overcome
with feelings of guilt, the film ends with her suicide.
Aka: 3 A.M.
A                             77 min (ort 90 min) Cut
B,V                                       TCX; CAL

## THREE AMIGOS **                             PG
John Landis              USA                  1986
*Steve Martin, Chevy Chase, Martin Short, Alfonso
Rau, Patrice Martinez, Jon Lovitz, Tony Plana, Joe
Mantegna, Fred Asparagus*
Three friends involved in a silent screen comedy act in
the 1920s, find themselves broke and out of work.
When they are offered a personal appearance at a
Mexican village, they soon realise the locals expect
them to be the heroes they portray, and fight a band of
desperadoes terrorising the area. A one-joke comedy
buoyed up by vigorous performances.
COM                           99 min (ort 105 min)
V/sh                                           RCA

## THREE BULLETS FOR A LONG GUN **            15
Peter Henkel             USA                  1973
*Beau Brummell, Keith Van Der Wat, Patrick
Mynhardt, Tulio Moneta*
A man joins forces with a Mexican bandit in a hunt for
some hidden treasure, but they soon fall out. Fair.
WES                           79 min (ort 89 min)
V                                            TURBO

## THREE CABALLEROS, THE ***                   U
Norman Ferguson          USA                  1945
*Aurora Miranda, Carmen Molina, Dora Luz, Nestor
Amarale, Almirante, Trio Calcaveras, Ascencio Del
Rio Trio, Padua Hill Players. Voices of: Sterling
Holloway, Clarence Nash, Jose Oliveira, Joaquin
Garay, Fred Shields*
A mixture of live-action and animation, and largely
consisting of a set of short features paying homage to
Latin America, with Donald Duck acting as tourist
and guide. Part of the 1940s Good Neighbour Policy
that also gave rise to the earlier and shorter "Saludos
Amigos" of 1943. Not really a film in the true sense,
but worth seeing for its fascinating combination of
superb cartoons and colourful performances.
JUV                                         85 min
V                                              WDV

## THREE CRAZY JERKS **
Franz Joseph Gottlieb    USA    15    1988
*Michael Winslow*
After a woman's car breaks down, three destitute actors who have just been fired set out to help her, and she returns the favour, eventually becoming pregnant by one of them. Without worrying too much as to which of them is the father, all three set out to provide for her and the child. A flimsy and mildly diverting slapstick comedy.
COM    90 min
V    RCA

## THREE FACES OF EVE, THE ***
Nunnally Johnson    USA    PG    1957
*Joanne Woodward, David Wayne, Nancy Culp, Lee J. Cobb, Edwin Jerome, Vince Edwards, Alistair Cooke (narration only)*
A female schizophrenic being treated by a psychiatrist is found to have three completely separate personalities in this intriguing but dated story. Cooke's introduction carries a conviction that's somewhat lacking in the script, but Woodward's powerful performance ensured the film enjoyed considerable success at the box office. Screenplay is by Johnson, who also produced. AA: Actress (Woodward).
Boa: book by Corbett H. Thigpen and Hervey M. Cleckley.
DRA    95 min B/W
V    CBS

## THREE FOR ALL *
Martin Campbell    UK    PG    1975
*Adrienne Posta, Lesley North, Cheryl Hall, Graham Bonnet, Robert Lindsay, Paul Nicholas, Christopher Neil, Richard Beckinsale, George Baker, Simon Williams, Cathy Collins, Diana Dors, Jonathan Adams, Arthur Mullard*
The trials and tribulations of a pop group on holiday in Spain, form the basis for this limp musical comedy, done in the style of a British "Carry On" film.
COM    86 min (ort 90 min)
V    MIA

## THREE FOR THE ROAD **
Bill W.L. Norton    USA    15    1987
*Charlie Sheen, Kerri Green, Alan Ruck, Sally Kellerman, Raymond J. Barry, Blair Tefkin, Alexa Hamilton, James Avery*
The selfish young daughter of a senator is packed off to boarding school, with the senator's aide and his buddy escorting her, but instead all three set forth on a series of wild adventures. A silly teen outing.
COM    88 min (ort 90 min)
B,V    CBS

## THREE FUGITIVES **
Francis Veber    USA    15    1989
*Nick Nolte, Martin Short, Sarah Rowland Doroff, James Earl Jones, Alan Ruck, Kenneth McMillan, Bruce McGill*
A reformed bank robber is forced to go on the run with an amateur thief and his 6-year-old daughter, when he inadvertently gets caught up in a bungled bank raid. Veber's first US film is largely a re-run of his earlier work "Les Fugitifs", and is little more than a fast-paced blend of knockabout slapstick and cloying sentimentality, that soon becomes quite tiresome.
COM    92 min (ort 96 min)
V    TOUCH

## THREE HATS FOR LISA **
Sidney Hayers    UK    U    1965
*Joe Brown, Sophie Hardy, Sidney James, Una Stubbs, Dave Nelson, Peter Bowles, Seymour Green, Josephine Blake, Jeremy Lloyd, Michael Brennan, Eric Barker*
A frothy, lightweight musical in which an Italian film star steals three typically English hats, namely: a bowler, busby and policeman's helmet, being helped in this task by a docker and a taxi driver.
MUS    95 min (ort 99 min)
V    WHV

## THREE IMMORAL WOMEN ***
Walerian Borowczyk    FRANCE    1978
*Marina Pierro, Gaelle Legrand, Pascale Christophe, Francois Guetany*
A well-made trio of stories about immoral women.
Aka: HEROINES OF EVIL, THE; LES HEROINES DU MAL
A    89 min
B,V,V2    WAL L/A; EIV; MMA

## THREE IN THE ATTIC *
Richard Wilson    USA    1968
*Yvette Mimieux, Christopher Jones, Judy Pace, Maggie Turett, Nan Martin, John Beck*
A brainless film about three girls who have their revenge on the fellow who has been dating them all at once. They lock him in an attic and use him till he is utterly exhausted. And if that sounds titillating it's not, just rather dull.
Boa: novel Paxton Quigley's Had The Course by Stephen Yafa.
COM    90 min (ort 92 min)
B,V,V2    GHV

## THREE IN THE CELLAR *
Theodore J. Flicker    USA    1970
*Larry Hagman, Joan Collins, Wes Stern, Judy Pace, David Arkin, Nira Barab*
A college student who lost his scholarship due to a computing error, takes revenge on the principal who refused to help him, by seducing his wife, daughter and mistress, in this laboured attempt to cash in on the success of THREE IN THE ATTIC. The script is by Flicker.
Aka: THREE IN A CELLAR; UP IN THE CELLAR
Boa: novel The Late Boy Wonder by A. Hall.
DRA    94 min
B,V    RNK

## THREE INTO SEX WON'T GO *
Guy Perol    FRANCE    1973
*Sandra Julien, Virginie Vignor, Jacques Cornet, Martine Drucker*
A dated and trite French sex farce.
Aka: BIRD IN THE HAND, A; LES GOURMANDINES
A    80 min
B,V    INT L/A

## THREE KINDS OF HEAT *
Leslie Stevens    USA    15    1987
*Robert Ginty, Victoria Barrett, Shakti Ghen, Sylvester McCoy, Barry Foster, Jack Hedley, Mary Tamm*
Warring criminal factions attract the attentions of Interpol, who send a couple of agents to London to nab a criminal mastermind. Very dull and uninspired.
A/AD    84 min (ort 87 min)
B,V    WHV

## THREE LIVES OF THOMASINA, THE ***
Don Chaffey    UK/USA    U    1963
*Susan Hampshire, Karen Dotrice, Patrick McGoohan, Vincent Winter, Laurence Naismith, Finlay Currie, Wilfrid Brambell, Jean Anderson, Francis De Wolff, Oliver Johnston, Elspeth March, Denis Gilmore, Ewan Roberts, Charles Carson*
A Scottish vet finds that a local girl has a much better success rate in curing sick animals. Filmed in England, this appealing but cloying story has one of the animals narrating. Scripted by Robert Westerby.
Boa: novel Thomasina, The Cat Who Thought She Was God by Paul Gallico.
JUV    97 min
B,V    WDV

## THREE MEN AND A BABY ***     PG
Leonard Nimoy     USA     1987
*Tom Selleck, Ted Danson, Steve Guttenberg, Nancy Travis, Margaret Colin, Philip Bosco, Celeste Holm*
A lively remake of the French film from 1985, "Three Men And A Cradle", with three bachelors suddenly finding themselves in possession of a baby and a parcel of heroin. They manage to get rid of the drugs but are less willing to give up the child. The film really has very little plot, but the three stars carry it all off most enjoyably.
COM     101 min
B,V     BUENA; TOUCH

## THREE MUSKETEERS, THE ***     U
George Sidney     USA     1948
*Gene Kelly, Lana Turner, June Allyson, Van Heflin, Angela Lansbury, Robert Coote, Frank Morgan, Vincent Price, Keenan Wynn, Gig Young, John Sutton, Reginald Owen, Ian Keith, Patricia Medina*
In France at the time of Louis XIII three friends become involved in intrigue, treachery and swordplay. A rumbustious version of the classic tale, done in burlesque style, and remarkable for its vigour if not its realism.
Boa: novel by Alexandre Dumas.
A/AD     125 min
V     MGM

## THREE MUSKETEERS, THE **
Richard Lester     UK     1973
*Oliver Reed, Michael York, Raquel Welch, Richard Chamberlain, Frank Finlay, Christopher Lee, Geraldine Chaplin, Jean-Pierre Cassel, Spike Milligan, Roy Kinnear, Gitty Djamel, George Wilson, Simon Ward*
Meant to be funny, this version of the famous tale sometimes goes well over the top in a desperate search for laughs. A good performance from Welch is a highlight. The second half of the film was released as a sequel – THE FOUR MUSKETEERS. Scripted by George MacDonald Fraser. Look out for Faye Dunaway, who appears briefly in a small part. See also THE RETURN OF THE MUSKETEERS.
Aka: THREE MUSKETEERS, THE: THE QUEEN'S DIAMONDS
Boa: novel by Alexandre Dumas.
COM     102 min (ort 107 min)
B,V     TEVP

## THREE MUSKETEERS, THE **     U
Rowland V. Lee     USA     1935
*Walter Abel, Paul Lukas, Moroni Olson, Ian Keith, Onslow Stevens, Ralph Forbes, Margot Grahame, Heather Angel, Rosamond Pinchot, John Qualen, Nigel De Brulier, Murray Kinnell, Lumsden Hare, Miles Mander*
Film version of famous novel with Abel miscast as D'Artagnan. The good supporting cast can do little in the lifeless rendition of this tale. The script is by Dudley Nichols and Rowland V. Lee.
Boa: novel by Alexandre Dumas.
A/AD     92 min; 47 min (VCC) (ort 97 min) B/W
B,V     KVD L/A; VCC

## THREE O'CLOCK HIGH **     15
Phil Joanou     USA     1987
*Casey Siemaszko, Ann Ryan, Richard Tyson, Jeffrey Tambor, Philip Baker Hall, John P. Ryan, Stacey Glick, Jonathan Wise, Liza Morrow*
HIGH NOON comes to teenage Southern California, when the class hero has to face up to the recently arrived bully whose legendary reputation has preceded him. Despite some great performances, this slight little effort has nothing of substance, and the stars have little material to work with.
COM     86 min (ort 101 min)
B,V     CIC

## THREE SISTERS, THE ****
Laurence Olivier/John Sichel     1970
UK     (released in USA 1974)
*Jeanne Watts, Joan Plowright, Alan Bates, Derek Jacobi, Louise Purnell, Laurence Olivier, Kenneth Mackintosh, Sheila Reid, Ronald Pickup, Frank Wylie, Daphne Heard*
An excellent version of Chekhov's famous play, about the three daughters of a deceased Russian colonel who dream of exchanging their dull provincial existence for life in the big city, at the turn of the century. Translated by Moura Budberg, this lavish and evocative film is one of the best adaptations of this writer's work.
Boa: play by Anton Chekhov.
DRA     158 min (ort 165 min)
B,V     CAN L/A; TEVP

## THREE SOVEREIGNS FOR SARAH: THE     15
## SALEM WITCH HUNT ***
Philip Leacock     USA     1985
*Vanessa Redgrave, Patrick McGoohan, Kim Hunter, Phyllis Thaxter, Ronald Hunter, Shay Duffin, Will Lyman*
A mini-series on the 17th century Salem witch hunts and subsequent trials, that tells of the survivor of a witchcraft trial who tries to clear the names of her two sisters, who were hanged as witches. A slow, careful and absorbing drama, with Redgrave giving one of her best perfomances.
DRA     128 min mTV
B,V     STABL

## THREE WARRIORS **
Keith Merrill     USA     1977
*Randy Quaid, Byron Patt, Charlie White Eagle, Lois Red Elk, McKee "Kiko" Red Wing*
The story of the cultural conflict between the modern world and life on an Indian reservation, forms the background to this tale of an Indian boy who is initially unwilling to let his grandfather teach him about his culture, but eventually learns the value of his grandfather's knowledge. Fair, but somewhat overlong.
WES     100 min (ort 105 min)
B,V     TEVP

## THREE WORLDS OF GULLIVER, THE **     U
Jack Sher     UK     1960
*Kerwin Mathews, Jo Morrow, June Thorburn, Lee Patterson, Gregoire Aslan, Basil Sydney, Mary Ellis, Charles Lloyd Pack, Martin Benson, Peter Bull*
Having been washed overboard, ship's doctor Gulliver first encounters the tiny folk of Liliput and then the giants of Brobdingnag. A well-mounted juvenile adaptation of Swift's classic satire, lacking the wonderful sharpness and vigour of the novel. The trick photography and special effects of Ray Harryhausen are adequate and the score is by Bernard Herrmann.
Boa: novel Gulliver's Travels by Jonathan Swift.
A/AD     95 min (ort 98 min)
V     RCA

## THREE-HUNDRED YEAR WEEKEND, THE *
Victor Stoloff     USA     1971
*William Devane, Sharon Laughlin, Michael Tolan, Roy Cooper, Gabriel Dell, M'el Dowd*
The saga of a marathon encounter group session, with a group of people endlessly discussing their personal problems. Neither entertaining nor instructive.
Aka: 300 YEAR WEEKEND, THE
DRA     80 min (ort 123 min)
B,V     RNK

## THREE-THOUSAND MILE CHASE, THE **     PG
Russ Mayberry     USA     1977
*Cliff De Young, Glenn Ford, Blair Brown, David Spielberg, Priscilla Pointer, Brendon Dillon, Lane*

Allan, John Zenda, Carmen Argenziano, Tom Bower,
Roger Aaron Brown, Titos Vandis, Marc Alaimo,
Michael J. London, Stephen Coit
A courier hired to ensure that a key witness in the
trial of a drugs gangster is delivered to court to testify,
finds himself being stalked by some thugs sent to stop
him. Average.
Aka: 3,000 MILE CHASE, THE
A/AD                              93 min (ort 100 min) mTV
V                                                       CIC

## THREE'S TROUBLE **                                   15
Chris Thomson          AUSTRALIA                       1987
John Waters, Jacki Weaver, Steven Vidler
A look at the battle of the sexes, with an arrogant
lecturer finding that his wife, who gave up her career
to look after their kids, has made plans to go back to
college. Problems arise when she hires a young man
from Denmark to be their "nanny". A pleasant and
unambitious little outing, scripted by David Williamson.
COM                                                 90 min
B,V                                                    NWV

## THRESHOLD ***                                        PG
Richard Pearce         CANADA                         1981
                                (released in USA 1983)
Donald Sutherland, John Marley, Jeff Goldblum,
Sharon Ackerman, Michael Lerner, Mare
Winningham, Allan Nichols, Paul Hecht, Stuart
Gillard, Mavor Moore, Lally Cadeau, James B.
Douglas, Barbara Gordon, Julie Armstrong
Not shown in the USA until 1983, when the first
artificial heart implantation took place (Barney Clark
being the real-life recipient), this is a sober and
restrained account of the process that led to its
invention by a biologist.
DRA                              92 min (ort 97 min)
B,V,V2                                                 GHV

## THRILL KILLERS, THE *                                18
Ray Dennis Steckler    USA                            1965
Cash Flagg (Ray Dennis Steckler), Liz Renay, Brick
Bardo, Carolyn Brandt, Ron Burr, Garay Kent, Keith
O'Brien, Herb Robins, Laura Benedict, Atlas King,
George J. Morgan, Erina Enyo, Titus Moede
Three maniacs escape from their asylum and subject
Los Angeles to a reign of terror. (Probably threatening
the populace with mass showings of this film.) See also
THE TEENAGE PSYCHO MEETS BLOODY MARY,
an earlier gem from this director.
Aka: MANIACS ARE LOOSE, THE; MONSTERS
ARE LOOSE, THE
HOR                                             90 min B/W
V                                                      PAL

## THRILLED TO DEATH **                                 18
Chuck Vincent          USA                            1988
Blake Bahner, Rebecca Lynn, Richard Maris,
Christine Moore
An author and his wife become friends with a
charming couple, but soon discover that they have
become deeply implicated in a game of deceit and
murder.
THR                      88 min (ort 90 min) Cut (1 min 11 sec)
V                                            HER L/A; CAST

## THRILLKILL **                                        15
Anthony Kramreither/Anthony D'Andrea
                       CANADA                          1983
Robin Ward, Gina Massay, Laura Robinson, Eugene
Clerk, Diana Reis, Kurt Reis, Frank Moore, Colleen
Embree, Joy Boushel, Grant Cowan
A female computer expert is murdered after having
hidden away the location of a large amount of money
in a computer games program.
THR                                                 87 min
B,V                                                    CBS

## THRONE OF FIRE, THE **                               15
Michael E. Lemick (Franco Prosperi)
                       ITALY                           1984
Peter McCoy (Pietro Torrisi), Sabrina Siani, Mario
Novelli, Harrison Muller, Peter Caine, Benny Carduso,
Dan Collins, Stefano Abbati, Roberto Lattanzio,
Amedo Leonardi, Isarco Ravailoi, Gianlorenzo Bernini
One of those typical Italian warrior adventure films –
watchable, but hardly memorable.
Aka: IL TRONO DI FUOCO
FAN                                                 89 min
B,V        MRV L/A; VIP6 L/A; MERL/CBS L/A; NET

## THROUGH NAKED EYES **                                PG
John Llewellyn Moxey   USA                            1983
David Soul, Pam Dawber, Fionnula Flanagan,
William Schallert, Dick Anthony Williams, Gerald
Castillo, Rod McCary, Amy Morton, Ward Ohrman,
Mike Miller, Arnold Kopek, Rick LeFevour, Rick
Cluckey, Roberta Baskin, Rolf Boettger
An offbeat thriller telling of a man who begins to spy
on his neighbours through binoculars. He discovers
that a woman is watching him through a telescope
and they meet, embarking on a torrid affair. Later,
they become involved in a murder and discover that
someone else is observing them. Unfortunately, despite the interesting premise, all this watching leaves
little room for a decent plot to evolve. Average.
THR                      95 min (ort 100 min) mTV
B,V                                              IVS; CHV

## THROUGH THE FIRE *                                   18
Gary Marcum            USA                            1988
Tamara Hext, Tom Campitelli, Randy Strickland
A grotesque creature appears in Texas and takes over
the bodies of a series of victims, as it searches for a
talisman that holds the key to its power.
HOR                                                 90 min
B,V                                                    CHV

## THROUGH THE LOOKING GLASS ***                        18
Jonas Middleton        USA                            1976
Catherine Burgess, Douglas Wood, Jamie Gillis, Mike
Jefferson, Maria Taylor, Laura Nicholson, Terri Hall
A demon lives on the other side of an old mirror kept
at the ancestral home of an elegant but restless
middle-aged woman. She develops a compulsion to
visit the attic where the mirror is kept, and the demon
beckons her to enter his world. Eventually she does so
and the last portion of the film merges sex and horror
genres for a 15-minute tour of madness. This repellent
but unusual adult film is highly unlikely to be
available in an uncut form in the UK.
A             61 min (ort 89 min) (Abridged at film release)
B,V TCX L/A; 18PLAT/TOW L/A; PHE L/A; NET L/A;
SHEP

## THROW MOMMA FROM THE TRAIN ***                       15
Danny DeVito           USA                            1987
Danny DeVito, Billy Crystal, Kim Greist, Anne
Ramsey, Kate Mulgrew, Rob Reiner, Branford
Marsalis, Bruce Kirby, Oprah Winfrey, Olivia Brown,
Philip Perlman, Stu Silver, J. Alan Thomas, Randall
Miller, Tony Ciccone
A comedy hostage to Hitchcock's STRANGERS ON A
TRAIN, with a creative writing professor finding that
one of his students has misunderstood his teaching
and is convinced the professor wants them to swap
murders. An entertaining and unusual film, of uneven
scripting and wild, overblown performances. Written
by Stu Silver. The photography is by Barry Son-
nenfield.
COM                              84 min (ort 88 min)
B,V                                                    VIR

## THUMB TRIPPING **                                    18
Quentin Masters        USA                            1972
Michael Burns, Meg Foster, Marianna Hill, Bruce

*Dern, Mike Conrad, Joyce Van Patten*
Story of teenagers Burns and Foster who spend all
their summers thumbing lifts on the highways. A
mildly interesting but dated outing, written by Mitch-
ell from his novel.
Boa: novel by Don Mitchell.
DRA                                        94 min
B,V,V2                                     EHE

## THUNDER ALLEY **                        18
J.S. Cardone         USA                  1984
*Roger Wilson, Jill Schoelen, Scott McGinnis, Leif
Garrett*
An aspiring rock group start their journey to stardom,
and encounter the usual joys and pitfalls along the
way.
DRA                       97 min (ort 102 min)
B,V                                        MGM

## THUNDER AND LIGHTNING **                15
Corey Allen          USA                  1978
*David Carradine, Kate Jackson, Roger C. Carmel,
Sterling Holloway, Ed Barth, Ron Feinberg*
Two rival moonshiners in the Florida Everglades,
fight it out in a struggle that offers ample scope for the
obligatory chase sequences.
A/AD                                       94 min
B,V                                        CBS

## THUNDER PRINCE **                       PG
Lenny Washington HONG KONG                1989
Produced by Joseph Lai (and making a pleasant
change from his usual animated space operas such as
CAPTAIN COSMOS and the like) this martial arts
tale tells of the master of a secret technique, whose
son vows to avenge his father when he is murdered by
three thugs. Despite being captured by one of those
responsible, he eventually escapes and has his revenge. Fair.
CAR                                        65 min
V                                          VPD

## THUNDER RUN **                          15
Gary Hudson          USA                  1985
*Forrest Tucker, John Ireland, John Shepherd, Jill
Whitlow, Wally Ward, Cheryl M. Lynn, Marilyn
O'Connor*
A retired lorry driver is given a large sum of money to
transport nuclear waste to a research centre, and
thereby act as a decoy in a plan to capture a gang of
international terrorists.
A/AD                                       86 min
B,V                                    GHV; VCC

## THUNDER WARRIOR **                      18
Larry Ludman (Fabrizio De Angelis)
                    ITALY                 1984
*Mark Gregory, Bo Svenson, Raymond Harmstorf*
A young Indian takes revenge for the desecration of a
sacred burial site in Arizona, when it is turned into a
building site. Followed by two sequels. Average.
Aka: THUNDER
A/AD                       79 min (ort 83 min)
B,V                                        EIV

## THUNDER WARRIOR 2 **                    15
Larry Ludman (Fabrizio De Angelis)
                    ITALY                 1986
*Mark Gregory, Karen Reel, Raymond Harmstorf, Bo
Svenson*
A sequel to the first film, with a young Navajo Indian
returning to his homeland as a police officer, and
investigating corruption in the local force. A crooked
sheriff frames him and he is sent to a desert prison
camp, but soon starts plotting his escape.
Aka: THUNDER 2
A/AD                                       89 min
B,V                                        MED

## THUNDER WARRIOR 3 *                     18
Larry Ludman (Farbizio de Angelis)
                    ITALY                 1988
*Mark Gregory, Horts Schon, Werner Pochath, Ingrid
Lawrence, John Philip Law*
Third in this series about a much-wronged Indian who
is pushed too far by his racist tormenters. Violent and
exploitative nonsense.
Aka: THUNDER 3
A/AD              82 min (ort 90 min) Cut (22 sec)
V                                          VPD

## THUNDERBALL ***                         PG
Terence Young        UK                   1965
*Sean Connery, Adolfo Celi, Claudine Auger, Luciana
Paluzzi, Rik Van Nutter, Martine Beswick, Bernard
Lee, Lois Maxwell, Guy Dolman, Molly Peters, Roland
Culver, Desmond Llewelyn, Earl Cameron, Paul
Stassino, Rose Alba*
The fourth Bond film, with our secret agent up against
the criminal organisation SPECTRE. There are some
memorable sequences, as Miami is threatened with
destruction, but the story does tend to lose out to the
effects. Written by Richard Maibum and John Hop-
kins, with music by John Barry. Followed by YOU
ONLY LIVE TWICE. Remade with Connery 18 years
later, as NEVER SAY NEVER AGAIN. AA: Effects
(Aud) (Tregoweth Brown).
Boa: novel by Ian Fleming.
A/AD                      125 min (ort 132 min)
V                                          WHV

## THUNDERBIRDS ARE GO: THE MOVIE **       U
David Lane           UK                   1966
*Voices of: Ray Barrett, Sylvia Anderson, Peter
Dyneley, Neil McCallum, Shane Rimmer, Charles
Tingwell, Bob Monkhouse, David Graham, Jeremy
Wilkin, Matt Zimmerman*
A lively but dated puppet animation inspired by a
popular TV series, that detailed the exploits of
International Rescue, a sophisticated and elite orga-
nisation. In this story, they are called on to save a
Martian exploration ship that's in danger of crashing.
The effects are by Derek Meddings, who worked on
SUPERMAN.
CAR                        89 min (ort 92 min)
V                                          MGM

## THUNDERBIRDS IN OUTER SPACE **          U
David Lane/Brian Burgess
                    UK         1966 (re-edited 1981)
*Voices of: Peter Dyneley, Shane Rimmer, David
Holliday, Matt Zimmerman, David Graham, Ray
Barrett, Sylvia Anderson*
Puppet animated feature about a professional high-
tech rescue organisation, which this time has to save a
spaceship from falling into the sun.
CAR                                   90 min mTV
B,V,LV              PRV L/A; CH5 (VHS only)

## THUNDERBIRDS SIX: THE MOVIE **          U
David Lane           UK                   1968
*Voices of: Peter Dyneley, Catherine Finn, Sylvia
Anderson, Keith Alexander, Jeremy Wilkin, John
Carson, David Graham, Shane Rimmer, Gary Files,
Matt Zimmermann, Geoffrey Keen*
Puppet animation based on a popular TV series,
telling of the efforts of a sophisticated scientific
organisation to combat crime and avert disasters. In
this tale International Rescue fights an old enemy, the
"Black Phantom". Fair for its time but now looking
distinctly dated. The effects are by Derek Meddings.
Aka: THUNDERBIRD SIX
CAR                                        89 min
V                                          MGM

## THUNDERBIRDS: ATTACK OF THE
ALLIGATORS!/THE DUCHESS
ASSIGNMENT **                              U

David Lane/David Elliott
UK                1966

Voices of: Peter Dyneley, Shane Rimmer, David Holliday, Matt Zimmerman, David Graham, Ray Barrett, Sylvia Anderson, Christine Finn
In the first of these tales a scientist invents a growth drug that inadvertently creates the threat of monster alligators and in the second story, Lady Penelope spots some crooks swindling a Duchess at a casino, and calls in International Rescue to restore justice.
CAR                97 min mTV
V                CH5

## THUNDERBIRDS: CITY OF FIRE **   U
David Elliott        UK         1966
Voices of: Peter Dyneley, Shane Rimmer, David Holliday, Matt Zimmerman, David Graham, Ray Barrett, Sylvia Anderson
One episode from the puppet animation series, telling of the rescue by Scott and Virgil of some people trapped in a burning shopping complex.
CAR                48 min mTV
V                CH5

## THUNDERBIRDS: CRY WOLF/DANGER AT
## OCEAN DEEP **                   U
David Elliot/Desmond Saunders
UK                1966
Voices of: Peter Dyneley, Shane Rimmer, David Holliday, Matt Zimmerman, David Graham, Ray Barrett, Sylvia Anderson, Christine Finn
In "Cry Wolf" two young Australian boys are kidnapped by the Hood after they inadvertently called out International Rescue in the course of their games. In the second adventure IR are called in to prevent a catastrophic explosion taking place when a failed launch causes a vessel to drift dangerously close to a polluted region of the ocean.
CAR                96 min mTV
V                CH5

## THUNDERBIRDS: DAY OF DISASTER/   U
## EDGE OF IMPACT **
David Elliott/Desmond Saunders
UK                1966
Voices of: Peter Dyneley, Shane Rimmer, David Holliday, Matt Zimmerman, David Graham, Ray Barrett, Sylvia Anderson
In "Day Of Disaster" Lady Penelope and Brains set out to rescue the crew of a rocketship when the collapse of a bridge traps it on a river bed. In "Edge Of Impact" an old enemy of International Rescue, the Hood, becomes involved in a plot to cause the crash of a fighter plane.
CAR                96 min mTV
V                CH5

## THUNDERBIRDS: DESPERATE INTRUDER/   U
## THIRTY MINUTES AFTER NOON **
David Lane/Alan Fennell
UK                1966
Voices of: Peter Dyneley, Shane Rimmer, David Holliday, Matt Zimmerman, David Graham, Ray Barrett, Sylvia Anderson
Two episodes from the popular puppet animation series of the 1960s. In the first tale a hunt for underwater treasure leads to danger for Brains and Tin Tin, and in the second story International Rescue sets out to save a man who has had a time bomb locked to his wrist.
CAR                97 min mTV
V                CH5

## THUNDERBIRDS: END OF THE ROAD/   U
## THE PERILS OF PENELOPE **
David Lane/Desmond Saunders
UK                1966
Voices of: Peter Dyneley, Shane Rimmer, David

Holliday, Matt Zimmerman, David Graham, Ray Barrett, Sylvia Anderson
In the first of these stories a member of a construction team is trapped on the edge of a cliff with a truck-load of explosives. The second tale has Lady Penelope attempting to discover the whereabouts of a missing scientist and being taken hostage by the fiendish Dr Godber.
CAR                97 min mTV
V                CH5

## THUNDERBIRDS: MARTIAN INVASION/BRINK
## OF DISASTER **                   U
David Elliott/David Lane
UK                1966
Voices of: Peter Dyneley, Shane Rimmer, David Holliday, Matt Zimmerman, David Graham, Ray Barrett, Sylvia Anderson, Christine Finn
In the first of these tales the Hood traps two actors in a flooded cave while they are making a Martian invasion movie, but only in order to film Thunderbird I as it makes its rescue attempt. The second story sees Lady Penelope being approached by a crooked businessmen who is looking for money to finance a monorail project.
CAR                100 min mTV
V                CH5

## THUNDERBIRDS: PIT OF PERIL **   U
Desmond Saunders     UK         1966
Voices of: Peter Dyneley, Shane Rimmer, David Holliday, Matt Zimmerman, David Graham, Ray Barrett, Sylvia Anderson
A US Army mobile fortress crashes into an underground pit and the crew are trapped in their control room. Another job for International Rescue.
CAR                48 min mTV
V                CH5

## THUNDERBIRDS: TERROR IN NEW      PG
## YORK CITY/ATLANTIC INFERNO **
David Lane and David Elliott/Desmond Saunders
UK                1966
Voices of: Peter Dyneley, Shane Rimmer, David Holliday, Matt Zimmerman, David Graham, Ray Barrett, Sylvia Anderson
Two episodes from TV puppet series "Thunderbirds". In the first adventure International Rescue swings into action to save the Empire State building from collapse, and in the second the accidental ignition of an undersea pocket of gas threatens the lives of the crew on a drilling platform.
Aka: COUNTDOWN TO DISASTER
CAR                90 min mTV
B,V            PRV L/A; CH5 (VHS only)

## THUNDERBIRDS: THE CHAN-CHAN/SECURITY
## HAZARD **                        U
Alan Pattillo/Desmond Saunders
UK                1966
Voices of: Peter Dyneley, Shane Rimmer, David Holliday, Matt Zimmerman, David Graham, Ray BArrett, Sylvia Anderson, Christine Finn
In "The Chan-Chan" Lady Penelope investigates a performing air-team whose dangerous act seems to always result in the destruction of their fighter planes. "Security Hazard" sees Thunderbirds I and II returning from a mission in England, but taking along a young stowaway who has concealed himself in Pod I.
CAR                96 min
V                CH5

## THUNDERBIRDS: THE IMPOSTERS/     U
## THE MAN FROM MI5 **
Desmond Saunders/David Lane
UK                1966
Voices of: Peter Dyneley, Shane Rimmer, David

*Holliday, Matt Zimmerman, David Graham, Ray Barrett, Sylvia Anderson*
Two more episodes from this lively puppet animation series. In the first the work of International Rescue is being hampered by the operations of some imposters and Jeff shuts down the organisation, but is forced to resume operations to save a lost astronaut. In the second tale British Intelligence, ask for help in retrieving a stolen nuclear weapon. This tape includes some Lyons Maid TV commercials made by Gerry Anderson.

| | |
|---|---|
| CAR | 98 min mTV |
| V | CH5 |

### THUNDERBIRDS: THE UNINVITED/    U
### THE MIGHTY ATOM **
Desmond Saunders/David Lane
           UK          1966
*Voices of: Peter Dyneley, Shane Rimmer, David Holliday, Matt Zimmermann, David Graham, Ray Barrett, Sylvia Anderson*
In the first of these puppet animations Scott is forced to land Thunderbird I in the Sahara after being shot down by creatures known as the Zombites. Later he meets two archaeologists and all three are soon taken prisoner. The second tale has their old enemy the Hood attempting to discover the secrets of a new atomic power station in the Sahara.

| | |
|---|---|
| CAR | 104 min mTV |
| V | CH5 |

### THUNDERBIRDS: VAULT OF DEATH/    U
### MOVE AND YOU'RE DEAD **
David Elliott/Alan Pattillo
           UK          1966
*Voices of: Peter Dyneley, Shane Rimmer, David Holliday, Matt Zimmerman, David Graham, Ray Barrett, Sylvia Anderson*
In "Vault Of Death" Parker becomes involved in an attempt to rescue a bank clerk who has become trapped in an impregnable vault. The second story has Alan winning a motor race in a car built by Brains, and then finding himself the victim of one of his rivals, who plants a bomb on a bridge and traps him there.

| | |
|---|---|
| CAR | 96 min mTV |
| V | CH5 |

### THUNDERBOLT AND LIGHTFOOT ***    18
Michael Cimino     USA        1974
*Clint Eastwood, Jeff Bridges, George Kennedy, Geoffrey Lewis, Catherine Bach, Gary Busey, Vic Tayback, Dub Taylor, Bill McKinney*
Two drifters team up to regain the loot stashed away by one of them from a previous robbery. A well-composed blend of comedy and action, written by Cimino in his debut as director, but slightly marred by the unexpectedly downbeat ending.

| | |
|---|---|
| A/AD | 110 min (ort 115 min) |
| V | WHV |

### THUNDERING MANTIS, THE ***
Yeh Yung-Tsu    HONG KONG    1980
*Liang Chia-Yen, Huang I Lung, Hsia Chun, Chao Tung Shan, Cheng Feng, Chien Yueh-Sheng*
After his best friend is killed, a delivery boy is inexplicably transformed into a giant mantis; a metamorphosis he is not slow to exploit in his thirst for revenge. A bizarre martial arts fantasy quite unlike any other film of this genre.
Aka: MANTIS FIST FIGHTER

| | |
|---|---|
| MAR | 85 min |
| B,V | VPD |

### THURSDAY'S CHILD ***
David Lowell Rich    USA     1982
*Gena Rowlands, Don Murray, Jessica Walter, Rob Lowe, Tracey Gold, Janet MacLachlan, Glenn Morrissey, Ken Stovitz, Heidi Bohay, Larry Poindexter,*

*Liz Keifer, Robin Gammell, Alan Fudge, Thomas Hill, Stephen Keep, Curt Lowens*
A teenage boy is found to have an enlarged heart and must undergo transplant surgery, in a story that looks at how his family copes with this. Scripted by Gwen Banig-Dubov. A restrained and interesting account.
Boa: book by Victoria Poole.

| | |
|---|---|
| DRA | 90 min (ort 100 min) mTV |
| B,V | VDB L/A; CAP |

### THX 1138 ****    15
George Lucas     USA       1970
*Robert Duvall, Donald Pleasance, Maggie McOmie, Don Pedro Colley, Ian Wolfe, Sid Haig, John Pearce, Marshall Efrom, Irene Forrest, Claudette Bessing, John Seaton, Eugene L. Sullivan, Gary Alan Marsh, Raymond J. Walsh*
A starkly brilliant look at an underground city of the future, with life so dehumanised that the inhabitants take drugs in order to work efficiently. Cutting and voice-over are used to great effect. Following an illegal love affair with his female room-mate, THX 1138 is imprisoned but escapes. An expanded version of a prize-winning feature Lucas made as a student at U.S.C. The script is by Lucas and Walter Murch, with music by Lalo Schifrin.

| | |
|---|---|
| FAN | 82 min (ort 95 min) |
| V | WHV |

### THY NEIGHBOUR'S WIFE **    18
Danielle Rogers    USA     1986
*Eric Edwards, Paul Thomas, Sheena Horne, Kimberly Carson, Tony Montana, Tami White, Rick Savage*
A famous columnist visits a writer to find out why his latest novel is so different, and discovers that his new wife is responsible. Mad with jealousy, he plots with a female big game huntress to kill the writer in a fake accident. But the huntress is caught seducing the wife, and our outraged writer shoots her instead. Just as she dies she tries to kill him, but misses and shoots his wife, thus ending this ludicrous tale.

| | |
|---|---|
| A | 50 min |
| V | ROXY; PYR; GLOB |

### TIARA TAHITI **    PG
William (Ted) Kotcheff   UK     1962
*James Mason, John Mills, Claude Dauphin, Herbert Lom, Rosenda Monteros, Jacques Marin, Libby Morris, Madge Ryan, Gary Cockrell, Peter Barkworth*
Conflict erupts between two army officers of different backgrounds, who settle on the island of Tahiti. An awkward blend of comedy and drama, that has engaging performances hampered by the shortcomings of the script. Written by Geoffrey Cotterell and Ivan Foxwell.
Boa: novel by Geoffrey Cotterell.

| | |
|---|---|
| DRA | 98 min (ort 100 min) |
| B,V | RNK; VCC |

### TICKET TO HEAVEN ***
Ralph L. Thomas    CANADA    1981
*Nick Mancuso, Meg Foster, Kim Cattrail, Saul Rubinek, R.H. Thomsom, Jennifer Dale, Guy Boyd, Paul Soles, Harvey Atkin, Robert Joy, Stephen Markle, Marcia Diamond, Timothy Webber, Patrick Brymer, Michael Zelniker, Denise Naples*
A youth joins a cult and undergoes brainwashing, but is subsequently snatched from its clutches by his friends, who mount a kidnapping attempt in order to rescue him. Absorbing and quite chilling, this is a thinly veiled attack on the Moonies. Written by Ralph L. Thomas and Anne Cameron.
Boa: novel Moonwebs by Josh Freed.

| | |
|---|---|
| DRA | 107 min |
| B,V | VCL/CBS |

### TIE ME UP! TIE ME DOWN! ***    18
Pedro Almodovar    SPAIN    1990

*Victoria Abril, Antonio Banderas, Loles Leon, Francisco Rabal, Julieta Serrano, Maria Barranco, Rossy De Palma*
Written by cult director Almodovar, this strange black comedy concerns a young man, his recent release from mental hospital, and his invasion of the apartment of a former porno movie star. Having tied her up, he keeps her as prisoner, convinced that she will eventually fall in love with him. Despite the distasteful premise, Almodovar's subdued approach and the explicit script give this film considerable impact. Music is by Ennio Morricone.

COM                                         102 min
V                                         ENTER

## TIFFANY **             18
WEST GERMANY
*Anna Zarni, Claire William, Sabine Schneider*
A top female photographer becomes caught up in a web of sex and intrigue when she is sent to Greece on a steamy photo assignment.
Aka: TIFFANY: TRIANGLE OF LUST
A                67 min (UK cinema version)
B,V                     ELV L/A; ATLAN

## TIFFANY JONES ***       18
Pete Walker        UK            1974
*Anouska Hempel, Ray Brooks, Eric Pohlmann, Susan Sheers, Damien Thomas, Ivor Salter, Lynda Baron, Martin Benson, Alan Curtis, John Clive, Martin Wyldeck, Geoffrey Hughes, Bill Kerr, Nick Zaran, Walter Randall, Kim Alexander*
Film version of the adventures of a character in the cartoon column of the Daily Mail. She gets entangled in a plot to depose the cruel president of Zirdania and return the young prince to the throne. After avoiding the advances of the president, she falls into the hands of an inept underground movement, and this utterly silly but quite entertaining romp ends with her semi-nude in London, being chased across an airfield.
A                   87 min (ort 90 min)
B,V     RNK L/A; AMB L/A; VMA L/A; STABL

## TIGER BAY ***           PG
J. Lee Thompson     UK          1959
*John Mills, Hayley Mills, Horst Buchholz, Yvonne Mitchell, Megs Jenkins, Anthony Dawson, George Selway, George Pastell, Marne Maitland, Meredith Edwards, Shari, Paul Stassino, Marianne Stone, Rachel Thomas, Brian Hammond*
A child witnesses a murder by a Polish seaman of his girlfriend, and is abducted by the seaman but proves to be more than a match for him. A box office success for Hayley Mills in her first major role. The script is by John Hawkesworth and Shelley Smith.
Boa: novel Rodolphe Et Le Revolveur by Noel Calef.
DRA       105 min; 102 min (MIA or PARK) B/W
B,V     RNK; MIA (VHS only); PARK (VHS only)

## TIGER GANG **
Harold Reinl
    ITALY/PAKISTAN/WEST GERMANY   1971
*Tony Kendall, Brad Harris, Mohd Ali, Gisella Hahn, Zeba, E.F. Furbringer*
A detective is sent to solve the murder of an Interpol agent in Pakistan, and meets an old friend who has been sent there on a similar mission by the family of another murdered agent.
Aka: F.B.I. OPERAZIONE PAKISTAN; KOMMISAR X JAGT DIE ROTEN TIGER
A/AD                              87 min
B,V                              VPD

## TIGER JOE **           15
Anthony M. Dawson (Antonio Margheriti)
           ITALY              1982
*David Warbeck, Anne Bell, Tony King, Antonella Interlenghi*
A former Vietnam pilot is shot down on a gun

smuggling operation over Cambodia and has to survive in the jungle.
A/AD                          92 min
V                   ALPHA/CBS; TRACKS

## TIGER OVER WALL *         18
          HONG KONG       1977
*Phillip Ko*
Following the collapse of the Ching Dynasty, various powerful warriors battle it out for dominance.
MAR            86 min (ort 88 min) Cut (7 sec)
B,V                              VPD

## TIGER SHARK **         18
M. Emmett Alston              1987
*John Quade, Pamela Bryant, Mike Stone, Vic Silayan, Roy Alvarez, Roland Dantes*
A martial arts instructor learns that his girlfriend and her friends have been kidnapped by a communist warlord, and are being ransomed for guns and ammunition. Together with an ex-Vietnam buddy, he mounts a rescue mission.
A/AD         98 min (ort 100 min) Cut (37 sec)
B,V                              TGP

## TIGER STRIKES AGAIN, THE **
Hwa I Hung      HONG KONG
*Bruce Li (Ho Tsung-Tao)*
Story of kung fu conflict between refugees and underworld figures.
MAR                           88 min
B,V,V2                            VPD

## TIGER TOWN ***          U
Alan Shapiro      USA           1983
*Roy Scheider, Justin Henry, Ron McLarty, Bethany Carpenter, Noah Moazezi, Mary Wilson*
A young fan of the Detroit Tigers, inspires an ageing ballplayer to have one last crack at the championship. A sensitive and warm story, totally free of mawkish sentiment and sugary cuteness. A fine work from first time writer and director Shapiro.
DRA                 90 min (ort 95 min) mCab
B,V                         RNK; WDV

## TIGER WALKS, A ***        U
Norman Tokar      USA          1963
*Brian Keith, Vera Miles, Pamela Franklin, Sabu, Kevin Corcoran, Una Merkel, Frank McHugh, Peter Brown, Edward Andrews, Arthur Hunnicutt, Connie Gilchrist, Theodore Marcuse, Merry Anders, Frank McHugh, Doodles Weaver*
A tiger escapes from the circus in a small Western town and engages the compassion of a young girl, in this unusually mature and effective Disney offering. Written by Lowell S. Hawley and Sabu's last film.
Boa: novel by Ian Niall.
DRA                   91 min; 85 min (WDV)
B,V                         RNK; WDV

## TIGER WARSAW **         15
Amin Q. Chaudhri    USA        1988
*Patrick Swayze, Barbara Williams, Lee Richardson, Mary McDonnell, Bobby Di Cicco, Piper Laurie, Jenny Chrisinger, Kaye Ballard*
A former junkie returns home with the intention of getting his life straightened out and healing an old wound, this being the fact that he nearly killed his father years ago. A murky and confused melodrama that neither convinces nor entertains.
DRA                          92 min
B,V                            CINE

## TIGERS DON'T CRY **
Peter Collinson   SOUTH AFRICA     1976
*Anthony Quinn, John Phillip Law, Ken Gampu, Simon Sabela, Marius Weyers, Sandra Prinsloo*
A South African male nurse with a terminal disease, plans to kidnap an African president being treated at

the hospital where he works, in a desperate attempt to find a way to provide for his daughter after his death. A competent thriller, well handled and paced.
Aka: AFRICAN RAGE; LONG SHOT, THE; TARGET OF AN ASSASSIN; TIGER DOESN'T CRY, THE
Boa: novel Running Scared by John Burmeister.
THR                                    98 min (ort 105 min)
B,V                                                      RNK

## TIGER'S TALE, A **                                    15
Peter Douglas              USA                   1987
C. Thomas Howell, Ann-Margret, Charles Durning, Kelly Preston, William Zabka, Ann Wedgeworth, Tim Thomerson, Steven Kampmann, Traci Lin, Linda Rae Favila, James Noble, Angel Tompkins, Steve Farrell, David Denney, Jo Perkins
An attractive lonely divorcee embarks on an affair with a high school senior, whose former girlfriend just happens to be her daughter. One of those irritatingly smug films that attempts to show just how prejudiced we all are about age differences in relationships. Written by Douglas, this was his directorial debut.
COM                                    95 min (ort 97 min)
B,V                                                      EIV

## TIGHTROPE **                                    18
Richard Tuggle             USA                   1984
Clint Eastwood, Genevieve Bujold, Dan Hedaya, Alison Eastwood, Jennifer Beck, Marco St John, Rebecca Perle, Regina Richardson, Randi Brooks, Janet MacLachlan, Margaret Howell, Rebecca Clemons, Graham Paul, Donald Barber
A New Orleans policeman discovers that he has the same inclinations as the sex murderer he is after. A sordid and generally unappealing effort, not helped by the fact that much of the story takes place in darkness. Written by Tuggle.
THR                                  110 min (ort 114 min)
V                                                        WHV

## TIGHTROPE TO TERROR **                           U
Robert Kellett             UK                    1982
Richard Owens, Rebecca Lacey, Eloise Ritchie, Mark Jeffries, Stuart Wilde, Peter Boom
Four children are stranded in the Alps when a helicopter damages their cable car. A fairly competent drama from the Children's Film Foundation.
DRA                                                53 min
B,V                                                      RNK

## TILL DEATH ***                                    
Walter Stocker             USA                   1972
Keith Atkinson, Belinda Balaski, Bert Freed, Marshall Reed, Jonathan Hole
A newly married couple have a road accident as they start on their honeymoon, and the wife is killed, but the husband refuses to accept her death and resurrects her from her crypt. A tense little film built around the two main characters.
HOR                                    80 min (ort 89 min)
B,V                                                      HER

## TILL DEATH US DO PART *                          
Norman Cohen               UK                    1968
Warren Mitchell, Dandy Nicholls, Anthony Booth, Una Stubbs, Liam Redmond, Bill Maynard, Sam Kydd, Brian Blessed
A wretched spin-off from a TV series, that looks at the life of an obnoxious bigot from the 1930s to the 1960s. A sequel, "The Alf Garnett Saga" followed in 1972. Written by Johnny Speight.
COM                                                99 min
B,V                                                      TEVP

## TILL WE MEET AGAIN: PARTS 1, 2 AND 3 *      PG
Charles Jarrott            USA                   1989
Bruce Boxleitner, Barry Bostwick, Mia Sara, Courteney Cox, Lucy Gutteridge, Michael York, Hugh Grant, Maxwell Caulfield, Juliet Mills

Overlong TV adaptation of Krantz's novel dealing with three French women: a former Paris music-hall star and her two daughters, and the major events in their lives over a period of 50 years. As one might expect, WW2 serves as little more than a backdrop to this artificial and saccharine confection.
Boa: novel by Judith Krantz.
DRA                         296 min (3 cassettes) mTV
V                                              CASPIC/TERRY

## TILT **                                          15
Rudy Durand                USA                   1978
Brooke Shields, Ken Marshall, Charles Durning, John Crawford, Gregory Walcott, Geoffrey Lewis
A girl pinball expert mounts a challenge to the reigning champion after she teams up with an aspiring rock singer. OK for pinball freaks for whom photography of the inside of one of these machines will no doubt be a real highlight. Later re-cut by Durand to 100 minutes.
DRA                                107 min (ort 111 min) mTV
B,V                                                      RNK

## TIM **                                           PG
Michael Pate               AUSTRALIA             1979
Mel Gibson, Piper Laurie, Alwyn Kurts, Pat Evison, Peter Gwynne, Deborah Kennedy, David Foster, Margo Lee, James Condon, Michael Caulfield, Brenda Senders, Brian Barrie, Kevin Leslie, Louise Pago, Arthur Faybes, Geoff Usher
The story of an affair between an older woman and a young, retarded man, who has started working for her as a gardener. Sincere and quite poignant, but a little too contrived to work. Written by Pate.
Boa: novel by Colleen McCullogh.
DRA                                104 min (ort 108 min)
B,V                                                      SHOW

## TIME AFTER TIME ***                              15
Nicholas Meyer             USA                   1980
Malcolm McDowell, David Warner, Mary Steenburgen, Charles Cioffi, Kent Williams, Patti D'Arbanville, Laurie Main, Andonia Katsaros, Leo Lewis, Keith McConnell, Geraldine Baron, James Garrett, Bryon Webster, Joseph Maher
Using his time machine, H.G. Wells pursues Jack the Ripper from 19th century England to present-day New York. An amusing fantasy with many loopholes in the story. Steenburgen's great performance, as the writer's 20th century girlfriend, is a highlight. The script is by Karl Alexander and Steve Hayes, with a memorable score by Miklos Rozsa.
Boa: novel by Karl Alexander and Steve Hayes.
FAN                                108 min (ort 112 min)
B,V                                                      WHV

## TIME BANDITS **                                  PG
Terry Gilliam              UK                    1981
John Cleese, Sean Connery, Shelley Duvall, David Warner, Ralph Richardson, Katherine Helmond, Ian Holm, Michael Palin, Peter Vaughan, Craig Warnock, David Rappaport, Jack Purvis, Malcolm Dixon, Kenny Baker, Mike Edmonds
Long and totally unfunny fantasy about some dwarfs who steal a cosmic plan from God to use for their own advantage. They take an 11-year-old boy on an adventure through space and time eventually culminating in a meeting with the Devil. Written by Michael Palin and Terry Gilliam of "Monty Python" TV fame.
COM                105 min; 111 min (CBS) (ort 116 min)
B,V                              TEVP; CBS (VHS only)

## TIME BOMB *                                      PG
Paul Krasny                USA                   1984
Morgan Fairchild, Billy Dee Williams, Merlin Olsen, Joseph Bottoms, Anne Kerry, Chad Redding, Dianne Shaw, Colin Lane, Alan Justin, Sandi Fish, Robert Ginnaven, Hugh Gorrian, Harlan Jordan, Tom

McMadden, Kenneth McLean
A terrorist group plans to seize a load of plutonium waste. Fairchild leads the terrorists in this mediocre and predictable actioner, a failed pilot for a TV series. Boa: story by Roderick Taylor.
A/AD                              91 min (ort 100 min) mTV
B,V                                                      CIC

## TIME BURST *                                        15
Peter Yuval              USA                         1988
David Scott King, Jay Richardson, Michiko, Gerald Okamura, Craig Ng, Chet Hood, Jack Vogel
A pseudo-mystical piece of low-budget claptrap, that opens with a character being trained in the art of combat by a Japanese samurai. It would appear that he has now become immortal, for the film then takes us to the 20th century, where he engages in battle with an assortment of enemies. Fairly mind-numbing and barely comprehensible.
A/AD                                               90 min
B,V                                                     SCRN

## TIME FOR DYING, A **                                PG
Bud Boetticher           USA                         1969
                                             (released 1982)
Richard Lapp, Anne Randall, Bob Random, Victor Jory, Audie Murphy
Produced by Audie Murphy (who appears as Jesse James), this obscure film tells of a young gunslinger who saves a girl from prostitution, but is forced to marry her by Judge Roy Bean. An adequate time-filler.
WES                                      69 min (ort 90 min)
B,V                                                      AVR

## TIME FOR MIRACLES, A **                             PG
Michael O'Herlihy        USA                         1980
Kate Mulgrew, Lorne Greene, Rossano Brazzi, John Forsythe, Jean-Pierre Aumont, Jean LeClerc, Leonard Mann, Robin Clarke, William Prince, Dominic Chianese, George Murdock, Milo O'Shea, Danny Moran, Todd Fine, Erika Katz
Average is probably the best way to describe this biography of the first native-born US saint, Elizabeth Bayley Seton (1774-1821) who founded the American Sisters of Charity as well as the first Catholic orphanage. The script is by Henry Denker.
DRA                                     95 min (ort 104 min) mTV
V                                                       HER

## TIME GAMES **                                       15
Donald Crombie    AUSTRALIA                          1985
Imogen Annersley, Peter Phelps, Mouche Phillips, Moya O'Sullivan, Sue Cruickshank
A young girl finds herself carried back 100 years to Sydney of 1873, when the spirit of a girl who lived in that period comes to her.
Aka: PLAYING BEATIE BOW
FAN                                                 86 min
B,V                                                    APOL

## TIME GUARDIAN, THE *                                PG
Brian Hannant      AUSTRALIA                         1987
Tom Burlinson, Nikki Coghill, Dean Stockwell, Carrie Fisher
In yet another post-nuclear holocaust world of the future (A.D. 4039 to be exact) scattered bands of survivors fight off man-made cyborgs who have rebelled against their masters. Burlinson is the tough guy leader in this one, who takes off with his followers back into the 20th century, only to find his enemies waiting there for his arrival. This is not SF for the discerning, but a lightweight adventure for the desperate.
FAN                                      84 min (ort 90 min)
B,V                                                      GHV

## TIME IN THE SUN ***                                 PG
Sergei Eisenstein        USSR                      1930/40

A collection of fragments of QUE VIVA MEXICO, consisting of some striking sequences following peasant and Indian life. In the final section "Death Day" is celebrated with appropriate displays of fireworks, skulls etc. Not so much a film as an incomplete set of visually pleasing images, some portions of which turned up in other works.
Osca: BEZHIN MEADOW
DRA                     60 min; 91 min (2 film cassette) B/W
V                                                      HEND

## TIME MACHINE, THE ***                               PG
George Pal               UK/USA                      1960
Rod Taylor, Yvette Mimieux, Alan Young, Sebastian Cabot, Tom Helmore, Whit Bissell, Doris Lloyd, Bob Barran
A Victorian scientist builds a time machine and travels forward to the year 802,701, where he finds human beings have evolved into two separate races. A lavish and entertaining version of Wells' story, but considerably simplified and lacking the social perspective of the original. The special effects are the film's highlight, and it was remade for TV in 1978. AA: Effects (Gene Warren/Tim Baar).
Boa: short story by H.G. Wells.
FAN                                      98 min (ort 103 min)
V                                                       MGM

## TIME OF DESTINY, A **                               15
Gregory Nava            USA                          1988
William Hurt, Timothy Hutton, Melissa Leo, Stockard Channing, Francisco Rabal, Conchata Hildalgo, Megan Follows
Set in 1943, this tells of the favourite daughter of Basque immigrants, who is forbidden by her strict father to marry her soldier boyfriend. The lovers elope, but their wedding night is interrupted by the girl's father, who bundles her into his car but is killed in a tragic accident. A dreary tale of passion and revenge. Written by Anna Thomas and with music by Ennio Morricone.
DRA                                     112 min (ort 118 min)
V                                                       VES

## TIME OF THE APES *                                  PG
Atsuo Okunaga/Kiyosumi Fukazawa
                         JAPAN                       1987
Reiko Tokunaga, Hiroko Saito, Masaaki Kaji, Hitoshi Omae, Tetsuya Ushid, Baku Hatakeyama, Kazue Takita, Noboru Nakaya
Children trapped by an earthquake, in underground chambers used for experiments in suspended animation, emerge many centuries later into a world ruled by apes. A blatant but uninspired copy of PLANET OF THE APES.
FAN                                                 96 min
V                                                      XTASY

## TIME SLIP *                                         18
Kossei Saito             JAPAN                        1983
SonnShinichi) Chiba, Isao Natsuki, Raita Ryu, Miyuki Ono, Jana Okada
A Japanese army unit on manoeuvres, gets sent back 400 years in time to the samurai era.
Aka: DAY OF THE APOCALYPSE; SENGOKU JIEITAI; TELE; TIME WARS (WARAD)
FAN                              88 min (ort 100 min) Cut (23 sec)
V                               AST L/A; WARAD; KRP

## TIME TO DIE, A *
Matt Cimber (Matteo Ottaviano)
                         USA          1979 (released 1983)
Rex Harrison, Rod Taylor, Edward Albert Jr, Raf Vallone, Linn Stokke
A man sets out for revenge on those who tortured and killed his wife during WW2, and his search takes him to the seamy side of Munich. A plodding waste of time and effort.

Aka: MARIO PUZO'S SEVEN GRAVES FOR
ROGAN; SEVEN GRAVES FOR ROGAN
Boa: short story by Mario Puzo.
DRA                                        92 min
B,V                                   VIP L/A; VPD

## TIME TO LIVE, A ***                          PG
Rick Wallace          USA              1985
*Liza Minnelli, Scott Schwartz, Swoosie Kurtz, Jeffrey
DeMunn, Corey Haim, Janine Manatis, Karen Shallo,
Francois Klanfer, Henry G. Sanders, David Connor,
Chuck Shamata, Ken Pogue, Samatha Langevin,
Alain Goulen, Kurt Reis*
Hollywood version of the true story of a woman writer
who has to come to terms with the fact that her
two-year-old son is suffering from muscular dystro-
phy. A fine performance from Minnelli saves this from
becoming just another tearjerker. Scripted by John
McGreevey. This was Minnelli's TV movie debut.
Boa: book Intensive Care by May-Lou Weisman
DRA                        91 min (ort 100 min) mTV
B,V                                   IVS L/A; CAST

## TIME TRACKERS *                              U
Howard R. Cohen        USA             1989
*Ned Beatty, Wil Shriner, Kathleen Beller, Bridget
Hoffman, Alex Hyde-White, Lee Bergere, Robert
Cornthwaite*
In the year 2033 a scientist succeeds in building a
time machine, but a jealous colleague uses it to go
back in time with the intention of preventing the birth
of all his rivals. A group from the future set out in
pursuit and wind up in medieval England, having
picked up a 20th century cop along the way. A film
that starts out with a few clever touches, but soon
degenerates into a dreary costumed farce.
FAN                                        86 min
V                                             MGM

## TIME TRAVELERS, THE ***                       PG
Ib Melchior           USA              1964
*Preston Foster, Philip Carey, Merry Anders, John
Hoyt, Steve Franken, Joan Woodbury, Dolores Wells,
Dennis Patrick, Forrest J. Ackerman, Gloria Leslie,
Margaret Seldeen, Peter Strudwick*
Scientists travel into the future to find the Earth
devastated by nuclear war and inhabited by mutants.
However, a colony of survivors live beneath the
surface and are building a spaceship to take them to
another planet. Quite enjoyable, if rather bleak. The
photography of Vilmos Zsigmond is an asset. Remade
as JOURNEY TO THE CENTRE OF TIME in 1967.
FAN                              80 min (ort 84 min)
B,V                                           RNK

## TIME WALKER *                                15
Tom Kennedy           USA              1982
*Ben Murphy, James Karen, Nina Axelrod, Kevin
Brophy, James Karen, Shari Belafonte-Harper, Austin
Stoker, Clint Young, Jason Williams, Sam Chew Jr,
Antoinette Bower, Melissa Prophet, Gerard
Prendergast, Jack Olsen*
An earthquake uncovers an alien buried in the tomb
of an Egyptian ruler, and the former comes to life after
being subjected to an overdose of gamma rays. A
shuffling and amateurish production demonstrating
the limitations of its budget, acting and direction.
HOR                             82 min (ort 86 min)
B,V                                           GHV

## TIMERIDER **                                 15
William Dear          USA              1983
*Fred Ward, Belinda Bauer, Peter Coyote, Ed Lauter,
Richard Masur, Tracey Walter, L.Q. Jones, Chris
Mulkey, Macon McCalman, Jonathan Banks, Laurie
O'Brien, William Dear, Susan Dear, Bruce Gordon,
Ben Zeller, Tommy Leyba*
A bike rider slips back in time to the days of the Old
West circa 1875, after he gets lost in the desert and

strays into a scientific experiment. Once there, his
bike attracts the attention of a mean group of outlaws
and their leader, all of whom are fascinated by this
example of 20th century technology. An interesting
story is let down by a bad script and slow pacing.
Aka: TIME RIDER; TIMERIDER: THE
ADVENTURE OF LYLE SWANN
FAN                              89 min (ort 93 min)
B,V                                           TEVP

## TIMES SQUARE *                               15
Alan Moyle            USA              1980
*Tim Curry, Trini Alvarado, Robin Johnson, Peter
Coffield, Herbert Berghof, David Margulies, Miguel
Pinero, Elizabeth Pena*
Two runaway girls in New York eventually make
good by forming their own rock band. Unpleasant and
unbelievable, with Times Square appearing a friendly
(and safe!) rendezvous. The music is by Blue Weaver
for those who are hard of hearing. Written by Jacob
Brackman.
MUS                            106 min (ort 113 min)
B, V/sh                                       TEVP

## TIMESTALKERS ***                             PG
Michael Schultz       USA              1986
*William Devane, Lauren Hutton, Klaus Kinski, John
Ratzenberger, Forrest Tucker, John Considine, James
Avery, Gail Youngs, Danny Pintauro, Tracey Walter,
R.D. Call, Patrik Baldauff, Ritch Brinkley, J. Michael
Flynn*
A professor comes across an authentic 1886 photo-
graph that shows a modern gun in a man's gunbelt,
and is mystified by this until he meets a girl from the
future. Together, they embark on a journey into the
past to track down a demented scientist from her time,
who is out to change the course of history. A bizarre
and highly imaginative tale, written by Brian Clemens. This was the last film for Tucker.
Boa: novel (unpublished) The Tintype by Ray Brown.
FAN                            87 min (ort 100 min) mTV
B,V                                           CBS

## TIMEWARP *
Robert Emenegger/Allan Sandler
                      USA              1981
*Gretchen Corbett, Peter Kastner, Steven Mond, Adam
West, Chip Johnson, Kirk Alyn, Karen Kondazian*
On his way to Jupiter, an astronaut gets caught in a
time warp in this obscure and rather tedious fantasy.
FAN                                        80 min
B,V                     VIDFOR L/A; BLAC L/A; HER

## TIN MAN, THE **                              15
John G. Thomas        USA              1982
*Timothy Bottoms, Deana Jurgens, Troy Donahue,
John Phillip Law*
A deaf boy invents a computer device for artificial
speech, that immediately attracts the attentions of a
ruthless salesman. An interesting drama with a
competent, fairly low-key script.
DRA                                        95 min
B,V                                       VCL/CBS

## TIN MEN ***                                  15
Barry Levinson        USA              1987
*Richard Dreyfuss, Barbara Hershey, Danny DeVito,
John Mahoney, Jackie Gayle, Stanley Brock, Seymour
Cassel, Bruno Kirby, J.T. Walsh, Richard Portnow,
Matt Craven, Alan Blumenfield, Brad Sullivan,
Michael Tucker*
Set in 1963, this tells of two "tin men" or aluminium
cladding salesmen, who meet by way of a traffic
accident and find their lives linked, when they both
engage in an obsessive series of tit-for-tat incidents. A
detailed work with sharp dialogue, good characterisa-
tions and totally implausible situations.
COM                            108 min (ort 112 min)
B,V                                           RNK

## TINTIN: RED RACKHAM'S TREASURE **   U
Raymond Le Blance
        BELGIUM/FRANCE     1987
Tintin and his pals set out to dscover the whereabouts of a treasure hidden by a notorious pirate. They experience hazards in the shape of headhunters, a vocano, a landslide and sharks, plus danger from a gang of crooks who are also after the loot.
Aka: ADVENTURS OF TINTIN, THE: RED RACKM'S TRESURE
Osca: TINTIN: THE SECRET OF THE UNICORN
CAR          60 min; 95 min (2 film cassette)
B,V                          VIR

## TINTIN: THE BLACK ISLAND **   U
Raymond Le Blance
        BELGIUM/FRANCE     1987
Another adventure based on the famous comic book character Tintin. In this tale he goes with his friends to the aid of the people on a plane that has crashed in the highlands. They are driven away from the aircraft by gunshots, and attempts to solve this puzzle lead them to a sinister island and an old castle that's reputed to be haunted.
Aka: ADVENTURES OF TINTIN, THE: THE BLACK ISLAND; BLACK ISLAND, THE
CAR          45 min; 40 min (VCC)
V                   JVC L/A; VCC

## TINTIN: THE CALCULUS AFFAIR **   U
Raymond Le Blance
        BELGIUM/FRANCE
Animated feature with comic-strip hero Tintin setting out to rescue a professor, who has been kidnapped by a foreign power and taken to an impregnable fortress, in an effort to discover to secrets of his ultrasonic invention.
Aka: ADVENTURES OF TINTIN, THE: THE CALCULUS AFFAIR; ADVENTURES OF TINTIN, THE; THE CALCULUS CASE (VIR); CALCULUS AFFAIR, THE
CAR          60 min; 58 min (VIR)
B,V         JVC; ART; VIR (VHS only)

## TINTIN: THE CRAB WITH THE GOLDEN   U
## CLAWS **
Raymond Le Blance
        BELGIUM/FRANCE     1987
Cartoon adventure with Tintin and Snowy setting out to rescue Captain Haddock, whose boat has been taken over by diamond smuggling crooks. They drug the Captain and he fails to recognise Tintin, who has a tough time saving both him and his vessel.
Aka: ADVENTURES OF TINTIN, THE: THE CRAB WITH THE GOLDEN CLAWS; CRAB WITH THE GOLDEN CLAWS, THE
JUV                     60 min
V           JVC L/A; ART L/A; VCC

## TINTIN: THE LAKE OF SHARKS **   U
Raymond Le Blance
        BELGIUM/FRANCE     1972
A pleasant animated story based on the popular comic book character, with Tintin and his friends becoming involved in an adventure which leads them to an underwater village, and a chase through the streets aboard some very strange vehicles. One of a number of Tintin adventures.
Aka: ADVENTURES OF TINTIN, THE: THE LAKE OF SHARKS; LAKE OF SHARKS, THE; TINTIN ET LE LAC AUX REQUINS
CAR                    75 min
B,V                   ART L/A

## TINTIN: THE SECRET OF THE UNICORN **   U
Raymond Le Blance
        BELGIUM/FRANCE     1987
Tintin buys a model ship as a present for his friend,

Captain Haddock. When a piece of parchment falls out of the ship, he becomes embroiled in a strange mystery revolving around a hoard of treasure hidden by one of the Captain's ancestors, and faces danger from sinister figures out to obtain the parchment.
Aka: ADVENTURES OF TINTIN, THE: THE SECRET OF THE UNICORN
Osca: TINTIN: RED RACKHAM'S TREASURE (asa)
CAR      37 min; 95 min (2 film cassette)
B,V                        VIR

## TINTIN: THE SEVEN CRYSTAL BALLS **   U
Raymond Le Blance
        BELGIUM/FRANCE
After his friend Cuthbert Calculus is kidnapped, Tintin and his friends set out to rescue him, finding that their search takes them to the jungles of Peru and the famous Temple of the Sun. Another enjoyable animation in this series, based on the popular comic book characters.
Aka: ADVENTURES OF TINTIN, THE: THE SEVEN CRYSTAL BALLS; SEVEN CRYSTAL BALLS, THE
Osca: TINTIN: PRISONERS OF THE SUN (asa)
CAR         71 min (2 film cassette)
V                         VIR

## TINTIN: THE SHOOTING STAR **   U
Raymond Le Blance
        BELGIUM/FRANCE     1987
As a great meteorite heads towards the Earth, Tintin goes to see his friend Professor Calculus, to see if tragedy can be averted. Together with Captain Haddock and the Thompson Twins, he races to the Arctic to find a comet fragment that may provide the information needed to prevent a catastrophe.
Aka: ADVENTURES OF TINTIN, THE: THE SHOOTING STAR; SHOOTING STAR, THE
CAR          43 min (ort 45 min)
V                         VIR

## TINTORERA *
Rene Cardona Jr    MEXICO/UK     1977
*Susan George, Fiona Lewis, Jennifer Ashley, Hugo Stiglitz, Andres Garcia, Priscilla Barnes, Robert Guzman, Laura Lyons, Pamela Garner, Erika Carlson*
Two Mexican shark hunters get involved with American and British women on holiday on a lush tropical island, but a deadly shark threatens their idyll. A rip-off of JAWS, with nudity and extra gore added in a forlorn attempt to sustain interest.
Aka: TINTORERA: TIGER SHARK
Boa: novel by Ramon Bravo.
DRA          86 min (ort 91 min)
B,V                    VCL/CBS

## TITAN FIND **   18
William Malone       USA        1984
*Klaus Kinski, Robert Jaffe, Wendy Schaal, Stan Ivar, Annette McCarthy, Lyman Ward, Marie Laurin, Diane Salinger*
ALIEN copy with two rival expeditions on a mission to Titan, to establish the fate of an expedition that took place several months ago. Average.
Aka: CREATURE
FAN         93 min; 89 min (CH5)
B,V         POLY; CH5 (VHS only)

## TITFIELD THUNDERBOLT, THE ***   U
Charles Crichton     UK       1952
*Stanley Holloway, George Relph, John Gregson, Naunton Wayne, Godfrey Tearle, Hugh Griffith, Sidney James, Edie Martin, Gabrielle Brune, Nancy O'Neil, Reginald Beckwith, Michael Trubshawe, Jack MacGowran, Ewan Roberts*
Villagers take over their threatened branch line and run it themselves. An Ealing comedy which was undervalued at the time but has some fine touches,

not least being the colour photography of Douglas Slocombe. Written by T.E.D. Clarke, with music by Georges Auric.

COM                 82 min; 80 min (WHV) (ort 84 min)
B,V                                      TEVP; WHV

### TITILLATION ***                                    R18
Damon Christian         USA                    1982
*Kitten Natividad, Heaven St John, Gina Gianetti,*
*Randy West, Eric Edwards, Angelique Pettyjohn,*
*Sandra Miller, Ray Simpson, Mike Zempter, Mike*
*Horner*
An eccentric millionaire has in his old age decided to add a large-breasted woman to his collection of artefacts, and for this purpose has had a large brass bra made which he insists must fit his choice. After seeing photos of Natividad his secretary hires a third-rate detective to find her. An utterly crazy spoof on detective films, with countless twists to the plot, and a Sam Spade-type voice-over for good measure. A tale even Russ Meyer would envy.

A                                          80 min
B,V                                          EVI

### TO ALL A GOODNIGHT *
David Hess              USA                    1980
*Jennifer Runyon, Forrest Swanson, Linda Gentile,*
*William Lauer, Katherine Herrington, Judith Bridges,*
*Buck West, Sam Shamshak, Denise Stearns, Angela*
*Bath, Solomon Trager*
Five girls at a finishing school smuggle their boyfriends in for a Christmas party, unaware that a crazy killer is on the loose and is about to dispatch them in a variety of gory ways.

HOR                                         90 min
B,V,V2                                       VPD

### TO BE OR NOT TO BE ***                             PG
Alan Johnson            USA                    1983
*Mel Brooks, Anne Bancroft, Charles Durning, Tim*
*Matheson, Jose Ferrer, Christopher Lloyd, George*
*Gaynes, James Haake, George Wyner, Jack Riley,*
*Lewis J. Stradlen*
Faithful remake of an earlier film of 1942, based on an Ernst Lubitsch story that follows the first film almost scene for scene, and tells of a Polish theatre troupe who use their talents to resist the Nazi invaders. Let down by an irritating degree of pretentiousness and rather flat direction, though both Brooks and Bancroft are in fine form. Written by Thomas Meehan and Ronnie Graham.

COM                              103 min (ort 108 min)
B,V                                          CBS

### TO BE OR NOT TO BE ****                            U
Ernst Lubitsch          USA                    1942
*Carole Lombard, Jack Benny, Robert Stack, Felix*
*Bressart, Lionel Atwill, Sig Ruman, Stanley Ridges,*
*Tom Dugan, Charles Halton, Peter Caldwell, Helmut*
*Dantine*
A Warsaw theatre troupe find their own way to resist the Nazis, culminating in a mass impersonation that allows great scope for their acting skills. A combination of witty dialogue, tip-top performances and finely balanced comedy, enable tragic events to be depicted in a light-hearted but sensitive way. Written by Edwin Justus Mayer and remade by Mel Brooks in 1983. This was Lombard's last film and was released after her death.

COM                             94 min (ort 99 min) B/W
V                                            VCC

### TO BE TWENTY *
Fernando Di Leo         ITALY                  1978
*Gloria Guida, Lilli Carati, Ray Lovelock, Vincenzo*
*Crocitti, Loria Lilli, Vittorio Caprioli*
Two girls hitch-hiking in Italy have various adventures, some fun and a little love. What more would one expect from a film like this?

Aka: AVERE VENT'ANI
DRA                                         90 min
B,V,V2                                       VPD

### TO BUILD A FIRE ***
David Cobham            UK                     1970
*Ian Hogg, Orson Welles (narration)*
Excellent adaptation of a story of a man who unwisely ventures out alone in the wilds of Alaska during a particularly cold spell. Simple, unadorned and extremely effective.
Boa: short story by Jack London.
DRA                                         50 min
B,V                                          QUA

### TO CATCH A KING *                                  PG
Clive Donner            USA                    1984
*Robert Wagner, Teri Garr, Horst Janson, Barbara*
*Parkins, John Standing, Jane Lapotaire, Barry Foster,*
*Marcel Bozzuffi, Peter Egan, John Patrick, John*
*Baron, Constantine Gregory, Edmund Kente, Peter*
*Woodthorpe, Lex Van Delden*
Spy thriller about a Nazi conspiracy to abduct the Duke and Duchess of Windsor from Lisbon in 1940, with Garr as a nightclub singer and Wagner as a cafe owner out to thwart this momentous occurrence. Very dull.
Boa; novel by Harry Patterson (Jack Higgins).
THR                                   113 min mCab
B,V                                          HER

### TO DIE FOR *                                       18
Deran Serafian          USA                    1989
*Brendan Hughes, Sydney Walsh, Amanda Wyss,*
*Duane Jones, Scott Jacoby, Steve Bond, Micah Grant*
Vlad Tepish, better known as Dracula, comes to L.A. to start a new life, but encounters an ancient adversary who threatens to put paid to his plans for good. A misguided and tepid effort.
HOR                              89 min (ort 94 min)
B,V                                          ACDV

### TO HAVE AND HAVE NOT ****                          PG
Howard Hawks            USA                    1945
*Humphrey Bogart, Lauren Bacall, Walter Brennan,*
*Hoagy Carmichael, Dolores Moran, Sheldon Leonard,*
*Dan Seymour, Marcel Dalio*
An American charter boat operator living on Vichy-run Martinique, is reluctantly drawn into the French resistance movement while becoming entangled with a young femme fatale. The plot has more holes than a Swiss cheese, but the sparkling performance of the leads (especially Bacall's catlike sensuality) and the great dialogue, make this a memorable film. Remade as "The Breaking Point" and "The Gun Runners".
Boa: novel by Ernest Hemingway.
DRA                            96 min (ort 100 min) B/W
V                                            WHV

### TO HAVE AND TO HOLD **
Herbert Wise            UK                     1963
*Ray Barrett, Katherine Blake, Nigel Stock, William*
*Hartnell, Patricia Bredin*
A police sergeant assigned to protection duties after a woman received threatening telephone calls finds himself falling in love with her. When she is murdered his interest becomes more than purely professional and he sets out to catch the killer.
DRA                                      68 min B/W
V                                            WHV

### TO HEAL A NATION ***                               U
Michael Pressman        USA                    1987
*Eric Roberts, Glynnis O'Connor, Scott Paulin,*
*Marshall Colt, Brock Peters, Lee Purcell, Laurence*
*Luckinbill, Linden Chiles*
The story of Vietnam veteran Jan Scruggs, and his campaign to have the Vietnam Veteran's War Memorial built in Washington. A sincere and effective film

that all too often is sidetracked by self-righteousness and histrionics. The script is by Lionel Chetwynd.
Boa: book by Jan Scruggs and Joel L. Swerdlow.

DRA 105 min mTV
B,V SONY

## TO KILL A JACKAL * 15
Joseph Warren 1970
*Klaus Kinski, John Ely*
A criminal gang heads for Mexico with a hoard of stolen gold, but the members squabble amongst themselves in this violent and bloody tale.
Mediocre.
Aka: SHOOT THE LIVING, PRAY FOR THE DEAD

WES 90 min
V VPD

## TO KILL A MOCKINGBIRD **** PG
Robert Mulligan USA 1962
*Gregory Peck, Mary Badham, Philip Alford, John Megna, Brock Peters, Robert Duvall, Frank Overton, Collin Wilcox, William Windom, Rosemary Murphy, Paul Fix, Ruth White, Alice Ghostley*
A white liberal lawyer in a small Southern town, defends a black man accused of rape, and finds that the locals are hostile to him and his family. A slow but careful and extremely absorbing study of bigotry and ignorance. This was Duvall's first film. The script is by Horton Foote and won a well-deserved Oscar. AA: Actor (Peck), Screen (Adapt) (Horton Foote), Art/Set (Alexander Golitzen and Henry Bumstead/Oliver Emert).
Boa: novel by Harper Lee.

DRA 124 min (ort 129 min) B/W
B,V RCA; CIC

## TO KILL A PRIEST ** 18
Agnieszka Holland FRANCE/USA 1988
*Christopher Lambert, Ed Harris, David Suchet, Joss Ackland, Tim Roth, Joanne Whalley-Kilmer, Peter Postlethwaite, Timothy Spall, Cherie Lunghi*
A drama inspired by the career and subsequent death of Polish priest Father Jerzy Popieluszko, who fought for trade unionists in his native country. An undoubtably sincere but shallow and unconvincing effort, with Lambert miscast as the priest caught up in the political troubles afflicting his country.

DRA 130 min
V RCA

## TO KILL A STRANGER * 18
Juan Lopez-Moctezuma MEXICO 1983
*Donald Pleasence, Dean Stockwell, Aldo Ray*
A girl singer takes refuge from a storm in the house of a respected war hero, but finds herself menaced by a rapist and killer in this Gothic mansion horror yarn. A tired formula offering.

HOR 84 min (ort 90 min) Cut (42 sec)
B,V VCL L/A; PVG; VIR

## TO KILL WITH INTRIGUE * 18
Lo Wei HONG KONG 1984
*Jackie Chan*
Kung fu violence and revenge tale, with a man being seriously injured by a gang and embarking on the expected vengeance-seeking mission.

MAR 103 min
B,V AVR; TGP (VHS only)

## TO LIVE AND DIE IN L.A. ** 18
William Friedkin USA 1985
*Willem Dafoe, William L. Peterson, John Pankow, Debra Feuer, John Turturro, Darlanne Fluegel, Dean Stockwell, Steve James, Robert Downey, Christopher Allport, Jack Hoar, Val De Vargas, Dwier Brown, Michael Chong, Michael Zand*
Tough, harsh portrayal of a federal agent looking for counterfeiters who murdered his partner. A depressingly realistic work from the director of THE

FRENCH CONNECTION, and slightly enlivened by the obligatory car chase. The script is by Friedkin and Petievich.
Boa: novel by Gerald Petievich.

THR 114 min (ort 116 min)
V VES

## TO RACE THE WIND *** PG
Walter Grauman USA 1980
*Steve Guttenberg, Randy Quaid, Barbara Barrie, Mark L. Taylor, Catherine Hicks, Lisa Eilbacher, Gregory Walcott, Norman Burton, Deborah Ryan, David James Carroll, David Hollander, Demetre Phillips, Cameron Young*
A law student is determined to continue his normal life after he goes blind, in this surprisingly cheerful and engaging story, based on the autobiography of the writer of BUTTERFLIES ARE FREE.
Boa: book by Harold Krents.

DRA 97 min (ort 105 min) mTV
B,V BWV

## TO SIR, WITH LOVE ** PG
James Clavell UK 1967
*Sidney Poitier, Judy Geeson, Suzy Kendall, Lulu, Christian Roberts, Faith Brook, Geoffrey Bayldon, Edward Burnham, Gareth Robinson, Graham Charles, Patricia Routledge, Fiona Duncan, Adrienne Posta, Ann Bell*
The story of a West Indian teacher who comes to a tough London school, and gradually wins the respect and affection of his unruly pupils. Somewhat over-sentimental and unrealistic, but mildly enjoyable. The film led to the creation of the British TV series "Please Sir". Written by James Clavell. See also THE CLASS OF MISS MACMICHAEL.
Boa: novel by E.R. Braithwaite.

DRA 101 min (ort 105 min)
V RCA

## TO THE DEVIL A DAUGHTER ** 18
Peter Sykes UK/WEST GERMANY 1976
*Richard Widmark, Christopher Lee, Nastassja Kinski, Denholm Elliott, Honor Blackman, Michael Goodliffe, Eva Marie Meineke, Anthony Valentine, Derek Francis, Isabella Telezynska, Irene Prador, Brian Wilde, Frances De La Tour*
A girl is promised to a group of Satanists who want to dedicate her to the Devil, but an American occultist novelist intervenes in the struggle for her soul, aided by the rituals he finds described in an ancient book. A muddled and cumbersome adaptation lacking both force and pace. Written by Chris Wicking.
Aka: DIE BRAUT DES SATANS
Boa: novel by Dennis Wheatley.

HOR 90 min; 89 min (WHV) (ort 93 min)
B,V TEVP; WHV (VHS only)

## TO THE LIGHTHOUSE *** PG
Colin Gregg UK 1983
*Rosemary Harris, Michael Gough, Suzanne Bertish, Pippa Guard, Lyndsey Baxter, T.P. McKenna, Kenneth Branagh*
A TV adaptation of Woolf's autobiographical novel about a family on holiday in Cornwall in the hot summer of 1914, when the Edwardian era was soon to come to a brutal end with the advent of WW1.
Boa: novel by Virginia Woolf.

DRA 116 min mTV
B,V BBC

## TOBRUK ** PG
Arthur Hiller USA 1967
*Rock Hudson, George Peppard, Nigel Green, Guy Stockwell, Jack Watson, Leo Gordon, Liam Redmond, Norman Rossington, Percy Herbert*
A wildly inaccurate WW2 North African action film, based on the British raid on the port of Tobruk, in a desperate bid to destroy Rommel's fuel dumps. This

factual basis is however, soon left behind in favour of a fictional view of how Hollywood won the war. As German Jews, Peppard and Stockwell are never less than ludicrous, the other characters faring little better. Battle footage was later used in RAID ON ROMMEL. The screenplay is by Leo Gordon.

WAR                           105 min (ort 110 min)
B,V                                              CIC

**TOBY McTEAGUE ***                           PG
Jean-Claude Lord      CANADA                 1985
*Yannick Bisson, Andrew Bednarski, Winston Rekert, George Clutesi, Liliane Clune, Timothy Webber, Stephanie Morgenstern, Evan Adams, Hamish McEwan, Tom Rack, Anthony Levinson, Mark Kulik, Joanne Vannicola, Doug Price, Ian Finlay*
A boy living in the Canadian wilds takes an interest in dog-sled racing, while his widowed father finds a new romance. A pleasant outdoors adventure.

A/AD                                        92 min
B,V                                            VIR

**TOBY TYLER ***                              Uc
Charles Barton       USA                     1959
*Kevin Corcoran, Henry Calvin, Gene Sheldon, Bob Sweeney, Richard Eastham, James Drury*
A young orphan boy runs away to join a travelling circus and becomes a star, following a series of adventures. A turn-of-the-century Disney offering that offers pleasant enjoyment of an undemanding nature.
Aka: TOBY TYLER, OR TEN WEEKS WITH A CIRCUS
Boa: novel by James Otis Kaler.

COM                           90 min (ort 96 min)
B,V                             RNK L/A; WDV

**TODD KILLINGS, THE ***
Barry Shear          USA                     1970
*Richard Thomas, Robert F. Lyons, Edward Asner, Belinda Montgomery, Barbara Bel Geddes, Gloria Grahame, Sherry Miles*
Factually based psychological study of a bisexual, whose behaviour drove him to commit acts of murder and rape. Not a pleasant film, but tautly made and fairly absorbing. Written by Dennis Murphy and Joe L. Oliansky. The music is by Leonard Rosenman.
Aka: DANGEROUS FRIEND, A

THR                                         93 min
B,V                                            VDM

**TOGETHER? ***                               18
Armenia Balducci     ITALY                   1979
*Jacqueline Bisset, Maximilian Schell, Terence Stamp, Monica Guerritore, Gian Luca Venantini, Pietro Biondi, Birgita Hamer, Francesa DeSapio, Carla Tato*
Charts the stormy course of a couple's relationship during a single weekend, in which they argue and talk incessantly, in this unpatented (as yet) certain cure for insomnia. However, more sensitive souls may merely be left with a headache. Originally the film was entitled "I Love You, I Love You Not". I think not.
Aka: I LOVE YOU, I LOVE YOU NOT

DRA                           86 min (ort 100 min)
B,V                                            CBS

**TOM BROWN'S SCHOOL DAYS ***                  U
Gordon Parry         UK                      1951
*John Howard Davies, Robert Newton, Diana Wynyard, Hermione Baddeley, James Hayter, Kathleen Byron, John Charlesworth, John Forrest, Michael Hordern, Max Bygraves, Francis De Wolff, Amy Veness, Brian Worth, Rachel Gurney*
A later version of this novel of Victorian school life, with a youngster finding his first years at Rugby harsh and brutal, but eventually exerting a civilising influence on those around him. Quite competently made, but clinical and somewhat stilted; the 1940 film is the better of the two. Written by Noel Langley.

Boa: novel by Thomas Hughes.
DRA                           93 min (ort 96 min) B/W
V                                            BRAVE

**TOM HORN ***                                15
William Wiard        USA                     1979
*Steve McQueen, Linda Evans, Richard Farnsworth, Billy Green Bush, Slim Pickens, Peter Canon, Elisha Cook Jr, Roy Jenson, James Kline, Geoffrey Lewis, Harry Northup, Steve Oliver*
An ex-cavalry scout gets a job working with cattle, and suffers an unjust end when he is hanged for murder after being framed. A kind of semi-Western with the film revolving around the last days of the title character. McQueen lacks much of his old charisma in this, his penultimate role, but the film is beautifully shot. Written by Thomas McGuane and Bid Shrake, and to some extent based on the alleged autobiography of Tom Horn. See also MISTER HORN.
Boa: book by Tom Horn.
WES 93 min (ort 97 min) (Cut at film release by 39 sec)
B,V                                            WHV

**TOM JONES ****
Tony Richardson      UK                      1963
*Albert Finney, Susannah York, Hugh Griffith, Edith Evans, Joyce Redman, Joan Greenwood, Diane Cilento, David Tomlinson, Rosalind Atkinson, David Warner, George A. Cooper, Angela Baddeley, Joyce Redman, Rosalind Knight*
A bawdy romp through 17th century England, with foundling Finney marrying the daughter of the squire after many adventures. An excellent cast and superb settings made this the huge box office success it deserved to become. Written by John Osborne. AA: Pic, Dir, Screen (Adapt) (John Osborne), Score (Orig) (John Addison).
Boa: novel by Henry Fielding.
COM                           122 min (ort 129 min)
B,V                                            TEVP

**TOM SAWYER ***                               U
Don Taylor           USA                     1973
*Johnnie Whitaker, Jeff East, Jodie Foster, Warren Oates, Celeste Holm, Noah Keen, Lucille Benson, Henry Jones, Dub Taylor, Richard Eastham, Susan Joyce, Sandy Kenyon, Joshua Hill Lewis, Steve Hogg, Sean Summers, Kevin Jefferson*
A slow, careful, detailed and unmoving version of this classic tale of boyhood adventures. This fourth adaptation of Twain's yarn is given the dubious benefit of Richard and Robert Sherman songs to help the action along.
Boa: novel The Adventures Of Tom Sawyer by Mark Twain.
JUV                           95 min (ort 103 min)
V                                              WHV

**TOM, DICK AND HARRY ***                      U
Garson Kanin         USA                     1941
*Ginger Rogers, George Murphy, Alan Marshal, Burgess Meredith, Joe Cunningham, Jane Seymour, Phil Silvers, Lenore Lonergan*
A sharp and lively comedy about a girl so popular that she has no less than three boyfriends, and they all want to marry her. A highlight of the film is Silvers, memorable as an offensive ice-cream seller. Written by Paul Jarrico and later remade in 1957 as THE GIRL MOST LIKELY.
COM                           83 min (ort 86 min) B/W
V                                              VCC

**TOMB, THE ***                               15
Fred Olen Ray        USA                     1985
*Cameron Mitchell, John Carradine, Richard Alan Hench, Susan Stokey, Michelle Bauer, David Pearson, George Hoth, Sybil Danning (Sybelle Danninger), Stu Weltman, Victor Von Wright, Frank MacDonald, Jack Frankel, Peter Conway*

Loosely based on Stoker's horror story, this tells of an Egyptian princess who reincarnates in order to obtain a magic amulet she needs to ensure her survival. A campy horror yarn of three parts tedium to one part chills. See also BLOOD FROM THE MUMMY'S TOMB and THE AWAKENING, two other versions of this story.
Boa: novel Jewel Of The Seven Stars by Bram Stoker.
HOR                                          89 min; 84 min (VCC)
B,V                                 FRON/GHV; VCC (VHS only)

## TOMBOY *                                                15
Herb Freed                  USA                          1984
*Betsy Russell, Jerry Dinome, Kristi Somers, Richard Erdman, Philip Sterling, Cynthia Ann Thompson, Eric Douglas, Toby Iland*
A female garage mechanic takes on the local racing champion outracing him in an attempt to win his romantic interest. A standard teen sex comedy with neither wit nor imagination.
COM                                          90 min (ort 92 min)
V                                                         RCA

## TOMBS OF THE BLIND DEAD ***                             18
Amando de Ossario
                          PORTUGAL/SPAIN                  1971
*Cesar Burner, Lone Fleming, Helen Harp, Maria Silva, Joseph Telman, Juan Cortes, Rufino Ingles, Antonio Orengo, Veronica Limera, Simon Arriaga Garibaldi, Francisco Sanz, Carmen Gir, Andres Speizer*
Devil worshipping Knights Templars were executed in the 13th century, and initially left unburied so that birds pecked out their eyes. When some youngsters stray into an abandoned cemetery, the Templars rise from their graves in search of blood, locating their victims by sound. An effective film of uneven scripting but chilling detail. Followed by THE RETURN OF THE EVIL DEAD, the first of three sequels. See also NIGHT OF THE SEAGULLS.
Aka: A NOITE DO TERROR CEGO; BLIND DEAD, THE: CRYPT OF THE BLIND DEATH, THE; LA NOCHE DE LA MUERTA CIEGA; LA NOCHE DEL TERROR CIEGO; NIGHT OF THE BLIND DEAD
HOR                               80 min Cut (1 min 57 sec)
B,V                                             PRV L/A; CH5

## TOMMY ***                                               15
Ken Russell                 UK                            1975
*Oliver Reed, Ann-Margret, Roger Daltrey, Elton John, Eric Clapton, Keith Moon, Robert Powell, Tina Turner, Jack Nicholson, Paul Nicholas, Victoria Russell, Barry Winch, Ben Aris, Mary Holland, Jennifer Blake, Susan Baker*
The idea for this film was developed from a rock opera album by the rock group The Who. It tells of a deaf blind and dumb boy who has an amazing ability to play on pinball machines, and who rises to the position of a kind of modern day saviour to the young. The use of multi-channel sound will be lost on TV, but the customary assault on the senses on the part of this director is thankfully muted. Written by Russell.
Boa: record album and rock opera by Pete Townsend and The Who.
MUS                                        108 min (ort 111 min)
B, V/sh                                    TEVP; WHV (VHS only)

## TOMMY THE TOREADOR **                                    U
John Paddy Carstairs        UK                           1959
*Tommy Steele, Janet Munro, Sidney James, Noel Purcell, Kenneth Williams, Warren Mitchell*
Lightweight musical-comedy in which Steele plays a sailor who's stranded in Seville and takes the place of a bullfighter who has been framed on smuggling charges. Pleasant enough in its way, and largely sustained by Steele's chirpy personality.
MUS                                                     83 min
V                                                        WHV

## TOMORROW NEVER COMES *                                   15
Peter Collinson             CANADA/UK                    1977
*Oliver Reed, Raymond Burr, Susan George, John Ireland, Stephen McHattie, Donald Pleasence, John Osborne, Paul Koslo, Cec Linder, Richard Donat, Dolores Etienne, Sammy Snyder, Jane Eastwood*
A young man goes crazy when he discovers his girlfriend has been unfaithful and a shooting takes place, with a police chief finding himself confronted with a siege on his last day in the force. A violent melodrama of little appeal.
DRA                                      109 min; 86 min (VIR)
B,V                                            VCL/CBS; VIR

## TONGS **
Alan Metzger                USA                          1989
*Louis Gossett Jr*
An anthropology professor gets a Chinese student to apply for a prestigious fellowship. However, gang warfare breaks out in Chinatown and the police call in the professor, as his expertise is of value in solving a Tong murder. Meanwhile, the student has returned to his Tong godfather and when the professor contacts him he is drawn into the conflict. One of several films in a series. See also SLEEP WELL, PROFESSOR OLIVER and GIDEON'S WAR.
A/AD                                                 90 min mTV
V                                                        CIC

## TONGS: A NEW YORK CHINATOWN                              18
STORY **
Philip Y.P. Chan            HONG KONG                    1986
*Simon Yam, Larry Tan, Anthony Gioia, Christopher O'Connor, Ovima Han, Daisy Yong, Peter C.M. Chan, Felipe Luciano, Neil Mauriellio, Ian Anthony Leung*
Story set against the background of New York's Chinatown and Hong Kong, and telling of a series of gang wars that are fought over drug dealing. A violent and brutal tale. Cut before video submission by 13 sec.
Aka: TONGS; TONGS: A CHINATOWN STORY
A/AD                                        87 min (ort 90 min)
B,V                                             IVS L/A; BRAVE

## TONKA **                                                  U
Lewis R. Foster             USA                          1958
*Sal Mineo, Philip Carey, Jerome Courtland, Rafael Campos, H.M. Wynant, Joy Page, Britt Lomond, Herbert Rudley, Sydney Smith, John War Eagle, Gregg "Buzz" Henry*
A young Sioux Indian becomes attached to a white stallion after taming him, but they are parted and he is only re-united with him at Little Big Horn. A low-budget version of Custer's Last Stand that is spoilt by weak plotting and poor action sequences. Written by Lewis R. Foster and Lillie Hayward.
Aka: HORSE NAMED COMANCHE, A
Boa: novel Comanche by David Appel.
JUV                                        93 min (ort 97 min)
B,V                                                      WDV

## TOO BEAUTIFUL TO DIE ***                                 18
Dario Piana                 ITALY                        1989
*Francois Gendron, Florence Guerin, Randy Ingermann*
A video producer in Milan holds a party to celebrate the end of a project, but during the celebrations a young model is raped while everyone looks on and applauds. The victim flees in the producer's car, but the following day her remains are found in the abandoned and burnt-out vehicle. Soon all the party guests find their lives in danger in this stylish and clever thriller that never reveals its hand until the very end.
THR                                                     95 min
V                                                        CFD

## TOO GOOD TO BE TRUE **                                   15
Christian I. Nyby II        USA                          1988
*Loni Anderson, Patrick Duffy, Glynnis O'Connor,*

*Julie Harris, Larry Drake, James B. Sikking*
Ignoring the warnings of his friends, a lonely widow
becomes involved with a seductive blonde who soon
begins to show possessive tendencies, and whose
beauty masks a murderous nature. A competent but
overstretched remake of the 1945 film "Leave Her To
Heaven".
Boa: novel Leave Her To Heaven by Ben Ames
Williams.
DRA                              95 min (ort 100 min) mTV
B,V                                                    CBS

## TOO HOT TO HANDLE *
Don Schain              USA                      1976
*Cheri Caffaro, Sharon Ipale, John van Dreelen, Vic
Diaz, Jordan Rosengarten, Corinne Calvet, Butz
Aquino*
A detective gets involved with a hit-lady he is
investigating, and they become embroiled in various
adventures in Manila. A low-grade mixture of action
and sexploitation. The music is by Hugo Montenegro.
A/AD                              84 min (ort 90 min)
B,V,V2                                                 VPD

## TOO LATE THE HERO **                            15
Robert Aldrich          USA                      1969
*Michael Caine, Cliff Robertson, Henry Fonda, Ian
Bannen, Harry Andrews, Denholm Elliott, Ronald
Fraser, Percy Herbert*
Two soldiers are sent on a suicide mission, to an island
held partly by the Japanese and partly by the Allied
troops during WW2. A cat-and-mouse game takes
place between them and a Japanese officer, in this
well-handled but unremarkable actioner. The script is
by Aldrich and Lukas Heller.
Aka: SUICIDE RUN
Boa: novel by W. Hughes.
WAR           133 min; 127 min (VCC) (ort 144 min)
B,V                              GHV; VCC (VHS only)

## TOO MANY CROOKS ***                             U
Mario Zampi             UK                        1958
*George Cole, Sidney James, Bernard Bresslaw, Brenda
De Banzie, Terry-Thomas, Vera Day, Delphi
Lawrence, John Le Mesurier, Sydney Tafler, Rosalie
Ashley, Nicholas Parsons, Terry Scott, John Stuart,
Vilma Ann Leslie, Edie Martin*
A gang of inept crooks plot a kidnapping in an effort to
get a businessman to part up with some money. A
lightweight black comedy with a good chase sequence
and a nice performance from Terry-Thomas. Written
by Michael Pertwee.
COM                            82 min (ort 87 min) B/W
V                                                      VCC

## TOO MUCH *                                      U
Eric Rochat             USA                       1987
*Masao Fukazawa, Bridgette Anderson, Hiroyuki
Watanabe, Char Fontana*
Set in Japan, this empty and insufferably cute tale
follows the adventures of a young girl and her robot
friend, an invention of her scientist uncle.
JUV                              85 min (ort 89 min)
B,V                                                    WHV

## TOO YOUNG THE HERO **                           15
Buzz Kulik              USA                       1988
*Ricky Schroder, John De Vries, Debra Mooney, Mary
Louise Parker, Rick Warner*
A dramatised account of the exploits of Calvin Gra-
ham, who joined the US Navy at the age of 12 and saw
a good deal of action during WW2. Despite recreating
some of Calvin's more harrowing experiences, includ-
ing a brutal sexual attack whilst in prison, the film
conveys little more than a sense of blandness –
Schroder simply fails to convince in the lead role.
WAR                             90 min (ort 100 min) mTV
B/h, V/h                                               ODY

## TOO YOUNG TO DIE: A TRUE STORY ***            18
Robert Markowitz        USA                       1989
*Michael Tucker, Juliette Lewis, Michael O'Keefe*
Harrowing account (based on a true story) of a
15-year-old girl who was raped by her stepfather and
abused by just about everyone else, and finally found
herself in a condemned cell after her murder of her
soldier boyfriend. Told by the girl's lawyer in a series
of flashbacks, this is a solid and well-handled drama.
DRA                                               88 min
V/h                                                    ODY

## TOOLBOX MURDERS, THE *
Dennis Donnelly         USA                       1978
*Cameron Mitchell, Pamelyn Ferdin, Wesley Evre,
Nicholas Beauvy, Kelly Nichols, Tim Donnelly, Aneta
Coraut, Evelyn Guerrero, Marcie Drake, Faith
McSwain, Mariane Walter*
This violent and gory effort features graphic murders
of women with various hardware appliances. The
culprit is a demented caretaker who blames the death
of his daughter on the "corruption" of women in
general, and pretty ones in particular. Not a reward-
ing film, nor a particularly well made one.
HOR                                               93 min
B,V                                                    HOK

## TOOTSIE ***                                     15
Sydney Pollack          USA                       1982
*Dustin Hoffman, Teri Garr, Jessica Lange, Dabney
Coleman, Charles Durning, Bill Murray, Sydney
Pollack, Geena Davis, George Gaynes, Estelle Getty,
Christine Ebersole*
A failed actor is desperate to raise money to finance
his buddy's play. He dresses as a woman and lands a
role in a hospital soap. He falls for one of the stars, but
doesn't dare tell the girl he's not half the woman she
thinks he is. Entertaining and lightweight, with
Hoffman giving a fine performance, but Lange a
somewhat less memorable one. The script is by Larry
Gelbart and Murray Shisgal. See also HOLLYWOOD
SUPERSTAR. AA: S. Actress (Lange).
Boa: story by Don McGuire.
COM                                              115 min
V                                                      RCA

## TOP GUN ***                                     15
Tony Scott              USA                       1986
*Tom Cruise, Kelly McGillis, Anthony Edwards, Val
Kilmer, Tom Skerritt, John Stockwell, Michael
Ironside, Barry Tubb, Rick Rossovich, James Tolkan,
Meg Ryan*
Action tale filmed at the Miramar Naval Base in San
Diego, where a bunch of F-14 pilots compete for the
honour of becoming "Top Gun". Cruise as one such
pilot, falls for McGillis whilst training at the weapons
school. A contrived blend of memorable action sequ-
ences and stilted romantic ones. Written by Jim Cash
and Jack Epps Jr, with music by Harold Faltermeyer.
AA: Song ("Take My Breath Away" – Giorgio Moroder
– music/Tom Whitlock – lyrics).
A/AD                             105 min (ort 110 min)
V/sh                                                   CIC

## TOP HAT ****                                    U
Mark Sandrich           USA                       1935
*Fred Astaire, Ginger Rogers, Helen Broderick,
Edward Everett Horton, Eric Blore, Erik Rhodes*
The charming story of a couple and their romance,
which suffers various complications arising from
mistaken identity. A classic musical with Astaire and
Rogers at their liveliest. Memorable numbers include
"Cheek To Cheek", "Top Hat, White Tie, And Tails"
and "Isn't This A Lovely Day To Be Caught In The
Rain". Music and lyrics are by Irving Berlin, with
choreography by Hermes Pan. The script is by Dwight
Taylor and Allan Scott.
Boa: play by Alexander Farago and Alasdar Laszlo.

MUS      97 min; 93 min (CH5) (ort 101 min) B/W
B,V      HER; TEVP; CH5 (VHS only)

## TOP KIDS ***      U
Michael Pfleghar    USA    1987
*Niki Lauda, Ross Harris, Jared Rushton, Anthony Ko,
Scott Neames*
When one of three young computer hackers wins a
competition to an international car show, that has on
display a sophisticated computer on wheels, they
attempt to exploit the situation by tapping into its
data banks. However, the computer takes over and
carries the youngster off on an exciting adventure.
A/AD      75 min
V      HER

## TOP LINE **      18
Ted Archer    USA    1987
*Franco Nero, George Kennedy, Deborah B. Moore,
William Berger*
A boozy journalist tries to sell some jewels from a
hoard of Aztec treasure he found, but a series of
strange murders starts. Fair.
A/AD      90 min
B,V      TGP

## TOP OF THE HEAP *
Christopher St John    USA    1972
*Christopher St John, Paula Kelly, Florence St Peter*
A black policeman tires of his job and home life and
runs off with his mistress, but then changes his mind
and tries to make a fresh start.
THR      79 min (ort 91 min)
B,V      ATA L/A; APX

## TOP SECRET! *      15
Jim Abrahams/David Zucker/Jerry Zucker
    USA    1984
*Val Kilmer, Lucy Gutteridge, Christopher Villiers,
Jeremy Kemp, Omar Sharif, Warren Clarke, Peter
Cushing, Michael Gough, Harry Ditson, Jim Carter*
A rock star on tour in East Germany becomes involved
in espionage, in this uninventive and patchy spoof
that has Kilmer embroiled in the schemes of spies
from both sides of the Iron Curtain. From the team
that produced the far superior AIRPLANE! and
written by Jerry and David Zucker, Abrahams and
Martin Burke.
COM      86 min (ort 90 min) Cut (8 sec)
B,V      CBS L/A; CIC (VHS only)

## TOPKAPI **      U
Jules Dassin    USA    1964
*Melina Mercouri, Peter Ustinov, Maximilian Schell,
Robert Morley, Akim Tamiroff, Gilles Segal, Jess
Hahn, Despo Diamantidou*
An international gang of thieves try to steal a jewelled
dagger from an Istanbul museum. An overlong and
only slightly amusing comedy caper, filmed in Istan-
bul, with initial excitement soon evaporating until a
finale that is reminiscent of "Rififi". The attractive
score is by Manos Hadjidakis. Written by Monja
Danischewsky. AA: S. Actor (Ustinov).
Boa: novel The Light Of Day by Eric Ambler.
COM      119 min (ort 122 min)
B,V      WHV

## TOPPER **
Charles S. Dubin    USA    1979
*Kate Jackson, Andrew Stevens, Jack Warden, Rue
McClanahan, James Karen, Macon McCalman,
Charles Siebert, Larry Gelman, Gloria LeRoy, Estelle
Omens, Lois Areno, Frances Bay, Gregory Chase, Ellen
March, Mary Peters*
Remake of the 1937 film about a rich couple who die in
a car crash, and find that if they're going to get to
heaven they have to do at least one good deed. So they
decide to help their lawyer regain his self respect and
resist his domineering wife. A sugary, silly confection

that leaves no aftertaste.
Boa: novel by Thorne Smith.
COM      93 min (ort 100 min) mTV
B,V      VTC L/A

## TOR: MIGHTY WARRIOR *      PG
Antonio Leonviola
    FRANCE/ITALY    1983
*Joe Robinson, Bella Cortez, Harry Baird, Susy
Anderson, Janine Hendy, Carla Foscari, Antonio
Leonviola, Ermino Spalla, Claudia Capone, Alberto
Cevenini, Thea Fleming, Jose Torres*
A warrior uses his powers to rescue his peaceful
people from a strange tribe in yet another low-budget
costumed epic.
Aka: TARZAN, KING OF BRUTE FORCE; TARZAN,
ROI DE LA FORCE BRUTALE; TAUR THE
MIGHTY; THAUR, KING OF BRUTE FORCE;
THOR AND THE AMAZON WOMEN; TOR
FAN      93 min
B,V,V2      VPD

## TORA! TORA! TORA! ****      U
Richard Fleischer/Ray Kellogg/Toshio Masuda/Kinji
Fukasuki    JAPAN/USA    1970
*Martin Balsam, Joseph Cotten, James Whitmore,
Jason Robards, E.G. Marshall, Soh Yamamura,
Takahiro Tamura, Edward Andrews, Leon Ames,
George Macready, Toshio Masuda, Kinji Fukasuki,
Tatsuya Mihashi, Wesley Addy*
Pearl Harbour as seen from both viewpoints. An
overlong and over-elaborate recreation of the actual
attack, that badly needed the light touch of Kurosawa.
(He wanted to do the Japanese parts but was not given
the chance.) Written by Larry Forrester, Hideo Oguni
and Ryuzo Kikushima. AA: Effects (Vis) (A.D. Flow-
ers/L.B. Abbott).
WAR      144 min
V/h      CBS

## TORCH SONG TRILOGY ***      15
Paul Bogart    USA    1988
*Matthew Broderick, Anne Bancroft, Harvey Fierstein,
Brian Kerwin, Karen Young, Charles Pierce*
An examination of nine years in the life of gay New
York female impersonator Arnold Beckoff and his
search for understanding in the heterosexual world. A
touching drama that follows his struggles with his
domineering mother, his unfaithful lover and his
adopted son. Adapted by Fierstein from his Broadway
play.
Boa: play by Harvey Fierstein.
DRA      115 min (ort 117 min)
B,V      RCA

## TORCHLIGHT *      18
Tom Wright    USA    1984
*Pamela Sue Martin, Ian McShane, Steve Railsback, Al
Corley, Rita Taggart, Rudy Ramos*
A couple's happy marriage is threatened when the
husband becomes hooked on cocaine. A sincere but
cliched film that is ruined by melodramatic treatment
and a self-righteous tone.
DRA      93 min
B,V      AVA

## TORMENT, THE **      15
Marcello Andrei    ITALY    1974
*Bradford Dillman, Marina Malfatti, Gig Young, Delia
Boccardo, Lucretia Love, Adriano Amidei Migano,
Gigi Casellato, Vittorio Mangano, Mario Garibba,
Luigi Antonio Guerra*
A woman who has psychic powers witnesses a fatal car
crash, and finds that she has "inherited" the dead
woman's pregnancy.
Aka: BLACK RIBBON FOR DEBORAH; DEBORAH;
UN FIOCCO NERO PER DEBORAH
HOR      85 min (ort 101 min)
B,V      CBS

**TORMENTORS, THE \***       18
Boris Eagle     USA       1986
*James Craig, Chris Noel, Anthony Eisley, William Dooley*
A man joins a gang of murderous neo-Nazi thugs, to get his revenge for the death of his girlfriend at their hands. A debased wallow in violence and meaningless death, disguised as entertainment.
DRA       77 min (ort 85 min) Cut (1 min 57 sec)
B,V       IVS L/A; TOW

**TORN ALLEGIANCE \*\***       15
Alan Nathanson     USA       1984
*Jonathan Morris, Marius Weyers, Shelagh Halliday, Ronald France, Trevyn McDowell, Ron Smerczak, Joe Maytham*
The Boer War between the British and the descendants of the Dutch settlers in South Africa at the turn of the century, forms the historical background to this tale of divided families and loyalties.
DRA       92 min (ort 105 min)
B,V,V2       MED

**TORN BETWEEN TWO LOVERS \*\***       PG
Delbert Mann     USA       1979
*Lee Remick, Joseph Bologna, George Peppard, Giorgio Tozzi, Molly Cheek, Kay Hawtrey, Derrick Jones, Murphy Cross, Martin Shakar, Andrea Martin, Mary Long, Lois Markle, Tom Harvey, Jess Osuna, Sean McCann, David Hughes*
A married woman meets a man at an airport, and an affair develops which threatens her marriage. A pleasant but undemanding romantic drama.
Boa: story by Doris Silverton and Rita Lakin.
DRA       97 min (ort 100 min) mTV
B,V,V2       GHV; ODY (VHS only)

**TORN BETWEEN TWO VALUES \*\***       U
Buzz Kulik     USA       1968
*Lee Marvin, Bradford Dillman, Vera Miles, Peter Graves, Lloyd Nolan, Murray Hamilton*
Adapted from the TV film "The Case Against Sergeant Ryker", this follows the trial of a soldier accused of being a traitor during the Korean War. A competent drama that would be unmemorable indeed were it not for Marvin's excellent performance in the role of the accused.
Aka: SERGEANT RYKER
DRA       85 min
V       MANHAT; GLOB; KRP

**TORNADO \*\***       18
Anthony M. Dawson (Antonio Margheriti)
      ITALY       1983
*Timothy Brent (Giancarlo Prete), Tony Marsina, Alan Collins*
Despite the fact that the Vietnam War is coming to an end, a helicopter captain continues to send his men out on suicide missions. When one GI decides to desert, a chase is mounted to bring him back. A mediocre war yarn.
Aka: TORNADO STRIKE FORCE
WAR       87 min (ort 90 min)
B,V,V2       MED

**TORPEDOED \*** 
Paul Donovan     CANADA       1979
*Alan MacGillivray, Lynette Louise, Jeff Pustil, Terry-David Despres, Mahar Boutros, Bill Papps, Richard Rebiere, Dug Rotstein, Lorna Ryan, Fred Wadden, Gary Vermeir, Andrea Zabudan, Sandy Abbass, Hiro Akiyama, Bob Backen*
An incompetent submarine captain torpedoes a liner after mistaking it for a Japanese aircraft carrier, and two girl survivors of the attack add further to the general chaos on board. A tasteless and unfunny comedy.
Aka: SOUTH PACIFIC 1942

COM       80 min (ort 85 min)
B,V       EIV

**TORTURE ZONE, THE \***       18
Juan Ibanez     MEXICO       1969
*Boris Karloff, Isela Vega, Carlos East, Andres Garcia, Julissa, Eva Muller, Yerye Beirute, Sandra Chavez, Rafael Munoz (Santanon), Pamela Rosas, Fuensanta*
A prehistoric rocklike life-form is discovered, which lives on a substance derived from the blood of women who have been frightened. The title refers to the chamber victims are taken to, by the obligatory mad scientist. Karloff is little in evidence in this dull offering, the film concentrating on the scientist's greedy underlings. One of Karloff's last performances and an unworthy end to a long and varied screen career.
Aka: CHAMBER OF FEAR; DANCE OF DEATH; FEAR CHAMBER, THE; LA CAMERA DEL TERROR
HOR       70 min (ort 90 min) Cut (1 min 3 sec)
B,V       CINE

**TOTAL DEFIANCE \*\***       15
Bruce Morrison     USA       1989
*Matthew Hunter, Pilisi Mark, Peter Bland*
Standard blend of tough urban action and romance, with a youngster giving up his old street-gang ways when his best friend is killed and he falls in love.
A/AD       89 min
V       BIGPIC

**TOTAL RECALL \*\*\***       18
Paul Verhoeven     USA       1990
*Arnold Schwarzenegger, Rachel Ticotin, Sharon Stone, Michael Ironside, Ronny Cox, Marshall Bell, Mel Johnson Jr*
A spectacular expansion of Dick's multi-layered story, that adds a dose of gory violence and some remarkable effects. Schwarzenegger plays a man whose urge to travel to Mars leads him to purchase a memory of one such trip, from which he learns that his true identity has been erased and that he must go to Mars to discover why. Visual effects are by Dream Quest, and Rob Bottin of ROBOCOP did the special make-up effects. The music is by Jerry Goldsmith.
Boa: short story We Can Remember It For You Wholesale by Philip K. Dick.
FAN       109 min
V       GHV

**TOUCH AND GO \***       15
Peter Maxwell     AUSTRALIA       1980
*Wendy Hughes, Chantal Contouri, Carmen Duncan, Jeanie Drynan, Liddy Clark, Jon English*
A group of women take to crime to aid their favourite charitable causes in a forgettable comedy that has little entertainment value or wit.
COM       88 min (ort 92 min)
B,V       MED

**TOUCH AND GO \*\***       15
Robert Mandel     USA       1985
*Michael Keaton, Maria Tucci, Maria Conchita Alonso, Ajay Naidu, Max Wright, Lara Jill Miller*
The story of an ice-hockey player who is mugged by a gang of youths, but catches one of the boys and escorts him home to his divorced mother, to whom he finds himself so attracted that a romance soon blossoms. Sincere performances sustain a thin and unconvincing blend of humour and sentiment.
COM       97 min (ort 101 min)
B,V       VES

**TOUCH ME NOT \*** 
Douglas Fifthian     UK       1974
*Lee Remick, Michael Hinz, Ivan Desny, Ingrid Garbo*
Thriller about an industrial spy exploiting a man's secretary to gather information about him. An undis-

tinguished and deservedly obscure film.
Aka: HUNTED, THE
THR                                      82 min (ort 84 min)
B,V,V2                                                    INT

## TOUCH OF CLASS, A **
Melvin Frank            UK                                 PG
                                                         1973
George Segal, Glenda Jackson, Paul Sorvino,
Hildegard Neil, Cec Linder, Mary Barclay, K. Callan,
Michael Elwyn, Samantha Weston, Michael McVey,
Edward Kemp, Lisa Vanderpump, Ian Thompson,
Donald Hewlett, David Healy
A married man has a casual affair with a dress
designer, but what was initially no more than a brief
fling becomes more complex when his passion deepens
into real love. A highly over-rated and contrived
romantic comedy, that leaves one curiously detached
from the proceedings. Written by Melvin Frank and
Jack Rose. AA: Actress (Jackson).
COM                                              106 min
B,V                              CBS; HOLLY (VHS only)

## TOUCH OF LOVE, A **                                    15
Waris Hussein           UK                               1969
Sandy Dennis, Ian McKellen, Michael Coles, John
Standing, Eleanor Bron, Deborah Stanford, Roger
Hammond, Margaret Denham, Rachel Kempson
A pregnant research graduate in London decides to
have an abortion but then has misgivings. A thought-
ful and surprisingly unsentimental view of this
formerly controversial subject.
Aka: THANK YOU VERY MUCH
Boa: novel The Millstone by Margaret Drabble.
DRA                                     102 min (ort 107 min)
V                                                        WHV

## TOUCH, THE **
Ingmar Bergman   SWEDEN/USA                              1970
Elliott Gould, Bibi Andersson, Max Von Sydow, Sheila
Reid, Steffan Hallerstam, Maria Nolgard, Barbro
Hiort Af Ornas, Ake Lindstrom, Mimi Wahlander,
Elsa Ebbesen.
Story of a woman who falls for an American academic
and leaves her husband. Gould is miscast and this
film, Bergman's first English language one, was not a
success. Unfortunately, the characters seem contrived
and out of place, mouthing their lines in a foreign
tongue and from a script that lacks the usual flair of
this director's writing.
Aka: BERORINGEN
DRA                                              112 min
B,V                                                      GHV

## TOUCHED BY LOVE ***                                     U
Gus Trikonis            USA                              1980
Deborah Raffin, Diana Lane, Michael Learned,
Cristina Raines, Mary Wickes, Clu Gulager, John
Amos, Clive Shalom
A nurse at a children's home becomes deeply involved
with a young girl suffering from cerebral palsy, who is
uncommunicative until she helps her establish a
pen-pal friendship with her idol Elvis Presley. A
sentimental but quite engrossing tale, based on the
memoirs of student nurse Lena Canada. Written by
Hesper Anderson.
Aka: TO ELVIS, WITH LOVE
DRA             92 min; 90 min (MOIRA) (ort 95 min)
B,V                              HOK L/A; MOIRA

## TOUGH *
Horace Jackson          USA                              1974
Dian Gossett, Renny Roker, Sandy Reed, Rich Holmes
Drama telling the story of an 11-year-old juvenile
delinquent and his home background.
DRA                                               87 min
B,V                                                      WAL

## TOUGH ENOUGH *                                          15
Richard Fleischer       USA        1981 (released 1983)

Dennis Quaid, Stan Shaw, Carlene Watkins, Pam
Grier, Warren Oates, Wilford Brimley, Bruce McGill,
Fran Ryan
An aspiring Country singer turns amateur boxer, as a
way of getting enough exposure to boost his singing
career. A bland and predictable musical clone of
ROCKY, that takes a fine cast, and does nothing with
it.
COM                                     102 min (ort 107 min)
B,V                                                      CBS

## TOUGH GUY *                                             18
Pao Houeh-Li       HONG KONG
Chia Ling, Chen Hsing, Chen Kuan-Tai, Ouyang Sha
Fei
Ching dynasty martial arts adventure with a tough
detective tracking down the killer of a concubine and
discovering a sinister political plot behind it all. A
very uninspired treatment of a fairly good idea.
Aka: CHUEH-TOU LAO-HU CHUANG; TOUGH
GUYS
MAR   82 min; 88 min (SHEP) Cut (3 sec in addition to
film cuts)
B,V                                      VPD L/A; SHEP

## TOUGH GUYS **                                           15
Jeff Kanew              USA                              1986
Kirk Douglas, Burt Lancaster, Charles Durning,
Alexis Smith, Dana Carvey, Darlanne Fluegel, Eli
Wallach, Monty Ash, Bill Barty
A blend of action and comedy that tells of two bank
robbers who are released on parole after 30 years and
have difficulties adjusting to the 1980s, so they set
about planning their next heist. Douglas and Lancas-
ter work well together, but the film slowly runs out of
steam and becomes both sentimental and puerile.
Written by James Orr and Jim Cruickshank.
COM                                     100 min (ort 104 min)
B,V                                                      RNK

## TOUGH GUYS DON'T DANCE ***                              18
Norman Mailer           USA                              1987
Ryan O'Neal, Isabella Rossellini, Debra Sandlund,
Wings Hauser, Lawrence Tierney, Frances Fisher,
John Bedford Lloyd, Penn Jillette, R. Patrick Sullivan,
John Snyder, Stephen Morrow, Clarence Williams III
A black comedy-thriller telling of a writer who is
unable to clear himself of murder charges with regard
to his wife and mistress, and sets out to discover those
responsible. An overwrought and self-indulgent dis-
play of purple prose and weird characterisations, but
held together by a manic logic all of its own.
Boa: novel by Norman Mailer.
THR                                     105 min (ort 110 min)
B/sh, V/sh                                               WHV

## TOUGH NINJA: THE SHADOW
## WARRIOR **                                              18
Larry Hutton                                             198-
Tony Gable, Judy Caine, Rod Penn, Philip Ko,
Raymond Chan, Lily Chen, Roger Lockhart, June
Hack, Ken Kuroda
Three recruits to a Ninjitsu training camp realise that
their instruction has a more sinister purpose and
escape to warn the city, using their skills to help the
inhabitants fight back.
MAR                              85 min Cut (1 min 9 sec)
B,V                                                      NINJ

## TOUGHER THAN LEATHER *                                  18
Rick Rubin              USA                              1988
Run DMC (Joseph Simmons, Darryl McDaniels, Jason
Mizell), Richard Edson, Jenny Lumet
Rappers avenge the murder of one of their group who
discovered that the booking agency which had signed
them was really a front for the laundering of drugs
money. A vehicle for Run DMC that combines low
production values with a disjointed and gratuitously
violent plot.

A/AD                        86 min (ort 92 min)
V/h                                          PAL

## TOUGHEST MAN IN THE WORLD, THE **   PG
Dick Lowry              USA              1984
*Mr T, Dennis Dugan, John P. Navin Jr, Peggy Pope,*
*Lynne Moody, Joe Greco, Tom Milanovich,*
*Englehardt, Jimmie Skaggs, Frank Rice, Tina*
*DeLeone, Ron Dean, Brian Finn, Diane Dorsey, Jobe*
*Cerny*
A kind-hearted tough guy takes on the Mob, when the
centre he runs for kids with problems is threatened by
closure. An amiable story that gave Mr T his first
starring role – he also gets to sing the title song. Fair.
Boa: story by Vincent Bono.
DRA              94 min (ort 96 min) Cut (26 sec) mTV
B,V                                          CBS

## TOUR OF DUTY **                          15
Bill L. Norton          USA              1987
*Terence Knox, Stephen Caffrey, Stan Foster, Joshua*
*Maurer, Steve Akahoshi, Tony Becker, Eric Bruskotter,*
*Kevin Conroy, Ramon Franco, Miguel A. Nunez Jr,*
*Bob Fimiani, Terry Cook, Brian Kenton, Anthony*
*Curry, James Walker*
Another nostalgic return to the horrors of the Viet-
nam War, with a platoon experiencing the rigours of
jungle warfare on a secret mission to destroy a North
Vietnamese base. Despite an attempt to show the
humanity of the enemy, this action tale is never more
than a contrived and unimaginative effort. A pilot for
a TV series that was followed by several sequels.
Aka: KILLZONE, THE: TOUR OF DUTY; NAM:
TOUR OF DUTY
WAR                            89 min (ort 93 min)
B,V                                          NWV

## TOUR OF DUTY 2: UNDER SIEGE **           15
Bill L. Norton          USA              1987
*Terence Knox, Stephen Caffrey, Joshua Maurer, Steve*
*Akahoshi, Tony Becker, Eric Bruskotter, Stan Foster,*
*Ramon Franco, Miguel A. Nunez Jr, Kevin Conroy*
In this story the men of Bravo Company find that they
are short of firepower when a North Vietnamese
attack threatens their base. Average.
WAR                                      94 min
B,V                                          NWV

## TOUR OF DUTY 3: THE HILL **              15
Bill L. Norton          USA              1987
*Terence Knox, Stephen Caffrey, Joshua Maurer, Steve*
*Akahoshi, Tony Becker, Eric Bruskotter, Stan Foster,*
*Ramon Franco, Miguel A. Nunez Jr, Kevin Conroy*
Another tale in this series. This one continues to
follow the exploits of Bravo Company, whose morale
sinks to an all-time low with the needless loss of three
men.
WAR                                      93 min
V/h                                          NWV

## TOUR OF DUTY 4: THE KILL ZONE **         15
Bill L. Norton          USA              1988
*Terence Knox, Steven Caffrey, Joshua Maurer, Steve*
*Akahoshi, Tony Becker, Eric Bruskotter, Stan Foster,*
*Ramon Franco, Miguel A. Nunez Jr, Kevin Conroy*
While the men of Bravo Company enjoy the pleasures
on offer in Saigon, their lieutenant learns that the
North Vietnamese are moving their troops into a
strong position prior to mounting the Tet Offensive.
Another tale in this seemingly endless series of films
following the exploits of one particular company.
WAR                                      92 min
B,V                                          NWV

## TOUR OF DUTY 5: THE ASSASSIN **          15
Ed Sherin/Stephen L. Posey
                        USA              1988
*Terence Knox, Steven Caffrey, Tony Becker, Stan*
*Foster, Ramon Franco, Miguel A. Nunez Jr*

Following an explosion that kills an army chaplain, a
sergeant is falsely accused. An officer has to betray a
confidence in order to prove the man's innocence and
catch the real culprit. Yet another tale in this glossy,
soap opera-style Vietnam War saga.
WAR                                      85 min
V                                            NWV

## TOUR OF DUTY 6: THE BORDER **            15
                        USA              1989
*Terence Knox, Stephen Caffrey*
Another story in this series, with the Viet Cong now
setting up a group of bases along the Cambodian
border. Despite the grave concern this causes, US
forces are instructed to avoid crossing into Cambodia.
However, when one of the men of Bravo Company is
trapped on the wrong side of the border, his comrades
mount a rescue operation. A competent action tale
with few surprises.
WAR                                      90 min
V                                            NWV

## TOURIST TRAP, THE **                     
David Schmoeller        USA              1978
*Chuck Connors, Jon Van Ness, Jocelyn Jones, Robin*
*Sherwood, Tanya Roberts, Keith McDermott, Dawn*
*Jeffory, Shailar Coby*
A group of people are menaced by sinister manne-
quins, at a seedy petrol station in a run-down desert
holiday resort. A restrained and generally gore-free
film, with no explanation offered for the ability of the
dummies to move, but several scary moments that
successfully exploit it.
Aka: NIGHTMARE OF TERROR
HOR                            85 min (ort 90 min)
B,V,V2                                    INT L/A

## TOWERING INFERNO, THE ***                15
Irwin Allen/John Guillermin
                        USA              1974
*Steve McQueen, Paul Newman, William Holden, Faye*
*Dunaway, Fred Astaire, Richard Chamberlain, Susan*
*Blakely, Jennifer Jones, O.J. Simpson, Robert*
*Vaughn, Robert Wagner, Susan Flannery, Gregory*
*Sierra, Dabney Coleman*
The world's tallest building catches fire on its inaugu-
ral night. A good idea is not helped by a lousy script.
The sets are excellent, but the pyrotechnics overpower
just about every other aspect of the film. The script is
by Stirling Silliphant and the music by John Wil-
liams. AA: Cin (Joseph Biroc/Fred Koenekamp), Edit
(Harold K. Kress/Carl Kress), Song ("We May Never
Love Like This Again" – Al Kasha/Joel Hirschhorn).
Boa: novels The Tower by Richard Martin Stern/The
Glass Inferno by Thomas M. Scortia and Frank M.
Robinson.
A/AD                           158 min (ort 165 min)
V                                            WHV

## TOWN CALLED BASTARD, A *                 
Robert Parrish         SPAIN/UK          1971
*Robert Shaw, Telly Savalas, Stella Stevens, Martin*
*Landau, Fernando Rey, Al Lerrieri, Michael Craig,*
*Dudley Sutton, Paloma Cela, Aldo Sambrelli, Maribel*
*Hildago, Cass Martin, Antonio Mayans, Tito Garcia,*
*Elizabeth Sands*
A young widow arrives at a town and starts a
manhunt, by offering a large reward in gold for the
killers of her husband, who was killed in a massacre
ten years earlier, when a priest and his entire
congregation were slaughtered by revolutionaries.
This event, which starts the film, sets the tone for the
series of killings that follow, but this relentless
emphasis on bloodletting, dulls any impact the story
might otherwise have had.
Aka: TOWN CALLED HELL, A
WES                                      97 min
B,V                                          HER

## TOWN CALLED BEAUTY, A ***  PG
E.W. Swackhamer        USA         1987
*Alex McArthur, Billy Dee Williams*
Second and better tale in a trilogy that began with
DESPERADO. A gunslinger searching for the man
who framed him for murder, is ambushed by a bounty
hunter, but his life is saved by a young black man who
later steals his horse. Our gunslinger follows him to a
corrupt town run by a self-appointed gang of thugs.
The inevitable shoot-out climaxes this enjoyable and
quite unusual tale.
Aka: RETURN OF THE DESPERADO
Boa: novel by Elmore Leonard.
WES                        89 min mTV
V/sh                              CIC

## TOWN LIKE ALICE, A ***  PG
Jack Lee               UK          1956
*Peter Finch, Virginia McKenna, Marie Lohr, Maureen
Swanson, Jean Anderson, Renee Houston, Vincent
Ball, Nora Nicholson, Takagi, Tran Van Khe, Marie
Lohr, Eileen Moore, John Fabian, Tim Turner, Vi
Ngoc Tuan, Geoffrey Keen*
A group of British women taken on a forced march
through the Malayan jungle by their Japanese captors
during WW2, face great privation and suffering, but
after the war the woman who led them is eventually
re-united with the Australian soldier who was tor-
tured when he stole food for them. A well-made and
harrowing film that enjoyed great success. Written by
W.P. Lipscomb and Richard Mason and later remade
as a TV mini-series in 1981.
Aka: RAPE OF MALAYA
Boa: novel by Nevil Shute.
DRA                111 min (ort 117 min) B/W
V                                 RNK

## TOWN THAT DREADED SUNDOWN, THE **  18
Charles B. Pierce      USA         1977
*Ben Johnson, Andrew Prine, Dawn Wells, Christine
Ellsworth, Charles B. Pierce*
The true story of a hooded serial killer who struck at
the Texas town of Texarkana in the 1940s, forms the
basis for this poor thriller in which the performance of
Johnson is largely wasted.
THR                    86 min (ort 90 min)
B,V                               GHV

## TOWN WITHOUT PITY **  15
Gottfried Reinhardt
           SWITZERLAND/USA/WEST GERMANY 1961
*Kirk Douglas, E.G. Marshall, Robert Blake, Richard
Jaeckel, Frank Sutton, Alan Gifford, Christine
Kaufmann, Barbara Rutting*
A German girl is raped and four American GIs are
accused, but the skilful tactics of their defence counsel
cause the girl to commit suicide. A grim melodrama
offering no surprises and generating little interest.
Written by Silvia Reinhardt and George Hurdalek.
Boa: novel The Verdict by Manfred Gregor.
DRA                99 min (ort 103 min) B/W
V                                 WHV

## TOXIC AVENGER, THE ***  18
Michael Herz/Sam Weil USA          1986
*Andree Maranda, Mitchell Cohen, Jennifer Baptist,
Cindy Manion, Mark Torgi, Robert Pritchard, Gary
Scjneider, Pat Ryan Jr, Dick Martinsen, Chris Liano,
David Weiss, Dan Snow, Doug Isbecque, Charles Lee
Jr, Pat Kilpatrick*
A deliciously funny SF spoof in which a weedy janitor
falls into a barrel of toxic waste and is turned into a
powerful, but incredibly good-natured monster. He
sets about doing good deeds, and cleaning up the
corrupt and lawless town. Followed by a sequel.
Aka: HEALTH CLUB
COM                    76 min (ort 100 min)
B,V                               PVG

## TOXIC AVENGER: PART 2, THE ***  18
Michael Herz/Lloyd Kaufman
                       USA         1989
*Ron Fazio, Phoebe Legere, John Altamura, Rick
Collins, Rikiya Yasuoka, Tsutomu Sekine, Lisa Gaye,
Mayako Katsuragi*
In this sequel to the first film, toxic hero Melvin Junko
goes after the Japanese conglomeration responsible
for destroying a home for the blind, and a trip to Japan
gives him the chance to locate the man who may be his
father. A zany comedy that exploits an issue of real
concern, but has some hilarious moments. Filmed at
the same time as "The Toxic Avenger 3: The Last
Temptation Of Toxie".
COM                    90 min (ort 96 min)
V/sh                              VIR

## TOY SOLDIERS **  18
David Fisher           USA         1984
*Jason Miller, Cleavon Little, Rodolfo De Anda, Terri
Garber, Douglas Warhit, Tracy Scoggins*
Four college students on holiday in Central America
are kidnapped by guerrillas, and have to be rescued by
an ex-marine and his associates. A formula guns and
fists action tale that's enjoyable enough to watch, but
almost impossible to remember.
A/AD                   92 min; 82 min (CBS)
B,V                         VTC L/A; CBS

## TOY, THE *  PG
Richard Donner         USA         1982
*Richard Pryor, Jackie Gleason, Ned Beatty, Scott
Schwarz, Teresa Ganzel, Wilfrid Hyde-White,
Annazette Chase, Tony King*
Remake of the French film "Le Joue" in which a
millionaire buys a black man to be a toy for his spoilt
son. A feeble and tasteless romp that yields neither
laughs nor social comment. Written by Carol Sobleski.
COM                    97 min (ort 102 min)
V                                 RCA

## TRACK 29 **  18
Nicolas Rocg           UK          1987
*Theresa Russell, Gary Oldman, Colleen Camp, Sandra
Bernhard, Seymour Cassel, Christopher Lloyd, Leon
Rippy, Vance Colvig*
An offbeat black comedy telling of a frustrated and
unloved woman, her selfish husband and a stranger
who turns up claiming to be her long lost son. Written
by Roeg and Dennis Potter, this bizarre film has a few
moments of mirth but nothing more. Filmed in
Carolina.
COM                    87 min (ort 90 min)
B/sh, V/sh                  CAN; PATHE

## TRACK OF THE MOON BEAST *
Richard Ashe           USA         1976
*Chase Cordell, Donna Leigh Drake, Gregorio Sala,
Patrick Wright, Joe Blasco, Francine Kessler,
Crawford MacCallum, Fred McCaffrey, Timothy
Wayne Brown, Alan Swain, Tim Butler, Jeanne Swain*
A man becomes a monster after being hit by a
meteorite fragment, and as such is obliged to go on the
expected campaign of mayhem and murder. The usual
rubber-suited creature just about passes muster, in an
otherwise rubbishy effort.
HOR                               93 min
B,V                               HER

## TRACKDOWN **  18
Richard T. Heffron     USA         1976
*Jim Mitchum, Karen Lamm, Anne Archer, Erik
Estrada, Cathy Lee Crosby, Vince Cannon*
The sister of a Montana rancher has run off to L.A.,
where she has fallen in with gangsters and has
suffered abuse at their hands. Her brother sets out to
rescue her and avenge her ill-treatment. Very much a
standard plot, but enlivened by a heavy dose of
realism and much violent action.

THR 94 min (ort 98 min) Cut (35 sec)
B,V WHV

## TRACKERS, THE **
Earl Bellamy USA 1971
*Sammy Davis Jr, Ernest Borgnine, Julie Adams,*
*Connie Kreski, Jim Davis, Arthur Hunnicutt, Caleb*
*Brooks, Norman Alden, Leo V. Gordon, Ross Elliott,*
*David Reynard*
A rancher is forced to team up with a black tracker,
after his son is murdered and his daughter kidnapped
by a gang of outlaws, and comes to rely on his ability,
the latter accepting the job but leaving Borgnine in no
doubt as to what he thinks of him. A formula Western
with the usual trimmings.
Boa: story by Aaron Spelling and Sammy Davis Jr.
WES 71 min (ort 73 min) mTV
B,V RNK

## TRADER HORNEE ** 18
Tsanusdi (David Friedman)
USA 1970
*Buddy Pantsari, Christine Murry, John Alderman,*
*Elisabeth Monica, Brandon Duffy, Lisa Grant, Deek*
*Sills*
A pair of private detectives have to find out whether
an heiress, missing in the jungle for the past 15 years,
is still alive. They travel to Africa to make a search.
Aka: LEGEND OF THE GOLDEN GODDESS, THE
COM 82 min (ort 105 min)
B,V,V2 DFS L/A; XTASY

## TRADING PLACES *** 15
John Landis USA 1983
*Dan Aykroyd, Eddie Murphy, Jamie Lee Curtis, Don*
*Ameche, Denholm Elliott, Paul Gleason, Ralph*
*Bellamy, Jim Belushi, Kristin Holby*
Two rich brothers conduct an experiment by making a
street punk and a rich kid swap places. Murphy in his
second film gives a great performance, but the film,
though often very funny, suffers badly from self-
indulgent direction. Written by Timothy Harris and
Herschel Weingrod.
COM 111 min (ort 116 min)
V CIC

## TRAFFIC ** 15
Jacques Tati/Bert Haanstra
FRANCE/ITALY/NETHERLANDS 1972
*Jacques Tati, Maria Kimberly, Marcel Fravel, Honore*
*Bostel, Tony Kneppers, Francois Maisongrosse*
Our hero transports his new and innovative car model
to a motor show and encounters various problems. A
mildy amusing outing that tends to meander too much
for its own good. This was the fourth and concluding
film in the "Monsieur Hulot" series and the last film
for Tati (excluding the dreary TV film "Parade").
Written by Tati and Jacques Legrange.
COM 89 min (ort 96 min)
B,V POLY; CH5 (VHS only)

## TRAIL OF THE PINK PANTHER * PG
Blake Edwards USA 1982
*David Niven, Richard Mulligan, Herbert Lom, Joanna*
*Lumley, Capucine, Burt Kwouk, Richard Mulligan,*
*Harvey Korman, Robert Loggia, Leonard Rossiter,*
*Peter Sellers, Graham Stark, Peter Arne, Andre*
*Maranne, Ronald Fraser*
A lousy attempt to cash in on the success of the PINK
PANTHER series after the death of Sellers, using
footage discarded from earlier films. Sellers' widow
strongly objected to this film – when you see it you'll
understand why. The story has journalists seeking out
Clouseau's colleagues for a TV feature. The film uses
previously unseen footage and linking material –
THE CURSE OF THE PINK PANTHER being filmed
at the same time.
COM 92 min (ort 97 min) Cut (21 sec)
V WHV

## TRAIN ROBBERS, THE ** U
Burt Kennedy USA 1973
*John Wayne, Ann-Margret, Rod Taylor, Ben Johnson,*
*Christopher George, Bobby Vinton, Ricardo*
*Montalban, Jerry Gatlin*
An outlaw's widow asks two cowboys to help her
recover some stolen gold so that she can clear the
family name. A low-key Western remarkably lacking
in action. Written by Kennedy and with music by
Dominic Frontiere.
WES 88 min (ort 92 min)
V WHV

## TRAIN, THE *** PG
Arthur Penn/John Frankenheimer
FRANCE/ITALY/USA 1964
*Burt Lancaster, Jeanne Moreau, Paul Scofield, Michel*
*Simon, Albert Remy, Wolfgang Preiss, Suzanne Flon*
Taut, well acted and highly realistic account of the
attempts by the French resistance, to prevent a train
loaded with national art treasures from going to
Germany during the last days of WW2. The music is
by Maurice Jarre.
WAR 128 min (ort 140 min) B/W
B,V WHV

## TRAINED TO KILL ** 18
H.K. Dyal 1988
*Chuck Connors, Robert Zdar, Ron O'Neal*
A Vietnam War hero made a lot of enemies when he
informed on a drug-running operation being carried
out by his buddies. Years later, some assassins arrive
to settle the score. Standard guns and action, made to
a well-tried formula.
A/AD 89 min
V MED

## TRAINKILLER, THE ** 15
Sandor Simo HUNGARY/USA 1983
*Michael Sarrazin, Towje Kleiner, Armin Mueller-*
*Stahl*
The story of a real-life maniac who had a compulsive
urge to blow up trains, including the Vienna to Paris
Orient Express in 1931. Average.
Aka: TRAIN KILLER, THE
DRA 87 min Cut (1 min 4 sec)
B,V TEVP

## TRANCERS *** 15
Charles Band USA 1984
*Tim Thomerson, Helen Hunt, Michael Stefani, Art La*
*Fleur, Thelma Hopkins, Richard Herd, Biff Manard,*
*Anne Seymour, Miguel Fernandez, Pete Schrum, Brad*
*Logan, Barbara Perry, Minnie Lindsay, Richard*
*Erdman, Valey Harker*
This low-budget variant of BLADE RUNNER, has a
cop from the 23rd century returning to L.A. of the
20th, and taking over the body of one of his ancestors
in order to prevent a charismatic megalomaniac from
creating a future totalitarian state. A visually satis-
fying and witty SF excursion.
Aka: FUTURE COP
FAN 73 min (ort 83 min)
B,V EIV

## TRANSFORMATIONS * 18
Jay Kamen 1989
*Rex Smith, Lisa Langlois, Patrick Macnee,*
*Christopher Neame*
An interplanetary smuggler discovers a girl hidden on
his ship by his friends as a birthday present, but after
an enjoyable night with her he finds himself slowly
mutating into a lizard-like creature.
HOR 77 min
V CBS

## TRANSFORMERS: ARRIVAL FROM CYBERTRON, THE ** U
John Walker USA 1985

Animated feature with characters based on toy robots. The Autobots and the Receptions exhaust their planet's resources in their struggle, and continue their conflict on Earth.

CAR 64 min
B,V VGM

## TRANSFORMERS: THE MOVIE ** U
Nelson Shin USA 1986
*Voices of: Eric Idle, Lionel Stander, Orson Welles, Leonard Nimoy, Robert Stack, Judd Nelson*
A spin-off film inspired by robot toys that are able to change their shape. This one has the mighty Autobots slugging it out with the Decepticons. When a sinister new planet appears, all Transformers, both good and bad, are placed in peril. Mediocre.

CAR 85 min
V VGM

## TRANSFORMERS: THE RETURN OF OPTIMUS PRIME ** U
Mediocre animation based on a series of popular toys. With the death of Optimus Prime, there is no-one to protect the autobots from a deadly alien plague. However, they devise a plan to revive their dead leader.

CAR 45 min
V MSD

## TRANSYLVANIA 6-5000 * PG
Rudy De Luca USA 1985
*Jeff Goldblum, Ed Begley Jr, Joseph Bologna, Carol Kane, Jeffrey Jones, John Byner, Geena Davis, Michael Richards, Norman Fell, Donald Gibb, Teresa Ganzel, Rudy DeLuca, Ino Apelt, Bozidar Smiljanovic*
A feeble attempt to produce a vampire spoof, with two journalists investigating rumours of vampires in modern day Transylvania. Shot in Yugoslavia.

COM 93 min
B,V NWV

## TRAP ON COUGAR MOUNTAIN **
Keith Larsen USA 1975
*Eric Larsen, Keith Larsen, Karen Steele, Alvin Keeswood, Randy Burt, Lawrence J. Rink, Gene Merlino (songs)*
A boy is befriended by a cougar and together they enjoy many adventures, and they struggle to survive in the mountains in this competent outdoors yarn. One of those likeable nature romps in which the grandeur of the scenery dwarfs both actors and plot.

A/AD 93 min
B,V,V2 VPD

## TRAP, THE ** 15
Sidney Hayers CANADA/UK 1966
*Oliver Reed, Rita Tushingham, Rex Sevenoaks, Barbara Chilcott, Linda Goranson, Blain Fairman, Walter Marsh, Jo Golland*
A rather stilted production, with the undeveloped story of a trapper in British Columbia who takes a mute girl as a wife. When he catches his leg in one of his own traps, she is obliged to amputate it. She then runs away but later returns to him. What could have been fine and touching, remains unexplored. The photography is by Robert Krasker.

DRA 102 min (ort 106 min)
B,V RNK; PARK (VHS only)

## TRAPPED ** 15
Frank De Felitta USA 1973
*James Brolin, Earl Holliman, Susan Clark, Robert Hooks, Ivy Jones, Bob Hastings, Tammy Harrington, Marco Lopez, Erica Hagen, Mary Robinson, Elliott Lindsey*
After being attacked in a department store washroom, a man recovers and finds that he has been locked in overnight, and is now at risk from vicious guard dogs. A sound idea never develops into more than a sluggish and unrewarding thriller.
Aka: DOBERMAN PATROL

THR 83 min (ort 88 min) mTV
B,V CIC

## TRAPPED **
William Fruet CANADA 1981
*Henry Silva, Nicholas Campbell, Barbara Gordon, Gina Dick, Joy Thompson, Ralph Benmergui, Allan Royal, John C. Rutter, Sam Malkin, Stuart Culpepper, Danone Camden, Jeff Toole, Jele Beery, Erwin Melton, Wallace Wilkinson*
Four university students on a camping holiday in the mountains, tangle with the hostile locals (or the local hostiles). Standard survival melodramatics.
Aka: BAKER COUNTY, USA; KILLER INSTINCT, THE

A/AD 90 min
B,V VFO L/A; VNET

## TRAPPED *** PG
Fred Walton USA 1989
*Kathleen Quinlan, Bruce Abbot*
When the building manageress of a new industrial office block decides to work late with a friend, they find themselves trapped there for the night. Unfortunately, so is a revenge-seeking killer, who blames the company for the death of his son. After her friend is murdered, a battle of wits ensues, made more complex when the woman stumbles across an industrial spy. Despite the hackneyed plot, this is a tense and highly absorbing thriller.

THR 88 min
V CIC

## TRAPPED BENEATH THE SEA ***
William A. Graham USA 1974
*Lee J. Cobb, Martin Balsam, Paul Michael Glaser, Joshua Bryant, Barra Grant, Warren Kemmerling, Cliff Potts, Laurie Prange, Phillip R. Allen, Redmond Gleeson, Roger Kern, S. John Launer, Rod Perry, William Wintersole*
The story of four men trapped in a mini-sub off the Florida coast. A tense and realistic account, based on events that took place in June 1973.

THR 96 min (ort 100 min) mTV
B,V GHV

## TRAPPER COUNTY WAR, THE ** 18
Worth Keeter USA 1988
*Robert Estes, Betsy Russell, Don Swayze*
Two city boys arrive at a town that's in the grip of a brutal and corrupt family. When one of them is murdered in a vicious attack, the other makes his escape. Helped by a Vietnam veteran and an honest sheriff, he forms a little band with the intention of fighting back. Average.

A/AD 94 min
V/sh GHV

## TRASH *
Paul Morrissey USA 1970
*Joe Dallesandro, Holly Woodlawn, Jane Forth, Michael Sklar, Geri Miller, Andrea Feldman*
The sleazy saga of a heroin addict and his efforts to raise the cash for his habit, that is neither edifying, entertaining nor instructive, but represents an exploitative look at New York low-lifes. Rarely was a film so aptly titled.

DRA 95 min (ort 110 min)
B,V PVG

## TRASHI * R18
Louie Lewis USA 1980
*Lisa De Leeuw, Loni Sanders, David Morris, Dorothy Le May, Carol Doda, Joey Civera, Serena, Michael Morrison, Sharon Mitchell*
A latter-day Dr Frankenstein has created an army of

female robots well versed in the arts of love. A detective is assigned to investigate the doctor, but eventually falls victim to his latest creation, the beautiful Trashi. Low-grade nonsense that's well titled.

A                    68 min (ort 90 min) Cut (2 min 15 sec)
B,V                                        XTACY/KRP; SEX

## TRAVELLING EXECUTIONER, THE *           18
Jack Smight         USA                    1970
*Stacy Keach, Marianna Hill, Bud Cort, Graham Jarvis, James J. Sloyan*
A man who travels the American South with a portable electric chair falls in love with an intended female victim. The music is by Jerry Goldsmith, and this is one of the better aspects of a bizarre, tasteless and unfunny tale.

DRA                                        94 min
B,V                                        MGM

## TRAVELLING MAN ***
Irvin Kershner      USA                    1989
*John Lithgow, Jonathan Silverman, John Glover, Chynna Phillips, Margaret Colin*
Lithgow is wonderful in this story of a burned-out salesman who travels the road selling foam insulation. When his ruthless boss decides that he isn't selling enough, he allocates him a young hotshot to train, but doesn't tell him that the young man is really a rival out to grab all his accounts. A downbeat comedy that tries to inject realism into its portrait of life on the road, and generally succeeds right up to the obligatory happy ending.

DRA                    100 min (ort 105 min) mCab
V                                          WHV

## TRAVELLING NORTH **                     15
Carl Schultz        AUSTRALIA             1988
*Leo McKern, Julia Blake, Graham Kennedy, Henri Szeps, Michele Fawdon, Diane Craig, Andrea Moor, Drew Forsythe, John Gregg, Rob Steele, John Black, Roger Oakley*
A crusty old retired civil engineer marries a divorcee, and the pair move to the idyllic surroundings of Northern Queensland, but his worsening heart condition casts a deep shadow over their future. Warm-hearted comedy-drama of no great depth.
Boa: play by David Williamson.

COM                                        97 min
V                                          COL

## TRAXX **                                18
Jerome Gary         USA                    1988
*Shadoe Stevens, Priscilla Barnes, Willard E. Pugh, Robert Davi, John Hancock*
An ex-mercenary and former policeman decides to try a more peaceful mode of life and moves to the country to set up his own cookie company. However, when the local sheriff pleads for help in dealing with a crime wave, our man cannot resist this opportunity and offers his services. Enter various mobsters who now arrange for him to be dealt with by a hit-man. A rather bizarre spoof on all those tough-cop-cleans-up-town movies.

A/AD                                       81 min
B,V                                        CBS

## TREASURE ISLAND **                      PG
John Hough
        FRANCE/SPAIN/UK/WEST GERMANY 1972
*Orson Welles, Kim Burfield, Walter Slezak, Lionel Stander, Angel Del Pozo, Rik Battaglia, Maria Rohm, Paul Muller, Jean Lefevbre, Michael Garland, Aldo Sambrelli, Alibe, Chinchilla*
Another version of the famous adventure story, in which the discovery of an old pirate map leads to a voyage in search of buried treasure and the adventure of a lifetime for a young boy. A feeble retelling of Stevenson's classic, that wastes the talents of a poorly

dubbed international cast and has Welles at his hammiest for good measure.
Boa: novel by Robert Louis Stevenson.

JUV                              85 min (ort 95 min)
B,V                                        GHV

## TREASURE ISLAND **                       U
Dave Heather        UK                     1982
*Christopher Cazenove, Piers Eady, John Judd, Bernard Miles, David Kernan, Roderick Horne, Harold Innocent, Norman Rossington*
A lively musical version of the famous story, with pleasant locations but fairly uninspiring songs.
Aka: TREASURE ISLAND: THE MUSICAL
Boa: novel by Robert Louis Stevenson.

MUS                       100 min; 118 min (VGM)
B,V                    BWV L/A; VGM (VHS only)

## TREASURE ISLAND ***                     15
Fraser Heston       USA                    1989
*Charlton Heston, Christian Bale, Oliver Reed, Christopher Lee, Julian Glover, Richard Johnson, Clive Woods, Michael Thoma*
A spirited and colourful adaptation of the classic story of buried treasure and a young boy's adventures. An enjoyable remake (bizarrely re-titled by Warner Brothers) that is notable for its strong characterisations. Heston is splendid as Long John Silver, and Reed and Lee as Captain Bones and Blind Pew are also memorable, but Bale as Jim Hawkins is a disappointment. Written and produced by Fraser Heston, Charlton's son.
Aka: DEVIL'S TREASURE
Boa: novel by Robert Louis Stevenson.

A/AD                      127 min (ort 131 min) mTV
V                                          WHV

## TREASURE ISLAND ***                      U
Z. Janzic           AUSTRALIA             1970
*Jon Pertwee (introduction only)*
A spirited adaptation of this rousing adventure, one in a series of illustration-style animations made for Australian TV.
Boa: novel by Robert Louis Stevenson.

CAR                                        46 min mTV
V                                          STYL

## TREASURE ISLAND ***                      U
Byron Haskin        USA                    1950
                                  (re-issued 1975)
*Bobby Driscoll, Robert Newton, Basil Sydney, Walter Fitzgerald, Dennis O'Dea, Ralph Truman, Finlay Currie, John Laurie, Francis de Wolff, Geoffrey Wilkinson, David Davies, Andrew Blackett, Paddy Brannigan, Ken Buckle*
A charming Disney version of the classic tale. Filmed in England, with Newton perfectly cast as Long John Silver and Driscoll good as Jim Hawkins. The script is by Lawrence Edward Watkin. Some "objectionable" violence was removed from the film when it was re-issued in 1975.
Boa: novel by Robert Louis Stevenson.

A/AD                                       96 min
B,V                                        WDV

## TREASURE ISLAND ***                      U
Victor Fleming      USA                    1934
*Wallace Beery, Jackie Cooper, Lewis Stone, Lionel Barrymore, Otto Kruger, Nigel Bruce, Douglass Dumbrille, Chic Sale*
Stevenson's tale of 18th century pirates, buried treasure and adventure receives a slow but careful treatment in this nicely mounted production. Beery makes a splendid Long John Silver, whose rumbustious presence is somewhat let down by Cooper's colourless performance as young Jim Hawkins.
Boa: novel by Robert Louis Stevenson.

A/AD                     99 min (ort 105 min) B/W
V                                          MGM

## TREASURE OF BRUCE LE *
Joseph Velasco    HONG KONG    1985
*Bruce Le (Huang Kin Lung), Chen Hsing, Chang Li, Chaing Tao, Mulo Tong*
A search for a missing martial arts manual brings a fighter into contact with a Shaolin traitor and a samurai. Another dreary Bruce Lee spin-off, using a clone of the late star to trade on his fame.
MAR    85 min (ort 89 min)
V    ICL

## TREASURE OF DOOM **    18
Rene Cardona Jr    MEXICO    1983
*Clark Jarett, Donald Pleasence, Stuart Whitman, Bradford Dillman, John Ireland, Ann Sidney, Pedro Armendariz Jr, Jorge Luke, Hugo Stiglitz, Sonia Infante*
Three fortune hunters go off in search of a cache of diamonds, in this violent, formula adventure.
Aka: EL TESORO DEL AMAZONES; TREASURE OF THE AMAZON
A/AD    90 min (ort 94 min)
B,V    EIV; MRD

## TREASURE OF JAMAICA REEF, THE *    U
Virginia Stone    USA    1974
*David Ladd, Cheryl Stoppelmoor (Ladd), Stephen Boyd, Chuck Woolery, Darby Hinton, Roosevelt Grier*
The story of a Caribbean hunt for buried treasure, that has little to offer except the presence of Stoppelmoor (Cheryl Ladd) in an early role, before she found fame in the TV series "Charlie's Angels".
Aka: EVIL IN THE DEEP
A/AD    96 min; 88 min (MAST)
B,V    CRYS/DFS; VMA; MAST (VHS only)

## TREASURE OF MATECUMBE **    U
Vincent McEveety    USA    1976
*Robert Foxworth, Peter Ustinov, Vic Morrow, Joan Hackett, Jane Wyatt, Johnny Duran, Billy "Pop" Attmore, Dub Taylor, Don Knight, Virginia Vincent, Dick Van Patten, Mills Watson, Val De Vargas, Robert Doqui*
Two boys armed with a treasure map, try to recover a fortune buried on an island off the Florida coast, and are helped by three goodies and pursued by Morrow. A competent but uninspired romp. Filmed in the Florida Keys.
Boa: novel Journey To Matecumbe by R.L. Taylor.
JUV    110 min (ort 116 min) Cut (40 sec)
B,V    WDV

## TREASURE OF PANCHO VILLA, THE **
George Sherman    USA    1955
*Rory Calhoun, Shelley Winters, Gilbert Roland, Joseph Calleia, Fanny Schiller, Tony Carvajal, Pasquel Pena, Carlos Mosquiz*
The story of a gold train robbery masterminded by the famous Mexican bandit leader, with an American adventurer involved, and with both seeking the gold consignment, although the latter has undertaken to deliver it safely to the rebels. A good cast is somewhat hampered by slow pacing.
WES    90 min (ort 96 min)
B,V    VCL/CBS

## TREASURE OF THE FOUR CROWNS *    15
Ferdinando Baldi    SPAIN    1983
*Tony Anthony (Roger Petitto), Ana Obregon, Gene Quintano, Francisco Rabal, Jerry Lazarus, Emiliano Redondo, Francisco Villena, Kate Levan, Lewis Gordon*
Five men set out to steal a legendary gold treasure in this 3-D copy of RAIDERS OF THE LOST ARK. They find their way to a haunted castle where they are attacked by a variety of wild animals, before discovering the hiding place of the treasure. Meaningless 3-D effects and poor production values make this one hard to sit through.

Aka: EL TESORO DE LAS CUATRO CORONAS
A/AD    95 min (ort 100 min)
B,V,V2    GHV; VCC (VHS only)

## TREASURE OF THE LOST DESERT *    15
Tony Zarindast    USA    1982
*Bruce Miller, Susan West, Larry Finish, Tony Zarindast, Danny Bonyadi, Rudal Daniela, Jim White*
A US officer is sent to crush a terrorist organisation in Dubai in this low-budget production that offers the usual violent action.
A/AD    88 min (ort 90 min) Cut (4 min 18 sec)
B,V    HER L/A; 21ST/CYC; COBRA

## TREASURE OF THE SIERRA MADRE ****    PG
John Huston    USA    1948
*Humphrey Bogart, Walter Huston, Tim Holt, Bruce Bennett, Barton MacLane, Alfonso Bedoya, Robert Blake, John Huston, Martin Garralaga, A. Soto Rangel, Manuel Donde, Jose Torvay, Margarito Luna, Jacqueline Dalya, Spencer Chan*
Excellent film adaptation of a story of three men who join up to search for gold in the wilds of Mexico, and of the difficulties and hazards they experience. Walter Huston is outstanding as the experienced old timer who leads the expedition. Written by John Huston, who appears briefly to give Bogart a series of hand-outs. Music is by Max Steiner with musical direction by Leo F. Forbstein. AA: Dir, S. Actor (Huston), Screen (John Huston).
Aka: TREASURE OF SIERRA MADRE, THE
Boa: novel by B. Traven.
A/AD    121 min (ort 126 min) B/W
V    WHV

## TREE OF HANDS **    18
Giles Foster    UK    1988
*Helen Shaver, Paul McGann, Peter Firth, Lauren Bacall*
A successful authoress and single parent is joined by her mother in London. When her young son dies tragically, the mother abducts a young boy in an effort to comfort her, telling her daughter that he is the son of a friend. By the time the daughter has realised this is untrue and that her mother is mentally unbalanced, she finds herself embroiled in a nasty blackmail attempt.
Boa: novel by Ruth Rendell.
THR    89 min
V/sh    PATHE

## TREMORS ***    15
Ron Underwood    USA    1989
*Kevin Bacon, Fred Ward, Finn Carter, Michael Gross, Reba McEntire, Rhonda Le Beck, Bobby Jacoby, Charlotte Stewart, Tony Genaros, Victor Wong*
This effective updating of the old-fashioned 1950s-style monster movies, combines a sharp and witty script with some genuinely suspenseful moments. Bacon and Ward are a couple of likeable handymen who live in a small Nevada town. The discovery of a decapitated sheep farmer and his partially devoured flock leads to the discovery of giant wormlike creatures that live in the sands and our duo lead the town's inhabitants in a battle against them.
HOR    92 min (ort 96 min)
V    CIC

## TRENCHCOAT **    PG
Michael Tuchner    USA    1983
*Margot Kidder, Robert Hays, Daniel Faraldo, Gila Von Weitershausen, David Suchet, Ronald Lacey*
A female stenographer with literary ambitions, takes a holiday on Malta in the hope of finding material for her novel, and gets more adventure than she bargained for when she finds a map that leads her into involvement with a gang of international terrorists. A lacklustre Disney studio production with little to recommend it.

COM                        90 min (ort 95 min)
B,V                                 RNK; WDV

**TRENCHCOAT IN PARADISE ★★**              PG
Martha Coolidge         USA            1989
*Dirk Benedict, Sydney Walsh, Bruce Dern, Catherine
Oxenberg, Michelle Phillips, Jeremy Slate, Kim
Zimmer*
A 1940s-style pilot for a prospective series, that
follows the adventures of a small-time detective who
has to flee New Jersey when he incurs the wrath of a
local crime boss. Arriving in Hawaii, he finds life
there no quieter and is soon involved in an investiga-
tion into a local land swindle. An amiable if unre-
markable detective story with a few amusing touches.
DRA                    89 min (ort 100 min) mTV
V                                        MGM

**TRENT'S LAST CASE ★★**                   U
Herbert Wilcox           UK            1952
*Michael Wilding, Margaret Lockwood, Orson Welles,
Hugh McDermott, John McCallum, Miles Malleson*
Despite appearing to have committed suicide, a
business tycoon may in fact have been murdered by
his secretary. An inquisitive journalist investigates. A
watery adaptation of a famous novel, its absorbing
moments are diluted by excessive dialogue. Filmed
once before in 1920.
Boa: novel by E.C. Bentley.
DRA                      86 min (ort 90 min) B/W
V                                        WHV

**TRESPASSER, THE ★★**
Colin Gregg              USA            1981
*Alan Bates, Pauline Moran, Dinah Stabb, Margaret
Whiting*
A musician and music teacher has an affair with a
young student in this TV adapaptation of the Lawr-
ence novel. Fair, but unmemorable.
Boa: novel by D.H. Lawrence.
DRA                          90 min mTV
B,V                                   VCL/CBS

**TRESPASSES ★**                           18
Adam Rourke              USA            1986
*Robert Kuhn, Thom Myers, Adam Rourke, Ben
Johnson, Mary Pillot, Van Brooks, Lou Diamond
Phillips*
The death of a popular and kindly banker in a small
Texas town causes hardship for many of the town-
sfolk, and when the new, and considerably more
ruthless replacement arrives, some of the locals
contemplate murder. An offbeat and unappealing
drama, that ambles along without ever developing a
clear direction.
Aka: TRESPASS
THR                    90 min (ort 97 min) Cut (59 sec)
B,V                                      EHE

**TRIAL BY TERROR ★★**                     15
Hildy Brooks             USA            1983
*Kay Lenz, Wayne Crawford, Martin Landau*
A couple are terrorised in a series of mysterious
attacks on their home and the husband shoots an
intruder, but they then find that their troubles are by
no means over.
HOR                     86 min (ort 90 min)
B,V                                      CBS

**TRIAL BY VENGEANCE ★★**                  18
Dean Lewis               USA            1989
*Walker Bonshor, Linda Singer, Laird Evans, Roberto
Ozores*
Routine tale of a vigilante who, sickened by police
inactivity and corruption, decides to clean up the
streets of L.A. in his own way. Eventually the
inevitable clash occurs when a special agent is
brought in to bring him to book and restore the rule of
law.

A/AD                             85 min
V                                   ARF

**TRIAL OF THE INCREDIBLE HULK, THE ★★★**    PG
Bill Bixby               USA            1989
*Bill Bixby, Lou Ferrigno, Rex Smith, John Rhys-
Davies, Marta DuBois, Nancy Everhard, Nicholas
Hormann, Joseph Mascolo*
The second full-length feature inspired by the popular
TV series, in which a brilliant scientist finds that after
conducting various experiments with himself as sub-
ject, he turns into an irascible green giant in moments
of rage. In this story the Hulk teams up with
Daredevil, another character from Marvel Comics,
and together they take on a powerful gangster.
Harmless, mindless, and fun.
A/AD                    93 min (ort 100 min) mTV
B,V                                      NWV

**TRIAL RUN ★★**                           15
Melanie Read       NEW ZEALAND         1984
*Annie Whittle, Judith Gibson, Christopher Broun,
Philippa Mayne, Stephen Tozer, Lee Grant, Martyn
Sanderson, Frances Edmond, Teresa Woodham,
Allison Roe, Karen Sims, Maggie Eyre, Margaret Blay*
A woman photographer has to stay in a deserted beach
house and starts to hear strange noises. Gradually she
comes to realise that her life is in danger. An opaque
and slightly disjointed thriller, with some tense
moments but a feeble climax. Written by Read.
THR                     85 min (ort 89 min)
B,V                                      EHE

**TRIAL, THE ★★★**
Orson Welles
        FRANCE/ITALY/WEST GERMANY       1963
*Anthony Perkins, Orson Welles, Jeanne Moreau, Romy
Schneider, Elsa Martinelli, Madeleine Robinson,
Akim Tamiroff*
A moody, atmospheric adaptation of Kafka's novel of a
man arrested for a crime that is never specified, yet
against which he must mount a defence. Not entirely
effective, yet full of touches of brilliance with an
intense performance from Perkins set against some
remarkable photography. Written and directed by
Welles, and very much aimed at admirers of Kafka.
The photography is by Edmond Richard.
Aka: LE PROCES
Boa: novel by Franz Kafka.
DRA                    118 min (ort 120 min) B/W
B,V                                      SCRN

**TRIALS OF TRACI, THE ★★**               R18/18
Gerry Ross               USA
*Traci Lords, John Leslie, Amber Lynn, Ginger Lynn*
A mermaid gets washed up on the beach of a nature
reserve and her first encounter is with a couple
making love. Thinking that this is the normal method
of communication between humans, she sets off to find
a man of her own. Average story slightly enlivened by
a more unusual setting.
A              64 min Cut (2 sec – R18 version); 53 min Cut
                              (41 sec – 18 version)
B,V                                      ELV

**TRIANGLE FACTORY FIRE SCANDAL, THE ★★**   PG
Mel Stuart               USA            1979
*Tom Bosley, Tovah Feldshuh, Janet Margolin, David
Dukes, Lauren Frost, Ted Wass, Stacey Nelkin,
Stephanie Zimbalist, Charlotte Rae, Erica Yohn,
Milton Selzer, Michael Mullins, Jerome Guardino,
Valerie Landsburg*
The story of a tragic factory fire in which 146 workers
died in New York in 1911, and which was in-
strumental in improving both working conditions and
fire regulations. A sincere but not terribly gripping
account of this event and its ultimate consequences.
DRA                          100 min mTV
B,V                                      GHV

## TRIANGLE OF LUST ** 18
Hubert Frank
AUSTRIA/SPAIN/WEST GERMANY 1977
*Barbara Rey, Patricia Adreani, Brigitte Stein, Jose
Antonio Ceinos, Miguel Angel Godo, Manu, Eric
Wedekind, Jose Luis Alexandre, Florentino Alonso,
Alexander Allerson, Andres Santana, Pedro Sopena,
Carmen Zorilla*
Fleeing from his insatiable girlfriend, a young man
parachutes into the jungle, but is followed by his
girlfriend. However, she is captured by two men and
two women when she inadvertently stumbles on a
gang hideout. She suffers various humiliations as they
all take a fancy to her, and make use of her to satisfy
their sexual desires. Routine sex film.
Aka: CAPTIVE WOMEN (GLOB); DAS
TEUFELSCAMP DER VERLORENEN FRAUEN;
DIRTY JOBS; TERRIFYING CONFESSIONS OF A
CAPTIVE WOMAN; TERRIFYING CONFESSIONS
OF CAPTIVE WOMEN (GLOB)
A 78 min (ort 80 min) Cut (GLOB: 43 sec SHEP:
18 sec in addition to film cuts)
B,V GOV L/A; NET; TCX; GLOB; SHEP

## TRIBES *** 15
Joseph Sargent USA 1970
*Darren McGavin, Jan-Michael Vincent, Earl
Holliman, John Gruber, Danny Goldman, Richard
Yniguez*
When a hippie is drafted into the US Marines, a tough
drill instructor finds he is unable to break his spirit,
and his problems mount when the hippie teaches his
meditation techniques to the other guys in the
barracks. An absorbing and convincingly portrayed
film, whose thoughtful, Emmy Award-winning script
(by Tracy Keenan Wynn and Marvin Schwartz)
combines drama with sharp social comment.
Aka: SOLDIER WHO DECLARED PEACE, THE
DRA 90 min mTV
V CBS

## TRICK OR TREAT ** 18
Charles Martin Smith USA 1986
*Marc Price, Tony Fields, Doug Savant, Gene Simmons,
Ozzy Osbourne, Elaine Joyce, Lisa Orgolini, Glen
Morgan, Elise Richards, Richard Pachorek, Clare
Nono, Alice Nunn, Claudia Templeton, Denny Price,
Ray Shaffer, Brad Thomas*
A dead heavy-rock singer is accidentally resurrected
by an ardent fan who then makes use of him as a
means of asserting himself against his bullying
classmates. Another supernatural revenge fantasy, no
better or worse than a hundred others.
HOR 93 min (ort 97 min)
V/sh PAL

## TRICKS OF THE TRADE *** 15
Jack Bender USA 1989
*Cindy Williams, Markie Post, Chris Mulkey, James
Whitmore Jr, Scott Paulin, John Ritter*
The pampered wife of a wealthy stockbroker is
shocked when her husband is found murdered at the
apartment of a high-class prostitute. However, she
teams up with the latter and they set out to find the
killer. An appealing and inventive odd-couple comedy
that starts off with great promise, unfortunately it
soon gets bogged down in the over-complex plot. A
highlight is a crazy shoot-out in a sex shop.
COM 90 min (ort 100 min) mTV
V CASVIS

## TRINITY IS STILL MY NAME! ** U
E.B. Clucher (Enzo Barboni)
ITALY 1972
*Terence Hill (Mario Girotti), Bud Spencer (Carlo
Pedersoli), Jessica Dublin, Harry Carey Jr, Yanti
Somer, Enzo Tarascio, Pupo De Luca*
Sequel to THEY CALL ME TRINITY with our comic
duo fighting their way through the usual stock

situations that form the basis for all their films, of
which this one is fairly typical, with much of the
broad, unsophisticated humour that has made them so
popular in a number of countries. Later recut to 101
minutes.
Aka: THEY STILL CALL ME TRINITY
WES 117 min; 107 min (EHE) (ort 124 min)
B,V EHE; CH5 (VHS only)

## TRIP TO BOUNTIFUL, THE *** U
Peter Masterton USA 1985
*Geraldine Page, John Heard, Rebecca De Mornay,
Carlin Glynn, Kevin Cooney, Richard Bradford,
Norman Bennett, Harvey Lewis, Kirk Sisco, Dave
Tanner, Gil Glasgow, Mary Kay Mars, Wezz Tildon,
Peggy Ann Byers, David Romo*
A widow living with her son and his wife in Houston
hankers after her home town, and decides to revisit it
before it is too late. Originally a play shown on US TV
in 1953 and later transferred to Broadway. Well acted,
and made with a good deal of warmth. AA: Actress
(Page).
Boa: play by Horton Foote.
DRA 103 min (ort 106 min)
B,V VES

## TRIP TO KILL ** 
Tom Stern USA 1971
*Telly Savalas, Robert Vaughn, John Marley*
The FBI use a Vietnam veteran to bust a Mafia
operated drugs ring. Average.
DRA 89 min
B,V VCL/CBS

## TRIPLE CROSS ** 
Terence Young FRANCE/UK 1967
*Christopher Plummer, Yul Brynner, Romy Schneider,
Trevor Howard, Gert Frobe, Claudine Auger, Harry
Meyen, George Lycan, Gil Barber, Jean-Claude Bercq,
Francis De Wolff*
Biopic of Eddie Chapman, who worked during WW2
as a safecracking double agent employed by both
Britain and Germany, and was decorated by both
sides. A loose and dullish film with too few moments of
excitement. Written by Rene Hardy.
Boa: book The Eddie Chapman Story by Frank Owen.
DRA 117 min (ort 140 min)
B,V VCL/CBS

## TRIPLE ECHO, THE ** 
Michael Apted UK 1972
*Glenda Jackson, Oliver Reed, Brian Deacon, Jenny
Lee Wright, Anthony May, Gavin Richards, Ken
Colley, Daphne Heard, Zelah Clarke, Colin Rix*
A lonely woman living on a farm in 1942, takes in an
army deserter and gets him to pose as her sister, but
her subsequent involvement with a tank sergeant
serves only to complicate matters, in this foolish and
fragile story. Written by Robin Chapman.
Aka: SOLDIER IN SKIRTS
Boa: novel by H.E. Bates.
DRA 93 min
B,V VCL/CBS

## TRIPWIRE * 18
James Lemmo USA 1988
*Terence Knox, David Warner, Isabella Hofmann,
Charlotte Lewis, Yaphet Kotto, Andras Jones, Sy
Richardson, Viggo Mortensen, Tommy Chong, Meg
Foster*
A federal agent foils a weapons robbery by the world's
most lethal terrorist, a deadly figure known as
"Tripwire". In revenge, the latter kills the agent's
ex-wife and kidnaps their son, thereby sparking off
the inevitable cycle of revenge and general destruc-
tion. One of those utterly predictable dime-a-dozen
action-thrillers.
THR 87 min
V MED

**TRIUMPH OF THE SPIRIT ***                        15
Robert M. Young          USA              1989
*Willem Dafoe, Edward James Olmos, Robert Loggia,*
*Wendy Gazelle, Kelly Wolf, Costas Mandylor, Kario*
*Salem*
A Jewish boxer and his family are transported from
Thessalonica in Greece to Auschwitz by the Nazis and
are separated. His captors discover that he is a boxer
and give him a chance of survival if he will fight an
endless series of bouts with other prisoners for their
amusement. The harrowingly true story of Salamo
Arouch receives a weak treatment that, for all its
location filming at Auschwitz and Bikenau, lacks both
conviction and force.
A/AD                       115 min (ort 121 min)
V                                           GHV

**TRIUMPHS OF A MAN CALLED HORSE ***        15
John Hough          MEXICO/USA            1982
*Richard Harris, Michael Beck, Ana De Sade, Vaughn*
*Armstrong, Anne Seymour, Buck Taylor, Simon*
*Andreu, Lautaco Murua, Roger Cudney, Jerry Gatlin,*
*John Chandler, Jacqueline Evans*
Third in the series of "Horse" films, about a man who
has been accepted by the Sioux as one of them. In this
disappointing sequel, Harris dies early on in the film,
leaving his half-breed son to defend the Yellow Hand
Sioux from the brutal and greedy prospectors who
threaten the tribe's very existence.
WES     89 min; 86 min (MAST or XTASY) Cut (7 sec)
V                            VTC; MAST; XTASY

**TROG ***                                        15
Freddie Francis          UK              1970
*Joan Crawford, Michael Gough, Bernard Kay, Joe*
*Cornelius (Trog), Kim Braden, David Griffith, John*
*Hamill, Thorley Walters, Jack May, Geoffrey Case,*
*Robert Hutton, Simon Lack*
An apeman is discovered living in a cave, and is
captured and subjected to experiments conducted by a
woman scientist. This poorly made low-budget film
was Crawford's last, and what a sad finale to her
career it is.
HOR                         91 min (ort 93 min)
B,V                                         WHV

**TROJAN WAR, THE ***
Giorgio Ferroni    FRANCE/ITALY           1961
*Steve Reeves, John Drew Barrymore, Juliette Mayniel,*
*Edy Vessel, Lidia Alfonsi*
Film version of the ancient story done in the custom-
ary heroic style. Worth seeing if only to appreciate
Reeves' splendidly proportioned physique, if not his
acting ability.
Aka: LA GUERRA DI TROIA; LA GUERRE DE
TROIE; WOODEN HORSE OF TROY, THE (DAV)
Boa: epic poem The Iliad by Homer.
WAR                    100 min; 105 min (DAV)
B,V,V2         DAV L/A (Betamax and VHS only); VPD

**TROLL ***                                       15
John Carl Buechler      USA              1985
*Michael Moriarty, Shelley Hack, Noah Hathaway,*
*Jenny Beck, Sonny Bono, June Lockhart, Anne*
*Lockhart, Phil Fondacaro, Brad Hall, Gary Sandy,*
*James Beck, Julia Louis-Dreyfus, Robert Hathaway,*
*Dale Wyatt, Barbara Sciorilli*
A family's home is invaded by trolls who possess their
younger daughter, and use a magical ring to turn
people into mythical creatures. A dullish horror
fantasy that attempts to incorporate elements of
GREMLINS.
HOR                         79 min (ort 82 min)
V                                           EIV

**TROLL 2 ***                                     18
Drago Floyd             USA              1989
*Connie McFarland, Michael Stephenson*
Sequel to the first film that has a family taking a

holiday in a small town that is not quite as it seems,
for the woods are inhabited by Trolls who disguised as
peasants, offer people food that turns them into
vegetables the creatures can eat. A strange blend of
horror and black humour that does justice to neither
genre.
HOR                                        95 min
V                                     PRISM L/A

**TROMA'S WAR ***                                 18
Samuel Weil (Lloyd Kaufman/Michael Herz)
                         USA              1988
*Carolyn Beauchamp, Sean Bowen, Michael Ryder*
One of the earliest films from Troma Studios, who
gave us THE TOXIC AVENGER and RABID GRAN-
NIES. A plane crashes on a Caribbean island and
most of the survivors are captured by soldiers. Those
remaining form themselves into an efficient combat
force and attack the army base to free their fellow-
passengers. A silly, overlong spoof on action movies,
with each actor taking at least two roles.
COM                        103 min (ort 105 min)
V                                           VIR

**TRON ***                                        PG
Steven Lisberger        USA              1982
*Jeff Bridges, Bruce Boxleitner, David Warner, Cindy*
*Morgan, Barnard Hughes, Dan Shor*
A computer whizz-kid who lives by writing games,
attempts to obtain some information contained within
a master computer. The machine resists and absorbs
him into an inner world full of strange electronic
marvels. Despite great effects, the film never progresses beyond the juvenile in its plotting and characterisation. Written and directed by Lisberger.
FAN                         92 min (ort 96 min)
V                                           WDV

**TROOP BEVERLY HILL$ ***                         PG
Jeff Kanew              USA              1989
*Shelley Long, Craig T. Nelson, Betty Thomas, Mary*
*Gross, Stephanie Beacham, Audra Lindley, Edd*
*Byrnes, Ami Foster, Jenny Lewis, Frankie Avalon, Pia*
*Zadora, Cheech Marin*
Long plays a silly Beverly Hills mom who agrees to
act as a troop leader for her daughter's Wilderness
group and ends up teaching her charges all about
self-respect and the things that really matter in
Beverly Hills. An amiable comedy vehicle for Long
that offers the occasional flash of wit.
COM                              106 min subH
V                                           RCA

**TROPICAL SNOW ***                               18
Ciro Duran              USA              1988
*Nick Lorri, Madeline Stowe, David Carradine*
A small-time crook and a waitress tire of life in the
slums of Bogota and hatch a scheme to smuggle
themselves into the USA.
DRA                                        84 min
B,V                                         CIC

**TROUBLE IN MIND ***                             15
Alan Randolph           USA              1985
*Kris Kristofferson, Divine (Glenn Milstead), Lori*
*Singer, Keith Carradine, Genevieve Bujold, Joe*
*Morton, George Kirby, John Considine, Albert Hall*
An ex-cop serves a jail sentence for several murders,
and on his release returns to the town where the
woman he killed for still lives, only to find himself
deeply involved with a group of youngsters. A strange,
highly charged drama, with a style that recalls 1940s
film noir.
A/AD                       107 min (ort 111 min)
V/h                                         CBS

**TROUBLE IN PARADISE ***                         15
Di Drew          AUSTRALIA/USA           1988
*Raquel Welch, Jack Thompson, Nicholas Hammond,*

*John Gregg*
The elegant widow of a diplomat sets out for the USA amd the promise of a new life, but when her ship is wrecked, she finds herself alone on a tropical island with a happy-go-lucky Australian seaman. Together they face various hazards, such as the arrival of drug smugglers. Welch is quite appealing in this undemanding tale, that has much in common with both "The Admirable Crichton" and "Swept Away".
DRA                             89 min (ort 100 min) mTV
V                                                    BRAVE

### TROUBLE IN STORE ***
John Paddy Carstairs    UK                      1953
*Norman Wisdom, Margaret Rutherford, Moira Lister,*
*Megs Jenkins, Lana Morris, Jerry Desmonde, Derek*
*Bond, Joan Sims, Michael Brennan, Michael Ward,*
*John Warwick, Perlita Nielson, Eddie Leslie, Cyril*
*Chamberlain, Ronan O'Casey*
Wisdom's film debut has him as an accident-prone department store assistant who finally makes good. Probably one of the best of his films. Though dated, Wisdom's comic talent ensures that the film retains a charm of its own. Written by Carstairs with Maurice Cowan and Ted Willis. The music is by Mischa Spoliansky.
Aka: NORMAN WISDOM: TROUBLE IN STORE
Osca: ON THE BEAT
COM                             85 min B/W
B,V                                                    RNK

### TROUBLE IN THE CITY OF ANGELS **            15
Steven H. Stern         USA                     1987
*George Peppard, Kathryn Harrold, Barry Corbin,*
*Stella Stevens, Max Gail*
A thriller set in the era of big bands and swing music, that follows the exploits of an honest cop who takes on the gangs running prostitution, gambling and gun-running rackets.
THR                                               92 min
V                                                    GHV

### TROUBLE WITH DICK, THE *                     15
Gary Walkow             USA                     1986
*Tom Villard, Susan Dey, Elaine Giftos, David Clennon*
A fantasy writer attempts to rescue his flagging career, but his efforts are curtailed when three women set out to seduce him.
COM                             82 min (ort 86 min)
V                                                    VES

### TROUBLE WITH HARRY, THE ***                  PG
Alfred Hitchcock        USA                     1955
*Shirley MacLaine, John Forsythe, Edmund Gwenn,*
*Mildred Natwick, Mildred Dunnock, Jerry Mathers,*
*Royal Dano, Parker Fennelly, Dwight Marfield, Leslie*
*Woolf, Philip Truex, Ernest Curt Bach*
A corpse found in a copse, causes problems in a peaceful rural community in New England, in this unusual black comedy, chiefly because several people believe themselves to be responsible for its demise. Among them is a young woman (MacLaine in her acting debut) who recognises it as her husband. A twee and unreal black comedy, with a musical score (the first to be used by Hitchcock) by Bernard Herrmann. Written by John Michael Hayes.
Boa: novel by Jack Trevor Story.
COM                             95 min (ort 99 min)
B,V                                                    CIC

### TROUBLE WITH SPIES, THE *                    PG
Burt Kennedy            USA     1984 (released 1987)
*Donald Sutherland, Ned Beatty, Lucy Gutteridge,*
*Ruth Gordon, Michael Hordern, Robert Morley,*
*Gregory Sierra*
A dreadful secret agent spoof that casts Sutherland as a bumbling spy who runs into the expected treachery and intrigue on an espionage mission. An inane comedy that has so many plot twists it rapidly becomes completely incomprehensible, and even Sutherland's charm fails to make it sparkle. The unsubtle script is the work of Kennedy.
Boa: novel Apple Spy In The Sky by Marc Lovell.
COM                             86 min (ort 91 min)
V                                                    VES

### TRUCK STOP **                                18
Jean-Marie Pallardy
                        FRANCE/ITALY            1978
*Jean-Marie Pallardy, Elizabeth Turner, Nikki Gentile,*
*Ajita Wilson*
A reworking of the Ulysses and Penelope legend, revolving around the sexual fantasies of a truck driver, and his girlfriend who owns a cafe.
Aka: EROTIC ENCOUNTERS; I GROSSI BESTIONI;
L'AMOUR CHEZ LES POIDS LOURDS
A                               87 min (ort 105 min)
V                                       XTASY; PICPAL

### TRUCK STOP WOMEN **
Mark Lester             USA                     1974
*Claudia Jennings, Lieux Dressler, Dennis Fimple,*
*Gene Drew, Dolores Doru, Jennifer Burton, Paul Carr,*
*John Martino*
A group of women use a truck stop as cover for their prostitution and robbery rackets, but the daughter of one of them consorts with hoodlums in order to ruin her mother's schemes. A tawdry sexploitation film with one or two good action sequences but little else on offer.
DRA                             84 min (ort 88 min)
B,V,V2                                   HOK L/A; VPD

### TRUCK TURNER *                               18
Jonathan Kaplan        USA                      1974
*Isaac Hayes, Yaphet Kotto, Alan Weeks, Annazette*
*Chase, Sam Laws, Nichelle Nichols*
A black detective who traces bail jumpers, avenges his partner's murder in this very violent and exploitative piece. Deservedly obscure, and a poor vehicle for a talented star.
THR                                               91 min
B,V                                                    STABL

### TRUE BLOOD **                                18
Frank Kerr              USA                     1989
*Jeff Fahey, Chad Lowe, James Tolkan, Sherilyn Fenn,*
*Billy Drago, Ken Foree*
Writer-director gives us the tale of a young thug and member of a street gang who is framed for the murder of a cop and forced to flee. Ten years later, after having served with the US Marines, he returns in time to save his kid brother from a life of crime in a gang that's led by an old enemy. However, his problems are exacerbated by the fact that he is still wanted for the cop's murder. A thinly-plotted action tale.
A/AD                                              89 min
V                                                    CBS

### TRUE CONFESSIONS ***                         15
Ulu Grosbard            USA                     1981
*Robert De Niro, Robert Duvall, Charles Durning, Ed*
*Flanders, Cyril Cusack, Burgess Meredith, Rose*
*Gregorio, Kenneth McMillan, Dan Hedaya, Gwen Van*
*Dam, Tom Hill, Jeanette Nolan, Jorge Cervera Jr,*
*Susan Meyers, Louisa Moritz*
An account of the complex relationship between two brothers, one a Catholic priest and the other a cop. Set in the late 1940s in California, and supposedly based on real life murder case the "Black Dahlia", which formed the basis for the TV movie WHO IS THE BLACK DAHLIA? Written by John Gregory Dunne and Joan Didion, who present a far from flattering view of the Catholic church and its servants.
Boa: novel by John Gregory Dunne.
DRA                             104 min (ort 108 min)
B,V                                                    WHV

**TRUE GAME OF DEATH *** 18
Chen Tien Tai Steve
                    HONG KONG            197-
*Bruce Le (Huang Kin Lung), Hsao Lung, Ali Taylor*
A martial arts master tries to form his own movie
production company, but runs into opposition from the
owners of the major studios, who hatch a plot to stop
him. A shoddy and exploitative copy of GAME OF
DEATH, with a Bruce Lee clone.
MAR            77 min (ort 90 min) Cut (3 min 33 sec)
B,V                      VTM L/A; NINCOL; MART; NET

**TRUE GRIT ****** PG
Henry Hathaway        USA            1969
*John Wayne, Kim Darby, Glen Campbell, Jeremy
Slate, Robert Duvall, Strother Martin, Dennis Hopper,
Alfred Ryder, Jeff Corey, Ron Soble, John Fielder,
James Westerfield, John Doucette, Donald Woods,
Edith Atwater, Carlos Rivas*
A plucky 14-year-old girl hires an ageing US marshal
with a reputation for doing things his own way, in
order to track down her father's killer. Wayne really
finds his form in this film, as the cynical hardbitten
marshal whose growing fondness for the girl brings
some joy into his life. Wayne's fine portrayal won him
his only Oscar. Written by Marguerite Roberts with
music by Elmer Bernstein. ROOSTER COGBURN
followed in 1975. AA: Actor (Wayne).
Boa: novel by Charles Portis.
WES                              128 min
V/h                               CIC

**TRUE STORIES *** PG
David Byrne        USA            1986
*David Byrne, John Goodman, Annie McEnroe,
Swoosie Kurtz, Spalding Gray, Roebuck "Pop" Staples,
Humberto "Tito" Larriva, John Ingle, Matthew Posey,
Jo Harvey Allen, Alix Elias*
Musical exploration of a fictional Texas town and the
lives of its more than averagely eccentric inhabitants,
with a narrator introducing a succession of figures. An
offbeat, aimless and curious blend of comedy, music
and social comment, all bundled up in the form of a set
of vignettes. The excellent score is by Byrne and New
Wave group Talking Heads.
MUS                        86 min (ort 89 min)
V/sh                              WHV

**TRUST ME *** 15
Robert Houston        USA            1988
*Adam Ant, Talia Balsam, David Packer*
The owner of an art gallery is heavily in debt, and has
hatched a scheme to solve his financial worries by
buying up the works of a great artist, and then killing
him so that the paintings will increase in value.
COM                              91 min
V                               FUTUR

**TUBBY THE TUBA *** Uc
Alexander Schure        USA            1977
*Voices of: Dick Van Dyke, Pearl Bailey, Jack Gilford,
Hermione Gingold, Ruth Enders, Ray Middleton*
Animated feature in which Tubby goes in search of a
melody of his own.
CAR                              81 min
B,V                      LOCUS L/A; CBS; VES

**TUCKER *** PG
Francis Ford Coppola   USA            1988
*Jeff Bridges, Martin Landau, Joan Allen, Frederic
Forrest, Dean Stockwell, Mako, Elias Koteas, Nina
Siemaszko, Christopher Slater, Corky Nemec,
Marshall Bell, Don Novello, Peter Donat, Dean
Goodman, Patti Austin*
The story of Preston Tucker, who attempted to build a
car for the future (he first conceived the seatbelt) in
the 1940s, but was crushed by opposition from the
giant automobile corporations. A big, wholesome and
stylish film in which the basically absorbing tale

tends to get swamped by flashy direction. The per-
formances are however, outstanding. The score is by
Joe Jackson.
Aka: TUCKER: THE MAN AND HIS DREAM
DRA                              110 min
B,V                              MGM

**TUFF TURF *** 18
Fritz Kierch        USA            1985
*James Spader, Kim Richards, Paul Mones, Robert
Downey, Matt Clark, Claudette Nevins, Olivia Barash,
Panchito Gomez, Michael Wyle, Catya Sassoon, Frank
McCarthy, Art Evans, Herb Mitchell, Cecil Cabot,
Donald Fullilove, Lou Fant*
A young boy falls for the girlfriend of a psychotic gang
leader and in so doing invites tragedy. Another
unimaginative reworking of a theme first successfully
explored in WEST SIDE STORY.
Aka: LOVE FIGHTERS; TOUGH TURF
DRA                        106 min (ort 112 min)
B,V                              CBS/FOX

**TULIPS** 15
Stan Ferris (Mark Warren/Rex Bromfield/Al
Waxman)               CANADA            1981
*Gabe Kaplan, Bernadette Peters, Henry Gibson, Al
Waxman, David Boxer, Harry Hill, Monique Belisle,
Richard Comar, Gregory Van Riel, Sean McCann,
Marilyn Innes, Elaine Labrie, Victor Desy, Terry
Coady, Gayle Garfinkle*
Two failed suicides meet and fall in love, a fortunate
event that gives them both a reason to go on living. A
trite and poorly directed attempt at an offbeat roman-
tic comedy.
COM                        89 min (ort 91 min)
B,V,V2                              EHE

**TUNES OF GLORY ****** PG
Ronald Neame        UK            1960
*Alec Guinness, John Mills, Dennis Price, Kay Walsh,
John Fraser, Gordon Jackson, Susannah York,
Duncan Macrae, Allan Cuthbertson*
A callous, hard-drinking and lazy colonel is replaced
by a younger, far more disciplined officer, and a battle
of wills takes place. A superb character study, with
fine performances and realistic confrontations. Set in
Scotland and written by Kennaway. Photography is
by Arthur Ibbetson.
Boa: novel by James Kennaway.
DRA                              106 min
V                               CH5

**TUNNEL, THE *** 15
Antonio Drove        SPAIN            1987
*Jane Seymour, Peter Weller, Fernando Rey*
This irritatingly pretentious offering tells of a painter
who, at an exhibition of his work, meets and becomes
obsessed with a woman. The two soon embark on an
intense relationship. An obscure and ponderous work
that will no doubt appeal to some. Filmed in Spain and
Argentina.
Boa: novel by Ernesto Sabato.
DRA                              110 min
V                               VES

**TUNNEL, THE *** 18
Massimo Pirri        ITALY            1983
*Helmut Berger, Corinne Clery, Marzio C. Honorato,
Franco Citti, Giorgio Ardisson*
The story of a heroin addict's long journey of self-
destruction, triggered off by his wife's desertion and
his meeting up with a female addict with the same
problems.
DRA                        88 min Cut (3 min 14 sec)
V                               ELE

**TUNNELS *** 15
Mark Byers        USA            1988
*Catherine Bach, Nicholas Guest, John Saxon, Vic*

*Tayback*
A woman reporter and photographer team up to investigate a series of murders and discover that the killings have been arranged by a property developer anxious to buy up property cheaply on behalf of a client. A flat and unconvincing story told very much in the style of a TV movie.

| | |
|---|---|
| THR | 89 min |
| V | VES |

## TUNNELVISION *
Brad Swirnoff/Neal Israel

USA 1976

*Brad Swirnoff, Phil Proctor, Howard Hesseman, Ernie Anderson, James Bacon, Edwina Anderson, Chevy Chase, Laraine Newman, Betty Thomas, Al Franken, Tom Davis, Gerrit Graham, Roger Bowen, Bill Schallert*
Satire on the future of TV, with examples of the kind of programmes we might expect to see but which with a little luck, will never be made. Many now famous names appear in bit parts. A limp and crude effort.

| | |
|---|---|
| COM | 65 min (ort 76 min) |
| B,V,V2 | INT |

## TURBO BLADE ***  PG
William A. Graham USA 1973

*David Janssen, Ralph Meeker, Elayne Heilveil, Sam Dawson, Harry Klekas, Don Wilbanks, Gavin James, Larry Doll, Wayne Wilkinson, Larry Peacey*
An air traffic controller, having witnessed an armed robbery and the taking of hostages, becomes involved in the hunt, using his WW2 pilot skills to mount an aerial chase. A taut and well-paced thriller.
Aka: BIRDS OF PREY
Boa: story by Rupert Hitzig and Robert Boris.

| | |
|---|---|
| THR | 81 min; 90 min (SID) mTV |
| B,V,V2 | IFS; SID (Betamax and VHS only); |
| NEWMED/SID | |

## TURK 182! **  15
Bob Clark USA 1985

*Timothy Hutton, Robert Urich, Robert Culp, Kim Cattrall, Darren McGavin, Peter Boyle, Steven Keats, Paul Sorvino, James Tolkan, Dick O'Neill*
A teenage boy mounts a graffiti campaign to protest against the shabby treatment of his fireman brother, injured in a fire but denied compensation and a pension. Given the vast expanse of graffiti (much highly artistic) that once covered the New York subway system, it's hard to accept the basic premise of this film, that it's OK to deface property provided it's in a good cause. In addition, neither Hutton nor the script provide much humour.

| | |
|---|---|
| COM | 92 min (ort 98 min) |
| B,V | CBS |

## TURN OF THE SCREW, THE ****
Jack Clayton UK/USA 1961

*Deborah Kerr, Michael Redgrave, Peter Wyngarde, Megs Jenkins, Pamela Franklin, Martin Stephens, Clytie Jessop, Isla Cameron*
Highly atmospheric tale of two children apparently possessed by evil spirits. Kerr is the newly-appointed governess, who suspects that their precocious and lascivious behaviour has its origin in a tragic love affair between two of the master's former employees. Remade as a TV movie in 1974. Written by William Archibald and Truman Capote with music by Georges Auric and photography by Freddie Francis. See also THE NIGHTCOMERS.
Aka: INNOCENTS, THE
Boa: story by Henry James.

| | |
|---|---|
| DRA | 100 min B/W |
| B,V | CBS |

## TURNAROUND **  15
Ola Solum USA 1986

*Tim Maier, Doug McKeon, Jonna Lee, Ed Bishop,*

*Eddie Albert, Gayle Hunnicutt, Edward McClarity*
A gang harasses a young boy out with his girlfriend in his dad's car, and the following night they gatecrash a party being given at his house and terrorise the guests. The girlfriend escapes and calls on the boy's uncle, a world famous illusionist, and he lures the gang to his mansion where he nearly frightens them to death by way of retribution. A thin little thriller rendered enjoyable by the attractive cast.

| | |
|---|---|
| THR | 87 min (ort 97 min) |
| V/sh | GHV |

## TURNER AND HOOCH **  PG
Roger Spottiswoode USA 1989

*Tom Hanks, Mare Winningham, Craig T. Nelson, Reginald VelJohnson, Scott Paulin, J.C. Quinn, John McIntire, Beasley the dog*
Hanks plays a fastidious detective whose one chance to catch a murderer resides in the only witness: the dead man's dog. Unfortunately, the beast is an ugly, slobbering mutt of voracious appetite and disagreeable habits. A kind of distant cousin to K-9, that's sustained by Hanks' likeable personality if not by the shallow plot, though there are one or two laughs to be had before the lame ending.

| | |
|---|---|
| COM | 96 min (ort 99 min) |
| V | TOUCH |

## TURNING POINT, THE **  PG
Herbert Ross USA 1977

*Shirley MacLaine, Anne Bancroft, Mikhail Baryshnikov, Leslie Browne, Tom Skerritt, Martha Scott, Marshall Thompson*
After many years have elapsed, two friends from the world of ballet meet up again. One has achieved stardom as a ballerina, while the other teaches dance and now has a daughter who has set her heart on a career in ballet. A tedious soap opera-style drama, partially redeemed by the excellent ballet sequences. This was Baryshnikov's debut. Written by Arthur Laurents.

| | |
|---|---|
| DRA | 114 min (ort 119 min) |
| B,V | CBS |

## TURTLE DIARY ***  PG
John Irvin UK 1985

*Glenda Jackson, Ben Kingsley, Richard Johnson, Michael Gambon, Eleanor Bron, Rosemary Leach, Harriet Walter, Jeroen Krabbe, Nigel Hawthorne, Michael Aldridge, Ron Anderson, Tony Melody, Gary Olsen, Peter Capaldi*
An odd couple are drawn together by their concern for the welfare of the giant turtles at the local zoo, and hatch a plan to return them to the ocean. An uneven but highly unusual character study, with offbeat dialogue and good performances. Scripted by Harold Pinter and produced by Richard Johnson. Look out for Pinter who appears very briefly as a customer in Kingsley's bookshop.
Boa: novel by Russell Hoban.

| | |
|---|---|
| DRA | 92 min (ort 97 min) |
| B,V | CBS |

## TUSKS *  15
Tara Moore UK 1987

*Lucy Gutteridge, Andrew Stevens, John Rhys-Davies, Julian Glover*
A curiously empty and simple-minded film, set in the African bush and telling of an American girl who arrives and immediately antagonises the local poachers, by publicly denouncing them as a menace to conservation. Our poachers set out to silence her in this predictable effort for which the location and natives serve as nothing more than a colourful backdrop.

| | |
|---|---|
| A/AD | 104 min |
| B,V | GHV |

## TUXEDO WARRIOR ** 15
Andrew Sinclair        USA         1985
*John Wyman, Carol Royle, James Coburn Jr, Holly
Palance, John Terry, Mike Samson, Beth Adams, Ken
Gampu*
Routine thriller set in an African country, with a hard
drinking, hard living anti-hero type, involved in a
hunt for stolen diamonds.
Aka: AFRICAN RUN, THE (ATLAS)
A/AD                                    93 min
B,V                          AVP L/A; ATLAS

## TWELFTH NIGHT *** U
John Gorrie          UK          198-
*Alec McCowen, Felicity Kendal, Sinead Cusack,
Annette Crosby, Robert Hardy*
An enjoyable TV version of Shakespeare's romantic
comedy of disguise, intrigue and passion with good
performances and direction.
Boa: play by William Shakespeare.
DRA                              130 min mTV
V/h                                    BBC

## TWELVE ANGRY MEN **** U
Sidney Lumet        USA         1957
*Henry Fonda, Lee J. Cobb, Ed Begley, E.G. Marshall,
Jack Warden, Martin Balsam, Jack Klugman, John
Fiedler, George Voskovec, Robert Webber, Edward
Binns, Joseph Sweeney*
After a jury retire to consider their verdict in an
apparently simple murder case, one man stands out
against the others, not because he believes the suspect
to be innocent, but simply because he is uncertain as
to his guilt. In the course of several hours, he
convinces them of the soundness of his position.
Despite the contrived script, this is a brilliant and
rewarding film, with memorable dialogue and performances. Written by Rose.
Boa: play by Reginald Rose.
DRA                    92 min (ort 95 min) B/W
V                                      WHV

## TWELVE CHAIRS, THE * U
Mel Brooks          USA         1970
*Ron Moody, Dom DeLuise, Mel Brooks, Frank
Langella, Bridget Brice, Robert Bernal, Diana
Coupland*
An unfunny comedy written and directed by Brooks,
but drawing its inspiration from a Russian satirical
novel of the 1920s. A poor Russian aristocrat sells a
set of twelve chairs only to discover that one of them
contains a fortune in jewels sewn into the seat,
thereby producing the perfect recipe for a frantic
chase. Filmed in Yugoslavia and most tiresome. See
also TWELVE PLUS ONE.
Boa: novel The Twelve Chairs by Ilf and Petroff
COM                      89 min (ort 93 min)
B,V                                    CBS

## TWELVE O'CLOCK HIGH ***
Henry King          USA         1949
*Gregory Peck, Hugh Marlowe, Gary Merrill, Millard
Mitchell, Dean Jagger, Paul Stewart, Robert Arthur,
John Kellogg*
The story of a US bomber group based in England
during WW2, and of the inevitable tensions the
alternating periods of combat and boredom cause
among the men. Peck gives an especially good per-
formance. Later recycled as a TV series. The script
was by Sy Bartlett and Beirne Lay Jr. AA: S. Actor
(Jagger), Sound (Fox Studios).
Boa: novel by Beirne Lay Jr and Sy Bartlett.
WAR                              132 min B/W
V/h                                    CBS

## TWELVE PLUS ONE **
Nicolas Gessner    FRANCE/ITALY      1971
*Sharon Tate, Orson Welles, Terry-Thomas, Vittorio
Gassman, Vittorio De Sica*

An Italian immigrant in New York sells some furniture he inherited and discovers too late that a fortune
has been hidden in one of the chairs. One of those
chase-type comedies that goes on for far too long and
has the laughs spread out far too thinly. The plot is
similar to Mel Brooks' film THE TWELVE CHAIRS
and was certainly inspired by the same novel. This
film has the last performance Tate gave before her
brutal murder.
Aka: 12 + 1; THIRTEEN CHAIRS, THE; UNA SU 13
COM                      90 min (ort 94 min)
B,V                                    ARF

## TWENTY DOLLAR STAR * 18
                     USA          1989
*Rebecca Holden, Eddie Barth, Marilyn Hassett, Steven
Ford, Dick Sargent*
A successful female movie star appears to enjoy a
totally fulfilled life, but in reality enjoys humiliation
and leads a double-life as a hooker, taking on
customers at $20 a time.
DRA                                    89 min
V                                      NEON

## TWENTY-ONE DAYS ** PG
Basil Dean/Alexander Korda
                     UK           1937
*Vivien Leigh, Laurence Olivier, Leslie Banks, Francis
L. Sullivan, David Horne, Esme Percy, Robert Newton,
William Dewhurst, Morris Harvey, Meinhart Maur,
Hay Petrie, Eliot Mason, Wallace Lupino, Muriel
George, Victor Rietti*
A man accidentally kills his girlfriend's husband but
is persuaded not to give himself up to the police by his
barrister brother, who is anxious to avoid a scandal. A
slow and stilted melodrama. The title refers to the
three weeks the culprit enjoys with his love before the
law catches up with him. Written by Graham Geeene.
Aka: 21 DAYS; FIRST AND THE LAST, THE;
TWENTY-ONE DAYS TOGETHER
Boa: play The First And The Last by John
Galsworthy.
DRA                              75 min B/W
V                                      PICK

## TWENTY-ONE HOURS AT MUNICH ** 15
William A. Graham     USA         1976
*William Holden, Shirley Knight, Franco Nero,
Anthony Quayle, Noel Willman, Georg Marischka,
Paul Smith, Martin Gilat, Else Quecke, Michael
Degen, James Hurley, Gunther-Maria Halmer,
Djamchid Soheli, Walter Kohout, Jan Niklas*
Dramatisation of the brutal murder of eleven Israeli
athletes and coaches by the PLO at the 1972 Munich
Olympics, with Holden miscast as the police chief in
charge of the operation. Fails to address the real
questions of possible collusion with the terrorists, or
other reasons for this fatal breach of security.
Aka: 21 HOURS AT MUNICH
Boa: book The Blood Of Israel by S. Groussard.
DRA                  97 min (ort 105 min) mTV
B,V                                    HER

## TWENTY-ONE JUMP STREET ** 15
Kim Manners         USA         1987
*Johnny Depp, Dustin Nguyen, Holly Robinson, Peter
DeLuise, Steven Williams*
A pilot for a TV series about a special group of young
police officers who fight crime in schools, with one
being sent there to investigate an extortion racket.
Not a bad effort, but a little too glossy to be
convincing.
Aka: 21 JUMP STREET
DRA                              95 min mTV
B,V                                    EIV

## TWENTY-THOUSAND LEAGUES UNDER U
THE SEA **
William Hanna/Joseph Barbera

USA 1973
A competent but unmemorable animated version of the famous story, that's set in New England of the 1860s and follows the exploits of a professor and a sailor who set out to hunt down a mysterious "sea beast".
Aka: 20,000 LEAGUES UNDER THE SEA
Boa: novel by Jules Verne.
CAR 48 min (ort 60 min)
V VES; VCC

## TWENTY-THOUSAND LEAGUES UNDER THE SEA ***
Richard Fleischer    USA    1954
Kirk Douglas, James Mason, Peter Lorre, Paul Lukas, Robert J. Wilke, Ted De Corsia, Carleton Young, Percy Helton, Fred Graham, J.M. Kerrigan, Edward Marr, Harry Harvey, Herb Vigran, Ted Cooper
An entertaining film version of the story of Captain Nemo, who uses his submarine to wage a personal battle against ships used for warfare. Douglas gives a vigorous performance as the harpooner in the group taken on board the vessel, when their own ship is sunk by the Nautilus. Mason is good as Nemo in an enjoyable Disney film with excellent effects. Written by Earl Felton. AA: Art/Set (John Meehan/Emil Kuri), Effects (Walt Disney Studios).
Aka: 20,000 LEAGUES UNDER THE SEA
Boa: novel by Jules Verne.
A/AD 122 min (ort 127 min)
B,V RNK

## TWICE A WOMAN **
George Sluizer    NETHERLANDS    1979
Anthony Perkins, Sandra Dumas, Bibi Andersson, Kitty Courbois, Tilly Perin-Bouwmeeste
A middle-aged woman falls for a young girl she picks up on the street and takes her to live with her in an openly lesbian relationship. However, the maternal urge proves so strong that the latter returns temporarily to her husband in order to have a child that they will be able to raise together.
Aka: SECOND TOUCH; TWEE VROUWEN
DRA 90 min (ort 113 min)
B,V,V2 VUL L/A; HVH

## TWICE DEAD *
Bert L. Dragin    USA    1988    18
Tom Breznahan, Jill Whitlow, Jonathan Chapin, Sam Melville, Christopher Burgard, Brooke Bundy, Todd Bridges
A wholesome all-American family moves into a mansion that's haunted by the ghost of a dead movie star and they clash, not with the ghost, but with a nasty gang of punks who were using the premises as their clubhouse. When they begin terrorising the family, the ghost helps them fight off the gang. Good performances and fair effects make this uninspired time-filler just about watchable.
FAN 85 min
V RCA

## TWICE IN A LIFETIME ***
Bud Yorkin    USA    1985    15
Gene Hackman, Ann-Margret, Ally Sheedy, Ellen Burstyn, Amy Madigan, Brian Dennehy, Stephen Lang, Darrell Larson, Chris Parker, Rachel Street, Kevin Bleyer, Nicole Mercurio, Doris Hugo Drewien, Lee Corrigan, Ralph Steadman
A comedy-drama telling of a middle-aged man with a dull marriage who falls in love with a younger woman, causing his family a great deal of pain. This powerful examination of the mid-life crisis generally avoids both cliche and over-sentimentality, and has memorable performances from all concerned. Written by Colin Welland.
DRA 106 min (ort 117 min)
B,V VES

## TWICE ROUND THE DAFFODILS **
Gerald Thomas    UK    PG    1962
Juliet Mills, Donald Sinden, Donald Houston, Kenneth Williams, Ronald Lewis, Jill Ireland, Joan Sims, Andrew Ray, Lance Percival, Sheila Hancock, Nanette Newman
This uneven collection of observations and misadventures revolves around the lives of the patients and staff at a male TB sanatorium, where an attractive nurse has a difficult time fending off her amorous patients. A bawdy adaptation of the stage play, done in appropriate "Carry On" style.
Boa: play Ring For Catty by Patrick Cargill and Jack Beale.
COM 85 min (ort 89 min) B/W
V WHV

## TWICE UNDER **
Dean Crow    USA    18    1987
Ian Border, Ron Spencer, Amy Lacy, Jack O'Hara
An ex-GI spent his time in Vietnam as a "tunnel rat", fighting the Vietcong in the network of underground tunnels they used as bolt-holes. After the war he takes a job working in a city's underground sewage system, but keeps in training by playing underground war games with his son. When a series of fellow workers are found murdered, he realises that an old enemy from the war is out to get him. Fair.
THR 82 min (ort 90 min)
V HIFLI

## TWILIGHT PEOPLE, THE *
Eddie Romero    PHILIPPINES/USA    15    1972
John Ashley, Pat Woodell, Pam Grier, Charles Macaulay, Eddie Garcia, Jan Merlin, Ken Metcalfe, Tony Gonsalves, Mona Morena, Kim Ramos, Letty Mirasol, Angelo Centenera, Cenon Gonzalez, Romeo Mabutol, Max Rojo, Roger Ocomapo
A mad scientist on a deserted island conducts experiments that result in the creation of half-human creatures. A feeble clone of "The Island Of Lost Souls".
HOR 76 min (ort 84 min)
B,V ATLAS

## TWILIGHT ZONE: THE MOVIE ***
Steven Spielberg/Joe Dante/George Miller/John Landis    USA    15    1983
Vic Morrow, John Lithgow, Scatman Crothers, Bill Quinn, Dan Aykroyd, Albert Brooks, Kevin McCarthy, Kathleen Quinlan, Selma Diamond, Jeremy Licht, Abbe Lane, Donna Dixon, Doug McGrath, Charles Hallahan, Martin Garner
Four tales (three of which were remakes from the TV series), of varying power on the theme of the unknown. In one old folk regain their youth, in another an odious bigot suffers racism, in the third a boy has horrifying powers and in the last a man on a plane sees a nasty creature perched outside. Narrated by Burgess Meredith, Dan Aykroyd and Albert Brooks.
Aka: TWILIGHT ZONE, THE
Boa: short stories Kick The Can by George Clayton Johnson/Nightmare At 20,000 Feet by Richard Matheson.
FAN 98 min (ort 101 min)
V/sh WHV

## TWILIGHT ZONE: VOLUME 1 **
Wes Craven/Tommy Lee Wallace    PG
USA    1986
Bruce Willis, Dan Gilvezan, Murukh, John Carlyle, Seth Isler, Anthony Gumbach, Melinda Dillon, Greg Mullavey, Virginia Keehne, Brittany Wilson, Robert Klein, Annie Potts, Adam Raber, Meg Foster, David Hayward
Four shorts that attempt to recapture the feeling of a popular TV series of the 1950s. Episodes are entitled: "Shatterday", "A Little Peace and Quiet", "Wordplay" and "Dreams for Sale". Followed by several more compilations.

Osca: TWILIGHT ZONE: VOLUME 2 (asa)
FAN          95 min; 191 min (2 film cassette) mTV
B,V                                              CBS

**TWILIGHT ZONE: VOLUME 2 ** **          PG
S. Neufeld Jr/R. Downey/J. Hancock/R. Friedberg/T.L.
Wallace          USA          1986
*Eric Bogosian, Vincent Gardenia, Robert Constanzo,
Steven Keats, Lorna Luft, Sydney Walsh, Jeffrey
DeMunn, Michael Greene, Arliss Howard, Season
Hubley, Scott Grimes, Nicolas Surovy, Dee Wallace-
Stone, Peter Land, Julie Carmen*
Five short tales inspired by the popular supernatural
TV series of the 1950s. Episodes are entitled: "Healer",
"Children's Zoo", "Kentucky Rye", "Little Boy Lost"
and "Wish Bank".
Osca: TWILIGHT ZONE: VOLUME 1 (asa)
FAN          96 min; 191 min (2 film cassette) mTV
B,V                                              CBS

**TWILIGHT ZONE: VOLUME 3 ** **          PG
John Hancock/Peter Medak/Paul Lynch
                 USA          1986
*Tony LoBianco, Jenny Lewis, Nan Martin, Andrea
Barber, David Dukes, Robert Morse, Carolyn Seymour,
David Mendenhall, Christopher Allport, Elizabeth
Normant, Ed Krieger, Kerry Noonan, Duncan McNeil,
Vanessa Brown*
Another four supernatural tales in this series – "If She
Dies", "Ye Gods", "Examination Day" and "Message
From Charity". Average.
Osca: TWILIGHT ZONE: VOLUME 4 (asa)
FAN          97 min; 194 min (2 film cassette) mTV
B,V                                              CBS

**TWILIGHT ZONE: VOLUME 4 ** **          15/PG
B.W.L. Norton/Alan Smithee/Theodore Flicker/J.D.
Feigelson          USA          1986
*Adrienne Barbeau, Adam Postil, Miguel Nunez, Josh
Richman, Danny Kaye, Glyn Thurman, John Bryant,
Corky Ford, Mike Reynolds, James Coco, Bob Dishy,
Avery Schreiber, Piper Laurie, Robert Blossom, Andre
Gower, Danny Cooksey*
The four tales of the supernatural in this volume are
entitled: "Teacher's Aide", "Paladin of the Lost Hour",
"Act Break" and "The Burning Man".
Osca: TWILIGHT ZONE: VOLUME 3 (asa)
FAN          95 min; 194 min (2 film cassette – PG) mTV
B,V                                              CBS

**TWIN DRAGON ENCOUNTER ***          15
Paul Dunlop          USA          1988
*Michael McNamara, Martin McNamara*
Twin brothers take on a mercenary group who
invaded their summer paradise and kidnapped their
girlfriends. Another violent martial arts story.
MAR                            78 min Cut (52 sec)
V                                              BRAVE

**TWIN PEAKS ** **
David Lynch          USA          198-
*Michael Ontkean, Joan Chen, Kyle MacLachlan, Piper
Laurie, Dan Ashbrook, Jim Marshall*
A bizarre story set in a small North American logging
town, where the discovery of the body of a dead girl is
a prelude to a series of sinister events. Pilot for an
opaque and over-hyped TV series.
THR                                              113 min
V/sh                                              WHV

**TWINKLE TWINKLE LUCKY STARS ** **          18
Samo Hung          HONG KONG          198-
*Jackie Chan, Samo Hung*
Chan heads a team of crime-fighters who take on the
task of destroying a powerful underworld organisa-
tion.
MAR                                              90 min
B,V                                              VPD

**TWINKY ** **          15
Richard Donner          ITALY/UK          1969
*Charles Bronson, Susan George, Trevor Howard,
Michael Craig, Honor Blackman, Lionel Jeffries,
Elspeth March, Eric Chitty, Cathy Jose, Robert Morley,
Jack Hawkins, Jimmy Tarbuck, Norman Vaughan,
Orson Bean, Eric Barker*
Story of a strange marriage between a teenage girl
and a 40-year-old author, who takes his young bride
back to New York and raises a few eyebrows. One of
those 1960s sex comedies that now looks very dated.
Aka: LOLA
COM          94 min (ort 98 min) (Cut at film release)
B,V                            RNK; MIA (VHS only)

**TWINS *** ***          PG
Ivan Reitman          USA          1988
*Arnold Schwarzenegger, Danny DeVito, Chloe Webb,
Kelly Preston, Bonnie Bartlett, Marshall Bell, Trey
Wilson, Hugh O'Brian*
A crazy and totally implausible comedy telling of
genetically designed twins who were separated at
birth and only learn of each other 35 years later,
whereupon they embark on a search for their mother.
Schwarzenegger and DeVito work perfectly together,
and it is their fine performances that largely sustain
the film.
COM                            102 min (ort 112 min)
V/sh                                              CIC

**TWINS OF EVIL ***          18
John Hough          UK          1971
*Peter Cushing, Dennis Price, Isobel Black, Mary
Collinson, Madeleine Collinson, Kathleen Byron,
David Warbeck, Damien Thomas, Alex Scott, Luan
Peters, Katya Keith, Harvey Hall, Roy Stewart, Maggie
Wright, Inigo Jackson*
Identical twins become victims of a vampire cult. Only
a crucifix-wielding vampire hunter can save them
before they are burnt alive by a Puritan sect. Hammer
used twin Playmates from Playboy magazine, but this
novel aspect adds little to a film whose only outstand-
ing asset is its excellent sets.
Aka: GEMINI TWINS, THE; TWINS OF DRACULA;
VIRGIN VAMPIRES
HOR          83 min (ort 86 min) (Cut at film release)
B,V                            RNK L/A; MIA (VHS only)

**TWIST, THE ***
Claude Chabrol
                 FRANCE/ITALY/WEST GERMANY          1976
*Bruce Dern, Stephane Audran, Ann-Margret, Sydne
Rome, Jean-Pierre Cassel, Curt Jurgens, Charles
Aznavour, Maria Schell*
An American writer living in Paris finds his marriage
is coming apart. An endlessly boring and dull attempt
to make something of an uninteresting story. Both an
English and a French version were filmed.
Aka: FOLIES BOURGEOISES
DRA                                              105 min
B,V                                              TEVP

**TWISTED ***          18
Adam Holender          USA          1985
*Lois Smith, Tandy Cronyn, Christian Slater, Brooke
Tracy, Dina Merrill*
Film version of a Broadway play about a highly
disturbed 14-year-old boy who directs his energies
towards terrorising his family and peers. Having
finished off the latest in a long line of nannies by
arranging an "accident", his parents hire a new nanny
to babysit for him and his baby sister. He sets about
giving her the full treatment, in a plodding film full of
sadistic scares but little else.
Boa: play Children! Children! by Jack Horrigan.
DRA                                              87 min
B,V                                              VIR

## TWISTED NERVE *
Roy Boulting          UK          1968
*Hayley Mills, Hywel Bennett, Billie Whitelaw, Phyllis
Calvert, Frank Finlay, Barry Foster, Salmaan Peer,
Gretchen Franklin, Christian Roberts, Thorley
Walters, Timothy West, Russell Napier*
A psychopathic young man with a retarded brother
disguises himself in order to kill his hated stepfather.
A tasteless and exploitative film that almost says that
mental retardation and psychopathic violence are
linked. A waste of a good cast. Written by Leo Marks
and Roy Boulting. The music is by Bernard Herr-
mann.
THR                          113 min (ort 118 min)
B,V                                          TEVP

## TWISTED NIGHTMARE *                      18
Paul Hunt             USA              1987
*Belinda Grey, Rhonda Gray, Cleve Hall, Brad
Bartrum, Robert Padilla*
A bunch of teens take a vacation at a seedy holiday
resort, and discover to their cost that it's haunted by a
deformed, maniacal killer. Bad dialogue and uncon-
vincing acting unite in this utterly predictable and
boring slasher tale. Cut before video submission by 6
sec.
HOR                          91 min Cut (20 sec)
B,V                                           RCA

## TWISTER *                                  15
Michael Almereyda    USA               1988
*Suzy Amis, Crispin Glover, Harry Dean Stanton,
Dylan McDermot, Jenny Wright, Charlaine Woodard,
Lois Chiles, Tim Robbins, William Burroughs*
Patriarch Stanton is the head of a large family of
spoilt brats and disagreeable misfits, and this rather
pointless film looks at a few days in their lives.
Written by Almereyda, this offbeat character study
has no central point of view to give it direction, nor
enough wit to make it enjoyable.
Boa: book Oh by Mary Robison.
COM                          88 min (ort 93 min)
V                                             VES

## TWO AND A HALF DADS **                     U
Tony Bill             USA              1986
*George Dzundza, Richard Young, Sal Viscuso, Lenore
Kasdorf*
Three Vietnam veterans and their families attempt to
live under the one roof in this typical Disney-style
comedy.
Aka: 2 1/2 DADS
Osca: LAST ELECTRIC KNIGHT, THE
JUV                          44 min (ort 60 min)
B,V                                           WDV

## TWO CRIPPLED HEROES **                     18
                HONG KONG              1980
A woman incurs the wrath of a powerful warlord when
she learns the secret source of his weapons, but is
saved from death by the two title characters, one of
whom has no legs and the other no arms. Apart from
the unusual spectacle of disabled fighters proving
their worth, this routine martial arts film has little
else of originality.
MAR                                        92 min
B,V                                           VPD

## TWO EVIL EYES *                            18
George A. Romero/Dario Argento          1989
*Adrienne Barbeau, Harvey Keitel*
Two perfectly good Poe stories are mangled in the
service of two directors. In the first tale a wife plots
the murder of her rich husband with the help of a
doctor and in the second a jealous husband kills his
musician wife and her beloved pet cat (or so he
thinks).
Boa: short stories: The Facts In The Case Of M.
Valdemar and The Black Cat By Edgar Allan Poe.

HOR                                       115 min
V                                             MED

## TWO FACES OF EVIL, THE **                  15
Alan Gibson           UK               1980
*Anna Calder-Marshall, Gary Raymond, Pauline
Delany, Paul Hawkins, Phillip Latham, Jenny Laird,
William Moore, Jeremy Longhurst, Brenda Cowling,
Mike Savage, Malcolm Hayes*
Strange things happen to a family as they set out on
their holidays during a storm. Driving through a
village, the father is attacked by a vampire-like
creature that seems to be his double. A standard
Hammer House of Horror production.
Osca: RUDE AWAKENING (CH5)
HOR      54 min (ort 60 min); 101 min (2 film cassette)
mTV
B,V,V2                        PRV; CH5 (VHS only)

## TWO FATHERS' JUSTICE **                    PG
Rod Holcomb           USA              1984
*Robert Conrad, George Hamilton, Brooke Bundy,
Catherine Corkill, Whitney Kershaw, Greg Terrell, Bo
Kapral, Ted Levine, Dean Hill, Stephen Dunn, David
Darlow, Mark Von Holstein, Will Zahn, Byrne Piven,
Richard Kind, Alan Wilder*
Two fathers plan to get revenge on the killers of their
children, murdered on the eve of their wedding in a
disagreement over drugs. Though one is an unem-
ployed steelworker and the other an inhibited execu-
tive, they are both obliged to forget their differences in
order to collaborate in the murder hunt. Average.
Boa: story by Begen Meggs.
A/AD                         95 min (ort 100 min) mTV
B,V                                           EHE

## TWO FOR THE ROAD ***                       PG
Stanley Donen         UK               1967
*Audrey Hepburn, Albert Finney, Eleanor Bron,
William Daniels, Nadia Gray, Claude Dauphin,
Jacqueline Bisset*
On a motoring holiday through France, an architect
and his wife reminisce over their 12 years of marriage,
doing their best to come to terms with what each has
come to dislike about the other. An absorbing comedy-
drama whose rather trite plot serves as little more
than a backdrop to splendid performances from the
leads. The score is by Henry Mancini.
DRA                          111 min (ort 113 min)
V/h                                           CBS

## TWO IDIOTS IN HOLLYWOOD *                   15
                USA                    1989
*Jim McGrath, Jeff Doucette*
Two losers leave their dreary lives in Ohio and try to
make it in Hollywood, but find that things do not go as
planned. Unsympathetic characterisations combine
with poor plotting and indifferent dialogue to produce
a film of minimal entertainment value.
Aka: 2 IDIOTS IN HOLLYWOOD
COM                                        82 min
V                                             RCA

## TWO LEFT FEET *                            15
Roy Baker             UK               1963
*Michael Crawford, Nyree Dawn Porter, Julia Foster,
David Hemmings, Bernard Lee, Dilys Watling, David
Lodge*
A callow and inexperienced teenager embarks on an
affair with a waitress, has a fight with his fiance but
eventually achieves some maturity. A rather pointless
stab at a comedy with sexual overtones, that looked
dated at the time.
Boa: novel In My Solitude by David Stuart Leslie.
COM                          90 min (ort 93 min) B/W
V                                             WHV

## TWO MOON JUNCTION *                        18
Zalman King           USA              1988

*Sherilyn Fenn, Richard Tyson, Louise Fletcher, Burl Ives, Kristy McNichol, Millie Perkins, Don Galloway, Herve Villechaize, Dabbs Greer, Screamin' Jay Hawkins*
Just two weeks before she is due to be married, a well-bred Southern girl falls for a handsome carnival worker and runs off with him. Her rich granny and the local sheriff conspire to stop them. A dumb romance with a lot of humour on offer, but most of it of the unintentional kind.

| DRA | 100 min (ort 104 min) |
|---|---|
| V | CBS |

## TWO MRS CARROLLS, THE ***

| Peter Godfrey | USA | 1945 (released 1947) |
|---|---|---|

*Humphrey Bogart, Barbara Stanwyck, Alexis Smith, Nigel Bruce, Isobel Elsom, Ann Carter, Creighton Hale, Peter Godfrey, Pat O'Moore, Anita Bolster, Colin Campbell, Leyland Hodgson, Barry Bernard*
Bogart stars as a psychopathic artist who paints his wives as the Angel of Death, then disposes of them with poisoned milk. This disjointed film climaxes with a fair degree of tension, but is hampered by implausible casting of the star. Written by Thomas Job.
Boa: play by Martin Vale.

| THR | 95 min (ort 99 min) B/W |
|---|---|
| V | WHV |

## TWO MRS GRENVILLES, THE: PARTS 1 AND 2 ***    15

| John Erman | USA | 1987 |
|---|---|---|

*Ann-Margret, Claudette Colbert, Stephen Collins, John Rubinstein, Elizabeth Ashley, Alan Oppenheimer, Margaret Courtney, Delena Kidd, Penny Fuller, Sian Philips, Peter Eyre, Sam Wanamaker, Kate Harper, Jana Shelden, Toria Fuller*
A chorus girl with a dubious past, marries a member of a wealthy and influential family, that's headed by a redoubtable matriarch who cannot accept her for her humble origins. Scandal erupts however, when the wife shoots her husband in what she claims is a tragic accident. Based on a true case, this fictionalised account offers great scope for a moving performance by Ann-Margret, in a restrained and well-crafted drama.
Boa: novel by Dominick Dunne.

| DRA | 190 min (2 cassettes) mTV |
|---|---|
| B,V | CBS |

## TWO MULES FOR SISTER SARA **    15

| Don Siegel | USA | 1969 |
|---|---|---|

*Clint Eastwood, Shirley MacLaine, Manolo Fabregas, Alberto Morin, Armando Silvestre, John Kelly, Enrique Lucero, Jose Chavez*
A tough American mercenary in Mexico meets a prostitute posing as a nun, and gradually becomes involved with her and the struggle against the French forces, who occupied the country in the 1860s. Together they embark on a daring scheme to seize control of the enemy's garrison, in this mildly entertaining but seriously overlong story. The script is by Albert Maltz.
Boa: story by Budd Boetticher.

| WES | 100 min (ort 116 min) |
|---|---|
| V/h | CIC |

## TWO OF A KIND *    PG

| John Herzfield | USA | 1983 |
|---|---|---|

*John Travolta, Olivia Newton-John, Charles Durning, Beatrice Straight, Scatman Crothers, Castulo Guerra, Oliver Reed, James Stephens, Gene Hackman (voice only)*
A fantasy about God's angels persuading him to give humanity another chance and sparing the Earth from a second flood, provided they can find two people prepared to make a great sacrifice for each other. A silly yarn that lacks the light touch of those 1930s and 1940s films of the same genre, such as "Here Comes Mr Jordan". Written by Herzfield.

| COM | 84 min (ort 87 min) |
|---|---|
| B,V | CBS |

## TWO RODE TOGETHER **    PG

| John Ford | USA | 1961 |
|---|---|---|

*James Stewart, Richard Widmark, Shirley Jones, Linda Crystal, Andy Devine, John McIntire*
A lawman and a cavalry officer form an uneasy alliance when they set out to rescue a group of settlers kidnapped by Comanches. A competent Western sustained by convincing performances rather than any intrinsic merits within the plot.

| WES | 105 min (ort 109 min) |
|---|---|
| V | RCA |

## TWO TO TANGO **    18

| Hector Olivera | ARGENTINA/USA | 1988 |
|---|---|---|

*Don Stroud, Adrienne Sachs, Michael Cavanaugh, Duilio Marzio*
A contract killer falls in love with the girlfriend of his intended victim, and decides to quit the profession without completing his assignment. An obscure and murky little thriller, but quite atmospheric.

| THR | 88 min |
|---|---|
| V | RCA |

## TWO WAY STRETCH ***

| Robert Day | UK | 1960 |
|---|---|---|

*Peter Sellers, Lionel Jeffries, Wilfrid Hyde-White, Liz Fraser, Beryl Reid, Maurice Denham, Bernard Cribbins, David Lodge, Irene Handl, Thorley Walters, Walter Hudd, George Woodbridge, Cyril Chamberlain, John Wood*
Amusing prison comedy with a certain period charm, that is blessed by the happy notion of prisoners devising a means of absenting themselves temporarily, in order to commit a robbery for which they will have a perfect alibi. Some of the plot is borrowed from the 1938 film "Convict 99".

| COM | 83 min (ort 87 min) B/W |
|---|---|
| B,V | TEVP; WHV (VHS only) |

## TWO WONDROUS TIGERS ***    15

| Cheung Sum | HONG KONG | 1980 |
|---|---|---|

*Philip Ko, John Chang, Tiger Young, Wilson Tong, Yang Pan Pan, Charlie Chan, Mung Kwun Ha, Kim Woo-Suk, Lee Suk-Koo, Jang Jung-Kuok, Ahn Jin-Soo*
A young man tries to kidnap a girl he wants to marry, but is opposed and told that only if he can defeat the girl, her sister and her brother will he gain her hand. When these three beat him, he posts a large reward to find some champions to fight on his behalf. A fast-paced action tale set in Nationalist China.

| MAR | 88 min Cut (38 sec) |
|---|---|
| B,V | VPD |

## TWO WORLDS OF JENNY LOGAN, THE ***    PG

| Frank De Felitta | USA | 1979 |
|---|---|---|

*Lindsay Wagner, Marc Singer, Alan Feinstein, Linda Gray, Henry Wilcoxon, Joan Darling, Irene Tedrow, Peter Hobbs, Constance McCashin, Charles Thomas Murphy, Allen Williams, Pat Corley, John Hawker, Gloria Stuart*
A woman and her husband move to their new home and she finds a 19th century dress in the attic. Putting it on transports her back to that period, where she finds she has a life in that time too, and where two bitter rivals vie for her affections. She returns to the present, but with research learns of an "imminent" tragedy in the 19th, and ultimately leaves her husband in an attempt to avert it. An unusual and entertaining fantasy.
Boa: novel Second Sight by David Williams.

| FAN | 92 min (ort 100 min) mTV |
|---|---|
| V | HER |

## 240 ROBERT **    U

| Paul Krasny | USA | 1979 |
|---|---|---|

*Joanna Cassidy, Mark Harmon, John Bennett Perry,*
*Lew Saunders, Joe Al Nicasio, Thomas Babson, Steve*
*Tabber, Peter J. Pitchess*
Pilot for a series detailing the exploits of a search-and-
rescue team working in Los Angeles county, using a
variety of special vehicles such as helicopters, motor-
bikes, boats etc. Nothing more than a gimmick-
ridden, formula action film.

| | |
|---|---|
| A/AD | 69 min (ort 73 min) |
| B,V | HER |

## TWO-HUNDRED MOTELS ** 18
Frank Zappa/Tony Palmer
                          USA                        1971
*Frank Zappa, Ringo Starr, Theodore Bikel, The*
*Mothers of Invention, Keith Moon, Flo and Eddie,*
*Janet Ferguson, Lucy Offerall, Don Preston, Dick*
*Barber, Jimmy Carl Black, Pamela Miller*
Rambling musical fantasy featuring Frank Zappa of
rock group fame, and his associates, that does not
really work as a movie, as no discipline is applied to
the filming. If you like the music of Zappa, this one is
worth hearing if not seeing.
Aka: 200 MOTELS

| | |
|---|---|
| MUS | 98 min |
| V/h | WHV |

## 2001: A SPACE ODYSSEY **** U
Stanley Kubrick        UK                        1968
*Keir Dullea, William Sylvester, Gary Lockwood,*
*Leonard Rossiter, Robert Beatty, Daniel Richter,*
*Margaret Tyzack, Frank Miller, Alan Gifford, Penny*
*Brahms, Edwina Carroll, Sean Sullivan, Douglas*
*Rain (voice of HAL 9000)*
A brilliantly innovative film spoilt by an incoherent
plot. The evolution of man has been subject to strange
forces which have waited until mankind has reached
the point at which space flight is possible. Great ideas,
such as "HAL" a super-computer, are contained in a
Clarke and Kubrick script. Scored by Ligeti, with
Richard Strauss's opening to "Also Spake Zarathus-
tra". Cut by 17 minutes after premiere. 2010 followed
in 1984. AA: Effects (Kubrick).
Boa: short story The Sentinel by Arthur C. Clarke.

| | |
|---|---|
| FAN | 139 min (ort 141 min) |
| V/sh | MGM |

## 2010 *** PG
Peter Hyams           USA                        1984
*Roy Scheider, John Lithgow, Helen Mirren, Bob*
*Balaban, Keir Dullea, Dana Elcar, James McEachin,*
*Madolyn Smith, Elya Baskin, Savely Kramarov,*
*Natasha Schneider, Oleg Rudnik, S. Newton*
*Anderson, Douglas Rain (voice of HAL 9000)*
Interesting sequel to Kubrick's famous original which
builds on some of the ideas explored in the earlier film.
A combined US/USSR mission is launched nine years
after Discovery's voyage, to find out what happened to
the first mission. By way of a subplot, both participat-
ing countries are drawing progressively closer to
nuclear war. Good effects, and a sound if uninspired
story, lead to a contrived ending. Written by Hyams.
Aka: 2010: THE YEAR WE MAKE CONTACT
Boa: novel 2010: Odyssey Two by Arthur C. Clarke.

| | |
|---|---|
| FAN | 112 min (ort 114 min) |
| V/sh | MGM |

## TWO-THOUSAND MANIACS * 18
Herschell Gordon Lewis
                          USA                        1964
*Connie Mason, Thomas Wood, Jeffrey Archer, Shelby*
*Livingston, Jerome Eden, Ben Moore, Vincent Santo,*
*Gary Bakeman, Mark Douglas, Michael Korb*
A legendary low-grade horror tale, telling of a sinister
Southern ghost town that comes to life 100 years after
it was sacked in the Civil War, and takes a grisly
revenge on six young swingers who find themselves
trapped there. As poorly supplied with acting talent as
it is well supplied with gore. Better than "Blood

Feast", an earlier Lewis film, but that's not saying
much.
Aka: 2,000 MANIACS

| | |
|---|---|
| HOR | 85 Min; 80 min (WIZ) (ort 88 min) |
| | Cut (4 min 27 sec) |
| B,V | WIZ/VPR; VPD; WIZ |

## TYCOON ** U
Richard Wallace       USA                        1947
*John Wayne, Anthony Quinn, Cedric Hardwicke,*
*Laraine Day, Judith Anderson, James Gleason, Grant*
*Withers, Paul Fix, Fernando Alvarado, Harry Woods,*
*Michael Harvey, Charles Trowbridge, Martin*
*Garralaga*
An engineer engaged to build a railway tunnel in the
Andes, comes into conflict with his boss when he falls
for the latter's daughter. An overlong but mildly
enjoyable tale. Written by Borden Chase and John
Twist.
Boa: novel by C.E. Scoggins.
Osca: SIX GUN GOLD (KVD); HELLO SUCKER or
TITANS DON'T CRY (CHAM)

| | |
|---|---|
| DRA | 123 min (ort 129 min) |
| B,V | KVD L/A; CHAM L/A; VCC (VHS only) |

## TYCOON: PARTS 1 AND 2 ** U
Doug Jackson/Denys Arcand
                          USA                        1983
*Kenneth Walsh, Jennifer Dale, Martha Henry,*
*Gabrielle Arcand*
Set in the years between WW1 and WW2, this
two-part tale follows the rise to power of a ruthless
Canadian tycoon. A glossy, superficial and rather
tedious story, originally shown in six 50 minute
episodes.
Aka: EMPIRE INC. (Part 1 only); TYCOON: HELLO
SUCKER/TITANS DON'T CRY

| | |
|---|---|
| DRA | 300 min (2 cassettes) mTV |
| B,V | KVD; |
| CAREY | |

# U

## U-2 INCIDENT, THE *** 
Delbert Mann          USA                        1976
*Lee Majors, Nehemiah Persoff, Noah Beery Jr,*
*William Daniels, Lew Ayres, Brooke Bundy, Jim*
*McMullen, Biff McGuire, James Gregory*
The story of the infamous U-2 incident of 1960, when
an American spy-plane was shot down over the Soviet
Union and the pilot captured. Majors is excellent as
Powers, and the pilot's interrogation at the hands of
his captors and subsequent exchange in a spy-swap is
convincingly chronicled in this restrained,
documentary-style drama. Powers later became a
helicopter pilot for an American radio station but was
killed in an air-crash in 1977.
Aka: FRANCIS GARY POWERS: THE TRUE STORY
OF THE U-2 INCIDENT

| | |
|---|---|
| DRA | 100 min mTV |
| V | PARK |

## U.F.O. – INVASION U.F.O. ** PG
Gerry Anderson/David Lane/David Tomblin
                          UK                         1972
*Ed Bishop, George Sewell, Michael Billington, Wanda*
*Ventham, Vladek Sheybal, Gabrielle Drake, Antonia*
*Ellis, Dolores Mantez, Peter Gordeno, Harry Baird,*
*Grant Taylor, Jeremy Wilkin*
A top-secret organisation is formed to protect Earth
from an alien invasion. A mediocre feature compiled
from TV series of similar virtues.
Aka: INVASION U.F.O.

| | |
|---|---|
| FAN | 95 min mTV |
| B,V | PRV; CH5 (VHS only) |

## U.F.O. – VOLUME 6 *

U

Ron Appleton/Alan Perry  UK
*Ed Bishop, George Sewell, Michael Billington, Wanda
Ventham, Vladek Sheybal, Gabrielle Drake, Antonia
Ellis, Dolores Mantez, Peter Gordeno, Harry Baird,
Grant Taylor, Jeremy Wilkin, Jack Hedley, Pippa
Steele, David Sumner*
Two episodes from a rather tedious space opera series.
"Court Martial" tells of a clash of loyalties when a
security leak leads to a sentence of death and in "Kill
Straker!" a lunar model is attacked by a UFO and
Commander Straker has to face the possibility that
one of his officers may have been taken over by the
aliens.

| FAN | 95 min mTV |
|---|---|
| V | CH5 |

## U.H.F. **

PG

Jay Levey            USA            1989
*Victoria Jackson, Weird Al Yankovic, Kevin
McCarthy, Michael Richards, David Bowe, Stanley
Brock, Anthony Geary, Trinidad Silva, Gedde
Watanabe, Billy Barty, John Paragon, Fran Drescher,
Sue Ann Langdon, Emo Philips*
Taking a break from his parodies of music videos,
Yankovic gets a starring feature film debut, when he
plays the new manager of Channel 62, a UHF station
with the lowest ratings in the country. The station
soon climbs the ratings ladder with its wacky programming, and this unfocused film provides some very
funny parodies and a good role for Richards as an
ex-janitor turned kiddie-show host. The disjointed
script is by Yankovic and Levey.

| COM | 93 min (ort 97 min) |
|---|---|
| V | VIR |

## UFORIA ***

PG

John Binder            USA            1981
*Cindy Williams, Harry Dean Stanton, Fred Ward,
Harry Carey Jr, Beverly Hope Atkinson, Darrell
Larson, Robert Gray, Peggy McCay, Ted Harris, Diane
Diefendorf, Hank Worden, Alan Beckwith, Andrew
Winner, Pamela Lamont*
Gentle look at a collection of Southwest misfits,
focusing on a checkout cashier who believes in UFOs
and is eagerly awaiting contact with visiting aliens.

| COM | 90 min (ort 92 min) |
|---|---|
| V | CIC |

## UGLY DACHSHUND, THE **

Uc

Norman Tokar            USA            1966
*Dean Jones, Suzanne Pleshette, Charlie Ruggles, Kelly
Thordsen, Parley Baer, Mako, Charles Lane*
A husband and wife each have a dog, and both
animals are trained to be entered in a competition.
(And if that doesn't set your adrenalin going then I'm
afraid there's no hope for you.) A silly and contrived
Disney comedy aimed at kids but an insult to their
intelligence. Written by Albert Aley.
Boa: novel by G.B. Stern.

| COM | 93 min; 90 min (WDV) |
|---|---|
| B,V | RNK; WDV |

## ULTIMATE NINJA, THE ***

18

Godfrey Ho      HONG KONG      1986
*Stuart Smith, Bruce Baron, Sorapong Chatri*
A twenty year old feud between an evil tyrant and the
benevolent leader of a village, results in the death of
the latter and the village falling under the control of
ruthless thugs. The eldest child of the murdered
leader returns one day to have his revenge. A kind of
Ninja version of YOJIMBO with the hero playing off
the two clans who now battle for supremacy.

| MAR | 83 min Cut (38 sec) |
|---|---|
| B,V | VPD |

## ULTIMATE THRILL, THE **

Robert Butler            USA            1974
*Eric Braeden, Britt Ekland, Barry Brown, Michael*

*Blodgett, John Davis Chandler*
A business executive becomes involved in murder due
to his paranoid fears. An undistinguished and unmemorable thriller.
Aka: ULTIMATE CHASE, THE

| THR | 84 min (ort 110 min) |
|---|---|
| B,V | GHV |

## ULTIMATE WARRIOR, THE **

15

Robert Clouse            USA            1975
*Yul Brynner, Max Von Sydow, Joanna Miles, William
Smith, Richard Kelton, Stephen McHattie, Lane
Bradbury, Darrell Zwerling, Mel Novak, Nate
Esformes, Mickey Caruso, Gray Johnson, Susan
Keener, Stevie Meyers, Fred Siyter*
In the 21st century, scattered bands eke out a meagre
existence following a worldwide ecological disaster.
One group has developed resistant plants that may
one day replenish the Earth, but is constantly
threatened by another. The arrival of an expert
fighter, who works as a kind of roving mercenary,
changes all that. Good ideas are badly let down by
stilted dialogue and poor acting. Written by Clouse.

| FAN | 94 min |
|---|---|
| B,V | WHV |

## ULTIMAX FORCE *

18

Wilfred Milan            USA            1986
*Arnold Nicholas, Jeremy Ladd, Patrick Scott, Vincent
Griffin*
Another formula action saga, with a commando group
being set up to rescue POWs being tortured in a
Vietnamese prison camp by a sadistic commander.
Despite the pretensions of the movie, whose long
rambling introduction takes pains to point out that
American POWs are still being held, this film is a
banal and stereotyped offering indeed.

| A/AD | 81 min (ort 85 min) Cut (1 min 39 sec) |
|---|---|
| B,V | A A |

## ULYSSES **

U

Mario Camerini      ITALY      1954
*Kirk Douglas, Silvana Mangano, Anthony Quinn,
Rosanna Podesta, Silvie*
Routine sword-and-sandal historical epic telling of the
adventures befalling Ulysses as he journeys home to
Ithaca after the Trojan War, returning to his wife
Penelope after an absence of twenty years. This is one
of Douglas' less successful independent productions
with dialogue winning over action. Watch him speak
dubbed Italian and then English. Photography is by
Harold Rosson with a script by Irwin Shaw, Ben Hecht
and about five others.
Boa: epic poem The Odyssey by Homer.

| A/AD | 104 min; 99 min (STABL) |
|---|---|
| B,V | VDM; VMA; STABL (VHS only) |

## ULZANA'S RAID ***

18

Robert Aldrich            USA            1972
*Burt Lancaster, Bruce Davison, Jorge Luke, Richard
Jaeckel, Lloyd Bochner, Joaquin Martinez, Karl
Swenson, Douglas Walton, Dran Hamilton, John
Pearce, Gladys Holland, Margaret Fairchild, Aimee
Eccles, Richard Bull, Otto Reichow*
The story of a violent conflict between Indians and the
US Cavalry with Lancaster as an experienced Indian
fighter being sent out with a raw officer and an Indian
scout, to destroy a marauding Apache band that is
terrorising the citizens. Written by Alan Sharp this
violent and bloody film benefits from a taut script and
has Lancaster giving one of his best performances.

| WES | 96 min (ort 103 min) Cut (45 sec) |
|---|---|
| V/h | CIC |

## UNBEARABLE LIGHTNESS OF
## BEING, THE ****

18

Philip Kaufman            USA            1987
*Daniel Day-Lewis, Juliette Binoche, Lena Olin, Erland
Josephson, Daniel Olbrychski, Derek De Lint, Paul*

Landovsky, Donald Moffat, Stellan Skarsgard, Tomek
Bork, Bruce Meyers, Pavel Slaby, Pascale Kalensky,
Jacques Ciron
This intelligent and absorbing adaptation of Kun-
dera's novel tells of a young Czech doctor of the 1960s
who is more interested in women than in politics, but
finds himself caught up in his country's turmoil. A
joyful, exuberant and zestful film, beautifully acted
and employing the talents of top photographer Sven
Nykvist. The script is by Kaufman and Jean-Claude
Carriere.
Boa: novel by Milan Kundera.
DRA                          165 min (ort 172 min)
V/sh                                           CBS

## UNCANNY, THE **                             18
Denis Heroux        CANADA/UK              1977
Peter Cushing, Joan Greenwood, Donald Pleasence,
Ray Milland, Roland Culver, Susan Penhaligon,
Simon Williams, Alexandra Stewart, Chloe Franks,
Katrina Holden, Donald Pilon, Samantha Eggar,
John Vernon, Sean McCann, Jean Leclerc
Three rather foolish tales, based around author
Cushing explaining to Milland his obsessive fear that
cats plot against and control humanity. Apart from
one rather funny moment when a cat really does "get
someone's tongue", this is a superficial and insipid
effort. The script is by Michael Parry.
HOR                                       84 min
B,V                           RNK; VCC (VHS only)

## UNCERTAIN GLORY *                            U
Raoul Walsh          USA                   1944
Errol Flynn, Paul Lukas, Jean Sullivan, Lucile
Watson, Faye Emerson, James Flavin, Douglass
Dumbrille, Dennis Hoey, Sheldon Leonard
In Occupied France a disreputable philanderer pre-
tends to be a saboteur, sacrificing himself for the
benefit of his country. Cliched WW2 heroics with a
lack of action and an uncertain script.
DRA                       98 min (Ort 102 min) B/W
V                                             WHV

## UNCHAINED ***                                15
Daniel Mann          USA                   1987
Val Kilmer, Charles Durning, Sonia Braga, Kyra
Sedgewick, William Sanderson, James Keach
A fictionalised account loosely based on the life of
Robert Burns, who was sentenced to a chain gang in
Georgia, after becoming an unwilling accomplice
during a robbery. After escaping, he started a new life
but was eventually recaptured. He escaped once
more, and eventually wrote a book that helped
expose the brutality of the chain gang system. A solid
and absorbing tale, made once before as the classic "I
Am A Fugitive From A Chain Gang".
Aka: MAN WHO BROKE 1,000 CHAINS, THE
Boa: Robert Elliott Burns.
DRA                           92 min (ort 113 min)
B,V                                           GHV

## UNCLE BUCK **                                15
John Hughes          USA                   1989
John Candy, Amy Madigan, Jean Louisa Kelly,
Macaulay Culkin, Gaby Hoffman, Elaine Bromka,
Garrett M. Brown, Laurie Metcalf, Jay Underwood
A fat slob of an uncle is called upon to look after his
brother's kids for a few days when their father dies.
His inability to cook and clean leads to the expected
slapstick humour, but his unexpected abilities as a
loving uncle add a note of warmth. Writer-director
Hughes provides an uneven and sentimental script
that blends light and dark humour; the flirtatious
behaviour of Candy's niece injects a rather sour note.
A TV series followed.
COM                           95 min (ort 100 min)
V                                             CIC

## UNCLE SCAM **
Mike Levanios/Tom Pileggi
                         USA                1981
James E. Meyers, Joan Rivers, Marvin Stafford, Tom
McCarthy
An investigative team have difficulty in finding
evidence to show the corruption of elected US officials.
COM                                       98 min
B,V                                           VIP

## UNCLE TOM'S CABIN ***                        PG
Stan Lathan          USA                   1987
Avery Brooks, Kate Burton, Bruce Dern, Paula Kelly,
Phylicia Rashad, Kathryn Walker, Edward
Woodward, Frank Converse, George Coe, Albert Hall,
Jenny Lewis
A competent if not unduly exciting film of Stowe's
landmark novel, that makes use of a contemporary
(and somewhat revisionist) script by John Gay, but
boasts performances of considerable strength. This
first American sound version of the novel manages to
tackle the issue of slavery with sincerity and insight.
Boa: novel by Harriet Beecher Stowe.
DRA                       108 min (ort 110 min) mTV
V                                           CASPIC

## UNCOMMON VALOR ***                           15
Ted Kotcheff         USA                   1983
Gene Hackman, Robert Stack, Fred Ward, Randall
"Tex" Cobb, Reb Brown, Tim Thomerson, Patrick
Swayze, Harold Sylvester
A grief stricken retired Army officer gathers together
a motley collection of Vietnam veterans, and mounts
an expedition to Laos when he learns that his son,
reported as missing in action, may in fact be alive in a
POW camp. Good performances lift this formula
Vietnam actioner above the usual run.
A/AD                                     100 min
V                                             CIC

## UNCONQUERED, THE **                          PG
Dick Lowry           USA                   1988
Peter Coyote, Dermot Mulroney, Tess Harper, Jenny
Robertson, Bud Gunton, Larry Riley
The family of a D.A. are caught up in the violence
surrounding the struggle to achieve desegregation, in
the Southern states of the USA in the 1960s. At the
same time the film follows the tale of the man's son,
who overcomes physical disabilities to become a
sporting star. An attempt to provide two stories for the
price of one, makes for a messy and disjointed affair.
The script is by Pat Conroy.
DRA                       113 min (ort 130 min) mTV
V                                             CBS

## UNDEFEATED, THE **                           PG
Andrew V. McLaglen    USA                  1969
John Wayne, Rock Hudson, Tony Aguilar, Roman
Gabriel, Marian McCargo, Lee Meriwether, Merlin
Olsen, Melissa Newman, Bruce Cabot, Michael
Vincent, Ben Johnson, Edward Faulkner, Harry Carey
Jr, Paul Fix, Royal Dano, Carlos Rivas
Routine post-Civil War Western. Former colonels
Wayne and Hudson from the Union and Confederate
Armies respectively, form an uneasy alliance as they
head for Mexico in order to start new lives. Apart from
the unusual pairing of the two leads, this one has little
new to say. Introduces former football stars Gabriel
and Olsen.
WES                                      119 min
B,V                                           CBS

## UNDER ACHIEVERS, THE *                       18
Jackie Kong          USA                   1987
Edward Albert Jr, Barbara Carrera, Michael Pataki,
Susan Tyrrell, Mark Blankfield, Vic Tayback, Garrett
Morris
Dim-witted comedy that's set at an evening-class
institute attended by a mixed group of rejects and

losers, all of whom believe passionately that they can make a success of themselves, if not of this film.

COM 90 min
V VES

## UNDER CAPRICORN ** PG
Rod Hardy AUSTRALIA 1983
*John Hallam, Lisa Harrow, Peter Cousens, Julia Blake, Peter Collingwood, Jim Holt, Catherine Lynch*
A remake of a classic Hitchcock film. A young Irish immigrant to Australia almost pays with his life when he uncovers a married couple's closely guarded secret. Stick to the original rather than this cut down version of a TV mini-series of 235 min.
Boa: novel by Helen Simpson.
DRA 112 min (ort 235 min) mTV
B,V ODY; VGM

## UNDER CAPRICORN *** 
Alfred Hitchcock UK 1949
*Joseph Cotten, Ingrid Bergman, Michael Wilding, Margaret Leighton, Cecil Parker, Jack Watling, Denis O'Dea, Harcourt Williams, John Ruddock, Ronald Adam, Francis De Wolff, G.H. Mulcaster, Olive Sloane, Maureen Delaney*
A love triangle set in 19th century Australia, with Bergman as Cotten's wife taking to drink and her bed as Leighton the housekeeper tries to help drive her insane. The unexpected visit of Wilding upsets their plans. A stilted drama bearing slight similarities to REBECCA but not a commercial success. Written by James Bridie with photography by Jack Cardiff and a score by Richard Addinsell. Remade for TV in 1983.
Boa: novel by Helen Simpson/play by John Colton and Margaret Linden.
DRA 117 min
B,V MEV L/A

## UNDER FIRE *** 15
Roger Spottiswoode USA 1983
*Nick Nolte, Gene Hackman, Joanna Cassidy, Jean-Louis Trintignant, Ed Harris, Richard Masur, Rene Enriquez, Hamilton Camp*
An account of the experiences of three American TV journalists in Nicaragua in 1979 before the fall of the Somoza dictatorship. The film has a few good moments but they are a long time coming. Trintignant and Harris are both excellent in support. Written by Ron Shelton and Clayton Frohman with music by Jerry Goldsmith.
DRA 123 min
B,V RNK; VIR (VHS only)

## UNDER MILK WOOD *** 15
Andrew Sinclair UK 1973
*Richard Burton, Elizabeth Taylor, Peter O'Toole, Glynis Johns, Sian Philips, Vivien Merchant, Victor Spinetti, Ryan Davies, Angharad Rees, Ray Smith, Glyn Edwards, Bridget Turner, Talfryn Thomas, Wim Wylton, Bronwen Williams*
A film version of a wonderfully evocative radio play, weaving a magical tapestry of words around the lives and dreams of the inhabitants of the tiny Welsh fishing village of Llareggub. The visual images add nothing to Thomas' marvellous writing, and in the end serve only as a distraction and an annoyance. Just close your eyes and listen as Burton narrates.
Boa: radio play by Dylan Thomas.
DRA 87 min
V/h CBS

## UNDER SIEGE ** 18
Rene E. Cardona Jr 198-
*Stuart Whitman, Marisa Mel, Hugo Stiglitz*
When a gang of terrorists take part in a large-scale robbery, to obtain the money for their organisation, the operation goes wrong and they take hostages in a bid to escape.

DRA 91 min
B,V IVS

## UNDER SIEGE *** 15
Roger Young USA 1986
*Peter Strauss, Hal Holbrook, E.G. Marshall, Lew Ayres, Fritz Weaver, Mason Adams, George Grizzard, Stan Shaw, Paul Winfield, Beatrice Straight, David Opatoshu, Frederick Coffin, Victoria Tennant, Ann Sweeny, David Opatoshu*
The US President has to deal with a series of terrorist outrages that culminate in an attack on the Capital Building in Washington. Despite the use of clever special effects (especially in blowing the dome off the State Building, the one in Arkansas being used), this remains a stilted and talky film. Scripted by a host of writers, among them being Bob Woodward of ALL THE PRESIDENT'S MEN fame.
A/AD 150 min mTV
B,V GHV

## UNDER THE CHERRY MOON ** 15
Prince USA 1986
*Prince, Jerome Benton, Kristin Scott-Thomas, Steven Berkoff, Francesca Annis, Victor Spinetti, Alexandra Stewart, Emmanuelle Sallet*
Empty-headed attempt to build a dramatic vehicle for this talented singing star. He plays an American entertainer on the French Riviera whom women find irresistable. An eminently resistible "vanity vehicle".
MUS 98 min B/W
V/sh WHV

## UNDER THE DOCTOR ** 18
Gerry Poulson UK 1981
*Barry Evans, Liz Fraser, Penny Spencer, Hilary Pritchard, Jonathan Cecil, Elizabeth Counsell, Peter Cleall*
Sex comedy about a Harley Street psychiatrist and his involvement with three female patients. A fairly routine British medi-com.
COM 82 min (ort 90 min) Cut (1 min 1 sec)
B,V INT L/A; IVS L/A; GLOB; NET

## UNDER THE GUN ** 18
James Sbardellati USA 1988
*Sam Jones, Vanessa Williams, John Russell, Michael Halsey, Sharon Williams, Bill McKinney, Rockne Tarkington, Don Stark, Nick Cassavetes*
A cop and a lawyer team up to go after the gangster who arranged the death of the brother of the former, and has stolen a supply of plutonium in order to sell it to the highest bidder. A competent if far-fetched thriller.
THR 87 min (ort 89 min)
V CINE

## UNDER THE RAINBOW * PG
Steve Rash USA 1981
*Chevy Chase, Carrie Fisher, Eve Arden, Mako, Pat McCormick, Joseph Maher, Robert Donner, Billy Barty, Adam Arkin*
A spy comedy set in a hotel during the filming of the "Wizard of Oz". Features midgets, undercover agents, assassination attempts on a duke and the nefarious activities of Nazi and Japanese spies, all parties concerned crossing paths at said hotel. A tasteless and breakneck trip to boredom.
COM 98 min
B,V WHV

## UNDER THE VOLCANO *** 15
John Huston USA 1984
*Albert Finney, Jacqueline Bisset, Anthony Andrews, Ignacio Lopez Tarso, Katy Jurado, James Villiers*
A love triangle story that involves an alcoholic diplomat, his wife and one of her former lovers, all of whom are in Mexico in 1938 on the eve of WW2. A sombre and disturbing story with a plum of a part for

Finney. Written by Guy Gallo with an Alex North score.
Boa: novel by Malcolm Lowry.

DRA 107 min
B,V CBS

## UNDERBOSS, THE *** PG
Robert Collins USA 1981
*Ted Danson, Deborah Carney, Steven Apostle, Chip Mayer, Vera Miles, David Morse, James O'Sullivan, Ayn Ruymen, James Luisini, Sam Wanamaker, Ray Milland, John Carter, Terry Alexander, Michael Currie, Ben Fuhrman*
A look at the life of a Canadian Mafia family, with Danson as the son who has been informing in exchange for police protection, and Morse as the vice president of a bank who would dearly like to cut away from the family. The unusual casting of Milland as an ailing mafia chief and the camerawork of Reynaldo Villalobos are assets in this above average production.
Aka: OUR FAMILY BUSINESS
Boa: TV play by Lane Slate.

DRA 71 min (ort 90 min) mTV
B,V POLY

## UNDERCOVER ** 15
John Stockwell USA 1987
*David Neidorf, Barry Corbin, Jennifer Jason Leigh, David Denny, Kathleen Wilhoite, David Harris*
An out-of-town policeman teams up with a female narcotics agent and goes undercover in a South Carolina high school, in order to break up a drugs ring and catch the murderers of a cop who was also working on the case. A cliched cops and drugs story that gave Stockwell his directorial debut.
Aka: UNDER COVER

A/AD 91 min
V/sh WHV

## UNDERGRADS, THE ** U
Steven Hilliard Stern USA 1984
*Art Carney, Chris Makepeace, Len Birman, Dawn Greenhall, Lesleh Donaldson, Jackie Burroughs, Alfie Scopp, Angela Fusco, Nerene Virgin, Adam Ludwig, Ron James, Peter Spence, Wendy Bushell, Gary Farmer, Pat Patterson*
An old man whose family want to put him in a home, gets to attend his son's college instead. This idea was later used in a TV series starring Mickey Rooney. Made by Disney for cable TV and a typically bland offering, though Carney's considerable comic talents go some way towards redeeming it.
Boa: story by Paul W. Shapiro and Michael Wisman.

COM 98 min mCab
B,V WDV

## UNDERGRADUATE GIRLS ** 18
Michele Massimo Tarantini
ITALY 1975
*Gloria Guida, Angela Darrion, Enzo Cannavale, Giuseppe Pambieri, Gianfranco d'Angelo, Gisella Sofio, Rodolfo Bigotti*
The story of a girl, her mother, and their sexual adventures and fantasies.
Aka: LA LICEALE

A 70 min
B,V 18PLAT/TOW; PRI; GLOB

## UNDERGROUND ACES ** 15
Robert Butler USA 1980
*Dirk Benedict, Melanie Griffith, Michael Winslow, Audrey Landers, Jerry Orbach, Robert Heyes, Frank Gorshin, Karlo Salem, Mimi Maynard*
Comedy about the adventures of a boorish and vulgar bunch of hotel parking attendants who work for a big Beverly Hills hotel. They relieve the tedium of their job by getting up to a variety of pranks, such as smashing up customers' cars and poking fun at the management. As stupid as it is tasteless.

COM 90 min
B,V STARB

## UNDERGROUND TERROR ** 18
James McCalmont USA 1988
*Doc Dougherty, Lenny Loftin*
A tough cop and a female reporter go after a gang of killers who live in an underground labyrinth beneath the subway system, and have formed a community led by a recently discharged psychotic.

HOR 87 min (ort 91 min)
V/h MED

## UNDERWATER! * U
John Sturges USA 1955
*Jane Russell, Richard Egan, Gilbert Roland, Lori Nelson, Jayne Mansfield, Robert Keith, Joseph Calleia, Eugene Iglesias, Ric Roman*
An underwater treasure hunt with all the usual dangers of the deep to be faced by intrepid skin divers out to locate a sunken galleon in the Caribbean. Jane and Jayne are the main attractions in a waterlogged tale. Produced by millionaire recluse Howard Hughes who originally planned on having it previewed underwater. Too bad he didn't.
Osca: BIG STEAL, THE

A/AD 95 min
B,V VCC (VHS only); KVD

## UNDERWORLD *** 18
George Pavlov UK 1985
*Denholm Elliott, Steven Berkoff, Larry Lamb, Miranda Richardson, Art Malik, Irina Brook, Roy Bain, Hugo Motherskille, Nicola Cowper, Ingrid Pitt, Paul Brown, Philip Davies, Gary Olsen, Brian Crocuher, Trevor Thomas, Paul Mari*
A group of underground mutants, disfigured by a cruel chemical experiment, kidnap a girl in order to obtain from the doctor responsible for their condition, the drug they need to stay alive. A retired gunman is hired to rescue her. Fair.
Aka: TRANSMUTATIONS

HOR 87 min (ort 103 min)
B,V VES

## UNE PARISIENNE * PG
Michel Boisrond FRANCE 1957
*Brigitte Bardot, Charles Boyer, Henri Vidal*
Gossamer-light, dated sex-comedy that's clearly intended as a vehicle for Bardot, who plays the daughter of the French Prime Minister. When she and his principal secretary are discovered in bed together, a quick and involuntary marriage seems inevitable.

COM 86 min
V CASPIC

## UNFAITHFUL WIVES **** 
Claude Chabrol FRANCE/ITALY 1969
*Stephane Audran, Michel Bouquet, Maurice Ronet, Stephen Di Napolo, Michel Duchaussoy*
This atmospheric and taut drama tells of how a wife comes to have more respect for her husband when he murders her lover. A near classic tale of adultery and murder; elegant, sensuous and dramatic.
Aka: LA FEMME INFIDELE; UNFAITHFUL WIFE

DRA 98 min
V INT

## UNFAITHFULLY YOURS *** 15
Howard Zieff USA 1984
*Dudley Moore, Nastassja Kinski, Armand Assante, Albert Brookes, Cassie Yates, Richard Libertini, Richard B. Shull*
A romantic comedy involving an orchestra conductor who plans to murder his wife whom he suspects of having an affair with a violinist. A remake of the 1948 Preston Sturges film that is funny at times but begins

to run down about half-way through.

COM 96 min
B,V CBS

## UNHINGED **
Don Gronquist USA 1982
*Laurel Munson, J.E. Penner, Sara Ansley, Virginia Settle*
After a car crash, three girls take refuge in a house inhabited by a strange mother and daughter. A pale imitation of PSYCHO that lacks the complexity and sheer force of the 1960s classic.

HOR 79 min
B,V CBS L/A

## UNHOLY, THE ** 18
Camilo Vila USA 1988
*Ben Cross, Hal Holbrook, Jill Carroll, William Russ, Trevor Howard, Claudia Robinson, Ned Beatty, Nicole Fortier*
A Catholic priest appointed to a parish where his two predecessors have been brutally murdered, discovers a welter of Satanic practices as well as a real-life demon, that sustains its existence by killing sinners in the act of sinning. An ambitious but somewhat ludicrous tale with rather good special effects. Scripted by Philip Yordan and Fernando Fonseca, the film's designer.

HOR 94 min
V VES

## UNINVITED, THE ** 18
Greydon Clark USA 1987
*George Kennedy, Alex Cord, Clu Gulager, Toni Hudson, Erik Larson*
A cat escapes from a research laboratory and finds its way aboard a yacht. Unfortunately for all those on it, this seemingly harmless feline has developed the knack of transforming itself into a mutant monster.

HOR 88 min
B,V IVS

## UNION CITY *** 15
Mark Reichert USA 1980
*Dennis Lipscomb, Deborah Harry, Irina Maleeva, Everett McGill, Taylor Mead, Tony Azito, Pat Benatar*
A man obsessed with the idea of trapping the vagrant who steals a drink from his milk each morning, eventually loses control and beats him to death. An interesting new wave thriller set in a large and oppressive industrial town. Written by Reichert, this was the debut for Harry who plays Lipscomb's neurotic wife, as well as for first-time cinematographer Ed Lachman.

THR 82 min (INT); 90 min (MIA or PARK)
B,V,V2 INT L/A; MIA (VHS only); PARK (VHS only)

## UNKNOWN POWERS * 
Don Como USA 1979
*Samantha Eggar, Jack Palance, Will Geer, Roscoe Lee Browne*
A rather contrived and muddled examination of mystical and paranormal phenomena such as astrology and spiritual healing, with each of the stars introducing a section of the film.

FAN 86 min
V INT

## UNMARRIED WOMAN, AN **** 18
Paul Mazursky USA 1978
*Jill Clayburgh, Alan Bates, Michael Murphy, Cliff Gorman, Pat Quinn, Kelly Bishop, Lisa Lucas, Michael Tucker, Jill Eikenberry*
A woman has to start life over again when her husband leaves her, and takes up with several men, but her daughter gives her trouble. Written by Mazursky who has a good eye for the problems that beset a single mother trying to cope in New York City. Clayburgh gives a memorable performance in the title

role.

DRA 119 min
B,V CBS

## UNMASKING THE IDOL ** 15
Worth Keeter USA 1986
*Ian Hunter, William T. Hicks, Charles K. Bibby*
Adventure spoof which sends up a variety of different heroes of the silver screen. The story is of a man having to recover a cache of stolen gold hidden on an island in the South China Sea.

COM 86 min (ort 90 min) Cut (7 sec)
B,V MED

## UNNAMEABLE, THE * 18
Jean-Paul Ouellette USA 1988
*Charles King, Alexandra Durrell, Mark Kinsey Stephenson*
Very loosely based on the Lovecraft tale, this tells of a haunted house, and a demonic creature that gained its freedom from a locked room there, when the former warlock owner foolishly released it 300 years ago. The excellent special effects are a poor compensation for the incoherent plot.
Boa: short story The Shuttered Room by H.P. Lovecraft.

HOR 84 min (ort 87 min) Cut (21 sec)
B,V CINE; PARK

## UNNATURAL ACT, AN: PART 2 ** 18
Ned Morehead USA 1986
*Nina Hartley, John Leslie, Colleen Brennan, Bunny Bleu, Keli Richards, Nikki Randall, Erica Boyer, Jerry Butler*
Rather silly "Topper"-style story of a wealthy woman who is being poisoned. Meeting an artist in her garden the two go to bed and indulge in a wild session of lovemaking. After this she dies, but her spirit is still able to communicate with him and he is instructed to find her murderers. Eventually the culprits are found to be her jealous relatives, but after bedding a maid the woman tells him that she will inherit her estate instead.

A 45 min (ort 80 min) Cut (14 sec)
V DREAM

## UNSEEN, THE * 18
Peter Foleg USA 1980
*Barbara Bach, Sidney Lassick, Stephen Furst, Lelia Goldoni, Karen Lamm, Doug Barr, Lois Young*
A three-woman TV crew are attacked, and two of them suffer horrible deaths at the hands of "Junior" (Furst), as the result of an incestuous relationship between Goldoni and Lassick. As moronic as it is unmemorable.

HOR 91 min; 83 min (ACAD or APX)
B,V VPD; ACAD; APX

## UNSINKABLE MOLLY BROWN, THE ** U
Charles Walters USA 1964
*Debbie Reynolds, Harve Presnell, Ed Begley, Jack Kruschen, Martita Hunt, Hermione Baddeley*
In Denver during the late 19th century, a girl rises from rags to riches. Broadway musical adaptation with Reynolds as the determined backwoods girl who knows what she wants out of life and aims to become accepted by Denver society. This lively musical comedy-western is likeable but unmemorable. Based on a true story (the lady in question survived the Titanic) and written by Helen Deutsch. The score is by Meredith Willson.
Boa: musical by Richard Morris.

MUS 128 min
V/sh MGM

## UNSPEAKABLE ACTS *** PG
Linda Otto USA 1989
*Jill Clayburgh, Brad Davis, Season Hubley, Gary Frank, Gregory Sierra, Valerie Landsburg, Bebe*

Neuwirth, Terence Knox
Clayburgh and Davis play real-life child advocates Laurie and Joe Braga in this powerful, fact-based dramatisation of a famous 1984 child abuse trial in Miami. The film focuses on the efforts made by child psychologists to gather evidence from their young witnesses, but although the Alan Landsburg script is based on both court transcripts and Hollingsworth's book, it raises important issues that it fails to explore.
Boa: book by Jan Hollingsworth.
DRA                           94 min (ort 100 min) mTV
V                                              BRAVE

## UNSUITABLE JOB FOR A WOMAN, AN ***   15
Christopher Petit          UK                 1981
Billie Whitelaw, Paul Freeman, Pippa Guard, Dominic Guard, David Horovitch, Elizabeth Spriggs, Dawn Archibald, Bernadette Short, James Gilbey, Kelda Holmes, Alex Guard
A secretary takes over the running of a detective agency after her boss commits suicide and investigates an unusual murder case. An interesting example of British film noir that is not without its moments.
Boa: novel by P.D. James.
THR                             90 min (ort 94 min)
V                                            PVG/PAL

## UNTAMED SEX *                              18
Michael Thomas (Erwin C. Dietrich)
                    FRANCE/SWITZERLAND       1980
Brigitte Lahaie, Daniela White, Nadine Pascal, Ande Mallois
European sex film of unbridled passions, intrigue etc. Very dull.
Aka: SECHS SCHWEDINNEN IM PENSIONAT
A       80 min Cut (2 min 43 sec in addition to film cuts)
B,V                     18PLAT/TOW; GLOB; SHEP

## UNTAMED, THE ***                          PG
Geoff Burrowes     AUSTRALIA                  1988
Tom Burlinson, Sigrid Thornton, Brian Dennehy, Nicholas Eadie, Bryan Marshall
This sequel to THE MAN FROM SNOWY RIVER has Burlinson once more having to prove himself, with the villainous Eadie engaged to his sweetheart. Not as good as the earlier film but full of good action shots, including more of those herds of galloping wild horses.
Aka: RETURN TO SNOWY RIVER; RETURN TO SNOWY RIVER PART 2
A/AD                                          99 min
V                                       WDV; TOUCH

## UNTIL DEATH *                             18
Lamberto Bava       ITALY                     1987
Gioia Scola
A clumsy reworking of Mario Bava's SHOCK, in which a woman murders her husband, the owner of a lakeside diner, and settles into a life of sin with her lover. The arrival of a mysterious stranger six years later heralds the start of a series of horrifying events. A flabby effort of stilted (and badly dubbed) dialogue and lacklustre performances.
HOR                              93 min mTV dubbed
B,V                                             AVA

## UNTIL SEPTEMBER **                        15
Richard Marquand    USA                       1984
Karen Allen, Thierry Lhermitte, Christopher Cazenove, Marie-Christina Conti, Nitza Saul, Hutton Hobb
Stranded temporarily in Paris, Allen meets married banker Lhermitte and falls in love with him. A predictable romantic drama that even manages to make Paris look boring.
DRA                                           95 min
B/h, V/h                                        WHV

## UNTOUCHABLES, THE ****                    15
Brian De Palma      USA                       1987
Kevin Costner, Sean Connery, Charles Martin Smith, Andy Garcia, Robert De Niro, Richard Bradford, Jack Kehoe, Brad Sullivan, Billy Drago, Patricia Clarkson
Writer David Mamet has updated the popular TV series that followed the career of FBI agent Eliot Ness, in his battle against organised crime in prohibition-era Chicago. A powerful and exciting production, with Connery getting an Oscar as an experienced cop and De Niro memorable as a gangster boss. AA: S. Actor (Connery).
A/AD                                         115 min
V/sh                                             CIC

## UP A TREE **
Serge Korber       FRANCE/ITALY               1971
Geraldine Chaplin, Louis de Funes, Olivier de Funes, Alice Sapritch, Hans Meyer
Men from the local garrison keep going AWOL to enjoy the delights of the local lady innkeeper. Drastic action is called for. Average.
Aka: SUR UN ARBRE PERCHE
COM                                           87 min
B,V                                         VCL/CBS

## UP AGAINST THE ODDS **                    PG
Lawrence Doheny     USA                       1979
Robert Conrad, Larry Monetti, Red West, Patricia Conwell, Joey Green, Peter Haskell, Michael Baselean, Daphne Maxwell, Fred Herrick, Percy Rodrigues
The pilot for a shortlived four-episode TV series about a boxing champ, who decides that being a private detective is a more appealing profession. Average.
Aka: DUKE, THE
A/AD                                     93 min mTV
B,V                                       EAG; GLOB

## UP AND COMING **
Sergio Bergonzelli   ITALY                    1976
Antinesca Nemour, Carlo de Mejo, Tiberio Mergia
A young bride tries hard to cure her husband's impotency.
Aka: BRIDE, THE; LA SPOSINA; YOUNG BRIDE, THE
A                                             90 min
B,V                                  IVS; ELV; PINVID

## UP IN ARMS ***                            U
Elliott Nugent      USA                       1944
Danny Kaye, Dinah Shore, Constance Dowling, Dana Andrews, Louis Calhern, Lyle Talbot, Margaret Dumont, Elisha Cook Jr
A reluctant hypochondriac recruit in the US Army eventually becomes a hero. Kaye's first film is an untidy mess that hasn't worn well; only his singing of some great patter songs such as "The Lobby Number" and "Melody In 4F" make it worth seeing. Shore is attractive as the woman he doesn't love, as is Dowling as the one he does. Look out for Virginia Mayo as one of the chorus girls. Filmed before as "Whoopee" with Eddie Cantor in 1930.
Boa: play The Nervous Wreck by Owen Davis.
COM                                    105 min B/W
B,V                                             VGM

## UP 'N' COMING ***                         R18/18
Godfrey Daniels     USA                       1982
Marilyn Chambers, Lisa De Leeuw, Herschel Savage, Loni Sanders, Sharon Mitchell, Jamie Gillis, Constance Money, Cody Nicole, Richard Pacheco, Gina Gianetti, John C. Holmes
A second-billed Country singer lands the job as the opening act for a female singer and proves to be the more popular of the two. Not unnaturally, this antagonises the latter who, hooked on booze and drugs, is coming to the end of her career. Chambers plays the aspiring singer who is out for success even if she has to use her body to get it. De Leeuw gives good

support as the singer she challenges. A better than average sex film.

A        61 min Cut (14 min 38 sec – 18);
            76 min (R18) (ort 83 min)
B,V      ELV L/A; ROGUE L/A; VPD

## UP POMPEII **
Bob Kellett      UK      1971
*Frankie Howerd, Patrick Cargill, Lance Percival,*
*Michael Hordern, Barbara Murray, Bill Fraser,*
*Adrienne Posta, Julie Ege, Bernard Bresslaw, Royce*
*Mills, Madeleine Smith, Rita Webb, Ian Trigger,*
*Aubrey Woods, Hugh Paddick*
Spin-off of a popular British TV series about a lascivious and lazy slave living in ancient Pompeii. Nero is outwitted and our slave effects his escape from Pompeii just before the volcano goes up. The comic acting talent of Howerd does not suffice. Written by Sid Colin with music by Carl Davis.
COM            90 min
B,V            TEVP

## UP THE ACADEMY *
                 15
Robert Downey    USA    1983
*Ron Leibman, Ralph Macchio, Wendell Brown, Tom*
*Citera, Tom Poston, Antonio Fargas, Stacey Nelkin,*
*Barbara Bach, Leonard Frey*
A truly awful teen comedy set in a military academy peopled by unbelievably gross slobs, whose antics are clearly modelled on films like those in the "National Lampoon" series. Mad Magazine financed this one, and although it was made for Pay-TV release, all references to the magazine and their mascot Alfred E. Neuman were excised. Note that Ron Leibman kept his name off the credits. This was Macchio's film debut.
Aka: MAD MAGAZINE PRESENTS UP THE ACADEMY
COM        85 min mPay
V/sh            WHV

## UP THE CHASTITY BELT **
Bob Kellett      UK      1971
*Frankie Howerd, Graham Crowden, Bill Fraser, Roy*
*Hudd, Hugh Paddick, Anna Quayle, Eartha Kitt, Dave*
*King, Fred Emney, Lance Percival, Nora Swinburne,*
*Godfrey Winn, David Batley, Royce Mills, Veronica*
*Clifford*
A serf and his master go off to the Crusades, in this broad and unfunny farce, that stumbles along with precious few gags but much vulgarity.
COM            94 min
V             WHV

## UP THE CREEK **
Val Guest      UK      1958
*David Tomlinson, Peter Sellers, Wilfrid Hyde-White,*
*Michael Goodliffe, Vera Day, Lionel Jeffries, Liliane*
*Sottane, Lionel Murton, Sam Kydd, John Warren,*
*David Lodge, Frank Pettingell, Tom Gill, Michael*
*Goodliffe, Howard Willliams*
A lieutenant is given command of a rundown ship in this broad naval farce. A sort of MISTER ROBERTS spoof with some good gags but it relies on too much slapstick to be really effective. Written by Guest, this was previously filmed as OH! MR PORTER. Followed by "Further Up The Creek".
COM        83 min B/W
B,V         WAL L/A

## UP THE CREEK ***
                 15
Robert Butler    USA    1984
*Tim Matheson, Stephen Furst, Dan Monatian,*
*Jennifer Runyon, Sandy Helberg, Jeff East, Blaine*
*Novak, James B. Sikking, John Hillerman*
A college team takes part in a desperate bid to win a white-water rafting race against teams of preppies and military cadets. Matheson and Furst cut their

teeth on NATIONAL LAMPOON'S ANIMAL HOUSE, and are reunited in this silly but generally entertaining college-kids comedy. The same level of brash humour is very much in evidence.
COM      92 min (ort 99 min)
B,V            RNK

## UP THE FRONT **
                 PG
Bob Kellett      UK      1972
*Frankie Howerd, Zsa Zsa Gabor, Stanley Holloway,*
*Hermione Baddeley, Robert Coote, Bill Fraser, Lance*
*Percival, Peter Bull, Jonathan Cecil, Percy Herbert,*
*William Mervyn, Linda Gray, Madeleine Smith,*
*Nicholas Bennett*
In 1914 the footman of a lord is hypnotised into enlisting in the army, and helps a spy steal German plans by getting them tattooed on his buttocks. A tired and dated romp. The script is by Sid Colin and Eddie Braben.
COM  85 min (ort 89 min) (Cut at film release)
V             WHV

## UP THE MILITARY **
                 18
Andrew Sugerman  USA  1983 (released 1985)
*Ann Dusenberry, Rhonda Shear, Angela Ames, Will*
*Nye, Walter Gotell, Marty Brill, Christopher Peenock*
Adult comedy about a secretary who gets a rapid series of rises in her job at the Pentagon. Made by Playboy Enterprises, this witless comedy has buxom Dusenberry turning the tables on her lecherous male colleagues. Its appeal is largely confined to its voyeuristic content.
Aka: BASIC TRAINING; UP THE PENTAGON
COM            85 min
B,V            MED

## UP THE NAVY *
                 15
Ed Forsyth      USA     197-
*Shari Eubank*
A well-endowed female recruit uses all her resources to work her way through training school; together with her friends they reduce everything to chaos in the process.
COM      80 min (ort 90 min)
B,V            CLOK

## UP THE SANDBOX ***
                 15
Irvin Kershner    USA    1972
*Barbra Streisand, David Selby, Jane Hoffman, Ariane*
*Heller, John C. Becher, Jacobo Morales*
A young mother living in New York is largely ignored by her piggish husband and finds that she needs her daydream world in order to survive. An uneasy blend of comedy and fantasy that's touching in parts and worth seeing for its surreal sequences. Not a great film, but Streisand's performance redeems it. Written by Paul Zindel.
Boa: novel by Anne Richardson Roiphe.
COM            97 min
B,V    VDM L/A; VMA; STABL

## UP WORLD **
                 PG
Stan Winston    USA    1990
*Anthony Michael Hall, Jerry Orbach, Claudia*
*Christian*
One of the most bizarre of recent cop-and-his-partner pairings, that teams a police detective with an endearing gnome, when both find themselves with a common enemy. A curious blend of comic, action and fantasy elements, that fails to blend its disparate parts into an effective whole.
COM            88 min
V             VES

## UP YOUR ALLEY **
                 18
Bob Logan      USA    1988
*Linda Blair, Murray Langston*
A young female reporter dons a disguise in order to

get a story on a murder case, but also finds herself drawn into a surprising relationship.

COM                                                    90 min
V                                                         BOX

## UP YOUR ANCHOR ** 18
Dan Wolman
          ISRAEL/WEST GERMANY           1985
*Yftach Katzur, Zachi Noy, Joseph Deborah Keidar, Yehuda Efroni, Alexandre Arelson, Petra Koglenik, Beah Fidler*
Teenage sex comedy in the interminable LEMON POPSICLE series. This time our three boys get jobs on board a cruise liner.
Aka: EIS AM STIEL, 6 TEIL; ESKIMO LIMON 6; HAREEMU OHGEN LEMON POPSICLE 6
COM                                                    87 min
B,V                                                GHV; VCC

## UP YOUR LADDER ** 18
Edward Ryder/John Hayes
                          USA                          1979
*Cindy Morgan, George Flower, Chuck McCann, Coleen Meeker, Lola French*
An L.A. apartment block is the scene of scandalous goings-on among its swinging tenants, with the building itself recounting the stories of its tenants.
Aka: UP YOURS; UP YOURS . . . A ROCKIN' COMEDY
COM                                     86 min (ort 115 min)
B,V                                  VCL/CBS; APX; INTMED

## UPHILL ALL THE WAY ** PG
Frank Q. Dobbs        USA                          1985
*Roy Clark, Mel Tillis, Burl Ives, Glen Campbell, Trish Van Devere, Burt Reynolds, Frank Gorshin, Sheb Wooley*
The story of two bungling con-artists and their attempts to get rich quick, set in the early 1900s. An empty-headed and mirthless chase caper.
COM                                                    91 min
B,V                                                       NWV

## UPTOWN SATURDAY NIGHT *** PG
Sidney Poitier        USA                          1974
*Sidney Poitier, Bill Cosby, Harry Belafonte, Calvin Lockhart, Flip Wilson, Richard Pryor, Rosalind Cash, Roscoe Lee Browne, Lee Chamberlain, Paula Kelly*
Two men trying to get a stolen lottery ticket back, run up against the local godfather. A broad and happy comedy with Belafonte hilarious as a gangster boss. Followed by "Let's Do It Again" and A PIECE OF THE ACTION.
COM                                                    104 min
B,V                                                       WHV

## URBAN COWBOY ** 15
James Bridges         USA                          1980
*John Travolta, Debra Winger, Scott Glenn, Madolyn Smith, Barry Corbin, Brooke Alderson, Mickey Gilley, Charles Daniel Band, Bonnie Raitt*
The story of a young Texan "cowboy" and his macho life style in Pasadena, with Travolta frequenting a honky-tonk bar and working hard to perfect his image. OK if you like Country music, others may find the mechanical bull that's taken on by would-be rodeo riders, one of the film's few highlights. Written by Aaron Latham and Bridges.
Boa: magazine story by Aaron Latham.
DRA                                    125 min (ort 135 min)
B,V                                                       CIC

## URSUS ** 
Carlo Campogalliani
                  ITALY/SPAIN                       1962
*Ed Fury, Cristina Gajoni, Maria Orfei, Mary Marlon, Mario Scaccia, Lus Prendez*
A warrior sets out to rescue his kidnapped fiancee, held captive on a mysterious island where she is to be sacrificed to a pagan goddess. Standard high-camp Italian sword-and-sandal adventure.
Aka: MIGHTY URSUS, THE
A/AD                                                   93 min
B,V                                                       VPD

## USED CARS *** 15
Robert Zemeckis       USA                          1980
*Kurt Russell, Jack Warden, Gerrit Graham, Frank McRae, Deborah Harmon, David L. Lander, Joseph P. Flaherty, Michael McKean, Michael Talbott, Andrew Duncan, Marvey Northup*
Two car dealers engage in great rivalry with no holds barred when it comes to pulling the customers in. The coarse but hilarious script is by Zemeckis and Bob Gale.
COM                                                    107 min
B,V                                                       RCA

## UTU ** 15
Geoff Murphy        NEW ZEALAND               1984
*Anzac Wallace, Bruno Lawrence, Tim Elliott, Kelly Johnson, Wi Kuki Kaa*
A realistic portrayal of the Maori uprising of the 1870s, that starts with a Maori tribesman going on a rampage following the slaughter of his family. Let down by a dull plot and poor characterisation; THE CHANT OF JIMMY BLACKSMITH handled this theme a lot better.
Aka: REVENGE
DRA                                                    104 min
B,V                                                       MGM

# V

## V: THE HOT ONE ** 
Robert McCallum       USA                          1978
*Annette Haven, John Leslie, Laurien Dominique, Paul Thomas, Joey Silvera, Kay Parker*
A woman does not make love to her husband because of a childhood experience but instead cruises the sleazier parts of San Francisco, offering herself as a way of gaining sexual satisfaction. She winds up working in a brothel where she services drunks and assorted perverts. A disagreeable film as unconvincing as it is inconclusive.
A                                       72 min (ort 95 min) Cut
B,V                                                       CAL

## VAGABOND LOVER, THE *** 
Marshall Neilan       USA                          1929
*Rudy Vallee, Sally Blane, Marie Dressler, Charles Sellon, Norman Peck*
The story of an orchestra crooner who impersonates an impressario, and falls for the niece of the wealthy man who hires his band. Vallee's singing makes up for the story's deficiencies in this pleasant little musical-comedy vehicle.
MUS                                 70 min B/W semi-silent
V                                                         HVS

## VALACHI PAPERS, THE *** 
Terence Young          ITALY                        1972
*Charles Bronson, Lino Ventura, Joseph Wiseman, Fred Valleca, Walter Chiari, Jill Ireland*
A tense retelling of the life of a Mafia godfather who told all to a crime commission. Despite its many merits, it was overshadowed by THE GODFATHER. Bronson as famed informer Joseph Valachi, spills the beans from his prison whilst we see his reminiscences as a series of flashbacks. Absorbing but untidy. Based on actual events and written by Stephen Geller with music by Riz Ortolani.
Boa: book by Peter Maas.
DRA                                                    129 min
B,V                                                       TEVP

## VALDEZ: THE HALF-BREED ***
John Sturges USA 1973 (released
in USA in 1976)
*Charles Bronson, Vincent Van Patten, Marcel Bozzoffi,
Jill Ireland, Melissa Chimenti, Fausto Tozzi, Ettore
Manni, Adolfo Thous, Florencia Amarilla, Corrado
Gaida, Diana Lorys*
Set in 1880, this tells of a half-breed who befriends a
teenage boy who helps him on his ranch. However, the
man falls in love with the sister of a neighbour who
vows to destroy him. An entertaining film that was
shot in Spain.
Aka: CHINO; VALDEZ
HORSES, THE
WES 94 min (ort 98 min)
B,V TEVP

## VALENTINO *** 18
Ken Russell USA 1977
*Rudolf Nureyev, Leslie Caron, Michelle Phillips,
Felicity Kendal, Carol Kane, Seymour Cassel, Peter
Vaughan, Anton Diffring, Alfred Marks, Jennie
Linden, John Justin*
Nureyev stars as Rudolph Valentino in this story of
the life of the famous silent screen actor who had an
immense female following. This lavish and painsta-
kingly made work has all the makings of a fine film,
except the merits which more disciplined, less self-
indulgent direction would have brought it. Also filmed
in 1951 as "Valentino" and in 1975 as THE LEGEND
OF VALENTINO.
Boa: book by Brad Steiger and Chaw Mane.
DRA 123 min (ort 127 min)
B,V WHV

## VALET GIRLS ** 18
Rafal Zielinski USA 1986
*Meri D. Marshall, April Stewart, Mary Kohnert,
Christopher Weeks, Patricia Scott Mitchell, John
Terlesky*
Three buxom college girls show their enterprising
spirit when they use the assets they were born with to
start their own business. Dressed in uniforms that
include spike-heeled shoes, hot pants and little else,
they hire themselves out together with a limousine to
serve at parties. A simple-minded and smutty sex
comedy.
COM 79 min (ort 89 min)
B,V VES

## VALLEY GIRL **
Martha Coolidge USA 1983
*Nicolas Cage, Deborah Foreman, Colleen Camp,
Elizabeth Bowen, Cameron Dye, Heidi Holicker,
Frederic Forrest, Elizabeth Daily, Lee Purcell*
This portrait of a typical California youth-culture is a
pleasant enough look at teenagers and their families,
but never really goes anywhere.
DRA 95 min
B,V AVA; CBS

## VALLEY GIRLS ** 15
James Polakof USA 1983 (released 1985)
*Chuck Connors, Elena Stratheros, Jill Carroll, Gina
Calabrese, John Carradine, Michell Laurita, Sony
Bono, Sue Ann Langdon, Tiffany Bolling, Jim
Greenleaf, Matthew Conlon, Adam Mills, Tony Longo,
Michael Leon*
Four Californian high school girls get up to the usual
zany antics when, having lost a large bet, they
attempt to con two drug dealers out of money to raise
cash for an orphanage.
Aka: VALS, THE
COM 97 min
B,V QUA; AVR

## VALLEY OF THE DOLLS * 15
Mark Robson USA 1967
*Barbara Parkins, Patty Duke, Sharon Tate, Susan*

*Hayward, Paul Burke, Martin Milner, Tony Scotti, Lee
Grant, Joey Bishop, George Jessel*
A story of corruption and drug-taking with a young
actress innocent of the dangers falling victim to the
system, intertwined with the stories of two other
women trying to cope. Ramade as a TV film in 1981,
this is a glossy and exploitative adaptation of a
similar novel. Written by Helen Deutsch and Dorothy
Kingsley with music by Andre Previn and musical
direction by John Williams.
Boa: novel by Jacqueline Susann.
DRA 118 min
B,V CBS

## VALLEY OF THE SUN **
George Marshall USA 1942
*Lucille Ball, Cedric Hardwicke, Dean Jagger, James
Craig, Billy Gilbert, Peter Whitney, Antonio Moreno,
Tom Tyler, George Cleveland, Hank Bell, Don Terry,
Richard Fiske, Chris Willow Bill, Fern Emmett, Al St
John*
A crooked Indian agent in Arizona engineers an
Indian uprising but he is outwitted by a government
agent, who pretends to be a renegade Indian scout in
order to spy on him. A slow-moving second-rate
Western, written by Horace McCoy.
Boa: book by Clarence Budington Kelland.
WES 75 min (ort 79 min) B/W
B,V KVD

## VALOR OF WAR, THE ** 15
Phil Karlson USA 1970
*Rock Hudson, Sylva Koscina, Sergio Fantoni, Jacques
Sernas, Giacomo Rossi Stuart, Tom Felleghi*
Hudson plays a WW2 explosives expert who after
being wounded, is nursed back to health by a group of
child partisans. With their aid, he embarks on a
mission to blow up a German-held dam. Intermittent-
ly exciting, the film's use of kids as a cute gimmick
detracts from its impact.
Aka: HORNET'S NEST
WAR 109 min; 103 min (KRP)
B,V FILV; KRP

## VAMP ** 18
Richard Jones USA 1986
*Grace Jones, Chris Makepeace, Robert Rusler, Gedde
Watanabe, Sandy Baron, Edee Pfeiffer, Billy Drago,
Brad Logan, Lisa Lyon, Jim Boyle, Larry Spinak, Eric
Welch, Stuart Rogers, Gary Swailes, Ray Ballard,
Paunita Nichols*
Two college boys visit a strange club looking for a
stripper for their fraternity party, and fall victim to
some modern-day female vampires. Starts out as a
very tongue-in-cheek comedy-horror, but this early
promise soon gives way to a kinky and ghoulish
nightmare. Disappointing, despite the best efforts of
Jones as outrageous head vampire/stripper Katrina.
HOR 93 min
B,V NWV

## VAMPING ** 15
Frederick King Keller USA 1985
*Patrick Duffy, Christine Hyland, Fred A. Keller, David
Booze*
An unemployed musician takes part in a robbery and
finds himself a murder target.
DRA 105 min
B,V EIV

## VAMPIRA **
Clive Donner UK 1974
*David Niven, Teresa Graves, Peter Bayliss, Jennie
Linden, Nicky Henson, Linda Hayden, Bernard
Bresslaw, Cathie Shirriff, Andrea Allen, Veronica
Carlson, Minah Bird, Christopher Sandford, Freddie
Jones, Frank Thornton*
A vampire organises a beauty contest in order to get
blood to resurrect his departed wife in this horror

spoof. A one joke movie that has him extracting samples from the necks of Playboy Bunnies in search of the correct type.
Aka: OLD DRACULA
COM                              86 min (ort 88 min)
B,V                                             RNK

**VAMPIRE AT MIDNIGHT **                        18
Gregory McClatchy       USA                   1987
*Jason Williams, Gustav Vintas, Lesley Milne, Jeanie Moore, Ester Alise, Robert Random, Tom Friedman*
Los Angeles witnesses the work of a grisly serial murderer, whose victims are found drained of blood and with their throats slashed. An excitable and unconventional cop is given the task of bringing the killer to justice, little realising what this will entail in this macabre tale.
HOR                                        92 min
V/h                                           PAL

**VAMPIRE BAT ***
Frank Strayer            USA                  1933
*Melvyn Douglas, Fay Wray, Lionel Atwill, Dwight Frye, Maude Eburne, George E. Stone, Carl Stockdale, Robert Frazer, Harrison Greene, Lionel Belmore, Rita Carlisle, Stella Adams, William Humphrey, William V. Mong, Fern Emmett*
A remote Bavarian village is the setting for a series of baffling murders of villagers. They have their origin in the efforts of mad doctor Atwill to find a blood substitute. A low budget horror tale that has a few eerie moments and benefits from a strong cast. Beware of the many shorter prints.
HOR                          60 min (ort 71 min) B/W
B,V                                        VCL/CBS

**VAMPIRE CIRCUS **                              18
Robert Young            UK                    1971
*John Moulder Brown, Adrienne Corri, Laurence Payne, Thorley Walters, Lynne Frederick, Elizabeth Seal, Anthony Corlan, Richard Owens, Domini Blythe, Robin Hunter, Robert Tayman, Mary Wimbush, Lalla Ward, Robin Sachs*
Set in 1825, this tells of a travelling circus entirely composed of vampires, including the animals. A slightly unusual Hammer film, but unfortunately the plot, which told of a vampire's curse and a subsequent plague, was spoilt by last minute cuts. The music is by Philip Martel.
Osca: COUNTESS DRACULA (VCC)
HOR         83 min (ort 87 min) (Cut at film release)
B,V                      RNK; FUTVI; VCC (VHS only)

**VAMPIRE HOOKERS **                             18
Cirio H. Santiago    PHILIPPINES             1978
*John Carradine, Karen Stride, Bruce Fairbairn, Trey Wilson, Lex Winter, Lenka Novak, Katie Dolan, Vic Diaz*
An ageing vampire retains a bevy of beautiful blood-suckers who frequent a port, enticing sailors to their doom. A film which unfortunately, never lives up to its tantalising title.
Aka: SENSUOUS VAMPIRES; TWICE BITTEN (ARF or NET)
HOR                       78 min; 76 min (NET)
B,V                            ARF; ABA; NET

**VAMPIRE IN VENICE ***                          18
Augusto Caminito      ITALY                   1988
*Klaus Kinski, Donald Pleasence, Christopher Plummer, Anne Knecht, Barbara De Rossi, Elvire Audray*
A slow-moving, unofficial sequel to NOSFERATU THE VAMPYRE, with Kinski now resurrected and haunting the canals of Venice during carnival time. As he works his way through various revellers, Plummer as our intrepid vampire hunter is not far behind. An arty exercise in glossiness that is well and truly overdone, with an irritating operatic score and a

ludicrous climax for good measure. This self-indulgent mess was written by Caminito.
HOR                                       106 min
B,V                                           VES

**VAMPIRE KNIGHTS **                             18
Daniel M. Peterson      USA                   1987
*Thomas Kingsley, Ann Michaels*
Three vampire girls enjoy ensnaring and killing young boys, but finally come up against an organisation that's out to put paid to their activities.
COM                  83 min (ort 90 min) Cut (11 sec)
B,V                                 CHV L/A; IVS

**VAMPIRE LOVERS, THE ***                        15
Roy Ward Baker          UK                    1970
*Ingrid Pitt, Peter Cushing, Madeleine Smith, George Cole, Kate O'Mara, Dawn Addams, Pippa Steel, Douglas Wilmer, Jon Finch, Ferdy Mayne, Harvey Hall, Charles Farrell, Janey Key, Kirsten Betts, John Forbes-Robertson*
A fairly faithful version of "Carmilla", with the voluptuous Pitt a lesbian vampire who seduces many a pretty female victim. The touch of eroticism that Hammer added to a dated formula helped prolong the life of this genre, but by this time the paucity of possible plot variations had become apparent. Followed by LUST FOR A VAMPIRE and TWINS OF EVIL.
Boa: short story Carmilla by Sheridan Le Fanu.
HOR                      91 min (Cut at film release)
B,V                                           RNK

**VAMPIRE MEN OF THE LOST PLANET **
Al Adamson              USA                   1971
*John Carradine, Robert Dix, Vicki Volantie, Joey Benson, Jennifer Bishop*
A laughable and pathetic film, in which Carrradine as the ageing Dr Rhining traces attacks of vampirism to Tubetan, home planet of the Vampire people. Ably assisted by some other scientists (and footage from several other duff movies), an expedition to this world is mounted. All the old SF cliches are here, plus a few more besides.
Aka: CREATURES OF THE PREHISTORIC PLANET; CREATURES OF THE RED PLANET; FLESH CREATURES (OF THE RED PLANET); HORROR CREATURES OF THE PREHISTORIC PLANET; HORROR OF THE BLOOD MONSTERS; SPACE MISSION OF THE LOST PLANET
FAN                         85 min Colour and B/W
B,V                              PORVI L/A; MMA

**VAMPYRES **                                    18
Joseph Larraz          UK                     1974
*Marianne Morris, Murray Brown, Sally Faulkner, Brian Deacon, Michael Byrne, Anulka, Karl Larchbury, Margaret Heald, Douglas Jones, Gerald Case, Bessie Love*
Two murdered lesbian hitch-hikers return as vampires and take their revenge on men drivers in this gruesome nonsense.
Aka: DAUGHTERS OF DRACULA; VAMPYRES, DAUGHTERS OF DARKNESS; VAMPYRE ORGY, THE
HOR                         82 min (ort 84 min)
B,V                            RNK; MIA (VHS only)

**VAN DER VALK: DESTROYING ANGEL **             15
Graham Evans            UK                    1972
*Barry Foster, Susan Travers, Joanna Dunham, Michael Latimer, Nigel Stock, James Cairncross, Patricia Quinn, Walter Brown*
Van Der Valk becomes concerned when he finds a link between a car crash that took place in France 20 years ago and a possible poisoning case at a sleazy boarding house.
DRA                                       51 min mTV
V                                          THAMES

## VAN DER VALK: ONE HERRING'S NOT ENOUGH **

Dennis Vance     UK     15     1972
*Barry Foster, Susan Travers, Joanna Dunham, Michael Latimer, Nigel Stock, Alain Haines*
The very first episode in a competent police detective series based on the books of Nicholas Freeling. The stories were generally set in Amsterdam, and concerned the exploits of the title character. In this tale he is called in to solve a murder mystery, made all the more puzzling by the fact that an innocent man has confessed to it.
DRA     51 min mTV
V     THAMES

## VAN, THE **

Sam Grossman     USA     1976
*Stuart Getz, Harry Moses, Debbie White, Nora Sanders, Connie Lisa Mari, Bill Adler, Danny DeVito, Marcie Barkin, Stephen Oliver*
Teen-comedy about a girl-mad but rather shy youth who puts his fancy new van to good use in seducing pretty girls. A witless but inoffensive comedy with a light and frothy plot.
COM     77 min; 92 min (CBS)
B,V     GOV L/A; CBS

## VANESSA ***

Hubert Frank     WEST GERMANY     18     1976
*Olivier Pascal, Anton Diffring, Uschi Zech, Gunther Clemens*
A convent-educated girl has no knowledge of sex except that gained from magazines. When a rich uncle in Hong Kong dies, she discovers on visiting his estate that she is now the owner of a string of brothels. Taken by a new acquaintance to the estate of a pervert, she is sexually abused but is soon rescued and returns to Paris to enjoy her new found wealth. A well-made and quite sophisticated sex fantasy in the EMMANUELLE mould.
A     88 min; 83 min (VPD)
B,V     WOV; ORANGE/STABL; VPD (VHS only)

## VANISHING ACT **

David Greene     USA     PG     1986
*Margot Kidder, Mike Farrell, Elliott Gould, Fred Gwynne, Graham Jarvis, John Bluethner, Heather Ward Siegel, Wally McSween, Paul Jolicoeur, Grant Lowe, Linda Mackay, Larry Musser, Tony Totino, Reg Glass*
A couple married one week have a row and the wife walks out. She returns in the company of the local priest after her husband has reported her as missing. However, he insists that the woman is not his wife. This third TV movie to be made from the play has a few moments of suspense but little else, while Kidder's mannerisms soon begin to irritate. The final resolution is disappointingly contrived. Scripted by Richard Levinson and William Link.
Boa: play Trap For A Lonely Man by Robert Thomas.
THR     93 min (or 134 min) Cut (30 sec) mTV
B,V     CBS

## VANISHING POINT **

Richard C. Sarafian     USA     18     1971
*Barry Newman, Cleavon Little, Dean Jagger, Victoria Medlin, Paul Koslo, Timothy Scott, Bob Donner, Gilda Texter, Anthony James, Karl Swenson, Severn Darden, Lee Weaver, Tom Reese*
Given the job of driving a car from Denver to San Francisco, Newman decides to do it in 15 hours. He is soon being chased across several states by an army of law enforcement agencies who finally mount a co-ordinated operation to stop him. A strange, moody and ultimately pointless film that remains a cult movie. Little as blind D.J. Super Soul and the rock score (with musical direction by Jimmy Brown) are high-spots in a fast journey to nowhere.

DRA     98 min (ort 107 min)
B,V,V2     CBS

## VASECTOMY: A DELICATE MATTER *

Robert Burge     USA     15     1986
*Paul Sorvino, Lorne Greene, Cassandra Edwards, Ina Balin, Gary Raff, Abe Vigoda, June Wilkinson, William Marshall*
After bearing him his eighth child, the wife of a bank executive tells him to have a vasectomy or say goodbye to sexual relations. While he is occupied overcoming his fear of the operation, he hires a detective to stop his family pilfering. A banal one-joke comedy that tries hard to shock but winds up being merely stupid.
Aka: VASECTOMY: A DELICATE OPERATION
COM     92 min mTV
B,V     IVS

## VATICAN CONSPIRACY, THE **

Marcello Aliprandi
ITALY/MEXICO/SPAIN     1982
*Terence Stamp, Angela Molina, Vittorio Mezzogiorno, Paolo Molina, Fabrizio Bentivoglio, Lopez Vasquez, Antonio Marsina, Roberto Antonelli, Patrick La Place, Adriano Amidei Migliano, Eduardo Fajardo, Franco Ferri, Pepi Munne*
The story of a conspiracy to murder the Pope, involving one of his former students.
Aka: DEATH IN THE VATICAN; MORTE IN VATICANO
THR     120 min
B,V     POLY

## VAULT OF HORROR **

Roy Ward Baker     UK     15     1973
*Terry-Thomas, Glynis Johns, Curt Jurgens, Daniel Massey, Anna Massey, Dawn Addams, Denholm Elliott, Michael Pratt, John Forbes-Robertson, Jasmina Hilton, Michael Craig, Edward Judd, Arthur Mullard, Tom Baker*
Another set of horror stories in this quasi-sequel to TALES FROM THE CRYPT, borrowed from the stories in E.C. Comics of the early 1950s. Screenplay is by Milton Subotsky with the five stories of murder, torture, vampirism and voodoo the work of Al Feldstein and William Gaines. A good cast works hard, but this poor effort is definitely short of atmosphere.
Aka: FURTHER TALES FROM THE CRYPT; TALES FROM THE CRYPT 2
Osca: TALES FROM THE CRYPT
HOR     87 min
B,V     CBS

## VEGAS STRIP WAR, THE **

George Englund     USA     PG     1984
*Rock Hudson, James Earl Jones, Noryuki "Pat" Morita, Sharon Stone, Robert Costanzo, Rick Wagner, Bryan Englund, Tony Russel, Madison Mason, Dennis Holahan, Robin Gammell, Chadda Battrell, J. Carlton Adair, George Englund Jr*
Hudson as a Las Vegas casino owner opens a run-down casino across the street, and becomes a rival to his ex-partners as his way off hitting back after being cheated by them. Hudson's last TV movie and one that perhaps, will be remembered on that account, if for nothing else.
Aka: VEGAS STRIP WARS, THE
DRA     93 min (ort 100 min) mTV
B,V     PRV L/A; CH5

## VELVET HOUSE, THE **

Viktors Ritelis     UK     1969
*Michael Gough, Yvonne Mitchell, Sharon Gurney, Simon Gough, Olaf Pooley, David Butler, Mary Hignett, Nicholas Jones*
A mother plots with her daughter to murder her tyrannical stockbroker husband, but their plans go awry when they find themselves haunted by his

corpse.
Aka: CORPSE, THE; CRUCIBLE OF HORROR;
VELVET HOUSE CORPSE, THE
THR                                          91 mi
B,V,V2                                  INT L/A

**VENDETTA ** **                                  18
Bruce Logan               USA               1985
*Karen Chase, Sandy Martin, Lisa Clarson, Lisa
Hullana, Linda Lightfoot, Kim Shriner, Michelle
Newkirk, Roberta Collins, Durga McBroom*
A woman gets herself put in prison to track down her
sister's killers. A real exploitative women-in-jail
movie with lashings of gratuitous sex and violence.
Aka: ANGELS BEHIND BARS
DRA                                       102 min
B,V                                           VES

**VENDETTA FOR THE SAINT ** **                    PG
James O'Connolly          UK                1968
*Roger Moore, Ian Hendry, Rosemary Dexter*
Compiled from a popular TV series "The Saint", which
in turn was based on the detective novels of Leslie
Charteris, this has our hero getting himself involved
with the Mafia.
DRA                                  94 min mTV
B,V                             PRV; CH5 (VHS only)

**VENGEANCE ***                                   18
Antonio Isasi             ITALY             1977
*Jason Miller, Lea Massari, Marisa Peredes, Manuel
DeBlas, Aldo Sambrell, Yolanda Farr, Francisco
Casares*
A prisoner on the run is pursued by a guard with a dog
in this forgettable melodrama.
DRA                            107 min Cut (25 sec)
B,V,V2                            INT L/A; XTASY

**VENGEANCE ** **                                  15
Anthony M. Dawson (Antonio Margheriti)
                         ITALY/WEST GERMANY
                  1968 (released in USA in 1971)
*Richard Harrison, Claudio Camaso, Allan Collins,
Sheyla Rozin, Werner Pochat, Guido Lollobrigida*
Routine Euro-Western. A man seeks revenge on the
outlaw gang who murdered his friend in this extreme-
ly violent but unmemorable tale.
Aka: JOKO, INVOCO DIO . . . E MUORI
WES                            96 min (ort 100 min)
B,V                                           GHV

**VENGEANCE IS MINE ** **
Joy Houck Jr              USA               1973
*Mickey Dolenz, James Ralston, Susan McCullough,
Chuck Patterson, Michael Anthony, Katie Tilley, Ann
Barrett*
The story of racial, social and family conflicts in New
Orleans with a black/white love affair providing the
trigger for a wave of killings of beautiful women.
Unpleasant and exploitative.
Aka: NIGHT OF THE STRANGLER
HOR                                        87 min
V                                  CIN L/A; CYC

**VENGEANCE OF THE ZOMBIES ** **
Leon Klimovsky   ITALY/SPAIN                1972
*Vic Winner (Victor Alcanzar), Mirta Miller, Paul
Naschy (Jacinto Molina), Luis Ciges, Romy, Maria
Kosti, Aurora de Alba, Pierre Besari, Antonio Pica,
Elsa Zabala, Monserrat Julio, Ramon Lillo, Norma
Kastell, Ingrid Rabel*
Zombies run amok in this routine continental zombie
pic.
Aka: LA REBELION DE LAS MUERTAS; LA
VENDETTA DEI MORTI VIVENTI; REBELLION
OF THE DEAD WOMEN, THE; REVOLT OF THE
DEAD ONES, THE
HOR                                        84 min
B,V,V2                                       VPD

**VENGEANCE, THE DEMON ***                        18
Stan Winston              USA               1987
*Lance Henriksen, John Di Aquino, Kerry Remsen,
Devon Odessa, Jeff East, Cynthia Bain, Joel Hoffman,
Kimberly Ross, Florence Schauffler, Buck Flower,
Madeleine Taylor Holmes, Tom Woodruff Jr*
When a man's child is killed in an accident caused by
a biker gang, the distraught father goes to a back-
woods witch for help, and a monstrous demon is called
up to execute revenge. However, the father begins to
have second thoughts about what he has done but
finds himself unable to control the creature. The
directorial debut of make-up expert Winston, is a film
rich in effects that's held back by a predictable script.
Aka: PUMPKINHEAD
HOR                            82 min (ort 86 min)
B,V                                           CBS

**VENGEANCE: THE STORY OF TONY CIMO ***  15
Marc Daniels              USA               1986
*Brad Davis, Roxanne Hart, Brad Dourif, William
Conrad, Michael Beach, Wayne Tippit, Frances
McDormand, Chuck Patterson, Cass Morgan, Joyce
O'Brien, Fritz Bronner, Jill Featherstone, Marcey
Leshay, Jody Wilson, Gregg Parrish*
Vigilante tale with a young bricklayer taking the law
into his own hands to avenge the brutal murder of his
parents, when he tires of waiting for the courts to give
him justice. A gritty and tense tale, based to some
extent on fact. Filmed in Jacksonville, Florida.
DRA                                  85 min mTV
B,V                               NEWMED/PVG

**VENOM ***                                       15
Piers Haggard             UK                1982
*Klaus Kinski, Oliver Reed, Susan George, Nicol
Williamson, Sterling Hayden, Sarah Miles, Cornelia
Sharpe, Lance Holcomb, Mike Gwilym, Rita Webb,
John Williamson, Michael Gough, Peter Porteous,
Maurice Colbourne, Moti Makan*
The 10-year-old son of a wealthy family has been
given a deadly black mamba snake as a present. The
story has an international terrorist group holding a
house full of hostages while the snake slithers
through the ventilation ducts, stalking its victims.
This clumsy combination of a police thriller and a
horror yarn was a waste of the talents of a good cast.
Watch it and you'll waste your time too. Written by
Robert Carrington.
Boa: novel by Alan Scholefield.
HOR                            89 min (ort 98 min)
B,V                              TEVP L/A; CAN

**VERBOTEN! ***
Samuel Fuller             USA               1959
*James Best, Susan Cummings, Tom Pittman, Paul
Dubov, Dick Kallman, Steven Geray*
An American soldier in Berlin just after WW2 falls in
love with a German girl who has become embittered
by her experiences. Interesting but rather overblown
WW2 melodrama.
DRA                                  93 min B/W
B,V.                             PACVI L/A; ODY

**VERDICT, THE ****                               15
Sidney Lumet              USA               1982
*Paul Newman, Charlotte Rampling, Jack Warden,
James Mason, Milo O'Shea, Lindsay Crouse, Edward
Binns, Julie Bovasso, Roxanne Hart, James Handy*
A lawyer who's gone to seed, gets a chance to recover
his self respect by fighting a medical incompetance
case. Newman gives a powerful performance as the
drunken Boston lawyer who has the chance to fight for
the values he still believes in; Mason is his wily
opponent. Written by David Mamet and one of
Lumet's best films.
Boa: novel by Barry Reed.
DRA                                       123 min
B,V                                           CBS

**VERONIKA VOSS** ***
Rainer Werner Fassbinder
　　　　WEST GERMANY　　　1982
*Rosel Zech, Hilmar Thate, Cornelia Froboess, Anne-Marie Duringer, Doris Schade, Volker Spengler*
The story of a faded film star of the 1940s who, allegedly a friend of Goebbels, has become a morphine addict ten years after the war. Written by Fassbinder, Pea Frohlich and Peter Marthesheimer, this was the last of the director's trilogy after THE MARRIAGE OF MARIA BRAUN and "Lola" that looked at post-war Germany. Good but not great, interesting but not engrossing.
DRA　　　　　　　　　　　105 min
B,V　　　　　　　　　　　VCL/CBS

**VERTIGO** ****　　　　　　　　　PG
Alfred Hitchcock　　USA　　　1958
*James Stewart, Kim Novak, Barbara Bel Geddes, Tom Helmore, Henry Jones, Ellen Corby, Raymond Bailey, Konstantin Shayne, Lee Patrick, Paul Bryar, William Remick, Julian Petruzzi, Sara Taft, Fred Graham, Mollie Dodd*
A retired policeman who has a fear of heights is drawn into a complex web of deceit and betrayal. Stewart plays the cop, hired to keep an eye on Novak, the wife of an old school friend. One of Hitchcock's best thrillers, this atmospheric film demands repeated viewing to unravel its complexities. Written by Alex Coppel and Samuel Taylor with a fine score by Bernard Herrmann.
Boa: novel D'Entre Les Morts by Pierre Boileau and Thomas Narcejac.
THR　　　　　　123 min (ort 128 min)
B,V　　　　　　　　　　　CIC

**VERY CLOSE ENCOUNTERS OF THE**　　　18
**FOURTH KIND** **
Roy Garrett (Maurio Garazzo)
　　　　ITALY　　　　　1979
*Maria Baxa, Monica Zanchi, Mario Maranzana, Marina D'Auria, Alessio Pigna*
Sex comedy spoof involving alien visitors to Earth, and their amorous pursuits.
Aka: COMING OF ALIENS, A (DRUM or GLOB); INCONTRI MOLTI RAVVICINATI DEL QUATRO TIPO
A　　　　　83 min (ort 105 min) Cut (32 sec)
B,V　　　　　VPD L/A; HTM; DRUM; GLOB

**VERY IMPORTANT PERSON** **　　　　U
Ken Annakin　　UK　　　1962
*James Robertson Justice, Leslie Phillips, Stanley Baxter, Eric Sykes, Colin Gordon, Richard Wattis, Godfrey Winn, Jean Cadell, John Le Mesurier, Peter Myers, Norman Bird, Ronnie Stevens, Jeremy Lloyd, Ronald Leigh Hunt*
A rescue plan is mounted to smuggle an important British scientist out of Germany, after he's been shot down and taken prisoner. Baxter impersonates the German Commandant to help Justice escape in this tame POW farce.
Aka: COMING-OUT PARTY, A; V.I.P.
COM　　　　　　　　　　98 min B/W
B,V　　　　　　　　　　RNK; VCC

**VERY LIKE A WHALE** **
Alan Bridges　　UK　　　1980
*Alan Bates, Gemma Jones, Ann Bell, Anna Cropper, Ian Hogg, Leslie Sands, Ann Stallybrass*
An outwardly successful businessman, with all the trappings of wealth and prestige, is in reality very lonely and disillusioned.
DRA　　　　　　　　　　　82 min
B,V　　　　　　　　　　　PRV

**VIBES** *　　　　　　　　　　PG
Ken Kwapis　　USA　　　1987
*Cyndi Lauper, Jeff Goldblum, Julian Sands, Googy*

*Gress, Peter Falk, Michael Lerner, Ramon Bieri, Elizabeth Pena, Bill McCutcheon, Karen Akers*
A silly adventure comedy, in which two psychics team up to hunt for a lost treasure in the mountains of Ecuador. Written by Lowell Ganz and Babaloo Mandel, this unfortunate excursion probably sounded funnier on paper.
COM　　　　　　　95 min (ort 99 min)
V　　　　　　　　　　　RCA

**VICE SQUAD** ***　　　　　　　18
Gary A. Sherman　　USA　　　1982
*Season Hubley, Gary Swanson, Wings Hauser, Pepe Serna, Beverly Todd, Stack Pierce, Nina Blackwood*
A prostitute agrees to work for the cops in an attempt to catch the sadistic pimp who mutilates the girls of rivals and killed one of her friends. She finds that she has herself become a target in this dull and sleazy offering, that's partially redeemed by a great performance from Hauser as the villain.
DRA　　　　　　87 min (ort 97 min) mTV
B,V,V2,LV　　　　　　　　　EHE

**VICE VERSA** ***　　　　　　　PG
Brian Gilbert　　USA　　　1988
*Judge Reinhold, Fred Savage, Swoozie Kurtz, David Proval, Corinne Bohrer, Jane Kaczmerek, David Proval, William Prince, Gloria Gifford*
A semi-remake of the 1947 British film with a magical Thai skull enabling a workaholic department store boss to swap bodies with his 11-year-old son. This idea has been done to death, but the Dick Clement and Ian La Frenais script plus the comical Reinhold-Savage duo help keep this one on its toes.
COM　　　　　　　95 min (ort 97 min)
B,V　　　　　　　　　　　RCA

**VICEBUSTERS** *
Rick Sloane　　USA　　　1988
*Linnea Quigley, Ginger Lynn Allen, Karen Russell*
Two attractive police cadets are prepared to use any means to ensure they graduate, and go undercover to break up a porno ring. A fairly mindless POLICE ACADEMY-style comedy.
COM　　　　　　　　　　86 min
V　　　　　　　　　　　FUTUR

**VICES IN THE FAMILY** **　　　　　18
Mariano Laurenti　　ITALY
*Susan Scott, Juliette Mayniel, Orchidea De Santis, Renzo Montagnani, Edwige Fenech, Gigi Ballista*
Italian melodrama mixing sex and intrigue in about equal proportions.
Aka: FAMILY VICES; IL VIZIO DI FAMIGLIA
A　　　　　　72 min; 79 min (SHEP)
B,V　　　　　　18PLAT/TOW; SHEP

**VICTIM** ***　　　　　　　　15
Basil Dearden　　UK　　　1961
*Dirk Bogarde, Sylvia Sims, Dennis Price, John Barrie, Derren Nesbitt, Peter McEnery, Donald Churchill, Nigel Stock, Anthony Nicholls, Hilton Edwards, Norman Bird, Alan McNaughton, Noel Howlett, Charles Lloyd Pack*
Tense and well-handled drama in which a group of homosexuals find themselves the victims of a nasty blackmailing couple. A successful barrister breaks off his relationship with a young boy, who later commits suicide. Soon a victim himself, he decides to co-operate with the police. Written by Janet Green and John McCormack this was a courageous film (for the time) that will now seem much less daring. Photography is by Otto Heller.
DRA　　　　　96 min (ort 100 min) B/W
B,V　　　　　　　　　　RNK; VCC

**VICTIM, THE** **
　　　　HONG KONG　　　197-
*Cheung Yick, Leung Ka Yan*

A martial arts student attaches himself to an unwilling master whose main concern is to get away from his new wife.

MAR 88 min
B,V POLY

## VICTIMS *** 15
Jerrold Freedman USA 1981
*Kate Nelligan, Ken Howard, Madge Sinclair, Jonelle Allen, Pamela Dunlap, Amy Madigan, Rose Portillo, Bert Remsen, Michael C. Gwynne, Sherry Hursey, Karmin Murcelo, Howard Hesseman, Alex Henteloff, Charles Sweigart*
When a rapist is freed by the courts on a technicality, his latest victim bands together with three former victims in order to stalk him. Nelligan is good as the woman intent on having her revenge, as is Hesseman as the villain. However, the poor story and plot development dissipate the tension as it develops.

THR 92 min (ort 100 min) mTV
B,V WHV

## VICTIMS FOR VICTIMS *** 15
Karen Arthur USA 1984
*Theresa Saldana, Adrian Zmed, Lelia Goldoni, Lawrence Pressman, Mariclare Costello, Linda Carlson, Stanley Kamel, Pierrino Mascarino, Patricia McAneny, Kenneth Phillips, Philip English, William Allen Young, Arva Holt*
Theresa Saldana plays herself, in this retelling of the true story of how this actress nearly lost her life in a brutal attack by a knife-wielding maniac. She went on to found an association to help the victims of violent crimes. Written by Arthur Heinemann, this is a harrowing and dramatic story.
Aka: VICTIMS FOR VICTIMS: THE THERESA SALDANA STORY

DRA 100 min mTV
B,V MGM

## VICTIMS OF PASSION *** 15
Henri Safran AUSTRALIA 1986
*Kerry Mack, Nicholas Eadie, Wayne Cull*
Set in the 1930s, this tells the story of the real-life affair between two aviators, Jessica "Chubbie" Miller and Bill Lancaster, that created a scandal and ended in tragedy. A glossy and absorbing tale, well scripted and acted.
Aka: LANCASTER MILLER AFFAIR, THE

DRA 169 min mTV
B,V CAN; AVS; SCRN

## VICTIMS OF VICE ** 18
Claude De Givray FRANCE 1964
*Jean Yanne, Perrette Pradier, Valeria Ciangottini, Patrice Valota, Odil Michel, Florence Cayrol, Patrick Oliver*
The story of a young girl who becomes a prostitute and her conflict with a racketeer.
Aka: L'ARMOUR A LA CHAINE

A 87 min Cut (2 min 22 sec)
B,V ARI L/A; BLUES; NET

## VICTOR FRANKENSTEIN *** 
Calvin Floyd EIRE/SWEDEN 1975
*Per Oscarsson, Nicholas Clay, Leon Vitali, Stacey Dorning, Jan Ohlsson, Olof Bergstrom, Archie O'Sullivan, Harry Brogan*
This careful adaptation of the Frankenstein legend is well made and literate but lacks power. Filmed partly in Ireland, this film is good to look at but dissipates its force in a psychological examination of the creature and its angst-ridden existence.
Aka: TERROR OF FRANKENSTEIN
Boa: novel Frankenstein; Or, The Modern Prometheus by Mary Shelley.

HOR 92 min
B,V ARF

## VICTOR/VICTORIA *** 15
Blake Edwards USA 1982
*Julie Andrews, James Garner, Robert Preston, Lesley Ann Warren, Alex Karras, John Rhys-Davies, Graham Stark, Peter Arne*
A struggling singer dresses up as a man and masquerades as a drag artist, becoming a great success in Paris. A stylish and often hilarious version of the 1933 German film "Viktor Und Viktoria", first remade in 1936 as "First A Girl". Preston gives a gem of a performance as the ageing drag queen who put her up to it. AA: Score (Henry Mancini/Leslie Bricusse)

COM 129 min (ort 133 min)
V MGM

## VICTORIA THE GREAT *** 
Herbert Wilcox UK 1937
*Anna Neagle, Anton Walbrook, H.B. Warner, Walter Rilla, Mary Morris, James Dale, Felix Aylmer, Charles Carson, C.V. France, Gordon McLeod, Arthur Young, Grete Wegener, Paul Leyssac, Percy Parsons, Derrick De Marney*
Biopic on the life of Britain's longest reigning monarch that examines some episodes in her life including her romance with Prince Albert. The Jubilee celebration in the final reel is in Technicolor. A solid film, well made and acted, with all the virtues (and faults) of those traditional stolid British biopics. Followed by "Sixty Glorious Years". Written by Robert Vansittart and Miles Malleson.
Boa: play Victoria Regina by Laurence Houseman.

DRA 112 min B/W and Colour
B,V TEVP L/A

## VICTORY AT ENTEBBE ** PG
Marvin J. Chomsky USA 1976
*Helmut Berger, Theodore Bikel, Linda Blair, Kirk Douglas, Richard Dreyfuss, Stefan Gierasch, David Groh, Julius Harris, Helen Hayes, Anthony Hopkins, Burt Lancaster, Christian Marquand, Elizabeth Taylor, Jessica Walter*
A poor treatment of the actual events surrounding the daring June 4 1976 rescue of hostages held, with the connivance of Idi Amin, by terrorists at Entebbe airport. A star cast cannot save a dull movie rushed out after the actual events, originally on tape and then transferred to film. Harris as Amin replaced Godfrey Cambridge who died during filming. See also the far better films OPERATION THUNDERBOLT and RAID ON ENTEBBE.

A/AD 150 min mTV
B,V WHV

## VIDEO DEAD ** 18
Robert Scott USA 1987
*Roxanna Augesen, Rocky Duvall, Michael St Michaels, Jennifer Munro, Cliff Watts, Vickie Bastel, Sam David McClelland, Libby Russler, Garrett Dressler, Mufie Greco, Walter Garrett, Jo Ann Peterson, Don McClelland, Thaddeus Golas*
A couple of kids discover an old TV set in the attic of their new home. They switch it on and find that it keeps showing the same monochrome horror film. They turn it off and go to bed, but at night it switches itself on again and releases hordes of moronic zombies, who climb out of the set and attack the living. A low-budget, semi-spoof treatment of an intriguing idea.

HOR 86 min (ort 90 min)
B,V MED

## VIDEODROME *** 18
David Cronenberg CANADA 1982
*James Woods, Sonya Smits, Debbie Harry, Peter Dvorsky, Les Carlson, Jack Creley, Lynne Gorman*
The boss of a cable TV station producing broadcasts for an underground market, picks up a series of strange, untraceable transmissions from his own TV set. These transmissions have the power to create

hallucinations that initially fascinate, but ultimately destroy him. Despite its intelligent start, this shocker gets slower (and sicker) as it develops. The repulsive special effects are by Rick Baker. Cut before video submission.

| HOR | 81 min (ort 90 min) |
|---|---|
| V/h | CIC |

### VIETNAM: PARTS 1 AND 2 ** 18
John Duigan/Chris Noonan
AUSTRALIA    1987
*Barry Otto, Veronica Noonan, Nicholas Eadie, Nicole Kidman, Noel Ferrier, Imogen Annersley, Mark Lee, John Polson, Graeme Blundell, Alan Cassell, Francesca Raft, Alyssa Cook*
An account of the Vietnam War as seen through the eyes of a young conscript and telling of the four years he spends fighting. A harsh and uncompromising tale, with a satisfactory but somewhat predictable script.

| WAR | 360 min (2 cassettes) |
|---|---|
| B,V | SCRN |

### VIETNAM, TEXAS * 18
Robert Ginty    USA    1990
*Robert Ginty, Tim Thomerson, Haing S. Ngor, Tamlyn Tomita, Kieu Chinh, Bert Remsen*
Ginty plays a priest who sets out to find the woman he abandoned (while pregnant) when he was in Vietnam. He finds her living in a Vietnamese community in Texas, where she has become the wife of the local drugs baron. One of those films that starts off with a social conscience and then rapidly descends into the standard cliches and violent action sequences.

| A/AD | 90 min |
|---|---|
| V | EIV |

### VIETNAM WAR STORY *** 15
1989
*Steve Astin, Haing S. Ngor, Chris Mulkey, Chau Mau Doan*
Three absorbing tales set in Vietnam in April 1975 when US soldiers and CIA agents were preparing to withdraw just before the fall of Saigon to the Communists. "Dirty Work" is set at a South Vietnamese army post, that must survive without its US advisors. "The Last Outpost" tels the same story, but from the Vietcong point of view. Finally, "The Last Soldier" takes place inside the American Embassy compound 24 hours before the final airlift.
Aka: VIETNAM WAR STORY: THE LAST DAYS

| WAR | 92 min |
|---|---|
| V | WHV |

### VIEW TO A KILL, A ** PG
John Glen    UK/USA    1985
*Roger Moore, Christopher Walken, Grace Jones, Tanya Roberts, Patrick Macnee, Lois Maxwell, Fiona Fullerton, Patrick Bauchau, David Yip, Manning Redwood, Alison Doody, Willoughby Gray, Desmond Llewelyn, Robert Brown, Walter Gotell*
A James Bond adventure with remarkably few gadgets but some memorable stunts as 007 battles it out with a madman out to dominate the world. Walken is a remarkably bland and unconvincing villain, out to destroy California's lucrative "Silicon Valley". This one really does drag, only the spectacular stunts keep it (and Bond) alive. A weak story and a poor note to bow out on for Roger Moore as our secret agent. Followed by LICENSE TO KILL.

| A/AD | 126 min (ort 131 min) |
|---|---|
| V/sh | WHV |

### VIGIL *** 15
Vincent Ward    NEW ZEALAND    1984
*Fiona Kay, Bill Kerr, Gordon Shields, Penelope Stewart, Frank Whitten*
An 11-year-old girl has a hard time accepting her father's death, which happened at about the same time as a stranger arrived at their farm. She gradual-

ly withdraws into an inner world of fantasy. A sparse and moody drama that often demands one's attention.
Aka: FIRST BLOOD, LAST RITES

| DRA | 86 min |
|---|---|
| B,V | MGM |

### VIGILANTE FORCE *** 18
George Armitage    USA    1976
*Kris Kristofferson, Victoria Principal, Bernadette Peters, Jan-Michael Vincent, Brad Dexter, David Doyle, Andrew Stevens*
A Vietnam veteran is hired to enforce order in a Californian oil boom town that has suffered from an influx of workers. However, having succeeded he begins to take over the town himself. A fast-paced but simple-minded action tale.

| A/AD | 86 min (ort 89 min) Cut (9 sec) |
|---|---|
| B,V | WHV |

### VIGILANTE, THE ** 18
William Lustig    USA    1982
*Robert Forster, Fred Williamson, Richard Bright, Rutanya Alda, Willie Colon, Joe Spinell, Carol Lynley, Woody Strode*
A man's son is killed and his wife disfigured in an attack by a bunch of degenerates. Inspired by the thirst for revenge (and no doubt the film DEATH-WISH), he decides to go on a vengeance-seeking rampage in this violent and distasteful offering.
Aka: STREET GANGS

| DRA | 89 min |
|---|---|
| B,V,V2 | INT L/A; SKP |

### VILLA RIDES! ** 15
Buzz Kulik    USA    1968
*Yul Brynner, Robert Mitchum, Charles Bronson, Grazia Buccella, Frank Wolff, Robert Viharo, Herbert Lom, Alexander Knox, Diana Lorys, Robert Carricart, Fernando Rey, Regina De Julian, Andres Monreal, Antonio Ruiz, John Ireland*
Superficial account of the Mexican Revolution and Pancho Villa's part in it. Set in 1912 this has Mitchum as a captured gunrunner deciding to throw in his lot with the rebels. An untidy and overblown action tale which offers us a rare chance to see a hirsute Brynner. Written by Sam Peckinpah and Robert Towne.

| WES | 117 min (ort 125 min) |
|---|---|
| B,V | CIC |

### VILLAGE OF THE GIANTS * PG
Bert I. Gordon    USA    1965
*Tommy Kirk, Johnny Crawford, Beau Bridges, Ronny Howard, Tisha Sterling, Tim Rooney, Joy Harmon*
Teenagers eat a strange potion and grow to a great height, in this utterly silly offering with poor effects. Re-filmed in 1976 by Gordon as FOOD OF THE GODS, the title of the original H.G. Wells novel which provided the idea if not the plot for this mediocre film. Howard puts in an early appearance before he shortened his name.

| FAN | 77 min |
|---|---|
| B,V | EHE |

### VILLAIN ** 18
Michael Tuchner    UK    1971
*Richard Burton, Ian McShane, Nigel Davenport, Donald Sinden, Fiona Lewis, T.P. McKenna, Joss Ackland, Cathleen Nesbitt, Elizabeth Knight, Colin Welland, Tony Selby, John Hallam, Del Henney, Ben Howard, James Cossins*
Burton plays a vicious homosexual cockney gangster, so feared that the police can never get anyone to testify against him. Heavy doses of gratuitous violence cannot hide the fact that Burton is woefully miscast; Reed does it so much better in SITTING TARGET. Written by Dick Clement and Ian La Frenais.

Boa: novel The Burden Of Proof by James Barlow.
DRA                          93 min (ort 98 min)
B,V                                TEVP; WHV

## VINDICATOR, THE **                          18
Jean-Claude Lord      CANADA              1984
*Terri Austin, Richard Cox, Pam Grier, David
McIlwraith, Maury Chaykin, John Zoboles, Mickie
Moore, Catherine Disher, Caroline Arnold, Trevor
Davies, Carl Knutson, Robert Stewart, Robert Parson,
Rob Roy, Jeremy Ratchford*
A scientist puts a badly injured man inside a specially
constructed suit, creating the inevitable monster that
obligingly goes on a rampage. The plot is reminiscent
of "The Colossus Of New York" but the latter film was
infinitely better. The metal monster is, however, quite
impressive.
Aka: FRANKENSTEIN 88; FRANKENSTEIN
FACTOR, THE
FAN              88 min (ort 90 min) Cut (24 sec)
B,V                        POLY; CH5 (VHS only)

## VINEYARD, THE **                           18
James Hong/Bill Rice/Michael Wong
                      USA                   1989
*James Hong, Karen Winter (Karren Witter), Michael
Wong*
A scientist who needs blood and bodies to remain
immortal, lures unsuspecting victims to his island,
drinking the blood of young women, and preparing
wine from vines fertilised by the bodies of young men.
Quite stylishly done but lacking in fresh ideas.
HOR                                        93 min
V                                            NWV

## VIOLATION OF THE BITCH **                   18
Jose Ramon Larrez      SPAIN              1978
*Patricia Granada, Lydia Zuazo, Rafael Machado,
Montserrat Julio*
A couple leave an orphan girl in the care of an artist
whilst they go on holiday to England. Attempted rape
and murder are the result.
Aka: LA VISITA DEL VICIO; SEX MANIAC
DRA 67 min (ort 85 min) Cut (28 sec in addition to film
cuts)
B,V,V2                       HOK L/A; SHAD; MIG

## VIOLENT BREED, THE **                       18
Fernando Di Leo      ITALY                1984
*Harrison Muller, Deborah Keith, Woody Strode, Henry
Silva, Carole Andre*
The CIA sends an agent into Vietnam to stop a
guerrilla gang that is importing drugs into America.
Lousy acting and gratuitous violence abound in this
badly made and totally unbelievable second-rate
actioner.
Aka: RAZZA VIOLENTA
A/AD                       86 min (ort 91 min) dubbed
B,V                                          GHV

## VIOLENT ENEMY, THE **
Don Sharp              UK                 1968
*Tom Bell, Susan Hampshire, Ed Begley, Jon
Laurimore, Michael Standing, Noel Purcell, Philip
O'Flynn*
An IRA explosives expert escapes from jail but
quarrels with the decision of his superiors to blow up a
power station. Written by Edmund Ward, this is a dull
political melodrama that in its own clumsy way,
attempts to examine the issues of this conflict.
Boa: novel A Candle For The Dead by Hugh Marlowe.
DRA                                        94 min
B,V,V2                                       INT

## VIOLENT RAGE **                             15
Anthony Carras
*Katy Jurado, Paul Picerni, Fernando Soler, Sonia
Amelio*
An opera star whose widowed father has just died

finds her younger sister has fallen under the influence
of a suitor with an ulterior motive, i.e. the family
fortune.
DRA                                        84 min
V                                          ATLAS

## VIOLENT STRANGERS: WETHERBY ***             15
David Hare            UK                  1984
*Vanessa Redgrave, Ian Holm, Judi Dench, Joely
Richardson, Tim McInnery, Suzanna Hamilton,
Stuart Wilson, Tom Wilkinson, Robert Hones, Penny
Downie, Marjorie Yates, Brenda Hall, Marjorie
Sudell, Patrick Blackwell, Katy Behan*
A young university student commits suicide in front of
a repressed female schoolteacher. Subsequent inves-
tigations reveal his reasons in a biting and intense,
but often gloomy tale. Written by Hare, in his
directorial debut.
Aka: WETHERBY
DRA                          97 min (ort 102 min)
B,V                                          PVG

## VIOLENT STREETS **                          18
Michael Mann          USA                 1981
*James Caan, Tuesday Weld, Willie Nelson*
A thief falls in with a mobster and finds himself
having to do things he dislikes.
DRA                                        118 min
B/s, V/s                                     WHV

## VIOLETS ARE BLUE **                          PG
Jack Fisk              USA                 1986
*Sissy Spacek, Kevin Kline, Bonnie Bedelia, John
Kellogg, Jim Standford, Kate McGregor-Stewart,
Augusta Dabney, Adrian Sparks*
A woman journalist returns to her home town and
becomes involved with an old boyfriend, following a
tough assignment in Belfast. Even though he is now
married and has a young son, they attempt to take up
where they left off. A dullish romantic-drama, not a
great deal removed from a TV soap opera.
DRA                                        87 min
B,V                                          RCA

## VIRGIN AMONG THE LIVING DEAD **             18
Jesse Franco          SPAIN               1985
*Christina Von Blanc, Britt Nichols, Paul Muller, Ann
Libert, Rose Kiekens, Howard Vernon*
A woman goes to British Honduras for the reading of
her father's will and discovers plenty of nasty things
in the eerie family house.
HOR                          88 min (ort 90 min)
B,V                                  CAREY; GLOB

## VIRGIN AND THE GYPSY, THE ***
Christopher Miles      UK                 1970
*Joanna Shimkus, Franco Nero, Honor Blackman,
Maurice Denham, Mark Burns, Fay Compton, Kay
Walsh, Harriet Harper, Norman Bird, Imogen Hassall,
Roy Holder*
The daughter of a priest falls in love with a vagabond
gypsy and suffers the consequences. A skilful and
thoroughly good adaptation of Lawrence's story of
tragic love. Written by Alan Plater. Miles later
directed his biopic on D.H. Lawrence – PRIEST OF
LOVE.
Boa: short story by D.H. Lawrence.
DRA                                        95 min
B,V                                      VCL/CBS

## VIRGIN OF BALI, THE **
Guido Zurli      INDONESIA/ITALY          1972
*George Ardisson, Lea Lander, Pedro Sanchez, Isarco
Ravaioli, Haydee Politoff*
A man dreams of finding an unspoilt South Sea island
on which he can escape from Western civilisation.
Aka: LA VERGINE DI BALI
DRA                                        94 min
B,V,V2                                       VPD

## VIRGIN QUEEN, THE ***     U
Henry Koster     USA     1955
*Bette Davis, Richard Todd, Joan Collins, Herbert
Marshall, Jay Robinson, Dan O'Herlihy, Rod Taylor,
Robert Douglas, Romney Brent*
Davis gives a pleasing performance as Queen Eli-
zabeth I, in this costume drama that examines her
relationship with Sir Walter Raleigh. Of little value
as a history lesson, but an engaging piece of cinema.
Written by Harry Brown and Mindret Lord. The
music is by Franz Waxman.
DRA     88 min (ort 92 min)
V/h     CBS

## VIRGIN SOLDIERS, THE ***     15
John Dexter     UK     1969
*Hywel Bennett, Lynn Redgrave, Nigel Davenport,
Nigel Patrick, Tsai Chin, Rachel Kempson, Michael
Gwynn, Jack Shepherd, Christopher Timothy,
Geoffrey Hughes, Don Hawkins, Roy Holder, Jolyon
Jackley*
The story of National Service recruits and their
experiences in Singapore, set during the time of the
Communist insurgency in Malaya. A frothy comedy-
drama, whose title refers to the recruits' lack of
experience in bed as well as in battle. Written by John
Hopkins and followed by the inferior sequel STAND
UP VIRGIN SOLDIERS in 1977.
Boa: novel by Leslie Thomas.
DRA     91 min (ort 96 min)
V     RCA; PREST

## VIRGIN SPRING, THE **** 
Ingmar Bergman     SWEDEN     1959
*Max Von Sydow, Brigitta Pettersson, Brigitta Valberg,
Gunnel Lindblom, Axel Duberg*
A medieval drama telling of the rape and murder of a
farmer's daughter by three brigands, and of her
father's revenge. The title refers to the spring that
gushes forth at the spot of her murder. Written by
Ulla Isaakson, this is a stark and beautiful rendition
of a medieval legend. The photography of Sven
Nykvist is no small asset. Remade (after a fashion), as
THE LAST HOUSE ON THE LEFT. AA: Foreign.
Aka: JUNGFRUKALLAN
DRA     88 min B/W
B,V     PVG; LNG

## VIRGIN WIFE **     18
Franco Martinelli     ITALY     1976
*Edwige Fenech, Carroll Baker, Ray Lovelock, Renzo
Montagnani*
A newly married couple have sexual problems when
the husband finds that he is impotent in this slight
Italian sex-comedy. Desperate to cure himself, he
enlists the aid of a variety of call girls, waitresses,
sexy girls etc., even turning for help to his twin
cousins.
Aka: LA MOGLIE VERGINE
A     94 min
B,V     VPD

## VIRGIN WITCH ** 
Ray Austin     UK     1970
*Ann Michelle, Vicki Michelle, Neil Hallett, James
Chase, Patricia Haines, Keith Buckley, Paula Wright,
Christopher Strain, Esme Smythe, Garth Watkins,
Helen Downing*
Two girls go to London to become models but get
involved in Satanism when one of them, a psychic
lesbian, tries to make her girlfriend a witch. Dull
nonsense.
Boa: novel by Klaus Vogel.
HOR     93 min
B,V,V2     INT L/A

## VIRUS **     PG
Kinji Fukasaku     JAPAN     1980
*Sonny (Shinichi) Chiba, Chuck Connors, Glenn Ford,*

*Stephanie Faulkner, Masao Kusakari, Robert Vaughn,
Olivia Hussey, George Kennedy, Henry Silva, Bo
Svenson, Cec Linder, Edward J. Olmos, Stuart Gillard*
Nuclear war and disease wipe mankind out except for
858 men and eight women. The sequences filmed in
the Antarctic are memorable and the special effects
are acceptable, but this is an overlong tale that lacks
pace and direction. One of Japan's biggest budgeted
films.
Aka: FUKKATSU NO HI; RESURRECTION DAY
A/AD     155 min; 100 min (APX) (ort 155 min)
B,V     INT L/A; ACAD; APX

## VISIONS OF CLAIR *** 
Thomas Erp     USA     1977
*Annette Haven, Bonnie Holiday, John Rolling, Susan
Bates, Jay Gamble*
A classic of its kind, this tells of a frustrated artist
who finds that he cannot capture a woman on canvas
because he sees her as somewhat ethereal and unattainable. She moves in to live with the artist and
finds that both she and a female artist living with
them come under the spell of Clair, the artist's wife. A
number of erotic scenes ensue, all of which may be no
more than visions taking place in the mind of Clair.
A     88 min
B,V     HAR

## VISITING HOURS *     18
Jean-Claude Lord     CANADA     1980
*Michael Ironside, Lee Grant, William Shatner, Linda
Purl, Harvey Atkin, Helen Hughes, Lenore Zann,
Michael J. Reynolds, Kirsten Bishopric, Dustin Waln,
Debra Kirschenbaum, Elizabeth Leigh Milne, Maureen
McRae, Neil Afflec*
Ironside as a psychopath stalks woman journalist
Grant inside a hospital. An utterly distasteful film
that's little more than an exploitative journey of
humiliation, degradation and mutilation.
DRA     99 min (ort 105 min) (Cut at film release)
B,V     CBS

## VISITOR FROM THE GRAVE **     15
Peter Sasdy     UK     1980
*Kathryn Leigh, Simon MacCorkindale, Gareth
Thomas, Mioa Nadasi, Stanley Labor, Gordan Reid*
A couple kill an intruder and bury him, but the body
refuses to stay in its grave. Fairly undistinguished
Hammer offering.
Osca: CHILDREN OF THE FULL MOON
HOR     60 min; 105 min (2 film cassette) mTV
V     CH5

## VISITOR, THE *     18
Michael J. Paradise (Giulio Paradisi)
    ITALY     1979
*John Huston, Glenn Ford, Sam Peckinpah, Shelley
Winters, Lance Henriksen, Joanne Nail, Mel Ferrer,
Paige Conner, Jo Townsend, Jack Dorsey, Johnny
Popwell, Steve Somers, Wallace Williamson, Lou
Walker, Walter Gordon Sr*
First-rate acting talent gets wasted on grade-Z films.
This copy of THE OMEN has Earth playing host to a
visitor on a mysterious mission. The real mystery is
how a feeble rip-off like this ever came to be made.
Aka: IL VISITATORE
HOR     97 min
B,V     INT L/A; WHV

## VISTA VALLEY P.T.A. **     18
Anthony Spinelli     USA     1980
*Jamie Gillis, John Leslie, Jesie St James, Dorothy Le
May, Desiree West, Aaron Stuart, Dewey Alexander,
Juliet Anderson, Shirley Woods, Kay Parker*
A new female English teacher arrives at a high school
where two former teachers have been raped. The film
now moves on to the sexual activities of the townsfolk
and their wayward kids. The new teacher tries to
make the kids study but doesn't have much success

and is eventually raped herself. A kind of spiced up version of "Blackboard Jungle". Cut before video submission by 24 min 6 sec.

A 53 min (ort 77 min) Cut (9 sec)
B,V CRAW

## VITAL SIGNS * 15
Marisa Silver USA 1990
*Adrian Pasdar, Diane Lane, Jimmy Smits, Norma Aleandro, Jack Gwaltney, Laura San Giacomo, Jane Adams, Tim Ransom, Bradley Whitford, Lisa Jane Persky, William Devane, James Kanre, Telma Hopkins*
A medical melodrama that focuses on the lives and traumas of a set of third-year students as they struggle with both private and professional pressures and compete for an internship post. Hardly incisive, barely entertaining and painfully cliched.
DRA 98 min (ort 103 min)
V CBS

## VIVA KNIEVEL! * PG
Gordon Douglas USA 1977
*Evel Knievel, Gene Kelly, Red Buttons, Lauren Hutton, Leslie Nielsen, Marjoe Gortner, Cameron Mitchell, Eric Shea, Frank Gifford, Albert Salmi, Dabney Coleman*
More a promo than a film, this vehicle for stunt-driver Knievel tells of a plan by drug dealers to have him killed, in order to use his car to ship drugs from Mexico to the USA. Plenty of stunt driving and little else in a mindless but unintentionally hilarious piece of junk. (The ludicrous opening has Knievel paying a midnight visit to an orphanage to distribute models of his car, and one boy throws down his crutches and walks!)
DRA 100 min
B,V WHV

## VIVA MAX! ** 
Jerry Paris USA 1969
*Peter Ustinov, John Astin, Pamela Tiffin, Jonathan Winters, Keenan Wynn, Henry Morgan, Alice Ghostley, Kenneth Mars, Ann Morgan Guilbert, Paul Sand*
A Mexican general decides to vindicate his nation's honour by re-taking the Alamo and claiming it as a tourist attraction, forcing the Americans to send a force to rout him out. A flat comedy whose forced humour becomes strained with time, though Winters as a bumbling National Guards officer is worth a look. Written by Elliott Baker with music by Hugo Montenegro.
Boa: novel by James Lehrer.
COM 93 min
B,V HER

## VIVA ZAPATA! **** PG
Elia Kazan USA 1952
*Marlon Brando, Jean Peters, Anthony Quinn, Joseph Wiseman, Arnold Moss, Alan Reed, Margo, Frank Silvera, Mildred Dunnock*
The career of Mexican revolutionary Emiliano Zapata, who rose from peasant to leader of his country, but met his death when betrayed by a friend. Scripted by John Steinbeck, this romanticised look at history serves as a fine star vehicle for Brando, who is on top form in the title role. The AAN score is by Alex North.
AA: S. Actor (Quinn).
A/AD 108 min (ort 113 min) B/W
V/h CBS

## VIVACIOUS LADY *** U
George Stevens USA 1938
*Ginger Rogers, Fred Astaire, James Stewart, Charles Coburn, Beulah Bonoi, Frances Mercer, James Ellison, Phyllis Kennedy, Franklin Pangborn, Grady Sutton, Jack Carson, Alec Craig, Willie Best*
This entertaining comedy has Rogers as a nightclub singer marrying Stewart, who plays a professor. He tries to break the news to his conservative family and

his fiancee back home. Overlong but quite good fun; the brawl between bride and ex-sweetheart is a little gem.
COM 87 min (ort 90 min) B/W
V VCC

## VIXEN * 18
Russ Meyer USA 1968
*Erica Gavin, Harrison Page, Garth Pillsbury, Jon Evans*
Another in a long series of unfunny Meyer spoofs in which the sex is as phoney as the humour, this time concerning a voluptuous young woman with an unlimited appetite for sex. The talents of Meyer were employed as writer, producer, director and cameraman.
COM 71 min
B,V VSP L/A; SUP

## VOICE OF THE HEART: PARTS 1 AND 2 ** 15
Tony Wharmby USA 1989
*Lindsay Wagner, Victoria Tennant, Honor Blackman, Richard Johnson, James Brolin, Stuart Wilson, Leigh Lawson, Neil Dickson, Kathryn Leigh Scott, Pip Torrens*
A long, lavish soap opera, telling of an actress who is destined for stardom and a novelist who becomes her friend, but falls in love with one of her leading men. A glossy piece of escapism.
DRA 186 min (2 cassettes)
V/h ODY

## VOICES *** 15
Robert Markowitz USA 1979
*Michael Ontkean, Amy Irving, Alex Rocco, Herbert Berghof, Viveca Lindfors, Barry Miller*
An aspiring rock singer falls in love with a woman who, though deaf and unable to hear him sing, appreciates him as a person and is able to return his love. A drama that starts off sensitively, but is ultimately let down by cliched development.
DRA 101 min (ort 107 min)
B,V MGM

## VOLTRON DEFENDER OF THE UNIVERSE Uc
## IN THE BATTLE OF ARUS **
JAPAN 1984
A banal kid's feature, based on a powerful robot that is constantly obliged to defend its planet from attack. In this tale Voltron and five youngsters engage in combat with the evil King Zarkon, who has hatched a plan to conquer Planet Arus.
Aka: VOLTRON DFENDER OF THE UNIVERSE: PLANET ARUS
CAR 77 min (ort 87 min)
B,V CBS

## VOLTRON DEFENDER OF THE UNIVERSE Uc
## IN THE CASTLE OF LIONS **
JAPAN 1984
Five young space explorers are sent on a mission by the Galactic Alliance to find the secret keys of the Castle of Lions, which they need to unleash the power of Voltron, their robot defender, and thus foil King Zarkon's plans for conquest of their planet.
Aka: VOLTRON DEFENDER OF THE UNIVERSE: CASTLE OF LIONS
CAR 77 min
B,V CBS

## VOLTRON DEFENDER OF THE UNIVERSE Uc
## IN THE INVASION OF THE ROBOBEASTS *
JAPAN 1984
Another animated space adventure set in the 25th century, and following the exploits of the title character, who this time has to defend his planet from an attack mounted by the evil Hazar, Emperor of the Drules.

Aka: VOLTRON DEFENDER OF THE UNIVERSE:
INVASION OF THE ROBOBEASTS
CAR                                77 min (ort 87 min)
B,V                                               CBS

## VOLTRON DEFENDER OF THE UNIVERSE
## VERSUS THE EMPIRE OF DRULE **            Uc
            JAPAN              1984
One more super-robot animated feature in the series,
with the title character battling it out with an evil
empire. Average.
CAR                                           78 min
B,V                                               CBS

## VOLUNTEERS **                                   15
Nicholas Meyer        USA               1986
Tom Hanks, John Candy, Rita Wilson, Tim
Thomerson, Gedde Watanabe, George Plimpton,
Ernest Harada, Allan Arbus, Ji-Tu Cumbaka,
Jacqueline Evans, Chick Hearn, Pamela Gula, Philip
Guilmann, Virginia Kiser, Clyde Kusatsu
A playboy joins the Peace Corps to escape his Mafia
creditors, and is sent to Thailand to educate the locals.
Set in 1962, this film has a few good moments for
Candy but lacks anything of real substance to hold it
together. A dull and dismal comedy that replaces
humour with profanity.
COM                                          102 min
B, V/sh                                      CAN; WHV

## VON RYAN'S EXPRESS ***                          PG
Mark Robson          USA                1965
Frank Sinatra, Trevor Howard, Raffaella Carra, Brad
Dexter, Sergio Fantoni, Edward Mulhare, John
Leyton, James Brolin, Wolfgang Preiss, Adolfo Celi,
Vito Scotti
An unpopular American captain leads a daring escape
of POWs from a WW2 Italian prison camp by taking
over a freight train. An exciting war thriller marred
by some flat spots and an unexpectedly downbeat
ending. Written by Wendell Meyers and Joseph
Landon.
Boa: novel by David Westheimer.
WAR                             112 min (ort 117 min)
V/h                                               CBS

## VOODOO DAWN *                                   15
Steven Fierburg       USA               1989
Raymond St Jacques, Theresa Merrit, Gina Gershon,
Kirk Baily, J. Grant Albrecht, Tony Todd
Two college friends travel to the Deep South to pay a
visit to a third, but find that he has vanished and that
his girlfriend believes him to be a victim of voodoo.
HOR                                           90 min
V                                              20VIS

## VOYAGE AROUND MY FATHER, A ***                  PG
Alvin Rakoff          UK                1982
Laurence Olivier, Alan Bates, Jane Asher, Elizabeth
Sellars
A skilful adaptation of John Mortimer's touching and
perceptive play about his relationship with his father.
Boa: play by John Mortimer.
DRA                                      81 min mTV
B,V                                            THAMES

## VOYAGE OF THE DAMNED **                         PG
Stuart Rosenberg     SPAIN/UK           1976
Max Von Sydow, Faye Dunaway, James Mason, Oskar
Werner, Orson Welles, Luther Adler, Katherine Ross,
Malcolm McDowell, Lee Grant, Ben Gazzara, Denholm
Elliott, Jose Ferrer, Julie Harris, Wendy Hiller,
Fernando Rey, Janet Suzman
In 1939 a liner carrying 937 Jewish refugees sailed
from Germany for Havana, but once there they were
denied asylum by the Cuban authorities. The liner
then returned to Germany where the passengers
subsequently met their deaths during the Holocaust.

A tragic and shameful story, poorly and insensitively
told. Written by Steve Shagan and David Butler, with
music by Lalo Schifrin.
Boa: book by Gordon Thomas and Max Morgan-Witts.
DRA                             174 min (ort 178 min)
B,V                           PRV L/A; CH5 (VHS only)

## VOYAGE OF THE ROCK ALIENS, THE *               15
James Fargo          USA                1984
Pia Zadora, Tom Nolan, Craig Sheffer, Ruth Gordon
A ludicrously unfunny SF musical-comedy that deals
with the misadventures of a bunch of dim-witted alien
rock musicians. From its flashy opening the film
rapidly degenerates into a dismal and tedious mess.
Aka: WHEN THE RAIN BEGINS TO FALL
FAN                               90 min (ort 97 min)
V                                            PRISM L/A

## VOYAGE TO THE BOTTOM OF THE SEA, A ***          U
Irwin Allen          USA                1961
Walter Pidgeon, Joan Fontaine, Barbara Eden, Peter
Lorre, Robert Sterling, Henry Daniell, Michael
Ansara, Frankie Avalon, Regis Toomey
A giant experimental submarine is sent to prevent the
Earth being destroyed by firing a missile at the Van
Allen radiation belts in space, these having caught
fire. Enjoyable and colourful nonsense, with Pidgeon
at his bullying best as the admiral out to save the
world from being fried. Written by Allen and Charles
Bennett, this was later made into a TV series.
FAN                             101 min (ort 105 min)
V/h                                               CBS

## VOYAGER FROM THE UNKNOWN **                     U
James D. Parriott/Rick Colby (Winrich Kolbe)
                     USA             1982/1983
Jon-Erik Hexum, Meeno Peluce, Faye Grant, Donald
Petrie, Ed Begley, Sondra Currie, Peter Frechette,
Jeanie Bradley, Terence O'Hara
SF adventure featuring two episodes from "Voyagers!"
– a TV series that ran from 1982 to 1983. A young
orphan becomes lost in time together with a time
traveller from the future. He accompanies him on his
travels, meeting a number of historical figures such as
Mary Pickford, the Wright Brothers and Louis Pas-
teur.
FAN                                      87 min mTV
B,V                                               CIC

# W

## W **                                            15
Richard Quine        USA                1973
Twiggy (Lesley Hornby), Dirk Benedict, John Vernon,
Michael Witney, Eugene Roche, Alfred Ryder, Michael
Conrad, Carmen Zapata, Dave Morick, Ken Lynch,
Peter Walker
A woman's ex-husband was convicted of her supposed
murder, but she is not dead and has since re-married.
She now finds that both she and her new husband are
being menaced by her former spouse. A flashy but not
terribly convincing thriller.
Aka: I WANT HER DEAD; W: TERROR IS ONE
LETTER
THR                               91 min (ort 95 min)
B,V                                  VES/PVG; VES

## W.B. BLUE AND THE BEAN *                        15
Max J. Kleven        USA                1989
David Hasselhoff, Tony Brubaker, Thomas Rosales,
Linda Blair
Adventure tale about a man with an unusual profession: a tennis pro who goes after bail-jumpers, ably
assisted by his sidekicks "Blue" and "The Bean". When
a suspect in a drugs case (an unusually demanding
role for Blair) is kidnapped after bail is posted, our trio
swing into action and mount a rescue. Mindless

entertainment that looks and sounds like a TV pilot.
A/AD                                                    84 min
V                                                        EIV

## W.H.I.F.F.S. **                                          15
Ted Post                    USA                        1975
*Elliott Gould, Eddie Albert, Harry Guardino, Godfrey
Cambridge, Jennifer O'Neill, Alan Manson*
Gould plays a guinea pig who has been working for
the Army Chemical Corps but is no longer needed.
However, the Army find that he is not got rid of so
easily. A very uneven and slightly manic comedy that
is sorely in need of firmer direction.
Aka: C.A.S.H.; STIFFS; WHIFFS
COM                          96 min; 89 min (HOLLY)
B,V                           ODY; CINE; HOLLY; PARK

## WACKIEST WAGON TRAIN IN THE WEST, THE *
                            USA                        1977
*Bob Denver, Ivor Francis, Lynn Wood, Forrest Tucker,
Jeanine Riley*
Western spoof comedy about a strange procession of
one wagon and a coach on its way West.
COM                                                     86 min
B,V                                                 MED; VPD

## WACKO **
Greydon Clark              USA                         1982
*Joe Don Baker, George Kennedy, Stella Stevens, Jeff
Altman, Anthony James*
Horror spoof about a cop hunting the dreaded "lawn-
mower killer" who was responsible for a wave of terror
ten years ago. Something of a spoof on all those
HALLOWEEN-type shockers, this one lacks enough
inventiveness to be really funny.
COM                                                     84 min
B,V                                                  AVA; CBS

## WACKY TAXI **
Alex Grashoff              USA                         1982
*Frank Sinatra Jr, John Astin, Allan Sherman*
An unemployed man buys an old heap and goes into
business as a taxi driver without any regard for legal
formalities. Fair.
COM                                                     87 min
B,V,V2                                                   INT

## WACKY WEEKEND **                                        15
Arthur Allan Seidelman
                            USA                         1987
*George Dzundza, Archie Hahn, Tim Thomerson,
Tawny Kitaen, Michael Fairman, Sandy Simpson,
Beau Starr, Donna Pescow, Donna Denton, Geofrey L.
Rivas, Rick Telles, Joey Bishop, Mamie Van Doren*
Three former high school friends meet up at a reunion
and decide to go on a spree with a scholarship fund
raised by their class, blowing the lot in Las Vegas, and
then attempting with increasing desperation to win it
back.
Aka: GLORY YEARS
COM                          120 min (ort 150 min) mTV
B,V                                                     MOG

## WAGON MASTER ***
John Ford                  USA                         1950
*Ben Johnson, Ward Bond, Harry Carey Jr, Joanne
Dru, Alan Mowbray, Charles Kemper, Jane Darwell,
Ruth Clifford, Russell Simpson, James Arness,
Kathleen O'Malley, Fred Libby, Hank Worden, Mickey
Simpson, Francis Ford, Cliff Lyons*
A Mormon wagon train en route for Utah is joined by
two cowboys. A good, solid Western helped along by
beautiful photography. Inspired the popular TV series
"Wagon Train" which ran from 1957. Written by
Frank Nugent and Patrick Ford.
WES                                                82 min B/W
B,V                                                     KVD

## WAITRESS! *                                             18
Samuel Weil/Michael Herz
                            USA                         1982
*Jim Harris, Carol Drake, Carol Bevar, June Martin,
David Hunt, Calvert DeForest, Renata Majer, Carl
Sturmer, Bonnie Horan*
A comedy about the strange staff of a high-class
restaurant. Unpleasant, tasteless and moronic in
roughly equal proportions.
COM                          82 min (ort 93 min)
V                                            WAL L/A; EIV

## WAKE OF THE RED WITCH ***                               PG
Edward Ludwig              USA                         1948
*John Wayne, Gail Russell, Luther Adler, Gig Young,
Adele Mara, Eduard Franz, Grant Withers, Henry
Daniell, Paul Fix*
An adventure story set in the East Indies and
involving a hunt for treasure and the rivalry between
an East Indies shipping boss and an adventurous
ship's captain. The good action sequences and fine
photography by Reggie Lanning are compensations
for the flashback style of the narrative, which is
confusing at times. Written by Harry Brown and
Kenneth Gamet.
Boa: novel by Garland Roark.
A/AD                         102 min (ort 106 min)
V                                                       VCC

## WAKING HOUR, THE **
Stephanie Rothman          USA                         1971
*Michael Blodgett, Sherry Miles, Celeste Yarnall, Jerry
Daniels, Paul Prokop, Gene Shane, Chris Woodley,
Sandy Ward, Bob Tessier*
A young couple stranded in the desert encounter a
woman who invites them to her home. Pleased to be
out of the hot sun, they are mercifully unaware that
their host is the local vampire. An updated version of
the legend of Countess Bathory, who is said to have
bathed in the blood of virgins to preserve her beauty.
Aka: CEMETERY GIRLS; VELVET VAMPIRE, THE
HOR                                                     82 min
B,V                                                PRIME; CBS

## WALK LIKE A MAN **                                      PG
Melvin Frank              USA                         1987
*Howie Mandel, Christopher Lloyd, Cloris Leachman,
Colleen Camp, Amy Steel, Stephen Elliott, George
DiCenzo, John McLiam, Earl Boen, Howard Platt,
Millie Slavin, William Bogert, Isabel Cooley, Asa
Lorre, Jeremy Gosch*
This highly unfunny attempt at a spoof on Kipling's
"The Jungle Book", has Mandel playing a young boy
lost in the woods and being raised by wolves. He
eventually returns to civilisation, making life difficult
for his creepy brother. The silly, overblown storyline
does little with what was basically a sound idea.
Aka: BOBO
COM                                                     89 min
B,V                                                     MGM

## WALK PROUD *
Robert Collins             USA                         1979
*Robby Benson, Sarah Holcomb, Domingo Ambriz,
Pepe Serna, Trinidad Silva*
An earnest but tiresome tale of a Chicano gang leader
who falls in love with a WASP girl at his high school.
One of those utterly contrived romantic dramas that
unfolds in a totally predictable way.
DRA                          94 min (ort 102 min)
V                                                       CIC

## WALK SOFTLY, STRANGER ***
Robert Stevenson           USA                         1950
*Joseph Cotten, Alida Valli, Spring Byington, Paul
Stewart, John McIntire, Jack Paar, Jeff Donnell*
The love of a crippled girl for a petty criminal, so
inspires him that he becomes a changed character, but
finds the road to redemption a rocky one. A touching

story that is only slightly hampered by its mawkishness.

DRA                          78 min (ort 81 min) B/W
B,V                                              KVD

## WALKER *                                        18
Alex Cox              USA                         1987
*Ed Harris, Richard Masur, Rene Auberjonois, Marlee
Martin, Peter Boyle, Migual Sandoval, Gerrit Graham,
Keith Szarabajka, Sy Richardson, Xander Berkeley,
John Diehl, Peter Boyle, Alfonso Arau, Pedro
Armendariz, Alan Bolt*
An account of one of the more bizarre cases of US
intervention in Central America, when a soldier of
fortune in 1855 briefly became the virtual ruler of
Nicaragua. This messy account of the exploits of
William Walker fails to make the most of its material.
The script is by Rudy Wurlitzer.

DRA   91 min (ort 95 min) (Cut at film release by 6 sec)
V                                                CIC

## WALKING TALL ***                                18
Phil Karlson          USA                        1973
*Joe Don Baker, Elizabeth Hartman, Gene Evans,
Rosemary Murphy, Noah Beery Jr, Felton Perry*
Dramatisation of the true-life story of a sheriff's lone
fight against crime based upon the story of baseball-
bat wielding sheriff Buford Pusser. Excessive violence
did not stand in the way of its huge commercial
success; two sequels followed with Svenson replacing
Baker. The film inspired the TV movie "A Real
American Hero" and a rather mediocre TV series.

DRA                       119 min (ort 125 min) Cut (29 sec)
B,V                                           VES/PVG

## WALKING TALL PART 2:                            15
## VENGEANCE TRAIL **
Earl Bellamy          USA                        1975
*Bo Svenson, Luke Askew, Noah Beery Jr, Robert
Doqui, Bruce Glover, Richard Jaeckel, Angel
Tompkins*
A club-wielding lawman takes on the criminals who
murdered his wife. First of two sequels to WALKING
TALL this one cut down considerably on the earlier
film's violence, with more cars than people being
demolished this time round. The lack of Baker in the
role of our lone vigilante is noticeable; Svenson is a
poor replacement.
Aka: LEGEND OF THE LAWMAN; PART 2:
WALKING TALL; WALKING TALL: PART 2

DRA                          105 min (ort 109 min)
B,V                                              VES

## WALKING TALL 3: THE FINAL CHAPTER **            18
Jack Starrett         USA                        1977
*Bo Svenson, Margaret Blye, Forrest Tucker, Lurene
Tuttle, Morgan Woodward, Libby Boone*
Another episode chronicling the career and ultimate
death of the legendary Tennessee sheriff Buford
Pusser. Much inferior to the first two films, this one
showed a definite trailing off of ideas, as our stoic
upholder of the law continued to battle criminal
figures even after his wife was murdered in retalia-
tion. Spawned a TV movie as well as a series.
Aka: FINAL CHAPTER: WALKING TALL

DRA                                          113 min
B,V                                              VES

## WALKING THE EDGE **                             18
Norbert Meissel       USA                        1983
*Nancy Kwan, Robert Foster, Joe Spinell, Aarika Wells,
A. Martinez, Jayne Woodson, James McIntire*
A housewife seeks revenge on the gang who murdered
her husband and son and ensures that those responsi-
ble meet an equally violent end, in this cliched and
brutal revenger.

THR                   87 min (ort 94 min) Cut (2 min 20 sec)
B,V                                              CBS

## WALL STREET ***                                 15
Oliver Stone          USA                        1987
*Michael Douglas, Charlie Sheen, Martin Sheen, Daryl
Hannah, James Spader, Terence Stamp, Sylvia Miles,
Hal Holbrook, Sean Young, Richard Dysart, Saul
Rubinek, Annie McEnroe, Tamara Tunie, Franklin
Cover, Josh Mostel*
A young broker whose career is going nowhere
manages to gain the confidence of a powerful Wall
Street broker, and thus gain admittance to the
exclusive world of financial dealing. However, in the
process he is forced to "sell his soul" and compromise
his principles. An absorbing if simplistic morality tale
updated to a modern setting. AA: Actor (Douglas).

DRA                                          120 min
V/sh                                             CBS

## WALLS *                                         18
Tom Shandel           CANADA                     1985
*Winston Rekert, Andree Pelletier, Alan Scarfe, John
Lord, Lloyd Berry*
A dreadfully stilted and earnest attempt to examine
the reasons why convicts come to take hostages. This
factual and well-meaning look at the ills of prison life,
fails on just about every count. Hopelessly shallow
and one-dimensional characterisation, and a preachy
and pompous script makes it an experience to be
avoided at all costs.

A/AD                                         90 min
B,V                                            PACEV

## WALLS OF GLASS **                               15
Scott Goldstein       USA                        1985
*Philip Bosco, Geraldine Page, Linda Thorson, Brian
Bloom, Olympia Dukakis, Steven Weber, William
Hickey, Louis Zorich, Phillip Astor, James Tolkan,
Jered Holmes, Gwyllum Evans, Pierre Epstein, E.R.
Davis, Cory Notrica*
An actor forced to work as a cab driver in order to
survive, has a difficult time relating to his wife and
children. A film that works as an engaging character
study if not as a story, with the lack of pace a serious
handicap.
Aka: FLANAGAN

DRA                          83 min (ort 85 min)
B,V                                              RCA

## WALTZ OF THE TOREADORS **                       15
John Guillermin       UK                         1962
*Peter Sellers, Dany Robin, Margaret Leighton, John
Fraser, Cyril Cusack, Prunella Scales, John Le
Mesurier, Raymond Huntley, Jean Anderson, Cardew
Robinson, Vanda Godsell, Denise Coffey, Guy
Middleton, Humphrey Lestocq*
Limp adaptation of a story of a retired general who is
unable to stop his son from taking over his mistress.
Not one of Seller's best films – a disappointing
experience all round.
Boa: play by Jean Anouilh.

COM                                         105 min
B,V                                          RNK; VCC

## WANDERERS, THE ****                             18
Philip Kaufman        USA                        1979
*Ken Wahl, John Friedrich, Karen Allen, Toni Kalem,
Alan Rosenberg, Erland Van Lidth de Jeude, Linda
Manz, Olympia Dukakis*
A wonderfully fresh and witty look at kids and their
street gangs in the early 1960s. Full of fine performances with the music of the period used to great effect,
often in highly apt ways. The story is really one of the
relationship between several friends, set against
attempts to stave off a conflict by holding a football
match between rival gangs. A little gem. The script is
by Rose and Phillip Kaufman.
Boa: novel by Richard Price.

DRA                       112 min; 109 min (VCC)
B,V               VIR; PVG/VCL; VCC (VHS only)

## WANTED DEAD OR ALIVE **                     18
Gary Sherman          USA            1986
*Rutger Hauer, Gene Simmons, Robert Guillaume, Mel
Harris, William Russ, Hugh Gillin, Susan McDonald,
Jerry Hardin, Robert Harper, Eli Danker, Joe Nasser,
Suzanne Wouk, Gerald Papasian, Nick Falatas,
Hamman Shafie, Tyler Tyhurst*
When an international terrorist begins a ruthless
bombing attack on Los Angeles, the CIA call on a
former operative. The terrorist discovers that he is
being followed and attempts to kill the operative, but
mistakenly kills one of his old friends from the CIA
days. Our CIA operative now goes after said terrorist
as a personal vendetta. A routine action-tale that
offers little of interest except the explosive finale.
Aka: WANTED: DEAD OR ALIVE
A/AD                                 102 min
B,V                                  NWV

## WAR AND LOVE **                            PG
Moshe Mizrahi        USA             1983
*Krya Sedgewick, Sebastian Keneas, David Spielberg,
Cheryl Gianini, Brita Youngblood, Eda Reiss-Merin,
Rueul Schiller, Eric Faber*
Based on Eisner's own experiences (he also produced
the film), this film attempts to follow the experiences
of a young Jewish man and his family, and tells of
their sufferings in the Warsaw Ghetto and the Nazi
death-camps of Poland. A sincere and commendable
effort, but lacking the impact it could have had.
Aka: CHILDREN'S WAR, THE; LOVE AND WAR
Boa: novel The Survivor by Jack Eisner.
DRA                             106 min (ort 112 min)
B,V                                  MGM

## WAR AND PEACE ***                           U
King Vidor      ITALY/USA            1956
*Henry Fonda, Herbert Lom, Audrey Hepburn, Mel
Ferrer, Vittorio Cassman, John Mills, Oscar Homolka,
Anita Ekberg, Helmut Dantine, Mai Britt, Milly Vitale*
Competent version of this epic which attempts to
condense both action and plot into manageable prop-
ortions, unlike the over-rated 1968 Soviet version. Not
completely successful, the awkward script (six writers
were credited, including Vidor) is a serious drawback
as is some of the casting. The spectacular battle scenes
are however, a compensating feature. Filmed once
more in 1968.
Boa: novel by Leo Nikolaevich Tolstoy.
DRA                                  211 min
B,V                                  CIC

## WAR BOY, THE *                              15
Allan Eastman       CANADA           1984
*Jason Hopley, Helen Shaver, Kenneth Walsh, Ingrid
Venninger, Derrick Hart*
Filmed in Yugoslavia, this ponderous and stilted
effort tells of a young boy who takes up arms against
the invading Germans, when his country is invaded
during WW2.
WAR                                  90 min
B,V                              CAN; GLOB

## WAR BRIDES **
Martin Lavut        CANADA           198-
*Elisabeth Richardson, Sharry Flett, Geoffrey Bowes,
Sonja Smits, Ken Pogue, Layne Coleman*
The story of both German and British WW2 brides in
Canada, and their difficulties in their new country.
DRA                                  105 min
B,V                                  EVI

## WAR OF THE MONSTERS *                       PG
Jun Fukada          JAPAN            1972
*Minoru Takashima, Hiroshi Ichikawa, Tomoko
Umeda, Yuriko Hishimi, Kunio Murai, Susumu
Fujita, Toshiaki Nishizawa*
Aliens from a planet dying from pollution, take over a
children's amusement park and summon two evil

monsters, Ghidorah and Gaigan to attack Earth. As
luck would have it, we have Godzilla fighting in our
corner so all ends happily. Despite the underlying
seriousness of the pollution theme, this is very
juvenile stuff indeed.
Aka: CHIKIYU KOGERI MEIREI; GODZILLA TAI
GAIGAN; GODZILLA VERSUS GIGAN; GODZILLA,
WAR OF THE MONSTERS; GOJIRA TAI GAIGAN
FAN                                  89 min
B,V                       DFS L/A; VMA; STABL

## WAR OF THE ROBOTS *
Al Bradley (Alfonso Brescia)
                     ITALY           1978
*Antonio Sabato, Yanti Somer, West Buchanan, Ines
Pellegrini, Melissa Long*
A woman is kidnapped by robot aliens and a rescue
mission encounters many adventures before she is
eventually rescued. An inept space opera from a
director who has plenty of experience in this area.
FAN                                  96 min
B,V                       ADB L/A; SVC L/A; APX

## WAR OF THE ROSES, THE ***                   15
Danny DeVito        USA             1989
*Michael Douglas, Kathleen Turner, Danny DeVito,
Marianne Sagebrecht, Sean Astin, Heather Fairfield,
G.D. Spradlin, Peter Donat*
A spiteful black comedy about an affluent couple
whose marriage goes sour and leads to a vicious and
escalating binge of destruction, when they are unable
to reach an amicable property settlement. Acting and
direction are superb, and the bitterness of it all is
softened by making the story a cautionary fable told
by divorce lawyer DeVito to a client. Unappealing
after the first hour, but the film's viewpoint is
certainly unusual.
COM                        111 min (ort 116 min) subH
V                                    CBS

## WAR OF THE WIZARDS                          PG
Sadama Arikawa/Richard Caan
                     TAIWAN          1978
*Richard Kiel, Betty Noonan, Charles Lang*
Adventure story about a quest by an alien woman to
recover her book of spells stolen by a fisherman and
avidly sought by a bevy of villains eager to use its
magic to gain wealth and power.
Aka: PHOENIX, THE
A/AD                                 92 min
B,V                                  HER

## WAR OF THE WIZARDS **                       PG
Richard Caan        TAIWAN           1978
*Richard Kiel, Betty Noonan, Charles Lang*
Adventure story about a quest to recover stolen
objects from a remote island.
Aka: PHOENIX, THE
A/AD                                 92 min
B,V                                  HER

## WAR OF THE WORLDS, THE ***                  PG
Bryon Haskin        USA             1953
*Gene Barry, Ann Robinson, Les Tremayne, Robert
Cornthwaite, Henry Brandon, Jack Kruschen, Sandro
Giglio, William Phipps, Paul Birch, Vernon Rich,
House Stevenson, Paul Frees, Carolyn Jones, Pierre
Cressoy, Nancy Hale*
A thoroughly disappointing attempt to film a famous
novel that tells of an alien invasion from Mars. The
action is transplanted from the UK to the USA and
brought forward to the 1950s – little of Wells' fine
novel remains. Produced by George Pal, it inspired a
later Canadian TV series. AA: Effects (George Pal).
Boa: novel by H.G. Wells.
FAN                                  85 min
B,V                                  CIC

## WAR OF THE WORLDS: THE RESURRECTION * 15
Colin Chilvers        CANADA        1988
*Jared Martin, Lynda Mason Green, Philip Akin,*
*Richard Chaves*
Pilot for the TV dull series that's remotely based on
the H.G. Wells novel. Thirty-five years after the
Martian invaders were destroyed by germs, a radia-
tion leak revives six of the original creatures, that
were unwisely being stored in canisters (an idea no
doubt borrowed from RETURN OF THE LIVING
DEAD: PART 2). Naturally, the man who has disco-
vered this unedifying piece of news cannot get anyone
to believe him.
FAN                                    91 min mTV
B,V                                         CIC

## WAR STORY **                                    15
Michael Toshiyuki Uno/Jack Sholder/Rick King
                      USA                    1988
*William Lawrence*
Three separate tales telling of incidents in the Viet-
nam War. In "An Old Ghost Walks The Earth", a
young GI is shocked by the attitude of his colleagues
to the locals, and befriends a young girl. "Dusk To
Dawn" tells of a youngster who has enlisted to fight
and enjoys a last evening with his family. Finally,
"The Fragging" has a platoon deciding to kill their
incompetent commanding officer. See also VIETNAM
WAR STORY.
WAR                                        87 min
V                                            ODY

## WAR STORY 2 ***                                 15
Todd Holland/David Burton Morris/Leslie Linka
Glatter               USA                    1989
*Todd Graff, Raymond Cruz, Cynthia Bain, Tate*
*Donnovan, Stacy Edwards, Laura Harrington*
A set of three stories written to illustrate the brutality
of the Vietnam War. In the first, a soldier finds
himself cut off from his unit, in the second, an officer
on leave is unable to tell his wife of his experiences,
and in the third a nurse sent to a front-line hospital,
encounters hostility from the colleague she is replac-
ing. Three short, sharp, literate tales.
Aka: VIETNAM WAR STORY 2
WAR                                        90 min
V                                            ODY

## WAR STORY, A **                                 15
Anne Wheel           CANADA                  1978
*David Edney, Frank C. Turner, Doug Kier, Doug*
*Bagot, W. Forrest MacDonald, Patrick McGuigan,*
*Dean Stoker, Alan Stebbings, Gerry Whelpton, Tom*
*Whitton, Cecil Grinstead, Rodrigue Deschenes, Brian*
*Laird, Grant Carmichael*
A dramatisation of the diaries of Dr Ben Wheeler, who
was a prisoner of the Japanese during WW2. A
well-made and moderately absorbing account.
DRA                                        88 min
V                                            COL

## WAR ZONE *                                      15
Nathaniel Gutman     USA                     1986
*Christopher Walken, Hywel Bennett, Marita*
*Marschall, Arnon Zadock, Amos Lavie, Etti Ankri,*
*Martin Umbach*
Two reporters, one American, the other English, are
sent to Beirut to cover the fighting, and the former
obtains an interview with a PLO spokesman. Howev-
er, his report is denounced by the PLO, who insist that
the interviewee was an imposter, and our intrepid
reporter sets out to get at the truth. A muddled and
pointless affair that offers neither entertainment nor
education.
Aka: WITNESS IN THE WAR ZONE
A/AD                                       95 min
B,V                                          GHV

## WARBIRDS *                                      18
Ulli Lommel          USA                     1988
*Jim Eldert, Curly Holland, Bill Brinsfield*
The USA sends a crack flying team to one of its allies
that's under attack from radical elements.
A/AD                                       88 min
B,V                                          GHV

## WARBUS **                                       18
Ted Kaplan           USA                     1985
*Daniel Stephen, Ron Kristoff, Urs Althaus,*
*Gwendoline Cook, Ernie Zarte, Don Gordon, Josephine*
*Sylva, Steve Elliott*
As South Vietnam collapses, three US Marines escape
from behind enemy lines in an old school bus and have
many hair-raising encounters before they finally
reach safety. A sequel followed in 1988.
Aka: WARBUS: RAW COURAGE
WAR                             85 min (ort 90 min)
B,V                                          MED

## WARDOG: THE KILLING MACHINE ***                 18
Bjorn Carlstrom/Daniel Hunenbecker
                   SWEDEN/USA                1986
*Tim Earle, Bill Redvers, David Gillies, Chris Masters,*
*Sydney Livingstone*
A man finds out that his brother did not really die in
Vietnam but has in fact been forced to join a squad of
brainwashed killers who are being trained in secret by
the American government. Armed with this know-
ledge he sets out on a daring rescue mission. Standard
high-action war yarn with few surprises.
Aka: ASSASSINATION TEAM, THE; WARDOG;
WARDOGS
WAR                       90 min Cut (1 min 29 sec)
B,V                                          AVA

## WARGAMES **                                     PG
John Badham          USA                     1983
*Matthew Broderick, Ally Sheedy, Dabney Coleman,*
*John Wood, Barry Corbin, Juanin Clay*
A youngster who spends most of his time playing with
his home computer, accidentally hacks into a military
computer that is both used to simulate nuclear war
and to control the conduct of a real one. When he
begins playing with the computer he unwittingly sets
in motion a chain of events that may lead to a nuclear
exchange. Corbin as a wilfully retired scientist, adds
some charm to an otherwise forgettable juvenile
effort.
A/AD                                      108 min
V/sh                                         WHV

## WARLOCK ***                                     15
Steve Miner          USA                     1989
*Julian Sands, Lori Singer, Richard E. Grant*
A 17th century warlock is about to be executed by the
town elders, when a thunderbolt strikes, and he is
catapulted into the 20th century. Once there, he
embarks on a frantic search for the missing parts of
the Devil's Bible, which would give him the power to
undo all creation. Fortunately, he is followed into the
20th century by a witchfinder, who thwarts his plans.
A lively and entertaining yarn. The music is by Jerry
Goldsmith.
A/AD                                       98 min
V/sh                                         MED

## WARLORDS *                                      18
Fred Olen Ray        USA                     1989
*David Carradine, Ross Hagen, Sid Haig, Dawn*
*Wildsmith, Fox Harris, Robert Quarry, Victoria*
*Sellers, Michelle Bauer*
In the usual devastated post-nuclear holocaust world
so beloved by low-budget SF film-makers, Carradine
plays a warrior out to rescue his wife from the clutches
of a local despot. Wildsmith adds a little colour as the
feisty woman he is accompanied by, but this dismal
film is one more low-budget exercise in tedium.
FAN                                        86 min
V                                           HIFLI

## WARLORDS FROM HELL *   18
Clark Henderson          USA          1987
*Brad Henson, Jeffrey D. Rice, Mark Merry, Anne Charlotte Elming*
Two dirt-bikers go south of the border and are captured by drug-runners who put them to work harvesting their crop.
A/AD                              80 min
V                                  CBS

## WARLORDS OF ATLANTIS ***   PG
Kevin Connor          UK          1978
*Doug McClure, Peter Gilmore, Shane Rimmer, Lea Brodie, Cyd Charisse, Daniel Massey, Michael Gothard, Hal Galili, John Ratzenberger, Derry Power, Donald Bisset, Ashley Knight, Robert Brown*
An expedition in search of an underwater city encounters a mixture of mystery and monsters, when McClure joins British scientists in the search for Atlantis. A wholesome but unremarkable adventure.
A/AD                              96 min
B,V                                TEVP

## WARM DECEMBER, A **
Sidney Poitier          USA          1973
*Sidney Poitier, Johnny Sekka, Esther Anderson, Yvette Curtis, George Baker, Earl Cameron*
A man falls in love with a woman who is dying from sickle cell anaemia. This one tries hard, but despite good acting does not really come over. Made in England and written by Lawrence Roman.
DRA                              103 min
B,V                                VDM

## WARM NIGHTS ON A SLOW MOVING   18
TRAIN ***
Bob Ellis          AUSRTRALIA          1987
*Wendy Hughes, Colin Friels, Norman Kaye, John Clayton, Lewis Fitz-Gerald, Rod Zuanic, Peter Whitford, Grant Tilly*
A schoolteacher makes some extra money as a part-time prostitute aboard a train, in order to support her sick brother, but her cosy set-up is disturbed when she meets a man who refuses to let her go. An engrossing drama, for which Hughes obtained the Best Actress Award at the 1987 Rio International Film Festival.
DRA                              90 min
V                                  VES

## WARM SUMMER RAIN **   18
Joe Gayton          USA          1989
*Kelly Lynch*
A small-town secretary with a botched suicide attempt behind her escapes from hospital and meets up with a romantic stranger. From a seedy bar they make their way to bed, and in between the steamy sex scenes the characters discuss their problems via a sequence of emotional monologues. An interesting idea for a drama that's hurt by self-indulgence and a lack of flow.
DRA                              79 min
V                                  EIV

## WARNING SIGN **   15
Hal Barwood          USA          1985
*Sam Waterson, Yaphet Kotto, Kathleen Quinlan, Jeffrey De Munn, Jerry Hardin, Richard Dysart, G.W. Bailey, Rick Rossovich, Cynthia Carle, Kavi Raz, Scott Paulin, Keith Szarabajka, Jack Thibeau, J. Patrick McNamara*
An accident in a research laboratory leads to the escape of a deadly virus. Reminiscent of Romero's THE CRAZIES, but the serious first half gives way to an unfunny parody that it would have been wiser to avoid. This was the directorial debut of screenwriter Barwood.
Aka: BIOHAZARD
FAN                              95 min
B,V                                CBS

## WARNING, THE **   15
Greydon Clark          USA          1980
*Jack Palance, Martin Landau, Cameron Mitchell, Tarah Nutter, Neville Brand, Christopher S. Nelson, Ralph Meeker, Larry Storch, Sue Ann Langdon, Lynn Theel, Darby Hinton, David Caruso*
Alien creatures attack four young people on a trip to a lake after they disregard warnings about strange happenings there. An utterly silly horror yarn which couples foolish ideas (the aliens make use of carnivorous disks) with a poor script and acting. The few shudders generated are soon dissipated.
Aka: IT CAME WITHOUT WARNING; WITHOUT WARNING
HOR                              96 min
B,V,V2,LV                          GHV

## WARP SPEED **
Allan Sandler          USA          1980
*Adam West, Camille Mitchell, David Chandler, Joanne Nail, Barry Gordon, Akosua Busia, Gela Jacobson, John Stinson, Jerry Prell, David Wiley, Reginald Dunn, Channing Mitchell, Stanley Wojno*
A man who possesses psychic powers discovers that there is something amiss aboard a spaceship.
FAN                              88 min
B,V                                HER

## WARRIOR AND THE NINJA, THE *   18
H. Jutt          HONG KONG
*Barry Prima, Terry Kosmin, Rita Zahara, Kim Chee, Unger Wu*
A Ninja teams up with a fighter known as "The Warrior", to fight colonial forces. The usual set-piece battles take place.
MAR                          94 min Cut (5 sec)
B,V              ECF/VIDLNE L/A; GLOB; TOW

## WARRIOR AND THE SORCERESS, THE **   18
John Broderick          USA          1984
*David Carradine, Luke Askew, Maria Socas, Anthony Delongis, Harry Townes, William Marin*
Routine sword-and-sorcery on a distant desert planet that circles two suns. A lone fighter battles injustice, playing one side off against the other in this transplanted copy of A FISTFUL OF DOLLARS. Leading lady Socas appears topless throughout, a small compensation in this unimaginative offering.
Aka: KAIN OF DARK PLANET
FAN                              76 min
B,V                              PVG; VES

## WARRIOR OF THE LOST WORLD **   18
David Worth          USA          1983
*Robert Ginty, Persis Khambatta, David Pleasance, Harrison Muller, Philip Dallas, Fred Williamson, Laura Nucci, Vinicio Recchi, Janna Ryan, Consuelo Marcaccini, Dan Stephen, Stefano Minor, Scott Coffey, Goffredo Marcaccini*
Good versus Evil in a post-WW3 world where a knight rides into his encounters on a supersonic cycle, and helps a woman rescue her father from captivity in the fortress of the evil Omegans. Plenty of non-stop action and loud music help cover the gaping holes in the plot.
Aka: WARRIOR LOST WORLD
FAN              87 min (ort 90 min) Cut (18 sec)
B,V                                TEVP

## WARRIOR QUEEN **   18
Chuck Vincent          USA          1985
*Sybil Danning (Sybelle Danninger), Donald Pleasence, Richard Hill, Josephine Jacqueline Jones, Tally Chanel, Stasia Micula (Samantha Fox), Suzanna Smith, David Cain Haughton, Mario Cruciani, Marco Tullio Cau*
Set against the impending destruction of Pompeii, this is a turgid attempt at a historical spectacular on the cheap. What plot there is involves a young slave girl and her rescue from a brothel by her tribal sister, a

famous warrior queen. Exploitative in the extreme, this film borrows heavily from the 1960s film THE LAST DAYS OF POMPEII for the finale.
Aka: POMPEII
DRA                67 min (ort 79 min) Cut (2 min 7 sec)
B,V                                                    VES

**WARRIORS OF THE WIND **                          U
Kazuo Komatsubara    JAPAN                        1984
Animated saga set in a bleak (is there any other variety?) post-nuclear future a thousand years hence, with good battling evil in the shape of a princess who fights to free her enslaved people.
CAR                                              91 min
B,V                              VES; PREST (VHS only)

**WARRIORS THREE **                                18
S.H. Lau          HONG KONG                       198-
Lawrence Tan, Laurens C. Postma, Mike Kelly, Rowena Cortes, Jenny Tamen, Michael James
A rough, tough actioner set in Hong Kong.
Aka: HEROES THREE
A/AD                             85 min Cut (58 sec)
B,V                          VTC L/A; XTACY/KRP

**WARRIORS, THE ***                                18
Walter Hill          USA                          1979
Michael Beck, James Remar, Thomas Waites, Dorsey Wright, Brian Tyler, David Harris, Deborah Van Valkenburgh
A New York youth gang is forced to cross enemy turf on its way home, in this violent and action-packed film. In the hands of the director, Yurick's powerful book becomes a simplified fast-paced actioner. However, the photography of Andrew Laszlo is an asset. Written by Hill and David Shaber.
Boa: novel by Sol Yurick. A/AD               90 min
B,V                                               CIC

**WASH, THE ***                                    PG
Michael Toshiyuki Uno  USA                        1988
Mako, Nobu McCarthy, Patty Yasutake
A simple and rather touching tale of the break-up of a marriage and a rekindling of love, that concerns the wife of a Japanese-American couple, who, after 40 years married to her morose husband, has decided to divorce him. The incisive script examines the cultural and sociological pressures brought to bear on the couple, and Mako is excellent as the introverted husband who cannot see what all the fuss is about.
DRA                                              94 min
V                                             AVALON

**WASHINGTON AFFAIR, THE ***
Victor Stoloff          USA                        1977
Tom Selleck, Barry Sullivan, Carol Lynley, Arlene Banas, Kathleen Gaffney
A corrupt businessman uses hidden cameras and a woman to trap a government engineer and thereby blackmail him into getting him an aircraft contract. A gripping and tense film, not a little claustrophobic due to being filmed in two rooms for most of the time. Unreleased to cinemas until after the start of Selleck's TV series "Magnum", this is very much a remake of the 1966 film "Intimacy", by the same director.
DRA                                              90 min
B,V                                               HER

**WATCH COMMANDER, THE **                          PG
                        USA                        1988
Jack Warden
A police sergeant is so closely involved with the men under him that his marriage is on the rocks, and eventually the hunt for a vicious killer brings matters to a head.
A/AD                                             97 min
V                                                 RCA

**WATCH ON THE RHINE ****                           U
Herman Shumlin          USA                        1943
Bette Davis, Paul Lukas, Geraldine Fitzgerald, Lucile Watson, Beulah Bond, George Coulouris, Donald Woods, Henry Daniell
A German man and his wife live in Washington but are harassed by Nazi spies. For once Davis is overshadowed by another actor as Lukas gives what was probably the finest performance of his career. This excellent adaptation of the Hellman play was written by Dashiell Hammett. The music was by Max Steiner. AA: Actor (Lukas).
Boa: play by Lillian Hellman.
DRA                                         114 min B/W
B,V                                               WHV

**WATCH OUT, WE'RE MAD *                            PG
Marcello Fondato    ITALY/SPAIN                    1976
Terence Hill (Mario Girotti), Bud Spencer (Carlo Pedersoli), John Sharp, Donald Pleasence, Deogratias Muerta, Manual de Blas
A tale about stock car racing, with our comic duo seeking revenge when their dune buggies are dented by crooks. Another dreary Hill-Spencer effort.
Aka: ALTRIMENTI CI ARRABBIAMO; Y SI NO ENFADAMOS
COM                             98 min (ort 102 min)
V                                                 RCA

**WATCH THE SHADOWS DANCE **                        15
Mark Joffe          USA                           1987
Tom Jennings, Nicole Kidman, Vince Martin
A group of students study by day, but relax at night by playing a bizarre series of war games that involve martial arts prowess. The mentor of the young hero turns out to be less than honest about his relationship with drug dealers when he is questioned by the latter, but all is resolved in the expected climax. A slow and muddled tale.
A/AD                                             87 min
V                                                 VES

**WATCH YOUR STERN *                                PG
Gerald Thomas          UK                          1960
Kenneth Connor, Eric Barker, Leslie Phillips, Joan Sims, Noel Purcell, Hattie Jacques, Spike Milligan, Eric Sykes, Sid James
A ship's steward fools an admiral when he pretends to be the inventor of a homing torpedo. A predictable navy lark with all the expected complications and farcical situations. A "Carry On" film in all but name.
Boa: play Something About A Sailor by Earle Couttie.
COM                             85 min (ort 88 min) B/W
V                                                 WHV

**WATCHED ***                                       15
John Parsons          USA                          1974
Stacy Keach, Harris Yulin, Bridget Polk, Turid Aarstad, Valeri Parker, Tony Serra, Denver John Collins
A former government lawyer has gone underground and befriends addicts, and fights a battle of wits with the head of a narcotics squad, who makes use of a mass of surveillance equipment. An interesting idea that generates tension, but relies too heavily on the almost constant presence of Keach on-screen.
DRA                                              93 min
B,V                                               VES

**WATCHER IN THE WOODS, THE ***                     PG
John Hough          USA                           1980
Bette Davis, Caroll Baker, David McCallum, Lynn-Holly Johnson, Ian Bannen, Richard Pasco, Kyle Richards, Frances Cuka, Benedict Taylor, Georgina Hale, Eleanor Summerfield, Katherine Levy
An American family buys a country home in Britain, but finds that it is haunted by the spirit of a young child, the missing daughter of the owner. This well-worn theme has few surprises, but the photography of

Alan Hume some way towards generating atmosphere. The ending was reworked for 1981 release by Vincent McEveety.
Boa: novel by F.E. Randall.
DRA                                        84 min (ort 100 min)
B,V                                                          WDV

## WATCHERS *                                                    18
Jon Hess                    USA                          1988
*Corey Haim, Barbara Williams, Michael Ironside, Lala*
An accident at a biological research station that was engaged in experiments to breed an efficient killing machine, causes the release of a highly intelligent canine and its bloodthirsty and telepathic "twin", which has been programmed to find and destroy the former. A low-grade and incoherent mess.
Boa: novel by Dean Koontz.
HOR                                        87 min (ort 99 min)
B,V                                                          GHV

## WATCHERS 2 **                                                 18
Thierry Notz                                             1990
*Tracy Scoggins, Marc Singer, Irene Miracle, Jonathan Farewell*
Despite the title, this film is not so much a sequel to the earlier work as an amplification, in which a misguided government-sponsored research project results in the creation of a rampaging monster. Average.
HOR                                                    94 min
V                                                            RCA

## WATER **                                                      15
Dick Clement                UK                           1985
*Michael Caine, Valerie Perrine, Brenda Vaccaro, Leonard Rossiter, Jimmie Walker, Billy Connolly, Fred Gwynne, Maureen Lipman, Dennis Dugan, Dick Shawn, George Harrison, Eric Clapton, Ringo Starr, Fulton McKay*
The discovery of a mineral water spring on a British Caribbean island on the eve of independence, results in international complications with Caine as the the embattled governor trying to rein in American oil interests, a rebellion and various malcontents. Slightly funny, more often not, this uneven film has Lipman giving a nasty caricature of Margaret Thatcher, and Vaccaro a pointless one of Carmen Miranda.
COM                                    97 min; 93 min (WHV)
B, V/sh                                        TEVP L/A; WHV

## WATER BABIES, THE **                                          U
Lionel Jeffries          POLAND/UK                       1978
*James Mason, Billie Whitelaw, Bernard Cribbins, Joan Greenwood, David Tomlinson, Tommy Pender, Samantha Gates, Paul Luty. Voices of: Jon Pertwee, Olive Gregg, Lance Percival, David Jason, Una Stubbs*
The story of a young chimney sweep who discovers a marvellous underwater world. Mixes animation with live-action. Written by Michael Robson, this bland adaptation of the Kingsley classic makes the error of adding a virtually unrelated tale of Victorian London to its underwater adventure.
Boa: novel by Charles Kingsley.
JUV                                    88 min; 95 min (PICK)
B,V                                        TEVP; PICK (VHS only)

## WATER UNDER THE BRIDGE **
Igor Auzins            AUSTRALIA                         1980
*Judy Davis, David Cameron, Robin Nevin, Jacki Weaver, Chris Milne*
A young foster mother has to make sacrifices for the child she has taken into her care. See IT'S MY LIFE TO LIVE, for part 2 of this story.
DRA                                                    80 min
B,V                                                    CAREY/PVG

## WATERHOLE 3 **                                                15
William A. Graham         USA                            1967
*James Coburn, Carroll O'Connor, Margaret Blye, Claude Akins, Bruce Dern, Timothy Carey, Roy Jenson, Joan Blondell, James Whitmore, Harry Davis, Robert Cornthwaite, Jim Boles, Steve Whitaker, Ted Markland, Robert Crosse*
Three Confederate soldiers steal a fortune in bullion from the Army and bury it in a desert waterhole in this Blake Edwards produced comedy-Western. No great movie but fairly amusing.
WES                                        91 min (ort 100 min)
B,V                                                          CIC

## WATERLOO **                                                   U
Sergei Bondarchuk ITALY/USSR                             1971
*Rod Steiger, Christopher Plummer, Orson Welles, Jack Hawkins, Virginia McKenna, Ian Ogilvy, Dan O'Herlihy, Rupert Davies, Michael Wilding*
Clumsy historical drama that concentrates on Napoleon's defeat at Waterloo. The spectacular recreation of the battle scenes cannot compensate for the lack of drama and the confused plot. The original Soviet version was nearly twice as long as this one. Written by Bondarchuk and H.A.L. Craig, with music by Nino Rota.
Boa: novel War And Peace by Leo Nikolaevich Tolstoy.
DRA                            127 min (ort 240 min) Cut (20 sec)
B/sh, V/sh                                                  RCA

## WATERSHIP DOWN ***                                            U
Martin Rosen             UK                              1978
*Voices of: John Hurt, Richard Briers, Roy Kinnear, Denholm Elliott, Michael Hordern, Ralph Richardson, Simon Cadell, Terence Rigby, Richard O'Callaghan, Lyn Farleigh, Mary Maddox, Zero Mostel, Harry Andrews, Joss Ackland*
Animated version of the highly successful novel about a community of rabbits and the dangers they face as they embark on a perilous journey in search of a new home. This excellent animation has a fine score by Angela Morley. Not really light-hearted enough to be regarded as wholly a children's film, the only comic element is provided by Zero Mostel's bird character.
Boa: novel by Richard Adams.
CAR                                        88 min (ort 92 min)
B,V                          TEVP; EVC L/A; GHV (VHS only)

## WAVELENGTH **                                                 15
Mike Gray                USA                             1982
*Robert Carradine, Cherie Currie, Keenan Wynn, Cal Bowman, James Hess, Terry Burns, Eric Morris, Bob McLean, Robert Glaudini, Eric Heath, George Skaff, George O. Petrie, Milt Kogan, Dov Young, Joshua Oreck, Christian Morris*
Aliens arrive from outer space, but are captured by the authorities who want to conduct experiments on them. A rock star and his psychic girlfriend discover this, and face great danger from the intelligence forces, who are determined to preserve secrecy at all costs. A rather cheap-looking SF film. The unusual score is by Tangerine Dream.
FAN                                        84 min (ort 90 min) Cut
B,V,V2                                                      MED

## WAVES OF LUST **                                              18
Ruggero Deodato          ITALY                           1975
*John Steiner, Elizabeth Turner, Al Cliver (Pier Luigi Conti), Silvia Dionisio*
Routine sex film.
Aka: UNA ONDATA DI PIACERE
A                              76 min; 88 min (SHEP) Cut (1 min 4 sec)
B,V                          18PLAT/TOW L/A; GLOB; SHEP

## WAXWORK *                                                     18
Anthony Hickox           USA                             1986
*Zach Galligan, Deborah Foreman, Michelle Johnson, Miles O'Keeffe, David Warner, Dana Ashbrook, Patrick Macnee, Charles McCaughan, J. Kenneth Campbell, John Rhys-Davies*

A group of teenagers inside a wax museum, fall victim to a killer in this patchy and generally unsatisfactory blend of comedy and horror. A highlight should have been the point at which the teenagers had to battle some of the famous fictitious monsters of history, but even this lacked impact.

HOR          90 min (ort 100 min) Colour and B/W (one sequence)
B,V                                                                    VES

### WAY AHEAD, THE ***                                         U
Carol Reed                 UK                       1944
*David Niven, Stanley Holloway, William Hartnell, Jimmie Hanley, John Laurie, Hugh Burden, Peter Ustinov, Raymond Huntley, Trevor Howard, Tessie O'Shea, Penelope Dudley Ward, James Donald, Leo Genn, Mary Jerrold, Renee Asherson*
Originally intended as a training film, this project grew into the exciting story of how civilians from varied backgrounds came together as a unit of raw recruits, and were then shaped into a fighting force. Written by Peter Ustinov and Eric Ambler, this film retains a strong documentary feel. The music is by William Alwyn with photography by Guy Green. Trevor Howard's screen debut.
Aka: IMMORTAL BATTALION, THE
DRA                   110 min (ort 115 min) B/W
V                                                                     VCC

### WAY OF THE DRAGON, THE ***                          18
Bruce Lee             HONG KONG              1973
*Bruce Lee, Nora Miao, Chuck Norris*
Bruce Lee arrives in Rome to help relatives, whose Chinese restaurant has attracted the unwelcome attentions of gangsters who run a protection racket. They soon learn the futility of trying to use normal methods to deal with him, and decide instead to engage a number a martial artists of their own to take him on. Some splendidly choreographed fights are embedded in a flabby script. A few humorous touches demonstrate Lee's unexplored comic gifts.
Aka: RETURN OF THE DRAGON (VPD)
MAR  86 min; 90 min (VPD) Cut (1 min 11 sec) dubbed
V                                                          RNK; VPD

### WAY WE WERE, THE ***                                   PG
Sydney Pollack             USA                      1973
*Barbra Streisand, Robert Redford, Bradford Dillman, Viveca Lindfors, Herb Edelman, Murray Hamilton, Patrick O'Neal, Lois Chiles, Allyn Ann McLerie, Sally Kirkland*
The story of a romance from the 1930s to the 1950s between two people of opposing political views, with Redford playing a good-natured square against Streisand's political activist. The intelligent script by Laurents survives despite some clumsy pre-release cutting that left Hamilton and Lindfors with only small parts. AA: Score (Orig) (Marvin Hamlisch), Song ("The Way We Were" – Hamlisch – music/Alan and Marilyn Bergman – lyrics).
Boa: novel by Authur Laurents.
DRA                                                      118 min
B,V                                                            RCA

### WAYS OF KUNG FU, THE *                                 18
                           HONG KONG
*Chik Kuen Kwan, Mong Fai*
A martial arts student discovers that a monk is the reincarnation of an evil bandit and so exposes himself to great danger.
MAR                                                       91 min
B,V                         NORM L/A; ACE L/A; XTASY

### WE DIVE AT DAWN ***                                      U
Anthony Asquith            UK                       1943
*Eric Portman, John Mills, Reginald Purdell, Joan Hopkins, Josephine Wilson, Niall MacGinnis, Louis Bradfield, Ronald Millar, Jack Watling, Caven Wilson, Leslie Weston, Norman Williams, Lionel*

*Grose, Beatrice Varley, Marie Ault*
A low-key submarine drama telling of a crew assigned to attack a German battleship, the Brandenberg, that concentrates on the tensions and pressures the men suffer after the attack leaves their vessel disabled, short of fuel and far from home. Written by J.P. Williams, Val Valentine and Frank Launder.
WAR                                                    97 min B/W
V                                                              RNK

### WE OF THE NEVER NEVER ***                            U
Igor Auzins            AUSTRALIA             1982
*Angela Punch McGregor, Arthur Dignam, Tony Barry, Tommy Lewis, Martin Vaughn, Lewis Fitz-Gerald, Donald Blitner, Sibina Willy*
A high-class Australian girl marries the manager of a cable station and has to prove her worth in the Outback. Based on the memoirs of the first white woman to venture into Australia's wilderness or "Never Never", this film has little dramatic tension or plot. The beautiful outback locations are its strongest asset.
Boa: book by Mrs Aeneas Gunn.
DRA                             128 min (ort 134 min)
B,V                     NUT L/A; ODY/CBS; VCC

### WEAK AND THE WICKED, THE **                         PG
J. Lee-Thompson            UK                       1953
*Glynis Johns, John Gregson, Jane Hylton, Diana Dors, Sidney James, A.E. Matthews, Anthony Nichols, Athene Seyler, Olive Sloane, Sybil Thorndike, Barbara Couper, Joyce Heron, Ursula Howells, Mary Merrall, Rachel Roberts*
A woman gambler is sent to prison for a year and in a series of flashbacks we learn how both she and several other inmates came to be there. An interesting look at prison life that adopts an optimistic stance and is sustained by convincing performances.
Boa: novel Who Lie In Gaol by Joan Henry.
DRA                          83 min (ort 88 min) B/W
V                                                              WHV

### WEDDING PARTY, THE *
Cynthia Munroe/Brian De Palma/Wilford Leach
                           USA                       1963
*Jill Clayburgh, Charles Pfluger, Valda Satterfield, Raymond McNally, Robert DeNero (De Niro), Jennifer Salt, John Braswell, Judy Thomas, William Finley*
This description of the people and events surrounding a marriage ceremony is something of a curiosity. Boring and corny, it really has very little going for it except perhaps, early appearances by Clayburgh and De Niro. Briefly released after production, it promptly sank without a trace.
DRA                                                  88 min B/W
B,V                                                           VPD

### WEDDING REHEARSAL **                                    U
Alexander Korda            UK                       1932
*Roland Young, George Grossmith, John Loder, Lady Tree, Wendy Barrie, Maurice Evans, Joan Gardner, Merle Oberon, Kate Cutler, Edmund Breon, Morton Selton, Diana Napier, Lawrence Hanray, Rodolfo Mele*
An aristocratic Guards officer survives his grand-mother's matchmaking attempts by introducing the young ladies in question to his friends, but he is finally hooked by his mother's secretary. A faltering attempt at comedy that is too trite to be more than mildly amusing. Written by Biro and Arthur Wimperis.
Boa: story by Lajos Biro and George Grossmith.
COM                          75 min (ort 84 min) B/W
V                                                             PICK

### WEDDING, A **                                             15
Robert Altman             USA                       1978
*Carol Burnett, Desi Arnaz Jr, Amy Stryker, Vittorio Gassman, Geraldine Chaplin, Mia Farrow, Lillian Gish, Dina Merrill, Lauren Hutton, Pam Dawber, Pat*

*McCormick, Paul Dooley, Nina Van Pallandt, Viveca Lindfors, Howard Duff*
An account of a wedding among the nouveau riche with a scattering of amusing moments, as the various participants muddle and intrigue their way through the event. Limp direction and lack of plot development get in the way of any points the film had to make. Very largely a waste of good talent.
DRA                                                              125 min
B,V                                                                    CBS

## WEEDS **                                                          18
John Hancock                     USA                            1987
*Nick Nolte, William Forsythe, Lane Smith, Joe Mantegna, Mark Rolston, John Tols-Bey, Ernie Hudson, Rita Taggart, Anne Ramsey, Charlie Rich, J.J. Johnson*
A lifer in San Quentin who is also an aspiring playwright, is released from prison following pressure from a newspaper critic on his behalf. He then goes on to form his own theatre troupe, employing ex-convicts. This strange and uneasy blend of comedy and drama came from the real-life experiences of Rick Cluchey and his San Quentin Drama Group. A brave but muddled portrayal.
DRA                                                              114 min
B,V                                                                  PRES

## WEEKEND AT BERNIE'S **                                          15
Ted Kotcheff                     USA                            1989
*Andrew McCarthy, Jonathan Silverman, Catherine Mary Stewart, Terry Kiser, Don Calfa, Louis Giambalvo*
Silverman and McCarthy play two ambitious young executives who get an invitation to spend the weekend at their boss' luxurious beach house. When they find he has been murdered, they realise they could be the next victims, and spend the rest of the movie trying to convince the unknown assassin that their boss is still alive. Written by Robert Klane, this raucous slapstick comedy lacks punch, but the two leads make the most of the simple script.
COM                                               94 min (ort 97 min)
V                                                                      MGM

## WEEKEND MURDERS **                                               15
Michel Lupo                      ITALY                          1970
*Anna Moffo, Peter Baldwin, Gastone Moschin, Lance Percival, Marisa Fabbri*
The reading of a will sparks off a series of murders among the surviving heirs.
DRA                                                               94 min
B,V                                                                    MGM

## WEEKEND PASS *                                                   18
Lawrence Bassoff                 USA                            1984
*Patrick Hauser, D.W. Brown, Chip McAllister, Peter Ellenstein, Hilary Shapiro, Pamela G. Kay, Graem McGavin, Daureen Collodel, Annette Sinclair, Grand L. Bush*
Four naval recruits celebrate the end of their basic training with a wild 72 hour fling in L.A. A pale imitation of ON THE TOWN with a poor script and worse direction.
COM                                                               92 min
B,V                                                                VES/PVG

## WEEKEND WAR **                                                   PG
Steven Hilliard Stern    USA                                   1988
*Stephen Collins, Daniel Stern, Evan Mirand, Michael Beach, Scott Paulin, James Tolkan, Charles Haid*
A unit of part-time soldiers find themselves engaged in an all too real war with guerilla fighters, whilst doing two weeks National Guard duty in Honduras. Competent action-film that makes a number of salient points about Central America.
A/AD                                                        91 min mTV
B,V                                                                    EIV

## WEIRD SCIENCE **                                                 15
John Hughes                      USA                            1985
*Kelly LeBrock, Anthony Michael Hall, Ian Mitchell-Smith, Bill Paxton, Judie Aronson, Suzanne Snyder, Robert Downey, Robert Rusler, Vernon Wells, Michael Berryman, Ivor Barry, Anne Coyle, Barbara Lang, Britt Leach*
Silly teen-comedy with two shy kids using their computer to create a woman from a Barbie Doll to fill the gap in their lives. Engaging dialogue and good performances get lost in the moronic plot. Written by Hughes.
FAN                                               90 min (ort 94 min)
V/sh                                                                    CIC

## WELCOME HOME **                                                  15
Franklin J. Schaffner    USA                                   1989
*Kris Kristofferson, JoBeth Williams, Sam Waterston, Brian Keith, Thomas Wilson Brown, Trey Wilson*
After 17 years spent in Kampuchea hiding from the Khmer Rouge, a US pilot who now has a second wife and two children, decides to return home to the first one. However, he finds she has since remarried and that he now has a teenaged son he never knew. Schaffner's final film is an earnest but underplotted affair that runs out of energy all too soon.
DRA                                               88 min (ort 96 min)
V/sh                                                                    WHV

## WELCOME TO 18 **                                                 15
Terry Carr                       USA                            1986
*Courtney Thorne-Smith, Jo Ann Willette, Mariska Hargitay, Cristen Kauffman, E. Erich Anderson, John Putch*
Jayne Mansfield's daughter Mariska Hargitay stars in this story of three beautiful High School graduates who spend their summer vacation in Lake Trahoe as employees of a wacky dude ranch. A stale teen-comedy that provides a particle of titillation buried in a muddled and confused plot.
COM                                                               87 min
B,V                                                                    VES

## WELCOME TO ARROW BEACH ***                                      18
Laurence Harvey                  USA                            1974
*Laurence Harvey, Joanna Pettet, Stuart Whitman, John Ireland, Meg Foster, Jesse Vint, Gloria LeRoy*
A teenage hitch-hiker cannot convince a sleepy community that she has discovered a mad killer on the loose. Harvey's last film (which he edited by telephone from his deathbed) has him as a crazed war veteran who kills to satisfy his newly-acquired craving for human flesh. An unpleasant but absorbing horror-film that has acquired a modicum of cult status.
Aka: AND NO-ONE WOULD BELIEVE HER; DERANGED (BRAVE); NO ONE WOULD BELIEVE HER (CBS); TENDER FLESH
HOR                                               80 min; 99 min (CBS)
B,V                                                    CBS; CINE; BRAVE

## WELCOME TO BLOOD CITY ***                                       15
Peter Sasdy                      USA                            1972
*Jack Palance, Samantha Eggar, Keir Dullea, Hollis McLaren, Chris Wiggins, Barry Morse, Allan Royal, Henry Ramer, Ken James, John Evans, Gary Reineke, Jack Creley, Chuck Shamata, Jack Crofoot, Mina E. Mina, Calvin Butler*
Four people who cannot remember anything about themselves are found on the outskirts of a sinister "Wild West" town, which employs bizarre rules to control survival of its inhabitants. It transpires that the town is really a computer generated illusion used to select people for use in real combat. A demanding film with some great ideas but opaque; almost certainly made as a comment of sorts on the Vietnam War.
FAN                                          92 min (Cut at film release)
B,V                                                                   TEVP

## WELCOME TO L.A. ** 15
Alan Rudolph            USA            1977
*Keith Carradine, Sally Kellerman, Geraldine Chaplin,*
*Harvey Keitel, Lauren Hutton, Viveca Lindfors, Sissy*
*Spacek, John Considine, Denver Pyle, Diahann*
*Abbott, Richard Baskin, Mike Caplan, Allan Nicholls,*
*Cedric Scott*
A star-studded cast cannot bring to life this rambling
account of the complex relations among a group of
assorted Californian musicians and hangers-on. This
overlong and pretentious nonsense has Carradine
playing a rock composer who, having spent the last
three years in London, has returned to Los Angeles
and is attempting to catch up musically on all that lost
time. Written by Rudolph and produced by Robert
Altman.
DRA                                      100 min
B,V                                      WHV

## WE'RE NO ANGELS ** 15
Neil Jordan            USA            1989
*Robert De Niro, Sean Penn, Demi Moore, Hoyt Axton,*
*Bruno Kirby, James Russo, Ray McAnally, Wallace*
*Shawn, John C. Reilly*
Two dumb cons inadvertently break out of jail and
find themselves being taken for priests on their way to
a local shrine. This parody of the earlier Bogart movie,
spoofs gangster films of the period, and Penn and De
Niro give nice restrained performances, but the
clumsy blending of comedy and drama and a violent
sequence near the end are serious flaws. Russo's
performance as a Cagney-style gangster is a highlight. Scripted by David Mamet.
COM                        102 min (ort 106 min)
V                                        CIC

## WEREWOLF ** 15
David Hemmings            USA            1987
*John J. York, Chuck Connors, Lance LeGault,*
*Michelle Johnson, Raphael Sbarge, John Quade,*
*Harold Ayer, Geraldine O'Brien, Robert Sutton, Ethan*
*Phillips, Robert Krantz, Stanley Grover, Gail O'Grady,*
*Linden Ashby*
A youngster learns that his best friend is a were-
wolf, and is forced to kill him after being attacked. As
well as being wanted for murder, he now has to find a
cure for his affliction, having become a werewolf
himself. Average.
HOR                          83 min (ort 90 min) mTV
B,V                                      EIV

## WEREWOLF'S SHADOW, THE * 18
Leon Klimorsky            SPAIN            1970
*Paul Naschy (Jacinto Molina), Paty Shepard, Gaby*
*Fuchs, Barbara Capell, Andrew Reese (Andres*
*Resino), Julio Pena, Yelena Samarina, Jose Marco,*
*Barta Barri*
Routine vampire mayhem with a reluctant werewolf
being revived by doctors who remove the silver bullet
he has in his body.
Aka: BLACK HARVEST OF COUNTESS
DRACULA; THE; LA NOCHE DE WALPURGIS;
NACHT DER VAMPIRE; SHADOW OF THE
WEREWOLF; WEREWOLF SHADOW; WEREWOLF
VERSUS THE VAMPIRE WOMEN, THE
HOR                  83 min (ort 85 min) Cut (34 sec)
B,V,V2                  INT L/A; SID L/A; XTASY

## WEST OF THE DIVIDE *** U
R.N. Bradbury            USA            1934
*John Wayne, Virginia Browne Faire, Yakima Canutt,*
*Gabby Hayes, Lafe McKee, Lloyd Whitlock, Billy*
*O'Brien, John Whiteford, Earl Dwire, Tex Palmer,*
*Dick Dickinson, Artie Ortego, Horace B. Carpenter,*
*Hal Price, Archie Ricks*
A young man discovers the identity of the outlaw who
murdered his parents and kidnapped his baby brother
years ago. He poses as an outlaw in order to infiltrate
the man's gang and have his revenge. A well-made

second feature, with Whitlock as the outlaw especially
memorable.
WES                    58 min; 52 min (CH5) B/W
B,V                                      VIV L/A

## WEST OF ZANZIBAR * U
Harry Watt            UK            1954
*Anthony Steel, Sheila Sim, Edric Connor, Orlando*
*Martins, William Simons, Martin Benson, Peter Illing,*
*Juma, Howard Marion-Crawford, R. Stuart Lindsell*
In Africa the work of a national park warden is
hampered by ivory smugglers and native tribesmen.
This weak follow-up to WHERE NO VULTURES FLY
has good locations but not much else.
A/AD                          90 min (ort 94 min)
V                                        WHV

## WEST SIDE STORY *** PG
Robert Wise/Jerome Robbins
                        USA            1961
*Natalie Wood, Russ Tamblyn, Rita Moreno, George*
*Chakaris, Richard Beymer, Tucker Smith, David*
*Winters, Tony Mordenete, Simon Oakland, John Astin*
This updated Romeo and Juliet tale, has a Puerto
Rican girl and white boy falling in love despite peer
pressures. The dancing and Leonard Bernstein score
are dynamic but characterisation is weak. Scripted by
Ernest Lehman, with Stephen Sondheim lyrics and
choreography by Robbins. AA: Pic, Dir, Cin (Fapp), S.
Actor (Chakiris), S. Actress (Moreno), Art/Set (Levin/
Gangelin), Score (Chaplin et al.), Cost (Sharaff),
Sound (Hynes), Hon Award (Robbins).
Boa: play by Arthur Laurents.
MUS                        115 min (ort 151 min)
V/sh                                    WHV

## WESTERNER, THE *** U
William Wyler            USA            1940
*Gary Cooper, Walter Brennan, Forrest Tucker, Doris*
*Davenport, Fred Stone, Paul Hurst, Chill Wills, Dana*
*Andrews, Tom Tyler, Lillian Bond, Charles Halton,*
*Arthur Aylesworth, Lupita Tovar, Julian Rivero,*
*Roger Gray*
A classic Western about the struggle over land claims
and the problems which this causes. Brennan won an
Oscar for his portrayal of Judge Roy Bean, and
deservedly so. The music is by Dimitri Tiomkin with
photography by Gregg Toland and the script by Jo
Swerling and Niven Busch. Tucker's film debut. AA:
S. Actor (Brennan).
Boa: short story by Stuart N. Lake.
WES                  100 min; 95 min (PARK) B/W
V                                  VGM; PARK

## WESTWARD HO, THE WAGONS ** U
William Beaudine            USA            1956
*Fess Parker, Kathleen Crowley, George Reeves, Jeff*
*York, David Stollery, Sebastian Cabot, Doreen Tracey,*
*Barbara Woodell, John War Eagle, Cubby O'Brien,*
*Tommy Cole, Leslie Bradley, Morgan Woodward, Iron*
*Eyes Cody*
A wagon train of settlers slowly moves West and has a
number of adventures along the way. Sugary Disney
confection liberally laced with songs but in need of a
story of real substance.
Boa: novel by Mary Jane Carr.
WES                          79 min (ort 94 min)
B,V                                      WDV

## WESTWARD PASSAGE ** 
Robert Milton            USA            1932
*Ann Harding, Laurence Olivier, Irving Pichel, ZaSu*
*Pitts, Irene Purchell, Bonita Granville, Ethel Griffies*
A woman accepts the need to make sacrifices when she
decides to divorce her husband and marry her lover.
Written by Bradley King and Humphrey King, this
dull romantic drama is sustained by the actors if not
by their lines. The music is by Max Steiner.
Boa: novel by Margaret Ayer Barnes.

DRA                        70 min B/W
B,V                          KVD

## WESTWORLD ***         15
Michael Crichton    USA           1973
*Richard Benjamin, Yul Brynner, James Brolin,
Norman Bartold, Victoria Shaw, Alan Oppenheimer,
Dick Van Patten, Majel Barrett, Steve Franken, Linda
Scott, Nora Marlowe, Terry Wilson, Norman Bartold,
Michael Mikler*
A futuristic holiday camp offers trips to three recre-
ated past periods, such as a Wild West town. Each
setting employs robots programmed to satisfy the
whims of the visitors, even to the point of staging
mock duels. All goes well until the robots start to
malfunction and the fights become real. An excellent
idea spoilt by lack of development. Written and
directed by Crichton. FUTUREWORLD followed in
1976.
FAN               85 min (ort 90 min)
V                         MGM

## WET GOLD **          PG
Dick Lowry       USA           1984
*Brooke Shields, Tom Byrd, Burgess Meredith, Brian
Kerwin, William Bronder, David Kass*
Routine story of a hunt for sunken treasure with
Shields and three men. The similarity to THE TREA-
SURE OF THE SIERRA MADRE is evident, with
Meredith having Walter Huston's role and Shields
Tim Holt's. Bogart's character is divided between
Byrd and Kerwin. Strictly average.
A/AD           95 min; 91 min (CH5) mTV
B,V         ODY/POLY; CH5 (VHS only)

## WHALE FOR A KILLING, A ***
Richard T. Heffron   USA        1981
*Peter Strauss, Richard Widmark, Dee Wallace,
Kathryn Walker, Bruce McGill, Ken James, David
Ferry, David Hollander, Bill Calvert, Larry Reynolds,
Kent Barrett, George Morner, Reuven Bar-Yotam,
Arthur Rosenberg, Colin Fox*
A stranded humpback whale is the object of one man's
care and attention, in the face of hostility from those
who want to use it for commercial gain. Strauss is the
campaigner, in this verbose but absorbing study of the
slaughter of whales off the Newfoundland coast.
Written by Lionel Chetwynd.
Boa: book by Farley Mowat.
DRA           136 min (ort 150 min) mTV
B,V                      HER

## WHALES OF AUGUST, THE ***    U
Lindsay Anderson    UK          1987
*Bette Davis, Lillian Gish, Vincent Price, Ann Sothern,
Harry Carey Jr, Frank Grimes, Frank Pitkin,
Margaret Ladd, Tisha Sterling, Mary Steenburgen*
Two elderly sisters live out their last days on an island
off the coast of Maine, in this gentle meditation on the
inevitability of old age and death. Screenplay is by
Berry from his touching play, with music by Alan
Price.
Boa: play by David Berry
DRA               87 min (ort 91 min)
V                     NELS; VES

## WHAM! BAM! THANK YOU SPACEMAN **
William Levey     USA          197-
*Jay Rasumny, Chet Norris, Dyanne Thorne*
Tedious sex film that's a kind of space spoof.
A                          87 min
B,V                       TCX

## WHAT A WAY TO GO *       18
Karl Rawicz    AUSTRALIA   198-
*Adrian Ayres, Adam Johnson, Stacey Abrahams,
Kathleen Johnson*
A gormless skinny mechanic is kidnapped by a group
of women to serve as a sex slave to an overweight

sex-starved woman. Arousing him for her takes the
combined efforts of all the women. Not to be confused
with a 1964 comedy of the same title.
Aka: BOTTOMS UP
COM                         85 min
B,V          IVS; MOV L/A; GLOB

## WHAT COMES AROUND **     PG
Jerry Reed       USA          1985
*Jerry Reed, Bo Hopkins, Barry Corbin, Arte Johnson,
Ernest Dixon*
A Country singer whose career seems to be doomed to
extinction from his drug addiction, receives unex-
pected help from his estranged brother, who holds him
captive at a remote cabin to wean him off his habit.
DRA                       92 min
B,V                       AVA

## WHAT MAD PURSUIT? **     PG
Tony Smith       UK           1985
*Carroll Baker, Paul Daneman, Neil Cunningham*
An author and actor badly in need of a rest is promised
a quiet weekend in the country, but finds on arriving
at his host's house that the opposite is the case.
Unwilling to appear rude, he begins to employ the
most bizarre strategems in order to get way. One of a
set of tales based on Noel Coward plays. See also ME
AND THE GIRLS, MISTER AND MRS EDGEHILL
and MRS CAPPER'S BIRTHDAY.
Boa: play by Noel Coward.
DRA                       55 min
V                         PICK

## WHAT NEXT? *
Claes Felbom    SWEDEN     1968
*Monica Nordquist, Ollegard Wellton, Erik Hell, Lissa
Alandin, Birger Malmsten*
A Swedish love story in which a young girl first
seduces her stepfather and then transfers her affec-
tions to the young couple who accidentally run him
over in their car. As bizarre (and tedious) as it sounds.
Aka: CARMILLA; SWEDISH LOVE PLAY
DRA                       78 min
B,V                   RNK L/A

## WHAT SCHOOLGIRLS DON'T TELL *   18
Clause Rott   WEST GERMANY   1974
*Susie Atkins*
Sex film done in that pseudo-documentary style used
in the 1970s, by German film-makers with such feeble
offerings.
Aka: SECRETS OF SWEET SIXTEEN: WHAT
SCHOOLGIRLS DON'T TELL
A       71 min (ort 77 min) Cut (3 min 20 sec)
B,V    WOV L/A; ORANGE/STABL; ORANGE

## WHATEVER HAPPENED TO AUNT ALICE? ***  15
Robert Aldrich    USA         1969
*Geraldine Page, Rosemary Forsyth, Ruth Gordon,
Robert Fuller, Mildred Dunnock, Valerie Allen, Peter
Brandon, Joan Huntingdon, Michael Barbera, Peter
Bonerz, Claire Kelly, Jack Bannon, Richard Angarola,
Martin Garralaga*
A woman's housekeepers have a strange habit of
disappearing. The latest in the series tries to solve the
mystery and avoid the same fate. Written by Theodore
Apstein, this has Page as the lady of the house and
Gordon as her next victim, both playing their parts
with considerable gusto. A most enjoyable murder
mystery.
Boa: novel The Forbidden Garden by Ursula Curtess.
HOR                       98 min
B,V                    VGM; RNK

## WHATEVER HAPPENED TO BABY JANE? ****  18
Robert Aldrich    USA         1962
*Bette Davis, Joan Crawford, Victor Buono, Marjorie
Bennett, Anna Lee, Dave Willock, Maidie Norman,
Wesley Add, Bert Freed, Gina Gillespie, Ann Barton,*

*Julie Allred, Barbara Merrill*
Crawford as a crippled film star is at the mercy of her
sadistic sister Davis. A macabre first venture into the
black-comedy genre for these two stars. Buono sup-
ports as a pianist accompanist for Davis' hoped for
return to films. Far-fetched, grisly and utterly absorb-
ing. Written by Lukas Heller. AA: Cost (Norma
Koch).
Boa: novel What Ever Happened To Baby Jane
Hudson by Henry Farrell.
HOR                          129 min (ort 132 min) B/W
B,V                                                    WHV

## WHAT'S NEW PUSSYCAT? **                          15
Clive Donner          USA                          1965
*Peter Sellers, Peter O'Toole, Woody Allen, Romy
Schneider, Capucine, Paula Prentiss, Ursula Andress,
Louise Lasser*
A silly, confused romp involving a disturbed fashion
editor who pays a visit to a psychiatrist but finds that
he is crazier than he is. Woody Allen's first film script
is heavily flawed with but the occasional flash of wit.
The catchy title song is by Burt Bacharach and Hal
David.
COM                                            108 min
B,V                                                    WHV

## WHAT'S UP DOC? ***                               U
Peter Bogdanovich     USA                          1972
*Barbra Streisand, Ryan O'Neal, Kenneth Mars, Austin
Pendleton, Madeline Kahn, Sorrell Booke, Mabel
Albertson, Randy Quaid, John Hillerman, Stefan
Geirasch, Michael Murphy, Graham Jarvis, Liam
Dunn, Phil Roth, Eleanor Zee*
A crazy female student latches onto a musicologist
and makes life unbearable for him and his dowdy
fiancee. A plot involving spies and a jewel theft adds to
the general confusion, culminating in an extremely
funny chase and a splendid courtroom scene. Written
by Buck Henry, David Newman and Robert Benton.
COM                                87 min (ort 94 min)
B,V                                                    WHV

## WHAT'S UP NURSE? **
Derek Ford            UK                            1977
*Nicholas Field, Felicity Devonshire, John Le Mesurier,
Graham Stark, Kate Williams, Cardew Robinson,
Barbara Mitchell, Angela Grant, Julia Bond, Peter
Butterworth, Ronnie Brody, Sheila Bernette, Keith
Smith, Chic Murrary*
A new doctor takes up his first hospital post. The fact
that the daughter of one of the consultants can only
have sex whilst on the move (e.g. in a car), helps
compound his problems. One more to add to the dated
and tedious collection of British doctor-nurse sex
comedies.
COM                                82 min (ort 84 min)
B,V,V2                                           HOK L/A

## WHAT'S UP TIGER LILY? ***                        PG
Compiled by Woody Allen
                      USA                          1966
*Tatsuya Mihashi, Miya Hana, Elko Wakabayashi,
Tadao Nakamura, Woody Allen, China Lee, Louise
Lasser (voice only)*
A Japanese agent film from 1964 was redubbed by
Allen into an international hunt for a recipe for egg
salad. An interesting project that provides a number
of laughs whilst poking fun at all those James Bond
movies. The music is by The Lovin' Spoonful who also
appear in the film. The original film was entitled
"Kagi No Kag" (or Key Of Keys) and was released in
1964.
COM                                 79 min Cut (4 sec)
B,V                          SPEC/POLY; CH5 (VHS only)

## WHEELS OF FIRE **                                18
Cirio H. Santiago     USA                          1984
*Gary Watkins, Laura Banks, Lynda Wiesmeier, Linda*

*Grovenor, Joseph Anderson, Joe Zaccharo, Jack S.
Daniels, Steve Parvin, Nigel Hodge, Dennis Cole, Don
Gordon, Gery Taylor, Linda Oball, Harry Sherman,
Debbie Pusa, Cathie Leckie*
Another post-nuclear holocaust epic in the MAD MAX
mould. No better or worse than a hundred others.
Aka: DESERT WARRIOR; VINDICATOR
A/AD                   75 min (ort 85 min) Cut (2 min 18 sec)
B,V                                                    MED

## WHEELS OF TERROR **                              15
Gordon Hessler        USA                          1987
*Bruce Davidson, David Patrick Kelly, D.W. Moffett,
Jay O. Sanders, Oliver Reed, David Carradine, Keith
Szarabajka*
A WW2 story that follows the exploits of some soldiers
from the German Penal Regiment, who are sent on a
suicidal mission behind the Russian lines. A brutal
and harsh account, scripted by Nelson Gidding from
Hassel's book.
Aka: MISFIT BRIGADE, THE
Boa: novel by Sven Hassel.
WAR                                            100 min
B,V                                                    MED

## WHEELS OF TERROR **                              15
Christopher Cain      USA                          1990
*Joanna Cassidy, Marcie Leeds, Carlos Cervantes,
Arlen Dean Snyder*
Having moved to Copper Valley from L.A. to escape
the pollution, a mother and her daughter are horrified
by the news of the abduction of two young girls, one of
whom is raped and the other murdered. When her own
daughter is kidnapped, the mother begins a desperate
chase to get her back.
THR                                             82 min
V                                                      CIC

## WHEELS ON MEALS **                               15
Samo Hung      HONG KONG                            1984
*Jackie Chan*
Another high-kicking mixture of good stunt-work and
martial arts action, as Chan and his brother are forced
to take time out from running their mobile food-bar to
deal with some villains who are after a girl.
MAR                                            103 min
B,V                                                    VPD

## WHEN A STRANGER CALLS **
Fred Walton           USA                          1979
*Carol Kane, Charles Durning, Colleen Dewhurst, Tony
Beckley, Rachel Roberts, Ron O'Neal, Carmen
Argenziano, Rutanya Alda, Kirsten Larkin, Bill
Boyett, Michael Champion, Heetu, Joe Beale, Ed
Wright, Louise Wright, Carol O'Neal*
A crazed killer who was incarcerated seven years ago
when he murdered two children and terrorised their
babysitter, escapes from his asylum with the intention
of repeating his crimes. A disagreeable and not really
convincing shocker, that rapidly runs out of steam
after the first 10 minutes.
Boa: short film The Sitter.
HOR                                79 min (ort 97 min)
B,V,V2                                                 GHV

## WHEN A WOMAN IS IN LOVE **                       18
                      FRANCE                        1976
*Sylvia Kristel, Nathalie Delon, Jon Finch, Gisele
Casadesus, Marie Lebee, Jean Mermet*
A mediocre film version of this classic 18th century
tale of seduction and sexual conquests among the
aristocracy. See also DANGEROUS LIAISONS.
Aka: UNE FEMME FIDELE
Boa: novel Les Liaisons Dangereuses by Choderlos de
Laclos.
DRA                                81 min (ort 85 min)
B,V                          VIP L/A; VUL L/A; CERT

## WHEN DINOSAURS RULED THE EARTH ***               PG
Val Guest             UK                            1969

Victoria Vetri, Patrick Allen, Robin Hawdon, Drewe Henley, Imogen Hassall, Sean Caffrey, Magda Konopka, Patrick Holt, Jan Rossini, Carol-Anne Hawkins

The story of a Stone Age romance between two people of different backgrounds who are themselves rejected by their respective tribes. The beautiful locations and good special effects (by Jim Danforth) help the J.G. Ballard story along nicely. See also ONE MILLION YEARS B.C.

DRA                 96 min (ort 100 min)
B,V                      WHV

### WHEN DREAMS COME TRUE **
             15
John Llewellyn Moxey   USA         1985
Cindy Williams, David Morse, Jessica Harper, Stan Shaw, Lee Horsley, Jeanne Cairns, Ouida White, Eli Cummins, Norma Young, Tommy Madden, Lou Hancock, Marjie Rynearson, John L. Martin, Chris Burton, Tyrees Allen, Gil Glasgow

A woman's dreams about a killer start to come true, but she finds it difficult to get anybody to take her seriously. An unexciting suspense cum horror yarn that is well below average for films of this genre.

THR             91 min (ort 100 min) mTV
B,V                      GHV

### WHEN EIGHT BELLS TOLL **
               15
Etienne Perier      UK          1971
Anthony Hopkins, Robert Morley, Jack Hawkins, Corin Redgrave, Ferdy Main, Derek Bond, Nathalie Delon

A naval secret agent, sent to investigate the piracy of gold bullion from ships in the Irish Sea, poses as a biologist. A clumsy adaptation of the novel, scripted by MacLean and devoid of wit or inspiration, but made a little more bearable by some beautiful locations.
Boa: novel by Alistair MacLean.

A/AD                     94 min
V                      VCC

### WHEN FATHER WAS AWAY ON BUSINESS ***15
Emir Kusturica    YUGOSLAVIA     1985
Moreno De Bartolli, Miki Manojlovic, Mirjana Karanovic, Mustafa Nadarevic, Mira Furlan, Pedrag Lakovic, Pavle Vujisic, Slobodan Aligrudic

The effect of the rift between Stalin and Tito as reflected in the fate of one family where the father is accused of pro-Stalinism and treated accordingly. These events are seen through the eyes of the young son, the film's central character. It won the Palme d'Or at Cannes and is a work of great charm, but criticism of the clear abuses that occur when the state is all-powerful are muted indeed. Set in early 1950s Sarajevo.
Aka: OTAC NA SLUZBENOM PUTU

COM              130 min (ort 136 min)
B,V                      CAN

### WHEN GIRLS UNDRESS *
Eberhard Schroeder
           WEST GERMANY     1972
Rinaldo Talamanti, Franz Muxeneder, Eva Matern, Dorothea Rau

A young racing cyclist is enjoined not to have sex for six weeks, but his opponents exploit his predicament for their own ends. A low-grade sex comedy.
Aka: MATRATZEN TANGO; SECRETS OF NAKED GIRLS (BEV)

COM                    80 min
B,V           GOV L/A; BEV; DFS

### WHEN HARRY MET SALLY ****
            15
Rob Reiner      USA         1989
Billy Crystal, Meg Ryan, Carrie Fisher, Bruno Kirby, Steven Ford, Lisa Jane Persky, Michelle Nicastro, Harley Kozak

A romantic comedy somewhat reminiscent of ANNIE HALL, that has Crystal and Ryan playing long-time acquaintances who drift from mild dislike through platonic friendship to love. Nora Ephron's semi-autobiographical script takes a funny and serious look at romantic relationships in a way that is both poignant and incisive. A topnotch cast and some great dialogue make it all the better.

COM                    95 min
V                      PAL

### WHEN HE'S NOT A STRANGER ***
          15
John Gray      USA         1989
Annabeth Gish, Kevin Dillon, John Terlesky, Kim Meyers, Stephen Elliott, Paul Dooley

A college girl suffers the trauma of being raped by her best friend's boyfriend – the top sportsman on the campus. Scripted by Gray and Beth Sullivan, and finely acted by Gish, this compelling drama attempts an honest look at a difficult and disturbing subject.

DRA             95 min (ort 100 min) mTV
V                   PRISM L/A

### WHEN MEN CARRIED CLUBS, WOMEN PLAYED DING DONG! *
Bruno Corbucci     ITALY        1970
Antonio Sabato, Aldo Guiffre, Vittorio Caprioli, Nadia Cassini, Senta Berger, Renzo Montagnani, Frank Wolff, Valeria Fabrizi, Ello Pandolfi, Renato Rossini, Anabella Incontrera

Satire on the arms race but set in prehistoric times and very loosely based on the play Lysistrata by Aristophanes. Full of fetching beauties clad in animal skins and little else. A sequel to "When Women Had Tails".
Aka: QUANDO GLI UOMINI AMARANO LA CLAVA . . . E CON LE DONNE FECERO DIN-DON; QUANDO LE DONNE PERSERO LA CODA; WHEN WOMEN LOST THEIR TAILS; WHEN WOMEN PLAYED DING DONG

FAN             98 min (ort 105 min)
B,V                MED; VPD

### WHEN NIGHT FALLS *
                  15
Eltan Green      ISRAEL       1985
Assaf Dayan, Yoseph Millo, Orna Dorath, Dani Roth, Maya Pick-Pardo, Irith Sheleg, Amos Lavi

A man and his wife break up after 40 years of marriage, at the same time their son is experiencing trouble with underworld figures. A confused and rather poorly made drama.
Aka: AD SOFF HALAYLA

DRA                    97 min
B,V                    MGM

### WHEN THE KUNG FU HERO STRIKES *
         HONG KONG
Betty Ting Pei
A martial artist uses his skills on a ruthless white slaver.

MAR                   80 min
V                    OCEAN

### WHEN THE NORTH WIND BLOWS ***
Stewart Raffill     USA        1974
Henry Brandon, Herbert Nelson, Dan Haggerty, Henry Olek, Sander Johnson, Jan Smithers

An old fur trapper living in Alaska attempts to protect Siberian snow tigers being hunted for their pelts but is not entirely successful. A simple and enjoyable outdoors tale, made more so by the beautiful scenery.

JUV             109 min (ort 113 min)
B,V                    RNK

### WHEN THE TIME COMES ***
                15
John Erman      USA        1987
Bonnie Bedelia, Brad Davis, Terry O'Quinn, Karen Austen, Donald Moffat

A 34-year-old woman discovers that she has terminal cancer and decides to kill herself, but is opposed by her husband and best friend. An engrossing drama with

Bedelia giving a fine performance.
DRA                                 104 min mTV
B,V                                        VIR

## WHEN THE WHALES CAME ***
Clive Rees              UK              1988
*Paul Scofield, Helen Pearce, Max Rennie, Helen*
*Mirren, John Hallam, David Threlfall*
The story of an old recluse who lives on an island and
spends his time whittling bird sculptures. A couple of
inquisitive children get to know him and learn of a
secret that has haunted him for years. An engaging
tale set on the Scilly Isles just before WW1.
Boa: story by Michael Morpurgo.
DRA                                    97 min
V                                          CBS

## WHEN THE WIND BLOWS **                  PG
Jimmy T. Murakami       UK              1986
*Voices of: Peggy Ashcroft, John Mills*
An adequate adaptation of Briggs' morbid semi-comic
tale of a rather naive middle-aged couple, and their
pathetic attempts to prepare for an imminent nuclear
conflict. Not quite the satire it was intended to be, but
not bad either.
Boa: book by Raymond Briggs.
CAR                                    85 min
V/sh                                       CBS

## WHEN TIME RAN OUT *                      PG
James Goldstone        USA              1980
*Paul Newman, Jacqueline Bisset, William Holden,*
*James Franciscus, Edward Albert, Red Buttons,*
*Ernest Borgnine, Burgess Meredith, Valentina*
*Cortesa, Veronica Hamel, Alex Karras, Barbara*
*Carrera*
Routine disaster movie about a volcanic eruption on a
tropical island peopled by the rich and famous. A
disaster movie in every sense of the word with a
rehashed and cliched plot courtesy of Carl Foreman
and Stirling Silliphant. The music is by Lalo Schifrin.
The original running-time is for versions that contain
extra footage not shown theatrically.
Boa: novel The Day The World Ended by Max Morgan
Witts and Gordon Thomas.
THR                              121 min (ort 144 min)
B,V                                        WHV

## WHEN WORLDS COLLIDE ***                   U
Rudolph Mate           USA              1951
*Barbara Rush, Richard Derr, Peter Hanson, Larry*
*Keating, John Hoyt, Stephen Chase, Hayden Rorke,*
*Sandro Giglio, Laura Elliot, Frank Cady, Judith*
*Ames, Jim Congdon, Frances Sanford, Freeman Lusk,*
*Joseph Nell*
Scientists prepare a spaceship to save a selected band
of people to start life on another world, before the
Earth is destroyed by a giant planetoid hurtling
towards it. Poor characterisation and pedestrian pac-
ing are flaws, but the special effects (including the
submerging of Manhattan) won a well-deserved
Oscar. Written by Sidney Boehm. AA: Effects (George
Pal).
Boa: novel by Philip Wylie and Edwin Balmer.
FAN                                    79 min
V/h                                        CIC

## WHEN YOU'RE IN LOVE ***                   U
Robert Riskin          USA              1937
*Grace Moore, Cary Grant, Aline MacMahon, Thomas*
*Mitchell, Henry Stephenson, Emma Dunn*
An Australian opera star finds herself unable to
obtain a visa to enter the United States, so she pays an
American artist $2,000 to marry her. However, the
scheme misfires as the thoroughly unsuited couple
embark on a series of disputes and wrangles. An
enjoyable comedy-singing vehicle for opera star Moore
that represents screenwriter Riskin's only film as
director.

Aka: FOR YOU ALONE
COM                                 99 min B/W
V                                          RCA

## WHERE DANGER LIVES ***
John Farrow            USA              1950
*Robert Mitchum, Faith Domergue, Claude Rains,*
*Maureen O'Sullivan, Charles Kemper*
A doctor falls in love with a murderous female patient
who is hovering on the edge of madness and finds
himself drawn into her schemes. A competent and
well-handled if somewhat depressing example of
1950s film noir.
Osca: SPLIT SECOND
DRA                                 78 min B/W
B,V                                        KVD

## WHERE DOES IT HURT? *
Ralph Amateau          USA              1972
*Peter Sellers, Jo Ann Pflug, Rick Lenz, Harold Gould,*
*Hope Summers, Eve Bruce, Kathleen Freeman*
The story of a corrupt hospital and its greedy and
incompetent staff. This sad attempt at comedy is as
unpleasantly tasteless as it is unfunny. A thorough
waste of good actors.
Boa: novel The Operator by Budd Robinson.
COM                                    85 min
B,V                                    VCL/CBS

## WHERE EAGLES DARE ***                    PG
Brian G. Hutton        USA              1969
*Richard Burton, Clint Eastwood, Mary Ure, Michael*
*Hordern, Patrick Wymark, Robert Beatty, Ferdy*
*Mayne, Anton Diffring, Donald Houston, Ingrid Pitt,*
*Derren Nesbitt, Peter Barkworth*
Commandos have to mount a rescue operation for an
American general who is being held in an impregn-
able Nazi mountain fortress. The tension in this one is
maintained throughout whilst the plot is serpentine to
say the least. Written by MacLean with music by Ron
Goodwin.
Boa: novel by Alistair MacLean.
WAR                                   148 min
V                                          MGM

## WHERE HAVE ALL THE PEOPLE GONE? *
John Llewellyn Moxey   USA              1974
*Peter Graves, Verna Bloom, George O'Hanlon Jr,*
*Kathleen Quinlan, Michael James Wixted, Noble*
*Willingham, Doug Chapin, Jay W. MacIntosh, Dan*
*Barrows, Ken Sansom*
A family survive a solar flare and earthquake that
appears to have killed off most of the world's popula-
tion. Try hard to care – the lousy acting and poor
script don't make it easy.
Boa: story by Lewis John Carlino.
FAN                                 78 min mTV
B,V                                        IFS

## WHERE NO VULTURES FLY ***                 U
Harry Watt             UK               1951
*Anthony Steel, Dinah Sheridan, Harold Warrender,*
*William Simons, Meredith Edwards, Orlando*
*Martins, Philip Birkinshaw*
In East Africa the game warden responsible for
starting up the Mount Kilimanjaro National Park,
faces a threat to the wildlife in his care from ivory
poachers. An enjoyable outdoors adventure, done in
restrained semi-documentary style. WEST OF ZAN-
ZIBAR followed.
Aka: IVORY HUNTER
A/AD                             103 min (ort 107 min)
V                                          WHV

## WHERE THE BOYS ARE ***                   PG
Henry Levin            USA              1960
*Dolores Hart, George Hamilton, Yvette Mimieux, Jim*
*Hutton, Barbara Nichols, Paula Prentiss, Connie*
*Francis, Frank Gorshin, Chill Wills*

Story of four girls on holiday in Florida during Easter looking for sexual conquests. Fairly enjoyable light-hearted nonsense, with Connie Francis in her first film (she also gets to sing the title song). Look out for Nichols in a funny role as a flashy blonde. Written by George Wells and remade in 1984.
Boa: novel by Glendon Swarthout.

MUS                              95 min (ort 99 min)
B,V                              MGM; CH5 (VHS only)

### WHERE THE BOYS ARE '84 **                    15
Hy Averback              USA                    1984
*Lisa Hartman, Lorna Luft, Wendy Schaal, Lynn-Holly Johnson, Russell Todd, Howard McGillin, Louise Sorel, Alana Stewart*
Remake of a 1960 film about four girls on holiday in Ft. Lauderdale Florida and on the look-out for sexual adventure. This clumsy remake has little in common with its predecessor apart from the title.
Boa: novel by Glendon Swarthout.

COM                              91 min (ort 97 min)
B,V,V2                           PRV L/A; HER

### WHERE THE BUFFALO ROAM *                     18
Art Linson               USA                    1980
*Bill Murray, Peter Boyle, Bruno Kirby, Rene Auberjonois, R.G. Armstrong, Rafael Campos, Leonard Frey, Mark Metcalf, Craig T. Nelson*
A journalist who has to meet a deadline asks a lawyer for help in this dismal movie, inspired by the adventures of real-life journalist and writer Hunter S. Thompson. Written by John Kaye with music by Neil Young.

COM                              95 min
B,V                              CIC

### WHERE THE BULLETS FLY **
John Gilling             UK                     1966
*Tom Adams, Dawn Addams, Sidney James, Wilfrid Brambell, Joe Baker, Tim Barrett, Michael Ripper, Suzan Farmer, Heidi Erich, Julie Martin, Maggie Kimberley, Ronald Leigh-Hunt, John Arnott, Michael Ward, Garry Marsh*
Routine spy spoof with a secret agent preventing the Russians from getting their hands on a nuclear power unit, for use in aircraft. Fast-moving and occasionally funny but otherwise quite forgettable.

COM                              88 min (ort 90 min)
B,V                              ABV L/A; PORVI; MARKET

### WHERE THE EAGLE FLIES ***                    15
John Florea              USA                    1972
*Jack Albertson, Lesley Anne Warren, Martin Sheen, Michael Ontkean, George Chandler, Hay Baylor*
A gentle road movie involving a female college student, a drifter and a musician who hit the road in search of fun and adventure.
Aka: PICKUP ON 101

DRA                              85 min
B,V                              AMBAS

### WHERE THE RIVER RUNS BLACK **                PG
Christopher Cain         USA                    1986
*Charles Durning, Peter Horton, Conchata Ferrell, Ajay Najdu, Alessandro Rabelo, Castulo Guerra, Dana Delaney, Chico Diaz, Divana Brandao, Marcelo Rabelo, Ariel Coelho, Paul Sergio, Mario Borges, Francois Thijm*
An orphaned boy raised by river dolphins in the jungles of the Amazon, becomes committed to avenging the death of his "mother" at the hands of gold prospectors. Meanwhile, a well-meaning priest who knew his father is intent on bringing him back to civilisation. Filmed in Brazil, this slow-moving tale loses its way roughly halfway through, but is worth seeing if only for the beauty of the locations.

A/AD                             92 min
B,V                              MGM

### WHEREVER YOU ARE **                          18
Krzysztof Zanussi
              POLAND/UK/WEST GERMANY           1988
*Julian Sands, Renee Soutendijk*
The story of a young newly-married couple who arrive in Poland in 1938 looking forward to setting up home, little realising that the country is soon to be invaded by the Germans.

DRA                              100 min
B,V                              BRAVE

### WHILE THE CITY SLEEPS **
Fritz Lang               USA                    1956
*Dana Andrews, Ida Lupino, Rhonda Fleming, George Sanders, Vincent Price, John Drew Barrymore, Thomas Mitchell, Sally Forrest, Howard Duff, Robert Warwick, Mae Marsh, Ralph Peters, Sandy White, Larry Blake, Celia Lovsky*
A mad killer is hunted by both police and reporters, with three papers competing to be first with the scoop. Despite the many stars, the plodding pace of this melodrama is a major drawback. Written by Casey Robinson.
Boa: novel The Bloody Spur by Charles Einstein.

DRA                              100 min B/W
B,V                              KVD; ODY

### WHISKY GALORE ***                            PG
Alexander Mackendrick UK                        1948
*Basil Radford, Joan Greenwood, James Robertson Justice, Jean Cadell, Gordon Jackson, John Gregson, A.E. Matthews, Catherine Lacey, Bruce Seton, Wylie Watson, Gabrielle Blunt, Morland Graham, Henry Mollison, Gabrielle Blunt,*
Scottish islanders plot to get hold of a load of whisky from a ship, that has foundered on a small island in the Hebrides during WW2. A fast-paced and witty comedy that helped establish the reputation of Ealing studios. Written by Compton Mackenzie and Angus MacPhail, and followed in 1957 by "Mad Little Island".
Aka: TIGHT LITTLE ISLAND
Boa: novel by Compton Mackenzie.

COM                              81 min B/W
B,V                              TEVP; WHV

### WHISPER KILL **                              18
Christian I. Nyby II     USA                    1988
*Loni Anderson, Joe Penny, June Lockhart, James Sutorius, Jeremy Slate*
The story of a nasty serial killer who terrorises a small town, using the telephone to intimidate his intended victims. Standard, contrived unpleasantness.
Aka: WHISPER KILLS, A

THR                              90 min (ort 96 min) mTV
B,V                              CHV

### WHISPERING DEATH **                          18
Jurgen Goslar
              SOUTH AFRICA/WEST GERMANY        1979
*Christopher Lee, Sybil Danning (Sybelle Danninger), Trevor Howard, Horst Frank, James Faulkner, Sam Williams, Sascha Hein, Erik Schumann, Geoffrey Atkins, Josh Du Toit, Reggie Khangela, Harry Makela*
An albino leads a terrorist group in darkest Africa, who use magic to gain the support of the local population in their attacks on white settlers.
Aka: ALBINO; DEATH IN THE SUN; NIGHT OF THE ASKARI

HOR                              91 min Cut (1 min 2 sec)
B,V                              HER

### WHISTLE BLOWER, THE ***                      PG
Simon Langton            UK                     1986
*Michael Caine, Nigel Havers, John Gielgud, James Fox, Gordon Jackson, Barry Foster, Felicity Dean, Kenneth Colley, David Langton, Dinah Stabb, James*

Simmons, Andrew Hawkins, Trevor Cooper, Katherine Reeve, Bill Wallis
Caine is well-cast as a former intelligence officer, whose son was a highly talented linguist working for British Intelligence until he met an untimely end. Caine attempts to get at the truth behind his son's death and uncovers a sinister secret in the process. A fairly gripping thriller – the literate script is by Julian Bond.
Boa: bovel by John Hale.
THR                         100 min (ort 104 min)
B,V                                         NELS

## WHISTLE DOWN THE WIND ***
Bryan Forbes          UK              1961
Hayley Mills, Alan Bates, Bernard Lee, Norman Bird, Alan Barnes, Hamilton Dyce, Elsie Wagstaff, Diane Holgate, Diane Clare, Patricia Heneghan, Roy Holder
An escaped murderer hides out in a barn and is discovered by a group of kids who, because of his beard, take him to be Jesus. A sad, poignant and sometimes funny look at childhood innocence and fantasy. Written by Willis Hall and Keith Waterhouse, with music by Malcolm Arnold. This was the directorial debut of Forbes.
Boa: novel by Mary Hayley Bell.
DRA                        97 min (ort 99 min) B/W
B,V                                          RNK

## WHITE BUFFALO, THE **                    15
J. Lee Thompson        USA              1977
Charles Bronson, Jack Warden, Kim Novak, Will Sampson, Clint Walker, Stuart Whitman, Slim Pickens, Cara Williams, John Carradine, Shay Duffin, Douglas V. Fowley, Cliff Pellow, Ed Lauter, Martin Kove, Scott Walker, Ed Bakey
Wild Bill Hickok is disturbed by a vision of a strange white buffalo that symbolises his fear of death, in this strange moody tale set at the time of the Dakota Gold Rush. The opaque and allegorical imagery does little to help the story whose deficiencies soon become apparent. The script is by Richard Sale.
Aka: HUNT TO KILL
Boa: novel by Richard Sale.
WES                        97 min; 93 min (VCC)
B,V,V2                                 GHV; VCC

## WHITE CARGO FOR HONG KONG *            15
Helmut Ashley
          FRANCE/ITALY/WEST GERMANY    1964
Horst Frank, Mario Perschy, Dietmar Schoenheur, Dorothy Parker, Brad Harris, Philipe Lemaire
Standard Euro thriller set in Hong Kong and revolving around the perils of drug smuggling. Undistinguished and dull.
Aka: WEISSE FRACHT FUER HONG KONG; WHITE CARGO (VIC); WHITE CARGO FROM HONG KONG
THR                                       74 min
B,V                    DAV L/A; GOV L/A; STR L/A

## WHITE CHRISTMAS **                        U
Michael Curtiz         USA              1954
Bing Crosby, Danny Kaye, Rosemary Clooney, Dean Jagger, Vera-Ellen, Mary Wikes, Sig Ruman, Grady Sutton, John Brascia, Ann Whitfield, George Chakiris
Two ex-army buddies team up and go into show business, helping to boost the popularity of a winter resort run by their ex-officer. More or less a vehicle for some fine Irving Berlin numbers (and some forgettable ones too), this partial reworking of the 1942 film HOLIDAY INN could have done with a stronger story. Written by Norman Krasna, Norman Panama and Melvin Frank.
MUS                                      115 min
V                                            CIC

## WHITE COMANCHE ***
Gilbert Kay (Jose Briz)

ITALY                  1968
Joseph Cotten, William Shatner, Perli Cristal, Rossana Yanni
A sheriff has his hands full trying to stop two feuding half-breed brothers from murdering each other. Slightly better than the usual run of 1960s European Westerns, with Cotten and Shatner as the brothers, the latter seen in a dual role.
Aka: COMANCHO BLANCO
WES                                       98 min
B,V,V2                                       INT

## WHITE DOG **                             15
Samuel Fuller          USA              1982
Kristy McNichol, Paul Winfield, Burl Ives, Jameson Parker, Lynn Moody, Paul Bartel, Marshall Thompson, Dick Miller, Parley Baer
A young actress tries to get her dog retrained when she discovers that it has been trained to attack black people on sight. The subject of ludicrous charges of racism kept this film, essentially a study of animal behaviour, from being released after production. The script is by Curtis Hanson and Fuller, who appears briefly in a cameo as McNichol's agent.
Boa: novel by Romain Gary.
DRA                                       89 min
B,V                                          CIC

## WHITE FIRE **                            18
Jean-Marie Pallardy
          FRANCE/TURKEY/UK             1984
Robert Ginty, Fred Williamson, Mirella Banti, Belinda Mayne, Jess Hahn, Gordon Mitchell, Diana Goodwin
Standard adventure yarn about various people and their attempts to get hold of a world-famous diamond and smuggle it out of Istanbul.
Aka: VIVRE POUR SURVIVRE
A/AD                       87 min (ort 98 min)
B,V                                  VTC; XTASY

## WHITE FORCE *                            18
Eddie Romero           USA              1987
Sam Jones, Kimberley Pistone
An undercover agent is shadowing a drugs network in the Far East, when his partner is killed and he is accused of treachery. Teaming up with the man's daughter, he sets out to nail those responsible and clear his name.
A/AD                                      96 min
B,V                                          EMP

## WHITE GHOST **                           18
B.J. Lewis             USA              1987
William Katt, Rosalind Chao, Wayne Crawford, Martin Hewitt, Reb Brown
A man's decision to give up his solitary life in the jungle and return to civilisation brings him into conflict with an old enemy.
A/AD                   89 min (ort 93 min) Cut (18 sec)
B,V                                          VIR

## WHITE HEAT ****                          15
Raoul Walsh            USA              1949
James Cagney, Virginia Mayo, Edmond O'Brien, Margaret Wycherly, Fred Clark, Steve Cochran, John Archer
Immensely powerful story of a callous psychopath with a mother-fixation. Cagney is brilliant as the vicious hoodlum; this film marked his explosive return in a gangster role. O'Brien plays the undercover cop who infiltrates his gang leading to a dramatic final reckoning. A remarkable film that improves with repeated viewing. Written by Ivan Goff and Ben Roberts with music by Max Steiner. Computer-coloured versions are available.
Boa: story by Virginia Kellogg.
DRA                       109 min (ort 114 min) B/W
V                                            WHV

## WHITE HORSES OF SUMMER, THE ***   15
Raimondo Del Balzo     ITALY              1975
*Jean Seberg, Frederick Stafford, Renato Cestie,*
*Alberto Terracina*
An American couple with a young son take an Italian
vacation to try to patch up their shaky marriage, but
once there marital unfaithfulness threatens to split
them up for good. Unable to cope with his parents'
disharmony the boy retreats progressively into a
fantasy world of his own.
Aka: BIANCHI CAVALLI D'AGOSTO; WHITE
HOUSES IN AUGUST
DRA                                      89 min
B,V                                        VMA

## WHITE HOT *                           18
Michel Le Blanc     FRANCE               1982
*Olinka, Gabriel Pontello, Lisa Shine, Danny Berger,*
*Myka, Sarah Claudia*
A businessman enjoys a dirty weekend in the Alps
with his mistress while his wife and daughter indulge
in similar pursuits in a nearby chalet. As more guests
arrive at the chalets, sundry couplings take place and
the story, such as it is, gets lost in a welter of
love-making.
Aka: ALPINE ROMANCE; WHITE HEAT
A                     47 min (ort 76 min) Cut dubbed
B,V                                         AVR

## WHITE LIES **                          PG
Anson Williams     USA                    1989
*Ann Jillian, Tim Matheson*
On holiday in Rome, two Americans meet and fall
madly in love, but each has failed to tell the other
what they really do for a living, for the woman is a
police detective and the man a cardiologist. When the
former goes to the latter's hospital to follow up a case,
the expected complications arise.
Aka: LITTLE WHITE LIES
COM                                       91 min
V                                          NWV

## WHITE LIGHTNING **                     15
Joseph Sargent     USA                    1973
*Burt Reynolds, Jennifer Billingsley, Ned Beatty, Bo*
*Hopkins, Matt Clark, Louise Lathay, Diane Ladd, R.G.*
*Armstrong*
A moonshiner goes after the crooked sheriff who
drowned his brother. This lively actioner is helped
along by a good cast, but is as predictable in outcome
as it is contrived in development. Followed by GATOR
in 1976.
A/AD                            97 min (ort 101 min)
B,V                                        WHV

## WHITE LINE FEVER **                    15
Jonathan Kaplan     USA                   1975
*Jan-Michael Vincent, Kay Lenz, Slim Pickens, L.Q.*
*Jones, Leigh French, Don Porter, Sam Laws, Johnny*
*Ray McGhee, Martin Kove, Jamie Anderson, Ron Nix,*
*Dick Miller, Neils Summers, Bud Brown, Arnold*
*Jeffers, Swede Johnson*
A trucker fights corruption and wrongdoing, both on
the road and off it, using his diesel truck as a weapon.
Written by Ken Friedman and Kaplan and a good deal
better than one might have expected.
DRA                                       92 min
B,V                                        RCA

## WHITE LIONS, THE **                    15
Mel Stuart     USA                        1981
*Michael York, Glynnis O'Connor, Donald Moffat, J.A.*
*Preston, Roger E. Mosley*
Life on an African game reserve with naturalist York
and his family working to protect and study the
threatened wildlife. A simple story, similar to many
others but enjoyable for the outdoor locations.
JUV                                       96 min
B,V                                        GHV

## WHITE MISCHIEF ***                     18
Michael Radford     UK                    1987
*Sarah Miles, Joss Ackland, John Hurt, Greta Scacchi,*
*Alan Dobie, Hugh Grant, Gregor Fisher, Ray*
*McAnally, Charles Dance, Susan Fleetwood, Trevor*
*Howard, Murray Head, Geraldine Chaplin, Catherine*
*Neilson, Jacqueline Pearce*
The tale of a bunch of British ex-pats living gloriously
hedonistic lives out in Kenya during WW2. Based on
true events, this charts the response of a husband to
his wife's infidelity and the scandal that arose at the
time. An elegantly bizarre story made with great care
and patience but in many ways rather unmoving.
Boa: book by James Fox.
DRA                                      104 min
V/sh                                       RCA

## WHITE NIGHTS ***                       15
Taylor Hackford     USA                   1985
*Mikhail Baryshnikov, Gregory Hines, Isabella*
*Rossellini, Jerzy Skolimowski, Helen Mirren,*
*Geraldine Page, John Glover, Stefan Gryff, Shane*
*Rimmer, David Savile, Florence Faure, Ian Liston,*
*Benny Young, Hilary Drake*
A Russian ballet dancer who defected finds himself
home again after a flight he was on makes an
emergency landing. He now has to find a way of
escaping in an unbelievable film, that's only redeemed
by some good dance sequences and a Lionel Richie
score. Film director Skolimowski appears as the KGB
agent who hounds Baryshnikov, and as ever there is a
part for Mirren as a Russian. AA: Song ("Say You, Say
Me" – Lionel Richie).
DRA                                      131 min
V/sh                                       RCA

## WHITE OF THE EYE ***                   18
Donald Cammell     UK                     1986
*David Keith, Cathy Moriarty, Alan Rosenberg,*
*Michael Green, Art Evans, China Cammell, Alberta*
*Watson, Mark Hayashi, William Schilling, David*
*Chow, Danko Gurovich, Danielle Smith, Fred Allison,*
*Bob Zache, John Diehl*
David Keith plays an apparently normal and loving
husband and father who in reality is a murderous
psycho, responsible for the savage dismemberment of
four wealthy women in Arizona's Valley of the Sun.
With the police closing in the pressure begins to
mount and his hitherto unsuspecting wife is able to
see his true nature. This offbeat and bizarre thriller
displays a fine touch and uses several interesting
techniques.
Boa: novel Mrs White by Margaret Tracy.
THR                             107 min (ort 111 min)
B,V                                        WHV

## WHITE PHANTOM: ENEMY OF DARKNESS *   15
Dusty Nelson     HONG KONG                1987
*Bo Svenson, Jay Roberts Jr, Page Leong, Jimmy Lee,*
*H.F. Chiang, Kathy McClure*
Some Ninja villains hijack a load of plutonium and
Svenson is sent after them to sort this difficulty out.
The muddled and disjointed plot seems to take forever
to unfold, and by the time it does one doesn't care
anymore.
Aka: WHITE PHANTOM
A/AD                            89 min Cut (42 sec)
B,V                                        MED

## WHITE STAR *                           18
Roland Kirk     USA                       1988
*Dennis Hopper, Terrance Robay, Ramona Sweeney,*
*David Hess*
A pop singer is exploited by his totally unscrupulous
manager, who hatches a number of disreputable
schemes to make him into a star. A sleazy and violent
tale that's generally unappealing.
THR                                       89 min
B,V                                        RCA

**WHITE TOWER, THE** ***
Ted Tetzlaff             USA              1950
*Glenn Ford, Alida Valli, Lloyd Bridges, Claude Rains,*
*Oscar Homolka, Cedric Hardwicke, June Clayworth,*
*Lotte Stein, Fred Essler, Edit Angold*
A motley collection of people climb a peak in the Swiss
Alps, risking their lives for a variety of reasons.
Heavy-going at times but ultimately worthwhile.
Written by Paul Jarrico.
Boa: novel by James Ramsay Ullman.
Osca: VALLEY OF THE SUN
DRA                                       94 min
B,V                                       KVD

**WHITE WATER SAM** **                        15
Keith Larsen           USA              1978
*Keith Larsen, Lorne Greene (narration)*
Routine epic of one man's survival in the wilderness
as he faces the hostile elements and Indians in the
great North-West. Standard outdoors adventure yarn
from writer/producer/director/star Larsen.
Aka: RUN OR BURN
A/AD                                      84 min
B,V                                VPD L/A; RCA

**WHITE WATER SUMMER** ***                     15
Jeff Bleckner          USA              1985
                                (released in 1987)
*Kevin Bacon, Sean Astin, Jonathan Ward, Matt Adler,*
*K.C. Martel, Caroline McWilliams, Charles Siebert*
Simple tale of an experienced and rather ruthless
wilderness guide who turns a bunch of city-kids into
men. Though they have suffered abuse from him as
part of their training, they find themselves placed in a
dilemma when he is injured and needs their help.
A/AD                                      86 min
B,V                                       RCA

**WHO DARES WINS** *                           18
Ian Sharp              UK               1982
*Lewis Collins, Judy Davis, Ingrid Pitt, Edward*
*Woodward, Richard Widmark, Robert Webber,*
*Kenneth Griffith, Tony Doyle, John Duttine, Rosalind*
*Lloyd, Norman Rodway, Maurice Reeves, Bob*
*Sherman, Albert Fortell, Mark Ryan*
Flat and dull account of how a lone SAS man foils a
terrorist plot to take over the American Embassy.
Undoubtedly inspired by the real-life incident when
the Iranian Embassy in London was taken over by
terrorists, this singularly inept piece of film-making is
almost embarrassing to watch. Look out for Widmark,
he had third billing but if you blink you might miss
him.
Aka: FINAL OPTION, THE
DRA                          120 min (ort 125 min)
V                                         RNK

**WHO FINDS A FRIEND FINDS A**            PG
**TREASURE** **
Sergio Corbucci        ITALY            1979
*Bud Spencer (Carlo Pedersoli), Terence Hill (Mario*
*Girotti), John Fujoka*
Another Spencer and Hill comedy with our inept duo
off treasure-hunting in the South Seas, but coming up
against opposition from assorted villains and
Japanese warriors still fighting WW2.
Aka: CHI TROUA UN AMICO TROUA UN TESORO;
WHO FINDS A FRIEND
COM                                      102 min
V                                         RCA

**WHO FRAMED ROGER RABBIT?** ****        PG
Robert Zemeckis        USA              1988
*Bob Hoskins, Christopher Lloyd, Joanna Cassidy,*
*Stubby Kaye, Alan Tilvern, Richard Le Parmentier,*
*Joel Silver. Voices of: Charles Fleischer, Lou Hirsch,*
*Mel Blanc, Mac Questel, Tony Anselmo, June Foray,*
*Wayne Allwine,*
This incredible mixture of live-action and animation

has Hoskins as a seedy detective investigating a
murder, with chief suspect Roger Rabbit along to help.
The weak story is forgotten in the face of the superb
animation, most especially the part where Hoskins
ventures into "Toontown". AA: Edit (Arthur Schmidt),
Effects (Aud) (Charles L. Campbell/Louis L. Ede-
mann), Effects (Vis) (Ken Ralston/Richard Williams/
Edward Jones/George Gibbs).
Boa: novel Who Censored Roger Rabbit by Gary K.
Wolf.
FAN                                      105 min
V                                       TOUCH

**WHO GETS THE FRIENDS?** ***            PG
Lila Garrett           USA              1988
*Jill Clayburgh, James Farentino, Lucie Arnaz, Leigh*
*Taylor-Young, Robin Thomas, James Sloyan, Greg*
*Mullavey*
A bitter-sweet comedy, that follows the changes in a
couple's relationship with their circle of friends after
they get divorced. Touches of despair are wrapped up
neatly in a happy, candyfloss ending. Scripted by
Garrett and Sandy Krinski.
COM                    90 min (ort 96 min) mTV
B,V                                       CBS

**WHO IS JULIA?** ***                    PG
Walter Grauman         USA              1986
*Mare Winningham, Jameson Parker, Jeffrey DeMunn,*
*Jonathan Banks, Bert Remsen, Mason Adams, James*
*Handy, Philip Baker Hall, Tracy Brooks Swope, Judy*
*Ledford, Ford Rainey, Joel Colodner, Bruce French,*
*Clare Nono*
Following a car crash, the brain of a beautiful model is
transplanted into the body of a plain housewife. Not as
silly as it sounds, this literate tale of double identity is
given credibility by the acting of Winningham in a
dual role.
Boa: novel by Barbara S. Harris.
DRA                               120 min mTV
B,V                                       CBS

**WHO MISLAID MY WIFE?** *               18
Ugo Tognazzi           ITALY            1976
*Ugo Tognazzi, Edwige French, Paolo Bonacelli, Orazio*
*Orlando, Luc Merenda, Massimo Serato*
When a man's wife is unfaithful suspicion falls on four
characters: a skier, a playboy, a business partner and
a brother.
Aka: CATTIVI PENSIERI; EVIL THOUGHTS
A                                        101 min
B,V                                       VPD

**WHO SLEW AUNTIE ROO?** ***
Curtis Harrington      UK/USA          1971
*Shelley Winters, Mark Lester, Chloe Franks, Ralph*
*Richardson, Hugh Griffith, Lionel Jeffries, Judy*
*Cornwell, Michael Gothard, Rosalie Crutchley,*
*Richard Beaumont, Pat Heywood, Jacqueline Cowper,*
*Charlotte Sayce*
An old woman takes in orphans but all is not quite as
it appears in this updated telling of the Hansel and
Gretel tale. An unpleasantly ghoulish horror yarn,
with Winters excellent as the demented murderess
who lures Lester and Franks into her clutches. Made
in England.
Aka: GINGERBREAD HOUSE; WHOEVER SLEW
AUNTIE ROO?
HOR                                       91 min
B,V                                       RNK

**WHO WILL LOVE MY CHILDREN?** ***       PG
John Ehrman            USA              1983
*Ann-Margret, Frederic Forrest, Cathryn Damon,*
*Donald Moffat, Lonny Chapman, Patricia Smith, Jess*
*Osuna, Christopher Allport, Patrick Brennan, Soleil*
*Moon Frye, Tracey Gold, Joel Graves, Rachel Jacobs,*
*Robbie Kiger*
A woman with only a year to live tries to find loving

homes for her ten children. Based on the true story of farm wife Lucille Fray, who finding that she had terminal cancer, tried to find homes for her children rather than leaving them to the care of her alcoholic husband. Written by Michael Bortman, this literate and moving film won ten Emmy awards. This was the TV film debut for Ann-Margret.

DRA                                    96 min mTV
B,V,V2                              VSP L/A; APX

## WHO WILL SAVE OUR CHILDREN? ***
George Schaefer           USA                  1978
Shirley Jones, Len Cariou, Cassie Yates, David Hayward, Conchata Ferrell, Frances Sternhagen, Lee Ann Mitchell, David Schott, Jordan Charney, Franz Russell, Stephen E. Miller, Janet Wright, Dale Wilson, Anna Hagan

A childless couple become foster parents to a couple of children who have been abandoned by their parents. Having cared for them for some time, they attempt to legally adopt them, but the natural parents now sue for custody. A well-made drama with an exceptionally strong cast.
Aka: WHO'LL SAVE OUR CHILDREN?
Boa: novel The Orchard Children by Rachel Maddox.
DRA                        92 min (ort 100 min) mTV
B,V                                     CAP/CBS

## WHODUNNIT? *
Bill Nauld                USA                  1982
Marie Alise, Rick Dean, Ron Gardner, Terry Goodman, Richard Helm, Jeanine Marie, Gary Phillips, Red McVay, Steven Tash, Bari Suber, Michael Stroka, Jim Williams

A female rock singer answers an advert and gets a part in a porno film on a remote island, but once there she finds that the actors are being murdered one by one.
Aka: ISLAND OF BLOOD
THR                                       83 min
B,V                                          EIV

## WHO'LL STOP THE RAIN? **                          18
Carl Reiss (Karel Reisz)
                          UK/USA                1978
Nick Nolte, Tuesday Weld, Michael Moriarty, Anthony Zerbe, Richard Masur, Ray Sharkey, David Opatoshu, Gail Strickland

A news correspondent gets involved in smuggling heroin from Vietnam to California. Written by Judith Roscoe and well-acted throughout, but let down by bland and unconvincing direction.
Aka: DOG SOLDIERS
Boa: novel Dog Soldiers by Robert Stone.
DRA                        121 min (ort 125 min)
B,V                                         WHV

## WHOLLY MOSES! **                                 15
Gary Weis                 USA                  1980
Dudley Moore, Laraine Newman, James Coco, Paul Sand, Jack Gilford, Richard Pryor, Dom DeLuise, John Houseman, Madeline Kahn, David L. Lander, John Ritter

A man suffers from the delusion that he is Moses and must lead the Jews out of Egypt. Written by Guy Thomas, this stale and tedious comedy attempts to poke fun at all those Hollywood biblical epics but never really comes off. Look out for Dom DeLuise, one of the film's few compensating features.
COM                                       99 min
V                                           RCA

## WHOOPEE BOYS, THE **                             15
John Byrum                USA                  1986
Michael O'Keefe, Paul Rodriguez, Lucinda Jenny, Denholm Elliott, Carole Shelley, Andy Bumantai, Eddie Deezen, Marsha Warfield, Joe Spinell, Dan O'Herlihy
Two down and out New Yorkers decide to seek

adventure and fortune in the ritzy city of Palm Beach, Florida, and attempt to save a school for needy children in the process. Stand-up comic Rodriguez teams up with O'Keefe in an unrelentingly foul-mouthed and tedious comedy.
COM                                       87 min
B,V                                          CIC

## WHOOPS APOCALYPSE **                             15
Tom Bussman               USA                  1986
Loretta Swit, Peter Cook, Michael Richards, Rik Mayall, Ian Richardson, Alexei Sayle, Herbert Lom, Joanne Pearce, Christopher Malcolm, Shane Rimmer, Ian McNeice, Daniel Benzali, Richard Wilson, Richard Pearson, Marc Smith

Based on a popular TV series, this satire follows the events leading up to a nuclear conflict and though fun is very occasionally made of the Russians, most of the barbs are reserved for British and American institutions. Quite amusing in places, but undeniably partisan.
COM                      88 min (Cut at film release)
B,V                                          VIR

## WHOOPS APOCALYPSE ***                            15
John Reardon              UK                    1982
John Barron, John Cleese, Richard Griffiths, Barry Morse, Alexei Sayle, Ed Bishop, Bruce Montague, David Kelley, Peter Jones, Charles Kay, Richard Davies, Geoffrey Palmer, Christopher Malcolm, Christopher Mincke, Ron Cook

Re-edited version of the satirical TV series, that chronicles the funny set of mishaps that result in WW3. Done in the form of spoof news reports detailing the events leading up to war, with highlights being a series of interviews with world leaders. Somewhat overlong, but good fun – the plot largely revolving around the theft of an American nuclear bomb.
Aka: MUSHROOM BUTTON, THE
COM                                   137 min mTV
B,V                           PVG; CH5 (VHS only)

## WHO'S AFRAID OF VIRGINIA WOOLF? ****            15
Mike Nichols              USA                  1966
Richard Burton, Elizabeth Taylor, George Segal, Sandy Dennis

Two couples engage in a complex session of all-night conversation that leads to much bitterness and recrimination. Burton and Taylor were never better together than in this utterly absorbing but ultimately depressing film. Written and produced by Ernest Lehman this was Nichols' first film as director. AA: Actress (Taylor), S. Actress (Dennis), Cin (Haskell Wexler), Art/Set (Richard Sylbert/George James Hopkins), Cost (Irene Sharaff).
Boa: play by Edward Albee.
DRA                                  129 min B/W
B,V                                         WHV

## WHO'S HARRY CRUMB? **                            PG
Paul Flaherty             USA                  1989
John Candy, Jeffrey Jones, Annie Potts, Tim Thomerson, Barry Corbin, Shawnee Smith, Valri Bromfield, Renee Coleman, Joe Flaherty, Lyle Alzado, James Belushi, Stephen Young

The story of a pompous and accident-prone private detective, who tries to solve a kidnapping case, in the face of opposition from his boss. With but a few funny moments, this creaky and empty-headed comedy wastes the talents of Candy on a plot that is more foolish than it is amusing.
COM                              87 min (ort 98 min)
V                                           RCA

## WHO'S THAT GIRL *                                PG
James Foley               USA                  1987
Madonna (Madonna Ciccone), Griffin Dunne, John Miles, Haviland Morris, John McMartin, Bibi Besch, Robert Swan, Drew Pillsbury, Coat Mundi, Jim Dietz,

*Dennis Birkley, Cecile Callan, Karen Baldwin,*
*Kimberlin Brown*
This trite and tiresome attempt at a screwball comedy
has Dunne being assigned to escort Madonna (who has
just been sprung from jail) out of town, and finding his
life turned upside down in the process. A film that
tries so hard one might award it points for effort, were
it not so unremittingly unfunny.
Aka: SLAMMER
COM        88 min (Cut at film release by 1 min 43 sec)
V/sh                                                  WHV

### WHOSE LIFE IS IT, ANYWAY? ***                    15
John Badham            USA                          1981
*Richard Dreyfuss, John Cassavetes, Christine Lahti,*
*Bob Balaban, Kenneth McMillan, Kaki Hunter,*
*Thomas Carter, George Wyner*
A disabled man argues for his right to decide to end
his own life, after he has become totally paralysed
following a car crash. Based on Clark's hit play, this
has Dreyfuss turning in an excellent performance,
ably supported by a fine cast. Written by Brian Clark
and Reginald Rose.
Boa: play by Brian Clark.
DRA                                              114 min
V                                                    MGM

### WHY DID YOU PICK ON ME? *                         PG
Michele Lupo           ITALY                        1981
*Bud Spencer (Carlo Pedersoli), Cary Guffey, Raimund*
*Harmstorf, Ferrucio Amendola, John Bartha, Robert*
*Hundar*
A sequel to THE SHERIFF AND THE SATELLITE
KID, with our space visitor being pursued by soldiers
who want to use him for secret experiments.
Aka: CHISSA PERCHE CAPITANO TUTTO A ME
COM               87 min (ort 90 min) Cut (9 sec)
B,V,V2                                               MED

### WHY DIDN'T THEY ASK EVANS? ***                    PG
John Davies/Tony Wharmby
                       UK                           1979
*Francesca Annis, Eric Porter, Leigh Lawson, James*
*Warwick, Madeleine Smith, Connie Booth, Robert*
*Longden, Joan Hickson, John Gielgud, Bernard Miles,*
*Doris Hare*
Two golfers find a dying man who appears to have
fallen off a cliff. One of them, a doctor, goes for help
leaving his companion alone with the man who utters
the title remark just before expiring. This intriguing
start to a highly convoluted mystery leads into a
well-crafted and highly enjoyable adaptation of
Christie's novel.
Boa: novel The Boomerang Clue by Agatha Christie.
DRA                                          144 min mTV
V                                                    MSD

### WHY NOT STAY FOR BREAKFAST? **
Terence Marcel         UK                           1978
*George Chakiris, Gemma Craven, Yvonne Wilder, Ray*
*Charleson, David Baxt, Carintha West, Vic Gallucci,*
*Baby Dale, Ted Shapiro, Herbert Leith Jr, Frank*
*Severino, Maggie Solomon, Tony Echevarria, Deborah*
*Dangerfield*
A divorced postal clerk becomes involved with a young
pregnant girl in New York, and provides her with
accommodation so that she can have her baby.
Screenplay is by Cooney and Terence Martel.
Boa: play by Gene Stone and Ray Cooney.
COM                                               95 min
B,V                                                  HVH

### WHY SHOOT THE TEACHER? ***                        PG
Silvio Narizzano       CANADA                       1977
*Bud Cort, Samantha Eggar, Chris Wiggins, Gary*
*Reineke, John Friesen, Michael J. Reynolds, Kenneth*
*Griffith, Scott Swan, Merrilyn Gann, Norma West,*
*Joanne McNeal, Margery Hill, George Gwin, Doug*
*Blake, Alan Stebbings, Joe Yasinsky*

An account of a young teacher who takes up a new
teaching post in a small rural Canadian community
during the Depression years. Written by James
DeFilice, this is a good-natured work of some warmth.
Boa: novel by Max Braithwaite.
DRA                                              101 min
B,V                                                  RNK

### WHY WOULD ANYONE WANT TO KILL A
### NICE GIRL LIKE YOU? **
Don Sharp              UK                           1968
*Eva Renzi, David Buck, Peter Vaughan, Paul*
*Hubschmid, Sophie Hardy, Kay Walsh*
A girl on holiday in the French Riviera reports a
man's murder to the police and claims that her own
life is in danger, but the police will not believe her.
Straightforward thriller yarn done in an unimagina-
tive and cliched way.
THR                                               99 min
B,V,V2                                                INT

### WHY WOULD I LIE? *                                15
Larry Peerce           USA                          1980
*Treat Williams, Lisa Eichhorn, Gabriel Swann, Susan*
*Heldfond, Anne Byrne, Valerie Curtin, Jocelyn*
*Brando, Nicolas Coster, Severn Darden*
An unpleasant and charmless dud that has Williams
as a social worker who is also a compulsive liar,
attempting to re-unite a hateful feminist with her
estranged ex-con mother, whilst all the while giving
vent to his half-baked views on life.
Aka: WHY SHOULD I LIE?
Boa: novel The Fabricator by H. Hodges.
COM                                              105 min
B,V                                                  MGM

### WICKED LADY, THE **                               18
Michael Winner         UK                           1983
*Faye Dunaway, Alan Bates, John Gielgud, Denholm*
*Elliott, Prunella Scales, Oliver Tobias, Jane Purcell,*
*Glynis Barber, Joan Hockson, Helena McCarthy,*
*Millie Maureen, Derek Francis, Nicholas Geeks, Hugh*
*Millais, John Savident*
Remake of the 1945 film about a lady highway robber
updated with nudity and violence. Intended to be a
costumed romp but lacking the style or wit to carry it
off, this has Dunaway camping up her role as the
wicked Lady Skelton, who robs the rich for the sheer
fun of it, in the over-acting experience of the decade.
The photography is by Jack Cardiff.
Boa: novel The Life And Death Of The Wicked Lady
Skeleton by Magdalen King-Hall.
A/AD              94 min (ort 99 min) Cut (13 sec)
B,V,V2                                     GHV L/A; VCC

### WICKED STEPMOTHER *                               PG
Larry Cohen            USA                          1989
*Barbara Carrera, Colleen Camp, Lionel Stander,*
*David Rasche, Bette Davis, Tom Bosley, Richard Moll*
An old woman with evil powers moves in with a
family and causes havoc in this lame horror spoof.
Reputedly intended to be a straight horror yarn, but a
disagreement between Davis and writer-producer
Cohen led to her replacement with Carrera and an
extensively re-written script. But this film is a mess,
and almost certainly would have been anyway. Davis'
final film.
COM                                               91 min
V                                                    MGM

### WICKER MAN, THE ****
Robin Hardy            UK                           1973
*Edward Woodward, Britt Ekland, Christopher Lee,*
*Ingrid Pitt, Diane Cilento, Lindsay Kemp, Ian*
*Campbell, Aubrey Morris, Russell Waters, Walter*
*Carr, Irene Carr, Irene Sunters, Geraldine Cowper,*
*Jennifer Martin, Roy Boyd*
A detective investigating the disappearance of a child
on a remote Scottish island is slowly drawn into a web

of intrigue by the inhabitants, who are worshippers of a strange and sinister cult. The original 103 minute version was believed lost, but still survives together with a 95 minute reconstruction made in 1980 by Hardy. This bizarre and erotic horror film has a strong script by Anthony Shaffer.

HOR          83 min (ort 103 min – available MHE or MAGNUM)
B,V                    TEVP; MHE; MAGNUM

## WIDOWS **                                      15
Ian Tonyton          UK                    1983
*Fiona Hendley, Maureen O'Farrell, Eva Mottley, Ann Mitchell, David Calder, Paul Jesson, Maurice O'Connell, Stanley Meadows*
Three widows of criminals killed while pulling off a job, decide to carry out what was to have been the gang's next robbery themselves, using the notes left behind by their leader. More clever than appealing, this unusual heist tale was sustained by good performances if not by a believable script. A sequel followed in 1985. Originally shown in seven 52-minute episodes.
DRA       288 min (ort 364 min) (2 cassettes) mTV
B,V                                        THAMES

## WIFE SWAPPERS, THE **                          18
Derek Ford           UK                    1970
*James Donnelly, Larry Taylor, Valerie St John, Denys Hawthorne, Bunty Garland, Sandra Satcl.with, Fiona Fraser, Joan Hayward*
A film masquerading as a documentary on the title subject and consisting of an episodic series of dramatisations of supposed case histories. Dull.
Aka: WIFE SWAPPER
A              82 min (ort 86 min) Cut (37 sec)
B,V                    MOV L/A; PHV L/A; SHEP

## WIFE/MISTRESS **                               18
Marco Vicario        ITALY                 1977
*Marcello Mastroianni, Laura Antonelli, Leonard Mann, Annie-Belle, Gastone Moschin, William Berger*
A woman discovers her husband's secret life after he goes into hiding. Set in Italy at the turn of the century, this is an untidy blend of comedy and drama – sometimes sensual but more often opaque.
Aka: MOGLIAMENTE
DRA 101 min (ort 110 min) (dubbed version available)
B,V                                          WHV

## WILBY CONSPIRACY, THE ***                      15
Ralph Nelson         USA                   1975
*Sidney Poitier, Michael Caine, Nicol Williamson, Persis Khambatta, Prunella Gee, Saeed Jaffrey, Rutger Hauer, Joseph De Graf, Ryk De Gooyer, Brian Epsom, Patrick Allen, Archie Duncan, Helmut Dantine*
A black African nationalist escapes across country with a white companion. Political thriller with action sequences, written by Rod Amateau and Harold Rosenthal and representing a version of sorts of Poitier's earlier film, THE DEFIANT ONES.
Boa: novel by Peter Driscoll.
DRA                                     101 min
B,V                                          WHV

## WILD AND THE FREE, THE ***                      U
James Hill           USA                   1980
*Granville Van Dusen, Linda Gray, Frank Logan, Ray Forchion, Sharon Anderson, Bill Gribble, Joan Murphy, Bruce McLaughlin, Fred Buch, Walter Zukowski, Jack McDermott, Shelly Spurlock, Kevan North, Sean Cunningham, Teddy Milford*
A group of chimps that have been raised in captivity are taken to Africa to be released into the wild by two scientists, who join forces to prevent them being used by the government in radiation research. A comical adventure tale filmed on location in Tampa, Florida and made by producer Paul Radin and director Hill,

who previously worked together on BORN FREE.
Boa: story by Michael Berk, Douglas Schwartz and Jack Couffer.
A/AD            92 min (ort 100 min) mTV
B,V                    PRV; CH5 (VHS only)

## WILD ANGELS, THE **
Roger Corman         USA                   1966
*Peter Fonda, Nancy Sinatra, Bruce Dern, Lou Procopio, Michael J. Pollard, Diane Ladd, Gayle Hunnicutt, Coby Denton, Marc Cavell, Buck Taylor, Norman Alden*
Story of a nasty motorbike gang and their escapades that predates the far more stylish EASY RIDER and has none of that later film's wit or charm. A film of considerable unpleasantness that was the subject of much work on the part of Peter Bogdanovich, who was responsible for a good deal of the writing and editing, and even turns up briefly in one of the fights.
DRA             83 min (ort 124 min) Cut
B,V,V2                                       GHV

## WILD AT HEART ***                              18
David Lynch          USA                   1990
*Nicolas Cage, Laura Dern, Willem Dafoe, Crispin Glover, Diane Ladd, Isabella Rossellini, Harry Dean Stanton*
Writer-director Lynch brings his own inimitable style to this adaptation of Gifford's offbeat novel. Newly released from prison after killing a man in a brawl, Cage takes off with a free-spirit Dern, hotly pursued by the mother's lover and a vicious hit-man she has hired. As they travel to New Orleans, they meet a succession of weirdos and misfits. A bizarre, violent and patchy film, but certainly unforgettable. It won the Palme d'Or at Cannes in 1990.
Boa: novel by Barry Gifford.
A/AD                                    120 min
V/sh                                         PAL

## WILD BUNCH, THE ***                            18
Sam Peckinpah        USA
             1969 (re-released in 1981 at 142 min)
*William Holden, Ernest Borgnine, Robert Ryan, Edmond O'Brien, Warren Oates, Ben Johnson, Jaime Sanchez, Strother Martin, L.Q. Jones, Emilio Fernandez, Albert Dekker, Bo Hopkins, Dub Taylor, Jorge Russek, Alfonso Arau*
A group of outlaws who realise that they are becoming an anachronism as the world is changing, decide to pull off one last robbery in 1913. An extremely violent film whose ending puts one in mind of an abattoir, all concerned getting shot to pieces and blood spraying out everywhere in true Peckinpah style. Made with infinite care and written by Peckinpah and Walon Green, this brutal actioner is a classic of sorts.
WES              135 min (ort 142 min)
V                                            WHV

## WILD COUNTRY, THE ***                           U
Robert Totten        USA                   1971
*Steve Forrest, Vera Miles, Ron Howard, Jack Elam, Frank DeKova, Morgan Woodward, Clint Howard, Dub Taylor, Woodrow Chambliss, Karl Swenson, Mills Watson*
The story of a family moving West to Wyoming in the 1880s and facing hardships as they settle on a ranch. A simple enjoyable tale set off by some splendid scenery. Written by Paul Savage and Calvin Clements Jr.
Boa: novel Little Britches by Ralph Moody.
WES              87 min (ort 100 min)
B,V                                          WDV

## WILD GEESE, THE ***                            15
Andrew V. McLaglen   UK                    1978
*Richard Burton, Roger Moore, Richard Harris, Hardy Kruger, Stewart Granger, Jack Watson, Winston Ntshona, Ronald Fraser, Frank Finlay, Kenneth*

*Griffith, Jeff Corey, Barry Foster, Patrick Allen, John Kani, Ian Yule, Brook Williams*
Action adventure yarn with a bunch of mercenaries being assembled, and trained for a mission to rescue a kidnapped African leader. The pace of the first half, in which our intrepid team are being trained, soon gives way to more plodding direction, as the implausible story quickly runs down. Not bad but definitely not great. Written by Reginald Rose with the first sequel following in 1985.
Boa: novel by Daniel Carney.
A/AD                           129 min (ort 134 min)
V                                          RNK

## WILD GEESE 2 *                                18
Peter Hunt                USA              1985
*Scott Glenn, Barbara Carrera, Edward Fox, Laurence Olivier, Robert Webber, Robert Freitag, Kenneth Haigh, Stratford Johns, Derek Thompson, Paul Antrim, John Terry, Ingrid Pitt, Patrick Stewart, Michael Harbour, David Lumsden*
In this sequel to the original our mercenaries set out on another mission, this time to spring Hess from Spandau Prison. A foolish and unbelievable film, burdened by a messy and disjointed script. A definite dud.
Boa: novel The Square Circle by Daniel Carney.
A/AD                           120 min (ort 125 min)
B,V                            TEVP L/A; CAN

## WILD HEART, THE ***                            PG
Michael Powell/Emeric Pressburger
                          UK               1950
*Jennifer Jones, David Farrar, Cyril Cusack, Sybil Thorndike, Edward Chapman, Esmond Knight, George Cole, Hugh Griffith, Beatrice Varley, Frances Clare, Raymond Rollett, Gerald C. Lawson, Valentine Dunn*
A 19th Century country romance, with a superstitious girl marrying a local minister whilst all the while being desired by the squire. Set in Victorian times with Jones well-cast as the wild and strange Shropshire lass. The beautiful photography is by Christopher Challis. Re-edited from an original and superior 110 minute version, which had extra scenes directed by Robert Mamoulian, and was first released in the UK under its alternative title.
Aka: GONE TO EARTH
Boa: novel by Mary Webb.
DRA                            82 min (ort 110 min)
B,V                                        GHV

## WILD HORSES **                                 PG
Derek Morton    NEW ZEALAND                1983
*Kevin J. Wilson, Keith Aberdain, John Bach, Bruno Lawrence, Robyn Gibbes, Kathy Rawlings, Tom Poata, Marshall Napier, Michael Haigh, Martyn Sanderson*
Violence erupts when wild horse-tamers come into conflict with commercial deer farmers in a national park.
A/AD                     85 min (ort 93 min) Cut (1 sec)
B,V                                        CBS

## WILD HORSES ***                                PG
Dick Lowry                USA              1985
*Kenny Rogers, Pam Dawber, Ben Johnson, David Andrews, Richard Masur, Karen Carlson, Richard Farnsworth, Richard Hamilton, Jack Rader, Ritch Brinkley, Buck Taylor, Kelly Yunkerman, Cathy Worthington, R.W. Hampton, Brian Rogers*
The lure of his former profession proves too strong for an ex-rodeo star to resist. He abandons his family to ride again. An enjoyable and competent piece carried along by Rogers' charm (and singing). Ex-rodeo wranglers Johnson and Farnsworth add a measure of colour.
DRA                            90 min (ort 100 min) mTV
B,V                            GHV; VCC (VHS only)

## WILD LIFE, THE **                              18
Art Linson                USA              1984
*Eric Stoltz, Christopher Penn, Lea Thompson, Rick Moranis, Randy Quaid, Hart Bochner, Jenny Wright, Ilan Mitchell-Smith*
Stoltz as an 18-year-old grows up and finds his expectations not being fulfilled. He leaves home to take up residence in an apartment for singles. A pale imitation of FAST TIMES AT RIDGEMOUNT HIGH (which had the same writer and producer) but with none of the earlier film's appeal or honesty.
COM                   91 min (ort 96 min) Cut (1 min 7 sec)
B,V                                        CIC

## WILD LITTLE BUNCH, THE **
David Hemmings           UK                1972
*Jack Wild, June Brown, John Bailey, Keith Buckley, Cheryl Hall*
When their mother dies a family of 14 kids have to fend for themselves in the east end of London. The oldest child tries everthing to keep the family together.
Aka: EXISTENCE; FOURTEEN, THE
DRA                                        86 min
B,V,V2                                     GHV; IFS

## WILD ONE, THE ***                              PG
Laslo Benedek            USA               1954
*Marlon Brando, Lee Marvin, Mary Murphy, Robert Keith, Jay C. Flippen, Jerry Paris, Alvy Moore, Gil Stratton*
A powerful performance from Brando as a motorbike gangleader terrorising a small town, helps keep this grand-daddy of all biker films from looking too dated. Produced by Stanley Kramer with a script by John Paxton.
DRA                                        76 min B/W
V                                          RCA

## WILD ORCHID *                                  18
Zalman King              USA               1990
*Mickey Rourke, Carre Otis, Jacqueline Bisset, Bruce Greenwood, Assumpta Serna*
A beautiful law graduate is hired by a major brokerage firm and goes to Rio de Janeiro to assist experienced lawyer Bisset. When the latter is called away she takes her place for a meeting with a wealthy businessman. She is soon embroiled in a strange, one-sided relationship with Rourke, an aloof weirdo who speaks in dull cliches and combines attention with indifference. An over-hyped film that's as short on plot as it is on eroticism.
DRA                                        107 min
V                                          EIV

## WILD PAIR, THE **                              18
Beau Bridges             USA               1987
*Beau Bridges, Bubba Smith, LLoyd Bridges, Gary Lockwood, Danny De La Paz, Raymond St Jacques, Lela Rochon, Ellen Geer*
Bridges' first theatrical film as director, is a highly forgettable little tale of a cop and FBI agent teaming up to bring some nasty drug dealers to justice. Disappointing in just about every area.
A/AD                                       92 min
B,V                                        EIV

## WILD PARTY, THE **
James Ivory              USA               1974
*James Coco, Raquel Welch, Perry King, Tiffany Bolling, David Dukes, Royal Dano, Dena Dietrich*
A comedian in Hollywood of the 1920s tries to save his failing reputation by throwing a party, in this uneven and disjointed homage to Hollywood of the 1920s. The film's strongest points are in its performances and casting (Coco's comedian is modelled on Fatty Arbuckle), but the lack of any clear direction is a serious handicap. Cut by the distributor on release, it was later restored to 107 minutes by Ivory.

Boa: narrative poem by Joseph Moncure March.
DRA                          88 min (ort 107 min)
B,V                                          RNK

**WILD ROVERS ✱✱**                             15
Blake Edwards          USA               1971
*Ryan O'Neal, William Holden, Karl Malden, Lynn*
*Carlin, Tom Skerritt, Joe Don Baker, James Olson,*
*Leora Dana, Moses Gunn, Victor French, Rachel*
*Roberts, Charles Gray, Sam Gilman, William Bryant,*
*Jack Garner, Caitlin Wyles*
Two bored cowboys rob a bank on the spur of the
moment for fun, but are then forced to make a run for
it when they find themselves being pursued by a
relentless posse. The uneven script hinders the de-
velopment of a good idea but the music by Jerry
Goldsmith is a definite plus. Written and directed by
Edwards.
WES                         105 min (ort 138 min)
B,V                                          MGM

**WILD STALLION, THE ✱✱**
Kevin Sullivan         USA               1983
*Art Hindle, Josh Byrne, Kelsey McLeod, Murray Ord,*
*Paul Jolicoeur, Marilyn Lightstone*
After his father is killed in a quarrel with a neigh-
bour, the son becomes obsessed with a wild stallion.
Aka: WILD PONY, THE
DRA                                       84 min
B,V                                      CBS; KRP

**WILD STRAWBERRIES ✱✱✱✱**                      15
Ingmar Bergman      SWEDEN               1957
*Victor Sjostrom, Ingrid Thulin, Bibi Andersson,*
*Gunnar Bjornstrand, Folke Sundquist, Bjorn*
*Bjelvenstam, Naima Wifstrand, Gertrud Fridh, Ake*
*Fridell, Gunnel Brostrom, Gunnar Sjoberg, Per*
*Sjostrand, Sif Ruud, Yngve Nordwall*
An ageing professor reviews the past tragedies of his
rather empty life on a car journey to receive an
honorary degree at his old university. This sharp and
poignant look at life is not quite as bleak as it sounds,
and is regarded by many as being one of the director's
more joyful films. The script is by Bergman.
Aka: SMULTRONSTALLET
DRA                                   93 min B/W
B,V                                          VCC

**WILD STYLE ✱✱**
Charlie Ahearn         USA               1982
*"Lee" Quinones, Sandra "Pink" Fabara, Fred*
*Brathwaite, Patti Astor, Busy Bee, Grand Master*
*Flash, Cold Crush Brothers, Rock Steady Crew,*
*Electric Force, Charlie Ahearn*
A musical view of New York life with breakdancing,
aerosol graffiti, rapping etc. as a South Bronx graffiti
artist tries to both preserve his principles and realise
his ambitions.
MUS                                       82 min
B,V                                21ST; INT; PYRAM

**WILD THING ✱✱**                               15
Max Reid               USA               1987
*Rob Knepper, Kathleen Quinlan, Robert Davi, Maury*
*Chaykin, Betty Buckley, Gillaume Lemay-Thivierge,*
*Robert Bedarski, Clark Johnson, Sean Hewitt, Teddy*
*Abner, Cree Summer Francks, Shawn Levy, Rod*
*Torchia, Christine Jones*
A kind of urban variation on the Tarzan theme, with a
boy whose parents were murdered growing up wild on
the streets, and swinging down from tower blocks as
he protects the public from the depradations of
criminals. Badly scripted and directed, this untidy
effort has "Wild Thing" by The Troggs as its theme
tune; one of the better things in it.
A/AD                                      88 min
B,V                                          EIV

**WILD TIMES ✱✱✱**                              PG
Richard Compton        USA               1980
*Sam Elliott, Cameron Mitchell, Penny Peyser, Ben*
*Johnson, Bruce Boxleitner, Dennis Hopper, Harry*
*Carey Jr, Timothy Scott, Trish Stewart, Gene Evans,*
*Leif Erickson, Pat Hingle, L.Q. Jones, Buck Taylor,*
*Geno Silva, Sheryl Brown*
This star-studded biopic looks at the life of Hugh
Cardiff; famed marksman, buffalo hunter and Wild
West show organiser. A literate adaptation of the
Garfield book that was originally shown in two parts
but was shortened for its second run.
Boa: story by Brian Garfield.
WES                         179 min (ort 200 min) mTV
V                                            GHV

**WILD WOMEN ✱✱**
Don Taylor             USA               1970
*Hugh O'Brian, Anne Francis, Marilyn Maxwell, Marie*
*Windsor, Sherry Jackson, Cynthia Hall, Robert F.*
*Simon, Richard Kelton, Pepe Callahan, Ed Call, John*
*Neris, Lois Bridge, Troy Melton, Joseph Kaufman,*
*Chuck Hicks, Jim Boles*
US Army engineers on a delicate operation to map
trails in Texas, near the Mexican border in the 1840s,
travel disguised as a wagon train of settlers complete
with a contingent of "wives" from federal prisons. A
bland mixture of comedy and adventure that never
amounts to anything of substance.
Boa: novel The Trailmakers by Vincent Fotre.
WES                         73 min (ort 90 min) mTV
B,V                                          RNK

**WILD YOUTH ✱**                                15
Nick Foskos            USA               1985
*Dennis Anthony, John Constantine*
A street gangleader attempts to re-assert his author-
ity after a spell in prison but finds that another gang
member has other ideas.
DRA                                       75 min
B,V                              VIDLNE/ECF; GLOB

**WILDCAT ✱✱**
Don Taylor             USA               1976
*Lee Marvin, Oliver Reed, Elizabeth Ashley, Robert*
*Culp, Howard Platt, Kay Lenz, Strother Martin, Sylvia*
*Miles, Leticia Robles, Erika Carlson, Ana Verdugo*
A comedy Western set in Colorado in 1908, with an old
cowboy out to have his revenge on a former partner,
who absconded with the money from their gold strike,
and has become a respected citizen. Whilst setting out
to ruin his ex-partner our cowboy falls for a prostitute.
A few knockabout moments fail to dispel the general
tedium.
Aka: GREAT SCOUT AND CATHOUSE
THURSDAY, THE
COM                                      102 min
B,V                                      RNK; VES

**WILDCATS ✱✱✱**                                15
Michael Ritchie        USA               1986
*Goldie Hawn, James Keach, Swoosie Kurtz, Robyn*
*Lively, Brandy Gold, Jan Hooks, Bruce McGill, M.*
*Emmet Walsh, Nipsey Russell, Tab Thacker*
A woman P.E. teacher becomes coach to a football
team at a rough inner-city high school, thereby
fulfilling a long cherished dream of following in her
father's footsteps. Routine formula comedy with Hawn
gurgling and cooing her way through a film that's OK
for easy laughs but instantly forgettable.
COM                                      102 min
B,V                                          WHV

**WILDCATS OF ST TRINIANS, THE ✱**
Frank Launder          UK                1980
*Sheila Hancock, Michael Hordern, Rodney Bewes,*
*Maureen Lipman, Joe Melia, Thorley Walters, Julia*
*McKenzie, Veronica Quilligan, Deborah Norton, Rose*
*Hill, Luan Peters, Ambrosine Philpotts, Bernardette*

*O'Farrell, Barbara Hicks*
Another of these painfully unfunny comedies about an unruly girl's school, that started with THE BELLES OF ST TRINIANS. Each film in the series was less funny than the last, and all epitomised everything that's wrong with British cinema, namely: NO NEW IDEAS. In this tale, the girls form a union and abduct the daughter of an Arab prince. Written by Launder.
COM                                    92 min
B,V                                  HVH L/A

## WILDE'S DOMAIN *                     U
Charles Tingwell   AUSTRALIA          198-
*Kit Taylor, June Salter, Martin Vaughn*
The visit of a Russian ballet company to an Australian community triggers off opposition from the locals.
DRA                                    73 min
B,V                                     PRV

## WILL ANY GENTLEMAN . . .? **         U
Michael Anderson      UK              1953
*George Cole, Veronica Hurst, Jon Pertwee, Heather Thatcher, James Hayter, William Hartnell, Diana Decker, Joan Sims, Alan Badel*
Hypnosis turns a meek bank clerk into a philanderer, in this adequate adaptation of the successful stage play. The script is by Sylvaine.
Boa: play by Vernon Sylvaine.
COM                       80 min (ort 84 min)
V                                       WHV

## WILL OF EBENEZER GRIMSDYKE, THE *    18
Peter Kay              UK              1989
A lecherous old man gathers the children of his dead brother together at his palatial home and reveals details of his sordid past, and they slowly become aware of the fact that they have been made the unconscious participants in a set of debauched acts. Very dull.
A                        53 min Cut (1 min 4 sec)
V                                       SFI

## WILL THERE REALLY BE A MORNING? ***
Fielder Cook          USA             1983
*Susan Blakely, Lee Grant, Royal Dano, Joe Lambie, John Heard, Melanie Mayron, Leonard Cimino, Jack Creely, James Eckhouse, Jeanne Elias, Joseph Maher, Bruce Ornstein, Paul Perri, Madeleine Thornton-Sherwood, Ivor Francis*
Biopic on the tragic life of Hollywood actress Frances Farmer, that's a good deal closer to the truth than the film FRANCES. Adapted by Dalene Young from Farmer's autobiography, it traces her life from childhood in Seattle through college, and to her success and ultimate mental breakdown.
Boa: book by Frances Farmer.
DRA                    136 min (ort 150 min) mTV
B,V                                     RNK

## WILLA ***
Joan Darling/Claudio Guzman
                       USA            1979
*Deborah Raffin, Clu Gulager, Cloris Leachman, Diane Ladd, John Amos, Nancy Marchand, Mary Wickes, Bob Seagren, John Amos, Hank Williams Jr, Freddye Chapman, Gary Bisig, Gary Grubbs, Corey Feldman, Megan Jeffers, Four Scott*
A truck-stop waitress embarks on a new career as a trucker, driving her late father's rig after her husband abandons both her and her children. A few good moments in a pretty average offering.
DRA                    92 min (ort 100 min) mTV
B,V                                     HOK

## WILLARD ***
Daniel Mann           USA             1971
*Bruce Davison, Elsa Lanchester, Ernest Borgnine, Sondra Locke, Joan Shawlee, Michael Dante, J. Pat O'Malley, Jody Gilbert, Almira Sessions, Alan Baxter,*

*William Hansen, Pauline Drake, John Myhers, Helen Spring, Paul Bradley*
A withdrawn boy who can only relate to his pet rats, finds that he is able to train them to attack those who have incurred his wrath. Despite the fine work of animal-trainer Moe De Sesso, this thriller fails to really develop. Written by Gilbert Ralston and followed by "Ben".
Boa: novel Ratman's Notebook by Stephen Gilbert.
THR                                    95 min
B,V                                  BWV; IFS

## WILLIE AND PHIL ***                  18
Paul Mazursky         USA             1980
*Michael Ontkean, Margot Kidder, Ray Sharkey, Jan Miner, Tom Brennan, Julie Bovasso, Natalie Wood, Louis Guss, Kathleen Maguire, Kaki Hunter*
An examination of a love triangle over several years between two men and a woman. This American version of the 1961 film "Jules And Jim" has Ontkean and Sharkey meeting up after the screening of that classic, and becoming friends and lovers of Kidder. Perceptive and honest but for all that a trifle overlong. Written and directed by Mazursky.
DRA                                    115 min
B,V                                     CBS

## WILLIES, THE **                      15
Brian Peck            USA             1989
*James Karen, Sean Astin, Kathleen Freeman, Jeremy Miller*
A young boy's desire to be rid of his teachers and a gang of school bullies becomes a reality in an unexpected and horrible way.
HOR                                    90 min
V                                       BCB

## WILLOW ***                           PG
Ron Howard            USA             1988
*Val Kilmer, Joanne Whalley, Warwick Davis, Jean Marsh, Patricia Hayes, Billy Barty, Pat Roach, Gavan O'Herlihy*
Fantasy-adventure based on a George Lucas story, with an elf-like creature undertaking the task of taking an abandoned baby to its place of destiny, where it is to destroy the powers of evil. A high-spirited and exciting romp with numerous special effects and a fine performance from Marsh as the evil Queen Bavmorda.
FAN                    121 min (ort 125 min)
V                                       RCA

## WILLY MILLY ***                      15
Paul Schneider        USA             1986
*Pamela Segall, Eric Gurry, Patty Duke Astin, John Glover, Mary Tanner, Seth Green, Jeb Ellis-Brown, John David Callum*
A young girl who is of the opinion that boys have more fun, has her dearest wish granted when she utters an ancient spell during a rare solar eclipse. A light-hearted and pleasing comedy-fantasy with a spirited performance from Segall.
Aka: I WAS A TEENAGE BOY; SOMETHING SPECIAL
COM                    83 min (CBS); 90 min
B,V                                  CBS; MED

## WILLY WONKA AND THE                  U
## CHOCOLATE FACTORY **
Mel Stuart            USA             1971
*Gene Wilder, Jack Albertson, Peter Ostrum, Aubrey Woods, Michael Bollner, Roy Kinnear, Ursula Reit, Leonard Stone, Julie Dawn Cole, Denise Nickerson, Paris Themmen, Dodo Denny, Diana Sowle, David Battley*
Clever but only slightly amusing tale of the owner of a fabulous sweet factory who runs a competition the winners of which get to visit his premises. A nasty edge to this fantasy and the variable quality songs (by

Leslie Bricusse and Anthony Newley) spoil what might have been a most pleasing story. The script is by Dahl from his children's story.
Boa: novel Charlie And The Chocolate Factory by Roald Dahl.

| JUV | | 96 min |
| B,V | | WHV |

**WILT ***    15
Michael Tuchner    UK    1988
*Griff Rhys Jones, Mel Smith, A..son Steadman, Diana Quick*
Sharpe's satirical novel of black humour and zest is reduced to yet another failed British farce, that revolves around the pathetic figure of a liberal arts teacher who becomes suspected of having murdered his over-bearing wife when she mysteriously disappears. Given the comic possibilities of the novel, to see it made into such a dreary and woodenly directed failure is a major disappointment.
Boa: novel Henry Wilt by Tom Sharpe.

| COM | | 92 min |
| V | | GHV |

**WIMPS ***    18
Chuck Vincent    USA    1986
*Louie Bonnano, Deborah Blaisdell, Jim Abele, Jane Hamilton, Eddie Prevot, Derrick R. Roberts, Philip Campanaro, Michael Heintzman, Douglas Gibson, Edward K. Mallia, Steven Shaw, Jeanne Marie*
The weedy son of a football star tries to get into the same fraternity house his dad was in, and ends up helping the college's star quarterback woo a brainy sorority girl. A simple-minded college-comedy – and not an especially well-handled one.

| COM | | 90 min |
| B,V | | VES |

**WINCHESTER '73 *****    U
Anthony Mann    USA    1950
*James Stewart, Shelley Winters, Stephen McNally, Dan Duryea, Charles Drake, Millard Mitchell, John McIntire, Will Geer, J.C. Flippen, Rock Hudson, John Alexander, Steve Brodie, James Millican, Abner Biberman, Tony Curtis*
A cowboy wins a prize winchester rifle in a competition in Dodge City in 1873, only to have it stolen by the man who murdered his father. He embarks on a chase after the culprit that culminates in a shoot-out among the hills. A memorable Western that is beautifully photographed by William Daniels and scripted by Robert L. Richards and Borden Chase.
Boa: story by Stuart N. Lake.

| WES | | 82 min (ort 92 min) |
| V | | CIC |

**WIND IN THE WILLOWS, THE ***    Uc
1988
Competent animation based on the characters created by Kenneth Grahame, and following their exploits and adventures as they try to save Mr Toad from his own foolishness.
Boa: novel by Kenneth Grahame.

| CAR | | 49 min |
| V | | PARK |

**WIND IN THE WILLOWS, THE ***    U
Arthur Rankin Jr/Jules Bass
JAPAN/USA    1983
*Voices of: Charles Nelson Reilly, Roddy McDowall, Jose Ferrer, Paul Frees, Eddie Bracken, Robert McFadden, Ray Owens, Gerry Matthews, Ron Marshall, Alice Tweedie, Jeryl Jagoda*
An animated version of this children's classic, that introduces Grahame's famous characters and follows them on some of their better known exploits.
Boa: novel by Kenneth Grahame.

| CAR | 92 min; 78 min (VCC) (ort 97 min) mTV |
| B,V | POLY; CH5 (VHS only); VCC |

**WIND IN THE WILLOWS, THE ***    U
John Salway    198-
Yet another animated version of this tale that attempts to follow more closely, the events portrayed in Grahame's famous classic.
Boa: novel by Kenneth Grahame.

| CAR | | 236 min (2 cassettes) |
| B,V | | GHV |

**WIND IN THE WILLOWS, THE ****    U
Brian Cosgrave/Mark Hall
UK    1983
*Voices of: Ian Carmichael, Michael Horden, David Jason, Richard Pearson, Beryl Reid, Una Stubbs, Jonathan Cecil*
A lively puppet animation of this classic story, told with considerable zest.
Boa: novel by Kenneth Grahame.

| JUV | | 75 min; 78 min (VCC) |
| B,V | | TEVP; VCC |

**WINDMILLS OF THE GODS:**
**PARTS 1 AND 2 ***    PG
Lee Philips    USA    1987
*Robert Wagner, Jaclyn Smith, Christopher Cazenove, Jean-Pierre Aumont, Ruby Dee, Michael Moriarty, Jeffrey de Munn, Avi Meyers, John Standing, Susan Tyrell, J.T. Walsh, Dick Olsen, Franco Nero, Lisa Pelikan, Ian McKellen*
International adventure-thriller telling of a lady ambassador who finds that she is the target of assassins. The John Gay script weaves a tangled and somewhat unbelievable web of intrigue around what is in fact a rather pedestrian story.
Boa: novel by Sidney Sheldon.

| THR | 179 min (ort 200 min) mTV |
| B,V | CBS |

**WINDOWS ***    18
Gordon Willis    USA    1980
*Talia Shire, Elisabeth Ashley, Joseph Cortese, Kay Medford, Michael Gorrin, Russell Horton*
A rape victim finds herself in danger once more, but from an unexpected quarter when she becomes friends with her new neighbour, unaware that the woman is a homicidal lesbian. The directorial debut for Willis, this is a glum and disappointing first offering from a gifted cameraman.

| DRA | 88 min Cut (2 min 16 sec) |
| B,V | WHV |

**WINDRIDER ***    15
Vincent Monton    AUSTRALIA    1985
*Tom Burlinson, Nicole Kidman, Jill Perryman, Charles Tingwell, Simon Chilvers*
Although he is heir to an engineering empire, a man's only real interest is in board-sailing, and he has to fight against the odds when he encounters a series of setbacks at work, in his sport and in his love life all at the same time. May appeal to surfing fans but holds little interest for others.
Aka: MAKING WAVES

| DRA | | 88 min |
| B,V | | VES |

**WINDS OF JARRAH, THE ****    PG
Mark Egerton    AUSTRALIA    1983
*Susan Lyons, Terence Donovan, Emil Minty, Harold Hopkins, Steve Bisley, Martin Vaughn*
A love story set in post-WW2 Australia with a woman arriving to be the governess to a planter's three unruly children and finding that their father's frosty exterior hides his growing affection for her. A warm and meticulously detailed romantic drama.
Boa: novel The House In The Timberlands by Joyce Dingwall.

| DRA | | 78 min |
| B,V | | VSP L/A; CBS |

## WINDS OF KITTY HAWK, THE ***
E.W. Swackhamer          USA          1978
*Michael Moriarty, David Huffman, Tom Bower,*
*Eugene Roche, Scott Hylands, John Randolph, Robin*
*Gammell, Kathryn Walker, John Hoyt, Ari Zeltzer,*
*Lew Brown, Carole Tru Foster, Mo Malone, Dabbs*
*Greer, Ross Durfee, Robert Casper*
Dramatisation of the efforts of the Wright brothers, to
be the first to build a heavier-than-air flying machine.
At its very best when detailing their flying attempts,
this talky and stilted drama rapidly gets bogged down
once it's back on the ground.
DRA                              98 min mTV
B,V                                  HER

## WINDS OF WAR, THE: VOLUMES 1 TO 5 ***  PG
Dan Curtis          USA          1983
*Robert Mitchum, Ali McGraw, Jan-Michael Vincent,*
*John Houseman, Polly Bergen, Lisa Eilbacher, David*
*Dukes, Topol, Ben Murphy, Peter Graves, Jeremy*
*Kemp, Ralph Bellamy, Victoria Tennant*
An expensive, handsome and incredibly detailed
drama following the fortunes of a family at the time of
Hitler's rise to power and the Japanese Pearl Harbour
attack. Originally shown in eight 96-minute episodes,
the main story revolves around an American naval
officer (Mitchum) who finds himself taking part in
high-level discussions on the eve of WW2. Despite its
lack of depth and some tedious sub-plots, this remains
an effective and absorbing work.
Boa: novel by Herman Wouk.
DRA                    458 min (5 cassettes) mTV
V/h                                  CIC

## WINGS OF DESIRE ****  PG
Wim Wenders
              FRANCE/WEST GERMANY          1987
*Bruno Ganz, Solveig Dommartin, Otto Sander, Curt*
*Bois, Peter Falk*
Wenders' follow-up to PARIS, TEXAS tells of two
angels who wander West Berlin, observing and com-
forting humanity. When one of them tires of his role,
he slowly re-enters the world of mortals and his
monochrome view of life (for angels do not see in
colour) takes on human attributes. Scripted by Wenders and Peter Handke, this haunting and lyrical
fantasy was inspired by the poetry of Rainer Maria
Rilke. Photography is by Henri Alekan.
FAN          123 min (ort 130 min) Colour and B/W
V                                  CONNO

## WINGS OF THE APACHE ***  15
David Green          USA          1989
*Nicolas Cage, Tommy Lee Jones, Sean Young, Bryan*
*Kestner*
British director Green makes his Hollywood debut in
this helicopter-based adventure that inevitably reminds one think of TOP GUN. Having been nearly
shot down while on a anti-drugs reconnaissance
mission in Latin America, Cage gets to train in an
outfit of crack pilots put together by the Pentagon to
ensure the defeat of the drug barons. A fairly mindless
blend of action and occasional romantic interludes, yet
put together with considerable zest.
A/AD                              89 min
V                                  MED

## WINNERS AND LOSERS **  15
              UK          1989
*Leslie Grantham*
The story of a boxing promoter who travels to Glasgow
in order to sign up a promising young boxer, but
discovers that other parties are interested in him as
well.
DRA                              149 min mTV
V                                  TELS

## WINNERS AND SINNERS **  15
Samo Hung          HONG KONG          198-

*Jackie Chan*
When a group of former prisoners set up a cleaning
company, they inadvertently come into conflict with a
counterfeiting gang who have been using one of the
buildings they were hired to clean.
MAR                              102 min
B,V                                  VPD

## WINNERS TAKE ALL **  15
Fritze Kiersch          USA          1987
*Don Michael Paul, Kathleen York, Robert Krantz,*
*Deborah Richter, Brock Glover, Peter DeLuise, Marc*
*Price, Courtney Gains, Tony Longo*
Enjoyable film set in the dangerous world of motorcy-
cle supercross, where two young men become both
rivals and comrades, eventually competing in a
grudge race when they fall out over a girl.
Aka: SUPERCROSS
A/AD                              102 min
B,V                                  RCA

## WINNING ***  PG
James Goldstone          USA          1969
*Paul Newman, Joanne Woodward, Robert Wagner,*
*Richard Thomas, David Sheiner, Clu Gulager, Robert*
*Quarry, Bobby Unser*
A racing driver marries but finds his relationship with
his wife being put under strain when he hits a losing
streak. Above average.
DRA                              123 min
B,V                                  CIC

## WINNING STREAK *  PG
Jim Wilson          USA          1984
*Andra Millian, Kevin Connors*
A girl with a knack for gambling, teams up with an
experienced card-sharp to take on the casinos.
DRA                              94 min
B,V                    VDM L/A; VMA; STABL

## WINSLOW BOY, THE ***
Anthony Asquith          UK          1948
*Robert Donat, Cedric Hardwicke, Margaret Leighton,*
*Frank Lawton, Neil North, Jack Watling, Francis L.*
*Sullivan, Basil Radford, Walter Fitzgerald, Marie*
*Lohr, Wilfrid Hyde-White, Kynaston Reeves, Ernest*
*Thesiger, Lewis Casson*
A courtroom drama based on a real incident, where a
young naval cadet was expelled for the theft of a
postal order from one of his fellow cadets. His family
battled for years to clear his name, the case becoming
something of a cause celebre of the time. Written by
Terence Rattigan and Anatole De Grunwald with
music by William Alwyn.
Boa: play by Terence Rattigan.
DRA              112 min (ort 117 min) B/W
B,V                                  RNK

## WINTER COMES EARLY **
Geirge McCowan          CANADA          1977
*Trudy Young, Art Hindle, Frank Moore, John Vernon,*
*Austin Willis, Vivian Reis, Sean Sullivan, Weston*
*Gavin, Steve Pernie, Kay Hawtrey, George Armstrong,*
*Derek Sanderson, Bruce Armstrong, Eric Cryderman,*
*Don Allen*
A hockey player falls for a rock singer but their
conflicting lifestyles and unwillingness to compromise
puts their relationship under great strain.
DRA                              85 min
B,V,V2                                INT L/A

## WINTER KILLS ***  18
William Richert          USA          1979
                        (re-released in 1983)
*Jeff Bridges, John Huston, Anthony Perkins, Sterling*
*Hayden, Eli Wallach, Richard Boone, Toshiro Mifune,*
*Elizabeth Taylor, Belinda Bauer, Brad Dexter, Ralph*
*Meeker, Dorothy Malone, Thomas Milian, Peter*
*Brandon, Michael Thomas*

The younger brother of an assassinated US President tries to discover who was responsible, and comes up against a complex web of intrigue. A flop in 1979, it was re-edited and re-released in 1983 with an original ending restored and is now generally appreciated as a black comedy. Patchy and confusing but worth a look.
Boa: novel by Richard Condon.

| DRA | 97 min |
| B,V,V2 | CBS; CH5 (VHS only) |

## WINTER OF OUR DISCONTENT, THE ** PG
Waris Hussein   USA   1983
*Donald Sutherland, Teri Garr, Tuesday Weld, Michael Gazzo, Richard Masur, E.G. Marshall*
An honourable middle-class man compromises his principles in order to regain lost social standing. Badly adapted by Michael De Guzman from Steinbeck's last novel, this confused and disjointed effort does little with a good cast.
Boa: novel by John Steinbeck.

| DRA | 100 min mTV |
| B,V | POLY |

## WINTER OF OUR DREAMS ** 15
John Duigan   AUSTRALIA   1981
*Judy Davis, Bryan Brown, Cathy Downes, Baz Luhrmann, Peter Mochrie, Mervyn Drake*
A lonely female prostitute with a drug habit meets a bookshop-owner who is unhappily married, and the two become romantically involved. An interesting drama that moves along somewhat fitfully, with an unsatisfying and confused ending.

| DRA | 90 min |
| B,V | SPEC/POLY |

## WINTER PEOPLE **
Ted Kotcheff   USA   1989
*Kurt Russell, Kelly McGillis, Lloyd Bridges, Mitchell Ryan, Amelia Burnette, Eileen Ryan, Jeffrey Meek*
During the Depression, clockmaker Russell leaves his hometown in search of work and arrives at an Appalachian town, where he falls for single mother McGillis and inadvertently sparks off a feud between rival families. McGillis is excellent in this overheated and underplotted romantic drama, and contrives to sustain a film that is given no support by its weak script.
Boa: novel by John Ehle.

| DRA | 110 min |
| V | VES |

## WINTER'S TALE, THE **** PG
Jane Howell   UK   1981
*Jeremy Kemp, Anna Calder-Marshall, John Welsh, David Burke, Robert Stephens, Jeremy Dimmick, Merelina Kendall, Susan Brodrick, Leonard Kavanagh, John Bailey, Cyril Luckham, William Relton, Margaret Tyzack, John Benfield*
An excellent television production of this play, easily one of the best adaptations produced by the BBC.
Boa: play by William Shakespeare.

| DRA | 117 min mTV |
| V/h | BBC |

## WIRED * 18
Larry Peerce   USA   1989
*Michael Chiklis, Ray Sharkey, J.T. Walsh, Patti D'Arbanville, Lucinda Jenney, Alex Rocco, Gary Groomes, Jere Burns, Billy Preston*
Loosely based on Woodward's bestseller, this ill-conceived film purports to examine the life of John Belushi, offering us a cautionary tale of his self-destructive urges and death from a drugs overdose at 33. After his untimely death Chiklis (who does look a little like Belushi) is escorted through his past by an angel/taxi driver, but the film fabricates as much as it examines and this tasteless fantasy is neither funny nor instructive.
Boa: book by Bob Woodward.

| DRA | 104 min (ort 108 min) |
| V | EIV |

## WISDOM ** 18
Emilio Estevez   USA   1986
*Emilio Estevez, Demi Moore, Tom Skerritt, Veronica Cartwright, William Allen Young, Richard Minchenberg, Ernie Brown*
A young man who has recently graduated is unable to obtain work because of a past felony. Frustration drives him and his girlfriend into committing a series of bank robberies across the country, destroying the records of loans and mortgages as a way of helping debt-ridden farmers. First-time director Estevez was assisted by Robert Wise, but even so, this remains a shallow and unappealing effort.

| A/AD | 105 min (ort 109 min) |
| V/sh | WHV |

## WISE BLOOD *** 15
John Huston   USA   1979
*Harry Dean Stanton, Brad Dourif, Ned Beatty, Daniel Shor, John Huston, Amy Wright, Mary Nell Santacroce*
Uneven, offbeat and semi-comic tale of a moody young man, whose obsessive dislike of religion drives him to attempt to found a church without Christ. Various individuals exploit his beliefs for their own ends. The music is by Alex North.
Boa: novel by Flannery O'Connor.

| COM | 102 min |
| B,V | CIC |

## WISE GUYS ** 15
Brian De Palma   USA   1986
*Danny DeVito, Joe Piscopo, Harvey Keitel, Ray Sharkey, Dan Hedaya, Captain Lou Albamo, Julie Bovasso, Patti LuPone*
Two losers who work for a small-time crook attempt to steal his money, but in revenge he sets them up to kill each other. A lame black comedy that is largely sustained by the comic talents of DeVito.

| COM | 89 min |
| B,V | MGM |

## WISEGUY ** 15
Rod Holcomb   USA   1987
*Ken Wahl, Ray Sharkey, Jonathan Banks, Jim Byrnes*
An undercover cop infiltrates the Mob and befriends a top Mafia man, soon becoming one of his most trusted associates. A competent gangster thriller.

| THR | 95 min |
| B,V | EIV |

## WISH YOU WERE HERE *** 15
David Leland   UK   1987
*Emily Lloyd, Tom Bell, Jesse Birdsall, Geoffrey Durham, Clare Clifford, Barbara Durkin, Geoffrey Hutchings, Charlotte Barker, Chloe Leland, Pat Heywood, Charlotte Ball*
Inspired by the early life of celebrated brothel-keeper Cynthia Payne, this is a bittersweet tale of a young girl's sexual maturing set against the austere back-drop of post-war Britain. A good debut as director for Leland, who also wrote the screenplay for PERSONAL SERVICES.

| COM | 92 min |
| V/h | PAL |

## WITCH BITCH ** 18
Michael Fischa   USA   1988
*William Bumiller, Brenda Blake, Shari Shuttuck, Merritt Butrick*
A slick horror tale with a supernatural flavour, telling of a health club that is the scene for a number of grisly deaths, all caused by the equipment used there. It turns out that the equipment is all controlled by a computer, and this has become haunted by the ghost

of the owner's wife. An effective chiller with a predictable outcome.
Aka: DEATH SPA
HOR 87 min (ort 90 min)
B,V WATER; COL

## WITCH STORY *** 18
Alessandro Capone 1989
*Ian Bannen, Christopher Peacock*
A woman burnt at the stake as a witch many years ago cursed the village of those responsible and all their descendants. Sixty years later a bunch of teenagers arrive there for a holiday, and our dead witch has her opportunity to wreak a gruesome vengeance, with only an insane, defrocked priest able to link the two events. A well-constructed and effective tale.
HOR 93 min
V MED

## WITCHBOARD *** 15
Kevin S. Tenney USA 1986
*Tawny Kitaen, Todd Allen, Stephen Nichols, Kathleen Wilhoite, Rose Marie, Burke Byrnes, James W. Quinn, Judy Tatum, Gloria Hayes, J.P. Luebsen, Susan Nickerson, Ryan Carroll, Kenny Rhodes, Clare Bristol*
A trio of friends are having fun playing with a ouija board when they succeed in contacting the spirit of a young boy. However, their troubles really begin when they contact the spirit of an evil turn-of-the-century mass murderer, who takes over one of their bodies with the intention of finding fresh victims.
HOR 94 min (ort 97 min)
V GHV

## WITCHCRAFT ** 18
Robert Spera USA 1988
*Gary Sloan, Lee Kisman, Anat Topol-Barzilla, Deborah Scott*
A pregnant woman and her husband are burnt at the stake by an enraged mob who are convinced they are Satanists. Some 300 years later their spirits return to have their revenge. The slow script allows time for tension to build up in this satisfactory chiller. A sequel followed.
HOR 85 min (ort 90 min)
B,V CHV

## WITCHCRAFT 2 * 18
Mark Woods USA 1989
*Delia Sheppard, Charles Solomon, Mia Ruiz*
When Satan learns that his "heir" has been abducted, he despatches a beautiful but totally ruthless servant to find him. A disappointing effort that takes an interesting idea and does little with it.
Aka: WITCHCRAFT PART 2: THE TEMPTRESS
HOR 90 min
V BOX

## WITCHES, THE *** PG
Nicolas Roeg USA 1989
*Anjelica Huston, Mai Zetterling, Jasen Fisher, Charlie Potter, Rowan Atkinson, Bill Paterson, Brenda Blethyn, Jane Horrocks, Jenny Runacre, Rosamund Greenwood*
Thanks to his granny, a 9-year-old boy knows a witch when he sees one, and on a trip to London he stumbles on a convention of them, and overhears their dastardly plans to change all of the country's children into mice. This delightful collaboration between Roeg and Muppets-creator Jim Henson (who produced) is a spooky tale of excellent scripting and superb effects. Intended for children but perhaps a touch more scary than it need have been.
Boa: novel by Roald Dahl.
FAN 88 min (ort 92 min) subH
V/sh WHV

## WITCHES OF EASTWICK, THE *** 18
George Miller USA 1987
*Jack Nicholson, Cher, Susan Sarandon, Michelle Pfeiffer, Richard Jenkins, Veronica Cartwright, Keith Joachim, Carel Struycken, Helen Lloyd Breed, Caroline Struzik, Michele Savage, Heather Coleman, Carolyn Ditmars*
Three bored and sex-starved ladies living in a New England town get together with the intention of bringing some male company into their lives, but find that they have unwittingly conjured up the Devil in the shape of the town's newest arrival. This lively and inventive fantasy has a terrific part for Nicholson and is sustained throughout by fine performances, despite often veering wildly between comedy and horror. The score is by John Williams.
Boa: novel by John Updike.
COM 114 min (ort 118 min)
V/sh WHV

## WITCHFINDER GENERAL *** 18
Michael Reeves UK 1968
*Vincent Price, Ian Ogilvy, Rupert Davies, Patrick Wymark, Wilfrid Brambell, Robert Russell, Nicky Henson, Hilary Dwyer, Tony Selby, Michael Beint, Peter Haigh*
A superior horror film about a vindictive witch-hunter living at the time of Cromwell, who is not averse to using torture in order to extract confessions. Price as Matthew Hopkins is excellent in this atmospheric period film set in 1645. The script is by Reeves and Tim Baker.
Aka: CONQUEROR WORM, THE
Boa: novel by Ronald Bassett.
HOR 81 min (ort 87 min) (Cut at film release)
B,V,V2 HOK L/A; TAR

## WITCHING TIME ** 15
Don Leaver UK 1982
*Jon Finch, Patricia Quinn, Prunella Gee, Ian McCulloch, Lennard Pearce, Margaret Anderson*
A further instalment from Hammer's House of Horror. A man sees the ghost of a girl in his farmhouse, that proves to be the spirit of a 17th century witch. This episode was the first one shown in the series.
Aka: HAMMER HOUSE OF HORROR: WITCHING TIME
Osca: SILENT SCREAM, THE (CH5)
HOR 54 min; 108 min (2 film cassette) mTV
B,V,V2 PRV; CH5 (VHS only)

## WITCHING, THE * 
Bert I. Gordon USA 1972
*Orson Welles, Pamela Franklin, Michael Ontkean, Lee Purcell, Harvey Jason, Sue Bernard, Lisa James, Terry Quinn*
A routine horror film on the subject of a witches' coven with Welles as High Priest trying to make Franklin a witch. A tedious and badly edited piece of nonsense.
Aka: NECROMANCY; TOY FACTORY, THE
HOR 83 min
B,V AVA; CBS

## WITCHMAKER, THE ** 18
William O. Brown USA 1969
*John Lodge, Anthony Eisley, Thordis Brandt, Alvy Moore, Shelby Grant, Helene Winston, Warene Ott, Tony Benson, Robyn Millan, Larry Vincent, Diane Webber, Sue Bernard, Nancy Crawford, Carolyn Rhodimer, Gwen Lipscomb*
A series of horrible murders of young women in the Louisiana swamps are eventually traced to an outbreak of Satanism. As badly made as it is gory.
HOR 100 min; 90 min (NET)
B,V DFS; NET

## WITCHTRAP ** 18
Kevin S. Tenney USA 1988
*James W. Quinn, Kathleen Bailey, Judy Tatum, Rob*

*Zapple, Linnea Quigley*
A Satanist who practiced his dark rituals in his attic dies in mysterious cirmcumstances. However, his evil spirit continues to haunt the house, and when the new owner calls in a group of psychics to rid the building of its entity, their attempts to do so merely unleash a series of horrifying events. An adequate chiller with a few good moments but a general lack of conviction.
HOR                                           92 min
V                                              VPD

**WITHNAIL AND I ***                            15
Bruce Robinson          UK                    1986
*Paul McGann, Richard E. Grant, Richard Griffiths,*
*Ralph Brown, Michael Elphick, Daragh O'Malley,*
*Michael Wardle, Una Brandon-Jones, Noel Johnson,*
*Irene Sutcliffe*
Set in the closing months of 1969, this semi-autobiographical tale (the script is by Robinson) has two unemployed actors who share a room, setting off for what is to be a disastrous holiday in the country. Amusing in parts, but the lack of pace or direction eventually begins to tell.
COM                         103 min (ort 108 min)
B,V                                            CAN

**WITHOUT A CLUE ***                            PG
Thom Eberhardt       UK/USA                   1988
*Michael Caine, Ben Kingsley, Jeffrey Jones, Lysette*
*Anthony, Paul Freeman, Nigel Davenport, Pat Keen,*
*Peter Cook*
This unusual little farce starts with the premise that Sherlock Holmes was a fictitious character invented by Dr Watson. When the fame of the former begins to be such that people wish to meet him, Watson is forced to hire an actor to impersonate him. Mildly amusing, but by no means hilarious.
COM                         102 min (ort 106 min)
V                                              VIR

**WITHOUT A TRACE ***                           15
Stanley R. Jaffe        USA                   1983
*Kate Nelligan, Judd Hirsch, David Dukes, Stockard*
*Channing, Jacqueline Brookes, Kathleen Widdoes,*
*Keith McDermott, David Bryan Corkill*
A woman faces a terrible ordeal when her 6-year-old son disappears one day whilst on the way to school. The directorial debut for Jaffe, this has Nelligan giving a strangely unmoving portrayal of the mother, and is spoilt by a clumsy and contrived ending. Said to be based (apart from the ending), on a real incident that took place in New York City. The script is by Beth Gutcheon.
Boa: novel Still Missing by Beth Gutcheon.
DRA                         114 min (ort 119 min)
B,V                                            CBS

**WITHOUT HER CONSENT ***                       15
Sandor Stern            USA                   1989
*Melissa Gilbert, Scott Valentine, Bebe Neuwirth, Barry*
*Tubb, Crystal Bernard, Brooke Bundy, Madison*
*Mason, William Allen Young*
A girl who is new to the big city is raped when she unwisely accepts an invitation to visit the apartment of a new acquaintance. When the law is unable to help her ("date rape" is virtually impossible to prove) and she learns that her assailant has done this several times before, she sets out administer her own form of justice. An overwrought and exploitative melodrama that fails to deal with the issues it purportedly examines.
DRA                      93 min (ort 100 min) mTV
V                                              WHV

**WITHOUT RESERVATIONS ***
Mervyn Le Roy           USA                   1946
*John Wayne, Claudette Colbert, Don DeFore, Anne*
*Triola, Frank Puglia, Phil Brown, Louella Parsons*
This wartime comedy has a successful authoress

meeting a soldier, whom she decides is perfect to play the leading man in a forthcoming film of her book. A light and frothy comedy that has a number of guest appearances by assorted Hollywood celebrities.
Boa: novel Thanks God, I'll Take It From Here by J. Allen and M. Livingston. Osca: FOOTLIGHT VARIETIES (compilation film)
COM                                    102 min B/W
B,V                                            KVD

**WITNESS ***                                   15
Peter Weir              USA                   1985
*Harrison Ford, Lukas Haas, Kelly McGillis, Josef*
*Sommer, Alexander Gudonov, Jan Rubes, Danny*
*Glover, Patty LuPone*
A little Amish boy in the big city sees a murder and the cop assigned to protect him and his widowed mother has to hide in the Amish community, when his own life is threatened. The cultural clash between Harrison and the Amish and his growing affection for the boy's mother are skilfully handled, but the violent climax is thoroughly contrived. A flawed but enjoyable work. AA: Screen (Orig) (W. Kelley/P. Wallace/E.W. Wallace), Edit (T. Noble).
THR                         108 min (ort 112 min)
V/sh                                           CIC

**WITNESS FOR THE PROSECUTION ***               PG
Alan Gibson             USA                   1982
*Ralph Richardson, Deborah Kerr, Diana Rigg, Beau*
*Bridges, Wendy Hiller, Donald Pleasence, David*
*Langton, Richard Vernon, Peter Sallis, Frank Mills,*
*Patricia Leslie, Zulema Dean, Peter Copley, Barbara*
*New, John Kidd*
Passable remake of the 1957 film in which a crusty old barrister takes on the case of a man charged with the murder of a wealthy widow. Made for TV but not shown in the UK until 1985 on BBC. Adapted by John Gay from the Christie play and the original Billy Wilder/Harry Kurnitz screenplay. This was Kerr's TV debut.
Boa: play by Agatha Christie.
DRA                                     94 min mTV
B,V                                            MGM

**WITNESS FOR THE PROSECUTION ****              U
Billy Wilder            USA                   1957
*Charles Laughton, Marlene Dietrich, Tyrone Power,*
*Elsa Lanchester, John Williams, Henry Daniell, Una*
*O'Connor*
A powerful courtroom drama based on a Christie play with Laughton quite superb as a defence barrister intent on getting an acquittal for his client, an alleged murderer. Dietrich is excellent as the faithful wife, prepared to do anything to save Power from the gallows. Scripted by Wilder and Harry Kurnitz and remade in 1982.
Boa: play by Agatha Christie.
DRA                                    113 min B/W
V                                              WHV

**WIZ, THE ***                                  U
Sydney Lumet            USA                   1978
*Michael Jackson, Diana Ross, Richard Pryor, Nipsey*
*Russell, Ted Ross, Lena Horne, Thelma Carpenter,*
*Theresa Merritt, Stanley Greene, Mabel King, Clyde J.*
*Barrett, Carlton Johnson, Henry Madsen, Vicki*
*Baltimor, Glory Van Scott*
Despite many flaws, this updated version of THE WIZARD OF OZ with an all-black cast has many good things, not least some good music and dance routines. Undeservedly panned by the critics on release, this film version of the successful Brown/Smalls musical is an entertaining film, despite a poor performance from Ross. Written by Joel Schumacher with photography by Oswald Morris and musical direction by Quincy Jones.
Boa: novel The Wonderful Wizard Of Oz by Lyman Frank Baum/musical by William F. Brown and Charlie Smalls.

MUS                           127 min (ort 133 min)
V/sh                                           CIC

## WIZARD, THE *                               PG
Todd Holland            USA               1989
*Fred Savage, Luke Edwards, Jenny Lewis, Beau
Bridges, Christian Slater, Will Seltzer, Jackey Vinson,
Wendy Phillips, Sam McMurray*
A juvenile version of RAIN MAN that takes Savage
and his mentally disturbed brother (who is a video-
game wizard) on a cross-country trip to the Universal
Studios amusement park and the National Video
Game Championships. Meanwhile, various grown-ups
set off in pursuit. Not so much a film as a plug for the
Universal Studios Tour and Nintendo video games,
this vacuous movie combines a nasty view of adults
with a clumsy ROCKY-like finale.
JUV                            96 min (ort 99 min)
V/sh                                           GHV

## WIZARD OF LONELINESS, THE **           15
Jenny Bowen             USA               1988
*Lukas Haas, Lea Thompson, John Randolph, Anne
Pitoniak, Dylan Baker, Lance Guest, Jeremiah Warner*
During WW2 a young boy is sent to live with his
grandparents in Vermont when his father is away
fighting. He finds his new life difficult to adjust to at
first, but soon warms to the small town, especially
when it seems that his aunt and cousin are in danger
from a mysterious stranger. Fine acting is weakened
by the disorganised nature of the narrative.
Boa: novel by John Nichols.
DRA                          106 min (ort 110 min)
V                                              VIR

## WIZARD OF MARS, THE *
David L. Hewitt         USA               1964
*John Carradine, Roger Gentry, Vic McGee, Eve
Bernhardt, Jerry Rannow*
The first manned mission to Mars crash-lands and its
members, three men and a woman, begin a desperate
search for oxygen that leads them to the ruler of an
extinct Martian civilisation. An obvious reworking of
THE WIZARD OF OZ, whose ambitions in terms of
plot and effects far exceeded the meagre resources
available.
Aka: ALIEN MASSACRE, HORRORS OF THE RED
PLANET; HORROR OF THE RED PLANET
Osca: DESTINATION INNER SPACE
FAN                                         81 min
B,V                                            HER

## WIZARD OF OZ, THE ****                   U
Victor Fleming          USA               1939
*Judy Garland, Ray Bolger, Bert Lehr, Jack Haley,
Frank Morgan, Billie Burke, Margaret Hamilton,
Charley Grapewin, Clara Blandick, The Singer
Midgets*
This classic American fantasy is as enjoyable today as
when it was made. Garland is perfect as Dorothy who
finds herself taken to Oz by a tornado. Sequels are
"Journey Back To Oz" and RETURN TO OZ. Written
by E.A. Wolfe, F. Ryerson and N. Langley. MGM
originally wanted Shirley Temple for Dorothy but
luckily 20th Century Fox refused to release her. AA:
Score (H. Stothart), Song ("Over The Rainbow" – H.
Arlen – music/E.Y. Harburg – lyrics).
Boa: novel by Lyman Frank Baum.
MUS                                        101 min
B,V                                            MGM

## WIZARD OF SPEED AND TIME, THE ***       PG
Mike Jittlov             USA              1988
*Mike Jittlov, Paige Moore, Richard Kaye*
The partially true story of the work of special effects
man Jittlov, telling of how he made his own film
despite opposition from Hollywood, said film being
about how a special effects man succeeds in making
his own film. This film-within-a-film structure is

somewhat confusing, but there are some intriguing
effects and amusing moments.
COM                                         94 min
B,V                                            MED

## WIZARDS **                              PG
Ralph Bakshi             USA              1977
*Voices of: Mark Hamill, Bob Holt, Jesse Wells,
Richard Romanus, David Proval, James Connel,
Christopher Tayback, Barbara Sloane, Hyman Wien,
Tina Bowman, Angelo Grisanti, Peter Hobbs*
An animated view of Earth 3,000 years after a nuclear
war from the creator of FRITZ THE CAT, and telling a
turgid tale of warring factions that battle for control of
the planet. See also FIRE AND ICE, HEY GOOD-
LOOKIN' and HEAVY TRAFFIC, three other films by
this director.
CAR                                         80 min
B,V                                            CBS

## WIZARDS OF THE LOST KINGDOM *           PG
Hector Olivera   ARGENTINA/USA           1985
*Bo Svenson, Thom Christopher, Vidal Peterson,
Barbara Stock, Edward Murrow, Mari Socas, Dolores
Michaels, August Larreta, Michael Fontaine, Mark
Welles, Mary Gale, Norton Freeman, Arch Gallo, Mark
Peters, Rick Gallo*
Routine sword and sorcery adventure from the Roger
Corman studios. As ever, set in a mythical world of
the never-never, where a young man and his compan-
ion search for a magic ring, aided in their quest by a
wandering swordfighter known as Kor the Conqueror.
Other stock figures emerge, including an evil sorcerer
and sundry alien creatures. Apart from a larger
budget, there's little here that couldn't be found in a
1950s production.
Aka: LA GUERRA DE LOS MAGOS; WIZARD
WARS
A/AD                                        85 min
B,V                                            MED

## WIZARDS OF THE LOST KINGDOM 2 **        PG
Charles B. Griffith      USA             1989
*David Carradine, Bobby Jacoby, Lana Clarkson, Mel
Welles, Susan Lee Hoffman, Sid Haig*
This in-name-only sequel is set in medieval times,
where a young wizard sets out on a quest to free three
kingdoms from their domination by the powers of
darkness. Neither coherent enough nor exciting
enough to interest adults, but one or two colourful
sequences may give it some appeal for kids.
FAN                                         78 min
V                                            20VIS

## WOLF AT THE DOOR ***                    18
Henning Carlsen
            DENMARK/FRANCE               1987
*Donald Sutherland, Jean Yanne, Valerie Gladut, Max
Von Sydow, Sofi Grabol, Merete Voldstedlund, Jurgen
Reenberg, Valerie Morea, Fanny Bastin*
A depiction of the struggles of artist Paul Gauguin
during his middle period when he returned to Paris
after his sojourn in Tahiti, and fought to win accept-
ance for his work and resolve his relationships with
the women in his life. An interesting biographical film
that has Sutherland well-cast as the painter.
DRA                          87 min (ort 102 min)
V/sh                                           RCA

## WOLF LAKE ***                           18
Burt Kennedy             USA             1978
*Rod Steiger, David Huffman, Robin Mattson, Jerry
Hardin, Richard Herd, Paul Mantee*
A young Vietnam deserter running a Canadian
lakeside hunting lodge finds himself being terrorised
by one of his guests, a sadistic ex-sergeant from the
Marines who lost his son in that war. A dull revenge
drama held up by an intense and believable perform-
ance from Steiger as the former sergeant.

DRA                                      83 min
B,V                                         RNK

## WOLF MAN, THE ****                        PG
George Waggner          USA              1941
*Lon Chaney Jr, Evelyn Ankers, Claude Rains, Maria*
*Ouspenskaya, Ralph Bellamy, Patric Knowles, Warren*
*William, Bela Lugosi, Fay Helm*
One of the great original horror stories, this has
Chaney being bitten by werewolf Lugosi during the
full moon, and surviving to continue life as a werewolf
himself. His fate is foretold by a gypsy woman and
eventually he is released from the curse by death.
Numerous sequels followed but this one, with superb
make-up by Jack Pierce and a good score by Charles
Previn and Hans J. Salter, stands above them all.
Osca: FRANKENSTEIN MEETS THE WOLF MAN
HOR            70 min; 140 min (2 film cassette) B/W
V/h                                         CIC

## WOLFEN ***                                 18
Michael Wadleigh       USA               1981
*Albert Finney, Diane Venora, Edward James Olmos,*
*Gregory Hines, Tom Noonan, Dick O'Neill, Dehi Berti,*
*Peter Michael Goetz, Ralph Bell, Sam Gray, Max M.*
*Brown, Anne Marie Photamo, Sarah Felder, Reginald*
*Vel Johnson, Chris Manor*
A New York detective investigates strange attacks by
mysterious animals and starts to track them down,
eventually discovering that after they have mutilated
their victims they retreat underground. Scripted by
Wadleigh and David Eyre, this moody and atmospher-
ic horror tale is memorable for the fine photography of
Gerald Fisher.
Boa: novel by Whitley Strieber.
HOR                                     114 min
V/sh                                        WHV

## WOLFPACK *                                 15
William Milling        USA               1988
*Tony Carlin, Jim Abele*
A fanatical right-wing group of high school kids
appear to be out simply to clear their neighbourhood
of drugs and crime, but in reality are the tool of a
neo-Nazi organisation. Exploitative and muddled
dross.
A/AD                                     81 min
B,V                                       SHEER

## WOLVES OF WILLOUGHBY CHASE, THE ***  PG
Stuart Orme                              1989
*Stephanie Beacham, Mel Smith, Geraldine James,*
*Richard O'Brien, Emily Hudson, Aleks Darowska*
Two young girl cousins are cheated out of their
inheritance by a conniving governess and are sent to
live in a bleak, Dickensian orphanage, where they
endure much hardship, but ultimately win through in
the end. A charming children's film, shot in Czechoslo-
vakia, and imbued with a delightful, fairytale-like
quality.
Boa: novel by Joan Aiken.
JUV                                      89 min
V                                           EIV

## WOMAN AT PIER THIRTEEN, THE ***
Robert Stevenson       USA               1949
*Laraine Day, Robert Ryan, John Agar, Thomas*
*Gomez, Janis Carter*
An anti-communist drama in which a shipping execu-
tive finds himself being blackmailed over former
activities by a murderous communist. An interesting
example of a patriotic film of the time, this has a plot
far too contrived to really convince.
Aka: I MARRIED A COMMUNIST; WOMAN ON
PIER THIRTEEN, THE
Osca: CORNERED
DRA                                    70 min B/W
B,V                                         KVD

## WOMAN CALLED GOLDA, A ***                   U
Alan Gibson            USA               1982
*Ingrid Bergman, Leonard Nimoy, Judy Davis, Anne*
*Jackson, Ned Beatty, Barry Foster, Franklin Cover,*
*Robert Loggia, Jack Thompson, Bruce Boa, Anthony*
*Bate, Ron Berglas, David DeKeyser, Nigel Hawthorne,*
*Yossie Graber*
Traces the career of Golda Meir right up to her 1977
meeting with Egypt's Sadat. Bergman's last film, she
made this when she was already seriously ill with
cancer. Nevertheless, she gives a remarkable perform-
ance – one that earned her a posthumous Emmy
Award as Outstanding Actress. Written by Steven
Gethers and Harold Gast and originally shown in two
parts.
DRA                     180 min (ort 200 min) mTV
B,V                                         CIC

## WOMAN HE LOVED, THE **                     PG
Charles Jarrott        USA               1988
*Jane Seymour, Anthony Andrews, Olivia De*
*Havilland, Lucy Gutteridge, Julie Harris, Robert*
*Hardy, Phyllis Calvert*
An insipid account of the fateful relationship between
the Prince of Wales and Wallis Warfield Simpson that
eventually led to the former's abdication as Edward
VIII. Seen mostly though Simpson's eyes, the film
expends considerable energy recording the tedious
minutae of two rather dull individuals, but the leads
are extremely well cast and William Luce's script is
adequate if not inspired.
DRA                      95 min (ort 100 min) mTV
V                                           VGM

## WOMAN IN BLACK, THE ***                    15
Herbert Wise                             1989
*Adrian Rawlings, Bernard Hepton, David Daker*
A small-scale, highly effective ghost story, that's set
in the 1920s and eschews big-budget special effects in
favour of a convincing, doom-laden atmosphere. A
London-based solicitor is appointed to administer the
estate of a recently deceased woman, and discovers
that she was greatly feared by the locals. To solve this
mystery, he is obliged to visit her remote house, that
is situated on an isolated island. A splendidly absorbing drama.
DRA                                      99 min
V                                         FUTUR

## WOMAN IN RED, THE ***                      15
Gene Wilder            USA               1984
*Gene Wilder, Kelly LeBrock, Judith Ivey, Gilda*
*Radner, Joseph Bologna, Charles Grodin, Michael*
*Huddleston*
A middle-aged happily married executive falls in love
with a model and pursues her relentlessly. Nothing
more than a transplanted remake of the
1977 French film "Pardon Mon Affaire". Gilda Radner
was married to Wilder until her untimely death from
cancer.
AA: Song ("I Just Called To Say I Love You" – Stevie
Wonder).
COM                         86 min; 83 min (VIR)
B,V                        RNK; VIR (VHS only)

## WOMAN IN THE WINDOW, THE ***              PG
Fritz Lang             USA               1944
*Edward G. Robinson, Joan Bennett, Raymond Massey,*
*Dan Duryea, Bobby (Robert) Blake, Edmund Breon,*
*Thomas Jackson, Dorothy Peterson, Arthur Loft*
While his family is on holiday, a staid professor
becomes involved with a pretty girl whose portrait he
stopped to admire in a shop window. However, his new
friendship leads to murder and he witnesses an
investigation that can only lead to his certain
apprehension. An absorbing melodrama, its surprise
ending was criticised at the time, but should not be
seen as a cop out, being both logical and artistically
satisfying.

Boa: novel Once Off Guard by J.H. Wallis.
THR                         95 min (ort 99 min) B/W
V                                                     WHV

## WOMAN OF SUBSTANCE, A ***                    PG
Don Sharp              UK/USA              1984
*Jenny Seagrove, Barry Bostwick, Deborah Kerr, John*
*Mills, Peter Egan, Gayle Hunnicutt, Barry Morse,*
*Nicola Pagett, Miranda Richardson, Diane Baker,*
*John Duttine, George Baker, Peter Chelsom, Mick*
*Ford, Dominic Guard, Del Henny*
A better than average mini-series that examines the
life of an ill-treated kitchen maid who works her way
up to become the owner of a chain of department
stores. Seagrove is attractive as the young Emma
Hart in a performance that rises above the banality of
the script. Followed by the inferior HOLD THE
DREAM in 1986.
Boa: novel by Barbara Taylor Bradford.
DRA                     300 min (2 cassettes) mTV
B, V/h                        IPC/VSP; ODY (VHS only)

## WOMAN TIMES SEVEN **                          15
Vittorio De Sica
                    FRANCE/ITALY/USA          1967
*Shirley MacLaine, Peter Sellers, Rossano Brazzi,*
*Vittorio Gassman, Lex Barker, Michael Caine, Elsa*
*Martinelli, Robert Morley, Anita Ekberg, Alan Arkin,*
*Patrick Wymark, Adrienne Corri, Philippe Noiret*
This examination of the nature of women has Mac-
Laine showing seven different aspects in an episodic
and uneven film. Despite some interesting and funny
moments it remains a trivial and undeveloped exer-
cise.
DRA                          99 min; 95 min (CH5)
B,V                           EHE; CH5 (VHS only)

## WOMBLING FREE **                              U
Lionel Jeffries        UK                  1978
*David Tomlinson, Frances de la Tour, Bernard Spear,*
*Bonnie Langford, Jack Purvis, Kenny Baker, Yasuko*
*Nagazumi, John Junkin, Reg Lye, Marcus Powell,*
*Sadie Corrie, Eileen Baker, John Lumiss, Brian Jones,*
*Albert Wilkinson*
Musical comedy based on a popular TV series of the
1970s, and telling of strange furry creatures that live
on Wimbledon common and decide to make a protest
against man's pollution of the environment. Both
written and direct by Jeffries, this silly and pointless
film offers little of value. The Womble characters were
created by Elizabeth Beresford.
JUV                         96 min; 92 min (PARK)
B,V                           RNK; PARK (VHS only)

## WOMEN IN CAGES **                             18
Gerry De Leon    PHILIPPINES/USA          1972
*Judy Brown, Pam Grier, Roberta Collins, Jennifer*
*Gun*
A lurid and exploitative prison melodrama with Grier
as a sadistic lesbian guard whose pleasure it is to
torture prisoners in a chamber she has fitted up for the
purpose.
Aka: BAMBOO DOLLS HOUSE
THR            74 min (ort 78 min) Cut (3 min 19 sec)
B,V                                                   APX

## WOMEN IN CHAINS **                            15
Bernard L. Kowalski    USA                1971
*Ida Lupino, Lois Nettleton, Jessica Walter, Belinda J.*
*Montgomery, John Larch, Penny Fuller, Neile Adams,*
*Hazel Medina, Katherine Cannon, Lucille Benson,*
*Joyce Jameson, Barbara Luna, Judy Strangis, Alice*
*Baches, Noah Keen*
A probation officer arranges a false identity in order to
see life in a prison from the inside. However, she finds
herself in a tough situation when the only person who
knows about her scheme dies. Good attention to detail
helps in the face of what is basically an implausible
idea.

DRA                                       71 min mTV
B,V                                                   CIC

## WOMEN IN LOVE ****                            18
Ken Russell            UK                  1970
*Alan Bates, Glenda Jackson, Oliver Reed, Jennie*
*Linden, Eleanor Bron, Alan Webb, Michael Gough,*
*Vladek Sheybal, Catherine Wilmer, Norman*
*Shebbeare, Sarah Nicholls, Sharon Gurney,*
*Christopher Gable, Nike Arrighi*
The story of an intense and passionate love affair in a
small mining town is told with style and feeling, in
this full-blooded adaptation of the Lawrence novel. A
highlight is the nude wrestling scene between Bates
and Reed which broke new ground in the cinema.
Written by Larry Kramer and one of Russell's more
mature works. AA: Actress (Jackson).
Boa: novel by D.H. Lawrence.
DRA                     127 min (ort 130 min)
B,V                                                   WHV

## WOMEN OF SAN QUENTIN *                        15
William A. Graham      USA                 1983
*Stella Stevens, Amy Steel, Debbie Allen, Hector*
*Elizondo, Rosana DeSoto, Gregg Henry, William Allen*
*Young, Yaphet Kotto, Rockne Tarkington, Robert*
*Beauchamp, James Gammon, Ernie Hudson, Alex*
*Colon, Robert Carnegie*
A story not of prisoners this time, but of female
guards. And superior beings they are too; able to quell
a riot by merely issuing a verbal order, as Stevens so
ably demonstrates. With a little love interest between
Stevens and the captain of the guards thrown in for
good measure, this adds up to a laughable and idiotic
experience.
Boa: story by Mark Rodgers and Larry Cohen.
DRA                                       97 min mTV
B,V                                                  MGM

## WOMEN OF VALOR ***                            15
Buzz Kulik             USA                 1986
*Susan Sarandon, Kristy McNichol, Alberta Watson,*
*Valerie Mahaffey, Suzanne Lederer, Patrick Bishop,*
*Terry O'Quinn, Neva Patterson, Jay Acovone, John*
*Philbin, Jeff Allin, Marilyn Redfield, Go Awazu, Rey*
*Malonzo, Ken Metcalfe*
An account of the harrowing captivity of American
Army nurses taken captive by the Japanese in a POW
camp on Bataan, during their occupation of the
Philippines in WW2. A curiously old-fashioned and
unfashionably patriotic piece, that inevitably puts one
in mind of "So Proudly We Hail" or "Cry Havoc".
Filmed on the island of Luzon and written by Jonas
McCord.
DRA                                       95 min mTV
B,V                                                   VIR

## WOMEN'S CLUB, THE **                          15
Sandra Weintraub       USA                 1986
*Michael Pare, Maud Adams, Eddie Velez, Dotty*
*Colorso, Wiley Harker*
Having just been jilted by his girlfriend, a young man
is seduced by the glamorous owner of an exclusive
women's salon, who sets him up in business as a stud
for the wealthy but sexually frustrated women of
Beverly Hills. What initially seems like a great form
of employment, quickly turns into a nightmare in this
dull comedy. Velez as Pare's zany buddy provides a
few good moments.
COM                                          85 min
B,V                                                  SONY

## WONDERFUL WIZARD OF OZ, THE **               U
                       USA                 1987
*Narrated by Margot Kidder*
Dorothy and her dog Toto are carried away by a
tornado to the magical land of Oz, where they have
various adventures with good and bad witches, the
tin-man, scarecrow and cowardly lion before arriving

back home safely. An animated version of this classic tale.

Boa: novel by Lyman Frank Baum.

| | |
|---|---|
| CAR | 93 min |
| V/sh | RCA |

## WOO WOO KID, THE *** PG

Phil Alden Robinson    USA    1987
*Patrick Dempsey, Talia Balsam, Beverly D'Angelo,*
*Michael Constantine, Betty Jinnette, Kathleen*
*Freeman, Peter Hobbs, Tony Longo, Douglas Rowe,*
*Ernie Kim Meyers, Brian McNamara, Gillian Grant,*
*Lisanne Falk, Barbara Wint*

A story set in 1944 during the latter days of WW2, and telling of the amorous exploits of a 14-year-old who has an eye for older women. When his escapades reach the newspapers, the public follows his adventures avidly, as a way of escaping from the rigours of the war. Said to be based to some extent on a true story.

Aka: IN THE MOOD

| | |
|---|---|
| COM | 94 min |
| V/sh | GHV/PARK |

## WOODEN HORSE, THE *** U

Jack Lee    UK    1950
*Leo Genn, David Tomlinson, Anthony Steel, David*
*Greene, Michael Goodliffe, Bryan Forbes, Peter Finch,*
*Peter Burton, Patrick Waddington, Anthony Dawson,*
*Franz Schaftheitlin, Hans Meyer, Jacques Brunius,*
*Dan Cunningham, Ralph Ward*

Taut story of POWs escaping from their camp by digging a tunnel beneath a wooden horse they use in their gym. Exciting and dramatic with a good script by Eric Williams. The photography is by C. Pennington-Richards.

Boa: book by Eric Williams.

| | |
|---|---|
| WAR | 101 min; 98 min (WHV) B/W |
| B,V | TEVP; WHV (VHS only) |

## WOOF! * U

David Cobham    UK    1989
*Liza Goddard, John Ringham*

Rather silly tale of a normal ten-year-old who one day turns into a dog.

| | |
|---|---|
| JUV | 93 min |
| V | PICK |

## WORD, THE *** PG

Richard Lang    USA    1978
*David Janssen, Eddie Albert, Geraldine Chaplin,*
*Florinda Bolkan, Ron Moody, Kate Mulgrew, Janice*
*Rule, John Huston, James Whitmore, Hurd Hatfield,*
*John McEnery, Diana Muldaur, Martha Scott, Nicol*
*Williamson, David Ackroyd*

The discovery of what appears to be writings by Christ's younger brother plunges the religious world into turmoil. Janssen plays a public relations executive hired to promote a new version of the Bible. A cut-down version of a TV mini-series. This was Balkan's American acting debut. Alex North received an Emmy Award for his score.

Boa: novel by Irving Wallace.

| | |
|---|---|
| DRA | 225 min; 185 min (IVS) (ort 480 min) mTV |
| B,V | HER; IVS |

## WORKING GIRL *** 15

Mike Nichols    USA    1988
*Sigourney Weaver, Harrison Ford, Melanie Griffith,*
*Alec Baldwin, Joan Cusack, Philip Bosco, Nora Dunn,*
*Oliver Platt, James Lally, Kevin Spacey, Robert*
*Easton, Olympia Dukakis, Ricki Lake*

A working girl makes her way in Wall Street and discovers that this requires all her resourcefulness and cunning, when she finds herself involved in outsmarting her boss and closing a business deal. A likeable light comedy, with pleasing performances all round. AA: Song ("Let The River Run" – Carly Simon).

| | |
|---|---|
| COM | 108 min (ort 115 min) |
| B,V | CBS |

## WORKING GIRLS *** 18

Lizzie Borden    USA    1986
*Louise Smith, Amanda Goodwin, Ellen McElduff,*
*Marusia Zach, Jane Peters, Helen Nicholas*

A look at a day in the life of Molly, a photographer, who supplements her income working as a prostitute in a small New York brothel. A very laid-back account this one, with the sex shown more as a viable alternative to poorly paid jobs than as anything to be ashamed of. Not without its moments of humour and extremely well made.

| | |
|---|---|
| DRA | 89 min |
| B,V | PAL |

## WORKING GIRLS, THE ***

Stephanie Rothman    USA    1973
*Sarah Kennedy, Laurie Rose, Lynne Guthrie, Mark*
*Thomas, Solomon Sturges, Mary Beth Hughes,*
*Cassandra Peterson*

Adventures of a trio of working girls in the big city struggling to make it against great odds. An attractive comedy with a number of good moments, not least a striptease performed by Peterson (known on American TV as "Elvira").

| | |
|---|---|
| COM | 87 min |
| B,V | PPL L/A; VIV L/A; STV |

## WORLD ACCORDING TO GARP, THE *** 15

George Roy Hill    USA    1982
*Robin Williams, Mary Beth Hurt, Glenn Close, John*
*Lithgow, Hume Cronyn, Jessica Tandy, Swoosie*
*Kurtz, Amanda Plummer, James McCall, Peter*
*Michael Goetz, George Ede, Mark Soper, Nathan*
*Babcock, Ian MacGregor, Susan Browning*

The story of a young man making his way in the world, with his unusual views on life owing not a little to the influence of his unorthodox and unmarried mother. Absorbing and entertaining, this loose adaptation of Irving's novel, gave Close her acting debut. The script is by Steve Tesich. Lithgow appears as a transsexual.

Boa: novel by John Irving.

| | |
|---|---|
| DRA | 131 min |
| B,V | WHV |

## WORLD APART, A *** PG

Chris Menges    USA    1987
*Barbara Hershey, David Suchet, Joroen Krabbe, Paul*
*Freeman, Tim Roth, Jodhi May, Linda Mvusi*

A very personal look at the workings of apartheid in South Africa seen through the eyes of a young girl whose mother, a communist, is jailed under the 1963 90-day Detention Act. Both a look at state abuse and an examination of family pressures with May giving an excellent performance as the girl. Based to an extent on the experiences of Shawn Slovo, who wrote the script. The directorial debut for photographer Menges.

| | |
|---|---|
| DRA | 112 min |
| V/sh | PAL |

## WORLD CUP, THE: A CAPTAIN'S TALE ***

Tom Clegg    UK    1982
*Dennis Waterman, Nigel Hawthorne, Andrew Keir,*
*Derek Francis, Marjorie Bland, Richard Griffiths*

Loosely based on real events, this engaging drama follows the fortunes of a football team from a mining town who get their chance to represent Britain in the first World Cup competition of 1910.

| | |
|---|---|
| DRA | 90 min |
| V | STYL |

## WORLD GONE WILD ** 18

Lee H. Katzin    USA    1987
*Michael Pare, Bruce Dern, Adam Ant*

A post-nuclear holocaust tale set in a world where it hasn't rained for fifty years. Water is scarce and a small village that has preserved a meagre supply is attacked by a gang of murderers. The town leader survives the attack and, knowing the gang will return, sets out to find an old mercenary friend and persuades him to return and help defend the town. A brutal, high-action merging of MAD MAX and THE MAGNIFICENT SEVEN.

A/AD                                          90 min
V                                               WHV

### WORLD IS FULL OF MARRIED MEN, THE **    18
Robert Young            UK                   1979
*Anthony Franciosa, Carroll Baker, Anthony Steel, Sherrie Lee Cronin, Gareth Hunt, Georgina Hale, Paul Nicholas, John Nolan, Jean Gilpin, Moira Downie, Alison Elliott, Eva Louise, Joanne Ridley, Emma Ridley, Roy Scammell*
A model on her way to the top meets a 40-year-old advertising man who is married but cannot stop himself having affairs. A shoddy and exploitative drama based on a poor Collins screenplay, which is in turn based on a worse book.
Boa: novel by Jackie Collins.
DRA              84 min; 104 min (VGM or PARK)
                              (ort 107 min)
B,V    WOV L/A; VGM (VHS only); PARK (VHS only)

### WORLD OF THE TALISMAN, THE **           U
                                              198-
The story of a young brother and sister who embark on a magical journey to the Planet of the Gods, where they hope to find a great treasure.
CAR                                          80 min
V                                       MAST; XTASY

### WORLD WAR THREE ***
Boris Segal/David Greene
                       USA                   1982
*Rock Hudson, David Soul, Brian Keith, Cathy Lee Crosby, Jeroen Krabbe, Katherine Helmond, Robert Prosky, James Hampton, Harry Basch, Frank Dent, Rick Fitts, John Lehne, Marcus K. Mukai, William Traylor, Lee Wallace*
The Russian seizure of an Alaskan pipeline in retaliation for an American grain embargo threatens to lead to a nuclear exchange. Hudson and Keith as US President and Soviet General Secretary respectively find themselves hardpressed to avert a conflict. Segal died in a helicopter crash a few days into shooting in Alaska; the film was finished by Greene in Coppola's film studios. Written by Robert L. Joseph and shown on TV in two parts.
DRA               180 min (ort 200 min) mTV
B,V                                           HER

### WORLD'S GREATEST ATHLETE, THE ***       U
Robert Sheerer          USA                  1973
*John Amos, Jan-Michael Vincent, Tim Conway, Roscoe Lee Browne, Dayle Haddon, Howard Cosell, Billy De Wolfe, Nancy Walker, Frank Gifford, Jim McKay, Danny Goldman, Vito Scotti, Ivor Francis, Liam Dunn, Leon Askin*
A college coach on a safari holiday in Africa discovers a fantastic athlete, and takes this youngster back with him to the States. A mildly amusing Disney comedy with some great special effects, such as where Conway shrinks to Tom Thumb size. The music is by Marvin Hamlisch.
COM                                          89 min
B,V                                      WDV; RNK

### WORLD'S GREATEST LOVER, THE **          15
Gene Wilder             USA                  1977
*Gene Wilder, Carol Kane, Dom DeLuise, Carl Ballantine, Michael Huddleston, Fritz Feld, Ronny Graham, Matt Collins*
Inspired by Fellini's "The White Sheik", this period comedy is set in the 1920s and concerns the ambitions of a rival studio, which screen-tests a man they hope will replace Valentino. Unfortunately, his wife falls

for the star it's his ambition to supplant. An uneven slapstick romp with a few touching moments and a general over-abundance of energy. Written and produced by Wilder.
COM                                          88 min
V                                              CBS

### WORST WITCH, THE **                      U
Robert Young            UK                   1987
*Diana Rigg, Tim Curry, Fairuza Balk, Charlotte Rea, Su Elliot, Sabina Franklyn*
The story of an accident-prone apprentice witch who attends a school with others of her kind, but never seems able to do anything but create havoc with her spells. However, she eventually saves the day for all concerned in this pleasant children's fantasy.
Boa: book by Jill Murphy.
JUV                                     70 min mTV
V                                           CENTV

### WORTH WINNING *                          15
Will Mackenzie          USA                  1989
*Mark Harmon, Madeleine Stowe, Lesley Ann Warren, Maria Holvoe, Mark Blum, Andrea Martin, David Brenner*
A stale and tasteless farce that focuses on the exploits of an obnoxious and smugly successful TV weatherman, who is convinced he is God's gift to women. This leads to a wager with a friend that he can get a trio of attractive women to accept his proposal of marriage, and the expected set of humorous episodes unfold. A vapid and unappealing comedy that wastes both time and talent.
COM                          98 min (ort 102 min)
V                                              CBS

### WORZEL GUMMIDGE: A CUP O' TEA AN' A SLICE O' CAKE ***                              U
James Hill              UK                   1980
*John Pertwee, Una Stubbs, Geoffrey Bayldon, Billy Connolly, Barbara Windsor, Thorley Walters, Bill Maynard, Wayne Norman*
An enjoyable 1-hour special based on the popular children's programme that featured an adventurous scarecrow and his friends. This story sees Worzel being banned from the Christmas festivities and setting out in search of his girlfriend Aunt Sally. On the way he helps Santa find his way home, encounters pirates, fights a duel and attends the Scarecrow Ball. The script is by Keith Waterhouse and Willis Hall.
JUV                           52 min (ort 60 min) mTV
V                                             PICK

### WORZEL GUMMIDGE DOWN UNDER ***          U
James Hill          NEW ZEALAND             1981
*Jon Pertwee, Una Stubbs, Bruce Phillips*
Our scarecrow hero ups stakes and moves to New Zealand when his beloved Aunt Sally is sold to a museum. An enjoyable spin-off of the popular children's series shown on British TV.
JUV                                          94 min
B,V                                            IVS

### WOYZECK **
Werner Herzog    WEST GERMANY               1978
*Klaus Kinski, Eva Mattes, Wolfgang Reichmann, Willy Semmelrogge, Josef Bierbichler, Paul Burian*
The story of a soldier oppressed and abused by all and sundry who goes mad and becomes a murderer. Kinski gives his usual intense and staring performance in this minor Herzog feature.
Boa: play by Georg Buchner.
DRA                                          82 min
B,V                                            PVG

### WPINK TV: PART 2 **                     R18
Miles Kidder            USA                  1986

Kari Foxx, Nina Hartley, Jeremy Butler, Ron Jeremy,
Kristara Barrington, Don Hart, Amber Lynn, Jamie
Gillis, Bunny Bleu, Buck Adams, Troy Tanier
Sex spoof on a TV station and its passion-arousing
programmes. Ron Jeremy is the executive of the
station, and he spends most of his time on his yacht
whilst Gillis plots to blow the station up. An uneven
story, mostly taken up with the station's crude but
occasionally amusing shows.
A         58 min Cut (59 sec with some cuts substituted)
(ort 84 min)
V                                                    SHEP

## WRAITH, THE **                                      18
Mike Marvin          USA                             1986
Nick Cassavetes, Charlie Sheen, Randy Quaid,
Sherilyn Fenn, Griffin O'Neal, David Sherill, Jamie
Bozian, Clint Howard, Chris Nash, Vickie Benson,
Peter Methuse, Jeffrey Sudzin, Michael Hungerford,
Steven Echholdt
A small Arizona town is terrorised by a gang of thugs
led by a ruthless psychopath. One day the spirit of
someone he murdered returns in the shape of a sleek,
black car that challenges the gang members to deadly
duels. One by one they are eliminated to the sounds of
screeching tyres, excessive concentration on this
rather diluting any sense of the supernatural.
HOR                                                90 min
B,V                                                  MED

## WRECKING CREW, THE **                               PG
Phil Karlson         USA                             1968
Dean Martin, Elke Sommer, Nancy Kwan, Sharon
Tate, Nigel Green, Tina Louise
The final film in the "Matt Helm" series, with Martin
playing a secret agent who is out to recover a load of
bullion stolen from a hijacked train. As with the other
films, this uneven mixture of comedy and thrills is
little more than a dated and hammy spy spoof. Look
out for Chuck Norris, who appears briefly. See also
THE AMBUSHERS and THE SILENCERS. Written
by William McGivern.
Boa: novel by Donald Hamilton.
A/AD                              100 min (ort 104 min)
V                                                    RCA

## WRONG ARM OF THE LAW, THE ***                        U
Cliff Owen           UK                              1962
Peter Sellers, Lionel Jeffries, Bernard Cribbins, Davy
Kaye, Nanette Newman, John Le Mesurier, Dennis
Price, Bill Kerr, Irene Browne, John Boddey, Ed
Devereaux, Arthur Mullard, Reg Lye, Dermot Kelly,
Graham Stark, Dick Emery
British crooks collaborate with Scotland Yard in
tracking down three Aussie criminals, who disguise
themselves as policemen and are in the habit of
confiscating loot from apprehended criminals. A lively
comedy yarn with some very funny moments. Written
by John Warren and Len Heath with music by
Richard Rodney Bennett.
COM                                            94 min B/W
V                                                    VCC

## WRONG BOX, THE ***                                   U
Bryan Forbes         UK                              1966
Michael Caine, Peter Cook, Dudley Moore, Ralph
Richardson, Tony Hancock, John Mills, Nanette
Newman, Wilfred Lawson, Peter Sellers, Cicely
Courtneidge, Thorley Walters, Peter Graves, Irene
Handl, Norman Bird
Set in Victorian England, this black comedy has an
aged Mills attempting to bump off his brother
Richardson, so as to be the sole heir to an inheritance.
Sellers has a gem of a cameo as a not-quite-normal
doctor. The script is by Larry Gelbart and Burt
Shevelove.
Boa: novel by Robert Louis Stevenson and Lloyd
Osbourne.
COM                              102 min (ort 110 min)
V                                                    RCA

## WRONG GUYS, THE **                                   PG
Danny Bilson         USA                             1988
Louie Anderson, Richard Lewis, Richard Belzer,
Franklyn Ajaye, Brion James, Tim Thomerson, John
Goodman, Ernie Hudson, Alice Ghostley, Kathleen
Freeman
A tiresome and utterly tedious comedy, all about a
camping-trip reunion of a 1962 Cub Scout troop. When
the troop is taken for FBI agents by a crazy convict
complications are bound to occur. A cast of stand-up
comedians do their best with a banal script.
COM                                                82 min
B,V                                                  NWV

## WRONG MAN, THE ***                                   PG
Alfred Hitchcock     USA                             1956
Henry Fonda, Vera Miles, Anthony Quayle, Harold J.
Stone, Nehemiah Persoff, Esther Minciotti
A musician is accused of robbery but protests his
innocence. The semi-documentary style is spoilt by
jerky camerawork and inappropriate music. However,
it's not without its moments, especially Miles as the
wife who cracks up under the strain. Hitchcock based
this one on a true story. Written by Angus MacPhail
and Maxwell Anderson, with music by Bernard
Herrmann.
DRA                         101 min (ort 105 min) B/W
V                                                    WHV

## WUTHERING HEIGHTS ***                                U
Robert Fuest         UK                              1970
Anna Calder-Marshall, Timothy Dalton, Ian Ogilvy,
Harry Andrews, Pamela Brown, Judy Cornwell,
Hilary Dwyer, Hugh Griffith, Julian Glover, James
Cossins, Rosalie Crutchley, Peter Sallis
Another version of this famous tale, this is a solid and
competent work, making good use of authentic loca-
tions. Dalton and Calder-Marshall are good as doomed
lovers Heathcliff and Cathy but the film's compressed
pace is a drawback. Written by Patrick Tilley and
with music by Michel Legrand.
Boa: novel by Emily Bronte.
DRA                                               105 min
B,V,V2                                               GHV

## WUTHERING HEIGHTS ****                               U
William Wyler        USA                             1939
Merle Oberon, Laurence Olivier, David Niven, Flora
Robson, Donald Crisp, Geraldine Fitzgerald, Leo G.
Carroll, Cecil Kellaway, Miles Mander, Hugh
Williams
A splendid version of this classic romance, set in
Victorian England and telling of the passionate but
doomed love affair between a girl and a gypsy. The
story stops at chapter 17 of the novel, but the fine
direction and performances sustain it. Scripted by
Charles MacArthur and Ben Hecht and remade in
1953 and 1970. The atmospheric climax is a highlight,
and the photography won a well-deserved Oscar. AA:
Cin (Gregg Toland).
Boa: novel by Emily Bronte.
DRA                                          104 min B/W
V                                                    VGM

## WYNNE AND PENKOVSKY ***                              15
Paul Seed            UK/USA                          1984
David Calder, Christopher Rozycki, Fiona Walker,
Frederick Treves, Paul Geoffrey
A recreation of the career of Greville Wynne as a
secret agent working in the USSR during the 1960s,
and concentrating on his relationship with Oleg
Penkovsky, a high-ranking KGB officer who passed
secrets to him until he was exposed. Originally shown
in three 55-minute episodes, this is a good, solid and
unadorned account.
Boa: book The Man From Moscow by Greville Wynne.
DRA                         135 min (ort 165 min) mTV
B,V                                                  BBC

# X

## X-RAY **
Boaz Davidson          USA          1980
*Barbie Benton, Chip Lucia, Jon Van Ness, John
Warner Williams, Den Surles, Gay Austin*
A girl patient is said to be terminally ill, but her
medical records have been falsified and all her visitors
are being murdered.
Aka: BE MY VALENTINE, OR ELSE . . .;
HOSPITAL MASSACRE
THR                                    78 min
B,V                                    RNK

## X-TERMINATOR, THE *                   R18
Van Rogel              USA          1986
*Trinity Loren, Kari Foxx, Patti Petite, Rick Savage,
Tony Martin, Shanna McCullough, Chanel Price,
Steve Drake, Troy Tanner, Marc Wallace*
Sex film inspired by THE EXTERMINATOR with a
fugitive woman being stalked by a sex machine from
the future. Eventually he finds his way to a brothel
where he spends most of the time asking stupid
questions about the activities taking place. Finally, he
joins in. A bizarre spoof severely hampered by a lack
of ideas.
A                                      59 min
V                                      SHEP L/A

## X: THE UNKNOWN **
Leslie Norman          UK           1956
*Dean Jagger, Leo McKern, William Lucas, Edward
Chapman, Anthony Newley, Jameson Clark, Peter
Hammond, Marianne Brauns, Ian MacNaughton,
Michael Ripper, John Harvey, Edward Judd, Jane
Aird, Kenneth Cope, Michael Brooke*
Radioactive sludge escapes from the Earth's core and
swallows everthing in its path in this very cheap-
looking British offering. Filmed in Scotland and not
without a few good moments, but the lack of money
seriously reins it in. Written by Jimmy Sangster and
made by Hammer Films.
FAN                                80 min B/W
B,V                                    WAL L/A

## XANADU **                              PG
Robert Greenwald       USA          1980
*Olivia Newton-John, Gene Kelly, Michael Beck, James
Sloyan, Dimitra Arliss, Katie Hanley, Sandahl
Bergman*
A muse comes down to Earth to inspire a young
musician and the owner of a nightclub who are
planning to launch a roller-disco. Very much a vehicle
for Newton-John, this flashy and empty film only
serves to highlight her total lack of screen presence. A
saccharine sweet confection leaving no aftertaste,
that's essentially a remake of the 1947 film "Down To
Earth". Music is by The Electric Light Orchestra.
MUS                                    88 min
B,V,V2                                 CIC

## XTRO ***                               18
Harry Bromley Davenport
                       UK           1982
*Phillip Sayer, Bernice Stegers, Simon Nash, Danny
Brainin, Anna Wing, Maryam D'Abo, David Cardy,
Peter Mandell, Robert Fyfe, Arthur Whybrow,
Katherine Best, Robert Moreno, Anna Mottram, David
Henry, Robert Austin, Vanya Seager*
A man kidnapped by aliens is returned to Earth three
years later but is not quite human. Revolving around
a series of repulsive effects, this has our Mister
Average returning home where he infects his son,
kills countless people and turns the au pair into an
alien-breeding chamber. A grotesque and unpleasant
film.
Aka: JUDAS GOAT

FAN                           83 min (ort 86 min)
B, V/s, LV                             POLY

# Y

## YANKEE-DOODLE DANDY ****             U
Michael Curtiz         USA          1942
*James Cagney, Joan Leslie, Walter Huston, Rosemary
De Camp, Irene Manning, Richard Whorf, Jeanne
Cagney, S.Z. Sakall, Walter Cartlett, Eddie Foy Jr,
Frances Langford, George Tobias, Jack Young, Minor
Watson*
The life and times of one of America's most talented
songwriters George M. Cohan, as portrayed by Cag-
ney in one of his finest performances. A lavish,
enjoyable and patriotic production. Photographed by
James Wong Howe, written by Robert Buckner and
Edmund Joseph and with the songs by Cohan, natur-
ally. AA: Actor (Cagney), Score (Heinz Roemheld/Ray
Heindorf), Sound (Nathan Levinson).
MUS                                    126 min
B, V/h                      VCC; MGM; WHV

## YANKS ***                              15
John Schlesinger       USA          1979
*Richard Gere, Lisa Eichhorn, Vanessa Redgrave,
William Devane, Wendy Morgan, Chick Vennera,
Rachel Roberts, Joan Hickson, John Ratzenberger,
Anthony Sher*
Romantic story of three American GI's in Britain and
their love-lives whilst billeted in a Lancashire town.
An overlong and lavish production that would have
benefited from some judicious editing. Written by
Colin Welland and Walter Bernstein.
DRA                                    139 min
B,V                                    WHV

## YEAR MY VOICE BROKE, THE ***          PG
John Duigan         AUSTRALIA       1987
*Noah Taylor, Loene Carmen, Ben Mendelsohn,
Graeme Blundell, Lynette Curran, Malcolm Roberts,
Judi Farr*
An affectionate coming-of-age film set in a small
Australian town in the early 1960s and telling of a
young boy's friendship and growing infatuation with a
troubled girl. The intelligent script is by Duigan with
the fine performances and perceptive dialogue major
assets.
DRA                                    94 min
V/h                                    PAL

## YEAR OF LIVING DANGEROUSLY, THE ***   PG
Peter Weir          AUSTRALIA       1983
*Mel Gibson, Sigourney Weaver, Linda Hunt, Michael
Murphy, Bill Kerr, Noel Ferrier, Paul Sonkkila,
Bembol Roco, Domingo Landicho, Hermino De
Guzman, Ali Nur, Joel Agona, Mike Emperio,
Bernardo Nacilla, Coco Marantha*
An Australian journalist and a cameraman are
assigned to cover exciting but dangerous events in
Indonesia in 1965, just prior to the fall of Sukarno.
More effective as a political drama than as a romance,
with diminutive Hunt playing a man, a role for which
she deservedly won an Oscar.
AA: S. Actress (Hunt).
Boa: novel by C.J. Koch.
DRA                                    110 min
V                                      MGM

## YEAR OF THE DRAGON ***                18
Michael Cimino         USA          1985
*Mickey Rourke, John Lone, Ariane, Leonard Termo,
Ray Barry, Caroline Kava, Eddie Jones, Joey Chin,
Mr. Lee, Victor Wong, Pao Han Lin, Rosang, K. Dock
Yip, Dennis Dun, Way Dong Woo, Jimmy Sun, Daniel
Davin*
A former Vietnam veteran now working as a New

York cop mounts his own violent anti-drugs campaign in Chinatown. Overblown, unrealistic scenes of violence spoil what might have been a good film. Written by Oliver Stone. Interestingly, the New York settings were all recreated in North Carolina on location.
Boa: novel by Robert Daley.

DRA 129 min (ort 136 min)
B,V CAN; TEVP

### YEAR OF THE SEX DRAGON, THE ** R18
Ron Jeremy USA
*Tiffany Storm, Kristara Barrington, Mimi Kurosawa, Tom Byron, Peter North, Randy West*
Madame Tong manages a Chinese massage parlour which isn't doing too well, mainly because of her refusal to allow the girls to perform extras for the customers. She discovers that some of them have been ignoring her rule, but eventually sees the error of her ways in a standard hardcore offering certain to be cut for the UK.

A 60 min
V PRI; SHEP

### YELLOW EMMANUELLE **
Albert Thomas (Adalberto Albertini)
ITALY 1971
*Ilona Staller, Claudio Giorgi, Giuseppe Pambieri, Chai Lee*
Emmanuelle falls for an airline pilot but finds the course of true love is far from smooth (you would think she'd have learnt that by now). A kind of reworking of the Madame Butterfly theme, but adequate rather than inspired.
Aka: EMMANUELLE GIALLA

A 90 min (ort 105 min)
B,V,V2 VPD

### YELLOW PAGES *** 15
James Kenelm Clarke USA 1985
*Chris Lemmon, Lea Thompson, Jean Simmons, Viveca Lindfors, Mills Watson, Joe Michael Terry, Nancy Cartwright*
An incompetent private detective is given the job of bodyguard to a young girl who is vacationing with her friends in Europe. He soon finds himself out of his depth when she is kidnapped, as part of a plot to wrest a secret from her scientist father.
Aka: GOING UNDERCOVER

COM 90 min
B,V MED

### YELLOW WINTON FLYER, THE **
Mark Rydell USA 1969
*Steve McQueen, Sharon Farrell, Will Geer, Michael Constantine, Mitch Vogel, Rupert Crosse, Lonny Chapman, Clifton James, Juano Hernandez*
Meandering account of a young boy's adventures with a couple of hired hands, when they borrow the family's car for a little trip in search of fun and adventure. A none-too-profound road movie set in 1905 Mississippi. Written by Irving Ravetch and Harriet Frank Jr, with music by John Williams.
Aka: REIVERS, THE
Boa: novel by William Faulkner.

DRA 90 min (ort 107 min)
B,V SCAN

### YELLOWBEARD ** 15
Mel Damski UK 1983
*Graham Chapman, Peter Boyle, Peter Cook, John Cleese, Richard "Cheech" Marin, Tommy Chong, Marty Feldman, Michael Hordern, Eric Idle, James Mason, Kenneth Mars, Martin Hewitt, Madeline Kahn, Susannah York, David Bowie*
A laboured and unfunny zany pirate comedy written by Chapman, Cook and Bernard McKenna, all of whom should have been made to walk the plank after this. Damski's first role as director, Feldman's last as actor; and what a poor tribute to the latter it is.

COM 95 min; 93 min (VIR)
B,V RNK; ORION; VIR (VHS only)

### YELLOWHAIR AND THE FORTRESS 15
### OF GOLD **
Matt Cimber (Matteo Ottaviano)
SPAIN/USA 1984
*Laurene Landon, Ken Roberson, Luis Lorento, John Ghaffari, Aldo Sambrel, Luis Lorenzo, Claudia Grani, Eduardo Fajardo, Ramiro Oliveros, Suzannah Woodside, Concha Marquez Piquer, Tony Tarruella, Daniel Martin*
Spoof adventure with a female "Indiana Jones" (see RAIDERS OF THE LOST ARK), investigating the secret behind an Aztec cult and its strange temple.
Aka: YELLOWHAIR AND THE PECOS KID

A/AD 102 min Cut (15 sec)
B,V VES

### YENTL *** PG
Barbra Streisand USA 1983
*Barbra Streisand, Mandy Patinkin, Amy Irving, Nehemiah Persoff, Steven Hill, Allan Corduner, Ruth Goring, David De Peyser, Bernard Spear, Doreen Mantle, Jack Lynn, Anna Tzelniker, Miriam Margolyes*
In order to get an education, a young girl disguises herself as a boy in this tale of Eastern European Jewry. An unusual offering from Streisand, her first film as director/producer, and written by her and Jack Rosenthal. This loose adaptation of Singer's tale is made with great care, but suffers badly from excessive length.
AA: Score (Michel Legrand/Marilyn Bergman/Alan Bergman).
Boa: short story by Isaac Bashevis Singer.

DRA 128 min (ort 133 min)
V/sh WHV

### YES, GIORGIO ** PG
Franklin J. Schaffner USA 1982
*Luciano Pavarotti, Kathryn Harrold, Eddie Albert, Paolo Borboni, James Hong, Beulah Quo*
On a tour of America, an opera singer loses his voice and requires the services of a throat specialist. Smitten by the attractive woman doctor who helps him, he decides to court her. A dull romantic comedy that's only partially redeemed by the singing of the star.
Boa: novel by Anne Piper.

COM 106 min
V/sh MGM

### YIELD TO THE NIGHT ** 15
J. Lee Thompson UK 1956
*Diana Dors, Yvonne Mitchell, Michael Craig, Geoffrey Keen, Olga Lindo, Mary Mackenzie, Joan Miller, Marie Ney, Liam Redmond, Marjorie Rhodes, Athene Seyler, Molly Urquhart, Harry Locke, Michael Ripper*
A condemned woman ponders on the events that led to her shooting the rich mistress of her pianist lover. Both sombre and thoughtful, this sad little moral tale was loosely based on the story of Ruth Ellis.
Aka: BLONDE SINNER
Boa: novel by Joan Henry.

DRA 95 min (ort 99 min) B/W
V WHV

### YOGI BEAR AND THE MAGICAL
### FLIGHT OF THE SPRUCE GOOSE **
Ray Patterson USA 1984
*Voices of: Daws Butler, Peter Medak*
Yogi Bear and his friends become trapped on a plane as it takes off, but turn it to their advantage by mounting a rescue mission for some other animals. Fair.

CAR 91 min
V VCC

## YOGI BEAR: YOGI'S FIRST CHRISTMAS ** U
Ray Patterson          USA              1983
*Voices of: Daws Butler, Don Messick, Janet Waldo,*
*John Stephenson, Marilyn Schreffler, Hal Smith*
Yogi Bear awakes from hibernation to experience his
first Christmas in Jellystone Park, in this feature
spin-off from the popular TV series.
Aka: YOGI'S FIRST CHRISTMAS
CAR                                   99 min
V                                        VCC

## YOGI BEAR: YOGI'S GREAT ESCAPE ** U
Ray Patterson          USA              198-
*Voices of: Daws Butler, Don Messick*
Waking up from hibernation, Yogi and Boo Boo
discover that Jellystone Park is to close and that all
the bears are to be sent to a zoo. They begin to make
preparations to escape, taking along three young cubs.
Aka: YOGI'S GREAT ESCAPE
CAR                                   96 min
V                                        VCC

## YOJIMBO ****
Akira Kurosawa      JAPAN              1961
*Toshiro Mifune, Eijiro Tone, Seizaburo Kawazu, Izuzu*
*Yamada*
A fine film by Kurosawa, in which a wandering
samurai exploits two gangs who are fighting for
control of a village. Very much a tongue-in-cheek
samurai film, with Mifune quite superb as the warrior
who teaches both warring factions a lesson. Followed
by SANJURO and without a doubt the inspiration for
the infinitely poorer A FISTFUL OF DOLLARS.
DRA                                   110 min B/W
B,V                                     PVG; PAL

## YOL ****                              15
Serif Goren   SWITZERLAND/TURKEY       1982
*Tarik Akan, Serif Sezer, Halil Ergun, Necmettin*
*Cobanoglu, Meral Orhonsoy, Hikmet Celik, Sevda*
*Aktolga, Tuncay Akca, Hale Akinli, Turgut Savas,*
*Hikmet Tashdemir, Engin Celik, Osman Bardakci,*
*Envery Guney, Erdogan Seren*
A harrowing account of five prisoners out on a week's
parole, and of the circumstances that lead to tragedy.
The work of Turkish film-maker and political prisoner
Yilmaz Gurney (who worked secretly on the film from
prison and escaped to edit it), this is both a study of
the oppression of totalitarian governments and an
examination of the brutality that women can suffer at
the hands of men. Winner of the Cannes Film Festival
Grand Prix.
Aka: WAY, THE
DRA                        105 min (ort 111 min)
B,V                                     POLY

## YOR                                   15
Anthony M. Dawson (Antonio Margheriti)
                 ITALY/TURKEY           1983
*Reb Brown, Corinne Clery, John Steiner, Carole*
*Andre, Alan Collins, Ayshe Gul, Aytekin Akkaya,*
*Marina Rocchi, Sergio Nicolai*
Routine post-nuclear holocaust fantasy with muscle-
man Brown attempting to discover his true identity,
whilst trapped on a planet where both past and future
have merged. A gloriously bad film in which bad
acting is seamlessly united with worse dialogue.
Aka: YOR, THE HUNTER FROM THE FUTURE
FAN                    88 min; 85 min (VES)
B,V                                  PVG; VES

## YOU AND ME **
David Carradine        USA              1973
*David Carradine, Barbara Seagull (Hershey), Chipper*
*Chadbourne II, Bobbi Shaw*
A Hell's Angel teams up with a nine-year-old boy who
is also on the run from the law in this mediocre drama.
DRA                                   93 min
B,V                                    VCL/CBS

## YOU CAN'T HURRY LOVE **              18
Richard Martini        USA              1986
*David Packer, Scott McGinnis, Bridget Fonda, David*
*Leisure, Anthony Geary, Frank Bonner, Lu Leonard,*
*Meret Van Kemp, Sally Kellerman, Charles Grodin,*
*Kristy McNichol, Judy Balduzzi, Danitza Kingsley*
Trite little story of a young man's adventures on the
L.A. singles circuit. Shallow, predictable and dull, in
roughly that order.
COM                                   92 min
B,V                                      VES

## YOU CAN'T TAKE IT WITH YOU ***       U
Frank Capra            USA              1938
*Jean Arthur, Lionel Barrymore, James Stewart,*
*Edward Arnold, Mischa Auer, Ann Miller, Spring*
*Byington, Eddie "Rochester" Anderson, Donald Meek,*
*Dub Taylor, Halliwell Hobbes, Samuel S. Hinds,*
*Harry Davenport*
Entertaining if somewhat corny story of a highly
eccentric New York household, and of how the daugh-
ter falls for the son of a wealthy man. Lacking the wit
or warmth of the original play, this film tends to
concentrate too much on taking swipes at the world of
big business. AA: Pic, Dir.
Boa: play by G.S. Kaufman and Moss Hart.
COM                                   121 min B/W
V                                        RCA

## YOU LIGHT UP MY LIFE **              PG
Joseph Brooks          USA              1977
*Didi Conn, Joe Silver, Michael Zaslow, Stephen*
*Nathan, Melanie Mayron, Amy Letterman*
An aspiring woman singer finds her life and work
difficult, until she meets a young man who prompts
her into putting her life in order. A painfully thin
story produced, written and musically supervised by
Brooks. Followed by IF EVER I SEE YOU AGAIN.
AA: Song ("You Light Up My Life" – Joseph Brooks).
DRA                                   87 min
V                                        RCA

## YOU ONLY LIVE TWICE ***             PG
Lewis Gilbert          UK/USA           1967
*Sean Connery, Donald Pleasence, Karin Dor, Tetsuro*
*Tamba, Akiko Wakabayashi, Bernard Lee, Lois*
*Maxwell, Charles Gray, Mie Hama, Teru Shimada,*
*Karin Dor, Desmond Llewellyn, Tsai Chin, Alexander*
*Knox, Robert Hutton, Burt Kwouk*
The fifth Bond adventure, with Secret Service agent
007 fighting SPECTRE, a nasty organisation bent on
world domination. As always, the novels of Ian
Fleming form the basis (if not the plot) for these films.
Set in Japan and memorable for some exotic and
colourful locations. Written by Roald Dahl, with
music by John Barry and photography by Freddie
Young. The spectacular sets are by Ken Adam.
Followed by ON HER MAJESTY'S SECRET SER-
VICE.
Boa: novel by Ian Fleming.
A/AD                       108 min (ort 116 min)
V/sh                                    WHV

## YOU RUINED MY LIFE ***              U
David Ashwell          USA              1987
*Soleil Moon Frye, Paul Reiser, Mimi Rogers, Allen*
*Garfield, Tony Burton, Todd Susman*
An 11-year-old girl lives a life of considerable luxury,
thanks to her rich uncle who runs a flashy hotel in Las
Vegas. However, when a professor is brought in with
the intention of turning her into a refined young lady,
she decides to fight him all the way.
COM                        90 min (ort 100 min) mTV
B,V                                     WDV

## YOU'LL FIND OUT **                  15
David Butler           USA              1940
*Kay Kyser, Peter Lorre, Boris Karloff, Bela Lugosi,*
*Helen Parrish, Ginny Simms, Alma Kruger, Harry*

*Babbitt, Dennis O'Keefe, Ish Kabibble*
A band who find themselves having to spend the night in a haunted house after being hired for a 21st birthday party, discover a dastardly plot to defraud an orphan. On hand are the villainous characters of Karloff, Lugosi and Lorre. Written by James V. Kern and Butler and with songs by Johnny Mercer and James McHugh, this is a considerable disappointment all round.

| MUS | 92 min B/W |
| B,V | KVD |

### YOU'LL NEVER GET RICH ***     U
Sidney Lanfield     USA     1941
*Fred Astaire, Rita Hayworth, John Hubbard, Robert Benchley, Osa Massen, Frieda Inescort, Guinn Williams, Donald MacBride*
Astaire plays a dance director who is drafted at an inconvenient time, but is determined the show must go on. For good measure he becomes involved with his philandering producer's latest girlfriend. A charming musical comedy that conferred star status on young Hayworth. Songs are by Cole Porter and include "So Near And Yet So Far".

| MUS | 88 min B/W |
| V | RCA |

### YOUNG AGAIN **     U
Steven Hilliard Stern     USA     1986
*Lindsay Wagner, Robert Urich, Jack Gilford, Keanu C. Reeves, Jessica Steen, Jason Nicolof, Jeremy Ratchford, Peter Spence, Jonathan Welsh, Louise Vallance, Vincent Murray, John Friesen, Marshall Perlmutter, Barbara Kyle*
Angelic intervention transforms a thirty-year-old bachelor into a teenager, effectively placing his high-school sweetheart beyond reach as she is now twice his age. A cute idea that attempts to cash in on films like BACK TO THE FUTURE and PEGGY SUE GOT MARRIED, but lacking the real talent a 1940s Hollywood studio would have brought to such a film.
Boa: story by Steven Hilliard Stern and David Simon.

| COM | 85 min mTV |
| B,V | WDV |

### YOUNG AND INNOCENT ***     U
Alfred Hitchcock     UK     1937
*Derrick De Marney, Percy Marmont, Mary Clare, Edward Rigby, Basil Radford, Nova Pilbeam, George Curzon, John Longden, George Merritt, J.H. Roberts, Jerry Verno, H.F. Maltby, Pamela Carme, Torin Thatcher, Gerry Fitzgerald*
When a man finds himself implicated in a murder he attempts to find the real culprit, aided by a young girl with whom he goes on the run. Echoes THE THIRTY-NINE STEPS with a revelation taking place in a memorable nightclub scene. Written by Charles Bennett and Alma Reville with music by Louis Levy.
Aka: GIRL WAS YOUNG, THE
Boa: novel A Shilling For Candles by Josephine Tey.

| THR | 77 min (ort 82 min) B/W |
| B,V | RNK |

### YOUNG AT HEART ***     U
Gordon Douglas     USA     1954
*Frank Sinatra, Doris Day, Gig Young, Ethel Barrymorre, Dorothy Malone, Alan Hale Jr, Robert Keith, Elizabeth Fraser*
Romantic musical comedy all about a cynical musician who falls in love. Sinatra romances Day whilst other romances take place for the daughters of a small town music teacher. A musical remake of the 1938 film "Four Daughters" and written by Julius J. Epstein and Lenore Coffee.
Boa: novel by Fannie Hurst.

| MUS | 112 min |
| B,V,V2 | BBC; VCC (VHS only) |

### YOUNG AVENGER, THE **     18
HONG KONG     1989
A young man working in a funeral parlour is addicted to gambling, and often robs the dead to provide his stake. One night a ghost appears to him and relates such a tale of injustice that he vows to seek revenge on its behalf, and the spirit becomes his martial arts mentor. This unusual fantasy element does much to enliven the standard revenge-seeking plot.

| MAR | 86 min |
| B,V | VPD |

### YOUNG BRUCE LEE, THE *     
HONG KONG     1983
*Bruce Lee, Bruce Li (Ho Tsung-Tao), Hon Kwok Choi*
After defeat in a match, the young Bruce learns a style called "The Three Cobras" and puts it to good use when his friend is murdered.

| MAR | 90 min |
| B,V | AVA |

### YOUNG DOCTORS IN LOVE **     15
Garry Marshall     USA     1982
*Michael McKean, Hector Elizondo, Patrick Macnee, Sean Young, Harry Dean Stanton, Dabney Coleman, Pamela Reed, Demi Moore, Michael Richards, Taylor Negron, Saul Rubinek, Titos Vandis*
This spoof medical soap opera fires off so many gags in true AIRPLANE! fashion that a few hit home. Might have been good as a 20-minute short, but the gags are spread out too thinly to really sustain the feeble storyline. The debut for writer and producer Marshall.

| COM | 95 min |
| B,V,LV | RNK |

### YOUNG EINSTEIN ***     PG
Yahoo Serious (Greg Pead)
AUSTRALIA     1989
*Yahoo Serious, Odile Le Clezio, John Howard, Su Cruickshank, Pee Wee Wilson*
Silly, self-indulgent and childish, but this crazy screwball comedy has a lot going for it. Written by David Roach and Serious (who also produced), it details the career of young Albert, who when not discovering physics theorems, finds time to invent rock 'n' roll and surfing. The flimsy plot concerns the retrieval of his nuclear brewery before it blows the world up. Hilarious after a few beers and understandably a great success Down Under.

| COM | 88 min (ort 90 min) |
| V/sh | WHV |

### YOUNG EMMANUELLE, A ***     
Nelly Kaplan
FRANCE/WEST GERMANY     1976
*Sami Frey, Ann Zacharias, Nelly Kaplan, Francoise Brion, Micheline Presle, Heinz Bennent, Ingrid Caren*
Bearing no relation to all those other "Emmanuelle" films, this has a young girl anonymously writing erotic literature from first-hand experience as a way of escaping from the wealthy and stifling lifestyle of her parents. When her identity is betrayed, she devises a form of revenge in order to perfect her latest novel – "Nea". A relatively successful and entertaining adult comedy.
Aka: NEA
Boa: novel by Emmanuelle Arsan.

| A | 103 min |
| B,V | WOV |

### YOUNG FRANKENSTEIN ***     15
Mel Brooks     USA     1974
*Gene Wilder, Marty Feldman, Teri Garr, Peter Boyle, Madeline Kahn, Cloris Leachman, Gene Hackman, Richard Hadyn, Kenneth Mars, Leon Askin, Liam Dunn, Oscar Beregi Jr, Lou Cutell, Danny Goldman, Richard Roth, Rusty Blitz*
An uneven spoof on those monster films of the 1930s, with Wilder as young brain surgeon Frederick Frank-

enstein returning to his roots in Transylvania. Not terribly funny though Hackman's spoof on the blindman sequence from THE BRIDE OF FRANKENSTEIN is a joy, and the use of sets and lab equipment from the 1930s was a masterstroke. Scripted by Brooks and Wilder with photography by Gerald Hirschfield.

COM                                    106 min B/W
B,V                                           CBS

## YOUNG GIANTS **                          U
Terrill Tannen        USA               1983
*John Huston, Peter Fox, Pele, Lisa Wills, F. William Parker, Severn Darden*
A San Diego priest re-organises a football team as a way of helping a boys' home and thus enables an old priest to die contented. A kind of flimsy version of "Going My Way" with a guest appearance by top football star Pele. Written by Tom Moyer, Mike Lammers and director Tannen.
Aka: MINOR MIRACLE, A
JUV                                    97 min
B,V                                           ARF

## YOUNG GRADUATES, THE **
Robert Anderson       USA               1971
*Patricia Wymer, Tom Stewart, Jennifer Rist, Gary Rist, Dennis Christopher*
Formula college-kids comedy with a youngster falling in love with her teacher amidst assorted high school adventures. Dennis Christopher's first feature, but not any more memorable on that account.
COM                         88 min (ort 99 min)
B,V                                           VCL

## YOUNG GUNS ***                           18
Christopher Cain      USA               1988
*Emilio Estevez, Kiefer Sutherland, Lou Diamond Phillips, Dermot Mulroney, Charlie Sheen, Casey Siemaszko, Jack Palance, Terry O'Quinn, Terence Stamp, Sharon Thomas, Brian Keith, Patrick Wayne*
Set in New Mexico in 1878, this story tells of how a British ranch-owner befriends six young rebels and hires them to look after his property. When he is murdered and the law fails to act, the boys set out to avenge him, but their vendetta soon turns into a bloody rampage. Branded as outlaws they now find themselves the objects of a huge manhunt.
WES                         102 min (ort 107 min)
B,V                                           VES

## YOUNG HARRY HOUDINI ***                  U
James Orr             USA               1987
*Wil Wheaton, Jeffrey DeMunn, Kerri Green, Barry Corbin, Roy Dotrice, J. Reuben Silverbird, Ross Harris, Jose Ferrer*
A compelling film relating the early days of Harry Houdini, the world's foremost escape artist. As a 12-year-old he runs away from home intent on becoming a renowned magician. During his journey he falls in with a travelling carnival, an encounter which prepares him for his future feats of magic. Narrated by DeMunn, who plays the grown-up Houdini. Written by Jim Cruickshank and James Orr.
JUV                    89 min (ort 100 min) mTV
B,V                                           WDV

## YOUNG HERO **                            18
Lo Chia Po        HONG KONG             1982
*Wang Chiang, Wang Sha, Huang Cheng Li, Kwan Young Moon, Yuan Wu, Yuan Chu*
Two powerful criminal clans struggle for control of the same territory, with no holds (or kicks) barred. Fairly standard kung fu actioner.
MAR                                    88 min
B,V                                           VPD

## YOUNG JOE: THE FORGOTTEN KENNEDY ***
Richard T. Heffron    USA               1977

*Peter Strauss, Barbara Parkins, Stephen Elliott, Darleen Carr, Simon Oakland, Asher Brauner, Lance Kerwin, Peter Fox, Steve Kanaly, Robert Englund, Gloria Stroock, Tara Talboy, Ben Fuhrman, James B. Sikking*
This drama on the eldest Kennedy brother tells of how he undertook a dangerous WW2 mission and returned home a hero, thus paving the way for a Kennedy in the White House. Strauss gives a strong performance in a film somewhat hampered by a strong bias towards sentimentality.
Boa: book The Lost Prince: Young Joe, The Forgotten Kennedy by Hank Searls.
DRA                    97 min (120 min) mTV
B,V                                           HER

## YOUNG LADY CHATTERLEY **                 18
Alan Roberts          USA               1976
*Harlee McBride, Peter Ratray, William Beckley, Joi Stanton, Mary Forbes, Joi Patrick Wright, Henry Charles, Edgar Daniels, Lawrence Montaigne, Anne Michelle*
Lady C's niece inherits her estate and coming across her diary, decides to follow in her footsteps. A sequel followed in 1984.
A                      91 min (ort 100 min)
                              (Cut at film release)
B,V                   SLA L/A; PRI L/A; SHEP

## YOUNG LADY CHATTERLEY 2 **               18
Alan Roberts          USA               1984
*Harlee McBride, Sybil Danning, Adam West, Brett Clerk, Monique Gabriel*
Sequel to the 1976 film from the same director and with a largely identical cast. Here, Lady C fights to save the family estate, but still finds time for more athletic pursuits.
A                           82 min (ort 85 min)
B,V                                           MED

## YOUNG LIONS, THE ****                    PG
Edward Dmytryk        USA               1958
*Marlon Brando, Montgomery Clift, Dean Martin, Hope Lange, Barbara Rush, Mai Britt, Maximilian Schell, Lee Van Cleef, Arthur Franz*
A study of WW2 as seen from both sides with Martin and Clift as American soldiers, and Brando quite superb as a Nazi officer who has come to doubt his most cherished beliefs. Written by Edward Anhalt with a fine score by Hugo Friedhofer and photography by Joe MacDonald.
Boa: novel by Irwin Shaw.
DRA                                    167 min B/W
V/h                                           CBS

## YOUNG LOVE, FIRST LOVE **
Steven Hilliard Stern   USA             1979
*Valerie Bertinelli, Timothy Hutton, Arlen Dean Snyder, Fionnula Flanagan, Leslie Ackerman, Dee Wallace, James Gallery, Grant Wilson, Adam Gunn, Stoney Jackson, Charlie Brill, Michael Lang, Mitch Brown, Loren Lester, Mike Foster*
The story of a first-time romance between the daughter of a liberal family from California and the son of a conservative family from the mid-West. The burning question that is asked is whether Valerie should "go all the way". Originally entitled "A Boy And A Girl: The First Time" and far from riveting stuff.
DRA                                    95 min mTV
B,V                                    SPEC/POLY

## YOUNG MAN WITH A HORN ****               PG
Michael Curtiz        USA               1950
*Kirk Douglas, Lauren Bacall, Doris Day, Juano Hernandez, Hoagy Carmichael, Jerome Cowan, Nestor Paiva, Mary Beth Hughes*
A trumpet player is torn between his love for two women, one nice the other nasty. The story is based on the life of Bix Biederbecke, with Harry James dubbing

for Douglas. An excellent and beautifully acted film. Written by Edmund H. North and Carl Foreman with music by Ray Heindorf. On release in the UK it was retitled, the American title not being acceptable at that time.
Aka: YOUNG MAN OF MUSIC
Boa: novel by Dorothy Baker.
DRA                                            110 min B/W
B,V                                                    WHV

**YOUNG MASTER, THE ***                           15
Jackie CHan        HONG KONG                     1979
*Jackie Chan, Yuan Biao, Lily Li, Wei Pai, Whong In Sik*
A man tries to prevent his best friend from leading a life of crime and in the process finds himself on the wrong side of the law. He now is obliged to clear his name and bring the real criminals to justice.
MAR                                                87 min
B,V                                                    GHV

**YOUNG NURSES, THE ***                           18
Clinton Kimbro     USA                           1973
*Jean Manson, Ashley Porter, Angela Gibbs, Zack Taylor, Jack La Rue Jr, Dick Miller, Sally Kirkland, Allan Arbus*
The fourth in a series of five Roger Corman "nurse" movies, focuses on a hospital drug ring and offers the usual blend of broad comedy and forgettable shenanigans. Director Samuel Fuller has a memorable cameo as a villain and Mantan Moreland also appears in his final film. CANDY STRIPE NURSES followed and completed a series that began with SECRETS OF A STUDENT NURSE.
Aka: L.A. NURSES (XTASY)
COM                                    72 min (ort 77 min)
B,V                                  XTASY L/A; TURBO L/A

**YOUNG PIONEERS ***
Michael O'Herlihy    USA                         1976
*Roger Kern, Linda Purl, Robert Hays, Robert Donner, Shelly Juttner, Frank Marth, Brendan Dillon, Charles Tyner, Jonathan Kidd, Arnold Soboloff, Janis Famison, Bernice Smith, Dennis Fimple*
A newly-married teenage couple leave the comforts of their family home in Iowa and head West to settle for a rugged lifestyle in 1870s Dakota. A simple and wholesome tale, followed in 1976 by "Young Pioneer's Christmas".
Boa: novel by Rose Wilder Lane.
A/AD                                           120 min mTV
B,V                                                     CBS

**YOUNG SHERLOCK HOLMES AND THE PYRAMID OF FEAR ***                           PG
Barry Levinson     USA                           1985
*Nicholas Rowe, Alan Cox, Sophie Ward, Anthony Higgins, Nigel Stock, Susan Fleetwood, Freddie Jones, Michael Hordern, Earl Rhodes, Brian Oulton, Roger Ashton-Griffith, Patrick Newell, Donald Eccles, Matthew Ryan, Jonathan Lacy*
An interesting idea; Holmes and Watson meet at public school and together solve their first case – the deaths of the elderly members of a previous archaeological expedition to Egypt. Unfortunately the careful detail and intellectual appeal of the story is drowned in a welter of spectacular effects, reducing the film to the level of RAIDERS OF THE LOST ARK. Written by Chris Columbus, with Steven Spielberg as one of the executive producers.
Aka: YOUNG SHERLOCK HOLMES
A/AD                                               105 min
V/sh                                                   CIC

**YOUNG STRANGER, THE ***
John Frankenheimer   USA                         1957
*James MacArthur, Kim Hunter, James Daly, James Gregory, Whit Bissell, Marian Seldes*
A young boy who gets into trouble with the law, finds

that his relationship with his wealthy and somewhat neglectful father is put under strain. Written by Robert Dozier with music by Leonard Rosenman. A sincere and absorbing film. The debut for both Frankenheimer and MacArthur.
DRA                                            84 min B/W
B,V                                  MOV L/A; PORVI; ODY

**YOUNG VISITORS, THE ***
James Hill         UK                            1984
*Tracey Ullman, Alec McGowen, John Standing, John Harding, Kenny Ireland, Carina Radford*
This turn-of-the-century story of a butcher who is also a social-climber, effectively captures a child's innocent view of the world, being largely based on a short story written by a 9-year-old.
Boa: short story by Daisy Ashford.
DRA                                            90 min mTV
B,V                                                    SWAN

**YOUNG WARRIORS, THE ***                         18
Lawrence D. Foldes   USA                         1983
*Ernest Borgnine, Richard Roundtree, Lynda Day George, James Van Patten, Anne Lockhart, Mike Norris, Dick Shawn, Tom Reilly, Linnea Quigley, Ed DeStefane*
After his sister is raped and murdered, a young boy and his college chums decide to take their own revenge, in this violent exploitation movie. Written by Foldes and Russell W. Colgin, and a sequel of sorts to MALIBU HIGH.
DRA                                    98 min (ort 103 min)
B,V,V2                                                 GHV

**YOUNG WINSTON ***                               PG
Richard Attenborough   UK                        1972
*Simon Ward, Robert Shaw, Anne Bancroft, John Mills, Jack Hawkins, Anthony Hopkins, Patrick Magee, Edward Woodward, Ian Holm, Peter Cellier, Ronald Hines, Raymond Huntley, Russell Lewis, Pat Heywood, Laurence Naismith*
A careful and enjoyable if somewhat glamorised account of the early years of Churchill, told in the form of a series of flashbacks and taking us up to his election to Parliament. The semi-narrative style and use of contrived "interviews", are flaws in an otherwise excellent film. Ward is well-chosen (he also narrates) and the film is scripted and produced by Carl Foreman.
Boa: book My Early Life by Winston Spencer Churchill.
DRA                                   123 min (ort 157 min)
V                                                      RCA

**YOUNGBLOOD ***                                  15
Peter Markle       USA                           1986
*Rob Lowe, Patrick Swayze, Cynthia Gibb, Ed Lauter, Eric Nesterenko, George Finn, Fionnula Flanagan, Jim Youngs*
Dull account of a country lad who joins a Canadian hockey team and receives a fierce baptism. Writer/director Markle adds a few contrived comedy bits and some love interest, but this remains very much a production-line effort, and one very clearly aimed at the teen market.
DRA                                                106 min
B,V                                                    WHV

**YOUR TICKET IS NO LONGER VALID ***              18
George Kaczender    CANADA                       1979
*Richard Harris, George Peppard, Jeanne Moreau, Jennifer Dale, Alexandra Stewart, Winston Reckert, Jan Rubes, Michael Kane, Peter Hutt, Many Hallson, Victor Desy, Michelle Martin, Lesley Rae Robinson, Roger Garceau*
An international business tycoon faces ruin as he struggles to raise the cash to stave off the collapse of his inherited empire. And if this wasn't enough to occupy him, he also suffers from impotency and is

plagued by a recurrent series of nightmares. Lurid and garish junk based on a novel of similar attributes.
Aka: FINISHING TOUCH; SLOW DESCENT INTO HELL, A (VIDAGE)
Boa: novel by Romain Gary.
DRA 91 min; 88 min (VIDAGE)
B,V VTC L/A; CBS; VIZ; VIDAGE

## YOU'VE COME A LONG WAY, KATIE **
Vic Sarin CANADA 1982
Lolly Cadeau, Irene Mayeska, Tim Henry, Booth Savage, Norma Renault, Scot Denton, David Calderisi
A TV show hostess struggles to overcome her alcoholism but finds it an uphill struggle.
DRA 153 min
B,V,V2 INT L/A

## YUM-YUM GIRLS, THE **
Barry Rosen USA 1976
Judy Landers, Tanya Roberts, Barbara Tully, Michelle Dawn, Carey Poe, Stan Bernstein
Set in New York, this purports to be an in-depth look at the world of the fashion model, and follows the careers of some young girls who come to the city to make their fortune. A sporadically amusing but otherwise forgettable softcore tour of the fashion world.
DRA 89 min (ort 98 min)
B,V RNK

## YUMA ***
Ted Post USA 1970
Clint Walker, Barry Sullivan, Edgar Buchanan, Kathryn Hays, Morgan Woodward, Peter Mark Richman, John Kerr, Robert Phillips, Miguel Alejandro, Neil Russell, Bruce Glover, Rudy Diaz, Bill McLean, Napoleon Whiting
A plot is hatched to discredit a tough lawman, with the brother of an imprisoned badman stalking the marshal, to prevent him from finding out who is trying to discredit him. An old-fashioned Western that lacks pace and verve but is worth seeing nonetheless.
WES 73 min mTV
B,V VCC; GHV

# Z

## Z.I.T.S. ** PG
Arthur Sherman USA 1988
Danielle Du Clos, Jason Kristofer, Cameron Johann, Kimble Joyner, Devin Ratray, Elya Baskin
A lightweight espionage romp in which a bunch of kids become embroiled in a complex $100,000 plot to sell Pentagon secrets to the Russians, which must then be recovered from the KGB.
Aka: ZITS
A/AD 84 min Cut (7 min 54 sec)
V FUTUR

## ZABRISKIE POINT * 15
Michelangelo Antonioni USA 1970
Mark Frechette, Daria Halpin, Rod Taylor, Paul Fix, Harrison Ford
A boring and utterly meaningless series of loosely connected images that passes for a film, following a couple and their meanderings in the desert. Endless slow-motion shots were raved over by certain critics who, as ever, saw deep hidden meanings, too obscure to be spotted by lesser mortals. The exasperating script is by Antonioni and Sam Shepard. Harrison Ford is credited but his scenes were deleted.
DRA 112 min
B,V MGM

## ZACHARIAH *** 15
George Englund USA 1971
John Rubinstein, Pat Quinn, Don Johnson, Country Joe and The Fish, Elvin Jones, The James Gang, Dick Van Patten, Doug Kershaw
A satirical and offbeat rock Western containing elements of a morality play, with little real direction but a host of songs to suit every taste. Now a minor cult classic. Co-scripted by members of the Firesign Theater.
MUS 93 min
B,V RNK; VGM

## ZAPPED! ** 15
Robert J. Rosenthal USA 1982
Scott Baio, Willie Aames, Felice Schachter, Heather Thomas, Robert Mandan, Greg Bradford, Scatman Crothers, Sue Ann Langdon.
An accident in a school chemistry lab gives a boy strange powers that he uses in really adolescent ways (like undressing his girlfriend). Written by Rosenthal and Bruce Rubin, this is a kind of spoof on CARRIE and similar high school movies. A waste of good talent.
COM 96 min
B,V,V2 EHE; NELSN

## ZARDOZ *** 15
John Boorman UK 1974
Sean Connery, Charlotte Rampling, Sara Kestelman, Sally Anne Newton, John Alderton, Niall Buggy, Bosco Hogan, Reginald Jarman, Bairbe Dowling, Christopher Casson, Jessica Swift
In 2293 most of the world has reverted to barbarism following a cataclysm, and civilisation is preserved in small enclaves inhabited by self-indulgent groups. An inhabitant of the outer wastelands gains entry to one of these sheltered enclaves, ultimately finding that he was brought there on purpose. A visually impressive film whose many ideas needed a stronger story. Scripted by Boorman, with the haunting and highly unusual scoring of Beethoven's 7th by David Munrow.
FAN 105 min
B,V CBS

## ZEBRA FORCE **
Joe Tornatore USA 1977
Mike Lane, Richard X. Slattery, Rockne Tarkington, Glenn Wilder, Anthony Caruso
Let's hear it again for the Vietnam-vets. This time they use their military expertise to combat organised crime and line their own pockets at the same time. Scripted and co-produced by Tornatore. Low-budget actioner let down by poor acting.
A/AD 100 min
B,V,V2 HOK L/A; VPD

## ZED AND TWO NOUGHTS, A *** 15
Peter Greenaway NETHERLANDS/UK 1986
Andrea Ferreol, Brian Deacon, Eric Deacon, Joss Ackland, Frances Barber, Jim Davidson, Geoffrey Palmer, Agnes Brulet, Guusje Van Tilborgh, Ken Campbell, Wolf Kahler, Gerard Thoolwn, David Attenborough (narration)
Twin brothers lose their wives in an accident, and become obsessed with the driver of the car, who lost her leg in the accident. A strange and obsessive film that almost defies description, revolving around the study of decay. Beautifully photographed by Sacha Vierny and well worth a look, though never rising above the level of an interminable intellectual game.
Aka: ZOO: A ZED AND TWO NOUGHTS
DRA 115 min
V/h PAL

## ZELIG *** PG
Woody Allen USA 1983
Woody Allen, Mia Farrow, Garrett Brown, Stephanie Farrow, Will Holt, Sol Lomita, John Buckwalter, Marvin Chatinover, Stanley Swerdlow, Paul Nevens,

*Ellen Garrison, Mary Louise Wilson, Howard Erskine*
A phoney documentary making good use of photomontage techniques, this tells of a man who has the ability to change his appearance to merge with whatever surroundings he is placed in. More clever than it is funny, the Gordon Willis photography and Dick Hyman music are assets. As ever, Allen writes and directs.

DRA                          76 min B/W and Colour
V                                            WHV

### ZELLY AND ME *** 15
Tina Rathborne          USA              1988
*Isabella Rossellini, Glynis Johns, Alexandra Johnes, Kaiulani Lee, David Lynch, Joe Morton*
A perceptive but highly introspective study of the strains suffered by a wealthy but over-protected orphan. Intense and compelling but ultimately unsatisfying.

DRA                          88 min (ort 90 min)
V                                             RCA

### ZERO BOYS, THE ** 18
Nico Mastorakis         USA              1985
*Daniel Hirsch, Jared Moses, Crystal Carson, Nicole Rio, Tom Shell, Kelli Maroney, Joe Phelan, Gary Jochimsen, John Michaels, Elise Turner, T.K. Webb, Steve Shaw, Jason Pickets, Stephen Kay, Neil Weiss, Dennis Ott, Trudy Adams*
Six teenagers in the Californian forests on a camping holiday are menaced by a couple of murderous psychos, who play a nasty game of hide-and-seek armed with a variety of weapons. A dull and plodding exploiter in the DELIVERANCE mould but lacking the credibilty of that earlier film.

A/AD                        90 min Cut (15 sec)
B/sh, V/sh                                   POLY

### ZERO OPTION * PG
Sarah Hellings          UK               1988
*Stephen Hattersly, John Walton*
An action thriller in which an SAS team is called in to end a siege at a London embassy. When the operation goes wrong, the leader of the unit is blamed and he leaves the service in disgust, joining an agency that specialises in the protection of VIPs. A lacklustre and unconvincing yarn.

THR                                       105 min
V                                            PICK

### ZERO POPULATION GROWTH **
Michael Campus          UK               1972
*Oliver Reed, Geraldine Chaplin, Don Gordon, Diane Cilento, Aubrey Woods, David Markham, Sheila Reid, Bill Nagy, Lotte Tholander, Ditte Maria, Wayne John Rhodda, Lone Lindorff, Belinda Donkin, Birgitte Federspiel, Paul Sceon*
In an over-populated world of the future, tough government acts have been passed to control childbirth; the penalty for flouting these laws is death. In spite of this a couple have an illegal baby, and threatened with exposure by their neighbours, are forced to share it with them, but ultimately flee to an island. A silly and unworkable basic premise is made more so by the use of android-dolls that serve as substitutes in a child-starved world.
Aka: Z.P.G.

FAN                                        95 min
B,V                          VUL L/A; HVP; VDB

### ZERO TO SIXTY ** 15
Don Weis                USA              1978
*Darren McGavin, Sylvia Miles, Joan Collins, Denise Nickerson, The Hudson Brothers, Lorraine Gary*
In the aftermath of a divorce in which he has lost everything to his former wife, a man becomes involved with a crowd of young people who earn their living by repossessing cars. A clumsy mixture of thin comedy and car chase thrills.

COM                                       100 min
B,V                            HVP L/A; HVH

### ZERTIGO DIAMOND CAPER, THE ** U
Paul Asselin            USA              1980
*Adam Rich, David Groh, Jane Elliott, Jeffrey Tambor*
When a priceless diamond is stolen from a museum, a young blind boy, who was present at the time, finds that his museum administrator mother is suspected. He embarks on a scheme to clear her name.

A/AD                                       45 min
V                                            PICK

### ZIEGFELD FOLLIES *** U
Vincente Minnelli       USA              1946
*William Powell, Judy Garland, Lucille Ball, Fred Astaire, Fanny Brice, Lena Horne, Red Skelton, Victor Moore, Virginia O'Brien, Cyd Charisse, Edward Arnold, Gene Kelly, Esther Williams*
A musical extravaganza in which Ziegfeld mounts a spectacular revue in Heaven (!). Powell plays Ziegfeld, with a good supporting cast who mount a number of entertaining numbers. Of variable quality but bursting at the seams with life. Some segments were directed by George Sidney, Norman Taurog, Roy Del Ruth and others.

MUS                                       105 min
V                                            MGM

### ZOLTAN, HOUND OF HELL * 18
Albert Band             USA              1977
*Jose Ferrer, Reggie Nalder, Michael Pataki, Jan Shutan, Libbie Chase, John Levin, Arleen Martell, Simmy Bow, Jojo D'Amore, Roger Schumacher, Cleo Harrington, Katherine Fitzpatrick*
The Count's dead servant comes back to life and tries to find the last member of the Dracula family. This takes him and the Count's dog, which has acquired the tastes of its dead master, on a trip to Los Angeles. A silly, tedious and totally unfrightening piece of nonsense.
Aka:
DRACULA'S DOG, ZOLTAN; ZOLTAN, HOUND OF DRACULA

HOR                                        83 min
B,V                                          TEVP

### ZOMBIE CREEPING FLESH ** 18
Vincent Dawn (Bruno Mattei)
                        ITALY/SPAIN      1981
*Robert O'Neil, Frank Garfield, Selan Karr*
An industrial accident in a factory turns the workers into blood-lusting zombies in this low-budget shocker from the Continent.
Aka: INFERNO DEI MORTI-VIVENTI

HOR                                        81 min
B,V                              VCL L/A; APX

### ZOMBIE HIGH * 15
Ron Link                USA              1987
*Virginia Madsen, Richard Cox, Kay E. Kuter, James Wilder, Sherilyn Fenn, Paul Feig, T. Scott Coffey, Paul Williams, Henry Sutton, Clare Carey, John Sack, Christopher Crews, Susan Barnes, Abigail Hanness, Arvid Holmberg*
Ridiculous shocker with the students at a sleepaway academy being lobotomised, by their teachers and turned into zombies. Sit through this one and you'll think it happened to you.

HOR                                        87 min
B,V                                          VES

### ZOMBIE NIGHTMARE ** 18
Jack Bravman            USA              1986
*Adam West, John Mikl Thor, Tia Carrere, Manuska Rigaud, Frank Dietz, Linda Singer, Linda Smith, Francesca Bonacorsa, John Fasano*

A man foils a robbery at a local grocery store, only to be run over and killed by a group of suburban punks. But following a weird voodoo ceremony in his backyard, he is resurrected as a superhuman avenger. A film that tries hard to be mystical rather than gory, but never develops enough of an atmosphere to succeed.

HOR                                    80 min (ort 90 min)
B,V                                                     IVS

## ZOMBIES: DAWN OF THE DEAD ***                    18
George A. Romero        USA                        1979
*David Emge, Ken Foree, Scott H. Reiniger, Gaylen Ross, Tom Savini*
The zombie community increases and threatens to engulf the entire US population. Four people take refuge in a barricaded shopping mall. The grisly effects and genuinely frightening moments should please zombie-lovers everywhere. A film of considerable power if not charm, and both a sequel and a remake of the 1968 film NIGHT OF THE LIVING DEAD. Followed by DAY OF THE DEAD.
Aka: DAWN OF THE DEAD
HOR            121 min; 95 min (EIV) (ort 140 min)
B,V,V2                        INT; EIV (VHS only)

## ZONE TROOPERS **                                 15
Danny Bilson            USA                         1985
*Tim Thomerson, Timothy Van Patten, Art La Fleur, Biff Manard, Peter Boom, William Paulsen, Max Turilli, Eugene Brell, John Leamer, Bruce McGuire, Mike Manderville, Alviero Martin, Archille Brunini, Ole Jorgensen, Peter Hinz*
In Italy in 1943 an American Army unit is trapped behind German lines, until it receives help from aliens off a ship that has crash-landed in the woods. The soldiers are now faced with the task of preventing the aliens being captured by the Germans. Little more than a gimmicky WW2 story, in which the plain fact of aliens being around during the war rapidly becomes somewhat irrelevant.

FAN                                               82 min
B,V                                                   EIV

## ZOO GANG, THE **                                 15
Pat Densham/John Watson
                        USA                         1985
*Jackie Earle Haley, Eric Gurry, Tiffany Helm, Jason Gedrick, Ben Vereen, Bobby Jacoby, Ty Hardin, Roman Bieri*
Youth action comedy revolving around the efforts of a bunch of five teenagers, to turn a dilapidated night eatery into a nightclub. Their new club is a roaring success and attracts the attention of another gang who decide to take it over. Not bad, but a kind of mishmash of two films, one being a straightforward teen-comedy and the other a plug for youthful enterprise.

COM                                               96 min
B,V                                                  POLY

## ZORBA THE GREEK ****                              PG
Michael Cacoyannis      USA                        1964
*Anthony Quinn, Alan Bates, Irene Papas, Lila Kedrova, Sofiris Moustakas, Anna Kyriakou, Eleni Anousaki, George Viyadjis, Takis Emmanuel, George Foundas*
Excellent adaptation of a novel about a stuffy young Englishman, who becomes involved with the title character on his arrival in Crete to open a family mine. Quinn is excellent as Zorba, a man with a sad past but a wonderful zest for life, which he attempts to instil into Bates. A rich, lively and joyful film. Written by Cacoyannis with a memorable Mikis Theodorakis score. AA: S. Actress (Kedrova), Cin (Walter Lassally), Art/Set (V. Fotopoulos).
Boa: novel by Nikos Kazantzakis.

DRA                                              146 min
B,V                                                   CBS

## ZORRO AND THE THREE MUSKETEERS *
Marino Vacca            ITALY                       1962
*Gordon Scott, Jose Greci, Giacomo Rossi Stuart, Livio Lorenzon, Franco Fantasia, Nazzareno Zamperla*
Aided by the Three Musketeers, Zorro tries to free the cousin of the Spanish King. One of a series of silly costume adventures inspired by this famous character. For fans only.
A/AD                                 90 min (ort 99 min)
B,V,V2                                                VPD

## ZORRO AT THE SPANISH COURT **
Luigi Capuano           ITALY                       1962
*Giorgio Ardisson, Alberto Lupo, Maria Grazia Spina, Nadia Marlowe, Livio Lorenzon*
Zorro places the rightful heir on the throne of Spain in this standard Italian costumer.
Aka: ZORRO ALLA CORTE DI SPAGNA
A/AD                                              90 min
B,V,V2                                                VPD

## ZORRO, THE GAY BLADE ***                          PG
Peter Medak             USA                         1981
*George Hamilton, Lauren Hutton, Brenda Vaccaro, Ron Leibman, Donovan Scott, James Booth*
A spoof on the Zorro films with some hints of homosexuality. This odd idea for a comedy has Hamilton playing Don Diego Vega, the foppish son of the famous adventurer plus his gay brother Bunny Wigglesworth. Dedicated to the director of THE MARK OF ZORRO – Rouben Mamoulian, this loving send-up of the Zorro films delivers a few laughs but never really gets into its stride. A high-spot is the villainous Leibman who over-acts outrageously.
COM                                               93 min
B,V                                                   CBS

## ZULU ****                                         PG
Cy Endfield             UK                          1963
*Stanley Baker, Jack Hawkins, Ulla Jacobbson, James Booth, Michael Caine, Nigel Green, Ivor Emmanuel, Paul Daneman, Glynn Edwards, Neil McCarthy, David Kernan, Gary Bond, Patrick Magee, Chief Buthelezi*
The story of how a handful of British soldiers resisted a ferocious Zulu attack at Rorke's Drift in 1879. The bulk of the film is taken up with the massive battle, when wave after wave of warriors were driven back, and on that level it is hard to fault. Characterisation tends towards the standard cliches, but for all that it remains a truly spectacular and exciting film. Written by Endfield and John Prebble and followed by ZULU DAWN in 1979.
A/AD                                133 min (ort 135 min)
V/h                                                   CIC

## ZULU DAWN ***
Douglas Hickox
                  NETHERLANDS/USA                  1979
*Burt Lancaster, Peter O'Toole, Simon Ward, John Mills, Nigel Davenport, Michael Jayston, Denholm Elliott, Ronald Lacey, Freddie Jones, Bob Hoskins*
A prequel to the film ZULU, describing a famous engagement in which British troops were decimated by Zulus in a ferocious battle at Isandhlwana; the defence of Rorke's Drift following soon after. No great insights from the Endfield/Anthony Storey script but this is a solid and competent account, the spectacular locations of which may be lost on TV. The score is by Elmer Bernstein.
DRA                                115 min (ort 121 min)
B,V                                                   INT

# ALTERNATIVE TITLES

**"10"**
See TEN
**$1,000,000 DUCK**
See MILLION DOLLAR DUCK
**077: FURY IN ISTANBUL**
See FURY IN ISTANBUL
**077: MISSION BLOODY MARY**
See MISSION BLOODY MARY
**077: SPECIAL MISSION LADY CHAPLIN**
See SPECIAL MISSION LADY CHAPLIN
**10½ WEEKS**
See TEN AND A HALF WEEKS
**10 TO MIDNIGHT**
See TEN TO MIDNIGHT
**100 RIFLES**
See ONE-HUNDRED RIFLES
**1001 NIGHTS**
See BED OF A THOUSAND PLEASURES
**11 DAYS 11 NIGHTS: PART 3 – THE FINAL CHAPTER**
See ELEVEN DAYS ELEVEN NIGHTS: PART 3
**11,000 SEXES, THE**
See BISEXUAL
**12 + 1**
See TWELVE PLUS ONE
**13TH FLOOR, THE**
See THIRTEENTH FLOOR, THE
**14 GOING ON 30**
See FOURTEEN GOING ON THIRTY
**18 AGAIN!**
See EIGHTEEN AGAIN!
**18 BRONZE GIRLS OF SHAOLIN, THE**
See EIGHTEEN BRONZE GIRLS OF SHAOLIN, THE
**1922: A MINER'S STRIKE**
See CORONATION DEEP 1922
**1990: THE BRONX WARRIORS**
See BRONX WARRIORS
**1001 ARABIAN NIGHTS**
See MISTER MAGOO: 1001 ARABIAN NIGHTS
**2 IDIOTS IN HOLLYWOOD**
See TWO IDIOTS IN HOLLYWOOD
**2½ DADS**
See TWO AND A HALF DADS
**2,000 MANIACS**
See TWO-THOUSAND MANIACS
**20,000 LEAGUES UNDER THE SEA**
See TWENTY-THOUSAND LEAGUES UNDER THE SEA
**20,000 LEAGUES UNDER THE SEA**
See TWENTY-THOUSAND LEAGUES UNDER THE SEA
**200 MOTELS**
See TWO-HUNDRED MOTELS
**2010: THE YEAR WE MAKE CONTACT**
See 2010
**2019**
See AFTER THE FALL OF NEW YORK
**2019: AFTER THE FALL OF NEW YORK**
See AFTER THE FALL OF NEW YORK
**2019: DOPO LA CAPUTA DI NEW YORK**
See AFTER THE FALL OF NEW YORK
**2020 TEXAS FREEDOM FIGHTERS**
See TEXAS GLADIATORS 2020
**2020 TEXAS GLADIATORS**
See TEXAS GLADIATORS 2020
**2084**

See LORCA AND THE OUTLAWS
**21 DAYS**
See TWENTY-ONE DAYS
**21 HOURS AT MUNICH**
See TWENTY-ONE HOURS AT MUNICH
**21 JUMP STREET**
See TWENTY-ONE JUMP STREET
**3 A.M.**
See THREE A.M.
**3,000 MILE CHASE, THE**
See THREE-THOUSAND MILE CHASE, THE
**3.15**
See MOMENT OF TRUTH
**3.15: MOMENT OF TRUTH**
See MOMENT OF TRUTH
**300 YEAR WEEKEND, THE**
See THREE-HUNDRED YEAR WEEKEND, THE
**353 AGENTE ESPECIAL**
See HUNTER OF THE UNKNOWN
**36TH CHAMBER OF SHAOLIN, THE**
See THIRTY-SIXTH CHAMBER OF SHAOLIN, THE
**37.2 DEGREES IN THE MORNING**
See BETTY BLUE
**37.2 DEGRES LE MATIN**
See BETTY BLUE
**37.2 LE MATIN**
See BETTY BLUE
**40 CARATS**
See FORTY CARATS
**42ND STREET**
See FORTY-SECOND STREET
**52 PICK-UP**
See FIFTY-TWO PICK-UP
**55 DAYS AT PEKING**
See FIFTY-FIVE DAYS IN PEKING
**67 DAYS**
See SIXTY-SEVEN DAYS
**68**
See SIXTY-EIGHT
**72 DESPERATE REBELS, THE**
See SEVENTY-TWO DESPERATE REBELS, THE
**72 HOURS OR DIE**
See POWER GAME
**79 A.D. – THE DESTRUCTION OF HERCULANEUM**
See DESTRUCTION OF HERCULANEUM, THE
**8 TO 4**
See EIGHT TO FOUR
**80,000 SUSPECTS**
See EIGHTY-THOUSAND SUSPECTS
**84 CHARING CROSS ROAD**
See EIGHTY-FOUR CHARING CROSS ROAD
**9½ WEEKS**
See NINE AND A HALF WEEKS
**9 DEATHS OF THE NINJA**
See NINE DEATHS OF THE NINJA
**9 TO 5**
See NINE TO FIVE
**92 IN THE SHADE**
See NINETY-TWO IN THE SHADE
**976: EVIL**
See NINE SEVEN SIX: EVIL
**99 AND 44/100% DEAD**
See CALL HARRY CROWN
**A NOITE DO TERROR CEGO**
See TOMBS OF THE BLIND DEAD
**A-HAUNTING WE WILL GO**
See LAUREL AND HARDY: A-HAUNTING WE WILL GO

**A-TEAM, THE: TRIAL BY FIRE**
See A-TEAM, THE: THE COURT MARTIAL
**A.W.O.L. ABSENT WITHOUT LEAVE**
See A.W.O.L.
**ABDUCTION**
See ABDUCTED
**ABGERECHNET WIRD NACHTS**
See ALPHA CITY
**ABOVE THE LAW**
See NICO
**ABSURD**
See ANTHROPHAGUS 2
**ABU EL BANAT**
See DAUGHTERS, DAUGHTERS
**ABWARTS**
See OUT OF ORDER
**ABWARTS: DAS DUELL UBER DER TIEFE**
See OUT OF ORDER
**ACCIDENT, THE**
See ACCIDENT AT MEMORIAL STATION
**ACE, THE**
See GREAT SANTINI, THE
**ACES GO PLACES**
See MAD MISSION 2
**ACES GO PLACES 3**
See MAD MISSION THREE: OUR MAN IN BOND STREET
**AD SOFF HALAYLA**
See WHEN NIGHT FALLS
**ADAM AND NICOLE**
See EROTIC INFERNO
**ADAMSON OF AFRICA**
See KILLERS OF KILIMANJARO, THE
**ADDITION**
See L'ADDITION
**ADIEU L'AMI**
See CODE, THE
**ADIOS, TEXAS**
See TEXAS ADIOS
**ADOLF HITLER: THE BUNKER**
See BUNKER, THE
**ADULTERESS IN LOVE**
See HOT ACTS OF LOVE
**ADULTERIO ALL'ITALIANA**
See ADULTERY ITALIAN STYLE
**ADVANCE TO GROUND ZERO**
See NIGHTBREAKER
**ADVENTURES OF ARCHIE, THE**
See HOT TIMES
**ADVENTURES OF BUCKAROO BANZAI ACROSS THE EIGHTH DIMENSION**
See BUCKAROO BANZAI
**ADVENTURES OF CHOPPY AND THE PRINCESS, THE**
See CHOPPY AND THE PRINCESS
**ADVENTURES OF MARK TWAIN, THE**
See COMET QUEST
**ADVENTURES OF PINOCCHIO, THE**
See PINOCCHIO
**ADVENTURES OF SHERLOCK HOLMES, THE**
See SHERLOCK HOLMES
**ADVENTURES OF TAURA PART 1, THE**
See PRISON SHIP STAR SLAMMER
**ADVENTURES OF TEDDY RUXPIN, THE**
See TEDDY RUXPIN: THE ADVENTURES OF TEDDY RUXPIN
**ADVENTURES OF THE ACTION**

**HUNTERS, THE**
See ACTION HUNTERS
**ADVENTURES OF TINTIN, THE: RED RACKHAM'S TREASURE**
See TINTIN: RED RACKHAM'S TREASURE
**ADVENTURES OF TINTIN, THE: THE BLACK ISLAND**
See TINTIN: THE BLACK ISLAND
**ADVENTURES OF TINTIN, THE: THE CALCULUS AFFAIR**
See TINTIN: THE CALCULUS AFFAIR
**ADVENTURES OF TINTIN, THE: THE CALCULUS CASE**
See TINTIN: THE CALCULUS AFFAIR
**ADVENTURES OF TINTIN, THE: THE CRAB WITH THE GOLDEN CLAWS**
See TINTIN: THE CRAB WITH THE GOLDEN CLAWS
**ADVENTURES OF TINTIN, THE: THE LAKE OF SHARKS**
See TINTIN: THE LAKE OF SHARKS
**ADVENTURES OF TINTIN, THE: THE SECRET OF THE UNICORN**
See TINTIN: THE SECRET OF THE UNICORN
**ADVENTURES OF TINTIN, THE: THE SEVEN CRYSTAL BALLS**
See TINTIN: THE SEVEN CRYSTAL BALLS
**ADVENTURES OF TINTIN, THE: THE SHOOTING STAR**
See TINTIN: THE SHOOTING STAR
**AFFAIRE BERLINESE**
See BERLIN AFFAIR, THE
**AFRICA SCREAMS**
See ABBOTT AND COSTELLO: AFRICA SCREAMS
**AFRICAN RAGE**
See TIGERS DON'T CRY
**AFRICAN RUN, THE**
See TUXEDO WARRIOR
**AFTER DARK**
See AFTER DARKNESS
**AFTER MIDNIGHT**
See NEW YORK AFTER MIDNIGHT
**AFTER SCHOOL**
See QUEST FOR EDEN
**AFTERNOON DELIGHT**
See AFTERNOON DELIGHTS
**AFURIKA MOWOGATARI**
See GREEN HORIZONS
**AGATHA CHRISTIE HOUR, THE: IN A GLASS DARKLY**
See AGATHA CHRISTIE COLLECTION, THE: IN A GLASS DARKLY
**AGATHA CHRISTIE HOUR, THE: THE CASE OF THE MIDDLE-AGED WIFE**
See AGATHA CHRISTIE COLLECTION, THE: THE CASE OF THE MIDDLE-AGED WIFE
**AGATHA CHRISTIE'S DEAD MAN'S FOLLY**
See DEAD MAN'S FOLLY
**AGATHA CHRISTIE'S ENDLESS NIGHT**
See ENDLESS NIGHT
**AGATHA CHRISTIE'S ORDEAL BY INNOCENCE**
See ORDEAL BY INNOCENCE
**AGATHA CHRISTIE'S THIRTEEN AT DINNER**
See THIRTEEN AT DINNER
**AGENT 69**
See EMMANUELLE IN DENMARK
**AGENT 69 JENSEN I SKYTTENS TEGN**
See EMMANUELLE IN DENMARK

**AGENTE 077 DALL'ORIENTE CON FURORTE**
See FURY IN ISTANBUL
**AGENTE 353 ENVIADO SPECIAL**
See HUNTER OF THE UNKNOWN
**AGENTE 353, MASSACRO AL SOLE**
See HUNTER OF THE UNKNOWN
**AGENTE: MISSIONE BLOODY MARY**
See MISSION BLOODY MARY
**AGGRESSOR, THE**
See MAD BULL
**AGONIJA**
See RASPUTIN
**AGONY**
See RASPUTIN
**AGONY: DEATH THROES**
See RASPUTIN
**AIR RAID WARDENS**
See LAUREL AND HARDY: AIR RAID WARDENS
**AIRPORT 1975**
See AIRPORT '75
**AIRPORT '79**
See AIRPORT '80: THE CONCORDE
**AIRWOLF 2: DEADLY MISSION**
See AIRWOLF 2
**AIRWOLF 2: THE SEARCH**
See AIRWOLF 2
**AL DI LA DELLA LEGGE**
See GOOD DIE FIRST FOR A HANDFUL OF SILVER, THE
**ALADDIN AND HIS MAGIC LAMP**
See ALADDIN
**ALADDIN ET LA LAMPE MERVEILLEUSE**
See ALADDIN
**ALAMO, THE**
See ALAMO, THE: THIRTEEN DAYS TO GLORY
**ALAMO, THE: PARTS 1 AND 2**
See ALAMO, THE: THIRTEEN DAYS TO GLORY
**ALBINO**
See WHISPERING DEATH
**ALEXANDRA**
See ALEXANDRA: QUEEN OF SEX
**ALI: FEAR EATS THE SOUL**
See FEAR EATS THE SOUL
**ALICE, SWEET ALICE**
See COMMUNION
**ALIEN ATTACK**
See SPACE 1999: ALIEN ATTACK
**ALIEN CONTAMINATION**
See CONTAMINATION
**ALIEN MASSACRE, HORRORS OF THE RED PLANET**
See WIZARD OF MARS, THE
**ALIEN PREDATOR**
See MUTANT 2
**ALIEN PREDATORS**
See MUTANT 2
**ALIEN PREY**
See PREY
**ALIEN WARRIOR**
See KING OF THE STREETS
**ALIENS FROM SPACESHIP EARTH WANTED**
See ALIENS FROM SPACESHIP EARTH
**ALIENS: THIS TIME IT'S WAR**
See ALIENS
**ALIVE BY NIGHT**
See METAMORPHOSIS
**ALL 33 DI VIA OROLOGIO FA SEMPRE FREDDO**
See SHOCK
**ALL THE MARBLES**
See CALIFORNIA DOLLS, THE

**ALL THINGS BRIGHT AND BEAUTIFUL**
See IT SHOULDN'T HAPPEN TO A VET
**ALL YOU NEED IS CASH**
See COMPLEAT RUTLES, THE
**ALLEGHENY UPRISING**
See FIRST REBEL, THE
**ALLIGATOR ALLEY**
See FLORIDA CONNECTION, THE
**ALL'OMBRA DI UNA COLT**
See IN A COLT'S SHADOW
**ALL'ONOREVOLE PIACCIONO LE DONNE**
See EROTICIST, THE
**ALMOST HUMAN**
See SHOCK WAVES
**ALMOST SUMMER**
See DIRTY LOOKS
**ALPINE ROMANCE**
See WHITE HOT
**ALTER EGO**
See MURDER BY THE BOOK
**ALTER EGO**
See CLONUS
**ALTRIMENTI CI ARRABBIAMO**
See WATCH OUT, WE'RE MAD
**ALVIN RIDES AGAIN**
See FOREPLAY: THE PREQUEL
**ALWAYS**
See DEJA VU
**AMANTI MIEI**
See CINDY'S LOVE GAMES
**AMAZING GRACE AND CHUCK**
See SILENT VOICE
**AMAZONIA INFERNO VERDE**
See AMAZONIA
**AMAZONIA: THE CATHERINE MILES STORY**
See AMAZONIA
**AMERICAN COUSIN, THE**
See BLOOD TIES
**AMERICAN GOTHIC**
See HIDE AND SHRIEK
**AMERICAN JUSTICE**
See JACKALS
**AMERICAN NINJA 3**
See AMERICAN NINJA 3: BLOODHUNT
**AMERICAN ODDBALLS**
See CRY UNCLE
**AMERICAN PLAYHOUSE: ROOMMATES**
See ROOMMATE, THE
**AMERICAN SUCCESS**
See SUCCESS
**AMERICAN SUCCESS COMPANY, THE**
See SUCCESS
**AMERICAN TICKLER OR THE WINNER OF 10 ACADEMY AWARDS**
See EJECTION
**AMERICAN VOYEUR**
See GETTING IT ON
**AMERICAN WARRIOR**
See AMERICAN NINJA
**AMIN: THE RISE AND FALL**
See RISE AND FALL OF IDI AMIN, THE
**AMITYVILLE HORROR, THE: THE EVIL ESCAPES PART 4**
See AMITYVILLE 4: THE EVIL ESCAPES
**AMITYVILLE: THE DEMON**
See AMITYVILLE 3-D
**AMITYVILLE: THE EVIL ESCAPES**
See AMITYVILLE 4: THE EVIL ESCAPES
**AMOK**

See SCHIZO
**AMORE A PALERMO**
See SICILIAN CONNECTION, THE
**AMOROUS ADVENTURES OF A MILKMAN, THE**
See AMOROUS MILKMAN, THE
**AMOROUS ADVENTURES OF DON QUIXOTE AND SANCHO PANZA, THE**
See SUPERKNIGHTS
**AMY PRENTISS: BAPTISM OF FIRE**
See PRIME SUSPECT
**ANASTASIA: THE MYSTERY OF ANNA**
See ANASTASIA
**AND BABY COMES HOME**
See BABY COMES HOME
**AND NO-ONE WOULD BELIEVE HER**
See WELCOME TO ARROW BEACH
**AND ONCE UPON A LOVE**
See FANTASIES
**AND THEN THERE WERE NONE**
See TEN LITTLE INDIANS
**AND WOMAN WAS CREATED**
See AND GOD CREATED WOMAN
**AND YOU'LL LIVE IN TERROR! THE BEYOND**
See BEYOND, THE
**ANDERSON'S ANGELS**
See CHESTY ANDERSON, U.S. NAVY
**ANDREWS' RAIDERS**
See GREAT LOCOMOTIVE CHASE, THE
**ANDY AND THE AIRWAVE RANGERS**
See ANDY COLBY'S INCREDIBLE ADVENTURE
**ANDY WARHOL'S YOUNG DRACULA**
See ANDY WARHOL'S DRACULA
**ANGEL**
See ANGEL CLOUD
**ANGEL 3**
See ANGEL 3: THE FINAL CHAPTER
**ANGEL ABOVE, DEVIL BELOW**
See ANGEL ABOVE AND DEVIL BELOW
**ANGEL FROM H.E.A.T.**
See ANGEL OF HEAT
**ANGEL OF H.E.A.T.**
See ANGEL OF HEAT
**ANGEL, THE**
See HEAVENLY KID
**ANGELS BEHIND BARS**
See VENDETTA
**ANGELS NEVER SLEEP**
See IN THE AFTERMATH: ANGELS NEVER SLEEP
**ANIMAL HOUSE**
See NATIONAL LAMPOON'S ANIMAL HOUSE
**ANO 79 DOPO CRISTO**
See DESTRUCTION OF HERCULANEUM, THE
**ANTEFFATTO**
See LAST HOUSE ON THE LEFT PART 2, THE
**ANTICHRIST, THE**
See TEMPTER, THE
**ANTICRISTO**
See TEMPTER, THE
**ANTS**
See ANTS: PANIC AT LAKEWOOD MANOR
**APARTMENT ON THE 13TH FLOOR**
See CANNIBAL MAN, THE
**APOCALIPSE CANNIBAL**
See CANNIBAL APOCALYPSE
**APOCALISSE DOMANI**

See CANNIBAL APOCALYPSE
**APOCALYPSE DOMANI**
See CANNIBAL APOCALYPSE
**APOLOGY: FOR MURDER**
See APOLOGY
**APRIL FOOL'S DAY**
See SLAUGHTER HIGH
**AQUARIUS**
See STAGE FRIGHT
**ARCHER**
See ARCHER'S ADVENTURE
**ARCHER, THE: FUGITIVE FROM THE EMPIRE**
See ARCHER AND THE SORCERESS
**ARE YOU ALONE TONIGHT?**
See MIND OVER MURDER
**ARGOMAN SUPERDIABOLICO**
See FANTASTIC ARGOMAN
**ARGOMAN THE FANTASTIC SUPERMAN**
See FANTASTIC ARGOMAN
**ARK OF THE SUN GOD . . . TEMPLE OF HELL, THE**
See ARK OF THE SUN GOD
**ARMY WIVES**
See WHEN DUTY CALLS
**AROUND THE WORLD WITH DOT**
See DOT AND SANTA CLAUS
**AROUSERS, THE**
See SWEETKILL
**ARRIVA DORELLIK**
See HOW TO KILL 400 DUPONTS
**ARTHUR 2: ON THE ROCKS**
See ARTHUR 2
**ARTHUR THE KING**
See MERLIN AND THE SWORD
**AS DE PIL (OPERACION CONTRAESPIONAJE)**
See OPERATION COUNTERSPY
**AS I RODE DOWN TO LAREDO**
See RETURN OF THE GUNFIGHTER
**AS THE BEAST DIES**
See BEAST, THE
**ASHANTI: LAND OF NO MERCY**
See ASHANTI
**ASQUITH: THE TAX SCANDAL**
See SECRET LIVES OF THE BRITISH PRIME MINISTERS, THE: ASQUITH
**ASQUITHS, THE**
See SECRET LIVES OF THE BRITISH PRIME MINISTERS, THE: ASQUITH
**ASSASSINATION TEAM, THE**
See WARDOG: THE KILLING MACHINE
**ASSAULT FORCE**
See NORTH SEA HIJACK
**ASSAULT OF THE KILLER BIMBOS**
See SCUMBUSTERS
**ASSAULT ON PARADISE**
See RANSOM
**ASSIGNMENT: KILL CASTRO**
See CUBA CROSSING
**ASSO DI PICCHE OPERAZIONE CONTROSPIONAGGIO**
See OPERATION COUNTERSPY
**ASSO PIGLIA TUTTO**
See ACE UP MY SLEEVE
**ASTERIX CHEZ LES BRETONS**
See ASTERIX IN BRITAIN
**ASTERIX IN BRITAIN: THE MOVIE**
See ASTERIX IN BRITAIN
**ASTERIX LE GAULOIS**
See ASTERIX THE GAUL: 1
**ASTROLOGER, THE**
See SUICIDE CULT
**ATAQUE DE LOS ZOMBIES ATOMICOS**
See NIGHTMARE CITY
**ATLANTIC CITY, USA**

See ATLANTIC CITY
**ATOLL K**
See LAUREL AND HARDY: UTOPIA
**ATOR**
See ATOR, THE FIGHTING EAGLE
**ATOR L'INVINCIBLE**
See ATOR THE INVINCIBLE
**ATTACK OF THE MUSHROOM PEOPLE**
See MATANGO: FUNGUS OF TERROR
**ATTACK OF THE PHANTOMS**
See PHANTOM OF THE PARK, THE
**ATTACO ALLA PIOURA**
See SICILIAN CONNECTION, THE
**ATTACO ALLA PIOVRA**
See SICILIAN CLAN, THE
**ATTENTATO AI TRE GRANDI**
See DESERT COMMANDO
**ATTENTION LES YEUX!**
See LET'S MAKE A DIRTY MOVIE
**ATTILA**
See ATTILA THE HUN
**AU NOM DE TOUS LES MIENS**
See FOR THOSE I LOVED
**AU SERVICE DU DIABLE**
See DEVIL'S NIGHTMARE
**AURORA BY NIGHT**
See AURORA
**AUS DEM TAGEBUCH EINER SIEBZEHNJAEHRIGEN**
See COME MAKE LOVE WITH ME
**AUSTERLIZ**
See BATTLE OF AUSTERLITZ, THE
**AUSTRIA 1700**
See MARK OF THE DEVIL
**AUTOSTOP ROSSO SANGUE**
See DEATH DRIVE
**AUTUMN CHILD**
See REFLECTION OF FEAR, A
**AVENGERS, THE**
See LAST GLORY OF TROY, THE
**AVENUE O**
See MIXED BLOOD
**AVERE VENT'ANI**
See TO BE TWENTY
**B.L. STRYKER: THE DANCER'S TOUCH**
See DANCER'S TOUCH, THE
**BA-PAI CHUANO-SHIN**
See LONGEST BRIDGE, THE
**BAA BAA BLACKSHEEP**
See FLYING MISFITS, THE
**BABES IN TOYLAND**
See LAREL AND HARDY: BABES IN TOYLAND
**BABETTES GAESTEBUD**
See BABETTE'S FEAST
**BABY**
See BABY: SECRET OF THE LOST LEGEND
**BABY JOHN DOE**
See KIDNAPPING OF BABY JOHN, THE
**BABY, THE**
See DEVIL WITHIN HER, THE
**BACANALES ROMANAS**
See NIGHT WITH MESSALINA, A
**BACKWOODS**
See GEEK
**BACKWOODS MASSACRE**
See MIDNIGHT
**BAD**
See ANDY WARHOL'S BAD
**BAD TIMING: A SENSUAL OBSESSION**
See BAD TIMING
**BAKER COUNTY, USA**
See TRAPPED
**BALBOA: MILLIONAIRE'S**

**PARADISE**
See BALBOA
**BALLAD OF DEATH VALLEY**
See ANGRY GUN, THE
**BALLAD OF TAM-LIN**
See DEVIL'S WIDOW, THE
**BALLOON VENDOR, THE**
See MY YOUNG MAN
**BAMBOO DOLLS HOUSE**
See WOMEN IN CAGES
**BANDIDOS O CREPA TU . . . CHE VIVO IO**
See BANDIDOS
**BANG BANG**
See BANG BANG KID, THE
**BANG, BANG, YOU'VE GOT IT!**
See BANG BANG
**BAPTISM OF FIRE**
See AMERICAN ANGELS
**BARBARELLA, QUEEN OF THE GALAXY**
See BARBARELLA
**BARBARIANS, THE**
See BARBARIAN, THE
**BARON, THE**
See BARON AND THE KID, THE
**BASIC TRAINING**
See UP THE MILITARY
**BASKERVILLE CURSE, THE**
See SHERLOCK HOLMES: THE BASKERVILLE CURSE
**BAT. 21**
See BAT 21
**BATMAN: THE MOVIE**
See BATMAN
**BATTLE COMMAND**
See BATTLE SQUADRON
**BATTLE CREEK BRAWL**
See BIG BRAWL, THE
**BATTLE FOR ANZIO, THE**
See ANZIO
**BATTLE FORCE**
See BIGGEST BATTLE, THE
**BATTLE OF NERETVA**
See BATTLE ON THE RIVER NERETVA, THE
**BATTLE OF THE EAGLES**
See BATTLE SQUADRON
**BATTLE OF THE MARETHLINE**
See BIGGEST BATTLE, THE
**BATTLE RAGE**
See MISSING IN ACTION 2: THE BEGINNING
**BATTLE STRIPE**
See MEN, THE
**BATTLING BELLHOP**
See KID GALAHAD
**BATTLING HOOFER**
See SOMETHING TO SING ABOUT
**BAY COVEN**
See BAY COVE
**BAY OF BLOOD**
See LAST HOUSE ON THE LEFT PART 2, THE
**BE MY VALENTINE, OR ELSE . . .**
See X-RAY
**BEARTOOTH**
See BEARHEART OF THE GREAT NORTHWEST
**BEAST, THE**
See BEAST OF WAR, THE
**BEAST, THE**
See EQUINOX
**BEAUTIFUL AND WILD ON IBIZA**
See SEX ON THE ROCKS
**BEAUTIFUL BUT DEADLY**
See DON IS DEAD, THE
**BEAUTY AND THE BEAST, THE**
See LA BELLE ET LA BETE

**BEAUTY AND THE ROBOT, THE**
See SEX KITTENS GO TO COLLEGE
**BEDSIDE HEAD**
See DANISH BED AND BOARD
**BEDSIDE ROMANCE**
See DANISH PILLOW TALK
**BEFORE THE FACT**
See LAST HOUSE ON THE LEFT PART 2, THE
**BEHIND ENEMY LINES**
See P.O.W. – THE ESCAPE
**BEHIND THE CONVENT WALLS**
See BEHIND CONVENT WALLS
**BEHIND THE DOOR**
See DEVIL WITHIN HER, THE
**BEHIND THE DOOR**
See JAIL BIRD
**BEHIND THE SCENES OF AN X-RATED MOVIE**
See BEHIND THE SCENES OF AN ADULT MOVIE
**BELARUS FILE, THE**
See KOJAK: THE BELARUS FILE
**BELFAST ASSASSIN, THE**
See HARRY'S GAME
**BELL FROM HELL, A**
See BELL OF HELL, THE
**BELLE STARR**
See BELLE STARR STORY, THE
**BENJAMIN DISRAELI**
See SECRET LIVES OF THE BRITISH PRIME MINISTERS, THE: DISRAELI
**BENTLEY ACADEMY, THE**
See PRETTY SMART
**BERLIN INTERIOR**
See BERLIN AFFAIR, THE
**BERMUDAS: LA CUEVA DE LOS TIBURONES**
See SHARK'S CAVE, THE
**BERMUDE: LA FOSSA MALEDETTA**
See SHARK'S CAVE, THE
**BERRY GORDON'S THE LAST DRAGON**
See LAST DRAGON, THE
**BERSERKER: THE NORDIC CURSE**
See BERSERKER
**BETRAYED**
See LIFE IS BEAUTIFUL
**BEVERLY HILLS COWGIRL BLUES**
See BEVERLY HILLS CONNECTION
**BEWARE! THE BLOB**
See SON OF BLOB
**BEYOND OBSESSION**
See JAIL BIRD
**BEYOND THE BRIDGE**
See DOUBLE JEOPARDY
**BEYOND THE DOOR**
See JAIL BIRD
**BEYOND THE DOOR**
See DEVIL WITHIN HER, THE
**BEYOND THE DOOR 2**
See SHOCK
**BEYOND THE LAW**
See GOOD DIE FIRST FOR A HANDFUL OF SILVER, THE
**BEYOND THE LIMIT**
See HONORARY CONSUL, THE
**BEZHIN LUG**
See BEZHIN MEADOW
**BIANCHI CAVALLI D'AGOSTO**
See WHITE HORSES OF SUMMER, THE
**BIBLE . . . IN THE BEGINNING, THE**
See BIBLE, THE
**BICYCLE THIEF, THE**
See BICYCLE THIEVES
**BIG AND THE BAD, THE**
See CAN BE DONE AMIGO
**BIG BLACK PILL, THE**

See JOE DANCER VOL. 1
**BIG BOSS, THE**
See FISTS OF FURY
**BIG COUNTRY**
See GREAT OUTDOORS, THE
**BIG HOUSE, THE**
See DOIN' TIME
**BIG LOBBY, THE**
See ROSEBUD BEACH HOTEL, THE
**BIG RIP-OFF, THE**
See SHOT, THE
**BIG SHOWDOWN, THE**
See STORMRIDER
**BIG SLAMMER, THE**
See SLAMMER GIRLS
**BIG STORE, THE**
See MARX BROTHERS: THE BIG STORE
**BIG TIME OPERATORS**
See SMALLEST SHOW ON EARTH, THE
**BIGGLES**
See BIGGLES GETS OFF THE GROUND
**BIGGLES: ADVENTURES IN TIME**
See BIGGLES GETS OFF THE GROUND
**BILL JOHNSON STORY, THE**
See GOING FOR THE GOLD: THE BILL JOHNSON STORY
**BILLION DOLLAR BOY'S CLUB**
See BILLIONAIRE BOY'S CLUB
**BILLY**
See APACHE MASSACRE
**BILLY BRONCO**
See BRONCO BILLY
**BILLY ROSE'S DIAMOND HORSESHOE**
See DIAMOND HORSESHOE
**BIOHAZARD**
See WARNING SIGN
**BIONIC SHOWDOWN: THE SIX MILLION DOLLAR MAN AND THE BIONIC WOMAN**
See BIONIC SHOWDOWN, THE
**BIRD IN THE HAND, A**
See THREE INTO SEX WON'T GO
**BIRD WITH THE GLASS FEATHERS, THE**
See BIRD WITH THE CRYSTAL PLUMAGE, THE
**BIRDMEN, THE**
See OPERATION BRAINDRAIN
**BIRDS OF A FEATHER**
See LA CAGE AUX FOLLES
**BIRDS OF PREY**
See TURBO BLADE
**BITKA NA NERETVI**
See BATTLE ON THE RIVER NERETVA, THE
**BLACK CHRISTMAS**
See BLACK SABBATH
**BLACK ELIMINATOR, THE**
See DEATH DIMENSIONS
**BLACK EMMANUELLE NO. 2**
See BLACK EMMANUELLE 2
**BLACK FRANKENSTEIN**
See BLACKENSTEIN
**BLACK GESTAPO**
See GHETTO WARRIORS
**BLACK GODFATHER, THE**
See STREET WAR
**BLACK HARVEST OF COUNTESS DRACULA, THE**
See CURSE OF THE DEVIL
**BLACK HARVEST OF COUNTESS DRACULA, THE**
See WEREWOLF'S SHADOW, THE
**BLACK ISLAND, THE**

See TINTIN: THE BLACK ISLAND
**BLACK OAK CONSPIRACY**
See CONSPIRACY
**BLACK RIBBON FOR DEBORAH**
See TORMENT, THE
**BLACK STREETFIGHTER, THE**
See BLACK FIST
**BLACK TRASH**
See DEATH OF A SNOWMAN
**BLACKBOARD MASSACRE**
See MASSACRE AT CENTRAL HIGH
**BLACKFIRE**
See CODENAME: BLACKFIRE
**BLACKOUT**
See ATTIC, THE
**BLADE MASTER, THE**
See ATOR THE INVINCIBLE
**BLADES OF COURAGE**
See BLADES OF STEEL
**BLADESTORM**
See ATTACK OF THE NORMANS
**BLASTFIGHTER: L'EXECUTEUR**
See BLASTFIGHTER
**BLASTFIGHTER: THE FORCE OF VENGEANCE**
See BLASTFIGHTER
**BLAZING MAGNUM**
See BLAZING MAGNUMS
**BLESS 'EM ALL**
See ACT, THE
**BLIND DEAD, THE**
See TOMBS OF THE BLIND DEAD
**BLIND MAN'S BLUFF**
See CAULDRON OF BLOOD
**BLIND RAGE**
See BOYS NEXT DOOR, THE
**BLIND RAGE**
See SURROGATE, THE
**BLOCKHEADS**
See LAUREL AND HARDY: BLOCKHEADS
**BLONDE FROM PEKING, THE**
See PEKING BLONDE
**BLONDE SINNER**
See YIELD TO THE NIGHT
**BLOOD AND WINE**
See EQUALISER, THE: BLOOD AND WINE
**BLOOD BARON, THE**
See BARON BLOOD
**BLOOD BARRIER**
See BORDER, USA, THE
**BLOOD EVIL**
See DEMONS OF THE MIND
**BLOOD FARMERS**
See INVASION OF THE BLOOD FARMERS
**BLOOD FEAST OF THE BLIND DEAD**
See NIGHT OF THE SEAGULLS
**BLOOD FOR A SILVER DOLLAR**
See ONE SILVER DOLLAR
**BLOOD FOR DRACULA**
See ANDY WARHOL'S DRACULA
**BLOOD LEGACY**
See LEGACY OF BLOOD
**BLOOD MONEY**
See STRANGER AND THE GUNFIGHTER, THE
**BLOOD MONEY: THE STORY OF CLINTON AND NADINE**
See BLOOD MONEY
**BLOOD OF DR JEKYLL, THE**
See STRANGE CASE OF DOCTOR JEKYLL AND MISS OSBOURNE, THE
**BLOOD OF FRANKENSTEIN**
See DRACULA VERSUS FRANKENSTEIN
**BLOOD OF GHASTLY HORROR**
See MAN WITH THE SYNTHETIC

BRAIN, THE
**BLOOD SISTERS**
See SISTERS
**BLOOD SPLATTERED BRIDE, THE**
See BLOOD-SPATTERED BRIDE, THE
**BLOOD VOWS: THE STORY OF A MAFIA WIFE**
See BLOOD VOWS
**BLOOD VOYAGE**
See NIGHTMARE VOYAGE
**BLOOD WILL HAVE BLOOD**
See DEMONS OF THE MIND
**BLOODBATH**
See SKY IS FALLING, THE
**BLOODBATH BAY OF BLOOD**
See LAST HOUSE ON THE LEFT PART 2, THE
**BLOODBATH OF DR JEKYLL**
See STRANGE CASE OF DOCTOR JEKYLL AND MISS OSBOURNE, THE
**BLOODFIGHT**
See OPPONENT, THE
**BLOODLINE**
See SECRET LIVES OF THE BRITISH PRIME MINISTERS, THE: PITT
**BLOODSPELL**
See BOY FROM HELL, THE
**BLOODSUCKER**
See BLOODSUCKERS
**BLOODTIDE**
See BLOOD TIDE
**BLOODY BUSHIDO BLADE, THE**
See BUSHIDO BLADE, THE
**BLOODY CEREMONY**
See LEGEND OF BLOOD CASTLE, THE
**BLOODY CHE CONTRA**
See REBEL WITH A CAUSE
**BLOODY FIANCEE**
See BLOOD-SPATTERED BRIDE, THE
**BLOODY FIST, THE**
See BLOODY FISTS, THE
**BLOODY MARY**
See REBORN
**BLOODY SUNDAY**
See BLOODY BIRTHDAY
**BLUE EYES OF DEATH**
See PARAPSYCHICS
**BLUE FIN**
See SEA QUEST
**BLUE FYRE LADY**
See BLUE FIRE LADY
**BLUE HAWAII**
See ELVIS PRESLEY: BLUE HAWAII
**BLUE HOLOCAUST**
See BEYOND THE DARKNESS
**BLUE HOTEL: PRIVATE EYE**
See BLUE HOTEL
**BLUE MAN, THE**
See ETERNAL EVIL
**BLUE MONKEY**
See INVASION OF THE BODYSUCKERS
**BLUE MOVIE BLACKMAIL**
See SUPERBITCH
**BLUE MOVIE STAR**
See CONFESSIONS OF A BLUE MOVIE STAR
**BLUES FOR BUDER**
See B.L. STRYKER: BLUES FOR BUDER
**BLUETIGER FREITAG**
See BLOODY FRIDAY
**BLUT AN DEN LIPPEN**
See DAUGHTERS OF DARKNESS
**BOBBIE JOE AND THE OUTLAW**
See BOBBIE JO AND THE OUTLAW
**BOBBY JOE AND THE OUTLAW**
See BOBBIE JO AND THE OUTLAW

**BOBO**
See WALK LIKE A MAN
**BODY BEAT**
See DANCE ACADEMY
**BOGEYMAN 2**
See BOGEY MAN 2
**BOGIE: THE LAST HERO**
See BOGIE
**BOGUS BANDITS**
See LAUREL AND HARDY: BOGUS BANDITS
**BOHEMIAN GIRL, THE**
See LAUREL AND HARDY: THE BOHEMIAN GIRL
**BON VOYAGE, CHARLIE BROWN**
See CHARLIE BROWN: BON VOYAGE
**BON VOYAGE, CHARLIE BROWN (AND DON'T COME BACK!)**
See CHARLIE BROWN: BON VOYAGE
**BONES**
See PARKER
**BONNIE SCOTLAND**
See LAUREL AND HARDY: HEROES OF THE REGIMENT
**BOOBY TRAP**
See HOT, FAST AND LOOSE
**BOOGEY MAN, THE**
See BOGEY MAN, THE
**BOOGEYMAN 2**
See BOGEY MAN 2
**BOOTLEGGERS' ANGEL**
See BOOTLEGGERS
**BORDELLET: EN GLAEDESPIGES ERINDRINGER**
See BEST BIT OF CRUMPET IN DENMARK, THE
**BORDELLO**
See BEST BIT OF CRUMPET IN DENMARK, THE
**BORDER, THE**
See BORDER, USA, THE
**BORN AMERICAN**
See ARCTIC HEAT
**BOSAMBO**
See SANDERS OF THE RIVER
**BOSS**
See BLACK BOUNTY KILLER, THE
**BOSS NIGGER**
See BLACK BOUNTY KILLER, THE
**BOSTON AND KILBRIDE: THE CHINESE TYPEWRITER**
See CHINESE TYPEWRITER, THE
**BOTTOMS UP**
See WHAT A WAY TO GO
**BOUNTY KILLERS**
See BOUNTY KILLER, THE
**BOXER ADVENTURE**
See BOXER'S ADVENTURE, THE
**BOY NAMED CHARLIE BROWN, A**
See CHARLIE BROWN: A BOY NAMED CHARLIE BROWN
**BOYAR'S PLOT, THE: IVAN THE TERRIBLE – PART 2**
See IVAN THE TERRIBLE
**BRADDOCK: MISSING IN ACTION 3**
See MISSING IN ACTION 3
**BRAIN CREATURE**
See MIND KILLER
**BRAINKILL**
See SOMEONE BEHIND THE DOOR
**BRAT PATROL, THE**
See B.R.A.T. PATROL, THE
**BRAVE AND THE BEAUTIFUL, THE**
See MAGNIFICENT MATADOR, THE
**BRAVE FROG'S GREATEST ADVENTURE, THE**
See BRAVE FROG, THE: GREATEST ADVENTURE
**BRAVESTARR**

See BRAVESTARR: THE LEGEND
**BREAKDOWN**
See LOVELESS, THE
**BREAKFAST AT THE MANCHESTER MORGUE**
See LIVING DEAD AT THE MANCHESTER MORGUE, THE
**BREAKIN'**
See BREAKDANCE: THE MOVIE
**BREAKIN' 2 ELECTRIC BOOGALOO**
See BREAKDANCE 2: ELECTRIC BOOGALOO
**BREAKING THE RULES**
See BREAKING ALL THE RULES
**BREAKING THE SOUND BARRIER**
See SOUND BARRIER, THE
**BREAKOUT ON PRISON PLANET**
See SPACERAGE
**BRENN HEXE BRENN**
See MARK OF THE DEVIL
**BRIAN WALKER, PLEASE CALL HOME**
See INTO THIN AIR
**BRIDE, THE**
See HOUSE THAT CRIED MURDER, THE
**BRIDE, THE**
See UP AND COMING
**BROKEN BADGE, THE**
See POLICE IN ACTION 1: THE BROKEN BADGE
**BROKEN HEARTS AND MOSES**
See CRIMEWAVE
**BRONCO BUSTERS**
See GONE WITH THE WEST
**BRONENOSETS POTEMKIN**
See BATTLESHIP POTEMKIN, THE
**BRONZE GIRLS OF SHAOLIN**
See EIGHTEEN BRONZE GIRLS OF SHAOLIN, THE
**BROTHERS**
See HOUNDS OF WAR
**BRUCE AGAINST THE ODDS**
See BIG BOSS 2
**BRUCE AND THE SHAOLIN BRONZEMEN MASTER**
See BRUCE AND THE SHAOLIN BRONZEMEN
**BRUCE LEE, WE MISS YOU**
See DRAGON DIES HARD, THE
**BRUCE LEE: GAME OF DEATH**
See GAME OF DEATH
**BRUCE LEE: THE TRUE STORY**
See BRUCE LEE: THE MAN – THE MYTH
**BRUCE LI IN NEW GUINEA**
See BRUCE LEE IN NEW GUINEA
**BRUCE LI: THE INVINCIBLE**
See BRUCE LEE THE INVINCIBLE
**BRUCE LI'S GREATEST REVENGE**
See BRUCE LEE'S GREATEST REVENGE
**BRUCE'S DEADLY FINGERS**
See BRUCE'S FINGER
**BRUTE AND THE BEAST, THE**
See COLT CONCERT
**BUCK ROGERS**
See BUCK ROGERS IN THE 25TH CENTURY
**BUFFALO BILL**
See BUFFALO BILL AND THE INDIANS, OR SITTING BULL'S HISTORY LESSON
**BUILD MY GALLOWS HIGH**
See OUT OF THE PAST
**BUIO OMEGA**
See BEYOND THE DARKNESS
**BULLET FOR A GANGSTER**
See BULLET FOR PRETTY BOY, A

**BULLET TRAIN, THE**
See NEGATIVE CONTACT
**BULLFIGHTERS, THE**
See LAUREL AND HARDY: THE BULLFIGHTERS
**BUMMER**
See SADIST, THE
**BUNNY PICNIC, THE**
See TALE OF THE BUNNY PARK, THE
**BURGESS, PHILBY AND MACLEAN: SPY SCANDAL OF THE CENTURY**
See PHILBY, BURGESS AND MACLEAN
**BURN!**
See BATTLE OF THE ANTILLES
**BURN, WITCH, BURN!**
See NIGHT OF THE EAGLE
**BURNING CROSS, THE**
See KLANSMAN, THE
**BURNING MAN, THE**
See DANGEROUS SUMMER, A
**BURNING QUESTION, THE**
See REEFER MADNESS
**BURNING, THE**
See DON'T GO INTO THE HOUSE
**BUTCHER, THE**
See PSYCHO FROM TEXAS
**C.A.S.H.**
See W.H.I.F.F.S.
**C.H.U.D. 2: BUD THE CHUD**
See C.H.U.D. 2
**C.O.D.**
See SNAP
**CABIRIA**
See NIGHTS OF CABIRIA
**CAGE, THE**
See MAFU CAGE, THE
**CAGED HEART, THE**
See L'ADDITION
**CAHILL**
See CAHILL: U.S. MARSHAL
**CAIN'S WAY**
See CAIN'S CUT-THROATS
**CALCULUS AFFAIR, THE**
See TINTIN: THE CALCULUS AFFAIR
**CALHOUN**
See METAL FORCE
**CALIFORNIA DRIVE-IN GIRLS**
See CARHOPS, THE
**CALIFORNIA HOLIDAY**
See ELVIS PRESLEY: SPINOUT
**CALIGULA E MESSALINA**
See CALIGULA AND MESSALINA
**CALIGULA ET MESSALINA**
See CALIGULA AND MESSALINA
**CALIGULA'S HOT NIGHTS**
See CALIGULA EROTICA
**CALL ME A CAB**
See CARRY ON CABBY
**CALL ME GENIUS**
See HANCOCK: THE REBEL
**CALL TO GLORY**
See BLADE RIDER: ATTACK OF THE INDIAN NATION
**CALL TO GLORY: JFK**
See CALL TO GLORY
**CALLAN**
See THIS IS CALLAN
**CAMILLE**
See CAMILLE 2000
**CAMORRA MAN, THE**
See PROFESSOR, THE
**CAMORRA MEMBER, THE**
See PROFESSOR, THE
**CAMPANOS ROJAS**
See MEXICO IN FLAMES
**CAMPSITE MASSACRE**
See FINAL TERROR, THE

**CAMPUS CORPSE, THE**
See CURIOUS CASE OF THE CAMPUS CORPSE, THE
**CAN CAN**
See CAN-CAN
**CAN I COME AGAIN?**
See BLONDE AMBITION
**CAN I COME TOO?**
See BLONDE AMBITION
**CANDIDATO PER UN ASSASSINO**
See CANDIDATE FOR A KILLING
**CANDIDO EROTICA**
See CANDIDO EROTICO
**CANDY REGENTAG**
See KISS THE NIGHT
**CANICLE**
See DOG DAY
**CANNIBAL APOCALIPSIS**
See CANNIBAL APOCALYPSE
**CANNIBAL ORGY**
See SPIDER BABY
**CANNIBAL WOMEN IN THE AVOCADO JUNGLE OF DEATH**
See PIRANHA WOMEN
**CANNIBALS**
See EATEN ALIVE
**CANNIBALS ARE IN THE STREETS, THE**
See CANNIBAL APOCALYPSE
**CANNIBALS IN THE CITY**
See CANNIBAL APOCALYPSE
**CANNON MOVIE TALES: RED RIDING HOOD**
See RED RIDING HOOD
**CANNON MOVIE TALES: SLEEPING BEAUTY**
See SLEEPING BEAUTY
**CANNON MOVIE TALES: SNOW WHITE**
See SNOW WHITE AND THE SEVEN DWARFS
**CANNON MOVIE TALES: THE EMPEROR'S NEW CLOTHES**
See EMPEROR'S NEW CLOTHES, THE
**CANNONBALL**
See CARQUAKE
**CANNONBALL 2**
See CANNONBALL RUN 2
**CANON OPERATION, THE**
See CANNON OPERATION
**CANTONEN IRON KUNG FU**
See CANTON IRON KUNG FU
**CANTONESE IRON KUNG FU**
See CANTON IRON KUNG FU
**CAPTAIN APACHE**
See GUN OF APRIL MORNING, THE
**CAPTAIN LUST AND THE PIRATE WOMEN**
See CAPTAIN LUST
**CAPTAIN MIDNIGHT**
See ON THE AIR LIVE WITH CAPTAIN MIDNIGHT
**CAPTIVE HEARTS**
See FATE OF THE HUNTER
**CAPTIVE HEARTS**
See FIRE WITH FIRE
**CAPTIVE WOMEN**
See TRIANGLE OF LUST
**CARAVAN OF COURAGE**
See CARAVAN OF COURAGE: AN EWOK ADVENTURE
**CARMILLA**
See WHAT NEXT?
**CARNABY M.D.**
See DOCTOR IN CLOVER
**CARNACITA**
See CARNAL REVENGE
**CARNAGE**
See LAST HOUSE ON THE LEFT

PART 2, THE
**CARNE PER FRANKENSTEIN**
See ANDY WARHOL'S
FRANKENSTEIN
**CARNIVAL OF TERROR**
See FUNHOUSE, THE
**CAROSELLO NAPOLETANO**
See NEAPOLITAN CAROUSEL
**CARRY ON SAILOR**
See CARRY ON JACK
**CARRY ON TV**
See DENTIST ON THE JOB
**CARRY ON VAMPIRE**
See CARRY ON SCREAMING
**CARRY ON VENUS**
See CARRY ON JACK
**CASE OF THE MIDDLE-AGED WIFE, THE**
See AGATHA CHRISTIE
COLLECTION, THE: THE CASE OF
THE MIDDLE-AGED WIFE
**CASE OF THE NOTORIOUS NUN, THE**
See PERRY MASON: THE CASE OF
THE NOTORIOUS NUN
**CAST A GIANT SHADOW**
See EVASIVE PEACE
**CAT IN THE CAGE**
See CAT IN A CAGE
**CAT SQUAD: PYTHON WOLF**
See C.A.T. SQUAD 2: OPERATION
PYTHON WOLF
**CATCH THE HEAT**
See FEEL THE HEAT
**CATHERINE**
See CATHERINE CHERIE
**CATHERINE THE GREAT**
See RISE OF CATHERINE THE
GREAT, THE
**CATHOLICS, THE**
See CONFLICT, THE
**CATHY'S CHILD**
See CATHIE'S CHILD
**CATTIVI PENSIERI**
See WHO MISLAID MY WIFE?
**CAVE OF THE SHARKS**
See SHARK'S CAVE, THE
**CELESTINE, MAID AT YOUR SERVICE**
See CELESTINE
**CELLESTINE, BONNE A TOUT FAIRE**
See CELESTINE
**CEMETERY GIRLS**
See COUNT DRACULA'S GREAT
LOVE
**CEMETERY GIRLS**
See WAKING HOUR, THE
**CENT VINGT-DEUX RUE DE PROVENCE**
See NEVER LOVE A HOOKER
**CENTRESPREAD**
See CENTRE SPREAD
**C'ERA UNA VOLTA IL WEST**
See ONCE UPON A TIME IN THE
WEST
**CERCATI UN POSTO PER MORIRE**
See FIND A PLACE TO DIE
**CEREMONIA SANGRIENTA**
See LEGEND OF BLOOD CASTLE,
THE
**CERTAIN HEAT**
See SPOOK WHO SAT BY THE DOOR,
THE
**CHAIN REACTION**
See STATE OF EMERGENCY, A
**CHAINED WOMEN**
See BLACK MAMA, WHITE MAMA
**CHAINS OF HATE**
See BLACK MAMA, WHITE MAMA

**CHALLENGE OF THE TIGER**
See DRAGON BRUCE LEE
**CHALLENGE TO SURVIVE**
See LAND OF NO RETURN, THE
**CHAMBER OF FEAR**
See TORTURE ZONE, THE
**CHAMBER OF TORTURES**
See BARON BLOOD
**CHAMPAGNE FOR BREAKFAST**
See TALK NAUGHTY TO ME
**CHAMPION ON FIRE**
See NINJA OPERATION 8:
CHAMPION ON FIRE
**CHANDLERTOWN**
See MARLOWE: PRIVATE EYE
**CHARLEY HANNAH**
See CHARLEY HANNAH'S WAR
**CHARLEYS NICHTEN**
See CONFESSIONS OF A SEXY
PHOTOGRAPHER
**CHARLEY'S TANTE NACKT**
See SEXY DOZEN, THE
**CHARLIE AND THE GREAT BALLOON CHASE**
See CHARLIE'S BALLOON
**CHARLOTTE: A GIRL MURDERED**
See CHARLOTTE
**CHASE FOR THE GOLDEN NEEDLES, THE**
See GOLDEN NEEDLES
**CHECK IS IN THE MAIL, THE**
See CHEQUE IS IN THE POST, THE
**CHEERING SECTION**
See CRAZY CAMPUS
**CHEREZ TERNII K ZVEZDAM**
See HUMANOID WOMAN
**CHERYL HANSON: COVER GIRL**
See COVER GIRL
**CHESSGAME: ENTER HASSAN**
See ALAMUT AMBUSH, THE
**CHI SEI?**
See DEVIL WITHIN HER, THE
**CHI TROUA UN AMICO TROUA UN TESORO**
See WHO FINDS A FRIEND FINDS A
TREASURE
**CH'I-SOU SHIN ERH TAO**
See DYNAMITE TRIO
**CHIBIKO REMI TO MEIKEN KAPI**
See NOBODY'S BOY
**CHICKIE**
See CHICKIE TETTRAZZINI
**CHIKIYU KOGERI MEIREI**
See WAR OF THE MONSTERS
**CHIKYU BOIGUN**
See MYSTERIANS, THE
**CHILDREN OF BLOOD**
See CAULDRON OF BLOOD
**CHILDREN OF PARADISE**
See LES ENFANTS DU PARADIS
**CHILDREN'S WAR, THE**
See WAR AND LOVE
**CHILLING, THE**
See NIGHT OF THE ZOMBIES, THE
**CHIN-SE TAI YANG**
See DRAGON DIES HARD, THE
**CHINESE WEB, THE**
See SPIDERMAN: THE DRAGON'S
CHALLENGE
**CHING-WU MEW SU-TSI**
See FISTS OF FURY 2
**CHINO**
See VALDEZ: THE HALF-BREED
**CHISSA PERCHE CAPITANO TUTTO A ME**
See WHY DID YOU PICK ON ME?
**CHISSA PERSCHE . . . CAPITANO TUTTO A ME**
See SHERIFF AND THE SATELLITE

KID, THE
**CHLOE IN THE AFTERNOON**
See LOVE IN THE AFTERNOON
**CHOICE KILL**
See DANGEROUSLY CLOSE
**CHOKE CANYON**
See ON DANGEROUS GROUND
**CHOSEN, THE**
See HOLOCAUST 2000
**CHRISTINA AND SEXUAL RETRAINING**
See CHRISTINA
**CHRISTINA Y LA RECONVERSION SEXUAL**
See CHRISTINA
**CHRISTMAS AT THE BROTHEL**
See LOVE BY APPOINTMENT
**CHRISTMAS TIME IN A BROTHEL**
See LOVE BY APPOINTMENT
**CHRISTOFORO COLOMBO**
See CHRISTOPHER COLUMBUS
**CHUEH-TOU LAO-HU CHUANG**
See TOUGH GUY
**CHUMP AT OXFORD, A**
See LAUREL AND HARDY: A CHUMP
AT OXFORD
**CIAK MULL, L'UNO DELLA VENDETTA**
See CHUCK MOOL
**CICLON**
See CYCLONE
**CINDERELLA**
See OTHER CINDERELLA, THE
**CINDERELLA'S WONDERLAND**
See CINDERELLA'S WONDERWORLD
**CINQUE PER L'INFERNO**
See FIVE FOR HELL
**CINQUE TOMBE PER UN MEDIUM**
See CEMETERY OF THE LIVING
DEAD
**CIRCLE OF IRON**
See SILENT FLUTE, THE
**CIRCLE OF POWER**
See BRAINWASH
**CIRCUS WORLD**
See MAGNIFICENT SHOWMAN, THE
**CIRCUS, THE**
See CHARLIE CHAPLIN: THE
CIRCUS
**CITY LIGHTS**
See CHARLIE CHAPLIN: CITY
LIGHTS
**CITY OF NIGHT**
See NIGHTMARE CITY
**CITY OF SHADOWS**
See NIGHTMARE CITY
**CITY OF THE WALKING DEAD**
See NIGHTMARE CITY
**CITY ON ANGELS**
See COVER KILL
**CLAIRVOYANT, THE**
See KILLING HOUR, THE
**CLAMBAKE**
See ELVIS PRESLEY: CLAMBAKE
**CLARISSE**
See CLARISSA
**CLASH OF SWORDS**
See SWORD OF THE VALIANT
**CLASS OF 1984**
See CLASS OF '84
**CLASS REUNION**
See NATIONAL LAMPOON'S CLASS
REUNION
**CLAUDIA'S STORY**
See CLAUDIA
**CLINIC XCLUSIVE**
See SEX CLINIC
**CLONUS HORROR, THE**
See CLONUS

**CLOUD WALTZING**
See CLOUD WALTZER
**CLOUDS OVER EUROPE**
See Q PLANES
**COCAINA**
See COCAINE WARS
**COCAINE**
See MIXED BLOOD
**COCAINE: ONE MAN'S SEDUCTION**
See COCAINE: ONE MAN'S POISON
**COCOON 2**
See COCOON: THE RETURN
**CODA**
See SYMPHONY OF EVIL
**CODENAME: FIREFOX**
See CODENAME: FOXFIRE – SLAY IT
AGAIN SAM
**COLEGIALAS LESBIANAS Y EL
PLACER DE PERVERTIR**
See SEXUAL DESIRES
**COLLEGE**
See BUSTER KEATON: COLLEGE
**COLONEL BLIMP**
See LIFE AND DEATH OF COLONEL
BLIMP, THE
**COLORADO STONE**
See GOT IT MADE
**COLPI DI LUCE**
See LIGHTBLAST
**COLPI IN CANNA**
See LOADED GUNS
**COLPO MAESTRO AL SERVIZIO DI
SUA MAESTA BRITANNICA**
See GREAT DIAMOND ROBBERY,
THE
**COLUMBIA CONNECTION, THE**
See DEAD WRONG
**COMBAT ZONE**
See HOW SLEEP THE BRAVE
**COME AND GET IT**
See LUNCH WAGON
**COME RUBARE LA CORONA
D'INGHILTERRA**
See FANTASTIC ARGOMAN
**COME WITH ME MY LOVE**
See TAKE TIME TO SMELL THE
FLOWERS
**COMING ATTRACTIONS**
See LOOSE SHOES
**COMING OF ALIENS, A**
See VERY CLOSE ENCOUNTERS OF
THE FOURTH KIND
**COMING OF ANGELS, A: THE
SEQUEL**
See ANGELS
**COMING-OUT PARTY, A**
See VERY IMPORTANT PERSON
**COMMANCHO BLANCO**
See WHITE COMMANCHE
**COMMANDO ATTACK**
See PLACE IN HELL, A
**COMMANDO THE NINJA**
See AMERICAN COMMANDO NINJA
**COMPANY OF KILLERS**
See HIT TEAM, THE
**COMPLICATED INTRIGUE OF BACK
ALLEYS AND CRIMES**
See CAMORRA
**COMPUTER WIZARD**
See COMPUTER KID, THE
**CON MEN, THE**
See CON ARTISTS, THE
**CONCORDE AFFAIRE SEVENTY-
NINE**
See CONCORDE AFFAIR
**CONCORDE, THE: AIRPORT '79**
See AIRPORT '80: THE CONCORDE
**CONDOR MAN**
See CONDORMAN

**CONFESSIONAL, THE**
See CONFESSIONAL MURDERS, THE
**CONFESSIONS OF A MARRIED MAN**
See SUCCESS
**CONFESSIONS OF THE NAUGHTY
NYMPHOS**
See SEX WITH THE STARS
**CONFIDENTIALLY YOURS**
See FINALLY SUNDAY
**CONQUEROR WORM, THE**
See WITCHFINDER GENERAL
**CONQUERORS, THE**
See PIONEER BUILDERS
**CONQUEST OF MYCENAE, THE**
See HERCULES CHALLENGE
**CONQUEST OF THE NORMANS**
See ATTACK OF THE NORMANS
**CONTES PERVERS**
See EROTIC TALES
**CONTRABAND**
See FORTY MILLION BUCKS
**CONTRORAPINA**
See RIP-OFF, THE
**COOK AND PEARY: THE RACE TO
THE POLE**
See ONLY ONE WINNER
**COOKIE**
See STREETWALKIN'
**COOLANGATTA GOLD, THE**
See GOLD AND THE GLORY, THE
**COP KILLERS**
See ORDER OF DEATH
**COP OF HONOUR**
See COP'S HONOUR
**COPENHAGEN NIGHTS**
See CANDIDO EROTICO
**CORLEONE: FATHER OF THE
GODFATHERS**
See CORLEONE
**CORMACK OF THE MOUNTIES**
See CORMACK
**CORNETTI A COLAZIONE**
See COUNTRY NURSE
**CORPSE COLLECTORS, THE**
See CAULDRON OF BLOOD
**CORPSE, THE**
See VELVET HOUSE, THE
**CORRI, UOMO, CORRI**
See RUN, MAN, RUN
**CORRUPT**
See ORDER OF DEATH
**CORSICAN BROTHERS, THE**
See CHEECH AND CHONG'S THE
CORSICAN BROTHERS, THE
**CORVETTE SUMMER**
See HOT ONE, THE
**COSMIC PRINCESS**
See SPACE 1999: COSMIC PRINCESS
**COUNT DRACULA AND HIS
VAMPIRE BRIDE**
See SATANIC RITES OF DRACULA,
THE
**COUNT YOUR BLESSINGS**
See APACHE MASSACRE
**COL'NTDOWN TO DISASTER**
See THUNDERBIRDS: TERROR IN
NEW YORK CITY/ATLANTIC
INFERNO
**COUNTERFEIT COMMANDOS**
See INGLORIOUS BASTARDS, THE
**COUNTERFEIT KILLER, THE**
See CRACKSHOT
**COUNTESS DRACULA**
See LEGEND OF BLOOD CASTLE,
THE
**COUP DE TORCHON**
See CLEAN SLATE
**COURT MARTIAL**
See CARRINGTON V.C.

**COVERGIRL**
See COVERGIRLS
**COWBOY AND THE GIRL, THE**
See LADY TAKES A CHANCE, A
**CRAB WITH THE GOLDEN CLAWS,
THE**
See TINTIN: THE CRAB WITH THE
GOLDEN CLAWS
**CRACKERS**
See STREET GIRLS
**CRACKING UP**
See SMORGASBORD
**CRASH**
See CRASH OF FLIGHT 401, THE
**CRAZY JACK AND THE BOY**
See SILENCE
**CREATED TO KILL**
See EMBRYO
**CREATURE**
See TITAN FIND
**CREATURE WASN'T NICE, THE**
See SPACESHIP
**CREATURES OF THE PREHISTORIC
PLANET**
See VAMPIRE MEN OF THE LOST
PLANET
**CREATURES OF THE RED PLANET**
See VAMPIRE MEN OF THE LOST
PLANET
**CREEPER, THE**
See RITUALS
**CREEPING FLESH, THE**
See CRAZE
**CRIME AND PASSION**
See ACE UP MY SLEEVE
**CRIME OF HONOR**
See CRY FOR JUSTICE, A
**CRIME OF HONOUR**
See CRY FOR JUSTICE, A
**CRIMES IN THE WAX MUSEUM**
See NIGHTMARE IN WAX
**CRIMINAL ACT**
See TUNNELS
**CRIMSON CULT, THE**
See CURSE OF THE CRIMSON ALTAR
**CRITTERS 2: THE MAIN COURSE**
See CRITTERS 2
**CRONACA DI UNA MORTE
ANNUNCIATA**
See CHRONICLE OF A DEATH
FORETOLD
**CROSS SHOT**
See MARK
**CROSSWINDS**
See OUT OF COTROL
**CRUCIBLE OF HORROR**
See VELVET HOUSE, THE
**CRUISE MISSILE**
See MISSILE-X
**CRUNCH**
See KINKY COACHES AND THE
POM-POM PUSSYCATS, THE
**CRY DEMON**
See EVIL, THE
**CRY FOR JUSTICE, A**
See POLICE IN ACTION 5: A CRY FOR
JUSTICE
**CRY FOR LOVE, A**
See ADDICTION: A CRY FOR LOVE
**CRY FOR ME**
See APACHE MASSACRE
**CRY FOR ME, BILLY**
See APACHE MASSACRE
**CRY FOR STRANGERS**
See CRY FOR THE STRANGERS
**CRY OF INNOCENCE**
See PRIME SUSPECT
**CRYING BLUE SKY**
See EYES OF FIRE

**CRYPT OF DARK SECRETS**
See MARDI GRAS MASSACRE
**CRYPT OF THE BLIND DEATH, THE**
See TOMBS OF THE BLIND DEAD
**CURLEY**
See ADVENTURES OF CURLEY AND
HIS GANG, THE
**CURLEY AND HIS GANG**
See CURLEY AND HIS GANG IN THE
HAUNTED MANSION
**CURSE 2: THE BITE**
See BITE, THE
**CURSE OF THE VAMPIRES**
See CREATURES OF EVIL
**CURSE OF THE VOODOO**
See CURSE OF SIMBA, THE
**CUTTER AND BONE**
See CUTTER'S WAY
**D.C. CAB**
See STREET FLEET
**DA DUNKERQUE ALL VITTORIA**
See FROM HELL TO VICTORY
**DADAH IS DEATH**
See LONG WAY FROM HOME, A:
DADAH IS DEATH
**DADDY WANTED**
See LOOK WHO'S TALKING
**DAIKYOJU GAPPA**
See GAPPA THE TRIFIBIAN
MONSTER
**DALEKS: INVASION EARTH 2150
A.D.**
See DOCTOR WHO: INVASION
EARTH 2150 A.D.
**DALLE ARDENNE ALL'INFERNO**
See DIRTY HEROES
**DANCE OF DEATH**
See TORTURE ZONE, THE
**DANCING MASTERS, THE**
See LAUREL AND HARDY: THE
DANCING MASTERS
**DANDY, THE ALL-AMERICAN GIRL**
See SWEET REVENGE
**DANG KOU-TAN**
See BLOODY FISTS, THE
**DANGER DOWN UNDER**
See HARRIS DOWN UNDER
**DANGER GROWS WILD**
See POPPIES ARE ALSO FLOWERS
**DANGER IN THE SKIES**
See PILOT, THE
**DANGEROUS ENCOUNTERS OF
THE FIRST KIND**
See DON'T PLAY WITH FIRE
**DANGEROUS FRIEND, A**
See TODD KILLINGS, THE
**DANGEROUS LOVE, A**
See BLACK MARKET BABY
**DANISH DENTIST ON THE JOB**
See DENTIST ON THE JOB
**DANISH ESCORT GIRLS**
See ESCORT GIRLS
**DANNY BOY**
See ANGEL
**D'ARDENELLE**
See HAREM
**DARK POWERS**
See DARK POWER, THE
**DARK ROOM**
See DARKROOM, THE
**DARK SIDE OF MIDNIGHT, THE**
See CREEPER, THE
**DARLING I AM GROWING
YOUNGER**
See MONKEY BUSINESS
**D'ARTAGNAN L'INTREPIDE**
See GLORIOUS MUSKETEERS, THE
**DARYL**
See D.A.R.Y.L.

**DAS ARCHE NOAH PRINZIP**
See NOAH'S ARK PRINCIPLE, THE
**DAS AUGE DER SPINNE**
See DEADLY REVENGE
**DAS BOOT**
See BOAT, THE
**DAS CABINET DES DR CALIGARI**
See CABINET OF DOCTOR
CALIGARI, THE
**DAS GANZ GROSSE DING**
See WANTED BABYSITTER
**DAS GEHEIMIS DER JUNGEN
WITSE**
See BLACK VEIL FOR LISA, A
**DAS GEHEIMNIS DER SCHWARZEN
HANSCHUHE**
See BIRD WITH THE CRYSTAL
PLUMAGE, THE
**DAS TEUFELSCAMP DER
VERLORENEN FRAUEN**
See TRIANGLE OF LUST
**DAUGHTERS OF DRACULA**
See VAMPYRES
**DAVID CROCKETT, KING OF THE
WILD FRONTIER**
See DAVY CROCKETT
**DAVID E GOLIA**
See DAVID AND GOLIATH
**DAVID LLOYD GEORGE**
See SECRET LIVES OF THE BRITISH
PRIME MINISTERS, THE: LLOYD
GEORGE
**DAVY CROCKETT, KING OF THE
WILD FRONTIER**
See DAVY CROCKETT
**DAWN OF THE DEAD**
See ZOMBIES: DAWN OF THE DEAD
**DAY AFTER HALLOWEEN**
See SNAPSHOT: AUSTRALIAN
STYLE
**DAY AT THE RACES, A**
See MARX BROTHERS: A DAY AT
THE RACES
**DAY OF ANGER**
See GUN LAW
**DAY OF RECKONING**
See GUNS OF DIABLO, THE
**DAY OF TERROR, NIGHT OF FEAR**
See POLICE IN ACTION 6: DAY OF
TERROR, NIGHT OF FEAR
**DAY OF THE APOCALYPSE**
See TIME SLIP
**DAY OF THE WOMAN**
See I SPIT ON YOUR GRAVE
**DAY OF WRATH**
See GUN LAW
**DAY THE LORD GOT BUSTED, THE**
See MIRACLE MAN, THE
**DAY THE SCREAMING STOPPED,
THE**
See COMEBACK, THE
**DAYBREAK**
See LE JOUR SE LEVE
**DAYS OF WRATH**
See GUN LAW
**DE LA PART DES COPAINS**
See COLD SWEAT
**DE LIFT**
See LIFT, THE
**DE SCHORPIOEN**
See SCORPION, THE
**DE VERDE MAN**
See FOURTH MAN, THE
**DEAD AS A DOORMAN**
See DOORMAN
**DEAD END: CRADLE OF CRIME**
See DEAD END
**DEAD EVEN**
See DEAD-TIME STORIES: VOLUME 3

**DEAD KIDS**
See SMALL TOWN MASSACRE
**DEAD OF NIGHT**
See DEATHDREAM
**DEAD PEOPLE**
See MESSIAH OF EVIL
**DEAD PLANET, THE**
See DOCTOR WHO: THE DALEKS
**DEAD TIME**
See FREAKY FAIRY TALES
**DEAD TIME STORIES**
See DEAD-TIME STORIES: VOLUME 1
**DEADLINE MADRID**
See DEADLINE: MADRID
**DEADLY AVENGER**
See LOVELY BUT DEADLY
**DEADLY DECEPTION**
See DEADLY DECEPTIONS
**DEADLY EYES**
See RATS, THE
**DEADLY GAME, THE**
See STUNTS: THE DEADLY GAME
**DEADLY MISSION, THE**
See DIRTY DOZEN, THE: THE
DEADLY MISSION
**DEADLY SNAIL VERSUS KUNG FU
KILLERS**
See DEADLY SNAKE VERSUS KUNG
FU KILLERS
**DEADLY STING**
See METAMORPHOSIS
**DEADLY TREASURE OF THE
PIRANA**
See KILLERFISH
**DEADLY WARRIORS**
See NINE DEATHS OF THE NINJA
**DEADLY WHEN AROUSED**
See SEX HUNGRY GIRLS
**DEATH BITE**
See SPASMS
**DEATH CAR**
See DEATH CAR ON THE FREEWAY
**DEATH CARS**
See DEATH CAR ON THE FREEWAY
**DEATH COMES FROM THE DARK**
See CAULDRON OF BLOOD
**DEATH CORPS**
See SHOCK WAVES
**DEATH DIMENSION**
See DEATH DIMENSIONS
**DEATH DORM**
See PRANKS
**DEATH GAME**
See DEATHGAME
**DEATH HAS BLUE EYES**
See PARAPSYCHICS
**DEATH HOUSE**
See SILENT NIGHT, BLOODY NIGHT
**DEATH IN FULL VIEW**
See DEATHWATCH
**DEATH IN PERSEPOLIS**
See TEN LITTLE INDIANS
**DEATH IN THE SUN**
See WHISPERING DEATH
**DEATH IN THE VATICAN**
See VATICAN CONSPIRACY, THE
**DEATH IS CHILD'S PLAY**
See ISLAND OF DEATH
**DEATH LEGACY**
See GIRL'S SCHOOL SCREAMERS
**DEATH MERCHANTS, THE**
See ASSASSINATION, THE
**DEATH OF A CENTREFOLD: THE
DOROTHY STRATTEN STORY**
See DEATH OF A CENTREFOLD
**DEATH OF A STRANGER**
See ASSASSINATION, THE
**DEATH OF RICHIE, THE**
See RICHIE

**DEATH ON THE FREEWAY**
See DEATH CAR ON THE FREEWAY
**DEATH RACE**
See STATE OF DIVISION
**DEATH SCREAM**
See DEADLY TRAP, THE
**DEATH SPA**
See WITCH BITCH
**DEATH STALKER**
See DEATHSTALKER
**DEATH WATCH**
See DEATHWATCH
**DEATH WAVES**
See SHOCK WAVES
**DEATH WHEELERS, THE**
See PSYCHOMANIA
**DEATHMASK**
See DAMNING, THE
**DEATH'S DOOR**
See CONFESSIONAL MURDERS, THE
**DEATH'S ECSTASY**
See BEAST, THE
**DEATHSTALKER 2: DUEL OF THE TITANS**
See DEATHSTALKER 2
**DEATHSTALKER 3: THE WARRIORS FROM HELL**
See DEATHSTALKER
**DEBORAH**
See TORMENT, THE
**DECOY**
See MYSTERY SUBMARINE
**DEEP IN THE HEART**
See HANDGUN
**DEFENCE OF MINNIE DEAD, THE**
See HANLON: IN DEFENCE OF MINNIE DEAD
**DEFENSE CONDITION FOUR**
See DEF-CON 4
**DEFY TO THE LAST PARADISE**
See EATEN ALIVE
**DELINQUENT SCHOOLGIRLS**
See DELINQUENTS
**DELOS ADVENTURE, THE**
See DELOS FILE, THE
**DELTA PI**
See MUGSY'S GIRLS
**DELUSION**
See HOUSE WHERE DEATH LIVED, THE
**DEMON PLANET, THE**
See PLANET OF THE VAMPIRES
**DEMONI**
See DEMONS
**DEMONI 2**
See DEMONS 2
**DEMONS 1**
See DEMONS
**DEMONS 2: THE NIGHTMARE BEGINS**
See DEMONS 2
**DEMONS 2: THE NIGHTMARE CONTINUES**
See DEMONS 2
**DEMON'S MASK, THE**
See BLACK SUNDAY
**DEMONWORLD**
See DEMONWORLD, MESSENGER OF DEATH
**DENNIS THE MENACE MOVIE EXCLUSIVES: MEMORY MAYHEM**
See DENNIS: THE MOVIE – MEMORY MAYHEM
**DER AANSLAG**
See ASSAULT, THE
**DER AUFZUG**
See OUT OF ORDER
**DER BULLE UND DAS MADCHEN**
See COP AND THE GIRL, THE

**DER LIEBERSCHULER**
See JULIA
**DER MAFIA BOSS: SIE TOTEN WIE SCHAKALE**
See MANHUNT
**DER RICHTER UND SEIN HENKER**
See DECEPTION
**DER SCHREI DER SCHWARZEN WOLFE**
See CRY OF THE BLACK WOLVES
**DER SCHWARZE PANTHER VON RATANA**
See KILLER PANTHER, THE
**DER TOD EINES FREMDEN**
See ASSASSINATION, THE
**DER WURGER KOMMT AUF LEISEN SOCKEN**
See STRANGLER OF VIENNA, THE
**DER ZWEITE FRUHLING**
See SECOND SPRING, A
**DERANGED**
See WELCOME TO ARROW BEACH
**DERANGED**
See IDAHO TRANSFER
**DES TEUFELS PARADIES**
See DEVIL'S PARADISE, THE
**DESERT ATTACK**
See ICE-COLD IN ALEX
**DESERT TANKS**
See BATTLE OF EL ALAMEIN, THE
**DESERT WARRIOR**
See WHEELS OF FIRE
**DESIGN FOR LOVE**
See CONFESSIONS OF A SEX MANIAC
**DESIGN FOR LUST**
See CONFESSIONS OF A SEX MANIAC
**DESIRES OF A NAUGHTY NYMPHO**
See JACK 'N' JILL 2
**DESPERATE CHASE**
See BLOOD OF THE DRAGON
**DESTINATION MOONBASE ALPHA**
See SPACE 1999: DESTINATION MOONBASE ALPHA
**DESTROYER**
See DESTROYERS, THE
**DESTRUCTION FORCE**
See DIRTY GANG
**DESTRUCTORS, THE**
See MARSEILLE CONTRACT, THE
**DETSTVO GORKOVO**
See CHILDHOOD OF MAXIM GORKY, THE
**DEUX AFFREUX SUR LE SABLE**
See IT RAINED ALL NIGHT THE DAY I LEFT
**DEUX REQUINS SUR LE SABLE**
See IT RAINED ALL NIGHT THE DAY I LEFT
**DEVIATION**
See MAFU CAGE, THE
**DEVIL AND DR FRANKENSTEIN, THE**
See ANDY WARHOL'S FRANKENSTEIN
**DEVIL AND THE DEAD, THE**
See LISA AND THE DEVIL
**DEVIL FISH**
See DEVOURING WAVES
**DEVIL IN THE HOUSE OF EXORCISM**
See LISA AND THE DEVIL
**DEVIL IS A WOMAN, THE**
See TEMPTER, THE
**DEVIL OBSESSION, THE**
See SEXORCIST, THE
**DEVIL SLEEP**
See SLEEP OF DEATH
**DEVIL'S BROTHER, THE**

See LAUREL AND HARDY: BOGUS BANDITS
**DEVIL'S IMPOSTER, THE**
See POPE JOAN
**DEVIL'S PEOPLE, THE**
See DEVIL'S MEN, THE
**DEVIL'S THREE**
See MEAN BUSINESS
**DEVIL'S TREASURE**
See TREASURE ISLAND
**DEVIL'S UNDEAD, THE**
See NOTHING BUT THE NIGHT
**DIAMOND RUN**
See JAVA BURN
**DIARIO SEGRETO DI UN CARCERE FEMMINILE**
See LOVE IN A WOMEN'S PRISON
**DIARY OF A BED**
See BETWEEN THE SHEETS
**DIARY OF A SPACE VIRGIN**
See SEXPLORER, THE
**DIDN'T YOU KILL MY BROTHER?**
See COMIC STRIP PRESENTS: DIDN'T YOU KILL MY BROTHER?
**DIE ANGEL VON ST PAULI**
See ANGELS OF THE STREETS
**DIE ANGST ESSEN SEELE AUF**
See FEAR EATS THE SOUL
**DIE BLUTIGEN GEIER VON ALASKA**
See HELL HOUNDS OF ALASKA, THE
**DIE BRAUT DES SATANS**
See TO THE DEVIL A DAUGHTER
**DIE BRUT DES BOSEN**
See ROOTS OF EVIL
**DIE BUMSFIDELEN MADCHEN VON BIRKENHOF**
See RANCH OF THE NYMPHOMANIAC GIRLS
**DIE DIAMANTENHOHLE AM MEKONG**
See CAVE OF DIAMONDS
**DIE FLUSSPIRATEN DES MISSISSIPPI**
See PIRATES OF THE MISSISSIPPI
**DIE HERRENREITERIN**
See MISTRESS, THE
**DIE HOLLE VON MACAO**
See CORRUPT ONES, THE
**DIE INSEL DER 1000 FREUDEN**
See SEX SLAVES
**DIE LETZEN DREI DER ALBATROS**
See MUTINY IN THE SOUTH SEAS
**DIE NEUNSCHWANZIGE KATZE**
See CAT O'NINE TAILS
**DIE REBELLEN**
See FLASHPOINT AFRICA
**DIE SCHONEN WILDEN VON IBIZA**
See SEX ON THE ROCKS
**DIE SCHWARZE PANTHER VON RATANA**
See KILLER PANTHER
See BLACK EAGLES OF SANTA FE
**DIE SOELDNER**
See DIAMOND MERCENARIES, THE
**DIE TODESGOTTEN DES LIEBESCAMPS**
See LOVE CAMP
**DIE WIRTIN VON DER LAHN**
See SWEET SINS OF SEXY SUSAN, THE
**DIE, SISTER DIE!**
See DIE SISTER DIE
**DIEZ NEGRITOS**
See TEN LITTLE INDIANS
**DIGITAL KNIGHTS**
See RAGEWAR
**DILEMMA**
See CHOICES
**DIM SUM: A LITTLE BIT OF HEART**

**REEPERBAHN**
See NYMPHO GIRLS
**DREI VATERUNSER FUR VIER HALUNKEN**
See STORMRIDER
**DRESSED TO KILL**
See SHERLOCK HOMES: DRESSED TO KILL
**DROP DEAD DEAREST**
See I MISS YOU HUGS AND KISSES
**DROPS OF BLOOD**
See TALES OF TERROR 3: DROPS OF BLOOD
**DRUMS**
See DRUM, THE
**DUCK SOUP**
See MARX BROTHERS: DUCK SOUP
**DUCK, YOU SUCKER!**
See FISTFUL OF DYNAMITE, A
**DUEL OF THE SEVEN TIGERS**
See SHADOW OF THE TIGER
**DUEL OF THE TITANS**
See DEATHSTALKER 2
**DUKE OF WELLINGTON, THE**
See SECRET LIVES OF THE BRITISH PRIME MINISTERS, THE: THE IRON DUKE
**DUKE, THE**
See UP AGAINST THE ODDS
**DUNGEONMASTER, THE**
See RAGEWAR
**DYKKET**
See DIVE, THE
**DYNAMITE WOMEN**
See GREAT TEXAS DYNAMITE CHASE, THE
**DYNASTY OF FEAR**
See FEAR IN THE NIGHT
**E CONTINUANO A FREGARSI IL MILIONE DI DOLLARI**
See BAD MAN'S RIVER
**E POI LO CHIAMARONO IL MAGNIFICO**
See MAN OF THE EAST
**E TU VIVRAI NEL TERRORE! L'ALDILA**
See BEYOND, THE
**E.T: THE EXTRA-TERRESTRIAL NASTIE**
See NIGHTFRIGHT
**EAGER BEAVERS**
See SWINGING BARMAIDS, THE
**EAGLES OVER BRITAIN**
See BATTLE SQUADRON
**EAGLES OVER LONDON**
See BATTLE SQUADRON
**EAGLE'S SHADOW, THE**
See SNAKE IN THE EAGLE'S SHADOW
**EARTH 2**
See EARTH TWO
**EARTH DEFENSE FORCES**
See MYSTERIANS, THE
**EARTHQUAKE 7.9**
See MEGAFORCE 7.9
**EARTH'S DEFENCE**
See FORMATORS: EARTH'S DEFENCE
**EASTER SUNDAY**
See BEING, THE
**EATEN ALIVE BY THE CANNIBALS**
See EATEN ALIVE
**ECHOES**
See LIVING NIGHTMARE
**ECHOES OF THE ROAD**
See: WHERE THE EAGLE FLIES
**ECOLOGIA DEL DELITTO**
See LAST HOUSE ON THE LEFT

PART 2, THE
**ECOLOGY OF A CRIME, THE**
See LAST HOUSE ON THE LEFT PART 2, THE
**ECSTASY GIRLS**
See SMALL TOWN GIRLS
**ECSTASY INC.**
See SWEDISH SEX CLINIC
**EDGAR ALLAN POE'S BURIED ALIVE**
See BURIED ALIVE
**EDGE OF THE CITY**
See CITY'S EDGE, THE
**EDIPO RE**
See OEDIPUS REX
**EDUT ME ONESS**
See FORCED WITNESS
**EERIE MIDNIGHT HORROR SHOW, THE**
See SEXORCIST, THE
**EGGHEAD ON HILL 656, THE**
See RELUCTANT HEROES, THE
**EGYMASRA MEZRE**
See ANOTHER WAY
**EICHMANN**
See HOUSE ON GARIBALDI STREET, THE
**EIGHT DIAGRAM POLE FIGHTER, THE**
See INVINCIBLE POLE FIGHTER, THE
**EINE REISE INS LICHT**
See DESPAIR
**EINE SYMPHONIE DES GRAVENS**
See NOSFERATU
**EINS OG SKEPNAN DEYR**
See BEAST, THE
**EL ATAQUE DE LOS MUERTOS SIN OJOS**
See RETURN OF THE EVIL DEAD, THE
**EL CAZADOR DE LA MUERTE**
See DEATH STALKER
**EL CHE GUEVARA**
See REBEL WITH A CAUSE
**EL COLECCIONISTA DE CADAVERES**
See CAULDRON OF BLOOD
**EL DIABOLO SE LLEVA A LOS MUERTOS**
See LISA AND THE DEVIL
**EL GRAN AMOR DEL CONDE DRACULA**
See COUNT DRACULA'S GREAT LOVE
**EL HOMBRE DEL RIO MALO**
See BAD MAN'S RIVER
**EL MARQUES, LA MENOR Y EL TRAVESTI**
See INSATIABLE ALICIA AND THE MARQUIS
**EL MAS FABULOSO GOLPE DEL FAR-WEST**
See BOLDEST JOB IN THE WEST, THE
**EL PAESE DEL SESSO SELVAGGIO**
See DEEP RIVER SAVAGES
**EL RAPTO DE ELENA, LA DELENTE ITALIANA**
See HECTOR THE MIGHTY
**EL REFUGIO DEL MIEDO**
See REFUGE OF FEAR
**EL RETORNO DE WALPURGIS**
See CURSE OF THE DEVIL
**EL RIO DE LOS MALDITOS**
See BAD MAN'S RIVER
**EL SALVEJO**
See GREAT GUNDOWN, THE
**EL SALVEJO**

See GREAT GUNDOWN, THE
**EL TESORO DE LAS CUATRO CORONAS**
See TREASURE OF THE FOUR CROWNS
**EL TESORO DEL AMAZONES**
See TREASURE OF DOOM
**EL ULTIMO DIA DE LA GUERRA**
See DEATH ZONE
**EL VAMPIRO DE LA AUTOPISTA**
See HORRIBLE SEXY VAMPIRE, THE
**ELEMENTARY STUD, THE**
See EMMANUELLE GOES TO CANNES
**ELENI**
See ELENI: A SON'S REVENGE
**ELIMINATOR, THE**
See DEADLY GAMES
**ELVIS**
See ELVIS: THE MOVIE
**EMBALMED**
See MORTUARY
**EMBODIMENT OF FORBIDDEN PLEASURE, THE**
See CHINA GIRL
**EMERALD**
See CODENAME: EMERALD
**EMMANUELLE GIALLA**
See YELLOW EMMANUELLE
**EMMANUELLE IN BANGKOK**
See BLACK EMMANUELLE GOES EAST
**EMMANUELLE IN EGYPT**
See BLACK EMMANUELLE, WHITE EMMANUELLE
**EMMANUELLE IN THE COUNTRY**
See COUNTRY NURSE
**EMMANUELLE NERA**
See BLACK EMMANUELLE
**EMMANUELLE NERA NO. 2**
See BLACK EMMANUELLE 2
**EMMANUELLE NERA: ORIENT REPONTAGE**
See BLACK EMMANUELLE GOES EAST
**EMMANUELLE QUEEN BITCH**
See EMMANUELLE: QUEEN OF THE SADOS
**EMMANUELLE REPORTAGE DA UN CARCERE FEMMINILE**
See CAGED WOMEN
**EMMANUELLE REPORTS FROM A WOMEN'S PRISON**
See CAGED WOMEN
**EMMANUELLE, THE JOYS OF A WOMAN**
See EMMANUELLE 2
**EMMANUELLE: PERCHE VIOLENZA ALLE DONNE?**
See CONFESSIONS OF EMMANUELLE
**EMMANUELLE'S DAUGHTER**
See EMMANUELLE: QUEEN OF THE SADOS
**EMPEROR OF THE NORTH POLE**
See EMPEROR OF THE NORTH
**EMPIRE INC.**
See TYCOON: PARTS 1 AND 2
**EMPIRE OF PASSION**
See AI NO BOREI
**EN EFFLUEILLANT LA MARGUERITE**
See PLUCKING THE DAISY
**ENCUENTRO EN EL ABISMO**
See ENCOUNTERS IN THE DEEP
**END OF INNOCENCE, THE**
See BLUE BELLE
**END OF THE GAME**
See DECEPTION
**ENDGAMES**

See ENDGAME
**ENEMIES OF THE PUBLIC**
See PUBLIC ENEMY, THE
**ENFORCER 2**
See DEATH COLLECTOR
**ENOLA GAY: THE MEN, THE MISSION, THE ATOMIC BOMB**
See ENOLA GAY
**ENTEBBE: OPERATION THUNDERBOLT**
See OPERATION THUNDERBOLT
**ENTER THE DEVIL**
See SEXORCIST, THE
**ENTITY FORCE, THE**
See ONE DARK NIGHT
**ENTRAPMENT**
See DEAD WRONG
**ERCOLE AL CENTRO DELLA TERRA**
See HERCULES IN THE CENTRE OF THE EARTH
**ERCOLE ALLA CONQUISTA DI ATLANTIDE**
See HERCULES CONQUERS ATLANTIS
**ERCOLE E LA REGINA DI LIDIA**
See HERCULES UNCHAINED
**EROTIC ADVENTURES OF SIEGFRIED, THE**
See TERRIBLE QUICK SWORD OF SIEGFRIED, THE
**EROTIC ENCOUNTERS**
See TRUCK STOP
**EROTIC PLEASURES**
See EROTIC PLEASURES: THE BODIES DESIRE
**EROTIC RADIO WSSX**
See EROTIC RADIO WSEX
**EROTIC REVENGE**
See CARNAL REVENGE
**EROTIC THREE, THE**
See SCRATCH HARRY
**ERZEBETH**
See DAUGHTERS OF DARKNESS
**ES WAR NICHT DIE NACHTIGALL**
See JULIA
**ESCAPADE**
See CAR NAPPING
**ESCAPE FROM APARTHEID**
See GITANOS: ESCAPE FROM APARTHEID
**ESCAPE FROM HELL**
See SAVAGE ISLAND
**ESCAPE FROM SAFEHAVEN**
See INFERNO IN SAFEHAVEN
**ESCAPE FROM THE BRONX**
See BRONX WARRIORS 2: THE BATTLE OF MANHATTAN
**ESCAPE OF THE BIRDMEN**
See OPERATION BRAINDRAIN
**ESKIMO LIMON**
See LEMON POPSICLE
**ESTATE OF INSANITY**
See BLACK TORMENT, THE
**ET DIEU CREA LA FEMME**
See AND GOD CREATED WOMAN
**ETTORE LO FUSTO**
See HECTOR THE MIGHTY
**EUR WEG FUHRT DURCH DIE HOLLE**
See JUNGLE WARRIORS
**EVA NERA**
See EROTIC EVA
**EVE OF THE WILD WOMAN**
See KING OF KONG ISLAND
**EVERGLADE KILLINGS, THE**
See FLORIDA CONNECTION, THE
**EVERY MAN FOR HIMSELF AND GOD AGAINST ALL**
See ENIGMA OF KASPAR HAUSER,

THE
**EVERYBODY'S BABY: THE RESCUE OF JESSICA McCLURE**
See RESCUE OF JESSICA McCLURE, THE
**EVERYBODY'S CHEERING**
See TAKE ME OUT TO THE BALL GAME
**EVIL IN THE DEEP**
See TREASURE OF JAMAICA REEF, THE
**EVIL MIND, THE**
See CLAIRVOYANT, THE
**EVIL SPAWN**
See METAMORPHOSIS
**EVIL THOUGHT**
See WHO MISLAID MY WIFE?
**EVIL + HATE = KILLER**
See PSYCHO FROM TEXAS
**EWOK ADVENTURE, THE**
See CARAVAN OF COURAGE: AN EWOK ADVENTURE
**EXECUTION, THE**
See ASSASSINATION, THE
**EXECUTIONER 2**
See EXECUTIONER, THE
**EXECUTIONER OF VENICE, THE**
See EXECUTIONER, THE
**EXECUTIONER, PART 2**
See EXECUTIONER, THE
**EXECUTIVE HOUSEWIVES**
See HOT AND BLUE
**EXECUTORS, THE**
See SICILIAN CROSS
**EXISTENCE**
See WILD LITTLE BUNCH, THE
**EXORCISMO**
See EXORCISM
**EXPEDITIONS, THE**
See MARTIAN CHRONICLES, THE
**EXPRESS TO TERROR**
See SUPERTRAIN
**EXTRA-TERRESTRIAL NASTIE**
See NIGHTFRIGHT
**EYE OF THE EAGLE 2: INSIDE THE ENEMY**
See EYE OF THE EAGLE 2
**EYE OF THE EVIL DEAD, THE**
See POSSESSED, THE
**EYE OF THE SPIDER**
See DEADLY REVENGE
**EYES BEYOND THE STARS**
See EYES BEHIND THE STARS
**EYEWITNESS**
See JANITOR, THE
**F/X**
See FX: MURDER BY ILLUSION
**F.B.I. OPERAZIONE PAKISTAN**
See TIGER GANG
**F.I.S.T.**
See FIST
**FABULOUS ADVENTURES OF MARCO POLO, THE**
See KUBLAI KHAN
**FACE TO THE WIND**
See APACHE MASSACRE
**FACES OF FEAR**
See DOUBLE JEOPARDY
**FAIR TRADE**
See BLOOD RANSOM
**FAIRY TALES**
See ADULT FAIRYTALES
**FALCON'S GOLD**
See ROBBERS OF THE SACRED MOUNTAIN
**FALCON'S MALTESER, THE**
See JUST ASK FOR DIAMOND
**FALL AND RISE OF THE ROMAN EMPIRE, THE**

See CALIGULA AND MESSALINA
**FALLING, THE**
See MUTANT 2
**FALSE FACE**
See SCALPEL
**FAME**
See FAME: THE MOVIE
**FAMILY ENFORCER, THE**
See DEATH COLLECTOR
**FAMILY JEWELS**
See FRENCH BLUE
**FAMILY VICES**
See VICES IN THE FAMILY
**FANATIC, THE**
See LAST HORROR FILM, THE
**FANTASTIC SEVEN**
See STUNT SEVEN
**FANTASY**
See FASCINATION
**FAREWELL, FRIEND**
See CODE, THE
**FAREWELL, MY LOVELY**
See MURDER, MY SWEET
**FARM, THE**
See CURSE, THE
**FAST CARS**
See FAST CARS, FAST WOMEN
**FAST TIMES**
See FAST TIMES AT RIDGEMONT HIGH
**FAT CHANCE**
See PEEPER
**FAT MAN AND LITTLE BOY**
See SHADOW MAKERS
**FATAL GAMES**
See KILLING TOUCH, THE
**FATHER'S REVENGE, A: THE TERRORISTS**
See FATHER'S REVENGE, A
**FEAR**
See CITY OF THE LIVING DEAD
**FEAR CHAMBER, THE**
See TORTURE ZONE, THE
**FEARLESS**
See FEARLESS FUZZ
**FEARLESS VAMPIRE KILLERS OR: PARDON ME, BUT YOUR TEETH ARE IN MY NECK, THE**
See DANCE OF THE VAMPIRES
**FEARLESS YOUNG BOXER, THE**
See AVENGING BOXER
**FELLINI'S CASANOVA**
See CASANOVA
**FEMALE BUTCHER, THE**
See LEGEND OF BLOOD CASTLE, THE
**FERESTADEH**
See MISSION, THE
**FFOLKES**
See NORTH SEA HIJACK
**FFOULKES**
See NORTH SEA HIJACK
**FIELD OF HONOUR**
See FIELD OF HONOR
**FIEND WITH THE ATOMIC BRAIN, THE**
See MAN WITH THE SYNTHETIC BRAIN, THE
**FIEND WITH THE ELECTRONIC BRAIN, THE**
See MAN WITH THE SYNTHETIC BRAIN, THE
**FIFTH DAY OF PEACE, THE**
See CRIME OF DEFEAT
**FIGHTING BACK**
See DEATH VENGEANCE
**FIGHTING OF SHAOLIN MONK, THE**
See FIGHTING OF SHAOLIN MONKS, THE

**FIGHTING PIMPERNEL, THE**
See PIMPERNEL SMITH
**FIGURES IN A LANDSCAPE**
See HUNTED, THE
**FIN DE SEMANA PARA LOS MUERTOS**
See LIVING DEAD AT THE MANCHESTER MORGUE, THE
**FINAL CHAPTER: WALKING TALL**
See WALKING TALL 3: THE FINAL CHAPTER
**FINAL CONFLICT, THE**
See FINAL CONFLICT, THE: OMEN 3
**FINAL CRASH, THE**
See STEELYARD BLUES
**FINAL DEFEAT, THE**
See SEVEN WINCHESTERS FOR A MASSACRE
**FINAL EXECUTOR**
See FINAL EXECUTIONER
**FINAL OPTION, THE**
See WHO DARES WINS
**FINAL WAR, THE**
See LAST WAR, THE
**FINALMENTE . . . LE MILLE E UNA NOTTE**
See BED OF A THOUSAND PLEASURES
**FINDERS KEEPERS**
See FINDERS, KEEPERS
**FINE WHITE LINE, THE**
See COCAINE WARS
**FINISHING TOUCH**
See YOUR TICKET IS NO LONGER VALID
**FIONA**
See LET'S GET LAID
**FIRES OF YOUTH**
See DANNY JONES
**FIRST AND THE LAST, THE**
See TWENTY-ONE DAYS
**FIRST BLOOD, LAST RITES**
See VIGIL
**FIRST BORN**
See MOVING IN
**FIRST KINO, THE**
See DON'T PLAY WITH FIRE
**FIRST LOVE . . . MISTER LOVE**
See MISTER LOVE
**FIRST NUDIE MUSICAL, THE**
See DIRECTORS, THE
**FIRSTBORN**
See MOVING IN
**FISH MEN, THE**
See ISLAND OF MUTATIONS
**FIST**
See BLACK FIST
**FIST FIGHTER**
See FISTFIGHTER
**FIST OF FURY**
See FISTS OF FURY
**FIST OF FURY PART 2**
See FISTS OF FURY 2
**FIST OF POWER**
See KARATE WARRIOR
**FIST OF SHAOLIN**
See FISTS OF SHAOLIN
**FIST OF VENGEANCE**
See FISTS OF VENGEANCE, THE
**FISTFUL OF CHOPSTICKS, A**
See THEY CALL ME BRUCE?
**FISTS OF BLOOD**
See STRIKE OF THE PANTHER, THE
**FIVE FINGERS OF DEATH**
See KING BOXER
**FIVE GRAVES FOR THE MEDIUM**
See CEMETERY OF THE LIVING DEAD
**FIVE MILLION YEARS TO EARTH**

See QUATERMASS AND THE PIT
**FLAME OVER INDIA**
See NORTHWEST FRONTIER
**FLAMING STAR**
See ELVIS PRESLEY: FLAMING STAR
**FLANAGAN**
See WALLS OF GLASS
**FLASHING LIGHTS**
See NEW YORK AFTER MIDNIGHT
**FLATBED ANNIE AND SWEETIEPIE**
See LADY TRUCKERS
**FLATBED ANNIE AND SWEETIEPIE: LADY TRUCKERS**
See LADY TRUCKERS
**FLESH CREATURES (OF THE RED PLANET)**
See VAMPIRE MEN OF THE LOST PLANET
**FLESH FOR FRANKENSTEIN**
See ANDY WARHOL'S FRANKENSTEIN
**FLIGHT OF DRAGONS**
See FLIGHT OF THE DRAGON, THE
**FLIGHT OF THE WHITE STALLIONS, THE**
See MIRACLE OF THE WHITE STALLIONS, THE
**FLINTSTONE CHRISTMAS, A**
See FLINTSTONES: A FLINTSTONE CHRISTMAS
**FLOSSIE**
See SWEDISH SEX KITTEN
**FLOWER ANGEL, THE**
See ANGEL CLOUD
**FLYING ACES**
See LAUREL AND HARDY: THE FLYING DEUCES
**FLYING DEUCES, THE**
See LAUREL AMD HARDY: THE FLYING DEAUCES
**FOG**
See STUDY IN TERROR, A
**FOLIES BOURGEOISES**
See TWIST, THE
**FOLKS AT RED WOLF INN, THE**
See TERROR AT RED WOLF INN
**FOLLOW ME IF YOU DARE**
See MYSTERIOUS TWO
**FOLLOW THAT CAMEL**
See CARRY ON FOLLOW THAT CAMEL
**FOLLOW THAT DREAM**
See ELVIS PRESLEY: FOLLOW THAT DREAM
**FOLLOW YOUR DREAMS**
See LOVE, HONOR AND OBEY
**FOOL'S NIGHT**
See KILLER PARTY
**FOR A FEW BULLETS MORE**
See ANY GUN CAN PLAY
**FOR KEEPS**
See MAYBE BABY
**FOR YOU ALONE**
See WHEN YOU'RE IN LOVE
**FORBIDDEN PARADISE**
See HURRICANE
**FORBIDDEN SUN**
See BULLDANCE, THE
**FORCE BEYOND, THE**
See EVIL, THE
**FORCE FIVE**
See FINAL TACTIC
**FORCE OF DEATH**
See DEATH FORCE
**FORCED ENTRY**
See LAST VICTIM, THE
**FORD: HIS MISTRESS AND HIS MACHINE – PARTS 1 AND 2**
See FORD

**FORD: THE MAN AND THE MACHINE**
See FORD
**FORMULA UNO FEBBRE DELLA VELOCITA**
See SPEED FEVER
**FORTRESS EUROPE**
See FROM HELL TO VICTORY
**FORTUNE IN DIAMONDS**
See ADVENTURERS, THE
**FORTUNE IS STANDING AROUND IN THE STREETS, A**
See CAR NAPPING
**FORTY GRAVES FOR FORTY GUNS**
See GREAT GUNDOWN, THE
**FORTY MILLION BUCKS ON A DEAD MAN'S CHEST**
See FORTY MILLION BUCKS
**FORTY MILLION DOLLARS**
See FORTY MILLION BUCKS
**FOUR AGAINST FATE**
See DERBY DAY
**FOUR DAYS IN DALLAS**
See RUBY AND OSWALD
**FOUR FRIENDS**
See GEORGIA
**FOUR MUSKETEERS, THE: THE REVENGE OF MILADY**
See FOUR MUSKETEERS, THE
**FOURTEEN, THE**
See WILD LITTLE BUNCH, THE
**FOX AND HIS FRIENDS**
See FOX
**FOXTROT**
See FAR SIDE OF PARADISE, THE
**FRA DIAVOLO**
See LAUREL AND HARDY: BOGUS BANDITS
**FRANCIS GARY POWERS: THE TRUE STORY OF THE U-2 INCIDENT**
See U-2 INCIDENT, THE
**FRANKENSTEIN**
See ANDY WARHOL'S FRANKENSTEIN
**FRANKENSTEIN 88**
See VINDICATOR, THE
**FRANKENSTEIN EXPERIMENT**
See ANDY WARHOL'S FRANKENSTEIN
**FRANKENSTEIN FACTOR, THE**
See VINDICATOR, THE
**FRANKENSTEIN ISLAND**
See FRANKENSTEIN'S ISLAND
**FRANKENSTEIN'S SPUKSCHOSS**
See ACE UP MY SLEEVE
**FRANKIE AND JOHNNY**
See ELVIS PRESLEY: FRANKIE AND JOHNNY
**FRATERNALLY YOURS**
See LAUREL AND HARDY: SONS OF THE DESERT
**FREDDY'S REVENGE**
See NIGHTMARE ON ELM STREET, A: PART 2 – FREDDY'S REVENGE
**FREE SPIRIT**
See MAXIE
**FREE SPIRIT**
See BELSTONE FOX, THE
**FREEDOM FOR REBEL**
See BARBARIAN, THE
**FREEDOM TO LOVE**
See LIFE IS BEAUTIFUL
**FREEWAY KILLINGS, THE**
See POLICE STORY: THE FREEWAY KILLINGS
**FREEZE BOMB**
See DEATH DIMENSIONS
**FRENCH BLUE**
See ROOM SERVICE

**FRENCH LESSON**
See FROG PRINCE, THE
**FRENCH WOMAN, THE**
See MADAME CLAUDE
**FRESHMAN, THE**
See HAROLD LLOYD: THE
FRESHMAN
**FREUDE AM FLIEGEN**
See SEX AT 7000 FEET
**FRIEND, THE**
See HURRY UP OR I'LL BE THIRTY
**FRIGHTMARE**
See BODY SNATCHERS, THE
**FRITZ AND LILY**
See DOUBLE PLAY
**FROG DREAMING**
See GO KIDS, THE
**FROG, THE**
See PSYCHOMANIA
**FROM CHINA WITH DEATH**
See CHINESE HERCULES
**FROM THE MIXED-UP FILES OF MR
BASIL E. FRANKWEILER**
See HIDEAWAYS, THE
**FROM THE ORIENT WITH FURY**
See FURY IN ISTANBUL
**FROZEN TERROR**
See MACABRE
**FUGITIVE OF THE EMPIRE**
See ARCHER AND THE SORCERESS
**FUKKATSU NO HI**
See VIRUS
**FULL CIRCLE**
See HAUNTING OF JULIA, THE
**FUN IN ACAPULCO**
See ELVIS PRESLEY: FUN IN
ACAPULCO
**FUN LOVING**
See QUACKSER FORTUNE HAS A
COUSIN IN THE BRONX
**FUN PARK**
See BREAKING ALL THE RULES
**FUNF GEGEN CASABLANCA**
See DESERT COMMANDO
**FUNSEEKERS, THE**
See COMIC STRIP PRESENT: THE
FUNSEEKERS
**FUREUR SUR LE BOSPHORE**
See FURY IN ISTANBUL
**FURTHER ADVENTURES OF
TENNESSEE BUCK, THE**
See TENNESSEE BUCK
**FURTHER ADVENTURES OF THE
WILDERNESS FAMILY**
See ADVENTURES OF THE
WILDERNESS FAMILY, THE: PART 2
**FURTHER TALES FROM THE CRYPT**
See VAULT OF HORROR
**FUTURE COP**
See TRANCERS
**FUTURE KILL**
See NIGHT OF THE ALIEN
**G.I. BLUES**
See ELVIS PRESLEY: G.I. BLUES
**GABRIELLE**
See THIS TIME FOREVER
**GALACTICA 3: CONQUEST OF THE
EARTH**
See CONQUEST OF THE EARTH
**GALLERY MURDERS, THE**
See BIRD WITH THE CRYSTAL
PLUMAGE, THE
**GALYON: THE INDESTRUCTIBLE
MAN**
See GALYON
**GAMEKEEPER**
See STRONGHOLD
**GAMES THAT NURSES PLAY**
See SECRETS OF YOUNG NURSES

**GAMMA 693**
See NIGHT OF THE ZOMBIES, THE
**GANG WAR**
See ODD MAN OUT
**GARDENER, THE**
See GARDEN OF DEATH
**GAS-S-S-S**
See GAS
**GAS . . . OR IT MAY BECOME
NECESSARY TO DESTROY THE
WORLD IN ORDER TO SAVE IT**
See GAS
**GATES OF HELL, THE**
See CITY OF THE LIVING DEAD
**GATES OF NIGHT**
See LES PORTES DE LA NUIT
**GBH: GREVIOUS BODILY HARM**
See GREVIOUS BODILY HARM
**GEFAHRLICH SEXFRUMREIFE
MADCHEN**
See FINISHING SCHOOL
**GEMINI TWINS, THE**
See TWINS OF EVIL
**GENERAL, THE**
See BUSTER KEATON: THE
GENERAL
**GENERALNAYA LINYA**
See GENERAL LINE, THE
**GENETIC CONTACT**
See ANNA TO THE INFINITE
DEGREE
**GENIO, DUE COMPARI, UN POLLO**
See NOBODY'S THE GREATEST
**GENIUS, THE**
See NOBODY'S THE GREATEST
**GEORGIA'S FRIENDS**
See GEORGIA
**GERBOKEN SPIEGELS**
See BROKEN MIRRORS
**GET CHARLIE TULLY**
See OOH, YOU ARE AWFUL
**GET ON WITH IT**
See DENTIST ON THE JOB
**GETTING AWAY WITH MURDER**
See DECEPTION
**GETTING EVEN**
See HOSTAGE DALLAS
**GETTING SAM HOME**
See LAST OF THE SUMMER WINE:
GETTING SAM HOME
**GHARBAR**
See HOUSEHOLDER, THE
**GHIDRAH: THE THREE-HEADED
MONSTER**
See GHIDRAH: THE THREE-HEADED
DRAGON
**GHOST SOLDIERS**
See SUPERNATURALS, THE
**GHOST STORIES**
See KWAIDAN
**GHOULIES GO TO COLLEGE**
See GHOULIES 3
**GIFT OF FURY**
See GREAT SANTINI, THE
**GINGERBREAD HOUSE**
See WHO SLEW AUNTIE ROO?
**GIRL FROM STARSHIP VENUS**
See SEXPLORER, THE
**GIRL HAPPY**
See ELVIS PRESLEY: GIRL HAPPY
**GIRL NAMED JULIUS, A**
See GIRL CALLED JULES, A
**GIRL SCHOOL SCREAMERS**
See GIRL'S SCHOOL SCREAMERS
**GIRL STROKE BOY**
See GIRL/BOY
**GIRL WAS YOUNG, THE**
See YOUNG AND INNOCENT
**GIRL WITH GREEN EYES**

See GIRL WITH THE GREEN EYES,
THE
**GIRL-TOY**
See FOREPLAY
**GIRLS' HOTEL**
See SYNDICATE VICE
**GIRLS IN THE STREETS**
See SCREAM IN THE STREETS, A
**GIRL'S NIGHT OUT**
See SCAREMAKER, THE
**GIRL'S NITE OUT**
See SCAREMAKER, THE
**GIRLS OF THE WHITE ORCHID**
See DEATH RIDE TO OSAKA
**GIRLS! GIRLS! GIRLS!**
See ELVIS PRESLEY: GIRLS! GIRLS!
GIRLS!
**GIU LA TESTA**
See FISTFUL OF DYNAMITE, A
**GIVE US OUR DAILY SEX**
See AND GIVE US OUR DAILY SEX
**GLADSTONE: THE PROSTITUTE
SCANDAL**
See SECRET LIVES OF THE BRITISH
PRIME MINISTERS, THE:
GLADSTONE
**GLI AMORI DI ERCOLE**
See LOVES OF HERCULES, THE
**GLI ESECUTORI**
See SICILIAN CROSS
**GLI ORRORI DEL CASTELLO DI
NORIMBERGA**
See BARON BLOOD
**GLO FRIENDS: THE QUEST**
See GLO FRIENDS: THE MOVIE –
THE QUEST
**GLORY YEARS**
See WACKY WEEKEND
**GO KILL AND COME BACK**
See ANY GUN CAN PLAY
**GO TO THE LIGHT**
See GO TOWARD THE LIGHT
**GO WEST**
See MARX BROTHERS: GO WEST
**GOD TOLD ME TO**
See DEMON
**GODFATHER THE MASTER**
See NINJA OPERATION 5:
GODFATHER THE MASTER
**GODIVA GIRLS**
See GIRLS OF GODIVA HIGH, THE
**GODZILLA**
See GODZILLA: THE LEGEND IS
REBORN
**GODZILLA 1985**
See GODZILLA: THE LEGEND IS
REBORN
**GODZILLA TAI GAIGAN**
See WAR OF THE MONSTERS
**GODZILLA VERSUS GIGAN**
See WAR OF THE MONSTERS
**GODZILLA VERSUS
MECHAGODZILLA**
See GODZILLA VERSUS THE COSMIC
MONSTER
**GODZILLA VERSUS THE BIONIC
MONSTER**
See GODZILLA VERSUS THE COSMIC
MONSTER
**GODZILLA, WAR OF THE
MONSTERS**
See WAR OF THE MONSTERS
**GOING UNDERCOVER**
See YELLOW PAGES
**GOING UP**
See LIFT, THE
**GOJIRA**
See GODZILLA: THE LEGEND IS
REBORN

**GOJIRA TAI GAIGAN**
See WAR OF THE MONSTERS
**GOJIRA TAI MEKA GOJIRA**
See GODZILLA VERSUS THE COSMIC
MONSTER
**GOKE THE VAMPIRE**
See GOKE: BODYSNATCHER FROM
HELL
**GOLA PROFONDA NERA**
See BLACK DEEP THROAT
**GOLD**
See FORTY MILLION BUCKS
**GOLD RUSH, THE**
See CHARLIE CHAPLIN: THE GOLD
RUSH
**GOLD WING**
See GOLDWING
**GOLDEN GIRL**
See GOLDENGIRL
**GOLDEN HEIST, THE**
See INSIDE OUT
**GOLDEN MASK, THE**
See SOUTH OF ALGIERS
**GOLDEN MOMENT, THE: AN
OLYMPIC LOVE STORY**
See GOLDEN MOMENT, THE
**GOLDEN NINJA WARRIORS**
See GOLDEN NINJA WARRIOR
**GOLDFACE THE FANTASTIC
SUPERMAN**
See GOLDFACE
**GOLDFACE, IL FANTASTICO
SUPERMAN**
See GOLDFACE
**GOLDILOCKS AND THE THREE
BEARS**
See GOLDILOCKS
**GONE TO EARTH**
See WILD HEART, THE
**GOOD GIRLS OF GODIVA HIGH, THE**
See GIRLS OF GODIVA HIGH, THE
**GOOD GIRLS, BAD GIRLS**
See GOOD GIRL, BAD GIRL
**GOOD LIFE, THE**
See LA VIE DU CHATEAU
**GOOD MORNING, BABYLONIA**
See GOOD MORNING, BABYLON
**GOOD MOTHER, THE**
See PRICE OF PASSION, THE
**GOODBYE BRUCE LEE: HIS LAST
GAME OF DEATH**
See GOODBYE, BRUCE LEE
**GOODNIGHT, GOD BLESS**
See LUCIFER
**GOON SHOW MOVIE, THE**
See DOWN AMONG THE Z-MEN
**GORDON IL NERO PIRATA**
See BLACK PIRATE, THE
**GORDON THE BLACK PIRATE**
See BLACK PIRATE, THE
**GORE VIDAL'S LINCOLN**
See LINCOLN
**GOSH**
See ALICE GOODBODY
**GOSPEL ACCORDING TO VIC, THE**
See HEAVENLY PURSUITS
**GOSSIP FROM THE FRONT**
See GOSSIP FROM THE FOREST
**GOTHAM**
See DEAD CAN'T LIE, THE
**GOTT MIT UNS**
See CRIME OF DEFEAT
**GOTTERDAMMERUNG**
See DAMNED, THE
**GRACE KELLY**
See GRACE KELLY STORY, THE
**GRADUATION, THE**
See ROSEMARY'S KILLER
**GRAHAM MURDERS, THE**

See BAD BLOOD
**GRAN COLPE AL SERVICIO DE SU
MAJESTAD BRITANICA**
See GREAT DIAMOND ROBBERY,
THE
**GRAND DUEL, THE**
See STORMRIDER
**GRAND MANEUVER, THE**
See LES GRANDES MANOEUVRES
**GRANDMOTHER'S HOUSE**
See GRANDMA'S HOUSE
**GRAVE ROBBERS FROM OUTER
SPACE**
See PLAN 9 FROM OUTER SPACE
**GREAT ADVENTURE, THE**
See ADVENTURERS, THE
**GREAT BATTLE, THE**
See BIGGEST BATTLE, THE
**GREAT DICTATOR, THE**
See CHARLIE CHAPLIN: THE GREAT
DICTATOR
**GREAT ESCAPE 2, THE: THE
UNTOLD STORY – PARTS 1 AND 2**
See GREAT ESCAPE 2, THE
**GREAT GUNS**
See LAUREL AND HARDY: GREAT
GUNS
**GREAT HOUDINIS, THE**
See GREAT HOUDINI, THE
**GREAT RIDE, THE**
See GREAT RIDE, A
**GREAT SCOUT AND CATHOUSE
THURSDAY, THE**
See WILDCAT
**GREAT SPIDER INVASION, THE**
See GIANT SPIDER INVASION, THE
**GREAT SPY MISSION, THE**
See OPERATION CROSSBOW
**GREAT TRAIN ROBBERY, THE**
See FIRST GREAT TRAIN ROBBERY,
THE
**GREAT WALL IS A GREAT WALL,
THE**
See GREAT WALL, A
**GREAT WALL, THE**
See GREAT WALL, A
**GREEN HORIZON, THE**
See GREEN HORIZONS
**GREEN HORNET, THE**
See FURY OF THE DRAGON
**GREYSTOKE**
See GREYSTOKE: THE LEGEND OF
TARZAN, LORD OF THE APES
**GRIDLOCK**
See GREAT AMERICAN TRAFFIC
JAM, THE
**GROSS ANATOMY**
See CUT ABOVE, A
**GROWING PAINS**
See HOMEWORK
**GRUNT! THE WRESTLING MOVIE**
See GRUNT
**GRUPPO DI FAMIGLIA IN UN
INTERNO**
See CONVERSATION PIECE
**GUARDIAN OF THE WILDERNESS**
See MOUNTAIN MAN
**GUERRA SUCIA**
See DIRTY WAR
**GUESS WHAT!?!/I AIN'T NO
BUFFALO**
See GUESS WHAT WE LEARNT IN
SCHOOL TODAY
**GUIDE TO AMERICA**
See SEX O'CLOCK NEWS, THE
**GUNAN NO. 2: THE INVINCIBLE
SWORD**
See SWORD OF THE BARBARIANS
**GUNAN, KING OF THE**

**BARBARIANS**
See INVINCIBLE BARBARIAN, THE
**GUNAN, KING OF THE
BARBARIANS**
See SWORD OF THE BARBARIANS
**GUNANA RE BARBARO**
See INVINCIBLE BARBARIAN, THE
**GUNS AND FURY**
See GUNS AND THE FURY, THE
**GUNS OF SAN SEBASTIAN**
See GUNS FOR SAN SEBASTIAN
**GUNS, SIN AND BATHTUB GIN**
See LADY IN RED, THE
**GUYANA: CULT OF THE DAMNED**
See GUYANA: CRIME OF THE
CENTURY
**GYPSY GIRL**
See SKY WEST AND CROOKED
**HACK 'EM HIGH**
See SCUMBUSTERS
**HACK O'LANTERN**
See DAMNING, THE
**HADAKA NO JUKYUSAI**
See LIVE TODAY, DIE TOMORROW
**HAI-YUAN CH'I-HAO**
See SEVEN MAGNIFICENT FIGHTS
**HAKHOREF HAACHARON**
See LAST WINTER, THE
**HALLELUJAH, I'M A BUM**
See HALLELUJAH, I'M A TRAMP
**HALLMARK HALL OF FAME**
See RESTING PLACE
**HAMATRA TIRAN**
See SINAI COMMANDOS
**HAMBONE AND HILLIE**
See ADVENTURES OF HAMBONE
AND HILLIE, THE
**HAME'AHEV**
See LOVER, THE
**HAMER HOUSE OF HORROR:
SILENT SCREAM**
See SILENT SCREAM
**HAMMER HOUSE OF HORROR:
SILENT SCREAM**
See SILENT SCREAM, THE
**HAMMER HOUSE OF HORROR:
WITCHING TIME**
See WITCHING TIME
**HAMSTER OF HAPPINESS, THE**
See SECOND-HAND HEARTS
**HANLON**
See HANLON: IN DEFENCE OF
MINNIE DEAD
**HANNAH: QUEEN OF THE
VAMPIRES**
See CRYPT OF THE LIVING DEAD
**HANS BRINKER AND THE SILVER
SKATES**
See HANS BRINKER
**HANS BRINKER OF THE SILVER
SKATES**
See HANS BRINKER
**HAPPY GIGOLO, THE**
See PASSION HOTEL
**HAPPY HOUR**
See SOUR GRAPES
**HAPPY TIMES**
See INSPECTOR GENERAL, THE
**HARD DAY'S NIGHT, A**
See BEATLES: A HARD DAY'S NIGHT
**HARD DRIVER**
See LAST AMERICAN HERO, THE
**HARD SOAP**
See HARD SOAP, HARD SOAP
**HARD TIMES**
See STREETFIGHTER, THE
**HARDCORE LIFE, THE**
See HARDCORE
**HAREEMU OHGEN LEMON**

**POPSICLE 6**
See UP YOUR ANCHOR
**HAREM HOLIDAY**
See ELVIS PRESLEY: HAREM
HOLIDAY
**HAREM: THE LOSS OF INNOCENCE**
See HAREM: PARTS 1 AND 2
**HARMONIE**
See GREATEST ATTACK, THE
**HARRY PALMER RETURNS**
See FUNERAL IN BERLIN
**HARRY TRACY**
See HARRY TRACY: DESPERADO
**HARRY'S GAME: THE MOVIE**
See HARRY'S GAME
**HARUM SCARUM**
See ELVIS PRESLEY: HAREM
HOLIDAY
**HATIMOHNI**
See DREAMER, THE
**HAUNTED PLANET**
See PLANET OF THE VAMPIRES
**HAUNTED STRANGER, THE**
See GRIP OF THE STRANGLER
**HAVE GUN, WILL TRAVEL**
See ACE HIGH
**HAVEN CAN'T WAIT**
See HOT PURSUIT
**HAVING A WILD WEEKEND**
See CATCH US IF YOU CAN
**HAZING, THE**
See CURIOUS CASE OF THE CAMPUS
CORPSE, THE
**HE WALKS LIKE A TIGER**
See KING OF KUNG FU
**HE WHO SHOOTS FIRST**
See DJANGO SHOOTS FIRST
**HEAD**
See TALES OF TERROR 2: THE
IMPURE, WILD RIDERS
**HEAD ON**
See FATAL ATTRACTION
**HEADING FOR BROADWAY**
See HEADIN' FOR BROADWAY
**HEALTH CLUB**
See TOXIC AVENGER, THE
**HEARSAY**
See SEE CHINA AND DIE
**HEART AND SOUL**
See MISCHIEF
**HEART BEAT**
See HEARTBEAT
**HEART OF DRAGON**
See FIRST MISSION, THE
**HEART TO WIN**
See RICKY 1
**HEARTS IN ARMOUR**
See HEARTS AND ARMOUR
**HEAT AND LUST**
See SWEDISH SEX CLINIC
**HEAT AND LUST: DIARY OF A SEX
THERAPIST**
See SWEDISH SEX CLINIC
**HEATHCLIFF MOVIE, THE:
HEATHCLIFF AND ME**
See HEATHCLIFF: THE MOVIE
**HEAVEN FELL THAT NIGHT**
See LES BIJOUTIERS DU CLAIR DE
LUNE
**HEAVEN HELP US**
See CATHOLIC BOYS
**HEAVY METAL**
See RIDING HIGH
**HEAVY THUNDER**
See BLOOD AND GUTS
**HECTOR LE FORTICHE**
See HECTOR THE MIGHTY
**HEIR TO GENGHIS KHAN, THE**
See STORM OVER ASIA

**HEISSE SEX IN BANGKOK**
See HOT SEX IN BANGKOK
**HEIST, THE**
See DOLLARS
**HELENE, REINE DE TROIE**
See LION OF THEBES, THE
**HELL RACER**
See DEATH DRIVER
**HELL RACERS**
See DEATH DRIVER
**HELL TO MACAO**
See CORRUPT ONES, THE
**HELL, HEAVEN AND HOBOKEN**
See I WAS MONTY'S DOUBLE
**HELL, LIVE**
See CUT AND RUN
**HELLO MARY LOU: PROM NIGHT 2**
See PROM NIGHT 2: HELLO MARY
LOU
**HELL'S BELLES**
See BOSTON WARRIORS
**HELL'S BRIGADE**
See ATTACK FORCE NORMANDY
**HELL'S BRIGADE: THE FINAL
ASSAULT**
See ATTACK FORCE NORMANDY
**HELP!**
See BEATLES: HELP!
**HER SUMMER VACATION**
See GISELLE
**HERCULE A LA CONQUETE DE
L'ATLANTIDE**
See HERCULES CONQUERS
ATLANTIS
**HERCULES AND THE CAPTIVE
WOMEN**
See HERCULES CONQUERS
ATLANTIS
**HERCULES AND THE CONQUEST
OF ATLANTIS**
See HERCULES CONQUERS
ATLANTIS
**HERCULES AND THE HAUNTED
WORLD**
See HERCULES IN THE CENTRE OF
THE EARTH
**HERCULES AT THE CENTRE OF THE
WORLD**
See HERCULES IN THE CENTRE OF
THE EARTH
**HERCULES GOES BANANAS**
See HERCULES IN NEW YORK
**HERCULES IN THE HAUNTED
WORLD**
See HERCULES IN THE CENTRE OF
THE EARTH
**HERCULES THE MOVIE**
See HERCULES IN NEW YORK
**HERE COMES THE BRIDE**
See HOUSE THAT CRIED MURDER,
THE
**HERETIC, THE**
See EXORCIST 2: THE HERETIC
**HERO, THE**
See BLOOMFIELD
**HEROES OF THE REGIMENT**
See LAUREL AND HARDY: HEROES
OF THE REGIMENT
**HEROES THREE**
See WARRIORS THREE
**HEROES TWO**
See TEMPLE OF THE DRAGON
**HEROINE**
See CAPTIVE
**HEROINES OF EVIL, THE**
See THREE IMMORAL WOMEN
**HEXEN BIS AUFS BLUT GEQUAELT**
See MARK OF THE DEVIL
**HEY CINDERELLA**

See MUPPETS: HEY CINDERELLA
**HIDE AND GO SHRIEK**
See CLOSE YOUR EYES AND PRAY
**HIGH AND DRY**
See MAGGIE, THE
**HIGH COMMISSIONER, THE**
See NOBODY RUNS FOREVER
**HIGH ENCOUNTERS OF THE
ULTIMATE KIND**
See CHEECH AND CHONG'S NEXT
MOVIE
**HIGH SEASON**
See SEXUAL EXTASY
**HIGHEST HONOUR, THE**
See HIGHEST HONOUR, THE: A
TRUE STORY
**HIJACK**
See AIRPORT S.O.S. HIJACK
**HIJACKED TO HELL**
See NO TIME TO DIE
**HILL 171**
See HILL 171: TOUR OF DUTY
**HILLSIDE STRANGLERS, THE**
See CASE OF THE HILLSIDE
STRANGLERS, THE
**HISTOIRES EXTRAORDINAIRES**
See POWERS OF EVIL
**HISTOIRES EXTRAORDINAIRES**
See TALES OF MYSTERY AND
IMAGINATION
**HIT MAN**
See MAFIA WARFARE
**HIT MAN, THE**
See MEAN JOHNNY BURROWS
**HITCH-HIKE**
See DEATH DRIVE
**HITLER'S GOLD**
See INSIDE OUT
**HITLER'S SS: PORTRAIT IN EVIL**
See HITLER'S SS: PORTRAIT OF EVIL
**HITMAN**
See AMERICAN COMMANDOS
**HITTING HOME**
See OBSESSED
**HO TENTATO DI VIVERE**
See RIP-OFF, THE
**HOG WILD**
See GO HOG WILD
**HOLD THAT DREAM**
See HOLD THE DREAM
**HOLE, THE**
See ONIBABA
**HOLLYWOOD COWBOY**
See HEARTS OF THE WEST
**HOLLYWOOD HOOKERS**
See HOLLYWOOD CHAINSAW
HOOKERS
**HOLLYWOOD STRANGLER, THE**
See DON'T ANSWER THE PHONE
**HOLY TERROR**
See COMMUNION
**HOME IS WHERE THE HEART IS**
See SQUARE DANCE
**HOMECOMING, THE**
See ALL CREATURES GREAT AND
SMALL: THE HOMECOMING
**HONEY BOY**
See HONEYBOY
**HONEYBUNCH**
See HONEYBUN
**HONOR AMONG THIEVES**
See CODE, THE
**HOOKED GENERATION, THE**
See FLORIDA CONNECTION, THE
**HOOSIERS**
See BEST SHOT
**HOPLA PA SENGEKANTEN**
See ESCORT GIRLS
**HORNET'S NEST**

See VALOR OF WAR, THE
**HORRIBLE DOCTOR HICHCOCK, THE**
See TERROR OF DOCTOR
HICHCOCK, THE
**HORRIBLE HOUSE ON THE HILL, THE**
See DEVIL TIMES FIVE
**HORRIBLE MILL WOMEN, THE**
See TALES OF TERROR 3: DROPS OF BLOOD
**HORROR CHAMBER OF DR FAUSTUS, THE**
See EYES WITHOUT A FACE
**HORROR CREATURES OF THE PREHISTORIC PLANET**
See VAMPIRE MEN OF THE LOST PLANET
**HORROR HOTEL**
See CITY OF THE DEAD
**HORROR HOUSE**
See HAUNTED HOUSE OF HORROR, THE
**HORROR OF DEATH**
See ASPHYX, THE
**HORROR OF THE BLOOD MONSTERS**
See VAMPIRE MEN OF THE LOST PLANET
**HORROR OF THE RED PLANET**
See WIZARD OF MARS, THE
**HORROR OF THE STONE WOMEN**
See TALES OF TERROR 3: DROPS OF BLOOD
**HORROR PLANET**
See INSEMINOID
**HORSE NAMED COMANCHE, A**
See TONKA
**HOSPITAL MASSACRE**
See X-RAY
**HOSTAGE: THE CHRISTINE MARESCH STORY**
See HOSTAGE
**HOT BLUE**
See HOT AND BLUE
**HOT COWGIRLS**
See LIPPS AND McCAINE
**HOT NEON**
See LINDA LOVELACE FOR PRESIDENT
**HOT PLAYMATES**
See CARNAL REVENGE
**HOT SPOT**
See I WAKE UP SCREAMING
**HOT STUFF**
See FEAR IN THE CITY
**HOT SUMMER**
See HOT CHILI
**HOT, HARD AND MEAN**
See BLACK MAMA, WHITE MAMA
**HOTS**
See H.O.T.S.
**HOTS 2**
See H.O.T.S. 2
**HOTS 3**
See REVENGE OF THE CHEERLEADERS
**HOU HSING K'OU SHOU**
See SNAKE IN THE MONKEY'S SHADOW
**HOUND OF THE BASKERVILLES, THE**
See SHERLOCK HOLMES: THE HOUND OF THE BASKERVILLES
**HOUND OF THE BASKERVILLES, THE**
See ADVENTURES OF SHERLOCK HOLMES, THE: THE HOUND OF THE BASKERVILLES
**HOUSE AT THE END OF THE**

**WORLD, THE**
See DIE, MONSTER, DIE!
**HOUSE BY THE LAKE, THE**
See DEATH WEEKEND
**HOUSE OF CRAZIES**
See ASYLUM
**HOUSE OF DOOM**
See BLUE EYES OF THE BROKEN DOLL, THE
**HOUSE OF EVIL**
See EVIL, THE
**HOUSE OF EXORCISM, THE**
See LISA AND THE DEVIL
**HOUSE OF FRIGHT**
See BLACK SUNDAY
**HOUSE OF MORTAL SIN**
See CONFESSIONAL MURDERS, THE
**HOUSE OF PSYCHOTIC WOMEN, THE**
See BLUE EYES OF THE BROKEN DOLL, THE
**HOUSE OF SEVEN CORPSES, THE**
See SEVEN TIMES DEATH
**HOUSE OF THE DARK STAIRWAY**
See BLADE IN THE DARK, A
**HOUSE OF THE SEVEN CORPSES, THE**
See SEVEN TIMES DEATH
**HOUSE OF USHER**
See FALL OF THE HOUSE OF USHER, THE
**HOUSE ON SORORITY ROW, THE**
See HOUSE OF EVIL
**HOUSE ON STRAW HILL, THE**
See EXPOSE
**HOUSE OUTSIDE THE CEMETERY, THE**
See HOUSE BY THE CEMETERY, THE
**HOUSE THAT VANISHED, THE**
See SCREAM AND DIE
**HOUSEKEEPER, THE**
See JUDGEMENT IN STONE, A
**HOW COME NOBODY'S ON OUR SIDE?**
See CAPERS
**HOW I FLEW FROM LONDON TO PARIS IN 25 HOURS AND 11 MINUTES**
See THOSE MAGNIFICENT MEN IN THEIR FLYING MACHINES
**HOW MUCH LOVING DOES A NORMAL COUPLE NEED?**
See COMMON-LAW CABIN
**HOW SLEEP THE BRAVE**
See FORGOTTEN PARALLEL, THE
**HOW TO MAKE IT**
See TARGET: HARRY
**HOW TO STEAL A DIAMOND IN FOUR UNEASY LESSONS**
See HOT ROCK, THE
**HOW TO STEAL THE CROWN OF ENGLAND**
See FANTASTIC ARGOMAN
**HOWARD BEACH: MAKING A CASE FOR MURDER**
See MAKING A CASE FOR MURDER: THE HOWARD BEACH STORY
**HOWARD THE DUCK**
See HOWARD: A NEW BREED OF HERO
**HOWLING 2, THE: YOUR SISTER IS A WEREWOLF**
See HOWLING 2, THE
**HOWLING 3: THE MARSUPIALS**
See HOWLING 3
**HUCKLEBERRY FINN**
See ADVENTURES OF HUCKLEBERRY FINN, THE

**HUGGERS**
See CRAZY MOON
**HUGHES AND HARLOW: ANGELS IN HELL**
See ANGELS IN HELL
**HUGO OCH JOSEPHINE**
See HUGO AND JOSEPHINE
**HUMANOIDS FROM THE DEEP**
See MONSTER
**HUMANOIDS OF THE DEEP**
See MONSTER
**HUNGRY FOR SEX**
See LOVE GAMES OF YOUNG GIRLS
**HUNT TO KILL**
See WHITE BUFFALO, THE
**HUNTED, THE**
See TOUCH ME NOT
**HUNTED, THE**
See BENJI THE HUNTED
**HUNTERS, THE**
See DREAMSLAYER
**HURTING, THE**
See PSYCHO FROM TEXAS
**HUSTLER SQUAD**
See DOLL SQUAD, THE
**HYPERSPACE**
See GREMLOIDS
**I AM SARTANA: YOUR ANGEL OF DEATH**
See SARTANA, ANGEL OF DEATH
**I CALDI AMORI DI UNA NINOR ENNE**
See PERVERSION STORY
**I COME IN PEACE**
See DARK ANGEL
**I CRUDELI**
See HELLBENDERS, THE
**I DISMEMBER MAMA**
See POOR ALBERT AND LITTLE ANNIE
**I DISMEMBER YOU**
See CRAZED
**I DOLCI VIZI DELLA CASTA SUSANNA**
See SWEET SINS OF SEXY SUSAN, THE
**I DON'T WANT TO BE BORN**
See DEVIL WITHIN HER, THE
**I GIORNI DELL'IRA**
See GUN LAW
**I GIRASOLI**
See SUNFLOWER
**I GROSSI BESTIONI**
See TRUCK STOP
**I GUAPPI**
See BLOOD BROTHERS
**I HATE YOUR GUTS!**
See INTRUDER, THE
**I LED TWO LIVES**
See GLEN OR GLENDA?
**I LEOPARDI DI CHURCHILL**
See CHURCHILL'S LEOPARDS
**I LOVE YOU, I LOVE YOU NOT**
See TOGETHER?
**I MARRIED A COMMUNIST**
See WOMAN AT PIER THIRTEEN, THE
**I NUOVI BARBARI**
See NEW BARBARIANS, THE
**I PADRONI DELLA CITTA DI MISTER SCARFACE**
See RULERS OF THE CITY
**I PALADINI: STORIA D'ARMI E D'AMORI**
See HEARTS AND ARMOUR
**I PASCOLI ROSSI**
See MASSACRE AT GRAND CANYON
**I PREDATORI DEL COBRA D'ORO**
See HUNTERS OF THE GOLDEN

COBRA
**I QUATTRO DELL'AVE MARIA**
See ACE HIGH
**I SKYTTENS TEGN**
See EMMANUELLE IN DENMARK
**I TRE SERGENTI DEL BENGALA**
See ADVENTURES OF THE BENGAL
LANCERS
**I TRE VOLTI DELLA PAURA**
See BLACK SABBATH
**I WANT HER DEAD**
See W
**I WAS A TEENAGE BOY**
See WILLY MILLY
**I WON'T DANCE**
See JUST THE WAY YOU ARE
**IF YOU MEET SARTANA PRAY FOR
YOUR DEATH**
See SARTANA, PRAY FOR YOUR
DEATH
**IKE: THE WAR YEARS**
See IKE
**IL BOIA DI VENEZIA**
See EXECUTIONER, THE
**IL BOSS**
See BOSS, THE
**IL BUONO, IL BRUTO, IL CATTIUO**
See GOOD, THE BAD, AND THE
UGLY, THE
**IL CACCIATORE 2**
See LAST HUNTER, THE
**IL CAMORRISTA**
See PROFESSOR, THE
**IL COLOSSO DI ROMA**
See ARM OF FIRE
**IL COMMISSARIO VERRAZZANO**
See DEADLY CHASE
**IL CONQUISTATORE DI
MARACAIBO**
See CONQUEROR OF MARACAIBO,
THE
**IL CORSAREO NERO**
See BLACK PIRATE, THE
**IL CUGINO AMERICANO**
See BLOOD TIES
**IL DECAMERONE**
See DECAMERON, THE
**IL DIAVOLO E I MORTI**
See LISA AND THE DEVIL
**IL DIAVOLO E IL MORTO**
See LISA AND THE DEVIL
**IL DIRITTO D'AMARE**
See BRAINWASHED
**IL DISERTORE**
See DESERTER, THE
**IL DISPEZZO**
See CONTEMPT
**IL DITO NELLA PIAGA**
See DIRTY TWO, THE
**IL DOMINATORE DEL FERRO**
See IRON MASTER, THE
**IL GATTO A NOVE CODE**
See CAT O'NINE TAILS
**IL GATTO NERO**
See BLACK CAT, THE
**IL GINECOLOGO DELLA MUTUA**
See LADIES DOCTOR
**IL GIUDICE E I SUO BOIA**
See DECEPTION
**IL GRANDE ATTACCO**
See BIGGEST BATTLE, THE
**IL GRANDE DUELLO**
See STORMRIDER
**IL GRANDE RITORNO DI DJANGO**
See DJANGO STRIKES AGAIN
**IL LEONE DI TEBE**
See LION OF THEBES, THE
**IL LETTO IN PIAZZA**
See SEX DIARY

**IL MERCENARIO**
See DJANGO
**IL MIO CORPO PER UN POKER**
See BELLE STARR STORY, THE
**IL MIO NOME SHANGHAI JOE**
See FIGHTING FISTS OF SHANGHAI
JOE, THE
**IL MOSTRO E IN TAVOLA . . .
BARONE FRANKENSTEIN**
See ANDY WARHOL'S
FRANKENSTEIN
**IL MULINO DELLE DONNE DI
PIETRA**
See TALES OF TERROR 3: DROPS OF
BLOOD
**IL NAND E LA STREGA**
See KING DICK
**IL PADRONE DEL FERRO**
See IRON MASTER, THE
**IL PIACERE**
See PLEASURE, THE
**IL PORTIERE DI NOTTE**
See NIGHT PORTER, THE
**IL PREZZO DEL POTERRE**
See PRICE OF POWER, THE
**IL SERGENTE KLEMS**
See SERGEANT KLEMS
**IL SERVIZIO SEGRETO UCCIDE**
See SILENT ACTION
**IL SIGILLO DI PECHINO**
See CORRUPT ONES, THE
**IL SORRISO DEL GRANDE
TENTATORE**
See TEMPTER, THE
**IL STRANGOLATORE DI VIENNA**
See STRANGLER OF VIENNA, THE
**IL SUO MODO DI FARE**
See GIRL WHO COULDN'T SAY NO,
THE
**IL TEMPO DEGLI ASSASSINI**
See SEASON FOR ASSASSINS
**IL TESTIMONE DEVE TACERE**
See SILENCE THE WITNESS
**IL TRONO DI FUOCO**
See THRONE OF FIRE, THE
**IL VENDITORE DI MORTE**
See PRICE OF DEATH, THE
**IL VISITATORE**
See VISITOR, THE
**IL VIZIO DI FAMIGLIA**
See VICES IN THE FAMILY
**I'LL GO . . . I'LL KILL HIM AND COME
BACK**
See ANY GUN CAN PLAY
**IM LAUF DER ZEIT**
See KINGS OF THE ROAD
**I'LL MEET YOU IN HEAVEN**
See MAXIE
**IMI, HAGENERALIT**
See MY MOTHER, THE GENERAL
**IMMORAL**
See CONFESSIONS OF A
PROSTITUTE
**IMMORTAL BATTALION, THE**
See WAY AHEAD, THE
**IMPURE, THE**
See TALES OF TERROR 2: THE
IMPURE, WILD RIDERS
**IN A GLASS DARKLY**
See AGATHA CHRISTIE
COLLECTION, THE: IN A GLASS
DARKLY
**IN LOVE**
See STRANGERS IN LOVE
**IN PURSUIT OF D.B. COOPER**
See PURSUIT
**IN SAIGON, SOME MAY LIVE**
See SOME MAY LIVE
**IN THE AFTERNOON OF WAR**

See MOUSE AND THE WOMAN, THE
**IN THE DEVIL'S GARDEN**
See ASSAULT
**IN THE MOOD**
See WOO WOO KID, THE
**IN THE REALM OF THE SENSES**
See AI NO CORRIDA
**IN THE SHADOW OF A COLT**
See IN A COLT'S SHADOW
**INCENSE FOR THE DAMNED**
See BLOODSUCKERS
**INCHON**
See OPERATION INCHON
**INCIDENT IN CRESTRIDGE**
See INCIDENT AT CRESTRIDGE
**INCONTRI MOLTI RAVVICINATI DEL
QUATRO TIPO**
See VERY CLOSE ENCOUNTERS OF
THE FOURTH KIND
**INCREDIBLE CHESTY (72-32-36)
MORGAN AND HER DEADLY
WEAPONS, THE**
See DEADLY WEAPONS
**INCREDIBLE INVASION, THE**
See ALIEN TERROR
**INCREDIBLY STRANGE CREATURES
WHO STOPPED LIVING AND
BECAME MIXED-UP ZOMBIES**
See TEENAGE PSYCHO MEETS
BLOODY MARY, THE
**INCUBO SULLA CITTA
CONTAMINATA**
See NIGHTMARE CITY
**INDAGINE SU UN CITTADINO AL DI
SOPRA DI OGNI SOSPETTO**
See INVESTIGATION OF A CITIZEN
ABOVE SUSPICION
**INDAGINE SU UN DELITTO
PERFETTO**
See PERFECT GRIME, THE
**INDEPENDENCE DAY**
See LOVE, HONOR AND OBEY
**INDISCRETION**
See INDISCRETION OF AN
AMERICAN WIFE
**INDUCED SYNDROME**
See PLAGUE
**INFERNO '80**
See INFERNO
**INFERNO DEI MORTI-VIVENTI**
See ZOMBIE CREEPING FLESH
**INFERNO IN DIRETTA**
See CUT AND RUN
**INHERITORS, THE**
See INHERITANCE, THE
**INKRAKTARNA**
See SWEDISH SEX GAMES
**INN OF THE FLYING DRAGON, THE**
See SLEEP OF DEATH, THE
**INNOCENT SALLY**
See DIRTY MIND OF YOUNG SALLY,
THE
**INNOCENT SEX**
See TEENAGE INNOCENCE
**INNOCENTS, THE**
See TURN OF THE SCREW, THE
**INSECT**
See INVASION OF THE
BODYSUCKERS
**INSTANT JUSTICE**
See MARINE ISSUE
**INSURGENT MEXICO**
See MEXICO IN FLAMES
**INTELLIGENCE MEN, THE**
See MORECOMBE AND WISE: THE
INTELLIGENCE MEN
**INTERIOR OF A CONVENT**
See BEHIND CONVENT WALLS
**INTERNECINE PROJECT, THE**

See MANIPULATOR, THE
**INTERNO BERLINELE**
See BERLIN AFFAIR, THE
**INTIMATE MOMENTS**
See MADAME CLAUDE 2
**INTO THE FIRE**
See LEGEND OF WOLF LODGE, THE
**INTRIGO COMPLICATO DI VICOLI E
DELITTI**
See CAMORRA
**INTRIGUE**
See ADVENTURES OF ELIZA
FRASER, THE
**INTRUDER, THE**
See SWEDISH SEX GAMES
**INTRUDERS, THE**
See SWEDISH SEX GAMES
**INVADERS FROM THE DEEP**
See STINGRAY: INVADERS FROM
THE DEEP
**INVADERS, THE**
See ATTACK OF THE NORMANS
**INVADERS, THE**
See FORTY-NINTH PARALLEL, THE
**INVASION BY THE ATOMIC
ZOMBIES**
See NIGHTMARE CITY
**INVASION EARTH 2150 A.D.**
See DOCTOR WHO: INVASION
EARTH 2150 A.D.
**INVASION FORCE**
See HANGAR 18
**INVASION OF THE ATOMIC
ZOMBIES**
See NIGHTMARE CITY
**INVASION OF THE BODY STEALERS**
See BODY STEALERS, THE
**INVASION OF THE FLESH HUNTERS**
See CANNIBAL APOCALYPSE
**INVASION U.F.O.**
See U.F.O. – INVASION U.F.O.
**INVESTIGATION INTO A CITIZEN
ABOVE SUSPICION**
See INVESTIGATION OF A CITIZEN
ABOVE SUSPICION
**INVESTIGATION OF A PRIVATE
CITIZEN**
See INVESTIGATION OF A CITIZEN
ABOVE SUSPICION
**INVINCIBLE BOXER**
See KING BOXER
**INVINCIBLE KUNG FU LEGS, THE**
See LEG FIGHTERS, THE
**INVINCIBLE POLE FIGHTERS, THE**
See INVINCIBLE POLE FIGHTER,
THE
**INVINCIBLE, THE**
See BRUCE LEE THE INVINCIBLE
**IO, TU, LORO E GLI ALTRI**
See DOUBLE TROUBLE
**IRON DUKE, THE**
See SECRET LIVES OF THE BRITISH
PRIME MINISTERS, THE: THE IRON
DUKE
**IRON FIST OF KWANGTUNG**
See CANTON IRON KUNG FU
**IRON NECK**
See IRON NECK LI
**IRON OX, THE TIGER'S KILLER**
See IRON OX: THE TIGER KILLER
**IRONMASTER, THE**
See IRON MASTER, THE
**ISH RACHAEL**
See RACHEL'S MAN
**ISLAND OF BLOOD**
See WHODUNNIT?
**ISLAND OF MUTANTS**
See ISLAND OF MUTATIONS
**ISLAND OF PASSION**

See PASSION ISLAND
**ISLAND OF THE ALIVE**
See It'S ALIVE 3: ISLAND OF THE
ALIVE
**ISLAND OF THE BURNING DAMNED**
See NIGHT OF THE BIG HEAT
**ISLAND OF THE BURNING DOOMED**
See NIGHT OF THE BIG HEAT
**ISLAND OF THE DAMNED**
See ISLAND OF DEATH
**ISLAND OF THE FISHERMEN, THE**
See ISLAND OF MUTATIONS
**ISLAND OF THE SAVAGE SEX
SLAVES**
See CONFESSIONS OF THE SEX
SLAVES
**ISLAND OF THE SNAKE PEOPLE**
See CULT OF THE DEAD
**ISLAND, THE**
See LIFE AND DEATH (A STRUGGLE)
**ISLE OF THE SNAKE PEOPLE**
See CULT OF THE DEAD
**IT CAME FROM THE LAKE**
See MONSTROID
**IT CAME WITHOUT WARNING**
See WARNING, THE
**IT HAPPENED AT LAKEWOOD
MANOR**
See ANTS: PANIC AT LAKEWOOD
MANOR
**IT HAPPENED AT THE WORLD'S
FAIR**
See ELVIS PRESLEY: IT HAPPENED
AT THE WORLD'S FAIR
**IT HAPPENED ONE SUMMER**
See STATE FAIR
**IT LIVES AGAIN**
See IT'S ALIVE 2
**IT LIVES BY NIGHT**
See BAT PEOPLE, THE
**IT LIVES WITHIN HER**
See DEVIL WITHIN HER, THE
**IT ONLY HURTS WHEN I LAUGH**
See ONLY WHEN I LAUGH
**IT'S NOT SIZE THAT COUNTS**
See PERCY'S PROGRESS
**IT'S NOT THE SIZE THAT COUNTS**
See PERCY'S PROGRESS
**IT'S ONLY MONEY**
See DOUBLE DYNAMITE
**IVAN THE TERRIBLE: PART 1**
See IVAN THE TERRIBLE
**IVORY HUNTER**
See WHERE NO VULTURES FLY
**IZZY AND MOE**
See IZZY AND MOE, THE BOOTLEG
BUSTERS
**J:S, A CRIMINAL STORY OF THE
FAR WEST**
See BANDITS
**JACK AND THE BEANSTALK**
See ABBOTT AND COSTELLO: JACK
AND THE BEANSTALK
**JACK LONDON'S KLONDIKE FEVER**
See KLONDIKE FEVER
**JACK TILLMAN: THE SURVIVALIST**
See SURVIVALIST, THE
**JACKIE CHAN VERSUS JIMMY
WANG YU**
See KILLER METEORS, THE
**JACKIE CHAN'S POLICE STORY**
See POLICE STORY
**JACKSON COUNTY JAIL**
See INNOCENT VICTIM
**JACOBO TIMMERMAN: PRISONER
WITHOUT A NAME, CELL WITHOUT
A NUMBER**
See PRISONER WITHOUT A NAME,
CELL WITHOUT A NUMBER

**JADE CLAW, THE**
See CRYSTAL FIST
**JADE JUNGLE, THE**
See ARMED RESPONSE
**JADE PUSSYCAT, THE**
See SILKEN PUSSYCAT, THE
**JAG VILL LIGGA MED DIN AYSKARE
MAMMA**
See SWEDISH CONFESSIONS
**JAILBAIT**
See JAILBAIT BABYSITTER
**JAILBIRDS**
See LAUREL AND HARDY: PARDON
US
**JAILHOUSE ROCK**
See ELVIS PRESLEY: JAILHOUSE
ROCK
**JAMAICAN GOLD**
See FORTY MILLION BUCKS
**JAMES RAMSAY MACDONALD**
See SECRET LIVES OF THE BRITISH
PRIME MINISTERS, THE:
MACDONALD
**JANE'S SEXUAL AWAKENING**
See SWEET SEXUAL AWAKENING
**JASON LIVES: FRIDAY THE 13TH
PART 6**
See FRIDAY THE 13TH, PART 6:
JASON LIVES
**JATSZANI KELL**
See DOUBLE PLAY
**JAWS 3-D**
See JAWS 3
**JAWS OF DEATH, THE**
See MAKO: THE JAWS OF DEATH
**JAWS: THE REVENGE**
See JAWS 4
**JAYNE MANSFIELD: A SYMBOL OF
THE 50s**
See JAYNE MANSFIELD STORY, THE
**JEANNIE**
See PORTRAIT OF JENNIE
**JEANNOT INTREPIDE**
See JOHNNY AND THE WICKED
GIANT
**JEDER FUR SICH UND GOTT GEGEN
ALLE**
See ENIGMA OF KASPAR HAUSER,
THE
**JENNIFER, THE SNAKE GODDESS**
See JENNIFER
**JESSE AND LESTER**
See JESSIE AND LESTER: TWO
BROTHERS IN A PLACE CALLED
TRINITY
**JESSE E LESTER, DUE FRATELLI IN
UN POSTO CHIAMATO TRINITA**
See JESSIE AND LESTER: TWO
BROTHERS IN A PLACE CALLED
TRINITY
**JESUS**
See STORY OF JESUS, THE
**JET SEX**
See CANDI GIRL
**JETSONS MEET THE FLINTSTONES,
THE**
See FLINTSTONES: THE JETSONS
MEET THE FLINTSTONES
**JEUX POUR COUPLES INFIDELES**
See HOT AND BLUE
**JEZEBELS, THE**
See SWITCHBLADE SISTERS, THE
**JIM BUCK**
See PORTRAIT OF A HITMAN
**JIM IL PRIMO**
See LAST GUN, THE
**JINGCHA GOSHI**
See POLICE STORY
**JISHIN RETTO**

See MEGAFORCE 7.9
**JOE HILL**
See BALLAD OF JOE HILL, THE
**JOE, CERCATI UN POSTO PER MORIRE**
See FIND A PLACE TO DIE
**JOEY**
See MAKING CONTACT
**JOHN AND YOKO: A LOVE STORY**
See JOHN AND YOKO: THE COMPLETE STORY
**JOHN STEINBECK'S EAST OF EDEN**
See EAST OF EDEN
**JOHNNY THE GIANT KILLER**
See JOHNNY AND THE WICKED GIANT
**JOKO, INVOCO DIO . . . E MUORI**
See VENGEANCE
**JORDEN RUNT MED FANNY HILL**
See AROUND THE WORLD WITH FANNY HILL
**JORNADA DE MUERTE**
See DEATH JOURNEY
**JOUISSANCES A DOMICILE**
See MOBILE-HOME GIRLS
**JOUISSANCES ROULANTES**
See MOBILE-HOME GIRLS
**JOURNEY THROUGH THE BLACK SUN**
See SPACE 1999: JOURNEY THROUGH THE BLACK SUN
**JOY OF FLYING**
See SEX AT 7000 FEET
**JOY STICKS**
See JOYSTICKS
**JUDAS GOAT**
See XTRO
**JUDITH**
See CONFLICT
**JULCHEN UND JETTCHEN: DIE VERLIEBTEN APOTHEKERSTOECHTER**
See COME PLAY WITH ME 3
**JUMP**
See FURY ON WHEELS
**JUMPIN' AT THE BEDSIDE**
See ESCORT GIRLS
**JUNGFRUKALLAN**
See VIRGIN SPRING, THE
**JUNGLE FEVER**
See JUNGLE WARRIORS
**JUNGLE FIGHTERS**
See LONG AND THE SHORT AND THE TALL, THE
**JUNGLE HEAT**
See DANCE OF THE DWARFS
**JUNGLE RAIDERS**
See CAPTAIN YANKEE AND THE JUNGLE RAIDERS
**JUNIOR**
See HOT WATER
**JUNKMAN, THE**
See GONE IN 60 SECONDS 2
**JUST ANOTHER MIRACLE**
See HEAVENLY PURSUITS
**JUSTINE**
See CRUEL PASSION
**JUSTINE: LE DISAVVENTURE DELLA VIRTU**
See JUSTINE
**KADAICHA: THE DEATH STONE**
See KADAICHA
**KAGEMUSHA THE SHADOW WARRIOR**
See KAGEMUSHA
**KAIN OF DARK PLANET**
See WARRIOR AND THE SORCERESS, THE

See KARATE KID 3, THE
**KARLEKSSVINGEL**
See SWEDISH CONFESSIONS
**KARLEKSVIRVELN**
See SWEDISH CONFESSIONS
**KASPAR HAUSER**
See ENIGMA OF KASPAR HAUSER, THE
**KATY CATERPILLAR**
See KATY
**KEEP MY GRAVE OPEN**
See HOUSE WHERE HELL FROZE OVER, THE
**KEEPERS**
See SPOOK WHO SAT BY THE DOOR, THE
**KENNY ROGERS AS THE GAMBLER**
See GAMBLER, THE
**KENNY ROGERS AS THE GAMBLER: PART 2**
See GAMBLER, THE: PART 2
**KENNY ROGERS AS THE GAMBLER: PART 3**
See GAMBLER, THE: PART 3
**KENT CHRONICLES, THE**
See BASTARD, THE
**KGOD**
See PRAY TV
**KIA**
See EYE OF THE EAGLE 2
**KID BROTHER, THE**
See HAROLD LLOYD: THE KID BROTHER
**KID GALAHAD**
See ELVIS PRESLEY: KID GALAHAD
**KID, THE**
See CHARLIE CHAPLIN: THE KID
**KIDNAPPING OF BABY JOHN DOE, THE**
See KIDNAPPING OF BABY JOHN, THE
**KILL**
See DEATHDREAM
**KILL AND GO HIDE**
See CHILD, THE
**KILL CASTRO**
See CUBA CROSSING
**KILL FACTOR, THE**
See DEATH DIMENSIONS
**KILL POINT**
See KILLPOINT
**KILL, KILL, KILL**
See KILL
**KILLBOTS**
See CHOPPING MALL
**KILLBRAND**
See DEADLY TRACKERS, THE
**KILLER FISH**
See KILLERFISH
**KILLER FORCE**
See DIAMOND MERCENARIES, THE
**KILLER GRIZZLY**
See GRIZZLY
**KILLER INSTINCT, THE**
See TRAPPED
**KILLER MAN**
See MAFIA WARFARE
**KILLER OF KILLERS**
See MECHANIC, THE
**KILLERS**
See BOYS NEXT DOOR, THE
**KILLERS INVINCIBLE**
See NINJA SQUAD
**KILLER'S CANYON**
See LAST GUN, THE
**KILLING HEAT, THE**
See GRASS IS SINGING, THE
**KILLING KIND, THE**
See PSYCHOPATH, THE

**KILLING TIME**
See MACON COUNTY LINE
**KILLZONE, THE: TOUR OF DUTY**
See TOUR OF DUTY
**KING AND MISTER BIRD, THE**
See MISTER BIRD TO THE RESCUE
**KING AND THE BIRD, THE**
See MISTER BIRD TO THE RESCUE
**KING AND THE MOCKINGBIRD, THE**
See MISTER BIRD TO THE RESCUE
**KING CREOLE**
See ELVIS PRESLEY: KING CREOLE
**KING GUN**
See GATLING GUN, THE
**KING OF THE OLYMPICS: THE LIVES AND LOVES OF AVERY BRUNDAGE**
See KING OF THE OLYMPICS: PARTS 1 AND 2
**KING ROBOT**
See MY SON THE VAMPIRE
**KINGDOM OF SPIDERS**
See KINGDOM OF THE SPIDERS
**KINGS AND DESPERATE MEN: A HOSTAGE INCIDENT**
See KINGS AND DESPERATE MEN
**KINGS OF THE SUN**
See INCA
**KINGU KONGU TAI GOJIRA**
See KING KONG VERSUS GODZILLA
**KINJITE: FORBIDDEN SUBJECTS**
See KINJITE
**KIPPERBANG**
See P'TANG, YANG, KIPPERBANG
**KISS FROM EDDIE, A**
See SWEET KILL
**KISS ME . . . KILL ME**
See POLICE IN ACTION 4: KISS ME . . . KILL ME
**KISS MEETS THE PHANTOM OF THE PARK**
See PHANTOM OF THE PARK, THE
**KISS: THE PHANTOM OF THE PARK**
See PHANTOM OF THE PARK, THE
**KISSIN' COUSINS**
See ELVIS PRESLEY: KISSIN' COUSINS
**KISSOGRAM GIRLS**
See SEXY SECRETS OF THE KISSOGRAM GIRLS, THE
**KITTY CAN'T HELP IT**
See CARHOPS, THE
**KNIGHT AND WARRIOR**
See NINJA OPERATION: KNIGHT AND WARRIOR
**KNIGHT OF THE DRAGON, THE**
See STAR KNIGHT
**KNOCK OUT COP, THE**
See FLATFOOT
**KOMMANDO LEOPARD**
See COMMANDO LEOPARD
**KOMMANO SINAI**
See SINAI COMMANDOS
**KOMMISAR X JAGT DIE ROTEN TIGER**
See TIGER GANG
**KONG ISLAND**
See KING OF KONG ISLAND
**KONYETS SANKT-PETERBURGA**
See END OF SAINT PETERSBURG, THE
**KRASNYE KOLOKOLA**
See MEXICO IN FLAMES
**KRISH LELO MOTZA**
See DEAD END STREET
**KRUG AND COMPANY**
See LAST HOUSE ON THE LEFT, THE
**KRVAVI JASTREBOVI ALJASKE**
See HELL HOUNDS OF ALASKA, THE
**KUAI KO**

See STRANGER FROM CANTON
**KUNG FU COMMANDOS**
See INCREDIBLE KUNG FU
MISSION, THE
**KUNG FU MASTER NAMED DRUNK
CAT**
See KUNG FU MASTER
**KUNTA KINTE'S GIFT**
See ROOTS: KUNTA KINTE'S GIFT
**KYRKOHERDEN**
See LUSTFUL VICAR
**KYUKETSUKI GOKEMIDORO**
See GOKE: BODYSNATCHER FROM
HELL
**L.A. NURSES**
See YOUNG NURSES, THE
**L.A. THRILLER**
See SUNSET STRIP
**LA AMENALA**
See POWER GAME
**LA AMETRALLADORA**
See GATLING GUN
**LA BANDA**
See BANDITS
**LA BANDA J+S: CRONICA
CRIMINALA DEL WEST**
See BANDITS
**LA BATTAGLIA DI ALGERI**
See BATTLE OF ALGIERS, THE
**LA BATTAGLIA D'INGHILTERRA**
See BATTLE SQUADRON
**LA BATTALLA SOBRE BRETANA**
See BATTLE SQUADRON
**LA BETE**
See DEATH'S ECSTASY
**LA BIBLIA**
See BIBLE, THE
**LA CADUTA DEGLI DEI**
See DAMNED, THE
**LA CAGE AUX FOLLES 3: ELLES SE
MARIENT**
See LA CAGE AUX FOLLES 3
**LA CAGE AUX FOLLES 3: THE
WEDDING**
See LA CAGE AUX FOLLES 3
**LA CAMERA DEL TERROR**
See TORTURE ZONE, THE
**LA CAMPANA DEL INFIERNO**
See BELL OF HELL, THE
**LA CASA AI CONFINI DEL PARCO**
See HOUSE ON THE EDGE OF THE
PARK, THE
**LA CASA CON LA SCALA NEL BUIO**
See BLADE IN THE DARK, A
**LA CASA DELL'EXORCISMO**
See LISA AND THE DEVIL
**LA CASA NEL PARCO**
See HOUSE ON THE EDGE OF THE
PARK, THE
**LA CASA SPERDUTA DEL PARCO**
See HOUSE ON THE EDGE OF THE
PARK, THE
**LA CASSE**
See BURGLARS, THE
**LA COLLINA DEGLI STIVALI**
See BOOT HILL
**LA CROCE SICILIANA**
See SICILIAN CROSS
**LA DENTELLIERE**
See LACEMAKER, THE
**LA FABULEUSE AVENTURE DE
MARCO POLO**
See KUBLAI KHAN
**LA FEMME ECARLATE**
See SCARLET WOMAN, THE
**LA FEMME INFIDELE**
See UNFAITHFUL WIVES
**LA FINE DELL'INNOCENZA**
See BLUE BELLE

**LA FLUTE A SIX SCHTROUMPFS**
See SMURFS AND THE MAGIC
FLUTE, THE
**LA GUERRA DE LOS MAGOS**
See WIZARDS OF THE LOST
KINGDOM
**LA GUERRA DEL FERRO**
See IRON MASTER, THE
**LA GUERRA DI TROIA**
See TROJAN WAR, THE
**LA GUERRE DE TROIE**
See TROJAN WAR, THE
**LA GUERRE DES TUQUES**
See DOG WHO STOPPED THE WAR,
THE
**LA GUERRE DU FER**
See IRON MASTER, THE
**LA GUERRE DU FEU**
See QUEST FOR FIRE
**LA HISTORIA OFICIAL**
See OFFICIAL VERSION, THE
**LA HONTE DE LA JUNGLE**
See JUNGLE BURGER
**LA INVASION DE LOS ZOMBIES
ATOMICOS**
See NIGHTMARE CITY
**LA INVASION SINIESTRA**
See ALIEN TERROR
**LA ISLA DE LOS MUERTOS**
See CULT OF THE DEAD
**LA JEUNE FILLE ASSASSINEE**
See CHARLOTTE
**LA LEGGENDA DI ENEA**
See LAST GLORY OF TROY, THE
**LA LICEALE**
See UNDERGRADUATE GIRLS
**LA LUNE DANS LE CANIVEAU**
See MOON IN THE GUTTER, THE
**LA MALA ORDINA**
See MANHUNT
**LA MASCHERA DEL DEMONIO**
See BLACK SUNDAY
**LA MOGLIE VERGINE**
See VIRGIN WIFE
**LA MONTAGNA DEL DIO
CANNIBALE**
See PRISONER OF THE CANNIBAL
GOD
**LA MORTA NON CONTRA I DOLARI**
See DEATH AT ORWELL ROCK
**LA MORTE EN DIRECT**
See DEATHWATCH
**LA MORTE NON HA SESSO**
See BLACK VEIL FOR LISA, A
**LA MOTORCYCLETTE**
See GIRL ON A MOTORCYCLE
**LA MUERTE DE UN PRESIDENTE**
See PRICE OF POWER, THE
**LA MUERTE DEL CHE GUEVARA**
See REBEL WITH A CAUSE
**LA MUERTE ESPERA EN ATHENAS**
See MISSION BLOODY MARY
**LA MUERTE VIVIENTE**
See CULT OF THE DEAD
**LA NOCHE DE LA MUERTA CIEGA**
See TOMBS OF THE BLIND DEAD
**LA NOCHE DE LOS GAVIOTAS**
See NIGHT OF THE SEAGULLS
**LA NOCHE DE WALPURGIS**
See WEREWOLF'S SHADOW, THE
**LA NOCHE DEL TERROR CIEGO**
See TOMBS OF THE BLIND DEAD
**LA NOVIA ENSANGRETADA**
See BLOOD-SPATTERED BRIDE, THE
**LA NUIT AMERICAINE**
See DAY FOR NIGHT
**LA NUORA GIOVANE**
See INTIMATE RELATIONS
**LA PADRONA E SERVITA**

See MISTRESS, THE
**LA PAURA IN CITTA**
See FEAR IN THE CITY
**LA PLUS LONGUE NUIT DU DIABLE**
See DEVIL'S NIGHTMARE
**LA POLIZIA ACCUSA**
See SILENT ACTION
**LA POLIZIA INTERVIENE: ORDINE DI
UCCIDERE!**
See LEFT HAND OF THE LAW, THE
**LA POLIZIA STA A GUARDERE**
See GREAT KIDNAPPING, THE
**LA RAGAZZA DI NOME GUILIO**
See GIRL CALLED JULES, A
**LA RAGAZZA DI TRIESTE**
See GIRL FROM TRIESTE, THE
**LA REBELION DE LAS MUERTAS**
See VENGEANCE OF THE ZOMBIES
**LA REINA BARBARA**
See BARBARIAN QUEEN
**LA ROUGE AUX LEVRES**
See DAUGHTERS OF DARKNESS
**LA SAGA DE LOS DRACULA**
See DRACULA SAGA, THE
**LA SCHIAVA IO CE LINO E TU NO**
See MY DARLING SLAVE
**LA SCOUMOUNE**
See MAFIA WARFARE
**LA SEMANA DEL ASESINO**
See CANNIBAL MAN, THE
**LA SPADA BARBARA**
See SWORD OF THE BARBARIANS
**LA SPIA SENZA DOMANI**
See SELL-OUT, THE
**LA SPIAGGIA DEL DESIDERO**
See TABOO ISLAND
**LA SPINA DORSALE DEL DIAVOLO**
See DESERTER, THE
**LA SPOSINA**
See UP AND COMING
**LA TUMBA DE LA ISLA MALDITA**
See CRYPT OF THE LIVING DEAD
**LA VENDETTA DEI BARBARI**
See REVENGE OF THE BARBARIANS
**LA VENDETTA DEI MORTI VIVENTI**
See VENGEANCE OF THE ZOMBIES
**LA VERGINE DI BALI**
See VIRGIN OF BALI, THE
**LA VISITA DEL VICIO**
See VIOLATION OF THE BITCH
**LA VITA E BELLA**
See LIFE IS BEAUTIFUL
**LABYRINTH**
See REFLECTION OF FEAR, A
**LADIES CLUB, THE**
See SISTERHOOD, THE
**LADRI DI BICICLETTE**
See BICYCLE THIEVES
**LADY CHAPLIN STORY, THE**
See SPECIAL MISSION LADY
CHAPLIN
**LADY DRACULA**
See LEMORA
**LADY DRACULA**
See LEGEND OF BLOOD CASTLE,
THE
**LADY GODIVA MEETS TOM JONES**
See LADY GODIVA RIDES AGAIN
**LADY GODIVA RIDES**
See LADY GODIVA RIDES AGAIN
**LADY IN DANGER**
See LAST SONG, THE
**LADY IS A TRAMP, THE**
See THAT GIRL IS A TRAMP
**LADY LIBERTINE**
See FRANK AND I
**LADY OF BURLESQUE**
See G-STRING MURDERS, THE
**LADY VAMPIRE**

**L'ORRIBILE SEGRETO DEL DOTTORE HICHCOCK**
See TERROR OF DOCTOR HICHCOCK, THE

**LOS AMIGOS**
See DEAF SMITH AND JOHNNY EARS

**LOS BANDIDOS**
See BANDITS, THE

**LOS CORSARIOS DEL CARIBE**
See CONQUEROR OF MARACAIBO, THE

**LOS HIJOS DEL DIA Y DE LA NOCHE**
See BANDITS

**LOS LEOPARDOS DE CHURCHILL**
See CHURCHILL'S LEOPARDS

**LOS NUEVOS EXTRA TERRESTRES**
See EXTRA TERRESTRIAL VISITORS

**LOS OSOS AZULES DE LA MUNECA ROTA**
See BLUE EYES OF THE BROKEN DOLL, THE

**LOS TIGROS DEL DESIERTO**
See DESERT TIGERS, THE

**LOSS OF INNOCENCE**
See GREENGAGE SUMMER, THE

**L'OSSESSA**
See SEXORCIST

**LOST HONOR OF KATHRYN BECK, THE**
See ACT OF PASSION

**LOST! – A TRUE STORY**
See LOST!

**LOUIS L'AMOUR'S DOWN THE LONG HILLS**
See DOWN THE LONG HILLS

**LOUIS L'AMOUR'S THE SACKETTS**
See DAYBREAKERS, THE

**LOUISANE**
See LOUISIANA

**L'OURS**
See BEAR, THE

**LOVE AND THE MIDNIGHT AUTO SUPPLY**
See RIP OFF

**LOVE AND WAR**
See WAR AND LOVE

**LOVE AT THE TOP**
See FRENCH WAY, THE

**LOVE CAMP**
See LOVE BOX, THE

**LOVE FIGHTERS**
See TUFF TURF

**LOVE FOR RENT**
See LOVE FOR SALE

**LOVE GAMES FOR YOUNG GIRLS**
See LOVE GAMES OF YOUNG GIRLS

**LOVE HAPPY**
See MARX BROTHERS: LOVE HAPPY

**LOVE IN LAS VEGAS**
See ELVIS PRESLEY: VIVA LAS VEGAS

**LOVE IS FOREVER**
See COMEBACK, THE

**LOVE MADNESS**
See REEFER MADNESS

**LOVE MANIAC, THE**
See MAN WITH THE SYNTHETIC BRAIN, THE

**LOVE ME TENDER**
See ELVIS PRESLEY: LOVE ME TENDER

**LOVE ON A HORSE**
See CONFESSIONS OF A RIDING MISTRESS

**LOVE SCENES**
See ECSTASY

**LOVE TRAP**
See CURSE OF THE BLACK WIDOW

**LOVE YOU TO DEATH**
See DEADLY ILLUSION

**LOVE-HUNGRY GIRLS**
See DEADLY WHEN AROUSED

**LOVES OF LILY, THE**
See DOUBLE PLAY

**LOVESCENE**
See ECSTASY

**LOVING YOU**
See ELVIS PRESLEY: LOVING YOU

**L'UCCELLO D'ALLE PIUME DI CRISTALLO**
See BIRD WITH THE CRYSTAL PLUMAGE, THE

**LUCIFER PROJECT, THE**
See BARRACUDA

**LUCKY LUKE: DAISY TOWN**
See LUCKY LUKE

**LUCKY LUKE: THE BALLAD OF THE DALTONS**
See LUCKY LUKE AND THE DALTON GANG

**LUCKY NICK CAIN**
See I'LL GET YOU FOR THIS

**LUCKY STIFF**
See MISTER CHRISTMAS DINNER

**LUDAS MATYI**
See MATTIG THE GOOSEBOY

**L'ULTIMA ORGIA DEL III REICH**
See GESTAPO'S LAST ORGY

**L'ULTIMO SAPORE DELL'ARIA**
See LAST FEELINGS

**L'UMO, L'ORGOGLIO, LA VENDETTA**
See MAN, PRIDE AND VENGEANCE

**LUNCH WAGON GIRLS**
See LUNCH WAGON

**LUNE DE MIEL**
See HONEYMOON

**LUNG MU TOU**
See CHINESE BOXER, THE

**L'UOMO DALLE DUE OMBRE**
See COLD SWEAT

**LUSSURIA**
See LUST

**LUST AT FIRST BITE**
See DRACULA SUCKS

**LUST IN SPACE: CONTACT IS MADE**
See LUST IN SPACE

**LUSTFUL DESIRES**
See FUR TRAP, THE

**M.T.B.**
See HELL BOATS

**M3: THE GEMINI STRAIN**
See PLAGUE

**MACABRO**
See MACABRE

**MacARTHUR THE REBEL GENERAL**
See MacARTHUR

**MACCHERONI**
See MACARONI

**MACDONALD**
See SECRET LIVES OF THE BRITISH PRIME MINISTERS, THE: MACDONALD

**MACE**
See DEATH GAMES

**MACH 78**
See DAREDEVIL DRIVERS

**MACHISMO**
See GREAT GUNDOWN, THE

**MACHISMO: FORTY GRAVES FOR FORTY GUNS**
See GREAT GUNDOWN, THE

**MACK, THE**
See MACK AND HIS PACK, THE

**MAD BUTCHER OF VIENNA, THE**
See STRANGLER OF VIENNA, THE

**MAD BUTCHER, THE**
See STRANGLER OF VIENNA, THE

**MAD DOG MORGAN**
See MAD DOG

**MAD MAGAZINE PRESENTS UP THE ACADEMY**
See UP THE ACADEMY

**MAD MISSION 2: ACES GO PLACES**
See MAD MISSION 2

**MAD MISSION PART 2: ACES GO PLACES**
See MAD MISSION 2

**MAD TRAPPER OF THE YUKON**
See CHALLENGE TO BE FREE

**MADAME OLGA'S PUPILS**
See SEX ACADEMY

**MADDEST STORY EVER TOLD, THE**
See SPIDER BABY

**MADE IN L.A.**
See L.A. CRIMEWAVE

**MADMAN**
See CAMP 708

**MADMAN MARZ**
See MADMAN

**MAGEE AND THE LADY**
See MAGEE

**MAGICA AVENTURA**
See MAGIC ADVENTURE

**MAGICAL MYSTERY TOUR, THE**
See BEATLES: THE MAGICAL MYSTERY TOUR

**MAGNIFICENT TWO, THE**
See MORECOMBE AND WISE: THE MAGNIFICENT TWO

**MAIDEN QUEST**
See TERRIBLE QUICK SWORD OF SIEGFRIED, THE

**MAKAI TENSHO**
See SAMURAI REINCARNATION

**MAKING WAVES**
See WINDRIDER

**MALIBU BIKINI SHOP, THE**
See BIKINI SHOP, THE

**MALIZIA EROTICA**
See AND GIVE US OUR DAILY SEX

**MALOMBRA, LE PERVERSIONI SESSUALI DI UNA ADOLESCENTE**
See MALOMBRA

**MALOMBRA, THE SEXUAL PERVERSIONS OF AN ADOLESCENT**
See MALOMBRA

**MALPERTUIS: HISTOIRE D'UNE MAISON MAUDITE**
See MALPERTUIS

**MALTESE CONNECTION, THE**
See FINAL JUSTICE

**MALTESE PROJECT, THE**
See FINAL JUSTICE

**MAMA SANTISSIMA**
See CAMORRA

**MAMA'S BOY, THE**
See PSYCHO FROM TEXAS

**MAN ABOUT TOWN**
See LE SILENCE EST D'OR

**MAN FROM ATLANTIS: THE DEATH SCOUTS**
See MAN FROM ATLANTIS, THE

**MAN FROM DEEP RIVER, THE**
See DEEP RIVER SAVAGES

**MAN FROM S.E.X., THE**
See NUMBER ONE OF THE SECRET SERVICE

**MAN IN 5A, THE**
See KILLING 'EM SOFTLY

**MAN OF EVIL**
See FANNY BY GASLIGHT

**MAN ON A STRING**
See POLICE IN ACTION 2: MAN ON A STRING

**MAN ON THE RUN**
See MANHUNT
**MAN OUTSIDE**
See HIDDEN FEAR
**MAN WHO BROKE 1,000 CHAINS, THE**
See UNCHAINED
**MAN WHO COULDN'T GET ENOUGH, THE**
See CONFESSIONS OF A SEX MANIAC
**MAN WITH A MILLION**
See MILLION POUND NOTE, THE
**MAN WITHOUT A FACE**
See MAN IN THE STEEL MASK, THE
**MAN WITHOUT MERCY**
See GONE WITH THE WEST
**MANEATER**
See SHARK!
**MANEATER**
See EVASION
**MANGIA**
See EAT AND RUN
**MANGIATI VIVI**
See EATEN ALIVE
**MANGIATI VIVI DAI CANNIBALI**
See EATEN ALIVE
**MANHATTAN BABY**
See POSSESSED, THE
**MANHATTAN PROJECT, THE**
See DEADLY GAME
**MANHATTAN PROJECT, THE: THE DEADLY GAME**
See DEADLY GAME
**MANIA**
See EAT AND RUN
**MANIAC**
See RANSOM
**MANIACS ARE LOOSE, THE**
See THRILL KILLERS, THE
**MANKILLERS**
See FASTER PUSSYCAT, KILL . . . KILL
**MANNAJA**
See MAN CALLED BLADE, A
**MANON OF THE SPRING**
See MANON DES SOURCES
**MANTIS FIST FIGHTER**
See THUNDERING MANTIS, THE
**MANTIS VERSUS FALCON CLAWS**
See MANTIS UNDER FALCON CLAWS
**MANY-SPLENDORED THING, A**
See LOVE IS A MANY-SPLENDORED THING
**MARCH OF THE WOODEN SOLDIERS**
See LAUREL AND HARDY: BABES IN TOYLAND
**MARCO POLO**
See KUBLAI KHAN
**MARCO POLO EL AZIME**
See KUBLAI KHAN
**MARIANNE**
See MIRRORS
**MARIE**
See MARIE: A TRUE STORY
**MARIHUANA**
See MARIHUANA: THE DEVIL'S WEED
**MARIHUANA: DEVIL'S WEED WITH ROOTS IN HELL**
See MARIHUANA: THE DEVIL'S WEED
**MARILYN, MON ARMOUR**
See MARILYN, MY LOVE
**MARIO PUZO'S SEVEN GRAVES FOR ROGAN**
See TIME TO DIE, A

**MARIO PUZO'S THE FORTUNATE PILGRIM**
See FORTUNATE PILGRIM, THE
**MARK IL POLIZIOTTO**
See MARK
**MARK OF THE WITCH**
See MARK OF THE DEVIL
**MARQUIS DE SADE: JUSTINE**
See JUSTINE
**MARQUIS DE SADE'S JUSTINE**
See CRUEL PASSION
**MARRIAGE, A**
See BROKEN PROMISE
**MARSHAL BRAVESTARR**
See BRAVESTARR: THE LEGEND
**MARTIAL MONKS OF SHAOLIN TEMPLE**
See MARTIAL MONKS OF SHAOLIN
**MARTIAN CHRONICLES PART 1, THE: THE EXPEDITIONS**
See MARTIAN CHRONICLES, THE
**MARTIAN CHRONICLES PART 2, THE: THE SETTLERS**
See MARTIAN CHRONICLES, THE
**MARTIAN CHRONICLES PART 3, THE: THE MARTIANS**
See MARTIAN CHRONICLES, THE
**MARTIANS, THE**
See MARTIAN CHRONICLES, THE
**MARVELLOUS STUNTS OF KUNG FU**
See MARVELLOUS KUNG FU
**MARVIN AND TIGE**
See LIKE FATHER AND SON
**MARX BROTHERS GO WEST, THE**
See MARX BROTHERS: GO WEST
**MARY AND JOSEPH: A STORY OF FAITH**
See MARY AND JOSEPH
**MASADA**
See ANTAGONISTS, THE
**MASS MURDERER**
See MURDERLUST
**MASSACRE EN CONDOR PASS**
See MONTANA TRAP
**MASSAGE GIRLS**
See MASSAGE GIRLS IN BANGKOK
**MASTER KILLER**
See THIRTY-SIXTH CHAMBER OF SHAOLIN, THE
**MASTER OF THE GAME 1: JAMES MCGREGOR**
See MASTER OF THE GAME
**MASTER OF THE GAME 2: KATE BLACKWALL**
See MASTER OF THE GAME
**MASTER OF THE GAME 3: EVE AND ALEXANDRA**
See MASTER OF THE GAME
**MASTERS OF THE UNIVERSE**
See MASTERS OF THE UNIVERSE: THE MOTION PICTURE
**MAT**
See MOTHER
**MATA HARI'S DAUGHTER**
See DAUGHTER OF MATA HARI, THE
**MATANGO**
See MATANGO: FUNGUS OF TERROR
**MATI**
See BEYOND REASON
**MATRATZEN TANGO**
See WHEN GIRLS UNDRESS
**MATRIMONIO ALL'ITALIANA**
See MARRIAGE ITALIAN-STYLE
**MATT RIKER: MUTANT HUNT**
See MUTANT HUNT
**MATT THE GOOSEBOY**
See MATTIG THE GOOSEBOY
**MATTER OF RESISTANCE**

See LA VIE DU CHATEAU
**MATTIE THE GOOSEBOY**
See MATTIG THE GOOSEBOY
**MAUDITE: THE LEGEND OF DOOM HOUSE**
See MALPERTUIS
**MAX ET LES FERRAILLEURS**
See MAX
**MAX HEADROOM STORY, THE**
See MAX HEADROOM FILM, THE
**MAX HEADROOM: THE ORIGINAL STORY**
See MAX HEADROOM FILM, THE
**MAYBE BABY**
See MAYBE BABY . . . AGAIN?
**MEAN COMBAT**
See LOSERS, THE
**MEANING OF LIFE, THE**
See MONTY PYTHON'S MEANING OF LIFE
**MEAT IS MEAT**
See STRANGLER OF VIENNA, THE
**MEATBALLS 3: SUMMER JOB**
See MEATBALLS 3
**MEATBALLS: PART 2**
See MEATBALLS 2
**MEDIC, THE**
See GREATEST ATTACK, THE
**MEET CAPTAIN KIDD**
See ABBOTT AND COSTELLO MEET CAPTAIN KIDD
**MEET WHIPLASH WILLIE**
See FORTUNE COOKIE, THE
**MEIACHOREI HASORALIM**
See BEYOND THE WALLS
**MELANIE ROSE**
See HIGH STAKES
**MELIMOT BEYERUSHALAIM**
See SELL-OUT, THE
**MELVIN: SON OF ALVIN**
See FOREPLAY
**MEN OF STEEL**
See STEEL
**MENACE ON THE MOUNTAIN**
See MENACE OF THE MOUNTAIN
**MERCENARIES, THE**
See CUBA CROSSING
**MERCENARIES, THE**
See DARK OF THE SUN
**MERCENARY, THE**
See DJANGO
**MERRY-GO-ROUND, THE**
See LA RONDE
**MESMERISED**
See MESMERIZED
**MESSENGER, THE**
See MESSENGER OF DEATH
**METALFORCE**
See METAL FORCE
**METALSTORM: THE DESTRUCTION OF JARED-SYN**
See METALSTORM
**MEZZOGIORNO DE FUCCO PER AN HAO**
See FIGHTING FISTS OF SHANGHAI JOE, THE
**MICHAEL'S FRIGHT**
See PEANUT BUTTER SOLUTION, THE
**MICKEY SPILLANE'S MARGIN FOR MURDER**
See MARGIN FOR MURDER
**MIDDLE AGE CRAZY**
See GOING ON 40
**MIDNIGHT**
See CALL IT MURDER
**MIDNIGHT AUTO SUPPLY**
See RIP OFF
**MIDNIGHT PLOWBOY**

See LIVE A LITTLE, STEAL A LOT
**MUSHROOM BUTTON, THE**
See WHOOPS APOCALYPSE
**MUSSOLINI ULTIMO ATTO**
See MUSSOLINI
**MUSSOLINI, THE LAST ACT**
See MUSSOLINI
**MUSSOLINI: THE DECLINE AND FALL OF IL DUCE**
See MUSSOLINI AND I
**MUTANT**
See FORBIDDEN WORLD
**MY AFRICAN ADVENTURE**
See GOING BANANAS
**MY BIRD TO THE RESCUE**
See MISTER BIRD TO THE RESCUE
**MY LOVE LETTERS**
See LOVE LETTERS
**MY NEW CAR**
See IT TAKES TWO
**MY NIGHTS WITH MESSALINA**
See NIGHT WITH MESSALINA, A
**MY NIGHTS WITH SUSAN, SANDRA, OLGA AND JULIE**
See MY NIGHTS WITH SUSAN, ALBERT, OLGA, JULIE, PIET AND SANDRA
**MY PALIKARI**
See BIG SHOT
**MY SISTER, MY LOVE**
See MAFU CAGE, THE
**MY UNCLE**
See MON ONCLE
**MY UNCLE MISTER HULOT**
See MON ONCLE
**MYSTERIOUS ISLAND OF BEAUTIFUL WOMEN, THE**
See ISLAND OF SISTER TERESA, THE
**MYSTERY OF KASPAR HAUSER, THE**
See ENIGMA OF KASPAR HAUSER, THE
**MYSTERY OF MANON, THE**
See EQUALISER, THE: THE MYSTERY OF MANON
**MYSTERY SUBMARINES**
See MYSTERY SUBMARINE
**MYSTIQUE**
See BRAINWASH
**NACH DER FINSTERNIS**
See AFTER DARKNESS
**NACHT DER VAMPIRE**
See WEREWOLF'S SHADOW, THE
**NACKT UND HEISS AUF MYKONOS**
See SEXUAL EXTASY
**NAIROBI AFFAIR, THE**
See NAIROBI
**NAKED AND WILLING**
See EROTIC INFERNO
**NAKED EXORCISM**
See EXORCIST 3, THE: CRIES AND SHADOWS
**NAKED GUN, THE**
See NAKED GUN, THE: FROM THE FILES OF POLICE SQUAD
**NAKED STREET GIRLS**
See CONFESSIONS OF THE SEX SLAVES
**NAKED UNDER LEATHER**
See GIRL ON A MOTORCYCLE
**NAKED WARRIORS**
See ARENA, THE
**NAKED WEEKEND, THE**
See BRAINWASH
**NAM: TOUR OF DUTY**
See TOUR OF DUTY
**NAN-TZU HAN**
See KUNG FU GANG BUSTERS
**NAPLES CONNECTION, THE**

See CAMORRA
**NARC, THE**
See MARK
**NASTY HABITS**
See AVENGER, THE
**NASTY RABBIT, THE**
See SPIES A GO-GO
**NATALE IN CASA D'APPUNTAMENTO**
See LOVE BY APPOINTMENT
**NATAS**
See NATAS: THE REFLECTION
**NATHALIE COMES OF AGE**
See NATHALIE
**NATIONAL LAMPOON GOES TO THE MOVIES**
See NATIONAL LAMPOON'S MOVIE MADNESS
**NATTY GANN**
See JOURNEY OF NATTY GANN, THE
**NATURAL ENEMIES**
See HIDDEN THOUGHTS
**NAUGHTY NIGHTS**
See LADY IS A WHORE, THE
**NAUGHTY NURSES**
See TENDER LOVING CARE
**NAVIGATOR, THE**
See BUSTER KEATON: NAVIGATOR, THE
**NEA**
See YOUNG EMMANUELLE, A
**NECROMANCER: SATAN'S SERVANT**
See NECROMANCER
**NECROMANCY**
See WITCHING, THE
**NED KELLY, OUTLAW**
See NED KELLY
**NEIGHBOUR, THE**
See KILLING 'EM SOFTLY
**NEIGHBOURHOOD, THE**
See MISSION HILL
**NEIGHBOURHOOD, THE: MISSION HILL**
See MISSION HILL
**NEPTUNE FACTOR, THE**
See NEPTUNE DISASTER, THE
**NEUESBERICHT UBER EINE REISE IN EINE STRAHLENDE ZUKUNFT**
See NUCLEAR CONSPIRACY, THE
**NEVADA**
See BOLDEST JOB IN THE WEST, THE
**NEVER KILL A SCORPION**
See SCORPION, THE
**NEVER SO FEW**
See CAMPAIGN BURMA
**NEVER TO LOVE**
See BILL OF DIVORCEMENT, THE
**NEW ADVENTURES OF THE BIONIC BOY, THE**
See DYNAMITE JOHNSON
**NEW BLACK EMMANUELLE, THE**
See BLACK EMMANUELLE 2
**NEW GAME OF DEATH, THE**
See GAME OF DEATH 2
**NEW GLADIATORS, THE**
See ROME 2033: THE FIGHTER CENTURIONS
**NEW KID IN TOWN**
See PARADISE MOTEL
**NEW LIFE, A**
See SUICIDE'S WIFE, THE
**NEW YORK AFTER DARK**
See NEW YORK AFTER MIDNIGHT
**NEW YORK, AVENUE O**
See MIXED BLOOD
**NICE DREAMS**

See CHEECH AND CHONG'S NICE DREAMS
**NICO: ABOVE THE LAW**
See NICO
**NIGHT ANDY CAME HOME, THE**
See DEATHDREAM
**NIGHT AT THE OPERA, A**
See MARX BROTHERS: A NIGHT AT THE OPERA
**NIGHT CAPER**
See BERK, THE
**NIGHT CREW**
See INTRUDER, THE
**NIGHT FIGHTERS**
See NIGHTFORCE
**NIGHT FLIGHT FROM MOSCOW**
See SERPENT, THE
**NIGHT FLOWERS**
See NIGHT ANGELS
**NIGHT FRIGHT**
See NIGHTFRIGHT
**NIGHT HEAVEN FELL, THE**
See LES BIJOUTIERS DU CLAIR DE LUNE
**NIGHT IN THE LIFE OF JIMMY REARDON, A**
See JIMMY REARDON
**NIGHT KILLER**
See SILENT MADNESS
**NIGHT OF ANUBIS**
See NIGHT OF THE LIVING DEAD
**NIGHT OF DARKNESS**
See ONE DARK NIGHT
**NIGHT OF THE ASKARI**
See WHISPERING DEATH
**NIGHT OF THE BLIND DEAD**
See TOMBS OF THE BLIND DEAD
**NIGHT OF THE DARK FULL MOON**
See SILENT NIGHT, BLOODY NIGHT
**NIGHT OF THE DEATH CULT**
See NIGHT OF THE SEAGULLS
**NIGHT OF THE FLESH EATERS**
See NIGHT OF THE LIVING DEAD
**NIGHT OF THE LIVING DEAD**
See RETURN OF THE LIVING DEAD
**NIGHT OF THE STRANGLER**
See VENGEANCE IS MINE
**NIGHT OF THE WEHRMACHT ZOMBIES**
See NIGHT OF THE ZOMBIES, THE
**NIGHT ON THE TOWN, A**
See ADVENTURES IN BABYSITTING
**NIGHT PROWLER, THE**
See NIGHT OF THE PROWLER, THE
**NIGHT SCHOOL**
See TERROR EYES
**NIGHT SHADOWS**
See MUTANT
**NIGHT SHIFT**
See NIGHTSHIFT
**NIGHT STAR: GODDESS OF ELECTRA**
See ROME AGAINST ROME
**NIGHT TRAIN TO MURDER**
See MORECOMBE AND WISE: NIGHT TRAIN TO MURDER
**NIGHT VISITOR, THE**
See LUNATIC
**NIGHT WALK**
See DEATHDREAM
**NIGHT WATCH**
See FIREHOUSE
**NIGHTMARE**
See NIGHTMARE VACATION
**NIGHTMARE**
See NIGHTMARES IN A DAMAGED BRAIN
**NIGHTMARE IN BADHAM COUNTY**
See NIGHTMARE VACATION

**NIGHTMARE OF TERROR**
See TOURIST TRAP, THE
**NIGHTMARE OF TERROR**
See DEMONS OF THE MIND
**NIGHTMARE TRACKS**
See GREAT RIDE, A
**NIGHTSHIFT**
See STEPHEN KING'S NIGHT SHIFT
COLLECTION
**NIGHTSTALKER**
See DON'T GO NEAR THE PARK
**NIGHTSTICK**
See METAL FORCE
**NIGHTWARS**
See NIGHT WARS
**NIHONKAI DAIKAISEN**
See BATTLE OF THE JAPAN SEA
**NINGYO HIME**
See LITTLE MERMAID, THE
**NINJA CONNECTION**
See NINJA IN THE KILLING FIELDS
**NINJA KISS OF DEATH KIDS**
See NINJA KIDS: KISS OF DEATH
**NINJA MURDERS**
See DEATH MACHINES
**NINJA OF THE MAGNIFICENCE**
See AMERICAN NINJA THE
MAGNIFICENT
**NINJA TURF**
See L.A. STREETFIGHTERS
**NITTI**
See CAPONE'S ENFORCER
**NITTI: THE ENFORCER**
See CAPONE'S ENFORCER
**NO DRUMS, NO BUGLES**
See ALTERNATIVE WAR
**NO ONE CRIES FOREVER**
See DEATH THREAT
**NO ONE WOULD BELIEVE HER**
See WELCOME TO ARROW BEACH
**NO PROFANAR EL SUENO DE LOS
MUERTOS**
See LIVING DEAD AT THE
MANCHESTER MORGUE, THE
**NO SWEAT**
See ADIOS AMIGO
**NO WAY OUT**
See HOUSE THAT CRIED MURDER,
THE
**NO. 1 LICENSED TO LOVE AND KILL**
See LICENSED TO LOVE AND KILL
**NO. 1 OF THE SECRET SERVICE**
See NUMBER ONE OF THE SECRET
SERVICE
**NOAH**
See DELUGE, THE
**NON SI DEVE PROFANARE IL SONO
DEI MORTI**
See LIVING DEAD AT THE
MANCHESTER MORGUE, THE
**NONE BUT THE BRAVE**
See KUNG FU GIRL
**NORMAN WISDOM: GIRL TROUBLE**
See GIRL TROUBLE
**NORMAN WISDOM: ON THE BEAT**
See ON THE BEAT
**NORMAN WISDOM: PRESS FOR
TIME**
See PRESS FOR TIME
**NORMAN WISDOM: THE BULLDOG
BREED**
See BULLDOG BREED, THE
**NORMAN WISDOM: THE EARLY
BIRD**
See EARLY BIRD, THE
**NORMAN WISDOM: THE SQUARE
PEG**
See SQUARE PEG, THE
**NORMAN WISDOM: TROUBLE IN**

**STORE**
See TROUBLE IN STORE
**NORTH AVENUE IRREGULARS, THE**
See HILL'S ANGELS
**NOSFERATU, A SYMPHONY OF
TERROR**
See NOSFERATU
**NOSFERATU, EINE SYMPHONIE
DES GRAUENS**
See NOSFERATU
**NOSFERATU, THE VAMPIRE**
See NOSFERATU
**NOSFERATU: PHANTOM DER
NACHT**
See NOSFERATU THE VAMPYRE
**NOT QUITE PARADISE**
See NOT QUITE JERUSALEM
**NOTHING BUT TROUBLE**
See LAUREL AND HARDY: NOTHING
BUT TROUBLE
**NOTORIOUS BANDIT, THE**
See GODFATHER OF HONG KONG
**NOVEMBER PLAN, THE**
See COVER KILL
**NOW IS THE TIME**
See DEAREST LOVE
**NOZ W WOOZIE**
See KNIFE IN THE WATER
**NUCLEAR TERROR**
See GOLDEN RENDEVOUS
**NUKE 'EM HIGH**
See CLASS OF NUKE 'EM HIGH
**NUMBER 10: DIZZY**
See SECRET LIVES OF THE BRITISH
PRIME MINISTERS, THE: DISRAELI
**NURSE, THE**
See I WILL IF YOU WILL
**NUTCRACKER**
See NUTCRACKER FANTASY
**NUTCRACKER FANTASIES**
See NUTCRACKER FANTASY
**NUTCRACKER SUITE**
See NUTCRACKER
**NUTCRACKER, THE**
See NUTCRACKER: THE MOTION
PICTURE
**NUTRIA MAN**
See TERROR IN THE SWAMP
**NUTRIA MAN**
See TERROR IN THE SWAMP
**NYMPHO SUPERSTARS**
See DIRECTORS, THE
**NYMPHO, THE**
See ANDREA THE NYMPHO
**OBSESSED, THE**
See SEXORCIST, THE
**OBSESSION, THE**
See SEXORCIST
**OBSESSION: A TASTE FOR FEAR**
See TASTE FOR FEAR, A
**OBSZONITATEN**
See CONFESSIONS OF A MALE
ESCORT
**OCCHI DALLE STELLE**
See EYES BEHIND THE STARS
**ODDBALLS**
See ALL SHOOK UP!
**OFF BALANCE**
See PHANTOM OF DEATH
**OFF LIMITS**
See SAIGON
**OFF THE MARK**
See CRAZY LEGS
**OFFICIAL STORY, THE**
See OFFICIAL VERSION, THE
**OFFSPRING, THE**
See FROM A WHISPER TO A SCREAM
**OGRE, THE**
See DEMONS 3

**OH LUCKY MAN**
See O LUCKY MAN!
**OH, ALFIE**
See ALFIE DARLING
**OH, CAROL**
See COOL IT CAROL!
**OHANIAN**
See KILLER WHO WOULDN'T DIE,
THE
**OIL: THE BILLION DOLLAR FIRE**
See OIL
**OKTOBER-DAGE**
See ONLY WAY, THE
**OKTYABR**
See OCTOBER
**OLD AND NEW**
See GENERAL LINE, THE
**OLD DRACULA**
See VAMPIRA
**OLD GLAD EYES**
See SECRET LIVES OF THE BRITISH
PRIME MINISTERS, THE:
GLADSTONE
**OLD MOTHER RILEY MEETS THE
VAMPIRE**
See MY SON THE VAMPIRE
**OLIVIA**
See DOUBLE JEOPARDY
**OLLY OLLY OXEN FREE**
See GREAT BALLOON ADVENTURE,
THE
**OMAR MUKHTAR**
See LION OF THE DESERT
**OMEGA CONNECTION, THE**
See LONDON CONNECTION, THE
**OMEGA FACTOR**
See SILENT MADNESS
**OMEN 2**
See DAMIEN: OMEN 2
**OMEN 3**
See FINAL CONFLICT, THE: OMEN 3
**OMEN 3: THE FINAL CONFLICT**
See FINAL CONFLICT, THE: OMEN 3
**ON THE ROAD AGAIN**
See HONEYSUCKLE ROSE
**ONCE UPON A MURDER**
See CHIEFS
**ONCE UPON A TIME IN VIETNAM**
See HOW SLEEP THE BRAVE
**ONDSKANS VARDSHUS**
See SLEEP OF DEATH, THE
**ONE AWAY**
See GITANOS: ESCAPE FROM
APARTHEID
**ONE HOUR TO DOOMSDAY**
See CITY BENEATH THE SEA
**ONE OF ONE**
See TERRITORY, THE
**ONE TAKE TWO**
See FLASHPOINT AFRICA
**ONE TWO TWO**
See NEVER LOVE A HOOKER
**ONE TWO TWO RUE DE PROVENCE**
See NEVER LOVE A HOOKER
**ONE-ARMED BOXER VERSUS THE
FLYING GUILLOTINE**
See MASTER OF THE FLYING
GUILLOTINE
**OOH . . . YOU ARE AWFUL**
See OOH, YOU ARE AWFUL
**OPEN SEASON**
See RECON GAME
**OPENING OF MISTY BEETHOVEN,
THE**
See MISTY BEETHOVEN
**OPERACION LADY CHAPLIN**
See SPECIAL MISSION LADY
CHAPLIN
**OPERATION GANYMEDE**

See OPERATION GANYMED
**OPERATION NAM**
See COBRA MISSION
**OPERATION PETTICOAT**
See PETTICOAT AFFAIR
**OPERATION UNDERCOVER**
See REPORT TO THE
COMMISSIONER
**OPERATION: TAKE NO PRISONERS**
See TAKE NO PRISONERS
**OPERAZIONE LADY CHAPLIN**
See SPECIAL MISSION LADY
CHAPLIN
**OPPOSING FORCE**
See HELL CAMP
**OPTIMISTS, THE**
See OPTIMISTS OF NINE ELMS, THE
**ORAZI E CURIAZI**
See DUEL OF CHAMPIONS
**ORCA**
See ORCA: KILLER WHALE
**ORCA, THE KILLER WHALE**
See ORCA: KILLER WHALE
**ORCHID FOR NO. 1, AN**
See NUMBER ONE OF THE SECRET
SERVICE
**ORDINARY GUY, AN**
See ORDINARY HEROES
**ORGASMO**
See PARANOIA
**ORION'S BELTE**
See ORION'S BELT
**ORLOFF AND THE INVISIBLE MAN**
See INVISIBLE DEAD, THE
**ORLOFF Y EL HOMBRE INVISIBLE**
See INVISIBLE DEAD, THE
**ORO MALDITO**
See DJANGO KILL (IF YOU LIVE
SHOOT)
**ORPHEUS**
See ORPHEE
**OS DEMONIOS**
See DEMONS, THE
**OTAC NA SLUZBENOM PUTU**
See WHEN FATHER WAS AWAY ON
BUSINESS
**OTHER SIDE OF PARADISE, THE**
See FAR SIDE OF PARADISE, THE
**OUR FAMILY BUSINESS**
See UNDERBOSS, THE
**OUR HOSPITALITY**
See BUSTER KEATON: OUR
HOSPITALITY
**OUR MAN FROM BOND STREET**
See MAD MISSION THREE: OUR MAN
IN BOND STREET
**OUR RELATIONS**
See LAUREL AND HARDY: OUR
RELATIONS
**OUT IN THE WORLD**
See MY APPRENTICESHIP
**OUT OF ROSENHEIM**
See BAGDAD CAFE
**OUT OF SIGHT, OUT OF MIND**
See SIGHT UNSEEN
**OUT OF THE DARKNESS**
See NIGHT CREATURE
**OUTING, THE**
See SCREAM
**OUTLAW PLANET**
See PLANET OF THE VAMPIRES
**OVERKLASSENS HEMLIGE
SEXGLAEDER**
See SEXY SISTERS
**P.I. – PRIVATE INVESTIGATIONS**
See PRIVATE INVESTIGATIONS
**P.O.W. – PRISONERS OF WAR**
See P.O.W.
**PACE THAT KILLS, THE**

See COCAINE FIENDS, THE
**PACK UP YOUR TROUBLES**
See LAUREL AND HARDY: PACK UP
YOUR TROUBLES
**PANIC AT LAKEWOOD MANOR**
See ANTS: PANIC AT LAKEWOOD
MANOR
**PANIC ON THE TRANS-SIBERIAN
EXPRESS**
See HORROR EXPRESS
**PANICO**
See PANIC
**PARADISE, HAWAIIAN STYLE**
See ELVIS PRESLEY: PARADISE,
HAWAIIAN STYLE
**PARADOX: BACK TO THE FUTURE 2**
See BACK TO THE FUTURE: PART 2
**PARASITE MURDERS, THE**
See SHIVERS
**PARDON US**
See LAUREL AND HARDY: PARDON
US
**PARIS-ESTAMBUL SIN REGRESO**
See FURY IN ISTANBUL
**PARISIENNE, A**
See UNE PARISIENNE
**PAROLE DE FLIC**
See COP'S HONOUR
**PART 2: WALKING TALL**
See WALKING TALL PART 2:
VENGEANCE TRAIL
**PARTIZANI**
See PARTIZAN
**PARTS: THE CLONUS HORROR**
See CLONUS
**PARTY AT KITTY AND STUDS**
See ITALIAN STALLION, THE
**PASQUALINO SETTEBELLEZZE**
See SEVEN BEAUTIES
**PASSIONATE STRANGERS, THE**
See KLEINHOFF HOTEL
**PASSIONE D'AMORE**
See PASSION OF LOVE
**PASSIONS NOCTURNES**
See LADIES' NIGHT
**PATMAN**
See CROSSOVER
**PATTON: LUST FOR GLORY**
See PATTON
**PATTY HEARST**
See PATTY HEARST: HER OWN
STORY
**PAUL RAYMOND'S EROTICA**
See EROTICA
**PAVRA NELLA CITTA DEI MORTI
VIVENTI**
See CITY OF THE LIVING DEAD
**PAY-OFF TIME**
See DEATH PROMISE
**PECCATI IN FAMIGLIA**
See SINS WITHIN THE FAMILY
**PEKING MEDALLION, THE**
See CORRUPT ONES, THE
**PELLE SVANSLOS**
See PETER-NO-TAIL
**PENSIERI MORBOSI**
See DEEP THOUGHTS
**PEOPLE TOYS**
See DEVIL TIMES FIVE
**PEOPLETOYS**
See DEVIL TIMES FIVE
**PEPITA JIMENEZ**
See BRIDE TO BE
**PER ASPERA AD ASTRA**
See HUMANOID WOMAN
**PER QUAICHE DOLLARI IN PIU**
See FOR A FEW DOLLARS MORE
**PER SALDO MORD**
See SWISS CONSPIRACY, THE

**PER UN PUGNO DI DOLLARI**
See FISTFUL OF DOLLARS, A
**PER UNA BARA PIENA DI DOLLARI**
See BARREL FULL OF DOLLARS, A
**PERFECT STRANGERS**
See BLIND ALLEY
**PERILS OF GWENDOLINE IN THE
LAND OF THE YIK-YAK, THE**
See GWENDOLINE
**PERILS OF GWENDOLINE, THE**
See GWENDOLINE
**PET SHOP BOYS: IT COULDN'T
HAPPEN HERE**
See IT COULDN'T HAPPEN HERE
**PETER RABBIT AND THE TALES OF
BEATRIX POTTER**
See TALES OF BEATRIX POTTER
**PETROLEUM GIRLS**
See LEGEND OF FRENCHIE KING,
THE
**PEUR SUR LA VILLE**
See NIGHT CALLER, THE
**PEVERSE TALLES**
See EROTIC TALES
**PHANTOM OF TERROR, THE**
See BIRD WITH THE CRYSTAL
PLUMAGE, THE
**PHAR LAP: HEART OF A NATION**
See PHAR LAP
**PHASE IV**
See PHASE 4
**PHENOMENA**
See CREEPERS
**PHILIP MARLOWE: PRIVATE EYE**
See MARLOWE: PRIVATE EYE
**PHOBIA**
See NESTING, THE
**PHOENIX, THE**
See WAR OF THE WIZARDS
**PICK-UP SUMMER**
See PINBALL SUMMER
**PICKUP ON 101**
See WHERE THE EAGLE FLIES
**PIED PIPER, THE**
See PIED PIPER OF HAMELIN, THE
**PILLOW TALK**
See DANISH PILLOW TALK
**PILSKA JULIA PA BROLLOPSRESAN**
See HONEYMOON SWEDISH STYLE
**PINBALL PICK-UP**
See PINBALL SUMMER
**PINK MOTEL**
See MOTEL
**PINOCCHIO DANS L'ESPACE**
See PINOCCHIO IN OUTER SPACE
**PIRANHA 2: THE SPAWNING**
See PIRANHA 2: FLYING KILLERS
**PISTOL FOR RINGO, A**
See ANGRY GUN, THE
**PITT: THE YOUNGER GIRL
SCANDAL**
See SECRET LIVES OF THE BRITISH
PRIME MINISTERS, THE: PITT
**PIXOTE: LA LEY DEL MAS DEBIL**
See PIXOTE
**PIZAZ**
See PRONTO
**PIZZA CONNECTION**
See SICILIAN CONNECTION, THE
**PIZZAZ**
See PRONTO
**PLANET OF HORRORS**
See GALAXY OF TERROR
**PLANET OF TERROR**
See PLANET OF THE VAMPIRES
**PLATOON THE WARRIORS**
See PLATOON WARRIORS
**PLAYERS**
See CLUB, THE

**PLAYERS**
See DOUBLE PLAY
**PLAYGIRL GANG**
See SWITCHBLADE SISTERS, THE
**PLAYING BEATIE BOW**
See TIME GAMES
**PLAYING FOR KEEPS**
See DOUBLE PLAY
**PLUCK OF THE IRISH**
See GREAT GUY
**PLUTONIUM BABY**
See MUTANT KID
**POHADY TISICE A JEDNE NOCI**
See ADVENTURES OF SINBAD THE
SAILOR, THE
**POINT TWO TWO**
See STONE COLD DEAD
**POKOLENIE**
See GENERATION, A
**POLICE ACADEMY 2: THEIR FIRST
ASSIGNMENT**
See POLICE ACADEMY 2
**POLICE ACADEMY 3: BACK IN
TRAINING**
See POLICE ACADEMY 3
**POLICE ACADEMY 4: CITIZEN'S
PATROL**
See POLICE ACADEMY 4
**POLICE ACADEMY 5: ASSIGNMENT
MIAMI BEACH**
See POLICE ACADEMY 5
**POLICE ACADEMY 6: CITY UNDER
SIEGE**
See POLICE ACADEMY 6
**POLICE CALL 9000**
See DETROIT 9000
**POLICE CAN'T MOVE, THE**
See KILLER COP
**POLICE DES MOEURS: LES FILLES
DE SAINT TROPEZ**
See SAINT TROPEZ VICE
**POLICE FORCE**
See POLICE STORY
**POLICE IN ACTION: CONFESSIONS
OF A LADY COP**
See CONFESSIONS OF A LADY COP
**POLICE STORY: DAY OF TERROR,
NIGHT OF FEAR**
See POLICE IN ACTION 6: DAY OF
TERROR, NIGHT OF FEAR
**POLTERGEIST 2: THE OTHER SIDE**
See POLTERGEIST 2
**POMPEII**
See WARRIOR QUEEN
**POOR LITTLE RICH GIRL: THE
BARBARA HUTTON STORY**
See POOR LITTLE RICH GIRL: PARTS
1 AND 2
**POOR WHITE TRASH 2**
See POOR WHITE TRASH
**POPPY IS ALSO A FLOWER, THE**
See POPPIES ARE ALSO FLOWERS
**PORKY'S 2: THE NEXT DAY**
See PORKY'S 2
**PORN FLAKES**
See BANG BANG
**PORTRAIT, THE**
See GIRL'S SCHOOL SCREAMERS
**POTATO-FRITZ**
See MONTANA TRAP
**POTEMKIN**
See BATTLESHIP POTEMKIN, THE
**POTOMOK CHINGIS-KHANA**
See STORM OVER ASIA
**POULET AU VINAIGRE**
See COP AU VIN
**POUND PUPPIES AND THE LEGEND
OF BIG PAW**
See POUND PUPPIES: THE LEGEND

OF BIG PAW
**POUSSIERE D'ANGE**
See ANGEL DUST
**PREACHERMAN MEETS
WIDDERWOMAN**
See PREACHERMAN
**PRECINCT 45: LOS ANGELES
POLICE**
See NEW CENTURIONS, THE
**PRELAZ PREKO DJAVOLJE KICMA**
See DESERTER, THE
**PRELUDE TO APOCALYPSE**
See GREATEST ATTACK, THE
**PRENEZ LA QUEUE COMME TOUT
LE MONDE**
See LINE UP AND LAY DOWN
**PREPPIES**
See MAKING THE GRADE
**PRESIDENT'S WOMAN, THE**
See FOREPLAY
**PRICE OF FREEDOM**
See OPERATION DAYBREAK
**PRIMAL SCREAM**
See HELL FIRE
**PRIME 40**
See GOING ON 40
**PRIME TIME**
See AMERICAN RASPBERRY
**PRISON SHIP**
See PRISON SHIP STAR SLAMMER
**PRIVATE EYE**
See DAIN CURSE, THE
**PRIVATE EYE: BLUE HOTEL**
See BLUE HOTEL
**PRIVATE ROAD: NO TRESPASSING**
See PRIVATE ROAD
**PRIVATE SCHOOL FOR GIRLS**
See PRIVATE SCHOOL
**PROBABILITA ZERO**
See PROBABILITY ZERO
**PROFESSION: REPORTER**
See PASSENGER, THE
**PROFESSIONAL GUN, A**
See DJANGO
**PROFESSIONE: REPORTER**
See PASSENGER, THE
**PROGRAMMED TO KILL**
See RETALIATOR
**PROJECT GENOCIDE**
See ALIEN ENCOUNTERS
**PROMISE OF BED, A**
See THIS, THAT AND THE OTHER
**PROMISE OF RED LIPS**
See DAUGHTERS OF DARKNESS
**PROMOTER, THE**
See CARD, THE
**PRONTO AD UCCIDERE**
See PRONTO
**PROSTITUTE, THE**
See PROSTITUTION RACKET, THE
**PROTECTORS, THE: BOOK 1**
See ANGEL OF HEAT
**PROWLER, THE**
See ROSEMARY'S KILLER
**PSYCHIC KILLER, THE**
See DEATH DEALER, THE
**PSYCHO A GO-GO!**
See MAN WITH THE SYTHETIC
BRAIN, THE
**PSYCHO MANIA**
See PSYCHOMANIA
**PSYCHO PUPPET**
See DELIRIUM
**PSYCHO SEX FIEND**
See SCREAM AND DIE
**PUFNSTUF**
See H.R. PUFNSTUF
**PUMPKINHEAD**
See VENGEANCE, THE DEMON

**PUNCH AND JUDY MAN, THE**
See HANCOCK: THE PUNCH AND
JUDY MAN
**PUNCH AND JUDY MAN, THE**
See HANCOCK: THE PUNCH AND
JUDY MAN
**PURELY A LEGAL MATTER**
See QUESTION OF LOVE, A
**PURSUIT OF D.B. COOPER, THE**
See PURSUIT
**PURSUIT OF THE GRAF SPEE**
See BATTLE OF THE RIVER PLATE,
THE
**PUSSY TALK: LE SEXE QUI PARLE**
See PUSSY TALK
**PYRAMIDS OF MARS, THE**
See DOCTOR WHO: THE PYRAMIDS
OF MARS
**Q**
See Q: THE WINGED SERPENT
**QUALCOSA DI BLONDA**
See AURORA
**QUANDO GLI UOMINI AMARANO
LA CLAVA . . . E CON LE DONNE
FECERO DIN-DON**
See WHEN MEN CARRIED CLUBS,
WOMEN PLAYED DING DONG!
**QUANDO LE DONNE PERSERO LA
CODA**
See WHEN MEN CARRIED CLUBS,
WOMEN PLAYED DING DONG!
**QUEEN OF DIAMONDS**
See BELLE STARR STORY, THE
**QUEEN OF SEX**
See BLACK DEEP THROAT
**QUEEN OF THE NAKED STEEL**
See BARBARIAN QUEEN
**QUEIMADA**
See BATTLE OF THE ANTILLES
**QUEL CALDO MALE DETTO
GIORNO DI FUOCO**
See GATLING GUN
**QUELLA CASA CON LA SCALA AL
BUIO**
See BLADE IN THE DARK, A
**QUELLA VILLA ACCANTO AL
CIMITERO**
See HOUSE BY THE CEMETERY,
THE
**QUELQU'UN DERRIERE LA PORTE**
See SOMEONE BEHIND THE DOOR
**QUERELLE DE BREST**
See QUERELLE
**QUEST FOR PEACE, THE**
See SUPERMAN 4: THE QUEST FOR
PEACE
**QUEST FOR THE SEVEN CITIES**
See GOLD OF THE AMAZON WOMEN
**QUIEN PUEDO MATAR A UN NINO?**
See ISLAND OF DEATH
**QUIEN SABE?**
See BULLET FOR THE GENERAL,
THE
**QUIET VICTORY: THE CHARLIE
WEDEMEYER STORY**
See QUIET VICTORY
**QUILT OF HATHOR**
See FRIDAY'S CURSE 4: QUILT OF
HATHOR/THE AWAKENING
**R.O.B.O.T.**
See CHOPPING MALL
**RACE FOR YOUR LIFE, CHARLIE
BROWN**
See CHARLIE BROWN: RACE FOR
YOUR LIFE
**RACE TO THE POLE, THE**
See ONLY ONE WINNER
**RACE TO THE YANKEE ZEPHYR**
See RACE FOR THE YANKEE

ZEPHYR
See RETURN TO WATERLOO

**RAFFERTY AND THE HIGHWAY HUSTLERS**
See RAFFERTY AND THE GOLD DUST TWINS

**RAGE OF ANGELS: THE STORY CONTINUES**
See RAGE OF ANGELS 2: PARTS 1 AND 2

**RAGE OF HONOUR**
See RAGE OF HONOR

**RAGGEDY ANNE**
See SAVAGE HARBOUR

**RAGTIME SUMMER**
See AGE OF INNOCENCE, THE

**RAIDERS OF ATLANTIS**
See ATLANTIS INTERCEPTORS, THE

**RAIDERS OF THE GOLDEN COBRA**
See HUNTERS OF THE GOLDEN COBRA

**RAINBOW BOYS, THE**
See LOGAN

**RAINBOW GANG, THE**
See LOGAN

**RAINBOW PROFESSIONALS**
See COBRA MISSION

**RANA**
See CREATURE FROM SHADOW LAKE, THE

**RANA: CREATURE FROM SHADOW LAKE**
See CREATURE FROM SHADOW LAKE, THE

**RANA: THE LEGEND OF SHADOW LAKE**
See CREATURE FROM SHADOW LAKE, THE

**RANCH OF THE NYMPHOMANIACS**
See RANCH OF THE NYMPHOMANIAC GIRLS

**RANDY RIDES ALONE**
See SAGEBRUSH TRAIL

**RANSOM RUNNER**
See GOLDRUNNER

**RAPE AND MARRIAGE: THE RIDEOUT CASE**
See RIDEOUT CASE, THE

**RAPE OF MALAYA**
See TOWN LIKE ALICE, A

**RAPE OF THE THIRD REICH, THE**
See ENGLAND MADE ME

**RAPPORTO FULLER BASE A STOCCOLMA**
See FULLER REPORT

**RAPTUS**
See TERROR OF DOCTOR HICHCOCK, THE

**RASCALS AND ROBBERS: THE SECRET ADVENTURES OF TOM SAWYER AND HUCK FINN**
See RASCALS AND ROBBERS

**RASPOUTINE**
See SWEDISH SEX CLINIC

**RAT FINK AND BOBO**
See RAT PFINK A BOO-BOO

**RAT FINK AND BOO-BOO**
See RAT PFINK A BOO-BOO

**RATAS DE LA CIUDAD**
See CITY RATS

**RATS**
See RATS: NIGHT OF TERROR

**RAW COURAGE**
See COURAGE

**RAW MEAT**
See DEATH LINE

**RAWHEAD**
See RAWHEAD REX

**RAY DAVIES' RETURN TO WATERLOO**

**RAY OF LIGHT**
See LIGHTBLAST

**RAZZA VIOLENTA**
See VIOLENT BREED, THE

**REACHOUT**
See HOTLINE

**READY AND WILLING**
See KISS ME WITH LUST

**REAPER'S REVENGE**
See DANGER ZONE 2: REAPERS'S REVENGE

**REASON TO LIVE, A REASON TO DIE, A**
See MASSACRE AT FORT HOLMAN

**REAZIONE A CATENA**
See LAST HOUSE ON THE LEFT PART 2, THE

**REBEL**
See NO PLACE TO HIDE

**REBEL, THE**
See HANCOCK: THE REBEL

**REBELLION**
See RED BERETS, THE

**REBELLION OF THE DEAD WOMEN, THE**
See VENGEANCE OF THE ZOMBIES

**RECKLESS DISREGARD**
See JUDGEMENT, THE

**RECON HUNT**
See RECON GAME

**RED BARON, THE**
See BATTLE OF THE ACES

**RED BELLS**
See MEXICO IN FLAMES

**RED FLAG**
See RED FLAG: THE ULTIMATE GAME

**RED LIPS, THE**
See DAUGHTERS OF DARKNESS

**RED TIDE, THE**
See BLOOD TIDE

**REDEEMER . . . SON OF SATAN, THE**
See REDEEMER, THE

**REILLY: THE ACE OF SPIES**
See REILLY: ACE OF SPIES

**REINA SALVAJE**
See BARBARIAN QUEEN

**REINCARNATE, THE**
See DARK SIDE, THE

**REIVERS, THE**
See YELLOW WINTON FLYER, THE

**REJUVENATRIX**
See REJUVENATOR

**REJUVENATRIX: A CLASSIC TALE OF TERROR**
See REJUVENATOR

**REKTOR PA SENGEKANTEN**
See DANISH BED AND BOARD

**REKVIJEM**
See LAST TRAIN TO BERLIN

**REMO WILLIAMS: THE ADVENTURE BEGINS**
See REMO: UNARMED AND DANGEROUS

**REMO WILLIAMS: THE ADVENTURE CONTINUES**
See REMO: UNARMED AND DANGEROUS

**RENACER**
See REBORN

**RENACIDA**
See REBORN

**RENEE RICHARDS STORY, THE**
See SECOND SERVE

**RENEGADE GIRLS**
See CAGED HEAT

**RESURRECTION DAY**
See VIRUS

**RESURRECTION SYNDICATE, THE**
See NOTHING BUT THE NIGHT

**RETURN OF MAXWELL SMART, THE**
See NUDE BOMB, THE

**RETURN OF THE 38 GANG, THE**
See GANGSTERS

**RETURN OF THE ALIEN'S DEADLY SPAWN**
See DEADLY SPAWN, THE

**RETURN OF THE BIG**
See BIG CAT, THE

**RETURN OF THE BIONIC BOY, THE**
See DYNAMITE JOHNSON

**RETURN OF THE BLIND DEAD**
See RETURN OF THE EVIL DEAD, THE

**RETURN OF THE DESPERADO**
See TOWN CALLED BEAUTY, A

**RETURN OF THE DRAGON**
See WAY OF THE DRAGON

**RETURN OF THE INCREDIBLE HULK**
See INCREDIBLE HULK RETURNS, THE

**RETURN OF THE LIVING DEAD**
See MESSIAH OF EVIL

**RETURN OF WALPURGIS, THE**
See CURSE OF THE DEVIL

**RETURN TO AFRICA**
See ESCAPE FROM ANGOLA

**RETURN TO MACON COUNTY LINE**
See RETURN TO MACON COUNTY

**RETURN TO SNOWY RIVER**
See UNTAMED, THE

**RETURN TO SNOWY RIVER PART 2**
See UNTAMED, THE

**REVAK, LO SCHIAVO DI CARTHAGE**
See BARBARIAN, THE

**REVAK, SLAVE OF CARTHAGE**
See BARBARIAN, THE

**REVENGE**
See UTU

**REVENGE**
See DOUBLE DRAGON IN LAST DUEL

**REVENGE AT EL PASO**
See ACE HIGH

**REVENGE IN EL PASSO**
See ACE HIGH

**REVENGE IN THE SKY**
See BLUE THUNDER: REVENGE IN THE SKY

**REVENGE OF DOCTOR DEATH, THE**
See MADHOUSE

**REVENGE OF DRACULA**
See DRACULA VERSUS FRANKENSTEIN

**REVENGE OF MILADY, THE**
See FOUR MUSKETEERS, THE

**REVENGE OF THE DRAGON**
See REVENGE OF THE DRAGONS

**REVENGE OF THE INNOCENTS**
See SOUTH BRONX HEROES

**REVENGE OF THE NERDS 2: NERDS IN PARADISE**
See REVENGE OF THE NERDS 2

**REVENGE OF THE NINJA, THE**
See NINJA 2: THE REVENGE OF THE NINJA

**REVENGE OF THE SCREAMING DEAD**
See MESSIAH OF EVIL

**REVENGE OF THE VAMPIRE**
See BLACK SUNDAY

**REVENGE SQUAD**
See HIT AND RUN

**REVOLT OF THE DEAD ONES, THE**
See VENGEANCE OF THE ZOMBIES

**RHODE ISLAND MURDERS, THE**

VIRGIN
**SCHULMADCHEN: REPORT 12 TEIL**
See BLUE FANTASIES
**SCORING**
See THIS TIME FOREVER
**SCOUNDREL**
See MAFIA WARFARE
**SCREAM**
See NIGHT GOD SCREAMED, THE
**SCREAM OR DIE!**
See SCREAM AND DIE
**SCREAM SHOW**
See DEAD-TIME STORIES: VOLUME 2
**SCREAM TIME**
See SCREAMTIME
**SCREAMER**
See SCREAM AND SCREAM AGAIN
**SCREAMERS**
See ISLAND OF MUTATIONS
**SCUM OF THE EARTH**
See POOR WHITE TRASH
**SCUOLA DI BALLO**
See DANCE ACADEMY
**SE INCONTRI SARTANA PREGA PER LA TUA MORTE**
See SARTANA, PRAY FOR YOUR DEATH
**SE SEI VIVO SPARA**
See DJANGO KILL (IF YOU LIVE SHOOT)
**SEA GYPSIES, THE**
See SHIPWRECK!
**SEAGULL ISLAND**
See SECRET OF SEAGULL ISLAND, THE
**SEAMAN NUMBER SEVEN**
See SEVEN MAGNIFICENT FIGHTS
**SEARCH AND DESTROY**
See KILLER INSTINCT
**SEARCH FOR SPOCK, THE**
See STAR TREK 3: THE SEARCH FOR SPOCK
**SEARCH FOR THE MOTHER LODE**
See MOTHER LODE
**SEAWEED CHILDREN, THE**
See MALACHI'S COVE
**SECHS SCHWEDINNEN AUF IBIZA**
See MORE DESIRES WITHIN YOUNG GIRLS
**SECHS SCHWEDINNEN IM PENSIONAT**
See UNTAMED SEX
**SECOND BEST SECRET AGENT IN THE WHOLE WIDE WORLD, THE**
See LICENSED TO KILL
**SECOND COMING, THE**
See MESSIAH OF EVIL
**SECOND THUNDER**
See BLUE THUNDER: SECOND THUNDER
**SECOND TOUCH**
See TWICE A WOMAN
**SECRET LIVES OF THE BRITISH PRIME MINISTERS, THE: THE DUKE OF WELLINGTON**
See SECRET LIVES OF THE BRITISH PRIME MINISTERS: THE IRON DUKE
**SECRET LOVE LIVES OF ROMEO AND JULIET, THE**
See SECRET SEX LIVES OF ROMEO AND JULIET, THE
**SECRET OF BLOOD ISLAND, THE**
See P.O.W.
**SECRET OF DORIAN GRAY, THE**
See DORIAN GRAY
**SECRET OF THE PHANTOM KNIGHT**
See CHOPPY AND THE PRINCESS
**SECRET OF THE SWORD, THE**
See HE-MAN AND SHE-RA: THE

SECRET OF THE SWORD
**SECRET SEX LIFE OF ROMEO AND JULIET, THE**
See SECRET SEX LIVES OF ROMEO AND JULIET, THE
**SECRET SHAOLIN KUNG FU, THE**
See INVINCIBLE SHAOLIN KUNG FU
**SECRET WEAPONS**
See SEXPIONAGE
**SECRETS OF A GIRL FRIDAY**
See SEX WITH THE STARS
**SECRETS OF A PLAYGIRL**
See PLAYBIRDS, THE
**SECRETS OF A SENSUOUS NURSE**
See I WILL IF YOU WILL
**SECRETS OF A SEXY GAME**
See CONFESSIONS FROM THE DAVID GALAXY AFFAIR
**SECRETS OF NAKED GIRLS**
See WHEN GIRLS UNDRESS
**SECRETS OF SWEET SIXTEEN: WHAT SCHOOLGIRLS DON'T TELL**
See WHAT SCHOOLGIRLS DON'T TELL
**SECRETS OF THE RED BEDROOM**
See SEXPIONAGE
**SECRETS OF THE SATIN BLUES**
See NAUGHTY BLUE KNICKERS
**SEDUCER, THE**
See FRENCH WAY, THE
**SEDUCERS, THE**
See DEATH GAME
**SEDUCTION, THE**
See SEDUCTION, THE: A FATAL OBSESSION
**SEDUCTRESS, THE**
See TEACHER, THE
**SEE NO EVIL**
See BLIND TERROR
**SEX AND THE MARRIED DETECTIVE**
See COLUMBO: SEX AND THE MARRIED DETECTIVE
**SEX BOX, THE**
See LOVE BOX, THE
**SEX CRIME OF THE CENTURY**
See LAST HOUSE ON THE LEFT, THE
**SEX DEMONS, THE**
See DEMONS, THE
**SEX FEVER**
**SEEDS OF EVIL, THE**
See GARDEN OF DEATH
**SEI DONNE PER L'ASSASSINO**
See BLOOD AND BLACK LACE
**SEIMILLE CHILOMETRI DI PAURA**
See SAFARI RALLY
**SEIZURE!**
See QUEEN OF EVIL
**SEKAI DAISENSO**
See LAST WAR, THE
**SEKA'S CRUISE**
See ROCKING WITH SEKA
**SELLING OF AMERICA, THE**
See BEER
**SENGOKU JIEITAI**
See TIME SLIP
**SENSUOUS NURSE, THE**
See I WILL IF YOU WILL
**SENSUOUS VAMPIRES**
See VAMPIRE HOOKERS
**SENZA BUCCIA**
See SKIN DEEP
**SERENA, AN ADULT FAIRY TALE**
See SERENA
**SERGEANT BLUE**
See GATLING GUN, THE
**SERGEANT DEADHEAD, THE ASTRONAUT**
See SERGEANT DEADHEAD
**SERGEANT RYKER**

See TORN BETWEEN TWO VALUES
**SERGEANT STEINER**
See BREAKTHROUGH
**SERVIZIO DI SCORTA**
See SUPERBITCH
**SESAME STREET PRESENTS FOLLOW THAT BIRD**
See FOLLOW THAT BIRD
**SESSO PROFONDO**
See FLYING SEX
**SETTE WINCHESTER PER UN MASSACRO**
See SEVEN WINCHESTERS FOR A MASSACRE
**SETTIMA DONNA**
See TERROR
**SETTLERS, THE**
See MARTIAN CHRONICLES, THE
**SEVEN BROTHERS MEET DRACULA, THE**
See LEGEND OF THE SEVEN GOLDEN VAMPIRES, THE
**SEVEN CRYSTAL BALLS, THE**
See TINTIN: THE SEVEN CRYSTAL BALLS
**SEVEN DOORS OF DEATH**
See BEYOND, THE
**SEVEN GRAVES FOR ROGAN**
See TIME TO DIE, A
**SEVEN SISTERS**
See HOUSE OF EVIL
**SEVENTY-TWO HOURS OR DIE**
See POWER GAME
**SEVENTY-TWO HOURS TO DIE**
See POWER GAME
**SEX FEVER**
See SEX SLAVES
**SEX FEVER ON AN ISLAND OF 1,000 DELIGHTS**
See SEX SLAVES
**SEX GAMES**
See COMMUTER HUSBANDS
**SEX MANIAC**
See VIOLATION OF THE BITCH
**SEX ON THE BRAIN**
See SEX IN THE HEAD
**SEX RACKETEERS, THE**
See MAN OF VIOLENCE
**SEXORCISTS, THE**
See SEXORCIST, THE
**SEXY ADVENTURES OF LIPPS AND McCAINE, THE**
See LIPPS AND McCAINE
**SEXY SECRETS OF A SEX THERAPIST, THE**
See SEXY SECRETS OF THE SEX THERAPISTS, THE
**SHADOW MAN**
See STREET OF SHADOWS
**SHADOW OF DEATH**
See BRAINWAVES
**SHADOW OF THE WEREWOLF**
See WEREWOLF'S SHADOW, THE
**SHADOWS IN A ROOM**
See BLAZING MAGNUMS
**SHADOWS OF DARKNESS**
See CROSSOVER
**SHAME**
See INTRUDER, THE
**SHAME OF A NATION, THE**
See SCARFACE
**SHAMING, THE**
See GOOD LUCK, MISS WYCKOFF
**SHANGHAI JOE**
See FIGHTING FISTS OF SHANGHAI JOE, THE
**SHAOLIN DEVIL, SHAOLIN ANGEL**
See SHAOLIN DEVIL AND SHAOLIN ANGEL

**SHAOLIN DRUNK FIGHTER**
See SHAOLIN DRUNKEN FIGHTER
**SHAOLIN KIDS, THE**
See SHAOLIN DEATH SQUAD
**SHAOLIN TEMPLE STRIKES BACK**
See SHAOLIN TEMPLE 2
**SHAOLIN WOODEN MEN**
See SHAOLIN CHAMBER OF DEATH
**SHARON'S BABY**
See DEVIL WITHIN HER, THE
**SHATTER**
See CALL HIM MISTER SHATTER
**SHATTERED SILENCE**
See LOVE IS NEVER SILENT
**SHE FREAK**
See TALES OF TERROR 1: SHE FREAK
**SHE WAITS**
See NIGHT OF THE EXORCIST
**SHEENA: QUEEN OF THE JUNGLE**
See SHEENA
**SHE'LL BE SWEET**
See MAGEE
**SHERLOCK HOLMES AND THE BASKERVILLE CURSE**
See SHERLOCK HOLMES: THE BASKERVILLE CURSE
**SHERLOCK HOLMES AND THE SECRET CODE**
See SHERLOCK HOLMES: DRESSED TO KILL
**SHERLOCK HOLMES AND THE VALLEY OF FEAR**
See SHERLOCK HOLMES: THE VALLEY OF FEAR
**SHERLOCK HOLMES' GROSSTER FALL**
See STUDY IN TERROR, A
**SHERLOCK HOLMES' THE SIGN OF FOUR**
See SIGN OF FOUR, THE
**SHERLOCK JR**
See BUSTER KEATON: SHERLOCK JR
**SHE'S DRESSED TO KILL**
See CATWALK KILLER
**SHE'S SEVENTEEN AND ANXIOUS**
See CONFESSIONS OF EMMANUELLE
**SHE'S THE BOSS**
See RUNNING OUT OF LUCK
**SHIFSHUF NAIM**
See HOT BUBBLEGUM
**SHINKANSEN DAIBABUHA**
See NEGATIVE CONTACT
**SHIPWRECKED**
See SHIPWRECK!
**SHOCK (TRANSFER SUSPENSE HYPNOS)**
See SHOCK
**SHOOT THE LIVING, PRAY FOR THE DEAD**
See TO KILL A JACKAL
**SHOOT TO KILL**
See DEADLY PURSUIT
**SHOOTING STAR, THE**
See TINTIN: THE SHOOTING STAR
**SHOOTING, THE**
See BAD BLOOD
**SHORT FUSE**
See GOOD TO GO
**SHOUT!**
See SHOUT: PARTS 1 AND 2
**SHOUT: THE STORY OF JOHNNY O'KEEFE**
See SHOUT: PARTS 1 AND 2
**SHUDDERS**
See KISS OF THE TARANTULA
**SI DON JUAN ETAIT UNE FEMME**
See IF DON JUAN WERE A WOMAN

**SI PUO FARE, AMIGO**
See CAN BE DONE AMIGO
**SIDECAR RACERS**
See TEAM, THE
**SIDEKICKS**
See LAST ELECTRIC KNIGHT, THE
**SIDNEY SHELDON'S BLOODLINE**
See BLOODLINE
**SIEGFRIED UND DAS SAGENHAFTE LIEBESLEBEN DER NIBELUNGEN**
See TERRIBLE QUICK SWORD OF SIEGFRIED, THE
**SILENCE IS GOLDEN**
See LE SILENCE EST D'OR
**SILENCE OF THE NORTH**
See SILENCE IN THE NORTH
**SILENT KILLER FROM ETERNITY**
See RETURN OF THE TIGER
**SILENT REBELLION**
See BIG SHOT
**SILVER SKATES, THE**
See HANS BRINKER
**SIN, THE**
See GOOD LUCK, MISS WYCKOFF
**SINGLETON'S PLUCK**
See LAUGHTERHOUSE
**SINISTER HOUSE**
See CURLEY AND HIS GANG IN THE HAUNTED MANSION
**SINISTER INVASION, THE**
See ALIEN TERROR
**SINS IN THE FAMILY**
See SINS WITHIN THE FAMILY
**SIR HENRY ASQUITH**
See SECRET LIVES OF THE BRITISH PRIME MINISTERS, THE: ASQUITH
**SISTER STREET FIGHTERS**
See SISTER STREETFIGHTER
**SISTERHOOD**
See ADDICTED TO HIS LOVE
**SIX-SMURF FLUTE, THE**
See SMURFS AND THE MAGIC FLUTE, THE
**SIZZLE BEACH**
See MALIBU HOT SUMMER
**SIZZLE BEACH, USA**
See MALIBU HOT SUMMER
**SIZZLE PANTS**
See SIZZLE
**SKATE**
See BLADES OF STEEL
**SKULL: A NIGHT OF TERROR**
See NIGHT OF RETRIBUTION
**SKY BANDITS**
See GUNBUS
**SKY TERROR**
See SKYJACKED
**SKYDIVER**
See BLUE THUNDER: SKYDIVER
**SKY'S NO LIMIT, THE**
See STAR CHASERS
**SLAMMER**
See SHORT EYES
**SLAMMER**
See WHO'S THAT GIRL
**SLAPSTICK**
See SLAPSTICK OF ANOTHER KIND
**SLASH**
See BLOOD SISTERS
**SLATE, WYN AND MACBRIDE**
See SLATE, WYN AND ME
**SLAUGHTER**
See DOGS, THE
**SLAUGHTERERS, THE**
See CANNIBAL APOCALYPSE
**SLAUGHTERHOUSE ROCK**
See HELL ISLAND
**SLAVE OF THE CANNIBAL GOD**
See PRISONER OF THE CANNIBAL

GOD
**SLEEPAWAY CAMP**
See NIGHTMARE VACATION
**SLEEPAWAY CAMP 2**
See NIGHTMARE VACATION 2
**SLEEPAWAY CAMP 2: UNHAPPY CAMPERS**
See NIGHTMARE VACATION 2
**SLICE OF LIFE, A**
See SEVEN UP
**SLOW DESCENT INTO HELL, A**
See YOUR TICKET IS NO LONGER VALID
**SLUMBER PARTY MASSACRE**
See SLUMBER PARTY MURDERS
**SMART ALEC**
See HOLLYWOOD DREAMING
**SMOKEY AND THE BANDIT RIDE AGAIN**
See SMOKEY AND THE BANDIT 2
**SMOKEY AND THE GOOD-TIME OUTLAWS**
See GOOD-TIME OUTLAWS, THE
**SMOKEY IS THE BANDIT**
See SMOKEY AND THE BANDIT: PART 3
**SMUG FIT**
See NOT JUST ANOTHER AFFAIR
**SMUGGLERS**
See KUNG FU GANG BUSTERS
**SMULTRONSTALLET**
See WILD STRAWBERRIES
**SMUTSIGA FINGRAR**
See DIRTY FINGERS
**SNAKE CANYON PRISON**
See OFF THE WALL
**SNAKE IN EAGLE'S SHADOW**
See SNAKE IN THE EAGLE'S SHADOW
**SNAKE PEOPLE, THE**
See CULT OF THE DEAD
**SNAKES IN EAGLE SHADOW**
See SNAKE IN THE EAGLE'S SHADOW
**SNAPSHOT**
See SNAPSHOT: AUSTRALIAN STYLE
**SNAPSHOTS**
See SNAPSHOT: AUSTRALIAN STYLE
**SNEAKERS**
See SPRING FEVER
**SNO-LINE**
See DEATHLINE
**SNOW: THE MOVIE**
See SNOW BUNNIES: NERDS ON VACATION
**SNOWMAN**
See LAND OF NO RETURN, THE
**SO LONG FRIEND**
See CODE, THE
**SOBRENATURAL**
See SUPERNATURAL
**SOFT BALLS**
See SQUEEZE PLAY
**SOFT BEDS AND HARD BATTLES**
See SOFT BEDS, HARD BATTLES
**SOFT FOCUS**
See PERFECT TIMING
**SOHO BLUES**
See PERFECT TIMING
**SOLARBABIES**
See SOLARWARRIORS
**SOLDAT VAN ORANGE**
See SURVIVAL RUN
**SOLDIER IN SKIRTS**
See TRIPLE ECHO, THE
**SOLDIER OF ORANGE**
See SURVIVAL RUN

**SOLDIER, THE**
See CODENAME: THE SOLDIER
**SOLEIL ROUGE**
See RED SUN
**SOME GIRLS**
See SISTERS
**SOMERSET MAUGHAM'S QUARTET**
See QUARTET
**SOMETHING BIG**
See GUN THAT SHOOK THE WEST, THE
**SOMETHING BLONDE**
See AURORA
**SOMETHING FOR JOEY**
See QUESTION OF LIFE, A
**SOMETHING IS OUT THERE**
See DAY OF THE ANIMALS
**SOMETHING SPECIAL**
See WILLY MILLY
**SOMETHING WAITS IN THE DARK**
See ISLAND OF MUTATIONS
**SOMETIMES A GREAT NOTION**
See NEVER GIVE AN INCH
**SOMETIMES AUNT MARTHA DOES TERRIBLE THINGS**
See SOMETIMES AUNT MARTHA DOES DREADFUL THINGS
**SOMMAREN MED MONIKA**
See SUMMER WITH MONIKA
**SON RISE: A MIRACLE OF LOVE**
See MIRACLE OF LOVE
**SONG FOR EUROPE, A**
See CRY FOR JUSTICE, A
**SONNY + JED**
See BANDITS
**SONO SARTANA IL VOSTRO BECCHINO**
See SARTANA, ANGEL OF DEATH
**SONS OF THE DESERT**
See LAUREL AND HARDY: SONS OF THE DESERT
**SORCERER'S CURSE, THE**
See MAGIC SWORD, THE
**SORCERESS**
See DEVIL'S ADVOCATE, THE
**SORORITY BABES IN THE SLIME-A-RAMA**
See IMP, THE
**SOTTO GLI OCCHI DELL'ASSASSINO**
See TENEBRAE
**SOTTO IL VESTITO NIENTE**
See NOTHING UNDERNEATH
**SOUTH PACIFIC 1942**
See TORPEDOED
**SOUTHERN CROSS**
See HIGHEST HONOUR, THE: A TRUE STORY
**SPACE CAMP**
See SPACECAMP
**SPACE CRUISER**
See SPACE CRUISER: GUARDIAN OF THE GALAXY
**SPACE MISSION OF THE LOST PLANET**
See VAMPIRE MEN OF THE LOST PLANET
**SPACE VAMPIRES**
See ASTRO ZOMBIES
**SPACEHUNTER: ADVENTURES IN THE FORBIDDEN ZONE**
See SPACEHUNTER
**SPAWN OF THE SLITHIS**
See SLITHIS
**SPECTER ON THE BRIDGE**
See GOLDEN GATE MURDERS, THE
**SPECTRES**
See SPECTERS

**SPEEDWAY**
See ELVIS PRESLEY: SPEEDWAY
**SPETTRI**
See SPECTERS
**SPIDER BABY, OR THE MADDEST TALE EVER TOLD**
See SPIDER BABY
**SPIDER WOMAN**
See SHERLOCK HOLMES AND THE SPIDERWOMAN
**SPIDER-MAN**
See SPIDERMAN: THE MOVIE
**SPIDERMAN AND THE DRAGON'S CHALLENGE**
See SPIDERMAN: THE DRAGON'S CHALLENGE
**SPIES INC.**
See SPIES, LIES AND ALIBIS
**SPINOUT**
See ELVIS PRESLEY: SPINOUT
**SPIRIT OF THE DEAD**
See ASPHYX, THE
**SPIRITS OF THE DEAD**
See TALES OF MYSTERY AND IMAGINATION
**SPIRITS OF THE DEAD**
See POWERS OF EVIL
**SPITFIRE**
See FIRST OF THE FEW, THE
**SPITFIRE: THE FIRST OF THE FEW**
See FIRST OF THE FEW, THE
**SPLATTER**
See NIGHT OF THE ALIEN
**SPOGLIAMOCI COSI' SENZA PUDOR**
See LOVE IN FOUR EASY LESSONS
**SPOILERS, THE**
See S.T.A.B.
**SPOOKS**
See SPIES, LIES AND ALIBIS
**SPORT BILLY**
See ADVENTURES OF SPORTS BILLY, THE
**SPORTING CHANCE**
See PERSUADERS, THE: SPORTING CHANCE
**SPRINGBREAK**
See SPRING BREAK
**SPY BUSTERS**
See GUNS IN THE HEATHER
**SPYLARKS**
See MORECOMBE AND WISE: THE INTELLIGENCE MEN
**SQUADRA ANITSCIPPO**
See COP IN BLUE JEANS
**SSSSNAKE**
See SNAKE
**SSSSSSS**
See SNAKE
**SST: DEATH FLIGHT**
See DEATH FLIGHT
**SST: DISASTER IN THE SKY**
See DEATH FLIGHT
**STACEY AND HER GANGBUSTERS**
See STACEY
**STACHKA**
See STRIKE
**STACKING**
See SEASON OF DREAMS
**STAGEFRIGHT**
See STAGE FRIGHT
**STAIRCASE C**
See ESCALIER C
**STALKING MOON, THE**
See ELITE KILLER, THE
**STAMPEDED**
See BIG LAND, THE
**STAND EASY**
See DOWN AMONG THE Z-MEN

**STAR FORCE: FUGITIVE ALIEN 2**
See STAR FORCE
**STAR SEX**
See CONFESSIONS FROM THE DAVID GALAXY AFFAIR
**STAR SLAMMER**
See PRISON SHIP STAR SLAMMER
**STAR SLAMMER: THE ESCAPE**
See PRISON SHIP STAR SLAMMER
**STAR TREK: THE MOTION PICTURE**
See STAR TREK
**STARFLIGHT: THE PLANE THAT COULDN'T LAND**
See STARFLIGHT ONE
**STAROYE I NOVOYE**
See GENERAL LINE, THE
**STARSHIP**
See LORCA AND THE OUTLAWS
**STARSHIP INVASIONS**
See ALIEN ENCOUNTERS
**STATE OF SHOCK**
See POWER PLAY
**STAY AWAY, JOE**
See ELVIS PRESLEY: STAY AWAY, JOE
**STEPHEN KING'S SILVER BULLET**
See SILVER BULLET
**STEPTOE AND SON: THE FEATURE**
See STEPTOE AND SON
**STICK 'EM UP, DARLINGS**
See LOADED GUNS
**STICKFIGHTER**
See PACIFIC CONNECTION
**STIFFS**
See W.H.I.F.F.S.
**STIGMA**
See POLICE IN ACTION 3: STIGMA
**STILL SMOKIN'**
See CHEECH AND CHONG: STILL SMOKIN'
**STINGRAY**
See ABIGAIL WANTED
**STORIE DI VITA E MALAVITA**
See PROSTITUTION RACKET, THE
**STORMBRINGER**
See DAY OF JUDGEMENT, A
**STORY OF A CITIZEN ABOVE SUSPICION**
See INVESTIGATION OF A CITIZEN ABOVE SUSPICION
**STORY OF A MARRIAGE**
See ON VALENTINE'S DAY
**STORY OF DAVID, THE**
See KING DAVID
**STORY OF ROBIN HOOD, THE**
See STORY OF ROBIN HOOD AND HIS MERRIE MEN, THE
**STRAIGHT JACKET**
See DARK SANITY
**STRANGE BEHAVIOUR**
See SMALL TOWN MASSACRE
**STRANGE SHADOWS IN A ROOM**
See BLAZING MAGNUMS
**STRANGER, THE**
See INTRUDER, THE
**STRANGER IN OUR HOUSE**
See SUMMER OF FEAR
**STREET GANGS**
See VIGILANTE
**STREET HAWK**
See STREETHAWK
**STREET LAW**
See REVENGE
**STREET LOVE**
See SCARRED
**STREET OF THE LOST**
See STREET OF THE DAMNED
**STREET WARRIOR**
See HIT MAN, THE

**STREET WARRIOR**
See MEAN JOHNNY BURROWS
**STREETFIGHTER COUNTER-ATTACKS, THE**
See STREETFIGHTER'S LAST REVENGE, THE
**STRENG VERTRAULICH**
See CRY FOR JUSTICE, A
**STRIKE, THE**
See COMIC STRIP PRESENTS: THE STRIKE
**STRIKE, THE**
See COMIC STRIP PRESENTS: THE STRIKE
**STRIP POKER**
See BIG SWITCH, THE
**STRIPTEASE LADY**
See G-STRING MURDERS, THE
**STROMBOLI, TERRA DI DIO**
See STROMBOLI
**STUD BROWN**
See DYNAMITE BROTHERS, THE
**STUDENT NURSES, THE**
See SECRETS OF A STUDENT NURSE
**STUDENT UNION**
See HARRAD SUMMER
**STUNTS**
See STUNTS: THE DEADLY GAME
**SUBMISSION**
See PETS
**SUDDEN DEATH**
See TEXAS GLADIATORS 2020
**SUDDEN TERROR**
See EYEWITNESS
**SUICIDE RUN**
See TOO LATE THE HERO
**SUMMER CAMP MASSACRE**
See BUTTERFLY REVOLUTION, THE
**SUMMER CAMP NIGHTMARE**
See BUTTERFLY REVOLUTION, THE
**SUMMER HOLIDAY**
See CLIFF RICHARD: SUMMER HOLIDAY
**SUMMER OF INNOCENCE**
See BIG WEDNESDAY
**SUMMER MANOEUVRES**
See LES GRANDES MANOEUVRES
**SUMMER SCHOOL**
See SCREWBALLS 2: LOOSE SCREWS
**SUMMER SCHOOL TEACHERS**
See SUMMER HEAT
**SUMMERTIME KILLER, THE**
See TARGET REMOVED
**SUMMERTIME YANKS**
See CHILDREN IN THE CROSSFIRE
**SUMMONS, THE**
See SCORPION
**SUPER CHICK**
See SUPERCHIC
**SUPER COOL**
See BODY FEVER
**SUPER DICK**
See CRY UNCLE
**SUPER FUZZ**
See SUPERSNOOPER
**SUPERCROSS**
See WINNERS TAKE ALL
**SUPERDRAGON**
See BRUCE LEE STORY, THE
**SUPERKNIGHT**
See SUPERKNIGHTS
**SUPERMAN: THE MOVIE**
See SUPERMAN
**SUPERVIVIENTES DE LOS ANDES**
See SURVIVE!
**SUR UN ARBRE PERCHE**
See UP A TREE
**SURF NAZIS**
See SURF NAZIS MUST DIE

**SURVIVAL ELEMENT**
See LAND OF NO RETURN, THE
**SURVIVORS OF THE LAST RACE**
See REFUGE OF FEAR
**SUSANNE, DIE WIRTIN VON DER LAHN**
See SWEET SINS OF SEXY SUSAN, THE
**SUSPENSE**
See SHOCK
**SUTJESKA**
See FIFTH OFFENSIVE, THE
**SUZANNE: THE HOSTESS OF THE LAHN**
See SWEET SINS OF SEXY SUSAN, THE
**SVETLAWA UCCIDERA IL 28 SETTEMBRE**
See FULLER REPORT
**SWAMP BAIT**
See GATOR BAIT
**SWORDS OF BLOOD**
See CARTOUCHE
**SWEDISH DREAM**
See LOVE IS A SPLENDID ILLUSION
**SWEDISH LOVE PLAY**
See WHAT NEXT?
**SWEET 16**
See SWEET SIXTEEN
**SWEET LIFE, A**
See LA DOLCE VITA
**SWEET VIOLENT TONY**
See CUBA CROSSING
**SWEET VIRGIN**
See GOT IT MADE
**SWEETER SONG, A**
See SNAPSHOT
**SWEETHEARTS**
See DARLINGS
**SWEETHEARTS**
See PERFECT TIMING
**SWINGSHIFT**
See SWING SHIFT
**SWISS MISS**
See LAUREL AND HARDY: SWISS MISS
**SWITCH, THE**
See PERSUADERS, THE: THE SWITCH
**SWORD OF GIDEON**
See ELEVENTH COMMANDMENT, THE
**SYTTEN**
See SEVENTEEN
**T.A.G. – THE ASSASSINATION BUREAU**
See TAG: THE ASSASSINATION GAME
**T.A.P.S.**
See TAPS
**TA E KOU**
See GODFATHER OF HONG KONG
**TACTICAL GUERILLA**
See PARTIZAN
**TAFFIN: A DIFFERENT KIND OF HERO**
See TAFFIN
**TAKE ME HIGH**
See CLIFF RICHARD: TAKE ME HIGH
**TAKING OF FLIGHT 847, THE: THE ULI DERICKSON STORY**
See TAKING OF FLIGHT 847, THE
**TALE OF AFRICA, A**
See GREEN HORIZONS
**TALE OF THE BUNNY PICNIC, THE**
See TALE OF THE BUNNY PARK, THE
**TALE OF TIFFANY LUST, THE**
See BODY LUST

**TALES FROM THE CRYPT 2**
See VAULT OF HORROR
**TALES OF 1001 NIGHTS**
See ADVENTURES OF SINBAD THE SAILOR, THE
**TALES OF EROTIC FANTASIES**
See EROTIC TALES
**TALES OF MYSTERY**
See POWERS OF EVIL
**TALKING BACK**
See LISTEN TO ME
**TALL BLOND MAN WITH ONE BLACK SHOE, THE**
See MAN WITH ONE RED SHOE, THE
**TAM-LIN**
See DEVIL'S WIDOW, THE
**TANDLAEGE PA SENGEKANTEN**
See DENTIST ON THE JOB
**TANGERINE MAN, THE**
See CANDY TANGERINE MAN, THE
**TANTRUMS**
See DEVIL TIMES FIVES
**TANZERINNEN FUR TANGER**
See CONFESSIONS OF THE SEX SLAVES
**TARGET OF AN ASSASSIN**
See TIGERS DON'T CRY
**TARZAN, KING OF BRUTE FORCE**
See TOR: MIGHTY WARRIOR
**TARZAN, ROI DE LA FORCE BRUTALE**
See TOR: MIGHTY WARRIOR
**TARZOON LA HONTE DE LA JUNGLE**
See JUNGLE BURGER
**TARZOON THE SHAME OF THE JUNGLE**
See JUNGLE BURGER
**TAUR THE MIGHTY**
See TOR: MIGHTY WARRIOR
**TAXI**
See HIT AND RUN
**TAXI TO THE JOHN**
See TAXI TO THE TOILET
**TAXI TO THE LOO**
See TAXI TO THE TOILET
**TAXI ZUM KLO**
See TAXI TO THE TOILET
**TEA-LEAF, THE**
See RAGMAN'S DAUGHTER, THE
**TEEN WOLF 1**
See TEEN WOLF
**TEENAGE INNOCENTS**
See TEENAGE INNOCENCE
**TEENAGE MADAME**
See TEENAGE MADAM
**TEENAGE SLUMBER PARTY**
See SLUMBER PARTY '57
**TEHERAN '43**
See ELIMINATOR, THE
**TELE**
See TIME SLIP
**TELL YOUR CHILDREN**
See REEFER MADNESS
**TEMPO DI CHARLESTON: CHICAGO 1929**
See THEY PAID WITH BULLETS
**TEMPO DI MASSACRO**
See COLT CONCERT
**TEN DAYS THAT SHOOK THE WORLD**
See OCTOBER
**TEN LITTLE NIGGERS**
See TEN LITTLE INDIANS
**TENDER FLESH**
See WELCOME TO ARROW BEACH
**TENDRES COUSINES**
See COUSINS IN LOVE
**TENGOKU TO JIGOKU**

See HIGH AND LOW
**TEPEPA**
See BLOOD AND GUNS
**TERMINAL STATION**
See INDISCRETION OF AN
AMERICAN WIFE
**TERMINUS STATION**
See INDISCRETION OF AN
AMERICAN WIFE
**TERRIBLE JOE MORAN**
See ONE BLOW TOO MANY
**TERRIFYING CONFESSIONS OF A
CAPTIVE WOMAN**
See TRIANGLE OF LUST
**TERRIFYING CONFESSIONS OF
CAPTIVE WOMEN**
See TRIANGLE OF LUST
**TERROR BY NIGHT**
See SHERLOCK HOLMES: TERROR
BY NIGHT
**TERROR FROM SPACE**
See PLNAET OF THE VAMPIRES
**TERROR FROM THE SKY**
See TERROR OUT OF THE SKY
**TERROR HOUSE**
See TERROR AT RED WOLF INN
**TERROR IN TOYLAND**
See CHRISTMAS EVIL
**TERROR OF FRANKENSTEIN**
See VICTOR FRANKENSTEIN
**TERROR OF SHEBA, THE**
See PERSECUTION
**TERROR ON THE MENU**
See TERROR AT RED WOLF INN
**TERROR SQUAD**
See HIJACKING OF THE ACHILLE
LAURO, THE
**TERROR, THE**
See NIGHT OF THE TERROR, THE
**TERROR, THE**
See TERROR ON TOUR
**TERROR: CREATURES FROM THE
GRAVE**
See CEMETERY OF THE LIVING
DEAD
**TERRORE NELLO SPAZIO**
See PLANET OF THE VAMPIRES
**TERRORISTS, THE**
See RANSOM
**TERROR'S EDGE**
See EDGE OF TERROR, THE
**TERRORVISION**
See TERROR VISION
**TEST OF LOVE, A**
See ANNIE'S COMING OUT
**TEXAS, ADIO**
See TEXAS ADIOS
**THANK YOU ALL VERY MUCH**
See TOUCH OF LOVE, A
**THAT CHAMIONSHIP SEASON**
See CHAMPIONSHIP SEASON, THE
**THAT HAMILTON WOMAN**
See LADY HAMILTON
**THAT LADY IS A TRAMP**
See THAT GIRL IS A TRAMP
**THAT PRICKLY FEELING**
See FASCINATION
**THAT RIVIERA TOUCH**
See MORECAMBE AND WISE: THAT
RIVIERA TOUCH
**THAT'S THE WAY IT IS**
See ELVIS: THAT'S THE WAY IT IS
**THAT'S WHAT FRIENDS ARE FOR**
See MARSEILLE CONTRACT, THE
**THAUR, KING OF BRUTE FORCE**
See TOR: MIGHTY WARRIOR
**THEIR BREAKFAST MEANT LEAD**
See PUSHING UP DAISIES
**THEODORA, SLAVE EMPRESS**

See THEODORA, QUEEN OF
BYZANTIUM
**THEY CALL HIM AMEN**
See THEY CALLED HIM AMEN
**THEY CAME FROM WITHIN**
See SHIVERS
**THEY LOVED LIFE**
See KANAL
**THEY MADE HIM A CRIMINAL**
See LIFE IS BEAUTIFUL
**THEY PAID WITH BULLETS:
CHICAGO 1929**
See THEY PAID WITH BULLETS
**THEY STILL CALL ME TRINITY**
See TRINITY IS STILL MY NAME!
**THEY'RE PLAYING WITH FIRE**
See PLAYING WITH FIRE
**THIN AIR**
See BODY STEALERS, THE
**THING IN THE ATTIC, THE**
See GHOUL, THE
**THING, THE**
See THING FROM ANOTHER WORLD,
THE
**THINGS ARE TOUGH ALL OVER**
See CHEECH AND CHONG: THINGS
ARE TOUGH ALL OVER
**THINK DIRTY**
See EVERY HOME SHOULD HAVE
ONE
**THINK DIRTY**
See EVERY HOME SHOULD HAVE
ONE
**THIRST OF BARON BLOOD, THE**
See BARON BLOOD
**THIRTEEN CHAIRS, THE**
See TWELVE PLUS ONE
**THIS GIRL IS A TRAMP**
See THAT GIRL IS A TRAMP
**THOL IL CONQUISTATORE**
See THOR THE CONQUEROR
**THONG**
See S.T.A.B.
**THOR AND THE AMAZON WOMEN**
See TOR: MIGHTY WARRIOR
**THORNY WAY TO THE STARS, THE**
See HUMANOID WOMAN
**THOROUGHBRED**
See RUN FOR THE ROSES
**THOSE DARING YOUNG MEN IN
THEIR JAUNTY JALOPIES**
See MONTE CARLO OR BUST
**THOSE WERE THE HAPPY DAYS**
See STAR!
**THOSE WERE THE HAPPY TIMES**
See STAR!
**THREAT, THE**
See POWER GAME
**THREE FACES OF FEAR, THE**
See BLACK SABBATH
**THREE FACES OF TERROR, THE**
See BLACK SABBATH
**THREE IN A CELLAR**
See THREE IN THE CELLAR
**THREE MUSKETEERS, THE: THE
QUEEN'S DIAMONDS**
See THREE MUSKETEERS, THE
**THREE SWEDISH GIRLS IN
HAMBURG**
See NYMPHO GIRLS
**THREE SWEDISH GIRLS ON THE
REEPERBAHN**
See NYMPHO GIRLS
**THRILL SEEKERS**
See HOT AND NAKED
**THUNDER**
See THUNDER WARRIOR
**THUNDER 2**
See THUNDER WARRIOR 2

**THUNDER 3**
See THUNDER WARRIOR 3
**THUNDERBIRD SIX**
See THUNDERBIRDS SIX: THE
MOVIE
**THUNDERBOLT ANGELS**
See NINJA OPERATION 4:
THUNDERBOLT ANGELS
**THURSDAY THE 12TH**
See PANDEMONIUM
**THURSDAY'S GAME**
See BERK, THE
**TIDAL WAVE**
See PORTRAIT OF JENNIE
**T'IEH NIU FU HU**
See IRON OX: THE TIGER KILLER
**TIEMPOS DE CHICAGO**
See THEY PAID WITH BULLETS
**TIFFANY: TRIANGLE OF LUST**
See TIFFANY
**TIGER DOESN'T CRY, THE**
See TIGERS DON'T CRY
**TIGER IN THE SKY**
See McCONNELL STORY, THE
**TIGHT FIT**
See CINDY'S LOVE GAMES
**TIGHT LITTLE ISLAND**
See WHISKY GALORE
**'TIL DEATH DO US PART**
See BLOOD-SPATTERED BRIDE, THE
**TILL DEATH DO US PART**
See BLOOD-SPATTERED BRIDE, THE
**TILL SEX US DO PART**
See SEX TO THE END
**TIME FLYER**
See BLUE YONDER, THE
**TIME FOR A KILLING, A**
See LONG RIDE HOME, A
**TIME KILLER, THE**
See NIGHT STRANGLER, THE
**TIME RIDER**
See TIMERIDER
**TIME WARP TERROR**
See BLOODY NEW YEAR
**TIME WARS**
See TIME SLIP
**TIMERIDER: THE ADVENTURE OF
LYLE SWANN**
See TIMERIDER
**TINERETE FARA BATRINETE**
See KINGDOM IN THE CLOUDS
**TINTIN ET LE LAC AUX REQUINS**
See TINTIN: THE LAKE OF SHARKS
**TINTORERA: TIGER SHARK**
See TINTORERA
**TO CATCH A SPY**
See CATCH ME A SPY
**TO ELVIS, WITH LOVE**
See TOUCHED BY LOVE
**TO KILL OR TO DIE**
See FIGHTING FISTS OF SHANGHAI
JOE, THE
**TO LOVE A VAMPIRE**
See LUST FOR A VAMPIRE
**TO THE STARS**
See HUMANOID WOMAN
**TOBY TYLER, OR TEN WEEKS WITH
A CIRCUS**
See TOBY TYLER
**TODAY IS FOREVER**
See GRIFFIN AND PHOENIX: A LOVE
STORY
**TOKE**
See DANGEROUS TRAFFIC
**TOMORROW'S A KILLER**
See PRETTYKILL
**TONGS**
See TONGS: A NEW YORK
CHINATOWN STORY

**TONGS: A CHINATOWN STORY**
See TONGS: A NEW YORK
CHINATOWN STORY
**TONIGHT'S THE NIGHT**
See HAPPY EVER AFTER
**TOO SCARED TO SCREAM**
See DOORMAN
**TOP MODEL**
See ELEVEN DAYS ELEVEN
NIGHTS: PART 2
**TOR**
See TOR: MIGHTY WARRIOR
**TORMENTED, THE**
See SEXORCIST, THE
**TORMENTORS, THE**
See SEXORCIST, THE
**TORNADO STRIKE FORCE**
See TORNADO
**TORTURE CHAMBER OF BARON
BLOOD, THE**
See BARON BLOOD
**TOUCHDOWN**
See CHOICES
**TOUGH GUYS**
See TOUGH GUY
**TOUGH TURF**
See TUFF TURF
**TOWARDS THE DICTATORSHIP OF
THE PROLETARIAT**
See STRIKE
**TOWER OF TERROR**
See ASSAULT
**TOWN CALLED HELL, A**
See TOWN CALLED BASTARD, A
**TOY FACTORY, THE**
See WITCHING, THE
**TRACER, THE**
See MISTER MEAN
**TRACKERS**
See SPACERAGE
**TRACKERS: 2180**
See SPACERAGE
**TRAHISON A STOCKHOLM**
See FULLER REPORT
**TRAIN KILLER, THE**
See TRAINKILLER, THE
**TRAIN SPECIAL POUR HITLER**
See SPECIAL TRAIN FOR HITLER
**TRAIN SPECIAL POUR SS**
See SPECIAL TRAIN FOR HITLER
**TRAINED TO KILL**
See NO MERCY MAN, THE
**TRANSMUTATIONS**
See UNDERWORLD
**TRAPPED**
See BIRDS OF PREY
**TRAUMA**
See EXPOSE
**TRAVELLING PICTURE SHOW MAN,
THE**
See PICTURE SHOW MAN, THE
**TRE PASSI NEL DELIRIO**
See TALES OF MYSTERY AND
IMAGINATION
**TREACHERY GAME, THE**
See ASSASSINATION RUN, THE
**TREASURE ISLAND IN OUTER
SPACE**
See SPACE ISLAND
**TREASURE ISLAND: THE MUSICAL**
See TREASURE ISLAND
**TREASURE OF DEATH**
See FORTY MILLION BUCKS
**TREASURE OF SIERRA MADRE, THE**
See TREASURE OF THE SIERRA
MADRE, THE
**TREASURE OF THE AMAZON**
See TREASURE OF DOOM
**TREASURE OF THE MOON**

**GODDESS**
See RACE TO DANGER
**TREASURE OF THE WHITE
GODDESS**
See DEVIL HUNTER, THE
**TREASURE OF THE YANKEE
ZEPHYR**
See RACE FOR THE YANKEE
ZEPHYR
**TREASURE SEEKERS, THE**
See FORTY MILLION BUCKS
**TREE OF LIBERTY, THE**
See HOWARDS OF VIGINIA, THE
**TRESPASS**
See TRESPASSES
**TRESPASSES**
See OMEN OF EVIL
**TRINITY IS MY NAME**
See THEY CALL ME TRINITY
**TROJAN HORSE**
See BLUE THUNDER: TROJAN
HORSE
**TROLLS**
See SEX TO THE END
**TROPICAL EXPRESS**
See AFRICA EXPRESS
**TROUBLE WITH GIRLS, THE**
See ELVIS PRESLEY: THE TROUBLE
WITH GIRLS
**TRUE BELIEVER**
See FIGHTING JUSTICE
**TRUMAN CAPOTE'S THE GLASS
HOUSE**
See GLASS HOUSE, THE
**TRUTH ABOUT SPRING, THE**
See PIRATES OF SPRING COVE
**TRY AND GET ME!**
See SOUND OF FURY, THE
**TSUBAKI SANJURO**
See SANJURO
**TUAREG IL GUERRIERO DEL
DESERTO**
See DESERT WARRIOR
**TUAREG: THE DESERT WARRIOR**
See DESERT WARRIOR
**TUCKER: THE MAN AND HIS
DREAM**
See TUCKER
**TUREG**
See DESERT WARRIOR
**TURKEY SHOOT**
See ESCAPE 2000
**TURKISH DELIGHT**
See SENSUALIST, THE
**TURKS FRUIT**
See SENSUALIST, THE
**TURN OF THE BADGE**
See SANTEE
**TURNING TO STONE**
See CONCRETE HELL
**TWEE VROUWEN**
See TWICE A WOMAN
**TWELVE MILLION DOLLAR BOY,
THE**
See DYNAMITE JOHNSON
**TWELVE TASKS OF ASTERIX, THE**
See ASTERIX THE GAUL 2: THE
TWELVE TASKS OF ASTERIX
**TWENTY-ONE DAYS TOGETHER**
See TWENTY-ONE DAYS
**TWICE BITTEN**
See VAMPIRE HOOKERS
**TWILIGHT ZONE, THE**
See TWILIGHT ZONE: THE MOVIE
**TWILIGHT'S LAST GLEAMING**
See NUCLEAR COUNTDOWN
**TWINS OF DRACULA**
See TWINS OF EVIL
**TWIST OF SAND, A**

See GHOST OF WOLFPACK, THE
**TWISTED SOULS**
See SPOOKIES
**TWITCH OF THE DEATH NERVE**
See LAST HOUSE ON THE LEFT
PART 2, THE
**TWO FACES OF LOVE, THE**
See LADY IS A WHORE, THE
**TWO FISTS VERSUS SEVEN
SAMURAI**
See FISTS OF VENGEANCE, THE
**TWO MINDS FOR MURDER**
See SOMEONE BEHIND THE DOOR
**TWO SUPERCOPS**
See CRIME BUSTERS
**TYCOON: HELLO SUCKER/TITANS
DON'T CRY**
See TYCOON: PARTS 1 AND 2
**UCHUSENKAN YAMATO**
See SPACE CRUISER: GUARDIAN OF
THE GALAXY
**UGLY, MONSTROUS, MIND-
ROASTING SUMMER OF O.C. AND
STIGGS**
See O.C. AND STIGGS
**ULTIMATE CHASE, THE**
See ULTIMATE THRILL, THE
**ULTIMATE SOLUTION OF GRACE
QUIGLEY, THE**
See GRACE QUIGLEY
**ULTIMO TANGO A PARIGI**
See LAST TANGO IN PARIS
**UMBRELLA WOMAN, THE**
See GOOD WIFE, THE
**UN COMPLICATO INTRIGO DI
DONNE, VICOLI E DELITTI**
See CAMORRA
**UN DOLLAR TROUE**
See ONE SILVER DOLLAR
**UN DOLLARO BUCATO**
See ONE SILVER DOLLAR
**UN FIOCCO NERO PER DEBORAH**
See TORMENT, THE
**UN GENIE, DEUX ASSOCIES, UNE
CLOCHE**
See NOBODY'S THE GREATEST
**UN HOMME AMOUREUX**
See MAN IN LOVE, A
**UN HOMME ET UNE FEMME:
VINGT ANS DEJA**
See MAN AND A WOMAN, A:
TWENTY YEARS LATER
**UN KILLER PER SUA MAESTA**
See KILLER LIKES CANDY, THE
**UN POSTO ALL'INFERNO**
See PLACE IN HELL, A
**UN SUDARIO A LA MEDIA**
See CANDIDATE FOR A KILLING
**UN TIPO CON UNA FACCIA STRANA
TI CERCA PER UCCIDERTI**
See RICCO
**UN URLO DALLE TENEBRA**
See EXORCIST 3, THE: CRIES AND
SHADOWS
**UNA HISTORIA PERVERSA**
See ONE ON TOP OF THE OTHER
**UNA MAGNUM SPECIAL PER TONY
SAITTA**
See BLAZING MAGNUM
**UNA ONDATA DI PIACERE**
See WAVES OF LUST
**UNA PISTOLA PER RINGO**
See ANGRY GUN, THE
**UNA SU 13**
See TWELVE PLUS ONE
**UNA SULL'ALTRA**
See ONE ON TOP OF THE OTHER
**UNA VELA PARA EL DIABLO**
See CANDLE FOR THE DEVIL, A

**UNCLE HARRY**
See STRANGE AFFAIR OF UNCLE HARRY, THE
**UNCLE OF THE BRIDE**
See LAST OF THE SUMMER WINE: UNCLE OF THE BRIDE
**UNDER COVER**
See UNDERCOVER
**UNDERCOVER CAPER, THE**
See THEY WENT THAT-A-WAY AND THAT-A-WAY
**UNDERCOVER HERO**
See SOFT BEDS, HARD BATTLES
**UNDERCOVERS HERO**
See SOFT BEDS, HARD BATTLES
**UNDERDOG**
See SECRET LIVES OF THE BRITISH PRIME MINISTERS, THE: MACDONALD
**UNDERGROUND**
See RESISTANCE
**UNDERSTUDY, THE**
See GRAVEYARD SHIFT 2
**UNDERWATER ODYSSEY, AN**
See NEPTUNE DISASTER, THE
**UNDICI GIORNI, UNDICI NOTTI**
See ELEVEN DAYS ELEVEN NIGHTS
**UNE FEMME FIDELE**
See WHEN A WOMAN IS IN LOVE
**UNE FOLLE ENVIE D'AIMER**
See PARANOIA
**UNE INGENUE LIBERTINE**
See INTIMATE CONFESSIONS OF STELLA
**UNFAITHFUL WIFE**
See UNFAITHFUL WIVES
**UNIDENTIFIED FLYING ODDBALL**
See SPACEMAN AND KING ARTHUR, THE
**UNO SCERIFFO EXTRATERRESTRE . . . POCO EXTRA E MOLTO TERRESTRE**
See SHERIFF AND THE SATELLITE KID, THE
**UNSANE**
See TENEBRAE
**UP FRANKENSTEIN**
See ANDY WARHOL'S FRANKENSTEIN
**UP IN SMOKE**
See CHEECH AND CHONG'S UP IN SMOKE
**UP IN THE CELLAR**
See THREE IN THE CELLAR
**UP THE PENTAGON**
See UP THE MILITARY
**UP THE WORLD**
See GOODBYE CRUEL WORLD
**UP YOURS**
See UP YOUR LADDER
**UP YOURS . . . A ROCKIN' COMEDY**
See UP YOUR LADDER
**UPS AND DOWNS OF A HANDYMAN, THE**
See CONFESSIONS OF AN ODD-JOB MAN
**UTILITIES**
See GETTING EVEN
**UTOPIA**
See LAUREL AND HARDY: UTOPIA
**V.I.P.**
See VERY IMPORTANT PERSON
**VACATION**
See NATIONAL LAMPOON'S VACATION
**VADO . . . L'AMMAZO E TORNO**
See ANY GUN CAN PLAY
**VALDEZ HORSES, THE**
See VALDEZ: THE HALF-BREED

**VALLEY OF FEAR, THE**
See SHERLOCK HOLMES: THE VALLEY OF FEAR
**VAMPIRE AND THE ROBOT, THE**
See MY SON THE VAMPIRE
**VAMPIRE OVER LONDON**
See MY SON THE VAMPIRE
**VAMPIRE PLAYGIRLS**
See DEVIL'S NIGHTMARE
**VAMPIRE WOMEN**
See CRYPT OF THE LIVING DEAD
**VAMPIRE-BEAST CRAVES BLOOD, THE**
See BLOOD BEAST TERROR, THE
**VAMPYRE ORGY, THE**
See VAMPYRES
**VAMPYRES, DAUGHTERS OF DARKNESS**
See VAMPYRES
**VASECTOMY: A DELICATE OPERATION**
See VASECTOMY: A DELICATE MATTER
**VEGAS STRIP WARS, THE**
See VEGAS STRIP WAR, THE
**VELLUTO NERO**
See BLACK EMMANUELLE, WHITE EMMANUELLE
**VELVET HOUSE CORPSE, THE**
See VELVET HOUSE, THE
**VELVET VAMPIRE, THE**
See WAKING HOUR, THE
**VENDITORE DI PALLANCINI**
See MY YOUNG MAN
**VENGEANCE IS MINE**
See SUNDAY IN THE COUNTRY
**VENGEANCE OF THE BARBARIANS**
See GET MEAN
**VERNE MILLER**
See GANGLAND: THE VERNE MILLER STORY
**VERSTECKT**
See FORBIDDEN
**VERY BIG WITHDRAWAL, A**
See MAN, A WOMAN, A BANK, A
**VERY HEAVY METAL**
See RIDING HIGH
**VERY SPECIAL WOMAN, A**
See KISS ME WITH LUST
**VETERAN, THE**
See DEATHDREAM
**VICAR, THE**
See LUSTFUL VICAR
**VICOLO CIECO**
See BLACK VEIL FOR LISA, A
**VICTIM, THE**
See OUT OF CONTENTION
**VICTIMS FOR VICTIMS: THE THERESA SALDANA STORY**
See VICTIMS FOR VICTIMS
**VICTORY**
See ESCAPE TO VICTORY
**VICTORY, THE**
See THIS TIME FOREVER
**VIDEO MADNESS**
See JOYSTICKS
**VIENNA STRANGLER, THE**
See STRANGLER OF VIENNA, THE
**VIETNAM WAR STORY: THE LAST DAYS**
See VIETNAM WAR STORY
**VIETNAM WAR STORY 2**
See WAR STORY 2
**VIGILANTE 2**
See REVENGE
**VILLAIN, THE**
See CACTUS JACK
**VINDICATOR**
See WHEELS OF FIRE

**VIOLATORS, THE**
See ACT OF VENGEANCE
**VIOLENCE ET PASSION**
See CONVERSATION PIECE
**VIPER THREE**
See NUCLEAR COUNTDOWN
**VIRGIN CONFESSIONS**
See CHERRY HILL HIGH
**VIRGIN VAMPIRES**
See TWINS OF EVIL
**VIRUS**
See CANNIBAL APOCALYPSE
**VISION QUEST**
See CRAZY FOR YOU
**VISKINGAR OCH ROP**
See CRIES AND WHISPERS
**VIVA LA REVOLUCION**
See BLOOD AND GUNS
**VIVA LAS VEGAS**
See ELVIS PRESLEY: VIVA LAS VEGAS
**VIVA MARIA!**
See BANDIDA
**VIVEMENT DIMANCHE**
See FINALLY SUNDAY
**VIVRE POUR SURVIVRE**
See WHITE FIRE
**VIZI PRIVATI, PUBBLICHE VIRTU**
See PRIVATE VICES AND PUBLIC VIRTUES
**VOLTRON DEFENDER OF THE UNIVERSE: CASTLE OF LIONS**
See VOLTRON DEFENDER OF THE UNIVERSE IN THE CASTLE OF LIONS
**VOLTRON DEFENDER OF THE UNIVERSE: INVASION OF THE ROBOBEASTS**
See VOLTRON DEFENDER OF THE UNIVERSE IN THE INVASION OF THE ROBOBEASTS
**VOLTRON DEFENDER OF THE UNIVERSE: PLANET ARUS**
See VOLTRON DEFENDER OF THE UNIVERSE IN THE BATTLE OF ARUS
**VON RICHTHOFEN AND BROWN**
See BATTLES OF THE ACES
**VORTEX**
See DAY TIME ENDED, THE
**VOYAGE HOME, THE**
See STAR TREK 4: THE VOYAGE HOME
**VZICKA REPUBLIKA**
See SIXTY-SEVEN DAYS
**W: TERROR IS ONE LETTER**
See W
**WAITING FOR MORNING**
See PLACES IN THE HEART
**WAKE IN FRIGHT**
See OUTBACK
**WALKING TALL: PART 2**
See WALKING TALL PART 2: VENGEANCE TRAIL
**WALL, THE**
See PINK FLOYD: THE WALL
**WANG YU'S 7 MAGNIFICENT FIGHTS**
See SEVEN MAGNIFICENT FIGHTS
**WANT A RIDE, LITTLE GIRL?**
See IMPULSE
**WANTED WOMEN**
See JESSI'S GIRLS
**WANTED: DEAD OR ALIVE**
See WANTED DEAD OR ALIVE
**WAR CAT**
See ANGEL OF VENGEANCE
**WAR GAMES**
See SUPPOSE THEY GAVE A WAR

AND NOBODY CAME?
**WAR GODS OF THE DEEP**
See CITY UNDER THE SEA
**WAR OF THE TROJANS**
See LAST GLORY OF TROY, THE
**WAR OF THE ZOMBIES**
See ROME AGAINST ROME
**WARBUS: RAW COURAGE**
See WARBUS
**WARDOG**
See WARDOG: THE KILLING
MACHINE
**WARDOGS**
See WARDOG: THE KILLING
MACHINE
**WARHOL'S FRANKENSTEIN**
See ANDY WARHOL'S
FRANKENSTEIN
**WARRIOR LOST WORLD**
See WARRIOR OF THE LOST WORLD
**WARRIORS OF THE 21ST CENTURY**
See BATTLETRUCK
**WARRIORS OF THE WASTELAND**
See NEW BARBARIANS, THE
**WASHINGTON MISTRESS**
See BROKEN DREAMS
**WASP**
See W.A.S.P.
**WATCH OUT FOR THE EYES**
See LET'S MAKE A DIRTY MOVIE
**WATER WAR**
See THICKER THAN WATER
**WATUSI**
See QUEST FOR KING SOLOMON'S
MINES, THE
**WAY OF CHALLENGE**
See NINJA OPERATION 2: WAY OF
CHALLENGE
**WAY OUT WEST**
See LAUREL AND HARDY: WAY OUT
WEST
**WAY, THE**
See YOL
**WE ARE NO VIRGINS**
See COME AND PLAY
**WEB**
See MISSION MANILA
**WEDDING BELLS**
See ROYAL WEDDING
**WEDNESDAY'S CHILD**
See FAMILY LIFE
**WEEKEND WARRIORS**
See HOLLYWOOD AIR FORCE
**WEIRD TALES**
See KWAIDAN
**WEISSE FRACHT FUER HONG KONG**
See WHITE CARGO FOR HONG
KONG
**WELCOME TO THE SUICIDE CLUB**
See SUICIDE CLUB, THE
**WELLINGTON: THE DUEL SCANDAL**
See SECRET LIVES OF THE BRITISH
PRIME MINISTERS, THE: THE IRON
DUKE
**WEREWOLF SHADOW**
See WEREWOLF'S SHADOW, THE
**WEREWOLF VERSUS THE VAMPIRE WOMEN, THE**
See WEREWOLF'S SHADOW, THE
**WEREWOLF WOMAN**
See NAKED WEREWOLF WOMAN
**WET DREAMS**
See DREAMS OF THIRTEEN
**WETHERBY**
See VIOLENT STRANGERS:
WETHERBY
**WE'VE GOT A BONE TO PICK WITH YOU**

See PACK, THE
**WHAT ARE FRIENDS FOR?**
See MARSEILLE CONTRACT, THE
**WHAT LOLA WANTS**
See DAMN YANKEES
**WHAT WAITS BELOW**
See SECRETS OF THE PHANTOM
CAVERNS
**WHAT'S GOOD FOR THE GOOSE**
See GIRL TROUBLE
**WHAT'S IN IT FOR HARRY?**
See TARGET: HARRY
**WHEELER**
See PSYCHO FROM TEXAS
**WHEELS OF DEATH**
See DEATH CAR ON THE FREEWAY
**WHEN THE RAIN BEGINS TO FALL**
See VOYAGE OF THE ROCK ALIENS,
THE
**WHEN THE SCREAMING STOPS**
See LORELEI'S GRASP, THE
**WHEN TOMORROW COMES**
See INTERLUDE
**WHEN WOMEN LOST THEIR TAILS**
See WHEN MEN CARRIED CLUBS,
WOMEN PLAYED DING DONG!
**WHEN WOMEN PLAYED DING DONG**
See WHEN MEN CARRIED CLUBS,
WOMEN PLAYED DING DONG!
**WHERE THERE'S A WILL**
See GOOD MORNING, BOYS
**WHERE'S WILLIE?**
See COMPUTER KID, THE
**WHIFFS**
See W.H.I.F.F.S.
**WHITE AMAZON**
See AMAZONIA
**WHITE CARGO**
See WHITE CARGO FOR HONG
KONG
**WHITE CARGO FROM HONG KONG**
See WHITE CARGO FOR HONG
KONG
**WHITE HEAT**
See WHITE HOT
**WHITE HOUSES IN AUGUST**
See WHITE HORSES OF SUMMER,
THE
**WHITE PHANTOM**
See WHITE PHANTOM: ENEMY OF
DARKNESS
**WHITE SLAVE**
See AMAZONIA
**WHO CAN KILL A CHILD?**
See ISLAND OF DEATH
**WHO FINDS A FRIEND**
See WHO FINDS A FRIEND FINDS A
TREASURE
**WHO IS KILLING THE STUNTMEN?**
See STUNTS: THE DEADLY GAME
**WHO KILLED DOC ROBBINS?**
See CURLEY AND HIS GANG IN THE
HAUNTED MANSION
**WHO KILLED MARY MAGDELENE**
See DEATH OF A HOOKER
**WHO KILLED MARY WHAT'S'ERNAME?**
See DEATH OF A HOOKER
**WHO?**
See MAN IN THE STEEL MASK, THE
**WHOEVER SLEW AUNTIE ROO?**
See WHO SLEW AUNTIE ROO?
**WHO'LL SAVE OUR CHILDREN?**
See WHO WILL SAVE OUR
CHILDREN?
**WHY SHOULD I LIE?**
See WHY WOULD I LIE?
**WIFE SWAPPER**

See WIFE SWAPPERS, THE
**WILD IN THE COUNTRY**
See ELVIS PRESLEY: WILD IN THE
COUNTRY
**WILD JOE BASS**
See ANGRY JOE BASS
**WILD PONY, THE**
See WILD STALLION, THE
**WILD RIDERS**
See TALES OF TERROR 2: THE
IMPURE, WILD RIDERS
**WILD SIDE, THE**
See SUBURBIA
**WILD WHEELS**
See FAST LANE FEVER
**WILDERNESS FAMILY PART 2, THE**
See ADVENTURES OF THE
WILDERNESS FAMILY, THE: PART 2
**WILDERNESS FAMILY, THE**
See ADVENTURES OF THE
WILDERNESS FAMILY, THE: PART 1
**WILDSCHUT**
See STRONGHOLD
**WILL TO DIE**
See LEGACY OF BLOOD
**WIND, THE**
See EDGE OF TERROR, THE
**WINGED SERPENT, THE**
See Q: THE WINGED SERPENT
**WINNERS**
See MY WAY
**WINTER RATES**
See OUT OF SEASON
**WIRED TO KILL**
See BOOBY TRAP
**WISHBONE CUTTER**
See SHADOW OF CHIKARA, THE
**WITCH, THE**
See SUPERSTITION
**WITCHCRAFT**
See GHOSTHOUSE 2
**WITCHCRAFT PART 2: THE TEMPTRESS**
See WITCHCRAFT 2
**WITCHERY**
See GHOSTHOUSE 2
**WITH THESE HANDS**
See SEX CLINIC
**WITHOUT WARNING**
See WARNING, THE
**WITNESS IN THE WAR ZONE**
See WAR ZONE
**WIZARD WARS**
See WIZARDS OF THE LOST
KINGDOM
**WOLF**
See JUNGLE WOLF
**WOLF LARSEN**
See LEGEND OF THE SEA WOLF,
THE
**WOLF OF THE SEVEN SEAS**
See LEGEND OF THE SEA WOLF, THE
**WOMAN ALONE, A**
See SABOTAGE
**WOMAN ALONE, A**
See SABOTAGE
**WOMAN HUNT, THE**
See ESCAPE
**WOMAN IN GREEN, THE**
See SHERLOCK HOLMES AND THE
WOMAN IN GREEN
**WOMAN OF STYLE, A**
See SECRET LIVES OF THE BRITISH
PRIME MINISTERS, THE: LLOYD
GEORGE
**WOMAN ON PIER THIRTEEN, THE**
See WOMAN AT PIER THIRTEEN,
THE
**WOMEN IN CELL BLOCK 7**

See LOVE IN A WOMEN'S PRISON
**WONDERFUL LIFE**
See CLIFF RICHARD: WONDERFUL
LIFE
**WONDERFUL TO BE YOUNG**
See CLIFF RICHARD: THE YOUNG
ONES
**WOODEN HORSE OF TROY, THE**
See TROJAN WAR, THE
**WOODEN SOLDIERS**
See LAUREL AND HARDY: BABES IN
TOYLAND
**WORLD SONG, THE**
See LE CHANT DU MONDE
**WOULD YOU KILL A CHILD?**
See ISLAND OF DEATH
**WRATH OF KHAN, THE**
See STAR TREK 2: THE WRATH OF
KHAN
**WRONG IS RIGHT**
See MAN WITH THE DEADLY LENS,
THE
**WRONG KIND OF GIRL, THE**
See BUS STOP
**WU-TI T'IEH SHA CHANG**
See INVINCIBLE IRON PALM
**X: THE MAN WITH X-RAY EYES**
See MAN WITH X-RAY EYES, THE
**XYZ MURDERS, THE**
See CRIMEWAVE
**Y SI NO ENFADAMOS**
See WATCH OUT, WE'RE MAD
**YAB-YUM OP STELTEN**
See HOT PURSUIT
**YABU NO NAKA KURONEKO**
See KURONEKO
**YELLOW SUBMARINE**
See BEATLES: YELLOW SUBMARINE
**YELLOWHAIR AND THE PECOS KID**
See YELLOWHAIR AND THE
FORTRESS OF GOLD
**YESTERDAY**
See THIS TIME FOREVER
**YOB, THE**
See COMIC STRIP PRESENTS: THE

YOB
**YOGI'S FIRST CHRISTMAS**
See YOGI BEAR: YOGI'S FIRST
CHRISTMAS
**YOGI'S GREAT ESCAPE**
See YOGI BEAR: YOGI'S GREAT
ESCAPE
**YOR, THE HUNTER FROM THE
FUTURE**
See YOR
**YOTZ'IM KAVUA**
See GOING STEADY
**YOU BETTER WATCH OUT**
See CHRISTMAS EVIL
**YOU CAN'T STEAL LOVE**
See LIVE A LITTLE, STEAL A LOT
**YOU MUST BE JOKING**
See IF YOU DON'T STOP IT YOU'LL
GO BLIND
**YOUNG ANIMALS, THE**
See BORN WILD
**YOUNG BRIDE, THE**
See UP AND COMING
**YOUNG DRACULA**
See ANDY WARHOL'S DRACULA
**YOUNG HANNAH, QUEEN OF THE
VAMPIRES**
See CRYPT OF THE LIVING DEAD
**YOUNG MAN OF MUSIC**
See YOUNG MAN WITH A HORN
**YOUNG NURSE, THE**
See SECRETS OF YOUNG NURSES
**YOUNG ONES, THE**
See CLIFF RICHARD: THE YOUNG
ONES
**YOUNG SCARFACE**
See BRIGHTON ROCK
**YOUNG SHERLOCK HOLMES**
See YOUNG SHERLOCK HOLMES
AND THE PYRAMID OF FEAR
**YOUNG WARRIORS, THE**
See EAGLE WARRIORS
**YOUR PAST IS SHOWING**
See NAKED TRUTH, THE
**Z.P.G.**

See ZERO POPULATION GROWTH
**ZABOU**
See CRACK CONNECTION, THE
**ZEBRA KILLER, THE**
See PANIC CITY
**ZEISTERS**
See FAT GUY GOES NUTZOID
**ZENOBIA**
See MADAME ZENOBIA
**ZHAN SHEN TAN**
See BEACH OF THE WAR GODS
**ZHIZN PREKRASNA**
See LIFE IS BEAUTIFUL
**ZIGZAG**
See FALSE WITNESS
**ZITS**
See Z.I.T.S.
**ZOLTAN**
See ZOLTAN, HOUND OF HELL
**ZOLTAN, HOUND OF DRACULA**
See ZOLTAN, HOUND OF HELL
**ZOMBIE 3**
See NIGHTS OF TERROR, THE
**ZOMBIE AFTERMATH**
See AFTERMATH, THE
**ZOMBIE CHILD**
See CHILD, THE
**ZOMBIE HORROR**
See NIGHTS OF TERROR, THE
**ZOMBIE, THE**
See PLAGUE OF THE ZOMBIES, THE
**ZOMBIES ATOMICOS**
See NIGHTMARE CITY
**ZOMBIES, THE**
See PLAGUE OF THE ZOMBIES, THE
**ZOO: A ZED AND TWO NOUGHTS**
See ZED AND TWO NOUGHTS, A
**ZORA**
See SILENT NIGHT, BLOODY NIGHT
**ZORRO ALLA CORTE DI SPAGNA**
See ZORRO AT THE SPANISH COURT
**ZUCKER FUR DEN MORDER**
See KILLER LIKES CANDY, THE
**ZWEI SUPERTYPEN RAUMEN AUF**
See RULERS OF THE CITY

# DISTRIBUTORS LIST

The codes in the following list refer to both video distributors and video labels. Film companies are generally only included if they have been found to distribute videos as well.

Where the distributor code refers to a film or video company, the address of the company is given if known. This even applies where the products of that company are being handled by another distributor. Where this is the case, the code of the distributor handling that company's products is noted. Video/film companies often change their distributors, reference to the actual production company may be necessary in order to find out who is now handling the film.

As many distributor addresses have been supplied as it was possible to determine at the time of printing. Distributors change so frequently, that a list such as this must, of necessity, be incomplete. Many of the codes that have no address may be taken to be merely labels, for which details of the appropriate parent or handling company are given where known.

Distributors handling a given film often change, or sometimes merely change their name. For any given film they are generally listed in chronological order. Thus where a film is handled by several distributors, the last one noted is the most recent one found to be handling that film. Where the position with regard to availability of a given film is uncertain, old distributor codes are retained until the position is clarified.

| | |
|---|---|
| **18CAR** | 18 CARAT VIDEO |
| | also known as |
| | 18 Carat Solid Gold |
| | See INTCON |
| **18PLAT** | 18 PLATINUM COLLECTION |
| | also known as Eighteen |
| | (Platinum) Collection |
| **2020** | 20-20 VISION |
| | VIP Premiere |
| | First Floor, Acorn House |
| | Victoria Road |
| | London, W3 6UL |
| | (081-993 7705) |
| | Telex: 267069 |
| | Fax: 081-993 0209 |
| **20VIS** | 20-20 VISION VIDEO UK |
| | Horatio House |
| | 77-85 Fulham Palace Road |
| | London, W6 8JA |
| | (081-748 4034) |
| | Fax: 081-748 4546 |
| **21ST** | 21ST CENTURY |
| **3APX** | 3 APEX |
| | See APX |
| **3MVID** | 3M VIDEO |
| | also known as |
| | 3M UK Ltd. |
| | 3M House, PO Box 1 |
| | Bracknell, Berks. |
| | See PVG |
| **4BID** | 4-BIDDEN |
| | See FFV |
| **A&M** | A & M SOUND PICTURES |
| | also known as A & M |
| | Records Ltd. |
| | 136-140 Kings Road |
| | London, SW6 4LZ |
| | (071-736 3311) |
| | Telex: 916342 |
| | Fax: 071-731 4606 |
| | See CH5 for |
| | distribution |
| **ABA** | ABACUS |
| | Distributed by INT |
| **ABBEY** | ABBEY BROADCAST |
| | COMMS. PLC |

| | |
|---|---|
| | 53 Abbey Road |
| | London, NW8 0AD |
| | (071-372 0752) |
| | Fax: 071-372 0887 |
| | See PICK for |
| | distribution |
| **ABCVID** | ABC VIDEO |
| | See RNK |
| **ABC** | ABC FILMS (UK) LTD |
| | 77 Methyr Road, Whitchurch |
| | Cardiff, Glamorgan |
| | (0222-615676) |
| | No longer active |
| | See GLEN |
| **ABV** | ABBEY VIDEO |
| **ACAD** | ACADEMY VIDEO |
| | See INTMED for |
| | distribution |
| **ACDV** | ACADEMY/VIRGIN |
| | See HIFLY/CBDSIS for |
| | distribution |
| **ACE** | ACE PRODUCTIONS |
| **ACPHOT** | A & C PHOTOGRAPHICS |
| **ACTEL** | ACTION CHANNEL |
| | (081-997 1330) |
| **ACN** | ACTION FILMS |
| **ACT** | ACTIVE VIDEO |
| **ACTION** | ACTION ESSENTIAL |
| | See SFI for |
| | distribution |
| **ADAM** | ADULT AMUSEMENT |
| **ADB** | ADB DISTRIBUTION |
| **AFE** | AFE VIDEO |
| **AIP** | ACTION INTERNATIONAL |
| | PICTURES |
| **AJAX** | AJAX VIDEO |
| | See VAL |
| **ALB** | ALBANY VIDEO DISTRIBUTION |
| | Battersea Studios |
| | Television Centre |
| | Thackeray Road |
| | London, SW8 3TW |
| | (071-498 6811) |
| | Fax: 071-498 1494 |
| **ALLAM** | ALL-AMERICAN |
| | See MOG |

**ALLIED**   ALLIED VISION LTD.
See INTMED

**ALPHA**   ALPHA VIDEO
See INT

**AMARA**   AMARANTH PRODUCTIONS
See CLUB

**AMB**   AMBASSADOR VIDEO
See KRP

**AMBAS**   AMBASSADOR
See WOV

**AMBER**   AMBER VIDEO

**AMT**   A.M.T.
See VGM

**AMU**   AMUST VIDEO

**ANGLIA**   ANGLIA TELEVISION
Brook House
Park Lane, London W1
(071-408 2288/629 5082)

**APOL**   APOLLO ENTERTAINMENT CORP.
42 Maiden Lane
London, WC2E 7LM
(071-836 1844)

**APOLLO**   APOLLO FILM DISTRIBUTORS
14 Ensbury Park Raod
Bournemouth, BH9 2SJ
(0202-520962/533577)

**APV**   APPLE VIDEO

**APX**   APEX DISTRIBUTION LTD.
also known as Apex Video
3 Standard Road
Park Royal Ind. Park
London, NW10 6EX
See INTMED for
distribution

**ARC**   ARC VIDEO

**ARCADE**   ARCADE VIDEO
Arcade/PVG
Palace Video
8 Poland Street
London, W1
See VSP

**ARCH**   ARCHER VIDEO
See MOV

**ARCTIC**   ARCTIC VIDEO

**ARENA**   ARENA
See CIC

**ARF**   ARIEL FILMS LTD.
47a Elizabeth Avenue
Christchurch
Dorset, BH23 2DN
(0202-479868)
Telex: 41594
See CBSDIS for
distribution

**ARAMA**   ARAMA

**ARI**   ARION COMMUNICATIONS

**ARIES**   ARIES

**ARROW**   ARROW FILMS LTD.
69 Long Lane
London EC1
(071-600 5145/6945)
No longer active

**ART**   ARTEL HOME VIDEO

**ASCOT**   ASCOT VIDEO
See INT

**AST**   ASTRA VIDEO
9a Ribblesdale Place
Preston
Lancs., PR1 3NA
(0772-27546)

**ASV**   ASTRO VIDEO
also known as Astro
Supplies Ltd.
98 Cranbourne Avenue
London, E11 2BQ

**ATA**   ATA DISTRIBUTION
also known as
ATA Video

**ATLAS**   ATLAS HOME VIDEO

also known as
Atlas Video
29 Milkstone Road
Rochdale, Lancs.
(0706-47980)

**ATLAN**   ATLANTIC FILM
DISTRIBUTORS
First Floor
Paramount House
162 Wardour Street
London, W1V 3AT
(071-437 4415/9513)

**ATT**   ATTAR VIDEO PRODUCTIONS

**AUD**   AUDIO VISUAL

**AVA**   AVATAR COMMUNICATIONS LTD.
No longer active

**AVALON**   AVALON INTERNATIONAL
PICTURES
Unit 12, Brunswick
Industrial Park
Brunswick Way
New Southgate
London, N11 1HX
(081-368 7788)
Fax: 081-368 6298

**AVC**   ADULT VIDEO CENTRE

**AVI**   AVI VIDEO
Now part of VPD

**AVO**   AVO FILMS
See FFV

**AVP**   ATLANTIS VIDEO
PRODUCTIONS LTD.
See CYCLO

**AVR**   AVR HOME ENTERTAINMENT
27 Brigstock Road
Thornton Heath
Surrey, CR4 7JJ
(081-684 8455)
No longer active

**AVTON**   AVTON COMMUNICATIONS
19 Watford Road
Radlett, Herts.
WD7 8LF
(0923-853255)
Fax: 0923-855757

**BAG**   BAGSTER VIDEO
8-9 Embassy Court
Welling High Street
Welling
Kent, DA16 1TL
No longer active

**BANO**   BANO COMMUNICATIONS PLC
27 Old Gloucester Street
London, WC1 N3XX
See PRISM for
distribution

**BAR**   BARBER
See PRV

**BARBAR**   BARBARIAN THEATRE
label for AVR

**BBC**   BBC ENTERPRISES LTD.
also known as BBC
Enterprises Video Sales
Woodlands
80 Wood Lane
London, W12 0TT
(081-743 5588)
Telex: 934678
Fax: 081-749 0538
See PICK for
distribution

**BBHV**   BB HOME VIDEO
also known as
BB Video Productions

**BCB**   BCB ENTERTAINMENT GROUP PLC
1 Dundee Court
Dundee Wharfing Estate
73 Wapping High Street
London, E1 9YG

| | |
|---|---|
| | (071-480 5688) |
| | Fax: 071-481 4640 |
| BCM | BCM PUFF VIDEO |
| | Old Gloucester Street |
| | London WC1N 3XX |
| BCV | BEST OF BRITISH |
| | CINEMA ON VIDEO |
| BECK | BECKMANN HOME VIDEO |
| | PO Box 109 |
| | 1 Church Street, Douglas |
| | Isle of Man |
| | British Isles |
| | (0624-72193) |
| | Telex: 629888 |
| | Fax: 0624-20206 |
| BEG | BEGGAR'S BANQUET |
| | also known as Beggar's |
| | Banquet Records |
| | 17/19 Alma Road |
| | London, SW18 1AB |
| | (081-870 9912) |
| | Telex: 915733 |
| | Fax: 081-871 1766 |
| | See VIRVIS for |
| | distribution |
| BEV | BEVERLY'S PRODUCTIONS |
| | See KRP |
| BHV | BRITISH HOME VIDEO |
| BIGPIC | BIG PICTURES |
| | See HIFLI for |
| | distribution |
| BLABEL | BLACK LABEL VIDEO |
| BLAC | BLACK CAT |
| BLUEDO | BLUE DOLPHIN FILMS |
| | 15-17 Old Compton St. |
| | London, W1V 6JR |
| | (071-439 9511) |
| BLUES | BLUES |
| | See SHEP or DOV for |
| | distribution |
| BLUMO | BLUE MOVES |
| | See GOLD |
| BMGREC | BMG RECORDS (UK) LTD. |
| | Lyng Lane |
| | West Bromwich |
| | West Midlands, B70 7ST |
| | (021-500 5678) |
| | Telex: 21349 |
| | Fax: 021-553 6880 |
| BMGVID | BMG VIDEO |
| | Cavendish House |
| | 423 New Kings Road |
| | London, SW6 4RN |
| | (071-973 0011) |
| | Fax: 071-973 0345 |
| BOOK | BOOKWORM |
| | ADVERTISING LTD. |
| BOOLA | BOOLA BULA |
| | See BBHV |
| BOX | BOX OFFICE FILMS |
| | Unit 2 |
| | Highway Trading |
| | Centre |
| | Heckford Street |
| | London, E1 9HR |
| | (071-791 2000) |
| | Fax: 071-265 8114 |
| | See CFD |
| BRAT | BRATPACK PROGRAMME |
| | DISTRIBUTION CO. |
| | Canalot Studios |
| | 222 Kensal Road |
| | London, W10 5BN |
| | (081-969 7609) |
| BRAVE | BRAVEWORLD VIDEO |
| | Prestwich House |
| | Centre 1 |
| | Caxton Way, Watford |
| | Herts., WD1 8UF |

| | |
|---|---|
| | (0923-55558) |
| | Telex: 925430 |
| | Fax: 0923 816744 |
| | See CBSDIS for rental |
| | distribution |
| | See TERRY for sell-thru |
| | distribution |
| BRD | BORDER TELEVISION |
| | 33 Margaret Street |
| | London W1 |
| | (071-637 4363) |
| | No longer active |
| BRENO | BRENDA AND ROBERT GEORGE |
| BRIF | BRITISH FILMS |
| BRNX | BRONX VIDEO CO. |
| BRO | BROADWAY FILMS LTD. |
| BRONZ | BRONZE |
| | See POLY |
| BRT | BRITANNIA VIDEO |
| BRV | BARRY WILES VIDEO |
| | London Road Trading Est. |
| | Sittingbourne, Kent |
| BUDGE | BUDGET |
| BUDPAC | BUDGET PACK |
| | distributed by: |
| | Dealerpack Ltd. |
| | Trinity Business Centre |
| | 365-367 Rotherhithe St. |
| | London, SE16 1EY |
| | (071-232 8271) |
| BUENA | BUENA VISTA HOME |
| | VIDEO LTD. |
| | 3 Centaurs Business Park |
| | Grant Way, off Syon Lane |
| | Isleworth |
| | Middlesex, TW7 5QD |
| | (081-569 8080) |
| | Telex: 925662 |
| | Fax: 081-568 8983 |
| | See CBSDIS for |
| | distribution |
| BUVID | B.U. VIDEO |
| BVP | BB VIDEO PRODUCTIONS |
| BWV | BRENT WALKER VIDEO |
| | Knightsbridge House |
| | 197 Knightsbridge |
| | London, SW7 1RB |
| | (071-225 1941) |
| | Telex: 23639 |
| CAB | CABLE COMMUNICATIONS |
| CAB2 | CABLE 2 VIDEO |
| CAL | CAL VISTA |
| CAM | CAMERA CLUB VIDEO |
| CAN | CANNON VIDEO |
| | also known as Cannon |
| | Screen Entertainment |
| | and Cannon Film |
| | Distributors (UK) Ltd. |
| | 30-31 Golden Square |
| | London, W1A 4QX |
| | (071-437 9234) |
| | Telex: 22760 |
| | Fax: 071-439 1964 |
| | No longer active |
| | See PATHE for |
| | distribution |
| CANON | CANON |
| | See VPD |
| CAP | CAPRICORN |
| CAPIT | CAPITAL |
| | See STABL |
| CAPS | CAPSTAN VIDEO |
| | See PVG |
| CAR | CARDINAL |
| CAREY | CAREY COMMUNICATIONS |
| | also known as |
| | Careyvision Home Video |
| | and Careyvision Ltd. |
| | Unit 4 |

Whitworth Road Ind. Est.
Pin Green
Stevenage, SG1 4QS
(0438-318733)
Fax: 0438-353641
Now known as
HOLLYWOOD NITES
No longer active

**CARN**    CARNABY VIDEO
**CASH**    CASH 'N' CAREY
See CAREY
**CASS**    CASSEX
See AVR
**CASPIC**    CASTLE PICTURES
also known as
Castle Music Pictures
Unit A29
Barwell Business Park
Leatherhead Road
Chessington, Surrey
KT9 2NY
(081-974 1021)
Fax: 081-974 2674
See CBSDIS for rental
distribution
See BMGREC for music tapes
and sell-thru distribution
**CAST**    CASTLE COMMUNICATIONS PLC
also known as Castle
Communication
Unit 5, Ripon House
35-37 Station Lane
Hornchurch
Essex, RM12 6JL
**CASTLE**    CASTLE VIDEO
See IVS
**CASVIS**    CASTLE VISION
1. Units 5-7
Merton Road Ind. Est.
271 Merton Road
London, SW18 5JS
(081-877 1606)
Telex: 911515
Fax: 081-874 8273
2. Penthouse Suite
8 Northfields Prospect
Putney Bridge Road
London, SW18 1PE
(081-877 0922)
Fax: 081-877 0416
See POLY for
distribution
**CBS**    CBS
also known as
CBS/Fox Video Ltd.
Perivale Ind. Est.
Greenford, Middlesex
UB6 7RU
(081-997 2552)
Telex: 8951742
Fax: 081-997 2552 ext. 223
**CBSDIS**    CBS DISTRIBUTION
Rabans Lane
Aylesbury, Bucks.
HP19 3BX
(0296-26151)
Sales Desk: 0296-395151
**CCV**    CRYSTAL CLEAR VIDEO
**CDC**    CDC VIDEO (UK) LTD
36 Nottingham Road
Eastwood Common, Notts.
NG16 3NQ
(0773-530 316)
**CEN**    CENTRE VIDEO
**CENCOM**    CENTRAL COMMUNICATIONS
**CENTV**    CENTRAL TELEVISION
ENTERPRISES
Hesketh House
43-45 Portman Square

London, W1H 9FG
(071-486 6688)
Telex: 24337
Fax: 071-486 1707
See PICK for
distribution
**CENVID**    CENTRAL VIDEO
also known as Central
Independant Television
**CERT**    CERTJET LTD.
37 Stanmore Hill
Stanmore, Middlesex
HA7 3DS
**CFD**    COLOURBOX FILM
DISTRIBUTORS
also known as
Colourbox Video
1. Unit 3, St. Anne's Court
Wardour Street
London, W1V 3AS
(071-437 3901)
Fax: 071-799 1850
2. Unit 2
Highway Trading Estate
Heckford Street
London, E1 9HR
(071-791 2000)
Fax: 071-799 1850
**CH5**    CHANNEL 5 VIDEO
1 Rockley Road
London, W14 0DL
(081-743 3474)
Telex: 298816
Fax: 081-743 2074
See POLYREC for
distribution
**CHAM**    CHAMPAGNE VIDEO
**CHANX**    CHANNEL X
See EEC
**CHAR**    CHARLY RECORDS LTD.
156-166 Ilderton Road
London, SE15 1NT
(071-639 8603)
Telex: 8953184
**CHARLES**    CHARLES 2ND ENTERTAINMENT
**CHE**    CHESS VALLEY FILMS & VIDEO
Film House
Nightingales Corner
Little Chalfont
Bucks., HP7 9PY
(0494-762222)
**CHEQ**    CHEQUERBOARD
See WOV
**CHEREN**    CHERRYWOOD ENTERTAINMENT
10/12 Carlisle Street
London, W1V 5RF
(071-287 3018)
**CHERRY**    CHERRY RED
also known as Continental
Productions Ltd.
53 Kensington Garden
Square
London, W2 4BA
(071-229 8854)
No longer active
**CHEV**    CHEVRON VIDEO
**CHILD**    CHILDRENS' ANIMATED
CLASSICS
**CHILVID**    CHILDREN'S VIDEO LIBRARY
label for VES
**CHM**    CHAMPION
69-70 Long Lane
London, EC1
**CHP**    CHIPSTEAD FILM PRODUCTIONS
Kings House
12 Stratford Place
Cheltenham
Gloucestershire
No longer active

| | |
|---|---|
| **CHROME** | CHROME |
| | label for CINE |
| **CHRY** | CHRYSALIS RECORDS LTD. |
| | part of the Chrysalis |
| | Group PLC |
| | also known as Chrysalis |
| | Home Video |
| | 12 Statford Place |
| | London, W1N 9AF |
| | (071-221 2213) |
| | See VCC for |
| | distribution |
| **CHV** | CASTLE HOME VIDEO |
| | 1. Media House |
| | Abbs Cross Gardens |
| | Hornchurch, Essex |
| | RM12 4UN |
| | (04024-57025) |
| | Fax: 04024-43542 |
| | 2. Unit A29 |
| | Barwell Business Park |
| | Surrey |
| | See CBSDIS for |
| | distribution |
| **CIC** | CIC VIDEO |
| | 4th Floor |
| | Glenthorne House |
| | 5-17 Hammersmith Grove |
| | London, W6 0ND |
| | (081-846 9433) |
| | Telex: 268763 |
| | Fax: 081-741 9773 |
| | See CBSDIS for |
| | distribution |
| **CID** | CID-REX/CYCLO |
| | See CYCLO |
| **CIN** | CINEMA INDOORS |
| | 45 Kingswood Road |
| | London W4 |
| | (081-995 5253) |
| **CINE** | CINEPLEX DISTRIBUTION |
| | Unit 12 |
| | Brunswick Ind. Park |
| | Brunswick Way, |
| | London, N11 1HX |
| | (081-368 7788) |
| | Telex: 929195 |
| | Fax: 081-361 887 |
| | Sales: 081-361 8822 |
| **CINF** | CINEMA FEATURES |
| **CINGRO** | CINEMA GROUP |
| **CINHOL** | CINEHOLLYWOOD |
| | See VPD |
| **CINV** | CINEVIDEO |
| **CIRO** | CIROSHIRE |
| **CIV** | CHANNEL ISLAND VIDEO |
| **CLIM** | CLIMATIC VIDEO |
| **CLIMAX** | CLIMAX INTERNATIONAL |
| | See PPL |
| **CLM** | CLIMAX VIDEO |
| **CLOK** | CLOCKWORK FILMS |
| | 3 Meadowside |
| | Charterhouse Road |
| | Godalming, GU7 2AL |
| | (04868-24296) |
| **CLUB** | CLUB VIDEO |
| | 148 Merton High St. |
| | London SW19 |
| | (081-542 2858) |
| **CMV** | CMV ENTERPRISES |
| | 17-19 Soho Square |
| | London, W1V 6HE |
| | (071-734 8181) |
| | Telex: 24203 |
| | Fax: 071-734 4321 |
| | See CBSDIS for |
| | distribution |
| **CN7** | CINESPORT 7 |
| | also known as |

| | |
|---|---|
| | Cinesport Film Co. |
| **CNL** | CHANNEL VIDEO |
| **COBRA** | COBRA |
| | label for HOMCO |
| **COCK** | COCKNEY VIDEO |
| **COL** | COLLINS HOME VIDEO |
| | 8 Grafton Street |
| | London, W1X 3LA |
| | (071-493 7070) |
| | Fax: 071-493 3061 |
| | a division of MSD |
| | See CBSDIS/HIFLY for |
| | distribution |
| **COLISS** | COLISSEUM VIDEO |
| **COM** | COMMERCIAL VIDEO |
| **COMPTV** | COMPUTER TELEVISION |
| | 9 Cavendish Square |
| | London W1 |
| | (071-631 1801) |
| | No longer active |
| **COMVI** | COMMAND VISION (UK) LTD. |
| | Britannia House |
| | 1-11 Glenthorne Road |
| | London, W6 0LF |
| | (081-748 9898) |
| | Fax: 081-746 3675 |
| | See BECK for |
| | distribution |
| **CON** | CONDOR VIDEO |
| **CONCO** | CONCORDE VIDEO |
| **CONCOLL** | CONNOISSEUR COLLECTION |
| | (071-724 1502) |
| | Fax: 071-706 1754 |
| **CONNO** | CONNOISSEUR VIDEO |
| | British Film Institute |
| | Glenbuck House |
| | Glenbuck Road |
| | Surbiton, Surrey |
| | KT6 6BT |
| | (081-399 0022) |
| | See ROUGH for |
| | distribution |
| **CONQ** | CONQUEST VIDEO |
| **CONRAD** | CONRAD TELEVISION |
| | ASSOCIATES LTD. |
| | 28 Bells Hill |
| | Barnet, Herts. |
| | EN5 2RY |
| | (081-441 8044) |
| | Fax: 081-441 7466 |
| **CONVID** | CONNOISSEUR VIDEO |
| | See RIP |
| **COU** | COUGAR VIDEO |
| | No longer active |
| **COV** | COVENT GARDEN VIDEO |
| | 1/44 Monmouth Street |
| | London WC2 |
| | (071-836 6509) |
| **CRN** | CARNABY VIDEO |
| **CROS** | CROWN CREST |
| | See VDEL |
| **CROWN** | CROWN VIDEO |
| **CRS** | COCKNEY REBELS SPECIAL |
| **CRST** | CREST VIDEO FILM |
| | PRODUCTIONS |
| | See LIGHT for |
| | distribution |
| **CRAW** | CRESTSHAW LTD |
| | Unit 4 |
| | Montague Works |
| | Queensborough Road |
| | Wembley, Middlesex |
| | HAD 1QC |
| **CRYS** | CRYSTAL VIDEO |
| | See DFS |
| **CRZ** | CROZET |
| **CTL** | CATALYST VIDEO |
| | PUBLISHING |
| **CTVC** | CTVC |

Beeson's Yard
Bury Lane
Rickmansworth
Herts., WD3 1DS
(0923-777933)

**CURZON**   CURZON FILM
DISTRIBUTORS
38 Curzon Street
London, W1Y 8EY
(071-499 7571)

**CVL**   CVL
**CVP**   CVP
**CVV**   CVV
**CYC**   CYCLO
**DAPON**   DAPON
See PPL

**DARK**   DARK BROS.
**DARV**   DARVILL ASSOCIATES
280 Chartridge Lane
Chesham, Bucks.
HP5 2SG
(0494-783643)

**DD-D**   DD DISTRIBUTION
5 Churchill Court
58 Station Road
North Harrow
Middlesex
HA2 7SA
(081-863 8819)

**DDA**   DDA CREATIVE
**DECCA**   DECCA
PO Box 1420
1 Sussex Place
London, W6 9XS
(081-846 8515)
Telex: 916155/263828
Poly G
Fax: 081-748 4104
See POLYREC for
distribution

**DEL**   DELTA VIDEO
See VDEL

**DER**   DEERMARK VIDEO LTD.
**DEUT**   DEUTSCHE GRAMMOPHON
Sales: 081-994 9199
See POLYREC for
distribution

**DFS**   DERANN FILM SERVICES
99 High Street
Dudley, West Midlands
DY1 1QP
(0384-233191)

**DIAM**   DIAMOND FILMS
c/o Picture Box
Collection
Unit 4
Forest Hill Business
Centre
Forest Hill
London, 3JF
081-291 6000/4576)

**DIAVID**   DIAMOND VIDEO
**DIPLO**   DIPLOMAT
See HER

**DIRECT**   DIRECT ENTERTAINMENT LTD.
22 Little Portland Street
London, W1N 5AF
(071-580 0007)
Fax: 071-580 7771
See GRANT for
distribution

**DMS**   DMS VIDEO COMPANY
150 Coles Green Road
London, NW2 7HQ
(081-208 1699)
Fax: 081-208 2509
See TAY for
distribution

**DOV**   DOUBLE VISION DISTRIBUTORS

DVD House
8 Canons Corner
Edgware, Middlesex
HA8 8AE
(081-968 1088)
Fax: 081-958 1092

**DREAM**   DREAMLAND HOME VIDEO
See KRP

**DREVID**   DREAM VIDEO LTD.
**DRUM**   DRUMFIRE LTD.
10 Market Parade
Hanworth, Middlesex
TW13 6AL

**DUKE**   DUKE MARKETING LTD.
Milbourne House
Saint Georges Street
Douglas, Isle of Man
(0624-623634)
Telex: 946240
Fax: 0624-629745

**DUP**   DUPLIVISION
**DVS**   DIRECT VIDEO SUPPLIERS
**EAG**   EAGLE CREST VIDEO
See KRP

**ECF**   EUROPEAN CREATIVE FILMS
Business & Technology Centre
Bessemer Drive
Stevenage, Herts.
(0438-351992)
No longer active

**EEC**   EECO VIDEO
**EFD**   ENTERTAINMENT FILM DIST. LTD.
27 Soho Square
London W1
(071-439 1606)

**EHE**   EMBASSY HOME ENTERTAINMENT
Now known as NELSON

**EIPT**   ENTERTAINMENT IN PRIME TIME
See CBS

**EIV**   ENTERTAINMENT IN VIDEO
27 Soho Square
London, W1V 5FL
(071-439 1979)
Fax: 071-734 2483
See CBSDIS for
distribution

**ELBLU**   ELECTRIC BLUE
See ELV

**ELE**   ELEPHANT VIDEO LTD.
Tivoli Cinema
Station Street
Birmingham, B5 4DY
(021-616 1021)
Fax: 021-616 1019

**ELEC**   ELECTRO FILMS
**ELHOL**   ELECTRIC HOLLYWOOD
See ELV

**ELL**   ELLEM DISTRIBUTORS
**ELPIC**   ELECTRIC PICTURE PALACE
**ELV**   ELECTRIC VIDEO
10-14 Lonsdale Road
London, NW6 6RD
(071-935 7288)
Telex: 24583
Fax: 071-328 3215

**ELVIS**   ELVISLY YOURS LTD.
107 Shoreditch High St.
London, E1 6JN
(071-739 2001)

**EMIDIS**   EMI RECORDS DISTRIBUTION
1-3 Uxbridge Road
Hayes, Middx.
UB4 0SY
(081-848 9811)

**EMP**   EMPIRE VIDEO
6 Empire Road
Leicester, LE3 5HE

**EMPIR**   EMPIRE HOME VIDEO
Wynd-Up Distribution

Turntable House
Guinness Road Trading
Estate
Trafford Park
Manchester, M17 1SD
(061-872 5020)
See WYND for
distribution

**EMV**   EMV VIDEO
SALES PROMOTION
PO Box 732
London, SE26 4RR
No longer active

**ENT**   ENTERPRISE
See HVP

**ENTER**   ENTERPRISE PICTURES
See HIFLI for
distribution

**EOT**   EOTHEN FILMS
EMI Film Studios
Shenley Road
Borehamwood
(081-953 1600)
No longer active

**EPC**   ELECTRONIC
PUBLISHING CO.

**EQUIN**   EQUINOX
**EROS**   EROS
**EROT**   EROTIC COLLECTION
label for ATLAS

**EVC**   EUROPEAN VIDEO CO.
**EVI**   ESSEX VIDEO
INTERNATIONAL
Unit 10
Osiers Road Ind. Est.
Enterprise Way
London, SW18

**EVP**   EXTROVERT VIDEO
PRODUCTIONS

**EXC**   EXCALIBUR
COMMUNICATIONS LTD.

**EXCEL**   EXCEL
**EXEC**   EXECUTIVE
See GSP

**EXFIL**   EXECUTIVE FILMS
Weir House
62 King Street
Maidenhead
Berks., SL6 1EQ

**EXOTIC**   EXOTIC
label for VPD

**FALCON**   FALCON VIDEO LTD.
20 Charlotte Street
London W1
(071-636 8881)

**FAM**   FAMILY HOME
ENTERTAINMENT

**FAMCLA**   FAMILY CLASSICS
See DFS

**FAMOUS**   FAMOUS VIDEO
**FANVID**   FANCEY VIDEO
See CEN

**FAST**   FAST FORWARD
VIDEO SOFTWARE
Unit 10
Guardian Business Centre
Faringdon Avenue
Harold Hill, Essex
(04023-84171)

**FEED**   FEED THE WORLD
**FEST**   FESTELLE VIDEO
**FFC**   FILMFAIR COMMUNICATIONS
1-4 Jacobs Well Mews
London, W1
(071-935 1596)

**FFV**   FLETCHER FILM AND VIDEO
also known as
Fletcher Films

**FIFTH**   FIFTH DIMENSION VIDEO

also known as
Fifth Dimension Movies
See GLOB

**FIG**   FILMSGALORE
**FILFUN**   FILMFAIR FUN
See LIGHT

**FILINT**   FILMS INTERNATIONAL
See CBS

**FILV**   FILMVIEW
See KRP

**FISH**   FISHER PRICE
See CH5 for
distribution

**FLK**   FLK VIDEO
**FLV**   FILMLAND VIDEO WHOLESALERS
**FNF**   FRIGHT NITE FILMS
**FOD**   FILMS OF DISTINCTION
**FOTO**   FOTODISK VIDEO
PO Box 270
Wimborne, Dorset
(0202-823052)
Telex: 41126
Fax: 0202-826926

**FOU**   FOURMATT VIDEO
**FOURM**   FOURMOST VIDEOGRAM
See WOV

**FOX**   FOXTROT VIDCOM
See KRP

**FOXVID**   FOX VIDEO
**FREN**   FRENCH LABEL
See WOV

**FRM**   FRM
**FRON**   FRONTIER
**FTV**   FILMTOWN VIDEO
43-44 Great Windmill
Street, London
W1V 8EQ

**FTW**   FILM TO WIN
**FUTUR**   FUTURISTIC ENTERTAINMENT
87 Wellesley Road
London, W4 3AT
(081-995 9039)
Fax: 081-742 1952
See POLYREC for
distribution

**FUTVI**   FUTUREVISION LTD.
**FVC**   FILM VIDEO & CABLE UCL
**FVL**   FUTUREVISION LTD.
also known as
FVL Video

**GAL**   GALAXY
**GAM**   GAMM
**GCRST**   GOLDCREST
See ART

**GENEV**   GENEVIEVE
See VPD

**GENT**   GENTLEMAN'S CLUB, THE
**GHB**   GHB
See VCL

**GHV**   GUILD HOME VIDEO
Crown House
2 Church Street
Walton-On-Thames
Surrey, KT12 2QS
(081-546 3377)
Telex: 269651
Fax: 081-546 4568
Telesales: 0932-228899

**GLEN**   GLENBUCK FILMS
Glenbuck House
Glenbuck Road
Surbiton
Surrey, KT6 6BT
(081-399-0022/5266)

**GLOB**   GLOBAL SALES LTD.
351 Holloway Road
London, N7
(071-607 6780/700 5671)

**GMH**   GMH ENTERTAINMENTS LTD.

22 Manasty Road
Orton Southgate
Peterborough, Cambs.
PE2 0UP
(0733-233464)
Fax: 0733-238966

**GOLD** S.GOLD & SONS
(VIDEO DIVISION) LTD.
69 Flempton Road
London, E10 7NL
(081-539 3600)
Telex: 894793
Fax: 081-539 2176

**GOST** GOLDSTAR PUBLICATIONS
Gadoline House
2 Godstone Road
Whyteleafe
(071-600 0102)

**GOV** GO VIDEO

**GRA** GRAPHIC VIDEO

**GRANT** GRANTHAM BOOK
SERVICES LTD.
Isaac Newton Way
Alma Park Ind. Estate
Grantham, Lincs.
NG31 9SD
(0476-674421)
Fax: 0476-590223

**GRN** GRANADA VIDEO
also known as
Granada Television
International Ltd.
36 Golden Square
London, W1
See POLYREC

**GSCRN** GOLDEN SCREEN
See CIC

**GSV** GUILD SOUND AND
VISION LTD.
6 Royce Road
Peterborough
(0733-315315)

**GTO** GTO FILMS

**GVC** GULF VIDEO CENTRE

**GVI** GVI VIDEO

**GWV** GOLD WORLD VIDEO

**HANNA** HANNA BARBERA
HOME VIDEO
Premier House
313 Kilburn Lane
London, W9 3EG
(081-968 6633)
Fax: 081-968 0892
See VCC for
distribution

**HAR** HARMONY VIDEO
16 Frith Street
London W1

**HBL** HBL VIDEO
Hillbit Ltd.
547 Stockport Road
Longsight
Manchester 12
(061-256 2621)
Telex: 669755 G

**HBR** HOLIDAY BROTHERS
(AUDIO/VIDEO) LTD.
172 Finney Lane
Heald Green, Cheadle
Cheshire SK8 3PU
(061-437 0538/0539)

**HDA** HAZEL DOBRIAN AND
ASSOCIATES
49 Hallam Street
London, W1N 5LL
No longer active

**HEL** HELLO VIDEO
See KRP

**HEMD** HEMDALE

**HEND** See GHV
HENDRING LTD.
also known as
Castle Hendring
20a Eccleston Street
London, SW1W 9LT
(071-730 8691)
Fax: 071-823 4934
See BMGVID for
distribution

**HER** HERON HOME ENTERTAINMENT
also known as Heron
Films Ltd.
formerly known
as Videoform
Telford House
Woodside Lane
London, W12 8TP
(081-446 8441)
No longer active
See PARK

**HERAY** HERON RELAY

**HERIT** HERITAGE VIDEO LTD.
72 Moss Lane
Macclesfield
Cheshire, SK11 7TT
(0625-615910)

**HERO** HERO PRODUCTIONS
12 D'Arblay Street
London, W1

**HIFLI** HI-FLIERS
DISTRIBUTION LTD.
58 Waldeck Road
London, W4 3NP
(081-742 2023)
See CBSDIS for
distribution

**HIK** HIKON VIDEO

**HNU** HAWLEY NUSOUND

**HOK** HOKUSHIN
See KRP

**HOLLY** HOLLYWOOD NITES LTD.
a division of the
Parkfield Group PLC
Unit 4
Whitworth Road
Industrial Estate
Pin Green,
Stevenage, SG1 4QS
(0438-318733)
Fax: 0438 353641
formerly CAREY
See PARK for
distribution

**HOLVID** HOLLYWOOD HOUSE VIDEO

**HOM** HOME ENTERTAINMENT

**HOMCO** HOME COUNTIES VIDEO
Plumpton House
Plumpton Road
Hoddesdon, Herts
(0992-44693)
No longer active

**HOMEX** HOME VIDEO EXPRESS
See HVP

**HOR** HORROR TIME

**HOT** HOTLINE VIDEO

**HTM** HOT TAPE MACHINE

**HVH** HOME VIDEO HOLDINGS

**HVM** HOME VIDEO MERCHANDISERS

**HVP** HOME VIDEO PRODUCTIONS

**HVS** HOME VIDEO SUPPLIERS

**ICL** INTERCONTINENTAL

**ICV** INTERCITY VIDEO

**IDS** IDS

**IFD** IFD FILMS

**IFS** IVER FILM SERVICES
Pinewood Studios
Iver, Bucks SL0 0NH
(0753-651700)

No longer active

**IHM** IN-HOUSE MOVIES

**IKON** IKON FCL
also known as
Ikon Records
Suite 48
Atlantic Business Centre
Broadheath, Altrincham
Cheshire, WA14 5NQ
(061-928 7387)
Fax: 061-926 9520

**IMVID** IMAGINATION VIDEO
See ODY

**IMP** IMPALA

**IMPACT** IMPACT
See ODY

**IMPENT** IMPERIAL ENTERTAINMENT
See VPD

**IMPVID** IMPERIAL VIDEO

**INT** INTERVISION VIDEO LTD.
Unit 6/7
271 Merton Road Ind. Estate
271 Merton Road
London, SW18 5JS
(081-870 0159)
Fax: 081-874 8952

**INTCON** INTERCONTINENTAL
CORPORATE SERVICES
No longer active

**INTFF** INTERNATIONAL FEATURE
FILMS
See INT

**INTGOL** INTERNATIONAL
GOLDEN HITS
See FFV

**INTMED** INTERMEDIA SALES AND
DISTRIBUTION LTD.
Unit 4
90-92 Queensbury Road
Wembley, Middx.
HA0 1QG
(081-997 2366)
Fax: 081-991 9180

**IOVID** INTER-OCEAN VIDEO
See VPD

**IPC** IPC VIDEO
IPC Magazines
Kings Reach Tower
Stamford Street
London, SE1 9LS
See PVG

**ISLPIC** ISLAND PICTURES
also known as Island
Records Ltd.
22 St. Peters Square
London, W6
See PVG

**ITC** ITC
See PRV

**ITL** INTERLITE

**ITM** INTERMOVIES

**IVA** ISLAND VISUAL ARTS
334-336 King Street
London, W6 0RA
(081-846 9141)
Telex: 934541
Fax: 081-741 4038
See POLYREC for
distribution

**IVC** IVC
43 Westfield Road
Chandlers Ford
Eastleigh, Hants.

**IVL** INDEPENDENT VIDEO LTD.

**IVP** INTERVIDEO PRODUCTS
also known as Intervideo
Productions
87 Boundary Road
London NW8

(071-328 8922)

**IVN** INTERNATIONAL VIDEO
NETWORK LTD.
24 Scala Street
London, W1P 1LU
(071-631 4737)

**IVS** INDEPENDENT VIDEO
SERVICES LTD.
64 Yew House
Church Hill, Penn
Wolverhampton
(0902-341792)

**JAG** JAGUAR VIDEO

**JETS** JETSTAR RECORDS
155 Acton Lane
London, NW10 7NG
(081-965 5818)
Fax: 081-965 7008

**JETT** JETTISOUNDZ
28-30 The Square
Lytham St. Annes
Lancs., FY8 1RF
(0253-712453)
Telex: 94011783
Fax: 0253-712362
See ROUGH for
distribution

**JUB** JUBILEE FILM & VIDEO

**JUNG** JUNGLE MUSIK
Old Dairy Mews
62 Chalk Farm Road
London, NW1 8AN
(071-267 0171)
Fax: 071-267 0912
See ROUGH for
distribution

**JVC** JVC

**JVI** JVI

**K-TEL** K-TEL ENTERTAINMENT
(UK) LTD.
Windmill Courtenue
192 Windmill Lane
Greenford, Middlesex
UB6 9DW
(081-566 6789)
Fax: 081-566 2264

**KAS** KASINO

**KENT** KENTISH TOWN CAMERAS
See KTC

**KES** KESTREL GOLD VIDEO
See GOL for
distribution

**KFM** KF MOVIES

**KIDVID** KIDVID
See ART

**KJAZ** KAY JAZZ PRODUCTIONS
29 May Road
Rochester, Kent
ME1 2HY
(0634-405698)

**KLVID** KL VIDEO
also known as
KLV Video
See PPL

**KMV** KM VIDEO

**KNGFIL** KINGSTON FILMS
See VCC

**KONTI** KONTIKKI VIDEO

**KRP** KRYPTON
also known as
Kryptonforce
58/60 Berners Street
London, W1B 4JS

**KSV** KNIGHT SHIELD VIDEO
See KRP

**KTC** KTC FILMS
also known as
Kentish Town Cameras

**KVD** KINGSTON VIDEO

c/o HARRIS FILMS
Glenbuck Road
Surbiton, Surrey
KT6 6BT
(081-399 0022)

**LASGO** LASGO LTD.
Unit 2
Chapmans Park Ind. Est.
378-388 High Road
Willesden, London
NW10 2DY
(081-459 8800)
Telex: 22111
Fax: 081-451 6773

**LATE** LATE NIGHT VIDEO
**LEIS** LEISURE TIME
2-4 Church Street
Steeple Bumpstead
Haverhill, Suffolk

**LEISUR** LEISUREVIEW LTD
5 Churchill Court
58 Station Road
North Harrow
Middlesex, HA2 7SA
(081-863 8819)
Telex: 27972 TVUIN
Fax: 081-863 0463
See K-TEL for
distribution

**LIB** LIBERTY VIDEO
**LIFE** LIFE STYLE
See MIC

**LIGHT** LIGHTNING DISTRIBUTION
also known as Lightning
Records and Video
103 Bashley Road
London, NW10 6SD
(081-965 9292)
Telex: 927813
Fax: 081-961 8040

**LNG** LONGMAN VIDEO
21-27 Lambs Conduit St.
London, WC1N 3NJ
No longer active

**LNK** LINKED RING TELEVISION
FILMS LTD.

**LOCUS** LOCUS
**LON** LONESTAR VIDEO
**LONDON** LONDON LEISURE
DISTRIBUTION LTD.
Fulton House
Fulton Road
Wembley, Middlesex
HA9 0TF
(081-902 9416/9453)

**LOOK** LOOK
See PPL

**LOTUS** LOTUS
**LUN** LUNAR VIDEO
**LUPRO** LU PRODUCTIONS
See WOV

**LVC** LVC
See CEN

**LWT** LONDON WEEKEND
TELEVISION
also known as
Weekend Video
Seymour Mews House
Seymour Mews
London, W1

**LYDVID** LYDCARE VIDEO
See GSP

**LYNX** LYNX
See AST

**MAD** MADAM VIDEO
**MAG** MAGNETIC VIDEO
**MAGNUM** MAGNUM VIDEO
also known as
Magnum Entertainment

See GOLD
**MAGUS** MAGUS HOME ENTERTAINMENT
Unit 1, GEC Estate
East Lane
Wembley, Middlesex
HA9 7FG
See VPD

**MAIN** MAINLINE VIDEO
See VSP

**MALEK** MALEK FILM
DISTRIBUTORS LTD.
No longer active

**MANHAT** MANHATTAN VIDEO
See KRP

**MAR** MARE PRODUCTIONS
**MARC** MARC ON WAX
Wholesalers

**MARK1** MARK ONE FILMS
See CEN

**MARKET** MARKET VIDEO
See GOV

**MARKIN** MARKETING FILM INT.
See DFS

**MARKIV** MARK IV PICTURES VIDEO
**MART** MARTIAL ARTS COLLECTION
See XTASY

**MASS** MASTER CLASS
See FFV

**MAST** MASTERVISION LTD.
2-4 Vernon Yard
Portobello Road
London, W11 2DX
(071-727 8070)

**MATIN** MATINEE
See MGM

**MAUVE** MAUVE
label for CINE

**MAXVID** MAX VIDEO
See IDS

**MED** MEDUSA
COMMUNICATIONS LTD.
also known as Medusa
Pictures
Regal House
51 Bancroft
Hitchin, Herts.
SG5 1LL
(0462-421818)
Telex: 826552
Fax: 0462 420393
For "Medusa" label
see CBSDIS
For "Pegasus" label
see POLYREC
See CH5 for sell-thru
distribution

**MEDPER** MEDIA PERPETUITY
INVESTMENTS

**MHE** MEDIA HOME ENTERTAINMENT
See VPD

**MEGA** MEGA FILMS
**MEN** THE MEN'S CLUB
**MERC** MERCURY VIDEO LTD.
See VPD

**MERL** MERLIN VIDEO
See APX

**MET** METROMEDIA
**MEV** MOTION EPICS VIDEO
COMPANY LTD.

**MGM** MGM/UA HOME ENTERTAINMENT
GROUP (UK) LTD.
Hammer House
113-117 Wardour Street
London, W1V 3TD
(071-439 9932)
Telex: 28527
Fax: 071-437 8843
See CBSDIS for rental
distribution

| | |
|---|---|
| | See TERRY for sell-thru distribution |
| **MIA** | MISSING IN ACTION |
| | 18 Uppper Brook street |
| | London, W1Y 1PD |
| | (071-355 2066) |
| | Fax: 071-493 8780 |
| | See VCC for |
| | distribution |
| **MIC** | MICROMETRO |
| | 165/167 High Road |
| | Willesden |
| | London, NW10 |
| **MIDAS** | MIDAS VIDEO |
| **MIDBLU** | MIDNIGHT BLUES |
| **MIDTV** | MIDNIGHT TV |
| | see CEN |
| **MIG** | MIGHTYFAIR LTD. |
| | also known as |
| | Mighty Fair Ltd. |
| | Unit B11 |
| | Trinity Business Centre |
| | 305-307 Rotherhithe St. |
| | London, SE16 1BY |
| | (071-237 5768) |
| **MIL** | MILLS VIDEO |
| **MIN** | MINERVA SOUND |
| **MINST** | MINSTREL ENTERTAINMENTS |
| | See CBS |
| **MIRROR** | MIRROR VISION |
| | Athene House |
| | 66-73 Shoe Lane |
| | London, EC4 |
| | No longer active |
| **MKR** | MOVIEMAKERS |
| **MMA** | MOVIEMATIC |
| | 61 Princes Park Avenue |
| | London, NW11 |
| **MMG** | MAGNUM MUSIC GROUP |
| | Magnum House |
| | High Street |
| | Lane End, Bucks. |
| | HP14 3JG |
| | (0494-882858) |
| | Fax: 0494-882631 |
| | Wholesalers |
| **MOD** | MODERN FILMS |
| **MODVI** | MODERN VIDEO |
| | See MOV |
| **MOG** | MOGUL COMMUNICATIONS LTD. |
| | PO Box 4BT |
| | 35-37 Wardour Street |
| | London, W1A 4BT |
| | No longer active |
| **MOGP** | MOGUL PLUS |
| | See MOG |
| **MON** | MONTE VIDEO |
| **MOIRA** | MOIRA MAHER |
| **MOV** | MOUNTAIN VIDEO |
| | Albion Courtyard |
| | 3rd Floor |
| | Green Hill Rents |
| | London, EC1 |
| **MOVLAND** | MOVIELAND |
| **MOVTIM** | MOVIETIME VIDEO |
| | See MOV |
| **MPI** | M.P.I. VIDEO |
| **MPL** | MPL |
| | See TEVP |
| **MPV** | MOTION PICTURES ON VIDEO |
| | MDV Distribution |
| | 40 Queensway |
| | London, W2 |
| | (071-727 9442) |
| | Telex: 265905 |
| **MRD** | MEDIA RELEASING LTD. |
| | 27 Soho Square |
| | London W1 |
| | (071-437 2341) |

| | |
|---|---|
| **MRV** | MISTER VIDEO |
| **MSVP** | MSVP |
| | See VTV |
| **MSD** | MULTIPLE SOUND |
| | DISTRIBUTORS |
| | also known as MSD |
| | Holdings Ltd. |
| | 3 Standard Road, |
| | Park Royal Ind. Estate |
| | London, NW10 6EX |
| | (081-961 5646) |
| | Telex: 914382 |
| | Fax: 081-965 3047 |
| **MULTI** | MULTISQUASH |
| | See QUA |
| **MUSVID** | MUSIC VIDEO |
| | See WOV |
| **MVM** | MAGICAL VIDEO MOVIES |
| **MVX** | MVX |
| **MYTV** | MY-TV LTD. |
| | Unit 2 |
| | Endeavour Way |
| | Durnsford Road |
| | Industrial Estate |
| | London, SW19 8HX |
| | (081-946 5388) |
| | Fax: 081-879 7357 |
| **NARROW** | NARROWCAST |
| | 25 Blenheim Avenue |
| | London, W11 |
| | See PVG |
| **NATGE** | NATIONAL GEOGRAPHIC |
| | See STYL for |
| | distribution |
| **NCV** | NC VIDEO |
| **NDH** | NEW DIMENSION HOME VIDEO |
| | See GHV |
| **NEAT** | NEAT RECORDS |
| | 71 High Street |
| | Wallsend, Tyne & Wear |
| | NE28 7RJ |
| | (091-2624999) |
| | Telex: 537681 |
| | See PINN for |
| | distribution |
| **NELS** | NELSON ENTERTAINMENT |
| | INTERNATIONAL |
| | 8 Queen Street |
| | London, W1X 7PH |
| | (071-493 3362) |
| | See EHE |
| **NEON** | NEON EMPIRE LTD. |
| | See INT for |
| | distribution |
| **NET** | NETWORK DISTRIBUTION LTD. |
| | 64 Saint Mary's Road |
| | Market Harborough |
| | Leics. |
| | (0858-32461) |
| | Fax: 0858 410228 |
| **NEWDIR** | NEW DIRECTION VIDEO |
| | See AVR |
| **NEWMED** | NEW MEDIA (RELEASING) |
| | also known as New Media |
| | Entertainment |
| | See PVG |
| **NGV** | NEW GENERATION VIDEO |
| | See MSD |
| **NICK** | NICKELODEON PICTURES LTD. |
| | See MPV |
| **NINCOL** | NINJA COLLECTION |
| | See MKR |
| **NINJ** | NINJA THEATRE |
| | See VPD |
| **NORM** | NORMARK |
| **NOVA** | NOVA VIDEO |
| | 15 Dufours Place |
| | London, W1V 1FE |
| | (071-437 8251) |

Telex: 926326
Fax: 071-734 6941
See PVG for
distribution

**NOVEL**   NOVELLO AND CO. LTD.
8-10 Lower James Street
London, W1R 3PL
(071-287 5060)
Fax: 071-287 0816
Ansaphone: 071-287 5061
(24 hours)

**NUC**     NUCHRON
**NUT**     NUTLAND
**NVC**     NATIONAL VIDEO CORPORATION
31 Lancaster Gate
London, W2 3LP
(071-723 1133)
No longer active

**NWV**     NEW WORLD VIDEO
also known as New World
Entertainment and New World
Pictures
2nd Floor
27 Soho Square
London, W1V 6AX
(071-434 0499)
See CBSDIS/HIFLY for
distribution

**OASIS**   OASIS PICTURES
42 Maiden Lane
London, WC2E 7JL
(071-836 1844)
Telex: 418120
Fax: 071-240 2432
No longer active
See VES for
distribution

**OCEAN**   OCEAN SHORES GROUP
See GVC

**ODY**     ODYSSEY VIDEO LTD.
15 Dufours Place
London, W1V 1FE
(071-437 8251)
Telex: 926326
Fax: 071-734 6941
See CBSDIS for rental
distribution
See VIRVIS for sell-thru
distribution

**OLY**     OLYMPUS
**OMNI**    OMNI
See GVC

**OPP**     OPPIDANS
**OPX**     OPIX VIDEO
3rd Floor
Carlisle Street
London, W1V 5RG
(071-734 7365)
No loner active

**ORANGE**  ORANGE PEEL VIDEO
See STABL

**OREG**    OREGON
**ORION**   ORION
See RNK

**ORSCO**   ORANGE SCOPE LTD.
21 Beethoven Street
London, W10
(081-969 4781)

**OSC**     OSCAR VIDEO
**PACAR**   PACIFIC ART
See PLF

**PACE**    PACESETTER
**PACEV**   PACE VIDEO
See PVG

**PACVI**   PACIFIC VIDEO
See PCM

**PAE**     P.A. ENTERTAINMENTS
81 Winstanley Road
Sale, Cheshire

**PAL**     PALACE VIDEO LTD.
also known as
Palace Pictures
16-17 Wardour Mews
London, W1V 3FF
(071-734 7060)
Telex: 263900 Palace G.
Fax: 071-437 3248
See GHV for rental
distribution
See TERRY for Sell-Thru
distribution

**PALAN**   PALAN ENTERTAINMENT
CORPORATION LTD.
Prestwich House
Caxton Way
Watford, Herts
WD1 8VF

**PAN**     PANTHER ENTERTAINMENT
also known as
Panther And Chevron
Entertainment Ltd.

**PANA**    PANACHE VIDEO
**PARA**    PARAGON HOME
ENTERTAINMENT LTD.
115 Caerphilly Road
Birchgrave
Cardiff
CF4 4QA
(0222-617497)
Telex: 497244

**PARCOM**  PARAGON COMMUNICATIONS
**PARK**    PARKFIELD ENTERTAINMENT
also known as Parkfield
Publishing
a division of the
Parkfield Group PLC
1. For Sell-Thru:
Unit 12
Brunswick Ind. Park
Brunswick Way
London, N11 1HX
(081-368 7788)
Telex: 929195
Fax: 081-361 8877
Sales Desk: 081-361 8822
2. For Rental:
103 Bashley Road
London, NW10 6SD
(081-965 5555)
Telex: 927813
Fax: 081-961 8040

**PARVID**  PARK VIDEO
See WOV

**PATHE**   PATHE VIDEO LTD.
Pathe House
76 Hammersmith Road
London, W14 8YR
(071-603 4555)
Telex: 268840
Fax: 071-603 4277

**PATPRO**  PAT WYNN PROMOTIONS
Letchforth House
Headstone Lane
Harrow, HA3 6PE

**PAULR**   PAUL RAYMOND
See VSP

**PAUSE**   PAUSEROY LTD.
189 Brighton Road
South Croydon, Surrey
CR2 6EG

**PCM**     PACIFIC COMMUNICATIONS
**PCP**     PCP
See VSP

**PEACH**   PEACH VIDEO
See PACE

**PEGA**    PEGASUS
**PEND**    PENDULUM
COMMUNICATIONS LTD.

10 Market House
Market Square
Bromley, Kent
BR1 1NA
(081-460 5749)
Telex: 264036
Fax: 071-437 0885

**PENG** PENGUIN VIDEO CO. LTD.
Avica House
346 High street
Berkhamsted, Herts
HP4 1HT

**PFS** PHOENIX FILM SERVICE
**PHE** PHOENIX HOME
ENTERTAINMENTS
Old Station Works
31 Station Road
Harold Wood
RM3 0BP
(04023-81509)

**PHIL** PHILIPS
Sales: 081-994 9199
See POLYREC for
distribution

**PHV** PICADILLY HOME VIDEO
PO Box 288
Hove, Sussex
BN3 3QJ
formerly Strand Films
No longer active
See SHEP

**PICAD** PICCADILLY
**PICK** PICKWICK VIDEO LTD.
The Hyde Ind. Estate
The Hyde
London, NW9 6JU
(081-200 7000)
Telex: 922170

**PICMED** PICTUREMEDIA
See VFO

**PICPAL** PICTURE PALACE
PRODUCTIONS
71 Beak Street
London, W1
(071-439 9882)

**PICTV** PICTURE TIME VIDEO
See VCL

**PICVID** PICADILLY VIDEO
See GOV

**PINK** PINK CLIMAX
**PINN** PINNACLE RECORDS
Unit 2
Orpington Trading Estate
Sevenoaks Way
Orpington, Kent
BR5 3SR
(0689-73144)
Telex: 929053
Fax: 0689 78269

**PINVID** PINBALL VIDEO
**PIR** PIRATE VIDEO
**PLACE** PLACECROSS
**PLAVID** PLAYTIME VIDEO
**PLF** PACIFIC LEISURE FILMS
**PMA** PMA VIDEO
See CYCLO

**PMI** PICTURE MUSIC
INTERNATIONAL
20 Manchester Square
London, W1 1ES
(071-486 4488)
Telex: 22643
Fax: 071-935 3852
See EMIDIS for
distribution

**POLVID** POLESTAR VIDEO
See CEN

**POLY** POLYGRAM VIDEO
1 Rockley Road

London, W14 0DL
(081-743 3474)
Telex: 298816
Fax: 081-743 2074

**POLYREC** POLYGRAM RECORDS LTD.
also known as Polygram
Records Ops. Ltd.
Clyde Works, Grove Road
Chadwell Heath, Essex
RM6 4QR
(081-590 6044 Account
holders)
Sales Desk: 081-590 7790

**POR** PORTLAND FILMS LTD.
55 Shaftesbury Avenue
London, WC1
No longer active

**PORTO** PORTOBELLO
PRODUCTIONS LTD.
42 Tavistock Road
London, W11 1AW
(071-221 2426)
Telex: 268388 Porto G
Fax: 071-221 5991

**PORVI** PORTLAND VIDEO
See MOV

**POTPOU** POT POURRI LTD.
Unit 4
Whitworth Road
Pingreen
Stevenage, Herts
No longer active

**PPL** PROBE PRODUCTS LTD
**PRECOL** PRESTIGE COLLECTION
**PREM** PREMIER RELEASING
360 Oxford Street
London, W1N 9HA
(071-493 0440/1984)

**PRES** PRESIDENT HOME
ENTERTAINMENT
Unit 1
Perivale Ind. Park
Greenford, Middlesex
UB6 1RU
(081-997 2552)
Telex: 8951742
Fax: 081-992 0251
See CBS for
distribution

**PREST** PRESTWICH OPERATIONS LTD.
Prestwich House
Centre 1, Caxton Way
Watford, Herts.
WD1 8UF
(0923-55558)
Telex: 925430
Fax: 0923-816744

**PREVI** PREVIEW
See PRV

**PRI** PRIVATE VIDEO
See PHE

**PRIME** PRIME TIME
See VFM

**PRISCO** PRISM LEISURE CORP. PLC
Unit 1, Baird Road
Enfield, Middlesex
EN1 1SQ
(081-804 8100)
Fax: 081-805 8001

**PRISM** PRISM DISTRIBUTION PLC
28 Nottingham Place
London, W1M 3FD
No longer active

**PRISPY** PRIVATE SPY
See PRI

**PRK** PARK
See PPL

**PRO** PROLOGUE PRODUCTIONS
13 Mayfield Ind. Park

Fyfield Road
Andover, Hants.
No longer active

**PRV**   PRECISION VIDEO
Unit 4
Brunswick Park Ind. Est.
London, N11
No longer active

**PSYCH**   PSYCHO VIDEO
See CBS

**PUFF**   PUFF VIDEO
See BCM

**PUSSY**   PUSSY GALORE
See PPL

**PVE**   PAKEFIELD VIDEO EXCHANGE

**PVG**   PALACE, VIRGIN AND GOLD
DISTRIBUTION LTD.
also known as
Virgin/PVG Distribution
Grand Union Centre
Unit 23
338a Ladbroke Grove
London, W10 5AS
(081-968 4466/4472)
Fax: 081-968 9620
Sales Desk: 081-968 3333

**PYR**   PYRAMID PRODUCTIONS
also known as
Pyramid Distribution
See CBS

**PYRAM**   PYRAMID
See Home Counties Video

**QUA**   QUADRANT VIDEO
1. 37a High Street
Carshalton, Surrey
SM5 3BB
(081-669 1114)
Telex: 269556
Fax: 081-669 8831
2. 17 West Hill
London SW18
(081-870 9433)

**QLV**   QUALITY VIDEO

**QUICK**   QUICK VIDEO

**RACE**   RACE VIDEO

**RAD**   RADIAL CHOICE

**RAIN**   RAINBOW VIDEO
also known as Rainbow
Audio and Video Inc. Ltd.
See MOV

**RAP969**   RAPID 969 LTD.
No longer active

**RCA**   RCA/COLUMBIA PICTURES
VIDEO (UK)
Metropolis House
22 Percy Street
London, W1P 9FF
(071-636 8373)
Telex: 23876
See BMGREC for rental
distribution
See VCC for Sell-Thru
distribution

**RECREL**   RECORDED RELEASING LTD.
66-68 Margaret Street
London, W1N 7FL
(071-734 7477)

**RED**   RED LIGHT

**REDTAP**   RED TAPE PRODUCTION LTD
See EEC

**REED**   REED VISION

**REEVE**   REEVE AND PARTNERS
See HIFLI

**REGAL**   REGAL PICTURES

**REL**   RELAY VIDEO

**REN**   RENOWN VIDEO
See GLOB

**REP**   REPLAY
See VPD

**REV**   REVOLUTION FILMS

**REVIS**   REVISION
28/30 The Square
Lytham St. Annes
Lancs., FY8 1RF
(0253-712453/712244)
Fax: 0253-712362
See ROUGH for
distribution

**REWIND**   REWIND
See TEVP

**REX**   REX VIDEO

**RHIHOM**   RHINO HOME VIDEO

**RHINO**   RED RHINO DIST. LTD.
also known as Red Rhino
Records Ltd.
The Coach House
Fetter Lane
York, N. Yorkshire
YO1 1EH
(0904-27828)
Fax: 0904-644190

**RHV**   ROLF HARRIS VIDEO

**RIP**   RIPPLEDALE

**RITZ**   RITZ PRODUCTIONS LTD.
1, Grangeway
London, NW6 2BW
(071-328 9599)
Fax: 071-624 4471

**RL2**   REEL TWO

**RNK**   RANK HOME VIDEO
also known as Rank Video
Library
3 Centaurs Business Park
Grant Way, off Syon Lane
Isleworth, Middlesex
TW7 5QD
(081-568 9222)
Telex: 935064
Fax: 081-847 0370
No longer active
See BUENA

**ROGUE**   ROGUE
Owned by MAGUS HOME
ENTERTAINMENT
See VPD for address

**ROSA**   ROSALIND WOODS MAIL
ORDER LTD.
12 Little Street
Congleton, Cheshire
CW12 1AR

**ROSS**   ROSS RECORDS
29 Main Street
Turriff, Aberdeenshire
AB5 7AB
(0888-62403)

**ROUGH**   ROUGH TRADE DISTRIBUTION
339 Seven Sisters Road
London, N15
(081-802 8696)
Fax: 081-802 8142
Sales: 081-802 1155

**ROXY**   ROXY FILMS
102 Old Street
London, EC1
See HOMCO

**RPTA**   RPTA VIDEO LTD.
Seymour Mews House
Seymour Mews
Wigmore Street
London, W1H 9PE
(071-935 9000)

**RSPB**   ROYAL SOCIETY FOR THE
PROTECTION OF BIRDS
The Lodge, Sandy
Beds., SG19 2DL
(0767-80551)

**RSVP**   RED STAR VIDEO PUBLISHING

**RTF**   RT FILMS

| | |
|---|---|
| **RUSS** | RUSS MEYER |
| | See VSP |
| **RUST** | RUSTLER |
| **RVD** | RAPID VIDEO DISTRIBUTION |
| | 9a Embassy Court |
| | Welling High Street |
| | Welling, Kent |
| | DA16 1TH |
| | No longer active |
| **SAGE** | SAGEBRUSH PRODUCTIONS |
| **SAM** | SAMURAI RECORDS |
| | See LASGO for |
| | distribution |
| **SAPPH** | SAPPHIRE |
| | See AVI |
| **SAT** | SATELLITE FILMS |
| | 6 Parchmore House |
| | Thornton Heath, Surrey |
| | CR4 8LU |
| | (081-771 4591) |
| **SATPRO** | SATELLITE PRODUCTIONS |
| | Melrose Close, Hayes |
| | Middlesex |
| **SATUR** | SATURN VIDEO |
| **SCAN** | SCANEURO VIDEO |
| | See KRP |
| **SCILL** | SCILLONIA FILMS |
| | Little Wingletang |
| | Rams Valley, St. Mary's |
| | Isles of Scilly |
| | (0720-22659) |
| **SCO** | SCORPIO VISION |
| | 6 Stour Street |
| | Canterbury |
| | Kent, CT1 2NR |
| | See BMGREC for |
| | distribution |
| **SCREL** | SCREEN LEGENDS |
| **SCRIP** | SCRIPGLOW |
| | See ELV |
| **SCRN** | SCREEN ENTERTAINMENT LTD. |
| | PO Box 352 |
| | Harrow, Middx. |
| | HA3 0YH |
| | (081-863 9001) |
| | Telex: 265451 Ref: CQQ 08 |
| | Fax: 081-863 8490 |
| | No longer active |
| | See CBSDIS for |
| | distribution |
| **SCRT** | SCREEN TIME |
| **SCVID** | SC VIDEO LTD. |
| | HTN House, Thames Side |
| | off Water Lane |
| | Kingston-upon-Thames |
| | Surrey |
| | (081-541 1498) |
| | No longer active |
| **SEE** | SEE HEAR INDUSTRIES |
| **SEL** | SELECT VIDEO LTD. |
| | PO Box 111 |
| | Great Dulcie Street |
| | Manchester |
| | No longer active |
| **SENAT** | SENATOR RELEASING |
| | See PHE |
| **SEX** | SEX-CESS VIDEO |
| **SFI** | STRAND INTERNATIONAL |
| | /ACTION ESSENTIAL |
| | also known as Strand |
| | Films International |
| | Unit 4 |
| | Tentercroft Road |
| | Tentercroft Ind. Estate |
| | Lincoln, Lincolnshire |
| | LN2 4YL |
| | (0522-560919) |
| | Fax: 0522-567027 |
| **SGE** | SGE VIDEO |

| | |
|---|---|
| | See COL |
| **SHA** | SHAFTESBURY VIDEO |
| **SHAD** | SHADES OF BLUE |
| **SHADE** | SHADES RECORDS |
| | The Basement |
| | 9-12 Saint Annes Court |
| | Wardour Street |
| | London, W1V 3AX |
| | (071-434 1363) |
| **SHAP** | SHAPIRO GLICKENHAUS |
| | ENTERTAINMENT |
| | 3rd Floor, Maple House |
| | 2/6 High Street |
| | Potters Bar, Herts. |
| | EN6 5BH |
| | (0707-49963) |
| | Fax: 0707-47969 |
| **SHEER** | SHEER ENTERTAINMENT |
| | Prestwich House |
| | Caxton Way |
| | Watford, Herts. |
| | WD1 8UF |
| | (0923-55558) |
| | Telex: 925430 |
| | Fax: 081-361 2054 |
| | See CBSDIS/HIFLY for |
| | distribution |
| **SHEP** | SHEPTONHURST LTD. |
| | 19 West Hill |
| | London SW18 |
| | (081-874 0095) |
| **SHO** | SHOTGUN VIDEO |
| **SHOG** | SHOGUN VIDEO |
| **SHOVID** | SHOWVID |
| | See ART |
| **SHOW** | SHOWCHANNEL VIDEO |
| | See PVG |
| **SID** | SCREEN INDOORS |
| | 87 Wellesley Road |
| | London, W4 4AT |
| | (081-995 2726) |
| | No longer active |
| **SIL** | SHUTTLE |
| | INTERNATIONAL LTD. |
| | also known as |
| | Shuttle Video |
| **SILV** | SILVER VISION |
| | Suite 12a |
| | Millmead House |
| | Millmead Road |
| | London, N17 9QU |
| | (081-808 0833) |
| | Fax: 081-808 5312/0719 |
| | See VCC for |
| | distribution |
| **SIMIT** | SIMITAR ENTERTAINMENT UK |
| | 22/24 Corsham Street |
| | London, N1 6DR |
| | (071-490 2463) |
| | Fax: 071-490 2487 |
| | See CBSDIS for |
| | distribution |
| **SKP** | SK PRODUCTIONS |
| **SKY** | SKYLINE VIDEO |
| | See HER |
| **SLA** | SELECT-A-TAPE |
| **SONY** | SONY VIDEO SOFTWARE |
| | also known as Sony Video |
| | Software Europe Ltd. |
| | 2nd Floor |
| | 41-42 Berners Street |
| | London, W1P 3AA |
| | (071-631 4000) |
| | Telex: 268054 |
| | Fax: 071-631 4665 |
| | See CBSDIS for |
| | distribution |
| | No longer active |
| **SOUTH** | SOUTHERN STUDIOS |

|  | 10 Middleton Road |
|  | London, N22 4NS |
|  | (081-888 8949) |
|  | Telex: 268041 |
| SOV | SOVEREIGN VIDEO |
| SPA | SPARTAN |
| SPE | SPECTRE |
| SPEC | SPECTRUM |
|  | See POLY |
| SPECTA | SPECTACULAR VIDEO |
|  | also known as |
|  | Spectacular Films |
|  | Hammer House |
|  | Ground Floor |
|  | 113 Wardour Street |
|  | London, W1 |
| SQUARE | SQUARECAPE LTD. |
|  | No longer active |
| SQUIR | SQUIRREL VIDEO |
| SSVID | S&S VIDEO |
|  | See HIK |
| STABL | STABLECANE STUDIOS |
|  | also known as |
|  | Stablecane Home Video |
|  | See SCVID |
| STAG | STAG VIDEO |
| STARB | STARBLEND RECORDS LTD. |
|  | Wholesalers |
| STARL | STARLITE VIDEO |
|  | No longer active |
| START | START VIDEO |
|  | Unit 1B |
|  | The Hyde Ind. Estate |
|  | The Hyde |
|  | London, NW9 6JU |
|  | (081-200 5335) |
|  | Telex: 264597 Old |
|  | Gold G. |
|  | Fax: 081-205 0109 |
|  | See PICK for |
|  | distribution |
| STARX | STARBOX |
|  | See SEL |
| STAT | STATESIDE PRODUCTIONS |
| STI | STIRLING VIDEO |
| STJ | ST JAMES FILM |
|  | DISTRIBUTORS |
|  | 60-66 Wardour Street |
|  | London, W1 |
| STP | STANLEY PRODUCTIONS |
| STR | STARCURVE |
| STRAND | STRAND MAGNETICS LTD. |
| STUD | STUDIO INTERNATIONAL |
| STV | STARLINE VIDEO |
| STYL | STYLUS VIDEO |
|  | also known as Stylus |
|  | Music Video Ltd. |
|  | 21 Abbey Road Ind. Park |
|  | Abbey Road |
|  | London, NW10 7XF |
|  | (081-453 0886) |
|  | Fax: 081-453 0968 |
| SUN | SUNSET VIDEO LTD. |
| SUP | SUPREME FILM |
|  | DISTRIBUTORS LTD. |
|  | Paramount House |
|  | 162 Wardour Street |
|  | London, W1V |
|  | (071-437 4415/9513) |
| SURREY | SURREY VIDEO CO. |
|  | See SVC |
| SVC | SOUTHERN VIDEO COMPANY |
| SVS | STANMORE VIDEO SERVICE |
| SWAN | SWAN PRODUCTIONS LTD |
|  | 67 Glebe Place |
|  | London, SW3 5JB |
|  | (071-351 5311) |
| SWECOL | SWEDISH COLLECTION |
| SWISH | SWISH PUBLICATIONS LTD. |

|  | also known as |
|  | Swish Collection |
|  | 1. 47 Great Guildford St. |
|  | London, SE1 0ES |
|  | (071-928'5816) |
|  | 2. Retail: |
|  | 8 Greek Street |
|  | London W1 |
|  | (071-437 8132) |
| SYD | SYDNEY THOMPSON VIDEO |
|  | Eastcote Point |
|  | Cuckoo Hill |
|  | Pinner, Middlesex |
| TAB | TABOO FILMS |
| TAKE2 | TAKE 2 PLUS |
|  | 56 Great Northern Road |
|  | Aberdeen |
|  | (0224-482943) |
| TAME | TAMEHART ENTERPRISES LTD. |
| TAMO | TAMO VIDEO |
| TAR | TARGET INTERNATIONAL |
|  | FILMS LTD. |
|  | Avon House |
|  | 360 Oxford Street |
|  | London, W1N |
|  | (071-493 0440) |
| TARG | TARGET RECORDS SALES LTD. |
|  | Target House |
|  | Cornwall Road |
|  | Croydon, Surrey |
|  | CR9 2TG |
|  | (081-686 3322) |
|  | Fax: 081-681 6523 |
|  | See TAY for |
|  | distribution |
| TAY | TAYLOR'S DISTRIBUTION |
|  | 58 Rovex Business Park |
|  | Hay Hall Road |
|  | Tyseley, Birmingham |
|  | B11 2AQ |
|  | (021-765 4024) |
|  | Fax: 021-765 4451 |
|  | Sales: 021-765 4405 |
| TCE | TWENTY-FIRST CENTURY VIDEO |
|  | See CYCLO |
| TCR | TCR VIDEO |
| TCX | TELE CINE X |
|  | Mainsped House |
|  | 98-102 Ley Street |
|  | Ilford, Essex |
|  | (081-514 0768) |
|  | See CRAW |
| TECHNO | TECHNO FILM |
|  | See FFV |
| TEL | TELLTALE |
| TELS | TELSTAR VIDEO |
|  | ENTERTAINMENT |
|  | The Studios |
|  | 5 King Edward Mews |
|  | Byfield Gardens, Barnes |
|  | London, SW13 9HP |
|  | (081-846 9946) |
|  | See BMGREC for |
|  | distribution |
| TEM | TEMPLE VIDEO |
| TERRY | TERRY BLOOD DISTRIBUTION |
|  | Unit 18-20 |
|  | Rosevale Road |
|  | Parkhouse Industrial Estate |
|  | Newcastle-Under-Lyme |
|  | Staffs., 1ST5 7QT |
|  | (0782-566566) |
|  | Fax: 0782-565400 |
|  | Sales: 0782-566511 |
| TEVP | THORN-EMI VIDEO |
|  | See CANNON who now own |
|  | company |
|  | releases will be under |
|  | their name |

| | | | |
|---|---|---|---|
| | No longer active | | distribution |
| TFI | TFI LEISURE | TUV | TUFF VIDEO |
| TGP | TRANS-GLOBAL PICTURES | TVN | TVN LTD. |
| | (UK) LTD. | | Unit 23 |
| | PO Box 1 | | The Penthouse |
| | Consett, County Durham | | Chelsea Wharf |
| | DH8 5SF | | 15 Lots Road |
| | (0207-581514) | | London, SW10 0QJ |
| THAMES | THAMES VALLEY PRODUCTIONS | | (071-351 4155) |
| | also known as: Thames Video | | Telex: 266218 |
| | Collection, Thames Video | TVP | THAMES VALLEY |
| | Ltd., Thames Television | | PRODUCTIONS |
| | West Lodge | | West Lodge |
| | Hungerford Common | | Hungerford Common |
| | Hungerford, Berks. | | Hungerford |
| | RG17 0UP | | Berks., RG17 0UP |
| | See VCC for | | (0488-84451; 071-283 |
| | distribution | | 1030 ext. 503) |
| THERA | THERAPEUTIC VISUALISATION | TVTIM | TV TIMES/UPITN |
| THV | TIGER HOME VIDEO | | See VCL |
| TIG | TIGER FILMS | TVX | TVX |
| TMI | TMI | | See VCL |
| TOM | TOM HUSTLER VIDEO | TWE | TRANS WORLD |
| TOP | TOP HAT VIDEO | | ENTERTAINMENT |
| TOPART | TOPART FILM | | See VPD |
| | DISTRIBUTORS LTD. | TWENTY | TWENTY TWENTY VISION |
| | 90 Walworth Road | | Unit Seven |
| | London, SE1 6SW | | Hebden Court, Bakewell |
| TOUCH | TOUCHSTONE HOME VIDEO | | Derbyshire, DE4 1EE |
| | See BUENA for | | (0629-813907) |
| | distribution | TWF | TW FILMS |
| TOW | TOWER ENTERTAINMENT | UK | UK |
| | also known as Tower | | See TEM |
| | Entertainments | ULT | ULTRA VIDEO |
| | 102 Old Street | ULTRA | ULTRAVISION |
| | London, EC1 | | INTERNATIONAL LTD. |
| | (071-250 1720) | | Saxon Hall |
| | associated with ECF | | South Harling |
| TOWFIL | TOWERBELL FILMS | | Petersfield |
| | See PRV | | Hants., GU31 5LD |
| TOWN | TOWN AND COUNTRY | | (0730-85576) |
| | PRODUCTIONS | UMV | ULTRA MODERN VIDEO |
| | 21 Cheyne Row | UNDIST | UNIVERSAL DISTRIBUTOR CO. |
| | London, SW3 | | See GOLD |
| | No longer active | UNIV | UNIVERSAL VIDEO |
| TOWNCO | TOWNCORD LTD. | UNM | UNIT M |
| | 47 Great Guildford St. | UTTVID | UTTLEYVISION VIDEO |
| | London, SE1 | | See APV |
| | (071-928 0723) | UVV | ULTRAVISION VIDEO |
| TPL | TPL VIDEO | VAG | VIDEO MAGAZINE |
| TRACKS | TRACKS AMERICAN | VAH | VIDEO AT HOME |
| TRANS | TRANS OCEAN | VAI | VIDEO AID |
| | ENTERTAINMENT | VAL | VALUE VIDEO |
| | See POLY for | VALIV | VALIANT VIDEO |
| | distribution | VAMP | VAMPIX |
| TRAX | TRAX VIDEO | | See VDM |
| | 4-8 Greenland Place | VAYEL | VAYELLA PRODUCTIONS |
| | London, NW1 0AP | VBL | VIDEO BLUE |
| | See SCRN for | VCC | VIDEO COLLECTION, THE |
| | distribution | | also known as |
| TRB | TRAIL BLAZER | | Video Collection |
| TROPIC | TROPICAL FRUIT | | International Ltd. |
| TRS | TRADE SECRETS | | Prestwich House |
| | 15 Station Road | | Caxton Way |
| | Carlton, Nottingham | | Watford, Herts. |
| TRUE | TRUE WORLD VIDEO | | WD1 8UF |
| TTV | TAKE TWO VIDEO | | (0923-55558) |
| TURBO | TURBOPHASE LTD. | | Telex: 925430 |
| | Trafalgar House | | Fax: 0923-816744 |
| | Suite 123 | | Telesales: 0923-816511 |
| | Grenville Place | VCD | VIDEO CITY DISTRIBUTORS |
| | London, NW7 3SA | VCL | VCL VIDEO |
| | (081-959 3611) | | Now merged with VIRGIN |
| | Telex: 915765 | VCO | VIDEO CO |
| | Fax: 081-906 1700 | VCX | VCX |
| | No longer active | | See EEC |
| TURNER | TURNER HOME | VD1 | VIDEO ONE |
| | ENTERTAINMENT | | 42 Camberwell Road |
| | See VPD for | | London SE5 |

|  |  |
|---|---|
|  | (071-701 9266) |
|  | No longer active |
| VD7 | VIDEO 7 |
| VDB | VIDEO BROKERS |
|  | 43-44 Great Windmill |
|  | Street, London W1 |
| VDC | VIDEO DUPLICATING CENTRE |
| VDEL | VIDEO DELTA |
| VDF | VDF |
| VDM | VIDEOMEDIA |
|  | 48-70 Wardour Street |
|  | London, W1 |
| VDN | VIDEON |
| VDUP | VIDEO DUPLICATIONS |
| VDX | VIDEX |
| VER | VERTEX VIDEO |
| VES | VESTRON VIDEO (UK) LTD. |
|  | also known as Vestron |
|  | Video International and |
|  | Vestron Pictures (UK) Ltd. |
|  | 69 New Oxford Street |
|  | London, WC1A 1DG |
|  | (071-379 0406) |
|  | Fax: 071-528 7770 |
|  | See CBSDIS for |
|  | distribution |
| VEX | VIDEO EXCLUSIVE |
|  | DISTRIBUTORS |
| VEXCEL | VIDEO EXCELLENCE (UK) LTD. |
|  | 9 Easthampstead Road |
|  | Wokingham, Berks. |
|  | RG1 2EH |
|  | (0734-771133) |
|  | Fax: 0734-771114 |
| VFLY | VIDEO FLYERS |
| VFM | VIDEO FILM MERCHANDISERS |
| VFO | VIDEO FILM ORGANISATION |
|  | See KRP |
| VFP | VIDEO FILM PROMOTIONS |
|  | also known as Video Film |
|  | Productions |
| VGM | VIDEO GEMS |
|  | also known as A.M.T. |
|  | 1st Floor, Acorn House |
|  | Victoria Road |
|  | London, W3 6UL |
|  | (081-993 7705) |
|  | Fax: 081-993 0209 |
|  | See PARK for |
|  | distribution |
| VHS | VIDEO HOME SELECTIONS |
| VIC | VICTOR VIDEO |
| VIDAGE | VIDAGE |
|  | See GLOB |
| VIDCIN | VIDEOCINEMA |
|  | See CNL |
| VIDCLB | VIDEO COLLECTORS CLUB |
|  | See DIAM |
| VIDFIL | VIDEO FILM PARTNERSHIP |
|  | See CLUB |
| VIDFOR | VIDEOFORM |
|  | See HER |
| VIDGOL | VIDEO GOLD |
|  | See IFS |
| VIDKNG | VIDEO KING |
|  | See TEM |
| VIDLNE | VIDEOLINE |
|  | See ECF |
| VIDMER | VIDEO MERCHANDISERS |
|  | See HVM |
| VIDMID | VIDEO AT MIDNIGHT |
| VIDMO | VIDEO MOVIE COMPANY, THE |
| VIDMOV | VIDEO MOVIES |
|  | See HOK |
| VIDMQ | VIDEO MARQUEE |
| VIDPAC | VIDEO PACIFIC |
| VIDPLY | VIDEO PLAYBACK |
|  | See GOLD |
| VIDPRO | VIDEO INDEPENDENT |

|  |  |
|---|---|
|  | PRODUCTIONS (VIP) |
|  | See VHS |
| VIDPX | VIDEOPIX |
|  | See VDM |
| VIDRNG | VIDEORING |
|  | See PRV |
| VIDSAL | VIDEO TELE SALES LTD. |
|  | Unit E3 |
|  | Kemp Road, Dagenham |
|  | Esssex, RM8 1SL |
| VIDSCE | VIDEOSCENE |
|  | See PPL |
| VIDSI | VIDEOSINO LTD. |
|  | 1. 3 Earlham Street |
|  | London, WC2 |
|  | (071-497 2020/2030 |
|  | and 497 2591/2592) |
|  | and |
|  | 2. 114 Shaftesbury Avenue |
|  | London, W1 |
|  | (071-437 8802/9175) |
| VIDST | VIDEO 1ST |
|  | A label for MSD |
| VINTA | VINTAGE CLASSICS |
|  | See VCL |
| VIDTAP | VIDEO TAPES INTERNATIONAL |
| VIDVIC | VIDEO VICTORIA |
| VIDVIS | VIDEO VISION |
|  | See CEN |
| VIDVW | VIDEOVIEW |
|  | See VDM |
| VIP | VIP PREMIER LTD. |
|  | also known as VIP Video |
|  | 1st Floor, Acorn House |
|  | Victoria Road |
|  | London, W3 6UL |
|  | (081-993 7705) |
|  | Telex: 267067 |
|  | See INTMED |
| VIP6 | VIPCOUNT 6 |
| VIPCO | VIDEO INSTANT PICTURES CO. |
| VIR | VIRGIN VIDEO |
|  | also known as |
|  | Virgin Vision Ltd. |
|  | and Virgin Premiere |
|  | 328 Kensal Road |
|  | London, W10 5XJ |
|  | (081-968 8888) |
|  | Telex: 892890 |
|  | Fax: 081-968 8537 |
|  | See PVG for |
|  | distribution |
| VIRVIS | VIRGIN VISION DISTRIBUTION |
|  | Grand Union Centre |
|  | Unit 25 |
|  | 338a Ladbroke Grove |
|  | London, W10 5AH |
|  | (081-968 4466/4472) |
|  | Fax: 081-968 9620 |
|  | Sales: 081-968 3333 |
| VIS | VISION LINK |
| VIV | VISION ON VIDEO |
| VIZ | VIZ MOVIES |
|  | See GLOB |
| VMA | VIDEO MASTERPIECE |
|  | Budget sales only label |
| VMR | VIDEO MARKET |
| VNET | VIDEO NETWORK |
| VOR | VORTEX LTD. |
|  | Suite 14/15 |
|  | 2 Eastgate |
|  | Barnsley, South Yorks. |
|  | S70 2EP |
| VOV | VOV PICTURES/DARK BROS. |
| VOX | VOX |
| VP6 | VIPCOUNT 6 |
| VPB | VIDEO PAYBOX |
| VPD | VIDEO PROGRAMME |
|  | DISTRIBUTORS LTD. |

|  | VPD Building 1 |
|  | GEC Estate |
|  | East Lane, Wembley |
|  | Middlesex, HA9 7FF |
|  | (081-904 0921) |
|  | Telex: 295369 |
|  | Fax: 081-908 6785 |
| VPLAY | VIDEO PLAYBAL |
| VPM | VPM DISTRIBUTION LTD. |
| VPR | VPR VIDEO |
| VPS | VIDPICS INTERNATIONAL |
| VREL | VIDEO RELEASING |
| VRM | VIDEORAMA |
| VRO | VRO |
| VSA | VIDEOSCENE ASSOCIATION |
| VSP | VIDEOSPACE LTD. |
|  | 272 London Road |
|  | Wallington |
|  | Surrey, SM6 7DJ |
| VTC | VIDEO TAPE CENTRE LTD. |
|  | See STABL |
| VTEL | VIDEOTEL |
|  | 1 Ramilles Place |
|  | London W1 |
|  | (071-439 6301) |
| VTM | VIDEO TEAM |
| VTP | VIDEO TAPE |
| VTS | VIDEOTEST |
| VTV | VINTAGE TELEVISION |
| VTVSPO | VTV SPORT |
|  | 207 Dean Lane |
|  | Water, Rossendale |
|  | Lancashire |
| VUL | VIDEO UNLIMITED |
|  | See CYCLO |
| VVA | VIDNOVA |
| VWH | VIDEO WAREHOUSE |
| WAL | WALTON FILM AND VIDEO |
| WAR | WARWICK VIDEO |
| WARAD | WARAD MOVIES ON VIDEO |
|  | See KRP |
| WAT | WATCH AND WIPE |
| WATCH | WATCHWORD VIDEO |
|  | 2 Greys Road |
|  | Henloy-on-Thames |
|  | Oxfordshire, RG9 1RY |
|  | (0491-410015) |
|  | Fax: 0491-410016 |
| WATER | WATERSHED PICTURES |
|  | 2 St. George's Court |
|  | 131 Putney Bridge Road |
|  | London, SW15 2PA |
|  | See HIFLI/CBSDIS for rental |
|  | distribution |
|  | See VIR for sell-thru |
|  | distribution |
| WCP | WCP |
| WDV | WALT DISNEY HOME VIDEO |
|  | also known as Walt Disney |
|  | Productions |
|  | See BUENA for |
|  | distribution |
| WEA | WEA RECORDS |
|  | also known as WEA |
|  | Music Video |
|  | The Electric Lightning |
|  | Station |
|  | 42 Kensington Court |
|  | London, W8 5DP |
|  | (071-938 2181) |
|  | Telex: 261425 |
|  | Fax: 071-937 6662 |
|  | See WEADIS for |
|  | distribution |
| WEADIS | WEA RECORDS DISTRIBUTION |
|  | PO Box 59 |
|  | Alperton Lane |
|  | Wembley |
|  | Middlesex, HA0 1FJ |

|  | (081-998 5929) |
| WEC | WORLDWIDE |
|  | ENTERTAINMENT CORP. |
| WEEK | WEEKEND VIDEO |
| WEG | WEG VIDEO |
| WEST | WEST END |
| WESTRUM | WESTRUM |
| WEV | WESTERN ENTERPRISES |
|  | VIDEO |
| WHV | WARNER HOME VIDEO |
|  | also known as |
|  | Warner Brothers Video |
|  | and Warner Weintraub |
|  | 135 Wardour Street |
|  | London, W1V 4AP |
|  | (071-437 5600) |
|  | Telex: 8811577 |
|  | Fax: 071-494 3297 |
|  | Sales: 081-997 4450 |
| WIE | WIENERWORLD |
|  | 90 Old Church Lane |
|  | Stanmore, Middlesex |
|  | HA7 2RR |
|  | (081-954 8777) |
|  | Fax: 081-954 2999 |
|  | See VCC for |
|  | distribution |
| WIN | WINNING |
| WIND | WINDSONG INTERNATIONAL LTD. |
|  | Electron House |
|  | Cray Avenue |
|  | St. Mary Cray |
|  | Orpington, Kent |
|  | BR5 3RJ |
|  | (0689-36969) |
|  | Fax: 0689-890392/394 |
|  | See PINN for |
|  | distribution |
| WISE | WISE OWL INVESTMENTS LTD. |
| WIZ | WIZARD VIDEO |
|  | See VPD |
| WMV | WARNER MUSIC VISION |
|  | PO Box 59 |
|  | Alperton Lane |
|  | Wembley, Middlesex |
|  | HA0 1FJ |
|  | (081-998 8844) |
|  | Fax: 081-991 9628 |
|  | See WEA for |
|  | distribution |
| WOMAN | WOMAN'S OWN SELECTION |
|  | See PVG |
| WOOD | WOODSTOCK VIDEO |
| WOT | WOT PRODUCTIONS |
|  | 162 Regent Street |
|  | London W1 |
|  | (071-439 8504) |
| WOV | WORLD OF VIDEO 2000 |
|  | also known as Professional |
|  | Magnetics Ltd. |
|  | Cassette House |
|  | 329 Hunslet Road |
|  | Leeds, LS10 1NJ |
|  | (0532-706066) |
|  | Telex: 55293 |
| WTV | WYVERN TELEVISION LTD |
|  | 40 St. Martins Lane |
|  | London WC2 |
|  | (071-240 4961) |
| WWVI | WWVI |
| WYND | WYND UP RECORDS |
|  | also known as Wynd-Up |
|  | Distribution |
|  | Unit 11 |
|  | Turntable House |
|  | Guinness Road Trading |
|  | Estate, Trafford Park |
|  | Manchester, M17 1SD |
|  | (061-872 5020) |

**XSVID**    XS VIDEO
    See GSP

**XTACY**    XTACY VIDEO
    See XTASY

**XTASY**    XTASY VIDEO
    Unit 10
    Osiers Road Estate
    Enterprise Way
    London, SW18 1NL

**YAGO**    YAGO HOLDINGS
    Unit 18
    Roman Way
    Coleshill, Birmingham
    B46 1RL

**YELLOW**    YELLOWBILL
    See CLUB

**YORK**    YORKSHIRE TELEVISION LTD.
    The Television Centre
    Leeds, Yorkshire
    LS3 1JS
    (0532-438283)
    Fax: 0532-429522

**YOUNG**    YOUNG IS BEAUTIFUL

**ZOD**    ZODIAC
    See VDM